LAYMAN'S

ENGLISH - GREEK

CONCORDANCE

JAMES GALL

BAKER BOOK HOUSE
Grand Rapids, Michigan

Paperback edition issued 1975
by Baker Book House
ISBN: 0-8010-3686-0

Second printing, October 1976

Formerly published under the title:
*Bible Student's English-Greek Concordance
and Greek-English Dictionary*

PHOTOLITHOPRINTED BY CUSHING - MALLOY, INC.
ANN ARBOR, MICHIGAN, UNITED STATES OF AMERICA
1976

PREFACE.

HOLY SCRIPTURE, unlike all other books, will bear the most minute investigation, yielding up its treasures of wisdom and knowledge and beauty the more that it is examined: like all the other works of God it bears this stamp of its divine origin, distinguishing it from all human productions, and affording the most convincing internal evidence of its plenary inspiration. But it is only of the Hebrew and Greek originals that this can be fully and truly said; because any uninspired translation, however faithful it may be, is but a work of man, and depends for its value on the closeness of its conformity to the inspired originals, to which appeals can be made at any time for its explanation, supplementation, or correction. The picture of a flower may give a general and truthful representation of the work of nature; but for botanical research or microscopic study, the flower itself must be examined, and can have no substitute. And so it is with the Bible; for the analogy of faith, and for general and practical purposes, the authorised version of the Scriptures (with the originals in reserve) is amply sufficient; but he who would search the Scriptures and study them in the very words selected by the Holy Ghost, will seek to know in every passage what these words really are, and will search in other passages where the same words have been employed, to ascertain the very shade of meaning which the Spirit intended to convey. Hitherto this has been a luxury enjoyed only by the Hebrew and Greek student, who, with the original before him, and excellent Lexicons, as well as Concordances at his command, is able to pursue his investigations, and receive at the fountainhead the pure stream of inspiration.

In the study of any language there are two distinct departments, which are in a great measure independent of each other; the one is the Vocabulary, the other is the Grammar. Now, it is the former of these that presents the greatest difficulty to the translator. The extreme flexibility of the English language, with its auxiliary verbs and prepositions, enables him with tolerable precision to represent nearly all the inflections of the Greek; but whenever the Greek vocable has no corresponding word in English, but combines the ideas expressed by three or four of them, the translator feels that he has only a choice of evils; and it is here chiefly that the weakness of *any* translation appears. There is little difficulty in regard to moods and tenses, numbers and persons,—little difficulty, in short, regarding the *inflection* of the word, but great difficulty in the selection of the word to be inflected.

If for every Greek word in the New Testament there were one in English which exactly expressed its meaning, and if that word were always used as its equivalent in the authorised translation, there would be no need of such a Concordance as the present: the common Concordance would then enable us to ascertain the meaning of any word, by tracing it through all the passages in which it occurs. But this is far from being the case; for the structure of the two languages is so entirely different that there are very few of the Greek words which have an exact equivalent in English, and there are very few English words that have an exact equivalent in Greek. In numerous cases it is only by a number of English words, each of which contains a portion of the meaning of the Greek, that we are able to convey an accurate idea

of its meaning. The consequence is, that in our English translation the word which is the fittest rendering in one sentence would misrepresent the meaning of the same word in another; and therefore it is impossible always to use the same English for the same Greek, or to avoid giving more in one way and less in another than is t' be found in the original. The full and true meaning of such Greek words can only be expressed by a combination of English ones, and ascertained by an examination of all the various passages in which they occur. As the only way in which we can learn the great doctrines of Christianity is to compare Scripture with Scripture, so the only method by which we can ascertain the exact import of the words in which the Holy Ghost expressed them, is to compare passages with passages.

By means of our English New Testament, this is, of course, impossible; because for every English word there are, on an average, four or five Greek originals, and for every Greek word there are two or three English translations. The common English Concordance, therefore, would be a very treacherous guide, if we were to attempt any investigation of this kind by its aid; unless under each English heading we had a classification of the passages, according to the different words used in the Greek. This, indeed, is the desideratum which the present Concordance is intended to supply; and now by its means the Bible student, without any previous knowledge of Greek, will be able to ascertain, in any passage, the very word used in the original, and distinguish it from all the others in which the same English word is a translation from a different Greek.

To complete the apparatus of investigation a Glossary is appended, in which the signification of each Greek word is supplied, with all the different renderings which are given to it in the authorised translation. By this means, not only are its shades of meaning brought out, but, by turning up the passages in the Concordance under the various English words by which it is translated, the student is able to trace the same word in all its different renderings throughout the New Testament.

The author has to acknowledge the important help he has received in the compilation of this volume from various fellow-labourers both male and female; especially from two gentlemen, whose names he is not permitted to use, but whose labours in connection with it have been both great and valuable. The "Englishman's Greek Concordance"* also, a most precious contribution towards Bible study, has been of the greatest service.

EDINBURGH, *March* 1863.

* *Walton and Maberly.*—This would be a valuable companion to the present work : being a Greek Concordance, the headings are Greek, but the texts are in English. Under each Greek word all the texts are cited, whatever be their rendering, and exhibit at one view the true meaning and use of the word.

METHOD OF USING THE CONCORDANCE.

THE PURPOSE OF THE BOOK.

THIS Interpreting Concordance is not intended to enable the Bible student to retranslate for himself the New Testament, or even to correct or improve the Authorised Version. This, indeed, it may occasionally enable him to do; but it is necessary that the reader should understand that this is not the true purpose of the book; it is simply *to enable him to ascertain the true import of the words of the authorised version, when the English language did not enable the translators sufficiently to define or express it.*

The following is the plan of the work, which consists of two parts,—the CONCORDANCE and the GLOSSARY. By means of the Concordance the student finds the original Greek of the English words; by means of the Glossary he ascertains its meaning, and obtains a key to the passages in which it occurs:—

1. Under every English heading the passages are classified according to the Greek words, of which the English heading is a translation; each Greek word being placed at the head of the passages in which it occurs.

2. The Greek words are given throughout the book, each only in one form, whatever be the variety of inflexions which it assumes in the passages underneath. If it be a noun, it appears as a nominative singular; if it be a verb, it is in the first person singular indicative. The Greek inflexions are altogether ignored.

3. As it frequently requires two English words to translate one Greek one, the passages in which it occurs do not always appear under both headings; it is therefore sometimes necessary to turn to both headings before finding it. For example, the Greek word **merimnaō** is sometimes translated *"to take thought,"* and in this case the passages are found only under the heading "THOUGHT."

4. When the Greek word is translated by more than one English word, whether it be on account of the meaning or the inflection, all the English words which are covered by the Greek are printed in italic, to show that the one Greek word represents them all. For example, under the heading ABIDE, **menō**, the following passage occurs :—

John xii. 46—*Should* not *abide* in darkness.

This indicates that the words "*should abide*" are a translation of the word as it is inflected in this passage.

5. In most instances the italic words represent the inflection of the Greek, and show the cases and numbers of the nouns, and the voices, moods, tenses, numbers, persons, and participles of the verbs. All these are represented by a variety of forms of the Greek word: in the English they are represented by auxiliary words or by a circumlocution, all of which is printed in italic. To those who do not understand Greek, some of these italics may seem strange; for example, under ARISE, **anistēmi,** we find such quotations as—

Luke i. 39—Mary *arose* in those days *and* went,

so that "*arose, and,*" seems the translation of **anistēmi;** and so it is, because the passage, if translated literally, would run thus, "Mary, *having arisen* in those days, went." Were the object of this work either to communicate a knowledge of the Greek, or to supersede it, all this should be explained; but, as has already been stated, it is not so. Its purpose is sufficiently important without attempting or professing to do more; and the author, so far from disparaging the importance of a thorough acquaintance with Greek for the study of the Greek Testament, will be greatly disappointed if it does not induce many to attempt both.

6. The Greek words are printed in English letters according to the plan shown in page viii., and in the Glossary the arrangement is according to the English, not the Greek alphabet.

7. The Greek word, when a compound, is either divided by a hyphen, or there is added within brackets one or both of its constituents. The brackets also contain its derivation when it is not compound.

8. The explanations are in the order of their importance, the most characteristic being placed

first. The words within parentheses are not true equivalents of the Greek word, but indicate headings of the Concordance, under which also it may be found.

9. The words printed in italics are meanings which do not occur in the New Testament, and on that account are not to be found in the Concordance.

There are two ways in which this Concordance may be used, both of them most instructive. The first is to study a particular English word as it occurs in the various passages collected together under the various Greek originals, of which it is a translation. The other is to study a particular passage of Scripture, by examining the different words of which it is composed.

The First Method.

In adopting the first of these methods, which is perhaps the best, the student having turned up in its place the English word which is to be the subject of his study, will find under it the different Greek words of which it is a translation. These he turns up one by one, examining their composition, and observing the various shades of meaning by which they differ one from another. Each Greek word has probably several meanings attached to it; but as the first in order is that which is most characteristic, let him take it and substitute it for the authorised translation, observing the peculiar meaning which it is thus made to assume. If, however, the first meaning be also that of the authorised version, let him take the next in order, or even go over them all for the same purpose. It will be impossible to go over the passages in this way without his being frequently surprised and delighted with the new light that is thus thrown upon them; contrasts, coincidences, and unexpected associations, will present themselves, which not only were not observed before, but which were not likely to be observed except by such a method of study.

The Second Method.

The second method is the one which will probably be most frequently adopted: to illustrate it, therefore, a few examples may be given. Let us suppose that the passage to be investigated is Matt. vi. 25—"Take no thought for your life"; the student turns up the Concordance under the heading THOUGHT, and under the Greek **merimnaō**, page 282, he finds the passage,—

Matt. vi. 25—*Take* no *thought* for your life.

The words in italic show that **merimnaō** is translated by the two words "*take thought*," which appear in the sentence as the second person plural of the imperative. It may be presumed that it is so in Greek also; but, as has been already explained, no account is taken of this, or of any other grammatical point, because we go on the supposition that the Authorised Version is correct. What is wanted is first to know what is meant by "*taking thought*." Turning to the word **merimnaō** in the Glossary, he finds in page 18 as follows:—

> **merimnaō,** to be *anxiously* careful,
>   to take thought, to care.

He sees that the passage does not mean, "Pay no attention to your life," as our translation might suggest, but "*Do not be anxiously careful* for your life." The word "*anxiously*" being in italic, shows that this word is not used in the New Testament; but it is inserted to show the essential meaning of the Greek verb, as ascertained by careful research, and vouched by the best authorities.

It is important to notice, however, that Scripture is its own best interpreter; and therefore, although the classical use of any Greek word is that which generally should determine its meaning, its scriptural use is more authoritative for Scripture interpretation. The student may therefore proceed to examine the other passages in which it occurs, to verify or modify, as the result may be, the interpretation given in the Glossary. In the present instance, he will find other passages under the headings CARE and CAREFUL, which confirm the interpretation: for example,—

Luke x. 41—Thou *art careful* and troubled.
Phil. iv. 6—*Be careful* for nothing, &c.

3. For the same purpose, he may next look at the other words of the same family, which are sometimes very numerous and suggestive. Here, however, there is but one, viz.,—

> **merimna [merizō]**, *distracting thought,*
>   *anxiety,* care.

By reference to the Bible use of this word, under the heading CARE, he will have additional light cast on the meaning of the cognate verb.

Matt. xiii. 22—And the *care* of this world.
Luke viii. 14—Are choked with *cares.*
2 Cor. xi. 28—The *care* of all the churches.
1 Peter v. 7—Casting all your *care* upon.

In this manner we have ascertained the true import of "taking thought;" and now we turn to the word "life" for the same purpose. Under this heading, p. 161, we find several Greek words so translated, "**zŏē**," "**psuchē**," and "**bios;**" but on examining the passages under each, we find a very marked difference of meaning. Under **zŏē** we find such passages as these, "I am the bread of *life*," "As the Father hath *life* in himself, so hath

he given to the Son to have *life* in himself." Under **"psuchē"** we have such passages as these : "He gave his *life* a ransom for many," "Neither count I my *life* dear unto me." And under **"bios"** such passages as these : "A quiet and peaceable *life*," "The time past of our *lives*," &c.

Under which of these heads, then, do we find the present passage? It is under **psuchē.** "Take no thought for your **psuchē."** We therefore look up in the Glossary to know what the word **"psuchē"** means.

psuchē [psuchō] *animal life*, life, the soul, the mind ; the *animal nature*, the heart. (*See* heartily, us, you).

Here is a rich field for study. Under the headings, "SOUL," "MIND," "HEART," passages are found in which **"psuchē"** is translated by these words ; and in most cases their scope and connection will go far to cast great light upon the precise sense in which the word is used. If the student be inclined to extend his research, under the words **"psuchō"** and **"psuchikos"** still further materials for investigation will be found.

In the case selected, the passage will not be found cited under any of the other words, *no, for, your;* and the reason may be explained for the reader's guidance in all such cases. Under the heading "No" it is stated that the word is *generally represented by* **"ou"** *or* **"mē;"** and only the exceptions are cited. This passage, therefore, as it is not cited, must have **ou** or **mē,** both of which, as stated in the Glossary, are simple negatives ; but their occurrence is too frequent to allow the citation of the passages in which they appear.

Under the heading "FOR," also, this passage does not occur ; it is included, therefore, among those referred to at the end by "(*See words in connection*)," which means that there is no separate Greek word for it, but that the composition or inflection of some of the other words is such as to require its presence.

This sentence has been taken very much at random, as a short example of the method of investigation ; it would have been easy to select others much more interesting, and exhibiting more luminous and unexpected results, but each of them would require an exhibition either too large for admission here, or too superficial to be of use.

In conclusion, it may be remarked that light may be cast on some of the expressions in the Authorised Version, which in the intervening period have suffered a change of meaning : such as "atonement," "letteth," "prevent," "conversation," "sometimes," &c.

Turning to "ATONEMENT" in the Concordance, he finds the word in Rom. v. 11, to be **katallagē,** which the Glossary informs him has "reconciliation," or "at-one-ment" for its essential meaning. And turning to the cognate verb, **katallassō,** he finds what at once satisfies him that this was the sense in which the translators used the word, in the fact that this verb has "reconcile" for its essential meaning, and is so rendered by them more than once in the immediate context.

Again, in like manner, on turning to the word "LET," in the Concordance, he finds the Greek verb used to be **katechō,** which has for its proper meaning, "to hold down ;" and among its meanings he finds the similar one "to withhold ;" by searching under which, in the Concordance, he discovers that the same word which is rendered "let" in this text, is rendered "withhold" in the verse which immediately precedes. He thus sees that the translators used the word "let," not in the sense of "permit," but of "withhold," or "not permit."

In a similar way, he very easily discovers that "prevent," in 1 Thess. iv. 15, was used as an equivalent to "anticipate," or "get before," and not to "hinder ;" that "conversation" always means "manner of life or behaviour," and not "speech ;" that "sometimes" does not mean "occasionally," as in contrast with "always," but "once," or "at a former time," in contrast with "the present time ;" and that "of," in John xvi. 13, as in many other texts, means, "from ;" "He (the Holy Spirit) shall not speak of [*i.e.*, from] himself ; but," &c. In this way he will be able, in almost every instance, to clear away the obscurity that attaches to the Authorised Version in a number of passages, and to ascertain decisively the true meaning.

CONTENTS.

THE ALPHABET.

The Greek Alphabet is represented by the common Roman letters, as follows :—

A, a, = a.	H, η, = $\bar{\text{e}}$.	N, ν, = n.	T, τ, = t.
B, β, = b.	Θ, θ, = th.	Ξ, ξ, = x.	Υ, υ, = u.
Γ, γ, = g.	I, ι, = i.	O, o, = o.	Φ, ϕ, = ph.
Δ, δ, = d.	K, κ, = k.	Π, π, = p.	X, χ, = ch.
E, ϵ, = e.	Λ, λ, = l.	P, ρ, = r.	Ψ, ψ, = ps.
Z, ζ, = z.	M, μ, = m.	Σ, σ, ς, = s.	Ω, ω, = $\bar{\text{o}}$.

The aspirate of the vowels and diphthongs is represented by **h**.

These letters have nearly the same power as in English, with the following exceptions :—**g** is always hard, as in " go," **ch** is always hard, as in "chorus " or " loch," and **th** is always hard, as in " thin," never soft, as in " thus."

A small italic *n* is inserted before **g** when it is followed by another **g**, or by **k**, or **x**, or **ch** ; thus **aggelos**, *an angel*, is pronounced a*n*ggelos ; **agkura**, *an anchor*, is pronounced a*n*gkura, and so on, in accordance with a rule of Greek euphony.

The proper diphthongs are **ai, au, ei, eu, oi, ou.** When **ae, ea,** or **oo** occur, they are not diphthongs, but are pronounced as in two syllables.

When Greek words are Anglicised, it is usual to change the κ (kappa) into **c**, as **kritikos**, *critical*, and the υ (upsilon) into **y**, as in **hupokritēs**, *a hypocrite*, **sunagogē**, *a synagogue*, &c. In diphthongs the υ is changed into **u**, as in **autonomia**, *autonomy*, though sometimes it is made a **v**, as in **euanggelistos**, *an evangelist*. In the present work these transformations would have been inexpedient.

NOTE.

The insertion of " *bis*," " *ter*," &c., after a quotation, indicates that the word referred to occurs " *twice*," " *thrice*," &c., in the same verse.

AN
ENGLISH-GREEK CONCORDANCE
OF
THE NEW TESTAMENT
WITH
GREEK CLASSIFICATIONS

²Ti. 4.20. Erastus a-o at Corinth.
Heb. 7.3. a-*eth* a priest continually,
¹Pet.1.23. which liveth and a-*eth* for ever.
¹Jo. 2. 6. He that saith he a-*eth* in him
  10. a-*eth* n the light, and
  14. the word of God a-*eth* in you,
  17. doeth the will of God, a-*eth*
  24. *Let* that therefore a. in you,
  27. have received of him, a-*eth* in
    taught you, ye shall a. in
  28. now, little children, a. in
 3. 6. Whoso a-*eth* in him sinneth
  14. loveth not his brother a-*eth* in
  15. murd. hath eternal life a-*ing*
  24. we know that he a-*eth* in us.
2John 9. and a-*eth* not in the doctrine,
  He that a-*eth* in the doctrine,
  diatribō.
Act.12.19. to Cesarea, and a-*o* they
 14. 3. Long time therefore a-*o* they
  28. there they a-*o* long time with
 16.12. in that city a-*o* certain days
 20. 6. where we a-*o* seven days.
  epimenō.
Act.15.34. it pleased Silas *to* a. there,
Ro. 11.23. if they a. not *in* unbelief,
Gal. 1.18. and a-*o* with him fifteen days;
Phi. 1.24. to a. *in* the flesh is more
  paramenō.
¹Co. 16.6. it may be that I *will* a., yea
  katamenō.
Act. 1.13. wherein a-*o* both Peter and
  hupomenō.
Act 17.14. S. and Timotheus a-*o* there,
  aulizomai.
Lu.21.37. went out, and a-*o* in the mo.
  histēmi
Jo. 8.44. and a-*o* not in the truth,
  poieō.
Act.20.3. and there a-*o* three months,
  anastrephō.
Mat.17.22. *while* they a-*o* in Galilee,
  prosmenō.
¹Ti. 1. 3. thee *to* a. *still* at Ephesus.
  agrauleō.
Lu. 2. 8. shepherds a-*ing in the field,*

ABILITY.
  dunamis.
Mat.25.15. according to his several a.
  ischus.
¹Pet.4.11. as of the a. which God giveth,
  euporeomai.
Act.11.29. every man accord. to his a.
  (*as he was prosperous.*)

ABLE.
  dunamai.
Mat. 3.9. God *is* a. of these stones to raise
  9.28. Believe ye that I *am* a. to do
 10.28. but *are* not a. to kill the soul,
  which is a. to destroy both so.
 19.12. He *that is* a. to receive it
 20.22. *Are* ye a. to drink of the cup
  They say unto him, we *are* a.
 22.46. no man *was* a. to answer him
 26.61. I *am* a. to destroy the temple,
Mar.4.33. as they *were* a. to bear it.
Lu. 1.20. dumb, and not a. to speak
 3. 8. God *is* a. of these stones to raise
 12.26. If ye then *be* not a. to do
 21.15. advy. shall not *be* a. to gainsay
Jo. 10.29. no man *is* a. to pluck them
Act.20.32. word of his grace, *which is* a.
Ro. 8.39. creature *shall be* a. to separate
 15.14. a. also to admonish one anoth.
¹Co. 3. 2. ye *were* not a. to bear it.
  neither yet now *are* ye a.
 6. 5. not one that *shall be* a. to jud.
 10.13. tempted above that ye *are* a.
  that ye may *be* a. to bear it.
²Co. 1. 4. may be a. to comfort them

Eph.3.20. unto him *that is* a. to do
 6.11. ye may be a. to stand against
  13. *may be* a. to withstand in the
  16. ye *shall be* a. to quench all
Phil.3.21. he *is* a. even to subdue all
²Ti. 3. 7. never a. to come to the knowl.
  15. *which are* a. to make thee wise
Heb.2.18. he *is* a. to succour them that
 5. 7. him *that was* a. to save him,
 7.25. Wherefore he *is* a. also to save
Ja. 1.21. word *which is* a. to save you
 4.12. lawgiver *who is* a. to save
Jude 24. unto him *that is* a. to keep
Rev.5. 3. *was* a. to open the book,
 6.17. who *shall be* a. to stand
 13. 4. who *is* a. to make war with
 15. 8. no man *was* a. to enter
  ischuō.
Lu.13.24. enter in, and *shall* not *be* a.
 14.29. and *is* not a. to finish it, 30.
Jo. 21. 6. now they *were* not a. to draw
Act. 6.10. not a. to resist the wisdom
 15.10. fathers nor we *were* a. to bear
  exischuō.
Eph.3.18. *may be* a. to comprehend, with
  echō.
²Pet.1.15. ye may *be* a. after my decease
  hikanoō.
²Co. 3.6. hath also *made* us a. ministers
  (*qualified* us [to be] ministers)
  dunatos.
Act.25.5. which among you are a. go
Ro. 4.21. he was a. also to perform
 11.23. God is a. to graff them in
 14. 4. God is a. to make him stand
²Co. 9. 8. God is a. to make all grace
²Ti. 1.12. persuaded that he is a. to
Tit. 1. 9. may be a. by sound doctrine
Heb.11.19. God was a. to raise him up
Ja. 3. 2. a. also to bridle the whole
  hikanos.
²Ti. 2. 2. be a. to teach others also

ABOARD.
  epibainō.
Act. 21.2. we went a., and set forth

ABODE [*verb*], see *Abide.*

ABODE [*noun.*]
  monē.
Jo. 14.23. and make our a. with him.

ABOLISH,   -ed.
  katargeō.
²Co.3.13. to the end of that *which is* a-ed
Eph.2.15. *Having* a-ed in his flesh
²Ti.1.10. Christ, *who hath* a-ed death,

ABOMINABLE.
  bdeluktos.
Tit. 1.16. being a. and disobedient
  bdelussomai.
Rev.21.8. unbelieving and the a.
  athemitos.
¹Pet. 4.3. banquetings and a. idolatries

ABOMINATION,   -s.
  bdelugma.
Mat.24.15. a. of desolation, Mar.13.14.
Lu.16.15. is a. in the sight of God,
Rev.17.4. full of a-s and filthiness of
  5. mother of harlots and a-s of
 21.27. whatsoever worketh a., or

ABOUND,   -ed,-eth,-ing.
  perisseuō.
Ro. 3. 7. hath more a-ed through my lie;
 5.15. hath a-ed unto many,
 15.13. that ye may a. in hope,
¹Co.15.58. always a-*ing* in the work
²Co. 1. 5. sufferings of Christ a. in us

²Co. 1. 5. consolation also a-*eth* by Chr.
 8. 2. a-ed unto the riches of their
  7. as ye a. in every thing, in faith
  that ye a. in this grace also,
 9. 8. *make* all grace a. toward you,
  may a. to every good work,
Eph.1. 8. Wherein he *hath* a-ed toward
Phi. 1. 9. that your love *may* a. yet more
 4.12. and I know how to a.
  both *to* a. and to suffer need.
  18. I have all, and a. I am full,
Col. 2. 7. a-*ing* therein with thanksgiv.
¹Th. 3.12. make you to increase and a.
 4. 1. so ye *would* a. more and more
  pleonazō.
Ro. 5.20. that the offence *might* a.
  But where sin a-ed, grace
 6. 1. con. in sin that grace *may* a.
Phil.4.17. *that may* a. to your account:
²Th. 1. 3. charity towa. each other a-*eth*
²Pet.1. 8. these things be in you and a.
  plēthunomai.
Mat.24.12. because iniquity *shall* a.
  huperperisseuō.
Ro. 5.20. grace *did much more* a.

ABOUT [*preposition.*]
  peri, [*accu.*]
Mat.3. 4. leathern girdle a. his loins;
 8.18. great multitudes a. him,
 20. 3. went out a. the third hour.
  5. a. the sixth and ninth hour.
  6. And a. the eleventh hour.
  9. hired a. the eleventh hour.
 27.46. And a. the ninth hour, Jesus
Mar.1. 6. girdle of a skin a. his loins;
 3. 8. and they a. Tyre and Sidon,
  32. And the multitude sat a. him,
  34. on them which sat a. him,
 4.10. they that were a. him, with
 6.48. and a. the fourth watch of the
 9.14. a great multitude a. them
  42. were hanged a. his neck, and
Lu.10.40. was cumbered a. much ser.
  41. and troubled a. many things;
 13. 8. till I shall dig a. it, and dung
 17. 2. hanged a. his neck, and he
 22.49. When they which were a. him
Act.10.9. to pray a. the sixth hour.
 22.6. a. noon, suddenly there shone
  a great light round a. me
¹ Ti.6. 4. but doting a. questions, and
Jude 7. and the cities a. them, in like
  peri, [*gen.*]
Jo. 3.25. and the Jews a. purifying.
Act.15.2. apostles and elders a. this
 19.23. no small stir a. that way.
 25.15. a. whom when I was at Jeru.
  24. a. whom all the multitude
Jude 9. disputed a. the body of Moses.
  kata, [*accu.*]
Act.2.10. in the parts of Lybia a. Cyrene,
 12. 1. Now a. that time, Herod the
 27.27. Adria, a. midnight the shipm.
  pros, [*dat.*]
Rev.1.13. girt a. the paps with a golden
  pros, [*accu.*]
Mar. 2.2. not so much as a. the door
  epi, [*gen.*]
Mat.1.11. a. *the time* they were carried
  (*time of* their being carried.)
Mar.14.51. a linen cloth cast a. his
Jo. 20.7. napkin that *was* a. his head
  epi, [*dat.*]
Act.11.19. persecution that arose a. Step.
  epi, [*accu.*]
Mat.18.6. stone were hanged a. his neck
  en.
Lu. 2.49. I must be a. my father's bus.
(See *Round*, and also those *verbs of
which* "about" *forms a part.*)

2

kuklothen.
Rev. 4.3. a rainbow *round* a. the throne
4.4. and *round* a. the throne
8. six wings a. him
5.11. angels *round* a. the throne

ABOUT, [*adverb.*]
hōs.
Mar.5.13. they were a. two thousand
8. 9. eaten were a. four thousand
Lu. 2.37. a widow of a. fourscore and
8.42. a. twelve years of age
Jo. 1.39. for it was a. the tenth hour
6.19. rowed a. five and twenty or
11.18. a. fifteen furlongs off
Act. 1.15 a. an hundred and twenty
5. 7. a. the space of three hours aft.
13.18. And a. the time of forty years
20. a. the space of four hundred
19.34. a. the space of two hours cried
Rev.8. 1. a. the space of half an hour
16.21. every stone a. the weight of
Mat.14.21.were a. five thousand men
Mar.6.44.were a. five thousand men
Lu. 1.56. abode with her a.three months
3.23. began to be a. thirty years of
9.14. were a. five thousand men
28. a. an eight days after these
22.41. from them a. a stone's cast
22.59. a. the space of one hour after
23.44. And it was a. the sixth hour
Jo. 4. 6. it was a. the sixth hour
6.10. in number a. five thousand
19.14. and a. the sixth hour
39. a. an hundred pound weight
Act. 2.41. unto them a. three thousand
4. 4. of the men was a. five thous.
5.36. men, a. four hundred
10. 3. a. the ninth hour of the
19. 7. all the men were a. twelve

pou.
Ro. 4.19. when he was a. an hundred

zēteō.
Act.27.30.the shipmen *were* a. to flee

mellō.
Act.3. 3. seeing Peter and John a. to go
18.14. when Paul *was* now a. to open
20. 3. *as* he *was* a. to sail into
Heb. 8.5. *when* he *was* a. to make the
Rev.10.4. voices, I *was* a. to write
(See *verbs of which it forms a part.*)

ABOVE, [*preposition.*]
huper, [*accu.*]
Mat.10.24.a. his master, nor the servant
a. his lord; Lu.6.40
Act.26.13.a. the brightness of the sun
1Co. 4.6. not to think of men a. that
10.13. be tempted a. that ye are
2Co. 1.8. out of measure, a. strength
12.6. a. that which he seeth me to
Gal. 1.14. a. many my equals in mine
Phil. 2.9. name which is a. every name
Phile. 16. as a servant, but a. a serv.

epanō.
Jo. 3.31. cometh from above is a. all
cometh from heaven is a. all
1Co. 15.6. seen of a. five hundred breth.

para, [*accu.*]
Lu. 13.2. sinners a. all the Galileans
4. were sinners a. all men that
Ro. 14.5. esteemeth one day a. another
Heb. 1.9. oil of gladness a. thy fellows.

epi, [*dat.*]
Lu. 3.20. added yet this a. all that he
Eph.6.16. a. all, taking the shield of fa.
Col. 3.14. a. all these things put on char.

epi, [*accu.*]
1Th. 2.4. a. all that is called God

epi, [*gen.*];
Eph. 4.6. who is a. all and through

pro.
2Co. 12.2. a. fourteen years *ago*
Jas. 5.12. but a. all things, my brethren
1Pet. 4.8. a. all things have fervent cha.

peri, [*gen.*]
3Jo. 2. I wish a. all things that thou

pleiōn.
Act.2.22. the man was a. forty years

ABOVE, [*adverb.*]
anō.
Jo. 8.23. from beneath ; I am from a.
Act.2.19. will shew wonders in heavn. a.
Gal. 4.26. Jerusalem which is a. is free
Col. 3.1. seek those things which are a.
2. Set your affection on things a.

anōteron.
Heb.10.8. a., when he said sacrifice, and

anōthen.
Jo. 3.31. He that cometh *from* a. is
19.11. it were given thee *from* a.
Jas. 1.17. every perfect gift is *from* a.
3.15. descendeth not *from* a. but
17. the wisdom that is *from* a. is
(See *Measure, Far, Abundantly.*)

ABROAD.
phaneros.
Mar. 4.22. but that it should come a.
6.14. for his name was spread a.
Lu. 8.17. be known and come a.
(See *Blaze, Come, Disperse, Go,
Noise, Scatter, Shed, Spread.*)

ABSENCE.
apousia.
Phi.2.12. now much more in my a.

ater.
Lu. 22.6. *in the* a. *of* the multitude

ABSENT.
apeimi.
1Co. 5.3.For I verily, as a. in body, but
2Co. 10.1. *being* a. am bold toward you
11. by letters *when* we *are* a., such
13.2. *being* a. now I write to them
15. I write these things *being* a.
Phil.1.27. come and see you, else be a.
Col. 2.5. though I *be* a. in the flesh

ekdēmeō.
2Co. 5.6. we are a. from the Lord
8. rather to *be* a. from the body
9. that whether present or a.

ABSTAIN.
apechomai. (*Mid.*)
Act. 15.20.that they a. from pollutions
29. That ye a. from meats offered
1Th. 4. 3. that ye should a. from forni.
5,22. a. from all appearance of evil
1Ti. 4. 3. commanding *to* a. from meats
1Pet.2.11. a. from fleshly lusts, which

ABSTINENCE.
asitia.
Act. 27.21.After long a. Paul stood

ABUNDANCE.
perisseia.
Ro. 5.17. which receive a. of grace
2Co. 8. 2. the a. of their joy

perisseuma.
Mat.12.34. out of the a. of the heart
Lu. 6.45. for of the a. of the heart
2Co. 8.14. your a. may be a supply
that their a. also may be

perisseuō, (*Pas.*)
Mat.13.12. and he shall *have* more a.
25.29. and he shall *have* a.

Mar.12.44.did cast in of their a.
(of that which *abounded* to them.
Lu.12.15. consisteth not in the a. of the
(*abounding* of the things.,
21. 4. these have of their a.

huperbolē.
2Co. 12.7. the a. of the revelations

hadrotēs.
2Co.8.20. blame us in this a.

dunamis.
Rev.18.3. the a. of her delicacies

ABUNDANT.
perissoteros.
1Co.12.23.we bestow *more* a. honour
have *more* a. comeliness
24. given *more* a. honour

perissoterōs.
2Co. 7.15. affection is *more* a. toward
11.23. in labours *more* a.

polus.
1Pet.1.3. according to his a. mercy

perisseuō. (*Part.*)
2Co. 9.12. *is* a. also by many thanksgiv.
Phil.1.26. rejoicing may *be more* a. in

pleonazō. (*Part.*)
2Co. 4.15. that the a. grace might

huperpleonazō.
1Ti. 1.14. grace of our L. *was exceed.* a.

ABUNDANTLY.
plousiōs.
Tit. 3. 6. which he shed on us a.
2Pet.1.11. be ministered unto you a.

perissoterōs.
2Co.1.12. and *more* a. to you-ward
2. 4. I have *more* a. unto you

perissoteros.
1Co. 15.10.I laboured *more* a. than they
Heb.6.17. willing *more* a. to shew

perissos.
Jo. 10.10. might have it *more* a.

huper ek perissos.
Eph.3.20. do *exceeding* a. above all

eis perisseia.
2Co.10.15.according to our rule a.

ABUSE,   -ing.
katachraomai. (*Mid.*)
1Co. 7.31. use this world as not a-*ing* it
9.18. that I a. not my power in

ABUSER.
arsenokoitēs.
1Co. 6. 9. a-*s of themselves with mankind*

ACCEPT,   -ed, -est, -eth, -ing.
lambanō.
Lu.20.21. neither a-*est* thou the person
Gal. 2. 6. God a-*eth* no man's person.

dechomai. (*Mid.*)
2Co. 8.17.indeed he a-*ed* the exhortation
11. 4. gospel which ye have not a-*ed*

prosdechomai. (*Mid.*)
Heb.11.35.not a-*ing* deliverance that

apodechomai. (*Mid.*)
Act. 24.3.We a. it always and in all

euarestos.
2Co. 5. 9. we may be a-*ed* of him.
(*well-pleasing* to him.)

dektos.
Lu. 4.24. No prophet is a-*ed* in his own
Act.10.35.worketh righteousness is a-*ed*
2Co. 6.2. I have heard thee in a time a-*ed*

euprosdektos.
Ro.15.31. may be a-*ed* of the saints
(*well received* by.)
2Co. 6. 2. behold now is the a-*ed* time
8.12. is a-*ed* according to that a man

charitoō.
Eph. 1.6. wherein he hath made us a-*ed*
(*exercised grace toward* us.)

3

ACCEPTABLE.
euarestos.
Ro. 12.1. living sacrifice, holy, **a.** unto
   2. what is that good, and **a.**, and
14.18. **a.** to God, approved of
Eph.5.10. what is **a.** unto the Lord.
dektos.
Lu. 4.19. preach the **a.** year of the Lord
Phil.4.18. of a sweet smell, a sacrifice **a.**
apodektos.
1Tim.2.3. for this is good and **a.** in the
   5.4. good and **a.** before God
euprosdektos.
Ro. 15.16. offer. up of the G. might be **a.**
charis.
1Pet.2.20. patiently, this is **a.** with God

ACCEPTABLY.
euarestōs.
Heb.12.28. we may serve God **a.**

ACCEPTATION.
apodochē.
Tim.1.15.worthy of all **a.**, that Christ
   4.9. saying, and worthy of all **a.**

ACCESS.
prosagōgē.
Ro. 5.2. we have **a.** by faith into this
Eph.2.18. both have **a.** by one Spirit
   3.12. **a.** with confidence by the faith

ACCOMPANY,   -ied.
sunepomai.
Act.20.4. there a-ed him into Asia
sunerchomai.
Act.10.23.breth. from Joppa a-ed him
propempō.
Act.20.38.they a-ed him unto the ship.
echō.
Heb. 6.9. things that **a.** salvation
      (are connected with.)
erchomai sun.
Act.11.12.six brethren a-ed me
      (came with me.)

ACCOMPLISH,   -ed, -ing.
teleō.
Lu.12.50. straitened till it be a-ed
18.31. the Son of man shall be a-ed
22.37. must yet be a-ed in me
Jo. 19.28. that all things were now a-ed
plēthō.
Lu. 1.23. days of his ministra. were a-ed
   2. 6 days were a-ed that she should
21. eight days were a-ed for the cir.
22. days of her purifica. were a-ed.
epiteleō.
Heb. 9.6. a-ing the service of God
1 Pet. 5.9. are a-ed in your brethren
plēroō.
Lu. 9.31. which he should **a.** at Jerusa.
exartizō.
Act.21.5. when we had a-ed those days

ACCOMPLISHMENT.
ekplērōsis.
Act.21.26. the **a.** of the days

ACCORD.
automatos.
Act.12.10. opened to them of his own **a.**
homothumadon.
Act. 1.14. continued with one **a.** in
   2. 1. all with one **a.** in one place
46. daily with one **a.** in the tem.
4.24. their voice to God with one **a.**
5.12. they were all with one **a.**
7.57. and ran upon him with one **a.**
8. 6. people with one **a.** gave heed
12.20. they came with one **a.** to him
15.25. being assembled with one **a.**
4

Act.18.12.made insurrection with one **a.**
19.29. rushed with one **a.** into the
authairetos.
2Co. 8.17. of his own **a.** he went unto

ACCORDING,
kata, [accu.]
Mat.2.16. **a.** to the time which
9.29. **a.** to your faith be it unto you
16.27. reward every man **a.** to his
25.15. to every man **a.** to his several
Mar.7. 5. thy disciples **a.** to the tradit.
Lu. 1. 9. **a.** to custom of priest's office
38. be it unto me **a.** to thy word
2.22. **a.** to the law of Moses
24. **a.** to that which is said
29. in peace **a.** to thy word.
39. **a.** to the law of the Lord
23.56. **a.** to the commandment
Jo. 7.24. Judge not **a.** to the appearance
18.31. judge him **a.** to your law
Act. 2.30. **a.** to the flesh, he would raise
7.44. make it **a.** to the fashion
13.23. **a.** to his promise raised unto
22. 3. taught **a.** to the perfect
12. a devout man **a.** to the law
24. 6. would have judged **a.** to our
Ro. 1. 3. seed of David **a.** to the flesh
4. **a.** to the spirit of holiness
2. 2. judgment of God is **a.** to truth
6. every man **a.** to his deeds
16. Jesus Christ **a.** to my gospel
4.18. **a.** to that which was
8.27. **a.** to the will of God
28. the called **a.** to his purpose
9. 3. my kinsmen **a.** to the flesh
11. **a.** to election might
10. 2. but not **a.** to knowledge
11. 5. **a.** to the election of
12. 6. differing **a.** to the grace
   a. to the proportion of
15. 5. like minded **a.** to Christ Jesus
16.25. **a.** to my gospel ; 2Tim.2.8.
   a. to the revelation
26. **a.** to the commandment
1Co. 3. 8. **a.** to his own labour
10. **a.** to the grace of God
15. 3. died for our sins **a.** to the
4. third day **a.** to the scriptures
2Co. 1.17. do I purpose **a.** to the flesh
4.13. **a.** as it is written, I believed
10. 2. as if we walked **a.** to the flesh
13. but **a.** to the measure
15. **a.** to our rule abundantly
11.15. end shall be **a.** to their works
13.10. **a.** to the power which
Gal. 1. 4. **a.** to the will of God
3.29. heirs **a.** to the promise
Eph.1. 5. **a.** to the good pleasure
7. **a.** to the riches of his grace
9. **a.** to his good pleasure
11. **a.** to the purpose of him
19. **a.** to the working of his
2. 2. **a.** to the course of this
   a. to the prince of the
3. 7. **a.** to the gift of the grace of
11. **a.** to the eternal purpose
16. **a.** to the riches of his glory
20. **a.** to the power that
4. 7. grace **a.** to the measure
16. **a.** to the effectual working
22. **a.** to the deceitful lusts
6. 5. **a.** to the flesh ; Col.3.22.
Phi. 3.21. **a.** to the working whereby
4.19. **a.** to his riches in glory
Col. 1.11. **a.** to his glorious power
25. **a.** to the dispensation
29. striving **a.** to his working
2Th. 1.12. **a.** to the grace of our God
1Ti. 1.11. **a.** to the glorious gospel
18. **a.** to the prophecies
1Ti. 6. 3. which is **a.** to godliness

2Ti. 1. 1. **a.** to the promise of
8. **a.** to the power of God
9. not **a.** to our works
   but **a.** to his own purpose
4.14. reward him **a.** to his works
Tit. 1. 1. **a.** to the faith of God's
3. **a.** to the commandment
3. 5. but **a.** to his mercy
7. **a.** to the hope of eternal life
Heb.2. 4. **a.** to his own will
7. 5. the people **a.** to the law; 9.19.
8. 4. gifts **a.** to the law
5. **a.** to the pattern shewed to
9. Not **a.** to the covenant
Jas. 2. 8. royal law **a.** to the scripture
1Pet.1. 2. Elect **a.** to the foreknowledge
3. **a.** to his abundant mercy
17. judgeth **a.** to every man's
3. 7. **a.** to knowledge, giving
4. 6. judged **a.** to men in the flesh
   but live **a.** to God in the spirit
19. that suffer **a.** to the will
2Pet.3.13. we, **a.** to his promise
15. Paul also **a.** to the wisdom
1Jo. 5.14. any thing **a.** to his will
Rev.2.23. **a.** to your works
18. 6. double **a.** to her works
20.12,13. **a.** to their works
kathōs.
Act.11.29. every man **a.** to his ability
Ro. 11.8. **a.** as it is written ; 1Co.1.31.
2Co. 9. 7. **a.** as he purposeth in his heart
Eph.1. 4. **a.** as he hath chosen us in
hōs.
Ro. 12.3. **a.** as God hath dealt to every
2Pet. 1. 3. **a.** as his divine power
Rev.22.12.**a.** as his work shall be
pros.
Lu.12.47. neither did **a.** to his will
Gal. 2.14. **a.** to the truth of the gospel
kathoti.
Act. 4.35. unto every man **a.** as he had
katho.
2Co.8.12. accepted **a.** to that a man hath
   not **a.** to that he hath not
   (See Fashion.)

ACCOUNT, [noun.]
logos.
Mat.12.36. they shall give **a.** thereof
18.23. take **a.** of his servants
Lu. 16. 2. give an **a.** of thy stewardship
Act. 19.40. give an **a.** of this concourse
Ro. 14.12. every one of us shall give **a.**
Phi. 4.17. may abound to your **a.**
Heb.13.17.as they that must give **a.**
1Pet. 4. 5. Who shall give **a.** to him
ellogeō.
Phile. 18. aught, put that on mine **a.**

ACCOUNT, [verb]   -ed, -ing.
logizomai.
Ro. 8.36. we are a-ed as sheep for
1Co. 4. 1. Let a man so **a.** of us
Gal.3. 6. it was a-ed to him for
Heb.11.19.a-ing that God was able to
kataxioomai.
Lu.20.35. shall be a-ed worthy to obtain
21.36. may be a-ed worthy to escape
dokeō.
Mar.10.42.they which are a-ed to rule
Lu.22.24. them which should be a-ed
hēgeomai.
2Pet.3.15. and a- that the long-suffer.

ACCURSED.
anathema.
Ro. 9. 3. that myself were **a.** from
1Co. 12.3. calleth Jesus **a.** and that no
Gal.1. 8. preached to you let him be **a.**
9. have received, let him be **a.**

ACCUSATION.
katēgoria.
Lu. 6. 7. might find an **a.** against him
Jo. 18.29. What **a.** bring ye against this
¹Ti. 5.19. an elder, receive not an **a.**
aitia.
Mat.27.37.over his head his **a.** written
Mar.15.26.his **a.** was written over
Act.25.18.they brought none **a.** of
krisis.
²Pet.2.11. bring not railing **a.** against
Jude ɤ 9. him a railing **a.**, but said
sukophanteō.
Lu. 19.8. *have taken* anything *by false* **a.**

ACCUSE, -ed, -eth, -ing.
katēgoreō.
Mat.12.10. that they *might* **a.** him
27.12. when he *was* a-ed of the
Mar. 3.2. that they *might* **a.** him
15.3. the chief priests a-ed him of
Lu.11.54. that they *might* **a.** him
23. 2. they began to **a.** him
10. and vehemently a-ed him
14. whereof ye **a.** him
Jo. 5.45. Do not think that I *will* **a.**
there is one *that* a-eth you
8. 6. that they might have to **a.** him
Act.22.30. wherefore he *was* a-ed of the
24. 2. Tertullus began to **a.** him
8. whereof we **a.** him
13. whereof they now **a.** me
25. 5. go down and **a.** this man
11. whereof these **a.** me
16. before that he *which is* a-ed
28.19. had ought *to* **a.** my nation of
Ro. 2.15. thoughts the mean while a-ng
Rev.12.10.*which* a-ed them before our G.
engkaleō.
Act.23.28.cause wherefore they a-ed
29. *to be* a-ed of questions of their
26.2. whereof I am a-ed of the Jews
7. king Agrippa, I am a-ed of
diaballō.
Lu. 16.1. the same *was* a-ed unto him
en katēgoria.
Tit. 1. 6. not a-ed of riot, or unruly
(not under *accusation.*)
epēreazō.
¹Pet.3.16 ashamed *that falsely* **a.** your
sukophanteō.
Lu. 3.14. neither **a.** any *falsely*

ACCUSER, -s.
katēgoros.
Jo. 8.10. where are those thine a-s
Act.23.30.gave commandment to his a-s
35. when thine a-s are also come
24. 8. Commanding his a-s to come
25.16. have the a-s face to face
18. when the a-s stood up
Rev.12.10. the **a.** of our brethren is cast
diabolos.
²Ti. 3. 3. truce-breakers, *false* a-s, inco.
Tit. 2. 3. not *false* a-s, not given to mu.

ACKNOWLEDGE, -ed, -ing.
epiginōskō.
¹Co.14.37. *let* him **a.** that the things
16.18. therefore **a.** ye them that
²Co. 1.13. than what ye read or **a.**
ye shall **a.** even to the end
14. ye *have* a-ed us in part
epignōsis.
²Ti. 2.25. repentance to the a-ing of the
Tit. 1. 1. the a-ing of the truth
Phile. 6. by the a-ing of every

ACKNOWLEDGMENT.
epignōsis.
Col. 2. 2. to the **a.** of the mystery

ACQUAINTANCE.
gnōstos.
Lu. 2.44. among their kinsfolk **and a.**
23.49. all his **a.**, and the women
idios.
Act.24.23.should forbid none of his **a.**

ACT.
epautophōrō.
Jo. 8. 4. taken in adultery *in the very* **a.**

ADD, -ed, -eth, -ing.
prostithēmi.
Mat.6.27. can **a.** one cubit unto his
33. all these things *shall be* a-ed
Lu. 3.20. a-ed yet this above all
12.25. can **a.** to his stature one cubit
31. all these things *shall be* a-ed
19.11. he a-ed and spake a parable
Act. 2.41. there *were* a-ed unto them
47. and the Lord a-ed to the chur.
5.14. believers *were* the more a-ed
11.24. and much people *was* a-ed
Gal. 3.19. It *was* a-ed because of trans.
epipherō.
Phi. 1.16. to **a.** affliction to my bonds
epichorēgeō.
²Pet. 1.5. **a.** to your faith virtue, and to
epidiatassomai.
Gal. 3.15. disannulleth, or a-eth *thereto*
epitithēmi.
Rev.22.18. If any man shall **a.** unto these
God *shall* **a.** unto him the
prosanatithēmi.
Gal.2. 6. *in conference* a-ed nothing to

ADDICTED.
tassō.
¹Co.16.15.they *have* a-ed themselves to

ADJURE.
horkizō.
Mar. 5.7. I **a.** thee by God that thou
Act.19.13.We **a.** you by Jesus whom Pa.
exorkizō.
Mat.26.63.I **a.** thee by the living God

ADMINISTERED.
diakoneō.
²Co. 8.19. *which* is a-d by us to the glory
20. abundance *which* is a-d by us

ADMINISTRATION, -s.
diakonia.
¹Co. 12.5. are differences of a-s
²Co. 9.12. For the **a.** of this service

ADMIRATION.
thauma.
Rev.17.6. I wondered with great **a.**
thaumazō.
Jude 16. *having* men's persons *in* **a.**

ADMIRE.
thaumazō.
²Th.1.10. and to be a-ed in all them that

ADMONISH, -ing.
noutheteō.
Ro.15.14. able also *to* **a.** one another
Col. 3.16. and a-ing one another in psal.
¹Th. 5.12. over you in the Lord, and **a.**
²Th. 3.15. but **a.** him as a brother
paraineō.
Act.27.9. already past, Paul a-ed them
chrēmatizō.
Heb. 8.5. as Moses *was* a-ed of God

ADMONITION.
nouthesia.
¹Co.10.11.they are written for our **a.**
Eph. 6.4. and **a.** of the Lord
Tit. 3.10. after the first and second **a.**

ADO.
thorubeomai.
Mar.5.39. Why *make* ye this **a.** and weep

ADOPTION.
huiothesia.
Ro. 8.15. have received the spirit of **a.**
23. waiting for the **a.** to wit the
9.4. to whom pertaineth the **a.**
Gal. 4.5. we might receive the **a.** *of sons*
Eph. 1.5. us unto the **a.** *of children*

ADORN, -ed.
kosmeō.
Lu.21.25. how it *was* a-ed with goodly
¹Ti. 2. 9. that women a-ed themselves
2.10. that they *may* **a.** the doctrine
¹Pet.3. 5. **a.** themselves, being in subje.
Rev.21.2. as a bride a-ed for her

ADORNING, [*noun.*]
kosmos.
¹ Pet.3.3. Whose **a.** let it not be

ADULTERER, -s.
moichos.
Lu.18.11. extortioners, unjust, a-s
¹Co. 6. 9. nor idolaters, nor a-s
Heb. 13.4. whoremongers and a-s God
Ja. 4. 4. Ye a-s and adulteresses

ADULTERESS, -es.
moichalis.
Ro. 7. 3. she shall be called an **a.**
so that she is no **a.**
Ja. 4. 4. Ye adulterers and a-s

ADULTEROUS.
moichalis.
Mat. 12.39. An evil and **a.** generation
16. 4. A wicked and **a.** generation
Mar. 8. 38. in this **a.** and sinful genera.

ADULTERY, -ies.
moicheia.
Mat.15.19.murders, a-s, fornications
Mar. 7.21. evil thoughts, a-s, fornicatio.
Jo. 8. 3. with a man woman taken in a.
Gal. 5.19. **a.**, fornication, uncleanness
moichalis.
²Pet.2.14. Having eyes full of **a.**,
(full of *an adulteress.*)
moicheuō.
Mat.5.27. Thou *shalt* not *commit* **a.**
28. *hath* committed **a.** with her
19.18. Thou *shalt* not *commit* **a.**
Mar.10.19.Do not *commit* **a.**
Lu.16.18. marrieth anoth. committeth **a.**
her husband committeth **a.**
18.20. *Do* not *commit* **a.**
Jo. 8. 4. woman was taken *in* **a.**
(being committed adultery with.)
Ro. 2.22. a man *should* not *commit* **a.**
dost thou commit **a.**
13. 9. Thou *shalt* not *commit* **a.**
Ja. 2.11. *Do* not *commit* **a.**
Now if thou *commit* no **a.**
Rev.2.22. them *that commit* **a.** with her
moichaomai.
Mat.5.32. causeth her *to commit* **a.**
that is divorced *committeth* **a.**
19. 9. marry another, *committeth* **a.**
is put away *doth commit* **a.**
Mar.10.11. *committeth* **a.** against her
12. to another, she *committeth* **a.**

ADVANTAGE, [*noun.*]
ōpheleia.
Jude 16. in admiration because of **a.**
perissos.
Ro. 3. 1. What **a.** then hath the Jew
(what *more abundant* belongs to.

5

pleonekteō.
¹Co. 2.11. lest Satan should get an **a**.
(we *should be taken advantage of by*.)

ADVANTAGE, [*verb*]-*ed*,-*eth*.
ōpheleō.
Lu. 9.25. what is a man **a**-*ed* if he gain
ophelos.
¹Co.15.32. What **a**-*eth* it me if the dead
(what is the *profit* to me.)

ADVENTURE.
didōmi.
Act.19.31.not **a**. himself into the theatre

ADVERSARY,   -*ies*.
antidikos.
Mat.5.25. Agree with thine **a**. quickly
at any time the **a**. deliver
Lu.12.58. goest with thine **a**. to the
18. 3. Avenge me of mine **a**.
¹Pet. 5.8. because your **a**. the devil
antikeimai.
Lu.13.17. all his **a**-*s* were ashamed.
21.15. which all your **a**-*s* shall
¹Co.16. 9. and there are many **a**-*s*
Phi. 1.28. nothing terrified by your **a**-*s*
¹Ti. 5.14. give none occasion to the **a**.
hupenantios.
Heb.10.27.which shall devour the **a**-*s*

ADVERSITY.
kakouchoumenos.
Heb.13.3. and them *which suffer* **a**. as

ADVICE.
gnōmē.
² Co.8.10. herein I give my **a**.; for this is

ADVISE,   -*ed*
tithēmi boulē.
Act.27.12.the more part **a**-*ed* to depart
(*gave counsel*.)

ADVOCATE.
paraklētos.
¹Jo. 2. 1. an **a**. with the Father, Jesus

AFFAIR,   -*s*.
pragmateia.
²Ti. 2. 4. entangl. himself with the **a**-*s*
ho peri.
Eph.6.22. that ye might know our **a**-*s*
(*the* [*things*] *concerning* us.)
Phil.1.27. absent I may hear of your **a**-*s*
ho kata.
Eph.6.21. ye also may know my **a**-*s*
(*the* [*things*] *respecting* me.)

AFAR.
makrothen.
Mat.26.58.Peter followed him **a**. *off*
27.55. women there beholding **a**. *off*
Mar.5. 6. when he saw Jesus **a**. *off*
11.13. seeing a fig-tree **a**. *off*
14.54. Peter followed him **a**. *off*
15.40. women looking on **a**. *off*
Lu.16.23. and seeth Abraham **a**. *off*
18.13. the publican, standing **a**. *off*
22.54. Peter followed **a**. *off*
23.49. stood **a**. *off*, beholding these
Rev.18.10.Standing **a**. *off* for the fear
15. shall stand **a**. *off* for the fear
17. as trade by sea, stood **a**. *off*
makran.
Act. 2.39. and to all that are **a**. *off*
Eph.2.17. to you which were **a**. *off*
porrōthen
Lu.17.12. ten lepers, which stood **a**. *off*
Heb.11.but having seen them **a**. *off*
muōpazō.
²Pet. 1. 9. is blind, and *cannot see* **a**. *off*
(*not seeing afar off*.)

AFFECT,   -*ed*.
zēloō.
Gal. 4.17. they *zealously* **a**. you, but not
that ye might **a**. them
18. good to be *zealously* **a**-*ed*
kakoō.
Act. 14.2. *made* their minds *evil* **a**-*ed*

AFFECTION,   -*s*.
pathēma.
Gal. 5.24. cruci. the flesh, with the **a**-*s*
pathos.
Ro. 1.26. gave them up unto vile **a**-*s*
Col.3. 5. uncleanness, *inordinate* **a**.
splangchna.
²Co. 7.15. And his *inward* **a**. is more
phroneō.
Col. 3. 2. *Set* your **a**. *on* things above
astorgos.
Ro. 1.31.*without natural* **a**., implacable
²Ti. 3. 3. *Without natural* **a**.,truce-brea

AFFECTIONATELY.
himeiromai.
¹Th. 2. 8. So *being* **a**. *desirous* of you

AFFECTIONED.
philostorgos.
Ro.12.10. *Be kindly* **a**. one to another

AFFIRM,   -*ed*.
phaskō.
Act.25.19.whom Paul **a**-*ed* to be alive
phēmi.
Ro. 3. 8. and as some **a**. that we say
diabebaioomai.
²Ti. 1. 7. they say, nor whereof they **a**.
Tit. 3. 8. I will that thou **a**. *constantly*
diischurizomai.
Lu.22.59. another *confidently* **a**-*d*, saying
Act.12.15.she *constantly* **a**-*d* that it was

AFFLICT,   -*ed*.
thlibō.
²Co. 1. 6. And whether we be **a**-*d*
¹Ti. 5.10. if she have relieved the **a**-*d*
Heb.11.37.being destitute, **a**-*d*.,torment.
talaipōreō.
Ja. 4.9. *Be* **a**-*d*, and mourn and weep
kakopatheō.
Ja. 5.13. Is any among you **a**-*d*, let
thlipsis.
Mat.24.9. deliver you up to be **a**-*d*
(*to affliction*.)

AFFLICTION,   *s*.
thlipsis.
Mar.4.17. afterward, when **a**. or perse.
13.19. in those days shall be **a**.
Act. 7.10. delivered him out of all his **a**-*s*
11. and Chanaan, and great **a**.
20.23. that bonds and **a**-*s* abide me
²Co. 2. 4. For out of much **a**.
4.17. our light **a**. which is
6. 4. in **a**-*s*, in necessities
8. 2. in a great trial of **a**.
Phil.1.16. to add **a**. to my bonds
4.14. did communicate with my **a**-*s*
Col. 1.24. that which is behind of the **a**.
¹Th. 1. 6. received the word in much **a**.
3. 3. should be moved by these **a**-*s*
7. in all our **a**. and distress
Heb.10.33.both by reproaches and **a**-*s*
Ja. 1. 27. and widows in their **a**.
pathēma.
²Ti. 3.11. Persecutions, **a**-*s* which came
Heb.10.32.endured a great fight of **a**-*s*
¹Pet. 5.9. the same **a**-*s* are accomplished
kakōsis.
Act.7.34. I have seen the **a**.of my people

kakopatheia.
Ja. 5 10. for an example of *suffering* **a**.
(*the suffering of affliction*.)
kakopatheō.
²Ti. 4. 5. *endure* **a**-*s*, do the work of
sungkakoucheomai.
Heb.11.25.rather to *suffer* **a**. *with* the
sungkakopatheō.
²Ti. 1. 8. *be thou partaker of the* **a**-*s* of

AFFRIGHTED.
emphobos.
Lu.24.37. they were terrified and **a**.
Rev.11.13.and the remnant were **a**. and
ekthambeō.
Mar.16.5. white garm., and they were **a**.
6. he saith unto them, *Be* not **a**.

AFOOT.
pezē.
Mar.6.33. knew him, and ran **a**. thither
pezeuō.
Act.20.13.minding himself *to go* **a**.

AFORE.
proepanggellomai.
Ro. 1. 2. which he *had promised* **a**. by
prographō.
Eph. 3.3. as I *wrote* **a**. in few words

AFOREHAND.
prolambanō.
Mar.14.8. she *is come* **a**. to anoint

AFORETIME.
pote.
Jo. 9. 13. to the Pharisees, him that **a**.
prographō.
Ro. 15.4. things *were written* **a**. were

AFRAID.
phobeomai.
Mat.2.22. he *was* **a**. to go thither
14.27. I,*be* not **a**.; Mar.6.50.; Jo.6.20.
30. the wind boisterous, he *was* **a**.
17. 6. their face, and *were* sore **a**.
7. and said, Arise, and *be* not **a**.
25.25. And I *was* **a**. and went and
28.10. *Be* not **a**. ; go tell my breth.
Mar.5.15. and they *were* **a**.; Lu.8.35.
36. *Be* not **a**., only believe
9.32. and *were* **a**. to ask him
10.32. they followed, they *were* **a**.
16. 8. to any man, for they *were* **a**.
Lu. 2. 9. and they *were* sore **a**.
8.25. And they *being* **a**. wondered
12. 4. *Be* not **a**. of them that kill
Jo. 6.19. the ship, and they *were* **a**.
19. 8. saying, he *was* the more **a**.
Act. 9.26. but they *were* all **a**. of him
18. 9. *Be* not **a**., but speak, and hold
22.29. the chief captain also *was* **a**.
Ro. 13.3. Wilt thou then not *be* **a**.
4. do that which is evil, *be* **a**.
Gal. 4.11. I am **a**. of you, lest I have
Heb.11.23. and they *were* not **a**. of the
¹Pet. 3.6. and *are* not **a**. with any
14. and *be* not **a**. of their terror
emphobos.
Lu.24. 5. as they were **a**. and bowed
Act.10.4. looked on him, he was **a**.
22. 9. indeed the light, and were **a**.
deiliaō.
Jo. 14.27. be troubled, neither *let* it *be* **a**.
tremō.
²Pet.2.10. they *are* not **a**. to speak evil
ekphobos.
Mar. 9. 6. to say, for they were *sore* **a**.
phobeō phobos megas.
Lu. 2. 9. and they *were sore* **a**.
(*were afraid with great fear*.)

AFRESH.
anastauroō.
Heb. 6.6. *crucify* to them. the S. of G. **a.**

AFTER, [*prep.*]
meta, [*accu.*]
Mat.17.1. And **a.** six days Jesus taketh
24.29. Immediately **a.** the tribulati.
25.19. **a.** a long time the lord of
26. 2. ye know that **a.** two days
73. And **a.** a while came unto
27.53. out of the graves **a.** his resur.

(*Also every other passage in the New Test. in which the word occurs as a preposition, except where it is part of a verb, and also the following*):—

opisō.
Mat.3.11. but he that cometh **a.** me
10.38. and followeth **a.** me
16.24. If any man will come **a.** me
Mar. 1. 7. one mightier than I **a.** me
17. Come ye **a.** me, and I will
20. servants, and went **a.** him
8.34. Whosoever will come **a.** me
Lu. 9.23. If any man will come **a.** me
14.27. and come **a.** me, cannot be
19.14. and sent a message **a.** him
21. 8. go ye not therefore **a.** them
Jo. 1.15. He that cometh **a.** me is
27. He it is, who coming **a.** me is
30. **a.** me cometh a man which is
12.19. the world is gone **a.** him.
Act. 5.37. drew away much people **a.**him
20.30. to draw away disciples **a.**them
1Ti. 5. 15. are already turned aside **a.**
2Pe. 2.10. that walk **a.** the flesh in
Jude 7. and going **a.** strange flesh
Re.12.15. as a flood **a.** the woman
13. 3. the world wondered **a.** the

opisthen.
Mat.15.23. her away, for she crieth **a.** us
Lu.23.26. that he might bear it **a.** Jesus

kata, [*accu.*]
Mat.23.3. but do not ye **a.** their works
Lu. 2.27. **a.** the custom of the law
42. **a.** the custom of the feast
Jo. 2. 6. **a.** *the manner of* the purifying
8.15. Ye judge **a.** the flesh
Act.13.22.a man **a.** mine own heart
23. 3. to judge me **a.** the law
24.14. that **a.** the way which they
26. 5. that **a.** the most straitest
Ro. 2. 5. But **a.** thy hardness and im.
7.22. law of G. **a.** the inward man
8.1,4. walk not **a.** the flesh, but **a.**
5. that are **a.** the flesh do mind
they that are **a.** the Spirit
12. the flesh to live **a.** the flesh
13. if ye live **a.** the flesh ye shall
1Co. 1.26. wise men **a.** the flesh
7.40. so abide **a.**, my judgment
10.18. Behold Israel **a.** the flesh
15.32. If **a.** *the manner of* men I have
2Co. 5.16. know we no man **a.** the flesh
known Christ **a.** the flesh
7. 9. made sorry **a.** a godly manner
11. ye sorrowed **a.** a godly sort
10. 3. we do not war **a.** the flesh
7. **a.** the outward appearance
11.17. I speak it not **a.** the Lord
18. that many glory **a.** the flesh
Gal. 1.11. preached of me is not **a.** man
3.15. I speak **a.** *the manner of* men
4.23. was born **a.** the flesh
29. born **a.** the flesh persecuted
Eph.1.11. worketh all things **a.** the
4.24. which, **a.** God, is created
Col. 2. 8. **a.** the tradition of men
a. the rudiments of the world
and not **a.** Christ
22. **a.** the commandments and

Col. 3.10. **a.** the image of him that
2Th. 2. 9. is **a.** the working of Satan
3. 6. and not **a.** the tradition
2Ti. 4. 3. but **a.** their own lusts
Tit. 1. 1. the truth which is **a.** godliness
4. own son **a.** the common faith
Heb.5.6.10. **a.** the order of Melchisedec
ch. 6. 20., 7. 11. 15. 21.
7.11. called **a.** the order of Aaron
15. **a.** the similitude of Melchise.
16. not **a.** the law of a carnal
but **a.** the power of an
12.10. chastened us **a.** their own
Ja. 3. 9. **a.** the similitude of God
2Pet.3. 3. walking **a.** their own lusts
2Jo. 6. we walk **a.** his command.
Jude 18. who should walk **a.** their own

epi, [*dat.*]
Lu. 1.59. **a.** the name of his father
Ro. 5.14. **a.** the similitude of Adam's

epi, [*accu.*]
Lu.15. 4. go **a.** that which is lost until

dia, [*gen.*]
Mar. 2. 1. into Capernaum **a.** certain da.

en.
Heb.4.11. **a.** the same example of unbe.

ouketi.
Mar.12.34.no man **a.** *that* durst ask
Lu.20.40. **a.** *that* they durst *not* ask

eita.
Mar.4.28. **a.** *that* the full corn
8.25. **a.** *that* he put his hands again
Jo. 13. 5. **a.** *that* he poureth water into

epeita.
1Co.12.28.**a.** *that* miracles, then gifts
15. 6. **a.** *that* he was seen of above
7. **a.** *that* he was seen of James
Heb. 7.2. **a.** *that* also king of Salem

eti.
Lu.20.40. And **a.** *that* they durst not ask
(durst not *any longer.*)

mellō.
Lu. 13.9. **a.** *that* thou shalt cut it down
(*at a future* [time].)

hōsautōs.
1Co.11.25. **a.** *the same manner* he took

ethnikōs.
Gal. 2.14. livest **a.** *the manner of* Genti.

diaginomai.
Act.25.13.**a.** certain days king Agrippa
(when certain days *were past*)

plēroō.
Act.24.27.**a.** two years Porcius Festus
(when..*were fulfilled.*)

huparchō.
Act.27.21.**a.** long abstinence Paul stood
(when *there was.*)

periechō.
Act. 23.25.wrote a letter **a.** this manner
(*having* this form.)

AFTER, [*adv. and conj.*]
meta, [*accu.*]
Mat.1.12. **a.** they were brought to B.
Mar.1.14. **a.** that John was put in pri.
14.28. and **a.** that I am risen
70. a little **a.** they that stood by
16.19. **a.** the Lord had spoken unto
Lu. 12. 5. which **a.** he hath killed
15.13. And not many days **a.**
Act.10.41.**a.** he rose from the dead
15.13. and **a.** they had held their
19.21. **a.** I have been there
27.14. not long **a.** there arose
Gal. 3.17. and thirty years **a.**, cannot
Heb.10.15. for **a.** that he had said befo.
26. **a.** that we have received
Act.9.23. And **a.** *that* many days were
16.10. And **a.** he had seen the vision
19.21. **a.** these things were ended

hote.
Mat.27.31.**a.** *that* they had mocked him
Jo. 13.12. So **a.** he had washed their feet
Tit. 3. 4. But **a.** *that* the kindness and

epeidē.
1Co. 1.21. For **a.** *that* in the wisdom

hexēs.
Lu. 7. 11. it came to pass the day **a.**

kathexēs.
Act.3.24. Sam. and those that follow **a.**

mellō.
Heb.11.8. which he *should* **a.** receive
2Pet. 2.6. *that* **a.** *should* live ungodly

dia, [*gen.*]
Gal. 2.1. fourteen years **a.** I went up

epaurion.
Jo. 1.35. *the next day* **a.** John stood

AFTERWARD, -s.
husteron.
Mat.4. 2. he was **a.** an hungered
21.29. but **a.** he repented and went
32. had seen it, repented not **a.**
25.11. **a.** came also the other virgins
Mar.16.14. **a.** he appeared unto the
Lu. 4. 2. he **a.** hungered
Jo. 13.36. but thou shalt follow me **a-s**
Heb.12.11.**a.** it yieldeth the peaceable

meta houtos.
Lu.17. 8. and **a.** thou shalt eat and
18. 4. but **a.** he said within himself
Jo. 5.14. **a.** Jesus findeth him in the
Heb.4. 8. then would he not **a.** have

epeita.
1Co.15.23. first-fruits, **a.** they that are
46. and **a.**, that which is spiritual
Gal. 1.21. **a-s** I came into the regions

eita.
Mar.4.17. **a.** when affliction or persecu.

kathexēs.
Lu. 8. 1. And it came to pass **a.** that

metepeita.
Heb.12.17.For ye know how that **a.**when

deuteros.
Jude 5. **a.** destroyed them that believ.

kakeithen.
Act.13.21.*And* **a.** they desired a king

AGAIN.
palin.
Mat. 4. 7. It is written **a.**, Thou shalt not
8. **a.** the devil taketh him up
5.53. **a.** ye have heard that it hath
13.44. **a.** the kingdom of heaven is
18.19. **a.** I say unto you, That if
19.24. and **a.** I say unto you, if

(*And in all other passages, except where it is part of a verb, and also the following*):—

deuteros.
Jo. 9.24. Then **a.** called they the man
Act.11. 9. voice answered me **a.** from
Rev.19.3. **a.** they said, Alleluiah

dis.
Phi. 4.16. sent once and **a.** unto my
1Th. 2.18. you, even I Paul, once and **a.**

anōthen.
Jo. 3. 3. Except a man be born **a.** he
7. unto thee, ye must be born **a.**

palin anōthen.
Gal. 4. 9. whereunto ye desire **a.** to be

prostithēmi pempō.
Lu.20,11,12.And **a.** *he sent* another ser.
(he *added to send.*)

(See *Remembrance, Set at One.*)

AGAINST.
kata, [*gen.*]
Mat.5.11. say all manner of evil **a.** you
23. that thy brother hath ought **a.**

7

Mat.10.35.man at variance a. his father
    daughter a. her mother
    a. her mother-in-law
  12.14. held a council a. him
    25. kingdom divided a. itself
    house divided a. itself
    30. He that is not with me is a.
    32. speaketh a word a. the Son of
    whoso speaketh a. the Holy
  20.11. murmured a. the goodman of
  26.59. witness a. Jesus; Mar.14.55.
  27. 1. took counsel a. Jesus to put
Mar.3. 6. with the Herodians a. him
  9.40. he that is not a. us is on
  11.25. if ye have ought a. any
  14.56, 57.bare false witness a. him
Lu. 9.50. he that is not a. us is for us
  11.23. is not with me is a. me
Jo. 18.29. bring ye a. this man
  19.11. no power at all a. me
Act. 4.26. gathered together a. the Lord
    and a. his Christ
  6.13. a. this holy place, and the law
  14. 2. evil affected a. the brethren
  16.22. rose up together a. them
  19.16. and prevailed a. them.
  21.28. everywhere a. the people
  24. 1. informed the governor a. Paul
  25. 2. informed him a. Paul
    3. desired favour a. him
    7. grievous complaints a. Paul
    15. to have judgment a. him
    27. the crimes laid a. him
  27.14, arose a. it a tempestuous
Ro. 8.31. G. be for us, who can be a. us
  11. 2. to God a. Israel, saying
1Co. 4. 6. for one a. another
2Co.10. 5. exalteth itself a. the know.
  13. 8. we can do nothing a. the
Gal. 3.21. is the law then a. the pro.
  5.17. the flesh lusteth a. the Spirit
    and the Spirit a. the flesh
    23. a. such there is no law
Col. 2.14. of ordinances that was a. us
1Ti. 5.19. a. an elder receive not
Ja. 3.14. and lie not a. the truth
  5. 9. Grudge not one a. another
1Pet.2.11. which war a. the soul
2Pet.2.11. accusation a. them
Jude 15. sinners have spoken a.
Rev.2. 4. I have somewhat a. thee
  14.20. I have a few things a. thee
  12. 7. fought a. the dragon
    epi, [*accu.*]
Mat.10.21.children shall rise up a. their
  12.26. he is divided a. himself
  24. 7. nation shall rise a. nation
    and kingdom a. kingdom
    Mar.13. 8; Luke 21.10.
  26.55. come out as a. a thief
Mar.3.24. kingdom be divided a. itself
    25. a house be divided a. itself
    26. if Satan rise up a. himself
  10.11. committeth adultery a. her
  13.12. shall rise up a. their parents
  14.48. Are ye come out as a. a the
Lu. 9. 5. for a testimony a. them if
  11.17. Every kingdom divided a.
    a house divided a. a house
    18. Satan also be divided a. him
  12.53. mother-in-law a. her
    daughter-in-law a. her
  14.31. him that cometh a. him
  21.52. Be ye come out as a. a thief
    53. stretched forth no hands a.
Jo. 13.18. lifted up his heel a. me
Act.4.27. For of a truth a. thy holy
  8. 1. persecution a. the church
  13.50. raised persecution a. Paul
  51. dust of their feet a. them
Ro. 1.18. heaven a. all ungodliness
  2. 2. a. them which commit
  8

2Co.10. 2. I think to be bold a. some
1Pet.3.12. a. them that do evil
    epi, [*dat.*]
Lu.12.52. divided, three a. two, and two
    53. a. the son, and the son a. the
    father; the mother a. the
    daugh., and the daugh. a. the
    mother
    eis.
Mat.18.15. brother shall trespass a.
    21. oft shall my brother sin a.
Mar. 3.29. blaspheme a. the Holy Gh.
Lu. 7. 30. counsel of God a. themselves
  12.10. speak a word a. the Son of
    blasphemeth a. the Holy G.
  15.18,21. I have sinned a. heaven
  17. 3. If thy brother trespass a.
    4. If he trespass a. thee seven
  22.65. blasphemously spake they a.
Jo. 12. 7. a. the day of my burying
  13.29. have need of a. the feast
Act. 6. 11. blasphemous words a. Moses
  9. 1. a. the disciples of the Lord
  25. 8. a. the law of the Jews,
    neither a. the temple, nor
    a. Cæsar
Ro. 8. 7. carnal mind is enmity a.
1Co. 6.18. sinneth a. his own body
  8.12. ye sin so a. the brethren
    ye sin a. Christ
1Ti. 6. 19. a. the time to come
2Ti. 1. 12. committed unto him a. that
Heb.12. 3. contradiction of sinners a.
2Pet. 3. 7. a. the day of judgment
    pros.
Mat.4. 6. dash thy foot a. a st.; Lu.4.11.
Mr.12.12. spoken the parable a. them
Lu. 5.30. murmured a. his disciples
  20.19. spoken this parable a. them
Act. 6. 1. the Grecians a. the Hebrews
  9. 5. for thee to kick a. the pricks
  29. and disputed a. the Grecians
  19.38. have a matter a. any man
  23.30. what they had a. him
  24.19. if they had ought a. me
  25.19. certain questions a. him of
  26.14. for thee to kick a. the pricks
1Co. 6. 1. having a matter a. another
Eph.6.11. able to stand a. the wiles of
    12. wrestle not a. flesh and blood,
    but a.principalities, a.powers
    a. rulers, a. spiritual
Col. 3.13. man have a quarrel a. any
    19. be not bitter a. them
Heb.12.4. unto blood striving a. sin
Rev.13.6. in blasphemy a. God
    enantios.
Mar.15.39. which stood *over* a. him.
Act.28.17. committed nothing a. the
    meta, [*gen.*]
Rev. 2.16. will fight a. them with the
  11. 7. will make war a. them and
  19.19. make war a. him..and a. his
    para, [*accu.*]
Ro. 1.26. into that which is a. nature
  4.18. Who a. hope believed in hope
    peri, [*gen.*]
Mat.20.24. indignation a. the two bret.
Act.25.18. a. whom when the accusers
    emprosthen.
Mat.23.13. up the kingdom of heaven a.
    en.
Ro. 2. 5. to thyself wrath a. the day

(See *Mad, Over, Will, and also*
  verbs followed by "against.")

AGE.
    hēlikia.
Jo. 9.21. we know not: he is of a. ask
  23. said his parents, He is of a.
He.11.11. of a child when she was past a.

    hēmera.
Lu. 2. 36. she was of a great a. and had
    teleios.
Heb.5.14. to them that are *of full* a.
    probainō hēmera polus.
Lu. 2.36. she *was of great* a. and had
    gēras.
Lu. 1.36. conceived a son in her *old* a.
    huperakmos.
1Co. 7.36. if she *pass the flower* of her a.

AGED.
    presbutēs.
Tit. 2. 2. That the a. *men* be sober
Phile. 9. being such an one as Paul the a.
    presbutis.
Tit. 2.3. The a. *women* likewise that

AGES.
    aiōn.
Eph. 2.7. That in the a. to come he
Col. 1.26. hid from a. and from genera.
    genea.
Eph. 3.5. Which in other a. was not
  21. throughout all a., world with.

AGO.
    apo.
Act.10.30. Four days a. I was fasting
  15.7. know how that a goodwhile a.
2Co. 8.10. also to be forward a year a.
  9. 2. Achaia was ready a year a.
    pro.
2Co. 12.2. Christ above fourteen years a.
    perusi.
2Co.8.10,9.2. *a year* a.

AGONY.
    agōnia.
Lu.22.44. and being in an a. he prayed

AGREE,   -d.
    sumphōneō.
Mat.18.19. That if two of you *shall* a.
  20. 2. And when he *had* a-d with
    13. *didst* not thou a. *with* me
Lu. 5.36. a-*eth* not *with* the old
Act. 5. 9. ye *have* a-d together to tempt
  15.15. to this a. the words of the
    suntithēmi.
Jo. 9.22. for the Jews *had* a-d already
Act.23.20. The Jews *have* a-d to desire
    eimi.
1Jo. 5. 8. these three a. in one
    (*are* into one.)
    eunoeō.
Mat.5.25. a. with thine adversary
    eimi isos.
Mar.14.56,59. their witness a-d not
    (*were* not *equal.*)
    homoiazō.
Mar.14.70.and thy speech a-*th thereto*
    peithō.
Act. 5.40. And to him they a-*d;* and when
    poieō heis gnōmē.
Re.17.17. to fulfil his will and to a.
    asumphōnos.
Act.28.25. *when* they a-d. not among
    (*were not harmonious.*)

AGREEMENT.
    suŋgkatathesis.
2Co. 6.16. what a. hath the temple of

AGROUND.
    epokellō.
Act.27.41. They *ran* the ship a.

AH.
    oua.
Mar.15.29. a., thou that destroyest the

AIR.
aēr.
Act.22.23. threw dust into the **a.**
¹Co. 9.26. not as one that beateth the **a.**
   14. 9. for ye shall speak into the **a.**
Eph.2. 2. prince of the power of the **a.**
¹Th. 4.17. to meet the Lord in the **a.**
Rev.9. 2. the sun and the **a.** were dark.
  16.17. poured out his vial into the **a.**
ouranos.
Mat.8.20. the birds of the **a.** have nests
Mar.4. 4. the fowls of the **a.** came and
    32. the fowls of the **a.** may lodge
Lu. 8. 5. the fowls of the **a.** devoured it
  9.58. and birds of the **a.** have nests
 13.19. the fowls of the **a.** lodged in
Act.10.12.and fowls of the **a.**; 11.6.

ALABASTER.
alabastron.
Mat.26.7. having an **a.** *box* of very pre.
Mar.14.3. having an **a.** *box* of ointment.
Lu. 7.37. brought an **a.** *box* of ointme.

ALAS.
ouai.
Re.18.10. **a. a.** that great city Babylon
  16. **a. a.** that great city, that was
  19. **a. a.** that great city, wherein

ALBEIT.
hina
Phile. 19. **a.** I do not say to thee how

ALIEN,   -s.
allotrios.
Heb.11.34. flight the armies of the **a**-*s.*
apallotrioō.
Eph.2.12. being **a**-*s* from the common.
   (*having been excluded* from.)

ALIENATED.
apallotrioō.
Eph.4.18. **a**-*d* from the life of God.
Col. 1.21. that were sometimes **a**-*d* and

ALIVE.
zaō.
Mat.27.63.said, *while* he *was* yet **a.**
Mar.16.11. they had heard that he *was* **a.**
Lu. 24.23.which said that he *was* **a.**
Act. 1. 3. he shewed himself **a.**
  9.41. widows, he presented her **a.**
 20.12. brought the young man **a.**
 25.19. whom Paul affirmed *to be* **a.**
Ro. 6.11. dead indeed unto sin, but **a.**
  13. as *those that are* **a.** from the
   7. 9. I *was* **a.** without the law once
¹Th.4.15,17. *which are* **a.** and remain
Rev.1.18. and, behold, I *am* **a.**
   2. 8. which was dead, and *is* **a.**
 19.20. both were cast **a.** into a lake
anazaō.
Lu.15.24. son dead and *is* **a.** *again*
   32. brother dead and *is* **a.** *again*
zōopoieō.
¹Co.15.22. in Christ *shall* all *be made* **a.**

ALL.
pas.
Mat.1.17. so **a.** the generations from A.
  2. 3. and **a.** Jerusalem with him
   4. gathered **a.** the chief priests
  16. slew **a.** the children that were
   and in **a.** the coasts thereof
  3. 5. **a.** Judea and **a.** the region

(And all other passages except the following:—)

holos.
Mat.1.22. Now **a.** this was done, that
 4.23. Jesus went about **a.** Galilee

Mat.4.24. his fame went throughout **a.**
  9.26. hereof went abroad into **a.**
   31. his fame in **a.** that country
 14.35. they sent out into **a.** that
 20. 6. Why stand ye here **a.** the day
 21. 4. **a.** this was done, that
 22.37. love the Lord thy God with **a.**
   with **a.** thy soul, and with **a.**
  40. hang **a.** the law and the pro.
 24.14. in **a.** the world for a witness
 26.56. But **a.** this was done, that
  59. and **a.** the council, sought
Mar.1.28. throughout **a.** the region
  33. **a.** the city was gathered
  39. synagogues throughout **a.**
 12.30,33. love the L. thy God with **a.**
   thy heart, and with **a.** thy
   soul, and with **a.** thy mind,
   and with **a.** thy strength
  44. even **a.** her living
 14.55. and **a.** the council sought
Lu. 1.65. throughout **a.** the hill coun.
 4.14. a fame of him through **a.** the
 5. 5. we have toiled **a.** the night
 7.17. went forth throughout **a.**
 8.43. had spent **a.** her living upon
 10.27. love the Lord thy God with
   a. thy heart, and with **a.**
   thy soul, and with **a.** thy
   strength, and with **a.** thy
   mind
 23. 5. teaching throughout **a.** Jewry
  44. darkness over **a.** the earth
Act. 2. 2. and it filled **a.** the house
  47. favour with **a.** the people
 5.11. fear came upon **a.** the church
 7.10. over Egypt and **a.** his house
  11. a dearth over **a.** the land of
 8.37. If thou believest with **a.** thine
 9.31. churches rest throughout **a.**
  42. it was known throughout **a.**
 10.22. among **a.** the nation of the
  37. was published throughout **a.**
 11.28. throughout **a.** the world
 13.49. throughout **a.** the region
 18. 8. believed on the Lord with **a.**
 19.27. whom **a.** Asia and the world
 21.30. And **a.** the city was moved
  31. that **a.** Jerusalem was in an
 22.30. And **a.** their council to appear
Ro. 8.36. we are killed **a.** the day long
 10.21. **a.** day long I have stretched
²Co. 1. 1. which are in **a.** Achaia
Phi. 1.13. are manifest in **a.** the palace
¹Th. 4.10. which are in **a.** Macedonia
Heb.3. 2. Moses was faithful in **a.** his
  5. verily was faithful in **a.** his
Rev.3.10. which shall come upon **a.** the
 13. 3. **a.** the world wondered after
hapas.
Mat.6.32. ye have need of **a.** these things
 24.39. flood came, and took them **a.**
 28.11. unto the chief priests **a.** the
Mar.5.40. when he had put them **a.** out
 11.32. for **a.** men counted John, that
 16.15. Go ye unto **a.** the world, and
Lu. 2.39. had performed **a.** things acco.
 3.16. John answered, saying unto **a.**
 21. when **a.** the people were bap.
 4. 6. **a.** this power will I give thee
 5.11. they forsook **a.**, and followed
 26. were **a.** amazed, and they
 28. he left **a.**, rose up, and fol.
 7.16. there came a fear on **a.**; and
 9.15. they did so, and made them **a.**
 15.13. younger son gathered **a.** to.
 17.27. came and destroyed them **a.**
  29. from heaven, and destroyed **a.**
 19. 7. when they saw it, they **a.**
  48. for **a.** the people were very
 21. 4. For **a.** these have of their
   hath cast in **a.** the living that

Lu.21.12. before **a.** these, they shall lay
Act. 2. 1. they were **a.** with one accord
   4. they were **a.** filled with the
  14. **a.** ye that dwell at Jerusalem
  44. together, and had **a.** things
 4.31. they were **a.** filled with the
  32. they had **a.** things common
 5.12. they were **a.** with one accord
 6.15. **a.** that sat in the council
 10. 8. had declared **a.** these *things*
 11.10. **a.** were drawn up again into
 13.29. had fulfilled **a.** that was writ.
 16. 3. they knew **a.** that his father
  20. thyself no harm: for we are **a.**
 27.33. Paul besought them **a.** to
Eph.6.13. having done **a.**, to stand
Ja. 3. 2. in many things we offend **a.**
hosos.
Lu. 9.10. told him **a.** *that* they had
Act. 4.23. and reported **a.** *that* the chief
 14.27. **a.** *that* God had done with
 15. 4. declared **a.** things *that* God
²Co. 1.20. For **a.** the promises of God in
Rev.1. 2. and of **a.** things *that* he saw
pantos.
Act.18.21. I must *by* **a.** *means* keep this
¹Co. 9.22. that I might *by* **a.** *means* save
 16.12. his will was not *at* **a.** to come
holos.
Mat.5.34. swear not *at* **a.**; neither by
¹Co.15.29.if the dead rise not *at* **a.**, why
tis.
Act.25. 8.have I offended *anything at* **a.**
katholou.
Act. 4.18. not to speak *at* **a.** nor teach
prōton.
Lu.12. 1. unto his disciples *first of* **a.**
¹Co.11.18.For first of **a.** when ye come
malista.
Act.20.38.sorrowing *most of* **a.** for the
mēpote.
Heb.9.17.it is of *no* strength at **a.** while
ou mē.
Rev.18.14.shalt find them no more *at* **a**
  21. shall be found *no* more *at* **a.**
 22.23. heard *no* more *at* **a.** in thee
ephapax.
Heb.10.10.offer. body of J.C. *once for* **a.**
houtō.
¹Co.14.21.*for* **a.** *that* will they not hear
panoiki.
Act.16.34. be. in God *with* **a.** his *house*
pantachou.
Act.24. 3. always and *in* **a.** *places* most
hōs tachista.
Act.17.15. to come to him *with* **a.** *speed*
pamplēthei.
Lu.23.18. they cried out **a.** *at once*, say
panoplia.
Lu.11.22. from him **a.** *his armour*
dianuktereuō.
Lu. 6.12. *continued* **a.** *night* in prayer

ALL *manner.*
pas.
Mat.4.23. healing **a.** *manner of* sickness
  and **a.** *manner*; 10.11.
 12.31. **a.** *manner of* sin and
Act.10.12.Wherein were **a.** *manner of*
Ro. 7. 8. in me **a.** *manner of* concupi.
¹Pet.1.15. holy in **a.** *manner of* conver.
Rv.18.12. and **a.** *manner* vessels of ivory,
  and **a.** *manner* vessels of
 21.19. with **a.** *manner of* precious

ALLEDGE,   -*ing.*
paratithēmi.
Act.17. 3. Opening and **a**-*ing* that

ALLEGORY.
allēgoreō.
Gal. 4.24. Which things are *an* **a.** for

ALLELUIA.
allēlouia.
Rev.19.1. people in heaven, saying, a.
  3. again they said, a. And her
  4. the throne, saying, Amen ; a.
  6. mighty thunderings, saying, a.

ALLOW,   -ed, -eth.
suneudokeō.
Lu.11.48. that ye a. the deeds of your
    prosdechomai.
Act.24.15. which they themselves also a.
    ginōskō.
Ro. 7.15 that which I do I a. not : for
    dokimazō.
Ro.14.22. in that thing which he a-eth
1Th. 2. 4. as we were a-ed of God to

ALLURE.
deleazō.
2Pet.2.18. they a. through the lusts of

ALMIGHTY.
pantokratōr.
2Co. 6.18. saith the Lord A.
Rev.1. 8. and which is to come, the A.
  4. 8. Holy, holy, holy, Lord God A.
  11.17. O Lord God A., which
  15. 3. thy works, Lord God A.
  16. 7. Lord God A., true and
  14. that great day of God A.
  19.15. and wrath of A. God.
  21.22. the Lord God A. and the L.

ALMOST.
schedon.
Act.13.44. came a. the whole city
  19.26. but a. throughout all Asia
Heb.9.22. And a. all things are by the
    en oligos.
Act.26.28. a. thou persuadest me.
  29. were both a. and altogether.
    mellō.
Act.21.27. the seven days were a. ended

ALMS.
eleēmosunē.
Mat.6. 1. do not your a. before men,
  2. Ther. when thou doest thine a.
  3. when thou doest a., let not
  4. That thine a. may be in sec.
Lu.11.41. rather give a. of such things
  12.33. Sell that ye have, and give a.
Act.3. 2. to ask a. of them that entered
  3. into the temple asked an a.
  10. it was he which sat for a.
  10. 2. gave much a. to the people,
  4. Thy prayers and thine a. are
  31. thine a. are had in remem.
  24.17. I came to bring a. to my na.

ALMSDEED.
eleēmosunē.
Act.9.36. full of good works and a.

ALOES.
aloē.
Jo. 19.39. a mixture of myrrh and a.

ALONE.
monos.
Mat.4. 4. shall not live by bread a.
  14.23. he was there a.
  18.15. between thee and him a.
Mar.6.47. and he a. on the land.
Lu. 4. 4. not live by bread a., but
  5.21. can forgive sins, but God. a.
  6. 4. but for the priests a.
  9.36. Jesus was found a.
  10.40. hath left me to serve a.
Jo. 6.15. into a mountain himself a.
  22. his disciples were gone away a.
10

Jo. 8. 9. and Jesus was left a.
  16. for I am not a. but I and
  29. the Father hath not left me a.
  12.24. and die, it abideth a.
Jo. 16.32. and shall leave me a.; and yet
    I am not a.
Ro.11. 3. and I am left a., and they
Gal. 6. 4. have rejoicing in himself a.
1Th. 3. 1. to be left at Athens a.
Heb.9. 7. went the high priest a.
    aphiēmi.
Mat.15.14. Let them a., they be blind
Mar.14.6. Jesus said, Let her a., why
  15.36. saying, Let a., let us see
Lu.13. 8. Lord, let it a. this year also
Jo. 11.48. If we let him thus a., all
  12. 7. Then said Jesus, Let her a.
    monon.
Jo. 17.20. pray I for these a. but for
Act.19.26. not a. at Ephesus, but
Ro. 4.23. not written for his sake a.
    katamonas.
Mar.4.10. And when he was a. they
Lu. 9.18. as he was a. praying, his
    kata [accu.] heautos
Jas. 2.17. not works is dead being a.
    kata idios.
Mar.4.34. and when they were a. he
    eaō.
Mar.1.24. saying, Let us a.
Lu. 4.34. Let us a.; what have we to do
Act. 5.38. fr. these men, and let them a.

ALOUD.
anaboaō.
Mar15.8. the multitude crying a.

ALPHA.
Rev. 1.8. I am a. and Omega ; 1.11, 21.
  6, 22. 13.

ALREADY.
ēdē.
Mat.5.28. commit. adultery with her a.
  17.12. Elias is come a. and they
Mar.15.44. if he were a. dead
Lu.12.49. if it be a. kindled?
Jo. 3.18. believeth not is condemned a.
  4.35. they are white a. to harvest
  9.22. for the Jews had agreed a.,
  27. I have told you a.
  11.17. lain in the grave four days a.
  19.33. that he was dead a.
Act.27.9. the fast was now a. past
1Co. 5. 3. have judged a., as though I
Phi.3.12. Not as though I had a. at.
    either were a. perfect
2Th.2. 7. of iniquity doth a. work
1Ti. 5.15. For some are a. turned aside
2Ti. 2.18. the resurrection is past a.
1Jo.4. 3. a. is it in the world.
    phthanō.
Phil.3.16. whereto we have a. attained
    proamartanō.
2Co.12.21. many which have sinned a.

ALSO.
kai.
Mat.5.40. let him have thy cloak a.
  6.14. heavenly Fa. will a. forgive
  21. there will your heart be a.
  10.4. Jud. Isc. who a. betrayed

(And in all other passages in which it
occurs, with the following exceptions:—)
    mentoi.
Jo. 12.42. among the chief rulers a.
Jude 8. Likewise a. these filthy
    hama.
Act24.26. He hoped a. that money shou.
    dē.
Mat.13.23. which a. beareth fruit and

---

    eti.
Lu.14.26. yea and his own life a. he
    te
Heb11.32. of David a. and Samuel, and
    kan.
Mat21.21. but a. if ye shall say unto
    oude.
Ro.11.21. take heed lest he a. spare no

ALTAR.
thusiastērion.
Mat.5.23. bring thy gift to the a.
  24. thy gift before the a.
  23.18. shall swear by the a.
  19. the gift, or the a.
  20. shall swear by the a.
  35. the temple and the a.
Lu. 1. 11. of the a. of incense
  11.51. between the a. and the tem.
Ro. 11. 3. and digged down thine a.
1Co.9. 13. and they which wait at the a.
    are partakers with the a.
  10.18. partakers of the a.
Heb7.13. man gave attendance at the a.
  13.10. We have an a. whereof
Jas.2. 21. Isaac his son upon the a.
Rev. 6. 9. under the a. the souls
  8.3. stood at the a.
    upon the golden a.
  5. with fire of the a.
  9. 13. horns of the golden a.
  11. 1. the temple of God, and the a.
  14.18. came out from the a.
  16. 7. I heard another out of the a.
    bōmos.
Act.17.23. I found an a. with this in.

ALTERED.
heteros.
Lu. 9.29. of his countenance was a.
    (was another; i.e. not the same.)

ALTHOUGH.
ei.
Mar.14.29. a. all shall be offended, yet
    kaitoi.
Heb.4. 3. a. the works were finished

ALTOGETHER.
holos.
Jo. 9.34. Thou wast a. born in sins
    pantōs.
1Co. 5.10. Yet not a. with the fornicat.
  9.10. Or saith he it a. for our sakes
    en polus.
Act.26.29. were both almost and a.
    (both in little, and in much.)

ALWAY,   -s
pantote.
Mat.26.11. ye have the poor a-s with
    but me ye have not a-s
Mar.14.7. ye have the poor with you a-s
    but me ye have not a-s
Lu. 18. 1. that men ought a-s to pray
Jo. 7. 6. but your time is a. ready
  8. 29. for I do a-s those things that
  11. 42. knew that thou hearest me a-s
  12. 8. the poor a-s ye have with
    you; but me ye have not a-s
  18. 20. whither the Jews a-s resort
Ro. 1. 9. a-s in my prayers
1Co. 1. 4. thank my God a-s on your
  15. 58. a-s abounding in the work
2Co. 2. 14. which a. causeth us to
  4. 10. a-s bearing about in the
  5. 6. Therefore we are a-s confi.
  9. 8. that ye, a-s having
Gal.4. 18. to be zealously affected a-s
Eph.5.20. Giving thanks a-s for all
Phi. 1. 4. a-s in every prayer of mine

Phi. 20. with all boldness, as a-s so
2. 12. my beloved as ye have a-s
4. 4. Rejoice in the Lord a.
Col. 1. 3. praying a-s for you
4. 6. Let your speech be a. with
12. a-s labouring fervently for
1Th. 1. 2. We give thanks to God a-s
2. 16. to fill up their sins a.
3. 6. good remembrance of us a-s
2Th. 1. 3. are bound to thank God a-s
11. Wherefore also we pray a-s
2. 13. bound to give thanks a. to
Phile. 4. mention of thee a-s in my
aei.
Act. 7.51. ye do a-s resist the Holy Gh.
2Co. 4.11. we which live are a. delivered
6.10. As sorrowful, yet a. rejoicing
Tit. 1.12. The Cretians are a. liars
Heb.3.10. They do a. err in their hearts
1Pet.3.15. be ready a-s to give an
2Pet.1.12. to put you a-s in remembra.
diapantos.
Mar. 5.5. a-s night and day, he was
(through the whole [time.])
Act.10.2. and prayed to God a.
24.16. to have a-s a conscience void
Ro.11.10. and bow down their back a.
Heb.9.6. the priests went a-s into
dia [gen.] pas.
Mat.18.10. their angels do a-s behold
Act.2.25. the Lord a-s before my face
1Th.3.16. you peace a-s by all means
en pas kairos.
Lu.21.36. and pray a-s that ye may be
(in every season.)
Eph.6.18. Praying a-s with all prayer
pas ho hēmera.
Mat.28.20. and lo I am with you a.
hekastote.
2Pet.1.15. to have these things a-s
pantē.
Act.24.3. We accept it a-s, and in all

AMAZED.
existēmi.
Mat.12.23. all the people *were* a.
Mar.2. 12. that they *were* all a.
6. 51. they *were* sore a. in them.
Acts. 2. 7.12. they *were* all a.
9.21. all that heard him *were* a.
ekplēssō.
Mat.19.25. they *were* exceedingly a.
Lu. 2.48. they saw him they *were* a.
9.43. And they were all a. at the
lambanō ekstasis.
Mar.16.8. for they trembled and were a.
Lu. 5.26. And they were all a., and they
(astonishment seized them.)
thambeō.
Mar.1.27.And they *were* all a.,insomuch
10.32. before them, and they *were* a.
ekthambeō.
Mar.9.15. beheld him, *were greatly* a.
14.33. and began to *be sore* a. and to
thambos.
Lu.4.36. And they were all a., and spake
(amazement was upon them.)

AMAZEMENT.
ekstasis.
Act.3.10. filled with wonder and a.
ptoēsis.
1Pet. 3.6. and are not afraid with any a.

AMBASSADOR.
presbeuō.
2Co.5.20. now then we *are* a-s for Christ
Eph.6.20. For which I *am an* a. in

AMBASSAGE.
presbeia.
Lu.14.32. he sendeth an a. and desireth

AMEN.
amēn.
Mat.6.13. and the glory, for ever. a.
28.20. the end of the world. a.
Mar.16.20. with signs following. a.
Lu.24.53. praising and blessing God. a.
Jo.21.25. that should be written. a.
Ro. 1.25. who is blessed for ever. a.
9. 5. God blessed for ever. a.
11.36. be glory for ever. a.
15.33. peace be with you all. a.
16. 20.24. be with you. a.
27. Jesus Christ for ever. a.
1Co.14.16. unlearned say a. at thy giv.
16.24. you all in Christ Jesus. a.
2Co. 1.20. are yea, and in him a., unto
13.14. Holy Gh. be with you all. a.
Gal. 1. 5. glory for ever and ever. a.
6.18. Christ be with your spirit. a.
Eph.3.21. ages, world without end. a.
6.24. Jesus Christ in sincerity. a.
Phi. 4.20. be glory for ever and ever. a.
23. be with you all. a.
Col. 4.18. Grace be with you. a.
1Th. 5.28. Christ be with you. a.
2Th. 3.18. Christ be with you all. a.
1Ti. 1.17. glory for ever and ever. a.
6.16. and power everlasting. a.
21. Grace be with thee. a.
2Ti. 4.18. be glory for ever and ever. a.
22. Grace be with you. a.
Tit. 3.15. Grace be with you all. a.
Phile. 25. Christ be with your spirit. a.
Heb.13.21.glory for ever and ever. a.
25. Grace be with you all. a.
1Pet.4.11. for ever and ever. a. 5.11.
5.14. that are in Christ Jesus. a.
2Pet.3.18. both now and for ever. a.
1Jo. 5.21. yourselves from idols. a.
2Jo. 13. thy elect sister greet thee. a.
Jude 25. both now and ever. a.
Rev.1. 6. dom. for ever and ever. a.
7. because of him. Even so, a.
18. I am alive for evermore, a.
3.14. These things saith the A.
5.14. And the four beasts said, a.
7.12. Saying a.: Blessing, and glory
our God for ever and ever. a.
19. 4. throne, saying, a.
22.20. a. Even so come, Lord J.
21. Jesus C. be with you all. a.

AMEND.
echō kompsoteron.
Jo. 4.52. the hour when he began to a.
(had [himself] *i.e., was better.)*

AMETHYST.
amethustos.
Re.21.20. a jacinth; the twelfth, an a.

AMISS.
atopos.
Lu.23.41. this man hath done nothing a.
kakōs.
Jas. 4.3. receive not, because ye ask a.

AMONG.
en
Mat. 2.6. not the least a. the princes
4.23. disease a. the peo.; 9. 35.
11.11. a. them that are born of
16.7. they reasoned a. yourselves
8. why reason ye a. yourselves
20.26. it shall not be so a. you
*(And in all other passages in which it
occurs except the following:—)*
pros.
Mar.1.27. they questioned a. themselves

Mar.8.16. they reasoned a. themselves
9.33. that ye disputed a. yourselves
34. had disputed a. themselves
10.26. saying a. themselves
12. 7.15.31,16.3. said a. themselves
Lu. 4.36. and spake a. themselves
20.14. they reasoned a. themselves
22.23. began to inquire a.themselves
Jo. 6.52. strove a. themselves
7.35. said the Jews a. themselves
12.19. said a. themselves
16.17. of his disciples a. themselves
19.24. said therefore a. themselves
Act.4.15. they conferred a. themselves
28. 4. they said a. themselves
25. agreed not a. themselves
2Co.12.21. my God will humble me a. you
eis.
Mat.13.22.He also that received seed a.
Mar.4. 7. some fell a. thorns
18. they which are sown a. thorns
8.19. I brake the five loaves a.
20. when the seven a. four thous.
13.10. first be published a. all nati.
Lu. 8.14. that which fell a. thorns
10.36. him that fell a. the thieves
24.47. in his name a. all nations
Jo. 6. 9. what are they a. so many
21.23. this saying abroad a. the breth.
Act.2.22. a man approved of God a. you
4.17. spread no further a. the peo.
14.14. ran *in* a. the people crying
20.29. wolves enter *in* a. you.
2Co. 11.6. manifest a. you in all things
1Th. 5.15. both a. yourselves, and to all
1Pet.4. 8. fervent charity a. yourselves
mesos.
Mat.13.25.sowed tares a. the wheat
49. sever the wicked from a. the
Lu. 8. 7. And some fell a. thorns
10. 3. as lambs a. wolves
22.27. I am a. you as he that serveth
22.55. Peter sat down a. them
Jo. 1.26. there standeth one a. you
Act.17.33. Paul departed from a. them
23.10. by force from a. them
1Co. 5. 2. be taken away from a. you
2Co. 6.17. come out from a. them
1Th. 2. 7. But we were gentle a. you
meta, [gen.]
Lu. 22.37. reckoned a. the transgressors
24. 5. the living a. the dead
Jo. 6.43. Murmur not a. yourselves
11.56. and spake a. themselves
16.19. Do ye inquire a. yourselves
ek.
Mat.12.11. What man shall there be a.
Jo. 12.20. Greeks a. them that came
42. a. the chief rulers also many
Act.3.23. destroyed *from* a. the people
27.22. no loss of any man's life a.
1Co.5.13. put away *from* a. yourselves
Heb.5.1. high priest taken *from* a. men
Act. 6.3. look ye *out* a. you seven men
epi, [accu.]
Mat.13.7. And some fell a. thorns
Act.1.21. Lord Jesus went in and out a.
2Th.1.10. because our testimony a. you
Re. 7.15. on the throne shall dwell a.
para, [dat.]
Mat.28.15. commonly reported a. the
Col. 4.16. when this epistle is read a.
Rev.2.13. martyr, who was slain a.
kata, [accu.]
Act.21.21. all the Jews which are a.
26.3. questions which are a. the
hupo.
Act.10.22. of good report a. all the
sungkrinō.
2Co.10.12. *comparing* themselves a.

engkatoikeð.
²Pet. 2.8. righteous man *dwelling* **a.**
  dia. [*gen.*]
²Tim.2.2. heard of me **a.** many witness
  sullaleð.
Lu. 4.36. and *spake* **a.** themselves.
  peripiptō.
Lu.10.30. and *fell* **a.** thieves
  empiptō.
Lu.10.36. him that *fell* **a.** thieves.

ANATHEMA.
anathema.
¹Co.16.22. let him be **a.** maranatha

ANCHOR.   -s.
angkura.
Act.27.29. they cast four **a-**s out of the
  30. would have cast **a-**s out of the
  40. they had taken up the **a-**s
Heb.6.19. which hope we have as an **a.**

ANKLE-BONE.
sphuron.
Act. 3.7. his feet and **a-**s received

AND.
de, (*and, then, but, now.*)
Mat. 1.2. **a.** Isaac begat Jacob, **a.** Jacob
  begat Judas, &c.
  12. **a.** after they were brought
  21. **a.** she shall bring forth a son
  &c.
(*When* "and" *occurs at the beginning of
a sentence (as above) de (not* dē) *is
the word most generally so translated.*)

kai, (*and, even, also.*)
Mat. 1.2. Jacob begat Judas **a.** his
  3. Judas begat Phares, **a.** Zara
  11. begat Jechonias **a.** his breth.
  17. **a.** from David until the car.
  a. from the carrying away
  19. being a just man, **a.** not will.
(*This word,* kai, *is the true Greek for
and. It differs from* de, *in being
used to connect* thoughts, *rather than
to introduce* them. *Its occurrence is
too frequent for quotation. The following are the exceptions to the above
general rules :—*)
te.
Mt.23. 6. **a.** love the uppermost rooms
27.48. **a.** filled it with vinegar
28.12. **a.** had taken counsel
Mr.15.36. vinegar, **a.** put it on a reed
Lu.21.11. **a.** great earthquakes shall be
  a. fearful sights and great
  24.20. **a.** how the chief priests and
Jo. 4.42. **a.** said unto the woman
6.18. **a.** the sea arose by reason of
Act.2. 3. **a.** it sat upon each of them
  9. **a.** in Judæa, and Cappadocia
  10. Phrygia **a.** Pamphilia in
  33. **a.** having received of the Fa.
  37. **a.** said unto Peter and to the
  40. **a.** with many other words did
  43. **a.** many wonders and signs
  46. **a.** they, continuing daily with
  a. breaking bread from house
3.10. **a.** they knew that it was he
4.13. **a.** they took knowledge of
  33. **a.** great grace was upon them
5.19. **a.** brought them forth, and
  35. **a.** said unto them, Ye men of
  42. **a.** daily in the temple, and in
6. 7. **a.** a great company of the
  12. **a.** they stirred up the
  13. **a.** set up false witnesses
7.26. **a.** the next day he shewed
8. 1. **a.** they were all scattered
  3. **a.** hailing men and women
12

Act. 8. 6. **a.** the people with one accord
  13. **a.** wondered, beholding the
  25. **a.** preached the gospel in
  31. **a.** he desired Philip that he
9. 6. **a.** he trembling and
  15. kings, **a.** the children of Is.
  18. **a.** he received sight forthwith
  24. **a.** they watched the gates
10.22. **a.** of good report among all
  28. **a.** he said unto them, Ye
  33. **a.** thou hast well done that
  48. **a.** he com. them to be bap.
11.13. **a.** he shewed us how he had
  21. **a.** a great number believed
  26. **a.** the disciples were called
12. 6. **a.** the keepers before the door
  8. **a.** the angels said unto him
  12. **a.** when he had considered the
13. 1. **a.** Manaen, which had been
  4. **a.** from thence they sailed
14.12. **a.** they called Barnabas Jupi.
  21. **a.** when they had preached
15. 4. **a.** they declared all things
  5. **a.** to command them to keep
  39. **a.** so Barnabas took Mark
16.11. **a.** the next day to Neapolis
  12. **a.** from thence to Philippi
  13. **a.** on the Sabbath we went
  23. **a.** when they had laid many
  26. **a.** immediately all the doors
  34. **a.** when he had brought them
17. 4. **a.** of the devout Greeks a
  a. of the chief women
  5. **a.** assaulted the house of
  19. **a.** they took him, and brought
  26. **a.** hath made of one blood all
18. 4. **a.** persuaded the Jews and
  11. **a.** he continued there a year
  26. **a.** he began to speak boldly in
19. 3. **a.** he said unto them, Unto
  6. **a.** they spake with tongues
  11. **a.** God wrought special mira.
  12. **a.** the evil spirits went out of
  18. **a.** many that believed
  29. **a.** having caught Gaius and
20. 3. **a.** there abode three months
  7. **a.** continued his speech until
  11. **a.** talked a long while, even
  35. **a.** to remember the words of
21.11. **a.** bound his own hands and
  18. **a.** all the elders were present
  20. **a.** said unto him, Thou seest
  28. **a.** further brought Greeks
  30. **a.** all the city was moved, and
  37. **a.** as Paul was to be led into
22. 7. **a.** I fell unto the ground, and
  8. **a.** he said unto me, I am Jesus
  28. **a.** the chief captain answered
23.10. **a.** to bring him into the castle
  24. **a.** provide them beasts, that
  35. **a.** he commanded him to be
24.5. **a.** a ringleader of the sect of
  23. **a.** he commanded a centurion
    to keep Paul, **a.** to let
  27. **a.** Felix, willing to shew the
26.10. **a.** when they were put to
  11. **a.** being exceedingly mad
  16. seen, **a.** of those things in
  30. **a.** Bernice, and they that sat
27. 3. **a.** the next day we touched
  5. **a.** when we had sailed over
  8. **a.**, hardly passing it, came
  17. **a.**, fearing lest they should
  20. **a.** no small tempest lay on us
  21. **a.** to have gained this harm
  43. **a.** commanded that they
Ro. 1.27. **a.** likewise also the men
  2.19. **a.** art confident that thou
14. 8. **a.** whether we die, we die unto
16.26. **a.** by the scriptures of the
¹Co. 1.30. wisdom, **a.** righteousness
  4.21. **a.** in the spirit of meekness

Eph.3.19. **a. to** know the love of Christ
Heb.1. 3. **a.** upholding all things by the
  6. 2. **a.** of laying on of hands
    a. of resurrection of the dead
  4. **a.** have tasted of the heavenly
  5. **a.** the powers of the world to
  9. 1. **a.** a worldly sanctuary
  11.32. **a.** of Barak, and of Samson,
  12. 2. **a.** is set down at the right
Jude 6. **a.** the angels which kept not
Rev.1. 2. **a.** of all things that he saw
  21.12. **a.** had a wall great and high
  te kai.
Lu. 2.16. **a.** found Mary and Joseph
  12.45. **a.** to eat and drink, and
Act.26.20. **a.** thr. all the c. of Judæa, and
Heb.4.12. **a.** of the joints and marrow
Ja. 3. 7. **a.** of serpents, and of things
  oun men.
Lu. 3.18. **a.** many other things in his
Act. 8.25. **a.** they when they had tes.
  15. 3. **a.** being brought on their way
  17.30. **a.** the times of this ignorance
  28. 5. **a.** he shook off the beast
  oun.
Mat.18.29. **a.** his fellow servant, fell
Jo.20.11. **a.** as she wept she stooped
Act.15.39. **a.** the contention was so sharp
  25.23. **a.** on the morrow when Ag.
  gar.
Jo. 4.37. **a.** herein is that saying true
Act. 8.39. **a.** he went on his way rejoicing
²Ti. 2. 7. **a.** the Lord give thee underst.
  alla.
Lu. 12.16. **a.** will not rather say
  24.21. **a.** besides all this
  ē.
Mar.6.11. **a.** for Sodom **a.** Gomorrha, in
¹Co.11.27. eat this bread **a.** drink this
¹Pet.1.18. as silver **a.** gold from your
  hama.
Act.27.40. sea, **a.** loosed the rudder bands
  dē.
Act.15.36. Let us go again **a.** visit our
  ana.
Lu. 10.1. sent them two **a.** two, before
  meta, [*gen.*]
Jo. 3.25. **a.** the Jews about purifying
  hostis.
Act. 9.35. **a.** (*who*) turned to the Lord

(See *also other words of which*
"and" *is a part translation.*)]

ANGEL.
anggelos.
Mat.1.20. the **a.** of the Lord appeared
  24. as the **a.** of the Lord had
  2.13. **a.** of the Lord appeareth to
  19. an **a.** of the Lord appeareth
  4.6. He shall give his **a.** charge
  11. behold, **a-**s came and minist.
  13.39. and the reapers are the **a-**s
  41. Son of man send forth his **a-**s
  49. the **a-**s shall come forth, and
  16.27. glory of his Fath. with his **a-**s
  18.10. That in heaven their **a-**s do
  22 30. as the **a-**s of God; Mar. 12.25.
  24.31. And he shall send his **a-**s
  36. no, not the **a-**s of heaven
  25.31. all the holy **a-**s with him
  41. prep. for the devil and his **a-s**
  26.53. than twelve legions of **a-**s
  28. 2. the **a.** of the Lord descended
  5. the **a.** answered and said
Mar.1.13. the **a-**s ministered unto him
  8.38. of his Father with the holy **a-s**
  13.27. then shall he send his **a-s**
  32. not the **a-**s which are in
Lu. 1.11. appeared unto him an **a.**
  13. the **a.** said unto him, Fear
  18. Zacharias said unto the **a.**

Luk.1.19. the a. answering said unto
26. the sixth month the a. Gab.
28. And the a. came in unto her
30. a. said unto her, Fear not,
34. Then said Mary unto the a.
35. the a. answered and said unto
38. And the a. departed from her
2. 9. the a. of the Lord came upon
10. the a. said unto them, Fear
13. with the a. a multitude of
15. as the a-s were gone away
21. which was so named of the a.
4.10. shall give his a-s charge over
9.26. Father's, and of the holy a-s
12. 8. confess before the a-s of God
9. denied before the a-s of God
15.10. presence of the a-s of God
16.22. by the a-s into Abraham's
22.43. there appeared an a. unto
24.23. had also seen a vision of a-s
Jo. 1. 51. the a-s of God ascending and
5. 4. For an a. went down at
12.29. others said, An a. spake to
20.12. seeth two a-s in white sitting
Act. 5.19. the a. of the Lord by night
6.15. as it had been the face of an a.
7.30. mount Sinia an a. of the Lord
35. by the hand of the a. which
38. with the a. which spake to
53. law by the disposition of a.
8.26. a. of the Lord spake unto
10. 3. an a. of God coming in to
7. the a. which spake unto Cor.
22. warned from God by an holy a.
11.13. had seen an a. in his house
12. 7. the a. of the Lord came upon
8. the a. said unto him, Gird
9. which was done by the a.
10. forthwith the a. departed
11. the Lord had sent his a.
15. said they, It is his a.
23. the a. of the Lord smote him
23. 8. no resurrection, neither a.
9. if a spirit or an a. hath spoken
27.23. by me this night the a. of God
Ro. 8.38. life, nor a-s, nor principalities
1Co. 4.9. the world, and to a-s, and to
6. 3. Know that we shall judge a-s
11.10. on her head because of the a-s
13. 1. the tongues of men and of a-s
2Co.11.14.transformed into an a. of light
Gal. 1.8. we, or an a. from heaven
3.19. and it was ordained by a-s in
4.14. received me as an a. of God
Col. 2.18. and worshipping of a-s
2Th. 1.7. heaven with his mighty a-s
1Ti. 3.16. in the Spirit, seen of a.s
5.21. Jesus Christ, and the elect a-s
Heb. 1.4. so much better than the a-s
5. unto which of the a-s said he
6. all the a-s of God worship him
7. a-s he saith, Who mak. his a-s
13. to which of the a-s said he at
2. 2. word spoken by a-s was stedf.
5. unto the a-s hath he not put
7. a little lower than the a-s
9. made a lit. lower than the a-s
16. not on him the nature of a-s
12.22. innumerable company of a-s
13. 2. have entertained a-s unawares
1Pet.1.12. which things the a-s desire to
3.22. a-s and authorities and powers
2Pet.2. 4. spared not the a-s that sinned
11. Whereas a-s, which are greater
Jude 6. the a-s which kept not their
Rev. 1.1. sent and signified by his a.
20. the a-s of the seven churches
2. 1. Unto the a. of the ch. of Eph.
ve. 3. 8. 12. 18. *ch.* 3. 1. 7. 14.
5. my Father, and before his a-s
5. 2. I saw a strong a. proclaiming
11. I heard the voice of many a-s

Rev.7. 1. I saw four a-s standing
7.2. I saw another a. ascending
a loud voice to the four a-s
11. all the a-s stood round
8.2. I saw the seven a-s which
3. another a. came and stood at
4. before God out of the a-s hand
5. the a. took the censer, and
6. seven a-s which had the seven
7. first a. sounded, and there followed ; 8. the second a. ; 10.
third a. ; 12. fourth a.
13. an a. flying through the midst
the trumpet of the three a-s
9. 1. the fifth a. sounded, and I saw
11. the a. of the bottomless pit
13. And the sixth a. sounded,
14. Saying to the sixth a., Loose
the four a-s which are
15. And the four a-s were loosed
10. 1. And I saw another mighty a.
5. the a. which I saw stand
7. of the voice of the seventh a.
8. open in the hand of the a.
9. I went unto the a., and said
10. little book out of the a-'s hand
11. 1. and the a. stood, saying, Rise
15. And the seventh a. sounded
12. 7. Michael and his a-s fought ;
the dragon fought and his a-s
9. his a-s were cast out with him
14. 6. I saw another a. fly in the
8. there followed another a.
9. the third a. followed them
10. in the presence of the holy a-s
15. another a. came out of ; 17.
18. another a. came out from the
19. the a. thrust in his sickle
15. 1. seven a-s having the seven
6. the seven a-s came out of
7. gave unto the seven a-s seven
8. plagues of the seven a-s were
16. 1. saying to the seven a-s, Go
3. second a. poured out his vial
4. third a. poured out his vial
5. I heard the a. of the waters
8. fourth a. ; 10. fifth a. ; 12.
sixth a. ; 17. seventh a.
17. 1. one of the seven a. which
7. And the a. said unto me
18. 1. I saw another a. come down
21. a mighty a. took up a stone
19.17. I saw an a. standing in the sun
20. 1. And I saw an a. come down
21. 9. one of the seven a-s which
12. at the gates twelve a-s
17. of a man, that is, of the a.
22. 6. sent his a. to shew unto
8. before the feet of the a.
16. have sent mine a. to testify
isanggelos.
Lu.20.36. for they are *equal unto the* a-s

ANGER. [*noun.*]
orgē.
Mar. 3.5. round about on them with a.
Eph.4.31. and wrath, and a., and clam.
Col. 3.8. put off all these, a., wrath

ANGER, [*verb.*]
parorgizō.
Ro.10.19. by a foolish nation I *will* a.

ANGRY.
orgizomai.
Mat.5.22. *who* soever *is* a. with his
Lu.14.21. master of the house *being* a.
15.28. he *was* a. and would not go
Eph.4.26. *Be* ye a. and sin not
Re.11.18. the nations *were* a.
cholaō.
Jo. 7.23. *are* ye a. at me because I

---

orgilos.
Tit. 1.7. not *soon* a., not given to

ANGUISH.
thlipsis.
Jo.16.21. remembereth no more the a.
stenochōria.
Ro. 2. 9. Tribulation and a. upon
sunochē.
2Co. 2.4. out of much affliction and a.

ANISE.
anēthon.
Mat.23.23. tithe of mint, and a., and

ANOINT,   -*ed*
aleiphō.
Mat.6.17. a. thine head, and wash
Mar.6.13. a-*ed* with oil many that were
16.1. they might come and a. him
Lu. 7. 38. a-*ed* them with the ointment
46. with oil thou *didst* not a. but
this woman *hath* a-*ed* my feet
Jo. 11. 2. Mary *which* a-*ed* the Lord
12.3. a-*ed* the feet of Jesus, and
Jas. 5. 14. a-*ing* him with oil in the
chriō.
Lu. 4. 18. he *hath* a-*ed* me to preach
Act.4.27. Jesus, whom thou *hast* a-*ed*
10.38. How God a-*ed* Jesus of Naz.
2Co. 1.21. and *hath* a-*ed* us, is God
Heb. 1.9. *hath* a-*ed* thee with the oil of
engchriō.
Re. 3.18. a. thine eyes with eye salve
epichriō.
Jo. 9. 6. he a-*ed* the eyes of the blind
11. and a-*ed* mine eyes and said
murizō.
Mar.14.8. to a. my body to the burying

ANOINTING.
chrisma.
1Jo. 2.27. But the a. which ye have but
but as the same a. teacheth

ANON.
eutheōs.
Mar.1.30. fever, and a. they tell him of
euthus.
Mat.13.20. word, and a. with joy

ANOTHER.
allos.
Mat.2.12. their own country a. way
8. 9. and to a. Come, and he com. ;
Lu. 7.8.
10.23. this city, flee ye into a.
13.24.31. a. par. put he forth unto
33. a. parable spake he unto them
19. 9. fornication, and shall marry a.
21.33. Hear a. parable : There was
26.71. into the porch a. maid saw
Mar.10.11.away his wife, and marry a.
12. husband, and be married to a.
12. 4. he sent unto them a. servant
5. again he sent a. ; and him
14.19. Is it I? and a. said, is it I?
58. three days I will build a.
Lu.7.19. 19.20. come? or look we for a.
22.59. one hour after a. confidently
Jo. 5. 7. a. steppeth down before me
32. There is a. that beareth wit.
43. if a. shall come in his
14.16. he shall give you a. Comforter
18.15. and so did a. disciple
21.18. a. shall gird thee, and carry
Act.19.32.one thing, and some a.
21.34. some cried one thing, some a.
1Co. 3.10. foundation, and a. buildeth
10.29. liberty judged of a. man's
12. 8. to a. the word of knowledge
9. to a. the gifts of healing by

13

¹Co.12.10. To a. the working of miracles;
    to a. prophecy; to a. dis-
    cerning of spirits
    to a. the interpretation of ton.
14.30. revealed to a. that sitteth by
15.39. one kind of flesh of men, a.
    flesh of beasts, a. of fishes,
    and a. of birds
    41. one glory of the sun, and a.
    glory of the moon, and a.
    glory of the stars
²Co. 11.4. he that cometh preacheth a.
Gal. 1. 7. Which is not a.; but there
Heb.8. 4. have spoken of a. day
Rev.6. 4. there went out a. horse
    7. 2. I saw a. angel ascending
    8. 3. a. angel came and stood at
    10. 1. I saw a. mighty angel
    12. 3. there appeared a. wonder in
    13.11. I beheld a. beast coming
    14. 6. I saw a. angel fly in the
    8. there followed a. angel, saying
    15.17. a. angel came out of the
    18. a. angel came out from
    15. 1. I saw a. sign in heaven
    16. 7. I heard a. out of the altar
    18. 1. I saw a. angel come down
    4. I heard a. voice from heaven
    20.12. a. book was opened, which

heteros.

Mat.8.21. And a. of his disciples said
    11.3. or do we look for a.
Mar.16.12. he appeared in a. form
Lu. 6. 6. also on a. sabbath that he
    9.56. And they went to a. village
    59. And he said unto a., Follow
    61. And a. also said, Lord, I will
    14.20. And a. said, I have married
    31. to make war against a. king
    16. 7. said he to a., And how much
    18. and marrieth a. committeth
    19.20. And a. came, saying, Lord
    20.11. he sent a. servant: and they
    22.58. a. saw him, and said
Jo. 19.37. again a. scripture saith
Act. 1.20. his bishoprick let a. take
    7.18. a. king arose, which
    12.17. and went into a. place
    13.35. Wherefore he said also in a.
    17. 7. that there is a. king, one
Ro. 2. 1. thou judgest a., thou con.
    21. therefore which teaches a.
    7. 3. she be married to a. man
    though she be married to a.
    4. that ye should be married to a.
    23. a. law in my members
    13. 8. he that loveth a. hath fulfill.
¹Co. 3. 4. and a. I am of Apollos
    4. 6. puffed up for one against a.
    6. 1. having a matter against a.
    10.24. but every man a's wealth
    12. 9. To a. faith by the same
    10. to a. divers kinds of tongues
    15.40. glory of the terrestrial is a.
²Co. 11.4. or if ye receive a. spirit
    or a. gospel which ye have
Gal. 1. 6. of Christ unto a. gospel
    6. 4. in himself alone, and not in a.
Heb.5. 6. As he saith also in a. place
    7.11. that a. priest should rise
    13. pertaineth to a. tribe
    15. there ariseth a. priest
Jas. 2.25. and had sent them out a.
    4.12. who art thou that judgest a.

allotrios.

Lu.16.12. in that which is a. man's
Ro.14. 4. that judgest a. man's servant
    15.20. build upon a. man's founda.
²Co.10.16.not to boast in a. man's line

allophulos.

Act.10.28. come unto one of a. nation

(See *Compassion, One, Prefer.*)

14

ANSWER, [*noun.*]   -s.
apokrisis.
Lu. 2.47. at his understanding and a-s
    20.26. they marvelled at his a.
Jo. 1.22. that we may give an a.
    19. 9. Jesus gave him no a.

apologia.
¹Co. 9. 3. Mine a. to them that
²Ti. 4.16. At my first a. no man
¹Pet.3.15. to give an a. to every

eperōtēma.
¹Pet.3.21. the a. of a good conscience

chrēmatismos.
Ro.11. 4. what saith the a. *of God* unto

ANSWER, [*verb.*]   -ing, -ed.
apokrinomai.
Mat.3.15. Jesus a-*ing*, and said unto him
    4. 4. he a-*ed* and said, It is written

(*And all other passages in which the
word is found except the following:—*)

apologeomai.
Lu.12.11. how or what thing ye *shall* a.
    21.14. medi. before what ye shall a.
Act.24.10.more cheerfully a. for myself
    25. 8. *While* he a-*ed for* him *self*
    26. 1. the hand, and a-*ed for* him *self*
    2. I shall a. *for* my *self* this

epō.
Lu.20. 3. ask you one thing; and a. me

hupolambanō.
Lu.10.30. And Jesus a-*ing* said, A cer.

antapokrinomai.
Lu.14. 6. could not a. him *again*

antilegō.
Tit. 2. 9. in all things not a-*ing again*

apologia.
Act.25.16.have licence to a. *for* him *self*
    (opportunity *to make a defence.*)

sustoicheō.
Gal. 4.25. and a-*eth to* Jerusalem which

ANTICHRIST,   -s.
antichristos.
¹Jo. 2.18. heard that a. shall come
    now are there many a-s
    22. He is a. that denieth the F.
    4. 3. this is that spirit of a. where.
²Jo. 7. This is a deceiver and an a.

ANY.   (See *If*.)
tis, (*some one.*)
Mat.11.27. neither knoweth a. man the
    12.19. neither shall a. man hear his
    21. 3. And if a. man say ought unto
    22.46. neither durst a. man from
    24.17. to take a. thing out of his
    23. if a. man shall say unto you
Mar.8.26. nor tell it to a. in the town
    9.30. that a. man should know it
    11. 3. And if a. man say unto you
    13. he might find a. thing thereon
    16. that a. man should carry any
    25. if ye have ought against a.
    13. 5. Take heed lest a.man deceive
    15. to take a. thing out of his
    21. And then if a. man shall say
    16.18. and if they drink a. deadly
Lu. 9. 23. If a. man will come after me
    14. 8. thou art bidden of a. man
    19. 8. taken a. thing from a. man
    31. And if a. man ask you
    20.28. If a. man's brother die
    22.35. lacked ye a. thing
    24.41. Have ye here a. meat
Jo. 1. 46. Can there a. good thing come
    2.25. that a. should testify of man
    4.33. Hath a. man brought him
    6.46. Not that a. man hath seen
    51. if a. man eat of this bread

Jo. 7. 4. that doeth a. thing in secret
    17. If a. man will do his will
    37. If a. man thirst, let him come
    48. Have a. of the rulers or of the
    9. 22. if a. man did confess that he
    31. if a. man be a worshipper of
    32. that a. man opened the eyes
    10. 9. by me if a. man enter in
    28. neither shall a. man pluck
    11. 9. if a. man walk in the day
    57. if a. man knew where he
    12.26. If a. man serve me, let him
    if a. man serve me, him will
    47. And if a. man hear my words
    14.14. shall ask a. thing in my name
    16.30. that a. man should ask thee
Act.4.34. Neither was there a. among
    9. 2. that if he found a. of this
    10.47. Can a. man forbid water
    17.25. as though he needed a. thing
    19.38. have a matter against a. man
    39. if ye enquire a. thing concer.
    24.12. temple disputing with a. man
    20. have found a. evil doing in
    25.8. have I offended a. thing at all
    11. committed a. thing worthy
    16. to deliver a. man to die
    27.42. lest a. of them should swim
    28.21. neither a. of the brethren
    shewed or spake a. harm of
Ro. 8. 9. if a. man have not the Sp. of
    39. nor depth, nor a. other creat.
    9.11. having done a. good or evil
    14.14. esteemeth a. thing to be un.
    15.18. dare to speak of a. of those
¹Co. 1.15. Lest a. should say that I had
    2. 2. not to know a. thing among
    3. 7. ne. is he that planteth a-thing
    12. Now if a. man build upon
    14. If any man's work abide
    17. If a. man defile the temple of
    5.11. if a. man that is called a bro.
    6. 1. Dare a. of you having a mat.
    12. brought under the power of a.
    7.12. If a. brother hath a wife
    18. Is a. man called being circu.
    Is a. called in uncircumcision
    36. But if a. man think that he
    8. 2. And if a. man think that he
    knoweth a. thing.
    3. But if a. man love God, the
    10. For if a. man see thee which
    9.15. than that a. man should ma.
    10.19. that the idol is a. thing, or
    sacrifice to idols is a. thing
    27. If a. of them that believe not
    28. But if a. man say unto you
    11.16. if a. man seem to be conten.
    34. And if a. man hunger, let
    14.27. If a. man speak in an unkno.
    35. And if they will learn a. thing
    38. But if a. man be ignorant
    16.22. If a. man love not the L. Je.
²Co. 2. 5. But if a. have caused grief
    10. ye forgive a. thing, I forgive
    also; for if I forgave a. thing
    3. 5. to think a. thing as of oursel.
    10.7. If a. man trust to himself
    11.21. whereinsoever a. is bold
    12. 6. lest a. man should think of
    17. by a. of them whom I sent
Gal. 5. 6. circumcision availeth a. thing
    15. circumcision availeth a. thing
Eph. 2.9. Not of works, lest a. man
    5.27. spot, or wrinkle. or a. such
Phi. 2. 1. If there be therefore a. cons.
    a. comfort, a. fellowship, a.
    3.15. if in a. thing ye be otherwise
    4. 8. a. virtue, and if a. praise
Col. 2. 4. lest a. man should beguile
    8. Beware lest a. man spoil you
    23. not in a. honour to the satisf.

Col. 3.13. if a. *man* have a quarrel ag. a.

¹Th. 1. 8. we need not to speak a. *thing*

2. 9. not be chargeable unto a. of

5.15. render evil for evil unto a.

²Th. 3. 8. did we eat a. *man's* bread for

not be chargeable to a. of

14. And if a. *man* obey not our

¹Ti. 5. 4. But if a. widow have childre.

8. But if a. provide not for his

Heb. 3.12. lest there be in a. of you

13. lest a. of you be hardened

4. 1. a. of you should seem to come

11. lest a. *man* fall after the same

12.15. lest a. *man* fail of the grace of

a. root of bitterness

Jas. 1. 5. if a. of you lack wisdom

7. that he shall receive a. *thing*

26. If a. *man* among you seem

5.12. neither by a. other oath

13. Is a. among you afflicted

Is a. merry, let

14. Is a. sick among you, let him

19. if a. of you do err from the

¹Pet. 3. 1. if a. obey not the word, they

4.11. If a. *man* speak, let him sp.

if a. *man* minister, let him

²Pet. 3.9. not willing that a. should

¹Jo. 2.1. if a. *man* sin, we have an

15. If a. *man* love the world, the

27. and ye need not that a. *man*

4.20. if a. man say I love

5.14. if we ask a. *thing* according

16. If a. *man* see his brother sin

²Jo. 10. If there come a. unto you

Rev. 3.20. if a. *man* hear my voice

11. 5. and if a. *man* will hurt them

13. 9. If a. *man* have an ear, let

14. 9. If a. *man* worship the beast

22.18. If a. *man* shall add unto

19. And if a. *man* shall take

pas.

Mat.18.19. as touching a. thing that they

Act.10.14. I have never eaten a. thing

²Co. 1. 4. them which are in a. trouble

Heb.4.12. sharper than a. two-edged

Rev.7. 1. nor on the sea, nor on a. tree

16. sun light on them, nor a. heat

9. 4. nei. a. green thing, neither a.

21.27. into it a. thing that defileth

eti.

Mar.14.63. What need we a. *further* wit.

Lu.20.36. can they die a. *more*

22.71. What need we a. *further* wit.

Ro. 6. 2. dead to sin, live a. *longer*

Rev.12.8. there place found a. *more* in

18.22. shall be found a. *more* in thee

21. 4. shall there be a. *more* pain

heis.

Jo. 1.3. was not a. thing made that

Act. 4.32. neither said a. of them that

hekastos.

Eph. 6.8. whats. good thing a. *man*

mē.

Lu.20.27. deny that there is a. resurrec.

oudeis, (*with another negative.*)

(*In English a double negative is equal to an affirmative; but in Greek it makes the negation stronger.*)

Mat.22.16. neither carest thou for a. *man*

(neither carest thou for *no man*)

Mar.16.8. said they a. *thing* to a. *man*

Lu. 8.43. neither could be healed of a.

9.36. told no man a. of those things

20.40. not ask him a. *question at all*

(durst not ask him *nothing*.)

Jo.18.31. not lawful to put a. *man* to

Act. 4.12. neither is there sal. in a. other

(not salvation in *no* other.)

mēdeis, (*with another negative.*)

Mar.1.44. say nothing to a. *man*

(nothing to *no man*.)

Act.10.28. not call a. man common

Ro. 13.8. Owe no man a. thing, but

²Cor. 6.3. Giving no offence in a. thing

²Th. 2.3. no man deceive you by a.

¹Pet. 3.6. not afraid with a. amazement

ouketi, (*with another negative.*)

Mat.22.46. man ask him a. more quest.

(question him *no longer*.)

Mar. 9.8. they saw no man a. *more*

Lu.22.16. will not a. *more* eat thereof

Rev.18.11. brought them mer. a. *more*

mēketi, (*with another negative.*)

Act.25.24. he ought not to live a. *longer*

Ro. 14.13. not judge one anoth. a. *more*

oudeis, [*without another nega.*]

Mar. 5. 4. *neither* could a man tame

Jo. 8.33. were *never* in bond. to a. *man*

(were in b. to *no man* at any time.)

Act.27.22. *no* loss of a. man's life

34. *not* a hair fall from head of a.

Ja. 1.13. *neither* tempteth he a. *man*

mēdeis, (*without another nega.*)

Act.25.17. *without* a. delay on the mor.

mētis.

Jo. 4.33. Hath a. man brought him

7.48. Have a. of the rulers..believ.

21.5. children have ye a. meat

ou mē eti.

Rev.18.22. *no* craftsman found a. *more*

(any c. *not* found *no more*)

prostithēmi.

Heb.12.19. not *spoken* to them a. more

(should not be *added* to them)

(See *Lest, Means, Time, While.*)

APART.

kata idios.

Mat.14.13. into a desert place a.

23. into a mountain a.

17. 1. into an high mountain a.

19. the disciples to Jesus a.

20.17. took the twelve disciples a. in

Mar.6.31. a. into a desert place

9. 2. a high mountain a. by them.

apotithēmi.

Ja. 1.21. Wherefore lay a. all filthi.

APIECE.

ana.

Lu. 9. 3. neither have two coats a.

Jo. 2. 6. two or three firkins a.

APOSTLE.

apostolos.

Mat.10.2. the names of the twelve a-s

Mar.6.30. the a-s gathered themselves

Lu. 6.13. whom also he named a-s

9.10. the a-s, when they were

11.49. send them prophets and a-s

17. 5. the a-s said unto the Lord

22.14. the twelve a-s with him

24.10. told these things unto the a-s

Act. 1. 2. commandments unto the a-s

26. numbered with the eleven a-s

2.37. Peter, and to the rest of the a-s

42. in the a-s' doctrine and fellow.

43. were done by the a-s

4.33. gave the a-s witness of the

35. laid them down at the a-s' feet

36. who by the a-s was surnamed

37. laid it at the a-s' feet

5. 2. laid it at the a-s' feet

12. by the hands of the a-s were

18. laid their hands on the a-s

29. Peter and the other a-s answ.

5.34. to put the a-s forth a little

40. they had called the a-s

6. 6. Whom they set before the a-s

8. 1. Jud. and Sam., except the a-s

14. Now when the a-s which

18. laying on of the a-s' hands

9.27. brought him to the a-s, and

Act.11. 1. the a-s and brethren that were

14. 4. with Jews, part with the a-s

14. Which when the a-s, Barnabas

15. 2. unto the a-s and elders about

4. of the a-s and elders, and they

6. the a-s and elders came toget.

22. Then pleased it the a-s and

23. the a-s and elders and breth.

33. the brethren unto the a-s

16. 4. were ordained of the a-s and

Ro. 1. 1. called to be an a., separated

11.13. as I am the a. of the Gentiles

16. 7. are of note among the a-s

¹Co. 1. 1. called to be an a. of Jesus

4. 9. set forth us the a-s last

9. 1. Am I not an a. ? am I not

2. If I be not an a. unto others

5. as well as other a-s, and

12.28. first a., secondarily

29. Are all a. ? are all

15. 7. of James ; then of all the a-s

9. I am the least of the a-s,

not meet to be called an a.

²Co. 1. 1. Paul, an a. of Jesus Christ

11. 5. behind the very chiefest a-s

13. themselves into the a-s of

12.11. the very chiefest a-s

12. the signs of an a. were

Gal. 1. 1. Paul, an a., not of men

17. to them which were a-s

19. others of the a-s saw I none

Eph.1. 1. Paul, an a. of Jesus Christ

2.20. the foundation of the a-s and

3. 5. revealed unto his holy a-s and

4.11. he gave some, a-s; and some

Col. 1. 1. Paul, an a. of Jesus Christ

¹Th. 2. 6. as the a-s of Christ

¹Ti. 1. 1. Paul, an a. of Jesus Christ

2. 7. ordained a preacher, and an a.

²Tim.1. 1. Paul, an a. of Jesus Christ

11. appointed a prea., and an a.

Tit. 1. 1. an a. of Jesus Christ

Heb.3. 1. consider the a. and high pr.

¹Pet.1. 1. Peter, an a. of Jesus Christ

²Pet.1. 1. a servant and an a. of Jesus

3. 2. us the apostles of the Lo. and

Jude 17. before of the a-s of our Lord

Rev. 2. 2. them which say they are a-s

18.20. ye holy a-s and prophets

21.14. the names of the twelve a-s

pseudapostolos.

²Co.11.13. such are *false* a-s deceitful

APOSTLESHIP.

apostolē.

Act. 1.25. of this ministry and a.

Ro. 1. 5. received grace and a., for

¹Co. 9. 2. the seal of mine a. are ye

Gal. 2. 8. to the a. of the circumcision

APPAREL.

esthēs.

Act.1.10. stood by them in white a.

12.21. Herod, arrayed in royal a.

Ja. 2. 2. gold ring in goodly a.

himation.

¹Pet. 3. 3. or of putting on of a.

himatismos.

Act.20.33. no man's silver or gold or a.

katastolē.

¹Ti. 2. 9. adorn themselves in modest a.

APPARELLED.

himatismos.

Lu.7. 25. they which are gorgeously a.

APPEAL.   -ed.

epikaleomai.

Act.25.11. I a. *unto* Cesar.

12. hast thou a-*ed* unto Cesar

21. But when Paul had a-*ed*

25. himself hath a-*ed to* Augus.

Act.26.32. if he *had* not **a**-ed unto C.
28.19. constrained *to* **a.** *unto* Cesar

APPEAR,   -ed, -eth.
phainō.
Mat.1.20. angel of the Lord **a**-ed unto
2. 7. what time the star **a**-ed
13. **a**-eth to Joseph in a dream
19. **a**-eth in a dream to Joseph
6.16. *may* **a.** unto men to fast
18. thou **a.** not unto men to fast
13.26. then **a**-ed the tares also
23.27. which indeed **a.** beautiful
28. ye also outwardly **a.** righteous
24.30. then *shall* **a.** the sign of the S.
Mar.16.9. he **a**-ed first to Mary Magda.
Lu. 9. 8. of some, that Elias *had* **a**-ed
Ro. 7.13. But sin, that it *might* **a.** sin
2Co.13. 7. not that we *should* **a.** approv.
Heb.11.3. not made of things *which do* **a.**
Ja. 4.14. a vapour *that* **a**-eth for a little
1Pet.4.18. ungodly and the sinner **a.**
optomai.
Mat.17.3. there **a**-ed unto them Moses
Mar. 9.4. there **a**-ed unto them Elias
Lu. 1.11. there **a**-ed unto him an angel
9.31. Who **a**-ed in glory, *and* spake
22.43. And there **a**-ed an angel
24.34. and hath **a**-ed to Simon
Act. 2. 3. there **a**-ed unto them cloven
7. 2. The God of glory **a**-ed unto
30. there **a**-ed to him in the wil.
35. angel which **a**-ed to him in
9.17. Jesus, *that* **a**-ed unto thee
16. 9. a vision **a**-ed to Paul in the
26.16. I *have* **a**-ed unto thee for this
in the which I *will* **a.** unto
Heb.9.28. that look for him *shall* he **a.**
Rev.12.1. And there **a**-ed a great wond.
3. there **a**-ed another wonder iu
phaneroō.
Mar.16.12. After that he **a**-ed in anoth.
14. Afterward he **a**-ed unto the
2Co. 5.10. we must all **a.** before the
7.12. our care might **a.** unto you
Col. 3. 4. Christ who is our life, *shall* **a.**
then *shall* ye also **a.**
Heb.9.26. *hath* he **a**-ed to put away sin
1Pet. 5. 4. the chief Shepherd *shall* **a.**
1Jo. 2.28. then when he *shall* **a.**, we
3. 2. it *doth* not yet **a.** what we
when he *shall* **a.** we shall be
Rev. 3.18. of thy nakedness *do* not **a.**
epiphainō.
Act.27.20. nor stars in many days **a**-ed
Tit. 2.11. bringeth salvation *hath* **a**-ed
3. 4. of G. our S. toward man **a**-ed
emphanizō.
Mat.27.53. into the holy city and **a**-ed
Heb. 9.24. now *to* **a.** in the presence of
anaphainomai.
Lu.19.11. of G. should immediately **a.**
erchomai.
Act.22.30. com. all their council *to* **a.**
eimi phaneros.
1Tim.4.15. that thy profiting may **a.**
adēlos.
Lu.11.44. are as graves which **a.** *not*

APPEARANCE.
prosōpon.
2Co. 5.12. which glory in **a.** and not
10. 7. things after the *outward* **a.**
eidos.
1Th.5.22. Abstain from all **a.** of evil
opsis.
Jo. 7.24. Judge not according to the **a.**

APPEARING, [*noun.*]
epiphaneia.
1Ti. 6.14. the **a.** of our Lord Jesus Ch.
2Ti. 1.10. the **a.** of our Saviour.
16

2Ti. 4. 1. at his **a.** and his kingdom
8. them also that love his **a.**
Tit. 2.13. glorious **a.** of the great
apokalupsis.
1Pet. 1.7. glory at the **a.** of Jesus

APPEASED.
katastellō,
Act.19.35. *when* the town clerk *had* **a.**

APPOINT,   -ed.
tithēmi.
Mat.24.51.shall cut him asunder, and **a.**
Lu.12.46. and *will* **a.** him his portion
1Th. 5. 9. God *hath* not **a**-ed us to wrath
2Ti. 1.11. Whereunto I am **a**-ed a prea.
Heb.1. 2. whom he *hath* **a**-ed heir of all
1Pet.2. 8. whereunto also they *were* **a**-ed
diatassō.
Lu. 3.13. than that *which is* **a**-ed you
Act. 7.44. as he *had* **a**-ed speaking unto
20.13. for so had he **a**-ed, minding
Tit. 1. 5. every city, as I *had* **a**-ed thee
tassō.
Mat.28.16.where Jesus *had* **a**-ed them
Act.22.10. which *are* **a**-ed for thee to do
28.23. And *when* they *had* **a**-ed him
suntassō.
Mat.26.19.did as Jesus *had* **a**-ed them
27.10.field as the Lord **a**-ed me
histēmi.
Act.1.23. they **a**-ed two, Joseph, called
17.31. Because he *hath* **a**-ed a day in
diatithēmi.
Lu.22.29. I **a.** unto you a kingdom, as
my Father *hath* **a**-ed unto me
anadeiknumi.
Lu.10. 1. the Lord **a**-ed other seventy
apokeimai.
Heb.9.27. as it *is* **a**-ed unto men once to
poieō.
Heb.3. 2. faithful to him *that* **a**-ed him
kathistēmi.
Act. 6. 3. whom we may **a.** over this
protassomai.
Act.17.26.deter. the times *before* **a**-ed
keimai.
1Th. 3. 3. know that we *are* **a**-ed there.
prothesmia.
Gal. 4. 2. until the *time* **a**-ed of the Fa.
epithanatios.
1Co. 4. 9. as it were **a**-ed *to death;* for

APPREHEND,   -ed.
katalambanō.
Phi. 3.12. if that I *may* **a.** that for which
also I *am* **a**-ed
13. count not myself *to have* **a**-ed
piazō.
Act.12. 4. And *when* he *had* **a**-ed him, he
2Co.11.32. garrison, desirous *to* **a.** me

APPROACH,   -eth, -ing.
enggizō.
Lu.12.33. where no thief **a**-eth, neither
Heb.10.25.more, as ye see the day **a**-ing
aprositos.
1Ti. 6.16. light *which no man can* **a.**

APPROVE,   -ed, -est, -ing.
dokimos.
Ro.14.18. acceptable to God, and **a**-ed
16.10. Salute Apelles **a**-ed in Christ
1Co.11.19.they *which are* **a**-ed may be
2Co.10.18. commendeth himself is **a**-ed
13. 7. that we should appear **a**-ed
2Ti. 2.15. Study to shew thyself **a**-ed
dokimazō.
Ro. 2.18. **a**-est the things that are more
1Co.16. 3. whomsoever ye shall **a.** by
Phi. 1.10. That ye may **a.** things that
sunistēmi.
2Co. 6. 4. But in all things **a**-ing our.

2Cor.7.11. In all things ye *have* **a**-ed your
apodeiknumi.
Act. 2.22. man **a**-ed of God among you

APRON.
simikinthion.
Act.19.12. handkerchiefs or **a**-s, and the

APT.
didaktikos.
1Ti. 3. 2. to hospitality, **a.** *to teach*
2Ti. 2.24. unto all men, **a.** *to teach*

ARCHANGEL.
archanggelos.
1Th. 4.16. with the voice of the **a.**, and
Jude 9. yet Michael the **a.**, when

ARE. (See *Be.*)

ARISE,   -ose, -eth.
anistēmi.
Mat.9. 9. he **a**-ose and follow.Mar.2.14.
26.62. the high priest **a**-*ose, and* said
Mar.5.42. the damsel **a**-*ose,* and walked
7.24. from thence he **a**-*ose,* and
9.27. lifted him up; and he **a**-*ose*
10. 1. he **a**-*ose* from thence, and
14.57. there **a**-*ose* certain, *and* bare
Lu. 1.39. Mary **a**-*ose* in those days, and
4.38. he **a**-*ose* out of the syna., and
39. she **a**-*ose and* ministered unto
6. 8. midst. And he **a**-*ose and*
8.55. came again, and she **a**-*ose*
15.18. I will **a.** *and* go to my father
20. he **a**-*ose and* came to his fa.
17.19. said unto him **a.**, go thy way
23. 1. multitude of them **a**-*ose and*
24.12. Then **a**-*ose* Peter, *and* ran
Act. 5. 6. young men **a**-*ose,* wound..*and*
6. 9. Then there **a**-*ose* certain of
7.18. Till another king **a**-*ose,* which
8.26. **a.**, and go toward the south
27. he **a**-*ose and* went: and, be.
9. 6. **a.**, and go into the city, and
11. **a.**, *and* go into the street wh.
18. and **a**-*ose, and* was baptized
34. **a.**, make thy bed. And
he **a**-*ose* immediately
39. *Then* Peter **a**-*ose and* went
40. the body, said, Tabitha, **a.**
10.20. **a.** therefore, and get thee
11. 7. me, **a.**, Peter, slay and eat
12. 7. raised him up, saying, **a.** *up*
20.30. your own selves *shall* men **a.**
22.10. said unto me, **a.**, *and* go
16. **a.** *and* be baptized, and wash
23. 9. the Pharisees' part **a**-*ose, and*
Eph.5.14. **a.** from the dead, and Christ
Heb.7.15. there **a**-*eth* another priest
egeirō.
Mat.2.13. **a.**, *and* take the young child
14. *When he* **a**-*ose,* he took the
20. **a.**, *and* take the young child
21. he **a**-*ose, and* took the young
8.15. she **a**-*ose, and* ministered unto
26. Then he **a**-*ose, and* rebuked
9. 5. thee; or to say, **a.**, and walk
6. **a.**, take up thy bed, and go
7. he **a**-*ose, and* departed to his
19. Jesus **a**-*ose, and* followed his
25. the hand, and the maid **a**-*ose*
17. 7. said, **a.**, and be not afraid
24.24. For there *shall* **a.** false Ch.
25. 7. then all those virgins **a**-*ose*
27.52. bodies of saints wh. slept **a**-*ose*
Mar.2. 9.11. **a.**, and take up thy bed
12. immediately he **a**-*ose,* took up
5.41. Damsel, I say unto thee, **a.**
Lu. 5.24. I say unto thee, **a.**, and take
7.14. Young man, I say unto thee, **a.**
8.24. Then he **a**-*ose, and* rebuked

Lu. 8.54. and called, saying, Maid, **a.**
Jo. 7.52. for out of Galilee **a**-*eth* no
11.29. she **a**-*ose* quickly, and came
14.31. even so I do. **a.**, let us go
Act.9. 8. Saul **a**-*ose* from the earth
  ginomai.
Mat.8.24. there **a**-*ose* a great tempest in
13.21. *when* tribula. or perse. **a**-*eth*
Mar.4.17. *when* afflic. or persecu. **a**-*eth*
37. there **a**-*ose* a great storm of
Lu. 6.48. *when* the flood **a**-*ose*, the
15.14. there **a**-*ose* a mighty famine
Jo. 3.25. there **a**-*ose* a question between
Act. 6. 1. there **a**-*ose* a murmuring of
11.19. the persecution *that* **a**-*ose*
19.23. same time there **a**-*ose* no small
23. 7. there **a**-*ose* a dissension betw.
9. there **a**-*ose* a great cry: and
10. *when* there **a**-*ose* a great dis.
  anabainō.
Lu.24.38. why do thoughts **a.** in your
Rev.9. 2. there **a**-*ose* a smoke out of
  diegeirō.
Mar.4.39. And he **a**-*ose, and* rebuked
Jo. 6.18. the sea **a**-*ose* by reason of a
  eiserchomai.
Lu. 9.46. there **a**-*ose* a reasoning among
  anatellō.
2Pet.1.19. the day-star **a.** in your hearts
  ballō.
Act.27.14. there **a**-*ose* against it a temp.

ARK.
  kibōtos.
Mat.24.38. that Noe entered ínto the **a.**
Lu.17.27. Noe entered into the **a.**, and
Heb.9. 4. the **a.** of the covenant over.
11. 7. prepared an **a.** to the saving
2Pet.3.20. while the **a.** was a preparing
Rev.11.19. was seen in his temple the **a.**

ARM, [noun] -s.
  brachiōn.
Lu. 1.51. shewed strength with his **a.**
Jo.12.38. to whom hath the **a.** of the L.
Act.13.17. with an high **a.** brought he
  enangkalizomai.
Mar.9.36. *wh.* he had *taken* him *in* his **a**-*s*
10.16. he *took* them *up in* his **a**-*s*
  angkalē.
Lu. 2.28. Then took him up in his **a**-*s*

ARM, [verb] -ed.
  hoplizomai.
1Pet.4. 1. **a.** *yourselves* likewise *with* the
  kathoplizomai.
Lu.11.21. When a strong man **a**-*ed* keep.

ARMOUR.
  panoplia.
Lu.11.22. taketh from him *all* his **a.**
Eph.6.11. Put on the *whole* **a.** of God
13. take unto you the *whole* **a.** of
  hopla.
Ro.13.12. let us put on the **a.** of light
2Co. 6. 7. by the **a.** of righteousness

ARMY, -ies.
  strateuma.
Mat.22.7. and he sent forth his **a**-*ies*
Act.23.27. then came I with an **a.**, and
Rev. 9.16. the number of the **a.** of horse
19.14. And the **a**-*ies* which were in
19. and their **a**-*ies* gathered tog.
  the horse and against his **a.**
  stratopedon.
Lu.21.20. Jerusa. compassed with **a**-*ies*
  parembolē.
Heb.11.34. turned to flight the **a**-*ies* of

ARRAY, [noun.]
  himatismos.
1Ti. 2. 9. or gold, or pearls, or costly **a.**

ARRAY, [verb] ed.
  periballō.
Mat.6.29. Lu. 12.27., *was* not **a**-*ed* like
Lu. 23.11. **a**-*ed* him in a gorge. robe, *and*
Rev. 7.13. these *which are* **a**-*ed* in white
17. 4. And the woman was **a**-*ed* in
19. 8. that she *should be* **a**-*ed* in fine
  enduō.
Act.12.21. Herod **a**-*ed* in royal apparel

ARRIVE, -ed.
  paraballō.
Act.20.15. next day we **a**-*ed* at Samos
  katapleō.
Lu. 8. 26. And they **a**-*ed* at the country

ART, [noun] -s.
  technē.
Act.17.29. stone graven by **a.** and man's
  periergon.
Act.19.19. also, which used *curious* **a**-*s*

ART, [verb] see Be.

AS.
  hōs.
Mat.1.24. did **a.** the angel of the Lord
6.10. done in earth **a.** it is in
12. debts, **a.** we forgive our debt.
7.29. taught them **a.** one having
  and not **a.** the scribes
8.13. **a.** thou hast believed, so be

*(And all other passages in which it
occurs except the following :—)*

  kathōs.
Mat.21.6. and did **a.** Jesus commanded
26.24. Mar. 9.13, 14.21, **a.** it is writ.
28. 6. he is risen, **a.** he said. Come
Mar.4.33. **a.** they were able to hear it
11. 6. *even* **a.** Jesus had commanded
14.16. found **a.** he had said unto
15. 8. **a.** he had even done unto
16. 7. see him, **a.** he said unto you
Lu. 1. 2. *Even* **a.** they delivered them
55. **a.** he spake to our fathers, to
70. **a.** he spake by the mouth of
2.20. seen **a.** it was told unto them
23. **a.** it is written in the law of
5.14. **a.** Moses commanded, for a
6.31. **a.** ye would that men should
36. **a.** your Father also is mercif.
11. 1. **a.** John also taught his disci.
30. For **a.** Jonas was a sign unto
17.26. And **a.** it was in the days of
19.32. *even* **a.** he had said unto them
22.13. found **a.** he had said unto
29. **a.** my father hath appointed
24.24. *even* so **a.** the women had
39. and bones **a.** ye see me have
Jo. 1.23. the Lord, **a.** said the prophet
3.14. And **a.** Moses lifted up the
5.23. *even* **a.** they honour the Fath.
30. **a.** I hear, I judge: and my
6.31. **a.** it is written, 12,14; Acts 7.
  42, 15.15; Ro. 1.17, 2.24, 3.4,
  10, 4.17, 8.36, 9.13, 33, 10.15,
  11.26, 15. 3, 9, 21 ; 1Co. 2. 9;
  2Co. 8.15, 9.9.
57. **a.** the living Father hath sent
58. not **a.** your fathers did eat
7.38. **a.** the scripture hath said
8.28. but **a.** my Father hath taught
10.15. **a.** the Father knoweth me
26. not of my sheep, **a.** I said unto
50. *even* **a.** the Father said unto
13.15. shoulḋ do **a.** I have done to

Jo.13. 33. and **a.** I said unto the Jews
34. 15.12, **a.** I have loved you
14.27. not **a.** the world giveth, give I
31. **a.** the Father gave me com.
15. 4. **a.** the branch cannot bear
9. **a.** the Father hath loved me,
10. *even* **a.** I have kept my Fath.
17. 2. **a.** thou hast given him power
11. that they may be one, **a.** we
14. 16. *even* **a.** I am not of the
18. **a.** thou hast sent me into the
21. **a.** thou, Father, art in me,
22. be one, *even* **a.** we are one
23. loved them **a.** thou hast loved
19.40. **a.** the manner of the Jews is
20.21. **a.** my Father hath sent me
Act. 2. 4. **a.** the Spirit gave them utter.
22. you **a.** ye yourselves also
7.44. **a.** he had appointed, speaking
48. with hands, **a.** saith the prop.
10.47. received the Holy Ghost **a.**
15. 8. even **a.** he did unto us
22. 3. toward God **a.** ye all are this
Ro. 1.13. even **a.** among other Gentiles
28. And *even* **a.** they did not like
8. **a.** we be slanderously report.
  and **a.** some affirm that we say
9.29. And **a.** Esaias said before
11.8. *According* **a.** it is written
15.7. **a.** Christ also received us to
1Co. 1. 6. *Even* **a.** the testimony of Ch.
31. *according* **a.** it is written
4.17. **a.** I teach everywhere in
5. 7. **a.** ye are unleavened. For
8. 2. nothing yet **a.** he ought to
10. 6. evil things **a.** they also lusted
7. **a.** were some of them; as it
8. **a.** some of them committed
9. **a.** some of them also tempted
10. **a.** some of them also murmu.
33. *Even* **a.** I please all men in
11. 1. *even* **a.** I also am of Christ
2. **a.** I delivered them to you
12.11. to every man severally **a.** he
18. body **a.** it hath pleased him
13.12. *even* **a.** also I am known
14.34. obedience **a.** also saith the
15.38. a body **a.** it hath pleased him
49. And **a.** we have borne the
2Co. 1. 5. For **a.** the sufferings of Christ
14. **a.** also ye have acknowledged
4. 1. **a.** we have received mercy, we
6.16. **a.** God hath said, I will dwell
8. 5. And this they did, not **a.** we
6. that **a.** he had begun, so he
9. 3. that, **a.** I said, ye may be rea.
7. *according* **a.** he purposeth in
10. 7. **a.** he is Christ's, even so are we
11.12. they may be found even **a.** we
Gal. 2. 7. the gospel of the circumcis.
3. 6. *Even* **a.** Abraham believed
5.21. **a.** I have also told you in time
Eph.1. 4. *According* **a.** he hath chosen
3. 3. **a.** I wrote afore in few words
4. 4. even **a.** ye are called in one
17. walk not **a.** other Gentiles
21. by him, **a.** the truth is in
32. even **a.** God for Christ's sake
5. 2. **a.** Christ also hath loved us,
3. among you, **a.** becometh
25. even **a.** Christ also loved the
29. even **a.** the Lord the church
Phil.1. 7. *Even* **a.** it is meet for me to
2.12. **a.** ye have always obeyed, not
3.17. **a.** ye have us for an ensample
Col. 1. 6. **a.** it is in all the world; and
  a. it doth also in you, since
7. **a.** ye also learned of Epaphr.
2. 7. **a.** ye have been taught, abou
3.13. even **a.** Christ forgave you
1Th. 1. 5. **a.** ye know what *manner* of
2. 2. **a.** ye know, at Philippi, we

17

1Th. 2. 4. But a. we were allowed of
5. a. ye know, nor a cloke of
13. a. it is in truth, the word of
14. even a. they have of the Jews
3. 4. even a. it came to pass, and
4. 1. that a. ye have received of us
6. a. we also have forewarned
11. hands, a. we commanded you
13. even a. others which have no
5.11. one another, even a. also ye
2Th. 1. 3. a. it is meet, because that
3. 1. glorified, even a. it is with
1Ti. 1. 3. a. I besought thee to abide
Heb.3. 7. a. the Holy Ghost saith, To-
4. 3. a. he said, As I have sworn
7. a. it is said, To-day if ye will
5. 3. a. for the people, so also for
6. a. he saith also in another
8. 5. a. Moses was admonished of
10.25. a. the manner of some is
11.12. a. the stars of the sky in mul.
1Pe. 4.10. a. every man had received
2Pe. 1.14. even a. our Lord Jesus
3.15. even a. our beloved brother
1Jo. 2. 6. so to walk, even a. he walked
18. a. ye have heard that antich.
27. even a. it hath taught you, ye
3. 2. for we shall see him as he is
3. himself, even a. he is pure
7. righteous, even a. he is right.
12. Not a. Cain, who was of that
23. a. he gave us commandment
4.17. because a. he is, so are we in
2Jo. 4. a. we have received a com.
6. a. ye have heard from the
3Jo. 2. even a. thy soul prospereth
3. even a. thou walkest in the

hŏsper.

Mat.5.48. even a. your Father which is
6. 2. a. the hypocrites do in the
5. thou shalt not be a. the hypo.
7. vain repetitions, a. the heath.
16. be not, a. the hypocrites, of
12.40. For a. Jonas was three days
13.40. a. therefore the tares are
18.17. let him be unto thee a. an
20.28. Even a. the Son of man came
24:27. For a. the lightning cometh
37. But a. the days of Noe were
38. a. in the days that were
25.14. the kingdom of heaven is a. a
32. a. a shepherd divideth his
Lu.17.24. For a. the lightning, that
18.11. that I am not a. other men
Jo. 5.21. For a. the Father raiseth up
26. For a. the Father hath life in
Act. 2. 2. a. of a rushing mighty wind
3.17. did it, a. did also your rulers
11.15. them a. on us at the begin.
Ro. 5.12. Wherefore, a. by one man sin
19. For a. by one man's disobedi.
21. That a. sin hath reigned unto
6. 4. that like a. Christ was raised
19. a. ye have yielded your mem.
11.30. For a. ye in times past have
1Co. 8. 5. a. there be gods many, and
11.12. For a. the woman is of the
15.22. For a. in Adam all die, even
16. 1. a. I have given order to the
2Co. 1. 7. a. ye are partakers of the suff.
8. 7. Therefore, a. ye abound in
9. 5. and not a. of covetousness
Gal. 4.29. But a. then, he that was born
Eph.5.24. Therefore a. the church is
1Th. 5. 3. a travail upon a woman with
Heb.4.10. works, a. God did from his
7.27. needeth not daily, a. those
9.25. a. the high priest entereth
Jas. 2.26. For a. the body without the
Rev.10.3. a. when a lion roareth : and

hosos.

Mat.9.15. a. long as the bridegroom is
18

Mat.14.36. a. many as touched were
22. 9. a. many as ye shall find, bid
10. a. many as they found, both.
25.40. In a. much as ye have done it
45. In a. much as ye did it not to
Mar.2.19. a. long as they have the bride.
3.10. touch him, a. many as had
6.56. a. many as touched him were
11. 8. give him a. many as he
Jo. 1.12. But a. many as received him
6.11. of the fishes a. much as they
Act.2.39. a. many as the Lord our God
3.24. a. many as have spoken, have
4. 6. a. many as were of the kind.
34. for a. many as were possess.
5.36,37. a. many as obeyed him
10.45. a. many as came with Peter
13.48. and a. many as were ordained
Ro. 2.12. a. many as have sinned with.
and a. many as have sinned
7. 1. a man, a. long as he liveth
8.14. For a. many as are led by the
11.13. in a. much as I am the apostle
1Co. 7.39. a. long as her husband liveth
Gal. 3.10. For a. many as are of the
27. For a. many of you as have
4. 1. the heir, a. long as he is a c.
6.12. a. many as desire to make a
16. a. many as walk according to
Phil.3.15. a. many as be perfect, be thus
Col. 2. 1. and for a. many as have not
1Ti. 6. 1. Let a. many servants as are
Heb.1. 4. a. he hath by inheritance
3. 3. in a. much as he who hath
7.20. And in a. much as not without
9.27. And a. it is appointed unto
10.25. so much the more, a. ye see
2Pet.1.13. a. long as I am in this taber.
Rev.2.24. a. many as have not this doc.
3.19. a. many as I love, I rebuke
13.15. that a. many as would not
18.17. a. many as trade by sea, stood
21.16. the length is a. large as the

kathaper.

Ro. 4. 6. Even a. David also describeth
12. 4. For a. we have many memb.
1Co.12.12. For a. the body is one, and
2Co. 1.14. even a. ye also are ours in
3.13. And not a. Moses, which put
18. even a. by the Spirit of the
8.11. that a. there was a readiness
1Th. 2.11. a. ye know how we exhorted
3. 6. see us a. we also to see you
12. even a. we do toward you
4. 5. even a. the Gentiles which
Heb.4. 2. a. well as unto them : but the
5. 4. called of God, a. was Aaron

kata, [accu.]

Lu. 4.16. And a. his custom was, he
(according to his custom.)
22.22. a. it was determined, but woe
39. a. he was wont to the mount
Act.15.11. We shall be saved, even a.
17. 2. And Paul, a. his manner was
27.25. it shall be even a. it was told
Ro. 3. 5. vengeance. I speak a. a man
4. 1. father a. pertaining to the
9. 5. whom a. concerning the flesh
11.28. a. concerning the gospel, they
but a. touching the election
1Co. 3. 3. ye not carnal, and walk a.
9. 8. say I these things a. a man
2Co. 4.13. of faith, according a. it is
11.21. I speak a. concerning reproach
Gal. 4.28. Now we, brethren, a. Isaac
Phi. 3. 5. a. touching the law, a Pharis.
Tit. 1. 9. a. he hath been taught, that
Heb.4.15. all points tempted like a.
9. 9. a. pertaining to the consc.

en.

Mar.2.15. to pass a. Jesus sat
4. 4. came to pass a. he sowed

Lu. 2.43. a. they returned, the child
5. 1. to pass a. the people pressed
8. 5. a. he sowed, some fell
42. a. he went the people
9.18. a. he was alone praying
29. a. he prayed the fashion
33. a. they departed from him
11. 1. a. he was praying in a
27. it came to pass a. he spake
37. a. he spake, a certain Pharis.
24. 4. a. they were much perplexed
30. to pass a. he sat at meat
Act. 9. 3. a. he journeyed, he came near
11.15. a. I began to speak, the H. G.
(*In the above passages, the en is used
with the infinitive of the verb* "in his
sitting," "in his sowing," &c.)

hōsei.

Mat.9.36. a. sheep having no shepherd
28. 3. and his raiment white a. snow
4. spake and became a. dead
Mar.9.26. and he was a. one dead ; inso.
Lu.22.44. was a. it were great drops of
24.11. seemed to them a. idle tales
Act. 2. 3. cloven tongues like a. of fire
6.15. a. it had been the face of an
9.18. from his eyes a. it had been
Heb.1.12. And a. a vesture shalt thou
11.12. and a. the sand which is by

hoios.

Mat.24.21. tribulation, such a. was not
Mar.9. 3. so a. no fuller on earth can
13.19. affliction such a. was not
Ro. 9. 6. Not a. though the word of
1Co.15.48.a. is the earthy, such are they
a. is the heavenly, such are
2Co.10.11. such a. we are in words by
12.20. I shall not find you such a.
unto you such a. ye would
Rev.16.18.such a. was not since men

hos tropos.

Mat.23.37.even a. a hen gathereth her
Lu.13.34. a hen doth gather her brood
Act. 7.28. a. thou diddest the Egyptian
15.11. we shall be saved, even a. they
27.25. it shall be even a. it was told
2Ti. 3. 8. Now a. Jannes and Jambres

peri, [gen.]

Mat.18.19.agree on earth a. touching
22.31. But a. touching the resurrec.
Mar.12.26.a. touching the dead, that
Act.21.25.a. touching the Gentiles which
1Co. 8. 1. a. touching things offered
4. a. concerning therefore the
16.12. a. touching our brother Apol.
2Co. 9. 1. a. touching the ministering to
1Th. 4. 9. a. touching brotherly love ye

hostis.

Mar.4.20. such a. hear the word, and
1Co. 5. 1. such fornication a. is not so
16. 2. a. God hath prospered him

hōste.

Mat.15.33. a. to fill so great a multitude
Act. 1.19. insomuch a. that field is called

kathoti.

Lu.19. 9. forsomuch a. he also is a son
Act. 2.45. a. every man had need
4.35. every man according a. he had

katho.

Ro. 8.26. what we should pray for a. we
1Pet.4.13. But rejoice inasmuch a. ye

hōsperei.

1Co.15. 8. a. of one born out of due time

katha.

Mat.27.10.the potter's field, a. the Lord

houtō.

2Pet.3. 4. all things continue a. they

eis.

Phi. 4.15. a. concerning giving and rec.

gar.

Mat.1.18. When a. his mother Mary was

hoti.
Act.13.34.And **a.** *concerning that* he
Phi. 3.12. not **a.** *though* I had already
   achri.
Act.28.15. meet us **a.** *far as* Apii Forum
²Cor.10.14.we are come **a.** *far as to* you
   heōs.
Lu.24.50. them out **a.** *far as* to Bethany
Act.11.19.travelled **a.** *far as* Phenice
   22.he should go **a.** *far as* Antio.
   tosoutos.
Rev.21.16.length is **a.** *large as* the brea.
   hotan.
Jo. 9. 5. **a.** *long as* I am in the world
   16.21. but **a.** *soon as* she is delivered
   epi, [*accu.*]
Act. 5.35. to do **a.** *touching* these men
   epi hosos.
Mat.9.15. **a.** *long as* the bridegroom is
   pas hos.
Jo. 17. 2. eternal life to **a.** *many as*
   isos.
Lu. 6.34. to sinners, to receive **a.** *much*
   hosakis.
¹Co.11.25. **a.** *oft as* ye drink it in rem.
   26. For **a.** *often as* ye eat this b.
Rev.11.6. all plagues **a.** *often as* they
   hote.
Lu.15.30. But **a.** *soon as* this thy son was
Rev.10.10.and **a.** *soon as* I had eaten it
   eutheōs.
Mar.5.36. **a.** *soon as* Jesus heard the
   11. 2. **a.** *soon as* ye be entered into it
   ouketi.
²Co. 1.23. I came *not* **a.** *yet* unto Corinth
   oupō.
Act. 8.16. For **a.** *yet* he was fallen upon
Rev.17.12.received *no* kingdom **a.** *yet*
   oudepō.
Jo. 20. 9. For **a.** *yet* they knew *not* the

(See *Become, Behold, Crystal,*
   Forasmuch, So.)

ASCEND,   -ed, -eth, -ing.
   anabainō.
Lu.19.28. he went before, **a**-*ing up* to
Jo. 1.51. the angels of God **a**-*ing* and
   3.13. no man *hath* **a**-*ed up* to hea.
   6.32. see the Son of man **a.** *up*
   20.17. for I am not yet **a**-*ed* to my
   I **a.** unto my Father, and your
Act. 2.34. For David is not **a**-*ed* into the
   25. I he **a**-*ed* from Cesarea to Jer.
Ro.10. 6. Who shall **a.** into heaven?
Eph.4. 8. When he **a**-*ed up* on high, he
   9. Now that he **a**-*ed*, what is it
   10. the same also *that* **a**-*ed up* far
Rev.7. 2. another angel **a**-*ing* from the
   8. 4. **a**-*ed up* before God out of the
   11. 7. the beast *that* **a**-*eth* out of the
   12. And they **a**-*ed up* to heaven in
   14.11. their torment **a**-*eth up* for
   17. 8. shall **a.** out of the bottomless

ASHAMED.
   epaischunomai.
Mar.8.38. therefore *shall be* **a.** of me, and
   shall the Son of man *be* **a.**
Lu. 9.26. whosoever *shall be* **a.** of me, and
   him shall the Son of man *be* **a.**
Ro. 1.16. For I *am* not **a.** of the gospel
   6.21. whereof ye *are* now **a.**? for
³Ti. 1. 8. *Be* not thou therefore **a.** of
   12. nevertheless I *am* not **a.**; for
   16. and *was* not **a.** of my chain
Heb.2.11.*is* not **a.** to call them brethren
   11.16. God *is* not **a.** to be called their
   kataischunō.
Lu.13.17. all his adversaries *were* **a.**
Ro. 5. 5. hope *maketh* not **a.**; because
   9.33,10.11. on him *shall* not *be* **a.**

---

²Co. 7.14. I *am* not **a.**; but as we spake
   9. ♪. we..*should be* **a.** in this same
¹Pet.3 .6. they *may be* **a.** that falsely
   aischunomai.
Lu.16. 3. I cannot dig; to beg I *am* **a.**
²Co.10. 8. destruction, I *should* not *be* **a.**
Phil.1.20. in nothing I *shall be* **a.**, but
¹Pet.4.16. a Christian, *let* him not *be* **a.**
¹Jo. 2.28. not *be* **a.** before him at his
   anepaischuntos.
²Ti. 2.15. *that needeth* not to be **a.**

ASHES.
   spodos.
Mat.11.21.long ago in sackcloth and **a.**
Lu.10.13. sitting in sackcloth and **a.**
Heb.9.13. the **a.** of an heifer sprinkling
   tephroō.
²Pet.2. 6. *turning* the cities of Sodom
   and Gomorrha *into* **a.**

ASIDE.
   idios.
Mar.12.to.they **a.** from the multi.
Lu. 9.10. and went **a.** privately into a
   kat idian.
Mar.7.33. took him **a.** from the multi.
   anachōreō.
Act.23.19.*went* with him **a.** privately
   26.31.*when* they *were gone* **a.**, they
   ektrepō.
¹Ti. 1. 6. *have turned* **a.** unto vain
   5.15. some *are* already *turned* **a.**

(See *Lay.*)

ASK,   -ed, -est, -eth, -ing.
   eperōtaō.
Mat.12.10.they **a**-*ed* him, saying, Is it
   17.10. his disciples **a**-*ed* him; Mar.
   7.17; Lu. 8.9.
   22.23. is no resurrection, and **a**-*ed*
   35. a lawyer, **a**-*ed* him a question
   41. gathered together, Jesus **a**-*ed*
   46. man from that day forth **a.**
   27.11. the governor **a**-*ed* him, saying
Mar.5. 9. he **a**-*ed* him, What is thy na.
   7. 5. Pharisees and scribes **a**-*ed*
   8. 5. he **a**-*ed* them, How many loa.
   23. he **a**-*ed* him if he saw ought
   27. by the way he **a**-*ed* his disci.
   9.11. they **a**-*ed* him, saying, Why
   16. he **a**-*ed* the scribes, What qu.
   21. he **a**-*ed* his father, How long
   28. his disciples **a**-*ed* him private.
   32. saying, and were afraid to **a.**
   33. in the house he **a**-*ed* them
   10. 2. came to him, and **a**-*ed* him
   10. his disciples **a**-*ed* him again of
   17. kneeled to him, and **a**-*ed* him
   11.29. I *will* also **a.** of you one ques.
   12.18. they **a**-*ed* him, sayi.; Lu.21.7.
   28. **a**-*ed* him, Which is the first
   34. no man after that durst **a.**
   13. 3. John and Andrew **a**-*ed*
   14.60. in the midst, and **a**-*ed* Jesus
   61. Again the high priest **a**-*ed*
   15. 2. Pilate **a**-*ed* him, Art thou the
   4. Pilate **a**-*ed* him again, saying
   44. he **a**-*ed* him whether he had
Lu. 2.46. them, and **a**-*ing* them *quest.*
   3.10. the people **a**-*ed* him, saying
   6. 9. I *will* **a.** you one thing, Is it
   8.30. Jesus **a**-*ed* him, saying, What
   9.18. he **a**-*ed* them, saying, Whom
   18.18. a certain ruler, **a**-*ed* him, say.
   40. was come near, he **a**-*ed* him
   20.21. they **a**-*ed* him, saying, Master
   27. resurrection, and they **a**-*ed* hi.
   40. they durst not **a.** him any qu.
   22.64. him on the face, and **a**-*ed* him
   23. 6. he **a**-*ed* whether the man were

Jo. 18. 7. Then **a**-*ed* he them again
   21. Why **a**-*est* thou me? **a.** them
Act.1. 6. they **a**-*ed* of him, saying
   5.27. the high priest **a**-*ed* them
   23.34. he **a**-*ed* of what province he
Ro.10.20. them *that* **a**-*ed* not *after* me
²Co.14.35.*let* them **a.** their husbands at
   aiteō.
Mat.5.42. Give to him *that* **a**-*eth* thee
   6. 8. have need of, before ye **a.** him
   7. 7. **a.**, and it shall begi.; Lu.11.9.
   8. one *that* **a**-*eth* rece.; Lu.11.10.
   9. if his son **a.** bread, will he give
   10. Or if he **a.** a fish, will he give
   11. good things to them *that* **a.**
   14. 7. her whatsoever she *would* **a.**
   18.19. anything that they *shall* **a.**, it
   20.22. said, Ye know not what ye **a.**
   21.22. whatsoever ye *shall* **a.** in pra.
   27.20. that they *should* **a.** Barabbas
Mar.6.22. **a.** of me whatsoever thou wilt
   23. Whatsoever thou *shalt* **a.** of
   24. her mother, What *shall* I **a.**
   25. unto the king, and **a**-*ed*, sayi.
   10.38. Ye know not what ye **a.**: can
Lu. 1.63. he **a**-*ed* for a writing table, *and*
   6.30. to every man *that* **a**-*eth* of
   11.11. If a son *shall* **a.** bread of any
   12. or if he *shall* **a.** an egg, will
   13. Holy Spirit to them *that* **a.**
   12.48. of him they *will* **a.** the more
Jo. 4. 9. being a Jew, **a**-*est* drink of me
   10. thou *wouldest have* **a**-*ed* of
   11.22. whatsoever thou *wilt* **a.** of G.
   14.13. whatsoever ye *shall* **a.** in my
   14. If ye *shall* **a.** anything in my
   15. 7. abide in you, ye *shall* **a.** what
   16. whatsoever ye *shall* **a.** of the
   16.23. Whatsoever ye *shall* **a.** the F.
   24. *have* ye **a**-*ed* nothing in my
   a., and ye shall receive
   26. At that day ye *shall* **a.** in my
Act. 3. 2. to **a.** alms of them that enter.
Eph.3.20. above all that we **a.** or think
Ja. 1. 5. lack wisdom, *let* him **a.** of G.
   6. But *let* him **a.** in faith, noth.
   4. 2. ye have not, because ye **a.** not
   3. Ye **a.**, and receive not, beca.
   ye **a.** amiss, that ye may
¹Pet.3.15. every man *that* **a**-*eth* you a
¹Jo. 3.22. whatsoever we **a.**, we receive
   5.14. if we **a.** anything according
   15. we **a.** we know that we have
   16. not unto death, he *shall* **a.**
   erōtaō.
Mat.16.13.he **a**-*ed* his disciples, saying
   21.24. I also will **a.** you one; Lu.20.3.
Mar.4.10. him with the twelve **a**-*ed of*
Lu. 9.45. they feared *to* **a.** him of that
   19.31. if any man **a.** you, Why do ye
   22.68. And if I also **a.** you, ye will
Jo. 1.19. from Jerusalem to **a.** him
   21. And they **a**-*ed* him, What
   25. they **a**-*ed* him, and said unto
   5.12. Then **a**-*ed* they him, What
   8. 7. So when they continued **a**-*ing*
   9. 2. his disciples **a**-*ed* him, saying
   15. the Pharisees also **a**-*ed* him
   19. they **a**-*ed* them, saying, Is this
   21. he is of age; **a.** him: he shall
   23. his parents, He is of age: **a.**
   16. 5. none of you **a**-*eth* me, Whi.
   19. they were desirous *to* **a.** him
   23. ye *shall* **a.** me nothing. Veri.
   30. that any man *should* **a.** thee
   18.19. The high priest **a**-*ed* Je.
Act. 3. 3. to go into the temple, **a**-*ed* an
   exetazō.
Jo. 21.12. of the disciples durst **a.**
   legō.
Act.25.20. I **a**-*ed* him whether he would

epaiteō.
Lu. 6.30. thy goods **a.** them not again
anakrinō.
¹Co.10.25. 27. a-ing no *question* for con.
punthanomai.
Lu.15.26. and a-*ed* what these things
18.36. pass by, he a-*ed* what it meant
Jo.13.24. that he should **a.** who it shd.
Act. 4. 7. they a-*ed*, By what power, or
10.18. and a-*ed* whether Simon, wh.
29. I **a.** therefore for what intent
23.19. aside privately, and a-*ed* him

ASLEEP.
koimaomai.
Act.7.60. he had said this, he *fell* **a.**
¹Co.15.6. present, but some *are fallen* **a.**
18. they also *which are fallen* **a.**
¹Th. 4.13. concerning them *which are* **a.**
15. not prevent them *which are* **a.**
²Pet. 3.4. since the fathers *fell* **a.** all
katheudō.
Mat.8.24. the waves, but he *was* **a.**
26.40. and findeth them **a.**, and saith
43. came and found them **a.**
Mar.4.38. **a.** on a pillow, and they
14. 40. he found them **a.** again, for
aphupnoō.
Lu. 8.23. as they sailed he *fell* **a.**

ASP.
aspis.
Ro.3.13. poison of a-*s* is under their lips

ASS.
onos.
Mat.21.2. ye shall find an **a.** tied, and a
5. meek, and sitting upon an **a.**
7. and brought the **a.**, and the
Lu.13.15. loose his ox or his **a.** from
14. 5. Which of you shall have an **a.**
Jo.12.15. cometh, sitting on an a-'*s*
hupozugion.
Mat.21.5. and a colt the foal of an **a.**
²Pet.2.16. dumb **a.** speaking with man's
onarion.
Jo.12.14. he had found a *young* **a.**

ASSAULT,　　　　-ed.
ephistēmi.
Act.17.5. a-*ed* the house of Jason, and
hormē.
Act.14.5. when there was an **a.** made

ASSAY,　　　　-ed, -ing.
peiraō.
Act.9.26. he a-*ed* to join himself to the
peirazō.
Act.16.7. tries　a-*ed* to go into Bithynia
lambanō peira.
Heb.11.29. which the Egyptians a-*ing*

ASSEMBLED.
sunagō.
Mat.26.3. Then a-*ed together* the chief
57. and the elders *were* a-*ed*
28.12. And *when* they *were* a-*ed*
Jo. 20.19. where the disciples were a-*ed*
Act. 4.31. where they were a-*ed togeth.*
11.26. they a-*ed* them *selves* with
sunerchomai.
Mar.14.53. and *with* him *were* a-*ed* all
ginomai.
Act.15.25. *being* a-*ed* with one accord
sunalizomai.
Act. 1. 4. And *being* a-*ed together* with

ASSEMBLING, [noun.]
episunagōgē.
Heb.10.25. the **a.** of ourselves *together*

ASSEMBLY.
sunagōgē.
Jas. 2. 2. if there come unto *your* **a.**
20

ekklēsia.
Act.19.32. for the **a.** was confused.
39. determined in a lawful **a.**
41. spoken; he dismissed the **a.**
panēguris.
Heb.12.23. To the *general* **a.** and church

ASSENTED.
suntithēmi.
Act.24.9. And the Jews also a-*ed* saying

ASSIST.
paristēmi.
Ro. 16. 2. and that ye **a.** her in whatso.

ASSURANCE.
plērophoria.
Col. 2. 2. of the *full* **a.** of understanding
¹Th. 1. 5. and in much **a.**; as ye know
Heb.6.11. to the *full* **a.** of hope unto
10.22. in *full* **a.** of faith, having
pistis.
Act.17.31. he hath given **a.** unto all

ASSURE,　　　　-ed.
peithō.
¹Jo. 3.19. and *shall* **a.** our hearts before
pistoō.
²Ti. 3.14. and *hast been* a-*ed of*, knowing

ASSUREDLY.
asphalōs.
Act.2.36. house of Israel know **a.**
sumbibazō.
Act.16.10. **a.** *gathering* that the Lord

ASTONISH,　　　　-ed
ekplēssō.
Mat.7.28. the people *were* a-*ed* at his
13.54. insomuch that they *were* a-*ed*
22.33. Mar. 1.22. Lu.4.32. *were* a-*ed*
Mar. 6.2. many hearing him *were* a-*ed*
7.37. *were* beyond measure a-*ed*
10.26. they *were* a-*ed* out of measu.
11.18. the people *was* a-*ed* at his
Act.13.12. *being* a-*ed* at the doctrine
existēmi.
Mar.5.42. they *were* a-*ed* with a great
Lu. 2.47. *were* a-*ed* at his understandi.
8.56. her parents *were* a-*ed*: but he
24.22. *made* us a-*ed*, which were
10.45. *were* a-*ed*, as many as came
12.16. and saw him, they *were* a-*ed*
thambeomai.
Mar.10.24. disciples *were* a-*ed* at his
Act. 9. 6. And he, trembling and a-*ed*
periechō thambos.
Lu. 5. 9. For he was a-*ed*, and all that

ASTONISHMENT.
ekstasis.
Mar.5.42. astonished with a great **a.**

ASTRAY.
planaō.
Mat.18.12. and one of them *be gone* **a.**
seeketh that *which is gone* **a.**
13. and nine which *went* not **a.**
¹Pet. 2.25. ye were as sheep *going* **a.**
²Pet. 2.15. and *are gone* **a.**, following

ASUNDER.
(See *Verbs which it follows*.)

AT.
en.
Mat.8. 6. my servant lieth **a.** home
11.22. **a.** the day of judgment
25. **a.** that time Jesus answered
12. 1. **a.** that time Jesus went on
13.49. **a.** the end of the world

Mat.14.1. **a.** that time Herod the tetra.

(And all other passages in which it occurs except the following:—)

epi, [dat.]
Mat.7.28. 22.33. Mar. 1.22. Lu. 4.32.
astonished **a.** his doctrine
24.33. is near even **a.** the doors
Mar.10.22. he was sad **a.** that saying
24. were astonished **a.** his words
12.17. And they marvelled **a.** him
13.29. it is nigh, even **a.** the doors
Lu. 1.14. many shall rejoice **a.** his birth
29. was troubled **a.** his saying
2.33. marvelled **a.** those things
47. astonished **a.** his understand.
4.22. wondered **a.** the gracious
5. 5. nevertheless **a.** thy word I will
9. **a.** the draught of the fishes
9.43. **a.** the mighty power of God
a. all things which Jesus did
20.26. they marvelled **a.** his answer
Jo. 8. 7. let him first cast a stone **a.**
Act. 3.10. **a.** the Beautiful gate of the
a. that which had happened
12. why marvel ye **a.** this? or why
5. 9. are **a.** the door, and shall
13.12. **a.** the doctrine of the Lord
¹Co.14.16.**a.** thy giving of thanks, seeing
Rev.21.12.**a.** the gates twelve angels
epi, [gen.]
Lu.20.37. even Moses shewed **a.** the
22.30. may eat and drink **a.** my
40. when he was **a.** the place, he
Jo. 6.21. immediately the ship was **a.**
21. 1. disciples **a.** the sea of Tiberi.
Act.25.10.I stand **a.** Cesar's judgment
epi, [accu.]
Mat. 9.9. **a.** the receipt of custom.
Mar. 2.14 ; Lu.5.27.
Lu.24.22. were early **a.** the sepulchre
Jo. 8.59. took they up stones to cast **a.**
Act.10.25.him, and fell down **a.** his feet
Rev.3.20. Behold, I stand **a.** the door
8. 3. came and stood **a.** the altar
eis.
Mat.12.41. Lu.11.32. they repented **a.**
18.29. his fellowservant fell down **a.**
Lu. 8.26. **a.** the country of the Gadare.
9.61. which are at home **a.** my ho.
Jo.11.32. she fell down **a.** his feet
Act. 4. 6. gathered together **a.** Jerusal.
7.26. have set them **a.** one again
8.40. Philip was found **a.** Azotus
18.22. when he had landed **a.** Caesa.
20.14. when he met with us **a.** Assos
15. next day we arrived **a.** Samos
21. 3. sail. *into* Syria, and landed **a.**
13. also to die **a.** Jerusalem for
23.11. thou bear witness also **a.** Ro.
25.15. when I was **a.** Jerusalem, the
27. 3. next day we touched **a.** Sidon
28.12. landing **a.** Syracuse, we tarr.
Ro. 4.20. staggered not **a.** the promise
²Ti. 2.26. taken captive by him **a.** his
para, [accu.]
Mat.15.30. and cast them down **a.**
7.38. And stood **a.** his feet behind
35. sitting **a.** the feet of Jesus
41. and he fell down **a.** Jesus'
10.39. which also sat **a.** Jesus' feet
Lu.17.16. fell down on his face **a.** his
Act. 4.35. laid them down **a.** the apost.
37. 5.2. and laid it **a.** the apostles
5.10. **a.** his feet, and yielded up
7.58. **a.** a young man's feet, whose
22. 3. **a.** the feet of Gamaliel, and
pros, [accu.]
Mat.26.18.keep the passover **a.** thy ho.)
Mar.1.33. was gathered together **a.** the
5.22. saw him, he fell **a.** his feet

Mar.7.25. and came and fell **a.** his
   11. 1. **a.** the mount of Olives, he
   14.54. and warmed himself **a.** the
Lu 16.20. which was laid **a.** his gate
   19.29. **a.** the mount called the mou.
Jo. 20.11. without **a.** the sepulchre
Act. 3. 2. daily **a.** the gate of the temp.
Rev.1.17. I fell **a.** his feet as dead
   pros, [*dat.*]
Lu.19.37. **a.** the descent of the mount
Jo. 18.16. But Peter stood **a.** the door
   20.12. **a.** the head, and the other **a.**
   apo.
Mat.19.4. made them **a.** the first
Lu.24.27. beginning **a.** Moses and
   24.47. all nations, beginning **a.** Jer.
Jo. 8. 9. beginning **a.** the eldest, even
Act. 8.35. began **a.** the same scripture
   23.23. the third hour of the night
   26. 4. from my youth, which was **a.**
1Pet.4.17. must begin **a.** the house of
   and if it first begin **a.** us
   kata, [*accu.*]
Mat.27.15. Now **a.** that feast the gover.
Mar.15.6. Now **a.** that feast he released
Lu.10.32. when he was **a.** the place
   23.17. release one unto them **a.** the
Jo. 5. 4. an angel went down **a.** a
Act.16.25.And a. midnight Paul and
Ro. 9. 9. **a.** this time will I come
2Ti. 4. 1. and the dead **a.** his appear.
   peri, [*gen.*]
Lu.2.18. wondered **a.** those things
Jo. 6.41. The Jews then murmured **a.**
   61. his disciples murmured **a.** it
   dia, [*gen.*]
Mat.7.13. Enter ye in **a.** the strait gate
   there be which go in there **a.**
Lu.13.24. Strive to enter in **a.** the strait
   emprosthen.
Rev.19.10. I fell **a.** his feet to worship
   ek.
Jo. 16. 4. said not unto you **a.** the beg.
(See *other words with which it is*
   connected.)

ATHIRST.
dipsaō.
Mat.25.44.saw we thee an hungered,or **a.**
Rev.21. 6.I will give unto him *that is* **a.**
   22.17.And let him *that is* **a.** come

ATONEMENT.
katallagē.
Ro. 5.11. we have now received the **a.**

ATTAIN,   *-ed.*
phthanō.
Ro. 9.31. *hath* not **a**-*ed* to the law of
Ph. 3.16. whereto we *have already* **a**-*ed*
   katantaō.
Act.27.12.by any means they might **a.**
Ph. 3.11. by any means I *might* **a.** unto
   lambanō.
Ph. 3.12. as though I *had* already **a**-*ed*
   parakoloutheō.
1Ti. 4. 6. doc.,whereunto thou *hast* **a**-*ed*
   katalambanō.
Ro. 9.30. *have* **a**-*ed* to righteousness

ATTEND,   *-ed, -ing.*
proskartereō.
Ro.13. 6. **a**-*ing continually upon* this
   prosechō.
Act.16.14. that she **a**-*ed unto* the things
   euprosedros.
1Co. 7.35. that ye may **a.** upon the Lord
   (and for your *attending.*)

ATTENDANCE.
prosechō.
1Ti. 4.13. Till I come, *give* **a.** *to* reading

Heb.7.13. no man *gave* **a.** *at* the altar

ATTENTIVE.
ekkremamai.
Lu.19.48. the people were very **a.** to he.

AUDIENCE.
akoē.
Lu. 7. 1. sayings in the **a.** of the people
Lu.20.45. *in the* **a.** *of* all the people
Act.13.16.ye that fear God, *give* **a.**
   15.12. *gave* **a.** *to* Barnabas and Paul
   22.22. they *gave* him **a.** unto this

AUSTERE.
austēros.
Lu.19.21. because thou art an **a.** man
   22. Thou knewest that I was an **a.**

AUTHOR.
aitios.
Heb.5. 9. he became the **a.** of eternal
   archēgos.
Heb.12.2. Jesus, the **a.** and finisher of

AUTHORITY.   *-ies.*
exousia.
Mat.7.29. as one having **a.**, and not
   8. 9. For I am a man under **a.**
   21.23. By what **a.** doest; Mar.11.28.
   and who gave thee this **a.**
   24.27. by what **a.** I do these things
   Mar.11.29,33; Lu.20.8.
Mar.1.22. as one that had **a.**, and not
   27. for with **a.** commandeth he
   13.34. gave **a.** to his servants, and
Lu. 4. 36. for with **a.** and power he
   7. 8. am a man set under **a.**, having
   9. 1. gave them power and **a.** over
   19.17. have thou **a.** over ten cities
   20. 2. by what **a.** doest thou these
   things? or who is he that
   gave thee this **a.**?
   20. power and **a.** of the governor
Jo. 5.27. hath given him **a.** to execute
Act. 9.14. here he hath **a.** from the chief
   26.10. having received **a.** from the
   12. with **a.** and commission from
1Co.15.24. all rule and all **a.** and power
2Co.10. 8. somewhat more of our **a.**
1Pet. 3.22. **a**-*ies* and powers being made
Rev.13.2. pow. and his seat, and great **a.**
   huperochē.
1Ti. 2. 2. and for all that are in **a.**
   epitagē.
Tit. 2.15. exhort and rebuke with all **a.**
   katexousiazō.
Mat.20.25. are great, *exercise* **a.** upon
Mar.10.42. great ones *exercise* **a.** upon
   exousiazō.
Lu.22.25. they *that exercise* **a.** *upon* th.
   dunastēs.
Act. 8.27. an eunuch *of great* **a.** under
   authenteō.
1Ti. 2.12. not *to usurp* **a.** *over* the man

AVAILETH.
ischuō.
Gal. 5. 6,6.15. neith. circumcision **a.**
Ja. 5.16. prayer of a righte. man **a.**

AVENGE,   *-ed.*
ekdikeō.
Lu.18. 3. saying, **a.** me of mine advers.
   5. I *will* **a.** her, lest by her
Ro.12.19. Dearly beloved, **a.** not yoursel.
Rev.6.10. dost thou not judge and **a.** our
   19. 2. *hath* **a**-*ed* the blood of his ser.
   poieō ekdikēsis.
Lu.18. 7. shall not God **a.** his own elect
   8. that he will **a.** them speedily
Act. 7.24. **a**-*ed* him that was oppressed

---

krinō krima.
Rev.18.20.for God hath **a**-*ed* you on her

AVENGER.
ekdikos.
1Th. 4. 6. the Lord is the **a.** of all such

AVOID,   *-ing.*
ekklinō.
Ro.16.17. ye have learned; and **a.** them
   ektrepomai.
1Ti. 6.20. **a**-*ing* profane and vain babb.
   stellomai.
2Co. 8.20. **a**-*ing* this, that no man shou.
   periistēmi.
Ti. 3. 9. But **a.** foolish questions and
   paraiteomai.
2Ti. 2.23. and unlearned questions **a.**
   dia, [*accu.*]
1Co. 7. 2. Nevertheless to **a.** fornication
   (*because of* fornication.)

AWAKE,   *-ing.*
egeirō.
Mat.8.25. **a.** him, saying, Lord save us
Ro.13.11. high time to **a.** out of sleep
Eph.5.14. he saith, **a.** thou that sleep.
   eknēphō.
1Co.15.34. **a.** to righteous., and sin not
   diegeirō.
Mar.4.38. they **a.** him, and say unto
   diagrēgoreō.
Lu. 9.32. *when* they *were* **a.**, they saw
   exupnizō.
Jo. 11.11. that I *may* **a.** him *out of sleep*
   ginomai exupnos.
Act.16.27.**a**-*ing* out of his *sleep*, and see.

AWARE.
ginōskō.
Mat.24.50.an hour that he *is* not **a.** *of*
Lu.12.46. at an hour when he *is* not **a.**
   eideō.
Lu.11.44. walk over them *are* not **a.** of

AWAY.
exō.
Mat.13.48.vessels, but cast the bad **a.**
   airō.
Lu.23.18. saying, **a.** *with* this man
Jo. 19.15. **a.** *with* him, **a.** *with* him
Pet.21.36. followed after, crying, **a.** *with*
   22.22. said, **a.** *with* such a fellow

(See *verbs which it follows*—Cast
   away, Fall *away*, &c.)

AXE.
axinē.
Mat.3.10. also the **a.** is laid unto; Lu.3.9.

BABBLER.
spermologos.
Act.17.18. some said, What will this **b.**

BABE,   *-s.*
nēpios.
Mat.11.25.hast revealed them unto **b**-*s*
   21.16. Out of the mouth of **b**-*s* and
Lu.10.21. hast revealed them unto **b**-*s*
Ro. 2.20. a teacher of **b**-*s*, which hast
1Co. 3. 1. carnal, even as unto **b**-*s* in
Heb.5.13. of righteousness; for he is a **b.**
   brephos.
Lu. 1.41. the **b.** leaped in her womb
   44. the **b.** leaped in my womb for
   2.12. the **b.** wrapped in swaddling
   16. Mary, and Joseph, and the **b.**
1Pet.2. 2. As newborn **b**-*s*, desire the

BACK,   [*noun.*]
nōtos.
Ro.11.10. and bow down their **b.** alway

BACK, [*adverb.*]
opisō.
Mat.24.18. return **b.** to take his clothes
  13.16. that is in the field not turn **b.**
Lu. 9.62. and looking **b.** is fit for the
  17.31. let him likewise not return **b.**
Jo. 6.66. many of his disciples went **b.**
  20.14. she turned herself **b.** and

(See *verbs which it follows*—Draw
  back, Roll *back*, &c.)

BACKBITERS.
katalalos.
Ro. 1.30. **b-s**, haters of God, despiteful

BACKBITINGS, [*noun.*]
katalalia.
Co.12.20. wraths, strifes, **b.** whisper.

BACKSIDE.
opisthen.
Rev.5. 1. written within, and on the **b.**

BACKWARD.
eis ho opisō.
Jo. 18. 6. they went **b.**, and fell to the

BAD.
kakos.
²Co. 5.10. done, whether it be good or **b.**
poneros.
Mat.22.10.many as they found, both **b.**
sapros.
Mat.13.48. into vessels, but cast the **b.**

BAG,   *-s.*
glōssokomon.
Jo. 12.6. was a thief, and had the **b.**
  13.29. because Judas had the **b.** that
balantion.
Lu.12.33. provide yourselves **b-s** which

BALANCES.
zugos.
Rev.6. 5. had a *pair of* **b.** in his hand

BAND,   *-s.*
speira.
Mat.27.27.gather unto him the whole **b.**
Mar.15.16.call together the whole **b.**
Jo. 18. 3. having received a **b.** of men
  12. Then the **b.** and the captain
Act.10. 1. a centurion of the **b.** called
  21.31. the chief captain of the **b.**
  27. 1. a centurion of Augustus' **b.**
desmos.
Lu. 8.29. he brake the **b-s**, and was
Act. 16.26. and every one's **b-s** were
  22.30. he loosed him from his **b-s**
zeuktēria.
Act.27.40.and loosed the rudder-**b-s**
sundesmos.
Col. 2.19. the body by joints, and **b-s**

BANDED.
poieō sustrophē.
Act.23.12. certain of the Jews **b.** toget,

BANK.
trapeza.
Lu.19.23. thou my money into the **b.**

BANQUETINGS.
potos.
¹Pet. 4. 3. **b.** and abominable idolatries

BAPTISM.   *-s.*
baptisma.
Mat. 3. 7. and Sadducees come to his **b.**
22

Mat.20.22,23. the **b.** that ; Mar.10.38,39
  21.25. The **b.** of John, whence was
Mar. 1.4. preach the **b.** of repentance
  11.30. Lu.20.4. The **b.** of John, was
Lu. 3. 3. preaching the **b.** of repentan.
  7.29. baptized with the **b.** of John
  12.50. I have a **b.** to be baptized
Act. 1.22. Beginning from the **b.** of John
  10.37. the **b.** which John preached
  13.24. the **b.** of repentance to all
  18.25. knowing only the **b.** of John
  19. 3. they said, Unto John's **b.**
  4. with the **b.** of repentance
Ro. 6. 4. with him by **b.** into death
Eph.4. 5. One Lord, one faith, one **b.**
Col. 2.12. Buried with him in **b.**
¹Pet.3.21. even **b.**, doth also now save us
baptismos.
Heb. 6.2. Of the doctrine of **b-s**, and of

BAPTIST.
baptistēs.
Mat. 3.1. In those days came John the **b.**
  11.11. a greater than John the **b.**
  12. from the days of John the **b.**
  14. 2. This is John the **b.**; he is
  8. Give me here John **b's** head
  16.14. that thou art John the **b.**
  17.13. unto them of John the **b.**
Mar.6.24. 25. The head of John the **b.**
  8.28. they answered, John the **b.**
Lu. 7.20. John **b.** had sent us unto
  28. prophet than John the **b.**
  33. John the **b.** came neither
  9.19. answering said, John the **b.**
baptizō.
Mar.6.14. That John the **b.** was risen

BAPTIZE,   *-ed, -est, -ing.*
baptizō.
Mat.3. 6. were **b-ed** of him in Jordan
  11. indeed **b.** you with water
  he *shall* **b.** Mar.1.8; Lu.3.16.
  13. unto John, to be **b-ed** of him
  14. I have need to be **b-ed** of thee
  16. Jesus, *when he was* **b-ed**, went
  20.22, 23. *to be* **b-ed**, with the bapti.
  that I *am* **b-ed** with; Mar.10.38
  28.19. **b-ing** them in the name of
Mar. 1.4. John did **b.** in the wilderness
  5. *were* all **b-ed** of him in the
  8. I indeed *have* **b-ed** you with
  9. *was* **b-ed** of John in Jordan
  10.39. **b-ed** withal *shall* ye be **b-ed**
  16.16. He that believeth and is **b-ed**
Lu. 3. 7. came forth *to be* **b-ed** of him
  12. came also publicans *to be* **b-ed**
  16. I indeed **b.** you with water
  21. were **b-ed** it came to pass, that
  Jesus also *being* **b-ed**
  7.29. *being* **b-ed** with the baptism
  30. themselves, *being* not **b-ed** of
  12.50. I have a baptism *to be* **b-ed**
Jo. 1. 25. said unto him, Why **b-est**
  26. saying, I **b.** with water
  28. Jord. where John *was* **b-ing**
  31. therefore am I come **b-ing**
  33. sent me *to* **b.** with water, but
  which **b-eth** with the Holy G.
  3.22. tarried with them, and **b-ed**
  23. John also was **b-ing** in Ænon
  they came, and *were* **b-ed**
  26. behold, the same **b-eth**, and
  4. 1. that Jesus made and **b-ed**
  2. Though Jesus himself **b-ed**
  10.40. place where John at first **b-ed**
Act. 1. 5. John truly **b-ed** with water
  ye *shall be* **b-ed** with; 11.16.
  2.38. Repent, and *be* **b-ed** every one
  41. received his word *were* **b-ed**
  8.12. *were* **b-ed**, both men and

Act. 8.13. *when he was* **b-ed**, he contin
  16. only they were **b-ed** in the
  36. what doth hinder me *to be* **b-ed**
  38. the eunuch; and he **b-ed** him
  9.18. forth. and arose, and *was* **b-ed**
  10.47. that these should not *be* **b-ed**
  48. commanded them *to be* **b-ed**
  11.16. John indeed **b-ed** with water
  16.15. when she *was* **b-ed**, and her
  33. *was* **b-ed**, he and all his
  18. 8. heari. believed, and *were* **b-ed**
  19. 3. Unto what then *were* ye **b-ed**
  4. John verily **b-ed** with the ba.
  5. they *were* **b-ed** in the name
  22.16. arise, and *be* **b-ed**, and wash
Ro. 6. 3. so many of us as *were* **b-ed**
  into Jesus Christ *were* **b-ed**
¹Co. 1.13. *were* ye **b-ed** in the name of
  14. that I **b-ed** none of you, but
  15. that I *had* **b-ed** in mine own
  16. I **b-ed** also the household of
  I know not whether I **b-ed** any
  17. Christ sent me not *to* **b.**, but
  10. 2. were all **b-ed** unto Moses in
  12.13. by one Spirit *are* we all **b-ed**
  15.29. which are **b-ed** for the dead
  why *are* they then **b-ed** for
Gal. 3.27. *have been* **b-ed** into Christ ha.

BARBARIAN,   *-s.*
barbaros.
Act.28.4. when the **b-s** saw the venom.
Ro. 1.14. to the Greeks, and to the **b-s**
¹Co.14.11.unto him that speaketh a **b.**
  speaketh shall be a **b.** unto
Col. 3.11. **b.**, Scythian, bond nor free

BARBAROUS.
barbaros.
Act.28.2. the **b.** people shewed us no

BARE.
gumnos.
¹Co.15.37. body that shall be, but **b.**

BARLEY.
krithē.
Rev.6. 6. three measures of **b.** for a
krithinos.
Jo. 6. 9. which hath five **b.** loaves, and
  13. fragments of the five **b.** loav.

BARN,   *-s.*
apothēkē.
Mat.6.26. they reap, nor gather into **b-s**
  13.30. gather the wheat into my **b.**
Lu.12.18. I will pull down my **b-s**, and
  24. neither have storehouse nor **b.**

BARREN.
steira.
Lu. 1. 7. because that Elisabeth was **b.**
  36. with her, who was called **b.**
  23.29. Blessed are the **b.**, and the
Gal.4.27. Rejoice, thou **b.** that bearest
argos.
²Pet.1. 8. neither be **b.** nor unfruitful

BASE.
tapeinos.
²Co.10.1. who in presence am **b.** among
agenēs.
¹Co. 1.28. **b.** *things* of the world, and

BASER.
agoraios
Act.17. 5. lewd fellows of the **b.** *sort*

BASKET,   *-s.*
kophinos.
Mat.14.20.that remained **twelve b** *s*ful

Mat.16.9. and how many b-s ye took up
Mar.6.43. twelve b-s full of the fragms.
  8.19. how many b-s full of fragms.
Lu. 9.17. remained to them twelve b-s
Jo. 6.13. and filled twelve b-s with the
    spuris.
Mat.15.37.meat that was left seven b-s
  16.10.and how many b-s ye took up?
Mar.8. 8. meat that was left seven b-s
  20. how many b-s full of fragms.
Act. 9.25. down by the wall in a b.
    sarganē.
2Co.11.33. in a b. was I let down by the

BASON.
niptēr.
Jo.13. 5. he poureth water into a b.

BASTARDS.
nothos.
Heb.12.8. then are ye b., and not sons

BATTLE.
polemos.
1Col.14. 8. shall prepare himself to the b.
Rev.9. 7. horses prepared unto b.; and
  9. of many horses running to b.
  16.14. to the b. of that great day of
  20. 8. to gather them together to b.

BE, -en, -ing, am, are, art, is, was, were.

(*When this verb is printed in italics in our English version, there is no corresponding Greek. It is also sometimes a mere auxiliary to other words. When it is represented by a Greek word, that word is generally eimi, "to be," and is of too frequent occurrence to be quoted. The following are the exceptions:)—*

ginomai.
Mat.5.45. ye may be the children of your
  6.16. when ye fast, be not, as the
  8.26. the sea; and there was a great
  9.29. According to your faith be it
  10.16. be ye therefore wise as serpts.
  25. the disciple that he be as his
  12.45. the last state of that man is
  14.15. when it was evening, his disc.
  15.28. be it unto thee even as thou
  16. 2. said unto them, When it is
  17. 2. his raiment was white as the
  18.13. if so be that he find it, verily
  19. 8. from the beginning, it was not
  20.26. whosoever will be; Mar.10.43.
  24.26. the outside of them may be
  23.20. that your flight be not in the
  21. such as was not since the begi.
  this time, no, nor ever shall be
  32. When his branch is yet tender
  44. Therefore be ye also ready
26. 2. after two days is the feast of
  5. lest there be an uproar among
  6. when Jesus was in Bethany, in
  54. fulfilled, that thus it must be
  27.45 there was darkness over all
  28. 2. behold there was a great
Mar.4.10. when he was alone, they that
  39. wind ceased, and there was a
  6.14. for his name was spread abd.
  26. the king was exceeding sorry
  35. when the day was now far
  9. 7. there was a cloud that oversh.
  26. out of him; and he was as one
  33. being in the house he asked
  10.44. whosoever of you will be the
  13. 7. for such things must needs be
  18. that your flight be not in the
  19. such as was not from the
  unto this time, neither shall be

Mar.13.28. When her branch is yet ten.
  15.53. hour was come, there was
  16.10. them that had been with
Lu. 1. 2. which from the beginning were
  5. There was in the days of He.
  38. be it unto me according to thy
  2. 2. when Cyrenius was governor
  6. so it was, that, while they
  13. suddenly there was with the
  42. when he was twelve years old
  4.25. great famine was throughout
  36. they were all amazed, and
  42. when it was day, he departed
  6.13. when it was day, he called
  16. Judas Iscariot, which also was
  36. be ye therefore merciful, as
  49. the ruin of that house was
  8.24. they ceased, and there was a.
  9.29. of his countenance was
  10.32. a'Levite, when he was at the
  36. was neighbour unto him that
  11.26. last state of that man is worse
  30. as Jonas was a sign unto the
  12.40. be ye therefore ready also: for
  54. cometh a shower; and so it is
  13. 2. were sinners above all the Gal.
  4. think ye that they were sinn.
  15.10. there is joy in the presence of
  16.11. If therefore ye have not been
  12. if ye have not been faithful in
  17.26. as it was in the days of Noe
  28. also as it was in the days of
  18. 23, 24. heard this, he was very
  19. 17. because thou hast b. faithful
  19. be thou also over five cities
  20.14. that the inheritance may be
  33. whose wife of them is she? for
  22.24. there was also a strife among
  25. let him be as the younger; and
  40. when he was at the place, he
  44. being in an agony he prayed
  and his sweat was as it were
  66. as soon as it was day, the eld.
  23.24. that it should be as they requ.
  44. there was a darkness over
  24. 5. as they were afraid, and bow.
  19. which was a prophet mighty
  22. which were early at the sepul.
  37. were terrified and affrighted
Jo. 1. 6. There was a man sent from
  15.27. after me is preferred before
  30. a man which is preferred bef.
  2. 1. the third day there was a
  3. 9. him, How can these things be
  4.14. shall be in him a well of water
  6.17. it was now dark, and Jesus
  21. immediately the ship was at
  7.43. there was a division among
  8.58. Before Abraham was, I am
  9.22. he should be put out of the
  27. will ye also be his disciples
  10.16. there shall be one fold, and
  19. There was a division therefore
  22. it was at Jerusalem the feast
  36. that ye may be the children of
  42. lest they should be put out of
  14.22. Lord, how is it that thou wilt
  15. 8. fruit, so shall ye be my disci.
  20,27. be not faithless, but believing
Act. 1.16. Judas, which was guide to
  19. it was known unto all the
  20. Let his habitation be desolate
  22. one be ordained to be a witn.
  26. when this was noised abroad
  4. 4. the number of the men was
  5. 7. it was about the space of thr.
  7.29. was a stranger in the land of
  38. This is he, that was in the
  52. of whom ye have been now the
  8. 1. at that time there was a great
  8. there was great joy in that
  9.19. Then was Saul certain days

Act. 9.42. it was known throughout all
  10. 4. looked on him, he was afraid
  25. as Peter was coming in. Cor.
  12.18. as soon as it was day, 16.35
  23. he was eaten of worms, and
  13. 5. when they were at Salamis,
  15. 7. there had been much dispu.
  39. the contention was so sharp
  16.26. suddenly there was a great
  35. when it was day, the magist.
  19.17. this was known to all the
  21. After I have been there, I must
  28. they were full of wrath, and
  20.16. to be at Jerusalem the day of
  18. I have been with you at all
  22. 9. saw indeed the light, and were
  17. in the temple, I was in a
  23.12. when it was day, certain of
  25.15. About whom, when I was at
  26. 4. which was at the first among
  19. I was not disobedient unto
  28. thou persuadest me to be a
  29. were both almost, and altoge
  27.36. Then were they all of good
  39. when it was day, they knew
  42. the soldiers' counsel was to
Ro. 3. 4. God forbid: let God be true
  6. 5. if we have been planted toge.
  9.29. we had been as Sodoma, and
  11. 5. there is a remnant according
  16. otherwise grace is no more
  34. or who hath been his counsel.
  12.16. be not wise in your own con.
  15. 8. Jesus Christ was a minister
  16. offer. up of Gentiles might be
  31. may be accepted of the saints
  16. 2. she hath been a succourer of
  7. who also were in Christ before
1Co. 2. 3. I was with you in weakness
  3.18. become a fool, that he may be
  4.16. I beseech you, be ye followers
  7.23. be not ye the servants of men
  9.23. that I might be partaker there.
  27. I myself should be a castaway
  10. 6. these things were our exam.
  7. Neither be ye idolaters, as
  11. 1. be ye followers of me, even as
  14.20. be not children in understand.
  in understanding be men
  15.10. bestowed upon me was not in
  37. not that body that shall be
  58. my beloved brethren, be ye
  16. 2. that there be no gatherings
  10. that he may be with you with
2Cor.1.18. our word toward you was not
  19. was not yea, nay, but in him
  3. 7. engraven in stones, was glori.
  6.14. be ye not unequally yoked
  8.14. their abundance also may be
  that there may be equality
Gal. 3.17. the law, which was four hun.
  24. the law was our schoolmaster
  4.12. Brethren, I beseech you, be as
  5.26. Let us not be desirous of vain
Eph.4.32.be ye kind one to another,
  5. 1. be ye therefore followers of
  7. be not ye therefore partakers
  17. Wherefore be ye not unwise
  6. 3. That it may be well with thee
Phi. 1.13. my bonds in Christ are mani.
  15. That ye may be blameless and
  17. Brethren, be followers togeth.
  21. that it may be fashioned like
Col. 3.15. called in one body; and be ye
  4.11. which have been a comfort
1. 5. what manner of men we were
  7. So that ye were ensamples to
  2. 1. unto you, that it was not in
  7. we were gentle among you
  8. because ye were dear unto us
  3. 5. and our labour be in vain
1Ti. 2.14. deceived, was in the transgr

23

¹Ti. 4.12. **be** thou an example of the
    5. 9. *having* been the wife of one
²Ti. 1.17. *when* he **was** in Rome, he
    3. 9. all men, as theirs also **was**
Heb.2. 2. word spoken by angels **was**
    17. that he *might* **be** a merciful
    5.11. seeing ye **are** dull of hearing
    6.12. That ye **be** not slothful, but
    7.18. For there **is** verily a disannul.
    9.22. without shedding of blood **is**
    11. 6. he **is** a rewarder of them that
    12. 8. whereof all *are* partakers, then
Jas. 1.12. for *when* he **is** tried, he shall
    22. **be** ye doers of the word, and
    25. *being* not a forgetful hearer
    2.10. in one point, he **is** guilty of
    3.10. these things ought not so to **be**
    5. 2. your garments **are** motheaten
¹Pet.1.15. so **be** ye holy in all manner of
    16. Because it is written, **be** ye
    3. 6. whose daughters ye **are**, as
    13. if ye **be** followers of that which
    4.12. the fiery trial *which* **is** to try
    5. 3. *being* ensamples to the flock
²Pet.1. 4. by these ye *might* **be** partakers
    16. **were** eyewitnesses of his maj.
    20. prophecy of the scripture **is** of
    2. 1. there **were** false prophets also
    20. the latter end **is** worse with
¹Jo. 2.18. even now **are** there many an.
³Jo. 8. that we *might* **be** fellowhelpers
Rev. 1. 9. **was** in the isle that is called
    10. I **was** in the Spirit on the
    18. I am he that liveth, and **was**
    19. the things which shall **be**
    2. 8. which **was** dead, and is alive
    10. **be** thou faithful unto death
    3. 2. **be** watchful, and strengthen
    4. 1. things which must **be** hereafter
    2. immediately I **was** in the spi.
    6.12. *there* **was** a great earthquake
    8. 1. there **was** silence in heaven
    5. there **were** voices, and thund.
    11.13. same hour **was** there a great
    the remnant **were** affrighted
    15. there **were** great voices in
    19. there **were** lightnings, and
    12. 7. there **was** war in heaven
    16.10. his kingdom **was** full of dark.
    18. there **were** voices, and thund.
    there **was** a great earthquake,
    as **was** not since men **were**
    huparchō.
Lu. 8.41. and he **was** a ruler of the
    9.48. for he *that* **is** least among you
    11.13. If ye then, *being* evil, know
    16.14. the Pharisees also, *who* **were**
    23. he lifted up his eyes, *being* in
Act.2.30. Therefore *being* a prophet
    Neither **was** there any among
    as many as **were** possessors
    5. 4. **was** it not in thine own power
    7.55. But he, *being* full of the H. G.
    8.16. only they **were** baptized in the
    10.12. Wherein **were** all manner of
    14. 8. *being* a cripple from his moth.
    16. 3. all that his father **was** a Greek
    20. These men, *being* Jews, do
    37. openly uncondemned, *being*
    17.24. *seeing* that he **is** Lord of heav.
    27. though he **be** not far from
    then *as* we **are** the offspring
    19.36. ye ought to **be** quiet, and to do
    40. These **being** no cause whereby
    21.20. and they **are** all zealous of the
    22. 3. *and* **was** zealous toward God
    27.12. And *because* the heaven **was**
    34. for this **is** for your health : for
    28. 7. In the same quarters **were**
    18. because there **was** no cause of
Ro. 4.19. when he **was** about an hund.
¹Co. 7.26. that this **is** good for the pres.
24

---

¹Co.11. 7. *forasmuch as* he **is** the image
    18. I hear that there **be** divisions
    12.22. which seem to **be** more feeble
²Co. 8.17. but *being* more forward, of
    12.16. *being* crafty, I caught you wi.
Gal. 1.14. *being* more exceedingly zeal.
    2.14. If thou, *being* a Jew, livest
Phi. 2. 6. Who, *being* in the form of
    3.20. For our conversation **is** in
Jas. 2.15. If a brother or sister **be** naked
²Pet.1. 8. For *if* these things **be** in you
    (For, these things *being* yours.)
    2.19. themselves **are** the servants
    3.11. of persons ought ye to **be**
    keimai.
²Co.3.15. read, the veil **is** upon their
    apechō.
Mat.15.8.Mar.7.6. their heart **is** far from
Lu. 7. 6. *when* he **was** now not far from
    15.20. *when* he **was** yet a great way
    24.13. *which* **was** from Jerusalem
    echō.
Jo. 8.57. **art** not yet fifty years old
    (*hath not yet fifty years.*)
    9.21. he **is** of age (*hath* full age.)
Act.7. 1. **are** these things so, *ch.* 17. 11.
    24. 9. that these things **were** so
    kathistēmi.
Jas. 3. 6. so **is** the tongue among our
    4. 4. of the world **is** the enemy of
    suneimi.
Lu. 9.18. his disciples **were** with him
Act.22.11. of them *that* **were** with me
    pherō.
Heb.9.16. must also of necessity **be** the
    prosmenō.
Mar.8. 2. bec. they *have* now **been** with
    poieō.
²Co.11.25. night and a day I *have* **been** in
    sumbainō.
Act.21.35. *so* it **was** that he was borne of
    tungchanō.
¹Co.14.10. there are it *may* **be** so many
    16. 6. And it *may* **be** that I will abi.
    mellō.
Act.21.27. the seven days **were** almost
    agō.
Lu.24.21. to-day **is** the third day since
    diatribō.
Act.25.14. when they *had* **been** there
    eis.
Act.13.22. David to **be** their king

BEAM.
dokos.
Mat.7. 3. considerest not the **b.** that is
    4. behold, a **b.** is in thine own
    5. first cast out the **b.** out of
Lu.6. 41. perceivest not the **b.** that is
    42. beholdest not the **b.** that is in
    cast out first the **b.** out of

BEAR, [*noun.*]
arktos.
Rev.13.2. feet were as the feet of a **b.**

BEAR, [*verb.*] *-are, -orne, -est,*
-eth, -ing.
bastazō.
Mat.3.11. shoes I am not worthy to **b.**
    8.17. our infirmities, and **b-e** our
    20.12. *which have* **b-o** the burden and
Mar.14.13. a man **b-**ing a pitcher of
Lu. 7.14. they *that* **b-e** him stood still
    11.27. Blessed is the womb *that* **b-e**
    14.27. whosoever *doth* not **b.** his
    22.10. a man meet you, **b-**ing
Jo 12. 6. had the bag, and **b-e** what was
    16.12. but ye cannot **b.** them now
    19.17. he **b-**ing his cross went forth
    20.15. Sir, if thou *have* **b-o** him

Act.9.15. to **b.** my name before the
    15.10. fathers nor we were able to **b.**
    21.35. that he was **b-**o of the soldiers
Ro.11.18. thou **b-**est not the root, but
    15. 1. ought to **b.** the infirmities of
Gal.5.10. shall **b.** his judgment, who.
    6. 5. **b.** ye one another's burdens
    5. every man *shall* **b.** his own
    6.17. for I **b.** in my body the marks
Rev.2. 2. how thou canst not **b.** them
    3. *hast* **b-**o and hast patience
    pherō.
Lu.23.26. that he might **b.** it after Jes.
Jo. 2. 8. and **b.** unto the governor of
    And they **b-e** it
    15. 2. branch in me *that* **b-**eth not
    every branch that **b-**eth fruit
    4. As the branch cannot **b.** fruit
    8. that ye **b.** much fruit; so
    airō.
Mat.4. 6. in their hands they shall **b.**
    27.32. they compelled to **b.** his
Mar.2. 3. palsy, which was **b-**o of four
    15.21. of Alexander and Rufus, to **b.**
    poieō.
Lu. 8. 8. sprang up, and **b-e** fruit an
    13. 9. And if it **b.** fruit well; and if
Jas.3.12. my brethren, **b.** olive berries
Rev.22.2. which **b-e** twelve manner of
    phoreō.
Ro.13. 4. for he **b-**eth not the sword in
¹Co.15.49. as we have **b-**o the image of
    earthly, we *shall* also **b.** the
    anechomai.
Act.18.14. would that I *should* **b.** with
²Co.11. 1. could **b.** with me a little in
    my folly: and indeed **b.** with
    4. ye might well **b.** with him
    anapherō.
Heb.9.28. once offered to **b.** the sins of
¹Pet.2.24. Who his own self **b-e** our sins
    gennaō.
Lu. 1.13. wife, Elizabeth, *shall* **b.** thee
    23.29. and the wombs that never **b-e**
    tiktō.
Gal.4.27. thou barren *that* **b-**est not
    ekpherō.
Heb.6. 8. But that *which* **b-**eth thorns
    hupopherō.
¹Co.10.13. that ye may be able to **b.** it
    stegō.
¹Co. 13.7. **b-**eth all things, believeth all
    peripherō.
²Co.4.10. Always **b-**ing about in the body
    karpophoreō.
Mat.13.23. which also **b-**eth *fruit,* and
    makrothumeō.
Lu.18. 7. him, though he **b.** *long* with
    antophthalmeō.
Act.27.15. and could not **b.** up *into* the

(See *Born, Borne, Children, Witness.*)

BEAST, -s.
thērion.
Mar.1.13. was with the *wild* **b-**s; and
Act.10.12. 11.6. *wild* **b-**s, and creeping
    28. 4. *the venomous* **b.** hang on his
    5. shook off the **b.** into the fire
Tit. 1.12. alway liars, evil **b-**s, slow belli.
Heb 12.20.And if so much as a **b.** touch
Jas. 3. 7. of **b-**s, and of birds, and of
Rev.6. 8. death, and with the **b-**s of the
    11.7. the **b.** that ascendeth out of
    13.1. a **b.** rise up out of the sea
    2. the **b.** which I saw was like
    3. world wondered after the **b.**
    4. power unto the **b.**: and they
    worshipped the **b.**, saying,
    Who is like unto the **b.**? who
    11. I beheld another **b.** coming

Rev.13.12.all the power of the first **b**.
    to worship the first **b**., whose
  14. to do in the sight of the **b**.
    shou. make an image to the **b**.
  15. unto the image of the **b**., that
    the image of the **b**. should
    worship the image of the **b**.
  17. or the name of the **b**. or the
  18. count the number of the **b**.
  14. 9. If any man worship the **b**.
  11. who worship the **b**. and his
  15. 2. over the **b**., and over his
  16. 2. the mark of the **b**., and upon
  10. upon the seat of the **b**.; and
  13. out of the mouth of the **b**.
  17. 3. upon a scarlet coloured **b**.
    7. of the **b**. that carrieth her
    8. The **b**. that thou sawest was
    the **b**. that was, and is not
  11. And the **b**. that was, and is
  12. as kings one hour with the **b**.
  13. power and strength unto the **b**.
  16. which thou sawest upon the **b**.
  17. their kingdom unto the **b**.
  19.19. A d I saw the **b**., and the
  20. the **b**. was taken, and with
    the mark of the **b**., and them
  20. 4. had not worshipped the **b**.
  10. where the **b**. and the false
    zōon.
Heb.13.11. of those **b**-s, whose blood is
²Pet. 2.12. as natural brute **b**-s made to
Jude 10. know naturally, as brute **b**-s
Rev.4. 6. were four **b**-s full of eyes
    7. the first **b**. was like a lion
    and the second **b**. like a calf
    and the third **b**. had a face as
    a man, and the fourth **b**. was
    8. And the four **b**-s had each of
    9. when those **b**-s give glory and
  5. 6. and of the four **b**-s and in the
    8. the four **b**-s and four and
  11. about the throne and the **b**-s
  14. And the four **b**-s said, Amen
  6. 1. I heard one of the four **b**-s
    3. I heard the second **b**. say
    5. I heard the third **b**. say, Come
    6. in the midst of the four **b**-s
    7. the voice of the fourth **b**.
  7.11. the elders and the four **b**-s
  14. 3. before the four **b**-s, and the
  15. 7. one of the four **b**-s gave unto
  19. 4. elders and the four **b**-s fell
    ktēnos.
Lu.10.34. and set him on his own **b**.
Act.23.24. And provide them **b**-s, that
¹Co.15.39. another flesh of **b**-s, another
Rev.18.13. and **b**-s, and sheep, and

    tetrapous.
Act.10.12. manner of *four-footed* **b**-s
  11. 6. and saw *four-footed* **b**-s of
Ro. 1.23. *four-footed* **b**-s and creeping

    sphagion.
Act.7.42. ye offered to me *slain* **b**-s

    thēriomacheō.
¹Co.15.32. I *have fought with* **b**-s at

BEAT,   -en, -ing.
    derō.
Mat.21.35. took his servants, and **b**.
Mar.12.3. they caught him, and **b**. him
    5. many others, **b**-ing some, and
  13. 9. synagogues ye *shall be* **b**-en
Lu.12.47. *shall be* **b**-en with many
  48. *shall be* **b**-en with few stripes
  20.10. the husbandmen **b**. him, *and*
  11. another servant, *and* they **b**.
Act. 5.40. called the apostles, *and* **b**-en
  16.37. *have* **b**-en us openly unconde.
  22.19. imprisoned *and* **b**. in every
¹Co. 9.26. not as *one that* **b**-eth the air

    tuptō.
Lu.12.45. shall begin *to* **b**. the men-ser.
Act.18.17.and **b**. him before the judg.
  21.32. soldiers, they left **b**-ing of
    prosrēgnumi.
Lu. 6.48. stream, **b**. *vehemently* upon
  49. *against* wh. the stream *did* **b**.
    vehemently, and
    rabdizō.
Act.16.22. and commanded *to* **b**. them
²Co.11.25. Thrice *was I* **b**-en *with rods*
    epiballō.
Mar.4.37. and the waves **b**. *into* the
    proskoptō.
Mat.7.27. winds blew, and **b**. *upon* that
    prospiptō.
Mat.7.27. winds blew, and **b**. *upon* that

BEAUTIFUL.
    hōraios.
Mat.23.27.indeed appear **b**. outwardly
Act. 3. 2. which is called **b**., to ask alms
  10. sat for alms at the **b**. gate
Ro.10.15. How **b**. are the feet of them

BECAUSE.
    hoti.
Mat.2.18. be comforted **b**. they are not
  5.36. **b**. thou canst not make
  7.14. **b**. strait is the gate and nar.
  9.36. **b**. they fainted, and were scat.
  11.20. were done **b**. they repented
  25. **b**. thou hast hid these things
  (And all other passages in which it occurs,
    with the following exceptions :—)
    dia. [*accu.*]
Mat.13.5. **b**. they had no deepness of
    6. **b**. they had no root, they
  21. persecution ariseth **b**. *of* the
  58. works there, **b**. *of* their unbe.
  17.20. said unto them, **b**. *of* your
  24.12. **b**. iniquity shall abound
  27.19. this day in a dream **b**. *of* him
Mar.3. 9. wait on him **b**. *of* the multi.
    4. 5. **b**. it had no depth of earth
    6. **b**. it had no root, it withered
    5. 4. **b**. that he had been often
    6. he marvelled **b**. *of* their unbe.
Lu. 2. 4. **b**. he was of the house and
    5.19. bring him in **b**. *of* the multi.
    8. 6. withered away, **b**. it lacked
    9. 7. **b**. that it was said of some
  11. 8. give him, **b**. he is his friend
    yet **b**. *of* his importunity he
  18. 5. Yet **b**. this widow troubleth
  19.11. **b**. he was nigh to Jerusalem
  23. 8. **b**. he had heard many things
Jo. 2.24. unto them, **b**. he knew
    3.29. **b**. *of* the bridegroom's voice
    4.41. more believed **b**. *of* his own
    42. we believe, not **b**. *of* thy say.
    7.43. division among people **b**. *of*
  11.42. **b**. *of* the people which stand
  12.42. **b**. *of* the Pharisees they did
  19.42. **b**. *of* the Jews' preparation
Act. 4.21. punish them, **b**. *of* the people
    8.11. **b**. *that* of long time he had
  12.20. **b**. their country was nourish.
  16. 3. circumcised him **b**. *of* the
  18. 2. **b**. *that* Claudius had comma.
    3. he was of the same craft
  27. 4. **b**. the winds were contrary
    9. **b**. the fast was now already
  28. 2. **b**. *of* present rain, and **b**. *of*
  18. **b**. there was no cause of death
Ro. 6.19. **b**. *of* the infirmity of your
  8.10. the body is dead **b**. *of* sin ; but
    the Spirit is life **b**. *of* righteo.
  15.15. **b**. *of* the grace that is given
¹Co.11.10. her head **b**. *of* the angels
Gal. 2. 4. that **b**. *of* false brethren una.
Eph.4.18. them, **b**. *of* the blindness of

Eph.5. 6. for **b**. *of* these things cometh
Phi. 1. 7. **b**. I have you in my heart
Heb.3.19. could not enter in **b**. *of* unbe.
    4. 6. entered not in **b**. *of* unbelief
  7.23. **b**. they were not suffered
  24. this man **b**. he continueth
Jas. 4. 2. ye have not **b**. ye ask not
    dioti.
Lu. 2. 7. **b**. there was no room for them
Act.17.31.**b**. he hath appointed a day
Ro. 1.19. **b**. that which may be known
  21. **b**. *that* when they knew God
    8. 7. **b**. the carnal mind is enmity
¹Co.15. 9. **b**. I persecuted the church of
Phi.2.26. **b**. *that* ye had heard that he
¹Th. 2. 8. **b**. ye were dear unto us
    4. 6. **b**. *that* the Lord is the avenger
Heb.11.5. **b**. God had translated him
  23. **b**. they saw he was a proper
Jas. 4. 3. receive not, **b**. ye ask amiss
¹Pet.1.16. **b**. it is written, Be ye holy
    epei.
Mat.18.32. **b**. thou desiredst me
  27. 6. **b**. it is the price of blood
Mar. 15.42. **b**. it was the preparation
Jo. 13.29. **b**. Judas had the bag
  19.31. **b**. it was the preparation
Heb. 6.13. **b**. he could swear by no
  11.11. **b**. she judged him faithful
    gar.
Jo. 3.19. **b**. their deeds were evil
  10.26. **b**. ye are not of my sheep, as
Act.28.20.**b**. *that* for the hope of Israel
Ro. 4.15. **b**. the law worketh wrath
³Jo. 7. **b**. that for his name's sake
    en. [*accu.*]
Mat.26.31. ye shall be offended **b**. *of*
  33. shall be offended **b**. *of* thee
Mar.14.27. offended **b**. *of* me this night
    epeidē.
Mat.21.46. **b**. they took him for a pro.
Act.14.12. **b**. he was the chief speaker
    kathoti.
Lu. 1. 7. **b**. *that* Elizabeth was barren
Act.2. 24. **b**. it was not possible that he
    heneka.
Lu. 4.18. **b**. he hath anointed
    hina.
Mat.20.31. **b**. they should hold their
    hopōs.
Act.20.16. **b**. he would not spend the
    apo.
Mat.18.7. Woe unto the world **b**. *of*
    ek.
Rev.16.21. **b**. *of* the plague of the hail
    epi, [*accu.*]
Rev.1. 7. the earth shall wail **b**. *of* him
    pros.
Mat.19.8. **b**. *of* the hardness of your
    charin.
Gal.3. 19. it was added **b**. *of* transgres.
Jude 16. in admiration **b**. *of* advantage

BECKON,   -ed, -ing.
    kataseiō.
Act.12.17. **b**-*ing* unto them with the
  13.16. Paul stood up, and **b**-*ing* with
  19.33. and Alexander **b**-*ed* with the
  21.40. stood on the stairs and **b**-*ed*
    neuō.
Jo.13. 24. Peter therefore **b**-*ed* to him
Act.24.10. *after that* the gov. *had* **b**-*ed*
    dianeuō.
Lu. 1.22. for he **b**-*ed* unto them, and
    kataneuō.
Lu. 5. 7. they **b**-*ed* unto their partners

BECOME, [*to be*]-eth, -ing, -ame.
    ginomai.
Mat.13.22. choke the word, and he **b**-*eth*
  32.among herbs, and **b**-*eth* a tree
  18. 3.converted, and **b**. as little

25

Mat.28.4. keepers did shake, and **b**-*ame*
Mar.1.17. I will make you *to* **b**. fishers
  4.19. choke the word, and it **b**-*eth*
  32. **b**-*eth* greater than all herbs
Lu.20.17. the same *is* **b**. the head of the
Jo. 1.12. power *to* **b**. the sons of God
Act.4.11. *which is* **b**. the head of the
  7.40. we wot not what *is* **b**. of him
  10.10. he **b**-*ame* very hungry, and
  12.18. the soldiers, what *was* **b**. of
Ro. 3.19. all the world *may* **b**. guilty
  4.18. that he might **b**. the father
  7.13. *might* **b**. exceeding sinful
1Co. 1.15. a fool that he may be wise
  8. 9. **b**. a stumblingblock to them
  9.20. unto the Jews I **b**-*ame* as a
  22. To the weak **b**-*ame* I as weak
  13. 1. I am **b**. as sounding brass
  11. when I **b**-*ame* a man, I put
  15.20. and **b**. the first-fruits of them
2Co.5. 17. behold all things *are* **b**. new
  12.11. I am **b**. a fool in glorying
Gal. 4.16. *Am* I therefore **b**. your ene.
Phi. 2. 8. *and* **b**-*ame* obedient unto
1Th. 1. 6. ye **b**-*ame* followers of us, and
  2.14. ye, brethren, **b**-*ame* followers
Phile. 6. thy faith *may* **b**. effectual by
Heb.5. 9. he **b**-*ame* the author of eter.
  12. *are* **b**. such as have need of
  10.33. *whilst* ye **b**-*ame* companions
  11. 7. **b**-*ame* heir of the righteousn.
Jas. 2. 4. *are* **b**. judges of evil thoughts
  11. thou *art* **b**. a transgressor of
Rev.6.12. **b**-*ame* black as sackcloth of
  and the moon **b**-*ame* as blood
  8. 8. third part of the sea **b**-*ame*
  11. part of the waters **b**-*ame*
  11.15. kingdoms of this world *are* **b**.
  16. 3. it **b**-*ame* as the blood of a
  4. of waters ; and they **b**-*ame*
  18. 2. *is* **b**. the habitation of devils

(See words with which it is con-
nected.)

BECOME, [*to be fitting,*] -*ame,*
    -eth.
  prepei.
Mat.3.15. for thus it **b**-*eth* us to fulfil
Eph.5. 3. named among you as **b**-*eth*
1Ti. 2.10. which **b**-*eth* women profes.
Tit. 2. 1. the things which **b**. sound
Heb.2.10. For it **b**-*ame* him, for whom
  7.26. such an high priest **b**-*ame* us
  axiōs.
Ro.16. 2. her in the Lord, *as* **b**-*eth* sal.
Phi. 1.27. be *as it* **b**-*eth* the gospel of
  hieroprepēs.
Tit. 2. 3. behaviour *as* **b**-*eth* holiness

BED,   -s.
  krabbatos.
Mar.2. 4. they let down the **b**. wherein
  9. 11. Arise, and take up thy **b**.
  12. he arose, took up the **b**. and
  6.55. began to carry about in **b**-*s*
Jo. 5. 8. Rise, take up thy **b**.,and walk
  9. and took up his **b**.,and walked
  10. lawful for thee to carry thy **b**.
  11.12. take up thy **b**., and walk
Act. 9.33. Eneas, which had kept his **b**.
  klinē.
Mat.9. 2. sick of the palsy, lying on a **b**.
  6. take up thy **b**., and go unto
Mar.4.21. or under a **b**., and not to be
  7.30. her daughter laid upon the **b**.
Lu. 5.18. men brought in a **b**. a man
  8.16. or putteth it under a **b**. ; but
  17.34. shall be two men in one **b**.
Act.5.15. and laid them on **b**-*s*, and
Rev.2.22. I will cast her into a **b**., and
26

---

    koitē.
Lu.11. 7. children are with me in **b**.
Heb.13.4. and the **b**. undefiled ; but
  strōnnumi.
Act. 9.34. whole ; arise, and *make* thy **b**.

BEFALL,   -ell.
  ginomai.
Mar.5.16. **b**-*ell* to him that was possess.
  sumbainō.
Act.20.19. temptations, *which* **b**-*ell* me
  sunantaō.
Act.20.22. the things *that shall* **b**. me

BEFORE. (See *Appendix*)
  pro.
Mat.5.12. the prophets which were **b**.
  6. 8. ye have need of, **b**. ye ask
  8.29. to torment us **b**. the time
  11.10. send my messeng. **b**. thy face
    Mar.1.2; Lu.7.27.
  24.38. in the days that were **b**. the
Lu. 1.76. thou shalt go **b**. the face of
  2.21. **b**. he was conceived in the
  9.52. And sent messengers **b**. his
  10. 1. two and two **b**. his face into
  11.38. he had not first washed **b**.
  21.12. But **b**. all these, they shall
  22.15. this passover with you **b**. I
Jo. 1.48. **b**. that Philip called thee
  5. 7. another steppeth down **b**. me
  10. 8. All that ever came **b**. me are
  11.55. up to Jerusalem **b**. the passo.
  12. 1. Then Jesus six days **b**. the
  13. 1. Now **b**. the feast of the pass.
  19. Now I tell you **b**. it come
  17. 5. which I had with thee **b**. the
  24. **b**. the foundation of the world
    Eph.1.4. 1Pe.1.20.
Act. 5.23. standing without **b**. the doors
  36. For **b**. these days rose up
  12. 6. and the keepers **b**. the door
  14. told how Peter stood **b**. the
  13.24. John had preached **b**. his
  14.13. which was **b**. their city
  21.38. which **b**. these days madest
Ro. 16.7. who also were in Christ **b**. me
1Co. 2. 7. God ordained **b**. the world
  4. 5. judge nothing **b**. the time
Gal. 1.17. which were apostles **b**. me
  2.12. For **b**. that certain came from
  3.23. But **b**. faith came we were
Col. 1.17. And he is **b** all things, and
2Ti. 1. 9. **b**. the world began; Tit.1.2.
  4.21. Do thy diligence to come **b**.
Heb.11.5. for **b**. his translation he had
Ja. 5. 9. the judge standeth **b**. the
  emprosthen.
Mat.5.16. Let your light so shine **b**.
  24. Leave there thy gift **b**. the
  6. 1. do not your alms **b**. men
  2. do not sound a trumpet **b**.
  7. 6. cast ye your pearls **b**. swine
  10.32. shall confess me **b**. men, him
    will I confess also **b**. my Fa.
  33. shall deny me **b**. men, him
    will I also deny **b**. my
  11.10. shall prepare thy way **b**. thee
  17. 2. was transfigured **b**.; Mar.9.2.
  25.32. **b**. him shall be gathered all
  26.70. he denied **b**. them all
  27.11. Jesus stood **b**. the governor
  29. they bowed the knee **b**. him
Mar.1. 2. shall prepare thy way **b**. thee
Lu. 5.19. into the midst **b**. Jesus
  7.27. shall prepare thy way **b**. thee
  12. 8. confess me **b**. men, him shall
    the Son of man also confess **b**.
  14. 2. there was a certain man **b**.
  19. 4. he ran **b**., and climbed up into
  27. bring hither, and slay them **b**.
  28. had thus spoken, he went **b**.
  21.36. to stand **b**. the Son of man

Jo. 1.15. 27. after me is preferred **b**. me
  30. a man which is preferred **b**.
  3.28. but that I am sent **b**. him
  10. 4. he goeth **b**. them, and the
  12.37. done so many miracles **b**.
Act.18.17. beat him **b**. the judgment
2Co. 5. 10. all appear **b**. the judgment
Gal. 2.14. I said unto Peter **b**. them all
Phi. 3.14. those things which are **b**.
1Th. 3. 9. for your sakes **b**. our God
  13. unblameable in holiness **b**.
1Jo. 3.19. shall assure our hearts **b**. him
Rev. 4. 6. full of eyes **b**. and behind
  22. 8. **b**. the feet of the angel which
  epi, [*gen.*]
Mar.13.9. brought **b**. rulers and kings
Act.23.30. also to say **b**. thee what they
  24.19. to have been here **b**. thee
  20. while I stood **b**. the council
  25. 9. judged of these things **b**. me
  26. brought him forth **b**. you
    and specially **b**. thee, O king
  26. 2. for myself this day **b**. thee
1Co. 6. 1. against another, go to law **b**.
    the unjust, and not **b**. the
  6. and that **b**. the unbelievers
2Co. 7.14. which I made **b**. Titus, is
1Ti. 5.19. but **b**. two or three witnesses
  6.13. who **b**. Pontius Pilate witn.
  epi, [*accu.*]
Mat.10.18. brought **b**. governors and
Lu.21.12. brought **b**. kings and rulers
Act.10.17.house, and stood **b**. the gate
  epi, [*dat.*]
Rev.10.11. must prophesy again **b**. many
  prin ē.
Mat.1.18. **b**. they came together, she
Mar.14.30. **b**. the cock crow twice
Lu. 2. 26. **b**. he had seen the Lord's
  22.34. **b**. *that* thou shalt thrice
Act. 2.20. **b**. that great and notable
  7. 2. **b**. he dwelt in Charran
  25.16. **b**. *that* he which is accused
  prin.
Mat.26.34.75. **b**. the cock crow
    Mar. 14. 72; Lu. 22. 61.
Jo. 8.58. **b**. Abraham was, I am
  14.29. I have told you **b**. it come to
  enantion.
Mar.2.12. and went forth **b**. them all
Lu.20.26. his words **b**. the people: and
  24.19. **b**. God and all the people
Act. 8.32. like a lamb dumb **b**. his
  eis.
Act.22.30. Paul down, and set him **b**.
2Co. 8. 24. to them, and **b**. the churches
Jas. 2. 6. draw you **b**. the judgment
  katenōpion.
2Co.12.19. we speak **b**. God in Christ
Eph.1. 4. and without blame **b**. him in
Jude 24. faultless **b**. *the presence* of his
  para.
Ro. 2.13. are just **b**. God, but the doers
Jas. 1.27. **b**. God and the Father is this
2Pet.2.11. against them **b**. the Lord
  apenanti.
Mat.27.24. washed his hands **b**. them
Ro. 3. 18. There is no fear of God **b**.
  en.
Mat.14.6. danced **b**. them, and pleased
Act. 5.27. them, they set them **b**. the
  kata. [*accu.*]
Lu. 2.31. prepared **b**. the face of all
Gal. 3. 1. **b**. whose eyes Jesus Christ
  pros.
Act.26.26. things, **b**. whom also I speak
Ro. 4. 2. to glory; but not **b**. God
  apo.
Act.7.45. God, drave out **b**. the face of
1Jo. 2.28. ashamed **b**. him at his coming
  ean mē.
Jo. 7.51. judge any man **b**. it hear him

enanti.
Lu. 1. 8. **b.** God in the order of his
    katenanti.
Ro. 4.17. **b.** him whom he believed
    ean mē proteron.
Jo. 7. 51. judge **b.** it hear him
        (*unless previously.*)
    ho proteron.
Jo. 6. 62. ascend up where he was **b.**
  9. 8. they which **b.** had seen him
1Ti. 1.13. who was **b.** a blasphemer
    proteron.
2Co.1. 15. minded to come unto you **b.**
    prōton.
Jo.15. 18. hated me **b.** it hated you
    prōtos.
Jo.1.15.30. before me, for he was **b.** me
        (was *first* of me.)
    pro prosōpon.
Act.13.24. preached **b.** his coming
    eis prosōpon.
2Co.8.24. and **b.** the churches the proof
    prouparchō.
Lu.23.12. for **b.** they *were* at enmity
    mesos.
Mat.14.6. of Herodias danced **b.** them

(See verbs which it follows; also
Day, Never.)

BEFOREHAND.
prodēlos.
1Ti. 5.24. Some men's sins are *open* **b.**
  25. of some are *manifest* **b.**
    prokatartizō.
2Co. 9. 5. and *make up* **b.** your bounty
    promarturomai.
1Pet.1.11. *when it testified* **b.** the
    promerimnaō.
Mar.13.11. *take no thought* **b.** what ye

BEFORETIME.
prouparchō.
Act. 8. 9. which **b.** in the same city used

BEG,   -ed,-ing.
prosaiteō.
Mar.10.46. by the highwayside **b**-ing
Lu. 18.35. man sat by the wayside **b**-ing
Jo. 9. 8. not this he that sat and **b**-ed
    aiteō.
Mat.27.58. **b**-ed the body; Lu.23.52.
    epaiteō.
Lu.16. 3. I cannot dig; to **b.** I am asha.

BEGET,   -at, otten.
gennaō.
Mat.1. 2. Abraham **b**-at Isaac; and
    Isaac **b**-at Jacob, &c.
  16. Jacob **b**-at Joseph the husba.
Act. 7. 8. so Abraham **b**-at Isaac
  29. Madian, where he **b**-at two
  13.33. my Son, this day *have I* **b**-otten
1Co. 4.15. I *have* **b**-otten you through the
Phile.10. whom I *have* **b**-otten in my
Heb.1. 5. my Son, this day *have I* **b**-otten
  5. 5. my Son, to day *have I* **b**-otten
1Jo. 5. 1. one that lcveth him *that* **b**-at
    loveth him also *that is* **b**-otten
  18. but he that is **b**-otten of God
    apokueō.
Jas. 1.18. Of his own will **b**-at he us
    anagennaō.
1Pet.1. 3. *which hath* **b**-ten us *again*

BEGGAR.
ptōchos.
Lu.16.20. there was a certain **b.** named
  22. came to pass that the **b.** died

BEGGARLY.
ptōchos.
Gal.4. 9. to the weak and **b.** elements

BEGIN,   -an, -un, -ing.
archomai.
Mat.4.17. Jesus **b**-an to preach, and to
  11. 7. Jesus **b**-an to say unto the
  20. Then **b**-an he to upbraid the
  12. 1. **b**-an to pluck the ears of corn
  14.30. **b**-ing to sink, he cried, saying
  16.21. **b**-an Jesus to shew unto his
  22. **b**-an to rebuke him, saying
  18.24. *when* he *had* **b**-un to reckon
  20. 8. **b**-ing from the last unto the
  24.49. *shall* **b.** to smite his fellow-se.
  26.22. **b**-an every one of them to
  37. **b**-an to be sorrowful and very
  74. Then **b**-an he to curse and to
Mar.1.45. **b**-an to publish it much, and
  2.23. his disciples **b**-an, as they
  4. 1. he **b**-an again to teach by the
  5.17. they **b**-an to pray him to dep.
  20. **b**-an to publish in Decapolis
  6. 2. he **b**-an to teach in the syna.
  7. **b**-an to send them forth by
  34. **b**-an to teach them many
  55. **b**-an to carry about in beds
  8.11. **b**-an to question with him
  31. he **b**-an to teach them, that
  32. Peter took him, and **b**-an to
  10.28. Then Peter **b**-an to say unto
  32. **b**-an to tell them what things
  41. they **b**-an to be much disple.
  47. he **b**-an to cry out and say
  11.15. he **b**-an to cast out them that
  12. 1. he **b**-an to speak unto them
  13. 5. Jesus answering them **b**-an
  14.19. they **b**-an to be sorrowful
  33. **b**-an to be sore amazed, and
  65. some **b**-an to spit on him, and
  14.69. he **b**-an to say to them that
  71. he **b**-an to curse and to swear
  15. 8. crying aloud, **b**-an to desire
  18. **b**-an to salute him, Hail, king
Lu. 3. 8. **b.** not to say within yoursel.
  23. Jesus himself **b**-an to be abo.
  4.21. he **b**-an to say unto them
  5.21. scribes and the Pharisees **b**-an
  7.15. that was dead sat up and **b**-an
  24. he **b**-an to speak unto the
  38. **b**-an to wash his feet with
  49. **b**-an to say within themselves
  9.12. when the day **b**-an to wear
  11.29. thick together, he **b**-an to say
  53. scribes and the Pharisees **b**-an
  12. 1. he **b**-an to say unto his disci.
  45. *shall* **b.** to beat the menserv.
  13.25. ye **b.** to stand without, and
  26. Then *shall* ye **b.** to say, We
  14. 9. thou **b.** with shame to take
  18. with one consent **b**-an to ma.
  29. that behold it, **b.** to mock him
  30. Saying, This man **b**-an to
  15.14. land; and he **b**-an to be in
  24. found. And they **b**-an to
  19.37. multitude of the disciples **b**-an
  45. **b.** to cast out them that sold
  20. 9. Then **b**-an he to speak to the
  21.28. *when* these things **b.** to come
  22.23. they **b**-an to enquire among
  23. 2. they **b**-an to accuse him, say.
  5. **b**-ing from Galilee to this
  30. Then *shall* they **b.** to say to
  24.27. he **b**-an at Moses and all the
  47. among all nations, **b**-ing at
Jo. 8. 9. **b**-ing at the eldest even unto
  13. 5. **b**-an to wash the disciples'
Act.1. 1. all that Jesus **b**-an both to do
  22. **b**-ing from the baptism of
  2. 4. **b**-an to speak with other
  8.35. **b**-an at the same scripture
  10.37. *and* **b**-an from Galilee, after
  11.15. as I **b**-an to speak, the H.G.
  18.26. he **b**-an to speak boldly in

Act. 24.2. Tertullus **b**-an to accuse him
  27.35. had broken it, he **b**-an to eat
2Co. 3. 1. *Do* we **b.** again to commend
1Pet.4.17. judgment must **b.** at the
    enarchomai.
Gal. 3. 3. *having* **b**-un *in* the spirit, are
Phil.1. 6. that he *which hath* **b**-un a
    proenarchomai.
2Co. 8. 6. that as he *had* **b**-un, so he
  10. who *have* **b**-un *before*, not
    mellō.
Rev.10.7. when he *shall* **b.** to sound
    echō kompsoteron.
Jo. 4.52. when he **b**-an *to amend*
    epiphōskō.
Mat.28.1. *as it* **b**-an *to dawn* toward
    buthizō.
Lu. 5. 7. so that they **b**-an *to sink*
    aiōn.
Lu. 1.70. been since the *world* **b**-an
Jo. 9.32. since the *world* **b**-an was it
Act.3. 21. prophets since the *world* **b**-an
    aiōnos.
Ro.16.25. secret since the *world* **b**-an
2Ti. 1. 9. Jesus before the *world* **b**-an

BEGINNING [*noun*].   -s.
archē.
Mat.19.4. which made them at the **b.**
  8. from the **b.** it was not so
  24. 8. these are the **b.** of sorrows
  21. since the **b.** of the world
Mar.1. 1. The **b.** of the gospel of Jesus
  10. 6. from the **b.** of the creation
  13. 8. these are the **b**-s of sorrows
  19. as was not from the **b.** of the
Lu. 1. 2. from the **b.** were eyewitnesses
Jo. 1. 1. In the **b.** was the Word, and
  2. The same was in the **b.** with
  2.11. This **b.** of miracles did Jes.
  6.64. Jesus knew from the **b.** who.
  8.25. I said unto you from the **b.**
  44. was a murderer from the **b.**
  15.27. been with me from the **b.**
  16. 4. not unto you at the **b.**, beca.
Act.11.15. on them, as on us at the **b.**
Phil.4.15. that in the **b.** of the gospel
Col. 1.18. who is the **b.**, the firstborn
2Th. 2.13. God hath from the **b.** chosen
Heb.1.10. Thou, Lord, in the **b.** hast
  3.14. if we hold the **b.** of our con.
  7. 3. having neither **b.** of days
2Pet.3. 4. from the **b.** of the creation
1Jo. 1. 1. which was from the **b.**, which
  2. 7. which ye had from the **b.**
    have heard from the **b.** 24.; 2Jo.6.
  13.14. him that is from the **b.**
  3. 8. the devil sinneth from the **b.**
  11. that ye heard from the **b.**
2Jo. 5. which we had from the **b.**
Rev. 1. 8. the **b.** and the ending, with
  3.14. the **b.** of the creation of God
  21. 6. the **b.** and the end, I will give
  22.13. Alpha and Omega, the **b.** and
    prōtos.
2Pet.2.20. worse with them than the **b.**
    prōton.
Jo. 2.10. Every man at the **b.** doth set
    anōthen.
Act.26. 5.knew me from the **b.** if they
    archomai.
Act.11. 4.rehearsed the mat. *from the* **b.**
    aiōn.
Act.15.18.the **b.** *of the world*; Eph. 3.9.

BEGOTTEN. (See *Beget*)
monogenēs.
Jo. 1.14. as of the *only* **b.** of the Father
  18. the *only* **b.** Son, which is in
  3.16. his *only* **b.** Son, that whosoev.

27

Jo. 3.18. of the *only* **b**. Son of God
Heb.11.17.offered up his *only* **b**. son
¹Jo. 4. 9. God sent his *only* **b**. Son into

BEGUILE,   -ed, -ing.
deleazō.
²Pet.2.14.**b**-*ing* unstable souls : an heart
exapataō.
²Co. 11.3. as the serpent **b**-*d* Eve through
paralogizomai.
Col. 2. 4. lest any man should **b**. you
katabrabeuō.
Col. 2.18. no man **b**. you *of* your *reward*

BEHALF.
huper.
²Co. 1.11. be given by many *on* our **b**.
  5.12. occasion to glory *on* our **b**.
  8.24. and of our boasting *on* your **b**.
Phi.1.29. it is given *in* the **b**. *of* Christ
meros.
²Co. 9. 3. you should be vain in this **b**.
¹Pet.4.16. him glorify God on this **b**.
epi, [*dat.*]
Ro.16.19. I am glad therefore *on* your **b**.
peri, [*gen.*]
¹Co.1.4.thank my God always *on* your **b**.

BEHAVE,   -ed, -eth.
anastrephō.
¹Ti. 3.15. *to* **b**. thy *self* in the house of
ginomai.
¹Th. 2.10. unblameably we **b**-*ed* ourselves
aschēmoneō.
¹Co. 7.36. he **b**-*eth* him *self uncomely*
  13. 5. *Doth* not **b**. it *self unseemly*
atakteō.
²Th. 3. 7. **b**-*ed* not our *selves disorderly*

BEHAVIOUR.
katastēma.
Tit. 2. 3. that they be in **b**. as becometh
kosmios.
¹Ti. 3. 2. vigilant, sober, *of good* **b**.

BEHEADED.
apokephalizō.
Mat.14.10.he sent, and **b**. John in the
Mar.6.16. It is John, whom I **b**. : he
  27. he went and **b**. him in the
Lu. 9. 9. Herod said, John have I **b**.
pelekizō.
Rev.20.4. souls of them *that were* **b**.

BEHIND.
opisthen.
Mat.9.20. came **b**. him, and ; Lu.8.44.
Mar.5.27. came in the press **b**., and
Rev. 4. 6. full of eyes before and **b**.
opisō.
Mat.16.23.thee **b**. me, Satan ; Mar. 8.33.
  Lu.4.8.
Lu. 7.38. And stood at his feet **b**. him
Phi. 3.13. those things which are **b**.
Rev.1.10. and heard **b**. me a great voice
husterēma.
Col. 1.24. fill up *that which is* **b**. of the
hustereō.
¹Co. 1. 7. So that ye *come* **b**. in no gift
²Co.11.5.suppose I *was* not a whit **b**. the
  12.11. for in nothing *am* I **b**. the very
hupomenō.
Lu. 2.43. child Jesus *tarried* **b**. in Jeru.

BEHOLD,   -eld, -est, -ing.
eideō.
Mar.9.15. the people, *when* they **b**-*e*
Lu.19.41. he **b**-*e* the city, and wept over
  21.29. **b**. the fig-tree, and all the
  22.56. a certain maid **b**-*e* him
  24.39. **b**. my hands and my feet, that
Jo. 20.27. hither thy finger, and **b**. my

28

Act.13.41.**b**., ye despisers, and wonder
Ro.11.22. **b**. therefore the goodness and
¹Jo. 3. 1. **b**., what manner of love the
Rev.5. 6. **b**-*e*, and, lo, in the midst of
  11. I **b**-*e*, and I heard the voice of
  6. 5. I **b**-*e*, and lo a black horse ;
  12. I **b**-*e* when he had opened the
  7. 9. After this I **b**-*e*, and, lo, a
  8.13. I **b**-*e*, and heard an angel fly.
  13.11. **b**-*e* another beast coming up
theōreō.
Mat.27.55. women were there **b**-*ing*
Mar.12.41. and **b**-*e* how the people cast
  15.47. Joses **b**-*e* where he was laid
Lu.10.18. I **b**-*e* Satan as lightning fall
  14.29. all *that* **b**. it begin to mock
  21. 6. for these things which ye **b**.
  23.35. the people stood **b**-*ing*. And
  48. **b**-*ing* the things which were
Jo. 17.24. that they *may* **b**. my glory
Act. 8.13. **b**-*ing* the miracles and signs
Rev.11.12.cloud; and their enemies **b**-*e*
blepō.
Mat. 7. 3. **b**-*est* thou the mote; Lu.6.41.
  18.10. do always **b**. the face of my
Lu. 6. 42. *when* thou thyself **b**-*est* not the
Act. 1. 9. *while* they **b**-*e*, he was taken
  4.14. **b**-*ing* the man which was
¹Co.10.18.**b**. Israel after the flesh : are
Col. 2. 5. joying and **b**-*ing* your order
emblepō.
Mat.6.26. **b**. the fowls of the air ; for
  19.26. Jesus **b**-*e* them, and said unto
Mar.10.21.Jesus **b**-*ing* him, loved him
Lu.20.17. he **b**-*e* them, and said, What
Jo. 1.42. when Jesus **b**-*e* him, he said
katanoeō.
Act.7.31. and as he drew near *to* **b**. it
  32. trembled, and durst not **b**.
Jas. 1.23. like unto a man **b**-*ing* his
  24 For he **b**-*eth* himself, and
atenizō.
Act.14.9. who *stedfastly* **b**-*ing* him, and
  23. 1. Paul, *earnestly* **b**-*ing* the
²Co. 3. 7. could not *stedfastly* **b**. the
epopteuō.
¹Pet.2.12. works, which they shall **b**.
  3. 2. *While* they **b**. your chaste
theaomai.
Lu.23.55. and **b**-*e* the sepulchre, and
Jo. 1. 14. we **b**-*e* his glory, the glory as
anatheōreō.
Act.17.23. *as* I passed by, and **b**-*e* your
ephoraō.
Act.4.29. Lord, **b**. their threatenings
horaō.
Lu.23.49. stood afar off **b**-*ing* these

BEHOLD, [*interjection.*]
idou.
Mat.1.20. **b**., the angel of the L.; 2.13.
  (*And all other passages, except*)
ide.
Mar.3.34. **b**. my mother and my breth.
  16.6. **b**. the place where they laid
Jo. 1. 29. 36. **b**. the Lamb of God
  48. **b**. an Israelite indeed, in
  19. 5. saith unto him, **b**. the man
  14 unto the Jews, **b**. your king
  also
Mat.25.20.22 ; 26.65 ; Mar.2.24 ; 11.21 ;
  15.4 ; Jo.3.26 ; 5.14 ; 11.3,36 ; 12.19 ;
  18.21 ; 19.4 ; Ro.2.17 ; Gal.5.2.

BEHOVED.
dei.
Lu.24.46. thus it **b**. Christ to suffer
opheilō.
Heb.2.17. in all things it **b**. *him* to be

BEING, [*noun*.] See *Have*.

BELIEF.
pistis.
²Th.2.13. the Spirit, and **b**. of the truth

BELIEVE,   -ed, -est, -eth, -ing.
pisteuō.
Mat.8.13. as thou *hast* **b**-*ed*, so be it
  9.28. **b**. ye that I am able to do
  18. 6. little ones *which* **b**. in me
  21.22. ye shall ask in prayer **b**-*ing*
  25. Why *did* ye not then **b**. him
    Mar.11.31; Lu.20.5.
  32. ye **b**-*ed* him not : but the
    harlots **b**-*ed* him..ye mig. **b**.
  24.23. 26. here is C., or there; **b**. it
  27.42. the cross, and we *will* **b**. him
Mar.1.15. repent..and **b**. the gospel
  5.36. Be not afraid, only **b**.
  9.23. If thou canst **b**., all things
    are possible to him *that* **b**-*eth*
  24. Lord, I **b**.; help thou mine un.
  42. little ones *that* **b**. in me
  11.23. but *shall* **b**. that those
  24. **b**. that ye receive them
  13.21. he is there; **b**. him not
  15.32. that we may see and **b**.
  16.13. neither **b**-*ed* they them
  14. because they **b**-*ed* not them
  16. He *that* **b**-*eth* and is baptized
  17. signs shall follow them *that* **b**.
Lu. 1.20. because thou **b**-*est* not my
  45. blessed is she *that* **b**-*ed*
  8.12. lest they should **b**. *and* be
  13. no root; which for a while **b**.
  50. **b**. only, and she shall be
  22.67. ye will not **b**. ; Jo.4.48
  24.25. fools, and slow of heart *to* **b**.
Jo. 1. 7. men through him *might* **b**.
  12. to them *that* **b**. on his name
  50. beca. I said unto thee..**b**-*est*
  2.11. his disciples **b**-*ed* on him
  22. and they **b**-*ed* the scripture
  23. many **b**-*ed*; 4.41; 7.31; 8.30;
    10.42; 12.42; Act.9.42; 17.12.
  3.12. and ye **b**. not, how *shall* ye **b**.
  15, 16. *who* soever **b**-*eth* in him
    Act.10.43; Ro.9.33; 10.11
  18. He *that* **b**-*eth* on him is not
    but he *that* **b**-*eth* not is con.
    because he *hath* not **b**-*ed*
  36. He *that* **b**-*eth* on the Son
  4.21. Woman, **b**. me, the hour
  39. the Samarit. of that city **b**-*ed*
  42. Now we **b**., not because of
  50. the man **b**-*ed* the word that
  53. himself **b**-*ed*, and his whole
  5.24. and **b**-*eth* on him that sent
  38. he hath sent, him ye **b**. not
  44. How can ye **b**., which receive
  46. *had* ye **b**-*ed* Moses, ye would
    have **b**-*ed* me
  47. if ye **b**. not his writings, how
    shall ye **b**. my words
  6.29. that ye **b**. on him whom he
  30. that we may see, and **b**. thee
  35, 47. he *that* **b**-*eth* on me; 7.38;
    11.25; 12.44; 14.12
  36. ye also have seen me, and **b**.
  40. and **b**-*eth* on him, may have
  64. some of you that **b**. not
    who they were *that* **b**-*ed* not
  69. And we **b**. and are sure that
  7. 5. neither *did* his brethren **b**.
  39. which they *that* **b**. on him
  48. or of the Pharisees **b**-*ed* on
  8.24. if ye **b**. not that I am he
  31. to those Jews *which* **b**-*ed* on
  45. you the truth ye **b**. me not
  46. truth, why *do* ye not **b**. me
  9.18. concern. the Jews *did* not **b**.
  35. *Dost* thou **b**. on the Son of

Jo. 9.36. that I *might* b. on nim
38. Lord, I b.; and he worshipped
10.25, 26. and ye b-ed not
37. works of my Fa., b. me not
38. though ye b. not me, b. the
that ye may know, and b.
11.15. to the intent ye *may* b.
26. b-eth in me..b-est thou this
27. I b. that thou art the Christ
40. that if thou *wouldst* b.
42. that they *may* b. that thou
45. which Jesus did, b-ed on him
48. all men *will* b. on him
12.11. went away and b-ed on Jesus
36. have light, b. in the light
37. yet they b-ed not on him
38. who *hath* b-ed our report
39. Therefore they could not b.
46. that *who*soever b-eth on me
47. and b. not, I judge him not
13.19. ye *may* b. that I am he
14. 1. ye b. in God, b. also in me
10. b-est thou not that I am in
11. b. me that I am in the Fath.
or else b. me for the very
29. it is come to pass, ye *might* b.
16. 9. because they b. not on me
27. and *have* b-ed that I came
30. by this we b. that thou cam.
31. answered them, *Do* ye now b.
17. 8. and they *have* b-ed that thou
20. for them also *which shall* b.
21. that the world *may* b. that
19.35. saith true, that ye *might* b.
20. 8. and he saw, and b-ed
25. into his side I *will* not b.
29. thou *hast* b-ed: blessed are
seen and yet *have* b-ed
31. that ye *might* b. that Jesus
and that b-ing ye might have
Act. 2.44. And all *that* b-ed were toge.
4. 4. which heard the word b-ed
32. of them *that* b-ed were of
8.12. But when they b-ed Philip
13. Then Simon himself b-ed
37. If thou b-est with all thine
I b. that Jesus Christ is the
9.26. *and* b-ed not that he was a
11.17. b-ed on the Lord; 18.8
21. a great number b-ed, and
13.12. he saw what b-ed, and
39. by him all *that* b. are justified
41. which ye shall in no wise b.
48. ordained to eternal life b-ed
14. 1. and also of the Greeks b-ed
23. Lord on whom they b-ed
15. 5. certain of the Ph. *which* b-ed
7. the word of the gospel, and b.
11. But we b. that through the
16.31. b. on the Lord Jesus Christ
34. b-ing in God with all his
17.34. clave unto him, and b-ed
18. 8. of the Corinth. hearing b-ed
27. them much *which had* b-ed
19. 2. rece. the Ho. Gh. *since* ye b-ed
4. that they *should* b. on him
18. And many *that* b-ed came
21.20. of Jews there are *which* b.
25. touching the Gen. *which* b.
22.19. them *that* b-ed on thee
24.14. b-ing all things which are
26.27. King Agrippa, b-est thou the
I know that thou b-est
27.25. for I b. God, that it shall
Ro. 1.16. to every one *that* b-eth
3.22. all, and upon all them *that* b.
4. 3. Abraham b-ed God, and it
5. but b-eth on him that
11. the father of all them *that* b.
17. before him whom he b-ed
18. against hope b-ed in hope
24. *if* we b. on him that raised

Ro. 6. 8. we b. that we shall also
10. 4. to every one *that* b-eth
9. and shalt b. in thine heart
10. with the heart man b-eth
14. in whom they *have* not b-ed
and how *shall* they b.
16. who *hath* b-ed our report
13.11. nearer than when we b-ed
14. 2. For one b-eth that he may
15.13. all joy and peace in b-ing
1Co. 1.21. to save them *that* b.
3. 5. ministers by whom ye b-ed
11.18. and I partly b. it
13. 7. b-eth all things, hopeth all
14.22. not to them *that* b., but
but for them *which* b. not
15. 2. unless ye *have* b-ed in vain
11. so we preach, and so ye b-ed
2Co. 4.13. I b-ed, and therefore have I
we also b., and therefore
Gal. 2.16. even we *have* b-ed in Jesus
3. 6. as Abraham b-ed God
22. mig. be given to them *that* b.
Eph.1.13. whom also *after that* ye b-ed
19. power to us-ward *who* b.
Phi. 1.29. not only *to* b. on him, but
1Th. 1. 7. ensamples to all *that* b.
2.10. ourselves among you *that* b.
13. worketh also in you *that* b.
4.14. For if we b. that Jesus died
2Th. 1.10. admired in all them *that* b.
our test. among you *was* b-ed
2.11. that they should b. a lie
12. *who* b-ed not the truth, but
1Ti. 1.16. should hereafter b. on him
3.16. b-ed *on* in the world
2Ti. 1.12. I know whom I *have* b-ed
Tit. 3. 8. that they *which have* b-ed
Heb.4. 3. we *which have* b-ed do enter
11. 6. must b. that he is, and
Jas. 2.19. Thou b-est that there is one
the devils also b., and trem.
23. Abraham b-ed God, and it
1Pet.1. 8. yet b-ing, ye rejoice
21. *Who* by him do b. in God
2. 6. and he *that* b-eth on him
7. Unto you therefore *which* b.
1Jo.3.23. That we *should* b. on the
4. 1. Beloved, b. not every spirit
16. we have known and b-ed
5. 1. *Who*soever b-eth that Jesus
5. he *that* b-eth that Jesus is
10. He *that* b-eth on the Son of
he *that* b-eth not God hath
because he b-eth not the rec.
13. unto you *that* b. on the name
that ye *may* b. on the name
Jude 5. destroyed them *that* b-ed not
Act.17.4. some of them b-ed; 28.24
pistos.
Jo. 20.27. be not faithless, but b-ing
Act.10.45. circumci., *which* b-ed were
16. 1. which was a Jewess, *and* b-ed
2Co. 6.15. he that b-eth with an infidel
1Ti. 4. 3. *which* b. and know the truth
10. specially of those *that* b.
5.16. If any man or wo. *that* b-eth
6. 2. they that have b-ing masters
pistis.
Ro. 3.26. of him which b-eth in Jesus
Heb.10.39. but of them that b. to the
apeitheō.
Jo. 3.36. he *that* b-eth *not* the Son shall
Act.17. 5. the Jews *which* b-ed not, mo.
19. 9. were hardened, and b-ed not
Ro.11.30. in times past *have* not b-ed
31. have these also now *not* b-ed
15.31. from them *that do* not b. in
Heb. 3.18.them *that* b-ed *not*; 11.31
apisteō.
Mar.16.11.been seen of her, b-ed *not*

Mar.16.16.he *that* b-eth *not* shall be
Lu. 24.11.tales, and they b-ed them *not*
41.*while* they yet b-ed *not* for
Act. 28.24.spoken, and some b-ed *not*
Ro. 3. 3.what if some *did* not b.
2Ti. 2.13.If we b. *not*, yet he abideth
apistos.
1Co. 7.12,13. a wife *that* b-eth not
10.27. them *that* b. *not*; 14.24
14.24. come in one *that* b-eth not
2Co. 4. 4. minds of them *which* b. *not*
(See *Surely*.)

BELIEVERS.
pisteuō.
Act. 5.14. And b. were the more added
pistos.
1Ti. 4.12. an example of the b.

BELLY,   -ies.
koilía.
Mat.12.40. three nights in the whale's b.
15.17. the mouth goeth into the b.
Mar. 7.19. his heart, but into the b.
Lu. 15.16. would fain have filled his b.
Jo. 7.38. out of his b. shall flow rivers
Ro. 16.18. Jesus Christ, but their own b.
1Co. 6.13. for the b., and the b. for
Phi. 3.19. whose God is their b., and
Rev.10.9,10.make thy b. bitter
gastēr.
Tit. 1.12. liars, evil beasts, slow b-ies

BELONG,   -ed.
eimi.
Mar. 9.41. because ye b. to Christ
Lu. 23. 7. he b-ed to Herod's jurisdict.

BELOVED.
agapētos.
Mat. 3.17. is my b.Son; 17.5
Mar.9.7; Lu.9.35; 2Pet.1.17
12.18. whom I have chosen; my b.
Mar. 1.11. Thou art my b. Son; Lu.3.22
12. 6. one son, his *well* b., he sent
Lu. 20.13. I will send my b. son
Act. 15.25. chos. men..with our b. Bar.
Ro. 1. 7. To all that be in Rome, b.
11.28. the election, they are b.
12.19. *Dearly* b., avenge not your.
16. 5. Salute my *well* b. Epinetus
8,9,12. Greet Amplias, my b. in
1Co. 4.14. as my b. sons I warn you
17. who is my b. son, and
10.14. *dearly* b., flee from idolatry
15.58. b. brethren; Jas.1.16,19; 2.5
2Co. 7. 1. *dearly* b., let us cleanse our.
12.19. we do all things, *dearly* b.
Eph. 6.21. b. brother; Col.4.7,9
Phil. 4. 1. breth. *dearly* b. and longed
fast in the Lo. my *dearly* b.
Col. 4.14. Luke, the b. physician, and
1Ti. 6. 2. bec. they are faithful and b.
2Ti. 1. 2. To Tim. my *dearly* b. son
Phile. 1. unto Philemon our *dearly* b.
2. and to our b. Apphia and
16. above a servant, a brother b.
1Pet. 2.11. *Dearly* b., I beseech you
2Pet. 3.15. even as our b. brother Paul
3John 1. The elder unto the *well* b. G.
See also Phil.2.12; Heb.6.9; 1Pet.4.12;
2Pet. 3.1,8,14,17; 1Jo. 3.2,21; 4.1,7,11;
3Jo. 2,5,11; Ju.3,17,20
(See *Dearly*.)
agapaō.
Ro. 9.25. her b. which was not b.
Eph.1. 6. made us accepted in the b.
Col. 3.12. the elect of God, holy and b.
1Th. 1. 4. brethren b.; 2Th.2.13
Rev.20.9. saints about, and the b. city
29

BENEATH.
katō.
Mar.14.66.Peter was **b**. in the palace
Jo. 8.23.Ye are from **b**.; I am from

BENEFACTORS.
euergetēs.
Lu.22.25. upon them, are called **b**.

BENEFIT.
charis.
²Co. 1.15. ye might have a second **b**.
euergesia.
¹Ti. 6. 2. beloved, partakers of the **b**.
agathos.
Phile. 14. that thy **b**. should not be as

BENEVOLENCE.
eunoia.
¹Co. 7. 3. render unto the wife due **b**.

BERRIES, See *Olive*.

BERYL.
bērullos.
Rev.21.20. chrysolite ; the eighth, **b**.

BESEECH,   *-ing, -ought*.
deomai.
Lu. 5.12. fell on his face, and **b**-*o* him
   8.28. I **b**. thee, torment me not
     38. **b**-*o* him that he might be
   9.38. **b**. thee, look upon my son
     40. I **b**-*o* thy disciples to cast him
Act.21.39.I **b**. thee suffer me to speak
   26. 3. **b**. thee to hear me patiently
²Co. 10. 2. I **b**. you that I may not
Gal. 4.12. I **b**. you, be as I am
erōtaō.
Mat.15.23.disciples came and **b**-*o* him
Mar.7.26. she **b**-*o* him that he would
Lu. 4.38. they **b**-*o* hin¦for her
   7. 3. **b**-*ing* him that he would
   8.37. **b**-*o* him to depart from them
   11.37. a certain Pharisee **b**-*o* him
Jo. 4.40. **b**-*o* him that he would tarry
     47. **b**-*o* him that he would come
   19.31, 38. **b**-*o* Pilate
¹Th. 4. 1. we **b**. you bre.; 5.12; ²Th.2.1
²John 5. And now I **b**. thee lady
parakaleō.
Mat.8. 5. a centurion, **b**-*ing* him
     31. the devils **b**-*o* him ; Mar.5.12
   18.29. **b**-*o* him,saying,Have patience
Mar.1.40. a leper to him, **b**-*ing* him
   5.23. **b**-*o* him greatly, saying
Act.13.42.Gentiles **b**-*o* that these
   16.15. she **b**-*o* us, saying, If ye
   21.12. **b**-*o* him not to go up to
   27.33. Paul **b**-*o* them all to take
Ro.12. 1. I **b**. you therefore brethren
²Co. 5.20. as *though* God did **b**. you
   12. 8. I **b**-*o* the Lord thrice
Phi. 4. 2. I **b**. Euodias, and **b**. Syntyche
Phile. 9. for love's sake I rather **b**.

BESET.
euperistatos.
Heb.12.1. *which doth so easily* **b**. us

BESIDE, [*preposition*.]   *-s*.
epi, (*dat*.)
Mat.25.20. I have gained **b**-*s* them five
     22. two other talents **b**-*s* them
Lu. 16.26. **b**-*s* all this, to day is the third
     sun.
Lu.24.21. **b**-*s* all this, to day is the third
chōris.
Mat.14.21. **b**-*s* wom. and children ; 15.38
²Co. 11.28. **b**-*s* those things that are
mainomai.
Act.26.24. Paul, thou art **b**. *thyself*
existēmi.
²Co. 5.13. whether we be **b**. ourselves
30

---

     alla ge sun.
Lu.24.21. *and* **b**. all this, to day is

BESIDE, [*adverb*.]
loipon.
¹Co. 1.16. **b**. I know not whether I
prosopheilō.
Phile. 19. *owest*..thine own self **b**.

BEST.
kreittōn.
¹Co.12.31. covet earnestly the **b**. gifts
prōtos.
Lu.15.22. Bring forth the **b**. robe, and

BESTOW,   *-ed*.
kopiaō.
Jo. 4.38. whereon ye **b**-*ed* no *labour*
Ro.16. 6. who **b**-*ed* much *labour* on us
Gal. 4.11. I *have* **b**-*ed* upon you *labour*
didōmi.
²Co. 8. 1. grace of God **b**-*ed* on the chu.
¹Jo. 3. 1. the Father *hath* **b**-*ed* upon us
sunagō.
Lu.12.17. no room, where to **b**. my fr.
     18. there *will* I **b**. all my fruits
psōmizō.
¹Co.13. 3. I **b**. all my goods *to feed*
peritithēmi.
¹Co.12.23. *upon* these we **b**. more abund.

BETRAY,   *-ed, -est, -eth*.
paradidōmi.
Mat.10.4. Iscariot *who* also **b**-*ed* him
   17.22. Son of man shall *be* **b**-*ed*; 20.18
   24.10. and *shall* **b**. one another
   26. 2. Son of man *is* **b**-*ed*; Mar.14.21
     16. oppor. to **b**. him ; Lu.22.6
     21. of you *shall* **b**. me; Jo.13.21
     23. dish, the same *shall* **b**. me
     24. the Son of man is **b**-*ed* ; 14.21
     25. *wh*. **b**-*ed* him ; Mr.3.19; Jo.18.2
     45. *is* **b**-*ed* into the hands of
     46. he is at hand *that doth* **b**. me
     48. he *that* **b**-*ed* him; Mar.14.44
   27. 3. Judas, *which had* **b**-*ed* him
     4. have sinned *in that* I have **b**-*ed*
Mar.13.12.brother *shall* **b**. the brother
   14.10. priests, to **b**. him unto them
     11. he *might* conveniently **b**. him
     18. eateth with me *shall* **b**. me
     42. he *that* **b**-*eth* me is at hand
Lu.21.16. And ye *shall be* **b**-*ed* both by
   22. 4. how he *might* **b**. him unto
     21. the hand of him *that* **b**-*eth* me
     22. that man by whom he is **b**-*ed*
     48. **b**-*est* thou the Son of man
Jo. 6.64. and who should **b**. him
     71. he it was that should **b**. him
   12. 4. Simon's son, which should **b**.
   13. 2. Simon's son, to **b**. him
     11. he knew *who* should **b**. him
   18. 5. *which* **b**-*ed* him, stood with
   21.20. which is he *that* **b**-*eth* thee
¹Co.11.23. night in which he *was* **b**-*ed*

BETRAYERS.
prodotēs.
Act.7.52. ye have been now the **b**.

BETTER, [*verb*,]   *-ed*.
ōpheleō.
Mar.5.26. *was* nothing **b**-*ed* but rather

BETTER, [*adj, and adv*.]
kreissōn.
¹Co. 7. 9. it is **b**. to marry than to burn
   11.17. not for the **b**., but for the
Phi. 1.23. with Christ; which is far **b**.
Heb.1. 4. Being made so much **b**. than
   6. 9. we are persuaded **b**. things of
   7. 7. the less is blessed of the **b**.
     19. the bringing in of a **b**. hope
     22. a surety of a **b**. testament
   8. 6. mediator of a **b**. covenant

Heb.8. 6. established upon **b**. promises
   9.23. with **b**. sacrifices than these
   10.34. ye have in heaven a **b**. and an
   11.16. now they desire a **b**. country
     35. might obtain a **b**. resurrection
     40. some **b**. thing for us
   12.24. **b**. things than that of Abel
¹Pet.3.17. it is **b**., if the will of God be
²Pet.2.21. For it had been **b**. for them
kreisson.
¹Co.7.38. her not in marriage doeth **b**.
kalos mallon.
Mar.9.42. is **b**. for thee to enter into life
¹Co. 9.15. it were **b**. for me to die
chrēstos.
Lu. 5.39. for he saith, The old is **b**.
huperechō.
Phil.2. 3. each esteem other **b**. than
diapherō.
Mat.6.26. *Are* ye not much **b**. than they
   12.12. *is* a man **b**. than a sheep
Lu.12.24. more, *are* ye **b**. than the fowls
proechomai.
Ro. 3. 9. What then, *are* we **b**. than
sumpherō.
Mat.18.6. it were **b**. for him that a
perisseuō.
¹Co. 8. 8. neither if we eat *are* we *the* **b**
lusiteleō.
Lu.17. 2. It were **b**. for him that a

BETWEEN.
metaxu.
Mat.18.15. tell him his fault **b**. thee
   23.35. **b**. the temple and the altar
Lu.11.51. **b**. the altar and the temple
   16.26. **b**. us and you there is a great
Act.12. 6. sleeping **b**. two soldiers
   15. 9. no difference **b**. us and them
pros.
Lu.23.12. were at enmity **b**. themselves
Act.26.31. they talked **b**. themselves
en.
Ro. 1.24. thine own bodies **b**. themsel.
ana mesos.
¹Co. 6. 5. able to judge **b**. his brethren
merizō.
¹Co.7.34. *There is difference* also **b**. a

BETWIXT.
ek.
Phil. 1.23. I am in a strait **b**. two

BEWAIL,   *-ed*.
koptō.
Lu. 8.52. And all wept, and **b**-*ed* her
   23.27. which also **b**-*ed* and lamented
klaiō.
Rev.18.9. *shall* **b**. her, and lament for
pentheō.
²Co.12.21. and that I *shall* **b**. many

BEWARE.
prosechō.
Mat.7.15. **b**. of false prophets, which
   10.17. But **b**. of men for they will
   16. 6. Take heed and **b**. of ; 11, 12.
Lu.12. 1. **b**. ye of the leaven of the
   20.46. **b**. of the scribes, which
blepō.
Mar.8.15. Take heed, **b**. of the leaven
   12.38. **b**. of the scribes, which love
Act.13.40.**b**. therefore, lest that come
Phi. 3. 2. **b**. of dogs, **b**. of evil worker
     b. of the concision
phulassō.
Lu.12.15. and **b**. of covetousness: for a
²Pet.3.17. know these things before, **b**.

BEWITCHED.
existēmi.
Act. 8. 9. **b**. the people of Samaria
     11. he *had* **b**. them with sorce.

baskainō.
al. 3.1. Galatians, who *hath* **b**. you

BEWRAYETH.
poieō dēlos.
Mat.26.73. of them; for thy speech **b**.

BEYOND.
peran.
Mat.4.15.the way of the sea, **b**. Jordan
    25. and from **b**. Jordan
   19. 1. coasts of Judeæ **b**. Jordan
Mar.3. 8. and from **b**. Jordan
Jo. 1.28. in Bethabara **b**. Jordan
   3.26. he that was with thee **b**. Jor.
  10.40. went away again **b**. Jordan
ek perissos.
Mar.6.51. in themselves **b**. *measure*
huperperissōs.
Mar.7.37. And were **b**. *measure* aston.
epekeina.
Act.7.43. will carry you away **b**. Baby.
kata huperbolē. [*accu.*]
Gal. 1.13. **b**. *measure* I persecuted the
huper.
[2]Co. 8.3. yea, and **b**. their power, they
huperekeina.
[2]Co.10.16. gospel in the reigons **b**. you

(See *Go, Stretch.*)

BID,   -ade, -den.
kaleō.
Mat.22.3. to call them *that were* **b-den**
   4. Tell them *which are* **b-den**
   8. they *which were* **b-den** were
   9. shall find, **b**. to the marriage
Lu. 7.39. the Pharisee *which had* **b-den**
  14. 7. par. to those *which were* **b-den**
   8. When thou *art* **b-den** of any
    than thou be **b-den** of
   9. And he *that* **b-a** thee and
  10. when thou *art* **b-den**, go and
    when he *that* **b-a** thee com.
  12. said he also to him *that* **b-a**
  16. a great supper, and **b-a**
  17. to say to them *that were* **b-den**
  24. of those men *which were* **b-den**
[1]Co.10.27. of them that believe not **b**.
epō.
Mat.16.12.thee how that he **b-a**
  23. 3. whatsoever they **b**. yo[r] obser.
Lu.10.40. **b**. her therefore that sne help
Act.11.12.And the Spirit **b-a** me go
  22.24. and **b-a** that he should be
keleuō.
Mat.14.28. **b**. me come unto thee on the
prostassō.
Mat.1.24. angel of the Lord *had* **b-den**
antikaleō.
Lu.14.12. lest they also **b**. thee *again*
apotassomai.
Lu. 9.61. me first go **b**. them *farewell*
Act.18.21. **b-a** them *farewell*, saying
legō.
[2]Jo. 10. 11. house, neither **b**. him God

BIER.
soros.
Lu. 7.14. he came and touched the **b**.

BILL.
biblion.
Mar.10.4. to write a **b**. of divorcement
gramma.
Lu.16.6.7. he said unto him, Take thy **b**.

BIND.   -ing, bound.
deō.
Mat.12.29. except he first **b**. the strong
  13.30. **b**. them in bundles to burn
  14. 3. laid hold on John, and **b-o**

Mat.16.19.18.18.**b**.on earth shall be **b-o**
  22.13. **b**. him hand and foot, *and*
  27. 2. *when* they *had* **b-o** hi**m**
Mar.3.27. except he will first **b**. the
  5. 3. no man could **b**. him, no, not
  4. had often been **b-o** with
  6.17. hold upon John, and **b-o**
  15. 1. **b-o** Jesus, *and* carried him
  7. Barabbas, which lay **b-o**
Lu.13.16. whom Satan *hath* **b-o**, lo
Jo.11.44. **b-o** hand and foot with
  18.12. Jews took Jesus, and **b-o**
  24. Annas had sent him **b-o**
Act.9. 2. bring them **b-o** unto
  14. *to* **b**. all that call on thy name
  21. he might bring them **b-o**
  12. 6. **b-o** with two chains : and
  20.22. I go **b-o** in the spirit unto
  21.11. **b-o** his own hands and feet
    Jews at Jerusalem **b**. the man
  13. I am ready not *to be* **b-o**
  33. commanded him *to be* **b-o**
  22. 5. **b-o** unto Jerusalem, for to
  29. and because he had **b-o** him
  24.27. a pleasure, left Paul **b-o**
Rom.7.2. hath an husband *is* **b-o** by
[1]Co.7.27. *Art* thou **b-o** unto a wife
  39. the wife *is* **b-o** by the law
[2]Ti. 2. 9. the word of God *is* not **b-o**
Rev.9.14. four angels *which are* **b-o**
  20. 2. Satan, and **b-o** him a thou.
desmeuō.
Mat.23.4. For they **b**. heavy burdens
Act.22.4. **b-ing** and delivering into pri.
katadeō.
Lu.10.34. and **b-o** *up* his wounds
proteinō.
Act.22.25. And as they **b-o** him with
hupodeomai.
Act. 12.8. Gird thyself, and **b**. *on* thy
anathematizō.
Act.23.12. **b-o** themselves *under a curse*
  14. **b-o** oursel. *under a great curse*
    (cursed with a curse.)
  21. *have* **b-o** themsel. *with an oath*
(See *Bound.*)

BIRD,   s.
peteinon.
Mat.8.20. **b-s** of the air have; Lu.9.58.
  13.32. **b-s** of the air come and lodge
Ro. 1.23. corruptible man, and to **b-s**
Jas.3. 7. every kind of beasts, and of **b-s**
orneon.
Rev.18.2. every unclean and hateful **b**.
ptēnon.
[1]Co.15.39. of fishes, and another of **b-s**

BIRTH.
gennēsis.
Mat.1.18. Now the **b**. of Jesus Christ
Lu. 1.14. many shall rejoice at his **b**.
ōdinō.
Gal. 4.19. whom I *travail in* **b**. again
Rev.12.2. cried, *travailing in* **b**., and
genetē.
Jo. 9. 1. which was blind from his **b**.

BIRTH-DAY.
genesia.
Mat.14.6. when Herod's **b**. was kept
Mar.6.21. Herod on his **b**. made supper

BIRTH-RIGHT.
prōtotokia.
Heb.12.16. morsel of meat sold his **b**.

BISHOP,   -s.
episkopos.
Phi. 1. 1. with the **b-s** and deacon**s**
[1]Ti. 3. 2. A **b**. then must be blameless

Tit. 1. 7. For a **b**. must be blameless
[1]Pet.2.25. Shepherd and **b**. of your soul**s**
episkopē.
[1]Ti. 3.1. a man desire the *office of a* **b**.

BISHOPRICK.
episkopē.
Act.1.20. and, His **b**. let another take

BITS.
chalinos.
Jas. 3.3. we put **b**. in the horses mou.

BITE.
daknō.
Gal.5.15. if ye **b**. and devour one anoth.

BITTER.
pikros.
Jas. 3.11. same place sweet water and **b**.
  14. if ye have **b**. envying and
pikrainō.
Col. 3.19. and be not **b**. against them
Rev.8.11. because they *were made* **b**.
  10. 9. it *shall make* thy belly **b**.
  10. eaten it, my belly *was* **b**.

BITTERLY.
pikrōs.
Mat.26.75. And he went out and wept **b**.
Lu. 22.62. Peter went out, and wept **b**.

BITTERNESS.
pikria.
Act.8.23. thou art in the gall of **b**.
Ro. 3.14. is full of cursing and **b**.
Eph.4.31. Let all **b**., and wrath, and
Heb.12.15.lest any root of **b**. springing

BLACK.
melas.
Mat.5.36. not make one hair white or **b**.
Rev. 6. 5. I beheld, and lo a **b**. horse
  12. sun became **b**. as sackcloth

BLACKNESS.
gnophos.
Heb.12.18.nor unto **b**., and darkness
zophos.
Jude 13. to whom is reserved the **b**.

BLADE.
chortos.
Mat.13.26. But when the **b**. was sprung
Mar. 4.28. first the **b**., then the ear, aft.

BLAME, [*verb*],   -ed.
mōmaomai.
[2]Co. 6. 3. that the ministry *be* not **b-ed**
  8.20. that no ma**n** *should* **b**. us in
kataginōskō.
Gal.2.11. face, because he was *to be* **b-ed**

BLAME, [*noun*.]
amōmos.
Eph.1. 4. *without* **b**. before him in love

BLAMELESS.
ane**n**klētos.
[1]Co. 1. 8. that ye may be **b**. in the day
[1]Ti. 3.10. of a deacon, being found **b**.
Tit. 1. 6. If any be **b**., the husband of
  7. For a bishop must be **b**., as
amemptos.
Lu. 1. 6. and ordinances of the Lord **b**.
Phil.2.15. That ye may be **b**. and harm.
  3. 6. which is in the law, **b**.
amemptōs.
[1]Th. 5.23. be preserved **b**. unto the
amōmētos.
[2]Pet.3.14. in peace, without spot, and **b**.

anaitios.
Mat.12.5. the Sabbath, and are **b**.
anepilēptos.
¹Ti. 3. 2. A bishop then must be **b**., the
5. 7. charge, that they may be **b**.

BLASPHEME. -ed, -est, -eth.
blasphēmeō.
Mat.9. 3. themselves, This man **b**-*eth*
Mar.3.28. wherewithsoever they *shall* **b**.
29. he that *shall* **b**. against the
Lu.12.10. unto him that **b**-*eth* against
Jo. 10.36. Thou **b**-*est;* because I said, I
Act.13.45. Paul contradicting and **b**-*ing*
18. 6. opposed themselves, and **b**-*ed*
26.11. compelled them *to* **b**. ; and
Ro. 2.24. the name of God *is* **b**-*ed*
¹Ti. 1.20. that they may learn not *to* **b**.
6. 1. and his doctrine *be* not **b**-*ed*
Tit. 2. 5. the word of God *be* not **b**-*ed*
Jas. 2. 7. *Do* not *they* **b**. that worthy
Rev.13. 6.*to* **b**. his name, and his taber.
16. 9. **b**-*ed* the name of God, which
11. **b**-*ed* the God of heaven beca.
21. men **b**-*ed* God because of the

BLASPHEMER, -s.
blasphēmeō. [*part.*]
Act.19.37. nor yet **b**-*s* of your goddess
blasphēmos.
¹Ti. 1.13. Who was before a **b**. and a
²Ti. 3. 2. covetous, boasters, proud, **b**-*s*

BLASPHEMOUS.
blasphēmos.
Act. 6.11. heard him speak **b**. words
13. to speak **b**. words against this

BLASPHEMOUSLY.
blasphēmeō.
Lu.22.65. **b**. spake they against him

BLASPHEMY, -ies.
blasphēmia.
Mat.12.31.All manner of sin and **b**.
the **b**. *against* the Holy Ghost
(*blasphemy* of the Spirit.)
15.19. thefts, false witness, **b**-*s*
26.65. now ye have heard his **b**.
Mar.2. 7. doth this man thus speak **b**-*s*
3.28. **b**-*s* wherewith soever they
7.22. an evil eye, **b**., pride, foolish.
14.64. Ye have heard the **b**.
Lu. 5.21. Who is this which speak **b**-*s*
Jo. 10.33. for **b**. ; and because that thou
Col. 3. 8. anger, wrath, malice, **b**., filth.
Rev.2. 9. I know the **b**. of them which
13. 1. upon his heads the name of **b**.
5. speaking great things and **b**-*s*
6. opened his mouth in **b**.against
17. 3. full of names of **b**., having
blasphēmeō.
Mat.26.65. saying, He *hath spoken* **b**.

BLAZE
diaphēmizō.
Mar.1.45. *to* **b**. abroad the matter, inso.

BLEMISH, -es.
mōmos.
²Pet.2.13. spots they are and **b**-*es*, sport.
amōmos.
Eph.5.27. should be holy and *without* **b**.
¹Pet.1.19. as of a lamb *without* **b**. and

BLESS, [*verb.*] -ed, -eth, -ing.
eulogeō.
Mat.5.44. **b**. them that curse you, do
14.19. to heaven, he **b**-*ed*, and brake,
25:34. ye **b**-*ed* of my Father, inherit
26.26. **b**-*ed* it, *and* brake it, and gave
Mar.6.41. to heaven, and **b**-*ed*, and
32

Mar.8. 7. and he **b**-*ed*, *and* commanded
10.16. hands upon them, and **b**-*ed*
14.22. and **b**-*ed*, *and* brake it, and
Lu. 2.28. him up in his arms, and **b**-*ed*
34. And Simeon **b**-*ed* them, and
6.28. **b**. them that curse you, and
9.16. he **b**-*ed* them, and brake, and
24.30. he took bread, and **b**-*ed* it
50. lifted up his hands, and **b**-*ed*
51. while he **b**-*ed* them
53. praising and **b**-*ing* God. Amen
Act.3.25. in thy seed *shall* all the kindr.
of the earth *be* **b**-*ed*
26. sent him to **b**. you, in turn.
Ro.12.14. **b**. them which persecute you
b., and curse not
¹Co. 4.12. being reviled, we **b**.; being
10.16. cup of blessing which we **b**.
14.16. Else when thou *shalt* **b**. with
Gal. 3. 8. thee *shall* all nations *be* **b**-*ed*
9. *are* **b**-*ed* with faithful Abrah.
Eph. 1 3. Lord Jesus Christ, *who hath* **b**.
Heb.6.14.Saying, Surely **b**-*ing I will*
7. 1. slaughter of the kings, and **b**-*ed*
6, and **b**-*ed* him that had the
7. the less *is* **b**-*ed* of the better
11.20. Isaac **b**-*ed* Jacob and Esau
21. **b**-*ed* both the sons of Joseph
Jas. 3. 9. Therewith **b**. we God, even
¹Pet.3. 9. but contrariwise **b**-*ing;* know.

BLESSED, [*adjective*].
makarios.
Mat.5. 3. **b**. are the poor in spirit : for
4. **b**. are they that mourn: for
5. meek ; 6. hunger ; 7. merciful
8. pure in heart ; 9. peacemakers
10. persecuted
11. **b**. are ye when men shall
11. 6. And **b**. is he, whosoever shall
13.16. But **b**. are your eyes, for they
16.17. **b**. art thou, Simon Barjona
24.46. **b**. is that servant, whom his
Lu. 1.45. **b**. is she that believed: for
6.20. **b**. be ye poor: for yours is the
21. **b**. are ye that hunger now
b. are ye that weep now: for
6.22. **b**. are ye, when men shall
7.23. And **b**. is he, whosoever shall
10.23. **b**. are the eyes which see the
11.27. **b**. is the womb that bare thee
28. Yea rather, **b**. are they that
12.37. **b**. are those servants, whom
38. them so **b**. are those servants
43. **b**. is that servant, whom his
14.14. And thou shalt be **b**. : for
15. **b**. is he that shall eat bread
23.29. they shall say, **b**. are the bar.
Jo. 20.29. **b**. are they that have not
Act.20.35.It is more **b**. to give than to
Ro. 4. 7. **b**. are they whose iniquities
8. is the man to whom
¹Ti. 1.11. the glorious gospel of the **b**.
6.15. the **b**. and only Potentate
Tit. 2.13. Looking for that **b**. hope
Jas. 1.12. **b**. is the man that endureth
25. this man shall be **b**. in his
Rev. 1. 3. **b**. is he that readeth, and
14.13. Write, **b**. are the dead which
16.15. **b**. is he that watcheth, and
19. 9. Write, **b**. are they which are
20. 6. **b**. and holy is he that hath
22. 7. **b**. is he that keepeth the say.
14. **b**. are they that do his comm.
eulogētos.
Mar.14.61. the Christ the Son of the **b**.
Lu. 1. 68. **b**. be the Lord God of Israel
Ro. 1. 25. the Creator who is **b**. for ever
9. 5. who is over all, God **b**. for ever
²Co. 1. 3. **b**. be God, even the Father of
11. 31. which is **b**. for evermore
Eph. 1. 3. ¹Pet. 1. 3. **b**. be the God and

---

eulogeō.
Mat.21. 9.**b**. is he that cometh ; 23 **29**.
Mar.11.9 ; Lu.13.35.
Mar.11.10.**b**. be the kingdom of our
Lu. 1.28.42.**b**. art thou among wom.
42. and **b**. is the fruit of thy
19.38. **b**. be the King that cometh
Jo.12.13. **b**. is the King of Israel that
eneulogeō.
Act.3.25. *shall* all kindr. of earth *be* **b**.
Gal.3. 8. In thee *shall* all nations *be* **b**
makarizō.
Lu. 1.48. generations *shall* call me **b**.

BLESSEDNESS.
makarismos.
Ro. 4. 6. describeth the **b**. of the man
9. Cometh this **b**. then upon the
Gal. 4.15. Where is then the **b**. ye spake

BLESSING, [*noun.*]
eulogia.
Ro.15.29. in the fulness of the **b**. of the
¹Co.10.16. The cup of **b**. which we bless
Gal. 3.14. That the **b**. of Abraham mi.
Eph. 1. 3. with all spiritual **b**. in heave.
Heb. 6. 7. dressed, receiveth **b**. from G.
12.17. would have inherited the **b**.
Jas. 3.10. proceedeth **b**. and cursing
¹Pet.3. 9. that ye should inherit a **b**.
Rev.5.12. honour, and glory, and **b**.
13. **b**., and honour, and glory
7.12. **b**., and glory, and wisdom

BLIND, [*adjective.*]
tuphlos.
Mat.9.27. two **b**. men followed him, cry.
28. the **b**. men came to him : and
11.5. The **b**. receive their sight, and
12.22. one possessed with a devil, **b**.
insomuch that the **b**. and
15.14. they be **b**. leaders of the **b**.
the **b**. lead the **b**., both shall
30. lame, **b**., dumb, maimed, and
31. and the **b**. to see : and they
20.30. And, behold, two **b**. men
21.14. And the **b**. and the lame
23.16. Woe unto you, ye **b**. guides
17. Ye fools and **b**. : for
24. Ye **b**. guides, which strain at
26. Thou **b**. Pharisee, cleanse
Mar.8.22. they bring a **b**. man unto
23. he took the **b**. man by the
10.46. **b**. Bartimæus, the son of Tim.
10.49. And they call the **b**. man
51. The **b**. man said unto him
Lu. 4. 18. recovering of sight to the **b**.
6.39. Can the **b**. lead the **b**. ? shall
7.21. unto many that were **b**. he
22. how that the **b**. see, the lame
14.13. the maimed, the lame, the **b**.
21. and the halt, and the **b**.
18.35. a certain **b**. man sat by the
Jo. 5. 3. of **b**., halt, withered, waiting
9. 1. which was **b**. from his birth
2, 6, 8, 13, 17, 18, 19, 20, 24.
25. whereas I was **b**., now I see
32. eyes of one that was born **b**.
39. which see might be made **b**.
40. unto him, are we **b**. also ?
41. If ye were **b**., ye should have
10.21. a devil open the eyes of the **b**.
11.37. opened the eyes of the **b**.
Act.13.11.and thou shalt be **b**., not
Ro. 2. 19. thyself art a guide of the **b**.
²Pet. 1. 9. that lacketh these things is **b**.
Rev.3.17. and poor, and **b**., and naked

BLINDED, [*verb.*]
tuphloō.
Jo. 12.40. He hath **b**. their eyes
²Co. 4. 4. god of this world hath **b**.
¹Jo. 2.11. darkness hath **b**. his eyes

pōroō.
Ro.11. 7. and the rest *were* b.
²Co. 3.14. But their minds *were* b.

BLINDFOLDED.
perikaluptō.
Lu.22.64. And *when tʰʸy had* b. him

BLINDNESS.
pōrōsis.
Ro.11.25. that b. in part is happened
Eph.4.18. because of the b. of their

BLOOD.
haima.
Mat.16.17. for flesh and b. hath not
   23.30. with them in the b. of the
    35. the righteous b. shed upon
    from the b. of righteous Abel
    unto the b. of Zacharias
   26.28. this is my b. of ; Mar.14.24.
   27. 4. have betrayed the innocent b.
   6. because it is the price of b.
   8. was called, The field of b.
   24. I am innocent of the b. of
   25. His b. be on us, and on our
Mar.5.25. which had an issue of b.
   29. the fountain of her b. was
Lu. 8. 43. having an issue of b. twelve
   44. immediately her issue of b.
   11.50. the b. of all the prophets
   51. the b. of Abel unto the b.
   13. 1. whose b. Pilate had mingled
   22.20. new testament in my b.
   44. great drops of b. falling down
Jo. 1.13. Which were born, not of b.
   6.53. Son of man, and drink his b.
   54. 56. flesh, and drinketh my b.
   55. indeed, and my b. is drink
   9.34. forthwith came thereout b.
Act. 1.19. that is to say, The field of b.
   2.19. b., and fire, and vapour of
   20. dark., and the moon into b.
   5.28. bring this man's b. upon us
   15.20. things strangled, and from b.
   29. offered to idols, and from b.
   17.26. hath made of one b. all natl.
   18. 6. Your b. be upon your own
   20.26. pure from the b. of all men
   28. purchased with his own b.
   21.25. from b., and from strangled
   22.20. when the b. of thy martyr
Ro. 3. 15. Their feet are swift to shed b.
   25. through faith in his b., to
   5. 9. being now justified by his b.
¹Co.10.16. communion of the b. of
   11.25. the new testament in my b.
   27. of the body and b. of the
   15.50. that flesh and b. cannot
Gal. 1.16. conferred not with flesh and b.
Eph. 1. 7. redemption through his b.
   2.13. as made nigh by the b. of
   6.12. wrestle not against flesh and b.
Col. 1.14. redemption through his b.
   20. peace through the b. of his
Heb.2.14. partakers of flesh and b., he
   9. 7. every year, not without b.
   12 Neither by the b. of goats
    calves, but by his own b.
   13. For if the b. of bulls and of
   14. more shall the b. of Christ
   18. was dedicated without b.
   19. he took the b. of calves and
   20. Saying, This is the b. of the
   21. sprinkled with b. both the
   22. are by the law purged with b.
   25. place every year with b. of
   10. 4. that the b. of bulls and of
   19. into the holiest, by the b. of
   29. counted the b. of the coven.
   11.28. and the sprinkling of b.
   12. 4. not yet resisted unto b.

Heb.12.24.to the b. of sprinkling, that
   13.11. those beasts, whose b. is
   12. the people with his own b.
   20. through the b. of the ever.
¹Pet. 1.2. sprinkling of the b. of Jesus
   19. with the precious b. of Christ
Jo. 1. 7. the b. of Jesus Christ his Son
   5. 6. came by water and b.
   but by water and b.
   8. and the water, and the b.
Rev. 1.5. from our sins in his own b.
   5. 9. redeemed us to God by thy b.
   6.10. not judge and avenge our b.
   12. and the moon became as b.
   7.14. white in the b. of the Lamb
   8. 7. hail and fire mingled with b.
   8. third-part of the sea became b.
   11. 6. waters to turn them to b.
   12.11. by the b. of the Lamb and
   14.20. b. came out of the winepress
   16. 3. it became as the b. of the
   4. waters ; and they became b.
   6. shed the b. of saints
   and thou hast given them b.
   17. 6. drunken with the b. of the
   and with the b. of the mar.
   18.24. was found the b. of prophets
   19. 2. avenged the b. of his servants
   13. with a vesture dipped in b.
haimorroeō.
Mat.9.20. *diseased with an issue of* b.
haimatekchusia.
Heb.9.22. without *shedding of* b. is no

BLOODY.
dusenteria.
Act. 28.8. of a fever and of a b-*flux*

BLOT,   -ed, -ing.
exaleiphō.
Act. 3.19. your sins may *be* b-ed *out*
Col. 2.14. b-*ing out* the handwriting of
Rev. 3.5. I *will* not b. *out* his name out

BLOW,   -eth, -blew.
pneō.
Mat.7.25.27.the winds b-*e*, and beat up.
Lu.12.55. when ye see the south wind b.
Jo. 3. 8. The wind b-*eth* where it list.
   6.18. reason of a great wind *that* b-*e*
Rev.7. 1. that the wind *should* not b.
epiginomai.
Act. 28.13. one day the south wind b-*e*
hupopneō.
Act.27.13.*when* the south wind b-*e softly*

BOARDS.
sanis.
Act.27.44.And the rest, some on b.

BOAST, [verb.] -ed, -eth, -ing.
kauchaomai.
Ro. 2.17. the law and *makest* thy b. of
   23. Thou that *makest* thy b. of
²Co. 7.14. if I *have* b-ed any thing to
   9. 2. for which I b. of you to them
   10. 8. though I *should* b. somewhat
   13. we *will* not b. of things with.
   15. Not b-*ing* of things without
   16. *not to* b. in another man's
   11.16. that I *may* b. myself a little
Eph.2. 9. works, lest any man *should* b.
katakauchaomai.
Ro.11.18. b. not *against* the branches
   if thou b., thou bearest not
legō.
Act. 5.36. b-*ing* himself to be somebody
megalaucheō.
Jas. 3. 5. and b-*eth great things.*

BOASTERS.
alazōn.
Ro. 1.30. spiteful, proud, b., inventors
²Ti. 3. 2. covetous, b., proud, blasph.

BOASTING, [noun.]   -s.
kauchēsis.
Ro. 3.27. Where is b. then? It is excl.
²Co. 7.14. even so our b., which I made
   8.24. and of our b. on your behalf
   9. 4. in this same confident b.
   11.10. man shall stop me of this b.
   17. in this confidence of b.
alazoneia.
Jas. 4.16. now ye rejoice in your b-*s*
kauchēma.
²Co.9. 3. lest our b. of you should be

BOAT.   -s.
ploiarion.
Jo. 6.22. there was none other b. there
   with his disciples into the b.
   23. there came other b-s from
skaphē.
Act.27.16. much work to come by the b.
   30. when they had let down the b.
   32. cut off the ropes of the b., and

BODILY.
sōmatikos.
Lu. 3.22. descended in a b. shape
¹Ti. 4. 8. For b. exercise profiteth little
sōmatikōs.
Col. 2. 9. the fulness of the Godhead b.
sōma.
²Co.10.10. but his b. presence is weak
   (presence *of his body.*)

BODY,   -ies.
sōma.
Mat.5.29.30. that thy whole b. should
   6.22. the light of the b. is Lu.11.34.
   thy whole b. shall be full of; 23.
   25. for your b., what ye shall put
   meat, and the b. than raim.
   10.28. not them which kill the b.
   to destroy both soul and b.
   14.12. came, and took up the b., and
   26.12. poured this ointment on my b.
   26. Take, eat ; this is my b.
   Mar. 14. 22 ; ¹Co. 11. 24.
   27.52. and many b-s of the saints
   58. begged the b. of Jesus. Then
   Pilate commanded the b. to
   59. when Joseph had taken the b.
Mar.5.29. and she felt in her b. that she
   14. 8. to anoint my b. to the buryi.
   15.43. Pilate, and craved the b. of
   45. centurion, he gave the b. to
Lu.11.34. thy whole b. also is full of
   thy b. also is full of darkness
   36. If thy whole b. therefore be
   12. 4. afraid of them that kill the b.
   22. for the b. what ye shall put
   23. and the b. is more than raim.
   17.37. Wheresoever the b. is, thith.
   22.19. This is my b. which is given
   23.52. unto Pilate, and begged the b.
   55. sepulchre, and how his b. was
   24. 3. found not the b. of the Lord
   23. when they found not his b.
Jo. 2.21. spake of the temple of his b.
   19.31. the b-s should not remain
   38. he might take away the b. of
   therefore, and took the b. of
   40. Then took they the b. of Jes.
   20.12. where the b. of Jesus had lain
Act. 9.40. and turning him to the b.
Ro. 1.24. to dishonour their own b-s
   4.19. he considered not his own b.
   6. 6. that the b. of sin might be
   12. reign in your mortal b., that
   7. 4. dead to the law by the b. of
   24. deliver me from the b. of this
   8.10. the b. is dead because of sin
   11. also quicken your mortal b-s
   13. do mortify the deeds of the b.

33

Ro. 8.23. the redemption of our **b**.
12. 1. that ye present your **b**-*s* a
   4. have many members in one **b**.
   5. we, being many, are one **b**.
¹Co. 5. 3. For I verily, as absent in **b**.
6.13. Now the **b**. is not for fornica.
    Lord, and the Lord for the **b**.
   15. your **b**-*s* are the members of
   16. joined to an harlot is one **b**.
   18. that a man doeth is without
    sinneth against his own **b**.
   19. your **b**. is the temple of the
   20. therefore glorify God in your
7. 4. hath not power of her own **b**.
    hath not power of his own **b**.
   34. she may be holy both in **b**.
9.27. But I keep under my **b**., and
10.16. the communion of the **b**. of
   17. are one bread, and one **b**.
   27. shall be guilty of the **b**. and
   29. not discerning the Lord's **b**.
12.12. For as the **b**. is one, and hath
    the members of that one **b**.
    are one **b**. : so also is Christ
   13. are we all baptized into one **b**.
   14. For the **b**. is not one member
   15, 16. I am not of the **b**. ; is it
    therefore not of the **b**.
   17. If the whole **b**. were an eye
   18. every one of them in the **b**.
   19. member, where were the **b**.
   20. many members, yet but one **b**.
   22, 23. those members of the **b**.
   24. but God hath tempered the **b**.
   25. should be no schism in the **b**.
   27. Now ye are the **b**. of Christ
13. 3. though I give my **b**. to be
15.35. and with what **b**. do they co.
   37. thou sowest not that **b**. that
   38. But God giveth it a **b**. as it
    and to every seed his own **b**.
   40. also celestial **b**-*s*, and **b**-*s* ter.
   44. It is sown a natural **b**. ; it is
    spiritual **b**. There is a nat. **b**.
    and there is a spiritual **b**.
²Co. 4.10. bearing about in the **b**. the
    be made manifest in our **b**.
5. 6. whilst we are at home in the **b**.
   8. rather to be absent from the **b**.
   10. the things done in his **b**.
12. 2. the **b**., I cannot tell ; or
    whether out of the **b**.
   3. in the **b**., or out of the **b**. I
Gal. 6.17. I bear in my **b**. the marks of
Eph.1.23. Which is his **b**., the fulness
2.16. unto God in one **b**. by the
4. 4. There is one **b**., and one Spi.
   12. for the edifying of the **b**. of
   16. From whom the whole **b**. fitly
    maketh increase of the **b**.
5.23. and he is the saviour of the **b**.
   28. their wives as their own **b**-*s*
   30. For we are members of his **b**.
Phi.1.30. shall be magnified in my **b**.
3.21. Who shall change our vile **b**.
    like unto his glorious **b**.
Col. 1.18. And he is the head of the **b**.
   22. In the **b**. of his flesh through
   24. in my flesh for his **b**-'*s* sake
2.11. putting off the **b**. of the sins
   17. to come ; but the **b**. is of
   19. from which all the **b**., by joints
   23. and neglecting of the **b**.
3.15. also ye are called in one **b**.
¹Th. 5.23. and **b**. be preserved blameless
Heb.10.5. but a **b**. hast thou prepared
   10. through the offering of the **b**.
   22. our **b**-*s* washed with pure
13. 3. being yourselves also in the **b**.
   11. For the **b**-*s* of those beasts
Jas. 2.16. which are needful to the **b**.
   26. as the **b**. without the spirit
34

Jas. 3. 2. also to bridle the whole **b**.
   3. we turn about their whole **b**.
   6. that it defileth the whole **b**.
¹Pet.2.24. bare our sins in his own **b**.
Jude   9. he disputed about the **b**. of
    sussōma.
Eph.3. 6. felw.-heirs, and *of the same* **b**.
    chrōs.
Act.19.12.So that from his **b**. were
    ptōma.
Rev.11.8. And their *dead* **b**-*s* shall lie
   9. shall see their *dead* **b**-*s* three
    not suffer their *dead* **b**-*s* to

BOISTEROUS.
    ischuros.
Mat.14.30. when he saw the wind **b**., he

BOLD.
    tolmaō.
²Co.10. 2. wherewith I think *to be* **b**.
11.21. whereinsoever any *is* **b**.
    (I speak foolishly,) I *am* **b**. also
    apotolmaō.
Ro.10.20. Esaias *is very* **b**., and saith, I
    parrēsiazomai.
Act.13.46.and Barnabas *waxed* **b**., *and*
¹Th. 2. 2. we *were* **b**. in our God to
    echō parrēsia.
Phile. 8. though I might *be* much **b**. in
    tharreō.
²Co. 10.1. being absent, *am* **b**. toward
   2. that I may not be **b**. when I

BOLDLY.
    parrēsiazomai.
Act. 9.27. how he had *preached* **b**. at
   29. And he *spake* **b**. in the
14. 3. *speaking* **b**. in the Lord, wh.
18.26. began *to speak* **b**. in the syna.
19. 8. and *spake* **b**. for the space of
Eph.6.20. I *may speak* **b**., as I ought to
    parrēsia.
Jo. 7.26. But, lo, he speaketh **b**., and
Eph.6.19. may open my mouth **b**., to
Heb.4.16.Let us therefore come **b**. unto
    tharreō.
Heb.13.6. So that we may **b**. say, The
    tolmaō.
Mar.15.43. and went in **b**. unto Pilate
    tolmēroteron.
Ro.15.15. I have written *the more* **b**.

BOLDNESS.
    parrēsia.
Act.4.13. when they saw the **b**. of Peter
   29. with all **b**. they may
   31. spake the word of God with **b**.
²Co. 7. 4. Great is my **b**. *of speech* towa.
Eph.3.12. In whom we have **b**. and acc.
Phi. 1.20. but that with all **b**., as alwa.
¹Ti. 3.13. and great **b**. in the faith
Heb.10.19.**b**. to enter into the holiest
¹Jo. 4.17. that we may have **b**. in the

BOND, [*noun*.]   -*s*.
    desmos.
Lu.13.16. be loosed from this **b**. on the
Act.20.23.saying that **b**-*s* and afflictions
   23.29. cha. worthy of death or of **b**-*s*
   26.29. such as I am, except these **b**-*s*
   31. worthy of death or of **b**-*s*
Phi. 1. 7. inasmuch as both in my **b**-*s*
   13. So that my **b**-*s* in Christ are
   14. waxing confident by my **b**-*s*
   16. to add affliction to my **b**-*s*
Col. 4.18. Remember my **b**-*s*.   Grace
²Ti. 2. 9. an evil doer, even unto **b**-*s*

Phile. 10. I have begotten in my **b**-*s*
   13. ministered unto me in the **b**-*s*
Heb.10.34.compassion of me in my **b**-*s*
11.36. moreover of **b**-*s* and impriso.
    sundesmos.
Act.8.23. and in the **b**. of iniquity
Eph. 4.3. unity of the spirit, in the **b**. o.
Col. 3.14. which is the **b**. of perfectness
    desmios.
Act.25.14. certain man, left *in* **b**-*s* by
Heb. 13.3. Remem. *them that are in* **b**-*s*
    (Remember *the prisoners*)
    halusis.
Eph.6.20. I am an ambassador in **b**-*s*
    deō.
Col. 4. 3. for which I *am* also *in* **b**-*s*

BOND, [*adjective*.]
    doulos.
¹Co.12.13. whether we be **b**. or free
Gal. 3.28. there is neither **b**. nor free
Eph. 6. 8. Lord, whether he be **b**. or
Col. 3.11. Barbarian, Scythian, **b**. nor
Rev.13.16. rich and poor, free and **b**.
   18. of all men, both free and **b**.

BONDAGE.
    douleia.
Ro. 8.15. received the spirit of **b**. again
   21. be delivered from the **b**. of
Gal.4.24. which gendereth to **b**., which
5. 1. again with the yoke of **b**.
Heb.2.15. their lifetime subject to **b**.
    douleuō.
Jo. 8. 33. *were* never *in* **b**. to any man
Act. 7. 7. to whom they *shall be in* **b**.
Gal. 4. 9. ye desire again *to be in* **b**.
   25. and *is in* **b**. with her children
    douloō.
Act. 7.6. should *bring* them *into* **b**.
¹Co. 7.15. *is not under* **b**. in such cases
Gal. 4.3. were *in* **b**. under the elements
²Pet.2.19. the same *is he brought in* **b**.
    katadouloō.
²Co.11.20. if a man *bring* you *into* **b**. if
Gal. 2. 4. they *might bring* us *into* **b**.

BONDMAID.
    paidiskē.
Gal. 4.22. two sons; the one by a **b**., the

BONDMAN.
    doulos.
Rev.6.15. the mighty men, and every **b**.

BONDWOMAN.
    paidiskē.
Gal. 4.23. But he who was of the **b**.
   30. Cast out the **b**. and her son
    the son of the **b**. shall not be
   31. we are not children of the **b**.

BONE,   -*s*.
    osteon.
Mat.23.27.full of dead men's **b**-*s* and
Lu.24.39. hath not flesh and **b**-*s*, as y
Jo.19.36. A **b**. of him shall not be
Eph.5.30.of his flesh, and of his **b**-*s*
Heb.11.22.comman. concerning his **b**-*s*
    sphuron.
Act.3. 7. his feet and *ancle* **b**-*s* received

BOOK,   -*s*.
    biblos.
Mat.1. 1. The **b**. of the generation of
Mar.12.26.have ye not read in the **b**. of
Lu. 3. 4. As it is written in the **b**. of
   20.42. David himself saith in the **b**.
Act. 1.20. it is written in the **b**. of Psa.
   7.42. written in the **b**. of the proph.
   19.19. brought their **b**-*s* together
Phi. 4. 3. whose names are in the **b**. of
Rev.3. 5. out his name out of the **b**.

Rev.13. 8. not written in the **b.** of life
20.15. found written in the **b.** of life
22.19. away from the words of the **b.**
    away his part out of the **b.**
biblion.
Lu. 4.17. the **b.** of the prophet Esaias
    when he had opened the **b.**
20. he closed the **b.** and he gave
Jo. 20.30. are not written in this **b.**
21.25. could not contain the **b-s** that
Gal. 3.10. which are written in the **b.**
²Ti. 4.13. bring with thee, and the **b-s**
Heb.9.19. sprinkled both the **b.**, and all
10. 7. in the volume of the **b.** it is
Rev.1.11. What thou seest, write in a **b.**
5. 1. on the throne a **b.** written
2. Who is worthy to open the **b.**
3. was able to open the **b.**, neit.
4. to open and to read the **b.**
5. hath prevailed to open the **b.**
7. he came and took the **b.** out
8. when he had taken the **b.**, the
9. Thou art worthy to take the **b.**
17. 8. were not written in the **b.**
20.12. the **b-s** were opened : and
    another **b.** was opened
    which were written in the **b-s**
21.27. written in the Lamb's **b.** of
22. 7. 10. of the prophecy of this **b.**
9. keep the sayings of this **b.**
18. of the prophecy of this **b.**
    that are written in this **b.**
19. which are written in this **b.**
biblaridion.
Rev.10.2. had in his hand a *little* **b.**
8. Go and take the *little* **b.** which
9. unto him, Give me the *little* **b.**
10. I took the *little* **b.** out of the

BORDER,   -s.
kraspedon.
Mat.23.5. enlarge the **b-s** of their garm.
Mar.6.56. touch if it were but the **b.** of
Lu. 8.44. touched the **b.** of his garment
methoria.
Mar.7.24. went into the **b-s** of Tyre and
horia.
Mat.4.13. coast, in the **b-s** of Zabulon

BORN, (See *Bear.*)
gennaō.
Mat.1.16. of whom *was* **b.** Jesus, who is
2. 1. *when* Jesus *was* **b.** in Bethle.
4. them where Christ *should be* **b.**
19.12. which *were* so **b.** from their
26.24. that man if he *had* not *been* **b.**
Mar.14.21.man if he *had* never *been* **b.**
Lu. 1.35. holy thing which *shall be* **b.**
Jo. 1.13. Which *were* **b.**, not of blood
3. 3. Except a man *be* **b.** again, he
4. How can a man be **b.** when
    his mother's womb, and be **b.**
5. Except a man *be* **b.** of water
6. That *which is* **b.** of the flesh
    and that *which is* **b.** of the
7. unto thee, ye must *be* **b.** again
8. every one *that is* **b.** of the Sp.
8.41. We *be* not **b.** of fornication
9. 2. or his parents, that he *was* **b.**
19. your son, who ye say *was* **b.**
20. our son, and that he *was* **b.**
32. the eyes of one *that was* **b.**
34. Thou *wast* altogether **b.** in
16.21. that a man *is* **b.** into the w.
18.37. To this end *was* I **b.**, and for
Act.2. 8. tongue, wherein we *were* **b.**
7.20. In which time Moses *was* **b.**
22. 3. a man which am a Jew, **b.** in
28. Paul said, But I *was* free **b.**
Ro. 9.11. the children *being* not yet **b.**
Gal. 4.23. bondwoman *was* **b.** after the
29. he *that was* **b.** after the flesh

Heb.11.23.faith Moses *when* he *was* **b.**
¹Jo. 2.29. doeth righteousness *is* **b.** of
3. 9. Whosoever is **b.** of God doth
    cannot sin, because he *is* **b.**
4. 7. every one that loveth *is* **b.** of
5. 1. Jesus is the Christ *is* **b.** of
4. For whatsoever is **b.** of God
18. whosoever is **b.** of God sinn.
tiktō.
Mat.2. 2. Where is he *that is* **b.** king of
Lu. 2.11. For unto you *is* **b.** this day in
Rev.12.4. her child as soon as it was **b.**
genos.
Act.18. 2. Aquila **b.** in Pontus, lately
24. named Apollos **b.** at Alexan.
gennētos.
Mat.11.11. Among *them that are* **b.** of
Lu. 7.28. Among *those that are* **b.** of
ektrōma.
¹Co.15. 8. as of one **b.** *out of due time*
anagennaō.
¹Pet.1.23. *Being* **b.** *again*, not of corru.

BORNE, (See *Bear.*)
dusbastaktos.
Mat.23.4. and *grievous to be* **b.**; Lu.11.46.

BORROW.
daneizō.
Mat.5.42. from him that would **b.** of

BOSOM.
kolpos.
Lu. 6.38. shall men give into your **b.**
16.22. the angels into Abraham's **b.**
23. afar off, and Lazarus in his **b.**
Jo. 1.18. which is in the **b.** of the Fat.
13.23. there was leaning on Jesus' **b.**

BOTH.
kai.
Mat.10.28.destroy **b.** soul and body in
12.22. and dumb **b.** spake and saw
(*And in all other passages except the
following :—*)
te.
Mat.22.10.many as they found, **b.** bad
Act. 1. 1. Jesus began **b.** to do and
8. b. in Jerusalem, and in all
13. **b.** Peter, and James, and Jo.
4.27. **b.** Herod, and Pontius Pilate
5.14. to the Lord, multitudes **b.** of
8.12. they were baptized, **b.** men
38. **b.** Philip and the eunuch
10.39. **b.** in the land of the Jews
14. 1. **b.** of the Jews and also of the
5. **b.** of the Gentiles, and also of
19.10. Lord Jesus, **b.** Jews and Gr.
20.21. **b.** to the Jews, and also to
21.12. **b.** we, and they of that place
22. 4. into prisons **b.** men and wo.
24.15. of the dead, **b.** of the just
25.24. **b.** at Jerusalem, and also here
26.16. a witness **b.** of these things
22. witnessing b. to small and
28.23. them concerning Jesus, **b.** out
Ro. 1.12. the mutual faith **b.** of you and
14. **b.** to the Greeks, and to the
    b. to the wise, and to the un.
3. 9. **b.** Jews and Gentiles, that
¹Co. 1. 2. Jesus Christ our Lord, **b.**
24. **b.** Jews and Greeks, Christ
Eph.1.10. **b.** which are in heaven, and
Phi. 1. 7. inasmuch as **b.** in my bonds
Heb.2. 4. **b.** with signs and wonders
11. For **b.** he that sanctifieth and
5. 1. that he may offer **b.** gifts and
14. to discern **b.** good and evil
6.19. an anchor of the soul, **b.** sure
9. 9. were offered **b.** gifts and sacr.
9.19. sprinkled **b.** the book, and all
10.33. **b.** by reproaches and afflict.

amphoteros.
Mat.9.17. and **b.** are preserved ; Lu.5.33
13.30. Let **b.** grow together until
15.14. blind, **b.** shall fall ; Lu.6.39.
Lu. 1. 6. they were **b.** righteous before
7. they **b.** were now well strick.
5. 7. they came, and filled **b.** the
7.42. he frankly forgave them **b.**
Act.8.38. went down **b.** into the water
23. 8. but the Pharisees confess **b.**
Eph.2.14. our peace, who hath made **b.**
16. he might reconcile **b.** unto G.
18. through him we **b.** have acce.
duo.
Jo. 20. 4. So they ran **b.** together ; and
Rev.19.20.These **b.** were cast alive into
hekastos.
Heb.11.21. blessed **b.** the sons of Joseph

BOTTLES.
askos.
Mat.9.17. put new wine into old **b.**
Mar.2.22. Lu.5.37,38. else the **b.** break

BOTTOM.
katō.
Mat.27.51. Mar.15.38. the top to the **b**

BOTTOMLESS.
abussos.
Rev. 9. 1. was given the key of the **b.**
2. And he opened the **b.** *pit*
11. the angel of the **b.** *pit*, whose
11. 7. that ascendeth out of the **b.**
17. 8. shall ascend out of the **b.** *pit*
20. 1. having the key of the **b.** *pit*
3. cast him into the **b.** *pit*, and

BOUGHT. See *Buy.*

BOUNDS, [*noun.*]
horothesia.
Act.17.26.and the **b.** of their habitat.

BOUND, [*verb.*] See *Bind.*
opheilō.
²Th. 1. 3. We *are* **b.** to thank G.; 2.13.
desmeō.
Lu. 8.29. he *was* kept **b.** with chains
perideomai.
Jo.11.44. his face *was* **b.** *about* with a
perikeimai.
Act.28.20. of Israel I am **b.** *with* this
sundeomai.
Heb.13.3. that are in bonds, as **b.** *with*

BOUNTIFULLY.
eulogia.
²Co. 9. 6. soweth **b.** shall reap also **b.**

BOUNTIFULNESS.
haplotēs.
²Co. 9.11. in every thing to all **b.**,which

BOUNTY.
eulogia.
²Co. 9. 5. as a *matter of* **b.**, and not as

BOW, [*noun.*]
toxon.
Rev.6. 2. he that sat on him had a **b.**

BOW, [*verb*]   -ed, -ing.
kamptō.
Ro.11. 4. who *have* not **b-ed** the knee
14.11. every knee *shall* **b.** to me, and
Eph.3.14. For this cause I **b.** my knees
Phi.2.10. of Jesus every knee *should* **b.**
klinō.
Lu.24. 5. they were afraid, and **b-ed**
Jo. 19.30. he **b-ed** his head, *and* gave **up**
35

tithēmi.

Mar.15.19. b-*ing* their knees worshipp.

su*n*gkamptō.

Rc.11.10. and b. *down* their back alw.

gonupeteō

Mat.27.29. b-*ed the knee* before him

su*n*gkuptō.

Lu.13.11. and was b-*ed together*, and

BOWELS.
splangchna.

Act.1.18. midst, and all his b. gushed

²Co.6.12. are straitened in your own b.

Phi.1.8. after you all in the b. of Jes.

   2.1. the spirit, if any b. and mer.

Col.3.12. b. of mercies, kindness, hum.

Phile.7. the b. of the saints are refres.

   12. him, that is, mine own b.

   20. refresh my b. in the Lord

¹Jo.3.17. shutteth up his b. of compas.

BOX.
alabastron.

Mat.26.7. having an *alabaster* b. of

Mar.14.3. having an *alabaster* b. of

   she brake the b., and poured

Lu.7.37. brought an *alabaster* b. of

BRAMBLE.
batos.

Lu.6.44. nor of a b. *bush* gather they

BRANCH,   -es.
klados.

Mat.13.32.and lodge in the b-s thereof

   21.8. others cut down b-s from the

   24.32. When his b. is yet tender, and

Mar.4.32. shooteth out great b-s: so

   13.28. When her b. is yet tender

Lu.13.19. the air lodged in the b-s of it

Ro.11.16. root be holy, so are the b-s

   17. if some of the b-s be broken

   18. Boast not against the b-s. But

   19. The b-s were broken off, that

   21. God spared not the natural b.

klēma.

Jo.15.2. Every b. in me that beareth

   4. as the b. cannot bear fruit of

   5. I am the vine, ye are the b-s

   6. he is cast forth as a b. and is

stoibas.

Mar.11.8. and others cut down b-s off

baion.

Jo 12.13. took b-s of palm-trees, and

BRASS.
chalkos.

Mat.10.9. gold, nor silver, nor b. in

¹Co.13.1. I am become as sounding b.

Rev.18.12.and of b., and iron, and

chalkolibanon.

Rev.1.15. And his feet like unto *fine* b.

   2.18. and his feet are like *fine* b.

chalkeos.

Rev.9.20. of gold, and silver, and b.

BRAWLER,   -s.
amachos.

¹Ti.3.3. patient, *not a* b., nor coveto.

Tit.3.2. evil of no man, to be *no* b-s

BRAZEN.
chalkion.

Mar.7.4. of cups, and pots, b. *vessels*

BREAD.
artos.

Mat.4.3. that these stones be made b.

   4. shall not live by b.; Lu.4.4

   6.11. Give us this day our daily b.

   7.9. whom if his son ask b., will

   12.4. did eat the shew b.; Mar.2.26.

36

Mat.15.2. their hands, when they eat b.

   26. the children's b.; Mar.7.27

   33. should we have so much b.

  16.5. they had forgotten to take b.

   7. because we have taken no b.

   8. because ye have brought no b.

   11. not to you concerning b.

   12. not beware of the leaven of b.

  26.26. Jesus took b., and; Mar.14.22

Mar.3.20. could not so much as eat b.

  6.8. no scrip, no b., no money in

   36. villages, and buy themsel. b.

   37. pennyworth of b.; Jo.6.7.

  7.2. some of his disciples eat b.

   5. eat b. with unwashen hands

  8.4. satisfy these men with b.

   14. disci. had forgotten to take b.

   16. It is because we have no b.

   17. because ye have no b.? perce.

Lu.4.3. this stone that it be made b.

   6.4. did take and eat the shew b.

   7.33. neither eating b. nor drinking

   9.3. nor scrip, neither b., neither

   11.3. us day by day our daily b.

   11. If a son shall ask b. of his

  14.1. to eat b. on the sabbath day

   15. he that shall eat b. in the

  15.17. serva. of my father's have b.

  22.19. he took b., and; Act.27.35

  24.30. he took b., and blessed it

   35. known of them in break. of b.

Jo.6.5. Whence shall we buy b., that

   23. place where they did eat b.

   31. He gave them b. from heaven

   32. Moses gave you not that b.

   my father giveth you true b.

   33. For the b. of God is he

   34. Lord, evermore give us this b.

   35. I am the b. of life: he that

   41. I am the b. which came down

   48. I am that b. of life

   50. This is the b. which cometh

   51. I am the living b. which came

   if any man eat of this b. he

   the b. that I will give is my

   58. This is that b. which came

   he that eateth of this b. shall

  13.18. He that eateth b. with me

  21.9. and fish laid thereon, and b.

   13. then cometh, and taketh b.

Act.2.42. in breaking of b., and in

   46. breaking b. from house to

  20.7. came together to break b.

   11. had broken b. and eaten, and

¹Co.10.16. The b. which we break, is it

   17. we being many are one b.

   all partakers of that one b.

  11.23. which he was betray. took b.

   26. as often as ye eat this b.

   27. whosoever shall eat this b.

   28. so let him eat of that b.

²Co.9.10. minister b. for your food

²Th.3.8. Neit. did we eat any man's b.

   12. work, and eat their own b.

Heb.9.2. the table, and the shew b.

azumos.

Mat.26.17. of *unleavened* b.; Lu. .1.

Mar.14.1. passo., and of *unleavened* b.

   12. first day of *unleavened* b.

Lu.22.7. the day of *unleavened* b.

Act.12.3. 20.6. days of *unleavened* b.

BREADTH.
platos.

Eph.3.18. what is the b. and length

Rev.20.9. they went up on the b. cf

  21.16. the length is as large as the b.

   and the b. and the height

BREAK.   -ake, -ing, -oken.
klazō.

Mat.14.19. he blessed, and b-e, and

Mat.15.36.and gave thanks, and b-e

  26.26. and blessed it, and b-e

   Mar.14.22 ; Lu.24.30

Mar.8.6. and gave thanks, and b-e

   Lu.22.19

   19. When I b-e the five loaves

Act.2.46. and b-*ing* bread from house

  20.7. came together *to* b. bread

   11. and *had* b-en bread, ana

  27.35. *when* he *had* b-en it, he

¹Co.10.16. The bread which we b., is

  11.24. he b-*e* it, and said, Take

   my body, *which is* b-en for

luō.

Mat.5.19. *shall* b. one of these least

Jo.5.18. he not only *had* b-en the

   7.23. law of M. *should* not *be* b-en

   10.35. the scripture cannot *be* b-en

Act.13.43.*when* the congr. *was* b-en up

  27.41. the hinder part *was* b-en

Eph.2.14. and *hath* b-en down the

suntribō.

Mar.5.4. and the fetters b-en *in pieces*

   14.3. and she b-*e* the box, and pour.

Lu.4.18. sent me to heal the b-en-hear.

Jo.19.36. bone of him *shall* not *be* b-en

Rev.2.27. *shall* they *be* b-en *to* shivers

katagnumi.

Mat.12.20. A bruised reed *shall* he not b.

Jo.19.31. that their legs *might be* b-en

   32. and b-*e* the legs of the first

   33. dead already, they b-*e* not

diorussō.

Mat.6.19. where thieves b. *through* and

   20. where thieves *do* not b. *thro.*

  24.43. suffered his ho. *to be* b-en up

Lu.12.39. his house *to be* b-en *through*

ekklazō.

Ro.11.17. some of the bran. *be* b-en *off*

   19. The branches *were* b-en *off*

   20. of unbelief they *were* b-en *off*

rēgnumi.

Mat.9.17. else the bottles b., and the

Gal.4.27. b. *forth* and cry, thou that

diarrēgnumi.

Lu.5.6. of fishes; and their net b-*e*

  8.29. he b-*e* the bands, *and* was

kataklaō.

Mar.6.41. and b-*e* the loaves, and gave

Lu.9.16. he blessed them, and b-*e*

sunthlaō.

Mat.21.44. on this stone *shall be* b-en

Lu.20.18. that stone *shall be* b-en

sunthruptō.

Act.21.13. ye to weep and to b. mine

schizō.

Jo.21.11. many, yet was not the net b-en

exoruttō.

Mar.2.4. *when* they *had* b-en it *up*

BREAK, [noun.]
augē.

Act.20.11. long while even till b. *of day*

BREAKER,   -s.
parabatēs.

Ro.2.25. but if thou be a b. of the law

asunthetos.

Ro.1.31. *covenant* b-s, without natural

BREAKING, [noun.]
klasis.

Lu.24.35. was known of them in b. of

Act.2.42. and in b. of bread, and in

parabasis.

Ro.2.23. through b. the law dishon.

BREAST,   -s.
stēthos.

Lu.18.13. but smote upon his b , saying

Lu.23.48. smote their **b**-s and returned
Jo.13.25. He then lying on Jesus' **b**.
21.20. which also leaned on his **b**.
Rev.15.6. their **b**-s girded with golden

BREASTPLATE, -s.
thōrax.
Eph.6.14. having on the **b**. of righteou.
1Th.5. 8. putting on the **b**. of faith and
Rev.9. 9. **b**-s, as it were **b**-s of iron ; and
17. **b**-s of fire, and of jacinth, and

BREATH.
pnoē.
Act.17.25. he giveth to all life, and **b**.

BREATHED, -ing.
empneō.
Act. 9. 1. Saul, yet **b**-ing out threaten.
emphusaō.
Jo.20.22. had said this, he **b**. on them

BRETHREN. (See Brother.)
adelphos. [plural]
Mat.1. 2. begat Judas and his **b**.
11. begat Jechonias and his **b**.
4.18. Galilee, saw two **b**.
21. he saw other two **b**.
5.47. if ye salute your **b**. only
12.46. his mother and his **b**.; Lu.8.19.
Jo.2.12.
47. mother and thy **b**.; Lu. 8.20.
48. mother, and who are my **b**.
49. mother and my **b**.; Mar.3.34.
13.55. his **b**., James, and Joses, and
19.29. houses, or **b**., or sisters, or
20.24. indignation against the two **b**.
22.25. there were with us seven **b**.
Mar. 12. 20 ; Lu. 20. 20.
23. 8. Christ ; and all ye are **b**.
25.40. the least of these my **b**.
28.10. go tell my **b**. that they go
Mar.3.31. There came then his **b**. and
32. mother and thy **b**. without
33. Who is my mother, or my **b**.
10.29. left house, or **b**., or sisters,
30. houses, and **b**., and sisters
Lu. 8.21. My mother and my **b**. are
14.12. not thy friends, nor thy **b**.
26. children, and **b**., and sisters
16.28. For I have five **b**. ; that
18.29. or parents, or **b**., or wife, or
21.16. parents, and **b**., and kinsfolks
22.32. converted, strengthen thy **b**.
Jo. 7. 3. His **b**. therefore said unto
5. neither did his **b**. believe in
10. when his **b**. were gone up
20.17. go to my **b**., and say unto
21.23. saying abroad among the **b**.
Act.1.14. of Jesus, and with his **b**.
16. Men and **b**.; 2.29,37 ; 13.26;
15.13 ; 23.1,6 ; 28.17.
(men, brethren.)
3.22. unto you of your **b**., like
7. 2. Men, **b**., and fathers ; 22.1.
13. was made known to his **b**.
23. to visit his the children
25. his **b**. would have understood
26. saying, Sirs, ye are **b**. ; why
37. unto you of your **b**., like unto
9.30. Which when the **b**. knew
10.23. certain **b**. from Joppa accom.
11. 1 the apostles and **b**. that were
12. these six **b**. accompanied me
29. to send relief unto the **b**.
12.17. unto James, and to the **b**.
13.15. saying, Ye men and **b**. ; 38.
14. 2. evil affected against the **b**.
15. 1. from Judæa taught the **b**. and
3. caused great joy unto all the **b**.
7. said unto them, Men and **b**.
22. chief men among the **b**.

Act.15.23.**b**. send greeting unto the **b**.
32. exhorted the **b**. with many
33. from the **b**. unto the apostles
36. go again and visit our **b**. in
40. being recommended by the **b**.
16. 2. reported of by the **b**. that
40. and when they had seen the **b**.
17. 6. they drew Jason and certain **b**.
10. the **b**. immediately sent away
14. the **b**. sent away Paul, to go
18.18. then took his leave of the **b**.
27. the **b**. wrote, exhorting the
21. 7. saluted the **b**., and abode with
17. Jerusalem, the **b**. received us
22. 5. I received letters unto the **b**.
28.14. Where we found **b**., and were
15. And from thence, when the **b**.
21. any of the **b**. that came
Ro. 8.29. the firstborn among many **b**.
9. 3. accursed from Christ for my **b**.
16.14. the **b**. which are with him
1Co. 6. 5. able to judge between his **b**.
8. defraud, and that your **b**.
8.12. ye sin so against the **b**., and
9. 5. as the **b**. of the Lord, and
15. 6. above five hundred **b**. at once
58. Therefore, my beloved **b**., be
16.11. for I look for him with the **b**.
12. unto you with the **b**. : but
20. All the **b**. greet you. Greet
2Co. 8.23. or our **b**. be enquired of
9. 3. Yet have I sent the **b**., lest
5. necessary to exhort the **b**.
11. 9. the **b**. which came from
Gal. 1. 2. all the **b**. which are with me
Eph.6.23. Peace be to the **b**., and love
Phil.1.14. many of the **b**. in the Lord
4. 1. my **b**. dearly beloved and
21. The **b**. which are with me
Col. 1. 2. saints and faithful **b**. in Chr.
4.15. Salute the **b**. which are in
1Th. 4.10. toward all the **b**. which are
5.26. Greet all the **b**. with an holy
27. read unto all the holy **b**.
1Ti. 4. 6. put the **b**. in remembrance
5. 1. and the younger men as **b**.
6. 2. because they are **b**. ; but
2Ti. 4.21. and Claudia, and all the **b**.
Heb.2.11. not ashamed to call them **b**.
12. declare thy name unto my **b**.
17. made like unto his **b**.
3. 1. Wherefore, holy **b**., partakers
7. 5. that is, of their **b**., though
1Jo. 3.14. because we love the **b**. He
16. lay down our lives for the **b**.
3John 3. when the **b**. came and testified
5. thou doest to the **b**., and
10. he himself receive the **b**.
Rev.6.11. fellowserv. also and their **b**.
12.10. the accuser of our **b**. is cast
19.10. **b**. that have the testimony
22. 9. of thy **b**. the prophets, and

(And all other passages in which it
occurs, except the following :—)

adelphotēs.
1Pet.5.9. accomplished in your **b**. that

(See also Love, False.)

BRIDE.
numphē.
Jo. 3.29.He that hath the **b**. is the
Rev.18.23.and of the **b**. shall be heard
21. 2. prepared as a **b**. adorned for
9. shew thee the **b**., the Lamb's
22.17. the Spirit and the **b**. say

BRIDECHAMBER.
numphōn.
Mat.9.15. of the **b**.; Mar.2.19; Lu.5.34.

BRIDEGROOM.
numphios.
Mat.9.15. as long as the **b**. is with them
when the **b**.;Mar.2.20 ;Lu.5.35
25.1. and went forth to meet the **b**.
5. While the **b**. tarried, they
6. Behold, the **b**. cometh ; go
10. went to buy, the **b**. came
Mar.2.19. while the **b**. is with them
long as they have the **b**.
Lu. 5.34. fast while the **b**. is with them
Jo. 2. 9. of the feast called the **b**.
3.29. that hath the bride is the **b**.
the friend of the **b**.
because of the **b**-'s voice
Rev.18.23.and the voice of the **b**. and

BRIDLES, [noun.]
chalinos.
Rev.14.20. even unto the horse **b**., by

BRIDLE, [verb.] -eth
chalinagōgeō.
Jas. 1.26. and **b**-eth not his tongue
3. 2. able also to **b**. the whole

BRIEFLY.
dia oligos.
1Pet.5.12. I suppose, I have written **b**.
anakephalaioomai.
Ro. 13.9. it is **b**. comprehended in this

BRIERS.
tribolos.
Heb.6. 8. which beareth thorns and **b**.

BRIGHT.
lampros.
Act. 10.30. stood before me in **b**. cloth.
Rev.22.16. and the **b**. and morning
phōteinos.
Mat.17.5. a **b**. cloud overshadowed
astrapē.
Lu.11.36. as when the **b**. shining of a

BRIGHTNESS.
apaugasma.
Heb.1. 3. Who being the **b**. of his glory
epiphaneia.
2Th. 2. 8. with the **b**.of his coming.
lamprotēs.
Act.26.13. from heaven, above the **b**.

BRIM.
anō.
Jo. 2. 7. they filled them up to the **b**.

BRIMSTONE.
theion.
Lu.17.29. fire and **b**. from heaven, and
Rev.9.17. issued fire and smoke and **b**.
18. the smoke, and by the **b**.
14.10. with fire and **b**. in the prese.
19.20. lake of fire burning with **b**.
20.10. the lake of fire and **b**., where
21. 8. burneth with fire and **b**.
theiōdes.
Rev.9.17. of fire, and of jacinth, and **b**.

BRING, -est, -eth, -ing.
(See Brought.)
pherō.
Mat.14.18.He said, **b**. them hither to
17.17. suf. you **b**. him hither to
Mar.2. 3. **b**-ing one sick of the palsy
7.32. they **b**. unto him one that
8.22. and they **b**. a blind man unto
9. suffer you **b**. him unto me
12.15. **b**. me a penny, that I may
15.22. they **b**. him unto the place
Lu.15.23. **b**. hither the fatted calf, and
24. 1. **b**-ing the spices which they
37

Jo. 12.24. **b**-*eth forth* much fruit ; 15.5.
15. 2. purgeth it, that it *may* **b.** *forth*
16. that ye should go and **b.** *forth*
18.29. What accusation **b.** ye against
21.10. **b.** of the fish which ye have
Act. 5.16. unto Jerusalem, **b**-*ing* sick
²Ti. 4.13. **b.** with thee, and the books
²Pet.2.11. **b.** not railing accusation aga.
²Jo. 10. and **b.** not this doctrine, rec.
Rev.21.24. *do* **b.** their glory and honour
26. they *shall* **b.** the glory and
eisphero.
Lu. 5.18. sought means *to* **b.** him *in*
19. they *might* **b.** him *in* because
Act.17.20.**b**-*est* certain strange things to
prophero.
Lu. 6.45. **b**-*eth forth* that which is good
b-*eth forth* that which is evil
prosphero.
Mat.5.23. if thou **b.** thy gift *to* the
Lu. 12.11. when they **b.** you *unto* the
¹Co.16.3. them will I send *to* **b.** your
epiphero.
Jude 9. durst not **b.** *against* him a
ekphero.
Lu.15.22. **b.** *forth* the best robe, and
anaphero.
Mat.17.1. and **b**-*eth* them *up* into an
ago.
Mat.21.2. loose them and **b.** them
Mar.11.2. loose him, and **b.**; Lu.19.30
Lu.19.27. reign over them, **b.** hither
Jo. 10.16. this fold: them also I must **b.**
19. 4. Behold, I **b.** him forth to
Act. 9. 2. 21. he *might* **b.** them bound
17. 5. sought *to* **b.** them out to the
22. 5. *to* **b.** them which were there
23.10. *to* **b.** him into the castle
18. *to* **b.** this young man unto
¹Th. 4.14. in Jesus *will* God **b.** with
²Ti. 4.11. Take Mark, and **b.** him with
Heb.2.10. **b**-*ing* many sons unto glory
eisago.
Lu.14.21. **b.** *in* hither the poor, and the
Heb.1. 6. when he **b**-*eth in* the firstbeg.
epago.
Act. 5.28. *to* **b.** this man's blood *upon*
²Pet.2. 1. *and* **b.** *upon* themselves swift
5. **b**-*ing in* the flood *upon* the
prosago.
Lu. 9.41. suffer you? **b.** thy son hither
¹Pet.3.18. that he *might* **b.** us *to* God
anago.
Act.12. 4. after Easter *to* **b.** him *forth* to
Ro. 10. 7. *to* **b.** *up* Christ *again* from the
katago.
Act.23.15.that he **b.** him *down* unto you
20. that thou *wouldest* **b.** *down*
apago.
Act.23.17. **b.** this young man unto the
pareisago.
²Pet.2. 1. *privily shall* **b.** *in* damnable
poieo.
Mat. 3.8. **b.** *forth* therefore fruits meet
10. *which* **b**-*eth* not *forth;* Lu.3.9
7.17. good tree **b**-*eth forth* good
a corrupt tree **b**-*eth forth*
18. A good tree cannot **b.** *forth*
a corrupt tree **b.** *forth* good
19. Every tree *that* **b**-*eth* not *forth*
13.23. **b**-*eth forth,* some an hundred.
21.43. given to a nation **b**-*ing forth*
Lu. 3. 8. **b.** *forth* therefore fruits
Lu. 6.43. **b**-*eth* not *forth* corrupt fruit
a corrupt tree **b.** *forth* good
Act.24.17.I came *to* **b.** alms to my
tikto.
Mat.1.21, 23. *shall* **b.** *forth* a son
Lu. 1.31. **b.** *forth* a son, and shalt call
Heb.6. 7. and **b**-*eth forth* herbs meet for
Jas. 1.15 hath conceived, it **b**-*eth forth*
38

propempo.
¹Co.16. 6. ye *may* **b.** me *on my journey*
Tit. 3.13. **b.** Ze. and Ap. *on their jour.*
³John 6. *if* thou **b.** *forward on journey*
apokueo.
Jas. 1.15. is finished, **b**-*eth forth* death
ekballo.
Mat.12.35.the heart, **b**-*eth forth* good
treasure, **b**-*eth forth* evil
13.52. **b**-*eth forth* out of his treasu.
diasozo.
Act.23.24.**b.** him *safe* unto Felix the
ektrepho.
Eph.6. 4. **b.** *them up* in the nurture and
atheteo.
¹Co. 1.19. *will* **b.** *to nothing* the under.
katargeo.
¹Co. 1.28. to **b.** *to nought* things that are

(See *other words with which it is connected.*)

BRINGING, [*noun.*]
epeisagoge.
Heb.7.19. but the **b.** *in* of a better hope

BROAD.
euruchoros.
Mat.7.13. and **b.** is the way, that lead.
platuno.
Mat.23.5. they *make* **b.** their phylacter.

BROIDERED.
plegma.
¹Ti. 2. 9. not with **b.** *hair,* or gold, or

BROILED.
optos.
Lu.24.42. gave him a piece of a **b.**

BROKEN-HEARTED.
kardia suntribo.
Lu. 4.18. he hath sent me to heal the **b.**

BROOD.
nossia.
Lu.13.34. as a hen doth gather her **b.**

BROOK.
cheimarros.
Jo. 18. 1. his disciples over the **b.** Ced.

BROTHER.
adelphos.
Mat.4.18. Simon and Andrew his **b.**
21. of Zebedee, and John his **b.**
5.22. whosoever is angry with his **b.**
whosoever shall say to his **b.**
23. thy **b.** hath ought against
24. first be reconciled to thy **b.**
7. 3. is in thy **b**-*'s* eye ; Lu. 41.42.
4. wilt thou say to thy **b.**, Let
5. out the mote out of thy **b**-*'s*
10.21. **b.** shall deliver up **b.**
12.50. the same is my **b.** and sister
18.15. if thy **b.** shall trespass against
thee, thou hast gained thy **b.**
21. how oft shall my **b.** sin again.
35. forgive not every one his **b.**
22.24. his **b.** shall marry his wife
up seed unto his **b.**; Mar.12.19;
Lu. 20.28.
25. issue, left his wife unto his **b.**
Mar.3.17. and John the **b.** of James
35. will of God, the same is my **b.**
6. 3. son of Mary, the **b.** of James
17. Herodias' sake, his **b.** Philip's
18. for thee to have thy **b**-*'s* wife
13.12. the **b.** shall betray the **b.**
Lu. 3. 1. and his **b.** Philip, tetrarch of
19. Herodias his **b.** Philip's wife

Lu. 6.42. say to thy **b.**, **b.**, let me
12.13. Master, speak to my **b.**, that
15.27. said unto him, Thy **b.** is come
32. for this thy **b.** was dead, and
17. 3. If thy **b.** trespass against thee
Jo. 1.41. findeth his own **b.** Simon, and
11. 2. whose **b.** Lazarus was sick
19. them concerning their **b.**
21.32. been here, my **b.** had not
23. unto her, thy **b.** shall rise
Act. 9.17. said, **b.** Saul, the Lord, even
12. 2. he killed James the **b.** of Jo.
21.20. Thou seest, **b.**, how many
22.13. **b.**Saul, receive thy sight. And
Ro.14.10. dost thou judge thy **b.** ? or why
dost thou set at nought thy **b.**
13. occasion to fall in his **b**-*'s* way
15. if thy **b.** be grieved with thee
21. anything whereby thy **b.**stum.
16.23. salut. you, and Quartus a **b.**
¹Co. 1. 1. of God, and Sosthenes our **b.**
5.11. that is called a **b.** be a forni.
6. 6. **b.** goeth to law with **b.**
7.12. If any **b.** hath a wife that
15. a **b.** or a sister is not under
8.11. shall the weak **b.** perish, for
13. make my **b.** to offend
16.12. As touching our **b.** Apollos
²Co. 1. 1. of God, and Timothy our **b.**
2.13. I found not Titus my **b.**
8.18. have sent with him the **b.**
22. have sent with them our **b.**
12.18. with him I sent a **b.**
Gal. 1.19. save James the Lord's **b.**
Eph.6.21. a beloved **b.** and faithful min.
Phil.2.25. to you Epaphroditus my **b.**
Col. 1. 1. God, and Timotheus our **b.**
4. 7. you who is a beloved **b.**, and
9. a faithful and beloved **b.**, who
¹Th. 3. 2. sent Timotheus, our **b.**, and
6. defraud his **b.** in any matter
²Th.3. 6. from every **b.** that walketh
15. but admonish him as a **b.**
Phile. 1. Timothy our **b.**, unto Philem.
7. saints are refreshed by thee,**b**
16. above a servant, a **b.** beloved
20. Yea, **b.**, let me have joy of
Heb.8.11. neighb., and every man his **b.**
13.23. Know ye that our **b.** Timothy
Jas. 1. 9. Let the **b.** of low degree rejo.
2.15. If a **b.** or sister be naked, and
4.11. of his **b.**, and judgeth his **b.**
¹Pet.5.12. a faithful **b.** unto you, as I
²Pet 3.15. as our beloved **b.** Paul also
¹Jo. 2. 9. in the light, and hateth his **b.**
10. He that loveth his **b.** abideth
11. he that hateth his **b.** is in
3.10. he that loveth not his **b.**
12. wicked one, and slew his **b.**
works were evil, and his **b**-*'s*
14. loveth not his **b.** abideth
15. Whosoever hateth his **b.** is a
17. seeth his **b.** have need, and
4.20. hateth his **b.**, he is a liar : for
he that loveth not his **b.**
21. loveth God love his **b.** also
5.16. If any man see his **b.** sin a sin
Jude 1. of Jesus Christ, and **b.** of Jas.
Rev.1. 9. I John, who also am your **b.**

BROTHERHOOD.
adelphotes.
¹Pet.2.17. love the **b.** Fear God. Honour

BROTHERLY.
philadelphia.
Ro.12.10. one to another with **b.** *love*
¹Th. 4. 9. But as touching b. *love* ye
Heb.13.1. Let **b.** *love* continue
²Pet. 1.7. And to godliness **b.** *kindness*
to **b.** *kindness* charity

BROUGHT. (See *Bring*.)
ago.

Mat.10.18.ye *shall be* **b.** before govern.
21. 7. **b.** the ass, and the colt, and
Mar.11.7. they **b.** the colt to Jesus, and
Lu. 4. 9. And he **b.** him to Jerusalem
40. diseases **b.** them unto him
10.34. **b.** him to an inn, and took
18.40. comm. him *to be* **b.**; Act.22.24
19.35. And they **b.** him to Jesus
21.12. *being* **b.** before kings and
Jo. 1.42. he **b.** him to Jesus. And
7.45. them, Why *have* ye not **b.**
8. 3. scribes and Pharisees **b.** unto
9.13. They **b.** to the Pharisees him
19.13. Jesus forth, and sat down
Act. 5.21. to the prison *to have* them **b.**
26. officers, and **b.** them without
27. And *when* they *had* **b.** them
6.12. caught him and **b.** him to
9.27. took him, and **b.** him; 23. 18.
11.26. had found him, he **b.**
17.15. conducted Paul, **b.** him unto
19. took him, and **b.** him unto
18.12. against Paul, and **b.** him to
19.37. ye *have* **b.** hither these men
20.12. they **b.** the young man alive
21.16. **b.** with them one Mnason of
23.31. Paul, and **b.** him by night
25. 6. seat, commanded Paul *to be* **b.**
17. com. the man *to be* **b.** *forth*
23. command. Paul *was* **b.** *forth*
eisago.

Lu. 2.27. when the parents **b.** *in* the
22.54. **b.** him *into* the high priest's
Jo. 18.16. the door, and **b.** *in* Peter
Act. 7.45. our fathers. . **b.** *in* with Jesus
9. 8. **b.** him *into* Damascus
21.28. **b.** Greeks also *into* the temp.
29. Paul had **b.** *into* the temple
exago.

Act.5.19. and **b.** them *forth*, and said
7.36. He **b.** them *out*, after that
40. Moses, which **b.** us *out* of the
12.17. the Lord *had* **b.** him *out* of
13.17. high arm **b.** he them *out* of
16.39. **b.** them *out, and* desired
anago.

Lu. 2.22. they **b.** him to Jerusalem
Act.9.39. they **b.** him into the upper
16.34. *when* he *had* **b.** them into
Heb.13.20.*that* **b.** *again* from the dead
katago.

Lu. 5.11. when they *had* **b.** their ships
Act. 9.30. they **b.** him *down* to Cesar.
22.30. **b.** Paul *down*, and set him
23.28. I **b.** him *forth* into their
proago.

Act.12.6. Her. would have **b.** him *forth*
16.30. And **b.** them *out, and* said
25.26. I *have* **b.** him *forth* before
prosago.

Act.16.20. And **b.** them to the magist.
phero.

Mat.14.11.his head *was* **b.** in a charger
and she **b.** it to her mother
Mar.1.32. they **b.** unto him all that
4. 8. and **b.** *forth*, some thirty
6.27. and comm. his head *to be* **b.**
28. And **b.** his head in a charger
9.17. I *have* **b.** unto thee my son
20. And they **b.** him unto him
12.16. And they **b.** it. And he
Lu. 5.18. And, behold, men **b.** in a bed
Jo. 4.33. *Hath* any man **b.** him ought
19.39. *and* **b.** a mixture of myrrh
Act. 4.34. and **b.** the prices of the thin.
37. and **b.** the money, and laid
5. 2. and **b.** a certain part, and
14.13. **b.** oxen and garlands unto
²Pet.1.13. the grace of God *that is to be* **b.**

prosphero.

Mat.4.24. they **b.** *unto* him all sick
8.16. they **b.** *unto* him many that
9. 2. they **b.** *to* him a man sick of
32. they **b.** *to* him a dumb man
12.22. Then *was* **b.** *unto* him one
14.35. and **b.** *unto* him all that were
17.16. And I **b.** him *to* thy disciples
18.24. one *was* **b.** *unto* him, which
19.13. Then *were* there **b.** *unto* him
22.19. they **b.** *unto* him a penny
25.20. came and **b.** other five talen.
Mar.10.13.they **b.** young children *to*
disciples rebuk. those *that* **b.**
Lu.18.15. And they **b.** *unto* him also
23.14. Ye *have* **b.** this man *unto*
epiphero.

Act.19.12. So that from his body *were* **b.**
25.18. they **b.** none accusation of
eisphero.

¹Ti. 6. 7. we **b.** nothing *into* this
Heb.13.11. whose blood *is* **b.** *into* the
ekphero.

Act.5.15. they **b.** *forth* the sick into the
sumphero.

Act.19.19. **b.** their books *together, and*
histemi.

Mar.13.9. ye *shall be* **b.** before rulers
paristemi.

Act.27.24. thou must be **b.** *before*
trepho.

Lu. 4.16. where he had been **b.** *up*
apostrepho.

Mat.27.3. and **b.** *again* the thirty
anatrepho.

Act.22.3. yet **b.** *up* in this city at the
didomi.

Mat.13.8. good ground, and **b.** *forth*
paradidomi.

Mar.4.29. But when the fruit *is* **b.** *forth*
gennao.

Lu.1.57. delivered; and she **b.** *forth* a
ginomai.

Act.5.36. scattered *and* **b.** to nought
teknotropheo.

¹Ti. 5.10. if she *have* **b.** *up children*
suntrophos.

Act.13.1. *which had been* **b.** *up with*
erchomai.

Mar.4.21. *Is* a candle **b.** to be put
propempo.

Act.15.3. And *being* **b.** *on* their *way by*
21. 5. *and* they all **b.** us *on* our *way*
Ro.15.24. and *to be* **b.** *on* my *way* thith.
²Co. 1.16. of you *to be* **b.** *on* my *way*
tikto.

Mat.1.25. till she *had* **b.** *forth* her
Lu. 2. 7. she **b.** *forth* her firstborn son
Rev.12.5. she **b.** *forth* a man child
13. the woman which **b.** *forth*
komizo.

Lu. 7.37. house, **b.** an alabaster box
lambano.

Mat.16.8. because ye *have* **b.** no bread
parecho.

Act.16.16. which **b.** her masters much
19.24. **b.** no small gain unto the
poieo.

Mat.13.26. and **b.** *forth* fruit, then
blastano.

Jas. 5.18. the earth **b.** *forth* her fruit
euphoreo.

Lu.12.16. man **b.** *forth plentifully*
tapeinoo.

Lu. 3. 5. and hill *shall be* **b.** low
metoikesia.

Mat.1.12. after they were **b.** to Babylon
(the Babylonian *emigration.*)
katabibazo.

Mat.11.23. shalt be **b.** *down* to hell: for
pareisaktos.

Gal. 2. 4. false brethren, *unawares* **b.** *in*

BROW.
ophrus.

Lu. 4.29. led him unto the **b.** of the

BRUISE,   *-ed, -ing.*
suntribo.

Mat.12.20. A **b-***ed* reed shall he not
Lu. 9.39. **b-***ing* him, hardly departeth
Ro. 16.20. *shall* **b.** Satan under your
thrauo.

Lu. 4.18. at liberty them *that are* **b-***ed*

BRUTE.
alogos.

²Pet.2.12. as natural **b.** beasts, made
Jude 10. know naturally, as **b.** beast

BUDDED.
blastano.

Heb. 9.4. Aaron's rod *that* **b.**, and the

BUFFET,   *-ed.*
kolaphizo.

Mat.26.67. spit in his face, and **b-***ed*
Mar.14.65. to cover his face, and to **b.**
¹Co. 4.11. and *are* **b-***ed*, and have no
²Co. 12. 7. the messenger of Satan to **b.**
¹Pet. 2.20. *when* ye be **b-***ed* for your

BUILD,   *-ed, -est, -ing, built,*
oikodomeo.

Mat.7.24. 26. which **b-***t* his house upon
16.18. upon this rock I *will* **b.** my
21.33. a winepress in it, and **b-***t* a
23.29. because ye **b.** the tombs of
26.61. and *to* **b.** it in three days
27.40. **b-***est* it in three; Mar.15.29
Mar.12. 1. and **b-***t* a tower, and let it
14.58. within three days I *will* **b.**
Lu. 4.29. whereon their city *was* **b-***t*
6.48. like a man *which* **b-***t* an hou.
49. *that* **b-***t* an ho. upon the earth
7. 5. and he *hath* **b-***t* us a synago.
11.47. for ye **b.** the sepulchres of
48. and ye **b.** their sepulchres
12.18. pull down my barns, and **b.**
14.28. intending *to* **b.** a tower, sitt.
30. This man began *to* **b.**, and
17.28. sold, they planted, they **b-***ed*
Jo. 2.20. *was* this temple *in* **b-***ing*, and
Act. 7.47. But Solomon **b-***t* him an
49. what house *will* ye **b.** me
Ro.15.20. lest I *should* **b.** upon another
Gal. 2.18. if I **b.** again the things which
¹Pet.2. 5. as lively stones, *are* **b-***t* up
kataskeuazo.

Heb. 3.3. as he *who hath* **b-***ed* the hou.
4. every house *is* **b-***ed* by some
he *that* **b-***t* all things is God
epoikodomeo.

Act.20.32. *to* **b.** you *up*, and to give you
¹Co. 3.10. and another **b-***eth thereon*
heed how he **b-***eth thereupon*
12. Now if any man **b.** upon this
14. which he *hath* **b-***t thereupon*
Eph. 2.20.*And are* **b-***t upon* the founda.
Col. 2. 7. Rooted and **b-***t up* in him
Jude 20. **b-***ing up* yourselves *on* your
anoikodomeo.

Act.15.16.*will* **b.** *again* the tabernacle
I *will* **b.** *again* the ruins the.
sunoikodomeo.

Eph.2.22. ye also *are* **b-***ed together* for an

BUILDER,   *-s.*
oikodomeo.

Mat.21.42.The stone which the **b-***s* rejec.
Mar. 12.10; Lu. 20.17.
Act. 4.11. was set at nought of you **b-***s*
¹Pet.2. 7. stone which the **b-***s* disallow.
technites.

Heb.11.10.whose **b.** and maker is God

BUILDING, [*noun.*]   -*s.*
  oikodomē.
Mat.24.1. to shew him the **b**-*s* of the
Mar.13.1. and what **b**-*s* are here
   2. Seest thou these great **b**-*s*
1Co. 3. 9. husbandry, ye are God's **b**.
2Co. 5. 1. we have a **b**. of God, an house
Eph 2.21. In whom all the **b**. fitly
  endomēsis.
Rev.21.18.And the **b**. of the wall of it
  ktisis.
Heb.9.11. that is to say, not of this **b**.

BULLS.
  tauros.
Heb.9.13. if the blood of **b**. and of goats
  10. 4. possible that the blood of **b**.

BUNDLE,   -*s.*
  desmē.
Mat.13.30 bind them in **b**-*s* to burn
  plēthos.
Act. 28.3. had gathered a **b**. of sticks.

BURDEN, [*noun.*]   -*s.*
  baros.
Mat.20.12.have borne the **b**. and heat
Act. 15.28. upon you no greater **b**. than
Gal. 6. 2. Bear ye one another's **b**-*s*
Rev. 2.24. put upon you none other **b**.
  phortion.
Mat.11.30.is easy and my **b**. is light
  23. 4. For they bind heavy **b**-*s* and
Lu.11.46. with **b**-*s* grievous to be borne
   yourselves touch not the **b**-*s*
Gal. 6. 5. man shall bear his own **b**.
  gomos.
Act.21. 3. the ship was to unlade her **b**.

BURDEN, [*verb.*]   -*ed.*
  katabareō.
2Co.12.16. be it so, I did not **b**. you
  thlipsis.
2Co.8.13.other men be eased, and ye **b**-*ed*
   (but *a burden* to you.)
  bareō.
2Co. 5. 4. do groan,*being* **b**-*ed* : not for

BURDENSOME.
  katanarkaō.
2Co.12.13. that I myself *was* not **b**. to
  14. I *will* not *be* **b**. to you : for
  baros.
1Th. 2. 6. we might have been **b**., as
  abarēs.
2Co. 11.9. kept myself *from being* **b**.

BURIAL.
  entaphiazō.
Mat.26.12. body, she did it for my **b**.

BURN,   -*ed*, -*eth*, -*ing*, *burnt.*
  kaiō.
Lu.12.35. about and your lights **b**-*ing*
  24.32. Did not our hearts **b**. within
Jo. 5. 35. He was a **b**-*ing* and a shining
  15. 6. the fire, and they are **b**-*ed*
1Co.13. 3. I give my body to *be* **b**-*ed*
Heb.12.18.and *that* **b**-*ed* with fire, nor
Rev.4. 5. seven lamps of fire **b**-*ing* bef.
  8. 8. a great mountain **b**-*ing* with
  10. **b**-*ing* as it were a lamp, and
  19.20. lake of fire **b**-*ing* with brims.
  21. 8. in the lake *which* **b**-*eth* with
  katakaiō.
Mat.3.12. but he *will* **b**. *up* the chaff
  13.30. bind them in bundles *to* **b**.
  40. tares are gathered and **b**.
Lu. 3.17. but the chaff he *will* **b**. with
Act.19.19.and **b**-*ed* them before all
1Co. 3.15. any man's work *shall be* **b**-*ed*
40

Heb.13.11.*are* **b**-*ed* without the camp
2Pet.3.10. are therein *shall be* **b**-*ed up*
Rev.8. 7. third part of trees *was* **b**-*t up*
  all green grass *was* **b**-*t up*
  17.16. her flesh and **b**. her with fire
  18. 8. she *shall be utterly* **b**-*ed* with
  puroomai.
1Co. 7. 9. it is better to marry than *to* **b**.
2Co.11.29. who is offended, and I **b**. not
Rev.1.15. as if they **b**-*ed* in a furnace
  holokautōma.
Mar.12.33. more than all *whole* **b**-*t offer.*
Heb.10.6. In **b**-*t offerings* and sacrifices
  8. and **b**-*t offerings* and offering
  ekkaiomai.
Ro. 1.27. **b**-*ed* in their lust one toward
  emprēthō.
Mat.22.7. murderers, and **b**-*ed up* their
  thumiaō.
Lu. 1. 9. his lot was *to* **b**. *incense* when
  kausis.
Heb.6. 8. whose end is to *be* **b**-*ed*
  kausōn.   (for *burning.)*
Jas. 1.11. sooner risen with a **b**-*ing heat*

BURNING, [*noun.*]
  purōsis.
Rev.18.9.18. the smoke of her **b**.

BURST.
  rēgnumi.
Mar.2.22. new wine *doth* **b**. the bottles
Lu. 5.37. new wine *will* **b**. the bottles
  lakeō.
Act.1.18. he **b**. *asunder* in the midst

BURY,   -*ied.*
  thaptō.
Mat.8.21. first to go and **b**. my ; Lu.9.59,
  22. let the dead **b**. their ; Lu.9.60.
  14.12. and **b**-*ed* it, and went and
Lu.16.22. man also died, and *was* **b**-*ed*
Act. 2.29. he is both dead and **b**-*ed*, and
  5. 6. carried him out, and **b**-*ed* him
  9. feet of them *which have* **b**-*ed*
  10. **b**-*ed* her by her husband
1Co.15. 4. And that he *was* **b**-*ed*, and
  sunthaptō.
Ro. 6. 4. we are **b**-*ed with* him by bap.
  (we *were buried with.*)
Col. 2.12. **b**-*ed with* him in baptism
  entaphiazō.
Jo. 19.40. the manner of the Jews is *to* **b**.
  taphē.
Mat.27.7. field to **b**. strangers in
  (for *burial* to the strangers.)

BURYING, [*noun.*]
  entaphiasmos.
Mar.14.8. to anoint my body to the **b**.
Jo. 12. 7. against the day of my **b**.

BUSH.
  batos.
Mar.12.26. how in the **b**. God spake
Lu. 6.44. nor of a *bramble* **b**. gather
  20.37. even Moses shewed at the **b**.
Act. 7.30. in a flame of fire in a **b**.
  35. appeared to him in the **b**.

BUSHEL.
  modios.
Mat.5.15. candle, and put it under a **b**.
Mar.4.21. brought to be put under a **b**.
Lu.11.33. neither under a **b**., but on a

BUSINESS.
  pragma.
Ro.16. 2. in whatsoever **b**. she hath
  spoudē.
Ro.12.11. Not slothful in **b**. : fervent

  chreia.
Act.6. 3. we may appoint over this **b**.
  idios.
1Th. 4.11. to do *your own* **b**., and to

BUSYBODY,   -*ies.*
  periergos.
1Ti. 5.13. but tattlers also, and **b**-*s* spe.
  allotrioepiskopos.
1Pet.4.15. *a* **b**. *in other men's matters*
  periergazomai.
2Th. 3.11. working not at all, but *are* **b** *s*

BUT.
  de.
Mat.1.20. **b**. while he thought on
  2.19. **b**. when Herod was dead
  22. **b**. when he heard that Ar.
  3. 7. **b**. when he saw many of
  14. **b**. John forbade him, saying

(*And generally in other passages in
which* **but** *introduces a sentence. This
occurs too frequently for quotation.*)

  alla.
Mat.4. 4. not by bread alone, **b**. by
  5.15. not under a bushel, **b**. on
  17. not come to destroy, **b**. to
  39. resist not evil; **b**. whosoever
  6.13. not into temptation, **b**. deliver
  18. not unto men to fast, **b**. unto

(*And in all other passages in which*
but *comes between a negative and a
positive, or between opposite ideas. The
following are exceptions :—*)

  ei mē.
Mat.5.13. good for nothing, **b**. to be cast
  11.27. knoweth the Son, **b**. the Fath.
  12. 4. with him, **b**. only for the
  24. **b**. by Beelzebub the prince of
  39. **b**. the sign of the prophet
  14.17. We have here **b**. five loaves
  15.24. I am not sent **b**. unto the lost
  16. 4. **b**. the sign of the prophet
  17.21. goeth not out **b**. by prayer
  19.17. there is none good **b**. one
  21.19. found nothing thereon, **b**.
  24.36. of heaven, **b**. my Father only
Mar.2. 7. who can forgive sins **b**. God
  26. not lawful to eat **b**. for the
  6. 4. without honour, **b**. in his own
  9.29. by nothing, **b**. by prayer and
  10.18. there is none good **b**. one,
  11.13. he found nothing **b**. leaves
  13.32. neither the Son, **b**. the Father
Lu. 5.21. Who can forgive sins, **b**. God
  6. 4. not lawful to eat **b**. for the
  10.22. knoweth who the Father is,**b**.
  and who the Father is, **b**. the
  11.29. **b**. the sign of Jonas the prop.
Jo. 3.13. **b**. he that came down from
  10.10. The thief cometh not, **b**. for
  14. 6. cometh unto the Father, **b**.
  17.12. is lost, **b**. the son of perdition
  19.15. we have no king **b**. Cesar
Act.11.19.to none **b**. unto the Jews
Ro. 7. 7. I had not known sin, **b**. by
  11.15. of them be, **b**. life from the
  13. 1. For there is no power **b**. of
  8. any thing, **b**. to love one ano.
  14.14. **b**. to him that esteemeth any
1Co. 1 14. none of you, **b**. Crispus and
  2.11. knoweth no man, **b**. the Spirit
  7.17. **b**. as God hath distributed
  8. 4. there is none other God **b**.
  10.13. **b**. such as is common to mac.
  12. 3. the Lord, **b**. by the Holy
2Co. 2. 2. **b**. the same which is made
  12. 5. I will not glowr, **b**. in mine

Gal. 1. 7. **b.** there be some that trouble
Eph.4. 9. what is it **b.** that he also des.
Phi.4.15. giving and receiving, **b.** ye
    b. before two or three witnes.
Heb.3.18. **b.** to them that believed not
1Jo. 2.22. Who is a liar, **b.** he that de.
  5. 5. **b.** he that believeth that
Rev.9. 4. **b.** only those men which have
  14. 3. **b.** the hundred and forty and
  19.12. that no man knew, **b.** he him.
  21.27. **b.** they which are written in
plēn.
Mat.11.22,24. **b.** I say unto you
  18. 7. **b.** woe to that man by whom
Mar.12.32.and there is none other **b.**
Lu. 6.24. **b.** woe unto you that are rich
  35. **b.** love ye your enemies
  10.14. **b.** it shall be more tolerable
  11.41. **b.** *rather* give alms of such
  21.31. **b.** *rather* seek ye the kingdom
  19.27. **b.** those mine enemies, which
  22.21. **b.**, behold, the hand of him
  22. **b.** woe unto that man by
  23.28. **b.** weep for yourselves, and
Jo. 8.10. and saw none **b.** the woman
Act.27.22.life among you, **b.** of the ship
Rev.2.25. **b.** that which ye have already
oun.
Lu 21. 7. **b.** when shall these things be
Jo. 8. 5. be stoned : **b.** what sayest
  9.18. **b.** the Jews did not believe
Act.23.21.**b.** do not thou yield unto
  25. 4. **b.** Festus answered, that Paul
ean mē.
Mar.10.30. **b.** he shall receive an hund.
Jo. 5.19. **b.** what he seeth the Father
Gal. 2.16. **b.** by the faith of Jesus Chr.
gar.
1Pet.4.15. **b.** let none of you suffer as a
2Pet.1. 9. **b.** he that lacketh these things
kan.
Mar.5.28. *If* I may touch **b.** his clothes
  6.56. *if* it were **b.** the border of
ektos ei mē.
1Ti. 5. 19. accusation, **b.** before two or
  ē.
Act.17.21. **b.** *either* to tell, or to hear
mentoi.
Jo. 21. 4. **b.** the disciples knew not that
  mē.
Act. 4.20. For we cannot **b.** speak the
monon.
Mat.9.21. If I may **b.** touch his garment
alla ē.
1Co. 3. 5. who is Apollos, **b.** ministers
menounge.
Ro. 9.20. *Nay* **b.**, O man, who art thou
ou pleiōn ē.
Act.24.11. there are *yet* **b.** twelve days
    (not more than twelve.)
parautika.
2Co. 4.17. afflic.which is **b.** *for a moment*
tanun.
Act.17.30. **b.** *now* commandeth all men

BUY,   *-eth, bought.*
agorazō.
Mat.13.44.hath, and **b-**eth that
  46. all that he had, and **b-**o it
  14.15. and **b.** themselves victuals
  21.12. sold and **b-**o in ; Mar.11.15
  25. 9. that sell, and **b.** for yourselv.
  10. while they went to **b.**, the
  27. 7. **b-**o with them the potter's
Mar.6.36. villages, and **b.** themselv.bre.
  37. **b.** two hundred pennyworth
  15.46. he **b-**o fine linen, and took
  16. 1. *had* **b-**o sweet spices, that
Lu. 9.13. we should go and **b.** meat
  14.18. I *have* **b-**o a piece of ground
  19. I *have* **b-**o five yoke of oxen
  17.28. eat, they drank, they **b-**o

Lu.19.45. therein, and them *that* **b-**o
  22.36. sell his garment, and **b.** one
Jo. 4. 8. away unto the city to **b.** meat
  6. 5. Whence *shall* we **b.** bread
  13.29. **b.** those things that we have
1Co. 6.20. ye *are* **b-**o with a price ; 7.23
  7.30. they *that* **b.**, as though they
2Pet.2. 1. denying the Lord *that* **b-**o
Rev.3.18. I counsel thee *to* **b.** of me
  13.17. that no man might **b.** or sell
  18.11. no man **b-**eth their merchan.
ōneomai.
Act. 7.16. that Abraham **b-**o for a sum
emporeuomai.
Jas. 4.13. and **b.** *and sell,* and get gain

BY.
dia.   *[gen.]*
Mat.1.22. of the Lord **b.** the pro.; 2.15
  2. 5. for thus it is written **b.** the
  23. which was spoken **b.** the pro.
  4.14. spoken **b.** Esaias the ; 8.17
  8.28. no man might pass **b.** that

(And all other passages in which it occurs
    except the following :—)

en.
Mat.5.34. Swear not at all ; neither **b.**
  35. Nor **b.** the earth ; for it is
  36. Neither shalt thou swear **b.**
  12.24. **b.** Beelzebub the prince of
  27. **b.** Beelzebub cast out devils
  b. whom do your; Lu.11.19
  28. cast out devils **b.** the Spirit
  14.13. he departed thence **b.** ship
  17.21. goeth not out but **b.** prayer
  21.23. **b.** what authority doest thou ;
    Mar.11.28 ; Lu.20.2.
  24. I will tell you **b.**; Mar.11.29
  27. Neither tell I you **b.** what
  22. 1. spake unto them again **b.** pa.
  23.16,18.Whosoever shall swear **b.**
  whosoever sweareth **b.** the
  20. shall swear **b.** the altar
  sweareth **b.** it and **b.** all
  21. swear **b.** the temple, sweareth
  b. it, and **b.** him that dwell.
  22. swear **b.** heaven, sweareth **b.**
  the throne of God, and **b.**him
Mar.3.22. **b.** the prince of the devils
  4. 2. them many things **b.** parabl.
  5.21. was passed over again **b.** ship
  8. 3. they will faint **b.** the way
  27. **b.** the way he asked his disci.
  9.29. come forth **b.** nothing, but **b.**
  33. disputed among yourselves **b.**
  34. **b.** the way they had disputed
  11.33. **b.** what authority I ; Lu.20.8
  12. 1. to speak unto them **b.** parab.
  36. himself said **b.** the Holy
  14. 1. might take him **b.** craft, and
Lu. 1.77. **b.** the remission of their sins
  2.27. he came **b.** the Spirit into
  4. 1. was led **b.** the Spirit into
  24.32. talked with us **b.** the way
Jo. 13.35. **b.** this shall all men know
  16.30. **b.** this we believe that thou
Act.1. 3. **b.** many infallible proofs
  4. 7. the midst, they asked, **b.**
  what power, or **b.** what name
  9. **b.** what *means* he is made
  10. **b** the name of Jesus Christ
  b. him doth this man stand
  30. **b.** stretching forth thine
  7.35. **b.** the hand of the angel
  13.39. **b.** him all that believe are
  justified **b.** the law of Moses
  17.31. the world in righteousness **b.**
  20.19. **b.** the lying in wait of the
Ro. 1.10. **b.** the will of God to come
  5. 9. now justified **b.** 1.is blood
  10. we shall be saved **b.** his life

Ro. 5.15. the gift **b.** grace which is by
  10. 5. those things shall live **b.**
  14.14. persuaded **b.** the Lord Jesus
  15.16. sanctified **b.** the Holy Ghost
  19. mighty signs and wonders **b.**
1Co. 1. 4. is given you **b.** Jesus Christ
  5. thing ye are enriched **b.**
  3.13. it shall be revealed **b.** fire
  6. 2. shall be judged **b.** you, are
  11. name of Lord Jesus, and **b.**
  7.14. is sanctified **b.** the wife, and
  wife is sanctified **b.** the hus.
  12. 3. speaking **b.** the Spirit of God
  calleth the lord, but **b.** the
  9. faith **b.** the same Spirit ; to
  another the gifts of healing **b.**
  13. for **b.** one Spirit are we all
  14. 6. **b.** revelation, or **b.** know., or
  b. proph., or **b.** doctrine
  16. 7. will not see you now **b.** the
2Co. 1.12. with fleshly wisdom, but **b.**
  6. 6. **b.** pureness, **b.** knowledge,
  b. long-suffering, **b.** kindness
  b. the Holy Ghost, **b.** love
  7. **b.** the word of truth, **b.** the
  7. 6. comforted us **b.** the coming
  7. not **b.** his coming only, but **b.**
  10.12. measuring themselves **b.** the.
  15. we shall be enlarged **b.** you
Gal. 2.17. seek to be justified **b.** Christ
  20. live in the flesh I live **b.**
  3.11. no man is justified **b.** the
  5. 4. are justified **b.** the law ; ye
Eph.2.13. nigh **b.** the blood of Christ
  18. have access **b.** one Spirit unto
  3. 5. apostles and prophets **b.** the
  21. glory in the church **b.** Christ
  4.14. **b.** the sleight of men, and
  21. taught **b.** him, as the truth
  5.26. washing of water **b.** the
Phi. 4.19. riches in glory **b.** Christ
Col. 1.16. **b.**him were all things created
  17. **b.** him all things consist
  21. in your mind **b.** wicked
  2.11. the circumcision of Christ
1Th. 3. 3. moved **b.** these afflictions
  4. 1. exhort you **b.** the Lord
  15. unto you **b.** the word of the
2Th. 3.16. peace always **b.** all means
1Ti. 1.18. that thou **b.** them mightest
Tit. 1. 9. may be able **b.** sound doctri.
Phile. 6. **b.** the acknowledging of
Heb.1. 1. unto the fathers **b.** the proph.
  2. spoken unto us **b.** his Son
  10.10. **b.** the which will we are
  19. the holiest, **b.** the blood of
  11. 2. For **b.** it the elders obtained
1Pet.1. 5. kept **b.** the power of God
  3.19. **b.** which also he went and
  5.10. his eternal glory **b.** Christ Je.
2Pet.1.13. **b.** putting you in remembr.
1Jo. 5. 2. **b.** this we know that we love
  6. not **b.** water only, but **b.** wat.
Jude 1. sanctified **b.** God the Father
Rev.5. 9. redeemed us to God **b.** thy
  9.20. were not killed **b.** these pla.
  10. 6. sware **b.** him that liveth for
  18.23. for **b.** thy sorceries were all
ek.
Mat.12.33.the tree is known **b.** his
  37. **b.** thy words thou shalt be
  and **b.** thy words thou shalt
  15.5. be profited **b.** me ; Mar.7.11
Lu. 6.44. tree is known **b.** his own
Jo. 3.34. giveth not the Spirit **b.** mea.
Act.19.25.ye know that **b.** this craft
Ro. 1. 4. **b.** the resurrection from the
  17. the just shall live **b.** faith
  Gal.3 11 ; Heb.10.38.
  2.27. uncircumcision which is **b.**
  3.20. **b.** the deeds of the law there
  30. justify the circumcision **b.**

41

Ro. 4. 2. if Abraham were justified **b.**
5. 1. Therefore being justified **b.**
16. the judgment was **b.** one to
9.10. Rebecca also had conceived **b.**
32. not **b.** faith, but as it were **b.**
10.17. So then faith cometh **b.** hear.
¹Co. 2. 2. same which is made sorry **b.**
7. 9. receive damage **b.** us in noth.
8.14. **b.** an equality, that now
11.26. in perils **b.** mine own count.
in perils **b.** the heathen
13.4. liveth **b.** the power of God
live with him **b.** the power
Gal. 2.16. **b.** the works of the law
justified **b.** faith of Christ
and not **b.** the works of the
law : for **b.** the works of the
3.2,5. **b.** the works of the law, or **b.**
21. should have been **b.** the law
22. the promise **b.** faith of Jesus
24. we might be justified **b.** faith
4.22. **b.** a bondmaid, the other **b.**
5. 5. hope of righteousness **b.** fai.
Tit. 3. 5. Not **b.** works of righteousness
Jas. 2.18. I will shew thee my faith **b.**
21. our father justified **b.** works
22. **b.** works was faith made per.
24. see then how that **b.** works
a man is justified, and not **b.**
25. Rahab the harlot justified **b.**
¹Pet.2.12. they may **b.** your good
¹Jo. 3.24. **b.** the Spirit which he hath
Rev.9.18. **b.** the fire, and **b.** the smoke,
and **b.** the brimstone, which
hupo, [*gen.*]
Mat.2.17. spoken **b.** Jeremy the prophet
3. 3. that was spoken of **b.** the
22.31. was spoken unto you **b.** God
27.35. which was spoken **b.** the
Mar.5. 4. had been plucked asunder **b.**
13.14. spoken of **b.** Daniel the pro.
Lu. 2.18. which were told them **b.** the
26. revealed unto him **b.** the
3.19. being reproved **b.** him for
5.15. to be healed **b.** him of their
9. 7. heard of all that was done **b.**
13.17. things that were done **b.** him
16.22. carried **b.** the angels into
21.16. ye shall be betrayed both **b.**
23. 8. seen some miracle done **b.**
Jo. 8. 9. being convicted **b.** their own
Act. 4.36. who **b.** the apostles was sur.
10.22. was warned from God **b.**
13. 4. being sent forth **b.** the Holy
45. which were spoken **b.**; 27.11
15. 3. brought on their way **b.** the
40. being recommended **b.** the
16. 2. well reported of **b.** the breth.
24.21. I am called in question **b.**
25.14. certain man left in bonds **b.**
Ro. 3.21. witnessed **b.** the law and the
15.24. on my way thitherward **b.**
¹Co. 1.11. **b.** them which are of the ho.
²Co. 3. 3. ministered **b.** us, written not
which is administ. **b.** us; 20.
Eph.2.11. **b.** that which is called the
5.13. are made manifest **b.** the
Phi. 1.28. in nothing terrified **b.** your
Col. 2.18. vainly puffed up **b.** his fleshly
²Ti. 2.26. who are taken captive **b.** him
Heb.2. 3. confirmed unto us **b.** them
3. 4. For every house is builded **b.**
²Pet.1.21. spake as they were moved **b.**
3. 2. were spoken before **b.** the
Rev.9.18. **b.** these three was the third
para, [*accu.*]
Mat.4.18. walking **b.** the sea of Galilee
13. 1. house, and sat **b.** the sea *side*
4. fell **b.** the way *side*, and the
19. received seed **b.** the way *side*
20.30. sitting **b.** the way *side*, when
Mar.1.16. as he walked **b.** the sea of

Mar.2.13. forth again **b.** the sea *side*
4. 1. to teach **b.** the sea *side :* and
4. fell **b.** the way *side ;* Lu.8.5
15. these are they **b.** the way *side*
10.46. sat **b.** the highway *side* beg.
Lu. 5. 1. he stood **b.** the lake of Genn.
2. two ships standing **b.** the
8.12. Those **b.** the way *side* are
18.35. blind man sat **b.** the way *side*
Act. 10.6. whose house is **b.** the sea *side*
32. a tanner **b.** the sea *side*
16.13. out of the city **b.** a river *side*
Heb.11.12. which is **b.** the sea shore
para, [*dat.*]
Lu. 9.47. a child, and set him **b.** him
Jo. 19.25. Now there stood **b.** the cross
¹Co.16. 2. every one of you lay **b.** him
apo,
Mat.7.16. Ye shall know them **b.** their
20. Wherefore **b.** their fruits ye
Act. 9.13. I have heard **b.** many of
12.20. was nourished **b.** the king's
²Co. 3.18. even as **b.** the Spirit of the
7.13. his spirit was refreshed **b.** you
Heb.5. 8. **b.** the things which he suffer.
Jude 23. the garment spotted **b.** the
Rev.14.20. **b.** *the space of* a thousand
18.15. **b.** her, shall stand afar off
kata, [*accu.*]
Lu. 10.4. and salute no man **b.** the
31. And **b.** chance there came
11.3. Give us day **b.** day our daily
Jo. 10.3. he calleth his own sheep **b.**
19.7. and **b.** our law he ought to
Act. 27.2. meaning to sail **b.** the
Ro. 4.16. that it might be **b.** grace
kata, [*gen.*]
Mat.26.63. I adjure thee **b.** the living
epi, [*dat.*]
Mat.4. 4. not live **b.** bread alone, but
b. every word ; Lu.4.4
Jo. 5. 2. the sheep market a pool
Ro.10.19. to jealousy **b.** them that are
no people, and **b.** a foolish
pros.
Mar.4. 1. multitude was **b.** the sea on
11. 4. found the colt tied **b.** the
Lu.25.56. him as he sat **b.** the fire, and
Act. 5.10. buried her **b.** her husband
eis.
Mat.5.35. neither **b.** Jerusalem ; for it
Act. 7.53. **b.** the disposition of angels
huper.
²Th. 2. 1. we beseech you brethren **b.**
ina mē.
Lu. 18.5. *lest* **b.** her continual coming
ana, [*adverb.*]
Mar.6.40. ranks, **b.** hundreds, and **b.**
Lu. 9.14. sit down **b.** fifties in a comp.
eutheōs.
Lu. 17.7. will say unto him **b.** *and* **b.**
21.9. but the end is not **b.** *and* **b.**
euthus, [*adverb.*]
Mat.13.21. the word, **b.** *and* **b.** he is
exautēs.
Mar.6.25. that thou give me **b.** *and* **b.**
(See *other words which follow it.*)

CAGE.
phulakē.
Rev.18.2. and a **c.** of every unclean and

CALF, -ves.
moschos.
Lu.15.23. And bring hither the fatted **c.**
27. father hath killed the fatted **c.**
30. hast kill. for him the fatted **c.**
Heb.9.12. the blood of goats and **c-ves**
19. the blood of **c-ves** and of goats
Rev. 4.7. the second beast like a **c.**

moschopoieō.
Act.7.41. And they *made a* **c.** in those

CALL, -ed, -est, -eth, -ing.
kaleō.
Mat.1.21. and thou shalt **c.** his name
23. they shall **c.** his name Emma.
25. and he **c-ed** his name Jesus
2. 7. privily **c-ed** the wise men
15. Out of Egypt *have* I **c-ed** my
23. He shall be **c-ed** a Nazarene
4.21. their nets, and he **c-ed** them
5. 9. they shall be **c-ed** the childre n
19. he shall be **c-ed** the least in
the same shall be **c-ed** great in
9.13. I am not come to **c.** the right.
10.25. If they have **c-ed** the master
20. 8. **c.** the labourers, and give
21.13. My house shall be **c-ed** the
22. 3. *to* **c.** them that were bidden
43. *doth* David in spirit **c.** him
45. If David then **c.** him Lord
23. 7. and *to be* **c-ed** of men, Rabbi
8. *be* not ye **c-ed** Rabbi : for one
9. And **c.** no man your father
10. Neither *be* ye **c-ed** masters
25.14. **c-ed** his own servants and
27. 8. that field *was* **c-ed**, The field
Mar.1.20. straightway he **c-ed** them
2.17. not *to* **c.** the righteo.; Lu.5.32
11.17. My house shall be **c-ed** of all
Lu. 1.13. thou shalt **c.** his name John
31. and shalt **c.** his name Jesus
32. and shall be **c-ed** the Son of
35. shall be **c-ed** the Son of God
36. with her, *who was* **c-ed** barren
59. and they **c-ed** him Zacharias
60. not so; but he shall be **c-ed**
61. kindred that *is* **c-ed** by this
62. how he would have him **c-ed**
76. shalt be **c-ed** the prophet of
2. 4. which is **c-ed** Bethlehem
21. his name *was* **c-ed** Jesus
23. shall be **c-ed** holy to the Lord
6.15. and Simon **c-ed** Zelotes
46. And why **c.** ye me, Lord
7.11. he went into a city **c-ed** Nain
8. 2. Mary **c-ed** Magdalene, out of
9.10. belonging to the city **c-ed**
10.39. she had a sister **c-ed** Mary
14.13. when thou makest a feast, **c.**
15.19, 21. no more worthy *to be* **c-ed**
19.13. And he gave his ten servants
29. at the mount **c-ed** the mount
20.44. David therefore **c-eth** him
21.37. *that is* **c-ed** the mount of
22.25. upon them *are* **c-ed** benefact.
33. *which is* **c-ed** Calvary, there
Jo. 1.42. thou shalt be **c-ed** Cephas
2. 2. Jesus *was* **c-ed**, and his disci.
10. 3. and he **c-eth** his own sheep
Act. 1.12. from the mount **c-ed** Olivet
19. insomuch as that field *is* **c-ed**
23. Joseph **c-ed** Barsabas, who
3.11. the porch *that is* **c-ed** Solom.
4.18. And they **c-ed** them, and com.
9.11. the street *which is* **c-ed** Straig,
10. 1. band **c-ed** the Italian band
13. 1. and Simeon *that was* **c-ed**
14.12. they **c-ed** Barnabas, Jupiter
24. 2. And *when* he *was* **c-ed** forth
27. 8. a place *which is* **c-ed** The fair
14. tempestuous wind, **c-ed** Euro.
16. island *which is* **c-ed** Clauda
28. 1. that the island *was* **c-ed** Meli.
Ro. 4.17. and **c-eth** those things which
8.30. also **c-ed**: and whom he **c-ed**
9. 7. In Isaac *shall* thy seed *be* **c-ed**
11. of works, but of him *that* **c-eth**
24. Even us, whom he *hath* **c-ed**
25. I *will* **c.** them my people

Ro. 9.26. there *shall* they *be* c-ed the
¹Co. 1. 9. by whom ye *were* c-ed unto
   7 15. but God *hath* c-ed us to
     17. as the Lord *hath* c-ed every
     18. *Is* any man c-ed being cir.
        Is any c-ed in uncircumcision
     2c. calling wherein he *was* c-ed
     21. *Art* thou c-ed being a servant
     22. For he *that is* c-ed in the
        he *that is* c-ed being free, is
     24. wherein he *is* c-ed, therein
  15. 9. am not meet *to be* c-ed an
Gal. 1. 6. from him *that* c-ed you into
    15. and c-ed me by his grace
     5. 8. cometh not of him *that* c-eth
    13 ye *have been* c-ed unto liberty
Eph. 4.1. vocation wherew. ye *are* c-ed
    4. even as ye *are* c-ed in one
Col. 3.15. to the which also ye *are* c-ed
¹Th. 2.12. worthy of God, *who hath* c-ed
    4. 7. God *hath* not c-ed us unto
    5.24. Faithful is he *that* c-eth you
²Th. 2.14. he c-ed you by our gospel, to
¹Ti. 6.12. whereunto thou *art* also c-ed
²Ti. 1. 9. and c-ed us with an holy
Heb.2.11. not ashamed *to* c. them bret.
    3.13. while it *is* c-ed To-day; lest
    5. 4. but he *that is* c-ed of God, as
  9.15. they *which are* c-ed might
  11. 8. Abraham, *when* he *was* c-ed
    18. in Isaac *shall* thy seed *be* c-ed
Jas. 2.23. he *was* c-ed the Friend of G.
¹Pet.1.15. as he *which hath* c-ed you is
    2. 9. of him *who hath* c-ed you out
    21. hereunto *were* ye c-ed: becau.
    3. 6. Sara obeyed Abraham, c-ing
    9. that ye *are* thereunto c-ed
    5.10. God of all grace, *who hath* c-ed
²Pet. 1.3. of him *that hath* c-ed us to
¹Jo. 3. 1. that we *should be* c-ed the
Rev.1. 9. the isle *that is* c-ed Patmos
  11. 8. which spiritually *is* c-ed S.
  12. 9. that old serpent, c-ed the D.
  16.16. c-ed in the Hebrew tongue
  19. 9. are they *which are* c-ed unto
    11. was c-ed Faithful and True
    13. his name *is* c-ed The Word of
     proskaleomai.
Mat.10.1. And *when* he *had* c-ed unto
  15.10. And he c-ed the multitude
    32. c-ed his disciples *unto* him
  18. 2. c-ed a little child *unto* him
    32. *after that* he *had* c-ed him
  20.25. Jesus c-ed them *unto; Lu.*18.16
Mar.3.13. and c-eth *unto* him whom he
    23. And he c-ed them *unto* him
    6. 7. And he c-ed *unto* him the
  7.14. *when* he *had* c-ed all the peo.
  8. 1. Jesus c-ed his disciples *unto*
    34. *when* he *had* c-ed the people
  10.42. But Jesus c-ed them to him
  12.43. c-ed *unto* him his disciples
  15.44. and c-ing *unto* him the cent.
Lu. 7.19. And John c-ing *unto* him two
  15.26. he c-ed one of the servants
  16. 5. he c-ed his lord's debtors *unto*
Act. 2.39. as the Lord our God *shall* c.
  5.40. *when* they *had* c-ed the apos.
  6. 2. the twelve c-ed the...*unto*
  13. 2. where *unto* I *have* c-ed them
    7. c-ed *for* Barnabas and Saul
  16.10. that the Lord *had* c-ed us for
  20. 1. Paul c-ed *unto* him the discip.
  23.17. c-ed one of the centurio. *unto*
    18. Paul the pris. c-ed me *unto*
    23. And he c-ed *unto* him two
Jas. 5.14. *let* him c. *for* the elders of the
    epikaleomai.
Act.2.21. whosoever *shall* c. on the
  7.59. stoned Stephen, c-ing *upon*
  9.14. to bind all *that* c. on thy
  21. them *which* c-ed on this name

Act.15.17. upon whom my name *is* c-ed
  22.16. c-ing *on* the name of the
Ro.10.12. unto all *that* c. *upon* him
    13. whosoever *shall* c. *upon* the
    14. How then *shall* they c. on
¹Co. 1. 2. all *that* in every place c. *upon*
²Co. 1.23. I c. God for a record upon
²Ti. 2.22. with them *that* c. on the
Heb.11.16. ashamed *to* c. their God
Jas. 2. 7. name by the which ye *are* c-ed
¹Pet.1.17. And *if* ye c. *on* the Father
    sungkaleō.
Mar.15.16. and they c-ed *together* the
Lu. 9. 1. c-ed his twelve disciples *toge.*
  15. 6. he c-eth *together* his friends
    9. c-eth her fr. and her ne. *toget.*
  23.13. *when* he *had* c-ed *together* the
Act. 5.21. and c-ed the council *together*
  10.24. and *had* c-ed *together* his
  28.17. c-ed chief of the Jews *together*
    metakaleō.
Act.7.14. and c-ed his father Jacob *to*
  10.32. and c. *hither* Simon, whose
  20.17. and c-ed the elders of the
  24.25. conv. season I *will* c. *for* thee
    eiskaleō.
Act.10.23. Then c-ed he them *in, and*
    parakaleō.
Act.28.20. have I c-ed *for* you, to see
    phōneō.
Mat.20.32. Jesus stood still, and c-ed
  27.47. This man c-eth *for* Elias
Mar.3.31. without, sent unto him, c-ing
  9.35. and c-ed the twelve, and
  10.49. and commanded him *to be* c-ed
    And *they* c. the blind man
    good comfort, rise; he c-eth
  15.35. said, Behold, he c-eth Elias
Lu. 8.54. and c-ed, saying, Maid, arise
  14.12. c. not thy friends, nor thy
  16. 2. And he c-ed him, *and* said
  19.15. these servants *to be* c-ed unto
Jo. 1.48. Before that Philip c-ed thee
  2. 9. of the feast c-ed the bridegro.
  4.16. c. thy husband, and come
  9.18. until they c-ed the parents of
  24. Then again c-ed they the man
  11.28. and c-ed Mary her sister sec.
    master is come, and c-eth *for*
  12.17. when he c-ed Lazarus out of
  13.13. Ye c. me Master and Lord
  18.33. c-ed Jesus, and said unto him
Act.9.41. *when* he *had* c-ed the saints
  10. 7. he c-ed two of his household
    18. And c-ed, and asked whether
    prosphōneō.
Mat.11.16. and c-ing *unto* their fellows
Lu. 6.13. he c-ed *unto* him his disciples
  7.32. c-ing one *to* another, and say.
  13.12. he c-ed her *to* him, and said
    prosagoreuomai.
Heb.5.10. c-ed of God an high priest
    aiteō.
Act.16.29. Then he c-ed *for* a light and
    metapempō.
Act.10. 5. c. *for* Simon, whose surname
    sunathroizō.
Act.19.25. Whom he c-ed *together*, with
    lambanō.
²Ti. 1.5. *When* I c. *to* remembrance the
    legō.
Mat.1.16. born Jesus, *who is* c-ed Christ
  2.23. dwelt in a city c-ed Nazareth
  4.18. Simon c-ed Peter, and Andr.
  10. 2. Simon, *who is* c-ed Peter, and
Mat.13.55. *is* not his mother c-ed Mary
  19.17. Why c-est thou me good
  26. 3. high priest, *who was* c-ed
    14. Then one of the twelve, c-ed
    36. unto a place c-ed Gethsemane
  27.16. notable prisoner, c-ed Barab.
    17. or Jesus, *which is* c-ed Christ

Mat.27.22. then with Jesus *which is* c-ed
    33. unto a place c-ed Golgotha
Mar.10.18. c-*est* thou me good ; Lu.18.19
  12.37. David therefore himself c-*eth*
  15.12. whom ye c. the King of the
Lu.20.37. when he c-*eth* the Lord the
  22. 1. nigh, *which is* c-ed the passov.
    47. he *that was* c-ed Judas, one
Jo. 4. 5. to a city of Sam., *which is* c-ed
    25. Messias com-*h, which is* c-ed
  9.11. A man *that is* c-ed Jesus
  11.16. Thomas, *which is* c-ed Didym.
    54. into a city c-ed Ephraim
  15.15. Henceforth I c. you not serv.
  19.13. in a place *that is* c-ed the Pa.
    17. a place c-ed the place of a
    is c-ed in the Hebrew Golgot.
  20.24. c-ed Didymus, was not with
  21. 2. and Thomas c-ed Didymus
Act. 3. 2. of the temple *which is* c-ed
  6. 9. the synagogue, *which is* c-ed
  9.36. by interpretation *is* c-ed Dor.
  24.14. which they c. heresy, so wor.
¹Co. 8. 5. there be *that are* c-ed gods
  12. 3. c-*eth* Jesus accursed: and that
Eph.2.11. *who are* c-ed Uncircumcision
    which is c-ed the Circumcision
Col. 4.11. Jesus, *which is* c-ed Justus
²Th. 2. 4. above all *that is* c-ed God
Heb.7.11. and not *be* c-ed after the¶
  9. 2. which is c-ed the sanctuary
    3. the tabernacle which *is* c-ed
  11.24. refused *to be* c-ed the son of
Rev.2.20. *which* c-*eth* herself a prophet.
  8.11. the star *is* c-ed Wormwood
    klētos.
Mat.20.16.many *be* c-ed, but few chosen
  22.14. many *are* c-ed, but few are
Ro. 1. 1. c-ed to be an apostle, separa.
    6. are ye also the c-ed of Jesus
    7. c-ed to be saints : Grace to
  8.28. to them who are the c-ed acc.
¹Co. 1. 1. Paul, c-ed to be an apostle
    2. sanctified in Christ Jesus, c-ed
    24. But unto them which are c-ed
Jude 1. in Jesus Christ, and c-ed
Rev.17.14. that are with him are c-ed
    onoma.
Lu.24.13. to a village c-ed Emmaus
Act. 8. 9. a certain man c-ed Simon
        (*by name* Simon.)
  9.11. for one c-ed Saul of Tarsus
  10. 1. c-ed Cornelius, a centurion of
    chrēmatizō.
Act.11.26. the disciples *were* c-ed Chri.
Ro. 7. 3. she *shall be* c-ed an adulteress
    onomazō.
Act.19.13. to c. over them which had
¹Co. 5.11. if any man *that is* c-ed a
    eponomazō.
Ro. 2.17. Behold thou *art* c-ed a Jew
    epilegō.
Jo. 5. 2. *which is* c-ed in the Hebrew
    epō.
Jo.10.35. If he c-ed them gods unto
    ereō.
Jo.15.15. but I *have* c-ed you friends
    hos eimi.
Mar.15.16. into the hall c-ed Praetorium
        (*which is* Praetorium.)
    pseudōnumos.
¹Ti. 6.20. of science *falsely* so c-ed

(See *Blessed, Common, Mind, Question, Remembrance.*)

CALLING.
    klēsis.
Ro.11.29. the gifts and c. of God are
¹Co. 1.26. For ye see your c., brethren
  7.20. abide in the same c. wherein
Eph.1.18. what is the hope of his c.

Eph.4. 4. called in one hope of your **c.**
Phi.3.14. for the prize of the high **c.**
²Th.3.14. count you worthy of this **c.**
²Ti. 1. 9. called us with an holy **c.**
Heb.3. 1. partakers of the heavenly **c.**
²Pet.1.10. give diligence to make your **c.**

CALM.
galēnē.
Mat.8.26. there was a great **c.**; Mar.4.39
Lu. 8.24. ceased, and there was a **c.**

CAMEL.
kamēlos.
Mat.3. 4. his raiment of **c.**'s hair, and
  19.24. a **c.** to go through; Mar.10.25.
               Lu.18.25.
  23.24. at a gnat, and swallow a **c.**
Mar.1. 6. clothed with **c.**'s hair, and

CAMP.
parembolē.
Heb.13.11. are burned without the **c.**
  13. unto him without the **c.**, bear.
Rev.20. 9. and compassed the **c.** of the

CAN, (See *Could*.)   -st.
dunamai.
Mat.5.36. thou **c-st** not make one hair
  27. by taking thought **c.** add one
   8. 2. if thou wilt, thou **c-st** make
   9.15. the children of; Mar.2.19
  12.29. how **c.** one enter into a strong
  34. how **c.** ye, being evil, speak
  16. 3. **c.** ye not discern the signs of
  19.25. saying, Who then **c.** be saved
          Mar.10.26; Lu.18.26
Mar 1.40. **c-st** make me clean; Lu.5.12
   7. **c.** forgive sins but G.; Lu.5.21
   3.23. How **c.** Satan cast out Satan
  27. No man **c.** enter into a strong
   7.15. that entering into him **c.** defi.
   8. 4. whence **c.** a man satisfy these
   9. 3. as no fuller on earth **c.** white
  22. If thou **c-st** do anything, have
  23. If thou **c-st** believe, all things
  29. This kind **c.** come forth by
  39. that **c** lightly speak evil of me
  38. **c.** ye drink of the cup that I
  39. they said unto him, We **c.**
   5.34. **c.** ye make the children of the
   6.39. **c.** the blind lead the blind
  42. how **c-st** thou say to thy bro.
  12.25. taking thought **c.** add to his
  16.13. No servant **c.** serve two mas.
  20.36. Neither **c.** they die any more
Jo. 1.46. **c.** there any good thing come
   3. 2. for no man **c.** do these mira.
   4. How **c.** a man be born when
      he is old? **c.** he enter the sec.
   9. him, How **c.** these things be
  27. A man **c.** receive nothing, ex.
   5.19. The Son **c.** do nothing of him.
  30. I **c.** of mine own self do noth.
  44. How **c.** ye believe, which rec.
   6.44. No man **c.** come to me, exce.
  52. How **c.** this man give us his
  60. an hard saying; who **c.** hear
  65. that no man **c.** come unto me
   9. 4. night cometh, when no man **c.**
  16. How **c.** a man that is a sinner
  10.21. **c.** a devil open the eyes of the
  13.36. Whither I go, thou **c-st** not
  14. 5. how **c.** we know the way
  15. 5. without me ye **c.** do nothing
Act.8.31. How **c.** I, except some man
  10.47. **c.** any man forbid water, that
  24.13. Neither **c.** they prove the th.
Ro. 8. 7. law of God, neither indeed **c.**
¹Co. 2.14. neither **c.** he know them, bec.
   3.11. other foundation **c.** no man
  12. 3. that no man **c.** say that Jesus
44

²Co.13. 8. we **c.** *do* nothing against the
¹Th. 3. 9. what thanks **c.** we render to
¹Ti. 6. 7. certain we **c.** carry nothing
  16. who. no man hath seen, nor **c.**
Heb.5. 2. *Who* **c.** have compassion on
  10. 1. **c.** never with those sacrifices
  11. which **c.** never take away sins
Jas. 2.14. have not works? **c.** faith save
   3. 8. the tongue **c.** no man tame
  12. **c.** the fig-tree, my brethren
¹Jo. 4.20. how **c.** he love God whom he
Rev.2. 2. how thou **c-st** not bear them
   3. 8. an open door, and no man **c.**
   9.20. which neither **c.** see, nor hear
eideō.
Mat.27.65. way, make it as sure as ye **c.**
Lu. 12.56. ye **c.** discern the face of the
Jo. 3. 8. **c-st** not *tell* whence it cometh
ischuō.
Phi. 4.13. I **c.** *do* all things through Ch.
     (See *Cannot*.)

CANDLE.
luchnos.
Mat.5.15. Neither do men light a **c.**
Mar.4.21. Is a **c.** brought to be put under
Lu. 8.16. he hath lighted a **c.**; 11.33
  11.36. the bright shining of a **c.** doth
  15. 8. doth not light a **c.** and sweep
Rev.18.23. And the light of a **c.** shall
  22. 5. they need no **c.**, neither light

CANDLESTICK,   -s.
luchnia.
Mat.5.15. but on a **c.**; and it giveth
Mar.4.21. bed? and not to be set on a **c.**
Lu. 8.16. but setteth it on a **c.**, that
  11.33. but on a **c.**, that they which
Heb.9. 2. wherein was the **c.**, and the
Rev.1.12. turned, I saw seven golden **c-s**
  13. in the midst of the seven **c-s**
  20. the seven golden **c-s**; 2.1
     and the seven **c-s** which those
   2. 5. remove thy **c.** out of his place
  11. 4. and the two **c-s** standing befo.

CANKER, [*noun*.]
ganggraina.
²Ti. 2.17. word will eat as doth a **c.**

CANKERED.
katioomai.
Jas. 5. 3. Your gold and silver *is* **c.**

CANNOT.
dunamai, [*with negative*.]
Mat.5.14. A city that is set on an hill **c.**
   6.24. Ye **c.** serve God and mammon
   7.18. A good tree **c.** bring forth
  26.53. that I **c.** now pray to my Fa.
  27.42. himself he **c.** save; Mar.15.31
Mar.2.19. bridegroom with them, they **c.**
   3.24. itself, that kingdom **c.** stand
  25. against itself, that house **c.**
  26. he **c.** stand, but hath an end
   7.18. into the man, it **c.** defile him
Lu.11. 7. in bed, I **c.** rise and give thee
  14.20. and therefore I **c.** come
  26,27,33. **c.** be my disciple
  16.26. they which would pass **c.**
Jo. 3. 3. he **c.** see the kingdom of God
   5. he **c.** enter into the kingdom
   7. 7. The world **c.** hate you; but
  34,36. where I am, thither ye **c.**
   8.21,22. whither I go, ye **c.** come; 13.33
  43. because ye **c.** hear my word
  10.35. the scripture **c.** be broken
  37. Lord, why **c.** I follow thee
  14.17. whom the world **c.** receive
  15. 4. the branch **c.** bear fruit of it.

Jo. 16.12. but ye **c.** bear them now
Act. 4.16. in Jerusalem; and we **c.** deny
   5.39. be of God, ye **c.** overthrow it
  15. 1. the manner of Moses, ye **c.** be
  27.31. abide in the ship, ye **c.** be
Ro. 8. 8. they that are in the flesh **c.**
¹Co.10.21. drink the cup of the L.
    ye **c.** be partakers of the L.'s
  12.21. the eye **c.** say unto the hand
  15.50. flesh and blood **c.** inherit the
¹Ti. 5.25. that are otherwise **c.** be hid
²Ti. 2.13. faithful: he **c.** deny himself
Heb.4.15. an high priest *which* **c.** be
Jas. 4. 2. desire to have, and **c.** obtain
¹Jo. 3. 9. he **c.** sin, because he is born
eideō, [*with negative*.]
Mat.21.27. We **c.** *tell*; Mar.11.33;
Jo. 8.14. but ye **c.** *tell* whence
  16.18. while? we **c.** *tell* what he saith
²Co.12. 2. in the body I **c.** tei
    out of the body, I **c.** tei
   3. I **c.** *tell*: God knoweth
echō, [*with negative*.]
Lu.14.14. for they **c.** recompense thee
    (*have* not to recompense.)
ischuō, [*with negative*.]
Lu.16. 3. I **c.** dig; to beg I am ashamed
endechomai, [*with negative*.]
Lu.13.33. for it **c.** be that a prophet
    (See *Cease, Moved*.)

CAPTAIN,   -s.
chiliarchos.
Mar.6.21. a supper to his lords, *high* **c-s**
Jo. 18.12. Then the band and the **c.** and
Act.21.31. tidings came unto the *chief* **c.**
  32. they saw the *chief* **c.** and the
  33. Then the *chief* **c.** came; 22.27
  37. he said unto the *chief* **c.**, May
  22.24. The *chief* **c.** commanded him
  26. he went and told the *chief* **c.**
  28. the *chief* **c.** answered, With
  29. the *chief* **c.** also was afraid
  23.10. the *chief* **c.**, fearing lest Paul
  15. signify to the *chief* **c.** that he
  17. young man unto the *chief* **c.**
  18. brought him to the *chief* **c.**
  19. the *chief* **c.** took him by the
  22. *chief* **c.** then let the young man
  24. 7. But the *chief* **c.** Lysias came
  22. When Lysias the *chief* **c.** shall
  25.23. the *chief* **c-s**, and principal
Rev.6.15. rich men, and the *chief* **c-s**
  19.18. of kings, and the flesh of **c-s**
stratēgos.
Lu.22. 4. with the chief priests and **c-s**
  52. and **c-s** of the temple, and the
Act. 4. 1. and the **c.** of the temple; 5.24
   5.26. Then went the **c.** with the
archēgos.
Heb.2.10. make the **c.** of their salvation
stratopedarchēs.
Act.28.16. prisoners to the **c.** *of the guard*

CAPTIVE,   -s.
aichmalōtos.
Lu. 4.18. preach deliverance to the **c-s**
aichmalōteuō.
Eph.4. 8. on high he *led* captivity **c.**
²Ti. 3. 6. *lead* **c.** silly women laden
aichmalōtizō.
Lu.21.24. *shall* be led *away* **c.** into all
zōgreō.
²Ti. 2.26. *who are taken* **c.** by him at

CAPTIVITY.
aichmalōsia.
Eph. 4. 8. he led **c.** captive and gave
Rev.13.10. into **c.** shall go into **c.**: he

aichmalōtizō.

Ro. 7.23. *bringing* me *into* **c.** to the
²Co.10.5. *bringing into* **c.** every thou.

CARCASE,   -s.
kōlon.

Heb.3.17. whose **c**-s fell in the wildern.

ptōma.

Mat.24.28. For wheresoever the **c.** is

CARE, [noun,]   -s.
merimna.

Mat.13.22. and the **c.** of this world, and
Mar. 4.19. the **c**-s of this world, and
Lu. 8. 14. are choked with **c**-s and
21.34. and **c**-s of this life, and so
²Co. 11.28. the **c.** of all the churches
¹Pet. 5. 7. Casting all your **c.** upon

spoudē.

²Co. 7.12. our **c.** for you in the sight of
8.16. put the same *earnest* **c.** into

epimeleomai.

Lu.10.34. to an inn and *took* **c.** of him
35. *Take* **c.** *of* him; and whatsoe.
¹Ti. 3. 5. how shall he *take* **c.** *of* the

merimnaō.

¹Co.12.25. *should have* the same **c.** one

CARE, [verb,]   -ed,, -est -eth.
melei.

Mat.22.16.neither **c**-*st* thou for any
Mar.4.38. Master, **c**-*st* thou not that we
12.14. and **c**-*st* for no man : for thou
Lu.10.40. Lord, *dost* thou not **c.** that
Jo. 10.13. and **c**-*th* not for the sheep
12. not that he **c**-*ed* for the poor
Act.18.17.And Gallio **c**-*ed* for none of
¹Co. 7.21. **c.** not for it : but if thou
9. 9. *Doth* God *take* **c.** for oxen ?
¹Pet.5. 7. upon him, for he **c**-*th* for you

merimnaō.

¹Co. 7.32. He that is unmarried **c**-*th*
33. he that is married **c**-*th* for
34. **c**-*th* for the things of the L.
c-*th* for the things of the wo.
Phi. 2.20. who *will* naturally **c.** for

phroneō.

Phi. 4.10. your **c.** of me hath flourished

CAREFUL.
merimnaō.

Lu.10.41. thou *art* **c.** and troubled
Phi. 4. 6. *Be* **c.** for nothing ; but in

phroneō.

Phi. 4.10. wherein ye *were* also **c.** but

phrontizō.

Tit. 3. 8. *might be* **c.** to maintain good

CAREFULLY.
spoudaioterōs.

Phi.2.28. sent him therefore *the more* **c.**

ekzēteō.

Heb.12.17. though he *sought* it **c.** with

CAREFULNESS.
spoudē.

²Co. 7.11. what **c.** it wrought in you

amerimnos.

¹Co. 7.32. I would have you *without* **c.**

CARNAL.
sarkikos.

Ro. 7.14. but I am **c.**, sold under sin
15.27. to minister unto him in **c.**
¹Co. 3. 1. but as unto **c.**, even as unto
3. For ye are yet **c.**: for whereas
are ye not **c.**, and walk as
4. I am of Apollos, are ye not **c.**
9.11. if we shall reap your **c.** things
²Co.10. 4. of our warfare are not **c.**
Heb.7.16. not after the law of a **c.** com.

---

sarx.

Ro. 8. 7. the **c.** mind is enmity against
(the minding *of the flesh.*)
Heb.9.10. and **c.** ordinances imposed
(ordinances *of the flesh.*)

CARNALLY.
sarx.

Ro. 8. 6. to be **c.** minded is death
(the minding *of the flesh.*)

CARPENTER.
tektōn.

Mat.13.55. Is not this the **c.**'s son ? is
Mar. 6. 3. Is not this the **c.**, the son of

CARRIAGES.
aposkeuazomai.

Act.21.15. We *took up* our **c.** *and* went

CARRY.   -ied, -eth.
bastazō.

Lu.10. 4. **c.** neither purse, nor scrip
Act. 3. 2. his mother's womb was **c**-*ed*
Rev.17.7. and of the beast that **c**-*eth*

pherō.

Jo. 21.18. shall gird thee and **c.** thee

apopherō.

Mar.15.1. bound Jesus, and **c**-*ed* him
Lu.16.22. and was **c**-*ed* by the angels
Rev.17.3. he **c**-*ed* me *away* in the; 21.10

ekpherō.

Act. 5. 6. **c**-*ed* him *out, and* buried him
9. the door, and *shall* **c.** thee *out*
10. *c*-*ing* her *forth*, buried her
¹Ti. 6. 7. certain we can **c.** nothing *out*

peripherō.

Mar.6.55. *to* **c.** *about* in beds those
Eph.4.14. and **c**-*ed about* with every
Heb.13.9. *Be* not **c**-*ed about* with divers
Jude 12. **c**-*ed about* of winds ; trees

anapherō.

Lu.24.51. from them and **c**-*ed up* into

diapherō.

Mar.11.16. that any man *should* **c.** any

airō.

Jo. 5.10. not lawful for thee *to* **c.** thy

agō.

Act.21.34. commanded him *to be* **c**-*ed*

sunapagō.

Gal. 2.13. Bar. also *was* **c**-*ed away with*

apagō.

¹Co.12. 2. **c**-*ed away* unto these dumb

metatithēmi.

Act. 7.16. And *were* **c**-*ed over* into Syc.

sunkomizō.

Act. 8. 2. and devout men **c**-*ed* Stephen

ekkomizō.

Lu. 7.12. there *was* a dead man **c**-*ed*

metoikizō.

Act. 7.43. *I will* **c.** you *away* beyond

metoikesia.

Mat.1.11. *time they were* **c**-*ed away to*
(the Babylonian *emigration.*)
17. until the **c**-*ing away into*
and from the **c**-*ing away into*

elaunō.

²Pet.2.17. clouds that are **c**-*ed* with a

potamophorētos.

Rev.12.15. to be **c**-*ed away of the flood*

CASE.
aitia.

Mat.19.10. If the **c.** of the man be so

ou mē.

Mat.5.20. ye shall *in no* **c.** enter into

CAST,   -ing.
ballō.

Mat.3.10. hewn down, and **c.** into the
4. 6. the Son of God **c.** thyself
18. **c**-*ing* a net into ; Mar.1.16

Mat.5.13. good for nothing, but *to be* **c**
25. to the officer, and thou *be* **c.**
29. pluck it out, and **c.** it ; 18.9
whole body *should be* **c.** into
30. cut it off, and **c.** it from thee
6.30. to morrow *is* **c.** into the oven
7. 6. neither **c.** ye your pearls
19. hewn down, and **c.** into the
13.42. *shall* **c.** them into a furnace
47. a net, that *was* **c.** into the
48. good into vessels, but **c.** the
50. *shall* **c.** them into the furnace
15.26. bread, and to **c.** it to; Mar.7.27
17.27. go thou to the sea, and **c.** an
18. 8. cut them off, and **c.** them
to be **c.** into everlasting fire
two eyes *to be* **c.** ; Mar.9.47
30. went and **c.** him into prison
21.21. *be* thou **c.** into the; Mar.11.23
27.35. his garments, **c**-*ing*; Mar.15.24
upon my vesture *did* they **c.**
Mar.4.26. a man *should* **c.** seed into
9.22. it *hath* **c.** him into the fire
42. his neck, and he *were* **c.** into
45. two feet *to be* **c.** into hell
12.41. people **c.** money into the
and many that were rich **c.**
43. this poor widow *hath* **c.** more
in, than all they *have* **c.** into
44. they *did* **c.** in of their abund.
but she of her want *did* **c.** in
Lu. 3. 9. is hewn down, and **c.** into
4. 9. **c.** thyself down from hence
12.28. to morrow *is* **c.** into the oven
58. the officer **c.** thee into prison
13.19. a man took, and **c.** into his
14.35. dunghill ; but men **c.** it *out*
21. 1. the rich men **c**-*ing* their gifts
2. a certain poor widow **c**-*ing* in
3. this poor widow *hath* **c.** in
4. of their abundance **c.** in unto
she of her penury *hath* **c.** in
23.19. for murder, *was* **c.** into prison
25. sedition and murder *was* **c.**
34. parted his raiment, and **c.**
Jo. 3.24. John *was* not yet **c.** into
8. 7. *let* him first **c.** a stone at her
59. took they up stones *to* **c.** at
15. 6. he *is* **c.** forth as a branch
c. them into the fire, and
19.24. and for my vesture they *did* **c.**
21. 6. **c.** the net on the right side of
They **c.** therefore, and now
7. *did* **c.** himself into the sea
Act.16.23.they **c.** them into prison
37. *have* **c.** us into prison ; and
¹Jo. 4.18. perfect love **c**-*eth* out fear
Rev.2.10. the devil *shall* **c.** some of you
14. Balac *to* **c.** a stumblingblock
22. Behold, I *will* **c.** her into a
4.10. **c.** their crowns before the
6.13. as a fig tree **c**-*eth* her untimely
8. 5. **c.** it into the earth ; and
7. they *were* **c.** upon the earth
8. with fire *was* **c.** into the sea
12. 4. stars of heaven, and *did* **c.**
9. the great dragon *was* **c.** *out*
he *was* **c.** *out* into the earth
and his angels *were* **c.** *out*
13. dragon saw that he *was* **c.**
15. the serpent **c.** out of his
16. the dragon **c.** out of his
14.19. **c.** it into the great winepress
18.19. they **c.** dust on their heads
21. millstone, and **c.** it into the
19.20. These both *were* **c.** alive into
20. 3. **c.** him into the bottomless pit
10. *was* **c.** into the lake of fire, and
14. death and hell *were* **c.** into
15. *was* **c.** into the lake of fire

ekballō.

Mat.7. 5. first **c.** *out* the beam out of

Mat.7. 5. see clearly to **c.** *out* the mote
   22. in thy name have **c.** *out* devils
8.12. *shall be* **c.** *out* into outer dark.
   16. he **c.** *out* the spirits with his
   31. saying, If thou **c.** us *out*, suff.
9.33. *when* the devil *was* **c.** *out*
   34. He **c**-*eth out* devils ; Lu.11.15
10. 1. unclean spirits, *to* **c.** them *out*
   8. raise the dead, **c.** *out* devils
12.24. *doth* not **c.** *out* devils, but by
   26. if Satan **c.** *out* Satan, he is
   27. if I by Beelzebub **c.** *out* devils
      Lu.11.19
      do your children **c.** them *out*
   28. if I **c.** *out* devils by the Spirit
15.17. *is* **c.** *out* into the draught
17.19. Why could not we **c.** him *out*
      Mar.9.28.
21.12. **c.** *out* all them that sold and
   39. they caught him, and **c.** him
22.13. **c.** him into outer darkness
25.30. **c.** ye the unprofitable servant
Mar.1.34. and **c.** *out* many devils ; and
   39. throughout all Galilee, and **c.**
3.15. sicknesses, and *to* **c.** *out* devils
   22. of the devils **c**-*eth* he *out* dev.
   23. How can Satan **c.** *out* Satan
6.13. they **c.** *out* many devils, and
7.26. he *would* **c.** *forth* the devil
9.18. that they *should* **c.** him *out*
   38. we saw one **c**-*ing out* devils
      Lu. 9.49.
11.15. *to* **c.** *out* them that ; Lu.19.45.
12. 8. **c.** him *out* of the vineyard
16. 9. out of whom he *had* **c.** seven
   17. *shall* they **c.** *out* devils ; they
Lu. 6.22. reproach you, and **c.** *out* your
   42. **c.** *out* first the beam out of
9.40. thy disciples to **c.** him *out*
11.14. he was **c**-*ing out* a devil, and
   18. I **c.** *out* devils through Beelz.
   19. *do* your sons **c.** them *out*
   20. if I with the finger of God **c.**
13.32. Behold, I **c.** *out* devils, and I
20.12. him also, and **c.** him *out*
   15. **c.** him out of the vineyard
Jo   6.37. to me I *will* in no wise **c.** out
9.34. teach us ? And they **c.** him
   35. that they *had* **c.** him *out*
12.31. prince of this world be **c.** *out*
Act.7.58. **c.** him out of the city, *and*
 27.38. *and* **c.** *out* the wheat into the
Gal. 4.30. **c.** *out* the bondwoman, and
3John 10. **c**-*eth* them out of the church
   periballō.
Mar.14.51.having a linen *cloth* **c.** *about*
   (*enveloped* with linen upon.)
Lu.1.).43. enemies *shall* **c.** a trench *about*
Act.12. 8. **c.** thy garment *about* thee
   apoballō.
Mar.10.50. he, **c**-*ing away* his garment
Heb.10.35. **c.** not *away* therefore your
   kataballō.
2Co. 4. 9. **c.** *down* but not destroyed
Rev.12.10. of our brethren *is* **c.** *down*
   emballō.
Lu. 12. 5. hath power *to* **c.** *into* hell
   epiballō.
Mar.11. 7.and **c.** their garments *on* him
1Co. 7.35.that I *may* **c.** a snare *upon*
   riptō.
Mat.15.30.and **c.** them *down* at Jesus'
   27. 5. And he **c.** *down* the pieces of
Lu.17. 2. and he **c.** *into* the sea, than
Act.22.23.as they cried out, and**c.** *off*
 27.19. we **c.** *out* with our own hands
   29. they **c.** four anchors out of
   apotithēmi.
Ro.13.12. **c.** *off* the works of darkness
   ektithēmi.
Act.7.12. *when* he was **c.** *out*, Pharaoh's
46

---

   apōthomai.
Ro.11. 1. *Hath* God **c.** *away* his **people**
   2. God *hath* not **c.** *away* his peo.
   zēmioō.
Lu. 9.25. lose himself, or *be* **c.** *away*
   ekpiptō.
Act.27.26.we must *be* **c.** upon a certain
   kathaireō.
2Co.10. 5. **c**-*ing down* imaginations and
   aporriptō.
Act.27.43.should **c.** *themselves* first into
   epirriptō.
Lu.19.35. they **c.** their garments *upon*
1Pet.5. 7. **c**-*ing* all your care *upon* him
   atheteō.
1Ti. 5.12. they *have* **c.** *off* their first faith
   ekteinō.
Act.27.30.though they would have **c.**
   (as intending *to cast*.)
   paradidōmi.
Mat.4.12. that John *was* **c.** *into* prison
   katakrēmnizō.
Lu. 4.29. might **c.** him *down* headlong
   tapeinos.
2Co. 7. 6. those *that are* **c.** *down*
   oneidizō.
Mat.27.44.him, **c.** the same *in his teeth*
   dialogizomai.
Lu. 1.29. **c.** *in her mind* what manner
   poieō ekthetos.
Act. 7.19. **c.** *out* their young children
   lithoboleō.
Mar.12.4. *at* him they **c.** *stones and*
   langchanō.
Jo.19.24. us not rend it, but **c.** *lots* for
   apobolē.
Ro.11.15. if the **c**-*ing away* of them be
   tartaroō.
2Pet.2. 4. but **c.** them *down to hell, and*

CAST, [noun.]
   bolē.
Lu.22.41. from them about a stone's **c.**

CASTAWAY.
   adokimos.
1Co.9.27. others, I myself should be a **c.**

CASTLE.
   parembolē.
Act.21.34. to be carried into the **c.**
   37. Paul was to be led into the **c.**
22.24. to be brought into the **c.**
23.10. to bring him into the **c.**
   16. entered into the **c.**, and told
   32. him, and returned to the **c.**

CATCH,   -eth, caught.
   harpazō.
Mat.13.19. the wicked one, and **c**-*eth*
Jo. 10.12. the wolf **c**-*eth* them, and
Act. 8.39. Spirit of the Lord **c**-*t away*
2Co. 12. 2 such an one **c**-*t up* to the
   4. that he *was* **c**-*t up* into
1Th. 4.17. *shall be* **c**-*t up* together with
Rev.12. 5. her child *was* **c**-*t up* unto
   sunarpazō.
Lu. 8.29. For oftentimes it *had* **c**-*t* him
Act.6.12. **c**-*t* him, and brought him
   19.29. and *having* **c**-*t* Gaius and
   27.15. And *when* the ship *was* **c**-*t*
   lambanō.
Mat.21.39. And they **c.** him ; Mar.12.3
2Co. 12.16. being crafty I **c.** you with
   epilambanomai.
Mat.14.31. **c**-*t* him, and said unto him
Act. 16.19. they **c**-*t* Paul and Silas, *and*
   sullambanō.
Act.26.21. the Jews **c**-*t* me in the temple
   piazō.
Jo. 21. 3. that night they **c.** nothing
   10. fish which ye have now **c.**

---

   zōgreō.
Lu.5.10. henceforth thou shalt **c.** men
   (be *a catcher of*.)
   thēreuō.
Lu.11.54. seeking *to* **c.** something out of
   agreuō.
Mar.12.13. Herodians, *to* **c.** him in his

CATTLE.
   thremma.
Jo.4.12. and his children and his **c.**
   poimainō.
Lu.17.7. a servant plowing or *feeding* **c.**

CAUSE, [noun,]   -s, -ed, -eth.
   aitia.
Mat.19. 3. away his wife for every **c.**
Lu. 8.47. for what **c.** she had touched
Act.10.21. what is the **c.** wherefore
   13.28. they found no **c.** of death in
   23.28. I would have known the **c.**
   28.18. there was no **c.** of death in
   20. For this **c.** therefore have I
2Ti. 1.12. For the which **c.** I also suffer
Heb. 2.11. for which **c.** he is not ashamed
   aition.
Lu. 23. 22. I have found no **c.** of death
Act. 19.40. there being no **c.** whereby
   logos.
Mat.5.32. saving for the **c.** of fornication
   dia. [accu.]
Jo. 12.18. For this **c.** the people also
   27. for this **c.** came I unto this
Ro.13. 6. For *for* this **c.** pay ye tribute
   15.9. For this **c.** I will confess to
1Co. 4.17. For this **c.** have I sent unto
   11.10. For this **c.** ought the woman
   30. For this **c.** many are weak
Col. 1. 9. For this **c.** we also, since the
1Th. 2.13. For this **c.** also thank we God
   3. 5. For this **c.** when I could no
2Th. 2.11. *for* this **c.** God shall send
1Ti. 1.16. *for* this **c.** I obtained mercy
Heb.9.15. *for* this **c.** he is the mediator
   heneka.
Mat.19.5. For this **c.** shall a ; Mar.10.7
Act.26.21. *For* these **c**-*s* the Jews caug.
2Co. 7.12. not *for* his **c.** that had done
   the wrong, nor *for* his **c.** that
   charin.
Eph.3. 1. *For* this **c.** I Paul the prison.
   14. *For* this **c.** I bow my knees
Tit. 1. 5. *For* this **c.** left I thee in Crete
   dio.
Ro.15.22. *For which* **c.** also I have been
2Co. 4.16. *For which* **c.** we faint not
   dōrean.
Jo. 15.25. They hated me *without a* **c.**
   eikē.
Mat.5.22. his brother *without a* **c.**
   lupeō.
2Co. 2. 5. if any *have* **c**-*ed* grief, he
   thriambeuō.
2Co. 2.14. *which* . . **c**-*eth* us *to triumph*

CAUSE, [verb,]   -ed, -eth.
   poieō.
Mat. 5.32.**c**-*eth* her to commit adultery
Jo. 11.37.*have* **c**-*ed* that even this man
Act.15. 3.they **c**-*ed* great joy unto all
Ro. 16.17.mark them *which* **c.** division*s*
Col. 4.16.**c.** that it be read also in
Rev.12.15.that he *might* **c.** her to be
   13.12. beast before him and **c**-*eth*
   15. and **c.** that as many as
   16. And he **c**-*eth* all, both small
   katergazomai.
2Co. 9.11. **c**-*eth* through us thanksgiving
   thanatoō.
Mat.10.21.**c.** them *to be put* ; Mar.13.1,
Lu. 21.16.*shall* they **c.** *to be put to death*

CAVE,   -s.
opē.
Heb.11.38. in dens and c-s of the earth
     spēlaion.
Jo.11.38. It was a c. and a stone lay

CEASE,   -ed,-eth,-ing.
pauomai.
Lu. 8.24. and they c-ed, and there was
   11. 1. when he c-ed, one of his disc.
Act. 5.42. they c-ed not to teach and
   6.13. This man c-eth not to speak
13.10. wilt thou not c. to pervert
20. 1. And after the uproar was c-ed
31. I c-ed not to warn every one
1Co. 13.8. there be tongues, they shall c.
Eph.1.16. c. not to give thanks for you
Col. 1. 9. do not c. to pray for you
Heb.10.2. would they not have c-ed to
1Pet.4. 1. suffered in the flesh hath c-ed
     akatapaustos.
2Pet.2.14. cannot c. from sin ; beguiling
     dialeipō.
Lu. 7.45. hath not c-ed to kiss my feet
     hēsuchazō.
Act.21.14. not be persuaded, we c-ed
     katapauō.
Heb.4.10. he also hath c-ed from his
     katargeō.
Gal. 5.11. is the offence of the cross c-ed
     kopazō.
Mat.14.32. the wind c-ed ; Mar.4.39,6.51
     adialeiptos.
2Ti. 1. 3. that without c-ing I have
     adialeiptōs.
Ro. 1. 9. without c-ing I make mention
1Th. 1. 3. Remembering without c-ing
2.13. thank we God without c-ing
5.17. Pray without c-ing
     ektenēs.
Act.12.5. prayer was made without c-ing

CELESTIAL.
epouranios.
1Co.15.40. There are also c. bodies, and
     but the glory of the c. is one

CENSER.
libanōton.
Rev.8. 3. the altar, having a golden c.
   5. angel took the c., and filled
     thumiatērion.
Heb.9. 4. Which had the golden c., and

CENTURION,   -s.
hekatontarchos.
Mat.8. 5. there came unto him a c.
   8. The c. answered and said
   13. Jesus said unto the c., Go thy
27.54. when the c., and they that
Lu. 7. 2. a certain c.'s servant, who was
   6. the c. sent friends to him
23.47. when the c. saw what was
Act.21.32.took soldiers and c-s
22.25. Paul said unto the c. that
26. When the c. heard that, he
23.17. Paul called one of the c-s
23. he called unto him two c-s
27. 6. there the c. found a ship of
11. the c. believed the master and
43. the c., willing to save Paul
28.16. the c. delivered the prisoners
     hekatontarchēs.
Act.10. 1. a c. of the band called the
22. they said, Cornelius the c.
24.23. commanded a c. to keep Paul
27. 1. a c. of Augustus' band
31. Paul said to the c. and to
     kenturiōn.
Mar.15.39. when the c., which stood
44. and calling unto him the c.
45. when he knew it of the c.

CERTAIN (Sure.)
asphalēs.
Act.25.26. Of whom I have no c. thing
     dēlos.
1Ti. 6. 7. it is c. we can carry nothing
     astateō.
1Co. 4.11. and have no c. dwelling place

CERTAIN, (Particular.)
tis.
Mat.20.20.and desiring a c. thing of
Mar.14.57.And there arose c., and bare
Lu. 8.27. a c. man, which had devils
   9.57. a c. man said unto him, Lord
10.30. a c. man went down from
13. 6. a c. man had a fig-tree
14. 2. there was a c. man before him
16. A c. man made a great supper
15.11. he said, A c. man had two
18. 9. this parable unto c. which
20. 9. A c. man planted a vineyard
24. 1. and c. others with them
24. And c. of them which were
Jo. 5. 5. And a c. man was there, whic.
11. 1. Now a c. man was sick, nam.
Act.3. 2. And a c. man lame from his
8. 9. But there was a c. man, called
12. 1. to vex c. of the church
15. 2. Barnabas, and c. other of th.
24. that c. which went out from
17.28. as c. also of your own poets
34. c. men clave unto him
18. 7. entered into a c. man's house
19.13. Then c. of the vagabond Jews
31. And c. of the chief of Asia   s
23.17. hath a c. thing to tell him
25.14. There is a c. man left in bon d
Gal. 2.12. before that c. came from Jas.
Heb.10.27.But a c. fearful looking for
Jude 4. For there are c. men crept in
(And all other passages in which it oc-
     curs, except the following :—)
     heis.
Mat.8.19. a c. scribe came, and said
Mar.12.42.there came a c. poor widow
Lu. 5.12. when he was in a c. city
17. came to pass on a c. day ; 8.22
     anthrōpos.
Mat.18.23. likened unto a c. king ; 22.2
21.33. There was a c. householder
     (a man, a householder.)
     pou.
Heb.2. 6. one in a c. place testified
4. 4. spake in a c. place of the

CERTAINLY.
ontōs.
Lu.23.47. c. this was a righteous man

CERTAINTY.
asphalēs.
Act. 21.34. he could not know the c. for
22.30. he would have known the c.
     asphaleia.
Lu. 1. 4. mightest know the c. of those

CERTIFY.
gnōrizō.
Gal.1.11. I c. you, brethren, that the

CHAFF.
achuron.
Mat.3.12. he will burn up the c. with
Lu. 3.17. but the c. he will burn with

CHAIN,   -s.
halusis.
Mar. 5. 3. bind him, no, not with c-s
4. fetters and c-s, and the c-s
Lu. 8.29. he was kept bound with c-s
Act. 12. 6. bound with two c-s : and the
7. his c-s fell off from his

Act.21.33. to be bound with two c-s
28.20. I am bound with this c.
2Ti. 1.16. was not ashamed of my c.
Rev.20. 1. bottomless pit and a great c.
     desmos.
Jude 6. reserved in everlasting c-s
     seira.
2Pet.2.4. them into c-s of darkness

CHALCEDONY.
chalkēdōn.
Rev.21.19. the third, a c., the fourth an

CHAMBER,   -s.
huperōon.
Act. 9.37. they laid her in an upper c.
39. brought him into the upper c.
20. 8. many lights in the upper c.
     tameion.
Mat.24.26. behold, he is in the secret c-s

CHAMBERING.
koitē.
Ro.13.13. not in c. and wantonness

CHAMBERLAIN.
koitōn.
Act.12.20. made Blastus the king's c.
     (that was over the bed-chamber.)
     oikonomos.
Ro.16.23. Erastus the c. of the city

CHANCE, [noun.]
sungkuria.
Lu.10.31. by c. there came down a

CHANCE, [verb.]
tungchanō.
1Co.15.37. bare grain, it may c. of wheat

CHANGE, [noun.]
metathesis.
Heb. 7.12. of necessity a c. also of the

CHANGE, [verb,]   -ed.
allattō.
Act. 6.14. shall c. the customs which
Ro. 1.23. c-ed the glory of the
1Co. 15.51. sleep, but we shall all be c-ed
52. and we shall be c-ed
Gal. 4.20. with you now, and to c. my
Heb. 1.12. them up and they shall be c-ed
     metallattō.
Ro. 1.25. Who c-ed the truth of God
26. even their women did c. the
     metaschēmatizō.
Phi.3. 21. Who shall c. our vile body
     metatithēmi.
Heb.7.12. the priesthood being c-ed
     metaballomai.
Act.28.6. they c-ed their minds, and
     metamorphoomai.
2Co.3.18. are c-ed into the same image

CHANGERS.
kollubistēs.
Jo. 2.15. and poured out the c. money
     kermatistēs.
Jo. 2.14. and the c. of money sitting

CHARGE, [noun,]   -s.
paranggelia.
Act.16.24. having received such a c.
1Ti. 1.18. This c. I commit unto thee
     engklēma.
Act.23.29. have nothing laid to his c.
     entellomai.
Mat. 4.6. shall give his ang. c.; Lu.4.10
     eimi epi.
Act.8.27. who had the c. of all her
     engkaleō kata, [gen.]
Ro. 8.33. shall lay anything to the c. of

47

opsōnion.

¹Co. 9. 7. warf. any time at his own c-*s*

dapanaō.

Act.21.24. *be at* c-*s* with them, that

adapanos.

¹Co. 9.18. gospel of Christ *without* c.

CHARGE, [*verb*,]   -*ed*, -*ing.*
paraⁿggellō.

Lu. 5.14. And he c-*ed* him to tell no

8.56. but he c-*ed* them that they

Act.16.23. c-*ing* the jailor to keep them

23.22. *and* c-*ed* him, See thou

¹Ti. 1. 3. that thou *mightest* c. some

7. And these things *give in* c.

6.13. I *give* thee c. in the sight of

17. c. them that are rich in this

diastellomai.

Mat.16.20. Then c-*ed* he his disciples

Mar. 5.43. he c-*ed* them straitly that no

7.36. he c-*ed* them that they should

the more he c-*ed* them, so

8.15. he c-*ed* them, saying, Take

9. 9. he c-*ed* them that they should

Mat.12.16. And c-*ed* them that they

Mar. 3.12. And he straitly c-*ed* them

8.30. And he c-*ed* them that they

10.48. many c-*ed* him that he should

Lu. 9.21. And he *straitly* c-*ed* them

diamarturomai.

¹Ti.5.21. I c. thee before God and the

²Ti.2.14. c-*ing* them before the Lord

4. 1. I c. thee therefore before God

embrimaomai.

Mat.9.30. Jesus *straitly* c-*ed* them

epitassō.

Mar.9.25. I c. thee come out of him, and

martureō.

¹Th.2.11. and c-*ed* every one of you, as a

horkizō.

¹Th. 5.27. I c. you by the Lord that this

bareō.

¹Ti. 5.16. let not the church *be* c-*ed*

CHARGEABLE.
katanarkaō.

²Co.11.9. I *was* c. to no man: for that

epibareō.

¹Th.2. 9. not *be* c. *unto* any; ²Th.3.8.

CHARGER.
pinax.

Mat.14.8. John Baptist's head in a c.

11. was brought in a c., and

Mar.6.25. by and by in a c. the head

28. brought his head in a c. and

CHARIOT,   -*s.*
harma.

Act. 8.28. and sitting in his c. read

reda

Rev.18.13. and horses, and c-*s*, and

CHARITABLY.
kata [*accu.*] agapē.

Ro.14.15. now walkest thou not c.

CHARITY.
agapē.

¹Co. 8. 1. Knowledge puffeth up, but c.

13. 1. of angels, and have not c.

2. mountains, and have not c.

3. to be burned, and have not c.

4. c. suffereth long ; c. envieth

not ; c. vaunteth not itself

8. c. never faileth : but whether

13. now abideth faith, hope, c.

the greatest of these is c.

14. 1. Follow after c., and desire

16.14. your things be done with c.

Col. 3.14. above all these things put on c.

48

---

²Th. 3. 6. tidings of your faith and c.

²Th. 1. 3. the c. of every one of you

¹Ti. 1. 5. command is c. out of a

2.15. in faith and c. and holiness

4.12. in conversation, in c., in spirit

²Ti. 2.22. follow righteousness, faith, c.

3.10. longsuffering, c., patience

Tit. 2. 2. in faith, in c., in patience

¹Pet.4. 8. have fervent c. among your.

c. shall cover the multitude

5.14. one another with a kiss of c.

²Pet.1. 7. to brotherly kindness c.

³John 6. have borne witness of thy c.

Jude 12. spots in your *feasts of* c.

Rev.2.19. I know thy works, and c.

CHASTE.
hagnos.

²Co.11. 2. present you as a c. virgin

Tit. 2. 5. discreet, c., keepers at home

¹Pet.3. 2. behold your c. conversation

CHASTEN,   -*ed*, -*eth.*
paideuō.

¹Co.11.32. we *are* c-*ed* of the Lord, that

²Co. 6. 9. we live ; as c-*ed*, and not

Heb.12.6. the Lord loveth he c-*eth*

7. is he whom the father c-*eth*

10. for a few days c-*ed* us after

Rev. 3.19. as I love, I rebuke and c.

CHASTENING.
paideia.

Heb.12.5. despise not thou the c. of

7. If ye endure c., God dealeth

11. Now no c. for the present

CHASTISE.
paideuō.

Lu.23.16,22. I will therefore c. him

CHASTISEMENT.
paideia.

Heb.12.8. But if ye be without c.

CHEEK.
siagōn.

Mat.5.39. smite thee on the right c.

Lu. 6.29. smiteth thee on the one c.

CHEER.
tharseō.

Mat. 9.2. Son, *be of good* c.; thy sins

14.27. *Be of good* c.; it is I; Mar.6.50.

Jo. 16.33. but *be of good* c.; I have over.

Act.23.11.*Be of good* c., Paul : for as

euthumeō.

Act.27.22. I exhort you *to be of good* c.

25. Wherefore, sirs, *be of good* c.

euthumos.

Act.27.36. Then were they all *of good* c.

CHEERFUL.
hilaros.

²Co. 9. 7. for God loweth a c. giver

CHEERFULLY.
euthumoteron.

Act.24.10. *more* c. answer for myself

CHEERFULNESS.
hilarotēs.

Ro.12. 8. that sheweth mercy, with c.

CHERISHETH.
thalpō.

Eph.5.29. but nourisheth and c. it, even

¹Th. 2. 7. even as a nurse c. her

CHERUBIMS.
cheroubim.

Heb.9. 5. c. of glory shadowing the

CHICKENS.
nossion.

Mat.23.37. as a hen gathereth her c.

CHIEF,
prōtos.

Mat.20.27.whosoever will be c. among

Mar. 6.21. and c. estates of Galilee

Lu. 19.47. and the c. of the people so.

Act.13.50. and the c. men of the city

16.12. which is the c. city of that

17. 4. and of the c. women not a

25. 2. and the c. of the Jews infor.

28. 7. of the c. man of the island

17. Paul called the c. of the Jews

¹Ti. 1. 15. sinners ; of whom I am c.

archōn.

Lu.11.15. through Beelzebub the c. of

14. 1. house of one of the c. Phari.

Jo. 12.42. among the c. *rulers* also many

hēgeomai.

Lu. 22.26. he *that is* c., as he that doth

Act.14.12. he was the c. speaker, the

15.22. c. men among the brethren

asiarchēs.

Act.19.31. certain of the c. *of Asia*

(*See other words with which it is
connected.*)

CHIEFEST.
prōtos.

Mar.10.44.will be the c., shall be serv.

huper lian.

²Co.11. 5. the *very* c. apostles ; 12.11.

CHIEFLY.
prōton.

Ro. 3. 2. c., because that unto them

malista.

Phi. 4.22. c. they that are of Cesar's

²Pet.2.10. But c. them that walk after

CHILD,   -*ren.*
teknon.

Mat.2.18. Rachel weeping for her c-*n*

3. 9. to raise up c-*n* unto; Lu.3.8

7.11. give good gifts unto your c-*n*

10.21. the father the c.: and the c-*n*

11.19. is justified of her c-*n*; Lu.7.35

15.26. not meet to take the c-*n's*

18.25. be sold, and his wife, and c-*n*

19.29. or c-*n*, or lands; Mar.10.29

22.24. If a man die, having no c-*n*

23.37. have gathered thy c-*n* togeth.

27.25. blo. be on us, and on our c-*n*

Mar.7.27. Let the c-*n* first be filled

not meet to take the c-*n's*

10.24. c-*n*, how hard is it for them

30. and c-*n*, and lands, and

12.19. and leave no c-*n*, that his

13.12. and c-*n* shall rise up against

Lu. 1. 7. And they had no c., because

17. hearts of the fathers to the c-*n*

11.13. give good gifts unto your c-*n*

13.34. have gathered thy c-*n* togeth.

14.26. c-*n*, and brethren, and sisters

18.29. or c-*n* for the kingdom of

19.44. and thy c-*n* within thee; and

20.31. and they left no c-*n*, and

23.28. yourselves, and for your c-*n*

Jo. 8.39. If ye were Abraham's c-*n*

11.52. in one, the c-*n* of God that

Act. 2.39. is unto you, and to your c-*n*

7. 5. when as yet he had no c.

13.33. fu. the same unto us their c-*n*

21. 5. our way, with wives and c-*n*

21. not to circumcise their c-*n*

Ro. 8.16. that we are the c-*n* of God

17. And if c-*n* then heirs; heirs

21. the glorious liberty of the c-*n*

Ro. 9. 7. of Abraham, are they all c-n
   8. They which are the c-n of
      these are not the c-n of God
      but the c-n of the promise
1Co. 7.14. else were your c-n unclean
2Co. 6.13. I speak as unto my c-n
  12.14. the c-n ought not to lay up
      but the parents for the c-n
Gal. 4.25. and is in bond. with her c-n
   27. desolate hath many more c-n
   28. as Isaac was, are the c-n of
   31. we are not c-n of the bondw.
Eph.2. 3. were by nature the c-n of
  5. 1. followers of God, as dear c-n
   8. Lord, walk as c, of the light
  6. 1. c-n obey your par.; Col.3.20
   4. provoke not your c-n to
Col. 3.21. Fathers, prov. not your c-n
1Th. 2. 7. as a nurse cherisheth her c-n
  11. as a father doth his c-n
1Ti. 3. 4. having his c-n in subjection
  12. ruling their c-n and their
  5. 4. But if any widow have c-n
Tit. 1. 6. having faithful c-n, not
1Pet.1.14. As obedient c-n, not fashion.
¶Pet.2.14. covetous practices; cursed c-n
1Jo. 3.10. In this the c-n of God and
      and the c-n of the devil
  5. 2. we know that we love the c-n
2John 1. the elect lady and her c-n
   4. that I found of thy c-n walk.
  13. The c-n of thy elect sister
3John 4. to hear that my c-n walk in
  12. 4. to devour her c. as soon as it
   5. c. was caught up unto God

teknion.
Jo. 13.33. Little c-n, yet a little while I
Gal. 4.19. My little c-n, of whom I
1Jo. 2. 1. My little c-n, these things
  12. I write unto you, little c-n
  28. And now, little c-n, abide in
  3. 7. Little c-n, let no man deceive
  18. My little c-n, let us not love
  4. 4. Ye are of God, little c-n, and
  5.21. Little c-n, keep yourselves

huios.
Mat.5. 9. for they shall be called the c-n
  45. that ye may be the c-n of your
  8.12. But the c-n of the kingdom
  13. Can the c-n of the ; Mar.2. 19
  12.27. by whom do your c-n cast
  13.38. the good seed are the c-n of
      but the tares are the c-n
  17.25. of their own c-n, or of strang.
  26. him, then are the c-n free
  20.20. the mother of Zebedee's c-n
  23.15. twofold more the c. of hell
  31. that ye are the c-n of them
  27. 9. they of the c-n of Israel did
  56. the mother of Zebedee's c-n
Lu. 1.16. many of the c-n of Israel shall
  5.34. Can ye make the c-n of the
  6.35. ye shall be the c-n of the
  16. 8. for the c-n of this world are
      wiser than the c-n of light
  20.34. The c-n of this world marry
  36. c-n of God, being the c-n of
Jo. 4.12. and his c-n, and his cattle
  12.36. that ye may be the c-n of
Act. 3.25. Ye are the c-n of the prophets
  5.21. the senate of the c-n of Israel
  7.23. visit his brethren the c-n of
  37. which said unto the c-n of
  9.15. and kings, and the c-n of Isra.
  10.36. God sent unto the c-n of
  13.10. thou c. of the devil, thou
  26. c-n of the stock of Abraham
Ro. 9.26. called the c-n of the living G.
  27. Though the number of the c-n
1Co. 3. 7. so that the c-n of Israel could
  13. that the c-n of Israel could

Gal. 3. 7. the same are the c n of Abra.
  26. ye are all the c-n of God
Eph.2. 2. c-n of disob.; 5.6; Col.3.6
1Th. 5. 5. the c-n of light, and the c-n of
Heb.11.22.the departing of the c-n of
  12. 5. unto you as unto c-n
Rev.2.14. before the c-n of Israel, to
  7. 4. of all the tribes of the c-n of
  12. 5. she brought forth a man c.
  21.12. the twelve tribes of the c-n of

paidion.
Mat. 2. 8. diligently for the young c.
  9. over where the young c. was
  11. they saw the young c. with
  13, 20.Arise, and take the young c.
      Herod will seek the young c.
  14, 21. took the young c. and his
  20. which sought the young c.'s
  14.21. beside women and c-n; 15.38
  18. 2. And Jesus called a little c.
  3. and become as little c-n, ye
  4. humble himself as this little c.
  5. receive one such little c. in
  19.13. brought unto him little c-n
  14. Jesus said, Suffer little c-n
Mar.7.28. table eat of the c-n's crum.
  9.24. straight. the father of the c.
  36. And he took a c.,and set him
  37. receive one of such c-n in
  10.13. brought young c-n to him
  14. Suffer the little c-n ; Lu.18.16
  15. of God as a little c. ; Lu.18.17
Lu. 1.59. to circumcise the c.; and th.
  66. What manner of c. shall this
  76. And thou, c., shalt be called
  80. And the c. grew, and ; 2.40
  2.17. told them concerning this c.
  21. for the circumcising of the c.
  27. parents brought in the c. Jes.
  7.32. unto c-n sitting in the
  9.47. took a c.,and set him by him
  48. Whosoever shall receive this c.
  11. 7. my c-n are with me in bed
Jo. 4.49. Sir, come down ere my c. die
  16.21. as she is delivered of the c.
  21. 5. c-n, have ye any meat
1Co.14.20. be not c-n in understanding
Heb.2.13. Behold I and the c-n which
  14. Forasmuch then as the c-n
  11.23. they saw he was a proper c.
1Jo. 2.13. I write unto you, little c-n
  18. Little c-n, it is the last

pais.
Mat.2.16. and slew all the c-n that
  17.18. and the c. was cured from
  21.15. and the c-n crying in the
Lu. 2.43. the c. Jesus tarried behind in
  9.42. and healed the c., and deliv.
Act.4.27. against thy holy c. Jesus
  30. name of thy holy c. Jesus

paidiothen.
Mat.11.16. It is like unto c-n sitting

paidiothen.
Mar.9.21. unto him? And he said, Of a c.

nēpios.
1Co.13.11. I was a c., I spake as a c.,
      as a c., I thought as a c.
Gal. 4. 1. the heir, as long as he is a c.
  3. when we were c-n, were in
Eph.4.14. be no more c-n, tossed to

brephos.
Act.7.19. they cast out their young c-n
2Ti. 3.15. from a c. thou hast known

echō en gastēr.
Mat. 1.18. she was found with c.
  23. Beh., a virgin shall be with c.
  24.19. with c.; Mar. 13.17; Lu.21.23
1Th. 5. 3. travail upon woman with c.
Rev.12. 2. she being with c. cried

engkuos.
Lu. 2. 5. wife, being great with c.

nēpiazō.
1Co.14.20. howbeit in malice be ye c-n

huiothesia.
Eph.1. 5. us unto the adoption of c-n

teknogoneō.
1Ti. 5.14. youn. women marry, bear c-n

teknotropheō.
1Ti. 5.10. if she have brought up c-n

ateknos.
Lu.20.28. he die without c-n that his
  29. a wife, and died without c-n

philoteknos.
Tit. 2. 4. husbands, to love their c-n

CHILDBEARING.
teknogonia.
1Ti. 2.15. she shall be saved in c., if

CHILDISH.
nēpios.
1Co. 13.11. a man I put away c. things
      (the [things] of the child.)

CHILDLESS.
ateknos.
Lu.20.30. to wife, and he died c.

CHOICE.
eklegomai.
Act.15. 7. God made c. among us, that

CHOKE,   -ed.
sumpnigō.
Mat.13.22.deceitfulnees of riches c. the
Mar.4. 7. and c-ed it, and it yielded no
  19. entering in, c. the word, and
Lu. 8.14. go forth, and are c-ed with car.

apopnigō.
Mat.13.7. thorns sprung up, and c-ed
Lu. 8. 7. sprang up with it, and c-ed it
  33. into the lake, and were c-ed

pnigō.
Mar.5.13. thousand, and were c-ed in

epipnigō.
Lu. 8. 7. sprang up with it, and c-ed it

CHOOSE,   -ing, -ose, -osen.
eklegomai.
Mar.13.20.elect's sake, whom he hath c-n
Lu. 6.13. of them he c-o twelve, whom
  10.42. Mary hath c-n that good part
  14. 7. they c-o out the chief rooms
Jo. 6.70. Have not I c-n you twelve
  13.18. I know whom I have c-n : but
  15.16. have not c-n me, but I have c-n
  19. I have c-n you out of the wor.
Act. 1. 2. the apostles whom he had c-n
  24. of these two thou hast c-n
  6. 5. they c-o Stephen, a man full
  13.17. c-o our fathers, and exalted ;
  25. to send c-n men
1Co. 1.27. God hath c-n the foolish things
      God hath c-n the weak
  28. are despised, hath God c-n
Eph.1. 4. as he hath c-n us in him befo.
Jas. 2. 5. Hath not God c-n the poor of

epilegomai.
Act.15.40.Paul c-o Silas, and departed

eklektos.
Mat.20.16.many be called, but few c-n
  22.14. are called, but few are c-n
Lu.23.35. if he be Christ, the c-n of God
Ro. 16.13.Salute Rufus c-n in the Lord
1Pet.2. 4. but c-n of God, and precious
  9. ye are a c-n generation, a roy.
Rev.17.14.are called, and c-n, and faith.

eklogē.
Act. 9.15. he is a c-n vessel unto me
      (a vessel of choice to me.)

haireomai.
Phil. 1.22.yet what I shall c. I wot not

49

Th. 2.13.*hath* from the beginning **c**-*n*
Heb.11.25.**c**-*ing* rather to suffer afflicti.
hairetizō.
Mat.12.18.my servant, whom I *have* **c**-*n*
procheirizomai.
Act.22.14.*hath* **c**-*n* thee, that thou sh.
cheirotoneō.
2Co. 8.19. *who was* also **c**-*n* of the chur.
procheirotoneō.
Act.10.41.unto witnesses **c**-*n before* of
stratologeō.
2Ti. 2. 4. *who hath* **c**-*n* him *to be a soldi.*

CHRIST,   -'s.
christos.
Mat.1.16. Jesus, who is called **c**.
  Mat.27.17.22.
  17. unto **c**. are fourteen generat.
 2. 4. them where **c**. should be bo.
11. 2. in the prison the works of **c**.
16.16. Thou art the **c**.
  Mar.8.29; Lu.22.67.
  20. that he was Jesus the **c**.
22.42. What think ye of **c**.? whose
23. 8,10.one is your Master, even **c**.
24. 5. my name, saying, I am **c**.
  23. Lo, here is **c**., or there
26.63. whether thou be the **c**., the
  68. Prophesy unto us, thou **c**.
Mar.9.41. because ye belong to **c**., veri.
12.35. How say the scribes that **c**. is
13.21. Lo, here is **c**.; or, lo, he is
14.61. Art thou the **c**., the Son of
15.32. Let **c**. the King of Israel des.
Lu. 2.11. a Saviour, which is **c**. the Lo.
  26. he had seen the Lord's **c**.
 3.15. whether he were the **c**., or
 4.41. for they knew that he was **c**.
 9.20. answering, said, The **c**. of G.
20.41. they that **c**. is David's son
23. 2. saying that he himself is **c**.
  35. if he be **c**., the chosen of God
  39. If thou be **c**., save thyself
24.26. Ought not **c**. to have suffered
  46. thus it behoved **c**. to suffer
Jo. 1.20. I am not the **c**.; 3.28
  25. if thou be not that **c**., nor
  41. being interpreted, the **c**.
 4.25. cometh, which is called **c**.
  29. ever I did, is not this the **c**.
  42. this is indeed the **c**., the Sav.
 6.69. sure that thou art that **c**.
 7.26. indeed that this is the very **c**.
  27. when **c**. cometh, no man
  31. When **c**. cometh, will he do
  41. This is the **c**. But some
     Shall **c**. come out of Galilee
  42. **c**. cometh of the seed of
 9.22. confess that he was **c**.
10.24. If thou be the **c**., tell us
11.27. I believe that thou art the **c**.
12.34. that **c**. abideth for ever; and
20.31. believe that Jesus is the **c**.
Act.2.30. raise up **c**. to sit on his
  36. crucified, both Lord and **c**.
 3.18. prophets, that **c**. should suffer
 4.26. the Lord, and against his **c**.
 8. 5. and preached **c**. unto them
 9.20. preached **c**. in the synagogues
  22. proving that this is very **c**.
17. 3. **c**. must needs have suffered
    whom I preach unto you, is **c**.
18. 5,28. that Jesus was **c**.
24.24. concerning the faith in **c**.
26.23. That **c**. should suffer, and
Ro. 1.16. ashamed of the gospel of **c**.
 5. 6. in due time **c**. died for the
  8. yet sinners, **c**. died for us
 6. 4. that like as **c**. was raised up
  8. if we be dead with **c**., we bel.
  9. Knowing that **c**. being raised
 7. 4. law by the body of **c**.; that ye
50

Ro. 8. 9. have not the Spirit of **c**., he is
  10. if **c**. be in you, the body
  11. he that raised up **c**. from the
  17. joint-heirs with **c**.; if so be
  34. It is **c**. that died, yea, rather
  35. from the love of Christ? shall
 9. 1. say the truth in **c**., I lie not
  3. accursed from **c**. for my breth.
  5. **c**. came, who is over all, God
10. 4. **c**. is the end of the law for
  6. to bring **c**. down from above
  7. bring up **c**. again from the
12. 5. one body in **c**., and every
14. 9. **c**. both died, and rose, and
  10. judgment-seat of **c**.; 2Co.5.10.
  15. for whom **c**. died; 1Co.8.11.
  18. that in these things serveth **c**.
15. 3. **c**. pleased not himself; but
  7. as **c**. also received us, to the
  18. which **c**. hath not wrought
  19. fully preached the gospel of **c**.
  20. where **c**. was named, lest
  29. blessing of the gospel of **c**.
16. 5. first-fruits of Achaia unto **c**.
  7. also were in **c**. before me
  9. our helper in **c**., and Stachys
  10. Salute Apelles approved in **c**.
  16. churches of **c**. salute you
1Co. 1. 6. testimony of **c**. was confirmed
  12. and I of Cephas; and I of **c**.
  13. Is **c**. divided? was Paul cruci.
  17. **c**. sent me not to baptize, but
    lest the cross of **c**. should
  23. But we preach **c**. crucified
  24. **c**. the power of God, and the
 2.16. But we have the mind of **c**.
 3. 1. even as unto babes in **c**.
  23. ye are **c**.'s; and **c**. is God's
 4. 1. ministers of **c**., and stewards
  10. for **c**.'s sake, but ye are wise
    in **c**.; we are weak, but ye
  15. instructors in **c**., yet have ye
  17. which be in **c**., as I teach
 5. 7. **c**. our passover is sacrificed
 6.15. members of **c**.? shall I then
    take the members of **c**. and
 7.22. being free, is **c**.'s servant
 8.12. conscience, ye sin against **c**.
 9.12. should hinder the gospel of **c**.
  18. make the gospel of **c**. without
  21. but under the law to **c**.
10. 4. them; and that Rock was **c**.
  9. Neither let us tempt **c**., as
  16. the blood of **c**.? The bread
    communion of the body of **c**.
11. 1. even as I also am of **c**.
  3. of every man is **c**.; and the
    and the head of **c**. is God
12.12. are one body, so also is **c**.
  27. ye are the body of **c**., and
15. 3. **c**. died for our sins, according
  12. if **c**. be preached that he rose
  13. dead, then is **c**. not risen
  14. if **c**. be not risen, then is
  15. he raised up **c**.: whom he
  16. rise not, then is not **c**. raised
  17. if **c**. be not raised, your faith
  18. which are fallen asleep in **c**.
  19. only we have hope in **c**., we
  20. now is **c**. risen from the
  22. in **c**. shall all be made alive
  23. **c**. the first-fruits; afterward
    they that are **c**.'s at his coming
2Co. 1. 5. sufferings of **c**. abound in us
    consolat. also aboundeth by **c**.
  21. with you in **c**., and hath ano.
2.10. gave I it in the person of **c**.
  12. **c**.'s gospel, and a door was
  14. causeth us to triumph in **c**.
  15. unto God a sweet savour of **c**.
  17. of God speak we in **c**.
 3. 3. epistle of **c**. ministered by us

2Co. 3. 4. we through **c**. to God-ward
  14. which vail is done away in **c**.
 4. 4. the glorious gospel of **c**., who
 5.14. the love of **c**. constraineth
  16. known **c**. after the flesh, yet
  17. man be in **c**., he is a new
  19. God was in **c**., reconciling
  20. we are ambassadors for **c**.
    in **c**.'s stead, be ye reconciled
 6.15. hath **c**. with Belial? or what
 8.23. churches, and the glory of **c**.
 9.13. unto the gospel of **c**., and for
10. 1. meekness and gentleness of **c**.
  5. thought to the obedience of **c**.
  7. trust to himself that he is **c**.'s
    is **c**.'s, even so are we **c**.'s
  14. preaching the gospel of **c**.
11. 2. you as a chaste virgin to **c**.
  3. the simplicity that is in **c**.
  10. truth of **c**. is in me, no man
  13. themselves into the apo. of **c**.
  23. Are they ministers of **c**.
12. 2. a man in **c**. above fourteen
  9. power of **c**. may rest upon
  10. distresses for **c**.'s sake; for
  19. before God in **c**.: but we do
13. 3. of **c**. speaking in me, which
Gal. 1. 6. grace of **c**. unto another gosp.
  7. would pervert the gospel of **c**.
  10. should not be the serva. of **c**.
  22. of Judea which were in **c**.
 2.16. justified by the faith of **c**.
  17. we seek to be justified by **c**.
    is therefore **c**. the minister
  20. I am crucified with **c**.: never.
    c. liveth in me: and the life
  21. law, then **c**. is dead in vain
 3.13. **c**. hath redeemed us from
  16. And to thy seed, which is **c**.
  17. of God in **c**., the law, which
  24. bring us unto **c**., that we
  27. baptiz. into **c**. have put on **c**.
  29. if ye be **c**.'s, then are ye
 4. 7. then an heir of God throu. **c**.
  19. until **c**. be formed in you the
 5. 1. in the liberty wherewith **c**.
  2. **c**. shall profit you nothing
  4. **c**. is become of no effect unto
  24. are **c**.'s have crucified the
 6. 2. and so fulfil the law of **c**.
  12. persecution for the cross of **c**.
Eph.1. 3. in heavenly places in **c**.
  10. all things in **c**., both which
  12. glory, who first trusted in **c**.
  20. Which he wrought in **c**.
 2. 5. quickened us together with **c**.
  12. without **c**., being aliens from
  13. made nigh by the blood of **c**.
 3. 4. knowledge in the myst. of **c**.
  6. partakers of his promise in **c**.
  8. unsearchable riches of **c**.
  17. **c**. may dwell in your hearts
  19. know the love of **c**., which
 4. 7. measure of the gift of **c**.
  12. edifying of the body of **c**.
  13. stature of the fulness of **c**.
  15. which is the head, even **c**.
  20. ye have not so learned **c**.
  32. God for **c**.'s sake hath forgiv.
 5. 2. as **c**. also hath loved us
  5. kingdom of **c**. and of God
  14. **c**. shall give thee light
  23. **c**. is the head of the church
  24. the church is subject unto **c**.
  25. even as **c**. also loved the
  32. concerning **c**. and the church
 6. 5. singl. of your heart, as unto **c**.
Eph.6. 6. but as the servants of **c**., do.
Phi. 1.10. offence till the day of **c**.
  13. So that my bonds in **c**. are
  15. Some indeed preach **c**. even
  16. The one preach **c**. of content.

Phi. 1.18. in truth, **c.** is preached; and
20. **c.** shall be magnified in my
21. For to me to live is **c.**, and
23. and to be with **c.**, which
27. becometh the gospel of **c.**
29. given in the behalf of **c.**
2. 1. therefore any consolation in **c.**
16. rejoice in the day of **c.**
30. Because for the work of **c.**
3. 7. those I counted loss for **c.**
8. but dung, that I may win **c.**
9. is through the faith of **c.**
18. enemies of the cross of **c.**
4.13. **c.** which strengtheneth me
Col. 1. 2. and faithful brethren in **c.**
7. a faithful minister of **c.**
24. the afflictions of **c.** in my
27. **c.** in you, the hope of glory
2. 2. and of the Father, and of **c.**
5. stedfastness of your faith in **c.**
8. of the world, and not after **c.**
11. flesh by the circumcision of **c.**
17. but the body is of **c.**
20. if ye be dead with **c.** from
3. 1. If ye then be risen with **c.**
where **c.** sitteth on the right
3. life is hid with **c.** in God
4. When **c.**, who is our life
11. but **c.** is all, and in all
13. even as **c.** forgave you, so also
16. Let the word of **c.** dwell in you
4. 3. to speak the mystery of **c.**
12. a servant of **c.**, saluteth you
¹Th. 2. 6. burden. as the apostles of **c.**
3. 2. labourer in the gospel of **c.**
4.16. the dead in **c.** shall rise first
²Th. 2. 2. as that the day of **c.** is at hand
3. 5. into the patient waiting for **c.**
¹Ti. 2. 7. I speak the truth in **c.**, and lie
5.11. wax wanton against **c.**, they
²Ti. 2.19. nameth the name of **c.**, depart
Phile. 8. might be much bold in **c.**
Heb.3. 6. but **c.** as a son over his own.
14. we are made partakers of **c.**
5. 5. So also **c.** glorified not
6. 1. of the doctrine of **c.**, let us
9.11. But **c.** being come an High
14. more shall the blood of **c.**
24. For **c.** is not entered into the
28. So **c.** was once offered to bear
11.26. Esteeming the reproach of **c.**
¹Pet.1.11. the Spirit of **c.** which was in
beforehand the sufferings of **c.**
19. with the precious blood of **c.**
2.21. because **c.** also suffered for
3.16. your good conversation in **c.**
18. For **c.** also hath once suffered
4. 1. Forasmuch then as **c.** hath
13. partakers of **c.**'s sufferings
14. for the name of **c.**, happy
5. 1. of the sufferings of **c.**, and
¹Jo. 2.22. denieth that Jesus is the **c.**
²Jo. 9. not in the doctrine of **c.**
abideth in the doctrine of **c.**
Rev.11.15.our Lord, and of his **c.**
12.10. and the power of his **c.**
20. 4. lived and reigned with **c.**
6. priests of God and of **c.**

pseudochristos.
Mat.24.24. For there shall arise *false* **c-s**
Mar.13.22. For *false* **c-s** and false prop.
(See *Jesus*, in Appendix.)

CHRISTIAN,   -s.
christianos.
Act. 11.26. disciples were called **c-s** first
Act. 26.28. persuadest me to be a **c.**
¹Pet. 4.16. if any man suffer as a **c.**

CHRYSOLITE.
chrusolithos.
Rev.21.20. the seventh, **c.**; the eighth

CHRYSOPRASUS.
chrusoprasos.
Rev.21.20. the tenth a **c.**; the eleventh

CHURCH,   -es.
ekklēsia.
Mat.16.18.this rock I will build my **c.**
18.17.hear them tell it unto the **c.**
if he neglect to hear the **c.**
Act. 2.47. the Lord added to the **c.**daily
5.11. fear came upon all the **c.**
7.38. this is he, that was in the **c.**
8. 1. the **c.** which was at Jerusalem
3. he made havock of the **c.**
9.31. Then had the **c-es** rest throu.
11.22. the **c.** which was in Jerusalem
26. assemb.themselves with the **c.**
12. 1. to vex certain of the **c.**
5. without ceasing of the **c.** unto
13. 1. Now there were in the **c.**
14.23. elders in every **c.**, and had
27. had gathered the **c.** together
15. 3. brought on their way by the **c.**
4. they were received of the **c.**
22. and elders, with the whole **c.**
41. Cilicia, confirming the **c-es**
16. 5. so were the **c-es** established
18.22. gone up, and saluted the **c.**
20.17. called the elders of the **c.**
28. to feed the **c.** of God, which
Ro.16. 1. sister wh. is a servant of the **c.**
4. all the **c-es** of the Gentiles
5. the **c.** that is in their house
16. The **c-es** of Christ salute you
23. mine host, and of the whole **c.**
¹Co. 1. 2. Unto the **c.** of God which is
4.17. teach every where in every **c.**
6. 4. are least esteemed in the **c.**
7.17. and so ordain I in all **c-es**
10.32. Gentiles, nor to the **c.** of God
11.16. neither the **c-es** of God
18. ye come together in the **c.**
22. or despise ye the **c.** of God
12.28. God hath set some in the **c.**
14. 4. prophesieth edifieth the **c.**
5. the **c.** may receive edifying
12. excel to the edifying of the **c.**
19. in the **c.** I had rather speak
23. the whole **c.** be come togeth.
28. let him keep silence in the **c.**
33. as in all **c-es** of the saints
34. keep silence in the **c-es**: for
35. for women to speak in the **c.**
15. 9. I persecuted the **c.** of God
16. 1. order to the **c-es** of Galatia
19. The **c-es** of Asia salute you
with the **c.** that is in their
²Co. 1. 1. unto the **c.** of God which is
8. 1. on the **c-es** of Macedonia
18. gospel throughout all the **c-es**
19. also chosen of the **c-es** to
23. the messengers of the **c-es**
24. to them, and before the **c-es**
11. 8. I robbed other **c-es**, taking
28. daily the care of all the **c-es**
12.13. were inferior to other **c-es**
Gal. 1. 2. unto the **c-es** of Galatia
13. I persecuted the **c.** of God
22. face unto the **c-es** of Judæa
Eph.1.22. head over all things to the **c.**
3.10. might be known by the **c.**
21. glory in the **c.** by Christ Jes.
5.23. Christ is the head of the **c.**
24. the **c.** is subject unto Christ
25. as Christ also loved the **c.**
27. to himself a glorious **c.**, not
29. it even as the Lord the **c.**
32. concerning Christ and the **c.**
Phi.3. 6. Concern. zeal, persec. the **c.**
4.15. no **c.** communicated with me
Col. 1.18. the head of the body, the **c.**

Col. 1.24. body's sake, which is the **c.**
4.15. the **c.** which is in his house
16. in the **c.** of the Laodiceans
¹Th. 1. 1. **c.** of the Thessal.; ²Th.1.1
2.14. followers of the **c-es** of God
²Th. 1. 4. in you in the **c-es** of God
¹Ti. 3. 5. take care of the **c.** of God
15. the **c.** of the living God
5.16. and let not the **c.** be charged
Phile. 2. and to the **c.** in thy house
Heb.2.12. in the midst of the **c.** will I
12.23. assembly and **c.** of the firstb.
Jas. 5.14. call for the elders of the **c.**
³John 6. of thy charity before the **c.**
9. I wrote unto the **c.**, but Dio.
10. casteth them out of the **c.**
Rev.1. 4. John to the seven **c-es** in Asia
11. unto the seven **c-es**'which are
20. the angels of the seven **c-es**
sawest, are the seven **c-es**
2. 1. the angel of the **c.** of Ephesus
8. Smyr.; 12. Perg.; 18. Thya.
3.1.Sard.; 7.Philad.; 14.the La.
7. Spirit sayeth unto the **c-es**;
17, 29; 3. 6, 13, 22
23. all the **c-es** shall know that I
22.16. you these things in the **c-es**
hierosulos.
Act.19.37. are neither *robbers of* **c-es**

CINNAMON.
kinamōmon.
Rev.18.13. And **c.**, and odours, and

CIRCUMCISE,   -ed, -ing.
peritemnō.
Lu. 1.59. they came *to* **c.** the child; and
2.21. accomplished for the **c-**ing of
Jo. 7.22. ye on the sabbath day **c.** a man
Act. 7. 8. and **c-ed** him the eighth day
15. 1. Except ye be **c-ed** after the
5. That it was needful *to* **c.** them
24. saying, Ye must be **c-ed** and
16. 3. and took and **c-ed** him because
21.21. saying that they ought not *to* **c.**
¹Co. 7.18. Is any man called *being* **c-ed**
uncircum.? *let* him not be **c-ed**
Gal. 2. 3. Greek, was compelled *to be* **c-ed**
5. 2. that if ye *be* **c-ed**, Christ shall
3. to every man *that is* **c-ed**, that
6.12. they constrain you *to be* **c-ed**
13. they themselves *who are* **c-ed**
desire *to have* you **c-ed** that
Col. 2.11. In whom also ye are **c-ed** with
peritomē.
Phil.3. 5. **c-ed** the eighth day of the
akrobustia.
Ro. 4.11. though they be *not* **c-ed**: that

CIRCUMCISION.
peritomē.
Jo. 7.22. gave unto you **c.**; not because
23. on the sabbath day receive **c.**
Act. 7. 8. gave him the covenant of **c.**
10.45. of the **c.** which believed
11. 2. they that were of the **c.**
Ro. 2.25. For **c.** verily profiteth, if thou
thy **c.** is made uncircumcision
26. uncircum. be counted for **c.**
27. by the letter and **c.** dost
28. is that **c.**, which is outward
29. and **c.** is that of the heart
3. 1. what profit is there of **c.**
30. shall justify the **c.** by faith
4. 9. upon the **c.** only, or upon
10. when he was in **c.** or in
not in **c.** but in uncircumcision
11. received the sign of **c.** a seal
12. of **c.** to them who
are not of the **c.** only
15. 8. was a minister of the **c.** for the
¹Co. 7.19. **c.** is nothing, and uncircum.

51

Gal. 2. 7. the gospel of the c. was
     8. to the apostleship of the c.
     9. heathen, and they unto the c.
    12. them which were of the c.
   5. 6. c. availeth anything; 6.15
    11. if I yet preach c., why do
Eph.2.11. called the c. in the flesh, made
Phi. 3. 3. For we are the c., which
Col. 2.11. with the c. made without
      of the flesh by the c. of Christ
   3.11. c. nor uncircum., Barbarian
   4.11. who are of the c. These only
Tit. 1.10. specially they of the c.

CIRCUMSPECTLY.
akribōs.
Eph.5.15. that ye walk c., not as fools

CITIZEN,   -s.
politēs.
Lu.15.15. joined himself to a c. of that
   19.14. But his c-s hated him, and
Act.21.39.a c. of no mean city : and I

CITIES.
polis.
Mat.9.35. went about all the c. and
   10.23. over the c. of Israel, till
   11. 1. teach and to preach in their c.
    20. began he to upbraid the c.
   14.13. him on foot out of the c.
Mar.6.33. ran afoot thither out of all c.
    56. into villages, or c., or country
Lu. 4.43. the kingdom of God to other c.
   13.22. he went through the c. and
   19.17. have thou authority over ten c.
    19. Be thou also over five c.
Act. 5.16. out of the c. round about
   8.40. he preached in all the c.
   14. 6. Lystra and Derbe, c. of
   16. 4. they went through the c.
   26.11. them even unto strange c.
²Pet.2. 6. turning the c. of Sodom and
Jude   7. and the c. about them
Rev.16.19.and the c. of the nations fell

CITY.
polis.
Mat.2.23. c. Nazareth ; Lu.2.4,39
   4. 5. holy c.; 27.53; Rev.21.2,22.19
   5.14. A c. that is set on an hill
    35. for it is the c. of the great
   8.33. went their ways into the c.
    34. behold, the whole c. came out
   9. 1. into his own c.; Lu.2.3
   10. 5. into any c. of the Samaritans
    11. into whatsoever c.; Lu.10.8,10
    14. depart out of that house or c.
    15. for that c.; Mar.6.11; Lu.10.12
    23. they persecute you in this c.
   12.25. and every c. or house divided
   21.10. all the c. was moved, saying
    17. went out of the c.; Mar.11.19
    18. as he returned into the c.
   22. 7. and burned up their c.
   23.34. persecute them from c. to c.
   26.18. Go into the c.; Mar.14.13
   28.11. of the watch came into the c.
Mar.1.33. And all the c. was gathered
    45. openly enter into the c.
   5.14. told it in the c.; Lu.8.34
   14.16. and came into the c. and
    26. a c. of Galilee; 4.31
Lu. 1.39. with haste, into a c. of Juda
   2. 4. into Judea, unto the c. of Da.
    11. in the c. of David a Saviour
   4.29. and thrust him out of the c.
     hill whereon their c. was bui.
   5.12. when he was in a certain c.
   7.11. he went into a c. called Nain
    12. nigh to the gate of the c.
     much people of the c. was
52

Lu. 7.37. behold, a woman in the c.
   8. 1. throughout every c. and vill.
    4. come to him out of every c.
    27. there met him out of the c.
    39. pub. throughout the whole c.
   9. 5. when ye go out of that c.
    10. belonging to the c. called Be.
   10. 1. into every c. and place
    11. Even the very dust of your c.
   14.21. streets and lanes of the c.
   18. 2. There was in a c. a judge
    3. there was a widow in that c.
   19.41. beheld the c., and wept over
   22.10. when ye are enter. into the c.
   23.19. certain sedit. made in the c.
    51. Arimathea, a c. of the Jews
   24.49. tarry ye in the c. of Jerusalem
Jo. 1.44. the c. of Andrew and Peter
   4. 5. Then cometh he to a c. of Sa.
    8. unto the c. to buy meat
    28. and went her way into the c.
    30. Then they went out of the c.
    39. the Samaritans of that c. be.
   11.54. into a c. called Ephraim
   19.20. crucified was nigh to the c.
Act.7.58. And cast him out of the c.
   8. 5. went down to the c. of Sam.
    8. there was great joy in that c.
    9. in the same c. used sorcery
   9. 6. Arise, and go into the c.
   10. 9. and drew nigh unto the c.
   11. 5. I was in the c. of Joppa pray.
   12.10. that leadeth unto the c.
   13.44. came almost the whole c. to.
    50. and the chief men of the c.
   14. 4. But the multitude of the c.
    13. which was before their c.
    19. drew him out of the c.
    20. rose up, and came into the c.
    21. preached the gospel to that c.
   15.21. in every c. them that preach
    36. visit our brethren in every c.
   16.12. the chief c. of that part of
     we were in that c. abiding
    13. we went out of the c. by a
    14. purple of the c. of Thyatira
    20. exceedingly trouble our c.
    39. depart out of the c.
   17. 5. set all the c. on an uproar
    16. when he saw the c. wholly
   18.10. I have much people in this c.
   19.29. And the whole c. was filled
    35. how that the c. of the Ephe.
   20.23. H.Ghost witnesseth in every c.
   21. 5. till we were out of the c.
    29. with him in the c., Trophimus
    30. And all the c. was moved
    39. a citizen of no mean c.
   22. 3. brought up in this c., at the
   24.12. in the synagog., nor in the c.
   25.23. principal men of the c.
   27. 8. whereunto was the c. of Lasea
Ro.16.23. Erast. the chamberl. of the c.
²Co.11.26. in perils in the c., in perils
    32. kept the c. of the Damascenes
Tit. 1. 5. ordain elders in every c.
Heb.11.10.For he looked for a c. which
    16. hath prepared for them a c.
   12.22. unto the c. of the living God
   13.14. here have we no continuing c.
Jas. 4.13. we will go into such a c.
Rev.3.12. the name of the c. of my God
   11. 2. and the holy c. shall they
    8. the street of the great c.
    13. and the tenth part of the c.
   14. 8. is fallen, that great c.
    20. trodden without the c.
   16.19. great c. was divided into three
   17.18. is that great c., which reigne.
   18.10,16,19. alas that great c. Bab.
    18. c. is like unto this great c.
    21. that great c. Babylon be thro.

Rev. 20.9.and the beloved c., and fire
   21.10. and shewed me that great c.
    14. And the wall of the c.
    15. golden reed to measure the c.
    16. And the c. lieth foursquare
     he measured the c. with the
    18. the c. was pure gold
    19. founda. of the wall of the c.
    21. and the street of the c. was
    23. the c. had no need of the sun
   22.14. through the gates into the c.
politarchēs.
Act. 17. 6. unto the *rulers of the* c.
    8. and the *rulers of the* c. when

CLAMOUR.
kraugē.
Eph.4.31. and anger, and c., and evil

CLAY.
pēlos.
Jo. 9. 6. and made c. of the spittle, and
     of the blind man with the c.
    11. that is called Jesus, made c.
    14. when Jesus made the c., and
    15. He put c. upon mine eyes, and
Ro. 9.21. the potter power over the c.

CLEAN.
katharos.
Mat.23.26.the outside of them may be c.
   27.59. he wrapped it in a c. linen
Lu. 11.41. behold all things are c. unto
Jo. 13.10. c. every whit : and ye are c.
    11. said he, Ye are not all c.
    15. 3. Now ye are c. through the
Act. 18.6. upon your own heads ; I am c.
Rev.19.8. fine linen, c. and white : for
    14. in fine linen, white and c.
katharizō.
Mat.8. 2. wilt, thou canst *make* me c.
    3. *be* thou c.; Mar.1.41; Lu.5.13
   23.25. for ye *make* c. the outside of
Mar.1.40. canst *make* me c.; Lu.5.12
   11.39. ye Pharisees *make* c. the
ontōs.
²Pet.2.18. those that were c. escaped

CLEANSE,   -ed, -eth, -ing.
katharizō.
Mat.8. 3. imme. his leprosy *was* c-ed
   10. 8. c. the lepers, raise the dead
   11. 5. the lepers *are* c-ed ; Lu.7.22
   23.26. c. first that which is within
Mar.1.42. from him and he *was* c-ed
Lu. 4.27. and none of them *was* c-ed
   17.14. as they went, they *were* c-ed
    17. *Were* there not ten c-ed? but
Act.10.15.What God *hath* c-ed ; 11.9
²Co.7. 1. *let* us c. ourselves from all
Eph.5.26. That he might sanctify *and* c.
Jas. 4. 8. c. your hands, ye sinners
Jo. 1. 7. of Jesus Christ his Son c-*eth*
    9. and to c. us from all unrighte.
katharismos.
Mar.1.44. offer for thy c-*ing*; Lu.5.14

CLEAR,   -ing.
lampros.
Rev.22.1. water of life, c. as crystal
hagnos.
²Co. 7.11. yourselves to be c. in this
katharos.
Rev.21.18. gold, like unto c. glass
apologia.
²Co. 7.11. yea, what c-*ing* of your *selves*
krustallizō.
Rev.21.11. a jasper stone, c. *as crystal*

CLEARLY.
tēlaugōs.
Mar.8.25. restored,and saw every man c.

diablepō.

Mat. 7.5. then *shalt* thou *see* **c**.; Lu.6.42
kathoraō.

Ro. 1.20. *are* **c**. *seen*, being understood

CLEAVE,   *-eth, -ave.*
kollaō.

Lu.10.11. dust out of your city, *which* **c**-*eth*
Act.17.34.certain men **c**-*a* unto him
Ro. 12. 9.is evil; **c**. to that which is
proskollaomai.
Mat.19.5. mother, and *shall* **c**. *to* his
Mar.10.7. mother, and **c**. *to* his wife
prosmenō.
Act.11.23. they would **c**. *unto* the Lord

CLEMENCY.
epieikeia.

Act.24.4. thou wouldst hear us of thy **c**.

CLIMBETH.
anabainō.

Jo. 10.1. **c**. *up* some other way, the

CLOKE.
himation.

Mat.5.40. let him have thy **c**. also
Lu. 6.29. him that taketh away thy **c**.
prophasis.
Jo.15.22. they have no **c**. for their sin
[1]Th. 2. 5. nor a **c**. of covetousness
epikalumma.
[1]Pet.2.16. using your liberty for a **c**. of
phailonēs.
[2]Ti. 4.13. The **c**. that I left at Troas

CLOSE,   *-ed.*
kammuō.

Mat.13.15. their eyes they *have* **c**-*ed*
Act. 28.27. their eyes *have* they **c**-*ed*
ptussō.
Lu. 4.20. And he **c**-*ed* the book, and he
asson.
Act.27.13. thence they sailed **c**. by Crete

CLOSET,   *-s.*
tameion.

Mat.6. 6. prayest, enter into thy **c**.
Lu.12. 3. have spoken in the ear in **c**-*s*

CLOTH,   *-es.*
rakos.

Mat.9.16. new **c**. unto an old garment
Mar.2.21. piece of new **c**. on an old
himation.
Mat.21.7. put on them their **c**-*es*, and
24.18. return back to take his **c**-*es*
26.65. Then the high pr. rent his **c**-*es*
Mar.5.28. If I may touch but his **c**-*es*
30. said, Who touched my **c**-*es*
15.20. and put his own **c**-*es* on him
Lu. 8.27. and ware no **c**-*es*, neither
19.36. they spread their **c**-*es* in the
Act. 7.58. witnesses laid down their **c**-*es*
14.14. they rent their **c**-*es*, and ran
16.22. magistrates rent off their **c**-*es*
22.23. and cast off their **c**-*es*, and
chitōn.
Mar.14.63. the high priest rent his **c**-*es*
sparganoō.
Lu. 2. 7.*wrapped* him *in swaddling* **c**-*es*
12.*wrapped in swaddling* **c**-*es*
sindōn
Mat.27.59. wrapped it in a clean *linen* **c**.
Mar.14.51. having a *linen* **c**. cast about
52. left the *linen* **c**. and fled
othonion.
Lu.24.12. beheld the *linen* **c**-*es* laid by
Jo.19.40. and wound it in *linen* **c**-*es*
20. 5, 6. saw the *linen* **c**-*es* lying
7. not lying with the *linen* **c**-*es*

CLOTHE,   *-ed.*
periballō.

Mat.6.31. Wherewithal shall we be **c**-*ed*
25.36, 38,43. Naked, and ye **c**-*ed*
Mar.16.5. **c**-*ed* in a long white garment
Rev.3. 5. the same *shall be* **c**-*ed* in white
18. raim., that thou *mayest be* **c**-*ed*
4. 4. sitting **c**-*ed* in white raiment
7. 9. Lamb, **c**-*ed* with white robes
10. 1. from heaven, **c**-*ed* with a clo.
11. 3. threescore days, **c**-*ed* in sack.
12. 1. a woman **c**-*ed* with the sun
18.16. city, *that was* **c**-*ed* in fine lin.
19.13. he was **c**-*ed* with a vesture
enduō.
Mar.15.17.They **c**-*ed* him with purple
[2]Co. 5. 3. If so be that *being* **c**-*ed*, we sh.
Rev.1.13. **c**-*ed with* a garment down to
15. 6. **c**-*ed in* pure and white linen
19.14. **c**-*ed in* fine linen, white and
ependuomai.
[2]Co. 5. 2. desiring *to be* **c**-*ed upon*
4. be unclothed, but **c**-*ed upon*
amphiennumi.
Mat.6.30. God so **c** the grass ; Lu.12.28
11. 8. A man **c**-*ed* in soft ; Lu.7.25
himatizomai.
Mar.5.15. sitting, and **c**-*ed*, and in his
Lu. 8.35. sitting at the feet of Jesus **c**-*ed*
endiduskomai.
Lu.16.19. which *was* **c**-*ed* in purple and
engkomboomai.
[1]Pet. 5.5. *be* **c**-*ed with* humility, for G.

CLOTHES, (See *Cloth*.)

CLOTHING, [*noun*.]
esthēs.

Act.10.30. stood before me in bright **c**.
Jas. 2. 3. him that weareth the gay **c**.
enduma.
Mat.7.15. come to you in sheep's **c**.
stolē.
Mar.12.38. which love to go in *long* **c**.

CLOVEN.
diamerizō.

Act. 2. 3. app. unto them **c**. tongues

CLOUD,   *-s.*
nephelē.

Mat.17.5. bright **c**. ov.; Mar.9.7; Lu.9.34
out of the **c**.; Mar.9.7; Lu.9.35
24.30. coming in the **c**-*s* of heaven
Lu. 9.34. as they entered into the **c**.
12.54. When ye see a **c**. rise out of
21.27. coming in a **c**., with power
Act.1. 9. a **c**. received himout of their
1Co. 10.1. fathers were under the **c**.
2. unto Moses in the **c**., and in
1Th. 4.17. together with them in the **c**-*s*
2Pet.2.17. **c**-*s* that are carried with a
Jude 12. **c**-*s* they are without water
Rev. 1. 7. Behold, he cometh with **c**-*s*
10. 1. fr. heaven, clothed with a **c**.
11.12. ascended up to heaven in a **c**.
14.14. white **c**., and upon the **c**.
nephos.
Heb.12.1. so great a **c**. of witnesses

CLUSTERS.
botrus.

Rev.14.18. gather the **c**. *of the vine* of

COALS.
anthrax.

Ro.12.20. heap **c**. *of fire* on his head
anthrakia.
Jo.18.18. who had made a *fire* of **c**.
21.9. they saw a *fire* of **c**. there

COAST,   *-s.*
meros.

Mat.15.21. departed unto the **c**-*s* of
16.13. Jesus came unto the **c**-*s* of
Act. 19. 1. passed through the upper **c**-*s*
horia.
Mat.2.16. and in all the **c**-*s* thereof
8.34. would depart out of their **c**-*s*
15.22. out of the same **c**-*s*, and
39. came into the **c**-*s* of Magdala
19. 1. and came into the **c**-*s* of
Mar.5.17. to depart out of their **c**-*s*
7.31. from the **c**-*s* of Tyre and
the midst of the **c**-*s* of Deca.
10. 1. and cometh into the **c**-*s* of
Act.13.50.expelled them out of their **c**-*s*
chōra.
Act.26.20. throughout all the **c**-*s* of
topos.
Act.27. 2. to sail by the **c**-*s* of Asia
paralios.
Lu. 6.17. from *the sea* **c**. *of* Tyre
parathalassios.
Mat.4.13. Cap.,*which is upon* the sea **c**.

COAT,   *-s.*
chitōn.

Mat.5.40. law, and take away thy **c**.
10.10. neither two **c**-*s*, neither shoes
Mar.6. 9. and not put on two **c**-*s*
Lu. 3.11. He that hath two **c**-*s*, let him
6.29. forbid not to take thy **c**. also
3. neither have two **c**-*s* apiece
Jo. 19.23. **c**. : now the **c**. was without
Act. 9.39. shewing the **c**-*s* and garments
ependutēs.
Jo. 21. 7. girt his *fisher's* **c**. unto him

COCK.
alektōr.

Mat.26.34,75.bef. the **c**. crow; Lu.22.61
74. the **c**. crew ; Mar.14.68 ;
Lu.22.60 ; Jo.18.27
Mar.14.30,72.before the **c**. crow twice
72. the second time the **c**. crew
Lu.22.34. the **c**. shall not crow ; Jo.13.38
alektorophōnia.
Mar.13.35.midnight, or at the **c**-*crowing*

COLD.
psuchos.

Jo. 18.18. a fire of coals ; for it was **c**.
Act. 28 2. rain, and because of the **c**.
2Co.11.27. in fastings often, in **c**. and
psuchros.
Mat.10.42.little ones a cup of **c**. water
Rev.3.15. thou art neither **c**. nor hot
I would thou wert **c**. or hot
16. and neither **c**. nor hot, I will
psuchomai.
Mat.24.12.the love of many *shall wax* **c**.

COLLECTION.
logia.

1Co.16. 1. Now concerning the **c**. for

COLONY.
kolōnia.

Act.16.12.part of Macedonia, and a **c**.

COLOUR,   *-ed.*
kokkinos.

Rev.17.3. sit upon a *scarlet* **c**-*ed* beast
4. in purple and *scarlet* **c**.
prophasis.
Act.27.30. under **c**. as though they wou.

COLT.
pōlos.

Mat.21.2. an ass tied, and a **c**. with her
5. and a **c**. the foal of an ass
7. and the **c**., and put on them

Mar.11.2. shall find a **c.** tied ; Lu. 19.30
  4. found the **c.** tied by the door
  5. What do ye, loosing the **c.**
  7. they brought the **c.** to Jesus
Lu.19.33. as they were loosing the **c.**
  35. cast their garmen. upon the **c.**
Jo. 12.15. cometh sitting on an ass's **c.**

COMB.
kērĭŏn.
Lu. 24.42.broiled fish and of an *honey* **c.**

COME, -est, -eth, -ing, -ame.
erchomai.
Mat.2. 2, 8. and *are* **c.** to worship him
  21. and **c-a** into the land of Israel
 3. 7. the Phar. and Sad. **c.** to his
  11. but he *that* **c-eth** after me is
  14. of thee, and **c-est** thou to me
 5.17. that I *am* **c.** to destroy the
  I *am* not **c.** to destroy, but
  24. and then **c.** *and* offer thy gift
 6.10. Thy kingdom **c.**; Lu.11.2
 7.15. which **c.** to you in sheep's
  25,27.and the floods **c-a**, and the
 8. 9. **c.**, and he **c-eth** ; Lu.7.8
  29. *art* thou **c.** hither to torment
 9.13. for I *am* not **c.** to call the ri.
    Mar.2.17; Lu.5.32
  15. the days *will* **c.**; Mar.2.20
10.13. *let* your peace **c.** upon it
  23. till the Son of man *be* **c.**
  34. that I *am* **c.** to send peace on
  c-a not to send peace, but a
  35. I *am* **c.** to set a man at vari.
11. 3. Art thou he *that should* **c.**
  14. is Elias which was for *to* **c.**
  18. For John **c-a** neither eating
  19. S. of man **c-a** eating; Lu.7.34
12.42. she **c-a** fr. the ut.; Lu.11.31
  44. *when* he is **c.**, he findeth it
13.19. then **c-eth** the wicked one
  25. his enemy **c-a** and sowed
  32. so that the birds of the air **c.**
14.28. bid me **c.** unto thee on the
  29. and he said **c.** And when
16.24. If any m. *will* **c.** af.; Lu.9.23
  27. Son of man shall **c.**; 25.31
  28. see the Son of man **c-ing** in
    24.30 ; Mar.13..6 ; Lu.21.27
17.10. that Elias must first **c.**
  11. Elias truly shall first **c.**, and
  12. that Elias is **c.**; Mar.9.13
18. 7. that offences **c**...by whom
  the offence **c-eth**; Lu.17.1
  11. Son of man is **c.**; Lu.19.10
19.14. forbid them not, *to* **c.**unto me
20.28. **c-a** not to be ministered unto
21. 5. **c-eth** unto thee, meek, and
  9. blessed is he *that* **c-eth** in the
    23,39; Mar.11.10; Lu.13.35;
    19.38; Jo.12.13
  32. For John **c-a** unto you in
  40. lord of the vineyard **c-eth**
22. 3. wed. and they would not **c.**
23.35. That upon you *may* **c.** all the
24. 5. For many shall **c.** in my
  39. until the flood **c-a** and took
  42. what hour your Lord *doth* **c.**
  43. what watch the thief would **c.**
  44. the Son of man **c-eth** ; 25.13
    Lu.12.40; 18.8
  46. whom his lord *when* he **c-eth**
  48. lord del. his **c-ing**; Lu.12.45
25. 6. Behold, the bridegroom **c-eth**
  10. to buy, the bridegroom **c-a**
  27. at my **c-ing** I should have
  36,39.prison, and ye **c-a** unto me
26.64. **c-ing** in the clouds; Mr.14.62
27.49. whetherElias*will***c.**;Mar.15.36
  64. lest his disciples **c.** by night
Mar.1. 7. There **c-eth** one mightier than
  54

Mar.4.22. that it *should* **c.** abroad
 6.31. for there were many **c-ing**
 8.34. Whosoever will **c.** after me
  38. when he **c-eth** in the glory
 9. 1. kingdom of God **c.** with pow.
10.14. the little ch. *to* **c.**; Lu.18.16
  30. in the world *to* **c.** eternal life
  45. **c-a** not to be ministered unto
11. 9. he *that* **c-eth** in the name of
13. 6. For many shall **c.** in my
  36. Lest, **c-ing** suddenly, he find
14.41. it is enough; the hour is **c.**
  45. And *as soon as* he *was* **c.**, he
Lu. 3.16. but one mightier than I **c-eth**
 6.47. *Who* soever **c-eth** to me
 7. 9,20.Art thou he *that should* **c.**
  33. For John the Baptist **c-a** nei.
 8.17. not be known and **c.** abroad
 9.26. when he shall **c.** in his own
  56. *is* not **c.** to destroy men's
10. 1. whither he himself would **c.**
12.36. *when* he **c-eth** and knocketh
  37. lord *when* he **c-eth** shall find
  38. **c.** in the second watch, or **c.**
  43. whom his lord *when* he **c-eth**
  49. I *am* **c.** to send fire on the
14.17. **c.**; for all things are now
  20. and therefore I cannot **c.**
  26. If any man **c.** to me, and hate
  27. bear his cross, and **c.** after
  31. meet him *that* **c-eth** against
15.17. And *when* he **c-a** to himself
  30. as soon as this thy son *was* **c.**
16.28. also **c.** into this place of tor.
17.20. the kingdom of God should **c.**
  The kingdom of God **c-eth** not
  27. the flood **c-a** and destroyed
18. 5. by her continual **c-ing** she
  30. in the world *to* **c.** life everlas.
19.13. unto them, Occupy till I **c.**
  23. at my **c-ing** I might have re.
21. 8. for many shall **c.** in my name
22.18. the kingdom of God shall **c.**
Jo. 1. 7. The same **c-a** for a witness
  9. *that* **c-eth** into the world
  11. He **c-a** unto his own, and
  15,27. He *that* **c-eth** after me
39,46. saith unto them, **c.** and
  They **c-a** and saw where
 3. 2. art a teacher **c.** from God
  8. canst not tell whence it **c-eth**
  19. light is **c.** into the world
  20. neither **c-eth** to the light
  21. he that doeth truth **c-eth** to
  26. all men **c.** to him
  31. He *that* **c-eth** from above all
  he *that* **c-eth** from heaven
 4.16. call thy husband and **c.** hither
  21, 23. the hour **c-eth**, when ye
  25. I know that Messias **c-eth**
  is called Christ : when he *is* **c.**
 5. 7. but while I *am* **c-ing** another
  24. shall not **c.**unto condemnaticn
  25, 28. The hour is **c-ing**
  40. ye will not **c.** to me that ye
  43. I *am* **c.** in my Father's name
  if another shall **c.** in his own
 6.14. prophet *that should* **c.** into
  35. he *that* **c-eth** to me shall never
  37. him *that* **c-eth** to me I will in
  44, 65. No man can **c.** unto me
  45. learned of the Father, **c-eth**
 7.27. when Christ **c-eth**, no man
  28. I am not **c.** of myself, but he
  30. his hour *was* not yet **c.**
  31. When Christ **c-eth**, will he do
34,36. thither ye cannot **c.**
  37. *let* him **c.** unto me, and
  41. shall Christ **c.** out of Galilee
 8.14. for I know whence I **c-a**
  ye cannot tell whence I **c.**
 9. 4. the night **c-eth**, when no man

Jo. 9.39. I *am* **c.** into this world 12.46
  10. 8. All that ever **c-a** before me
  11.27. *which should* **c.** into the
  34. said unto him, Lord, **c.** and see
 14. 6. no man **c-eth** unto the Father
  18. comfortless, I will **c.** *to* you
  23. we *will* **c.** unto him, and
 16.13. he will shew you things *to* **c.**
  18.37. for this cause **c-a** I into the
 21.22, 23. that he tarry till I **c.**
Act. 1.11. shall so **c.** in like manner as
 2.20. notable day of the Lord **c.**
 3.19. times of refreshing shall **c.**
 16.37. but let them **c.** themselves
  39. they **c-a** *and* besought them
 19. 5. the Holy Ghost **c-a** on them
Ro. 3. 8. us do evil, that good *may* **c.**
 7. 9. *when* the commandment **c-a**
1Co.11.26. the Lord's death till he **c.**
  34. will I set in order when I **c.**
 13.10. that which is perfect *is* **c.**
 15.35. with what body do they **c.**
 16. 2. be no gatherings when I **c.**
2Co.12. 1. I *will* **c.** to visions and revel.
Gal. 3.25. But *after that* faith is **c.**
Eph.5. 6. **c-eth** the wrath of G.; Col.3.6
1Th. 1.10. deliv. us from the wrath *to* **c.**
 5. 2. the day of the Lord so **c-eth**
2Th. 1.10. When he shall **c.** to be glori.
 2. 3. except there **c.** a falling away
1Ti. 1.15. Christ Jesus **c-a** into the wo.
 2. 4. *to* **c.** unto the knowledge of
 4.13. Till I **c.**, give attendance to
2Ti. 3. 7. never able *to* **c.** to the know.
Heb.6. 7. drinketh in the rain *that* **c-eth**
 10.37. and he *that* shall **c.** will **c.**
2Pet.3. 3. there shall **c.** in the last days
1Jo. 2.18. heard that antichrist shall **c.**
 4. 2,3. J.Ch.is **c.** in the flesh ; 2Jo.7
 5. 6. This is he that **c-a** by water
Jude 14. the Lord **c-eth** with ten thou.
Rev.1. 4. and *which is* to **c.**; 4.8; 11.17
  7. Behold he **c-eth** with clouds
 2. 5, 16. or else I will **c.** unto thee
3.10. of temptation which shall **c.**
  11. Behold, I **c.** quickly: hold fast
 6. 1, 3, 5, 7. saying, **c.** and see
  17. great day of his wrath is **c.**
 7.13. in white robes? & whence **c-a**
  14. These are they *which* **c-a** out
 11.18. thy wrath is **c.**, and the time
 14. 7. the hour of his judgment is **c.**
 16.15. Behold, I **c.** as a thief. Blessed
 17.10. the other is not yet **c.** ; and
  when he **c-eth** he must cont.
 19. 7. the marriage of the Lamb is **c.**
 22. 7, 12, 20. Behold, I **c.** quickly
  17. and the bride say, **c.** And
  let him that heareth say, **c.**
  And *let* him that is athirst **c.**
  20. Even so **c.**, Lord Jesus
exerchomai.
Mat.2. 6. out of thee shall **c.** a Govern.
 5.26. shalt by no means **c.** *out*
 8.28. **c-ing** out of the tombs
  32. *when* they were **c.** out, they
  34. city **c-a** out to meet Jesus
 12.44. from whence I **c-a** *out*
 13.49. the angels shall **c.** *forth*
 15.18. **c.** *forth* from the heart
  22. of Canaan **c-a** out *of* the same
 24.27. lightning **c-eth** *out of* the east
 26.55. **c.** *out* as against a; Lu.22.52
 27.32. *as* they **c-a** out, they found
  53. **c-a** out of the graves..and
Mar.1.25. **c.** out of him.; 9.25. Lu.4.35
  26. **c-a** out of him; 9.26; Lu.4.35
  29. *when* they were **c.** out of the
  38. for therefore **c-a** I *forth*
 5. 2. *when* he was **c.** *out* of the ship
  8. **c.** *out* of the man, thou unclea.
 6.34. Jesus, *when* he **c-a** out, saw

Mar.6.54. *when they were* c. *out* of the
8.11. the Pharisees c-a *forth*
9.29. This kind can c. *forth by*
11.12. *when they were* c. from Beth.
14.48. *Are* ye c. out, as against
Lu. 1.22. *when* he c-a *out*, he could
4.36. uncl. spirits, and they c-a out
41. devils also c-a *out* of many
8.29. *to* c. out of the man
11.24. my house whence I c-a *out*
15.28. therefore c-a his father *out*
22.39. he c-a out, and went, as he
Jo. 11.44. he that was dead c-a *forth*
13. 3. that he *was* c. from God
16.27. that I c-a out from God
28. I c-a *forth* from the Father
30. that thou c-a-*est forth* from G.
17. 8. that I c-a *out* from thee
19. 5. Then c-a Jesus forth, wearing
34. forthwith c-a there *out* blood
Act.7. 4. Then c-a he *out* of the land
7. after that *shall* they c. *forth*
8. 7. c-a out of many that were
16.18. J.C.to c.out of her,& he c-a *out*
28. 3. c-a viper *out* of the heat, and
15. they c-a to meet us as far
1Co.14.36. c-a the word of God *out* from
2Co. 6.17. c. out from among them
Heb.3.16. howbeit not all *that* c-a *out*
7. 5. though they c. *out* of the loins
11.15. from whence they c-a *out*
Rev.9. 3. there c-a *out* of the smoke
14.15. another angel c-a *out* of the
17. And another angel c-a *out* of
18. another angel c-a *out* from
20. blood c-a *out* of the winepress
15. 6. seven angels c-a *out* of the
16.17. c-a a great voice *out* of the
18. 4. saying, c. *out* of her
19. 5. a voice c-a *out* of the throne
    proserchomai.
Mat.4. 3. when the tempter c-a *to* him
11. angels c-a and ministered un.
5. 1. his disciples c-a *unto* him
8.25; 13.10,36; 14.15; 15.12,23;
17.19; 18.1; 21.1,3; 26.17;
Mar.6.35.
8. 5. there c-a *unto* him a centurion
19. And a certain scribe c-a, and
9.14. Then c-a *to* him the disciples
20. c-a behind him, *and;* Lu.8.44
28. the blind men c-a *to* him
13.27. c-a and said unto him, Sir
14.12. his disciples c-a and took up
15. 1. Then c-a *to* Jesus scribes and
30. great multitudes c-a *unto* him
16. 1. Sadducees c-a, and tempting
17. 7. Jesus c-a and touched them
14. there c-a *to* him a certain man
24. c-a *to* Peter, and said, Doth
18.21. Then c-a Peter to him, and
19. 3. also c-a *unto* him ; Mar.10.2
16. And, behold, one c-a *and* said
20.20. Then c-a *to* him the mother
21.14. the blind and the lame c-a *to*
23. elders of the people c-a *unto*
28. and he c-a *to* the first, *and*
30. he c-a *to* the second, *and* said
22.23. same day c-a *to* him the Sad.
25.20. c-a and brought other five
22, 24. c-a *and* said, Lord, thou
26.49. he c-a *to* Jesus, *and* said, Hail
50. Then c-a they, *and* laid hands
60. *tho.* many false witnesses c-a
the last c-a two false witnesses
69. a damsel c-a *unto* him
73. c-a *unto* him they that stood
8. 2. c-a and rolled back the stone
9. c-*n* and held him by the feet
18. Jesus c-a and spake unto
Mar.1.31. c-a and took her by the hand
12.28. one of the scribes c-a, *and*

Lu. 7.14. he c-a *and* touched the bier
8.24. they c-a *to* him, and awoke
9.12. then c-a the twelve, *and* said
42. And *as* he was yet a c-*ing*
13.31. there c-a certain ; 20.27
23.36. c-*ing to* him, and offering him
Jo. 12.21. same c-a therefore to Philip
Act.10.28. c. *unto* one of another nation
12.13. a damsel c-a *to* hearken
18. 2. fro. Rome, and c-a *unto* them
22.27. the chief captain c-a, *and*
23.14. they c-a to the chief priests
24.23. to minister or c. *unto* him
28. 9. others..c-a, and were healed
Heb.4.16. *Let* us therefore c. boldly *unto*
7.25. *that* c. *unto* God by him
11. 6. for he *that* c-*eth to* God
12.18. ye *are* not c. *unto* the mount
22. ye *are* c. *unto* mount Sion
1Pet.2. 4. c-*ing*, as unto a living stone
    sunerchomai.
Mat.1.18. before they c-a *together*, she
Mar.3.20. multitude c-*eth together*
6.33. and c-a *together* unto him
Lu. 5.15. multit. c-a *together;* Act.2.6
23.55. women also, *which* c-a *with*
Jo. 11.33. weeping *which* c-a *with* her
Act.1. 6. *When* they *were* c. *together*
5.16. There c-a also a multitude
10.27. many *that were* c. *together*
45. as many as c-a *with* Peter
19.32. wherefore they *were* c. *toget.*
21.22. must needs c. *together*
25.17. *when* they *were* c. *hither*
28.17. *when* they *were* c. *together*
1Co. 7. 5. and c. *together* again
11.17. c. *together* not for the better
18, 20,33. *when* ye c. *togeth.;* 14.26
34. that ye c. *not together unto*
14.23. the whole church be c. *toget.*
    eperchomai.
Lu. 1.35. Holy Ghost *shall* c. *upon* thee
11.22. shall c. *upon* him, *and* over.
21.26. things *which are* c-*ing* on the
35. as a snare *shall it* c. on all
Act. 1. 8. *after that* the H.G. *is* c. *upon*
8.24. which ye have sp. c. *upon* me
14.19. there c-a *thither* certain Jews
Eph.2. 7. in the ages *to* c. he might
Jas. 5. 1. miseries *that shall* c. *upon*
    katerchomai.
Lu. 4.31. And c-a *down* to Capernaum
9.37. *when* they *were* c. *down* from
Act.9.32. he c-a *down* also to the saints
11.27. c-a prophets from Jerusalem
15. 1. certain man *which* c-a *down*
18. 5. and Timotheus *were* c. *from*
21.10. there c-a *down* from Judæa
27. 5. we c-a to Myra, a city of
    eiserchomai.
Mat. 8. 8. shouldest c. under my roof
Lu. 17. 7. *when* he *is* c. *from* the field
Act.11.20. *when* they *were* c. to Antioch
23.33. *when* they c-a to Cæsarea
Jas. 2. 2. if there c. unto your assem.
    aperchomai.
Mar.3.13. whom he would, and they c-a
Lu.23.33. when they *were* c. to the place
Ro.15.28. I *will* c. by you into Spain
    parerchomai.
Lu.12.37. will c. *forth* and serve them
Act.24.7. the chief captain Lysias c-a
    dierchomai.
Act.9.38. would not delay to c. to them
    epanerchomai.
Lu.10.35. when I c. *again* I will repay
    ginomai.
Mat.8.16. *When* the even *was* c. they
14.23,20.8,26.20,27.57; Mar.4.
35,6.47,11.19,15.42; Jo.6.16
Mat.27.1. *When* the mo. was c.;Jo.12.4

Mar.1.11. there c-a a voice from heaven
6. 2. *when* the Sabbath day *was* c
21. *when* a convenient day *was* c.
9.21. since this c-a unto him ? And
15.33. sixth hour was c., there was
Lu.1. 65. fear c-a on all; Act.5.5,11
3. 2. the word of God c-a unto Jo.
22. a voice c-a from heaven which
9.34. there c-a a cloud, and over.
35. there c-a a voice; Act.10.13
19. 9. This day *is* salvation, c. to
22.14. when the hour *was* c., he sat
Jo. 1.17. grace and truth c-a by Jesus
5.14. lest a worse thing c. unto thee
6.25. Rabbi, when c-*est* thou hith.
10.35. unto whom the word of G. c-a
12.30. This voice c-a not because of
13.19. NowI tell you before it c.,that
Act. 2. 2. suddenly there c-a a sound
43. fear c-a upon every soul: and
7.31. voice of the Lord c-a unto
9. 3. as he journeyed, he c-a near
12.11. *when* Peter was c. to himself
21.17. *when* we *were* c. to Jerusalem
35. when he c-a upon the stairs
26.22. and Moses did say should c.
27. 7. scarce were c. over against
27. the fourteenth night *was* c.
28. 6. saw no harm c. to him
2Co. 1. 8. trouble *which* c-a to us in
Gal. 3.14. blessing of Abraham *might* c.
1Th. 1. 5. our gospel c-a not unto you
1Ti. 6. 4. of words, whereof c-*eth* envy
3.11. afflictions, which c-a unto me
Heb.11.24.Moses,*when* he *was* c. to years
Rev.12.10.Now *is* c. salvation, and
    paraginomai.
Mat.2. 1. there c-a wise men from
3. 1. In those days c-a John the B.
13. Then c-*eth* Jesus from Galilee
Mar.14.43.while he yet spake, c-*eth* Ju.
Lu. 7. 4. And *when* they c-a to Jesus
20. *When* the men *were* c. unto
8.19. c-a to him his mother and
11. 6. in his journey *is* c. to me
12.51. Suppose ye that I *am* c. to
14.21. that servant c-a, *and* shewed
19.16. Then c-a the first, saying, Lo
22.52. elders, *which were* c. to him
Jo. 3.23. they c-a, and were baptized
8. 2. morning he c-a again into
Act. 5.21. high priest c-a, and they tha;
22. But when the officers c-a, an=
25. Then c-a one *and* told them
9.26. And *when* Saul *was* c. to Jer.
39. *When* he *was* c., they broug.
10.32. *when* he c-*eth*, shall speak
33. well done that thou *art* c.
11.23. *when* he c-a, and had seen
13.14. they c-a to Antioch in Pisid.
14.27. And *when* they *were* c.; 15.4
17.10. c-*ing* thither went into the
18.27. who, *when* he *was* c., helped
20.18. And when they *were* c. to
23.35. thine accusers *are* also c.
24.17. I c-a to bring alms to my
24. *when* Felix c-a with his wife
25. 7. *when* he *was* c., the Jews
28.21. any of the brethren *that* c-a
1Co. 16.3. And when I c., whomsoever
Heb.9.11. Christ *being* c. an high pries
    sumparaginomai.
Lu.23.48. the people *that* c-a *together*
    ginomai perikratēs.
Act.27.16. much work to c. by the boat
    katabainō.
Mat.8. 1. *When* he *was* c. *down* from
14.29. *when* Peter was c. *down* out
17. 9. *as* they c-a *down* from the
24.17. on housetop, not c. *down*
27.40, 42. c. *down* from the cross
Mar.15.30

53

Mar.3.22. scribes *which* c-*a down* from
9. 9. *as* they c-*a down* from the
Lu. 6.17. he c-*a down* with them, *and*
8.23. and there c-*a down* a storm
9.54. command fire *to* c. *down*
10.31. by chance there c-*a down*
17.31. *let* him not c. *down* to take
19. 5, 6. make haste, and c. *down*
Jo. 3.13. but he *that* c-*a down* from
4.47. that he *would* c. *down*
49. c. *down* ere my child die
6.33. is he *which* c-*eth down* from
38, 42. I c-*a down* from heaven
41, 50, 51, 58, bread *wh.* c-*a down*
Act. 7.34. and *am* c. *down* to deliver
8.15. *when* they *were* c. *down*
14.11. The gods *are* c. *down* to us
16. 8. by Mysia, c-*a down* to Troas
24.22. the chief captain shall c. *down*
25. 7. the Jews *which* c-*a down*
Jas. 1.17. *and* c-*eth down* from the Fa.
Rev.3.12. which c-*eth down* out of hea.
10. 1. another mighty angel c. *down*
12.12. the devil *is* c. *down* unto you
13.13. he maketh fire c. *down ;* 20.9
18. 1. I saw another angel c. *down*
20. 1. I saw an angel c. *down*
21. 2. city, new Jerusalem, c-*ing do.*
   anabainō.
Mat.17.27.the fish that first c-*eth up*
Mar.1.10. c-*ing up* out of the water
Jo. 12.20. Gre. among them *that* c-*a up*
Act. 7.23. it c-*a* into his heart to visit
8.31. that he *would* c. *up* and sit
39. *were* c. *up* out of the water
10. 4. thine alms *are* c. *up* for a
11. 2. when Peter *was* c. *up* to Jer.
20.11. therefore *was* c. *up* again, and
31. tidings c-*a* unto the chief cap.
Rev.4. 1. c. *up* hither, and ; 11.12
13.11. another beast c-*ing up* out of
   epibainō.
Act.20.18.first day that I c-*a* into Asia
25. 1. *when* Festus *was* c. *into* the
   embainō.
Mat.14.32.*when* they *were* c. *into* the
Mar. 5.18.*when* he *was* c. *into* the ship
   diabainō.
Jo. 21.9. then as they *were* c. to land
   diabainō.
Act.16. 9. c. *over* into Macedonia, and
   hēkō.
Mat.8.11. shall c. from the; Lu.13.29
23.36. All these things *shall* c. upon
24.14. then *shall* the end c.
50. of that ser. *shall* c. ; Lu.12.46
Mar. 8.3. divers of them c-*a* from far
Lu.13.35. until the time c. when ye
15.27. Thy brother *is* c.; and they
19.43. the days *shall* c. upon thee
Jo. 2. 4. mine hour is not yet c.
4.47. he heard that Jesus *was* c.
6.37. Fa. giveth me *shall* c. to me.
8.42. forth and c-*a* from God
Act.28.23.there c-*a* many to him
Ro.11.26. There *shall* c. out of Sion
Heb.10.7, 9. Then said I, Lo, I c.
37. and he that shall come *will* c.
2Pet.3.10. day of the Lord *will* c. as a
1Jo. 5.20. that the Son of God *is* c.
Rev. 2.25. hold fast till I c.
3. 3. I *will* c. on thee as a thief
what hour I *will* c. upon
9. make them to c. and worshi.
15. 4. all nations *shall* c. and wor.
18. 8. *shall* her plagues c. in one
   deuro, deute.
Mat.11.28. c. unto me, all ye
19.21. tre. in hea. : and c.; Lu.18.22
21.38. c., let us kill him, and let us
22. 4. things are ready : c. unto the
25.34. c., ye blessed of my Father
56

Mat.28. 6. c., see the place where the L.
Mat. 1.17. c. ye after me,and I will make
6.31. c. ye yourselves apart into
10.21. c., take up the cross, and fol.
12. 7. the heir ; c., let us ; Lu.20.14
Jo. 4.29. c., see a man which
11.43. loud voice, Lazarus, c. forth
21.12. Jesus saith unto them, c. and
Act. 7. 3. c. into the land which I shall
34. c., I will send thee into Egy.
Rev.17. 1. c. *hither :* I will shew unto
19.17. c. and gather yourselves tog.
21. 9. c. *hither,* I will shew thee the
   mellō.
Mat. 3. 7. from the wrath *to* c.; Lu.3.7
12.32. the world *to* c. ; Heb.2.5 ; 6.5
Act.24.25.temperance, and judgm. *to* c.
27.33. while the day *was* c-*ing* on
Ro. 5.14. figure of him *that was to* c.
8.38. pres., nor *things to* c.;1Co.3.22
Eph.1.21. but also in *that which is to* c.
Col. 2.17. a shadow of *things to* c.
1Ti. 4. 8. and of *that which is to* c.
6.19. against the *time to* c., that
Heb.9.11. of good things *to* c. ; 10.1
11.20. Esau concerning *things to* c.
13.14. city, but we seek one *to* c.
   mellō erchomai.
Mat.11.14. is Elias which was for *to* c.
   katantaō.
Act.16. 1. Then c-*a* he to Derbe and
18.19. And he c-*a* to Ephesus, and
24. mighty in the scriptures, c-*a*
20.15. c-*a* the next day over against
21. 7. we c-*a* to Ptolemais, and sa.
25.13. Ag. and Bern. c-*a* unto Cæs.
26. 7. day and night, hope *to* c.
28.13. compass, and c-*a* to Rhegium
1Co.10.11. the ends of the world *are* c.
14.36. or c-*a* it unto you only
Eph.4.13. Till we all c. in the unity
   ekporeuomai.
Mat.15.11.that which c-*eth* out of the
Mar.7.15. the things *which* c. out of him
20. That *which* c-*eth* out of the
23. these evil things c. from
Lu. 3. 7. to the multitude *that* c-*a* forth
Jo. 5.29. *shall* c. forth ; they that have
   epiporeuomai.
Lu. 8. 4. and *were* c. to him out of
   prosporeuomai.
Mar.10.35. sons of Zebedee, c. *unto*
   eimi.
Jo. 1.46. can any good thing c. out of
Act.24.25.temperance, and judg. to c.
2Ti. 4. 3. For the time *will* c. when they
   pareimi.
Mat.26.50.Friend, wherefore *art* thou c.
Jo. 7. 6. My time is not yet c.
11.28. The master *is* c., and calleth
Act.10.21.the cause wherefore ye *are* c.
12.20. they c-*a* with one accord to
17. 6. *are* c. hither also
Col. 1. 6. *Which* is c. unto you
   sunagō.
Mat.27.62.priests and Pharisees c-*a* toge.
Mar.7. 1. c-*a together* unto him the
Lu. 22.66. and the scribes c-*a together*
Act.13.44.c-*a* almost the whole city toge.
15. 6. apostles and elders c-*a* togeth.
20. 7. *when* the disciples c-*a* togeth.
   ephistēmi.
Lu. 2. 9. angel of the Lord c-*a upon*
38. And she c-*ing in* that instant
10.40. and c-*a* to him, and said
20. 1. scribes c-*a upon* him; Act.6.12
21.34. day c. *upon* you unawares
Act. 4. 1. the Sadducees, c-*a upon*
11.11. *were* three *men* already c. *unto*
12. 7. angel of the Lord c-*a upon*
23.27. then c-*a* I with an army, and
1Th. 5. 3. destruction c-*eth upon* them

   paristēmi.
Mar.4.29. because the harvest is c.
   enistēmi.
2Ti. 3. 1. days, perilous times *shall* c.
   phthanō.
Mat.12.28.king. of God *is* c.; Lu.11.20
2Co.10.14. for we *are* c. as far as to
1Th. 2.16. for the wrath *is* c. upon
   pherō.
2Pet.1.17. when there c-*a* such a voice
18. And this voice which c-*a* from
21. For the prophecy c-*a* not in
   hustereō.
Ro. 3.23. and c. *short* of the glory of G.
1Co. 1. 7. so that ye c. *behind* in no
Heb.4. 1. should seem to c. *short* of it
   lambanō.
Lu. 7. 16. And there c-*a* a fear *on* all
(fear *took* all.)
Act.24.27. Festus c-*a into* Felix' room
   sumplēroomai.
Lu. 9.51. when the time *was* c. that he
Act. 2. 1. the day of Pent. *was fully* c.
   suntunchanō.
Lu. 8.19. could not c. *at* him for the
   epistrephō.
Lu. 8.55. And her spirit c-*a again*
   hupostrephō.
Act.22.17. when I *was* c. *again* to Jeru.
   diadechomai.
Act.7.45. also our fathers *that* c-*a after*
   sunanabainō.
Mar.15.41. c-*a up with ;* Act.13.31
   episustasis.
2Co.11.28. *that which* c-*eth upon* me
   katalambanō.
Jo. 12.35. lest darkness c. *upon* you
   chōreō.
2Pet. 3.9. all should c. to repentance
   aphikneomai.
Ro.16.19. your obedience *is* c. abroad
   (See *Nought*)
COME *to pass,*   *Came to pass.*
   ginomai.
Mat.7.28. it c-*a to pass,* wh. ; 9.10 ; 11.1
24. 6. these things must c. *to pass*
Mar.11.23.which he saith *shall* c. *to pass*
13.29. shall see these things c. *to pass*
Lu.21.7,36.these things shall c. *to pass*
9. things must first c. *to pass*
28. these things begin to c. *to pass*
24.12. at that *which was* c. *to pass*
18. things *which are* c. *to pass*
Jo. 13.19. when *it is* c. *to pass,* ye may
Act.11.28.which c-*a to pass* in the days
1Th. 3. 4. even as it c-*a to pass,* and ye
Rev.1. 1. which must shortly c. *to pass*
(And all other passages in which it oc-
curs, except the following :—)
   eimi, [*future.*]
Act.2.17. it shall c. *to pass ;* 21 ; 3.23 ;
Ro.9.26

COMELINESS.
   euschēmosunē.
1Co.12.23. have more abundant c.

COMELY.
   euschēmōn.
1Co. 7.35. but for that which is c., and
12.24. For our c. parts have no need
   prepei.
1Co.11.13. is it c. that a woman pray

COMERS.
   proserchomai.
Heb.10.1. make the c. there *unto* perfect

COMFORT, [*noun.*]
   paraklēsis.
Act.9.31. and in the c. of the Holy Gh.
Ro.15. 4. and c. of the Scriptures might

²Co. 1. 3. mercies, and the God of all c.
4. by the c., wherewith we ourse.
7. 4. I am filled with c., I am
13. we were comforted in your c.
paramuthia.
¹Co.14. 3. and exhortation, and c.
paramuthion.
Phi. 2. 1. if any c. of love, if any
parēgoria.
Col.4.11. which have been a c. unto
eupsucheō.
Phi.2.19. that I also *may be of good* c.
tharseō.
Mat. 9.22. Daug. *be of good* c. ; Lu.8.48
Mar.10.49. *Be of good* c.; rise, he calleth
parakaleō.
²Co.13.11. Be perfect, *be of good* c.

COMFORT, [verb,]   -ed, -eth.
parakaleō.
Mat.2.18. would not *be* c-ed, because
5. 4. for they *shall be* c-ed
Lu.16.25. but now he *is* c-ed, and thou
Act.16.40.the brethren, they c-ed them
20.12. and *were* not a little c-ed
¹Co.14.31. learn, and all *may be* c-ed
²Co. 1. 4. *Who* c-eth us in all our trib.
that we may be able to c.
wherewith we oursel. *are* c-ed
6. or whether we *be* c-ed, it is
2. 7. to forgive him, and c. him
7. 6. God, *that* c-eth those that are
cast down, c-ed us by the co.
7. wherewith he *was* c-ed in you
13. we *were* c-ed in your comfort
Eph.6.22. *might* c. your hearts ; Col.4.8
Col. 2. 2. That their hearts *might be* c-ed
¹Th. 2.11. c-ed and charged every one of
3. 2. and *to* c. you concerning
7. we *were* c-cd over you
4.18. Wherefore c. one another
5.11. Wherefore c. yourselves tog.
²Th. 2.17. c. your hearts, and stablish
paramutheomai.
Jo. 11.19. Martha and Mary, to c. them
31. in the house and c-ed her
¹Th. 2.11. how ye exhorted, and c-ed
5.14. c. the feeble-minded, support
sumparakaleomai.
Ro. 1.12. That I may be c-ed together

COMFORTER.
paraklētos.
Jo. 14.16. he shall give you another c.
26. the c., which is the Holy Gh.
15.26. But when the c. is come
16. 7. the c. will not come unto

COMFORTLESS.
orphanos.
Jo.14.18. I will not leave you c.: I will

COMING, [noun.]
parousia.
Mat.24. 3. shall be the sign of thy c.
27,37,39.so shall also the c. of the
¹Co.15.23. that are Christ's at his c.
16.17. glad of the c. of Stephanas
²Co. 7. 6. comforted us by the c. of Tit.
7. And not by his c. only, but
Phi. 1.26. for me by my c. to you again
¹Th. 2.19. Lord Jesus Christ at his c.
3.13. at the c. of our Lord Jesus
4.15. and remain unto the c. of
5.23. the c. of our Lord J.; ²Th.2.1
²Th. 2. 8. with the brightness of his c.
9. Even him, whose c. is after
Jas. 5. 7. unto the c. of the Lord. Beh.
8. for the c. of the Lord draweth
²Pet.1.16. the power and c. of our Lord
3. 4. Where is the promise of his c.
12. and hasting unto the c. of the

¹Jo. 2.28. ashamed before him at his c.
eleusis.
Act.7.52. of the c. of the Just One
eisodos.
Act.13.24. first preached before his c.
apokalupsis.
¹Co. 1. 7. waiting for the c. of our L.

COMMAND, [verb,] -ed, -est, -eth, -ing.
keleuō.
Mat.14.9. he c-ed it to be given her
19. he c-ed the multitude ; 15.35
18.25. his lord c-ed him to be sold
27.58. Pilate c-ed the body to be
64. c. therefore that tne sepulchre
Lu.18.40. and c-ed him to be brought
Act. 4.15. *when* they *had* c-ed them to
5.34. c-ed to put the apostles forth
8.38. he c-ed the chariot to stand
12.19. c-ed that they should be put
16.22. clothes, and c-ed to beat them
21.33. and c-ed him to be bound
34. he c-ed him to be carried into
22.24. The chief captain c-ed him
30. c-ed the chief priests and all
23. 3. and c-*est* me to be smitten
10. c-ed the soldiers to go down
35. he c-ed him to be kept in He.
24. 8. c-*ing* his accusers to come
25. 6. seat, c-ed Paul to be brought
17. c-ed the man to be brought
21. I c-ed him to be kept, till I
27.43. c-ed that they which could
paranggellō.
Mat.10.5. *and* c-ed them, saying, Go not
Mar.6. 8. c-ed them that they ; Act.1.4
8. 6. And he c-ed the people to sit
Lu. 8.29. For he had c-ed the unclean
9.21. straitly char. them, and c-ed
Act. 4.18. and c-ed them not to speak
5.28. *Did* not we straitly c. you
40. they c-ed that they should not
10.42. he c-ed us to preach unto the
15. 5. and *to* c. them to keep the
16.18. I c. thee in the name of Jesus
17.30. but now c-*eth* all men every
¹Co. 7.10. unto the married I c., yet not
¹Th. 4.11. own hands, as we c-ed you
²Th. 3. 4. do the things which we c.
6. Now we c. you, brethren, in
10. this we c-ed you, that if any
12. them that are such we c. and
¹Ti. 4.11. These things c. and teach
entellomai.
Mat. 15.4. God c-ed, saying, Honour
19. 7. Why *did* Moses then c. to
28.20. whatsoever I *have* c-ed you
Mar. 10.3. What did Moses c. you
11. 6. them, even as Jesus *had* c-ed
13.34. c-ed the porter to watch
Jo. 8. 5. Moses in the law c-ed us
15.14. do whatsoever I c. you
17. These things I c. you, that
Act.13.47. so hath the Lord c-ed us
epitassō.
Mar.1.27. c-*eth* he even the unclean
6.27. c-ed his head to be brought
39. he c-ed them to make all sit
Lu. 4.36. he c-*eth* the unclean spirits
8.25. he c-*eth* even the winds
31. that he *would* not c. them
14.22. it is done as thou *hast* c-ed
Act. 23.2. Ananias c-ed them that stood
diatassō.
Mat.11.1. of c-*ing* his twelve disciples
Lu. 8.55. he c-ed to give her meat
17. 9. things *that were* c-ed him
10. things *which are* c-ed you
Act. 18.2. Claudius *had* c-ed all
23.31. the soldiers, as it *was* c-ed

Act.24.23. he c-ed a centurion to keep
prostassō.
Mat.8. 4. offer the gift that Moses c-ed
21. 6. and did as Jesus c-ed them
Mar.1.44. those things which Moses c-ed
Lu. 5.14. according as Moses c-ed, for a
Act.10.33.*that are* c-ed thee of God
48. he c-ed them to be baptized
epō.
Mat.4. 3. c. that these stones be made
Mar.5.43. c-ed that something should
8. 7. c-ed to set them also before
10.49. c-ed him to be called. And
Lu. 4. 3. c. this stone that it be made
9.54. Lord, wilt thou that we c.
19.15. he c-ed these servants to be
²Co. 4. 6. For God, *who* c-ed the light to
reō.
Rev.9. 4. it *was* c-ed them that they
diastellō.
Heb.12.20.endure *that which was* c-ed

COMMANDMENT,   -s.
entolē.
Mat.5.19. break one of these least c-s
15. 3. do ye also trangress the c.
6. made the c. of God of none
19.17. enter into life keep the c-s
22.36. which is the great c. in the
38. this is the first c.; Mar.12.30
40. On these two c-s hang
Mar. 7. 8. laying aside the c. of God
9. full well ye reject the c.
10.19. knowest the c-s; Lu.18.20
12.28. which is the first c. of all
29. The first of all the c-s is
31. is none other c. greater
Lu. 1. 6. walking in all the c-s
15.29. trans. I at any time thy c.
23.56. same day according to the c
Jo. 10.18. This c. have I received of
11.57. had given a c., that if any
12.49. he gave me a c., what I
50. his c. is life everlasting
13.34. A new c. I give unto you
14.15. if ye love me keep my c-s
21. He that hath my c-s, and
15.10. If ye keep my c-s, ye shall
I have kept my Father's c-s
12. This is my c., that ye love
Act.17.15.receiving a c. unto Silas
Ro. 7. 8, 11. taking occasion by the c.
9. when the c. came, sin
10. the c., which was ordained
12. the c. holy, and just, and
13. that sin by the c. might
13. 9. if there be any other c., it
¹Co. 7.19. but the keeping of the c-s
14.37. are the c-s of the Lord
Eph.2.15. the law of c-s contained
6. 2. which is the first c. with **pr.**
Col. 4.10. touch. whom ye received c-s
¹Ti. 6.14. keep this c. without spot
Tit. 1.14. c-s of men, that turn fro.
Heb. 7.5. have a c. to take tithes
16. the law of a carnal c.
18. a disannulling of the c.
²Pet.2.21. to turn from the holy c.
3. 2. the c. of us the apostles
¹Jo. 2. 3. him, if we keep his c-s
4. keepeth not his c-s, is a liar
7. I write no new c. unto you
but an old c. which ye
The old c. is the word
8. Again a new c. I write
3.22. because we keep his c-s
23. this is his c., That we should
another as he gave us c.
24. keepeth his c-s dwelleth
4.21. this c. have we from him
5. 2, 3. God, and keep his c-s

57

¹Jo. 5. 3. **c**-s are not grievous
²Jo. 4. as ye have received a **c.**
   5. as though I wrote a new **c.**
   6. after his **c**-s. This is the **c.**
Rev.12.17.keep the **c**-s of God; 14.12
  22.14. that do his **c**-s that they
   epitagē.
Ro.16.26. the **c.** of the everlasting God
¹Co. 7. 6. permission, and not of **c.**
  25. I have no **c.** of the Lord
²Co. 8. 8. I speak not by **c.**, but by
¹Ti. 1. 1. by the **c.** of God our Saviour
Tit. 1. 3. according to the **c.** of God
   keleuō.
Mat. 8.18. he *gave* **c.** to depart to the
Act.25.23. *at* Festus **c.** Paul was broug.
   entalma.
Mat.15.9. the **c**-s of men; Mar.7.7
Col. 2.22. the **c**-s and doctrines of men
   paranggellia.
¹Th. 4. 2. ye know what **c**-s we gave
¹Ti. 1. 5. Now the end of the **c.** is
   diatagma.
Heb.11.23.not afraid of the king's **c.**
   diastellomai.
Act.15.24. we *gave* no such **c.**
   paranggellō.
Act.23.30. *and gave* **c.** to his accusers
   entellomai.
Heb.11.22. *gave* **c.** concerning his bones

COMMEND,   -ed, -eth, -ing.
   sunistēmi.
Ro. 3. 5. But if our unrighteousness **c.**
  5. 8. But God **c**-eth his love toward
  16. 1. I **c.** unto you Phebe our
²Co. 4. 2. **c**-*ing* ourselves to every
  10.18. For not he *that* **c**-eth himself
    but whom the Lord **c**-eth
  12.11. I ought *to have been* **c**-ed
   paratithēmi.
Lu. 23.46. into thy hands I **c.** my spirit
Act.14.23. they **c**-ed them to the Lord
  20.32. brethren, I **c.** you to God
   sunistanō.
²Co. 3. 1. Do we begin again *to* **c.** our.
  5.12. we **c.** not ourselves again
  10.12. with some *that* **c.** themselves
   epaineō.
Lu.16. 8. the lord **c**-ed the unjust stew.
   paristēmi.
¹Co. 8. 8. But meat **c**-eth us not to God

COMMENDATION.
   sustatikos.
²Co. 3. 1. epistles of **c.** to you, or letters
   of **c.** from you

COMMISSION.
   epitropē.
Act.26.12. with authority and **c.** from

COMMIT,   -ed, -eth, -ing.
   poieō.
Mar.15.7. who *had* **c**-ed murder in the
Lu.12.48. *did* **c.** things worthy of stripes
Jo. 8.34. Who soever **c**-eth sin is the
Act.28.17.though I have **c**-ed nothing
²Co.11. 7. *Have* I **c**-ed an offence in aba.
Jas. 5.15. if he *have* **c**-ed sins, they sh.
¹Jo. 3. 4. Whosoever **c**-eth sin transg.
  8. He *that* **c**-eth sin is of the de.
  9. born of God *doth* not **c.** sin
   pisteuō.
Lu.16.11. who *will* **c.** to your *trust*
Jo. 2.24. Jesus *did* not **c.** himself unto
Ro. 3. 2. *were* **c**-ed the oracles of God
¹Co. 9.17. a disp. of the gospel *is* **c**-ed
Gal. 2. 7. *was* **c**-ed unto me
¹Ti. 1.11. which *was* **c**-ed to my trust
Tit. 1. 3. which *is* **c**-ed unto me

   prassō.
Act. 25.11.or *have* **c**-ed any thing worthy
  25. that he *had* **c**-ed nothing wo.
Ro. 1.32. they *which* **c.** such thin.; 2.2.
²Co. 12.21. lascivi. which they *have* **c**-ed
   paratithēmi.
Lu.12.48. to whom men *have* **c**-ed much
¹Ti. 1.18. This charge I **c.** unto thee
²Ti. 2. 2. the same **c.** thou to faithful
¹Pet.4.19. *let* them..**c.** *the keeping of*
   tithēmi.
²Co. 5.19. and *hath* **c**-ed unto us the w.
   paradidōmi.
Act. 8. 3. men and women **c**-ed them to
¹Pet.2.23. but **c**-ed himself to him that
   didōmi.
Jo. 5.22. *hath* **c**-ed all judgment unto
   parakatathēkē.
¹Ti. 6.20. *that which is* **c**-ed *to* thy *trust*
²Ti. 1.14. *that* good *thing which was* **c**-ed
   parathēkē.
²Ti. 1.12. *that which* I have **c**-ed *unto*
   eaō.
Act.27.40. **c**-ed themselves unto the sea
   hierosuleō.
Ro. 2.22. idols, dost thou **c.** *sacrilege*
   ergazomai.
Jas. 2. 9. ye **c.** sin, and are convinced
   asebeō.
Jude 15. which they *have ungodly* **c**-ed
(See other words which it precedes.)

COMMODIOUS.
   aneuthetos.
Act.27.12. the haven was *not* **c.** to

COMMON.
   koinos.
Act. 2.44. had all things **c.**; 4.32
  10.14. eaten anything that is **c.** or
  28. should not call any man **c.** or
  11. 8. for nothing **c.** or unclean
Tit. 1. 4. mine own son after the **c.**
Jude 3. to write unto you of the **c.**
   praitōrion.
Mat.27.27. took Jesus into the **c.** *hall*
   polus.
Mar.12.37. And the **c.** people heard him
   dēmosios.
Act. 5.18. put them in the **c.** prison
   koinoō.
Act.10.15. that *call* not thou **c.**; 11.9
   anthrōpinos.
¹Co.10.13. but such as is **c.** *to man:* but

COMMONLY.
   diaphēmizō.
Mat.28.15. this saying is **c.** *reported*
   holōs.
¹Co. 5. 1. It is reported **c.** that there is

COMMONWEALTH.
   politeia.
Eph.2.12. aliens from the **c.** of Israel

COMMOTIONS.
   akatastasia.
Lu. 21. 9. shall hear of wars and **c.**

COMMUNED.
   homileō.
Lu. 24.15. that, while they **c.** together
Act. 24.26. the oftener, and **c.** with
   dialaleō.
Lu.6.11. **c.** one with another what
   sullaleō.
Lu.22. 4. and **c**-ed *with* the chief priests

COMMUNICATE,   -ed.
   anatithēmi.
Gal. 2. 2. **c**-ed unto them that gospel

   koinōneō.
Gal. 6. 6. *Let* him that is taught . . **c.**
   sungkoinōneō.
Phi. 4.14. *that* ye *did* **c.** *with* my afflict
   koinōnikos.
¹Ti. 6.18. to distribute, *willing to* **c.**
   koinōnia.
Heb.13.16. do good and *to* **c.**, forget not

COMMUNICATION,   -s.
   logos.
Mat.5.37. let your **c.** be Yea, yea
Lu.24.17. What manner of **c**-s are
   homilia.
¹Co.15.33. evil **c**-s corrupt good manners
   aischrologia.
Col. 3. 8. *filthy* **c.** out of your mouth
   koinōnia.
Phile. 6. That the **c.** of thy faith

COMMUNION.
   koinōnia.
¹Co.10.16.is it not the **c.** of the blood
   is it not the **c.** of the body
²Co. 6.14. what **c.** hath light with dark.
  13.14. the **c.** of the Holy Ghost

COMPACTED.
   sumbibazō.
Eph.4.16. **c.** by that which every joint

COMPANION,   -s.
   sunekdēmos.
Act.19.29. Paul's **c**-s *in travel,* they
   sunergos.
Phi. 2.25. my brother, and **c.** *in labour*
   koinōnos.
Heb.10.33. ye became **c**-s of them that
   sungkoinōnos.
Rev.1. 9. and **c.** in tribulation, and

COMPANY, [*noun,*]   -ies.
   ochlos.
Lu. 5.29. a great **c.** of publicans and
  6.17. and the **c.** of his disciples
  9.38. a man of the **c.** cried out
  11.27. a certain woman of the **c.**
  12.13. one of the **c.** said unto him
Jo. 6. 5. saw a great **c.** come unto
Act.6. 7. and a great **c.** of the priests
   sumposion.
Mar.6.39. make all sit down *by* **c**-s
   (*sit down, companies, companies.*)
   sunodia.
Lu. 2.44. him to have been in the **c.**
   klisia.
Lu. 9.14. sit down by fifties in a **c.**
   ek egō.
Lu.24.22. certain women also *of our* **c.**
   (*from among us.*)
   homilos.
Rev.18.17. and all the **c.** in ships, and
   ho peri.
Act. 13.13. when Paul and his **c.**
  21. 8. we that were of Paul's **c.**
   sunanamignumi.
²Co. 5.11. written unto you not *to keep* **c.**
¹Th. 3.14. and *have no* **c.** *with* him
   plēthos.
Lu.23.27. him, a great **c.** of people
   kollaō.
Act.10.28. man that is a Jew to keep **c.**
   ochlopoieō.
Act.17. 5. *gathered a* **c.**, *and* set all the

COMPANY, [*verb,*]   -ied.
   sunanamignumi.
¹Co. 5. 9. not to **c.** *with* fornicators
   sunerchomai.
Act.1.21. men which *have* **c**-ied *with us*

COMPARE, *-ing,*
sungkrinō.
¹Co. 2. 13. c-*ing* spiritual things *with*
²Co. 10.12. or c. ourselves *with* some
   c-*ing*themselves *among*them.
paraballō.
Mar.4.30. what comparison shall we c.

COMPARISON.
parabolē.
Mar.4.30. or with what c. shall we

COMPASS, *-ed.*
Lu. 21.20. see Jerusalem c-*ed* with
Heb.11.30. *after they were* c-*ed about*
Rev.20. 9. c-*ed* the camp of saints *about*
perikeimai.
Heb.5. 2. himself also *is* c-*ed with*
  12. 1. we also are c-*ed about* with so
periagō.
Mat.23.15. for ye c. sea and land to
perikukloō.
Lu.19.43. about thee, and c. thee *round*
perierchomai.
Act.28.13. thence we *fetched a* c., *and*

COMPASSION.
splangchnizomai.
Mat.9.36. he *was moved with* c.; 14.14
  18.27 ; Mar.1.41
  15.32. I *have* c. on the multitude
  20.34. Jesus *had* c. on them, *and*
  9.22. *have* c. on us, *and* help us
Lu. 7.13. he *had* c. on her, and said
  10.33. saw him, he *had* c. on him
  15.20. saw him, and *had* c., and ran
eleeō.
Mat.18.33. also *have had* c. on thy
Mar. 5.19. and *hath had* c. on thee
Jude   22. And *of some have* c., making
oikteirō.
Ro. 9.15, I *will have* c. *on* whom I
  will *have* c.
metriopatheō.
Heb.5.2. can *have* c. on the ignorant
sumpatheō.
Heb.10.34. *had have* c. *of* me in my bonds
sumpathēs.
¹Pet.3. 8. *having* c. *one of another*
splangchna.
¹Jo. 3.17. shutteth up his *bowels* of c.

COMPEL, *-ed, -est.*
anangkazō.
Lu. 14.23. c. them to come in, that my
Act.26.11. c-*ed* them to blaspheme; and
²Co. 12.11. in glorying; ye *have* c-*ed* me
Gal. 2. 3. being a Greek, *was* c-*ed* to be
  14. why c-*est* thou the Gentles to
anggareuō.
Mat. 5.41. shall c. thee *to go* a mile
  27.32. they c-*ed* to bear his cross
Mar.15.21. they c. one Simon a Cyren.

COMPLAINERS.
mempsimoiros.
Jude 16. These are murmurers, c.

COMPLAINTS.
aitiama.
Act.25.7. many and grievous c. against

COMPLETE.
plēroō.
Col.2.10. And ye are c. in him, which
  4.12. perfect and c. in all the will

COMPREHEND, *-ed.*
katalambanō.
Jo. 1. 5. and the darkness c-*ed* it not
Eph. 3.18. able *to* c. with all saints

---

anakephalaioomai.
Ro. 13.9. it *is briefly* c-*ed* in this saying

CONCEITS.
heautou.
Ro.11.25. wise in *your own* c.; 12.:6

CONCEIVE, *-ed.*
sullambanō.
Lu. 1.24. his wife Elisabeth c-*ed*, and
  31. thou *shalt* c. in thy womb
  36. she hath also c-*ed* a son in
  2.21. before he *was* c-*ed* in the
Jas. 1.15. Then *when* lust *hath* c-*ed*, it
gennaō.
Mat.1.20. that which is c-*ed* in her is
echō koitē.
Ro. 9.10. when Rebecca also had c-*ed*
katabolē.
Heb.11.11. received strength to c. seed
tithēmi.
Act.5. 4. why *hast* thou c-*ed* this

CONCERN.
peri. [*gen.*]
Act.28.31. things *which* c. the Lord J. C.

CONCERNING.
peri.
Mat.4. 6. his angels charge c. thee
  11. 7. unto the multitudes c. John
  16.11. spake not to you c. bread
Mar.5.16. and also c. the swine
  7.17. asked him c. the parable
Lu. 2.17. was told them c. this child
  7.24. unto the people c. John
  22.37. things c. me have an end
  24.19. c. Jesus of Nazareth, which
  27. scriptures the things c. hims.
  44. and in the psalms, c. me
Jo.7. 12. murm. among people c. him
  32. murm. such things c. him
  9.18. believe c. him, that he had
  11.19. comfort them c. their broth.
Act. 1.16. c. Judas, which was guide
  8.12. things c. the kingdom ; 19.8
  19.39. enquire anything c. other
  21.24. informed c. thee, are nothing
  22.18. receive they testimony c. me
  23.15. more perfectly c. him: and
  24.24. him c. the faith in Christ
  25.16. c. the crime laid against him
  28.21. letters out of Judæa c. thee
  22. *as* c. this sect, we know
  23. persuading them c. Jesus
Ro. 1. 3. c. his Son Jesus Christ
¹Co. 7.25. Now c. virgins I have no
  8. 4. *as* c. therefore the eating
  12. 1. Now c. spiritual gifts
  16. 1. c. the collection for the saints
¹Th. 3. 2. comfort you c. your faith
  4.13. c. them which are asleep
  13. c. faith have made shipwreck
¹Ti. 1.19. c. the truth have erred
  6.21. have erred c. the faith
²Ti. 2.18. c. the truth have erred
  3. 8. minds, reprobate c. the faith
Heb.7.14. spake nothing c. priesthood
  11.20. and Esau c. things to come
  22. commandment c. his bones
¹Jo. 2.26. c. them that seduce you
kata, [*accu.*]
Ro. 9. 5. of whom *as* c. the flesh
  11.28. *As* c. the gospel, they are
²Co.11.21. I speak *as* c. reproach
Eph.4.22. c. the former conversation
Phi. 3. 6. c. zeal, persecuting the ch.
eis.
Act. 2.25. for David speaketh c. him
²Co. 8.23. and fellowhelper c. you
Eph.5.32. speak c. Christ, and the chu.
¹Th. 5.18. of God, in Christ Je. c. you

---

hoti.
Act.13.34. And *as* c. *that* he raised
huper.
Ro. 9.27. Esaias also crieth c. Israel
eis logos.
Ph. 4.15. *as* c. giving and receiving
  (as far as [taking] *account* of.)

CONCISION.
katatomē.
Phi. 3. 2. workers, beware of the c.

CONCLUDE, *-ed.*
sungkleiō.
Ro.11.32. For God *hath* c-*ed* them all
Gal. 3.22. But the scripture *hath* c-*ed*
krinō.
Act.21.25. have written *and* c-*ed* that
logizomai.
Ro. 3.28. Therefore we c. that a man

CONCORD.
sumphōnēsis.
²Co. 6.15. what c. hath Christ with B.

CONCOURSE.
sustrophē.
Act.19.40. may give an acco. of this c.

CONCUPISCENCE.
epithumia.
Ro. 7. 8. wrought in me all man. of c.
Col. 3. 5. evil c., and covetousness
¹Th. 4. 5. Not in the lust of c., even as

CONDEMN, *-ed, -est.*
katakrinō.
Mat.12.41, 42. and *shall* c. it; Lu.11.32
  20.18. they *shall* c. him; Mar.10.33
  27. 3. when he saw that he *was* c-*ed*
Mar.14.64. they all c-*ed* him to be guilty
Lu. 11.31. this generation, and c. them
Jo. 8. 10. accusers? *hath* no man c-*ed*
  11. Neither *do* I c. thee: go, and
Ro. 2. 1. another, thou c-*est* thyself
  8. 3. for sin, c-*ed* sin in the flesh
  34. Who is he *that* c-*eth?* It is
¹Co. 11.32. that we should not be c-*ed*
Heb.11. 7. by the which he c-*ed* the
Jas. 5. 9. lest ye *be* c-*ed:* behold, the
²Pet. 2. 6. c-*ed* them with an overthrow
krinō.
Jo. 3.17. into the world to c. the wor.
  18. believeth on him *is* not c-*ed*
  that believeth not *is* c-*ed* alr.
Ro.14.22. Happy is he *that* c-*eth* not
katadikazō.
Mat.12.7. ye would not *have* c-*ed* them
  37. by thy wo. thou *shalt* be c-*ed*
Lu. 6.37. c. not, and ye *shall* not be c-*ed*
Jas. 5. 6. Ye *have* c-*ed* and killed the
krima.
Lu.24.20. delivered him to *be* c-*ed* to
  (to the *condemnation* of.)
katakrisis.
²Co. 7. 3. I speak not this to c. you
akatagnōstos.
Tit. 2. 8. speech, that *cannot be* c-*ed*
autokatakritos.
Tit. 3.11. sinneth, being c-*ed* of him*self*
kataginōskō.
¹Jo. 3.20, 21. if our heart c. us ; God is

CONDEMNATION.
krima.
Lu.23.40. seeing thou art in the same c.
¹Co. 11.34.come not together unto c.
¹Ti. 3. 6. he fall into the c. of the dev.
Jas. 3. 1. shall receive the greater c.
Jude 4. of old ordained to this c.
katakrima.
Ro. 5.16. judgment was by one to c.
  18. came upon all men to c.
  8. 1. now no c. to them which are

59

krisis.
Jo. 3.19. And this is the **c.**, that light
5.24. shall not come into **c.**; but is
katakrisis.
²Co. 3. 9. ministration of **c.** be glory
hupokrisis.
Jas. 5.12. nay; lest ye fall into **c.**

CONDESCEND.
sunapagomai.
Ro.12.16. but **c.** to men of low estate

CONDUCT,   -ed.
kathistĕmi.
Act.17.15. And they *that* **c**-ed Paul
propempō.
¹Co.16.11. but **c.** him *forth* in peace

CONFERRED.
sumballō.
Act.4.15. they **c.** among themselves
sullaleō.
Act.25.12. Festus, *when* he had **c.**
prosanatithĕmi.
Gal.1.16. I **c.** not with flesh and bl.

CONFERENCE.
prosanatithĕmi.
Gal. 2. 6. *in* **c.** added nothing to me

CONFESS,   -ed, -eth, -ing.
homologeō.
Mat.10.32.*shall* **c.** me before men
him *will* I **c.** also before my
Lu. 12.8. *shall* **c.** me before men, him
shall the Son of man also **c.**
Jo. 1.20. **c**-ed, and denied not; but **c**-ed
9.22. that if any man did **c.** that
12.42. Pharisees they did not **c.**
Act. 23.8. spirit, but the Pharisees **c.**
24.14. But this I **c.** unto thee, that
Ro.10. 9. if thou *shalt* **c.** with thy
Heb.11.13.and **c**-ed that they were
¹Jo. 1. 9. If we **c.** our sins, he is faith.
4. 2, 3. Every spirit that **c**-eth
15. Whosoever *shall* **c.** that Jesus
²Jo. 7. *who* **c.** not that Jesus Christ
exomologeō.
Mat. 3. 6. Jordan, **c**-*ing* their; Mar 1.5
Act.19.18. came, *and* **c**-ed, and shewed
Ro. 14.11. every tongue *shall* **c.** to God
15. 9. I *will* **c.** to thee among the
Phi. 2.11. every tongue *should* **c.** that
Jas. 5.16. **c.** your faults one to anoth.
Rev. 3. 5. I *will* **c.** his name before my

CONFESSION.
homologia.
¹Ti. 6.13. Pilate witnessed a good **c.**
homologeō.
Ro.10.10. with the mouth **c.** *is made*

CONFIDENCE.
parrēsia.
Act.28.31. with all **c.**, no man forbidding
Heb. 3. 6. if we hold fast the **c.** and the
10.35. your **c.**, which hath great
¹Jo. 2.28. we may have **c.**, and not
3.21. then have we **c.** toward
5.14. this is the **c.** that we have
peithō.
²Co. 2. 3. *having* **c.** in you all
Gal. 5.10. I *have* **c.** in you through the
Phi.1.25. And *having* this **c.**, I know
3. 3. and *have* no **c.** in the flesh
²Th. 3. 4. we *have* **c.** in the Lord
Phile. 21. *Having* **c.** in thy obedience
pepoithēsis.
²Co. 1.15. And in this **c.** I was minded
8.22. the great **c.** which I have in
10. 2. with that **c.**, wherewith I
60

Eph. 3.12. access with **c.**, by the faith
Phi. 3. 4. might also have **c.** in the flesh
hupostasis.
²Co.11.17. foolishly, in this **c.** of boast.
Heb. 3.14. hold the beginning of our **c.**
tharreō.
²Co. 7.16. I *have* **c.** in you in all things

CONFIDENT.
peithō.
Ro. 2.19. And *art* **c.** that thou thyself
Phi.1. 6. *Being* **c.** of this very thing
14. *waxing* **c.** by my bonds, are
tharreō.
²Co. 5. 6. Therefore we are always **c.**
8. We *are* **c.**, I say, and willing
hupostasis.
²Co. 9. 4. in this same **c.** boasting

CONFIDENTLY.
diischurizomai.
Lu.22.59. another **c.** *affirmed*, saying

CONFIRM,   -ed, -ing.
bebaioō.
Mar.16.20. **c**-*ing* the word with signs
Ro. 15. 8. to **c.** the promises made unto
¹Co. 1. 6. testimony of Christ *was* **c**-ed
8. Who *shall* also **c.** you unto
Heb. 2. 3. *was* **c**-ed unto us by them
epistērizō.
Act.14.22. **c**-*ing* the souls of the discip.
15.32. with many words, and **c**-ed
41. Cilicia, **c**-*ing* the churches
kuroō.
²Co. 2. 8. that ye would **c.** your love
Gal. 3.15. covenant, yet if it be **c**-ed, no
prokuroō.
Gal. 3.17. covenant *that was* **c**-ed *before*
mesiteuō.
Heb.6.17. counsel, **c**-ed it by an oath

CONFIRMATION.
bebaiōsis.
Phi.1. 7. defence and **c.** of the gospel
Heb.6.16. an oath for **c.** is to them

CONFLICT.
agōn.
Phi. 1.30. Having the same **c.** which
Col. 2. 1. what great **c.** I have for you

CONFORMABLE.
summorphoō.
Phi. 3.10. *being made* **c.** *unto* his death

CONFORMED.
suschēmatizō.
Ro.12. 2. And *be* not **c.** *to* this world
summorphos.
Ro. 8.29. to be **c.** *to* the image of his

CONFOUND,   -ed.
kataischunō.
¹Co. 1.27. of the world to **c.** the wise
to **c.** the things which are
¹Pet.2. 6. belie. on him *shall* not *be* **c**-ed.
sungchunō.
Act. 2. 6. together and *were* **c**-ed because
9.22. and **c**-ed the Jews which dwelt

CONFUSED.
sungchunō.
Act.19.32. for the assembly was **c.**

CONFUSION.
akatastasia.
¹Co. 14.33. God is not the author of **c.**
Jas. 3.16. there is **c.** in every evil work
sungchusis.
Act.19.29. whole city was filled with **c.**

CONGREGATION.
sunagōgē.
Act.13.43. when the **c.** was broken up

CONQUER,   -ing.
nikaō.
Rev.6. 2. went forth **c**-*ing* and to **c.**

CONQUERORS.
hupernikaō.
Ro. 8.37. we *are more than* **c.** through

CONSCIENCE,   -s.
suneidēsis.
Jo. 8. 9. convicted by their own **c.**
Act.23. 1. I have lived in all good **c.**
24.16. to have always a **c.** void of
Ro. 2.15. their **c.** also bearing witness
9. 1. my **c.** also bearing me witness
13. 5. wrath, but also for **c.** sake
¹Co. 8. 7. for some with **c.** of the idol
their **c.** being weak is defiled
10. **c.** of him which is weak
12. and wound their weak **c.**, ye
10.25,27. asking no ques. for **c.** sake
28. and for **c.** sake: for the earth
29. **c.**, I say, not thine own, but
judged of another man's **c.**
²Co. 1.12. the testimony of our **c.**, that
4. 2. ourselves to every man's **c.**
5.11. made manifest in your **c**-s
¹Ti. 1. 5. of a good **c.**, and of a
19. Holding faith, and a good **c.**
3. 9. of the faith in a pure **c.**
4. 2. having their **c.** seared with a
²Ti. 1. 3. with pure **c.**, that without
Tit. 1.15. their mind and **c.** is defiled
Heb.9. 9. as pertaining to the **c.**
14. purge your **c.** from dead works
10. 2. had no more **c.** of sins
22. sprinkled from an evil **c.**
13.18. we trust we have a good **c.**
¹Pet.2.19. if a man for **c.** toward God
3.16. Having a good **c.**; that
21. but the answer of a good **c.**

CONSECRATED.
teleioō.
Heb.7.28. the Son, *who is* **c.** for everm.
engkainizō.
Heb.10.20.way, which he *hath* **c.** for

CONSENT, [noun.]
sumphōnos.
¹Co. 7. 5. except it be with **c.** for a time

CONSENT, [verb,]   -ed, -ing.
sungkatatithēmi.
Lu.23.51. had not **c**-ed to the counsel
suneudokeō.
Act. 8. 1. And Saul was **c**-*ing* unto his
22.20. and **c**-*ing* unto his death, and
epineuō.
Act.18.20. time with them, he **c**-ed not
sumphēmi.
Ro. 7.16. I **c.** *unto* the law that it is
proserchomai.
¹Ti. 6. 3. and **c.** not to wholesome word

CONSIDER,   -ed, -est, -ing.
katanoeō.
Mat.7. 3. but **c**-*est* not the beam that
Lu.12.24. **c.** the ravens: for they neither
27. **c.** the lilies how they grow
Act. 11.6. I **c**-ed, and saw fourfooted
Ro. 4.19. he **c**-ed not his own body now
Heb.3. 1. **c.** the apostle and high priest
10.24. us **c.** one another to provoke
katamantlanō.
Mat.6.28. **c.** the lilies of the field

suniēmi.
Mar.6.52. For they c-ed not the miracle
  dialogizomai.
Jo.11.50. Nor c. that it is expedient
  suneideō.
Act.12.12. And when he had c-ed the
  eideō.
Act.15. 6. came together for to c. of this
  skopeō.
Gal. 6. 1. c-ing thyself, lest thou also
  noeō.
²Ti. 2. 7. c. what I say; and the Lord
  theōreō.
Heb.7. 4. Now c. how great this man
  analogizomai.
Heb.12.3. For c. him that endured such
  anatheōreō.
Heb.13.7. c-ing the end of their conver.

CONSIST, -eth.
eimi.
Lu.12.15. a man's life c-eth not in the
  sunistēmi.
Col. 1.17. and by him all things c.

CONSOLATION.
paraklēsis.
Lu. 2.25. waiting for the c. of Israel
6.24. ye have received your c.
Act.4.36. The son of c., a Levite
15.31. they rejoiced for the c.
Ro. 15.5. the God of patience and c.
²Co. 1. 5. so our c. also aboundeth
6. for your c. and salvation
7. shall ye be also of the c.
7. 7. but by the c. wherewith
Phi. 2. 1. any c. in Christ, if any
²Th. 2.16. given us everlasting c.
Phile. 7. great joy and c. in thy love
Heb.6.18. we might have a strong c.

CONSORTED.
prosklēroō.
Act.17.4. and c. with Paul and Silas

CONSPIRACY.
sunōmosia.
Act.23.13. which had made this c.

CONSTANTLY.

(See *Affirm*.)

CONSTRAIN, -ed, -eth.
anangkazō.
Mat.14.22. c-ed his disciples; Mar 6.45
Act.28.19. I was c-ed to appeal unto
Gal. 6.12. they c. you to be circumcised
  parabiazomai.
Lu. 24.29. But they c-ed him, saying
Act. 16.15. abide there. And she c-ed
  sunechō.
²Co. 5.14. the love of Christ c-eth us

CONSTRAINT.
anangkastōs.
¹Pet. 5.2. not by c., but willingly

CONSULTED, -eth.
bouleuō.
Lu.14.31. c-eth whether he be able with
Jo. 12.10. the chief priests c. that
  sumbouleuō.
Mat.26.4. And c. that they might

CONSULTATION.
sumboulion.
Mar.15.1. the chief priests held a c.

CONSUME, -ed, -ing.
analiskō.
Lu. 9.54. from heaven, and c. them

Gal. 5.15. that ye be not c-ed one of
²Th. 2. 8. whom the Lord shall c. with
  katanaliskō.
Heb.12.29. For our God is a c-ing fire
  dapanaō.
Jas. 4. 3. that ye may c. it upon your

CONTAIN, -ing.
chōreō.
Jo. 2. 6. c-ing two or three firkins
21.25. world itself could not c. the
  engkrateuomai.
¹Co. 7. 9. if they can not c., let them
  periechō.
¹Pet.2. 6. also it is c-ed in the scripture

CONTEMPTIBLE.
exoutheneō.
²Co.10.10. is weak, and his speech c.

CONTEND, -ed, -ing.
diakrinō.
Act. 11.2. of the circumcision c-ed with
Jude 9. when c-ing with the devil
  epagōnizomai.
Jude 3. should earnestly c. for the

CONTENT.
arkeō.
Lu. 3.14. and be c. with your wages
¹Ti. 6. 8. raiment let us be therewith c.
Heb.13.5. be c. with such things as ye
³John 10. malicious words; and not c.
  poieō hikanos.
Mar.15.15.Pilate willing to c. the peop.
  autarkēs.
Phi.4.11. I am, therewith to be c.

CONTENTION, -s.
eris.
¹Co. 1.11. there are c-s among you
  eritheia.
Phi. 1.16. The one preach Christ of c.
  agōn.
¹Th. 2. 2. gospel of God with much c.
  paroxusmos.
Act.15.39. And the c. was so sharp

CONTENTIOUS.
eritheia.
Ro. 2. 8. But unto them that are c.
  philoneikos.
¹Co.11.16. But if any man seem to be c.

CONTENTMENT.
autarkeia.
¹Ti. 6. 6. godliness with c. is great

CONTINUAL.
eis telos.
Lu.18. 5. lest by her c. coming she
  adialeiptos.
Ro. 9. 2. heaviness and c. sorrow

CONTINUALLY.
diapantos.
Lu. 24.53. And were c. in the temple
Heb.13.15. sacrifice of praise to God c.
  diēnekes.
Heb. 7.3. of God; abideth a priest c.
10.1. offered year by year c., make
(*See verbs which it follows.*)

CONTINUANCE.
hupomonē.
Ro. 2. 7. by *patient* c. in well doing

CONTINUE, -ed, -eth, -ing.
menō.
Jo. 2.12. they c-ed there not many
8.31. If ye c. in my word, then

Jo. 15.9. loved you: c. ye in my love
¹Ti. 2.15. if they c. in faith and charity
²Ti. 3.14. c. thou in the things which
Heb.7.24. because he c-eth ever, hath
13. 1. Let brotherly love c.
14. here have we no c-ing city
¹Jo. 2.19. no doubt have c-ed with us
24. remain in you, ye also shall c.
Rev.17.10.he must c. a short space
  epimenō.
Jo. 8. 7. So when they c-ed asking
Act.12.16.But Peter c-ed knocking
13.43. them to c. in the grace of
Ro. 6. 1. Shall we c. in sin, that grace
11.22. if thou c. in his goodness
Col. 1.23. If ye c. in the faith grounded
¹Ti. 4.16. c. in them: for in doing this
  diamenō.
Lu.22.28. they which have c-ed with
Gal. 2. 5. truth of the gospel might c.
²Pet.3. 4. all things c. as they were
  paramenō.
Heb.7.23. they were not suffered to c.
Jas. 1.25. law of liberty, and c-eth
  emmenō.
Act.14.22. them to c. in the faith, and
Gal. 3.10. every one that c-eth not in
Heb.8. 9. they c-ed not in my covenant
  prosmenō.
Mat.15.32. because they c. *with* me
¹Ti. 5. 5. c-eth *in* supplications and
  sumparamenō.
Phi. 1.25. shall abide and c. *with* you
  proskartereō.
Act.1.14. These all c-ed with one accord
2.42. And they c-ed stedfastly in
46. And they, c-ing daily with
8.13. he c-ed with Philip, and
Ro.12.12. c-ing instant in prayer
Col. 4. 2. c. in prayer, and watch
  poieō.
Jas. 4.13. and c. there a year, and buy
Rev.13.5. to c. forty and two months
  diatribō.
Jo. 11.54. there c-ed with his disciples
Act.15.35. Paul also and Barnabas c-ed
  histēmi.
Act.26.22. I c. unto this day, witnessing
  kathizō.
Act.18.11. And he c-ed there a year
  parateinō.
Act.20.7. and c-ed his speech until
  ginomai.
Act.19.10. this c-ed by the space of two
  diateleō.
Act.27.33. c-ed fasting, having taken
  dianuktereuō.
Lu. 6.12. c-ed all night in prayer to G.

CONTRADICTING.
antilegō.
Act.13.45. Paul, c. and blaspheming

CONTRADICTION.
antilogia.
Heb.7. 7. without all c. the less is
12. 3. him that endured such c. of

CONTRARIWISE.
tounantion.
²Co. 2. 7. so that c., ye ought rather
Gal. 2. 7. But c., when they saw that
¹Pet.3. 9. but c. blessing; knowing

CONTRARY. (See *Law*.)
enantios.
Mat.14.24. for the wind was c.; Mr.6.43
Act. 26. 9. many things c. to the name
27. 4. because the winds were c.
¹Th. 2.15. God, and are c. to all men
Tit. 2. 8. he that is of the c. part may

para, [accu.]
Act. 18.13. worship God c. to the law
Ro. 11.24. and were graffed c. to nature
    16.17. c. to the doctrine which ye
antikeimai.
Gal. 5.17. these are c. the one to the
1Ti. 1.10. that is c. to sound doctrine
apenanti.
Act.17.7. these all do c. to the decrees

CONTRIBUTION.
koinōnia.
Ro.15.26. make a certain c. for the poor

CONTROVERSY.
homologoumenōs.
1Ti.3.16. And without c., great is the

CONVENIENT.
anēkō.
Eph.5. 4. nor jesting, which are not c.
Phile. 8. enjoin thee that which is c.
eukairos.
Mar.6.21. And when a c. day was come
kairos.
Act.24.25. when I have a c. season I will
kathēkon.
Ro. 1.28. those things which are not c.
eukaireō.
1Co.16.12. when he shall have c. time

CONVENIENTLY.
eukairōs.
Mar.14.11. how he might c. betray him

CONVERSATION.
anastrophē.
Gal. 1.13. ye have heard of my c. in
Eph.4.22. concerning the former c.
1Ti. 4.12. in word, in c., in charity
Heb.13.7. consider. the end of their c.
Jas. 3.13. shew out of a good c. his
1Pet.1.15. ye holy in all manner of c.
    18. from your vain c., received
    2.12. Having your c. honest
    3. 1. won by the c. of the wives
    2. they behold your chaste c.
    16. accuse your good c. in Christ
2Pet.2. 7. the filthy c. of the wicked
    3.11. in all holy c. and godliness
anastrephō.
2Co. 1.12. have had our c. in the world
Eph.2. 3. we all had our c. in times
politeuō.
Phi. 1.27. let your c. be as it becometh
politeuma.
Phi. 3.20. For our c. is in heaven; from
tropos.
Heb.13. 5. Let your c. be without covet.

CONVERSION.
epistrophē.
Act.15. 3. declaring the c. of the Gent.

CONVERT, -ed, -eth.
epistrephō.
Mat.13.15. and should be c-ed; Act.28.27
Mar. 4.12. lest..they should be c-ed
Lu. 22.32. and when thou art c-ed
Jo. 12.40. and be c-ed, and I should heal
Act. 3.19. Rep. ye therefore, and be c-ed
Jas. 5.19. from the truth, and one c.
    20. he which c-eth the sinner fr.
strephō.
Mat.18.3. Except ye be c-ed, and become

CONVEYED.
ekneuō.
Jo. 5.13. Jesus had c. himself away .

CONVICTED.
elengchō.
Jo. 8. 9. being c. by their own conscie.
62

CONVINCE, -ed, -eth.
elengchō.
Jo. 8.46. which of you c-eth me of sin
1Co.14.24. unlearned, he is c-ed of all
Tit. 1. 9. and to c. the gainsayers
Jas. 2. 9. and are c-ed of the law as
diakatelengchomai.
Act.18.28. he mightily c-ed the Jew
exelengchō.
Jude 15. to c. all that are ungodly

COOL.
katapsuchō.
Lu.16.24. in water, and c. my tongue

COPPERSMITH.
chalkeus.
2Ti. 4.14. Alexander the c. did me

CORBAN.
korban.
Mar.7.11. It is c., that is to say, a gift

CORDS.
schoinion.
Jo. 2.15. made a scourge of small c.

CORN.
stachus.
Mat.12.1. pluck the ears of c.; Mar.2.23
Lu. 6. 1. disciples plucked the ears of c.
sporima.
Mat.12.1. sabbath day through the c.
Mar.2.23. through the c. fields; Lu.6.1
sitos.
Mar.4.28. after that, the full c. in the
Act.7.12. heard that there was c. in
kokkos.
Jo.12.24. Except a c. of wheat fall into
(See *Tread.*)

CORNER, -s.
gōnia.
Mat.6. 5. in the c-s of the streets, that
    21.42. is become the head of the c.
    Mar.12.10; Lu.20.17; Act.4.11
Act.26.26.this thing was not done in a c.
1Pet. 2.7. is made the head of the c.
Rev.7. 1. standing on the four c-s of
archē.
Act.10.11. knit at the four c-s and let
    11. 5. down from heav. by four c-s
akrogōniaios.
Eph.2.20. himself being the chief c. sto.
1Pet.2. 6. I lay in Sion a chief c. stone

CORPSE.
ptōma.
Mar.6.29. they came and took up his c.

CORRECTED.
paideutēs.
Heb.12.9. fathers of our flesh which c.

CORRECTION.
epanorthōsis.
2Ti. 3.16. doctrine, for reproof, for c.

CORRUPT.
sapros.
Mat.7.17. but a c. tree bringeth forth
    18. neither can a c. tree bring
    12.33. tree corrupt, and his fruit c.
Lu. 6.43. tree bringeth not forth c.
    fruit; neither doth a c. tree
Eph.4.29. Let no c. communication
phtheirō.
Eph.4.22. old man, cometh which is c.

CORRUPT, [verb,] -ed, -eth.
phtheirō.
1Co.15.33. evil communications c. good
2Co. 7. 2. we have c-ed no man, we
    11. 3. so your minds should be c-ed

Jude 10. things they c. themselves
Rev.19.2. which did c. the earth with
aphanizō.
Mat.6.19. where moth and rust doth c.
    20. neither moth nor rust doth c.
diaphtheirō.
Lu.12.33. approach, neither moth c-eth
1Ti. 6. 5. disputings of men of c. minds
kapēleuō.
2Co. 2.17. not as many which c. the wo.
kataphtheirō.
2Ti. 3. 8. men of c. minds, reprobate
sēpō.
Jas.5. 2. your riches are c-ed, and your

CORRUPTIBLE.
phthartos.
Ro. 1.23. an image made like to c. man
1Co. 9.25. to obtain a c. crown, but we
    15.53. this c. must put on incorrup.
    54. So when this c. shall have
1Pet.1.18. ye were not redeemed with c.
    23. again, not of c. seed, but of
aphthartos.
1Pet. 3.4. that which is not c. even the

CORRUPTION.
phthora.
Ro. 8.21. delivered from the bond. of c.
1Co.15.42.It is sown in c.; it is raised
    50. neither doth c. inherit incor
Gal. 6. 8. shall of the flesh reap c.
2Pet.1. 4. having escaped the c. that is
    2.12. utterly perish in their own c.
    19. themselves are the ser. of c.
diaphthora.
Act.2.27. Holy One to see c.; 13.35
    31. neither his flesh did see c.
    13.34. no more to return to c.
    36. laid unto his fath., and saw c.
    37. God raised again, saw no c.

COST.
dapanē.
Lu.14.28. first, and counteth the c.

COSTLINESS.
timiotēs.
Rev.18.19. by reason of her c.; for in

COSTLY.
polutimos.
Jo.12. 3. ointment of spikenard, very c.
polutelēs.
1Ti. 2. 9. or gold, or pearls, or c. array

COUCH, -es.
klinidion.
Lu. 5.19. through the tiling with his c.
    24. take up thy c., and go unto
krabbatos.
Act. 5.15. laid them on beds and c-es

COULD. See Can.

COUNCIL, -s
sunedrion.
Mat.5.22. shall be in danger of the c.
    10.17. you up to the c-s; Mar.13.9
    26.59. and elders, and all the c.
    14.55. the chief priests and all the c.
    15. 1. scribes and the whole c.
Lu.22.66. and led him into their c., say.
Jo.11.47. priests and the Pharisees a c.
Act. 4.15. to go aside out of the c., they
    5.21. and called the c. together, and
    27. they set them before the c.
    34. stood there up one in the c.
    41. from the presence of the c.
    6.12. and brought him to the c.
    15. And all that sat in the c.
    22.30. and all their c. to appear

Act. 23.1. Paul, earnestly behold. the **c.**
   6. he cried out in the **c.**, Men
  15. Now therefore ye with the **c.**
  20. Paul to-morrow into the **c.**
  28. broug. him forth into their **c.**
24.20. while I stood before the **c.**
sumboulion.
Mat.12.14. and held a **c.** against him
Act. 25.12. had conferred with the **c.**

COUNSEL, [noun,]   -s.
boulē.
Lu. 7.30. lawyers rejected the **c.** of God
 23.51. consented to the **c.** and deed
Act. 2.23. by the determinate **c.** and
  4.28. whatsoev. thy hand and thy **c.**
  5.38. for if this **c.** or this work be
 20.27. unto you all the **c.** of God
 27.42. the soldiers' **c.** was to kill
¹Co. 4. 5. manifest the **c**-s of the heart
Eph.1.11. after the **c.** of his own will
Heb.6.17. the immutability of his **c.**
sumboulion.
Mat.22.15. and took **c.** how they might
 27. 1. elders of the people took **c.**
  7. And they took **c.**, and boug.
 28.12. and had taken **c.**, they gave
Mar. 3. 6. and straightway took **c.** with
sumbouleuō.
Jo. 11.53. they *took* **c.** *together* for to
18.14. Caiaphas was he, *which gave* **c.**
Act. 9.23. the Jews *took* **c.** to kill him
bouleuomai.
Act. 5.33. heart, and *took* **c.** to slay

COUNSEL, [verb,]   -ed.
sumbouleuō.
Rev.3.18. I **c.** thee to buy of me gold

COUNSELLOR.
bouleutēs.
Mar.15.43. Arimathea, an honourable **c.**
Lu. 23.50. a man named Joseph, a **c.**
sumboulos.
Ro.11.34. Lord? or who hath been his **c.**

COUNT,   -ed, -eth.
hēgeomai.
Phi. 3. 7. those I **c**-ed loss for Christ
  8. I **c.** all things but loss for
  do **c.** them but dung, that I
²Th. 3.15. **c.** him not as an enemy, but
¹Ti. 1.12. for that he **c**-ed me faithful
  6. 1. *Let* as many servants . . . **c.**
Heb.10.29. and *hath* **c**-ed the blood of
Jas. 1. 2. **c.** it all joy when ye fall into
¹Pet. 2.13. as they *that* **c.** it pleasure to
 3. 9. as some men **c.** slackness
logizomai.
Ro. 2.26. not his uncircumcision *be* **c**-ed
 4. 3. it *was* **c**-ed unto him for
 5. his faith *is* **c**-ed for righteous.
 9. 8. promise *are* **c**-ed for the seed
Phi.3.13. Brethren, I **c.** not myself to
echō.
Mat 14. 5. because they **c**-ed him as a
Mar.11.32. **c**-ed John that he was a pro.
Act. 20.24. neither **c.** I my life dear unto
Phile. 17. If thou **c.** me therefore a
psēphizō.
Lu.14.28. and **c**-*eth* the cost, whether
Rev.13.18. Let him . . **c.** the number of
sumpsēphizō.
Act.19.19. they **c**-ed the price of them

(See other words with which it is
connected.)

COUNTENANCE.
prosōpon.
Lu. 9.29. the fashion of his **c.** was

Act. 2.28. me full of joy with thy **c.**
²Co. 3. 7. of Moses for the glory of his **c.**
skuthrōpos.
Mat.6.16. as the hypocrites, *of a sad* **c.**
idea.
Mat.28.3. His **c.** was like lightning
opsis.
Rev.1.16. his **c.** was as the sun shineth

COUNTRY,   -ies.
chōra.
Mat. 2.12. into their own **c.** another
 8.28. the **c.** of the Gergesenes
Mar. 5. 1. the **c.** of the Gadar.; Lu.8.26
 10. send them away out of the **c.**
Lu. 2. 8. were in the same **c.** shepher.
 15.13. took his journey into a far **c.**
 15. to a citizen of that **c.**; and
 19.12. went into a far **c.** to receive
 21.21. them that are in the **c**-s enter
Jo. 11.54. unto a **c.** near to the wilder.
 55. many went out of the **c.** up
Act.12.20. their **c.** was nourished by
 18.23. over all the **c.** of Galatia
 27.27. they drew near to some **c.**
perichōros.
Mat.14.35. into all that **c.** *round about*
Lu. 3. 3. into all the **c.** *about* Jordan
 4.37. place of the **c.** *round about*
 8.37. the **c.** of the Gad. *round abo.*
agros.
Mar.5.14. city, and in the **c.**; Lu.8.34
 6.36. go into the **c.** round about
 56. into villages, or cities, or **c.**
 15.21. coming out of the **c.**, the fat.
 16.12. walked, and went into the **c.**
Lu. 9.12. into the towns and **c.** round
 23.26. coming out of the **c.**, and on
patris.
Mat.13.54. into his *own* **c.**; Mar.6.1
 57. save in his *own* **c.**; Mar.6. 4
Lu. 4.23. Caper., do also here in thy **c.**
 24. pro. is accepted in his *own* **c.**
Jo. 4.44. hath no honour in his own **c.**
Heb.11.14. plainly that they seek a **c.**
gē.
Mat.9.31. abroad his fame in all that **c.**
Act. 7. 3. Get thee out of thy **c.**, and
apodēmeō.
Mat.21.33. *went into a far* **c.**; Mar.12.1;
    Lu.20.9
 25.14. man *travelling into a far* **c.**
genos.
Act. 4.36. a Levite, and of the **c.** of

COUNTRYMEN.
genos.
²Co.11.26. in perils by mine own **c.**
sumphuletēs.
¹Th.2.14. like things of your own **c.**

COURAGE.
tharsos.
Act.28.15. he thanked God, and took **c.**

COURSE.
dromos.
Act.13.25. as John fulfilled his **c.**, he
 20.24. I might finish my **c.** with
²Ti. 4. 7. I have finished my **c.** I
ephēmeria.
Lu. 1. 5. Zacharias, of the **c.** of Abia
 8. bef. God in the order of his **c.**
ploos.
Act.21.7. finished our **c.** from Tyre
meros.
¹Co.14.27. and that by **c.**; and let one
trechō.
²Th. 3. 1. of the Lord *may have* free **c.**
trochos.
Jas. 3. 6. setteth on fire the **c.** of
(See other words with which it is
connected.)

COURT,   -s.
basileion.
Lu. 7.25. delicately, are in Kings' **c**-s
aulē.
Rev.11.2. the **c.** which is without th.

COURTEOUS.
philophrōn.
¹Pet.3. 8. brethren, be pitiful, be **c.**

COURTEOUSLY.
philanthrōpōs.
Act.27.3. Julius **c.** entreated Paul
philophronōs.
Act.28.7. and lodged us three days **c.**

COUSIN,   -s.
sunggenēs.
Lu. 1.36. And, behold, thy **c.** Elisabeth
 58. her neighbours and her **c**-s

COVENANT, [noun,]   -s.
diathēkē.
Lu. 1.72. and to remember his holy **c.**
Act. 3.25. of the **c.** which God made
 7. 8. And he gave him the **c.** of
Ro. 9. 4. the glory, and the **c**-s, and
 11.27. this is my **c.** unto them, when
Gal. 3.15. Though it be but a man's **c.**
 17. the **c.**, that was confirmed
 4.24. for these are the two **c**-s; the
Eph.2.12. strangers from the **c**-s of
Heb. 8.6. the mediator of a better **c.**
 8. when I will make a new **c.**
 9. Not according to the **c.** that
 they continued not in my **c.**
 10. is the **c.** that I will; 10.16
 9. 4. the ark of the **c.** overlaid
 and the tables of the **c.**
 10.29. counted the blood of the **c.**
 12.24. the mediator of the new **c.**
 13.20. the blood of the everlasting **c.**
asunthetos.
Ro. 1.31. **c.** *breakers*, without natural

COVENANT, [verb.]   -ed
histēmi.
Mat.26.15. they **c**-ed with him for
suntithēmi.
Lu.22. 5. and **c**-ed to give him money

COVER,   -ed, -eth.
kaluptō.
Mat.8.24. the ship was **c**-ed with the
 10.26. there is nothing **c**-ed, that
Lu. 8.16. **c**-*eth* it with a vessel, or
 23.20. on us; and to the hills, **c.** us
¹Pet.4. 8. *shall* **c.** the multitude of sins
katakaluptomai.
¹Co.11. 6. For if the woman *be* not **c**-ed
 or shaven, *let* her *be* **c**-ed
perikaluptō.
Mar.14.65. to spit on him, and *to* **c.** his
sungkaluptō.
Lu.12. 2. there is nothing **c**-ed, that sh.
epikaluptō.
Ro. 4. 7. forg., and whose sins *are* **c**-ed
kata [gen.] **kephalē.**
¹Co.11. 4. proph., having *his head* **c**-ed

COVERING, [noun.]
peribolaion.
¹Co.11.15. hair is given her for a **c.**

COVET,   -ed.
epithumeō.
Act. 20.33. I *have* **c**-ed no man's silver
Ro. 7. 7. Thou shalt not **c.**; 13.9
zēloō.
¹Co.12.31. But **c.** earnestly the best gift
 14.39. **c.** to prophesy, and forbid

oregomai.
¹Ti. 6.10. which *while* some **c**-*ed after*

COVETOUS.
pleonektēs.
¹Co. 5.10. this world, or with the **c**.
    11. or **c**., or an idolater, or a
    6.10. Nor thieves, nor **c**., nor
Eph.5. 5. nor **c**. man, who is an idolater
philarguros.
Lu.16.14. Pharisees also, who were **c**.
²Ti. 3. 2. lovers of their own selves, **c**.
pleonexia.
²Pet.2.14. exercised with **c**. *practices*

COVETOUSNESS.
pleonexia.
Mar.7.22. **c**., wickedness, deceit
Lu.12.15. and beware of **c**.: for a man's
Ro. 1.29. wickedness, or **c**., maliciousness
²Co. 9. 5. of bounty, and not as of **c**.
Eph.5. 3. all uncleanness, or **c**., let it
Col. 3. 5. and **c**., which is idolatry
¹Th. 2. 5. nor a cloak of **c**.; God is
²Pet.2. 3.through **c**. shall they with
aphilarguros.
Heb.13.5. conversation be *without* **c**.

CRAFT.
dolos.
Mar.14.1. they might take him by **c**.
homotechnos.
Act.18.3. because he was *of the same* **c**.
ergasia.
Act.19.25. by this **c**. we have our wealth
meros.
Act.19.27. not only this our **c**. is in
technē.
Rev.18.22. craftsmen, of whatsoever **c**.

CRAFTINESS.
panourgia.
Lu.20.23. perceived their **c**., and said
¹Co. 3.19. the wise in their own **c**.
²Co. 4. 2. walking in **c**., nor handling
Eph.4.14. sleight of men, and *cunning* **c**.

CRAFTSMAN,   -*men*.
technitēs.
Act. 19.24. no small gain unto the **c**-*e*
    38. and the **c**-*e* which are with
Rev.18.22. no **c**., of whatsoever craft

CRAFTY.
panourgos.
²Co.12.16. nevertheless, being **c**., I

CRAVED.
aiteō.
Mar.15.43. unto Pilate, and **c**. the body

CREATED.
ktizō.
Mar.13.19. which God **c**. unto this time
¹Co. 11. 9. Neither *was* the man **c**. for
Eph. 2.10. **c**. in Christ Jesus unto good
    3. 9. hid in God, *who* **c**. all things
    4.24. man, *which* after God *is* **c**.
Col. 1.16. by him *were* all things **c**.
    all things *were* **c**. by him, and
    3.10. the image of him *that* **c**. him
¹Ti. 4. 3. which God *hath* **c**. to be
Rev. 4.11. for thou *hast* **c**. all things
    pleasure they are and *were* **c**.
    10. 6. who **c**. heav., and the things

CREATION.
ktisis.
Mar.10.6. beginning of the **c**.; 13.19;
    ²Pet.3.4 ; Rev.3.14
Ro. 1.20. from the **c**. of the world are
    8.22. that the whole **c**. groaneth
64

CREATOR.
ktizō.
Ro. 1.25. more than the **c**., who is
ktistēs.
¹Pet. 4.19. w.-doing, as unto a faithf. **c**.

CREATURE,   -*s*.
ktisis.
Mar.16.15. preach the gospel to every **c**.
Ro. 1.25. and served the **c**. more than
    8.19. expectation of the **c**. waiteth
    20. For the **c**. was made subject
    21. bec. the **c**. itself also shall be
    39. nor any other **c**., shall be
²Co. 5.17. be in Christ, he is a new **c**.
Gal. 6.15. uncircumcision, but a new **c**.
Col. 1.15. God, the firstborn of every **c**.
    23. was preached to every **c**.
Heb. 4.13. Neither is there any **c**. that
ktisma.
¹Ti. 4. 4. For every **c**. of God is good
Jas. 1.18. a kind of first-fruits of his **c**-*s*
Rev.5.13. and every **c**. which is in heav.
    8. 9. third part of the **c**-*s* which

CREDITOR.
daneistēs.
Lu. 7.41. There was a certain **c**. which

CREEK.
kolpos.
Act.27.39. certain **c**. with a shore, into

CREEP,   -*ing*, -*ept*.
herpeton.
Act.10.12. beasts, and **c**-*ing things*
    11.6; Ro.1.23
endunō.
²Ti. 3. 6. they *which* **c**. into houses
pareisdunō.
Jude 4. *are* cert. men **c**-*t in unawares*

CRIME,   -*s*.
engklēma.
Act.25.16. conc. the **c**. *laid against*
aitia.
Act.25.27. signify the **c**-*s* laid against

CRIPPLE.
chōlos.
Act. 14.8. impotent in his feet, being a **c**.

CROOKED.
skolios.
Lu. 3. 5. the **c**. shall be made straight
Phi. 2.15. midst of a **c**. and perverse

CROSS.
stauros.
Mat.10.38. And he that taketh not his **c**.
    16.24. and take up his **c**.;
    Mar.8.34; Lu.9.23
    27.32. they compelled to bear his **c**.
    40, 42. from the **c**.; Mar.15.32.
Mar.10.21. and come, take up the **c**.
    15.21. Alex. and Ru., to bear his **c**.
    32. descend now from the **c**.
Lu. 14.27. whoso. doth not bear his **c**.
    23.26. and on him they laid the **c**.
Jo. 19.17. And he bearing his **c**., went
    19. and put it on the **c**. And
    25. Now there stood by the **c**. of
    31. should not rem. upon the **c**.
¹Co. 1.17. lest the **c**. of Christ should
    18. For the preaching of the **c**.
Gal. 5.11. then is the offence of the **c**.
    6.12. persecution for the **c**. of
    14. save in the **c**. of our Lord
Eph. 2.16. God in one body by the **c**.
Phi. 2. 8. even the death of the **c**.
    3.18. the enemies of the **c**. of Ch.
Col. 1.20. peace thr. the blood of his **c**.

Col. 2.14. the way, nailing it to his **c**.
Heb. 12.2. endured the **c**., despising the

CROW, [*verb*,]   -*ew*.
phōneō.
Mat.26.34. this night, before the cock **c**.
    74. im. the cock **c**-*ew*; Jo.18.27
    75. Before the cock **c**.; Lu.22.61
Mar.14.30, 72. before the cock **c**. twice
    68. the porch, and the cock **c**-*ew*
    72. the sec. time the cock **c**-*ew*
Lu. 22.34. cock *shall* not **c**.; Jo.13.38
    60. he yet spake the cock **c**-*ew*

CROWN, [*noun*,]   -*s*.
stephanos.
Mat.27.29.platted a **c**. of thorns
    Mar.15.17; Jo.19.2
Jo. 19.5. wearing the **c**. of thorns
¹Co. 9.25. to obtain a corruptible **c**.
Phi. 4. 1. my joy and **c**., so stand fast
¹Th. 2.19. our hope, or joy, or **c**. of
²Ti. 4. 8. for me a **c**. of righteousness
Jas. 1.12. he shall receive the **c**. of life
¹Pet. 5.4. a **c**. of glory that fadeth not
Rev.2.10. I will give thee a **c**. of life
    3.11. hast, that no man take thy **c**.
    4. 4. on their heads **c**-*s* of gold
    10. cast their **c**-*s* before the
    6. 2. and a **c**. was given unto him
    9. 7. as it were **c**-*s* like gold, and
    12. 1. upon her head a **c**. of twelve
    14.14. having on his head a golden **c**.
diadēma.
Rev.12.3. and seven **c**-*s* upon his heads
    13. 1. upon his horns ten **c**-*s*, and
    19.12. on his head were many **c**-*s*

CROWNED,   -*est*.
stephanoō.
²Ti. 2. 5. yet *is* he not **c**., except he
Heb.2. 7. thou **c**-*st* him with glory and
    9. **c**. with glory and honour

CRUCIFY,   -*ed*.
stauroō.
Mat.20.19.and to scourge, and *to* **c**.
    23.34. of them ye shall kill and **c**.
    26. 2. Son of man is betr. *to be* **c**-*ed*
    27.22, 23. *Let* him *be* **c**-*ed*
    26. he delivered him to *be* **c**-*ed*
    31. and led him away *to* **c**. him
    35. they **c**-*ed* him, *and* parted
    38. Then *were* there two thi. **c**-*ed*
    28. 5. ye seek Jes., *which was* **c**-*ed*
Mar.15.13.they cried out again, **c**. him
    14. out the more exceedingly, **c**.
    15. delivered Jesus,..to *be* **c**-*ed*
    20. him, and led him out to **c**.
    24. And *when* they *had* **c**-*ed* him
    25. third hour, and they **c**-*ed*
    27. And with him they **c**. two
    16. 6. Je. of Naz. *which was* **c**-*ed*
Lu.23.21. saying, **c**. him, **c**.; Jo.19.6
    23. repair. that he might *be* **c**-*ed*
    33. Calvary, there they **c**-*ed* him
    24. 7. and *be* **c**-*ed*, and the third
    20. to death, and *have* **c**-*ed* him
Jo.19. 6. Take ye him, and **c**. him: for
    10. I have power *to* **c**. thee, and
    15. with him, away with him, **c**.
    Shall I **c**. your King? The
    16. unto them to *be* **c**-*ed*. And
    18. Where they **c**-*ed* him, and
    20. the place where Jes. *was* **c**-*ed*
    23. when they *had* **c**-*ed* Jesus
    41. the place where he *was* **c**-*ed*
Act. 2.36. Jesus, whom ye *have* **c**-*ed*
    4.10. of Nazareth, whom ye **c**-*ed*
¹Co. 1.13. *was* Paul **c**-*ed* for you? or
    23. But we preach Christ **c**-*ed*
    2. 2. Jesus Christ, and him **c**-*ed*

¹Co. 2. 8. would not have c-ed the Lord
²Co.13. 4. he was c-ed through weakness
Gal. 3. 1. set forth, c-ed among you
   5.24. have c-ed the flesh with the
   6.14. by whom the world is c-ed
Rev.11.8. where also our Lord was c-ed
   sustauroō.
Mat.27.44. also, which were c-ed with
Mar.15.32. they that were c-ed with him
Jo. 19.32. other which was c-ed with
Ro. 6. 6. our old man is c-ed with
Gal. 2.20. I am c-ed with Christ: neve.
   prospēgnumi.
Act.2.23. wicked hands have c-ed and
   anastauroō.
Heb.6. 6. c. to th. the Son of G. afresh

CRUMBS.
   psichion.
Mat.15.27. eat of the c. which fall from
Mar. 7.28. eat of the children's c.
Lu. 16.21. to be fed with the c. which

CRY, [noun,]   -ies.
   kraugē.
Mat.25. 6. at midnight there was a c.
Act.23. 9. And there arose a great c.
Rev.14.18. and cried with a loud c. to
   boē.
Jas. 5. 4. c-s of them which have reaped

CRY, [verb,]   -ied, -eth, -ing.
   krazō.
Mat.8.29. behold, they c-ed out, saying
   9.27. c-ing, and saying, Thou son
  14.26. is a spirit : they c-ed out for
  30. he c-ed, saying, Lord, save me
  15.23. her away, for she c-eth after
  20.30. c-ed out, saying, Have mercy
  31. but they c-ed the more, saying
  21. 9. c-ed, saying, Hosanna to the
  15. and the children c-ing in the
  27.23. they c-ed out the ; Mar. 15.14
  50. when he had c-ed again with
Mar.1.26. c-ed with a loud voice ; 5. 7 ;
   Act.7.60 ; Rev.6.10 ; 7.2,10 ;
   10.3 ; 19.17
  3.11. c-ed, saying, Thou art the Son
  5. 5. and in the tombs, c-ing, and
  9.24. c-ed out, and said with tears
  26. And the spirit c-ed, and rent
  10.47. he began to c. out, and say
  48. but he c-ed the more a great
  11. 9. that followed, c-ed, saying
  15.13. And they c-ed out again, Cru.
  39. saw that he so c-ed out, and
Lu. 4.41. came out of many, c-ing out
  9.39. and he suddenly c-eth out
  18.39. but he c-ed so much the more
  19.40. stones would immed. c. out
Jo. 1.15. and c-ed, saying, This was he
  7.28. Then c-ed Jesus in the temple
  37. Jesus stood and c-ed, saying
  12.13. to meet him, and c-ed, Hosa.
  44. Jesus c-ed and said, He that
  19.12. the Jews c-ed out, saying, If
Act. 7.57. they c-ed out with a loud voi.
  14.14. in among the peo., c-ing out
  16.17. and c-ed, saying, These men
  19.28. and c-ed out, saying, Great is
  32. Some therefore c-ed one thing
  34. c-ed out, Great is Diana of the
  21.28. c-ing out, Men of Israel, help
  36. after, c-ing, Away with him
  23. 6. he c-ed out in the council
  24.21. I c-ed standing among them
Ro. 8.15. whereby we c., Abba, Father
  9.27. Esaias also c-eth concerning
Gal. 4. 6. into your hearts, c-ing, Abba
Jas.5. 4. you kept back by fraud, c-eth
Rev.10.3. when he had c-ed, seven thun.
  12. 2. And she being with child c-ed

Rev.14.15. c-ing with a loud voice to him
  18. 2. And he c-ed mightily with a
  18. And c-ed when they saw the
  19. and c-ed, weeping and wailing
   kraugazō.
Mat.12.19. He shall not strive, nor c.
  15.22. and c-ed unto him, saying
Jo. 11.43. spoken, he c-ed with a loud
  18.40. Then c-ed they all again, sa.
  19. 6. they c-ed out, saying, Crucify
  15. they c-ed out, Away with
Act. 22.23. And as they c-ed out, and
   anakrazō.
Mar.1.23. uncle. spirit ; and he c-ed out
  6.49. been a spirit, and c-ed out
Lu. 4.33. and c-ed out with a loud voice
  8.28. he saw Jesus, he c-ed out, and
  23.18. they c-ed out all at once, say.
   boaō.
Mat. 3. 3. voice of one c-ing in the ;
    Mar.1.3 ; Lu.3.4 ; Jo. 1.23
Mar.15.34. ninth hour Jesus c-ed with a
Lu. 18. 7. his own elect, which c. day
  38. he c-ed, saying, Jesus, thou
Act. 8. 7. unclean spirits, c-ing with
  17. the rulers of the city, c-ing
  21.34. some c-ed one thing, some
Gal. 4.27. break forth and c. thou that
   anaboaō.
Mat.27.46. Jesus c-ed with a loud voice
Mar.15. 8. the multitude c-ing aloud
Lu. 9.38. man of the company c-ed out
   epiboaō.
Act. 25.24. c-ing that he ought not to
   phōneō.
Lu. 8. 8. had said these things, he c-ed
  16.24. And he c-ed and said, Father
  23.46. when Jesus c-ed with a
Act.16.28. Paul c-ed with a loud voice
Rev.14.18. c-ed with a loud cry to him
   epiphōneō.
Lu. 23.21. But they c-ed, saying, Crucify
Act. 22.24. wherefo. they c-ed so against
   aphiēmi.
Mar.15.37. c-ed with a loud voice, and

CRYING, [noun.]
   kraugē.
Heb.5. 7. with strong c. and tears
Rev.21.4. neither sorrow, nor c., neither

CRYSTAL.
   krustallos.
Rev.4. 6. a sea of glass like unto c.
  22. 1. of water of life, clear as c.
   krustallizō.
Rev.21.11. a jasper stone, clear as c.

CUBIT,   -s.
   pēchus.
Mat. 6.27. add one c. unto his stature
Lu. 12.25. can add to his stature one c.
Jo. 21. 8. as it were two hundred c-s
Rev.21.17. hund. and forty and four c-s

CUMBER,   -ed, -eth.
   perispaomai.
Lu.10.40. Martha was c-ed about much
   katargeō.
Lu.13. 7. down; why c-eth it the ground

CUMI.
   koumi.
Mar.5.41. said unto her, Talitha c.

CUMMIN.
   kuminon.
Mat.23.23. tithe of mint and anise and c.

CUNNING.
   panourgia.
Eph. 4.14. of men, and c. craftiness

CUNNINGLY.
   sophizō.
²Pet. 1.16. not followed c. devised fable.

CUP,   -s,
   potērion.
Mat.10.42. a c. of cold water only, in the
  20.22. Are ye able to drink of the c.
  23. Ye shall drink indeed of my c.
  23.25. outside of the c. ; Lu.11.39
  26. that which is within the c.
  26.27. c., and gave thanks; Lu.22.17
  39. possible, let this c. pass from
  42. if this c. may not pass away
Mar. 7. 4, 8. as the washing of c-s and
  9.41. a c. of water to drink in my
  10.38. can ye drink of the c. that I
  39. Ye shall indeed drink of the c.
  14.23. And he took the c., and when
  36. take away this c. from me
Lu.22.20. Likewise also the c. after sup.
  c. is the new testa. ; ¹Co.11.25
  42. thou be willing, remove this c.
Jo. 18.11. the c. which my Father hath
¹Co.10.16. The c. of blessing which we
  21. the c. of the Lord, and the c.
  11.25. manner also he took the c.
  26. drink this c., ye do shew the
  27. this c. of the Lord, unworthily
  28. that bread, and drink of that c.
Rev.14.10. into the c. of his indignation
  16.19. the c. of the wine of the fierc.
  17. 4. having a golden c. in her
  18. 6. in the c. which she hath filled

CURES, [noun.]
   iasis.
Lu.13.32. I do c. to-day and to-morrow

CURE, [verb,]   -ed.
   therapeuō.
Mat.17.16. and they could not c. him
  18. the child was c-ed from that
Lu. 7.21. he c-ed many of their infirm.
  9. 1. all devils, and to c. diseases
Jo. 5.10. said unto him that was c-ed

CURIOUS.
   periergos.
Act.19.19. them also which used c. arts

CURSE, [noun,]   -ing.
   katara.
Gal. 3.10. are under the c.
  13. hath redeemed us from the c.
  law, being made a c. for us
Heb. 6.8. nigh unto c-ing; whose end
Jas. 3.10. proceedeth blessing and c-ing
   anathematizō anathema.
Act.23.14. bound..under a great c.
  (cursed ourselves with a curse.)
   katanathema.
Act.23.12. bound themselves under a c.
Rev. 22.3. there be no more c.

CURSE, [verb,] -ed, -eth, -edst, -ing.
   kataraomai.
Mat.5.44. bless them that c. ; Lu.6.28
  25.41. Depart from me, ye c-ed, into
Mar.11.21. the fig-tree which thou c-edst
Ro.12.14. perse. you, bless and c. not
Jas. 3. 9. and therewith c. we men
   kakologeō.
Mat.15.4. He that c-eth father or moth.
Mar.7.10. Whoso c-eth father or moth.
   anathematizō.
Mar.14.71. he began to c. and to swear
   katanathematizō.
Mat.26.74. Then began he to c. and to
   epikataratos.
Jo. 7.49. knoweth not the law are c-ed
Gal. 3.10, 13 c-ed is every one that

ara.

Ro. 3.14. Whose mouth is full· of c-*ing*
  katara.
²Pet.2.14. practices; c-*ed* children
  (children *of a curse.*)

CUSTOM,   -*s.*
  ethos.

Lu. 1. 9. According to the c. of the
  2.42. Jerusalem after the c. of the
Act. 6.14. change the c-*s* which Moses
  16.21. teach c-*s,* which are not law.
  21.21. neither to walk after the c-*s*
  26. 3. to be expert in all c-*s* and
  28.17. against the people, or c-*s*
  sunētheia.
Jo.18.39. But ye have a c. that I should
¹Co.11.16.we have no such c., neither
  ethō.
Lu. 4.16. as his c. *was,* he went into
  ethizō.
Lu. 2.27. for him after the c. of the
  telos.
Mat.17.25. kings of the earth take c.
Ro. 13.7. tribute is due; c. to whom c.
  telōnion.
Mat.9. 9. at the *receipt of* c.
  Mar.2.14; Lu.5.27

CUT,   -*ing.*
  apokoptō.

Mar.9.43. thy hand offend thee c. it *off*
  45. if thy foot offend thee, c. it *off*
Jo. 18.10. priest's servant, and c. *off* his
  26. kinsman whose ear Peter c. *off*
Act.27.32.the soldiers c. *off* the ropes of
Gal. 5.12. I would they were even c. *off*
  ekkoptō.
Mat.5.30. c. it *off,* and cast it; 18.8
Lu.13. 7. find none: c. it *down;* why
  9. that thou shalt c. it *down*
Ro.11.22. thou also shalt be c. *off*
  24. *vert* c. *out* of the olive tree
²Co.11.12.that I *may* c. *off* occasion
  katakoptō.
Mar. 5.5. crying, and c-*ing* himself
  koptō.
Mat.21.8. others c. *down* bra.; Mar.11.8
  dichotomeō.
Mat.24.51. *shall* c. him *asunder,* and
Lu. 12.46. *will* c. him *in sunder,* and
  suntemnō.
Ro. 9.28. c. it *short* in righteousness
  aphaireō.
Mar.14.47. priest, and c.*off* his; Lu.22.50
  diapriō.
Act.5.33. *were* c. to the heart; 7.54

CYMBAL.
  kumbalon.
¹Co.13. 1. sound. brass, or a tinkling c.

DAILY.
  kata hēmera. [*accu.*]
Mat.26.55. I sat c. with you teaching
Mar.14.49. I was c. with you in the ;
  Lu.22.53
Lu. 19.47. he taught c. in the temple
Act. 2.46. continuing c. with one acco.
  47. the Lord added to the ch. c.
  3. 2. whom they laid c. at the
  16. 5. and increased in number c.
  17.11. searched the scriptures c.
  17. in the market c. with them
  19. 9. disputing c. in the school of
¹Co. 15.31. Jesus our Lord, I die c.'
²Co. 11.28. which cometh upon me c.
Heb. 3.13. exhort one another c., while
  7.27. Who needeth not c., as those
  10.11. every priest standeth c. mi.
  kathēmerinos.
Act.6. 1. neglected in the c. ministra.
66

ephēmeros.

Jas. 2.15. and destitute of c. food
  pas hēmera.
Act.5.42. and c. in the temple, and
  epiousios.
Mat.6.11. Give us this day our c. bread
Lu. 11. 3. us day by day our c. bread

DAINTY.
  liparos.
Rev.18.14. all things which were c. and

DAMAGE.
  zēmia.
Act.27.10. be with hurt and much c.
  zēmioō.
²Co. 7. 9. ye might *receive* d. by us in

DAMNABLE.
  apōleia.
²Pet.2. 1. shall bring in c. heresies

DAMNATION.
  krima.
Mat.23.14. ye shall receive greater c.
Ro. 3. 8. may come? whose c. is just
  13. 2. shall receive to themselv. c.
¹Co.11.29. eateth and drinketh c. to
¹Ti. 5.12. Having c., because they have
  krisis.
Mat.23.33. how can ye escape the c. of
Mar. 3.29. is in danger of eternal c.
  apōleia.
²Pet.2. 3. their c. slumbereth not

DAMNED.
  katakrinō.
Mar.16.16. believeth not *shall be* d.
Ro. 14.23. he that doubteth *is* d. if he
  krinō.
²Th. 2.12. That they all *might be* d.

DAMSEL.
  korasion.
Mat.14.11. charger, and given to the d.
Mar. 5.41. d., I say unto thee, arise
  42. the d. arose, and walked ; for
  6.22. king said unto the d., Ask
  28. gave it to the d. : and the d.
  paidion.
Mar.5.39. the d. is not dead, but sleep.
  40. father and mother of the d.
  entereth in where the d. was
  41. he took the d. by the hand
  paidiskē.
Mat.26.69. and a d. came unto him
Jo. 18.17. Then saith the d. that kept
Act.12.13. a d. came to hearken, named
  16.16. a certain d. possessed with a

DANCED.
  orcheomai.
Mat.11.17. and ye have not d.; Lu.7.32
  14. 6. the daughter of Herodias d.
Mar. 6.22. came in, and d., and pleased

DANCING, [*noun.*]
  choros.
Lu.15.25. house, he heard music and d.

DANGER.
  enochos.
Mat.5.21,22. shall be *in* d. *of*
Mar.3.29. is *in* d. *of* eternal damnation
  kinduneuō.
Act.19.27. only this our craft *is in* d.
  40. we *are in* d. to be called in

DANGEROUS.
  episphalēs.
Act.27. 9. when sailing was now d.

DARE.
  tolmaō.
Ro. 5. 7. some would even d. to die
  15.18. For I *will* not d. to speak cf
¹Co. 6. 1. d. any of you having a matter
²Co.10.12. For we d. not make ourselves

DARK.
  skoteinos.
Lu.11.36. light, having no part d.
  skotia.
Jo. 6.17. And it was now d., and Jesus
  20. 1. early, when it was yet d., unto
  auchmēros.
²Pet.1.19. that shineth in a d. place

DARKENED.
  skotizomai.
Mat.24.29. *shall* the sun *be* d.; Mar.13.24
Lu. 23.45. the sun *was* d., and the veil
Ro. 1.21. their foolish heart *was* d.
  11.10. *Let* their eyes *be* d., that
Eph. 4.18. Having the understanding d.
Rev. 8.12. the third part of them *was* d.
  9. 2. the sun and the air *were* d.

DARKLY.
  ainigma.
¹Co.13.12. we see through a glass, d.

DARKNESS.
  skotos.
Mat. 4.16. The people which sat in d.
  6.23. be d., how great is that d.
  8.12. into outer d. ; 22.13 ; 25.30
  27.45. was d. over all ; Mar.15.33
Lu. 1.79. light to them that sit in d.
  11.35. which is in thee be not d.
  22.53. hour, and the power of d.
  23.44. there was a d. over all the
Jo. 3.19. men loved d. rather than
Act. 2.20. sun shall be turned into d.
  13.11. fell on him a mist and a d.
  26.18. to turn them from d. to light
Ro. 2.19. light of them which are in d.
  13.12. cast off the works of d., and
¹Co. 4. 5. the hidden things of d., and
²Co. 4. 6. the light to shine out of d.
  6.14. commun. hath light with d.
Eph. 5. 8. ye were sometimes d., but
  11. the unfruitful works of d.
  6.12. the rulers of the d. of this
Col. 1.13. deliv. us from the pow. of d.
¹Th. 5. 4. ye, brethren, are not in d.
  5. are not of the night, nor of d.
Heb.12.18. nor unto blackness, and d.
¹Pet. 2. 9. called you out of d. into his
²Pet. 2.17. mist of d. is reserved for ever
¹Jo. 1. 6. and walk in d., we lie, and
Jude 13. the blackness of d. for ever
  skotia.
Mat.10.27. What I tell you in d., that
Lu. 12. 3. whatso. ye have spoken in d.
Jo. 1. 5. shineth in d. ; and the d.
  8.12. shall not walk in d., but shall
  12.35. lest d. come upon you : for
  he that walketh in d.
  46. on me should not abide in d.
¹Jo. 1. 5. light, and in him is no d. at
  2. 8. because the d. is past, and
  9. brother, is in d. even until
  11. is in d., and walketh in d.
  because that d. hath blinded
  skoteinos.
Mat.6.23. whole-body shall be *full of* d.
Lu.11.34. evil, thy body also is *full of* d.
  zophos.
²Pet.2. 4. deliv. them into chains of d.
Jude 6. everlasting chains under d.
  skotoomai.
Rev.16.10. his kingdom was *full of* d.

DART, -s.
belos.
Eph.6.16. quench all the fiery **d**-s of the
bolis.
Heb.12.20. or thrust through with a **d**.

DASH.
proskoptō.
Mat. 4.6. thou **d**. thy foot ; Lu.4.11

DAUGHTER, -s.
thugatēr.
Mat. 9.18. My **d**. is even now dead ; but
  22. **d**., be of good comf.; Lu.8.48
  10.35. and the **d**. against her moth.
  37. loveth son or **d**. more than
  14. 6. the **d**. of Herodias danced
  15.22. my **d**. is grievously vexed
  28. And her **d**. was made whole
  21. 5. Tell ye the **d**. of Sion, Behold
Mar. 5.34. **d**., thy faith hath made
  35. Thy **d**. is dead ; Lu.8.49
  6.22. And when the **d**. of the said
  7.26. forth the devil out of her **d**.
  29. devil is gone out of thy **d**.
  30. and her **d**. laid upon the bed
Lu. 1. 5. of the **d**-s of Aaron, and her
  2.36. the **d**. of Phanuel, of the
  8.42. he had one only **d**., about
  12.53. against the **d**., and the **d**.
  13.26. being a **d**. of Abraham, whom
  23.28. **d**-s of Jerusalem, weep not
Jo. 12.15. Fear not, **d**. of Sion : behold
Act. 2.17. and your **d**-s shall prophesy
  7.21. Pharaoh's **d**. took him up
  21. 9. four **d**-s, virgins, which did
2Co. 6.18. ye shall be my sons and **d**-s
Heb.11.24.called the son of Pharaoh's **d**.
thugatrion.
Mar. 5.23. My *little* **d**. lieth at the point
  7.25. whose *young* **d**. had an uncl.
teknon.
1Pet.3. 6. whose **d**-s ye are, as long as
numphē.
Mat.10.35. **d**. in law against ; Lu.12.53
Lu. 12.53. against her **d**. *in law*, and

DAWN.
epiphōskō.
Mat.28.1. *as it began to* **d**. toward the
diaugazō.
2Pet.1.19. until the day **d**., and the day

DAY.
hēmera.
Mat.6.34. Sufficient unto the **d**. is the
  10.15. the **d**. of judgment; 11.22,24;
  12.36 ; Mar. 6.11 ; 2Pet. 2.9;
  3.7 ; 1Jo.4.17
  20. 2. for a penny a **d**., he sent them
  6. stand ye here all the **d**. idle
  12. the burden and heat of the **d**.
  24.38. the **d**. that Noe ent.; Lu.17.27
  50. in a **d**. when he looketh not
  25.13. ye know neither the **d**. nor
Mar.6.21. when a convenient **d**. was
  14.12. the first **d**. of unleavened bre.
Lu. 1.20. not able to speak, until the **d**.
  59. that on the eighth **d**. they
  80. was in the deserts till the **d**.
  2.44. went a **d**.'s journey ; and they
  4.42. when it was **d**. he departed
  5.17. on a certain **d**., as he was
  6.13. when it was **d**., he called
  8.22. it came to pass on a certain **d**.
  9.12. And when the **d**. began to
  37. that on the next **d**., when
  11. 3. Give us **d**. by **d**.
  12.46. in a **d**. when he looketh not
  16.19. fared sumptuously every **d**.
  17. 4. a **d**., and seven times in a **d**.
  24. the Son of man be in his **d**.
  30. in the **d**. when the Son of

Lu. 19.42. at least in this thy **d**., the
  21.37. And in the **d**. *time* he was
  22. 7. the **d**. of unleavened bread
  66. as soon as it was **d**., the elders
  24.29. the **d**. is far spent. And he
Jo. 6.39. raise it up again at the last **d**.
  40,44,54. him, at the last **d**.
  7.37. In the last **d**., that great day
  8.56. Abrah. rejoiced to see my **d**.
  9. 4. while it is **d**. : the night
  11. 9. **d**. ? If any man walk in the **d**.
  24. the resurrection at the last **d**.
  12. 7. against the **d**. of my burying
  48. shall judge him in the last **d**.
Act. 1. 2. Until the **d**. in which he was
  2. 1. the **d**. of Pentecost ; 20.16
  15. but the third hour of the **d**.
  20. that great and notable **d**. of
  29. sepul. is with us unto this **d**.
  7. 8. circumcised him the eighth **d**.
  26. And the next **d**. he shewed
  10. 3. the ninth hour of the **d**.
  12.18. Now as soon as it was **d**.
  21. And upon a set **d**., Herod
  17.31. Because he hath appoint. a **d**.
  20.18. from the first **d**. that I came
  26. I take you to record this **d**.
  21. 7. and abode with them one **d**.
  26. and the next day purifying
  23. 1. before God until this **d**.
  26.22. God, I continue unto this **d**.
  27.29. stern, and wished for the **d**.
  33. while the **d**. was coming on
  the fourteenth **d**. that ye
  28.13. after one **d**. the south wind
  23. they had appointed him a **d**.
Ro. 2. 5. wrath against the **d**. of wrath
  16. In the **d**. when God shall jud.
  8.36. we are killed all the **d**. long
  10.21. All **d**. long I have stretched
  11. 8. should not hear) unto this **d**.
  13.12. the **d**. is at hand : let us
  13. honestly, as in the **d**.; not it
  14. 5. esteemeth one **d**. above anot.
  another esteemeth every **d**.
  6. he that regardeth the **d**.
  he that regardeth not the **d**.
1Co. 1. 8. **d**. of our Lord ; 5.5 ; 2Co.1.14
  3.13. for the **d**. shall declare it
  10. 8. and fell in one **d**. three and
2Co. 4.16. man is renewed **d**. by **d**.
  6. 2. in the **d**. of salvation have I
  behold, now is the **d**. of salv.
Eph.4.30. unto the **d**. of redemption
  6.13. to withstand in the evil **d**.
Phi. 1. 5. from the first **d**. until now
  6. until the **d**. of Jesus Christ
  10. without offence till the **d**. of
  2.16. in the **d**. of Christ, that I
Col.1.6,9. since the **d**. ye heard of it
1Th. 5. 2. the **d**. of the Lord so cometh
  5. and the children of the **d**.
  8. But let us, who are of the **d**.
2Th. 2. 2. the **d**. of Christ is at hand
Heb.3. 8. in the **d**. of temptation in the
  4. 4. God did rest the seventh **d**.
  7. Again, he limiteth a certain **d**.
  8. have spoken of another **d**.
  8. 9. in the **d**. when I took them
  10.25. as ye see the **d**. approaching
Jas. 5. 5. your hearts, as in a **d**. of
1Pet.2.12. glorify God in the **d**. of visit.
2Pet.1.19. in a dark place, until the **d**.
  2. 8. righteous soul from **d**. to **d**.
  13. to riot in the **d**. time. Spots
  3. 8. one **d**. is with the Lord as a
  a thousand years as one **d**.
  10. But the **d**. of the Lord will
  12. unto the coming of the **d**. of
Jude 6. unto the judg. of the great **d**.
Rev.1.10. in the Spirit on the Lord's **d**.
  6.17. the great **d**. of his wrath is

Rev.8.12. the **d**. shone not for a third
  9.15. a **d**., and a month, and a year
  16.14. of that great **d**. of God Almi.
  18.18. her plagues come in one **d**.
  21.25. shall not be shut at all by **d**.
  Night and Day.
Mar.4.27. sleep, and rise night and **d**.
  5. 5. And always, night and **d**., he
Lu. 2.37. fast. and prayers night and **d**.
  18. 7. which cry **d**. and night unto
Act.9.24. watched the gates **d**. and nig.
  20.31. warn every one night and **d**.
  26. 7. serving God **d**. and night
1Th. 2. 9. for labouring night and **d**.
  3.10. Night and **d**. praying exceed.
2Th. 3. 8. labour and travail night and **d**.
1Ti. 5. 5. sup. and prayers night and **d**.
2Ti. 1. 3. in my prayers night and **d**.
Rev.4. 8. and they rest not **d**. and nig.
  7.15. and serve him **d**. and night
  12.10. before our God **d**. and night
  14.11. have no rest **d**. nor night
  20.10. **d**. and night for ever and ever
  Same Day.
Mat.13.1. The same **d**. went Jesus out
  22.23. The same **d**. came to him
Mar.4.35. the same **d**., when the even
Lu.13.31. The same **d**. there came cert.
  17.29. But the same **d**. that Lot went
  23.12. the same **d**. Pilate and Herod
  24.13. went that same **d**. to a village
Jo. 5. 9. on the same **d**. was the Sabb.
  20.19. the same **d**. at evening, being
Act. 1.22. unto that same **d**. that he was
  2.41. the same **d**. there were added
  That Day.
Mat.7.22. Many will say to me in that **d**.
  22.46. from that **d**. forth ask him
  24.36. But of that **d**. and ; Mar.13.32
  26.29. that **d**. when I ; Mar.14.25
Lu. 6.23. Rejoice ye in that **d**., and
  10.12. be more tolerable in that **d**.
  17.31. In that **d**., he which shall be
  21.34. and so that **d**. come upon
  23.54. that **d**. was the preparation
Jo. 1.39. abode with him that **d**. : for
  11.53. Then from that **d**. forth they
  14.20. At that **d**. ye shall know that
  16.23. in that **d**. ye shall ask me no.
  26. At that **d**. ye shall ask in my
1Th. 5. 4. that that **d**. should overtake
2Th. 1.10. you, was believed, in that **d**.
2Ti. 1.12. com. unto him against that **d**.
  18. mercy of the Lord in that **d**.
  4. 8. shall give me at that **d**.; and
  Third Day.
Mat.16.21.be raised again the third **d**.
  17.23. the third **d**. he shall be raised
  20.19. the third **d**. he shall rise again;
  Mar.10.34 ; Lu. 18.33
  27.64. until the third **d**., lest his
Mar.9.31. killed, he shall rise the third **d**.
Lu. 9.22. be raised the third **d**.
  24. 7. and the third **d**. rise again
  21. to-day is the third **d**. since
  46. from the dead the third **d**.
Jo. 2. 1. And the third **d**. there was a
Act.10.40. raised up the third **d**., and
1Co. 15. 4. he rose again the third **d**.
sēmeron.
Mat.6.11. Give us *this* **d**. our daily bre.
  11.23. have remained until *this* **d**.
  27. 8. The field of blood, unto this **d**.
  19. suffered many things *this* **d**.
  28.15. among the Jews until *this* **d**.
Mar.14.30.That *this* **d**., even in this
Lu. 2.11. For unto you is born *this* **d**.
  4.21. *This* **d**. is this Scripture fulfi.
  19. 9. *This* **d**. is salvation come
  22.34. the cock shall not crow *this* **d**.
Act.4. 9. If we *this* **d**. be examined
  13.33. *this* **d**. have I begot.; Heb.1.5

Act.19.40. called in question for *this* **d**-*'s*
20.26. I take you to record *this* **d**.
22. 3. towa. God, as ye are all *this* **d**.
24.21. called in ques. by you *this* **d**.
26. 2. I shall an. for myself *this* **d**.
29. also all that hear me *this* **d**.
27.33. *This* **d**. is the fourteenth **d**.
Ro.11. 8. should not hear; unto this **d**.
²Co. 3.14. for until *this* **d**. remaineth
15. But even unto *this* **d**., when
epaurion.
Mat.27.62. Now the *next* **d**., that follow.
Jo. 1.29. The *next* **d**. John seeth Jes.
35. the *next* **d**. *after* John stood
43. The **d**. *following* Jesus would
6.22. The **d**. *following*, when the
12.12. On the *next* **d**. much people
Act. 14.20. the *next* **d**. he departed with
21. 8. and the *next* **d**. we that were
25. 6. the *next* **d**. sitting on the
heteros.
Act.20.15. and the *next* **d**. we arrived
27. 3. And the *next* **d**. we touched
ennuchon.
Mar.1.35, up *a great while before* **d**.
hōra.
Mar.6.35. when the **d**. was now *far* spe.
aurion.
Act.4. 3. in hold unto the *next* **d**.
deuteraios.
Act.28.13. we came the *next* **d**. to Pute.
arti.
¹Co. 4.13. of all things unto *this* **d**.
nuchthēmeron.
²Co.11.25. *a night and a* **d**. I have been

(*See other words with which it is connected.*)

DAYS.
hēmera.
Mat.2. 1. in the **d**. of Herod; Lu.1 5
3. 1. In those **d**.; Mar.1.9; 2.20
9.15. the **d**. will come; Mar. 2.20;
Lu. 5.35
11.12. And from the **d**. of John the
17. 1. And after six **d**. Jesus taketh
23.30. If we had been in the **d**. of
24.19. that give suck in those **d**.;
Mar.13.17; Lu.21.23
22. except those **d**. should be
those **d**. shall be shortened
29. the tribulation of those **d**.
37. But as the **d**. of Noe were
38. For as in the **d**. that were
Mar.2. 1. into Capernaum after some **d**.
13.20. had shortened those **d**., no
he hath shortened them
Lu. 1.23. that as soon as the **d**. of his
24. And after those **d**. his wife
25. in the **d**. wherein he looked
75. before him all the **d**. of our
2.6,21. were accomplished that
22. when the **d**. of her purifica.
43. when they had fulfilled the **d**.
4.25. were in Israel in the **d**. of
5.35. But the **d**. will come, when
then shall they fast in those **d**.
17.22. The **d**. will come, when ye
desire to see one of the **d**.
26. as it was in the **d**. of Noe, so
also in the **d**. of the Son of
28. in the **d**. of Lot; they did eat
19.43. For the **d**. shall come upon
20. 1. that on one of those **d**., as
21. 6. the **d**. will come, in the which
22. For these be the **d**. of vengea.
23.29. behold, the **d**. are coming
24.18. come to pass there in these **d**.
Act. 2.17. come to pass in the last **d**.
3.24. likewise foretold of these **d**.
5.36. For before these **d**. rose up
68

Act. 5.37. in the **d**. of the taxing, and
7.45. fathers, unto the **d**. of David
9.19. then was Saul certain **d**. with
10.48. they him to tarry certain **d**.
11.27. And in these **d**. came proph.
12. 3. Then were the **d**. of unleav.
13.41. I work a work in your **d**.
15.36. And some **d**. after Paul said
16.12. that city abiding certain **d**.
20. 6. from Philippi after the **d**. of
21. 5. we had accomplished those **d**.
15. And after those **d**. we took
26. the accomplishment of the **d**.
38. Egypt., which before these **d**.
24.24. And after certain **d**.; 25.13
Gal. 4.10. Ye observe **d**. and months
Eph.5.16. because the **d**. are evil
²Ti. 3. 1. that in the last **d**. perilous
Heb.1. 2. Hath in these last **d**. spoken
5. 7. in the **d**. of his flesh, when
7. 3. neither beginning of **d**.
8. 8. Behold, the **d**. come, saith
10. house of Israel after those **d**.
10.16. make with them after those **d**.
32. to remembrance the former **d**.
12.10. For they verily for a few **d**.
Jas. 5. 3. treasure togeth. for the last **d**.
¹Pet.3.10. will love life, and see good **d**.
20. in the **d**. of Noah, while the
²Pet.3. 3. there shall come in the last **d**.
Rev.10.7. But in the **d**. of the voice of
Many Days.
Lu.15.13. not many **d**. after, the young.
Jo. 2.12. continued there not many **d**.
Act.1. 5. Holy Gho. not many **d**. hence
9.23. many **d**. were fulfilled, the
43. he tarried many **d**. in Joppa
13.31. he was seen many **d**. of them
16.18. did she many **d**. But Paul
21.10. as we tarried there many **d**.
25.14. they had been there many **d**.
27. 7. had sailed slowly many **d**.
20. sun nor stars in many **d**.
Two Days.
Mat.26.2. after two **d**. is the feast of the
Mar.14.1. After two **d**. was the feast of
Jo. 4.40. and he abode there two **d**.
43. Now after two **d**. he departed
11. 6. two **d**. still in the same place
Three Days, &c.
Mat.12.40. three **d**. and three nights
15.32. contin. with me now three **d**.
26.61. and to build it in three **d**.
27.40. it in three **d**.; Mar.15.29
63. After three **d**. I will rise again
Mar.8. 2. now been with me three **d**.
31. killed, and after three **d**. rise
14.58. within three **d**. I will build
Lu. 2.46. that after three **d**. they found
Jo. 2.19. in three **d**. I will raise it up
20. wilt thou rear it up in three **d**.
Act. 9. 9. three **d**. without sight, and
25.1. after three **d**. he ascended
28. 7. lodged us three **d**. courteously
12. we tarried there three **d**.
17. that after three **d**. Paul called
Rev.11.9. three **d**. and a half, and shall
11. after three **d**. and an half the
Jo. 11.17. had lain in the grave four **d**.
Act.10.30. Four **d**. ago I was fasting
20. 6. unto them to Troas in five **d**.
24. 1. And after five **d**. Ananias the
Mat.17.1. And after six **d**. Jesus taketh
9. 2. after six **d**. Jesus taketh with
Lu.13.14. There are six **d**. in which men
Jo. 12. 1. six **d**. before the passover
20. 6. where we abode seven **d**.
Act.21.4. we tarried there seven **d**.
27. the seven **d**. were almost
28.14. to tarry with them seven **d**.
Heb.11.30. compassed about seven **d**.

Lu. 9.28. about an eight **d**. after these
Jo. 20.26. And after eight **d**, again his
Act. 25.6. more than ten **d**., he went
Rev.2.10. shall have tribulation ten **d**.
Act.24.11. there are yet but twelve **d**.
Gal. 1.18. abode with him fifteen **d**.
Mat.4. 2. when he had fasted forty **d**.
Mar.1.13. in the wilderness forty **d**.
Lu. 4. 2. forty **d**. tempted of the devil
Act. 1. 3. being seen of them forty **d**.
Rev.11.3. hundred and threescore **d**.

DEACON, -s.
diakonos.
Phi. 1. 1. Ph., with the bishops and **d**-s
¹Ti. 3. 8. Likewise must the **d**-s be
12. **d**-s be the husbands of one
diakoneō.
Ti. 3.10. *let them use the office of a* **d**.
13. *that have used the office of a* **d**.

DEAD.
nekros.
Mat.8.22. the **d**. bury their **d**.; Lu.9.60
10. 8. raise the **d**., cast out devils
11. 5. the **d**. are raised up, and the
14. 2. risen from the **d**.; 27.64, 28.7;
Mar. 6.14,16, 9.9; Lu. 9.7;
Jo.2.22, 21.14; ¹Co.15.20
17. 9. be risen again from the **d**.
22.31. resurrection of the **d**.;
Lu.20.35; Act.4.2, 17.32, 23.6,
24.15,21; Ro.1.4; ¹Co.15.12.13.
21.42; Phil.3.11; Heb.6.2
32. the God of the **d**.; Mar.12.27
Lu.20.38
23.27. within, full of **d**. men's bones
28. 4. shake, and became as **d**. men
Mar.9.10. rising from the **d**. should me.
26. of him: he was as one **d**.
12.25. they shall rise from the **d**.
26. as touching the **d**., that they
Lu. 7.15. And he that was **d**. sat up
22. the deaf hear, the **d**. are
15.24. For this my son was **d**., and
32. for this thy brother was **d**.
16.30. went unto them from the **d**.
31. though one rose from the **d**.
20.37. Now that the **d**. are raised
24. 5. seek the living among the **d**.
46. rise from the **d**. the third
Jo. 5.21. the Father raiseth up the **d**.
25. when the **d**. shall hear the
12. 1, 9. whom he raised from the **d**.
Act. 3.15, 4.10; Ro.6.9, 7.4;
¹Th.1.10; ²Tim.2.8
17. raised him from the **d**.
Act.13.30.34, 17.31; Ro.10.9;
Gal.1.1; Eph.1.20; Col.2.12
20. 9. he must rise again from the **d**.
Act. 5.10. and found her **d**., and, car.
10.41. he rose from the **d**.; ¹Co.15.12
42. the Judge of quick and **d**.
17. 3. and risen again from the **d**.
20. 9. left, and was taken up **d**.
26. 8. that God should raise the **d**.
23. that should rise from the **d**.
28. 6. or fallen down **d**. suddenly
Ro. 4.17. who quickeneth the **d**., and
24. Jesus our Lord from the **d**.
6.11. to be **d**. indeed unto sin, but
13. that are alive from the **d**.
7. 8. For with. the law sin was **d**.
8.10. the body is **d**. because of sin
11. raised up Jesus from the **d**.
raised up Christ from the **d**.
10. 7. up Christ again from the **d**.
11.15. them be, but life from the **d**.
14. 9. be Lord both of the **d**. and
¹Co.15.15.16.32. that the **d**. rise not

DEA   DEA   DEA

¹Co.15.29. baptized for the **d.**, if the **d.**
    then baptized for the **d.**
  35. How are the **d.** raised up
  52. the **d.** shall be raised incorru.
²Co. 1. 9. but in God which ra. the **d.**
Eph.2. 1. who were **d.** in trespasses
   5. when we were **d.** in sins
  5.14. arise from the **d.**, and Christ
Col. 1.18. the firstborn from the **d.**
  2.13. And you, being **d.** in your
¹Th. 4.16. the **d.** in Christ shall rise
²Ti. 4. 1. judge the quick and the **d.**
Heb. 6.1. repentance from **d.** works
  9.14. your conscience from **d.** wor.
  17. of force after men are **d.**
    (confirmed upon the *dead*.)
  11.19. him up, even from the **d.**
  35. received their **d.** raised to
  13.20. brought again from the **d.**
Jas. 2.17. hath no works, is **d.**, being
  20. that faith without works is **d.**
  26. body without the spirit is **d.**
    so faith without works is **d.**
¹Pet.1. 3. of Jesus Christ from the **d.**
   4. 6. pr. also to them that are **d.**
Rev.1. 5. the first begotten of the **d.**
  17. I fell at his feet as **d.** And
  18. he that liveth, and was **d.**
   2. 8. which was **d.**, and is alive
   3. 1. that thou livest, and art **d.**
  11.18. the time of the **d.**, that they
  14.13. Blessed are the **d.** which die
  16. 3. became as the blood of a **d.**
  20. 5. the rest of the **d.** lived not
  12. And I saw the **d.**, small and
    and the **d.** were judged out of
  13. sea gave up the **d.** which
    hell delivered up the **d.**
nekroō.
Ro. 4. 19. not his own body now **d.**
Heb.11.12. of one, and him as good as **d.**
apothnēskō.
Mat.9.24. for the maid is not **d.**, but
Mar.5.35. which said, Thy daugh. *is* **d.**
  39. the damsel is not **d.**, but
  9.26. that many said, He is **d.**
  15.44. marvelled if he *were* alr. **d.**
  whe. he *had been* any while **d.**
Lu. 8.52. Weep not; she is not **d.**, but
  53. scorn, know. that she *was* **d.**
Jo. 6.49. in the wilderness, and are **d.**
  58. did eat manna, and are **d.**
  8.52. Abraham *is* dead, and the
  53. *is* **d.**? and prophets are **d.**
  11.14. them plainly, Lazarus is **d.**
  25. though he *were* **d.**, yet shall
Act. 7. 4. thence, when his fath. *was* **d.**
Ro. 5.15. the offence of one many *be* **d.**
   6. 2. how shall we that *are* **d.** to
   7. For he that *is* **d.** is freed from
   8. if we *be* **d.** with Ch.; Col.2.20
   7. 2. if the husband *be* **d.**, she
   6. that *being* **d.** wherein we
²Co. 5.14. for all, then were all **d.**
    (then all *died*.)
Gal. 2.19. I through the law *am* **d.** to
  21. then Christ *is* **d.** in vain
Col. 3. 3. For ye *are* **d.**, and your life
Heb.11.4. by it he *being* **d.** yet speaketh
Jude 12. without fruit, twice **d.**
thnēskō.
Mat.2.20. for they *are* **d.** which sought
Mar.15.44.if he *were* already **d.**: and
Lu. 7. 12. there was a **d.** man carried
  8.49. Thy daughter is **d.**; trouble
Jo. 11.39. the sister of him *that was* **d.**
  41. where the **d.** was laid. And
  44. And he *that was* **d.** came
  12. 1. Lazarus was *which had been* **d.**
  19.33. that he was **d.** *already*, they
Act.14.19.supposing he had been **d.**
  25.19. of one Jesus, *which was* **d.**

¹Ti. 5. 6. pleasure *is* **d.** while she liveth
sunapothnēskō.
²Ti. 2.11. For if we *be* **d.** *with* him, we
teleutaō.
Mat.2.19. But *when* Herod *was* **d.**
  9.18. My daughter is even now **d.**
Act. 2.29. that he *is* both **d.** and
thanatoō.
Ro. 7. 4. ye also *are become* **d.** to the
apoginomai.
¹Pet.2.24. that we *being* **d.** to sins
ptōma.
Rev.11.8. And their **d.** *bodies* shall lie
   9. shall see their **d.** *bodies* three
    shall not suffer their **d.** *bodies*
hēmithanēs.
Lu.10.30. departed, leaving him *half* **d.**
koimaomai.
¹Co.7.39. but if her husband *be* **d.** she

DEADLY.
thanasimos.
Mar.16.18. if they drink any **d.** thing
thanatēphoros.
Jas. 3. 8. unruly evil, full of **d.** poison
thanatos.
Rev.13.3, 12. **d.** wound was healed

DEADNESS.
nekrōsis.
Ro. 4.19. neither yet the **d.** of Sarah's

DEAF.
kōphos.
Mat.11.5. and the **d.** hear
Mar.7.32. one that was **d.**, and had an
  37. he maketh both the **d.** to
  9.25 Thou dumb and **d.** spirit, I
Lu. 7.22. the **d.** hear, the dead are

DEAL, [*verb*,]   -eth, -ealt.
poieō.
Lu. 1.25. Thus *hath* the Lord **d**-t with
  2.48. why *hast* thou thus **d**-t with
entungchanō.
Act.25.24. the Jews *have* **d**-t with me
merizō.
Ro.12. 3. as God *hath* **d**-t to every man
prospherō.
Heb.12.7. God **d**-*eth with* you as with
katasophizomai.
Act.7.19. **d**-t subtilely with our

DEAL, [*noun.*]
perissoteron.
Mar.7.36. so much the more *a great* **d.**

DEALINGS.
sungchraomai.
Jo. 4. 9. Jews *have* no **d.** *with* the Sa.

DEAR.
agapētos.
Eph.5. 1. followers of God, as **d.** child.
¹Th. 2. 8. because ye were **d.** unto us
agapē.
Col. 1.13. into the kingdom of his **d.**
entimos.
Lu. 7. 2. who was **d.** unto him, was
timios.
Act.20.24. neither count I my life **d.**

DEARLY.   See *Beloved.*
DEARTH.
limos.
Act. 7.11. there came a **d.** over all the
  11.28. there should be a great **d.**

DEATH,   -s.
thanatos.
Mat.4.16. the region and shadow of **d.**
  10.21. deliver up the brother to **d.**

Mat.15.4. let him die the **d.**; Mar.7.10
  16.28. shall not taste of **d.**
    Mar.9.1; Lu.9.27
  20.18. shall co. him to **d.**; Mar.10.33
  26.38. sor. even unto **d.**; Mar.14.34
  66. and said, He is guilty of **d.**
Mar.13.12.bro. shall betray broth. to **d.**
  14.64. cond. him to be guilty of **d.**
Lu. 1.79. and in the shadow of **d.**, to
  2.26. that he should not see **d.**
  22.33. both into prison, and to **d.**
  23.15. noth. worthy of **d.**; Act.25.25
  22. no cause of **d.** in him: I
  24.20. to be condemned to **d.**, and
Jo. 5.24. is passed from **d.** unto life
  8.51. saying, he shall never see **d.**
  52. he shall never taste of **d.**
  11. 4. This sickness is not unto **d.**
  13. Jesus spake of his **d.**: but
  12.33. what **d.** he should die; 18.32
  21.19. by what **d.** he should glorify
Act. 2.24. having loosed the pains of **d.**
  13.28. they found no cause of **d.** in
  22. 4. persec. this way unto the **d.**
  23.29. worthy of **d.** or of; 26.31
  25.11. committed any. worthy of **d.**
  28.18. there was no cause of **d.** in
Ro. 1.32. such things are worthy of **d.**
  5.10. by the **d.** of his Son, much
  12. and **d.** by sin; and so **d.**
  14. **d.** reigned from Adam to Mo.
  17. **d.** reigned by one; much
  21. sin hath reigned unto **d.** even
   6. 3. were baptized into his **d.**
   4. by baptism into **d.**; that like
   5. in the likeness of his **d.**, we
   9. **d.** hath no more dominion
  16. whether of sin unto **d.**, or of
  21. the end of those things is **d.**
  23. the wages of sin is **d.**; but
   7. 5. to bring forth fruit unto **d.**
  10. life, I found to be unto **d.**
  13. which is good made **d.** unto
    sin, working in me by that
  24. me from the body of this **d.**
   8. 2. free from the law of sin and **d.**
   6. to be carnally minded is **d.**
  38. neither **d.**, nor life, nor
¹Co.3.22. life, or **d.**, or things present
  11.26. ye do shew the Lord's **d.** till
  15.21. by man came **d.**, by man
  26. that shall be destroyed is **d.**
  54. **d.** is swallowed up in victory
  55. O **d.**, where is thy sting?
  56. The sting of **d.** is sin; and
²Co. 1. 9. we had the sentence of **d.** in
  10. delivered us from so great a **d.**
  2.16. are the savour of **d.** unto **d.**
   3. 7. the ministration of **d.**, written
  4.11. are alway delivered unto **d.**
  12. then **d.** worketh in us, but
  7.10. sorrow of the world wor. **d.**
  11.23. prisons more frequent, in **d**-s
Phi. 1.20. whether it be by life, or by **d.**
   2. 8. obedient unto **d.**, even the **d.**
  27. he was sick nigh unto **d.**
  30. nigh unto **d.**, not regarding
  3.10. made comformable unto his **d.**
Col. 1.22. body of his flesh through **d.**
²Ti. 1.10. who hath abolished **d.**, and
Heb. 2.9. for the suffering of **d.** crowned
    should taste **d.** for every man
  14. through **d.** he might destroy
    him that had the power of **d.**
  2.15. through fear of **d.** were all
   5. 7. to save him from death, and
  7.23. suffered to con. by reason of **d.**
  9.15. by means of **d.**, for the rede.
  16. also of necessity be the **d.**
  11. 5. that he should not see **d.**;
Jas. 1.15. finished, bringeth forth **d.**
  5.20. shall save a soul from **d.**

69

¹Jo. 3.14. we have passed from **d.**
     not his brother abideth in **d.**
  5.16. a sin which is not unto **d.**
     that sin not unto **d.**   There
     is a sin unto **d.**: I do not say
  17. and there is a sin not unto **d.**
Rev.1.18. the keys of hell and of **d.**
  2.10. be thou faithful unto **d.**, and
  11. not be hurt of the second **d.**
  23. I will kill her children with **d.**
  6. 8. name that sat on him was **d.**
     with hunger, and with **d.**
  9. 6. men seek **d.**, and shall not
     and **d.** shall flee from them
 12.11. not their lives unto the **d.**
 13. 3. as it were wounded to **d.**
 18. 8. **d.**, and mourning, and fam.
 20. 6. the second **d.** hath no power
  13. **d.** and hell delivered up the
  14. **d.** and hell were cast into the
     of fire.   This is the second **d.**
 21. 4. shall be no more **d.**, neither
  8. brims. which is the second **d.**
  teleutē.
Mat.2.15. was there until the **d.** of Her.
  eschatōs.
Mar.5.23. lieth *at the point of* **d.**
  anairesis.
Act.8. 1. consenting unto his **d.**; 22.20
  mellō apothnēskō.
Jo. 4.47. for he was *at the point of* **d.**
  apokteinō.
Mat.14.5. he would *have put* him *to* **d.**
Mar.14.1. by craft, and *put* him *to* **d.**
Jo. 11.53. together for to *put* him *to* **d.**
 12.10. *might put* Lazarus also to **d.**
 18.31. for us to *put* any man *to* **d.**
  thanatoō.
Mat.10.21. *cause* them *to be put to* **d.**
     Mar.13.12
  26.59. Jesus, to *put* him *to* **d.**; 27.1
     Mar.14.55
Lu. 21.16. *shall they cause to be put to* **d.**
¹Pet. 3.18. *being put to* **d.** in the flesh
  anaireō.
Lu. 23.32. led with him to *be put to* **d.**
Act.26.10. *when they were put to* **d.**, I
  apagō.
Act.12.19. that they should *be put to* **d.**
  epithanatios.
¹Co. 4. 9. as it were *appointed to* **d.**

DEBATE,   -s.
  eris.
Ro. 1.29. full of envy, murder, **d.**, de.
²Co.12.20. lest there be **d-s**, envyings

DEBT,   -s.
  opheilēma.
Mat.6.12. And forgive us our **d-s**, as we
Ro. 4. 4. reckoned of grace, but of **d.**
  daneion.
Mat.18.27. him, and forgave him the **d.**
  opheilē.
Mat.18.32. I forgave thee all that **d.**
  opheilō.
Mat.18.30. till he should pay the **d.**

DEBTOR,   -s.
  opheiletēs.
Mat.6.12. debts, as we forgive our **d-s**
Ro. 1.14. I am **d.** both to the Greeks
  8.12. we are **d-s** not to the flesh
 15.27. and their **d-s** they are.   For
Gal. 5. 3. he is a **d.** to do the whole
  chreōpheiletēs.
Lu. 7.41. creditor which had two **d-s**
  16. 5. every one of his lord's **d-s**
  opheilō.
Mat.23.16. the temple, he *is* a **d.**
70

DECAYETH.
  palaioō.
Heb. 8.13. Now that *which* **d.** and

DECEASE, (noun.)
  exodos.
Lu. 9.31. and spake of his **d.** which he
²Pet.1.15. ye may be able after my **d.**

DECEASED, (verb.)
  teleutaō.
Mat.22.25. he had married a wife, **d.**

DECEIT.
  dolos.
Mar.7.22. wickedness, **d.**, lasciviousness
Ro. 1.29. of envy, murder, debate, **d.**
  dolioō.
Ro. 3.13. tongues they *have used* **d.**
  apatē.
Col. 2. 8. philosophy and vain **d.**
  planē.
¹Th. 2 3. exhortation was not of **d.**

DECEITFUL.
  dolios.
²Co.11.13. false apostles, **d.** workers
  apatē.
Eph.4.22. corrupt according to the **d.**

DECEITFULLY. (See *Handle*.)

DECEITFULNESS.
  apatē.
Mat.13.22. the **d.** of riches; Mar.4.19
Heb. 3.13. hardened through the **d.** of

DECEIVABLENESS.
  apatē.
²Th. 2.10. all **d.** of unrighteousness in

DECEIVE,   -ed, -eth, -ing.
  planaō.
Mat.24.4. Take heed that no man **d.**
  5, 11. *shall* **d.** many; Mar.13.6
  24. they shall **d.** the very elect
Mar.13.5. Take heed lest any man **d.**
Lu. 21. 8. Take heed that ye *be* not **d**-*ed*
Jo. 7.12. Nay ; but he **d**-*eth* the peo.
  47. Pharisees, *are* ye also **d**-*ed*
¹Co. 6. 9. *Be* not **d**-*ed* ; 15.33. Gal.6.7.
²Ti. 3.13. worse, **d**-*ing* and *being* **d**-*ed*
Tit. 3. 3. **d**-*ed*, serving divers lusts and
¹Jo. 1. 8. we **d.** ourselves, and the
  3. 7. *let* no man **d.** you : he that
Rev.12.9. and Satan, *which* **d**-*eth* the
 13.14. And **d**-*eth* them that dwell
 18.23. sorceries *were* all nations **d**-*ed*
 19.20. with which he **d**-*ed* them
 20. 3. that he *should* **d.** the nations
  8. go out to **d.** the nations wh.
  10. the devil *that* **d**-*ed* them was
  apataō.
Eph.5. 6. *Let* no man **d.** you with vain
¹Ti. 2.14. Adam *was* not **d**-*ed*, but the
  woman *being* **d**-*ed* was in the
Jas. 1.26. his tongue, but **d**-*eth* his own
  exapataō.
Ro. 7.11. **d**-*ed* me, and by it slew me
 16.18. **d.** the hearts of the simple
¹Co. 3.18. *Let* no man **d.**; ²Th.2.3
  phrenapataō.
Gal. 6. 3. when he is nothing, he **d**-*eth*
  planē .
Eph.4.14. whereby they lie in wait *to* **d.**
  paralogizomai.
Jas. 1.22. only, **d**-*ing* your own selves

DECEIVER,   -s.
  planos.
Mat.27.63. remember that that **d.** said
²Co. 6. 8. report : as **d-s** and yet true

²Jo.   7. For many **d-s** are entered
     This is a **d.** and an antichrist
  phrenapatēs.
Tit. 1.10. and vain talkers and **d.** -s

DECEIVINGS.
  apatē.
²Pet.2.13. with their own **d.**, while

DECENTLY.
  euschēmonōs.
¹Co.14.40. Let all things be done **d.** and

DECKED.
  chrusoō.
Rev.17.4. and **d.** with gold, and ; 18.16

DECLARATION. (See *Ready*)
  diēgēsis.
Lu. 1. 1. to set forth in order a **d.**

DECLARE,   -ed, -ing.
  exēgeomai.
Jo. 1.18. of the Father, he *hath* **d**-*ed*
Act.10.8. *when* he *had* **d**-*ed* all these
 15.12. **d**-*ing* what miracles and won.
 14. Simeon *hath* **d**-*ed* how God
 21.19. he **d**-*ed* particularly what
  diēgeomai.
Act. 8.33. who shall **d.** his generation
 9.27. **d**-*ed* unto them how ; 12.17
  ekdiēgeomai.
Act.13.41. though a man **d.** it unto you
 15. 3. **d**-*ing* the conversion of the
  gnōrizō.
Jo. 17.26. I *have* **d**-*ed* unto them thy
  and *will* **d.** it : that the love
¹Co.15. 1. brethren, I **d.** unto you the
Col. 4. 7. *shall* Tychicus **d.** unto you
  ananggellō.
Act.15.4. they **d**-*ed* all things that God
 20.27. to **d.** unto you all the couns.
¹Jo. 1. 5. **d.** unto you that God is light
  apanggellō.
Lu. 8.47. she **d**-*ed* unto him before all
Heb.2.12. I will **d.** thy name unto my
¹Jo. 1. 3. seen and heard **d.** we unto
  katanggellō.
Act.17.23. worship, him **d.** I unto you
¹Co. 2. 1. **d**-*ing* unto you the testimo.
  dianggellō.
Ro. 9.17. that my name *might be* **d**-*ed*
  paranggellō.
¹Co.11.17. in this *that* I **d.** unto you
  euanggelizō.
Rev.10.7. as he *hath* **d**-*ed* to his servan.
  dēloō.
¹Co. 1.11. it *hath been* **d**-*ed* unto me of
 3.13. for the day *shall* **d.** it, because
Col. 1. 8. *Who* also **d**-*ed* unto us your
  endeixis.
Ro. 3.25. to **d.** his righteousness
 26. To **d.**, I say at this time
  anatithēmi.
Act.25.14. Festus **d**-*ed* Paul's cause
  phrazō.
Mat.13.36. **d.** unto us the parab.; 15.15
  horizō.
Ro. 1. 4. And **d**-*ed* to be the Son of
  phaneroō.
²Co. 3. 3. *manifestly* **d**-*ed* to be the
  emphanizō.
Heb.11.14. **d.** *plainly* that they seek a
  (See *Tidings*.)

DECREASE.
  elattoō.
Jo. 3.30. must increase, but I must **d.**

DECREE, (noun,)   -s
  dogma.
Lu. 2. 1. went out a **d.** from Caesar

Act.16. 4. they delivered them the **d**-*s*
   17. 7. contrary to the **d**-*s* of Caesar

DECREED, [*verb.*]
krinō.
¹Co. 7.37. *hath* so **d**. in his heart that

DEDICATED.
e_ngkainizō.
Heb.9.18. testament *was* **d**. without

DEDICATION.
e_ngkainia.
Jo. 10.22. Jerusalem the *feast of the* **d**.

DEED,   -s
ergon.
Lu.11.48. the **d**-*s* of your ; Jo.8.41
  24.19. mighty in **d**. and word before
Jo. 3.19. because their **d**-*s* were evil
  20. lest his **d**-*s* should be reprov.
  21. his **d**-*s* may be made mani.
Act.7.22. mighty in words and in **d**-*s*
Ro. 2. 6. every man accord. to his **d**-*s*
  3.20. by the **d**-*s* of the law there
  28. faith without the **d**-*s* of the
  15.18. obedient, by word and **d**.
¹Co. 5. 2. he that hath done this **d**.
²Co.10.11. also in **d**. when we are pres.
Col. 3.17. do in word or **d**., do all in
²Pet.2. 8. say with their unlawful **d**-*s*
¹Jo. 3.18. tongue ; but in **d**. and in
²Jo. 11. is partaker of his evil **d**-*s*
³Jo. 10. his **d**-*s* which he doeth, prat.
Jude. 15. of all their ungodly **d**-*s* which
Rev.2. 6. the **d**-*s* of the Nicolaitanes
  22. except they repent of their **d**-*s*
  16.11. and repented not of their **d**-*s*
euergesia.
Act. 4. 9. of the *good* **d**. *done* to the
praxis.
Lu.23.51. to the counsel and **d**. of them
Act.19.18.confess. and shewed their **d**-*s*
Ro. 8.13. do mortify the **d**-*s* of the
Col. 3. 9. off the old man with his **d**-*s*
prassō.
Lu.23.41. the due reward of our **d**-*s*
poiēsis.
Jas. 1.25. man shall be blessed in his **d**.

DEEMED.
huponoeō.
Act.27.27. the shipmen **d**. that they

DEEP.
bathos.
Lu. 5. 4. Launch out into the **d**., and
¹Co. 2.10. things, yea, the **d**. *things* of
²Co. 8. 2. and their **d**. poverty abound.
bathus.
Jo. 4.11. draw with, and the well is **d**.
Act.20.9. being fallen into a **d**. sleep.
abussos.
Lu. 8.31. them to go out into the **d**.
Ro.10. 7. Who shall descend into the **d**.
bathunō.
Lu. 6.48. built an house, and digged **d**.
buthos.
²Co.11.25. a day I have been in the **d**.

DEEPLY.
anastenazō.
Mar.8.12. he *sighed* **d**. in his spirit, *and*

DEEPNESS.
bathos.
Mat.13.5. because they had no **d**. of

DEFAMED.
blasphēmeō.
¹Co, 4.13. *Being* **d**., we entreat : we

DEFENCE.
apologia.
Act.22. 1. hear ye my **d**. which I make
Phi. 1. 7. in the **d**. and confirmation
  17. am set for the **d**. of the gosp.
apologeomai.
Act.19.33. would *have made* his **d**. unto

DEFENDED.
amunomai.
Act.7.24. suffer wrong, he **d**. him

DEFERRED.
anaballomai.
Act.24.22. of that way, he **d**. them

DEFILE,   -ed, -eth.
koinoō.
Mat.15.11. into the mouth **d**-*eth* a man
  of the mouth, this **d**-*eth* a
  18. the heart ; and they **d**. the
  20. These are the things *which* **d**.
  unwashen hands **d**-*eth* not a
Mar. 7.15. entering into him can **d**. him
  those are they *that* **d**. the
  18. into the man, it cannot **d**.
  20. of the man, that **d**-*eth* the
  23. come from within, and **d**.
Rev. 21.27. into it any thing *that* **d**-*eth*
miainō.
Jo. 18.28. lest they *should be* **d**-*ed*
Ti. 1.15. but unto them *that are* **d**-*ed*
  mind and conscience *is* **d**-*ed*
Heb.12.15. and thereby many *be* **d**-*ed*
Jude 8. these filthy dreamers **d**. the
moluno.
¹Co. 8. 7. conscience being weak *is* **d**-*ed*
Rev.3. 4. *have* not **d**-*ed* their garments
  14.4. which *were* not **d**-*ed* with
koinos.
Mar.7. 2. eat bread with **d**-*ed* (that is
phtheirō.
¹Co.3.17. If any man **d**. the temple of
spiloō.
Jas. 3. 6. that it **d**-*eth* the whole body
arsenokoitēs.
¹Ti. 1.10. that **d**. them *selves with man*.

DEFRAUD,   -ed.
apostereō.
Mar.10.19. **d**. not, Honour thy father
¹Co. 6. 7. suffer yourselves to be **d**-*ed*
  8. Nay, ye do wrong, and **d**.
  7. 5. **d**. ye not one the other
pleonekteō.
²Co. 7. 2. no man, we *have* **d**-*ed* no man
¹Th. 4. 6. and **d**. his brother in any

DEGREE.
bathmos.
¹Ti. 3.13. purchase to them. a good **d**.
tapeinos.
Lu. 1.52. and exalted them *of low* **d**.
Jas. 1. 9. the brother *of low* **d**. rejoice

DELAY, [*noun.*]
anabolē.
Act.25.17. without any **d**. on the mor.

DELAY, [*verb.*]   -eth.
chronizō.
Mat.24.48. My lord **d**-*eth* his; Lu.12.45
okneō.
Act.9.38. that he would not **d**. to come

DELICACIES.
strēnos.
Rev.18.3. thr. the abundance of her **d**.

DELICATELY.
truphē.
Lu. 7.25. and live **d**. are in king's cou.

DELICIOUSLY.
strēniaō.
Rev.18.7. glorified herself, and *lived* **d**.
  9. and *lived* **d**. with her, shall

DELIGHT.
sunēdomai.
Ro. 7.22. For I **d**. in the law of God

DELIVER,   -ed, -edst, -ing.
paradidōmi.
Mat.5.25. adversary **d**. thee to the
  judge and the judge **d**. thee
  10.17. will **d**. you *up* to the councils
  19. they **d**. you *up*; Mar.13.11
  21. the brother *shall* **d**. *up* the
  11.27. All things *are* **d**-*ed* unto me
  18.34. and **d**-*ed* him to the tormen.
  20.19. And *shall* **d**. him to the Gen.
  24. 9. Then *shall* they **d**. you *up* to
  25.14. and **d**-*ed* unto them his goods
  20, 22. Lord, thou **d**-*edst* unto
  26.15. and I will **d**. him unto you
  27. 2. and **d**-*ed* him to Pi.; Mar.15.1
  18. envy they *had* **d**-*ed; Mar.*15.10
  26. he **d**-*ed* him to be crucified
Mar.7.13. tradition, which *ye have* **d**-*ed*
  9.31. *is* **d**-*ed* into the hands of men
  10.33. S. of m. *shall be* **d**-*ed; Lu.*9.44
  and *shall* **d**. him to the Gent.
  13. 9. they *shall* **d**. you *up* to coun.
  15.15. and **d**-*ed* Jesus, when he had
Lu. 1. 2. Even as they **d**-*ed* them unto
  4. 6. of them: for that *is* **d**-*ed* unto
  10.22. All things *are* **d**-*ed* to me of
  12.58. and the judge **d**. thee to the
  18.32. For he *shall be* **d**-*ed* unto the
  20.20. that so they might **d**. him
  21.12. **d**-*ing* you *up* to the synagog.
  23.25. but he **d**-*ed* Jesus to their
  24. 7. must be **d**-*ed* into the hands
  20. and our rulers **d**-*ed* him to be
Jo. 18.30. we would not *have* **d**-*ed* him
  35. the chief priests *have* **d**-*ed*
  36. that I *should* not *be* **d**-*ed* to
  19.11. therefore he *that* **d**-*ed* me
  16. Then **d**-*ed* he him therefore
Act. 3.13. whom ye **d**-*ed* *up*, and denied
  6.14. the cust. which Moses **d**-*ed*
  12. 4. *and* **d**-*ed* him to four quater.
  16. 4. they **d**-*ed* them the decrees
  21.11. and *shall* **d**. him into the
  22. 4. and **d**-*ing* into prisons both
  27. 1. they **d**-*ed* Paul and certain
  28.16. the centurion **d**-*ed* the pris.
  17. yet *was* I **d**-*ed* prisoner from
Ro. 4.25. Who *was* **d**-*ed* for our offenc.
  6.17. form of doct. which was **d**-*ed*
    (*handed over.*)
  8.32. but **d**-*ed* him *up* for us all
¹Co.5. 5. *To* **d**. such an one unto Satan
  11. 2. ordinances, as I **d**-*ed* them
  23. which also I **d**-*ed* unto you
  15. 3. For I **d**-*ed* unto you first of
  24. when he shall *have* **d**-*ed* *up*
²Co. 4.11. *are* alway **d**-*ed* unto death
¹Ti. 1.20. whom I *have* **d**-*ed* unto Satan
²Pet.2. 4. and **d**-*ed* them into chains
  2.21. holy commandment **d**-*ed*
Jude 3. faith *which was* once **d**-*ed* unto
ruomai.
Mat.6.13. but **d**. us from evil; 11.4
  27.43. *let* him **d**. him now, if he
Lu. 1.74. that we *being* **d**-*ed* out of the
Ro. 7.24. who *shall* **d**. me from the
  15.31. That I *may be* **d**-*ed* from
²Co. 1.10. Who **d**-*ed* us from so great a
  de. and *doth* **d**.: in whom we
  trust that he *will* yet **d**. us
Col. 1.13. *hath* **d**-*ed* us from the power
¹Th.1.10. Jesus, *which* **d**-*ed* us from

²Th. 3. 2. *may be* d-*ed* from unreason.
²Ti. 3.11. of them all, the Lord d-*ed* me
  4.17. and I *was* d-*ed* out of the
    18. the Lord *shall* d. me from
²Pet. 2.7. And d-*ed* just Lot, vexed
  9. The Lord knoweth how *to* d.

exaireō.

Act.7.10. And d-*ed* him out of all his
  34. am come down *to* d. them
  12.11. *hath* d-*ed* me out of the
  26.17. d-*ing* thee from the people
Gal. 1. 4. that he *might* d. us from this

tiktō.

Lu. 1. 57. that she should *be* d-*ed*; 2.6
Heb.11.11. and *was* d-*ed of a child*
Rev. 12.2. birth, and pained *to be* d-*ed*
  4. which was ready *to be* d-*ed*

didōmi.

Lu. 7. 15. he d-*ed* him to his mother
  19.13. d-*ed* them ten pounds, and
Act. 7.25. God by his hand would d.
Rev.20.13. death and hell d-*ed up* the

epididōmi.

Lu. 4. 17. there *was* d-*ed unto* him
Act.15.30. together, they d-*ed* the epis.

apallassō.

Lu.12.58 that thou mayest *be* d-*ed* from
Heb.2.15. and d. them who through

charizomai.

Act.25.11. no man may d. me unto
  16. *to* d. any man to die, before

apodidōmi.

Mat.27.58. comm. the body *to be* d-*ed*

gennaō.

Jo.16.21. as soon as she *is* d-*ed of* the

ekdotos.

Act.2.23. being d-*ed* by the determinate

sōtēria.

Act.7.25. by his hand *would* d. them

anadidōmi.

Act.23.33. *when* . . d-*ed* the epistle to

katargeō.

Ro. 7. 6. now we *are* d-*ed* from the

eleutheroō.

Ro.8.21. shall be d-*ed* from the bond.

DELIVERANCE.

aphesis

Lu. 4.18. to preach d. to the captives

apolutrōsis.

Heb.11.35. tortured, not accepting d.

DELIVERER.

lutrōtēs.

Act.7.35. send to be a ruler and a d.

ruomai.

Ro.11.26. shall come out of Sion the d.

DELUSION.

planē.

²Th.2.11. God shall send them strong d.

DEMANDED.

punthanomai.

Mat. 2. 4. he d. of them where Christ
Act.21.33. and d. who he was, and

eperōtaō.

Lu. 3.14. soldiers likewise d. of him
  17.20. *when* he *was* d. of the Phar.

DEMONSTRATION.

apodeixis.

¹Co. 2. 4. in d. of the spirit and of

DEN,   -*s*.

spēlaion.

Mat.21.13. it a d. of thieves; Mar.11.17
    Lu.19.46
Heb.11.38. and in d-*s* and caves of the
Rev. 6.15. hid themselves in the d-*s*

DENY,   -*ed*, -*eth*, -*ing*.

arneomai.

Mat.10.33. whosoever *shall* d. me
  before men, him *will* I also d.
  26.70. he d-*ed* before them all
  72. again he d-*ed* with an oath
Mar.14.68. But he d-*ed*, saying, I know
  70. he d-*ed* it again. And a
Lu. 8.45. *When* all d-*ed*, Peter and
  12. 9. he *that* d-*eth* me before men
  22.57. he d-*ed* him, saying, Woman
Jo. 1.20. he confessed, and d-*ed* not
  18.25. He d-*ed* it, and said, I am
  27. Peter then d-*ed* again: and
Act. 3.13. d-*ed* him in the presence of
  14. ye d-*ed* the Holy One and
  4.16. Jerusalem; and we cannot d.
¹Ti. 5. 8. he *hath* d-*ed* the faith, and
²Ti. 2.12. we d. him, he also *will* d.
  13. faithful: he cannot d.
  3. 5. form of godliness, but d-*ing*
Tit. 1.16. in works they d. him, being
  2.12. d-*ing* ungodliness and
²Pet. 2. 1. even d-*ing* the Lord that
¹Jo. 2.22. he *that* d-*eth* that Jesus is
  that d-*eth* the Father and
  23. Whosoever d-*eth* the Son
Jude 4. d-*ing* the only Lord God
Rev. 2.13. *hast* not d-*ed* my faith, even
  3. 8. word, and *hast* not d-*ed* my

aparneomai.

Mat.16.24. *let* him d.; Mar.8.34.
    Lu.9.23.
  26.34, 75. cock crow, thou *shalt* d.
  35. with thee, yet *will* I not d.
Mar.14.31.I *will* not d. thee in any
  72. twice, thou *shalt* d. me thrice
Lu.12. 9. *shall be* d- *ed* before the
  22.34. thou *shalt* thrice d. that thou
Jo. 13.38. crow, till thou *hast* d-*ed* me

antilegō.

Lu. 20.27. *which* d. that there is any

DEPART,   -*ed*, -*eth*, -*ing*.

exerchomai.

Mat.9.31. *when* they *were* d-*ed*, spread
  10.14. *when* ye d. out *of* that house
  17.18. he d-*ed out of* him: and the
  28. 8. they d-*ed*. .*and* did run to
Mar.6.10. abide, till ye d. from that
  7.31. again, d-*ing* from the coasts
  9.30. they d-*ed* thence, *and* passed
Lu. 4.42. was day, he d-*ed and* went
  5. 8. saying, d. from me; for I am
  8.35, 38. whom the devils *were* d-*ed*
  9. 4. there abide, and thence d.
  6. they d-*ed*, and went through
  10.35. on the morrow *when* he d-*ed*
  12.59. thou *shalt* not d. thence, till
Jo. 4.43. after two days he d-*ed* thence
Act.11.25.Then d-*ed* Barnabas to Tarsus
  12.17. he d-*ed*, and went into anoth.
  14.20. he d-*ed* with Barnabas to
  15.40. Paul chose Silas and d-*ed*
  16.36. therefore d. *and* go in peace
  39. desired them *to* d. out *of* the
  40. they comfort. them, and d-*ed*
  17.33. Paul d-*ed* from among them
  18.23. he d-*ed*, and went over all
  20. 1. d-*ed* for to go into Macedonia
  11. till break of day, so he d-*ed*
  21. 5. we d-*ed* and went our way
  8. Paul's company d-*ed*, *and*
Phi. 4.15. when I d-*ed* from Macedonia

aperchomai.

Mat.8.18. commandment *to* d. unto the
  9. 7. he arose, and d-*ed* to his
  14.16. unto them, They need not d.
  16. 4. And he left them, and d-*ed*
  27.60. door of sepulchre, and d-*ed*

Mar.1.35. he went out and d-*ed* into a
  42. leprosy d-*ed* from; Lu.5.13
  5.17. to pray him *to* d. out of their
  20. he d-*ed*, and began to publish
  6.32. they d-*ed* into a desert place
  46. he d-*ed* into a mountain to
  8.13. again d-*ed* to the other side
Lu. 1.23. he d-*ed* to his own house
  38. And the angel d-*ed* from her
  5.25. d-*ed* to his own house glorify.
  7.24. *when* the mess. .were d-*ed*
  8.37. besought him *to* d. from
  10.30. d-*ed*, leaving him half dead
  24.12. laid by themselves, and d-*ed*
Jo. 4. 3. He left Judea, and d-*ed*
  5.15. The man d-*ed*, and told the
  12.36. things spake Jesus and d-*ed*
Act.10. 7. spake unto Cornel., *was* d-*ed*
  28.29. the Jews d-*ed*, and had great
Rev.18.14.lusted after *are* d-*ed* from
  goodly *are* d-*ed* from thee

aphistēmi.

Lu. 2.37. which d-*ed* not from the
  4.13. he d-*ed* from him for a season
  13.27. d. from me all ye workers of
Act.12.10.forthwith the angel d-*ed* from
  15.38. them, *who* d-*ed* from them
  19. 9. he d-*ed* from them, *and*
  22.29. straightway they d-*ed* from
²Co. 12.8. thrice, that it *might* d. from
¹Ti. 4. 1. some *shall* d. from the faith
²Ti. 2.19. name of Christ d. from
Heb.3.12. in d-*ing* from the living God

poreuomai.

Mat.2. 9. they d-*ed*; and, lo, the star
  11. 7. And *as* they d-*ed*, Jesus
  19.15. hands on them, and d-*ed*
  24. 1. and d-*ed* from the temple
  25.41. d. from me, ye cursed, into
Lu. 4.42. that he should not d. from
  13.31. Get thee out, and d. hence
  16. 7. but if I d. I will send
Act. 5.41. And they d-*ed* from the pres.
  22.21. d.: for I will send thee far
²Ti. 4.10. and *is* d-*ed* unto Thessalonica

anachōreō.

Mat.2.12. they d-*ed* into their own
  13. *when* they *were* d-*ed*, behold
  14. by night, and d-*ed* into Egypt
  4.12. into prison, he d-*ed* into Gal.
  14.13. he d-*ed* thence by ship into a
  15.21. d-*ed* into the coasts of Tyre
  27. 5. in the temple, and d-*ed*, and
Jo. 6.15. he d-*ed* again into a mount.

metabainō.

Mat.8.34. that he *would* d. out of their
  11. 1. he d-*ed* thence to teach and
  12. 9. *when* he *was* d-*ed* thence, he
  15.29. Jesus d-*ed* from thence, *and*
Jo. 7. 3. d. hence, and go into Judea
  13. 1. that he *should* d. out of this
Act. 18.7. he d-*ed* thence, *and* entered

chōrizō.

Act.1. 4. that they should not d. from
  18. 1. Paul d-*ed* from Athens, *and*
  2. commanded all Jews *to* d.
¹Co.7.10. Let not the wife d. from her
  11. But and if she d., let her
  15. unbelieving d., *let* him d.
Phile. 15. For perhaps he therefore d-*ed*

apochōreō.

Mat. 7.23. d. from me, ye that work
Lu. 9. 39. him hardly d-*eth* from him
Act.13.13. and John d-*ing* from them

ekporeuomai.

Mat.20.29. *as* they d-*ed* from Jericho
Mar. 6.11. *when* ye d. thence shake off
Act. 25. 4. he himself would d. shortly

apoluō.

Lu. 2. 29. *lettest* thou thy servant d. in
Act. 23.22. *let* the young man d., and
  28.25. among themselves, they d-*ed*

anagŏ.

Act. 27.12. part advised *to* d. thence
  28.10. when we d-*ed*, they laded
    11. we d-*ed* in a ship of Alexan.

metairŏ.

Mat.13.53. finished these para. he d-*ed*
  19. 1. he d-*ed* from Galilee, and

hupagŏ.

Mar.6.33. the people saw them d-*ing*
Jas. 2.16. say unto them, d. in peace

paragŏ.

Mat.9.27. And when Jesus d-*ed* thence

exeimi.

Act.17.15. him with all speed they d-*ed*
  20. 7. ready *to* d. on the morrow

apochōrizomai.

Act.15.39. they d-*ed asunder* one from
Rev. 6.14. the heaven d-*ed* as a scroll

diachōrizomai.

Lu. 9.33. as they d-*ed* from him, Peter

ekchōreŏ.

Lu.21.21. *let* them which are..d. *out*

katerchomai.

Act.13.4. d-*ed* unto Seleucia; and from

dierchomai.

Act.13.14. But *when* they d-*ed* from

apallassŏ.

Act.19.12. the diseases d-*ed* from them

analuŏ.

Phi. 1.23. having a desire *to* d., and to

DEPARTING, [*noun.*]

aphixis.

Act.20.29. I know this, that after my d.

exodos.

Heb.11.22. the d. of the children of

DEPARTURE.

analusis.

²Ti. 4. 6. the time of my d. is at hand

DEPTH,   -*s.*

bathos.

Mar.4. 5. because it had no d. of earth
Ro. 8.39. Nor height, nor d. nor any
  11.33. O the d. of the riches
Eph.3.18. breadth, and length, and d.
Rev.2.24. have not known the d-*s* of

pelagos.

Mat.18.6. drowned in the d. of the sea

DEPUTY,   -*s.*

anthupatos.

Act.13. 7. was with the d. of the count.
  8. to turn away the d. from
  12. Then the d. when he saw
  19.38. is open, and there are d-*s*

anthupateuo.

Act.18.12. *when* Gallio *was the* d. of

DERIDED.

ekmuktērizŏ.

Lu.16.14. things : and they d. him
  23.35. rulers also with them d.

DESCEND,   -*ed*, -*eth*, -*ing.*

katabainŏ.

Mat.3.16. d-*ing* like a dove, and light.
  7.25, 27. And the rain d-*ed*, and
  28. 2. for the angel of the Lord d-*ed*
Mar.1.10. the Spirit like a dove d-*ing*
  15.32. Christ the King of Israel d.
Lu. 3.22. the Holy Ghost d-*ed* in a
Jo. 1.32. I saw the Spirit d-*ing* from
  33. thou shalt see the Spirit d-*ing*
  51. ascending and d-*ing* upon
Act.10.11.a certain vessel d-*ing* unto
  11. 5. A certain vessel d., as it had
  24. 1. Ananias the high priest d-*ed*
Ro.10. 7. or, Who *shall* d. into the deep
Eph.4. 9. but that he also d-*ed* first
  10. He *that* d-*ed* is the same also
¹Th. 4.16. For the Lord himself *shall* d.
Rev.21.10.the holy Jerusalem, d-*ing*

katerchomai.

Jas. 3.15. This wisdom d-*eth* not from

DESCENT.

katabasis.

Lu.19.37. the d. of the mount of Olives

agenealogētos.

Heb.7. 3. without mother, *without* d.

genealogeŏ.

Heb.7. 6. whose d. *is* not *counted* from

DESCRIBETH.

legŏ.

Ro. 4. 6. Even as David also d. the

graphŏ.

Ro. 10.5. Moses d. the righteousness

DESERT,   -*s.*

erēmos.

Mat.24.26. Behold, he is in the d.
Lu. 1.80. and was in the d-*s* till the
Jo. 6.31. did eat manna in the d.

erēmia.

Heb.11.38. they wandered in d-*s*, and

DESIRE, [*noun,*]   -*s.*

epithumia.

Lu.22.15. With d. I have desired to
Phi. 1.23. having a d. to depart, and
¹Th. 2.17. endeavoured..with great d.

epipothēsis.

²Co. 7. 7. he told us your *earnest* d.
  11. yea, what *vehement* d., yea

eudokia.

Ro.10. 1. Brethren, my heart's d. and

epipothia.

Ro.15.23. having a *great* d. these many

thelēma.

Eph.2. 3. fulfilling the d-*s* of the flesh

DESIRE, [*verb,*] -*ed*, -*eth*, -*ing.*

aiteŏ.

Mat.20.20.d-*ing* a certain thing of him
Mar.10.35.for us whatsoever we *shall* d.
  11.24. What things soever ye d.
  15. 6. pris., whomsoever they d-*ed*
  8. began *to* d. him to do as he
Lu.23.25. prison, whom they *had* d-*ed*
Act. 3.14. the Just, and d-*ed* a murderer
  7.46. d-*ed* to find a tabernacle for
  9. 2. d-*ed* of him letters to Damas.
  12.20. their friend, d-*ed* peace ; bec.
  13.21. afterward they d-*ed* a king
  28. yet d-*ed* they Pilate that he
  25. 3. d-*ed* favour against him, that
  15. d-*ing* to have judgment agai.
Eph.3.13. I d. that ye faint not at my
Col. 1. 9. to d. that ye might be filled
¹Jo. 5.15. have the petitions that we d-*ed*

thelŏ.

Mar.9.35. If any man d. to be first
Lu. 5.39. straightway d-*eth* new : for
  8.20. stand without, d-*ing* to see
  10.24. prophets and kings *have* d-*ed*
  20.46. the scribes, *which* d. to walk
²Co.11.22. from them *which* d. occasion
  12. 6. For though I *would* d. to
Gal. 4. 9. ye d. again to be in bondage
  20. I d. to be present with
  21. Tell me, ye that d. to be
  6.12. As many as d. to make a
  13. d. to have you circumcised
¹Ti. 1. 7. d-*ing* to be teachers of the

epithumeŏ.

Mat.13.17.righteous men *have* d-*ed* to
Lu.16.21. d-*ing* to be fed with crumbs
  17.22. ye *shall* d. to see one of the
  22.16. desire I *have* d-*ed* to eat this
¹Ti. 3. 1. of a bishop, he d-*eth* a good
Heb.6.11. And we d. that every one
¹Pet.1.12. which things the angels d. to
Rev. 9. 6. and *shall* d. to die, and dea.

parakaleŏ.

Mat.18.32. debt; because thou d-*edst*

_____

Act. 8.31. And he d-*ed* Philip that he
  9.38. d-*ing* him that he ; 19.31
  28.14. and *were* d-*ed* to tarry with
¹Co.16.12. Apollos, I greatly d-*ed* him
²Co. 8. 6. Insomuch that we d-*ed*
  12.18. I d-*ed* Titus, and with him I

erōtaŏ.

Lu. 7.36. And one of the Pharisees d-*ed*
  14.32. and d-*eth* conditions of peace
Jo. 12.21. d-*ed* him, saying, Sir, we
Act.16.39.brought them out, and d-*ed*
  18.20. *When* they d-*ed* him to tarry
  23.20. The Jews have agreed *to* d.

epipotheŏ.

²Co. 5. 2. *earnestly* d-*ing* to be clothed
¹Th. 3. 6. d-*ing greatly* to see us, as
²Ti. 1. 4. *Greatly* d-*ing* to see thee
¹Pet.2. 2. d. the sincere milk of the

zēteŏ.

Mat.12.46, 47. d-*ing* to speak with
Lu. 9. 9. things ? And he d-*ed* to see

epizēteŏ.

Act. 13.7. and d-*ed* to hear the word of
Phi. 4.17. Not bec. I d. a gift : but I d.

zēloŏ.

¹Co.14. 1. and d. spiritual gifts, but
Jas. 4. 2. ye kill, and d. *to have*, and

oregŏ.

¹Ti. 3. 1. If a man d. the office of a
Heb.11.16.But now they d. a better

eperōtaŏ.

Mat.16.1. d-*ed* him that he would show

exaiteomai.

Lu.22.31. Satan *hath* d-*ed* to have you

axioŏ.

Act.28.22. we d. to hear of thee what

DESIROUS.

kenodoxos.

Gal. 5.26. Let us not be d. *of vain glory*

thelŏ.

Lu.23. 8. for he *was* d. to see him of a
Jo. 16.19. knew that they *were* d. to
²Co.11.32. garrison, d. to apprehend me

(See *Affectionately.*)

DESOLATE.

erēmos.

Mat.23.38. house is left unto you d.
Act. 1.20. Let his habitation be d.
Gal. 4.27. the d. hath many more

erēmoŏ.

Rev.17.16. shall make her d. and
  18.19. in one hour *is* she *made* d.

monoŏ.

¹Ti. 5. 5. is a widow indeed, and d.

DESOLATION.

erēmōsis.

Mat.24.15. abomina. of d.; Mar.13.14
Lu. 21.20. know that the d. thereof is

erēmoŏ.

Mat.12.25. kingdom..*is brought to* d.
Lu. 11.17. against itself *is brought to* d.

DESPAIR,   -*ed.*

exaporeomai.

²Co. 1. 8. insomuch that we d-*ed* even
  4. 8. are perplexed, but not in d.

DESPISE,   -*ed*, -*est*, -*ing.*

kataphroneŏ.

Mat.6.24. the one, and d. the ; Lu.16.13
  18.10. that ye d. not one of these
Ro. 2. 4. Or d-*est* thou the riches of his
¹Co.11.22. or d. ye the church of God
¹Ti. 4.12. *Let* no man d. thy youth ; but
  6. 2. *let* them not d. them, because
Heb.12.2. d-*ing* the shame, and is set
²Pet.2.10. and d. government. Presum.

exoutheneŏ.

Lu.18. 9. were righteous, and d-*ed* oth.

Ro.14. 3. *Let* not him that eateth **d**.
1Co. 1.28. thi. *which are* **d**-*ed*, hath God
    16.11. Let no man therefore **d**. him
Gal. 4.14. was in my flesh ye **d**-*ed* not
1Th. 5.20. **d**. not prophesyings
    atheteō.
Lu. 10.16. he *that* **d**-*eth* you **d**-*eth* me
        that **d**-*eth* me **d**-*eth* him that
1Th. 4. 8. therefore *that* **d**-*eth*, **d**-*eth*
Heb.10.28. He *that* **d**-*ed* Moses' law
Jude   8. defile the flesh, **d**. dominion
    logizomai eis oudeis.
Act. 19.27. goddess Diana *should be* **d**-*ed*
    atimos.
1Co.4.10. honourable, but we are **d**-*ed*
    periphroneō.
Tit. 2.15. authority. *Let* no man **d**.
    oligōreō.
Heb.12.5. **d**. not thou the chastening of
    atimazō.
Jas. 2. 6. ye *have* **d**-*ed* the poor. Do

DESPISERS.
kataphronētēs.
Act.13.41. Behold, ye **d**., and wonder
    aphilagathos.
2Ti. 3. 3. fierce, **d**. *of those that are good*

DESPITE.
enubrizō.
Heb.10.29. *hath done* **d**. *unto* the Spirit

DESPITEFUL.
hubristēs.
Ro. 1.30. Backbiters, haters of God, **d**.

DESPITEFULLY.
epēreazō.
Mat.5.44. them *which* **d**. *use*; Lu. 6. 28
    hubrizō.
Act.14.5. to *use* them **d**., and to stone

DESTITUTE.
apostereō.
1Ti. 6. 5. corrupt minds, and **d**. of
    hustereō.
Heb.11.37. *being* **d**., afflicted, torment.
    leipō.
Jas. 2.15. be naked, and **d**. of daily food

DESTROY,   *-ed, -est.*
apollumi.
Mat.2.13. the young child *to* **d**. him
    10.28. able *to* **d**. both soul and body
    12.14. *might* **d**. him; Mar.3.6; 11.18
    21.41. *will* miserably **d**. those wicked
    22. 7. **d**-*ed* those murderers, and
    27.20. ask Barabbas, and **d**. Jesus
Mar.1.24. art thou come *to* **d**.; Lu.4.34
    9.22. into the waters, to **d**. him
    12. 9. and **d**. the husband.; Lu.20.16
Lu. 6. 9. do evil? to save life, or *to* **d**.
    9.56. not come *to* **d**. men's lives
    17.27,29. and **d**-*ed* them all
    19.47. of the people sought *to* **d**. him
    10.10. to steal, and to kill, and to **d**.
Ro.14.15. **d**. not him with thy meat, for
1Co. 1.19. I *will* **d**. the wisdom of the
    10. 9. tempted, and *were* **d**-*ed* of ser.
    10. and *were* **d**-*ed* of the destroyer
2Co. 4. 9. forsak.; cast down, but not **d**.
Jas. 4.12. is able to save and *to* **d**.
Jude   5. afterward **d**-*ed* them that bel.
    kataluō.
Mat.5.17. not that I am come *to* **d**. the
      I am not come *to* **d**., but to
    26.61. I am able *to* **d**. the temple
    27.40. **d**-*est* the temple ; Mar.15.29
Mar.14.58. I *will* **d**. this temple that is
Act.6.14. Jesus of Nazareth *shall* **d**. the
Ro.14.20. For meat **d**. not the work
Gal. 2.18. the things which I **d**-*ed*, I
    katargeō.
Ro. 6. 6. the body of sin *might be* **d**-*ed*

1Co. 6.13. God *shall* **d**. both it and them
    15.26. last enemy that *shall be* **d**.
2Th. 2. 8. and *shall* **d**. with the bright.
Heb.2.14. through death he *might* **d**.
    luō.
Jo. 2.19. **d**. this temple, and in three
1Jo. 3. 8. that he *might* **d**. the works of
    portheō.
Act. 9.21. Is not this he that **d**-*ed* them
Gal. 1.23. the faith which once he **d**-*ed*
    kathaireō.
Act.13.19. And *when* he *had* **d**-*ed* seven
    19.27. magnificence should *be* **d**-*ed*
    diaphtheirō.
Rev.8. 9. part of the ships *were* **d**-*ed*
    11.18. **d**. them *which* **d**. the earth
    exolothreuō.
Act. 3.23. *shall be* **d**-*ed* from among
    phtheirō.
1Co. 3.17. of God, him *shall* God **d**.
    olothreuō.
Heb.11.28. lest he *that* **d**-*ed* the firstborn
    phthora.
2Pet.2.12. made to be taken and **d**-*ed*

DESTROYER.
olothreutēs.
1Co.10.10. were destroyed of the **d**.

DESTRUCTION.
apōleia.
Mat.7.13. that leadeth to **d**., and
Ro. 9.22. vessels of wrath fitted to **d**.
Phi. 3.19. Whose end is **d**., whose god
2Pet.2. 1. bring upon themselv. swift **d**.
    3.16. scriptures, unto their own **d**.
    olethros.
1Co. 5. 5. for the **d**. of the flesh, that
1Th. 5. 3. then sudden **d**. cometh upon
2Th. 1. 9. with everlasting **d**. from
1Ti. 6. 9. which drown men in **d**. and
    kathairesis.
2Co. 10.8. and not for your **d**., I should
    13.10. edification, and not to **d**.
    suntrimma.
Ro. 3.16. **d**. and misery are in their

DETERMINATE.
horizō.
Act. 2.23. delivered by the **d**. counsel

DETERMINE,   *-ed.*
krinō.
Act. 3.13. *when* he *was* **d**-*ed* to let him
    20.16. Paul *had* **d**-*ed* to sail by Eph.
    25.25. Augustus, I *have* **d**-*ed* to send
    27. 1. when it *was* **d**-*ed* that we sh.
1Co. 2. 2. For I **d**-*ed* not to know anyth.
2Co. 2. 1. But I **d**-*ed* this with myself
Tit. 3.12. for I *have* **d**-*ed* there to winter
    horizō.
Lu.22.22. goeth, as it *was* **d**-*ed*: but woe
Act.11.29. **d**-*ed* to send relief unto the
    17.26. *and hath* **d**-*ed* the times befo.
    proorizō.
Act.4.28. counsel **d**-*ed* before to be done
    tassō.
Act. 15.2. **d**-*ed* that Paul and Barnabas
    bouleuō.
Act.15.37. Barnabas **d**-*ed* to take with
    epiluō.
Act.19.39. it *shall be* **d**-*ed* in a lawful

DEVICE,   *-s.*
enthumēsis.
Act.17.29. graven by art and man's **d**.
    noēma.
2Co. 2.11. we are not ignorant of his **d**-*s*

DEVIL,   *-s.*
daimonion.
Mat.7.22. in thy name have cast out **d**-*s*
    9.33. when the **d**. was cast out

Mat. 9.34. out **d**-*s* through the prince
       of the **d**-*s*; Mar.3.22
    10. 8. raise the dead, cast out **d**-*s*
    11.18. hath a **d**.; Lu.7.33; Jo.10.20
    12.24. out **d**-*s*, but by Beelzebub
       prince of **d**-*s*
    27. Beelze. cast out **d**-*s*; Lu.11.19
    28. if I cast out **d**-*s* by the Spirit
    17.18. Jesus rebuked the **d**.; and he
Mar.1.34. dise., and cast out many **d**-*s*
       and suffered not the **d**-*s* to
    39. all Galilee, and cast out **d**-*s*
    3.15. sicknesses, and to cast out **d**-*s*
    6.13. they cast out many **d**-*s*, and
    7.26. that he would cast forth the **d**.
    29. the **d**. is gone out of thy
    30. she found the **d**. gone out
    9.38. one casting out **d**-*s*; Lu.9.49
    16. 9. whom he had cast seven **d**-*s*
    17. name shall they cast out **d**-*s*
Lu. 4.33. had a spirit of an unclean **d**.
    35. when the **d**. had thrown him
    41. **d**-*s* also came out of many
    8. 2. out of whom went seven **d**-*s*
    27. a certain man, which had **d**-*s*
    30. because many **d**-*s* were
    33. Then went the **d**-*s* out of the
    35. out of whom the **d**-*s* were
    38. the man out of whom the **d**-*s*
    9. 1. power and auth. over all **d**-*s*
    42. the **d**. threw him down, and
    10.17. Lord, even the **d**-*s* are subject
    11.14. he was casting out a **d**., and
       it was when the **d**. was gone
    15. out **d**-*s* through Beelzebub
       chief of **d**-*s*
    18. that I cast out **d**-*s* through
    20. finger of God cast out **d**-*s*
    13.32. Behold, I cast out **d**-*s*, and
Jo. 7.20. and said, Thou hast a **d**.
    8.48. art a Samaritan, and hast a **d**.
    49. Jesus ans., I have not a **d**.
    52. we know that thou hast a **d**.
    10.21. Can a **d**. open the eyes of the
1Co.10.20. they sacrifice to **d**-*s*, and not
       should have fellows. with **d**-*s*
    21. of Lord, and the cup of **d**-*s*
       table, and of the table of **d**-*s*
1Ti. 4. 1. spirits and doctrines of **d**-*s*
Jas. 2.19. the **d**-*s* also believe, and
Rev.9.20. they should not worship **d**-*s*
    daimōn.
Mat. 8.31. the **d**-*s* besought; Mar.5.12
Lu. 8.29. was driven of the **d**. into the
Rev.16.14. For they are the spirits of **d**-*s*
    18. 2. become the habitation of **d** *s*
    diabolos.
Mat.4. 1. wilde. to be tempted of the **d**.
    5, 8. the **d**. taketh him; Lu.4.5
    11. Then the **d**. leaveth him; and
    13.39. enemy that sowed them is **d**.
    25.41. prepared for the **d**. and his
Lu. 4. 2. forty days tempted of the **d**.
    3. the **d**. said unto him, If thou
    6. the **d**. said unto him, All
    13. when the **d**. had ended all
    8.12. then cometh the **d**., and tak.
Jo. 6. 70. twelve, and one of you is a **d**.
    8.44. Ye are of your father the **d**.
    13. 2. the **d**. having now put into
Act.10.38. that were oppressed of the **d**.
    13.10. thou child of the **d**., thou
Eph.4.27. Neither give place to the **d**.
    6.11. against the wiles of the **d**.
1Ti. 3. 6. the condemnation of the **d**.
    7. repr. and the snare of the **d**.
2Ti. 2.26. out of the snare of the **d**.
Heb.2.14. power of death, that is, the **d**.
Jas. 4. 7. Resist the **d**., and he will flee
1Pet. 5.8. because your adversary the **d**.
1Jo. 3. 8. is of the **d**.; for the **d**. sin.
       destroy the works of the **d**.

Jo. 3.10. mani., and children of the **d**.
Jude 9. when contending with the **d**.
Rev.2.10. the **d**. shall cast some of
12. 9. that old serpent called the **d**.
12. the **d**. is come down unto
20. 2. old serpent, which is the **d**.
10. the **d**. that deceived them

daimonizomai.
Mat.4.24. which were *possessed with* **d**-*s*
8.16. *possessed with* **d**-*s*; Mar.1.32
28. him two *possessed with* **d**-*s*
33. to the *possessed of the* **d**-*s*
9.32. dumb man *possessed with a* **d**
12.22. one *possessed with a* **d**., blind
15.22. is grievously *vexed with a* **d**.
Mar.5.15, 16. *was possessed with the* **d**.
18. *that had been pos. with the* **d**.
Lu. 8.36. he *that was possessed of the* **d**-*s*
Jo.10.21. words of him *that hath a* **d**.

DEVILISH.
daimoniōdēs.
Jas. 3.15. but is earthly, sensual, **d**.

DEVISED, (See *Cunningly*.)

DEVOTIONS.
sebasma.
Act.17.23. and beheld your **d**., I found

DEVOUR,   -eth, -ed.
kataphagō.
Mat.13.4. fowls came and **d**-ed them *up*
Mar.4. 4. of the air came and **d**-ed it *up*
Lu. 8. 5. the fowls of the air **d**-ed it
15.30. which *hath* **d**-ed thy living
Rev.12.4. for to **d**. her child as soon as
20. 9. out of heaven, and **d**-ed them
katesthiō.
Mat.23.14. up **d**. widows' houses, and
Mar.12.40. *Which* **d**. widows'; Lu.20.47
2Co. 11.20. if a man **d**. you, if a man
Gal. 5.15. if ye bite and **d**. one anoth.
Rev. 11.5. and **d**-eth their enemies
esthiō.
Heb.10.27. which shall **d**. the adversar.
katapinō.
1Pet. 5. 8. about, seek. whom he *may* **d**.

DEVOUT.
eulabēs.
Lu. 2.25. same man was just and **d**.
Act. 2 5. Jews, **d**. men, out of every
8. 2. And **d**. men carried Stephen
eusebēs.
Act. 10.2. A **d**. man, and one that fear.
7. and a **d**. soldier of them that
22.12. a **d**. man according to the law
sebomai.
Act.13.50. the **d**. and honourable wom.
17. 4. of the Greeks a great multitu.
17. and with the **d**. persons, and

DIE, (See *Dying*), -ed, -eth, -ing.
apothnēskō.
Mat.22.24.Moses said. If a man **d**.
27. woman **d**-ed also ; Mar,12.22
Lu.20.32.
26.35. Though I should **d**. with
Mar.12.19.man's brother **d**.; Lu.20.28
20. took a wife and **d**-ing left
21. the second took her, and **d**-ed
Lu. 8.42. of age, and she *lay a* **d**-ing
16.22. to pass, that the beggar **d**-ed
the rich man also **d**-ed, and
20.28. and he **d**. without children
29. took a wife, and **d**-ed without
30. her to wife, and he **d**-ed
31. they left no children, and **d**-ed
36. Neither can they **d**. any

Jo. 4.49. come down ere my child **d**.
6.50. may eat thereof, and not **d**.
8.21, 24. shall seek me, and *shall* **d**.
11.16. also go, that we *may* **d**. with
26. believeth in me *shall* never **d**.
32. here, my brother *had* not **d**-ed
37. this man should not *have* **d**-ed
50. one man *should* **d**. for the
51. that Jesus should **d**. for that
12.24. fall into the ground and **d**.
it abideth alone : but if it **d**.
33. death he should **d**.; 18.32
19. 7. and by our law he ought *to* **d**.
21.23. that disciple *should* not **d**.
not unto him, He *shall* not **d**.
Act. 9.37. that she was sick, and **d**-ed
21.13. also *to* **d**. at Jerusalem for
25.11. of death, I refuse not *to* **d**.
Ro. 5. 6. in due time Christ **d**-ed for
7. a righteous man *will* one **d**.
some would even dare *to* **d**.
8. yet sinners, Christ **d**-ed for
6. 9. raised from the dead, **d**-eth
10. For in that he **d**-ed, he **d**-ed
7. 9. came, sin revived, and I **d**-ed
8.13. live after the flesh, ye shall **d**.
34. It is Christ *that* **d**-ed, yea
14. 7. and no man **d**-eth to himself
8. whether we **d**., we **d**. unto
live therefore, or **d**., we are
9. to this end Christ both **d**-ed
15. meat, for whom Christ **d**-ed
1Co. 8.11. perish, for whom Christ **d**-ed
9.15. better for me *to* **d**., than that
15. 3. how that Christ **d**-ed for our
22. For as in Adam all **d**., even
31. Christ Jesus our Lord, I **d**.
32. drink ; for to morrow we **d**.
36. is not quickened, except it **d**.
2Co. 5.14. that if one **d**-ed for all, then
15. that he **d**-ed for all, that
unto him *which* **d**-ed for ⚊
6. 9. as **d**-ing, and, behold, we
Phi. 1.21. to live is Christ, and *to* **d**. is
1Th. 4.14. that Jesus **d**-ed and rose
5.10. *Who* **d**-ed for us, that, whet.
Heb.7. 8. here men *that* **d**. receive tit.
9.27. appoint. unto men once *to* **d**.
10.28. despised Moses' law **d**-ed
11.13. These all **d**-ed in faith, not
21. Jacob, when he was *a* **d**-ing
Rev.3. 2. remain, that are ready *to* **d**.
8. 9. in the sea, and had life **d**-ed
11. many men **d**-ed of the waters
9. 6. find it ; and shall desire *to* **d**.
14.13. Blessed are the dead *which* **d**.
16. 3. every living soul **d**-ed in the.
sunapothnēskō.
Mar.14.31. If I should **d**. *with* thee
2Co. 7. 3. hearts *to* **d**. and live *with*
thnēskō.
Jo. 11.21. my brother *had* not **d**-ed
teleutaō.
Mat.15.4. *let* him **d**. the ; Mar.7.10
Mar.9.44. 46,48.Where their worm **d**-eth
Lu. 7. 2. him, was sick and ready *to* **d**.
Act. 7.15. down into Egypt and **d**.
Heb.11.22.faith Joseph, *when* he **d**-ed
apōleia.
Act.25.16. to deliver any man to **d**.
apollumi.
Jo. 18.14. one man should **d**. for the

DIFFER,   -eth, -ing.
diapherō.
1Co.15.41. for one star **d**-eth *from* ano.
Gal. 4. 1. **d**-eth nothing *from* a servant
diaphoros.
Ro.12. 6. gifts **d**-ing according to the
diakrinō.
1Co. 4. 7. For who *maketh* thee to **d**.

DIFFERENCE,   -s.
diastolē.
Ro. 3.22. believe ; for there is no **d**.
10.12. no **d**. between the Jew and
diairesis.
1Co.12. 5. there are **d**-s of administra.
diakrinō.
Act.15.9. *put* no **d**. between us and
Jude 22. have compassion, *making* **d**.
merizō.
1Co. 7.34. There *is* **d**. also *between* a

DIG,   -ed.
orussō.
Mat.21.33. and **d**-ed a winepress in it
25.18. and **d**-ed in the earth, and
Mar.12. 1. and **d**-ed a place for the
skaptō.
Lu. 6.48. and **d**-ed deep, and laid the
13. 8. till I shall **d**. about it, and
16. 3. I cannot **d**.; to beg I am
kataskaptō.
Ro.11. 3. and **d**-ed *down* thine altars

DIGNITIES.
doxa.
2Pet.2.10. speak evil of **d**.; Jude 8.

DILIGENCE.
spoudē.
Ro. 12.8. he that ruleth, with **d**.; he
2Co. 8. 7. and knowledge, and in all **d**.
Heb.6.11. do shew the same **d**. to the
2Pet.1. 5. giving all **d**., add to your
Jude 3. when I gave all **d**. to write
spoudazō.
2Ti. 4. 9, 21. *Do* thy **d**. to come
2Pet. 1.10. *give* **d**. to make your calling
ergasia.
Lu.12.58. give **d**. that thou mayest be

DILIGENT.
spoudaios.
2Co. 8.22. proved **d**. in many things
now much *more* **d**. upon the
spoudazō.
Tit. 3.12. *be* **d**. to come unto me to
2Pet.3.14. *be* **d**. that ye may be found

DILIGENTLY.
akribōs.
Mat. 2. 8. Go and search **d**. for the
Act.18.25. he spake and taught **d**. the
epimelōs.
Lu. 15.8. and seek **d**. till she find it
spoudaioteron.
2Ti. 1.17. he sought me out *very* **d**.
spoudaiōs.
Tit. 3.13. Apollos on their journey **d**.

(*See verbs with which it is connected.*)

DIMINISHING.
hēttēma.
Ro.11.12. and the **d**. of them the riches

DINE,   -ed.
aristaō.
Lu.11.37. besought him to **d**. with him
Jo. 21.12. saith unto them, come and **d**.
15. So when they had **d**-ed, Jesus

DINNER.
ariston.
Mat.22.4. Behold, I have prepared my **d**.
Lu.11.38. had not first washed before **d**.
14.12. When thou makest a **d**. or a

DIP,   -ed, -eth.
baptō.
Lu. 16.24. that he *may* **d**. the tip of his

Jo. 13.26. give a sop *when I have* d-ed
Rev.19.13. with a vesture d-ed in blood
   embaptō.
Mat.26.23. He *that* d-eth his hand with
Mar.14.20. *that* d-eth with me in the
Jo. 13. 26. And *when he had* d-ed the

DIRECT.
kateuthunō.
¹Th. 3.11. Jesus Christ, d. our way
²Th. 3. 5. the Lord d. your hearts into

DISALLOWED.
apodokimazō.
¹Pet.2. 4. d. indeed of men, but chosen
   7. stone which the builders d.

DISANNUL,   *-eth.*
atheteō.
Gal. 3.15. it be confirmed, no man d-*eth*
   akuroō.
Gal. 3.17. years after, cannot d., that

DISANNULLING.
athetēsis.
Heb.7.18. For there is verily a d. of

DISCERN,   *-ed, -ing.*
diakrinō.
Mat.16.3. ye can d. the face of the sky
¹Co.11.29. not d-*ing* the Lord's body
   dokimazō.
Lu. 12.56. ye can d. the face of the sky
   that ye *do* not d. this time
   diakrisis.
¹Co.12.10. to another d-*ing* of spirits
Heb.5.14. exercised to d. both good
   anakrinō.
¹Co. 2.14. bec. they *are* spiritually d-ed

DISCERNER.
kritikos.
Heb.4.12. and is a d. of the thoughts

DISCIPLE,   *-s.*
mathētēs.
Mat.5. 1. was set, his d-s came unto
  8.23. into a ship, his d-s follow.
  9.10. down with him and his d-s
   14. came to him the d-s of John
   thy d-s fast not ; Mar.2.18
  10. 1. call. unto him his twelve d-s
   24. the d. is not above; Lu.6.40
   25. It is enough for the d. that
   42. only in the name of a d.
  11. 1. of commanding his twelve d-s
   2. two of his d-s; 21.1; Mar.11.1,
   14 13 ; Lu.7.19,19.29 ; Jo.1.35
  12. 1. d-s were an hungered, and
   2. Behold, thy d-s do that
  14.19. his d-s came, and took up
   19. d-s, and the d-s to the multi.;
   15.36; Mar.6.41, 8.6.; Jo.6.11
   22. constrained his d-s ; Mar.6.45
  15. 2. Why do thy d-s ; Mar.7.5
  16.13. asked his d-s, saying, Whom
  17.16. him to thy d-s ; Mar.9.18
  19.13. and the d-s rebu.; Mar.10.13
  20.17. took the twelve d-s apart in
  22.16. sent out unto him their d-s
  26.18. at thy house with my d-s
   26. brake it, and gave it to the d-s
   35. Likewise also said all the d-s
   56. Then all the d-s forsook him
  27.64. lest his d-s come by night
  28. 7. tell his d-s that he is risen
   8. did run to bring his d-s
   13. Say ye, His d-s came by night
   16. Then the eleven d-s went
Mar.2.18. d-s of John and of the Phar.
   the d-s of John ; Lu.5.33
  2.23. d-s began to pluck ; Lu.6.1
  4.34. expound. all things to his d-s
76

Mar.7. 2. when they saw some of his d-s
  8.10. enter. into a ship with his d-s
   27. and his d-s, into the towns of
  10.24. And the d-s were astonished
  14 14. pass. with my d-s ; Lu.22.11
  16. 7. tell his d-s and Peter, that he
Lu. 5.30. murmured against his d-s
  7.18. the d-s of John shewed him
  8.22. into a ship with his d-s : and
  9.16. and gave to the d-s to set
  40. thy d-s to cast him out ; and
  11. 1. as John also taught his d-s
  14.26, 27,33. he cannot be my d.
  19.37. the d-s began to rejoice and
  39. him, Master, rebuke thy d-s
Jo. 2. 2. and his d-s, to the marriage
   11. and his d-s believed on him
   17, 22. his d-s remembered that
  3.25. between some of John's d-s
  4. 1. baptiz. more d-s than John
   2. baptized not, but his d-s
   8. For his d-s were gone away
   31. his d-s prayed him, saying
  6.22. went not with his d-s
   24. neither his d-s, they also took
   60. Many therefore of his d-s
   61. that his d-s murmured at it
   66. many of his d-s went back
  7. 3. that thy d-s also may see the
  8.31. then are ye my d-s indeed
  9.27. again, will ye also be his d-s
   28. his d.; but we are Moses' d-s
  11.54. there continued with his d-s
  12.16. understood not his d-s at the
  13. 5. to wash the d-s' feet, and to
   22. then the d-s looked one on
   23. one of his d-s, whom Jesus
   35. know that ye are my d-s; if
  15. 8. fruit ; so shall ye be my d-s
  16.17. said some of his d-s among
  18. 1. went forth with his d-s over
   which he entered, and his d-s
   2. resorted thither with his d-s
   15. another d.; that d. was kno.
   16. that other d. ; 20.3,8
  19.26. d. standing by, whom he
   27. Then saith he to the d., Be.
   from that hour that d. took
   38. being a d. of Jesus, but sec.
  20.10. Then the d-s went away aga.
   18. came and told the d-s
   19. where the d-s were assembled
   20. Then were the d-s glad, when
   26. his d-s were within, and Tho.
   30. in the presence of his d-s
  21. 1. himself again to the d-s
   2. Zeb., and two other of his d-s
   8. the other d-s came in a little
   12. none of the d-s durst ask him
   14. shewed himself to his d-s
   24. This is the d. which testifieth
Act. 1.15. in the midst of the d-s, and
  6. 1, 7. the number of the d-s
   2. multitude of the d-s unto
  9. 1. against the d-s of the lord
   10. a certain d. at Damascus
   19. certain days with the d-s
   25. then the d-s took him by
   26. to join himself to the d-s
   believed not that he was a d.
   38. and the d-s had heard that
  11.26. the d-s were called Christians
   29. the d-s, every man according
  13.52. the d-s were filled with joy
  14.20. Howbeit, as the d-s stood
   28. Confirm. the souls of the d-s
   28. abode long timo with the d-s
  15.10. upon the neck of the d-s
  16. 1. a certain d. was there, named
  18.23. strengthening all the d-s
   27. exhorting the d-s to receive
  19. 1. Eph., and finding certain d-s

Act.19. 9. and separated the d-s, disput.
   30. people, the d-s suffered him
  20. 1. Paul called unto him the d-s
   7. when the d-s came together
   30. to draw away d-s after them
  21. 4. And finding d-s, we tarried
   16. of the d-s of Cesarea, and
   an old d., with whom we sh.
(*And all other passages in which it oc-*
curs, except the following :—)
   mathēteuō.
Mat.27.57. also himself *was* Jesus' d.
   mathētria.
Act. 9.36. a certain d. named Tabitha

DISCOURAGED.
athumeō.
Col. 3.21. to anger, lest they *be* d.

DISCOVERED.
anaphainomai.
Act.21. 3. *when* we *had* d- Cyprus
   katanoeō.
Act.27.39. they d- a certain creek

DISCREET.
sōphrōn.
Tit. 2. 5. To be d., chaste, keepers at

DISCREETLY.
nounechōs.
Mar.12.34. Jesus saw that he answer. d.

DISEASE,   *-s*
nosos.
Mat.4.24. were taken with divers d-s
Mar.1.34. that were sick of divers d-s
Lu. 4.40. had any sick with divers d-s
  6.17. and to be healed of their d-s
  9. 1. over all devils, and to cure d-s
Act.19.12.and the d-s departed from
   malakia.
Mat.4.23. all manner of d. among tho
  9.35. every sickness and every d.
  10. 1. sickness and all manner of d.
   nosēma.
Jo. 5. 4. made whole of whatsoever d.
   astheneia.
Act. 28. 9. which had d-s in the island

DISEASED.
echō kakōs.
Mat.14.35. all that were d.; Mar.1.32
   (those having themselves *sickly.*)
   astheneō.
Jo. 6. 2. he did on them *that were* d.
   (See *Blood.*)

DISFIGURE.
aphanizō.
Mat.6.16. for they d. their faces, that

DISH.
trublion.
Mat.26.23. his hand with me in the d.
Mar.14.20. dippeth with me in the d.

DISHONESTY.
aischunē.
²Co. 4. 2. the hidden things of d., not

DISHONOUR, [*noun.*]
atimia.
Ro. 9.21. honour, and another unto d.
¹Co.15.43. It is sown in d.; it is raised
²Co. 6. 8. By honour and d., by evil
²Ti. 2.20. to honour, and some to d.

DISHONOUR [*verb*], *-est, -eth.*
atimazō.
Jo. 8.49. my Father, and ye *do* d. me
Ro. 1.24. *to* d. their own bodies between
  2.23. breaking the law d-*est* thou

kataischunō.
1Co.11. 4. head covered, **d**-*eth* his head
    5. uncovered, **d**-*eth* her head

DISMISSED.
apoluō.
Act. 15.30. so *when* they *were* **d.**, they
    19.41. spoken, he **d.** the assembly

DISOBEDIENCE.
parakoē.
Ro. 5.19. For as by one man's **d.** many
2Co.10. 6. readiness to revenge all **d.**
Heb.2. 2. and every transgression and **d.**
apeitheia.
Eph. 2. 2. the child. of **d.**; 5.6; Col.3.6

DISOBEDIENT.
apeithēs.
Lu. 1.17. the **d.** to the wisdom of the
Act.26.19. I was not **d.** unto the heav.
Ro. 1.30. **d.** to parents; **2**Ti.3.2
Tit. 1.16. being abominable, and **d.**
    3. 3. were sometimes foolish, and **d.**
apeitheo.
Ro.10.21. unto a. **d.** and gainsaying peo.
1Pet. 2. 7. unto them *which be* **d.**, the
    8. stumble at the word, *being* **d.**
    3.20. Which sometime *were* **d.**
anupotaktos.
1Ti. 1. 9. for the lawless and **d.**, for the

DISORDERLY.
ataktōs.
2Th. 3. 6. every brother that walketh **d.**
    .11. which walk among you **d.**
atakteō.
2Th. 3. 7. we *behaved* not our *selves* **d.**

DISPENSATION.
oikonomia.
1Co. 9.17. my will, a **d.** of the gospel is
Eph.1.10. That in the **d.** of the fulness
    3. 2. If ye have heard of the **d.** of
Col. 1.25. according to the **d.** of God

DISPERSED.
skorpizō.
2Co. 9. 9. He *hath* **d.** *abroad;* he
diaskorpizō.
Act. 5.37. many as obeyed him, *were* **d.**
diaspora.
Jo. 7.35. unto the **d.** among the Gen.

DISPLEASED.
aganakteō.
Mat.21.15. of David: they *were sore* **d.**
Mar.10.14. Jes. saw it he *was much* **d.**
    41. they began *to be much* **d.**
thumomacheō.
Act.12.20. Herod was *highly* **d.** with

DISPOSED.
boulomai.
Act. 18.27. And *when* he *was* **d.** to pass
thelō.
1Co.10.27. to a feast, and ye *be* **d.** to go

DISPOSITION.
diatagē.
Act. 7.53. the law by the **d.** of angels

DISPUTATION,   -*s*.
suzētēsis.
Act.15. 2. no small dissension and **d.**
diakrisis.
Ro.14. 1. ye, but not to doubtful **d**-*s*

DISPUTE,   -*ed*, -*ing*.
dialegomai.
Mar. 9.34. they *had* **d**-*ed* among them.
Act.17.17. Therefore **d**-*ed* he in the syn.
    19. 8. three months, **d**-*ing* and per.

Act. 19.9. **d**-*ing* daily in the school of
    24.12. in the temple **d**-*ing* with any
Jude 9. he **d**-*ed* about the body of
    suzēteō.
Act. 6. 9. and of Asia, **d**-*ing with* Step.
    9.29. and **d**-*ed* against the Grecians
dialogizomai.
Mar.9.33. that ye **d**-*ed* among yourselves

DISPUTER.
suzētētēs.
1Co. 1.20. where is the **d.** of this world

DISPUTING, [*noun*,]   -*s*.
suzētēsis.
Act.15. 7. when there had been much **d.**
dialogismos.
Phi. 2.14. without murmurings and **d**-*s*
paradiatribē.
1Ti. 6. 5. *Perverse* **d**-*s* of men of corrupt

DISSEMBLED.
sunupokrinomai.
Gal. 2.13. other Jews **d.** likewise *with*

DISSENSION.
stasis.
Act.15.2. had no small **d.** and disputa.
    23. 7. there arose a **d.** between the
    10. when there arose a great **d.**

DISSIMULATION.
anupokritos.
Ro.12. 9. Let love be *without* **d.** Abhor
hupokrisis.
Gal. 2.13. was carried away with their **d.**

DISSOLVED.
luō.
2Pet.3.11. all these things shall be **d.**
    12. heav. being on fire *shall be* **d.**
kataluō.
2Co. 5. 1. of this tabernacle *were* **d.**

DISTINCTION.
diastolē.
1Co.14. 7. except they give a **d.** in the

DISTRACTION.
aperispastōs.
1Co. 7.35. upon the Lord *without* **d.**

DISTRESS,   -*ed*, -*es*.
ana*n*gkē.
Lu.21.23. there shall be great **d.** in the
1Co. 7.26. this is good for the present **d.**
1Th. 3. 7. in all our affliction and **d.** by
stenochōria.
Ro. 8.35. shall tribulation, or **d.**, or
2Co. 6. 4. afflict., in necessities, in **d**-*s*
    12.10. in **d**-*s* for Christ's sake; for
sunochē.
Lu.21.25. upon the earth **d.** of nations
stenochōreō.
2Co. 4. 8. on every side, yet not **d**-*ed*.

DISTRIBUTE,   -*ed*, -*ing*.
diadidōmi.
Lu.18.22. **d.** unto the poor, *and* those
Jo. 6.11. he **d**-*ed* to the disciples, and
merizō.
1Co. 7.17.as God *hath* **d**-*ed* to every
2Co. 10.13.which God *hath* **d**-*ed* to us
koinōneō.
Ro.12.13. **d**-*ing* to the necessity of saints
eumetadotos.
1Ti. 6.18. *ready to* **d.**, willing to com.

DISTRIBUTION.
koinōnia.
2Co. 9.13. for your liberal **d.** unto them
diadidōmi.
Act. 4.35. **d.** *was made* unto every man

DITCH.
bothunos.
Mat.15.14. shall fall into the **d.**; Lu.6.39

DIVERS.
poikilos.
Mat.4.24. with **d.** diseases and torments
Mar.1.34. sick of **d.** diseases; Lu.4.40
2Ti. 3. 6. with sins, led away with **d.**
Tit. 3. 3. serving **d.** lusts and pleasures
Heb.2. 4. and with **d.** miracles, and
    13. 9. with **d.** and strange doctrines
Jas. 1. 2. when ye fall into **d.** tempta.
    tis.
Mar.8. 3. for **d.** of them came from far
Act. 19.9. But when **d.** were hardened
polutropōs.
Heb.1. 1. times, and *in* **d.** *manners*
diaphoros.
Heb.9.10. and drinks, and **d.** washings
    (See *Places.*)

DIVERSITIES.
diairesis.
1Co. 12.4. Now there are **d.** of gifts, but
    6. there are **d.** of operations, but
genos.
1Co.12.28. governments, **d.** of tongues

DIVIDE,   -*ed*, -*eth*, -*ing*.
merizō.
Mat.12.25. Every kingdom **d**-*ed* against
    city or house **d**-*ed* against
    26. he is **d**-*ed* against himself
Mar. 3.24. if a kingdom *be* **d**-*ed* against
    25. if a house *be* **d**-*ed* against
    26. and *be* **d**-*ed*; he cannot stand
    6.41. the two fishes **d**-*ed* he among
Lu. 12.13. that he **d.** the inheritance
1Co. 1.13. *Is* Christ **d**-*ed*? was Paul
diamerizō.
Lu.11.17. Every kingdom **d**-*ed* against
    18. If Satan also *be* **d**-*ed* against
    12.52. shall be five in one house **d**-*ed*
    53. The fath. *shall be* **d**-*ed* against
    22.17. Take this, and **d.** it among
diaireō.
Lu.15.12. he **d**-*ed* unto them his living
1Co.12.11. **d**-*ing* to every man severally
schizō.
Act. 14.4. multitude of the city *was* **d**-*ed*
    23. 7. and the multitude *was* **d**-*ed*
aphorizō.
Mat.25.32. as a shepherd **d**-*eth* his sheep
diadidōmi.
Lu.11.22. he trusted, and **d**-*eth* his
kataklērodoteō.
Act.13.19. **d**-*ed* their land to them *by lot*
orthotomeō.
2Ti. 2.15. *rightly* **d**-*ing* the word of
ginomai.
Rev.16.19. the great city *was* **d**-*ed* into

DIVIDER.
meristēs.
Lu.12.14. made me a judge or a **d.** over

DIVIDING, [*noun.*]
merismos.
Heb.4.12. even to the **d.** *asunder* of

DIVINE.
theios.
2Pet. 1.3. According as his **d.** power
    4. be partakers of the **d.** nature
latreia.
Heb.9. 1. ordinances of **d.** *service,* and

DIVISION,   -*s*.
schisma.
Jo. 7.43. there was a **d.** among; 9.16
    10.19. There was a **d.** therefore

¹Co. 1.10. there be no **d**-s among you
    11.18. I hear that there be **d**-s among

diamerismos.
Lu.12.51. I tell you, Nay; but rather **d**.

dichostasia.
Ro.16.17. mark them which cause **d**-s

DIVORCED
apoluō.
Mat.5.32. shall marry her *that is* **d**.

DIVORCEMENT.
apostasion.
Mat.5.31. let him give her a *writing of* **d**.
    19.7. to give a writing of **d**., and to
Mar.10.4. to write a bill of **d**., and to put

DO, -*st*, -*th*, -*eth* -*ing*, Did, Done.
poieō.
Mat.1.24. **d**-*d* as the angel of the Lord
    5.19. but whosoever *shall* **d**. and
    44. **d**. good to them that hate you
    7.12. that men *should* **d**. to you, **d**.
    21. but he *that* **d**-*eth* the will of
    24. sayings of mine, and **d**-*eth*
    8. 9. **d**. this, and he -*eth* it;
        Lu. 7.8
    19.16. what good thing *shall* I **d**.
    20.15. Is it not lawful for me *to* **d**.
    23. 3. observe and **d**.; but **d**. not
    23. these ought ye *to have* **d**-*ne*
Mar.3.35. whosoever shall **d**. the will of
    6. 5. he could there **d**. no mighty
    20. he **d**-*d* many things, and
    10.17. what *shall* I **d**. that I may
    14. 8. She hath **d**-*ne* what she could
Lu. 6.46. and **d**. not the things which I
    47. heareth my sayings, and **d**-*eth*
    49. But he that heareth, and **d**-*eth*
    8.21. hear the word of God, and **d**.
    10.37. Go, and **d**. thou likewise
    11.42. these ought ye *to have* **d**-*ne*
    12. 4. no more that they can **d**.
    16. 3. What *shall* I **d**.? for my lord
    17.10. when ye *shall have* **d**-*ne* all
    18.18. what shall I **d**. to inherit
    22.19. this **d**. in remembrance of me
Jo. 3.21. But he *that* **d**-*eth* truth com.
    4.29. me all things that ever I **d**-*d*
    34. My meat is to **d**. the will of
    6. 6. hims. knew what he would **d**.
    38. not to **d**. mine own will, but
    7.17. If any man will **d**. his will
    8.28. I **d**. nothing of myself; but
    40. heard of God : this **d**-*d* not
    13.12. Know ye what I *have* **d**-*ne* to
    17. happy are ye if ye **d**. them
    27. That thou **d**-*est*, **d**. quickly
    14.10. dwelleth in me, he **d**-*eth* the
    14. thing in my name, I *will* **d**.
    15. 5. without me ye can **d**. nothing
    14. if ye **d**. whatsoever I comman.
    15. know. not what his lord **d**-*eth*
    17. 4. which thou gavest me to **d**.
Act.2.37. and breth., what shall we **d**.
    9. 6. what wilt thou have me to **d**.
    16.30. Sirs, what must I **d**. to be
Ro. 3. 8. *Let* us **d**. evil, that good may
    7.15. but what I hate, that **d**. I
    10. 5. the man *which* **d**-*eth* those
¹Co.10.31. or whatsoever ye **d**., **d**. all to
    11.24. this **d**. in remembrance of me
Gal. 3.10. the book of the law *to* **d**. them
    12. The man *that* **d**-*eth* them
Col. 3.23. whatsoever ye **d**., do it heart.
¹Th. 5.24. calleth you, who also *will* **d**.
Heb.10.7. I come..*to* **d**. thy will, O God
    13. 6. what man *shall* **d**. unto me
Jas. 2. 8. neighbour as thyself, ye **d**.
    19. thou **d**-*est* well : the devils
    4.17. knoweth *to* **d**. good, and **d**-*eth*
78

Rev.2. 5. and **d**. the first works; or else
    ginomai.
Mat.1.22. Now all this *was* **d**-*ne*, that it
    6.10. Thy will *be* **d**-*ne* in earth, as
        Lu.11.2.
    8.13. thou hast believed,so *be it* **d**-*ne*
    11.20. his mighty works *were* **d**-*ne*
    21. works, *which were* **d**-*ne* in you
    had been **d**-*ne* in ; Lu.10.13.
    23. *which have been* **d**-*ne* in thee
    had been **d**-*ne* in Sodom
    18.19. it *shall be* **d**-*ne* for them of my
    31. servants saw *what was* **d**-*ne*
    their lord all *that was* **d**-*ne*
    21. 4. this *was* **d**-*ne*, that it might
    21. into the sea ; it *shall be* **d**-*ne*
    26.42. I drink it, thy will *be* **d**-*ne*
    56. all this *was* **d**-*ne* that the
    27.54. those things *that were* **d**-*ne*
    28.11. all the things *that were* **d**-*ne*
Mar.1. 4. John **d**-*d* baptize in the wilder.
    4.11. all these things *are* **d**-*ne* in
    5.14. see what it was *that was* **d**-*ne*
    33. knowing *what was* **d**-*ne* in her
    13.30. till all these things *be* **d**-*ne*
Lu. 4.23. we have heard **d**-*ne* in Caper.
    8.34. fed them saw *what was* **d**-*ne*
    35. went out to see *what was* **d**-*ne*
    56. tell no man *what was* **d**-*ne*
    9. 7. of all *that was* **d**-*ne* by him
    10.13. Sidon *which have been* **d**-*ne*
    13.17. things *that were* **d**-*ne* by him
    14.22. Lord, it *is* **d**-*ne* as thou hast
    22.42. not my will, but thine *be* **d**-*ne*
    23. 8. seen some miracle *be* **d**-*ne* by him
    31. what *shall be* **d**-*ne* in the dry
    47. centurion saw *what was* **d**-*ne*
    48. the things *which were* **d**-*ne*
    24.21. since these things *were* **d**-*ne*
Jo. 1.28. things *were* **d**-*ne* in Bethabara
    15. 7. and it *shall be* **d**-*ne* unto you
    19.36. these things *were* **d**-*ne*, that
Act. 2.43. and signs *were* **d**-*ne* by the
    4.16. miracle *hath been* **d**-*ne* by
    21. God for that *which was* **d**-*ne*
    28. determined before to *be* **d**-*ne*
    30. and wonders may *be* **d**-*ne* by
    5. 7. not knowing *what was* **d**-*ne*
    8.13. and signs *which were* **d**-*ne*
    10.16. This *was* **d**-*ne* thrice ; and the
    11.10. this *was* **d**-*ne* three times
    12. 9. *which was* **d**-*ne* by the angel
    13.12. when he saw *what was* **d**-*ne*
    14. 3. signs and wonders to *be* **d**-*ne*
    21.14. The will of the Lord *be* **d**-*ne*
    24. 2. very worthy deeds are **d**-*ne*
    28. 9. So *when* this *was* **d**-*ne*, others
¹Co. 9.15. that it *should* be so **d**-*ne* unto
    14. 26, 40. *Let* all things *be* **d**-*ne*;16.14
Eph.5.12. those things *which are* **d**-*ne*
Rev.16.17.the throne, saying, It *is* **d**-*ne*
    21. 6. unto me, It *is* **d**-*ne*. I am
    22. 6. which must shortly *be* **d**-*ne*
    prassō.
Lu.22.23. that should **d**. this thing
    23.15. nothing worthy of death is **d**-*ne*
    41. but this man *hath* **d**-*ne* noth.
Jo. 3.20. every one *that* **d**-*eth* evil hat.
    5.29. and they *that have* **d**-*ne* evil
Act. 3.17. through ignorance ye **d**-*d* it
    5.35. what ye intend *to* **d**. as touch.
    15.29. ye *shall* **d**. well. Fare ye well
    16.28. **d**. thyself no harm : for we
    17. 7. these all **d**. contrary to the
    19.36. quiet, and *to* **d**. nothing rash.
    26. 9. that I ought *to* **d**. many things
    20. *and* **d**. works meet for repent.
    26. this thing was not **d**. in a
    31. This man **d**-*eth* nothing worthy
Ro. 1.32. have pleasure in them *that* **d**.
    2. 1. judgest **d**-*est* the same things
    3. *which* **d**. such things ; Gal.5.21

Ro. 7.15. what I would, that **d**. I not
    19. which I would not, that I **d**.
    9.11. neither *having* **d**-*ne* any good
    13. 4. wrath upon him *that* **d**-*eth*
¹Co. 9.17. For if I **d**. this thing willingly
²Co. 5.10. according to that he *hath* **d**-*ne*
Eph.6.21. affairs, and how I **d**., Tychicus
Phi. 4.9. and seen in me, **d**.; and the
¹Th. 4.11. and *to* **d**. your own business
    katargeō.
¹Co.13.10. which is in part *shall* be **d**-*ne*
²Co. 3. 7. *wh.* glo. *was to be* **d**-*ne away*
    11. if that *which is* **d**-*ne away*
    14. which vail *is* **d**-*ne away* in
    katergazomai.
Ro. 2. 9. every soul of man *that* **d**-*eth*
    7.15. For that which I **d**. I allow
    17, 20. it is no more I that **d**. it.
Eph.6.13. and *having* **d**-*ne* all to stand
    ergazomai.
Gal. 6.10. opportunity, *let* us **d**. good
Col. 3.23. **d**. it heartily, as to the Lord
³John 5. whatsoever thou **d**-*st* to the
    parechō.
Lu. 7. 4. worthy for whom he should **d**.
    epiteleō.
Lu.13.32. I **d**. cures to-day and to-mor.
    prospherō.
Jo. 16.2. think that he **d**-*eth* God ser.
    echō.
Act.15.36. Lord, and see how they **d**.
    katatithēmi.
Act.25.9. willing to **d**. the Jews a pleas.
    energeō.
Phi. 2.13. both to will and to **d**. of his
    ischuō.
Phi.4.13. I *can* **d**. all things through C.
    logos.
Heb.4.13. with whom we have to **d**.
    (to whom we [must give] *account*.)

(*See other words with which it is connected at o Doing.*)

DOCTOR,   -s.
nomodidaskalos.
Lu. 5.17. and **d**-*s of the law* sitting by
Act. 5.34. Gamaliel, a **d**. *of the law*, had
    didaskalos.
Lu. 2.46. sitting in the midst of the **d**-*s*

DOCTRINE,   -s.
didachē.
Mat.7.28. astonished at his **d**.; 22.33
    Mar.1.22,11.18.; Lu.4.32
    16.12. of the **d**. of the Pharisees and
Mar.1.27. what new **d**. is this? for
    4. 2. unto them in his **d**.; 12.38
Jo. 7.16. My **d**. is not mine, but his
    17. he shall know of the **d**., whe.
    18.19. of his disciples, and of his **d**.
Act. 2.42. in the apostles' **d**. and fellow.
    5.28. filled Jerusalem with your **d**.
    13.12. astonished at the **d**. of the
    17.19. what this new **d**., whereof
Ro. 6.17. form of **d**. which was deliver.
    16.17. offences contrary to the **d**.
¹Co.14. 6. or by prophesying, or by **d**.
    26. hath a psalm, hath a **d**., hath
²Ti. 4. 2. with all longsuffering and **d**.
Heb.6. 1. Of the **d**. of baptisms, and of
    13.9. with divers and strange **d**-*s*
²Jo. 9. abideth not in the **d**. of Chr.
    10. bring not this **d**., receive him
Rev.2.14, 15. that hold the **d**.
    24. as many as have not this **d**.
    didaskalia.
Mat.15.9. for **d**-*s* the com.; Mar.7.7
Eph.4.14. about with every wind of **d**.
Col. 2.22. commandments and **d**-*s* of
¹Ti. 1.10. that is contrary to sound **d**.

¹Ti. 4. 1. seducing spirits, and **d**-*s* of
   6. words of faith and of good **d**.
   13. reading, to exhortation, to **d**.
   16. thyself, and unto the **d**.
  5.17. who labour in the word and **d**.
   6. 1. the name of God and his **d**.
   3. to the **d**. which is according
²Ti. 3.10. thou hast fully known my **d**.
   16. profitable for **d**., for reproof
  4. 3. will not endure sound **d**.
Tit. 1. 9. may be able by sound **d**. both
  2. 1. things which become sound **d**.
   7. in **d**. shewing uncorruptness
   10. may adorn the **d**. of God
   logos.
Heb.6. 1. leav. the principles of the **d**.
   heterodidaskaleō.
¹Ti. 1. 3. that they *teach* no *other* **d**.

DOER,   -*s*.
   poiētēs.
Ro. 2.13. but the **d**-*s* of the law shall
Jas. 1.22. be ye **d**-*s* of the word, and
   23. and not a **d**., he is like unto
   25. but a **d**. of the work, this
  4.11. art not a **d**. of the law, but a
   (See *Evil*.)

DOG,   -*s*.
   kuōn.
Mat.7. 6. which is holy unto the **d**-*s*
Lu.16.21. the **d**-*s* came and licked his
Phi. 3. 2. Beware of **d**-*s*, beware of
²Pet.2.22. The **d**. is turned to his own
Rev.22.15.For without are **d**-*s*, and
   kunarion.
Mat.15.26. to cast it to **d**-*s*; Mar.7.27
   27. yet the **d**-*s* eat of the crumbs
Mar. 7.28. yet the **d**-*s* under the table

DOING, [*noun*.]
   poieō.
Mat.24.46. shall find so **d**. ; Lu.12.43
Ro. 12.20. for in so **d**. thou shalt
²Co. 8.11. therefore perform the **d**.
Gal. 6. 9. let us not be weary in well **d**.
Eph. 6. 6. **d**. the will of God from the
   ginomai.
Mat.21.42. This is the L's **d**.; Mar.12.11
   ergon.
Ro. 2. 7. patient continuance in well **d**.
   (See *Evil, Well*.)

DOMINION,   -*s*.
   kurieuō.
Ro. 6. 9. *hath* no more **d**. *over* him
   14. sin *shall* not *have* **d**. *over* you
  7. 1. the law hath **d**. *over* a man
²Co. 1.24. we *have* **d**. *over* your faith
   kuriotēs.
Eph.1.21. and **d**., and every name that
Col. 1.16. or **d**-*s*, or principalities, or
Jude   8. despise **d**., and speak evil
   kratos.
¹Pet.4.11. praise and **d**. for ever and
  5.11. him *be* glory and **d**.; Rev.1.6
Jude 25. **d**. and power, both now and
   katakurieuō.
Mat.20.25. Gentiles *exercise* **d**. *over*

DOOR,   -*s*.
   thura.
Mat.6. 6. when thou hast shut thy **d**.
  24.33. it is near, even at the **d**-*s*
  25.10. marriage ; and the **d**. was
  27.60. the **d**. of the sepulchre
         Mar.15.46, 16.3
   28. 2. the stone from the **d**., and sat
Mar.1.33. gathered together at the **d**.
  2. 2. not so much as about the **d**.
  11. 4. by the **d**. without, in a place
  13.29. it is nigh, even at the **d**-*s*
Lu.11. 7. the **d**. is now shut, and my
  13.25. hath shut to the **d**., and ye

Lu.13.25. to knock at the **d**., saying
Jo. 10. 1. by the **d**. into the sheepfold
   2. by the **d**. is the shepherd
   7. you, I am the **d**. of the sheep
   9. I am the **d**.; by me if any
  18.16. at the **d**. without. Then
  20.19. the **d**-*s* were shut; Act.21.30
   26. the **d**-*s* being shut, and stood
Act. 5. 9. are at the **d**., and shall carry
   19. opened the prison **d**-*s*, and
   23. without before the **d**-*s*; but
  12. 6. before the **d**. kept the prison
   13. the **d**. of the gate, a damsel
  14.27. the **d**. of faith unto the
  16.26. immediately all the **d**-*s* were
   27. seeing the prison **d**-*s* open
¹Co. 16.9. For a great **d**. and effectual
²Co. 2.12. and a **d**. was opened unto me
Col. 4. 3. would open unto us a **d**. of
Jas. 5. 9. Judge standeth before the **d**.
Rev.3. 8. set before thee an open **d**.
   20. I stand at the **d**., and knock
   my voice, and open the **d**.
  4. 1. a **d**. was opened in heaven
   thurōros.
Jo. 18.16. spake unto her *that kept the* **d**.
   17. the damsel *that kept the* **d**.

DOTING.
   noseō.
¹Ti. 6. 4. but **d**. about questions and

DOUBLE, [*adject*.]
   diplous.
¹Ti. 5.17. be counted worthy of **d**. hon.
Rev.18.6. double unto her **d**., according
   she hath filled, fill to her **d**.

DOUBLE, [*verb*.]
   diploō.
Rev.18.6. **d**. unto her double, according

DOUBLE-MINDED.
   dipsuchos.
Jas. 1. 8. A **d**. man is unstable in all
  4. 8. and purify your hearts, ye **d**.

DOUBLE TONGUED.
   dilogos.
¹Ti. 3. 8. not **d**., not given to much

DOUBT,   -*ed*, -*eth*, -*ing*.
   diakrinō.
Mat. 21.21. If ye have faith, and **d**. not
Mar.11.23. and shall not **d**. in his heart
Act. 10.20. them **d**-*ing* nothing ; 11.12
Ro. 14.23. he *that* **d**-*eth* is damned if
   distazō.
Mat.14.31. faith, wherefore didst thou **d**.
  28.17. worsh. him ; but some **d**-*ed*
   aporeō.
Jo. 13.22. another **d**-*ing* of whom he
Act.25.20.because I **d**-*ed* of such manner
   diaporeō.
Act.5.24. they **d**-*ed* of them whereunto
  10.17. while Peter **d**-*ed* in himself
   airō.
Jo. 10.24. dost thou make us to **d**.
        (*hold up* our souls.)
   dialogismos.
¹Ti. 2. 8. without wrath and **d**-*ing*

DOUBT, [*noun*.]
   ara.
Lu.11.20. *no* **d**. the kingdom of God is
   pantōs.
Act. 28.4. *No* **d**. this man is a murderer
   gar.
¹Co. 9.10. For our sakes, *no* **d**. this is
   diaporeō.
Act. 2.12. all amazed, and *were in* **d**.

   aporeō.
Gal. 4.20. voice ; for I *stand in* **d**. of

DOUBTFUL.
   dialogismos.
Ro.14. 1. but not to **d**. disputations
   meteōrizō.
Lu.12.29. drink, neither *be ye of* **d**. mind

DOUBTLESS.
   ge.
¹Co. 9. 2. apostle unto others, yet **d**. I
   dē.
²Co.12. 1. not expedient for me **d**. to
   menounge.
Phi. 3. 8. *yea* **d**., and I count all thing

DOVE,   *s*.
   peristera.
Mat.3.16. descending like a **d**., and
  10.16. serpents, and harmless as **d**-
  21.12. them that sold **d**-*s*; Mar.11.1
Mar.1.10. and the Spirit like a **d**. desce
Lu. 3.22. in a bodily shape like a **d**.
Jo. 1.32. descend. from heaven like a **d**.
  2.14. sold oxen and sheep and **d**-*s*
   16. said unto them that sold **d**-*s*

DOWN.
   katō.
Mat.4. 6. cast thyself **d**.: for it is writ.
Lu. 4. 9. cast thyself **d**. from hence
Jo. 8. 6. But Jesus stooped **d**., and
   8. again he stooped **d**. and wro.
Act.20.9. and fell **d**. from the third
   kata, [*gen*.]
Mat.8.32. violently **d**. a steep ; Mar.5.13;
         Lu.8.33
(*See other words which it follows*.)

DRAGGING.
   surō.
Jo.21. 8. cubits, **d**. the net with

DRAGON.
   drakōn.
Rev.12.3. behold a great red **d**., having
   4. the **d**. stood before the wom.
   7. angels fought against the **d**.
   the **d**. fought and his angels
   9. the great **d**. was cast out, that
   13. when the **d**. saw that he was
   16. the flood which the **d**. cast
   17. the **d**. was wroth with the
  13. 2. the **d**. gave him his power
   4. they worshipped the **d**. which
   11. a lamb, and he spake as a **d**.
  16.13. out of the mouth of the **d**.
  20. 2. he laid hold on the **d**., that

DRAUGHT.
   agra.
Lu. 5. 4. let down your nets for a **d**.
   9. at the **d**. of the fishes which
   aphedrōn.
Mat.15.17. out into the **d**.; Mar.7.19

DRAW,   -*eth*, -*ew*, -*awn*.
   enggizō.
Mat.15.8. **d**-*eth nigh* unto me with their
  21. 1. when they **d**-*e nigh* unto
   34. the time of the fruit **d**-*e near*
Lu.15. 1. Then **d**-*e near* unto him all
   25. as he came and **d**-*e nigh* to
  21. 8. the time **d**-*eth near*: go ye
   28. your redemption **d**-*eth nigh*
  22. 1. of unleavened bread **d**-*e nigh*
   47. **d**-*e near* unto Jesus to kiss
  24.15. **d**-*e near, and* went himself
   28. they **d**-*e nigh* unto the village
Act. 7.17. time of the promise **d**-*e nigh*
  10. 9. *as* they went..and **d**-*e nigh*

Heb.7.19. by the which we **d**. *nigh* unto
Jas. 4. 8. **d**. *nigh* to G., he will **d**. *nigh*
   5. 8. coming of the Lord **d**-*eth nigh*
     proserchomai.
Act. 7.31. *as* he **d**-*e near* to behold it
Heb.10.22.*Let us* **d**. *near* with a true
     ginomai.
Jo. 6.19. on the sea, and **d**-*ing nigh*
     prosagō.
Act.27.27. that they **d**-*e near* to some
     epiphōskō.
Lu.23.54. prepara., and the sabb. **d**-*e* on
     hupostellō.
Heb.10.38. but if any man **d**. *back*, my
     hupostolē.
Heb.10.39. are not of them who **d**. *back*
     helkuō.
Jo. 6.44. which hath sent me **d**. him
   12.32. earth, *will* **d**. all men unto
   18.10. Peter having a sword **d**-*e* it
   21. 6. they were not able *to* **d**. it for
   11. Peter went up, and **d**-*e* the
Act.16.19.they caught..and **d**-*e* them
     helkō.
Act. 21.30. took Paul, and **d**-*e* him out
Jas. 2. 6. Do not rich men..and **d**. you
     surō.
Act. 14.19. having stoned Paul, **d**-*e* him
   17. 6. **d**-*e* Jason and certain breth.
Rev.12. 4. his tail **d**-*e* the third part of
     probibazō.
Act.19.33. they **d**-*e* Alexander out of
     anabibazō.
Mat.13.48. they **d**-*e* to shore, and sat
     prosormizō.
Mar.6.53. Gennes., and **d**-*e to the shore*
     spaō.
Mat.14.47. that stood by **d**-*e* a sword
Act. 16.27. he **d**-*e out* his sword, *and*
     apospaō.
Mar.26.51. **d**-*e* his sword, and struck a
Act. 20.30. *to* **d**. *away* disciples after
     anaspaō.
Act. 11.10. all *were* **d**-*n up* again into
     antleō.
Jo. 2. 8. saith unto them, **d**. *out* now
    9. the servants *which* **d**-*e* the
   4. 7. woman of Samaria to **d**. water
   15. not, neither come hither *to* **d**.
     antlēma.
Jo. 4.11. thou hast nothing *to* **d**. *with*
     aphistēmi.
Act 5.37. **d**-*e away* much people after
     exelkō.
Jas. 1.14. *when* he is **d**-*n away* of his

DREAM, [noun,]   -s.
     enupnion.
Act.2.17. your old men shall dream **d**-s
     onar.
Mat.1.20. appeared unto him in a **d**.
   2.12,22. being warned of God in a **d**.
   13,19. appeareth to Joseph in a **d**.
   27.19. this day in a **d**. because of

DREAM, [verb,]
     enupniazomai.
Act.2.17. your old men *shall* **d**. dreams

DREAMERS.
     enupniazomai.
Jude 8. also these filthy **d**. defile

DRESSED.
     geōrgeō.
Heb.6. 7. them by whom it *is* **d**.

DRESSER.
     ampelourgos.
Lu.13. 7. unto the **d**. *of his vineyard*

DRINK, [noun,]   -s.
     posis.
Jo. 6.55. and my blood is **d**. indeed
80

Ro. 14.17. of God is not meat and **d**.
Col. 2.16. judge you in meat or in **d**.
     poma.
1Co.10. 4. drink the same spiritual **d**.
Heb.9.10. stood only in meats and **d**-*s*
     sikera.
Lu. 1.15. drink neit. wine nor *strong* **d**.
     potizō.
Mat. 25.35. and ye *gave* me **d**.: I was a
   37. or thirsty and *gave* thee **d**.
   42. thirsty and *gave* me no **d**.
Ro. 12.20. if he thirst, *give* him **d**.: for

DRINK, [verb,] -eth, -ing, -ank, -unk, -unken.
     pinō.
Mat.6.25. or what ye shall **d**.; Lu.12.29
   31. What shall we **d**.? wherewit.
   11.18. came neither eating nor **d**-*ing*
   19. came eating and **d**-*ing*, and
   20.22,23.*to* **d**. of the cup that I sh. **d**.
     Mar.10.38
   24.38. they were eating and **d**-*ing*
   49. to eat and **d**. with the drunk.
   26.27. to them saying,**d**. ye all of it
   29. I will not **d**. henceforth of
     when I **d**. it new with you in
   42. except I **d**. it, thy will be
   27.34. They gave him vinegar *to* **d**.
     tasted thereof he would not **d**.
Mar.2.16. eateth and **d**-*eth* with publi.
   10.39. Ye *shall* indeed **d**. of the cup
     that I **d**. of ; and the bapt.
   14.23. them and they all **d**-*a* of it
   25. I will **d**. no more of ; Lu.22.18
     vine, until that day that I **d**.
   15.23. they gave him *to* **d**. wine
   16.18. and if they **d**. any deadly
Lu. 1.15. and shall **d**. neither wine nor
   5.30. Why do you eat and **d**. with
   33. Phar.; but thine eat and **d**.
   39. No man also *having* **d**-*u*
   7.33. nor **d**-*ing* wine ; and ye say
   34. is come eating and **d**-*ing*
   10. 7. eating and **d**-*ing* such things
   12.19. take thine ease, eat, **d**., and
   45. to eat and **d**., and to be
   13.26. We have eaten and **d**-*u*
   17. 8. till I have eaten and **d**-*n*
     after. thou shalt eat and **d**.
   27, 28. They did eat, they **d**-*a*
   22.30. That ye may eat and **d**. at my
Jo. 4. 7, 10. Give me to **d**.
   9. askest **d**. of me, which am a
   12. and **d**-*a* thereof himself
   13. *Who*soever **d**-*eth* of this water
   14. But whosoever **d**-*eth* of the
   6.53. and **d**. his blood, ye have no
   54, 56. and **d**-*eth* my blood
   7.37. let him come unto me, and **d**.
   18.11. given me, shall I not **d**. it
Act. 9. 9. and neither did eat nor **d**.
   23.12, 21. would neither eat nor **d**.
Ro.14.21. nor *to* **d**. wine, nor any thing
1Co. 9. 4. we not power to eat and *to* **d**.
   10. 4. *did* all **d**. the same spiritual
     they **d**-*a* of that spiritual
   7. sat down to eat and **d**., and
   21. Ye cannot **d**. the cup of the
   31. Whether therefore ye eat,or **d**.
   11.22. houses to eat and *to* **d**. in
   25. this do ye, as oft as ye **d**. it
   26. as ye eat this bread, and **d**.
   27. and **d**. this cup of the Lord
   28. him eat of that bread, and **d**.
   29. For he that eateth and **d**-*eth*
     eateth and **d**-*eth* damnation
   15.32. let us eat and **d**.; for to-mor.
Heb.6. 7. the earth *which* **d**-*eth* in the
Rev.14.10.The same *shall* **d**. of the
   16. 6. hast given them blood *to* **d**.

Rev.18. 3. all nations have **d**-*u* of the
     sumpinō.
Act.10.41. who did eat and **d**. *with* him
     potizō.
Mat.10.42. whosoever shall *give to* **d**.
   27.48. *gave* him *to* **d**.; Mar.15.36
Mar. 9.41. *give* you a cup of water *to* **d**.
1Co. 12.13. and *have been* all *made to* **d**.
Rev. 14. 8. bec. she *made* all nations **d**.
     hudropoteō.
1Ti. 5.23. **d**. no longer *water*, but use a
     methuō.
Jo. 2.10. when men *have well* **d**-*u*

DRIVE, -eth, -en, -ave, -ove.
     ekballō.
Mar.1.12. **d**-*eth* him into the wilderness
Jo. 2.15. **d**-*o* them all out of the tem.
     elaunō.
Lu. 8.29. *was* **d**-*n* of the devil into
Jas. 3. 4. are **d**-*n* of fierce winds, yet
     exōthe.
Act. 7.45. whom God **d**-*a out* before
     epididōmi pherō.
Act.27.15. we let her **d**.
   (surrendering, we were carried along.)
     pherō.
Act.27.17. strake sail, and so *were* **d**-*n*
     diapherō.
Act.27.27. *as* we *were* **d**-*n up and down*
     anemizomai.
Jas. 1. 6. sea, **d**-*n with the wind* and
     apelaō.
Act.18.16. he **d**-*a* them from the jud.

DROPS.
     thrombos.
Lu.22.44. as it were *great* **d**. of blood

DROPSY.
     hudrōpikos.
Lu.14. 2. before him *which had the* **d**.

DROWN, -ed.
     katapontizō.
Mat.18.6. and that he were **d**-*ed* in the
     buthizō.
1Ti. 6. 9. which **d**. men in destruction
     katapinō.
Heb.11.29. assaying to do *were* **d**-*ed*

DRUNK, [adject.]
     methuskomai.
Eph.5.18. And *be* not **d**. with wine
     methuō.
Rev.17.2. *have been made* **d**. with the

DRUNKARD, -s.
     methusos.
1Co. 5.11. or a **d**., or an extortioner
   6.10. nor **d**-*s*, nor revilers, nor

DRUNKEN, [adject.]
     methuō.
Mat.24.49. and drink with the **d**.
Act. 2.15. these *are* not **d**., as
1Co. 11.21. and another *is* **d**.
1Th. 5. 7. *are* **d**. in the night
Rev.17. 6. **d**. with the blood of the sain.
     methuskomai.
Lu.12.45. eat and drink, and *to be* **d**.
1Th. 5. 7. they *that be* **d**. are drunken

DRUNKENNESS.
     methē.
Lu.21.34. and **d**., and cares of this life
Ro.13.13. not in rioting and **d**., not in
Gal. 5.21. murders, **d**., revellings, and

DRY, [adject.]
anudros.
Mat.12.43. walketh through d. places;
　　Lu.11.24
xēros.
Lu. 23.31. what shall be done in the d.
Heb.11.29. the Red sea as by d. land

DRIED.
xērainō.
Mar. 5.29. fo. of her blood was d. up
　11.20. saw the fig-tree d. up from
Rev.16.12. water thereof was d. up

DUE, (See Time)　　　-s.
opheilō.
Mat.18.34. he should pay all that was d.
¹Co. 7. 3. unto the wife d. benevolence
idios.
Gal. 6. 9. for in d. season we shall
¹Ti. 2. 6. to be testified in d. time
Tit. 1. 3. hath in d. times manifested
opheilē.
Ro.13. 7. Render theref. to all their d-s
(See other words with which it is
　　connected.)

DULL.
bareōs.
Mat.13.15. ears are d. of hear.; Act.28.27
nōthros.
Heb.5.11. seeing ye are d. of hearing

DUMB.
kōphos.
Mat.9.32. brought to him a d. man
　　33. the devil was cast out, the d.
　12.22. with a devil, blind and d.
　　that the blind and d. both
　15.30. blind, d., maimed, and many
　31. when they saw the d. to speak
Lu.11.14. cast. out a devil, and it was d.
　　devil was gone out, the d.
alalos.
Mar.7.37. to hear, and the d. to speak
　9.17. my son, which hath a d. spirit
　25. Thou d. and deaf spirit, I
aphōnos.
Act. 8.32. like a lamb d. before his she.
¹Co.12. 2. carried away unto these d.
²Pet.2.16. the d. ass speak. with man's
siōpaō.
Lu. 1.20. d. and not able to speak, until

DUNG.
ballō koprion.
Lu.13. 8. I shall dig about it, and d. it
skubalon.
Phi. 3. 8. and do count them but d.

DUNGHILL.
kopria.
Lu.14.35. the land, nor yet for the d.

DURETH.
eimi.
Mat.13.21. himself, but d. for a while

DURST, (See Dare.)
tolmaō.
Mat.22.46. neither d. any man from
Mar.12.34. no man after that d. ask
Lu. 20.40. they d. not ask him any que.
Jo. 21.12. none of the disciples d. ask
Act. 5.13. And of the rest d. no man
　7.32. Moses trembled, and d. not
Jude　9. d. not bring against him a

DUST.
koniortos.
Mat.10.14. shake off the d. of your feet

Lu. 9. 5. shake off the very d. from
　10.11. the very d. of your city, wh.
Act.13.51. But they shook off the d.
　22.23. and threw d. into the air
choos.
Mar. 6.11. shake off the d. under your
Rev.18.19. they cast d. on their heads

DUTY.
opheilō.
Lu.17.10. done that which was our d. to
Ro.15.27. their d. is also to minister

DWELL, 　-est, -eth, -lt, -ing.
katoikeō.
Mat.2.23. and d-lt in a city called Naza.
　4.13. he came and d-lt in Caperna.
　12.45. in and d. there; Lu.11.26
　23.21. and by him that d-eth therein
Lu.13. 4. above all men that d-lt in Je.
Act. 1.20. and let no man d. therein
　2. 5. there were d-ing at Jerusalem
　14. and all ye that d. at Jerusa.
　4.16. to all them that d. in Jerusa.
　7. 2. Mesopotamia, before he d-lt
　4. and d-lt in Charran: and from
　this land wherein ye now d.
　48. d-eth not in temples; 17.24
　9.22. the Jews which d-lt at Dam.
　32. to the saints which d-lt at
　35. all that d-lt in Lydda and Sa.
　11.29. unto the brethren which d-lt
　13.27. For they that d. at Jerusalem
　17.26. for to d. on all the face of
　19.10. all they which d-lt in Asia
　17. Greeks also d-ing at Ephesus
　22.12. of all the Jews which d-lt
Eph.3.17. That Christ may d. in your
Col. 1.19. in him should all fulness d.
　2. 9. in him d-eth all the fulness
Heb.11.9. d-ing in tabernacles with
Jas. 4. 5. The spirit that d-eth in us.
²Pet.3.13. wherein d-eth righteousness
Rev.2.13. and where thou d-est, even
　among you, where Satan d-eth
　3.10. that d. upon the earth; 6.10,
　13.8,14,14.6,17.8
　11.10. that d-lt on the earth
　13.12. and them which d. therein
oikeō.
Ro.7.17,20. but sin that d-eth in me
　18. d-eth no good thing: for to
　8. 9. be that the Spirit of God d.
　11. up Jesus from the dead, d. in
¹Co. 3.16. the Spirit of God d-eth in you
　7.12. and she be pleased to d. with
　13. if he be pleased to d. with her
¹Ti. 6.16. d-ing in the light which no
enoikeō.
Ro. 8.11. his Spirit that d-eth in you
²Co. 6.16. God hath said, I will d. in
Col. 3.16. Let the word of Christ d. in
²Ti. 1. 5. which d-lt first in thy grand.
　14. Holy Ghost which d-eth in us
perioikeō.
Lu. 1.65. on all that d-lt round about
sunoikeō.
¹Pet.3. 7. d. with them according to
engkatoikeō.
²Pet.2. 8. righteous man d-ing among
menō.
Jo. 1.38. Master,) where d-est thou
　39. came and saw where he d-lt
　6.56. blood, d-eth in me, and I in
　14.10. the Father that d-eth in me
　17. for he d-eth with you, and
Act.28.16.Paul was suffered to d. by
　30. Paul d-lt two whole years in
¹Jo.3.17. how d-eth the love of God in
　24. d-eth in him, and he in him
　4.12. God d-eth in us, and his love
　13. that we d. in him, and he in

¹Jo. 4.15. God d-eth in him, and he in
　16. he that d-eth in love d-eth in
²John. 2. the truth's sake, which d-eth
skēnoō.
Jo. 1.14. and d-lt among us, and we
Rev.7.15. the throne, shall d. among
　12.12. heavens, and ye that d. in
　13. 6. and them that d. in heaven
　21. 3. and he will d. with them, and
kathēmai.
Lu.21.35. on all them that d. on the

DWELLERS.
katoikeō.
Act.1.19. was known unto all the d. at
　2. 9. and the d. in Mesopotamia

DWELLING, [noun.]
katoikēsis.
Mar.5. 3. Who had his d. among the

DWELLING-PLACE.
astateō.
¹Co. 4.11. buffet., and have no certain d.

DYING, [noun.]
nekrōsis.
²Co. 4.10. about in the body the d. of

EACH.
hekastos.
Lu.13.15. doth not e. one of you on the
Act. 2. 3. and it sat upon e. of them
allēlōn.
Phi. 2. 3. let e. esteem other better than
²Th. 1. 3. all toward e. other aboundeth
ana.
Rev.4. 8. the four beasts had e. of them

EAGLE,　　　-s.
aetos.
Mat.24.28. e-s be gathered; Lu.17.37
Rev. 4. 7. beast was like a flying e.
　12.14. given two wings of a great e.

EAR,　　　-s.
ous.
Mat.10.27. what ye hear in the e., that
　11.15. hath e-s to hear; Mar.4.9;
　　Lu.8.8,14.35
　13. 9. hath e-s to hear; Mat.13.43
　15. their e-s are dull; Act.28.27
　hear with their e-s; Act.28.27
　16. and your e-s, for they hear
Mar. 4.23. If any man have e-s to; 7.16
　7.33. put his fingers into his e-s
　8.18. and having e-s, hear ye not
Lu. 1.44. saluta. sounded in mine e-s
　4.21. scripture fulfilled in your e-s
　9.44. sink down into your e-s
　12. 3. ye have spoken in the e.
　22.50. priest, and cut off his right e.
Act. 7.51. uncircum. in heart and e-s
　57. and stopped their e-s, and
　11.22. came unto the e-s of the ch.
Ro.11. 8. and e-s that they should not
¹Co. 2. 9. nor e. heard, neither have
　12.16. And if the e. shall say, Bec.
Jas. 5. 4. are entered into the e-s of
¹Pet. 3.12. and his e-s are open unto
Rev. 2. 7. He that hath an e., let him;
　　11.17.29,3.6,13,22
　13. 9. If any man have an e., let
ōtion.
Mat.26.51. priest, and smote off his e.
Mar.14.47. high priest, and cut off his e.
Lu. 22.51. he touched his e., and healed
Jo. 18.10. serv., and cut off his right e.
　26. his kinsman whose e. Peter.
akouē.
Mar. 7.35. straightway his e-s were
Act.17.20. cer. strange things to our e-s

²Ti. 4. 3. teachers, having itching e-s
    4. shall turn away their e-s
   akouō.
Mat.28.14. *come to* the governor's e-s
   stachus.
Mat.12.1. the e-s *of corn* ; Mar.2.23
Mar.4.28. first the blade, then the e.
    that the full corn in the e.
Lu. 6. 1. discip. plucked the e-s *of corn*

EARLY.
prōi.
Mat.20.1. went out e. *in the morning*
Mar.16.2. And very e. *in the morning*
    9. was risen e. the first day of
Jo. 20.1. cometh Mary Magdalene e.
   prōia.
Jo. 18.28. it was e. ; and they themselves
   prōimos.
Jas. 5. 7. receive the e. and latter rain
   orthros.
Lu.24. 1. very e. *in the morning*, they
Jo. 8. 2. e. *in the morning* he came
Act.5.21. the temple e. *in the morning*
   orthrios.
Lu. 24.22. which were e. at the sepulch.
   orthrizō.
Lu.21.38. people *came* e. *in the morning*
   bathus.
Lu.24. 1. *very* e. in the morning, they

EARNEST.
arrabōn.
²Co. 1.22. given the e. of the Spirit in
    5. 5. given unto us the e. of the
Eph.1.14. is the e. of our inheritance
   perissoterōs.
Heb.2. 1. to give the *more* e. heed
(See other words with which it is connected.)

EARNESTLY.
ektenesteron.
Lu.22.44. he prayed *more* e.: and his
(See other words with which it is connected.)

EARTH.
gē.
Mat.5. 5. for they shall inherit the e.
    13. Ye are the salt of the e.: but
    18. Till heaven and e. pass, one
    35. Nor by the e.; for it is his
    6.10. Thy will be done in e., as it
    19. yourselves treasures upon e.
    9. 6. man hath power on e. to
    10.34. I am come to send peace on e.
    11.25. Lord of heaven and e.;
       Lu.10.21.; Act.17.24
    12.40. nights in the heart of the e.
    42. uttermost parts of the e.;
       Mar.13.27 ; Act.1.8
    13. 5. had not much e.; Mar.4.5
    they had no deepness of e.
    16.19. thou shalt bind on e.; 18.18
    thou shalt loose on e.; 18.18
    17.25. whom do the kings of the e.
    18.19. if two of you shall agree on e.
    23. 9. man your father upon the e.
    35. right. blood shed upon the e.
    24.30. shall all the tribes of the e.
    35. Heaven and e. shall pass away;
       Mar.13.31 ; Lu.21.33
    25.18. one went and digged in the e.
    25. and hid thy talent in the e.
    27.51. the e. did quake, and the
    28.18. unto me in heaven and in e.
Mar.2.10. hath power on e. to ; Lu.5.24
    4. 5. because it had no depth of e.
    28. the e. bringeth forth fruit
82

Mar.4.31. when it is sown in the e., is
    all the seeds that be in the e.
    9. 3. as no fuller on e. can white
Lu. 2.14. on e. peace, good will toward
    6.49. built an house upon the e.
    11. 2. be done, as in heaven, so in e.
    31. the utmost parts of the e.
    12.49. am come to send fire on the e.
    51. come to give peace on e.
    56. face of the sky and of the e.
    16.17. easier for heaven and e. to
    18. 8. shall he find faith on the e.
    21.25. upon the e. distress of nati.
    35. on the face of the whole e.
    23.44. was a darkness over all the e.
    24. 5. down their faces to the e.
Jo. 3.31. he that is of the e. is earthly
    and speaketh of the e.
    12.32. if I be lifted up from the e.
    17. 4. I have glorified thee on the e.
Act.2.19. signs in the e. beneath; blood
    3.25. the kindreds of the e. be
    4.24. made heaven and e.; 14.15 ;
       Rev.14.7
    26. The kings of the e. stood up
    7.49. my throne, and e. is my foot.
    8.33. his life is taken from the e.
    9. 4. he fell to the e., and heard a
    8. Saul arose from the e.; and
    10.11. corn., and let down to the e.
    12. fourfoot. beasts of the e.; 11.6
    13.47. salva. unto the ends of the e.
    17.26. dwell on all the face of the e.
    22.22. with such a fellow from the e.
    26.14. we were all fallen to the e.
Ro. 9.17. declared throughout all the e.
    28. will the Lord make upon the e
    10.18. their sound went into all the e.
¹Co. 8. 5. whether in heaven or in e.
    10.26, 28. For the e. is the Lord's
    15.47. The first man is of the e.
Eph.1.10. heaven, and which are on e.
    3.15. family in heaven and e. is
    4. 9. into the lower parts of the e.
    6. 3. mayest live long on the e.
Col. 1.16. in heaven, and that are in e.
    20. whether they be things in e.
    3. 2. above, not on things on the e.
    5. memb. which are upon the e.
Heb.1.10. laid the foundation of the e.
    6. 7. For the e. which drinketh in
    8. 4. For if he were on e., he should
    11.13. strang. and pilgrims on the e.
    38. in dens and caves of the e.
    12.25. refused him that spake on e.
    26. Whose voice then shook the e.
    once more I shake not the e.
Jas. 5. 5. lived in pleasure on the e.
    7. the precious fruit of the e.
    12. by heaven, neither by the e.
    17. it rained not on the e. by
    18. he brought forth her fruit
²Pet.3. 5. the e. standing out of the
    7. the heavens and the e., wh.
    10. the e. also and the works
    13. for new heavens and a new e.
¹Jo. 5. 8. three that bear witness in e.
Rev.1. 5. prince of the kings of the e.
    7. all kindreds of the e. shall
    3.10. them that dwell upon the e.
       6.10, 13.8, 14.6, 17.8
    5. 3. in e., neither under the e.
    6. God sent forth into all the e.
    5.10. and we shall reign on the e.
    13. on the e., and under the e.
    6. 4. to take peace from the e.
    8. over the fourth part of the e.
    and with the beasts of the e.
    13. stars of heaven fell unto the e.
    15. kings of the e., and the great
    7. 1. on the four corners of the e.
    hold. the four winds of the e.

Rev. 7. 1. should not blow on the e.
    2. it was given to hurt the e.
    3. Saying, Hurt not the e., nei.
    8. 5. cast it into the e.: and there
    7. they were cast upon the e.
    13. the inhabiters of the e.; 12.12
    9. 1. fall from heaven unto the e.
    3. the smoke, locusts upon the e.
    as the scorpions of the e. have
    4. not hurt the grass of the e.
    10. 2. and his left foot on the e.
    5. 8. the sea and upon the e.
    6. the e., and the things that
    11. 4. before the God of the e.
    6. to smite the e. with all pla.
    10. they that dwell upon the e.
    them that dwell on the e.
    18. them which destroy the e.
    12. 4. did cast them to the e.: and
    9. he was cast out into the e.
    13. that he was cast unto the e.
    16. e. help. the woman and the e.
    13.11. beast coming up out of the e.
    12. causeth the e. and them wh.
    13. from heaven on the e. in the
    14. them that dwell on the e.
    14. 3. were redeemed from the e.
    15. for the harvest of the e. is
    16. sickle on the e.; and the e.
    18. clusters of the vine of the e.
    19. thrust in his sickle into the e.
    and gathered the vine of the e.
    16. 1. wrath of God upon the e.
    2. pour. out his vial upon the e.
    14. unto the kings of the e. and
    18. since men were upon the e.
    17. 2. With whom the kings of the e.
    the inhabitants of the e. have
    5. harlots and abomina. of the e.
    18. reign. over the kings of the e.
    18. 1. the e. was lightened with his
    3. the kings of the e. have com.
    the merchants of the e. are
    9. the kings of the e., who have
    11. the merchants of the e. shall
    23. were the great men of the e.
    24. that were slain upon the e.
    19. 2. which did corrupt the e. with
    19 beast, and the kings of the e.
    20. 8. in the four quarters of the e.
    9. up on the breadth of the e.
    11. the e. and the heaven fled
    21. 1. and a new e.: for the first
    heaven and the first e. were
    24. the kings of the e. do bring
   oikoumenē.
Lu.21.26. which are coming on the e.
   epigeios.
Phi. 2.10. things in e., and things
   katachthonios.
Phi. 2.10. earth, and things *under the* e.
   ostrakinos.
²Ti. 2.20. but also of wood and *of* e.

EARTHEN.
ostrakinos.
²Co. 4. 7. this treasure in e. vessels

EARTHLY.
epigeios.
Jo. 3.12. If I have told you e. thing₃
²Co. 5. 1. our e. house of this taberna
Phi. 3.19. shame, who mind e. things
Jas. 3.15. but is e., sensual, devilish
   gē.
Jo. 3.31. he that is of the earth is e.

EARTHQUAKE,   -s.
seismos.
Mat.24.7. and e-s in divers places
    27.54. saw the e., and those things
    28. 2. there was a great e.; Act.16.26
       Rev.6.12

Mar.13.8. there shall be e-s in divers
Lu.21.11. great e-s shall be in divers
Rev.8. 5. and lightnings, and an e.
  11.13. was there a great e., and the

EARTHY.
choikos.
¹Co.15.47. first man is of the earth, e.
    48. As is the e., such are they
       that are e.; and as is the
    49. have borne the image of the e.

EASE.
anapauō.
Lu.12.19. take thine e., eat, drink, and

EASED.
anesis.
²Co. 8.13. mean not that other men be e.

EASIER.
eukopōteros.
Mat.9. 5. whether is e.,to say; Mar.2.9
     Lu.5.23
  19.24. It is e. for a camel; Mar.10.25
     Lu.18.25
Lu.16.17. It is e. for heaven and earth

EASILY, (See *Beset, Provoke.*)

EAST.
anatolē.
Mat.2. 1. wise men from the e. to Jer.
     2. we have seen his star in the e.
     9. star which they saw in the e.
  8.11. come from the e.; Lu.13.29
  24.27. lightning cometh out of the e.
Rev.21.13.On the e. three gates ; on the
anatolē hēlios.
Rev.7. 2. angel ascending from the e.
  16.12. way of the kings of the e.

EASTER.
pascha.
Act.12.4. intending after e. to bring

EASY.
chrēstos.
Mat.11.30. For my yoke is e., and my
(*See other words with which it is connected.*)

EAT,   *Ate, -en, -eth, -ing.*
phagō.
Mat.6.25. what ye *shall* e., or what ye
    31. saying, What shall we e.
  12. 4. and *did* e. the shewbread,
     not lawful for him to e.
  14.16. give ye them *to* e.; Mar.6.37
     Lu.9.13
  20. *did* all e., and were fill.;15.37
     Mar.6.42; Lu.9.17
  15.20. but *to* e. with unwashen
    32. days, and have nothing to e.
  26.17. we prepare for thee *to* e.
    26. Take, e.; this is my body ;
     Mar. 14.22 ; ¹Co.11.24
Mar.2.26. and *did* e. the shewbread,
     to e. but for the prie.; Lu.6.4
  3.20. could not so much as e. bread
  5.43. should be given her *to* e.
  6.31. no leisure so much as *to* e.
    36. have nothing to e.; 8.1,2.
    37. of bread, and give them *to* e.
    44. And they *that did* e. of the
  8. 8. So they *did* e., and were filled
     9. And they *that had* e-n were
  11.14. No man e. fruit of thee here.
  14.12. prepare that thou *mayest* e.
    14. shall e. the passover; Lu.22.11
Lu. 4. 2. in those days he *did* e. noth.
  6. 4. and did take and e. the shew.

Lu. 7.36. desired him that he *would* e.
  12.19. take thine ease, e., drink, and
    22. for your life, what ye shall e.
    29. seek not ye what ye shall e.
  13.26. We *have* e-n and drunk in
  14. 1. *to* e. bread on the sabbath
    15. Blessed is he that *shall* e.
  15.23. and let us e. and be merry
  17. 8. till I have e-n and drunken
     afterward thou *shalt* e. and
  22. 8. the passover, that we *may* e.
    15. I have desired *to* e. this pass.
    16. I will not any more e. thereof
  24.43. he took it, and *did* e. before
Jo. 4.31. prayed him, saying, Master, e.
    32. I have meat *to* e. that ye kn.
    33. man brought him ought *to* e.
  6. 5. buy bread that these *may* e.
    23. where they *did* e. bread, aft.
    26. but because ye *did* e. of the
    31, 49, 58. fathers *did* e. manna
     them bread from heaven *to* e.
    50. that a man *may* e. thereof
    51. if any man e. of this bread
    52. this man give us his flesh *to* e.
    53. Except ye e. the flesh of the
  18.28. but that they *might* e. the
Act. 9. 9. and neither *did* e. nor drink
  10.13. him, Rise, Peter ; kill, and e.
    14. for I *have* never e-n anything
  11. 7. Arise, Peter ; slay and e.
  23.12. that they would neither e.
    21. oath, that they will neither e.
Ro.14. 2. believeth that he may e. all
    21. It is good neither *to* e. flesh
    23. doubteth is damned if he e.
¹Co. 8. 8. neither, if we e., are we the
     neither, if we e. not, are we
    13. I will e. no flesh while the
  9. 4. Have we not power *to* e. and
  10. 3. *did* all e. the same spiritual
     7. The people sat down *to* e. and
  11.20. this is not *to* e. the Lord's
    21. For in e-*ing* every one that
    33. when ye come together *to* e.
  15.32. *let* us e. and drink : for to.
²Th. 3. 8. Neither *did* we e. any man's
Heb.13.10.they have no right *to* e. wh.
Jas. 5. 3. and *shall* e. your flesh, as it
Rev.2. 7. will I give *to* e. of the tree
    14. 20. *to* e. things sacrificed unto
    17. will I give *to* e. of the hidden
  10.10. as soon as I *had* e-n it, my
    17.16. and *shall* e. her flesh, and
  19.18. That ye *may* e. the flesh of
kataphagō.
Jo. 2.17. thine house *hath* e-n me *up*
Rev.10.9. Take it, and e. it *up*; and it
    10. the little book..and *ate* it *up*
esthiō.
Mat.9.11. Why e-*eth* your Master with
  11.18. nei. e-*ing* nor drink.; Lu.7.33
    19. The Son of man came e-*ing*
  12. 1. the ears of corn, and *to* e.
  14.21. And they *that had* e-n
  15. 2. not their hands, when they e.
    27. the dogs e. of the crumbs
    38. And they *that did* e. were
  24.49. and *to* e. and drink with
  26.21. *as* they *did* e., he said, Ver.
    26. And *as* they *were* e-*ing*
Mar.1. 6. did e. locusts and wild
  2.16. saw him e. with publicans
     How is it that he e-*eth* and
  7. 2. saw some of his disciples e.
     3. e. not, holding the tradition
     4. except they wash, they e.
     5. but e. bread with unwashen
    28. dogs under the table e. of
  14.18. as they sat and *did* e., Jesus
     you, One of you *which* e-*eth*
    22. *as* they *did* e., Jesus took

Lu. 5.30. Why *do* ye e. and drink with
    33. Pharisees ? but thine e. and
  6. 1. and *did* e., rubbing them in
    34. The Son of man is come e-*ing*
  10. 7. remain, e-*ing* and drinking
     8. e. such things as are set bef.
  12.45. and *to* e. and drink, and to
  15.16. that the swine *did* e.; and
  17.27, 28. They *did* e., they drank
  22.30. That ye *may* e. and drink at
Act.27.35.had broken it, he began *to* e.
Ro.14. 2. another, who is weak, e-*eth*
     3. Let not him *that* e-*eth* despise
     him *that* e-*eth* not: and
     let not him which e-*eth*
     not judge him *that* e-*eth*
     6. He *that* e-*eth*, e-*eth* to the L.
     and he *that* e-*eth* not
     to the Lord he e-*eth* not
    20. for that man *who* e-*eth* with
¹Co. 8. 7. e. it as a thing offered unto
    10. *to* e. those things which are
  9. 7. and e-*eth* not of the fruit
     and e-*eth* not of the milk of
  10.18. they *which* e. of the sacrifi.
    25. sold in the shambles, that e.
    27. soever is set before you, e.
    28. e. not for his sake that shew.
    31. Whether therefore ye e., or
  11.22. have ye not houses *to* e. and
    26. as often as ye e. this bread
    27. whosoever shall e. this bread
    28. *let* him e. of that bread, and
    29. For he *that* e-*eth* and drink.
     e-*eth* and drinketh damnation
    34. *let* him e. at home ; that ye
²Th. 3.10. work, neither should he e.
    12. they work, and e. their own
sunesthiō.
Lu. 15. 2. rec. sinners, and e-*eth with*
Act. 10.41. who *did* e. and drink *with*
  11. 3. and *didst* e. *with* them
¹Co. 5.11. *with* such an one no not *to* e.
Gal. 2.12. he *did* e. *with* the Gentiles
trōgō.
Mat.24.38. they were e-*ing* and drink.
Jo. 6.54. *Whoso* e-*eth* my flesh, and
    56. He *that* e-*eth* my flesh, and
    57. so he *that* e-*eth* me, even he
    58. he *that* e-*eth* of this bread
  13.18. He *that* e-*eth* bread with me
geuomai.
Act.10.10. hungry, and would *have* e-n
  20.11. had broken bread, and e-n
  23.14. that we will e. nothing until
brōskō.
Jo. 6.13. unto them *that had* e-n
metalambanō.
Act.2.46. *did* e. their meat with glad.;
echō nomē.
²Ti. 2.17. their word will e. as doth
(See *Enough, Worms.*)

EATING, [noun.]
brōsis.
¹Co. 8. 4. the e. of those things that

EDGE,   -s
stoma.
Lu. 21.24. fall by the e. of the sword
Heb.11.34. escaped the e. of the sword
distomos.
Rev.2.12. the sharp sword *with two* e-s

EDGED.
distomos.
Heb.4.12. sharper than any *two* e. sword
Rev. 1.16.went a sharp *two* e. sword

EDIFICATION.
oikodomē.
Ro.15. 2. neighbour for his good *to* e.

¹Co.14. 3. speaketh unto men to e., and
²Co.10.8. the Lord hath given us for e.
   13.10. the Lord hath given me to e.

EDIFY,   *-ed, -eth, -ing.*
oikodomeō.
Act.9.31. churches rest..*and were* e-*ed*
¹Co.8. 1. puffeth up, but charity e-*eth*
  10.23. for me, but all things e. not
  14. 4. unkno. tongue e-*eth* himself
      but he that prophesi. e-*eth*
    17. well, but the other *is* not e-*ed*
¹Th.5.11. and e. one another, even as
oikodomē.
Ro.14.19. things *wherewith one may* e.
      (*things of edification.*)
¹Co.14. 5. the church may receive e-*ing*
   12. excel to the e-*ing* of the ch.
   26. all things be done unto e-*ing*
²Co.12.19. dearly beloved, for your e-*ing*
Eph.4.12. for the e-*ing* of the body of
  16. unto the e-*ing* of itself in love
  26. whi. is good to the use of e-*ing*
oikonomia.
¹Ti. 1. 4. rather than godly e-*ing* whi.

EFFECT.
katargeō.
Ro. 3. 3. *make* the faith of G. *without* e.
  4.14. the promise *made of none* e.
Gal. 3.17. *make* the promise *of none* e.
  5. 4. Christ is *become of no* e. unto
akuroō.
Mat.15.6. Thus *have* ye *made* the command. of God *of none* e.
Mar.7.13. *making* t. word of G. *of none* e.
ekpiptō.
Ro. 9. 6. word of God *hath taken none* e.
kenoō.
¹Co. 1.17. Ch. *should be made of none* e.

EFFECTUAL.
energēs.
¹Co.16. 9. great door and e. is opened
Phile. 6. bec. e. by the acknowledging
energeō.
²Co. 1. 6. *which is* e. in the enduring
Jas. 5.16. The e. *fervent* prayer of a
energeia.
Eph.3. 7. by the e. *working* of his pow.
  4.16. the e. *working* in the measure

EFFECTUALLY.
energeō.
Gal. 2. 8. For he *that wrought* e. *in* Pe.
¹Th.2.13. which e. *worketh* also *in* you

EFFEMINATE.
malakos.
¹Co. 6. 9. nor adulterers, nor e., nor

EGG.
ōon.
Lu.11.12. if he shall ask an e., will he

EIGHT.
oktō.
Lu. 2.21. when e. days were accompl.
  9.28. about an e. days after these
Jo. 5. 5. an infirmity thirty and e. ye.
  20.26. after e. days again his disci.
Act. 9.33. which had kept his bed e.
¹Pet. 3.20. e. souls were saved by water

EIGHTEEN.
oktō deka.
Lu.13. 4. Or those e. upon whom the
  11. spirit of infirmity e. years
  16. Satan hath bound, lo, these e.

EIGHTH.
ogdoos.
Lu. 1.59. the e. day they came to cir.
Act.7. 8. and circumcised him the e.
84

²Pet.2. 5. but sáved Noah the e. person
Rev.17.11.even he is the e., and is of
  21.20. the e., beryl · the ninth, a
oktaēmeros.
Phi. 3. 5. Circumcised *the* e. *day,* of the

EITHER.
ē.
Mat.6.24. for e. he will hate ; Lu.16.13
  12.33. e. make the tree good, and
Lu. 6.42. e. how canst thou say to thy
  15. 8. e. what woman having ten
Act.17.21. *but* e. to tell, or to hear some
¹Co.14. 6. e. by revelation, or by know.
Phi. 3.12. e. were already perfect
Jas. 3.12. e. a vine, figs? so can no
enteuthen.
Jo. 19.18. others with him, *on* e. side
Rev.22.2. *on* e. *side* of the river, was
      (*hence and hence.*)

ELDER,   *-s.*
presbuteros.
Mat.15.2. tradi. of the e-*s ;* Mar.7.3,5
  16.21. suffer many things of the e-*s*
  21.23. the e-*s* of the ; 26.3,47,27.1
  26.57. and the e-*s* were assembled
  59. priests, and e-*s ;* 27.3,12,20
      Act.23.14,25.15
  27.41. scri. and e-*s ;* Mar.11.27,14.43
  28.12. were assembled with the e-*s*
Mar.8.31. be rejected of the e-*s ;* Lu.9.22
  14.53. the e-*s* and the scribes ; 15.1
      Act.6.12
Lu. 7. 3. he sent unto him the e-*s* of
  15.25. Now his e. son was in the
  20. 1. came upon him with the e-*s*
  22.52. capt. of the tem., and the e-*s*
Act. 4. 5. that the rulers, and e-*s*, and
  8. rulers of the people, and e-*s*
  23. and e-*s* had said unto them
  11.30. and sent it to the e-*s* by the
  14.23. ordained them e-*s* in every
  15. 2, 4. apos. and e-*s ;* 6.22,23,16.4
  20.17. the e-*s* of the church ; Jas.5.14
  21.18. and all the e-*s* were present
  24. 1. priest descended with the e-*s*
¹Ti. 5. 1. Rebuke not an e., but intreat
  2. The e. women as mothers
  17. Let the e-*s* that rule well be
  19. Against an e. receive not an
Tit. 1. 5. ordain e-*s* in every city, as I
Heb.11.2. For by it the e-*s* obtained a
¹Pet. 5. 1. The e-*s* which are among
  5. submit yourselves unto the e.
²John 1. The e. unto the elect lady
³John 1. The e. unto the wellbeloved
Rev.4. 4, 10. four and twenty e-*s*
      5.8,14,11.16,19.4
  5. And one of the e-*s* saith unto
  6. and in the midst of the e-*s*
  11. and the beasts and the e-*s*
  7.11. and about the e-*s* and the
  13. And one of the e-*s* answered
  14. the four beasts, and the e-*s*
sumpresbuteros.
¹Pet.5. 1. who am *also* an e., and a
presbuterion.
Lu.22.66. the e-*s* of the people, and the
Act. 22.5. and all the *estate of the* e-*s*
mei zōn.
Ro. 9.12. The e. shall serve the young.

ELDEST.
presbuteros.
Jo. 8. 9. beginning at the e., even

ELECT.
eklektos.
Mat.24.22. for the e-'s sake those days
  24. shall deceive the very e.
  31. together his e.; Mar.13.27
Mar.13.20. for the e-'s sake whom he

Mar.13.22. it were possible, even the e.
Lu. 18. 7. not God avenge his own e.
Ro. 8. 33. to the charge of God's e.
Col. 3.12. therefore, as the e. of God
¹Ti. 5.21. Jesus Christ, and the e. ang.
²Ti. 2.10. all things for the e-'s sakes
Tit. 1. 1. to the faith of God's e., and
¹Pet. 1. 2. e. according to the forekno.
  2. 6. a chief corner stone, e., pre.
²John 1. The elder unto the e. lady
  13. The children of thy e. sister

ELECTED.
suneklektos.
¹Pet.5.13. e. *together with* you, saluteth

ELECTION.
eklogē.
Ro. 9.11. purpose of God according to e.
  11. 5. according to the e. of grace
  7. the e. hath obtained it, and
  28. as touching the e., they are
¹Th.'1. 4. breth. beloved, your e. of
²Pet.1.10. your calling and e. sure

ELEMENTS.
stoicheion.
Gal. 4. 3. in bondage under the e. of
  9. to the weak and beggarly e.
²Pet.3.10, 12. e. shall melt with fervent

ELEVEN.
hendeka.
Mat.28.16. Then the e. disciples went
Mar.16.14. he appeared unto the e. as
Lu. 24. 9. all these things unto the e.
  33. found the e. gathered toget.
Act. 1.26. numbered with the e. apos.
  2.14. Pet., standing up with the e

ELEVENTH.
hendekatos.
Mat.20.6. about the e. hour he went
  9. were hired about the e. hour
Rev.21.20.the e., a jacinth ; the twelf.

ELI.
ēli.
Mat.27.46. e., e., lama sabachthani

ELOI.
eloī.
Mar.15.34. e., e., lama sabachthani

ELOQUENT.
logios.
Act.18.24. An e. man, and mighty in

ELSE.
ei de mē.
Mat.9.17. e. the bottles break, and the
Mar.2.21. e. the new piece that filled it
  22. e. the new wine doth burst
      Lu.5.37.
Lu.14.32. *Or* e., while the other is yet
Jo.14.11. *or* e. believe me for the very
Rev.2. 5. *or* e. I will come unto thee
  16. Repent ; *or* e. I will come
epei.
¹Co. 7.14. e. were your children unclean
  14.16. e. when thou shalt bless with
  15.29. e. what shall they do which
heteros.
Act.17.21. their time in nothing e., but

EMBOLDENED.
oikodomeō.
¹Co. 8.10. *shall* not the consc...*be* e.

EMBRACE,   *-ed, -ing.*
aspazomai.
Act.20. 1. him the disciples, and e.

sumperilambanō.
Act.20.10. and fell on him, and **e-ing**

EMERALD.
smaragdinos.
Rev.4. 3. throne, in sight like unto an **e.**
smaragdos.
Rev.21.19. chalcedony ; the fourth an **e.**

EMPTY, [adject.]
kenos.
Mar.12.3. sent him away **e.** ; Lu.20.10,11
Lu. 1.53. the rich he hath sent **e.** away
scholazō.
Mat.12.44. come, he findeth it **e.**, swept

EMULATION,   -s.
parazēloō.
Ro.11.14. I *may provoke to* **e.** them
zēlos.
Gal. 5.20. variance, **e-s**, wrath, strife

ENABLED.
endunamoō.
1Ti. 1.12. Jesus our Lord, *who hath* **e.**

ENCOUNTERED.
sumballō.
Act.17.18. and of the Stoicks, **e.** him

END,   -s.
telos.
Mat.10.22. he that endureth to the **e.**
24. 6. to pass, but the **e.** is not yet
13. endu. unto the **e.**; Mar.13.13
14. and then shall the **e.** come
26.58. the servants, to see the **e.**
Mar. 3.26. he cann.stand, but hath an **e.**
13. 7. but the **e.** shall not be yet
Lu. 1.33. kingdom there shall be no **e.**
21. 9. but the **e.** is not by and by
22.37. things concern.me have an **e.**
Jo. 13. 1. he loved them unto the **e.**
Ro. 6.21. for the **e.** of those things is
22. and the **e.** everlasting life
10. 4. For Christ is the **e.** of the
1Co. 1. 8. also confirm you unto the **e.**
10.11. upon whom the **e-s** of the
15.24. Then cometh the **e.**, when he
2Co. 1.13. shall acknow. even to the **e.**
13. to the **e.** of that which is
11.15. whose **e.** shall be according
Phi. 3.19. Whose **e.** is destruction
1Ti. 1. 5. Now the **e.** of the command.
Heb. 3. 6. of the hope firm unto the **e.**
14. confid., stedfast unto the **e.**
6. 8. whose **e.** is to be burned
11. assurance of hope unto the **e.**
7. 3. beginning of days, nor **e.** of
Jas. 5.11. and have seen the **e.** of the
1Pet. 1. 9. Receiving the **e.** of your faith
4. 7. But the **e.** of all things is at
17. what shall the **e.** be of them
Rev. 2.26. keep. my works unto the **e.**
21. 6. the begin. and the end ; 22.13
sunteleia.
Mat.13.39,40,49. the **e.** of the world ;
24.3, 28.20
teleiōs.
1Pet.1.13. and hope *to the* **e.** for the gra.
teleō.
Mat.11.1. when Jesus *had made an* **e.** of
eis ho or houtos.
Act. 7.19. *to the* **e.** they might not live
Ro. 1.11. *to the* **e.** ye may be established
4.16. *to the* **e.** the promise might
14. 9. For *to* this **e.** Christ both died
2Co. 2. 9. *to* this **e.** also did I write
2Th. 3.13. *To the* **e.** he may stablish

eschatos.
Act. 13.47. salvation unto the **e-s** of the
2Pet.2.20. the *latter* **e.** is worse with th.
akron.
Mat.24.31. *one* **e.** of heaven to the other
(from *end* to *end* of heaven.)
peras.
Ro.10.18. their words unto the **e-s** of
Heb.6.16. is to them an **e.** of all strife
ekbasis.
Heb.13.7. considering the **e.** of their
opse.
Mat.28.1. *In the* **e.** of the sabbath, as it
pros. [accu.] ho.
Lu. 18.1. unto them *to this* **e.**, *that* men

ENDED, [verb.]
sunteleō.
Mat.7.28. when Jesus *had* **e.** these
Lu. 4. 2. and *when* they *were* **e.**, he
13. And *when* the devil *had* **e.**
Act. 21.27. seven days were almost **e.**
plēroō.
Lu. 7. 1. when he *had* **e.** all his say.
Act. 19.21. After these things *were* **e.**
ginomai.
Jo. 13. 2. supper *being* **e.** the devil

ENDEAVOUR,   -ed, -ing.
spoudazō.
Eph.4. 3. **e-ing** to keep the unity of the
1Th. 2.17. **e-ed** the more abundantly to
2Pet.1.15. I *will* **e.** that ye may be able
zēteō.
Act. 16.10. we **e-ed** to go unto Macedonia

ENDING, [noun.]
telos.
Rev.1. 8. the beginning and the **e.**, saith

ENDLESS.
akatalutos.
Heb.7.16. after the power of an **e.** life
aperantos.
1Ti. 1. 4. to fables and **e.** genealogies

ENDUED.
enduō.
Lu.24.49. until ye *be* **e.** with power
epistēmōn.
Jas. 3.13. **e.** *with knowledge* among you

ENDURE,   -ed, -eth, -ing.
hupomenō.
Mat.10.22.but he *that* **e-eth** to the end
24.13.*that shall* **e.** unto ; Mar.13.13
1Co. 13.7.hopeth all things ; **e-eth** all
2Ti. 2.10.Therefore I **e.** all things for
Heb.10.32.ye **e-ed** a great fight of afflic.
12. 2. **e-ed** the cross, despising the
3.him *that* **e-ed** such contradic.
7.If ye **e.** chastening, God deal.
Jas. 1.12.Blessed is the man that **e-eth**
5.11.we count them happy *which* **e.**
menō.
Jo. 6.27. for that meat *which* **e-eth** un.
Heb.10.34.better and an **e-ing** subst.
1Pet. 1.25.word of the Lord **e-eth** for
pherō.
Ro. 9.22. **e-ed** with much longsuffering
Heb.12.20.For they could not **e.** that
hupopherō.
2Ti. 3.11. what persecutions I **e-ed** : but
1Pet.2.19. for conscience toward God **e.**
anechomai.
2Th. 1. 4. and tribulations that ye **e.**
2Ti. 4. 3. when they *will* not **e.** sound
proskairos.
Mar.4.17. so **e.** *but for a time*; afterwa.

hupomonē.
2Co. 1. 6. which is effectual in the **e-ing**
kartereō.
Heb.11.27. he **e-ed**, as seeing him who
(*See other words with which it is connected.*)

ENEMY,   -ies.
echthros.
Mat.5.43. neighbour, and hate thine **e.**
44. Love your **e-s**, bless them
13.25. his **e.** came and sowed tares
28. An **e.** hath done this. The
39. The **e.** that sowed them is the
22.44. till I make thine **e-s** thy;
Mar.12.36;Lu.20.43;Heb.1.13.
Lu. 1.71. should be saved from our **e-s**
74. out of the hand of our **e-s**
6.27. Love your **e-s**, do good to
35. love ye your **e-s**, and do
10.19. over all the power of the **e.**
19.27. But those mine **e-s**, which
43. that thine **e-s** shall cast a
Act.13.10. thou **e.** of all righteousness
Ro. 5.10. For if, when we were **e-s**
11.28. they are **e-s** for your sakes
12.20. if thine **e.** hunger, feed him
1Co.15.25. till he hath put all **e-s** un.
26. The last **e.** that shall be dest.
Gal. 4.16. I therefore become your **e.**
Phi. 3.18. that they are the **e-s** of the
Col. 1.21. **e-s** in your mind by wicked
2Th. 3.15. count him as an **e.**, but
Heb.10.13. his **e-s** be made his foot.
Jas. 4. 4. a friend of the world is the **e.**
Rev.11.5. and devoureth their **e-s**
12. and their **e-s** beheld them

ENGRAFTED.
emphutos.
Jas. 1.21. with meekness the **e.** word

ENGRAVEN.
entupoō.
2Co. 3. 7. written and **e.** in stones

ENJOY.
tungchanō.
Act.24.2. *Seeing that* by thee we **e.**
apolausis.
1Ti. 6.17. to us richly all things to **e.**
echō apolausis.
Heb.11.25. than *to* **e.** the pleasures of

ENLARGE,   -ed, -ing.
megalunō.
Mat.23.5. and **e.** the borders of their
2Co.10.15. that we shall *be* **e-ed** by you
platunō.
2Co. 6.11. unto you, our heart *is* **e-ed**
13. my children,) *be* ye also **e-ed**

ENLIGHTENED.
phōtizō.
Eph.1.18. your understanding *being* **e.**
Heb. 6.4. for those *who were* once **e.**

ENMITY.
echthra.
Lu.23.12. they were at **e.** between them.
Ro. 8. 7. the carnal mind is **e.** against
Eph.2.15. abolished in his flesh the **e.**
16. having slain the **e.** thereby
Jas. 4. 4. friendship of the world is **e.**

ENOUGH.
arketos.
Mat.10.25. It is **e.** for the disciple that
hikanos.
Lu.22.38. he said unto them, It is **e.**
perisseuō.
Lu.15.17. have bread **e.** *and to spare*
85

korennumi.

Act.27.38. *when* they *had eaten* e., they

   arkeō.

Mat.25.9. lest there *be* not e. for us and

   apechei.

Mar.14.41. *it is* e., the hour is come

ENQUIRE,   -ed.
   zēteō.

Jo. 16.19. *Do* ye e. among yourselves

Act.9.11. e. in the house of Judas, *for*

   ekzēteō.

¹Pet.1.10. *have* e-ed and searched dilig.

   epizēteō.

Act.19.39. if ye e. anything concerning

   suzēteō.

Lu.22.23. began to e. among themselves

   akriboō.

Mat.2. 7. e-ed *of them diligently* what'

   16. he *had diligently* e-ed of the

   punthanomai.

Jo. 4. 52. Then e-ed he of them the

Act.23.20. as though they would e.

   diaginōskō.

Act.23.15. ye would e. something more

   exetazō.

Mat.10.11. e. who in it is worthy ; and

ENQUIRY.
   dierōtaō.

Act.10.17. *had made* e. for Simon's hou.

ENRICHED.
   ploutizō.

¹Co. 1. 5. in every thing ye *are* e. by

²Co. 9.11. *Being* e. in every thing to all

ENSAMPLE,   -s.
   tupos.

¹Co.10.11. happened unto them for e-ş

Phi. 3.17. as ye have us for an e.

¹Th. 1. 7. So that ye were e-s to all that

²Th. 3. 9. but to make ourselves an e.

¹Pet.5. 3. but being e-s to the flock

   hupodeigma.

²Pet.2. 6. making them an e. unto

ENSUE.
   diōkō.

¹Pet.3.11. let him seek peace, and e. it

ENTANGLE,   -ed, -eth.
   emplekō.

²Ti. 2. 4. e-*eth himself with* the affairs

²Pet.2.20. are again e-ed there *in, and*

   pagideuō.

Mat.22.15. how they *might* e. him in

   enechō.

Gal. 5. 1. be not e-ed again *with* the

ENTER,   -ed, -eth, -ing.
   eiserchomai.

Mat.5.20. ye shall in no case e. *into*

   6. 6. when thou prayest, e. *into*

   7.13. e. ye in at the strait gate

   21. *shall* e. *into* the kingdo m of

   8. 5. *when* Jesus *was* e-ed *into*

   10. 5. city of the Samaritans e. ye

   11. what. city or town ye shall e.

   12. 4. How he e-ed *into* the house

   29. how can one e. *into* a strong

   45. *they* e. *in and* dwell there

   18. 3. ye shall not e. *into* the king.

   8. *to* e. *into* life halt or maimed

   9. *to* e. *into* life with one eye

   19.17. if thou wilt e. *into* life, keep

   23. *shall* hardly e. *into* the king.

   24. *to* e. *into* the king.; Mar.9.47,

   10.24,25 ; Lu.18.25

   23.13. ye them *that are* e-*ing* to go

   24.38. e-ed *into* the ark ; Lu.17.27

   25.21, 23. e. thou into the joy of

   26.41. that ye e. not into temptation

Mar.1.21. he e-*ed into* the synagogue

   Lu.6.6; Act.18.19

   45. no more openly e. *into* the

   2. 1. he e-*ed into* Capern.; Lu.7.1

   3. 1. he e-*ed* again *into* the syna.

   27. e. *into* a strong man's house

   5.12. swine, that we *may* e. *into*

   13. went out, and e-ed into the

   6.10. place scever ye e. *into* an

   7.17. when he *was* e-ed *into* the

   24. e-ed into an house, *and* wou.

   9.25. him, and e. no more *into*

   43. *to* e. *into* life maimed, than

   45. for thee *to* e. halt *into* life

   10.15. child, he shall not e. therein

   23. *shall.* .e. *into* the kingdom of

   11.11. Jesus e-*ed into* Jerusalem

   13.15. neither e. therein, to take

   14.38. lest ye e. *into* tem.; Lu.22.46

   16. 5. e-*ing into* the sepulchre, they

Lu. 1.40. e-ed *into* the house of Zach.

   4.38. e-ed into Simon's house

   7. 6. thou *shouldest* e. under my

   44. I e-ed *into* thine house, thou

   8.30. many devils *were* e-ed *into*

   32. suffer them *to* e. *into* them

   33. e-ed *into* the swine : and the

   9. 4. whatsoever house ye e. *into*

   34. feared as they e-*ed into* the

   52. they went, and e-ed into a

   10. 5. into whatsoever house ye e.

   8. 10. into whatsoever city ye e.

   38. he e-ed *into* a certain village

   11.26. they e. *in, and* dwell there

   52. ye e-ed not in yourselves, and

   that were e-*ing in* ye hinder

   13.24. Strive *to* e. *in* at the strait

   will seek *to* e. *in*, and shall

   17.12. *as* he e-ed *into* a certain villa.

   18.17. shall in no wise e. therein

   24. they that have riches e. *into*

   19. 1. Jesus e-ed *and* passed throu

   21.21. *let* not them. .countries e.

   22. 3. Then e-ed Satan into Judas

   10. *when* ye are e-ed *into* the city

   40. that ye e. not into temptation

   24. 3. they e-ed *in, and* found not

   26. things, and *to* e. *into* his glo.

Jo. 3. 4. can he e. the second time

   5. he cannot e. *into* the king.

   4.38. ye *are* e-ed into their labour.

   10. 1. He *that* e-*eth* not by the door

   2. he *that* e-*eth in* by the door

   9. by me if any man e. *in*, he

   13.27. Satan e-ed *into* him. Then

   18. 1. garden, into the which he e-ed

   33. Pilate e-ed *into* the judgment

Act. 3. 8. e-ed with them *into* the tem.

   5.21. they e-ed *into* the temple

   9.17. went his way, and e-ed *into*

   10.24. after they e-ed *into* Cesarea

   11. 8. at any time e-ed *into* my mo.

   12. we e-ed *into* the man's house

   14.22. e. *into* the kingdom of God

   16.40. e-ed *into* the house of Lydia

   19.30. have e-ed *in* unto the people

   20.29. *shall* grievous wolves e. *in*

   21. 8. we e-ed *into* the house. .*and*

   23.16. e-*ed into* the castle, *and* told

   25.23. *when.* .*was* e-ed *into* the pla.

   28. 8. to whom Paul e-ed *in*,. .*and*

Ro. 5.12. sin e-ed *into* the world, and

Heb.3.11. They *shall* not e. *into* my

   18. should not e. *into* his rest

   19. that they could not e. *in*

   4. 1. left us of e-*ing into* his rest

   3. have believed *do* e. *into* rest

   5. if they *shall* e. *into* my

   6. that some must e. therein

   e-ed not in because of unbe.

   10. he *that is* e-ed *into* his rest

   4.11. therefore *to* e. *into* that rest

Heb.6.19. and *which* e-*eth into* that wi.

   20. the forerunner *is* for us e-ed

   9.12. e-ed *in* once into the holy pl,

   24. For Christ is not e-ed *into*

   25. as the high priest e-*eth into*

Jas. 5. 4. *are* e-ed into the ears of the

²Jo. 7. deceivers are e-ed *into* the

Rev.11.11.life from God e-ed into them

   15. 8. was able to e. *into* the tem.

   21.27. shall in no wise e. *into* it

   22.14. *may* e. *in* through the gates

   erchomai.

Mar.1. 29. they e-ed into the house of

Act.18.7. and e-ed into a certain man's

   pareiserchomai.

Ro. 5.20. Moreover the law e-ed, that

   eisporeuomai.

Mat.15.17. *what* soever e-*eth in* at the

Mar. 4.19. lusts of other things e-*ing in*

   5.40. e-*eth in* where the damsel

   6.56. whithersoever he e-ed, *into*

   7.15. *that* e-*ing into* him can defi.

   18. *what* so. .without e-*eth into*

   19. it e-*eth* not *into* his heart

   11. 2. as soon *as* ye *be* e-ed *into* it

Lu. 8.16. they *which* e. *in* may see

   19.30. in the which *at* your e-*ing*

   22.10. the house where he e-*eth in*

Act. 3. 2. of them *that* e-ed *into* the

   8. 3. As for Saul,. .e-*ing into* eve.

   embainō.

Mat.8.23. *when* he *was* e-ed into a ship

   9. 1. he e-ed *into* a ship, *and* pas.

Mar. 4. 1. e-ed into a ship; 8.10.;Jo.6.17

   8.13. and e-*ing into* the ship again

Lu. 5. 3. he e-ed *into* one of the ships

Jo. 6.22. where. his disciples *were* e-ed

   anabainō

Jo. 21. 3. They went forth, and e-ed

¹Co. 2. 9. neither *have* e-ed into the

   epibainō.

Act.27. 2. And e-*ing into* a ship of

   eisodos.

¹Th. 1. 9. what manner of e-*ing in* we

Heb.10.19. boldness to e. *into* the holi.

   eiseimi.

Act.21.26. with them e-ed *into* the tem.

ENTERTAIN,   -ed.
   xenizō.

Heb.13. 2. *have* e-ed angels unawares

   philoxenia.

Heb.13. 2. not forgetful to e. *strangers*

ENTICED,   -ing.
   peithos.

¹Co. 2. 4. not with e-*ing* words of man's

   pithanologia.

Col. 2. 4. beguile you with e-*ing words*

   deleazō.

Jas. 1.14. away of his own lust, and e.

ENTIRE.
   holoklēros.

Jas. 1. 4. that ye may be perfect and e.

ENTRANCE.
   eisodos.

¹Th. 2. 1. know our e. *in* unto you, that

²Pet.1.11. an e. shall be ministered unto

ENTREAT,   -ed.
   hubrizō.

Mat.22.6. e-ed them *spitefully*, and

Lu. 18.32. be mocked, and *spitefully* e-ed

¹Th. 2. 2. and *were shamefully* e-ed

   kakoō.

Act. 7. 6. and e. them *evil* four hund,

   19. and *evil* e-ed our fathers, so

   atimazō.

Lu.20.11. e-ed him *shamefully*, and

   chraō.

Act.27. 3. Julius courteously e-ed Paul

ENVY, [noun,]   *-ies.*
  phthonos.
Mat.27.18. that for **e.** they had deliver.
Mar.15.10. had delivered him for **e.**
Ro. 1.29. full of **e.**, murder, debate
Phi. 1.15. preach Christ even of **e.** and
[1]Ti. 6. 4. whereof cometh **e.**, strife
Tit. 3. 3. living in malice and **e.**, hate.
Jas. 4. 5. dwelleth in us lusteth to **e.**
[1]Pet. 2. 1. guile, and hypocri., and **e**-*s*
  zēloō.
Act. 7. 9. the patriarchs, *moved with* **e.**
  17. 5. believed not, *moved with* **e.**
  zēlos.
Act.13.45. they were filled with **e.**, and

ENVY, [verb,]   *-eth, -ing.*
  zēloō.
[1]Co.13. 4. charity **e**-*eth* not, charity
  phthoneō.
Gal. 5.26. another, **e**-*ing* one another

ENVYING,   *-s.*
  zēlos.
Ro.13.13. wanton, not in strife and **e.**
[1]Co. 3. 3. **e.**, and strife, and divisions
[2]Co.12.20. debates, **e**-*s*, wraths, strifes
Jas. 3.14. But if ye have bitter **e.** and
  16. For where **e.** and strife is
  phthonos.
Gal. 5.21. **e**-*s*, murders, drunkenness

EPHPHATHA.
  ephphatha.
Mar.7.34. unto him, **e.**, that is, Be op.

EPISTLE,   *-s.*
  epistolē.
Act. 15.30. togeth., they delivered the **e.**
  23.33. and delivered the **e.** to the
Ro. 16.22. I Tertius, who wrote this **e.**
[1]Co. 5. 9. I wrote unto you in an **e.**
[2]Co. 3. 1. **e**-*s* of commendation to you
  2. Ye are our **e.**, written in your
  3. declared to be the **e.** of Ch.
  7. 8. I perceive that the same **e.**
Col. 4 16. when this **e.** is read among
[1]Th. 5.27. that this **e.** be read unto all
[2]Th. 2.15. whether by word, or our **e.**
  3.14. our word by this **e.**, note
  17. which is the token in every **e.**
[2]Pet. 3. 1. This second **e.**, beloved, I
  16. also in all his **e**-*s*, speaking

EQUAL,   *-s.*
  isos.
Mat.20.12. thou hast made them **e.** unto
[T]o. 5.18. making himself **e.** with God
Phil. 2. 6. not robbery to be **e.** with G.
Rev.21.16, and the height of it are **e.**
  sunēlikiōtēs.
Gal. 1.14. above many my **e**-*s* in mine
  isotēs.
Col. 4. 1. that which is just and **e.**
  isanggelos.
Lu.20.36. they are **e.** *unto the angels*

EQUALITY.
  isotēs.
[2]Co. 8.14. But by an **e.**, that now at this
  want : that there may be **e.**

ERE.
  prin.
Jo. 4.49. come down **e.** my child die

ERR,   *-ed.*
  planaō.
Mat.22.29. Ye do **e.**, not knowing the
Mar.12.24. *Do* ye not therefore **e.**, beca.
  27. ye therefore *do* greatly **e.**
Heb. 3.10. They *do* alway **e.** in their
Jas. 1.16. *Do* not **e.**, my beloved breth.
  5.19. Brethren, if any of you *do* **e.**

  astocheō.
[1]Ti. 6.21. *have* **e**-*ed* concerning the faith
[2]Ti. 2.18. concerning the truth *have* **e**-*ed*
  apoplanaō.
[1]Ti. 6.10. they *have* **e**-*ed* from the faith

ERROR,   *-s.*
  agnoēma.
Heb.9. 7. and for the **e**-*s* of the people
  planē.
Mat.27.64. so the last **e.** shall be worse
Ro. 1.27. that recompence of their **e.**
Jas. 5.20. from the **e.** of his way
[2]Pet. 2.18. from them who live in **e.**
  3.17. being led away with the **e.**
[1]Jo. 4. 6. of truth and the spirit of **e.**
Jude 11. ran greedily after the **e.** of

ESCAPE, (See *Way*)   *-ed.*
  pheugō.
Mat.23.33. how *can* ye **e.** the damna.
Heb.11.34. **e**-*ed* the edge of the sword
  12.25. if they **e**-*ed* not who refused
  ekpheugō.
Lu.21.36. worthy *to* **e.** all these things
Ro. 2. 3. thou *shalt* **e.** the judgment of
[2]Co.11.33. down by the wall, and **e**-*ed*
[1]Th. 5. 3. child ; and they shall not **e.**
Heb.2. 3. How *shall* we **e.**, if we neg.
  apopheugō.
[2]Pet. 1. 4. *having* **e**-*ed* the corruption
  2.18. *that were* clean **e**-*ed* from
  20. For if *after* they *have* **e**-*ed*
  diapheugō.
Act.27.42. them should swim out, and **e.**
  diasōzō.
Act.27.44. that they **e**-*ed* all *safe* to land
  28. 1. *when* they *were* **e**-*ed*, then
  4. *though* he *hath* **e**-*ed* the sea,
  exerchomai.
Jo. 10.39 but he **e**-*ed* out of their hand

ESCHEW.
  ekklinō.
[1]Pet.3.11. Let him **e.** evil, and do good

ESPECIALLY.
  malista.
Act.26. 3. **e.** because I know thee to be
Gal. 6.10. **e.** unto them who are of the
[1]Ti. 5.17. **e.** they who labour in the
[2]Ti. 4.13. books, but **e.** the parchmen.

ESPOUSED.
  mnēsteuomai.
Mat.1.18. *When* as his mother..*was* **e.**
Lu. 1.27. To a virgin **e.** to a man, whose
  2. 5. taxed with Mary his **e.** wife
  harmozō.
[2]Co.11. 2. I *have* **e.** you to one husband

ESTABLISH,   *-ed.*
  histēmi.
Mat.18.16.wit. every word *may be* **e**-*ed*
Ro. 3.31. God forbid : yea, we **e.** the
  10. 3. *to* **e.** their own righteousness
[2]Co.13. 1. *shall* every word *be* **e**-*ed*
Heb.10.9. that he *may* **e.** the second.
  stērizō.
Ro. 1.11. gift to the end ye may *be* **e**-*ed*
[1]Th. 3. 2. *to* **e.** you, and to comfort you
[2]Pet.1.12. *be* **e**-*ed* in the present truth
  stereoō.
Act.16.5. so *were* the churches **e**-*ed* in
  nomotheteō.
Heb. 8.6. which *was* **e**-*ed* upon better
  bebaioō.
Heb.13.9. the heart *be* **e**-*ed* with grace

ESTATE,   *-s.*
  prōtos.
Mar.6.21. and *chief* **e**-*s* of Galilee
  tapeinos.
Ro.12.16. condescend to men *of low* **e.**

  ho peri.
Col. 4. 8. that he might know your **e.**
  (the [things] *about* you.)
  archē.
Jude 6. which kept not their *first* **e.**
  presbuterion.
Act. 22.5. and all the **e.** *of the elders*

ESTEEM,   *-ed, -eth, -ing.*
  hēgeomai.
Phi. 2. 3.*let* each **e.** other better than
[1]Th. 5.13.And *to* **e.** them very highly
Heb.11.26.**e**-*ing* the reproach of Christ
  krinō.
Ro.14. 5. One man **e**-*eth* one day above
  another **e**-*eth* every day alike
  logizomai.
Ro.14.14. but to him *that* **e**-*eth* any
  exoutheneō.
[1]Co. 6. 4. to judge *who are* least **e**-*ed*
  hupsēlos.
Lu.16.15. that which is *highly* **e**-*ed*

ETERNAL.
  aiōnios.
Mat.19.16.I do ; that I may have **e.**
  25.46. the righteous into life **e.**
Mar.3.29. in danger of **e.** damnation
  10.17. that I may inherit **e.** life
  30. in the world to come **e.** life
Lu.10.25. I do to inherit **e.** life ; 18.18
Jo. 3.15. not perish, but have **e.** life
  4.36. gathereth fruit unto life **e.**
  5.39. ye think ye have **e.** life : and
  6.54. drinketh my blood, hath **e.**
  68. thou hast the words of **e.** life
  10.28. I give unto them **e.** life ; and
  12.25. world shall keep it unto life **e.**
  17. 2. he should give **e.** life to as
  3. this is life **e.**, that they might
Act.13.48. as were ordained to **e.** life
Ro. 2. 7. and immortality, **e.** life
  5.21. righteousness unto **e.** life
  6.23. the gift of God is **e.** life
[2]Co. 4.17. and **e.** weight of glory
  18. which are not seen are **e.**
  5. 1. with hands, **e.** in the heavens
[1]Ti. 6.12. 19. lay hold on **e.** life
[2]Ti. 2.10. in Christ Jesus with **e.** glory
Tit. 1. 2. hope of **e.** life, which God
  3. 7. according to the hope of **e.**
Heb.5. 9. the author of **e.** salvation
  6. 2. the dead, and of **e.** judgment
  9.12. having obtained **e.** redempt.
  14. who through the **e.** Spirit
  15. the promise of **e.** inheritance
[1]Pet.5.10. called us unto his **e.** glory
[1]Jo. 1. 2. shew unto you that **e.** life
  2.25. promised us, even **e.** life
  3.15. no murderer hath **e.** life
  5.11. God hath given to us **e.** life
  13. know that ye have **e.** life
  20. This is the true God, and **e.**
Jude 7. suffering vengeance of **e.** fire
  21. Lord Jesus Christ unto **e.**
  aiōn.
Eph.3.11. According to the **e.** purpose
[1]Ti. 1.17. unto the king **e.**, immortal
  aidios.
Ro. 1.20. his **e.** power and Godhead

ETHIOPIANS.
  aithiops.
Act. 8.27. Candace, queen of the **e.** *-s*

EUNUCH,   *-s.*
  eunouchos.
Mat.19.12.there are some **e**-*s*, which
  and there be **e**-*s*, which have
Act. 8.27. an **e.** of great authority under
  34. and the **e.** answered Philip
  36. the **e.** said, See, here is water

Act.8. 38. water, both Philip and the e.
    39. the e. saw him no more
eunouchizŏ.
Mat.19.12. which *were made* e-*s* of men
    have made themselves e-*s* for

EVANGELIST,   -s.
eua*n*ggelistēs
Act.21. 8. the house of Philip the e.
Eph.4.11. and some e-*s*; and some
2Ti. 4. 5. do the work of an e., make

EVEN, [*noun.*]
opsia.
Mat.8.16. When the e. was come; 26.20,
    27.57 ; Mar.4.35 ; 15.42.
    20. 8. So when e. was come, the
Mar.1.32. And at e., when the sun did
    6.47. And when e. was come, the
Jo. 6.16. And when e. was now come
opse.
Mar.11.19. And when e. was come, he
    13.35. *at* e., or at midnight, or at

EVEN, [*adverb.*]
kai.
Mat.5.46. do not e. the publicans the
    47. do not e. the publicans so
    7.12. do ye e. so to them, for
    8.27. that e. the winds and the
    12.45. e. so shall it be also unto
    13.12. taken away, e. that he hath
(*And all other passages in which it occurs, except the following :—*)
houtō, and houtōs
Mat.7.12. do ye e. *so* to them : for this
    17. e. *so* every good tree bringeth
    12.45. e. *so* shall it be also unto this
    18.14. e. *so* it is not the will of your
    23.28. e. *so* ye also outwardly appear
Jo. 3.14. e. *so* must the Son of man be
    5.21. e. *so* the Son quicken. whom
    14.31. gave me commandment, e. *so*
Act.12.15. affirmed that it was e. *so*
    27.25. it shall be e. as it was told
Ro. 5.18. e. *so* by the righteousness of
    21. e. *so* might grace reign throu.
    6. 4. e. *so* we also should walk in
    19. e. *so* now yield your members
    11. 5. e. *so* then at this present
    31. e. *so* have these also now not
1Co. 2.11. e. *so* the things of God know.
    9.14. e. *so* hath the Lord ordained
    11.12. e. *so* is the man also by the
    14.12. e. *so* ye, forasmuch as ye are
    15.22. e. *so* in Christ shall all be
    16. 1. church of Galatia, e. *so* do ye
2Co. 7.14. e. *so* our boasting, which I
    10. 7. Christ's, e. *so* are we Christ's
Gal. 4. 3. e. *so* we, when we were child.
    29. the Spirit, e. *so* it is now
1Th. 2. 4. e. *so* we speak ; not as pleas.
    4.14. e. *so* them also which sleep
Jas. 2.17. e. *so* faith, if it hath not wor.
    3. 5. e. *so* the tongue is a little
hōs.
Mat.15.28. be it unto thee e. as thou
Mar. 4.36. they took him e. *as* he was
1Co. 3. 5. e. *as* the Lord gave to every
Eph. 5.33. so love his wife e. *as* himself
1Pet. 3. 6. e. *as* Sara obeyed Abraham
Jude 7. e. *as* Sodom and Gomorrha
Rev.21.11. e. *like* a jasper stone
nai.
Mat.11.26. e. *so* Father: for; Lu. 10.21
Rev. 1. 7. because of him, e. *so*, Amen
    16. 7. e. *so*, Lord God Almighty
    22.20. Amen. e. *so*, come Lord Je.
heōs.
Mat.26.38. exceeding sorrowful, e. *unto*
Mar.14.54. e. into the palace of the high
1Co. 8.15. But e. *unto* this day, when
88

1Jo. 2. 9. is in darkness, e. *until* now
achri.
Act.11.5. corners ; and it came e. *to* me
Heb. 4.12. e. *to* the dividing asunder of
eti.
Lu. 1.15. e. from his mother's womb
te.
Ro. 1.26. e. their women did (for *both*)
homōs.
1Co.14.7. *And* e. things without life
men.
1Th. 2.18. e. I Paul, once and again
hōsautōs.
1Ti. 3.11. e. *so* must their wives be gra.
gar.
Jas. 4.14. It is e. a vapour, that appea.
oude. (*with a negative*).
Mat. 6.29. That e. Solomon in all his
Jo. 21.25. e. the world itself could *not*
1Co. 11.14. Doth *not* e. nature itself
(See *As, Now, Thus.*)

EVENING.
opsia.
Mat.14.15. And when it was e., his disc.
    23. and when the e. was come
    16. 2. When it is e., ye say, It
Mar.14.17. in the e. he cometh with the
Jo. 20.19. the same day at e., being the
hespera.
Lu. 24.29. it is toward e., and the day
Act.28.23. proph., from morning till e.

EVENTIDE.
opsia hōra.
Mar.11.11. and now the e. was come
hespera.
Act. 4. 3. next day: for it was now e.

EVER.
[eis] ho aiōn. (*to the age.*)
Mat.21.19. on thee henceforward for e.
Mar.11.14. fruit of thee hereafter for e.
Lu. 1.55. Abra., and to his seed for e.
Jo. 6.51. this bread, he shall live for e.
    58. of this bread shall live for e.
    8.35. abid. not in the house for e.
    but the Son abideth e.
    12.34. that Christ abideth for e.
    14.16. he may abide with you for e.
2Co. 9. 9. righteous. remaineth for e.
Heb. 5. 6. art a priest for e. ; 7.17,21
    6.20. made an high priest for e.
    7.24. man, beca. he continueth e.
1Pet. 1.23. which liveth and abid. for e.
    25. of the Lord endureth for e.
1Jo. 2.17. the will of God abideth for e.
2Jo. 2. and shall be with us for e.
Jude 13. blackness of darkness for e.
[eis] ho aiōn. (*to the ages.*)
Mat. 6.13. power, and the glory, for e.
Lu. 1.33. over the house of Jacob for e.
Ro. 1.25. Creator, who is blessed for e.
    9. 5. over all, God blessed for e.
    11.36. whom be glory for e. Amen
    16.27. through Jesus Christ for e.
Heb.13. 8. yester., and to day, and for e.
[eis] ho aiōn ho aiōn.
(*to the ages of the ages.*)
Gal. 1. 5. glory for e. and e. ; Phi.4.20;
    1Ti.1.17;2Ti.4.18;Heb.13.21
1Pet. 4 11. for e. and e.; 5.11 ; Rev.1.6
Rev.4.9,10. for e. and e. ; 5.14,10.6,15,7
    5.13. unto the Lamb for e. and e.
    7.12. unto our God for e. and e.
    11.15. he shall reign for e. and e.
    19. 3. smoke rose up for e. and e.
    20.10. day and night for e. and e.
    22. 5. they shall reign for e. and e.
[eis] ho aiōn ho aiōn.
(*to the age of the age.*)
Heb. 1. 8. throne O God is for e. and e.

[eis] aiōn. (*to ages.*)
2Pet. 2.17. of darkness is reserved for e.
[eis] aiōn aiōn.
(*to ages of ages.*)
Rev.14.11. ascendeth up for e. and e.
[eis] pas ho aiōn.
(*to all the ages.*)
Jude 25. and power both now and e.
[eis] hēmera aion.
(*to a day of an age.*)
2Pet. 3.18. glory both now and for e.
aiōnios.
Phile.15. shouldest receive him for e.
Lu.15.31. Son, thou art e. with me, and
Jo.18.20. I e. taught in the synagogue
1Th. 4.17. and so shall we e. be with the
    5.15. e. follow that which is good
2Ti. 3. 7. e. learning, and never able
Heb.7.25. he e. liveth to make interces.
dienekes.
Heb.10.12. *for* e. sat down on the right
    14. he hath perfected for e.
aei.
Mar.15.8. as he had e. done unto them
hosos.
Jo. 4.29. told me all things that e.
    39. He told me all *that* e. I did
    10. 8. All *that* e. came before me
pote.
Eph.5.29. no man e. *yet* hated his own
ou mē. (*with a negative*).
Mat.24.21. this time, no, *nor* e. shall be
pro.
Act.23.15. and we, *or* e. he come near

EVERLASTING.
aiōnios.
Mat.18.8. feet, to be cast into e. fire
    19.29. fold, and shall inherit e. life
    25.41. from me, ye cursed, into e.
    46. go away into e. punishment
Lu.16. 9. receive you into e. habita.
    18.30. in the world to come life e.
Jo. 3.16. not perish, but have e. life
    36. believeth on the Son hath e.
    4.14. springing up into e. life
    5.24. that sent me, hath e. life
    6.27. which endureth unto e. life
    40. on him, may have e. life
    47. believeth on me hath e. life
    12.50. his commandment is life e.
Act.13.46. unworthy of e. life, lo, we
Ro. 6.22. holiness, and the end e. life.
    16.26. commandment of the e. God
Gal. 6. 8. shall of the Spirit reap life e.
2Th. 1. 9. be punished with e. destruc.
    2.16. hath given us e. consolation
1Ti. 1.16. believe on him to life e.
    6.16. be honour and power e.
Heb.13.20. blood of the e. covenant
2Pet.1.11. into the e. kingdom of our
Rev.14.6. having the e. gospel to preach
aidios.
Jude 6. reserved in e. chains under

EVERMORE.
aiōn.
2Co.11.31. Christ, which is blessed for e.
Heb.7.28. Son, who is consecrated for e.
Rev.1.18. and, behold, I am alive for e.
pantote.
Jo. 6.34. Lord, e., give us this bread
1Th.5.16. Rejoice e.

EVERY.
pas.
Mat.4. 4. but by e. word that proceed.
    7. 8. For e. *one* that asketh receiv.
    19. 3. put away his wife for e. cause
Mar.7.14. Hearken unto me e. *one* of

Lu. 4.37. of him went out into e. place
  11.10. For e. one that asketh receiv.
  19.26. That unto e. one which hath
Jo. 3. 8. so is e. one that is born of the
  18.37. e. one that is of the truth
Act. 2.43. And fear came upon e. soul
  15.21. read in the synagogues e. sab.
Ro.14.11. e. knee shall bow to me, and
     e. tongue shall confess to God
1Co. 4.17. teach every where in e. church
2Co.10. 5. and e. high thing that exalt.
Gal. 3.10. e. one that continueth not in
Eph.1.21. and e. name that is named
  4.16. by that which e. joint sup.
Phi. 2. 9. a name which is above e.
  4.21. Salute e. saint in Christ J.
1Ti. 4. 4. For e. creature of God is
2Ti. 2.19. Let e. one that nameth
Heb.12.1. let us lay aside e. weight
Jas. 1.17. e. good gift and e. perfect
1Pet.2.13. to e. ordinance of man
1Jo. 4. 1. believe not e. spirit
  7. and e. one that loveth

*(And in all other passages in which
it occurs except the following:—)*

hekastos.
Mat.16.27.e. man according to his; 25.15
  18.35. forgive not e. one his brother
  26.22. began e. one of them to say
Mar.13.34.and to e. man his work, and
Lu. 2. 3. taxed, e. one into his own city
  4.40. his hands on e. one of them
  6.44. For e. tree is known by his
  16. 5. called e. one of his lord's
Jo. 6. 7. that e. one of them may take
  7.53. e. man went unto his own
  16.32. scattered, e. man to his own
  19.23. four parts, to e. soldier a part
Act. 2. 6. e. man heard them speak in
  8. how hear we e. man in our
  38. be baptized e. one of you in
  3.26. turning away e. one of you
  4.35. made unto e. man according
  11.29. e. man according to his ability
  17.27. he be not far from e. one of
  20.31. to warn e. one night and day
  21.26. be offered for e. one of them
Ro. 2. 6. render to e. man according to
  12. 3. as God hath dealt to e. man
  14. 5. Let e. man be fully persuaded
  12. So then e. one of us shall give
  15. 2. Let e. one of us please his
1Co. 1.12. that e. one of you saith, I am
  3. 5. as the Lord gave to e. man
  8. e. man shall receive his own
  10. let e. man take heed how he
  13. e. man's work shall be made
     fire shall try e. man's work of
  4. 5. e. man have praise of God
  7. 2. let e. man have his own wife
     e. woman have her own hus.
  7. e. man hath his proper gift
  17. hath distributed to e. man
     the Lord hath called e. one
  20. Let e. man abide in the same
  24. let e. man, wherein he is call.
  10.24. but e. man another's wealth
  11.21. in eating e. one taketh before
  12. 7. given to e. man to profit
  11. dividing to e. man severally
1Co12.18. e. one of them in the body
  14.26. e. one of you hath a psalm
  15.23. e. man in his own order
  38. and to e. seed his own body
  16. 2. let e. one of you lay by him
2Co. 5.10. that e. one may receive the
  9. 7. e. man according as he purp.
Gal. 6. 4. let e. man prove his own|
  5. e. man shall bear his own
Eph.4. 7. unto e. one of us is given

Eph.4.16. measure of e. part, maketh
  25. speak e. man truth with his
  5.33. let e. one of you in particular
Phi.2. 4. Look not e. man on his own
     but e. man also on the things
Col. 4. 6. how ye ought to answer e.
1Th.2.11. charged e. one of you, as a
  4. That e. one of you should
2Th.1. 3. the charity of e. one of you
Heb.6.11.we desire that e. one of you
  8.11. teach e. man his neighbour
     and e. man his brother
Jas.1.14. e. man is tempted, when he
1Pet.1.17.according to e. man's work
  4.10. As e. man hath received the
Rev.2.23.I will give unto e. one of you
  5. 8. having e. one of them harps
  6.11. given unto e. one of them
  20.13. were judged, e. man according
  22. yielded her fruit e. month
  12. to give e. man according as

kata. *[accu.]*
Lu. 8. 1. that he went *throughout* e.
  4. were come to him *out of* e.
  16.19. and fared sumptuously e.
Jo. 21.25. if they should be written e.
Act. 8. 3. entering into e. house, and
  14.23. ordained..elders *in* e.church
  15.21. *in* e. city, them that preach
  20.23. Holy Gh. witnesseth *in* e. city
  22.19. beat *in* e. synagogue them
Tit. 1. 5. ordain elders *in* e. city, as I
Heb.3.13. high priest entereth..e. year
  10.3. again made of sins e. year
Rev.22.2. yielded her fruit e. month

pantachou.
Mar.16.20.forth, and preached e. *where*
Lu. 9. 6. and healing e. *where*
Act.17.30. command. all men e. *where*
  21.28. that teacheth all men e. *where*
  28.22. that e. *where* it is spoken
1Co. 4.17. as I teach e. *where* in every

ana.
Mat.20.9, 10. received e. man a penny
Rev.21.21.e. several gate was of one

hapas.
Mar.5.25. restored, and saw e. man
Act.5.16. and they were healed e. *one*

holos.
Jo. 7.23. made a man e. *whit* whole
  13.10. but is clean e. *whit :* and ye

tis, *[what.]*
Lu.15.15. might know *how much* e.

tis, *(a certain.)*
Act.2.45. all men, as e. man had need

katheis.
Ro.12. 5. e. *one* members one of anoth.

(See Day, Go, Quarter, Side.)

EVIDENCE.
elengchos.
Heb.11.1. fai., the e. of things not seen

EVIDENT.
dēlos.
Gal.3.11. it is e.: for, The just shall
endeixis.
Phi.1.28. to them an e. *token* of perdit.
prodēlos.
Heb.7.14. For it is e. that our Lord
katadēlos.
Heb.7.15. And it is yet far more e.

EVIDENTLY.
phanerōs.
Act.10.3. He saw in a vision e., about
prographō.
Gal. 3. 1. Christ *hath been* e. *set forth*

EVIL,   -s.
ponēros.
Mat.5.11. shall say all manner of e.
  37. more than these cometh of e.
  39. you, That ye resist not e.; but
  45. mak. his sun to rise on the e.
  6.13. but deliv. us from e.; Lu.11.4
  23. But if thine eye be e., thy
  7.11. If ye then, being e., know
  17. corrupt tree bringeth forth e.
  18. bring forth e. fruit, neither
  9. 4. Wherefore think ye e. in your
  12.34. how can ye, being e., speak
  35. an e. man out of the e. treas.
     bringeth forth e. things
  39. An e. and adulterous genera.
  15.19. of the heart proceed e. thou.
  20.15. Is thine eye e., because I am
Mar.7.22. lasciviousness, an e. eye, blas.
  23. All these e. things come from
Lu. 3.19. for all the e-s which Herod
  6,22. cast out your name as e., for
  35. the unthankful and to the e.
  45. and an e. man out of the e.
     bring. forth that which is e.
  7.21. and plagues, and of e. spirits
  8. 2. healed of e. spirits and infir.
  11.13. If ye then, being e., know
  29. This is an e. generation
  34. but when thine eye is e., thy
Jo. 3.19. because their deeds were e.
  7. 7. that the works thereof are e.
  17.15. should. keep them from the e.
Act.19.12.and the e. spirits went out of
  13. call over them which had e.
  15. And the e. spirit answered
  16. the man in whom the e. spirit
Ro.12. 9. Abhor that which is e.; cleave
Gal. 1. 4. deliver us from this present e.
Eph.5.16. time, because the days are e.
  6.13. to withstand in the e. day
1Th. 5.22. Abs. from all appearance of e.
2Th. 3. 3. you, and keep you from e.
1Ti. 6. 4. strife, railings, e. surmisings
2Ti. 3.13. But e. men and seducers shall
  4.18. from every e. work, and will
Heb.3.12. you an e. heart of unbelief
  10.22. sprinkled from an e. conscien.
Jas. 2. 4. are become judges of e.
  4.16. boastings, all such rejoic. is e.
1Jo. 3.12. Because his own works were e.
2Jo. 11. speed, is partaker of his e.

kakos.
Mat.24.48. if that e. servant shall say
  27.23. What e. hath he done?
     Mar.15.14 ; Lu.23.22
Mar. 7.21. e. thoughts, adulteries, for.
Lu. 16.25. likewise Lazarus e. things
Jo. 18.23. bear witness of the e. : but
Act. 9.13. of this man, how much e. he
  23. 9. We find no e. in this man
Ro. 1.30. inventors of e. things, dis.
  2. 9. soul of man that doeth e.
  3. 8. that we say, Let us do e.
  7.19. but the e. which I would not
  21. good, e. is present with me
  9.11. done any good or e. that the
  12.17. Recom. to no man e. for e.
  21. Be not overcome of e., but
     overcome e. with good
  13. 3. to good works, but to the e.
  4. if thou do that which is e.
Ro. 13. 4. wrath upon him that doeth e.
  14.20. but it is e. for that man who
  16.19. good, and simple concern. e.
1Co. 10. 6. should not lust after e. things
  13. 5. easily provoked, think. no e.
  15.33. e. communications corrupt
2Co. 13. 7. that ye do no e. ; not that
Phi. 3. 3. beware of e. workers, beware
Col. 3. 5. e. concupiscence, and covet.

89

¹Th. 5.19. See that none render **e.** for **e.**
¹Ti. 6.10. of money is the root of all **e.**
²Ti. 4.14. did me much **e.** ; the Lord
Tit. 1.12. liars, **e.** beasts, slow bellies
Heb. 5.14. to discern both good and **e.**
Jas. 1.13. God can. be tempted with **e.**
     3. 8. an unruly **e.**, full of deadly
¹Pet. 3.9. Not rendering **e.** for **e.**, or
     10. refrain his tongue from **e.**
     11. Let him eschew **e.**, and do
     12. is against them that do **e.**
³John 11. follow not that which is **e.**
Rev. 2. 2. not bear them which are **e.**
   kakōs.
Jo. 18.23. If I have spoken **e.**, bear
Act. 23.5. Thou shalt not speak **e.** of
   kakia.
Mat.6.34. unto the day is the **e.** thereof
   kakopoieō.
Mar.3. 4. sabbath days, or to do **e.**
Lu. 6. 9. to do good, or to do **e.** ? to
¹Pet.3.17. well-doing, than for **e.** doing
³John 11. that doeth **e.** hath not seen
   phaulos.
Jo. 3.20. every one that doeth **e.** hate.
   5.29. and they that have done **e.**
Tit. 2. 8. having no **e.** thing to say of
Jas. 3.16. confusion, and every **e.** work
   adikēma.
Act.24.20. have found any **e.** doing in
(See other words with which it is connected.)

EVILDOER,   -s.
   kakopoios.
¹Pet.2.12. speak against you as **e-s**, they
   14. for the punishment of **e-s**, and
   3.16. they speak evil of you,as of **e-s**
   4.15. as a thief, or as an **e.**, or as a
   kakourgos.
²Ti. 2. 9. as an **e.**, even unto bonds

EXACT.
   prassō.
Lu. 3.13. **e.** no more than that which

EXALT,   -ed, -eth.
   hupsoō.
Mat.11.23. which art **e-ed** un.; Lu.10.15
   23.12. And whosoever shall **e.** him.
     humb. himself shall be **e-ed**
     Lu.14.11,18.14
Lu 1.52. and **e-ed** them of low degree
   14.11. For who soever **e-eth** himself
   18.14. every one that **e-eth** himself
Act. 2.33. being by. .hand of God **e-ed**
   5.31. Him hath God **e-ed** with his
   13.17. and **e-ed** the people when
²Co. 11. 7. myself that ye might be **e-ed**
¹Pet. 5. 6. that he may **e.** you in due
   epairō.
²Co.10. 5. high thing that **e-eth** itself
   11.20. if a man **e.** himself, if a man
   huperairomai.
²Co.12. 7. I should be **e-ed** above measure
   huperupsoō.
Phi.2. 9. God also hath highly **e-ed** him
   hupsos.
Jas. 1. 9. rejoice in that he is **e-ed**

EXAMINATION.
   anakrisis.
Act.25.26. that, after **e.** had, I might

EXAMINE,   -ed, -ing.
   anakrinō.
Lu. 23.14. having **e-ed** him before you
Act. 4. 9. If we this day be **e-ed** of the
   12.19. him not, he **e-ed** the keepers
   24. 8. by **e-ing** of whom thyself
   28.18. Who, when they had **e-ed** me
¹Co. 9. 3. to them that do **e.** me is this
90

   anetazō.
Act.22.24. should be **e-ed** by scourging
   29. which should have **e-ed** him
   dokimazō.
¹Co.11.28. But let a man **e.** himself, and
   peirazō.
²Co.13. 5. **e.** yourselves, whether ye be

EXAMPLE,   -s.
   hupodeigma.
Jo. 13.15. For I have given you an **e.**
Heb.4.11. after the same **e.** of unbelief
   8. 5. Who serve unto the **e.** of
Jas. 5.10. for an **e.** of suffering affliction
   deigma.
Jude 7. set forth for an **e.**, suffering
   paradeigmatizō.
Mat.1.19. to make her a publick **e.**, was
   tupos.
¹Co.10. 6. Now these things were our **e-s**
¹Ti. 4.12. thou an **e.** of the believers
   hupogrammos.
¹Pet.2.21. leaving us an **e.**, that ye sho.

EXCEED.
   perisseuō.
Mat.5.20. your righteousness shall **e.**
²Co. 3. 9. of righteousness, **e.** in glory
   perisseuō pleiōn.
Mat.5.20. shall **e.** the righteousness of

EXCEEDING.
   lian.
Mat.2.16. of the wise men, was **e.**
   4. 8. into an **e.** high mountain
   8.28. out of the tombs, **e.** fierce
Mar 9. 3. **e.** white as snow; so as no
Lu.23. 8. he was **e.** glad : for he was
   sphodra.
Mat. 2.10. they rejoiced with **e.** great joy
   17.23. And they were **e.** sor.; 26.22
Rev.16.21. plague thereof was **e.** great
   huperballō.
²Co. 9.14. for the **e.** grace of God in you
Eph.1.19. what is the **e.** greatness of his
   2. 7. shew the **e.** riches of his grace
   kata huperbolē.
Ro. 7.13. might become **e.** sinful
   kata huperbolē eis huperbolē.
²Co. 4.17. a far more **e.**, and eternal
   huper.
Eph.3.20. to do **e.** abundantly above all
   theos.
Act.7.20. and was **e.** fair (fair to God.)
   huperperisseuō.
²Co. 7. 4. I am **e.** joyful in all our
(See other words with which it is connected.)

EXCEEDINGLY.
   perissōs.
Act.26.11. being **e.** mad against them
   perissoterōs.
Mar.15.14. they cried out the more **e.**
²Co. 7.13. **e.** the more joyed we for the
Gal. 1.14. being more **e.** zealous of the
   huper ek perissos.
¹Th. 3.10. Night and day praying **e.**
   sphodra.
Mat.19.25. they were **e.** amazed, saying
   sphodrōs.
Act.27.18. And we being **e.** tossed with
   megas phobos.
Mar.4.41. And they feared **e.**, and said
(See other words with which it is connected.)

EXCEL,   -eth.
   perisseuō.
¹Co.14.12. that ye may **e.** to the edifying

   huperballō.
²Co. 3.10. reason of the glory that **e-th**

EXCELLENCY.
   huperochē.
¹Co. 2. 1. came not with **e.** of speech
   huperbolē.
²Co. 4. 7. that the **e.** of the power may
   huperechō.
Phi. 3. 8. for the **e.** of the knowledge of

EXCELLENT.
   kata huperbolē.
¹Co.12.31.I unto you a more **e.** way
   kratistos.
Lu. 1. 3. in order, most **e.** Theophilus
Act.23.26. unto the most **e.** governor F.
   diapherō.
Ro. 2.18. the things that are more **e.**
Phi.1.10. may approve things that are **e.**
   diaphoros.
Heb. 1.4. obtained a more **e.** name that
   8.6. obtained a more **e.** ministry
   pleiōn.
Heb.11.4. a more **e.** sacrifice than Cain
   megaloprepēs.
²Pet.1.17. voice to him from the **e.** glory

EXCEPT.
   ean mē.
Mat.5.20. **e.** your righteousness shall
   12.29. he first bind the; Mar.3.27
   18. 3. **e.** ye be converted, and become
   26.42. **e.** I drink it, thy will be done
Mar.7. 3. **e.** they wash their hands oft
   4. **e.** they wash, they eat not
Lu.13. 3, 5. but, **e.** ye repent, ye shall
Jo. 3. 2. doest, **e.** God be with him
   3. **e.** a man be born again, he
   5. **e.** a man be born of water and
   27. **e.** it be given him from heaven
   4.48. **e.** ye see signs and wonders
   6.44. **e.** the Father which hath sent
   53. **e.** ye eat the flesh of the Son
   65. **e.** it were given unto him of
   12.24. **e.** a corn of wheat fall into
   15. 4. **e.** it abide in the vine ; no
     more can ye, **e.** ye abide in me
   20.25. **e.** I shall see in his hands the
Act. 8.31. How can I, **e.** some man sh.
   15. 1. **e.** ye be circumcised
   27.31. **e.** these abide in the ship
Ro.10.15. they preach, **e.** they be sent
¹Co.14. 6. **e.** I shall speak to you either
   7. **e.** they give a distinction in
   9. **e.** ye utter by the tongue
   15.36. is not quickened, **e.** it die
²Th. 2. 3. **e.** there come a falling away
²Ti. 2. 5. crowned, **e.** he strive lawfully
Rev.2. 5. out of his place, **e.** thou rep.
   22. **e.** they repent of their deeds
   ei mē.
Mat. 19. 9.**e.** it be for fornication, and
   24.22. **e.** those days should be short.
Mar.13.20.**e.** that the Lord had shorten.
Jo. 19.11.**e.** it were given thee from
Ro. 7. 7.**e.** the law had said, Thou
   9.29.**e.** the Lord of Sabaoth had
²Co. 12.13.**e.** it be that I myself was not
   ei mē ti.
Lu. 9.13. **e.** we should go and buy meat
¹Co. 7. 5. **e.** it be with consent for a
²Co.13. 5. Christ is in you, **e.** ye be rep.
   ektos ei mē.
¹Co.14.5. with tongues, **e.** he interpret
   parektos.
Act.26.29. such as I am, **e.** these bonds
   plēn.
Act. 8. 1. and Samaria, **e.** the apostles
   ē.
Act. 24.21. **e.** it be for this one voice

EXCEPTED.
ektos.
¹Co.15.27. that he is e. which did put

EXCESS.
akrasiā.
Mat.23.25. are full of extortion and e.
asōtia.
Eph.5.18. dru. with wine, wherein is e.
anachusis.
¹Pet.4. 4. to the same e. of riot, speak.
(See *Wine*.)

EXCHANGE.
antallagma.
Mat.16.26. a man give *in* e.; Mar.8.37

EXCHANGERS.
trapezitēs.
Mat.25.27. have put my money to the e.

EXCLUDE,   -ed.
ekkleiō.
Ro. 3.27. is boasting then? It *is* e-ed
Gal. 4.17. yea, they would e. you, that

EXCUSE,   -ed, -ing.
paraiteomai.
Lu.14.18. one consent began *to make* e.
19. I pray thee have me e-ed
apologeomai.
Ro. 2.15. accusing or else e-ing one
²Co.12.19. that we e. our *selves* unto you
anapologētos.
Ro.1. 20. so that they are *without* e.

EXECUTE,   -ed.
poieō.
Jo. 5.27. authority *to* e. judgment also
Jude 15. *To* e. judgment upon all, and
hierateuō.
Lu. 1. 8. while he e-ed *the priest's office*

EXECUTIONER.
spekoulatōr.
Mar.6.27. the king sent an e., and com.

EXERCISE, [noun.]
gumnasia.
¹Ti. 4. 8. For bodily e. profiteth little

EXERCISE, [verb,]   -ed, -eth.
gumnazō.
¹Ti. 4. 7. e. thyself rather unto godline.
Heb.5.14. their senses e-ed to discern
12.11. them *which are* e-ed thereby
²Pet. 2.14. an heart they have e-ed with
askeō.
Act.24.16. herein *do* I e. myself, to
poieō.
Rev.13.12. he e-eth all the power of the
(*See other words with which it is
connected.*)

EXHORT,   -ed, -eth, -ing.
parakaleō.
Act. 2.40. did he testify and e., saying
11.23. and e-ed them all, that with
14.22. e-ing them to continue in the
15.32. e-ed the brethren with many
Ro.12. 8. Or he *that* e-eth, on exhorta.
²Co. 9. 5. I thought it necessary *to* e.
¹Th. 4. 1. and e. you by the Lord Jesus
5.14. Now we e. you, brethren
²Th. 3.12. e. by our Lord Jesus Christ
¹Ti. 2. 1. e. therefore, that, first of all
6. 2. These things teach and e.
²Ti. 4. 2. e. with all long-suffering
Tit. 1. 9. both *to* e. and to convince
2. 6. likewise e. to be sober mind.
15. speak, and e., and rebuke

Heb.3.13. But e. one another daily
10.25. but e-ing one another: and
¹Pet.5. 1. I e., who am also an elder
12. I have written briefly, e-ing
Jude 3. me to write unto you, *and* e.
protrepomai.
Act.18.27. wrote. e-ing the disciples to
paraineō.
Act.27.22. And now I e. you to be of

EXHORTATION.
paraklēsis.
Act.13.15. any word of e. for the people
Ro. 12. 8. Or he that exhorteth, on e.
¹Co. 14. 3. edification, and e., and com.
²Co. 8.17. he accepted the e.; but being
¹Th. 2. 3. For our e. was not of deceit
¹Ti. 4.13. to reading, to e., to doctrine
Heb.12. 5. forgotten the e. which sp.
13.22. suffer the word of e.: for I
parakaleō.
Lu. 3.18. other things *in* his e. preached
Act. 20.2. and *had given* them much e.

EXORCISTS.
exorkistēs.
Act.19.13. cer. of the vagabond Jews, e.

EXPECTATION.
apokaradokia.
Ro. 8.19. the *earnest* e. of the creature
Phi. 1.20. According to my *earnest* e.
prosdokia.
Act.12.11. and from all the e. of the
prosdokaō.
Lu. 3.15. as the people *were in* e., and

EXPECTING.
prosdokaō.
Act. 3. 5. e. to receive something of
ekdechomai.
Heb.10.13. e. till his enemies be made

EXPEDIENT.
sumpherō.
Jo. 11.50. Nor consider that it *is* e. *for*
16. 7. It *is* e. *for* you that I go away
18.14. that it *was* e. that one man
¹Co. 6.12. but all things *are* not e.; 10.23
²Co. 8.10. for this *is* e. *for* you, who
12. 1. It *is* not e. *for* me doubtless

EXPELLED.
ekballō.
Act.13.50. and e. them out of their co.

EXPERIENCE.
dokimē.
Ro. 5. 4. And patience, e.; and e., hope

EXPERIMENT.
dokimē.
²Co. 9.13. by the e. of this ministration

EXPERT.
gnōstēs.
Act.26. 3. to be e. in all customs and

EXPIRED.
plēroō.
Act.7.30. *when* forty years *were* e.
teleō.
Rev.20.7. the thousand years'are e.

EXPOUNDED.
ektithēmi.
Act.11.4. and e. it by order unto
18.26. and e. unto him the way
28.23. to whom he e. and testi.
epiluō.
Mar.4.34. e. all things to his discip.
diermēneuō.
Lu.24.27. he e. unto them in all the

EXPRESS.
charaktēr.
Heb. 1. 3. and the e. *image* of his per.

EXPRESSLY.
rētōs.
¹Ti. 4. 1. Now the Spirit speaketh

EXTORTION.
harpagē.
Mat.23.25. they are full of e. and excess

EXTORTIONER,   -s
harpax.
Lu.18.11. as other men are, e-s, unjust
¹Co. 5.10. with the covetous, or e-s, or
11. railer, or a drunkard, or an e.
6.10. revilers, nor e-s, shall inherit

EYE,   -s.
ophthalmos.
Mat.5.29. if thy right e. offend thee
38. An e. for an e., and a tooth
6.22. The light of the body is the e
thine e. be single; Lu.11.34
23. But if thine e. be evil, thy
7. 3. thy brother's e.; Lu.6.41,42
is in thine own e.; Lu.6.41
4. the mote out of thine e.; and
a beam is in thine own e.
5. out of thine own e.; Lu.6.42
mote out of thy brother's e.
9.29. Then touched he their e-s
30. And their e-s were; Lu.24.31
13.15. their e-s they have closed
see with their e-s; Act.28.27
16. But blessed are your e-s, for
17. 8. they had lifted up their e-s
18. 9. And if thine e. offe.; Mar.9.47
than having two e-s; Mar.9.47
20.15. Is thine e. evil, because I am
33. Lord, that our e-s may be
34. them; and touched their e-s
their e-s received sight, and
21.42. marvel. in our e-s; Mar.12.11
26.43. e-s were heavy; Mar.14.40
Mar.7.22. an evil e., blasphemy, pride
8.18. Having e-s, see ye not? and
25. hands again upon his e-s
Lu. 2.30. For mine e-s have seen thy
4.20. And the e-s of all them that
6.20. he lifted up his e-s;
Jo.6.5,11.41,17.1
42. the mote that is in thine e.
beam that is in thine own e.
10.23. Blessed are the e-s which see
16.23. in hell he lifted up his e-s
18.13. so much as his e-s unto hea.
19.42. they are hid from thine e-s
24.16. But their e-s were holden that
Jo. 4.35. Lift up your e-s, and look on
9. 6. he anointed the e-s of the bl.
10. How were thine e-s opened
11. and anointed mine e-s, and
14, 21. and opened his e-s
15. He put clay upon mine e-s
17, 26. he hath opened thine e-s
30. yet he hath opened mine e-s
32. that any man opened the e-s
10.21. Can a devil open the e-s of
11.37. which opened the e-s of the
12.40. He hath blinded their e-s
should not see with their e-s
Act. 9. 8. when his e-s were opened, he
18. there fell from his e-s as it
40. and she opened her e-s; and
26.18. To open their e-s, and to turn
28.27. their e-s have they closed
Ro. 3.18. fear of God before their e-s
11. 8. e-s that they should not see
10. Let their e-s be darkened
¹Co. 2. 9. e. hath not seen, nor ear

91

¹Co.12.16. Because I am not the e., I
17. If the whole body were an e.
21. And the e. cannot say unto
15.52. in the twinkling of an e., at
Gal. 3. 1. before whose e-s Jesus Christ
4.15. have plucked out your own e-s
Eph.1.18. The e-s of your understand.
Heb.4.13. opened unto the e-s of him
¹Pet.3.12. For the e-s of the Lord are
²Pet.2.14. Having e-s full of adultery
¹Jo. 1. 1. wh. we have seen with our e-s
2.11. darkness hath blinded his e-s
16. and the lust of the e-s, and
Rev.1. 7. and every e. shall see him
14. his e-s were as a flame of fire
2.18. who hath his e-s like unto
3.18. anoint thine e-s with eyesalve
4. 6. four beasts full of e-s before
8. and they were full of e-s
5. 6. and seven e-s which are the
7.17. all tears from their e-s; 21.4
19.12. His e-s were as a flame of fire

omma.
Mar.8.23. when he had spit on his e-s

monophthalmos.
Mat.18.9. to enter into life *with one* e.
Mar.9.47. kingdom of God *with one* e.

trumalia.
Mar.10.25. through the e. of a needle
Lu. 18.25. camel..through a needle's e.

trupēma.
Mat.19.24. through the e. of a needle
(See *Fasten, Set.*)

EYESALVE.
kollourion.
Rev.3.18. anoint thine eyes with e., that

EYESERVICE.
ophthalmodouleia.
Eph.6. 6. Not with e. as men; Col.3.22

EYEWITNESSES.
autoptēs.
Lu. 1. 2. from the beginning were e.

epoptēs.
²Pet.1.16. but were e. of his majesty

FABLES.
muthos.
¹Ti. 1. 4. Neither give heed to f. and
4. 7. refuse profane and old wives' f.
²Ti. 4. 4. and shall be turned unto f.
Tit. 1.14. Not giving heed to Jewish f.
²Pet.1.16.followed cunningly devised f.

FACE,   -s.
prosōpon.
Mat.6.16. for they disfigure their f-s
17. thine head, and wash thy f.
11.10. before thy f.; Mar.1.2; Lu.7.27
16. 3. disc. the f. of the sky; Lu.12.56
17. 2. and his f. did shine as the sun
6. they fell on their f., and were
18.10. do always behold the f. of my
26.39. and fell on his f. and prayed
67. Then did they spit in his f.
Mar.14.65.cover his f., and to buffet
Lu. 1.76. shalt go before the f. of the
2.31. prepared before the f. of all
5.12. seeing Jesus, fell on his f.
9.51. he stedfastly set his f. to go
52. sent messengers before his f.
53. because his f. was as though
10. 1. two and two before his f.
17.16. And fell down on his f. at his
21.35. on the f. of the whole earth
22.64. they struck him on the f.
24. 5. bowed down their f-s to the
Act. 6.15. saw his f. as it had been the f.
7.45. before the f. of our fathers
17.26. dwell on all the f. of the earth
92

Act.20.25, 38. they shall see my f. no
25.16. have the accusers f. to f.
¹Co.13.12. but then f. to f.: now I know
14.25. and so falling down on his f.
²Co. 3. 7. not stedfastly behold the f.
13. which put a vail over his f.
18. with open f. beholding as in
4. 6. glory of God in the f. of J. C.
11.20. if a man smite you on the f.
Gal. 1.22. And was unknown by f. unto
2.11. I withstood him to the f., be.
Col.2. 1. as have not seen my f. in the
¹Th. 2.17. to see your f. with great; 3.10
Jas. 1.23. beholding his natural f. in
¹Pet.3.12. the f. of the Lord is against
Rev.4. 7. third beast had a f. as a man
6.16. hide us from the f. of him
7.11. before the throne on their f-s
9. 7. there f-s as the f-s of men
10. 1. his f. as it were the sun
11.16. fell upon their f-s, and
12.14. from the f. of the serpent
20.11. from whose f. the earth and
22. 4. And they shall see his f.; and

opsis.
Jo. 11.44. his f. was bound about with

stoma.
²John 12. and speak f. to f., that our
³John 14. and we shall speak f. to f.

apo.
Act. 7.45. drave out *before the* f. of

FADE,   -eth.
marainomai.
Jas. 1.11. *shall* the rich man f. *away*

amarantos.
¹Pet. 1. 4. unde., and *that* f-eth *not away*

amarantinos.
¹Pet. 5. 4. of glory, *that* f-eth *not away*

FAIL,   -eth.
ekleipō.
Lu.16. 9. when ye f. they may receive
22.32. for thee, that thy faith f. not
Heb.1.12. and thy years *shall* not f.

piptō.
Lu.16.17. one tittle of the law *to* f.

ekpiptō.
¹Co.13. 8. Charity never f-eth: but whe.

katargeō.
¹Co.13.8. be prophecies, they *shall* f.

epileipō.
Heb.11.32. for the time *would* f. to tell

hustereō.
Heb.12.15. lest any man f. of the grace

anekleiptos.
Lu.12.33. in the heavens *that* f-eth *not*
(See *Hearts.*)

FAIN.
epithumeō.
Lu.15.16. he *would* f. have filled his

FAINT,   -ed.
ekluō.
Mat.9.36. because they f-ed and
15.32. fasting, lest they f. in the
Mar. 8. 3. they *will* f. by the way: for
Gal. 6. 9. we shall reap, *if* we f. not
Heb. 12.3. wearied *and* f. in your minds
5. nor f. when thou art rebuked

ekkakeō.
Lu.18. 1. always to pray, and not to f.
²Co. 4. 1. received mercy, we f. not
16. For which cause we f. not
Eph.3.13. I desire that ye f. not at my

kamnō.
Rev. 2. 3. laboured, and *hast* not f-ed

FAIR.
eudia.
Mat.16.2. ye say, it will be f. *weather*

asteios.
Act. 7.20. born, and was exceeding f.

kalos.
Act. 27.8. which is called the f. havens
(See *Shew, Speech.*)

FAITH.
pistis, (*without the article.*)
(*The passages in which my faith, your
faith, &c., occur, have the article; but it
is used only to indicate the possessive—
thus, the faith of me, the faith of you.*)

Mat.8.10. I have not found so great f.
9. 2. Jesus seeing their f. said
22. thy f. hath made thee whole
Mar.5.34,10.52;Lu.8.48,17.19
29. According to your f. be it
15.28. O woman, great is thy f.
17.20. If ye have f. as a; Lu.17.6
21.21. If ye have f., and doubt not
Mar.2. 5. When Jesus saw their f., he
4.40. how is it that ye have no f.
11.22. unto them, Have f. in God
Lu. 5.20. when he saw their f., he said
7. 9. I have not found so great f.
50. Thy f. hath saved thee; 18.42
8.25. Where is your f.? And they
17. 5. the Lord, Increase our f.
22.32. that thy f. fail not: and when
Act. 6. 5. full of f. and of the H. G.; 11.24
8. Stephen, full of f. and power
14. 9. that he had f. to be healed
27. he had opened the door of f.
20.21. and toward our Lord Jesus
26.18. sanctified by f. that is in me
Ro. 1. 5. for obedience to (of) the f.
8. that your f. is spoken of
17. revealed from f. to f.: as it
just shall live by f.; Gal.3.11
3.22. which is by f. of Jesus Christ
27. Nay; but by the law of f.
28. justified by f.; 5.1.; Gal.3.24
30. justify the circumcision by f.
4. 5. his f. is counted for righteous.
13. through the righteousness of f.
16. Therefore it is of f., that it
which is of the f. of Abraham
9.30. righteousn.which is of f.; 10.6
32. Bec. they sought it not by f.
12. 3. every man the measure of f.
14.22. Hast thou f.? have it to
23. because he eateth not of f.
whatsoever is not of f. is
16.26. nations for the obedience of f.
¹Co. 2. 5. That your f. should not stand
12. 9. To another f. by the same
13.13. And now abideth f., hope
15.14. and your f. is also vain
17. your f. is vain; ye are yet
²Co. 1.24. have dominion over your f.
5. 7. we walk by f., not by sight
8. 7. in f., and utterance, and kn.
10.15. when your f. is increased
Gal. 2.16. but by the f. of Jesus Christ
justified by the f. of Christ
20. I live by the f. of the Son
3. 2, 5. or by the hearing of f.
7. they which are of f., the
8. justify the heathen through f.
9. they which be of f. are bless.
12. the law is not of f.: but
22. the promise by f. of Jesus C.
5. 5. hope of righteousness by f.
6. but f. which worketh by love
22. gentleness, goodness, f.
Eph.1.15. after I heard of your f. in
4. 5. One Lord, one f., one bapti.
6.23. and love with f., from God
Phi. 2.17. sacrifice and service of your f.
3. 9. which is through the f. of

Col. 1. 4. since we heard of your f. in
2. 5. and the stedfastn. of your f..
Th. 1. 3. your work of f., and labour
8. your f. to God-ward is spread
3. 2. comfort you concern. your f.
5. I sent to know your f., lest
6. good tidings of your f. and
7. afflic. and distress by your f.
10. which is lacking in your f.
5. 8. the breastplate of f. and love
Th. 1. 3. your f. groweth exceedingly
4. for your patience and f. in
11. and the work of f. with power
Ti. 1. 2. my own son in the f.: grace
4. godly edifying which is in f.
5. and of f. unfeigned
14. with f. and love which is in
19. Holding f., and a good consc.
2. 7. of the Gentiles in f. and ver.
15. if they continue in f. and
3.13. great boldness in the f. which
4.12. in spirit, in f., in purity
5.12. they have cast off their first f.
6.11. godliness, f., love, patience
Ti. 1.13. in f. and love which is in Ch.
2.22. follow righteousness, f.
3.15. through f. which is in Christ
Tit. 1. 1. according to the f. of God's
3.15. that love us in the f. Grace
Phile. 5. of thy love and f., which
6. the communication of thy f.
Heb.6. 1. works, and of f. toward God
12. who through f. and patience
10.22. in full assurance of f., having
11. 1. Now f. is the substance of th.
3. Through f. we understand
4. By f. Abel offered unto God
5. By f. Enoch was translated
6. But without f. it is impossi.
7. By f. Noah, being warned of
righteousness which is by f.
8. By f. Abraham, when he was
9. By f. he sojourned in the
11. Through f. also Sara herself
13. These all died in f., not hav.
17. By f. Abraham ; 20. Isaac ;
21. Jacob ; 22. Joseph ; 23,
24. Moses
27. By f. he forsook Egypt, not
28. Through f. he kept the pass.
29. By f. they passed through the
30. By f. the walls of Jericho fell
31. By f. the harlot Rahab perish.
33. through f. subdued kingdoms
12. 2. and finisher of our f.; who
13. 7. whose f. follow, considering
Jas. 1. 3. the trying of your f. worketh
6. But let him ask in f., nothing
2. 5. rich in f., and heirs of the
14. though a man say he hath f.
18. Thou hast f., and I have wo.
shew me thy f. without thy
I will shew thee my f. by
24. justified, and not by f. only
*Pet.*1. 7. That the trial of your f. being
9. Receiving the end of your f.
21. that your f. and hope might
*Pet.*1. 1. obtained like precious f. with
5. add to your f. virtue ; and to
Jo. 5. 4. the world, even our f.
Jude 20. on your most holy f., praying
Rev.2.13. and hast not denied my f.
19. charity, and service, and f.
pistis, *(with the article.)*
Mat.23.23. judgment, mercy, and f.
Lu.18. 8. shall he find f. on the earth
Act. 3.16. through f. in his name hath
yea, f. which is by him
6. 7. priests were obedient to the f.
13. 8. away the deputy from the f.
14.22. to continue in the f., and
15. 9. purifying their hearts by f.

Act.16. 5. established in the f., and
24.24. concerning the f. in Christ
Ro. 1.12. by the mutual f. both of you
3. 3. make the f. of God without
25. a propitiation through f.
30. uncircumcision through f.
31. make void the law through f.
4. 9. for we say that f. was reckon.
11. of the righteousness from f.
12. walk in the steps of that f.
14. f. is made void, and the pro.
19. And being not weak in f., he
20. but was strong in f., giving
5. 2. we have access by f. into
10. 8. that is, the word of f., which
17. So then f. cometh by hearing
11.20. and thou standest by f. Be
12. 6. to the proportion of f.
14. 1. Him that is weak in the f.
*Co.*13. 2. though I have all f., so that
16.13. stand fast in the f., quit you
Co. 1.24. your joy: for by f. ye stand
4.13. having the same spirit of f.
5. 7. whether ye be in the f.; pro.
Gal. 1.23. now preacheth the f. which
3.14. prom. of the Spirit through f.
23. But before f. came, we were
shut up unto the f. which
25. But after that f. is come
26. children of God by f. in Ch.
6.10. who are of the household of f.
Eph.2. 8. are ye saved through f.
3.12. with confidence by the f. of
17. dwell in your hearts by f.
4.13. in the unity of the f., and of
6.16. all, taking the shield of f.
Phi. 1.25. your furtherance and joy of f.
27. for the f. of the gospel
3. 9. which is of God by f.
Col. 1.23. If ye continue in the f., grou.
2. 7. and stablished in the f., as ye
12. through the f. of the operation
*Th. 3. 2. for all men have not f.
Ti. 1.19. concerning f. have made ship.
4. 1. some shall depart from the f.
6. in the words of f. and of good
5. 8. he hath denied the f., and is
6.10. they have erred from the f.
12. Fight the good fight of f.
21. have erred concerning the f.
*Ti. 1. 5. the unfeigned f. that is in thee
2.18. and overthrow the f. of some
3. 8. reprobate concerning the f.
10. f., longsuffering, charity
4. 7. my course, I have kept the f.
Tit. 1. 4. own son after the common f.
13. they may be sound in the f.
2. 2. sound in f., in charity, in
Heb.4. 2. not being mixed with f. in
11.39. a good report through f.
Jas. 2. 1. have not the f. of our Lord
14. have not works ? can f. save
17. so f., if it hath not works
20,26. f. without works is dead
22. Seest thou how f. wrought
his works, and by works was f.
5.15. the prayer of f. shall save
*Pet.5. 9. stedfast in the f., knowing
Jude 3. contend for the f. which was
Rev.13.10. the patience and the f. of the
14.12. of God, and the f. of Jesus
elpis.
Heb.10.23. the profession of our f.
oligopistos.
Mat.6.30. O ye *of little* f.; 8.26,16.8 ;
Lu.12.28
14.31. O thou *of little* f., wherefore

FAITHFUL.
pistos.
Mat.24.45. Who then is a f. ; Lu.12.42

Mat.25.21, 23. thou good and f. servant
thou hast been f. ; Lu.19.17
Lu.16.10. He that is f. in that which
is least is f. also in much
11, 12. ye have not been f. in the
Act.16.15. If ye have judged me to be f.
*Co. 1. 9. God is f., by whom ye were
4. 2. that a man be found f.
17. and f. in the Lord, who shall
7.25. mercy of the Lord to be f.
10.13. but God is f., who will not
Gal. 3. 9. are blessed with f. Abraham
Eph. 1. 1. and to the f. in Christ Jesus
6.21. and f. minister in the Lord
Col. 1. 2. To the saints and f. brethren
7. a f. minister of Christ
4. 7. and a f. minister and fellow
9. a f. and beloved brother
*Th. 5.24. f. is he that calleth you
*Th. 3. 3. But the Lord is f., who shall
*Ti. 1.12. for that he counted me f.
15. is a f. saying, and worthy
4.9 ; *Ti.2.11 ; Tit.3.8
3.11. sober, f. in all things
6. 2. because they are f. and
*Ti. 2. 2. commit thou to f. men, who
13. he abideth f., he cannot
Tit. 1. 6. having f. children, not
9. Holding fast the f. word
Heb.2.17. a merciful and f. high priest
3. 2. f. to him that appointed
5. Moses verily was f. in all
10.23. he is f. that promised
*Pet.4.19. welldoing, as unto a f. Crea.
5.12. By Silvanus, a f. brother
*Jo. 1. 9. he is f. and just to forgive
Rev.1. 5. who is the f. witness, and
2.10. be thou f. unto death, and
13. Antipas was my f. martyr
3.14. the f. and true witness, the
17.14. called, and chosen, and f.
19.11. was called f. and True
21. 5. are true and f. ; 22.6

FAITHFULLY.
pistos.
*John 5. thou doest f. whatsoever

FAITHLESS.
apistos.
Mat.17.17. f. and perverse gen. ; Lu.9.41
Jo. 20.27. and be not f., but believing

FALL, [*noun.*]
ptōsis.
Mat.7.27. and great was the f. of it
Lu. 2.34. this child is set for the f. and
paraptōma.
Ro.11.11. through their f., salvation is
12. Now if the f. of them be the

FALL,   -en, -eth, -ing, Fell.
piptō.
Mat. 2.11. and fe down, *and* worshipp.
4. 9. if thou wilt f. *down and* wor.
7.25. and it fe not : for it was
27. and it fe : and great was the
10.29. *shall* not f. on the ground
13. 4. fe by the way side ; 5,7,8
Mar.4.4,5,7,8 ; Lu.8.5,6,7,8
15.14. both *shall* f. into the ditch
27. crumbs *which* f. from their
17. 6. they fe on their face, and
15. ofttimes he f-*eth* into the fire
18.26. fe *down* worshipped him
29. fe *down* at his feet, *and* beso.
21.44. *who* soever *shall* f. on this
on whomsoever it *shall* f.
24.29. the stars *shall* f. from heaven
26.39. and fe on his face, and prayed
Mar.5.22. when he saw him, he fe at his
9.20. he fe on the ground, and wal.
14.35. and fe on the ground, and

93

Lu. 5.12. ſe on his face, *and* besought
6.39. *shall*..both f. into the ditch
49. and immediately it ſe; and
8.14. that *which* ſe among thorns
41. he ſe *down* at Jesus' feet, *and*
10.18. Satan as lightning f. from he.
11.17. divided against a house f-*eth*
13. 4. whom the tower in Siloam ſe
16.21. with the crumbs *which* ſe
17.16. And ſe *down* on his face at
20.18. *Who*soever shall f. upon that
on whomsoever it shall f.
21.24. And they *shall* f. by the edge
23.30. f. on us; and to the hills, Co.
Jo. 11.32. she ſe *down* at his feet, saying
12.24. f. into the ground *and* die
18. 6. backward, and ſe to the grou.
Act. 1.26. and the lot ſe upon Matthias
5. 5. ſe *down, and* gave up the gho.
10. Then ſe she *down* straightway
9. 4. he ſe to the earth, *and* heard
10.25. and ſe *down* at his feet, *and*
15.16. of David, *which is* f-*en down*
20. 9. and ſe *down* from the third
22. 7. And I ſe unto the ground
27.34. there *shall* not an hair f. from
Ro.11.11. stumbled that they *should* f.
22. on them *which* ſe, severity
14. 4. master he standeth or f-*eth*
¹Co.10. 8. committed, and ſe in one day
12. he stand. take heed lest he f.
14.25. and so f-*ing down* on his face
Heb.3.17. whose carcases ſe in the wild.
4.11. lest any man f. after the
11.30. the walls of Jericho ſe *down*
Jas. 5.12. lest ye f. into condemnation
Rev.1.17. I ſe at his feet as dead. And
4.10. elders f. *down* before him
5. 8. ſe *down* before the Lamb
14. ſe *down* and worshipped him
6.13. the stars of heaven ſe unto
16. and rocks, f. on us, and hide
7.11. and ſe before the throne on
8.10. and there ſe a great star from
and it ſe upon the third part
9. 1. and I saw a star f. from hea.
11.11. and great fear ſe upon them
13. the tenth part of the city ſe
16. ſe upon their faces, and wor.
14. 8. Babylon *is* f-*n, is* f-*n;* 18.2
16.19. the cities of the nations ſe
17.10. five *are* f-*n*, and one is, and
19. 4. and the four beasts ſe *down*
10. And I ſe at his feet to worship
22. 8. I ſe *down* to worship before
epipiptō.
Lu. 1.12. troubled, and fear ſe upon
15.20. and ran, and ſe *on* his neck
Act. 8.16. he was f-*n upon* none of
10.10. made ready, he ſe *into* a tra.
44. the Holy Ghost ſe *on*; 11.15
13.11. there ſe *on* him a mist and
19.17. and fear ſe *on* them all, and
20.10. Paul went down, and ſe *on*
37. and ſe *on* Paul's neck, and
Ro. 15. 3. them that repro. thee ſe *on*
ekpiptō.
Act.12. 7. his chains ſe *off* from his
27.17. lest they *should* f. into the
29. lest we *should have* f-*n upon*
32. of the boat, and let her f. *off*
Gal. 5. 4. the law; ye *are* f-*n* from grace
Jas. 1.11. the flower thereof f-*eth, and*
¹Pet. 1.24. the flower thereof f-*eth away*
²Pet. 3.17. Lest ye also..f. from your
Rev. 2. 5. from whence thou *art* f-*n*
eimi ekpiptō.
Mar.13.25.the stars of heaven *shall* f.
empiptō.
Mat.12.11.if it f. *into* a pit on the sab.
Lu. 10.36. unto him *that* ſe among the
14. 5. an ass or an ox f-*n into* a pit
94

¹Ti. 3. 6. he f. *into* the condemnation
7. lest he f. *into* reproach and
6. 9. f. *into* temptation and a snare
Heb.10.31. *to* f. *into* the hands of the
prospiptō.
Mar. 3.11. ſe *down before* him; 5.33;
Lu.8.28
7.25. and came and ſe *at* his feet
Lu. 5. 8. he ſe *down at* Jesus' knees
8.47. and f-*ing down before* him
Act. 16.29. and ſe *down before* Paul and
peripiptō.
Lu. 10.30. and ſe *among* thieves, which
Act.27.41. and f-*ing into* a place where
Jas. 1. 2. f. *into* divers temptations
katapiptō.
Act. 26.14. *when we were* all f-*n* to the
28. 6. or f-*n down* dead suddenly
apopiptō.
Act. 9.18. there ſe *from* his eyes as it
parapiptō.
Heb. 6.6. *If* they shall f. *away*, to ren.
katabainō.
Lu. 22.44. drops of blood f-*ing down*
Rev.16.21. ſe upon men a great hail
ginomai.
Act. 1.18. f-*ing headlong*, he burst
Rev.16.2. there ſe a noisome and griev.
aphistēmi.
Lu. 8.13. time of temptation f. *away*
epiballō.
Lu.15.12. portion of goods *that* f-*eth* to
katapherō.
Act.20.9. *being* f-*n* into a deep sleep
erchomai.
Phi. 1.12. *have* f-*n out* rather unto
ptaiō.
²Pet.1.10. things, ye shall never f.
(See *Asleep, Occasion, Transgression*.)

FALLING, [noun.]
apostasia.
²Th. 2. 3. there come a f. *away* first
aptaistos.
Jude 24. is able to keep you *from* f.

FALSE.
pseudēs.
Act.6.13. And set up f. witnesses, which
(*See other words in connection*.)

FALSELY.
pseudomai.
Mat.5.11. manner of evil against you f.
(*See words in connection*.)

FAME.
akoē.
Mat.4.24. his f. went throughout all
14. 1. heard of the f. of Jesus
Mar.1.28. immediately his f. spread
phēmē.
Mat.9.26. the f. thereof went abroad
Lu. 4.14. there went out a f. of him
ēchos.
Lu. 4.37. the f. of him went out into
logos.
Lu. 5.15. went there a f. abroad of him
(See *Spread*.)

FAMILY.
patria.
Eph.3.15. whom the whole f. in heaven

FAMINE, -*s*.
limos.
Mat.24.7. there shall be f-*s*; Mar.13.8
Lu. 4.25. when great f. was throughout
15.14. arose a mighty f. in that land

Lu.21.11. and f-*s*, and pestilences; and
Ro. 8.35. or f., or nakedness, or peril
Rev.18.8. death, and mourning, and f.

FAN.
ptuon.
Mat.3.12. Whose f. is in his; Lu.3.17

FAR.
makran.
Mar.12.34. Thou art not f. from the
Lu. 7. 6. when he was now not f. from
Jo. 21. 8. they were not f. from land
Act. 17.27. though he be not f. from
22.21. I will send thee f. hence
Eph. 2.13. ye who sometimes were f. *of*
makros.
Lu.15.13. his journey into a f. country
19.12. went into a f. country to rec.
makrothen.
Mar.8. 3. divers of them came *from* f.
huperanō.
Eph.1.21. f. *above* all principality, and
4.10. ascended up f. *above* all heav.
porrō.
Mat.15.8. heart is f. from me; Mar. 7.6
hileōs.
Mat.16.22. saying, Be it f. from thee
heōs houtos.
Lu.22.51. and said, Suffer ye *thus* f.
polus mallon.
Phil.1.23. with Ch., which is f. better
(*See words in connection*.)

FARE, -*ed*.
euphrainō.
Lu.16.19. *and* f-*eā* sumptuously every
rōnnumai.
Act.15.29.ye shall do well. f. ye *well*

FAREWELL.
rōnnumai.
Act.23.30.they had against him. f.
chairō.
²Co.13.11. Finally, brethren, f. Be per.
(*See Bid*.)

FARM.
agros.
Mat.22.5. went their ways, one to his f.

FARTHER, (See *Go, Side*.)

FARTHING, -*s*.
kodrantēs.
Mat. 5.26. hast paid the uttermost f.
Mar.12.42. two mites, which make a f.
assarion.
Mat.10.29. two sparrows sold for a f.
Lu. 12.6. five sparrows sold for two f-*s*

FASHION, [noun.]
schēma.
¹Co. 7.31. the f. of this world passeth
Phi. 2. 8. being found in f. as a man.
eidos.
Lu. 9.29. the f. of his countenance was
tupos.
Act. 7.44. make it according to the f.
prosōpon.
Jas. 1.11. grace of the f. of it perisheth
houtōs.
Mar.2.12. We never saw it *on this* f.

FASHIONED, [verb.] -*ing*.
summorphos.
Phi. 3.21. f. *like unto* his glorious
suschēmatizomai.
¹Pet.1.14. f-*ing* your *selves* according to

FAST, [noun.]
nēsteia.
Act. 27.9. the f. was now already past

FAST, [verb.]   -ed, -est, -ing.
nēsteuō.
Mat 4. 2. when he had **f**-ed forty days
 6.16. Moreover when ye **f**., be not
   may appear unto men to **f**.
 17. when thou **f**-est, anoint thine
 18. appear not unto men to **f**.
 9.14. Why do we and the Phar. **f**.
   thy disciples **f**. not; Mar.2.18
 15. then shall they **f**.; Mar.2.20
   Lu.5.35
Mar. 2.18. the Pharisees used to **f**.
   Why do the disc..the Phar. **f**.
 19. of the bridechamb. **f**.; Lu.5.34
   with them, they cannot **f**.
Lu. 5.33. Why do the disc. of John **f**.
 18.12. I **f**. twice in the week, I give
Act.10.30. Four days ago I was **f**-ing
 13. 2. ministered to the L., and **f**-ed
 3. when they had **f**-ed and prayed

FAST, [adject. or adverb.]
asphalizō.
Act.16.24. made their feet **f**. in the sto.
(See words with which it is connected.)

FASTEN,   -ed, -ing.
atenizō.
Lu. 4.20. them that..were **f**-ed on him
Act. 3. 4. Peter **f**-ing his eyes upon him
 11. 6. when I had **f**-ed mine eyes
kathaptō.
Act.28. 3. heat, and **f**-ed on his hand

FASTING,   -s.
nēsteia.
Mat.17.21. by prayer and **f**.; Mar.9.29
Lu. 2.37. with **f**-s and prayers, night
Act 14.23. and had prayed with **f**., they
1Co. 7. 5. give yourself to **f**. and prayer
2Co. 6. 5. labours, in watchings, in **f**-s
 11.27. thirst, in **f**-s often, in cold
nēstis.
Mat.15.32. send them away **f**.; Mar.8.3
asitos.
Act.27.33. have tarried and continued **f**.

FATHER,   -s
patēr.
Mat. 2.22. in the room of his **f**. Herod
 3. 9. We have Abraham to our **f**.
 4.21. ship with Zebedee their **f**.
 22. left the ship and their **f**.
 6. 4. thy **f**. wh. seeth in secret; 18
 6. thy **f**. which is in secret
 9. Our **f**. which art; Lu.11.2
 10.35. man at variance against his **f**.
 37. he that loveth **f**. or mother
 11.25. I thank thee, O **f**.; Lu.10.21
 26. Even so, **f**.: for so; Lu.10.21
 13.43. in the kingdom of their **f**.
 15. 4. Honour thy **f**. and mother;
   19.9; Mar.7.10, 10.19;
   Lu.18.20; Eph.6.2
   He that curseth **f**. or mother
 5. Who. shall say to **f**.; Mar.7.11
 6. And honour not his **f**. or his
 16.27. come in the glory of his **f**.;
   Mar.8.38; Lu.9.26
 19. 5. shall a man leave **f**. and mo.
 20. breth., sisters, or **f**.;Mar.10.29
 21.31. twain did the will of his **f**.
Mar. 1.20. they left their **f**. Zebedee in
 7.10. Whoso curseth **f**. or mother
 12. no more to do ought for his **f**.
 9.21. And he asked his **f**., How
 10. 7. shall a man leave **f**. and
 11.10. the kingdom of our **f**. David
 14.36. And he said, Abba, **f**., all
Lu. 1.32. the throne of his **f**. David
 59. after the name of his **f**.
 62. made signs to his **f**., how
 67. And his **f**. Zacharias was

Lu. 1. 73. sware to our **f**. Abraham
 2.48. behold, thy **f**. and I have
 3. 8. We have Abraham to our **f**.
 9.42. delivered him again to his **f**.
 11.11. of any of you that is a **f**., will
 14.26. hate not his **f**., and mother
 15.12. said to his **f**., **f**., give me
 18, 21. **f**., I have sinned against
 20. he arose, and came to his **f**.
   his **f**. saw him, and had com.
 27. and thy **f**. hath killed the
 28. therefore came his **f**. out, and
 29. said to his **f**., Lo, these many
 16.24. **f**. Abraham, have mercy on
 27. I pray thee therefore, **f**., that
 30. And he said, Nay, **f**. Abrah.
 22.42. Saying, **f**., if thou be willing
 23.34. **f**., forgive them ; for they
 46. **f**., into thy hands I commend
Jo. 4.12. greater than our **f**.; 8.53
 5.18. said also that God was his **f**.
 6.42. whose **f**. and mother being
 57. As the living **f**. hath sent me
 8.19. Where is thy **f**.? Jesus ans.
 39. Abraham is our **f**. Jesus
 41. we have one **f**., even God
 11.41. **f**., I thank thee that thou
 12.27. **f**., save me from this hour
 28. **f**., glorify thy name. Then
 17. 1. **f**., the hour is come
 5. And now, O **f**., glorify thou
 11. Holy **f**., keep through thine
 21. as thou, **f**., art in me, and
 24. **f**., I will that they also, whom
 25. O righteous **f**., the world
Act. 7. 2. appeared unto our **f**. Abraha.
 4. thence, when his **f**. was dead
 14. and called his **f**. Jacob to him
 20. nourished up in his **f**-'s house
 16. 1, 3. but his **f**. was a Greek
 28.25. the prophet unto our **f**-s
Ro. 1. 7. from God our **f**.; 1Co.1.3 ;
   2Co.1.2 ; Eph.1.2; Phi.1.2;
   Col.1.2 ; 1Th.1.1 ; 2Th.1.2 ;
   1Tim.1.2 ; Phile.3
 4. 1. our **f**. as pertaining to the fle.
 12. faith of our **f**. Abraham
 17, 18. I have made thee a **f**. of
 8.15. we cry, Abba, **f**.; Gal.4.6
 9.10. even by our **f**. Isaac
1Co. 5. 1. one should have his **f**-'s wife
2Co. 6.18. And will be a **f**. unto you
Gal. 1. 4. the will of God and our **f**.
Eph. 4. 6. One God and **f**. of all, who is
 5.31. leave his **f**. and mother, and
Phi. 4.20. unto God and our **f**. be glory
1Th. 1. 3. in the sight of God and our **f**.
 2.11. as a **f**. doth his children
 3.11. Now God himself and our **f**.
 13. God, even our **f**.; 2Th.2.16
2Th. 1. 1. in God our **f**. and the Lord
1Ti. 5. 1. but entreat him as a **f**.
Heb. 1. 5. I will be to him a **f**., and he
 7.10. in the loins of his **f**., when
Jas. 2.21. Was not Abraham our **f**. jus.
Rev. 1. 6. priests unto God and his **f**.
 14. 1. having his **f**-'s name written

My Father.
Mat. 7.21. the will of my **f**.; 12.50
 8.21. go and bury my **f**.; Lu.9.59
 10.32, 33. my **f**. which is in hea.;16.17
 11.27. delivered unto me of my **f**.
 15.13. my heavenly **f**. hath not
 18.10. behold the face of my **f**.
 19. be done for them of my **f**.
 35. shall my heavenly **f**. do also
 20.23. whom it is prepared of my **f**.
 24.36. of heaven, but my **f**. only
 25.34. Come, ye blessed of my **f**.
 26.29. with you in my **f**-'s kingdom
 39. O my **f**., if it be possible
 42. O my **f**., if this cup may not

Mat.26.53. I cannot now pray to my **f**.
Lu. 2.49. must be about my **f**-'s busin.
 9.59. first to go and bury my **f**.
 10.22. delivered to me of my **f**.
 15.17. servants of my **f**-'s have bread
 18. arise and go to my **f**., and
 16.27. wouldest send him to my **f**-'s
 22.29. as my **f**. hath appointed unto
 24.49. I send the promise of my **f**.
Jo. 2.16. make not my **f**-'s house an
 5.17. My **f**. worketh hitherto
 43. I am come in my **f**-'s name
 6.32. but my **f**. giveth you the true
 8.19. know me, nor my **f**., if ye
   ye should have known my **f**.
 28. as my **f**. hath taught me, I
 38. I have seen with my **f**.: and
 49. but I honour my **f**., and ye
 54. it is my **f**. that honoureth
 10.17. Therefore doth my **f**. love me
 18. have I received of my **f**.
 25. that I do in my **f**-'s name
 29. My **f**., which gave them me
   them out of my **f**-'s hand
 30. I and my **f**. are one
 32. I shewed you from my **f**.; for
 37. the works of my **f**., believe
 12.26. him will my **f**. honour
 14. 2. In my **f**-'s house are many
 7. have known my **f**. also : and
 12. because I go unto my **f**.
 20. I am in my **f**., and ye in
 21. shall be loved of my **f**., and
 23. and my **f**. will love him, and
 28. my **f**. is greater than I
 15. 1. and my **f**. is the husbandman
 8. Herein is my **f**. glorified
 10. kept my **f**-'s commandments
 15. that I have heard of my **f**.
 23, 24. hateth my **f**. also
 16.10. because I go to my **f**., and
 18.11. the cup which my **f**. hath
 20.17. not yet ascended to my **f**.
   ascend unto my **f**., and your **f**.
 21. as my **f**. hath sent me, even
Rev. 2.27. as I received of my **f**.
 3. 5. before my **f**., and before his
 21. set down with my **f**. in his

The Father.
Mat.10.21. the **f**. the child ; Mar.13.12
 11.27. knoweth the Son, but the **f**.
   knoweth any man the **f**.
 28.19. in the name of the **f**., and of
Mar. 5.40. the **f**. and moth. of ; Lu.8.51
 9.24. And straightway the **f**. of the
 13.32. neither the Son, but the **f**.
 15.21. the **f**. of Alexander and Ruf.
Lu. 10.22. but the **f**.; and who the **f**. is
 12.53. The **f**. shall be divided agai.
   and the son against the **f**.
 15.22. But the **f**. said to his serva.
Jo. 1.14. of the only begotten of the **f**.
 18. in the bosom of the **f**., he
 3.35. The **f**. loveth the Son; 5.20
 4.21. at Jerusalem, worship the **f**.
 23. shall worship the **f**. in spirit
   truth : for the **f**. seeketh such
 53. So the **f**. knew that it was
 5.19. but what he seeth the **f**. do
 21. For as the **f**. raiseth up the
 22. For the **f**. judgeth no man
 23. as they honour the **f**. He
   honoureth not the **f**. which
 26. For as the **f**. hath life in
 30. but the will of the **f**. which
 36. which the **f**. hath given me
   me, that the **f**. hath sent me
 37. himself, which hath sent;
   8.16,18., 12.49., 14.24
 45. I will accuse you to the **f**.
 6.27. for him hath God the **f**. sealed
 37. All that the **f**. giveth me shall

Jo. 6.39. And this is the f.'s will which
44. except the f. which hath sent
45. hath learned of the f., cometh
46. that any man hath seen the f. is of God, he hath seen the f.
57. and I live by the f.
7.27. he spake to them of the f.
29. the f. hath not left me alone
8.44. for he is a liar, and the f. of
10.15. As the f. knoweth me, even so know I the f.: and I lay
36. whom the f. hath sanctified
38. that the f. is in me and I
12.50. even as the f. said unto me
13. 1. this world unto the f., hav.
3. that the f. had given all thin.
14. 6. cometh unto the f., but by
8. Lord, shew us the f., and it
9. hath seen the f.; and how thou then, Shew us the f.
10, 11. I am in the f., and the f. but the f. that dwelleth in
13. that the f. may be glorified
16. I will pray the f.; 16.26
26. whom the f. will send in my
28. because I said, I go unto the f.
31. love the f.; and as the f.
15. 9. As the f. hath loved me, so
16. ask of the f. in my ; 16.23
26. send unto you from the f. which proceedeth from the f.
16. 3. not known the f., nor me
15. All things that the f. hath
16, 17. because I go to the f.
25. shew you plainly of the f.
27. For the f. himself loveth
28. I came forth from the f. the world, and go to the f.
32. because the f. is with me
Act. 1. 4. the promise of the f., which
7. which the f. hath put in his
2.33. having received of the f. the
28. 8. that the f. of Publius lay
Ro. 4.11. the f. of all them that believe
12. And the f. of circumcision
16. who is the f. of us all
6. 4. by the glory of the f.
11.28. are beloved for the f-s' sakes
15. 6. God, even the f. of our Lord ²Co.1.3, 11.31; Eph.1.3; ¹Pet.1.3
Co. 8. 6. one God, the f., of whom are
15.24. kingdom to God, even the f.
Co. 1. 3. the f. of mercies, and the
Gal. 1. 1. and God the f., who raised
3. peace from God the f., and ; ²Ti.1.2; Tit.1.4; Eph.6.23 ; ²John 3
4. 2. the time appointed of the f.
Eph. 1.17. the f. of glory, may give
2.18. by one Spirit unto the f.
3.14. my knees unto the f. of our
5.20. thanks unto God and the f. Col.1.3,12; 3.17
Phi. 2.11. to the glory of God the f.
2.22. as a son with the f., he has
Col. 2. 2. and of the f., and of Christ
¹Th. 1. in God the f. and in the Lord
Heb.12. 7. what son is he whom the f.
9. unto the f. of spirits, and live
Jas. 1.17. from the f. of lights, with
27. before God and the f. is this
3. 9. bless we God, even the f.
¹Pet. 1. 2. foreknowledge of God the f.
17. And if ye call on the f., who
¹Pet. 1.17. he received from God the f.
¹Jo. 1. 2. life, which was with the f.
3. with the f., and with his Son
2. 1. an advocate with the f., Jes.
13. because ye have known the f.
15. the love of the f. is not in
16. is not of the f., but is of the
96

¹Jo. 2.22. that denieth the f. and the
23. the same hath not the f.
24. cont. in the Son, and in the f.
3. 1. love the f. hath bestowed
4.14. that the f. sent the Son
5. 7. the f., the Word, and the
²John 3. the Son of the f., in truth
4. rece. a command. from the f.
9. hath both the f. and the Son
Jude 1. sanctified by God the f.

Your Father.

Mat. 5.16, 45,48. your f. which is in; 6.1
6. 8, 32. your f. knoweth; Lu.12.30
14. your heavenly f.; 26,32
15. neither will your f. forgive ; Mar.11.25,26
7.11. how much more shall your f.
10.20. but the spirit of your f. which
29. on the ground without your f.
18.14. it is not the will of your f.
23. 9. And call no man your f. for one is your f., which is
Lu. 6.36. as your f. also is merciful
11.13. more shall your heavenly f.
12.32. it is your f.'s good pleasure
Jo. 8.38. ye have seen with your f.
41. Ye do the deeds of your f.
42. God were your f., ye would
44. Ye are of your f. the devil lusts of your f. ye will do
56. Your f. Abraham rejoiced

Fathers.

Mat. 23.30.been in the days of our f-s
32. then the measure of your f-s
Lu. 1.17. to turn the hearts of the f-s
55. As he spake to our f-s, to
72. mercy promised to our f-s
6.23. did their f-s unto the proph.
26. did their f-s to the false
11.47. and your f-s killed them
48. allow the deeds of your f-s
Jo. 4.20. Our f-s worshipped in this
6.31, 49,58. f-s did eat manna in
7.22. of Moses, but of the f-s; and
Act. 3.13. God of our f-s; 5.30, 22.14
22. Moses truly said unto the f-s
25. which God made with our f-s
7. 2. Men, brethren, and f-s; 22.1
11. and our f-s found no susten.
12. Egypt, he sent out our f-s
15. and died, he, and our f-s
19. and evil entreated our f-s, so
32. I am the God of thy f-s, the
38. Sina, and with our f-s: who
39. To whom our f-s would not
44. Our f-s had the tabernacle
45. Which also our f-s that came before the face of our f-s
51. as your f-s did, so do ye
52. have not your f-s persecuted
13.17. chose our f-s, and exalted
32. promise made unto the f-s
36. and was laid unto his f-s
15.10. which neither our f-s nor we
26. 6. made of God unto our f-s
Ro. 9. 5. Whose are the f-s, and of who.
11.28. are beloved for the f-s' sakes
15. 8. promises made unto the f-s
¹Co. 4.15. yet have ye not many f-s
10. 1. all our f-s were under the clo.
Eph. 6. 4. f-s, provoke not ; Col.3.21
Heb. 1. 1. spake in time past unto the f-s
3. 9. When your f-s tempted me
8. 9. that I made with their f-s in
12. 9. Furthermore we have had f-s
²Pet. 3. 4. since the f-s fell asleep, all
¹Jo. 2.13, 14. I write unto you, f-s

patroös.

Act.22. 3. manner of the law *of* the f-s
24.14. worship I the God *of* my f-s
28.17. people, or customs *of* our f-s

patrikos.
Gal. 1.14. of the traditions *of* my f-s
patroparadotos.
¹Pet.1.18. *received by tradi. from* your f-s
apatōr.
Heb. 7.3. *Without* f., without mother
pentheros.
Jo. 18.13. he was f. *in law* to Caiaphas (See *Murderer*.)

FATHERLESS.
orphanos.
Jas. 1.27. To visit the f. and widows

FATHOMS.
orguia.
Act.27.28. and found it twenty f. and found it fifteen f.

FATLINGS.
sitistos.
Mat.22.4. oxen and my f. are killed

FATNESS.
piotēs.
Ro.11.17. root and f. of the olive tre

FATTED.
siteutos.
Lu.15.23. And bring hither the f. ca
27. father hath killed the f. cal
30. hast killed for him the f. cal

FAULT, -s.
elengchō.
Mat.18.15. go and *tell* him his f. between
memphomai.
Mar. 7. 2. unwash.,hands, they *found* f.
Ro. 9.19. Why *doth* he yet *find* f.? for
Heb. 8. 8. For *finding* f. with them, he
aition.
Lu.23.4,14.find no f. in this man
aitia.
Jo. 18.38. I find in him no f.;19.4,6
hēttēma.
¹Co. 6. 7. there is utterly a f. among
paraptōma.
Gal. 6. 1. if a man be overtaken in a f.
Jas. 5.16. Confess your f-s one to anoth.
hamartanō.
¹Pet.2.20. ye be buffeted *for your* f-s
amōmos.
Rev.14.5. they are *without* f. before

FAULTLESS.
amemptos.
Heb.8. 7. first covenant had been f.
amōmos.
Jude 24. present you f. before the

FAVOUR.
charis.
Lu. 1.30. for thou hast found f. with
2.52. and in f. with God and man
Act. 2.47. and having f. with all the
7.10. gave him f. and wisdom in
46. Who found f. before God, and
25. 3. And desired f. against him

FAVOURED.
charitoō.
Lu. 1.28. Hail, thou that art *highly* f.

FEAR, [*noun.*] -ed, -s.
phobos.
Mat.14.26. and they cried out for f.
28. 4. for f. of him the keepers did
8. from the sepulchre with f.
Mar. 4.41. And they f-ed exceedingly
Lu. 1.12. troubled, and f. fell upon
65. And f. came on all that
5.26. and were filled with f., say.
7.16. And there came a f. on all
8.37. they were taken with great f

Lu.21.26. for f., and for looking after
Jo. 7.13. f. of the Jews ; 19.38,20.19
Act. 2.43. And f. came upon every soul
  5.5,11. great f. came on all
  9.31. and walking in the f. of the
  19.17. and f. fell on them all, and
Ro. 3.18. There is no f. of God before
  8.15. spirit of bondage again to f.
  13. 7. f. to whom f.; honour to
¹Co. 2. 3. and in f., and in much tremb.
²Co. 7. 1. perfecting holiness in the f. of
  5. fightings, within were f-s
  11. indignation, yea, what f.
  15. with f. and trembling ;
    Eph.6.5 ; Phi.2.12
Eph.5.21. one to another in the f. of God
Heb.2.15. who through f. of death were
¹Pet.1.17. of your sojourning here in f.
  2.18. to your masters with all f.
  3. 2. conversation coupled with f.
  15. in you with meekness and f.
¹Jo. 4.18. There is no f. in love; but
    perfect love casteth out f. :
    because f. hath torment
Jude 23. And others save with f., pu.
Rev.11.11.great f. fell upon them which
  18.10,15.afar off for the f. of her tor.
  eulabeomai.
Heb.11.7. moved with f., prepared an
  eulabeia.
Heb.12.28. with reverence and godly f.
  deilia.
²Ti. 1. 7. not given us the spirit of f.
  aphobos.
Lu. 1.74. might serve him without f.
¹Co.16.10.he may be with you without f.
Phi. 1.14. to speak the word without f.
Jude 12. feeding themselves without f.

FEAR, [verb,]   -ed, -eth, -ing.
  phobeomai.
Mat.1.20. f. not to take unto thee Mary
  10.26. f. them not therefore : for
    28. And f. not them which kill
    but rather f. him which is
    31. f. ye not therefore, ye are of
  14. 5. f-ed the multitude, bec.;21.46
  21.26. we f. the people ; for all hold
  27.54. they f-ed greatly, saying, Tru.
  28. 5. f. not ye: for I know that ye
Mar.5.33. But the woman f-ing and tre.
  6.20. For Herod f-ed John, know.
  11.18. for they f-ed him, because all
    32. they f-ed the people ; 12.12 ;
    Lu.20,19,22,2 : Act.5.26
Lu. 1.13. f. not, Zacharias : for thy
    30. f. not, Mary : for thou hast
    50. mercy is on them that f. him
  2.10. f. not : for, behold, I bring
  5.10. And Jesus said unto Simon, f.
  8.50. f. not : believe only, and she
  9.34. f-ed as they entered into the
    45. they f-ed to ask him of that
  12. 5. whom ye shall f. : f. him
    yea, I say unto you, f. him
  7. f. not therefore : ye are of
    32. f. not, little flock ; for it is
  18. 2. a judge, which f-ed not God
  4. Though I f. not God, nor
  19.21. For I f-ed thee, because thou
  23.40. Dost not thou f. God, seeing
Jo. 9.22. because they f-ed the Jews
  12.15. f. not, daughter of Sion : be.
Act.10. 2. that f-ed God with all his
  22. one that f-eth God, and of
  35. in every nation he that f-eth
  13.16.and ye that f. God, give audi.
  26. and whosoever among you f-eth
  16.38. they f-ed, when they heard
  27.17. and, f-ing lest they should
  24. Saying, f. not, Paul ; thou
  29. f-ing lest we should have fall.

Ro.11.20. Be not highminded, but f.
²Co.11. 3. But I f., lest by any means
  12.20. For I f., lest, when I come, I
Gal.2.12. f-ing them which were of the
Col. 3.22. singleness of heart, f-ing God
Heb.4. 1. Let us therefore f., lest, a pro.
  11.27. not f-ing the wrath of the
  13. 6. I will not f. what man shall
¹Pet.2.17. f. God. Honour the king
¹Jo. 4.18. He that f-eth is not made per.
Rev.1.17. saying unto me, f. not ; I am
  2.10. f. none of those things which
  11.18. saints, and them that f. thy
  14. 7. f. God, and give glory to him
  15. 4. Who shall not f. thee, O Lord
  19. 5. and ye that f. him, both small
  phobeomai megas phobos.
Mar.4.41. they f-ed exceedingly, and
  echo phobos.
¹Ti. 5.20. all, that others also may f.
  eimi ekphobos.
Heb.12.21. I exceedingly f. and quake
  eulabeomai.
Act.23.10. chief captain, f-ing lest Paul
  eulabeia.
Heb.5. 7. and was heard in that he f-ed
    (for his reverent fear.)

FEARFUL.
  deilos.
Mat.8.26. Why are ye f.; Mar.4.40
Rev.21.8. the f., and unbelieving, and
  phobetron.
Lu.21.11. and f. sights and great signs
  phoberos.
Heb.10.27. f. looking for of judgment
  31. It is a f. thing to fall into

FEAST, [noun,]   -s.
  heorte.
Mat.26. 5. Not on the f. day ; Mar.14.2
  27.15. at that f. the governor was
Mar.15. 6. Now at that f. he released
Lu. 2.41. the f. of the passov.; Jo.13.1
  42. after the custom of the f.
  22. 1. the f. of unleavened bread
  23.17. relea. one unto them at the f.
Jo. 2.23. at the passover, in the f. day
  4.45. at Jerusalem at the f.: for
    they also went unto the f.
  5. 1. a f. of the Jews ; 6.4
  7. 2. the Jews' f. of tabernacles
  8. f.: I go not up yet unto this f.
  10. went he also up unto the f.
  11. Jews sought him at the f.
  14. about the midst of the f.
  37. that great day of the f., Jes.
  11.56. he will not come to the f.
  12.12. were come to the f., when
  20. came up to worship at the f.
  13.29. need of against the f.; or
Act.18.21. by all means keep this f.
  deipnon.
Mat.23.6. upper.rooms at f-s ; Mar.12.39
Lu.20.46. and the chief rooms at f-s
  doche.
Lu. 5.29. Levi made him a great f. in
  14.13. when thou makest a f., call
  heortazo.
¹Co. 5. 8. Therefore let us keep the f.
(See Charity, Dedication, Governor, Ruler.)

FEAST, [verb.]
  suneuocheomai.
²Pet.2.13. deceivings while they f. with
Jude 12. charity, when they f. with you

FEEBLE.
  asthenes.
¹Co.12.22. which seem to be more f., are
  paraluomai.
Heb.12.12.hang down, and the f. knees

FEEBLEMINDED.
  oligopsuchos.
¹Th. 5.14. comfort the f., support the

FEED,   -eth, -ing, Fed.
  poimaino.
Lu. 17. 7. serv. plowing or f-ing cattle
Jo. 21.16. He saith unto him f. my
Act. 20.28. to f. the church of God, wh.
¹Co. 9. 7. who f-eth a flock, and eateth
¹Pet. 5. 2. f. the flock of God which is
Jude 12. f-ing themselves without
Rev. 7.17. midst of the throne shall f.
  bosko.
Mat.8.30. of many swine f-ing ; Lu.8.32
Mar.5.11. a great herd of swine f-ing
  14. they that f-d the swine fled
Lu. 8.34. they that f-d them saw what
  15.15. sent him into his fields to f.
Jo. 21.15, 17. saith unto him, f. my
  trepho.
Mat.6.26. heavenly Father f-eth them
  25.37. thee an hungered, and f-d
Lu.12.24. nor barn ; and God f-eth
Rev.12.6. that they should f. her there
  psomizo.
Ro.12.20. thine enemy hunger, f. him
¹Co.13. 3. I bestow all my goods to f.
  chortazo.
Lu.16.21. desiring to be f-d with the
  potizo.
¹Co. 3. 2. I have f-d you with milk

FEEL,   Felt.
  ginosko.
Mar.5.29. she f-t in her body that
  pselaphao.
Act.17.27. haply they might f. after
  pascho.
Act.28.5. into the fire, and f-t no harm

FEELING, [noun.]
  apalgeo.
Eph.4.19. Who being past f., have given
  sumpatheo.
Heb.4.15. be touched with the f. of our

FEIGN.
  hupokrinomai.
Lu.20.20. forth spies which should f.

FEIGNED.
  plastos.
²Pet.2. 3. with f. words make merchan

FELLOWS.
  hetairos
Mat.11.16. and calling unto their f.
  aner.
Act.17. 5. certain lewd f. of the baser
  metochos.
Heb.1. 9. oil of gladness above thy f.

FELLOW-CITIZENS.
  sumpolites.
Eph.2.19. but f. with the saints, and

FELLOW-DISCIPLES.
  summathetes.
Jo. 11.16. unto his f., Let us also go

FELLOW-HEIRS.
  sungkleronomos.
Eph.3. 6. the Gentiles should be f.

FELLOW-HELPER,   -s.
  sunergos.
²Co. 8.23. my partner and f. concerning
³John 8. we might be f-s to the truth

FELLOW-LABOURER,   -s.
  sunergos.
Phi. 4. 3. with other my f-s, whose

¹Th. 3. 2. our **f.** in the gospel of Christ
Phile. 1. our dearly beloved, and **f.**
  24. Aristarchus..Lucas, my **f**-s

FELLOW-PRISONER, -s.
sunaichmalōtos.
Ro.16. 7. my kinsmen, and my **f**-s, who
Col. 4.10. Aristarchus my **f.** saluteth you
Phile. 23. Epaphras, my **f.** in Christ

FELLOW-SERVANT, -s.
sundoulos.
Mat.18.28. and found one of his **f**-s, wh.
  29. And his **f.** fell down at his
  31. So when his **f**-s saw what was
  33. had compassion on thy **f**
  24.49. shall begin to smite his **f**-s
Col. 1. 7. Epaphras our dear **f.**, who
  4. 7. minister and **f.** in the Lord
Rev. 6.11. until their **f**-s also and their
  19.10. I am thy **f.**, and of thy ; 22.9
  (a *fellow-servant* of thee and of.)

FELLOWSHIP.
koinōnia.
Act. 2.42. and **f.**, and in breaking of br.
¹Co. 1. 9. called unto the **f.** of his Son
¹Co. 8. 4. and take upon us the **f.** of the
Gal. 2. 9. the right hands of **f.**; that we
Eph.3. 9. what is the **f.** of the mystery
Phi.1. 5. For your **f.** in the gospel, from
  2. 1. if any **f.** of the Spirit, if any
  3.10. and the **f.** of his sufferings
¹Jo. 1. 3. may have **f.** with us : and
  truly our **f.** is with the fath.
  6. If we say that we have **f.** with
  7. we have **f.** one with another
koinōnos.
¹Co.10.20. ye should have **f.** with devils
metochē.
²Co. 6.14. what **f.** hath righteousness
sungkoinōneō.
Eph.5.11. *have* no **f.** *with* the unfruitful

FELLOW-SOLDIER.
sustratiōtēs.
Phi. 2.25. companion in labour, and **f.**
Phile. 2. and Archippus our **f.**, and to

FELLOW-WORKERS.
sunergos.
Col. 4.11. These only are my **f.** unto

FEMALE.
thēlu.
Mat.19.4. them male and **f.**; Mar.10.6
Gal. 3.28. there is neither male nor **f.**

FERVENT.
ektenēs.
¹Pet.4. 8. **f.** charity among yourselves
zeō.
Act. 18.25. *being* **f.** in the spirit, he spa.
Ro. 12.11. **f.** in spirit ; serving the Lord
zēlos.
²Co. 7. 7. your **f.** *mind* toward me ; so
kausoō.
²Pet.3.10,12. shall melt *with* **f.** *heat*
  (melt, *being set on fire.*)
  (See *Effectual.*)

FERVENTLY.
agōnizomai.
Col. 4.12. labouring **f.** for you in prayers
ektenōs.
¹Pet.1.22. another, with a pure heart **f.**

FETCH, (See *Compass.*)
exagō.
Act.16.37. themselves and **f.** us *out*

FETTERS.
pedē.
Mar.5. 4. with **f.** and chains ; Lu.8.29
  and the **f.** broken in pieces

98

FEVER.
puretos.
Mat.8.15. and the **f.** left her ; Mar.1.31
Lu. 4.38. was taken with a great **f.**
  39. rebuked the **f.**; and it left her
Jo. 4.52. at the seventh hour the **f.** left
Act. 28.8. sick of a **f.** and of a bloody
puressō.
Mat.8.14. laid and *sick of a* **f.**; Mar.1.30

FEW.
oligos.
Mat.7.14. and **f.** there be that find it
  9.37. the labourers are **f.**; Lu.10.2
  15.34. and a **f.** little fishes ; Mar.8.7
  20.16. be called, but **f.** chosen; 22.14
  25.21, 23. hast been faithful over a **f.**
Mar.6. 5. he laid his hands upon a **f.**
Lu. 12.48. shall be beaten with **f.** stripes
  13.23. Lord, are there **f.** that be
Act. 17.4. of the chief women not a **f.**
  12. Greeks, and of men, not a **f.**
Eph.3. 3. as I wrote afore in **f.** words
Heb.12.10.for a **f.** days chastened us
¹Pet.3.20. wherein **f.**, that is, eight
Rev. 2.14, 20. I have a **f.** things against
  3. 4. Thou hast a **f.** names even in
suntomōs.
Act.24. 4. of thy clemency *a* **f.** *words*
brachus.
Heb.13.22. letter unto you in **f.** *words*

FIDELITY.
pistis.
Tit. 2.10. but shewing all good **f.**

FIELD, (See *Abide, Corn.*) -s.
agros.
Mat.6.28. Consider the lilies of the **f.**
  30. so clothe the grass of the **f.**
  13.24, 27. sowed good seed in his **f.**
  31. took, and sowed in his **f.**
  36. parable of the tares of the **f.**
  38. The **f.** is the world ; the good
  44. like unto treasure hid in a **f.**
  he hath, and buyeth that **f.**
  24.18. which is in the **f.**; Mar.13.16;
  Lu.17.31
  40. Then shall two be in the **f.**
  27. 7. bought with them potter's **f.**
  8. that **f.** was called, The **f.**
  10. gave them for the potter's **f.**
Lu.12.28. which is to day in the **f.**
  15.15. sent him into his **f**-s to feed
  25. his elder son was in the **f.**
  17. 7. when he is come from the **f.**
  36. Two men shall be in the **f.**
chōrion.
Act. 1.18. purchased a **f.** with the rewa.
  19. that **f.** is called in their prop.
  that is to say, The **f.** of blood
chōra.
Jo. 4.35. look on the **f**-s ; for they are
Jas. 5. 4. who have reaped down your **f**-s

FIERCE.
chalepos.
Mat.8.28. exceeding **f.**, so that no man
epischuō.
Lu.23. 5. they *were the more* **f.**, saying
anēmeros.
²Ti. 3. 3. accusers, incontinent, **f.**
sklēros.
Jas. 3. 4. and are driven of **f.** winds

FIERCENESS.
thumos.
Rev.16.19. of the wine of the **f.** of his
  19.15. of the **f.** and wrath of Almi.

FIERY.
puroomai.
Eph.6.16. the **f.** darts of the wicked

pur.
Heb.10.27. and **f.** indignation, which
purōsis.
¹Pet.4.12. concerning the **f.** *trial*

FIFTEEN.
dekapente.
Jo. 11.18. Jerusalem, about **f.** furlongs
Act.27.28.and found it **f.** fathoms
Gal. 1.18. and abode with him **f.** days

FIFTEENTH.
pentekaidekatos.
Lu. 3. 1. Now in the **f.** year of the

FIFTH.
pemptos.
Rev.6. 9. when he had opened the **f.**
  9. 1. And the **f.** angel sounded
  16.10. the **f.** angel poured out his
  21.20. The **f.**, sardonyx ; the sixth

FIFTY, -ies.
pentēkonta.
Mar.6.40. by hundreds, and by **f**-s
Lu. 7.41. pence, and the other **f.**
  9.14. sit down by **f**-s in a company
  16. 6. down quickly, and write **f.**
Jo. 8.57. Thou art not yet **f.** years old
  21.11. an hundred and **f.** and three
Act.13.20. four hundred and **f.** years
pente murias.
Act.19.19. **f.** *thousand* pieces of silver

FIG, -s.
sukē.
Mat.21.19. And when he saw a **f.** *tree* in
  20. the **f.** *tree* withered away
  21. which is done to the **f.** *tree*
  24.32. a parable of the **f.** *tree*
  Mar.13.28
Mar.11.13. And seeing a **f.** *tree* afar off
  20. they saw the **f.** *tree* dried up
  21. behold, the **f.** *tree* which
Lu. 13. 6. A certain man had a **f.** *tree*
  7. seeking fruit on this **f.** *tree*
  21.29. Behold the **f.** *tree*, and all
Jo. 1.48, 50. under the **f.** *tree*
Jas. 3.12. Can the **f.** *tree*, my brethren
Rev. 6.13. as a **f.** *tree* casteth her un.
sukon.
Mat. 7.16. grapes of thorns, or **f**-s of
Mar.11.13. the time of **f**-s was not yet
Lu. 6.44. thorns men do not gather **f**-s
Jas. 3.12. either a vine, **f**-s ? so can
olunthos.
Rev.6.13. tree casteth her *untimely* **f**-s

FIGHT, [*noun.*]
agōn.
¹Ti. 6.12. Fight the good **f.** of faith
²Ti. 4. 7. I have fought a good **f.**, I have
athlēsis.
Heb.10.32.endured a great **f.** of afflicts.
polemos.
Heb.11.34.waxed valiant in **f.**, turned to

FIGHT, [*verb.*] -Fought.
agōnizomai.
Jo. 18.36. then *would* my servants **f.**
¹Ti. 6.12. **f.** the good fight of faith
²Ti. 4. 7. I *have* **f**-o a good fight, I have
polemeō.
Rev.2.16. and *will* **f.** against them with
Rev. 12.7. Michael and his angels **f**-o
  and the dragon **f**-o and his
machomai.
Jas. 4. 2. ye **f.** and war, yet ye have not
pukteuō.
¹Co. 9.26. so **f.** I, not as one that beateth
theomacheō.
Act. 23.9. *let* us not **f.** *against* God
theomachos.
Act 5.39. found even *to* **f.** *against* God
  (See *Beast.*)

FIGHTINGS.
machē.
²Co. 7. 5. without were **f.**, within were
Jas. 4. 1. come wars and **f.** among you

FIGURE,   -s.
tupos.
Act. 7.43. **f**-s which ye made to worship
Ro. 5.14. who is the **f.** of him that was
    antitupon.
Heb.9.24. which are the **f**-s of the true
¹Pet. 3.21. The like **f.** whereunto, even
    parabolē.
Heb.9. 9. Which was a **f.** for the time
  11.19. also he received him in a **f.**
    metaschēmatizō.
¹Co. 4. 6. I have in a **f.** transferred to

FILL,   -ed, -eth, -ing.
plēroō.
Mat.23.32. **f.** ye up then the measure of
Lu. 2.40. strong in spirit, **f**-ed with
  3. 5. Every valley shall be **f**-ed
Jo. 12. 3. the house was **f**-ed with the
  16. 6. sorrow hath **f**-ed your heart
Act. 2. 2. and it **f**-ed all the house
  5. 3. why hath Satan **f**-ed thine
  28. and, behold, ye have **f**-ed Je.
  13.52. the disciples were **f**-ed with
Ro. 1.29. Being **f**-ed with all unright.
  15.13. **f.** you with all joy and peace
  14. **f**-ed with all knowledge
²Co. 7. 4. I am **f**-ed with comfort, I am
Eph. 1.23. of him that **f**-eth all in all
  3.19. might be **f**-ed with all the
  4.10. that he might **f.** all things
  5.18. but be **f**-ed with the Spirit
Phi. 1.11. Being **f**-ed with the fruits of
Col. 1. 9. that ye might be **f**-ed with
²Ti. 1. 4. that I may be **f**-ed with joy
    sumplēroō.
Lu. 8.23. they were **f**-ed with water
    anaplēroō.
¹Th. 2.16. to **f.** up their sins alway: for
    antanaplēroō.
Col. 1.24. **f.** up that which is behind of
    plēthō.
Mat.27.48. and **f**-ed it with vinegar
Lu. 1.15,41,67. **f**-ed with the Holy G.;
    Act.2.4, 4.8,31, 9.17, 13.9
  4.28. heard these things were **f**-ed
  5. 7. and **f**-ed both the ships, so
  26. and were **f**-ed with fear, say.
  6.11. they were **f**-ed with madness
Jo. 19.29. and they **f**-ed a spunge with
Act. 3.10. and they were **f**-ed with won.
  5.17. and were **f**-ed with indigna.
  13.45. they were **f**-ed with envy
  19.29. the whole city was **f**-ed with
    emplēthō.
Lu. 1.53. He hath **f**-ed the hungry with
Jo. 6.12. when they were **f**-ed, he said
Ro. 15.24. **f**-ed with your company
    gemizō.
Mar. 15.36. one ran and **f**-ed a spunge
Lu. 14.23. that my house may be **f**-ed
  15.16. he would fain have **f**-ed his
Jo. 2. 7. **f.** waterpots with water
    they **f**-ed them up to the brim
  6.13. **f**-ed twelve baskets with the
Rev. 8. 5. **f**-ed it with fire of the altar
  15. 8. the temple was **f**-ed with
    chortazō.
Mat. 5. 6. righte.: for they shall be **f**-ed
  14.20. all eat, and were **f**-ed ; 15.37 ;
    Mar.6.42, 8.8 ; Lu.9.17
  15.33. as to **f.** so great a multitude
Mar. 7.27. Let the children first be **f**-ed
Lu. 6.21. hun. now : for ye shall be **f**-ed
Jo. 6.26. of the loaves, and were **f**-ed
Jas. 2.16. peace, be ye warmed and **f**-ed
Rev.19.21. fowls were **f**-ed with their fle.

---

empiplaō.
Act.14.17. **f**-ing our hearts with food
    teleō.
Rev.15.1. in them is **f**-ed up the wrath
    kerannumi.
Rev.18.6. cup which she hath **f**-ed **f.**
    plērōma.
Mat.9.16. which is put in to **f.** it up
Mar.2.21. the new piece that **f**-ed it up
    (See Piece.)

FILTH.
perikatharma.
¹Co. 4.13. made as the **f.** of the world
    rupos.
¹Pet.3.21. putting away of the **f.** of the

FILTHINESS.
molusmos.
²Co. 7. 1. from all **f.** of the flesh and
    aischrotēs.
Eph. 5. 4. Neither **f.**, nor foolish talking
    ruparia.
Jas. 1.21. lay apart all **f.** and superflu.
    akathartēs.
Rev.17.4. and **f.** of her fornication

FILTHY.
aischros.
Tit. 1.11. ought not, for **f.** lucre's sake
    aselgeia.
²Pet. 2.7. vexed with the **f.** conversation
    rupoō.
Rev.22.11. he which is **f.**, let him be **f.**
    (See Communication, Lucre.)

FINALLY.
loipon.
²Co.13.11. **f.**, brethren, farewell. Be
Eph. 6.10. **f.**, my brethren, be strong in
Phi. 3. 1. **f.**, my brethren, rejoice in the
  4. 8. **f.**, brethren, whatsoever thi.
²Th. 3. 1. **f.**, brethren, pray for us, that
    telos.
¹Pet. 3. 8. **f.**, be ye all of one mind

FIND,   -eth, -ing, Found.
heuriskō.
Mat.1.18. she was **f**-o with child of the
  2. 8. and when ye have **f**-o him
  7. 7. seek, and ye shall **f.**; Lu.11.9
  8. he that seeketh **f**-eth; Lu.11.10
  14. and few there be that **f.** it
  8.10. have not **f**-o so great ; Lu.7.9
  10.39. He that **f**-eth his life shall
    his life for my sake shall **f.** it
  11.29. ye shall **f.** rest unto your souls
  12.43. seeking rest, and **f**-eth none
  44. he **f**-eth it empty ; Lu.11.25
  13.44. the which when a man hath **f**-o
  46. Who, when he had **f**-o one
  16.25. his life for my sake shall **f.** it
  17.27. thou shalt **f.** a piece of money
  18.13. if so be that he **f.** it, verily
  28. **f**-o one of his fellow-servants
  20. 6. and **f**-o others standing idle
  21. 2. ye shall **f.** an ass tied; Mar.11.2
    Lu.19.30
  19.**f**-o nothing thereon; Mar.11.13
    Lu.13.6
  22. 9. as many as ye shall **f.** bid to
  10. all as many as they **f**-o, both
  24.46. when he cometh shall **f.** so ;
    Lu.12.37,43
  26.40. **f**-eth them asleep; Mar.14.37
  43. **f**-o them asleep ag.; Mar.14.40
    Lu.22.45
  60. But **f**-o none : yea, though
    came, yet **f**-o they; Mar.14.55
  27.32. they **f**-o a man of Cyrene
Mar.1.37. And when they had **f**-o him
  7.30. she **f**-o the devil gone out

Mar.11.4. and **f**-o the colt tied by the
  13.if haply he might **f.** any
  13.36. suddenly, he **f.** you sleeping
  14.16. **f**-o as he had said unto them
Lu. 1.30. for thou hast **f**-o favour with
  2.12. Ye shall **f.** the babe wrapped
  45. And when they **f**-o him not
  46. they **f**-o him in the temple
  4.17. he **f**-o the place where it was
  5.19. when they could not **f.** by
  6. 7. that they might **f.** an accusat.
  7.10. the servant whole that had
  8.35. and **f**-o the man, out of whom
  9.36. Jesus was **f**-o alone. And
  11.24. and **f**-ing none, he saith, I will
  12.38. and **f.** them so, blessed are
  13. 7. on this fig tree, and **f.** none
  15. 4. which is lost, until he **f.** it
  5. when he hath **f**-o it, he layeth
  6. I have **f**-o my sheep which
  8. diligently till she **f.** it
  9. when she hath **f**-o it, she call.
    for I have **f**-o the piece which
  24, 32. he was lost, and is **f**-o
  17.18. There are not **f**-o that return.
  18. 8. shall he **f.** faith on the earth
  19.32. and **f**-o even as he had ; 22.13
  48. could not **f.** what they might
  23. 2. We **f**-o this feLow perverting
  4. I **f.** no fault in this man ;
    Jo.18.38, 19.4,6
  14. have **f**-o no fault in this man
  22. I have **f**-o no cause of death in
  24. 2. And they **f**-o the stone rolled
  3. and **f**-o not the body of the
  23. And when they **f**-o not his bod.
  24. and **f**-o it even so as the wom.
  33. **f**-o the eleven gathered toget.
Jo. 1.41. He first **f**-eth his own brother
    unto him, We have **f**-o; 45
  43. and **f**-eth Philip, and saith
  45. Philip **f**-eth Nathanael, and
  2.14. And **f**-o in the temple those
  5.14. Afterward Jesus **f**-eth him in
  6.25. when they had **f**-o him on
  7.34, 36. and shall not **f.** me
  35. go, that we shall not **f.** him
  9.35. and when he had **f**-o him, he
  10. 9. shall go in and out, and **f.**
  11.17. he **f**-o that he had laid in the
  12.14. Jesus, when he had **f**-o a you.
  21. 6. of the ship, and ye shall **f.**
Act. 4.21. **f**-ing nothing how they might
  5.10. came in, and **f**-o her dead
  22. **f**-o them not in the prison
  23. The prison truly **f**-o we shut
    opened, we **f**-o no man within
  39. ye be **f**-o even to fight against
  7.11. and our fathers **f**-o no susten.
  46. Who **f**-o favour before God
    to **f.** a tabernacle for the God
  8.40. But Philip was **f**-o at Azotus
  9. 2. if he **f**-o any of this way
  33. And there he **f**-o a certain man
  10.27. **f**-o many that were come tog.
  11.26. when he had **f**-o him, he bro.
  12.19. and **f**-o him not, he examined
  13. 6. they **f**-o a certain sorcerer,
  22. I have **f**-o David the son of
  28. And though they **f**-o no cause
  17. 6. And when they **f**-o them not
  23. I **f**-o an altar with this inscrip.
  27. might feel after him, and **f.**
  18. 2. And **f**-o a certain Jew named
  19. 1. and **f**-ing certain disciples
  19. and **f**-o it fifty thousand pieces
  21. 2. And **f**-ing a ship sailing over
  23. 9. We **f.** no evil in this man
  24. 5. For we have **f**-o this man
  12. they neither **f**-o me in the
  18. Jews from Asia **f**-o me purifi.
  20. if they have **f**-o any evil doing

Act.27. 6. And there the centurion f-o
28. and f-o it twenty fathoms
2S.14. Where we f-o brethren, *and*
Ro. 4. 1. pertain. to the flesh, *hath* f-o
7.10. the commandment . . I f-o
18. that which is good I f. not
21. I f. then a law, that, when I
10.20. I *was* f-o of them that sought
¹Co. 4. 2. that a man *be* f-o faithful
15.15. Yea, and we *are* f-o false wit.
²Co. 2 13. because I f-o not Titus
5. 3. we *shall* not *be* f-o naked
9. 4. come with me, and f. you un.
11,12. they *may be* f-o even as we
12.20. lest, . . I shall not f. you such
that I shall *be* f-o unto you
Gal. 2.17. we ourselves also *are* f-o
Phi. 2. 8. *being* f-o in fashion as
3. 9. And *be* f-o in him, not having
²Ti. 1.17. very diligently, and f-o me
18. that he may f. mercy of me
Heb.4.16. we may obtain mercy, and f.
11. 5. and *was* not f-o because God
12.17. for he f-o no place of repent.
¹Pet.1. 7. *might be* f-o unto praise and
2.22. neither *was* guile in his
²Pet.3.14. that ye may *be* f-o of him in
²John 4. I f-o of thy children walking
Rev. 2. 2. and *hast* f-o them liars
3. 2. for I *have* not f-o thy works
5. 4. no man *was* f-o worthy to
9. 6. seek death, and *shall* not f.
12. 8. neither *was* their place f-o
14. 5. in their mouth *was* f-o no
16.20. the mountains *were* not f-o
18.14. thou *shalt* f. them no more
21. and *shall be* f-o no more at
22. *shall be* f-o any more in thee
24. *was* f-o the blood of prophets
20.11. there *was* f-o no place for
15. And whosoever *was* not f-o

aneuriskō.
Lu. 2.16. with haste, and f-o Mary, and
Act.21. 4. f-*ing* disciples, we tarried

katalambanō.
Act.25.25. But *when* I f-o that he had

anexichniastos.
Ro.11.33. and his ways *past* f-*ing out*

FINE, (See *Brass, Flour, Linen.*)

FINGER,   -*s.*

daktulos.
Mat.23.4. them with one of their f-s
Mar.7.33. put his f-s into his ears and
Lu.11.20. if I with the f. of God cast
46. burdens with one of your f-s
16.24. may dip the tip of his f. in
Jo. 8. 6. with his f. wrote on the gro.
20.25. put my f. into the print of
27. Reach hither thy f., and beh.

FINISH,   -*ed.*

teleō.
Mat.13.53. Jesus *had* f-ed; 19.1,26.1
Jo. 19.30. he said, it *is* f-ed : and he
²Ti. 4. 7. I *have* f-ed my course
Rev.10. 7. mystery of God *should be* f-ed
11. 7. And when they*shall have* f-ed
20. 5. thousand years *were* f-ed

teleioō.
Jo. 4.34. sent me, and to f. his work
5.36. Father hath given me to f.
17. 4. I *have* f-ed the work which
Act. 20.24. that I might f. my course

ekteleō.
Lu.14.29, 30. not able *to* f. it

sunteleō.
Ro. 9.28. he will f. the work, and cut

epiteleō.
²Co. S. 6. so he *would* also f. in you

apoteleō.
Jas. 1.15. sin, *when* it is f-ed, bringeth
100

---

dianuō.
Act.21. 7. *when* we *had* f-ed our course

ginomai.
Heb.4. 3. the works *were* f-ed from

apartismos.
Lu.14.28. he have sufficient to f. it

FINISHER.

teleiōtēs.
Heb.12. 2. Jesus the author and f. of

FIRE.

pur.
Mat.3.10. and cast into the f.; 7.19 ;
Lu.3.9 ; Jo.15.6
11. H. Ghost, and with f.; Lu.3.16
12. the chaff with unquenchable f.
5.22. shall be in danger of hell f.
13.40. gathered and burned in the f.
42, 50. into a furnace of f : there
17.15. he falleth into the f. ; Mar.9.22
18. 8. to be cast into everlasting f.
9. to be cast into hell f.; Mar.9.47
25.41. ye cursed, into everlasting f.
Mar.9.43. into the f. that ; 44,45,47,48
49. every one shall be salt. with f.
Lu. 3.17. he will burn with f. unquen.
9.54. that we command f. to come
12.49. I am come to send f. on the
17.29. it rained f. and brimstone
22.55. when they had kindled a f.
Act. 2. 3. cloven tongues like as of f.
19. blood, and f., and vapour of
7.30. in a flame of f. in a bush
28. 5. shook off the beast into the f.
Ro.12.20. heap coals of f. on his head
¹Co. 3.13. revealed by f.; and the f. sh.
15. shall be saved; yet so as by f.
²Th. 1. 8. In flaming f. taking vengean.
Heb.1. 7. his ministers a flame of f.
11.34. Quenched the violence of f.
12.18. and that burned with f.
29. our God is a consuming f.
Jas. 3. 5. matter a little f. kindleth
6. And the tongue is a f., a
5. 3. shall eat your flesh as it were f.
¹Pet.1. 7. though it be tried with f.
²Pet.3. 7. reserved unto f. against
Jude 7. the vengeance of eternal f.
23. pulling them out of the f.
Rev.1.14. eyes were as a flame of f.; 2.18,
19.12
3.18. gold tried in the f., that thou
4. 5. seven lamps of f. burning
8. 5. and filled it with f. of the alt.
7. hail and f. mingled with blo.
8. mountain burning with f.
9.17. their mouths issued f.; 11.5
18. by the f., and by the smoke
10. 1. his feet as pillars of f.
13.13. he maketh f. come down from
14.10. with f. and brimstone ; 21.8
18. which had power over f.; and
15. 2. a sea of glass mingled with f.
16. 8. un. him to scorch men with f.
17.16. her flesh and burn her with f.
18. 8 shall be utterly burned with f.
19.20. into a lake of f. burning with
20. 9. and f. came down from God
10. into the lake of f. and brim.
14, 15. cast into the lake of f.

phlogizō.
Jas. 3. 6. *setteth on* f. the course of
and it is *set on* f. of hell

puroomai.
²Pet.3.12. the heavens *being on* f. shall

pura.
Act.28.2. they kindled a f., and receiv.
3. and laid them on the f.

phōs.
Mar.14.54. warmed himself at the f.
Lu. 22.56. be. him as he sat by the f.

(See Coals.)

FIRKINS.

metrētēs.
Jo. 2. 6. containing two or three f.

FIRM.

bebaios.
Heb.3. 6. of the hope f. unto the end

FIRST.

prōtos.
Mat.10.2. The f., Simon, who is called
12.45. is worse than the f.; Lu.11.26
17.27. the fish that f. cometh up
19.30. many that are f. shall be last
and the last shall be f.; 20.16
Mar.10.31 ; Lu.13.30
20. 8. begin.from the last unto the f.
10. But when the f. came, they
21.28. and he came to the f., and
31. They say unto him, The f.
36. servants more than the f.
22.25. the f., when . . married ;
Mar.12.20 ; Lu.20.29
38. This is the f. . . commandment;
Mar.12,28,29,30
26.17. Now the f. day of the feast of
27.64. error shall be worse than the f.
Mar.9.35. If any man desire to be f.
14.12. And the f. day of unleavened
16. 9. early the f. day of the week
Lu. 2. 2. this taxing was f. made when
14.18. The f. said unto him
16. 5. and said unto the f., How
19.16. Then came the f., saying
Jo. 1.41. He f. findeth his own brother
5. 4. whosoever then f. after the
8. 7. let him f. cast a stone at her
19.32. and brake the legs of the f.
20. 4, 8. and came f. to the sepul.
Act.12.10.When they were past the f.
20.18. Ye know, from the f. day
26.23. he should be the f. that
27.43. should cast themselves f. into
Ro.10.19. f. Moses saith, I will provoke
¹Co.14.30. let the f. hold his peace
15. 3. I delivered unto you f. *of all*
45. The f. man Adam was made
47. The f. man is of the earth
Eph.6. 2. which is the f. commandment
Phi. 1. 5. from the f. day until now
¹Ti. 1.16. that in me f., Jesus Christ
2.13. For Adam was f. formed
5.12. they have cast off their f.
²Ti. 2. 6. must be f. partaker of the
4.16. At my f. answer no man
Heb.8. 7, 13. For if that f. covenant; 9.1
9. 2. the f.,wherein was the candl.
6. 8. went always into the f.
15. under the f. testament
18. neither the f. testament was
10. 9. He taketh away the f., that
1Jo. 4.19. him, because he f. loved us
Rev.1.11, 17. the f. and the f. ; 2.8,22.13
2. 4. thou hast left thy f. love
5. and do the f. works ; or else
19. the last to be more than the f.
4. 1. and the f. voice which I hea.
7. And the f. beast was like
8. 7. The f. angel sounded, and
13.12. all the power of the f. beast
to worship the f. beast, who.
16. 2. And the f. went, and poured
20. 5. This is the f. resurrection
6. part in the f. resurrection
21. 1. the f. heaven and the f. earth
19. The f. foundation was jasper

prōton.
Mat.5.24. f. be reconciled to thy broth.
6.33. But seek ye f. the kingdom
7. 5. f. cast out the beam ; Lu.6.42
8.21. suffer me f. to go ; Lu.9.59
12.29. f. bind the strong ; Mar.3.27

Mat.13.30.Gather ye together f. the
  17.10, 11. that Elias must f. come ;
          Mar.9.11,12
  23.26. cleanse f. that which is with.
Mar.4.28. f. the blade, then the ear
  7.27. Let the children f. be filled
  13.10. the gospel must f. be publish.
  16. 9. he appeared f. to Mary Mag.
Lu. 9.61. let me f. go bid them farewell
  10. 5. f. say, Peace be to this house
  11.38. that he had not f. washed
  12. 1. unto his disciples f. of all
  14.28, 31. sitteth not down f., and
  17.25. But f. must he suffer many
  21. 9. these things must f. come to
Jo. 10.40. when John at f. baptized
  12.16. not his disciples at the f.
  18.13. to Annas ; for he was fath.
  19.39. which at the f. came to Jesus
Act. 3.26. Unto you f., God, having
  7.12. he sent out our fathers f.
  11.26. called Christians f. in Antio.
  13.46. should f. have been spoken
  15.14. how God at the f. did visit
  26.20. But shewed f. unto them of
Ro. 1. 8. f., I thank my God through
  16. to the Jew f., and ; 2,9,10
  15.24. if f. I be somewhat filled
1Co.11.18. For f. of all, when ye come
  12.28. f.,apostles ; secondarily,prop.
  15.46. that was not f. which is spirit.
2Co. 8. 5. but f. gave their own selves
Eph.4. 9. he also descended f. into the
1Th. 4.16. the dead in Christ shall rise f.
2Th. 2. 3. there come a falling away f.
1Ti. 2. 1. that, f. of all, supplications
  3.10. let these also f. be proved
  5. 4. let them learn f.to shew piety
2Ti. 1. 5. which dwelt f. in thy grand.
Heb.7. 2. f. being by interpretation
Jas. 3.17. is f. pure, then peaceable
1Pet.4.17. if it f. begin at us, what
2Pet.1.20. Knowing this f., that ; 3.3
      proteron.
Gal. 4.13. the gospel unto you at the f.
Heb.4. 6. to whom it was f. preached
  7.27. f. for his own sins, and then
    heis.
Mat.28.1. f. day of the week; Mar.16.2;
      Lu.24.1; Jo.20.1,19;
      Act.20.7; 1Co.16.2
Tit. 3.10. after the f. and second
    archē.
Act. 26. 4. which was at the f. among
Heb. 2. 3. which at the f. began to be
  5.12. the f. principles of the oracl.
Jude 6. kept not their f. estate
    anŏthen.
Lu. 1. 3. of all things from the very f.
    prodidōmi.
Ro.11.35. Or who hath f. given to him
    prokeimai.
2Co. 8.12. if there be f. a willing mind
    (See Trust, Second.)

FIRST-BEGOTTEN.
    prōtotokos.
Heb. 1.6. bringeth in the f. into the
Rev. 1.5. the f. of the dead, and the

FIRST-BORN.
    prōtotokos, [singular.]
Mat.1.25. broug. forth her f. son; Lu.2.7
Ro. 8.29. the f. among many brethren
Col. 1.15. the f. of every creature
  18. the f. from the dead ; that in
    prōtotokos, [plural.]
Heb.12.23. and church of the f. which
    prōtotokos, [plu. neuter.]
Heb.11.28. he that destroyed the f.

FIRST-FRUIT,   -s,
    aparchē.
Ro. 8.23. which have the f-s of the Spi.

Ro. 11.16. For if the f. be holy, the
  16. 5. the f-s of Achaia; 1Co.16.15
1Co.15.20.become the f-s of them that
  23. Christ the f-s; afterward
Jas. 1.18. a kind of f-s of his creatures
Rev.14.4. being the f-s unto God and

FISH, [noun,]   -es.
    ichthus.
Mat. 7.10. Or if he ask a f., will he give
  14.17, 19. five loaves, and two f-es ;
      Mar.6.38,41; Lu.9.13,16
  15.36. the seven loaves and the f-es
  17.27. take up the f. that first
Mar. 6.41. the two f-es divided he amo.
  43. the fragments and of the f-es
Lu. 5. 6. a great multitude of f-es
  9. at the draught of the f-es
  11.11. if he ask a f., will he for a f.
  24.42. him a piece of a broiled f.
Jo. 21. 6. it for the multitude of f-es
  8. dragging the net with f-es
  11. net to land full of great f-es
1Co. 15.39. another of f-es, and another
    opsarion.
Jo. 6. 9. loaves, and two small f-es
  11. and likewise of the f-es
  21. 9. and f. laid thereon, and bread
  10. Bring of the f. which ye have
  13. giveth them, and f. likewise
    ichthudion.
Mat.15.34. Seven, and a few little f-s
Mar. 8. 7. they had a few small f-es

FISHING, [verb.]
    halieuō.
Jo. 21. 3. saith unto them I go a f.

FISHER,   -s.
    halieus.
Mat.4.18. for they were f-s ; Mar.1.16
  19. will make you f-s of; Mar.1.17
    ependutēs.
Jo. 21.7. he girt his f.'s coat unto him

FISHERMEN.
    halieus.
Lu. 5. 2. but the f. were gone out of

FIT,   -ed.
    euthetos.
Lu. 9.62. looking back, is f. for the
  14.35. It is neither f. for the land
    kathēkon.
Act.22.22. it is not f. that he should
    katartizō.
Ro. 9.22. ves. of wrath f-ed to destruct.
    anēkō.
Col. 3.18. husbands, as it is f. in the

FITLY, (See Framed, Joined.)

FIVE.
    pente.
Mat.14.17, 19. but f. loaves, and two fis.;
      Mar.6.38; Lu.9.13,16
  16. 9. neither remember the f. loa.
  25. 2. And f. of them were wise
    and f. were foolish
  15. unto one he gave f. talents
  16, 20. that had received the f.
    and made them other f. tal.
  20. thou deliveredst unto me f.
    beside them f. talents more
Mar. 6.41. when he had taken the f.
  8.19. When I brake the f. loaves
Lu. 1.24. and hid herself f. months
  12. 6. Are not f. sparrows sold
  52. there shall be f. in one house
  14.19. I have bought f. yoke of oxen
  16.28. For I have f. brethren ; that
  19.18. thy pound hath gained f.
  19. Be thou also over f. cities
Jo. 4.18. For thou hast had f.husbands
  5. 2. Bethesda, having f. porches

Jo. 6. 9, 13. which hath f.barley loaves
  19. had rowed about f. and
Act. 4. 4. of the men was about f. thou.
  20. 6. unto them to Troas in f. days
  24. 1. And after f. days Ananias
1Co. 14.19. I had rather speak f. words
Rev. 9. 5. be tormented f. months: and
  10. was to hurt men f. months
  17.10. f. are fallen, and one is, and
    pentakis.
2Co.11.24. f. times received I forty
    (See Hundred, Thousand.)

FIXED.
    stērizō.
Lu.16.26. there is a great gulph f.

FLAME.
    phlox.
Lu. 16.24. for I am tormented in this f.
Act. 7.30. in a f. of fire in a bush
Heb.1. 7. and his ministers a f. of fire
Rev. 1.14. eyes were as a f. of fire; 2.18,
      19.12

FLAMING.
    phlox.
2Th. 1. 8. In f. fire, taking vengeance

FLATTERING.
    kolakeia.
1Th. 2. 5. any time used we f. words

FLAX.
    linon.
Mat.12.20. and smoking f. shall he not

FLEE,   -eth, Fled.
    pheugō.
Mat.2.13. and f. into Egypt, and be
  3. 7. to f. from the wrath to come ;
      Lu.3.7
  8.33. And they that kept them f-d
  10.23. f. ye into another : for verily
  24.16. let them which be in Jud. f.;
      Mar.13.14; Lu.21.21
  26.56. disciples forsook him and f-d;
      Mar. 14.50
Mar.5.14. they that fed the swine f-d
  14.52. cloth, and f-d from them na.
  16. 8. and f-d from the sepulchre
Lu. 8.34. they f-d, and went and told
Jo.10. 5. but will f. from him : for
  12. leaveth the sheep, and f-eth
  13. The hireling f-eth, because he
Act. 7. 29. Then f-d Moses at this saying
  27.30. were about to f. out of th
1Co. 6.18. f. fornication. Every sin that
  10.14. my dearly beloved, f. from
1Ti. 6.11. O man of God, f. these things
2Ti. 2.22. f. also youthful lusts : but
Jas. 4. 7. devil, and he will f. from you
Rev.9. 6. and death shall f. from them
  12. 6. the woman f. into the wilder.
  16.20. And every island f-d away
  20.11. earth and the heaven f-d aw.
    katapheugō.
Act.14. 6. and f-d unto Lystra and Der.
Heb.6.18. who have f-d for refuge to lay
    ekpheugō.
Act.16.27. the prisoners had been f-d

FLESH.
    sarx.
Mat.16.17. f. and blood hath not reveal.
  19.5, 6. shall be one f.; Mar.10.18 ;
      1Co.6.16 ; Eph.5.31
  24.22. should no f. be ; Mar.13.20
  26.41. the f. is weak ; Mar.14.38
Lu. 3. 6. And all f. shall see the salv.
  24.39. a spirit hath not f. and bones
Jo. 1.13. nor of the will of the f.
  14. And the Word was made f.
  3. 6. which is born of the f. is f.
  6.51. bread that I will give is my f.
  52. man give us his f. to eat

Jo. 6.53. Except ye eat the f. of the
54, 56. Whoso eateth my f., hath
55. For my f. is meat indeed, and
63. the f. profiteth notning : the
8.15. Ye judge after the f.; I jud.
17. 2. given him power over all f.

Act. 2.17. out of my Spirit upon all f.
26. also my f. shall rest in hope
30. according to the f.; Ro.1.3
31. neither his f. did see corrup.

Ro. 2.28. which is outward in the f.
3.20. shall no f. be justi.; Gal.2.16
4. 1. father as pertaining to the f.
6.19. of the infirmity of your f.
7. 5. For when we were in the f.
18. in me, that is, in my f.
25. but with the f. the law of sin
8. 1. 4. who walk not after the f.
3. it was weak through the f.
in the likeness of sinful f.
sin, condemned sin in the f.
5. they that are after the f. do
mind the things of the f.
8. they that are in the f cannot
9. ye are not in the f., but in
12. the f. to live after the f.
13. For if ye live after the f., ye
9. 3. kinsmen according to the f.
5. whom as concerning the f.
8. are the children of the f.
11.14. them which are my f.
13.14. make not provision for the f.

¹Co. 1.26. many wise men after the f.
29. That no f. should glory in
5. 5. for the destruction of the f.
7.28. shall have trouble in the f.
10.18. Behold Israel after the f.
15.39. All f. is not the same f.: but
is one kind of f. of men
another f. of beasts, another
50. f. and blood cannot inherit

²Co. 1.17. I purpose according to the f.
4.11. made manifest in our mor. f.
5.16. no man after the f. : yea
have known Christ after the f.
7. 1. from all filthiness of the f.
5. our f. had no rest, but we
10. 2. walked according to the f.
3. f., we do not war after the f.
11.18. that many glory after the f.
12. 7. a thorn in the f., the messe.

Gal. 1.16. I conferred not with f. and
2.20. which I now live in the f.
3. 3. now made perfect by the f.
4.13. through infirmity of the f. I
14. tempta. which was in my f.
23, 29. was born after the f.
5.13. liberty for an occa. to the f.
16. not fulfil the lust of the f.
17. the f. lusteth against the Sp.
and the Spirit against the f.
19. the works of the f. are man.
24. have crucified the f. with
6. 8. to his f. shall of the f. reap
12. to make a fair shew in the f.
13. they may glory in your f.

Eph. 2. 3. in the lusts of our f., fulfill.
the desires of the f. and of
11. time past Gentiles in the f.
the Circumcision in the f.
15. Having abolished in his f.
5.29. ever yet hated his own f.
30. of his f., and of his bones
6. 5. masters according to the f.;
Col.3.22
12. we wrestle not against f. and

Phi. 1.22. But if I live in the f., this
24. Neverthel. to abide in the f.
3. 3. have no confidence in the f.
4. also have confidence in the f.
he might trust in the f.

Col. 1.22. In the body of his f. through
102

Col. 1. 24. in my f. for his body s sake
2. 1. not seen my face in the f.
5. absent in the f., yet am I
11. the body of the sins of the f.
13. the uncircumcision of your f.
23. to the satisfying of the f.

¹Ti. 3.16. God was manifest in the f.

Phile. 16. both in the f., and in the L.

Heb. 2.14. children are partakers of f.
5. 7. Who in the days of his f.
9.13. to the purifying of the f.
10.20. the vail, that is to say, his f.
12. 9. we have had fathers of our f.

Jas. 5. 3. shall eat your f. as it were

¹Pet. 1.24. For all f. is as grass, and
3.18. put to death in the f., but
21. away of the filth of the f.
4. 1. hath suffered for us in the f.
2. rest of his time in the f.
6. according to men in the f.

²Pet. 2.10. that walk after the f. in the
18. through the lusts of the f.

¹Jo. 2.16. the lust of the f., and the
4. 2, 3. Jesus C. is come in the f.
²John 7

Jude 7. going after strange f., are set
8. dreamers defile the f., desp.
23. the garment spotted by the f.

Rev. 17.16. and shall eat her f., and burn
19.18. f. of kings, and the f. of cap.
f. of mighty men, and the f.
and the f. of all men, both
21. fowls were filled with their f.

kreas.
Ro. 14.21. It is good neither to eat f.
¹Co. 8.13 I will eat no f. while the world

FLESHLY.
sarkikos.
²Co. 1.12. not with f. wisdom, but by.
¹Pet.2.11. abstain from f. lusts which

sarkinos.
²Co. 3. 3. but in f. tables of the heart

sarx.
Col. 2.18. vainly puffed up by his f.

FLIGHT.
phugē.
Mat.24.20. f. be not in the ; Mar.13.18

klinō.
Heb.11.34. turned to f. the armies of

FLOCK.
poimnion.
Lu. 12.32. Fear not, little f.; for it is
Act.20.28. and to all the f., over the
29. among you, not sparing the f.
¹Pet. 5. 2. Feed the f. of God which is
3. but being ensamples to the f.

poimnē.
Mat.26.31. and the sheep of the f. shall
Lu. 2. 8. watch over their f. by night
¹Co. 9. 7. who feedeth a f., and eateth
not of the milk of the f.

FLOOD, -s.
kataklusmos.
Mat.24.38. before the f. they were eat.
39. until the f. came ; Lu.17.27

²Pet. 2. 5. bringing in the f. upon the

potamos.
Mat.7.25,27. descend., and the f-s came
Rev. 12.15. of his mouth water as a f.
16. and swallowed up the f.

plēmmura.
Lu. 6.48. when the f. arose, the stream
(See Carry.)

FLOOR.
halōn.
Mat.3.12. thoro. purge his f.; Lu.3.17

FLOUR.
semidalis.
Rev.18.13. oil, and fine f., and wheat

FLOURISHED.
anathallō.
Phi. 4.10. care of me hath f. again

FLOW.
reō.
Jo. 7.38. shall f. rivers of living water

FLOWER.
anthos.
Jas. 1.10. as the f. of the grass; ¹Pet.1.24
11. the f. thereof falleth; ¹Pet.1.24

huperakmos.
¹Co.7.36. she [pass the f. of her age

FLUX, (See Bloody.)

FLY, -ing.
petaomai.
Rev. 4. 7. beast was like a f-ing eagle
8.13. an angel f-ing through the
14. 6. saw another angel f. in the
19.17. saying to all the fowls that f.

petomai.
Rev.12.14. might f. into the wilderness

FOAL.
huios.
Mat.21.5. and a colt the f. of an ass

FOAMETH, -ing.
aphrizō.
Mar. 9.18. he f. and gnasheth with
20. ground, and wallowed, f-ing

aphros.
Lu. 9.39. him, that he f. again

epaphrizō.
Jude 13. f-ing out their own shame

FOES.
echthros.
Mat.10.36. a man's f. shall be they of
Act. 2.35. I make thy f. thy footstool

FOLD, [noun.]
aulē.
Jo. 10. 1. the door into the sheep f.
16. which are not of this f.: them

poimnē.
Jo. 10.16. be one f., and one shepherd
(See Four.)

FOLD, [verb.]
helissō.
Heb.1.12. vesture shalt thou f. them up

FOLK, (See Impotent, Sick.)

FOLLOW, -ed, -eth, -ing.
akoutheō.
Mat. 4.20, 22. their nets, and f-ed him ;
Mar.1.18
25. there f-ed him great multi.;
8.1, 12.15, 19.2, 20.29 ;
Mar.3.7 ; Jo.6.2
8.10. said to them that f-ed, Veri.
19. I will f. thee whithersoever ;
Lu.9.57,61
22. Jesus said unto him, f. me ;
Lu.5.27; Jo.1 43, 21,19
23. his discip. f-ed him; Lu.22.39
9. 9. f. me. And he arose, and f-ed ;
Mar.2.14
19. Jesus arose and f-ed him
27. two blind men f-ed him, cry.
10.38. not his cross, and f-eth after
14.13. they f-ed him on foot out or
16.24. take up his cross, and f. me ;
Mar.8.34, 10.21.
19.21. in heaven: and come and f.
27. have forsaken all, and f-ed
28. That ye which have f-ed me
20.34. received sight, and they f-ed
21. 9. went before, and that f-ed
26.58. Peter f-ed him afar off unto:
Mar.14.54; Lu.22.54

Mat. 27.55. which f-ed Jesus from Gali.
Mar. 2.15. were many, and they f-ed
   5.24. him; and much people f-ed
   6. 1. country; and his disciples f.
   9.38. in thy name, and he f-eth
     him, because he f-eth not;
      Lu.9.49
   10.28. left all, and have f-ed thee;
      Lu.18.28
     32. as they f-ed, they were afraid
     52. received his sight, and f-ed;
      Lu.18 43
   11. 9. went bef., and they that f-ed
   14.13. bearing a pitcher of water: f.
     51. there f-ed him a certain you.
   15.41. he was in Galilee, f-ed him
Lu. 5.11, 28.they forsook all, and f-ed
   7. 9. unto the people that f-ed
   9.11. when they knew it, f-ed him
   23. up his cross daily, and f. me
   59. he said unto another, f. me
   18.22. heaven: and come, f. me
   22.10. f. him into the house where
   23.27. there f-ed him a great comp.
Jo. 1.37. him speak, and they f-ed
     38. turned, and saw them f-ing
     40. heard John speak, and f-ed
   8.12. he that f-eth me shall not
   10. 4. them, and the sheep f. him
     5. a stranger will they not f.
     27. I know them, and they f.
   11.31. up hastily and went out, f-ed
   12.26. any man serve me, let him f.
   13.36. f. me now; but thou shalt f.
     37. why cannot I f. thee now
   18.15. Simon Peter f-ed Jesus, and
   20. 6. cometh Simon Peter f-ing
   21.20. disc. whom Jesus loved f-ing
   22. is that to thee? f. thou me
Act. 12. 8. thy garme. about thee, and f.
   9. he went out, and f-ed him
   13.43. religious proselytes f-ed Paul
   21.36. multitude of the people f-ed
1Co. 10. 4. spiritual Rock that f-ed them
Rev. 6. 8. Death, and hell f-ed with
   14. 4. are they which f. the Lamb
     8. there f-ed another angel,
     9. the third angel f-ed them
     13. and their works do f. them
   19.14. f-ed him upon white horses
     epakoloutheō.
Mar.16.20. the word with signs f-ing
1Ti. 5.10. if she have diligently f-ed
   24. and some men they f. after
1Pet. 2.21. that ye should f. his steps
     exakoloutheō.
2Pet.1.16. For we have not f-ed cunnin.
   2. 2. many shall f. their pernicious
   15. f-ing the way of Balaam the
     sunakoloutheō.
Mar. 5.37. suffered no man to f. him
Lu. 23.49. the women that f-ed him
     katakoloutheo.
Lu. 23.55. f-ed after, and beheld the
Act.16.17. same f-ed Paul and us, and
     parakoloutheō.
Mar.16.17. And these signs shall f. them
     diōkō.
Lu. 17.23. go not after them, nor f.
Ro. 9.30. which f-ed not after righteo.
   31. Israel, which f-ed after the la.
   14.19. therefore f. after the things
1Co.14. 1. f. after charity, and desire
Phi. 3.12. but I f. after, if that I may
1Th. 5.15. ever f. that which is good
1Ti. 6.11. f. after righteousness, godli.
2Ti. 2.22. f. righteousness, faith, chari.
Heb.12.14.f. peace with all men, and
     katadiōkō.
Mar. 1.36. were with him f-ed after him
     mimeomai.
2Th. 3. 7. how ye ought to f. us: for

2Th. 3. 9. an ensample unto you to f.
Heb.13. 7. whose faith f., considering
3John 11. f. not that which is evil, but
     deute opisō.
Mat. 4.19. saith unto them, f. me
     ginomai.
Rev. 8. 7. there f-ed hail and fire ming.
     echō.
Lu. 13.33. to-morrow, and the day f-ing
     hexēs.
Act. 21. 1. the day f-ing unto Rhodes
     epiousa.
Act. 21.18. the day f-ing Paul went in
   23.11. And the night f-ing the Lord
     meta houtos.
1Pet.1.11. glo. that should f. (after these)
     eimi meta.
Mat.27.62. that f-ed the day of (is after)
     eimi.
Lu.22.49. saw what would f. (was to be)
     (See Day.)

FOLLOWERS.
     mimētēs.
1Co. 4.16. be ye f. of me; 11.1
Eph.5. 1. Be ye therefore f. of God.
1Th. 1. 6. And ye became f. of us, and
   2.14. ye, brethren, became f. of the
Heb.6.12. but f. of them who through
1Pet.3.13. if ye be f. of that which is
     summimētēs.
Phi. 3.17. Brethren, be f. together of

FOLLY.
     aphrosunē.
2Co.11. 1. bear with me a little in my f.
     anoia.
2Ti. 3. 9. their f. shall be manifest

FOOD.
     trophē.
Act.14.17. filling our hearts with f. and
Jas. 2.15. and destitute of daily f.
     brōsis.
2Co. 9.10. minister bread for your f.
     diatrophē.
1Ti. 6. 8. having f. and raiment, let us

FOOL,   -s.
     aphrōn.
Lu. 11.40. Ye f-s, did not he that made
   12.20. Thou f., this night thy soul
1Co. 15.36. Thou f., that which thou
2Co. 11.16. Let no man think me a f.; if
     yet.as a f. receive me, that I
     19. For ye suffer f-s gladly, seeing
   12. 6. I shall not be a f.; for I will
     11. I am become a f. in glorying
     mōros.
Mat. 5.22. whosoever shall say, Thou f.
   23.17, 19. Ye f-s and blind: for
1Co. 3.18. let him become a f., that he
   4.10. We are f-s for Christ's sake
     anoētos.
Lu.24.25. O f-s, and slow of heart to
     mōrainō.
Ro. 1.22. to be wise, they became f-s
     paraphroneō.
2Co.11.23. I speak as a f., I am more
     asophos.
Eph.5.15. circumspectly, not as f-s, but

FOOLISH.
     mōros.
Mat.7.26. be likened unto a f. man
   25. 2. were wise, and five were f.
     3. They that were f. took their
     8. the f. said unto the wise
2Ti. 2.23. f. and..questions avoid;
     Tit.3.9
     anoētos.
Gal. 3. 1. O f. Galatians, who hath
     3. Are ye so f.? having begun
1Ti. 6. 9. into many f. and hurtful

Tit. 3. 3. also were sometimes f.
     asunetos.
Ro. 1.21. their f. heart was darkened
   10.19. by a f. nation I will anger
     aphrōn.
Ro. 2.20. An instructor of the f., a
1Pet.2.15. silence the ignorance of f.
     mōrainō.
1Co. 1.20. hath not God made f. the
     mōrologia.
Eph.5. 4. nor f. talking, nor jesting

FOOLISHLY.
     aphrosunē.
2Co.11.17. as it were f. (in foolishness)
   21. I speak f., I am bold also

FOOLISHNESS.
     aphrosunē.
Mar.7.22. evil eye, blasphemy, pride, f.
     mōria.
1Co. 1.18. to them that perish f.; but
   21. by the f. of preaching to save
   23. and unto the Greeks f.
   2.14. for they are f. unto him
   3.19. wisdom of this world is f.
     mōros, [neuter.]
1Co. 1.25. the f. of God is wiser than

FOOT,   Feet.
     pous.
Mat.4. 6. time thou dash thy f.; Lu.4.;
   7. 6. trample them under their f.
   10.14. shake off the dust of your f.
     Mar.6.11.; Lu.9.5
   15.30. cast them down at Jesus' f-e
   18. 8. or thy f. offend thee; Mar.9.45
     having two hands or two f-e;
     Mar.9.45
   29. fellower. fell down at his f-e
   22.13. Bind him hand and f., and
   28. 9. and held him by the f-e, and
Mar.5.22. fell at his f-e; 7.25; Lu.8.41:
     Jo.11.32; Act.5.10, 10.25
Lu. 1.79. to guide our f-e into the way
   7.38. stood at his f-e behind him
     began to wash his f-e with
     and kissed his f-e, and anoint.
     44. gavest me no water for my f-e
     she hath washed my f-e with
     45. hath not ceased to kiss my f-e
     46. anointed my f-e with ointment
   8.35. sitting at the f-e of Jesus
   10.39. which also sat at Jesus' f-e
   15.22. hand, and shoes on his f-e
   17.16. down on his face at his f-e
   24.39. Behold my hands and my f-e
   40. them his hands and his f-e
Jo.11. 2. wiped his f-e with her; 12.3
     44. bound hand and f. with gra.
   12. 3. and anointed the f-e of Jesus
   13. 5, 12. to wash the disciples' f-e
     6, 8. Lord; dost thou wash my f-e
     9. Lord, not my f-e only, but
     10. save to wash his f-e, but is
     14. Master, have washed your f-e
     ought to wash one anothers' f-e
   20.12. and the other at the f-e, where
Act. 4.35, 37. at the apostles' f-e; 5.2
   5. 9. behold, the f-e of them which
   7. 5. so much as to set his f. on
     33. Put off thy shoes from thy f-e
     58. at a young man's f-e, whose
   13.25. whose shoes of his f-e I am
   51. shook off the dust of their f-e
   14. 8. impotent in his f-e, being a
     10. Stand upri. on thy f-e; 26.16
   16.24. made their f-e fast in the sto.
   21.11. bound his own hands and f-e
   22. 3. at the f-e of Gamaliel, and
Ro. 3.15. Their f-e are swift to shed blo.
   10.15. How beautiful are the f-e of
   16.20. bruise Satan under your f-e

¹Co.12.15. If the **f.** shall say, Because
  21. nor again the head to the **f-e**
15.25, 27. put all..under his **f-e** ;
  Eph.1.22
Eph.6.15. And your **f-e** shod with the
¹Ti. 5.10. she have washed the saints' **f-e**
Heb.2. 8. in subjection under his **f-e**
  12.13. make strai. paths for your **f-e**
Rev.1.15. And his **f-e** like unto fine
  17. I fell at his **f-e** as dead. And
2.18. and his **f-e** are like fine brass
3. 9. and worship before thy **f-e**
10. 1. and his **f-e** as pillars of fire
  2. and he set his right **f.** upon
11.11. and they stood upon their **f-e**
12. 1. and the moon under her **f-e**
13. 2. and his **f-e** were as the feet of
19.10. I fell at his **f-e** to worship
22. 8. before the **f-e** of the angel wh.
peze.
Mat.14.13. followed him on **f.** out of
basis.
Act. 3. 7. his **f-e** and ancle bones receiv.
(See *Garment, Tread.*)

FOOTSTOOL.
hupopodion.
Mat.5.35. by the earth ; for it is his **f.**
  22.44. I make thine enemies thy **f.**
  Mar.12.36; Lu.20.43
  Act.2.35; Heb.1.13 ; 10.13
Act. 7.49. and earth is my **f.** : what hou.
Jas. 2. 3. there, or sit here under my **f.**

FOR, [*preposition.*]
eis.
Mat. 5.13. is thenceforth good **f.** noth.
6.13. power, and the glory, **f.** ever
  34. no thought **f.** the morrow
8. 4. **f.** a testimony ; Mat.10.18;
  Mar.1.44,6.11,13.9 ; Lu.5,
  14.9.5,21.13 ; Heb.3.5
10.10. **f.** your journey ; Mar.6.8;
  Lu.9.3
21.19. thee henceforward **f.** ever
24.14. a witness unto all nations
26.13. be told **f.** a memorial of her ;
  Mar.14.9
  28. **f.** the remission of sins ;
  Mar.1.4 ; Lu.3.3 ; Act.2.38
27.10. gave them **f.** the potter's
Mar.11.14. fruit of thee hereafter **f.** ever
Lu. 1.33. over the house of Jacob **f.**
  55. and to his seed **f.** ever
2.34. **f.** the fall and rising again of
  f. a sign which shall be spok.
5. 4. let down your nets **f.** a drau.
9.13. buy meat **f.** all this people
  62. and looking back, is fit **f.** the
12.19. goods laid up **f.** many years
14.35. fit **f.** the land, nor yet **f.** the
Jo. 1. 7. The same came **f.** a witness
6.51,58. shall live **f.** ever
8.35. not in the house **f.** ever : but
12.34. that Christ abideth **f.** ever
14.16. he may abide with you **f.** ever
18.37. this end was I born, and **f.**
Act. 7. 5. give it to him **f.** a possession
21. nourished him **f.** her own son
10. 4. are come up **f.** a memorial
13. 2. **f.** the work whereunto I
  47. that thou shouldest be **f.**
14.26. **f.** the work which they fulfi.
23.30. the Jews laid wait **f.** the
Ro. 1. 5. **f.** obedience to the fai. ; 16.26
  25. who is blessed **f.** ever. Amen
2.26. be counted **f.** circumcision
4. 3, 5,9,22. unto him **f.** righteous.;
  Gal.3.6 ; Jas.2.23
8.28. all things work together **f.**
9. 5. over all, God blessed **f.** ever
  8 are counted **f.** the seed
104

Ro. 10. 4. the law **f.** righteousness to
11.11. **f.** to provoke them to jealo.
  36. be glory **f.** ever ; Gal.1.5 ;
  Phi.4.20 ; ¹Ti.1.17; ²Ti.4.18 ;
  Heb.13.21 ; ²Pet.3.18
13. 4. minister of God to thee **f.**
15. 2. **f.** his good to edification
  4. were written **f.** our learning
26. contribution **f.** the poor sai.
31. which I have **f.** Jerusalem
16,27. through Jesus Christ **f.** ever
¹Co. 5. 5. **f.** the destruction of the flesh
11.17. not **f.** the better, but **f.** the
14.22. Wherefore tongues are **f.** a
16. 1. the collection **f.** the saints
²Cor. 5. 5. **f.** the selfsame thing is God
8.14. may be a supply **f.** their wa.
9. 9. his righteous. remaineth **f.**
  10. both minister bread **f.** your
10. 8. **f.** edification, and not **f.** your
11.31. Christ, which is blessed **f.**
Gal. 5.13. liberty **f.** an occasion to the
Eph. 2.22. **f.** an habitation of God
4.12. **f.** the work . .**f.** the edifying
5. 2. **f.** a sweet smelling savour
6.22. I have sent unto you **f.** the
Phi. 1.17. **f.** the defence of the gospel
25. **f.** the furtherance and joy of
Col. 1.16. were created by him, and **f.**
25. which is given to me **f.** you
²Ti. 4.11. profitable to me **f.** the minis.
Tit. 3.14. good works **f.** necessary uses
Heb. 1. 3. Thy throne, O God, is **f.** ever
5. 6. art a priest **f.** ever ; 7.17,21
6.16. an oath **f.** confirmation is to
20. made an high priest **f.** ever
7.28. who is consecrated **f.** everm.
9. 9. a figure **f.** the time then pre.
15. **f.** the redemption of the
10.12. **f.** ever sat down on the right
14. perfected **f.** ever them that
11. 8. after receive **f.** an inheritan.
13. 8. and to-day, and **f.** ever
¹Pet.1. 4. reserved in heaven **f.** you
23. which liveth and abideth **f.**
25. word of the Lord endureth **f.**
2.14. **f.** the punishment of evildo.
4.11. dominion **f.** ever ; 5.11 ;
  Rev.1.6   [Jude 13
²Pet. 2.17. darkness is reserved **f.** ever ;
¹Jo. 2.17. will of God abideth **f.** ever
²John 2. shall be with us **f.** ever
Rev. 1.18. behold, I am alive **f.** everm.
4. 9, 10. who liveth **f.** ever and ;
  5.14,10.6,15.7
5.13. unto the Lamb **f.** ever and
7.12. unto our God **f.** ever and
9.15. were prepared **f.** an hour
11.15. shall reign **f.** ever and ; 22.5
14.11. ascendeth up **f.** ever and
19. 3. her smoke rose up **f.** ever
20.10. day and night **f.** ever and
22. 2. **f.** the healing of the nations
huper.
Mat. 5.44. pray **f.** them which despite.;
  Lu.6.28
Lu. 9.50. that is not against us is **f.** us
22.19. body which is given **f.** you
20. blood, which is shed **f.** you
Jo. 6.51. I will give **f.** the life of the
11. 4. but **f.** the glory of God, that
50. one man should die **f.** the ;
  18.14
51. that Jesus should die **f.** that
52. And not **f.** that nation only
15.13. lay down his life **f.** his frien.
Act. 5.41. to suffer shame **f.** his name
8.24. Pray ye to the Lord **f.** me
12. 5. of the church unto God **f.**
15.26. **f.** the name of our L.; 21.13
21,26. should be offered **f.** every
26. 1. art permitted to speak **f.**

Ro. 1. 5. among all nations, **f.** his
8. through Jesus Christ **f.** you
5. 6. time Christ died **f.** the un.
7. For scarcely **f.** a righteous
  yet peradventure **f.** a good
8. yet sinners, Christ died **f.** us
8.26, 27,34. maketh intercession **f.**
31. If God be **f.** us, who can be
32. but delivered him up **f.** us
9. 3. accursed from Christ **f.** my
10. 1. and prayer to God **f.** Israel
14.15. with thy meat, **f.** whom Ch.
15. 8. of the circumcision **f.** the
9. might glorify God **f.** his mer
30. in your prayers to God **f.** me
16. 4. Who have **f.** my life laid
¹Co. 1.13. was Paul crucified **f.** you
4. 6. be puffed up **f.** one against
5. 7. our passover is sacrificed **f.**
10.30. that **f.** which I give thanks
11.24. my body, which is broken **f.**
12.25. have the same care one **f.** an.
15. 3. how that Christ died **f.** our
29. which are baptized **f.** the
²Co. 1. 6. **f.** your consolation and
11. helping together by prayer **f.**
5.14,15.that if one died **f.** all, then
15. unto him which died **f.** them
20. we are ambassadors **f.** Christ
21. made him to be sin **f.** us
7.12. but that our care **f.** you
8.16. care into the heart of Titus **f.**
9.14. And by their prayer **f.** you
12. 8. **f.** this thing I besought the
15. spent **f.** you (*for* your souls)
19. things, dearly beloved, **f.** yo.
13. 8. against the truth, but **f.** the
Gal. 1. 4. gave himself **f.** our sins ;
  Tit.2.14
2.20. me, and gave himself **f.** me
3.13. being made a curse **f.** us : for
Eph. 1.16. Cease not to give thanks **f.**
3. 1. prisoner of Jesus Christ **f.**
13. at my tribulations **f.** you
5. 2. and hath given himself **f.** us
20. thanks always **f.** all things
25. church, and gave himself **f.**
6.19. And **f.** me, that utterance
20. **f.** which I am an ambassador
Phi. 1. 4. in every prayer of mine **f.**
Col. 1. 7. who is **f.** you a faithful min.
9. do not cease to pray **f.** you
24. rejoice in my sufferings **f.**
4.12. labouring fervently **f.** you in
13. that he hath a great zeal **f.**
¹Th. 5.10. Who died **f.** us, that, whether
²Th. 1. 4. **f.** your patience and faith in
5. kingdom of God, **f.** which ye
¹Ti. 2. 1. of thanks, be made **f.** all men
2. **f.** kings, and for all that are
6. Who gave him. a ransom **f.**
Heb. 2. 9. should taste death **f.** every
5. 1. is ordained **f.** men in things
  gifts and sacrifices **f.** sins
3. so also for himself, to offer **f.**
6.20. the forerunner is **f.** us enter.
7.25. liveth to make intercess. **f.**
27. first **f.** his own sins, and
9. 7. which he offered **f.** himself
24. in the presence of God **f.** us
10.12. had offered one sacrifice **f.**
13.17. for they watch **f.** your souls
Jas. 5.16. and pray one **f.** another, that
¹Pet. 2.21. Christ also suffered **f.** us ; 4.1
3.18. the just **f.** the unjust, that
¹Jo. 3.16. he had laid down his life **f.**
  to lay down our lives **f.** the
dia. [*accu.*]
Mat.27.18 **f.** envy they had delivered ;
  Mar.15.10
Mar. 2. 4. nigh unto him **f.** the press;
  Lu.8.19

Mar. 2.27. made **f.** man, and not man **f.**
    7.29. **f.** this saying go thy way
Lu. 8.47. **f.** what cause she had touch.
    23.19, 25. Who **f.** a certain sedition
Jo. 4.39. **f.** the saying of the woman
    7.13. **f.** fear of the Jews ; Jo.19.38, 20.19
    10.19. among the Jews **f.** these say.
    32. **f.** which of those works do
    16.21. **f.** joy that a man is born into
Act. 21.34. the certainty, **f.** the tumult
    35. **f.** the violence of the people
    28.20. **f.** this cause therefore have I
Ro. 1.26. **f.** this cause God gave them
    3.25. **f.** the remission of sins
    4.24. **f.** us also, to whom it shall
    25. Who was delivered **f.** our was raised again **f.** our justi.
    13. 5. be subject, not only **f.** wrath
    15.30. **f.** the L. J. Ch.'s sake, and **f.**
1Co. 7. 5. Satan tempt you not **f.** your
    26. this is good **f.** the present
    8.11. brother perish, **f.** whom Ch.
    11. 9. man created **f.** the woman ; but the woman **f.** the man
2Co. 3, 7. **f.** the glory of his countena.
    9.14. **f.** the exceeding grace of G.
Eph. 2. 4. **f.** his great love wherewith
Phil. 1.24. flesh is more needful **f.** you
    2.30. Because **f.** the work of Chri
    3. 7. those I counted loss **f.** Christ
    8. **f.** the excellency of the kno. **f.** whom I have suffered the
Col. 1. 5. **f.** the hope which is laid up
    4. 3. **f.** which I am also in bonds
2Ti. 1.12. **f.** the which cause I also
Heb. 1.14. sent forth to minister **f.** them
    2. 9. **f.** the suffering of death
    10. **f.** whom are all things, and
    11. **f** which cause he is not ash.
    5.12. **f.** the time ye ought to be
    7.18. **f.** the weakness and unprofi.
1Pet. 1.20. in these last times **f.** you
    2.19. a man **f.** conscience toward
Rev. 1. 9. **f.** the word of God, and **f.**
    4.11. **f.** thy pleasure they are and
    6. 9. **f.** the word of God, and **f.**
    18.10, 15. afar off **f.** the fear of her
    20. 4. **f.** the witn. of Jesus, and **f.**
peri.
Mat. 2. 8. search diligently **f.** the young
    6.28. take ye thought **f.** raiment
    22.16. neither carest thou **f.** any
    26.28. is shed **f.** many ; Mar.14.24
Mar.1.44. offer **f.** thy cleansing ; Lu.5.14
    12.14. and carest **f.** no man : for
Lu. 2.27. to do **f.** him after the custom
    3.19. reproved by him **f.** Herodias and **f.** all the evils which He.
    4.38. they besought him **f.** her
    12.26. why take ye thought **f.** the
    19.37. **f.** all the mighty works that
    22.32. I have prayed **f.** thee, that
Jo. 9.21. he shall speak **f.** himself
    10.13. and careth not **f.** the sheep
    33. **f.** a good work we stone thee not ; but **f.** blasphemy
    12. 6. not that he cared **f.** the poor
    15.22. they have no cloke **f.** their
    16.26. I will pray the Father **f.** you
    17. 9. I pray **f.** them : I pray not **f.** but **f.** them which thou hast
    20. Neither pray I **f.** these alone but **f.** them also which shall
    19.24. but cast lots **f.** it, whose
Act. 8.15. prayed **f.** them, that they
    19.40. **f.** this day's uproar, there
    24.10. cheerfully answer **f.** myself
    21. Except it be **f.** this one voice
Ro. 8. 3. likeness of sinful flesh, and **f.**
Eph.6.18. and supplication **f.** all saints
Col. 1. 3. pray. always **f.** you ; 2Th.1.11

Col. 2. 1. great conflict I have **f.** you
    4. 3. praying also **f.** us, that God
1Th. 1. 2. always **f.** you all ; 1Th.1.3,2.13
    3. 9. render to God again **f.** you
    5.25. Brethren, pray **f.** us ; 2Th.3.1 ; Heb.13.18
Phile. 10. I beseech thee **f.** my son One.
Heb.5. 3. as **f.** the people, so also **f.**
    10. 6. offerings and sacrifices **f.** sin
    8. and offering **f.** sin thou would.
    18, 26. no more offering **f.** sin
    11.40. some better thing **f.** us, that
    13.11. by the high priest **f.** sin
1Pet.3.18. hath once suffered **f.** sins
    5. 7. upon him ; for he careth **f.**
1Jo. 2. 2. the propitiation **f.** our sins and not **f.** ours only, but also **f.** the sins of the
    4.10. the propitiation **f.** our sins
    5.16. say that he shall pray **f.** it
epi.
Mat.19. 9. except it be **f.** fornication
Mar. 3. 5. grieved **f.** the hardness of
Lu. 2.20. **f.** all the things that they
    7.44. gavest me no water **f.** my
    13.17. **f.** all the glorious things that
    18. 4. he would not **f.** a while
    23.28. weep not **f.** me, but weep **f.** yourselves and **f.** your child.
Jo. 19.24. **f.** my vesture they did cast
Act. 4.21. glorified God **f.** that which
    15.14. of them a people **f.** his name
    31. they rejoiced **f.** the consolat.
    20.38. **f.** the words which he spake
    26. 6. **f.** the hope of the promise
1Co. 1. 4. **f.** the grace of God which is
2Co. 7.13. **f.** the joy of Titus, because
    9.13. **f.** your professed subjection
    15. God **f.** his unspeakable gift
Phi. 1. 5. **f.** your fellowship in the gos.
    3.12. that **f.** which also I am appre.
    14. **f.** the prize of the high calli.
1Th. 3. 9. **f.** all the joy wherewith we
Heb.12.10. he **f.** our profit, that we
Jas. 5. 1. **f.** your miseries that shall
    7. hath long patience **f.** it, until
1Pet.1.13. hope to the end **f.** the grace
Rev.18. 9. bewail her, and lament **f.** her
pros.
Mat.26.12. body, she did it **f.** my burial
Mar.10. 5. **f.** the hardness of your heart
Lu. 8.13. which **f.** a while believe, and
Jo. 5.35. ye were willing **f.** a season
Act. 3.10. which sat **f.** alms at the
    13.15. of exhortation **f.** the people
    27.34. for this is **f.** your health
1Co. 7. 5. except it be with consent **f.** a
    35. this I speak **f.** your own but **f.** that which is comely
    10.11. are written **f.** our admonition
2Co. 2.16. who is sufficient **f.** these
    7. 8. though it were but **f.** a season
Gal. 2. 5. no, not **f.** an **our** ; that the
Eph. 4.12. **f.** the perfecting of the saints
1Ti. 1.16. **f.** a pattern to them which
2Ti. 3.16. profitab. **f.** doctrine, **f.** reproof **f.** correction, **f.** instruction
Phile. 15. he therefore departed **f.** a
Heb.12.10. they verily **f.** a few days
    11. no chastening **f.** the present
Jas. 4.14. that appeareth **f.** a little time
apo.
Mat.13.44. **f.** joy thereof goeth and sell.
    14.26. and they cried out **f.** fear
    28. 4. **f.** fear of him the keepers did
Lu. 19. 3. could not **f.** the press, beca.
    21.26. hearts failing them **f.** fear
    22.45. them sleeping **f.** sorrow
    24.41. yet believed not **f.** joy, and
Jo. 21. 6. to draw it **f.** the multitude of
Act. 12. 6. opened not the gate **f.** glad.
    21.11. I could not see **f.** the glory

anti.
Mat.5.38. An eye **f.** an eye, and a tooth
    17.27. give unto them **f.** me and
    20.28. a ransom **f.** many ; Mar.10.45
Lu. 11.11. **f.** a fish give him a serpent
Jo. 1.16. all we received, and grace **f.**
Ro.12.17. no man evil **f.** evil ; 1Th.5.15
    1 Pet.3.9
1Co.11.15. her hair is given her **f.** a cov.
Eph.5.31. **f.** this cause shall a man leave
Heb.12.2. who **f.** the joy that was set
    16. who **f.** one morsel of meat
en.
Mat. 6. 7. heard **f.** their much speaking
Lu. 1.44. leaped in my womb **f.** joy
Phi. 1.26. abundant in Jesus Ch. **f.** me
1Ti. 5.10. Well reported of **f.** good works
Jas. 5. 3. treasure together **f.** the last
1Pet.4.14. reproached **f.** the name of Ch.
hōs.
Mat.21.46. they took him **f.** a prophet
1Pet. 2.16. using your liberty **f.** a cloke
ek.
Mat.20.2. labourers **f.** a penny a day
Rev.16.10. gnawed their tongues **f.** pain
achri.
Lu. 4.13. departed from him **f.** a seas.
Act.13.11. not seeing the sun **f.** a seas.
heneka.
Act.28.20. that **f.** the hope of Israel
Ro.14.20. **f.** meat, destroy not the work
kata.
Mat.19.3. away his wife **f.** every cause
houtō.
1Co.14.21. and yet **f.** *all that* will they
    (See words in connection.)

FOR, [*conjunction.*]
    gar *and* **hoti.**
Mat.1.20. **f.** that which is concei. (gar.)
    21. **f.** he shall save his peo. (gar.)
    2. 5, 6. **f.** thus it is written (gar.)
    13. **f.** Herod will seek the (gar.)
    20. they are dead that (gar.)
    8. 2. **f.** the kingd. of h. ; 4.17 (gar.)
    3. **f.** this is he that was sp. (gar.)
    9. **f.** I say unto you (gar.)
    15. **f.** thus it becometh us (gar.)
    4. 6, 10. **f.** it is written (gar.)
    18. **f.** they were fishers (gar.)
    5. 3. **f.** theirs is the kingd. (hoti)
    4. **f.** they ; 5, 6, 7, 8, 9, 10 (hoti)
    12. **f.** great is your reward (hoti)
    f. so persecuted they (gar.)
    (And in all other passages in which it occurs except the following :—)
dioti.
Lu. 1.13. **f.** thy prayer is heard : and
    21.28. **f.** your redemption draweth
Act.10.20. doubting nothing : **f.** I have
    18.10. **f.** I am with thee, and no man **f.** I have much people in this
    22.18. **f.** they will not receive thy
Gal. 2.16. **f.** by the works of the law
1Pet. 1 24. **f.** all flesh is as grass, and all
epei.
Ro. 3. 6. **f.** *then* how shall God judge
1Co. 5.10. **f.** *then* must ye needs go out
Heb.9.26. **f.** *then* must he often have
    10. 2. **f.** *then* would they not have
epeidē.
Lu. 11. 6. **f.** a friend of mine in his
1Co. 1.22. **f.** the Jews require a sign
Phi. 2.26. **f.** he longed after you all
anti.
Jas. 4.15. **f.** that ye ought to say
epi.
Ro. 5.12. **f.** that all have sinned
hina.
Mar. 3.10. pressed upon him **f.** *to touch*
Jo. 10.10. cometh not, but **f.** *to steal*

105

Act. 17.15. f. *to* come to him with all
  22. 5. unto Jerusalem, f. *to* be
Eph. 2.15. f. *to* make in himself of
Rev. 9.15. f. *to* slay the third part of
  12. 4. f. *to* devour her child as soon
  pros.
Mat.23. 5. they do f. to be seen of men

FORASMUCH.
ei.
Act. 11.17. f. then *as* God gave them
  epeidē.
Act. 15.24. f. *as* we have heard, that
  epei.
¹Co. 14.12. f. *as* ye are zealous of spirit.
Heb. 2.14. f. then *as* the children are
  epeidēper.
Lu. 1. 1. f. *as* many have taken

FORBEAR,   -ing.
mē.
¹Co. 9. 6. to f. working (*not* to work)
  pheidomai.
²Co.12. 6. I f., lest any man should
  anechomai.
Eph.4. 2. f-*ing* one another; Col.3.13
  aniēmi.
Eph. 6. 9. unto them, f-*ing* threatening
  stegō.
¹Th. 3.1, 5. *when* we *could* no longer f.

FORBEARANCE.
anochē.
Ro. 2. 4. riches of his goodness and f.
  3.25. past, through the f. of God

FORBID, -en, -eth, -ing, -bade.
kōluō.   [Lu.18.16
Mat.19.14. and f. them not; Mar.10.14;
Mar. 9.38. and we f-*a* him; Lu.9.49
  39. Jesus said, f. him not; Lu.9.50
Lu. 6.29. f. not to take thy coat also
  23. 2. f-*ing* to give tribute to Cesar
Act.10.47. Can any man f. water, that
  16. 6. *and were* f-*en* of the H. Ghost
  24.23. and that he should f. none
¹Co. 14.39. and f. not to speak with
¹Th. 2.16. f-*ing* us to speak to the Gent.
¹Ti. 4. 3. f-*ing* to marry, and command.
²Pet. 2.16. f-*a* the madness of the prophet
⁵John 10. and f-*eth* them that would
  diakōluō.
Mat.3.14. John f-*a* him, saying, I have
  akōlutōs.
Act.28.31. confidence, *no man* f-*ing* him
  mē ginomai.
Lu.20.16 God f. (*let it not be*); Ro.3.4,6,31,
  6.2,15, 7.7,13, 9.14, 11.1,11;
  ¹Co.6.15; Gal.2.17,21, 6.14

FORCE.
harpazō.
Mat.11.12. the violent *take* it *by* f.
Jo. 6.15. come and *take* him *by* f.
Act. 23.10. *to* take him *by* f. from among
  bebaios.
Heb. 9.17. a testament is *of* f. after men

FOREFATHERS.
progonos.
²Ti 1. 3. whom I serve from my f.

FOREHEAD,   -s.
metōpon.
Rev. 7. 3. servants of our God in their f-*s*
  9. 4. not the seal of God in their f-*s*
  13.16. right hand, or in their f-*s*
  14. 1. name writ. in their f-*s*; 22.4
  9. *and* receive his mark in his f.
  17. 5 And upon her f. was a name
  20. 4 his mark upon their f-*s*

FOREIGNERS.
paroikos,
Eph.2.19. are no more strangers and f.
106

FOREKNOW,   -knew.
proginōskō.
Ro. 8.29. For whom he did f., he also
  11. 2. away his people which he f-*e*

FOREKNOWLEDGE.
prognōsis.
Act. 2.23. counsel and f. of God, ye
¹Pet.1. 2. Elect according to the f. of

FOREORDAINED.
proginōskō.
¹Pet.1.20. *Who* verily was f. before

FOREPART.
prōra.
Act.27.41. the f. stuck fast and remained

FORERUNNER.
prodromos.
Heb.6.20. Whither the f. is for us ent.

FORESEEING,   -saw.
proeideō.
Gal. 3. 8. And the scripture, f. that
  prooraō.
Act. 2.25. I f-*a* the Lord always before

FORESHIP.
prōra.
Act.27.30. cast anchors out of the f.

FORETELL,   -told.
proereō.
Mar 13.23. I have f-*o* you all things
  prokatanggellō.
Act. 3.24. have likewise f-*o* of these days
  prolegō.
²Co. 13.2. and f. you, as if I were present

FOREWARN,   -ed.
hupodeiknumi.
Lu. 12. 5. But I *will* f. you whom ye
  proepō.
¹Th. 4. 6. as we also *have* f-*ed* you and

FORGET,   -eth, -ing, -gotten.
epilanthanomai.
Mat.16.5. had f-*en* to take bread ;
  Mar.8.14
Lu. 12. 6. not one of them is f-*en* before
Phi. 3.13. f-*ing* those things which are
Heb.6.10. *to* f. your work and labour
  13.16. and to communicate f. not
Jas. 1.24. f-*eth* what manner of man
  eklanthanomai.
Heb.12.5. ye *have* f-*en* the exhortation
  lambanō lēthē.
²Pet. 1.9. *hath* f-*en* that he was purged

FORGETFUL,
epilanthanomai.
Heb.13.2. *Be* not f. to entertain strangers
  epilēsmonē.
Jas.1.25. not a f. hearer (*of forgetfulness*)

FORGIVE, -eth, -en, -ing, -gave.
apoluō.
Lu.6.37. f., and ye *shall* be f-*en*
  aphiēmi.
Mat.6.12. f. us our debts, as we f. ; Lu.11.4
  14. For if ye f. men their trespas.
  heavenly Father *will* also f.
  15. ye f. not men their; Mar.11.26
  will your Father f. your tres. ;
  Mar.11.26
  9. 2, 5. thy sins *be* f-*en* thee ;
  Mar.2.5,9; Lu.5.20,23, 7.48
  6. power on earth *to* f. sins ;
  Mar.2.10; Lu.5.24
  12.31, 32. blasphemy *shall* be f-*en* ;
  Mar.3.28
  shall not be f-*en* unto men ;
  Lu.12.10
  18.21. sin against me, and I f. him

Mat.18.27.loosed him, and f-*a* him the
  32. I f-*a* thee all that debt, beca.
  35. f. not every one his brother
Mar.2. 7. who can f. sins but God ;
  Lu.5.21
  4. 12. their sins *should be* f-*en* them
  11.25. f. if ye have ought against
  may f. you your trespasses
Lu. 7.47. sins, which are many, *are* f-*en*
  to whom little *is* f-*en*, the
  49. Who is this that f-*eth* sins
  17. 3, 4. if he repent, f. him
  23.34. said Jesus, Father, f. them
Act. 8.22. of thine heart *may be* f-*en*
Ro. 4. 7. they whose iniquities *are* f-*en*
Jas. 5.15. sins, they *shall* be f-*en* him
¹Jo. 1. 9. faithful and just to f. us our
  2.12. because your sins *are* f-*en*
  charizomai.
Lu. 7.42. he *frankly* f-*a* them both
  43. he, to whom he f-*a* most
²Co. 2. 7. ye ought rather to f. him
  10. To whom ye f. any thing
  I f-*a* any thing, to whom I f-*a*
  12.13. to you, f. me this wrong
Eph.4.32. f-*ing* one another; Col.3.13
  Christ's sake *hath* f-*en* you ;
  Col.3.13
Col. 2.13. *having* f-*en* you all trespasses

FORGIVENESS.
aphesis.
Mar.3.29. hath never f., but is in danger
Act. 5.31. repentance to Israel, and f. of
  13.38. preached unto you the f. of
  26.18. may receive f. of sins
Eph.1. 7. the f. of sins, according ;
  Col.1.14

FORM, [*noun.*]
morphē.
Mar.16.12. he appeared in another f.
Phi. 2. 6. Who being in the f. of God
  7. took upon him the f. of a
  morphōsis.
Ro. 2.20. which hast the f. of knowled.
²Ti. 3. 5. Having a f. of godliness, but
  tupos.
Ro. 6.17. that f. of doctrine which was
  hupotupōsis.
²Ti. 1.13. Hold fast the f. of sound wo.

FORM, [*verb,*]   -ed.
plassō.
Ro. 9.20. say to him *that* f-*ed* it, Why
¹Ti. 2.13. For Adam *was* first f-*ed*, then
  morphoō.
Gal. 4.19. until Christ be f-*ed*, in you
  plasma.
Ro. 9.20. shall the *thing* f-*ed* say to him

FORMER.
prōtos.
Act. 1. 1. The f. treatise have I made
Rev. 21.4. the f. things are passed away
  proteron.
Heb.10.32. to remembrance the f. days
¹Pet. 1.14. according to the f. lusts
  proteros.
Eph.4.22. concerning the f. conversation

FORNICATION,   -s.
porneia.
Mat.5.32. saving for the cause of f. ; 19.9
  15.19. adulter., f-*s*, thefts ; Mar.7.21
Jo. 8.41. We be not born of f. ; we
Act.15.20,29. and from f., and ; 21.25
Ro. 1.29. f., wickedness, covetousness
¹Co. 5. 1. that there is f. among you
  and such f. as is not so much
  6.13. Now the body is not for f.
  18. Flee f. Every sin that
  7. 2. to avoid f., let every
²Co.12.21.and f. and lasciviousness

Gal. 5.19. **f.**, uncleanness ; Eph.5.3 ;
     Col.3.5
¹Th. 4. 3. ye should abstain from **f.**
Rev. 2.21. to repent of her **f.**; and she
     9.21. nor of their **f.**, nor of their
     14. 8. wine of the wrath of her **f.**;18.3
     17. 2. drunk with the wine of her **f.**
     4. and filthiness of her **f.**
     19. 2. corrupt the earth with her **f.**
     porneuō.
¹Co. 6.18. but he that commiteth **f.**
     10. 8. Neither let us commit **f.**, as
Rev.2.14, 20. unto idols, and to commit **f.**
     17. 2. earth have committed **f.**; 18.3
     18. 9. who have committed **f.** and
     ekporneuō.
Jude   7. giving themselves over to **f.**

FORNICATOR,   -s.
     pornos.
¹Co. 5. 9, 10. not to company with **f-s**
     11. is called a brother be a **f.**, or
     6. 9. neither **f-s**, nor idolaters, nor
Heb.12.16.Lest there be any **f.**, or prof.

FORSAKE. -eth,-en,-ing,-sook.
     engkataleipō.   [Mar.15.34
Mat.27.46. why hast thou **f-ēn** me ;
²Co. 4. 9. Persecuted, but not **f-en**
²Ti. 4.10. Demas hath **f-en** me, having
     16. with me, but all men **f-o** me
Heb.10.25. Not **f-ing** the assembling of
     13. 5. never leave thee, nor **f.** thee
     kataleipō.
Heb.11.27. By faith he **f-o** Egypt, not
²Pet. 2.15. which have **f-en** the right
     aphiēmi.
Mat.19.27. Behold, we have **f-en** all
     29. every one that hath **f-en** ho.
     26.56. disci. **f-o** him, and fled ;
              Mar.14.50
Mar.1. 18. straightway they **f-o** their
Lu. 5. 11. they **f-o** all, and followed
     apo tassō.
Lu.14.33. that **f-eth** not all that he hath
     apostasia.
Act.21.21. the Gentiles to **f.** Moses

FORSOMUCH.
     kathoti.
Lu.19. 9. house, **f.** as he also is a son

FORSWEAR.
     epiorkeō.
Mat.5.33. Thou shalt not **f.** thyself

FORTH.
     exō.
Jo. 11.43. loud voice, Lazarus, come **f.**
     15. 6. he is cast **f.** as a branch, and
     19. 4. Pilate therefore went **f.** again
         I bring him **f.** to you that, ye
     5. Then came Jesus **f.**, wearing
     13. he brought Jesus **f.**, and sat
Act. 5.34. to put the apostles **f.** a little
     9.40. Peter put them all **f.**, and
     ek.
Jas. 3.11. send **f.** at the same place
     eisho mesos
Mar.3. 3. the withered hand, stand **f.**
     apo.
Mat.16.21. From that time **f.** began Je.
     (See words in connection.)

FORTHWITH.
     eutheōs.
Mat.13. 5. **f.** they sprung up, because
     26.49. And **f.** he came to Jesus, and
Mar. 1.29. **f.**, when they were come out
     43. him, and **f.** sent him away
     5.13. **f.** Jesus gave them leave
Act. 12.10. **f.** the angel departed from
     21.30. and **f.** the doors were shut

     euthus.
Jo. 19.34. **f.** came thereout blood and
Act. 9.18. and he received sight **f.**, and

FORTY.
     tessarakonta.
Mat.4. 2. he had fasted **f.** days and **f.**
Mar.1.13. in the wilderness **f.** days ;
           Lu.4.2
Jo. 2.20. **f.** and six years was this
Act. 1. 3. being seen of them **f.** days
     4.22. the man was above **f** years
     7.30. And when **f.** years were expi.
     36, 42. and in the wilderness **f.**
     13.21. by the space of **f.** years
     23.13. they were more than **f** which
     21. of them more than **f.** men
²Co.11.24. received I **f.** stripes save one
Heb.3. 9. and saw my works **f.** years
     17. whom was he grieved **f.** years
Rev.7. 4. an hundred and **f.** and four ;
          14.1,3
     11. 2. foot **f.** and two months ; 13.5
     21.17. an hundred and **f.** and four
     tessarakontaetēs.
Act. 7.23. when he was full **f.** years old
     13.18. about the time of **f.** years

FORWARD.
     thelō.
²Co. 8.10. but also to be **f.** a year ago
     spoudazō.
Gal.2.10. which I also was **f.** to do
     spoudaios.
²Co.8.17. but being more **f.**, of his own
     (See words in connection.)

FORWARDNESS.
     spoudē.
²Co. 8. 8. by occasion of the **f.** of others
     prothumia.
²Co. 9. 2. I know the **f.** of your mind

FOUL.
     akathartos.
Mar.9.25. he rebuked the **f.** spirit
Rev. 18.2. the hold of every **f.** spirit
     cheimōn.
Mat.16.3. It will be **f.** weather to day

FOUND, (See Find,)   -ed.
     themelioō.
Mat.7.25. it was **f-ed** upon a ; Lu.6.48
     ginomai.
²Co. 7.14. before Titus, is **f.** a truth

FOUNDATION,   -s.
     themelios.
Lu. 6. 48. laid the **f.** on a rock: And
     49. without a **f.**, built an house
     14.29. after he had laid the **f.**, and
Act. 16.26. the **f-s** of the prison were
Ro. 15.20. build upon another man's **f.**
¹Co. 3. 10. I have laid the **f.**, and ano.
     11. For other **f.** can no man lay
     12. upon this **f.**, gold, silver
Eph. 2.20. upon the **f.** of the apostles
¹Ti. 6. 19. for themselves a good **f.** aga.
²Ti. 2. 19. the **f.** of God standeth sure
Heb. 6. 1. not laying again the **f.** of
     11.10. a city which hath **f-s**, whose
Rev.21.14. wall of the city had twelve **f-s**
     19. the **f-s** of the wall of the
        The first **f.** was jasper ; the
     katabolē
Mat.13.35. from the **f.** of the wo.; 25.34
         Lu.11.50; Heb.4.3; Rev.13.8,
         17.8
Jo. 17.24. thou lovedst me before the **f.**
Eph. 1. 4. chosen us in him before the **f.**

Heb. 9.26. have suffered before the **f.**
¹Pet.1. 20. foreordained before the **f.**
     themelioō.
Heb.1.10. hast laid the **f.** of the earth

FOUNTAIN,   -s.
     pēgē.
Mar.5.29. the **f.** of her blood was dried
Jas. 3.11. Doth a **f.** send forth at the
     12. so can no **f.** both yield salt
Rev.7.17. unto living **f-s** of waters: and
     8.10. rivers, and upon the **f-s** of
     14. 7. the sea, and the **f-s** of waters
     16. 4. upon the rivers and **f-s** of
     21. 6. of the **f.** of the water of life

FOUR.
     tessares.   [Mar.13.27
Mat.24.31. elect from the **f.** winds ;
Mar. 2. 3. palsy, which was borne of **f.**
Lu. 2.37. of about fourscore and **f**
Jo. 11.17. lain in the grave **f.** days
     19.23. **f.** parts, to every soldier a
Act.10.11. sheet knit at the **f.** corners
     11. 5. down from heaven by **f.**
     12. 4. delivered him to **f.** quatern.
     21. 9. the same man had **f.** daugh.
     23. We have **f.** men which have
     27.29. cast **f.** anchors out of the
Rev. 4. 4. were **f.** and twenty seats
        f. and twenty elders; 10,5.14,
        11.16
     6. **f.** beasts full of eyes before
     8. And the **f.** beasts had each
     5. 6. of the throne and of the **f.**
     8. the **f.** beasts and **f.** and; 19.4
     14. And the **f.** beasts said, Amen
     6. 1. one of the **f.** beasts ; 15.7
     6. in the midst of the **f.** beasts
     7. 1. after these things I saw **f.**
        on the **f.** corners of the earth
        holding the **f.** winds of the
     2. with a loud voice to the **f.**
     4. and forty and **f.** thousand ;
        14.1,3
     11. about the elders and the **f.**
     9.13. I heard a voice from the **f.**
     14, 15. Loose the **f** angels which
     14. 3. and before the **f.** beasts
     20. 8. are in the **f.** quarters of the
     21.17. hundred and forty and **f.**
     tetartos.
Act.10.30. **f.** days ago I was fasting
     tetartaios.
Jo.11.39. he hath been dead **f.** days
     tetramēnon.
Jo.4.35. There are yet **f.** months
     (See Hundred, Thousand.)

FOURFOLD.
     tetraploos.
Lu.19.8. accusation, I restore him **f.**

FOURFOOTED.
     tetrapous.
Act.10.12. of **f.** beasts of the earth ; 11.6
Ro. 1.23. **f.** beasts, and creeping things

FOURSCORE.
     ogdoēkonta.
Lu. 2.37. a widow of about **f.** and four
     16. 7. Take thy bill, and write **f.**

FOUR-SQUARE.
     tetragōnos.
Rev.21.16. the city lieth **f.**, and the

FOURTEEN.
     dekatessares.
Mat.1.17. are **f.** generations
²Co.12. 2. man in Christ, about **f.** years
Gal. 2. 1. **f.** years after I went up again
                     107

FOURTEENTH.
tessareskaidekatos.
Act.27.27. when the f. night was come
33. This day is the f. day that

FOURTH.
tetartos.   [Mar.6.48
Mat.14.25. the .f watch of the night;
Rev. 4. 7. f. beast was like a flying eagle
6. 7. opened the f. seal, I heard
of the f. beast say, Come
8. over the f. part of the earth
8.12. And the f. angel sounded
16. 8. the f. angel poured out his
21.19. chalcedony; the f., an emer.

FOWLS.
peteinon.
Mat. 6.26. Behold the f. of the air: for
13. 4. the f. came and devoured
Mar. 4. 4,32. and the f. of the air came;
Lu.8.5,13.19;Act.10.12,11.6
Lu. 12.24. are ye better than the f.
orneon.
Rev.19.17. saying to all the f. that fly
21. all the f. were filled with

FOX,   -es.
alōpēx.
Mat.8.20. f-es have holes, and ; Lu.9.58
Lu.13.32. Go ye, and tell that f., Behold

FRAGMENTS.
klasma.
Mat.14.20. they took up of the f. that ;
Mar.6.43; Lu.9.17; Jo.6.13
Mar. 8.19, 20. many baskets full of f.

FRAMED.
sunarmologeō.
Eph.2.21. building fitly f. together
katartizō.
Heb.11.3. worlds were f. by thy word

FRANKINCENSE.
libanos.
Mat.2.11. gifts, gold, and f., and myrrh
Rev.18.13.ointments, f., and wine, and

FRANKLY, (See *Forgive*.)

FRAUD.
apostereō.
Jas. 5. 4. which is of you kept back by f.

FREE,   -d.
eleutheros.
Mat.17.26. Then are the children f.
Jo. 8.33. thou, Ye shall be made f.
36. you free, ye shall be f.indeed
Ro. 6.20. ye were f. from righteousness
7. 3. she is f. from that law : so
1Co. 7.21. if thou mayest be made f.
22. he that is called, being f.
9. 1. an apostle? am I not f.
19. though I be f. from all men
12.13. whether we be bond or f.;
Eph.6.8
Gal. 3.28. there is neither bond nor f.
4.26. Jerusalem which is above is f.
31. bondwoman, but of the f.
Col. 3.11. Scythian, bond nor f.
1Pet. 2.16.As f., and not using your
Rev. 6.15. bondman, and every f. man
13.16. rich and poor, f. and; 19.18
eleutheroō.
Jo. 8.32, 36. the truth shall make you f.
Ro. 6.18, 22. Being then made f.from sin
8. 2. hath made me f. from the law
Gal.5. 1. where. Christ hath made us f.
dikaioō.
Ro. 6. 7. he that is dead is f-ed from sin
(See *Gift*.)
108

FREEDOM.
politeia.
Act.22.28. great sum obtained I this f.

FREELY.
dōrean.
Mat.10.8. f. ye have received, f. give
Ro. 3.24. Being justified f. by his grace
2Co.11. 7. to you the gospel of God f.
Rev.21.6. fountain of the water of life f.
22.17. him take the water of life f.
charizomai.
Ro. 8.32. how shall he not..also f. give
1Co. 2.12. things that are f. given to us
parrēsia.
Act. 2.29. let me f. speak unto you
parrēsiazomai.
Act.26.26. before whom also I speak f.

FREEMAN.
apeleutheros.
1Co. 7.22. a servant, is the Lord's f.

FREEWOMAN.
eleutheros. [fem.]
Gal. 4.22. bond maid, the other by a f.
23. he of the f. was by promise
30. heir with the son of the f.

FREQUENT.
perissoterōs.
2Co.11.23. in prisons more f., in deaths

FRESH.
glukus.
Jas. 3.12. both yield salt water and f.

FRIEND,   -s.
philos.   [Lu.7.34
Mat.11.19. a f. of publicans and sinners ;
Lu. 7. 6. the centurion sent f-s to him
11. 5. Which of you shall have a f.
f., lend me three loaves
6. For a f. of mine in his jour.
8. give him, because he is his f.
12. 4. And I say unto you my f-s
14.10. f., go up higher : then shalt
12. call not thy f-s, nor thy bret.
15. 6, 9. calleth together his f-s and
29. might make merry with my f-s
16. 9. Make to yourselves f-s of the
21.16. brethren,and kinsfolks,and f-s
23.12. and Herod were made f-s
Jo. 3. 29. but the f. of the bridegroom
11.11. Our f. Lazarus sleepeth
15.13. lay down his life for his f-s
14. Ye are my f-s, if ye do what.
15. but I have called you f-s
19.12. go, thou art not Cesar's f.
Act.10.24. his kinsmen and near f-s
19.31. of Asia, which were his f-s
27. 3. to go unto his f-s to refresh
Jas. 2.23. and he was called the f. of
4. 4. therefore will be a f. of the
3John 14. f-s salute thee. Greet the f-s
hetairos.
Mat.20.13. f., I do thee no wrong : didst
22.12. f., how camest thou in hith
26.50. f., wherefore art thou come
sos.
Mar.5.19. Go home to thy f-s, and tell
ho para autos.
Mar.3.21. when his f-s heard of it
peithō.
Act.12.20. having made Blastus..f.

FRIENDSHIP.
philia.
Jas. 4. 4. that the f. of the world is

FROGS.
batrachos.
Rev.16.13. three unclean spirits like f

FROM.
apo.
Mat.1.17. all the generations f. Abrah.
f. David..f. the carrying
21. save his people f. their sins
(And other passages except the
following :—)
ek.
Mat.3.17. a voice f. heaven, saying ;
Mar.1.11 ; Lu.3.22
12.42. f. the uttermost parts of ;
Lu.11.31
13.49. the wicked f. among the just
15.18. out of the mouth come forth f.
16. 1. them a sign f. heav.; Lu.11.16
17. 9. risen again f. the dead ;
Mar.6.14.16, 9.9 ; Lu.9.7 ;
Jo.2.22,21.14 ; Act.17.3 ;
1Co.15.20
19.12. f. their mother's womb ;
Lu.1.15 ; Act.3.2,14.8 ;
Gal.1.15
20. have I kept f. my youth up
21.25. f. heaven, or of men ;
Mar.11.30 ; Lu.20.4
If we shall say, f. heaven ;
Mar.11.31 ; Lu.20.5
24.31. his elect f. the four winds ;
Mar.13.27
28. 2. descended f. heaven, and
Mar.7.31. departing f.the coasts of Tyre
9.10. rising f. the dead should mean
10.20. have I observed f. my youth
11.20. fig tree dried up f. the roots
12.25. shall rise f. the dead ; Jo.20.9
16. 3. roll us away the stone f. the
Lu. 1.71. saved f. our enemies, and f.
78. the dayspring f. on high
10. 7. Go not f. house to house
18. Satan as lightning fall f.
12.36. he will return f. the wedding
16.31. though one rose f. the dead ;
Act.10.41
17. 7. when he is come f. the field
18.21. these have I kept f. my youth
20.35. the resurrection f. the dead ;
Act.4.2
23.55. which came with him f. Gal.
24.46. to rise f. the dead the third
49. endued with power f. on high
Jo. 1. 19. priests and Levites f. Jerusa.
32. descending f. heaven like
3.13, 31. came down f. heaven ;
6.33,38,41,42,51,58
27. it be given him f. heaven
5.24. passed f. death unto life ;
1Jo.3.14
6.23. came other boats f. Tiberias
31, 32. bread f. heaven to eat
50. which cometh down f. heaven
64. For Jesus knew f. the begin.
66. f. that time many of his
8.23. Ye are f. beneath ; I am f.
42. proceeded forth and came f.
9. 1. which was blind f. his birth
10.32. I shewed you f. my Father
12. 1. rais. f. the dead;9.17;Act.3.15,
4.10,13.30,34,17.31;Ro.4.24,
6.4,9,7.4,8.11,10.9 ; Gal.1.1;
Eph.1.20 ; Col.2.12; 2Ti.2.8;
Heb.11.19 ; 1Pet.1.21
27. Father, save me f. this hour
28. came there a voice f. heaven
32. if I be lifted up f. the earth
13. 4. He riseth f. supper, and laid
17.15. shouldest keep them f. the
18. 3. f. the chief priests and Phar.
19.12. f. thenceforth Pilate sought
23. woven f. the top throughout
20. 1. stone taken away f. the sep.

Act. 1.25. **f.** which Judas by transgres.
2. 2. there came a sound **f.** heaven
3.23. destroyed **f.** *among* the peop.
7. 3. country, and **f.** thy kindred
11. 5. a great sheet, let down **f.** hea.
9. answered me again **f.** heaven
12. 7. his chains fell *off* **f.** his hands
25. and Saul returned **f.** Jerusal.
15.24. certain which went *out* **f.** us
29. **f.** which if ye keep yourselves
17.33. Paul departed **f.** among them
18. 1. Paul departed **f.** Athens, and
2. all Jews to depart **f.** Rome
22. 6. there shone **f.** heaven a great
23.10. by force **f.** among them, and
26. 4. My manner of life **f.** my you.
17. Delivering these **f.** the people
23. first that should rise **f.** the
27.34. not an hair fall **f.** the head
28.17. was I delivered prisoner **f.**
Ro. 1.17. revealed **f.** faith to faith
6.13. those that are alive **f.** the
17. ye have obeyed **f.** the heart
7.24. deliver me **f.** the body of this
10. 7. bring up Christ again **f.** the
11.15. them be, but life **f.** the dead
1Co. 5. 2. be taken away **f.** among you
13. put away **f.** *among* yourselves
9.19. though I be free **f.** all men
15.12. that he rose **f.** the dead, how
47. the second man is the Lord **f.**
2Co. 1.10. delivered us **f.** so great a dea.
3. 1. letters of commendation **f.**
5. 2. our house which is **f.** heaven
8. rather to be absent **f.** the body
6.17. come out **f.** among them
Gal. 1. 4. **f.** this present evil world
8. though we, or an angel **f.** hea.
3.13. hath redeemed us **f.** the curse
Eph.4.16. **f.** whom the whole body
5.14. that sleepest, and arise **f.** the
6. 6. the will of God **f.** the heart
Phi. 3.20. **f.** whence also we look for
Col. 1.13. delivered us **f.** the power of
18. the firstborn **f.** the dead
2.19. **f.** which all the body by joints
4.16. read the epistle **f.** Laodicea
1Th. 1.10. **f.** heaven, whom he raised **f.**
Heb.5. 1. high priest taken **f.** *among*
7. able to save him **f.** death
7. 6. descent is not counted **f.** them
13.20. **f.** the dead our Lord Jesus
Jas. 5.20. the sinner **f.** the error of his
way shall save a soul **f.** death
1Pet.1. 3. of Jesus Christ **f.** the dead
18. **f.** your vain conversation
2Pet.1.18. this voice which came **f.** hea.
2.21. turn **f.** the holy command.
1Jo. 2.19. They went out **f.** us, but
Rev.3.10. thee **f.** the hour of temptation
8.10. fell a great star **f.** heaven; 9.1
9.13. I heard a voice **f.** the four
10. 1. come down **f.**; 20.1,13.13,18.1
4, 8. I heard a voice **f.** heaven ;
11.12,14.2,13,18.4
11.11. the Spirit of life **f.** God
14.13. they may rest **f.** their labours
18. angel came out **f.** their altar
15. 8. **f.** the glory of God, and **f.** his
para.
Mar.12.2. might receive **f.** the husband.
14.43. **f.** the chief priests and
Lu. 1.45. which were told her **f.** the
2. 1. there went out a decree **f.**
8.49. **f.** the ruler of the synagogue's
Jo. 1. 6. a man sent **f.** God, whose
5.34. I receive not testimony **f.** man
41. I receive not honour **f.** men
44. honour that cometh **f.** God
7.29. I am **f.** him, and he hath
15.26. send unto you **f.** the Father
16.27, 28. that I came out **f.**; 17.8

Act. 9.14. authority **f.** the chief priests
22. 5. **f.** whom also I received letters
26.10, 12. authority **f.** the chief
Phi. 4.18. things which were sent **f.** you
2Pet.1.17. **f.** God the Father ; 2Jo.3,4
2John 3. and **f.** the Lord Jesus Christ
hupo.
Lu. 1.26. Gabriel was sent **f.** God
2Pet.1.17. to him **f.** the excellent glory
enggus.
Act. 1.12. **f.** Jerusalem a sabbath day's
dia.
2Th. 2. 2. nor by letter as **f.** us, as that
kata, [*accus.*]   [20.20
Act. 2.46. breaking bread **f.** house *to* ho.
(breaking bread *by* house)
(*See words in connection.*)

FROWARD.
skolios.
1Pet.2.18. and gentle, but also to the **f.**

FRUIT,   -8.
karpos.
Mat.3. 8. Bring forth..**f-s** meet; Lu.3.8
10. bringeth not forth good **f.**;
7.19; Lu.3.9.
7.16, 20.ye shall know them by their
f-s; Lu.6.44
17, 18. tree bringeth forth good **f.**
tree bringeth forth evil **f.**
12.33. tree good, and his **f.** good
tree corrupt, and his **f.** corrupt
for the tree is known by his **f.**
13. 8, 26. and brought forth **f.**
21.19. Let no **f.** grow on thee
34. when the time of the **f.** drew
might receive the **f-s** of it
41. render him the **f-s** in their
43. bringing forth the **f-s** thereof
Mar.4. 7. it, and it yielded no **f.**
8. and did yield **f.** that sprang
29. when the **f.** is brought forth
11.14. No man eat **f.**of thee hereafter
12. 2. from the husbandmen the **f.**
Lu. 1.42. blessed is the **f.** of thy womb
6.43. bringeth not forth corrupt **f.**
doth a corrupt tree..good **f.**
8. 8. sprang up, and bare **f.** an
12.17. room where to bestow my **f-s**
13. 6. he came and sought **f.** thereon
7. three years I come seeking **f.**
9. And if it bear **f.**, well
20.10. should give him of the **f.**
Jo. 4.36. and gathereth **f.** unto life ete.
12.24. bringeth forth much **f.**, 15.5.8
15. 2. that beareth not **f.** he taketh
that beareth **f.**, he purgeth
that it may bring forth more **f.**
4. As the branch cannot bear **f.**
16. should go and bring forth **f.**
and that your **f.**should remain
Act.2.30. that of the **f.** of his loins
Ro. 1.13. that I might have some **f.**
6.21. What **f.** had you then in those
22. ye have your **f.** unto holiness
15.28. have sealed to them this **f.**
1Co. 9. 7. and eateth not of the **f.**thereof
Gal. 5.22. the **f.** of the Spirit is; Eph.5.9
Phi. 1.11. Being filled with the **f-s** of
22. this is the **f.** of my labour
4.17. but I desire **f.** that may abou.
2Ti. 2. 6. be first partaker of the **f-s**
Heb.12.11.it yieldeth the peaceable **f.**of
13.15. the **f.** of our lips giving thanks
Jas. 3.17. full of mercy and good **f-s**
18. And the **f.** of righteousness
5. 7. waiteth for the precious **f.** of
18. the earth brought forth her **f.**
Rev.22.2. twelve manner of **f-s**
and yielded her **f.** every month

karpophoreō.
Mat.13.23. which also *beareth* **f.**, some
Mar. 4.20. and *bring forth* **f.**, some
28. the earth *bringeth forth* **f.** of
Lu. 8.15. keep it, and *bring forth* **f.**
Ro. 7. 4. that we *should bring forth* **f.**
5. *to bring forth* **f.**, unto death
Col. 1. 6. and *bringeth forth* **f.**,as it doth
akarpos.
Jude 12. fruit withereth, *without* **f.**
gennēma.
Mat.26.29. not drink..this **f.**of the vine ;
Mar.14.25; Lu.22.18
Lu. 12.18. will I bestow all my **f-s** and
2Co. 9.10. increase the **f-s** of your righ.
opōra.
Rev.18.14. the **f-s** that thy soul lusted
(See *Perfection, Withereth.*)

FRUITFUL.
karpophoros.
Act.14.17. and **f.** seasons, filling our
Col. 1.10. *being* **f.** in every good work

FRUSTRATE.
atheteō.
Gal.2.21. I *do not* **f.** the grace of God

FULFIL,   -ed, -ing.
plēroō.
Mat.1.22. that it *might be* **f-ed**, 2.15,23,
4.14, 8.17,12.17, 13.35, 21.4,
26.56, 27.35;Jo.12.38,15.25,
17.12, 18.9,32, 19.24,36
2.17. Then *was* **f-ed** that which was;
27.9
3.15. us *to* **f.** all righteousness
5.17. not come to destroy, but *to* **f.**
26.54. shall the scriptures *be* **f-ed**
Mar.1.15. The time *is* **f-ed**, and the
14.49. but the scriptures *must be* **f-ed**
15.28. scripture *was* **f-ed**; Jas.2.23
Lu. 1.20. which *shall be* **f-ed** in their
4.21. This day *is* this scripture **f-ed**
21.22. which are written may *be* **f-ed**
24. times of the Gentiles *be* **f-ed**
22.16. until it *be* **f-ed** in the kingdom
24.44. that all things must *be* **f-ed**
Jo. 3.29. this my joy therefore *is* **f-ed**
13.18. that the scripture *may be* **f-ed**
17.13. might have my joy **f-ed** in
Act. 1.16. must needs have been **f-ed**
3.18. suffer, he hath so **f-ed**
9.23. after that many days *were* **f-ed**
12.25. *when* they *had* **f-ed** their
13.25. as John did **f.** his course, he
27. they *have* **f-ed** them in cond.
14.26. for the work which they **f-ed**
Ro. 8. 4. the law *might be* **f-ed** in us
13. 8. another *hath* **f-ed** the law
2Co. 10.6. when your obedience *is* **f-ed**
Gal. 5.14. all the law *is* **f-ed** in one word
Phi.2. 2. **f.** ye my joy, that ye be like
Col. 1.25. for you, *to* **f.** the word of God
4.17. in the Lord, that thou **f.** it
2Th. 1.11. and **f.** all the good pleasure
Rev.6.11. as they were, should *be* **f-ed**
anaplēroō.
Mat.13.14. in them *is* **f-ed** the prophecy
Gal. 6. 2. and so **f.** the law of Christ
ekplēroō.
Act.13.33. God *hath* **f-ed** the same unto
teleō.
Act.13.29. when they *had* **f-ed** all that
Ro. 2.27. if it **f.** the law, judge thee
Gal. 5.16. ye *shall not* **f.** the lust of the
Jas. 2. 8. If ye **f.** the royal law accord.
Rev.15. 8. of the seven angels *were* **f-ed**
17.17. the words of God *shall be* **f-ed**
20. 3. thousand years *should be* **f-ed**

sunteleō.

Mar.13.4. all these things shall be f-ed
  teleioō.
Lu. 2.43. when they had f-ed the days
Jo.19.28. that the scripture might be f-ed
  poieō.
Act.13.22. which shall f. all my will
Eph. 2. 3. f-ing the desires of the flesh
Rev.17.17.to f. his will, and to agree
  ginomai.
Mat.5.18. till all be f-ed; 24.34; Lu.21.32

FULFILLING, [noun.]
  plērōma.
Ro.13.10. love is the f. of the law

FULL.
  plērēs.
Mat.14.20. twelve baskets f.; Mar.6.43
  15.37. was left seven baskets f.
Mar. 4.28. that the f. corn in the ear
  8.19. how many baskets f. of
Lu. 4. 1. f. of the Holy Ghost;
     Act.6.3,8,11.24
  5.12. behold a man f. of leprosy
Jo. 1.14. Father, f. of grace and truth
Act. 6.5,8. a man f. of faith and of
  9.36. this woman was f. of good
  13.10. O f. of all subtilty and all
  19.28. they were f. of wrath, and
2John 8. that we receive a f. reward
  plēroō.
Mat.13.48. Which, when it was f., they
Jo. 7. 8. my time is not yet f. come
  15.11. that your joy might be f.
  16.24. that your joy may be f.;
     1Jo.1.4; 2John 12
Act. 2.28. thou shalt make me f. of joy
  7.23. when he was f. forty years
Phi. 4.18. I am f., having received
  plērōma, [plural.]
Mar.8.20. how many baskets f. of frag.
  plēthō.
Lu. 1.57. Elisabeth's f. time came
  emplēthō.
Lu. 6.25. Woe unto you that are f.
  gemō.
Mat.23.25. within they are f. of extort.
  27. are within f. of dead men's
Lu. 11.39. your inward part is f. of
Ro. 3.14. Whose mouth is f. of cursing
Rev. 4. 6. f. of eyes before and behind
  8. they were f. of eyes within
  5. 8. harps, and golden vials f. of
  15. 7. f. of the wrath of God, who
  17. 3. f. of names of blasphemy
  4. cup in her hand f. of abomi.
  21. 9. seven vials f. of the seven
  mestos.
Mat.23.28. within ye are f. of hypocrisy
Jo. 19.29. was set a vessel f. of vinegar
  21.11. f. of great fishes, an hundred
Ro. 1.29. f. of envy, murder, debate
  15.14. that ye also are f. of good.
Jas. 3. 8. unruly evil, f. of deadly poi.
  17. f. of mercy and good fruits
2Pet. 2.14. Having eyes f. of adultery
  mestoō.
Act.2.13. These men are f. of new wine
  gemizō.
Mar.4.37. ship, so that it was now f.
  korennumi.
1Co. 4. 8. Now ye are f., now ye are
  helkoomai.
Lu.16.20. laid at his gate, f. of sores
  phōteinos.   [Lu.11.34,36
Mat.6.22. body shall be f. of light;
Lu. 11.36. the whole shall be f. of light

(See Age, Assurance, Darkness,
  Glory, Heaviness, Proof,
  Well.)
110

FULLER.
  gnapheus.
Mar.9. 3. so as no f. on earth can white

FULNESS.
  plērōma.
Jo. 1.16. of his f. have all we received
Ro.11.12. how much more their f.
  25. until the f. of the Gentiles
  15.29. come in the f. of the blessing
1Co.10.26,28. the Lord's, and the f. the.
Gal. 4. 4. when the f. of the time was
Eph.1.10. dispensation of the f. of times
  23. the f. of him that filleth
  3.19. filled with all the f. of God
  4.13. stature of the f. of Christ
Col. 1.19. him should all f. dwell; 2.9

FULLY.   (See connected words.)

FURLONGS.
  stadios.
Lu.24.13. threescore f.; Jo.6.19. five and
    twenty, or thirty f.
  11.18. fifteen f.; Rev.14.20. sixteen
    hundred f.; 21.16. twelve
    thousand f.

FURNACE.
  kaminos.
Mat.13.42,50. cast them into a f. of fire
Rev.1.15. as if they burned in a f.; and
  9. 2. as the smoke of a great f.

FURNISHED.
  plēthō.
Mat.22.10. wedding was f. with guests
  strōnnumi.
Mar.14.15. a large upper room f.;
    Lu.22.12
  exartizō.
2Ti. 3.17. throughly f. unto all good

FURTHER.
  eti.
Mat.26.65. what f. need have we of
Mar. 5.35. troub. thou the Master any f.
  14.63. any f. witnesses; Lu.22.71
Act. 21.28. and f. brought Greeks also
Heb. 7.11. what f. need was there that
  epi pleiōn
Act. 4.17. that it spread no f. among
  24. 4. that I be not f. tedious
2Ti. 3. 9. they shall proceed no f.
  porrō.
Lu.24.28. though he would have gone f.
  diistēmi.
Act.27.28. when they had gone a little f.
  (See Proceed, Threaten.)

FURTHERANCE.
  prokopē.
Phi.1.12. unto the f. of the gospel
  25. for your f. and joy of faith

FURTHERMORE.
  ho loipos.
1Th. 4. 1. f. then we beseech you, breth.
  eita.
Heb.12.9. f. we have had fathers of our

GAIN, [noun.]   -s.
  ergasia.
Act. 16.16. broug. her masters much g.
  19. the hope of their g-s was gone
  19.24. brought no small g. unto the
  kerdos.
Phi. 1.21. is Christ, and to die is g.
  3. 7. what things were g. to me
  kerdainō.
Jas. 4.13. and buy and sell, and get g.
  porismos.
1Ti. 6.5,6. supposing that g. is godliness
  (godliness is gain)

  pleonekteō.
2Co.12.17,18. Did I make a g. of you

GAIN, [verb.]   -ed.
  kerdainō.
Mat.16.26. if he shall g. the whole wor.;
    Mar.8.36; Lu.9.25
  18.15. thou hast g-ed thy brother
  25.17,22. he also g-ed other two
  20. I have g-ed beside them five
Act.27.21. and to have g-ed this harm
1Co. 9.19. all that I might g. the more
  20. that I might g. the Jews; to
  21. that I might g. them that are
  22. that I might g. the weak: I
  poieō.
Lu.19.18. thy pound hath g-ed five
  prosergazomai.
Lu.19.16. thy pound hath g-ed ten
  diapragmateuomai.
Lu.19.15. every man had g-ed by tradi.

GAINSAY,   -ing.
  antepō.
Lu.21.15. shall not be able to g., nor
  antilegō.
Ro.10.21. disobedient and g-ing people

GAINSAYERS.
  antilegō.
Tit. 1. 9. exhort and to convince the g.

GAINSAYING, [noun.]
  antilogia.
Jude 11. perished in the g. of Core
  anantirrētōs.
Act.10.29. came I unto you without g.

GALL.
  cholē.
Mat.27.34. to drink mingled with g.

GARDEN.
  kēpos.
Lu.13.19. and cast into his g.; and it
Jo.18. 1. where was a g., into the
  26. Did I not see thee in the g.
  19.41. there was a g.; and in the g.

GARDENER.
  kēpouros.
Jo. 20.15. supposing him to be the g.

GARLANDS.
  stemma.
Act.14.13. brought oxen and g. unto

GARMENT,   -s.
  himation.
Mat.9.16. new cloth unto an old g.;
    Mar.2.21; Lu.5.36
    fill it up taketh from the g.
  20. touched the hem of his g.;
    14.36; Mar.5.27; Lu.8.44
  21. If I may but touch his g.;
  21. 8. spread their g-s in the way;
    Mar.11.8
  23. 5. enlarge the borders of their g-s
  27.35. parted his g-s, cast.;Mar.15.24
    parted my g-s among them
Mar.6.56. were but the border of his g.
  10.50. And he, casting away his g.
  11. 7. and cast their g-s on him
  13.16. again for to take up his g.
Lu.19.35. cast their g-s upon the colt
  22.36. sell his g., and buy one
Jo.13. 4. And laid aside his g-s; and
  12. and had taken his g-s, and
  19.23. took his g-s, and made four
Act. 9.39. shewing the coats and g-s
  12. 8. Cast thy g. about thee, and
Heb.1.11. shall wax old as doth a g.
Jas. 5. 2. and your g-s are motheaten
Rev.3. 4. have not defiled their g-s
  16.15. watcheth, and keepeth his g-s

stolē.
Mar.16.5. clothed in a *long* white **g.**
    enduma.
Mat.22.11, 12. had not on a wedding **g.**
    esthēsis.
Lu. 24.4. stood by them in shining **g-s**
    chitōn.
Jude 23. hating even the **g.** spotted
    podērēs.
Rev.1.13. with a **g.** *down to the foot*

GARNER.
    apothēkē.
Mat.3.12. his wheat into the **g.**; Lu.3.17

GARNISH,   *-ed.*
    kosmeō.
Mat.12.44. empty, swept, and **g-ed** ;
    Lu.11.25
   23.29. and **g.** the sepulchres of the
Rev. 21.19. wall of the city were **g-ed**

GARRISON.
    phroureō.
²Co.11.32. *kept* the city of..*with a* **g.**

GATE,   *-s.*
    pulōn.
Lu.16.20. which was laid at his **g.**, full
Act.10.17.and stood before the **g.**, 12.14
   12.13. knocked at the door of the **g.**
   14. she opened not the **g.** for
   14.13. oxen and garlands unto the **g-s**
Rev.21.12.twelve **g-s**, and at the **g-s**
   13. east three **g-s**; north three **g-s**
    south three **g-s**; west three **g-s**
   15. and the **g-s** thereof, and the
   21. And the twelve **g-s** were twe.
    pearls; every several **g.** was
   25. And the **g-s** of it shall not be
  22.14. enter in through the **g-s** into
    pulē.
Mat.7.13. Enter ye in at the strait **g** ;
    Lu.13.24 ; for wide is the **g.**
   14. Because strait is the **g.**
   16.18. the **g-s** of hell shall not prevail
Lu. 7.12. when he came nigh to the **g.**
Act. 3.10. at the Beautiful **g.** of the
   9.24. And they watched the **g·s**
   12.10. they came unto the iron **g.**
Heb.13.12.suffered without the **g.**
    thura.
Act. 3. 2. daily at the **g.** of the temple

GATHER,   *-ed, -eth, -ing.*
    sunagō.
Mat. 2. 4. *when* he *had* **g-ed** all
   3.12. and **g.** his wheat ; 13.30 :
    Lu.3.17
   6.26. nor **g.** into barns ; yet your
   12.30. he *that* **g-eth** not with me ;
    Lu.11.23
   13. 2. multitudes *were* **g-ed** *together*
   47. the sea, and **g-ed** of every
  18.20. are **g-ed** *together* in my name
  22.10. and **g-ed** *together* all as many
   34. they were **g-ed** *together*
   41. Pharisees *were* **g-ed** *together*
  24.28. eagles be **g-ed** *together* ;
    Lu.17.27
  25.24. and **g-ing** where thou hast
   26. and **g.** where I have not
   32. before him *shall be* **g-ed** all
  27.17. *when* they *were* **g-ed** *together*
   27. and **g-ed** unto him the whole
Mar. 2. 2. many *were* **g-ed** *together*, in.
   4. 1. and there *was* **g-ed** unto him
  5.21. much people **g-ed** unto him
  6.30. **g-ed** themselves *together*
Lu. 15.13. younger son **g-ed** all *together*
Jo. 4.36. and **g-eth** fruit unto life eter.
   6.12. **g.** *up* the fragments that
   13. they **g-ed** them *together*
  11.47. Then **g-ed** the chief priests

Jo. 11. 52. he *should* **g.** *together* in one
   15. 6. and men **g.** them, and cast
Act. 4. 6. *were* **g-ed** *together* at Jerusa.
   26. and the rulers were **g-ed** tog.
   27. of Israel *were* **g-ed** *together*
  14.27. and *had* **g-ed** the church *tog.*
  15.30. *had* **g-ed** the multitude *toge.*
  20. 8. where they were **g-ed** *togeth.*
¹Co. 5. 4. *when* ye *are* **g-ed** *together*
Rev.16.14. *to* **g.** them to the battle of
   16. And he **g-ed** them *together*
  19.17. Come and **g.** *yourselves toge.*
  19. and their armies, **g-ed** *toge.*
  20. 8. *to* **g.** them *together* to battle
    episunagō.
Mat.23.37. would I *have* **g-ed** thy child.
    together, even as a hen **g-eth**
  24.31. *shall* **g.** *together* his elect ;
    Mar.13.27
Mar. 1.33. was **g-ed** *together* at the door
Lu. 12. 1. *when* there *were* **g-ed** *together*
  13.34. *have* **g-ed** thy children *togeth.*
Mat.7.16. *Do* men **g.** grapes of thorns ;
    Lu.6.44
  13.28. that we go and **g.** them *up*
   29. Nay ; lest *while* ye **g.** them *up*
   30. **g.** ye *together* first the tares
   40. As therefore the tares *are* **g-ed**
   41. And they *shall* **g.** out of his
   48. and **g-ed** the good into vessels
    trugaō.
Lu. 6.44. nor of a bramble bush **g.** they
Rev.14.18. **g.** the clusters of the vine
   19. and **g-ed** the vine of the earth
    suneimi.
Lu. 8. 4. much people *were* **g-ed** *together*
    epathroizō.
Lu.11.29. people *were* **g-ed** *thick together*
    sustrephō.
Act.28.3. *when* Paul *had* **g-ed** a bundle
    anakephalaiooomai.
Eph.1.10. he *might* **g.** *together* in one

GATHERING, [*noun,*]   *-s.*
    episunagōgē.
¹Co. 16.2. that there be no **g-s** when I
    episunagōgē.
²Th. 2. 1. by our **g.** *together* unto him

GAY.
    lampros.
Jas. 2. 3. that weareth the **g.** clothing

GAZING.
    emblepō.
Act.1.11. stand ye **g.** *up* into heaven

GAZINGSTOCK.
    theatrizomai.
Heb.10.33. *whilst* ye *were* made a **g.**

GENDER,   *-eth.*
    gennaō.
Gal. 4.24. *which* **g-eth** to bondage, which
²Ti. 2.23. knowing that they *do* **g.** stri.

GENEALOGIES.
    genealogia.
¹Ti. 1. 4. heed to fables and endless **g.**
Tit. 3. 9. avoid foolish ques., and **g.**

GENERAL, (See *Assembly.*)

GENERATION,   *-s.*
    genea.
Mat.1.17. all the **g-s** from Abraham
    to David are fourteen **g-s**
    into Babylon are fourteen **g-s**
    unto Christ are fourteen **g-s**
  11.16. shall I liken this **g.**; Lu.7.31
  12.39. An evil and adulte. **g.** ; 16.4 ;
    Mar.8.38 ; Lu.11.29
   41, 42. in judgment with this **g.** ;
    Lu.11.31,32

Mat.12.45.also unto this wicked **g.**
  17.17. O faithless and perverse **g.** ;
    Mar.9.19 ; Lu.9.41
  23.36. things shall come upon this **g.**
  24.34. This **g.** shall not pass ;
    Mar.13.30 ; Lu.21.32
Mar.8.12. Why doth this **g.** seek after
    sign be given unto this **g.**
Lu. 1.48. all **g-s** shall call me blessed
   50. that fear him from **g.** to **g.**
  11.30. the Son of man be to this **g.**
   50, 51. may be required of this **g.**
  16. 8. are in their **g.** wiser than
  17.25. and be rejected of this **g.**
Act. 2.40. your. from this untoward **g.**
   8.33. who shall declare his **g.**? for
  13.36. he had served his own **g.** by
Col. 1.26. hid from ages and from **g-s**
Heb.3.10. I was grieved with that **g.**
    gennēma.
Mat:3. 7. O **g.** of vipers ; 12.34 ; Lu.3.7
  23.33. ye serpents, ye **g.** of vipers
    genesis.
Mat.1. 1. The book of the **g.** of Jesus
    genos.
¹Pet.2. 9. ye are a chosen **g.**, a royal

GENTILE,   *-s.*
    ethnos.
Mat.4.15. beyond Jor., Galilee of the **g-s**
   6.32. all these things do the **g-s**
  10. 5. Go not into the way of the **g-s**
   18. testi. agai. them and the **g-s**
  12.18. shall shew judgment to the **g-s**
   21. his name shall the **g-s** trust ;
    Ro.15.12
  20.19. deliver him to the **g-s** ;
    Mar.10.33 ; Lu.18.23
   25. princes of the **g-s** exercise ;
    Lu.22.25
Mar.10.42.accounted to rule over the **g-s**
Lu. 2.32. A light to lighten the **g-s**
  21.24. **g-s** until the times of the **g-s**
Act. 4.27. with the **g-s**, and the people
   7.45. into the possession of the **g-s**
   9.15. to bear my name before the **g-s**
  10.45. on the **g-s** also was poured
  11. 1. the **g-s** had also received the
   18. hath God also to the **g-s** gra.
  13.42. the **g-s** besought that these
   46. lo, we turn to the **g-s** ; 18.6
   47. thee to be a light of the **g-s**
   48. when the **g-s** heard this, they
  14. 2. Jews stirred up the **g-s**, and
   5. of the **g-s**, and also of the
   27. the door of faith unto the **g-s**
  15. 3. the conversion of the **g-s**
   7. that the **g-s** by my mouth
   12. wrought among the **g-s** by
   14. did visit the **g-s** to take out
   17. all the **g-s**, upon whom my
   19. which from among the **g-s**
   23. brethren which are of the **g-s**
  21.11. him into the hands of the **g-s**
   19. had wrought among the **g-s**
   21. Jews which are among the **g-s**
   25. As touching the **g-s** which
  22.21. thee far hence unto the **g-s**
  26.17. people, and from the **g-s**
   20. then to the **g-s** that they
   23. unto the people, and to the **g-s**
  28.28. of God is sent unto the **g-s**
Ro. 1.13. also, even as among other **g-s**
  2.14. the **g-s**, which have not the
   24. blasphemed among the **g-s**
  3.29. also of the **g-s**? Yes, of the **g-s**
  9.24. Jews only, but also of the **g-s**
   30. That the **g-s**, which followed
  11.11. salvation is come unto the **g-s**
   12. of them the riches of the **g-s**
   13. For I speak to you **g-s**, inas.
    I am the apostle of the **g-s**

Ro.11.25. until the fulness of the **g-s**
15. 9. that the **g-s** might glorify
     confess to thee among the **g-s**
10. he saith, Rejoice, ye **g-s**, with
11. Praise the Lord, all ye **g-s**
12. shall rise to reign over the **g-s**
16. of Jesus Christ to the **g-s**
     offering up of the **g-s** might
18. to make the **g-s** obedient
27. if the **g-s** have been made
16. 4. all the churches of the **g-s**
1Co. 5. 1. much as named among the **g-s**
10.20. things which the **g-s** sacrifice
12. 2. Ye know that ye were **g-s**
Gal. 2. 2. which I preach among the **g-s**
8. mighty in me toward the **g-s**
12. he did eat with the **g-s**: but
14. the **g-s** to live as do the Jews
15. and not sinners of the **g-s**
3.14 might come on the **g-s** throu.
Eph. 2.11. ye being in times past **g-s**
3. 1. of Jesus Christ for you **g-s**
6. That the **g-s** should be fellow.
8. should preach among the **g-s**
4.17. way not as other **g-s** walk
Col. 1.27. this mystery among the **g-s**
1Th. 2.16. Forbid. us to speak to the **g-s**
4. 5. as the **g-s** which know not
1Ti. 2. 7. a teacher of the **g-s** in faith
3.16. preached unto the **g-s**, believ.
2Ti. 1.11. apos., and a teacher of the **g-s**
4.17. that all the **g-s** might hear
1Pet.2.12. conver. honest among the **g-s**
4. 3. wrought the will of the **g-s**
3John 7. taking nothing of the **g-s**
Rev.11.2. for it is given unto the **g-s**

Hellēn.

Jo. 7.35. *the* **g-s**, and teach the **g-s**
Ro. 2.9,10.Jew first, and also of the **g.**
3. 9. proved both Jews and **g-s**
1Co.10.32. to the Jews, nor to the **g-s**
12.13. whether we be Jews or **g-s**

ethnikōs.

Gal. 2.14. *after the manner of* **g-s**

GENTLE.
epieikēs.

Tit. 3. 2. to be no brawlers, but **g.**
Jas. 3.17 **g.**, and easy to be entreated
1Pet.2.18. not only to the good and **g.**

ēpios.

1Th. 2. 7. But we were **g.** among you
2Ti. 2.24. must not strive; but be **g.**

GENTLENESS.
epieikeia.

2Co. 10.1. the meekness and **g.** of Ch.

chrēstotēs.

Gal.5.22. longsuffering, **g.**, goodness

GET,   *Gotten.*
heuriskō.

Lu.9.12. and lodge, and **g.** victuals

exerchomai.

Lu.13.31. **g.** *out,* and depart hence
Act.7. 3. **g.** thee *out* of thy country
22.18. **g.** thee quickly *out* of Jerusa.

hupagō.

Mat.4.10. **g.** thee *hence,* Satan; for it
16.23. **g.** thee behind me; Mar.8.33;
     Lu.4.8

embainō.

Mat.14.22. disciples *to* **g.** *into* a ship;
     Mar.6.45

katabainō.

Act.10.20. **g.** thee *down,* and go with

apospaō.

Act.21.1. *after* we *were* **g-en** from them
(See *Advantage, Behind, Gain, Land, Victory.*)
112

GHOST.
pneuma.

Mat. 1.18. with child of the Holy **g.**
20. in her is of the Holy **g.**
3.11. baptize you with the Ho. **g.**;
     Mar.1.8; Lu.3.16; Jo. 1.33
12.31,32. against the Holy **g.**;
     Mar.3.29; Lu.12.10
27.50. yielded up the **g.**; Jo.19.30
28.19. the Son, and of the Holy **g.**
Mar.12.36.himself said by the Holy **g.**
13.11. that speak, but the Holy **g.**
Lu.1.15,41,67. filled with the H. **g.**; 4.1
Act.2.4,4.8,31,6.3,5,7.55,9.17,
     11.24,13.9,52
35. The Holy **g.** shall come upon
2.25. and the Holy **g.** was upon
26. unto him by the Holy **g.**
3.22. And the Holy **g.** descended
12.12. For the Holy **g.** shall teach
Jo. 7.39. for the Holy **g.** was not yet
14.26. the Holy **g.**, whom the Fath.
20.22. Receive ye the Holy **g.**
     Act.2.38
Act. 1. 2. he through the Holy **g.** had
5. baptiz. with the Ho. **g.**; 11.16
8. after that the Holy **g.** is come
16. which the Holy **g.** by the
2.33. the promise of the Holy **g.**
5. 3. heart to lie to the Holy **g.**
32. and so is also the Holy **g.**
7.51. do always resist the Holy **g.**
8.15, 17,19. might rec. the Holy **g.**
18. the Holy **g.** was given, he
9.31. the comfort of the Holy **g.**
10.38. with the Holy **g.**, and with
44. the Holy **g.** fell on all them
45. out the gift of the Holy **g.**
47. have receiv. the Holy **g.**; 19.2
11.15. the Holy **g.** fell on them
13. 2. the Holy **g.** said, Separate
4. being sent forth by the Ho. **g.**
15. 8. giving them the Holy **g.**
28. it seemed good to the Ho. **g.**
16. 6. were forbidden of the Ho. **g.**
19. 2. whether there be any Ho. **g.**
6. the Holy **g.** came on them
20.23. Save that the Holy **g.** witne.
28. the Holy **g.** made you over.
21.11. Thus saith the Holy **g.**, so
28.25. Well spake the Holy **g.** by
Ro. 5. 5. by the Holy **g.** which is given
9. 1. me witness in the Holy **g.**
14.17. peace, and joy in the Holy **g.**
15.13. the power of the Holy **g.**
16. being sanctified by the Ho. **g.**
1Co. 2.13. but which the Holy **g.** teach.
6.19. the temple of the Holy **g.**
12. 3. the Lord, but the Holy **g.**
2Co. 6. 6. by the Holy **g.**, by love
13.14. the communion of the Ho. **g.**
1Th. 1. 5. in power, and in the Holy **g.**
6. with joy of the Holy **g.**
2Ti. 1.14. keep by the Holy **g.** which
Tit. 3. 5. and renewing of the Holy **g.**
Heb. 2. 4. and gifts of the Holy **g.**
3. 7. as the Holy **g.** saith, To-day
6. 4. made partakers of the Holy **g.**
9. 8. The Holy **g.** this signifying
10.15. the Holy **g.** also is a witness
1Pet.1.12. with the Holy **g.** sent down
2Pet.1.21. were moved by the Holy **g.**
1Jo.5. 7. and the Holy **g.** : and these
Jude 20. praying in the Holy **g.**

ekpsuchō.

Act. 5. 5. fell down, and *gave up the* **g.**
10. his feet, and *yielded up the* **g.**
12.23. of worms, and *gave up the* **g.**

ekpneō.

Mar15.37, 39. and *gave up the* **g.**;
     Lu.23.46

GIFT,   -s.
charisma.

Ro. 1.11. unto you some spiritual **g.**
5.15. so also is the *free* **g.** For if
16. but the *free* **g.** is of many
6.23. the **g.** of God is eternal life
11.29. For the **g-s** and calling of
12. 6. Having then **g-s** differing
1Co. 1. 7. that ye come behind in no **g.**
7. every man hath his proper **g.**
12. 4. there are diversities of **g-s**
9. to another the **g-s** of healing
28. then **g-s** of healings, helps
30. Have all the **g-s** of healing
31. covet earnestly the best **g-s**
2Co. 1.11. for the **g.** bestowed upon us
1Ti. 4.14. Neglect not the **g.** that is in
2Ti. 1. 6. stir up the **g.** of God, which
1Pet. 4.10. man hath received the **g.**

charis.

2Co. 8. 4. we would receive the **g.**, and

dōron.

Mat. 2.11. They presented unto him **g-s**
5.23. if thou bring thy **g.** to the
24. Leave there thy **g.** before the
     then come and offer thy **g.**
8. 4. offer the **g.** that Moses com.
15. 5. It is a **g.**, by whatsoever;
     Mar.7.11
23.18. whosoev. sweareth by the **g.**
19. whether is greater, the **g.**, or
     the altar that sanctifi. the **g.**
Lu. 21. 1. casting their **g-s** into the
Eph. 2. 8. yourselves: it is the **g.** of
Heb. 5. 1. offer both **g-s** and sacrifices
     8.3,9.9
8. 4. there are priests that offer **g-s**
11. 4. God testifying of his **g-s**
Rev.11.10. shall send **g-s** one to anoth.

dōrea.

Jo. 4.10. If thou knewest the **g.** of G.
Act. 2.38. the **g.** of the Holy Gh.; 10.45
8.20. hast thought that the **g.** of
11.17. as God gave them the like **g.**
Ro. 5.15. the grace of God, and the **g.**
17. of the **g.** of righteousness
2Co. 9.15. God for his unspeakable **g.**
Eph. 3. 7. according to the **g.** of the
4. 7. the measure of the **g.** of
Heb. 6. 4. tasted of the heavenly **g.**

doma.

Mat.7.11. give good **g-s** unto your;
     Lu.11.13
Eph.4. 8. captive, and gave **g-s** unto
Phi. 4.17. Not because I desire a **g.**

merismos.

Heb.2.4. and **g-s** of the Holy Ghost

anathēma.

Lu.21.5. with goodly stones and **g-s**

dōrēma.

Ro. 5.16. one that sinned, so is the **g.**
Jas. 1.17. gift, and every perfect **g.**

dosis.

Jas.1.17. Every good **g.** and every perf.

GIRD,   -ed, -edst, -ing, Girt.
zōnnuō.

Jo.21.18. thou wast young, thou **g-edst**
     and another *shall* **g.** thee

perizōnnumi.

Lu. 12.35. Let your loins be **g-ed** *about*
37. that he *shall* **g.** him*self,* and
17. 8. and **g.** thy*self, and* serve me
Act.12. 8. **g.** thy*self,* and bind on thy
Eph. 6.14. having your loins **g-t** about
Rev. 1.13. **g-t** about the paps with a *go*
15. 6. their breasts **g-ed** with gold.

diazōnnumi.

Jo. 13. 4. took a towel, and **g-ed** him.
5. the towel where. he was **g-ed**
21. 7. he **g-t** his fisher's coat unto

anazōnnumi.

¹Pet.1.13. Wherefore **g.** *up* the loins of

GIRDLE,   -s.
zōnē.

Mat. 3. 4. **g.** about his loins; Mar.1.6
Act. 21.11.he took Paul's **g.**, and
     the man that owneth this **g.**
Rev. 1.13. about the paps with a gold. **g.**
     15. 6. girded with golden **g-s**

GIVE, *-en, -est, -eth, -ing, Gave,*
didōmi.   [*Gavest*
       Give.

Mat. 4. 9. All these things *will* I **g.**
   5.31. *let* him **g.** her a writing of
     42. **g.** to him that asketh thee
   6.11. **g.** us this day our daily ;
          Lu.11.3
   7. 6. **g.** not that which is holy
     11. how to **g.** good gifts; Lu.11.13
       shall your Fa...heaven **g.**;
          Lu.11.13
   10. 8. ye have received, freely **g.**
   14. 7. *to* **g.** her whatsoever she
     8. **g.** me here John Baptist's
     16. **g.** ye them to eat ; Mar.6.37;
          Lu.9.13
   16.19. I *will* **g.** unto thee the keys
     26. *shall* a man **g.** in exchange ;
          Mar.8.37
   17.27. that take, and **g.** unto them
   19. 7. command *to* **g.** writing of
     21. **g.** to the poor, and thou ;
          Mar.10.21
   20. 4. whatsoever is right I *will* **g.**
     14. I will **g.** unto this last, even
     23. my left, is not mine *to* **g.**;
          Mar.10.40
     28. *to* **g.** his life a ransom for
   22.17. Is it lawful *to* **g.** tribute unto
   24.29. the moon *shall* not **g.** her
     45. *to* **g.** them meat in due sea.
   25. 8. **g.** us of your oil ; for our
     28. **g.** it unto him which hath ;
          Lu.19.24
   26.15. them, What will ye **g.** me
Mar. 6.22, 23. thou wilt, and I *will* **g.** it
     25. I will that thou **g.** me by and
   10.45. *to* **g.** a life a ransom for
   12. 9. *will* **g.** the vineyard unto
     14. it is lawful *to* **g.** tribute to
     15. Shall we **g.**,or shall we not **g.**
   13.24. the moon *shall* not **g.** her
   14.11. promised *to* **g.** him money
Lu. 1.32. the Lord God *shall* **g.** unto
     77. *To* **g.** knowledge of salvation
   4. 6. All this power *will* I **g.** you
     to whomsoever I will I **g.** it
   6.30. **g.** to every man that asketh
     38. **g.**, and it *shall be given* unto
       shall men **g.** into your bosom
   8.55. he commanded *to* **g.** her
   10.19. I **g.** unto you power to tread
   11. 7. I cannot rise and **g.** thee
     8. Tho. he will not rise and **g.**
     he will rise and **g.** him
     41. **g.** alms of such things ; 12.33
   12.32. Father's good pleasure to **g.**
     42. *to* **g.** them their portion of
     51. that I am come *to* **g.** peace
     58. **g.** diligence that thou may.
   14. 9. say to thee, **g.** this man pla.
   15.12. Father, **g.** me the portion of
   16.12. who *shall* **g.** you that which
     17.18. that returned *to* **g.** glory to
   19. 8. my goods I **g.** to the poor
   20.10. they *should* **g.** him of the fr.
     16. *shall* **g.** the vineyard to oth.
     22. Is it lawful for us *to* **g.** tribu.
   21.15. For I *will* **g.** you a mouth
   22. 5. covenanted *to* **g.** him money
   23. 2. forbidding *to* **g.** tribute to

Jo. 1.22. that we *may* **g.** an answer
   4. 7, 10. Jesus saith unto her, **g.**
     14. the water that I *shall* **g.** him
     15. Sir, **g.** me this water, that
   6.27. the Son of man *shall* **g.** unto
     34. Lord, evermore **g.** us this
     51. bread that I *will* **g.** is my fl.
     which I *will* **g.** for the life of
     52. How can this man **g.** us his
   7.19. *Did* not Moses **g.** you the
   9.24. said unto him, **g.** God the
   10.28. I **g.** unto them eternal life
   11.22. of God, God *will* **g.** it thee
   13.29. that he *should* **g.** something
     34. a new commandment I **g.**
   14.16. he *shall* **g.** you anotherCom.
     27. my peace I **g.** unto you
     the world *giveth*, **g.** I unto
   15.16. my name, he *may* **g.** it you ;
          16.23
   17. 2. that he *should* **g.** eternal life
Act. 3. 6. such as I have **g.** I thee : In
   5.31. for *to* **g.** repentance to Israel
   7. 5. promised that he would **g.** it
     38. the lively oracles *to* **g.** unto
   8.19. Saying, **g.** me also this pow.
   13.34. I *will* **g.** you the sure mercies
   20.32. *to* **g.** you an inheritance
     35. It is more blessed *to* **g.** than
Ro. 12.19. **g.** place unto wrath : for it
   14.12. *shall* **g.** account of himself
¹Co. 7.25. yet I **g.** my judgment as one
   14. 7. except they **g.** a distinction
     8. if the trumpet **g.** an uncertain
²Co. 5.12. **g.** you occasion to glory on
   8.10. herein I **g.** my advice : for
Eph. 1.17. *may* **g.** unto you the spirit of
   4.27. Neither **g.** place to the devil
²Th. 3.16. **g.** you peace always by all
¹Ti. 5.14. **g.** none occasion to the adv.
²Ti. 1.16. The Lord **g.** mercy unto the
   2. 7. the Lord **g.** thee understand.
     25. if God preadventure will **g.**
Jas. 2.16. notwithstanding ye **g.** them
¹Jo. 5.16. he *shall* **g.** him life for them
Rev. 2. 7. *will* I **g.** to eat of the tree of
     10. I *will* **g.** thee a crown of life
     17. him that overcometh *will* I **g.**
     and *will* **g.** him a white stone
     23. I *will* **g.** unto every one of
     26. to him *will* I **g.** power over
     28. I *will* **g.** him the morning
   4. 9. when those beasts **g.** glory
   10. 9. said unto him, **g.** me the
   11. 3. I *will* **g.** power unto my two
     18. that thou shouldest **g.**reward
   13.15. he had power to **g.** life unto
   14. 7. Fear God, and **g.** glory to
   16. 9. they repented not *to* **g.** him
     19. *to* **g.** unto her the cup of the
   17.17. and **g.** their kingdom unto
   18. 7. so much tor. and sorrow **g.**
   19. 7. rejoice, and **g.** honour to
   21. 6. I *will* **g.** unto him that is
       Gave. [Mar.6.7; Lu.9.1
Mat.10. 1. he **g.** them power against ;
   14.19. **g.** the loaves to his ; 15.36;
   26.26,27; Mar.6.41,8.6 ; Lu.9.16
   21.23. who **g.** thee this authority ;
          Mar.11.28; Lu.20.2
   25.15. unto one he **g.** five talents
     35, 42. an hungered, and ye **g.**
   26.48. he that betrayed him **g.** th.
   27.10. **g.** them for the potter's field
     34. They **g.** him vinegar to drink
Mar. 2.26. **g.** also to them which were
   6.28. in a charger, and **g.** it to the
     and the damsel **g.** it to her
   13.34. **g.** authority to his servants
   14.22, 23. and **g.** to them, and said;
          Lu.22.19
   15.23. they **g.** him to drink wine

Lu. 6. 4. **g.** also to them that were
   10.35. two pence, and **g.** them **to**
   15.16. eat, and no man **g.** unto him
   18.43. when they saw it, **g.** praise
Jo. 1.12. to them he **g.** power to bec.
   3.16. that he **g.** his only begotten
   4. 5. that Jacob **g.** to his son Jos.
     12. Jacob, which **g.** us the well
   6.31. He **g.** them bread from hea.
     32. Moses **g.** you not that bread
   7.22. Moses therefore **g.** unto you
   10.29. My Father, which **g.** them
   12.49. he **g.** me a commandment
   13.26. the sop, he **g.** it to Judas Isc.
   19. 9. Jesus **g.** him no answer
Act. 1.26. they **g.** forth their lots ; and
   2. 4. as the Spirit **g.** them utter.
   7. 5. he **g.** him none inheritance
     8. he **g.** him the covenant of
     9. **g.** him favour and wisdom
   9.41. he **g.** her his hand, *and* lift.
   11.17. as God **g.** them the like gift
   12.23. because he **g.** not God the
   13.20. after that he **g.** unto them
     21. God **g.** unto them Saul the
   14.17. *and* **g.** us rain from heaven
¹Co. 3. 5. even as the Lord **g.** to every
²Co. 8. 5. first **g.** their own selves to
Gal. 1. 4. *Who* **g.** himself for our sins
   2. 9. **g.** to me and Barnabas the
Eph. 1.22. **g.** him to be the head over
   4. 8. captivity captive, and **g.**
     11. he **g.** some, apostles ; and
¹Th. 4. 2. we **g.** you by the Lord Jesus
¹Ti. 2. 6. *Who* **g.** himself a ransom
Tit. 2.14. Who **g.** himself for us, that
Heb. 7. 4. Abraham **g.** the tenth of
Jas. 5.18. the heaven **g.** rain, and the
¹Pet. 1.21. from the dead, and **g.** him
¹Jo. 3.23. as he **g.** us commandment
Rev. 1. 1. which God **g.** unto him, to
   2.21. I **g.** her space to repent of
   11.13. **g.** glory to the God of heaven
   13. 2. dragon **g.** him his power
     4. which **g.** power unto the
   15. 7. **g.** unto the seven angels sev.
   20.13. the sea **g.** *up* the dead which
       Gavest, Giveth, Giving, Given.
Mat.7. 7. Ask, and it *shall be* **g-en** you ;
          Lu.11.9
   9. 8. *which had* **g-en** such power
   10.19. it *shall be* **g-en** you in that
   12.39. there *shall* no sign *be* **g-en** ;
       16.4; Mar.8.12 ; Lu.11.29
   13.11. it *is* **g-en** unto you to know ;
          Mar.4.11; Lu.8.10
     but to them it *is* not **g-en**
     12. hath, to him *shall be* **g-en** ;
          Lu.19.26
   14. 9. he commanded it *to be* **g-en**
     11. in a charger, and **g-en** to the
   19.11. save they to whom it *is* **g-en**
   21.43. taken from you, and **g-en** to
   25.29. one that hath *shall be* **g-en**
   26. 9. and **g-en**to the poor;Mar.14.5;
          Jo.12.5
   28.18. All power *is* **g-en** unto me in
Mar.5.43. something should *be* **g-en** her
   6. 2. this *which is* **g-en** unto him
   13.11. shall *be* **g-en** you in that hour
   14.44. betrayed him *had* **g-en** them
Lu. 6.38. it shall be **g-en** unto you
   7.44. thou **g-**est me no water for
     45. Thou **g-**est me no kiss : but
   12.48. unto whomsoev. much *is* **g-en**
   15.29. yet thou never **g-**est me a kid
   19.15. to whom he *had* **g-en** the
     23. Wherefore then **g-**est not thou
   22.19. This is my body *which is* **g-en**
Jo. 1.17. the law *was* **g-en** by Moses
   3.27. except it be **g-en** him from
   34. God **g-**eth not the Spirit by

113

Jo. 3.35. hath g-en all things into his
4.10. he would have g-en thee living
5.26. so hath he g-en to the Son to
27. hath g-en him authority to
36. which the Father hath g-en
6.32. My Father g-eth you the true
33. g-eth life unto the world
37. All that the Father g-eth me
39. of all which he hath g-en me
65. were g-en unto him of my
11.57. the Pharisees had g-en a
13. 3. the Father had g-en all things
15. For I have g-en you an exam.
17. 2. As thou hast g-en him power
many as thou hast g-en him
4. work which thou g-est me to
6. which thou g-est me out of
they were, and thou g-est the.
7. whatsoever thou hast g-en
8. I have g-en unto them the
which thou g-est me
9, 11,24. which thou hast g-en
12. those that thou g-est me ; 18.9
14. I have g-en them thy word
22. g-est me I have g-en them
24. glory, which thou hast g-en
18.11. which my Father hath g-en
19.11. except it were g-en thee
21.13. taketh bread, and g-eth them
Act.3.16. hath g-en him this perfect
4.12. name under heaven g-en am.
5.32. whom God hath g-en to them
S.18. the Holy Ghost was g-en, he
15. 8. g-ing them the Holy Ghost
17.25. seeing he g-eth to all life, and
24.26. money should have been g-en
Ro. 4.20. strong in faith, g-ing glory to
5. 5. H. Gh. which is g-en unto us;
1Th.4.8; 1Jo.3.24, 4.13
11. 8. God hath g-en them the spirit
12. 3. the grace g-en unto me, 15.15;
1Co.3.10; Gal.2.9; Eph.3.7
6. the grace that is g-en to us
Co. 1. 4. grace of God which is g-en
11.15. hair is g-en her for a covering
12. 7. of the Spirit is g-en to every
8. to one is g-en by the Spirit
24. having g-en more abundant
14. 7. things without life g-ing
15.38. God g-eth it a body as it hath
57. God, which g-eth us the vict.
2Co. 1.22. and g-en the earnest of the
5. 5. who also hath g-en unto us
18. and hath g-en to us the mini.
6. 3. g-ing no offence in any thing
9. 9. he hath g-en to the poor : his
10. 8. the Lord hath g-en us for
12. 7. there was g-en to me a thorn
13.10. which the Lord hath g-en me
Gal.3.21. if there had been a law g-en
22. might be g-en to them that
4.15. your own eyes, and have g-en
Eph. 3. 2. which is g-en me to you-ward
8. is this grace g-en, that I should
4. 7. unto every one of us is g-en
6.19. that utterance may be g-en
Col. 1.25. which is g-en to me for you
2Th. 2.16. and hath g-en us everlasting
1Ti. 4.14. which was g-en thee by proph.
2Ti. 1. 7. God hath not g-en us the spi.
9. grace which was g-en us in Ch.
Heb.2.13. children which God hath g-en
Jas. 1. 5. ask of God, that g-eth to all
not ; and it shall be g-en him
4. 6. he g-eth more grace. Wheref.
g-eth grace to the humble ;
1Pet.5.5
2Pet.3.15. according to the wisdom g-en
1Jo. 5.11. God hath g-en to us eternal
20. hath g-en us an understand.
Rev.6. 2. a crown was g-en unto him
4, 8. power was g-en to him
114

Rev.6. 4. there was g-en unto him a
11. white robes were g-en unto
7. 2. to whom it was g-en to hurt
8. 2. to them were g-en seven
3. there was g-en unto him
9. 1. to him was g-en the key of
3. unto them was g-en power
5. to them it was g-en that they
11. 1. there was g-en me a reed like
2. for it is g-en unto the Gentil.
12.14. to the women were g-en two
13. 5. there was g-en unto him a
7. it was g-en unto him to make
pow. was g-en unto him ; 16.8
16. 6. thou hast g-en them blood to
20. 4. judgment was g-en unto them
apodidōmi.
Mat.12.36.they shall g. account thereof
20. 8. Call the labourers, and g.
Lu. 4.20. he g-a it again to the minist.
16. 2. g. an account of thy steward.
Act. 4.33. g-a the apostles witness of
19.40. we may g. an account of this
2Ti. 4. 8. shall g. me at that day : and
Heb.13.17.as they that must g. account
1Pet. 4. 5. Who shall g. account to him
Rev.22.12. to g. every man according
paradidōmi.
Jo. 19.30. head, and g-a up the ghost
47.42. and g-a them up to worship
Ro. 1.24, 26. Wherefore G. also g-a
28. God g-a them over to a repr.
1Co. 13. 3. though I g. my body to be
Gal. 2.20. who loved me, and g-a hims.
Eph. 4.19. feeling have g-en themselves
5. 2. and hath g-en himself for us
25. the church, and g-a himself
epididōmi.
Mat. 7. 9. will he g. him a stone ;
Lu.11.11.
10. will he g. him a serpent ;
Lu.11.11
Lu. 24.30. and brake, and g-a to them
42. g-a him a piece of a broiled
Jo. 13.26. to whom I shall g. a sop
metadidōmi.
Ro.12. 8. he that g-eth, let him do it
Eph.4.28. he may have to g. to him
diadidōmi.
Rev.17.13. shall g. their power and
charizomai
Lu. 7.21. many that were blind he g-a
Act.27.24. and, lo, God hath g-en thee
Ro. 8.32. shall he not..also freely g.
1Co. 2.12. that are freely g-en to us of
Gal. 3.18. but God g-a it to Abraham
Phi. 1.29. you it is g-en in the behalf
2. 9. and g-en him a name which
Phile. 22. prayers I shall be g-en unto
prosechō.
Act. 8. 6. g-a heed unto those things
10. To whom they all g-a heed
1Ti. 1. 4. Neither g. heed to fables and
3. 8. not g-en to much wine, nor
4. 1. g-ing heed to seducing spirits
13. g. attendance to reading
Tit. 1.14. Not g-ing heed to Jewish fab.
Heb. 2. 1. to g. the more earnest heed to
7.13. no man g-a attendance at
parechō.
Act.17.31. whereof he hath g-en assur.
Col. 4. 1. g. unto your servants than
1Ti. 6.17. who g-eth us richly all things
epitrepō.
Mar.5.13. forthwith J. g-a them leave
Jo. 19.38. and Pilate g-a him leave
Act.21.40.when he had g-en him licence
27. 3. and g-a him liberty to go
dōreō.
Mar.15.45. he g-a the body to Joseph
2Pet. 1. 3. his divine power hath g-en
4. Whereby are g-en unto us

pareispherō.
2Pet.1.5. g-ing all diligence, add to
kataipherō.
Act.26.10. I g-a my voice against them
tithēmi.
Jo.10.11. the good shep. g-eth his life
prostithēmi.
Mar.4.24. unto you..shall more be g-en
aponemō.
1Pet.3.7. g-ing honour unto the wife, as
paraggellō.
1Ti. 5. 7. and these things g. in charge
6.13. I g. thee charge in the sight
matureō.
1Jo.5.10. record that God g. of his Son
(that God witnessed.)
poieō.
Act.10.2. which g-a much alms to the
Jude 3. when I g-a all diligence to write
chorēgeō.
1Pet.4.11. of the ability which God g-eth
diōkō.
Ro.12.13. of saints ; g-en to hospitality
scholazō.
1Co. 7. 5. may g. your selves to fasting
legō.
Act.8.9. g-ing out that himself was some
proskartereō.
Act.6.4. will g. our selves continually to
eimi en.
1Ti.4.15. g. thyself wholly to them
ho para autos.
Lu.10.7.such things as they g. (the [things]
by them, or, such as they have.)
douloō.
Tit. 2. 3. not g-en to much wine, teach
(See words in connection.)

GIVER.
dotēs.
2Co.9. 7. for God loveth a cheerful g.

GIVING, [noun.]
dosis.
Phi.4.15. concerning g. and receiving
nomothesia.
Ro. 9. 4. and the g. of the law, and

GLAD.
chairō.
Mar.14.11. they heard it, they were g.
Lu. 15.32. should make merry and be g.
22. 5. And they were g., and cove.
23. 8. Jesus, he was exceeding g.
Jo. 8.56. and he saw it, and was g.
11.15. And I am g. for your sakes
20.20. Then were the disciples g.
Act.11.23. was g., and exhorted them all
13.48. Gent. heard this, they were g.
Ro. 16.19. I am g. therefore on your
1Co.16.17. I am g. of the coming of
2Co.13. 9. For we are g., when we are
1Pet. 4.13. ye may be g. also with exceed.
Rev.19. 7. Let us be g. and rejoice, and
agalliaō.
Mat.5.12. Rejoice, and be exceeding g.
Act. 2.26. rejoice, and my tongue was g.
euaggelizō.
Lu. 1.19. to shew thee these g. tidings
8. 1. and shewing the g. tidings
13.32. we declare unto you g. tidings
Ro.10.15.and bring g. tidings of good
euphrainō.
2Co.2.2. he then that maketh me g.

GLADLY.
hēdeōs.
Mar. 6.20. things, and heard him g.
12.37. common people heard him g.
2Co.11.19. For ye suffer fools g., seeing
12. 9. Most g.therefore will I rather
15. I will very g. spend and be

asmenŏs.
Act.2.41. they that **g.** received his word
21.17. the brethren received us **g.**
  (See *Receive.*)

GLADNESS.
chara.
Mar. 4.16. immediate. receive it with **g.**
Act.12.14. opened not the gate for **g.**
Phi. 2.29. in the Lord with all **g.**
agalliasis.
Lu. 1.14. thou shalt have joy and **g.**
Act. 2.46. with **g.** and singleness of heart
Heb.1. 9. anoint. thee with the oil of **g.**
euphrosunē.
Act.14.17. hearts with food and **g.**

GLASS.
hualos.
Rev.21.18. pure gold, like unto clear **g.**
  21. gold, as it were transparent **g.**
esoptron.
1Co.13.12. see through a **g.**, darkly
Jas. 1.23. his natural face in a **g.**
hualinos.
Rev. 4.6. a sea *of* **g.** like unto crystal
  15.2. as it were a sea *of* **g.** mingled
    stand on the sea *of* **g.**, having
katoptrizomai.
2Co.3.18. *beholding as in a* **g.** the glory

GLISTERING.
exastraptō.
Lu.9.29. raiment was white and **g.**

GLORIFY,   -ed, -ing.
doxazō.
Mat. 5.16. see your good works, and **g.**
  9. 8. marvelled, and **g**-ed God;
    Mar.2.12 ; Lu.5.26
  15.31. they **g**-ed the God of Israel
Lu. 2.20. **g**-ing and praising God for
  4.15. synagogues, *being* **g**-ed of all
  5.25. to his own house, **g**-ing God
  7.16. they **g**-ed God, saying, That
  13.13. made straight, and **g**-ed God
  17.15. *and* with a loud voice **g**-ed
  18.43. followed him, **g**-ing God
  23.47. what was done, he **g**-ed God
Jo. 7.39. that Jesus *was* not yet **g**-ed
  11. 4. Son of God *might be* **g**-ed
  12.16. when Jesus *was* **g**-ed, then
    23. Son of man *should be* **g**-ed
    28. Father, **g.** thy name. Then
    have both **g**-ed it, and *will* **g.**
  13.31. Now *is* the Son of man **g**-ed
    32. and God *is* **g**-ed in him
    God *shall* also **g.** him in
    and *shall* straightway **g.** him
  14.13. Father *may be* **g**-ed in the
  15. 8. Herein *is* my Father **g**-ed
  16.14. He *shall* **g.** me: for he shall
  17. 1. is come; **g.** thy Son, that
    thy Son also *may* **g.** thee
    4. I *have* **g**-ed thee on the earth
    5. O Father, **g.** thou me with
    10. are mine; *I am* **g**-ed in them
  21.19. by what death he should **g.**
Act. 3.13. *hath* **g**-ed his Son Jesus
  4.21. for all men **g**-ed God for that
  11.18. held their peace, and **g**-ed
  13.48. **g**-ed the word of the Lord
  21.20. they **g**-ed the Lord, and said
Ro. 1.21. they **g**-ed him not as God
  8.30. justified, them he also **g**-ed
  15. 6. mind and one mouth **g.** God
  9. the Gentiles might **g.** God
1Co. 6.20. therefore **g.** God in your
2Co. 9.13. *Whiles.* .they **g.** God for
Gal. 1.24. And they **g**-ed God in me
2Th. 3. 1. *be* **g**-ed, even as it is with
Heb. 5. 5. Christ **g**-ed not himself
1Pet. 2 12. they *may.* .**g.** God in the day

1Pet. 4.11. *may be* **g**-ed through Jesus C.
  14. but on your part he *is* **g**-ed
  16. *let* him **g.** God on this behalf
Rev.15. 4. thee, O Lord, and **g.** thy
  18. 7. How much she *hath* **g**-ed
endoxazō.
2Th.1.10.he shall come *to be* **g**-ed in
  12.name of our L.J.Ch.*may be* **g**-ed
sundoxazō.
Ro.8.17. we *may be* also **g**-ed *together*

GLORIOUS.
doxa.
Ro. 8.21. into the **g.** liberty of the chil.
    (liberty of the *glory.*)
2Co. 3. 7. engraven in stones, was **g.**
  8. minis.of the spirit be rather **g.**
  11. which is done away was **g.**
    which remaineth is **g.**
  4. 4. the light of the **g.** gospel of
Phi.3.21. fashioned like unto his **g.**
Col. 1.11. according to his **g.** power
1Ti. 1.11. According to the **g.** gospel
Tit. 2.13. the **g.** appearing of the great
endoxos.
Lu.13.17. for all the **g.** things that were
Eph.5.27. it to himself a **g.** church
doxazō.
2Co.3.10. that *which was made* **g.** had no

GLORY, [noun.]
doxa.
Mat.4. 8. and the **g.** of them; Lu.4.6
  6.13. the power, and the **g.**, for
    29. S. in all his **g.** was ; Lu.12.27
  16.27. in the **g.** of his Fa.; Mar.8.38
  19.28. the throne of his **g.**; Lu. 9.26
  24.30. with power and great **g.**;
    Mar.13.26; Lu.21.27
  25.31. Son of man shall come in his **g.**
    sit upon the throne of his **g.**
Mar.10.37.on thy left hand, in thy **g.**
Lu. 2. 9. the **g.** of the Lord shone rou.
  14. **g.** to God in the highest ; 19.38
  32. the **g.** of thy people Israel
  9.31. Who appeared in **g.**, and
  32. they saw his **g.**, and the two
  17.18. returned to give **g.** to God
  24.26. and to enter into his **g.**
Jo. 1.14. we beheld his **g.**, the **g.** as of
  2.11. and manifested forth his **g.**
  7.18. himself seeketh his own **g.**
    he that seeketh his **g.** that
  8.50. I seek not mine own **g.**
  11. 4. for the **g.**of God, that the Son
  40. thou shouldest see the **g.** of
  12.41. said Esai., when he saw his **g.**
  17. 5. with the **g.** which I had with
  22. the **g.** which thou gavest me
  24. that they may behold my **g.**
Act. 7. 2. The God of **g.** appeared unto
  55. saw the **g.** of God, and Jesus
  12.23. because he gave not God the **g.**
  22.11. for the **g.** of that light, being
Ro. 1.23. the **g.** of the uncorruptible
  2. 7. doing seek for **g.** and honour
  10. **g.**, honour,and peace, to every
  3. 7. through my lie unto his **g.**
  23. come short of the **g.** of God
  4.20. strong in faith, giving **g.** to
  5. 2. rejoice in hope of the **g.** of
  6. 4. by the **g.** of the Father, even
  8.18. the **g.**which shall be revealed
  9. 4. adoption, and the **g.**, and the
  23. known the riches of his **g.**
    had afore prepared unto **g.**
  11.36. to whom be **g.** for ever;
    Gal.1.5;2Ti.4.18;Heb.13.21;
    1Pet.5.11
  15. 7. received us to the **g.** of God.
  16.27. To God only wise, be **g.**;
    1Ti.1.17
1Co. 2. 7. before the world unto our **g.**

1Co. 2. 8. not have crucified the L. of **g.**
  10.31. ye do, do all to the **g.** of God
  11. 7. as he is the image and **g.** of
    the woman is the **g.** of the
  15. have long hair, it is a **g.** to
  15.40. the **g.** of the celestial is one
  41. **g.** of the sun, and another **g.**
    another **g.** of the stars ; for
    from another star in **g**
  43. in dishonour; it is raised in **g**
2Co. 1.20. unto the **g.** of God by us
  3. 7. for the **g.** of his countenance
  9. of condemnation be **g.**, much
    of righteousness exceed in **g.**
  10. by reason of the **g.** that exce.
  18. as in a glass the **g.** of the L.
    same image from **g.** to **g.**
  4. 6. the knowledge of the **g.** of G.
  15. redound to the **g.** of God
  17. and eternal weight of **g.**
  8.19. to the **g.** of the same Lord
  23. the churches, and the **g.** of
Eph.1. 6, 12,14.To the praise of the **g.**
  17. the Father of **g.**, may give
  18. the riches of the **g.**; Col.1.27
  3.13. for you, which is your **g.**
  16. accord. to the riches of his **g.**
  21. Unto him be **g.** in the church
Phi. 1.11. unto the **g.** and praise of God
  2.11. to the **g.** of God the Father
  3.19. whose **g.** is in their shame
  4.19. his riches in **g.** by Ch. Jesus
  20. our Father, be **g.** for ever and
Col. 1.27. Christ in you, the hope of **g.**
  3. 4. ye also appear with him in **g.**
1Th. 2. 6. Nor of men sought we **g.**
  12. you unto his kingdom and **g.**
  20. For ye are our **g.** and joy
2Th. 1. 9. from the **g.** of his power
  2.14. the **g.** of our Lord Jesus Ch.
1Ti. 3.16. the world, received up into **g.**
2Ti. 2.10. in Ch. Jesus with eternal **g.**
Heb.1. 3. being the brightness of his **g.**
  2. 7. thou crownedst him with **g.**
  9. of death, crowned with **g.**
  10. in bringing many sons unto **g.**
  3. 3. counted worthy of more **g.**
  9. 5. over it the cherubims of **g.**
Jas. 2. 1. Jesus Christ, the Lord of **g.**
1Pet.1. 7. praise and honour and **g.** at
  11. the **g.** that should follow
  21. the dead, and gave him **g.**
  24. the **g.** of man as the flower
  4.13. when his **g.** shall be revealed
  14. for the spirit of **g.** and of God
  5. 1. a partaker of the **g.** that shall
  4. ye shall receive a crown of **g.**
  10. called us unto his eternal **g.**
2Pet.1. 3. hath called us to **g.** and virt.
  17. God the Father honour and **g.**
    to him from the excellent **g.**
Jude 24. before the presence of his **g.**
  25. God our Saviour, be **g.** and
Rev.4. 9. when those beasts give **g.** and
  11. to receive **g.** and honour ; 5.12
  5.13. Blessing, and honour, and **g.**
  7.12. Say., Amen: Blessing, and **g.**
  11.13. gave **g.** to the God of heaven
  14. 7. Fear God, and give **g.** to him
  15. 8. with smoke from the **g.** of
  16. 9. repented not to give him **g.**
  18. 1. earth was lightened with his **g.**
  19. 1. Salvation, and **g.**, and honour
  21.11. Having the **g.** of God : and
  23. the **g.** of God did lighten it
  24, 26.do bring their **g.** and hon.
kauchēma.
Ro. 4. 2. he hath *whereof to* **g.**; but
1Co. 9.16. I have nothing *to* **g.** *of*: for
2Co. 5.12. give you occasion *to* **g.** on
kleos.
1Pet 2.20. For what **g.** is it, if, when

doxazō.

Mat. 6. 2. that they *may have* g. of
²Co. 3.10. *had* no g. in this respect
¹Pet. 1. 8. joy unspeak. and *full of* g.

kenodoxos.

Gal. 5.26. not be *desirous of vain* g.

kenodoxia.

Phi. 2. 3. done through strife or *vain* g.

GLORY, [*verb,*] -*ing.*

kauchaomai.

Ro. 5. 3. but we g. in tribulations
¹Co. 1.29. That no flesh *should* g. in
  31. *that glorieth let* him g. in ;
    ²Co.10.17
  3.21. *let* no man g. in men. For
  4. 7. why *dost* thou g., as if thou
²Co. 5.12. them *which* g. in appearance
  11.12. that wherein they g., they
  18. g. after the flesh, I *will* g.
  30. If I must needs g., I *will* g.
  12. 1. expedient for me doubt. *to* g.
  5. Of such an one *will* I g.
    I *will* not g., but in mine
  6. though I would desire to g.
  9. *will* I rather g. in my infir.
  11. I am become a fool in g-*ing*
Gal. 6.13. that they *may* g. in your fle.
  14. God forbid that I should g.
²Th. 1. 4. So that we ourselves g. in

katakauchaomai.

Jas. 3.14. g. not, and lie not against

kauchēsis.

Ro. 15.17. therefore *whereof I may* g.

GLORYING, [*noun.*]

kauchēma.

¹Co. 5. 6. your g. is not good. Know
  9.15. man should make my g. void

kauchēsis.

²Co. 7. 4. great is my g. of you : I am

GLUTTONOUS.

phagos.

Mat.11.19. Behold a man g.; Lu.7.34

GNASHED, -*eth.*

trizō.

Mar. 9.18. foameth and g-*eth with* his

bruchō.

Act.7.54. they g. on him with their

GNASHING, [*noun.*]

brugmos.

Mat. 8.12. weeping and g. of teeth
  22.13,24.51,25.30 ; Lu.13.28
  13.42, 50. wailing and g. of teeth

GNAT.

kōnōps.

Mat.23.24. strain at a g., and swallow

GNAWED.

massaomai.

Rev.16.10. g. their tongues for pain

GO, -*est,* -*eth,* -*ing, Gone, Went, Wentest.*

poreuomai.

Mat.2. 8. g. *and* search diligently for
  20. and g. into the land of Israel
  8. 9. man, g. and he g-*eth ;* Lu.7.8
  9.13. But g. ye *and* learn what
  10. 6. But g. rather to the lost
    . And *as* ye g., preach, saying
  11. 4. g. *and* shew John again those
  12. 1. At that time Jesus w-*t* on the
  45. Then g-*eth* he, and taketh
  17.27. g. thou to the sea, *and* cast
  18.12. g-*eth* into the mountains *and*
  21. 2. g.into the village over against
  2. And the disciples w-*t,* and
  22. 9. g. ye therefore into the high.
116

Mat.22.15.Then w-*t* the Pharisees, *and*
  25. 9. but g. ye rather to them that
  16. w-*t and* traded with the same
  26.14. w-*t* unto the chief priests
  27.66. So they w-*t, and* made the
  28. 7. And g. quickly, *and* tell his
  9. And as they w-*t* to tell his
  11. Now *when* they *were* g-*ing*
  16. eleven disciples w-*t away*
  19. g. ye therefore, *and* teach all
Mar.16.10.she w-*t and* told them that
  12. as they walked, and w-*t* into
  15. g. ye into all the world, *and*
Lu. 1.39. and w-*t* into the hill country
  2. 3. And all w-*t* to be taxed every
  41. Now his parents w-*t* to Jeru.
  4.30. midst of them w-*t* his *way*
  42. he departed and w-*t* into a
  5.24. couch, and g. unto thine
  7. 6. Then Jesus w-*t* with them
  11. that he w-*t* into a city called
  22. g. your *way, and* tell John
  50. Thy faith hath saved thee ; g.
  8.14. g.*forth, and* are choked with
  48. made thee whole ; g. in peace
  9.13. except we should g. *and* buy
  51. set his face to g. to Jerusalem
  52. and *they* w-*t, and* entered
  53. *as though* he *would* g. to
  56. And they w-*t* to another
  57. *as* they w-*t* in the way, a cer.
  10.37. g., and do thou likewise
  38. as they w-*t,* that he entered
  11. 5. and *shall* g. unto him at mid.
  26. Then g-*eth* he, and taketh to
  13.32. g. ye, *and* tell that fox, Beh.
  14.10. g. *and* sit down in the lowest
  19. and I g. to prove them : I
  31. g-*ing* to make war against
  15. 4. and g. after that which is lost
  15. And he w-*t and* joined him.
  18. I will arise and g.to my father
  16.30. but if one w-*t* unto them
  17.11. as he w-*t* to Jerusalem, that
  14. g. shew yourselves unto the
  19. Arise, g. thy *way :* thy faith
  19.12. w-*t* into a far country to
  28. he w-*t* before, ascending up
  36. And as he w-*t,* they spread
  21. 8. g. ye not therefore after them
  22. 8. g.*and* prepare us the passover
  22. the Son of man g-*eth,* as it
  33. I am ready to g. with thee
  39. and w-*t,* as he was wont, to
  24.13. two of them w-*t* that same
  28. the village, whither they w-*t*
    as though he would have g-*n*
Jo. 4.50. g. thy *way ;* thy son liveth
    unto him, and he w-*t* his *way*
  7.35. Whither will he g., that we
    will he g. unto the dispersed
  53. every man w-*t* unto his own
  8. 1. Jesus w-*t* unto the mount of
  11. condemn thee : g., and sin no
  10. 4. he g-*eth* before them, and the
  11.11. but I g., that I may awake
  14. 2, 3. I g. to prepare a place for
  12. because I g. unto my Father
  28. I g. unto the Father ; 16.28
  20.17. but g. to my brethren, and
Act.1.10. *as* he w-*t* up, behold, two
  11. as ye have seen him g. into
  25. that he might g. to his own
  5.20. g., stand and speak in the
  8.26. Arise, and g. toward the
  27. And he arose and w-*t :* and
  36. And as they w-*t* on their way
  39. and he w-*t* on his way rejoic.
  9.11. Arise, and g. into the street
  15. g. thy *way :* for he is a chosen
  10.20. get thee down, and g. with
  12.17. and w-*t* into another place

Act.16. 7.they assayed *to* g. into Bithy.
  16. *as* we w-*t* to prayer, a certain
  36. therefore depart, and g. in
  17.14. *to* g. as it were to the sea
  18. 6. I *will* g. unto the Gentiles
  19.21. *to* g. to Jerusalem, saying
  20. 1. departed for *to* g. into Mace.
  22. behold, I g. bound in the
  21. 5. we departed and w-*t* our *way*
  22. 5. and w-*t* to Damascus, to
  10. Arise, and g. into Damascus
  23.23. two hundred soldiers to g. to
  32. left the horsemen *to* g. with
  24.25. g. thy *way* for this time
  25.12. unto Cesar *shalt* thou g.
  20. whether he would g. to Jeru.
  26.12. *as* I w-*t* to Damascus with
  27. 3. gave him liberty to g. unto
  28.26. g. unto this people, and say
Ro.15.25. now I g. unto Jerusalem
¹Co.10.27. and ye be disposed *to* g.
  16. 4. that I g. also, they *shall* g.
  6. on my journey whitherso. I g.
¹Ti. 1. 3. *when* I w-*t* into Macedonia
Jas. 4.13. we will g. into such a city
¹Pet.3.19. By which also he w-*t and*
  22. Who *is* g-*n* into heaven, *and*
Jude 11. they *have* g-*n* in the way of

ekporeuomai.

Mat. 3. 5. Then w-*t out* to him Jerusa.
  17.21. this kind g-*eth* not *out* but
Mar. 1. 5. there w-*t out* unto him all
  7.19. g-*eth out* into the draught
  10.17. *when* he *was* g-*n forth* into
  46. *as* he w-*t out* of Jericho with
  11.19. come, he w-*t out* of the city
  13. 1. *as* he w-*t out* of the temple
Lu. 4.37. the fame of him w-*t out* into
Act. 9.28. them coming in and g-*ing out*
Rev. 1.16. out of his mouth w-*t*
  16.14. which g. *forth* unto the
  19.15. out of his mouth g-*eth* a

paraporeuomai.

Mar.2.23. to pass that he w-*t* through

sumporeuomai.

Lu. 7. 11. of his disciples w-*t with* him
  14.25. there w-*t* great multi. *with*
  24.15. drew near, and w-*t* with them

proporeuomai.

Lu.1. 76. thou *shalt* g. *before* the face
Act.7.40. Make us gods to g. *before* us

diaporeuomai.

Lu. 6. 1. he w-*t through* the corn fields
  13.22. w-*t through* the cities ;
    Act.16.4

eisporeuomai.

Mar.1.21. they w-*t into* Capernaum

erchomai.

Mat.12. 9. he w-*t* into their synagogue
  13.36. and w-*t* into the house : and
  14.12. and w-*t and* told Jesus
  29. walked on the water, *to* g. to
Mar. 3.19. they w-*t* into an ; Lu.14.1
Lu. 2.44. in the company, w-*t* a day's
Jo. 4.45. for they also w-*t* unto the
  6.17. and w-*t* over the sea toward
  21. 3. We also g. with thee. They
Act. 4.23. they w-*t* to their own comp.
  28.14. we w-*t* toward Rome
Heb. 11.8. not knowing whither he w-*t*

exerchomai.

Mat. 9.26. fame hereof w-*t abroad* into
  32. *As* they w-*t out,* behold
  10.11. there abide till ye g. *thence*
  11. 7, 8, 9. What w-*t* ye *out* into ;
    Lu.7.24,25,26
  12.14. Then the Pharisees w-*t out*
  43. unclean spirit *is* g-*n out* of
  13. 1. w-*t* Jesus *out* of the house
  3. Behold, a sower w-*t* *forth to*
  14.14. Jesus w-*t* *forth, and* saw a

Mat.15.21. Then Jesus **w**-*t* thence, *and*
18.28. the same servant **w**-*t out, and*
20. 1. which **w**-*t out* early in the
3, 5,6.he **w**-*t out* about the third
21.17. **w**-*t out of* the city into Beth.
22.10. those servants **w**-*t out..and*
24. 1. Jesus **w**-*t out, and* departed
26. is in the desert; **g**. not *forth*
25. 1. **w**-*t forth* to meet the bride.
6. cometh ; **g**. ye *out* to meet
26.30. they **w**-*t out* into the mount
71. *when he was* **g**-*n out* into the
75. he **w**-*t out, and* wept bitterly ;
Lu.22.62
Mar. 1.35. before day, he **w**-*t out, and*
45. he **w**-*t out, and* began to
2.12. **w**-*t forth* before them all
13. he **w**-*t forth* again by the
3. 6. the Pharisees **w**-*t forth, and*
21. they **w**-*t out* to lay hold on
4. 3. there **w**-*t out* a sower to sow;
Lu.8.5
5.13. the unclean spirits **w**-*t out*
14. they **w**-*t out* to see what it
30. *that* virtue had **g**-*n out* of;
Lu.8.46
6. 1. he **w**-*t out* from thence, and
6.12. they **w**-*t out, and* preached
24. she **w**-*t forth, and* said unto
7.29, 30. the devil *is* **g**-*n out* of ;
Lu.11.14
8.27. Jesus **w**-*t out, and* his disci.
11.11. he **w**-*t out* unto Bethany
14.16. his disciples **w**-*t forth, and*
26. sung an hymn, they **w**-*t out*
68. he **w**-*t out* into the porch
16. 8. they **w**-*t out* quickly, *and*
20. they **w**-*t forth, and* preached
Lu. 2. 1. that there **w**-*t out* a decree
4.14. there **w**-*t out* a fame of him
5.27. after these things he **w**-*t forth*
6.12. he **w**-*t out* into a mountain
19. there **w**-*t* virtue *out* of him
7.17. this rumour of him **w**-*t forth*
8. 2. *out* of whom **w**-*t* seven devils
27. *when* he **w**-*t forth* to land
33. **w**-*t* the devils *out* of the man
35. they **w**-*t out* to see what was
9. 5. *when* ye **g**. *out* of that city
10.10. **g**. your ways *out* into the
11.24. unclean spirit *is* **g**-*n out* of a
14.18. I must needs **g**. and see it
21, 23. **g**. *out* quick. into the stre.
17.29. same day that Lot **w**-*t out*
21.37. at night he **w**-*t out, and* abode
Jo. 1.43. Jesus would **g**. *forth* into
4.30. Then they **w**-*t out* of the city
8. 9. **w**-*t out* one by one, beginn.
59. and **w**-*t out* of the temple
10. 9. shall **g**. in and *out*, and find
11.31. rose up hastily and **w**-*t out*
12.13. and **w**-*t forth* to meet him
13.30. the sop **w**-*t* immediately *out*
31. Theref., when he *was* **g**-*n out*
18. 1. he **w**-*t forth* with his discip.
4. **w**-*t forth* and said unto
16. Then he **w**-*t out* that other disc.
29. Pilate then **w**-*t out* unto
38. he **w**-*t out* again unto the
19. 4. Pilate therefore **w**-*t forth*
17. **w**-*t forth* into a place called
20. 3. Peter therefore **w**-*t forth*
21. 3. They **w**-*t forth*, and entered
23. Then **w**-*t* this saying *abroad*
Act. 1.21. **w**-*t* in and *out* among us
10.23. Peter **w**-*t away* with them
12. 9. he **w**-*t out, and* followed him
10. they **w**-*t out, and* passed on
15.24. certain *which* **w**-*t out* from us
16. 3. Paul have to **g**. *forth* with
10. to **g**. into Macedonia, assur.
13. on the sabbath we **w**-*t out* of

Act.16.19. hope of their gains *was* **g**-*n*
40. they **w**-*t out* of the prison
19.12. the evil spirits **w**-*t out* of
Ro. 10.18. their sound **w**-*t* into all the
1Co. 5.10. needs **g**. *out* of the world
2Co. 2.13. I **w**-*t from thence* into Mace.
8.17. his own accord he **w**-*t* unto
Heb. 11.8. he was called *to* **g**. *out* into
he **w**-*t out*, not knowing
13.13. *Let* us **g**. *forth* therefore unto
1Jo. 2.19. They **w**-*t out* from us, but
4. 1. false prophets *are* **g**-*n out*
3John 7. his name's sake they **w**-*t forth*
Rev. 3 12. he *shall* **g**. no more *out :* and
6. 2. he **w**-*t forth* conquering and
there **w**-*t out* another horse
20. 8. *shall* **g**. *out* to deceive the

aperchomai.

Mat. 2.22. he was afraid *to* **g**. thither
4.24. his fame **w**-*t* throughout all
8.19. whithersoever thou **g**-*est;*
Lu.9.57   [Lu.9.59
21. *to* **g**. and bury my father;
31. suffer us *to* **g**. *away* into the
32. they **w**-*t* into the herd of
33. **w**-*t* their *ways* into the city
10. 5. **g**. not into the way of the
13.25. the wheat, and **w**-*t* his *way*
28. that we **g**. *and* gather them
46. **w**-*t and* sold all that he had
14.15. they *may* **g**. into the villages
25. Jesus **w**-*t* unto them, walk.
16.21. how that he must **g**. unto
18.30. **w**-*t and* cast him into prison
19.22. **w**-*t away* sorrowf.; Mar.10.22
20. 4. And they **w**-*t* their *way;*
22.22 ; Mar.11.4,12.12
21.29. afterw. he repented, and **w**-*t*
30. said, I go, sir; and **w**-*t* not
22. 5. **w**-*t* their *ways*, one to his
25.10. *while* they **w**-*t* to buy, the
18. **w**-*t and* digged in the earth
25. **w**-*t and* hid thy talent in
46. these *shall* **g**. *away* into
26.36. here, while I **g**. *and* pray
42, 44. **w**-*t away* again the seco.
27. 5. departed, and **w**-*t and* hang.
28.10. my breth., that they **g**. into
Mar. 1.20. hired servants, and **w**-*t after*
5.24. Jesus **w**-*t* with him ; and
6.27. he **w**-*t and* beheaded him in
36. that they *may* **g**. into the
37. Shall we **g**. *and* buy two
7.24. he arose, and **w**-*t* his way
9.43. having two hands *to* **g**. into
14.10. one of the twelve, **w**-*t* unto
12. Where wilt thou *that* we **g**.
39. again he **w**-*t away*, and
16.13. they **w**-*t and* told it unto the
Lu. 2.15. as the angels *were* **g**-*n away*
5.14. **g**., *and* shew thyself to the
8.31. command them *to* **g**. *out* into
34. **w**-*t and* told it in the city
39. he **w**-*t* his *way*, and publish.
9.12. they *may* **g**. into the towns
60. **g**. thou *and* preach the
17.23. **g**. not after them, nor follow
19.32. that were sent **w**-*t* their *way*
22. 4. he **w**-*t* his *way, and* comm.
13. they **w**-*t*, *and* found as he
24.24. **w**-*t* to the sepulchre, and
Jo. 4. 8. For his disci. *were* **g**-*n away*
28. and **w**-*t* her *way ;* 11.28
43. thence, and **w**-*t* into Galilee
47. he **w**-*t* unto him, and besou.
6. 1. Jesus **w**-*t* over the sea of
22. that his disc. *were* **g**-*n away*
66. many of his disciples **w**-*t*
68. Lord, to whom *shall* we **g**.
9. 7. He **w**-*t* his *way* therefore
11. I **w**-*t and* washed, and I
10.40. **w**-*t away* again beyond Jor.

Jo. 11.46. some of them **w**-*t* their *ways*
54. **w**-*t* thence unto a country
12.19. behold, the world *is* **g**-*n* after
16. 7. I **g**.*away;* for if I **g**. not *away*
18. 6. they **w**-*t* backward, and fell
20.10. the disciples **w**-*t away* again
Act. 4.15. commanded them *to* **g**. *aside*
5.26. Then **w**-*t* the captain with
9.17. Ananias **w**-*t* his *way*, and
Gal. 1.17. I **w**-*t* into Arabia, and retu.
Jas. 1.24. himself, and **g**-*eth* his *way*
Jude 7. **g**-*ing* after strange flesh, are
Rev.10. 9. I **w**-*t* unto the angel, and
12.17. **w**-*t* to make war with the
16. 2. the first **w**-*t*, and poured out

eiserchomai.

Mat. 7.13. many there be *which* **g**. *in*
9.25. put forth, he **w**-*t in*, and
15.11. Not that *which* **g**-*eth into*
21.12. **w**-*t into* the temple of God ;
Mar.11.15 ; Lu.1.9, 19.45
23.13. ye neither **g**. *in* yourselves
that are entering *to* **g**. *in*
25.10. **w**-*t in* with him to the mar
26.58. priest's palace, and **w**-*t in*
27.53. **w**-*t into* the holy city, and
Mar. 2.26. How he **w**-*t into* the house
8.26. Neither **g**. *into* the town
10.25. a camel *to* **g**. *through* the ;
Lu.18.25
14.14. wheresoever he shall **g**. *in*
15.43. came, and **w**-*t in* boldly
Lu. 4.16. he **w**-*t into* the synagogue
6. 4. How he **w**-*t into* the house
7.36. **w**-*t into* the Pharisee's hou.
8.51. suffered no man *to* **g**. *in*
11.37. he **w**-*t in*, and sat down to
15.28. angry, and would not **g**. *in*
19. 7. he *was* **g**-*n* to be guest with
24.29. he **w**-*t in* to tarry with them
Jo. 10. 9. shall **g**. *in* and out, and
18.28. **w**-*t* not *into* the jud.; 19.9
20. 5. lying ; yet **w**-*t* he not *in*
6. **w**-*t into* the sepulchre, and
8. **w**-*t in* also that other discip.
Act. 1.21. the Lord Jesus **w**-*t in* and
9. 6. Arise, and **g**. *into* the city
10.27. talked with him he **w**-*t in*
11. 3. Thou **w**-*est in* to men uncir.
13.14. **w**-*t into* the synagogue; 19.3
14. 1. they **w**-*t* both together *into*
17. 2. as his manner was, **w**-*t in*

dierchomai.

Mat.19.24. **g**.*through* the eye; Mar.10.25
Lu. 2.15. *Let* us now **g**. even unto Be.
5.15. **w**-*t* their a fame *abroad*
8.22. *Let* us **g**. *over* unto the other
9. 6. departed, and **w**-*t through*
Jo. 4. 4. he must needs **g**. *through*
8.59. **g**-*ing through* the midst of
Act. 8. 4. **w**-*t every where* preaching
10.38. who **w**-*t about* doing good
11.22. that he should **g**. *as far as*
13. 6. *when* they had **g**-*n through*
15.41. he **w**-*t through* Syria and
16. 6. *when* they had **g**-*n througho.*
18.23. and **w**-*t over* all the country
20. 2. *when* he had **g**-*n over* those
25. among whom I *have* **g**-*n*

proerchomai.

Mat.26.39. he **w**-*t* a little *farther, and*
Mar.14.35. And he **w**-*t forward* a little
Lu. 1.17. he *shall* **g**. *before* him in the
22.47. one of the twelve, **w**-*t before*
Act. 20. 5. These **g**-*ing before* tarried for
13. And we **w**-*t before* to ship
2Co. 9. 5. that they *would* **g**. *before*

proserchomai.

Mat.27.58.He **w**-*t to* Pilate, *and* begged:
Lu.23.52
Mar.14.45.he **g**-*eth* straightway *to* him
Lu. 10.34.**w**-*t to* him, *and* bound up

Act. 8.29. **g.** *near*, and join thyself to
  9. 1.Lord, **w-t** *unto* the high priest
22.26. **w-t** *and* told the chief captain

sunerchomai.

Act. 9.39. Then Pet. arose and **w-t** *with*
  11.12. the spirit bade me **g.** *with*
  15.38. and **w-t** not *with* them to
  21.16. There **w-t** *with* us also cert.

anerchomai.

Jo. 6. 3. Jesus **w-t** *up* into a mountain
Gal. 1.17. Neither **w-t** I *up* to Jerusa.
  18. after three years I **w-t** *up* to

suneiserchomai.

Jo. 6.22. **w-t** not *with* his disciples *into*
18.15. **w-t** *in* with Jesus into the

katerchomai.

Act. 8. 5. Philip **w-t** *down* to the city of
12.19. he **w-t** *down* from Judea

parerchomai.

Lu.17. 7. **g.** *and* sit down to meat

agō.

Mat. 26.46. *let* us be **g**-*ing* : Mar.14.42
Mar. 1.38. *Let* us **g.** into the next
Jo. 11. 7. *Let* us **g.** into Judea again
  15. nevertheless, *let* us **g.** unto
  16. *Let* us also **g.**, that we may
14.31. I do.   Arise, *let* us **g.** hence

hupagō.

Mat.5.24. the altar, and **g.** thy *way*
  41. to go a mile, **g.** with him tw.
8. 4. but **g.** thy *way*, shew thyself;
      Mar.1.44   [Mar.10.52
  13. **g.**thy *way* ; and as thou hast :
  32. And he said unto them, **g.**
9. 6. thy bed, and **g.** unto thine
13.44. and for joy thereof **g**-*eth* and
18.15. **g.** and tell him his fault bet.
19.21. **g.** and sell that thou hast ;
      Mar.10.21
20. 4, 7. **g.** ye also into the vineyard
  14. thine is, and **g.** thy *way*
21.28. Son, **g.** work to day in my
26.18. **g.** into the city to such a man
  24. The Son of man **g**-*eth* as it is ;
      Mar.14.21
27.65. Ye have a watch : **g.** your way
28.10. Be not afraid: **g.** tell my bret.
Mar.2.11. and **g.** thy *way* into thine
5.19. **g.** home to thy friends, and
  34. **g.** in peace, and be whole of
6.31. were many coming and **g**-*ing*
  38. How many loaves have ye? **g.**
7.29. For this saying **g.** thy *way*
11. 2. **g.** your *way* into the village
14.13. **g.** into the city, and there
16. 7. But **g.** your *way*, tell his disc.
Lu. 8.42. But as he **w-t** the people
10. 3. **g.** your *ways*: behold, I send
12.58. When thou **g**-*est* with thine
17.14. as they **w-t**, they were clean.
19.30. **g.** ye into the village over
Jo. 3. 8. cometh, and whither it **g**-*eth*
4.16. **g.**, call thy husband, and
6.21. at the land whither they **w-t**
  67. twelve, Will ye also **g.** *away*
7. 3. Depart hence, and **g.** into
  33. and then I **g.** unto him that
8.14. I came, and whither I **g.**
  21. I **g.** my *way*, and ye shall
  22. whither I **g.**, ye cannot come;
      13.33,36
9. 7, 11. **g.**, wash in the pool of
11. 8. and **g**-*est* thou thither again
  31. She **g**-*eth* unto the grave to
44. Loose him, and let him **g.**
12.11. of the Jews **w-t** *away*, and
  35. knoweth not whither he **g**-*eth*;
      [1]Jo.2.11
13. 3. come from God, and **w-t** to
  36. Lord, whither **g**-*est* thou? J.
14. 4. And whither I **g.** ye know
  5. know not whither thou **g**-*est*
118

Jo.14.28. I **g.** *away*, and come again
15.16. that ye should **g.** and bring
16. 5. I **g.** my *way* to him that sent
  asketh me, Whither **g**-*est* thou
  10, 16,17.because I **g.** to my Fath.
18. 8. ye seek me, let these **g.** their
21. 3. Peter saith unto him, I **g.** a
Rev. 10.8. **g.** and take the little book
13.10. into captivity shall **g.** into
14. 4. Lamb whithersoever he **g**-*eth*
16. 1. **g.** *your ways*, and pour out
17. 8, 11. and **g.** into perdition

proagō.

Mat. 2. 9. **w-t** *before* them, till it came
14.22. to **g.** *before* him unto the
21. 9. the multitudes *that* **w-t** *before*
  31. **g.** into the king. of God *before*
26.32. will **g.** *before* you into Galilee;
     28.7 ; Mar.14.28,16.7
Mar. 6.45. to **g.** to the other side *before*
10.32. and Jesus **w-t** *before* them
11. 9. And they *that* **w-t** *before*
Lu. 18.39. they *which* **w-t** *before* rebuk.
[1]Ti. 1.18. prophecies *which* **w-t** *before*
5.24. **g**-*ing before* to judgment
Heb. 7.18. the command. **g**-*ing before*

periagō.

Mat. 4.23. And Jesus **w-t** *about* ; 9.35
Mar. 6. 6. he w. *round about* the villa.
Act. 13.11. he w. *about* seeking some

anabainō.

Mat. 3.16. **w-t** *up* straightway out of
5. 1. he **w-t** *up* into a mountain ;
  14.23,15.29; Mar.3.13; Lu.9.28
20.17,18. **g**-*ing up* to Jerusalem ;
     Mar.10.32,33 ; Lu.18.31 ;
     Act.15.2,21.4,12,25.9
Mar. 6.51. he **w-t** *up* unto them into
Lu. 2. 4. Joseph also **w-t** *up* from ;
  42. they **w-t** *up* to Jerusalem ;
     Jo.2.13,5.1,11.55 ;
     Act.21.15,24.11
5.19. they **w-t** *up* on the housetop
18.10. Two men **w-t** *up* into the
Jo. 7. 8. **g.** ye *up* unto this feast : I
  g. not *up* yet unto this feast
  10. when his breth. *were* **g**-*n up*
  then **w-t** he also *up* unto
  14. Jesus **w-t** *up* into the temple
21.11. Simon Peter **w-t** *up*, and
Act. 1.13. they **w-t** *up* into an upper
3. 1. Peter and John **w-t** *up* toge.
10. 9. Peter **w-t** *up* upon the house.
18.22. landed at Cæsa., *and* **g**-*n up*
Gal. 2. 1. I **w-t** *up* again to Jerusalem
  2. I **w-t** *up* by revelation, and
Rev.20. 9. they **w-t** *up* on the breadth

katabainō.

Mar.13.15. housetop, not **g.** *down* into
Lu. 2.51. And he **w-t** *down* with them
10.30. man **w-t** *down* from Jerusa.
18.14. this man **w-t** *down* to his
Jo. 2.12. he **w-t** *down* to Capernaum
4.51. And *as* he was now **g**-*ing* do.
5. 4. an angel **w** *t down* at a cert.
6.16. his disciples **w-t** *down* unto
Act. 7.15. So Jacob **w-t** *down* into Egy.
8.26. the way *that* **g**-*eth down* from
  33. they **w-t** *down* both into the
10.21. Then Peter **w-t** *down.* *and*
14.25. they **w-t** *down* into Attalia
18.22. church, he **w-t** *down* to Anti.
20.10. And Paul **w-t** *down*, and
23.10. the soldiers to **g.** *down*, *and*
25. 6. he **w-t** *down* unto Cæsarea

probainō.

Mat. 4.21. And **g**-*ing* on from thence
Mar. 1.19. *when* he had **g**-*n* a little *far.*

embainō.   [Lu.8.22,37

Mat.13. 2. he **w-t** *into* a ship, *and* ;

apobainō.

Lu. 5. 2. the fishermen *were* **g**-*n out*

metabainō.

Lu. 10.7. **g.** not from house to house

prosanabainō.

Lu.14.10. Friend, **g.** *up* higher : then

sungkatabainō.

Act. 25.5. **g.** *down with* me, *and* accuse

huperbainō.

[1]Th. 4. 6. That no man **g.** *beyond* and

apoluō.

Lu. 14. 4. healed him, and *let* him **g.**
22.68. not answer me, nor *let* me **g.**
23.22. chastise him, and *let* him **g.**
Jo. 19.12. If thou *let* this man **g.**, thou
Act. 3.13. determined to *let* him **g.**
4.21. they *let* them **g.**, finding
  23. *being let* **g.**, they went to
5.40. name of J., and *let* them **g.**
15.33. they *were let* **g.** in peace
16.35. saying, *Let* those men **g.**
  36. have sent to *let* you **g.**: now
17. 9. of the other, they *let* them **g.**
28.18. would *have let* me **g.**, because

planaō.

Mat.18.12. one of them be **g**-*n astray*
  seeketh ..*which is* **g**-*n astray*
  13. and mine wh. **w-t** not *astray*
[1]Pet. 2.25. ye were as sheep **g**-*ing astray*
[2]Pet. 2.15. and *are* **g**-*n astray*, following

eiseimi.

Act. 3. 3. about *to* **g.** *into* the temple
21.18. Paul **w-t** *in* with us unto
Heb. 9. 6. priests **w-t** always *into* the

exeimi.

Act.13.42. when the Jews *were* **g**-*n out*

apeimi.

Act.17.10. **w-t** into the synagog. of the

zēteō.

Jo. 7.19, 20. Why **g.** ye *about* to kill
Act. 21.31. *as* they **w-t** *about* to kill him
Ro. 10. 3. **g**-*ing about* to establish their

teleō.

Mat.10.23. ye *shall* not *have* **g**-*n over*

diaperaō.

Mat.14.34. *when* they *were* **g**-*n over*

chōreō.

Mat.15.17. **g**-*eth* into the belly, and is

sbennumi.

Mat.25.8. for our lamps *are* **g**-*n out*

peripateō.

Mar.12.38. love *to* **g.** in long clothing

diodeuō.

Lu. 8. 1. he **w-t** *throughout* every city

hupochōreō.

Lu. 9.10. **w-t** *aside* privately into a

hupantaō.

Jo. 11.20. **w-t** *and* met him : but Mary

epicheireō.

Act. 9.29. they **w-t** *about* to slay him

epistrephō.

Act.15.36. *Let* us **g.** *again* and visit

anachōreō.

Act.23.19. **w-t** with him *aside* privately
26.31. when they *were* **g**-*n aside*

peirazō.

Act. 24.6. Who also *hath* **g**-*n about*

peiraō.

Act.26.21. and **w-t** *about* to kill me

ekklinō.

Ro. 3.12. *are* all **g**-*n out of the way*

epiduō.

Eph.4.26. *let* not the sun **g.** *down* upon

pherō.

Heb. 6.1. *let* us **g.** *on* unto perfection

age.   (*let us be brought.*)

Jas. 4.13. **g.** *to* now, ye that say, To day
5. 1. **g.** *to* now ye rich men, weep

paraginomai.

Act.23.16. **w-t** and entered into the cas.

(See *Aboard, Compel, Country,*
Further, Journey, Law, Let,
Warfare.)

GOAT,   -s.
   eriphos.
Mat.25.32. his sheep from the g-s
   eriphion.
Mat.25.33. hand, but the g-s on the left
   tragos.
Heb. 9.12, 19. blood of g-s and calves
   13. blood of bulls and of g-s; 10.4
   aigeios.
Heb.11.37. in sheep skins and g. skins

GOD,   -s.
   Theos.
Mat. 1.23. being interpreted is, g. with
   3. 9. g. is able of these sto.; Lu.3.8
   6.24. serve g. and mam.; Lu.16.13
   31. they glorified the g. of Israel
  16.16. Son of the living g.; Jo.6.69
   23. things that be of g.; Mar.8.33
  19.17. good but one, that is g.;
      Mar.10.18; Lu.18.19
   26. with g.all things are possible;
      Mar.10.27; Lu.1.37, 18.27
  22.21. g. the things that are g.'s;
      Mar.12.17; Lu.20.25
   32. g. is not the g. of the dead
  26.63. I adjure thee by the living g.
Mar. 5. 7. of the most high g.; Lu.8.28
   I adjure thee by g.
  12.32. for there is one g.; and
Lu. 1. 6. both righteous before g.
   30. hast found favour with g.
  2.52. favour with g. and man
  12. 6. them is forgotten before g.
  24.19. before g. and all the people
Jo. 1. 1. g. and the Word was g.
   13. were born, not..but of g.
  3. 2. art a teacher come from g.
   33. his seal that g. is true
  4.24. g. is a Spirit : and they that
  5.18. making himself equal with g.;
      Phi.2.6
  6.46. save he which is of g., he
  7.17. whether it be of g., or
  8.41. we have one Father, even g.
   42. If g. were your Father, ye
   47. He that is of g. heareth g.'s
   because ye are not of g.
   54. ye say, that he is your g.
  9.16. This man is not of g., because
   33. If this man were not of g.
  12.43. more than the praise of g.
  13. 3. come from g., and went to g.
   31. and g. is glorified in him
  17. 3. know thee the only true g.
  20.17. and to my g., and your g.
   28. him, My Lord and my g.
Act. 2.22. approved of g. among you
  4.19. unto you more than unto g.
  5. 4. lied unto men, but unto g.
   29. We ought to obey g. rather
   39. But if it be of g., ye cannot
  6.11. against Moses, and against g.
  7. 9. but g. was with him
   46. favour before g., and desired
  10. 4. for a memorial before g.
   33. we all here present before g.
   34. g. is no respecter of persons
  14.15. unto the living g., which
  16.17. servants of the most high g.
  23. 1. all good conscience before g.
  26.18. of Satan unto g., that they
   20. repent and turn to g., and
Ro. 1. 8. I thank my g.through Jesus;
      1Co.1.4,14.18;Phi.1.3;Phile.4
   9. For g. is my witness, whom
  2.11. respect of persons with g.
   13. are just before g., but the
   29. is not of men, but of g.
  3. 4. yea, let g. be true, but every
   19. may become guilty before g.
  4. 2. glory but not before g.

Ro. 5. 1. we have peace with g.through
  6.10. he liveth, he liveth unto g.
   11. but alive unto g. through J.
   13. yield yourselves unto g.
  7. 4. bring forth fruit unto g.
  8. 7. is enmity against g.: for it is
   31. If g. be for us, who can
  9.14. there unrighteousness with g.
   16. but of g. that sheweth mercy
   20. that repliest against g.
   26. the children of the living g.
  11.23. for g. is able to graff them
  12. 1. acceptable unto g. which
  13. 1. power but of g.: the powers
   that be are ordained of g.
  14. 4. g. is able to make him stand
   12. give account of himself to g.
   22. have it to thyself before g.
  15. 5. Now the g. of patience and
  16.26. command. of the everlast. g.
1Co. 1. 9. g. is faithful, by whom ye
   30. of g.is made unto us wisdom
  3. 9. labourers together with g.
   19. is foolishness with g. For it
  6.11. and by the Spirit of our g.
   19. which ye have of g., and ye
  7.24. called therein abide with g.
  10.13. but g. is faithful, who will
  11.12. but all things of g.; 2Co.5.18
  14. 2. not unto men, but unto g.
   25. that g. is in you of a truth
   33. g. is not the author of conf.
  15.24. the kingdom to g., even the
   28. that g. may be all in all
2Co. 1.18. But as g. is true, our word
   21. and hath anointed us, is g.
  2.17. as of g., in the sight of g.
  3. 3. the Spirit of the living g.
   5. our sufficiency is of g.
  6.16. of the living g.; as g. hath
  9. 8. And g. is able to make
  12.19. before g. in Christ : but we
   21. my g. will humble me among
  13.11. and the g. of love and peace
Gal. 1.20. behold, before g., I lie not
  3.20. of one ; but g. is one
  6. 7. deceived; g. is not mocked
Eph. 2. 4. But g., who is rich in mercy
Phi. 1. 8. For g. is my record, how
   28. salvation, and that of g.
  3. 9. righteousness which is of g.
   19. whose g. is their belly
  4.19. But my g. shall supply
   20. Now unto g. and our Father
1Th. 1. 9. serve the living and true g.
  2. 5. covetousness; g. is witness
  3.13. before g., even our Father
2Th. 1. 6. is a righteous thing with g.
  2. 4. that is called g., or that is
   so that he as g. sitteth in
1Ti. 3.15. church of the living g.
   16. g. was manifest in the flesh
  4.10. we trust in the living g.;6.17
  5. 4. good and acceptable before g.
   21. charge thee before g.; 2Ti.4.1
Tit. 1.16. profess that they know g.
Heb. 3. 4. that built all things is g.
   12. departing from the living g.
  5. 4. is called of g., as was Aaron
  6.10. For g. is not unrighteous
  7.25. unto g. by him, seeing he
  8.10. I will be to them a g., and
  9.14. works to serve the living g.
  10. 7, 9. to do thy will, O g.
   31. into the hands of the living g.
  11. 6. he that cometh to g. must
   16. g. is not ashamed to be called
  12.22. unto the city of the living g.
   23. to g. the Judge of all, and to
   29. For our g. is a consuming
  13.16. sacrifices g. is well pleased
Jas. 1.27. before g. and the Father

Jas. 4. 4. world is enmity with g.
   7. yourselves therefore to g.
1Pet. 2.20. this is acceptable with g.
  3.18. might bring us to g., being
  4. 6. but live according to g. in
1Jo. 1. 5. that g. is light, and in him
  3.10. is not of g., neither he
   20. g. is greater than our heart
  4. 1. whether they are of g.:because
   3. is not of g.: and this is
   6. of g.: he that knoweth g
   8. knoweth not g.; for g. is
   12. No man hath seen g. at
  5.19. that we are of g., and the
3John 11. He that doeth good is of g.
Rev. 3. 2. thy works perfect before g.
   12. the name of my g., and the
  5. 9. hast redeemed us to g. by
   10. unto our g. kings and
  7. 2. the seal of the living g.: and
   10. Salvation to our g. which
   12. and might, be unto our g.
  9.13. altar which is before g.
  11.13. glory to the g. of heaven
  12. 5. unto g., and to his throne
   10. before our g. day and night
  13. 6. in blasphemy against g.
  14. 4. unto g. and to the Lamb
  16.11. blasphemed the g. of heaven
   19. in remembrance before g.
  20.12. and great, stand before g.
  21. 3. and g. himself shall be with
   4. g. shall wipe away all tears
   7. I will be his g., and he shall

*(And all other passages except the
      following :—)*
   ho kurios.
Act.19.20. mightily grew the word of g.
   daimonion.
Act.17.18. setter forth of strange g-s
   ophelon.
1Co. 4.8. I *would to* g. ye did reign
2Co. 11.1. *would to* g. ye could bear
   atheos.
Eph.2.12. and *without* g. in the world
   theomachomai.
Act.23.9. let us not fight against g.

(See *Admonish, Answer, Fight,
Forbid, Hater, Inspiration, Lover,
Speed, Taught, Worshipper.*)

GODDESS.
   thea.
Act.19.27, 35. of the great g. Diana
   37. yet blasphemers of your g.

GODHEAD.
   theios.
Act.17.29. that the g. is like unto
   theiotēs.
Ro. 1.20. even his eternal power and g.
   theotēs.
Col. 2. 9. all the fulness of the g. bodily

GODLINESS.
   eusebeia.
1Ti. 2. 2. life, in all g. and honesty
  3.16. great is the mystery of g.
  4. 7. thyself rather unto g.
   8. but g. is profitable unto all
  6. 3. which is according to g.
   5. that gain is g.; from such
   6. g.,with contentment, is great
   11. g., faith, love, patience
2Ti. 3. 5. Having a form of g., but
Tit. 1. 1. of the truth which is after g.
2Pet. 1. 3. unto life and g., through the
   6. patience; and to patience g.
   7. And to g. brotherly kindness
  3.11. all holy conversation and g.

theosebeia.
¹Ti. 2.10. women professing g.

GODLY, (See *Fear, Sort.*)
   kata Theos.
²Co. 1.12. simplicity and g. sincerity
  7. 9. made sorry after a g. manner
  10. For g. sorrow worketh
  11. ye sorrowed after a g. sort
  11. 2. jealous over you with g.
¹Ti. 1. 4. g. edifying which is in faith
²John 6. after a g. sort
   eusebōs.
²Ti. 3.12. all that will live g. in Christ
Tit. 2.12. soberly, righteously, and g.
   eusebēs.
²Pet. 2.9. knoweth how to deliver the g.
   eulabeia.
Heb.12.28. with reverence and g. *fear*

GOD-WARD.
   pros ho Theos.
²Co. 3. 4. have we through Christ to g.
¹Th. 1. 8. your faith to g. is spread

GOLD, (See *Ring.*)
   chrusos.
Mat. 2.11. unto him gifts ; g., and frank.
  10. 9. Provide neither g., nor silver
  23.16. swear by the g. of the temple
   17. whether is greater, the g., or
     temple that sanctifieth the g.
Act.17.29. Godhead is like unto g., or
¹Co. 3.12. upon this foundation, g.
¹Ti. 2. 9. not with broidered hair, or g.
Jas. 5. 3. Your g. and silver is canker.
Rev. 9. 7. as it were crowns like g.
  17. 4. decked with g. and ; 18.16
  18.12. The merchandise of g., and
   chrusion.
Act. 3. 6. Silver and g. have I none
  20.33. coveted no man's silver, or g.
Heb. 9. 4. overlaid round about with g.
¹Pet. 1. 7. more precious than of g. that
  18. corrupt. things, as sil. and g.
  3. 3. the hair, and of wearing of g.
Rev. 3.18. to buy of me g. tried in the
  21.18,21.and the city was pure g.
   chruseos.
²Ti. 2.20. not only vessels *of* g. and of
Rev. 4. 4. on their heads crowns *of* g.
  9.20. devils and idols of g. and

GOLDEN.
   chruseos.
Heb. 9. 4. Which had the g. censer
   the g. pot that had manna
Rev. 1.12. I saw seven g. candlesticks
  13. about the paps with a g.
  20. the seven g. candlesticks ; 2.1
  5. 8. and g. vials full of odours
  8. 3. having a g. censer ; and
   upon the g. altar which was
  9.13. the four horns of the g. altar
  14.14. having on his head a g.
  15. 6. breasts girded with g. girdles
  7. seven g. vials full of the
  17. 4. having a g. cup in her hand
  21.15. had a g. reed to measure the

GOOD.
   agathos.
Mat. 5.45. rise on the evil and on the g.
  7.11. g. gifts unto your children ;
   Lu.11.13
   wh. is in heaven give g. *things*
  17,18. every g. tree bring. forth
12.34. ye, being evil, speak g.
  35. A g. man out of the g. trea.
   bringeth forth g. *things ;*
   Lu. 6.45
  19.16. g. Master, what g. *thing ;*
   Mat.10.17 ; Lu.18.18

Mat.19.17. Why callest thou me g.
  none g.; Mar.10.18 ; Lu.18.19
  20.15. thine eye evil, because I am g.
  22.10. they found, both bad and g.
  25.21. Well done, g. and faithf.; 23
Lu. 1.53. fill. the hungry with g. *things*
  8. 8. And other fell on g. ground
  15. which is an honest and g.
  10.42. Mary hath chosen that g.
  16.25. receivedst thy g. *things*
  19.17. Well, thou g. servant : bec.
  23.50. he was a g. man, and a just
Jo. 1.46. Can any g. *thing* come out
  5.29. they that have done g., unto
  7.12. some said, He is a g. man
Act. 9.36. this woman was full of g.
  11.24. For he was a g. man, and
  23. 1. I have lived in all g. consci.
Ro. 2.10. every man that worketh g.
  3. 8. Let us do evil, that g. may
  5. 7. for a g. man some would
  7.12. commandment holy, just, g.
  13. that which is g. made death
   in me by that which is g.
  18. flesh, dwelleth no g. *thing*
  19. the g. that I would I do not
  8.28. all things work togeth. for g.
  9.11. having done any g. or evil
  10.15. bring glad tidings of g. *things*
  12. 2. prove what is that g., and
  9. cleave to that which is g.
  21. but overcome evil with g.
  13. 3. rulers not a terror to g. works
   do that which is g., and thou
  4. minister of God to thee for g.
  14.16. your g. be evil spoken of
  15. 2. please his neighbour for his g.
  16.19. wise unto that which is g.
²Co. 5.10. done, whether it be g. or
  9. 8. may abound to every g.
Gal. 6. 6. that teacheth in all g. *things*
  10. let us do g. unto all men
Eph. 2.10. created in Ch. Je. unto g.
  4.28. hands the thing which is g.
  29. but that which is g. to the
  6. 8. whatsoever g. thing any man
Phi. 1. 6. he which hath begun a g.
Col. 1.10. being fruitful in every g.
¹Th. 3. 6. ye have g. remembrance of
  5.15. ever follow that which is g. ;
   ³John 11
²Th. 2.16. and g. hope through grace
  17. stablish you in every g.
¹Ti. 1. 5. pure heart, and of a g. cons.
  19. Holding faith, and a g. cons.
  2.10. professing godliness with g.
  5.10. diligently followed every g.
²Ti. 2.21. prepared unto every g. work
  3.17. furnished unto all g. works
Tit. 1.16. unto every g. work reprobate
  2. 5. keepers at home, g., obedie.
  10. shewing all g. fidelity ; that
  3. 1. to be ready to every g. work
Phile. 6. acknowled. of every g. *thing*
Heb. 9.11. high priest of g. *things* to
  10. 1. a shadow of g. *things* to
  13.21. Make you perfect in every g.
Jas. 1.17. Every g. gift, and every perf.
  3.17. full of mercy and g. fruits
¹Pet. 2.18. not only to the g. and gentle
  3.10. that will love life, and see g.
  11. Let him esch. evil, and do g.
  13. be follow. of that which is g.
  16. Having a g. conscience ; that
   falsely accuse your g. conve.
  21. the answer of a g. conscience
   kalos.   [Lu.3.9
Mat. 3.10. bringeth not forth g. ; 7.19 ;
  5.16. that they may see your g.
  7.17,18. bringeth forth g. fruit ;
   Lu.6.43
  12.33. the tree g., and his fruit g.

Mat.13. 8, 23. fell into g. ground ;
   Mar.4.8 ; Lu.8.15
  24, 27,37,38. sowed g. seed
  48. gathered the g. into vessels
  17. 4. g. for us to be here ; Mar.9.5 :
   Lu.9.33
  26.10. hath wrought a g. work
   Mar.14.6   [Mar.14.21
  24. it had been g. for that man ;
Mar. 4.20. which are sown on g. ground
  9.50. Salt is g. ; Lu.14.31
Lu. 6.38. g. measure, pressed down
  43. For a g. tree bringeth not
Jo. 2.10. set forth g. wine . . kept the g.
  10.11, 14. I am the g. shep. : the g.
  32, 33. Many g. works. . For a g.
Ro. 7.16. unto the law that it is g.
  18. to perform that which is g.
  21. when I would do g., evil is
  14.21. It is g. neither to eat flesh
¹Co. 5. 6. Your glorying is not g.
  7. 1. It is g. for a man not
  8. It is g. for them if they
  26. that this is g. for the present
Gal. 4.18. g. to be zealously affect. in g.
¹Th. 5.21. hold fast that which is g.
¹Ti. 1. 8. we know that the law is g.
  18. mightest war a g. warfare
  2. 3. is g. and acceptable ; ¹Ti.5.4
  3. 1. bishop, he desireth a g. work
  7. must have a g. report of
  13. to themselves a g. degree
  4. 4. every creature of God is g.
  6. thou shalt be a g. minister
   of faith and of g. doctrine
  5.10. Well reported of for g. works
  25. also the g. works of some
  6.12. Fight the g. fight of faith
   professed a g. profession
  13. witnessed a g. confession
  18. that they be rich in g. works
  19. a g. foundation against the
²Ti. 1.14. That g. thing which was
  2. 3. as a g. soldier of Jesus Ch.
  4. 7. I have fought a g. fight, I
Tit. 2. 7. a pattern of g. works : in
  14. people zealous of g. works
  3. 14. maintain g. works . . g.
Heb. 5.14. to discern both g. and evil
  6. 5. have tasted the g. word
  10.24. provoke unto love and to g.
  13. 9. a g. thing that the heart be
  18. we trust we have a g. consc.
Jas. 3.13. out of a g. conversation
  4.17. to him that knoweth to do g.
¹Pet. 2.12. they may by your g. works
  4.10. as g. stewards of the manifo.
   chrēstotēs.
Ro. 3.12. there is none that doeth g.
   chrēstos.
¹Co.15.33. evil communica. corrupt g.
   bios.
¹Jo. 3.17. whoso hath this world's g.
   kalōs.
Mat.5.44. do g. to them which hate ;
   Lu.6.27
Jas. 2. 3. Sit thou here in *a* g. *place*
   eu.
Mar.14.7. ye will ye may do th*e*m g.
   hikanos.
Act.18.18. tarried there yet a g. while
   agathopoieō.
Mar. 3. 4. to do g. on the sab ; Lu.6.9
Lu. 6.33. ye do g. to them *which do* g.
  35. and do g., and lend, hoping
Act.14.17. in that he did g., and gave us
³John 11. He *that doeth* g. is of God
   eupoia.
Heb.13.16. *to do* g. and to communicate
   agathoergeō.
¹Ti. 6.18. *That they do* g., that they be

ischuŏ.

Mat.5.13. *is* thenceforth **g.** for nothing

sumpherŏ.

Mat.19.10. his wife, it *is* not **g.** to

euergeteŏ.

Act.10.38. who went about *doing* **g.**

(See *Behaviour, Cheer, Comfort, Deed, Despiser, Increase, Lover, Olive, Report, Seem, Teacher, Think, Tidings, Way, Will, Words.*)

GOODLY.

kalos.

Mat.13.45. man, seeking **g.** pearls
Lu. 21. 5. adorned with **g.** stones

lampros.

Jas. 2. 2. if there come..in **g.** apparel
Rev.18.14.which were dainty and **g.** are

GOODMAN.

oikodespotēs.

Mat.20.11. against the **g.** *of the house*
  24.43. if the **g.** *of the house* had ;
        Lu.12.39
Mar.14.14. say ye to the **g.** *of the house*
Lu. 22.11. shall say unto the **g.** of the

GOODNESS.

agathōsunē.

Ro.15.14. ye also are full of **g.**, filled
Gal. 5.22. longsuffering, gentleness, **g.**
Eph.5. 9. fruit of the Spirit in all **g.**
²Th. 1.11. the good pleasure of his **g.**

chrēstotēs.

Ro. 2. 4. thou the riches of his **g.**
  11.22. Behold therefore the **g.** and
     g. if thou continue in his **g.**

chrēstos.

Ro. 2. 4. that the **g.** of God leadeth

GOODS.

huparchonta.

Mat.24.47. make him ruler over all his **g.**
  25.14. delivered unto them his **g.**
Lu 11.21. palace, his **g.** are in peace
  16. 1. that he had wasted his **g.**
  19. 8. the half of my **g.** I give to
¹Co.13. 3. I bestow all my **g.** to feed
Heb.10.34.joyfully the spoil. of your **g.**

skeuos.

Mat.12.29. spoil his **g.**, except ; Mar.3.27

agathos.

Lu.12.18. bestow all my fruits and my **g.**
  19. thou hast much **g.** laid up

ousia.

Lu.15.12. give me the portion of **g.**

huparxis.

Act.2.45. sold their possessions and **g.**

GORGEOUS.

lampros.

Lu.23.11. arrayed him in a **g.** robe.

GORGEOUSLY.

endoxos.

Lu. 7.25. they which are **g.** apparelled

GOSPEL, (See *Preach.*)

euaⁿggelion.

Mat. 4.23. preaching the **g.** of the ;
    9.35 ; Mar.1.14
  24.14. this **g.** of the kingdom ;
    26.13 ; Mar.14.9
Mar. 1. 1. beginning of the **g.** of ;
    Phi.4.15
  15. repent ye, and believe the **g.**
  8.35. for my sake and the **g.**'s ;
    10.29
  13.10. the **g.** must first be published
  16.15. preach the **g.** to every creat.
Act.15. 7. hear the word of the **g.**

Act.20.24. to testify the **g.** of the grace
Ro. 1. 1. separated unto the **g.** of God
  9. in the **g.** of his Son, that
  16. I am not ashamed of the **g.**
  2.16. Christ, according to my **g.**
  10.16. have not all obeyed the **g.**
  11.28. As concerning the **g.**, they
  15.16. ministering the **g.** of God
  19. I have fully preached the **g.**
  29. of the blessing of the **g.**
  16.25. according to my **g.**, and the
¹Co. 4.15. begotten you through the **g.**
  9.12. lest we should hinder the **g.**
  14. the **g.** should live of the **g.**
  18. I may make the **g.** of Christ
    not my power in the **g.**
  23. I do for the **g.**'s sake, that
  15. 1. the **g.** which I preached
²Co. 2.12. to preach Christ's **g.**
  4. 3. if our **g.** be hid, it is hid to
  4. the light of the glorious **g.**
  8.18. whose praise is in the **g.**
  9.13. unto the **g.** of Christ
  10.14. in preaching the **g.** of Christ
  11. 4. or another **g.** ; Gal.1.6
  7. I have preached to you the **g.**
Gal. 1. 7. would pervert the **g.** of Christ
  11. that the **g.** which was preach.
  2. 2. communic. unto them that **g.**
  5. that the truth of the **g.** might
  7. the **g.** of the uncircumcision
  14. accord. to the truth of the **g.**
Eph.1.13. the **g.** of your salvation
  3. 6. promise in Christ by the **g.**
  6.15. with the preparation of the **g.**
  19. known the mystery of the **g.**
Phi. 1. 5. For your fellowship in the **g.**
  7, 17.and confirmation of the **g.**
  12. the furtherance of the **g.**
  27. as it becometh the **g.** of Ch.
    for the faith of the **g.**
  2.22. hath served with me in the **g.**
  4. 3. laboured with me in the **g.**
Col. 1. 5. the word of the truth of the **g.**
  23. from the hope of the **g.**
¹Th. 1. 5. For our **g.** came not unto
  2, 2, 9. unto you the **g.** of God
  4. to be put in trust with the **g.**
  8. not the **g.** of God only
  3. 2. fellowlabourer in the **g.** of
²Th. 1. 8. obey not the **g.** of ; ¹Pet.4.17
  2.14. he called you by our **g.**, to
¹Ti. 1.11. According to the glorious **g.**
²Ti. 1. 8. of the afflictions of the **g.**
  10. immo. to light through the **g.**
  2. 8. dead, according to my **g.**
Phile. 13. me in the bonds of the **g.**
Rev.14. 6. having the everlasting **g.**

GOVERNMENT,   -s.

kubernēsis.

¹Co.12.28. helps, **g-s**, diversities of

kuriotēs.

²Pet.2.10. uncleanness, and despise **g.**

GOVERNOR,   -s.

hēgemōn.

Mat.10.18. shall be brought before **g-s**
  27. 2. him to Pontius Pilate the **g.**
  11. before the **g.**: and the **g.**
  14. the **g.** marvelled greatly
  15. the **g.** was wont to release
  21, 23. The **g.** answered and said
  27. Then the soldiers of the **g.**
  28.14. if this come to the **g.**'s ears
Lu. 20.20. power and authority of the **g.**
Act.23.24. him safe unto Felix the **g.**
  26. unto the most excellent **g.**
  33. delivered the epistle to the **g.**
  34. And when the **g.** had read
  24. 1. who informed the **g.** against
  10. after that the **g.** had beckoned
  26.30. the king rose up, and the **g.**

¹Pet. 2.14. Or unto **g-s**, as unto them

ethnarchēs.

²Co.11.32. the **g.** under Aretas the king

oikonomos.

Gal. 4. 2. But is under tutors and **g-s**

architriklinos.

Jo. 2. 8. bear unto the **g.** *of the feast*
  9. the **g.** *of the feast* called the

hēgeomai.

Mat.2. 6. out of thee shall come a **g.**
Act. 7.10. made him **g.** over Egypt

hēgemoneuŏ.

Lu. 2. 2. *when* Cyrenius *was* **g.** of Syria
  3. 1. Pontius Pilate *being* **g.** of Jud.

GRACE.

charis.

Lu. 2.40. and the **g.** of God was upon
Jo. 1.14. Father, full of **g.** and truth
  16. received, and **g.** for **g.**
  17. **g.** and truth came by J. Ch.
Act. 4.33. and great **g.** was upon them
  11.23. and had seen the **g.** of God
  13.43. to continue in the **g.** of God
  14. 3. testi. unto the word of his **g.**
  26. recom. to the **g.** of God ; 15.40
  15.11. through the **g.** of the Lord J.
  18.27. which had believed throu. **g.**
  20.24. testify the gospel of the **g.** of
  32. God, and to the word of his **g.**
Ro. 1. 5. By whom we have received **g.**
  7. **g.** to you and peace from ;
    ¹Co.1.3 ; ²Co.1.2 ; Gal.1.3 ;
    Eph.1.2 ; Phi.1.2 ; Col.1.2 ;
    ¹Th.1.1 ; ²Th.1.2 ; Phile.3
  3.24. Being justified freely by his **g.**
  4. 4. reward not reckoned of **g.**
  16. faith, that it might be by **g.**
  5. 2. by faith into this **g.** wherein
  15. the **g.**of God, and the gift by **g.**
  17. which receive abundance of **g.**
  20. **g.** did much more abound
  21. even so might **g.** reign throu.
  6. 1. continue in sin, that **g.** may
  14, 15.under the law, but under **g.**
  11. 5. according to the election of **g.**
  6. if by **g.**, then it is no more
    otherwise **g.** is no more **g.**
    works, then is it no more **g.**
  12. 3. the **g.** given unto me ; 15.15
    ¹Co.3.10
  6. according to the **g.** that is
  16.20, 24.The **g.** of our L. J. Christ ;
    ¹Co.16.23; ²Co.13.14; Gal.6.18;
    Phi.4.23 ; ¹Th.5.28 ; ²Th.3.18 ;
    Phile.25 ; Rev.22.21
¹Co. 1. 4. for the **g.** of God which is
  10.30. For if I by **g.** be a partaker
  15.10. But by the **g.** of God I am
    and his **g.** which was bestow.
    not I, but the **g.** of God which
²Co. 1.12. but by the **g.** of God, we have
  4.15. that the abundant **g.** might
  6. 1. ye receive not the **g.** of God
  8. 1. do you to wit of the **g.** of
  6. finish in you the same **g.** also
  7. see that ye abound in this **g.**
  9. ye know the **g.** of our L. J.
  19. to travel with us with this **g.**
  9. 8. is able to make all **g.** abound
  14. for the exceeding **g.** of God
  12. 9. My **g.** is sufficient for thee
Gal. 1. 6. that called you into the **g.**
  15. and called me by his **g.**
  2. 9. perceived the **g.** that was
  21. I do not frustrate the **g.** of
  5. 4. law ; ye are fallen from **g.**
Eph.1. 6. praise of the glory of his **g.**
  7. accord. to the riches of his **g.**
  2. 5, 8. by **g.** ye are saved
  7. the exceeding riches of his **g.**
  3. 2. of the dispensation of the **g.**

Eph.3. 7. according to the gift of the g.
8. is this g. given, that I should
4. 7. every one of us is given g.
29. it may minister g. unto the
6.24. g. be with all them that love
Phi.1. 7. ye all are partakers of my g.
Col. 1. 6. and knew the g. of God in
3.16. singing with g. in your hearts
4. 6. your speech be alway with g.
18. g. be with you ; 1Ti.6.21 ;
2Ti.4.22 ; Tit.3.15 ; Heb.13.25
1Th.1.12. according to the g. of our
2.16. and good hope through g.
1Ti. 1. 2. g., mercy, and peace, from ;
2Ti.1.2 ; Tit.1.4 ; 2John 3
14. And the g. of our Lord was
2Ti. 1. 9. to his own purpose and g.
2. 1. be strong in the g. that is in
Tit. 2.11. For the g. of God that bring.
3. 7. That being justified by his g.
Heb.2. 9. that he by the g. of God
4.16. boldly unto the throne of g.
and find g. to help in time
10.29. despite unto the Spirit of g.
12.15. lest any man fail of the g.
28. let us have g., whereby we
18. 9. heart be established with g.
Jas. 4. 6. But he giveth more g. Wher.
giveth g. unto the humble ;
1Pet.5.5 [2Pet.1.2 ; Rev.1.4
1Pet.1. 2. g. unto you, and peace ;
10. who prophesied of the g. that
13. for the g. that is to be brought
3. 7. heirs together of the g. of
4.10. stewards of the manifold g. of
5.10. But the God of all g., who
12. that this is the true g. of God
2Pet.3.18. But grow in g., and in the
Jude 4. turning the g. of our God
euprepeia.
Jas.1.11. the g. of the fashion of it

GRACIOUS.
charis.
Lu.4.22. wondered at the g. words
chrēstos.
1Pet.2.3. tasted that the Lord is g.

GRAFF,   -ed.
engkentrizō.
Ro.11.17. wert g-ed in among them
19. off, that I might be g-ed in
23. unbelief, shall be g-ed in
for God is able to g. them in
24. and wert g-ed contrary to their
shall these..be g-ed into their

GRAIN.
kokkos.
Mat.13.31. like to a g. of mustard seed ;
Mar.4.31 ; Lu.13.19
17.20. faith as a g. of mustard ;
Lu.17.6
1Co. 15.37. bare g., it may chance of

GRANDMOTHER.
mammē.
2Ti. 1. 5. dwelt first in thy g. Lois

GRANT,   -ed.
didōmi.
Mar.10.37. g. unto us that we may sit
Lu. 1.74. That he would g. unto us
Act. 4.29. g. unto thy servants, that
11.18. to the Gentiles g-ed repent.
14. 3. and g-ed signs and wonders
Ro. 15. 5. g. you to be likeminded one
Eph 3.16. That he would g you, accor.
1Ti. 1.18. The Lord g. unto him that
Rev. 3.21. that overcometh, will I. g.
19. 8. to her was g-ed that she
epō.
Mat.20.21. g. that these my two sons
122

charizomai.
Act.3.14. desired a murderer to be g-ed

GRAPES.
staphulē.
Mat.7.16. men gather g. of thorns
Lu. 6.44. bramble bush gather they g.
Rev.14.18.for her g. are fully ripe

GRASS.
chortos.   [Lu.12.28
Mat. 6.30. if God so clothe the g.;
14.19. to sit down on the g., and
Mar. 6.39. companies upon the green g.
Jo. 6.10. there was much g. in the
Jas. 1.10. as the flower of the g. he
11. but it withereth the g., and
1Pet. 1.24. For all flesh is as g., and all
man as the flower of g.
The g. withereth, and the
Rev. 8. 7. all green g. was burnt up
9. 4. should not hurt the g. of the

GRAVE, [noun,]   -s.
mnēmeion.
Mat.27.52. And the g-s were opened
53. And came out of the g-s
Lu. 11.44. for ye are as g-s which appear
Jo. 5.28. all that are in the g-s shall
11.17. he had lain in the g. four
31. She goeth unto the g. to
38. cometh to the g. It was
Jo. 12.17. called Lazarus out of his g.
mnēma.
Rev.11.9. dead bodies to be put in g-s
hadēs.
1Co.15.55. O g., where is thy victory

GRAVE, [adject.]
semnos.
1Ti. 3. 8. must the deacons be g.
11. so must their wives be g.
Tit. 2. 2. the aged men be sober, g.

GRAVEN.
charagma.
Act.17.29. stone, g. by art, and man's

GRAVECLOTHES.
keiriai.
Jo.11.44. bound hand and foot with g.

GRAVITY.
semnotēs.
1Ti.3.4. in subjection with all g.
Tit.2.7. uncorruptness, g., sincerity

GREAT.
megas.
Mat. 2.10. with exceeding g. joy
4.16. sat in darkness saw g. light
5.19. shall be called g. in the
35. in the city of the g. King
7.27. g. was the fall of it ; Lu.6.49
8.24. there arose a g. tempest ;
Mar.4.37 [Mar.4.39
26. and there was a g. calm ;
15.28. O woman, g. is thy faith
20.25. and they that are g. exercise
26. whosoever will be g.;
Mar.10.43
22.36, 38.which is the g. command
24.21. then shall be g. tribulation
24. and shall shew g. signs
31. with a g. sound of a trumpet
27 60. he rolled a g. stone to the
28 2. there was a g. earthquake;
Act.16.26; Rev.6.12, 11.13,
16.18
8. with fear and g. joy ; and
Mar. 4.32. and shooteth out g. branches
5.11. a g. herd of swine feeding
5.42. with a g. astonishment
10.42. and their g. ones exercise

Mar. 13. 2. Seest thou these g. buildings
16. 4. away : for it was very g.
Lu. 1.15, 32. he shall be g. in the
2.10. you good tidings of g. joy
4.25. g. famine was throughout
38. was taken with a g. fever
5.29. Levi made him a g. feast
7.16. That a g. prophet is risen
8.37. they were taken with g. fear
9.48. you all the same shall be g.
13.19. and waxed a g. tree ; and
14.16. certain man made a g. sup.
16.26. there is a g. gulf fixed
21.11. And g. earthquakes shall be
and g. signs shall there be
23. there shall be g. distress
24.52. to Jerusalem with g. joy
Jo. 6.18. by reason of a g. wind that
7.37. that g. day of the feast
21.11. the net to land full of g.fishes
Act. 2.20. before that g. and notable
4.33. And with g. power gave the
and g. grace was upon them
5. 5, 11. and g. fear came on all ;
Rev.11.11
6. 8. did g. wonders and miracles
7.11. and Chanaan, and g. affict.
8. 1. there was g. persecution
2. and made g. lamentation
8. there was g. joy in that city
9. that himself was some g.
10. man is the g. power of God
10.11. it had been a g. sheet ; 11.5
11.28. that there should be g. dear.
15. 3. they caused g. joy unto all
19.27, 35. of the g. goddess Diana
28, 34. g. is Diana of the Eph.
23. 9. And there arose a g. cry
26.22. to small and g.; Rev.11.18,
13.16, 19.5
Ro. 9. 2. That I have g. heaviness
1Co. 9.11. is it a g. thing if we shall
16. 9. For a g. door and effectual
2Co. 11.15. it is no g. thing if his min.
Eph. 5.32. This is a g. mystery : but I
1Ti. 3.16. g. is the mystery of godliness
6. 6. with contentment is g. gain
2Ti. 2.20. But in a g. house there are
Tit. 2.13. glorious appear. of the g. G.
Heb. 4.14. that we have a g. high priest
10.35. which hath g. recompence
13.20. that g. Shepherd of the sheep
Jude 6. unto the judgment of the g.
Rev. 1.10. and heard behind me a g.
2.22. into g. tribulation, except
6. 4. was given unto him a g. sw.
17. the g. day of his wrath is
7.14. which came out of g. tribu.
8. 8. as it were a g. mountain
10. there fell a g. star from hea.
9. 2. as the smoke of a g. furnace
14. bound in the g. river Euph.
11. 8. in the street of the g. city
12. they heard a g. voice from
15. there were g. voices in heav.
17. hast taken to thee thy g.
19. an earthquake, and g. hail
12. 1. a g. wonder in heaven
3. a g. red dragon, having
9. the g. dragon was cast out
12. having g. wrath, because he
14. two wings of a g. eagle
13. 2. and his seat, and g. authority
5. a mouth speaking g. things
13. he doeth g. wonders, so that
14. 2. as the voice of a g. thunder
8. that g. city, because she
19. into the g. winepress of the
15. 1, 3. g. and marvellous, seven
16. 1. I heard a g. voice out of
9. scorched with g. heat, and
2. his vial upon the g. river

Rev. 16.14. of that g. day of G. Almighty
17. a g. voice out of the temple
18. an earthquake, and so g.
19. the g. city was divided
g. Babylon came in remem.
21. upon men a g. hail out of
thereof was exceeding g.
17. 1. judgment of the g. whore
5. BABYLON THE g.; 18.2
6. I wondered with g. admira.
18. is that g. city, which reign.
18. 1. having g. power ; and the
10, 16,19,21. that g.city Babylon
18. What city is like unto this g.
21. a stone like a g. millstone
19. 1. I heard a g. voice of much
2. hath judged the g. whore
17. unto the supper of the g. G.
18. bond, both small and g.
20. 1. and a g. chain in his hand
11. I saw a g. white throne
12. I saw the dead, small and g.
21. 3. I heard a g. voice out of
10. to a g. and high mountain
and shewed me that g. city
12. had a wall g. and high, and
polus.
Mat. 2.18. and g. mourning, Rachel
4.25. g. multitudes of people from
5.12. for g. is your reward
8. 1. g. multitudes followed ;
12.15,19.2,20.29
18. when Jesus saw g. multitu.
13. 2. And g. multitudes were
14.14. and saw a g. multitude
15.30. And g. multitudes came
19.22. for he had g. possessions
24.30. with power and g. glory
26.47. and with him a g. multitude
Mar. 3. 7. a g. multitude from Galilee
3. S. a g. multitude, when they
4. 1. gathered unto him a g. mul.
9.14. he saw a g. multitude
10.22. for he had g. possessions
10.48. he cried the more a g. deal
13.26. with g. power and glory
14.43. and with him a g. multitude
Lu. 2.36. she was of a g. age, and had
5. 6. they inclosed a g. multitude
15. and g. multitudes came tog.
29. and there was a g. company
6.17. and a g. multitude of people
23. your reward is g. in heaven
35. and your reward shall be g.
10. 2. The harvest truly is g.
14.25. there went g. multitudes
21.27. with power and g. glory
23.27. a g. company of people
Jo. 5. 3. a g. multitude of impotent
6. 2. And a g. multitude followed
5. and saw a g. company come
Act. 6. 7. a g. company of the priests
11.21. and a g. number believed
14. 1. that a g. multitude both
17. 4. devout Greeks a g. multitude
21.40. there was made a g. silence
22.28. With a g. sum obtained I
23.10. there arose a g. dissension
24. 2. by thee we enjoy g. quietness
7. with g. violence took him
25.23. and Bernice, with g. pomp
28. 6. they had looked a g. while
29. and had g. reasoning among
1Co. 3.12. we use g. plainness of speech
7. 4. g. is my boldness of speech
you, g. is my glorying of you
8. 2. How that in a g. trial of
22. upon the g. confidence whi.
Eph. 2. 4. for his g. love wherewith he
Col. 4.13. that he hath a g. zeal for
1Th. 2.17. to see your face with g. desire
1Ti. 3.13. and g. boldness in the faith

Phile. 7. For we have g. joy and con.
Heb.10.32.ye endured a g. fight of affli.
Rev. 7. 9. and, lo, a g. multitude
19. 6. the voice of a g. multitude
pampolus.
Mar.8. 1. the multitude being very g.
pleistos.
Mat.21. 8. a very g. multitude spread
megaleia.
Lu. 1.49. hath done to me g. things
megistos.
2Pet. 1. 4. exceeding g. and precious
megistanes.
Rev. 6.15. and the g. men, and the rich
18.23. thy merch. were the g. men
hikanos.
Mar.10.46. and a g. number of people
Act. 22. 6. from heaven a g. light
lian.
Mar.1.35. rising up a g. while before
tosautos. [Lu.7.9
Mat. 8.10. I have not found so g. faith ;
15.33. as to fill so g. a multitude
Heb.12. 1. with so g. a cloud of witness.
Rev.18.17. so g. riches is come to noug.
tēlikoutos.
2Co. 1.10. delivered us from so g. a
Heb. 2. 3. if we neglect so g. salvation
Jas. 3. 4. which though they be so g.
hosos.
Mar. 3. 8. had heard what g. things
5.19, 20. tell them how g. things ;
Lu.8.39
Act. 9.16. how g. things he must suffer
posos.
Mat. 6.23. how g. is that darkness
hēlikos.
Col. 2. 1. ye knew what g. conflict
Jas. 3. 5. how g. a matter a little fire
pēlikos.
Heb.7. 4. consider how g. this man
(See Authority, Boast, Child,
Curse, Deal, Desire, Drop,
Noise, Price, Shew, Swelling,
Way, While.)

GREATER.
meizōn.
Mat.11.11.not risen a g. than ; Lu.7.28
is g. than he ; Lu.7.28
12. 6. is one g. than the temple
23.17,19.for whether is g.; Lu. 22.27
Mar. 4.32. becometh g. than all herbs
12.31. commandment g. than these
Lu. 12.18. down my barns, and build g.
Jo. 1.50. thou shalt see g. things than
4.12. Art thou g. than ; 8.53
5.20. g. works than these ; 14.12
36. But I have g. witness than
10.29. is g. than all ; and none
13.16. servant is not g. than ; 15.20
neither he that is sent g.
14.28. for my Father is g. than I
15.13. g. love hath no man than
19.11. unto thee hath the g. sin
1Co. 14. 5. for g. is he that prophesieth
Heb. 6.13. could swear by no g., he
16. men verily swear by the g.
9.11. by a g. and more perfect
11.26. the reproach of Christ g.
Jas. 3. 1. receive the g. condemnation
2Pet. 2.11. which are g. in power and
1Jo. 3.20. God is g. than our heart
4. 4. g. is he that is in you, than
5. 9. the witness of God is g.
pleiōn. [Lu.11.32
Mat.12.41. a g. than Jonas is here ;
42. a g.than So. is here; Lu.11.31
Act. 15.28. to lay upon you no g. bur.
1Co. 15. 6. the g. part remain unto

perissoteros.
Mat.23.14. receive the g. damnation ;
Mar.12.40 ; Lu.20.47
meizoteros.
3John 4. I have no g. joy than to

GREATEST.
meizōn.
Mat. 13.32. is the g. among herbs
18.1,4. g. in the kingdom [Lu.22.26
23.11. But he that is g. among
Mar. 9.34. should be the g.; Lu.9.46
Lu. 22.24. should be accounted the g.
1Co. 13.13. but the g. of these is chari.
megas.
Act. 8.10. the least to the g.; Heb.8.11

GREATLY.
polus.
Mar. 5.23. And besought him g., say.
38. that wept and wailed g.
12.27. ye therefore do g. err
1Co. 16.12. I g. desired him to come
lian.
Mat.27.14. the governor marvelled g.
2Ti. 4.15. he hath g. withstood our
2John 4. I rejoiced g., that ; 3John 3
sphodra.
Mat. 27.54. they feared g., saying, Truly
Act. 6. 7. disciples multi. in Jeru. g.
megalōs.
Phi. 4.10. I rejoiced in the Lord g.
hōs.
Phi. 1. 8. how g. I long after you all
chairō chara.
Jo. 3.29. rejoiceth g. (rej. with joy.)
(See Amazed, Desire, Long,
Rejoice, Wonder.)

GREATNESS.
megethos.
Eph.1.19. exceeding g. of his power to

GREEDILY.
ekchunō.
Jude 11. and ran g. after the error

GREEDINESS.
pleonexia.
Eph.4.19. work all uncleanness with

GREEDY.
aphilarguros.
1Ti. 3. 3. striker, not g. of filthy lucre

GREEN.
chlōros.
Mar. 6.39. companies upon the g. grass
Rev. 8. 7. all g. grass was burnt
9. 4. neither any g. thing, neither
hugros.
Lu.23.31. these things in a g. tree

GREET, -eth, -ing.
aspazomai.
Ro. 16. 3. g. Priscilla and Aquila
6. g. Mary, who bestowed
8. g. Amplias, my beloved in
11. g. them that be of the hous.
1Co.16.20. g. you. g. ye one another
2Co.13.12 ; 1Pet.5.14
Phi. 4.21. which are with me g. you
Col. 4.14. physician, and Demas, g.
1Th. 5.26. g. all the brethren with an
2Ti. 4.21. Eubulus g-eth thee, and
Tit. 3.15. g. them that love us in the
2John 13. children of thy elect sister g.
3John 14. g. the friends by name
chairō.
Act. 15.23. send g-ing unto the brethren
23.26. unto . .Felix sendeth g-ing
Jas. 1. 1. are scattered abroad, g-ing

GREETINGS.
aspasmos. [20.46
Mat.23. 7. g. in the markets ; Lu.11.43,
128

GRIEF.
lupē.
¹Pet. 2.19. consc. toward God endure **g.**
lupeō.
²Co. 2. 5. if any *have caused* **g.**, he
stenazō.
Heb.13.17. joy, and not *with* **g.**

GRIEVE,   -ed.
lupeō.
Mar.10.22. and went away **g-**ed : for he
Jo. 21.17. Peter *was* **g-**ed because he
Ro. 14.15. if thy brother *be* **g-**ed with
²Co. 2. 4. not that ye *should be* **g-**ed
5. *hath* not **g-**ed me, but in
Eph. 4.30. And **g.** not the holy Spirit
sullupeomai.
Mar. 3. 5. *being* **g-**ed for the hardness
diaponeomai.
Act. 4. 2. *Being* **g-**ed that they taught
16.18. Paul, *being* **g-**ed, turned and
prosochthizō.
Heb. 3.10. I *was* **g-**ed *with* that genera.
17. *with* whom *was* he **g-**ed forty

GRIEVOUS.
barus.
Act.20.29. shall **g.** wolves enter in
25. 7. many and **g.** complaints
¹Jo. 5. 3. commandments are not **g.**
oknēros.
Phi. 3. 1. to me indeed is not **g.**
dusbastaktos.   [Lu.11.46
Mat.23.4. burdens and **g.** *to be borne ;*
ponēros.
Rev.16.2. a noisome and **g.** sore upon
lupē.
Heb.12.11. joyous, but **g.**   (*of grief.*)

GRIEVOUSLY.
deinōs.
Mat.8.6. of the palsy, **g.** tormented
kakōs.
Mat.15.22. is **g.** vexed with a devil

GRIND,   -ing.
likmaō.   [Lu.20.18
Mat.21.44. *will* **g.** him *to powder ;*
alēthō.
Mat.24.41.wom. shall be **g-**ing ; Lu.17.35

GROAN,   -ed, -eth, -ing.
stenazō.
Ro. 8.23. even we ourselves **g.** within
²Co. 5. 2. For in this we **g.**, earnestly
4. in this tabernacle *do* **g.**
sustenazō.
Ro.8.22. **g-**eth and travaileth..*together*
embrimaomai.
Jo.11.33. *he* **g-**ed in the spirit, and
38. therefore again **g-**ing in him.

GROANING, [noun,]   -s.
stenagmos.
Act.7.34. and I have heard their **g.**
Ro. 8.26. with **g-**s which cannot be

GROSS.
pachunomai.
Mat.13.15. heart *is waxed* **g.**;Act.28.27

GROUND, [noun.]
gē.
Mat.10.29. shall not fall on the **g.** with.
13. 8. other fell into good **g.**;
Mar.4.8 ; Lu.8.8
23. received seed into good **g.**
15.35. sit down on the **g.** ; Mar.8.6
Mar. 4.20. which are sown on good **g.**
26. should cast seed into the **g.**
9.20. he fell on the **g.**, and wallo.
14.35. fell on the **g.**, and prayed|
Lu. 8.15. that on the good **g.** are they
13. 7. why cumbereth it the **g.**
124

Lu. 22.44. blood falling down to the **g.**
Jo. 8. 6. his finger wrote on the **g.**
8. down, and wrote on the **g.**
12.24. of wheat fall into the **g.** and
Act. 7.33. where thou standest is h. **g.**
chōra.
Lu.12.16. The **g.** of a certain rich man
chōrion.
Jo.4.5. near to the *parcel of* **g.** that
agros.
Lu.14.18. I have bought a *piece of* **g.**
edaphos.
Act.22.7. I fell unto the **g.**, and heard
hedraiōma.
¹Ti.3.15. the pillar and **g.** of the truth
edaphizō.
Lu.19.44. *shall lay* thee *even with the* **g.**
chamai.
Jo. 9.6. he spat *on the* **g.**, and made
18.6. backward, and fell *to the* **g.**

GROUNDED.
themelioō.
Eph.3.17. being rooted and **g.** in love
Col. 1.23. continue in the faith **g.**

GROW,   -eth, Grew, Grown.
auxanō.
Mat. 6.28. lilies..how they **g.**; Lu.12.27
13.32. when it *is* **g-**n, it is the grea.
Lu. 1.80. the child **g-**e, and waxed; 2.40
13.19. it **g-**e, and waxed a great
Act. 7.17. the people **g-**e and multiplied
12.24. the word of God **g-**e and
19.20. So mightily **g-**e the word of
Eph. 2.21. **g-**eth unto an holy temple
4.15. *may* **g.** up into him in
¹Pet.2. 2. the word, that ye *may* **g.**
²Pet. 3.18. **g.** in grace, and in the know.
sunauxanomai.
Mat.13.30. Let both **g.** *together* until
huperauxanō.
²Th.1.3. your faith **g-**eth *exceedingly*
mēkunomai.
Mar.4.27. seed should spring and **g.** up
ginomai.
Mat.21.19. *Let* no fruit **g.** on thee hence.
Act. 5.24. whereunto this *would* **g.**
anabainō.
Mar.4. 7. thorns **g-**e up, and choked
32. when it is sown, it **g-**eth up
erchomai.
Mar.5.26. bettered, but rather **g-**e worse

GRUDGE.
stenazō.
Jas.5.9. **g.** not one against another

GRUDGING, [noun.]
gonggusmos.
¹Pet.4.9. one to another without **g.**

GRUDGINGLY.
ek lupē.
²Co.9.7. not **g.**, or of necessity : for

GUARD, (See *Captain.*)

GUEST,   -s.
anakeimai.
Mat.22.10. wed. was furnished with **g-**s
11. king came in to see the **g-**s
kataluō.
Lu.19.7. gone *to be* **g.** with a man

GUESTCHAMBER.
kataluma.
Mar.14.14. Where is the **g.**; Lu.22.11

GUIDE, [noun,]   -s.
hodēgos.
Mat.23.16. Woe unto you, ye blind **g-**s
24. Ye blind **g-**s, which strain
Act. 1.16. which was **g.** to them that
Ro. 2.19. art a **g.** of the blind, a light

GUIDE, [verb.]
hodēgeō.
Jo.16.13. he *will* **g.** you into all truth
Act.8.31. except some man *should* **g.**
kateuthunō.
Lu.1.79. *to* **g.** our feet into the way
oikodespoteō.
¹Ti.5.14. **g.** *the house*, give none occasion

GUILE.
dolos.
Jo. 1.47. indeed, in whom is no **g.**
²Co.12.16. crafty, I caught you with **g.**
¹Th. 2. 3. nor of uncleanness, nor in **g.**
¹Pet. 2. 1. aside malice, and all **g.**
22. neither was **g.** found ;Rev.14.5
3.10. his lips that they speak no **g.**

GUILTLESS.
anaitios.
Mat.12.7. not have condemned the **g.**

GUILTY.
enochos.
Mat.26.66. and said, He is **g.** *of* death
Mar.14.64. condemned him to be **g.** *of*
¹Co. 11.27. shall be **g.** *of* the body and
Jas. 2. 10. in one point, he is **g.** *of* all
opheilō.
Mat.23.18. gift that is upon it, *he is* **g.**
hupodikos.
Ro.3.19. world may become **g.** before

GULF.
chasma.
Lu.16.26. there is a great **g.** fixed : so

GUSHED.
ekchunō.
Act.1.18. and all his bowels **g.** *out*

HABITATION,   -s.
skēnē.
Lu. 16. 9. you into everlasting **h-**s
epaulis.
Act. 1.20. Let his **h.** be desolate, and
katoikia.
Act.17.26. and the bounds of their **h.**
katoikētērion.
Eph. 2.22. for an **h.** of God through
Rev.18. 2. is become the **h.** of devils
oikētērion.
Jude 6. but left their own **h.**, he

HAIL, [verb.]
chairō.
Mat.26.49. **h.** Master ! and kissed him
27.29. **h.**, King of the Jews
Mar.15.18 ; Jo.19.3
28. 9. Jes. met them, saying, *All* **h.**
Lu. 1.28. **h.**, thou that art highly fav.

HAIL, [noun.]
chalaza.
Rev. 8. 7. followed **h.** and fire mingled
11.19. earthquake, and great **h.**
16.21. there fell upon men a great **h.**
becau. of the plague of the **h.**

HAIR,   -s.
thrix.
Mat. 3. 4. raiment of camel's **h.**; [Mar. 1.6
5.36. make one **h.** white or black
10.30. the very **h-**s of your ; Lu.12.7
Lu. 7.38, 44. with the **h-**s of her head;
Jo.11.2,12.3
21.18. But there shall not an **h.** of
Act.27.34. an **h.** fall from the head of
¹Pet. 3. 3. of plaiting the **h.**, and of
Rev. 1.14. and his **h-**s were white like
9. 8. And they had **h.** as the **h.** of
komaō.
¹Co. 11.14. if a man *have long* **h.**, it is
15. But if a woman *have long* **h.**
komē.
¹Co. 11.15. for her **h.** is given her for a

plegma.
¹Ti. 2. 9. not with *broidered* **h**. or gold
trichinos.
Rev. 6.12. black as sackcloth *of* **h**.

HALE,   -*ing.*
katasurō.
Lu. 12.58. lest he **h**. thee to the judge
surō.
Act. 8. 3. and **h**-*ing* men and women

HALF ,(See *Dead, Hour.*)
hēmisu.
Mar. 6.23. unto the **h**. of my kingdom
Lu. 19. 8. the **h**. of my goods I give to
Rev.11. 9, 11. three days and an **h**.
  12.14. a time, and times, and **h**. a

HALL,(See *Common, Judgment.*)
aulē.
Mar.15.16.into the **h**., called Praetori.
Lu. 22.55.a fire in the midst of the **h**.

HALLOWED.
hagiazō.
Mat. 6. 9. **h**. *be* thy name; Lu.11.2

HALT.
chōlos.
Mat.18. 8. enter into life **h**. ; Mar.9.45
Lu. 14.21. and the **h**., and the blind
Jo. 5. 3. of blind, **h**., withered, wait.

HAND,   -*s.*
cheir.   [3.17
Mat. 3.12. Whose fan is in his **h**.; Lu.
  4. 6. **h**-*s* they shall bear ; Lu.4.11
  5.30. if thy right **h**. offend thee
  8. 3. Jesus put forth his **h**.;
          Mar.1.41; Lu.5.13
  15. he touched her **h**., and the
  9.18. lay thy **h**. upon her, and she
  25. took her by the **h** ; Mar.1.31,
          5.41 ; Lu.8.54
  12.10. which had his **h**. withered ;
          Mar.3.1,3; Lu.6.6,8
  13. Stretch forth thine **h**.;
          Mar.3.5; Lu.6.10
  49. stretched forth his **h**.; 14.31
  15. 2. for they wash not their **h**-*s*
  20. to eat with unwashen **h**-*s* ;
          Mar.7.2,5
  17.22. betrayed into the **h**-*s*; 26.45;
          Mar.9.3,14.41 ; Lu.9.44,24.7
  18. 8. **h**. or thy foot offe.; Mar.9.43
          than hav. two **h**-*s* ; Mar.9.43
  19.13. his **h**-*s* on them ; Mar.10.16
  15. he laid his **h**-*s* on them, and
  22.13. Bind him **h**. and foot, and
  26.23. He that dippeth his **h**. with
  50. laid **h**-*s* on Jes.; Mar.14.46
  51. stretched out his **h**., and
  27.24. washed his **h**-*s* before the
Mar. 3. 5. his **h**. was restored ; Lu.6.10
  5.23. come and lay thy **h**-*s* on her
  6. 2. works are wrought by his **h**-*s*
  5. laid his **h**-*s* upon a few sick
  7. 3. except they wash their **h**-*s*
  32. him to pút his **h**. upon him
  8.23. took the blind man by the **h**.
  25. and put his **h**-*s* upon him
  9.27. took him by the **h**., and
  16.18. they shall lay **h**-*s* on the
Lu. 1.66. And the **h**. of the Lord
  71. and from the **h**. of all that
  74. delivered out of the **h**. of
  4.40. laíd his **h**-*s* on every one of
  6. 1. rubbing them in their **h**-*s*
  9.62. No man, having put his **h**.
  13.13. And he laid his **h**-*s* on her
  15.22. and put a ring on his **h**.
  20.19. sought to lay **h**-*s* on him
  21.12. they shall lay their **h**-*s* on
  22.21. the **h**. of him that betrayeth

Lu. 22.53. ye stretched forth no **h**-*s*
  23.46. into thy **h**-*s* I commend my
  24.39. Behold my **h**-*s* and ; Jo.20.27
  40. shew. them his **h**-*s*; Jo.20.20
  50. he lifted up his **h**-*s*, and
Jo. 3.35. all things into his **h**.; Jo.13.3
  7.30, 44. but no man laid **h**-*s* on
  10.28. pluck them out of my **h**.
  29. them out of my Father's **h**.
  39. he escaped out of their **h**.
  11.44. bound **h**. and foot with gra.
  13. 9. but also my **h**-*s* and my head
  20.25. Except I shall see in his **h**-*s*
          and thrust my **h**. into his
  27. and reach hither thy **h**., and
  21.18. shalt stretch forth thy **h**-*s*
Act. 2.23. by wicked **h**-*s* have crucified
  3. 7. took him by the right **h**.
  4. 3. they laid **h**-*s* on them ; 6.6,
          8.17,13.3
  28. whatsoever thy **h**. and thy
  30. stretching forth thine **h**. to
  5.12. by the **h**-*s* of the apostles
  18. laid their **h**-*s* on the apostles
  7.25. how that God by his **h**. would
  35. by the **h**. of the angel which
  41. in the works of their own **h**-*s*
  50. Hath not my **h**. made all
  8.18. laying on of the apostles' **h**-*s*
  19. that on whomsoever I lay **h**-*s*
  9.12, 17. and putting his **h**. on
  41. he gave her his **h**., and
  11.21. And the **h**. of the Lord was
  30. by the **h**-*s* of Barnabas and
  12. 1. king stretched forth his **h**-*s*
  7. chains fell off from his **h**-*s*
  11. me out of the **h**. of Herod
  17. beckoning..with the **h**.;
          13.16,19.33,21.40
  13.11. behold, the **h**. of the Lord
  14. 3. won. to be done by their **h**-*s*
  17.25. is worshipped with men's **h**-*s*
  19. 6. when Paul had laid his **h**-*s*
  11. special miracles by the **h**-*s* of
  26. gods, wh. are made with **h**-*s*
  20.34. these **h**-*s* have ministered
  21.11. bound his own **h**-*s* and feet
          shall deliver him into the **h**-*s*
  27. all the people, and laid **h**-*s*
  23.19. captain took him by the **h**.
  24. 7. him away out of our **h**-*s*
  26. 1. Paul stretched forth the **h**.
  28. 3. heat, and fastened on his **h**.
  4. beast hang on his **h**., they
  8. laid his **h**-*s* on him, and
  17. into the **h**-*s* of the Romans
Ro. 10.21. I have stretched forth my **h**-*s*
¹Co. 4.12. working with our own **h**-*s*
  12.15. Because I am not the **h**., I
  21. eye cannot say unto the **h**.
  16.21. with mine own **h**.; Gal.6.11 ;
          Col.4.18 ; ²Th.3.17 ; Phile.19
²Co. 11.33. wall, and escaped his **h**-*s*
Gal. 3.19. by angels, in the **h**. of a
Eph. 4.28. working with his **h**-*s* the
¹Th. 4.11. to work with your own **h**-*s*
¹Ti. 2. 8. lifting up holy **h**-*s*, without
  4.14. laying on of the **h**-*s*; Heb.6.2
  5.22. Lay **h**-*s* suddenly on no
²Ti. 1. 6. by the putting on of my **h**-*s*
Heb. 1.10. are the works of thine **h**-*s*
  2. 7. over the works of thy **h**-*s*
  8. 9. I took them by the **h**. to lead
  10.31. to fall into the **h**-*s* of the
  12.12. lift up the **h**-*s* which hang
Jas. 4. 8. Cleanse your **h**-*s*, ye sinners
¹Pet. 5. 6. under the mighty **h**. of God
¹Jo. 1. 1. and our **h**-*s* have handled
Rev. 1.16. he had in his right **h**. seven
  17. he laid his right **h**. upon me
  6. 5. pair of balances in his **h**.
  7. 9. robes, and palms in their **h**-*s*

Rev. 8. 4. God out of the angel's **h**.
  9.20. not of the works of their **h**-*s*
  10. 2. he had in his **h**. a little
  5. lifted up his **h**. to heaven
  8. which is open in the **h**. of
  10. book out of the angel's **h**.
  13.16. a mark in their right **h**., or
  14. 9. in his forehead, or in his **h**.
  14. and in his **h**. a sharp sickle
  17. 4. a golden cup in her **h**. full
  19. 2. blood of his serv. at her **h**.
  20. 1. and a great chain in his **h**.
  4. their foreheads,or in their **h**-*s*
dexios.
Mat. 6. 3. know what thy *right* **h**. doeth
  20.21. one on thy *right* **h**.; 27.38 ;
          Mar.10.37 ; Lu.23.33
  23. to sit on my *right* **h**.;
          Mar.10.40
  22.44. Sit thou on my *right* **h**. ;
          Mar.12.36 ; Lu 20.42 ;
          Act.2.34; Heb 1.13
  25.33. set the sheep on his *right* **h**.
  34. say unto them on his *right* **h**.
  26.64. the *right* **h**. of power ;
          Mar.14.62 ; Lu.22.69
  27.29. a reed in his *right* **h**.: and
Mar.15.27.the one on his *right* **h**., and
  16.19. on the *right* **h**. of God ;
          Act.7.55,56 ; Col.3.1 ;
          Heb 10.12 ; ¹Pet.3.22
Lu. 6. 6. a man whose *right* **h**. was
Act. 2.25. for he is on my *right* **h**., that
  33. being by the *right* **h**. of God
  5.31. God exalted with his *right* **h**.
Ro. 8.34. even at the *right* **h**. of God
²Co. 6. 7. on the *right* **h**. and on the
Gal. 2. 9. the *right* **h**-*s* of fellowship
Eph. 1.20. set him at his own *right* **h**.
Heb. 1. 3. the *right* **h**. of the Majesty
  8. 1. set on the *right* **h**. of the
  12. 2. is set down at the *right* **h**.
Rev. 1.20. thou sawest in my *right* **h**.
  2. 1. the seven stars in his *right* **h**.
  5. 1. I saw in the *right* **h**. of him
  7. the book out of the *right* **h**.

cheiropoiētos.
Mar.14.58. temple that is *made with* **h**-*s*
Act. 7.48. tem. *made with* **h**; 17.24
Eph. 2.11. in the flesh *made by* **h**-*s*.
Heb. 9.11. taber., not *made with* **h**-*s*
  24. holy places *made with* **h**-*s*
acheiropoiētos.
Mar.14.58. another *made without* **h**-*s*
²Co. 5. 1. an house *not made with* **h**-*s*
Col. 2.11. circumcis. *made without* **h**-*s*
autocheir.
Act.27.19. we cast out *with* our *own* **h**-*s*
cheiragōgos.
Act.13.11. *some* to lead him *by the* **h**.
krateō.
Mat.18.28. and he *laid* **h**-*s* on him, and
  21.46. they sought *to lay* **h**-*s* *on*
piazō.
Jo. 8.20. and no man *laid* **h**-*s* on him
enggus.
Mat.26.18. Mast. saith, My time is *at* **h**.
Lu. 21.30. summer is now *nigh at* **h**.
  31. kingdom of God is *nigh at* **h**.
Jo. 2.13. the Jews' passover was *at* **h**.
  7. 2. feast of tabernacles was *at* **h**.
  11.55. Jews' passov. was *nigh at* **h**.
  19.42. the sepulchre was *nigh at* **h**.
Phi. 4. 5. all men. The Lord is *at* **h**.
Rev. 1. 3. for the time is *at* **h**.; 22.10
enggizō.
Mat. 3. 2. the king. of heaven *is at* **h**.
          Mat.4.17,10.7
  26.45. behold, the hour *is at* **h**.
  46. he *is at* **h**. that doth betray
Mar. 1.15. the kingdom of God *is at* **h**.
  14.42. he that betrayeth me *is at* **h**.

Ro. 13.12. far spent, the day *is at* h.
¹Pet. 4. 7. the end of all things *is at* h.
    enistēmi.
²Th. 2. 2 the day of Christ *is at* h.
    ephistēmi.
²Ti. 4. 6 of my departure *is at* h.
    epicheireō.
Lu. 1. 1. many *have taken in* h. to set
    (See *Lead, Palm, Smite, Strike.*)

HANDKERCHIEFS.
    soudarion.
Act.19.12. brought unto the sick, h.

HANDLE,   -ed.
    psēlaphaō.
Lu. 24.39. h. me, and see ; for a spirit
¹Jo. 1. 1. and our hands *have* h-ed
    thigō.
Col. 2.21. Touch not ; taste not ; h.
    doloō.
²Co. 4. 2. h. the word of God *deceitful.*
    (See *Shamefully.*)

HANDMAID,   -en, -s.
    doulē.
Lu. 1.38. Behold the h. of the Lord
    48. the low estate of his h-en
Act. 2.18. servants, and on my h-ens

HANDWRITING.
    cheirographon.
Col. 2.14. Blotting out the h. of ordin.

HANG,   -ed, -eth.
    kremamai.
Mat.18. 6. a millstone *were* h-ed about
    22.40. h. all the law and the prop.
Lu. 23.39. malefactors *which were* h-ed
Act. 5.30. *and* h-ed on a tree ; 10.39
    28. 4. venomous beast h. on his
Gal. 3.13. Cursed is every one *that* h-eth
    apangchomai.
Mat.27. 5. went and h-ed himself
    perikeimai.   [Lu.17.2
Mar. 9.42. millstone were h-ed *about* ;
    pariemai.
Heb.12.12. up the hands *which* h. *down*

HAPLY, (See *Lest.*)
    ara.
Mar.11.13. if h. he might find anything
Act. 17.27. if h. they might feel after
    pōs.
²Co. 9. 4. Lest h. if they of Macedonia

HAPPEN,   -ed.
    sumbainō.
Mar.10.32. what things should h. *unto*
Lu. 24.14. these things *which had* h-ed
Act. 3.10. at that*which had* h-ed *unto*
¹Co. 10.11. all these things h-ed *unto*
Pet. 4.12. strange thing h-ed *unto*
Pet. 2.22. But it *is* h-ed unto them
    ginomai.
Ro. 11.25. blindness in part *is* h-ed to

HAPPIER.
    makarios.
¹Co.7.40. But she is h. if she so abide

HAPPY.
    makarios.
Jo. 13.17. things, h. are ye if ye do
Act.26. 2. I think myself h., king Agri.
Ro. 14.22. h. is he that condemneth
¹Pet. 3.14. righteousness' sake, h. are
    4.14. name of Christ, h. are ye
    makarizō.
Jas.5.11. we *count* them h. which endu.

HARD, (See *Join.*)
    sklēros.
Mat.25.24. that thou art an h. man
Jo. 6.60. This is an h. saying ; who
126

Act. 9. 5. h. for thee to kick ; 26.14
Jude 15. and of all their h. speeches
    duskolos.
Mar.10.24. how h. is it for them that
    dusermēneutos.
Heb.5.11. to say, and h. *to be uttered*
    dusnoētos.
²Pet.3.16. things h. *to be understood*

HARDEN,   -ed, -eth.
    sklērunō.
Act.19. 9. But when divers *were* h-ed
Ro. 9.18. and whom he will he h-eth
Heb.3. 8, 15. h. not your hearts ; 4.7
    13. lest any of you *be* h-ed thro.
    pōroō.
Mar.6.52. loav.: for their heart was h-ed
    8.17. have ye your heart yet h-ed
Jo. 12.40. blinded their eyes, and h-ed

HARDLY.
    duskolōs.
Mat.19.23. a rich man shall h. enter
Mar.10.23. How h. shall they that ;
    mogis.   [Lu.18.24
Lu. 9.39. bruising him, h. departeth
    molis.
Act.27.8. h. passing it, came unto

HARDNESS.
    sklērokardia.
Mat.19. 8. bec. of the h. *of your hearts*
Mar.10. 5. For the h. *of your heart*
    16.14. unbelief and h. *of heart*
    pōrōsis.
Mar.3.5. for the h. of their hearts
    sklērotēs.
Ro.2.5. thy h. and impenitent heart
    kakopatheō.
²Ti.2.3. therefore endure h., as a good

HARLOT,   -s.
    pornē.
Mat.21.31. and the h-s go into the
    32. and the h-s believed him
Lu. 15.30. devoured thy living with h-s
¹Co. 6.15. them the members of an h.
    16. is joined to an h. is one
Heb.11.31. By faith the h. Rahab peris.
Jas. 2.25. was not Rahab the h. justi.
Rev.17. 5. THE MOTHER OF h-s AND

HARM, [*noun.*]
    kakos.
Act.16.28. Do thy self no h.; for we are
    28. 5. into the fire, and felt no h.
    hubris.
Act.27.21. to have gained this h. and
    atopos.
Act.28.6. saw no h. come to him, they
    ponēros.
Act.28.21. shewed or spake any h. of

HARM, [*verb.*]
    kakoō.
¹Pet.3.13. Who is he *that will* h. you

HARMLESS.
    akeraios.
Mat.10.16. as serpents, and h. as doves
Phil. 2.15. ye may be blameless and h.
    akakos.
Heb.7.26. who is holy, h., undefiled

HARP, [*noun,*]   -s.
    kithara.
¹Co.14. 7. sound, whether pipe or h.
Rev.5. 8. having every one of them h-s
    14. 2. harpers harp. with their h-s
    15. 2. glass, having the h-s of God

HARP, [*verb,*]   -ing.
    kitharizō.
¹Co. 14.7. known what is piped or h-ed
Rev. 14.2. harpers h-ing with their

HARPERS.
    kitharōdos.
Rev.14. 2. I heard the voice of h. harp.
    18.22. And the voice of h. and

HARVEST.
    therismos.
Mat. 9.37. The h. truly is ; Lu.10.2
    38. the Lord of the h. ; Lu.10.2
         labourers into his h.; Lu.10.2
    13.30. the h.: and in the time of h.
    39. the h. is the end of the wor.
Mar. 4.29. because the h. is come
Jo. 4.35. and then cometh h.? behold
         they are white already to h.
Rev. 14.15. the h. of the earth is ripe

HASTE, [*noun.*]
    spoudē.
Mar.6.25. came in straightway with h.
Lu. 1.39. the hill country with h.
    speudō.
Lu.2.16. And they came *with* h. and

HASTE, [*verb,*]   -ed, -ing.
    speudō.
Lu. 19. 5. Zaccheus, *make* h., *and* co.
    6. And he *made* h., *and* came
Act. 20.16. for he h-ed, if it were possi.
    22.18. *Make* h., and get thee quick.
²Pet. 3.12. and h-ing unto the coming

HASTILY.
    tacheōs.
Jo.11.31. she rose up h. and went

HATE,   -ed, -est, -eth, -ing.
    miseō.
Mat. 5.43. love thy neighbour, and h.
    44. good to them *that* h. you ;
         Lu.6.27;   [Lu.16.13
    6.24. either he *will* h. the one ;
    10.22. ye shall be h-ed of all men ;
         24.9 ; Mar.13.13 ; Lu.21.17
    24.10. and *shall* h. one another
Lu. 1.71. from the hand of all *that* h.
    6.22. when men *shall* h. you, and
    14.26. and h. not his father, and
    19.14. But his citizens h-ed him
Jo. 3.20. h-eth the light, neither
    7. 7. h. you ; but me it h-eth
    12.25. he *that* h-eth his life in this
    15.18. If the world h. you, ye know
         it h-ed me before it hated you
    19. therefore the world h-eth
    23. He *that* h-eth me h-eth my
    24. they both seen and h-ed both
    25. They h-ed me without a
    17.14. the world *hath* h-ed them
Ro. 7.15. not ; but what I h., that do
    9.13. Esau *have* I h-ed
Eph. 5.29. no man ever yet h-ed his
Tit. 3. 3. hateful, and h-ing one anot.
Heb. 1. 9. and h-ed iniquity ; therefore
¹Jo. 2. 9. and h-eth his brother ; 4.20
    11. But he *that* h-eth his brother
    3.13. brethren, if the world h. you
    15. *Whosoever* h-eth his brother
Jude 23. h-ing even the garment spot.
Rev. 2. 6. that thou h-est the deeds of
         Nicolaitanes, which I also h.
    15. Nicolaitanes, which thing I h.
    17.16. these *shall* h. the whore

HATEFUL.
    stugētos.
Tit.3.3. h., and hating one another
    miseō.
Rev.18.2. of every unclean and h. bird

HATERS.
    theostugēs.
Ro.1.30. h. *of God*, despiteful, proud

HATRED.
echthra.

Gal.5.20. witchcraft, **h.**, variance

HAVE, -ing, Had, Hast, Hath.
echō.

Mat. 3. 4. **h**-d his raiment of camel's
  9. We **h.** Abraham to our fath.;
    Lu.3.8
  14. I **h.** need to be baptized of
  5.23. **h**-th ought against thee
  46. what reward **h.** ye? do not
  6. 1. otherwise ye **h.** no reward
  8. what things ye **h.** need of
  7.29. as one **h**-ing authority
  8. 9. **h**-ing soldiers under ; Lu.7.8
  20. foxes **h.** holes, and ; Lu.9.58
    h-th not where to lay;Lu.9.58
  9. 6. the Son of man **h**-th power ;
    Mar.2.10 ; Lu.5.24
  36. sheep **h**-ing no sh.; Mar.6.34
  11.15. He that **h**-th ears to hear ;
    13.9,43 ; Mar.4.9,23,7.16 ;
    Lu.8.8,14.35;Rev.2.7,11,17,
    29,3.6,13,22
  18. and they say, He **h**-th a de.;
    Lu.7.33 ; Jo.10.20
  12.10. which **h**-d his hand wither.;
    Mar.3.1,3 ; Lu.6.8
  11. that shall **h.** one sheep
  13. 5. **h**-d not much earth ; Mar.4.5
    because they **h**-d no deepn.;
    Mar.4.5   [Mar.4.6
  6. because they **h**-d no root ;
  12. For whosoever **h**-th, to him
    whosoever **h**-th not, from
    taken away even that he **h**-th;
    25.29 ; Mar.4.25 ; Lu.8.18,
    19.26
  21. Yet **h**-th he not root in him.
  27. from whence then **h**-th it
  44. selleth all that he **h**-th, and
  46. sold all that he **h**-d, and
  14. 4. for thee to **h.** her ; Mar.6.18
  17. We **h.** here but five loaves
  15.30. came unto him, **h**-ing with
  32. and **h.** nothing to eat ;
    Mar.6.36, 8.1,2
  34. How many loaves **h.** ye ;
    Mar.6.38, 8.5
  17.20. If ye **h.** faith as a grain ;
    21.21 ; Lu.17.6
  18. 8, 9. rather than **h**-ing two ;
    Mar.9.43,45,47
  25. But forasmuch as he **h**-d not
    and all that he **h**-d, and
  19.16. that I may **h.** eternal life
  21. thou shalt **h.** treasure in
  22. for he **h**-d great ; Mar.10.22
  21. 3. The Lord **h**-th need of them ;
    Mar.11.3 ; Lu.19.31,34
  28. A certain man **h**-d two sons
  22.12. not **h**-ing a wedding garment
  24. If a man die, **h**-ing no child.
  25. **h**-ing no issue, left his wife
  28. for they all **h**-d her ;
    Mar.12.44 ; Lu.20.38
  25.25. lo, there thou **h**-st that is
  28. unto him which **h**-th ten ta.
  26. 7. **h**-ing an alabaster ; Mar.14.3
  11. ye **h.** the poor always with
    but me ye **h.** not always ;
    Mar.14.7 ; Jo.12.8
  65. what further need **h.** we of
  27.16. And they **h**-d then a notable
  65. unto them, Ye **h.** a watch
Mar. 1.22. as one that **h**-d authority
  2.17. They that are hole **h.** no
  19. as long as they **h.** the bride.
  25. David did, when he **h**-d
  3.10. him, as many as **h**-d plagues
  15. And to **h.** power to heal

Mar. 3.22. He **h**-th Beelzebub, and by
  26. he cannot stand, but **h**-th an
  29. **h**-th never forgiveness
  30. He **h**-th an unclean spirit
  4.17. **h.** no root in themselves
  40. how is it that ye **h.** no faith
  5. 3. Who **h**-d his dwelling amo.
  15. and **h**-d the legion, sitting
  7.25. daughter **h**-d an unclean
  8. 7. they **h**-d a few small fishes
  14. neither **h**-d they in the ship
  16, 17. because we **h.** no bread
    h. ye your heart yet harden.
  18. **h**-ing eyes, see ye not ? and
  9.17. my son, which **h**-th a dumb
  50. **h.** salt in yourselves, and
  10.21. sell whatsoever thou **h**-st ;
    and thou shalt **h.** treasure ;
    Lu.18.22
  23. shall they that **h.** riches
  11.13. see. a fig tree afar off **h**-ing
  22. unto them, **h.** faith in God
  25. if ye **h.** ought against any
  12. 6. **h**-ing yet therefore one son
  44. ca.in all that she **h**-d;Lu.21.4
  14. 8. She **h**-th done what she could
Lu. 3.11. He that **h**-th two coats, let
    h-th none ; and he that **h**-th
  4.33. a man, which **h**-d a spirit of
  40. all they that **h**-d any sick
  7.40. I **h.** somewhat to say unto
  42. And when they **h**-d nothing
  8.13. and these **h.** no root, which
  27. man, which **h**-d devils long
  9. 3. neither **h.** two coats apiece
  11. healed them that **h**-d need
  11. 5. Which of you shall **h.** a
  6. I **h.** nothing to set before
  36. full of light, **h**-ing no part
  12. 4. and after that **h.** no more
  5. wh. after he hath killed **h**-th
  17. I **h.** no room where to best.
  19. Soul, thou **h**-st much goods
  50. But I **h.** a baptism to be
  13. 6. A certain man **h**-d a fig tree
  11. a woman which **h**-d a spirit
  14.18, 19. I pray thee **h.** me excus.
  28. whether he **h.** sufficient to
  15. 4. **h**-ing an hundred sheep, if
  8. **h**-ing ten pieces of silver
  11. A certain man **h**-d two sons
  16. 1. rich man, which **h**-d a stew.
  28. For I **h.** five brethren ; that
  29 They **h.** Moses and the pro.
  17. 7. which of you, **h**-ing a serv.
  18.24. hardly shall they that **h.**
  19.17. **h.** thou authority over
  24, 25.him that **h**-th ten pounds
  20.24. image and superscrip. **h**-th
  28. man's brother die, **h**-ing a
  22.36. he that **h**-th a purse, let him
    he that **h**-th no sword, let
  37. concerning me **h.** an end
  24.39. for a spirit **h**-th not flesh
    and bones, as ye see me **h.**
  41. **h.** ye here any meat; Jo.21.5
Jo. 2. 3. unto him, They **h.** no wine
  3.15, 16.not perish, but **h.** eternal
  29. He that **h**-th the bride is
  36. on the Son **h**-th everlasting ;
    5.24, 6.47,54
  4.11. thou **h**-st nothing to draw
    from whence then **h**-st thou
  17. and said, I **h.** no husband
  18. For thou **h**-st **h**-d five husb.
    whom thou now **h**-st is not
  32. I **h.** meat to eat that ye
  44. **h**-th no honour in his own
  5. 2. Bethesda, **h**-ing five porches
  5. which **h**-d an infirmity thirty
  6. he **h**-d been now a long time
  7. I **h.** no man, when the water

Jo. 5.26. Father **h**-th life in himself
    given to the Son to **h.** life
  36. I **h.** greater witness than
  38. ye **h.** not his word abiding
  39. ye **h.** eternal life : and they
  40. to me, that ye might **h.** life
  42. ye **h.** not the love of God
  6. 9. which **h**-th five barley loaves
  40. may **h.** everlasting life : and
  53. blood, ye **h.** no life in you
  68. thou **h**-st the words of eter.
  7.20. Thou **h**-st a devil ; 8.48,52
  8. 6. that they might **h.** to accuse
  12. but shall **h.** the light of
  26. I **h.** many things to say and
  41. we **h.** one Father, even God
  49. I **h.** not a devil ; but I hon.
  9.41. should **h.** no sin : but now
  10.10. that they might **h.** life, and
    might **h.** it more abundantly
  16. And other sheep I **h.**, which
  18. I **h.** power to lay it down
    I **h.** power to take it again
  11.17. he found that he **h**-d lain in
  12. 6. **h**-d the bag, and bare what
  35, 36. while ye **h.** the light
  48. **h**-th one that judgeth him
  13. 8. thou **h**-st no part with me
  29. because Judas **h**-d the bag
    that we **h.** need of against
  35. if ye **h.** love one to another
  14.21. He that **h**-th my command.
  30. cometh, and **h**-th nothing
  15.13. Greater love **h**-th no man
  22, 24. they **h**-d not **h**-d sin
    they **h.** no cloak for their
  16.12. I **h.** yet many things to say
  15. things that the Father **h**-th
  21. **h**-th sorrow, because her
  22. ye now therefore **h.** sorrow
  33. ye might **h.** peace. In the
    world ye shall **h.** tribulation
  17. 5. which I **h**-d with thee before
  13. that they might **h.** my joy
  18.10. Simon Peter **h**-ing a sword
  19. 7. We **h.** a law, and by our
  10. knowest thou not that I **h.**p.
    to crucify thee, and **h.** pow.
  11. couldest **h.** (hadst) no power
    unto thee, **h**-th the greater
  15. We **h.** no king but Cesar
  20.31. believing ye might **h.** life
Act. 2.44. were together, and **h**-d all
  45. men, as every man **h**-d need
  47. **h**-ing favour with all the
  3. 6. but such as I **h.** give I thee
  4.35. according as he **h**-d need
  9.14. he **h**-th authority from the
  31. Then **h**-d the churches rest
  13. 5. and they **h**-d also John to
  14. 9. that he **h**-d faith to be heal.
  15.21. **h**-th in every city them that
  18.18. Cenchrea : for he **h**-d a vow
  19.13. over them which **h**-d evil
  38. **h.** a matter against any
  21.23. men which **h.** a vow on
  23.17, 18. for he **h**-th a certain
  19. that thou **h**-st to tell me
  29. to **h.** nothing laid to his
  24.15. And **h.** hope toward God
  16. to **h.** always a conscience
  19. if they **h**-d ought against
  23. and to let him **h.** liberty
  25.16. **h.** the accusers face to face
  19. But **h**-d certain questions
  26. I **h.** no certain thing to
    I might **h.** somewhat to
  28. 9. others also, which **h**-d dis.
  19. not that I **h**-d ought to
  29. and **h**-d great reasoning
Ro. 1.13. that I might **h.** some fruit
  2.14. the Gentiles, which **h.** not
                 127

Ro. 2.14. these, **h**-*ing* not the law, are
20. *which* **h**-*st* the form of kno.
4. 2. he **h**-*th* whereof to glory
5. 1. we **h**. peace with God thro.
2. By whom also we **h**. access
6.21. What fruit **h**-*d* ye then in
22. ye **h**. your fruit unto holin.
8. 9. if any man **h**. not the Spirit
23. ourselves also, *which* **h**. the
9. 21. **h**-*th* not the potter power
10. 2. they **h**. a zeal of God, but
12. 4. we **h**. many members in one
all members **h**. not the same
6. **h**-*ing* then gifts differing
13. 3. thou *shalt* **h**. praise of the
14.22. **h**-*st* thou faith? **h**. it to
15. 4. that we..*might* **h**. hope
17. I **h**. therefore whereof I may
23. **h**-*ing* no more place in these
and **h**-*ing* a great desire
2.16. we **h**. *the* mind of Christ
4. 7. and what **h**-*st* thou that
15. For though ye **h**. ten thous.
5. 1. that one should **h**. his fath.
6. 1. **h**-*ing* a matter against ano.
4. If then ye **h**. judgments of
19. in you, which ye **h**. of God
7. 2. *let* every man **h**. his own
and *let* every woman **h**. her
7. every man **h**-*th* his proper
12. If any brother **h**-*th* a wife
13. which **h**-*th* an husband that
25. I **h**. no commandment of
28. Nevertheless such *shall* **h**.
29. that both they *that* **h**. wives
be as though they **h**-*d* none
37. **h**-*ing* no necessity, but **h**-*th*
40. that I **h**. the Spirit of God
8. 1. that we all **h**. knowledge
10. any man see thee *which* **h**-*st*
9.4,5,6. **h**. we not power to
17. willingly, I **h**. a reward
11. 4. **h**-*ing* his head covered
10. *to* **h**. power on her head
16. we **h**. no such custom
22. **h**. ye not houses to eat and
and shame them *that* **h**.
12.12. is one, and **h**-*th* many
21. I **h**. no need of thee: nor
23. **h**. more abundant comelin.
24. our comely parts **h**. no need
30. **h**. all the gifts of healing
13.1,2,3. and **h**. not charity
2. though I **h**. the gift of pro.
though I **h**. all faith, so
14.26. **h**-*th* a psalm, **h**-*th* a doctri.
h-*th* a tongue, **h**-*th* a revela.
h-*th* an interpretation
15.31. which I **h**. in Christ Jesus
34. for some **h**. not the knowle.
2Co. 1. 9. we **h**-*d* the sentence of death
15. that ye *might* **h**. a second
2. 3. when I came, I should **h**.
4. which I **h**. more abundant
13. I **h**-*d* no rest in my spirit
3. 4. And such trust **h**. we thro.
12. *Seeing* then that we **h**. such
4. 1. *seeing* we **h**. this ministry
7. But we **h**. this treasure in
13. We **h**-*ing* the same spirit
5. 1. we **h**. a building of God
12. that ye *may* **h**. somewhat to
6.10. as **h**-*ing* nothing, and yet
7. 1. **h**-*ing* therefore these prom.
5. our flesh **h**-*d* no rest, but we
8.11. out of that which ye **h**.
12. according to that a man **h**-*th*
according to that he **h**-*th* not
9. 8. that ye, always **h**-*ing* all
10. 6. And **h**-*ing* in a readiness
15. but **h**-*ing* hope, when your
Gal. 2. 4. which we **h**. in Christ Jesus
128

Gal. 4.22. that Abraham **h**-*d* two sons
27. than she *which* **h**-*th* an hus.
6. 4. *shall* he **h**. rejoicing
10. As we **h**. therefore opportu.
Eph. 1. 7. In whom we **h**. redemption
2.12. **h**-*ing* no hope, and without
18. we both **h**. access by one
3.12. In whom we **h**. boldness
4.28. that he *may* **h**. to give to
5. 5. **h**-*th* any inheritance in the
27. a glorious church, not **h**-*ing*
Phi. 1. 7. because I **h**. you in my
23. **h**-*ing* a desire to depart
30. **h**-*ing* the same conflict
2. 2. **h**-*ing* the same love, being
20. For I **h**. no man likeminded
27. lest I *should* **h**. sorrow upon
3. 4. I might also **h**. confidence
9. not **h**-*ing* mine own righteo.
17. as ye **h**. us for an ensample
Col. 1.14. In whom we **h**. redemption
2. 1. what great conflict I **h**. for
23. Which things **h**. indeed a
3.13. if any man **h**. a quarrel
4. 1. ye also **h**. a Master in heav.
13. he **h**-*th* a great zeal for you
1Th. 1. 9. of entering in we **h**-*d* unto
3. 6. that ye **h**. good remembra.
4.12. ye *may* **h**. lack of nothing
13. as others *which* **h**. no hope
5. 1. ye **h**. no need that I write
2Th. 3. 9. Not because we **h**. not power
1Ti. 3. 4. **h**-*ing* his children in subjec.
7. he must **h**. a good report
4. 8. **h**-*ing* promise of the life
5. 4. But if any widow **h**. child.
12. **h**-*ing* damnation, because
16. woman that believeth **h**.
6. 2. they that **h**. believing mas.
8. And **h**-*ing* food and raim.
16. *Who* only **h**-*th* immortality
2Ti. 1. 3. without ceasing I **h**. remem.
2.19. standeth sure, **h**-*ing* this
3. 5. **h**-*ing* a form of godliness, but
Tit. 1. 6. **h**-*ing* faithful children, not
2. 8. **h**-*ing* no evil thing to say of
Phile. 5. faith, which thou **h**-*st* towa.
7. For we **h**. great joy and
Heb. 2.14. might destroy him that **h**-*d*
3. **h**-*th* more honour than the
4.14. *Seeing* then that we **h**. a
15. we **h**. not an high priest
5.12. ye **h**. need that one teach
are become *such as* **h**. need
14. *who* by reason of use **h**. their
6.18. we *might* **h**. a strong conso.
19. we **h**. as an anchor of the
7. 3. **h**-*ing* neither beginning of
5. **h**. a commandment to take
6. blessed him that **h**-*d* the pro.
24. **h**-*th* an unchangeable priest.
28. high priests *which* **h**. infirm.
8. 1. We **h**. such an high priest
3. that this man **h**. somewhat
9. 1. the first covenant **h**-*d* also
4. *Which* **h**-*d* the golden censer
the golden pot *that* **h**-*d* man.
10. 1. For the law **h**-*ing* a shadow
2. worshippers *should* **h**. **h**-*d*
19. **h**-*ing* therefore, brethren
34. knowing in your. that ye **h**.
35. which **h**-*th* great recompence
36. For ye **h**. need of patience
11.10. city *which* **h**-*th* foundations
15. they might have **h**-*d* oppor.
12. 9. we **h**. **h**-*d* fathers of our
28. *let* us **h**. grace, whereby we
13.10. **h**. an altar, whereof they **h**.
14. For here we **h**. no continu.
18. **h**. a good consci.; ¹Pet.3 16
Jas. 1. 4. *let* patience **h**. her perfect
2. 1. **h**. not the faith of our Lord

Jas. 2. 14. say he **h**-*th* faith, and **h**. not
17. faith, if it **h**-*th* not works, is
18. Thou **h**-*st* faith, and I **h**.
3.14. if ye **h**. bitter envying and
4. 2. Ye lust, and **h**. not: ye kill
yet ye **h**. not, because ye ask
¹Pet. 2.12. **h**-*ing* your conversation
4. 8. *And* above all things **h**. fer.
²Pet. 1.19. We **h**. also a more sure word
2.14. **h**-*ing* eyes full of adultery
an heart they **h**. exercised
¹Jo. 1. 3. that ye also *may* **h**. fellowsh.
6. we **h**. fellowship with him
7. we **h**. fellowship one with
8. If we say that we **h**. no sin
2. 1. we **h**. an advocate with
7. which ye **h**-*d* from the begin.
20. ye **h**. an unction from
23. the same **h**-*th* not the Fath.
28. we *may* **h**. confidence
3. 3. And every man *that* **h**-*th*
15. murderer **h**-*th* eternal life
17. But whoso **h**-*th* this world's
and seeing his brother **h**. need
21. then **h**. we confidence towa.
4.16. the love that God **h**-*th* to us
17. perfect, that we *may* **h**. bold
18. because fear **h**-*th* torment
21. this commandment, we
5.10. **h**-*th* the witness in himself
12. He that **h**-*th* the Son **h**-*th*
h-*th* not the S. of God **h**-*th*
13. may know that ye **h**. eternal
14. the confidence that we **h**. in
15. we know that we **h**. the
²John 5. that which we **h**-*d* from the
9. **h**-*th* not God. He that
doctr. of Christ, he **h**-*th* both
12. **h**-*ing* many things to write
³John 4. I **h**. no greater joy than to
13. I **h**-*d* many things to write
Jude 19. sensual, **h**-*ing* not the Spirit
Rev. 1.16. he **h**-*d* in his right hand
18. and **h**. the keys of hell and
2. 3. And hast borne, and **h**-*st*
4. Nevertheless I **h**. somewhat
6. But this thou **h**-*st*, that
10. and ye *shall* **h**. tribulation
12. he *which* **h**-*th* the sharp sw.
14. I **h**. a few things against
thee, because thou **h**-*st* there
15. So **h**-*st* thou also them that
18. the Son of God, *who* **h**-*th*
20. I **h**. a few things against
24. as many as **h**. not this doc.
25. that which ye **h**. already
3. 1. he *that* **h**-*th* the seven Spir.
thou **h**-*st* a name that; 4
7. he *that* **h**-*th* the key of Dav.
8. thou **h**-*st* a little strength
11. that fast which thou **h**-*st*
17. and **h**. need of nothing
4. 4. they **h**-*d* on their heads
7. the third beast **h**-*d* a face
8. beasts **h**-*d* each of them six
5. 6. **h**-*ing* seven horns and seven
8. **h**-*ing* every one of them
6. 2. he that sat on him **h**-*d* a
5. **h**-*d* a pair of balances in his
7. 2. **h**-*ing* the seal of the living
8. 3. **h**-*ing* a golden censer; and
6. angels *which* **h**-*d* the seven
9. wh. were in the sea, *and* **h**-*d*
9. 3. scorpio. of the earth **h**. pow.
4. which **h**. not the seal of G.
8. they **h**-*d* hair as the hair of
9. And they **h**-*d* breastplates
10. they **h**-*d* tails like unto scor.
11. they **h**-*d* a king over them
h-*th* his name Apollyon
14. which **h**-*d* the trumpet, Lo
17. **h**-*ing* breastplates of fire

Rev. 9.19. and h-d heads, and with
10. 2. he h-d in his hand a little
11. 6. These h. power to shut
    and h. power over waters to
12. 3. red dragon, h-ing seven hea.
    6. where she h-th a place pre.
    12. h-ing great wrath, because
    he knoweth that he h-th but
    17. h. the testimony of Jes. Ch.
13. 1. h-ing seven heads and ten
    11. he h-d two horns like a
    14. which h-d the wound by a
    17. or sell, save he that h-d the
    18. Let him that h-th under.
14. 1. thousand, h-ing his Father's
    6. h-ing the everlasting gospel
    11. they h. no rest day nor night
    14. h-ing on his head a golden
    17. he also h-ing a sharp sickle
    18. which h-d power over fire
    to him that h-d the sharp
15. 1. angels h-ing the seven last
    2. glass, h-ing the harps of G.
    6. h-ing the seven plagues, clo.
16. 2. upon the men which h-d the
    9. of God, which h-th power
17. 1. the seven angels which h-d
    3. h-ing seven heads and ten
    4. h-ing a golden cup in her
    7. which h-th the seven heads
    9. the mind which h-th wisdom
    13. These h. one mind, and sh.
18. 1. from heaven, h-ing great,
    19. all that h-d ships in the sea
19.10. brethren that h. the testi.
    12. and he h-d a name written
    16. he h-th on his vesture and
20. 1. h-ing the key of the bottom.
    6. and holy is he that h-th part
    such the second death h-th
21. 9. the seven angels which h-d
    11. h-ing the glory of God : and
    12. And h-d a wall great and
    14. wall of the city h-d twelve
    15. h-d a golden reed to measure
    23. the city h-d no need of the
apechō.
Mat.6. 2, 5,16.They h. their reward
Phi. 4.18. But I h. all, and abound
antiballō.
Lu. 24.17. these that ye h. one to another
katechō.
Jo. 5. 4. of whatsoever disease he h-d
eimi, (is to me, were to him, &c.)
Mat.19.22. he h-d great poss.; Mar.10.22
    27. what shall we h. therefore
Mar. 5.25. h-d an issue of blood
             (being in a flow.)
    11.23. he shall h. whatsoever he
    24. them, and ye shall h. them
Lu. 1. 7. they h-d no child, because
    14. And thou shalt h. joy
    6.32, 33, 34. what thank h. ye
    7.41. certain creditor which h-d
    8.42. he h-d one only daughter
    43. a woman h-ing an issue
    10.39. And she h-d a sister called
    12.24. which neither h. storehouse
    14.10. then shalt thou h. worship
Jo. 8.39. But ye h. a custom, that I
Act. 4.32. they h-d all things common
    7. 5. as yet he h-d no child
    44. Our fathers h-d the tabern.
    8.21. Thou h-st neither part nor
    18.10. I h. much people in this
    19.25. craft we h. our wealth
    20.13. for so h-d he appointed
    21. 9. same man h-d four daugh.
    33. he h-d done (was the doer)
Ro. 9. 2. I h. great heaviness
    9. and Sarah shall h. a son
1Co. 9.16. I h. nothing to glory of

Rev. 22.14. may h. right to the tree
eimi epi.
Act. 8.27. who h-d the charge of all
pareimi.
Heb.13.5. with such things as ye h.
    (things that are present.)
ginomai.
Mat.18.12.if a man h. an hundred
Act.25.26. after examination h-d, I
1Co. 4. 5. then shall every man h. prai.
    10. 2. h. fellowship (be partakers)
Col. 1.18. he might h. the pre-eminence
lambanō.
Mar.12.22. the seven h-d her, and left
Act. 25.16. and h. licence to answer
Heb.11.36. others h-d trial of cruel
metalambanō.
Act.24.25. when I h. a convenient sea.
enduō.
Mat.22.11. which h-d not on a wedding
Eph. 6.14. h-ing on the breastplate of
huparchō.
Act. 3. 6. Silver and gold h. I none
    4.37. h-ing land sold it, and brou.
aphiēmi.
Mat.5.40. let him h. thy cloke also
pleonazō.
2Co. 8.15. much h-d nothing over
poieō.
2Pet.1.15. to h. these things always in
(See words in connection.)

HAVEN,   -s.
limēn.
Act.27.8. which is called The fair h-s
    12. the h. was not commodious
    which is an h. of Crete, and

HAVOCK.
lumainomai.
Act. 8. 3. As for Saul, he made h. of

HAY.
chortos.
1Co. 3.12. precious stones, wood, h.

HAZARDED.
paradidōmi.
Act.15.26. Men that have h. their lives

HE,   She, It, They.
When any of these words is not em-
phatic, it is represented, sometimes by
ho, sometimes by autos, but most frequently by the mere form of the verb
of which it is the nominative. When
it is empathic the following words are
employed.
ekeinos or kakeinos.
Mat.15.18. heart ; and t. defile the man
Mar.16.10. s. went and told them that
    11. And t., when they had hea.
    13. And t. went and told it
    20. t. went forth, and preached
Lu. 9.34. as t. entered into the cloud
    11. 7. And h. from within shall
    22.12. And h. shall shew you a
Jo. 1. 8. h. was not that Light, but
    18. Father, h. hath declared
    2.21. h. spake of the temple of
    3.30. h. must increase, but I
    4.25. when h. is come, he will
    5.19. what things soever h. doeth
    35. h. was a burning and a
    38. for whom h. hath sent
    39. t. are they which testify of
    46. believed me : for h. wrote
    6.29. on him whom h. hath sent
    57. even h. shall live by me
    7. 11. and said, Where is h.; 9.12
    29. him, and h. hath sent me
    45. t. said unto them, Why ha.
    8.42. of myself, but h. sent me

Jo. 8.44. h. was a murderer from the
    9. 9. him ; but h. said, I am he
    11, 25, 36. h. answered and said
    37. it is h. that talketh with
    10. 6. t. understood not what
    11.13. t. thought that he had spo.
    29. as soon as s. heard that
    13.25. h. then lying on Jesus' bre.
    26. h. it is, to whom I shall give
    30. h. then having received the
    14.12. that I do shall h. do also
    21. h. it is that loveth me
    26. h. shall teach you all things
    15.26. h. shall testify of me
    16. 8. is come, h. will reprove
    13. Howbeit when h., the Spirit
    14. h. shall glorify me : for he
    17.24. I will that t. also whom
    18.17. disciples ? h. saith, I am
    25. h. denied it, and said, I am
    19.21. that h. said, I am King of
    35. and h. knoweth that he
    20.13. t. say unto her, Woman
    15. s., supposing him to be the
    16. s. turned herself, and saith
Act. 3.13. h. was determined to let
    5.37. h. also perished ; and all
    10. 9. as t. went on their journey
    10. while t. made ready, he
    15.11. shall be saved, even as t.
    21. 6. t. returned home again
Ro. 11.23. t. also, if they abide not in
1Co. 9.25. t. do it to obtain a corrup.
    10. 6. things, as t. also lusted
    15.11. whether it were I or t., so
2Co. 10.18. not h. that commendeth
2Ti. 2.12. him, h. also will deny us
    2.13. believe not, yet h. abideth
Heb.12.25. For if t. escaped not who
1Jo. 2. 6. to walk, even as h. walked
    3. himself, even as h. is pure
    5. ye know that h. was mani.
    7. righteous, even as h. is
    16. h. laid down his life for us
    4.17. because as h. is, so are we
    5.16. say that he shall pray for i.
houtos.
Mat.13.22, 23. is h. that heareth the
    27.58. h. went to Pilate, and begged
Mar.6. 16. i. is John, whom I beheaded
Lu. 1. 32. h. shall be great, and shall
    8.14. are t., which, when they
    15. are t., which in an honest
    13. 4. think ye that t. were sinners
    19. 2. publicans, and h. was rich
    20.28. and h. die without children
    30. to wife, and h. died childless
    23.22. Why, what evil hath h.
    35. if h. be Christ, the chosen
Jo. 1.41. h. first findeth his own bro.
    4.47. When h. heard that Jesus
    6.42. how is it then that h. saith
    46. God, h. hath seen the Father
    71. for h. it was that should
    7.35. Whither will h. go, that we
    18.21. behold, t. know what I said
    30 If h. were not a malefactor
Act. 3.10. they knew that it was h. wh.
    4. 9. by what means h. is made
    7.36. h. brought them out, after
    9.15. for h. is a chosen vessel unto
    20. that h. is the Son of God
    10. 6. h. lodgeth with one Simon
    h. shall tell thee what thou
    32. h. is lodged in the house of
    36. Jesus Christ : h. is Lord of
    13. 4. So t., being sent forth by
    17.24. seeing that h. is Lord of
    18.26. And h. began to speak bold.
    24.15. which t. themselves also
Ro. 8. 9. of Christ, h. is none of his
    14. of God, t. are the sons of

Rom. 9. 6. For *t.* are not all Israel, wh.
¹Co. 16.17. on your part *t.* have supp.
Gal. 6.12. *t.* constrain you to be circu.
Jas. 1.23. h. is like unto a man beho.
   25. h. being not a forgetful hea.
¹Jo. 2.22. h. is antichrist, that denieth
²John 9. h. hath both the Father and
   ei tis.
Rev.13.10. h. *that* leadeth into captiv.
   h. *that* killeth with the swo.
   tis.
Act. 4.35. according as h. had need
Heb.10.28. h. that despised Moses'
   hode.
Lu.10.39. And s. had a sister called
   16.25. but now h. is comforted, and
   hostis.
Mat.23.12. and h. *that* shall humble
   25. 3. *t. that* were foolish took
Act. 5.16. *and t.* were healed every
   17.11. *in that t.* received the word
   23.14. *And t.* came to the chief
Rev. 1. 7. and *t.* also *which* pierced

HEAD, -s
kephalē.
Mat.5.36. shalt thou swear by thy h.
   ,6.17. thou fastest, anoint thine h.
   8.20. where to lay his h.; Lu.9.58
   10.30. hairs of your h. are ; Lu.12.7
   14. 8. me here John Baptist's h.
   11. And his h. was bro.; Mar.6.28
   21.42. the same is become the h. of ;
      Mar.12.10;Lu.20.17;Act.4.11
   26. 7. poured it on his h.; Mar.14.3
   27.29. put it upon his h.; Jo.19.2
   30. sm. him on the h.; Mar.15.19
   37. And set up over his h. his
   39. him, wag. their h-s; Mar.15.29
Mar.6.24. The h. of John the Baptist
   25. in a charger the h. of John
   27. commanded his h. to be bro.
Lu. 7.38, 44. with the hairs of her h.
   46. My h. with oil thou didst not
   21.18. shall not an hair of your h.
   28. lift up your h-s; for your
Jo. 13. 9. but also my hands and my h.
   19.30. and he bowed his h., and
   20. 7. napkin, that was about his h.
   12. the one at the h., and the
Act. 18.6. blood be upon your own h-s
   18. having shorn his h. in
   21.24. that they may shave their h-s
   27.34. not an hair fall from the h. of
Ro.12.20. heap coals of fire on his h.
¹Co. 11.3. the h. of every man is Christ
   and the h. of the woman is
   and the h. of Christ is God
   4. h. covered, dishonour. his h.
   5. h. uncovered, dishon. her h.
   7. ought not to cover his h.
   10. wo. to have power on her h.
   12.21. nor again the h. to the feet
Eph.1.22. gave him to be h. over all
   4.15. which is the h., even Christ
   '5.23. the husband is the h. of the
      as Christ is the h. of the chu.
Col. 1.18. he is the h. of the body, the
   2.10. the h. of all principality and
   19. And not holding the h.
Rev.1.14. His h. and his hairs were wh.
   4. 4. had on their h-s crowns; 9.7
   9.17. h-s of the horses. .h-s of lions
   19. and had h-s, and with them
   10. 1. a rainbow was upon his h.
   12. 1. and upon her h. a crown of
   3. having seven h-s; 13.1,17.3,7
      seven crowns upon his h-s
   13. 1. upon his h-s the name of
   3. And I saw one of his h-s as
   14.14. having on his h. a golden cr.
   17. 9. The seven h-s are seven mo.

Rev.18.19. they cast dust on their h-s
   19.12. on his h. were many crowns
kephalaioō.
Mar.12.4. and *wounded* him in the h.

HEADLONG.
prēnēs.
Act. 1.18. and falling h., he burst
katakrēmnizō.
Lu. 4.29. they might *cast* him *down* h.

HEADY.
propetēs.
²Ti. 3. 4. Traitors, h., highminded

HEAL, -ed, -ing.
therapeuō.
Mat.4.23. h-ing all manner of ; 10.1
   24. and he h-ed them; 12.15,15.30,
      19.2, 21.14; Mar.6.13;
      Lu.4.40
   8. 7. him, I *will* come and h. him
   16. and h-ed all that were sick
   9.35. h-ing every sickness and eve.
   10. 8. h. the sick, cleanse the lepers
   12.10. Is it lawful *to* h. on; Lu.14.3
   22. and he h-ed him, insomuch
   14.14. them, and he h-ed their sick
Mar.1.34. he h-ed many that were sick
   3. 2. whether he would h. him on
   10. For he *had* h-ed many ; inso.
   15. *to* h. sickness, and to cast
   6. 5. upon a few sick folk, and h-ed
Lu. 4.23. proverb, Physician, h. thyself
   5.15. to hear, and *to be* h-ed by
   6. 7. whether he would h. on the
   18. and they *were* h-ed ; Act.5.16
   8. 2. women, which had been h-ed
   43. neither could *be* h-ed of any
   9. 6. gospel, and h-ing every whe.
   10. 9. h. the sick that are therein
   13.14. because that Jesus *had* h-ed
      therefore come and *be* h-ed
Act. 4.14. beh. the man *which was* h-ed
   8. 7. and that were lame, *were* h-ed
   28. 9. island, came, and *were* h-ed
Rev.13.3, 12. deadly wound *was* h-ed
iaomai.
Mat. 8. 8. servant *shall be* h-ed ; Lu.7.7
   13. And his servant *was* h-ed
   13.15. and I *should* h.; Jo.12.40;
      Act.28.27
Mar. 5.29. that she was h-ed of that
Lu. 4.18. he hath sent me *to* h. the
   5.17. the Lord was present *to* h.
   6.17. *to be* h-ed of their diseases
   19. of him, and h-ed them all
   8.47. and how she *was* h-ed imm.
   9. 2. of God, and *to* h. the sick
   11. and h-ed them that had need
   42. h-ed the child, and delivered
   14. 4. and h-ed him, and let him
   17.15. when he saw that he *was* h-ed
   22.51. touched his ear, and h-ed
Jo. 4.47. would come down, and h. his
   5.13. And he *that was* h-ed wist
Act. 3.11. the lame man *which was* h-ed
   10.38. and h-ing all that were opp.
   28. 8. hands on him, and h-ed him
Heb.12.13. way ; but let it rather *be* h-ed
Jas. 5.16. that ye *may be* h-ed. The
¹Pet. 2.24. by whose stripes ye *were* h-ed
sōzō.
Mar.5.23. on her, that she *may be* h-ed
Lu. 8.36. possess. of the devils *was* h-ed
Act. 14.9. that he had faith *to be* h-ed
diasōzō.
Lu. 7. 3. come and h. his servant
iasis.
Act. 4.30. forth thine hand *to* h.

HEALING, [noun.]
iama.
¹Co. 12.9. to another the gifts of h.

¹Co.12.28. miracles, then gifts of h.
   30. Have all the gifts of h.
iasis.
Act.4.22. on whom this miracle of h.
therapeia.
Lu. 9.11. them that had need of h.
Rev.22.2. were for the h. of the nations

HEALTH.
sōtēria.
Act.27.34. for this is for your h.: for
hugiainō.
³John 2. mayest prosper and *be in* h.

HEAP, (See Treasure.)
sōreuō.
Ro.12.20. thou shalt h. coals of fire on
episōreuō.
²Ti. 4 3. *shall* they h. to themselves

HEAR, -est, -eth, -ing, Heard.
akouō.
Mat. 7.24, 26. whosoever h-eth these say.
   10.14. receive you, nor h. your
   27. ye h. in the ear, that preach
   11.4. things which ye *do* h. and
   5. and the deaf h.; Mar.7.37
      Lu.7.22
   15. hath ears to h., *let* him h.;
      13.9,43; Mar.4.9,23,7.16;
      Lu.8.8,14.35
   12.19. *shall* any man h. his voice in
   42. *to* h. the wisdom of Solomon
   13.13. and h-ing they h. not
   14. hear. ye *shall* h.; Act.28.26
   15. are dull of h-ing; Act.28.27
      h. with their ears ; Act.28.27
   13.16. and your ears, for they h.
   17. *to* h. those thi. which ye h.
   18. h. ye therefore the parable
   19. *When* any one h-eth the wo.
   20, 22,23. is he *that* h-eth the wo.
   15.10. said unto them, h., and und.
   17. 5. h. ye him; Mar.9.7; Lu.9.35
   18.15. if he *shall* h. thee, thou
   16. if he *will* not h. thee, then
   21.16. said unto him, h-est thou
   33. h. another parable : There
   24. 6. h. of wars; Mar.13.7; Lu.21.9
   27.13. h-est thou not how many
Mar. 4.12. h-ing they *may* h., and und.
   18, 20. such *as* h. the;Lu.8.12,13
   24. Take heed what ye h.: with
      unto you *that* h. shall more
   33. as they were able to h. it
   6. 2. many h-ing him were aston.
   11. not receive you, nor h. you
   8.18. see ye not ? having ears, h.
   12.29. h., O Israel ; The Lord our
Lu. 2.46. both h-ing them, and asking
   5. 1. upon him *to* h. the word of
   15. came together to h.; 6.17
   6.27. say unto you *which* h., Love
   47. to me, and h-eth my sayings
   49. he *that* h-eth, and doeth not
   8.10. h-ing they might not under.
   18. heed therefore how ye h.
   21. are these *which* h.; 11.28
   9. 9. who is this, of whom I h.
   10.16. He *that* h-eth you h-eth me
   11.31. *to* h. the wisdom of Solomon
   15. 1. publi. and sinners for *to* h.
   16. 2. How is it that I h. this of
   29. the prophets;*let* them h.them
   31. If they h. not Moses and the
   18. 6. h. what the unjust judge
   36. h-ing the multitude pass by
   19.48. were very attentive to h.
   21.38. in the temple, for *to* h. him
Jo. 3. 8. thou h-est the sound thereof
   29. which standeth and h-eth
   5.24. He *that* h-eth my word, and
   25. when the dead *shall* h. the

Jo. 5.25. and they *that* h. shall live
28. in the graves *shall* h. his
♦ 30. as I h., I judge: and my
6.60. an hard saying; who can h.
7.51. any man, before it h. him
8.43. because ye cannot h. my
47. He that is of God h-*eth* God's
words: ye therefore h. them
9.27. already, and you *did* not h.
wherefore would ye h. it
31. know that God h-*eth* not
doeth his will, him he h-*eth*
10. 3. the sheep h. his voice: and
8. the sheep *did* not h. them
16. they *shall* h. my voice; and
20. and is mad; why h. ye him
27. My sheep h. my voice, and
11.42. I knew that thou h-*est* me
12.47. if any man h. my words
14.24. the word which ye h. is not
16.13. whatsoever he *shall* h., that
18.37. one that is of the truth h-*eth*
Act. 2. 8. how h. we every man in our
11. we *do* h. them speak in our
22. men of Israel, h. these wo.
33. which ye now see and h.
3.22. him *shall* ye h. in all; 7.37
23. which *will* not h. that pro.
5. 5. Ananias h-*ing* these words
8. 6. Philip spake, h-*ing* and
9. 7. stood speechless, h-*ing* a
10.22. house, and *to* h. words of
33. *to* h. all things that are
13. 7, 44. *to* h. the word of God
15. 7. should h. the word of the
17.21. to tell, or to h. some new
17.32. We *will* h. thee again of
18. 8. the Corinthians h-*ing* belie.
19.26. ye see and h., that not alone
21.22. for they *will* h. that thou
22. 1. and fathers, h. ye my defen.
14. shouldest h. the voice of
24. 4. thou wouldest h. us of thy
25.22. I would also h. the man
To-mo., said he, thou *shalt* h.
26. 3. I beseech thee *to* h. me pat.
29. also all *that* h. me this day
28.22. we desire to h. of thee what
28. and that they *will* h. it
Ro. 11. 8. *shall* they h. without a
8. that they should not h.; unto
1Co. 11.18. I h. that there be divisions
2Co. 12. 6. to be, or that he h-*eth* of me
Gal. 4.21. the law, *do* ye not h. the
Phi. 1.27. I may h. of your affairs
30. me, and now h. to be in me
2Th. 3.11. For we h. that there are
1Ti. 4.16. thyself, and them *that* h.
2Ti. 4.17. that all the Gen. *might* h.
Phile. 5. h-*ing* of thy love and faith
Heb. 3. 7, 15. To day if ye *will* h.; 4.7
Jas. 1.19. let every man be swift *to* h.
1Jo. 4. 5. world, and the world h-*eth*
6. he that knoweth God h-*eth*
is not of God h-*eth* not us
5.14. according to his will, he h-*eth*
15. if we know that he h. us
3John 4. no greater joy than to h.
Rev. 1. 3. they *that* h. the words of
2. 7. He that hath an ear *let* him h.
11,17,29,3.6,13,22,13.9
3.20. if any man h. my voice, and
9.20. neither can see, nor h., nor
22.17. let him *that* h-*eth* say, Come
18. every man *that* h-*eth* the
Heard.
Mat. 2. 3. *When* Her. the king *had* h-*d*
9. *When* they *had* h-*d* the king
18. Rama *was* there a voice h-*d*
22. *when* he h-*d* that Archelaus
4.12. *when* Jesus *had* h-*d* that
5.21. Ye *have* h-*d*; 27, 33, 38, 43

Mat. 8.10. *When* Jesus h-*d* it; Mar.2.17; Lu.8.50
9.12. *when* Jes. h-*d* that; Jo.11.4,6
11. 2. *when* John *had* h-*d* in the
12.24. *when* the Pharisees h-*d* it
13.17. *have* not h-*d* them; Lu.10.24
14. 1. the tetrarch h-*d* of; Lu.9.7
13. *When* Jesus h-*d* of it, he
when the people *had* h-*d*
15.12. offended, *after they* h-*d* this
17. 6. *when* the discip. h-*d*; 19.25; Mar.6.29
19.22. *when* the young man h-*d*
20.24. *when* the ten h-*d* it; 10.41
30. *when* they h-*d* that Jesus
21.45. *when* the ch...*had* h-*d*; 22.34
22. 7. *when* the king h-*d* thereof
22. *When* they *had* h-*d* these
33. *when* the multitude h-*d* this
26.65. *have* h-*d* his blas.; Mar.14.64
27.47. *when* they h-*d* that, said
Mar. 3. 8. *when* they *had* h-*d* what
21. *when* his friends h-*d* of it
4.15, 16. *when* they *have* h-*d*; 8.14
5.27. *Wh.* she *had* h-*d*; Jo.11.20,29
36. As soon as Jesus h-*d* the wo.
6.14. king Herod h-*d* of him; for
16. *when* Herod h-*d* thereof, he
20. *when* he h-*d* him, he did ma.
things, and h-*d* him gladly
55. were sick, where they h-*d*
7.25. an unclean spirit, h-*d* of
10.47. *when* he h-*d* that it was Jes.
11.14. And his disciples h-*d* it
18. scribes and chief priests h-*d*
12.28. *having* h-*d* them reasoning
37. common people h-*d* him
14.11. *when* they h-*d* it, they were
58. We h-*d* him say, I will dest.
15.35. *when* they h-*d* it, said, Beh.
16.11. *when* they *had* h-*d* that he
Lu. 1.41. Elisabeth h-*d* the salutation
58. her cousins h-*d* how the Lo.
66. all they that h-*d*; 2.18,47
2.20. that they *had* h-*d* and seen
4.23. whatsoever we *have* h-*d* done
28. *when* they h-*d* these things
7. 3. *when* he h-*d* of Jesus, he
9. *When* Jesus h-*d*; 18.22,23
22. things ye *have* seen and h-*d*
29. all the people *that* h-*d* him
8.15. *having* h-*d* the word, keep it
10.39. sat at Jesus' feet, and h-*d* his
12. 3. in darkness *shall be* h-*d* in
14.15. meat with him, h-*d* these thi.
15.25. he h-*d* musick and dancing
16.14. were covetous, h-*d* all these
18.26. they *that* h-*d* it said, Who
19.11. *as* they h-*d* these things, he
20.16. *when* they h-*d* it, they said
22.71. ourselves *have* h-*d* of his own
23. 6. *When* Pilate h-*d* of Galilee
8. he had h-*d* many things of
Jo. 1.37. the two disciples h-*d* him
40. One of the two *which* h-*d*
3.32. what he hath seen and h-*d*
4. 1. Pharisees *had* h-*d* that Jes.
42. we *have* h-*d* him ourselves
47. *When* he h-*d* that Jesus was
5.37. Ye *have* neither h-*d* his voice
6.45. man therefore that *hath* h-*d*
60. *when* they *had* h-*d*; 7.40
7.32. Pharisees h-*d* that the peo.
8. 9. they *which* h-*d* it, being
26. things which I *have* h-*d* of
40. truth, which I *have* h-*d* of G.
9.32. *was* it not h-*d* that any man
35. Jesus h-*d* that they had cast
40. Ph. which were with him h-*d*
11.41. I tha. thee that thou *hast* h-*d*
12.12. *when* they h-*d* that Jesus
18. for that they h-*d* that he

Jo. 12.29. that stood by, and h-*d* it
34. We *have* h-*d* out of the law
14.28. Ye *have* h-*d* how I said unto
15.15. things that I *have* h-*d* of my
18.21. ask them *which* h-*d* me
19. 8, 13. Pilate therefore h-*d* that
21. 7. *when* Simon Peter h-*d* that
Act. 1. 4. which, saith he, ye *have* h-*d*
2. 6. every man h-*d* them speak
37. *when* they h-*d* this, they
4. 4. many of them *which* h-*d*
20. have seen and h-*d*; 1Jo.1.1,3
24. *when* they h-*d* that; 5.21,33, 7.54, 11.18, 17.8, 19.5.28, 21.12,20
5. 5, 11. on all them *that* h-*d* these
24. the chief priests h-*d* these
6.11. We *have* h-*d* him speak blas.
14. For we *have* h-*d* him say
7.12. *when* Jacob h-*d* that there
34. I *have* h-*d* their groaning
8.14. at Jerusalem h-*d* that Sama.
30. h-*d* him read the prophet
9. 4. and h-*d* a voice say.; 11.7, 22.7, 26.14
13. I *have* h-*d* by many of this
21. all *that* h-*d* him were amaz.
38. the disciples had h-*d* that
10.44. fell on all them *which* h-*d*
46. For they h-*d* them speak with
11. 1. in Judea h-*d* that the Gent
13.48. *when* the Gentiles h-*d* this
14. 9. The same h-*d* Paul speak
14. Barnabas and Paul, h-*d* of
15.24. as we *have* h-*d*, that certain
16.14. which worshipped God, h-*d*
38. *when* they h-*d* that they were
Act.17.32. *when* they h-*d* of the resur.
18.26. *when* Aqu. and Prisc. *had* h-*d*
19. 2. We *have* not so much as h-*d*
10. Asia h-*d* the word of the Lo.
22. 2. *when* they h-*d* that he spake
9. they h-*d* not the voice of
15. what thou hast seen and h-*d*
26. *When* the centurion h-*d* that
23.16. *when* Paul's sister's son h-*d*
24.22. *when* Felix h-*d* these things
24. sent for Paul, and h-*d* him
28.15. *when* the brethren h-*d* of us
Ro. 10.14. of whom they *have* not h-*d*
18. I say, *Have* they not h-*d*
15.21. they that *have* not h-*d* shall
1Co. 2. 9. hath not seen, nor ear h-*d*
2Co. 12. 4. paradise, and h-*d* unspeak.
Gal. 1.13. ye *have* h-*d* of my conversa.
23. they had h-*d* only, That he
Eph. 1.13. *after that* ye h-*d* the word
15. *after* I h-*d* of your faith in
3. 2. If ye *have* h-*d* of the dispen.
4.21. If so be that ye *have* h-*d* him
Phi. 2.26. because that ye *had* h-*d* that
4. 9. and received, and h-*d*, and
Col. 1. 4. *Since* we h-*d* of your faith in
6, 9. since the day ye h-*d* of it
23. the gospel, which ye *have* h-*d*
2Ti. 1.13. thou *hast* h-*d* of me; 2.2
Heb. 2. 1. the things *which we have* h-*d*
3. unto us by them *that* h-*d*
3.16. some, *when* they *had* h-*d*
4. 2. with faith in them *that* h-*d*
12.19. which voice they *that* h-*d*
Jas. 5.11. Ye *have* h-*d* of the patience
2Pet. 1.18. came from heaven we h-*d*
1Jo. 1. 5. message which we *have* h-*d*
2. 7. word which ye *have* h-*d* fr.
18. ye *have* h-*d* that anti.; 4.3
24. ye *have* h-*d* from the begin.
3.11; 2John 6
Rev. 1.10. h-*d* beh. me; 16.1,19.1,21.3
3. 1. thou hast received and h-*d*
4. 1. the first voice which I h-*d*
5.11. I h-*d* the voice of many

Rev. 5.13. that are in them, h-d I say.
6. 1. I h-d, as it were the noise of
3. I h-d the second beast say
5. I h-d the third beast say, Co.
6. I h-d a voice in the midst of
7. I h-d the voice of the fourth
7. 4. I h-d the number of; 9.16
8.13. I beheld, and h-d an angel
9.13. I h-d a voice from the four
10. 4, 8. I h-d a voice from; 11.12,
14.2,13,18.4
12.10. I h-d a loud voice saying in
14. 2. I h-d the voice of harpers
16. 5. I h-d the angel of the waters
7. I h-d another out of the alt.
18.22. trumpeters, shall be h-d no
millstone shall be h-d no
23. the bride shall be h-d no
19. 6. I h-d as it were the voice of
22. 8. Jo. saw these things, and h-d
And when I had h-d and seen
eisakouō.
Mat. 6. 7. think that they shall be h-d
Lu. 1.13. thy prayer is h-d; Act.10.31
1Co.14.21. for all that, will they not h.
Heb. 5. 7. was h-d in that he feared
parakouō.
Mat.18.17. if he shall neglect to h. them
he neglect to h. the church
proakouō.
Col. 1. 5. whereof ye h-d before in the
epakouō.
2Co. 6. 2. I have h-d thee in a time
diakouomai.
Act.23.35. I will h. thee, said he, when
epakroaomai.
Act.16.25. the prisoners h-d them
akoē.
1Th. 2.13. of God which ye h-d of us

HEARER,   -s.
akroatēs.
Ro. 2.13. For not the h-s of the law
Jas. 1.22. the word, and not h-s only
23. be a h. of the word, and not
25. being not a forgetful h., but
akouō.
Eph. 4.29. minister grace unto the h-s
2Ti. 2.14. to the subverting of the h-s

HEARING.
akoē.
Mat.13.14. h. ye shall hear; Act.28.26
Ro. 10.17. cometh by h., and h.
1Co.12.17. h.? If the whole were h.
Gal. 3. 2, 5. or by the h. of faith
Heb. 5.11. seeing ye are dull of h.
2Pet. 2. 8. among them, in see. and h.
diagnōsis.
Act. 25.21. reserved unto the h. of Au.
akroatērion.
Act. 25.23. entered into the place of h.

HEARKEN,   -ed.
akouō.
Mar. 4. 3. h.; Behold, there went out
7.14. h. unto me every one of you
Act. 4.19. the sight of God to h. unto
7. 2. brethren, and fathers, h.
15.13. Men and brethren, h. unto
Jas. 2. 5. h., my beloved brethren
enōtizomai.
Act. 2.14. unto you, and h. to my
hupakouō.
Act. 12.13 a damsel came to h., named
peithakeō.
Act.27.21. have h-ed unto me, and

HEART, (See Cut, Hardness) -s.
kardia.
Mat. 5. 8. Blessed are the pure in h.
28. with her already in his h.
132

Mat. 6.21. will your h. be.; Lu.12.34
9. 4. think ye evil in your h-s
11.29. I am meek and lowly in h.
12.34. the h. the mouth; Lu.6.45
35. treasure of the h.; Lu.6.45
40. nights in the h. of the earth
13.15. this people's h. is waxed
understand with their h.
19. which was sown in his h.
15. 8. their h. is far from; Mar.7.6
18. come forth from the h.: and
19. of the h. proceed; Mar.7.21
18.35. if ye from your h-s forgive
22.37. Lord thy God with all thy h.
24,48. shall say in his h.; Lu.12.45
Mar. 2. 6. and reasoning in their h-s
8. ye these things in your h-s
3. 5. for the hardness of their h-s
4.15. that was sown in their h-s
6.52. their h. was hard.; Ro.1.21
7.19. it entereth not into his h.
8.17. have ye your h. yet harden.
11.23. and shall not doubt in his h.
12.30, 33. with all thy h.; Mar.10.27
Lu. 1.17. to turn the h-s of the fathers
51. the imagination of their h-s
66. laid them up in her h.
2.19, 51. ponder. them in her h.
35. the thoughts of many h-s
3.15. all men mused in their h-s
5.22. What reason ye in your h-s
6.45. the evil treasure of his h.
8.12. the word out of their h-s
15. in an honest and good h.
9.47. per. the thought of their h.
16.15. God knoweth your h-s: for
21.14. Settle it therefore in your h-s
34. lest at any time your h-s be
24.25. slow of h. to believe all that
32. Did not our h-s burn within
38. do thoughts arise in your h-s
Jo. 12.40. and hardened their h.; that
understand with their h.
13. 2. now put into the h. of Judas
14.1,27. Let not your h. be troubled
16. 6. sorrow hath filled your h.
22. and your h. shall rejoice
Act. 2.26. Therefore did my h. rejoice
37. they were pricked in their h.
46. gladness and singleness of h.
4.32. were of one h. and of one
5. 3. why hath Satan filled thine h.
conceiv. this thing in thine h.
7.23. it came into his h. to visit
39. in their h-s turned back again
51. and uncircumcised in h.
54. they were cut to the h., and
8.21. thy h. is not right in the
22. the thought of thine h. may
37. believest with all thine h.
11.23. that with purpose of h. they
13.22. a man after mine own h.
14.17. filling our h-s with food and
15. 9. purifying their h-s by faith
16.14. whose h. the Lord opened
21.13. weep and to break mine h.
28.27. For the h. of this people
understand with their h.
Ro. 1.24. the lusts of their own h-s
2. 5. hardness and impenitent h.
15. the law written in their h-s
29. circumcision is that of the h.
5. 5. shed abroad in our h-s by
6.17. have obeyed from the h.
8.27. he that searcheth the h-s
9. 2. continual sorrow in my h.
10. 1. my h.'s desire and prayer
6. Say not in thine h., Who
8. in thy mouth, and in thy h.
9. and shalt believe in thine h.
10. For with the h. man believ.
16.18. deceive the h-s of the simple

1Co. 2. 9. have entered into the h. of
4. 5. the counsels of the h-s: and
7.37. standeth stedfast in his h.
and hath so decreed in his h.
14.25. are the secrets of his h. made
2Co. 1.22. earn. of the Spirit in our h-s
2. 4. and anguish of h. I wrote
3. 2. written in our h-s, known
3. but in fleshy tables of the h.
15. read, the vail is upon their h.
4. 6. hath shined in our h-s, to
5.12. in appearance, and not in h.
6.11. unto you, our h. is enlarged
7. 3. ye are in our h-s to die and
8.16. care into the h. of Titus for
9. 7. as he purposeth in his h.
Gal. 4. 6. of his Son into your h-s
Eph. 3.17. Christ may dwell in your h-s
4.18. of the blindness of their h.
5.19. making melody in your h.
6. 5. singlen. of your h.; Col.3.22
22. he might comfort your h-s;
Col.4.8; 2Th.2.17
Phi. 1. 7. I have you in my h.; inasmu.
4. 7. shall keep your h-s and min.
Col. 2. 2. That their h-s might be com.
3.15. peace of God rule in your h-s
16. sing. with grace in your h-s
1Th. 2. 4. but God, which trieth our h-s
17. in presence, not in h.
3.13. he may stablish your h-s
2Th. 3. 5. the Lord direct your h-s into
1Ti. 1. 5. is charity out of a pure h.
2Ti. 2.22. on the Lord out of a pure h.
Heb.3. 8,15.Harden not your h-s; 4.7
10. They do alway err in their h.
12. an evil h. of unbelief, in
4.12. though. and intents of the h.
8.10. and write them in their h-s
10.16. put my laws unto their h-s
22. us draw near with a true h.
having our h-s sprinkled
13. 9. a good thing that the h. be
Jas. 1.26. but deceiveth his own h.
3.14. and strife in your h-s, glory
4. 8. and purify your h-s, ye
5. 5. ye have nourished your h-s
8. stablish your h-s: for the
1Pet. 1.22. one another with a pure h.
3. 4. the hidden man of the h.
15. sanctify the L. G. in your h-s
2Pet. 1.19. the day star arise in your h-s
2.14. an h. they have exercised
1Jo. 3.19. shall assure our h-s before
20. For if our h. condemn us
God is greater than our h.
21. if our h. condemn us not
Rev. 2.23. searcheth the reins and h-s
17.17. For God hath put in their h-s
18. 7. saith in her h., I sit a queen
psuchē.
Eph. 6. 6. will of God from the h.
kardiognōstēs.
Act. 1.24. which knowest the h-s; 15.8
apopsuchō.
Lu. 21.26. Men's h-s failing them for

HEARTED, (See Tender.)
HEARTILY.
ek psuchē.
Col. 3.23. whatsoever ye do, do it h.
HEAT, (See Fervent.)
kausōn.
Mat.20.12. the burden and h. of the
Lu. 12.55. ye say, There will be h.; and
Jas. 1.11. risen with a burning h.
kauma.
Rev. 7.16. light on them, nor any h.
16. 9. were scorched with great h.
thermē.
Act.28. 3. came a viper out of the h.

HEATHEN.
ethnos.
Act. 4.25. Why did the **h.** rage, and
²Co. 11.26. in perils by the **h.**, in perils
Gal. 1.16. preach him among the **h.**
  2. 9. we should go unto the **h.**
  3. 8. that God would justify the **h.**
ethnikos.
Mat. 6. 7. vain repetitions, as the **h.**
 18.17. unto thee as an **h.** *man*

HEAVEN, -s.
ouranos.   [4.17,10.7
Mat. 3. 2. kingdom of **h.** is at hand ;
 16. and,lo, the **h-**s were; Lu.3.21
 17. And lo a voice from **h.**, say.
 5. 3, 10. their's is the king. of **h.**
 12. is your reward in **h.**; Lu.6.23
 16. your Father which is in **h.**;
    45,48,6.1,7.11,18.14,23.9 ;
    Mar.11.25,26
 18. Till **h.** and earth pass, one
 19. least in the king. of **h.**; 11.11
    great in the king. of **h.**; 18.1,4
 20. enter into the kingdom of **h.**;
    7.21,18.3,19.23
 34. neither by **h.**; for it is G.'s ;
    Jas.5.12
 6. 9. Our F. wh. art in **h.**; Lu.11.2
 10. earth, as it is in **h.**; Lu.11.2
 20. treasures in **h.**, where neither
 7.21. my Father which is in **h.**;
    10.32,33,12.50,16.17,18.10,19
 8.11. Jacob, in the kingdom of **h.**
 11.12. the kingdom of **h.** suffereth
 23. art exalted unto **h.**, shalt be
 25. Lord of **h.** and earth ;
    Lu.10.21 ; Act.17.24
 13.11. mysteries of the king. of **h.**
 24. 31,33.The king. of **h.** is liken.
    44,45,47,18.23,20.1,22.2,25.1
 52. instruct. unto the king. of **h.**
 14.19. looking up to **h.**; Mar.6.41,
    7.34 ; Lu.9.16
 16. 1. shew them a sign from **h.**
 19. the keys of the king. of **h.**
    bo. in **h.**:. loosed in **h.**;18.18
 18.10. That in **h.** their angels do
 19.12. the kingdom of **h.**'s sake
 14. of such is the kingdom of **h.**
 21. shalt have treasure in **h.**;
    Mar.10.21 ; Lu.18.22
 21.25. from **h.**, or of men ;
    Mar.11.30; Lu.20.4
    From **h.**; he will say unto ;
    Mar.11.31; Lu.20.5
 22.30. angels of G. in **h.**; Mar.12.25
 23.13. shut up the kingdom of **h.**
 22. that shall swear by **h.**, swear.
 24.29. the stars shall fall from **h.**;
    Mar.13.25   [21.26
    powers of the **h-**s; Mar.13.25,
 30. sign of the Son of man in **h.**
    coming in the clouds of **h.**;
    26.64 ; Mar.14.62
 31. from one end of **h.** to the
 35. **h.** and earth shall pass ;
    Mar.13.35; Lu.21.33
 36. the angels of **h.**; Mar.13.32
 28. 2. descended from **h.**, and
    Rev.10.1,18.1,20.1
 18. is given unto me in **h.** and
Mar. 1.10. he saw the **h-**s opened, and
 11. there came a voice from **h.**;
    Lu.3.22 ; Jo.12.28
 8.11. him a sign from **h.**; Lu.11.16
 13.27. to the uttermost part of **h.**
 16.19. he was received up into **h.**
Lu. 2.15. gone away from them into **h.**
 4.25. when the **h.** was shut up
 9.54. fire to come down from **h.**
 10.15. which art exalted to **h.**, shalt

Lu. 10.18. S. as lightning fall from **h.**
 20. your names are written in **h.**
 12.33. a treasure in the **h-**s that
 15. 7. joy shall be in **h.** over one
 18, 21. I have sinned against **h.**
 16.17. it is easier for **h.** and earth
 17.24. out of the one part under **h.**
    unto the other part undur **h.**
 29. and brimstone from **h.**, and
 18.13. so much as his eyes unto **h.**
 19.38. peace in **h.**, and glory in the
 21.11. signs shall there be from **h.**
 22.43. an angel unto him from **h.**
 24.51. them, and carried up into **h.**
Jo. 1.32. from **h.** like a dove, and it
 51. ye shall see **h.** open, and
 3.13. man hath ascended up to **h.**
    that came down from **h.**; 31,
    6.33,41,50,51,58
    the Son of man which is in **h.**
 27. except he be giv. him from **h.**
 6.31. He gave them bread from **h.**
 32. not that bread from **h.**; but
    you the true bread from **h.**
 38, 42. I came down from **h.**
 17. 1. lifted up his eyes to **h.**, and
Act. 1.10. look. stedfastly tow. **h.**; 7.55
 11. gazing up into **h.**? this same
    taken up from you into **h.**
    ye have seen him go into **h.**
 2. 2. there came a sound from **h.**
 5. of every nation under **h.**
 19. shew wonders in **h.** above
 34. not ascended into the **h-**s
 3.21. Whom the **h.** must receive
 4.12. none other name under **h.**
 24. wh. hast made **h.**,and ;14.15;
    Rev.14.7
 7.42. to worship the host of **h.**
 49. **h.** is my throne, and earth
 56. Behold, I see the **h-**s opened
 9. 3. a light from **h.**: 22.6
 10.11. saw **h.** opened ; Rev.19.11
 16. receiv. up again into **h.**; 11.10
 11. 5. let down from **h.** by four
 9. answered me again from **h.**
Ro. 1.18. is revealed from **h.**; ²Th.1.7
 10. 6. Who shall ascend into **h.**
¹Co. 8. 5. whether in **h.** or in earth
 15.47. man is the Lord from **h.**
²Co. 5. 1. with hands, eternal in the **h-**s
 2. our house which is from **h.**
 12. 2. caught up to the third **h.**
Gal. 1. 8. or an angel from **h.**, preach
Eph. 1.10. both which are in **h.**, and
 3.15. in **h.** and earth is named
 4.10. far above all **h-**s, that he
 6. 9. your M. also is in **h.**; Col.4.1
Phi. 3.20. our conversation is in **h.**
Col. 1. 5. laid up for you in **h.**, whereof
 16. that are in **h.**, and that are
 20. in earth or things in **h.**
 23. which is under **h.**; whereof I
¹Th. 1.10. to wait for his Son from **h.**
 4.16. shall descend from **h.** with a
Heb. 1.10. and the **h-**s are the works of
 4.14. that is passed into the **h-**s
 7.26. made higher than the **h-**s
 8. 1. the Majesty in the **h-**s
 9.23. patterns of things in the **h-**s
 24. but into **h.** itself, now to
 10.34. that ye have in **h.** a better
 12.23. written in **h.**, and to God
 25. him that speaketh from **h.**
 26. not the earth only,but also **h.**
Jas. 5.18. and the **h.** gave rain, and the
¹Pet. 1. 4. away, reserved in **h.** for you
 12. H. Ghost sent down from **h.**
 3.22. Who is gone into **h.**, and is
²Pet. 1.18. this voice which came from **h.**
 3. 5. the **h-**s were of old, and the
 7. But the **h-**s and the earth

²Pet. 3.10. the **h-**s shall pass away with
 12. the **h-**s being on fire shall
 13. for new **h-**s and a new earth
¹Jo. 5. 7. three that bear record in **h.**
Rev. 3.12. out of **h.** from my God : and
 4. 1. a door was opened in **h.**
 2. a throne was set in **h.**, and
 5. 3. no man in **h.**, nor in earth
 13. every creature which is in **h.**
 6.13. And the stars of **h.** fell unto
 14. the **h.** departed as a scroll
 8. 1. there was silence in **h.** about
 10. there fell a great star from **h.**
 9. 1. I saw a star fall from **h.** unto
 10. 4, 8. I heard a voice from **h.**;
    11.12.14.2,13,18.4,21.3
 5. lifted up his hand to **h.**
 6. who created **h.**, and the thin.
 11. 6. have power to shut **h.**, that
 12. they ascended up to **h.** in a
 13. gave glory to the God of **h.**
 15. great voices in **h.**, saying
 19. was opened in **h.**, and there
 12. 1, 3. a great wonder in **h.**; and
 4. third part of the stars of **h.**
 7. And there was war in **h.**
 8. place found any more in **h.**
 10. loud voice saying in **h.**, Now
 12. Therefore rejoice, ye **h-**s
 13. 6. and them that dwell in **h.**
 13. fire come down from **h.** on
 14.17. the temple which is in **h.**, he
 15. 1. I saw another sign in **h.** gr.
 5. of the testimony in **h.** was
 16.11. blasphemed the God of **h.**
 17. out of the temple of **h.**
 21. a great hail out of **h.**, from
 18. 5. have reached unto **h.**, and
 20. Rejoice over her, thou **h.**
 19. 1. of much people in **h.**, saying
 14. which were in **h.** followed
 20. 9. from God out of **h.**; 21.2,10
 11. the earth and the **h.** fled
 21. 1. I saw a new **h.** and a new
    for the first **h.** and the first
ouranothen.
Act.14.17. and gave us rain *from* **h.**
 26.13. in the way a light *from* **h.**
epouranios.
Phi. 2.10. of things *in* **h.**, and things
mesouranēma.
Rev. 8.13. flying through the *midst of* **h.**
 14. 6. fly in the *midst of* **h.**; 19.17

HEAVENLY.
epouranios.
Mat.18.35.shall my **h.** Father do also
Jo. 3.12. if I tell you of **h.** things
¹Co. 15.48. **h.**, such are they also..**h.**
 49. bear the image of the **h.**
Eph. 1. 3. in **h.** places in Christ ; 2.6
 20. right hand in the **h.** places
 3.10. powers in **h.** places might
²Ti. 4.18. unto his **h.** kingdom : to
Heb. 3. 1. partakers of the **h.** calling
 6. 4. tasted of the **h.** gift, and
 8. 5. example and shadow of **h.**th.
 9.23. but the **h.** things themselves
 11.16. better country, that is, an **h.**
 12.22. the **h.** Jerusalem, and to an
ouranios.
Mat. 6.14. your **h.** Father will also for.
 26. yet your **h.** Father feedeth
 32. for your **h.** Father knoweth
 15.13. my **h.** Father hath not plan.
Lu. 2.13. a multitude of the **h.** host.
Act.26.19. not disobe. unto the **h.** vision
ek ouranos.
Lu. 11.13. shall your **h.** Father give

HEAVINESS.
lupē.
Ro. 9. 2. I have great **h.** and continual

²Co. 2. 1. not come again to you in **h.**
  lupeð.
¹Pet. 1. 6. *though* now . . ye *are in* **h.**
  katēpheia.
Jas. 4. 9. mourning, and your joy to **h.**
  adēmoneð.
Phi. 2.26. you all, and was *full of* **h.**

HEAVY, (See *Lade*.)
barus.
Mat.23. 4. they bind **h.** burdens and
  bareð.
Mat.26.43. their eyes were **h.**; Mar.14.40
Lu. 9.32. him, were **h.** with sleep
  adēmoneð.
Mat.26.37. be sorrowful and *very* **h.**
Mar.14.33. amazed, and *to be very* **h.**

HEDGE, [*noun.*]   s.
phragmos.
Mar.12 1. and set an **h.** about it
Lu. 14.23. the highways and **h-s**

HEDGED, [*verb.*]
peritithemi phragmos.
Mat.21.33. and **h.** it round about, and

HEED.
blepð.   [Mar.13.5; Lu.21.8
Mat.24. 4. *Take* **h.** that no man deceive
Mar. 4.24. *Take* **h.** what ye hear: with
  13. 9. *take* **h.** to yourselves: for
  23. *take* ye **h.**: behold, I have
  33. *Take* ye **h.**, watch and pray
Lu. 8.18. *Take* **h.** therefore how ye
¹Co. 3.10. *let* every man *take* **h.** how
  8. 9. *take* **h.** lest by any means
  10.12. *let* . . standeth *take* **h.** lest he
Gal. 5.15. *take* **h.** that ye be not consu.
Col. 4.17. *Take* **h.** to the ministry whi.
Heb. 3.12. *Take* **h.**, brethren, lest there
  prosechð.
Mat. 6. 1. *Take* **h.** that ye do not your
Lu. 17. 3. *Take* **h.** *to* yourselves;
  21.34; Act.5.35,20.28
Act. 8. 6. *gave* **h.** *unto* those things
  10. *To* whom they all *gave* **h.**
¹Ti. 1. 4. Neither *give* **h.** *to* fables and
  4. 1. *giving* **h.** *to* seducing spirits
Tit. 1.14. Not *giving* **h.** *to* Jewish fab.
Heb. 2. 1. *to give* the more earnest **h.** *to*
²Pet. 1.19. ye do well *that* ye *take* **h.**
  horað.   [Lu.12.15
Mat.16. 6. *Take* **h.** and bew.; Mar.8.15;
  18.10. *Take* **h.** that ye despise not
Act.22.26. *Take* **h.** what thou doest
  skopeð.
Lu. 11.35. *Take* **h.** therefore that the
  epechð.
Act. 3. 5. And he *gave* **h.** *unto* them
¹Ti. 4.16. *Take* **h.** *unto* thyself, and

HEEL.
pterna.
Jo. 13.18. lifted up his **h.** against me

HEIFER.
damalis.
Heb.9.13. ashes of an **h.** sprinkling

HEIGHT.
hupsos.
Eph. 3.18. length, and depth, and **h.**
Rev.21.16. and the **h.** of it are equal
  hupsōma.
Ro. 8.39. Nor **h.**, nor depth, nor any

HEIR,   -s.
klēronomos.
Mat.21.38. This is the **h.**; come, let us;
  Mar.12.7; Lu.20.14
Ro. 4.13. he should be the **h.** of the
  14. which are of the law be **h-s**
  8.17. if children, then **h-s**; **h-s** of
134

Gal. 3.29. and **h-s** acoording to the
  4. 1. Now I say, That the **h.**, as
  7. then an **h.** of God through
Tit. 3. 7. we should be made **h-s** acc.
Heb. 1. 2. appointed **h.** of all things
  6.17. to shew unto the **h-s** of pro.
  11. 7. and became **h.** of the right.
Jas. 2. 5. rich in faith, and **h-s** of the
  sungklēronomos.
Heb.11.9. *the* **h-s** *with* him of the same
¹Pet.3. 7. **h-s** *together* of the grace of
  klēronomeð.
Gal. 4.30. *shall* not *be* **h.** with the son
Heb.1.14. who shall *be* **h-s** *of* salvation

HELL.
geenna.
Mat.5.22. shall be in danger of **h.** fire
  29, 30. body should be cast into **h.**
  10.28. both soul and body in **h.**
  18. 9. to be cast into **h.**; Mar.9.47
  23.15. more the child of **h.** than
  33. escape damnation of **h.**
Mar.9.43. having two hands to go into **h.**
  45. two feet to be cast into **h.**
Lu.12. 5. hath power to cast into **h.**
Jas. 3. 6. and it is set on fire of **h.**
  hadēs.
Mat.11.23. be bro. down to **h.**; Lu.10.15
  16.18. the gates of **h.** shall not
Lu. 16.23. in **h.** he lift up his eyes
Act. 2.27, 31. not leave my soul in **h.**
Rev. 1.18. have the keys of **h.** and of
  6. 8. was Death, and **h.** followed
  20.13. death and **h.** delivered up
  14. death and **h.** were cast into
  tartaroð.
²Pet.2. 4. *cast* them *down to* **h.**, *and*

HELM.
pēdalion.
Jas. 3. 4. about with a very small **h.**

HELMET.
perikephalaia.
Eph.6.17. And take the **h.** of salvation
¹Th. 5. 8. and for an **h.**, the hope of

HELP, [*noun*,]   -s.
boētheia.
Act.27.17. had taken up, they used **h-s**
  epikouria.
Act.26.22. therefore **obtained h.** of God
  antilēpsis.
¹Co.12.28. gifts of healings, **h-s**, govern.

HELP, [*verb*,]   -ed, -eth, -ing,
        Holpen.
boētheð.
Mat.15.25. worsh. him, saying, Lord **h.**
Mar. 9.22. have compass. on us, and **h.**
  24. I believe; **h.** thou mine
Act.16. 9. over into Macedonia, and **h.**
  21.28. Crying out, Men of Israel, **h.**
Rev.12.16. the earth **h-ed** the woman
  boētheia.
Heb.4.16. find grace to **h.** in time of
  sullambanð.
Lu. 5. 7. they should come and **h.** them
Phi. 4. 3. **h.** those women which lab.
  sunantilambanomai.
Lu.10.40. therefore that she **h.** me
Ro. 8.26. the Spirit also **h-eth** our
  sumballð.
Act.18.27. **h-ed** them much which had
  antilambanomai.
Lu. 1.54. he *hath* **h-o** his servant
  sunergeð.
¹Co.16.16. every one *that* **h-eth** *with* us
  sunupourgeð.
²Co. 1.11. ye also **h-**ing *together* by pra.

HELPER,   -s.
sunergos.
Ro. 16. 3. and Aquila my **h-s** in Christ
  9. Urbane, our **h.** in Christ
²Co. 1.24. but are **h-s** of your joy; for
  boēthos.
Heb.13.6. The Lord is my **h.**, and I

HEM.
kraspedon.
Mat. 9.20. touched the **h.** of his; 14.36

HEN.
ornis.
Mat.23.37. as a **h.** gathereth; Lu.13.34

HENCE, (See *Get*.)
enteuthen.
Mat.17.20. Remove **h.** to yonder place
Lu. 4. 9. cast thyself down *from* **h.**
  13.31. Get thee out, and depart **h.**
  16.26. would pass *from* **h.** to you
Jo. 2.16. Take these things **h.**; make
  7. 3. Depart **h.**, and go into Judea
  14.31. so I do. Arise, let us go **h.**
  18.36. is my kingdom not *from* **h.**
Jas. 4. 1. come they not **h.**, even of
  meta [*accus.*] **houtos,**
Act. 1. 5. Holy Ghost not many days **h.**
  hupagð.
Mat.4.10. Get thee **h.** Satan; for

HENCEFORTH.
loipon.
²Ti. 4. 8. **h.** there is laid up for me
Heb.10.13. *From* **h.** expecting till his
  ho loipos.
Gal. 6.17. *From* **h.** let no man trouble
  nun.
Lu. 1.48. from **h.** all generations
  5.10. from **h.** thou shalt catch men
  12.52. from **h.** there shall be five
Act.18. 6. from **h.** I will go unto the
²Co. 5.16. **h.** know we no man after
  eti.
²Co. 5.16. **h.** know we him no *more*
  arti.
Mat.23.39. Ye shall not see me **h.**
  26.29. I will not drink **h.** of
Jo. 14. 7. from **h.** ye know him
  aparti.
Rev.14.13. die in the Lord from **h.**
  mēketi.
Act. 4.17. *speak* **h.** to no man in this
Ro. 6. 6. that **h.** we should *not* serve
²Co. 5.15. should *not* **h.** live unto them
Eph. 4.17. that ye **h.** walk *not* as other
  ouketi.
Jo. 15.15. **h.** I call you *not* servants

HENCEFORWARD.
mēketi.
Mat.21.19. Let *no* fruit grow on thee **h.**

HER, [*accus.*]
autos [*accu. fem.*] is generally translated **her**, and is too frequent for quotation. The following is an exception :—
hautos.
Rev.12.15. cause **h.** to be carried away

HER, [*possessive.*]
The genitive of **autos** [*feminine*] is generally so translated, and is too frequent for quotation. The following are exceptions :—
hautou.
Mat. 1.25. forth **h.** firstborn; Lu.2.7
  2.18. Rachel weeping for **h.** child.
  11.19. justified of **h.** child.; Lu.7.3
  14. 8. before instructed of **h.** moth.

Mat.14.11.broug. it to h. mo.; Mar.6.28
　　20.20. of Z.'s children with h. sons
　　24.29. not give h. light ; Mar.13.24
Mar. 6.24. forth, and said unto h. moth.
　　7.26. the devil out of h. daughter
　　30. when she was come to h. ho.
　　10.12. a woman shall put away h.
　　12.44. she of h. want, did cast in all
　　　she had, even all h. living
Lu. 1.36. conceived a son in h. old age
　　56. returned to h. own house
　　2.19. pondered them in h. heart
　　36. seven years from h. virginity
　　51. all these sayings in h. heart
　　7.38, 44. with the hairs of h. head
　　10.38. received him into h. house
　　12.53. against h. daughter-in-law
　　　against h. mother-in-law
Jo. 4.28. The woman then left h.
　　11. 2. wiped his feet with h. ; 12.3
　　28. called Mary h. sister secretly
Act. 9.40. she opened h. eyes : and wh.
　　16.16. brought h. masters much ga.
Gal. 4.25. is in bondage with h. child.
Jas. 5.18. earth brought forth h. fruit
Rev. 2.21. to repent of h. fornication
　　6.13. a fig tree casteth h. untimely
　　12.14. into h. place, where she is
　　16. the earth opened h. mouth
　　14. 8. the wrath of h. fornication
　　17. 4. a golden cup in h. hand, full
　　　filthiness of h. fornication
　　5. upon h. forehead was a name
　　18. 7. for she saith in h. heart
　　19. 2. the earth with h. fornication
　　21. 2. a bride adorned for h. husb.
　　22. 2. yielded h. fruit every month

heautou.
Mat.23.37. gathereth h. chickens under
Lu. 13.34. hen doth gather h, brood
Act. 7.21. nourished him for h. own
1Co. 11. 5. dishonoureth h. head
　　13. 5. seeketh not h. own, is not
1Th. 2. 7. nurse cherisheth h. children

HERBS.
　　lachanon.
Mat.13.32. great. among h.; Mar.4.32
Lu. 11.42. rue and all manner of h.
Ro. 14. 2. who is weak, eateth h.
　　botanē.
Heb. 6. 7. bringeth forth h. meet for

HERD.
　　agelē. 　[Mar.5.11 ; Lu.8.32
Mat. 8.30. h. of many swine feeding;
　　31. go away into the h. of swine
　　32. went into the h. of swine
　　　the whole h. of swine ran ;
　　　Mar.5.13 ; Lu.8.33

HERE, (See *Present, Stand.*)
　　hōde.
Mat.12.41. than Jonas is h.; Lu.11.32
　　42. gr.than Sol. is here ; Lu.11.31
　　14. 8. Give me h. John Baptist's
　　17. We have h. but five loaves
　　16.28. There be some standing h.;
　　　Mar.9.1 ; Lu.9.27
　　17. 4. it is good for us to be h.;
　　　Mar.9.5 ; Lu.9.33
　　　let us make h. three tabern.
　　20. 6. Why stand ye h. all the day
　　24. 2. There shall not be left h. one
　　23. unto you, Lo, h. is Christ;
　　　Mar.13.21 ; Lu.17.21
　　26.38. ye h., and watch ; Mar.14.34
　　28. 6. He is not h.; for he; Lu.24.6
Mar. 6. 3. are not his sisters h. with us
　　8. 4. with bread h. in the wildern.
　　14.32. Sit ye h., while I shall pray
　　16. 6. he is not h.: behold the pl.

Lu. 4.23. do also h. in thy country
　　9.12. for we are h. in a desert pla.
　　17.23. they shall say to you, See h.
　　22.38. behold, h. are two swords
Jo. 6. 9. There is a lad h., which hath
　　11.21, 32. if thou hadst been h.
Act. 9.14. And h. he hath authority
Col. 4. 9. all things which are done h.
Heb. 7. 8. And h. men that die receive
　　13.14. For h. have we no continu.
Jas. 2. 3. Sit thou h. in a good place
　　　or sit h. under my footstool
Rev.13.10. h. is the patience and the
　　18. h. is wisdom. Let him that
　　14.12. h. is the patience of the
　　　h. are they that keep the
　　17. 9. And h. is the mind which
　　　enthade.
Lu. 24.41. them, Have ye h. any meat
Act.16.28. no harm: for we are all h.
　　25.24. at Jerusalem, and also h.
　　　autou.
Mat.26.36. Sit ye h., while I go and

HEREAFTER.
　　meta [*accu.*] houtos.
Jo. 13. 7. now ; but thou shalt know h.
Rev.1.19. things which shall be h.; 4.1
　　9.12. come two woes more h.
　　　apo arti.
Mat.26.64. h. ye shall see the Son of
Jo. 1.51. h. ye shall see heaven
　　　mēketi.
Mar.11.14. No man eat fruit of thee h.
　　　apo nun.
Lu.22.69. h. shall the son of man sit
　　　eti.
Jo. 14.30. h. I will not talk much with

HEREBY.
　　en houtos.
1Co. 4. 4. yet am I not h. justified
1Jo. 2. 3. And h. we do know that we
　　5. h. know we that we are in
　　3.16. h. perceive we the love of G.
　　19, 24. And h. we know that we
　　4. 2. h. know ye the Spirit of God
　　13. h. know we that we dwell in
　　　ek houtos.
1Jo. 4. 6. h. know we the spirit of tru.

HEREIN.
　　en houtos.
Jo. 4.37. And h. is that saying true
　　9.30. Why h. is a marvellous thing
　　15. 8. h. is my Father glorified
Act.24.16.And h. do I exercise myself
2Co. 8.10. And h. I give my advice
1Jo. 4.10. h. is love, not that we loved
　　17. h. is our love made perfect

HEREOF.
Mat.9.26. the fame h. went abroad
Heb.5. 3. by reason h., he ought as for

HERESY,　　　　　　*-ies.*
　　hairesis.
Act.24.14. the way which they call h.
1Co. 11.19. there must be also h-s amo.
Gal. 5.20. wrath, strife, seditions, h-s
2Pet. 2. 1. shall bring in damnable h-s

HERETICK.
　　hairetikos.
Tit. 3.10. A man that is an h. after

HERETOFORE, (See *Sin.*)

HEREUNTO.
　　eis houtos.
1Pet.2.21. For even h. were ye called

HERITAGE.
　　klēros.
1Pet.5. 3. as being lords over God's h.

HERSELF.
　　heautou, [*fem.*]
Mat.9.21. For she said within h., If I
Lu. 1.24. hid h. five months, saying
Rev. 2.20. which calleth h. a prophetess
　　18. 7. much she hath glorified h.
　　19. 7. his wife hath made h. ready

HEWN.
　　latomeō.
Mat. 27.60. new tomb, which he *had* h.
Mar. 15.46. *which was* h. out of a rock
　　ekkoptō.
Mat.3.10. *is* h. *down* and ; 7.19 ; Lu.3.9
　　laxeutos.
Lu.23.53. sepulchre that was h. *in stone*

HIDE,　　　　*-eth, Hid, Hidden.*
　　kruptō.
Mat. 5.14. on an hill cannot be h-d
　　13.44. unto treasure h-d in a field
　　　a man hath found, he h-eth
　　25.25. and h-d thy talent in the
Lu. 18.34. this saying was h-d from
　　19.42. now they *are* h-d from thine
Jo. 8.59. but Jesus h-d himself
　　12.36. and *did* h. himself from
Col. 3. 3. your life *is* h-d with Christ
1Ti. 5.25. are otherwise cannot be h-d
Heb.11.23. *was* h-d three months of
Rev. 2.17. give to eat of the h-en man.
　　6.15. h-d themselves in the dens
　　16. h. us from the face of him
　　　apokruptō.
Mat.11.25. thou *hast* h-d the.; Lu.10.21
　　25.18. in the earth, and h-d his
1Co. 2. 7. even the h-en wisdom, wh.
Eph. 3. 9. *hath been* h-d in God, who
Col. 1.26. which *hath been* h-d from
　　　engkruptō. ⁎
Mat.13.33. took and h-d *in ;* Lu.13.21
　　　perikruptō.
Lu. 1.24. and h-d herself five months
　　　kruptos.　　　　　[Lu.12.2
Mat.10.26. h-d that shall not; Mar.4.22;
1Co. 4. 5. bring to light the h-en thi.
2Co. 4. 2. renounced the h-en things
1Pet. 3. 4. the h-en man of the heart
　　　apokruphos.
Lu. 8.17. neither any thing h-d, that
Col. 2. 3. In whom are h-d all the trea.
　　　lanthanō.
Mar. 7.24. but he could not be h-d
Lu. 8.47. saw that she *was* not h-d
Act.26.26. none of these things *are* h-en
　　　kaluptō.
2Co. 4. 3. our gospel be h-d, it is h-d to
Jas. 5.20. and *shall* h. a multitude of
　　　parakaluptō.
Lu. 9.45. it was h-d from them, that

HIGH, (See *Captain, Exalt.*)
　　hupsēlos.
Mat. 4. 8. into an exceeding h.; 17.1;
　　　Mar.9.2 ; Lu.4.5
Act. 13.17. and with an h. arm brought
Ro. 12.16. Mind not h. things, but
Heb. 1. 3. hand of the Majesty on h.
Rev. 21.10. spirit to a great and h. mou.
　　12. And had a wall great and h.
　　　hupsos.
Lu. 1.78. dayspring from *on* h. hath
　　24.49. endued with power from *on* h.
Eph.4. 8. when he ascended up on h.
　　　hupsistos.
Mar.5. 7. Son of the *most* h.; Lu.8.28
Act. 7.48. Howbeit the *most* h. dwell.
　　16.17. the servants of the *most* h.,
Heb.7. 1. priest of the *most* h. God

135

epouranios.

Eph.6.12. wickedness in **h.** places

anō.

Phi. 3.14. prize of the **h.** calling of God

megas.

Jo. 19.31. sabbath day was an **h.** day

Heb.10.21. having an **h.** priest over

hupsōma.

²Co.10. 5. every **h.** *thing* that exalteth

tuphoomai.

²Ti. 3. 4. Traitors, heady, **h.** *minded*

HIGH PRIEST,   -s.
archiereus.

Mat.26.3, 58. the palace of the **h.**;
     Mar.14.54 ; Jo.18.15
   51. struck a servant of the **h.**'s;
     Mar.14.47; Lu.22.50; Jo.18.10
   57. away to Caiaphas the **h.**
   62, 63. the **h.** arose, and said
   65. the **h.** rent his clo.; Mar.14.63

Mar.2.26. days of Abiathar the **h.**
   14.53. led Jesus away to the **h.**
   60. the **h.** stood up in the midst
   61. Again the **h.** asked ; Jo.18.19
   66. one of the maids of the **h.**

Lu. 3. 2. and Caiaphas being the **h.**-s
   22.54. into the **h.**'s house

Jo. 11.49, 51. being the **h.** that ; 18.15
   18.15, 16. known unto the **h.**, and
   22. Answerest thou the **h.** so
   24. bound unto Caiaphas the **h.**
   26. the servants of the **h.**

Act. 4. 6. Annas the **h.**, and Caiaphas
   5.17. the **h.** rose up, and all they
   21. the **h.** came, and they that
   27. the **h.** asked them
   7. 1. Then said the **h.**, Are
   9. 1. went unto the **h.**, and desired
   22. 5. also the **h.** doth bear
   23. 2. the **h.** Ananias commanded
   4. Revilest thou God's **h.**
   5. that he was the **h.**
   24. 1. Ananias the **h.** descended
   25. 2. the **h.** and the chief of the

Heb.2.17. merciful and faithful **h.**
   3. 1. apostle and **h.** of our
   4.14. we have a great **h.**, that
   15. we have not an **h.** which
   5. 1. every **h.** taken from
   5. himself to be made an **h.**
   10. Called of God an **h.**
   6.20. made an **h.** for ever
   7.26. For such an **h.** became
   27. not daily, as those **h.**-s
   28. maketh men **h.**-s which
   8. 1. We have such an **h.**
   3. For every **h.** is ordained
   9. 7. went the **h.** alone once
   11. Christ being come an **h.**
   25. as the **h.** entereth into
   13.11. by the **h.** for sin, are

hiereus.

Act. 5.24. the **h.** and the captain

HIGHER.
anōteron.

Lu.14.10. unto thee, Friend, go up **h.**

huperechō.

Ro.13. 1. subject unto the **h.** powers

hupsēloteros.

Heb.7.26. made **h.** than the heavens

HIGHEST, (See *Room, Seat.*)
hupsistos.

Mat.21.9. Hosanna in the **h.**; Mar.11.10

Lu. 1.32. be called the Son of the **h.**
   35. the power of the **h.** shall
   76. be called the prophet of the **h.**
   2.14. Glory to God in the **h.**, and
   6.35. shall be the children of the **h.**
   19.38. in heaven, and glory in the **h.**
136

HIGHLY, (See *Displease, Esteem*)
huperphroneō.

Ro.12. 3. *to think* of himself *more* **h.**

huperupsoō.

Phi. 2. 9. also *hath* **h.** *exalted* him

huper ek perissos.

¹Th. 5.13. esteem them *very* **h.** in love

HIGHMINDED.
hupsēlophroneō.

Ro.11.20. by faith. Be not **h.**, but

¹Ti. 6.17. they *be* not **h.**, nor trust

HIGHWAY,   -s.
hodos.

Mat. 22.10. serv. went out into the **h.**-s

Mar. 10.46. sat by the **h.** side begging

Lu. 14.23. Go out into the **h.**-s and

diexodos ho hodos.

Mat.22. 9. Go ye therefore into the **h.**-s
     (*crossings of the ways.*)

HILL,   -s.
oros.

Mat.5.14. A city that is set on an **h.**

Lu. 4.29. him unto the brow of the **h.**
   9.37. were come down from the **h.**

oreinos.

Lu. 1.39. and went into the **h.** country
   65. throughout all the **h.** country

bounos.

Lu. 3. 5. every mountain and **h.** shall
   23.30. and to the **h.**-s, Cover us

HIM,

Generally represents autos in some
of its oblique cases, although sometimes there is no corresponding word in
Greek. The following are exceptions :—

houtos.

Mat.27.32. **h.** they compelled to bear his

Lu. 9.26. of **h.** shall the Son of man be
   12. 5. yea, I say unto you, Fear **h.**
   19. 9. And he said likewise to **h.**
   20.12. and they wounded **h.** also
   13. rever. him when they see **h.**

Jo. 5. 6. When Jesus saw **h.** lie, and
   38. hath sent, **h.** ye believe not
   6.27. for **h.** hath God the Father
   9.31. doeth his will, **h.** he heareth
   10. 3. To **h.** the porter openeth
   13.24. therefore beckoned to **h.**
   21.21. Peter seeing **h.**, saith to Jes.

Act. 2.23. **h.** being delivered by the
   4.10. by **h.** doth this man stand
   5.31. **h.** hath God exalted with
   10.40. **h.** God raised up the third
   43. To **h.** give all the prophets
   13.27. because they knew **h.** not
   39. And by **h.** all that believe
   15.38. not good to take **h.** with
   16. 3. **h.** would Paul have to go
   17.23. **h.** declare I unto you
   25. 5. there be any wickedn. in **h.**

¹Co. 2. 2. Jesus Ch. and **h.** crucified
   3.17. of God, **h.** shall God destroy

Phi. 2.23. **h.** therefore I hope to send

Heb.11.12. of one, and **h.** as good as

¹Jo. 2. 4. and the truth is not in **h.**
   5. in **h.** verily is the love of G.

hautou, *or* heautou.

Mat. 8.18. great multitudes about **h.**

Mar. 3.34. on them which sat about **h.**
   5.30. that virtue had gone out of **h.**
   14.33. taketh with **h.** Peter and Ja.

Lu. 9.47. a child, and set him by **h.**
   18.40. him to be brought unto **h.**
   19.15. servants to be called unto **h.**

Jo. 1.47. saw Nathanael coming to **h.**
   6. 5. great company come unto **h.**

Act. 5.37. away much people after **h.**
   9. 4. heard a voice saying unto **h.**
   16. 3. Paul have to go forth with **h.**

Act. 23. 2. them that stood by **h.** to
   25.21. I commanded **h.** to be kept

¹Co. 16. 2. every one of you lay by **h.** in

Eph. 1.17. revela. in the knowledge *of* **h.**

Heb.12. 2. the joy that was set before **h.**

kakeinos.

Mar.12. 4. *and* at **h.** they cast stones
   5. *and* **h.** they killed, and many

Lu. 20.11. and they beat **h.** *also*, and

HIMSELF.
heautou.

Mat.12.26.he is divided against **h.**
   45. taketh with **h.** seven other
     spirits more wicked than **h.**
   13.21. Yet hath he not root in **h.**
   16.24. let him deny **h.**, and take up
     Mar.8.34 ; Lu.9.23
   18. 4. shall humble **h.**; 23.12 ;
     Lu.14.11,18.14
   23.12. shall exalt **h.**; Lu.14.11,18.14
   27.42. others ; **h.** he can.; Mar.15.31

Mar. 3.26. rise up against **h.**; Lu.11.18
   5. 5. crying, and cutting **h.** with
   30. immediately knowing in **h.**
   12.33. to love his neighbour as **h.**

Lu. 7.39. spake with. **h.**, saying ; 12.17
   9.25. the whole world, and lose **h.**
   10.29. he, willing to justify **h.**
   11.26. spirits more wicked than **h.**
   12.21. that layeth up treasure for **h.**
   15.17. when he came to **h.**, he said
   16. 3. the steward said within **h.**
   18. 4. afterward he said within **h.**
   11. stood and pray. thus with **h.**
   19.12. to receive for **h.** a kingdom
   23. 2. saying that *he* **h.** is Christ
   35. saved others ; let him save **h.**
   24.12. departed, wondering in **h.** at
   27. the things concerning **h.**

Jo. 2.24. Jesus did not commit **h.** unto
   5.18. making **h.** equal with God
   19. Son can do nothing of **h.**
   26. as the Father hath life in **h.**
     the Son to have life in **h.**
   6.61. When Jesus knew in **h.** that
   7.18. He that speaketh of **h.** seek.
   8.22. said the Jews, Will he kill **h.**
   11.38. therefore again groan. in **h.**
   51. this spake he not of **h.**: but
   13. 4. took a towel, and girded **h.**
   32. shall also glorify him in **h.**
   16.13. for he shall not speak of **h.**
   19. 7. he made **h.** the Son of God
   21. 1. Jesus shewed **h.** again to the
   7. and did cast **h.** into the sea

Act. 1. 3. whom also he shewed **h.**
   5.36. Theudas, boasting **h.** to be
   8. 9. that **h.** was some great one
   34. of **h.**, or of some other man
   10.17. while Peter doubted in **h.**
   12.11. when Peter was come to **h.**
   14.17. he left not **h.** without witne.
   16.27. and would have killed **h.**
   19.31. not adventure **h.** into the
   25. 4. that *he* **h.** would depart
   28.16. Paul was suff. to dwell by **h.**

Ro. 14. 7. **h.**, and no man dieth to **h.**
   12. shall give account of **h.** to G.
   22. he that condemneth not **h.**
   15. 3. For even Ch. pleased not **h.**

¹Co. 3.18. Let no man deceive **h.** If any
   11.28. let a man examine **h.**, and so
   29. drinketh damnation to **h.**
   14. 4. unknown tongue edifieth **h.**
   28. Let him speak to **h.**, and to

²Co. 5.18. reconciled us to **h.** by Jesus
   19. reconciling the world unto **h.**
   10. 7. If any man trust to **h.** that
     let him of **h.** think this again
   18. not he that commendeth **h.**

Gal. 1. 4. Who gave **h.** for our sins
   2.12. he withdrew and separat. **h.**

Gal. 2.20. loved me, and gave **h.** for
  6. 3. he is nothing, he deceiveth **h.**
    4. have rejoicing in **h.** alone
Eph. 2.15. for to make in **h.** of twain
  5. 2. hath given **h.** for us an offer.
  25. the church, and gave **h.** for
  27. present it to **h.** a glorious
  28. loveth his wife loveth **h.**
  33. love his wife even as **h.**; and
Phi. 2. 7. made **h.** of no reputation
  8. he humbled **h.**, and became
  3.21. to subdue all things unto **h.**
²Th. 2. 4. shewing **h.** that he is God
¹Ti. 2. 6. Who gave **h.** a ransom for
²Ti. 2.13. faithful : he cannot deny **h.**
  21. If a man therefore purge **h.**
Tit. 2.14. Who gave **h.** for us, that he
    purify unto **h.** a peculiar
Heb. 1. 3. had by **h.** purged our sins
  5. 3. so also for **h.**, to offer for
  4. taketh this honour unto **h.**
  5. Christ glorifieth not **h.**
  6.13. by no greater, he sware by **h.**
  7.27. once, when he offered up **h.**
  9. 7. which he offered for **h.**, and
  14. offered **h.** without spot to
  25. that he should offer **h.** often
Jas. 1.24. For he beholdeth **h.**, and
  27. to keep **h.** unspotted from
¹Jo. 3. 3. purifieth **h.**, even as he is
  5.10. hath the witness in **h.**: he
  18. begotten of God keepeth **h.**
  hautou.
Jo. 9.21. ask him ; he shall speak for **h.**
  19.12. whosoever maketh **h.** a king
Eph. 1. 5. by Jesus Ch. to **h.**, according
  9. whic. he hath purposed in **h.**
Col. 1.2c. reconcile all things unto **h.**
Heb. 9.26. sin by the sacrifice *of* **h.**
  12. 3. contra. of sinners against **h.**
(*See those verbs which this word*
follows in connection.)

HINDER, [*verb*,]   -ed.
engkoptō.
Ro. 15.22. I *have been* much **h-ed** from
Kal. 5. 7. Ye did run well ; who *did* **h.**
¹Th. 2.18. and again ; but Satan **h-ed**
  anakoptō.
Gal. 5. 7. who *did* **h.** you that ye should
  ekkoptō.
¹Pet. 3. 7. that your prayers *be* not **h-ed**
  didōmi engkopē.
·Co. 9.12. lest we *should* **h.** the gospel
  kōluō.
Lu. 11.52. that were entering in ye **h-ed**
Act. 8.36. what *doth* **h.** me to be bapti.

HINDER, [*adjective.*]
prumna.
Mar. 4.38. he was in the **h.** *part* of the
Act.27.41. but the **h.** *part* was broken

HIRE, [*noun.*]
misthos.
Mat. 20. 8. and give them their **h.**
Lu. 10. 7. labourer is worthy of his **h.**
Jas. 5. 4. Behold, the **h.** of the labour.

HIRE, [*verb*,]   -ed.
misthoomai.
Mat.20. 1. to **h.** labourers into his vine.
  7. Because no man *hath* **h-ed** us
  misthōtos.
Mar.1.20. ship with the **h-ed** *servants*
  misthios.
Lu.15.17. How many **h-ed** servants of
  19. as one of thy **h-ed** servants
  misthōma.
Act.28.30. years in his own **h-ed** *house*

HIRELING.
misthōtos.
Jo.10.12. But he that is an **h.**, and not

Jo. 10.13. **h.** fleeth, because he is an **h.**

HIS,
hautou and the genitive of **autos**
are the words generally so translated.
The following are exceptions :—
  idios.
Mat. 9. 1. and came into **h.** *own; Lu.*2.3
  22. 5. one to **h.** farm, another to
  25.14. who called **h.** *own* servants
  15. according to **h.** *several* abil.
Mar.15.20. and put **h.** *own* clothes on
Lu. 6.44. is known by **h.** *own* fruit
  10.34. and set him on **h.** *own* beast
Jo. 1.11. He came unto **h.** *own*, and
  h. *own* received him not
  41. findeth **h.** *own* brother Sim.
  4.44. honour in **h.** *own* country
  5.18. said also that God was **h.** F.
  43. in **h.** *own* name, him ye will
  7.18. seeketh **h.** *own* glory : but he
  8.44. he speaketh of **h.** *own :* for
  10. 3. he calleth **h.** *own* sheep
  4. when he putteth forth **h.** *own*
  13. 1. having loved **h.** own which
  15.19. the world would love **h.** *own*
  16.32. scattered, every man to **h.** *own*
  19.27. disciple took her unto **h.** *own*
Act. 1. 7. the Father hath put in **h.** *own*
  25. that he might go to **h.** *own*
  2. 6. speak in **h.** *own* language
  4.32. which he possess. was **h.** *own*
  13.36. after he had served **h.** *own*
  20.28. hath purchased with **h.** *own*
  24.23. forbid none of **h.** *acquaint.*
  28.30. in **h.** *own* hired house
Ro. 8.32. spared not **h.** *own* Son
  14. 4. to **h.** *own* master he standeth
  5. be fully persuaded in **h.** *own*
¹Co. 3. 8. eve. man shall receive **h.** *own*
  according to **h.** *own* labour
  6.18. sinneth against **h.** *own* body
  7. 4. hath not power of **h.** *own*
  7. every man hath **h.** *proper*
  37. power over **h.** *own* will
  9. 7. warfare any time at **h.** *own*
  11.21. taketh before other **h.** *own*
  15.23. in **h.** *own* order : Christ the
  38. to every seed **h.** *own* body
Gal. 6. 5. shall bear **h.** *own* burden
¹Ti. 3. 4. One that ruleth well **h.** *own*
  5. know not how to rule **h.** *own*
  8. if any provide not for **h.** *own*
  6.15. Which in **h.** *times* he shall
²Ti. 1. 9. according to **h.** *own* purpose
Heb. 4.10. works, as God did from **h.**
  7.27. first for **h.** *own* sins, and
  9.12. but by **h.** *own* blood he ent.
  13.12. sanctify the peo. with **h.** *own*
Jas. 1.14. drawn away of **h.** *own* lust
²Pet.2.22. turned to **h.** *own* vomit aga.
  heautou.
Lu. 11.21. man armed keepeth **h.** palace
  12.47. servant, which knew **h.** lord's
  13.19. took, and cast into **h.** garden
  14.26. to me, and hate not **h.** fath.
  yea, and **h.** *own* life also, he
  15. 5. he layeth it on **h.** shoulders
  20. arose, and came to **h.** father
  16. 5. called every one of **h.** lord's
  19.13. he called **h.** ten servants
Ro. 4.19. considered not **h.** *own* body
  5. 8. God commendeth **h.** love
  8. 3. God sending **h.** *own* Son in
¹Co. 7. 2. let every man have **h.** *own*
  37. heart that he will keep **h.** v.
  10.24. Let no man seek **h.** *own*, but
²Co. 3.13. which put a vail over **h.** face
Gal. 6. 4. let every man prove **h.** *own*
  8. he tnat soweth to **h.** flesh
Eph. 5.28. loveth **h** wife loveth himself
  29. man ever yet hated **h.** *own*

Eph. 5.33. love **h.** wife even as himself
Phi. 2. 4. Look not every man on **h.** *own*
¹Th. 2.11. as a father doth **h.** children
  12. hath called you unto **h.** king.
  4. 4. know how to possess **h.** ves.
²Th. 2. 6. might be revealed in **h.** time
Rev.10. 7. declared to **h.** servants the

HITHER, (See *Call, Come.*)
hōde.
Mat. 8.29. art thou come **h.** to torment
  14.18. He said, Bring them **h.** to
  17.17. bri. him **h.** to me; Lu.9.41
  22.12. Frie., how camest thou in **h.**
Mar.11. 3. straight. he will send him **h.**
Lu. 14.21. bring in **h.** the poor, and the
  19.27. bring **h.** ,and slay them before
Jo. 6.25. Rabbi, when camest thou **h.**
  20.27. Reach **h.** thy finger, and
Act. 9.21. and came **h.** for that intent
Rev. 4. 1. which said, Come up **h.**, and
  11.12. say. unto them, Come up **h.**
  enthade.
Jo. 4. 5. not, neither come **h.** to draw
  16. call thy husba., and come **h.**
Act.17. 6. upside down are come **h.** also
  25.17. when they were come **h.**
  deuro.
Rev.17. 1. Come **h.**; I will shew; 21.9

HITHERTO.
heōs arti.
Jo. 5.17. My Father worketh **h.**, and
  16.24. **h.** have ye asked nothing
  achri ho deuro.
Ro. 1.13. unto you, but was let **h.**
  oupō.
¹Co. 3. 2. for **h.** ye were *not* able to

HOISED.
epairō.
Act.27.40. **h.** *up* the mainsail to the

HOLD, [*noun.*]   (See *Strong.*)
tērēsis.
Act. 4. 3. put them in **h.** unto the
  phulakē.
Rev.18. 2. the **h.** of every foul spirit

HOLD, [*verb*,] -en, -ing, *Held.*
krateō.   [Mar.6.17
Mat.12.11. *will* he not *lay* **h.** on it, and ;
  14. 3. *had laid* **h.** on John, *and*
  26.48. that same is he ; **h.** him *fast*
  55. temple, and ye *laid* no **h.** *on*
  57. they *that had laid* **h.** on Jes.
  28. 9. and **h.** him *by* the feet, and
Mar. 3.21. they went out *to lay* **h.** *on*
  7. 3. **h-***ing* the tradition of the
  4. wh. they have received *to* **h.**
  8. ye **h.** the tradition of men
  12.12. they sought *to lay* **h.** on him
  14.51. the young men *laid* **h.** on him
Lu. 24.16. But their eyes *were* **h-***en*
Act. 2.24. that he should be **h-***en* of it
  3.11. *as* the lame. .was healed **he.**
Col. 2.19. And not **h-***ing* the Head
²Th. 2.15. stand fast, and **h.** the trad.
Heb. 4.14. *let* us **h.** *fast* our profession
  6.18. *to lay* **h.** *upon* the hope set
Rev. 2. 1. saith he *that* **h-***eth* the seven
  13. and thou **h-***est fast* my name
  14, 15. them *that* **h.** the doctrine
  25. ye have already **h.** *fast* till I
  3.11. **h.** *that fast* which thou hast
  7. 1. **h-***ing* the four winds of the
  20. 2. And he *laid* **h.** *on* the dragon
Mat.21.26. for all **h.** John as a prophet
Phi. 2.29. **h.** such in reputation
¹Ti. 1.19. **h-***ing* faith, and a good con.
  3. 9. **h-***ing* the myste. of the faith
²Ti. 1.13. **h.** *fast* the form of sound

katechō.
Ro. 1.18. *who* h. the truth in unright.
  7. 6. dead wherein we *were* he.
¹Th. 5.21. h. *fast* that which is good
Heb. 3. 6. if we h. *fast* the confidence
  14. if we h. the beginning of
  10.23. *Let us* h. *fast* the profession
sunechō.
Lu.22.63. the men *that* he. Jesus mock.
epechō.
Phi. 2.16. h-*ing forth* the word of life
antechomai.
Mat.6.24. else he *will* h. *to* ; Lu.16.13
Tit. 1. 9. h-*ing fast* the faithful word
epilambanomai.
Lu.20.20. that they *might take* h. *of* his
  26. they could not *take* h. *of* his
  23.26. they *laid* h. *upon* one Simon
¹Ti. 6.12, 19. *lay* h. *on* eternal life
lambanō.
Mat.12.14. and he. a council against
poieō.
Mar.15. 1. chief priests he. a consult.
eimi.
Act.14. 4. part he. with the Jews, and
histēmi.
Ro.14. 4. yea, he *shall be* h-*en up :* for
tēreō.
Rev.3. 3. heard ; and h. *fast,* and rep.
  (See *Peace.*)

HOLES.
phōleos.
Mat.8.20. foxes have h., and ; Lu.9.58

HOLIEST.
hagion. [*plu.***]**
Heb.9. 8. the way into the h. *of all*
  10.19. to enter into the h. by the
hagios hagiōn.
Heb.9. 3. which is called the h. *of all*

HOLILY.
hosiōs.
¹Th. 2.10. also, how h. and justly, and

HOLINESS, (See *Become.*)
hagiasmos.
Ro. 6.19. serv. to righteousness unto h.
  22. ye have your fruit unto h.
¹Th. 4. 7. unto uncleanness, but unto h.
¹Ti. 2.15. charity and h. with sobriety
Heb.12.14.peace with all men, and h.
hagiōsunē
Ro. 1. 4. according to the spirit of h.
²Co. 7. 1. perfecting in the fear of
¹Th. 3.13. unblameable in h. before
hagiotēs.
Heb.12.10. might be partakers of his h.
hosiotēs,
Lu. 1.75. In h. and righteousness befo.
Eph.4.24. in righteousness and true h.
eusebeia.
Act. 3.12. tho. by our own power or h.

HOLY.
hagios.
Mat. 1.18. found with child of the h. G.
  20. in her is of the h. Ghost
  3.11. baptize you with the h. Gh.;
    Mar.1.8 ; Lu.3.16 ; Jo.1.33;
    Act.1.5,11.16
  4. 5. up into the h. city ; 27.53
  7. 6. Give not that which is h.
  12.32. speaketh against the h. Gho.
  24.15. prophet, stand in the h. pla.
  25.31. all the h. angels with him
  28.19. of the Son, and of the h. Gh.
Mar. 1.24. thou art, the h. *One ;* Lu.4.34
  3.29. blasp. ag. the h. G.; Lu.12.10
  6.20. was a just man and an h.
  8.38. with the h. angels ; Lu.9.26
  12.36. said by the h. G.; Act.1.16
  13.11. ye that speak,)ut the h. G.
138

Lu. 1.15, 41. filled with the h. Ghost ;
    67 ; Act.2.4,4.8,31,9.17,13.9
  35. The h. Gh. shall come upon
    also that h. *thing* which sh.
  49. great things ; and h. is his
  70. mouth of his h. pro.; Act.3.21
  72. to remember his h. covenant
  2.23. shall be called h. to the Lord
  25. and the h. Ghost was upon
  26. unto him by the h. Ghost
  3.22. the h. Ghost descended in
  4. 1. full of the h. G.; Act.6.3,7.55
  11.13. give the h. Spirit to them
  12.12. For the h. Ghost shall teach
Jo. 7.39. for the h. Ghost was not yet
  14.26. Comforter, wh. is the h. Gh.
  17.11. h. Father, keep through
  20.22. Receive ye the h. G.; Act.2.38
Act. 1. 2. that he through the h. Ghost
  8. that the h. Ghost is come
  2.33. the promise of the h. Ghost
  3.14. denied the h. *One* and the
  4.27. against thy h. child Jesus
  30. name of thy h. child Jesus
  5. 3. heart to lie to the h. Ghost
  32. so is also the h. Ghost, whom
  6. 5. of faith and of the h. Ghost
  13. words against this h. place
  7.33. where thou standest is h. gr.
  51. do always resist the h. Gho.
  8.15, 19. might receive the h. Gh.
  17. they received the h. Ghost
  18. the h. Ghost was given, he
  9.31. in the comfort of the h. Gho.
  10.22. warned from God by an h.
  38. with the h. Gh. and with
  44. the h. Gh. fell on all ; 11.15
  45. poured out..gift of the h. G.
  47. have received the h. Gh. as
  13. 2. the h. Gh. said, Separate me
  4. sent forth by the h. Ghost
  52. with joy, and with the h. G.
  15. 8. giving them the h. Ghost
  28. seemed good to the h. Ghost
  16. 6. were forbidden of the h. Gh.
  19. 2. Have ye received the h. Gh.
    whether there be any h. Gh.
  6. the h. Gh. came on them
  20.23. Save that the h. Gh. witnes.
  28. the h. Ghost hath made you
  21.11. Thus saith the h. Ghost
  28. and hath polluted this h. pl.
  28.25. Well spake the h. Gh. by Es.
Ro. 1. 2. his prophets in the h. scrip.
  5. 5. our hearts by the h. Ghost
  7.12. law is h., and the comma. h.
  9. 1. me witness in the h. Ghost
  11.16. For if the first fruit be h.
    if the root be h., so are
  12. 1. a living sacrifice, h., accept.
  14.17. peace, and joy in the h. Gh.
  15.13. through..power of the h. G.
  16. sanctified by the h. Ghost
  16.16. Salu. one another with an h.;
    ¹Co.16.20 ; ²Co. 13.12 ;
    ¹Th.5.26
¹Co. 2.13. which the h. Gh. teacheth
  3.17. for the temple of God is h.
  6.19. is the temple of the h. Gho.
  7.14. unclean ; but now are they h.
  34. may be h. both in body and
  12. 3. is the Lord, but by the h.
²Co. 6. 6. by kindness, by the h. Ghost
  13.14. communion of the h. Ghost
Eph. 1. 4. we should be h. and ; 5.27
  13. with that h. Spirit of prom.
  2.21. groweth unto an h. temple
  3. 5. unto his h. apostles and pro.
  4.30. grieve not the h. Spirit
Col. 1.22. thr. death, to present you h.
  3.12. elect of God, h. and beloved
¹Th. 1. 5. in power, and in the h. Gh.

¹Th. 1. 6. with joy of the h. Ghost
  4. 8. given unto us his h. Spirit
  27. unto all the h. brethren
²Ti. 1. 9. called us with an h. calling
  14. by the h. Ghost which dwell
Tit. 3. 5. and renewing of the h. Ghost
Heb. 2. 4. and gifts of the h. Ghost
  3. 1. Wherefore, h. brethren, par.
  7. as the h. Ghost saith, To day
  6. 4. made partakers of the h. Gh.
  9. 8. The h. Ghost this signifying
  10.15. the h. Ghost also is a witness
¹Pet. 1.12. with the h. Ghost sent down
  15, 16. call. you is h., so be ye h.
  2. 5. spiritual house, an h. priest.
  9. a royal priesthood, an h. na.
  3. 5. in the old time the h. women
²Pet. 1.18. with him in the h. mount
  21. h. men of God spake as
    they were moved by the h. G.
  2.21. h. commandment delivered
  3. 2. spoken before by the h. pro.
  11. in all h. conversation and
¹Jo. 2.20. an unction from the h. *One*
  5. 7. the Word, and the h. Ghost
Jude 20. yours,.on your most h. faith
    praying in the h. Ghost
Rev. 3. 7. saith he that is h., he that
  4. 8. and night, saying, h., h., h.
  6.10. How long, O Lord, h. and
  11. 2. the h. city shall they tread
  14.10. the presence of the h. angels
  18.20. ye h. apostles and prophets
  20. 6. Blessed and h. is he that
  21. 2. And I John saw the h. city
  10. great city, the h. Jerusalem
  22. 6. God of the h. prophets sent
  11. that is h., let him be holy
  19. of life, and out of the h. city
hagion.
Heb.9.12. in once unto the h. *place*
  24. the h. *places* made with hands
  25. into the h. *place* every year
hagiazō.
Rev.22.11. is holy, *let him be* h. still
hosios.
Act. 2.27. thine h. One to see ; 13.35
¹Ti. 2. 8. lifting up h. hands, without
Tit. 1. 8. sober, just, h., temperate
Heb.7.26. who is h., harmless, undefiled
Rev.15.4. for thou only art h.
hieros.
¹Co. 9.13. which minister about h. thi.
²Ti. 3.15. hast known the h. scriptures

HOLYDAY.
heortē
Col.2.16. or in respect of an h., or of

HOME.
oikos.
Mar.5.19. Go h. to thy friends, and
Lu. 15. 6. when he cometh h., he call.
¹Co.11.34. let him eat at h.; that ye
  14.35. ask their husbands at h.
¹Ti. 5. 4. first to shew piety at h.
oikia.
Mat.8. 6. my servant lieth at h. sick
oikouros.
Tit. 2. 5. *keepers at* h., good, obedient
idios.
¹Ti. 5. 4. born first to shew piety at h.
endēmeō.
²Co. 5. 6. *whilst we are at* h. in the

HONEST, (See *Report.*)
kalos.
Lu. 8.15. which in an h. and good heart
Ro.12.17. Provide things h. in the
²Co. 8.21. Providing for h. things
  13. 7. ye should do that which is h.
¹Pet.2.12. conversation h. among the

semnos.

Phi. 4. 8. whatsoever things are **h**.

HONESTLY.

euschēmonōs.

Ro.13.13. Let us walk **h**., as in the day
1Th. 4.12. That ye may walk **h**. toward
     kalōs.

Heb.13.18. things, willing to live **h**.

HONESTY.

semnotēs.

1Ti. 2. 2. in all godliness and **h**.

HONEY.

meli.

Mat.3. 4. locusts and wild **h**.; Mar.1.6
Rev.10.9, 10. in thy mouth sweet as **h**.
     melissios.

Lu.24.42. broiled fish, and of an **h**. co.

HONOUR, [noun,]   -s.

timē.

Jo. 4.44. hath no **h**. in his own country
Act.28.10. honoured us with many **h**-s
Ro. 2. 7. seek for glory and **h**., and
    10. But glory, **h**., and peace to
  9.21. to make one vessel unto **h**.
  12.10. in **h**. preferring one another
  13. 7. to whom fear, **h**. to whom **h**.
1Co.12.23. we bestow more abundant **h**.
  24. having given more abund. **h**.
Col. 2.23. not in any **h**. to the satisfy.
1Th. 4. 4. vessel in sanctifica. and **h**.
1Ti. 1.17. be **h**. and glory for ever and
  5.17. counted worthy of double **h**.
  6. 1. own masters worthy of all **h**.
  16. to whom be **h**. and power
2Ti. 2.20. some to **h**., and some to dish.
  21. he shall be a vessel unto **h**.
Heb.2. 7, 9. cro. him with glory and **h**.
  3. 3. hath more **h**. than the house
  5. 4. taketh this **h**. unto himself
1Pet. 1. 7. be found unto praise and **h**.
  3. 7. giving **h**. unto the wife, as
2Pet. 1.17. from God the Father, **h**. and
Rev. 4. 9. those beasts give glory and **h**.
  11. to receive glory and **h**. and
  5.12. and **h**., and glory, and bless.
  13. Blessing, and **h**., and glory
  7.12. and **h**., and power, and mig.
  19. 1. Salvation, and glory, and **h**.
  21.24. bring their glory and **h**. into
  26. glory and **h**. of the nations
     doxa.

Jo. 5.41. I receive not **h**. from men
  44. which receive **h**. one of anot.
    the **h**. that cometh from God
  8.54. If I honour myself, my **h**. is
2Co. 6. 8. By **h**. and dishonour, by evil
Rev.19.7. and rejoice, and give **h**. to
    atimos.   [Mar.6.4

Mat.13.57. prophet is not *without* **h**.;

HONOUR, [verb,] -ed, -eth.

timaō.

Mat.15. 4. **h**. thy father and mo.;19.19;
    Mar.7.10,10.19; Lu.18.20 ;
    Eph.6.2
  5. And **h**. not his father or his
  8. **h**-*eth* me with their; Mar.7.6
Jo. 5.23. That all men *should* **h**. the
    Son, even as they **h**. the
    Father. He *that* **h**-*eth* not
    the Son **h**-*eth* not the Father
  8.49. but I **h**. my Father, and ye
  12.26. me, him *will* my Father **h**.
Act.28.10. Who also **h**-*ed* us with many
1Ti. 5. 3. **h**. widows that are widows
1Pet. 2.17. **h**. all men. Love the brot.
    Fear God. **h**. the king.
    doxazō.

Jo. 8.54. If I **h**. myself, my honour

Jo. 8.54. is my Father that **h**-*eth* me
1Co.12.26. or one member *be* **h**-*ed*, all

HONOURABLE.

euschēmōn.

Mar.15.43. Arimathea, an **h**. counsellor
Act. 13.50. the devout and **h**. women
  17.12. also of **h**. women, which we.
    entimos.

Lu.14. 8. lest a *more* **h**. man than thou
    endoxos.

1Co. 4.10. ye are strong; ye are **h**.
    atimos.

1Co.12.23. which we think to be *less* **h**.
    timios.

Heb.13. 4. Marriage is **h**. in all, and

HOOK.

angkistron.

Mat.17.27. to the sea, and cast an **h**.

HOPE, [noun.]

elpis.

Act. 2.26. also my flesh shall rest in **h**.
  16.19. the **h**. of their gains was go.
  23. 6. of the **h**. and resurrection of
  24.15. have **h**. toward God, which
  26. 6. for the **h**. of the promise
  7. For which **h**.'s sake, king
  27.20. all **h**. that we should be
  28.20. that for the **h**. of Israel
Ro. 4.18. Who against **h**. believed in **h**.
  5. 2. rejoice in **h**. of the glory of
  4. experience ; and experien. **h**.
  5. And **h**. maketh not ashamed
  8.20. subjected the same in **h**.
  24. we are saved by **h**.: but **h**.that
    is seen is not **h**.: for what
  12.12. Rejoicing in **h**.; patient in
  15. 4. the scriptures, might have **h**.
  13. Now the God of **h**. fill you
    that ye may abound in **h**.
1Co. 9.10. should plow in **h**.; and that
    h. should be partak. of his **h**.
  13.13. now abide. faith, **h**., charity
2Co. 1. 7. our **h**. of you is stedfast
  3.12. then that we have such **h**.
  10.15. having **h**., when your faith
Gal. 5. 5. the Spirit wait for the **h**. of
Eph. 1.18. what is the **h**. of his calling
  2.12. having no **h**., and without G.
  4. 4. called in one **h**. of your call.
Phi. 1.20. earnest expecta. and my **h**.
Col. 1. 5. the **h**. which is laid up for
  23. from the **h**. of the gospel
  27. Christ in you, the **h**. of glory
1Th. 1. 3. and patience of **h**. in our Lo.
  2.19. For what is our **h**., or joy
  4.13. as others which have no **h**.
  5. 8. an helmet, the **h**. of salvation
2Th. 2.16. consolation and good **h**. thro.
1Ti. 1. 1. Jesus Christ, which is our **h**.
Tit. 1. 2. In **h**. of eternal life, which
  2.13. Looking for that blessed **h**.
  3. 7. accord. to the **h**.of eternal life
Heb. 3. 6. and the rejoicing of the **h**.
  6.11. full assurance of **h**. unto the
  18. upon the **h**. set before us
  7.19. bringing in of a better **h**.
1Pet. 1. 3. a lively **h**. by the resurrection
  21. your faith and **h**. might be
  3.15. a reason of the **h**. that is in
1Jo. 3. 3. every man that hath this **h**.
    eimi elpizō.

1Co. 15.19. have **h**. in Christ (*are hoping*)

HOPE, [verb,] -ed, -eth, -ing.

elpizō.

Lu. 6.34. of whom ye **h**. to receive
  23. 8. he **h**-*ed* to have seen some
Act.24.26. He **h**-*ed* also that money sh.
  26. 7. God day and night, **h**. to co.
Ro. 8.24. why doth he yet **h**. *for*

Ro. 8.25. if we **h**. *for* that we see not
1Co.13. 7. believeth all things, **h**-*eth* all
2Co. 8. 5. not as we **h**-*ed*, but first gave
Phi. 2.23. Him therefore I **h**. to send
1Ti. 3.14. **h**-*ing* to come unto thee shor.
Heb.11. 1. substance of *things* **h**-*ed for*
1Pet. 1.13. **h**. to the end, for the grace
    apelpizō.

Lu. 6. 35. lend, **h**-*ing for* nothing *again*

HORN,   -s.

keras.

Lu. 1.69. hath raised up an **h**. of salva.
Rev. 5. 6. having seven **h**-s and seven
  9.13. a voice from the four **h**-s of
  12. 3. hav. seven heads and ten **h**-s
    13.1,17.3,7
  13. 1. and upon his **h**-s ten crowns
  11. he had two **h**-s like a lamb
  17.12,16. the ten **h**-s which thou

HORSE,   -s.

hippos.

Jas. 3. 3. we put bits in the **h**-s' mouths
Rev. 6. 2. I saw, and behold a white **h**.
  4. another **h**.; 5. a black **h**.;
  8. I looked, and behold a pale **h**.
  9. 7. the locusts were like unto **h**-s
  9. chariots of many **h**-s running
  17. thus I saw the **h**-s in the vis.
    and the heads of the **h**-s were
  14.20. even unto the **h**. bridles
  18.13. and **h**-s, and chariots, and
  19.11. opened, and beho. a white **h**.
  14. followed him upon white **h**-s
  18. and the flesh of **h**-s, and of
  19, 21. him that sat on the **h**.

HORSEMEN

hippeus.

Act.23.23. and **h**. threescore and ten
  32. left the **h**. to go with him
    hippikon.

Rev. 9.16. of the army of the **h**.

HOSANNA.

hōsanna.

Mat.21. 9, 15. **h**. to the son of David
    h. in the highest; Mar.11.10
Mar.11. 9. **h**.; Blessed is he that cometh
Jo. 12.13. **h**.: Blessed is the King of

HOSPITALITY.

philoxenia.

Ro. 12.13. necess. of saints ; given to **h**.
    philoxenos.

1Ti. 3. 2. *given* to **h**., apt to teach
Tit. 1. 8. But a *lover* of **h**., a lover of
1Pet.4. 9. *Use* **h**. one to another, with.

HOST, (*of Guests*.)

pandocheus.

Lu. 10.35. and gave them to the **h**.
    xenos.

Ro. 16.23. Gaius mine **h**., and of the

HOST, (*of Soldiers*.)

stratia.

Lu. 2.13. multitude of the heavenly **h**.
Act. 7.42. to worship the **h**. of heaven

HOT, (See *Seared*.)

zestos.

Rev. 3.15, 16. neither cold nor **h**.
    I would thou wert cold or **h**.

HOUR,   -s.

hōra.

Mat.8.13. healed in the selfsame **h**.
  9.22. made whole from that **h**.
    15.28,17.18
  10.19. be given you in that same **h**.
  20. 3. went out about the third **h**.
  5. sixth and ninth **h**.; 6.9.11th **h**.
  12. last have wrought but one **h**.

Mat.24.36, 42,44.that lay and **h.** know.;
　25.13　　Mar. 13.32 ; Lu.12.40
　30. **h.** that he is not aw. ; Lu.12.46
26.40. with me one **h.**, Mar.14.37
　45. the **h.** is at hand, and the Son
　55. that same **h.** said Jesus to tho
27.45. sixth **h.** there was dark. over
　　all the land unto the ninth **h.**;
　　Mar.15.33 ; Lu.23.44
　46. ninth **h.** Jes. cried ; Mar.15.34
Mar.13.11.shall be given you in that **h.**
　14.35. the **h.** might pass from him
　41. it is enough, the **h.** is come
　15.25. it was the third **h.**, and they
Lu. 7.21. And in the same **h.** he cured
　10.21 In that **h.** Jesus rejoiced
　12.12. shall teach you in the same **h.**
　39. had known what **h.** the thief
　20.19. the scribes the same **h.** sought
　22.14. when the **h.** was come, he sat
　53. but this is your **h.**, and the
　59. about the space of one **h.** after
24.33. they rose up the same **h.**, and
Jo. 1.39. for it was about the tenth **h.**
　2. 4. mine **h.** is not yet come
　4. 6. it was about the sixth **h.** ; 19.14
　21. the **h.** cometh when ye shall
　23. the **h.** cometh,and now is ; 5.25
　52. enquired he of them the **h.**
　　Yesterday at the seventh **h.**
　53. that it was the same **h.**, in
　5.28. the **h.** is coming, in the which
　7.30. his **h.** was not yet come ; 8.20
　11. 9. there not twelve **h-s** in the day
　12.23. The **h.** is come, that the S. of
　27. Father, save me from this **h.**
　　this cause came I unto this **h.**
　13. 1. when Jesus knew that his **h.**
　16.21. because her **h.** is come : but
　32. Behold, the **h.** cometh, yea
　17. 1. Father, the **h.** is come ; glorify
　19.27. that **h.** that disciple took her
Act.2.15. is but the third **h.** of the day
　3. 1. **h.** of prayer, being the ninth
　5. 7. the space of three **h-s** after
　10. 3. about the ninth **h.** of the day
　9, to pray about the sixth **h.**
　30. was fasting until this **h.** ; and
　　at the ninth **h.** I prayed in
　16.18. And he came out the same **h.**
　33. them the same **h.** of the night
　19.34. the space of two **h-s** cried out
　22.13. And the same **h.** I looked up
　23.23. at the third **h.** of the night
¹Co. 4.11. Even unto this present **h.** we
　15.30. stand we in jeopardy every **h.**
Gal. 2. 5. by subjection, no,not for an **h.**
Rev.3. 3. not know what **h.** I will come
　10. from the **h.** of temptation
　9.15. prepared for an **h.**, and a day
　11.13. And the same **h.** was there a
　14. 7. for the **h.** of his judgment is
　17.12. kings one **h.** with the beast
　18.10. one **h.** is thy judgment come
　17. in one **h.** so great riches
　19. one **h.** is she made desolate

hēmiōrion.

Rev. 8. 1. about the space of half an **h.**

heōs arti.

¹Co. 8. 7. of the idol *unto this* **h.**

HOUSE, -*s*.

oikos.

Mat. 9. 6. thy bed, and go unto thine **h.**
　7. depar. to his **h.** ; Lu.1.23,5.25
　10. 6. lost sheep of the **h.** of I. ; 15.24
　11. 8. soft clothing are in kings' **h-s**
　12. 4. entered into the **h.** of God
　44. return into my **h.** ; Lu.11.24
　21.13. My **h.** shall be called the **h.**
　23.38. your **h.** is left unto you des.
140

Mar. 2. 1. noised that he was in the **h.**
　11. way into thine **h.** ; Lu.5.24
　26. he went into the **h.** ; Lu.6.4
　3.19. they went into an **h.**
　5.38. he cometh to the **h.** of the
　7.17. he was entered into the **h.**
　30. when she was come to her **h.**
　8. 3. fasting to their own **h-s**
　26. he sent him away to his **h.**
　9.28. when he was come into the **h.**
　11.17. My **h.** shall be called of all
　　nations the **h.** of prayer
Lu. 1.27. Joseph, of the **h.** of David
　33. reign over the **h.** of Jacob
　40. entered into the **h.** of Zach.
　56. and returned to her own **h.**
　69. in the **h.** of his servant Dav.
　2. 4. he was of the **h.** and lineage
　7.10. returning to the **h.**, found
　8.39. Return to thine own **h.**
　41. that he wo. come into his **h.**
　9.61. which are at home at my **h.**
　10. 5. say, Peace be to this **h.**
　38. received him into her **h.**
　11.17. a **h.** divided against a **h.** fal.
　12.39. not have suffered his **h.** to be
　52. five in one **h.** divided, three
　13.35. Behold, your **h.** is left unto
　14. 1. as he went into the **h.** of
　23. that my **h.** may be filled
　16. 4. may receive me into their **h-s**
　27. send him to my father's **h.**
　18.14. this man went down to his **h.**
　19. 5. to day I must abide at thy **h.**
　9. is salvation come to this **h.**
　46. My **h.** is the **h.** of prayer
　22.54. into the high priest's **h.**
Jo. 2.16. not my Father's an **h.** of
　17. The zeal of thine **h.** hath
　7.53. man went unto his own **h.**
　11.20. but Mary sat still in the **h.**
Act. 2. 2. it filled all the **h.** where they
　36. let all the **h.** of Israel know
　46. break. bread from house to **h.**
　5.42. and in every **h.**, they ceased
　7.10. over Egypt and all his **h.**
　20. in his father's **h.** three mon.
　42. O ye **h.** of Israel, have ye
　47. Solomon built him an **h.**
　49. what **h.** will ye build me
　8. 3. entering into every **h.**, and
　10. 2. feared God with all his **h.**
　22. to send for thee into his **h.**
　30. I prayed in my **h.**, and, beho.
　11.12. we entered into the man's **h.**
　13. he had seen an angel in his **h.**
　14. whereby thou and all thy **h.**
　16.15. come into my **h.**, and abide
　31. thou shalt be sav., and thy **h.**
　34. brought them into his **h.**
　18. 8. on the Lord with all his **h.**
　19.16. they fled out of that **h.** naked
　20.20. publickly,and from hou.to **h.**
　21. 8. entered into the **h.** of Philip
Ro. 16. 5. the chur. that is in their **h.** ;
　　¹Co.16.19 ; Col.4.15 ; Phile.2
¹Ti. 3. 4. that ruleth well his own **h.**
　5. not how to rule his own **h.**
　12. children and their own **h-s**
　15. to behave thyself in the **h.**
²Ti. 1.16. Lord give mercy unto the **h.**
Tit. 1.11. who subvert whole **h-s**
Heb. 3. 2, 5. was faithful in all his **h.**
　3. hath more hono. than the **h.**
　4. every **h.** is builded by some
　6. over his own **h.** ; whose **h.**
　8. 8. of Israel and with the **h.**
　10. I will make with the **h.** of
　10.21. an high priest over the **h.** of
　11. 7. to the saving of his **h.** ; by
¹Pet. 2. 5. are built up a spiritual **h.**
　4.17. must begin at the **h.** of God

oikia.

Mat.2.11. were come into the **h.**, they
　5.15. light unto all that are in the **h.**
　7.24, 26.bui. his **h.**upon ; Lu.6.48,49
　25. 27. beat upon that **h.** ; Lu.6.48
　8.14. Jes. was come into Peter's **h.**
　9.10. as Jesus sat at meat in the **h.**
　23. Jesus came into the ruler's **h.**
　28. he was come into the **h.** ; 17.25
　10.12. come into an **h.**, salute it
　13. And if the **h.** be worthy
　14. when ye depart out of that **h.**
　12.25. city or **h.** divided ; Mar. 3.25
　29. a strong man's **h.** ; Mar.3.27
　　he will spoil his **h.** ; Mar.3.27
　13. 1. went Jesus out of the **h.**
　36. and went into the **h.** : and
　57. and in his own **h.** ; Mar. 6.4
　19.29. hath forsaken **h-s** ; Mar.10.29 ;
　　＇ Lu.18.29
　23.14. ye devour widows' **h-s** ;
　　Mar. 12.40 ; Lu. 20.47
　24.17. to take anything out of his **h.**
　43. not have suffered his **h.**
　26. 6. in Sim. the leper ; Mar.14.3
Mar.1.29. they entered into the **h.** of
　2.15. as Jesus sat at meat in his **h.**
　3.25. itself, that **h.** cannot stand
　6.10. ye enter into an **h.** there
　7.24. entered into an **h.** ; Act. 9.17
　9.33. and being in the **h.** he asked
　10.10. And in the **h.** his disciples
　30. **h-s**, and brethren, and sisters
　13.15. not go down into the **h.**, neit.
　　to take anything out of his **h.**
　34. left his **h.**, and gave authority
　35. the master of the **h.** cometh
Lu. 4.38. and entered into Simon's **h.**
　5.29. a great feast in his own **h.**
　6.49. the ruin of that **h.** was great
　7. 6. was now not far from the **h.**
　36, 37. went into the Pharis.'s **h.**
　44. I entered into thine **h.**
　8.27. neither abode in any **h.**
　51. when he came into the **h.**
　9. 4. whatso. **h.** ye enter into ; 10.5
　10. 7. And in the same **h.** remain
　　Go not from **h.** to **h.**
　15.8. and sweep the **h.**, and seek
　25. and drew nigh to the **h.**, he
　17.31. and his stuff in the **h.**, let
　22.10. follow him into the **h.** where
　11. unto the goodman of the **h.**
Jo. 4.53. believed, and his whole **h.**
　8.35. abideth not in the **h.** for ever
　11.31. which were with her in the **h.**
　12. 3. **h.** was filled with the odour
　14. 2. In my Father's **h.** are many
Act.4.34. of lands or **h-s** sold them
　9.11. enquire in the **h.** of Judas
　10. 6. whose **h.** is by the sea side
　17. made enquiry for Simon's **h.**
　32. in the **h.** of one Simon
　11.11. come unto the **h.** where I was
　12.12. he came to the **h.** of Mary
　16.32. to all that were in his **h.**
　17. 5. and assaulted the **h.** of Jason
　18. 7. into a certain man's **h.**
　　whose **h.** joined hard to the
¹Co.11.22. have ye not **h-s** to eat and to
　16.15. ye know the **h.** of Stephanas
²Cor.5. 1. we know that if our earthly **h.**
　　build. of God, an **h.** not made
¹Ti. 5.13. wandering ..from **h.** to **h.**
　　（going about the *houses.*）
²Ti. 2.20. But in a great **h.** there are
　3. 6. are they which creep into **h-s**
²John10. receive him not into your **h.**

oikētērion.

²Co. 5. 2. be clothed upon with our **h.**

pros [*accu.*] **su.**

Mat.26.18. keep thy passover *at thy* **h.**

panoiki.
Act.16.34. believ. in God *with all* his **h**.
oikeios.
¹Ti. 5. 8. specia. for *those of his own* **h**.
oikodespotēs.
Mat.10.25. have called the *mas. of the* **h**.
20.11. again. the *goodman of the* **h**.
24.43. the *good. of the* **h**.; Lu.12.39
Mar.14.14. say ye to the *good. of the* **h**.
Lu. 13.25. onee the *master of the* **h**. is
14.21. Then the *master of the* **h**.
22.11. say unto the *good.* of the **h**.
(See *Guide, Hire*.)

HOUSETOP,   -s.
dōma.
Mat.10.27. that preach ye upon the **h**-s
24.17. him which is on the **h**. not;
        Mar.13.15; Lu.17.31
Lu. 5.19. they went upon the **h**.
12. 3. be proclaimed upon the **h**-s
Act.10. 9. Peter went up upon the **h**.

HOUSEHOLD.
oikos.
Act.16.15. she was baptized, and her **h**.
¹Co. 1.16. I baptized also the **h**. of
²Ti. 4.19. and the **h**. of Onesiphorus
oikiakos.
Mat.10.25. shall they call *them of* his **h**.
36. shall be *they* of his own **h**.
oikeios.
Gal. 6.10. who are *of the* **h**. of faith
Eph. 2.19. saints, and of the **h**. of God
oiketēs.
Act.10. 7. called two of his **h**. *servants*
oikia.
Phi. 4.22. they that are of Cesar's **h**.
therapeia.   [Lu.12.42
Mat.24.45. made ruler over his **h**.;

HOUSEHOLDER.
oikodespotēs.
Mat.13.27. servants of the **h**. came
52. a man that is an **h**.; 20.1
21.33. There was a certain **h**., whi.

HOW.
pōs.
Mat. 6.28. **h**. they grow; they toil not
7. 4. Or **h**. wilt thou say to thy
10.19. **h**. or what ye shall; Lu.12.11
12. 4. **h**. he entered into; Mar.2.36
26. **h**. shall then his; Lu.11.18
29. **h**. can one enter into a stro.
34. **h**. can ye, being evil, speak
16.11. **h**. is it that ye do; Mar.8.21
21.20. **h**. soon is the fig-tree wither.
22.12. **h**. camest thou in hither
43. **h**. then doth David in spirit
45. L., **h**. is he his son; Lu.20.44
23.33. **h**. can ye escape the damna.
26.54. **h**. then shall the scriptures
Mar. 3.23. **h**. can Satan cast out Satan
4.13. **h**. then will ye know all par.
40. **h**. is it that ye have no faith
5.16. told them **h**. it befell to him
9.12. and **h**. it is written of the S.
10.23, 24. **h**. hardly shall; Lu.18.24
11.18. sought **h**. they might destroy
12.35. **h**. say the scribes that Christ
41. beheld **h**. the people cast
14. 1. sought **h**. they might take
11. sought **h**. he might; Lu.22.4
Lu. 1.34. **h**. shall this be, seeing
6.42. **h**. canst thou say to thy bro.
8.18. Take heed therefore **h**. ye
10.26. in the law? **h**. readest thou
12.27. Consider the lilies **h**. they
50. and **h**. am I straitened till it
56. **h**. is it that ye do not discern
14. 7. **h**. they choose out the chief
20.41. **h**. say they that Christ is

Lu. 22. 2. sought **h**. they might kill
Jo. 3. 4. **h**. can a man be born when
9. **h**. can these things be
12. **h**. shall ye believe, if I tell
4. 9. **h**. is it that thou, being a
5.44. **h**. can ye believe, which
47. **h**. shall ye believe my words
6.42. **h**. is it then that he saith, I
52. **h**. can this man give us his
7.15. **h**. knoweth this man letters
8.33. **h**. sayest thou, Ye shall be
9.10. **h**. were thine eyes opened
15. **h**. he had received his sight
16. **h**. can a man that is a sinner
19. **h**. then doth he now see
26. **h**. opened he thine eyes
11.36. Behold **h**. he loved him
12.34. and **h**. sayest thou; 14.9
14. 5. **h**. can we know the way
Act. 2. 8. And **h**. hear we every man
4.21. **h**. they might punish them
8.31. **h**. can I, except some man
9.27. **h**. he had seen the Lord in
and **h**. he had preached
11.13. **h**. he had seen an angel
12.17. **h**. the Lord had brought him
15.36. Lord, and see **h**. they do
Ro. 3. 6. for then **h**. shall God judge
4.10. **h**. was it then reckoned
6. 2. **h**. shall we, that are dead to
8.32. **h**. shall he not with him also
10.14. **h**. then shall they call on
and **h**. shall they believe in
and **h**. shall they hear with.
15. And **h**. shall they preach
¹Co. 3.10. take heed **h**. he buildeth
7.32. **h**. he may please the Lord
33. **h**. he may please his wife
34. **h**. she may please her husb.
14. 7, 9. **h**. shall it be known what
16. **h**. shall he that occupieth
15.12. **h**. say some among you that
35. **h**. are the dead raised up
²Co. 3. 8. **h**. shall not the ministration
Gal. 4. 9. **h**. turn ye again to the weak
Col. 4. 6. **h**. ye ought to answer every
¹Th. 1. 9. **h**. ye turned to God from
4. 1. **h**. ye ought to walk and
²Th. 3. 7. **h**. ye ought to follow us
¹Ti. 3. 5. **h**. shall he take care of the
15. **h**. thou oughtest to behave
Heb. 2. 3. **h**. shall we escape, if we ne.
¹Jo. 3.17. **h**. dwelleth the love of God
4.20. **h**. can he love God whom he
Rev. 3. 3. Remember therefore **h**. thou
posos.
Mat. 6.23. **h**. *great* is that darkness
7.11. **h**. *much* more shall; Lu.11.13
10.25. **h**. *much* more shall they call
12.12. **h**. *much* then is a; Lu.12.24
15.34. **h**. *many* loaves have ye;
        Mar.6.38,8.5
16. 9, 10. and **h**. *many* baskets ye;
        Mar.8.19,20
27.13. Hearest thou not **h**. *many*
Mar. 9.21. **h**. *long* is it ago since this
15. 4. **h**. *many* things they witness
Lu. 12.28. **h**. *much* more will he clothe
15.17. **h**. *many* hired servants of
16. 5, 7. **h**. *much* owest thou unto
Act.21.20. **h**. *many* thousands of Jews
Ro. 11.12. **h**. *much* more their fulness
24. **h**. *much* more shall these
Phile. 16. but **h**. *much* more unto thee
Heb. 9.14. **h**. *much* more shall the blood
10.29. Of **h**. *much* sorer punishme.
hoti.
Mat.12. 5. **h**. *that* on the sabbath days
16.21. **h**. *that* he must go unto Jer.
Lu. 1.58. **h**. *that* the Lord had shewed gre.
7.22. **h**. *that* the blind see, the
21. 5. **h**. *that* it was adorned with good.

Jo. 4. 1. When theref. the L. knew **h**.
12.19. Perceive ye **h**. ye prevail no.
14.28. Ye have heard **h**. I said unto
Act. 7.25. **h**. *that* God by his hand wo.
13.32. glad tidings, **h**. *that* the pro.
14.27. and **h**. he had opened the
15. 7. ye know **h**. *that* a good while
20.35. **h**. *that* so labouring ye ought
h. he said, It is more blessed
Ro. 7. 1. **h**. *that* the law hath domin.
¹Co. 1.26. **h**. *that* not many wise men
10. 1. be ignorant, **h**. *that* all our
15. 3. **h**. *that* Christ died for our
²Co. 8. 2. **h**. *that* in a great trial of
12. 4. **h**. *that* he was caught up in.
13. 5. **h**. *that* Jesus Christ is in
Gal. 1.13. **h**. *that* beyond measure I
4.13. Ye know **h**. through infirmi.
Eph. 3. 3. **h**. *that* by revelation he
Phile. 19. I do not say to thee **h**. thou
Heb.12.17. For ye know **h**. *that* afterw.
Jas. 2.22. Seest thou **h**. faith wrought
24. Ye see then **h**. *that* by works
Jude 5. **h**. *that* the Lord, having sav.
18. **h**. *that* they told you there
Rev. 2. 2. and **h**. thou canst not bear
hōs.
Mar. 4.27. grow up, he knoweth not **h**.
12.26. **h**. in the bush God spake
Lu. 6. 4. **h**. he went into the house of
8.47. and **h**. she was healed imme.
22.61. **h**. he had said unto him
23.55. and **h**. his body was laid
24. 6. remember **h**. he spake unto
35. and **h**. he was known of
Act.10.28. Ye know **h**. that it is an
38. **h**. God anointed Jesus of
11.16. **h**. that he said, John indeed
20.20. And **h**. I kept back nothing
Ro. 10.15. **h**. beautiful are the feet of
11. 2. **h**. he maketh intercession to
33. **h**. unsearchable are his jud.
²Co. 7.15. **h**. with fear and trembling
Phi. 1. 8. **h**. greatly I long after you
¹Th. 2.10. **h**. holily and justly and
11. ye know **h**. we exhorted and
hosos.   [Lu.8.39
Mar. 5.19, 20. tell them **h**. *great* things;
Act. 9.13. **h**. *much* evil he hath done
16. **h**. *great* things he must suffer
²Ti. 1.18. and in **h**. *many* things he
Heb. 8. 6. by **h**. *much* also he is the
tis.
Mat.18.12. **h**. think ye? if a man have
Mar. 2.16. **h**. is it that he eateth and
Lu. 1.62. **h**. he would have him called
2.49. **h**. is it that ye sought me
16. 2. **h**. is it that I hear this of
Jo. 14.22. Lord, **h**. is it that thou wilt
Act. 5. 9. **h**. is it that ye have agreed
¹Co. 7.16. or **h**. knowest thou, O man
14.26. **h**. is it then, brethren
Eph. 6.21. know my affairs, and **h**. I do
hopōs.   [Mar.3.6
Mat.12.14. **h**. they might destroy him;
22.15. **h**. they might entangle him
Lu. 24.20. And **h**. the chief priests and
kathōs.
Act.15.14. **h**. God at the first did visit
heōs pote. [Mar.9.19; Lu.9.41
Mat.17.17. **h**. *long* shall I be with;
h. *long* shall I suf.; Mar.9.19
Jo. 10.24. **h**. *long* dost thou make
Rev. 6.10. **h**. *long*, O Lord, holy and
mēti ge.
¹Co. 6. 3. **h**. *much more* things that
(See *Great, Large, Oft, Often*.)

HOWBEIT.
alla.
Jo. 7.27. **h**. we know this man whence

Act. 7.48. **h.** the most High dwelleth
¹Co. 8. 7. **h.** there is not in every man
    14.20. **h.** in malice be ye children
    15.46. **h.** that was not first which is
Gal. 4. 8. **h.** then, when ye knew not
¹Ti. 1.16. **h.** for this cause I obtained
Heb. 3.16. **h.** not all that came out of
    mentoi.
Jo. 7.13. **h.** no man spake openly of

HOWL.
ololuzō.
Jas. 5. 1. weep *and* **h.** for your mise.

HUMBLE, [*adject.*]
tapeinos.   [¹Pet.5.5
Jas. 4. 6. giveth grace to the **h.**;

HUMBLE, [*verb,*]   -*ed.*
tapeinoō. [23.12 ; Lu.14.11,18.14
Mat.18. 4. Whosoever *shall* **h.** himself ;
²Co. 12.21. my God *will* **h.** me among
Phi. 2. 8. he **h-**ed himself, and became
Jas. 4.10. **h.** yourselves in the sight of
¹Pet. 5. 6. **h.** *yourselves* therefore under

HUMBLENESS.
tapeinophrosunē.
Col. 3.12. kindness, **h.** *of mind*, meek.

HUMILIATION.
tapeinōsis.
Act. 8.33. In his **h.** his judgment was

HUMILITY.
tapeinophrosunē.
Act.20.19. the Lord with all **h.** *of mind*
Col. 2.18. reward in a voluntary **h.** and
    23. and **h.**, and neglecting of the
¹Pet. 5. 5. and be clothed with **h.** ; for

HUNDRED (See *Thousand*), -*s.*
hekaton.
Mat.18.12. man have an **h.** sh.; Lu.15.4
    28. owed him an **h.** pence : and
Mar. 4. 8, 20. so. sixty, and some an **h.**
    6.40. in ranks by **h-s**, and by fifties
Lu. 16. 6. An **h.** measures of oil. And
    7. An **h.** measures of wheat
Jo. 19.39. about an **h.** pound weight
    21.11. fishes, an **h.** and fifty and
Act. 1.15. were about an **h.** and twenty
Rev. 7. 4. an **h.** and forty ; 14.1,3,21.17
    diakosioi.   [Jo.6.7
Mar. 6.37. *two* **h.** pennyworth of bread ;
    21. 8. but as it were *two* **h.** cubits
Act.23.23. Make ready *two* **h.** soldiers
    spearmen *two* **h.**, at the third
    27.37. *two* **h.** threescore and sixteen
Rev.11. 3. a thousand *two* **h.** and ; 12.6
    triakosioi.
Mar.14. 5. for more than *three* **h.** pence
Jo. 12. 5. sold for *three* **h.** pence, and
    tetrakosioi.
Act. 5.36. num. of men, about *four* **h.**
    7. 6. entreat them evil *four* **h.** ye.
    13.20. space of *four* **h.** and fifty
Gal. 3.17. *four* **h.** and thirty years after
    pentakosioi.
Lu. 7.41. the one owed *five* **h.** pence
¹Co. 15. 6. seen of above *five* **h.** brethr.
    hexakosioi.
Rev.13.18. *Six* **h.** threescore and six
    14.20. thousand and *six* **h.** furlong
    hekatontaetēs.
Ro. 4.19. was about an **h.** *years old*

HUNDREDFOLD.
hekatontaplasiōn.
Mat.19.29 shall receive an **h.** ; Mar.10.30
Lu. 8. 8. up, and bear fruit an **h.**
    hekaton.
Mat.13. 8, 23. forth fruit, some an **h.**
142

HUNGER, [*noun.*]
limos.
Lu. 15.17. to spare, and I perish with **h.**
²Co. 11.27. in **h.** and thirst, in fastings
Rev. 6. 8. kill with sword, and with **h.**

HUNGER, [*verb,*]   *Hungred.*
peinaō.   [Lu.4.2.
Mat. 4. 2. he *was* afterward *an* **h-**ed :
    5. 6. are they *which do* **h.**; Lu.6.21
    12. 1. his disciples *were an* **h-**ed
    3. when he *was an* **h-**ed ;
        Mar.2.25 ; Lu.6.3
    21.18. return into the city, *he* **h-**ed
    25.35, 42. I *was an* **h-**ed, and ye
    37, 44. when saw we thee *an* **h-**ed
Lu. 6.25. that are full ! for ye *shall* **h.**
Jo. 6.35. *shall* never **h.**; and he that
Ro. 12.20. Therefore if thine enemy **h.**
¹Co. 4.11. we both **h.**, and thirst, and
    11.34. And if any man **h.**, let him
Rev. 7.16. They *shall* **h.** no more, neit.

HUNGRY.
peinaō.
Mar.11.12. come from Beth., he *was* **h.**
Lu. 1.53. He hath filled the **h.** with
¹Co. 11.21. and one *is* **h.**, and another
Phi. 4.12. both to be full and *to be* **h.**
    prospeinos.
Act.10.10. And he became *very* **h.**, and

HURT, [*noun.*]
hubris.
Act.27.10. be with **h.** and much damage
    adikeō.
Rev. 9.19. and with them they *do* **h.**

HURT, [*verb.*]
adikeō.
Lu. 10.19. *shall* by any means **h.** *you*
Rev. 2.11. *shall* not be **h.** of the second
    6. 6. see thou **h.** not the oil and
    7. 2. it was given *to* **h.** the earth
    3. Saying, **h.** not the earth
    9. 4. *should* not **h.** the grass of the
    10. was *to* **h.** men five months
    11. 5. if any man *will* **h.** them
    blaptō.
Mar.16.18. thing, it *shall* not **h.** them
Lu. 4. 35. out of him, and **h.** him not
    kakoō.
Act.18.10. shall set on thee *to* **h.** thee

HURTFUL.
blaberos.
¹Ti. 6. 9. into many foolish and **h.**

HUSBAND,   -*s.*
anēr.
Mat. 1.16. begat Joseph the **h.** of Mary
    19. Then Joseph her **h.**, being
Mar.10.12.wom. shall put away her **h.**
Lu. 2.36. lived with an **h.** seven years
    16.18. is put away from her **h.**
Jo. 4.16. Go, call thy **h.**, and come
    17. and said, I have no **h.**
    18. For thou hast had five **h-**s
    thou now hast is not thy **h.**
Act. 5. 9. have buried thy **h.** are at the
    10. forth, buried her by her **h.**
Ro. 7. 2. by the law to her **h.** so long
    the **h.** be dead, she is loos.; 3
    from the law of her **h.**
    3. if, while her **h.** liveth
¹Co. 7. 2. every wom. have her own **h.**
    3. Let the **h.** render unto the
    also the wife unto the **h.**
    4. of her own body, but the **h.**
    likewise also the **h.** hath not
    10. the wife depart from her **h.**
    11. or be reconciled to her **h.**
    not the **h.** put away his wife

¹Co. 7.13. woman which hath an **h.**
    14. unbelieving **h.** is sanctified
    wife is sanctified by the **h.**
    16. thou shalt save thy **h.**
    34. how she may please her **h.**
    39. **h.** liveth ; but if her **h.** be
    14.35. let them ask their **h-s** at ho.
²Co. 11. 2. have espoused you to one **h.**
Gal. 4.27. than she which hath an **h.**
Eph. 5.22. your. to yo.own **h-s** ; Col.3.18
    23. the **h.** is the head of the wife
    24. be to their own **h-s** in every
    25. **h-s**, love your wives; Col.3.19
    33. that she reverence her **h.**
¹Ti. 3. 2, 12.the **h.** of one wife ; Tit.1.6
Tit. 2. 5. obedient to their own **h-s**
¹Pet. 3. 1, 5. subjection to your own **h-s**
    7. Likewise, ye **h-s**, dwell with
Rev.21. 2. a bride adorned for her **h.**
    hupandros.
Ro. 7. 2. the woman *which hath an* **h.**
    philandros.
Tit. 2. 4. to *love their* **h-s**, to love their

HUSBANDMAN,   -*men.*
geōrgos. [Mar.12.1 ; Lu.20.9
Mat.21.33.iet it out to **h-**e, and went ;
    34. sent his servants to the **h-**e ;
        Mar.12.2 ; Lu.20.10
    35. the **h-**e took his servants, and
    38. when the **h-**e saw ; Lu.20.14
    40. what will he do unto those **h-**e
    41. vineyard unto other **h-**e
Mar.12. 2. might receive from the **h-**e
    7. those **h-**e said among them.
    9. and destr. the **h-**e ; Lu.20.16
Lu. 20.10. the **h-**e beat him, and sent
Jo. 15. 1. vine, and my Fa. is the **h.**
²Ti. 2. 6. The **h.** that laboureth must
Jas. 5. 7. the **h.** waiteth for the precio

HUSBANDRY.
geōrgion.
¹Co. 3. 9. with God : ye are God's **h.**

HUSKS.
keration.
Lu. 15.16. filled his belly with the **h-s**

HYMNS, (See *Sing.*)
humnos.
Eph. 5.19. in psalms, and **h.** ; Col.3.16

HYPOCRISY,   -*ies.*
hupocrisis.
Mat.23.28. within ye are full of **h.** and
Mar.12.15. But he, knowing their **h.**
Lu. 12. 1. of the Pharisees, which is **h.**
¹Ti. 4. 2. Speaking lies in **h.** ; having
¹Pet. 2. 1. and all guile, and **h-s**, and
    anupokritos.
Jas. 3.17. partiality, and *without* **h.**

HYPOCRITE,   -*s.*
hupokritēs.
Mat. 6. 2. as the **h-s** do in the synagog.
    5, 16. shalt not be as the **h-s**
    7. 5. Thou **h.**, first cast out the
    15. 7. Ye **h-s**, well did Esaias pro.
    16. 3. O ye **h-s**, ye can discern the
    22.18. Why tempt ye me, ye **h-s**
    23.13. scribes and Pharisees, **h-s** ;
        14,15,23,25,27,29; Lu.11.44
    24.51. him his portion with the **h-s**
Mar. 7. 6. Esaias prophesied of you **h-s**
Lu. 6.42. Thou **h.**, cast out first the
    12.56. Ye **h-s**, ye can discern the fa.
    13.15. Thou **h.**, doth not each one

HYSSOP.
hussōpos.
Jo. 19.29. and put it upon **h.**, and
Heb. 9.19. and scarlet wool, and **h.**

I.

egō.

Mat. 3.11. is mightier than I; Mar.1.7
14.27. is I, be not afraid; Mar.6.50; Jo.6.20
16.13. men say that I, the Son of
18.20. two or three, there am I in
24. 5. saying I am Ch.; Lu.21.8
26.22. began to say, Lord, is it I
Mar.14.29. be offended, yet will not I
Lu. 2.48. thy father and I have sought
11.19. if I by Beelzeb. cast out de.
20. if I, with the finger of God
22.67. but I am among you as he
24.39. that it is I myself, handle me
Jo. 1.20. conf., I am not the Ch.; 3.28
33. I knew him not; but he
4.26. I that speak unto thee, am he
8.16. I am not alone, but I and
23. I am from above, I am not
28. know that I am he, I do no.
58. before Abraham was, I am
10.30. I and my Father are one
38. Father in me, and I in him; 15.5,17.21
12.32. and I, if I be lifted up, will
13.14. if I then your Lord and Ma.
14.20. I am in my Father, and ye
15. 4. Abide in me, and I in you
28. I go unto my Father, for my Father is greater than I
17.23. I in them, and thou in me
25. but I have known thee, and
18.35. Pilate answered, am I a Jew
Act.11.17. what was I, that I could
22.28. obtained I this freedom
said, But I was free-born
Ro. 7.17, 20. it is no more I, but sin
¹Co. 1.12. I am of Paul, I of Apollos · 3.4
2. 1. and I, brethren, when I ca.
3. 1. I, brethren, could not speak
7. 7. I would that all men were
8. them if they abide even as I
10. yet not I but the Lord, Let
9. 6. or I only and Barnabas, have
26. I therefore so run, so fight I
11. 1. of me, even as I am of Christ
15.10. I am what I am, yet not I
11. whether it were I or they, so
16.10. the work of Christ, even as I
²Co. 11.22. are they Hebrews? so am I
23. I am more: in labours more
29. who is offended, I burn not
Gal. 2.19. I through the law am dead
20. I live; yet not I, but Christ
4.12. be as I am, for I am as ye
5.11. I, brethren, if I yet preach
6.14. that I should glory, save in unto me, and I unto the wor.
Eph. 1.15. I also, after I heard of your
4. 1. I therefore, the prisoner of
¹Pet. 1.16. be ye holy, for I am holy
²John 1. whom I love in the truth
Rev. 1. 8. I am Alpha and Omega, the
3.19. as many as I love I rebuke
21. even as I also overcame
21. 2. I John saw the holy city
22. 8. I John saw these things
9. I am thy fellow-servant
16. I Jesus have sent my angel
I am the root and offspring

(*And all other passages in which a nominative is expressed.*)

IDLE, (See *Tale.*)

argos.

Mat.12.36. That every i. word that men
20. 3. saw others standing i. in the
6. standing i., and saith unto
stand ye here all the day i.
¹Ti. 5.13. withal they learn to be i.
not only i., but tattlers also

IDOL, -*s.*

eidōlon.

Act. 7.41. offered sacrifice unto the i.
15.20. abstain from pollutions of i-*s*
Ro. 2.22. thou that abhorrest i-*s*, dost
¹Co. 8. 4. we know that an i. is nothing
7. with conscience of the i. unto
10.19. that the i. is any thing, or
12. 2. car. away unto these dumb i-*s*
²Co. 6.16. hath the tem. of G. with i-*s*
¹Th. 1. 9. how ye turned to G. from i-*s*
¹Jo. 5.21. keep yourselves from i-*s*
Rev. 9.20. i-*s* of gold, and silver, and

eidōlothuton.

Act.15.29. abst. from *meats offered to* i-*s*
Act.21.25. from things *offered to* i-*s*, and
¹Co. 8. . touch. *things offered unto* i-*s*
4. *that are off. in sacri. unto* i-*s*
7. as a *thing offered unto an* i.
10. *things which are offered to* i-*s*
10.19, 28. *wh. is offer. in sacri. to* i-*s*
Rev.2.14, 20. eat *things sacrific. unto* i-*s*

eidōleion.

¹Co. 8.10. at meat in the i.'s *temple*

IDOLATER, -*s.*

eidōlolatrēs.

¹Co. 5.10. or extortioners, or with i-*s*
11. fornicator, covetous, or an i.
6. 9. neither fornicators, nor i-*s*
10. 7. Neither be ye i-*s*, as were
Eph. 5. 5. nor covet. man, who is an i.
Rev.21. 8. i-*s*, and all liars, shall have
22.15. and murderers, and i-*s*, and

IDOLATRY, -*ies.*

eidōlolatreia.

¹Co. 10.14. dearly beloved, flee from i.
Gal. 5.20. i., witchcraft, hatred, varian.
Col. 3. 5. and covetousness, which is i.
¹Pet. 4. 3. banquetings, and abomin. i-*s*

kateidōlos.

Act.17.16. the city *wholly given to* i.

IF.

ei *or* **ean.** [27.40; Lu.4.3

Mat. 4. 3. i. thou be the Son of God;
14.28. i. it be thou, bid me come to
27.43. deliver him, i. he will have
Mar. 1.40. i. thou wilt, thou canst make
11.32. i. we shall say, Of men; they
Lu. 10. 6. but i. not, it shall turn to
23.35, 39. i. he be Christ; Jo.10.24
Jo. 1.25. i. thou be not Elias, nor that
15.18. . the wor. hate you; ¹Jo.3.13
19.12. cried out, i. thou let this m.
Act. 5.39. i. it be of God ye cannot
¹Co. 15.19. i. in this life only we have
Gal. 4. 7. i. a son, then an heir of God
Heb. 4. 3, 5. i. they shall enter into my
¹Jo. 2.19. i. they had been of us, they

(*And all other passages, except the following:—*)

ei tis.

Mat.16.24. i. *any* man will come after
Mar. 4.23. i. *any* man have ears to hear; 7.16; Rev.13.9
8.23. he asked him i. he saw *ought*
9.22. i. thou canst do *any thing*
35. i. *any* man desire to be first
Lu. 14.26. i. *any* man come to me, and
19. 8. i. I have tak. . . *from any*
Act.24.19. i. they had *ought* against me
20. i. they have found *any* evil
25. 5. i. there be *any* wickedness in
Ro. 13. 9. i. there be *any* other comm.
¹Co. 3.14. i. *any man's* work abide wh.
15. i. *any man's* work shall be
17. i. *any* man defile the temple
18. i. *any* man among you seem.
¹Co. 7.12. i. *any* brother hath a wife
14.37. i. *any* man think himself to
16.22. i. *any* man love not the Lord
²Co. 2.10. for i. I forgave *any thing*, to
5.17. Therefore i. *any* man be in
7.14. i. I have boasted *any thing*
10. 7. i. *any* man trust to himself
11.20. i. *a man* bring you into bon.
i. *a man* devour you
i. *a man* take of you, i. *a man*
exalt himself, i. *a man* smite
Gal. 1. 9. i. *any* man preach any other
Ph. 2. 1. i. there be therefore *any* con.
i. *any* comfort of love, i. *any*
of the Spirit, i. *any* bowels
3. 4. i. any other man thinketh
15. i. in *any thing* ye be otherw.
4. 8. i. *any* virtue, and i. *any* pra.
²Th. 3.10. that i. *any* would not work
¹Ti. 1.10. i. there be *any* other thing
3. 1. i. *a man* desire the office of
5.16. i. *any* man or woman that
6. 3. i. *any* man teach otherwise
Tit. 1. 6. i. *any* be blameless, the hus.
Jas. 1.23. For i. *any* be a hearer of the
3. 2. i. *any* man offend not in wo.
¹Pet. 3. 1. that, i. *any* obey not the wo.
4.11. i. *any* man speak, let him
i. *any* man minister, let him
²John 10. i. there come *any* unto you
Rev. 11.5. i. *any* man will hurt them
14. 9. i. *any* man worship the beast

ei ge.

²Co. 5. 3. i. *so be that* being clothed we
Gal. 3. 4. in vain? i. it be *yet* in vain
Eph. 3. 2. i. ye have heard of the disp.
4.21. i. *so be that* ye have heard
Col. 1.23. i. ye continue in the faith

ei per.

Ro. 8. 9. i. *so be that* the Spirit of God
17. i. *so be that* we suffer with
¹Co.15.15. i. *so be that* the dead rise not
¹Pet. 2. 3. i. *so be* ye have tasted that

mēpote.

²Ti. 2.25. i. God *peradventure* will give

IGNORANCE.

agnoia.

Act. 3.17. wot that through i. ye did
17.30. the times of this i. God wink.
Eph. 4.18. through the i. that is in them
¹Pet. 1.14. to the former lusts in your i.

agnōsia.

¹Pet. 2.15. silence the i. of foolish men

IGNORANT.

agnoeō. [¹Co.12.1; ¹Th.4.13

Ro. 1.13. I would not have you i.;
10. 3. For they *being* i. of God's
11.25. that ye *should be* i.; ¹Co.10.1
¹Co.14.38. if any man *be* i., *let* him *be* i.
²Co. 1. 8. brethren, have you i. of
2.11. we *are* not i. of his devices
Heb. 5. 2. have compassion on the i.

lanthanō.

²Pet. 3. 5. they willingly are i. of
(this *escapes* them willing.)
8. be not i. of this one thing

idiōtēs.

Act. 4.13. they were unlearned and i.

IGNORANTLY.

agnoeō.

Act.17.23. Whom therefore ye i. worsh.
¹Ti. 1.13. I did it i. in unbelief

ILL.

kakos.

Ro. 13.10. Love worketh no i. to his

ILLUMINATED.

phōtizō.

Heb.10.32. in which, after ye were i.

IMAGE, (See *Express.*)
eikōn.   [Mar.12.16; Lu.20.24
Mat.22.20. Whose is this i. and super.;
Ro.   1.23. into an i. made like to corr.
    8.29. conformed to the i. of his S.
¹Co.11. 7. as he is the i. and glory of
    15.49. have borne the i. of the earth.
       also bear the i. of the heav.
²Co. 3.18. into the same i. from glory
    4. 4. of Christ, who is the i. of God
Col. 1.15. Who is the i. of the invisible
    3.10. the i. of him that created him
Heb.10. 1. not the very i. of the things
Rev.13.14. should make an i. to the be.
    15. i. of the beast, that the i. of
       as would not worship the i.
    14. 9, 11. wor. the beast and his i.
    15. 2. over the beast, and over his i.
    16. 2. which worship. his i.; 19.20
    20. 4. the beast, neither his i.

IMAGINATION,   -s
dianoia.
Lu. 1.51. in the i. of their hearts
dialogismos.
Ro. 1.21. but became vain in their i-s
logismos.
²Co.10. 5. Casting down i-s, and every

IMAGINE.
meletaō.
Act. 4.25. and the people i. vain things

IMMEDIATELY.
eutheōs.
Mat. 4.22. i. left the ship and their
    8. 3. i. his leprosy was cleansed;
       Mar.1.42; Lu.5.13
    14.31. And i. Jesus stretched forth
    20.34. i. their eyes received sight
    24.29. i. after the tribulation
    26.74. i. the cock crew; Jo.18.27
Mar. 1.31. i. the fever left her, and she
    2. 8. i. when Jesus perceived
    12. And i. he arose; Act.9.34
    4. 5. and i. it sprang up, because
    15. Satan cometh i., and taketh
    16. i. receive it with gladness
    17. sake, i. they are offended
    29. i. he putteth in the sickle
    5. 2. i. there met him out of the
    30. Jesus, i. knowing in himself
    6.27. And i. the king sent an
    50. i. he talked with them
    10.52. And i. he received his sight
    14.43. i., while he yet spake,cometh
Lu. 6.49. and i. it fell; and the ruin
    12.36. they may open unto him i.
Jo. 5. 9. i. the man was made whole
    6.21. i. the ship was at the land
    13.30. received the sop went i. out
    31. i. there fell from his eyes
Act. 16.10. i. we endeavoured to go
    17.10. the brethren i. sent away
    14. And then i. the brethren
Gal. 1.16. i. I conferred not with flesh
Rev. 4. 2. i. I was in the spirit : and
parachrēma.
Lu. 1.64. mouth was opened i., and
    4.39. i. she arose and ministered
    5.25. and i. he rose up before them
    8.44. and i. her issue of blood
    47. and how she was healed i.
    13.13. and i. she was made straight
    18.43. And i. he received his sight
    19.11. king. of God should i. appear
    22.60. And i., while he yet spake
Act. 3. 7. and i. his feet and ankle
    12.23. And i. the angel of the Lord
    13.11. And i. there fell on him a
    16.26. and i. all the doors were
144

---

exautēs.
Act.10.33. i. therefore I sent to thee
    11.11. i. there were three men alrea.
    21.32. Who i. took soldiers and
euthus.
Mar. 1.12. i. the spirit driveth him into
    28. i. his fame spread abroad
Jo. 21. 3. and entered into a ship i.

IMMORTAL.
aphthartos.
¹Ti. 1.17. Now unto the King eternal, i.

IMMORTALITY.
aphtharsia.
Ro. 2. 7. for glory, and honour, and i.
²Ti. 1.10. brought life and i. to light
athanasia.
¹Co.15.53, 54. this mortal must put on i.
¹Ti. 6.16. Who only hath i., dwelling

IMMUTABILITY.
ametathetos.
Heb. 6.17. the i. of his counsel, confirm.

IMMUTABLE.
ametathetos.
Heb. 6.18. That by two i. things, in wh.

IMPART,   -ed.
metadidōmi.
Lu. 3.11. *let* him i. to him that hath
Ro. 1.11. that I *may* i. unto you some
¹Th. 2. 8. willing *to have* i-ed unto you

IMPEDIMENT.
mogilalos.
Mar.7.32. and *had an* i. *in his speech*

IMPENITENT.
ametanoētos.
Ro. 2. 5. thy hardness and i. heart

IMPLACABLE.
aspondos.
Ro. 1.31. without natural affection, i.

IMPLEAD.
engkaleō.
Act.19.38. *let* them i. one another

IMPORTUNITY.
anaideia.
Lu. 11. 8. because of his i. he will rise

IMPOSED.
epikeimai.
Heb. 9.10. i. *on* them until the time

IMPOSSIBLE.
adunatos.   [Mar.10.27
Mat.19.26. With men this is i.;
Lu. 18.27. things which are i. with men
Heb. 6. 4. For it is i. for those who
    18. in which it was i. for God to
    11. 6. without faith it is i. to please
adunateō.
Mat.17.20. nothing *shall be* i. unto you
Lu. 1.37. with God nothing *shall be* i.
anendektos.
Lu. 17. 1. It is i. but that offences will

IMPOTENT.
asthenēō.
Jo. 5. 3. a great multitude of i. *folk*
    7. The i. *man* answer. him, Sir
asthenēs.
Act. 4. 9. deed done to the i. man, by
adunatos.
Act.14. 8. man at Lystra, i. in his feet

IMPRISONED.
phulakizō.
Act.22.19. that I i. and beat in every

IMPRISONMENT,   -s.
phulakē.
²Co. 6. 5. In stripes, in i-s, in tumults
Heb.11.36. moreover of bonds and i.

IMPUTE,   -ed, -eth, -ing.
logizomai.
Ro. 4. 6. unto whom God i-*eth* righte.
    8. the Lord *will* not i. sin
    11. that righteous. might *be* i-ed
    22, 23. *was* i-ed to him; Jas.2.23
    24. to whom it shall *be* i-ed, if we
²Co. 5.19. not i-*ing* their trespasses un.
ellogeō.
Ro. 5.13. sin is not i-ed when there

IN.   (*See words in connection.*)
en.
Mat. 1.20. which is conceived i. her
    2. 1. born i. Bethl. of Ju. i. the
    2. have seen his star i. the east
(*And all other passages in which
it occurs, except the following :*)—
eis.
Mat. 2.23. came and dwelt i. a city call.
    4.13. he came and dwelt i. Caper.
    10. 9. nor silver, nor brass i. your
    27. what ye hear i. the ear, that
    41. receiveth a prophet i. the
    i. the name of a righteous
    42. water only i. the name of a
    12.18. i. whom my soul is well ple.
    13.30. bind them i. bundles to burn
    33. hid i. three measures of meal
    15.17. entereth i. *at* the mouth
    18. 6. little ones which believe i. me
    20. are gathered together i. my
    26.67. Then did they spit i. his face
    27.51. temple was rent i.; Mar.15.38
    28.19. baptizing them i. the name
Mar. 1. 9. was baptized of John i. Jor.
    2. 1. noised that he was i. the ho.
    5.14. i. the city, and i. the; Lu.8.34
    34. go i. peace, and be whole of
    6. 8. no bread, no money i. their
    9.42. little ones that believe i. me
    11. 8. spread their garments i. the
       and strawed them i. the way
    13. 9. up to councils; and i. the syn.
    16. him that is i. the field not turn
    14.20. that dippeth with me i. the
    60. the high priest stood up i. the
Lu. 1.20. shall be fulfilled i. their seas.
    44. salutation sounded i. mine
    2.28. took he him up i. his arms
    4.35. had thrown him i. the midst
    6. 8. stand forth i. the midst
    7. 1. i. audience of people, entered
    50. saved thee; go i. peace; 8.48
    11. 7. children are with me i. bed
    33. putteth it i. a secret place
    13.11. together, and could i. no wise
    21. hid i. three measures of meal
    14. 8. sit not down i. the highest
    10. sit down i. the lowest room
    16. 8. are i. their generation wiser
    21. 4. cast i. *unto* the offerings of G.
    14. Settle it therefore i. your he.
    37. went out, and abode i. the
    22.19. this do i. remembrance of me
Jo. 1.18. which is i. the bosom of the
    2.23. many believed i. his name
    3.15. whoso. believeth i. him; 16
    18. not believed i. the name of
    5.45. even Moses, i. whom ye trust
    7. 5. his brethren believe i. him.
    9. 7. Go, wash i. the pool of Siloam
    11.25,26. believeth i. me; Act.10.43
    52. should gather together i. one
    12.36. believe i. the light, that ye
    14. 1. believe i. God, believe also i.

Jo. 17.23. may be made perfect i. one
19.13. i. a place that is called the
20. 7. wrapped together i. a place
19, 26. and stood i. the midst
Act. 2.27. wilt not leave my soul i. hell
31. his soul was not left i. hell.
4. 3. put them i. hold unto the
8.16. i. the name of the Lord Jesus
23. thou art i. the gall of bitter.
12. 4. put him i. prison, and deliv.
13.29. laid him i. a sepulchre
14.14. ran i. among the people
16.24. and made their feet fast i. the
17.21. spent their time i. nothing
18.21. this feast that cometh i. Jer.
19. 5. i. the name of the Lord Jesus
22. he himself stayed i. Asia
30. entered i. unto the people
20.29. wolves enter i. among you
23.11. testified of me i. Jerusalem
24.24. concerning the faith i. Christ
26.18. sanctified by faith that is i.
Ro. 8.18. which shall be revealed i. us
10.14. i. whom they have not belie.
11.32. concluded them all i. unbel.
1Co. 1.13. baptized i. the name of Paul
15. baptized i. mine own name
8. 6. are all things, and we i. him
11.24, 25. this do i. remembrance of
15.54. Death is swallowed up i. vic.
2Co. 1. 5. sufferings of Christ abound i.
10. 1. whom we trust that he will
21. stablisheth us with you i.
2. 9. ye be obedient i. all things
6. 1. not the grace of God i. vain
8. 6. finish i. you the same grace
22. confidence which I have i.
10.16. the gospel i. the regions bey.
11. 3. the simplicity that is i. Chr.
Gal. 2. 2. run, or had run, i. vain
16. we have believed i. Jesus
3.17. confirmed before of God i.
5.10. I have confidence i. you thr.
6. 4. i. himself alone, and not i.
Eph. 1.10. That i. the dispensation of
3.16. his Spirit i. the inner man.
4.13. all come i. the unity of the
Phi. 1. 5. your fellowship i. the gospel
2.16. that I may rejoice i. the day
run i. vain, neither labour. i.
22. served with me i. the gospel
Col. 1.10. increasing i. the knowledge
2. 5. stedfastness of your faith i.
3.10. renewed i. knowledge after
1Th. 3. 5. our labour be i. vain.
4.17. to meet the Lord i. the air
2Th. 2. 4. sitteth i. the temple of God
1Ti. 6. 9. which drown men i. destruc.
Phile. 6. is in you i. Christ Jesus
Heb.11. 9. sojourned i. the land of pro.
Jas. 3. 3. we put bits i. the horses' mo.
1Pet. 1. 8. i. whom, though now ye see
21. Who by him do believe i. G
faith and hope might be i. G.
2Pet. 1. 8. i. the knowledge of our Lord
17. i. whom I am well pleased
1Jo. 5. 8. these three agree i. one
Rev. 1.11. thou seest, write i. a book
6.15. i. the dens and i. the rocks
11. 9. dead bodies to be put i. gra.
13. 6. i. blasphemy against God.
17.17. God hath put i. their hearts
epi, [gen.]
Mat. 2.22. Archelaus did reign i. Jud.
4. 6. i. their hands they ; Lu.4.11
6, 10. will be done i. earth, as
13.14. i. them is fulfilled the proph.
14. 8, 11. Jo. Bap. head i. a charger ;
Mar.6.25,28
18. 5. such little chil. i. my name
16. that i. the mouth of two or
19.28. sit i. the throne of his glory

Mat.21.19.a fig tree i. the way, he came
23. 2. Pharisees sit i. Moses' seat
24. 5. many shall come i. my name
24.30. coming i. the clouds of ; 26.64
27.29. and a reed i. his right hand
43. He trusted i. God ; let him
28.18. me in heaven and i. earth
Mar. 2.26. i. the days of Abiathar
4.31. when it is sown i. the earth
the seeds that be i. the earth
38. was i. the hinder part of the
5.33. knowing what was done i. her
6.55. began to carry about i. beds
8. 4. bread here i. the wilderness
9.37. one of such children i. my
39. shall do a miracle i.my name
10.24. for them that trust i. riches
12.14. the way of God i. truth
26. how i. the bush God spake
13. 6. many shall come i. my ; 21.8
15. 1. straightway i. the morning
Lu. 1. 47. hath rejoiced i. God my Sa.
4.27. i. the time of Eliseus the
5.18. men brought i. a bed a man
6.17. with them and stood i. the
9.48. receive this child i. my name
49. casting out devils i. my name
11. 2. be done,as in heaven, so i. ea.
17.34. shall be two men i. one bed
18. 9. which trusted i. themselves
21.23. great distress i. the land
24.47. should be preach. i. his name
Jo. 19.13. sat down i. the judgment seat
Act. 2. 1. with one accord i. one place
19. signs i. the earth beneath
26. my flesh shall rest i. hope
38. i. the name of Jesus Christ
3.11. i. the porch that is called
4.17, 18. no man i. this n. ; 5.28,40
8.28. sitting i. his chariot
9.42. many believed i. the Lord
11.28. i. the days of Claudius Cesar
14. 3. speaking boldly i. the Lord
20. 9. there sat i. a window a certain
27.20. nor stars i. many days appear.
Ro. 1. 9. of you always i. my prayers
4.18. against hope believed i. hope
5. 2. rejoice i. hope of the glory
8.20. subjected the same i. hope
15.12. i. him shall the Gentiles trust
1Co. 8. 5. whether in heaven or i. earth
9.10. should plow i. hope ; and
he that thresheth i. hope
13. 6. Rejoiceth not i. iniquity
2Co. 1. 4. i. all our tribulation, that we
9. not trust i. ourselves, but i.
2. 3. having confidence i. you all
3.14. i. the reading of the old testa.
7. 4. joyful i. all our tribulation
7. he was comforted i. you, wh.
13. were comforted i. your com.
9.14. exceeding grace of God i. you
13. 1. i. the mouth of two or three
Eph. 1.16. ment. of you i.my pr. ; Phile.4
Col. 1. 16, 20. and that are i. earth
1Th. 1. 2. mention of you i. our prayers
3. 7. you i. all our affliction
1Ti. 4.10. we trust i. the living God
5. 5. trusteth i. God, and continu.
6.17. nor trust i. uncertain riches
Tit. 1. 2. i. hope of eternal life, which
Phile. 7. consolation i. thy love, beca.
Heb. 1. 2. Hath i. these last days spok.
2.13. I will put my trust i. him
8.10. write them i. their hearts
9.10. stood only i. meats and drin.
26. i. the end of the world hath he
10.16. i. their minds will I write th.
1Pet.1.20. i. these last times for you
3. 5. women also, who trusted i.G.
2Pet. 3. 3. shall come i. the last days
Jo. 3. 3. that hath this hope i. him

Rev. 1.20. sawest i. my right hand, and
2.17. i. the stone a new name writ.
5. 1. And I saw i. the right hand of
3. no man in heaven nor i. earth
13. such as are i. the sea, and all
7. 3. servants of our God i. their f.,
9.4,13.16,14.1.9,22.4
9.14. are bound i. the great river
11. 8. i. the street of the great city
13.16. i. their right hand, or ; 14.1,9
14. 9. forehead, or i. his hand ; 20.4
17. 8. not written i. the book of life
18.17. all the company i. ships
20. 1. a great chain i. his hand
22.16. these things i. the churches
kata, [accu.]   [2.12,13,19,22
Mat. 1. 20. appeared unto him i. a dre.;
27.19. many things this day i. a dr.
Lu. 6.23. i. the like manner did their
15.14. a mighty famine i. that land
Act. 3.13. denied him i. presence of Pi.
22. i. all things whatsoever he
5.42. and i. every house they ceas.
11. 1. and brethren that were i. Ju.
13. 1. Now there were i.the church
15.23. i. Antioch and Syria and Ci.
36. i. every city where we have
17.22. I perceive that i. all things
24.14. which are written i. the law
25. 3. laying wait i. the way to kill
26.11. oft i. every synagogue, and
13. I saw i. the way a light from
Ro. 5. 6. yet without strength, i. due
16. 5. ch. that is i. their house ;
1Co.16.19 ; Col.4.15 ; Phile. 2
1Co.14.40. be done decently and i. order
2Co.10. 1. who i. presence am base
Col. 3.20. obey your parents i. all thin.
22. Servants, obey i. all things
Heb. 1.10. And, Thou, Lord, i. the be.
2.17. Wherefore i. all things it
3. 8. i. the day of temptation
9. 9. i. which were offered both g.
11.13. These all died i. faith
dia, [gen.]
Mat.26.61. to build it i. three days
Act.16. 9. appeared to Paul i. the night
2Co. 5.10. the things done i. his body
1Th. 4.14. them also which sleep i. Jes.
1Ti. 2.15. she shall be saved i. childbe.
Heb. 7. 9. tithes, payed tithes i. Abra.
2.22. a letter unto you i. few words
2Pet. 3. 5. out of the water and i. the
apo,
Ro. 11.25. blindness i. part is happened
15.15. boldly unto you i. some sort
2Co. 1.14. have acknowledged us i. part
2. 5. not grieved me, but i. part
2Th. 2. 2. be not soon shaken i. mind
Heb. 5. 7. was heard i. that he feared
ek.
Lu. 11. 6. a friend of mine i. his journ.
1Co.12.27. body of Ch., and members i.
13. 9. i. part, and we prophesy i.
10. then that which is i. part
12. now I know i. part
Rev. 3.18. of me gold tried i. the fire
esō.
Mat.26.58. went i., and sat with the ser.
meta, [gen.]
Mar.14.62. coming i. the clouds of hea.
pros, [accu.]
Lu. 12. 3. ye have spoken i. the ear
24.12. wondering i. himself at that
hupo, [accu.]
Act. 5.21. temple early i. the morning
hostis
Act.17.11. i. that they received the word
achri.
Act.20. 6. them to Troas i. five days
hoti.
Ro. 5. 8. i. that while we were yet sin.

para, [dat.]
Ro. 11.25. wise i. your own con.; 12.16
Gal. 3.11. by the law i. the sight of God
   huper, [gen.]
Phi. 1.29. given i. the behalf of Christ
Phile. 13. that i. thy stead he might
   peri, [accu.]
Tit. 2. 7. i. all things shewing thyself
   ana.
Rev. 7.17. the Lamb which is i. the

INASMUCH.
epi hosos.
Mat.25.40, 45. i. as ye have done it
Ro. 11.13. i. as I am the apostle of the
   kata hosos.
Heb. 3. 3. i. as he who hath builded
   7.20. And i. as not without an

INCENSE.
thumiama.
Lu. 1.10. without, at the time of i.
   11. right side of the altar of i.
Ro. 8. 3. was given unto him much i.
   4. smoke of the i.,..ascend. up
   thumiaō.
Lu. 1. 9. his lot was to burn i. when

INCLOSED.
sungkleiō.
Lu. 5. 6. they i. a great multitude of

INCONTINENCY.
akrasia.
1Co. 7. 5. tempt you not for your i.

INCONTINENT.
akratēs.
2Ti. 3. 3. false accusers, i., fierce

INCORRUPTIBLE.
aphthartos.
1Co. 9.25. corrupt. crown ; but we an i.
   15.52. the dead shall be raised i.
1Pet. 1. 4. To an inheritance i., and un.
   23. but of i., by the word of God

INCORRUPTION.
aphtharsia.
1Co. 15.42. corruption ; it is raised in i.
   50. doth corruption inherit i.
   53, 54. must put on i., and this

INCREASE, [noun.]
auxanō.
1Co. 3. 6. gave the i.; 7. giveth the i.
   auxēsis.
Eph. 4.16. maketh i. of the body unto
Col. 2.19. increaseth with the i. of God

INCREASE, [verb.] -ed, -eth, -ing.
auxanō.
Mar. 4. 8. fruit that sprang up and i-ed
Jo. 3.3o. He must i., but I must decr.
Act. 6. 7. the word of God i-ed; and
2Co. 9.10. i. the fruits of your righteo.
   10.15. when your faith is i-ed, that
Col. 1.10. i-ing in the knowledge of G.
   2.19. i-eth with the increase of G.
   prokoptō.
Lu. 2.52. Jesus i-ed in wisdom and
2Ti. 2.16. for they will i. unto more
   perisseuō.
Act.16. 5. and i-ed in number daily
1Th. 4.10. that ye i. more and more
   prostithēmi.
Lu. 17. 5. unto the Lord, i. our faith
   endunamoō.
Act. 9.22. Saul i-cd the more in strength
   pleonazō.
1Th. 3.12. the Lord make you to i. and
   ploutēo.
Rev. 3.17. am rich, and i-ed with goods

146

INCREDIBLE.
apistos.
Act.26. 8. thought a thing i. with you

INDEBTED.
opheilō.
Lu. 11. 4. every one that is i. to us

INDEED, (See Neither.)
men.   [Mar.1.8; Lu.3.16
Mat. 3.11. I i. baptize you with water ;
   13.32. Which i. is the least of all
   20.23. drink i. of my cup : Mar.10.39
   23.27. which i. appear beautiful
   26.41. the spirit i. is willing
Mar.14.21.The Son of man i. goeth
Lu. 11.48. for they i. killed them, and
   23.41. And we i. justly ; for we
Act. 4.16. for that i. a notable miracle
   11.16. John i. baptized with water
   22. 9. they that were with me saw i.
Ro. 6.11. to be dead i. unto sin
   14.20. All things i. are pure ; but
1Co.11. 7. For a man i. ought not to
2Co. 8.17. For i. he accepted the exhor.
Phi. 1.15. Some i. preach Christ even of
   3. 1. to me i. is not grievous
Col. 2.23. Which things have i. a shew
1Pet. 2. 4. disallowed i. of men, but
   ontōs.
Mar.11.32. that he was a prophet i.
Lu. 24.34. The Lord is risen i., and
Jo. 8.36. you free, ye shall be free i.
1Ti. 5. 3, 16. wido. that are widows i.
   5. Now she that is a widow i.
   alēthōs.
Jo. 1.47. Behold an Israelite i., in
   4.42. this is i. the Christ, the Sav.
   6.55. i., and my blood is drink i.
   7.26. know i. that this is the very
   8.31. then are ye my disciples i.
   gar.
Ro. 8. 7. of God, neither i. can be
1Th. 4.10. And i. ye do it toward all
   alla.
2Co.11. 1. my folly ; and i. bear with

INDIGNATION.
aganakteō.
Mat.20.24. were moved with i. against
   26. 8. they had i., saying, To what
Mar.14. 4. some that had i. within
Lu. 13.14. answered with i., because
   aganaktēsis.
2Co. 7.11. yea, what i., yea, what fear
   zēlos.
Act. 5.17. and were filled with i.
Heb.10.27. fiery i., which shall devour
   thumos.
Ro. 2. 8. obey unrighteousness, i., and
   orgē.
Rev.14.10. into the cup of his i.; and

INEXCUSABLE.
anapologētos.
Ro. 2. 1. Therefore thou art i., O man

INFALLIBLE.
tekmērion.
Act. 1. 3. by many i. proofs, being seen

INFANTS.
brephos.
Lu. 18.15. brought unto him also i.

INFERIOR.
hēttaomai.
2Co. 12.13. is it wherein you were i.

INFIDEL.
apistos.
2Co. 6.15. he that believeth, with an i.
1Ti. 5. 8. faith, and is worse than an i.

INFIRMITY, -ies.
astheneia.
Mat. 8.17. Himself took our i-s, and
Lu. 5.15. healed by him of their i-s
   8. 2. healed of evil spirits and i-s
   13.11. which had a spirit of i.
   12. thou art loosed from thine i.
Jo. 5. 5. had an i. thirty and eight ye.
Ro. 6.19. because of the i. of your flesh
   8.26. Spirit also helpeth our i-s
2Co. 11.30. things which concern mine i-s
   12. 5, 9. not glory, but in mine i-s
   10. I take pleasure in i-s
Gal. 4.13. through i. of the flesh
1Ti. 5.23. sake, and thine often i-s
Heb. 4.15. with the feeling of our i-s
   5. 2. also is compassed with i.
   7.28. high priests which have i.
   asthenēma.
Ro. 15. 1. to bear the i-s of the weak
   nosos.
Lu. 7.21. cured many of their i-s

INFORMED.
emphanizō.
Act.24. 1. who i. the governor against
   25. 2. the Jews i. him against Paul
   15. elders of the Jews i. me
   katēcheō.
Act.21.21. they are i. of thee, that thou
   24. they were i. concerning thee

INHABITANTS.
katoikeō.
Rev.17. 2. the i. of the earth have been

INHABITERS.
katoikeō.   [12.12
Rev. 8.13. Woe, woe, woe, to the i. of;

INHERIT, -ed.
klēronomeō.
Mat. 5. 5. for they shall i. the earth
   19.29. and shall i. everlasting life
   25.34. i. the kingdom prepared
Mar.10.17. that I may i. eternal life
Lu. 10.25. what shall I do to i.; 18.18
1Co. 6. 9. the unrighteous shall not i.
   10. shall i. the kingdom; Gal.5.21
   15.50. flesh and blood cannot i. the
   neither doth corruption i.
Heb. 6.12. who through faith.. i. the
   12.17. when he would have i-ed
1Pet. 3. 9. that ye should i. a blessing
Rev. 21. 7. that overcometh shall i. all

INHERITANCE, (See Obtain.
klēronomia.
Mat.21.38. him, and let us seize on his i.
Mar.12. 7. the i. shall be ours ; Lu.20.14
Lu. 12.13. brother, that he divide the i.
Act. 7. 5. gave him none i. in it, no
   20.32. and to give you an i. among
Gal. 3.18. if the i. be of the law, it is
Eph. 1.14. the earnest of our i. until the
   18. the riches of the glory of his i.
   5. 5. hath any i. in the kingdom
Col. 3.24. the reward of the i.: for ye
Heb. 9.15. the promise of eternal i.
   11. 8. after receive for an i., obeyed
1Pet. 1. 4. To an i. incorruptible, and
   klēros.
Act.26.18. and i. among them which are
Col. 1.12. to be partakers of the i. of

INIQUITY, -ies.
anomia.
Mat. 7.23. dep. from me, ye that work i.
   13.41. offend, and them which do i.
   23.28. are full of hypocrisy and i.
   24.12. because i. shall abound, the
Ro. 4. 7. they whose i-s are forgiven

Ro. 6.19. uncleanness and *to* ı. unto ı.
²Th. 2. 7. the myste. of ı. doth already
Tit. 2.14. might redeem us from all ı.
Heb. 1. 9. righteousness, and hated ı.
        8.12. their ı-*s* will I remember no
        10.17. their sins and ı-*s* will I reme.
adikia.
Lu. 13.27. from me, all ye workers of ı.
Act. 1.18. a field with the reward of ı.
        8.23. bitter. and in the bond of ı.
¹Ti. 2.19. of Christ depart from ı.
Jas. 3. 6. tongue is a fire, a world of ı.
ponēria.
Act. 3.26. every one of you from his ı-*s*
paranomia.
²Pet. 2.16. But was rebuked for his ı.
adikēma.
Rev.18. 5. hath remembered her ı-*s*

INJOIN,   -*ed.*
entellomai.
Heb. 9.20. which God *hath* ı-*ed* unto
epitassō.
Phile. 8. *to* ı. thee that which is conv.

INJURED.
adikeō.
Gal. 4.12. ye *have* not ı. me at all

INJURIOUS.
hubristēs.
¹Ti. 1.13. and a persecutor, and ı.; but

INK.
melan.
²Co. 3. 3. written not with ı., but with
²John 12. not write with paper and ı.
³John 13. will not with ı. and pen write

INN.
kataluma.
Lu. 2. 7. no room for them in the ı.
pandocheion.
Lu. 10.34. brought him to an ı., and

INNER.
esōteros.
Act.16.24. thrust them into the ı. prison
esō.
Eph. 3.16. by his Spirit in the ı. man

INNOCENT.
athōos.
Mat.27. 4. I have betrayed the ı. blood
        24. I am ı. of the blood of this

INNUMERABLE.
anarithmētos.
Heb.11.12. which is by the seashore ı.
murias.
Lu. 12. 1. an ı. *multitude* of people
Heb.12.22. to an ı. *company* of angels

INORDINATE.
pathos.
Col. 3. 5. uncleanness, ı. *affection*

INSCRIPTION.
epigraphō.
Act.17.23. found an altar with this ı.

INSOMUCH.
hōste.
Mat. 8.24. ı. *that* the ship was covered
        12.22. ı. *that* the blind and dumb
        13.54. ı. *that* they were astonished
        15.31. ı. *that* the multitude wonder.
        24.24. ı. *that*, if it were possible
        27.14. ı. *that* the governor marvell.
Mar. 1.27. ı. *that* they questioned
        45. ı. *that* Jesus could no
        2. 2. ı. *that* there was no room
        12. ı. *that* they were all amazed
        3.10. ı. *that* they pressed upon him
        9.26. ı. *that* many said, He is dead

Lu. 12. 1. ı. *that* they trode one
Act. 1.19. ı. *as* that field is called
        5.15. ı. *that* they brought forth
²Co. 1. 8. ı. *that* we despaired even
Gal. 2.13. ı. *that* Barnabas also was
eis.
²Cq. 8. 6. ı. *that* we desired Titus

INSPIRATION.
theopneustos.
²Ti. 3.16. scripture is *given by* ı. *of* God

INSTANT. (See *Continue.*)
hōra.
Lu. 2. 38. she coming in that ı.
epikeimai.
Lu. 23.23. they *were* ı. with loud voices
ephistēmi.
²Ti. 4. 2. *be* ı. in season, out of season

INSTANTLY.
spoudaiōs.
Lu. 7. 4. they besought him ı., saying
en ekteneia.
Act.26. 7. ı. serving God day and night

INSTRUCT,   -*ed,* -*ing.*
katēcheo.
Lu. 1. 4. Wherein thou *hast been* ı-*ed*
Act.18.25. This man was ı-*ed* in the way
Ro. 2.18. *being* ı-*ed* out of the law
mathēteuō.
Mat.13.52.every scribe *which is* ı-*ed*
probibazō.
Mat.14. 8.*being before* ı-*ed* of her moth.
sumbibazō.
¹Co. 2.16. the Lord, that he *may* ı. him
mueomai.
Phi. 4.12. in all things I *am* ı-*ed* both
²Ti. 2.25. In meekness ı-*ing* those that
paideuō.

INSTRUCTER,   -*s*
paideutēs.
Ro. 2.20. An ı. of the foolish, a teacher
paidagōgos.
¹Co. 4.15. ten thousand ı-*s* in Christ

INSTRUCTION.
paideia.
²Ti. 3.16. for ı. in righteousness

INSTRUMENTS.
hopla.
Ro. 6.13. ı. of unright.., ı. of righteous.

INSURRECTION.
sustasiastēs.
Mar.15. 7.that had made ı. *with* him
stasis.
Mar.15. 7. committed murder in the ı.
katephistēmi.
Act.18.12. *made* ı. with one accord *agai.*

INTEND,   -*ing.*
boulomai.
Act. 5.28. ı. to bring this man's blood
        12. 4. ı-*ing* after Easter to bring
mellō.
Act. 5.35. what ye ı. to do as touching
        20.13. there ı-*ing* to take in Paul
thelō.
Lu.14.28. ı-*ing* to build a tower, sitteth

INTENT,   -*s*
hina.
Jo. 11.15. *to the* ı. ye may believe
Eph. 3.10. *To the* ı. *that* now unto the
pros, [*accu.*]
Jo. 13.28. *for* what ı. he spake this
eis houtos.
Act. 9.21. and came hither *for that* ı.
eis ho.
¹Co.10. 6. *to the* ı. we should not lust
logos.
Act.10.29. for what ı. ye have sent for

ennoia
Heb. 4.12. thoughts and ᵤ-*s* of the heart

INTERCESSION,   -*s*
entungchanō.
Ro. 8.27. he *maketh* ı. for the saints
        34. who also *maketh* ı. for us
        11. 2. he *maketh* ı. to God against
Heb. 7.25. liveth *to make* ı. for them
huperentungchanō.
Ro. 8.26. Spirit itself *maketh* ı. *for* us
enteuxis.
¹Ti. 2. 1. ı-*s,* and giving of thanks

INTERPRET,   -*ed*
methermēneuomai.
Mat. 1.23. *being* ı-*ed* is, God with us
Mar. 5.41. which is, *being* ı-*ed*; 15.34;
        Act. 4.36
        15.22. *being* ı.*ed,* the place of a sku.
Jo. 1.41. which is, *being* ı-*ed,* the Christ
diermēneuō.
¹Co.12.30. speak with tongues? *do* all ı.
        14. 5. except he ı., that the church
        13. tongue pray that he *may* ı.
        27. by course ; and *let* one ı.
hermēnouō.
Jo. 1.38. which is to say, *being* ı-*ed*

INTERPRETATION.
hermēneuō.
Jo. 1.42. which *is by* ı. ; 9.7
Heb. 7. 2. being by ı., king of righteous.
diermēneuō.
Act. 9.36. which *by* ı. is called Dorcas
methermēneuomai.
Act.13. 8. for so *is* his name *by* ı.
hermēneia.
¹Co. 12.10. another the ı. of tongues
        14.26. hath a revelation, hath an ı.
epilusis.
²Pet. 1.20. Scripture is of any private ı.

INTERPRETER.
diermēneutēs.
¹Co. 14.28. if there be no ı., let him keep

INTO.
eis.
Mat. 2.11. they were come ı. the house
        12. they departed ı. their own
        13. flee ı. Egypt, and be thou th.
        14. night, and departed ı. Egypt
        20, 21. ı. the land of Israel
(*And all other passages except
the following :—*)
epi, [*accu.*]
Mat.13. 8, 23. other fell ı. good ground
        20. received the seed ı. stony pl.
        18.12. ı. the mountains ; 24.16
        22. 9. therefore ı. the highways
Mar. 4.26. should cast seed ı. the ground
        6.53. they came ı. the land of Gen.
Lu. 19. 4. climbed up ı. a sycamore tree
        23. my money ı. the bank
Act. 7.23. it came ı. his heart to visit
        9.11. go ı. the street which is
¹Co. 2. 9. ı. the heart of man, the thin.
        11.20. together therefore ı. one pla.
        14.23. be come together ı. one place
Heb.10.16. my laws ı. their hearts, and
Rev.11.11. life from God entered ı. them
en.
Mar. 1.16. casting a net ı. the sea
Lu. 5.16. withdrew himself ı. the wild.
        23.42. thou comest ı. thy kingdom
Jo. 3.35. given all things ı. his hand
        5. 4. at a certain season ı. the pool
Act. 7.45. ı. the possession of the Gent.
Ro. 1.23. ı. an image made like to
        25. the truth of God ı. a lie
²Co. 8.16. ı. the heart of Titus for you
Gal. 1. 6. ı. the grace of Christ unto
147

'Ti. 3.16. world, received up i. glory
Rev.14.10. i. the cup of his indignation
kata, [accu.]
Act. 5.15. the sick i. the streets
16. 7. assayed to go i. Bithynia
esō.
Mar.14.54. even i. (esō eis) the palace
15.16. led him away i. the hall
achri.
Act.20. 4. accompanied him i. Asia
(See words in connection.)

INTREAT, -ed.
parakaleō.
Lu. 15.28. his father out, and i-ed him
1Co. 4.13. Being defamed, we i.; we are
1Ti. 5. 1. elder, but i. him as a father
erōtaō.
Phi. 4. 3. I i. thee also, true yokefellow
paraiteomai.
Heb.12.19. i-ed that the word should not
eupeithēs.
Jas. 3.17. easy to be i-ed, full of mercy

INTREATY.
paraklēsis.
2Co. 8. 4. praying us with much i.

INTRUDING.
embateuō.
Col. 2.18. i. into those things which

INVENTORS.
epheuretēs.
Ro. 1.30. boasters, i. of evil things.

INVISIBLE.
aoratos.
Ro. 1.20. for the i. things of him from
Col. 1.15. who is the image of the i.God
16. are in earth, visible and i.
1Ti. 1.17. King eternal, immortal, i.
Heb.11.27. as seeing him who is i.

INWARD. (See Affection.)
esōthen.
Lu. 11.39. your i. part is full of ravening
2Co. 4.16. yet the i. man is renewed
esō.
Ro. 7.22. law of God after the i. man

INWARDLY.
esōthen.
Mat. 7.15. i. they are ravening wolves
en kruptos.
Ro. 2.29. he is a Jew, which is one i.

IRON. (See Seared.)
sidēreos.
Act.12.10. they came unto the i. gate
Rev. 2.27. rule them with a rod of i.;19.15
9. 9. as it were breastplates of i.
12. 5. rule all nations with a rod of i.
sidēros.
Rev.18.12. and of brass, and i., and

ISLAND.
nēsos.
Act. 27.26. be cast upon a certain i.
28. 1. that the i. was called Melita
7. the chief man of the i., whose
9. in the i., came, and were he.
Rev. 6.14. mountain and i. were moved
16.20. And every i. fled away, and
nēsion.
Act.27.16. running under a certain i.

ISLE.
nēsos.
Act.13. 6. had gone through the i. unto
28.11. which had wintered in the i.
Rev. 1. 9. was in the i. that is called.

ISSUE, [noun.]
haimorreō.
Mat. 9.20. diseased with an i. of blood
148

rusis.
Mar. 5.25. had an i. of blood; Lu. 8.43.
Lu. 8.44. her i. of blood stanched
sperma.
Mat.22.25. having no i., left his wife.

ISSUED, [verb.]
ekporeuomai.
Rev.9.17. out of their mouths i. fire
18. which i. out of their mouths

IT. (See He.)

ITCHING.
knēthō.
2Ti. 4. 3. teachers, having i. ears

ITSELF. (See Shew.)
heautou.
Mat. 6.34. thought for the things of i.
12.25. kingdom divided against i.;
Mar.3.24; Lu.11.17
house divided ag.i.; Mar.3.25.
Jo. 15. 4. branch cannot bear fruit of i.
Ro. 14.14. there is nothing unclean of i.
Eph. 4.16. unto the edifying of i. in love
autos.
Ro. 8.16. The Spirit i. beareth witness
3John 12. all men and of the truth i.
chōris.
Jo. 20. 7. together in a place by i.

IVORY.
elephantinos.
Rev.18.12. and all manner vessels of i.

JACINTH.
huakinthinos.
Rev. 9.17. breastplates of fire and of j.
huakinthos.
Rev.21.20. chrysopra.; the eleventh a j.

JAILOR.
desmophulax.
Act.16.23. charging the j. to keep them

JANGLING.
mataiologia.
1Ti. 1. 6. turned aside into vain j.

JASPER.
iaspis.
Rev. 4. 3. a j. and a sardine stone: and
21.11. even like a j. stone, clear as
18. of the wall of it was of j.
19. The first foundation was j.

JEALOUS.
zēloō.
2Co. 11. 2. For I am j. over you with

JEALOUSY, (See Provoke.)
zēlos.
2Co. 11. 2. jealous over you with godly j.

JEOPARDY.
kinduneuō.
Lu. 8.23. with water, and were in j.
1Co. 15.30. why stand we in j. every ho.

JESTING.
eutrapelia.
Eph. 5. 4. foolish talking, nor j. which

JEW, -s.
Ioudaikos.
Gal. 2.14. Gent., and not as do the j-s
Ioudaizō.
Gal. 2.14. Gentiles to live as do the j-s
Ioudaismos.
Gal. 1.13. time past in the j.'s religion
14. profited in the j.'s religion
(See proper names.)

JEWISH.
Ioudaikos.
Tit. 1.14. Not giving heed to j. fables

JEWRY.
Ioudaia.
Lu. 23. 5. teaching throughout all J.

JOIN, -ed.
kollaō.
Lu. 15.15. and j-ed himself to a citizen
Act. 5.13. durst no man j. himself to
8.29. Go near, and j. thyself to
9.26. he assayed to j. himself to
1Co. 6.16. he which is j-ed to an harlot
17. But he that is j-ed unto the
proskollaomai.
Act. 5.36. four hundred j-ed themselves
Eph. 5.31. and shall be j-ed unto his wife
suzeugnumi. [Mar.10.]
Mat.19. 6. God hath j-ed together;
sunomoreō.
Act.18. 7. whose house j-ed hard to the
katartizō.
1Co. 1.10. ye be perfectly j-ed together
sunarmologeomai.
Eph. 4.16. whole body fitly j-ed together

JOINT, -s.
haphē.
Eph. 4.16. that which every j. supplieth
Col. 2.19. all the body by j-s and bands
harmos.
Heb.4.12. of the j-s and marrow, and
sungklēronomos.
Ro. 8.17. heirs of G. and j. heirs with

JOT,
iōta.
Mat. 5.18. one j. or one tittle shall in

JOURNEY, [noun.](See Bring.)
hodos.
Mat.10.10. Nor scrip for your j., neither
Mar. 6. 8. nothing for their j.; Lu. 9. 3.
Lu. 2.44. went a day's j.; and they
11. 6. in his j. is come to me, and I
Act. 1.12. Jerusa.; a sabbath day's j.
hodoiporia.
Jo. 4. 6. being wearied with his j.
hodoiporeō.
Act.10. 9. as they went on their j.
poreuomai.
Act.22. 6. as I made my j., and was
Ro. 15.24. Whensoever I take my j. into
diaporeuomai.
Ro. 15.24. for I trust to see you in my j.
apodēmeō.
Mat.25.15.and straightway took his j.
Lu. 15.13. took his j. into a far country
apodēmos.
Mar.13.34. is as a man taking a far j.
euodoomai.
Ro. 1.10. might have a prosperous j.

JOURNEYED, [verb.] -ing.
poreuomai.
Act. 9. 3. And as he j., he came near
26.13. them which j. with me
hodeuō.
Lu. 10.33. certain Samaritan, as he j.
poieō poreia.
Lu. 13.22. and j-ing toward Jerusalem
sunodeuō.
Act. 9. 7. the men which j. with him

JOURNEYINGS.
hodoiporia.
2Cor.11.26. in j. often, in perils

JOY, [noun.] (See Leap.)
chara.
Mat. 2.10. rejoi. with exceeding great j.
13.20. and anon with j. receiveth it
44. and for j. thereof goeth and
25.21, 23. enter thou into the j. of
28. 8. sepul. with fear and great j.
Lu. 1.14. thou shalt have j. and gladn.

Lu. 2.10. you tidings of great j.
8.13. receive the word with j.
10.17. seventy returned again with j.
15. 7. likewise j. shall be in heaven
10. there is j. in the presence of
24.41. they yet believed not for j.
52. to Jerusalem with great j.
Jo. 3.29. my j. therefore is fulfilled
15.11. that my j. might remain in that your j. might be full ;
16.24 ; ¹Jo. 1.4 ; ²Jo. 12
16.20. sorrow shall be turned into j.
21. for j. that a man is born into
22. your j. no man taketh from
17.13. might have my j. fulfilled
Act. 8. 8. And there was great j. in that
13.52. the disciples were filled with j.
15. 3. caused great j. unto all the
20.24. might finish my course with j.
Ro. 14.17. peace, and j. in the Holy Gh.
15.13. fill you with all j. and peace
32. may come unto you with j.
¹Co. 1.24. but are helpers of your j.
2. 3. that my j. is the joy of you all
7.13. joyed we for the j. of Titus
8. 2. the abundance of their j. and
Gal. 5.22. fruit of the Spirit is love, j.
Phi. 1. 4. all making request with j.
25. for your furtherance and j. of
2. 2. Fulfil ye my j., that ye be
4. 1. my j. and crown, so stand fa.
¹Th. 1. 6. with j. of the Holy Ghost
2.19. For what is our hope, or j., or
20. For ye are our glory and j.
3. 9. for all the j. wherewith we
²Ti. 1. 4. that I may be filled with j.
Heb. 12.2. who for the j. that was set
13.17. that they may do it with j.
Jas. 1. 2. My brethren, count it all j.
4. 9. and your j. to heaviness
¹Pet. 1. 8. ye rejoice with j. unspeakable
³John 4. I have no greater j. than to
charis.
Phile. 7. have great j. and consolation
agalliasis.
Lu. 1.44. leaped in my womb for j.
Jude 24. of his glory with *exceeding* j.
agalliaō.
¹Pet. 4.13. be glad also *with exceeding* j.
euphrosunē.
Act. 2.28. thou shalt make me full of j.
onēmi.
Phile. let me *have* j. of thee in the
JOY, [*verb*,]   -*ed*, -*ing*.
chairō.
²Co. 7.13. exceedingly the more j-*ed* we
Phi. 2.17. I j., and rejoice with you all
18. *do* ye j. and rejoice with me
Col. 2. 5. j-*ing* and beholding your or.
¹Th. 3. 9. wherewith we j. for your
kauchaomai.
Ro. 5.11. we also j. in God through
JOYFUL.
chara.
²Co. 7. 4. I am exceeding j. (*in joy*.)
JOYFULLY.
chairō.
Lu. 19. 6. down, and received him j.
meta [*gen*.] **chara.**
Heb.10.34. took j. the spoiling of your
JOYFULNESS.
chara.
Col. 1.11. and long-suffering with j.
JOYOUS.
chara.
Heb.12.11. seemeth to be j.   (*of joy*.)
JUDGE, [*noun*,]   -*s*.
kritēs.   [Lu.12.58
Mat. 5.25. to the j., and the j. deliver;

Mat.12.27. they sh. be your j-*s* ; Lu.11.19
Lu. 18. 2. There was in a city a j., which
6. Hear what the unjust j. saith
Act.10.42. to be the j. of quick and dea.
13.20. that he gave unto them j-*s*
18.15. I will be no j. of such matters
24.10. hast been of many years a j.
²Ti. 4. 8. the Lord, the righteous j.
Heb.12.23.to God the j. of all, and to
Jas. 2. 4. are becom. j-*s* of evil thoughts
4.11. not a doer of the law, but a j.
5. 9. the j. standeth before the do.
dikastēs.
Lu. 12.14. who made me a j. or a divider
Act. 7.27, 35. thee a ruler and a j. over
JUDGE, [*verb*,] -*ed*, -*est*, -*eth*, -*ing*.
krinō.   [Lu.6.37
Mat. 7. 1. j. not, that ye be not j-*ed*
2. judg. ye j., ye shall be j-*ed*
19.28. j-*ing* the twelve tribes of Is. ; Lu. 22.30.
Lu. 7. 43. him. Thou *hast* rightly j-*ed*
12.57. j. ye not what is right
19.22. own mouth *will* I j. thee
Jo. 5.22. the Father j-*eth* no man, but
30. as I hear, I j. ; and my judg.
7.24. j. not according to the appe. but j. righteous judgment
51. *Doth* our law j. any man
8.15. Ye j. after the flesh ; I j. no
16. And yet if I j., my judgment
26. things to say and to j. of you
50. is one that seeketh and j-*eth*
12.47. I j. him not : for I came not to j. the world, but to save
48. hath one that j-*eth* him the same shall j. him in the
16.11. the prince of this world is j-*ed*
18.31. Take ye him, and j. him acc.
Act. 4.19. more than unto God, j. ye
7. 7. *will* I j., said God : and after
13.46. and j. yourselves unworthy
16.15. If ye *have* j-*ed* me to be faith.
17.31. will j. the world in righteous.
23. 3. for sittest thou to j. me after
24. 6. and would have j-*ed* accordi.
25. 9. there be j-*ed* of these things
10. where I ought to be j-*ed*
20. and there be j-*ed* of these
26. 6. And now I stand *and* am j-*ed*
Ro. 2. 1. whosoever thou art *that* j-*est* wherein thou j-*est* another for thou that j-*est* doest the
3. O man, *that* j-*est* them which
12. law, *shall* be j-*ed* by the law
16. when God *shall* j. the secrets
27. *shall* not uncircumcision . . j.
3. 4. overcome when thou art j-*ed*
6. how *shall* God j. the world
7. why yet *am* I also j-*ed* as a
14. 3. *let* not him which eateth not j.
4. Who art thou *that* j-*est* anot.
10. why *dost* thou j. thy brother
13. *Let* us not therefore j. one another any more : but j. this
¹Co. 4. 5. j. nothing before the time
5. 3. *have* j-*ed* already, as though I
12. what have I to do *to* j. them are without? *do* not ye j. th.
13. that are without God j-*eth*
6. 2. the saints *shall* j. the world the world *shall* be j-*ed* by you
3. that we *shall* j. angels? how
10.15. wise men : j. ye what I say
29. why *is* my liberty j-*ed* of an.
11.13. j. in yourselves : is it comely
31. ourse., we should not be j-*ed*
32. But *when* we are j-*ed*, we are
²Co. 5.14. *because* we thus j., that if one
Col. 2.16. *Let* no man therefore j. you

²Ti. 4. 1. who shall j. the quick and
Heb.10.30.The Lord shall j. his people
13. 4. and adulterers God *will* j.
Jas. 2.12. as they that shall be j-*ed* by
4.11. and j-*eth* his brother, speak. of the law, and j-*eth* the law but if thou j. the law
12. who art thou that j-*est* anot.
¹Pet. 1.17. *who* without . . of persons j-*eth*
2.23. to him *that* j-*eth* righteously
4. 5. that is ready *to* j. the quick
6. that they *might be* j-*ed* accor.
Rev. 6.10. *dost* thou not j. and avenge
11.18. dead, that they should be j-*ed*
16. 5. because thou *hast* j-*ed* thus
18. 8. is the Lord God *who* j-*eth* her
19. 2. for he *hath* j-*ed* the great wh.
11. in righteousness he *doth* j.
20.12. the dead *were* j-*ed* out of
13. and they *were* j-*ed* every man
anakrinō.
¹Co. 2.15. he that is spiritual j-*eth* all he himself *is* j-*ed* of no man
4. 3. that I *should be* j-*ed* of you yea, I j. not mine own self
4. he *that* j-*eth* me is the Lord
14.24. convinced of all, he *is* j-*ed* of
diakrinō.
¹Co. 6. 5. able to j. between his breth.
11.31. For if we *would* j. ourselves
14.29. or three, and let the other j.
kritērion.
¹Co. 6. 2. are ye unworthy *to* j. the
hēgeomai.
Heb.11.11.she j-*ed* him faithful who had

JUDGMENT,   -*s*.
krisis.
Mat. 5.21, 22.shall be in danger of the j.
10.15. the day of j. than for that ;
11.22,24;Mar.6.11;Lu.10.14
12.18. he shall shew j. to the Gen.
20. he send forth j. unto victory
36. acc. thereof in the day of j.
41, 42. shall rise in j. ; Lu.11.31,32
23.23. j., mercy, and faith : these
Lu. 11.42. pass over j. and the love of
Jo. 5.22. ha. committed all j. unto the
27. to execute j. also, because he
30. and my j. is just ; because I
7.24. but judge righteous j.
8.16. my j. is true : for I am not
12.31. Now is the j. of this world
16. 8. of righteousness, and of j.
11. Of j. because the prince of
Act. 8.33. his j. was taken away ; and
²Th. 1. 5. token of the righteous j. of
¹Ti. 5.24. going before to j. ; and some
Heb. 9.27. to die, but after this the j.
10.27. fearful looking for of j. which
Jas. 2.13. he shall have j. without mercy rejoiceth against j.
²Pet. 2. 4. dark., to be reserved unto j.
9. unjust, unto the day of j. to
3. 7. fire against the day of j.
¹Jo. 4.17. boldness in the day of j.
Jude 6. unto the j. of the great day
15. To execute j. upon all
Rev 14. 7. the hour of his j. is come
16. 7. and righteous are thy j-*s*
18.10. in one hour is thy j. come
19. 2. true and righteous are his j-*s*
krima.
Mat. 7. 2. For with what j. ye judge
Jo. 9.39. For j. I am come into this
Act.24.25. and j. to come, Felix tremb.
Ro. 2. 2. we are sure that the j. of God
3. thou shalt escape the j. of G.
5.16. for the j. was by one to
11.33. unsearchable are his j-*s*
Gal. 5.10. shall bear his j., whosoever
Heb. 6. 2. the dead, and of eternal j.

149

¹Pet. 4.17. For the time is come that **J.**
²Pet. 2. 3. whose **J.** now of a long time
Rev.17. 1. I will shew unto thee the **J.**
   20. 4. and **j.** was given unto them
     dikaiōma.
Ro. 1.32. Who knowing the **J.** of God
Rev.15. 4. thy **J-s** are made manifest
     dikē.
Act.25.15. desiring to have **J.** against
     kritērion.
¹Co. 6. 4. if then ye have **J-s** of things
Jas. 2. 6. draw you before the **J.** seats
     gnōmē.
¹Co. 1.10. same mind and in the same **J.**
   7.25. yet I give my **J.**, as one that
    40. if ye so abide, after my **J.**
     aisthēsis.
Phi. 1. 9. in knowledge and in all **J.**
     hēmera.
¹Co. 4. 3. judged of you, or of man's **J.**
     bēma.   [Jo.19.13
Mat.27.19. set down on the **J.** seat ;
Act.18.12. brought him to the **J.** seat
   16. drave them from the **J.** seat
   17. beat him before the **J.** seat
  25. 6. day sitting on the **J.** seat
   10. I stand at Cesar's **J.** seat, wh.
   17. morrow I sat on the **J.** seat
Ro. 14.10. be. the **J.** seat of Ch. ; ²Co.5.10
   (See *Hall, Righteous.*)

JURISDICTION.
     exousia.
Lu. 23. 7. belonged unto Herod's **J.**

JUST.
     dikaios.
Mat.1.19. her husband being a **J.** man
  5.45. sendeth rain on the **J.** and
  13.49. wicked from among the **J.**
  27.19. nothing to do with that **J.**
   24. inno. of the blood of this **J.**
Mar.6.20. knowing that he was a **J.** man
Lu. 1.17. diso. to the wisdom of the **J.**
  2.25. the same man was **J.** and
  14.14. at the resurrection of the **J.**
  15. 7. over ninety and nine **J.** per.
  20.20. should feign them. **J.** men
  23.50. he was a good man, and a **J.**
Jo. 5.30. my judgment is **J.** ; because I
Act. 3.14. denied the H. One and the **J.**
  7.52. of the coming of the **J.** One
  10.22. Cornelius the centurion, a **J.**
  22.14. know his will, and see that **J.**
  24.15. dead, both of the **J.** and unj.
Ro. 1.17. The **J.** shall live by faith ;
   Gal. 3.11 ; Heb. 10.38
  2.13. hearers of the law are **J.** befo.
  3.26. might be **J.**, and the justifier
  7.12. holy, and **J.**, and good
Phi. 4. 8. whatsoever things are **J.**, wh.
Col. 4. 1. that which is **J.** and equal
Tit. 1. 8. lover of good men, sober, **J.**
Heb.12.23.to the spirits of **J.** men made
Jas. 5. 6. condemned and killed the **J.**
¹Pet.3.18. suffered for sins, the **J.** for the
²Pet. 2. 7. delivered **J.** Lot, vexed with
¹Jo. 1. 9. he is faithful and **J.** to forgive
Rev.15. 3. **J.** and true are thy ways, thou
     endikos.
Ro. 3. 8. come? whose damnation is **J.**
Heb.2. 2. received a **J.** recompense of

JUSTIFICATION.
     dikaiōsis.
Ro. 4.25. was raised again for our **J.**
  5.18. upon all men unto **J.** of life
     dikaiōma.
Ro. 5.16. of many offences unto **J.**

JUSTIFIER.
     dikaioō.
Ro. 3.26. the **J.** *of* him which believeth
158

JUSTIFY,   *-ied, -eth.*
     dikaioō.   [Lu.7.35.
Mat.11.19. wisdom *is* **J-**ed of her child.
  12.37. thy words thou *shalt be* **j-**ed
Lu. 7.29. the publicans, **J-**ed God,being
  10.29. he, willing *to* **J.** himself, said
  16.15. Ye are they *which* **J.** yourse.
  18.14. went down to his house **J-**ed
Act. 13.39. him all that believe *are* **J-**ed
   ye could not *be* **J-**ed by the
Ro. 2.13. doers of the law *shall be* **J-**ed
  3. 4. That thou *mightest be* **J-**ed in
  20. there *shall* no flesh *be* **J-**ed;
   Gal. 2.16.
  24. *Being* **J-**ed freely by his grace
  28. that a man is **J-**ed by faith
  30. one God, which *shall* **J.** the
  4. 2. if Abra. *were* **J-**ed by works
  5. believeth on him *that* **J-**eth
  5. 1. Therefore *being* **J-**ed by faith
  9. *being now* **J-**ed by his blood
  8.30. **J-**ed: and whom he **J-**ed,them
  33. elect? It is God *that* **J-**eth
¹Co. 4. 4. yet *am* I not hereby **J-**ed
  6.11. ye *are* **J-**ed in the name of
Gal. 2.16. a man *is* not **J-**ed by the works
   that we *might be* **J-**ed by the
  17. we seek to be **J-**ed by Christ
  3. 8. that G. *would* **J.** the heathen
  11. no man *is* **J-**ed by the law
  24. that we *might be* **J-**ed by faith
  5. 4. whosoever of you *are* **J-**ed by
¹Ti. 3.16. manifest in the flesh, **J-**ed in
Tit. 3. 7. That *being* **J-**ed by his grace
Jas. 2.21. *Was* not Abra. our father **J-**ed
  24. that by works a man *is* **J-**ed
Jas. 2.25. *was* not Rah. the harlot **J-**ed

JUSTLY,
     dikaiōs.
Lu. 23.41. we indeed **J.**; for we receive
¹Th. 2.10. how holily, and **J.**, and

KEEP,   *-est, -eth, -ing, Kept,*
     tēreō.   [Ro.12.17,14.12
Mat.19.17.**k.** the commandments ;
Mar.7. 9. that ye *may* **k.** your own tr.
Jo. 2.10. thou *hast* **k-**t the good wine
  8.51, 52. If a man **k.** my saying
  55. but I know him, and **k.** his
  9.16. because he **k-**eth not the sab.
  12. 7. of my burying *hath* she **k-**t
  14.15. If ye love me, **k.** my comma.
  21. and **k-**eth them, he it is that
  23. If a man love me, he *will* **k.**
  24. loveth me not **k-**eth not my
  15.10. If ye **k.** my commandments
   even as I *have* **k-**t my Fath.
  20. **k-**t my saying, they *will* **k.**
  17. 6. and they *have* **k-**t thy word
  11. Holy Fath. **k.** through thine
  12. I **k-**t them in thy name ;
  15. *shouldest* **k.** them from the
Act.12. 5. Peter therefore *was* **k-**t in pr.
  6. keepers before the door **k-**t
  15. 5. to command them to **k.** the
  24. be circumcised, and **k.** the
  16.23. charging the jailor to **k.** them
  24.23. commanded a centurion to **k.**
  25. 4. that Paul should *be* **k-**t at
  21. I commanded him to *be* **k-**t
¹Co. 7.37. that he will **k.** his virgin
²Co. 11. 9. in all things I *have* **k-**t myse.
   and so *will* I **k.** myself
Eph. 4. 3. Endeavouring to **k.** the unity
¹Ti. 5.22. men's sins : **k.** thyself pure
  6.14. That thou **k.** this command.
²Ti. 4. 7. course, I *have* **k-**t the faith
Jas. 1.27. and *to* **k.** himself unspotted
  2.10. whosoever *shall* **k.** the whole
¹Jo. 2. 3. **k.** his commandments ;
   3.22,24,5.2,3

¹Jo. 2. 4. and **k-**eth not his command.
  5. But whoso **k-**eth his word, in
  5.18. begotten of God **k-**eth himse.
Jude 6. And the angels *which* **k-**t not
  21. **k.** yourselves in the love of
Rev. 1. 3. and **k.** those things which are
  2.26. and **k-**eth my works unto the
  3. 8. and *hast* **k-**t my word, and
  10. thou *hast* **k-**t the word of my
   patience, I also *will* **k.** thee
  16.15. *that* watcheth, and **k-**eth his
  22. 7, 9. is he *that* **k-**eth the sayings
     diatēreō.
Lu. 2.51. his mother **k-**t all these
Act.15.29. from which *if* ye **k.** yoursel.
     suntēreō.
Lu. 2.19. Mary **k-**t all these things
     phulassō.   [Lu.18.21
Mat.19.20. these things *have* I **k-**t from;
Lu. 2. 8. **k-**ing watch over their flock
  8.29. he was **k-**t bound with chains
  11.21. a strong man armed **k-**eth
  28. hear the word of God, and **k.**
Jo. 12.25. *shall* **k.** it unto life eternal
  17.12. thou gavest me I *have* **k-**t
Act. 7.53. of angels, and *have* not **k-**t
  12. 4. quaternions of soldiers to **k.**
  16. 4. them the decrees *for to* **k.**
  21.24. walkest orderly, and **k-**est
  25. only that they **k.** them*selves*
  22.20. **k-**t the raiment of them that
  23.35. *to be* **k-**t in Herod's judgment
  28.16. with a soldier *that* **k-**t him
Ro. 2.26. **k.** the righteousness of the
Gal. 6.13. who are circumcised **k.** the
²Th. 3. 3. *shall* stablish you, and **k.** you
¹Ti. 6.20. **k.** that which is committed
²Ti. 1.12. that he is able to **k.** that wh.
  14. committed unto thee **k.** by
¹Jo. 5.21. **k.** yourselves from idols
Jude 24. that is able *to* **k.** you from
     diaphulassō.
Lu. 4.10. charge over thee, *to* **k.** thee
     sigaō.
Lu. 9.36. And they **k-**t it *close,* and
Act.15.12. all the multitude **k-**t *silence*
Ro. 16.25. mystery, *which* *was* **k-**t secret
¹Co. 14.28. *let* him **k.** *silence* in the chu.
  34. *Let* your women **k.** *silence* in
     phroureō.
²Co. 11.32. **k-**t the city. .*with a garrison*
Gal. 3.23. we *were* **k-**t under the law
Phi. 4. 7. *shall* **k.** your hearts and
¹Pet. 1. 5. Who *are* **k-**t by the power of
     poieō.
Mat.26.18. I will **k.** the passover at thy
Jo. 7.19. none of you **k-**eth the law
Act. 18.21. must by all means **k.** this
Heb.11.28. Through faith he **k-**t the
     echō.
Lu. 19.20. pound, which I *have* **k-**t laid
     katechō.
Lu. 8.15. having heard the word, **k.** it
¹Co.11. 2. and **k.** the ordinances, as I
  15. 2. if ye **k.** *in memory* what I
     sunechō.
Lu. 19.43. and **k.** thee *in* on every side
     parechō.
Act.22. 2. they **k.** the more silence
     agō.
Mat. 14.6. wh. Herod's birthday *was* **k-**t
     ginomai.
Mar. 4.22. neither *was* anything **k-**t sec.
     krateō.
Mar. 9.10. they **k-**t that saying within
     nosphizomai.
Act. 5. 2, 3. **k-**t back part of the price
     hupostellō.
Act.20.20. And how I **k-**t back nothing
     katakeimai.
Act. 9.33. *which had* **k-**t his bed eight

kŏluŏ.
Act.27.43. k-t them from their purpose
prassō.
Ro. 2.25. profiteth, if thou k. the law
boskō.
Mat.8.33. they that k-t them fled, and
hupo-piazō.
¹Co. 9.27. But I k. under my body
(See *Company, Door, Feast, Fraud,*
Secret, Store.)

KEEPER, (See *Home*,)   -s.
phulax.
Act. 5.23. and the k-s standing without
12. 6. and the k-s before the door
19. he examined the k-s, and
desmophulax.
Act.16.27,36. the k. *of the prison* awak.
tēreō.
Mat.28. 4. for fear of him the k-s did

KEEPING, [noun.]
tērēsis.
¹Co. 7.19. the k. of the commandments
paratithēmi.
¹Pet. 4.19. *let..commit the* k. *of* th. so.

KEY,   -s.
kleis.
Mat.16.19.I will give unto thee the k-s
Lu. 11.52. ye have taken away the k.
Rev. 1.18. and have the k-s of hell and
3. 7. he that hath the k. of David
9. 1. to him was given the k. and
20. 1. having the k. of the bottom.

KICK,
laktizō.   [26.14
Act. 9. 5. for thee *to* k. against the ;

KID.
eriphos.
Lu. 15.29. thou never gavest me a k.

KILL,   -ed, -est, -eth, -ing.
apokteinō.
Mat.10.28.fear not them *which* k. the
are not able *to* k. the soul
16.21. be k-ed, and be raised again
17.23. they *shall* k. him, and the
21.35. beat one, and k-ed another
38. come *let* us k. him; Mar.12.7;
Lu. 20.14
23.34. some of them ye *shall* k. and
37. *that* k-est the pro.; Lu. 13.34
24. 9. to be afflicted, and *shall* k.
26. 4. take Jesus by subtilty and k.
Mar. 3. 4. to save life or *to* k. ? But
6.19. would *have* k-ed him; but
8.31. pri., and scribes, and *be* k-ed
9.31. *shall* k. him ; and *after that*
he *is* k-ed, he shall rise the
10.34. spit upon him, and *shall* k.
12. 5. him they k-ed, and many ot.
beating some, and k-*ing* some
8. they took him, and k-ed him
Lu. 11.47. prop., and your fathers k-ed
48. for they indeed k-ed them
12. 4. afraid of them *that* k. the bo.
5. after he *hath* k-ed hath power
13.31. hence : for Herod will k. thee
20.15. out of the vineyard, and k-ed
Jo. 5.18. sought the more *to* k. him
7. 1. the Jews sought *to* k. him
19. law ? Why go ye about *to* k.
20. devil : who goeth about *to* k.
25. this he, whom they seek *to* k.
8.22. *Will* he k. himself ? because
37. ยo. ye seek *to* k. me
16. 2. that whosoever k-eth you will
Act. 3.15. and k-ed the Prince of life
21.31. they went about *to* k. him
ย3.12. drink till they *had* k-ed Paul

Act.27.42. counsel was to k. the prison.
Ro. 11. 3. Lord, they *have* k-ed thy pro.
²Co. 3. 6. for the letter k-*eth*, but the
¹Th. 2.15 *Who* both k-ed the Lord Jes.
Rev. 2.23. I *will* k. her children with
6. 8. *to* k. with sword, and with
11. that should be k-ed as they
9. 5. that they *should* not k. them
18. *was* the thi. part of men k-ed
20. men which *were* not k-ed by
11. 5. must in this manner be k-ed
7. shall overcome them, and k.
13.10. k-*eth* with the sword must be
k-ed with the sword
15. of the beast *should* be k-ed
anaireō.
Lu. 22. 2. sought how they *might* k.
Act. 7.28. thou k. me, as thou diddest
9.23. the Jews took counsel *to* k.
24. gates day and night to k. him
12. 2. he k-ed James the brother of
16.27. sword, and would *have* k-ed
23.15. he come near, are ready *to* k.
21. nor drink till they *have* k-ed
27. should *have been* k-ed of them
25. 3. laying wait in the way *to* k.
thuō.
Mat.22. 4. and my fatlings are k-ed
Mar.14.12.when they k-ed the passover
Lu. 15.23. the fatted calf, and k. it
27. thy father *hath* k-ed the fatt.
30. thou *hast* k-ed for him the
22. 7. the passover must be k-ed
Jo. 10.10. but for to steal, and to k.
Act.10.13. to him, Rise, Peter, k., and
phoneuō.   [Ro. 13.9
Mat. 5.21. Thou *shalt* not k. ; and ;
whosoever *shall* k. shall be in
23.31. of them *which* k-ed the prop.
Mar.10.19.*Do* not k.; Lu.18.20; Jas.2.11
Jas. 2.11. yet if thou k., thou art beco.
4. 2. ye k., and desire to have
5. 6. have condemned and k-ed
diacheirizomai.
Act.26.21. temple, and went about *to* k.
sphattō.
Rev. 6. 4. that they *should* k. one anot.
thanatoō.
Ro. 8.36. For thy sake we *are* k-ed
²Co. 6. 9. as chastened, and not k-ed

KIN.
sunggenēs.
Mar. 6. 4. among his own k., and in

KIND, [noun,]   -s.
genos.
Mat.13.47. sea, and gathered of every k.
17.21. Howbeit this k. ; Mar. 9.29
¹Co.12.10. to another divers k-s of tong.
14.10. many k-s of voices in the wo.
tis.
Jas. 1.18. *a* k. *of* first fruits of his crea.
phusis.
Jas. 3. 7. every k. of beasts and of bir.

KIND, [adjective.]
chrēstos.
Lu. 6.35. he is k. unto the unthankful
Eph. 4.32. And be ye k. one to another
chrēsteuomai.
¹Co. 13. 4. suffereth long, and *is* k.

KINDLED,   -eth.
anaptō.
Lu. 12.49. will I, if it *be* already k.
Act.28. 2. for they k. a fire, *and* rece.
Jas. 3. 5. great a matter a little fire k-eth
haptō.
Lu. 22.55. *when* they had k. a fire in

KINDLY, (See *Affectioned*.)

KINDNESS.
chrēstotēs.
²Co. 6. 6. by longsuffering, by k., by
Eph. 2. 7. in his k. toward us through
Col. 3.12. k., humbleness of mind
Tit. 3. 4. after that the k. and love
philadelphia.
²Pet. 1. 7. And to godliness *brotherly* k.
and to *brotherly* k. charity
philanthrōpia.
Act.28. 2. people shewed us no little k.

KINDRED,   -s.
phulē.
Rev. 1. 7. and all k-s of the earth shall
5. 9. out of every k., and tongue
7. 9. and k-s, and people, and to.
11. 9. k-s and tongues and na.; 13.7
14. 6. and to every nation, and k.
sunggeneia.
Lu. 1.61. is none of thy k. that is
Act. 7. 3. thy country, and *from* thy k.
14. and all his k., threescore and
genos.
Act. 4. 6. of the k. of the high priest
7.13. Joseph's k. was made known
19. dealt subtilly with our k.
patria.
Act. 3.25. thy seed shall all the k-s of

KING, (See *Court*,)   -s.
basileus.
Mat. 1. 6. David the k.;and David the k.
2. 1. days of Her. the k.; Lu.1.5
2. he that is born k. of the Je.
3. When Herod the k. had hea.
9. When they had heard the k.
5.35. it is the city of the great k.
10.18. before governors and k-s for
11. 8. soft clothing are in k-s' hous.
14. 9. k. was sorry : nev.; Mar.6.26
17.25. the k-s of the earth take cus.
18.23. likened unto a cert. k.; 22.2
21. 5. Behold, thy k. cometh unto
22. 7. when the k. heard thereof
11. when the k. came in to see
13. Then said the k. to the serv.
25.34. Then sh.the k. say unto them
40. the k. shall answer and say
27.11. Art thou the k. of the Jews ?
Mar.15.2 ; Lu.23.3 ; Jo.18.33
29. saying, Hail, k. of the Jews ;
Mar.15.18 ; Jo.19.3
37. THIS IS JESUS THE k. OF ;
Mar.15.26; Lu.23.38; Jo.19.19
42. If he be the k. of Israel
Mar. 6.14. k. Herod heard of him ; for
22. the k. said unto the damsel
25. with haste unto the k., and
27. immediately the k. sent an
13. 9. bef. rulers and k-s fcr ; 21.12
15. 9. rel. unto you the k.; Jo.18.36
12. whom ye call the k. of the J.
32. Let Christ the k. of Israel
Lu. 10.24. many prophets and k-s have
14.31. Or what k., going to make
war against another k.
19.38. Blessed be the k. thatcometh
22.25. The k-s of the Gentiles exer.
23. 2. that,he himself is Christ a k.
37. If thou be the k. of the Jews
Jo. 1.49. thou art the k. of Israel
6.15. by force, to make him a k.
12.13. Blessed is the k. of Israel
15. thy k. cometh, sitting on an
18.37. Art thou a k. then ? Jesus
an., Thou say. that I am a k.
19.12. whosoever maketh him. a k.
14. unto the Jews, Beh. your k.
15. Shall I crucify your k.
We have no k. but Cesar

Jo. 19.21. Write not, The k. of the Je.
but that he said, I am k. of
Act. 4.26. The k-s of the earth stood up
7.10. sight of Pharaoh k. of Egypt
18. Till another k. arose, which
9.15. before the Gentiles, and k-s
12. 1. Herod the k. stretched forth
20. Blastus the k.'s chamberlain
13.21. afterward they desired a k.
22. them David to be their k.
17. 7. say. that there is another k.
25.13. k. Agrippa and Bernice came
14. decl. Paul's cause unto the k.
24. Festus said, k. Agrippa, and
26. before thee, O k. Agrippa
26. 2. I think myself happy, k. A.
7. For which hope's sake, k. A.
13. At midday, O k., I saw in
19. Whereupon, O k. Agrippa
26. the k. knoweth of these thin.
27. k. Agrippa, believest thou
30. the k. rose up, and the gov.
2Co. 11.32. the gover. under Aretas the k.
1Ti. 1.17. unto the k. eternal, immor.
2. 2. For k-s, and for all that are
6.15. k. of kings, and Lo. of lords;
Rev. 17.14,19.16
Heb. 7. 1. Melchisedec, k. of Salem
from the slaughter of the k-s
2. k. of righteousness, and
k. of Salem, which is k. of
11.23. afraid of the k.'s command.
27. fearing the wrath of the k.
1Pet. 2.13. whether it be to the k., as
17. Fear God. Honour the k.
Rev. 1. 5. the prince of the k-s of the
6. made us k-s and priests; 5.10
6.15. the k-s of the earth, and the
9.11. they had a k. over them
10.11. nations, and tongues, and k-s
15. 3. true are thy ways, thou k. of
16.12. the way of the k-s of the east
14. go forth unto the k-s of the
17. 2. With whom the k-s of the
10. there are seven k-s; five are
12. which thou sawest are ten k-s
receive power as k-s one ho.
17. reigneth over the k-s of the e
18. 3. the k-s of the earth have
9. the k-s of the earth, who ha.
19.18. ye may eat the flesh of k-s
19. I saw the beast, and the k-s
21.24. the k-s of the earth do bring
basileuō.
1Ti. 6.15. the King of k-s and Lord of
(of them that reign.)
basilikos.
Act.12.20. nourished by the k.'s country

KINGDOM,   -s.
basileia.   [10.7
Mat. 3. 2. k. of heaven is at hand; 4.17
4. 8. all the k-s of the wo.; Lu.4.5
23. preach. the gospel of the k.;
9.35; Mar.1.14
5. 3, 10. theirs is the k. of heav.
19. least in the k. of heav.; 11.11
called great in the k. of hea.
20. enter into the k. of heaven;
7.21,18.3,19.23
6.10. Thy k. come. Thy; Lu.11.2
13. For thine is the k., and the
33. seek ye first the k.; Lu.12.31
8.11. and Jacob, in the k. of heav.
12. the children of the k.; 13.38
11.12. until now the k. of heaven
12.25. Every k. divided against;
Mar.3.24; Lu.11.17
26. shall then his k. st.; Lu.11.18
28. the k. of God is co.; Lu.11.20
13.11. mysteries of the k. of heav.
19. heareth the word of the k.

152

Mat.13.24, 31, 33. The k. of heaven is;
44,45,47,18.23,20.1
41. shall gather out of his k. all
43. the sun in the k. of their Fa.
52. instructed unto the k. of
16.19. the keys of the k. of heaven
28. Son of man coming in his k.
18. 1, 4. greatest in the k. of heav.
19.12. for the k. of heaven's sake
14. for of such is the k. of heav.
24. enter into the k. of God;
Mar.9,47,10.23,24,25; Lu.18.
24,25; Jo.3.5; Act.14.22
20.21. other on the left, in thy k.
21.31. go into the k. of God before
43. The k. of God shall be taken
23.13. ye shut up the k. of heaven
24. 7. and k. against k.; Mar.13.8;
Lu.21.10
14. this gospel of the k. shall
25.34. inherit the k. prepared for
26.29. with you in my Father's k.
Mar. 1.15. k. of G. is at han.; Lu.21.31
3.24. itself, that k. cannot stand
4.11. myst. of the k. of G.; Lu.8.10
26. So is the k. of God, as if a
30. we liken the k. of; Lu.13.20
6.23. thee, unto the half of my k.
9. 1. have seen the k. of God co.
10.14. such is the k. of G.; Lu.18.16
15. not receive the k.; Lu.18.17
11.10. Blessed be the k. of our fa.
12.34. not far from the k. of God
14.25. I drink it new in the k. of G.
15.43. also waited for the k. of Go.
Lu. 1.33. of his k. there shall be no
4.43. preach the k. of God; 9.2,60;
Act.20.25,28,31
6.20. for yours is the k. of God
7.28. he that is least in the k. of
8. 1. glad tidings of the k. of God
9.11. spake unto them of the k. of
27. till they see the k. of God
62. back, is fit for the k. of God
10. 9, 11. The k. of God is come
12.32. pleasure to give you the k.
13.18. what is the k. of God like
28. the prophets, in the k. of G.
29. shall sit down in the k. of
14.15. shall eat bread in the k. of
16.16. the k. of God is preached
17.20. when the k. of God should
The k. of God cometh not
21. the k. of God is within you
18.29. children, for the k. of God's
19.11. thought that the k. of God
12. to make for himself a k.
15. returned, hav. receiv. the k.
22.16. fulfilled in the k. of God
18. until the k. of God shall co.
29. I appoint unto you a k., as
30. drink at my table in my k.
23.42. when thou comest into thy k.
51. waited for the k. of God
Jo. 3. 3. he cannot see the k. of God
18.36. My k. is not of this world
if my k. were of this world
now is my k. not from hence
Act. 1. 3. pertaining to the k. of God
6. restore again the k. to Israel
8.12. concerning the k. of G.; 19.8
28.23. testified the k. of God
Ro. 14.17. For the k. of God is not me.
1Co. 4.20. the k. of God is not in word
6. 9, 10. inherit the k. of God;
15.50; Gal.5.21
15.24. delivered up the k. to God
Eph 5. 5. inheritance in the k. of Ch.
Col. 1.13. into the k. of his dear Son
4.11. into the k. of God, which
Th. 2.12. called you unto his k. and
2Th. 1. 5. worthy of the k. of God, for

2Ti. 4. 1. at his appearing and his k.
18. unto his heavenly k.: to wh.
Heb. 1. 8. the sceptre of thy k.
11.33. through faith subdued k-s
12.28. receiving a k. which cannot
Jas. 2. 5. heirs of the k. which he
2Pet. 1.11. the everlasting k. of our Lo.
Rev. 1. 9. in the k. and patience of
11.15. The k-s of this world are
12.10. strength, and the k. of our
16.10. his k. was full of darkness
17.12. have received no k. as yet
17. give their k. unto the beast

KINSFOLK,   -s.
sunggenēs.
Lu. 2.44. sought him among their k.
21.16. brethren and k-s, and friends

KINSMAN,   -men.
sunggenēs.
Lu. 14.12. thy k-e, nor thy rich neigh.
Jo. 18.26. being his k. whose ear Peter
Act.10.24. and had called toget. his k-e
Ro. 9. 3. for my brethren, my k-e acc.
16. 7. Androni. and Junia, my k-e
11. Salute Herodion my k. Greet
21. Jason, and Sosipater, my k-e

KISS, [noun.]
philēma.
Lu. 7.45. Thou gavest me no k.: but
22.48. the Son of man with a k.
Ro. 16.16. one another with an holy k;
1Co.16.20; 2Co.13.12
1Th. 5.26. brethren with an holy k.
1Pet. 5.14. one another with a k. of cha.

KISS, [verb,]   -ed.
kataphileō.   [14.45
Mat.26.49. master; and k-ed him; Mar.
Lu. 7.38. k-ed his feet, and anointed
45. hath not ceased to k. my feet
15.20. his neck, and k-ed; Act.20.37
phileō.   [14.44
Mat.26.48. Whomsoev. I shall k.; Mar.
Lu. 22.47. drew near unto Jesus to k.

KNEE, (See Bow,)   -s.
gonu.
Mar.15.19. bowing their k-s worshipped
Lu. 5. 8. he fell down at Jesus' k-s
Ro. 11. 4. who have not bowed the k. to
14.11. every k. shall bow to me
Eph. 3.14. I bow my k-s unto the Fath.
Phi. 2.10. name of Jesus every k. sho.
Heb.12.12. hang down, and the feeble k-s

KNEEL,   -ed, -ing.
gonupeteō.
Mat.17.14. a certain man, k-ing down
Mar. 1.40. beseech. him and k-ing down
10.17. and k-ed to him, and asked
tithēmi gonu.
Lu. 22.41. k-ed down, and prayed; Act.
Act. 7.60. And he k-ed down, and cried
21. 5. and we k-ed down on the sh.

KNIT.
deō.
Act.10.11. a great sheet k. at the four
sumbibazō.
Col. 2. 2. being k. together in love, and
19. and k. together, increaseth

KNOCK,   -ed, -eth, -ing.
krouō.   [Lu.11.9.
Mat. 7. 7. k., and it shall be opened;
8. to him that k-eth it; Lu.11.10
Lu. 12.36. that when he com. and k-eth
13.25. and to k. at the door, saying
Act.12.13. And as Peter k-ed at the do.
16. But Peter continued k-ing
Rev. 3.20. I stand at the door, and k.

KNOW,   -est, -eth, &c.
eideō.

Know.

Mat. 7.11. If ye then..k. how to
   9. 6. that ye *may* k. that the Son;
     Mar. 2.10; Lu. 5.24
20.22. said, Ye k. not; Mar. 10.38
   25. Ye·k. that the princes of the
22.16. Master, we k. that thou art
24.42. ye k. not what hour; 25.13
25.12. Verily I say unto you, I k.
26. 2. Ye k. that after two days is
   70. I k. not what thou sayest;
   72, 74. I *do* not k. the; Mar. 14.71
28. 5. for I k. that ye seek Jesus
Mar. 1.24. I k. thee who thou; Lu.4.34
   4.13. k. ye not this parable? and
10.42. Ye k. that they which are ac.
12.14. Master, we k. that thou art
   24. *because* ye k. not the scriptu.
13.33. for ye k. not when the time is
   35. ye k. not when the master of
Lu. 9. 55. Ye k. not what manner of sp.
11.13. k. *how* to give good gifts unto
13.25, 27. I k. you not whence ye are
20.21. we k. that thou sayest and tea.
22.57. saying, Woman, I k. him not
23.34. for they k. not what they do
Jo. 1.26. one among you, whom ye k.
3. 2. we k. that thou art a teacher
   11. We speak that we *do* k., and
4.22. ye k. not what : we k. what
   25. I k. that Messias cometh, wh.
   32. meat to eat that ye k. not *of*
   42. heard him ourselves, and k.
5.32. I k. that the witness which
6.42. whose father and moth. we k.
7.27. we k. this man whence he is
   28. Ye both k. me, and ye k. wh.
     sent me is true, whom ye k.
   29. I k. him : for I am from him
8.14. I k. whence I came, and wh.
   19. Ye neither k. me, nor my Fa.
   37. I k. that ye are Abraham's
   55. I k. him : and if I should
     say I k. him not, I shall be
     I k. him, and keep his saying
9.12. Where is he? He said, I k.
   20. We k. that this is our son, and
   21. means he now seeth, we k.
     hath opened his eyes, we k.
   24. we k. that this man is a sinn.
   25. I k. not : one thing I k., that
   29. We k. that God spake unto
   29, 30. k. not from whence he is
   31. we k. that God heareth not
10. 4. sheep follow him ; for they k.
   5. they k. not the voice of stran.
11.22. I k., that even now, whatsoe.
   24. I k. that he shall rise again
   49. unto them, Ye k. nothing at
12.50. I k. that his commandment
13.17. If ye k. these things, happy
   18. I k. whom I have chosen
14. 4. I go ye k., and the way ye k.
   5. Lord, we k. not whither thou
     and how can we k. the way
15.21. they k. not him that sent me
18.21. behold, they k. what I said
20. 2, 13. k. not where they have la.
21.24. we k. that his testimony is
Act. 2.22. you as ye yourselves also k.
3.16. strong, whom ye see and k.
10.37. That word, I say, ye k., whi.
12.11. Now I k. of a surety, that the
20.25. now, behold, I k. that ye all
   29. I k. this, that after my depa.
26.27. I k. that thou believest
Ro. 3.19. Now we k. that what things
6.16. k. ye not, that to whom ye
7.14. we k. that the law is spiritual

Ro. 7.18. For I k. that in me, that is
8.22. we k. that the whole creation
   26. we k. not what we should pr.
   28. we k. that all things work to.
14.14. I k., and am persuaded by the
1Co. 1.16. I k. not whether I baptized
2. 2. not *to* k. any thing among you
   12. that we *might* k. the things
3.16. k. ye not that ye are the tem.
5. 6. k. ye not that a little leaven
6. 2. *Do* ye not k. that the saints
3. k. ye not that we shall judge
9. k. ye not that the unrighteo.
15. k. ye not that your bodies are
16. k. ye not that he which is jo.
19. k. ye not that your body is
8. 1. we k. that we all have know.
4. we k. that an idol is nothing
9.13. *Do* we k. that they which
24. k. ye not that they which
11. 3. I would have you k., that
12. 2. Ye k. that ye were Gentiles
14.11. if I k. not the meaning of the
15.58. forasmuch as ye k. that your
16.15. ye k. the house of Stephanas
2Cor. 5. 1. we k. that if our earthly ho.
16. henceforth k. we no man af.
9. 2. I k. the forwardness of your
Gal. 4.13. Ye k. how through infirmity
Eph. 1.18. that ye may k. what is the
6.21. that ye also *may* k. my affai.
Phi. 1.19. For I k. that this shall turn
25. I k. that I shall abide and
2. 1. I k. both how to be abased
     and I k. how to abound
15. Now ye Philippians k. also
Col. 4. 6. that ye may k. how ye ought
1Th. 1. 5. ye k. what manner of men
2. 1. selves, brethren, k. our entr.
2. shamefully entreated, as ye k.
5. we flattering words, as ye k.
11. As ye k. how we exhorted
3. 3. yourselves k. that we are ap.
4. as it came to pass, and ye k.
4. 2. ye k. what commandments
4. every one of you should k.
5. the Gentiles *which* k. not G.
5. 2. yourselves k. perfectly that
12. *to* k. them which labour am.
2Th. 1. 8. vengeance on them *that* k.
2. 6. now ye k. what withholdeth
3. 7. yourselves k. how ye ought
1Ti. 1. 8. we k. that the law is good, if
3. 5. if a man k. not how to rule
15. that thou *mayest* k. how thou
2Ti. 1.12. for I k. whom I have believ.
Tit. 1.16. They profess that they k. G.
Heb. 8.11. for all *shall* k. me, from the
10.30. For we k. him that hath said
Jas. 4. 4. k. ye not that the friendship
1Pet. 1.18. *Forasmuch as* ye k. that ye
2Pet. 1.12. these things, though ye k. th.
1Jo. 2.20. the Holy One, and ye k. all
21. k. not truth, but beca. ye k.
29. If ye k. that he is righteous
3. 2. we k. that, when he shall ap.
5. ye k. that he was manifested
14. We k. that we have passed
15. ye k. that no murderer hath
5.13. that ye *may* k. that ye have
15. And if we k. that he hear us
     we k. that we have the petit.
18. We k. that whosoever is bo.
19. we k. that we are of God
20. we k. that the Son of God is
3John 12. ye k. that our record is true
Jude 10. those things which they k.
Rev. 2. 2, 9,13,19. I k. thy wor.; 3.1,8,15

Knew, -est

Mat.12.25. Jes. k-e their thoughts; Lu.6.8
25.26. thou k-e-est that I reap where

Mat.27.18. For he k-e that for envy they
Mar. 1.34. speak, bec. they k-e; Lu. 4.41
Lu. 19.22. Thou k-e-est that I was an au.
Jo. 1. 31, 33. I k-e him not : but that
2. 9. k-e not whence it was : but
     serv. wh. drew the water k-e
4.10. If thou k-e-est the gift of God
6. 6. he himself k-e what he would
61. *When* Jesus k-e in himself th.
64. For Jesus k-e from the begin.
11.42. I k-e that thou hearest me al.
13. 1. *when* Jesus k-e that his hour
11. For he k-e who should betray
18. 2. also, which betrayed him, k-e
20. 9. as yet they k-e not the script.
14. k-e not that it was Jes. ; 21.4
Act. 7.18. another king arose, which k-e
16. 3. they k-e all that his father was
19.32. the more part k-e not where.
2Co.12. 2. I k-e a man in Christ above
3. I k-e such a man, whether in
Gal. 4. 8. then, *when* ye k-e not God
Col. 2. 1. I would that ye k-e what gre.
Rev.19.12. that no man k-e, but he him.
Jude 5. *though* ye once k-e this, how

Knowest, -eth.

Mat. 6. 8. your Father k-eth what thin.
32. your hea. Fa. k-eth ; Lu.12.30
15.12. k-est thou that the Pharisees
24.36. day and hour k-eth; Mar.13.32
Mar. 4.27. grow up, he k-eth not how
10.19. Thou k-st the com. ; Lu.18.20
Lu. 22.34. sh.thrice deny that thou k-est
Jo. 7.15. saying, How k-eth this man
12.35. in darkness k-eth not whither
13. 7. What I do thou k-est not now
15.15. the servant k-eth not what
16.30. are we sure that thou k-est
19.10. k-est thou not that I have po.
35. he k-eth that he saith true
21.15, 16. Lord ; thou k-est that I
17. Lord, thou k-est all things
Ro. 8.27. k-eth what is the mind of the
1Co. 2.11. what man k-eth the things of
     the things of God k-eth no m.
7.16. For what k-est thou, O wife
     or how k-est thou, O man,
8. 2. any man think that he k-eth
2Co. 11.11. I love you not? God k-eth
31. evermore, k-eth that I lie not
12. 2. body, I cannot tell: God k-eth
3. I cannot tell : God k-eth
2Ti. 1.15. This thou k-est that all they
Jas. 4.17. to him that k-eth to do good
2Pet. 2. 9. The Lord k-eth how to deliver
1Jo. 2.11. k-eth not whither he goeth
Rev. 3.17. k-est not that thou art wretc
7.14. said unto him, Sir, thou k-est
12.12. *because* he k-eth that he hath

Knowing, &c.

Mat. 9. 4. Jes. k-ing their tho. ; Lu.11.17
22.29. Ye do err, not k-ing the scri.
24.43. goodman of the ho. *had* k-n ;
     Lu.12.39
Mar. 5.33. k-ing what was done in her
6.20. k-ing that he was a just man
12.15. he, k-ing their hypocrisy
Lu. 8.53. sco., k-ing that she was dead
9.33. one for Elias : not k-ing what
Jo. 8.19. *had* k-n me, ye sho. *have* k-n
13. 3. Jesus k-ing that the Father
18. 4. k-ing all things that should
19.28. Jesus k-ing that all things
21.12. k-ing that it was the Lord
Act. 2.30. k-ing, that God had sworn
5. 7. his wife, not k-ing what was
20.22. not k-ing the things that sh.
Ro. 5. 3. k-ing that tribulation worke.
6. 9. k-ing that Christ being raised
7. 7. for I *had* not k-n lust, **except**
13.11. k-ing the time, that now it is
153

²Co. 1. 7. k-*ing*, that as ye are partakers
4.14. k-*ing* that he which raised
5. 6. k-*ing* that, whilst we are at.
11. k-*ing* therefore the terror of
Gal. 2.16. k-*ing* that a man is not just
Eph. 6. 8. k-*ing* that whatsoever good
9. k-*ing* that your Master also
Phi. 1.17. k-*ing* that I am set for the
Col. 3.24. k-*ing* that of the Lord ye sh.
4. 1. k-*ing* that ye also have a M.
¹Th. 1. 4. k-*ing*, brethren beloved, your
¹Ti. 1. 9. k-*ing* this, that the law is not
²Ti. 2.23. k-*ing* that they do gender st.
3.14. k-*ing* of whom thou hast lea.
15. thou *hast* k-*n* the holy scrip.
Tit. 3.11. k-*ing* that he that is such
Phile. 21. k-*ing* that thou wilt also do
Jas. 1. 3. k-*ing* that ye shall receive
¹Pet. 3. 9. k-*ing* that ye are thereunto
5. 9. k-*ing* that the same afflictions
²Pet. 1.14. k-*ing* that shortly I must put
suneideō.
¹Co. 4. 4. For I k. nothing by myself
ginōskō.
Mat. 1.25. k-*e* her not till she had brou.
6. 3. *let* not thy left hand k. what
7.23. profess unto them, I never k-*e*
9.30. saying, See that no man k. it
10.26. hid, that *shall* not *be* k-*n*;
Lu. 8.17; 12.2
12. 7. if ye *had* k-*n* what this mea.
15. *when* Jesus k-*e* it, he withdr.
33. the tree *is* k-*n* by; Lu. 6.44
13.11. given to you to *k.* the myst.;
Lu. 8.10   [Mar.13.28
24.32. ye k. that summer is nigh;
33. k. that it is near; Mar. 13.29
39. k-*e* not until the flood came
43. k. this, that if the; Lu. 12.39
25.24. Lord, I k-*e* thee that thou art
Mar. 4.11. to k. the mystery of the king.
13. how then *will* ye k. all para.
5.43. no man *should* k. it; 7.24,9.30
6.38. And *when* they k-*e*, they say
8.17. *when* Jesus k-*e* it, he saith
12.12. they k-*e* that he had spoken
15.10. he k-*e* that the chief priests
45. *when* he k-*e* it of the centurion
Lu 1.18. Whereby *shall* I k. this? for
34. this be, seeing I k. not a man
2.43. Joseph and his mother k-*e* not
7.39. would *have* k-*n* who and what
9.11. the people, *when* they k. it
10.22. no man k-*eth* who the Son is
12.47. servant, *which* k-*e* his lord's
48. he *that* k-*e* not, and did com.
16.15. God k-*eth* your hearts: for
18.34. neither k-*e* they the things
19.15. that he *might* k. how much
42. Saying, If thou *hadst* k-*n*
44. thou k-*e-est* not the time of
21.20. then k. that the desolation
30. ye see and k. of your own sel.
31. k. ye that the kingdom of G.
24.18. *hast* not k-*n* the things which
35. and how he *was* k. of them in
Jo. 1.10. and the world k-*e* him not
49. him, Whence k-*est* thou me
2.24. because he k-*e* all men
25. for he k-*e* what was in man
3.10. of Israel, and k-*est* not these
4. 1. When therefore the Lord k-*e*
53. So the father k-*e* that it was
5. 6. and k-*e* that he had been now
42. I k. you, that ye have not
7.17. he *shall* k. of the doctrine
26. Do the rulers k. indeed that
27. no man k-*eth* whence he is
49. this people *who* k-*eth* not the
51. bef. it hear him, and k. what
8.28. then *shall* ye k. that I am he
32. ye *shall* k. the truth, and the
154

Jo. 8. 52. Now we k. that thou hast a
55. Yet ye *have* not k-*n* him; but
10.14. k. my sheep, and *am* k-*n* of
15. k-*eth* me, even so k. I the
27. I k. them, and they follow
10.38. the works : that ye *may* k.
11.57. if any man k-*e* where he were
12. 9. therefore k-*e* that he was the.
13. 7. now; but thou *shalt* k. here.
12. k. ye what I have done to you
28. no man at the table k-*e* for
35. by this *shall* all men k. that
14. 7. If ye *had* k-*n* me, ye .. *have*
k-*n* my Father also : and from
henceforth ye k. him, and
9. *hast* thou not k-*n* me, Philip
17. neither k-*eth* him : but ye k.
20. At that day ye *shall* k. that
31. that the world *may* k.; 17.23
15.18. ye k. that it hated me before
16. 3. they *have* not k-*n* the Father
19. Jesus k-*e* that they were des.
17. 3. that they *might* k. thee the
7. they *have* k-*n* that all things
8. and have k-*n* surely that I
25. *hath* not k-*n* thee : but I
have k-*n* thee, .. *have* k-*n*
19. 4. that ye *may* k. that I find no
21.17. thou k-*est* that I love thee
Act. 1. 7. not for you *to* k. the times
2.36. *let* all the house of Israel k.
9.24. their laying await *was* k-*n*
17.19. May we k. what this new do.
20. we would k. therefore what
19.15. Jesus I k., and Paul I know
19.35. that k-*eth* not how that the
34. ye yourselves k., that these
21.24. all *may* k. that those things
34. when he could not k. the cer.
22.14. that thou *shouldest* k. his
30. would *have* k-*n* the certainty
23.28. when I would *have* k-*n* the
Ro. 1.21. *when* they k-*e* God, they glo.
2.18. k-*est* his will, and approvest
3.17. of peace *have* they not k-*n*
6. 6. k-*ing* this, that our old man
7. 1. I speak to them *that* k. the
7. I *had* not k-*n* sin, but by the
10.19. I say, *Did* not Israel k.? Fir.
11.34. who *hath* k-*n* the mind of the
¹Co. 1.21. the world by wisdom k-*e* not
2. 8. world k-*e*: for *had* they k-*n*
14. neither can he k. them, beca.
16. who *hath* k-*n* the mind of the
3.20. The Lord k-*eth* the thoughts
4.19. *will* k., not the speech of them
8. 2. anything he k-*eth* nothing yet
as he ought to k.
3. love God the same *is* k-*n*
13. 9. For we k. in part, and we pr.
12. now I k. in part; but then
14. 7, 9. how *shall* it *be* k-*n* what is
²Co. 2. 4. that ye *might* k. the love wh.
9. that I *might* k. the proof of
3. 2. hearts, k-*n* and read of all
5.16. we *have* k-*n* Christ after the
21. *who* k-*e* no sin ; that we mig.
8. 9. ye k. the grace of our Lord
13. 6. I trust that ye *shall* k.
Gal. 3. 7. k. ye therefore that they wh.
4. 9. *after* that ye *have* k-*n* God, or
rather *are* k-*n* of God, how
Eph. 3.19. *to* k. the love of Christ, which
5. 5. this ye k., that no whoremon.
6.22. that ye *might* k. our affairs
Phi. 2.19. good comfort, *when* I k. your
22. ye k. the proof of him, that
3.10. That I may k. him, and the
4. 5. *Let* your moderation *be* k-*n*
Col. 4. 8. that he *might* k. your estate
¹Th. 3. .5. I sent *to* k. your faith, lest by

²Ti. 1.18. at Ephesus, thou k-*est* very
2.19. The Lord k-*eth* them that are
3. 1. This k. also, that in the last
Heb. 3.10. they *have* not k-*n* my ways
8.11. his brother, saying, k. the L.
Heb.10.34. k-*ing* in yourselves that ye
13.23. k. ye that our brother Timo.
Jas. 1. 3. k-*ing* this, that the trying of
2.20. wilt thou k., O vain man, tha.
5.20. *Let* him k., that he which co.
²Pet. 1.20. k-*ing* this first, that ; 3.3
¹Joh. 2. 3. we *do* k. that we k. him
4. He that saith, I k.
5. hereby k. we that we are in
13, 14. bec. ye *have* k-*n* him that
14. because ye *have* k-*n* the Fath.
18. we k. that it is the last time
29. ye k. that every one that doe.
3. 1. k-*eth* us not, because it k-*e*
6. not seen him, neither k-*n* him
19. hereby we k. that we are of
20. than our heart, and k-*eth* all
24. hereby we k. that he abideth
4. 2. Hereby k. ye the Spirit of G.
6. he *that* k-*eth* God heareth us
Hereby k. we the spirit of tr.
7. is born of God, and k-*eth* God
8. He that loveth not k-*eth* not
(*hath* not *known*)
13. Hereby k. we that we dwell
16. we *have* k-*n* and believed the
5. 2. By this we k. that we love
20. that we *may* k. him that is
²John 1. they *that have* k-*n* the truth
Rev. 2.17. which no man k-*eth*, saving
23. all the churches *shall* k. that
24. which *have* not k-*n* the dept.
3. 3. thou shalt not k. what hour
9. and *to* k. that I have loved
epiginōskō.
Mat.7.16, 20. Ye *shall* k. them by their
11.27. no man k-*eth* the Son, but
neither k-*eth* any man the
17.12. and they k-*e* him not, but
Mar. 5.30. Jesus, immediately k-*ing* in
6.33. and many k-*e* him, and ran
54. ship, straightway they k-*e*
Lu. 1. 4. That thou *mightest* k. the
7.37. *when* she k-*e* that Jesus sat
23. 7. And *as soon as* he k-*e* that he
24.16. holden that they sho. not k.
31. opened, and they k-*e* him
Act. 3.10. And they k-*e* that it was he
9.30. Which *when* the brethren k-*e*
12.14. And *when* she k-*e* Peter's vo.
19.34. *when* they k-*e* that he was a
22.24. that he *might* k. wherefore
29. *after* he k-*e* that he was a Ro.
25.10. wrong, as thou very well k-*est*
27.39. they k-*e* not the land : but
28. 1. then they k. that the island
Ro. 1.32. Who k-*ing* the judgment of
¹Co. 13.12. *shall* I k...as also I *am* k-*n*
²Co. 6. 9. unknown, and yet *well* k-*n*
13. 5. k. ye not your own selves
Col. 1. 6. and k-*e* the grace of God in
¹Ti. 4. 3. which believe and k. the
²Pet. 2.21. for them not *to have* k-*n* the
than, *after* they *have* k-*n* it
proginōskō.
Act.26. 5. *Which* k-*e* me from the beg.
²Pet. 3.17. *seeing* ye k. these things befo.
diaginōskō.
Act.24.22. I *will* k. the *uttermost* of yo.
epistamai.
Act.10.28. Ye k. how that it is an unla.
15. 7. Men and brethren, ye k. how
18.25. k-*ing* only the baptism of Jo.
19.15. and Paul I k.; but who are
25. ye k. that by this craft we
20.18. Ye k., from the first day
22.19. they k. that I imprisoned

Jude 10. but what they k. naturally
  agnoeō.
Act.13.27. because they k-e him not
Ro. 2. 4. not k-ing that the goodness
  6. 3. k. ye not, that so many of us
  7. 1. k. ye not, brethren, for I sp.
  isēmi.
Act.26. 4. manner of life. k. all the J.
Heb.12.17.For ye k. how that afterward
  gnōstos.
Jo. 18.15. that disciple was k-n unto
  16. which was k-n unto the high
Act. 1.19. it was k-n unto all the dwel.
  2.14. be this k-n unto you, and
  4.10. Be it k-n unto you all, and
  9.42. it was k-n throughout all
  13.38. Be it k-n unto you; 28.28
  15.18. k-n unto G. are all his works
  19.17. this was k-n to all the Jews
  28.22. we k. that everywhere it is
Ro. 1.19. that which may be k-n of G.
  gnōrizō.
Lu. 2.15. which the Lo. hath made k-n
Jo. 15.15. I have made k-n unto you
Act. 2.28. Thou hast made k-n to me
Ro. 9.22. to make his power k-n, endu.
  23. that he might make k-n the
  16.26. made k-n to all nations for
Eph. 1. 9. Having made k-n unto us
  3. 3. he made k-n unto me the
  5. was not made k-n unto the
  10. might be k-n by the church
  6.19. to make k-n the mystery of
  21. shall make k-n to; Col.4.9
Phi. 4. 6. let your requests be made k-n
Col. 1.27. To whom G. would make k-n
²Pet.1.16. when we made k-n unto you
  phaneros. [3.12
Mat.12.16. sho. not make him k-n; Mar.
Act. 7.13. Joseph's kind. was made k-n
  diagnōrizō.
Lu. 2.17. they made k-n abroad the
  anagnōrizō.
Act. 7.13. Joseph was made k-n to his
  plērophoreō.
²Ti. 4.17. the preach. might be fully k-n
  (See Fully, Heart.)

KNOWLEDGE, (See Endued.)
  gnōsis.
Lu. 1.77. To give k. of salvation unto
  11.52. have taken away the key of k.
Ro. 2.20. which hast the form of k.
  11.33. of the wisdom and k. of God
  15.14. filled with all k., able also to
¹Co. 1. 5. all utterance, and in all k.
  8. 1. we all have k. k. puffeth
  7. not in every man that k.
  10. see thee which hast k. sit at
  11. through thy k, shall the we.
  12. 8. to another the word of k. by
  13. 2. all mysteries, and all k.
  [8. whether there be k., it shall
  14. 6. either by revelation, or by k.
¹Co. 2.14. manifest the savour of his k.
  4. 6. the light of the k. of the glo.
  6. 6. by k., by longsuffering, and k.
  8. 7. faith, and utterance, and k.
  10. 5. against the k. of God, and
  11. 6. rude in speech, yet not in k.
Eph. 3.19. love of Ch., which passeth k.
Phi. 3. 8. excellency of the k. of Christ
Col. 2. 3. treasures of wisdom and k.
¹Pet.3. 7. dwell with them accord. to k.
²Pet.1. 5. faith, virtue; and to vir. k.
  6. And to k. temperance; and
  3.18. in the k. of our Lord and Sa.
  epignōsis.
Ro. 1.28. to retain God in their k.
  3.20. by the law is the k. of sin
  10. 2. but not according to k.
Eph.1.17. revelation in the k. of him

Eph. 4.13. and of the k. of the Son of
Phi. 1. 9. in k. and in all judgment
Col. 1. 9. with the k. of his will in all
  10. increasing in the k. of God
  3.10. renewed in k. after the image
¹Ti. 2. 4. the k. of the truth; ²Th.3.7
Heb.10.26.received the k. of the truth
²Pet. 1. 2. through the k. of God, and
  3. through the k. of him that
  8. in the k. of our Lord Jesus
  2.20. the k. of the Lord and Savi.
  agnōsia.
¹Co. 15.34. some have not the k. of God
  sunesis.
Eph. 3. 4. my k. in the mystery of Ch.
  epiginōskō.
Act. 4.13. they took k. of them, that
  24. 8. thyself mayest take k. of all
  ginōskō.
Act. 17.13. Jews of Thessalonica had k.
  eideō.
Act.24.22. having more perfect k. of

LABOUR, [noun,]   -s.
  kopos.
Jo. 4.38. ye are entered into their l-s
¹Co. 3. 8. according to his own l.
  15.58. that your l. is not in vain
²Co. 6. 5. in l-s, in watchings
  10.15. of other men's l-s
  11.23. in l-s more abundant
¹Th. 1. 3. your work of faith, and l. of
  2. 9. our l. and travail
  3. 5. and our l. be in vain
²Th. 3. 8. but wrought with l. and tra.
Heb. 6.10. your work and l. of love
Rev. 2. 2. I know thy works, and thy l.
  14.13. they may rest from their l-s
  ergon.
Phi. 1.22. this is the fruit of my l.
  (See Bestow, Companion.)

LABOUR, [verb,] -ed, -eth, -ing.
  kopiaō.
Mat. 11.28.Come unto me, all ye that l.
Jo. 4,38. other men l-ed, and ye are
Act.20.35. how that so l-ing ye ought to
Ro. 16.12. and Tryphosa, who l. in the
  which l-ed much in the Lord
¹Co. 4.12. And l., working with our
  15.10. I l-ed more abundantly than
  16.16. helpeth with us, and l-eth
Eph. 4.28. but rather let him l., working
Phi. 2.16. in vain, neither l-ed in vain
Col. 1.29. Whereunto I also l., striving
¹Th. 5.12. to know them which l. amo.
¹Ti. 4.10. we both l. and suffer reproa.
  5.17. they who l. in the word and
²Ti. 2. 6. husbandman that l-eth must
Rev. 2. 3. for my name's sake hast l-ed
  ergazomai.
Jo. 6.27. l. not for the meat which
¹Th. 2. 9. l-ing night and day, because
  philotimeomai.
²Co. 5. 9. Wherefore we l., that wheth.
  sunathleō.
Phi. 4. 3. which l-ed with me in the
  spoudazō.
Heb. 4.11. Let us l. therefore to enter
  (See Fervently.)

LABOURER,   -s.
  ergatēs.
Mat. 9.37. but the l-s are few; Lu. 10.2
  38. will send forth l-s; Lu.10.2
  20. 1. to hire l-s into his vineyard
  2. agreed with the l-s for a pen.
  8. Call the l-s, and give them
Lu. 10. 7. the l. is worthy of; ¹Ti. 5.18
Jas. 5. 4. the hire of the l-s which have
  sunergos.
¹Co. 3. 9. we are l-s together with God

LACK, [noun.]
  elattoneō.
²Co. 8.15. had gathered little had no l.
  husterēma.
Phi.2.30. supply your l. of service tow.
  chreia.
¹Th.4.12. ye may have l. of nothing
LACK, [verb,]   -ed, -est, -eth.
  hustereō.
Mat. 19.20.from my youth up: what l.
Mar. 10.21.One thing thou l-est: go thy
Lu. 22.35. l-ed ye any thing? And they
¹Co.12.24. hon. to that part which l-ed
  leipō.
Lu. 18.22. yet l-est thou one thing: sell
  (one thing is wanting to thee.)
Jas. 1. 5. If any of you l. wisdom, let
  mē echō.
Lu. 8. 6. because it l-ed moisture
  endeēs.
Act. 4.34. any among them that l-ed
  mē pareimi.
²Pet.1. 9. But he that l-eth these things
  (See Opportunity.)

LACKING, [adjective.]
  husterēma.
¹Co. 16.17. for that which was l. on your
²Co.11. 9. for that which was l. to me
¹Th. 3.10. that which is l. in your faith

LAD.
  paidarion.
Jo. 6. 9. There is a l. here, which hath
LADE,   -ed, -en.
  phortizō.
Mat.11.28.that lab., and are heavy l-en
Lu. 11.46. for ye l. men with burdens
  epitithēmi.
Act.28.10. they l-ed us with such things
  sōreuō.
²Ti. 3. 6. captive silly women l-en with
LADING, [noun.]
  phortos.
Act.27.10. not only of the l. and ship
LADY.
  kuria.
²John 1. elder unto the elect l. and
  5. I beseech thee, l., not as tho.
LAID. (See Lay.)
LAKE.
  limnē.
Lu. 5. 1. he stood by the l. of Gennes.
  2. two ships standing by the l.
  8.22. unto the other side of the l.
  23. a storm of wind on the l.
  33. steep place into the l., and
Rev.19.20. cast alive into a l. of fire
  20.10, 14,15. was cast into the l. of
  21. 8. their part in the l. which bu.
LAMA, [a Hebrew word,] Why
  lama or lamma.
Mat.27.46.Eli, Eli, l. sabac.; Mar. 15.34
LAMB,   -s.
  arnion.
Jo. 21.15. saith unto him, Feed my l-s
Rev. 5. 6. midst of the elders stood a l.
  8. elders fell down before the l.
  12. Worthy is the l. that was sl.
  13. throne, and unto the l.; 7.10
  6. 1. when the l. opened one of
  16. and from the wrath of the l.
  7. 9. before the l. clothed with
  14. white in the blood of the l.
  17. For the l. which is in the
  12.11. by the blood of the l., and
  13. 8. book of life of the l. slain
  11. he had two horns like a l.

Rev.14. 1. lo, a **l**. stood on the mount
4. are they which follow the **l**. unto God and to the **l**.
10. in the presence of the **l**.
15. 3. of God, and the song of the **l**
17.14. with the **l**., and the **l**. shall
19. 7. the marriage of the **l**. is come
9. the marriage supper of the **l**.
21. 9. shew thee the bride, the **l**.'s
14. the twelve apostles of the **l**.
22. God Almighty, and the **l**.
23. the **l**. is the light thereof
27. written in the **l**.'s book of li.
22. 1, 3. throne of God and of the **l**.

amnos.

Jo. 1.29, 36. Behold the **l**. of God
Act. 8.32. like a **l**. dumb before his
1Pet.1.19. blood of Ch., as of a **l**. witho.

arēn.

Lu. 10. 3. send you forth as 1-s among

LAME.

chōlos.   [7.22

Mat.11. 5. the **l**.walk,the lepers are; Lu.
15.30. **l**., blind, dumb, maimed
31. the **l**, to walk, and the blind
21.14. the blind and the **l**. came to
Lu. 14.13. the maimed, the **l**., the blind
Act. 3. 2. man **l**. from his mother's
11. as the **l**. man which was hea.
8. 7. and that were **l**., were healed
Heb.12.13.lest that which is **l**. be

LAMENT,   -ed

koptō.

Mat.11.17. you, and ye have not 1-ed
Rev.18. 9. bewail her, and **l**. for her

thrēneō.

Lu. 23.27. also bewailed and 1-ed him
Jo. 16.20. ye shall weep and **l**., but

LAMENTATION.

thrēnos.

Mat. 2.18. was there a voice heard, **l**.

kopetos.

Act.8.2. and made great **l**. over him

LAMP,   -s.

lampas.

Mat.25.1. which took their 1-s, and went
3. that were foolish took their 1-s
4. in their vessels with their 1-s
7. arose, and trimmed their 1-s
8. oil, for our 1-s are gone out
Rev.4. 5. and there were seven 1-s of fire
8.10. burning as it were a **l**.

LAND, [noun,]   -s.

gē.

Mat. 2. 6. thou Bethl., in the **l**. of Juda
20, 21. into the **l**. of Israel
4.15. **l**. of Zabulon, and the **l**. of N.
9.26. went abroad into all that **l**.
10.15. tolera. for the **l**. of Sod.;21.24
14.34. came into the **l**. of Gennes.;
Mar.6.53
27.45. was darkness over all the **l**.
Mar. 4. 1. multitu. was by sea on the **l**.
6.47. sea, and he alone on the **l**.
15.33. was dark. over the whole **l**.
Lu. 4.25. famine was through. all the **l**.
5. 3. thrust out a little from the **l**.
11. had brought their ships to **l**.
8.27. when he went forth to **l**., th.
14.35. It is neither fit for the **l**., nor
21.23. shall be great distress in the **l**.
Jo. 3.22. his disciples into the **l**. of J.
6.21. the ship was at the **l**. whither
21. 8. they were not far from **l**., but
9. then as they were come to **l**.
11. drew the net to **l**. full of great
Act. 7. 3. come into the **l**. which I shall
4. Then came he out of the **l**.
he removed him into this **l**.

156

Act. 7. 6. should sojourn in a strange **l**.
11. a dearth over all the **l**.of;13.17
29. was a stranger in the **l**. of Ma.
36. signs in the **l**. of Egypt, and
7.40. out of the **l**. of Egypt;
Heb.8.9; Jude 5
13.19. seven nations in the **l**. of C. divided their **l**. to them by
27.39. was day, they knew not the **l**.
43. first into the sea, and get to **l**.
44. that they escaped all safe to **l**.
Heb.11. 9. he sojourned in the **l**. of pro.

chōra.

Mar. 1. 5. unto him all the **l**. of Jud.
Lu. 15.14. a mighty famine in that **l**.
Act. 10.39. he did both in the **l**. of the

chōrion.

Act.4.34. as were possessors of 1-s or
5. 3. part of the price of the **l**.
8. ye sold the **l**. for so much

agros.   [Mar.10.29

Mat.19.29.wife, or children, or 1-s;
Mar.10.30.mothers, and children, and 1-s
Act. 4.37.Having **l**., sold it, and broug.

xēros.

Mat. 23.15.ye compass sea and **l**. to
Heb.11.29.thro. the Red sea, as by dry **l**.

exeimi epi ho gē.

Act.27.43. into the sea, and get to **l**.

LANDED, [verb,]   -ing.

katagō.

Act. 21. 3. into Syria, and **l**. at Tyre
28.12. And 1-ing at Syracuse, we

katerchomai.

Act.18.22. when he had **l**. at Cesarea

LANES.

rumē.

Lu. 14.21. into the streets and **l**. of the

LANGUAGE.

dialektos.

Act. 2. 6. them speak in his own **l**.

LANTERNS.

phanos.

Jo. 18. 3. thither with **l**. and torches

LARGE. (See As.)

hikanos.

Mat.28.12. gave **l**. money unto the

megas.   [22.12

Mar.14.15. you a **l**. upper room; Lu.

pēlikos.

Gal. 6.11. see how **l**. a letter I have

LASCIVIOUSNESS.

aselgeia.

Mar. 7.22. deceit, **l**., an evil eye, blas.
2Co.12.21. **l**. which they have committ.
Gal. 5.19. fornication, uncleanness, **l**.
Eph. 4.19. themselves over unto **l**., to
1Pet. 4. 3. when we walked in **l**., lusts
Jude 4. grace of our God into **l**.

LAST.

eschatos.

Mat.12.45. the **l**. state of that man is
19.30. first shall be **l**. and the **l**.;
20.16; Mar.10.31; Lu.13.30
20. 8. beginning from the **l**. unto
12. These **l**. have wrought but
14. I will give unto this **l**., even
27.64. the **l**. error shall be worse
Mar. 9.35. the same shall be **l**. of all
12. 6. he sent him also **l**. unto them
22. 1. of all the woman died also
Lu. 11.26. the **l**. state of that man is
12.59. thou hast paid the very **l**.
Jo. 6.39. raise it up again at the **l**. day
40, 44, 54. raise him up at the **l**.
7.37. In the **l**. day, that great day
8. 9. at the eldest, even unto the **l**.
11.24. in the resurrection at the **l**.

Jo. 12.48. shall judge him in the **l**. day
Act. 2.17. shall come to pass in the **l**.
1Co. 4. 9. forth us the apostles **l**., as it
15. 8. And **l**. of all he was seen of
26. The **l**. enemy that shall be
45. the **l**. Adam was made a
52. at the **l**. trump : for the tru.
2Ti. 3. 1. in the **l**. days perilous times
Heb. 1. 2. Hath in these **l**. days spoken
Jas. 5. 3. treasure together for the **l**.
1Pet. 1. 5. ready to be revealed in the **l**.
20. was manifest in these **l**. times
2 Pet.3. 3. shall come in the **l**. days sco.
1Jo. 2.18. children, it is the **l**. time
we know that it is the **l**. time
Jude 18. should be mockers in the **l**.
Rev. 1.11. Om.,the first and the **l**.; 22.13
17. I am the first and the **l**.
2. 8. saith the first and the **l**.
19. the **l**. to be more than the first
15. 1. having the seven **l**. plagues
21. 9. vials full of the seven **l**. pla.

husteron.

Mat.21.37. **l**. of all he sent unto them
22.27. **l**. of all the woman; Lu.20.32
26.60. At the **l**. came two false

pote.

Phi. 4.10. now at the **l**. your care of

LATCHET.

himas.   [Lu.3.16; Jo.1.27

Mar. 1. 7. the **l**. of whose shoes I am ;

LATE.

nun.

Jo. 11. 8 Jews of **l**. sought to stone

LATELY.

prosphatōs.

Act.18. 2. **l**. come from Italy, with his

LATIN.

Rōmaisti.

Jo. 19.20. Hebrew, and Greek, and **l**.

LATTER. (See End.)

opsimos.

Jas. 5. 7. receive the early and **l**. rain

husteros.

1Ti. 4. 1. in the **l**. times some shall

LAUD.

epaineō.

Ro. 15.11. and **l**. him, all ye people

LAUGH,   -ed.

gelaō.

Lu. 6.21. weep now: for ye shall **l**.
25. Woe unto you that **l**. now

katagelaō.

Mat. 9.24. they 1-ed him to scorn ;
Mar.5.40; Lu.8.53

LAUGHTER.

gelōs.

Jas. 4. 9. let your **l**. be turned to mou.

LAUNCH,   -ed.

anagō.

Lu. 8.22. the lake. And they 1-ed forth
Act.21. 1. got. from them and had 1-ed
27. 2. we 1-ed, meaning to sail by
4. when we had 1-ed from then.

epanagō.

Lu. 5. 4. **l**. out into the deep, and let

LAW.

nomos.

Mat. 5.17. I am come to destroy the **l**.
18. in no wise pass from the **l**.
7.12. for this is the **l**. and the pro.
11.13. the **l**. pro. until Jo.; Lu.16.16
12. 5. have ye not read in the **l**., ho.
22.36. great commandment in the **l**.
40. hang all the **l**. and the pro.
23.23. weightier matters of the **l**.
Lu. 2.22. according to the **l**. of Moses

Lu. 2.23, 24. in the l. of the Lord
27. him, after the cus. of the l
39. according to the l. of the L.
10.26. What is written in the l.
16.17. than one tittle of the l. to
24.44. written in the l. of Moses
Jo. 1.17. For the l. was given by Mos.
45. of whom Moses in the l., and
7.19. Did not Moses give you the l.
none of you keepeth the l.
23. that the l. of Moses should
49. peo. who knoweth not the l.
51. Doth our l. judge any man
8. 5. Now Moses in the l. comma.
17. is also writ. in your l.; 10.34
12.34. We have heard out of the l.
15.25. that is written in their l.
18.31. judge him accord. to your l.
19. 7. We have a l., and by our l.
Act. 6.13. this holy place, and the l.
7.53. Who have received the l. by
13.15. after the reading of the l.
39. could not be justifi. by the l.
15. 5. them to keep the l. of Mos.
24. be circum., and keep the l.
18.13. to wor. G. contrary to the l.
15. and of your l., look ye to it
21.20. are all zealous of the l.
24. orderly, and keepest the l.
28. against the people, and the l.
22. 3. the perfect manner of the l.
12. a devout man accord. to the l.
23. 3. to judge me after the l., and
29. accused of quest. of their l.
24. 6. have judged accord. to our l.
14. in the l. and in the prophets
25. 8. Neither against the l. of the
28.23. both out of the l. of Moses
Ro. 2.12. the l.,shall be judged by the l.
13. For not the hearers of the l.
God, but the doers of the l.
74. which have not the l., do by
the things contained in the l.
the l., are a l. unto themsel.
15. the work of the l. written in
17. and resteth in the l., and
18. being instructed out of the l.
20. and of the truth in the l.
23. and the l., through break. the l.
25. if thou keep the l.: but if
thou be a breaker of the l.,
26. keep the righteous. of the l.,
27. if it fulfil the l., judge thee
circum. dost transgress the l.
3.19. soever the l. saith, it saith to
them who are under the l.
20. Theref. by the deeds of the l.
for by the l. is the knowledge
21. of God without the l. is man.
being witnessed by the l. and
27. By what l.? of works? Nay
but by the l. of faith
28. without the deeds of the l.
31. make void the l. through
yea, we establish the l.
4.13. or to his seed, through the l.
14. For if they which are of the l.
15. Because the l. worketh wrath
where no l. is, there is no
16. which is of the l., but to that
5.13. until the l. sin was in the
imputed when there is no l.
20. Moreover the l. entered, that
6.14, 15. are not under the l., but
7. 1. to them that know the l.
how that the l. hath domin.
2. is bound by the l. to her hus.
is loosed from the l. of her
3. she is free from that l.; so
4. become dead to the l. by the
5. which were by the l., did
6. we are delivered from the l.

Ro. 7. 7. Is the l. sin? God forbid
not known sin, but by the l.
except the l. had said, Thou
8. For without the l. sin was
9. I was alive without the l.
12. Wherefore the l. is holy
14. we know that the l. is spirit.
16. unto the l. that it is; 1Ti.1.8
21. I find then a l., that, when I
22. I delight in the l. of God
23. But I see another l. in my
warring against the l. of my
into captivity to the l. of sin
25. with the mind I..serve the l.
but with the flesh the l. of
8. 2. For the l. of the Spirit of life
free from the l. of sin and
3. For what the l. could not do
4. the righteousness of the l.
7. it is not subject to the l. of
9.31. after the l. of righteousness
attained to the l. of righteo.
32. by the works of the l.: for
10. 4. Christ is the end of the l.
5. righteous. which is of the l.
13. 8. another hath fulfilled the l.
10. love is the fulfilling of the l.
1Co. 7.39. The wife is bound by the l.
9. 8. saith not the l. the same also
9. it is written in the l. of Mos.
20. under the l., as under the l.
14.21. In the l. it is written, With
34. obedience, as also saith the l.
15.56. the strength of sin is the l.
Gal. 2.16. justify. by the works of the l.
and not by the works of the l.
the works of the l. shall no
19. thr. the l., am dead to the l.
21. righteousness come by the l.
3. 2. Spirit by the works of the l.
5. by the works of the l., or
10. as are of the works of the l.
in the book of the l. to do
11. no man is justified by the l.
12. And the l. is not of faith
13. from the curse of the l., bei.
17. the l., which was four hund.
18. the inheritance be of the l.
19. Wherefore then serveth the l.
21. Is the l. then against the
for if there had been a l. giv.
should have been by the l.
23. we were kept under the l.
24. Wherefore the l. was our
4. 4. woman, made under the l.
5. them that were under the l.
21. the l., do ye not hear the l.
5. 3. is a debtor to do the whole l.
4. of you are justified by the l.
14. For all the l. is fulfilled in
18. spirit, ye are not under the l.
23. against such there is no l.
6. 2. and so fulfil the l. of Christ
13. are circumcised keep the l.
Eph. 2.15. enmity, even the l. of com.
Phi. 3. 5. as touching the l., a Pharisee
6. which is in the l., blameless
9. righteous., which is of the l.
1Ti. 1. 9. that the l. is not made for a
Heb. 7. 5. of the people accord. to the l.
12. neces. a change also of the l.
16. after the l. of a carnal com.
19. the l. made nothing perfect
28. l. maketh men high priests
which was since the l. mak.
8. 4. offer gifts according to the l.
10. I will put my l-s into their
9.19. people according to the l.
22. things are by the l. purged
10. 1. For the l. having a shadow
8. which are offered by the l.
16. I will put my l-s into their

Heb.10.28.He that despised Moses' l.
Jas. 1.25. into the perfect l. of liberty
2. 8. If ye fulfil the royal l.
9. and are convinced of the l.
10. whoso. shall keep the whole l.
11. beco. a transgressor of the l.
12. be judged by the l. of liberty
4.11. speaketh evil of the l., and
judgeth the l.: but if thou
judge the l., thou art not a
doer of the l., but a judge
nomikos.
Tit. 3. 9. and strivings about the l.
paranomeō.
Act.23. 3. to be smit. contrary to the l.
nomotheteō.
Heb. 7.11. the people received the l.
krinō.
Mat. 5.40. man will sue thee at the l.
1Co. 6. 1. go to l. before the unjust
6. brother goeth to l. with bro.
echō krima.
1Co. 6. 7. because ye go to l. one with
anomos.
1Co. 9.21. are without l., as without l.
being not without l. to God
gain them that are without l
anomōs.
Ro. 2.12. withoutl.sh...perish witho.l.
agoraios.
Act.19.38. against any man, the l. is
(See Daughter, Doctor, Giving, Mother,
Teacher, Transgress, Transgression.)

LAWFUL.
exeimi, [impersonal.]
Mat. 12. 2. that which is not l.;
Mar.2.24; Lu. 6.2
4. was not l. for him to eat:
Mar.2.26.; Lu.6.4 [Lu.14.3
10. Is it l.to heal on the sabbath;
12. Wherefore it is l. to do well
14. 4. It is not l. for thee; Mar.6.18
19. 3. Is it l. for a man to; Mar.10.2
20.15. Is it not l. for me to do
22.17. Is it l. to give tribute;
Mar.12.14; Lu.20.22
27. 6. It is not l. for to put them
Mar. 3. 4. Is it l. to do good on; Lu.6.9
Jo. 5.10. it is not l. for thee to carry
18.31. It is not l. for us to put any
Act.16.21. which are not l. for us to re.
22.25. Is it l. for you to scourge
1Co. 6.12. All things are l. unto me
all things are l. for me; 10.23
2Co.12. 4. which it is not l. for a man
ennomos.
Act.19.39. determined in a l. assembly
LAWFULLY.
nomimōs.
1Ti. 1. 8. good, if a man use it l.
2Ti. 2. 5. crowned, except he strive l.
LAWGIVER.
nomothetēs.
Jas. 4.12. There is one l., who is able
LAWLESS.
anomos.
1Ti. 1. 9. for the l. and disobedient
LAWYER, -s.
nomikos.
Mat.22.35. one of them, which was a l.
Lu. 7.30. the Pharisees and l-s rejected
10.25. a certain l. stood up, and
11.45. Then answered one of the l-s
46, 52. Woe unto you also, ye l-s
14. 3. spake unto the l-s and Pha.
Tit. 3.13. Bring Zenas the l. and Apol.
LAY, -ing, Laid, Lain.
tithēmi.
Mat.27.60. And l-d it in his own new to.

Mar. 6.29. his corpse, and l-d it in a to.
  56. they l-d the sick in the streets
15.47. Joses beheld where he was l-d
16. 6. the place where they l-d him
.u. 1.66. l-d them *up* in their hearts
  5.18. in, and *to* l. him before him
  6.48. and l-d the foundation on a
14.29. *after he hath* l-d the founda.
19.21. up that thou l-*dst* not *down*
  22. taking up that I l-*d* not *down*
23.53. and l-d it in a sepulchre
  55. sepu.,..how his body *was* l-d
Jo. 10.15. I l. *down* my life for the sh.
  17. because I l. *down* my life
  18. but I l. it *down* of myself
  power for l. it *down*, and I
11.34. Where *have* ye l-d him? Th.
13. 4. and l-d *aside* his garments
  37. I *will* l. *down* my life for thy
  38. *Wilt* thou l. *down* thy life
15.13. that a man l. *down* his life
19.41. whe. *was* never man yet l-d
  42. There l-d they Jesus therefo.
20. 2, 13. not where they *have* l-d
  15. tell me where thou *hast* l-d
Act. 3. 2. whom they l-d daily at the
  4.35. And l-d them money at the
  37. l-*d* it at the apostles' feet; 5.2
  5.15. and l-d them on beds and
  7.16. over into Sychem, and l-d in
  9.37. they l-d her in an upper ch.,
13.29. and l-d him in a sepulchre
Ro. 9.33. I l. in Sion a stumblingstone
1Co. 3.10. I *have* l-d the foundation
  11. oth. foundation can no man l.
  16. 2. *let* every one of you l. by him
1Pet. 2. 6. I l. in Sion a chief corner st.
1Jo. 3.16. because he l-d *down* his life
  and we ought *to* l. *down*
epitithēmi.   [Mar.5.23
Mat. 9.18. and l. thy hand *upon* her;
19.15. he l-d his hands *on* them
23. 4. and l. them *on* men's shoul.
Mar. 6. 5. l-d his hands *upon* a few sick
16.18. they *shall* l. hands *on* the
Lu. 4.40. l-d hands *on* every one of
13.13. And he l-d his hands *on* her
15. 5. he l-*eth* it *on* his shoulders
23.26. *on* him they l. the cross
Act. 6. 6. they l-d their hands *on* them;
  8.17,13.3
8.19. *on* whomsoever I l. hands
15.28. *to* l. *upon* you no greater
16.23. they *had* l-d many str. *upon*
19. 6. Paul *had* l-d his hands *upon*
28. 3. and l-d them *on* the fire
  8. and l-d his hands *on* him
1Ti. 5.22. l. hands suddenly *on* no man
Rev. 1.17. he l-d his right hand *upon*
apotithēmi.
Act. 7.58. the witnesses l-d *down* their
Heb.12. 1. let us l. *aside* every weight
Jas. 1.21. Wherefore l. *apart* all filthi.
1Pet. 2. 1. Wherefore l-*ing aside* all
katatithēmi.
Mar.15.46. and l-d him in a sepulchre
prostithēmi.
Act.13.36. *was* l-d *unto* his fathers, and
hupotithēmi.
Ro. 16. 4. *have* for my life l-d *down*
keimai.   [Lu.3.9
Mat. 3.10. the axe *is* l-d *unto* the root;
Lu. 12.19. thou hast much goods l-d *up*
23.53. wherein nev. man bef. was l-d
24.12. the linen clothes l-d by them.
Jo. 11.41. place where the dead *was* l-d
epikeimai.
Jo. 21. 9. and fish l-d *thereon*, and bre.
1Co. 9.16. for necessity *is* l-d *upon* me
ballō.
Mat. 8.14. his wife's mother l-d, and
158

Mar. 7.30. her daughter l-d *upon* the
Lu. 16.20. which *was* l-d at his gate
epiballō.
Mat.26.50. Then came they, and l-d ha.
Mar.14.46. they l-d their hands *on* him
Lu. 20.19. *to* l. hands *on* him; and they
21.12. they *shall* l. their hands *on*
Jo. 7.30, 44. no man l-d hands *on*
Act. 4. 3. they l-d hands *on* them, and
  5.18. And l-d their hands *on* the
21.27. people, and l-d hands *on*
epiboulē.
Act.20. 3. when the Jews l-d *wait* for
23.30. how that the Jews l-d *wait*
kataballō.
Heb. 6. 1. not l-*ing* again the founda.
thēsaurizō.
Mat. 6.19. l. not *up* for yourselves trea.
  20. But l. *up* for yourselves trea.
Lu. 12.21. he *that* l-*eth up treasure* for
2Co. 12.14. ought not to l. *up* for the
apothēsaurizō.
1Ti. 6.19. l-*ing up in store* for themse.
klinō.   [9.58
Mat. 8.20. not where to l. his head ;Lu.
anaklinō.
Lu. 2. 7. l-d him in a manger; becau.
aphiēmi.
Mar. 7. 8. l-*ing aside* the commandme.
pherō.
Act.25. 7. *and* l-d many and grievous
logizomai.
2Ti. 4.16. may not *be* l-d *to* their char.
poieō enedra.
Act.25. 3. l-*ing wait* in the way to kill
enedreuō.
Lu. 11.54. l-*ing wait for* him, and seek.
apokeima.
Lu. 19.20. which I have kept l-d *up* in
Col. 1. 5. hope *which is* l-d *up* for you
2Ti. 4. 8. there *is* l-d *up* for me a crown
(See *Charge, Die, Foundation, Ground,*
Hand, Hold.)

LAYING, [noun.]
epithesis.
Act.8.18. through l. *on* of the apostles'
1Ti. 4.14. with the l. *on* of the hands
Heb.6. 2. and of l. *on* of hands, and of
epiboulē,
Act.9.24. their l. *await* was known of

LEAD,   -eth, Led, -est.
agō.
Mar.13.11.But when they *shall* l. you
Lu. 4. 1. *was* l-d by the Spirit into the
  29. l-d him unto the brow of the
22.54. took they him, and l-d
23. 1. arose, and l-d him unto Pilate
  32. malefactors, l-d with him to
Jo. 18.28. Then l-d they Jesus from Cai.
Act. 8.32. He *was* l-d as a sheep to the
Ro. 2. 4. God l-*eth* thee to repentance
  8.14. many as *are* l-d by the Sp.of G.
1Co. 12. 2. idols, even as ye *were* l-d.
Gal. 5.18. if ye *be* l-d of the Spirit, ye
2Ti. 3. 6. sins, l-d *away* with divers
apagō.
Mat. 7.13. the way, *that* l-*eth* to destr.
  14. nar. is the way, *which* l-*eth*
26.57. laid hold on J. l-d him *away*
27. 2. bound him, they l-d him aw.
  31. l-d him *away* to crucify him
Mar.14.44. take him, and l. him *away*
  53. they l-d Jesus *away* to the
15.16. soldiers l-d him *away* into
Lu. 13.15. stall, and l. him *away* to
Jo. 23.26. as they l-d him *away*, they
18.13. l-d him *away* to Annas first
19.16. took Jesus, and l-d him aw.

exagō.
Mar. 8.23. and l-d him *out* of the town
15.20. l-d him *out* to crucify him
Lu. 24.50. he l-d them *out* as far as to B.
Jo. 10. 3. by name, and l-*eth* them *out*
Act.21.38. *which before.* .l-*est out* into
Heb. 8. 9. *to* l. them *out* of the land of
anagō.
Mat.4. 1. *was* Jesus l-d *up* of the spirit
Lu.22.66. l-d him into their council, say.
eisagō.
Act.21.37. as Paul *was to be* l-d into the
periagō.
1Co. 9. 5. power *to* l. *about* a sister, a
diagō.
1Ti. 2. 2. that we *may* l. a quiet and
sunagō.
Rev.13.10. He that l-*eth into* captivity
eispherō.
Mat.6.13. l. us not *into* tempta.;Lu.11.4
anapherō.
Mar.9.2. and l-*eth* them *up* into an high
pherō.
Act.12.10. iron gate *that* l-*eth* unto the
hodēgeō.
Mat.15.14. the blind l. the blind;Lu.6.39
Rev. 7.17. and *shall* l. them unto living
sunapagō.
2Pet.3.17. *being* l-d *away with* the
cheiragōgeō.
Act. 9. 8. they l-d him *by the hand, and*
22.11. *being* l-d *by the hand* of them
cheiragōgos.
Act.13.11.seek some to l. him *by the hand*
  (See *Captive.*)

LEADERS,
hodēgos.
Mat.15.14. they be blind l. of the blind.

LEAF,   -ves.
phullon.
Mat.21.19.nothing thereon, but l-*ves*
24.32.tender, and putteth forth l-*ves*;
  Mar.13.28
Mar.11.13.a fig tree afar off having l-*ves*
  he found nothing but l-*ves*
Rev.22. 2.and the l-*ves* of the tree were

LEANED,   -ing.
anakeimai.
Jo.13.23.there was l-*ing* on Jesus' bosom
anapiptō.
Jo.21.20. which also l. on his breast

LEAP,   -ed, -ing.
skirtaō.
Lu.1.41, 44. the babe l. in her womb
hallomai.
Act. 3. 8. temple, walking, and l-*ing*
14.10. on thy feet. And he l. and
exallomai.
Act.3.8. he l-*ing up* stood and walked
ephallomai.
Act.19.16. l. on them..*and* prevailed

LEARN,   -ed, -ing.
manthanō.
Mat. 9.13. But go ye and l. what that
11.29. my yoke upon you, and l. of
24.32. Now l. a para. of the figtree;
  Mar.13.28
Jo. 6.45. hath heard, and *hath* l-*ed* of
7.15. man letters, *having* never l-*ed*
Ro. 16.17. doctrine which ye *have* l-*ed*
1Co. 4. 6. that ye *might* l. in us not to
14.31. that all *may* l., and all *may*
  35. And if they will l. any thing
Gal. 3. 2. This only would I l. of you
Eph. 4.20. But ye *have* not so l-*ed* Christ
Phi. 4. 9. which ye *have* both l-*ed*, and
  11. for I *have* l-*ed*, in whatsoever
Col. 1. 7. As ye also l-*ed* of Epaphras

¹Ti. 2.11. *Let* the woman **l**. in silence
   5. 4. *let* them **l**. first to shew piety
   13. And withal they **l**. to be idle
²Ti. 3. 7. Ever **l**-*ing*, and never able to
   14. things which thou *hast* **l**-*ed*
   know. of whom thou *hast* **l**-*ed*
Tit. 3.14. *let* our's also **l**. to maintain.
Heb.5. 8. yet **l**-*ed* he obedience by the
Rev.14. 3. no man could **l**. that song
   paideuō.
Act.7.22. And Moses *was* **l**-*ed* in all the
¹Ti. 1.20. they *may* **l**. not to blaspheme

LEARNING, [*noun.*]
   gramma, [*plural.*]
Act.26.24. much **l**. doth make thee mad
   didaskalia.
Ro.15.4. afore. were written for our **l**.

LEAST, (See *Esteem, Less.*)
   elachistos.
Mat. 2. 6. art not the **l**. among the pri.
   5.19. one of these **l**. commandmen.
   he shall be called the **l**. in
   25.40, 45. unto one of the **l**. of these
Lu. 12.26. to do that thing which is **l**.
   16.10. faithful in that which is **l**., is
   he that is unjust in the **l**. is
⁴Co. 15. 9. I am the **l**. of the apostles
   mikros.   [Lu.7.28
Mat.11.11. he that is **l**. in the kingdom;
   13.32. is the **l**. of all seeds : but
Lu. 9.48. he that is **l**. among you all
Act. 8.10. from the **l**. to the greatest ;
   ge.   [Heb.8.11
Lu.19.42. even thou, *at* **l**. in this thy
   kan.
Act.5.15. that *at the* **l**., the shadow

LEATHERN.
   dermatinos.
Mat.3.4. and a **l**. girdle about his loins

LEAVE, [*noun.*]
   epitrepō.
Mar.5.13. forthwith Jesus *gave* them **l**.
Jo. 19.38. Jesus : and Pilate *gave* him **l**.
   apotassomai.
Act.18.18. *then took* his **l**. of the breth.
²Co. 2.13. *taking* my **l**. of them, I went
   aspazomai.
Act.21.6. *when* we *had taken* our **l**. one

LEAVE, [*verb,*] -*eth,* -*ing, Left.*
   aphiēmi.
Mat. 4.11. Then the devil **l**-*eth* him, and
   20. straightway **l**-*ft* nets, *and*
   22. immediately **l**-*ft* the ship *and*
   5.24. **l**. there thy gift before the
   8.15. the fever **l**-*ft* her ; Mar.1.31
   18.12. *doth* he not **l**. the ninety and
   22.22. **l**-*ft* him, *and* went their way
   25. **l**-*ft* his wife unto his brother
   23.23. not *to* **l**. the other undone ;
   Lu.11.42   [Lu.13.35
   38. house *is* **l**-*ft* unto you desol.;
   24. 2. There shall not *be* **l**-*ft* here ;
   Mar.13.2 ; Lu.21.36
   40, 41. the one and the other **l**-*ft*;
   Lu.17.34,35,36
   26.44. he **l**-*ft* them, *and* went away
Mar. 1.20. they **l**-*ft* their father Zebedee
   8.13. he **l**-*ft* them, *and* entering
   10.28. Lo, we *have* **l**-*ft* all, and have
   29. no man that *hath* **l**-*ft* house;
   Lu.18.29
   12.12. they **l**-*ft* him, *and* went their
   19. wife behind him, and **l**. no
   20, 21,22. dying **l**-*ft* no seed
   13.34. who **l**-*ft* his house, *and* gave
Lu. 4.39. rebuked the fever ; and it **l**-*ft*
   10.30. departed, **l**-*ing* him half dead
   18.28. Peter said, Lo, we *have* **l**-*ft*

Lu. 19.44. they *shall* not **l**. in thee one
Jo. 4. 3. He **l**-*ft* Judea, and departed
   28. The woman then **l**-*ft* her wa.
   52. seventh hour the fever **l**-*ft*
   8.29. the Father *hath* not **l**-*ft* me
   10.12. **l**-*eth* the sheep, and fleeth
   14.18. I *will* not **l**. you comfortless
   27. Peace, I **l**. with you, my pe.
   16.28. again, I **l**. the world, and go
   32. *shall* **l**. me alone : and yet I
Act.14.17. he **l**-*ft* not himself without
Ro. 1.27. **l**-*ing* the natural use of the
¹Co. 7.13. dwell with her, *let* her not **l**.
Heb. 2. 8. he **l**-*ft* nothing that is not
   6. 1. **l**-*ing* the principles of the
Rev. 2. 4. thou *hast* **l**-*ft* thy first love
   aniēmi.
Heb.13.5. said, I *will* never **l**. thee
   kataleipō.
Mat. 4.13. And **l**-*ing* Nazareth, he came
   16. 4. And he **l**-*ft* them, *and* depa.
   19. 5. this cause *shall* a man **l**.;
   Mar.10.7
   21.17. he **l**-*ft* them, *and* went out
Mar.12.19.If a man's brother die, and **l**.
   14.52. And he **l**-*ft* the linen cloth
Lu. 5.28. And he **l**-*ft* all, rose up, *and*
   10.40. that my sister *hath* **l**-*ft* me
   15. 4. *doth* not **l**. the ninety and
   20.31. and they **l**-*ft* no children, and
Jo. 8. 9. and Jesus *was* **l**-*ft* alone, and
Act. 2.31. that his soul *was* not **l**-*ft* in
   6. 2. that we should **l**. the word
   18.19. and **l**-*ft* them there : but he
   21. 3. we **l**-*ft* it on the left hand *and*
   24.27. Jews a pleasure, **l**-*ft* Paul
   25.14. a certain man **l**-*ft* in bonds
Eph. 5.31. *shall* a man **l**. his father and
¹Th. 3. 1. thought it good *to be* **l**-*ft* at
Tit. 1. 5. For this cause **l**-*ft* I thee in
Heb.4. 1. lest, a promise *being* **l**-*ft* us
   engkataleipō.
Act.2.27. Thou *wilt* not **l**. my soul in
Ro. 9.29. of Sabaoth *had* **l**-*ft* us a seed
²Ti.4.13. The cloak that I **l**-*ft* at Troas
   20. Trophimus *have* I **l**-*ft* at Milet.
Jude 6. but **l**-*ft* their own habitation
   hupoleipō.
Ro.11.3. I *am* **l**-*ft* alone, and they seek
   pauomai.
Lu. 5. 4. How when he *had* **l**-*ft* speak.
Act.21.32.soldiers, they **l**-*ft* beating of P.
   eaō.
Act.23.32. **l**-*ft* the horsemen to go..*and*
   hupolimpanō.
¹Pet.2.21. suffered for us, **l**-*ing* us an
   perisseuō.
Mat.15.37. broken meat *that was* **l**-*ft*
   perisseuma.
Mar.8.8. the broken meat *that was* **l**-*ft*
   ekballō.
Rev.11. 2. without the temple **l**. out

LEAVEN, [*noun.*]
   zumē,
Mat.13.33. unto **l**., which a woman took
   16. 6, 11. beware of the **l**. of the ;
   Mar.8.15; Lu.12.1
   12. not beware of the **l**. of bread
Mar. 8.15. Pharisees, and of the **l**. of H.
Lu. 13.21. is like **l**., which a woman
¹Co. 5. 6. little **l**. leaven. the ; Gal.5.11
   7. Purge out therefore the old **l**.
   8. keep the feast, not with old **l**.
   neither with the **l**. of malice

LEAVEN, [*verb,*]   -*ed,* -*eth.*
   zumoō.   [13.21
Mat.13.33. till the whole *was* **l**-*ed* ; Lu.
¹Co. 5. 6. leav. **l**-*eth* the whole; Gal.5.9

LEFT, (*left hand.*)
   euōnumos.   [10.37
Mat.20.21.and the other on the **l**.; Mar.
   23. right hand, and on my **l**.·
   Mar.10.40
   25.33. hand, but the goats on the **l**.
   41. also unto them on the **l**. hand
   27.38. and another on the **l**.; Mar.
   15.27
Act.21. 3. we left it *on the* **l**. hand, and
Rev.10.2. and his **l**. foot on the earth
   aristeros.
Mat.6. 3. let not thy **l**. *hand* know wh.
Lu.23.33. hand, and the other on the **l**.
²Co. 6. 7. the right hand, and on the **l**.

LEGS.
   skelos.
Jo. 19.31. that their **l**. might be broken
   32. brake the **l**. of the first, and
   33. already, they brake not his **l**.

LEGION,   -*s.*
   legeōn.
Mat.26.53. give me more than twelve **l**-*s*
Mar. 5. 9. My name is **l**.: for ; Lu.8.30
   15. and had the **l**., sitting, and

LEISURE.
   eukaireō.
Mar.6.31. they *had* no **l**. so much as to

LEND.
   daneizō.
Lu.6.34. if ye **l**. to them of whom ye
   for sinners also **l**. to sinners
   35. do good, and **l**., hoping for
   chraō.
Lu.11.5. Friend, **l**. me three loaves

LENGTH.
   mēkos.
Eph. 3.18. and **l**., and depth, and hieg.
Rev.21.16. **l**. is as large as the breadth
   The **l**. and the breadth and
   pote.
Ro. 1.10. means now *at* **l**. I might have

LEOPARD.
   pardalis.
Rev.13.2. which I saw was like unto a **l**.

LEPER,   -*s.*
   lepros.   [Mar.1.40
Mat. 8. 2. And, behold, there came a **l**.:
   10. 8. cleanse the **l**-*s*, raise the dead
   11. 5. the **l**-*s* are cleansed ; Lu.7.22
   26. 6. in the house of Simon the **l**.;
   Mar.14.3
Lu. 4.27. many **l**-*s* were in Israel in the
   17.12. ten men that were **l**-*s*, which

LEPROSY.
   lepra.
Mat. 8. 3. And immediately his **l**. was
Mar. 1.42. immediately the **l**. departed ;
   Lu.5.13
Lu. 5.12. behold a man full of **l**.: who

LESS.
   mikros.
Mat. 4.31. is **l**. than all the seeds that
   15.40. the mother of James the **l**.
   hēttōn.
²Co.12.15. I love you, the **l**. I be loved
   elassōn.
Heb.7.7. the **l**. is blessed of the better
   elachistoteros.
Eph.3.8. who am I. *than the least* of
   (See *Honourable, Sorrowful.*)

LEST.
   hina mē.
Mat.17.27.Notwithstanding, **l**. we sho.

Mat.26. 5. **l.** there be an uproar among
Mar. 3. 9. **l.** they should throng him
  14.38. **l.** ye enter into temptation ;
       Lu.22.46
Lu. 8.12. **l.** they should believe and be
  16.28. **l.** they also come into this
  18. 5. **l.** by her continual coming
Jo. 3.20. **l.** his deeds should be repro.
  5.14. **l.** a worse thing come unto
  12.35. **l.** darkness come upon you
  42. **l.** they should be put out of
  18.28. **l.** they should be defiled
Act. 5.26. **l.** they should have been sto.
Ro. 11.25. **l.** ye should be wise in your
  15.20. **l.** I should build upon anoth.
¹Co. 1.15. **l.** any should say that I had
  17. **l.** the cross of Christ should
  8.13. **l.** I make my brother to off.
  9.12. **l.** we should hinder the gos.
-Co. 2. 3. **l.**, when I came, I should ha.
  11, I. Satan should get an adva.
  9. . **l.** our boasting of you should
  12. 7. And **l.** I should be exalted
Gal. 6.12. only **l.** they should suffer
Eph. 2. 9. **l.** any man should boast
Phi. 2.27. **l.** I should have sorrow upon
Col. 2. 4. **l.** any man should beguile you
  3.21. anger, **l.** they be discouraged
¹Ti. 3. 6. **l.** being lifted up with pride
  7. **l.** he fall into reproach and
Heb. 3.13. **l.** any of you be hardened
  4.11. **l.** any man fall after the same
  11.28. **l.** he that destroyed the first.
  12. 3. **l.** ye be wearied and faint
  13. **l.** that which is lame be
Jas. 5. 9. **l.** ye be condemned : behold
  12. **l.** ye fall into condemnation
²Pet. 3.17. beware **l.** ye also, being led
Rev.16.15. **l.** he walk naked, and they
       mēpote.   [Lu.4.11
Mat. 4. 6. **l.** *at any time* thou dash thy;
  5.25. **l.** *at any time* the adversary
  7. 6. **l.** they trample them under
  13.15. **l.** *at any time* they should
  29. Nay **l.** while ye gather up
  15.32. fasting, **l.** they faint in the
  25. **l.** there be not enough for us
  27.64. **l.** his disciples come by night
Mar. 4.12. **l.** *at any time* they should be
  14. 2. **l.** there be an uproar of the
Lu. 12.58. **l.** he hale thee to the judge
  14. . **l.** a more honourable man
  12. **l.** they also bid thee again
  29. **l.** *haply*, after he hath laid
  21.34. **l.** *at any time* your hearts be
Act. 5.39. **l.** *haply* ye be found even to
  28.27. **l.** they should see with their
Heb. 2. 1. **l.** *at any time* we should let
  3.12. **l.** there be in any of you an
  4. 1. Let us therefore fear, **l.**, a
       mē.
Mar.13. 5. Take heed **l.** any man decei.
  36. **l.** coming suddenly he find
Act.13.40. **l.** that come upon you, whi.
  23.10. fearing **l.** Paul should have
  27.17. and, fearing **l.** they should
  42. **l.** any of them should swim
¹Co. 10.12. standeth take heed **l.** he fall
²Co. 4. 4. **l.** the light of the glorious
  12. 6. **l.** any man should think of
  21. **l.**, when I come again, my G.
  13.10. **l.** being present I should use
Gal. 6. 1. thyself, **l.** thou also be temp.
Col. 2. 8. Beware **l.** any man spoil you
Heb.12.15. **l.** any man fail of the grace
     of God ; **l.** any root of bitter.
  16. **l.** there be any fornicator
       mēpōs.
Act.27.29. fearing **l.** we should have fal.
Ro. 11.21. **l.** he also spare not thee
¹Co. 8. 9. take heed **l.** *by any means*
  9.27. **l.** that *by any means*, when I
160

²Co. 2. 7. **l.** *perhaps* such a one should
  9. 4. **l.** *haply* if they of Macedonia
  11. 3. But I fear, **l.** *by any means*
  12.20. For I fear, **l.**, when I come, I
     l. there be debates, envyings
Gal. 2. 2. **l.** *by any means* I should run
  4.11. **l.** I have bestowed upon you
¹Th. 3. 5. **l.** *by some means* the tempter

LET.
       aphiēmi.   [Lu.6.42
Mat. 7. 4. **l.** me pull out the mote out ;
  8.22. **l.** the dead bury their dead ;
       Lu.9.60
  13.30. **l.** both grow together until
  27.49. The rest said, **l.** *be*, let us see
Mar. 7.27. **l.** the children first be filled
  11. 6. com.: and they **l.** them *go*
Jo. 11.44. them, loose him, and **l.** him
  18. 8. seek me, **l.** these go their
       kathiēmi.
Lu. 5.19. and **l.** him *down* through the
Act. 9.25. and **l.** him *down* by the wall
  10.11. corners, and **l.** *down* to the
  11. 5. a great sheet, **l.** *down* from
       chalaō.
Mar. 2. 4. they **l.** *down* the bed where.
Lu. 5. 4. and **l.** *down* your nets for a
  5. at thy word I *will* **l.** *down* the
Act. 9.25. and **l.** him *down* by the wall
  27.30. *when* they had **l.** *down* the
²Co. 11.33. in a basket *was* I **l.** *down* by
       ekdidōmi.   [Mar.12.1
Mat.21.33. **l.** it *out* to husbandmen ;
  41. *will* **l.** *out* his vineyard unto
Lu. 20. 9. **l.** it *forth* to husbandmen
       exeimi.
Act.2.29. **l.** me freely speak unto you
       epitrepō.
Lu. 9.61. but **l.** me first go bid them
       eaō.
Act.27.32. of the boat, and **l.** her fall
     (*See words in connection.*)

LET, (*hinder,*)   -*teth.*
       kōluō.
Ro. 1.13. unto you, but *was* **l.** hitherto
       katechō.
²Th. 2. 7. only he *who* now **l**-*eth* will let

LETTER, (See *Write*,)   -*s.*
       gramma.
Lu. 23.38. written over him in **l**-*s* of
Jo. 7.15. How knoweth this man **l**-*s*
Act.28.21. We neither received **l**-*s* out
Ro. 2.27. who by the **l.** and circumcis.
  29. the spirit, and not in the **l.**
  7. 6. not in the oldness of the **l.**
²Co. 3. 6. not of the **l.**, but of the spirit
     for the **l.** killeth, but the spi.
Gal. 6.11. Ye see how large a **l.** I have
       epistolē.
Act. 9. 2. **l**-*s* to Damascus to the syna.
  22. 5. I received **l**-*s* unto the breth.
  23.25. he wrote a **l.** after this man.
¹Co.16. 3. ye shall approve by your **l**-*s*
²Co. 7. 8. I made you sorry with a **l.**
  10. 9. if I would terrify you by **l**-*s*
  10. For his **l**-*s*, say they, are wei.
  11. by **l**-*s* when we are absent
²Th. 2. 2. nor by **l.** as from us, as that

LEVITICAL.
       Leuitikos.
Heb.7.11. were by the **l.** priesthood

LEWD.
       ponēros.
Act.17.5. **l.** fellows of the baser sort

LEWDNESS.
       radiourgēma.
Act.18.14. matter of wrong or wicked **l.**

LIAR,   -**s.**
       pseustēs.
Jo. 8.44. for he is a **l.**, and the father
  55. I shall be a **l.** like unto you
Ro. 3. 4. G. be true, but every man a **l.**
¹Ti. 1.10. for **l**-*s*, for perjured persons
Tit. 1.12. The Cretians are alway **l**-*s*
¹Jo. 1.10. not sinned, we make him a **l.**
  2. 4. not his commandments, is a **l.**
  22. Who is a **l.** but he that deni.
  4.20. hateth his brother, he is a **l.**
  5.10. not God hath made him a **l.**
       pseudēs.
Rev. 2. 2. not, and hast found them **l**-*s*
  21. 8. sorcerers, idolaters, and all **l**-*s*

LIBERAL.
       haplotēs.
²Co. 9.13. for your **l.** distribution unto

LIBERALITY.
       charis.
¹Co.16. 3. to bring your **l.** unto Jerus
²Co. 8. 2. unto the riches of their **l.**

LIBERALLY.
       haplōs.
Jas. 1. 5. that giveth to all men **l.**

LIBERTY.
       eleutheria.
Ro. 8.21. glorious **l.** of the children of
¹Co. 10.29. why is my **l.** judged of ano.
²Co. 3.17. the Lord is, there is **l.**
Gal. 2. 4. to spy out our **l.** which we
  5. 1. in the **l.** wherewith Christ
  13. unto **l.** ; only use not **l.** for
Jas. 1.25. the perfect law of **l.**, and
  2.12. be judged by the law of **l.**
¹Pet. 2.16. free, and not using your **l.**
²Pet. 2.19. While they promise them **l.**
       eleutheros.
¹Co. 7.39. she is at **l.** to be married to
       apoluō.
Act. 26.32. man might *have been set at* **l.**
Heb.13.23. brother Timothy *is set at* **l.**
       aphesis.
Lu. 4.18. to set at **l.** them that are
       anesis.
Act.24.23. to let him have **l.**, and that
       epitrepō.
Act.27. 3. and *gave* him **l.** to go unto his
       exousia.
¹Co. 8. 9. lest by any means this **l.** of

LICENSE.
       epitrepō.
Act.21.40. *when* he *had given* him **l.**
       topos.
Act.25.16. and have **l.** to answer for

LICKED.
       apoleichō.
Lu. 16.21. dogs came and **l.** his sores

LIE, [*noun.*]
       pseustos.
Jo. 8.44. When he speaketh a **l.**, he
Ro. 1.25. the truth of God into a **l.**
²Th. 2.11. that they should believe a **l.**
¹Jo. 2.21. and that no **l.** is of the truth
  27. and is truth, and is no **l.**
Rev.21.27. abomination, or maketh a **l.**
  22.15. who. loveth and maketh a **l.**
       pseusma.
Ro. 3. 7. abounded through my **l.** unto

LIE, (*to speak lies.*)   -*d.*
       pseudomai.
Act. 5. 3. Satan filled thine heart *to* **l.**
  4. thou *hast* not **l**-*d* unto men
Ro. 9. 1. I say the truth in Ch., I **l.** not
²Co. 11.31. knoweth that I **l.** not
Gal. 1.20. behold, before God, I **l.** not

Col. 3. 9. **l.** not one to another, seeing
¹Ti. 2. 7. truth in Christ, and **l.** not
Heb. 6.18. impossible for God *to* **l.**
Jas. 3.14. glory not, and **l.** not against
¹Jo. 1. 6. we **l.**, and do not the truth
Rev. 3. 9. Jews, and are not, but *do* **l.**

apseudēs.

Tit. 1. 2. which God, *that cannot* **l.**

LIE, [*to rest,*]-*eth, -ing, Lain, Lay.*

keimai.

Mat.28. 6. see the place where the L.**l**-*a*
Lu. 2.12, 16. **l**-*ing* in a manger
Jo. 20. 5. saw the linen clothes **l**-*ing*
   6. and seeth the linen clothes **l.**
   7. not **l**-*ing* with the linen clo.
  12. where the body of Je. *had* **l**-*n*
¹Jo. 5.19. the whole world **l**-*eth* in wic.
Rev.21.16. the city **l**-*eth* foursquare, and

anakeimai.

Mar. 5.40. in where the dams. *was* **l**-*ing*

katakeimai.

Mar. 1.30. Simon's wife's mother **l**-*a* sick
  2. 4. where. the sick of the palsy **l**-*a*
Lu. 5.25. took up that whereon he **l**-*a*
Jo. 5. 3. In these **l**-*a* a great multitude
  6. When Jesus saw him **l**-*a*, and
Act.28. 8. that the father of Publius **l**-*a*

epikeimai.

Jo. 11.38. a cave, and a stone **l**-*a* upon
Act.27.20. *when.* .no small tempest **l**-*a on*

ballo, [*passive.*]

Mat. 8. 6. my servant **l**-*eth* at home sic.
  9. 2. sick of the palsy, **l**-*ing* on a

echō.

Mar. 5.23. **l**-*eth at* the point of death : I

epipiptō.

Jo. 13.25. He then, **l**-*ing* on Jesus' bre.

enedreuō.

Act.23.16. heard of their **l**-*ing in wait*

blepō.

Act.27.12. **l**-*eth* toward the southwest

LIFE, *Lives.*

zōē.

Mat. 7.14. way, which leadeth unto **l.**
  18. 8, 9. to enter into **l.**; Mar.9.43
  19.16. that I may have eternal **l.**
   17. but if thou wilt enter into **l.**
  29. shall inherit everlasting **l.**
  25.46. the righteous into **l.** eternal
Mar. 9.45. to enter halt into **l.**, than
  10.17. that I may inherit eternal **l.**
  30. worl.to come eter. **l.**;Lu.18.30
Lu. 1.75. him, all the days of our **l.**
  10.25. I do to inherit eter. **l.**; 18.18
  12.15. a man's **l.** consisteth not in
Jo. 1. 4. In him was **l.**; and the **l.** was
  3.15, 16. perish, but have eternal **l.**
  36. the Son hath ever. **l.**; 6.47
   shall not see **l.**; but the wrath
  4.14. springeth up into everlast. **l.**
  36. fruit unto **l.** eternal : that
  5.24. sent me hath everlasting **l.**
   is passed from death unto **l.**
  26. Father hath **l.** in himself ; so
   given to the Son to have **l.** in
  29. unto the resurrection of **l.**
  39. ye think ye have eternal **l.**
  40. to me, that ye might have **l.**
  6.27. endureth unto everlasting **l.**
  33. and giveth **l.** unto the world
  35. I am the bread of **l.**: he that
  40. may have everlasting **l.**: and
  48. I am that bread of **l.**
  51. give for the **l.** of the world
  53. blood, ye have no **l.** in you
  54. hath eternal **l.**; and I will
  63. are spirit, and they are **l.**
  68. hast the words of eternal **l.**
  8.12. shall have the light of **l.**
  10.10. that they might have **l.**
  28. give unto them eternal **l.**

Jo. 11.25. the resurrection, and the **l.**
  12.25. shall keep it unto **l.** eternal
  50. his commandment is **l.** ever.
  14. 6. the way, the truth, and the **l.**
  17. 2. he should give eternal **l.** to
  3. And this is **l.** eternal, that
  20.31. believing ye might have **l.**
Act. 2.28. known to me the ways of **l.**
  3.15. And killed the Prince of **l.**
  5.20. people all the words of this **l.**
  8.33. his **l.** is taken from the earth
  11.18. granted repentance unto **l.**
  13.46. unworthy of everlasting **l.**
  48. were ordained to eternal **l.**
  17.25. he giveth to all **l.**, and breath
Ro. 2. 7. who by patient. .eternal **l.**
  5.10. we shall be saved by his **l.**
  17. shall reign in **l.** by one, Jes.
  18. men unto justification of **l.**
  21. righteousness unto eternal **l.**
  6. 4. should walk in newness of **l.**
  22. and the end everlasting **l.**
  23. is eternal **l.** through Jes. Ch.
  7.10. comm., which was orda. to **l.**
  8. 2. the law of the Spirit of **l.**
  6. spiritually mlnded is **l.** and
  10. is **l.** because of righteousness
  38. that neith. death, nor **l.**, nor
  11.15. be, but **l.** from the dead
¹Co. 3.22. or **l.**, or death, or things pre.
  15.19. If in this **l.** only we have
²Co. 2.16. the savour of **l.** unto **l.**
  4.10, 11.that the **l.** also of J. might
  12. worketh in us, but **l.** in you
  5. 4. might be swallowed up of **l.**
Gal. 6. 8. shall of the Spirit reap **l.** ev.
Eph. 4.18. alienated from the **l.** of God
Phi. 1.20. whether it be by **l.**, or by
  2.16. Holding forth the word of **l.**
  4. 3. names are in the book of **l.**
Col. 3. 3. and your **l.** is hid with Christ
  4. When Christ, who is our **l.**
¹Ti. 1.16. believe on him to **l.** everlast.
  6.12, 19. lay hold on eternal **l.**
²Ti. 1. 1. of **l.** which is in Christ Jesus
  10. brought **l.** and immort. to
Tit. 1. 2. In hope of eternal **l.**, which
  3. 7. accord. to the hope of eter. **l.**
Heb. 7. 3. beginn. of days, nor end of **l.**
  16. the power of an endless **l.**
Jas. 1.12. he shall recei. the crown of **l.**
  4.14. For what is your **l.**? It is
¹Pet. 3. 7. together of the grace of **l.**
  10. For he that will love **l.**, and
²Pet. 1. 3. that pertain unto **l.** and god.
¹Jo. 1. 1. handled of the Word of **l.**
  2. the **l.** was manifested, and
   shew unto you that eternal **l.**
  2.25. promised us, even eternal **l.**
  3.14. passed from death unto **l.**
  15. hath eternal **l.** abiding in
  5.11. us eternal **l.**, and this **l.** is in
  12. that hath the Son hath **l.**
   not the Son of God hath not **l.**
  13. that ye have eternal **l.**, and
  16. and he shall give him **l.** for
  20. the true God, and eternal **l.**
Jude 21. Jesus Christ unto eternal **l.**
Rev. 2. 7. I give to eat of the tree of **l.**
  10. I will give thee a crown of **l.**
  3. 5. out of the book of **l.**, but I
  11.11. the Spirit of **l.** from God
  13. 8. written in the book of **l.**;
   17.8,20.15
  20.12. which is the book of **l.**: and
  21. 6. the water of **l.** freely ; 22.17
  27. writ. in the Lamb's book of **l.**
  22. 1. river of water of **l.**, clear as
  2. was there the tree of **l.**, whi.
  14. have right to the tree of **l.**
  17. let him take the water of **l.**

Rev.22.19. his part out of the book of **l.**

psuchē.

Mat. 2.20. sought the young child's **l.**
  6.25. thought for your **l.**; Lu.12.22
   Is not the **l.** more ; Lu.12.23
  10.39. He that findeth his **l.** shall
   he that loseth his **l.** for my ;
   Mat.16.25; Mar.8.35; Lu.9.24
  16.25. whosoever will save his **l.** ;
   Mar.8.35; Lu.9.24,17.33
  20.28. give his **l.** a ran.; Mar.10.45
Mar. 3. 4. to save **l.**, or to kill ? But
Lu. 6. 9. to save **l.**, or to destroy it
  9.56. come to destroy men's **l**-*s*
  14.26. yea, and his own **l.** also, he
Jo. 10.11. good shepherd giveth his **l.**
  15. I lay down my **l.** for the she.
  17. because I lay down my **l.**
  12.25. He that loveth his **l.** shall
   lose it : and he that hat. his **l.**
  13.37. I will lay down my **l.** for thy
  38. Wilt thou lay down thy **l.**
  15.13. that a man lay down his **l.**
Act.15.26. that have hazarded their **l** *s*
  20.10. yourselves; for his **l.** is in
  24. neither count I my **l.** dear
  27.10. and ship, but also of our **l**-*s*
  22. be no loss of any man's **l.**
Ro. 11. 3. alone, and they seek my **l.**
  16. 4. have for my **l.** laid down
Phi. 2.30. not regard. his **l.**, to supply
¹Jo. 3.16. he laid down his **l.** for us
   ought to lay down our **l**-*s*
Rev. 8. 9. in the sea, and had **l.**, died
  12.11. they loved not their **l**-*s* unto

bios.

Lu. 8.14. riches and pleasures of this **l.**
¹Ti. 2. 2. a quiet and peaceable **l.** in all
²Ti. 2. 4. with the affairs of this **l.**
¹Pet. 4. 3. the time past of our **l.** may
¹Jo. 2.16. the pride of **l.**, is not of the

pneuma.

Rev.13.15. had power to give **l.** unto

zaō.

²Co. 1. 8. despaired even *of* **l.** (*to live.*)

biōtikos.

Lu. 21.34. drunken. and cares *of this* **l.**
¹Co. 6. 3. *things that pertain to this* **l.**
  4. of things *pertaining to this* **l.**

zōopoieō.

²Co. 3. 6. killeth, but the spirit *giveth* **l.**
Gal. 3.21. given which cou. *have given* **l.**

apsuchos.

¹Co. 14. 7. things *without* **l.** giving sou.

biōsis.

Act.26. 4. *manner of* **l.** from my youth

agōgē.

²Ti. 3.10. my doctrine, *manner of* **l.**

LIFETIME.

zōē.

Lu. 16.25. thou in thy **l.** receivedst thy

zaō.

Heb. 2.15. were all their **l.** subject to

LIFT, -*ed, -ing.*

epairō.

Mat.17. 8. *when* they *had* **l**-*ed* up their
Lu. 6.20. **l**-*ed up* his eyes. .*and* said
  11.27. **l**-*ed up* her voice, *and* said
  16.23. **l.** *up* his eyes, being in tor.
  18.13. would not **l.** *up* so much as
  21.28. **l.** *up* your heads; for your
  24.50. **l**-*ed up* his hands, *and* bless.
Jo. 4.35. **l.** *up* your eyes, and look on
  6. 5. *When* Jesus *then* **l**-*ed up* his
  13.18. *hath* **l**-*ed up* his heel against
  17. 1. **l**-*ed up* his eyes to heaven
Act. 2.14. **l**-*ed up* his voice, and said
  14.11. they **l**-*ed up* their voices, sa.
  22.22. and then **l**-*ed up* their voices
¹Ti. 2. 8. **l**-*ing up* holy hands, without

hupsoō.
Jo. 3.14. as Moses 1-ed up the serpent
    the S. of man be 1-ed up; 12.34
   8.28. When ye have 1-ed up the S.
  12.32. if I be 1-ed up from the earth
Jas. 4.10. Lord, and he shall 1. you up
    airō.
Lu. 17.13. they 1-ed up their voices, and
Jo. 11.41. Jesus 1-ed up his eyes, and
Act. 4.24. they 1-ed up their voice to
Rev.10. 5. 1-ed up his hand to heaven
    egeirō.
Mat.12.11.lay hold on it, and 1. it out
Mar. 1.31. by the hand, and 1-ed her up
   9.27. and 1-ed him up; and he
Act. 3. 7. right hand, and 1-ed him up
    anakuptō.
Lu. 13.11. could in no wise 1. up herself
Jo. 8. 7. he 1-ed up himself, and said
   10. When Jesus had 1-ed up him.
    anistēmi.
Act. 9.41. his hand, and 1-ed her up
    anorthoō.
Heb.12.12. 1. up the hands which hang
    tuphoomai.
1Ti. 3. 6. being 1-ed up with pride

LIGHT, (not heavy).
    elaphros.
Mat.11.30. easy, and my burden is 1.
2Co. 4.17. For our 1. affliction, which
    ameleō.
Mat.22. 5. they made 1. of it, and went

LIGHT, [noun,] (See Full.) -s.
    phōs.
Mat. 4.16. sat in darkness saw great 1.
    of death 1. is sprung up
   5.14. Ye are the 1. of the world
   16. Let your 1. so shine before
   6.23. If therefo. the 1. that is in thee
  10.27. that speak ye in 1.: and
   17. 2. raiment was white as the 1.
Lu. 2.32. A 1. to lighten the Gentiles
   0.16. which enter in may see the 1.
  11.35. that the 1. which is in thee
   12. 3. shall be heard in the 1.; and
   16. 8. wiser than the children of 1.
Jo. 1. 4. and the life was the 1. of men
   5. And the 1. shineth in darkn.
   7. 8. to bear witness of the 1.
   8. He was not that 1., but was
   9. That was the true 1., which
   3.19. that 1. is come into the world
    loved darkness rather than 1.
   20. that doeth evil hateth the 1.
    neither cometh to the 1.
   21. doeth truth cometh to the 1.
  5.35. for a season to rejoice in his 1.
  8.12. I am the 1. of the world; 9.5
    but shall have the 1. of life
  11. 9. because he seeth the 1. of this
   10. because there is no 1. in him
  12.35. Yet a little while is the 1.
    Walk while ye have the 1.
   36. While ye ha. 1., beli. in the 1.
    ye may be the children of 1.
   46. I am come a 1. into the world
Act. 9. 3. round about him a 1. from
  12. 7. and a 1. shined in the prison
  13 47. I have set thee to be a 1. of
  16.29. he called for a 1., and sprang
  22. 6. a great 1. round about me
   9. saw indeed the 1., and were
   11. not see for the glory of that 1.
  26.13. I saw in the way a 1. from
   18. them from darkness to 1.
   23. should shew 1. unto the peo.
Ro. 2.19. a 1. of them which are in da.
  13.12. put on the armour of 1.
Co. 4. 6. who commanded the 1. to
  6.14. what communion hath 1. wi h
162

2Co. 11.14. transform. into an angel of 1.
Eph. 5. 8. 1. in the Lord : walk as . .of 1.
   13. are made manifest by the 1.:
    doth make manifest is 1.
Col. 1.12. inheritance of the saints in 1.
1Th. 5. 5. Ye are all the children of 1.
1Ti. 6.16. dwelling in the 1. which no
Jas. 1.17. down from the Father of 1-s
1Pet. 2. 9. darkness into his marvell. 1.
1Jo. 1. 5. that God is 1., and in him is
   7. 1., as he is in the 1., we have
   2. 8. and the true 1. now shineth
   9. He that saith he is in the 1.
   10. abideth in the 1., and there
Rev.18.23. the 1. of a candle shall shine
  21.24. shall walk in the 1. of it
  22. 5. need no candle, neither 1. of
    phōtizō.
Lu. 11.36. of a candle doth give thee 1.
1Co. 4. 5. who both will bring to 1. the
2Ti. 1.10. hath brought life and . .to 1.
Rev.22. 5. the Lord God giveth them 1.
    phōtismos.
2Co. 4. 4. lest the 1. of the glorious go.
   6. to give the 1. of the knowle.
    phōstēr.
Phi. 2.15. among whom ye shine as 1-s
Rev.21.11. her 1. was like unto a stone
    luchnos.   [Lu.11.34
Mat. 6.22. The 1. of the body is the eye ;
Lu. 12.35. about, and your 1-s burning
Jo. 5.35. a burning and a shining 1.
2Pet.1.19. as unto a 1. that shineth in
Rev.21.23.the Lamb is the 1. thereof
    phenggos.   [Mar.13.24
Mat.24.29. moon shall not give her 1. ;
Lu. 11.33. which come in may see the 1.
    lampas.
Act.20. 8. there were many 1-s in the
    lampō.
Mat. 5.15. it giveth 1. unto all that are
    epiphainō.
Lu. 1.79. To give 1. to them that sit in
    epiphauō.
Eph. 5.14. and Christ shall give thee 1.

LIGHT, (to enlighten,) -ed, -eth.
    haptō.
Lu. 8.16. man, when he hath 1-ed ; 11.33
   15. 8. doth not 1. a candle, and
    kaiō.
Mat. 5.15. Neither do men 1. a candle
    phōtizō.
Jo. 1. 9. which 1-eth every man that

LIGHT, (to descend,)   -ing.
    erchomai.
Mat. 3.16. like a dove, and 1-ing upon
    piptō.
Rev. 7.16. neither shall the sun 1. on

LIGHTEN, (to enlighten,) -eth.
    eis apokalupsis.
Lu.2.32. A light to 1. (of) the Gentiles, and
    astraptō.
Lu.17.24. the lightning, that 1-eth out

LIGHTENED, (to unburden.)
    poieō ekbolē.
Act.27.18. next day they 1. the ship
    kauphizō.
Act.27.38. they 1. the ship, and cast

LIGHTLY.
    tachu.
Mar.9.39. than can 1. speak evil of me

LIGHTNESS.
    elaphria.
2Co.1.17. thus minded, did I use 1.

LIGHTNING,   -s.
    astrapē.
Mat.24.27. For as the 1. cometh out of

Mat.28. 3. His countenance was like 1.
Lu. 10.18. I beheld Satan as 1. fall
   17.24. For as the 1. that lighteneth
Rev. 4. 5. proceeded 1-s and thunderings
   8. 5. thunderings, and 1-s, and an
  11.19. there were 1-s, and voices
  16.18. voices, and thunders, and 1-s

LIKE, [adjec.]
    homoios.
Mat.11.16.It is 1. unto children sitting
  13.31. kingdom of heaven is 1. to a ;
    33,44,45,47,52,20, 1
  22.39. And the second is 1.; Mar.12.31
Lu. 6.47. will shew you to whom he is 1.
   48. He is 1. a man which built
   49. 1. a man that without a fou.
  7.31. and to what are they 1.
   32. They are 1. unto children sit.
  12.36. 1. unto men that wait for
  13.18. Unto what is the king. of G. 1.
   19. It is 1. a grain of mustard
   21. It is 1. leaven, which a woman
Jo. 8.55. I shall be a liar 1. unto you
   9. 9. others said, He is 1. him
Act. 17.29. that the Godhead is 1. unto
Gal. 5.21. revellings, and such 1.: of
1Jo. 3. 2. shall appear, we shall be 1.
Jude 7. in 1. manner, giving themse.
Rev. 1.13. one 1. unto the Son of man
   15. his feet 1. unto fine brass; 2.18
  4. 3. was to look upon 1. a jasper
    in sight 1. unto an emerald
   6. a sea of glass 1. unto crystal
   7. the first beast was 1. a lion
    and the second beast 1. a calf
    the fourth beast was 1. a flyi.
   9. 7. were 1. unto horses prepared
    as it were crowns 1. gold, and
   10, 19. they had tails 1. unto scor.
  11. 1. a reed 1. unto a rod ; and
  13. 2. was 1. unto a leopard, and
   4. Who is 1. unto the beast
   11. he had two horns 1. a lamb
  14.14. one sat 1. unto the Son of
  16.13. three unclean spirits 1. frogs
  18.18. What city is 1. unto this gre.
  21.11. her light was 1. unto a stone
   18. pure gold, 1. unto clear glass
    paromoios.
Mar.7.8,13. many other such 1. things
    paromoiazō.
Mat.23.27. for ye are 1. unto whited
    homoioō.
Mat. 6. 8. Be not ye therefore 1. unto
   22. 2. is 1. unto a certain king, wh.
Ro. 9.29. and been made 1. unto Gomo.
Heb. 2.17. to be made 1. unto his breth.
    homoiōma.
Ro.1.23. into an image made 1. to
    kata homoiotēs.
Heb.4.15. all points tempted 1. as we
    (after our similitude.)
    aphomoioō.
Heb. 7.3. made 1. unto the Son of God
    hōs.
Mat. 6.29. not arrayed 1. one of; Lu.12.27
  12.13. restored whole, 1. as the oth.
  28. 3. His countenance was 1. light.
Mar. 4.31. It is 1. a grain of mustard
Jo. 7.46. Never man spake 1. this man
Act. 3.22. 1. unto me ; him shall ; 7.37
   8.32. and 1. a lamb dumb before
Rev. 2.18. his eyes 1. unto a flame of fire
  18.21. a stone 1. a great millstone
  21.11. even 1. a jasper stone, clear
    hōsei.   [Lu.3.22 ; Jo.1.32
Mat.3.16. descending 1. a dove; Mar.1.10
Act. 2. 3. cloven tongues, 1. as of fire
Rev.1.14. white 1. wool, as white as sn
    hōsper.
Ro. 6. 4. that 1. as Christ was raised

houtō kai.
Mar.13.29. *So* ye *in* l. *manner*, when ye
houtos
Lu. 6.23. in the l. *manner* did their
1Th. 2.14. have suffered l. *things* of your
toioutos
Act.19.25. the workmen of l. occupation
isos.
Act.11.17. God gave them the l. gift
eikō.
Jas.1. 6. wavereth, *is* l. a wave of the
23. he *is* l. unto a man beholding
kagō, (kai egō.)
Mat.21.24. *I in* l. *wise* will tell you
(See *words in connection.*)

LIKE, [*verb.*]
dokimazō.
Ro.1.28. they *did* not l. to retain God

LIKEMINDED.
isopsuchos.
Phi.2.20. For I have no man l., who will
phroneō ho autos.
Ro. 15.5. *to be* l. one toward another
Phi. 2.2. that ye *be* l., having the same

LIKEN,   -ed.
homoioō.
Mat.7.24. I *will* l. him unto a wise man
26. *shall be* l-ed unto a foolish man
11.16. whereunto *shall I* l. this gener.
13.24. is l-ed unto a man which sow.
18.23. is the kingdom of heav. l-ed
25. 1. Then *shall..be* l-ed unto ten
Mar.4.30. Whereunto *shall* wel.; Lu.13.20
Lu. 7.31. *shall I* l. the men of this gen.

LIKENESS.
homoiōma.
Ro. 6.5. in the l. of his death, we shall
8.3. in the l. of sinful flesh, and for
Phi.2.7. was made in the l. of men
homoioō.
Act.14.11. down to us *in the* l. of men

LIKEWISE.
homoiōs.
Mat.22.26.l. the second also, and the
26.35. l. also said all the disciples
27.41. l. also the chief p.; Mar.15.31
Mar. 4.16. these are they l. which are
Lu. 3.11. hath meat, let him do l.
5.33. and l. the disciples of the
6.31. to you, do ye also to them l.
10.32. And l. a Levite, when he
37. unto him, Go, and do thou l.
13. 5. repent, ye shall all l. perish
16.25. l. Lazarus evil things: but
17.28. l. also as it was in the days
31. let him l. not return back
22.36. and l. his scrip: and he that
Jo. 5.19. these also doeth the Son l.
6.11. and l. of the fishes as much
21.13. and giveth them, and fish l.
Ro. 1.27. l. also the men, leaving the
1Co. 7. 3. and l. also the wife unto the
4. l. also the husband hath not
22. l. also he that is called, being
Jas. 2.25. l. also was not Rahab the
1Pet. 3. 1. l., ye wives, be in subjection
7. l., ye husbands, dwell with
5. 5. l., ye younger, submit your.
Jude 8. l. also these filthy dreamers
Rev. 8.12. part of it, and the night l.
hōsautōs.
Mat.20. 5.the ninth hour, and did l.
21.30. to the second, and said l.
36. and they did unto them l.
25.17. And l. he that had received
Mar.12.21.any seed: and the third l.
14.31. any wise. l. also said they all
Lu. 13. 3. repent, ye shall all l. perish
22.20. l. also the cup after supper

Ro. 8.26. l. the Spirit also helpeth our
1Ti. 3. 8. l. must the deacons be grave
5.25. l. also the good works of
Tit. 2. 3. The aged women l., that
6. Young men l. exhort to be
houtō.
Mat.17.12. l.'shall also the Son of man
Lu. 15. 7, 10. l. joy shall be in heaven
Ro. 6.11. l. reckon ye also yourselves
paraplēsiōs.
Heb.2.14. he also himself l. took part
oun.
Lu.14.33. So, l., whosoever he be of you

LILIES.
krinon.   [Lu.12.27
Mat.6.28.Consider the l. of the fields;

LIMITETH.
horizō.
Heb.4.7. Again, he l. a certain day, say.

LINE.
kanōn.
2Co.10.16. in another man's l. of things

LINEAGE,
patria.
Lu. 2. 4. of the house and l. of David

LINEN, (See *Cloth.*)
bussinos.
Rev.18.16. that was clothed in *fine* l.
19. 8. should be arrayed in *fine* l.
and white: for the *fine* l. is
14. clothed in *fine* l., white and
sindōn.
Mar.15.46.And he bought *fine* l., and
and wrapped him in the l.
Lu. 23.53. and wrapped it in l., and la.
bussos.
Lu. 16.19. clothed in purple and *fine* l.
Rev.18.12. pearls, and *fine* l., and pur.
linon.
Rev.15.6. clothed in pure and white l.

LINGERETH.
argeō.
2Pet.2.3. now of a long time l. not

LION,   -s.
leōn.
2Ti. 4.17. out of the mouth of the l.
Heb.11.33.stopped the mouths of l-s
1Pet. 5. 8. as a roaring l., walketh about
Rev. 4. 7. the first beast was like a l.
5. 5. the l. of the tribe of Juda
9. 8. teeth were as the teeth of l-s
17. as the heads of l-s; and out
10. 3. as when a l. roareth: and
13. 2. mouth as the mouth of l.

LIPS.
cheilos.   [Mar.7.6
Mat.15. 8. honoureth me with their l.;
Ro. 3.13. of asps is under their l.
1Co. 14.21. other tongues and other l.
Heb.13.15. the fruit of our l. giving th.
1Pet. 3.10. and his l. that they speak no

LISTED,   -eth.
thelō.
Mat.17.12.whatsoev. they l.; Mar.9.13
Jo. 3. 8. The wind blow. where it l-eth
euthunō.
Jas. 3. 4. whithersoev. the govern. l-eth
boulomai.
Jas. 3. 4. whithersoev. the govern. l-eth

LITTLE.
mikros.
Mat.10.42.unto one of these l. ones a
18. 6. offend one of these l. ones;
Mar.9.42; Lu.17.2
10. despise not one of these l.
14. one of these l. ones should

Lu. 12.32. Fear not, l. flock; for it is
19. 3. because he was l. of stature
Jo. 7.33. Yet a l. while am I with you
12.35. Yet a l. while is the light
1Co. 5. 6. Know ye not that a l. leaven
2Co. 11. 1. bear with me a l. in my folly
16. that I may boast myself a l.
Gal. 5. 9. A l. leaven leaveneth the wh.
Heb.10.37.For yet a l. while, and he
Jas. 3. 5. the tongue is a l. member
Rev. 3. 8. for thou hast a l. strength
6.11. they should rest yet *for a* l.
20. 3. must be loosed a l. season
mikron.
Mat.26.39. And he went *a* l. farther, and
Mar.14.35. And he went forward *a* l.
70. And a l. after, they that st.
Jo. 13.33. Little children, yet *a* l. *while*
14.19. Yet *a* l. *while*, and the world
16.16, 17,19. *A* l. *while*, and ye shall
and again, a l. *while*, and ye
18. this that he saith, *A* l. *while*
oligos.
Mar. 1.19. when he had gone *a* l. farther
Lu. 5. 3. thrust out *a* l. from the land
7.47. much: but to whom l. is
forgiven, the same loveth l.
2Co. 8.15. that had gathered l. had no
1Ti. 4. 8. bodily exercise profiteth l.
5.23. but use a l. wine for thy
Jas. 3. 5. how great a matter a l. fire
4.14. appeareth for a l. time, and
brachus.
Lu.22.58. after a l. *while* anot..er saw
Jo. 6. 7. one of them may take a l.
Act. 5.34. the apostles forth a l. *space*
27.28. when they had gone a l. fur.
Heb.2. 7, 9. a l. lower than the angels
elachistos.
Lu.19.17. hast been faithful in a *very* l.
Act.28.2. shewed us no l. kindness
metriōs.
Act.20.12. were not *a* l. comforted
(See *Book, Child, Daughter, Faith, Fish,
Ship.*)

LIVE,   -ed, -est, -eth, -ing.
zaō.   [4.4
Mat. 4. 4. Man *shall* not l. by bread; Lu.
9.18. upon her, and she *shall* l.
Mar.5.23. be healed; and she *shall* l.
Lu. 2.36. *and had* l-ed with an husba.
18. this do, and thou *shalt* l.
15.13. substance with riotous l-*ing*
20.38. but of the living: for all l.
Jo. 4.50. Go thy way; thy son l-*eth*
51. 53.him, saying, Thy son l-*eth*
5.25. G.; and they that hear *shall* l.
6.51. he *shall* l. for ever; and the
57. me, and I l. by the Father
me, even he *shall* l. by me
58. eateth of this bread *shall* l.
11.25. he were dead, yet *shall* he l.
26. *who* soever l-*eth* and believeth
14.19. because I l., ye *shall* l. also
Act.17.28. For in him we l., and move
22.22. it is not fit that he should l.
25.24. that he ought not *to* l. any
26. 5. religion, I l-*ed* a Pharisee
28. 4. vengeance suffereth not to l.
Ro. 1.17. The just *shall* l. by faith;
Gal.3.11; Heb.10.38
6. 2. How *shall* we..any longer l.
10. but in that he l-*eth*, he l-*eth*
7. 1. over a man as long as he l-*eth*
2. her husba. *so long as* he l-*eth*
3. then if, *while* her husb. l-*eth*
8.12. the flesh, *to* l. after the flesh
13. For if ye l. after the flesh, ye
deeds of the body, ye *shall* l.

Ro. 10. 5. doeth those things *shall* **l.** by
14. 7. For none of us **l.**-*eth* to hims.
  8. For whether we **l.**, we **l.** un.
    whether we **l.** therefore, or
  11. As I **l.**, saith the Lord, every
1Co. 7.39. as long as her husband **l.**-*eth*
  9.14. gospel should **l.** of the gospel
2Co. 4.11. For we *which* **l.** are always de.
  5.15. that they *which* **l.** *should* not
    henceforth **l.** unto themselves
  6. 9. as dying, and, behold, we **l.**
  13. 4. yet he **l.**-*eth* by the power of
    we *shall* **l.** with him by the
Gal. 2.14. **l.**-*est* after the manner of Gen.
  19. law, that I *might* **l.**, if ye stand
  20. nevertheless I **l.**; yet not I
    but Christ **l.**-*eth* in me
    the life which I now **l.** in the
    flesh I **l.** by the faith of the
  3.12. man that doeth them *shall* **l.**
  5.25. If we **l.** in the Spirit, let us
Phi. 1.21. For to me *to* **l.** is Christ
  22. But if I **l.** in the flesh, this is
Col. 2.20. why, as though **l.**-*ing* in the
  3. 7. some time, when ye **l.**-*ed* in
1Th. 3. 8. For now we **l.**, if ye stand
  5.10. we *should* **l.** together with
1Ti. 5. 6. pleas. is dead *while* she **l.**-*eth*
2Ti. 3.12. and all that will **l.** godly in
Tit. 2.12. we *should* **l.** soberly, righteo.
Heb. 7. 8. whom it is witnes. that he **l.**-*eth*
  25. *seeing* he ever **l.**-*eth* to make
  9.17. at all, while the testator **l.**-*eth*
  12. 9. the Father of spirits, and **l.**
Jas. 4.15. If the Lord will, we *shall* **l.**
1Pet. 1.23. the word of God, *which* **l.**-*eth*
  2.24. *should* **l.** unto righteousness
  4. 6. but **l.** according to God in
1Jo. 4. 9. that we *might* **l.** through him
Rev. 1.18. I am he *that* **l.**-*eth*, and was
  3. 1. that thou **l.**-*est*, and art dead
  4. 9, 10. *who* **l.**-*eth* for ever and ev';
    5.14, 15.7
  10. 6. sware by him *that* **l.**-*eth* for
  13.14. wound by a sword, and *did* **l.**
  20. 4. they **l.**-*ed* and reigned with

suzaō.   *[2.11
Ro. 6. 8. we *shall* also **l.** *with* him ;²Ti.
²Co. 7. 3. hearts to die and **l.** *with* you

anazaō.
Rev.20.5.rest of the dead **l.**-*ed* not *again*

huparchō.
Lu.7.25. and **l.** delicately, and are in

zōogoneō.
Act.7.19. to the end they might not **l.**

politeuomai.
Act.23.1. I *have* **l.**-*ed* in all good consc.

esthiō.
1Co.9.13. **l.** of the things of the temple

anastrephō.
Heb.13.18. things willing *to* **l.** honestly
²Pet. 2.18. from them *who* **l.** in error

bioō.
1Pet.4.2. should **l.** the rest of his time

diagō.
Tit.3.3. **l.** in malice and envy, hateful

eimi makrochronios.
Eph. 6. 3. *mayest* **l.** *long* on the earth
(See *Deliciously, Jews, Peaceably, Peace,
  Pleasure, Ungodly.*)

LIVELY.
zaō.
Act. 7.38. the **l.** oracles to give unto us
1Pet. 1.3. us again unto a **l.** hope
  2. 5. also, as **l.** stones, are built up

LIVING, [*adjec. and noun.*]
zaō.
Mat.16.16. the Son of the **l.** God;Jo.6.69
  22.32. God of the dead, but of the **l.**
  26.63. I adjure thee by the **l.** God
164

Mar.12.27.but the God of the **l.**; ye
  20.38. but of the **l.**: for all live unto
  24. 5. seek ye the **l.** among the dead
Jo 4.10. he would have given thee **l.**
  11. then hast thou that **l.** water
  6.51. I am the **l.** bread which came
  57. As the **l.** Father hath sent
  7.38. shall flow rivers of **l.** water
Act.14.15. unto the **l.** God, which made
Ro. 9.26. the children of the **l.** God
  12. 1. present your bodies a **l.** sac.
  14. 9. Lord both of the dead and **l.**
1Co.15.45. first man Adam was made a **l.**
²Co. 3. 3. with the Spirit of the **l.** God
  6.16. ye are the temple of the **l.** G.
1Th. 1. 9. to serve the **l.** and true God
1Ti. 3.15. the church of the **l.** God, the
  4.10. we trust in the **l.** God, who
  6.17. but in the **l.** God, who giveth
Heb. 3.12. in departing from the **l.** God
  9.14. works to serve the **l.** God
  10.20. By a new and **l.** way, which
  31. into the hands of the **l.** God
  12.22. unto the city of the **l.** God
1Pet. 2. 4. To whom coming, as unto a **l.**
Rev. 7. 2. the seal of the **l.** God : and
  17. unto **l.** fountains of waters
  16. 3. every **l.** soul died in the sea

bios.   [21.4
Mar.12.44. she had, even all her **l.**; Lu.
Lu. 8.43. spent all her **l.** upon physic.
  15.12. he divided unto them his **l.**
  30. hath devoured thy **l.** with

LO!
idou.
Mat. 2. 9. and, **l.**, the star, which they
  3.16. **l.**, the heavens were opened
  17. And **l.** a voice from heaven
  24.23. **l.**, here is Christ, or there
  26.47. **l.**, Judas, one of the twelve
  28. 7. see him : **l.**, I have told you
  20. and, **l.**, I am with you alway
Mar.10.28. **l.**, we have left all, and have
  13.21. **l.**, here is Christ ; or, **l.**, he
  14.42. **l.**, he that betrayeth me
Lu. 1.44. For, **l.**, as soon as the voice
  2. 9. And, **l.**, the angel of the L.
  9.39. And, **l.**, a spirit taketh him
  13.16. **l.**, these eighteen years, be
  15.29. **l.**, these many years do I ser.
  17.21, **l.** here ! or, **l.** there ! for
  18.28. **l.**, we have left all, and foll.
  23.15. and, **l.**, nothing worthy of
Act.13.46. **l.**, we turn to the Gentiles
  27.24. and, **l.**, God hath given thee
Heb.10. 7. **l.**, I come, in the volume of
  9. **l.**, I come to do thy will, O G.
Rev. 5. 6. and **l.**, in the midst of the
  6. 5. and **l.** a black horse ; and he
  12. **l.**, there was a great earthqu.
  7. 9. and, **l.**, a great multitude
  14. 1. And I looked, and, **l.**, a La.

ide.
Mat.25.25. **l.**, there thou hast that is
Jo. 7.26. But, **l.**, he speaketh boldly
  16.29. **l.**, now speakest thou plain.

LOAF,
artos.   *Loaves.*
     [9.13
Mat.14.17. We ha. here but five **l.**-*s*; Lu.
  19. took the five **l.**-*s*, and ; Lu.9.16
    gave the **l.**-*s* to his disciples
  15.34. How many **l.**-*s* have ye; Mar.
    6.38,8.5
  36. he took the sev. **l.**-*s*; Mar.8.6
  16. 9. neither remember the five **l.**-*s*
  10. Neither the seven **l.**-*s* of the
Mar. 6.41. when he had taken the five **l.**-*s*
  blessed, and brake the **l.**
  44. they that did eat of the **l.**-*s*

Mar. 6.52. not the miracle of the **l.**-*s*
  8.14. with them more than one **l.**
  19. When I brake the five **l.**-*s*
Lu. 11. 5. Friend, lend me three **l.**-*s*
Jo. 6. 9. which hath five barley **l.**-*s*
  11. Jesus took the **l.**-*s* ; and when
  13. frag. of the five barley **l.**-*s*
  26. because ye did eat of the **l.**-*s*

LOCUSTS.
akris.
Mat.3. 4. meat was **l.** and wild ; Mar.1.6
Rev. 9. 3. out of the smoke **l.** upon the
  7. shapes of the **l.** were like

LODGE,   *-ed, -eth.*
xenizō.
Act.10. 6. He **l.**-*eth* with one Simon a
  18. whi. was sur. Peter *were* **l.**-*ed*
  23. called he them in, and **l.**-*ed*
  32. he *is* **l.**-*ed* in the house of one
  21.16. with whom we *should* **l.**
  28. 7. and **l.**-*ed* us three days court.

xenodocheō.
1Ti. 5.10. if she *have* **l.**-*ed strangers*

kataskēnoō.
Mat.13.32. come and **l.** in the branches
Mar. 4.32. the fowls of the air may **l.**
Lu. 13.19. fowls of the air **l.**-*ed* in the

kataluō.
Lu. 9.12. and **l.**, and get victuals : for

aulizomai.
Mat.21.17. Bethany ; and he **l.**-*ed* there

LODGING.
xenia.
Act.28.23. many to him unto his **l.**
Phile. 22. prepare me also a **l.**: for I

LOINS.
osphus.
Mat. 3. 4. a leathern girdle about his **l.**
Mar. 1. 6. girdle of a skin about his **l.**
Lu. 12.35. Let your **l.** be girded about
Act. 2.30. that of the fruit of his **l.**
Eph. 6.14. having your **l.** girt about
Heb. 7. 5. come out of the **l.** of Abra.
  10. he was yet in the **l.** of his
1Pet. 1.13. gird up the **l.** of your mind

LONG, [*adjec. and adv.*]
hikanos.
Lu. 8.27. man, which had devils **l.**
  20. 9. a far country for a **l.** time
  23. 8. desirous to see him of a **l.**
Act. 8.11. of **l.** time he had bewitched
  14. 3. **l.** time therefore abode they
  20.11. talked a **l.** *while*, even till

polus.
Mat.25.19. After a **l.** time the lord of
Jo. 5. 6. he had been now a **l.** time
Act. 27.14. But not **l.** after there arose
  21. But after **l.** abstinence Paul

palai.
Mat.11.21. would have repented **l.** *ago*

makros.
Mat.23.14. for a pretence make **l.** pray.;
    Mar.12.40; Lu.20.47

hotan.
Jo. 9. 5. As **l.** *as* I am in the world

ouk oligos.
Act.14.28. there they abode **l.** time with

pleiōn.
Act.20. 9. as Paul was **l.** preaching

heōs pote.
Mat.17.17. *how* **l.** shall I be with you
    Mar.9.19; Lu.9.41 [9.19
Jo. 10.24. *how* **l.** dost thou make us to
Rev. 6.10. *how* **l.**, O Lord, holy and

tosoutos.
Jo. 14. 9. Have I been *so* **l.** time with
Heb. 4. 7. To-day, after *so* **l.** a time ; *as*

hosos.

Mar. 2.19. *as* **l.** *as* they have the bride.
Ro. 7. 1. a man *as* **l.** *as* he liveth
¹Co. 7.39. *as* **l.** as her husband liveth
Gal. 4. 1. the heir, as **l.** *as* he is a child
²Pet. 1.13. *as* **l.** *as* I am in this taberna.

posos.

Mar. 9.21. *How* **l.** is it ago since this

epi hosos.

Mat. 9.15. *as* **l.** *as* the bridegroom is

makrothumeō.

~u. 18. 7. though he *bear* **l.** with them
Co. 13. 4. Charity *suffereth* **l.**, and is
Jas. 5. 7. and *hath* **l.** *patience* for it
(See *Clothing, Garment, Hair, Live, Patience, Robe, Suffer, Time.*)

LONG, [*verb*,] -ed.

epipotheō.

Ro. 1.11. For I **l.** to see you, that I
²Co. 9.14. for you, *which* **l.** *after* you
Phi. 1. 8. how *greatly* I **l.** *after* you all
2.26. For he **l.**-*ed after* you all, and

epipothētos.

Phi. 4. 1. dearly beloved and **l.**-ed *for*

LONGER.

eti.

Lu. 16. 2. thou mayest be no **l.** steward
Ro. 6. 2. dead to sin, live *any* **l.** there.
Gal. 3.25. we are no **l.** under a school.
Rev. 10.6. there should be time no **l.**

mēketi.

Act.25.24. he ought not to live *any* **l.**
¹Th. 3. 1, 5. could *no* **l.** forbear
¹Ti. 5.23. Drink *no* **l.** water, but use
¹Pet. 4. 2. That he *no* **l.** should live the

ouketi.

Gal. 3.25. we are *no* **l.** under a schoolm.

pleiōn.

Act.18.20. to tarry **l.** time with them

LONGSUFFERING.

makrothumia.

Ro. 2. 4. and forbearance and **l.**; not
9.22. endured with much **l.** the
²Co. 6. 6. by **l.**, by kindness, by the
Gal. 5.22. Spirit is love, joy, peace, **l.**
Eph. 4. 2. with **l.**, forbearing one anot.
Col. 1.11. patience, and **l.** with joyfuln.
3.12. humble.of mind, meekness,**l.**
¹Ti. 1.16. might shew forth all **l.**, for a
²Ti. 3.10. faith, **l.**, charity, patience
4. 2. with all **l.** and doctrine
¹Pet. 3.20. when once the **l.** of God
²Pet. 3.15. account that the **l.** of our

makrothumeō.

²Pet. 3. 9. but *is* **l.** to usward, not willing

LOOK, -ed, -eth, -ing.

blepō.

Mat. 5.28. whosoever **l.**-*eth on* a woman
Lu. 9.62. hand to the plough, and **l.**-*ing*
Jo. 13.22. the disciples **l.**-ed one on ano.
Act. 3. 4. him with John, said, **l.** on
²Co.10. 7. *Do* ye **l.** *on* things after the
²John 8. 1. to yourselves, that we lose
Rev. 5. 3, 4. the book, neither *to* **l.** th.

anablepō. [Mar.6.41;Lu.9.16

Mat.14.19.**l.**-*ing up* to heaven, he ble.;
Mar. 7.34. **l.**-*ing up* to heaven, he sighed
8.24. he **l.**-ed *up, and* said, I see
25. his eyes, and made him **l.** *up*
16. 4. when they **l.**-*ed*,they saw that
Lu. 19. 5. to the place, he **l.**-ed *up, and*
21. 1. he **l.**-ed *up, and* saw the rich
Act.22.13.the same hour I **l.**-ed *up* upon

periblepō. [*on;* 11.11

Mar. 3. 5. *when*he had **l.**-ed round about
34. he **l.**-ed round about on them
5.32. And he **l.**-ed round about to
9. 8. *when* they had**l.**-ed round abo.
10.23. Jesus **l.**-ed round about, and

Lu. 6.10. And **l.**-*ing round about upon*

emblepō.

Mar.10.27. Jesus **l.**-*ing upon* them, saith
14.67. she **l.**-ed *upon* him, *and* said
Lu. 22.61. Lord turned, and **l.**-ed *upon*
Jo. 1.36. **l.**-*ing upon* Jesus as he walk.

epiblepō.

Lu. 9.38. **l.** *upon* my son : for he is

eideō.

Lu. 10.32. came and **l.**-ed *on* him, *and*
Jo. 7.52. Search, and **l.**: for out of Gal.
Rev. 4. 1. After this I **l.**-ed, and, behold
6. 8. I **l.**-ed, and behold a pale hor.
14. 1. I **l.**-ed, and, lo, a Lamb stood
14. I **l.**-ed, and behold a white cl.
15. 5. after that I **l.**-ed, and, behold

atenizō.

Lu. 22.56. *earnestly* **l.**-ed upon him, *and*
Act. 1.10. they **l.**-ed *stedfastly* toward
3.12. why **l.** ye so *earnestly* on us
6.15. **l.**-*ing stedfastly* on him, saw
7.55. **l.**-ed *up stedfastly* in to h. and
10. 4. *when* he **l.**-ed *on* him, he was
²Co. 3.13. could not *stedfastly* **l.** to the

prosdokaō.

Mat.11. 3. do we **l.** *for* anot.: Lu.7.19,20
24.50. whe. he **l.**-*eth* not *for*;Lu.12.46
Act.28. 6. they **l.**-ed *when* he should ha.
but *after* they had **l.**-ed a gr.
²Pet. 3.12. **l.**-*ing for* and hasting unto the
13. **l.** *for* new heavens and a new
14. *seeing* that ye **l.** *for* such

prosdechomai.

Lu. 2.38. to all them *that* **l.**-ed *for* red.
Act.23.21. **l.**-*ing for* a promise from thee
Tit. 2.13. **l.**-*ing for* that blessed hope
Jude 21. **l.**-*ing for* the mercy of our L.

ekdechomai.

¹Co. 16.11.I **l.** *for* him with the brethren
Heb.11.10.he **l.**-ed *for* a city which hath

apekdechomai.

Phi. 3.20.whence also we **l.** *for* the Sav.
Heb.9.28.unto them *that* **l.** *for* him shall

skopeō.

²Co. 4.18. *While* we **l.** not *at* the things
Phi. 2. 4. **l.** not every man *on* his own

episkopeō.

Heb.12.15.**l.**-*ing diligently* lest any man

parakuptō.

Jas. 1.25. But *whoso* **l.**-*eth* into the per.
¹Pet. 1.12. the angels desire *to* **l.** into

anakuptō.

Lu.21.28. then **l.** *up,* and lift up your

theaomai.

Jo. 4.35. and **l.** on the fields, for they
¹Jo.1. 1. which we *have* **l.**-ed *upon,* and

optomai.

Jo. 19.37.They *shall* **l.** on him whom
Act.18.15.**l.** ye to it ; for I will be no

theoreō.

Mar.15.40. also women **l.**-*ing on* afar off

episkeptomai.

Act. 6. 3. ye *out* among you seven men

aphoraō.

Heb.12. 2.**l.**-*ing* unto Jesus the author

ephoraō.

Lu. 1.25. wherein he **l.**-ed *on* me, to take

horasis.

Rev. 4. 3. was *to* **l.** *upon* like a jasper

prosdokia.

Lu. 21.26. and for **l.**-*ing after* those thi.

LOOKING, [*noun.*]

ekdochē.

Heb.10.27.fearful **l.** *for* of judgment

LOOSE, [*verb*,] -ed, -ing.

luō. [18.18

Mat.16.19.*shalt* **l.** on earth shall be **l.**-ed;
21. 2. **l.** them, *and* bring them un.
Mar. 7.35. string of his tongue was **l.**-ed
11. 2. **l.** him, *and* bring ; Lu.19.30
4. and they **l.** him

Mar.11. 5. What do ye, **l.**-*ing* the colt
Lu. 13.15. *doth* not each . on the sab. **l**
16. *be* **l.**-ed from this bond
19.31. Why *do* ye **l.** him
33. *as* they *were* **l.**-*ing* the
Why **l.** ye the colt
Jo. 11.44. **l.** him, and let him go
Act. 2.24. *having* **l.**-ed the pains of death
13.25. I am not worthy *to* **l.**
22.30. he **l.**-ed him from his bands
24.26. that he *might* **l.** him
¹Co. 7.27. *Art* thou **l.**-ed from a wife
Rev. 5. 2. and *to* **l.** the seals thereof
5. and *to* **l.** the seven seals
9.14. **l.** the four angels which
15. the four angels *were* **l.**-ed
20. 3. he must *be* **l.**-ed a little season
7. Satan *shall* be **l.**-ed out of his

apoluō.

Mat.18.27.**l.**-ed him, and forgave him
Lu. 13.12.thou *art* **l.**-ed from thine

lusis.

¹Co. 7.27. to a wife? seek not *to* be **l.**-ed

aniēmi.

Act.16.26. every one's bands *were* **l.**-ed
27.40. **l.**-ed the rudder bands, and

airō.

Act.27.13. **l.**-*ing* thence, they sailed close

anagō.

Act.13.13. *when* Paul and his comp. **l.**-ed
16.11. Therefore **l.**-*ing* from Troas
27.21. not *have* **l.**-ed from Crete, and

katargeō.

Ro. 7. 2. she *is* **l.**-ed from the law of

LORD, -s.

kurios.

Mat.10.24.nor the servant above his **l.**
25. and the servant as his **l.**
18.31. told unto their **l.** all that
22.44. The **l.** said unto my **l.** ; Mar.
12.36 ; Lu.20.42 ; Act.2.34
24.42. what hour your **l.** doth come
46. whom his **l.** when ; Lu.12.42
48. My **l.** delayeth his ; Lu.12.45
25.21, 23. His **l.** said unto him
23. thou into the joy of thy **l.**
Mar. 2.28. is **l.** also of the sab. ; Lu.6.5
Lu. 1.43. the mother of my **l.** should
12.36. men that wait for their **l.**,
14.21. and shewed his **l.** these th.
16. 3. my **l.** taketh away from me
5. called every one of his **l.**'s
much owest thou unto my **l.**
Jo. 13.13. Ye call me Master and **l.**
15.15. knoweth not what his **l.**
20. is not greater than his **l.**
20.13. they have taken away my **l.**
28. My **l.** and my God
Act. 2.36. that same Jesus..both **l.** and
10.36. by Jesus Christ : he is **l.** of
25.26. thing to write unto my **l.**
Ro. 10.12. the same **l.** over all is rich
¹Co. 8. 5. be gods many, and **l.**-s many
12. 5. of adminis., but the same **l.**
Gal. 4. 1. servant, though he be **l.** of
Eph. 4. 5. One **l.**, one faith, one baptism
Phi. 2.11. confess that Jesus Christ is **l.**
3. 8. of Christ Jesus my **l.**
²Th. 1.12. the name of our **l.** Jesus ; 3.6
¹Ti. 6.15. K. of kings, and **l.** of lords
¹Pet. 3. 6. obeyed Abrah., calling him **l.**
²Pet. 3.15. the longsuffering of our **l.** is
Rev. 4. 8. **l.** God Almighty ; 11.17, 16.7
11. 8. where also our **l.** was cruci.
15. beco. the kingdoms of our **l.**
15. 3. thy works, **l.** God Almighty
17.14. for he is **l.** of **l.**-s ; 19.16

The **l.**

Mat. 1.22. spoken of the **l.** by the ; 2.15
3. 3. Prepare ye the way of the **l.**
Mar.1.3 ; Lu.3.4

Mat. 4. 7. shalt not tempt the l.;Lu.4.12
5.33. shalt perform unto the l.
21. 3. The l. hath need of them ;
Mar.11.3 ; Lu.19.31,34
9. cometh in the name of the l.;
23.39 ; Mar.11.9,10 ; Lu.
13.35, 19.38 ; Jo.21.13
24.50. The l. of that serv.; Lu.12.46
28. 6. the place where the l. lay
Mar. 5.19. how great things the l. hath
16.19. So then after the l. had spo.
20. the l. working with them
Lu. 1. 9. into the temple of the l.
15. great in the sight of the l.
16. shall he turn to the l. their
17. a people prepared for the l.
25. Thus hath the l. dealt with
45. wh. were told her from the l.
68. Blessed be the l. God of Israel
2.11. Saviour, which is Ch. the l.
22. to present him to the l.
23. shall be called holy to the l.
4.18. The Spirit of the l. is upon
17. 5. said unto the l., Increase our
20.13. Then said the l. of the viney.
22.61. the word of the l.; Act.11.16.
24.34. The l. is risen indeed, and
Jo. 1.23. Make strai. the way of the l.
20. 2. They have taken away the l.
25. We have seen the l.
21. 7. It is the l. Now when Simon
Peter heard that it was the l.
12. knowing that it was the l.
Act. 2.39. as many as the l. our God
3.22. A prophet shall the l.; 7.37
4.26. against the l., and against
5. 9. to tempt the Spirit of the l.
14. were the more added to the l.
7.31. the voice of the l. came unto
8.24. Pray ye to the l. for me
25. preached the word of the l.;
13.49, 15.35,36, 16,32
39. the Spirit of the l. caught aw.
9.10. said the l. in a vision, Anan.
17. the l., even Jesus, that ap.
27. how he had seen the l. in the
29. the name of the l. Jesus ;
19.13,17, 21.13
42. and many believed in the l.
10.48. baptiz. in the name of the l.
11.23. they would cleave unto the l.
12.11. of a surety, that the l. hath
13. 2. As they ministered to the l.
10. perv. the right ways of the l.
48. glorified the word of the l.
14. 3. speaking boldly in the l.
23. commended them to the l.
15.17. might seek after the l.
saith the l., who doeth all
16.15. me to be faithful to the l.
17.27. That they should seek the l.
18. 9. Then spake the l. to Paul
25. instruct. in the way of the l.
19.10. heard the word of the l.
21.14. The will of the l. be done
22.10. And the l. said unto me
16. calling on the name of the l.
Ro. 9.28. a short work will the l.
12.19. I will repay, saith the l.
14. 6. regardeth it unto the l.
eateth to the l., for he giveth
8. live un. the l., we die un. the l.
we are the l.'s
16. 2. That ye receive her in the l.
8. Amplias my beloved in the l.
12. which laboured much in the l.
13. Rufus chosen in the l.
22. epistle salute you in the l.
1Co. 1.31. him glory in the l.; 2Co.10.17
2. 8. crucified the l. of glory
3. 5. even as the l. gave to every
4. 4. he that judgeth me is the l.
166

1Co. 4.17. and faithful in the l., who
19. if the l. will ; Jas.4.15
6.13. but for the l.; and the l. for
7.10. yet not l, but the l.
22. that is called in the l., being
39. whom she will ; only in the l.
9. 1. are not ye my work in the l.
2. mine apostles. are ye in the l.
10.26. the earth is the l.'s, and the
11.11. without the man, in the l.
23. I have received of the l.
14.21. they not hear me, saith the l.
15.47. second man is the l. from hea.
58. abound. in the work of the l.
16.10. he worketh the work of the l.
2Co. 2.12. was opened unto me of the l.
3.17. Now the l. is that Spirit
where the Spirit of the l. is
18. even as by the Spirit of the l.
5. 6. we are absent from the l.
8. to be present with the l.
6.17. be ye separate, saith the l.
8. 5. gave their own selves to the l.
21. in the sight of the l.; Jas.4.10
11.17. I speak it not after the l.
Eph. 2.21. an holy temple in the l.
4.17. and testify in the l., that
5. 8. now are ye light in the l.
10. what is acceptable unto the l.
22. own husbands, as unto the l.;
6.7 ; Col.3.23
29. even as the l. the church
6. 1. obey your parents in the l.
8. shall he receive of the l.
10. be strong in the l., and in
21. and faithful minister in the l.
Phi. 1.14. brethren in the l., waxing
2.24. I trust in the l. that I also
29. Recei. him therefore in the l.
4. 1. so stand fast in the l.;1Th.3.8
2. be of the same mind in the l.
5. all men. The l. is at hand
10. I rejoiced in the l. greatly
Col. 3.18. husbands, as it is fit in the l.
20. is well pleasing unto the l.
24. Knowing that of the l. ye
for ye serve the l. Christ
4. 7. and fellowservant in the l.
17. thou hast received in the l.
1Th. 1. 8. sound. out the word of the l.
4. 6. because that the l. is the av.
15. you by the word of the l.
17. shall we ever be with the l.
5.12. and are over you in the l.
2Th. 3. 1. that the word of the l. may
3. the l. is faithful, who shall
4. confidence in the l. touching
2Ti. 1.18. The l. grant unto him that
mercy of the l. in that day
2.14. charging them before the l.
22. with them that call on the l.
3.11. out of them all the l. deliver.
4. 8. which the l., the righteous j.
17. the l. stood with me, and
Phile. 16. both in the flesh, and in the l.
20. me have joy of thee in the l.
refresh my bowels in the l.
Heb. 2. 3. began to be spoken by the l.
8. 9. regard. them not, saith the l.
11. saying, Know the l.: for all
10.30. I will recompense, saith the l.
13. 6. The l. is my helper
Jas. 1. 7. receive any thing of the l.
5.10. spoken in the name of the l.
11. have seen the end of the l.
that the l. is very pitiful
14. with oil in the name of the l.
15. the l. shall raise him up; and
1Pet. 1.25. the word of the l. endureth
2. 3. tasted that the l. is gracious
3.15. sanctify the l. God in your
2Pet. 2.11. against them before the l.

2Pet. 3. 8. one day is with the l. as
9. The l. is not slack concern.
Jude 9. but said, The l. rebuke thee
Rev. 1. 8. and the ending, saith the l.
14.13. the dead which die in the l.
18. 8. for strong is the l. God
19. 1. power, unto the l. our God
6. for the l. God omnipotent
21.22. for the l. God Almighty and
22. 5. for the l. God giveth them

Lord [*vocative*].
Mat. 7.21, 22. that saith unto me, l., .l;
Lu.13.25   [Lu.5.12
8. 2. l., if thou wilt, thou canst;
25. saying, l. save us : we perish
9.28. said unto him, Yea, l.; 13.51
14.30. cried, saying, l., save me
15.22. O l.,thou son of Dav.;20.30,31
25. him, saying, l., help me
27. Truth, l.: yet the dogs eat of
18.26. saying, l., have patience with
20.33. l., that our eyes may be ope.
22.43, 45.David in spirit call him l ;
Mar.12.37 ; Lu.20.44
25.11. saying, l., l.. open to us
37, 44. l., when saw we thee an
Mar. 9.24. l., I believe ; Jo.9.38, 11.27
Lu. 5. 8. I am a sinful man, O l.
6.46. why call ye me, l., l.
9.57, 61. l., I will follow thee
11. 1. l., teach us to pray, as John
13. 8. l., let it alone this year also
17.37. Where, l.? And he said unto
23.42. l., remember me when thou
Jo. 6.68. l., to whom shall we go
8.11. She said, No man, l.
9.36. Who is he, l., that I might
11.34. to him, l., come and see
13.25. l., who is it
21.21. l., and what shall this man
Act. 4.29. l., behold their threatenings
9. 5. Who art thou, l.; 26.15
10. 4. What is it, l.
14. Not so, l., for I have ; 11.8
22.10. What shall I do, l.? And the l.
Rev. 4.11. Thou art worthy, O l., to re.
15. 4. Who shall not fear thee, O l.
16. 5. Thou art righteous, O l.
(*And all other passages in which it
occurs, except the following :—*)
despotēs.
Lu. 2.29. l., now lettest thou thy serv.
Act. 4.24. l., thou art God, which hast
2Pet.2. 1. denying the l. that bought
Jude 4. denying the only l. God, and
Rev.6.10. How long, O l., holy and true
rabboni.
Mar.10.51. l., that I might receive my
kurieuō.
Ro.14. 9. that he *might be* l. both *of* the
1Ti. 6.15. of kings, and Lord of l-*s*
katakurieuō.
1Pet.5.3. Neither as *being* l-*s over* God's
kuriakos.
1Co. 11.20. is not to eat the l.'s supper
Rev. 1.10. in the Spirit on the l.'s day
megistanes.
Mar. 6.21. made a supper to his l-*s*
26.22. say unto him, l. is it I

LORDSHIP.
kurieuō.
Lu.22.25. Gentiles *exercise* l. *over* them
katakurieuō.
Mar.10.42. Gentiles *exercise* l. *over* them

LOSE,   -eth, Lost.
apollumi.
Mat.10. 6. to the l-*t* sheep of the; 15.24
39. *shall* l. it : and he that l-*eth* ;
16.25;Mar.8.35;Lu.9.24,17.33
42. *shall* in no wise l.;Mar.9.14

Mat.18.11. that *which was* l-*t*; Lu.19.10
Lu. 9.25. *and* l. himself, or be cast
   15. 4. *if* he l. one of them, doth not
       go after that *which is* l-*t*
     6. found my sheep *which was* l-*t*
     8. if she l. one piece, doth not
     9. fou. the piece which I *had* l-*t*
   24, 32. he was l-*t*, and is found
Jo. 6.12. that remain, that noth. *be* l-*t*
   39. given me, I *should* l. nothing
  12.25. that loveth his life shall l. *it*
  17.12. kept, and none of them *is* l-*t*
  18. 9. thou gavest me *have* I I l-*t*
²Co. 4. 3. it is hid to them *that are* l-*t*
²John 8. that we l. not those things
       zēmioō.   [Mar.8.36
Mat.16.26. whole world, and l. his own
    (See *Saltness, Savour*.)

LOSS.
     zēmia.
Act.27.21. have gained this harm and l.
Phi. 3. 7. those I counted l. for Christ
     8. I count all things but l.
     zēmioō.
¹Co. 3.15. he *shall suffer* l.: but he him.
Phi. 3. 8. I *have suffered the* l. of all
     apobolē.
Act.27.22.there shall be no l. of any

LOT,   -*s*.
     klēros.
Mat.27.35.parted his garm., casting l-*s*
     vest.did they cast l-*s*;Jo.19.24
Mar.15.24.casting l-*s* upon them, what
Lu. 23.34.part. his raiment, and cast l-*s*
Act. 1.26.And they gave forth their l-*s*
     the l. fell upon Matthias
   8.21.Thou hast neither part nor l.
     lagchanō.
Lu. 1. 9. *his* l. *was* to burn incense
Jo.19.24. not rend it, but *cast* l-*s* for it

LOUD.
     megas.
Mat.27.46.cried with a l. voice ;
       Mar.1.26, 5.7, 15.34,37 ;
       Lu.23.46; Jo.11.43;Act.7.60
       16.28; Rev.7.2,10, 10.3, 19.17
Lu. 1.42. she spake out with a l. voice
   4.33. cried out with a l.;Act.7.57
   8.28. and with a l. voice said
  17.15. and with a l. voice glorified
  19.37. and praise God with a l. voi.
  23.23. were instant with l. voices
Act. 8. 7. crying with a l. voice, came
  14.10. Said with a l. voice, Stand
  26.24. Festus said with a l. voice
Rev. 5. 2. proclaiming with a l. voice
   12. Saying with a l. voice ; 6.10
       8.13, 14.7,9
  12.10. I heard a l. voice saying in
  14.15. crying with a l. voice to
  18. cried with a l. voice cry to

LOVE, [*noun*.]
     agapē.
Mat.24.12. the l. of many shall wax col.
Lu. 11.42. judgment and the l. of God
Jo. 5.42. have not the l. of God in you
  13.35. if ye have l. one to another
  15. 9. continue ye in my l.
    10. ye shall abide in my l.; even
       command.,and abide in his l.
   13. Greater l. hath no man than
  17.26. the l. wherewith thou hast
Ro. 5. 5. because the l. of God is shed
     8. God commendeth his l. tow.
   8.35, 39. separate us from the l. of
  12. 9. Let l. be without dissimula.
  13.10. l. worketh no ill to his neig.
     l. is the fulfilling of the law
  15.30. Ch.'s sake, and for the l. of
¹Co. 4.21. with a rod, or in l., and in

---

¹Co. 16.24. My l. be with you all in Ch.
²Co. 2. 4. ye might know the l. which I
     8. confirm your l. toward him
   5.14. the l. of Christ constraineth
   6. 6. by the H. Gh., by l. unfeign.
   8. 7. diligence, and in your l. to
     8. to prove the since. of your l.
   24. churches, the proof of your l.
  13.11. the God of l. and peace sha.
   14. and the l. of God, and the
Gal. 5. 6. faith which worketh by l.
   13. but by l. serve one another
   22. fruit of the Spirit is l., joy
Eph. 1. 4. without blame bef. him in l.
   15. faith in the L. Jesus, and l.
   2. 4. for his great l. wherewith he
   3.17. rooted and grounded in l.
   19. to know the l. of Christ, wh.
   4. 2. forbearing one another in l.
   15. speaking the truth in l., may
   16. the edifying of itself in l.
   5. 2. walk in l., as Christ also ha.
   6.23. the brethren, and l. with fa.
Phil. 1. 9. that your l. may abound yet
   17. the other of l., knowing that
   2. 1. in Christ, if any comfort of l.
     2. likeminded, hav. the same l.
Col. 1. 4. the l. which ye have to all
     8. also declared unto us your l.
   2. 2. be comf.,..knit togeth. in l.
¹Th. 1. 3. work of faith, and labour of l.
   3.12. abound in l. one toward an.
   5. 8. the breastplate of faith and l.
   13. highly in l. for their work's
²Th. 2.10. received not the l. of the tru.
   3. 5. your hearts into the l. of G.
¹Ti. 1.14. abundant with faith and l.
   6.11. faith, l., patience, meekness
²Ti. 1. 7. of power, and of l., and of a
   13. faith and l. which is in Ch.
Phile. 5. Hearing of thy l. and faith
     7. joy and consolation in thy l.
     9. for l.'s sake I rather beseech
Heb. 6.10. your work and labour of l.
  10.24. to provoke unto l. and to
¹Jo. 2. 5. verily is the l. of God perfec.
   15. l. of the Father is not in him
   3. 1. what manner of l. the Fath.
   16. Hereby perceive we the l. of
   17. how dwelleth the l. of God
   4. 7. love one another : for l. is of
     8. knoweth not G.; for G. is l.
     9. manifested the l. of God to.
   10. Herein is l., not that we lov.
   12. and his l. is perfected in us
   16. l. that G. hath to us. G. is l.
     that dwelleth in l. dwelleth
   17. Herein is our l. made perfect
   18. There is no fear in l.; but
     perfect l. casteth out fear
     fear. is not made perfect in l.
   5. 3. this is the l. of God, that we
²John 3. Son of the F., in truth and l.
     6. this is l., that we walk after
Jude 2. unto you, and peace, and l.
   21. Keep yourselves in the l. of
Rev. 2. 4. thou hast left thy first l.
     philadelphia.
Ro. 12.10. one to anot. with *brotherly* l.
¹Th. 4. 9. But as touching *brotherly* l.
Heb.13. 1. Let *brotherly* l. continue
¹Pet. 1.22. unfeigned l. *of the brethren*
     philanthrōpia.
Tit. 3. 4. l. of God our Saviour toward
     philarguria.
¹Ti. 6.10. For the l. *of money* is the

LOVE, [*verb*,] -*ed*,-*edst*, -*est*,-*eth*.
     agapaō.
Mat. 5.43. Thou *shalt* l. thy neighbour ;
     19.19,22.39; Mar.12.31 ;
     Ro.13.9; Gal.5.14 ; Jas.2.8

Mat. 5.44. I say unto you, l.yo.; Lu.6.35
  46. l. them *which* l. you ; Lu.6.32
   6.24. hate the one, and l. the oth. ;
     Lu.16.13   [12.30
  22.37. *shalt* l. the L. thy God ; Mar.
Mar.10.21.Jesus beholding him l-*ed* him
  33. *to* l. him with all the heart
     to l. his neighbour as himself
Lu. 6.27. l. your enemies
   32. sinners also l. those *that* l.
   7. 5. he l-*eth* our nation, and he
   42. which of them *will* l. him
   47. are forgiven ; for she l-*ed*
     little is forgiven, l-*eth* little
  10.27. *shalt* l. the Lord thy God
  11.43. for ye l. the uppermost seats
Jo. 3.16. God so l-*ed* the world, that
   19. l-*ed* darkness rather than
   35. Father l-*eth* the Son, and
   8.42. If G...your Fat., ye would l.
  10.17. Therefore *doth* my Fa. l. me
  11. 5. Now Jesus l-*ed* Martha, and
  12.43. they l-*ed* the praise of men
  13. 1. *having* l-*ed* his own which
     he l-*ed* them unto the end
   23. of his discip. whom Jes. l-*ed*
   34. That ye l. one another
     as I *have* l-*ed* you
     that ye also l. one another
  14.15. If ye l. me, keep my comma.
   21. he it is *that* l-*eth* me : he
     that l-*eth* me *shall be* l-*ed* of
     my Father, and I *will* l. him
   23. If a man l. me, he will keep
     and my Father *will* l. him
   24. He *that* l-*eth* me not keepeth
   28. If ye l-*ed* me, ye would rejo.
   31. may know that I l. the Fath.
  15. 9. *hath* l-*ed* me, so have I l-*ed*
   12. l. one another, as I *have* l-*ed*
   17. I command you, that ye l.
  17.23. *hast* l-*ed*..as thou *hast* l-*ed*
   24. thou l-*edst* me before the
   26. love wherewith thou *hast* l-*ed*
  19.26. disci.stand. by, whom he l-*ed*
  21. 7. disciple whom Jesus l-*ed*
   15. l-*est* thou me more than these
     thou knowest that I love thee
   16. l-*est* thou me?..thou knowest
     that I love thee
   20. the disciple whom Jesus l-*ed*
Ro. 8.28. for good to them *that* l. God
   37. conquers. thro. him *that* l-*ed*
   9.13. As it is writ., Jacob *have* I l-*ed*
  13. 8. to l. one another : for he
     that l-*eth* another hath fulfil.
¹Co. 2. 9. prepared for them *that* l. him
   8. 3. if any man l. God, the same
²Co. 9. 7. for God l-*eth* a cheerful giver
  11.11. Wherefore? because I l. you
  12.15. I l. you, the less I *be* l-*ed*
Gal. 2.20. the Son of God, who l-*ed* me
Eph. 2. 4. great l. wherewith he l-*ed* us
   5. 2. love, as Christ also *hath* l-*ed*
   25. Husb., l. your wives; Col.3.19
     as Christ also l-*ed* the church
   28. So ought men to l. their wives
     He *that* l-*eth* his wife l-*eth*
   33. so l. his wife even as himself
     all them *that* l. our Lord Je.
¹Th 4. 9. taught of God *to* l. one ano.
²Th. 2.16. our Father, which *hath* l-*ed*
²Ti. 4. 8. them also *that* l. his appear.
   10. *having* l-*ed* this present wor.
Heb. 1. 9. Thou *hast* l-*ed* righteousness
  12. 6. whom the Lord l-*eth* he chas.
Jas. 1.12. pro. to them *that* l. him ; 2.5
¹Pet. 1. 8. Whom having not seen, ye l.
   22. that ye l. one another with a
   2.17. l. the brotherhood. Fear G.
   3.10. For he that will l. life, and
²Pet. 2.15. who l-*ed* the wages of *unrigh-*
                  167

Jo. 2.10. He *that* l-*eth* his brother abi.
15. l. not the world, neither the
If any man l. the world, the
3.10. neither he *that* l-*eth* not his
11. that we *should* l. one another
14. because we l. the brethren
He *that* l-*eth* not his brother
18. children, *let* us not l. in word
23. his Son Je. Ch., and l. one
4. 7. Beloved, *let* us l. one another
every one *that* l-*eth* is born of
8 He *that* l-*eth* not knoweth
10. not that we l-*ed* God, but
that he l-*ed* us, and sent his
11. if God so l-*ed* us, we ought
also *to* l. one another
12. If we l. one another, God
19. We l. him, beca. he first l-*ed*
20. If a man say, I l. God, and
for he *that* l-*eth* not his bro.
how can he l. God whom he
21. he *who* l-*eth* God l. his broth.
5. 1. every one *that* l-*eth* him that
begat l-*eth* him also that is
2. we know that we l. the child.
of God, when we l. God
2John 1. children, whom I l. in the
5. from the beginning, that we l.
3John 1. Gaius, whom I l. in the truth
Rev. 1. 5. Unto him *that* l-*ed* us, and
3. 9. to know that I *have* l-*ed* thee
12.11. they l-*ed* not their lives unto
Mat. 6. 5. for they l. to pray standing
10.37. He *that* l-*eth* father or moth.
he *that* l-*eth* son or dau.
23. 6. And l. the uppermost rooms
Lu. 20.46. and l. greetings in the mark.
Jo. 5.20. For the Father l-*eth* the Son
11. 3. he whom thou l-*est* is sick
36. Jews, Behold how he l-*ed* him
12.25. He *that* l-*eth* his life shall
15.19. the world would l. his own
16.27. l-*eth* you, becau. ye *have* l-*ed*
20. 2. other disciple, whom Je. l-*ed*
21.15. lovest thou me more than th.
thou knowest that I l. thee
16. lovest thou me?..thou knowest that l. thee
17. l-*est* thou me? P. was gr. be.
he said the 3d time, l-*est* th.
me?..thou kn. that I l. thee
1Co. 16.22. If any man l. not the L. Je.
Tit. 3.15. Greet them *that* l. us in the
Rev. 3.19. As many as I l., I rebuke
22.15. and whosoever l-*eth* and ma.

philandros.
Tit. 2. 4. to l. *their husbands*, to love

philoteknos.
Tit. 2. 4. husbands, to l. *their children*

philadelphos.
1Pet. 3. 8. l. *as brethren*, be pitiful

philoprōteuō.
3John 9. *who* l-*eth* *to have the pre-emi.*

thelō.
Mar.12.38. l. to go in long clothing

LOVELY.

prosphilēs.
Phi. 4. 8. whatsoever things are l.

LOVER, (See *Hospitality*.) -*s.*

philautos.
2Ti. 3. 2. l-*s of their own selves*, covet.

philēdonos.
2Ti. 3. 4. l-*s of pleasures* more than lo.

philotheos.
2Ti. 3. 4. pleasures more than l-*s of* G.

philagathos.
Tit. 1. 8. hospitality, a l. *of good men*

168

LOW. (See *Degree, Estate.*)

tapeinōsis.
Lu. 1.48. hath regarded the l. *estate* of
Ja. 1.10. rich, in *that he is made* l.

tapeinoō.
Lu. 3. 5. and hill *shall be brought* l.

LOWER, [*comparative.*]

elattoō.
Heb. 2. 7. Thou *madest* him a little l.
9. Jes., *who was made* a little l.

katōteros.
Eph. 4. 9. descended first into the l.

LOWERING.

stugnazō.
Mat.16. 3. for the sky is red and l.

LOWEST.

eschatos.
Lu. 14. 9. shame to take the l. room
10. sit down in the l. room

LOWLINESS.

tapeinophrosunē.
Eph. 4. 2. With all l. and meekness
Phi. 2. 3. but in l. *of mind* let each

LOWLY.

tapeinos.
Mat.11.29. I am meek and l. in heart

LUCRE. (See *Greedy*.)

kerdos.
Tit. 1.11. ought not, for filthy l.'s sake

aischrokerdēs.
1Ti. 3. 3, 8. not *greedy of filthy* l.
Tit. 1. 7. striker, not *given to filthy* l.

aischrokerdōs.
1Pet.5. 2. willingly ; not *for filthy* l.

LUKEWARM.

chliaros.
Rev.3.16. So then because thou art l.

LUMP.

phurama.
Ro. 9.21. same l. to make one vessel
11.16. be holy, the l. is also holy
1Co. 5. 6. leaven, the whole l. ; Gal.5.9
7. that ye may be a new l., as

LUNATICK.

selēniazomai.
Mat. 4.24. and those *which were* l., and
17.15. mercy on my son, for he *is* l.

LUST, [*noun,*] -*s.*

epithumia.
Mar. 4.19. the l-*s* of other things
Jo. 8.44. the l-*s* of your father ye will
Ro. 1.24. through the l-*s* of their own
6.12. shou. obey it in the l-*s* thereof
7. 7. for I had not known l. except
13.14. to fulfil the l-*s* thereof
Gal. 5. 6. shall not fulfil the l. of the
24. with the affections and l-*s*
Eph. 2. 3. in the l-*s* of our flesh, fulfill.
4.22. according to the deceitful l-*s*
1Ti. 6. 9. many foolish and hurtful l-*s*
2Ti. 2.22. Flee also youthful l-*s* : but
3. 6. sins, led away with divers l-*s*
4. 3. after their own l-*s* shall they
Tit. 2.12. ungodliness and worldly l-*s*
3. 3. serving divers l-*s* and pleasu.
Jas. 1.14. is drawn away of his own l.
15. Then when l. hath conceived
1Pet. 1.14. according to the former l-*s*
2.11. abstain from fleshly l-*s*, whi.
4. 2. should live..to the l-*s* of men
3. l-*s*, excess of wine, revellings
2Pet. 1. 4. that is in the world throu. l.
2.10. in the l. of uncleanness
18. allure through the l-*s* of the
3. 3. walk.after their..l-*s* ; Jude16
1Jo. 2.16. l. of the flesh, and the l. of
17. world pass. away, and the l.
Jude 18. after their own ungodly l-*s*

orexis.
Ro. 1.27. burned in their l. one toward

pathos.
1Th. 4. 5. Not in the l. of concupiscenc
hēdonē.
Jas. 4. 1. not hence, even of your l-*s*
3. consume it upon your l-*s*

LUST, [*verb,*] -*ed*, -*eth.*

epithumeō.
Mat. 5.28. look. on a woman *to* l. *after*
1Co. 10. 6. after evil.., as they also l-*ed*
Gal. 5.17. For the flesh l-*eth* against the
Jas. 4. 2. Ye l., and have not : ye kill

epipotheō.
Jas. 4. 5. dwelleth in us l-*eth* to envy

eimi epithumētēs.
1Co.10. 6. we *should* not l. after evil

epithumia.
Rev.18.14. fruits *that* thy soul l-*ed after*

LYING, [*deceiving.*]

pseudos.
Eph. 4.25. Wherefore putting away l.
2Th. 2. 9. and signs and l. wonders

LYING IN WAIT.

enedra.
Act.23.16. sister's son heard of their l.

epiboulē.
Act.20.19. befell me by the l. of the Jews

MAD.

mainomai.
Jo. 10.20. He hath a devil, and *is* m.
Act.12.12. said unto her, Thou *art* m.
26.25. I am not m., most noble F.
1Co. 14.23. they not say that ye are m.

emmainomai.
Act.26.11. *being* exceedingly m. *against*

peritrepō eis mania.
Act.26.24. learning *doth make* thee m.

MADNESS.

anoia.
Lu. 6.11. And were filled with m.

paraphronia.
2Pet.2.16. forbad the m. of the prophet

MAGISTRATE, -*s.*

stratēgos.
Act.16.20.And brought them to the m-*s*
22.and the m-*s* rent off their clo.
35.the m-*s* sent the serjeants
36.The m-*s* have sent to let you
38.told these words unto the m-*s*

archē.
Lu.12.11. the synagogues, and unto m-*s*

archōn.
Lu.12.58. with thine adversary to the m.

peitharcheō.
Tit. 3. 1. to *obey* m-*s*, to be ready to

MAGNIFICENCE.

megaleiotēs.
Act 19.27. her m. should be destroyed

MAGNIFY, -*ed.*

megalunō.
Lu. 1.46. My soul *doth* m. the Lord
Act. 5.13. but the people m-*ed* them
10.46. speak with tongues, and m.
19.17. of the Lord J. Ch. *was* m-*ed*
Phi. 1.20. also Christ *shall be* m-*ed* in

doxazō.
Ro.11.13. Gentiles, I m. mine office

MAID, -*s.*

korasion.
Mat. 9.24. the m. is not dead, but sle.
25. the hand, and the m. arose

paidiskē.
Mar.14.66.there cometh one of the m-*s*
69. And a m. saw him again, and
Lu. 22.56. But a certain m. beheld him

pais.
Lu. 8.54. and called, saying, m. arise

MAIDEN, -s.
paidiskē.
Lu.12.45. beat the menservants and **m**-s
pais.
Lu. 8.51. and the mother of the **m**.

MAIMED.
kullos.
Mat.15.30.dumb, **m**., and many others
    31. the **m**. to be whole, the lame
18. 8. into life halt or **m**.;Mar.9.43
anapēros.
Lu.14.13, 21. call the poor, the **m**., the

MAINSAIL.
artemōn.
Act.27.40. hoised up the **m**. to the wind

MAINTAIN.
proistēmi.
Tit. 3. 8. be careful to **m**. good works
    14. also learn to **m**. good works

MAJESTY.
megalōsunē.
Heb.1. 3. on the right hand of the **m**.
  8. 1. throne of the **m**. in the hea.
Jude 25. be glory and **m**., dominion
megaleiotēs.
2Pet.1.16. were eyewitnesses of his **m**.

MAKE, -est, -eth, -ing, Made.
poieō.
Mat. 3. 3. Lord, **m**. his paths straight ;
    Mar.1.3 ; Lu.3.4 [1.17
  4.19. I *will* **m**. you fishers of ; Mar.
  5.36. thou canst not **m**. one hair
 12.16. *sh*.not **m**.him know;Mar.3.12
    33. Either **m**. the tree good, and
    or else **m**. the tree corrupt
17. 4. *let us* **m**. here three tabern. ;
    Mar.9.5 ; Lu.9.33
19. 4. that he *which* **m**-de them at
    m-de them male and;Mar.10.6
20.12. thou *hast* **m**-de them equal
21.13. ye *have* **m**-de it a den of thie.;
    Mar.11.17 ; Lu.19.46
22. 2. which **m**-de a marriage for
23.15. compass sea and land to **m**.
    ye **m**. him twofold more the
25.16. and **m**-de them other five ta.
Mar. 6.21. **m**-de a supper to his lords
  7.37. he **m**-eth both the deaf to
  8.25. his eyes, and **m**-de him look
Lu. 5.29. Levi **m**-de him a great feast
    33. fast often, and **m**. prayers
    34. Can ye **m**. the children of
11.40. *did* not he *that* **m**-de that
    which is without, **m**. that
14.12. When thou **m**-*est* a dinner
    13. when thou **m**-*est* a feast
    16. A certain man **m**-de a great
15.19. **m**. me as one of thy hired
 16. 9. **m**. to yourselves friends of
Jo. 2.15. *when* he *had* **m**-de a scourge
    16. **m**. not my Father's house an
4. 1. that Jesus **m**-de and baptiz.
    46. where he **m**-de the water wi.
 5.11. He *that* **m**-de me whole, the
    15. Jesus, *which had* **m**-de him
    18. **m**-*ing* himself equal with G.
6.10. **m**. the men sit down. Now
    15. by force to **m**. him a king
7.23. because I *have* **m**-de a man
8.53. whom **m**-*est* thou thyself
9. 6. and **m**-de clay of the spittle
    11. A man that is called J. **m**-de
    14. when Jesus **m**-de the clay
10.33. being a man, **m**-*est* thyself G.
12. 2. There they **m**-de him a sup.
14.23. and **m**. our abode with him
18.18. *who had* **m**-de a fire of coals
19. 7. because he **m**-de himself the
  12. *who* soever **m**-*eth* himself a
  33. and **m**-de four parts, to ev.

Act. 1. 1. former treatise *have* I **m**-de
 2.36. God *hath* **m**-de that same J.
 3.12. we *had* **m**-de this man to
 4.24. *which hast* **m**-de heaven and
 7.40. **m**. us gods to go before us
    43. which ye **m**-de to worship
    44. that he should **m**. it accord.
    50. *Hath* not my hand **m**-de all
8. 2. and **m**-de great lamentation
9.39. garments which Dorcas **m**-de
14.15. living God, which **m**-de hea.
17.24. God *that* **m**-de the world and
    26. And *hath* **m**-de of one blood
19.24. *which* **m**-de silver shrines for
23.13. *which had* **m**-de this conspl.
Ro. 1. 9. I **m**. mention of you always
9.20. Why *hast* thou **m**-de me thus
    21. *to* **m**. one vessel unto honour
    28. a short work *will* the Lord **m**.
13.14. and **m**. not provision for
15.26. *to* **m**. a certain contribution
1Co. 6.15. and **m**. them the members
10.13. *will* with the tempt. also **m**.
2Co. 5.21. he *hath* **m**-de him to be sin
Eph. 1.16. **m**-*ing* menti. of you;1Th.1.2
 2.14. *who hath* **m**-de both one, and
    15. one new man, so **m**-*ing* pea.
 4.16. **m**-*eth* increase of the body
Phi. 1. 4. you all **m**-*ing* request with
1Ti. 2. 1. giving of thanks, *be* **m**-de for
Phile. 4. **m**-*ing* mention of thee alwa.
Heb. 1. 2. by whom also he **m**-de the
    7. *Who* **m**-*eth* his angels spirits
8. 5. See,..thou **m**. all things ac.
    9. that I **m**-de with their fathers
12.13. **m**. straight paths for your
    27. as of things *that are* **m**-de
Jas. 3.18. peace of them that **m**. peace
2Pet. 1.10. *to* **m**. your calling and elect.
1Jo. 1.10. we **m**. him a liar, and his
5.10. *hath* **m**-de him a liar ; beca.
Rev. 1. 6. And *hath* **m**-de us kings and
3. 9. I *will* **m**. them to come and
    12. that overcometh *will* I **m**. a
5.10. And *hast* **m**-de us unto our
11. 7. *shall* **m**. war against them
12.17. and went *to* **m**. war with the
13. 7. *to* **m**. war with the saints
    13. he **m**-*eth* fire come down
    14. *that* they *should* **m**. an ima.
14. 7. worship him *that* **m**-de hea.
17.16. and *shall* **m**. her desolate and
19.19. *to* **m**. war against him that
21. 5. Behold, I **m**. all things new
22.15. whosoever loveth and **m**-*eth*
prospoieomai.
Lu. 24.28. he **m**-de *as though* he would
poiēma.
Ro. 1.20. by the *things that are* **m**-de
ginomai.
Mat. 4. 3. that these stones *be* **m**-de
9.16. rent is **m**-de worse;Mar.2.21
23.15. when he *is* **m**-de, ye make
25. 6. midnight the. *was* a cry **m**-de
27.24. rather a tumult *was* **m**-de
Mar.14. 4. waste of the ointment **m**-de
Lu. 4. 3. stone that it *be* **m**-de bread
8.17. *shall* not be **m**-de manifest
14.12. and a recompence *be* **m**-de
23.12. and Herod *were* **m**-de friends
    19. a certain sedition **m**-de in the
Jo. 1. 3. All things *were* **m**-de by him
    thing **m**-de *that was* **m**-de
    10. the world *was* **m**-de by him
    14. the Word *was* **m**-de flesh
2. 9. the water *that was* **m**-de wine
5. 4. *was* **m**-de whole of whatsoev.
    9. Wilt thou be **m**-de whole
    immed. the man *was* **m**-de
    14. Behold, thou *art* **m**-de whole
8.33. sayest.., Ye *shall be* **m**-de free
9.39. which see *might be* **m**-de bli.

Act. 7.13. Joseph's kindred *was* **m**-de
12. 5. prayer *was* **m**-de without
13.32. the promise which *was* **m**-de
14. 5. there *was* an assault **m**-de
19.26. no gods, *which are* **m**-de with
21.40. *when* there *was* **m**-de a great
26. 6. hope of the promise **m**-de of
Ro. 1. 3. *which was* **m**-de of the seed
2.25. circumcision *is* **m**-de uncir.
7.13. **m**-de death unto me? God
10.20. I *was* **m**-de manifest unto
11. 9. *Let* their table *be* **m**-de a sna.
1Co. 1.30. who of God *is* **m**-de unto us
3.13. man's work *shall be* **m**-de
4. 9. we *are* **m**-de a spectacle unto
    13. we *are* **m**-de as the filth of
7.21. if thou mayest *be* **m**-de free
9.22. I *am* **m**-de all things to all
11.19. *may be* **m**-de manifest among
14.25. *are* the secr. of his heart **m**-de
15.45. Adam *was* **m**-de a living soul
2Co. 5.21. we *might be* **m**-de the righte.
Gal. 3.13. *being* **m**-de a curse for us : for
4. 4. Son, **m**-de of a woman, **m**-de
Eph. 2.13. *are* **m**-de nigh by the blood
Phi. 2. 7. *and was* **m**-de in the likeness
Col. 1.23. whereof I Paul am **m**-de a.
    25. Whereof I *am* **m**-de a minis.
Tit. 3. 7. we *should be* **m**-de heirs ac.
Heb. 1. 4. *Being* **m**-de so much better
3.14. we *are* **m**-de partakers of
5. 5. himself *to be* **m**-de an high
6. 4. *were* **m**-de partakers of the
    20. Jesus, **m**-de an high priest
7 12. there *is* **m**-de of necessity a
    16. Who *is* **m**-de, not after the
    21. those priests *were* **m**-de with.
    22. By so much *was* Jesus **m**-de
    26. **m**-de higher than the heav.
11. 3. *were* not **m**-de of things whi.
Jas. 3. 9. *which are* **m**-de after the
1Pet. 2. 7. the same *is* **m**-de the head of
gennaō.
2Pet.2.12. beasts, **m**-e to be taken and
kathistēmi.
Mat.25.45.whom his lord *hath* **m**-de ru.
    47. *shall* **m**. him ruler ; Lu.12.44
25.21, 23.I *will* **m**. thee ruler over
Lu. 12.14. who **m**-de me a judge or a
    42. his lord *shall* **m**. ruler over
Act. 7.10. he **m**-de him governor over
    27, 35. Who **m**-de thee a ruler
Ro. 5.19. many *were* **m**-de sinners, so
    shall many *be* **m**-de righteo.
Heb.7.28. the law **m**-*eth* men high pri.
2Pet. 1. 8. they **m**. you that ye shall
tithēmi.
Mat.22.44.till I **m**. thine enemies thy;
    Mar.12.36;Lu.20.43;Heb.1.13
Act. 2.35. Until I **m**. thy foes thy foot.
20.28. the Holy Ghost *hath* **m**-de
Ro. 4.17. I *have* **m**-de thee a father of
1Co. 9.18. I *may* **m**. the gospel of Christ
Heb.10.13.till his enemies *be* **m**-de his
2Pet. 2. 6. **m**-*ing* them an ensample
diatithemai.
Act. 3.25. the covenant which God **m**-de
Heb. 8.10. covenant that I *will* **m**.;10.16
sumballō eis polemos.
Lu.14.31. to **m**. war against another
eimi.
Mar.12.42.two mites, which **m**. a farth.
Act.16.13. wh. pray.was wont *to be* **m**-de
procheirizomai.
Act.26.16. *to* **m**. thee a minister and a
katechō.
Act.27.40. wind, and **m**-de *toward* shore
sunistaō.
Gal. 2.18. I **m**. myself a transgressor
reō.
Gal.3.16. his seed *were* the promises **m**-de

ktizō.
Eph.2.15. for to **m**. in himself of twain
  epiteleō.
Heb. 8. 5. was about *to* **m**. the tabern.
  sunteleō.
Heb.8. 8.I *will* **m**. a new covenant with
  kataskeuazō.
Heb. 9. 2. there was a tabernacle **m**-*de*
  keimai.
¹Ti. 1. 9. law *is* not **m**-*de* fo. a righteous
  didōmi.
²Th. 3. 9. to **m**. ourselves an ensample
Rev. 3. 9. Behold, I will **m**. them of
  (*See words in connection.*)

MAKER.
  dēmiourgos.
Heb.11.10. whose builder and **m**. is G.

MALE.
  arsēn.   [Mar.10.6
Mat.19. 4. made them **m**. and female;
Lu. 2.23. Every **m**. that openeth the
Gal. 3.28. there is neither **m**. nor fem.

MALEFACTOR,   -*s*.
  kakourgos.
Lu.23.32. two others, **m**-*s*, led with
  33. crucified him, and the **m**-*s*
  39. one of the **m**-*s* which were
  kakopoios.
Jo. 18.30. If he were not a **m**., we wou.

MALICE.
  kakia.
¹Co. 5. 8. leaven of **m**. and wickedness
  14.20. howbeit in **m**. be ye children
Eph. 4.31. away from you, with all **m**.
Col. 3. 8. anger, wrath, **m**., blasphemy
Tit. 3. 3. living in **m**. and envy, hate.
¹Pet. 2. 1. laying aside all **m**., and all

MALICIOUS.
  ponēros.
³John 10. against us with **m**. words

MALICIOUSNESS.
  kakia.
Ro. 1.29. covetous, **m**.; full of envy
¹Pet. 2.16. liberty for a cloke of **m**.

MALIGNITY.
  kakoētheia.
Ro. 1.29. murder, debate, deceit, **m**.

MAMMON.
  mammōnas.   [Lu.16.13
Mat. 6.24. cannot serve God and **m**.;
Lu. 16. 9. friends of the **m**. of unright.
  11. faith. in the unrighteous **m**.

MAN. (See *Son of*.)   *Men*.
  anthrōpos.
       Man.   [Lu.4.4
Mat.4. 4. **m**. shall not live by bread ;
  7. 9. what **m**. is there of you, who
  9.32. brought to him a dumb **m**.
  12.11. What **m**. shall there be amo.
  13. Then saith he to the **m**., Str.
  35. A good **m**. out of the good ;
      Lu.6.45   [Lu.6.45
  an evil **m**. out of the evil ;
  45. state of that **m**. is ; Lu.11.26
  13.45. is like unto a merchant **m**.
  15.18. heart ; and they defile the **m**.
  17.14. came to him a certain **m**.
  18. 7. woe to that **m**. by whom ;
      26.24 ; Mar.14.21 ; Lu.22.22
  19.10. If the case of the **m**. be so
  21.28. A. . **m**. had two so.; Lu.15.11
  25.24. that thou art an hard **m**.
  26.24. it had been good for that **m**.;
      Mar.14.21   [Mar.14.71
  72, 74. I do not know the **m**.;
Mar 2.27. made for **m**., and not for
170

Mar. 3. 3, 5. he saith unto the **m**. wh.;
      Lu.6.8,10
  5. 8. unto him, Come out of the **m**.
  7.15. are they that defile the **m**.
  18. without entereth into the **m**.
  20. out of the **m**., that defileth
  23. from with., and defile the **m**.
  11. 2. whereon never **m**.; Lu.19.30
  12. 1. A cer. **m**. planted a ; Lu.20.9
Lu. 2.25. the same **m**. was just and
  52. and in favour with G. and **m**.
  5.20. said unto him, **m**., thy sins
  7.34. Behold a gluttonous **m**., and
  8.29. spirit to come out of the **m**.
  33. went the devils out of the **m**.
  35. came to Jes. and fou. the **m**.
  10.30. A certain **m**.went down from
  12.14. said unto him, **m**., who made
  16. ground of a certain rich **m**.
  14. 2. there was a certain **m**. before
  16. A certain **m**. made a great
  30. Saying, This **m**. began to
  15. 4. What **m**. of you, having an
  16. 1, 19. There was a cer. rich **m**.
  18. 2. not God, neither regarded **m**.
  4. I fear not God, nor regard **m**.
  19.21. beca. thou art an austere **m**.
  22. knewest. .I was an auste. **m**.
  22.58. Peter said, **m**., I am not
  60. Peter said, **m**., I know not
  23. 4. I find no fault in this **m**.
  6. whether the **m**. were a Gali.
  14. Ye have brought this **m**.unto
  ha. found no fault in this **m**.
  47. Certa. this was a righteo. **m**.
Jo. 1. 9. which lighteth every **m**. that
  2.10. Every **m**. at the beginning
  25. **m**.: for he knew. .was in **m**.
  4.50. the **m**. believed the word
  5. 5. a certain **m**. was there, which
  7. Sir, I have no **m**., when the
  9. immediately the **m**. was ma.
  12. What **m**. is that which said
  15. The **m**. departed, and told
  34. I receive not testi. from **m**.
  7.46. Never **m**. spake like this **m**.
  51. our law judge any **m**., before
  9.16. This **m**. is not of God, beca.
  24. again called they the **m**. that
  we know that this **m**. is a
  30. The **m**. answered and said
  11.47. this **m**. doeth many miracles
  50. that one **m**. shou. die ; 18.14
  18.17. also one of this **m**.'s discip.
  29. accusa. bring ye aga. this **m**.
  19. 5. saith. .them, Behold the **m**.
Act. 4. 9. de done to the impotent **m**.
  14. beholding the **m**. which was
  17. henceforth to no **m**. in this
  22. the **m**. was above forty years
  5.28. to bring this **m**.'s blood upon
  6.13. This **m**. ceaseth not to speak
  9.33. he found a certain **m**. named
  10.28. should not call any **m**. com.
  17.29. graven by art and **m**.'s devi.
  19.16. the **m**. in whom the evil spi.
  35. what **m**. is there that know.
  21.28. This is the **m**., that teacheth
  22.26. thou doest : for this **m**. is a
  23. 9. We find no evil in this **m**.
  25.16. to deliver any **m**. to die
  22. I would also hear the **m**.
  26.31. This **m**. doeth nothing wort.
  32. This **m**. might have been set
  28. 4. No doubt this **m**. is a murd.
Ro. 2. 1. image. .like to corruptib. **m**.
  2. 1. inexcusable, O **m**., whosoev.
  3. thinkest thou this, O **m**., th.
  9. every soul of **m**. that doeth
  3. 4. God be true, and every **m**. a
  4. 6. the blessedness of the **m**.
  5.12. as by one **m**. sin entered into

Ro. 5.15. gift by gra. wh. is by one **m**.
  19. as by one **m**.'s disobedience
  6. 6. that our old **m**. is crucified
  7.22. law of God after the ıw. **m**.
  24. O wretched **m**. that I am
  9.20. O **m**., who art thou that re.
  10. 5. the **m**. which doeth these
  14.20. it is evil for that **m**. who
¹Co. 2. 9. entered into the heart of **m**.
  11. what **m**. knoweth the things
  of a **m**. save the spirit of **m**.
  14. the natural **m**. receiveth not
  15.21. since by **m**. came death
  by **m**.came also the resurrec.
¹Co.15.45. The·first **m**. Adam was made
  47. The first **m**. is of the earth
  the second **m**. is the Lord
²Co. 4. 2. to every **m**.'s conscience in
  16. though our outward **m**. per.
Gal. 1. 1. not of **m**e., neither by **m**.
  11. preached of me is not after **m**.
  12. I neither received'it of **m**.
  2. 6. God accepteth no **m**.'s person
  3.12. The **m**. that doeth them sh.
  5. 3. I testify again to every **m**.
Eph. 2.15. himself of twain one new **m**.
  3.16. by his Spirit in the inner **m**.
  4.22. the old **m**., which is corrupt
  24. that ye put on the new **m**.
Col. 1.28. Whom we preach, warn. . .**m**.
  and teaching every **m**. in all
  that we may present every **m**.
  3. 9. ye have put off the old **m**.
  8. despiseth not **m**., but God
¹Th. 2. 3. that **m**. of sin be revealed
²Th. 2. 3. that **m**. of sin be revealed
¹Ti. 2. 5. the **m**. Christ Jesus
  6.11. But thou, O **m**. of God, flee
  16. whom no **m**. hath seen, nor
²Ti. 3.17. That the **m**. of God may be
Heb. 2. 6. What is **m**., that thou art
  r the son of **m**., that thou
  8. 2. the Lord pitched, and not **m**.
  13. 6. I will not fear what **m**. shall
Jas. 1. 7. let not that **m**. think that he
  19. let every **m**. be swift to·hear
  2.20. wilt thou know, O vain **m**.
  3. 8. the tongue can no **m**. tame
¹Pet. 1.24. all the glory of **m**. as the flo.
  3. 4. the hidden **m**. of the heart
²Pet. 1.21. in old time by the will of **m**.
  2.16. dumb ass speaking with **m**. s

       A Man.
Mat. 8. 9. For I am a **m**. under author.
  9. 9. he saw a **m**., named Matth.
  10.35. to set a **m**. at variance again.
  36. a **m**.'s foes shall be they of
  11. 8. a **m**. clothed in soft raiment
  19. and they say, Behold a **m**.
  12.10. behold, there was a **m**. which
  12. then is a **m**. better than a
  43. when the unclean spir. is gone
  out of a **m**.; Lu.11.24.
  13.24. is likened unto a **m**. which
  31. which a **m**. took, and sowed
  44. which when a **m**. hath found
  52. like unto a **m**. that is an ; 20.1
  15.11. into the mouth defileth a **m**.
  out of the **m**., this defil. a **m**.
  20. defile a **m**.: but to eat with
  unwash. hands defil. not a **m**.
  16.26. For what is a **m**. profited, if ;
      Mar.8.36   [Mar.8.37
  or what shall a **m**. give in ;
  18.12. if a **m**. have an hundred sh.
  19. 3. Is it lawful for a **m**. to put
  5. for this cause shall a **m**.
  leave ; Mar.10.7
  22.11. saw there a **m**. which had
  25.14. as a **m**. travelling into a far
  27.32. they found a **m**. of Cyrene
Mar. 1.23. a **m**. with an unclean spirit

Mar. 3. 1. there was a **m.** there which
4.26. as if a **m.** should cast seed
5. 2. out of the tombs a **m.** with
7.11. If a **m.** shall say to his fath.
15. is nothing from without a **m.**
13.34. Son of man is as a **m.** taking
14.13. sha. meet you a **m.**; Lu.22.10
2.25. there was a **m.**, which had a
4.33. there was a **m.**, which had a
5.18. brought in a bed a **m.** which
6. 6. there was a **m.** whose right
48. He is like a **m.** which built
49. is like a **m.** that without a
7. 8. I also am a **m.** set under au.
Lu. 7. 25. A **m.** clothed in soft raiment
9.25. For what is a **m.** advantaged
13.19. mustard seed, which a **m.**
Jo. 1. 6. There was a **m.** sent from G.
3. 1. There was a **m.** of the Phar.
4. How can a **m.** be·born when
27. A **m.** can receive nothing
4.29. Come, see a **m.**, which told
7.22. sabbath-day circumcise a **m.**
23. If a **m.** on the sabbath day
I have made a **m.** every whi
8.40. a **m.** that hath told you the
9. 1. he saw a **m.** which was blind
11. A **m.** that is called Jesus
16. said, How can a **m.**, that
10.33. thou, being a **m.**, makest
16.21. for joy that a **m.** is born into
Act.10.26. up; I myself also am a **m.**
12.22. of a god, and not of a **m.**
21.39. Paul said, I am a **m.** which
22.25. scourge a **m.** that is a Rom.
Ro. 3. 5. vengeance? I speak as a **m.**
28. that a **m.** is justified by faith
7. 1. dominion over a **m.** as long
1Co. 2.11. of a **m.**, save the spirit of **m.**
4. 1. Let a **m.** so account of us
6.18. Every sin that a **m.** doeth
7. 1. It is good for a **m.** not to
26. it is good for a **m.** so to be
9. 8. Say I these things as a **m.**
11.28. let a **m.** examine himself
Cor.12. 2. I knew a **m.** in Christ above
3. I knew such a **m.**, whether
4. is not lawful for a **m.** to utter
Gal. 2.16. a **m.** is not justified by the
3.15. Though it be but a **m.'s** cov.
6. 1. if a **m.** be overtaken in a
7. for whatsoever a **m.** soweth
Eph. 5.31. shall a **m.** leave his father
Phi. 2. 8. being fou. in fashion as a **m.**
Tit. 3.10. A **m.** that is an heretick after
Jas. 5.17. Elias was a **m.** subject to like
Rev. 4. 7. third beast had a face as a **m.**
9. 5. scor., when he striketh a **m.**
13.18. for it is the number of a **m.**

Men.   [Mar.1.17
Mat. 4.19. I will make you fish. of **me.**;
5,13. be trodden under foot of **me.**
16. your light so shine bef. **me.**
19. shall teach **me.** so, he shall
6. 1. do not your alms before **me.**
2. that they..have glory of **me.**
5. that they may be seen of **me.**
14. if ye forgive **me.** their trespa.
15. if ye forgive not **me.** their
16. they may appear unto **me.**
18. thou appear not unto **me.**
7.12. ye would that **me.** should do
8.27. the **me.** marvelled, saying
9. 8. given such power unto **me.**
10.17. beware of **me.**; for they will
32. shall confess **me.** before **me.**
33. shall deny **me.** before **me.**
12.31. blas. shall be forgi. unto **me.**
shall not be forgiv. unto **me.**
36. idle word that **me.** shall sp.
13.25. while **me.** slept, his enemy

Mat.15. 9. command. of **me.**; Mar.7.7
16.23. G., but those that be of **me.**
17.22. betray. into the hands of **me.**
19.12. were made eunuchs of **me.**
26. With **me.** this is impossible ;
Mar.10.27 [11.30; Lu.20.4
21.25. from heaven, or of **me.**; Mar.
26. if we shall say, Of **me.**; Mar.
11.32 ; Lu.20.6   [12.14
22.16. reg. not the per. of **me.**; Mar.
23. 4. lay them on **me.'s** shoulders
5. they do for to be seen of **me.**
7. to be called of **me.**, Rabbi
13. kingdom of hea. against **me.**
28. appear righteous unto **me.**
Mar 9.28. forgiven unto the sons of **me.**
7. 8. ye hold the tradition of **me.**
21. out of the heart of **me.** pro,
8.24. said, I see **me.** as trees, walk.
27. Whom do **me.** say that I am
33. the things that be of **me.**
9.31. the hands of **me.**; Lu.22.22
Lu. 1.25. away my reproach amo. **me.**
2.14. peace, good will'toward **me.**
5.10. hencef. thou shalt catch **me.**
6.22. Blessed are ye, when **me.** sh.
26. when all **me.** shall speak well
31. as ye would that **me.** should
7.31. shall I liken the **me.** of this
9.44. deliv. into the hands of **me.**
56. is not come to destroy **me.'s**
11.44. the **me.** that walk over them
46. ye lawyers ! for ye lade **me.**
12. 8. shall confess me before **me.**
9. he that denieth me befo. **me.**
36. ye yourselves like unto **me.**
13. 4. they were sin. above all **me.**
16.15. justify yourselves before **me.**,
esteemed among **me.** is abo.
18.10. Two **me.** went up into the
11. that I am not as other **me.**
27. which are inpossi. with **me.**
21.26. **me.'s** hearts failing them for
Jo. 1. 4. the life was the light of **me.**
3.19. **me.** loved darkness rather
4.28. the city, and saith to the **me.**
5.41. I receive not hon. from **me.**
6.10. Said, Make the **me.** sit down
14. Then those **me.**, when they
8.17. the testimony of two **me.** is
12.43. loved the praise of **me.** more
17. 6. mani. thy name unto the **me.**
Act. 4.12. given among **me.** whereby we
13. unlearned and ignorant **me.**
16. Wh. shall we do to these **me.**
5. 4. hast not lied unto **me.**, but
29. to obey God rather than **me.**
35. to do as touching these **me.**
38. Refrain from these **me.**, and
coun. or this work be of **me.**
14.11. to us in the likeness of **me.**
15. We also are **me.** of like pas.
15.17. the residue of **me.** might
26. **me.** that have hazarded their
16.17. These **me.** are the servants
20. saying, These **me.**, being Je.
35. serje., saying, Let those **me.**
17.25. Neither is worsh.with **me.'s**
26. one blood all nations of **me.**
30. commandeth all **me.** every.
18.13. This fellow persuadeth **me.**
22.15. be his witness unto all **me.**
24.16. toward God, and toward **me.**
Ro. 1.18. and unrighteousness of **me.**
2.16. shall judge the secrets of **me.**
29. whose praise is not of **me.**
5.12. so death passed upon all **me.**
18. judgment came upon all **me.**
free gift came upon all **me.**
12.17. honest in the sight of all **me.**
18. live peaceably with all **me.**
14.18. to God, and approved of **me.**

1Co. 1.25. foolish.of G.is wiser than **me.**
of God is stronger than **me.**
2. 5. stand in the wisdom of **me.**
3. 3. not carnal, and walk as **me.**
21. let no man glory in **me.**
4. 9. and to angels, and to **me.**
7. 7. I would that all **me.** were
23. be not ye the servants of **me.**
13. 1. with the tongues of **me.** and
14. 2. speaketh not unto **me.**, but
3. speaketh unto **me.** to edifica.
15.19. we are of all **me.** most mise.
32. If after the manner of **me.**
39. is one kind of flesh of **me.**
2Co. 3. 2. known and read of all **me.**
5.11. we persuade **me.**; but we are
8.21. but also in the sight of **me.**
Gal. 1. 1. an apostle, not of **me.**, nei.
10. For do I now persuade **me.**
do I seek to please **me.**,
for if I yet pleased **me.**, I
3.15. of **me.**; Though it be but a
Eph. 3. 5. known unto the sons of **me.**
4. 8. cap., and gave gifts unto **me.**
14. by the sleight of **me.** and cu.
6. 7. to the Lord, and not to **me.**
Phi. 2. 7. made in the likeness of **me.**
4. 5. mode. be known unto all **me.**
Col. 2. 8. deceit, after the tradi. of **me.**
22. command. and doctr. of **me.**
3.23. the Lord, and not unto **me.**
1Th. 2. 4. not as pleasing **me.**, but God
6. Nor of **me.** sought we glory
13. it not as the word of **me.**
15. G., and are contr. to all **me.**
2Th. 3. 2. from unrea. and wicked **me.**
1Ti. 2. 1. thanks, be made for all **me.**
4. Who will have all **me.** to be
5. between God and **me.**, the
4.10. who is the saviour of all **me.**
5.24. Some **me.'s** sins are open bef.
6. 5. disputings of .. of corrupt
9. which drown **me.** in destruc.
2Ti. 2. 2. commit thou to faithful **me.**
3. 2. For **me.** shall be lovers of
8. **me.** of corrupt minds, repro.
13. evil **me.** and seducers shall
Tit. 1.14. commandments of **me.**, that
2.11. sal. hath appeared to all **me.**
3. 2. shew. all meek. unto all **me.**
8. are good and profit. unto **me.**
Heb. 5. 1. among **me.** is ordain. for **me.**
6.16. For **me.** verily swear by the
7. 8. here **me.** that die receive
28. maketh **me.** high priests wh.
9.27. as it is appointed unto **me.**
Jas. 3. 9. therewith curse we **me.**, wh.
1Pet. 2. 4. disallowed indeed of **me.**
15. silence the igno.of foolish **me.**
4. 2. in the flesh to the lusts of **me.**
6. according to **me.** in the flesh
2Pet. 1.21. but holy **me.** of God spake
3. 7. and perdition of ungodly **me.**
1Jo. 5. 9. If we receive the wit. of **me.**
Jude there are certain **me.** crept
Rev. 8.11. many **me.** died of the waters
9. 4. only those **me.** which have
6. those days shall **me.** seek
7. faces were as the faces of **me.**
10. their power was to hurt **me.**
15. to slay the third part of **me.**
18. was the third part of **me.**
20. the rest of the **me.** which
11.13. were slain of **me.** seven tho.
13.13. the earth in the sight of **me.**
14. 4. redeemed from among **me.**
16. 2. grievous sore upon the **me.**
8. unto him to scorch **me.** with
9. **me.** were scorched with great
18. as was not since **me.** were
21. there fell upon **me.** a great
and **me.** blasphemed God

Rev.18.13. slaves, and souls of m*e*.
　21. 3. tabernacle of God is with m*e*.

anēr.

Mat. 7.24. will liken him unto a wise m.
　26. be likened unto a foolish m.
　12.41. The m*e*. of Nineveh shall;
　　　　Lu.11.32 [Mar.6.44 ;Lu.9.14
　14.21. about five thousand m*e.;*
　35. when the m*e*. of that place
　15.38. eat were four thousand m*e*.
Mar. 6.20. that he was a just m. and an
　10. 2. Is it lawful for a m. to put
Lu. 1.27. espoused to a m. whose
　34. ɒe, seeing I know not a 'm.
　5. 8. for I am a sinful m., O Lord
　12. behold a m. full of leprosy
　18. behold, m*e*. brought in a bed
　7.20. When the m*e*. were come un.
　8.27. a certain m., which had dev.
　38. Now the m. out of whom the
　41. there came a m. named Jai.
　9.30. talked with him two m*e*.
　32. the two m*e*. that stood with
　38. behold, a m. of the company
　11.31. with the m*e*. of this generat.
　14.24. none of those m*e*. which were
　17.12. ten m*e*. that were lepers
　19. 2. there was a m. named Zac.
　7. guest with a m. that is a
　22.63. the m*e*. that held Jesus moc.
　23.50. there was a m. named Joseph
　　　and he was a good m., and
　24. 4. two m*e*. stood by them in
Jo. 1.13. nor of the will of m., but of
　30. After me cometh a m. which
　6.10. So the m*e*. sat down, in num.
Act. 1.10. two m*e*. stood by them in
　11. Ye m*e*. of Galilee, why stand
　16. m*e*. and brethren ; 2.29,37,
　13.15,26,38, 15.7,13, 23.1,6,28.17
　21. these m*e*. which have comp.
　2. 5. Jews, devout m*e*., out of ev.
　14. Ye m*e*. of Judea, and all ye
　22. Ye m*e*. of Israel, hear these
　　　J. of Nazareth,a m. approved
　3. 2. a certain m. lame from his
　12. Ye m*e*. of Israel, why marvel
　4. 4. the number of the m*e*. was
　5. 1. a certain m. named Ananias
　14. multitudes both of m*e*. and
　25. the m*e*. whom ye put in pris.
　35. Ye m*e*. of Israel, take heed to
　36. to whom a number of m*e*.
　6. 3. seven m*e*. of honest report
　5. a m. full of faith and of the
　11. Then they suborned m*e*., wh.
　7. 2. m*e*., brethren, and fath.;22.1
　8. 2. devout m*e*. carried Stephen
　3. haling me. and women com.
　9. was a certain m., called Sim.
　12. baptized, both m*e*. and wom.
　27. behold, a m. of Ethiopia, an
　9. 2. whether they were m*e*. or
　7. m*e*. which journeyed with
　12. a m. named Ananias coming
　13. heard by many of this m.
　38. they sent unto him two m*e*.
　10. 1. There was a certain m. in
　5. now send m*e*. to Joppa, and
　17. m*e*. which were sent from
　19. Behold, three m*e*. seek thee
　21. down to the m*e*. which were
　22. the centurion, a just m., and
　28. for a m. that is a Jew to keep
　30. behold, a m. stood before
　11. 3. in to m*e*. uncircumcised
　11. there were three m*e*. already
　12. we entered into the m.'s ho.
　13. to him, Send m*e*. to Joppa
　20. were m*e*. of Cyprus and Cyr.
　24. he was a good m., and full
13. 7. Sergius Paulus, a prudent m.

Act. 13.16. said, m*e*. of Israel, and ye
　21. a m. of the tribe of Benjamin
　22. a m. after mine own heart
　14. 8. there sat a certain m. at Lys.
　15.22. to send chosen m*e*. of their
　　　chief m*e*. among the brethr.
　25. send chosen m*e*. unto you
　16. 9. There stood a m. of Macedo.
　17.12. were Greeks, and of m*e*., not
　22. Ye m*e*. of Athens, I perceive
　31. by that m. whom he hath
　34. certain m*e*. clave unto him
　18.24. an eloquent m., and mighty
　19. 7. all the m*e*. were about twelve
　35. he said, Ye m*e*. of Ephesus
　37. have brought hither these m*e*.
　20.30. of your own selves shall m*e*.
　21.11. bind the m. that owneth this
　23. We have four m*e*. which have
　26. Then Paul took the m*e*., and
　28. Cry. out, m*e*. of Israel, help
　38. four thousand m*e*. that were
　22. 3. I am verily a m. which am a
　4. into prisons both m*e*. and
　12. a devout m. according to the
　23.21. of them more than forty m*e*.
　27. This m. was taken of the Jews
　30. the Jews laid wait for the m.
　24. 5. we have found this m. a pest.
　25. 5. with me, and accuse this m.
　14. There is a certain m. left in
　17. commanded the m. to be
　23. captains, and principal m*e*.
　24. m*e*. which are here present
Ro. 4. 8. Blessed is the m. to whom
　7. 3. she be married to another m.
　11. 4. myself seven thousand m*e*.
1Co. 7.16. or how knowest thou, O m.
　11. 3. the head of every m. is Ch.
　　　head of the woman is the m.
　4. Every m. praying or prophe.
　7. For a m. indeed ought not
　　　woman is the glory of the m.
　8. For the m. is not of the wo.
　　　but the woman of the m.
　9. Neither was the m. created
　　　but the woman for the m.
　11. neither is the m. without the
　　　woman without the m.
　12. of the m., even so is the m.
　14. that, if a m. have long hair
　13.11. when I became a m., I put
Eph. 4.13. unto a perfect m., unto the
　5.28. So ought m*e*. to love their
1Ti. 2. 8. that m*e*. pray every where
　12. usurp authority over the m.
　5. 9. having been the wife of one m.
Jas. 1. 8. A double minded m. is uns.
　12. Blessed is the m. that endu.
　20. the wrath of m. worketh not
　23. he is like unto a m. behold.
　2. 2. assembly a m. with a gold
　3. 2. the same is a perfect m., and

oudeis.

Mat. 6.24. *No* m. can serve two masters
　9.16. *No* m. putt. a piece ; Lu.5.36
　11.27. and *no* m. knoweth the Son
　17. 8. they saw *no* m., save Jesus
　20. 7. Because *no* m. hath hired us
　22.46. *no* m. was able to answer him
　24.36. hour know. *no* m.; Mar.13.32
Mar. 2.21. *No* m. also seweth a piece
　22. *no* m. putteth new ; Lu.5.37
　3.27. *No* m. can enter into a stro.
　5. 3. *no* m. could bind him, no
　4. neither could *any* m. tame
　37. he suffered *no* m. to follow
　7.24. would have *no* m. know it
　9. 8. they saw *no* m. any more
　39. for there is *no* m. which sh.
　10.29. The. is *no* m. that ; Lu.18.29
　11. 2. wh. *never* m. sat ; Lu.19.30

Mar.12.14. true, and carest for *no* m.
　34. And *no* m. after that durst
Lu. 5.39. *No* m. also having drunk old
　8.16. *No* m., when he hath ; 11.33
　51. he suffered *no* m. to go in
　9.36. *no* m. in those days any of
　62. *No* m., having put his hand
　10.22. *no* m. knoweth who the Son
　15.16. and *no* m. gave unto him
　23.53. wherein never m.; Jo. 19.41
Jo. 1.18. *No* m. hath seen God at any
　3. 2. for *no* m. can do these mira.
　13. And *no* m. hath ascended up
　32. and *no* m. receiveth his
　4.27. yet *no* m. said, What seekest
　5.22. For the Father judgeth *no* m.
　6.44, 65. *No* m. can come to me
　7. 4. *no* m. that doeth any thing
　13. *no* m. spake openly of him
　27. *no* m. knoweth whence he is
　30, 44. *no* m. laid hands ; 8.20
　8.10. hath *no* m. condemned thee
　11. She said, *No* m., Lord. And
　15. after the flesh ; I judge *no* m.
　33. never in bondage to *any* m.
　9. 4. when *no* m. can work
　10.18. *No* m. taketh it from me, but
　29. and *no* m. is able to pluck
　13.28. Now *no* m. at the table knew
　14. 6. *no* m. cometh unto the Fath.
　15.13. Greater love hath *no* m. than
　16.22. your joy *no* m. taketh from
　18.31. lawful for us to put *any* m.
Act. 5.13. of the rest durst *no* m. join
　23. opened, we found *no* m. wi.
　18.10. *no* m. shall set on thee to
　20.33. I have coveted *no* m.'s silver
　25.11. *no* m. may deliver me unto
Ro. 14. 7. and *no* m. dieth to himself
1Co. 2.11. things of God knoweth *no* m.
　15. he himself is judged of *no* m.
　3.11. can *no* m. lay than that is
　12. that *no* m. speaking by the
　　　no m. can say that Jesus is
　14. 2. for *no* m. understandeth him
2Co. 5.16. know we *no* m. after the fle.
　7. 2. have wronged *no* m. we have
　　　no m., we have defrau. *no* m.
　11. 9. I was chargeable to *no* m.
Gal. 3.11. But that *no* m. is justified by
　15. *no* m. disannulleth, or addeth
Eph. 5.29. For *no* m. ever yet hated his
Phi. 2.20. I have *no* m. likeminded
1Ti. 6.16. whom *no* m. hath seen, nor
2Ti. 2. 4. *No* m. that warreth entangl.
　4.16. *no* m. stood with me, but all
Heb. 7.13. of which *no* m. gave attend.
　12.14. without which *no* m. shall
Jas. 1.13. *neither* tempteth he *any* m.
　3. 8. the tongue can *no* m. tame
1Jo. 4.12. *No* m. hath seen God at any
Rev. 2.17. which *no* m. knoweth saving
　3. 7. openeth, and *no* m. shutteth
　　　shutteth, and *no* m. openeth
　8. and *no* m. can shut it : for
　5. 3. And *no* m. in heaven, nor
　4. because *no* m. was found
　7. which *no* m. could number
　14. 3. and *no* m. could learn that
　15. 8. and *no* m. was able to enter
　18.11. for *no* m. buyeth their merc.
　19.12. that *no* m. knew, but he hi.

tis.

Mat. 8.28. that *no* m. might pass by that
　18.12. if a m have an hundred
　22.24. If a m. die, having no child.
　24. 4. Take heed that *no* m. deceive
Mar. 8. 4. whence can a m. satisfy those
　12.19. If a m.'s brother die, and
Lu. 12.15. a m.'s life consisteth not
Jo. 3. 3. Except a m. be born again
　5 Except a m. be born of water

Jo. 6.50. that a **m.** may eat thereof
   8.51, 52. If a **m.** keep my saying
  11.10. But if a **m.** walk in the night
  14.23. If a **m.** love me, he will keep
  15. 6. If a **m.** abide not in me he
     13. that a **m.** lay down his life
  13.41. though a **m.** declare it unto
Ro. 8.24. for what a **m.** seeth, why
¹Co. 4. 2. that a **m.** be found faithful
  16.11. Let no **m.** therefore despise
²Co. 8.12. according to that a **m.** hath
    20. that no **m.** should blame us
  11.16. Let no **m.** think me a fool
    20. if a **m.** bring you into bond.
      if a **m.** devour you, if a **m.**
      take of you, if a **m.** exalt
      himself, if a **m.** smite you
Gal. 6. 3. For if a **m.** think himself to
Col. 2.16. Let no **m.** therefore judge
²Th. 2. 3. Let no **m.** deceive you
¹Ti. 1. 8. good, if a **m.** use it lawfully
   3. 1. If a **m.** desire the office of a
     5. if a **m.** know not how to rule
²Ti. 2. 5. if a **m.** also strive for master.
    21. If a **m.** therefore purge him.
Heb.5. 4. no **m.** taketh this honour
Jas. 2.14. though a **m.** say he hath fai.
    18. Yea, a **m.** may say, Thou h.
¹Pet.2.19. if a **m.** for conscience toward
²Pet.2.19. of whom a **m.** is overcome
Rev.13.17.that no **m.** might buy or sell
    mēdeis.
Mat. 8. 4. See thou tell *no* **m.**; Lu.5.14
   9.30. See that *no* **m.** know it
  16.20. that they should tell *no* **m.**;
      Mar.7.36,8.30,9.9 ; Lu.8.56
  17. 9. Tell the vision to *no* **m.**, un.
Mar. 5.43. that *no* **m.** should know it
  11.14. *No* **m.** eat fruit of thee here.
Lu. 3.14. Do violence to *no* **m.**, nei.
   9.21. to tell *no* **m.** that thing
  10. 4. and salute *no* **m.** by the way
Act. 9. 7. a voice, but seeing *no* **m.**
  10.28. should *not* call *any* **m.** com.
  23.22. See thou tell *no* **m.** that
Ro. 12.17. Recompense to *no* **m.** evil
  13. 8. Owe *no* **m.** *any thing*, but to
¹Co. 3.18. Let *no* **m.** deceive himself
    21. let *no* **m.** glory in men : for
  10.24. Let *no* **m.** seek his own, but
Gal. 6.17. let *no* **m.** trouble me: for I
Eph. 5. 6. Let *no* **m.** deceive ; ¹Jo.3.7
Col. 2.18. Let *no* **m.** beguile you of your
¹Th. 3. 3. That *no* **m.** should be moved
¹Ti. 4.12. Let *no* **m.** despise thy youth
   5.22. Lay hands suddenly on *no* **m.**
Tit. 2.15. Let *no* **m.** despise thee
   3. 2. To speak evil of *no* **m.**, to
Jas. 1.13. Let *no* **m.** say when he is
Rev. 3.11. that *no* **m.** take thy crown
    anthrōpinos.
Ro. 6.19. speak *after the manner of* me.
¹Co. 2. 4. enticing words *of* **m.**'s wisdo.
    13. not in the words which **m.**'s
   4. 3. of you, or of **m.**'s judgment
  10.13. but such as is *common to* **m.**
¹Pet.2.13. to every ordinance of **m.**
    heis.
Act. 2. 6. because that every **m.** heard
Col. 4. 6. ought to answer every **m.**
    arrēn.
Ro. 1.27. likewise also the **m**e., leaving
Rev.12. 5, 13. brought forth a **m.** child
    arsēn.
Ro. 1.27. **m**e. with **m**e., working that
    teleios.
¹Co.14.20. but in understanding be **m**e.
    andrizomai.
¹Co.16.13. *quit* you *like* **m**e., be strong
    prosōpon.
Jude 16. having **m**e.'s *persons* in ad.
   (See words in connection.)

MANGER.
    phatnē.
Lu. 2. 7. laid him in a **m.**; because
Lu. 2.12. clothes, lying in a **m.**
    16. and the babe lying in a **m.**

MANIFEST, [*adjec.*]
    phaneroō.
Jo. 1.31. that he *should be made* **m.**
   3.21. his deeds *may be made* **m.**
   9. 3. of God *should be made* **m.** in
Ro. 16.26. But now *is made* **m.**, and by
¹Co. 4. 5. and *will make* **m.** the couns.
²Co. 2.14. and *maketh* **m.** the savour of
   4.10, 11.*might be made* **m.** in our
   5.11. but we are *made* **m.** unto G.
     I trust also *are made* **m.** in
  11. 6. *have been throughly made* **m.**
Eph. 5.13. reproved *are made* **m.** by the
     for *what*soever *doth make* **m.**
Col. 1.26. but now *is made* **m.** to his
   4. 4. That I *may make* it **m.**, as I
¹Ti. 3.16. God *was* **m.** in the flesh, jus.
²Ti. 1.10. But *is now made* **m.** by the
Heb. 9. 8. of all *was not yet made* **m.**
¹Pet.1.20. but *was* **m.** in these last tim.
¹Jo. 2.19. that they *might be made* **m.**
Rev.15. 4. thy judgments *are made* **m.**
    phaneros.
Lu. 8.17. that shall not be made **m.**
Act. 4.16. is **m.** to all them that
Ro. 1.19. is **m.** in them; for God
¹Co. 3.13. shall be made **m.**: for the
  11.19. may be made **m.** among you
  14.25. secrets of his heart made **m.**
Gal. 5.19. works of the flesh are **m.**
Phi. 1.13. my bonds in Christ are **m.** in
¹Jo. 3.10. the children of God are **m.**
    emphanēs.
Ro. 10.20. I was made **m.** unto them
    dēlos.
¹Co.15.27. it is **m.** that he is excepted
    prodēlos.
¹Ti. 5.25. of some are **m.** *beforehand*
    ekdēlos.
²Ti. 3. 9. folly shall be **m.** unto all
    aphanēs.
Heb.4.13. *that is not* **m.** in his sight
    (See *Token.*)

MANIFEST, [*verb,*]   -*cd.*
    phaneroō.
Mar. 4.22. hid, which *shall not be* **m**-ed
Jo. 2.11. and **m**-ed *forth* his glory
  17. 6. I *have* **m**-ed thy name unto
Ro. 3.21. of God with. the law *is* **m**-ed
Tit. 1. 3. *hath* in due times **m**-ed his
¹Jo. 1. 2. the life *was* **m**-ed, and we
     Father, and *was* **m**-ed unto
   3. 5. that he *was* **m**-ed to take
    8. the Son of God *was* **m**-ed
   4. 9. In this *was* **m**-ed the love of
Jo.14.21. and *will* **m.** myself to him
   22. that thou wilt **m.** thyself unto

MANIFESTATION.
    phanerōsis.
¹Co.12.7. the **m.** of the Spirit is given
²Co. 4. 2. by **m.** of the truth, commend.
    apokalupsis.
Ro. 8.19. for the **m.** of the sons of God

MANIFESTLY.
    phaneroō.
²Co. 3. 3. *are* **m.** *declared* to be the epi.

MANIFOLD.
    pollaplasiōn.
Lu. 18.30. shall not receive **m.** *more* in
    polupoikilos.
Eph. 3.10. church the **m.** wisdom of G.
    poikilos.
Pet. 1. 6. heaviness through **m.** temp.

MANKIND.
    arsenokoitēs.
¹Co. 6. 9. *abusers of* them*selves with* **m.**
¹Ti. 1.10. *that defile* them*selves with* **m.**
    phusis anthrōpinos.
Jas. 3. 7. and hath been tamed of **m.**

MANNA.
    manna.
Jo. 6.31, 49. fathers did eat **m.** in the
   58. not as your fathers did eat **m.**
Heb. 9. 4. the golden pot that had **m.**
Rev. 2.17. give to eat of the hidden **m.**

MANNER,   -*s.*
    houtō.
Mat. 6. 9. *After this* **m.** therefore pray
Mar.13.29.*So ye in like* **m.**, when ye
¹Co. 7. 7. one *after this* **m.**, and ano.
¹Pet.3. 5. For *after this* **m.** in the old
Rev.11. 5. he must *in this* **m.** be killed
    ethos.
Jo. 19.40. as the **m.** of the Jews is to
Act.15. 1. circumcised after the **m.** of
   25.16. It is not the **m.** of the Rom.
Heb.10.25.together, as the **m.** of some
    hōsautōs.
Lu. 20.31. and *in like* **m.** the seven also
¹Co.11.25. *After the same* **m.** also he
¹Ti. 2. 9. *In like* **m.** also, that women
    kata. [*accu.*]
Jo. 2. 6. *after the* **m.** of the purifying
¹Co.15.32. If *after the* **m.** *of* men I have
Gal. 3.15. I speak *after the* **m.** *of* men
    tis ara.   [8.25
Mar. 4.41. *What* **m.** *of man* is this ; Lu.
Lu. 1.66. *What* **m.** *of* child shall this
    houtos.
Lu. 6.23. for in *the like* **m.** did their
    tropos.
Act. 1.11. shall so come in like **m.** as
Jude 7. in like **m.**, giving themselves
    tropophoreō.
Act.13.18. *suffered* he their **m**-s in the
    hode.
Act.15.23. letters by them *after this* **m.**
    ethō.
Act.17. 2. Paul, as his **m.** *was*, went in
    pōs.
Act.20.18. *after what* **m.** I have been
    tupos.
Act.23.25. he wrote a letter after this **m.**
    peri houtos.
Act.25.20. doubted *of such* **m.** of quest.
    ēthos.
¹Co.15.33. communica. corrupt good **m**-s
   (See words in connection.)

MANSIONS.
    monē.
Jo.14. 2. my Father's house are many **m.**

MANSLAYERS.
    androphonos.
¹Ti. 1. 9. murderers of mothers, for **m.**

MANY, (See *How.*)
    polus.
Mat. 3. 7. when he saw **m.** of the Phar.
   7.13. and **m.** there be which go in
    22. **m.** will say to me in that day
     done **m.** wonderful works
   8.11. **m.** shall come from the east
    16. unto him **m.** that were poss.
    30. an herd of **m.** swine feeding
   9.10. **m.** publicans and sinners ca.
  10.31. more value than **m.** ; Lu.12.7
  13. 3. he spake **m.** things unto th.
    17. That **m.** prophets and right.
    58. did not **m.** mighty works th.
  15.30. dumb, maimed, and **m.** oth.
  16.21. and suffer **m.** things of the
  19.30. But **m.** that are ; Mar.10.31
  20.16. for **m.** be called, but ; 22.14

Mat.20.28.a ransom for m.; Mar.10.45
24. 5. For m. shall come in my na.;
    Mar. 13.6; Lu. 21.8
    shall deceive m.; Mar. 13.6
  10. And then shall m. be offend.
  11. And m. false prophets shall
    rise, and shall deceive m.
  12. the love of m. shall wax cold
  21, 23. make thee ruler over m.
26.28. which is shed for m. for the
  60. tho. m. false wit.; Mar.14.56
27.19. for I have suffered m. things
  52. and m. bodies of the saints
  53. city, and appeared unto m.
  55. And m. women were there
Mar. 1.34. healed m. that were sick of
    diseases, and cast out m. de.
2. 2. m. were gathered together
  15. m. publicans and sinners sat
    for there were m., and they
3.10. For he had healed m.; inso.
4. 2. he taught them m. th.; 6.34
  33. And with m. such parables
5. 9. is Legion: for we are m.
  26. suffered m. things of m. ph.
6. 2. and m. hearing him were as.
  13. they cast out m. devils, and
    anointed with oil m. that
  20. he did m. things, and heard
  31. there were m. coming and
  33. and m. knew him, and ran
7. 4. And m. other things there
  8, 13. m. other such like things
8.31. must suffer m. things; 9.12.
9.26. insomuch that m. said, He
10.48. m. charged him that he sho.
11. 8. And m. spread their garme.
12. 5. him they killed, and m. oth.
  41. and m. that were rich cast
14.24. testa., which is shed for m.
15. 3. priests accused him of m. th.
  41. and m. other women which
Lu. 1. 1. Forasmuch as m. have taken
  14. and m. shall rejoice at his
  16. And m. of the children of
2.34. and rising again of m. in Is.
  35. that the thoughts of m. hea.
3.18. And m. other things in his
4.25. m. widows were in Israel in
  27. And m. lepers were in Israel
  41. devils also came out of m.
7.21. he cured m. of their infirmi.
    and unto m. that were blind
  47. Her sins, which are m.
8. 3. Susanna, and m. others, wh.
  30. because m. devils were ente.
9.22. So. of m. must suff. m.; 17.25
10.24. that m. prophets and kings
  41. troubled about m. things
12.19. much goods laid up for m.
  47. shall be beaten with m. stri.
13.24. for m., I say unto you, will
14.16. a great supper, and bade m.
15.13. not m. days after the young.
22.65. m. other things blaspheno.
23. 8. he had heard m. things of
Jo. 2.12. continued there not m. days
  23. m. believed in his name
4.39. And m. of the Samaritans
  41. And m. more believed beca.
6.60. m. therefore of his disciples
  66. m. of his disciples went back
7.31. And m. of the people believ.
  40. m. of the people therefore
8.26. I have m. things to say and
  30. m. believed on; 10.42, 12.42
10.20. And m. of them said, He
  32. m. good works have I shew.
  41. And m. resorted unto him
11.19. And m. of the Jews came to
  45. Then m. of the Jews which
  47. this man doeth m. miracles
174

Jo. 11.55. and m. went out of the cou.
12.11. m. of the Jews went away
14. 2. In my Father's house are m.
16.12. I have yet m. things to say
19.20. This title then read m. of
20.30. And m. other signs truly did
21.25. there are also m. other thin.
Act. 1. 3. by m. infallible proofs, being
  5. the Holy Ghost not m.·days
2.43. and m. wonders and; 5.12
4. 4. m. of them which heard the
8. 7. came out of m. that were
    and m. taken with palsies
  25. in m. villages of the Samar.
9.13. I have heard by m. of this
10.27. and found m. that were co.
13.43. m. of the Jews and religious
15.32. exhor. the brethren with m.
  35. the Lord with m. others also
16.18. And this did she m. days
  23. when they had laid m. stri.
17.12. Therefore m. of them believ.
18. 8. and m. of the Corinthians
19.18. And m. that believed came
20.19. and with m. tears, and tem.
24.10. thou hast been of m. years
25. 7. laid m. and grievous compl.
26. 9. I ought to do m. things con.
  10. and m. of the saints did I sh.
28.10. honoured us with m. honou.
Ro. 4.17, 18. a father of m. nations
5.15. the offence of one, m. be dead
  Ch., hath abounded unto m.
  16. of m. offences unto justifica.
  19. m. were made sinners; so by
    shall m. be made righteous
8.29. the firstborn among m. bret.
12. 4. have m. members in one bo.;
    ¹Co.12.12   [12.12
  5. being m., are one body; ¹Co.
15.23. these m. years to come unto
16. 2. hath been a succourer of m.
¹Co. 1.26. how that not m. wise men
    not m. mighty, not m. nob.
4.15. yet have ye not m. fathers
8. 5. be gods m., and lords m.
10.17. For we being m. are one br.
  33. but the profit of m., that
11.30. For this cause m. are weak
12.14. is not one member, but m.
  20. But now are they m. memb.
  22. and there are m. adversaries
²Co. 1.11. by the means of m. persons
    thanks may be given by m.
2. 4. I wrote unto you with m. te.
  17. For we are not as m.
6.10. as poor, yet making m. rich
8.22. proved diligent in m. things
9.12. by m. thanksgivings unto G.
11.18. Seeing that m. glory after
12.21. I shall bewail m. which have
Gal. 1.14. above m. my equals in mine
3.16. And to seeds, as of m.; but
4.27. hath m. more children than
Phi. 3.18. For m. walk, of whom I have
¹Ti. 6. 9. m. foolish and hurtful lusts
  10. themselves through with m.
  12. good profession before m.
²Ti. 2. 2. among m. witnesses, the sa.
Tit. 1.10. For there are m. unruly and
Heb. 2.10. in bringing m. sons unto gl.
5.11. we have m. things to say
9.28. offered to bear the sins of m.
12.15. and thereby m. be defiled
Jas. 3. 1. My brethren, be not m. mas.
  2. For in m. things we offend
²Pet. 2. 2. And m. shall follow their
¹Jo. 2.18. now are there m. antichrists
4. 1. because m. false prophets
²John 7. For m. deceivers are entered
  12. Having m. things to write
³John 13. I had m. things to write

Rev. 1.15. as the sound of m. waters
5.11. I heard the voice of m. ang
8.11. and m. men died of the wa.
9. 9. of m. horses running to bat.
10.11. before m. peoples, and nati.
14. 2. as the voice of m. wa.; 19.6
17. 1. that sitteth upon m. waters
19 12. on his head were m. crowns
    hosos.
Mat.14.36. as m. as touched were made
22. 9. as m. as ye shall find, bid
  10. as m. as they found, both
Mar. 3.10. touch him, as m. as had pla.
6.56. as m. as touched him were
Lu. 11. 8. give him as m. as he need.
Jo. 1.12. But as m. as received him
Act. 2.39. as m. as the Lord our God
3.24. as m. as have spoken, have
4. 6. as m. as were of the kindred
  34. for as m. as were possessors
5.36, 37. as m. as obeyed him
10.45. as m. as came with Peter
13.48. and as m. as were ordained
Ro. 2.12. as m. as have sinned with.
    and as m. as have sinned in
6. 3. so m. of us as were baptized
8.14. For as m. as are led by the
  27. For as m. of you as have
6.12. As m. as desire to make a
16. as m. as walk according to
Phi. 3.15. as m. as be perfect, be thus
Col. 2. 1. and for as m. as have not
¹Ti. 6. 1. Let as m. servants as are
Rev. 2.24. as m. as have not this doct.
3.19. As m. as I love, I rebuke
13.15. that as m. as would not
18.17. as m. as trade by sea, stood
    pleiōn.
Lu. 11.53. him to speak of m. things
Act. 2.40. And with m. other words
13.31. he was seen m. days of them
21.10. as we tarried there m. days
24.17. Now after m. years I came
25.14. when they had been there m.
27.20. nor stars in m. days appear.
28.23. there came m. to him unto
¹Co. 10. 5. But with m. of them God
²Co. 2. 6. which was inflicted of m.
4.15. through the thanksgiv. of m.
9. 2. zeal hath provoked very m.
Phi. 1.14. m. of the brethren in
Heb. 7.23. they truly were m. priests
    hikanos.
Lu. 7.11. m. of his disciples went with
8.32. an herd of m. swine feeding
23. 9. questioned with him in m.
Act. 9.53. after that m. days were ful.
  43. he tarried m. days in Joppa
12.12. m. were gathered together
14.21. and had taught m., they
19.19. m. of them also which used
20. 8. m. lights in the upper cham.
27. 7. we had sailed slowly m. days
¹Co. 11.30. sickly am. you, and m. sleep
    tosoutos.
Lu. 15.29. Lo, these m. years do I serve
Jo. 6. 9. what are they among so m.
12.37. had done so m. miracles bef.
21.11. and for all there were so m.
¹Co. 14.10. so m. kinds of voices in the
Gal. 3. 4. Have ye suffered so m. thi.

MARAN-ATHA.
    maran atha.
¹Co.16.22.Ch., let him be Anathema m.

MARBLE.
    marmaros.
Rev.18.12. of brass, and iron, and m.

MARK, [noun,]   -s.
    charagma.
Rev.13.16. to receive a m. in their right

Rev.13.17. save he that had the **m.**, or
14. 9. and receive his **m.** in his
11. whosoever receiveth the **m.**
15. 2. his image, and over his **m.**
16. 2. men which had the **m.** of
19.20. had received the **m.** of the
20. 4. neither had received his **m.**
stigma.
Gal.6.17. the **m**-*s* of the Lord Jesus
skopos.
Phi.3.14. I press toward the **m.**, for the

MARK, [*verb*,]   -ed.
epechō.
Lu.14. 7. *when* he **m**-*ed* how they chose
skopeō.
Ro. 16.17. **m.** them which cause divis.
Phi. 3.17. **m.** them which walk so as

MARKET,   -s.
agora.
Mat.11.16. children sitting in the **m**-*s*
20. 3. standing idle in the **m**-*place*
23. 7. greetings in the **m**-*s*;Lu.11.43
20.46
Mar. 7. 4. when they come from the **m.**
12.38. salutations in the **m**-*places*
Lu. 7.32. child. sitting in the **m**-*place*
Act.16.19. drew them into the **m**-*place*
17.17. in the **m.** daily with them

MARRED.
apollumi.
Mar.2.22.spil., and the bottles *will be* **m.**

MARRIAGE.
gamos.
Mat.22. 2. certain king, wh. made a **m.**
4. are ready : come unto the **m.**
9. ye shall find, bid to the **m.**
25.10. went in with him to the **m.**
Jo. 2. 1. the third day there was a **m.**
2. and his disciples, to the **m.**
Heb.13. 4. **m.** is honourable in all, and
Rev.19. 7. for the **m.** of the Lamb is
9. unto the **m.** supper of the L.
ekgamizō.
Mat.22.30. marry, nor *are given in* **m.**
24.38. marrying and *giving in* **m.**
Lu. 17.27. they *were given in* **m.**, until
¹Co. 7.38. he *that giveth* her in **m.** do.
that giveth her not *in* **m.**
gamiskomai.
Mar.12.25. marry, nor *are given in* **m.**
ekgamiskomai.
Lu.20.34,35.marry, and *are given in* **m.**

MARROW.
muelos.
Heb.4.12. and of the joints and **m.**

MARRY,   -ied, -ieth, -ing.
gameō.
Mat. 5.32. whosoever *shall* **m.** her that
19. 9. and *shall* **m.** another ; Mar.
10.11 ; Lu.16.18
whoso **m**-*eth* her wh.;Lu.16.18
10. his wife, it is not good to **m.**
22.25. first, *when* he *had* **m**-*ed a*
30. resurrection they neither **m.**;
Mar.12.25; Lu.20.35
24.38. **m**-*ing* and giving in marriage
Mar. 6.17. Phi. wife : for he *had* **m**-*ed*
10.12. her husband, and *be* **m**-*ed* to
Lu. 14.20. another said, I *have* **m**-*ed a*
17.27. they drank, they **m**-*ed wives*
20.34. The children of this world **m.**
¹Co. 7. 9. *let* them **m.** for it is better
to **m.** than to burn
10. unto the **m**-*ed* I command
28. if thou **m.**, thou hast not
if a virgin **m.**, she hath not
33, 34. *that is* **m**-*ed* careth for
36. he sinneth not : *let* them **m.**

---

¹Co. 7.39. she is at liberty *to be* **m**-*ed*
¹Ti. 4. 3. Forbidding *to* **m.**, and com.
5.11. against Christ, they will **m.**
14. that the younger women **m.**
ginomai.
Ro. 7. 3. she *be* **m**-*ed* to another man
though she *be* **m**-*ed* to anot.
4. ye should *be* **m**-*ed* to anoth.
epigambreuō.
Mat.22.24. his brother *shall* **m.** his wife

MARTYR,   -s.
martus.
Act.22.20. when the blood of thy **m.**
Rev. 2.13. Antipas was my faithful **m.**
17. 6. with the blood of thy **m**-*s*

MARVEL, [*noun*.]
thaumastos.
²Co. 11.14. And no **m.**; for Satan hims.

MARVEL, [*verb*,]   -ed.
thaumazō.
Mat. 8.10. Jesus heard it, he **m**-*ed*, and
27. But the men **m**-*ed*, saying
9. 8. the multitu. saw it, they **m**-*ed*
33. the multitudes **m**-*ed*, saying
21.20. they **m**-*ed*, saying, How soon
22.22. heard these words, they **m**-*ed*
27.14. inso. that the gover. **m**-*ed*
Mar. 5.20. for him : and all men *did* **m.**
6. 6. he **m**-*ed* because of their unb.
12.17. are God's. And they **m**-*ed*
15. 5. nothing ; so that Pilate **m**-*ed*
44. Pilate **m**-*ed* if he were alrea.
Lu. 1.21. and **m**-*ed* that he tarried so
63. is John. And they **m**-*ed* all
2.33. Joseph and his mother **m**-*ed*
7. 9. he **m**-*ed* at him, and turned
11.38. the Pharisee saw it, he **m**-*ed*
20.26. they **m**-*ed* at his answer, *and*
Jo. 3. 7. **m.** not that I said unto thee
4.27. **m**-*ed* that he talked with
5.20. than these, that ye *may* **m.**
28. **m.** not at this : for the hour
7.15. And the Jews **m**-*ed*, saying
21. done one work and ye all **m.**
Act. 2. 7. and **m**-*ed*, saying one to ano.
3.12. why **m.** ye at this? or why
4.13. they **m**-*ed* ; and they took
Gal. 1. 6. I **m.** that ye are so soon
¹Jo. 3.13. **m.** not, my brethren, if the
Rev.17. 7. Wherefore *didst* thou **m.**

MARVELLOUS.
thaumastos.
Mat.21.42. it is **m.** in our ; Mar.12.11
Jo. 9.30. Why herein is a **m.** thing
¹Pet. 2. 9. out of darkness into his **m.**
Rev. 15. 1. sign in heaven, great and **m.**
3. Great and **m.** are thy works

MASTER, (See *House*,)   -s.
didaskalos.
Mat. 8.19. unto him, **m.**, I will follow
9.11. Why eateth your **m.** with
10.24. disciple is not above his **m.**
25. disciple that he be as his **m.**
12.38. **m.**, we would see a sign from
17.24. Doth not your **m.** pay tribute
19.16. Good **m.**, what good thing
22.16. **m.**, we know that; Mar.12.14
24. Saying, **m.**, Moses said, If a
36. **m.**, which is the great com.
26.18. say unto him, The **m.** saith
Mar. 4.38. **m.**, carest thou not that we
5.35. why troublest thou the **m.**
9.17. said, **m.**, I have brought
38. **m.**, we saw one casting out
10.17. Good **m.**, what shall I do ;
Lu.10.25, 18.18
20. **m.**, all these have I observed

Mar.10.35.saying, **m.**, we would that
12.19. **m.**, Moses wrote unto us
32. Well, **m.**, thou hast said the
13. 1. **m.**, see what manner of sto.
14.14. The **m.** saith, Where is the
Lu. 3.12. him, **m.**, what shall we do
6.40. perfect shall be as his **m.**
7.40. And he saith, **m.**, say on
8.49. is dead : trouble not the **m.**
9.38. saying, **m.**, I beseech thee
11.45. **m.**, thus saying thou repro.
12.13. **m.**, speak to my brother
19.39. **m.**, rebuke thy disciples
20.21. **m.**, we know that thou say.
28. Saying, **m.**, Moses wrote
39. said, **m.**, thou hast well said
21. 7. saying, **m.**, but when shall
22.11. The **m.** saith unto thee
Jo. 1.38. to say, being interpreted, **m.**
3.10. Art thou a **m.** of Israel, and
8. 4. **m.**, this woman was taken in
11.28. saying, The **m.** is come, and
13.13. Ye call me **m.** and Lord
14. If I then, your Lord and **m.**
20.16. Rabboni ; which is to say,**m.**
Jas. 3. 1. My breth., be not many **m**-*s*
rabbi.
Mat.26.25. **m.**, is it I ? He said unto
49. said, Hail, **m.**, and kissed
Mar. 9. 5. **m.** it is good for us to be
11.21. **m.**, behold, the fig tree wh.
14.45. **m.**, **m.**, and kissed him
Jo. 4.31. prayed him, saying, **m.**, eat
9. 2. **m.**, who did sin, this man
11. 8. **m.**, the Jews of late sought
kurios.   [Lu.16.13
Mat. 6.24. No man can serve two **m**-*s*;
15.27. which fall from their **m.**'s
Mar. 13.35. when the **m.** of the house
Act. 16.16. brought her **m**-*s* much gain
19. when her **m**-*s* saw that the
Ro. 14. 4. to his own m. he standeth
Eph. 6. 5. to them that are your **m**-*s*
9. And, ye **m**-*s*, do the same
that your **m.** also is in hea.
Col. 3.22. obey in all things your **m**-*s*
4. 1. **m**-*s*, give unto your servants
ye also have a **m.** in heaven
epistatēs.
Lu. 5. 5. **m.**, we have toiled all the
8.24. saying, **m.**, **m.**, we perish
45. **m.**, the multitude throng
9.33. **m.**, it is good for us to be
49. **m.**, we saw one casting out
17.13. Jesus, **m.**, have mercy on us
despotēs.
¹Ti. 6. 1. their own **m**-*s* worthy of all
2. they that have believing **m**-*s*
²Ti. 2.21. and meet for the **m.**'s use
Tit. 2. 9. obedient unto their own **m**-*s*
¹Pet. 2.18. be subject to your **m**-*s* with
kathēgētēs.
Mat.23. 8, 10. for one is your **m.**, even
10. Neither be ye called **m**-*s*
kubernētēs.
Act.27.11. believed the **m.** and the own.

MASTER-BUILDER.
architektōn.
¹Co. 3.10. as a wise **m.**, I have laid the

MATTER.
logos.
Mar. 1.45. and to blaze abroad the **m.**
Act. 8.21. nei. part nor lot in this **m.**
15. 6. for to consider of this **m.**
19.38. have a **m.** against any man
pragma.
¹Co. 6. 1. having a **m.** against another
²Co. 7.11. yoursel. to be clear in this **m.**
¹Th. 4. 6. defraud his brother in any **m**

hulē.

Jas. 3. 5. how great a **m**. a little fire
diapherō

Gal. 2. 6. were, it *maketh* no **m**. to me
(See *Busybody, Wrong*.)

MAY, *-est, Might.*
dunamai.

Mat.26. 9. this ointment **m**-*t* have been
42. if this cup **m**. not pass away
Mar. 4.32. the fowls of the air **m**. lodge
14. 5. it **m**-*t* have been sold for
7. whensoever ye will, ye **m**. do
Lu. 16. 2. thou **m**-*est* be no longer ste.
Act.17.19. m. we know what this new
19.40. we **m**. give an account of this
24. 8. thyself **m**-*est* take knowledge
11. *Because that* thou **m**-*est* un.
25.11. no man **m**. deliver me unto
26.32. This man **m**-*t* have been set
27.12. if by any means they **m**-*t*
¹Co. 7.21. if thou **m**-*est* be made free
14.31. ye **m**. all prophesy one by
Eph. 3. 4. when ye read, ye **m**. under.
¹Th. 2. 6. *when* we **m**-*t* have been bur.
Rev.13.17. that no man **m**-*t* buy or sell
exeimi, [*impersonal*.]

Act. 8.37. all thine heart, thou **m**-*est*
21.37. captain, **m**. I speak unto thee
ischuō.

Mat. 8.28. no man **m**-*t* pass by that
isōs.

Lu. 20.13. *it* **m**. *be* they will reverence

ME, (See *I*.)

MEAL.
aleuron. [Lu.13.21
Mat.13.33.hid in three measures of **m**.;

MEAN, [*adjec*.]
asēmos.

Act.21.39.Cilicia, a citizen of no **m**. city

MEAN, [*verb*,] *-eth, -ing, Meant*.
eimi.

Mat. 9.13. learn what that **m**-*eth*, I will
12. 7. had known what this **m**-*eth*
Mar. 9.10. rising from the dead shou. **m**.
Lu. 15.26. asked what these things **m**-*t*
18.36. by, he asked what it **m**-*t*
thelō.

Act. 2.12.to another, What **m**-*eth* this
17.20.therefore what these things **m**.
poieō.

Act.21.13. What **m**. ye to weep and br.
mellō.

Act.27. 2. **m**-*ing* to sail by the coasts of

MEANWHILE.
metaxu.

Jo. 4.31. In the **m**. his disciples
Ro. 2.15. their thoughts the **m**. accus.

MEANING.
dunamis.

¹Co. 14.11. know not the **m**. of the voi.

MEANS, (See *Seek*.)
pōs, [*indefinite*.]

Act.27.12. if by any **m**. they might
Ro. 1.10. if by any **m**. now at length
11.14. If by any **m**. I may provoke
¹Co. 8. 9. lest by any **m**. this liberty
9.27. lest that by any **m**., when I
²Co. 11. 3. lest by any **m**., as the serpe.
Gal. 2. 2. lest by any **m**. I should run
Phi. 3.11. If by any **m**. I might attain
¹Th. 3. 5. lest by some **m**. the tempter
pōs, [*definite*.]

Lu. 8.36. told them *by what* **m**. he th.
Jo. 9.21. *by what* **m**. he now seeth
176

ou mē.

Mat. 5.26. Thou shalt *by no* **m**. come
Lu. 10.19. *nothing* shall *by any* **m**. hurt
pantōs.

Act.18.21. I must *by all* **m**. keep this
¹Co. 9.22. might *by all* **m**. save some
ek.

²Co. 1.11. *by the* **m**. *of* many persons
en pas tropos.

²Th. 3.16. you peace always *by all* **m**.
kata tropos.

²Th. 2. 3. man deceive you *by any* **m**.

MEASURE, [*noun*,] *-s*.
metron.

Mat. 7. 2. and with what **m**. ye mete ;
Mar.4.24; Lu.6.38
23.32. Fill ye up then the **m**. of
Lu. 6.38. good **m**., pressed down, and
Jo. 3.34. G. giveth not the Spirit by **m**.
Ro. 12. 3. to every man the **m**. of faith
²Co. 10.13. according to the **m**. of the
a **m**. to reach even unto you
Eph. 4. 7. according to the **m**. of the
13. unto the **m**. of the stature
16. in the **m**. of every part, mak.
Rev.21.17.the **m**. of a man, that is, of
saton. [13.21
Mat.13.33.hid in three **m**-*s* of meal ;Lu.
choinix.

Rev. 6. 6. A **m**. of wheat for a penny
and three **m**-*s* of barley for a
batos.

Lu. 16. 6. said, An hundred **m**-*s* of oil
koros.

Lu. 16. 7. said, An hundred **m**-*s* of wh.
ek perissos.

Mar. 6.51. amazed in them. *beyond* **m**.
huperperissōs.

Mar. 7.37. were *beyond* **m**. astonished
perissōs.

Mar.10.26. were astonished *out of* **m**.
kata huperbolē.

¹Co. 1. 8. we were pressed *out of* **m**.
Gal. 1.13. *beyond* **m**. I persecuted the
ametros.

²Co.10.13, 15. of *things without* our **m**.
huperballontōs.

²Co. 11.23. in stripes *above* **m**., in pris.
(See *Exalted*.)

MEASURE, [*verb*,] *-ed, -ing*.
metreō.

Mar. 4.24. meas. ye mete,it *shallbe* **m**-*ed*
²Co. 10.12. they **m**-*ing* themselves by
Rev.11. 1. Rise, and **m**. the temple of
2. leave out, and **m**. it not ; for
21.15. a golden reed to **m**. the city
16. he **m**-*ed* the city with the
17. he **m**-*ed* the wall thereof, an
antimetreō. [Lu.6.38
Mat. 7. 2. *shall be* **m**-*ed* to you *again* ;

MEAT, *-s*.
brōma.

Mar. 7.19. the draught, purging all **m**-*s*
Lu. 3.11. he that hath **m**., let him do
9.13. we should go and buy **m**. for
Jo. 4.34. My **m**. is to do the will of
Ro. 14.15. bro. be grieved with thy **m**.
Destroy not him with thy **m**.
20. For **m**. destroy not the work
¹Co. 3. 2. with milk, and not with **m**.
6.13. **m**-*s* for belly, and belly for
m-*s* : but God shall destroy
8. 8. **m**. commendeth us not to
13. if **m**. make my brother to
10. 3. all eat the same spiritual **m**.
¹Ti. 4. 3. comman. to abstain from **m**-*s*
Heb.13. 9. not with **m**-*s* and **m**
13. 9. not with **m**-*s*, which have
trophē.

Mat. 3. 4. his **m**. was locusts and wild

Mat. 6.25. life more than **m**.; Lu.12.23
10.10. workman is worthy of his **m**.
24.45. to give them **m**. in due seas.
Jo. 4. 8. away unto the city to buy **m**
Act. 2.46. did eat their **m**. with gladn.
9.19. And when he had received **m**.
27.33. besought them all to take **m**.
34. I pray you to take some **m**.
36. they also took some **m**.
Heb. 5.12. milk, and not of strong **m**.
14. But strong **m**. belongeth to
brōsis.

Jo. 4.32. I have **m**. to eat that ye kn.
6.27. Labour not for the **m**. which
but for that **m**. which endu.
55. For my flesh is **m**. indeed
Ro. 14.17. the kingdom of God is not **m**.
Col. 2.16. man there. judge you in **m**.
Heb.12.16.for one *morsel of* **m**. sold his
phagō, [*infinitive*.]

Mat.25.35.hungered, and ye gave me **m**.
42. hung., and ye gave me no **m**.
Lu. 8.55. commanded to give her **m**
brōsimos.

Lu. 24.41. them, Have ye here any **m**.
prosphagion.

Jo. 21. 5. Children, have ye any **m**.
trapeza.

Act.16.34. he set **m**. before them, and
klasma. [Mar.8.8
Mat.15.37. took up of the *broken* **m**.;
(See *Idol, Portion, Sit*.)

MEDIATOR.
mesitēs.

Gal. 3.19. angels in the hand of a **m**.
20. Now a **m**. is not a mediator
¹Ti. 2. 5. one **m**. between God and **m**.
Heb. 8. 6. is the **m**. of a better covena.
9.15. he is the **m**. of the new test.
12.24. And to Jesus the **m**. of the

MEDITATE.
promeletaō.

Lu. 21.14. not *to* **m**. *before* what ye sh.
meletaō.

¹Ti. 4.15. **m**. upon these things ; give

MEEK.
praus.

Mat. 5. 5. Blessed are the **m**. : for
21. 5. King cometh unto thee, **m**.
¹Pet. 3. 4. of a **m**. and quiet spirit
praos.

Mat.11.29. for I am **m**. and lowly in

MEEKNESS.
praotēs.

¹Co. 4.21. and in the spirit of **m**.;Gal.6.1
²Co.10. 1. by the **m**. and gentleness of
Gal. 5.23. **m**., temperance : against su.
Eph. 4. 2. With all lowliness and **m**.
Col. 3.12. of mind, **m**., longsuffering
¹Ti. 6.11. faith, love, patience, **m**.
²Ti. 2.25. In **m**. instructing those that
Tit. 3. 2. shewing all **m**. unto all men
prautēs.

Jas. 1.21. receive with **m**. the engrafted
3.13. his works with **m**. of wisdom
¹Pet.3.15. is in you with **m**. and fear

MEET, [*adjec*.]
axios.

Mat. 3. 8. fruits **m**. for repentance
Act.26.20. do works **m**. for repentance
¹Co.16. 4. if it be **m**. that I go also, th.
²Th. 1. 3. for you, brethren, as it is **m**.
dei.

Lu. 15.32. It *was* **m**. that we should
Ro. 1.27. of their error which *was* **m**.
dikaios.

Phi. 1. 7. Even as it is **m**. for me to
²Pet. 1.13. Yea, I think it **m**., as long

kalos.   [Mar.7.27
Mat.15.26. not **m**. to take the children's
     hikanos.
1Co. 15. 9. not **m**. to be called an apostle
     hikanoō.
Col. 1.12. *which hath made* us **m**. to be
     euchrēstos.
2Ti. 2.21. and **m**. *for* the master's *use*
     euthetos.
Heb. 6. 7. bringeth forth herbs **m**. for

MEET, [*verb*,] (See *Sea*,)   *Met*.
     apantaō.
Mat.28. 9. behold, Jesus **m**-*t* them, say.
Mar. 5. 2. there **m**-*t* him out of the to.
   14.13. there *shall* **m**. you a man
Lu. 14.31. *to* **m**. him that cometh agai.
   17.12. there **m**-*t* him ten men that
Jo. 4.51. his servants **m**-*t* him, and
Act.16.16. with a spirit of divina. **m**-*t*
     apantēsis.
Mat.25. 1. went forth to **m**. the brideg.
   6. cometh ; go ye out to **m**. him
Act.28.15. they came to **m**. us as far as
1Th. 4.17. to **m**. the Lord in the air
     hupantaō.
Mat. 8.28. there **m**-*t* him two possessed
Lu. 8.27. there **m**-*t* him out of the city
Jo. 11.20. *u ent and* **m**-*t* him ; but Mary
   30. that place where Martha **m**-*t*
   12.18. cause the people also **m**-*t* him
     eis hupantēsis.
Jo. 12.13. and went forth to **m**. him
     sunantaō
Lu. 9.37. the hill, much people **m**-*t*
   22.10. there *shall* a man **m**. you
Act.10.25. Cornelius **m**-*t* him, and fell
Heb. 7. 1. *who* **m**-*t* Abraham returning
   10. father when Melchisedec **m**-*t*
     sunantēsis.
Mat. 8.34. whole city came out to **m**.
     paratungchanō.
Act.17.17. with them *that* **m**-*t with* him
     sumballō.
Act.20.14. And when he **m**-*t with* us at
     amphodon.
Mar.11. 4. in a place *where two ways* **m**-*t*

MELODY.
     psallō.
Eph. 5.19. and *making* **m**. in your heart

MELT.
     luō.
2Pet. 3.10. *shall* **m**. with fervent heat
     tēkomai.
2Pet. 3.12. elements *shall* **m**. with ferv.

MEMBER,   -*s*.
     melos.
Mat. 5.29, 30.that one of thy **m**-*s* shou.
Ro. 6.13. Neither yield ye your **m**-*s*
   and your **m**-*s* as instruments
   19. as ye have yielded your **m**-*s*
   now yield your **m**-*s* servants
   7. 5. did work in our **m**-*s* to bring
   23. another law in my **m**-*s*, war.
   law of sin whi. is in my **m**-*s*
   12. 4. as we have many **m**-*s* in one
   body, and all **m**-*s* have not
   5. every one **m**-*s*, one; Eph.4.25
1Co. 6.15. your bodies are the **m**-*s* of
   shall I then take the **m**-*s* of
   and make them the **m**-*s* of
   12.12. many **m**-*s*, and all the **m**-*s*
   14. the body is not one **m**., but
   18. now hath God set the **m**-*s*
   19. if they were all one **m**., wh.
   20. now are they many **m**-*s*, yet
   22. those **m**-*s* of the body, which
   25. but that the **m**-*s* should have
   26. And whether one **m**. suffer
   all the **m**-*s* suffer with it
   m. be honoured, all the **m**-*s*

1Co.12.27. of Christ, and **m**-*s* in partic.
Eph. 5.30. we are **m**-*s* of his body, of
Col. 3. 5. Mortify therefore your **m**-*s*
Jas. 3. 5. the tongue is a little **m**., and
   6. so is the tongue amo. our **m**-*s*
   4. 1. lusts that war in your **m**-*s*

MEMORIAL.
     mnēmosunon.
Mat. 26.13. done, be told for a **m**. of her
Mar.14. 9. shall be spoken of for a **m**.
Act. 10. 4. alms are come up for a **m**.

MEMORY.
     katechō.
1Co. 15. 2. if ye *keep in* **m**. what I prea.

MENDING.
     katartizō.
Mat. 4.21. **m**. their nets ; Mar.1.19

MENPLEASERS.
     anthrōpareskos.   [Col.3.22
Eph. 6. 6. Not with eyeservice, as **m**.;

MENSERVANTS.
     pais.
Lu.12.45. shall begin to beat the **m**. and

MENSTEALERS.
     andrapodistēs.
1Ti. 1.10. for **m**., for liars, for perjured

MENTION.
     mnēmoneuō.
Heb.11.22. when he died, *made* **m**. of
     mneia.   [Eph.1.16 ; Phile.4
Ro. 1. 9. making **m**. of you always in;
1Th. 1. 2. making **m**. of you in our pr.

MERCHANDISE.
     gomos.
Rev.18.11. no man buyeth their **m**.
   12. The **m**. of gold, and silver
     emporia.
Mat. 22. 5. his farm, another to his **m**.
     emporion.
Jo. 2.16. Father's house an house of **m**.
     emporeuomai.
2Pet. 2. 3. *shall* they ..make **m**. *of* you

MERCHANT,   -*s*.
     emporos.
Mat.13.45. like unto a **m**. man, seeking
Rev.18. 3. the **m**-*s* of the earth are wa.
   11. the **m**-*s* of the earth shall
   15. The **m**-*s* of these things
   23. thy **m**-*s* were the great men

MERCIFUL.
     eleēmōn.
Mat. 5. 7. Blessed are the **m**.: for they
Heb. 2.17. a **m**. and faithful high priest
     hileōs.
Heb. 8.12. For I will be **m**. to their
     oiktirmōn.
Lu. 6.36. **m**., as your Father also is **m**.
     hilaskomai.
Lu. 18.13. God *be* **m**. to me a sinner

MERCY,   -*ies*.
     eleos.   [12.7
Mat. 9.13. I will have **m**., and not sacri.;
   23.23. judgment, **m**., and faith
Lu. 1.50. his **m**. is on them that fear
   54. in remembrance of his **m**.
   58. shewed great **m**. upon her
   72. To perform the **m**. promised
   10.37. He that shewed **m**. on him
Ro. 9.23. glory on the vessels of **m**.
   11.31. that through your **m**. they
   15. 9. might glorify God for his **m**.
Gal. 6.16. peace be on them, and **m**.
Eph. 2. 4. God, who is rich in **m**., for
1Ti. 1. 2. Grace, **m**., and peace, from ;
     2Ti.1.2 ; Tit.1.4

2Ti. 1.16. The Lord give **m**. unto the
   18. may find **m**. of the Lord in
Tit. 3. 5. according to his **m**. he saved
Heb. 4.16. that we may obtain **m**., and
Jas. 2.13. shewed no **m**.; and **m**. rejoi.
   3.17. full of **m**. and good fruits
1Pet. 1. 3. according to his abundant **m**.
2John 3. Grace be with you, **m**., and
Jude 2. **m**. unto you, and peace, and
   21. the **m**. of our Lord Jes. Chr.
     eleeō.
Mat. 5. 7. merci.; for they *shall obta*. **m**.
   9.27. son of David, have **m**. *on* us
   15.22. *Have* **m**. *on* me, O Lord
   17.15. Lord, *have* **m**. *on* my son
   20.30, 31. *Have* **m**. *on* us, O Lord
Mar.10.47, 48. son of David, *have* **m**. *on* ·
     Lu.18.38,39
Lu. 16.24. Father Abraham, *have* **m**. *on*
   17.13. Jesus, Master, *have* **m**. *on* us
Ro. 9.15. *have* **m**. *on* wh. I *will have* **m**.
   16. but of God *that sheweth* **m**.
   18. Therefore *hath* he **m**. *on*
   11.30. yet *have* now *obtained* **m**.
   31. **m**. they also *may obtain* **m**.
   32. that he *might have* **m**. *upon*
   12. 8. he *that sheweth* **m**., with
1Co. 7.25. as one *that hath obtained* **m**.
2Co. 4. 1. as we *have received* **m**., we
Phi. 2.27. God *had* **m**. *on* him ; and
1Ti. 1.13. I *obtained* **m**., because I did
   16. for this cause I *obtained* **m**.
1Pet. 2.10. *which had* not *obtained* **m**.
   but now *have obtained* **m**.
     oiktirmos.
Ro. 12. 1. by the **m**-*s* of God, that ye
2Co. 1. 3. the Father of **m**-*s*, and the
Phi. 2. 1. spirit, if any bowels and **m**-*s*
Col. 3.12. bowels of **m**-*s*, kindness, hu.
Heb.10.28.Moses' law died without **m**.
     oiktirmōn.
Jas. 5.11. very pitiful, and *of tender* **m**.
     hosios.
Act.13.34. will give you the sure **m**-*s* of
     anileōs.
Jas. 2.13. have judgment *without* **m**.

MERCY-SEAT.
     hilastērion.
Heb. 9. 5. shadowing the **m**.; of which

MERRY.
     euphrainō.
Lu. 12.19. ease, eat, drink, and *be* **m**.
   15.23. and let us eat, and *be* **m**.
   24. And they began *to be* **m**.
   29. I *might make* **m**. with my fr.
   32. that we *should make* **m**., and
Rev.11.10. rej. over them, and *make* **m**.
     euthumeō
Jas. 5.13. *Is* any **m**.? let him sing psa.

MESSAGE.
     presbeia.
Lu. 19.14. and sent a **m**. after him, say.
     epanggelia.
1Jo. 1. 5. This then is the **m**. which
     anggelia.
1Jo. 3.11. this is the **m**. that ye heard

MESSENGER,   -*s*.
     anggelos.   [1.2. ; Lu. 7.27
Mat.11.10. Behold, I send my **m**.; Mar.
Lu. 7.24. when the **m**-*s* of John were
   9.52. And sent **m**-*s* before his face
2Co. 12. 7. in the flesh, the **m**. of Satan
Jas. 2.25. wh. she had received the **m**-*s*
     apostolos.
2Co. 8.23. they are the **m**-*s* of the chur.
Phi. 2.25. your **m**., and he that minis.

METE.
     metreō.   [Mar. 4.24 ; Lu. 6.38
Mat. 7. 2. with what measure ye **m**.;

MID-DAY.
mesos hēmera.
Act.26.13. At **m.**, O king, I saw in the

MIDDLE.
mesotoichon.
Eph. 2.14. broken down the **m.** *wall*

MIDNIGHT.
mesonuktion.
Mar.13.35. at even, or at **m.**, or at the
Lu. 11. 5. and shall go unto him at **m.**
Act.16.25. at **m.** Paul and Silas prayed
20. 7. continu. his speech until **m.**
mesos nux.
Mat. 25. 6. And at **m.** there was a cry

MIDST. (See *Heavens.*)
mesos.
Mat.10.16. as sheep in the **m.** of wolves
14.24. the **m.** of the sea; Mar. 6.47
18. 2. in the **m.** of them; Mar.9.36
20. there am I in the **m.** of them
Mar. 7.31. through the **m.** of the coasts
14.60. high pri. stood up in the **m.**
Lu. 2.46. sitting in the **m.** of the doc.
4.30. passing through the **m.** of '
35. had thrown him in the **m.**
5.19. into the **m.** before Jesus
6. 8. and stand forth in the **m.**
17.11. he passed through the **m.** of
21.21. in the **m.** of it, depart out
22.55. a fire in the **m.** of the hall
23.45. the vail..was rent in the **m.**
24.36. Jesus himself stood in the **m.**
Jo. 8. 3. they had set her in the **m.**
9. woman standing in the **m.**
59. through the **m.** of them, and
19.18. one, and Jesus in the **m.**
20.19, 26. and stood in the **m.**, and
Act. 1.15. Peter stood up in the **m.**
18. he burst asunder in the **m.**
2.22. God did by him in the **m.**
4. 7. had set them in the **m.**, they
17.22. Paul stood in the **m.** of Mars'
27.21. Paul stood forth in the **m.** of
Phi. 2.15. in the **m.** of a crooked and
Heb. 2.12. in the **m.** of the church will
Rev. 1.13. in the **m.** of the seven; 2. 1
7. which is in the **m.** of the pa.
4. 6. in the **m.** of the throne; 5.6,
7.17
5. 6. the four bea., and in the **m.**
6. 6. in the **m.** of the four beasts
22. 2. In the **m.** of the street of it
mesoō.
Jo. 7.14. *about the* **m.** *of* the feast

MIGHT, [*noun.*]
dunamis.
Eph. 1.21. princip., and power, and **m.**
3.16. be strengthened with **m.** by
Col. 1.11. Strengthened with all **m.**
²Pet.2.11. greater in power and **m.**
ischus.
Eph. 6.10. and in the power of his **m.**
Rev. 7.12. power and **m.** be unto our

MIGHT, [*verb.*] (See *May.*)

MIGHTIER.
ischuros.
Mat. 3.11. that cometh after me is **m.**
Mar. 1. 7. come. one **m.** than; Lu.3.16

MIGHTILY.
eutonōs.
Act.18.28. For he **m.** convinced the Je.
kata [*accu.*] kratos.
Act.19.20. So **m.** grew the word of God
dunamis.
Col. 1.29. which worketh in me **m.**
en ischus.
Rev.18 2. he cried **m.** with a strong
178

MIGHTY. (See *Power.*)
dunamis.
Mat.11.20.most of his **m.** *works* were
21, 23.for if the **m.** *wo.*; Lu.10.13
13.54. wisdom, and these **m.** *works*
58. did not many **m.** *works* there
14. 2. therefo. **m.** *works*; Mar.6.14
Mar. 6 2. even such **m.** *works* are wro.
5. could there do no **m.** *work*
Lu. 19.37. the **m.** *works* that they had
Ro. 15.19. through **m.** signs and wond.
(in the *power* of signs.)
²Co. 12.12. and wonders, and **m.** *deeds*
²Th. 1. 7. from heaven with his **m.** an.
(with angels *of his power.*)
dunatos.
Lu. 1.49. he *that is* **m.** hath done to
24.19. a prophet **m.** in deed and
Act. 7.22. was **m.** in words and in
18.24. man, and **m.** in the scriptu.
¹Co. 1.26. not many **m.**, not many no.
²Co.10. 4. **m.** through God to the pul.
Rev. 6.15. captains, and the **m.** *men*
dunastēs.
Lu. 1.52. put down the **m.** from their
dunateō.
²Co.13. 3. nct weak, but *is* **m.** in you
ischuros.
Lu. 15.14. there arose a **m.** famine
¹Co. 1.27. confound the th. whi. are **m.**
Rev.10. 1. I saw another **m.** angel
18.10. Babylon, that **m.** city ! for
21. a **m.** angel took up a stone
19. 6. as the voice of **m.** thunder.
18. and the flesh of **m.** men, and
ischus.
Eph. 1.19. the working of his **m.** power
biaios.
Act. 2. 2. as of a rushing **m.** wind, and
energeō.
Gal. 2. 8. the same *was* **m.** *in* me
krataios.
¹Pet. 5. 6. under the **m.** hand of God
megas.
Rev. 6.13. she is shaken of a **m.** wind
tēlikoutos.
Rev.16.18. *so* **m.** an earthquake, and so

MILE.
milion.
Mat. 5.41. shall compel thee to go a **m.**

MILK.
gala.
¹Co. 3. 2. I have fed you with **m.**, and
9. 7. eateth not of the **m.** of the
Heb.5.12. be. such as have need of **m.**
13. every one that useth **m.** is
¹Pet. 2. 2. desire the sincere **m.** of the

MILL.
mulōn.
Mat.24.41.grinding at the **m.**; the one

MILLSTONE.
lithos mulikos.
Mar. 9.42. that a **m.** were hanged about
mulos onikos. [17.2
Mat.18. 6. that a **m.** were hanged ; Lu.
mulos.
Rev.18.21. up a stone like a great **m.**
22. the sound of a **m.** shall be

MIND, [*noun,*] -*s.*
nous.
Ro. 1.28. them over to a reprobate **m.**
7.23. warring ag. the law of my **m.**
25. with the **m.** I myself serve
11.34. hath known the **m.**; ¹Co.2.16
12. 2. by the renewing of your **m.**
14. 5. fully persuad. in his own **m.**
¹Co. 1.10. joined toge. in the same **m.**
2.16. But we have the **m.** of Christ

Eph. 4.17. in the vanity of their **m.**
23. rene. in the spirit of your **m.**
Col. 2.18. puffed up by his fleshly **m.**
²Th. 2. 2. be not soon shaken in **m.**
¹Ti. 6. 5. men of corrupt **m-s**; ²Ti. 3.8
6. even their **m.** and conscience
Rev.17. 9. And here is the **m.** which
dianoia. [Lu.10.27
Mat.22.37.and with all thy **m.**;Mar.12.30
Eph. 2. 3. des. of the flesh and of the **m**
Col. 1.21. enemies in your **m.** by wick
Heb. 8.10. put my laws into their **m.**
10.16. in their **m-s** will I write them
¹Pet. 1.13. gird up the loins of your **m.**
²Pet. 3. 1. I stir up your pure **m-s** by
ennoia.
¹Pet. 4. 1. likewise with the same **m.**
noēma.
²Co. 3.14. But their **m-s** were blinded
4. 4. hath blinded the **m-s** of them
11. 3. so your **m-s** should be cor.
Phi. 4. 7. sh. keep your hearts and **m-s**
phroneō.
Ro. 12.16. *Be of* the same **m.** one to.
²Co.13.11. *be of* one **m.**, live in peace
Phi. 2. 2. being of one accord, *of* one **m.**
3. 5. *Let* this **m.** *be* in you, which
4. 2. *that* they *be of* the same **m.**
phronēma.
Ro. 8. 7. Bec. the carnal **m.** is enmity
27. knoweth what is the **m.** of
homophrōn.
¹Pet. 3. 8. Finally, be ye all *of one* **m.**
sōphroneō. [Lu.8.35
Mar. 5.15. clothed, and *in his right* **m.**
psuchē.
Act.14. 2. made their **m-s** evil affected
Phi. 1.27. with one **m.** striving togeth.
Heb.12. 3. weari. and faint in your **m-s**
gnōmē.
Phile. 14. without thy **m.** would I do
Rev.17.13.These have one **m.**, and shall
anamimnēskō.
Mar.14.72.Peter *called to* **m.** the word
hupomimnēskō.
Tit. 3. 1. *Put* them *in* **m.** to be subject
homothumadon.
Ro. 15. 6. That ye may *with one* **m.**
(*See words in connection.*)

MIND, [*verb,*] -ing.
phroneō.
Ro. 8. 5. *do* **m.** the things of the flesh
12.16. **m.** not high things
Phi. 3.16. *let* us **m.** the same thing
19. *who* **m.** earthly things
mellō.
Act.20.13. **m**-*ing* himself to go afoot

MINDED. (See *High.*)
phroneō.
Gal. 5.10. *will* be none otherwise **m.**
Phi. 3.15. as be perfect, be thus **m.**
thing ye be otherwise **m.**
phronēma.
Ro. 8. 6. *to be* carnally **m.** is death
but *to be* spiritually **m.** is
(*the mind* of the flesh,) (the m. of the sp.)
sōphroneō.
Tit. 2. 6. like. exhort *to be* sober **m.**
boulomai.
Mat. 1.19. *was* **m.** to put her away pri.
²Co. 1.15. I *was* **m.** to come unto you
bouleuomai.
Act. 27.39.unto the which they *were* **m.**
²Co. 1.17. *When* I therefore *was* thus **m.**

MINDFUL.
mnaomai.
²Ti. 1. 4. see thee, *being* **m.** of thy tea.
²Pet. 3. 2. ye may *be* **m.** of the words
mnēmoneuō.
Heb.11.15. if they *had been* **m.** of that

mimnēskomai.
ꟸeb. 2. 6. man, that thou *art* m. of

MINE.
egō *and* emos.
Mat. 7.24, 26. these sayings of m.
20.23. my left, is not m.; Mar.10.40
Lu. 11. 6. a friend of m. in his journey
Jo. 2. 4. Jesus saith m. hour is not
.7.16. my doctrine is not m.
10.14. am known of m.
14.24. word which ye hear is not m.
16.14. he shall receive of m., and
15. that the Father hath are m.
17.10. m. are thine, and thi. are m.
Ro. 12.19. vengeance is m., I will repay
(for me, vengeance.)
Phi. 1. 4. in every prayer of m. making
(*And all others in which it occurs.*)

MINE-OWN.
emos.
Mat. 20.15.do what I will with m.
25.27. received m. with usury
Jo. 5.30. bec. I seek not m. will ; 6.38
¹Co. 1.15. had baptized in m. name
16.21. Paul with m. hand ; ²Th.3.17
Gal. 6.11. you with m. hand ; Phile. 19
Phi. 3. 9. not having m. righteousness
Phile. 12. receive him, that is, m. bow.
egō, [*gen.*]
Jo. 8.50. I seek not m. glory ; there is
Act.13.22. a man after m. heart, which
26. 4. at the first among m. nation
Gal. 1.14. my equals in m. nation
emautou.
Jo. 5.30. I can of m. *self* do nothing
¹Co. 4. 3. yea, I judge not m. *self*
10.33. not seeking m. profit, but
autos.
Lu. 19.23. have required m. (*it*) with

MINGLED, (See *Myrrh.*)
mignumi.
Mat.27.34.vinegar to drink m. with gall
Lu. 13. 1. whose blood Pilate *had* m.
Rev. 8. 7. hail and fire m. with blood
15. 2. a sea of glass m. with fire

MINISTER, [*noun,*]   -*s.*
diakonos.
Mat 20.26.let him be your m.;Mar.10.43
Ro. 13. 4. For he is the m. of God to
he is the m. of God, a reven.
15. 8. a m. of the circumcision for
¹Co. 3. 5. m-*s* by whom ye believed
²Co. 3. 6. also hath made us able m-*s*
6. 4. ourselves as the m-*s* of God
11.15. if his m-*s* be also transformed
as the m-*s* of righteousness
23. Are they m-*s* of Christ?
Gal. 2.17. is therefore Christ the m. of
Eph. 3. 7. Whereof I was made a m.
6.21. belo. brother and faithful m.
Col. 1. 7. for you a faithful m. of Chri.
23, 25. I Paul am made a m.
4. 7. a faithful m. and fellowserv.
¹Th. 3. 2. our brother, and m. of God
¹Ti. 4. 6. thou shalt be a good m. of
hupēretēs.
Lu. 1. 2. eyewitnesses and m-*s* of the
4.20. he gave it again to the m.
Act. 13.5. had also John to their m.
26.16. to make thee a m. and a
¹Co. 4. 1. account of us, as of the m-*s*
leitourgos.
Ro. 13. 6. they are God's m-*s*, attending
15.16. That I should be the m. of
ꟸeb.1. 7. and his m-*s* a flame of fire
8. 2. A m. of the sanctuary, and

MINISTER,[*verb*]-*ed,-eth,-ing*
diakoneō   [Mar.1.13
Mat. 4.11. angels came and m-*ed unto* ;

Mat. 8.15. she arose, and m-*ed unto* ;
Mar.1.31 ; Lu.4.39
20.28. *to be* m-*ed unto,* but *to* m.;
Mar.10.45
25.44. in pri., and *did* not m. *unto*
27.55. from Galilee, m-*ing unto*
Mar.15.41.followed him, and m-*ed unto*
Lu. 8. 3. others, which m-*ed unto*
Act.19.22. of them *that* m-*ed unto* him
Ro. 15.25. unto Jerusalem to m. *unto*
²Co. 3. 3. the epistle of Christ m-*ed by*
²Ti. 1.18. many things he m-*ed unto*
Phile. 13. he *might have* m-*ed unto* me
Heb. 6.10. name, *in that* ye have m-*ed*
to the saints, and do m.
¹Pet. 1.12. *unto* us they did m. the thi.
4.10. even so m. the same one to
11. if any man m., let him do it
diakonia.
Heb. 1.14. spirits, sent forth to m. for
leitourgeō.
Act. 13. 2. *As* they m-*ed* to the Lord
Ro. 15.27. their duty is also *to* m. unto
Heb.10.11. priest stand. daily m-*ing*
leitourgos.
Phi. 2.25. *he that* m-*ed* to my wants
epichorēgeō.
²Co. 9.10. he *that* m-*eth* seed to the
Gal. 3. 5. He therefore *that* m-*eth* to
Col. 2.19. *having* nourishment m-*ed*
²Pet. 1.11. entrance *shall be* m-*ed unto*
hupēreteō.
Act.20.34. these hands *have* m-*ed unto*
24.23. *to* m. or come unto him
chorēgeō.
²Co. 9.10. both m. bread for your food
hierourgeō.
Ro. 15.16. m-*ing* the gospel of God
ergazomai.
¹Co. 9.13. they *which* m. about holy
didōmi.
Eph. 4.29. that it *may* m. grace unto
parechō.
¹Ti. 1. 4. genealogies, which m. ques.

MINISTERING, [*no. & adj.*]
diakonia.
Ro. 12. 7. let us wait on our m.
²Co. 8. 4. the fellowship of the m.
9. 1. touching the m. to the
leitourgikos.
Heb. 1.14. Are they not all m. spirits

MINISTRATION.
diakonia.
Act. 6. 1. neglected in the daily m.
²Co. 3. 7. if the m. of death, written
8. shall not the m. of the spirit
9. if the m. of condemnation
doth the m. of righteousness
9.13. the experiment of this m.
leitourgia.
Lu. 1.23. as the days of his m. were

MINISTRY.
diakonia.
Act. 1.17. had obtained part of this m.
25. he may take part of this m.
6. 4. prayer, and to the m. of the
12.25. they had fulfilled their m.
20.24. the m., which I have receiv.
21.19. among the Gentiles by his m.
Ro. 12. 7. Or m., let us wait on our
¹Co. 16.15. themselves to the m. of the
²Co. 4. 1. seeing we have this m., as
5.18. to us the m. of reconciliation
6. 3. that the m. be not blamed
Eph. 4.12. for the work of the m., for
Col. 4.17. Take heed to the m. which
¹Ti. 1.12. faithful, put. me into the m.
²Ti. 4. 5. make full proof of thy m.
11. profitable to me for the m.

leitourgia.
Heb. 8. 6. obtained a more excellent m
9.21. and all the vessels of the m

MINSTRELS.
aulētēs.
Mat. 9.23. saw the m. and the people

MINT.
hēduosmon.
Mat.23.23. ye pay tithe of m., and
Lu. 11.42. tithe m. and rue and all

MIRACLE,   -*s,*
sēmeion.
Lu. 23. 8. to have seen some m.
Jo. 2.11. This beginning of m-*s*
23. saw the m-*s* which he did
3. 2. can do these m-*s*
4.54. This is again the second m.
6. 2. because they saw his m-*s*
14. they had seen the m. that
26. not because ye saw the m-*s*
7.31. will he do more m-*s*
9.16. that is a sinner do such m-*s*
10.41. John did no m.
11.47. this man doeth many m-*s*
12.18. he had done this m.
37. he had done so many m-*s*
Act. 4.16. a notable m. hath been done
22. on whom this m. of healing
8. 6. seeing the m-*s* which he did
15.12. declaring what m-*s* and won.
Rev.13.14.those m-*s* which he had po.
16.14. spirits of devils,working m-*s*
19.20. false prop. that wrought m-*s*
dunamis.
Mar. 9.39. no man which shall do a m.
Act. 2.22. by m-*s* and wonders and
8.13. the m-*s* and signs which were
19.11. And God wrought special m-*s*
¹Co. 12.10. To ano. the working of m-*s*
28. thirdly teach., after that m-*s*
29. are all *workers* of m-*s*
Gal. 3. 5. and worketh m-*s* among you
Heb. 2. 4. wonders, and with divers m-*s*

MIRE.
borboros.
²Pet. 2.22. to her wallowing in the m,

MISCHIEF.
radiourgia.
Act. 13.10. of all subtility and all m.

MISERABLE.
eleeinos.
¹Co. 15.19. we are of all men *most* m.
(*more miserable* than all men.)
Rev. 3.17. thou art wretched, and m.

MISERABLY.
kakōs.
Mat.21.41. He will m. destroy those

MISERY,   -*ies.*
talaipōria.
Ro. 3.16. Destruction and m. are in
Jas. 5. 1. weep and howl for your m-*s*

MIST.
achlus.
Act.13.11. there fell on him a m. and a
zophos.
²Pet. 2.17. to whom the m. of darkness

MITE,   -*s.*
lepton.
Mar.12.42.she threw in two m-*s* which
Lu. 12.59. hast paid the very last m.
21. 2. casting in thither two m-*s*

MIXED.
sungkerannumi.
Heb. 4. 2. not *being* m. *with* faith in

MIXTURE.
migma.
Jo. 19.39. brought a **m**. of myrrh and
  akratos.
Rev.14.10.wh. is poured out *without* **m**.

MOCK,   *-ed, -ing.*
empaizō.
Mat. 2.16. he *was* **m**-ed of the wise men
  20.19. him to the Gentiles *to* **m**.
  27.29. before him, and **m**-ed him
    31. after that they *had* **m**-ed him
    41. priests **m**-*ing* him; Mar.15.31
Mar.10.34.they *shall* **m**. him, and shall
  15.20. when they *had* **m**-*ed* him
Lu. 14.29. that behold it begin *to* **m**.
  18.32. *shall be* **m**-*ed*, and spitefully
  22.63. men that held Jesus **m**-ed
  23.11. set him at nought, and **m**-ed
    36. the soldiers also **m**-ed him
chleuazō.
Act. 2.13. Others **m**-*ing* said, These m.
  17.32. resur. of the dead, some **m**-ed
muktērizō.
Gal. 6. 7. not deceiv.; God *is* not **m**-ed

MOCKERS.
empaiktēs.
Jude 18. should be **m**. in the last time

MOCKINGS.
empaigmos.
Heb.11.36.trials of cruel **m**. and scourg.

MODERATION.
epieikēs.
Phi. 4. 5. Let your **m**. be known unto

MODEST.
kosmios.
¹Ti. 2. 9. adorn themselves in **m**. app.

MOISTURE.
ikmas.
Lu. 8. 6. away, because it lacked **m**.

MOMENT.
stigmē.
Lu. 4. 5. of the world in a **m**. of time
atomos.
¹Co.15.52. In a **m**., in the twinkling of
parautika.
²Co.4.17. afflict., which is *but for a* **m**.

MONEY, (See *Changers.*)
argurion.
Mat.25.18.earth, and hid his lord's **m**.
  27. therefore to have put my **m**.
  28.12. they gave large **m**. unto the
    15. So they took the **m**., and did
Mar.14.11.and promised to give him **m**.
Lu. 9. 3. neither bread, neither **m**.
  19.15. whom he had given the **m**.
  23. gavest not thou my **m**. into
  22. 5. covenanted to give him **m**.
Act. 7.16. Abra. bought for a sum of **m**.
  8.20. Thy **m**. perish with thee, be.
chrēma.
Act. 4.37. and brought the **m**. and laid
  8.18. given, he offered them **m**.
  20. may be purchased with **m**.
  24.26. He hoped also that **m**. shou.
chalkos.
Mar. 6. 8. no bread, no **m**. in their pu.
  12.41. people cast **m**. into the trea.
statēr.
Mat.17.27.thou shalt find a *piece of* **m**.
nomisma.
Mat.22.19. Shew me the tribute **m**.
kerma.
Jo. 2.15. poured out the changers' **m**.
philarguria.
¹Ti. 6.10. the *love of* **m**. is the root of
180

MONEY-CHANGERS.
kollubistēs.   [Mar. 11.15
Mat.21.12. overth. the tables of the **m**.

MONTH,   *-s.*
mēn.
Lu. 1.24. and hid herself five **m**-s
  26. And in the sixth **m**. the an.
  36. this is the sixth **m**. with her
  56. ab. with her about three **m**-s
  4.25. up three years and six **m**-s
Act. 7.20. his father's house three **m**-s
  18.11. a year and six **m**-s, teaching
  19. 8. for the space of three **m**-s
  20. 3. and there abode three **m**-s
  28.11. and after three **m**-s we depa.
Gal. 4.10. Ye observe days, and **m**-s
Jas. 5.17. sp. of three years and six **m**-s
Rev. 9. 5. sho. be tormented five **m**-s
  10. was to hurt men five **m**-s
  15. and a day, and a **m**., and a
  11. 2. under foot forty and two **m**-s
  13. 5. continue forty and two **m**-s
  22. 2. yielded her fruit every **m**.
trimēnon.
Heb.11.23. was hid *three* **m**-s of his
tetramēnon.
Jo. 4.35. ye, There are yet *four* **m**-s

MOON.
selēnē.   [Mar.13.24
Mat.24.29. the **m**. shall not give her ;
Lu. 21.25. in the sun, and in the **m**.
Act. 2.20. and the **m**. into blood, bef.
¹Co. 15.41. and another glory of the **m**.
Rev. 6.12. and the **m**. became as blood
  8.12. and the third part of the **m**.
  12. 1. and the **m**. under her feet
  21.23. of the sun neither of the **m**.
noumēnia.
Col. 2.16. or of the *new* **m**. or of the

MORE.
mallon.
Mat. 6.30. shall he not much **m**. clothe
  7.11. how much **m**. shall your F.;
            Lu.11.13.
  10.25. how much **m**. shall they
  18.13. he rejoiceth **m**. of that sheep
Mar. 7.36. so much *the* **m**. a great deal
  10.48. but he cried *the* **m**. a great
  14.31. But he spake *the* **m**. vehem.
Lu. 5.15. But *so much the* **m**. went
  12.24. how much **m**. are ye better
  28. how much **m**. will he clothe
  18.39. but he cried so much *the* **m**.
Jo. 5.18. There. the Jews sou. *the* **m**.
  12.43. the praise of men **m**. than
  19. 8. saying, he was *the* **m**. afraid
Act. 4.19. to hearken unto you **m**. than
  5.14. believers were *the* **m**. added
  9.22. Saul increased *the* **m**. in str.
  20.35. **m**. blessed to give than to
  22. 2. to them, they kept *the* **m**.
  27.11. **m**. than those things which
Ro. 5. 9. Much **m**. then, being now
  10. much **m**., being reconciled
  15. much **m**. the grace of God
  17. much **m**. they which receive
  11.12. how much **m**. their fulness
  24. how much **m**. shall these
¹Co. 12.22. Nay, much **m**. those mem.
  14.18. with tongues **m**. than ye all
²Co. 3. 9. much **m**. doth the ministra.
  11. much **m**. that which remain.
  7. 7. so that I rejoiced *the* **m**.
  13. and exceedingly *the* **m**. joyed
Gal. 4.27. hath many **m**. child. *than*
Phi. 1. 9. may abound yet **m**. and **m**.
  2.12. but now much **m**. in my abs.
  3. 4. might trust in the flesh, I **m**.
¹Th. 4. 1. ye would abound **m**. *and* **m**.
  10. that ye increase **m**. *and* **m**.

²Ti. 3. 4. lovers of pleasures **m**. than
Phile. 16. but how much **m**. unto thee
Heb. 9.14. How much **m**. shall the blo.
  10.25. and so much *the* **m**., as ye
  12.25. much **m**. shall not we escape
eti.
Mat.18.16. take with thee one or two **m**.
Lu. 20.36. Neither can they die *any* **m**.
Jo. 11.54. no **m**. openly among the J.
  14.19. the world seeth me no **m**.
  16.10. Father, and ye see me no **m**.
  21. remembereth no **m**. the ang.
  25. no **m**. speak unto you in pro.
  17.11. I am no **m**. in the world, but
Ro. 6. 9. dieth no **m**.; death hath no
  m. dominion over him
  7.17, 20. then it is no **m**. I that
  11. 6. then is it no **m**. of works :
  otherwise grace is no **m**. gra.
  of works then it is no **m**. gra.
  otherwise work is no **m**. wo.
²Co. 5.16. *henceforth* kn. we him no **m**.
Gal. 3.18. it is no **m**. of promise : but
  4. 7. thou art no **m**. a servant
Heb. 8.12. will I remember no **m**.;10.17
  10. 2. should have had no **m**. cons.
  18. there is no **m**. offering for
  26. remaineth no **m**. sacrifice
  11.32. And what shall I **m**. say
  12.26. saying, *Yet* once **m**. I shake
  27. And this word, *Yet* once **m**.
Rev. 3.12. and he shall go no **m**. out
  7.16. no **m**. neither thirst *any* **m**.
  9.12. there come two woes **m**. here.
  12. 8. place found *any* **m**. in heav.
  18.21. shall be found no **m**. at all
  22, 23. shall be heard no **m**. at
  shall be found *any* **m**. in
  23. shall shine no **m**. at all in
  20. 3. sh. deceive the nations no **m**.
  21. 1. and there was no **m**. sea
  4. there shall be no **m**. death
  shall there he *any* **m**. pain
  22. 3. there shall be no **m**. curse
pleiōn.   [Lu.12.23
Mat. 6.25. is not the life **m**. than meat
  20.10. they should have received **m**.
  21.36. other servants **m**. than the
  26.53. **m**. than twelve legions of
Mar.12.33. is **m**. than all whole burnt
  43. cast **m**. in, than all; Lu.21.3
Lu. 3.13. Exact no **m**. than that wh.
  9.13. We have no **m**. but five loa.
Jo. 4. 1. baptized **m**. disciples than
  41. And many **m**. believed bec.
  7.31. will he do **m**. miracles than
  15. 2. it may bring forth **m**. fruit
  21.15. lovest thou me **m**. than th.
Act.23.13. they were **m**. than forty wh.
  21. **m**. than forty men which
  25. 6. among them **m**. than ten
¹Co. 9.19. that I might gain the **m**.
²Ti. 2.16. they will increase unto **m**.
Heb.3. 3. counted worthy of **m**. glory
  hath **m**. honour than the
Rev. 2.19. and the last to be **m**. than
perissos.
Mat. 5.37. for whatsoever is **m**. than
  47. what do ye **m**. than others
  11. 9. unto you, and **m**. than a pr.
Lu. 7.26. and *much* **m**. than a prophet
  12. 4. have no **m**. that they can do
  48. of him they will ask the **m**.
²Co.10. 8. I should boast somewhat **m**.
perissoterōs.
²Co. 1.12. and **m**. *abundantly* to you
  2. 4. I have **m**. *abundantly* unto
  12.15. *the* **m**. *abundantly* I love
Phi. 1.14. are *much* **m**. bold to speak
¹Th. 2.17. endeavoured *the* **m**. abund.
Heb.2. 1. we ought to give *the* **m**. ear.

perissōs.
Mat.27.23.they cried out *the* m., saying
    perissoteron.
Heb. 7.15. it is yet *far* m. evident
    huper.
Mat.10.37.lov. father or mother m. *than*
    lov. son or daughter m., *than*
¹Co.11.23. I speak as a fool I am m.
Phile. 21. thou wilt also do m. *than* I
    para, [*accu.*]
Ro. 1.25. creature m. *than* the Creator
  12. 3. m. highly *than* he ought to
    allos.
Mat.25.20.beside them five talents m.
    hosos.
Mar.7.36. but *the* m. he charged them
    ei mē.
Mar.8.14. with them m. *than* one loaf
    epanō.
Mar.14.5. m. *than* three hundred pence
    houtōs oude.
Jo. 15. 4. *no* m. can ye except ye abide
    meizōn.
Jas. 4. 6. But he giveth m. grace
  (*See words in connection.*)

MOREOVER. (See *Appendix*.)
    eti.
Act. 2.26. m. also my flesh shall rest in
Heb.11.36.yea, m. of bonds and impris.
    alla kai.
Lu. 16.21. m. the dogs came and licked
    ho loipos.
¹Co. 4. 2. m. it is required in stewards

MORNING. (See *Early*.)
    prōi.
Mat.16. 3. And *in the* m., It will be fo.
Mar. 1.35. *in the* m., rising up a great
  11.20. And *in the* m., as they pas.
  13.35. at the cockcro., or *in the* m.
  15. 1. And straightway *in the* m.
Act.28.23. prophets from m. till even.
    prōia.
Mat.21.18. Now *in the* m. as he return.
  27. 1. when the m. was ; Jo.21.4
    orthrizō.
Lu. 21.38. people *came early in the* m.
    prōinos.
Rev. 2.28. I will give him the m. star
    orthrinos.
Rev.22.16. and the bright and m. star

MORROW.
    epaurion.
Mar.11.12.on the m., when they were
Act.10. 9. On the m., as they went on
  23. on the m. Peter went away
  24. the m. *after* they entered in.
  20. 7. ready to depart on the m.
  22.30. On the m., because he would
  23.32. On the m. they left the
  25.23. On the m., when Agrippa
    aurion.
Mat. 6.30. *to* m. is cast into ; Lu.12.28
  34. for the m. : for the m. shall
Lu. 10.35. on the m. when he departed
  13.32. I do cures to day and *to* m.
  33. I must walk to day, and *to* m.
Act. 4. 5. it came to pass on the m.
  23.15. him down unto you *to* m.
  20. bring down Paul *to* m.
  25.22. *To* m., said he, thou shalt
¹Co.15.32. eat and drink ; for *to* m. we
Jas. 4.13. To day or *to* m. we will go
  14. what shall be on the m.
    hexēs.
Act.25.17. delay *on the* m. I sat on the

MORSEL.
    brōsis.
Heb.12.16.for one m. *of meat* sold his

MORTAL.
    thnētos.
Ro. 6.12. reign in your m. body, that
  8.11. also quicken your m. bodies
¹Co.15.53. and this m. must put on
  54. this m. shall have put on
²Co. 4.11. manifest in our m. flesh

MORTALITY.
    ho thnētos, [*neut.*]
²Co. 5. 4. m. might be swallowed up

MORTIFY.
    thanatoō.
Ro. 8.13. *do* m. the deeds of the body
    nekroō.
Col. 3. 5. m. therefore your members

MOST.
    pleiōn.
Mat.11.20.wherein m. of his mighty w.
¹Co.14.27. by two, or at the m. by three
    malista.
Act.20.38.sorrowing m. *of all* for the
    hagios, [*superl.*]
Jude 20. on your m. *holy* faith, pray.
  (*See words in connection.*)

MOTE.
    karphos.
Mat. 7. 3. the m. that is in ; Lu. 6.41
  4. pull out the m. ; Lu.6.42
  5. to cast out the m. out of

MOTH.
    sēs.
Mat. 6.19. where m. and rust doth cor.
  20. where neither m. nor rust
Lu. 12.33. neither m. corrupteth

MOTH-EATEN.
    sētobrōtos.
Jas. 5. 2. and your garments are m.

MOTHER, (See *Murderer*,) -s
    mētēr.
Mat. 1.18. When as his m. Mary was
  2.11. yo. child with Mary his m.
  13, 14,20,21. yo. child and his m.
  10.35. daugh. aga. her m.; Lu.12.53
  37. He that loveth father or m.
  12.46. behold, his m. and his breth.
  47. thy m. and thy brethren ;
    Mar. 3.32 ; Lu.8.20
  48. Who is my m. ? Mar. 3.33
  49. my m. and my brethren ;
    Mar. 3.34 ; Lu. 8.21
  50. and sister and m.; Mar. 3.33
  13.55. is not his m. called Mary
  14. 8. before instructed of her m.
  11. bro. it to her m. ; Mar. 6.28
  15. 4. Honour thy father and m. ;
    19.19 ; Mar. 7.10, 10.19 ;
    Lu. 18.20 ; Eph. 6. 2.
    curse. fath. or m. ; Mar.7.10
  5, 6. father or his m. ; Mar.7.11
  19. 5. a man leave father and m.;
    Mar. 10.7 ; Eph. 5.31
  12. so born from their m.'s wo.
  29. or m., or wife, or children
  20.20. Then came to him the m. of
  27.56. Mary the m. of ; Mar.15.40
    and the m. of Zebedee's
Mar. 3.31. then his brethren and his m.
  5.40. taketh the father and the m.
  6.24. and said unto her m., What
  7.12. ought for his fath. or his m.
  10.29. or sisters, or father, or m.
  30. and sisters, and m-s, and
Lu. 1.15. even from his m.'s womb
  43. that the m. of my Lord sho.
  60. And his m. answered and sa.
  2.33. Joseph and his m. marvelled

Lu. 2.34. and said unto Mary his m.
  43. and Joseph and his m. knew
  48. and his m. said unto him, S.
  51. but his m. kept all these sa.
  7.12. the only son of his m., and
  15. he delivered him to his m.
  8.19. Then came to him his m.
  51. and the m. of the maiden
  12.53. the m. against the daughter
  14.26. hate not his father, and m.
Jo. 2. 1. and the m. of Jesus was the.
  3. the m. of Jesus saith unto
  5. His m. saith unto the serva.
  12. he, and his m., and his bret.
  3. 4. the second time into his m.'s
  6.42. whose father and m. we kn.
  19.25. his m., and his m.'s sister
  26. When Jes. there saw his m.
    he saith unto his m., Woman
  27. the disciple, Behold thy m.
Act. 1.14. and Mary the m. of Jesus
  3. 2. lame from his m.'s womb
  12.12. to the house of Mary the m.
  14. 8. a cripple from his m.'s womb
Ro. 16.13. the Lord, and his m. and m.
Gal. 1.15. separated me from my m.'s
  4.26. which is the m. of us all
¹Ti. 5. 2. The elder women as m-s; the
²Ti. 1. 5. Lois, and thy m. Eunice
Rev.17. 5. THE m. OF HARLOTS AND
    penthera. [Mar. 1.30; Lu. 4.38
Mat. 8.14. saw his *wife's* m. laid, and;
Mat.10.35.daugh. against her m.-*in-law*
Lu. 12.53. m.-*in-law* against her daugh.
    amētōr.
Heb. 7. 3. Without father, *without* m.

MOTIONS.
    pathēma.
Ro. 7. 5. the m. of sins, which were

MOUNT.
    oros.
Mat.21. 1. unto the m. of Olives, then
  24. 3. up. the m. of Olives; Mar.13.3
  26.30. they went out into the m. ;
    Mar. 14.26; Jo. 8.1
Mar.11. 1. at the m. of Olives, he send.
Lu. 19.29. at the m. called the m. of O.
  37. at the descent of the m. of
  21.37. and abode in the m. that is
  22.39. to the m. of Olives ; and his
Act. 1.12. from the m. called Olivet, wh.
  7.30. in the wilderness of m. Sina
  38. spake to him in the m. Sina
Gal. 4.24. the one from the m. Sinai
  25. For this Agar is m. Sinai in
Heb. 8. 5. pat. shewed to thee in the m.
  12.18. unto the m. that might be
  22. ye are come unto m. Sion
²Pet. 1.18. we. with him in the holy m.
Rev.14. 1. a Lamb stood on the m. Sion

MOUNTAIN, -s.
    oros. [Jo. 6.3,15
Mat. 4. 8. into an exceeding high m.;
  5. 1. he went up into a m.; 14.23,
    15.29 ; Lu. 9.28
  8. 1. was come down from the m.
  17. 1. an high m. apart; Mar. 9.2
  9. down from the m.; Mar. 9.9
  20. ye shall say unto this m.;
    21.21 ; Mar. 11.23
  18.12. goeth unto the m-s, and seek.
  24.16. be in Judæa flee into the m-s
  28.16. into a m. where Jesus had
Mar. 3.13. And he goeth up into a m.
  5. 5. he was in the m-s, and in the
  11. nigh unto the m-s a great he.
  6.46. he departed into a m. to pr.
  13.14. Jud. flee to the m-s; Lu. 21.21
Lu. 3. 5. every m. and hill shall be br.
  4. 5. taking him up into a high m.

Mar. 6.12. he went out into a **m**. to
   8.32. swine feeding on the **m**.
  23.30. to say to the **m**-s, Fall on us
Jo. 4.20. worshipped in this **m**.; and
   21. neither in this **m**., nor yet at
¹Co.13. 2. so that I could remove **m**-s
Heb.11.38.and in **m**-s, and in dens
  12.20. as a beast touch the **m**., it
Rev. 6.14. every **m**. and island were m.
   15. and in the rocks of the **m**-s
   16. said to the **m**-s and rocks,
   8, 8. as it were a great **m**. burning
   6.20. and the **m**-s were not found
   17. 9. seven heads are seven **m**-s
  21.10. to a great and high **m**., and

MOURN,   -ed.
pentheō.
Mat. 5. 4. Blessed are they *that* **m**.
   9.15. chil. of the bridechamber **m**.
Mar.16.10.with him, *as they* **m**-*ed* and
Lu. 6.25. for ye *shall* **m**. and weep
¹Co. 5. 2. and *have* not rather **m**-*ed*, th.
Jas. 4. 9. and **m**., and weep: let your
Rev.18.11.*shall* weep and **m**. over her
thrēneō.
Mat.11.17. *have* **m**-*ed* unto you; Lu.7.32
koptō.
Mat.24.30. *shall* all tribes of earth **m**.

MOURNING.
odurmos.
Mat. 2.18. and great **m**., Rachel weep.
²Co. 7. 7. your **m**., your fervent mind
penthos.
Jas. 4. 9. your laugh. be turned to **m**.
Rev.18. 8. death, and **m**., and famine

MOUTH,   -s.
stoma.
Mat. 4. 4. that proceedeth out of the **m**.
   5. 2. And he opened his **m**. and
  12.34. heart the **m**. speak.; Lu.6.45
  13.35. I will open my **m**. in para.
  15. 8. nigh unto me with their **m**.
    11. that which goeth into the **m**.
      which cometh out of the **m**.
   17. whatsoever enter.in at the **m**.
   18. which proceed out of the **m**.
  17.27. wh. thou hast opened his **m**.
  18.16. that in the **m**. of two or thr.
  21.16. Out of the **m**. of babes and
Lu. 1.64. And his **m**. was opened im.
   70. by the **m**. of his; Act.3.18,21
  11.54. catch someth. out of his **m**.
  19.22. Out of thine own **m**. will I
  21.15. For I will give you a **m**. and
  22.71. have heard of his own **m**.
Jo. 19.29. hyssop, and put it to his **m**.
Act. 1.16. by the **m**. of David spake
   4.25. by the **m**. of thy servant
   8.32. so opened he not his **m**.
   35. Then Philip opened his **m**.
  10.34. Then Peter opened his **m**.
  11. 8. at any time enter.into my **m**.
  15. 7. that the Gentiles by my **m**.
  18.14. now about to open his **m**.
  22.14. sh. hear the voice of his **m**.
  23. 2. him to smite him on the **m**.
Ro. 3.14. Whose **m**. is full of cursing
  19. that every **m**. may be stopp.
  10. 8. nigh thee, even in thy **m**.
   9. confess with thy **m**. the Lo.
   10. and with the **m**. confession
  15. 6. with one mind and one **m**.
¹Co. 6.11. our **m**. is open unto you
  13. 1. In the **m**. of two or three
Eph. 4.29. proceed out of your **m**., but
  6.19. I may open my **m**. boldly
Col. 3. 8. communica. out of your **m**.
²Th. 2. 8. con. with the spirit of his **m**.
²Ti. 4.17. delivered out of the **m**. of
Heb.11.33.stopped the **m**-s of lions
182

Jas. 3. 3. put bits in the horses' **m**-s
   10. out of the same **m**. proceed.
¹Pet. 2.22. was guile found in his **m**.
Jude 16. and their **m**. speaketh great
Rev. 1.16. and out of his **m**. went a sh.
  2.16. with the sword of my **m**.
  3.16. I will spue thee out of my **m**.
  9.17. and out of their **m**-s issued
  18. which issued out of their **m**-s
  19. their power is in their **m**.
  10. 9. it shall be in thy **m**. sweet
  10. it was in my **m**. sweet as ho.
  11. 5. proceedeth out of their **m**.
  12.15. cast out of his **m**.water as a
  16. and the earth opened her **m**.
     the dragon cast out of his **m**.
  13. 2. and his **m**. as the **m**. of a
   5. a **m**. speaking great things
   6. And he opened his **m**. in
  14. 5. And in their **m**. was found
  16.13. out of the **m**. of the dragon
     out of the **m**. of the beast
     out of the **m**. of the false pro.
Rev.19.15. out of his **m**. goeth a sharp
  21. sword pro. out of his **m**.
logos.
Act. 15.27. you the same things by **m**.
epistomizō.
Tit. 1.11. Whose **m**-s must *be stopped*

MOVE,   -ed.
kineō.
Mat.23. 4.will not **m**. them with one of
Act.17.28. in him we live, and **m**., and
  21.30. all the city was **m**-ed, and
Rev. 6.14. moun. and island *were* **m**-*ed*
splangchnizomai.
Mat. 9.36. he *was* **m**-*ed with* compassion
  14.14. *was* **m**-*ed with comp*.;Mar.6.34
  18.27. *was* **m**-*ed with compassion*
Mar. 1.41. Jesus, **m**-*ed with compassion*
seiō.
Mat.21.10. all the city *was* **m**-*ed*, saying
anaseiō.
Mar.15.11. chief priests **m**-*ed* the peo.
saleuō.
Act. 2.25. that I *should* not *be* **m**-*ed*
poieō logos oudeis.
Act.20.24. *none of these things* **m**. me
  (*I make account of none of these th.*)
metakineō.
Col. 1.23. be not **m**-*ed away* from the
sainō.
¹Th. 3. 3. no man *should* be **m**-*ed* by
eulabeomai.
Heb.11. 7. **m**-*ed with fear*, prepared an
asaleutos.
Heb.12.28. kingd. *which cannot be* **m**-*ed*
pherō.
²Pet. 1.21. *as they were* **m**-*ed* by the
  (See *Envy, Indignation*.)

MOVER.
kineō.
Act.24. 5. and a **m**. *of* sedition among

MOVING, [*noun*.]
kinēsis.
Jo. 5. 3. waiting for the **m**. of the wa.

MUCH.
polus.
Mat. 6.30. shall he not **m**. more clothe
  13. 5. had not **m**. earth; Mar. 4.5
  26. 9. might have been sold for **m**.
Mar. 1.45. and began to publish it **m**.
  5.10. And he besought him **m**. th.
  21. **m**. people gathered unto hi.
  24. and **m**. people followed him
  6.34. saw **m**. people, and was
Lu. 7.11. went with him, and **m**. peo.
  47. are forgiv.; for she loved **m**.

Lu. 8. 4. **m**. people were gathered to.
  9.37. the hill **m**. people met him
  10.40. cumbered about **m**. serving
  12.19. thou hast **m**. goods laid up
  48. unto whomsoever **m**. is given
     of him shall be **m**. required
     whom men have commit. **m**.
  16.10. least, is faithful also in **m**.
     least, is unjust also in **m**.
  18.39. but he cried *so* **m**. the more
Jo. 3.23. because there was **m**. water
     (*many* waters.)
  6.10. Now there was **m**. grass in
  7.12. there was **m**. murmuring am.
  12. 9. **m**. people of the Jews there.
  12. **m**. people that were come to
  24. die, it bringeth forth **m**. fru.
  14.30. I will not talk **m**. with you
  15. 5. the same bringeth forth **m**.
  8. glorified, that ye bear **m**. fr.
Act.10. 2. which gave **m**. alms to the
  14.22. we must through **m**. tribula.
  15. 7. when there had been **m**. dis.
  16.16. brought her masters **m**. gain
  18.10. I have **m**. people in this city
  27. helped them **m**. which had
  20. 2. had given them **m**. exhortat.
  26.24. **m**. learning doth make thee
  27.10. will be with hurt and **m**. da.
Ro. 3. 2. **m**. every way: chiefly because
  5. 9. **m**. more then, being now jus.
  10. **m**. more, being reconciled
  15. **m**. more the grace of God
  17. **m**. more they which receive
  9.22. endured with **m**. longsuffer.
  15.22. I have been **m**. hindered
  16. 6. who bestowed **m**. labour on
  12. which laboured **m**. in the L.
¹Co. 2. 3. and in fear, and in **m**. trem.
  12.22. Nay, **m**. more those membe.
  16.19. salute you **m**. in the Lord
²Co. 2. 4. For out of **m**. affliction and
  3. 9. **m**. more doth the ministrat.
  11. **m**. more that which remain.
  6. 4. in **m**. patience, in afflictions
  8. 4. Praying us with **m**. intreaty
  15. He that had gathered **m**.
  22. but now **m**. more diligent
Phi. 2.12. but now **m**. more in my ab.
¹Th. 1. 5. in the Holy Ghost, and in **m**.
  6. received the word in **m**. affl.
  2. 2. gospel of God with **m**. conte.
¹Ti. 3. 8. given to **m**. wine; Tit. 2. 3
²Ti. 4.14. the coppersmith did me **m**.
Phile. 8. I might be **m**. bold in Christ
Heb.12. 9. shall we not **m**. rather be in
  25. **m**. more shall not we escape
Jas. 5.16. of a righte. man availeth **m**.
¹Pet. 1. 7. being **m**. more precious than
Rev. 5. 4. And I wept **m**., because no
  8. **m**. incense, that he should
  19. 1. I heard a great voice of **m**.
tosoutos.
Mat.15.33.*so* **m**. bread in the wilderness
Act. 5. 8. ye sold the land for *so* **m**.
    And she said, Yea, for *so* **m**.
Heb. 1. 4. made *so* **m**. better than the
  7.22. By *so* **m**. was Jesus made a
  10.25. and *so* **m**. the more, as ye see
Rev.18. 7. *so* **m**. torment and sorrow
hikanos.
Lu. 7.12. a widow: and **m**. people of
Act. 5.37. drew away **m**. people after
  11.24. **m**. people was added unto
  26. church, and taught **m**. peop.
  19.26. and turned away **m**. people
  27. 9. Now when **m**. time was spent
oude.
Mar. 6.31. they had no leisure, *so* **m**. *as*
Lu. 6. 3. Have ye *not* read *so* **m**. *as* th.
  18.13. would not lift up *so* **m**. *as*
Act.19. 2. We have *not so* **m**. *as* heard

¹Co. 5. 1. as is *not so* **m.** *as* named
   hosos.
Jo. 6.11. of the fishes *as* **m.** *as* they
Act. 9.13. *how* **m.** evil he hath done
Heb.8. 6. by *how* **m.** also he is the me.
Rev.18. 7. *How* **m.** she hath glorified
   mallon.
Mat. 6.26. Are ye not **m.** better than
   mēde.
Mar. 2. 2. *not so* **m.** *as* about the door
   isos.
Lu. 6.34. to receive *as* **m.** again
   kan.
Heb.12.20.*And if so* **m.** *as* a beast
(See *Abound, Displeased, How, More
Perplexed, Speaking, Work.*)

MULTIPLY,   *-ed, -ing.*
   plēthunō.
Act. 6. 1. numb. of..discip. *was* **m**-ed
   7. the number of the dis, **m**-ed
   7.17. people grew and **m**-ed in Eg.
   9.31. of the Holy Ghost, *were* **m**-ed
   12.24. word of God grew and **m**-ed
²Co. 9.10. and **m.** your seed sown, and
Heb. 6.14. and **m**-*ing* I *will* **m.** thee
¹Pet. 1. 2. and peace, *be* **m**-ed; ²Pet.1.2
Jude   2. and peace, and love, *be* **m**-ed

MULTITUDE,   *-s.*
   ochlos.   [12.15, 19.2, 20.29
Mat. 4.25. followed him great **m**-*s*; 8.1
   5. 1. and seeing the **m**-*s*, he went
   8.18. when Jesus saw great **m**-*s*
   9. 8. But when the **m**-*s* saw it
   33. and the **m**-*s* marvelled, say.
   36. when he saw the **m**-*s*, he
   11. 7. began to say unto the **m**-*s*
   13. 2. And great **m**-*s* were gathered
      and the whole **m.** stood on
   34. spake Jesus unto the **m.** in
   36. Jes. sent the **m.** away; 15.39;
      Mar.4.36
   14. 5. he feared the **m.**, because
   14. and saw a great **m.**, and
   15. send the **m.** away ; Lu.9.12
   19. command. the **m.** to sit; 15.35
      and the disciples to the **m.**
   22, 23. while he sent the **m**-*s* aw.
¹5.10. he called the **m.**, and said
   30. and great **m**-*s* came ; Lu.5.15
   31. Insomuch that the **m.** wond.
   32. compas. on the **m.** ; Mar.8.2
   33. wild. as to fill so great a **m.**
   36. and the disciples to the **m.**
   17.14. were come to the **m.**, there
   20.31. And the **m.** rebuked them
   21. 8. and a very great **m.** spread
   9. and the **m**-*s* that went before
   11. and the **m.** said, This is Jes.
   46. they feared the **m.**, because
   22.33. And when the **m.** heard this
   23. 1. then spake Jesus to the **m.**
   26.47. with him a great **m.** with
   55. said Jesus to the **m**-*s*, Are ye
   27.20. persuaded the **m.** that they
   24. hands before the **m.**, saying
Mar. 2.13. and all the **m.** resorted unto
   3. 9. because of the **m.**, lest they
   20. And the **m.** cometh together
   32. And the **m.** sat about him
   4. 1. unto him a great **m.**, so that
      and the whole **m.** was by the
   5.31. Thou seest the **m.** thronging
   7.33. aside from the **m.**, and put
   8. 1. the **m.** being very great, and
   9.14. he saw a great **m.** about th.
   17. And one of the **m.** answered
   14.43. with him a great **m.** with
   15. 8. And the **m.** crying aloud
Lu. 3. 7. Then said he to the **m.** that
   5.19. because of the **m.**, they went
   6.19. And the whole **m.** sought

Lu. 8.45. the **m.** throng thee and press
   9.16. disciples to set before the **m.**
   14.25. there went great **m**-*s* with
   18.36. hearing the **m.** pass by, he
   19.39. from among the **m.**, said unto
   22. 6. in the absence of the **m.**
   47. yet spake, behold a **m.**, and
Jo. 5.13. away, a **m.** being in that pl.
   6. 2. And a great **m.** followed him
Act.13.45. when the Jews saw the **m** -*s*
   16.22. And the **m.** rose up together
   19.33. drew Alexander out of the **m.**
   21.34. some another, among the **m.**
   24.18. neither with **m.**, nor with tu.
Rev. 7. 9. and, lo, a great **m.**, which no
   17.15. peoples, and **m**-*s*, and nations
   19. 6. the voice of a great **m.**, and
Mar. 3. 7. and a great **m.** from Galilee
   8. a great **m.**, when they had
Lu. 1.10. And the whole **m.** of the peo.
   2.13. a **m.** of the heavenly host
   5. 6. a great **m.** of fishes : and
   6.17. and a great **m.** of people out
   8.37. Then the whole **m.** of the
 `19.37. the whole **m.** of the disciples
   23. 1. the whole **m.** of them arose
Jo. 5. 3. In these lay a great **m.** of
   21. 6. draw it for the **m.** of fishes
Act. 2. 6. the **m.** came together, and
   4.32. and the **m.** of them that bel.
   5.14. **m**-*s* both of men and women
   16. There came also a **m.** out
   6. 2. the twelve called the **m.** of
   5. pleased the whole **m.**: and
   14. 1. a great **m.** both of the Jews
   4. But the **m.** of the city was
   15.12. Then all the **m.** kept silence
   30. gathered the **m.**, together
   17. 4. devout Greeks a great **m.**
   19. 9. evil of that way bef. the **m.**
   21.22. the **m.** must needs come tog.
   36. the **m.** of the people followed
   23. 7. and the **m.** was divided
   25.24. all the **m.** of the Jews have
Heb.11.12.the stars of the sky in **m.**
Jas. 5.20. shall hide a **m.** of sins
¹Pet. 4. 8. shall cover the **m.** of sins
   murias.
Lu. 12. 1. an *innumerable* **m.** of people

MURDER,   *-s.*
   phonos.
Mat.15.19.proceed evil thoughts, **m**-*s*
Mar. 7.21. adulteries, fornications, **m**-*s*
   15. 7. committed **m.** in the insurr.
Lu. 23.19. in the city, and for **m.**, was
   25. him that for sedition and **m.**
Ro. 1.29. full of envy, **m.**, debate, dec.
Gal. 5.21. Envyings, **m**-*s*, drunkenness
Rev. 9.21. repented they of their **m**-*s*
   phoneuō.
Mat.19.18. Thou *shalt do* no **m.**

MURDERER,   *-s.*
   phoneus.
Mat.22. 7. and destroyed those **m**-*s*, and
Act. 3.14. desired a **m.** to be granted
   7.52. now the betrayers and **m**-*s*
   28. 4. No doubt this man is a **m.**
¹Pet. 4.15. none of you suffer as a **m.**
Rev. 2. 8. and **m**-*s* and whoremongers
   22.15. and **m**-*s* and idolaters, and
   anthrōpoktonos.
Jo. 8.44. He was a **m.** from the beg.
¹Jo. 3.15. a **m.**: and ye know that no **m.**
   sikarios.
Act.21.38. thousand men that were **m**-*s*
   patraloēs.
¹Ti. 1. 9. for **m**-*s of fathers* and mur.
   mētraloēs.
¹Ti. 1. 9. and **m**-*s of mothers*, for

MURMUR,   *-ed.*
   gongguzō.
Mat.20.11.they **m**-ed against the good.
Lu. 5.30. scribes and Pharisees **m**-ed
Jo. 6.41. The Jews then **m**-ed at him
   43. **m.** not among yourselves
   61. that his disciples **m**-ed at it
   7.32. heard that the people **m**-ed
¹Co. 10.10. Neither **m.** ye, as some of
   them also **m**-ed, and were
   diagongguzō.
Lu. 15. 2. Pharisees and scribes **m**-ed
   19. 7. they saw it, they all **m**-ed
   embrimaomai.
Mar.14. 5. And they **m**-ed *against* her

MURMURERS.
   gonggustēs.
Jude 16. These are **m.**, complainers

MURMURING, [*noun,*]   -s
   gonggusmos.
Jo. 7.12. there was much **m.** among
Act. 6. 1. there arose a **m.** of the
Phi. 2.14. Do all things without **m**-*s*

MUSED.
   dialogizomai.
Lu. 3.15. *as*..all men **m.** in their hea.

MUSICIANS.
   mousikos.
Rev.18.22. harpers, and **m.**, and of pip.

MUSIC.
   sumphōnia.
Lu. 15.25. he heard **m.** and dancing

MUST.
   dei.
Mat.16.21. how that he **m.** go unto Jer.
   17.10. Elias **m.** first come; Mar.9.11
   24. 6. all these things **m.** come to
   26.54. be fulfilled, that thus it **m.**
Mar. 8.31. the Son of man **m.** suffer
   13. 7. for such things **m.** *needs* be
   10. the gospel **m.** first be publis.
Lu. 2.49. I **m.** be about my Father's
   4.43. I **m.** preach the kingdom of
   9.22. The Son of man **m.** suffer
   13.33. Nevertheless I **m.** walk to
   17.25. first **m.** he suffer many thi.
   19. 5. to day I **m.** abide at thy ho.
   21. 9. these things **m.** first come to
   22. 7. when the passover **m.** be
   37. that is written **m.** yet be ac.
   24. 7. The Son of man **m.** be deliv.
   44. that all things **m.** be fulfilled
Jo. 3. 7. thee, Ye **m.** be born again
   14. so **m.** the Son of man be lift.
   30. He **m.** increase, but I must
   4. 4. he **m.** *needs* go through Sam.
   24. **m.** worship him in spirit and
   9. 4. I **m.** work the works of him
   10.16. them also I **m.** bring, and
   12.34. The Son of man **m.** be lifted
   20. 9. that he **m.** rise again from
Act. 1.16. scripture **m.** *needs* have been
   22. **m.** one be ordained to be a
   3.21. Whom the heaven **m.** receive
   4.12. among men, whereby we **m.**
   9. 6. be told thee what thou **m.**
   16. he **m.** suffer for my name's
   14.22. we **m.** through much tribula.
   16.30. Sirs, what **m.** I do to be saved
   17. 3. that Christ **m.** *needs* have
   18.21. I **m.** by all means keep this
   19.21. there, I **m.** also see Rome
   23.11. so **m.** thou bear witness also
   27.24. thou **m.** be brought before
   26. we **m.** be cast upon a certain
¹Co.11.19. For there **m.** be also heresies
   15.25. For he **m.** reign, till he hath
   53. this corruptible **m.** put on
                   183

²Co. 5.10. we **m.** all appear before the
11.30. If I **m.** *needs* glory [Tit.1.7
¹Ti. 3. 2. A bishop then **m.** be blame.;
　　7. he **m.** have a good report
²Ti. 2. 6. that laboureth **m.** be first
　　24. the servant of the Lord **m.**
Tit. 1.11. Whose mouths **m.** be stop.
Heb. 9.26. then **m.** he often have suff.
　　11. 6. he that cometh to God **m.**
Rev. 1. 1. things which **m.** shortly co.
　　4. 1. things which **m.** be hereafter
　　10.11. said unto me, Thou **m.** pro.
　　11. 5. he **m.** in this manner be
　　13.10. **m.** be killed with the sword
　　17.10. he **m.** continue a short space
　　20. 3. after that he **m.** be loosed a
　　22. 6. the things which **m.** shortly
　　　　　blēteos.　　　　　[Lu.5.38
Mar. 2.22. new wine **m.** *be put* into new
　　　　　dei pantōs.
Act.21.22. the multitude **m.** *needs* come
　　　　　opheilō.　　(*by all means must.*)
¹Co. 5.10. then **m.** ye *needs* go out of
　　　　　anangke eimi.
Mat.18. 7. it **m.** *needs* be that offences
　　　　　echō anangke.
Lu. 14.18. I **m.** *needs* go and see it

MUSTARD-SEED.
　　　　　sinapi.
Mat.13.31.is like to a grain of **m.** ; Mar.
　　　　4.31 ; Lu. 13.19
　　17.20. fa. as a grain of **m.**; Lu.17. 6

MUTUAL.
　　　　　allēlōn.
Ro. 1.12. by the **m.** faith both of you

MUZZLE.
　　　　　phimoō.　　　　　　[¹Ti.5.18
¹Co. 9. 9. Thou *shalt* not **m.** the mou.

MY.
　　　　　egō, [*gen.*]
Mat.18.20.gathered together in **m.** name
Mar. 8.38. ashamed of me and **m.** words
Jo. 4.34. **m.** meat is to do the will of
　　7. 6. **m.** time is not yet come
　　　　(*And all other passages in which it*
　　　　　occurs.)

MYRRH.
　　　　　smurna.
Mat. 2.11. gold, and frankince., and **m.**
Jo. 19.39. a mixture of **m.** and aloes
　　　　　smurnizomai.
Mar.15.23.wine *mingled with* **m.**; but

MYSELF.
　　　　　emautou.
Lu. 7. 7. neither thought I **m.** worthy
Jo. 5.31. If I bear witness of **m.**, my
　　7.17. or whether I speak of **m.**
　　28. I am not come of **m.**, but he
　　(*And all others except the following.*)
　　　　　egō.
Phile. 17. partner, receive him as **m.**

MYSTERY,　　　　　　*-ies.*
　　　　　mustērion.
Mat.13.11.to know the **m-**s of ; Lu.8.10
Mar. 4.11. the **m.** of the kingdom of G.
Ro. 11.25. should be ignorant of this **m.**
　　16.25. of the **m.** which was kept se.
¹Co. 2. 7. the wisdom of God in a **m.**
　　4. 1. stewards of the **m-**s of God
　　13. 2. and understand all **m-**s, and
　　14. 2. in the spirit he speaketh **m-**s
　　15.51. Behold, I shew you a **m.**; We
Eph. 1. 9. unto us the **m.** of his will
　　3. 3. made known unto me the **m.**
　　4. knowledge in the **m.** of Chri.
　　9. the fellowship of the **m.**
　　5.32. This is a great **m.**: but I sp.
　　6.19. to make known the **m.** of the
184

Col. 1.26. the **m.** which hath been hid
　　27. this **m.** among the Gentiles
　　2. 2. **m.** of God, and of the Father
　　4. 3. to speak the **m.** of Christ
²Th. 2. 7. For the **m.** of iniquity doth
¹Ti. 3. 9. Holding the **m.** of the faith
　　16. great is the **m.** of godliness
Rev. 1.20. The **m.** of the seven stars
　　10. 7. the **m.** of God should be fin.
　　17. 5. **m.**, BABYLON THE GRE.
　　7. the **m.** of the woman, and of

NAILS.
　　　　　hēlos.
Jo. 20.25. his hands the print of the **n.**
　　　　　finger into the print of the **n.**

NAILING.
　　　　　prosēloō.
Col. 2.14. of the way, **n.** it *to* his cross

NAKED.
　　　　　gumnos.
Mat.25.36,43.**n.**, and ye clothed me
　　38. took thee in? or **n.**, and clo.
　　44. a stranger, or **n.**, or sick, or
Mar.14.51.linen cloth cast about his **n.**
　　52. cloth, and fled from them **n.**
Jo. 21. 7. for he was **n.**, and did cast
Act.19.16. out of that house, **n.** and wo.
²Co. 5. 3. we shall not be found **n.**
Heb. 4.13. all things are **n.** and opened
Jas. 2.15. If a brother or sister be **n.**
Rev. 3.17. and poor, and blind, and **n.**
　　16.15. lest he walk **n.**, and they see
　　17.16. shall make her desol. and **n.**
　　　　　gumnēteuomai.
¹Co. 4.11. hung., and thirst, and *are* **n.**

NAKEDNESS.
　　　　　gumnotēs.
Ro. 8.35. famine, or **n.**, or peril, or
²Co. 11.27. fastings often. in cold and **n.**
Rev. 3.18. the shame of thy **n.** do not

NAME, [*noun,*]　　　　　*-s.*
　　　　　onoma.　　　　　　[Lu.1.31
Mat. 1.21. thou shalt call his **n.** JESUS;
　　23. they shall call his **n.** Emma.
　　25. called his **n.** JESUS; Lu.2.21
　　6. 9. Hallowed be thy **n.** ; Lu.11.2
　　7.22. pro. in thy **n.** ? and in thy **n.**
　　　　　devils, and in thy **n.** done
　　10. 2. Now the **n-**s of the twelve
　　22. for my **n.**'s sake; 19.29,24.9;
　　　　　Mar. 13.13; Lu. 21.12,17;
　　　　　Jo. 15.21 ; Act. 9.16
　　41. in the **n.** of a prophet shall
　　　　　in the **n.** of a righteous man
　　42. in the **n.** of a disciple, verily
　　12.21. And in his **n.** shall the Gent.
　　18. 5. one such little child in my **n.**
　　20. are gathered toge. in my **n.**
　　21. 9. that cometh in the **n.** of the ;
　　　　　23.39; Mar. 11.9,10; Lu.
　　　　　13.35,19,38; Jo. 12.13
　　24. 5. many shall come in my **n.** ;
　　　　　Mar. 13.6; Lu. 21.8
　　27.32. a man of Cyre., Simon by **n.**
　　28.19. in the **n.** of the Father, and
Mar. 5. 9. What is thy **n.**? and ; Lu.8.30
　　　　　saying, My **n.** is Legion: for
　　22. the synagogue, Jairus by **n.**
　　6.14. for his **n.** was spread abroad
　　9.37. one of such children in my **n.**
　　38. out devils in my **n.** ; Lu.9.49
　　39. shall do a miracle in my **n.**
　　41. of water to drink in my **n.**
　　16.17. In my **n.** shall they cast out
Lu. 1. 5. and her **n.** was Elizabeth
　　13. thou shalt call his **n.** John
　　27. to a man whose **n.** was Jose.
　　　　　the virgin's **n.** was Mary
　　49. things ; and holy is his **n.**

Lu. 1.59. after the **n.** of his father
　　61. that is called by this **n.**
　　63. wrote, saying, His **n.** is John
　　2.25. whose **n.** was Simeon
　　6.22. and cast out your **n.** as evil
　　9.48. this child in my **n.** receiveth
　　10.17. subj. unto us through thy **n.**
　　20. because your **n-**s are written
　　24.18. whose **n.** was Cleopas, answ.
　　47. should be preached in his **n.**
Jo. 1. 6. from God, whose **n.** was John
　　12. to them that belie. on his **n.**
　　2.23. many believed in his **n.**
　　3.18. hath not believed in the **n.** of
　　5.43. I am come in my Father's **n.**
　　　　　ano. shall come in his own **n.**
　　10. 3. calleth his own sheep by **n.**
　　25. that I do in my Father's **n.**
　　12.28. Father, glorify thy **n.** Then
　　14.13. whats. ye shall ask in my **n.**;
　　　　　15.16,16.23,26
　　14. shall ask any thing in my **n.**
　　26. the Father will send in my **n.**
　　16.24. have ye asked noth. in my **n.**
　　17. 6. I have manifested thy **n.** un.
　　11. keep through thine own **n.**
　　12. I kept them in thy **n.**
　　26. I have dec. unto them thy **n.**
　　18.10. The servant's **n.** was Malchus
　　20.31. might have life through his **n.**
Act. 1.15. the number of the **n-**s toget.
　　2.21. shall call on the **n.** of the L.
　　38. the **n.** of Jes. Chr. ; 3.6,16,18
　　3.16. And his **n.** through faith in
　　　　　his **n.** hath made this man
　　4. 7. or by what **n.**, have ye done
　　10. that by the **n.** of Jesus Chri.
　　12. there is none other **n.** under
　　17. hence. to no man in this **n.**
　　18. nor teach in the **n.** of Jesus
　　30. by the **n.** of thy holy child
　　5.28. ye shou. not teach in this **n**
　　40. should not speak in the **n.** of
　　41. to suffer shame for thy **n.**,
　　8.12. and the **n.** of Jesus Christ
　　16. baptized in the **n.** of the L. ;
　　　　　10.48, 19.5
　　9.14. to bind all that call on thy **n.**
　　15. to bear my **n.** before the Ge.
　　21. which called on this **n.** in J.
　　27. at Damascus in the **n.** of Je.
　　29. spake boldly in the **n.** of the
　　10.43. that through his **n.** whosoe.
　　13. 6. a Jew, whose **n.** was Bar-jes.
　　8. for so is his **n.** by interpreta.
　　15.14. out of them a peo. for his **n.**
　　17. upon whom my **n.** is called
　　26. for the **n.** of our Lord Jesus
　　18.15. a question of words and **n-**s
　　19.13. which had evil spirits the **n.**
　　17. and the **n.** of the Lord Jesus
　　21.13. for the **n.** of the Lord Jesus
　　22.16. calling on the **n.** of the Lord
　　26. 9. contrary to the **n.** of Jesus of
　　28. 7. whose **n.** was Publius; who
Ro. 1. 5. among all nations, for his **n.**
　　2.24. For the **n.** of God is blasph.
　　9.17. that my **n.** might be declared
　　10.13. call upon the **n.** of; ¹Co. 1.2
　　15. 9. Genti., and sing unto thy **n.**
¹Co. 1.10. the **n.** of our Lord Jesus ; 5.4
　　　　　6.11; Eph.5.20; ²Th.1.12,3.6
　　13. were ye baptized in the **n.** of
　　15. I had baptized in mine own **n.**
Eph. 1.21. and every **n.** that is named
Phi. 2. 9. a **n.** which is above every **n.**
　　10. That at the **n.** of Jesus every
　　4. 3. whose **n-**s are in the book of
Col. 3.17. do all in the **n.** of the Lord
¹Ti. 6. 1. that the **n.** of God and his
²Ti. 2.19. that nameth the **n.** of Christ
Heb. 1. 4. a more excellent **n.** than they

Heb. 2.12. I will declare thy **n.** unto
  6.10. ye have shewed towa. his **n.**
 13.15. giving thanks to his **n.**
Jas. 2. 7. that worthy **n.** by the which
  5.10. who have spoken in the **n.** of
  14. with oil in the **n.** of the Lord
1Pet. 4.14. If ye be reproached for the **n.**
1Jo. 2.12. forgiven you for his **n.**'s sake
  3.23. we should believe on the **n.**
  5.13. believe on the **n.** of the Son
  may believe on the **n.** of the
2John 7. for his **n.**'s sake they went
  14. Greet the friends by **n.**
Rev. 2. 3. for my **n.**'s sake hast labour.
  13. thou holdest fast my **n.**
  17. and in the stone a new **n.**
 3. 1. thou hast a **n.** that thou liv.
  4. Thou hast a few **n**-s even in
  5. I will not blot out his **n.**
  but I will confess his **n.** bef.
  8. and hast not denied my **n.**
  12. the **n.** of my God, and the **n.**
  write upon him my new **n.**
 6. 8. his **n.** that sat upon him was
 8.11. the **n.** of the star is called
 9.11. whose **n.** in the Hebrew ton.
  hath his **n.** Apollyon
 11.18. and them that fear thy **n.**
 13. 1. upon his heads, the **n.** of bl.
  6. to blaspheme his **n.**, and his
  8. whose **n**-s are not written in
  17. had the mark, or the **n.** of
  or the number of his **n.**
 14. 1. having his Father's **n.** writt.
  11. receiveth the mark of his **n.**
 15. 2. and over the numb. of his **n.**
  4. O Lord, and glorify thy **n.**
 16. 9. and blasphemed the **n.** of G.
 17. 3. full of **n**-s of blasphemy
  5. upon her forehead was a **n.**
  8. whose **n**-s were not written
 19.12. he had a **n.** written, that no
  13. his **n.** is called The Word of
  16. and on his thigh a **n.** written
 21.12. and **n**-s written thereon
  14. in them the **n**-s of the twelve
 22. 4. his **n.** shall be in their foreh.
  kaleō.
Act. 7.58. man's feet, whose **n.** was Sa.

NAME, [*verb*,]   *-ed, -eth.*
  onoma.
Mat.27.57.man of Arimathæa, **n**-ed Jos.
Mar.14.32.which was **n**-ed Gethsemane
Lu. 1. 5. a certain priest **n**-ed Zachari.
  26. a city of Galilee, **n**-ed Nazar.
 5.27. saw a publican, **n**-ed Levi
 8.41. there came a man **n**-ed Jair.
 10.38. woman **n**-ed Martha received
 16.20. a certain beggar **n**-ed Lazarus
 23.50. a man **n**-ed Joseph, a couns.
Jo. 3. 1. **n**-ed Nicodemus, a ruler of
Act. 5. 1. a certain man **n**-ed Ananias
  34. a Pharisee, **n**-ed Gamaliel, a
 9.10. at Damascus, **n**-ed Ananias
  12. a man **n**-ed Ananias coming
  33. a certain man **n**-ed Æneas
  36. a certain disci. **n**-ed Tabitha
 11.28. one of them **n**-ed Agabus
 12.13. came to hearken, **n.** ed Rhoda
 16. 1. disciple was there, **n**-ed Tim.
  14. **n**-ed Lydia, a seller of purple
 17.34. and a woman **n**-ed Damaris
 18. 2. **n**-ed Aquila, born in Pontus
  7. **n**-ed Justus, one that worsh.
  24. **n**-ed Apollos, born at Alexa.
 19.24. **n**-ed Demetrius, a silversmith
 20. 9. **n**-ed Eutychus, being fallen
 21.10. a certain prophet, **n**-ed Aga.
 27. 1. one **n**-ed Julius, a centurion
  onomazō.
Lu. 6.13. whom also he **n**-ed apostles

Lu. 6.14. Simon, whom he also **n**-ed
Ro. 15.20. not where Christ was **n**-ed
1Co. 5. 1. as is not so much as **n**-ed
Eph. 1.21. and every name that is **n**-ed
  3.15. in heaven and earth is **n**-ed
 5. 3. let it not be once **n**-ed among
2Ti. 2.19. Let every one that **n**-eth the
  kaleō.
Lu. 2.21. which was so **n**-ed of the an.
 19. 2. there was a man **n**-ed Zacch.
  legō.
Mar.15. 7. there was one **n**-ed Barabbas

NAPKIN.
  soudarion.
Lu. 19.20. have kept laid up in a **n.**
Jo. 11.44. was bound about with a **n.**
 20. 7. the **n.**, that was about his

NARROW.
  thlibō.
Mat. 7.14. gate, and **n.** is the way

NATION,   -s.
  ethnos.
Mat.21.43. given to a **n.** bringing forth
 24. 7. **n.** shall rise against **n.** ; Mar.
  13.8 ; Lu. 21.10
  9. ye shall be hated of all **n**-s
  14. for a witness unto all **n**-s
 25.32. him shall be gathered all **n**-s
 28.19. Go ye. .and teach all **n**-s
Mar.11.17.called of all **n**-s the house of
 13.10. first be publis. among all **n**-s
Lu. 7. 5. For he loveth our **n.**, and he
 12.30. do the **n**-s of the world seek
 21.24. led away captive into all **n**-s
  25. upon the earth distress of **n**-s
 23. 2. this fellow perverting the **n.**
 24.47. in his name among all **n**-s
Jo. 11.48. away both our place and **n.**
  50. that the whole **n.** perish not
  51. Jesus should die for that **n.**
  52. not for that **n.** only, but that
 18.35. Thine own **n.** and the chief
Act. 2. 5. out of every **n.** under heaven
 7. 7. the **n.** to whom they shall be
 10.22. among all the **n.** of the Jews
  35. in every **n.** he that feareth
 13.19. he had destroyed seven **n**-s
 14.16. all **n**-s to walk in their own
 17.26. made of one blood all **n**-s of
 24. 2. deeds are done unto this **n.**
  10. years a judge unto this **n.**
  17. came to bring alms to my **n.**
 26. 4. among mine own **n.** at Jeru.
 28.19. had ought to accuse my **n.** of
Ro. 1. 5. to the faith among all **n**-s
 4.17. made thee father of many **n**-s
  18. beco. the father of many **n**-s
 10.19. and by a foolish **n.** I will
 16.26. made known to all **n**-s for
Gal. 3. 8. In thee shall all **n**-s be bless.
1Pet. 2. 9. a royal priesthood, an holy **n.**
Rev. 2.26. I give power over the **n**-s
 5. 9. and tong., and peop., and **n.**
 7. 9. man could number, of all **n**-s
 10.11. many peoples, and **n**-s, and
 11. 9. kind. and tong. and **n**-s ; 13.7
  18. the **n**-s were angry, and thy
 12. 5. was to rule all **n**-s with a rod
 14. 6. to every **n.**, and kindred, and
  8. she made all **n**-s drink of the
 15. 4. all **n**-s shall come and wors.
 16.19. the cities of the **n**-s fell
 17.15. peo. and multitudes, and **n**-s
 18. 3. For all **n**-s have drunk of the
  23. by thy sorceries were all **n**-s
 19.15. it he should smite the **n**-s
 20. 3. should deceive the **n**-s no m.
  8. shall go out to deceive the **n**-s
 21.24. the **n**-s of them which are
  26. glory and honour of the **n**-s

Rev.22. 2. were for healing of the **n**-s
  genos.
Mar. 7.26. Greek, a Syrophenician by **n.**
Gal. 1.14. my equals in mine own **n.**
  genea.
Phi. 2.15. of a crooked and perverse **n.**
  allophulos.
Act. 10.28. come unto one of another **n.**

NATURAL, (See *Affection.*)
  phusikos.
Ro. 1.26. women did change the **n.** use
  27. leaving the **n.** use of the wo.
2Pet. 2.12. But these as **n.** brute beasts
  kata [*accu.*] **phusis.**
Ro. 11.21. if God spared not the **n.** bra.
  24. these which be the **n.** bran.
  psuchikos.
1Co. 2.14. But the **n.** man receiveth
 15.44. It is sown a **n.** body ; it is
  There is a **n.** body, and there
  46. but that which is **n.**; and
  genesis, [*gen.*]
Jas. 1.23. a man beholding his **n.** face

NATURALLY.
  gnēsiōs.
Phi. 2.20. who will **n.** care for your
  phusikōs.
Jude 10. but what they know **n.**, as

NATURE.
  phusis.
Ro. 1.26. into that which is against **n.**
 2.14. do by **n.** the things contained
  27. uncircumcision which is by **n.**
 11.24. olive tree which is wild by **n.**
  wert graffed contrary to **n.**
1Co. 11.14. Doth not even **n.** itself teach
Gal. 2.15. We who are Jews by **n.**
 4. 8. which by **n.** are no gods
Eph. 2. 3. and were by **n.** the children
2Pet. 1. 4. be partakers of the divine **n**
  genesis.
Jas. 3. 6. on fire the course of **n.**

NAUGHTINESS.
  kakia.
Jas. 1.21. filthi. and superfluity of **n.**

NAY.
  ou.
Mat. 5.37. comm. be, Yea, yea ; **n.**, **n.**
 13.29. But he said, **n.**; lest while
Jo. 7.12. **n.**; but he deceiveth the peo.
Act. 16.37. **n.** verily; but let them come
2Co. 1.17. should be yea yea, and **n.** **n.**
 18, 19. was not yea and **n.**
Jas. 5.12. yea be yea, and your **n.**, **n.**
  ouchi.
Lu. 12.51. I tell you, **n.**; but rather div.
 13. 3, 5. **n.**: but, except ye repent
 16.30. And he said, **n.**, father Abr.
Ro. 3.27. **n.**: but by the law of faith
  alla.
Ro. 7. 7. **n.**, I had not known sin, but
 8.37. **n.**, in all these things we are
1Co. 6. 8. **n.**, ye do wrong, and defraud
 12.22. **n.**, much more those mem
  menounge.
Ro. 9.20. **n.** but, O man, who art thou

NEAR, (See *Draw.*)
  enggus.
Mat.24.33. know that it is **n.**, even at
Mar.13.28. ye know that summer is **n.**
Jo. 3.23. baptizing in Ænon **n.** to
 11.54. unto a country **n.** to the
  enggizō.
Lu. 18.40. when he was come **n.**; 19.41
Act. 9. 3. as he journeyed, he came **n.**
 21.33. chief captain came **n.**, and
 23.15. we, or ever he come **n.**, are
  anangkaios.
Act.10.24. his kinsmen and **n.** friends

plēsion.

Jo. 4. 5. n. to the parce of ground

NEARER.
engguteron.

Ro. 13.11. for now is our salvation n.

NECESSARY.
anangkaios.

Act.13.46. It was n. that the word of
1Co.12.22. to be more feeble, are n.
2Co. 9. 5. I thought it n. to exhort
Phi. 2.25. Yet I supposed it n. to send
Tit. 3.14. good works for n. uses
epanangkēs.

Act.15.28. burden than these n. things
anangkē.

Heb. 9.23. therefore n. that the patterns
pros [accu.] chreia.

Act. 28.10. with such things as were n.

NECESSITY, -ies.
anangkē.

Lu. 23.17. For of n. he must release
1Co. 7.37. in his heart, having no n.
 9.16. for n. is laid upon me ; yea
2Co. 6. 4. patience, in afflictions, in n-s
 9. 7. not grudgingly, or of n.: for
 12.10. in n-s, in persecutions
Phile. 14. not be as it were of n., but
Heb. 7.12. there is made of n. a change
 9.16. there must also of n. be the
anangkaios.

Heb. 8. 3. it is of n. that this man
echō anangkē.

Lu. 23. 17. For of n. he must release
chreia.

Act.20.34. have ministered unto my n-s
Ro. 12.13. Distributing to the n. of sai.
Phi. 4.16. once and again unto my n.

NECK, -s.
trachēlos.

Mat.18. 6. were hanged about his n. ;
 Mar.9.42 ; Lu.17.2
Lu. 15.20. fell on his n., and kissed
Act.15.10. a yoke upon the n. of the
 20.37. and fell on Paul's n., and
Ro. 16. 4. life laid down their own n-s

NEED, [noun.]
chreia.

Mat. 3.14. I have n. to be baptized of
 6. 8. what things ye have n. of
 21. 3. The Lord hath n. of them ;
  Mar.11.3 ; Lu.19.31,34.
 27.65. what further n. have we of
Mar. 2.17. that are whole have no n. of
 25. when he had n. and was an
Lu. 9.11. healed them that had n. of
Jo. 13.29. that we have n. of against
Act. 2.45. men, as every man had n.
 4.35. man according as he had n.
1Co. 12.21. I have no n. of thee : nor
 the feet I have no n. of you
 24. our comely parts have no n.
Phi. 4.19. God shall supply all your n.
1Th. 5. 1. ye have no n. that I write
Heb. 5.12. ye have n. that one teach
 become such as have n. of
 7.11. what further n. was there
 10.36. For ye have n. of patience
1Jo. 3.17. seeth his brother have n.
Rev. 3.17. goods, and have n. of noth.
 21.23. the city had no n. of the sun
chrēzō. [Lu.12.30
Mat. 6.32. that ye have n. of all these ;
Ro. 16. 2. whatso. business she hath n.
opheilō.

1Co. 7.36. and n. so require, let him
hustereō. (it needs so to be.)
Phi. 4.12. to abound and to suffer n.

186

eukairos.

Heb. 4.16. grace to help in time of n.
dei. (for seasonable help.)
1Pet. 1. 6. now for a season, if n. be

NEED, [verb,] -ed, -est, -eth.
echō chreia. [Lu.5.31
Mat. 9.12. They that be whole n. not a
 14.16. They n. not depart ; give ye
Mar.14.63. What n. we any ; Lu.22.71
Lu. 15. 7. just persons, which n. no
Jo. 2.25. n-ed not that any should
 13.10. n-eth not save to wash his
 16.30. n-est not that any man sho.
Eph. 4.28. have to give to him that n-eth
1Th. 1. 8. we n. not to speak anything
 4. 9. ye n. not that I write unto
1Jo. 2.27. ye n. not that any man tea.
Rev.22. 5. they n. no candle, neither
chrēzō.

Lu. 11. 8. give him as many as he n-eth
2Co. 3. 1. or n. we, as some others
prosdeomai.

Act.17.25. as though he n-ed anything
echō anangkē.

Heb. 7.27. who n-eth not daily, as those
 (See Ashamed.)

NEEDFUL.
chreia.

Lu. 10.42. But one thing is n., and M.
dei.

Act.15. 5. That it was n. to circumcise
anangkaios.

Phi. 1.24. in the flesh is more n. for
epitēdeios.

Jas. 2.16. things which are n. to the
echō anangkē.

Jude 3. it was n. for me to write un.

NEEDLE.
raphis.

Mat.19.24. to go through the eye of a n.
 Mar.10.25 ; Lu.18.25

NEEDS, (See Must.)

NEGLECT, (See Hear,) -ed.
ameleō.

1Ti. 4.14. n. not the gift that is in
Heb. 2. 3. if we n. so great salvation
paratheōreō.

Act. 6. 1. their widows were n-ed in

NEGLECTING, [noun.]
apheidia.

Col. 2.23. humanity, and n. of the

NEGLIGENT.
ameleō.

2Pet. 1.12. I will not be n. to put you

NEIGHBOUR, -s.
ho plēsion.

Mat. 5.43. shalt love thy n., and hate
 19.19. shalt love thy n. as thyself ;
 22.39; Mar.12.31; Lu.10.27;
 Ro.13.9; Gal.5.14; Jas.2.8.
Mar.12.33. to love his n. as himself
Lu. 10.29. unto Jes., And who is my n.
 36. was n. unto him that fell
Act. 7.27. But he that did his n. wrong
Ro. 13.10. Love worketh no ill to his n.
 15. 2. please his n. for his good in
Eph. 4.25. every man truth with his n.
Heb. 8.11. not teach every man his n.
geitōn.

Lu. 14.12. kinsmen, nor thy rich n-s
 15. 6, 9. toget. his friends and n-s
Jo. 9. 8. The n-s therefore, and they
perioikos.

Lu. 1.58. And her n-s and her cousins

NEITHER
Generally represents ou, oude, oute,
mē, mēde, mēte. The following are
exceptions :—
oudeis.

Mar. 5. 4. n. could any man tame him
 16. 8. n. said they anything to
Jas. 1.13. n. tempteth he any man
oudepō.

Lu. 15.29. n. transgressed I at any time
ē.

Act.24.12. n. raising up the people
Jas. 1.17. variable., n. shadow of turn.
ou mē.

Mar.13.19. unto this time, n. shall be
Lu. 1.15. drink n. wine nor strong

NEPHEWS.
ekgona.

1Ti. 5. 4. widow have children or n.

NESTS.
kataskēnōsis. [Lu.9.58
Mat. 8.20. birds of the air have n.

NET, -s.
diktuon. [Mar.1.18
Mat. 4.20. they straight. left their n-s ;
 21. mending their n-s ; and he
Mar. 1.19. in the ship mending their n-s
Lu. 5. 2. and were washing their n-s
 4. let down your n-s for a dra.
 5. thy wo, I will let down the n.
 6. of fishes : and their n. brake
Jo. 21. 6. Cast the n. on the right side
 8. dragging the n. with fishes
 11. drew the n. to land full of
 yet was not the n. broken
amphiblēstron. [Mar.1.16
Mat. 4.18. casting a n. into the sea ;
sagēnē.

Mat.13.47. of heaven is like unto a n.

NEVER.
oudepote.

Mat. 7.23. I n. knew you : depart from
 9.33. It was n. so seen in Israel
 21.16. have ye n. read, Out of the
 42. Did ye n. read in the scrip.
 26.33. yet will I n. be offended
Mar. 2.12. We n. saw it on this fashion
 25. Have ye n. read what David
Lu. 15.29. and yet thou n. gavest me a
Jo. 7.46. n. man spake like this man
Act.10.14. I have n. eaten any thing
 14. 8. womb, who n. had walked
1Co.13. 8. Charity n. faileth : but whe.
Heb.10. 1. can n. with those sacrifices
 11. which can n. take away sins
oudepō.

Lu. 23.53. wherein n. man before was
Jo. 19.41. wherein was n. man yet laid
oudeis pōpote.

Lu. 19.30. whereon yet n. man sat
Jo. 8.33. were n. in bondage to any
ou mē pōpote.

Jo. 6.35. believ. on me shall n. thirst
ou mē pote.

2Pet. 1.10. these things ye shall n. fall
mēdepote.

2Ti. 3. 7. n. able to come to the know.
ou mē eis aiōn.

Jo. 4.14. shall give him shall n. thirst
 8.51, 52. my saying he shall n. see
 10.28. they shall n. perish, neither
 11.26. believeth in me shall n. die
 13. 8. Thou shalt n. wash my feet
ou.

Mar. 3.29. hath n. forgiveness, but is in
 14.21. if he had n. been born
Lu. 23.29. the wombs that n. bare, and
 the paps which n. gave suck

mē.

Jo. 7.15. man letters, having **n.** learn.
ou mē.

Jo. 6.35. to me shall **n.** hunger
Heb.13. 5. I will **n.** leave thee nor for**s.**
oude hen.

Mat.27.14. answered him *to* **n.** *a* word
           (*not even one* word.)
oudeis.

Mar.11. 2. colt tied, whereon **n.** man
NEVERTHELESS.
alla.

Mar.14.36.cup from me : **n.** not what I
Jo. 11.15. believe ; **n.** let us go unto
   16. 7. **n.** I tell you the truth
Ro. 5.14. **n.** death reigned from Adam
1Co. 9.12. **n.** we have not used this
2Co. 7. 6. God that comforteth th.
   12.16. **n.**, being crafty, I caught
Gal. 4.30. **n.** what saith the scripture
2Ti. 1.12. **n.** I am not ashamed
Rev. 2. 4. **n.** I have somewhat against
plēn.

Mat.26.39.**n.** not as I will ; Lu.22.42
    64. **n.** I say unto you, hereafter
Lu. 13.33. **n.** I must walk to day, and
   18. 8. **n.** when the Son of man com.
1Co. 11.11. **n.** neither is the man which.
Eph. 5.33. **n.** let every one of you in
Phi. 3.16. **n.** whereto we have already
homōs mentoi kai.

Jo. 12.42. **n.** among the chief rulers
kai-toige.

Act.14.17. **n.** he left not himself with.
toi.

2Ti. 2.19. **n.** the foundation of God
NEW.   (See *Moon, Wine.*)
kainos.

Mat. 9.17. they put new wine into **n.**
   13.52. treasure things **n.** and old
   26.28. blo. of the **n.** test.; Mar.14.24
   29. when I drink it **n.**;Mar.14.25
   27.60. in his own **n.** tomb which
Mar. 1.27. what **n.** doctrine is this
   2.21. else the **n.** piece that filled
   22. be put into **n.** bottles;Lu.5.38
   16.17. shall speak with **n.** tongues
Lu. 5.36. No man putt. a piece of a **n.**
   both the **n.** maketh a rent
   out of the **n.** agreeth not wi.
   22.20. the **n.** testament in my blo.
Jo. 13.34. A **n.** commandment I give
   19.41. in the garden a **n.** sepluchre
Act.17.19. what this **n.** doctrine, wh.
   21. or to her some **n.** thing
1Co. 11.25. This cup is the **n.** testament
2Co. 3. 6. able ministers of the **n.** test.
   5.17. he is a **n.** creature : old thi.
   all things are become **n.**
Gal. 6.15. uncircumcision, but a **n.** cre.
Eph. 2.15. of twain one **n.** man, so
   4.24. put on the **n.** man, which
Heb. 8. 8. I will make a **n.** covenant
   13. In that he saith, A **n.** cove.
   9.15. the mediator of the **n.** test.
2Pet. 3.13. for **n.** heavens and a **n.** earth
1Jo. 2. 7. I write no **n.** commandment
   8. Again, a **n.** commandment
2John 5. as though I wrote a **n.** com.
Rev. 2.17. and in the stone a **n.** name
   3.12. in Jerusalem, which cometh
   write upon him my **n.** name
   5. 9. And they sung a **n.** song
   14. 3. they sung as it were a **n.** so.
   21. 1. And I saw a **n.** hea. and a **n.**
   2. I John saw the holy city, **n.**
   5. Behold I make all things **n.**
neos.

Mat. 9.17. Nei. do men put **n.**; Mar.2.22
   but they put **n.** wine into
Mar. 2 22. else the **n.** wine ; Lu.5.37

Mar. 2.22. but **n.** wine must ; Lu.5.38
Lu. 5.39. wine straightway desireth **n.**
1Co. 5. 7. that ye may be a **n.** lump
Col. 3.10. And have put on the **n.** man
Heb.12.24. mediator of the **n.** covenant
   agnaphos.   [Mar.2,21
Mat.9.16. **n.** cloth unto an old garment;
   prosphatos.
Heb.10.20. By a **n.** and living way, wh.
NEWBORN.
artigennētos.

1Pet. 2. 2. As **n.** babes, desire the sin.
NEWNESS.
kainotēs.

Ro. 6. 4. should walk in **n.** of life
   7. 6. should serve in **n.** of spirit
NEXT.   (See *Day.*)
echō, [*participle.*]

Mar.1.38. Let us go unto the **n.** towns
Act.21.26. the **n.** day purifying himself
   epeimi, [*part.*]
Act. 7.26. the **n.** day he shewed hims.
   16.11. and the **n.** day to Neapolis
   20.15. came the **n.** day over against
   hexēs.
Lu. 9. 37. to pass, that on the **n.** day
Act.27.18. the **n.** *day* they lightened
   metaxu.
Act.13.42. preached to them the **n.** sab.
   erchomai.
Act.13.44. And the **n.** sabbath day ca.
NIGH, (See *Draw, Hand.*)
enggus.

Mat.24.32.ye know that summer is **n.**
Mar.13.29.know that it is **n.**, even at
Lu. 19.11. because he was **n.** to Jerus.
Jo. 6. 4. a feast of the Jews, was **n.**
   19. on the sea, and drawing **n.**
   23. **n.** unto the place where th.
   11.18. Bethany was **n.** unto Jerus.
   19.20. was crucified was **n.** to the
Act. 9.38. as Lydda was **n.** to Joppa
   27. 8. **n.** whereunto was the city
Ro. 10. 8. The word is **n.** thee, even
Eph. 2.13. are made **n.** by the blood of
   17. off and to them that were **n.**
Heb. 6. 8. rejected, and is **n.** *unto* curs.
   enggizō.
Mar.11. 1. when they *came* **n.** to Jerus.
Lu. 7.12. when he *came* **n.** to the gate
   10. 9, 11. kingd. of God *is come* **n.**
   18.35. as he was *come* **n.** unto Jeri.
   19.29. when he *was come* **n.** to Bet.
   37. *when he was come* **n.**, even
   21.20. that thedesola, thereof *is* **n.**
Act.22. 6. *as* I made . .and *was come* **n.**
Phi. 2.30. work of Christ he *was* **n.** un.
   prosenggizō.
Mar. 2. 4. could not come **n.** unto him
   para, [*accu.*]
Mat.15.29. came **n.** *unto* the sea of
Mar. 5.21. and he was **n.** *unto* the sea
   pros, [*accu.*]
Mar. 5.11. there, **n.** *unto* the mountains
   paraplēsion.
Phi. 2.27. he was sick **n.** *unto* death
NIGHT, (See *Continue.*)   -s.
nux.

Mat. 2.14. child and his mother by **n.**
   4. 2. forty days and forty **n**-s
   12.40. was three days and three **n**-s
   and three **n**-s in the heart of
   14.25. watch of the **n.** ; Mar. 6.48
   26.31. offended beca. of me this **n.**
   34. That this **n.**, before the cock
   27.64. lest his disciples come by **n.**
   28.13. His disciples came by **n.**
Mar. 4.27. and rise **n.** and day, and the
   5. 5. And always, **n.** and day

Mar.14.27. offended beca. of me this **n.**
   30. this day, even in this **n.**
Lu. 2. 8. over their flock by **n.**
   37. fastings and prayers **n.** and
   5. 5. we have toiled all the **n.**
   12.20. this **n.** thy soul shall be req.
   17.34. in that **n.** there shall be two
   18. 7. which cry day and **n.** unto
   21.37. and at **n.** he went out, and
Jo. 3. 2. The same came to Jes. by **n.**
   7.50. he that came to Jesus by **n.**
   9. 4. the **n.** cometh, when no man
   11.10. if a man walk in the **n.**
   13.30. immediat. out, and it was **n.**
   19.39. the first came to Jesus by **n.**
   21. 3. and that **n.** they caught noth.
Act. 5.19. the angel of the Lord by **n.**
   9.24. gates day and **n.** to kill him
   25. the disciples took him by **n.**
   12. 6. the same **n.** Peter was sleep.
   16. 9. appeared to Paul in the **n.**
   33. the same hour of the **n.**
   17.10. away Paul and Silas by **n.**
   18. 9. the Lord to Paul in the **n.**
   20.31. to warn every one **n.** and day
   23.11. And the **n.** following the Lo.
   23. at the third hour of the **n.**
   31. him by **n.** to Antipatris
   26. 7. serving God day and **n.**
   27.23. For there stood by me this **n.**
   27. But when the fourteenth **n.**
Ro. 13.12. The **n.** is far spent, the day
1Co. 11.23. the same **n.** in which he was
1Th. 2. 9. for labouring **n.** and day,be.
   3.10. **n.** and day praying exceedin.
   5. 2. a thief in the **n.** ; 2Pet. 3.10
   5. we are not of the **n.**, nor of
   7. they that sleep,sleep in the **n.**
   are drunken in the **n.**
2Th. 3. 8. with labour and travail **n.**
1Ti. 5. 5. and prayers **n.** and day
2Ti. 1. 3. in my prayers **n.** and day
Rev. 4. 8. they rest not day and **n.**, sa.
   7.15. serve him day and **n.** in his
   8.12. part of it, and the **n.** likewi.
   12.10. before our God day and **n.**
   14.11. they have no rest day nor **n.**
   20.10. tormented day and **n.** for
   21.25. shall be no **n.** there ; 22.5
   nuchthēmeron.
2Co. 11.25. *a* **n.** *and a* day I have been
NINE.
ennea.

Lu. 17.17. clean. ? but where are the **n.**
NINETY-NINE.
ennenēkontaennea.

Mat.18.12. he not leave the **n.** ; Lu.15.4
   13. the **n.** which went not astray
Lu. 15. 7. than over **n.** just persons
NINTH.
ennatos.

Mat.20. 5. about the sixth and **n.** hour
   27.45. all the land unto the **n.** hour;
   Mar. 15.33 ; Lu. 23.44
   46. **n.** hour Je. cried; Mar.15.34
Act. 3. 1. prayer, being the **n.** hour
   10. 3. about the **n.** hour of the day
   30. at the **n.** hour I prayed in
Rev.21.20.the **n.**, a topaz ; the tenth, a
NO

Generally represents ou *or* mē. *The*
following are exceptions :—
   ouketi.

Mat.19. 6. are **n.** *more* twain ; Mar.10.8
Mar. 7.12. **n.** *more* to do ought for his
   14.25. I will drink **n.** *more* of the
Lu. 15.19, 21. am **n.** *more* worthy to be
Jo. 6.66. and walked **n.** *more* with him
   11.54. Jesus there. walked **n.** *more*
   14.19. the world seeth me **n.** *more*

Jo. 16.10. Fath., and ye see me **n.** *more*
     21. she remembereth **n.** *more* the
     25. when I shall **n.** *more* speak
   17.11. And now I am **n.** *more* in the
Act. 8.39. the eunuch saw him **n.** *more*
   20.25. shall see my face **n.** *more*
     38. should see his face **n.** *more*
Ro. 6. 9. **n.** *more*; death hath **n.** *more*
   7.17, 20. it is **n.** *more* I that do it
   11. 6. then is it **n.** *more* of works
     grace is **n.** *more* grace. But
     of works, then is it **n.** *more*
     otherwise work is **n.** *more*
²Co. 5.16. hence. know we him **n.** *more*
Gal. 3.18. it is **n.** *more* of promise
   4. 7. thou art **n.** *more* a servant
Eph. 2.19. ye are **n.** *more* strangers
Heb.10.18. there is **n.** *more* offering for
   26. **n.** *more* sacrifice for sins
Rev.18.14 shalt find them **n.** *more* at
mēketi.
Mat.21.19.Let **n.** fruit gr. on thee *hence.*
Mar. 1.45. Jesus could **n.** *more* openly
   2.. that there was **n.** *room* to
   9.25. and enter **n.** *more* into him
Jo. 5.14. sin **n.** *more*, lest a worse th.
   8.11. thee; go, and sin **n.** *more*
Act.13.34. **n.** *more* to return to corrup.
Ro. 15.23. But now having **n.** *more*
Eph. 4.14. Th. we *henceforth* be **n.** *more*
   28. him that stole steal **n.** *more*
oudeis.
Mar. 6. 5. he cŏuld there do **n.** mighty
Lu. 4.24. **n.** prophet is accepted in his
   16.13. **n.** servant can serve two
   23. 4, 14. I find **n.** fault in this man;
     Jo.18.38, 19.4
   22. I have found **n.** cause of
Jo. 10.41. and said, John did **n.** mir.
   16.29. and speakest **n.** proverb
   19.11. Thou couldest have **n.** pow.
Act. 9. 8. were opened, he saw **n.** *man*
   15. 9. And put **n.** difference betw.
   23. 9. We find **n.** evil in this man
   25.10. to the Jews have I done **n.**
   27.22. **n.** loss of any man's life
   28. 5. into the fire, and felt **n.** har.
Ro. 8. 1. now **n.** condemnation to
   14. 7. and **n.** *man* dieth to himself
²Co. 7. 5. our flesh had **n.** rest, but we
Gal. 2. 6. it maketh **n.** matter to me
Phi. 4.15. **n.** church communicated
²Ti. 2.14. about words to **n.** profit
Heb. 6.13. he could swear by **n.** greater
Jas. 3.12. so can **n.** fountain both yield
¹Jo. 1. 5. and in him is **n.** darkness
mēdeis.
Lu. 3.13. Exact **n.** more than that wh.
Act. 4.17. to **n.** man in this name
   13.28. though they found **n.** cause
   15.28. to lay upon you **n.** greater
   16.28. Do thyself **n.** harm: for we
   19.40. there being **n.** cause whereby
   21.25. that they observe **n.** such
   28. 6. and saw **n.** harm come to
   18. there was **n.** cause of death
¹Co. 1. 7. So that ye come behind in **n.**
   10.25, 27. asking **n.** ques. for con.
²Co. 6. 3. Giving **n.** offence in any th.
   13. 7. I pray to God that ye do **n.**
Tit. 2. 8. having **n.** evil *thing* to say
Heb.10. 2. have had **n.** more conscience
oude.   [Lu.7.9
Mat. 8.10. great faith, **n.**, *not* in Isra.;
   24.36. **n.**, *not* the angels;Mar.13.32
Mar. 6.31. they had **n.** leis. *so much as*
Lu. 23.15. **n.**, *nor* yet Herod: for I sent
Act. 7. 5. **n.**, *not* so much as to set his
Ro. 3.10. There is none right., **n.** *not*
   4.15. there is **n.** transgressi.n
¹Co. 6. 5. **n.**, *not* one that shall be able
²Co. 3.10. which was made glor. had **n.**
188

Gal. 2. 5. **n.**, *not* for an hour
oute.
Mar. 5. 3. bind him, **n.**, *not* with cha.
mēde.
¹Co. 5.11. with such an one **n.** *not* to
mē tis.
Lu. 11.36. having **n.** part dark, the wh.
   12. 4. after that have **n.** more
mēpote.
Heb. 9.17. it is of **n.** strength *at all* wh.
ou mē.
Mat. 5.18. or one tittle shall *in* **n.** *wise*
   20. ye shall *in* **n.** *case* enter into
   26. Thou shalt *by* **n.** *means* come
   10.42. he shall *in* **n.** *wise* lose his
Lu. 18.17. shall *in* **n.** *wise* enter there.
Jo. 6.37. I will *in* **n.** *wise* cast out
Act.13.41. which ye shall *in* **n.** *wise*
¹Co. 8.13. I will eat **n.** flesh while the
Heb. 8.12. will I remem. **n.** more; 10.17
Rev. 3.12. and he shall go **n.** more out
   18. 7. and shall see **n.** sorrow
   21.27. there shall *in* **n.** *wise* enter
ou pas.
Mat.24.22. **n.** flesh be saved; Mar.13.20
Ro. 3.20. **n.** flesh be justified; Gal.2.16
¹Co. 1.29. That **n.** flesh should glory
Eph. 4.29. **n.** corrupt communication
   5. 5. that **n.** whoremonger
Heb.12.11.Now **n.** chastening
²Pet. 1.20. that **n.** prophecy of the
¹Jo. 2.21. that **n.** lie is of the truth
   3.15. that **n.** murderer hath
Rev.18.22.and **n.** craftsman of whatso.
oupō.
Rev.17.12.received **n.** kingdom *as yet*
oude houtō.
Jo. 15. 4. **n.** *more* can ye except ye
alla.
Lu. 23.15. **n.**, nor yet Herod; for I se.
   (*See words in connection.*)

NOBLE.
    anthrōpos eugenēs.
Act.17.11. These were *more* **n.** than
¹Co. 1.26. not many **n.**, are called
    kratistos.
Act.24. 3. *most* **n.** Felix, with all tha.
   26.25. I am not mad, *most* **n.** Fest.

NOBLEMAN.
    basilikos.
Jo. 4.46. there was a certain **n.**, whose
   49. the **n.** saith unto him, Sir
    anthrōpos eugenēs.
Lu. 19.12. A certain **n.** went into a far

NOISE.
    thorubeomai.
Mat. 9.23. and the people *making* a **n.**
    roizēdon.
²Pet. 3.10. sh. pass away *with* a great **n.**
    phōnē.
Rev. 6. 1. were the **n.** of thunder *was*

NOISED.
    akouō.   [*was heard.*]
Mar. 2. 1. it *was* **n.** that he was in the
    dialaleō.
Lu. 1.65. these sayings *were* **n.** abroad
    phōnē ginomai.
Act 2. 6. when this *was* **n.** abroad

NOISOME.
    kakos.
Rev.16. 2. there fell a **n.** and grievous

NONE.
    oudeis   [Lu.18.19.
Mat.19.17.there is **n.** good; Mar.10.18;
Lu. 1.61. There is **n.** of thy kindred
   4.26. But unto **n.** of them was Eli.
   27. and **n.** of them was cleansed
   14.24. That **n.** of those men which

Lu. 18.34. they understood **n.** of these
Jo. 7.19. and yet **n.** of you keepeth
   15.24. works which **n.** other man
   16. 5. and **n.** of you asketh me
   17.12. and **n.** of them is lost, but
   18. 9. gavest me have I lost **n.**
   21.12. And **n.** of the disciples durst
Act. 8.16. he was fallen upon **n.** of them
   18.17. Gallio cared for **n.** of those
   20.24. But **n.** of these things move
   25.11. but if there be **n.** of these th.
   18. they brought **n.** accusation
   26.22. saying **n.** other things than
   26. that **n.** of these things are
Ro. 14. 7. For **n.** of us liveth to hims.
¹Co. 1.14. that I baptized **n.** of you
   2. 8. Which **n.** of the princes of
   8. 4. and that there is **n.** other
   9.15. I have used **n.** of these th.
   14.10. **n.** of them is without signi.
Gal. 5.10. that ye will be **n.** otherwise
    mēdeis.
Jo. 8.10. and saw **n.** but the woman
Act. 8.24. that **n.** of these things wh.
   11.19. the word to **n.** but unto the
   24.23. that he should forbid **n.** of
¹Ti. 5.14. give **n.** occasion to the adv.
Rev. 2.10. Fear **n.** of those things wh
    ou.
Mat.12.43.seeking rest, and findeth **n.**
   26.60. But found **n.**: yea though
    came yet found they **n.**
Mar.12.31.There is **n.** other command.
   32. and there is **n.** other but he
   14.55. him to death; and found **n.**
Lu. 13. 6. fruit thereon, and found **n.**
   7. on this fig tree, and found **n.**
Jo. 6.22. that there was **n.** other boat
Act. 3. 6. Silver and gold have I **n.**
   7. 5. And he gave him **n.** inherit.
Ro. 3.10. There is **n.** righteous, no, not
    (*not* a righteous man.)
   11. There is **n.** that understand.
    is **n.** that seeketh after God
   12. **n.** that doeth good, no, not
   8. 9. Spirit of Ch., he is **n.** *of* his
²Co. 1.13. For we write **n.** other things
Gal. 1.19. other of the apostles saw I **n.**
¹Jo. 2.10. there is **n.** occasion of stum.
Rev. 2.24. I will put upon you **n.** other
    mē.
Lu. 3.11. impart to him that hath **n.**
¹Co. 7.29. wives, be as tho. they had **n.**
    mē tis.
¹Th. 5.15. See that **n.** render evil for
¹Pet. 4.15. let **n.** of you suffer as a
    ou tis.
Act.26.26. I am persuaded that **n.** of
    oute.
Act. 4.12. for there is **n.** other name
   (*See words in connection.*)

NOON.
    mesēmbria.
Act.22 6. nigh unto Damas. about **n.**

NOR

Generally represents **oude, oute,**
mēde *or* **mēte,** having nearly the same
meaning. The following are exceptions :
    ē.
Lu. 22.68. not answer me, **n.** let me go
¹Co. 15.21. **n.** again the head to the feet
Eph. 5. 4. foolish talking **n.** jesting
    5. **n.** unclean person, **n.** covet.
    oude ou mē.
Heb.13. 5. never leave thee **n.** forsake
    kai ou.
¹Co. 2. 9. Eye hath not seen, **n.** ear

NORTH.
    borras.
Lu. 13.29. from the **n.**, and from the

Rev.21.13. on the **n.** three gates; on the

NORTH-WEST.
chŏros.
Act.27.12. toward the south-west and **n.**

NOT.
This word is represented by **ouk** *or* **ou** *and also by* **mē,** *which have nearly the same meaning. They are also modified by combination with other words, without affecting their negative power; but when* **ou** *and* **mē** *are combined, as in the following passages, the negation is stronger.*

ou mē.
Mat.10.23. Ye shall **n.** have gone over
 13.14. and shall **n.** understand
  and shall **n.** perceive
 15. 6. And honour **n.** his father or
 16.22. this shall **n.** be unto thee
  28. which shall **n.** taste of death
 18. 3. ye shall **n.** enter into the
 ·3.39. Ye shall **n.** see me henceforth
 24. 2. n. be left here one; Mar.13.2
   n. be thro. down; Mar. 13.2
  34. This generation shall **n.** pass;
   Mar. 13.30; Lu. 21.32
  35. but my words shall **n.** pass;
   Mar. 13.31; Lu. 21.33
 26.29. I will **n.** drink henceforth of
  35. yet will I **n.** deny thee
Mar. 9. 1. which shall **n.** taste of death
  41. he shall **n.** lose his reward
 10.15. he shall **n.** enter therein
 14.31. will **n.** deny thee *in any wise*
  18. it shall **n.** hurt them
Lu. 6.37. and ye shall **n.** be judged
  and ye shall **n.** be condemned
 9.27. which shall **n.** taste of death
 12.59. thou shalt **n.** depart thence
 13.35. Ye shall **n.** see me, until
 18. 7. And shall **n.** God avenge his
  30. Who shall **n.** receive manifo.
 21.18. there shall **n.** an hair of your
 22.16. I will **n.** any more eat there.
  18. I will **n.** drink of the fruit
  34. n. crow this day; Jo. 13.38
  67. ye will **n.** believe
  68. ye will **n.** answer me, nor let
Jo. 4.48. and wonders, ye will **n.** beli.
 8.12. shall **n.** walk in darkness
 10. 5. a stranger will they **n.** follow
 11.56. that he will **n.** come to the
 18.11. given me, shall I **n.** drink it
 20.25. his side, I will **n.** believe
Act.28.26. and shall **n.** understand; and
  shall see, and **n.** perceive
Ro. 4. 8. to whom the Lord will **n.**
Gal. 4.30. shall **n.** be heir with the son
 5.16. and ye shall **n.** fulfil the lust
¹Th. 4.15. shall **n.** prevent them which
 5. 3. and they shall **n.** escape
Heb. 8.11. they shall **n.** teach every man
¹Pet. 2. 6. shall **n.** be confounded
Rev. 2.11. shall **n.** be hurt of the second
 3. 3. thou shalt **n.** know what ho.
 5. I will **n.** blot out his name
 15. 4. Who shall **n.** fear thee, O L.
 21.25. shall **n.** be shut *at all* by day
(See words in connection.)

NOTABLE.
episēmos.
Mat.27.16.a n. prisoner, called Barnab.
Act. 2.20. that great and **n.** day of
gnōstos.
Act. 4.16. a **n.** miracle hath been done
NOTE.
episēmos.
Ro. 16. 7. who are *of* **n.** among the ap.

---

sēmeioō.
²Th. 3.14. n. that man, and have no
  (note for yourselves.)
NOTHING. (See *Bring.*)
oudeis.
Mat. 5.13. it is thenceforth good for **n.**
 10.26. there is **n.** covered; Lu.12.2
 17.20. and **n.** shall be impossible
 21.19. and found **n.** thereon
 23.16. swear by the temple, it is **n.**
  18. swear by the altar, it is **n.**
 26.62. Answerest thou **n.**;
   Mar.14.60,15.4
 27.12. and elders, he answered **n.**
  24. saw that he could prevail **n.**
Mar. 7.15. There is **n.** from without
 9.29. can come forth by **n.**, but
 11.13. he found **n.** but leaves
 14.61. held his peace, and ans. **n.**
 15. 5. Jesus yet answered **n.**
Lu. 4. 2. in those days he did eat **n.**
 5. all night, and have taken **n.**
 10.19. and **n.** shall by any means
 22.35. anything? And he said, **n.**
 23. 9. but he answered him **n.**
  15. n. worthy of death is done
  41. this man hath done **n.** amiss
Jo. 3.27. A man can receive **n.**, exce.
 5.19. The Son can do **n.** of hims.
 30. I can of mine own self do **n.**
 6.63. the flesh profiteth **n.**
 7.26. and they say **n.** unto him
 8.28. and that I do **n.** of myself
 54. my honour is **n.**
Jo. 9.33. not of God, he could do **n.**
 11.49. unto them, Ye know **n.** at all
 12.19. perceive ye how ye preva. **n.**
 14.30. cometh, and hath **n.** in me
 15. 5. without me ye can do **n.**
 16.23. that day ye shall ask me **n.**
  24. Hitherto have ye asked **n.**
 18.20. and in secret have I said **n.**
 21. 3. that night they caught **n.**
Act. 4.14. they could say **n.** against it
 17.21. spent their time in **n.** else
 20.20. how I kept back **n.** that
 21.24. concerning thee, are **n.**
 26.31. This man doeth **n.** worthy
 28.17. I have committed **n.** against
Ro. 14.14. that there is **n.** unclean of
¹Co. 4. 4. I know **n.** by myself; yet
 7.19. Circum. is **n.**, and uncir. is **n.**
 8. 2. he knoweth **n.** yet as he
 4. an idol is **n.** in the world
 13. 2. have not charity, I am **n.**
 3. charity, it profiteth me **n.**
²Co. 12.11. for in **n.** am I behind the
  apostles, though I be **n.**
Gal. 2. 6. in conference added **n.** to
 4. 1. differeth **n.** from a servant
 5. 2. Christ shall profit you **n.**
Phi. 1.20. that in **n.** I shall be asham.
¹Ti. 4. 4. and in **n.** to be refused, if it
 6. 7. For we brought **n.** into this
Tit. 1.15. unbelieving is **n.** pure
Phile. 14. thy mind would I do **n.**
Heb. 2. 8. he left **n.** that is not put
 7.14. Moses spake **n.** concerning
 19. the law made **n.** perfect
Rev. 3.17. and have need of **n.**; and
mēdeis.
Mat.27.19. Have thou **n.** to do with
Mar. 1.44. See thou say **n.** to any man
 5.26. and was **n.** bettered, but
 6. 8. take **n.** for their jour.;Lu.9.3
Lu. 6.35. lend, hoping for **n.** again
Act. 4.21. finding **n.** how they might
 10.20. go with them doubt. **n.**;11.12
 19.36. quiet, and to do **n.** rashly
 23.14. that we will eat **n.** until
 29. but to have **n.** laid to his
 25.25. committed **n.** worthy of

Act.27.33. fasting, having taken **n.**
²Co. 6.10. as having **n.**, and yet
 7. 9. receive damage by us in **n.**
Gal. 6. 3. be something, when he is **n.**
Phi. 1.28. in **n.** terrified by your
 2. 3. Let **n.** be done through
 4. 6. Be careful for **n.**; but in
¹Th. 4.12. that ye may have lack of **n.**
¹Ti. 5.21. doing **n.** by partiality
 6. 4. He is proud, knowing **n.**
Tit. 3.13. that **n.** be wanting unto
Jas. 1. 4. perf. and entire, wanting **n.**
 6. let him ask in faith, **n.** wav.
³John 7. taking **n.** of the Gentiles
ou tis.
Mar. 4.22. For there is **n.** hid, which
 6.36. for they have **n.** to eat
 8. 2. three days, and have **n.** to
²Co. 13. 8. can do **n.** against the truth
mē tis.
Jo. 6.12. that remain, that **n.** be lost
¹Co. 4. 5. judge **n.** before the time
mē.
Mar. 8. 1. and having **n.** to eat, Jesus
Lu. 7.42. And when they had **n.** to pay
Jo. 6.39. given me I should lose **n.**
ou.
Lu. 8.17. For **n.** is secret, that shall
¹Co. 9.16. I have **n.** to glory of : for ne.
²Co. 8.15. gathered much had **n.** over
oude tis.
¹Ti. 6. 7. certain we can carry **n.** out
oute.
Jo. 4.11. thou hast **n.** to draw with
pas ouk.
Lu. 1.37. with God **n.** shall be imposs.
 (every thing shall be not impossible.)
oudepote pas.
Act.11. 8. n. common or unclean hath
ou hos.
Lu. 11. 6. I have **n.** to set before him

NOTICE.
prokatanggellō.
²Co. 9. 5. whereof ye had **n.** *before*
 (which have been announced before.)

NOTWITHSTANDING.
plēn.
Lu. 10.11. in **n.** be ye sure of this, that
 20. n. in this rejoice not, that
Phi. 1.18. What then? **n.**, every way,
 4.14. n. ye have well done that
alla.
Rev. 2.20. n. I have a few things aga.

NOUGHT. (See *Bring, Sct.*)
oudeis.
Act. 5.36. scattered, and brought to **n.**
kataluō.
Act. 5.38. of men, it *will come to* **n.**
apelegmos.
Act.19.27. is in danger to be *set at* **n.**
dōrean.
²Th. 3. 8. eat any man's bread *for* **n.**
erēmoō.
Rev.18.17. so great riches *is come to* **n.**

NOURISH,   -ed, -eth.
trephō.
Act.12.20. bec. their country *was* **n**-ed
Jas. 5. 5. ye *have* **n**-ed your hearts, as
Rev.12.14. where she *is* **n**-ed for a time
anatrephō.
Act. 7.20. n-ed up in his father's house
 21. and **n**-ed him for her own son
ektrephō.
Eph. 5.29. n-eth and cherisheth it, even
entrephō.
¹Ti. 4. 6. n-ed up in the words of faith

NOURISHMENT.
(See Minister.)

189

NOVICE.
neophutos.
¹Ti. 3. 6. Not a n., lest being lifted up

NOW.
nun.
Mat.26.65. n. ye have heard his blasph.
27.42. let him n. come down from
43. let him deliver him n., if he
Mar.10.30.an hundredfold n. in this ti.
15.32. descend n. from the cross
Lu. 2.29. Lord, n. lettest thou thy ser.
6.21. Blessed are ye that hunger n.
Blessed are ye that weep n.
25. Woe unto you that laugh n.
11.39. n. do ye Pharisees make cle.
16.25. but n. he is comforted
19.42. but n. they are hid from th.
22.36. But n., he that hath a purse
Jo. 2. 8. Draw out n., and bear unto
4.18. he whom thou n. hast is not
23. hour cometh, and n. is; 5.25,
16.32
8.40. But n. ye seek to kill me
52. n. we know that thou hast a
9.21. But by what means he n. se.
41. no sin: but n. ye say, Wc
11.22. I know, that even n., whats.
12.27. n. is my soul troubled
31. n. is the judgment of this
n. shall be the prince of this w.
13.31. n. is the Son of man glorified
36. thou canst not follow me n.
14.29. And n. I have told you befo.
15.22. but n. they have no cloke
24. but n. have they both seen
16. 5. But n. I go my way to him
22. And ye n. therefore have so.
29. Lo, n. speakest thou plainly
30. n. are we sure that thou kn.
17. 5. And n., O Father, glorify th.
7. n. they have known that all
13. And n. come I to thee
18.36. but n. is my kingdom not
21.10. fish which ye have n. caught
Act. 2.33. this, which ye n. see and he.
3.17. And n., brethren, I wot that
7. 4. land, wherein ye n. dwell
34. And n. come, I will send th.
52. of whom ye have been n. the
10. 5. And n. send men to Joppa
33. n. therefore are we all here
12.11. n. I know of a surety, that
13.11. And n., behold, the hand of
15.10. n. therefore why tempt ye
16.36. n. therefore depart, and go
37. and n. do they thrust us out
20.22. And n., behold, I go bound
25. And n., behold, I know that
22. 1. my defence which I make n.
16. And n. why tarriest thou
23.15. n. therefore ye with the cou.
21. and n. are they ready, looki.
24.13. things whereof they n. accu.
26. 6. And n. I stand and am jud.
17. unto whom n. I send thee
Ro. 3.21. But n. the righteousness of
5. 9. being n. justified by his blo.
11. by whom we have n. received
6.19. even so n. yield your memb.
21. whereof ye are n. ashamed
8. 1. n. no condemnation to them
22. in pain together until n.
11.30. yet have n. obtained mercy
31. so have these also n. not be.
13.11. for n. is our salvation nearer
16.26. But n. is made manifest
¹Co. 3. 2. neither yet n. are ye able
7.14. unclean; but n. are they ho.
12.20. But n. are they many memb.
²Co. 5.16. yet n. henceforth know we
6. 2. behold, n. is the accepted ti.
190

²Co. 6. 2. behold, n. is the day of salv.
7. 9. n. I rejoice, not that ye were
13. 2. and being absent n. I write
Gal. 1.23. n. preacheth the faith
2.20. life which I n. live in the fle.
3. 3. are ye n. made perfect by
4. 9. But n., after that ye have kn.
25. to Jerusalem which n. is
29. the Spirit, even so it is n.
Eph. 2. 2. the spirit that n. worketh in
3. 5. as it is n. revealed unto his
10. To the intent that n. unto
5. 8. but n. are ye light in the Lo.
Phi. 1. 5. from the first day until n.
20. as always, so n. also Christ
30. and n. hear to be in me
2.12. but n. much more in my ab.
3.18. and n. tell you even weeping
Col. 1.24. Who n. rejoice in my suffer.
¹Th. 3. 8. For n. we live, if ye stand
²Th. 2. 6. And n. ye know what with.
¹Ti. 4. 8. promise of the life that n. is
²Ti. 1.10. But is n. made manifest
Heb. 2. 8. But n. we see not yet all th.
9. 5. of which we cannot n. speak
24. n. to appear in the presence
26. but n. once in the end of the
12.26. but n. he hath promised
Jas. 4.13. Go to n., ye that say, To-day
16. But n. ye rejoice in your bo.
5. 1. Go to n., ye rich men
¹Pet. 1.12. which are n. reported unto
2.10. but are n. the people of God
but n. have obtained mercy
25. but are n. returned unto the
3.21. baptism doth also n. save us
²Pet. 3. 7. and the earth, which are n.
18. To him be glory both n. and
¹Jo. 2.18. even n. are there many anti.
28. And n., little children, abide
3. 2. n. are we the sons of God
4. 3. even n. already is it in the
²John 5. And n. I beseech thee, lady
Jude 25. and power, both n. and ever
ho nun. [present circumstances.]
Act. 4.29. And n., Lord, behold their
5.38. And n. I say unto you, Refr.
17.30. but n. commandeth all men
20.32. And n., brethren, I commend
27.22. And n. I exhort you to be of
nuni.
Ro. 6.22. But n. being made free from
7. 6. But n. we are delivered from
17. n. then it is no more I that
15.23. But n. having no more place
25. But n. I go unto Jerusalem
¹Co. 5.11. But n. I have written unto
12.18. But n. hath God set the
13.13. And n. abideth faith, hope
14. 6. n., brethren, if I come unto
15.20. But n. is Christ risen from
²Co. 8.11. n. therefore perform the do.
22. but n. much more diligent
Eph. 2.13. But n. in Christ Jesus ye
Col. 1.21. yet n. hath he reconciled
26. but n. is made manifest to
3. 8. But n. ye also put off all
Phile. 9. and n. also a prisoner of Jes.
11. but n. profitable to thee and
Heb. 8. 6. But n. hath he obtained a
11.16. But n. they desire a better
ēdē.
Mat. 3.10. And n. also the axe; Lu .3.9
14.15. and the time is n. past
24. was n. in the midst of the
15.32. with me n. three; Mar. 8.2
Mar. 4.37. ship, so that it was n. full
6.35. when the day was n. far spe.
and n. the time is far passed
11.11. and n. the eventide was come
15.42.And n. when the even was
Lu. 7. 6. And when he was n. not far

Lu. 11. 7. the door is n. shut, and my
14.17. for all things are n. ready
19.37. was come nigh, even n. at the
21.30. When they n. shoot forth
that summer is n. nigh at
Jo. 4.51. And as he was n. going dowɳ
5. 6. that he had been n. a long
6.17. it was n. dark, and Jesus
7.14. n. about the midst of the fe.
13. 2. the devil having n. put
15. 3. n. ye are clean through the
19.28. all things were n. accomplis.
21. 4. when the morning was n. co.
14. This is n. the third time that
Act. 4. 3. day: for it was n. eventide
27. 9. when sailing was n. dangero.
the fast was n. already past
Ro. 1.10. if by any means n. at length
4.19. conside. not his own body n.
13.11. n. it is high time to awake
¹Co. 4. 8. n. ye are full, n. ye are rich
6. 7. n. therefore there is utterly
Phi. 4.10. that n. at the last your care
²Ti. 4. 6. For I am n. ready to be off.
²Pet.3. 1. This second epistle, bel., I n.
¹Jo. 2. 8. the true light n. shineth
arti.
Mat. 3.15. Suffer it to be so n. : for thus
9.18. My daughter is even n. dead
11.12. until n. the kingdom of hea.
26.53. that I cannot n. pray to my
Jo. 2.10. kept the good wine until n.
9.19. how then doth he n. see
25. whereas I was blind, n. I see
13. 7. What I do thou know. not n.
19. n. I tell you before it come
33. cannot come; so n. I say to
37. why cannot I follow thee n.
16.12. ye cannot bear them n.
31. answered them, Do ye n. be.
¹Co. 13.12. For n. we see through a glass
n. I know in part; but then
16. 7. I will not see you n. by the
Gal 1. 9. we said before, so say I n.
10. For do I n. persuade men, or
4.20. des. to be present with you n.
¹Th. 3. 6. when Timotheus came
²Th. 2. 7. only he who n. letteth, will
¹Pet. 1. 6. though n. for a season, if ne.
8. whom, though n. ye see him
¹Jo. 2. 9. is in darkness even until n.
Rev.12.10.n. is come salvation, and str.
oun.
Lu. 10.36. Which n. of these three
Jo. 16.19. n. Jesus knew that they were
19.29. n. there was set a vessel full
21. 7. n. when Simon Peter heard
Act. 1.18. n. this man purchased a field
11.19. n. they which were scattered
25. 1. n. when Festus was come
¹Co. 9.25. n. they do it to obtain a cor.
²Co. 5.20. n. then we are ambassadors
Eph. 2.19. n. therefore ye are no more
ouketi.
Jo. 4.42. n. we believe, not because of
17.11. And n. I am no more in the
21. 6. and n. they were not able to
Ro. 14.15. n. walkest thou not charita.
Phile. 16. Not n. as a servant, but
Mat.26.45. Sleep on n., and take your; [Mar.14.41
dē.
Lu. 2.15. Let us n. go even unto Beth.

NUMBER, [noun.]
arithmos.
Lu. 22. 3. being of the n. of the twelve
Jo. 6.10. in n. about five thousand
Act. 4. 4. the n. of the men was about
5.36. a n. of men, about four hun.
6. 7. the n. of the disciples multi.
11.21. a great n. believed, and turn.

Act.16. 5. and increased in **n.** daily
Ro. 9.27. Though the **n.** of the children
Rev. 7. 4. I heard the **n.** of them ; 9.16
   9.16. the **n.** of the army of the
  13.17. the beast, or the **n.** of his
    18. count the **n.** of the beast
     the **n.** of a man ; and his **n.**
   15. 2. over the **n.** of his name
  20. 8. the **n.** of whom is as the sand
  ochlos.
Mar.10.46. and a great **n.** *of people*
Act. 1.15. the **n.** of names together
  engkrinō.
2Co.10.12. not *make* ourselves *of the* **n.**
  katalegō.
1Ti. 5. 9. *Let* not..*be taken into the* **n.**

NUMBER, [*verb*,]   -*ed*.
  arithmeō.   [Lu.12.7
Mat.10.30. of your head are all **n**-*ed ;*
Rev. 7. 9. mult., whi. no man could **n.**
  logizomai.
Mar.15.28. he *was* **n**-ed with the trans.
  katarithmeō.
Act. 1.17. For he *was* **n**-*ed with* us, and
  sungkatapsēphizō.
Act. 1.26. he *was* **n**-ed with the eleven

NURSE.
  trophos.
1Th. 2. 7. as a **n.** cherisheth her chil.

NURTURE.
  paideia.
Eph. 6. 4. in the **n.** and admonition

O, *or* **OH**, [*interjection*,]
  *Generally represents the vocative case
  in Greek, or the definite article. The
  following are exceptions :—*
  ō.
Mat. 15.28. **o** woman, great is thy faith
  17.17. **o** faith. and per. gen.;Lu.9.41
Mar. 9.19. **o** faithless generation, how
Lu. 24.25. **o** fools, and slow of heart to
Act. 1. 1. treatise have I made, **o** The.
  13.10. **o** full of all subtilty and all
  18.14. **o** ye Jews, reason would that
Ro. 2. 1. **o** man, whosoever thou art
   3. And thinkest thou this, **o**
  9.20. Nay but, **o** man, who art
  11.33. **o** the depth of the riches
Gal. 3. 1. **o** foolish Galatians, who
1Ti. 6.20. **o** Timothy, keep that which
Jas. 2.20. But wilt thou know, **o** vain

OATH,   -**s**.
  horkos.
Mat. 5.33. perform unto the L. thine **o**-*s*
  14. 7. promised with an **o.** to give
   9. for the **o.**'s sake, and them
  26.72. again he denied with an **o.**
Mar. 6.26. yet for his **o.**'s sake, and
Lu. 1.73. The **o.** which he sware to our
Act. 2.30. God had sworn with an **o.**
Heb. 6.16. an **o.** for confirmation is to
  17. counsel confirmed it by an **o.**
Jas. 5.12. neither by any other **o.**; but
  horkōmosia.
Heb. 7.20. inasmu, as not without an **o.**
  21. without an **o.**; but this with
  28. but the word of the **o.**, which
  anathematizō.
Act.23.21. *have bound* them. *with an* **o.**

OBEDIENCE.
  hupakoē.
Ro. 1. 5. for **o.** to the faith among all
  5.19. so by the **o.** of one shall ma.
  6.16. or of **o.** unto righteousness
  16.19. For your **o.** is come abroad
  26. to all nations for the **o.** of
2Co. 7.15. whilst he remembereth the **o.**
  10. 5. every thought to the **o.** of

2Co.10. 6. all disobedi., when your **o.** is
Phile. 21. Having confidence in thy **o.**
Heb. 5. 8. yet learned he **o.** by the thi.
1Pet. 1. 2. unto **o.** and sprinkling of the
  hupotassō.
1Co.14.34. *to be under* **o.**, as also saith

OBEDIENT.
  hupakouō.
Act. 6. 7. priests *were* **o.** *to* the faith
Eph. 6. 5. Servants, *be* **o.** to them that
  hupēkoos.
2Co. 2. 9. whether ye be **o.** in all things
Phi. 2. 8. and became **o.** unto death
  hupakoē.
Ro. 15.18. to make the Gentiles **o.**
  (towards *obedience* of Gentiles.)
1Pet. 1.14. As **o.** children, not fashion.
  hupotassō.
Tit. 2. 5. **o.** *to* their own husbands
  9. servants *to be* **o.** *unto* their

OBEY,   -*ed*, -*ing*.
  hupakouō.   [Mar. 4.41
Mat. 8.27. the winds and the sea **o.** him ;
Mar. 1.27. spirits, and they do **o.** him
Lu. 8.25. and water, and they **o.** him
  17. 6. in the sea ; and it should **o.**
Ro. 6.12. that ye should **o.** it in the
  16. serva. ye are to whom ye **o.**
  17. but ye have **o**-*ed* from the
10.16. But they *have* not all **o**-*ed*
Eph. 6. 1. Children **o.** your parents
Phi. 2.12. belo., as ye *have* always **o**-*ed*
Col. 3.20. Children, **o.** your parents
  22. Servants, **o.** in all things yo.
2Th. 1. 8. know not God, and *that* **o.**
  3.14. And if any man **o.** not our
Heb. 5. 9. salvat. unto all them *that* **o.**
  11. 8. -*ed ;* and he went out, not
1Pet. 3. 6. Even as Sara **o**-*ed* Abraham
  hupakoē.
Ro. 6.16. yield yourselv. servants.to **o.**
1Pet. 1.22. your souls in **o**-*ing* the tr.
  hupēkoos.
Act. 7.39. fathers would not **o.** (be *ob-
  peithō.   edient.*)
Act. 5.36, 37. and all, as many as **o**-*ed*
Ro. 2. 8. but **o.** unrighteousness
Gal. 3. 1. ye *should* not **o.** the tr. ; 5.7
Heb.13.17.**o.** them that have the rule
Jas. 3. 3. mouths, that they *may* **o.** us
  apeitheō.
Ro. 2. 8. *do not* **o.** the truth, but
1Pet. 3. 1. if any **o.** *not* the word, they
  4.17. them *that* **o.** *not* the gospel
  peitharcheō.
Act. 5.29. We ought *to* **o.** God rather
  32. given to them *that* **o.** him
  (See *Magistrates*.)

OBJECT.
  katēgoreō.
Act.24.19. and **o.**, if they had ought

OBSERVATION.
  paratērēsis.
Lu. 17.20. of God cometh not with **o.**

OBSERVE,   -*ed*.
  tēreō.
Mat.23. 3. they bid you **o.**, that **o.**
  28.20. Teaching them *to* **o.** all thin.
Act.21.25. *that* they **o.** no such thing
  suntēreō.
Mar. 6.20. **o**-*ed* him ; and when he hea.
  paratēreō.
Gal. 4.10. Ye **o.** days, and months, and
  phulassō.
Mar.10.20.all these *have* I **o**-*ed* from
1Ti. 5.21. that thou **o.** these things
  poieō.
Act.16.21.neither to **o.**, being Romans

OBTAIN,   -*ed*, -*ing*.
  tungchanō.
Lu. 20.35. worthy *to* **o.** that world, and
Act.26.22. *Having* therefore **o**-*ed* help
2Ti. 2.10. they *may* also **o.** the salvati.
Heb. 8. 6. But now *hath* he **o**-*ed* a more
  11.35. that they *might* **o.** a better
  epitungchanō.
Ro. 11. 7. Israel *hath* not **o**-*ed* that
  but the election *hath* **o**-*ed* it
Heb. 6.15. endured, he **o**-*ed* the promi.
  11.33. **o**-*ed* promises, stopped the
Jas. 4. 2. desi. to have, and cannot **o.**
  langchanō.
Act. 1.17. *had* **o**-*ed* part of this ministry
2Pet. 1. 1. to them *that have* **o**-*ed* like
  ktaomai.
Act.22.28. With a great sum **o**-*ed* I this
  krateō.
Act.27.13. supposing *that* they *had* **o**-*ed*
  katalambanō.
1Co. 9.24. prize ? So run that ye *may* **o.**
  lambanō.
1Co. 9.25. to **o.** a corruptible crown
Heb. 4.16. that we *may* **o.** mercy, and
  klēroomai.
Eph. 1.11. also we *have* **o**-*ed* an inher.
  klēronomeō.
Heb. 1. 4. he *hath by inheritance* **o**-*ed*
  peripoiēsis.
1Th. 5. 9. but to **o.** salvation by our
2Th. 2.14. to the **o**-*ing* of the glory of
  heuriskō.
Heb. 9.12. *having* **o**-*ed* eternal redem.
  (See *Mercy, Report, Witness*.)

OCCASION.
  aphormē.
Ro. 7. 8, 11. taking **o.** by the comm.
2Co. 5.12. give you **o.** to glory on our
  11.12. **o.** from them wh. desire **o.**
Gal. 5.13. use not liberty for an **o.** to
1Ti. 5.14. give none **o.** to the adversary
  skandalon.
Ro. 14.13. or an **o.** *to fall* in his bro.
1Jo. 2.10. none **o.** of *stumbling* in him
  dia, [*gen.*]
2Co. 8. 8. *by* **o.** *of* the forwardness of

OCCUPATION.
  technē.
Act.18. 3. by their **o.** they were tent.

OCCUPY,   -*eth*, -*ied*.
  pragmateuomai.
Lu. 19.13. unto them, **o.** till I come
  anaplēroō.
1Co. 14.16. shall he *that* **o**-*eth* the room
  peripateō.
Heb.13. 9. them *that have* been **o**-*ed*

ODOUR,   -*s*
  osmē.
Jo. 12. 3. filled with the **o.** of the
Phi. 4.18. an **o.** of a sweet smell, a
  thumiama.
Rev. 5. 8. full of **o**-*s*, which are the
  18.13. cinnamon, and **o**-*s*, and

OF
  *In general represents the genitive of
  the Greek ; it is also used to translate
  the following :—*
  ek.
Mat. 1. 3. begat Phares and Zara **o.**
  5. begat Booz **o.** Rachab
  Booz begat Obed **o.** Ruth
  6. the king begat Solomon **o.**
  16. **o.** whom was born Jesus
  18. with child **o.** the Holy Gh.
  20. in her is **o.** the Holy Ghost
  3. 9. God is able **o.** these stones

Mat. 5.37. more than these cometh o.
6.27. Which o. you by taking
7. 9. Or what man is there o. you
10.29. one o. them shall not fall on
13.47. gathered o. every kind
18.12. one o. them be gone astray
21.25. from heaven, or o. men;
     Mar.11.30; Lu.20.4
    26. if we shall say, o. men; Mar.
     11.32 ; Lu.20.6
    31. Whether o. them twain did
22.35. Then one o. them which
23.25. are full o. extortion and
    34. some o. them ye shall kill
     Some o. them shall ye scour.
25. 2. five o. them were wise, and
    8. Give us o. your oil; for our
26.21. that one o. you shall betray
    27. saying, Drink ye all o. it
    29. henceforth o. this fruit of
    73. Surely thou also art one o.
Mar. 9.17. one o. the multitude answ.
11.14. No man eat fruit o. thee
12.44. o. their abund.; but she o.
14.18. One o. you which eateth
    20. one o. the twelve, that dip.
    23. they all drank o. it
    25. I will drink no more o. the
    69. that stood by, This is one o.
    70. Surely thou art one o. them
16.12. another form unto two o.
Lu. 1. 5. Zacharias, o. the course of
     and his wife was o. the dau.
    27. was Joseph, o. the house of
    35. which shall be born o. thee
2. 4. o. the house and lineage of
    35. that the thoughts o. many
    36. of Phanuel, o. the tribe of
3. 8. God is able o. these stones
6.44. For o. thorns men do not
     gather figs. nor o. a bramble
    45. for o. the abundance of the
10.11. the very dust o. your city
11. 5. Which o. you shall have a
    15. some o. them said, He cast.
    27. a certain woman o. the
    49. some o. them they shall slay
12. 6. not one o. them is forgotten
    13. one o. the company said unto
    15. in the abundance o. the
    25. which o. you with taking
14.28. which o. you, intending to
    33. whosoever he be o. you that
15. 4. What man o. you having an
     hund. sheep, if he lose one o.
16. 9. o. the mammon of unright.
17. 7. which o. you, having a serv.
    15. one o. them, when he saw
21. 4. these have o. their abund.
     she o. her penury hath cast
    16. some o. you shall they
    18. not an hair o. your head
22. 3. being o. the number of the
    23. which o. them it was that
    50. one o. them smote the serv.
    58. Thou art also o. them
23. 8. desirous to see him o. a
24.13. two o. them went that same
    22. certain women also o. our
Jo. 1.13. not o. blood, nor o. wi. of fl.
     o. the will of man, but o. G.
    16. o. his fulness have all we
    24. sent were o. the Pharisees
    35. John stood, and two o. his
    40. One o. the two which heard
2.15. made a scourge o. small
3. 1. There was a man o. the Ph.
    5. Except a man be born o. wa.
    6. That which is born o. the
     that which is born o. the
    8. every one that is born o.
    25. question between some o.
192

Jo. 3.31. he that is o. the earth is
     and speaketh o. the earth
4. 7. There cometh a woman o.
    13, 14. Whosoever drinketh o.
    22. for salvation is o. the Jews
    39. the Samaritans o. that city
6. 8. One o. his disciples, Andrew
    11. likewise o. the fishes as
    13. fragments o. the five barley
    26. because ye did eat o. the
    51. if any man eat o. this
    60. Many therefore o. his disci.
    64. some o. you that believe not
    65. given unto him o. my Father
    70. one o. you is a devil
    71. being one o. the twelve
7.17. whether it be o. God, or
    19. none o. you keepeth the law
    22. it is o. Moses, but o. the
    25. some o. them of Jerusalem
    31. many o. the people believed
    40. Many o. the people therefore
    42. cometh o. the seed of David
    44. some o. them would have
    48. Have any o. the rulers, or o.
    50. Jesus by night, being one o.
    52. Art thou also o. Galilee
8.23. o. this world ; I am not o.
    41. We be not born o. fornica.
    44. Ye are o. your father the
     he speaketh o. his own
    46. Which o. you convinceth me
    47. He that is o. God heareth
     because ye are not o. God
9. 6. made clay o. the spittle, and
    16. said some o. the Pharisees
    40. some o. the Pharisees which
10.16. which are not o. this fold
    20. many o. them said, He hath
    26. because ye are not o. my
11.19. many o. the Jews came to
    37. some o. them said, Could
    45. many o. the Jews which
    46. some o. them went their
    49. one o. them, named Caiap.
12. 4. Then saith one o. his discip.
    9. Much people o. the Jews
    49. I have not spoken o. myself
13.21. that one o. you shall betray
15.19. If we were o. the world, the
     because ye are not o. the
16. 5. none o. you asketh me
    14. for he shall receive o. mine
    15. that he shall take o. mine
    17. Then said some o. his discip.
17.12. none o. them is lost, but the
    14, 16. o. the world, even as _
     am not o. the world
18. 9. o. them which thou gavest
    17. also one o. this man's discip.
    25. Art not thou also one o. his
    26. One o. the servants of the
    36. My kingdom is not o. this
     if my kingdom were o. this
    37. Every one that is o. the
19. 2. soldiers platted a crown o.
20.24. Thomas, one o. the twelve
21. 2. two other o. his disciples
Act. 1.24. shew whether o. these two
2.30. that o. the fruit of his loins
3.22. raise up unto you o. your
4. 6. o. the kindred of the high
5.38. counsel or this work be o.
    39. if it be o. God, ye cannot
6. 9. arose certain o. the syna.
7.37. unto you o. your brethren
10. 1. a centurion o. the band
    45. they o. the circum.; 11.2
11.20. some o. them were men of
    28. there stood up one o. them
13.21. a man o. the tribe of Benja.
15. 2. certain other o. them, should

Act.15.21. Moses o. old time hath in
    22. to send chosen men o. their
    23. which are o. the Gentiles in
17. 4. some o. them believed, and
    12. Therefore many o. them
    26. hath made o. one blood all
20.30. Also o. your own selves sh.
21. 8. which was one o. the seven
22.14. hear the voice o. his mouth
23.21. o. them more than forty
    34. asked o. what province he
24.10. thou hast been o. many
Ro. 1. 3. made o. the seed of David
2.29. is not o. men, but o. God
4.12. not o. the circumcision only
    14. they which are o. the law
    16. Therefore it is o. faith, that
     not to that only which is o.
     to that also which is o. the
5.16. the free gift is o. many
9. 5. Wh. are the fathers, and o.
    6. not all Israel, which are o.
    11. not o. works, but o. him
    21. o. the same lump to make
    24. o. the Jews only, but also o.
    30. right. which is o. faith; 10.6
10. 5. which is o. the law; Phi. 3.9
11. 1. o. the seed of Abraham
    6. then is it no more o. works
     if it be o. works, then is it
    14. might save some o. them
    36. For o. him, and through him
13. 3. thou shalt have praise o. the
14.23. because he eateth not o. fai.
     whatsoever is not o. faith
16.10. which are o. Aristobulus'
    11. be o. the household of Nar.
1Co. 1.30. o. him are ye in Christ Jes.
2.12. the spirit which is o. God
7. 7. hath his proper gift o. God
8. 6. the Father, o. whom are all
9. 7. eateth not o. the fruit there.
     eateth not o. the milk of the
    13. live of the things o. the
    14. should live o. the gospel
10. 4. they drank o. that spiritual
    17. all partakers o. that one
11. 8. o. the wo.; but the woman o.
    12. as the woman is o. the man
     woman ; but all things o. G.
    28. o. that bread, and drink o.
12.15, 16. I am not o. the body
     is it therefore not o. the
15. 6. o. whom the greater part
    47. The first man is o. the earth
2Co. 2.17. as o. sincerity, but as o. G.
3. 5. think any thing as o. oursel.
     but our sufficiency is o. G.
4. 7. may be of God, and not o.
5. 1. we have a building o. God
    18. all things are o. God, who
9. 7. not grudgingly, or o. necess.
12. 6. or that he heareth o. me
Gal. 2.12. which were o. the circum.
    15. not sinners o. the Gentiles
3. 7. that they which are o. faith
    9. then they which be o. faith
    10. as are o. the works of the
    12. the law is not o. faith
    18. if the inheritance be o. the
     it is no more o. promise
4. 4. his Son, made o. a woman
    23. he who was o. the bondwo.
     he o. the freewoman was by
5. 8. cometh not o. him that
6. 8. shall o. the flesh reap corru.
     shall o. the Spirit reap life
Eph. 2. 8. that not o. yourselves, it is
    9. Not o. works, lest any man
3.15. o. whom the whole family
5.30. o. his flesh, and o. his bones
Phi. 1.16. one preach Christ o. conten

Phi. 1.17. the other o. love, knowing
3. 5. o. the stock of Israel
an Hebrew o. the Hebrews
9. righteousness which is o. God
4.22. they that are o. Cæsar's
Col. 4. 9. brother, who is one o. you
11. who are o. the circumcison
12. who is one o. you, a servant
¹Th. 2. 3. was not o. deceit, nor o.
6. Nor o. men sought we glory
²Ti. 2. 8. Jesus Christ o. the seed of
3. 6. For o. this sort are they wh.
Tit. 1.10. specially they o. the circum.
12. One o. themselves, even a
2. 8. he that is o. the contrary
Heb. 2.11. sanctified are all o. one
3.13. lest any o. you be hardened
4. 1. any o. you should seem to
7. 5. they that are o. the sons of
12. there is made o. necessity
11. 3. not made o. things which
Jas. 2.16. one o. you say unto them
4. 1. o. your lusts that war in
¹Pet. 1.23. not o. corruptible seed, but
4.11. as o. the ability which God
¹Jo. 2.16. is not o. the Father, but is o.
19. o. us; for if they had been o.
that they were not all o. us
21. that no lie is o. the truth
29. doeth righteousn. is born o.
3. 8. that committeth sin is o. the
9. whoso. is born o. God; 5.18
because he is born o. God
10. not righteousn. is not o. God
12. Cain, who was o. that wicked
19. we know that we are o. the
4. 1. whether they are o. God
2. come in the flesh is o. God
3. in the flesh is not o. God
4. Ye are o. God, little child.
5. They are o. the world: th.
speak they o. the world
6. We are o. God: he that
he that is not o. God hear.
7. love one ano.: for love is o.
that loveth is born o. God
13. he hath given us o. his Spirit
5. 1. is the Christ is born o. God
also that is begotten o. him
4. whatsoever is born o. God
18. but he that is begotten o.
19. we know that we are o. God
²John 4. that I found o. thy children
³John 11. He that doeth good is o. God
Rev. 1. 5. the first begotten o. the dead
2. 7. to eat o. the tree of life, wh.
10. the devil shall cast some o.
11. shall not be hurt o. the
17. I give to eat o. the hidden
21. to repent o. her fornication
22. except they repent o. their
3. 9. them o. the synagogue of
5. 5. one o. the elders saith unto
the Lion o. the tribe of Juda
6. 1. the Lamb opened one o. the
one o. the four beasts saying
7. 4. o. all the tribes of the child.
5, 6,7,8. o. the tribe of Juda
o. the tribe of Reuben, &c.
9. o. all nations, and kindreds
13. one o. the elders answered
8.11. many men died o. the waters
9.20. repented not o. the works of
21. o. their murders, nor o.
o. their fornication, nor o.
11. 9. they o. the people and kind.
14. 8. made all nations drink o.
10. same shall drink o. the wine
15. 7. one o. the four beasts gave
16.11. because o. their pains and th.
and repented not o. of their
17. 1. came one o. the seven angels

Rev.17.11. is o. the seven, and goeth
18. 3. have drunk o. the wine of
4. receive not o. her plagues
12. vessels o.most precious wood
21. 6. o. the fountain of the water
21. every several gate was o. one
peri, [gen.]
Mat.11.10.o. whom it is written; Lu.7.27
15. 7. did Esaias prophesy o. you
17.13. spake unto them o. John the
21.45. perceived that he spake o.
22.42. What think ye o. Christ
24.36. But o. that day and hour
26.24. it is written o.him;Mar.14.21
Mar. 1.30. anon they tell him o. her
4.19. and the lusts o. other things
5.27. When she had heard o. Jes.
7. 6. prophesied o. you hypocrites
25. heard o. him, and came and
8.30. should tell no man o. him
10.10. asked him again o. the same
13.32. But o. that day and that
Lu. 1. 1. a declaration o. those things
2.33. things which were spoken o.
38. spake o. him to all them
3.15. mused in their hearts o. Jo.
4.14. fame o. him through all the
37. fame o. him went out into
5.15. there a fame abroad o. him
7. 3. when he heard o. Jesus, he
17. this rumour o. him went for.
18. shewed him o. all these thin.
9. 9. o. whom I hear such things
11. spake unto them o. the king.
45. to ask him o. that saying
11.53. provoke him to speak o.
13. 1. told him o. the Galilæans
16. 2. How is it that I hear this o.
21. 5. And as some spake o. the
23. 8. had heard many things o.
24.14. talked together o. all these
Jo. 1. 7, 8. to bear witness o. the Light
15. John bare witness o. him
22. What sayest thou o. thyself
30. This is he o. whom I said
47. saith o. him, Behold an Isr.
2.21. spake o. the temple of his
25. testify o. man; for he knew
5.31. If I bear witness o. myself
32. ano. that bear. witness o.me;
36,37; 8.18; 10.25
39. they which testify o. me
46. for he wrote o. me
7. 7. I testify o. it, that the works
13. no man spake openly o. him
17. he shall know o. the doctrine
39. this spake he o. the Spirit
8.13. Thou bearest record o. thy.
14. Though I bear record o. my.
18. one that bear witness o. my.
26. to say and to judge o. you
46. of you convinceth me o. sin
9.17. What sayest thou o. him
10.41. that John spake o. this man
11.13. Jesus spake o. his death
spoken o. taking of rest in
12.41. his glory and spake o. him
13.18. I speak not o. you all
22, 24. doubting o. whom he
15.26. he shall testify o. me
16. 8. he will reprove the world o.
and o. righteo., and o. jud.
9. o. sin, because they believe
10. o. righteousness, because I
11. o. judgment, because the
19. among yourselves o. that I
25. I shall shew you plainly o.
18.19. o. his disciples, and o. his
23. bear witness o. the evil
34. did others tell it thee o. me
21.24. which testifieth o. these th.
Act. 1. 1. have I made, O Theo., o. all

Act. 2.29. unto you o. the patriarch
31. spake o. the resurrection
5.24. they doubted o. them
7.52. shewed before o. the coming
8.34. o. whom speaketh the pro.
o. himself, or o. some
9.13. heard by many o. this man
11.22. Then tidings o. these things
13.29. all that was written o. him
15. 6. to consider o. this matter
17.32. hear thee again o. this
18.15. a question o. words and
25. diligently the things o. the
21.21. And they are informed o.
22.10. told thee o. all things wh.
23. 6. o. the hope and resurrection
11. thou hast testified o. me in
20. enquire somewhat o. him
29. accused o. questions of their
24. 8. take knowledge o. all these
22. more perfect knowledge o.
25. reasoned o. righteousness
25. 9. there be judged o. these
19. o. their own super. and o.
20. I doubted of such manner o.
(as to the question concerning this.)
and there be judged o
26. o. whom I have no certain
26.26. knoweth o. these things
28.15. the brethren heard o. us
21. or spake any harm o. thee
Ro. 14.12. shall give account o. himself
15.14. am persuaded o. you, my
¹Co. 1.11. declared unto me o. you
²Co. 10. 8. boast somewhat more o. our
¹Th. 1. 9. they themselves shew o. us
4. 6. the avenger o. all such
5. 1. But o. the times and the
²Ti. 1. 3. I have remembrance o. thee
Tit. 2. 8. no evil thing to say o. you
Heb. 4. 4. spake in a certain place o.
8. have spoken o. another day
5.11. o. whom we have many
6. 9. persuaded better things o.
9. 5. o. which we cannot now
10. 7. it is written o. me
11. 7. warned of God o. things not
22. mention o. the departing of
32. would fail me to tell o. Ged.
¹Pet. 1.10. o. which salvation the pro.
prophesied o. the grace that
3.15. a reason o. the hope that
²Pet. 1.12. in remembrance o. these
3.16. speaking in them o. these
¹Jo. 1. 1. have handled, o. the Word
2.27. teacheth you o. all things
5. 9. he hath testified o. his Son
10. that God gave o. his Son
Jude 3. to write unto you o. the
15. o. all their ungodly deeds
and o. all their hard speech.
apo.
Mat. 3. 4. had his raiment o. camel's
5.42. him that would borrow o.
7.15. Beware o. false prophets
16. Do..grapes o. thorns, or figs
10.17. But beware o. men: for they
11.19. justified o. her child.;Lu.7.35
29. yoke upon you, and learn o.
15. 1. which were o. Jerusalem
27. eat o. the crumbs which fall
16. 6, 11.bew.o. the leaven; Lu.12.1
12. o. the leaven of bread, but o.
21. suffer many things o. the
17.25. o. whom do the kings of the
o. their own children, or o.
26. Peter saith unto them, o.
21.11. the prophet o. Nazareth of
24.32. learn a parable o. the fig
27. 9. they o. the children of Isra.
21. Whether o. the twain will
24. I am innocent o. the blood

Mat.27.57.came a rich man o. Arima.
Mar. 5.29. that she was healed o. that
34. in peace, and be whole o.
6.43. of the fragments, and o. the
7.28. under the table eat o. the
8.31. be rejected o. the ; Lu.9.22
12. 2. o. the fruit of the vineyard
38. Beware o. the scribes, wh.
15.43. Joseph o. Arimathæa, an
45. when he knew it o. the cen.
Lu. 5.15. healed by him o. their infir.
6.13. o. them he chose twelve
17. to be healed o. their diseases
30. o. him that taketh away thy
7.21. cured many o. their infirm.
8. 2. had been healed o. evil sp.
9.38. behold, a man o. the comp.
11.50, 51. be required o. this gen.
12. 4. Be not afraid o. them that
15. Take heed, and beware o.
20. thy soul shall be required o.
57. why even o. yourselves judge
17.25. be rejected o. this generation
18. 3. Avenge me o. mine adver.
20.10. should give him o. the fruit
46. Beware o. the scribes, which
21.30. know o. your own selves
22.18. not drink o. the fruit of the
71. ourselves have heard o. his
23.51. he was o. Arimathæa, a
24.42. broiled fish, and o. an honey.
Jo. 1.44. Philip was o. Bethsaida, the
45. Jesus o. Nazareth the son
5.19. The Son can do nothing o.
30. I can o. mine own self do
7.17. or whether I speak o. myself
18. He that speaketh o. himself
28. I am not come o. myself
8.28. that I do nothing o. myself
42. neither came I o. myself
10.18. I lay it down o. myself
11. 1. named Lazarus, o Bethany
51. this spake he not o. himself
12.21. which was o. Bethsaida, of
14.10. unto you I speak not o. my.
15. 4. the branch can. bear fruit o.
16.13. for he shall not speak o.
18.34. Sayest thou this thing o.
19.38. after this Joseph o. Arima.
21. 2. Nathanael o. Cana in Galil.
10. Bring o. the fish which ye
Act. 2.17. I will pour out o. my Spirit
18. in those days o. my Spirit
22. a man approved o. God
5. 2, 3. back part o. the price
6. 9. Alexan., and of them o. Cil.
8.22. Repent therefore o. this thy
10.38. God anointed Jesus o. Naz.
12. 1. to vex certain o. the church
13.23. o. this man's seed hath God
15. 5. certain o. the sect of the Pha.
17.13. when the Jews o. Thessalo.
19.13. Then certain o. the vagabo.
21.16. certain of the disciples o.
27. the Jews which were o. Asia
23.34. under. that he was o. Cilicia
27.44. some on broken pieces o. the
Ro. 13. 1. there is no power but o. God
1Co. 1.30. who o. God is made unto us
4. 5. every man have praise o.
6.19. which ye have o. God, and
11.23. I have received o. the Lord
2Co. 2. sorrow from them o. whom
3. 5. to think any thing as o. our.
10. 7. let him o. himself think
Gal. 1. 1. Paul, an apostle, not o. men
2. 6. o. those who seemed to be
3. 2. This only would I learn o.
Phi. 1.28. of salvation, and that o. G.
Col. 1. 7. As ye also learned o. Epap.
3.24. that o. the Lord ye shall
1Th. 2. 6. neither o. you, nor yet o.

1Ti. 3. 7. a good report o. them which
Heb. 7. 2. Abra. gave a tenth part o. all
13. o. which no man gave atten.
11.12. sprang there even o. one
12.15. lest any man fail o. the gra.
13.24. They o. Italy salute you
Jas. 1.13. tempted, I am tempted o.
5. 4. which is o. you kept back
1Jo. 1. 5. mes. which we have heard o.
2.27. which ye have received o.
3John 7. taking nothing o. the Gent.
Rev. 2.17. I give to eat o. the hidden
12. 6. hath a place prepared o. God
16.12. the way of the kings o. the
hupo, [gen.]
Mat. 1.22. spoken o. the Lord by ; 2.15
2.16. that he was mocked o. the
3. 6. And were bapti. o. ; Mar.1.5
13. unto John, to be baptized o.
14. I have need to be baptized o.
4. 1. led up o. the spirit ; Lu.8.29
to be tempted o. the devil
5.13. trodden under foot o. men
6. 2. that they may have glory o.
10.22. and ye shall be hated o. all
11.27. are delivered unto me o. my
14. 8. being before instructed o. her
17.12. also the Son of man suffer o.
19.12. which were made eunuchs o.
20.23. for whom it is prepared o.
23. 7. to be called o. men, Rabbi
24. 9. ye shall be hated o. all natio.
27.12. And when he was accused o.
Mar. 1. 9. and was baptized o. John in
13. forty days, tempt. o. ; Lu.4.2
2. 3. which was borne o. four
5.26. suffered many things o. ma.
13.13. ye shall be hated o. ; Lu.21.17
16.11. and had been seen o. her, be.
Lu. 2.21. which was so named o. the
3. 7. came forth to be baptized o.
4.15. synagogues, being glorified o.
7.30. being not baptized o. him
8.43. neither could be healed o.
9. 7. it was said o. some, that Jo.
8. And o. some, that Elias had
10.22. are delivered to me o. my F.
14. 8. art bidden o. any man to a
than thou be bidden o. him
17.20. when he was demanded o.
21.24. be trodden down o. the Gen.
Jo. 10.14. sheep, and am known o. m.
14.21. shall be loved o. my Father
Act. 2.24. that he should be holden o.
4.11. which was set at nought o.
10.33. that are commanded thee o.
38. all that were oppressed o. the
41. unto witnes. chosen before o.
42. it is he which was ordain. o.
12. 5. without ceasing o. the chur.
15. 4. they were received o. the ch.
16. 4. that were ordained o. the ap.
6. and were forbidden o. the
14. things which were spoken o.
17.13. word of God was preached o.
21.35. that he was borne o. the sol.
22.11. led by the hand o. them that
12. having a good report o. all
23.10. have been pulled in pieces o.
27. This man was taken o. the
should have been killed o.
24.26. have been given him o. Paul
26. 2, 7. I am accused o. the Jews
6. of the promise made o. God
Ro. 12.21. Be not overcome o. evil, but
13. 1. that be are ordained o. God
15.15. grace that is given to me o.
1Co. 2.12. that are freely given to us o.
15. yet he himself is judged o.
4. 3. should be judg. o. you, or o.
6.12. brought under the power o.
7.25. that hath obtained mercy o.

1Co. 8. 3. the same is known o. him
10. 9. and were destroyed o. serp.
10. destroyed o. their destroyer
29. judged o. another man's con.
11.32. we are chastened o. the Lord
14.24. convinced o. all, he is judg. o.
2Co. 1. 4. we ourselves are comfort. o.
16. and o. you to be brought on
2. 6. which was inflicted o. many
11. should get an advantage o.
(be taken advantage of by.)
3. 2. known and read o. all men
5. 4. might be swallowed up o. life
8.19. who was also chosen o. the
11.24. o. the Jews five times receiv.
12.11. to have been commended o.
Gal. 1.11. gospel which was preached o.
3.17. confirmed before o. God in
4. 9. or rather are known o. God
5.15. ye be not consumed one o.
Eph. 5.12. which are done o. them in
Phi. 3.12. I am apprehended o. Christ
1Th. 1. 4. beloved, your election o. God
2. 4. But as we were allowed o. G.
14. like things o. your own cou.
as they have o. the Jews
2Th. 2.13. brethren beloved o. the Lord
Heb. 5. 4. but he that is called o. God
10. Called o. God an high priest
7. 7. the less is blessed o. the bet.
11.23. hid three months o. his pare.
12. 3. endured such contradiction o.
5. when thou art rebuked o. him
Jas. 1.14. he is drawn away o. his own
2. 9. and are convinced o. the law
3. 4. and are driven o. fierce win.
6. and it is set on fire o. hell
1Pet. 2. 4. disallowed indeed o. men
3John 12. o. all men, and o. the truth
Jude 12. carried about o. winds
17. were spoken before o. the
Rev. 6.13. when she is shaken o. a mi.
para, [gen.]
Mat. 2. 4. demanded o. them where C.
7. enquired o. them diligently
16. enquired o. the wise men
6. 1. no reward o. your Father
18.19. be done for them o. my Fat.
20.20. desiring a certain thing o.
Mar. 8.11. seeking o. him a ; Lu. 11.16
Lu. 6.19. there went virtue out o. him
34. ye lend to them o. whom ye
12.48. o. him shall be much requir.
Jo. 1.14. the only begotten o. the Fat.
4. 9. askest drink o. me, which
52. Then enquired he o. them
5.44. receive honour one o. anoth.
6.45. and hath learned o. the Fat.
46. save he which is o. God
8.26. which I have heard o. him
40. which I have heard o. God
9.16. This man is not o. God
33. If this man were not o. God
10.18. have I received o. my Father
15.15. that I have heard o. my Fat.
17. 7. thou hast given me are o. th.
Act. 2.33. having received o. the Father
3. 2. to ask alms o. them that
5. to receive something o. them
7.16. money o. the sons of Emmor
9. 2. And desired o. him letters
10.22. and to hear words o. thee
17. 9. they had taken security o.
20.24. I have received o. the Lord
22.30. he was accused o. the Jews
26.22. obtained help o. God, I
28.22. we desire to hear o. thee wh.
Gal. 1.12. I neither received it o. man
Eph. 6. 8. the same shall he receive o.
Phi. 4.18. received of Epaphroditus the
1Th. 2.13. which ye heard o. us
4. 1. as ye have received o. us

²Th. 3. 6. which he received **o**. us
²Ti. 1.13. whi. thou hast heard **o**. ; 2.2
   18. may find mercy **o**. the Lord
   3.14. knowing **o**. whom thou hast
Jas. 1. 5. let him ask **o**. God, that
   7. receive any thing **o**. the Lord
¹Pet. 2. 4. chosen **o**. God, and precious
¹Jo. 3.22. we ask, we receive **o**. him
   5.15. that we desired **o**. him
Rev. 2.27. as I received **o**. my Father
   3.18. to buy **o**. me gold tried in
epi.
Mat.18.13.more **o**. that sheep, than
   o. the ninety and nine
Mar. 6.52. not the miracle **o**. the
   9.12. how it is written **o**. the Son
   13. as it is written **o**. him
Lu. 4.25. I tell you **o**. a truth
   22.59. **o**. a truth this fellow also
Jo. 12.16. these things were written **o**.
Act. 4. 9. examined **o**. the good deed
   27. For **o**. a truth against thy
   10.34. **o**. a truth I perceive that
¹Co. 16.17. I am glad **o**. the coming of
²Co. 12.21. not repented **o**. the unclean.
Gal. 3.16. as **o**. many; but as **o**. one
Heb. 7.13. For he **o**. whom these things
   8. 1. Now **o**. the things which we
   11. 4. God testifying **o**. his gifts
Rev. 8.13. to the inhabiters **o**. the earth
huper, [gen.]
²Co. 1. 7. And our hope **o**. you is sted.
   8. have you ignorant of our tro.
   7. 4. great is my glorifying **o**. you
   14. boasted any thing to him **o**.
   8.23. Whether any do enquire **o**.
   9. 2. for which I boast **o**. you to
   3. lest our boasting **o**. you sho.
   12. 5. **o**. such an one will I glory
   yet **o**. myself I will not glory
Phi. 1. 7. to think this **o**. you all
   2.13. to do **o**. his good pleasure
   4.10. your care **o**. me hath flouris.
en.
Lu. 1.61. There is none **o**. thy kind.
Act.26.20. first unto them **o**. Damascus
Ro. 2.17. makest thy boast **o**. God
   23. makest thy boast **o**. the law
   11. 2. the scripture saith **o**. Elias
²Co. 2.12. opened unto me **o**. the Lord
   10.15. Not boasting..**o**. other men's
Gal. 4.20. for I stand in doubt **o**. you
Eph. 4. 1. the prisoner **o**. the Lord
Tit. 3. 5. Not by works **o**. righteous.
Jas. 5.19. if any **o**. yeu do err from the
²Pet. 2.12. speak evil **o**. the things that
eis.
Mat. 5.22. shall be in danger **o**. hell fire
Act.25.20. **o**. such manner of questions
²Co.10.13. not boast **o**. things without
   15. boasting **o**. things without
   16. **o**. things made ready to our
   12. 6. should think **o**. me above
Heb. 7.14. **o**. which tribe Moses spake
¹Pet. 1.11. beforehand the sufferings **o**.
kata, [accu.]
Act.18.15. **o**. your law, look ye to it
   27. 5. sailed over the sea **o**. Cilicia
Ro. 4. 4. reckon. **o**. grace, but **o**. debt
¹Co. 7. 6. and not **o**. commandment
   15.15. we have testified **o**. God
Phile. 14. as it were **o**. necessity, but
dia, [gen.]
Mat. 4. 4. proceedeth out **o**. the mouth
Ro. 14.14. nothing unclean **o**. itself
Phi. 1.15. pre. Ch. even **o**. [accu.] envy
   some **o**. [accu.] good will
pros, [accu.]
Heb. 1. 7. And **o**. the angels he saith
   11.18. **o**. whom it was said, That
meta, [gen.]
Mat.18.23. take account **o**. his servants

OFF.
apo.   [Mar.14.54
Mat.26.58.Peter followed him afar **o**.
   27.55. were there beholding afar **o**.
Mar. 5. 6. when he saw Jesus afar **o**.
   15.40. also women look. on afar **o**.
Lu. 16.23. seeth Abraham afar **o**., and
Jo. 11.18. about fifteen furlongs **o**.
Rev.18.10. Standing afar **o**. for fear of
   17. as trade by sea, stood afar **o**.
ek.
Mar. 11.8. cut down branches **o**. the
(See words in connection.)

OFFENCE,   -s.
skandalon.
Mat.16.23.thou art an **o**. unto me : for
   18. 7. the world because of **o**-s..
   that **o**-s come..the **o**. cometh
Lu. 17. 1. but that **o**-s will come ; but
Ro. 9.33. stumbl...rock of **o**. ; ¹Pet.2.8
   16.17. which cause divisions and **o**-s
Gal. 5.11. then is the **o**. of the cross ce.
paraptōma.
Ro. 4.25. Who was delive. for our **o**-s
   5.15. But not as the **o**., so also is
   For if through the **o**. of one
   16. free gift is of many **o**-s unto
   17. For if by one man's **o**. death
   18. Therefore as by the **o**. of one
   20. the law entered, that the **o**.
aproskopos.
Act.24.16. a conscience *void of* **o**. towa.
¹Co.10.32. Give *none* **o**., neither to the
Phi. 1.10. *without* **o**. till the day of Ch.
proskomma.
Ro. 14.20. that man who eateth with **o**.
proskopē.
²Co. 6. 3. giving no **o**. in anything
hamartia.
²Co. 11. 7. Have I committed an **o**. in

OFFEND,   -ed.
skandalizō.
Mat. 5.29. if thy right eye **o**. thee
   30. right hand **o**. thee ; Mar.9.43
   11. 6. shall not *be* **o**-ed ; Lu. 7.23
   13.21. word, by and by he *is* **o**-ed
   57. And they *were* **o**-ed in him
   15.12. that the Pharisees *were* **o**-ed
   17.27. lest we *should* **o**. them, go ≠
   18. 6. whoso shall **o**. one ; Mar.9.42
   8. if thy hand or thy foot **o**. th.
   9. And if thine eye **o**.; Mar.9.47
   24.10. And then *shall* many *be* **o**-ed
   26.31. ye *shall be* **o**-ed ; Mar. 14.47
   33. men *shall be* **o**-ed ; Mar.14.29
   thee, yet *will* I never be **o**-ed
Mar. 4.17. immediately they *are* **o**-ed
   6. 3. And they *were* **o**-ed at him
   9.45. And if thy foot **o**. thee, cut
Lu. 17. 2. than that he *should* **o**. one
Jo. 6.61. unto them, *Doth* this **o**. you
   16. 1. that ye *should* not be **o**-ed
Ro. 14.21. stumbleth, or *is* **o**-ed, or is
¹Co. 8.13. *make* my brother *to* **o**.
²Co.11.29. who *is* **o**-ed, and I burn not
skandalon.
Mat. 13.41. all *things that* **o**., and them
ptaiō.
Jas. 2.10. law, and yet **o**. in one point
   3. 2. many things we **o**. (all *offend*)
   If any man **o**. not in word
hamartano.
Act.25. 8. *have* I **o**-ed anything at all

OFFENDER.
adikeō.
Act.25.11. For if I *be an* **o**., or have

OFFER, (See *Idols*,)   -ed, -ing.
prospherō.
Mat. 5.24. then come and **o**. thy gift

Mat. 8. 4. and **o**. the gift that Moses
Mar. 1.44. and **o**. for thy clea. ; Lu.5.14
Lu. 23.36. him, and **o**-*ing* him vinegar
Act. 7.42. *have* ye **o**-ed to me slain bea.
   8.18. given, he **o**-ed them money
   21.26. that an offeri. *should be* **o**-ed
Heb. 5. 1. that he *may* **o**. both gifts and
   3. so also for himself, *to* **o**. for
   7. *when* he had **o**-ed up prayers
   8. 3. *to* **o**. gifts and sacrifices
   man have somewhat also to **o**.
   4. priests *that* **o**. gifts according
   9. 7. which he **o**-ed for himself
   9. in which *were* **o**-ed both gifts
   14. **o**-ed himself without spot
   25. yet that he *should* **o**. himself
   28. So Christ *was* once **o**-ed to
   10. 1. which they **o**-ed year by year
   2. not have ceased *to be* **o**-ed
   8. which *are* **o**-ed by the law
   11. and **o**-*ing* oftentimes the sa.
   12. *after* he had **o**-ed one sacrifi.
   11. 4. By faith Abel **o**-ed *unto* God
   17. when he was tried, **o**-ed *up*
   o. *up* his only begotten son
anapherō.
Heb. 7.27. high priests, *to* **o**. *up* sacrifice
   once, *when* he **o**-ed *up* hims.
   13.15. *let* us **o**. the sacrifice of prai.
Jas. 2.21. *when* he had **o**-ed Isaac his
¹Pet. 2. 5. *to* **o**. *up* spiritual sacrifices
didōmi.
Lu. 2.24. *to* **o**. a sacrifice according to
Rev. 8. 3. *should* **o**. it with the prayers
epididōmi.
Lu. 11.12. *will* he **o**. him a scorpion
spendō.
Phi. 2.17. yea, and if I *be* **o**-ed upon
²Ti. 4. 6. I am now *ready to be* **o**-ed
parechō.
Lu. 6.29. one cheek, **o**. also the other
anagō.
Act. 7.41. **o**-ed sacrifice unto the idol
prosphora.
Ro. 15.16. the **o**-*ing up* of the Gentiles

OFFERING, [noun,]   -s.
prosphora.
Act.21.26. until that an **o**. should be
   24.17. alms to my nation, and **o**-s
Eph. 5. 2. an **o**. and a sacrifice to God
Heb.10. 5. Sacrifice and **o**. thou would.
   8. Sacrifice and **o**. and burnt
   10. through the **o**. of the body
   14. by one **o**. he hath perfected
   18. there is no more **o**. for sin.
dōron.
Lu. 21. 4. cast in unto the **o**-s of God
   (See *Burnt*.)

OFFICE.
diakonia.
Ro. 11.13. Gentiles, I magnify mine **o**.
praxis.
Ro. 12. 4. all mem. have not the same **o**.
   (See *Bishop*, *Priest*, *Priesthood*.)

OFFICER,   -s.
hupēretēs.
Mat. 5.25. judge deliver thee to the **o**.
Jo. 7.32. and the chief priests sent **o**-s
   45. Then came the **o**-s to the ch.
   46. The **o**-s answered, Never man
   18. 3. receiv. a band of men and **o**-s
   12. band and the captain and **o**-s
   18. And the servants and **o**-s sto.
   22. one of the **o**-s which stood
   19. 6. chief priests theref. and **o**-s
Act. 5.22. But when the **o**-s came, and
   26. went the captain with the **o**
praktōr.
Lu. 12.58. to the **o**., and the **o**. cast

OFFSCOURING.
peripsēma.
¹Co. 4.13. the o. of all things unto this

OFFSPRING.
genos.
Act.17.28. said, For we are also his o.
29. then as we are the o. of God
Rev.22.16. the root and o. of David

OFT, (See *At.*)
pollakis.
Mat.17.15.fire, and o. into the water
Act.26.11. punished them o. in every
²Co.11.23. more frequent, in deaths o.
²Ti. 1.16. for he o. refreshed me, and
Heb.6. 7. rain that cometh o. upon it
polus.
Mat. 9.14. we and the Pharisees fast o.
posakis.
Mat.18.21. *how* o. shall my brother sin
pugmē.
Mar. 7. 3. they wash their hands o.
(with the fist.)

OFTEN, (See *As.*)
pollakis.
Mar. 5. 4. had been o. bound with fet.
²Co. 11.26. In journeyings o., in perils
27. in watchings o., in hunger
in fastings o., in cold and
Phi. 3.18. of whom I have told you o.
Heb. 9.25. he should offer himself o.
26. For then must he o. have
posakis. [Lu.13.34
Mat.23.37.*how* o. would I have gather.;
puknos, [*compar.*]
Lu. 5.33. the disciples of John fast o.
¹Ti. 5.23. and thine o. infirmities

OFTENER.
puknos.
Act.24.26. he sent for him *the* o., and

OFTENTIMES.
pollakis.
Ro. 1.13. that o. I purposed to come
²Co. 8.22. whom we o. proved
Heb.10.11.offering o. the same sacrifice
polus chronos.
Lu. 8.29. for o. it had caught him

OFTTIMES.
pollakis.
Mat.17.15.for o. he falleth into the fire
Mar. 9.22. And o. it hath cast him into
Jo. 18. 2. for Jesus o. resorted thither

OIL.
elaion.
Mat.25. 3. and took no o. with them
4. the wise took o. in their ves.
8. Give us of your o.; for our
Mar. 6.13. anointed with o. many that
Lu. 7.46. My head with o. thou didst
10.34. pouring in o. and wine, and
16. 6. An hundred measures of o.
Heb.1. 9. with the o. of gladness above
Jas. 5.14. anointing him with o. in the
Rev. 6. 6. hurt not the o. and the wine
18.13. wine, and o., and fine flour

OINTMENT, -s.
muron.
Mat.26. 7. of very precious o., and
9. For this o. might have been
12. hath poured this o. on my
Mar.14. 3. an alabas. box of o.; Lu.7.37
4. this waste of the o. made
Lu. 7.38. anointed them with the o.
46. anointed my feet with o.
196

Lu. 23.56. and prepared spices and o-s
Jo. 11. 2. anointed the Lord with o.
12. 3. took Mary a pound of o.
filled with the odour of the o.
5. Why was not this o. sold
Rev.18.13. odours, and o-s, and frank.

OLD.
palaios.
Mat. 9.16. new cloth unto an o. garm.;
Mar.2.21; Lu.5.36
17. new wine into o. bottles ;
Mar.2.22; Lu.5.37
13.52. treasure things new and o.
Mar. 2.21. taketh away from the o.
Lu. 5.36. agreeth nôt with the o.
39. No man also having drunk o.
for he saith, The o. is better
Ro. 6. 6. our o. man is crucified with
¹Co. 5. 7. Purge out therefore the o.
8. not with o. leaven, neither
²Co. 3.14. in the reading of the o. test.
Eph. 4.22. the o. man, which is corrupt
Col. 3. 9. ye have put off the o. man
¹Jo. 2. 7. but an o. commandment
The o. commandment is the
archaios.
Mat. 5.21, 27,33. said by *them of* o. time
Lu. 9. 8, 19. one of the o. prophets
Act.15.21. For Moses of o. time hath
21.16. Mnason of Cyprus, an o.
²Co. 5.17. o. things are passed away
²Pet. 2. 5. spared not the o. world, but
Rev.12. 9. that o. serpent, 20.2
palai.
²Pet. 1. 9. purged from his o. sins
Jude 4. were before *of* o. ordained to
ekpalai.
²Pet. 3. 5. the heavens were *of* o., and
palaioō.
Lu. 12.33. bags *which wax* not o., a
Heb.1.11. they all *shall wax* o. as doth
8.13. he *hath made* the first o.
gerōn.
Jo. 3. 4. man be born when he is o.
presbuteros.
Act. 2.17. your o. men shall dream
presbutēs.
Lu. 1.18. for I am an o. *man*, and my
gēras.
Lu. 1.36. conceived a son in her o. *age*
gēraskō.
Jo. 21.18. when thou *shalt be* o., thou
Heb. 8.13. wh. decayeth and *waxeth* o.
chronos.
Act. 7.23. full forty years o., it came
pote.
¹Pet. 3. 5. this manner *in the* o. time
²Pet. 1.21. prophesy came not *in* o. time

OLDNESS.
palaiotēs.
Ro. 7. 6. not in the o. of the letter

OLIVE BERRIES.
elaia.
Jas. 3.12. fig tree, my brethren, bear o.

OLIVE TREE, -s.
elaia.
Ro. 11.17. root and fatness of the o.
24. graffed into their own o.
Rev.11. 4. These are the two o-s and
agrielaios.
Ro. 11.17. thou, being a *wild* o. wert
24. out of the o. *which is wild*
kallielaios.
Ro. 11.24. nature into a *good* o.

OLIVES.
elaia.
Mat.21. 1. unto the mount of o. [13.
24. 3. upon the mount of o.; Mar.3

Mar.26.30. out into the mount of o.;
Mar.14.26; Lu.22.39; Jo.8.1
Mar.11, 1. at the mount of o., he send.
Lu. 19.29. called the mount of o.; 21.37
37. the descent of the mount of o.

OMEGA.
ō.
Rev. 1, 8, 11. I am Alpha and o.; [21.6,22.13

OMITTED.
aphiēmi.
Mat.23.23. and *have* o. the weightier

OMNIPOTENT.
pantokratōr.
Rev.19. 6. the Lord God o. reigneth

ON.
epi.
Mat. 4. 5. o. a pinnacle of the temple
5.15. but o. a candlestick
39. smite thee o. thy right cheek
45. sun to rise o. the evil
(*And all other passages in which it occurs, except the following :—*)
eis.
Mat.27.30.reed, and smote him o. the
Mar. 4. 8. other fell o. good ground, and
8.23. when he had spit o. his eyes
14. 6. hath wrought a good work o.
Lu. 6.20. he lifted up his eyes o. his
8.23. a storm of wind o. the lake
12.49. come to send fire o. the earth
15.22. o. his hand, and shoes o. his
Jo. 1.12. them that believe o. his
2.11. his disciples believed o. him
3.18, 36.He that believeth o.; 6.35,
47, 7.38, 12.46, 14.12; ¹Jo.5.10
4.39. believed o. him for the say.
6.29. believe o. him whom he
40. the Son, and believeth o.
7.31. of the people believed o. him;
8.30, 10.42, 12.42
39. they that believe o. him
48. Pharisees believed o. him
8, 6, 8. wrote o. the ground
9.35. thou believe o. the Son of G.
36. that I might believe o. him
11.45. which Jesus did, believed o.
48. all men will believe o. him
12.11. went away, and believed o.
37. yet they believed not o. him
44. believe. o. me, believe. not o.
but o. him that sent me
13.22. disciples looked one o. anot.
16. 9. bec. they believe not o. me
17.20. which shall believe o. me
19.37. They shall look o. him whom
21. 4. Jesus stood o. the shore
6. Cast the net o. the right side
Act. 6.15. looking stedfastly o. him
13. 9. Holy Ghost, set his eyes o.
14.23. the Lord, o. whom they bel.
19. 4. believe o. him which should
him, that is, o. Christ Jesus
Ro. 16. 6. bestowed much labour o. us
²Co.11.20. if a man smite you o. the fa.
Gal. 3.14. might come o. the Gentiles
Eph. 4. 8. When he ascended up o. high
Phi. 1.29. not only to believe o. him
¹Jo. 5.13. believe o. the name of the
Rev.13.13.down from heaven o. the
en.
Mat.22.40.o. these two commandments
24.20. neither o. the sabbath day
26. 5. o. the feast day ; Mar.14.2
Mar. 2.23. through the corn fields o. the
24. why do they o. the sabbath
16. 5. man sitting o. the right side
Lu. 1.59. that o. the eighth day they
4.16. o. the sabbath day, and stood
31. taught them o. the sabbath

Lu. 5.17. pass o. a certain day ; Lu.8.22
6. 1. came to pass o. the second
2. to do o. the sabbath days
6. came to pass also o. another
7. would heal o. the sabbath
8.15. that o. the good ground are
32. swine feeding o. the mounta.
9.37. came to pass, that o. the
12.51. come to give peace o. earth
13. 7. seeking fruit o. this fig-tree
10. of the synagogues o. the sab.
14. 5. pull him out o. the sabbath
20. 1. that o. one of those days, as
Jo 5. 9. and o. the same day was the
16. these things o. the sabbath
7.22. ye o. the sabbath day circum.
23. If a man o. the sabbath day
whole o. the sabbath day
13.23. was leaning o. Jesus' bosom
19.31. the cross o. the sabbath day
Ro. 12. 7. let us wait o. our ministering
or he that teacheth, o. teach.
8. that exhorteth, o. exhorta.
²Co. 4. 8. We are troubled o. every
7. 5. we were troubled o. every
8. 1. bestowed o. the churches of
Col. 3. 1. o. the right hand of God ;
Heb.10.12 ; ¹Pet.3.22
Heb. 1. 3. o. the right. Majesty o. high
8. 1. who is set o. the right hand
¹Pet. 4.16. glorify God o. this behalf
Rev. 1.10. the Spirit o. the Lord's day
5.13. in heaven, and o. the earth

ek.

Mat.20.21.one o.thy right..the other o.;
Mar.10.27 ; Lu.23.33
23. sit o. my right hand, and o.;
Mar.10.40
21.19. o. thee henceforward for
22.44. Sit thou o. my right hand ;
Mar.12.36 ; Lu.20.42 ; Act.
2.34 ; Heb.1.13
25.33. sheep o. his right hand, but
the goats o. the left
34. unto them o. his right hand
41. unto them o. the left hand
26.64. sitting o. the right hand of
27.38. o. the right..another o. the
left ; Mar.15.27
Mar.14.62.sitting o. the right hand of
16.19. sat o. the right hand of God
Lu. 1.11. o. the right side of the altar
22.69. the Son of man sit o. the
Act. 2.25. for he is o. my right hand
7.55, 56. standing o. the right ha.
28. 4. beast hang o. his hand
Rev.18.20. God hath avenged you o. her

epanō.

Mat. 5.14. A city that is set o. an hill
21. 7. put o. them their clothes
Lu. 10.19. to tread o. serpents and
Rev. 6. 8. his name that sat o. him

apo.

Rev. 6.10. avenge our blood o. them
21.13. o. the east three gates ; o.
o. the south 3 gates ; and o.

peri, [gen.]

Mat. 9.36. with compassion o. them
Act. 10.19. thought o. the vision

kata, [gen.]

Mar.14. 3. poured it o. his head

kata, [accu.]

Act. 8.36. went o. their way

meta, [gen.]

Lu. 10.37. that shewed mercy o. him
(See words in connection.)

ONCE.

hapax.

¹Co. 11.25. beaten with rods, o. was I
Phi. 4.16. ye sent o. and again unto my
¹Th. 2.13. even I Paul, o. and again

Heb. 6. 4. those who were o. enlighten.
9. 7. the high priest alone o. eve.
26. now o. in the end of the wo.
27. appointed unto men o. to die
28. Christ was o. offered to bear
10. 2. worshippers o. purged shou.
12.26. Yet o. more I shake not the
27. this word, Yet o. more, sig.
¹Pet. 3.18. Christ also hath o. suffered
20. when o. the longsuffering of
Jude 3. faith which was o. delivered
5. though ye o. knew this, how

ephapax.

Ro. 6.10. he died unto sin o. : but in
¹Co. 15. 6. five hundred brethren at o.
Heb. 7.27. for this he did o., when he
9.12. he entered in o. into the ho.
10.10. the body of J. Ch. o. for all

pote.

Ro. 7. 9. alive without the law o.
Gal. 1.23. preacheth the faith which o.

apo hos.

Lu. 13.25. When o. the master of the

pamplēthei.

Lu. 23.18. they cried out all at o., say.

mēde.

Eph. 5. 3. let it not be o. named amo.

ONE.

heis.

Mat. 5.18. o. jot or o. tittle shall in no
19. shall break o. of these least
29, 30. that o. of thy members
36. thou canst not make o. hair
6.24. he will hate the o. ; Lu.16.13
will hold to the o. ; Lu.16.13
27. can add o. cubit ; Lu.12.25
29. not arrayed like o. ; Lu.12.27
10.29. o. of them shall not fall on
42. o. of these little ones ; 18.6,
10,14 ; Lu. 17.2
12.11. that shall have o. sheep, and
13.46. when he had found o. pearl
16.14. Jeremias, or o. of the proph.
17. 4. o. for thee, o. for M., and o.;
Mar. 9.5 ; Lu. 9.33
18. 5. receive o. such little child
12. o. of them be gone astray
16. take with thee o. or two mo.
24. o. was brought unto him
28. found o. of his fellowservan.
19. 5. and they twain shall be o. ;
Mar. 10.8 ; Eph. 5.31
6. more twain, but o.; Mar.10.8
16. behold, o. came and said un.
17. none good but o., that is ;
Mar. 10.18 ; Lu. 18.19
20.12. last have wrought but o. ho.
13. he answered o. of them, and
21. o. on thy right ; Mar. 10.37
21.24. I also will ask you o. thing
22.35. Then o. of them, which was
23. 8, 10. for o. is your Master, ev.
9. for one is your Father, which
15. sea and land to make o. pro.
24.40. o. shall be taken ; Lu. 17.34
41. o. shall be taken ; Lu.17.35
25.15. anot. two, and to another o.
18, 24. he that had received o.
40, 45. unto o. of the least of th.
26.14. Then o. of the twelve, called
21. o. of you shall bet.; Jo.13.21
40. cou. ye not watch with me o.
47. Judas, o. of the twelve ; Mar.
14.43 ; Lu. 22.47
51. o. of them which were with
27.48. straightway o. of them ran
Mar. 5.22. there cometh o. of the rulers
6.15. a prophet, or as o. of the
8.14. with them more than o. loaf
28. others, o. of the prophets
9.17. o. of the multitude answered

Mar. 9.37. shall receive o. of such chil.
42. whosoever shall offend o. of
10.17. there came o. running, and
21. said unto him, o. thing thou
11.29. I will also ask of you o. que.
12. 6. Having yet therefore o. son
28. o. of the scribes came, and
29. The Lord our God is o. Lord
32. for there is o. God ; and the.
13. 1. o. of his disciples saith unto
14.10. Judas Iscariot, o. of the twe.
18. o. of you which eateth with
20. It is o. of the twelve, that
37. couldest not thou watch o.
47. o. of them that stood by dr.
66. there cometh o. of the maids
15. 6. he released unto them o. pr.
27. o. on his right hand,the other
36. o. ran and filled a spunge
Lu. 4.40. laid his hands on every o. of
5.. 3. he entered into o. of the ships
7.41. the o. owed five hundred pe.
9. 8. that o. of the old prophets
10.42. o. thing is needful : and Ma.
11.46. with o. of your fingers
12. 6. not o. of them is forgotten
52. there shall be five in o. hou.
13.10. he was teaching in o. of the
14.18. they all with o. consent be.
15. 4. if he lose o. of them, doth
7, 10. over o. sinner that repen.
8. if she lose o. piece, doth not
19. as o. of thy hired servants
26. he called o. of the servants
16. 5. every o. of his lord's debtors
17. than o. tittle of the law to
17.15. o. of them, when he saw
22. shall desire to see o. of the
34. there shall be two men in o.
18.10. the o. a Pharisee, and the
22. Yet lackest thou o. thing
20. 1. on o. of those days, as he
3. I will also ask you o. thing
22.50. o. of them smote the servant
59. about the space of o. hour
23.17. he must release o. unto them
39. o. of the malefactors which
24.18. the o. of them, whose name
Jo. 1.40. o. of the two which heard
6. 8. o. of his disciples, Andrew
22. save that o. whereinto his
70. o. of you is a devil
71. betray him, being o. of the
7.21. I have done o. work, and ye
50. to Jesus by night, being o. of
8.41. we have o. Father, even God
9.25. o. thing I know, that, wher.
10.16. shall be o. fold, and o. sheph.
30. I and my Father are o.
11.49. o. of them, named Caiaphas
50. that o. man should die for
52. together in o. the children of
12. 2. Lazarus was o. of them that
4. Then saith o. of his disciples
13.23. on Jesus' bosom o. of his dis.
17.11. that they may be o., as we
21. That they all may be o.
that they also may be o. in
22. be o., even as we are o.
23. may be made perfect in o.
18.14. o. man should die for the
22. o. of the officers which stood
26. o. of the servants of the high
39. release unto you o. at the
19.34. o. of the soldiers with a spe.
20.24. Thomas, o. of the twelve
21.25. should be written every o.
Act. 1.22. must o. be ordained to be
4.32. were of one heart and of o.
11.28. there stood up o. of them
12.10. and passed on through o. st.
17.26. hath made of o. blood all

197

Act.17.27. not far from every o. of us
19.34. all with o. voice about the
20.31. to warn every o. night and
21. 7. and abode with them o. day
26. offered for every o. of them
23. 6. that the o. part were Sadduc.
17. Paul called o. of the centuri.
24.21. Except it be for this o. voice
28.13. and after o. day the south
25. Paul had spoken o. word
Ro. 3.10. none righteous, no, not o.
12. that doeth good, no, not o.
30. Seeing it is o. God, which
5.12. as by o. man sin entered into
15. if through the offence of o.
which is by o. man, Jesus Ch.
16. not as it was by o. that sinn.
the judgment was by o. to
17. For if by o. man's offence
death reigned by o.
shall reign in life by o., Jes.
18. as by the offence of o.
by the righteousness of o.
19. as by o. man's disobedience
by the obedience of o. shall
9.10. also had conceived by o.
12. 4. many members in o. body
5. being many, are o. body in
15. 6. with one mind and o. mouth
1Co. 3. 8. and he that watereth are o.
4. 6. o. of you be puffed up for o.
6.16. joined to an harlot is o. body
for two, saith he, shall be o.
17. joined unto the Lo. is o. sp.
8. 4. the. is none other God but o.
6. to us there is but o. God
o. Lord Jesus Christ, by wh.
9.24. run all, but o. receiveth the
10. 8. fell in o. day three and twe.
17. being many are o. bread
and o. body: for we are all
partakers of that o. bread
11. 5. for that is even all o. as if
12.11. that o. and the selfsame Spi.
12. For as the body is o.
o. body, being many, are o.
13. o. Spir. are we bapti. into o.
all made to drink into o. Sp.
14. the body is not o. member
18. every o. of them in the body
19. if they were all o. member
20. many members, yet but o.
26. whether o. member suffer
or o. member be honoured
14.27. by course; and let o. interp.
31. may all prophesy one by o.
2Co. 5.14. that if o. died for all, then
11. 2. have espoused you to o. hus.
24. receiv. I forty stripes save o.
Gal. 3.16. as of many; but as of o.
20. mediator of o., but God is o.
28. ye are all o. in Christ Jesus
4.22. the o. by a bondmaid, the
24. the o. from the mount Sinai
5.14. the law is fulfilled in o. word
Eph. 2.14. who hath made both o., and
15. in himself of twain o. new
16. both unto God in o. body by
18. by o. Spirit unto the Father
4. 4. There is o. body, and o. Spi.
ye are called in o. hope of
5. o. Lord, o. faith, o. bap.
6. o. God and Father of all, who
7. unto every o. of us is given
5.33. every o. of you in particular
Phi. 1.27. that ye stand fast in o. spirit
with o. mind striving togeth.
2. 2. being of one accord, of o. m.
3.13. this o. thing I do, forgetting
Col. 3.15. also ye are called in o. body
1Th. 2.11. comfor. and charged every o.
2Th. 1. 3. the charity of every o. of you
198

1Ti. 2. 5. there is o. God, and o. medi.
3. 2, 12. the husba. of o.; Tit.1.6
5. 9. having been the wife of o.
Heb. 2.11. sanctified are all of o.
10.12. after he had offered o. sacri.
14. For by o. offering he hath
11.12. sprang there even of o.
12.16. who for o. morsel of meat
Jas. 2.10. yet offend in o. point, he is
19. believest that there is o. God
4.12. There is o. lawgiver, who is
2Pet. 3. 8. be not ignorant of this o.
that o. day is with the Lord
and a thousand years as o.
1Jo. 5. 7. and these three are o.
8. these three agree in o.
Rev. 5. 5. o. of the elders saith unto me
6. 1. when the Lamb opened o. of
o. of the four beasts; 15.7
7.13. o. of the elders answered, sa.
9.12. o. woe is past; and, behold
13. 3. I saw o. of his heads
17. 1. came o. of the seven angels
10. five are fallen, and o. is
12. as kings o. hour with the be.
13. These have o. mind
18. 8. shall her plagues come in o.
10, 17, 19. for in o. hour
21. 9. came unto me o. of the seven
21. several gate was of o. pearl
tis.
Mat 12.29. how can o. enter into a strong
47. Then o. said unto him, Beho.
Mar. 9.38. o. casting out devils;Lu.9.49
15.21. And they compel o. Simon
Lu. 7.36. o. of the Pharisees desired
8.49. there cometh o. from the
9.19. o. of the old prophets is
11. 1. when he ceased, o. of his
45. Then answered o. of the
12.13. And o. of the company said
13.23. Then said o. unto him, Lord
14. 1. house of o. of the chief Pha.
15. And when o. of them that
16.30. if o. went unto them from
31. though o. rose from the
23.26. laid hold upon o. Simon, a
Act. 5.25. Then came o. and told them
34. Then stood there up o. in
7.24. seeing o. of them suffer wr.
9.43. with o. Simon a tanner; 10.6
19. 9. daily in the school of o. Tyr.
21.16. with them o. Mnason of Cyp.
22.12. o. Ananias, a devout man
25.19. of o. Jesus, which was dead
Ro. 5. 7. a righteous man will o. die
1Co. 3. 4. For while o. saith, I am of
5. 1. that o. should have his fath.
14.24. there come in o. that believ.
Tit. 1.12. o. of themselves, even a pro.
Heb. 2. 6. But o. in a certain place
Jas. 2.16. And o. of you say unto them
5.19. truth, and o. convert him
allos.
Jo. 4.37. o. soweth, and another reap.
Act. 2.12. in doubt, saying o. to anoth.
1Co.15.39. o. kind of flesh of men
41. o. glory of the sun, and
houtos.
Lu. 7. 8. I say unto o., Go, and he
heteros.
1Co.15.40. glory of the celestial is o.
(See words in connection.)

ONE *with* Another. (See *Prefer.*)
allēlos.
Mar.24.10.bet. o. a., and sh. hate o. a.
25.32. separate them o. from a.
4.41. exceedingly, and said o. to a.
9.50. and have peace o. with a.
Lu. 2.15. the shepherds said o. to a.
6.11. communed o. with a. what

Lu. 7.32. and calling o. to a.
8.25. wondered, saying o. to a.
12. 1. that they trode o. upon a.
24.17. that ye have o. to a., as
32. they said o. to a., Did not
Jo. 4.33. said the disciples o. to a.
5.44. receive honour o. of a.
13.14. ought to wash o. a.'s feet
22. disciples looked o. on a.
34. That ye love o. a.; 15.12,17;
1Pet.1.22
that ye also love o. a.
35. if ye have love o. to a.
Act. 2. 7. marvelled, saying o. to a.,
7.26. why do ye wrong o. to a.
19.38. let them implead o. a.
21. 6. had taken our leave o. of a.
Ro. 1.27. in their lust o. toward a.
2.15. accusing or else excus. o. a.
12. 5. every one members o. of a.
10. affectioned o. to a. with
in honour preferring o. a.
16. the same mind o. toward a.
13. 8. to love o. a.: for he that
14.13. therefore judge o. a. any
19. wherewith o. may edify a.
15. 5. be likeminded o. toward a.
7. Wherefore receive ye o. a.
14. able also to admonish o. a.
16.16. Salute o. a. with an holy
1Co. 11.33. together to eat, tarry o. for a.
12.25. have the same care o. for a.
16.20. Greet ye o. a. with an holy;
2Co.13.12; 1Pet.5.14
Gal. 5.13. but by love serve o. a.
15. if ye bite and devour o. a.
be not consumed o. of a.
26. provok. o. a., envying o. a.
6. 2. Bear ye o. a.'s burdens, and
Eph 4. 2. forbearing o. a. in love
25. for we are members o. of a.
32. kind o. to a., tenderhearted
5.21. Submitting yourselv. o. to a.
Col. 3. 9. Lie not o. to a., seeing that
13. Forbearing o. a., and forgiv.
1Th. 3.12. abound in love o. toward a.
4. 9. taught of God to love o. a.
18. comfort o. a. with these
Tit. 3. 3. hateful, and hating o. a.
Heb.10.24. consider o. a. to provoke
Jas. 4.11. Speak not evil o. of a.
5. 9. Grudge not o. against a.
16. your faults o. to a., and
pray o. for a. that ye may
1Pet. 4. 9. Use hospitality o. to a. with.
5. 5. all of you be subject o. to a.
1Jo. 1. 7. have fellowship o. with a.
3.11. we should love o. a.; 2Jo. 5
23. love o. a., as he gave us
4. 7. Beloved, let us love o. a.
11. we ought also to love o. a.
12. If we love o. a., God dwell.
Rev. 6. 4. that they should kill o. a.
10.10. shall send gifts o. to a.
heautou.
1Co. 6. 7. ye go to law o. with a.
Eph. 4.32. tenderhearted, forgiv. o. a
Col. 3.13. forgiving o. a., if any man
16. and admonishing o. a. in
Heb. 3.13. exhort o. a. daily, while
1Pet. 4.10. minister the same o. to a.
heis.
Mat.27.38. o. on the right hand, and a.
1Th. 5.11. edify o. a., even as also
ONLY.
monon.
Mat. 5.47. if ye salute your brethren o.
8. 8. but speak the word o., and
10.42. a cup of cold water o.
14.36. that they might o. touch the
21.19. nothing thereon, but lea. o.
21. not o. do this which is done

Mar. 5.36. Be not afraid : **o.** believe
6. 8. their journey, save a staff **o.**
Lu. 8.50. Fear not : believe **o.**, and
Jo. 5.18. not **o.** had broken the
11.52. not for that nation **o.**, but
12. 9. not for Jesus' sake only, but
13. 9. not my feet **o.**, but also my
Act. 8.16. **o.** they were baptized in the
11.19. none but unto the Jews **o.**
18.25. knowing **o.** the baptism of
19.27. So that not **o.** this our craft
21.13. not to be bound **o.**, but also
26.29. not **o.** thou, but also all that
27.10. not **o.** of the lading and ship
Ro. 1.32. not **o.** do the same, but have
3.29. the God of the Jews **o.**? is he
4.12. not of the circumcision **o.**
16. not to take that **o.** which is
5. 3, 11. And not **o.** so, but we gl.
8.23. And not **o.** they, but oursel.
9.10. And not **o.** this ; but when
24. not of the Jews **o.**, but also
13. 5. not **o.** for wrath, but also
¹Co. 7.39. to whom she will ; **o.** in the
15.19. If in this life **o.** we have hope
²Co. 7. 7. And not by his coming **o.**
8.10. not **o.** to do, but also to be
19. And not that **o.**, but who
21. not **o.** in the sight of the Lo.
9.12. not **o.** supplieth the want of
Gal. 1.23. But they had heard **o.**, That
2.10. **o.** they would that we should
3. 2. This **o.** would I learn of you
4.18. not **o.** when I am present
5.13. **o.** use not liberty for an
6.12. **o.** lest they should suffer
Eph. 1.21. not **o.** in this world, but also
Phi. 1.27. **o.** let your conversation be
29. not **o.** to believe on him, but
2.12. not as in my presence **o.**,
27. and not on him **o.**, but on
¹Th. 1. 5. not unto you in word **o.**
8. not **o.** in Macedonia and
2. 8. not the gospel of God **o.**, but
²Th. 2. 7. **o.** he who now letteth will
¹Ti. 5.13. not **o.** idle, but tattlers also
²Ti. 2.20. there are not **o.** vessels of
4. 8. and not to me **o.**, but unto
Heb. 9.10. **o.** in meats and drinks, and
12.26. I shake not the earth **o.**, but
Jas. 1.22. and not hearers **o.**, deceiving
2.24. justified, and not by faith **o.**
¹Pet. 2.18. not **o.** to the good and gen.
¹Jo. 2. 2. and not for our's **o.**, but also
5. 6. not by water **o.**, but by water
monos.
Mat. 4.10. him **o.** shalt thou : Lu.4.8
12. 4. with him : but **o.** for the
17. 8. saw no man, save Jesus **o.**
24.36. of heaven, but my Father **o.**
Mar. 9. 8. save Jesus **o.** with themsel.
Lu. 24.18. Art thou **o.** a stranger in
Jo. 5.44. that cometh from God **o.**
17. 3. the **o.** true God, and Jesus
Ro. 16. 4. unto whom not **o.** I give
27. To God **o.** wise, be glory
¹Co. 9. 6. Or I **o.** and Barnabas, have
14.36. you ? or came it unto you **o.**
Phi. 4.15. giving and receiv., but ye **o.**
Col. 4.11. These **o.** are my fellow-work.
¹Ti. 1.17. the **o.** wise God, be honour
6.15. the blessed and **o.** Potentate
16. Who **o.** hath immortality
²Ti. 4.11. **o.** Luke is with me. Take
²John 1. and not I **o.**, but also all
Jude 4. and denying the **o.** Lord God
25. To the **o.** wise God our Sav.
Rev.9. 4. but **o.** those men which have
15. 4. for thou **o.** art holy : for
monogenēs.
Lu. 7.12. the **o.** son of his mother
8.42. he had one **o.** daughter

Lu. 9.38. for he is mine **o.** child
heis.   [(but *one*, God.)
Mar. 2. 7. can forgive sins but God **o.**
(See *Begotten, Save.*)

OPEN,   -ed, -eth, -ing.
anoigō.
Mat. 2.11. *when* they *had* **o**-ed their
3.16. the heavens *were* **o**-ed unto
5. 2. he **o**-ed his mouth, *and*
7. 7. knock, and it *shall* be **o**-ed :
Lu.11.9   [Lu.11.10
8. that knocketh it *shall be* **o**-ed;
9.30. their eyes *were* **o**-ed ; and
13.35. I *will* **o.** my mouth in para.
17.27. *when* thou *hast* **o**-ed his
20.33. that our eyes *may be* **o**-ed
25.11. Lord, Lord, **o.** to us; Lu.13.25
27.52. the graves *were* **o**-ed; and
Lu. 1.64. his mouth *was* **o**-ed immed.
3.21. praying, the heaven was **o**-ed
12.36. they *may* **o.** unto him imme.
Jo. 1.51. ye shall see heaven **o.**, and
9.10. How *were* thine eyes **o**-ed
14. Jesus made the clay, and **o**-ed
17. that he *hath* **o**-ed thine eyes
21. or who *hath* **o**-ed his eyes
26. how **o**-ed he thine eyes
30. yet he *hath* **o**-ed mine eyes
32. that any man **o**-ed the eyes
10. 3. To him the porter **o**-eth
21. Can a devil **o.** the eyes of
11.37. *which* **o**-ed the eyes of the
Act. 5.19. by night **o**-ed the prison
23. *when* he *had* **o**-ed, we found
7.56. Behold, I see the heavens **o.**
8.32. so **o**-ed he not his mouth
35. Then Philip **o**-ed his mouth
9. 8. *when* his eyes *were* **o**-ed, he
40. she **o**-ed her eyes ; and when
10.11. saw heaven **o**-ed, and a cer.
34. Then Peter **o**-ed his mouth
12.10. which **o**-ed to them of his
14. she **o**-ed not the gate for
16. *when* they *had* **o**-ed the door
14.27. how he *had* **o**-ed the door of
16.26. all the doors *were* **o**-ed, and
27. seeing the prison doors **o.**
18.14. was now about to **o.** his
26.18. To **o.** their eyes, and to turn
Ro. 3.13. Their throat is an **o.** sepul.
¹Co.16. 9. door and effectual *is* **o**-ed
²Co. 2.12. *when . . a* door *was* **o**-ed unto
6.11. our mouth *is* **o.** unto you
Col. 4. 3. that God *would* **o.** unto us
Rev. 3. 7. he *that* **o**-eth, and no man
shutteth, and no man **o**-eth
8. I have set before thee an **o.**
20. hear my voice, and **o.** the
4. 1. a door was **o**-ed in heaven
5. 2. Who is worthy *to* **o.** the book
3. was able *to* **o.** the book
4. found wort. *to* **o.** and to read
5. hath prevailed *to* **o.** the book
9. *to* **o.** the seals thereof ; for
6. 1. when the Lamb **o**-ed one of
3, 5,7,9,12. wh. he *had* **o**-ed the
Rev. 8. 1. when he *had* **o**-ed the seventh
9. 2. he **o**-ed the bottomless pit
10. 2. in his hand a little book **o.**
8. the little book which is **o.**
11.19. temple of God *was* **o**-ed in
12.16. the earth **o**-ed her mouth
13. 6. he **o**-ed his mouth in blasp.
15. 5 testimony in heaven *was* **o**-ed
19.11. I saw heaven **o**-ed, and beh.
20.12. books *were* **o**-ed; and ano.
book was **o**-ed, which is
dianoigō.
Mar. 7.34. Ephphatha, that is, *Be* **o**-ed
35. straightway his ears *were* **o**-ed
Lu. 2.23. Every male *that* **o**-eth the

Lu. 24.31. their eyes *were* **o**-ed, and
32. while he **o**-ed to us the scri.
45. Then **o**-ed he their understa.
Act.16.14. whose heart the Lord **o**-ed
17. 3. **o**-ing and alledging, that
en anoixis.
Eph. 6.19. may **o.** my mouth boldly
anaptussō.
Lu. 4.17. *when* he *had* **o**-ed the book
schizō.
Mat.1.10. he saw the heavens **o**-ed
Heb. 4.13. naked and **o**-ed unto the

OPEN, [*adjec.*,] (See *Shame.*)
agō.   [(law courts *are* held.)
Act.19.38. agai. any man, the law *is* **o.**
prodēlos.
¹Ti. 5.24. men's sins are **o.** *beforehand*
anakaluptō.
²Co. 3.18. with **o.** face beholding as

OPENLY.
parrēsia.   (*with openness.*)
Mar. 8.32. And he spake that saying **o.**
Jo. 7. 4. seeketh to be known **o.**
13. no man spake **o.** of him
11.54. walked no more **o.** among
18.20. I spake **o.** to the world
Col. 2.15. he made a shew of them **o.**
phaneros.
Mar. 1.45. could no more **o.** enter
Jo. 7.10. not **o.**, but as it were in
en phaneros.
Mat. 6. 4, 6, 18. shall reward thee **o.**
emphanēs.
Act.10.40. third day, and shewed him **o.**
(gave him to be *manifest.*)
dēmosios.
Act.16.37. They have beaten us **o.**

OPERATION,   -s.
energēma.
¹Co. 12. 6. there are diversities of **o**-s
energeia.
Col. 2.12. through the faith of the **o.**

OPPORTUNITY.
eukairia.   [Lu.22.6
Mat.26.16. he sought **o.** to betray him ;
kairos.
Gal. 6.10. As we have therefore **o.**, let
Heb.11.15.have had **o.** to have returned
akaireomai.
Phi. 4.10. careful, but ye *lacked* **o.**

OPPOSE,   -ed, -eth.
antitassō.
Act.18. 6. *when* they **o**-ed them *selves*
antikeimai.
²Th. 2. 4. who **o**-eth and exalteth him.
antidiatithēmi.
²Ti. 2.25. those *that* **o.** *themselves*

OPPOSITIONS.
antithesis.
¹Ti. 6.20. **o.** of science falsely so called

OPPRESS.
katadunasteuō.
Act.10.38. healing all *that were* **o**-ed of
Jas. 2. 6. *Do* not rich men **o.** you
kataponeō.
Act. 7.24. avenged him *that was* **o**-ed

OR.   (See *Ever.*)
ē.   [Lu. 16.13
Mat. 6.24. **o.** *else* he will hold to the one;
12.29. **o.** *else* how can one enter
33. **o.** *else* make the tree corrupt
Act.24.20. **o.** *else* let these same here say
{*And all other passages in which it*
occurs, except the following :—)
eite.
Ro. 12. 7. **o.** ministry, let us wait on

Ro. 12. 7. **o.** he that teacheth, on
     8. **o.** he that exhorteth, on exh.
¹Co. 3.22. Wheth. Paul, **o.** Apollos, **o.**
     o. the world, **o.** life, **o.** dea.
     o. things present, **o.** things
     8. 5. whether in heaven **o.** in earth
     10.31. therefore ye eat, **o.** drink, **o.**
     12.13. whether we be Jews **o.** Gent.
     whether we be bond **o.** free
     26. **o.** one member be honoured
     14. 7. whether pipe **o.** harp, except
     15.11. Theref. whether it were I **o.**
²Co. 1. 6. **o.** whether we be comforted
     5. 9. whether present **o.** absent
     10. done, whether it be good **o.**
     13. it is to God, **o.** whether we be
     8.23. **o.** our brethren be enquired
     12. 2. body, I cannot tell; **o.** whet.
     3. whether in the body, **o.** out
Eph. 6. 8. whether he be bond **o.** free
Phi. 1.18. whether in pretence, **o.** in tr.
     20. whether it be by life, **o.** by
     27. I come and see you, **o.** else
Col. 1.16. **o.** domin., **o.** principal., **o.**
     20. whether things in earth, **o.**
¹Th. 5.10. whether we wake **o.** sleep, we
²Th. 2.15. taught, whether by word, **o.**
¹Pet. 2.14. **o.** unto governors, as unto
     mēte.
²Th. 2. 2. **o.** be troubled, neither by

ORACLES.
logion.
Act. 7.38. received the lively **o.** to give
Ro. 3. 2. committed the **o.** of God
Heb. 5.12. principles of the **o.** of God
¹Pet. 4.11. speak as the **o.** of God

ORATION.
dēmēgoreō.
Act.12.21. his throne, and *made an* **o.**

ORATOR.
rētōr.
Act.24. 1. with a certain **o.** named

ORDAIN,   -ed.
poieō.
Mar. 3.14. And he **o-**ed twelve, that th.
tithēmi.
Jo. 15.16. chosen you, and **o-**ed you, th.
¹Ti. 2. 7. Whereunto I *am* **o-**ed a pre.
ginomai.
Act. 1.22. *must* one *be* **o-**ed *to be* a wit.
horizō.
Act.10.42. *which was* **o-**ed of God to be
     17.31. that man whom he *hath* **o-**ed
proorizō.
¹Co. 2. 7. which God **o-**ed before the
diatassō.
¹Co. 7.17. And so **o.** I in all the churc.
     9.14. Even so hath the Lord **o-**ed
Gal. 3.19. it was **o-**ed by angels in the
tassō.
Act.13.48. as were **o-**ed to eternal life
Ro. 13. 1. powers that be are **o-**ed of
cheirotoneō.
Act.14.23. *when* they *had* **o-**ed them
krinō.
Act.16. 4. *that were* **o-**ed of the apostles
proetoimazō.
Eph. 2.10. which God *hath before* **o-**ed
kathistēmi.
Tit. 1. 5. and **o.** elders in every city
Heb. 5. 1. high priest. *is* **o-**ed for men
     8. 3. every high priest *is* **o-**ed to
kataskeuazō.
Heb. 9. 6. these things *were* thus **o-**ed
prographō.
Jude 4. *who were* before of old **o-**ed

ORDER.
taxis.
Lu 1. 8. before God in the **o.** of his
200

---

¹Co. 14.40. **be** done decently and in **o.**
Col. 2. 5. joying and beholding your **o.**
Heb. 5. 6, 10. after the **o.** of Melchise.;
     6.20, 7.11,17,21
     7.11. called after the **o.** of Aaron
     kathexēs.
Lu. 1. 3. to write unto thee *in* **o.**
Act.11. 4. expounded it *by* **o.** unto
     15.23. of Galatia and Phrygia *in* **o.**
     diatassō.
¹Co. 11.34. the rest *will* I *set in* **o.** when
     16. 1. as I *have given* **o.** to the ch.
     tagma.
¹Co.15.23. every man in his own **o.**

ORDERLY. (See *Walk.*)

ORDINANCE,   -s.
dikaiōma.
Lu. 1. 6. commandme. and **o-**s of div. serv.
Heb. 9. 1. had also **o-**s of divine serv.
     10. divers wash., and carnal **o-**s
dogma.
Eph. 2.15. command. contained in **o-**s
Col. 2.14. the handwriting of **o-**s that
dogmatizō.
Col. 2.20. world, *are ye subject to* **o-**s
diatagē.
Ro. 13. 2. resisteth the **o.** of God : and
paradosis.
¹Co. 11. 2. keep the **o-**s, as I delivered
ktisis.
¹Pet. 2.13. to every **o.** of man for the

OTHER, (See *Side,*)   -s.
allos.
Mat. 4.21. he saw **o.** two brethren, Ja.
     5.39. cheek, turn to him the **o.**;
     Lu.6.29 [Mar.3.5 ; Lu.6.10
     12.13. restored whole, like as the **o.**;
     13. 8. **o.** fell into good ; Mar.4.8
     20. 3, 6. saw **o-**s standing idle in
     21. 8. **o-**s cut down branches from;
     Mar.11.8
     36. Again, he sent **o.** serv.; 22.4
     41. vineyard unto **o.** husband.
     25.16. made them **o.** five talents
     17. two, he also gained **o.** two
     20. brought **o.** five talents, say.
     22. I have gained two **o.** talents
     27.42. He saved **o-**s; Mar.15.31
     61. Mary Mag., and the **o.**; 28.1
Mar. 4.36. were also with him **o.** little
     6.15. **o-**s said, That it is Elias
     and **o-**s said, That it is a ;
     8.28 ; Lu.9.19
     7. 4. many **o.** things there be
     8. many **o.** such like things
     12. 5. they killed, and many **o-**s
     9. give the vineyard unto **o-**s ;
     Lu.20.16
     31. There is none **o.** command.
     32. and there is none **o.** but he
     15.41. many **o.** women which came
Lu. 5.29. publicans and of **o-**s that sat
     9. 8. Elias had appear.; and of **o-**s
     23.35. He saved **o-**s ; let him save
Jo. 4.38. **o.** men laboured, and ye are
     6.22. there was none **o.** boat there
     23. there came **o.** boats from
     7.12. He is a good man : **o-**s said
     41. **o-**s said, This is the Christ
     9. 9. said, This is he : **o-**s said
     16. **o-**s said, How can a man
     10.16. **o.** sheep I have, which are
     21. **o-**s said, These are not the
     12.29. **o-**s said, An angel spake to
     15.24. works which none **o.** man
     18.16. Then went out that **o.** disc.
     34. or did **o-**s tell it thee of
     19.18. crucified him, and two **o.**
     32. the first, and of the **o.** which

Jo. 20. 2. to the **o.** disciple,whom Jesus
     3. went forth, and that **o.** dis.
     4. the **o.** disciple did outrun
     8. Then went in also that **o.**
     25. The **o.** disciples therefore
     30. many **o.** signs truly did Jes.
     21. 2. of Zebedee, and two **o.** of
     8. the **o.** disciples came in a
     25. there are also many **o.** thi.
Act. 4.12. is there salvation in any **o.**
     15. 2. Barnabas, and certain **o.** of
¹Co. 1.16. whether I baptized any **o.**
     3.11. For **o.** foundation can no
     9. 2. If I be not apostle unto **o-**s
     12. If **o-**s be partakers of this
     27. when I have preached to **o-**s
     14.19. my voice I might teach **o-**s
     29. two or three, and let the **o.**
²Co. 1.13. For we write none **o.** things
     8.13. I mean not that **o.** men be
     11. 8. I robbed **o.** churches, taking
Phi. 3. 4. If any **o.** man thinketh that
¹Th. 2. 6. neither of you, nor yet of **o.**
Heb.11.35. **o-**s were tortured, not accep.
Jas. 5.12. earth, neither by any **o.** oath
Rev. 2.24. put upon you none **o.** burd.
     17.10. one is, and the **o.** is not
     allotrios.
²Co.10.15. that is of **o.** *men's* labours
¹Ti. 5.22. be partaker of **o.** *men's* sins
Heb. 9.25. every year with blood *of* **o-**s
     heteros.   [Lu.16.13
Mat. 6.24. and love the **o.**: or else he
     the one and despise the **o.**;
     Lu.16.13
     12.45. with himself seven **o.** spirits
     15.30. dumb, maim., and many **o-**s
     16.14. and **o-**s, Jeremias, or one of
Lu. 3.18. And many **o.** things in his
     4.43. to **o.** cities also : for there.
     5. 7. which were in the **o.** ship
     7.41. hundred pence, and the **o.**
     8. 3. and many **o-**s, which minis.
     8. And **o.** fell on good ground
     10. 1. appointed **o.** seventy also
     11.16. And **o-**s, tempting him
     26. seven **o.** spirits more
     17.34, 35. and the **o.** shall be left
     18.10. and the **o.** a publican
     22.65. many **o.** things blasphem.
     23.32. there were also two **o.**, male.
     40. But the **o.** answering rebuk.
Act. 2. 4. to speak with **o.** tongues
     13. **o-**s mocking said, These men
     40. And with many **o.** words
     4.12. there is none **o.** name under
     8.34. himself, or of some **o.** man
     15.35. Lord, with many **o-**s also
     17.34. Damaris, and **o-**s with them
     19.39. any thing concerning **o.** mat.
     23. 6. Sadducees, and the **o.** Phar.
     27. 1. and certain **o.** prisoners
Ro. 8.39. nor any **o.** creature, shall
     13. 9. if there be any **o.** command.
¹Co. 8. 4. there is none **o.** God
     10.29. not thine own, but of the **o.**
     14.17. but the **o.** is not edified
     21. and **o.** lips will I speak unto
²Co. 8. 8. of the forwardness of **o-**s
Gal. 1.19. But **o.** of the apostles saw
Eph. 3. 5. Which in **o.** ages was not
Phi. 2. 4. man also on the things of **o-**s
¹Ti. 1.10. and if there be any **o.** thing
²Ti. 2. 2. who shall be able to teach **o-**s
Heb.11.36. And **o-**s had trial of cruel
     loipos.
Mat.25.11. Afterward came also the **o.**
Mar. 4.19. and the lusts of **o.** things
Lu. 8.10. but to **o-**s in parables ; that
     18. 9. righteous, and despised **o-**s
     11. that I am not as **o.** men
     24.10. and **o.** women that were with

Act.17. 9. secur. of Jason, and of the **o.**
28. 9. **o**-*s* also, which had diseases
Ro. 1.13. even as among **o.** Gentiles
¹Co. 7. 5. as well as **o.** apostles
15.37. of wheat, or of some **o.** grain
²Co.12.13. were inferior to **o.** churches
13. 2. sinned, and to all **o.**, that
Gal. 2.13. And the **o.** Jews dissembled
Eph. 2. 3. children of wrath, even as **o**-*s*
4.17. walk not as **o.** Gentiles
Phi. 1.13. palace, and in all **o.** places
4. 3. and with **o.** my fellowlabour.
¹Th. 4.13. even as **o**-*s* which have no
5. 6. let us not sleep, as do **o**-*s*
¹Ti. 5.20. that **o**-*s* also may fear

allēlōn.
Act.15.39. asunder *one* from the **o.**
¹Co. 7. 5. Defraud ye not *one the* **o.**
Gal. 5.17. are contrary *the one to the* **o.**
Phi. 2. 3. let *each* esteem **o.** better
²Th. 1. 3. you all toward *each* **o.** abo.

heis.   [Mar.10.37
Mat.20.21. thy right hand, and the **o.**;
24.40, 41. be taken and the **o.** left
Mar.15.27. his right hand, and the **o.** at
Jo. 20.12. the head, and the **o.** at the
Gal. 4.22. by a bondmaid, the **o.** by

ekeinos.   [Lu.11.42
Mat.23.23. not to leave *the* **o.** undone;
Lu. 18.14. justified rather than *the* **o.**

autos.
Lu. 14 32. while *the* **o.** is yet a great

allachothen.
Jo. 10. 1. but climbeth up *some* **o.** *way*

ektos.
Act.26.22. none **o.** things *than* those
(See Busybody, One, Pass, Side, Tongue.)

OTHERWISE. (See *Teach.*)
epei.
Ro. 11. 6. **o.** grace is no more grace
o. work is no more work
22. **o.** thou also shalt be cut off
Heb. 9.17. **o.** it is of no strength

ei de mē.
Mat. 6. 1. **o.** ye have no reward of your
Lu. 5.36. *if* **o.**, then both the new
²Co.11.16. *if* **o.**, yet as a fool receive

allos.
Gal. 5.10. ye will be none **o.** minded

heterōs.
Phi. 3.15. in any thing ye be **o.** minded

allōs.
¹Ti. 5.25. that are **o.** cannot be hid

OUGHT, [*noun.*]
tis.
Mat. 5.23. brother hath **o.** against
21. 3. if any man say **o.** unto you
Mar.11.25. if ye have **o.** against any
Act. 4.32. said any of them that **o.**
28.19. not that I had **o.** to accuse
Phile. 18. wrong. thee, or oweth thee **o.**

oudeis.
Mar. 7.12. suffer him no more to do **o.**

OUGHT, [*verb,*]   -*est.*
dei.
Mat.23.23. these **o.** ye to have; Lu.11.42
25.27. Thou **o**-*est* therefore to have
Mar.13.14. standing where it **o.** not
Lu. 12.12. in the same hour what ye **o.**
13.14. in which men **o.** to work
16. **o.** not this woman, being a
18. 1. that men **o.** always to pray
24.26. **o.** not Christ to have suffered
Jo. 4.20. where men **o.** to worship
Act. 5.29. We **o.** to obey God rather
10. 6. tell thee what thou **o**-*est* to do
19.36. ye **o.** to be quiet, and to do
20.35. labouring ye **o.** to support

Act.24.19. Who **o.** to have been here
25.10. where I **o.** to be judged
24. crying that he **o.** not to live
26. 9. that I **o.** to do many things
Ro. 8.26. should pray for as we **o.**
12. 3. more highly than he **o.** to
¹Co. 8. 2. nothing yet as he **o.** to know
²Co. 8. 3. them of whom I **o.** to rejoice
Eph. 6.20. may speak boldly as I **o.** to
Col. 4. 4. manifest, as I **o.** to speak
6. how ye **o.** to answer every
¹Th. 4. 1. how ye **o.** to walk and please
²Th. 3. 7. know how ye **o.** to follow us
¹Ti. 3.15. how thou **o**-*est* to behave th.
5.13. speaki. things which they **o.**
Tit. 1.11. things which they **o.** not
Heb. 2. 1. we **o.** to give the more earn.
²Pet. 3.11. manner of persons **o.** ye to be

opheilō.
Jo. 13.14. ye also **o.** to wash one ano.'s
19. 7. by our law he **o.** to die, bec.
Act.17.29. we **o.** not to think that the
Ro. 15. 1. that are strong **o.** to bear the
¹Co. 11. 7. a man indeed **o.** not to cover
10. For this cause **o.** the woman
²Co.12.11. for I **o.** to have been comme.
14. the children **o.** not to lay up
Eph. 5.28. So **o.** men to love their wives
Heb. 5. 3. by reason hereof he **o.**, as for
12. *when* for the time ye **o.** to be
¹Jo. 2. 6. **o.** himself also so to walk
3.16. we **o.** to lay down our lives
4.11. we **o.** also to love one anoth.
³John 8. We therefore **o.** to receive ¯
chrē.
Jas. 3.10. these things **o.** not so to be

OUR, (See *Own*,)   -*s.*
*Generally represents the genitive plural
or some other inflection of* **egō.** *The
following are exceptions :—*

hēmeteros.
Act. 2.11. hear them speak in **o.** tongu.
24. 6. judged according to **o.** law
26. 5. straitest sect of **o.** religion
Ro. 15. 4. were written for **o.** learning
²Ti. 4.15. he hath greatly withstood **o.**
Tit. 3.14. And let **o.**'s also learn to ma.
¹Jo. 1. 3. and truly **o.** fellowship is wi.
2. 2. and not for **o.**'s only, but al.

ho agapē meta egō, [*gen. plu.*]
¹Jo. 4.17. herein is **o.** *love* made perfect

OURSELVES.
heautos, [*plural.*]
Act.23.14. We have bound **o.** under a
Ro. 8.23. we ourselves groan within **o.**
15. 1. weak, and not to please **o.**
¹Co.11.31. if we would judge **o.**, we
²Co. 1. 9. the sentence of death in **o.**
that we shou. not trust in **o.**
3. 1. begin again to commend **o.**
5. Not that we are suffici. of **o.**
to think any thing as of **o.**
4. 2. commending **o.** to every man
5. we preach not **o.**, but Chris.
o. your servants for Jesus'
5.12. we commend not **o.** again
6. 4. approving **o.** as the ministers
7. 1. let us cleanse **o.** from all
10.12. or compare **o.** with some th.
14. we stretch not **o.** beyond
²Th. 3. 9. to make **o.** an ensample
Heb.10.25. the assembling of **o.** together
¹Jo. 1. 8. have no sin, we deceive **o.**

egō, [*plural.*]
²Th. 1. 4. So that *we* **o.** glory in you
Tit. 3. 3. For *we* **o.** also were sometim.

OUT.
ek.
Mat. 2. 6. for **o.** *of* thee shall come a
12.34. **o.** *of* the abundance of the

Mat.12.35. **o.** *of* the good treas.; Lu.6.45
man **o.** *of* the evil; Lu.6.45
15.19. **o.** *of* the heart proceed evil
Mar.13.15. take any thing **o.** *of* his hou.
Lu. 19.22. **o.** *of* thine own mouth will
Jo. 15.19. have chosen you **o.** *of* the w.
²Co. 2. 4. For **o.** *of* much affliction and
8.11. a performance also **o.** *of* that
²Ti. 2.26. **o.** *of* the snare of the devil
3.11. **o.** *of* them all the Lord deliv.
Jas. 3.10. **o.** *of* the same mouth proce.
(*And all other passages in which it is
not part of a compound word. The following are exceptions :—*)
exō.
Mat. 5.13. for nothing, but to be cast **o.**
21.17. went **o.** *of* the city into Bet.
39. cast him **o.** *of* the vineyard ;
Mar.12.8 ; Lu.20.15
26.75. he went **o.**, and wept bitterly;
Lu.22.62
Mar. 5.10. send them away **o.** *of* the
8.23. and led him **o.** *of* the town
11.19. come, he went **o.** *of* the city
14.68. he went **o.** into the porch
Lu. 4.29. thrust him **o.** *of* the city
8.54. he put them all **o.** and took
13.28. you yourselves thrust **o.**
33. a prophet perish **o.** *of* Jerus.
14.35. dunghill; but men cast it **o.**
24.50. he led them **o.** as far as to
Jo. 6.37. I will in no wise cast **o.**
9.34. us. And they cast him **o.**
35. that they had cast him **o.**
12.31. prince of this world be cast **o.**
Act. 4.15. aside **o.** *of* the council
7.58. cast him **o.** *of* the city
14.19. drew him **o.** *of* the city
16.13. we went **o.** *of* the city by a
30. brought them **o.**, and said
21. 5. till we were **o.** *of* the city
30. drew him **o.** *of* the temple
¹Jo. 4.18. perfect love casteth **o.** fear
Rev. 11. 2. and he shall go no more **o.**
11. 2. without the temple leave **o.**
ektos.
²Co. 12. 2. or whether **o.** *of* the body, I
3. in the body, or **o.** *of* the
apo.
Mat. 3.16. went up straightway **o.** *of*
7. 4. pull out the mote **o.** *of* thine
8.34. would depart **o.** *of* their
12.43. unclean spirit is gone **o.** *of*
13. 1. day went Jesus **o.** *of* the ho.
14.13. followed him on foot **o.** *of*
29. come down **o.** *of* the ship
15.22. came **o.** *of* the same coasts
17.18. and he departed **o.** *of* him
24.27. lightning cometh **o.** *of* the
Mar. 1.10. coming up **o.** *of* the water
5.17. him to depart **o.** *of* their
6.33. afoot thither **o.** *of* all cities
7.15. things which come **o.** *of* him
10.46. as he went **o.** *of* Jericho with
15.21. passed by, coming **o.** *of* the
16. 9. **o.** *of* whom he had; Lu.8.2
Lu. 4.35. in the midst, he came **o.** *of*
41. devils also came **o.** *of* many
5. 2. fishermen were gone **o.** *of*
36. that was taken **o.** *of* the new
6.17. multitude of people **o.** *of* all
8.12. the word **o.** *of* their hearts
29. unclean spirit to come **o.** *of*
33. went the devils **o.** *of* the
35, 38. **o.** *of* whom the devils
46. that virtue is gone **o.** *of* me
9. 5. when ye go **o.** *of* that city
11.24. unclean spirit is gone **o.** *of* a
12.54. ye see a cloud rise **o.** *of* the
17.29. day that Lot went **o.** *of* Sod.
23.26. coming **o.** *of* the country
24.31. he vanished **o.** *of* their sight

Jo. 7.42. **o.** *of* the town of Bethlehem
Act. 1. 9. a cloud received him **o.** *of*
2. 5. **o.** *of* every nation under hea.
13.50. expelled them **o.** *of* their
16.18. to come **o.** *of* her. And he
17. 2. with them **o.** *of* the scripture
19.12. evil spirits went **o.** *of* them
28.21. neither received letters **o.** *of*
23. both **o.** *of* the law of Moses
2Co. 1.16. to come again **o.** Macedo.
Heb.11.34. **o.** *of* weakness were made
Rev.16.17. **o.** *of* the temple of heaven
22.19. away his part **o.** *of* the book
kata, [*accu.*]
Lu. 18. 4. come to him **o.** *of every* city

OUTER.
exōteros.
Mat. 8.12. be cast out into **o.** darkness
22 13. cast him into **o.** darkness
25.30. unprofit. servant into **o.**

OUTRUN.
protrechō tachion
Jo. 20. 4. other disciple did **o.** Peter

OUTSIDE.
ektos.
Mat.23.26. that the **o.** of them may be
exōthen. [Lu.11.39
Mat.23.25. make clean the **o.** of the cup;

OUTWARD.
exōthen.
Mat.23.27. indeed appear beautiful **o.**
1Pet. 3. 3. adorning let it not be that **o.**
exō.
2Co. 4.16. though our **o.** man perish
phaneros.
Ro. 2.28. which is **o.** in the flesh
prosōpon.
1Co.10. 7. after the **o.** *appearance*

OUTWARDLY-
exōthen.
Mat.23.28. Even so ye also **o.** appear
en phaneros.
Ro. 2.28. not a Jew, which is one **o.**

OUTWENT.
proerchomai.
Mar.6.33. out of all cities, and **o.** them

OVEN.
klibanos. [Lu.12.28
Mat.6.30. to morrow is cast into the **o.**;

OVER.
epi.
Mat.24.45.hath made ruler **o.**; Lu.12.42
47. make him ruler **o.** all his go.
25.21, 23. faithful **o.** a few things
23. thee ruler **o.** many things
27.45. darkness **o.** all the land;
Mar. 15.33; Lu. 23.44
Lu. 1.33. reign **o.** the house of Jacob
2. 8. keeping watch **o.** their flock
9. 1. power and authority **o.** all
10.19. **o.** all the power of the enemy
12.14. a judge or a divider **o.** you
44. ruler **o.** all that he hath
15. 7, 10. **o.** one sinner that repen.
more than **o.** ninety and nine
19.14. this man to reign **o.** us
27. that I should reign **o.** them
41. beheld the city, and wept **o.**
23.38. also was written **o.** him
Act. 6. 3. may appoint **o.** this business
7.10. made him governor **o.** Egypt
11. a dearth **o.** all the land
27. a ruler and a judge **o.** us
8. 2. made great lamentation **o.**
19.13. to call **o.** them which had
Ro. 5.14. **o.** them that had not sinned

Ro. 9. 5. who is **o.** all, God blessed
2Co. 3.13. put a vail **o.** his face
1Th. 3. 7. we were comforted **o.** you
Heb. 2. 7. **o.** the works of thy hands
3. 6. as a son **o.** his own house
10.21. priest **o.** the house of God
Jas. 5.14. and let them pray **o.** him
1Pet. 3.12. eyes of the Lord are **o.** the
Rev. 2.26. will I give power **o.** the nat.
6. 8. **o.** the fourth part of the ear.
9.11. they had a king **o.** them
11. 6. have power **o.** waters to turn
10. earth shall rejoice **o.** them
13. 7. given him **o.** all kindreds
14.18. which had power **o.** fire
16. 9. hath power **o.** these plagues
17.18. **o.** the kings of the earth
18.11. shall weep and mourn **o.** her
20. Rejoice **o.** her, thou heaven
epanō.
Mat. 2. 9. stood **o.** where the young
27.37. And set up **o.** his head his
Lu. 4.39. he stood **o.** her, and rebuked
11.44. the men that walk **o.** them
19.17. have thou authority **o.** ten
19. Be thou also **o.** five cities
apenanti.
Mat.21. 2. into the village **o.** *against*
27.61. sitting **o.** *against* the sepul.
katenanti. [Lu.19.30
Mar.11. 2. the village **o.** *against* you;
12.41. Jesus sat **o.** *against* the trea.
13. 3. **o.** *against* the temple
ek enantios.
Mar.15.39. which stood **o.** *against* him
peran.
Jo. 6. 1. went **o.** the sea of Galilee
17. went **o.** the sea toward Cape.
18. 1. **o.** the brook Cedron, where
antiperan.
Lu. 8.26. which is **o.** *against* Galilee
antikru.
Act.20.15.next day **o.** *against* Chios
peri, [*gen.*]
Lu. 4.10. his angels charge **o.** thee
1Co. 7.37. hath power **o.** his own will
en.
Act.20.28.**o.** the which the Holy Ghost
kata, [*accus.*]
Act.27. 7. come **o.** *against* Cnidus
Crete, **o.** *against* Salmone
huper, [*accus.*]
Eph. 1.22. the head **o.** all things to the
proistēmi.
1Th. 5.12. and *are* **o.** you in the Lord
huperanō.
Heb. 9. 5. **o.** it the cherubims of glory
ek.
Rev.15. 2. **o.** the beast, and **o.** his ima.
o. his mark, and **o.** the num
(*See words which it follows.*)

OVERCHARGE, -ed.
barunō.
Lu. 21.34. any time your hearts be **o**-*ed*
epibareō.
2Co. 2. 5. that I *may* not **o.** you all

OVERCOME, -eth, -came.
nikaō.
Lu. 11.22. *shall* come upon him and **o.**
Jo. 16.33. I have **o.** the world
Ro. 3. 4. *mightest* **o.** when thou art
12.21. *be* not **o.** of evil, but **o.** evil
1Jo. 2.13, 14. ye have **o.** the wicked one
4. 4. and have **o.** them : because
5. 4. born of God **o**-*eth* the world
the victory that **o**-*eth* the wo.
5. Who is he that **o**-*eth* the wo.
Rev. 2. 7, 17. To him that **o**-*eth*; 3.21
11. He that **o**-*eth* shall not be

Rev. 2.26. And he that **o**-*eth*, and keep
3. 5. He that **o**-*eth*, the same shal
12. Him that **o**-*eth* will I make
21. even as I also **o**-*a*, and
11. 7. and *shall* **o.** them, and kill
12.11. And they **o**-*a* him by the
13. 7. and *to* **o.** them : and power
17.14. and the Lamb *shall* **o.** them
21. 7. He that **o**-*eth* shall inherit
katakurieuō.
Act.19.16. **o**-*a* them, *and* prevailed
hēttaomai.
2Pet. 2.19. for of whom a man *is* **o.**, of
20. *are* entangled therein, and **o.**

OVERFLOWED.
katakluzō.
2Pet. 3. 6. *being* **o.** with water, perished

OVERLAID.
perikaluptō.
Heb. 9. 4. **o.** round about with gold

OVERMUCH
perissoteros.
2Co. 2. 7. swallowed up with **o.** sorrow

OVERSEERS.
episkopos.
Act.20.28. Holy Ghost hath made you **o.**

OVERSHADOW, -ed.
episkiazō. [Lu. 9.34
Mat.17. 5. a bright cloud **o**-*ed*; Mar.9.7;
Lu. 1.35. of the Highest *shall* **o.** thee
Act. 5.15. *might* **o.** some of them

OVERSIGHT.
episkopeō, [*participle.*]
1Pet. 5. 2. *taking*·the **o.** thereof, not by

OVERTAKE, -en.
prolambanō.
Gal. 6. 1. if a man *be* **o**-*en* in a fault
katalambanō.
1Th. 5. 4. *should* **o.** you as a thief

OVERTHROW, [*noun.*]
katastrophē.
2Pet. 2. 6. condemned them with an **o.**

OVERTHROW, -n, -threw.
katastrephō.
Mat.21.12. **o**-*e* the tables; Mar. 11.15
anastrephō.
Jo. 2.15. money, and **o**-*e* the tables
anatrepō.
2Ti. 2.18. and **o.** the faith of some
kataluō.
Act. 5.39. be of God, ye cannot **o.** it
katastrōnnumi.
1Co. 10. 5. they *were* **o**-*n* in the wildern.

OWE, -ed, -est, -eth.
opheilō.
Mat.18.28.which **o**-*ed* him an hundred
saying,Pay me that thou **o**-*est*
Lu. 7.41. the one **o**-*ed* five hundred
16. 5, 7. How much **o**-*est* thou
Ro. 13. 8. **o.** no man any thing
Phile. 18. or **o**-*eth* thee ought, put that
prosopheilō.
Phile. 19. **o**-*est* unto me. .own self besi.
opheiletēs.
Mat.18.24.which **o**-*ed* him ten thousand

OWN, -eth.
idios.
Lu. 6.41. beam that is in *thine* **o.** eye
Jo. 10.12. whose **o.** the sheep are not
Act. 2. 8. every man in our **o.** tongue
3.12. as though by our **o.** power
4.23. they went to *their* **o.** comp.
25.19. of *their* **o.** superstition, and
Ro. 10. 3. about to establish *their* **o.**
11.24. be graffed into *their* **o.** olive

¹Co. 4.12. working with our o. hands
   7. 2. woman have her o. husband
    4. hath not power of her o. bo.
Eph. 5.22. yourselves unto your o. hus.
   24. to their o. husbands in every
Col. 3.18. submit yoursel. unto your o.
¹Th. 2.14. suffered like things of your o.
   15. and their o. prophets, and
   4.11. to do your o. business, and
    to work with your o. hands
¹Ti. 3.12. and their o. houses well
   6. 1. count their o. masters wort.
²Ti. 4. 3. after their o. lusts, shall they
Tit. 1.12. even a prophet of their o.
   2. 5. obedient to their o. husban.
   9. to be obedient unto their o.
¹Pet. 3. 1. be in subjection to your o.
   5. in subjection unto their o.
²Pet. 3. 3. walking after their o. lusts
   16. unto their o. destruction
Jude 6. but left their o. habitation
   heautou.
Lu. 14.26. yea, and his o. life also, he
   21.30. see and know of your o. selves
Jo. 20.10. aw. again unto their o. home
Act. 7.21. nourished him for her o. son
Ro. 4.19. considered not his o. body
   8. 3. God sending his o. Son in
   11.25. wise in your o. conceits; 12.16
   ·16. 4. laid down their o. necks
   18. their o. belly ; and by good
ᴬCo. 6.19. God, and ye are not your o.
   7. 2. let every man have his o.
   10.24. Let no man seek his o., but
   29. Consci., I say, not thine o.
   13. 5. seeketh not her o., is not
²Co. 8. 5. first gave their o. selves to
   13. 5. faith ; prove your o. selves
   Know ye not your o. selves
Gal. 6. 4. let every man prove his o.
Eph. 5.28. wives as their o. bodies
   29. no man ever yet hated his o.
Phi. 2. 4. not every man on his o. th.
   12. work out your o. salvation
   21. For all seek their o., not
¹Th. 2. 8. also our o. souls, because ye
²Th. 3.12. they work, and eat their o.
Jas. 1.22. only, deceiving your o. selves
Jude 13. foaming out their o. shame
   18. walk after their o. ungodly
   hautou.
Mat. 2.12. departed into their o. coun.
   13.54. he was come into his o. cou.;
     [Mar.6.4
   Mar.6.1
   57. his o. country, and in his o.;
   16.26. world, and lose his o. soul
     Mar.8.36
   17.25. of their o. children, or of
   27.60. laid it in his o. new tomb
Lu. 1.23. he departed to his o. house ;
     Lu.5.25
   56. returned to her o. house
   2.39. to their o. city Nazareth
   4.24. is accepted in his o. country
   5.29. a great feast in his o. house
   9.26. he shall come in his o. glory
   18. 7. not God avenge his o. elect
Jo. 7.53. went unto his o. house
Act. 7.41. in the works of their o. hands
   14.16. to walk in their o. ways
   21.11. bound his o. hands and feet
¹Co. 6.14. raise us up by his o. power
Eph. 1.11. after the counsel of his o.
   20. set him at his o. right hand
Heb. 3. 6. Christ as a son over his o.
   4.10. hath ceased from his o. wor.
   12.10. chastened us after their o.
Jas. 1.26. deceiveth his o. heart, this
¹Pet. 2.24. bare our sins in his o. body
²Pet. 2.12. perish in their o. corruption
   13. with their o. deceivings wh.
Jude 16. walking after their o. lusts

Rev. 1 5. from our sins in his o. blood
   autos.
Lu. 2.35. through thy o. soul also
   19.23. required mine o. with usury
   gnēsios.
¹Ti. 1. 2. Timothy, my o. son in the
Tit. 1. 4. Titus, mine o. son after the
   kata [accu.] su.
Act.17.28. certain also of your o. poets
  (See Accord, Conceits, Country, Hands,
    His, Mine, Thine.)

OWNERS.   (See Ship.)
   kurios.
Lu. 19.33. the o. thereof said unto

OWNETH.
   hos [gen.] eimi.
Act.21.11. the man that o. this girdle

OX,   -en.
   bous.
Lu. 13.15. loose his o. or his ass from
   14. 5. have an ass or an o. fallen
   19. have bought five yoke of o-en
Jo. 2.14. those that sold o-en and
   15. temple, and sheep, and o-en
¹Co. 9. 9. muzzle the mouth of the o.;
     ¹Ti.5.18
   Doth God take care for o-en
   tauros.
Mat.22. 4. my o-en and my fatlings
Act.14.13. brought o-en and garlands

PAIN,   (See Travail,) -s, -ed.
   ponos.
Rev.16.10.gnawed their tongues for p.
   11. because of their p-s and
   21. 4. there be any more p.
   ōdin.
Act. 2.24. having loosed the p-s of
   basanizō.
Rev.12. 2. in birth, and p-ed to be del.

PAINFULNESS.
   mochthos.
²Co.11.27. In weariness and p., in

PAIR.
   zeugos.
Lu. 2.24. A p. of turtle doves, or two
   zugos.
Rev. 6. 5. a p. of balances in his hand

PALACE.
   aulē.
Mat.26. 3, 58. the p. of the high priest;
   Mar.14.54 ; Jo.18.15
   69. Peter sat without in the p.
Mar.14.66.Peter was beneath in the p.
Lu. 11.21. man armed keepeth his p.
   praitōrion.
Phi. 1.13. are manifest in all the p.

PALE.
   chlōros.
Rev. 6. 8. looked, and behold a p. horse

PALM,   -s.
   phoinix.
Jo. 12.13. Took branches of p. trees
Rev. 7. 9. robes and p-s in their hands
   rapisma.
Mar.14.65.with the p-s of their hands
   rapizō.   [their hands
Mat.26 67. smote him with the p-s of
   didōmi ropisma.   [hand.
Jo. 18.22. struck Jes. with the p. of his

PALSY,   ·ies.
   paralutikos.
Mat. 4.24. and those that had the p.
   8. 6. lieth at home sick of the p.
   9. 2. to him a man sick of the p.
   6. said unto the sick of the p.;
     Mar. 2.5,10

Mar. 2. 3. bringing one sick of the p.
   4. bed wherein the sick of the p.
   9. to say to the sick of the p.
   paraluō.
Lu. 5.18. which was taken with a p.
   24. said unto the sick of the p.
Act. 8. 7. and many taken with p-ies
   9.33. years, and was sick of the p.

PAPER.
   chartēs.
²Jo. 12. not write with p. and ink.

PAPS.
   mastos.
Lu. 11.27. and the p. which thou hast
   23.29. the p. which never gave suck
Rev. 1.13. girt about the p. with a gold.

PARABLE,   -s.
   parabolē.
Mat.13. 3. many thin. unto them in p-s
   10. spea. thou unto them in p-s
   13. Ther. speak I to them in p-s
   18. Hear ye therefore the p. of
   24, 31, 33. Another p. put he ;
     Lu. 14.7
   34. Jes. unto the multitu. in p-s
   and without a p. spake he
   35. I will open my mouth in p-s
   36. Declare unto us the p.; 15.15
   53. Jesus had finished these p-s
   21.33. Hear another p.: There was
   45. Pharisees had heard his p-s
   22. 1. spake unto them again by p-s
   24.32. Now learn a p. of ; Mar.13.28
Mar. 3.23. and said unto them in p-s
   4. 2. tau. them many things by p-s
   10. twelve asked of him the p.
   11. these things are done in p-s
   13. Know ye not this p.? and
   then will ye know all p-s
   33. And with many such p-s spa.
   34. But without a p. spake he
   7.17. asked him concerning the p.
   12. 1. to speak unto them by p-s
   12. had spoken the p. against
Lu. 5 36. And he spake also a p. unto ;
   6.39, 12.16, 15.3, 18.1,9
   8. 4. every city, he spake by a p.
   9. saying, What might this p.
   10. but to others in p-s ; that
   11. Now the p. is this : The seed
   12.41. Lord, speakest thou this p.
   13. 6. He spake also this p.: A cer.
   19.11. he added and spake a p.
   20. 9. to speak to the people this p.
   19. had spoken this p. against
   21.29. And he spake to them a p.
   paroimia.
Jo. 10. 6. This p. spake Jesus unto th.

PARADISE.
   paradeisos.
Lu. 23.43. shalt thou be with me in p.
²Co. 12. 4. he was caught up into p.
Rev. 2. 7. in the midst of the p. of God

PARCEL.   (See Ground.)

PARCHMENTS.
   membrana.
²Ti. 4.13. books, but especially the p.

PARENTS.
   goneus.   [Mar.13.12
Mat.10.21.shall rise up agai. their p-s;
Lu. 2.27. when the p-s brought in the
   41. his p-s went to Jerusalem ev.
   8.56. her p-s were astonished : but
   18.29. hath left house, or p-s, or
   21.16. shall be betrayed both by p-s
Jo. 9. 2. did sin, this man, or his p-s

Jo. 9. 3. this man sinned, nor his **p**-s
18. they called the **p**-s of him
20. His **p**-s answered them and
22. These words spake his **p**-s
23. Therefore said his **p**-s, He is
Ro. 1.30. evil things, disobedient to **p**-s
²Co.12.14. lay up for **p**-s, but **p**-s for the
Eph. 6. 1. obey your **p**-s in the Lord
Col. 3.20. obey your **p**-s in all things
²Ti. 3. 2. blasphe., disobedient to **p**-s
   patēr.
Heb.11.23.hid three months of his **p**-s
   progonos.
¹Ti. 5. 4. and to requite their **p**-s

PART, [*noun,*]   -s.
   klēros.
Act. 1.17. had obtained **p**. of this min.
25. That he may take **p**. of this
   meris.
Lu. 10.42. Ma. hath chosen that good **p**.
Act. 8.21. Thou hast neither **p**. nor lot
16.12. the chief city of that **p**. of
²Co. 6.15. what **p**. hath he that believ.
   meros.
Mat. 2.22. aside into the **p**-s of Galilee
Mar. 8.10. came into the **p**-s of Dalman.
Lu. 11.36. full of light, having no **p**.
Jo. 13. 8. thee not, thou hast no **p**.
19.23. **p**-s, to every soldier a **p**.
Act. 2.10. and in the **p**-s of Libya
5. 2. brought a certain **p**. and
20. 2. he had gone over those **p**-s
23. 6. one **p**. were Sadducees, and
of the Pharisees' **p**. arose
Ro. 11.25. blindness in **p**. is happened
¹Co. 13. 9. in **p**., and we prophesy in **p**.
10. then that which is in **p**. shall
12. now I know in **p**.; but then
²Co. 1.14. acknowledged us in **p**. that
2. 5. not grieved me, but in **p**.
Eph. 4. 9. into the lower **p**-s of the earth
16. in the measure of every **p**.
Rev.16.19. was divided into three **p**-s
20. 6. hath **p**. in the first resurrec.
21. 8. shall have their **p**. in the
22.19. God shall take away his **p**.
   klima.
Ro. 15.23. no more place in these **p**-s
   pleiōn.
Act.19.32. and the *more* **p**. knew not
27.12. the *more* **p**. advised to depart
¹Co. 15. 6. the *greater* **p**. remain unto
   merizo.
Heb. 7. 2. Abraham *gave* a tenth **p**. of
   metechō.
Heb. 2.14. likewise *took* **p**. of the same
   (See *Hinder, Tenth, Uttermost.*)

PARTAKER,   -s.
   koinōnos.
Mat.23.30.we would not have been **p**-s
¹Co. 10.18. sacrifices **p**-s of the altar
¹Co. 1. 7. as ye are **p**-s of the sufferings
¹Pet. 5. 1. and also a **p**. of the glory
¹Pet. 1. 4. be **p**-s of the divine nature
   sungkoinōnos.
¹Co. 9.23. might be **p**. thereof *with*
Phi. 1. 7. ye all are **p**-s of my grace
   koinōneō.
Ro. 15.27. Gentiles *have been* **p**-s of
¹Ti. 5.22. neither be **p**. of other men's
Heb. 2.14. as the children *are* **p**-s of
¹Pet. 4.13. as ye *are* **p**-s of Christ's
John 11. speed, *is* **p**. of his evil deeds
   sungkoinōneō.
Rev.18. 4. that ye *be* not **p**-s *of* her sins
   metechō.
¹Co. 9.10. should *be* **p**. of his hope
12 If others *be* **p**-s of this power
10.17. we *are* all **p**-s of that one
21. ye cannot *be* **p**-s of the Lord's
204

¹Co.10.30. For if I by grace *be* a **p**., why
   metochos.
Heb. 3. 1. **p**-s of the heavenly calling
14. we are made **p**-s of Christ
6. 4. were made **p**-s of the Holy
12. 8. whereof all are **p**-s, then are
   summetochos.
Eph. 3. 6. **p**-s of his promise in Christ
5. 7. Be not ye therefore **p**-s with
   metalambanō.
²Ti. 2. 6. must *be* first **p**. of the fruits
Heb.12.10. that we might *be* **p**-s of his
   summerizō.
¹Co. 9.13. altar are **p**-s with the altar
   meris. ·[for the *share*] of the in.
Col. 1.12. us meet to be **p**-s (fitted us
   sungkakopatheō.
²Ti. 1. 8. *be* thou **p**. *of the afflictions* of
   antilambanomai.
¹Ti. 6. 2. beloved, **p**-s of the benefit

PARTAKEST.
   ginomai sungkoinōnos.
Ro. 11.17. *with* them **p**. of the root

PARTED.
   diamerizō.   [Lu.23.34
Mat.27.35. **p**. his garments : Mar.15.24;
They **p**. my garments amo.;
Jo.19.24
Act. 2.45. **p**. them to all men, as every
   diistēmi.
Lu. 24.51. he *was* **p**. from them, and

PARTIAL.
   diakrinō.
Jas. 2. 4. *Are* ye not then **p**. in yourse.

PARTIALITY.
   prosklisis.
¹Ti. 5.21. another, doing nothing by **p**.
   adiakritos.
Jas. 3.17. *without* **p**., and without hyp.

PARTICULAR.
   ek meros.
¹Co. 12.27. of Christ, and members *in* **p**.
   ho [*pl.*] kata heis, [*accu.*]
Eph. 5.33. let *every one* of you *in* **p**.

PARTICULARLY.
   kata [*accu.*] heis hekastos.
Act.21.19. he declared **p**. (*by each one.*)
   kata [*accu.*] meros.
Heb. 9. 5. we cannot now speak **p**.

PARTITION.
   phragmos.
Eph. 2.14. down the middle wall of **p**.

PARTLY.
   tis meros.
¹Co. 11.18. you; and I **p**. believe it
   houtos.
Heb.10.33.**p**., whilst ye were made a
and **p**., whilst ye became

PARTNER,   -s.
   koinōnos.
Lu. 5.10. which were **p**-s with Simon
²Co. 8.23. he is my **p**. and fellowhelper
Phile. 17. thou count me therefore a **p**.
   metochos.
Lu. 5. 7. they beckoned unto their **p**-s

PARTS.
   peras.   [Lu.11.31
Mat.12.42. from the *uttermost* **p**. of the;

PASS,   -cd, -eth, -ing.
   parerchomai.
Mat. 5.18. Till heav. and earth **p**. *away*
one tittle *shall* in no wise **p**.
8.28. that no man might **p**. by
24.34. This generation *shall* not **p**.;
Mar.13.30

Mat.24.35.Hea. and earth *shall* **p**. *away*;
Mar.13.31 ; Lu.21.33
my words *shall* not **p**. *away*;
Mar.13.31; Lu.21.33
26.39. *let* this cup **p**. from me
42. if this cup may not **p**. *away*
Mar. 6.48. and would *have* **p**-ed *by* them
14.35. the hour *might* **p**. from him
Lu. 11.42. and **p**. *over* judgment and
16.17. for heaven and earth *to* **p**.
18.37. Jesus of Nazareth **p**-eth *by*
21.32. This gener. shall not **p**. *away*
Act.16. 8. And they **p**-ing *by* Mysia
²Co. 5.17. old things *are* **p**-ed *away*
Jas. 1.10. of the grass he shall **p**. *away*
²Pet. 3.10. the heavens shall **p**. *away*
Rev.21. 1. first earth *were* **p**-ed *away*
   dierchomai.
Mar. 4.35. *Let* us **p**. *over* unto the
Lu. 4.30. he **p**-ing *through* the midst
17.11. he **p**-ed *through* the midst of
19. 1. Jesus entered and **p**-ed *thro.*
4. for he was *to* **p**. that way
Act. 8.40. **p**-ing *through* he preached
9.32. *as* Peter **p**-ed *throughout* all
14.24. *after* they had **p**-ed *through.*
15. 3. they **p**-ed *through* Phenice
17.23. For *as* I **p**-ed *by*, and beheld
18.27. when he was disposed *to* **p**.
19. 1. Paul *having* **p**-ed *through*
21. *when* he had **p**-ed *through*
Ro. 5.12. so death **p**-ed *upon* all men
¹Co. 10. 1. and all **p**-ed *through* the sea
16. 5. when I *shall* **p**. *through* Ma.
for I do **p**. *through* Macedo.
²Co. 1.16. *to* **p**. *by* you into Macedonia
Heb. 4.14. high priest *that is* **p**-ed *into*
   antiparerchomai.
Lu. 10.31, 32. **p**-ed *by* on the other side
   erchomai.
Act. 5.15. the shadow of Peter **p**-ing *by*
   proerchomai.
Act. 12.10. **p**-ed *on* through one street
   aperchomai.
Rev.21. 4. former things *are* **p**-ed *away*
   paragō.
Mat. 9. 9. And *as* Jesus **p**-ed *forth*
20.30. heard that Jesus **p**-ed *by*
Mar. 2.14. And *as* he **p**-ed *by*, he saw
15.21. Simon a Cyr., *who* **p**-ed *by*
Jo. 8.59. midst of th., and so **p**-ed *by*
9. 1. And *as* Jesus **p**-ed *by*, he
¹Co. 7.31. of this world **p**-eth *away*
¹Jo. 2.17. And the world **p**-eth *away*
   diaperaō.
Mat. 9. 1. into a ship, and **p**-ed *over*
Mar. 5.21. *when* Jesus *was* **p**-ed *over*
6.53. *when* they had **p**-ed *over*
Lu. 16.26. neither *can* they **p**. *to* us
   diabainō.
Lu. 16.26. *which* would **p**. *from* hence
Heb.11.29. By faith they **p**-ed *through*
   metabainō.   [¹Jo.3.14
Jo. 5.24. **p**-ed *from* death unto life ;
   paraporeuomai.   [Mar.15.29
Mat.27.39. And they *that* **p**-ed *by* revi.
Mar. 9.30. and **p**-ed *through* Galilee
11.20. *as* they **p**-ed *by*, they saw
   diaporeuomai.
Lu. 18.36. hearing the multitude **p**. *by*
   polus.
Mar. 6.35. and now the time is *far* **p**-ed
   diodeuō.
Act.17. 1. *when* they had **p**-ed *through*
   paralegomai.
Act.27. 8. And, hardly **p**-ing it, came
   huperakmos.
¹Co. 7.36. she **p**. the *flower of* her *age*
   ginomai.
¹Co. 15.54. then *shall* be brought to **p**.

huperballō.
Eph. 3.19. love of Ch., *which* p-*eth*
    huperechō.
Phi. 4. 7. peace of God, *which* p-*eth*
    anastrephō.
¹Pet. 1.17. p. the time of your sojourn.
      (See *Come, Past.*)

PASSION,   -*s.*
    paschō.   (*he had suffered.*)
Act. 1. 3. himself alive after *his* p.
    homoiopathēs.
Act.14.15. We also are men *of like* p-*s*
Jas. 5.17. a man *subject to like* p-*s* as

PASSOVER.
    pascha.
Mat.26. 2. days is the feast of the p.
    17. prepare for thee to eat the p.
    18. I will keep the p. at thy
    19. and they made ready the p.;
        Mar.14.16 ; Lu.22.13
Mar.14. 1. days was the feast of the p.
    12. when they killed the p., his
        that thou mayest eat the p.
    14. where I shall eat the p.;
        Lu.22.11
Lu. 2.41. year at the feast of the p.
    22. 1. nigh, which is called the p.
    7. when the p. must be killed
    8. Go and prepare us the p.
    15. desired to eat this p. with
Jo. 2.13. And the Jews' p. was at
    23. was in Jerusalem at the p.
    6. 4. And the p., a feast of the
    11.55. And the Jews' p. was nigh
        before the p., to purify
    12. 1. Jesus six days before the p.
    13. 1. Now bef. the feast of the p.
    18.28. that they might eat the p.
    39. unto you one at the p.
    19.14. was the preparation of the p.
¹Co. 5. 7. Christ our p. is sacrificed
Heb.11.28. Through faith he kept the p.

PAST, (See *Feeling.*)
    pote.
Ro. 11.30. For as ye *in times* p. have
Gal. 1.13. my conversation *in time* p.
    23. wh. persecuted us *in times* p.
Eph. 2. 2. Wherein *in time* p. ye walk.
    3. *in times* p. in the lusts of
    11. that ye being *in time* p. G.
Phile. 11. Which *in time* p. was to
¹Pet. 2.10. Which *in time* p. were not a
    parerchomai.
Mat.14.15. and the time *is* now p.; send
Act. 27. 9. the fast *was* now already p.
¹Pet. 4. 3. For the time p. of our life
    dierchomai.
Act. 12.10. *When they were* p. the first
    aperchomai.
Rev. 9.12. One woe *is* p.; and, behold
    11.14. The second woe *is* p.; and
    diaginomai.
Mar.16. 1. *when* the sabbath *was* p.
    ginomai.
Lu. 9.36. when the voice *was* p., Jesus
²Ti. 2.18. the resurrection *is* p. already
    paroichomai.
Act.14.16. Who in times p. suffered all
    proginomai.
Ro. 3.25. remission of sins *that are* p.
    anexichniastos.
Ro. 11.33. his ways p. *finding out*
    palai.
Heb. 1. 1. spake *in time* p. unto the
    para, [*accu.*]
Heb.11.11. child when she was p. age
    paragō.
¹Jo. 2. 8. because the darkness *is* p.

PASTORS.
    poimēn.
Eph. 4.11. and some, p. and teachers

PASTURE.
    nomē.
Jo. 10. 9. go in and out, and find p.

PATHS.
    tribos.   [Mar.1.3 ; Lu.3.4
Mat. 3. 3. make his p. straight ; *that*
    trochia.
Heb.12.13. make straight p. for your

PATIENCE.
    hupomonē.
Lu. 8.15. and bring forth fruit with p.
    21.19. In your p. possess ye your
Ro. 5. 3. that tribulation worketh p.
    4. And p., experience ; and
    8.25. do we with p. wait for it
    15. 4. through p. and comfort of
    5. Now the God of p. and cons.
²Co. 6. 4. in much p., in afflictions
    12.12. wrought among you in all p.
Col. 1.11. unto all p. and longsuffering
¹Th. 1. 3. and p. of hope in our Lord
²Th. 1. 4. for your p. and faith in all
¹Ti. 6.11. faith, love, p., meekness
²Ti. 3.10. fa., longsuffering, charity, p.
Tit. 2. 2. sou.in faith, in charity, in p.
Heb.10.36.For ye have need of p., that
    12. 1. and let us run with p. the
Jas. 1. 3. trying of your faith work. p.
    4. let p. have her perfect work
    5.11. Ye have heard of the p.
²Pet. 1. 6. temper. p.; and to p. godli.
Rev. 1. 9. in the kingdom and p. of Je.
    2. 2. and thy labour, and thy p.
    3. And hast borne, and hast p.
    19. and thy p., and thy works
    3.10. hast kept the word of my p.
    13.10. Here is the p. and the faith
    14.12. Here is the p. of the saints
    makrothumia.
Heb. 6.12. through faith and p. inherit
Jas. 5.10. suffering affliction, and of p.
    makrothumeō.
Mat.18.26,29. have p. with me, and I
Jas. 5. 7. *hath long* p. for it, until

PATIENT.
    makrothumeō.
¹Th. 5.14. weak, *be* p. toward all men
Jas. 5. 7. *Be* p. therefore, brethren, un.
    8. *Be* ye also p. ; stablish your
    hupomonē.
Ro. 2. 7. by p. *continuance* in welldo.
²Th. 3. 5. into the p. *waiting for* Christ
    hupomonō.
Ro. 12.12. p. in tribulation ; continuing
    epieikēs.
¹Ti. 3. 3. but p., not a brawler, not co.
    anexikakos.
²Ti. 2.24. unto all men, apt to teach, p.

PATIENTLY. (See *Take,*)
    makrothumōs.
Act.26. 3. I beseech thee to hear me p.
    makrothumeō.
Heb. 6.15. *after he had* p. endured, he

PATRIARCH,   -*s.*
    patriarchēs.
Act. 2.29. speak unto you of the p. Da.
    7. 8. Jacob begat the twelve p-*s*
    9. the p-*s*, moved with envy
Heb. 7. 4. even the p. Abraham gave

PATTERN,   -*s.*
    tupos.
Tit. 2. 7. shewing thyself a p. of good
Heb. 8. 5. according to the p. shewed

    hupotupōsis.
¹Ti. 1.16. for a p. to them which (*pat-*
    hupodeigma.   [*tern of them*)
Heb. 9.23. that the p-*s* of things in the

PAVEMENT.
    lithostrōtos.
Jo. 19.13. the p., but in the Hebrew

PAY, (See *Tithe,*)   *Paid.*
    apodidōmi.   [Lu.12.59
Mat. 5.26. till thou *hast* p-*d* the utter.;
    18.25. forasmuch as he had not *to* p.
    26, 29. with me, and I *will* p.
    28. saying, p. me that thou owe.
    30. till he *should* p. the debt
    34. till he *should* p. all that was
Lu. 7.42. when they had nothing *to* p.
    teleō.
Mat.17.24.*Doth* not your master p. trib.
Ro. 13. 6. for this cause p. ye tribute

PAYMENT.
    apodidōmi.
Mat.18.25.th. he had, and p. *to be made*

PEACE.
    eirēnē.
Mat.10.13.let your p. come upon it
        if it be.., let your p. return
    34. I am come to send p. on ear.
        I came not to send p.
Mar. 5.34. go in p., and be whole of thy
Lu. 1.79. our feet into the way of p.
    2.14. on earth p., good will toward
    29. thou thy servant depart in p
    7.50. faith..saved thee ; go in p.
    8.48. made thee whole ; go in p.
    10. 5. first say, p. be to this house
    6. son of p. be there, your p.
    11.21. palace, his goods are in p.
    12.51. I am come to give p. on earth
    14.32. and desireth conditions of p.
    19.38. p. in heaven, and glory in
    42. which belong unto thy p.
    24.36. p. be..you ; Jo.20.19,21,26
Jo. 14.27. p. I leave with you, my p. I
    16.33. that in me ye might have p.
Act.10.36. preaching p. by Jesus Christ
    12.20. their friend, desired p.
    15.33. they were let go in p. from
    16.36. therefo. depart, and go in p.
Ro. 1. 7. Grace to you, and p. from ;
        ¹Co.1.3 ; ²Co.1.2 ; Gal.1.3 ;
        Eph.1.2 ; Phi.1.2 ; Col.1.2 ;
        ¹Th.1.1 ; ²Th.1.2 ; Phile.3 ;
        ¹Pet.1.2 ; Rev.1.4
    2.10. glory, honour, and p., to ev.
    3.17. the way of p. have they not
    5. 1. by faith, we have p. with G.
    8. 6. spiritu. minded is life and p.
    10.15. them that preach..gosp.of p.
    14.17. righteousness, and p., and
    19. the things which make for p.
    15.13. with all joy and p. in believ.
    33. the God of p. be with you all
    16.20. the God of p. shall bruise S.
¹Co. 7.15. God hath called us to p.
    14.33. author of confus., but of p.
    16.11. conduct him forth in p., that
²Co.13.11. G. of love and p.; Phi.4.9
Gal. 5.22. love, joy, p., longsuffering
    6.16. p. be on them, and mercy
Eph. 2.14. For he is our p., who hath
    15. one new man, so making p.
    17. came and preached p. to you
    4. 3. unity of the Sin..bond of p.
    6.15. prepara. of the gospel of p.
    23. p. be to the brethren, and
Phi. 4. 7. the p. of God, which passeth
Col. 3.15. let the p. of God rule in your
¹Th. 5. 3. when they shall say, p. and
    23. the very God of p. sanctify

²Th. 3.16. Lord of **p.** himself give you **p.**
¹Ti. 1. 2. Grace, mercy, and **p.** from;
            ²Ti.1.2; Tit.1.4
²Ti. 2.22. righteous., faith, charity, **p.**
Heb. 7. 2. Salem, which is, King of **p.**
   11.31. had receiv. the spies with **p.**
   12.14. Follow **p.** with all men, and
   13.20. the God of **p.**, that brought
Jas. 2.16. say unto them, Depart in **p.**
   3.18. in **p.** of them that make **p.**
¹Pet..1. 2. Grace..you, and **p.**; ²Pet.1.2
   3.11. let him seek **p.**, and ensue it
   5.14. **p.** be with you all that are
²Pet. 3.14. ye may be found of him in **p.**
²John 3. be with you, mercy, and **p.**
³John 14. **p.** be to thee. Our friends
Jude 2. Mercy unto you, and **p.**, and
Rev. 1. 4. Grace be unto you, and **p.**
   6. 4. to take **p.** from the earth
      eirēneuō.
Mar. 9.50. have **p.** one with another
²Co. 13.11. be of one mind, *live in* **p.**
¹Th. 5.13. *be at* **p.** among yourselves
      eirēnopoieō.
Col. 1.20. *having made* **p.** through the
      siōpaō.
Mat. 20.31. bec. they *should hold* their **p.**
   26.63. But Jesus *held* his **p.** And
Mar. 3. 4. But they *held* their **p.**; 9.34
   4.39. unto the sea, **p.**, be still
   10.48. *should hold* his **p.**; Lu.18.39
   14.61. But he *held* his peace, and
Lu. 19.40. if these *should hold* their **p.**
Act.18. 9. speak, and *hold* not thy **p.**
      sigaō.
Lu. 20.26. his answer, and *held* their **p.**
Act.12.17. becko. unto..*to hold* their **p.**
   15.13. after they *had held* their **p.**
¹Co. 14.30. *let* the first *hold* his **p.**
      hēsuchazō.
Lu. 14. 4. they *held* their **p.**; Act.11.18
      phimoō. [Lu. 4.35
Mar. 1.25. *Hold* thy **p.**, and come out;

PEACEABLE.
eirēnikos.
Heb.12.11. the **p.** fruit of righteousness
Jas. 3.17. first pure, then **p.**, gentle
      hēsuchios.
¹Ti. 2. 2. may lead a quiet and **p.** life

PEACEABLY.
eirēneuō.
Ro. 12.18. in you, *live* **p.** with all men
PEACEMAKERS.
eirēnopoios.
Mat. 5. 9. Blessed are the **p.**: for they
PEARL, -s.
margaritēs.
Mat. 7. 6. neither cast ye your **p**-s bef.
   13.45. man, seeking goodly **p**-s
   46. found one **p.** of great price
¹Ti. 2. 9. gold, or **p**-s, or costly array
Rev.17. 4. and precious stones and **p**-s;
      18.12,16
   21.21. twelve gates were twelve **p**-s
      several gate was of one **p.**
PECULIAR.
periousios.
Tit. 2.14. unto himself a **p.** people
eis peripoiēsis.
¹Pet. 2. 9. an holy nation, a **p.** people
PEN.
kalamos.
³John 13. not with ink and **p.** write
PENNY, Pence.
dēnarion.
Mat.18.28.wh. owed him an hund. **p**-ce
206

Mat.20. 2. with the labourers for a **p.** a
   9, 10. received every man a **p.**
   13. thou agree with me for a **p.**
   22.19. they brought unto him a **p.**
Mar. 6.37. two hund. **p.** *worth*; Jo.6.7
   12.15. bring me a **p.** that I may see
   14. 5. more than three hundred **p**-ce
Lu. 7.41. the one owed five hund. **p**-ce
   10.35. took out two **p**-ce, and gave
   20.24. Shew me a **p.** Whose image
Jo. 12. 5. sold for three hundred **p**-ce
Rev. 6. 6. A measure of wheat for a **p.**
      measures of barley for a **p.**
PENTECOST.
pentēkostē.
Act. 2. 1. And when the day of **p.** was
   20.16. at Jerusalem the day of **p.**
¹Co.16. 8. tarry at Ephesus until **p.**
PENURY.
husterēma.
Lu. 21. 4. but she of her **p.** hath cast
PEOPLE, -s.
laos.
Mat. 1.21. shall save his **p.** from their
   2. 4. and scribes of the **p.** together
   6. shall rule my **p.** Israel
   4.16. The **p.** which sat in darkness
   23. disease among the **p.**; 9.35
   13.15. For this **p.**'s heart is waxed
   15. 8. This **p.** draweth nigh unto
   21.23. and the elders of the **p.**;
      26.3,47.27.1; Lu.22.66
   26. 5. be an uproar among the **p.**;
      Mar.14.2
   27.25. Then answered all the **p.**
   64. away, and say unto the **p.**
Mar. 7. 6. This **p.** honoureth me with
   11.32. they feared the **p.**; Lu.20.19,
      22.2; Act.5.26
Lu. 1.10. whole multitude of the **p.**
   17. to make ready a **p.** prepared
   21. And the **p.** waited for Zach.
   68. visited and redeemed his **p.**
   77. of salvation unto his **p.**
   2.10. which shall be to all **p.**
   31. before the face of all **p.**
   32. the glory of thy **p.** Israel
   3.15. And as the **p.** were in expec.
   18. preached he unto the **p.**
   21. when all the **p.** were baptiz.
   6.17. a great multitude of **p.**
   7. 1. the audience of the **p.**; 20.45
   16. God hath visited his **p.**
   29. And all the **p.** that heard
   8.47. before all the **p.** for what
   9.13. and buy meat for all this **p.**
   18.43. and all the **p.**, when they
   19.47. the chief of the **p.** sought to
   48. all the **p.** were very attentive
   20. 1. as he taught the **p.** in the
   6. all the **p.** will stone us: for
   9. speak to the **p.** this parable
   26. of his words before the **p.**
   21.23. land, and wrath upon this **p.**
   38. all the **p.** came early in the
   23. 5. He stirreth up the **p.**, teach.
   13. and the rulers and the **p.**
   14. as one that perverteth the **p.**
   27. a great company of **p.**, and
   35. And the **p.** stood beholding
   24.19. before God and all the **p.**
Jo. 8. 2. and all the **p.** came unto
   11.50. one man sh. die for the **p.**;
      18.14
Act. 2.47. having favour with all the **p.**
   3. 9. all the **p.** saw him walking
   11. all the **p.** ran together unto
   12. he answered unto the **p.**
   23. destroyed from among the **p.**
   4. 1. as they spake unto the **p.**
   2. griev. that they taught the **p.**

Act. 4. 8. Ye rulers of the **p.**, and eld.
   10. and to all the **p.** of Israel
   17. spread no further amo. the **p.**
   21. because of the **p.**; for all
   25. and the **p.** imagine vain
   27. and the **p.** of Israel, were
   5.12. won. wrought among the **p.**
   13. but the **p.** magnified them
   20. speak in the temple to the **p.**
   25. temple, and teaching the **p.**
   34. in reputa. among all the **p.**
   37. and drew away much **p.**
   6. 8. and miracles among the **p.**
   12. And they stirred up the **p.**
   7.17. the **p.** grew and multiplied
   34. the affliction of my **p.** which
   10. 2. gave much alms to the **p.**
   41. Not to all the **p.**, but unto
   42. to preach unto the **p.**, and
   12. 4. to bring him forth to the **p.**
   11. the expectation of the **p.** of
   13.15. exhortation for the **p.**, say
   17. The God of this **p.** of Israel
      and exalted the **p.** when
   24. repentance to all the **p.** of
   31. his witnesses unto the **p.**
   15.14. out of them a **p.** for his name
   18.10. I have much **p.** in this city
   19. 4. saying unto the **p.**, that they
   21.28. against the **p.**, and the law
   30. the **p.** ran together: and
   36. For the multitude of the **p.**
   39. suffer me to speak unto the **p.**
   40. with the hand unto the **p.**
   23. 5. evil of the ruler of thy **p.**
   26.17. Delivering thee from the **p.**
   23. sh. shew light unto the **p.**
   28.17. nothing against the **p.**, or
   26. Go unto this **p.**, and say
   27. For the heart of this **p.** as
Ro. 9.25. **p.**, which were not my **p.**
   26. Ye are not my **p.**; there
   10.21. disobedient and gainsay. **p.**
   11. 1. Hath God cast away his **p.**
   2. God hath not cast away his **p.**
   15.10. Rej., ye Gentiles, with his **p.**
   11. and laud him, all ye **p.**
¹Co.10. 7. The **p.** sat down to eat and
   14.21. will I speak unto this **p.**
²Co. 6.16. God, and they shall be my **p.**
Tit. 2.14. a peculiar **p.**, zealous of
Heb. 2.17. recon. for the sins of the **p.**
   4. 9. therefore a rest to the **p.** of
   5. 3. as for the **p.**, so also for
   7. 5. to take tithes of the **p.**
   11. under it the **p.** received
   27. and then for the **p.**'s: for
   8.10. and they shall be to me a **p.**
   9. 7. and for the errors of the **p.**
   19. every precept to all the **p.**
      both the book, and all the **p.**
   10.30. The Lord shall judge his **p.**
   11.25. affliction with the **p.** of God
   13.12. might sanctify the **p.** with
¹Pet. 2. 9. an holy nation, a peculiar **p.**
   10. not a **p.**, but are now the **p.**
²Pet. 2. 1. prophets also among the **p.**
Jude 5. having saved the **p.** out of
Rev. 5. 9. tongue, and **p.**, and nation
   7. 9. and **p.**, and tongues, stood
   10.11. prop. again before many **p**-s
   11. 9. And they of the **p.** and
   14. 6. kindred, and tongue, and **p.**
   17.15. the whore sitteth, are **p**-s
   18. 4. Come out of her, my **p.**, that
   21. 3. they shall be his **p.**, and
      ochlos.
Mat. 7.28. the **p.** were astonished at his
   9.23. and the **p.** making a noise
   25. But when the **p.** were put
   12.23. And all the **p.** were amazed
   46. While he yet talked to the **p**

Mat.14.13.and when the **p.** had heard
21.26. we fear the **p.**; for all hold
27.15. to release unto the **p.** a
Mar 5.21. much **p.** gathered unto him
24. much **p.** followed him, and
6.33. the **p.** saw them departing
34. saw much **p.**, and was moved
45. while he sent away the **p.**
7.14. when he had called the **p.**
17. into the house from the **p.**
8. 6. he commanded the **p.** to
set them before the **p.**
34. when he had called the **p.**
9.15. straightway all the **p.**, when
25. When Jesus saw that the **p.**
10. 1. and the **p.** resort unto him
46. and a great *number of* **p.**
11.18. because all the **p.** was aston.
12.12. but feared the **p.**: for they
37. the common **p.** heard him
41. and beheld how the **p.** cast
15.11. the chief priests moved the **p.**
15. willing to content the **p.**
Lu. 3.10. And the **p.** asked him, saying
4.42. and the **p.** sought him, and
5. 1. as the **p.** pressed upon him
3. and taught the **p.** out of the
7. 9. and said unto the **p.** that
11. went with him, and much **p.**
12. much **p.** of the city was with
24. began to speak unto the **p.**
8. 4. And when much **p.** were
40. the **p.** gladly received him
42. went, the **p.** thronged him
9.11. And the **p.**, when they knew
18. Whom say the **p.** that I am
37. the hill, much **p.** met him
11.14. spake ; and the **p.** wondered
29. And when the **p.** were gather.
12. 1. innumerable multitude of **p.**
54. And he said also to the **p.**
13.14. and said unto the **p.**, There
17. and all the **p.** rejoiced for all
23. 4. chief priests and to the **p.**
48. And all the **p.** that came to.
Jo. 6.22. when the **p.** which stood
24. When the **p.** therefore saw
7.12. among the **p.** concerning him
Nay ; he deceiveth the **p.**
20. The **p.** answered and said
31. And many of the **p.** believed
32. heard that the **p.** murmured
40. Many of the **p.** therefore
43. was a division among the **p.**
49. But this **p.** who knoweth not
11.42. because of the **p.** which stand
12. 9. Much **p.** of the Jews therefo.
12. On the next day much **p.**
17. The **p.** therefore that was
18. For this cause the **p.** also
29. The **p.** therefore, that stood
34. The **p.** answered him, We
Act. 8. 6. And the **p.** with one accord
11.24. and much **p.** was added unto
26. church, and taught much **p.**
14.11. when the **p.** saw what Paul
13. done sacrifice with the **p.**
14. and ran in among the **p.**
18. restrained they the **p.**, that
19. who persuaded the **p.**, and
17. 8. And they troubled the **p.** and
13. and stirred up the **p.**
19.26. and turned away much **p.**
35. had appeased the **p.**, he said
21.27. also stirred up all the **p.**
35. for the violence of the **p.**
24.12. neither raising up the **p.**
Rev.19. 1. a great voice of much **p.**
dēmos.
Act.12.22. the **p.** gave a shout, saying
17. 5. to bring them out to the **p.**
19.30. have entered in unto the **p.**

Act.19.33. made his defence unto the **p.**
ethnos.
Act. 8. 9. bewitched the **p.** of Samaria
Ro. 10.19. no **p.**, and by a foolish nat.

PERADVENTURE.
tacha.
Ro. 5. 7. yet **p.** for a good man some
mēpote.
²Ti. 2.25. *if* God **p.** will give them

PERCEIVE,   -ed, -est, -ing.
ginōskō.
Mat.16. 8. Which *when* Jesus **p**-*ed*, he
21.45. they **p**-*ed* that he spake of
22.18. Jes. **p**-*ed* their wicked., *and*
Lu. 8.46. for I **p.** *(did* **p.**) that virtue
20.19. they **p**-*ed* that he had spoken
Jo. 6.15. *When* Jesus therefore **p**-*ed*
Act.23. 6. *when* Paul **p**-*ed* that the one
Gal. 2. 9. *when*. . **p**-*ed* the grace that
¹Jo. 3.16. Hereby **p.** we the love of God
epiginōskō.   [*we have* **p**-*ed*)
Mar. 2. 8. immediately *when* Jesus **p**-*ed*
Lu. 1.22. they **p**-*ed* that he had seen a
5.22. *when* Jesus **p**-*ed* their thoug.
theōreō.
Jo. 4.19. I **p.** that thou art a prophet
12.19. **p.** ye how ye prevail nothing
Act.17.22. I **p**. . .ye are too superstitious
27.10. I **p.** that this voyage will be
eideō.
Mat.13.14.ye shall see, and shall not **p.**;
Mar. 4.12 ; Act.28.26
Mar.12.28.**p**-*ing* that he had answered
Lu. 9.47. Jesus, **p**-*ing* the thought of
Act.14. 9. **p**-*ing* that he had faith to be
noeō.
Mar. 7.18. Do ye not **p.**, that whatsoever
8.17. **p.** ye not yet, neither under.
katanoeō.
Lu. 6.41. but **p**-*est* not the beam that
20.23. he **p**-*ed* their craftiness, and
katalambanō.
Act. 4.13. **p**-*ed* that they were unlearn.
10.34. I **p.** that God is no respecter
aisthanomai.
Lu. 9.45. them, that they **p**-*ed* it not
horaō.
Act. 8.23. I **p.** that thou art in the
heuriskō.
Act.23.29. Whom I **p**-*ed* to be accused
blepō.
²Co. 7. 8. for I **p.** that the same epistle

PERDITION.
apōleia.
Jo. 17.12. but the son of **p.** ; that the
Phi. 1.28. an evident token of **p.**, but
²Th. 2. 3. be revealed, the son of **p.**
¹Ti. 6. 9. men in destruction and **p.**
Heb.10.39.who draw back unto **p.**
²Pet. 3. 7. judgment and **p.** of ungodly
Rev.17. 8. bottomless pit,and go into **p.**
11. the seven, and goeth into **p.**

PERFECT, [*adjec.*]
teleios.
Mat. 5.48. Be ye therefore **p.**, even as
Fath. which is in heaven is **p.**
19.21. If thou wilt be **p.**, go and
Ro. 12. 2. acceptable, and **p.**, will of G.
¹Co. 2. 6. wis. among them that are **p.**
13.10. when that which is **p.** is co.
Eph. 4.13. unto a **p.** man, unto the me.
Phi. 3.15. therefore, as many as be **p.**
Col. 1.28. may present every man **p.** in
4.12. that ye may stand **p.** and co.
Heb. 9.11. greater and more **p.** taberna.
Jas. 1. 4. let patience have her **p.** work
ye may be **p.** and entire
17. and every **p.** gift is from ab.
25. looketh into the **p.**law of lib.

Jas. 3. 2. the same is a **p.** man, and
¹Jo. 4.18. but **p.** love casteth not fear
teleioō.
Jo. 17.23. that they may be *made* **p.**
²Co. 12. 9. my strength *is made* **p.** in
Phi. 3.12. either *were* already **p.** : but
Heb. 2.10. *to make* the cap. of their . .**p.**
5. 9. And *being made* **p.**, he beca.
7.19. For the law *made* nothing **p.**
9. 9. *make* him that did the ser. **p.**
10. 1. *make* the comers thereunto **p.**
11.40. us *should* not be *made* **p.**
12.23. spirits of just men *made* **p.**
Jas. 2.22. by works *was* faith *made* **p.**
¹Jo. 4.17. Herein *is* our love *made* **p.**
18. He that fear. *is* not *made* **p.**
epiteleō.
Gal. 3. 3. *are* ye now *made* **p.** by the
katartizō.
Lu. 6.40. every one *that is* **p.** shall be
²Co. 13.11. *Be* **p.**, be of good comfort
Heb.13.21.*Make* you **p.** in every good
¹Pet. 5.10. *make* you **p.**, stablish, stren.
akribōs.
Lu. 1. 3. having had **p.** understanding
akribeia.
Act.22. 3. according to the **p.** *manner*
akribesteron.
Act.24.22. having *more* **p.** knowledge
holoklēria.
Act. 3.16. given him this **p.** *soundness*
artios.
²Ti. 3.17. the man of God may be **p.**
pleroō.   [(works *made full.*)
Rev. 3. 2. have not found thy works **p.**

PERFECT, [*verb,*]   -ed, -ing.
katartizō.
Mat.21.16.sucklings thou *hast* **p**-*ed* pra.
¹Th. 3.10. and might **p.** that which is
katartismos.
Eph.4.12. For the **p**-*ing* of the saints
teleioō.
Lu. 13.32. third day I shall be **p**-*ed*
Heb.10.14.by one offering he *hath* **p**-*ed*
¹Jo. 2. 5. verily *is* the love of God **p**-*ed*
4.12. and his love is **p**-*ed* in us
epiteleō.
²Co. 7. 1. **p**-*ing* holiness in the fear of

PERFECTION.
telesphoreō.
Lu. 8.14. and *bring* no *fruit to* **p.**
katartisis.
²Co.13. 9. also we wish, even your **p.**
teleiotēs.
Heb.6. 1. let us go on unto **p.**; not
teleiōsis.
Heb.7.11. If therefore **p.** were by the

PERFECTLY.
akribesteron.
Act.18.26.him the way of God *more* **p.**
23.15, 20.enquire something *more* **p.**
akribōs.
¹Th. 5. 2. yourselves know **p.** that the
(See *Join, Whole.*)

PERFECTNESS.
teleiotēs.
Col. 3.14. which is the bond of **p.**

PERFORM,   -ed.
apodidōmi.
Mat. 5.33. *shalt* **p.** unto the Lord thine
teleō.
Lu. 2.39. when they *had* **p**-*ed* all thin.
epiteleō.
Ro. 15.28. *When* therefore I *have* **p**-*ed*
²Co. 8.11. Now therefore **p.** the doing
Phi. 1. 6. *will* **p.** it until the day
poieō.
Lu. 1.72. To **p.** the mercy promised
207

Ro. 4.21. promi., he was able also *to* p.
     ginomai.
Lu. 1.20. these things *shall be* p-ed
     katergazomai.
Ro. 7.18. how to p. that which is

PERFORMANCE.
teleiōsis.
Lu. 1.45. there shall be a p. of those
     epiteleō.
2Co. 8.11. there may be *a* p. also

PERHAPS. (See *Lest.*)
ara.
Act. 8.22. if p. the thought of thine
     pōs.
2Co. 2. 7. lest p. such a one should
     tacha.
Phile. 15. For p. he therefore departed

PERIL,   -s.
kindunos.
Ro. 8.35. or nakedness, or p., or swo.
2Co. 11.26. p-s of waters, in p-s of, &c.

PERILOUS.
chalepos.
2Ti. 3. 1. last days p. times shall come

PERISH,   -ed, -eth.
apollumi.
Mat. 5.29, 30. of thy members *shoulⁿ* p.
   8.25. saying, Lord, save us : we p.
   9.17. run. out, and the bottles p.
  18.14. of these little ones *should* p.
  26.52. *shall* p. with the sword
Mar. 4.38. carest thou not that we p.
Lu. 5.37. spill., and the bottles *shall* p.
   8.24. saying, Master, master, we p.
  11.51. *which* p-ed between the altar
  13. 3, 5. ye *shall* all likewise p.
     33. that a prophet p. out of Jer.
  15.17. to spare, and I p. with hun.
  21.18. not an hair of your head p.
Jo. 3.15, 16. belie. in him *should* not p.
   6.27. for the meat *which* p-eth
  10.28. they *shall* never p., neither
  11.50. that the whole nation p. not
Act. 5.37. he also p-ed ; and all, even
Ro. 2.12. *shall* also p. without law
1Co. 1.18. to them *that* p. foolishness
   8.11. *shall* the weak brother p.
  15.18. fallen asleep in Chr. *are* p-ed
2Co. 2.15. saved, and in them *that* p.
2Th. 2.10. unrighteous. in them *that* p.
Heb. 1.11. They *shall* p.; but thou re.
Jas. 1.11. grace of the fashion of it p-eth
1Pet. 1. 7. preci. than of gold *that* p-eth
2Pet. 3. 6. overflowed with water, p-ed
    9. willing that any should p.
Jude 11. p-ed in the gainsaying of
     apothnēskō.
Mat. 8.32. sea, and p-ed in the waters
     eimi eis apōleia.
Act. 8.20. Thy money p. with thee
     aphanizō.
Act.13.41. despisers, and wonder, and p.
     diaphtheirō.
2Co. 4.16. though our outward man p.
     eis phthora.
Col. 2.22. Which all are *to* p. with
     sunapollumi.
Heb.11.31. Rahab p-ed not *with* them
     kataphtheirō.
2Pet. 2.12. *shall utterly* p. in their own

PERJURED.
epiorkos.
1Ti. 1.10. for liars, for p. *persons*

PERMISSION.
sunggnōmē.
1Co. 7. 6. But I speak this by p., and
208

PERMIT,   -ed.
epitrepō.
Act.26. 1. Thou *art* p-ed to speak for
1Co. 14.34. for it *is* not p-ed unto them
   16. 7. wh. with you, if the Lord p.
Heb. 6. 3. this will we do, if God p.

PERNICIOUS.
apōleia.
2Pet. 2. 2. shall follow their p. *ways*

PERPLEXED.
diaporeō.
Lu. 9. 7. he *was* p., because that it
  24. 4. as they *were* much p.
     aporeomai.
2Co. 4. 8. we *are* p., but not in despair

PERPLEXITY.
aporia.
Lu. 21.25. distress of nations, with p.

PERSECUTE,   -ed, -est, -ing.
diōkō.
Mat. 5.10. which are p-ed for righteou.
    11. men shall revile you, and p.
    12. for so p-ed they the prophets
    44. despitefully use you, and p.
  10.23. when they p. you in this
  23.34. and p. them from city to
Lu. 21.12. hands on you, and p. you
Jo. 5.16. therefore *did* the Jews p.
  15.20. *have* p-ed me, they *will* p.
Act. 7.52. *have* not your fathers p-ed
   9. 4. Saul, Saul, why p-*est* thou ;
       22.7, 26.14   [22.8, 26.15
     5. I am Jesus whom thou p-*est;*
  22. 4. I p-ed this way unto the
  26.11. I p-ed them even unto stra.
Ro. 12.14. Bless them *which* p. you
1Co. 4.12. bless ; *being* p-ed, we suffer
    15. 9. because I p-ed the church of
2Co. 4. 9. p-ed, but not forsaken ; cast
Gal. 1.13. beyond measure I p-ed the
     23. he *which* p-ed us in times
    4.29. p-ed him that was born after
Phi. 3. 6. Concerning zeal, p-*ing* the
Rev.12.13. he p-ed the woman which
     ekdiōkō.
Lu. 11.49. them they *shall* slay and p.
1Th. 2.15. prophets, and *have* p-ed us

PERSECUTION,   -s.
diōgmos.   [Mar.4.17
Mat.13.21. or p. ariseth because of the ;
Mar.10.30. children, and lands, with p-s
Act. 8. 1. a great p. against the church
    13.50. raised p. against Paul and
Ro. 8.35. distress, or p., or famine
2Co.12.10. in necessities, in p-s, in dist.
2Th. 1. 4. faith in all your p-s and
2Ti. 3.11. p-s, afflictions, which came
    at Lystra; what p-s I endured
     diōkō.
Gal. 5.11. why do I yet *suffer* p.? then
   6.12. *should suffer* p. for the cross
2Ti. 3.12. in Ch. Jesus *shall suffer* p.
     thlipsis.
Act.11.19. upon the p. that arose about

PERSECUTOR.
diōktēs.
1Ti. 1.13. a blasphemer, and a p., and

PERSEVERANCE.
proskarterēsis.
Eph. 6.18. with all p. and supplication

PERSON,   -s.
prosōpon.   [Mar.12.14
Mat.22.16. regardest not the p. of men ;
Lu. 20.21. neither acceptest thou the p.
2Co. 1.11. by the means of many p-s
   2.10. forgave I it in the p. of Christ

Gal. 2. 6. God accepteth no man's p.
Jude 16. having *men's* p-s in admirat.
     prosōpolēptēs.
Act.10.34. God is no *respecter of* p-s
     prosōpolēpsia.   [Col. 3.25
Ro. 2.11. is no *respect. of* p-s; Eph.6.9,
Jas. 2. 1. the faith. . with *respect of* p-s
     prosōpolēpteō.
Jas. 2. 9. But if ye *have respect to* p-s
     aprosōpolēptōs.
1Pet. 1.17. who *without respect of* p-s
     hupostasis.
Heb. 1. 3. the express image of his p.
     (See *Perjured, Profane.*)

PERSUADE,   -ed, -est, -eth, -ing.
peithō.
Mat.27.20. priests and elders p-ed the
  28.14. we *will* p. him, and secure
Lu. 16.31. neither *will* they *be* p-ed
   20. 6. for they be p-ed that John
Act.13.43. p-ed them to continue in the
   14.19. who p-ed the people, and
   18. 4. and p-ed the Jews and the
   19. 8. and p-*ing* the things concer.
     26. this Paul hath p-ed and tur.
   21.14. *when* he would not *be* p-ed
   26.26. for I am p-ed that none of
     28. Almost thou p-*est* me to be
   28.23. p-*ing* them concerning Jesus
Ro. 8.38. For I *am* p-ed, that neither
   14.14. and *am* p-ed by the Lord Je.
   15.14. also *am* p-ed of you, my bre.
2Co. 5.11. we p. men ; but we are made
Gal. 1.10. For *do* I now p. men, or God
2Ti. 1. 5. and I *am* p-ed that in thee
     12. and *am* p-ed that he is able
Heb. 6. 9. we *are* p-ed better things of
   11.13. and *were* p-ed of them, and
     anapeithō.
Act.18.13. This fellow p-*eth* men to
     plērophoreō.
Ro. 4.21. *being fully* p-ed that, what
  14. 5. Let every man *be fully* p-ed

PERSUASION.
peismonē.
Gal. 5. 8. This p. cometh not of him

PERTAIN,   -eth, -ing.
pros, [*accu.*]
Ro. 15.17. those things *which* p. *to* God
Heb. 2.17. in things p-*ing to* God ; 5.1
2Pet. 1. 3. all things *that* p. *unto* life
     peri, [*gen.*]
Act. 1. 3. things p-*ing to* the kingdom
     kata, [*accu.*]
Ro. 4. 1. *as* p-*ing to* the flesh hath fou.
     metechō.
Heb. 7.13. p-*eth* to another tribe, of wh.
     (See *Life.*)

PERVERSE.
diastrephō.   [Lu.9.41
Mat.17.17. faithless and p. generation ;
Act.20.30. men arise speaking p. things
Phi. 2.15. midst of a crooked and p.
     paradiatribē.
1Ti. 6. 5. p. *disputings* of men of corr.

PERVERT,   -eth, -ing.
diastrephō.
Lu. 23. 2. found this fellow p-*ing* the
Act.13.10. cease to p. the right ways of
     apostrephō.
Lu. 23.14. as one *that* p-*eth* the people
     metastrephō.
Gal. 1. 7. would p. the gospel of Christ

PESTILENCES.
loimos.   [21.11.
Mat.24. 7. shall be famines and p.; Lu.

PESTILENT.
loimos.
Act.24. 5. found this man a **p.** *fellow*

PETITIONS.
aitēma.
¹Jo. 5.15. we have the **p.**that we desired

PHILOSOPHERS.
philosophos.
Act.17.18.certain **p.** of the Epicureans

PHILOSOPHY.
philosophia.
Col. 2. 8. spoil you, through **p.** and

PHYLACTERIES.
phulaktērion.
Mat.23. 5. they make broad their **p.**

PHYSICIAN,   -s.
iatros.   [Mar.2.17; Lu.5.31
Mat. 9.12. that be whole need not a **p.**;
Mar. 5.26. of many **p-s**, and had
Lu. 4.23. proverb, **p.**, heal thyself
8.43. spent all her living upon **p-s**
Col. 4.14. Luke, the beloved **p.**, and

PIECE,   -s.
epiblēma.   [Lu. 5.36
Mat. 9.16. put. a **p.** of new; Mar. 2.21;
Lu. 5.36. and the **p.** that was taken
plērōma.
Mar. 2.21. the new **p.** *that filled it up*
drachmē.
Lu. 15. 8. **p-s** *of silver*, if she lose one **p.**
9, have found the **p.** which I
meros.
Lu.24.42. gave him a **p.** of a broiled
(See *Break, Money, Pull, Silver.*)

PIERCE,   -ed, -ing.
ekkenteō.
Jo. 19.37. look on him whom they **p-ed**
Rev. 1. 7. they also which **p-ed** him
diiknenmai.
Heb. 4.12. **p-ing** even to the dividing
dierchomai.
Lu. 2.35. a sword *shall* **p.** *through* thy
nuttō.
Jo. 19.34. with a spear **p-ed** his side
peripeirō.
¹Ti. 6.10. **p-ed** themselves *through* with

PIETY.
eusebeō.
¹Ti. 5. 4. learn first *to shew* **p.** at home

PIGEONS.
peristera.
Lu. 2.24. turtledoves or two young **p.**

PILGRIMS.
parepidēmos.
Heb.11.13.they were strangers and **p.**
¹Pet. 2.11. as strangers and **p.**, abstain

PILLAR,   -s.
stulos.
Gal. 2. 9. who seemed to be **p-s**, perce.
¹Ti. 3.15. the **p** and ground of the tru.
Rev. 3.12. a **p.** in the temple of my God
10. 1. and his feet as **p-s** of fire

PILLOW.
proskephalaion.
Mar. 4.38. of the ship, asleep on a **p.**

PINETH.
xērainō.
Mar. 9.18. with his teeth, and **p.** *away*

PINNACLE.
pterugion.   [Lu.4.9
Mat. 4. 5. him on a **p.** of the temple ;

PIPE,   -ed.
auleō.   [Lu.7.32
Mat.11.17. We *have* **p-ed** unto you ;
¹Co. 14. 7. known *what is* **p-ed** or har.
aulos.
¹Co. 14. 7. whether **p.** or harp, except

PIPERS.
aulētēs.
Rev.18.22. and musicians, and of **p.**

PIT.   (See *Bottomless.*)
phrear.
Lu. 14. 5. ass or an ox fallen into a **p.**
Rev. 9. 1. the key of the bottomless **p.**
2. opened the bottomless **p.**
arose a smoke out of the **p.**
reason of the smoke of the **p.**
bothunos.
Mat.12.11. fall into a **p.** on the sabbath

PITCHED.
pēgnumi.
Heb. 8. 2. which the Lord **p.**, and not

PITCHER.
keramion.   [22.10
Mar.14.13. bearing a **p.** of water; Lu.

PITIFUL.
eusplangchnos.
¹Pet. 3. 8. love as brethren, be **p.**, be
polusplangchnos.
Jas. 5.11. that the Lord is *very* **p.**

PITY.
eleeō.
Mat.18.33. even as I *had* **p.** *on* thee

PLACE.   -s.
topos.   [Lu.11.24
Mat.12.43. he walketh through dry **p-s** ;
14.13. by ship into a desert **p.** apa.
15. saying, This is a desert **p.**;
Mar.6.35
35. And when the men of that **p.**
24. 7. earthquakes, in divers **p-s**;
Mar.13.8 ; Lu.21.11
15. stand in the holy **p.**, whoso
26.52. again thy sword into his **p.**
27.33. unto a **p.** called Golgotha
say, a **p.** of a skull;Mar.15.22
28. 6. see the **p.** where the Lord ;
Mar.16.6
Mar. 1.35. departed into a solitary **p.**
45. but was without in desert **p-s**
6.31. apart into a desert **p.**, and
32. they depart. into a desert **p.**
Lu. 4.17. found the **p.** where it was
37. went out into every **p.** of the
42. and went into a desert **p.**
9.10. privately into a desert **p.**
12. we are here in a desert **p.**
10. 1. face into every city and **p.**
32. Lev., when he was at the **p.**
11. 1. was praying in a certain **p.**
14. 9. Give this man **p.**; aad thou
16.28. come into this **p.** of torment
19. 5. when Jesus came to the **p.**
22.40. And when he was at the **p.**
23.33. they were come to the **p.**
Jo. 4.20. that in Jerusal. is the **p.**
5.13. a multitude being in that **p.**
6.10. th. was much grass in the **p.**
23. nigh unto the **p.** where they
10.40. into the **p.** where John
11. 6. in the same **p.** where he was
30. was in that **p.** where Martha
48. take away both our **p.** and
14. 2, 3. prepare a **p.** for you
18. 2. betrayed him, knew the **p.**
19.13. in a **p.** that is called the Pa.
17. forth into a **p.** called the pl.
20. for the **p.** where Jesus was

Jo. 19.41. Now in the **p.** where he was
20. 7. wrapped together in a **p.** by
Act. 1.25. might go to his own **p.**
4.31. the **p.** was shaken where
6.13. against this holy **p.**, and the
14. of Naz. shall destroy this **p.**
7. 7. and serve me in this **p.**
33. for the **p.** where thou stand.
49. or what is the **p.** of my rest
12.17. and went into another **p.**
21.28. and the law, and this **p.**
hath polluted this holy **p.**
27. 8. came unto a **p.** which is
41. And falling into a **p.** where
Ro. 9.26. in the **p.** where it was said
12.19. rather give **p.** unto wrath
15.23. having no more **p.** in these
¹Co. 1. 2. with all that in every **p.**
²Co. 2.14. knowledge by us in every **p.**
Eph. 4.27. Neither give **p.** to the devil
¹Th. 1. 8. but also in every **p.** your
Heb. 8. 7. then should no **p.** have been
11. 8. was called to go out into a **p.**
12.17. for he found no **p.** of repent.
²Pet. 1.19. that shineth in a dark **p.**
Rev. 2. 5. thy candlestick out of his **p.**
6.14. were moved out of their **p-s**
12. 6. where she hath a **p.** prepared
8. neither was their **p.** found
14. into her **p.**, where she is
16.16. together into a **p.** called in
20.11. and there was found no **p.**
entopios.
Act.21.12. both we, and they *of that* **p.**
chōrion.   [Mar.14.32
Mat.26.36. unto a **p.** called Gethsema.;
chōreō.
Jo. 8.37. my word *hath* no **p.** in you
anachōreō.
Mat. 9.24. He said unto them, *Give* **p.**
hōde.
Mat.12. 6. *in this* **p.** is one greater
Lu. 23. 5. from Galilee *to this* **p.**
hopou.
Mar. 6.10. *In what* **p.** soever ye enter
ekeithen.
Mar. 6.10. till ye depart *from that* **p.**
epi [*gen.*] ho.
Mar.11. 4. *in a* **p.** where two ways met
periochē.
Act. 8.32. The **p.** of the scripture which
eikō.
Gal. 2. 6. To whom we *gave* **p.** by
pantachou.
Act.24. 3. alway, and *in all* **p-s** most
akroatērion.
Act.25.23. entered into the **p.** *of hear.*
opē.
Jas. 3.11. at the same **p.** sweet water
(See *Certain, Good, Holy, Market, Steep,*
Yonder.)

PLAGUE.   -s.
plēgē.
Rev. 9.20. were not killed by these **p-s**
11. 6. smite the earth with all **p-s**
15. 1, 6. having the seven last **p-s**
8. till the seven **p-s** of the seven
16. 9. hath power over these **p-s**
21. the **p.** of the hail; for the **p.**
18. 4. that ye receive not of her **p-s**
8. shall her **p-s** come in one day
21. 9. full of the seven last **p-s**
22.18. shall add unto him the **p-s**
mastix.
Mar. 3.10. tou. him, as many as had **p-s**
5.29. that she was healed of that **p.**
34. peace, and be whole of thy **p.**
Lu. 7.21. of their infirmities and **p-s**

PLAIN.
orthōs.
Mar. 7.35. loosed, and he spake **p.**
209

pedinos topos.
Lu. 6.17. and stood in the **p.**, and the

PLAINLY.   (See *Declare*.)
parrēsia.
Jo. 10.24. If thou be the Chr., tell us **p.**
   11.14. Then said Jesus unto them **p.**
   16.25. but I shall shew you **p.**
   29. Lo, now speakest thou **p.**

PLAINNESS.
parrēsia.
²Co. 3.12. we use great **p.** of speech

PLAIT,   -ed, -ing.
plekō.
Mat.27.28.*when* they *had* **p**-ed a crown
Mar.15.17.**p.**-ed a crown of tho. ; Jo.19.2
emplokē.
¹Pet. 3. 3. adorning of **p**-ing the hair

PLANT, [*noun*.]
phuteia.
Mat.15.13. Every **p.**,which my heavenly

PLANT, [*verb*,]   -eth.
phuteuō.
Mat.15.13.heaven. Father,*hath* not **p**-ed
   21.33. which **p**-ed a vineyard ; Mar.
      12.1 ; Lu. 20.9
Lu. 13. 6. man had a fig tree **p**-ed in
   17. 6. and *be* thou **p**-ed in the sea
   28. sold, they **p.**-ed, they builded
¹Co. 3. 6. I *have* **p**-ed, Apollos watered
   7. neither is he *that* **p**-*eth* any
   8. Now he *that* **p**-*eth* and he that
   9. 7. who **p**-*eth* a vineyard, and
sumphutos.
Ro. 6. 5. if we have been **p**-ed *together*

PLATTER.
paropsis.
Mat.23.25.outside of the cup and the **p.**
   26. is within the cup and **p.**
pinax.
Lu. 11.39. outside of the cup and the **p.**

PLAY.
paizō.
¹Co.10. 7. and drink, and rose up *to* **p.**

PLEASE,   -ed, -ing.
areskō.   [Mar. 6.22
Mat.14. 6. danced..and **p**-ed Herod
Act. 6. 5. the saying **p**-ed the whole
Ro. 8. 8. are in the flesh cannot **p.** G.
   15. 1. the weak, and not *to* **p.** our.
     2. *Let* every one of us **p.** his ne.
     3. even Christ **p**-ed not himself
¹Co. 7.32. how he *may* **p.** the Lord
     33. how he *may* **p.** his wife
     34. how she *may* **p.** her husband
   10.33. as I **p.** all men in all things
Gal. 1.10. *to* **p.** men? for if I yet **p**-ed
¹Th. 2. 4. not as **p**-ing men, but God
     15. persecuted us ; and they **p.**
     4. 1. ye ought to walk and *to* **p.**
²Ti. 2. 4. that he *may* **p.** him who ha.
areskeia.
Col. 1.10. of the Lord unto all **p**-ing
eudokeō.
Mat. 3.17. whom I *am well* **p**-ed ; 17.5 ;
     Mar.1.11 ; Lu.3.22 ; ²Pet.1.17
   12.18. in whom my soul *is well* **p**-ed
Ro. 15.26. it *hath* **p**-ed them of Maced.
   27. It *hath* **p**-ed them verily; and
¹Co. 1.21. it **p**-ed God by the foolishness
   10. 5. them God *was* not *well* **p**-ed
Gal. 1.15. But when it **p**-ed God, who
Col. 1.19. it **p**-ed the Father that in
dokeō.
Act.15 22. Then **p**-*ed* it the apostles and
   34. it **p**-ed Silas to abide there
210

suneudokeō.
¹Co. 7.12. and she *be* **p**-ed to dwell with
     13. and if he *be* **p**-ed to dwell
euaresteō.
Heb.11. 5. this testimony, that he **p**-ed
     6. it is impossible *to* **p.** him
   13.16. such sacrifi. God *is well* **p**-ed
eimi euaresteō. [*partic.*]
Tit. 2. 9. *to* **p.** them *well* in all things
     (*to be well pleasing* in all.)
arestos.
Jo. 8.29. always those *things that* **p.**
Act.12. 3. because he saw it **p**-ed the
¹Jo. 3.22. *things that are* **p**-ing in his
thelō.   [ed ; 5.38
¹Co. 12.18. *hath* **p**-ed him (he *hath will*-

PLEASURE, (See *Lover*.)   -s.
eudokia.
Eph. 1. 5. according to the *good* **p.** of
     9. according to his *good* **p.**
Phi. 2.13. will and to do of his *good* **p.**
²Th. 1.11. all the *good* **p.** of his goodn.
eudokeō.
Lu. 12.32. it is your Father's good **p.** to
²Co. 12.10. Therefore I *take* **p.** in infirm.
²Th. 2.12. but *had* **p.** in unrighteousn.
Heb.10. 6. for sin thou *hast had* no **p.**
     8. not, neither *hadst* **p.** therein
     38. my soul shall *have* no **p.** in
dokeō.
Heb.12.10.chasten. us after their *own* **p.**
suneudokeō.
Ro. 1.32. but have **p.** in them that do
hēdonē.
Lu. 8.14. riches and **p**-s of this life
Tit. 3. 3. serving divers lusts and **p**-s
²Pet. 2.13. as they that count it **p.** to
charis.   [25.9
Act.24.27. willing to shew the Jews a **p.**
spatalaō.
¹Ti. 5. 6. But she *that liveth in* **p.** is
truphaō.
Jas. 5. 5. ye *have lived in* **p.** on the
thelēma.
Rev. 4.11. for thy **p.** they are and were

PLENTEOUS.
polus.
Mat. 9.37. The harvest truly is **p.**

PLENTIFULLY.
(See *Brought*.)

PLOUGH.
arotron.
Lu. 9.62. having put his hand to the **p.**

PLOW,   -ing, -eth.
arotriaō.
Lu. 17. 7. you having a servant **p**-ing
¹Co. 9.10. *that* **p**-*eth* should **p.** in hope

PLUCK,   -ed.
exaireō.   [18.9
Mat. 5.29. **p.** it *out*, and cast it from ;
tillō.   [2.23 ; Lu.6.1
Mat.12. 1. *to* **p.** the ears of corn ; Mar.
diaspaō.
Mar. 5. 4. chains had been **p**-ed *asunder*
ekballō.
Mar. 9.47. eye offend thee, **p.** it *out*
ekrizoō.
Lu. 17. 6. *Be* thou **p**-ed *up by the root*
Jude 12. tw. dead, **p**-ed *up by the roots*
harpazō.
Jo. 10.28. any man **p.** them out of my
   29. to **p.** them out of my Father's
exoruttō.
Gal. 4.15. *would have* **p**-ed *out* your

POETS.
poiētēs.
Act.17.28. of your own **p.** have said

POINT, (See *Death*.)
mellō.
Jo. 4.47. for he *was at the* **p.** of death

POISON.
ios.
Ro. 3.13. the **p.** of asps is under their
Jas. 3. 8. evil, full of deadly **p.**

POLLUTED.
koinoō.
Act.21.28. and *hath* **p.** this holy place

POLLUTIONS.
alisgēma.
Act.15.20. abstain from **p.** of idols
miasma.
²Pet. 2.20. escaped the **p.** of the world

POMP.
phantasia.
Act.25.23. with great **p.**, and was

PONDERED.
sumballō.
Lu. 2.19. *and* **p.** them in her heart

POOL.
kolumbēthra.
Jo. 5. 2. by the sheep market a **p.**
     4. at a certa. season into the **p**
     7. to put me into the **p.** : but
     9. 7, 11. Go, wash in the **p.** of

POOR.
ptōchos.
Mat. 5. 3. Blessed are the **p.** in spirit
   11. 5. the **p.** have the go. ; Lu.7.22
   19.21. thou hast, and give to the **p.** ;
     Mar.10.21 [Mar.14.5;Jo.12.5
   26. 9. and given to the **p.** ;
     11. For ye have the **p.** always ;
     Mar.14.7 ; Jo.12.8
Mar.12.42. a certain **p.** widow, and she
     43. That this **p.** widow; Lu.21.3
Lu. 4.18. preach the gospel to the **p.**
   6.20. Blessed be ye **p.** : for your's
   14.13. makest a feast, call the **p.**
     21. bring in hither the **p.** and
   18.22. and distribute unto the **p.**
   19. 8. of my goods I give to the **p.**
Jo. 12. 6. not that he cared for the **p.**
   13.29. sh. give something to the **p.**
Ro. 15.26. contribution for the **p.** saints
²Co. 6.10. as **p.**, yet making many rich
Gai. 2.10. should remember the **p.**
Jas. 2. 2. there come in also a **p.** man
     3. and say to the **p.**, Stand
     5. Hath not God chosen the **p.**
     6. But ye have despised the **p.**
Rev. 3.17. and **p.**, and blind, and
   13.16. rich and **p.**, free and bond
penichros.
Lu. 21. 2. a certain **p.** widow casting
ptōcheuō.
²Co. 8. 9. for your sakes he *became* **p.**
penēs.
²Co. 9. 9. he hath given to the **p.**

PORCH.   -es.
stoa.
Jo. 5. 2. having five **p**-es
   10.23. the temple in Solomon's **p.**
Act. 3.11. in the **p.** that is called Solo.
   5.12. one accord in Solomon's **p.**
pulōn.
Mat.26.71. out into the **p.**, another
proaulion.
Mar.14.68. he went out into the **p.**

PORTER.
thurōros.
Mar.13.34. commanded the **p.** to watch
Jo. 10. 3. To him the **p.** openeth ; and

PORTION.
meros   [Lu.12.46]
Mat.24.51. appoint him his **p**. with ;
Lu. 15.12. give me the **p**. of goods that
sitometrion.
Lu. 12.42. them their **p**. *of meat* in

POSSESS,   *-ed, -ing·*
echō.
Act. 8. 7. of many that *were* **p**-*ed with*
16.16. **p**-*ed with* a spirit of divinat.
¹Co. 7.30. buy, as though they **p**-*ed* not
²Co. 6.10. nothing, and yet **p**-*ing* all
huparchō.
Lu. 12.15. of the *things which* he **p**-*eth*
Act. 4.32. of the *things which* he **p**-*ed*
ktaomai.
Lu. 18.12. give tithes of all that I **p**.
21.19. In your patience **p**. ye your
¹Th. 4. 4. how *to* **p**. his vessel in sanct.
(See *Devil*.)

POSSESSION,   *-s.*
ktēma.   [Mar. 10.22]
Mat.19.22.for he had great **p**-*s*;
Act. 2.45. And sold their **p**-*s* and goods
5. 1. with Sap. his wife, sold a **p**.
kataschesis.
Act. 7. 5. would give it to him for a **p**.
45. into the **p**. of the Gentiles
chōrion.
Act.28. 7. were **p**-*s* of the chief man of
peripoiēsis.
Eph. 1.14. redemp. of the *purchased* **p**.

POSSESSORS.
ktētōr.
Act. 4.34. as many as were **p**. of lands

POSSIBLE.
dunatos.   [Mat.10.27]
Mat.19.26.with God all things are **p**.;
24.24. if it were **p**., they ; Mar.13.22
26.39. O my Father, if it be **p**., let
Mar. 9.23. all things are **p**. to him that
14.35. if it were **p**., the hour might
36. Father, all things are **p**. unto
Lu. 18.27. impossible with men, are **p**.
Act. 2.24. it was not **p**. that he should
20.16. he hasted, if it were **p**. for
Ro. 12.18. if it be **p**., as much as lieth
Gal. 4.15. that, if it had been **p**., ye
dunamai.
Act.27.39. if it were **p**., to thrust in the
adunatos.
Heb.10. 4. it is *not* **p**. that the blood

POT,   *-s.*
xestēs.
Mar. 7. 4, 8. washing of cups and **p**-*s*
stamnos.
Heb. 9. 4. wherein was the golden **p**.

POTENTATE.
dunastēs.
¹Ti. 6.15. is the blessed and only **p**.

POTTER.
kerameus.
Mat.27. 7. bought with them the **p**.'s
10. gave them for the **p**.'s field
Ro. 9.21. Hath not the **p**. power over
keramikos.
Rev. 2.27. as the vessels *of a* **p**. shall

POUND,   *-s.*
mna.
Lu. 19.13. and delivered them ten **p**-*s*
16. thy **p**. hath gained ten **p**-*s*
18. thy **p**. hath gained five **p**-*s*
20. here is thy **p**., which I have
24. Take from him the **p**., and
it to him that hath ten **p**-*s*

Lu. 19.25. him, Lord, he hath ten **p**-*s*
litra.
Jo. 12. 3. Then took Mary a **p**. of oint.
19.39. about an hundred **p**. weight

POUR,   *-ed, -eth, -ing.*
ekcheō.
Jo. 2.15. **p**-*ed out* the changers' money
Act. 2.17. I *will* **p**. *out* of my Spirit up.
18. I *will* **p**. *out* in those days of
Rev.16. 1. **p**. *out* the vials of the wrath
2. **p**-*ed out* his vial ; 3,4,8,10,
12,17
katacheō.   [Mar. 14.3]
Mat.26. 7. and **p**-*ed* it on his head ;
epicheō.
Lu. 10.34. **p**-*ing in* oil and wine, and
ballō.
Mat.26.12.*in that* she *hath* **p**-*ed* this
Jo. 13. 5. he **p**-*eth* water into a bason
Act.10.45. also *was* **p**-*ed out* the gift of
kerannumi.
Rev.14.10. wr. of God, *which is* **p**-*ed out*

POVERTY.
ptōcheia.
²Co. 8. 2. their deep **p**. abounded unto
9. ye through his **p**. might be
Rev. 2. 9. works, and tribula., and **p**.

POWDER, (See *Grind*.)

POWER,   *-s.*
dunamis.
Mat. 6.13. is the kingdom, and the **p**.
22.29. the scriptures, nor the **p**. of;
Mar.12.24
24.29. the **p**-*s* of the heavens shall;
Mar.13.25 ; Lu.21.26
30. with **p**. and great glory ;
Mar.13.26 ; Lu.21.27
26.64. sit. on the right hand of **p**.;
Mar.14.62 ; Lu.22.69
Mar. 9. 1. kingd. of God come with **p**.
Lu. 1.17. in the spirit and **p**. of Elias
35. the **p**. of the Highest shall
4.14. Jesus returned in the **p**. of
36. with authority and **p**. he
5.17. the **p**. of the Lord was pre.
9. 1. gave them **p**. and authority
10.19. over all the **p**. of the enemy
24.49. until ye be endued with **p**.
Act. 1. 8. ye shall receive **p**., after
3.12. as though by our own **p**. or
4. 7. By what **p**., or by what
33. with great **p**. gave the apos.
6. 8. Stephen, full of faith and **p**.
8.10. This man is the great **p**. of
10.38. Holy Ghost and with **p**.
Ro. 1. 4. be the Son of God with **p**.
16. for it is the **p**. of God unto
20. even his eternal **p**. and God.
8.38. nor principalities, nor **p**-*s*
9.17. that I might shew my **p**. in
15.13. through the **p**. of the Holy
19. signs and wonders, by the **p**.
¹Co. 1.18. saved it is the **p**. of God
24. Christ the **p**. of God, and
2. 4. demonstra. of Spirit and **p**.
5. of men, but in the **p**. of God
4.19. wh. are puffed up, by the **p**.
20. is not in word, but in **p**.
5. 4. with the **p**. of our Lord Je.
6.14. raise up us by his own **p**.
15.24. and all authority and **p**.
43. in weak. ; it is raised in **p**.
²Co. 4. 7. excellency of the **p**. may be
6. 7. word of truth, by the **p**. of
8. 3. For to their **p**., I bear record
and beyond their **p**. they
12. 9. the **p**. of Christ may rest
13. 4. he liveth by the **p**. of God

---

²Co. 13. 4. by the **p**. of God toward you
Eph. 1.19. exceeding greatness of his **p**.
3. 7. the effectual work. of his **p**.
20. according to the **p**. that
Phi. 3.10. the **p**. of his resurrection
¹Th. 1. 5. in word only, but also in **p**.
²Th. 1.11. the work of faith with **p**.
2. 9. with all **p**. and signs and
²Ti. 1. 7. of **p**., and of love, and of a
8. according to the **p**. of God
3. 5. godliness, but deny. the **p**.
Heb. 1. 3. things by the word of his **p**.
6. 5. the **p**-*s* of the world to come
7.16. after the **p**. of an endless
¹Pet. 1. 5. Who are kept by the **p**. of
3.22. authorities and **p**-*s* being
²Pet. 1. 3. According as his divine **p**.
16. the **p**. and coming of our
Rev. 4.11. glory and honour and **p**.
5.12. to receive **p**., and riches
7.12. honour, and **p**., and might
11.17. taken to thee thy great **p**.
13. 2. the dragon gave him his **p**.
15. 8. of God and from his **p**.
17.13. shall give their **p**. and stren.
19. 1. honour, and **p**., unto the
ho dunatos. [*neut*.]
Ro. 9.22. and to make his **p**. known
exousia.
Mat. 9. 6. Son of man hath **p**. on ear.;
Mar.2.10 ; Lu.5.24
8. had given such **p**. unto men
10. 1. he gave them **p**. against
28.18. All **p**. is given unto me in
Mar. 3.15. to have **p**. to heal sicknesses
6. 7. gave them **p**. over unclean
Lu. 4. 6. All this **p**. will I give thee
32. for his word was with **p**.
10.19. I give unto you **p**. to tread
12. 5. hath **p**. to cast into hell
11. unto magistrates, and **p**-*s*
22.53. your hour, and the **p**. of
Jo. 1.12. to them gave he **p**. to bec.
10.18. I have **p**. to lay it down, and
have **p**. to take it again
17. 2. hast given him **p**. over all
19.10. I have **p**. to crucify thee, and
have **p**. to release thee
11. Thou couldest have no **p**.
Act. 1. 7. Fath. hath put in his own **p**.
5. 4. was it not in thine own **p**.
8.19. Give me also this **p**.
26.18. from the **p**. of Satan unto
Ro. 9.21. Hath not the potter **p**. over
13. 1. subject unto the higher **p**-*s*
for there is no **p**. but of God
the **p**-*s* that be are ordained
2. Who. there. resisteth the **p**.
3. not be afraid of the **p**.
¹Co. 7.37. hath **p**. over his own will
9. 4. Have we not **p**. to eat and
5. Have we not **p**. to lead about
6. have not we **p**. to forbear
12. partakers of this **p**. over you
we have not used this **p**.; but
18. that I abuse not my **p**. in
11.10. the woman to have **p**. on
²Co. 13.10. according to the **p**. which
Eph. 1.21. all principality, and **p**., and
2. 2. prince of the **p**. of the air
3.10. principalities and **p**-*s* in
12. principalities, against **p**-*s*
Col. 1.13. from the **p**. of darkness
16. dom., or principalities, or **p**-*s*
2.10. of all principality and **p**.
15. spoiled principalities and **p**-*s*
²Th. 3. 9. Not because we have not **p**.
Tit. 3. 1. to principalities and **p**-*s*
Jude 25. majesty, dominion and **p**.
Rev. 2.26. will I give **p**. over the nati.
6. 8. **p**. was given unto them
9. 3. unto them was given **p**., as

Rev. 9. 3. scorp. of the earth have **p.**
    10. their **p.** was to hurt men
    19. their **p.** is in their mouth
 11. 6. These have **p.** to shut hea.
     have **p.** over waters to turn
 12.10. the **p.** of his Christ : for the
 13. 4. which gave **p.** unto the beast
    5, 7. **p.** was given unto him
    12. he exerciseth all the **p.** of
 14.18. which had **p.** over fire ; and
 16. 9. hath **p.** over these plagues
 17.12. receive **p.** as kings one hour
 18. 1. from heaven, having great **p.**
 20. 6. second death hath no **p.**
    exousiazō.
¹Co. 6.12. not *be brought under the* **p.**
 7. 4. *hath* not **p.** *of* her own body
    husband *hath* not **p.** *of* his
    dunamai.
Ro. 16.25. to him *that is of* **p.** to stab.
    kratos.
Eph. 1.19. the working of his mighty **p.**
 6.10. and in the **p.** of his might
Col. 1.11. according to his glorious **p.**
¹Ti. 6.16. to whom be honour and **p.**
Heb. 2.14. that had the **p.** of death
Rev. 5.13. and glory, and **p.**, be unto
    megaleiotēs.
Lu. 9.43. amazed at the *mighty* **p.** of
    archē.
Lu. 20.20. mig. deliver him unto the **p.**
    ischus.
²Th. 1. 9. from the glory of his **p.**
²Pet. 2.11. which are greater in **p.** and
    didōmi.
Rev.13.14. miracles which he *had* **p.** to
 15. he *had* **p.** to give life unto
     (*it was given* him.)

POWERFUL.
    ischuros.
²Co.10.10. letters . . are weighty and **p.**
    energēs.
Heb. 4.12. word of God is quick, and **p.**

PRACTICES, (See *Covetous*.)

PRÆTORIUM.
    praitōrion.
Mar.15.16. into the hall, called **p.**

PRAISE, [*noun*,]   -s.
    epainos.
Ro. 2.29. whose **p.** is not of men
 13. 3. thou shalt have **p.** of the
¹Co. 4. 5. every man have **p.** of God
²Co. 8.18. whose **p.** is in the gospel
Eph. 1. 6. To the **p.** of the glory of his
    12, 14. to the **p.** of his glory
Phi. 1.11. the glory and **p.** of God
 4. 8. if there be any **p.**, think on
¹Pet. 1. 7. be found unto **p.** and honour
 2.14. the **p.** of them that do dwell
    ainos.
Mat.21.16. thou hast perfected **p.**
Lu. 18.43. saw it, gave **p.** unto God
    ainesis.
Heb.13.15. offer the sacrifice of **p.** to
    doxa.
Jo. 9.24. unto him, Give God the **p.**
 12.43. **p.** of men more than the **p.**
¹Pet. 4.11. to whom be **p.** and dominion
    aretē.
¹Pet. 2. 9. shew forth the **p-s** of him

PRAISE, [*verb*,]   -ed, -ing.
    aineō.
Lu. 2.13. the heavenly host, **p-ing** God
 20. glorifying and **p-ing** God for
 19.37. to rejoice and **p.** God with a
 24.53. temple, **p-ing** and blessing
Act. 2.47. **p-ing** God, and having favo.
 3. 8, 9. and leaping, and **p-ing** G.
Ro. 15.11. again, **p.** the Lord, all ye
212

Rev.19. 5. saying, **p.** our God, all ye
    epaineō.
¹Co.11. 2. Now I **p.** you, brethren, that
 17. I **p.** you not, that y- come
 22. *shall* I **p.** you in this ?   I **p.**
    eulogeō.
Lu. 1.64. he spake, *and* **p-ed** God
     (See *Sing.*)

PRATING.
    phluareō.
³John 10. **p.** *against* us with malicious

PRAY,   -ed, -est, -eth, -ing.
    proseuchomai.
Mat. 5.44. **p.** for them which despitefu.
 6. 5. And when thou **p-est**, thou
    for they love *to* **p.** standing
 6. when thou **p-est**, enter into
    p. to thy Father which is in
 7. But *when* ye **p.**, use not vain
 9. After this manner theref. **p.**
 14.23. into a mountain apart *to* **p.**;
     Mar.6.46 ; Lu.6.12,9.28
 19.13. his hands on them, and **p.**
 24.20. But **p.** ye that ; Mar. 13.18
 26.36. while I go and **p.** yonder
 39. and fell on his face, *and* **p-ed**
 41. Wat.and **p.**, that ; Mar.14.38
 42. and **p-ed**, saying, O my Fath.
 44. and **p-ed** the third time, say.
Mar. 1.35. solitary place, and there **p-ed**
 11.24. ye desire, *when* ye **p.**, believe
 25. And when ye stand **p-ing**
 13.33. watch and **p.**: for ye know
 14.32. Sit ye here, while I shall **p.**
 35. and **p-ed** that, if it were pos.
 39. and **p-ed**, and spake the sa.
Lu. 1.10. the people were **p-ing** witho.
 3.21. also being baptiz., and **p-ing**
 5.16. into the wilderness, and **p-ed**
 6.28. and **p.** for them which desp.
 9.18. as he was alone **p-ing**, his
 29. And as he **p-ed**, the fashion
 11. 1. as he was **p-ing** in a certain
    Lord, teach us *to* **p.**, as John
 2. When ye **p.**, say, Our Father
 18. 1. men ought always *to* **p.**, and
 10. into the temple *to* **p.**; the one
 11. and **p-ed** thus with himself
 22.40. **p.** that ye enter not into
 41. and kneeled down, and **p-ed**
 44. he **p-ed** more earnestly
 46. rise and **p.**, lest ye enter into
Act. 1.24. And they **p-ed**, *and* said, Th.
 6. 6. and *when* they *had* **p-ed**, th.
 8.15. **p-ed** for them, that they mi.
 9.11. Tarsus: for, behold, he **p-eth**
 40. and kneeled down, and **p-ed**
 10. 9. upon the housetop *to* **p.** abo.
 30. I **p-ed** in my house, and be.
 11. 5. in the city of Joppa **p-ing**
 12.12. were gathered together **p-ing**
 13. 3. wh. they had fasted and **p-ed**
 14.23. *and had* **p-ed** with fasting
 16.25. Paul and Silas **p-ed**, *and* sa.
 20.36. down, and **p-ed** with them
 21. 5. down on the shore, and **p-ed**
 22.17. *while* I **p-ed** in the temple
 28. 8. and **p-ed**, *and* laid his hands
Ro. 8.26. what we *should* **p.** *for* as we
¹Co.11. 4. Every man **p-ing** or prophe.
 5. But every woman *that* **p-eth**
 13. is it comely that a woman **p.**
 14.13. *let* him . . **p.** that he may int.
 14. For if I **p.** in an unknown
    tongue, my spirit **p-eth**, but
 15. I *will* **p.** with the spirit, and
    I *will* **p.** with the understan.
Eph. 6.18. **p-ing** always with all prayer
Phi. 1. 9. And this I **p.**, that your love
Col. 1. 3. Christ, **p-ing** always for you

Col. 1. 9. do not cease to **p.** for you
 4. 3. Withal **p-ing** also for us, th.
¹Th. 5.17. **p.** without ceasing
 25. Brethren, **p.** for us ; ²Th.3.1
²Th. 1.11. we **p.** always for you, that
¹Ti. 2. 8. that men **p.** every where
Heb.13.18.**p.** for us : for we trust we
Jas. 5.13. afflicted? *let* him **p.**   Is any
 14. *let* them **p.** over him, anoin.
 18. And he **p-ed** again, and the
Jude 20. **p-ing** in the Holy Ghost
    euchomai.
²Co.13. 7. I **p.** to God that ye do no
Jas. 5.16. **p.** one for another, that ye
    proseuchomai proseuchē.
Jas. 5.17. and he **p-ed** earnestly that it
    erōtaō.
Lu. 5. 3. **p-ed** him that he would thru.
 14.18, 19. I **p.** thee have me excus.
 16.27. I **p.** thee therefore, father
Jo. 4.31. his disciples **p-ed** him, saying
 14.16. I *will* **p.** the Father, and he
 16.26. that I *will* **p.** the Father for
 17. 9. I **p.** for them : I **p.** not for
 15. I **p.** not that thou shouldest
 20. Neither **p.** I for these alone
Act.10.48 **p-ed** they him to tarry certa.
 23.18. call. me unto him, and **p-ed**
¹Jo. 5.16. I do not say that he *shall* **p.**
    deomai.   [Lu.10.2
Mat. 9.38. **p.** ye therefore the Lord of ;
Lu. 21.36. Watch ye tnerefore, and **p.**
 22.32. I *have* **p-ed** for thee, that thy
Act. 4.31. *when* they *had* **p-ed**, the pla.
 8.22. **p.** God, if perhaps the thou.
 24. **p.** ye to the Lord for me, th.
 34. I **p.** thee, of whom speaketh
 10. 2. people, and **p-ed** to God alw.
²Co. 5.20. we **p.** you in Christ's stead
 8. 4. **p-ing** us with much intreaty
¹Th. 3.10. Night and day **p-ing** exceed.
    parakaleō.
Mat.26.53.I cannot now **p.** to my Fath.
Mar. 5.17. And they began *to* **p.** him to
 18. **p-ed** him that he might be
Act.16. 9. *and* **p-ed** him, saying, Come
 24. 4. I **p.** thee that thou wouldest
 27.34. I **p.** you to take some meat

PRAYER,   -s.
    proseuchē.   [Mar.9.29
Mat.17.21.but by **p.** and fasting ;
 21.13. the house of **p.** ; Mar.11.17
 22. whatsoever ye shall ask in **p.**
Lu. 6.12. continued all night in **p.** to
 19.46. My house is the house of **p.**
 22.45. when he rose up from **p.**
Act. 1.14. with one accord in **p.** and
 2.42. breaking of bread, and in **p-s**
 3. 1. at the hour of **p.**, being the
 6. 4. continually to **p.**, and to the
 10. 4. Thy **p-s** and thine alms are
 31. Cornelius, thy **p.** is heard
 12. 5. but **p.** was made without ce.
 16.13. where **p.** was wont to be ma.
 16. as we went to **p.**, a certain
Ro. 1. 9. me. of you always in my **p-s**
 12.12. continuing instant in **p.**
 15.30. in your **p-s** to God for me
¹Co. 7. 5. give yours. to fasting and **p.**
Eph. 1.16. mention of you in my **p-s** ;
    ¹Th. 1.2 ; Phile. 4
 6.18. Praying always with all **p.**
Phi. 4. 6. but in every thing by **p.** and
Col. 4. 2. Continue in **p.**, and watch
 12. fervently for you in **p-s**
¹Ti. 2. 1. supplications, **p-s**, intercess.
 5. in supplications and **p-s** nig.
Phile. 22. trust that through your **p-s**
¹Pet. 3. 7. that your **p-s** be not hindered
 4. 7. sober, and watch unto **p.**
Rev. 5. 8. which are the **p-s** of saints

Rev. 8. 3, 4. with the **p**-s of all saints
deēsis.
Lu. 1.13. Zacharias: for thy **p**. is hea.
  2.37. with fastings and **p**-s night
  5.33. Jo. fast often, and make **p**-s
Ro. 10. 1. my heart's desire and **p**. to
²Co. 1.11. helping together by **p**. for us
  9.14. by their **p**. for you, which
Phi. 1. 4. Always in every **p**. of mine
  19. my salvation through your **p**.
²Ti. 1. 3. of thee in my **p**-s night and
Heb. 5. 7. when he had offered up **p**-s
Jas. 5.16. fervent **p**. of a righteous man
¹Pet. 3.12. are open unto their **p**-s
proseuchomai.   [Lu.20.47
Mat.23.14.*make* long **p**-s; Mar. 12.40;
enteuxis.
¹Ti. 4. 5. by the word of God and **p**.
euchē.
Jas. 5.15. the **p**. of faith shall save

PREACH, *-ed, -est, -eth, -ing.*
euanggelizō.
Mat.11. 5. poor *have the gospel* **p**-*ed* to
Lu. 3.18. **p**-*ed* he unto the people
  4.18. *to* **p**. *the gospel to the poor*
  43. I must **p**. the kingdom of G.
  7.22. to the poor *the gospel is* **p**-*ed*
  9. 6. **p**-*ing the gospel,* and healing
  16.16. the kingdom of God *is* **p**-*ed*
  20. 1. temple, and **p**-*ed the gospel*
Act. 5.42. to teach and **p**. Jesus Christ
  8. 4. went every where **p**-*ing* the
  12. **p**-*ing* the things concerning
  25. **p**-*ed the gospel* in many vill.
  35. and **p**-*ed* unto him Jesus
  40. he **p**-*ed* in all the cities, till
  10.36. **p**-*ing* peace by Jesus Christ
  11.20. Grecians, **p**-*ing* the Lord Je.
  14. 7. And there they **p**-*ed the gos.*
  15. *and* **p**. unto you that ye sho.
  21. *when* they had **p**-*ed the gospel*
  15.35. and **p**-*ing* the word of the L.
  16.10. *to* **p**. *the gospel* unto them
  17.18. he **p**-*ed* unto them Jesus
Ro. 1.15. *to* **p**. *the gospel* to you that
  10.15. of them *that* **p**. *the gospel* of
  15.20. have I strived *to* **p**. *the gospel*
¹Co. 1.17. but *to* **p**. *the gospel*; not wi.
  9.16. For though I **p**. *the gospel*
  unto me, if I **p**. not *the gospel*
  18. *when* I **p**. *the gospel,* I may
  15. 1. which I **p**-*ed* unto you, whi.
  in memory what I **p**-*ed* unto
²Co.10.16. *To* **p**. *the gospel* in the regio.
  11. 7. I *have* **p**-*ed* to you the gospel
Gal. 1. 8. **p**. any other *gospel* unto you
  which we *have* **p**-*ed* unto you
  9. any man **p**. any other *gospel*
  11. the gospel *which was* **p**-*ed* of
  16. that I *might* **p**. him among
  23. now **p**-*eth* the faith which
  4.13. I **p**-*ed the gospel* unto you
Eph. 2.17. And came and **p**-*ed* peace
  3. 8. that I should **p**. among the
Heb. 4 2. unto us *was the gospel* **p**-*ed*
  5. to whom *it was* first **p**-*ed*
¹Pet. 1.12. th. *that have* **p**-*ed the gospel*
  25. *which by the gospel is* **p**-*ed*
  4. 6. *was the gospel* **p**-*ed* also to
Rev.14. 6. *to* **p**. unto them that dwell
katanggellō.
Act. 4. 2. **p**-*ed* through Jesus the resu.
  13. 5. they **p**-*ed* the word of God
  38. through this man *is* **p**-*ed* un.
  15.36. where we *have* **p**-*ed* the word
  17. 3. Jesus, whom I **p**. unto you
  13. the word of God *was* **p**-*ed* of
¹Co. 9.14. they which **p**. the gospel
Phi. 1.16. The one **p**. Christ of conten.
  18. or in truth, Christ *is* **p**-*ed*
Col. 1.28. Whom we **p**., warning every

diangellō.
Lu. 9.60. go thou and **p**. the kingdom
proeuanggelizomai.
Gal. 3. 8. **p**-*ed before the gospel* unto
kērussō.
Mat. 3. 1. **p**-*ing* in the wilderness of
  4.17. Jesus began *to* **p**., and to
  23. **p**-*ing* the gospel of the king
  9.35; Mar.1.14
  10. 7. as ye go, **p**., saying, The
  27. that **p**. ye upon the house.
  11. 1. and *to* **p**. in their cities
  24.14. *shall be* **p**-*ed* in all the world
  26.13. Wh. this gospel *shall be* **p**-*ed*;
  Mar.14.9   [Lu.3.3
Mar. 1. 4. and **p**. the baptism of repen.;
  7. And **p**-*ed*, saying, There
  38. that I *may* **p**. there also
  39. he **p**-*ed* in their ; Lu.4.44
  3.14. might send them forth *to* **p**.
  6.12. and **p**-*ed* that men should
  16.15. **p**. the gospel to every crea.
  20. 'and **p**-*ed* every where, the
Lu. 4.18. *to* **p**. deliverance to the cap.
  19. *To* **p**. the acceptable year
  8. 1. **p**-*ing* and shewing the glad
  9. 2. he sent them *to* **p**. the king.
  24.47. *should be* **p**-*ed* in his name
Act. 8. 5. and **p**-*ed* Christ unto them
  9.20. he **p**-*ed* Christ in the syna.
  10.37. the baptism which John **p**-*ed*
  42. he commanded us *to* **p**. unto
  15.21. in every city them *that* **p**.
  19.13. by Jesus whom Paul **p**-*eth*
  20.25. am. whom I have gone **p**-*ing*
  28.31. **p**-*ing* the kingdom of God
Ro. 2.21. thou that **p**-*est* a man should
  10. 8. word of faith, which we **p**.
  15. how *shall* they **p**., except
¹Co. 1.23. But we **p**. Christ crucified
  9.27. *when* I *have* **p**-*ed* to others
  15.11. so we **p**., and so ye believed
  12. if Christ *be* **p**-*ed* that he
²Co. 1.19. Jesus Christ, *who was* **p**-*ed*
  4. 5. we **p**. not ourselves
  11. 4. if he that cometh **p**-*eth* ano.
  Jes., whom we *have* not **p**-*ed*
Gal. 2. 2. that gospel which I **p**.
  5.11. if I yet **p**. circumcision
Phi. 1.15. Some indeed **p**. Christ even
Col. 1.23. *which was* **p**-*ed* to every cre.
¹Th. 2. 9. we **p**-*ed* unto you the gospel
¹Ti. 3.16. **p**-*ed* unto the Gentiles
²Ti. 4. 2. **p**. the word ; be instant in
¹Pet. 3.19. and **p**-*ed* unto the spirits
prokērussō.
Act. 3.20. *which before was* **p**-*ed* unto
  13.24. *When* John *had* first **p**-*ed*
laleō.
Mar. 2. 2. and he **p**-*ed* the word unto
Act. 8.25. and **p**-*ed* the word of the
  11.19. **p**-*ing* the word to none but
  13.42. might *be* **p**-*ed* to them the
  14.25. *when* they *had* **p**-*ed* the word
  16. 6. of the H. Gh. *to* **p**. the word
dialegomai.
Act.20. 7. Paul **p**-*ed unto* them, ready
  9. *as* Paul *was* long **p**-*ing,* he
parrēsiazomai.
Act. 9.27. how he had **p**-*ed* boldly at
plēroō.
Ro. 15.19. I *have fully* **p**-*ed* the gospel
akoē.
Heb. 4. 2. the word **p**-*ed* did not profit

PREACHER.
kērux.
¹Ti. 2. 7. I am ordained a **p**., and an
²Ti. 1.11. I am appointed a **p**., and an
²Pet. 2. 5. a **p**. of righteousness, bring.
kērussō.
Ro. 10.14. shall they hear without a **p**.

PREACHING, [*noun.*]
kērugma.
Mat.12.41.at the **p**. of Jonas; Lu.11.32
Ro. 16.25. and the **p**. of Jesus Christ
¹Co. 1.21. by the foolishness of **p**. to
  2. 4. my **p**. was not with enticing
  15.14. then is our **p**. vain, and
²Ti. 4. 7. by me the **p**. might be fully
Tit. 1. 3. mani. his word through **p**.
logos.
¹Co. 1.18. For the **p**. of the cross is to
PRECEPT.
entolē.
Mar.10. 5. heart, he wrote you this **p**.
Heb. 9.19. Moses had spoken every **p**.
PRECIOUS.
timios.
¹Co. 3.12. **p**. stones, wood, hay, stubble
Jas. 5. 7. waiteth for the **p**. fruit of the
¹Pet. 1. 7. being much *more* **p**. than of
  19. But with the **p**. blood of
²Pet. 1. 4. exceeding great and **p**. pro.
Rev.17. 4. deck. with gold and **p**.;18.16
  18.12. of gold, and silver, and **p**.
  vessels of *most* **p**. wood, and
  21.11. like unto a stone *most* **p**.
  19. with all manner of **p**. stones
entimos.
¹Pet. 2. 4. but chosen of God, and **p**.
  6. chief corner stone, elect, **p**.
ho timē.
¹Pet. 2. 7. there. which believe he is **p**.
barutimos.
Mat.26. 7. box of *very* **p**. ointment, and
isotimos.
²Pet. 1. 1. have obtained *like* **p**. faith
polutelēs.
Mar.14. 3. oint. of spikenard *very* **p**.
PREDESTINATE,   *-ed.*
proorizō.
Ro. 8.29. *did* **p**. to be conformed to
  30. whom he *did* **p**., them he
Eph. 1. 5. *Having* **p**-*ed* us unto the
  11. *being* **p**-*ed* according to the
PRE-EMINENCE.
prōteuō.
Col. 1.18. things he might *have the* **p**.
philoprōteuō.
³John 9. *who loveth* to *have the* **p**.
PREFER,   *-ing.*
proēgeomai.
Ro. 12.10. in honour **p**-*ing* one another
prokrima.
¹Ti. 5.21. **p**-*ing* one before another
PREMEDITATE.
meletaō.
Mar.13.11.shall speak, neither *do* ye **p**.
PREPARATION,
paraskeuē.
Mat.27.62.followed the day of the **p**.
Mar.15.42.because it was the **p**., that is
Lu. 23.54. that day was the **p**., and the
Jo. 19.14. it was the **p**. of the passover
  31. because it was the **p**., that
  42. because of the Jews' **p**. day
hetoimasia.
Eph. 6.15. with the **p**. of the gospel of
PREPARE,   *-ed, -ing.*
hetoimazō.   [Lu.3.4
Mat. 3. 3. **p**. ye the way of ; Mar. 1.3;
  20.23. whom it *is* **p**-*ed* ; Mar. 10.40
  22. 4. I *have* **p**-*ed* my dinner: my
  25.34. inherit the kingdom **p**-*ed* for
  41. **p**-*ed* for the devil and his
  26.17. that we **p**. for thee to eat
Mar.14.12.that we go and **p**. ; Lu. 22.9
Lu. 1.76. face of the Lord *to* **p**. his wa

Lu. 2.31. Which thou *hast* p-ed before
12.47. knew his lord's will, and p-ed
22. 8. Go and p. us the passover
23.56. p-ed spices and ointments
24. 1. spices which they *had* p-ed
Jo. 14. 2. I go to p. a place for you
3. if I go and p. a place for you
¹Co. 2. 9. God *hath* p-ed for them that
²Ti. 2.21. p-ed unto every good work
Phile. 22. p. me also a lodging: for I
Heb.11.16.for he *hath* p-ed for them a
Rev. 8. 6. p-ed themselves to sound
9. 7. like unto horses p-ed unto
15. *which were* p-ed for an hour
12. 6. a place p-ed of God, that
16.12. kings of the east *might be* p-ed
21. 2. out of heaven, p-ed as a bri.
proetoimazō.
Ro. 9.23. which he *had afore* p-ed unto
hetoimos.
Mar.14.15.room furnished and p-ed
kataskeuazō.   [Lu.7.27
Mat.11.10.which *shall* p. thy ; Mar.1.2 ;
Lu. 1.17. a people p-ed for the Lord
Heb.11. 7. p-ed an ark to the saving of
¹Pet. 3.20. *while* the ark *was a* p-ing
paraskeuazō.
¹Co.14. 8. who *shall* p. himself to the
katartizō.
Heb.10. 5. a body *hast* thou p-ed me

PRESBYTERY.
presbuterion.
¹Ti. 4.14. on of the hands of the p.

PRESENCE.
enōpion.
Lu. 1.19. that stand *in the* p. *of* God
13.26. have eaten and dru. *in thy* p.
14.10. *in the* p. *of* them that sit at
15.10. joy *in the* p. *of* the angels
Jo. 20.30. *in the* p. *of* his disciples
Act.27.35. to God *in* p. *of* them all
¹Co. 1.29. no flesh should glory *in* his p.
Rev.14.10.*in the* p. *of* the holy angels
and *in the* p. *of* the Lamb
katenōpion.
Jude 24. faultless *before the* p. *of* his
prosōpon.
Act. 3.13. and denied him in the p. of
19. shall come from the p. of the
5.41. from the p. of the council
²Co.10. 1. who in p. am base among
¹Th. 2.17. for a short time in p., not
²Th. 1. 9. from the p. of the Lord, and
Heb. 9.24. appear in the p. of God for
parousia.
²Co.10.10. but his bodily p. is weak
Phi. 2.12. not as in my p. only, but
apenanti.
Act. 3.16. soundness *in the* p. *of* you
emprosthen.
¹Th. 2.19. *in the* p. *of* our Lord Jesus

PRESENT, [adjec.]
pareimi.
Lu. 13. 1. There *were* p. at that season
Act.10.33. therefore we are all *here* p.
¹Co. 5. 3. but p. in spirit, have judged
already as though I *were* p.
²Co.10. 2. not be bold *when* I am p.
11. also in deed *when* we are p.
11. 9. And *when* I *was* p. with you
13. 2. as *if* I *were* p., the second
10. lest *being* p. I should use
Gal. 4.18. only when I *am* p. with you
20. I desire *to be* p. with you now
Heb.12.11.no chastening for the p. see.
²Pet. 1.12. established in the p. truth
sumpareimi.
Act.25.24. *which are here* p. *with* us
enistēmi.   [¹Co.3.22
Ro. 8.38. nor things p., nor things ;

214

---

¹Co. 7.26. good for the p. distress, I say
Gal. 1. 4. us from this p. evil world
Heb. 9. 9. for the time then p., in whi.
ephistēmi.
Act.28. 2. because of the p. rain, and
nun.
Ro. 8.18. the sufferings of this p. time
11. 5. Even so then at this p. time
²Ti. 4.10. having loved this p. world
Tit. 2.12. godly, in this p. world
endēmeō.
²Co. 5. 8. and *to be* p. with the Lord
9. whether p. or absent, we may
menō.
Jo. 14.25. you, *being yet* p. with you
paraginomai.
Act.21.18. and all the elders *were* p.
parakeimai.
Ro. 7.18. for to will *is* p. with me
21. do good, evil *is* p. with me
arti.
¹Co. 4.11. Even unto this p. hour we
15. 6. part remain unto this p.

PRESENT, [verb,]   -ed.
paristēmi.
Lu. 2.22. to p. him to the Lord
Act. 9.41. and widows, p-ed her alive
23.33. p-ed Paul also before him
Ro. 12. 1. *that* ye p. your bodies a livi.
²Co. 4.14. and *shall* p. us with you
11. 2. that I may p. you as a chaste
Eph. 5.27. That he *might* p. it to hims.
Col. 1.22. to p. you holy and unblame.
28. that we *may* p. every man
prospherō.
Mat. 2.11. they p-ed *unto* him gifts
histēmi.
Jude 24. *to* p. you faultless before the

PRESENTLY.
parachrēma.
Mat.21.19.And p. the fig tree withered
paristēmi.
Mat.26.53.he *shall* p. *give* me more
exautēs.
Phi. 2.23. therefore I hope to send p.

PRESERVE,   -ed.
suntēreō.
Mat. 9.17. and both *are* p-ed ; Lu.5.38
tēreō.
¹Th. 5.23. *be* p-ed blameless unto the
Jude 1. p-ed in Jesus Ch., and called
zōogoneō.
Lu. 17.33. lose his life *shall* p. it
sōzō.
²Ti. 4.18. *will* p. me unto his heavenly

PRESS, [noun.]
ochlos.
Mar. 2. 4. nigh unto him for the p.
5.27. came in the p. behind, and
30. turned him about in the p.
Lu. 8.19. not come at him for the p.
19. 3. and could not for the p.

PRESS, [verb,]   -ed, -eth.
epipiptō.
Mar. 3.10. insom. that they p-ed upon
epikeimai.
Lu. 5. 1. as the people p-ed upon him
piezō.
Lu. 6.38. good measure p-ed down, and
apothlibō.
Lu. 8.45. multit. throng thee, and p.
biazomai.
Lu. 16.16. and every·man p-eth into it
sunechō.
Act.18. 5. Paul *was* p-ed in the spirit
bareō.
²Co. 1. 8. we *were* p-ed out of measure

---

diōkō.
Phi. 3.14. I p. toward the mark for the

PRESUMPTUOUS.
tolmētēs.
²Pet. 2.10. p. are they, selfwilled, they

PRETENCE.
prophasis.   [Mar.12.40
Mat.23.14. for a p. make long prayers ;
Phi. 1.18. whether in p., or in truth

PREVAIL,   -ed.
ischuō.
Act.19.16. p-ed against them, so that
20. the word of God and p-ed
Rev.12. 8. And p-ed not ; neither was
katischuō.
Mat.16.18. of hell *shall* not p. *against*
Lu. 23.23. and of the chief priests p-ed
ōpheleō.
Mat.27.24. that he *could* p. nothing
nikaō.
Rev. 5. 5. *hath* p-ed to open the book

PREVENT,   -ed.
prophthanō.
Mat.17.25. Jesus p-ed him, saying
phthanō.
¹Th. 4.15. *shall* not p. them which are

PRICE,   -s.
timē.
Mat.27. 6. because it is the p. of blood
9. the p. of him that was valued
Act. 4.34. and brought the p-s of the
5. 2. kept back part of the p., his
3. part of the p. of the land
19.19. and they counted the p. of
¹Co. 6.20. ye are bought with a p. ; 7.23
polutimos.
Mat.13.46. found one pearl *of great* p.
polutelēs.
¹Pet. 3. 4. the sight of God *of great* p.

PRICKED.
katanussō.
Act. 2.37. they *were* p-ed in their heart

PRICKS.
kentron.   [26.14
Act. 9. 5. thee to kick against the p.;

PRIDE.
huperēphania.
Mar. 7.22. blasphemy, p., foolishness
alazoneia.
¹Jo. 2.16. of the eyes, and the p. of
tuphoō.
¹Ti. 3. 6. lest *being lifted up with* p.

PRIEST, (See *High Priest*,) -s.
hiereus.
Mat. 8. 4. shew thyself to the p.;
Mar.1.44 ; Lu.5.14
12. 4. but only for the p-s;Mat.2.26;
Lu.6.4
5. on the sabbath days the p-s
Lu. 1. 5. a certain p. named Zacharias
10.31. came down a certain p. that
17.14. shew yourselves unto the p-s
Jo. 1.19. p-s and Levites from Jerus.
Act. 4. 1. p-s, and the captain of the
6. 7. a great company of the p-s
14.13. Then the p. of Jupiter, wh.
Heb. 5. 6. Thou art a p. for ; 7.17,21
7. 1. p. of the most high God, who
3. abideth a p. continually
11, 15. another p. sh. rise after
21. those p-s were made without
23. they truly were many p-s
8. 4. p., seeing that there are p-s
9. 6. the p-s went always into
10.11. And every p. standeth daily

Heb.10.21. And having an high **p.** over
Rev. 1. 6. kings and **p**-s unto ; 5.10
  20. 6. they shall be **p**-s of God and

archiereus.

Mat. 2. 4. gathered all the *chief* **p**-s
 16.21. *chief* **p**-s and scribes ;
         21.15 ; Mar.8.31, 14.1,43 :
         Lu.9.22,19.47,20.1,19,22.2,
         66, 23.10
  20.18. betrayed unto the *chief* **p**-s
  21.23. the *chief* **p**-s and the elders ;
       26.47,59 ; 27.1,3,20 ;
       Act.4.23,25.15
    45. the *chief* **p**-s and Pharisees ;
       27.62; Jo.11.57, 18.3
  26. 3. assembled tog. the *chief* **p**-s;
       Mar.14.53   [Mar.14.10
    14. went unto the *chief* **p**-s;
  27. 6. the *chief* **p**-s took the silver
    12. was accused of the *chief* **p**-s;
       Mar.15.3   [Mar.15.31
    41. also the chief **p**-s mocking ;
  28.11. shewed unto the *chief* **p**-s
Mar.10.33. delivered unto the *chief* **p**-s
  11.18. the scribes and *chief* **p**-s
    27. come to him the *chief* **p**-s
  14.55. the *chief* **p**-s and all the
    15. 1. the *chief* **p**-s held a; Jo.12.10
    10. the *chief* **p**-s had delivered
    11. the *chief* **p**-s moved the peo.
Lu. 22. 4. communed with the *chief* **p**-s
    52. Jesus said unto the *chief* **p**-s
  23. 4. said Pilate to the *chief* **p**-s
    13. together the chief **p**-s and
    23. of them and of the *chief* **p**-s
  24.20. how the *chief* **p**-s and our
Jo. 7.32. Pharisees and the *chief* **p**-s
    45. the officers to the *chief* **p**-s
  11.47. gathered the *chief* **p**-s and
  18.35. own nation and the *chief* **p**-s
  19. 6. the *chief* **p**-s therefore and
    15. the *chief* **p**-s answered, we
    21. Then said the *chief* **p**-s of
Act. 9.14. authority from the *chief* **p**-s
    21. bound unto the *chief* **p**-s
  19.14. a Jew, and *chief of the* **p**-s
  22.30. commanded the *chief* **p**-s
  23.14. they came to the *chief* **p**-s
  26.10. authority from the *chief* **p**-s
    12. commis. from the *chief* **p**-s

archieratikos.

Act. 4. 6. of the kindred *of the high* **p.**

hierateuō.

Lu. 1. 8. *executed the* **p.**'*s office*

hierateia.

Lu. 1. 9. the custom of the **p.**'*s office*

PRIESTHOOD.

hierōsunē.

Heb. 7.11. perfec. were by the Levi. **p.**
    12. For the **p.** being changed
    14. Moses spake nothing con. **p.**
    24. hath an unchangeable **p.**

hierateuma.

1Pet. 2. 5. an holy **p.**, to offer up spiri.
    9. a royal **p.**, an holy nation

hierateia.

Heb. 7. 5. receive the office of the **p.**

PRINCE,   -s.

archōn.

Mat. 9.34. through the **p.** of the;12.24;
    Mar.3.22
  20.25. the **p.**-s of the Gentiles exer.
Jo. 12.31. now shall the **p.** of this
  14.30. the **p.** of this world cometh
  16.11. the **p.** of this world is judged
1Co. 2. 6, 8. of the **p**-s of this world
Eph. 2. 2. the **p.** of the power of the
Rev. 1. 5. the **p.** of the kings of the

archēgos.

Act. 3.15. killed the **p.** of life, whom
  5.31. to be a **p.** and a Saviour, for

hēgemōn.

Mat. 2. 6. not the least among the **p**-s

PRINCIPAL.

kata [*accu.*] **exochē.**

Act.25.23. and **p.** men of the city, at

PRINCIPALITY,   -ies.

archē.

Ro. 8.38. nor **p**-s, nor powers, nor thi.
Eph. 1.21. above all **p.**, and power, and
  3.10. now unto the **p**-s and powers
  6.12. against **p**-s, against powers
Col. 1.16. dominions, or **p**-s, or powers
  2.10. the head of all **p.** and power
    15. having spoiled **p**-s and pow.
Tit. 3. 1. subject to **p**-s and powers

PRINCIPLES.

stoicheion.

Heb. 5.12. the first **p.** of the oracles of

archē.

Heb. 6. 1. leaving the **p.** of the doctrine

PRINT.

tupos.

Jo. 20.25. in his hands the **p.** of the
    finger into the **p.** of the nails

PRISON, (See *Keeper*,)   -s.

phulakē.

Mat. 5.25. and thou be cast into **p.**
  14. 3. and put him in **p.**; Mar.6.17
    10. and beheaded John in the **p.**;
        Mar.6.28
  18.30. went and cast him into **p.**
  25.36. I was in **p.**, and ye came
    39. saw we thee sick, or in **p.**
    43, 44. sick, and in **p.**, and ye
Lu. 3.20. that he shut up John in **p.**
  12.58. the officer cast thee into **p.**
  21.12. to the syna., and into **p**-s
  22.33. both into **p.**, and to death
  23.19, 25. murder, was cast into **p.**
Jo. 3.24. John was not yet cast into **p.**
Act. 5.19. by night opened the **p.** do.
    22. and found them not in the **p.**
    25. the men whom ye put in **p.**
  8. 3. women committed them to **p.**
  12. 4. he put him in **p.**, and deliv.
    5. Peter there. was kept in **p.**
    6. before the door kept the **p.**
    17. brought him out of the **p.**
  16.23. they cast them into **p.**
    24. thrust them into the inner **p.**
    27. and seeing the **p.** doors open
    37. and have cast us into **p.**
    40. And they went out of the **p.**
  22. 4. and delivering into **p**-s both
  26.10. the saints did I shut up in **p.**
2Co. 11.23. in **p**-s more frequent
1Pet. 3.19. prea. unto the spirits in **p.**
Rev. 2.10. shall cast some of you into **p.**
  20. 7. shall be loosed out of his **p.**

desmōtērion.

Mat.11. 2. John had heard in the **p.**
Act. 5.21. sent to the **p.** to have them
    23. the **p.** truly found we shut
  16.26. foundations of the **p.** were

paradidōmi.

Mat. 4.12. that John *was cast into* **p.**
Mar. 1.14. after that John *was put in* **p.**

tērēsis.

Act. 5.18. put them in the common **p.**

oikēma.

Act.12. 7. a light shined in the **p.**

PRISONER,   -s.

desmios.

Mat.27.15. release unto the people a **p.**

Mat.27.16. they had then a notable **p.**
Mar.15. 6. released unto them one **p.**
Act.16.25. God: and the **p**-s heard
    27. supposing that the **p**-s had
  23.18. Paul the **p.** called me unto
  25.27. unreasonable to send a **p.**
  28.16. centurion delivered the **p**-s
    17. yet was I delivered **p.** from
Eph. 3. 1. Paul, the **p.** of; Phile. 1
    4. 1. I therefore, the **p.** of the
2Ti. 1. 8. our Lord, nor of me his **p.**
Phile. 9. now also a **p.** of Jesus Christ

desmōtēs.

Act.27. 1. Paul and certain other **p**-s
    42. counsel was to kill the **p**-s

PRIVATE.

idios.

2Pet. 1.20. is of any **p.** interpretation

PRIVATELY.

kata idios.

Mat.24. 3. disciples came unto him **p.**
Mar. 6.32. desert place by ship **p.**
  9.28. asked him **p.**, Why could
  13. 3. and Andrew asked him **p.**
Lu. 10.23. and said **p.**, Blessed are the
Act.23.19. went with him aside **p.**
Gal. 2. 2. but **p.** to them which were

PRIVILY.

lathra.

Mat. 1.19. minded to put her away **p.**
  2. 7. when he had **p.** called the
Act.16.37. do they thrust us out **p.**

pareiserchomai.

Gal. 2. 4. who *came in* **p.** to spy out

pareisagō.

2Pet. 2. 1. who **p.** *shall bring in* damn.

PRIVY.

suneideō.

Act. 5. 2. his wife also *being* **p.** to it

PRIZE.

brabeion.

1Co. 9.24. but one receiveth the **p.**
Phi. 3.14. toward the mark for the **p.**

PROCEED,   -ed, -eth.

ekporeuomai.

Mat. 4. 4. every word *that* **p**-eth *out of*
  15.18. *which* **p.** *out* of the mouth
Mar. 7.21. of men, **p.** evil thoughts
Lu. 4.22. *which* **p**-ed out of his mouth
Jo. 15.26. which **p**-eth from the Father
Eph. 4.29. *Let* no corrupt communi. **p.**
Rev. 4. 5. out of the throne **p**-ed light.
    11. 5. fire **p**-eth out of their mouth
  19.21. *which* sword **p**-ed out of his
  22. 1. clear as crystal, **p**-ing out of

exerchomai.

Mat.15.19. For out of the heart **p.** evil
Jo. 8.42. I **p**-ed *forth* and came from
Jas. 3.10. **p**-eth blessing and cursing

prostithēmi.

Act.12. 3. he **p**-ed *further* to take Peter

prokoptō.

2Ti. 3. 9. But they shall **p.** no further

PROCLAIM,   -ed, -ing.

kērussō.

Lu. 12. 3. shall be **p**-ed upon the house
Rev. 5. 2. I saw a strong angel **p**-ing

PROFANE.

bebēlos.

1Ti. 1. 9. sinners, for unholy and **p.**
    4. 7. refuse **p.** and old wives' fab.
    6.20. avoiding **p.** and vain babbli.
2Ti. 2.16. shun **p.** and vain babblings
Heb.12.16. any fornicator, or **p.** *person*

bebēloō.

Mat.12. 5. priests in the temple **p.** the
Act.24. 6. gone about *to* **p.** the temple

PROFESS,   -ed, -ing.
homologeō.
Mat. 7.23. then *will* I p. unto them
¹Ti. 6.12. *hast* p-*ed* a good profession
Tit. 1.16. They p. that they know God
homologia.
²Co. 9.13. for your p-*ed* subjection
epanggellomai.
¹Ti. 2.10. becometh women p-*ing* god.
6.21. Which some p-*ing* have err.
phaskō.
Ro. 1.22. p-*ing* themselves to be wise

PROFESSION
homologia.
¹Ti. 6.12. hast professed a good p.
Heb. 3. 1. and high priest of our p.
4.14. let us hold fast our p.
10.23. hold fast the p. of our faith

PROFIT, [noun.]
sumpherō.
¹Co. 7.35. I speak for your own p.
10.33. not seeking mine own p.
Heb.12.10.but he for our p., that we
ōpheleia.
Ro. 3. 1. what p. is there of circumci.
chrēsimos.
²Ti. 2.14. not about words to no p.

PROFIT, [verb,]   -ed, -eth.
ōpheleō.   [Mar.7.11
Mat.15. 5. thou *mightest be* p-*ed* by me;
16.26. what *is* a man p-*ed*; Mar.8.36
Jo. 6.63. the flesh p-*eth* nothing
Ro. 2.25. circumcision verily p-*eth*, if
¹Co.13. 3. it p-*eth* me nothing.
14. 6. what *shall* I p. you, except
Gal. 5. 2. Christ *shall* p. you nothing
Heb. 4. 2. the word preached did not p.
13. 9. which have not p-*ed* them
eimi ōphelimos.
¹Ti. 4. 8. bodily exercise p-*eth* little
sumpherō.
¹Co.12. 7. given to every man to p. wi.
prokoptō.
Gal. 1.14. p-*ed* in the Jews' religion
ophelos.
Jas. 2.14, 16. What doth it p., my bre

PROFITABLE.
sumpherō.
Mat. 5.29, 30. for it *is* p. *for* thee that
Act.20.20. nothing *that was* p. unto
ōphelimos.
²Ti. 3.16. and is p. for doctrine, for
Tit. 3. 8. These things are good and p.
euchrēstos.
²Ti. 4.11. p. to me for the ministry
Phile. 11. but now p. to thee and to me

PROFITING.
prokopē.
¹Ti. 4.15. that thy p. may appear to

PROMISE, [noun,]   -s.
epanggellia.
Lu. 24.49. I send the p. of my Father
Act. 1. 4. for the p. of the Father, wh.
2.33. the p. of the Holy Ghost
39. the p. is unto you, and to
7.17. the time of the p. drew nigh
13.23. according to his p. raised
32. the p. which was made unto
23.21. looking for a p. from thee
26. 6. for the hope of the p. made
Ro. 4.13. For the p., that he should
14. the p. made of none effect
16. the p. might be sure to all
20. not at the p. of God through
216

Ro. 9. 4. service of God, and the p-*s*
8. the children of the p. are
9. For this is the word of p.
15. 8. to confirm the p-*s* made unto
²Co. 1.20. For all the p-*s* of God in him
7. 1. Having therefore these p-*s*
Gal. 3.14. the p. of the Spirit through
16. his seed were the p-*s* made
17. make the p. of none effect
18. it is no more of p.: but God
gave it to Abraham by p.
21. then against the p-*s* of God
22. that the p. by faith of Jesus
29. and heirs according to the p.
4.23. the freewoman was by p.
28. was, are the children of p.
Eph. 1.13. with that holy Spirit of p.
2.12. from the covenants of p., ha.
3. 6. partakers of his p. in Christ
6. 2. first commandment with p.
¹Ti. 4. 8. having p. of the life that now
²Ti. 1. 1. according to the p. of life
Heb. 4. 1. lest, a p. being left us of
6.12. faith and patience inherit p-*s*
15. endured, he obtained the p.
17. to shew unto the heirs of p.
7. 6. blessed him that had the p-*s*
8. 6. established upon better p-*s*
9.15. might receive the p.; 10.36
11. 9. sojourned in the land of p.
with him of the same p.
13. not having received the p-*s*
17. that had received the p-*s*
33. obtained p-*s*, stopped the m.
39. th. faith, received not the p.
²Pet. 3. 4. Where is the p. of his coming
9. not slack concerning his p.
¹Jo. 2.25. this is the p. that he hath
epanggellomai.
Gal. 3.19. to whom the p. *was made*
Heb. 6.13. *when* God *made* p. to Abra.
epanggelma.
²Pet. 1. 4. exce. great and precious p-*s*
3.13. we, according to his p., look

PROMISE,   -ed.
epanggellomai.
Mar.14.11.they were glad, and p-*ed* to
Act. 7. 5. he p-*ed* that he would give
Ro. 4.21. that what he *had* p-*ed*, he
Tit. 1. 2. God, that cannot lie, p-*ed*
Heb.10.23.for he is faithful *that* p-*ed*
11.11. him faithful *who had* p-*ed*
12.26. but now he *hath* p-*ed*, saying
Jas. 1.12. which the Lord *hath* p-*ed* to
2. 5. which he *hath* p-*ed* to them
²Pet. 2.19. *While* they p. them liberty
¹Jo. 2.25. that he *hath* p-*ed* us, even
homologeō.
Mat.14. 7. he p-*ed* with an oath to give
exomologeomai.
Lu. 22. 6. he p-*ed*, and sought opportu.
proepanggellomai.
Ro. 1. 2. Which he *had* p-*ed* afore by

PROOF. (See *Infallible*.)
dokimē.
²Co. 2. 9. I might know the p. of you
13. 3. Since ye seek a p. of Christ
Phi. 2.22. But ye know the p. of him
endeixis.
²Co. 8.24. the p. of your love, and of
plērophoreō.
²Ti. 4. 5. *make full* p. of thy ministry

PROPER.
idios.
Act. 1.19. is called in their p. tongue
¹Co. 7. 7. every man hath *his* p. gift
asteios.
Heb.11.23.they saw he was a p. child

PROPHECY,   -ies.
prophēteia.
Mat.13.14.is fulfilled the p. of Esaias
Ro. 12. 6. whether p., let us prophesy
¹Co.12.10. to another p.; to another
13. 2. though I have the gift of p.
8. whether there be p-*s*, they
¹Ti. 1.18. according to the p-*s* which
4.14. which was given thee by p.
²Pet. 1.20. that no p. of the scripture
21. For the p. came not in old
Rev. 1. 3. that hear the words of this p.
11. 6. in the days of their p.: and
19.10. of Jesus is the spirit of p.
22. 7, 10. the sayings of the p. of
18. heareth the words of the p.
19. words of the book of this p.
prophētikos.
²Pet. 1.19. a more sure word *of* p.

PROPHESY, -ieth, -ied, -ing.
prophēteuō.
Mat. 7.22. *have* we nbt p-*ed* in thy name
11.13. prophets and the law p-*ed*
15. 7. well *did* Esaias p.; Mar. 7.6
26.68. Saying, p. unto us; Mar.
14.65.; Lu.22.64
Lu. 1.67. the Holy Ghost, and p-*ed*, sa.
Jo. 11.51. he p-*ed* that Jesus should die
Act. 2.17. your daughters *shall* p.
18. my Spirit; and they *shall* p.
19. 6. spake with tongues, and p-*ed*
21. 9. daugh., virgins, *which did* p.
¹Co. 11. 4. Every man praying or p-*ing*
5. that prayeth or p-*eth* with
13. 9. know in part, and we p. in
14. 1. but rather that ye *may* p.
3. But he *that* p-*eth* speaketh
4. he *that* p-*eth* edifieth the ch.
5. but rather than p. for
6. greater is he *that* p-*eth*
24. But if all p., and there come
31. For ye may all p. one by one
39. covet *to* p., and forbid not to
¹Pet. 1.10. *who* p-*ed* of the grace that
Jude 14. p-*ed* of these, saying, Behold
Rev.10.11.Thou must p. again before
11. 3. two witne., and they *shall* p.

PROPHESYING, [noun,] -s.
prophēteia.
¹Co. 14. 6. or by p., or by doctrine
22. but p. serveth not for them
¹Th. 5.20. Despise not p-*s*

PROPHET,   -s.
prophētēs.   [2.15
Mat. 1.22. spoken of the Lord by the p.:
2. 5. thus it is written by the p.
17. by Jeremy the p.; 27.9.
23. which was spoken by the p-*s*
3. 3. sp. of by the p. Esaias; 4.14,
8.17,12.17; Jo.1.23,12.38
5.12. so persecuted they the p-*s*
17. to destroy the law, or the p-*s*
7.12. this is the law and the p-*s*
10.41. He that receiveth a p. in the
a p. shall receive a p.'s rew.
11. 9. for to see? A p.? yea; Lu.7.26
and more than a p.; Lu.7.26
13. For all the p-*s* and the law
12.39. the sign of the p.Jonas; 16.4;
Lu. 11.29
13.17. That many p-*s* and righteous
35. spoken by the p., saying;
21.4,27.35
57. A p. is not without honour;
Mar. 6.4; Jo. 4.44
14. 5. they counted him as a p.
16.14. Jeremias, or one of the p-*s*
21.11. This is Jesus the p. of Naza.
26. for all hold John as a p.
46. beca. they took him for a p.

Mat. 22.40.hang all the law and the p-*s*
23.29. the tombs of the p-*s;* Lu.11.47
30. them in the blood of the p-*s*
31. of them which killed the p-*s*
34. I send unto you p-*s,* and wise
37. thou that killest the p-*s*
24.15. by Daniel the p.; Mar. 13.14
26.56. that the scriptures of the p-*s*
Mar. 1. 2. is written in the p-*s;* Jo. 6.45
6.15. is a p., or as one of the p-*s*
8.28. and others, One of the the p-*s*
11.32. that he was a p. indeed
Lu. 1.70. of his holy p-*s;* Act. 3.18,21
76. be called the p. of the High.
3. 4. the words of Esaias the p.
4.17. the book of the p. Esaias
24. No p. is accepted in his own
27. in the time of Eliseus the p.
6.23. did their fathers unto the p-*s*
7.16. That a great p. is risen up
28. there is not a greater p. than
39. This man, if he were a p.
9. 8, 19. that one of the old p-*s* was
10.24. that many p-*s* and kings ha.
11.49. I will send them p-*s* and ap.
50. That the blood of all the p-*s*
13.28. and all the p-*s,* in the kingd.
33. that a p. perish out of Jeru.
34. Jerusa., which killest the p-*s*
16.16. The law and the p-*s* were un.
29. They have Moses and the p-*s*
31. hear not Moses and the p-*s*
18.31. that are written by the p-*s*
20. 6. persuad. that John was a p.
24.19. which was a p. mighty in de.
25. all that the p-*s* have spoken
27. at Moses and all the p-*s,* he
44. law of Moses, and in the p-*s*
Jo. 1.21. Art thou that p.? And he
25. nor Elias, neither that p.
45. and the p-*s,* did write Jesus
4.19. I perceive that thou art a p.
6.14. that p. that should come in.
7.40. said, Of a truth this is the p.
52. out of Galilee ariseth no p.
8.52. Abraham is dead, and the p-*s*
53. and the p-*s* are dead: whom
9.17. eyes? He said, He is a p.
Act. 2.16. was spoken by the p. Joel
30. Therefore being a p., and
3.22. A p. shall the Lord your
23. which will not hear that p.
24. Yea, and all the p-*s* from
25. the children of the p-*s,* and
7.37. A p. shall the Lord your God
42. writ. in the book of the p-*s*
48. with hands; as saith the p.
52. Which of the p-*s* have not
8.28. his chariot read Esaias the p.
30. heard him read the p. Esaias
34. of whom speaketh the p.this
10.43. To him give all the p-*s* witn.
11.27. came p-*s* from Jerusalem
13. 1. certain p-*s* and teachers; as
15. read. of the law and the p-*s*
20. fifty years, until Sam. the p.
27. nor yet the voices of the p-*s*
40. which is spoken of in the p-*s*
15.15. agree the words of the p-*s*
32. being p-*s* also themselves
21.10. a certain p., named Agabus
24.14. wr. in the law and in the p-*s*
26.22. which the p-*s* and Moses did
27. believest thou the p-*s?* I kn.
28.23. and out of the p-*s,* from mo.
25. the Holy Gh.by Esaias the p
Ro. 1. 2. by his p-*s* in the holy script.
3.21. witn. by the law and the p-*s*
11. 3. Lo., they have killed thy p-*s*
1Co.12.28. first apostles, secondarily p-*s*
29. are all p-*s?* are all teachers
14.29. Let the p-*s* speak two or th.

1Co.14. 32. the p-*s* are subject to the p-*s*
37. man think himself to be a p.
Eph. 2.20. of the apostles and p-*s,* Jesus
3. 5. unto his holy apostles and p-*s*
4.11. some, p-*s;* and some, evang.
1Ti. 2.15. Lord Jes., and their own p-*s*
Tit. 1.12. even a p. of their own, said
Heb. 1. 1. unto the fathers by the p-*s*
11.32. and Samuel, and of the p-*s*
Jas. 5.10. the p-*s,* who have spoken in
1Pet. 1.10. Of which salvation the p-*s*
2Pet. 2.16. forbad the madness of the p.
3. 2. before by the holy p-*s*
Rev.10. 7. decl. to his servants the p-*s*
11.10. because these two p-*s* torme.
18. unto thy servants the p-*s*
16. 6. blo. of saints and p-*s;* 18.24
18.20. ye holy apostles and p-*s;* for
22. 6. the Lord God of the holy p-*s*
9. and of thy brethren the p-*s*

pseudoprophētēs.
Mat. 7.15. Beware of *false* p-*s,* which
24.11. many *false* p-*s;* Mar. 13.22
23. and *false* p-*s,* and shall shew
Lu. 6.26. their fathers to the *false* p-*s*
Act.13. 6. sorcerer, a *false* p., a Jew
2Pet. 2. 1. But there were *false* p-*s* also
1Jo. 4. 1. because many *false* p-*s* are
Rev.16.13.of the mouth of the *false* p.
19.20. and with him the *false* p. th.
20.10. the beast and the *false* p.

prophētikos.
Ro. 16.26 by the scriptures *of the* p-*s*

PROPHETESS.
prophētis.
Lu. 2.36. Anna, a p., the daughter of
Rev. 2.20. which calleth herself a p.

PROPITIATION.
hilastērion.
Ro. 3.25. a p. through faith in his
hilasmos.
1Jo. 2. 2. the p. for our sins; 4.10

PROPORTION.
analogia.
Ro. 12. 6. according to the p. of faith

PROSELYTE, -s.
prosēlutos.
Mat.23.15.sea and land to make one p.
Act. 2.10. stran. of Rome, Jews and p-*s*
6. 5. Nicolas a p. of Antioch
13.43. of the Jews and religious p-*s*

PROSPER, -ed, -eth.
euodoō.
1Co.16. 2. in store as God hath p-*ed*
(whatev he be *prospered* in.)
3John 2. *that* thou *mayest* p. and be
health even as thy soul p-*eth*

PROSPEROUS.
(See *Journey.*)

PROTEST.
nē.
1Co.15.31. *I* p. *by* your rejoicing which

PROUD.
huperēphanos.
Lu. 1.51. scattered the p. in the ima.
Ro. 1.30. p., boasters, inventors of
2Ti. 3. 2. boasters, p., blasphemers
Jas. 4. 6. God resisteth the p.;1Pet.5.5
tuphoō.
1Ti. 6. 4. He *is* p., knowing nothing

PROVE, -ed, -est, -ing.
dokimazō.
Lu. 14.19. yoke of oxen, and I go to p.
Ro. 12. 2. that ye may p. what is that
2Co. 8. 8. *to* p. the sincerity of your
22. whom we *have* oftenti. p-*ed*

2Co. 13. 5. in the faith; p. your own
Gal. 6. 4. *let* every man p. his own
Eph. 5.10. p-*ing* what is acceptable unt
1Th. 5.21. p. all things; hold fast that
1Ti. 3.10. And *let* these also first *be* p-*ed*
Heb. 3. 9. your fathers tempt. me, p-*ed*
peirazō.
Jo. 6. 6. And this he said *to* p. him
sumbibazō.
Act. 9.22. p-*ing* that this is very Christ
paristēmi.
Act.24.13. Neither can they p. the thi.
apodeiknumi.
Act.25. 7. which they could not p.
proaitiaomai.
Ro. 3. 9. we *have before* p-*ed* both

PROVERB, -s.
paroimia.
Jo. 16.25. have I spoken unto you in p-*s*
. more speak unto you in p-*s*
29. plainly, and speakest no p.
2Pet. 2.22. according to the true p.
parabolē.
Lu. 4.23. say unto me this p., Physi.

PROVIDE, -ed, -ing.
ktaomai.
Mat.10. 9. p. neither gold, nor silver
hetoimazō.
Lu. 12.20. be, which thou *hast* p-*ed*
poieō.
Lu. 12.33. p. yourselves bags which
paristēmi.
Act.23.24. And p. them beasts, that
pronoeō.
Ro. 12.17. p. things honest in the sight
2Co. 8.21. p-*ing for* honest things
1Ti. 5. 8. if any p. not *for* his own
problepō.
Heb.11.40.God *having* p-*ed* some better

PROVIDENCE.
pronoia.
Act.24. 2. unto this nation by thy p.

PROVINCE.
eparchia.
Act.23.34. he asked of what p. he was
25. 1. Festus was come into the p.

PROVISION.
pronoia.
Ro. 13.14. and make not p. *for* the flesh

PROVOCATION.
parapikrasmos.
Heb. 3. 8, 15. your hearts as in the p.

PROVOKE, -ed, -ing.
parazēloō.
Ro. 10.19. p. you *to* jealousy
11.11. for to p. them *to jealousy*
14. I may p. to emulation them
1Co. 10.22. *Do* we p. the Lord *to jealou.*
apostomatizō.
Lu. 11.53. *to* p. him *to speak* of many
paroxunomai.
1Co.13. 5. *is* not easily p-*ed,* thinketh
erethizō.
2Co. 9. 2. your zeal *hath* p-*ed* very
Col. 3.21. p. not your children *to anger*
prokaleomai.
Gal. 5.26. p-*ing* one another, envying
parorgizō.
Eph. 6. 4. p. not your children *to wrath*
parapikrainō.
Heb. 3.16. when they had heard, *did* p.
paroxusmos.
Heb.10.24. to p. unto love and to good

PRUDENCE.
phronēsis.
Eph. 1. 8. us in all wisdom and p

PRUDENT.
sunetos.
Mat.11.25.from the wise and **p.**;Lu.10.21
Act.13. 7. Sergius Paulus, a **p.** man
¹Co. 1.19. nothing the under. of the **p.**

PSALM,   -s.
psalmos.
Lu. 20.42. him. saith in the book of **p**-s
    24.44. and in the **p**-s concerning
Act. 1.20. is written in the book of **p**-s
    13.33. also written in the second **p.**
¹Co. 14.26. every one of you hath a **p.**
Eph. 5.19. Speaking to yourselves in **p**-s
Col. 3.16. admon. one another in **p**-s
psallō.
Jas. 5.13. any merry ? *let* him *sing* **p**-s

PUBLICAN,   -s.
telōnēs.
Mat. 5.46, 47. do not even the **p**-s the
    9.10. many **p**-s and sinners came
    11. eateth your Master with **p**-s
    10. 3. Thomas, and Matthew the **p.**
    11.19. a friend of **p**-s and; Lu.7.34
    18.17. as an heathen man and a **p.**
    21.31, 32. the **p**-s and the harlots
Mar. 2.15. many **p**-s and sinners sat
    16. **p**-s . .drinketh with **p**-s and
Lu. 3.12. Then came also **p**-s to be
    5.27. and saw a **p.**, named Levi
    29. was a great company of **p**-s
    30. drink with **p**-s and sinners
    7.29. and the **p**-s, justified God
    15. 1. all the **p**-s and sinners for to
    18.10. a Phari., and the other a **p.**
    11. adulterers, or even as this **p.**
    13. And the **p.**, standing afar off
architelōnēs.
Lu. 19. 2. was the *chief among the* **p**-s

PUBLIC.   (See *Example.*)

PUBLICLY.
dēmosios.
Act.18.28. convi. the Jews, and that **p.**
    20.20. have taught you **p.**, and

PUBLISH,   -ed.
kērussō.
Mar. 1.45. began *to* **p.** it much, and
    5.20. and began to **p.** in Decapolis
    7.36. more a great deal they **p**-ed
    13.10. must first *be* **p**-ed among all
Lu. 8.39. *and* **p**-ed throughout the wh.
ginomai.
Act.10.37. *which was* **p**-ed throughout
diapherō.
Act.13.49. word of the Lord *was* **p**-ed

PUFF.
phusioō.
¹Co. 4. 6. that no one of you *be* **p**-ed *up*
    18. Now some *are* **p**-ed *up*, as
    19. of them *which are* **p**-ed *up*
    5. 2. And ye are **p**-ed *up*, and
    8. 1. Knowledge **p**-*eth up*, but
    13. 4. not itself, *is* not **p**-ed *up*
Col. 2.18. vainly **p**-ed *up* by his fleshly

PULL,   -ed,-ing.
ekballō.
Mat. 7. 4. Let me **p.** *out* the mote out
Lu. 6.42. see clearly to **p.** *out* the
kathaireō.
Lu. 12.18. I will **p.** down my barns
anaspaō.
Lu. 14. 5. straightway **p.** *him out* on
diaspaō.
Act.23.10. *should have been* **p**-ed *in piec.*
harpazō.
Jude 23. **p**-*ing* them out of the fire
218

PULLING, [*noun.*]
kathairesis.
²Co.10. 4. to the **p.** down of strong

PUNISH,   -ed.
kolazō.
Act. 4.21. how they *might* **p.** them
²Pet. 2. 9. the day of judgme. *to be* **p**-ed
timōreō.
Act.22. 5. unto Jerusal., for *to be* **p**-ed
    26.11. I **p**-ed them oft in every syn.
tiō dikē.
²Th. 1. 9. *shall be* **p**-ed *with* everlast.

PUNISHMENT.
kolasis.
Mat.25.46. away into everlasting **p.**
epitimia.
²Co. 2. 6. to such a man is this **p.**
timōria.
Heb.10.29. Of how much sorer **p.**, sup.
ekdikēsis.
¹Pet.2.14. for the **p.** of evildoers, and

PURCHASE,   -ed.
ktaomai.
Act. 1.18. **p**-ed a field with the reward
    8.20. the gift of God may be **p**-ed
peripoieō.
Act.20.28. he *hath* **p**-ed with his own
¹Ti. 3.13. **p.** to themselves a good deg.
peripoiēsis.
Eph. 1.14. redemp. of the **p**-ed *possessi.*

PURE.
katharos.
Mat. 5. 8. Blessed are the **p.** in heart
Act.20.26. I am **p.** from the blood of
Ro. 14.20. All things indeed are **p.**
¹Ti. 1. 5. is charity out of a **p.** heart
    3. 9. of the faith in a **p.** conscie.
²Ti. 1. 3. with **p.** conscience, that
    2.22. on the Lord out of a **p.** hea.
Tit. 1.15. to the **p.** all things are **p.**
    unbelieving is nothing **p.**
Heb.10.22.bodies washed with **p.** water
Jas. 1.27. **p.** religion and undefiled
¹Pet. 1.22. with a **p.** heart fervently
Rev.15. 6. clothed in **p.** and white linen
    21.18. and the city was **p.** gold
    21. the street of the city was **p.**
    22. 1. And he shewed me a **p.** river
hagnos.
Phi. 4. 8. whatsoever things are **p.**
¹Ti. 5.22. men's sins : keep thyself **p.**
Jas. 3.17. from above is first **p.**, then
¹Jo. 3. 3. himself, even as he is **p.**
eilikrinēs.
²Pet. 3. 1. which I stir up your **p.** mi.

PURENESS.
hagnotēs.
²Co. 6. 6. By **p.**, by knowledge, by

PURGE,   -ed, -eth, -ing.
katharizō.
Mar. 7.19. the draught, **p**-*ing* all meats
Heb. 9.14. *shall* the blood of Ch . . **p.** yo.
    22. *arc* by the law **p**-ed with blo.
diakatharizō.   [Lu.3.17
Mat. 3.12. *will* thoroughly **p.** his floor;
kathairō.
Jo. 15. 2. he **p**-*eth* it, that it may bring
Heb.10. 2. that the worship. once **p**-ed
ekkathairō.
¹Co. 5. 7. **p.** *out* therefore the old leav.
²Ti. 2.21. If a man therefore **p.** himself
poieō katharismos.
Heb. 1. 3. *had* by himself **p**-ed our sins
    (havingmade a cleansing of.)
²Pet. 1. 9. forgot. *that he was* **p**-ed *from*

PURIFICATION.
katharismos.
Lu. 2.22. And when the days of her **p.**
hagnismos.
Act.21.26. of the days of **p.**, until that

PURIFY,   -ied, -ieth, -ing.
hagnizō.
Jo. 11.55. the passover, to **p.** themselv.
Act.21.24. Them take, and **p.** *thyself*
    26. next day **p**-*ing himself* with
    24.18. found me **p**-ed in the temple
Jas. 4. 8. and **p.** your hearts
¹Pet. 1.22. Seeing ye have **p**-ed your so.
¹Jo. 3. 3. **p**-*eth* himself, even as he
katharizō.
Act.15. 9. **p**-*ing* their hearts by faith
Tit. 2.14. **p.** unto himself a peculiar
Heb. 9.23. should *be* **p**-ed with these

PURIFYING, [*noun.*]
katharismos.
Jo. 2. 6. after the manner of the **p.**
    3.25. and the Jews about **p.**
katharotēs.
Heb. 9.13. to the **p.** of the flesh

PURITY.
hagneia.
¹Ti. 4.12. in spirit, in faith, in **p.**
    5. 2. youn. as sisters, with all **p.**

PURLOINING.
nosphizomai.
Tit. 2.10. Not **p.**, but shewing all good

PURPLE.
porphura.
Mar.15.17.And they cloth. him with **p.**
    20. they took off the **p.** from
Lu. 16.19. which was clothed in **p.** and
Rev.17. 4. was arrayed in **p.** and scarlet
    18.12. and **p.**, and silk, and scarlet
porphureos.
Jo. 19. 2. they put on him a **p.** robe
    5. crown of thorns, and the **p.**
Rev.18.16.fine linen, and **p.**, and scarlet
porphuropōlis.
Act.16.14. named Lydia, a *seller of* **p.** of

PURPOSE, [*noun.*]
prothesis.
Act.11.23. that with **p.** of heart they
    27.13. they had obtained their **p.**
Ro. 8.28. called according to his **p.**
    9.11. that the **p.** of God according
Eph. 1.11. according to the **p.** of him
    3.11. According to the eternal **p.**
²Ti. 1. 9. according to his own **p.**
    3.10. manner of life, **p.**, faith
eis.
Act.26.16. appear. unto thee *for* this **p.**
Ro. 9.17. Even *for* this same **p.** have
Col. 4. 8. *for* the same **p.**, that he
¹Jo. 3. 8. *For* this **p.** the Son of God
boulēma.
Act.27.43. kept them from their **p.**

PURPOSE, [*verb,*]   -ed, -eth.
protithēmi.
Ro. 1.13. I **p**-ed to come unto you
Eph. 1. 9. which he *hath* **p**-ed in hims.
tithēmi.
Act.19.21. Paul **p**-ed in the Spirit, whe.
gnōmē ginomai.
Act.20. 3. he **p**-ed to return through
bouleuomai.
²Co. 1.17. that I **p.**, *do* I **p.** according
proaireomai.
²Co. 9. 7. according as he **p**-*eth* in his
poieō.
Eph. 3.11. purpose which he **p**-ed in Ch.

PURSE,   -s.
zōnē.
Mat.10. 9. silver, ncr brass in your **p**-

Mar. 6. 8. bread, no money in their **p.**
  balantion.
Lu. 10. 4. Carry neither **p.** nor scrip
  22,35. sent you without **p.**, and
    36. he that hath a **p.**, let him

PUT,   *-eth, -ing.*
  tithēmi.
Mat. 5.15. and **p.** it under a bushel
  12.18. I *will* **p.** my spirit upon him
  14. 3. **p.** him in prison for Herodi.
Mar. 4.21. Is a candle brought to *be* **p.**
  10.16. **p.** his hands upon them, *and*
Lu. 8.16. or **p**-*eth* it under a bed
  11.33. **p**-*eth* it in a secret place
Jo. 19.19. wrote a title, and **p.** it on the
Act. 1. 7. which the Father *hath* **p.** in
  4. 3. and **p.** them in hold unto
  5.18. and **p.** them in common pri.
  25. the men whom ye **p.** in pri
  12. 4. he **p.** him in prison, and
Ro. 14.13. that no man **p.** a stumbling.
1Co. 15.25. till he *hath* **p.** all enemies
2Co. 3.13. **p.** a vail over his face
1Ti. 1.12. **p**-*ing* me into the ministry
Rev.11. 9. suffer their dead bod. *to be* **p.**
  epitithēmi.
Mat.19.13.that he *should* **p.** his hands *on*
  21. 7. and **p.** on them their clothes
  27.29. they **p.** it *upon* his ; Jo.19.2
Mar. 7.32. bes. him to **p.** his hand *upon*
  8.23, 25. *and* **p.** his hands *upon*
Jo. 9.15. He **p.** clay *upon* mine eyes
Act. 9.12, 17. **p**-*ing* his hand *on* him
  15.10. to **p.** a yoke *upon* the neck
  peritithēmi.
Mat.27.28.**p.** *on* him a scarlet robe
  48. **p.** it on a reed, *and ;*
    Mar.15.36
Mar.15.17.and **p.** it *about* his head
  apotithēmi.
Eph. 4.22. That ye **p.** *off* concerning
  25. Wherefore **p**-*ing away* lying
Col. 3. 8. now ye also **p.** *off* all these
  apothesis.
2Pet. 1.14. *must* **p.** *off* this my taberna.
Heb. 9.26. to **p.** *away* sin by the sacri.
  paratithēmi.
Mat.13.24,31. Another para. **p.** he *forth*
  enduō.   [Lu.12.22
Mat. 6.25. body, what ye *shall* **p.** *on;*
  27.31. and **p.** his own raiment *on*
Mar. 6. 9. and not **p.** *on* two coats
  15.20. **p.** his own clothes *on* him
Lu. 15.22. the best robe, and **p.** it *on*
Ro. 13.12. *let* us **p.** *on* the armour of
    14. **p.** ye *on* the Lord Jesus
1Co. 15.53. corruptible must **p.** *on* inco.
  must **p.** *on* immortality
  54. *shall have* **p.** *on* incorruption
  shall have **p.** *on* immortality
Gal. 3.27. into Christ *have* **p.** *on* Christ
Eph. 4.24. *that ye (have)* **p.** *on ;* Col.3.10
  6.11. **p.** *on* the whole armour of
Col. 3.12. **p.** *on* therefore, as the elect
1Th. 5. 8. **p**-*ing on* the breastplate of
  apekduomai.
Col. 3. 9. ye *have* **p.** *off* the old man
  ballō.   [Mar.2.22; Lu.5.37
Mat. 9.17. Neither *do* men **p.** new wine
  they **p.** new wine into new
  25.27. therefore *to have* **p.** my mon.
  27. 6. for *to* **p.** them into the trea.
Mar. 7.33. **p.** his fingers into his ears
Jo. 5. 7. to **p.** me into the pool : but
  12. 6. bag, and bare *what was* **p.**
  13. 2. devil *having* now **p.** into
  18.11. **p.** *up* thy sword into the
  20.25. **p.** my finger into the print
Jas. 3. 3. *we* **p.** bits in the horses'
Rev. 2.24. I *will* **p.** upon you none

ekballō.
Mat. 9.25. when the peo. *were* **p.** *forth*
Mar. 5.40. *when* he *had* **p.** them all *out*
Lu. 8.54. **p.** them all out, and took
Jo. 10. 4. he **p**-*eth forth* his own sheep
Act. 9.40. **p.** them all forth, and kneel.
  epiballō.
Mat. 9.16. **p**-*eth* a piece of new cl. unto
Lu. 5.36. No man **p**-*eth* a piece of a
  9.62. *having* **p.** his hand to the
  periballō.
Jo. 19. 2. **p.** *on* him a purple robe
  proballō.
Act.19.33. the Jews **p**-*ing* him *forward*
  apoluō.
Mat. 1.19. was minded *to* **p.** her *away*
  5.31, 32.Whos.*shall* **p.** *away;* 19.9;
    Mar. 10.11 ; Lu. 16.18
  19. 3. for a man *to* **p.** *away* his ;
    Mar.10.2
    7. divorce., and *to* **p.** her *away;*
    Mar.10.4
    8. you *to* **p.** *away* your wives
    9. marri. her *which is* **p.** *away;*
    Lu.16.18
Mar.10.12.if a woman *shall* **p.** *away*
  hupotassō.   [Eph.1.22
1Co.15.27. he *hath* **p.** all things *under ;*
  All things *are* **p.** *under* him
  which did **p.** all things und.
  28. him *that* **p.** all things *under*
Heb. 2. 8. yet all things **p.** *under* him.
  didōmi.
Lu. 15.22. **p.** a ring on his hand, and
2Co. 8.16. *which* **p.** the same earnest
Heb. 8.10. I *will* **p.** my laws ; 10.16
  poieō.
Jo. 16. 2. They *shall* **p.** you out of the
  (*shall make* you be *put* out.)
Act. 5.34. to **p.** the apostles forth a
  ekteinō.   [Mar.1.41 ; Lu.5.13
Mat. 8. 3. **p.** *forth* his hand, *and*
  chōrizō.   [Mar.10.9
Mat.19. 6. *let* not man **p.** *asunder*
  ekphuō.   [Mar.13.28
Mat.24.32.tender,and **p**-*eth forth* leaves;
  apostrephō.
Mat.26.52.**p.** *up again* thy sword into
  apostellō.
Mar. 4.29. immediate. he **p**-*eth in* the
  kathaireō.
Lu. 1.52. He *hath* **p.** *down* the mighty
  legō.
Lu. 14. 7. And he **p.** *forth* a parable
  methistanō.
Lu. 16. 4. when I *am* **p.** *out* of the
  prospherō.
Jo. 19.29. and **p.** it *to* his mouth
  luō.
Act. 7.33. **p.** *off* thy shoes from thy
  apōtheomai.
Act.13.46. seeing ye **p.** it *from* you
  embibazō.
Act.27. 6. Italy ; and he **p.** us therein
  epanamimnēskō.
Ro. 15.15. as **p**-*ing* you *in* mind becau.
  exairō.
1Co. 5.13. **p.** *away* from among yourse.
  aphiēmi.
1Co. 7.11. the husband **p.** *away* his
  12. *let* him not **p.** her *away*
  katargeō.
1Co. 13.11. I **p.** *away* childish things
  15.24. when he *shall have* **p.** *down*
  airō.
Eph. 4.31. evil speaking, be **p.** *away*
  apōtheō.
1Ti. 1.19. which some *having* **p.** *away*
  anupotaktos.
Heb. 2. 8. *that is* not **p.** *under* him
  (See *Account, Death, Difference, Fill,*
Mind, Must, Prison, Remembrance,

Shame, Silence, Subjection, Synagogue,
Trust.)

PUTTING, [*noun.*]
  apekdusis.
Col. 2.11. in **p.** *off* the body of the sins
  endusis.
1Pet. 3. 3. or of **p.** *on* of apparel
  apothesis.
1Pet. 3.21. not the **p.** *away* of the filth
  epithesis.
2Ti. 1. 6. by the **p.** *on* of my hands

QUAKE.
  seiō.
Mat.27.51.the earth *did* **q.**, and the
  entromos.
Heb.12.21.I exceedingly fear and **q.**

QUARREL.
  enechō.
Mar. 6.19. *had* a **q.** *against* him
  momphē.
Col. 3.13. if any man have a **q.** against

QUARTER,   *-s.*
  pantachothen.
Mar. 1.45. came to him *from every* **q.**
  topos.
Act.16. 3. Jews which were in those **q**-*s*
  28. 7. In the same **q**-*s* were posses.
    (parts round that *place.*)
  gōnia.
Rev.20. 8. in the four **q**-*s* of the earth

QUATERNIONS.
  tetradion.
Act.12. 4. delivered him to four **q.** of

QUEEN.
  basilissa.   [Lu.11.31
Mat.12.42.The **q.**of the south shall rise;
Act. 8.27. under Candace, **q.** of the
Rev.18. 7. saith in her heart, I sit a **q.**

QUENCH,   *-ed.*
  sbennumi.
Mat.12.20.smoking flax *shall* he not **q.**
Mar. 9.44, 46,48. and the fire *is* not **q**-*e*
Eph. 6.16. able *to* **q.** all the fiery darts
1Th. 5.19. **q.** not the Spirit
Heb.11.34.**q**-*ed* the violence of fire
  asbestos.
Mar. 9.43, 45. fire th. *never shall be* **q**-*ed*

QUESTION, [*noun,*]   *-s.*
  zētēsis.
Jo. 3.25. Then there arose a **q.** betwe
Act.25.20. doub. of such manner of **q**-*s*
  (hesitating about the *inquiry* of this
1Ti. 1. 4. genealo., which minister **q**-*s*
  6. 4. about **q**-*s* and strifes of wor.
2Ti. 2.23. foolish and unlearned **q**-*s*
Tit. 3. 9. But avoid foolish **q**-*s,* and
  zētēma.
Act.15. 2. apos. and elders about this **q.**
  18.15. But if it be a **q.** of words and
  23.29. accused of **q**-*s* of their law
  25.19. But had certain **q**-*s* against
  26. 3. expert in all customs and **q**-*s*
  logos.
Mar.11.29.I will also ask of you one **q.**
  engkaleō.
Act.19.40. in danger *to be called in* **q.**
  krinō.   [24.21
Act.23. 6. of the dead *I am called in* **q.**
  (See *Ask.*)

QUESTION, [*verb,*] *-ed, -ing.*
  suzēteō.
Mar. 1.27. they **q**-*ed* among themselves
  8.11. to **q.** *with* him
  9.10. **q**-*ing* one with another what
  14. and the scribes **q**-*ing with*
  16. scribes, What **q.** ye with th.

eperōtaō.
Lu. 23. 9. he q-*ed* with him in many

QUICK.
zaō.   [[1]Pet.4.5
Act.10.42. jud. of q. and dead ; [2]Ti.4.1 ;
Heb. 4.12. the word of God is q., and

QUICKEN,   -*ed*, -*eth*, -*ing*.
zōopoieō.
Jo.   5.21. rais. up the dead, and q-*eth*
          even so the Son q-*eth* whom
    6.63. It is the spirit *that* q-*eth*; the
Ro.   4.17. God, *who* q-*eth* the dead, and
    8.11. *shall* also q. your mortal bo.
[1]Co. 15.36. whi. thou sowest *is* not q-*ed*
     45. Adam was made a q-*ing* spi.
[1]Ti.   6.13. of God, *who* q-*eth* all things
[1]Pet. 3.18. flesh, but q-*ed* by the Spirit
suzōopoieō.
Eph. 2. 5. *hath* q-*ed* us *together with*
Col. 2.13. *hath* he q-*ed together* '*h*

QUICKLY.
tachu.
Mat. 5.25. Agree with thine adversary q.
   28. 7. And go q., and tell his disci.
     8. And they departed q. from
Mar.16. 8. And they went out q., and
Jo. 11.29. she arose q., and came unto
Rev. 2. 5, 16.I will come unto thee q.
   3.11. Behold, I come q.; 22.7,12
   11.14. the third woe cometh q.
   22.20. Surely I come q.; Amen
tacheōs.
Lu. 14.21. Go out q. into the streets
   16. 6. sit down q., and write fifty
tachion.
Jo. 13.27. him, That thou doest do q.
en tachos.
Act.12. 7. him up, saying, Arise up q.

QUICKSANDS.
surtis.
Act.27.17. they should fall into the q.

QUIET.
katastellō.
Act.19.36. ye ought to be q., and to do
hēsuchazō.
[1]Th. 4.11. And that ye study to be q.
ēremos.
[1]Ti. 2. 2. that we may lead a q. and
hēsuchios.
[1]Pet.3. 4. ornament of a meek and q.

QUIETNESS.
eirēnē.
Act.24. 2. by thee we enjoy great q.
hēsuchia.
[2]Th. 3.12. that with q. they work, and

QUIT.
andrizomai.
[1]Co. 16.13. q. you *like men*, be strong

RABBI.
rabbi.
Mat.23. 7. to be called of men, r., r.
     8. But be not ye called r.: for
Jo.   1.38. They said unto him r., which
     49. r., thou art the Son of God
    3. 2. r., we know that thou art a
     26. r., he that was with thee
   6.25. r., when camest thou hither

RABBONI.
rabbōni.
Jo. 20.16. r.; which is to say, Master

RACA.
raka.
Mat. 5.22. shall say to his brother, r.

RACE,
stadios.
[1]Co. 9.24. which run in a r. run all
220

agōn.
Heb.12. 1. r. that is set before us

RAGE.
phruassō.
Act. 4.25. Why *did* the heathen r., and

RAGING.
kludōn.
Lu. 8.24. wind and the r. of the water
agrios.
Jude 13. r. waves of the sea, foaming

RAILED.
blasphēmeō.
Mar.15.29.that passed by r. *on* him
Lu. 23.39. which were hanged r. *on* him

RAILER.
loidoros.
[1]Co. 5.11. or a r., or a drunkard, or an

RAILING,   -*s*.
blasphēmia.
[1]Ti. 6. 4. cometh envy, strife, r-*s*
Jude   9. against him a r. accusation
loidoria.
[1]Pet. 3. 9. evil for evil, or r. for r.
blasphēmos.
[2]Pet. 2.11. bring not r. accusation

RAIMENT.
himation.
Mat.11. 8. man clot. in soft r. ; Lu.7.25
   17. 2. his r. was white as the light
   27.31. and put his own r. on him
Mar. 9. 3. And his r. became shining
Lu. 23.34. And they parted his r., and
Jo. 19.24. They parted my r. among
Act.18. 6. he shook his r., and said
   22.20. and kept the r. of them that
Rev. 3. 5. clothed in white r. ; 4. 4.
     18. white r., that thou mayest
himatismos.
Lu. 9.29. his r. was white and glister.
enduma.
Mat. 3. 4. John had his r. of camel's
   6.25. the body than r.; Lu. 12.23
     28. why take ye thought for r.
   28. 3. and his r. white as snow
skepasma.
[1]Ti. 6. 8. having food and r. let us be
esthēs.
Jas. 2. 3. also a poor man in vile r.

RAIN, [*noun.*]
huetos.
Act.14.17. and gave us r. from heaven
   28. 2. because of the present r.
Heb. 6. 7. ear. which drinketh in the r.
Jas. 5. 7. recei. the early and latter r.
     18. again, and the heaven gave r.
brechō.
Mat. 5.45. *sendeth* r. on the just and
broche.
Mat. 7.25, 27. r. descended, and the flo.

RAIN, [*verb,*]   -*ed*.
brechō.
Lu. 17.29. *it* r-*ed* fire and brimstone fr.
Jas. 5.17. might not r.: and it r-*ed* not
brechō huetos.
Rev. 11. 6. that it r. not in the days of

RAINBOW.
iris.
Rev. 4. 3. a r. round about the throne
   10. 1. a r. was upon his head

RAISE,   -*ed*, -*eth*, -*ing*.
egeirō.
Mat. 3. 9. *to* r. up children un.; Lu.3.8
   10. 8. r. the dead, cast out devils
   11. 5. the dead *are* r-*ed up*, and the
   16.21. be r-*ed again* the third day ;
       17.23 ; Lu. 9.22

Lu.   1.69. *hath* r-*ed* up an horn of salv.
   7.22. deaf hear, the dead *are* r-*ed*
   20.37. Now that the dead *are* r-*ed*
Jo.   2.19. in three days I *will* r. it *up*
   5.21. as the Father r-*eth up* the
   12. 1, 9. whom he r-*ed* ; [1]Th. 1.10
     17. r-*ed* him from the dead, bare
Act. 3.15. whom God *hath* r-*ed*; 4.10
   5.30. God of our Fathers r-*ed up*
   10.40. Him God r-*ed up* the third
   12. 7. r-*ed* him *up*, saying, Arise
   13.22. he r-*ed up* unto them David
     23. r-*ed* unto Israel a Saviour Je.
     30. God r-*ed* him from the dead ;
       Ro.10.9; Gal.1.1 ; Col.2.12;
       [1]Pet. 1.21
     37. he, whom God r-*ed again*
   26. 8. that God should r. the dead
Ro. 4.24. believe on him *that* r-*ed up*
     25. and *was* r-*ed again* for our
   6. 4. as Christ *was* r-*ed up* from
     9. Christ *being* r-*ed* from the
   7. 4. to him *who is* r-*ed* from the
   8.11. spirit of him *that* r-*ed up* Je.
     he *that* r-*ed up* Christ from
[1]Co. 6.14. God *hath* both r-*ed up* the
   15.15. of God that he r-*ed up* Chr.
     whom he r-*ed* not *up*, if so
     16. not, then *is* not Christ r-*ed*
     17. if Christ *be* not r-*ed*, your fa.
     35. How *are* the dead r-*ed up*
     42. it *is* r-*ed* in incorruption
     43. it *is* r-*ed* in glory : it is sown
     weakness; it *is* r-*ed* in power
     44. it *is* r-*ed* a spiritual body
     52. the dead *shall be* r-*ed* incor.
[2]Co. 1. 9. in God *which* r-*eth* the dead
   4.14. he *which* r-*ed up* the Lord
     shall r. *up* us also by Jesus
Eph. 1.20. *when* he r-*ed* him from the
[2]Ti. 2. 8. was r-*ed* from the dead acco.
Heb.11.19.God was able *to* r. him *up*
Jas. 5.15. the Lord *shall* r. him *up*
epegeirō.
Act.13.50. r-*ed* persecution against Paul
anistēmi.
Mat.22.24.r. *up* seed unto his brother
Jo.   6.39. should r. it *up again* at the
     40, 44,54. I *will* r. him *up* at the
Act. 2.24. Whom God *hath* r-*ed up* ha.
     30. he would r. *up* Christ to sit
     32. This Jesus *hath* God r-*ed up*
   3.22. your God r. *up* unto you of
     26. God, *having* r-*ed up* his Son
   7.37. *shall* the Lord *your* God r. *up*
   13.33. he *hath* r-*ed up* Jesus *again*
     34. he r-*ed* him *up* from the de.
   17.31. he *hath* r-*ed* him from the
exanistēmi.   [Lu.20.28
Mar.12.19.and r. *up* seed unto his brot.;
anastasis.
Heb.11.35.their dead r-*ed to* life *again*
exegeirō.
Ro. 9.17. purpose *have* I r-*ed* thee *up*
[1]Co. 6.14. *will* also r. *up* us by his own
diegeirō.
Mat. 1.24. Joseph *being* r-*ed* from sleep
sunegeirō.
Eph. 2. 6. *hath* r-*ed* us *up together*
poieō episustasis.
Act.24.12. neither r-*ing* up the people

RANKS.
prasia.
Mar. 6.40. And they sat down *in* r.

RANSOM.
lutron.   [Mar.10.45
Mat.20,28.to give his life a r. for many;
antilutron.
[1]Ti. 2. 6. Who gave himself a r. for

RASHLY.
propetēs.
Act.19.36. quiet, and to do nothing **r.**

RATHER.
mallon
Mat.10. 6. But go **r.** to the lost sheep
    28. but **r.** fear him which is able
    25. 9. but go ye **r.** to them that
    27.24. but that **r.** a tumult was
Mar. 5.26. nothing bettered, but **r.** grew
    15.11. that he should **r.** release
Lu. 10.20. but **r.** rejoice, because your
Jo. 3.19. men loved darkness **r.** than
Act. 5.29. to obey God **r.** than men
Ro. 8.34. yea **r.**, that is risen again
    14.13. but judge this **r.**, that no
¹Co. 5. 2. and have not **r.** mourned
    6. 7. Why do ye not **r.** take wro.?
      why do ye not **r.** suffer your.
    7.21. be made free, use it **r.**
    9.12. over you, are not we **r.**
    14. 1. but **r.** that ye may prophesy
    5. but **r.** that ye prophesied
²Co. 2. 7. ye ought **r.** to forgive him
    3. 8. of the spirit be **r.** glorious
    5. 8. willing **r.** to be absent from
    12. 9. gladly therefore will I **r.** glo.
Gal. 4. 9. have known God, or **r.** are
Eph. 4.28. but **r.** let him labour, work.
    5. 4. but **r.** giving of thanks
    11. of darkness, but **r.** reprove
Phi. 1.12. fallen out **r.** unto the furth.
¹Ti. 1. 4. **r.** than godly edifying which
    6. 2. but **r.** do them service
Phile. 9. for love's sake I **r.** beseech
Heb.11.25. Choosing **r.** to suffer afflict.
    12. 9. shall we not much **r.** be in
    13. but let it **r.** be healed
²Pet. 1.10. Wherefore the **r.**, brethren
ē.
Mat.18. 8. **r.** than having two hands
    9. **r.** than having two eyes
Lu. 12.51. tell you, Nay ; but **r.** divi.
menounge.
Lu. 11.28. Yea **r.**, blessed are they that
plēn.
Lu. 11.41. But **r.** give alms of such
    12.31. But **r.** seek ye the kingdom
thelō.
¹Co. 14.19. I had **r.** speak five words
perissoterōs.
Heb.13.19. I beseech you the **r.** to do

RAVENING.
harpagē.
Lu. 11.39. inward part is full of **r.**
harpax.
Mat. 7.15. inwardly they are **r.** wolves

RAVENS.
korax.
Lu. 12.24. Consider the **r.**: for they

REACH,   -ed, -ing.
pherō.
Jo. 20.27. **r.** hither thy finger, and
    and **r.** hither thy hand
ephikneomai.
²Co.10.13. measure to **r.** even unto you
    14. as though we **r**-ed not unto,
epekteinomai.
Phi. 3.13. **r**-ing forth unto those things
akoloutheō.
Rev.18. 5. her sins have **r**-ed unto heav.

READ,   -est, -eth, -ing.
anaginōskō.   [Mar.2.25
Mat.12. 3. Have ye not **r.** what David;
    5. Or have ye not **r.** in the law
    19. 4. Have ye not **r.**, that he wh.
    21.16. have ye never **r.**, Out of the
    42. Did ye never **r.** in the scrip.
    22.31. have ye not **r.** that which

Mat.24.15. whoso **r**-eth, let ; Mar.13.14.
Mar.12.10. have ye not **r.** this scripture
    26. have ye not **r.** in the book of
Lu. 4.16. day, and stood up for to **r.**
    6. 3. Have ye not **r.** so much as
    10.26. written in the law? how **r**-est
Jo. 19.20. This title then **r.** many of
Act. 8.28. in his chariot **r.** Esaias the
    30. heard him **r.** the prophet
    under. thou what thou **r**-est
    32. the scripture which he **r.**
    13.27. the prophets which are **r.**
    15.21. being **r.** in the synagogues
    31. Which when they had **r.**
    23.34. when the governor had **r.**
²Co. 1.13. than what ye **r.** or acknow.
    3. 2. hearts, known and **r.** of all
    15. this day, when Moses is **r.**
Eph. 3. 4. when ye **r.**, ye may under.
Col. 4.16. when this epistle is **r.** among
    that it be **r.** also in the chur.
    that ye likewise **r.** the epis.
¹Th. 5.27. that this epistle be **r.** unto
Rev. 1. 3. Blessed is he that **r**-eth, and
    5. 4. worthy to open and to **r.** the
anagnōsis.
Act.13.15. after the **r**-ing of the law
²Co. 3.14. in the **r**-ing of the old testa.
¹Ti. 4.13. give attendance to **r**-ing, to

READINESS.
prothumia.
Act.17.11. the word with all **r.** of mind
²Co. 8.11. as there was a **r.** to will
hetoimos.
²Co.10. 6. having in a **r.** to revenge

READY.
hetoimos.
Mat.22. 4. and all things are **r.** ;Lu.14.17
    8. The wedding is **r.**, but they
    22.44. be ye also **r.** :for in; Lu.12.40
    25.10. they that were **r.** went in
Lu. 22.33. Lord, I am **r.** to go with
Jo. 7. 6. but your time is alway **r.**
Act.23.15. come near, are **r.** to kill
    21. and now are they **r.**, looking
²Co. 9. 5. that the same might be **r.**
    10.16. of things made **r.** to our hand
Tit. 3. 1. to be **r.** to every good work
¹Pet. 1. 5. unto salvation **r.** to be reve.
    3.15. and be **r.** always to give an
hetoimazō.
Mat.26.19.they made **r.** the passover ;
    Mar.14.16; Lu.22.13
Mar.14.15.there make **r.** for ; Lu.22.12
Lu. 1.17. to make **r.** a people prepared
    9.52. of the Samar. to make **r.** for
    17. 8. Make **r.** wherewith I may
Act.23.23. Make **r.** two hundred soldi.
Rev.19. 7. his wife hath made herself **r.**
echō hetoimōs.
Act.21.13. I am **r.** not to be bound
²Co.12.14. the third time I am **r.** to
¹Pet. 4. 5. to him that is **r.** to judge
mellō.
Lu. 7. 2. **r.** to die ; Rev.3.2
Act.20. 7. **r.** to depart on the morrow
Rev.12. 4. which was **r.** to be delivered
paraskeuazō.
Act.10.10. while they made **r.** he fell
²Co. 9. 2. Achaia was **r.**; 3. ye may be **r.**
prothumos.
¹Pet.5.2. filthy lucre, but of a **r. mind**
prothumos.
Mar.14.38.The spirit truly is **r.**, but
Ro. 1.15. I am **r.** to preach the gospel
prothumia.
²Co. 8.19. declaration of your **r.** mind
enggus.
Heb. 8.13. waxeth old is **r.** to vanish
    (See Distribute, Offer.)

REAP,   -ed, -eth, ing.
therizō.
Mat. 6.26. neither do they **r.** ; Lu.12.24
    25.24. **r**-ing where thou ; Lu.19.21
    26. I **r.** where I sowed ; Lu.19.22
Jo. 4.36. he that **r**-eth receiveth wages
    and he that **r**-eth may rejoice
    37. One soweth, and another **r**-eth
    38. I sent you to **r.** that whereon
¹Co. 9.11. if we shall **r.** your carnal
²Co. 9. 6. shall **r.** also sparingly ; and
    shall **r.** also bountifully
Gal. 6. 7. soweth, that shall he also **r.**
    8. shall of the flesh **r.** corrupt.
    shall of the Spirit **r.** life ever.
    9. for in due season we shall **r.**
Jas. 5. 4. cries of them which have **r**-ed
Rev.14.15.**r.**: for the time is..to **r.**
    16. and the earth was **r**-ed
amaō.
Jas. 5. 4. labourers who have **r**-ed down

REAPERS.
theristēs.
Mat.13.30.harvest I will say to the **r.**
    39. and the **r.** are the angels

REAR.
egeirō.
Jo. 2.20. wilt thou **r.** it up in three

REASON, [noun.]
dia, [accu.]
Jo. 12.11. Because that by **r.** of him m.
Ro. 8.20. by **r.** of him who hath subje.
Heb. 5. 3. by **r.** hereof he ought, as for
    14. those who by **r.** of use have
²Pet. 2. 2. by **r.** of whom the way of
arestos.
Act. 6. 2. It is not **r.** that we should
heneka or heneken.
²Co. 3.10. by **r.** of the glory that excel.
ek.
Rev. 8.13. by **r.** of the other voices
    9. 2. by **r.** of the smoke of the pit
    18.19. by **r.** of her costliness
logos.
Act. 18.14. **r.** would that I should bear
    (according to reason.)
¹Pet. 3.15. a **r.** of the hope that is in

REASON, [verb,]   -ed, -ing.
dialogizomai.
Mat.16. 7. they **r**-ed among themselves;
    21.25; Mar.8.16; Lu.20.14
    8. why **r.** ye among yourselves
Mar. 2. 6. sitting there, and **r**-ing in
    8. that they so **r**-ed within the.
    Why **r.** ye these things in
    8.17. Why **r.** ye, because ye have
Lu. 5.21. and the Pharisees began to **r.**
    22. What **r.** ye in your hearts
dialegomai.
Act.17. 2. he **r**-ed with them out of the
    18. 4. he **r**-ed in the synagogue ev.
    19. synagogue, and **r**-ed with the
    24.25. as he **r**-ed of righteousness
logizomai.
Mar.11.31.they **r**-ed with themselves
suzēteō.
Mar.12.28.heard them **r**-ing together
sullogizomai.
Lu. 20. 5. they **r**-ed with themselves

REASONABLE.
logikos.
Ro. 12. 1. which is your **r.** service

REASONING, [noun.]
dialogismos.
Lu. 9.46. there arose a **r.** among them.

suzētēsis.

Act.28.29. had great **r.** among themsel.

REBUKE, [noun.]
amōmētos.

Phi. 2.15. the sons of God *without* **r.**

REBUKE, [verb,] -ed, -ing.
epitimaō. [Mar.4.39; Lu.8.24

Mat. 8.26. he arose, and **r-ed** the winds;
16.22. and began to **r.** him; Mar.8.32
17.18. And Jesus **r-ed** the devil
19.13. the disciples **r-ed**; Mar.10.13
20.31. the multitude **r-ed** them, be.
Mar. 1.25. Jesus **r-ed** him, say.; Lu.4.35
8.33. he **r-ed** Peter, saying, Get
9.25. he **r-ed** the foul spirit, saying
Lu. 4.39. and **r-ed** the fever; and it
41. he **r-ing** them suffered them
9.42. Jesus **r-ed** the unclean spirit
55. he turned, and **r-ed** them
17. 3. trespass against thee, **r.** him
18.15. disciples saw it, they **r-ed**
39. which went before **r-ed** him
19.39. Master, **r.** thy disciples
23.40. answering, **r-ed** him, saying
2Ti. 4. 2. reprove, **r.**, exhort, with all
Jude 9. but said, The Lord **r.** thee

elengchō.

1Ti. 5.20. Them that sin **r.** before all
Tit. 1.13. Wherefore **r.** them sharply
2.15. and **r.** with all authority
Heb.12. 5. *when thou art* **r-ed** of him
Rev. 3.19. As many as I love, I **r.** and

epiplēttō.

1Ti. 5. 1. **r.** not an elder, but intreat

echō elengxis.

2Pet.2.16. But *was* **r-ed** for his iniquity

RECEIPT. (See *Custom.*)

RECEIVE, -ed, -edst, -eth, -ing.
lambanō. [Lu.11.10

Mat. 7. 8. every one that asketh **r-eth**;
10. 8. freely ye *have* **r-ed**, freely
41. *shall* **r.** a prophet's reward
shall **r.** a righteous man's
13.20. word, and anon with joy **r-eth**
17.24. they *that* **r-eth** tribute money
19.29. *shall* **r.** an hund.; Mar.10.30
20. 7. is right, that shall ye **r.**
9. they **r-ed** every man a penny
10. **r-ed** more; and they like.**r-ed**
11. *when* they had **r-ed** it, they
21.22. prayer believing, ye *shall* **r.**
34. that they might **r.** the fruits
23.14. *shall* **r.** the greater damna.;
Mar.12.40;Lu.20.47;Jas.3.1
25.16. Then he *that had* **r-ed** five
18, 24.But he *that had* **r-ed** one
20. so he *that had* **r-ed** five tale.
22. He also *that had* **r-ed** two
Mar. 4.16. immediately **r.** it with glad.
11.24. believe that ye **r.** them
12. 2. that he *might* **r.** from the
15.23. myrrh ; but he **r-ed** it not
Lu. 19.12. to **r.** for himself a kingdom
15. Was returned *having* **r-ed** the
Jo. 1.12. as many as **r-ed** him, to the.
16. have all we **r-ed**, and grace
3.11. and ye **r.** not our witness
27. A man can **r.** nothing, except
32. no man **r-eth** his testimony
33. He *that hath* **r-ed** his testi.
4.36. that reapeth **r-eth** wages
5.34. I **r.** not testimony from man
41. I **r.** not honour from men
43. name, and ye **r.** me not
his own name, him ye *will* **r.**
44. *which* **r.** honour one of ano.
6.21. Then they willingly **r-ed** him
7.23. a man on the sabbath day **r.**
222

Jo. 7.39. that believe on him should **r.**
10.18. This command. *have* I **r-ed**
12.48. and **r-eth** not my words
13.20. He *that* **r-eth** whomsoever I
r-eth me ; and he *that* **r-eth**
me **r-eth** him that sent me
30. He then *having* **r-ed** the sop
14.17. whom the world cannot **r.**
16.14. for he *shall* **r.** of mine, and
24. ask, and ye *shall* **r.**, that
17. 8. and they *have* **r-ed** them
18. 3. Judas then, *having* **r-ed** a
19.30. When Jesus there. *had* **r-ed**
20.22. them, **r.** ye the Holy Ghost
Act. 1. 8. But ye *shall* **r.** power, after
2.33. and having **r-ed** of the Father
38. ye *shall* **r.** the gift of the
3. 5. expecting to **r.** something
7.53. Who *have* **r-ed** the law by
8.15. that they *might* **r.** the H. Gh.
17. and they **r-ed** the Holy Gho.
19. he *may* **r.** the Holy Ghost
9.19. And *when* he *had* **r-ed** meat
10.43. *shall* **r.** remission of sins
47. which *have* **r-ed** the H. Gho.
16.24. Who, *having* **r-ed** such a ch.
17.15. and **r-ing** a commandment
19. 2. *Have* ye **r-ed** the Holy Ghost
20.24. which I *have* **r-ed** of the L.J.
35. more bless. to give than to **r.**
26.10. *having* **r-ed** authority from
18. that they may **r.** forgiveness
Ro. 1. 5. By whom we *have* **r-ed** grace
4.11. And he **r-ed** the sign of cir.
5.11. by whom we *have* now **r-ed**
17. much more they *which* **r.**
8.15. For ye *have* not **r-ed** the spi.
but ye *have* **r-ed** the Spirit of
13. 2. *shall* **r.** to themselves damn.
1Co. 2.12. Now we *have* **r-ed**, not the
3. 8. *shall* **r.** his own reward acco.
14. thereupon, he *shall* **r.** a rew.
4. 7. that thou *didst* not **r.**? now
didst **r.** it, why dost thou
as if thou *hadst* not **r-ed** it
9.24. all, but one **r-eth** the prize
14. 5. that the church *may* **r.** edif.
2Co. 11. 4. if ye **r.** another spirit, which
which ye *have* not **r-ed**
24. five times **r-ed** I forty stripes
Gal. 3. 2. **r-ed** ye the Spirit by the wo.
14. that we *might* **r.** the promise
Col. 4.10. whom ye **r-ed** commandmen.
1Ti. 4. 4. *if it be* **r-ed** with thanksgiving
Heb. 2. 2. **r-ed** a just recompence of
7. 5. *who* **r.** the office of the priest.
8. men that die **r.** tithes ; but
9. Levi also, *who* **r-eth** tithes
9.15. *might* **r.** the promise of eter.
10.26. after that we *have* **r-ed** the
11. 8. which he should after **r.** for
11. Sara herself **r-ed** strength
13. not *having* **r-ed** the promises
35. Women **r-ed** their dead raised
Jas. 1. 7. that he *shall* **r.** any thing of
12. he *shall* **r.** the crown of life
4. 3. Ye ask, and **r.** not, because
5. 7. until he **r.** the early and lat.
1Pet. 4.10. As every man *hath* **r-ed** the
2Pet. 1.17. For he **r-ed** from God the F.
1Jo. 2.27. anointing which ye *have* **r-ed**
3.22. whatsoever we ask, we **r.** of
5. 9. If we **r.** the witness of men
2John 4. as we *have* **r-ed** a command.
10. **r.** him not into your house
Rev. 2.17. knoweth saving he *that* **r-eth**
27. even as I **r-ed** of my Father
3. 3. how thou *hast* **r-ed** and hea.
4.11. to **r.** glory and honour and
5.12. to **r.** power, and riches, and
14. 9. and **r.** his mark in his foreh.
11. **r-eth** the mark of his name

Rev.17.12. which *have* **r-ed** no kingdom
but **r.** power as kings one ho.
18. 4. that ye **r.** not of her plagues
19.20. them *that had* **r-ed** the mark
20. 4. neither *had* **r-ed** his mark

paralambanō.

Mar. 7. 4. which they *have* **r-ed** to hold
Jo. 1.11. and his own **r-ed** him not
14. 3. I will come again, and **r.** you
1Co. 11.23. For I *have* **r-ed** of the Lord
15. 1. which also ye *have* **r-ed**, and
3. that which I also **r-ed**, how
Gal. 1. 9. than that ye *have* **r-ed**, let
12. For I neither **r-ed** it of man
Phi. 4. 9. ye *have* both learned, and **r-ed**
Col. 2. 6. As ye *have* therefore **r-ed** Ch.
4.17. ministry which thou *hast* **r-ed**
1Th. 2.13. *when* ye **r-ed** the word of God
4. 1. that as ye *have* **r-ed** of us how
2Th. 3. 6. tradition which he **r-ed** of us
Heb.12.28. Wherefore we **r-ing** a kingd.

apolambanō.

Lu. 6.34. of whom ye hope *to* **r.**, what
lend to sinners, *to* **r.**...*again*
15.27. because he *hath* **r-ed** him safe
16.25. in thy lifetime **r-edst** thy
18.30. Who *shall* not **r.** manifold
23.41. for we **r.** the due reward of
Ro. 1.27. and **r-ing** in themselves that
Gal. 4. 5. that we *might* **r.** the adoption
Col. 3.24. ye *shall* **r.** the reward of the
3John 8. but that *we* **r.** a full reward
3John 8. We therefore ought *to* **r.** such

proslambanō.

Act. 28. 2. and **r-ed** us every one, beca.
Ro. 14. 1. weak in the faith, **r.** ye, but
3. for God *hath* **r-ed** him
15. 7. **r.** ye one another, as Christ
also **r-ed** us to the glory
Phile. 12. thou therefore **r.** him, that
17. partner, **r.** him as myself

analambanō.

Mar.16.19.he *was* **r-ed** up into heaven
Act.10.16. vessel *was* **r-ed** up again
1Ti. 3.16. in the world, **r-ed** up into

hupolambanō.

Act. 1. 9. a cloud **r-ed** him out of their

metalambanō.

Heb. 6. 7. dressed, **r-eth** blessing from

lēpsis.

Phi. 4.15.as concerning giving and **r-ing**

analēpsis.

Lu. 9.51. that he *should be* **r-ed** up

proslēpsis.

Ro. 11.15. what shall the **r-ing** of them

eis metalēpsis.

1Ti. 4. 3. God hath created *to be* **r-ed**

dechomai.

Mat.10.14.whosoever *shall* not **r.** you,
Mar.6.11 ; Lu.9.5
40. He *that* **r-eth** me **r-eth** me
that **r-eth** me **r-eth** ; Lu.9.48
41. He *that* **r-eth** a prophet in
he *that* **r-eth** a righteous man
11.14. if ye will **r.** it, this is Elias
18. ʳ. *shall* **r.** one such little child
in my name **r-eth** me ; Mar.
9.37 ; Lu.9.48
Mar. 9.37. whosoever *shall* **r.** me, **r-eth**
10.15. Whosoever *shall* not **r.** the
Lu. 8.13. hear, **r.** the word with joy
9.11. he **r-ed** them, *and* spake un.
53. they *did* not **r.** him, because
10. 8, 10. city ye enter, and they **r.**
16. 4. they *may* **r.** me into their
9. they *may* **r.** you into everla.
18.17. Whosoever *shall* not **r.** the
Jo. 4.45. the Galileans **r-ed** him, havi.
Act. 3.21. Whom the heaven must **r.**
7.38. who **r-ed** the lively oracles
59. Lord Jesus, **r.** my spiri'
8.14. that Samaria *had* **r-ed** the

Act. 11. 1. Gentiles *had* also **r**-*ed* the
17. 11. in that they **r**-*ed* the word
21. 17. the brethren **r**-*ed* us gladly
22. 5. from whom also I **r**-*ed* letters
28. 21. We neither **r**-*ed* letters out
¹Co. 2. 14. the natural man **r**-*eth* not
²Co. 6. 1. **r.** not the grace of God in
7. 15. fear and trembling ye **r**-*ed*
8. 4. *that* we *would* **r.** the gift
11. 16. yet as a fool **r.** me, that I
Gal. 4. 14. **r**-*ed* me as an angel of God
Phi. 4. 18. *having* **r**-*ed* of Epaphroditus
Col. 4. 10. if he come unto you, **r.** him
¹Th. 1. 6. *having* 1-*ed*the word in much
2. 13. ye **r**-*ed* it not as the word of
²Th. 2. 10. they **r**-*ed* not the love of
Heb.11. 31.*when* she *had* **r**-*ed* the spies
Jas. 1. 21. **r.** with meekness the engraf.

paradechomai.

Mar. 4. 20. such as hear the word, and **r.**
Act. 16. 21. are not lawful for us to **r.**
22. 18. for they *will* not **r.** thy testi.
¹Ti. 5. 19. Against an elder **r.** not an
Heb.12. 6. every one whom he **r**-*eth*

apodechomai.

Lu. 8. 40. the people *gladly* **r**-*ed* him
Act. 2. 41. they *that gladly* **r**-*ed* his wo.
15. 4. they *were* **r**-*ed* of the church
18. 27. exhorting the disciples to **r.**
28. 30. **r**-*ed* all that came in unto

hupodechomai.

Lu. 10. 38. Martha **r**-*ed* him into her
19. 6. down, and **r**-*ed* him joyfully
Act. 17. 7. Whom Jason *hath* **r**-*ed*: and
Jas. 2. 25. *when* she *had* **r**-*ed* the mes.

prosdechomai.

Lu. 15. 2. This man **r**-*eth* sinners and
Ro. 16. 2. That ye **r.** her in the Lord
Phi. 2. 29. **r.** him therefore in the Lord

anadechomai.

Act. 28. 7. Publius; who **r**-*ed* us and
Heb. 11. 17. he *that had* **r**-*ed* the promises

epidechomai.

³John 9. but Diotrephes..**r**-*eth* us not
10. neither *doth* he himself **r.** the

eisdechomai.

²Co. 6. 17. unclean thing; and I *will* **r.**

komizō.

Mat.25. 27. I should *have* **r**-*ed* mine own
²Co. 5. 10. every one *may* **r.** the things
Eph. 6. 8. the same *shall* he **r.** of the
Col. 3. 25. *shall* **r.** for the wrong which
Heb. 10. 36. of God ye *might* **r.** the prom.
11. 19. from whence also he **r**-*ed* him
39. through faith, **r**-*ed* not the
¹Pet. 1. 9. **r**-*ing* the end of your faith
5. 4. ye *shall* **r.** a crown of glory
²Pet. 2. 13. *And shall* **r.** the reward of

chōreō.

Mat.19. 11. All men *cannot* **r.** this saying
12. to **r.** it, *let* him **r.** it
Mar. 2. 2. there *was* no room to **r.** them
²Co. 7. 2. us; we have wronged no

apechō.

Lu. 6. 24. ye *have* **r**-*ed* your consolation
Phile. 15. that thou *shouldest* **r.** him for

zēmioō.

²Co. 7. 9. ye *might* **r.** *damage* by us in

didōmi.

Rev. 13. 16. to **r.** a mark in their right
(See *Fathers, Law, Mercy, Seed, Sight,*
Strength, Tithe.)

RECKON,   -*ed*, -*eth*.

logizomai.

Lu. 22. 37. he *was* **r**-*ed* among the trans.
Ro. 4. 4. *is* the reward not **r**-*ed* of
9. faith *was* **r**-*ed* to Abraham
10. How *was* it then **r**-*ed*? when
6. 11. **r.** ye also yourselves to be
8. 18. For I **r.** that the sufferings

---

sunairō.
Mat.18. 24. And when he had begun *to* **r.**
sunairō logos.
Mat.25. 19. cometh and **r**-*eth* with them

RECOMMENDED.

paradidōmi.

Act. 14. 26. had been **r.** to the grace
15. 40. *being* **r.** by the brethren

RECOMPENCE.

misthapodosia.

Heb. 2. 2. received a just **r.** *of reward*
10. 35. which hath great **r.** *of rewa.*
11. 26. unto the **r.** *of the reward*

antapodoma.

Lu. 14. 12. again, and a **r.** be made thee
Ro. 11. 9. stumblingblock, and a **r.**

antimisthia,

Ro. 1. 27. that **r.** of their error which
²Co. 6. 13. Now for a **r.** in the same

RECOMPENSE,   -*ed*.

antapodidōmi.

Lu. 14. 14. **r.** thee: for thou *shalt be* **r**-*ed*
Ro. 11. 35. it *shall be* **r**-*ed* unto him *aga.*
²Th. 1. 6. with God *to* **r.** tribulation
Heb. 10. 30. I *will* **r.**, saith the Lord

apodidōmi.

Ro. 12. 17. **r.** to no man evil for evi

RECONCILE,   -*ed*, -*ing*.

katallassō.

Ro. 5. 10. we *were* **r**-*ed* to God by the
being **r**-*ed*, we shall be saved
¹Co. 7. 11. remain unmarried, or *be* **r**-*ed*
²Co. 5. 18. of God, *who hath* **r**-*ed* us to
19. **r**-*ing* the world unto himself
20. Christ's stead, *be* ye **r**-*ed* to

apokatallattō.

Eph. 2. 16. that he *might* **r.** both unto
Col. 1. 20. by him to **r.** all things unto
21. works, yet now *hath* he **r**-*ed*

diallattō.

Mat. 5. 24. first *be* **r**-*ed* to thy brother

RECONCILIATION.

katallagē.

²Co. 5. 18. given to us the ministry of **r.**
19. com. unto us the word of **r.**

hilaskomai.

Heb. 2. 17. to make **r.** *for* the sins of

RECONCILING, [noun.]

katallagē.

Ro. 11. 15. of them be the **r.** of the wor.

RECORD.

martureō.

Jo. 1. 32. And John bare **r.**, saying
34. I saw, and *bare* **r.** that this
8. 13. Thou *bearest* **r.** of thyself
14. Though I *bear* **r.** of myself
12. 17. him from the dead, *bare* **r.**
19. 35. he that saw it *bare* **r.**, and
Ro. 10. 2. For I *bear* them **r.** that they
²Co. 8. 3. I *bear* **r.**, yea, and beyond
Gal. 4. 15. for I *bear* you **r.**, that, if
Col. 4. 13. For I *bear* him **r.**, that he
¹Jo. 5. 7. three *that bear* **r.** in heaven
³John 12. yea, and we also *bear* **r.**
Rev. 1. 2. Who *bare* **r.** of the word

marturia.

Jo. 1. 19. this is the **r.** of John, when
8. 13. of thyself: thy **r.** is not true
14. my **r.** is true: for I know
19. 35. and his **r.** is true: and he
¹Jo. 5. 10. believeth not the **r.** that God
11. And this is the **r.**, that God
³John 12. ye know that our **r.** is true

martur.

²Co. 1. 23. I call God for a **r.** upon my
Phi. 1. 8. For God is my **r.**, how grea.

---

marturomai.
Act. 20. 26. I take you to **r.** this day

RECOVER,   -*ing*.

echō kalōs.

Mar. 61. 18. the sick, and they *shall* **r.**

anablepsis.

Lu. 4. 18. **r**-*ing of sight* to the blind

ananēphō.

²Ti. 2. 26. they *may* **r.** them*selves* out

RED.

purrazō.

Mat.16. 2, 3. weather: for the sky *is* **r.**

purros.

Rev. 6. 4. another horse that was **r.**
12. 3. behold a great **r.** dragon, ha.

REDEEM,   -*ed*, -*ing*.

agorazō.

Rev. 5. 9. **r**-*ed* us to God by thy blood
14. 3. *were* **r**-*ed* from the earth
4. These were **r**-*ed* from among

exagorazō.

Gal. 3. 13. Christ *hath* **r**-*ed* us from the
4. 5. To **r.** them that were under
Eph. 5. 16. **r**-*ing* the time, because the
Col. 4. 5. are without, **r**-*ing* the time

lutroō.

Lu. 24. 21. which should have **r**-*ed* Isra.
Tit. 2. 14. that he *might* **r.** us from
¹Pet. 1. 18. ye *were* not **r**-*ed* with corru.

poieō lutrōsis.

Lu. 1. 68. visited and **r**-*ed* his people

REDEMPTION.

apolutrōsis.

Lu. 21. 28. for your **r.** draweth nigh
Ro. 3. 24. through the **r.** that is in
8. 23. to wit, the **r.** of our body
¹Co. 1. 30. and sanctification, and **r.**
Eph. 1. 7. whom we have **r.**; Col. 1. 14
14. until the **r.** of the purchased
4. 30. sealed unto the day of **r.**
Heb. 9. 15. for the **r.** of the transgressio.

lutrōsis.

Lu. 2. 38. that looked for **r.** in Jerusa.
Heb. 9. 12. having obtained eternal **r.**

REDOUND.

perisseuō.

²Co. 4. 15. abundant grace *might*..**r.** to

REED.

kalamos.

Mat.11. 7. A **r.** shaken with; Lu. 7. 24
12. 20. A bruised **r.** shall he not br.
27. 29. and a **r.** in his right hand
30. took the **r.**, and; Mar.15. 19
48. and put it on a **r.**; Mar.15. 36
Rev. 11. 1. given me a **r.** like unto a rod
21. 15. had a golden **r.** to measure
16. he meas. the city with the **r.**

REFORMATION.

diorthōsis.

Heb. 9. 10. on them until the time of **r.**

REFRAIN.

aphistēmi.

Act. 5. 38. **r.** from these men, and let

pauō.

¹Pet. 3. 10. *let* him **r.** his tongue from

REFRESH,   -*ed*.

anapauō.

¹Co. 16. 18. they *have* **r**-*ed* my spirit and
²Co. 7. 13. his spirit *was* **r**-*ed* by you all
Phile. 7. bowels of the saints *are* **r**-*ed*
20. **r.** my bowels in the Lord

anapsuchō.

²Ti. 1. 16. for he oft **r**-*ed* me, and was

tungchanō epimeleia.

Act. 27. 3. unto his friends to **r.** himself
223

sunanapauō.

Ro. 15.32. and may *with* you be r-*ed*

REFRESHING.
anapsuxis.

Act. 3.19. when the times of r. shall

REFUSE,   -*ed.*
paraiteomai.

Act.25.11. I r. not to die : but if there
[1]Ti. 4. 7. r. profane and old wives' fa.
     5.11. But the younger widows r.
Heb.12.25.See that ye r. not him that
     who r-*ed* him that spake on

Act. 7.35. Moses whom they r-*ed*, sayi.
Heb.11.24.r-*ed* to be called the son of
arneomai.

Act. 7.35. Moses whom they r-*ed*, sayi.
Heb.11.24.r-*ed* to be called the son of
apoblētos.

[1]Ti. 4. 4. nothing *to be* r-*ed*, if it be

REGARD, -*ed, -est, -eth, -ing.*
blepō.   [Mar.12.14

Mat.22.16. thou r-*est* not the person ;
epiblepō.

Lu. 1.48. he *hath* r-*ed* the low estate
entrepō.

Lu. 18. 2,4. fear not God, neither r-*ed*
phroneō.

Ro. 14. 6. He *that* r-*eth* the day, r-*eth*
     and he *that* r-*eth* not the day
     to the Lord he *doth* not r. it
parabouleuomai.

Phi. 2.30. *not* r-*ing* his life, to supply
ameleō.

Heb. 8. 9. I r-*ed* them *not*, saith the L.

REGENERATION.
palinggenesia.

Mat.19.28. in the r.,when the Son of m.
Tit. 3. 5. by the washing of r., and re.

REGION,   -*s.*
chōra.

Mat. 4.16. to them which sat in the r.
Lu. 3. 1. and of the r. of Trachonitis
Act. 8. 1. throughout the r-*s* of Judea
     13.49. publis. throughout all the r.
     16. 6. and the r. of Galatia, and
perichōros.   [Lu. 4.14,7.17
Mat. 3. 5. the r.*round about;* Mar.1.28;
Mar. 6.15. that whole r. *round about*
Act.14. 6. the r. *that lieth round about*
klima.

[2]Co. 11.10. boasting in the r-*s* of Achaia
Gal. 1.21. I came into the r-*s* of Syria

REHEARSE.   -*ed.*
ananggellō.

Act.14.27. they r-*ed* all that God had
     (See *Beginning.*)

REIGN, [*noun.*]
hēgemonia.

Lu. 3. 1. of the r. of Tiberius Cæsar

REIGN, [*verb.*]   -*ed, -eth.*
basileuō.

Mat. 2.22. that Archelaus *did* r. in Ju.
Lu. 1.33. he *shall* r. over the house of
     19.14. will not have this man *to* r.
     27. not *that* I *should* r. over th.
Ro. 5.14. death r-*ed* from Adam to M.
     17. one man's offence death r-*ed*
     shall r. in life by one, Jesus
     21. as sin *hath* r-*ed* unto death
     even so *might* grace r. throu.
     6.12. *Let* not sin therefore r. in
[1]Co. 4. 8. ye *have* r-*ed* as kings without
     and I would to God ye *did* r.
     15.25. For he must r., till he hath
Rev. 5.10. we *shall* r. on the earth
     11.15. *shall* r. for ever and ; 22.5
     17. great power, and *hast* r-*ed*
     19. 6. Lord God omnipotent r-*eth*

224

Rev.20. 4. they lived and r-*ed* with Ch.
     6. *shall* r. with him a thousand
sumbasileuō.

[1]Co. 4. 8. we also *might* r. *with* you
[2]Ti. 2.12. we *shall* also r. *with* him
echō basileia.

Rev.17.18.which r-*eth* over the kings
archō.

Ro. 15.12. that shall rise *to* r. *over*

REINS.
nephros.

Rev. 2.23. he which searcheth the r.

REJECT,   -*ed, -eth.*
apodokimazō.

Mat.21.42.stone which the builders r-*ed*
     Mar.12.10; Lu.20.17
Mar. 8.31. *be* r-*ed* of the elders; Lu.9.22
Lu. 17.25. *be* r-*ed* of this generation
Heb.12.17. inheri. the bless.,he *was* r-*ed*
adokimos.

Heb. 6. 8. thorns and briers is r-*ed*
atheteō.

Mar. 6.26. with him, he would not r.
     7. 9. ye r. the commandment of
Lu. 7.30. lawyers r-*ed* the counsel of
Jo. 12.48. He *that* r-*eth* me, and
ekptuō.

Gal. 4.14. ye despised not, nor r-*ed*
paraiteomai.

Tit. 3.10. and second admonition r.

REJOICE,   -*ed, -eth, -ing.*
chairō.

Mat. 2.10. they r-*ed* with exceeding
     5.12. r., and be exceeding glad
     18.13. he r-*eth* more of that sheep
Lu. 1.14. and many *shall* r. at his
     6.23. r. ye in that day, and leap
     10.20. Notwithstanding in this r.
     but rather r., because your
     13.17. and all the people r-*ed* for
     15. 5. lay. it on his shoulders, r-*ing*
     19.37. began to r. *and* praise God
Jo. 3.29. r-*eth* greatly because of the
     4.36. he that reapeth *may* r. tog.
     14.28. ye *would* r., because I said
     16.20. lament, but the wor. *shall* r.
     22. and your heart *shall* r.
Act. 5.41. r-*ing* that they were counted
     8.39. he went on his way r-*ing*
     15.31. they r-*ed* for the consolation
Ro. 12.12. r-*ing* in hope ; patient in
     15. r. with them *that do* r.
[1]Co. 7.30. *that* r., as though they r-*ed*
     13. 6. r-*eth* not in iniquity, but
[2]Co. 2. 3. of whom I ought *to* r.
     6.10. sorrowful, yet alway r-*ing*
     7. 9. so that I r-*ed* the more
     9. Now I r., not that ye were
     16. I.r. therefore that I have
Phi. 1.18. therein *do* r., yea, and *will* r.
     2.28. ye see him again, ye *may* r.
     3. 1. Finally, my brethren, r. in
     4. 4. r. in the Lord alway : and
     again I say, r.
     10. But I r-*ed* in the Lord greatly
Col. 1.24. Who now r. in my sufferings
[1]Th. 5.16. r. evermore
[1]Pet. 4.13. r., inasmuch as ye are part.
[2]John 4. I r-*ed* greatly that I found
[3]John 3. For I r-*ed* greatly, when the
Rev.11.10. dwell upon the earth *shall* r.
sungchairō.

Lu. 1.58. her ; and they r-*ed with* her
     15. 6, 9. r. *with* me ; for I have
[1]Co.12.26. all the members r. *with* it
     13. 6. iniquity, but r-*eth in* the
Phi. 2.17. I joy, and r. *with* you all
     18. also do ye joy, and r. *with*
agalliaō.

Lu. 1.47. my spirit *hath* r-*ed* in God

Lu. 10.21. In that hour Jesus r-*ed* in
Jo. 5.35. for a season *to* r. in his light
     8.56. Your father Abraham r-*ed*
Act.16.34. meat before them, and r-*ed*
[1]Pet. 1. 6. Wherein ye *greatly* r., thou.
     8. ye r. with joy unspeakable
Rev.19. 7. *Let* us be glad and r., and
euphrainō.

Act. 2.26. Therefore *did* my heart r.
     7.41. unto the idol, and r-*ed* in
Ro. 15.10. r., ye Gentiles, with his
Gal. 4.27. r., thou barren that bearest
Rev.12.12. Therefore r., ye heavens
     18.20. r. over her, thou heaven and
kauchaomai.

Ro. 5. 2. r. in hope of the glory of
Phi. 3. 3. and r. in Christ Jesus, and
Jas. 1. 9. *Let* the bro. of low degree r.
     4.16. now ye r. in your boastings
katakauchaomai.

Jas. 2.13. mercy r-*eth against* judgmen.
eis kauchēma.

Phi. 2.16. *that* I *may* r. in the day of

REJOICING.
kauchēma.

[2]Co. 1.14. that we are your r., even as
Gal. 6. 4. shall he have r. in himself
Phi. 1.26. That your r. may be more
Heb. 3. 6. the r. of the hope firm unto
kauchēsis.

[1]Co.15.31. I protest by your r. which I
[2]Co. 1.12. For our r. is this, the testi.
[1]Th. 2.19. or crown of r.? Are not even
Jas. 4.16. boastings : all such r. is evil

RELEASE,   -*ed.*
apoluō.

Mat.27.15. was wont *to* r. unto the
     17, 21. will ye *that* I r.unto you ;
     Mar.15.9 ; Jo.18.39
     26. Then r-*ed* he Barabbas unto;
     Mar.15. 15
Mar.15. 6. he r-*ed* unto them one priso.
     11. he *should* rather r. Barabbas
Lu. 23.16. there. chastise him, and r.
     17. he must r. one unto them
     18. and r. unto us Barabbas
     20. therefore, willing *to* r. Jesus
     25. he r-*ed* unto them him
Jo. 18.39. *that* I r. unto you the King
     19.10. and have power *to* r. thee
     12. Pilate sought *to* r. him

RELIEF.
diakonia.

Act.11.29. determined to send r. unto

RELIEVE,   -*ed.*
eparkeō.

[1]Ti. 5.10. she *have* r-*ed* the afflicted
     16. *let* them r. them, and let
     that it *may* r. them that are

RELIGION. (See *Jews.*)
thrēskeia.

Act.26. 5. most straitest sect of our r.
Jas. 1.26. heart, this man's r. is vain
     27. Pure r. and undefiled before

RELIGIOUS.
sebomai.

Act.13.43. of the Jews and r. proselytes
thrēskos.

Jas. 1.26. man among you seem to be r.

REMAIN, -*ed, -est, -eth, -ing.*
menō.

Mat.11.23. it would *have* r-*ed* until
Lu. 10. 7. And in the same house r.
Jo. 1.33. and r-*ing* on him, the same
     9.41. therefore your sin r-*eth*
     15.11. that my joy *might* r. in you
     16. that your fruit *should* r.
     19.31. that the bodies *should* not r

Act. 5. 4. *Whiles* it **r-***ed*, was it not
  27.41. stuck fast, and **r-***ed* unmove.
1Co. 7.11. *let* her **r.** unmarried, or be
  15. 6. the greater part **r.** unto this
2Co. 3.11. much more that *which* **r-***eth*
  14. **r-***eth* the same vail untaken
  9. 9. his righteousness **r-***eth* for
Heb.12.27.wh. cannot be shaken *may* **r.**
1Jo. 2.24. **r.** in you, ye also shall con.
  3. 9. his seed **r-***eth* in him : and
    diameno.
Lu. 1.22. them, and **r-***ed* speechless
Heb. 1.11. shall perish ; but thou **r-***est*
    apoleipo.
Heb. 4. 6. Seeing therefore it **r-***eth* that
  9. There **r-***eth* therefore a rest
  10.26. there **r-***eth* no more sacrifice
    perileipomai.
1Th. 4.15. and **r.** unto the coming of
  17. which are alive and **r.** shall
    loipos.
Rev. 3. 2. strengthen the thin. *which* **r.**
    ho loipos eimi.
1Co. 7.29. it **r-***eth* that both they that
    (*as for the rest it is.*)
    perisseuo.   [Lu.9.17
Mat.14.20.of the fragments *that* **r-***ed* ;
Jo. 6.12. Gather up the frag. *that* **r.**
  13. which **r-***ed* over and above

REMEMBER,   -*ed*, -*est*, -*eth*,
             -*ing*.
    mnemoneuo.
Mat.16. 9. neither **r.** the five loaves of
Mar. 8.18. ye not ? and *do* ye not **r.**
Lu. 17.32. **r.** Lot's wife
Jo. 15.20. **r.** the word that I said unto
  16. 4. ye *may* **r.** that I told you
  21. she **r-***eth* no more the angui.
Act.20.31. *and* **r.**, that by the space of
  35. and *to* **r.** the words of the
Gal. 2.10. that we *should* **r.** the poor
Eph. 2.11. Wherefore **r.**, that ye being
Col. 4.18. **r.** my bonds. Grace be with
1Th. 1. 3. **r-***ing* without ceasing your
  2. 9. For ye **r.**, brethren, our
2Th. 2. 5. **r.** ye not, that, when I
2Ti. 2. 8. **r.** that Jesus Christ of the
Heb.13. 7. **r.** them which have the rule
Rev. 2. 5. **r.** therefore from whence
  3. 3. **r.** therefore how thou hast
  18. 5. God *hath* **r-***ed* her iniquities
    mnaomai.
Mat. 5.23. and there **r-***est* that thy bro.
  26.75. And Peter **r-***ed* the word
  27.63. Sir, we **r.** that that deceiver
Lu. 1.72. and *to* **r.** his holy covenant
  16.25. **r.** that thou in thy lifetime
  23.42. Lord, **r.** me when thou
  24. 6. **r.** how he spake unto you
  8. And they **r-***ed* his words
Jo. 2.17. And his disciples **r-***ed* that it
  22. his disciples **r-***ed* that he
  12.16. then **r-***ed* they that these
Act.11.16. Then **r-***ed* I the word of
1Co.11. 2. that ye **r.** me in all things
Heb. 8.12. iniquities *will* I **r.** ; 10.17
Jude 17. **r.** ye the words which were
    anamimnesko.
2Co. 7.15. he **r-***eth* the obedience of
    mimneskomai.
Heb.13. 3. **r.** them that are in bonds
    hupomimnesko.
Lu. 22.61. Peter **r-***ed* the word of the
3John 10. I *will* **r.** his deed which he

REMEMBRANCE.
    anamnesis.
Lu. 22.19. in **r.** of me ; 1Co.11.24,25
Heb.10. 3. there is a **r.** *again* made
    anamimnesko.
Mar.11.21. Peter *calling to* **r.** saith

4Co. 4.17. bring you *into* **r.** of my
2Ti. 1. 6. I *put* thee *in* **r.** that thou
Heb.10.32. call to **r.** the former days
    hupomnesis.
2Ti. 1. 5. When I call to **r.** the unfeign.
2Pet. 1.13. you up *by putting* you *in* **r.**
  3. 1. your pure minds by way of **r.**
    hupomimnesko.
Jo. 14.26. and *bring* all things *to* your **r.**
2Ti. 2.14. these things *put* them *in* **r.**
2Pet. 1.12. *to put* you always *in* **r.**
Jude 5. I will therefore *put* you *in* **r.**
    mnaomai.
Lu. 1.54. Israel, *in* **r.** *of* his mercy
Act.10.31. thine alms *are had in* **r.**
Rev.16.19. Babylon *came in* **r.** before
    mneia.
Phi. 1. 3. God upon every **r.** of you
1Th. 3. 6. that ye have good **r.** of us
2Ti. 1. 3. **r.** of thee in my prayers
    mneme.
2Pet. 1.15. these things always in **r.**
1Ti. 4. 6. *If* thou *put* the breth. *in* **r.**

REMISSION.
    aphesis.
Mat.26.28.for the **r.** of sins ; Mar.1.4 ;
              Lu.3.3 ; Act.3.38
Lu. 1.77. people by the **r.** of their sins
  24.47. repentance and **r.** of sins
Act.10.43. shall receive **r.** of sins
Heb. 9.22. shedding of blood is no **r.**
  10.18. Now where **r.** of these is
    paresis.
Ro. 3.25. for the **r.** of sins that are

REMIT,   -*ed*.
    aphiemi.
Jo. 20.23. sins ye **r.** they are **r-***ed*

REMNANT.
    loipos.
Mat.22. 6. And the **r.** took his servants
Rev.11.13. and the **r.** were affrighted
  12.17. to make war with the **r.** of
  19.21. And the **r.** were slain with
    kataleimma.
Ro. 9.27. of the sea, a **r.** shall be saved
    leimma.
Ro. 11. 5. there is a **r.** according to the

REMOVE,   -*ed*.
    metabaino.
Mat.17.20.**r.** hence to yonder place ; and
  it *shall* **r.** ; and nothing
    airo.   [Mar.11.23
Mat.21.21.*Be* thou **r-***ed*, and be thou ;
    paraphero.
Lu. 22.42. willing, **r.** this cup from me
    metoikizo.
Act. 7. 4. he **r-***ed* him into this land
    methistemi.
Act.13.22. And *when* he *had* **r-***ed* him
    methistano.
1Co.13. 2. so that I could **r.** mountains
    metatithemi.
Gal. 1. 6. that ye *are* so soon **r-***ed* from
    kineo.
Rev. 2. 5. and *will* **r.** thy candlestick

REMOVING, [*noun*.]
    metathesis.
Heb.12.27.the **r.** of those things that

REND,   *Rent*.
    schizo.   [Mar.15.38 ; Lu.23.45
Mat.27.51.veil of the temple *was* **r-***t* ;
  did quake, and the rocks **r-***t*
Jo. 19.24. *Let* us not **r.** it, but cast lots
    regnumi.
Mat. 7. 6. and turn again and **r.** you
    perirregnumi.
Act.16.22. mag. **r-***t off* their clothes, *and*

    diaresso.   [Mar.14.63
Mat.26.65. high priest **r-***t* his clothes ;
Act.14.14. they **r-***t* their clothes, *and*
    sparasso.
Mar. 9.26. cried, and **r-***t* him sore, *and*

RENDER,   -*ing*.
    apodidomi.
Mat.21.41.which *shall* **r.** him the fruits
  22.21. **r.** therefore unto Cesar the ;
        Mar.12.17 ; Lu.20.25
Ro. 2. 6. Who *will* **r.** to every man
  13. 7. **r.** therefore to all their dues
1Co. 7. 3. *Let* the husband **r.** unto the
1Th. 5.15. See that none **r.** evil for evil
1Pet. 3. 9. Not **r-***ing* evil for evil, or
    antapodidomi.
1Th. 3. 9. tha. can we **r.** to God *again*

RENEW,   -*ed*.
    anakainoo.
2Co. 4.16. inward man *is* **r-***ed* day by
Col. 3.10. *which is* **r-***ed* in knowledge
    ananeoo.
Eph. 4.23. *be* **r-***ed* in the spirit of your
    anakainizo.
Heb. 6. 6. *to* **r.** them again unto repent.

RENEWING.
    anakainosis.
Ro. 12. 2. transformed by the **r.** of your
Tit. 3. 5. and **r.** of the Holy Ghost

RENOUNCED.
    apeipon.
2Co. 4. 2. *have* **r.** the hidden things of

RENT.
    schisma.   [Mar.2.21
Mat. 9.16. and the **r.** is made worse ;
    schizo.
Lu. 5.36. both the new *maketh* a **r.**

REPAY.
    apodidomi.
Lu. 10.35. I come again, I *will* **r.** thee
    antapodidomi.
Ro. 12.19. I *will* **r.** saith the Lord
    apotio.
Phile. 19. mine own hand I *will* **r.** it

REPENT,   -*ed*.
    metanoeo.
Mat. 3. 2. **r.** ye: for the kingdom ; 4.17
  11.20. done, because they **r-***ed* not
  21. they would *have* **r-***ed* long
  12.41. because they **r-***ed* ; Lu.11.32
Mar. 1.15. **r.** ye, and believe the gospel
  6.12. preached that men *should* **r.**
Lu. 10.13. *had* a great while ago **r-***ed*
  13. 3, 5. but, except *ye* **r.**, ye shall
  15. 7, 10. over one sinner *that* **r-***eth*
  16.30. from the dead, they *will* **r.**
  17. 3. and if he **r.**, forgive him
  4. saying, I **r.** ; thou shalt forg.
Act. 2.38. **r.**, and be baptized every one
  3.19. **r.** ye therefore, and be conv.
  8.22. **r.** therefore of this thy wick.
  17.30. all men every where *to* **r.**
  26.20. *that they should* **r.** and turn
2Co.12.21. and *have* not **r-***ed* of the
Rev. 2. 5. **r.**, and do the first works
  of his place, except thou **r.**
  16. **r.** ; or else I will come unto
  21. I gave her space to **r.** of her
  fornication ; and she **r-***ed* not
  22. except they **r.** of their deeds
  3. 3. heard, and hold fast, and **r.**
  19. be zealous therefore, and **r.**
  9.20. **r-***ed* not of the works of their
  21. Neither **r-***ed* they of their
  16. 9. they **r-***ed* not to give him gl.
  11. and **r-***ed* not of their deeds
                      225

metamelomai.

Mat. 21.29. afterward he **r**-*ed*, *and* went
    32. **r**-*ed* not afterward, that ye
    27. 3. **r**-*ed himself*, and brought
²Co. 7. 8. I *do* not **r**., though I *did* **r**.
Heb. 7.21. Lord sware and *will* not **r**.

²Co. 7.10. to salvation *not to be* **r**-*ed of*

REPENTANCE.
metanoia.

Mat. 3. 8. fruits meet for **r**.; Lu. 3.8
    11. bapt. you with water unto **r**.
    9.13. but sinners to **r**.; Mar. 2.17 ;
        Lu. 5.32
Mar. 1. 4. pr. the baptism of **r**.; Lu.3.3
Lu. 15. 7. persons which need no **r**.
    24.47. And that **r**. and remission
Act. 5.31. for to give **r**. to Israel, and
    11.18. Gentiles granted **r**. unto life
    13.24. the baptism of **r**. to all the
    19. 4. bapti. with the baptism of **r**.
    20.21. **r**. toward God, and faith
    26.20. and do works meet for **r**.
Ro. 2. 4. of God leadeth thee to **r**.
²Co. 7. 9. but that ye sorrowed to **r**.
    10. worketh **r**. to salvation not
²Ti. 2.25. will give them **r**. to the
Heb. 6. 1. of **r**. from dead works, and
    6. to renew them again unto **r**.
    12.17. for he found no place of **r**.
²Pet. 3. 9. but that all should come to **r**.
ametamelētos.
Ro. 11.29. calling of.God are *without* **r**.

REPETITIONS.
battologeō.

Mat. 6. 7. when ye pray, *use* not *vain* **r**.

REPLIEST.
antapokrinomai.

Ro. 9.20. thou *that* **r**. *against* God

REPORT, [*noun*.]
martureō.

Act. 6. 3. seven men *of honest* **r**., full
    10.22. and *of good* **r**. mong all the
    22.12. *having a* good **r**. of all the J.
Heb.11. 2. by it elders *obtained a good* **r**.
    39. *having obtained a good* **r**. th.
³John 12. hath good **r**. of all men, and
marturia.
¹Ti. 3. 7. have a good **r**. of them which
    akoē.   [Ro. 10.16
Jo. 12.38. who hath believed our **r**.
euphēmia.
²Co. 6. 8. by evil report and *good* **r**.
euphēmos.
Phi. 4. 8. whatso. things are *of good* **r**.
dusphēmia.
²Co. 6. 8. by *evil* **r**. and good report

REPORT, [*verb*,]   -*ed*.
apanggellō.

Act. 4.23. **r**-*ed* all that the chief priests
¹Co.14.25. *and* **r**. that God is in you of
ananggellō.
¹Pet. 1.12. which *are* now **r**-*ed* unto you
martureō.
Act.16. 2. which *vas well* **r**-*ed of* by the
¹Ti. 5.10. *Well* **r**-*ed of* for good works
akouō.
¹Co. 5. 1. It *is* **r**-*ed* commonly that th.
blasphēmeō.
Ro. 3. 8. as we *be slanderously* **r**-*ed*
    (See *Commonly*.)

REPROACH, [*noun*,]   -*es*.
oneidismos.

Ro. 15. 3. The **r**-*es* of them that reproa.
¹Ti. 3. 7. lest he fall into **r**., and the
Heb.10.33.both by **r**-*es* and afflictions
    11.26. Esteeming the **r**. of Christ
    13.13. the camp, bearing his **r**.
226

oneidos.

Lu. 1.25. to take away my **r**. among
oneidizō.
¹Ti. 4.10. we both labour and *suffer* **r**.
hubris.
²Co. 12.10. pleas. in infirmities, in **r**-*es*
atimia.
²Co. 11.21. I speak as concerning **r**.

REPROACH, [*verb*,] -*ed*, -*est*.
oneidizō.

Lu. 6.22. and *shall* **r**. you, and cast
Ro. 15. 3. of them *that* **r**-*ed* thee fell
¹Pet. 4.14. If ye *be* **r**-*ed* for the name of
hubrizō.
Lu. 11.45. thus saying thou **r**-*est* us also

REPROACHFULLY.
charin loidoria.

¹Ti. 5.14. to the adversary to speak **r**.

REPROBATE,   -*s*.
adokimos.

Ro. 1.28. gave them over to a **r**. mind
²Co. 13. 5. is in you, except ye be **r**-*s*
    6. know that we are not **r**-*s*
    7. honest, though we be as **r**-*s*
²Ti. 3. 8. **r**. concerning the faith
Tit. 1.16. unto every good work **r**.

REPROOF.
elengchos.

²Ti. 3.16. for doctrine, for **r**., for corr.

REPROVE,   -*ed*.
elengchō.

Lu. 3.19. *being* **r**-*ed* by him for Herod.
Jo. 3.20. lest his deeds *should be* **r**-*ed*
    16. 8. he *will* **r**. the world of sin
Eph. 5.11. of darkness, but rather **r**. th.
    13. all things *that are* **r**-*ed* are
²Ti. 4. 2. **r**., rebuke, exhort with all

REPUTATION.
timios.

Act. 5.34. *had in* **r**. among all the peo.
dokeō.
Gal. 2. 2. pri. to them *which were of* **r**.
kenoō.
Phi. 2. 7. But *made* himself *of no* **r**.
entimos.
Phi. 2.29. gladness; and hold such *in* **r**.

REQUEST,   -*s*.
deomai.

Ro. 1.10. *Making* **r**. if by any means
deēsis.
Phi. 1. 4. you all making **r**. with joy
aitēma.
Phi. 4. 6. let your **r**-*s* be made known

REQUIRE,   -*ed*, -*ing*.
aiteō.

Lu. 23.23. **r**-*ing* that he might be cruci.
¹Co. 1.22. For the Jews **r**. a sign, and
apaiteō.
Lu. 12.20. soul *shall be* **r**-*ed* of thee
aitēma.
Lu. 23.24. it should be *as they* **r**-*ed*
    ekzēteō.   (their *request*.)
Lu. 11.50. *may be* **r**-*ed* of this generation
    51. It *shall be* **r**-*ed* of this gener.
zēteō.
Lu. 12.48. of him *shall be* much **r**-*ed*
¹Co. 4. 2. it *is* **r**-*ed* in stewards that
prassō.
Lu. 19.23. I might *have* **r**-*ed* mine own
ginomai.
¹Co. 7.36. need so **r**., let him do what
            (it ought so *to be*)

REQUITE.
apodidōmi amoibē.

¹Ti. 5. 4. home, and *to* **r**. their parents
    (return *recompences* to)

RESCUED.
exaireō.

Act.23.27. with an army, and **r**. him

RESEMBLE.
homoioō.

Lu. 13.18. and whereunto *shall* I **r**. it

RESERVE,   -*ed*.
tēreō.

Act.25.21. Paul had appealed *to be* **r**-*ed*
¹Pet. 1. 4. away, **r**-*ed* in heaven for you
²Pet. 2. 4. *to be* **r**-*ed* unto judgment
    9. and *to* **r**. the unjust unto the
    17. the mist of darkness *is* **r**-*ed*
    3. 7. **r**-*ed* unto fire against the day
Jude 6. he *hath* **r**-*ed* in everlasting
    13. to whom *is* **r**-*ed* the blackne.
kataleipō.
Ro. 11. 4. I *have* **r**-*ed* to myself seven

RESIDUE.
loipos.

Mar. 16.13. went and told it unto the **r**.
kataloipos.
Act.15.17. That the **r**. of men might se.

RESIST,   -*ed*, -*eth*.
anthistēmi.

Mat. 5.39. unto you, That ye **r**. not ev.
Lu. 21.15. not be able to gainsay nor **r**.
Act. 6.10. were not able to **r**. the wisd.
Ro. 9.19. For who *hath* **r**-*ed* his will
    13. 2. **r**-*eth* the ordinance of God
    and they *that* **r**. shall receive
²Ti. 3. 8. *do* these also **r**. the truth
Jas. 4. 7. **r**. the devil, and he will flee
¹Pet. 5. 9. Whom **r**. stedfast in the fai.
antikathistēmi.
Heb.12. 4. *have* not yet **r**-*ed* unto blood
antipiptō.
Act. 7.51. ye do always **r**. the Ho. Gh.
antitassō.
Ro. 13. 2. Whoso. therefore **r**-*eth* the
Jas. 4. 6. God **r**-*eth* the proud; ¹Pet.5.5
    5. 6. and he *doth* not **r**. you

RESOLVED.
ginōskō.

Lu. 16. 4. I *am* **r**. what to do, that wh.

RESORT,   -*ed*.
erchomai.

Mar. 2.13. the multitude **r**-*ed* unto him
Jo. 10.41. many **r**-*ed* unto him, and sa.
sunerchomai.
Jo. 18.20. whither the Jews always **r**.
Act.16.13. the women *which* **r**-*ed* thith.
sumporeuomai.
Mar.10. 1. the people **r**. unto him again
sunagō.
Jo. 18. 2. for Jesus ofttimes **r**-*ed* thith.

RESPECT. (See *Persons*.)
meros.

²Co. 3.10. had no glory in this **r**., by
Col. 2.16. or in **r**. of an holyday, or of
apoblepō.
Heb.11.26.he *had* **r**. unto the recompe.
epiblepō.
Jas. 2. 3. And ye *have* **r**. *to* him that
    kata, [*accu*.]
Phi. 4.11. Not that I speak *in* **r**. *of* wa.

REST. (*Remainder*.)
loipos.

Mat.27.49.The **r**. said, Let be, let us see
Lu. 12.26. why take ye thou. for the **r**.
    24. 9. the eleven, and to all the **r**.
Act. 2.37. unto Peter and to the **r**. of
    5.13. And of the **r**. durst no man
    27.44. And the **r**., some on boards
Ro. 11. 7. it, and the **r**. were blinded
¹Co. 7.12. But to the **r**. speak I, not the

¹Co.11.34. And the **r.** will I set in order
Rev. 2.24. and unto the **r.** in Thyatira
9.20. the **r.** of the men which were
20. 5. But the **r.** of the dead lived
epiloipos.
¹Pet. 4. 2. should live the **r.** *of his* time
(the *remaining* time.)

REST, [*noun.*]
katapausis.
Act. 7.49. what is the place of my **r.**
Heb. 3.11. shall not enter into my **r.**
18. should not enter into his **r.**
4. 1. of entering into his **r.**, any
3. have believed do enter into **r.**
5. if they shall enter into my **r.**
10. he that is entered into his **r.**
11. to enter into that **r.**, lest any
anapausis.
Mat.11.29.ye shall find **r.** unto your
12.43. dry places seek. **r.**; Lu.11.24
Rev.14.11.they have no **r.** day nor
anapauō.
Mat.11.28.laden, and I *will give* you **r.**
26.45. and *take* your **r.**; Mar.14.41
katapauō.
Heb. 4. 8. if Jesus *had given* them **r.**
anesis.
²Co. 2.13. I had no **r.** in my spirit
7. 5. our flesh had no **r.**, but we
²Th. 1. 7. you who are troubled **r.** with
eirēnē.
Act. 9.31. Then had the churches **r.**
sabbatismos.
Heb. 4. 9. There remaineth theref. a **r.**
koimēsis.
Jo. 11.13. had spoken of *taking of* **r.** in

REST, [*verb,*]   *-ed, -est, -eth.*
anapauō.
Mar. 6.31. into a desert place, and **r.** a
¹Pet. 4.14. of glory and of God **r**-*eth* up.
Rev. 6.11. they *should* **r.** yet for a little
14.13. that they may **r.** from their
epanapauomai.
Lu. 10. 6. your peace *shall* **r.** *upon* it
Ro. 2.17. a Jew, and **r**-*est* in the law
katapauō.
Heb. 4. 4. God *did* **r.** the seventh day
echō anapausis.
Rev. 4. 8. they **r.** not day and night
hezuchazō.
Lu. 23.56. and **r**-*ed* the sabbath day
kataskēnoō.
Act. 2.26. my flesh *shall* **r.** in hope
episkēnoō.
²Co. 12. 9. power of Christ *may* **r.** *upon*

RESTITUTION.
apokatastasis.
Act. 3.21. the times of **r.** of all things

RESTORE,   *-ed, -eth.*
apokathistēmi.   [Mar.3.5
Mat.12.13.it *was* **r**-*ed* whole, like as;
17.11. first come, and **r.** all things
Mar. 8.25. he *was* **r**-*ed*, and saw every
9.12. cometh first, and **r**-*eth* all th.
Lu. 6.10. his hand *was* **r**-*ed* whole as
Act. 1. 6. at this time **r.** *again* the ki.
Heb.13.19. that I *may be* **r**-*ed* to you the
apodidōmi.
Lu. 19. 8. accusation, I **r.** him fourfold
katartizō.
Gal. 6. 1. **r.** such an one in the spirit

RESTRAINED.
katapauō.
Act.14.18. scarce **r.** they the people

RESURRECTION.
anastasis.
Mat.22.23. say that there is no **r.**; Mar.
12.18; Lu.20.27; Act.23.8;
¹Co.15.12
28. in the **r.** whose wife; Mar.
12.23; Lu. 20.33
30. For in the **r.** they neither
31. touching the **r.** of; Act.24.21
Lu. 14.14. recompensed at the **r.** of the
20.35. that world, and the **r.** from
36. being the children of the **r.**
Jo. 5. 29. the **r.** of life; and they that
have done evil, unto the **r.**
11.24. rise again in the **r.** at the last
25. I am the **r.**, and the life
Act. 1.22. a witness with us of his **r.**
2.31. spake of the **r.** of Christ, that
4. 2. through Jesus the **r.** from
33. the **r.** of the Lord Jesus
17.18. unto them Jesus, and the **r.**
32. heard of the **r.** of the dead
23. 6. of the hope and **r.** of the de.
24.15. there shall be a **r.** of the de.
Ro. 1. 4. holiness, by the **r.** from the
6. 5. in the likeness of his **r.**
¹Co.15.13. if there be no **r.** of the dead
21. man came also the **r.** of the
42. So also is the **r.** of the dead
Phi. 3.10. the power of his **r.**, and the
²Ti. 2.18. that the **r.** is past already
Heb. 6. 2. and of **r.** of the dead, and of
11.35. might obtain a better **r.**
¹Pet. 1. 3. by the **r.** of Jesus Chr.; 3.21
Rev.20. 5. This is the first **r.**
6. that hath part in the first **r.**
exanastasis.
Phi. 3.11. unto the **r.** of the dead
egersis.
Mat.27.53.out of the graves after his **r.**

RETAIN,   *-ed.*
echō.
Ro. 1.28. *to* **r.** God in their knowledge
katechō.
Phile. 13. 1 would have **r**-*ed* with me
krateō.
Jo. 20.23. soev. sins ye **r.** they *are* **r**-*ed*

RETURN,   *-ed, -ing.*
hupostrephō.
Mar.14.40.And *when* he **r**-*ed*, he found
Lu. 1.56. and **r**-*ed* to her own house
2.39. they **r**-*ed* into Galilee, to the
43. as they **r**-*ed*, the child Jesus
4. 1. **r**-*ed* from Jordan, and was
14. And Jesus **r**-*ed* in the power
7.10. **r**-*ing* to the house, found
8.37. the ship, and **r**-*ed back aga.*
39. **r.** to thine own house, and
40. that, when Jesus *was* **r**-*ed*
9.10. apostles, *when* they *were* **r**-*ed*
10.17. the seventy **r**-*ed again* with
11.24. I *will* **r.** unto my house wh.
17.18. *that* **r**-*ed* to give glory to G.
19.12. himself a kingdom, and *to* **r.**
23.48. smote their breasts, and **r**-*ed*
56. they **r**-*ed*, and prepared spi.
24. 9. **r**-*ed* from the sepulchre, and
33. and **r**-*ed* to Jerusalem, and
52. **r**-*ed* to Jerusalem with great
Act. 1.12. Then **r**-*ed* they unto Jerus.
8.25. **r**-*ed* to Jerusalem, and prea.
28. Was **r**-*ing*, and sitting in his
12.25. Barnabas and Saul **r**-*ed* from
13.13. John depart. from them **r**-*ed*
14.21. they **r**-*ed again* to Lystra
20. 3. pur. *to* **r.** through Macedonia
21. 6. and they **r**-*ed* home *again*
23.32. with him, and **r**-*ed* to the
Gal. 1.17. and **r**-*ed again* unto Damas.
Heb. 7. 1. met Abraham **r**-*ing* from

mellō hupostrephō.
Act.13.34. no more *to* **r.** to corruption
epistrephō.
Mat.10.13.*let* your peace **r.** to you
12.44. I *will* **r.** into my house
24.18. Neither *let* him..**r.** back
Lu. 2.20. the shepherds **r**-*ed*, glorifying
17.31. *let* him likewise not **r.** back
¹Pet. 2.25. *are* now **r**-*ed* unto the shep.
anastrephō.
Act. 5.22. the prison, they **r**-*ed and*
15.16. After this I *will* **r.**, and will
anakamptō.
Mat. 2.12. that they should not **r.** to
Act.18.21. I *will* **r.** again unto you
Heb.11.15.had opportunity *to have* **r**-*ed*
epanagō.
Mat.21.18.*as* he **r**-*ed* into the city, he
analuō.
Lu. 12.36. when he *will* **r.** from the
epanerchomai.
Lu. 19.15. that when he *was* **r**-*ed*, havi.

REVEAL,   *-ed.*
apokaluptō.
Mat.10.26.that *shall* not *be* **r**-*ed*; and
11.25. *hast* **r**-*ed* them unto babes;
Lu.10.21   [Lu.10.22
27. whomsoever the Son will **r.**;
16.17. flesh and blood *hath* not **r**-*ed*
Lu. 2.35. of many hearts *may be* **r**-*ed*
12. 2. cover., that *shall* not *be* **r**-*ed*
17.30. when the Son of man *is* **r**-*ed*
Jo. 12.38. arm of the Lord *been* **r**-*ed*
Ro. 1.17. *is* the righteous. of God **r**-*ed*
18. the wrath of God *is* **r**-*ed*
8.18. glory which shall *be* **r**-*ed*;
¹Pet.5.1
¹Co. 2.10. God *hath* **r**-*ed* them unto us
3.13. because it *shall be* **r**-*ed* by
14.30. If any thing *be* **r**-*ed* to ano.
Gal. 1.16. *To* **r.** his son in me, that
3.23. which sh. afterwards *be* **r**-*ed*
Eph. 3. 5. as it *is* now **r**-*ed* unto his
Phi. 3.15. God *shall* **r.** even this unto
²Th. 2. 3. that man of sin *be* **r**-*ed*, the
6. that he *might be* **r**-*ed* in his
8. then *shall* that Wick. *be* **r**-*ed*
¹Pet. 1. 5. ready *to be* **r**-*ed* in the last
12. Unto whom it *was* **r**-*ed*, that
en apokalupsis.
²Th. 1. 7. *when* the Lord Jes *sh. be* **r**-*ed*
(*in the revelation of.*)
¹Pet. 4.13. *when* his glory shall *be* **r**-*ed*
chrēmatizō.
Lu. 2.26. it was **r**-*ed* unto him by the

REVELATION,   *-s.*
apokalupsis.
Ro. 2. 5. **r.** of the righteous judgment
16.25. according to the **r.** of the mys
¹Co.14. 6. speak to you either by **r.**
26. hath a tongue, hath a **r.**
²Co. 12. 1. to visions and **r**-*s* of the
7. the abundance of the **r**-*s*
Gal. 1.12. but by the **r.** of Jesus Christ
2. 2. And I went up by **r.**, and
Eph. 1.17. the spirit of wisdom and **r.**
3. 3. How that by **r.** he made kn.
¹Pet. 1.13. you at the **r.** of Jesus Christ
Rev. 1. 1. The **r.** of Jesus Christ, which

REVELLINGS.
kōmos.
Gal. 5.21. drunkenness, **r.**, and such
¹Pet. 4. 3. **r.**, banquetings, and abom.

REVENGE, [*noun.*]
ekdikēsis.
¹Co. 7.11. yea, what zeal, yea, what **r.**

REVENGE, [*verb.*]
ekdikeō.
²Co.10. 6. *to* **r.** all disobedience, when

227

REVENGER.
   ekdikos.
Ro. 13. 4. a **r.** to execute wrath upon

REVERENCE, [*noun.*]
   entrepō.
Heb.12. 9. and we *gave* them **r.**: shall
   aidōs.
Heb.12.28.acceptably with **r.** and

REVERENCE, [*verb.*]
   entrepō.   [12.6.
Mat.21.37. They *will* **r.** my son; Mar.
Lu. 20.13. may be they *will* **r.** him
   phobeomai.
Eph. 5.33. the wife see that she **r.** her

REVILE,   *-ed, -est.*
   loidoreō.
Jo. 9.28. Then they **r**-*ed* him, and said
Act.23. 4. **r**-*est* thou God's high priest
1Co. 4.12. *being* **r**-*ed*, we bless; being
1Pet. 2.23. Who, *when* he *was* **r**-*ed*, rev.
   antiloidoreō.
1Pet. 2.23. was reviled, **r**-*ed* not *again*
   oneidizō.
Mat. 5.11. are ye when men *shall* **r.** you
Mar.15.32.crucified with him **r**-*ed* him
   blasphēmeō.
Mat.27.39.that passed by **r**-*ed* him

REVILERS.
   loidoros.
1Co. 6.10. nor **r.**, nor extortioners, sh.

REVIVED.
   anazaō.
Ro. 7. 9. the command came, sin **r.**
   14. 9. both died, and rose, and **r.**

REWARD, [*noun.*]
   misthos.   [Lu.6.23
Mat. 5.12. for great is your **r.** in heaven;
   46. what **r.** have ye? do not even
   6. 1. ye have no **r.** of your Father
   2, 5,16. They have their **r.**
   10.41. shall receive a prophet's **r.**
      receive a righteous man's **r.**
   42. no wise lose his **r.**; Mar.9.41
Lu. 6.35. your **r.** shall be great
Act. 1.18. a field with the **r.** of iniquity
Ro. 4. 4. that worketh is the **r.** not
1Co. 3. 8. shall receive his own **r.**
   14. thereu., he shall receive a **r.**
   9.17. thing willingly, I have a **r.**
   18. What is my **r.** then? Verily
1Ti. 5.18. labourer is worthy of his **r.**
2Pet. 2.13. receive the **r.** of unrighteou.
2John 8. but that we receive a full **r.**
Jude 11. the error of Balaam for **r.**
Rev.11.18.that thou shouldest give **r.**
   22.12. and my **r.** is with me, to give
   axios, [*plur.*]
Lu. 23.41. we receive the *due* **r.** of
   antapodosis.
Col. 3.24. ye shall receive the **r.** of the
      (See *Beguile.*)

REWARD, [*verb,*]   *-ed.*
   apodidōmi.
Mat. 6. 4, 6, 18. *shall* **r.** thee openly
   16.27. then he *shall* **r.** every man
2Ti. 4.14. the Lord **r.** him according
Rev.18. 6. **r.** her even as she **r**-*ed*

REWARDER.
   misthapodotēs.
Heb.11. 6. that he is a **r.** of them that

RICH.
   plousios.
Mat.19.23.That a **r.** man shall hardly
   24. than for a **r.** man to enter;
      Mar.10.25; Lu.18.25
   27.75. there came a **r.** man of Arit.
228

Mat.12.41. and many that were **r.** cast
Lu. 6.24. woe unto you that are **r.**
   12.16. The ground of a certain **r.**
   14.12. nor thy **r.** neighbours; lest
   16. 1, 19. There was a certain **r.** m.
   21. which fell from the **r.** man's
   22. the **r.** man also died, and w.
   18.23. sorrowful: for he was very **r.**
   19. 2. the publicans, and he was **r.**
   21. 1. and saw the **r.** men casting
2Co. 8. 9. though he was **r.**, yet for yo.
Eph. 2. 4. God, who is **r.** in mercy
1Ti. 6.17. Charge them that are **r.** in
Jas. 1.10. But the **r.**, in that he is made
   11. so also shall the **r.** man fade
   2. 5. **r.** in faith, and heirs of
   6. Do not **r.** men oppress you
   5. 1. Go to now, ye **r.** men
Rev. 2. 9. but thou art **r.**, and I know
   3.17. Because thou sayest, I am **r.**
   6.15. and the **r.** men, and the ch.
   13.16. **r.** and poor, free and bond
   plouteō.
Lu. 1.53. the **r.** he hath sent empty
   12.21. and is not **r.** toward God
Ro. 10.12. is **r.** unto all that call upon
1Co. 4. 8. ye are full, now ye are **r.**
2Co. 8. 9. thro. his poverty *might* be **r.**
1Ti. 6. 9. they that will be **r.** fall into
   18. that they *be* **r.** in good works
Rev. 3.18. that thou *mayest* be **r.**; and
   18. 3. *are waxed* **r.** through the ab.
   15. *which were made* **r.** by her
   19. wherein *were made* **r.** all th.
   ploutizō.
2Co. 6.10. as poor, yet *making* many **r.**

RICHES.
   ploutos.
Mat.13.22.the deceitful. of **r.**; Mar.4.19
Lu. 8.14. choked with cares and **r.**
Ro. 2. 4. Or despisest thou the **r.** of
   9.23. make known the **r.** of his gl.
   11.12. fall of them be the **r.** of the
      of them the **r.** of the Gentiles
   33. O the depth of the **r.** both of
2Co. 8. 2. unto the **r.** of their liberality
Eph. 1. 7. according to the **r.** of his gr.
   18. what the **r.** of the glory of
   2. 7. the exceeding **r.** of his grace
   3. 8. the unsearchable **r.** of Christ
   16. according to the **r.** of his gl.
Phi. 4.19. according to his **r.** in glory
Col. 1.27. what is the **r.** of the glory
   2. unto all **r.** of the full assura.
1Ti. 6.17. nor trust in uncertain **r.**
Heb.11.26.greater **r.** than the treasures
Jas. 5. 2. Your **r.** are corrupted, and
Rev. 5.12. to receive power, and **r.**, and
   18.17. so great **r.** is come to nought
   chrēma.   [Lu.18.24
Mar.10.23.they that have **r.** enter;
   24. for them that trust in **r.**

RICHLY.
   plousiōs.
Col. 3.16. word of Ch. dwell in you **r.**
1Ti. 6.17. who giveth us **r.** all things

RIGHT (*Hand.*)   (See *Hand.*)
   dexios.
Mat. 5.29. if thy **r.** eye offend thee. plu.
   30. if thy **r.** hand offend thee
   39. shall smite thee on thy **r.**
Mar.16. 5. man sitting on the **r.** *side*
Lu. 1.11. standing on the **r.** *side* of the
   22.50. cut off his **r.** ear; Jo.18.10
Jo. 21. 6. Cast the net on the **r.** side
Act. 3. 7. he took him by the **r.** hand
Rev. 1.16. he had in his **r.** hand seven
   17. he laid his **r.** hand upon me
   10. 2. he set his **r.** foot upon the
   13.16. to receive a mark in their **r.**

RIGHT, (*Proper.*)
   dikaios.
Mat.20. 4, 7. whatsoever is **r.**
Lu. 12.57. judge ye not what is **r.**
Act. 4.19. Whether it be **r.** in the sight
Eph. 6. 1. in the Lord: for this is **r.**
   euthus.
Act. 8.21. thy heart is not **r.** in the
   13.10. cease to pervert the **r.** ways
2Pet. 2.15. have forsaken the **r.** way
   sophroneō.   [Lu.8.35
Mar. 5.15. clothed, and *in* his **r.** *mind*;
   orthōs.
Lu. 10.28. Thou hast answered **r.**

RIGHT, [*noun.*]
   exousia.
Heb.13.10 they have no **r.** to eat
Rev. 22.14.they may have **r.** to the

RIGHTEOUS.
   dikaios.
Mat. 9.13. not come to call the **r.**, but
   10.41. he that receiveth a **r.** man
      r. man shall receive a **r.** ma.
   13.17. many prophets and **r.** men
   43. Then shall the **r.** shine forth
   23.28. outwardly appear **r.** unto
   29. garnish the sepulch. of the **r.**
   35. the **r.** blood shed upon the
      from the blood of **r.** Abel
   25.37. Then shall the **r.** answer him
   25.46. the **r.** into life eternal
Mar. 2.17. not to call the **r.**; Lu.5.32
Lu. 1. 6. they were both **r.** before God
   18. 9. themselves that they were **r.**
   23.47. Certainly this was a **r.** man
Jo. 7.24. appearance, but judge **r.** jud.
   17.25. O **r.** Father, the world hath
Ro. 3.10. There is none **r.**, no, not one
   5. 7. scarcely for a **r.** man will one
   19. shall many be made **r.**
2Th. 1. 5. of the **r.** judgment of God
   6. Seeing it is a **r.** thing
1Ti. 1. 9. law is not made for a **r.** man
2Ti. 4. 8. which the Lord, the **r.** judge
Heb.11.4. obtained witn. that he was **r.**
Jas. 5.16. prayer of a **r.** man availeth
1Pet. 3.12. eyes of the L. are over the **r.**
   4.18. if the **r.** scarcely be saved
2Pet. 2. 8. For that **r.** man dwelling
      vexed his **r.** soul from day
1Jo. 2. 1. Father, Jesus Christ the **r.**
   29. If ye know that he is **r.**
   3. 7. is **r.**, even as he is **r.**
   12. were evil,and his brother's **r.**
Rev. 16.5. Thou art **r.**, O Lord, which
   7. true and **r.** are..judg.; 19.2
   22.11. he that is **r.**, let him be righ.
   dikaiokrisia.
Ro. 2. 5. revelation of the **r.** *judgment*
   dikaioō.
Rev.22.11.righteous, *let* him *be* **r.** still

RIGHTEOUSLY.
   dikaiōs.
Tit. 2.12. we should live soberly, **r.**
1Pet.2.23. to him that judgeth **r.**

RIGHTEOUSNESS.
   dikaiosunē.
Mat. 3.15. becometh us to fulfil all **r.**
   5. 6. do hunger and thirst after **r.**
   10. persecuted for **r.**' sake
   20. except your **r.** shall exceed
   6.33. kingdom of God, and his **r.**
   21.32. unto you in the way of **r.**
Lu. 1.75. In holiness and **r.** before him
Jo. 16. 8. and of **r.**, and of judgment
   10. Of **r.**, because I go to my
Act.10.35. feareth him, and worketh **r.**
   13.10. thou enemy of all **r.**, wilt
   17.31. will judge the world in **r** by

Act.24.25. as he reasoned of **r.**, tempe-
Ro. 1.17. therein is the **r.** of God reve-
  3. 5. commend the **r.** of God, wh.
    21. now the **r.** of God without
    22. Even the **r.** of God which
    25. to declare his **r.** for the
    26. at this time his **r.**: that he
  4. 3. cou. unto him for **r.**; Gal.3.6
    5. his faith is counted for **r.**
    6. God imputeth **r.** without
    9. reckoned to Abraham for **r.**
    11. a seal of the **r.** of the faith
      that **r.** might be imputed
    13. but through the **r.** of faith
    22. was inputed to him for **r.**
  5.17. of the gift of **r.** shall reign
    21. might grace reign through **r.**
  6.13. instruments of **r.** unto God
    16. death, or of obedien. unto **r.**
    18. became the servants of **r.**
    19. your members servants to **r.**
    20. of sin, ye were free from **r.**
  8.10. Spirit is life because of **r.**
  9.28. cut it short in **r.**: because
    30. which followed not after **r.**
      have attained to **r.**, even
      the **r.** which is of faith
    31. followed after the law of **r.**
      not attained to the law of **r.**
  10. 3. being ignorant of God's **r.**
      about to estab. their own **r.**
      submitted them. unto the **r.**
    4. of the law for **r.** to every
    5. Moses describeth the **r.** whi.
    6. the **r.** which is of faith spea.
    10. heart, man believeth unto **r.**
  14.17. but **r.**, and peace, and joy in
¹Co. 1.30. made unto us wisdom, and **r.**
²Co. 3. 9. the ministration of **r.** exceed.
  5.21. be made the **r.** of God in
  6. 7. by the armour of **r.** on the
    14. what fellowship hath **r.** with
  9. 9. his **r.** remaineth for ever
    10. increase the fruits of your **r.**
  11.15. as the ministers of **r.**; whose
Gal. 2.21. for if **r.** come by the law
  3.21. verily is. should have been
    5. the hope of **r.** by faith
Eph. 4.24. created in **r.** and true holine.
  5. 9. is in all goodness and **r.** and
  6.14. havi. on the breastplate of **r.**
Phi. 1.11. filled with the fruits of **r.**
  3. 6. touching the **r.** which is in
    9. not having mine own **r.**
      r. which is of God by faith
¹Ti. 6.11. follow after **r.**, godliness
²Ti. 2.22. follow **r.**, faith, charity
  3.16. correction, for instruct. in **r.**
  4. 8. laid up for me a crown of **r.**
Tit. 3. 5. Not by works of **r.** which
Heb. 1. 9. Thou hast loved **r.**, and hat.
  5.13. unskilful in the word of **r.**
  7. 2. King of **r.**, and after that
  11. 7. the **r.** which is by faith
    33. wrought by **r.**, obtained prom.
  12.11. the peaceable fruit of **r.**
Jas. 1.20. worketh not the **r.** of God
  2.23. imputed unto him for **r.**
  3.18. the fruit of **r.** is sown in
¹Pet. 2.24. should live unto **r.**: by
  3.14. if ye suffer for **r.**' sake
²Pet. 1. 1. through the **r.** of God and
  2. 5. a preacher of **r.**, bringing
    21. known the way of **r.** than
  3.13. new earth, wherein dwell. **r.**
¹Jo. 2.29. every one that doeth **r.**
  3. 7. he that doeth **r.** is born of
    10. whosoever doeth not **r.** is
Rev.19.11.in **r.** he doth judge and make
    dikaiōma.
Ro. 2.26. keep the **r.** of the law, shall
  5.18. by the **r.** of one, the free gift

Ro. 8. 4. That the **r.** of the law might
Rev.19.8. fine linen is the **r.** of saints
    dikaiōs.
¹Co.15.34. Awake to **r.**, and sin not; for
    euthutēs.
Heb. 1. 8. a sceptre of **r.** is the sceptre

RIGHTLY.   (See *Divide.*)
    orthōs.
Lu. 7.43. Thou hast **r.** judged
  20.21. thou sayest and teachest **r.**

RING.
    daktulios.
Lu. 15.22. put a **r.** on his hand, and
    chrusodaktulos.
Jas. 2. 2. a man *with a gold* **r.**, in

RINGLEADER.
    prōtostatēs.
Act.24. 5. and a **r.** of the sect of the

RIOT.
    asōtia.
Tit. 1. 6. not accused of **r.**, or unruly
¹Pet. 4. 4. to the same excess of **r.**
²Pet. 2.13. count it pleasure *to* **r.** in the

RIOTING.
    kōmos.
Ro. 13.13. not in **r.** and drunkenness

RIOTOUS.
    asōtōs.   [(living *riotously.*)
Lu. 15.13. his substance *with* **r.** living

RIPE.
    akmazō.
Rev.14.18.for her grapes *are fully* **r.**
    xērainō.
Rev.14.15.harvest of the earth is **r.**

RISE,   *-en, -eth, -ing, Rose.*
    anistēmi.
Mat.12.41.men of Nineveh shall **r.** in
    17. 9. the Son of man *be* **r**-en again
  20.19. third day he shall **r.** again;
       Mar.10.34; Lu.18.33,24.7
Mar. 1.35. **r**-ing *up* a great while before
    3.26. if Satan **r.** *up* against himse.
    8.31. and after three days **r.** again
    9. 9. the Son of man *were* **r**-en
    10. what the **r**-ing from the dead
    31. he shall **r.** the third day
  10.50. garment, **ro.**, and came to
  12.23. therefore, when they shall **r.**
    25. when they shall **r.** from the
  16. 9. *when* Jesus *was* **r**-en early
Lu. 4.29. **ro.** *up, and* thrust him out
    5.25. immediately he **ro.** *up* before
    28. he left all, **ro.** *up, and* follo.
  9. 8, 19.old proph. *was* **r**-en again
  11. 7. I cannot **r.** *and* give thee
    8. Though he will not **r.** *and*
    32. shall **r.** *up* in the judgment
  16.31. though one **ro.** from the dea.
  22.45. *when* he **ro.** *up* from prayer
    46. **r.** *and* pray, lest ye enter
  24.33. they **ro.** *up* the same hour
    46. *to* **r.** from the dead the third
Jo. 11.23. Thy brother *shall* **r.** again
    24. I know that he *shall* **r.** again
    31. that she **ro.** *up* hastily and
  20. 9. that he must **r.** *again* from
Act. 5.17. the high priest **ro.** *up, and*
    36. before these days **ro.** *up* Th.
    37. After this man **ro.** *up* Judas
  10.13. **r.**, Peter; kill, and eat
    41. after he **ro.** from the dead
  14.20. he **ro.** *up, and* came into the
  15. 7. Peter **ro.** *up, and* said unto
  17. 3. suffered, and **r**-en *again* from
  26.16. **r.**, and stand upon thy feet
    30. the king **ro.** *up,* and the gov.
Ro. 14. 9. Christ both died, and **ro.**

Ro. 15.12. he *that shall* **r.** to reign over
¹Co.10. 7. eat and drink, and **ro.** *up to*
¹Th. 4.14. Jesus died and **ro.** *again*
    16. the dead in Christ *shall* **r.**
Heb. 7.11. anoth. priest should **r.** after
    exanistēmi.
Act.15. 5. there **ro.** *up* certain of the
    sunephistēmi.
Act.16.22. the multitude **ro.** *up together*
    epanistamai.   [Mar.13.12
Mat.10.21.children *shall* **r.** *up against;*
    anastasis.
Lu. 2.34. the fall, and **r**-ing *again* of
Act.26.23. the first *that should* **r.** from
    egeirō.   (*of the resurrection.*)
Mat.11.11.there *hath* not **r**-en a greater
  12.42. queen of the south *shall* **r.**
  14. 2. John the Baptist; he *is* **r**-en
  24. 7. nation *shall* **r.** against nati.;
     Mar.13.8 ; Lu.21.10
    11. many false prophets *shall* **r.**;
     Mar.13.22
  26.32. after I *am* **r**-en *again*, I will
    46. **r.**, let us be going : behold
  27.63. Af. three days I *will* **r.** *again*
    64. He is **r**-en from ; Mar.6.16
  28. 6. here : for he *is* **r**-en : Lu.24.6
    7. tell his disci. that he *is* **r**-en
Mar. 4.27. should sleep, and **r.** night
  6.14. J. the Bap. *was* **r**-en ; Lu.9.7
  10.49. Be of good comfort, **r.**; he
  12.26. touc. the dead, that they **r.**
  14.28. after that I *am* **r**-en, I will
    42. **r.** *up*, let us go ; lo, he that
  16. 6. he *is* **r**-en; he is not here
    14. seen him *after he was* **r**-en
Lu. 5.23. or to say, **r.** *up* and walk
  6. 8. **r.** *up*, and stand forth in the
  7.16. a great prophet *is* **r**-en *up*
  11. 8. he will not **r.** *and* give him
    31. qu. of the south *shall* **r.** *up*
  13.25. master of the ho. *is* **r**-en *up*
  24.34. Saying, The Lord *is* **r**-en in.
Jo. 2.22. therefore he *was* **r**-en from
  5. 8. Jesus saith unto him, **r.**
  13. 4. He **r**-eth from supper, and
  21.14. *after that he was* **r**-en from
Act. 3. 6. Jes. Ch. of Nazareth **r.** *up*
Ro. 8.34. yea rather, *that is* **r**-en *again*
¹Co.15. 4. that he **ro.** *again* the third
    12. preached that he **ro.**
    13. the dead, then *is* C. not **r**-en
    14. if Christ be not **r**-en, then is
    15. if so be that the dead **r.** not
    16. For if the dead **r.** not, then
    20. now *is* Christ **r**-en from the
    29. the dead, if the dead **r.** not
    32. adva. it me, if the dead **r.** not
²Co. 5.15. died for them, and **ro.** *again*
Rev.11. 1. **r.**, and measure the temple
    sunegeirō.
Col. 2.12. wherein we also *are* **r**-en *with*
  3. 1. If ye then *be* **r**-en *with* Christ
    anatellō.
Mat. 5.45. *maketh* his sun *to* **r.** on the
Mar.16. 2. the sepul. *at the* **r**-ing *of* the
Lu. 12.54. When ye see a cloud **r.** out
Jas. 1.11. For the sun *is* no sooner **r**-en
    anabainō.
Rev.13. 1. saw a beast **r.** *up* out of the
    19. 3. her smoke **ro.** *up* for ever

RIVER,   *-s.*
    potamos.
Mar. 1. 5. baptized of him in the **r.** of
Jo. 7.38. shall flow **r**-s of living water
Act.16.13. went out of the city by a **r.**
Rev. 8.10. upon the third part of the **r**-s
  9.14. the great **r.** Euphrates ; 16.12
  16. 4. out his vial upon the **r**-s
  22. 1. a pure **r.** of water of life
    2. and on either side of the **r.**

ROAR,   *-eth, -ing.*
echeō.
Lu. 21.25. the sea and the waves **r**-*ing*
ōruomai.
1Pet. 5. 8. as a **r**-*ing* lion, walketh
mukaomai.
Rev.10. 3. voice, as when a lion **r**-*eth*

ROBBED.
sulaō.
2Co. 11. 8. I **r**. other churches, taking

ROBBER,   *-s.*
lēstēs.
Jo. 10. 1. the same is a thief and a **r**.
8. before me are thieves and **r**-*s*
18.40. Now Barabbas was a **r**.
2Co. 11.26. in perils of **r**-*s*, in perils by
hierosulos.
Act.19.37. are neither **r**-*s of churches*

ROBBERY.
harpagmos.
Phi. 2. 6. thought it not **r**. to be equal

ROBE,   *-s.*
stolē.
Lu. 15.22. Bring forth the best **r**.
20.46. wh. desire to walk in *long* **r**-*s*
Rev. 6.11. white **r**-*s* were given unto
7. 9. clothed with white **r**-*s*, and
13. which are arrayed in white **r**-*s*
14. have washed their **r**-*s* and
chlamus.
Mat.27.28.put on him a scarlet **r**.
31. they took the **r**. off from him
himation.
Jo. 19. 2. they put on him a purple **r**.
5. of thorns, and the purple **r**.
esthēs.
Lu. 23.11. arrayed him in a gorgeous **r**.

ROCK,   *-s.*
petra.
Mat. 7.24. built his house upon a **r**.
25. founded upon a **r**.; Lu.6.48
16.18. upon this **r**. I will build
27.51. did quake, and the **r**-*s* rent
60. hewn out in the **r**.;Mar.15.46
Lu. 6.48. laid the foundation on a **r**.
8. 6. And some fell upon a **r**.; and
13. They on the **r**. are they which
Ro. 9.33. a stumblingstone and **r**. of
1Co.10. 4. drank of that spiritual **r**. that
them : and that **r**. was Christ
1Pet. 2. 8. and a **r**. of offence, and to
Rev. 6.15. in the dens and in the **r**-*s* of
16. said to the mountains and **r**-*s*
trachus topos.
Act.27.29. should have fallen upon **r**-*s*

ROD,   *-s.*
rabdos.
1Co. 4.21. sh. I come unto you with a **r**.
Heb. 9. 4. and Aaron's **r**. that budded
Rev. 2.27. rule them with a **r**. of; 19.15
11. 1. a reed like unto a **r**.: and the
12. 5. to rule all nations with a **r**.
rabdizō.
2Co. 11.25. Thrice *was* I *beaten with* **r**-*s*

ROLL,   *-ed.*
apokulizō.
Mat.28. 2. came and **r**-*ed* back the stone
Mar.16. 3. Who *shall* **r**. us *away* the st.
4. that the stone *was* **r**-*ed away*
Lu. 24. 2. found the stone **r**-*ed away*
proskuliō.   [Mar.15.46
Mat.27.60.he **r**-*ed* a great stone *to* the ;
heilissō.
Rev. 6.14. a scroll *when* it is **r**-*ed togeth.*

ROOF.
stegē.   [Lu.7.6
Mat. 8. 8. shouldest come under my **r**.;
Mar.2. 4. they uncovered the **r**. where
230

ROOM,   *-s.*
topos.
Lu. 2. 7. no **r**. for them in the inn
14. 9. shame to take the lowest **r**.
10. sit down in the lowest **r**.
22. command., and yet there is **r**.
1Co.14.16. that occupieth the **r**. of
prōtoklisis.   [Mar.12.39
Mat.23. 6. love the *uppermost* **r**-*s* at ;
Lu. 14. 7. they chose out the *chief* **r**-*s*
8. sit not down in the *highest* **r**.
20.46. and the *chief* **r**-*s* at feasts
anti.
Mat. 2.22. *in the* **r**. *of* his father Herod
mēketi chōreō.
Mar. 2. 2. there *was no* **r**. *to receive*
anōgeon.   [Lu.22.12
Mar.14.15.a large *upper* **r**. furnished ;
huperōon.
Act. 1.13. went up into an *upper* **r**.
diadochos.   [*cessor* Por. Fes.
Act.24.27. *Came into* Felix' **r**. (got a *suc-*

ROOT,   *-ed, -s.*
riza.   [Lu.3.9
Mat. 3.10. the axe is laid unto the **r**.of ;
13. 6. because..had no **r**.; Mar.4 6
21. Yet hath he not **r**. in himse.
Mar. 4.17. And have no **r**. in themselv.
11.20. fig tree dried up from the **r**-*s*
Lu. 8.13. and these have no **r**., which
Ro. 11.16. and if the **r**. be holy, so are
17. partakest of the **r**. and fatn.
18. bearest not the **r**., but the **r**.
15.12. There shall be a **r**. of Jesse
1Ti. 6.10. the love of money is the **r**.
Heb.12.15.lest any **r**. of bitterness spri.
Rev. 5. 5. the **r**. of David, hath prevai.
22.16. I am the **r**. and the offspring
ekrizoō.
Mat.13.29. lest..ye **r**. *up* also the wheat
15.13. not planted, *shall be* **r**-*ed up*
Lu. 17. 6. *Be* thou *plucked up by the* **r**.
Jude 12. dead, *plucked up by the* **r**-*s*
rizooomai.
Eph. 3.17. *being* **r**-*ed* and grounded in
Col. 2. 7. **r**-*ed* and built up in him

ROPES.
schoinion.
Act.27.32. soldiers cut off the **r**. of the

ROUGH.
trachus.
Lu. 3. 5. **r**. ways shall be made sm.

ROUND.
kuklos.
Mar. 3.34. he looked **r**. *about* on them
6. 6. he went **r**. *about* the villages
36. into the country **r**. *about*
Lu. 9.12. and country **r**. *about*, and lo.
Ro. 15.19. from Jerusalem, and **r**. *about*
Rev. 4. 6. and **r**. *about* the throne
7.11. all the angels stood **r**. *about*
kukloō.
Jo. 10.24. came the Jews **r**. *about* him
Act.14.20. as the disciples *stood* **r**.*about*
kuklothen.
Rev. 4. 3, 4. **r**. *about* the throne ; 5.11
perix.
Act. 5.16. out of the cities **r**. *about*
pantothen.
Heb. 9. 4. overlaid **r**. *about* with gold
(*See words in connection.*)

ROW,   *-ed, -ing.*
elaunō.
Mar. 6.48. he saw them toiling in **r**-*ing*
Jo. 6.19. *when* they *had* **r**-*ed* about

ROYAL.
basilikos.
Act.12.21. Herod, arrayed in **r**. apparel

Jas. 2. 8. If ye fulfil the **r**. law accord.
basileios.
1Pet. 2. 9. a **r**. priesthood, an holy nat.

RUBBING.
psōchō.
Lu. 6. 1. did eat, **r**. them in their ha.

RUDDER.
pēdalion.
Act.27.40. and loosed the **r**. bands

RUDE.
idiōtēs.
2Co. 11. 6. though I be **r**. in speech, yet

RUDIMENTS.
stoicheion.
Col. 2. 8. after the **r**. of the world
20. dead with Christ from the **r**.

RUE.
pēganon.
Lu. 11.42. for ye tithe mint and **r**.

RUIN,   *-s.*
rēgma.
Lu. 6.49. the **r**. of that house was
kataskaptō.
Act.15.16. build again the **r**-*s* thereof

RULE, [*noun.*]
archē.
Co. 15.24. have put down all **r**. and
kanōn.
2Co.10.13. to the measure of the **r**. wh.
15. according to our **r**. abund.
Gal. 6.16. as walk according to this **r**.
Phi. 3.16. let us walk by the same **r**.
hēgeomai.
Heb.13. 7, 17, 24. *which have the* **r**. *ove*r

RULE, [*verb,*]   *-eth, -ing*
proistēmi.
Ro. 12. 8. he *that* **r**-*eth*, with diligence
1Ti. 3. 4. One *that* **r**-*eth* well his own
5. if a man know not how *to* **r**.
12. **r**-*ing* their children and
5.17. Let the elders *that* **r**. well be
poimainō.
Mat. 2. 6. *shall* **r**. my people Israel
Rev. 2.27. *shall* **r**. them with ; 19.15
12. 5. who was *to* **r**. all nations
archō.
Mar.10.42.accounted *to* **r**. *over* the
brabeuō.
Col. 3.15. peace of God **r**. in your hea.

RULER, (See *Synagogue,*)   *-s.*
archōn.
Mat. 9.18. there came a certain **r**., and
23. Jesus came into the **r**.'s hou.
Lu. 8.41. he was a **r**. of the synagogue
18.18. a certain **r**. asked him, say.
23.13. chief priests and the **r**-*s* and
35. the **r**-*s* also with them derid.
24.20. the chief priests and our **r**-*s*
Jo. 3. 1. Nicodemus, a **r**. of the Jews
7.26. Do the **r**-*s* know indeed that
48. Have any of the **r**-*s* or of the
12.42. among the *chief* **r**-*s* also
Act. 3.17. did it as did also your **r**-*s*
4. 5. that their **r**-*s* and elders
8. Ye **r**-*s* of the people, and
26. the **r**-*s* were gathered togeth.
7.27, 35. Who made thee a **r**. and
35. God send to be a **r**. and a
13.27. dwell at Jerus. and their **r**-*s*
14. 5. also of the Jews with their **r**-*s*
16.19. the marketplace unto the **r**-*s*
23. 5. not speak evil of the **r**. of
Ro. 13. 3. For **r**-*s* are not a terror to
hēgemōn.   [Lu.21,12
Mar. 13. 9. be brought before **r**-*s* and ;

kosmokratŏr.
Eph. 6.12. against the r-s of the darkn.
architriklinos.
Jo. 2. 9. When the r. *of the feast* had
politrachēs.
Act.17. 6, 8. the r-s *of the city*

RUMOUR,   -s.
     akoē.   [Mar.13.7
Mat.24. 6. hear of wars, and r-s of wars;
     logos.
Lu. 7.17. this r. of him went forth

RUN,   -eth, -ing, Ran.
     trechō.
Mat.27.48.straight. one of them ra. *and*
   28. 8. *did* r. to bring his disciples
Mar. 5. 6. he ra. and worshipped him
   15.36. And one ra. and filled a sp.
Lu. 15.20. and ra., *and* fell on his neck
   24.12. Then arose Peter, and ra.
Jo. 20. 2. Then she r-*eth*, and cometh
     4. So they ra. both together
Ro. 9.16. nor of him *that* r-*eth*, but of
¹Co. 9.24. they which r. in a race r. all
     So r., *that* ye may obtain
    26. I therefore so r., not as un.
Gal. 2. 2. I should r., or *had* r., in vain
   5. 7. Ye *did* r. well; who did hin.
Phi. 2.16. that I *have* not r. in vain
Heb.12. 1. and *let* us r. with patience
Rev. 9. 9. of many horses r-*ing* to battle
     suntrechō.
Mar. 6.33. he a. afoot thither out of all
Act. 3.11. all the people ra. *together*
¹Pet. 4. 4. *that* ye r. not *with* them
     episuntrechō.
Mar. 9.25. the people *came* r-*ing together*
     prostrechō.
Mar. 9.15. r-*ing to* him saluted him
   10.17. there came one r-*ing*, and
Act. 8.30. Philip ra. *thither to* him, *and*
     protrechō.
Lu. 19. 4. And he ra. *before, and* clim.
     katatrechō.
Act.21.32. and ra. *down* unto them
     eistrechō.
Act.12.14. opened not..but ra. *in, and*
     peritrechō.
Mar. 6.55. *And* ra. *through* that whole
     hupotrechō.
Act.27.16. And r-*ing under* a certain
     hormaō.   [Mar.5.13 ; Lu.8.33
Mat. 8.32. ra. *violently* down a steep;
Act. 7.57. ra.upon him with one accord
     ekcheō.
Mat. 9.17. break, and the wine r-*eth out*
     epokellō.
Act.27.41. they ra. the ship *aground*
     huperekchunomai.
Lu. 6.38. and r-*ing over*, shall men give
     eispēdaō.
Act.14.14. ra. in among the people, cry.
     sundromē.
Act.21.30. and the people ra. *together*
     ekchunō.
Jude 11. ra. *greedily* after the error of

RUSH,   -ed, -ing.
     pherō.
Act. 2. 2. as of a r-*ing* mighty wind
     hormaō.
Act.19.29. they r-*ed* with one accord in

RUST
     brōsis.
Mat. 6.19. where moth and r. doth cor.
   20. neither moth nor r. doth co.
     ios.
Jas. 5. 3. the r. of them shall be a wit.

SABACHTHANI.
     sabachthani.
Mat.27.46.Eli, Eli, lama s.; Mar. 15.34

SABAOTH,   sabaŏth.
Ro. 9.29. Except the Lord of s. had le.
Jas. 5. 4. in. the ears of the Lord of s.

SABBATH.
     sabbaton.
Mat.12. 2. lawful to do upon the s. *day*
     5. in the temple profane the s.
     8. is Lord even of the s. *day*
   24.20. winter, neither on the s. *day*
Mar. 2.27. The s. was made for man
     and not man for the s.
   28. is Lord also of the s.; Lu.6.5
   6. 2. And when the s. *day* was co.
   16. 1. And when the s. was past
Lu. 6. 1. on the second s. after the fir.
     6. to pass also on another s.
     7. he would heal on the s. *day*
   13.14. had healed on the s. *day*, and
     healed, and not on the s. day
     15. not each one of you on the s.
     16. from this bond on the s. day
   14. 1. to eat bread on the s. day
     3. lawful to heal on the s. *day*
     5. pull him out on the s. day
   23.54. preparation, and the s. drew
     56. and rested the s. *day* accord.
Jo. 5. 9. the same day was the s.
     10. It is the s. *day:* it is not
     16. these things on the s. *day*
     18. he not only had broken the s.
   7.22. ye on the s. *day* circumcise
     23. If a man on the s. *day* recei.
     whit whole on the s. *day*
   9.14. And it was the s. *day* when
     16. he keepeth not the s. *day*
   19.31. the cross on the s. *day* for
     that s. day was an high day
Act. 1.12. from Jerus., a s. *day's* journ.
   13.27. which are read every s. *day*
     42. preached to them the next s.
     44. And the next s. day came
   15.21. the synagogues every s. *day*
   18. 4. in the synagogue every s.
     sabbata.
Mat.12. 1. Jesus went on the s. *day* th.
     5. on the s. *days* the priests in
     10. lawful to heal on the s. *days*
     11. fall into a pit on the s. *day*
     12. well on the s. *days;* Mar.3.4
   28. 1. In the end of the s., as it be.
Mar. 1.21. on the s. *day* he entered in.
   2.23. the corn fields on the s. *day*
     24. why do they on the s. *day*
   3. 2. heal him on the s.*day;* that
Lu. 4.16. the synagogue on the s. day
     31. taught them on the s. *days*
   6. 2. lawful to do on the s. *days*
     9. lawful on the s. *days* to do
   13.10. one of the synagog. on the s.
Act.13.14. the synagogue on the s. day
   16.13. on the s. (the day of the s.)
     17. 2. three s. *days* reasoned with
Col. 2.16. new moon, or of the s. *days*
     prosabbaton.
Mar.15.42.that is, the *day* before the s.

SACKCLOTH.
     sakkos.
Mat.11.21.long ago in s. and ashes
Lu. 10.13. repent., sitting in s. and ash.
Rev. 6.12. became black as s. of hair
   11. 3. 1260 days, clothed in s.

SACRIFICE, [noun.]   -s.
     thusia.   [12. 7
Mat. 9.13. will have mercy, and not s.;
Mar. 9.49. and every s. shall be salted
   12.33. whole burnt offerings and s-s
Lu. 2.24. And to offer a s. according
   13. 1. mingled with their s-s
Act. 7.41. offered s. unto the idol
     42. to me slain beasts and s-s

Ro. 12. 1. a living s., holy, acceptable
¹Co. 10.18. they which eat of the s-s
Eph. 5. 2. an offering and a s. to God
Phi. 2.17. upon the s. and service of
     4.18. a s. acceptable, wellpleasing
Heb. 5. 1. both gifts and s-s for sins
   7.27. to offer up s., first for his
   8. 3. ordained to offer gifts and s-s
   9. 9. were offered both gifts and s-s
   23. with better s-s than these
   26. sin by the s. of himself
   10. 1. with those s-s which they
     5, 8. s. and offering thou
     11. offe. oftentimes the same s-s
     12. after he had offered one s.
     26. there remaineth no more s.
   11. 4. By faith..a more excellent s.
   13.15. let us offer the s. of praise
     16. for with such s-s God is well
¹Pet. 2. 5. to offer up spiritual s-s
     thuō.
Act.14.13. would *have done* s. with the
     18. that they *had* not *done* s.
     eidōlothuton.   [idols
¹Co. 10.19, 28. *which is offered* in s. *to*

SACRIFICE, [verb,]   -ed.
     thuō.
¹Co. 5. 7. Christ our passover *is* s-ed
   10.20. the Gentiles s. they s. to de.
     eidōlothuton.
Rev. 2.14, 20. eat *things* s-ed unto idols

SACRILEGE.
     hierosuleō.
Ro. 2.22. idols, dost thou *commit* s.

SAD.
     skuthrōpos.
Mat. 6.16. the hypo., *of a* s. *countenance*
Lu. 24.17. anoth., as ye walk and are s.
     stugnazō.
Mar.10.22. he *was* s. at that saying, *and*

SAFE.
     asphalēs.
Phi. 3. 1. grievous, but for you it is s.
     diasōzō.
Act.23.24. *bring* him s. unto Felix the
   27.44. they *escaped* all s. to land
     hugiainō.
Lu. 15.27. received him s. *and* sound

SAFELY.
     asphalōs.
Mar.14.44.him, and lead him away s.
Act.16.23. the jailor to keep them s.

SAFETY.
     asphaleia.
Act. 5.23. found we shut with all s.
¹Th. 5. 3. shall say, Peace and s.

SAID, [already mentioned.]
     autos.
Mar. 6.22. daughter of *the* s. Herodias

SAIL, [noun.]
     skeuos.
Act.27.17. strake s., and so were driven

SAIL, [verb,]   -ed, -ing.
     pleō.
Lu. 8.23. But *as* they s-ed, he fell asleep
Act.21. 3. it on the left hand, and s-ed
   27. 2. meaning *to* s. by the coasts
     6. a ship of Alexandria s-ing
     24. all them *that* s. with thee
     apopleō.
Act.13. 4. from thence they s-ed to Cy.
   14.16. thence s-ed to Antioch, from
   20.15. we s-ed thence, *and* came
   27. 1. that we *should* s. into Italy
     ekpleō.
Act.15.39. took Mark, and s-ed unto

Act.18.18. s-*ed thence* into Syria, and
   20. 6. we s-*ed away* from Philippi
     anagō.
Act.18.21. And he s-*ed* from Ephesus
   20. 3. he was about *to* s. into Syria
    13. to ship, and s-*ed* unto Assos
     parapleō.
Act.20.16. determined *to* s. *by* Ephesus
     diaperaō.
Act.21. 2. finding a ship s-*ing over*
     hupopleō.
Act.27. 4. we s-*ed under* Cyprus, beca.
    7. we s-*ed under* Crete, over
     diapleō.
Act.27. 5. *when* we *had* s-*ed over* the
     braduploeō.
Act.27. 7. *when* we *had* s-*ed slowly*
     paralegomai.
Act.27.13. they s-*ed* close *by* Crete

SAILING, [*noun.*]
     ploos.
Act.27. 9. when s. was now dangerous

SAILORS.
     nautēs.
Rev.18.17. s., and as many as trade by

SAINTS.
     hagios.
Mat.27.52. bodies of the s. which slept
Act. 9.13. he hath done to thy s. at
   32. came down also to the s.
   41. when he had called the s.
   26.10. many of the s. did I shut up
Ro. 1. 7. called to be s.; ¹Co.1.2
   8.27. maketh intercession for the s.
   12.13. to the necessity of s.
   15.25. Jerus. to minister unto the s.
   26. for the poor s. which are
   31. may be accepted of the s.
   16. 2. in the Lord, as becometh s.
   15. all the s. which are with th.
¹Co. 6. 1. and not before the s.
   2. the s. shall judge the world
   14.33. in all churches of the s.
   16. 1. the collection for the s. as I
   15. to the ministry of the s.
²Co. 1. 1. with all the s. which are
   8. 4. the ministering to the s.; 9.1
   9.12. supplieth the want of the s.
   13.13. All the s. salute you;Phi.4.22
Eph. 1. 1. to the s. which are at Ephes.
   15. and love unto all the s.
   18. his inheritance in the s.
   2.19. fellowcitizens with the s.
   3. 8. less than the least of all s.
   18. to comprehend with all s.
   4.12. For the perfecting of the s.
   5. 3. among you, as becometh s.
   6.18. supplication for all s.
Phi. 1. 1. to all the s. in Christ Jesus
   4.21. Salute every s. in Christ Jes.
Col. 1. 2. To the s. and faithful
   4. which ye have to all the s.
   12. inheritance of the s. in light
   26. made manifest to his s.
¹Th. 3.13. Jesus Christ with all his s.
²Th. 1.10. to be glorified in his s.
¹Ti. 5.10. if she have washed the s' feet
Phile. 5. Lord Jesus, and toward all s.
   7. the bowels of the s. are
Heb. 6.10. have ministered to the s.
   13.24. over you, and all the s.
Jude 3. once delivered unto the s.
   14. with ten thousands of his s.
Rev. 5. 8. which are the prayers of the s.
   8. 3, 4. with the prayers of all s.
   11.18. the prophets, and to the s.
   13. 7. to make war with the s.
   10. **pati.** and the faith of the s.
   14.12. Here is the pati. of the s.
   15. 3. thy ways, thou King of s.
232

Rev.16. 6. they have shed the blood of s.
   17. 6. drunk. with the blo. of the s.
   18.24. blood of prophets, and of s.
   19. 8. fine linen..righteousness of s.
   20. 9. compassed the camp of the s.

SAKE,   -*s.*
    dia, [*accu.*]
Mat.10.22. hated of all *for* my name's s.
   14. 3. in prison *for* Heriodas' s.
   9. *for* the oath's s. ; Mar.6.26
   24. 9. hated. *for* my name's s.;
     Mar.13.13 ; Lu.21.17
   22. *for* the elect's s. those days
Mar. 4.17. persecu. ariseth *for* word's s.
   13.20. *for* the elect's s., whom he
Jo. 11.15. I am glad *for* your s-s that I
   12. 9. they came not *for* Jesus' s.
   30. beca. of me, but *for* your s-s
   14.11. bel. me *for* the very works' s.
   15.21. unto you *for* my name's s.
Ro. 4.23. not written *for* his s. alone
   11.28. they are enemies *for* your s-s
     beloved for the fathers' s.
   13. 5. wrath, but also *for* conscie. s.
¹Co. 4. 6. myself and Apo. *for* your s-s
   10. We are fools *for* Christ's s.
   9.10. *for* our s-s ? *For* our s-s, no
   23. this I do *for* the gospel's s.
   10.25, 27.question *for* conscience' s.
   28. eat not *for* his s. that shewed
²Co. 2.10. *for* your s-s forgave I it in the
   4. 5. your servants *for* Jesus' s.
   11. deliver. unto death *for* J.'s s.
   15. all things are *for* your s-s
   8. 9. *for* your s-s he became poor
Col. 3. 6. *For* which things' s. the wra.
¹Th. 1. 5. were among you *for* your s.
   3. 9. we joy *for* your s-s before
   5.13. in love *for* their work's s.
¹Ti. 5.23. wine *for* thy stomach's s.
²Ti. 2.10. all things *for* the elect's s-s
Phile. 9. Yet *for* love's s. I rather
¹Pet. 2.13. ordin. of man *for* the L.'s s.
   3.14. if ye suffer *for* righteousn.' s.
¹Jo. 2.12. forgiv. you *for* his name's s.
²John 2. *For* the truth's s., which
Rev. 2. 3. patie., and *for* my name's s.
    heneka, *or* **heneken.**
Mat. 5.10. persecuted *for* righteous.' s.
   11. against you falsely, *for* my s.
   10.18. *for* my s., for a testimony
   39. loseth his life *for* my s. shall
   16.25. will lose his life *for* my s.;
     Mar.8.35; Lu.9.24
   19.29. *for* my name's s., shall rece.
Mar.10.29.*for* my s., and the gospel's
   13. 9. rulers and kings *for* my s.
Lu. 6.22. *for* the Son of man's s.
   18.29. *for* the kingdom of God's s.
   21.12. rulers *for* my name's s.
Ro. 8.36. *For* thy s. we are killed all
    huper, [*gen.*]   (*for* thee, &c.)
Jo. 13.37. lay down my life *for* thy s.
   38. lay down thy life *for* my s.
   17.19. And *for* their s-s I sanctify
Act. 9.16. must suffer *for* my name's s.
²Co. 12.10. in distresses *for* Christ's s.
Phi. 1.29. but also to suffer *for* his s.
Col. 1.24. in my flesh *for* his body's s.
³John 7. Beca. that *for* his name's s.
    peri, [*gen.*]
Act.26. 7. *For* which hope's s., king A
    charin.
Tit. 1.11. ought not *for* filthy lucre's s.
    en.   (*in* Christ hath.)
Eph. 4.32. as God *for* Christ's s. hath

SALT, [*noun and adjec.*]
    halas.
Mat. 5.13. Ye are the s. of the earth
    if the s. have lost his savour
Mar. 9.50. s. is..but if the s.; Lu.14.34

Mar. 9.50. Have s. in yourselves, and
Col. 4. 6. grace, seasoned with s., that
    hals.
Mar. 9.49. sacrifi. shall be salted with s.
    halukos.
Jas. 3.12. fountain both yield s. water

SALT, [*verb,*]   -*ed.*
    halizō.
Mat. 5.13. savour, wher. *shall it be* s-*ed*
Mar. 9.49. every one *shall be* s-*ed* with
    sacrifice *shall be* s-*ed* with sa.

SALTNESS.
    ginomai analos.
Mar. 9.50. if the salt *have* lost his s.

SALUTATION,   -*s.*
    aspasmos.
Mar.12.38.love s-s in the market places
Lu. 1.29. what manner of s. this shou.
   41. when Elisabeth heard the s.
   44. the voice of thy s. sounded
¹Co.16.21. The s. of me Paul ; ²Th. 3.17
Col. 4.18. The s. by the hand of me P.

SALUTE,   -*ed, -eth.*
    aspazomai.
Mat. 5.47. if ye s. your brethren only
   10.12. wh. ye come into an house, s.
Mar. 9.15. and running to him s-*ed* him
   15.18. began to s. him, Hail, King
Lu. 1.40. house of Zacharias, s-*ed* Eliz.
   10. 4. and s. no man by the way
Act.18.22. *when*..gone up, and s-*ed* the
   21. 7. s-*ed* the brethren, *and* abode
   19. And *when he had* s-*ed* them
   25.13. came unto Cæsarea, to s. F.
Ro. 16. 5. s. my wellbeloved Epenetus;
    s.; 7,9,10,11,12,13,14,15
   10. s. them which are of the
   16. s. one another with an holy
    kiss. The churches of Ch. s.
   21. Sosipater, my kinsmen, s. you
   22. who wrote this epistle, s. you
   23. of the whole church, s-*eth* you
    chamberlain of the city s-*eth*
¹Co.16.19. The churches of Asia s. you
    Aquila and Priscilla s. you
²Co.13.13. All the saints s. you; Phi.4.22
Phi. 4.21. s. every saint in Christ Jesus
Col. 4.10. my fellowprisoner s-*eth* you
   12. a servant of Christ, s-*eth* you
   15. s. the brethren which are
²Ti. 4.19. s. Prisca and Aquila, and the
Tit. 3.15. All that are with me s. thee
Phile. 23. There s. thee Epaphras, my
Heb.13.24. s. all them that have the rule
    They of Italy s. you
¹Pet. 5.13. elected toget. with you, s-*eth*
³John 14. Our friends s. thee

SALVATION.
    sōtēria.
Lu. 1.69. hath raised up an horn of s.
   77. To give knowledge of s. unto
   19. 9. This day is s. come to this
Jo. 4.22. worship : for s. is of the Jews
Act. 4.12. Neither is there s. in any ot.
   13.26. to you is the word of this s.
   47. for s. unto the ends of the
   16.17. shew unto us the way of s.
Ro. 1.16. is the power of God unto s.
   10.10. confession is made unto s.
   11.11. s. is come unto the Gentiles
   13.11. for now is our s. nearer than
²Co. 1. 6. for your consolation and s.
   6. 2. in the day of s. have I succo.
    behold, now is the day of s.
   7.10. worketh repentance to s. not
Eph. 1.13. the gospel of your s.: in wh.
Phi. 1.19. this shall turn to my s. thro.
   28. but to you of s., and that of

Phi. 2.12. work out your own **s.** with
¹Th. 5. 8. for an helmet, the hope of **s.**
　　9. to obtain **s.** by our Lord Je.
²Th. 2.13. chosen you to **s.** through
²Ti. 2.10. they may also obtain the **s.**
　　3.15. to make thee wise unto **s.**
Heb. 1.14. who shall be heirs of **s.**
　　2. 3. if we neglect so great **s.**
　　10. make the captain of their **s.**
　　5. 9. the author of eternal **s.**
　　6. 9. and things that accompany **s.**
　　9.28. sec. time without sin unto **s.**
¹Pet. 1. 5. of God through faith unto **s.**
　　9. even the **s.** of your souls
　　10. Of which **s.** the prophets ha.
²Pet. 3.15. longsuffering of our Lord is **s.**
Jude 3. unto you of the common **s.**
Rev. 7.10. **s.** to our God which sitteth
　　12.10. Now is come **s.**, and strength
　　19. 1. **s.**, and glory, and honour
　　sōtērion.
Lu. 2.30. mine eyes have seen thy **s.**
　　3. 6. all flesh shall see the **s.** of G.
Act.28.28. that the **s.** of God is sent un.
Eph. 6.17. And take the helmet of **s.**
　　sōtērios.
Tit. 2.11. grace of God *that bringeth* **s.**

SAME.
　houtos.
Mat. 5.19. *the* **s.** shall be called great
　　13.20. *the* **s.** is he that heareth the
　　18. 4. *the* **s.** is greatest in the king.
　　21.42. *the* **s.** is become the; Lu.20.17
　　24.13. *the* **s.** shall be sa.; Mar.13.13
　　26.23. dish, *the* **s.** shall betray me
Mar. 3.35. *the* **s.** is my brother, and my
　　8.35. *the* **s.** shall save it; Lu.9.24
Lu. 2.25. *the* **s.** man was just and
　　9.48. you all, *the* **s.** shall be great
　　16. 1. *the* **s.** was accused unto him
　　20.47. *the* **s.** shall receive greater
　　23.51. *The* **s.** had not consented to
Jo. 1. 2. *The* **s.** was in the beginning
　　7. *The* **s.** came for a witness
　　3. *the* **s.** is he which baptizeth
　　3. 2. *The* **s.** came to Jesus by nig.
　　26. behold, *the* **s.** baptizeth
　　7.18. sent him, *the* **s.** is true, and
　　12.21. *The* **s.** came therefore to Ph.
　　15. 5. *the* **s.** bringeth forth much
Act. 1.11. *this* **s.** Jesus, which is taken
　　7.19. *The* **s.** dealt subtilly with our
　　35. *the* **s.** did God send to be a
　　8.35. began at the **s.** scripture, and
　　13.33. God hath fulfilled *the* **s.**
　　14. 9. *The* **s.** heard Paul speak
　　16.17. *The* **s.** followed Paul and us
　　21. 9. And *the* **s.** man had four da.
¹Co. 7.20. abide in *the* **s.** calling where.
　　8. 3. God, *the* **s.** is known of him
　　9. 8. saith not the law *the* **s.** also
²Co. 8. 6. finish in you *the* **s.** grace also
　　9. 4. ashamed in *this* **s.** confident
　　5. that *the* **s.** might be ready
Gal. 3. 7. *the* **s.** are the children of
Eph. 6. 8. *the* **s.** shall he receive of the
Col. 4. 8. unto you for the **s.** purpose
²Ti. 2. 2. the **s.** commit thou to faith.
Jas. 3. 2. the **s.** is a perfect man
¹Pet. 2. 7. *the* **s.** is made the head of the
²Pet. 2.19. of the **s.** is he brought in bo.
Rev. 3. 5. *the* **s.** shall be clothed in wh.
　　ekeinos.
Mat.10.19. be given you in *that* **s.** hour
　　13. 1. *The* **s.** day went Jesus out
　　15.22. came out of the **s.** coasts
　　18. 1. At *the* **s.** time came the disc.
　　28. *the* **s.** servant went out, and
　　22.23. *The* **s.** day came to him the
　　26.55. In *that* **s.** hour said Jesus
Mar. 4.35. *the* **s.** day, when the even

Jo. 1.33. *the* **s.** said unto me; 5.11
　　4.53. at *the* **s.** hour, in the which
　　5. 9. on *the* **s.** day was the sabbath
　　10. 1. *the* **s.** is a thief and a robber
　　11.49. high priest *that* **s.** year; 18.13
　　12.48. *the* **s.** shall judge him in
　　20.19. *the* **s.** day at evening, being
Act. 2.41. *the* **s.** day there were added
　　12. 6. *the* **s.** night Peter was sleepi.
　　16.33. *the* **s.** hour of the night, and
　　19.23. *the* **s.** time there arose no sm.
　　28. 7. In *the* **s.** quarters were poss.
²Co. 7. 8. I perceive that *the* **s.** epistle
Rev.11.13. *the* **s.** hour was there a great
　　autos.
Mat.25.16.went and traded with *the* **s.**
Lu. 7.21. And in *the* **s.** hour he cured
　　10.10. into the streets of the **s.**
Ro. 9.17. for this **s.** purpose have I
　　12.16. be of the **s.** mind, one towa.
¹Co. 1.10. all speak the **s.** thing..in the
　　　　　s. mind..in the **s.** judgment
²Co. 2. 3. I wrote this **s.** unto you
Phi. 4. 2. of the **s.** mind in the Lord
¹Pet. 4. 1. arm yourselves..with the **s.**
(See *Body, Craft, Manner.*)

SANCTIFICATION.
　hagiasmos.
¹Co. 1.30. and **s.**, and redemption
¹Th. 3. will of God, even your **s.**
　　4. his vessel in **s.** and honour
²Th. 2.13. through **s.** of the ; ¹Pet. 1.2

SANCTIFY,　　*-ed, -eth.*
　hagiazō.
Mat.23.17. temple *that* **s-eth** the gold
　　19. or the altar *that* **s-eth** the gift
Jo. 10.36. whom the Father *hath* **s-ed**
　　17.17. **s.** them through thy truth
　　19. for their sakes I **s.** myself
　　also might be **s-ed** through
Act.20.32. them *which are* **s-ed**; 26.18
Ro. 15.16. *being* **s-ed** by the Holy Ghost
¹Co. 1. 2. *that are* **s-ed** in Christ Jesus
　　6.11. are washed, but ye *are* **s-ed**
　　7.14. husband is **s-ed** by the wife
　　the unbelieving wife *is* **s-ed**
Eph. 5.26. That he *might* **s.** and cleanse
¹Th. 5.23. God of peace **s.** you wholly
¹Ti. 4. 5. it *is* **s-ed** by the word of God
²Ti. 2.21. unto honour, **s-ed**, and meet
Heb. 2.11. *that* **s-eth**..they *who are* **s-ed**
　　9.13. unclean, **s-eth** to the purify.
　　10.10. By the which will we *are* **s-ed**
　　14. for ever them *that are* **s-ed**
　　29. cove., wherewith he *was* **s-ed**
　　13.12. that he *might* **s.** the people
¹Pet. 3.15. **s.** the Lord God in your hea.
Jude 1. them that are **s-ed** by God

SANCTUARY.
　hagion.
Heb. 8. 2. A minister of the **s.**, and
　　9. 1. service, and a worldly **s.**
　　2. which is called the **s.**
Heb.13.11.brought into the **s.** by the

SAND.
　ammos.
Mat. 7.26. built his house upon the **s.**
Ro. 9.27. Israel be as the **s.** of the sea
Heb.11.12.as the **s.** which is by the sea
Rev.13. 1. I stood upon the **s.** of the
　　20. 8. number of whom is as the **s.**

SANDALS.
　sandalion.
Mar. 6. 9. But be shod with **s.**; and not
Act. 12. 8. thyself, and bind on thy **s.**

SAPPHIRE.
　sappheiros.
Rev.21.19. jasper : the second **s.** ; the

SARDINE.
　sardios.
Rev. 4. 3. like a jasper and a **s.** stone
SARDIUS.
　sardios.
Rev.21.20.the sixth, **s.**; the seventh
SARDONYX.
　sardonux.
Rev.21.20.The fifth **s.**; the sixth
SATISFY.
　chortazō.
Mar. 8. 4. whence can a man **s.** these
SATISFYING, [*noun.*]
　plēsmonē.
Col. 2.23. honour to the **s.** of the flesh
SAVE, (*Except.*)
　ei mē.
Mat.11.27.any man the Father, **s.** the
　　13.57. without honour, **s.** in his
　　17. 8. they saw no man, **s.** Jesus
Mar. 5.37. no man to follow him, **s.** Pe.
　　6. 5. **s.** *that* he laid his hands up.
　　8. nothing for their journey, **s.**
Lu. 4.26. was Elias sent, **s.** unto Sarep.
　　8.51. no man to go in, **s.** Peter
　　17.18. to give glory to God, **s.** this
　　18.19. none is good, **s.** one, that is
Jo. 6.22. **s.** that one whereinto his dis.
　　46. **s.** he which is of G., he hath
Act.21.25. **s.** *only that* they keep them.
¹Co. 2. 2. **s.** Jesus Christ, and him cru.
　　11. **s.** the spirit of man which i.
Gal. 1.19. saw I none, **s.** James the Lo.
　　6.14. that I should glory, **s.** in the
Rev. 13.17.buy or sell, **s.** he that had
　　alla.
Mat.19.11. **s.** they to whom it is given
Mar. 9. 8. no man any more, **s.** Jesus
　　ē.
Jo. 13.10. needeth not **s.** to wash his
　　plēn.
Act.20.23. **s.** that the Holy Ghost witn.
　　para, [*accu.*]
²Co. 11.24. received I forty stripes **s.** one

SAVE,　　　　*-ed.*
　sōzō.
Mat. 1.21. for he *shall* **s.** his people from
　　8.25. saying, Lord, **s.** us : we per.
　　10.22. endu. to the end *shall* be **s-ed**;
　　24.13 ; Mar.13.13
　　14.30. he cried, saying, Lord, **s.** me
　　16.25. whosoever will **s.** his life sh. ;
　　Mar.8.35 ; Lu.9.24
　　18.11. to **s.** that whi. was ; Lu.19.10
　　19.25. saying, Who then can be **s-ed** ;
　　Mar.10.26 ; Lu.18.26
　　24.22. no flesh *be* **s-ed** ; Mar.13.13
　　27.40. buildest it in three days, **s.**
　　42. **s-ed** others ; him.he canno.**s.** ;
　　Mar.15.31
　　49. whether Elias will come to **s.**
Mar. 3. 4. to **s.** life, or to kill
　　8.35. the same *shall* **s.** it ; Lu.9.24
　　15.30. **s.** thyself, and come down
　　16.16. and is baptized *shall* be **s-ed**
Lu. 6. 9. to **s.** life, or to destroy it ?
　　7.50. Thy fa. *hath* **s-ed** thee ; 18.42
　　8.12. they should bel. and be **s-ed**
　　9.56. to destroy men's liv., but to **s.**
　　13.23. L., are there few *that be* **s-ed**
　　17.33. seek to **s.** his life shall lose it
　　23.35. **s-ed** others ; *let* him **s.** hims.
　　37. the king of the Jews, **s.** thy.
　　39. If thou be Christ, **s.** thyself
Jo. 3.17. wo. throu. him *might be* **s-ed**
　　5.34. I say, that ye *might be* **s-ed**
　　10. 9. he *shall be* **s-ed**, and shall go
　　12.27. Father, **s.** me from this hour

233

Jo. 12.47. the world, but to s. the wor.
Act. 2.21. name of the L. *shall be* s-ed
  40. s. *yourselves* from this unto.
  47. daily *such as should be* s-ed
  4.12. whereby we must *be* s-ed
  11.14. and all thy house *shall be* s-ed
  15. 1. of Moses, ye cannot *be* s-ed
  11. we shall *be* s-ed, even as they
  16.30. what must I do to *be* s-ed
  31. and thou *shalt be* s-ed, and
  27.20. hope that we should *be* s-ed
  31. in the ship, ye cannot *be* s-ed
Ro. 5. 9. we *shall be* s-ed from wrath
  10. we *shall be* s-ed by his life
  8.24. For we *are* s-ed by hope
  9.27. a remnant *shall be* s-ed
  10. 9. the dead, thou *shalt be* s-ed
  13. name of the Lo. *shall be* s-ed
  11.14. and might s. some of them
  26. And so all Israel *shall be* s-ed
¹Co. 1.18. unto us *which are* s-ed it is
  21. *to* s. them that believe
  3. 5. but he himself *shall be* s-ed
  5. 5. that the spirit *may be* s-ed
  7.16. thou *shalt* s, thy husband
  thou *shalt* s. thy wife
  9.22. I *might* by all means s. some
  10.33. many, that they *may be* s-ed
  15. 2. By which also ye *are* s-ed
²Co. 2. 15. of Ch., in them *that are* s-ed
Eph. 2. 5, 8. by grace ye are s-ed
¹Th. 2.16. that they *might be* s-ed
²Th. 2.10. truth, that they *might be* s-ed
¹Ti. 1.15. came into the world *to* s. sin.
  2. 4. will have all men to *be* s-ed
  15. Notwithsta. she *shall be* s-ed
  4.16. thou *shalt* both s. thyself and
²Ti. 1. 9. *Who hath* s-ed us, and called
  5. 3. accord. to his mercy he s-ed
Heb. 5. 7. unto him that was able *to* s.
  7.25. able also *to* s. them to the
Jas. 1.21. word, which is able *to* s. your
  2.14. have not works ? can faith s.
  4.12. who is able *to* s.and to des.
  5.15. the prayer of faith *shall* s.
  20. *shall* s. a soul from death
¹Pet. 3.21. even bapt. *doth* also now s.
  4.18. if the righteo. scarcely *be* s-ed
Jude 5. *having* s-ed the people out of
  23. And others s. with fear, pull.
Rev.21.24. natio. of them *which are* s-ed

diasōzō.
Act.27.43. centurion, willing *to* s. Paul
¹Pet. 3.20. eight souls *were* s-ed by wat.

sōtēria.   *(a salvation* from.)
Lu. 1.71. *That we should be* s-ed from
Ro. 10. 1. Isr. is, that they *might be* s-ed

phulassō.
²Pet. 2. 5. but s-ed Noa., the eighth per.

SAVING, [*excepting.*]
ei mē.
Lu. 4.27. was cleansed, s. Naaman the
Rev. 2.17. no man knoweth s. he that

parektos.
Mat. 5.32. s. *for* the cause of fornication

SAVING, [*noun.*]
peripoiēsis.
Heb.10.39.believe to the s. of the soul

sōtēria.
Heb.11. 7. prepared an ark to the s. of

SAVIOUR.
sōtēr.
Lu. 1.47. hath rejoiced in God my s.
  2.11. a s., which is Christ the Lord
Jo. 4.42. the Christ, the s. of the wor.
Act. 5.31. to be a Prince and a s., for to
  13.23. raised unto Israel a s., Jesus
Eph. 5.23. and he is the s. of the body
Phi. 3.20. we look for the s., the Lord
¹Ti. 1. 1. comm. of God our s.; Tit.1.3
234

¹Ti. 2. 3. in the sight of God our s.
  4.10. who is the s. of all men, sp.
²Ti. 1.10. by the appearing of our s. J.
Tit. 1. 4. the Lord Jesus Christ our s.
  2.10. the doctrine of God our s.
  13. the great God and our s. Je.
  3. 4. and love of God our s. towa.
  6. through Jesus Christ our s.
²Pet. 1. 1. of God and our s. Jesus Chr.
  11. of our Lord and s. Jes.; 3.18
  2.20. knowled. of the Lord and s.
  3. 2. the apost. of the Lord and s.
¹Jo. 4.14. sent the Son to be the s. of
Jude 25. To the only wise God our s.

SAVOUR.
osmē.
²Co. 2.14. the s. of his knowledge by us
  16. to the one we are the s. of
  to the other the s. of life un.
Eph. 5. 2. for a sweet smelling s.

morainō.
Mat. 5.13. salt *have* lost his s.; Lu.14.34

euōdia.
²Co. 2.15. we are..a *sweet* s. of Christ

SAVOUREST.
phroneō.   [Mar.8.33
Mat.16.23.s. not the things that be;

SAWN.
prizō.
Heb.11.37.they were s. *asunder,* were

SAY, -ing, Said, -st, Sayest, Saith.
legō.
Mat. 3. 9. think not *to* s. with.; Lu.3.8
  5.22. But I s.; 28,32,34,39,44,11.22,
  24,12.6,36,17.12,26,29; Lu.
  6.27
  7.21. Not every one *that* s-*ith* unto
  8. 9. I s. to this man, Go ; Lu.7.8
  11. 7. Jesus began *to* s. unto the
  15. 5. But ye s., Whosoever shall
  16.13. Whom do men s. that I the
  15. But whom s. ye that I am ;
  Mar.8.29; Lu.9.20
  17.10. Why then s. the scribes
  21.16. Hearest thou what these s.
  23. 3. for they s., and do not
  30. And s., If we had been
  24. 5. s-*ing,* I am Christ; and shall
  27.11. Je.said unto him, Thou s-*est* ;
  Mar.15.2 ; Lu.23.3
  33. is *to* s., a place of a skull
Mar. 5.41. Damsel, I s. unto thee, arise
  12.35. How s. the scribes that Ch.
Lu. 3. 8. begin not *to* s. within yours.
  13.26. Then shall ye begin *to* s.
  22.70. unto them, Ye s. that I am
Jo. 1.22. What s-*est* thou of thyself
  38. Rabbi, which *is to* s., being
  4.35. s. not ye, There are yet four
  8.48. s. we not well that thou art
  54. of whom ye s., that he is your
  18.37. Thou s-*est* that I am a king
Act.21.23. this that we s. to thee
Ro. 2.22. Thou *that* s-*est* a man should
  3.19. things soever the law s-*ith*
Gal. 3.17. And this I s., that the cove.
  4. 1. Now I s., That the heir
²Ti. 2. 7. Consider what I s.; and the
Phile. 19. albeit I *do* not s. to thee
  21. will also do more than I s.
Heb.11.14.For they *that* s. such things
  32. what shall I more s.? for the
13. 6. So that we *may* boldly s.
Jas. 1.13. *Let* no man s. when he is
  2.14. though a man s. he hath
  4.13. Go to now, ye *that* s., To-day
  15. For that ye ought *to* s.

Rev. 22.17.the Spi. and the bride s., Co.
(*And all others in which it occurs, except the following* :)—

epō.
Mat. 5.11. and shall s. all manner of ev.
  22. whosoever shall s. to his bro.
  but whosoever shall s., Thou
  9. 5. whether is easier, *to* s., Thy
  or *to* s., Arise, and walk?
  15. 5. Whosoever shall s. to his fa.
  21. 3. if any man s. ought unto you
  21. if ye shall s. unto this moun.
  25. If we shall s., From heaven ;
  Mar. 11.31 ; Lu. 20.5.
  26. But if we shall s., Of men ;
  Mar. 11.32 ; Lu. 20.6.
  23.39. till ye shall s., Blessed
  24.23. if any man shall s. unto you
  26. Wherefore if they shall s.
  48. and if that evil servant sh. s.
  26.44. tine, s-*ing* the same words
  64. Thou *hast* s-*id* : nevertheless
  27.21. unto you ? They s-*id,* Barab.
  25. all the people, and s-*id,* His
  43. for he s-*id,* I am the Son of
  63. remember that that de. s-*id*
  28. 6. for he is risen, as he s-*id*
  13. s. ye, His disciples came by
Mar. 1.44. See thou s. nothing to any
  2. 9. *to* s. to the sick of the palsy
  or *to* s., Arise, and take up
  4.39. and s-*id* unto the sea, Peace
  6.16. Herod..s-*id,* It is John, wh.
  24. And she s-*id,* The head of J.
  7.11. If a man shall s. to his father
  11. 3. if any man s. unto you, Why
  do ye this ? s. ye that the Lo.
  23. he shall have whats. he s-*ith*
  14.14. s. ye to the goodman of the
  16. and found as he *had* s-*id* un.
  16. 7. see him, as he s-*id* unto you.
  8. neither s-*id* they any thing
Lu. 5.23. Whether is easier, *to* s.
  or *to* s., Rise up and walk
  7. 7. but s. in a word, and my
  40. Simon, I have somew. *to* s.
  And he saith, Master, s. on.
  10.10. the streets of the sa., and s.
  12.11. answer, or what ye *shall* s.
  12. same hour, what ye oug. *to* s.
  45. But and if that servant s.
  13.35. time come when ye *shall* s.
  14.17. *to* s. to them that were bidd.
  20.39. s-*id,* Mas.,thou *hast* well s-*id*
  24.24. even so as the wom. *had* s-*id*
Jo. 1.30. he of whom I s-*id,* After me
  4.17. Thou *hast* well s-*id* I have
  5.12. What man is that *which* s-*id*
  8.55. and if I *should* s., I know hi.
  10.34. your law, I s-*id,* Ye are gods
  36. because I s-*id,* I am the Son
  11.28. And *when* she *had* so s-*id*
  s-*ing,* The Master is come
  40. s-*id* I not unto thee, that, if
  42. because of the people..I s-*id*
  12. 6. This he s-*id,* not that he car.
  27. and what *shall* I s. ? Father
  39. because that Esaias s-*id* aga.
  12.49. what I *should* s., and what I
  14.26. whatsoever I *have* s-*id* unto
  28. how I s-*id* unto you, I go
  ye would rejoice, beca. I s-*id*
  15.20. the word that I s-*id* unto
  16. 4. I s-*id* not unto you at the
  15. therefore s-*id* I, that he sha.
  18.21. they know what I s-*id*
Act. 2.34. The Lord s-*id* unto my Lord
  3.22. s-*id* unto the fathers, A pro.
  4.23. and elders *had* s-*id* unto the.
  25. mouth of..David *hast* s-*id*
  7.26. s-*ing,* Sirs, ye are brethren
  27. thrust him away, s-*ing,* Who

Act. 7.37. *which* s-*id* unto the children
  40. s-*ing* unto Aaron, Make us
Ro. 10. 6. s. not in thine heart, Who
1Co. 1.15. Lest any *should* s. that I had
  10.28. But if any man s. unto you
  11.22. What *shall* I s. to you
    24. he brake it, and s-*id*
  12. 3. no man can s. that Jesus is
    15. If the foot *shall* s.
    16. And if the ear *shall* s.
    21. the eye cannot s. unto the
  15.27. But when he s-*ith*, All things
2Co. 6.16. as God *hath* s-*id*, I will dwell
Gal. 2.14. I s-*id* unto Peter before them
Col. 4.17. And s. to Archippus, Take
Tit. 1.12. a prophet of their own, s-*id*
Heb. 1. 5. For unto which of the an. s-*id*
  3.10. that generation, and s-*id*, T.
  10. 7. Then s-*id* I, Lo, I come
    30. we know him *that hath* s-*id*
  12.21. Moses s-*id*, I exceedingly
Jas. 2. 3. and s. unto him, Sit thou
    and s. to the poor
    11. For he *that* s-*id*, Do not c5.
    adultery, s-*id* also, Do not
    16. And one of you s. unto them
1Jo. 1. 6. If we s. that we have fellows.
    8. If we s. that we have no sin
    10. If we s. that we have not si.
  4.20. If a man s., I love God
Jude 9. but s-*ith*, The Lord rebuke
Rev. 7.14. And he s-*id* to me, These are
  17. 7. And the angel s-*id* unto me
  21. 5. that sat upon the throne s-*id*
    6. And he s-*id* unto me, It is
  22. 6. And he s-*id* unto me, These
    17. And *let* him that heareth s.
(Also) Mat.2.5,8; 3.7,15; 4.3,4; 8.10,13,
19,21,22,32 ; 9.2,3,4,11,12,15,22 ; 11.3,4,
25; 12.2,3,11,24,25,39,47,48,49 ; 13.10,11,
27,28,37,52,57; 14. 2,16,18,28,29 ; 15.3,10,
12,13,15,16,24,26,27,28,32,34 ; 16.2,6,8,
14,16,17,23,24 ; 17.4,7,11,17,19,20,22,24 ;
18. 3,21 ; 19.4,5,11,14,16,17,18,23,26,27,
28; 20.4,13,17,21,22,25,32 ; 21. 6,16,21,24,
27,28,29,30,38 ;   22.13,18,24,29,37,44 ;
24.2, 4; 25.8, 12, 22, 24, 26; 26.1, 10, 15,
18, 21, 23,25,26, 33, 35, 49, 50, 55, 61, 62,
63,66,73; 27.4,6,17,21,64; 28.5. Mar.1.17;
2.8,19 ; 3.32 ; 4.40 ; 5.7,34 ; 6.22,24,31,
37 ; 7.6,10,27,29; 8.5,20,34; 9.17,21,23,
29,36,39 ; 10.3,4,5,14,18,20,21,29,36,37,
38,39,51,52; 11.6,14,23,29; 12.7,15,16,
17,24,32,34,36 ; 13.2,21 ; 14.6.18,20,22,
24,48,62,72 ; 15.2,12,39; 16.15. Lu.1.13,
18,19,28,30,34,35,38,42,46,60,61 ; 2.10,
15,28,34,48,49 ; 3.12,13,14 ; 4.3,6,8,9,12,
23,24,43 ; 5.4,5,10,13,20,22,24,27,31,33;
34 ; 6.2,3,8,9,10; 7.9,13,14,20,22,31,40,
43,48,50; 8.10,21,22,25,28,30,45,46,48,52;
9.3,9,12,13,14,19,20,29, 33, 41, 43, 48, 49,
50,54,55,57,58,59,60,61,62 ; 10.18,21,23,
26,27,28,29,30,35,37,40,41 ; 11.1,2,5,7,15,
17,27,28,39,46,49 ; 12.13,14,15,18,20,22,
41,42 ; 13.2,7,12,15,20,23,32 ; 14.5,10,15,
16,18,19,20,21,22,23,25 ; 15.11,12,17,21,
22,27,29,31; 16.2,3,6,7,15,24,25,27,30,31;
17.1,5,6,14,17,19, 20,22,37 ; 18.4,6,16,19,
21,22,24,26,27,28,29,31,41,42 ; 19.5,8,9,
12,13,17,19,24,25,30,32,33,34,39,40; 20.3,
8,13,16,17,23,24,25,34,41,42,45; 21.3,5,8;
22.8,9,10,15,17,25,31,33,34,35, 36, 38, 40,
46,48,49,51,52,56,58,60,61,67,70,71; 23.4,
14,22,28,43,46; 24.5,17,18,19,25,32,38,41.
44,46. Jo.1.22,23,25,33,38,42,46,48,50:2,
16,18,19,20,22;3.2,3,7,9,10,26,27,28;4.10,
13,17,27,32,48,52,53; 5.11,14,19; 6.10,25,
26,28,29,30,32,34,35, 36, 41,43, 53, 59, 60,
61,67; 7.3,9, 16, 20, 21, 33,35, 36,38, 42,
45,52 ; 8.7,10,11,13,14,21,23,24,25,28,39,
41,42,48,52,57,58; 9.7,11,12,15,17,20,23,
24,25,26,28,30,34,35,36,37,39,40,41; 10.7,

---

26 ; 11. 4,11,12,14,16,21,25,34,37,41,49,
12.7,19,30,35,41,44 ; 13.7,11,12,21,33 ;
14.23 ; 16.17,19 ;17.1 ; 18.4,6,7,11,25,29,
30,31,33,37,38 ; 19.21,24,30; 20.14,17,20,
21,22,25,26,28 ; 21.6,17,20,23 ; Act.1.7,
11,15,24; 2.37 ; 3.4,6 ; 4.8,19,24; 5.3,8,
9,19,29,35 ; 6.2 ; 7.1,3,7,33,35,56,60 ;
8.20,24,29,30,31,34,37; 9.5,6,10,15,17,34,
40 ; 10.3,4,14,19,21,22,34; 11.8,13 ; 12.8,
11,15,17 ; 13.2,10,16,22,46; 14.10 ; 15.7,
36; 16.18,20,31; 17.32; 18.6,14,21 ; 19.2,
3,4,15,21,25; 20.10,18,35; 21.11,14,20,
39; 22.8,10,13,14,19,21,25,27; 23.1,3,4,
11,14,20,23 ; 24.20,22 ; 25.9,10 ; 26.15,
29; 27.21,31 ; 28.21,26,29.
epō epos.   (*to say* the word.)
Heb.7. 9. And *as I may* so s., Levi also
antepō
Act. 4.14. could s. nothing *against* it
phēmi.   [26.34,27.11
Mat. 4. 7. Jesus s-*id* unto him ; 19.21,
  8. 8. The centurion ans. and s-*id*
  13.28. He s-*id* unto them, An enem.
    29. But he s-*id*, Nay ; lest while
  14. 8. s-*id*, Give me here John Bap.
  17.26. Jesus s-*ith* unto him, Then
  21.27. And he s-*id* unto them, Nei.
  25.21, 23. His lord s-*id* unto him
  26.61. This fellow s-*id*, I am able
  27.23. the governor s-*id*, Why, wh.
    65. Pilate s-*id* unto them, Ye ha.
Mar.14.29.But Peter s-*id* unto him, Al.
Lu. 7.40. And he s-*ith*, Master, say on
    44. s-*id* unto Simon, Seest thou
  22.58. another saw him, and s-*id*
    70. And he s-*id* unto them, Ye
  23. 3. he answered him and s-*id*
Jo. 1.23. He s-*id*, I am the voice of
  9.38. And he s-*id*, Lord, I believe
Act. 2.38. Peter s-*id* unto them, Repe.
  7. 2. And he s-*id*, Men, brethren
  8.36. and the eunuch s-*id*, See, he.
  10.28. he s-*id* unto them, Ye know
    30. And Cornelius s-*id*, Four da.
    31. and s-*id*, Cornelius, thy pra.
  16.30. and s-*id*, Sirs, what must I
    37. But Paul s-*id* unto them
  17.22. and s-*id*, Ye men of Athens
  19.35. he s-*id*, Ye men of Ephesus
  21.37. Who s-*id*, Canst thou speak
  22. 2. the more silence: and he s-*ith*
    27. art thou a Roman ? He s-*id*
    28. And Paul s-*id*, But I was fr.
  23. 5. Then s-*id* Paul, I wist not
    17. and s-*id*, Bring this young
    18. and s-*id*, Paul the prisoner
    35. I will hear thee, s-*id* he, who
  25. 5. Let them therefore, s-*id* he
    22. Then Agrippa s-*id* unto Fes.
    To morrow, s-*id* he, thou sh.
    24. And Festus s-*id*, King Agrip.
  26. 1. Then Agrippa s-*id* unto Paul
    24. Festus s-*id* with a loud voice
    25. But he s-*id*, I am not mad
    28. Then Agrippa s-*id* unto Pau.
    32. Then s-*id* Agrippa unto Fes.
1Co. 6.16. for two s-*ith* he, shall be one
  7.29. But this I s. brethren, the ti.
  10.15. wise men ; judge ye what I s.
    19. What s. I then ? that the id.
  15.50. Now this I s., brethren, that
2Co.10.10. For his letters, s. they, are
Heb. 8. 5. for, See, s-*ith* he, that thou
    ereō.
Mat. 7. 4. Or how *wilt* thou s. to thy
    22. Many *will* s. to me that
  13.30. I *will* s. to the reapers, Gath.
  17.20. ye *shall* s. unto this mounta.
  21. 3. ye *shall* s., The Lord hath
    25. he *will* s. unto us, Why
  25.34. Then *shall* the King s. unto
    40. *shall* answer and s.; Lu.13.25

Mat.25.41. Then *shall* he s. also unto
  26.75. of Jesus, *which* s-*id* unto hi.
Mar.11.31.he *will* s., Why then did ye
Lu. 2.24. accordi. to that *which* is s-*id*
  4.12. It *is* s-*id*, Thou shalt not te.
    23. Ye *will* surely s. unto me th.
  12.19. And I *will* s. to my soul
  13.27. he *shall* s., I tell you, I know
  14. 9. come and s. to thee, Give th.
  15.18. and *will* s. unto him, Father
  17. 7. *will* s. unto him by and by
    8. And *will* not rather s. unto
    21. Neither *shall* they s., Lo he.
    23. And they *shall* s. to you, See
  19.31. thus *shall ye* s. unto him
  20. 5. he *will* s., Why then believed
  22.11. And ye *shall* s. unto the go.
    13. and found as he *had* s-*id* un.
  23.29. in the which they *shall* s.
Jo. 4.18. in that s-*idst* thou truly
  6.65. Therefore s-*id* I unto you
  12.50. even as the Father s-*id* unte
Act.13.34. he s-*id* on this wise, I will
  17.28. of your own poets *have* s-*id*
Ro. 3. 5. of God, what *shall* we s.
  4. 1. What *shall* we then s. that
  6. 1. What *shall* we s. then ; 7.7,
    8.31,9,14,30
  9.19. Thou *wilt* s. then unto me
    20. *Shall* the thing formed s. to
  11.19. Thou *wilt* s. then, The bran.
1Co.14.16. *shall* he that..the unlearn. s.
    23. *will* they not s. that ye are
  15.35. But some man *will* s., How
2Co. 12. 6. for I *will* s. the truth
    9. And he s-*id* unto me,My gr.
Phi. 4. 4. and again I s., Rejoice
Heb.1.13. s-*id* he at any time, Sit on
  4. 3. as he s-*id*, As I have sworn
    7. as it *is* s-*id*, To day if ye wi.
  10. 9. Then he s-*id*, Lo, I come to
  13. 5. for he *hath* s-*id*, I will nev.
Jas. 2.18. Yea, a man *may* s.,Thou ha.
Rev. 7.14. And I s-*id* unto him, Sir, th.
  19. 3. And again they s-*id*, Allelu
    proereō.
Ro. 9.29. as Esaias s-*id* before, Except
2Co. 7. 3. I *have* s-*id* before, that ye are
Gal. 1. 9. As we s-*id before*, so say I
Heb.10.15.after that he *had* s-*id before*
    laleō.
Mar. 9. 6. For he wist not what *to* s.
Jo. 8.25. Even the same that I s-*id*
    26. I have many things to s. and
  16. 6. because I *have* s-*id* these th.
    18. we cannot tell what he s-*ith*
  18.20. in secret *have* I s-*id* nothing
    21. what I *have* s-*id* unto them
Act. 3.22. whatsoever he *shall* s. unto
  23. 7. And *when* he had so s-*id*
    18. hath something *to* s. unto
  26.22. and Moses *did* s. should co.
Ro. 3.19. it s-*ith* to them who are und.
1Co. 9. 8. s. I these things as a man
Heb. 5. 5. but he *that* s-*id* unto him
  11.18. Of whom it *was* s-*id*, That in
    reō.
Mat. 5.21, 27,33. it *was* s-*id* by them of
    31. It *hath been* s-*id*, Whosoever
    38. that it *hath been* s-*id*, An eye
    43. it *hath been* s-*id*, Thou shalt
Ro. 9.12. It *was* s-*id* unto her, The
    26. it *was* s-*id* unto; Rev.6.11
    phaskō.
Act.24. 9. s-*ing* that these things were
Rev. 2. 2. tried them *which* s. they are
apophthenggomai.
Act. 2.14. lifted up his voice, and s-*id*
polus logos.
Heb. 5.11. we have *many things to* s.
    hos eimi,   (*that is a* gift.
Mar. 7.11. Corban, *that is to* s., **a gift**

235

SAYING, [*noun,*]   -*s.*
logos.
Mat.7.24,26. heareth these s-s of mine
    28. Jesus had ended these s-s
    15.12. after they heard this s.
    19. 1. Je. had finish. these s-s ; 26.1
    11. All men cannot receive this s.
    22. the young man heard that s.
    28.15. this s. is commonly reported
Mar. 7.29. For this s. go thy way ; the
    8.32. And he spake that s. openly
    9.10. And they kept that s. with
    10.22. he was sad at that s., and
Lu.   1.29. she was troubled at his s.
    6.47. and heareth my s-s, and
    9.28. eight days after these s-s
    44. Let these s-s sink down
Jo.   4.37. And herein is that s. true
    39. for the s. of the woman, wh.
    6.60. This is an hard s.; who can
    7.36. What manner of s. is this
    40. when they heard this s.
    8.51, 52. If a man keep my s.
    55. know him, and keep his s.
    10.19. among the Jews for these s-s
    12.38. That the s. of Esaias the
    14.24. keepeth not my s-s: and the
    15.20. if they have kept my s.
    18. 9. That the s. might be fulfilled
    32. That the s. of Jesus might
    19. 8. Pilate therefo. heard that s.
    13. heard that s., he brought
    21.23. Then went this s. abroad
Act. 6. 5. the s. pleased the whole
    7.29. Then fled Moses at this s.
    16.36. told this s. to Paul, The
Ro.   3. 4. be justified in thy s-s, and
    13. 9. comprehended in this s.
1Co. 15.54. to pass the s. that is written
1Ti.   1.15. This is a fai. s.; 4.9; Tit.3.8
    3. 1. This is a true s.
2Ti.   2.11. It is a faithful s.: For
Rev.19. 9. These are the true s-s of God
    22. 6. These s-s are faithful and
    7. bless. is he that keep. the s-s
    9. of them which keep the s-s
    10. Seal not the s-s of the prop.
rēma.
Mar. 9.32. understo. not that s.; Lu.9.45
Lu.   1.65. and all these s-s were noised
    2.17. made known abroad the s.
    50. understood not the s. which
    51. his mother kept all these s-s
    7. 1. when he had ended all his s-s
    9.45. feared to ask him of that s.
    18.34. and this s. was hid from
lalia.
Jo.   4.42. not because of thy s.
legō.   (*speaking* these things.
Act.14.18. And with these s-s scarce

SCALES.
lepis.
Act. 9.18. his eyes as it had been s.

SCARCE.
molis.
Act.14.18. s. restrained they the people
    27. 7. s. were come over against

SCARCELY.
molis.
Ro.   5. 7. s. for a righteous man will
1Pet. 4.18. if the righteous s. be saved

SCARLET.
kokkinos.
Mat.27.28.and put on him a s. robe
Heb. 9.19. with water, and s. wool, and
Rev.17. 3. upon a s. coloured beast, full
    4. in purple and s. colour, and
    18.12. purple, and silk, and s., and
    16. purple, and s., and decked
236

SCATTER.   -*ed, -eth.*
skorpizō.
Mat. 12.30.not with me s-eth abroad
Lu. 11.23. gathereth not with me s-eth
Jo. 10.12. wolf catcheth them,and s-eth
    16.32. now come, that ye..be s-ed
diaskorpizō.
Mat. 26.31.the flock shall be s-ed abroad
Mar.14.27.and the sheep shall be s-ed
Lu.   1.51. he hath s-ed the proud in
Jo. 11.52. of G that were s-ed abroad
riptō.
Mat. 9.36. and were s-ed abroad, as
dialuō.
Act. 5.36. were s-ed, and brought to
diaspeirō.
Act. 8. 1. they were all s-ed abroad
    4. that were s-ed abroad ; 11.19
diaspora.   (in the dispersion.)
Jas. 1. 1. tribes which are s-ed abroad
1Pet. 1. 1. strangers s-ed throughout

SCEPTRE.
rabdos.
Heb. 1. 8. a s. of righteous. is the s. of

SCHISM.
schisma.
1Co.12.25. there should be no s. in

SCHOOL.
scholē.
Act.19. 9. daily in the s. of one Tyran.

SCHOOLMASTER.
paidagōgos.
Gal. 3.24. the law was our s. to bring
    25. we are no longer under a s.

SCIENCE.
gnōsis.
1Ti. 6.20. oppositions of s. falsely so

SCOFFERS.
empaiktēs.
2Pet. 3. 3. shall come in the last day s.

SCORCH,   -*ed.*
kaumatizō.
Mat.13. 6. sun was up, they were s-ed
Mar. 4. 6. it was s-ed ; and because it
Rev.16. 8. and to s. men with fire
    9. And men were s-ed with gre.

SCORPION,   -*s.*
skorpios.
Lu. 10.19. to tread on serpents and s-s
    11.12. will he offer him a s.
Rev. 9 3. as the s-s of the earth have
    5. as the torment of a s., when
    10. tails like unto s-s, and there

SCOURGE, [*noun.*]
phragellion.
Jo.   2.15. when he had made a s. of

SCOURGE, [*verb,*]   -*ed, -eth.*
mastigoō.
Mat.10.17.and they will s. you in their
    20.19. to mock, and to s., and
    23.34. some of them shall ye s.
Mar.10.34.and shall s. him, and shall
Lu. 18.33. And they shall s. him, and
Jo. 19. 1. took Jesus, and s-ed him
Heb.12. 6. and s-eth every son whom
mastizō.
Act.22.25. Is it lawful for you to s.
phragelloō.   [Mar.15.15
Mat.27.26.when he had s-ed Jesus ;

SCOURGING, [*noun,*]   -*s.*
mastix.
Act.22.24. should be examined by s.
Heb.11.36.of cruel mockings and s-s

SCRIBE,   -*s.*
grammateus.
Mat. 2. 4. chief priests and s-s ; 16.21,
    21.15,26,3 ; Mar.8.31,11.27,
    14.1,43; Lu.5.21,9.22,19.47,
    20.1,19,22.2,66,23.10
    5.20. righteousness of the s-s and
    7.29. authority, and not as the s-s
    8.19. a certain s. came, and said
    9. 3. behold, certain of the s-s sa
    12.38. certain of the s-s and of the
    13.52. every s. which is instructed
    15. 1. came to Jesus s-s and Phari.
    17.10. Why then say the s-s that
    20.18. chief priests and unto the s-s
    23. 2. The s-s and the Pharisees sit
    §13. woe unto you, s-s and Phar.;
    14,15,23,25,27,29 ; Lu.11.44
    34. prop., and wise men, and s-s
    26.57. the s-s and the elders ; 27.41
Mar. 1.22. authority, and not as the s-s
    2. 6. certain of the s-s sitting the.
    16. when the s-s and Pharisees
    3.22. the s-s which came down
    7. 1. certain of the s-s, which ca.
    5. the Pharisees and s-s asked
    9.11. Why say the s-s that Elias
    14. the s-s questioning with them
    16. he asked the s-s, What ques.
    10.33. chief priests, and unto the s-s
    11.18. the s-s and chief priests hea.
    12.28. one of the s-s came, and ha.
    32. the s. said unto him, Well
    35. How say the s-s that Christ
    38. Beware of the s-s, which love
    14.53. and the elders and the s-s ;
    15.1 ; Act.4.5,6.12
    15.31. among themsel. with the s-s
Lu.   5.30. their s-s and Pharisees mur.
    6. 7. the s-s and Pharisees watched
    11.53. the s-s and the Pharisees be.
    15. 2. the Pharisees and s-s murm.
    20.39. certain of the s-s answering
    46. Beware of the s-s, which des.
Jo.   8. 3. the s-s and Pharisees brought
Act.23. 9. the s-s that were of the Pha
1Co. 1.20. the wise? where is the s.

SCRIP.
pēra.
Mat.10.10.Nor s. for your journey
Mar. 6. 8. no s., no bread, no money
Lu.   9. 3. neither staves, nor s.
    10. 4. Carry neither purse, nor s.
    22.35. and s., and shoes, lacked ye
    36. him take it, and likew. his s

SCRIPTURE,   -*s.*
gramma.
2Ti. 3.15. thou hast known the holy s-s
graphē.
Mat.21.42.Did ye never read in the s-s
    22.29. Ye do err,not knowing the s-s
    26.54. shall the s-s be fulfilled
    56. that the s-s of the prophets
Mar.12.10.have ye not read this s.
    24. because ye know not the s-s
    14.49. the s-s must be fulfilled
    15.28. the s. was fulfilled, which
Lu.   4.21. This day is this s. fulfilled
    24.27. in all the s-s the things
    32. he opened to us the s-s
    45. they might understand the s-s
Jo.   2.22. they believed the s., and the
    5.39. Search the s-s ; for in them·
    7.38. as the s. hath said, out of
    42. Hath not the s. said
    10.35. the s. cannot be broken
    13.18. that the s. may be fulfilled ;
    17.12,19.24,28
    19.36. that the s. should be fulfilled
    37. again another s. saith
    20. 9. as yet they knew not the s.

Act. 1.16. this s. must needs have
8.32. The place of the s. which
35. began at the same s.
17. 2. rea. with them out of the s-*s*
11. searched the s-*s* daily
18.24. man, and mighty in the s-*s*
28. shewing by the s-*s* that
Ro. 1. 2. by his proph. in the holy s-*s*
4. 3. For what saith the s.
9.17. For the s.saith unto Pharaoh
10.11. For the s. saith, Whosoever
11. 2. Wot ye not what the s. saith
15. 4. pati. and comfort of the s-*s*
16.26. by the s-*s* of the prophets
¹Co. 15. 3. our sins according to the s-*s*
4. third day according to the s-*s*
Gal. 3. 8. the s., forseeing that God
22. the s. hath concluded all
4.30. Neverthe. what saith the s.
¹Ti. 5.18. For the s. saith, Thou shalt
²Ti. 3.16. All s. is given by inspiration
Jas. 2. 8. according to the s., Thou sh.
23. the s. was fulfilled which
4. 5. Do ye think that the s. saith
¹Pet. 2. 6. also it is contained in the s.
²Pet. 1.20. that no prophecy of the s. is
3.16. as they do also the other s-*s*

SCROLL.
biblion.
Rev. 6.14. heaven departed as a s. when

SEA, (See *Coast*,)   -s.
thalassa.
Mat. 4.15. by the way of the s., beyond
18. the s. of Galilee ; 15.29 ;
Mar. 1.16; Jo. 6.1
a net into the s.; Mar.1.16
8.24. aro. a great tempest in the s.
26. rebuked the winds and the s.
27. winds and the s.; Mar. 4.39
32. place into the s.; Mar. 5.13
13. 1. house, and sat by the s. side
47. that was cast into the s., and
14.24. the midst of the s.; Mar.6.47
25. unto them, walking on the s.
17.27. go thou to the s., and cast
18. 6. drown. in the depth of the s.
21.21. and be thou cast into the s.
23.15. for ye compass s. and land
Mar. 2.13. he went forth again by the s.
3. 7. with his disciples to the s.
4. 1. again to teach by the s. side
sat in the s.; and the whole
multitude was by the s.
39. and said unto the s., Peace
5. 1. unto the other side of the s.
13. and were choked in the s.
21. and he was nigh unto the s.
6.48, 49. walk.upon the s.; Jo.6.19
9.42. were cast into the s.; Lu.17.2
11.23. be thou cast into the s.
Lu. 17. 6. be thou planted in the s.
21.25. the s. and the waves roaring
Jo. 6.16. disci. went down unto the s.
17. and went over the s. toward
18. And the s. arose by reason
22, 25. the other side of the s.
21. 1. disciples at the s. of Tiberias
7. did cast himself into the s.
Act. 4.24. and earth, and the s.; 14.15
7.36. in the Red s., and in the wi.
10. 6. whose house is by the s. side
32. Simon a tanner by the s. side
17.14. to go as it were to the s.
27.30. the boat into the s., under
38. out the wheat into the s.
40. committed them. unto the s.
28. 4. tho. he hath escaped the s.
Ro. 9.27. the sand of the s.; Rev. 20.8
¹Co. 10. 1. and all passed through the s.
2. in the cloud and in the s.

²Co. 11.26. in perils in the s., in perils
Heb.11.12.by the s. shore innumerable
29. passed through the Red s.
Jas. 1. 6. wav. is like a wave of the s.
Jude 13. Raging waves of the s., foa.
Rev. 4. 6. a s. of glass like unto crystal
5.13. and such as are in the s.
7. 1. blow on the ear.,nor on the s.
2. hurt the earth and the s.
3. neither the s., nor the trees
8. 8. was cast into the s.; and the
part of the s. became blood
9. which were in the s., and had
10. 2. right foot upon the s., and
5. upon the s. and upon the
6. and the s., and the things
8. standeth upon the s. and
12.12. the earth and of the s.! for
13. 1. upon the sand of the s., and
a beast rise up out of the s.
14. 7. and earth, and the s., and
15. 2. as it were a s. of glass ming.
stand on the s. of glass, hav.
16. 3. his vial upon the s.; and it
every living soul died in the s.
18.17. as many as trade by s.,stood
19. that had ships in the s. by
21. and cast it into the s., saying
20.13. And the s. gave up the dead
21. 1. and there was no more s.
dithalassos.
Act.27.41. into a place *where two* s-*s met*
pelagos.
Act.27. 5. sailed over the s. of Cilicia
enalios.
Jas. 3. 7. and of *things in the* s., is

SEAL, [noun,]   -s.
sphragis.
Ro. 4.11. a s. of the righteousness of
¹Co. 9. 2. the s. of mine apostleship
²Ti. 2.19. having this s., The Lord kn.
Rev. 5. 1. backsi., sealed with seven s-*s*
2. and to loose the s-*s* thereof
5. loose the seven s-*s* thereof
9. and to open the s-*s* thereof
6. 1. Lamb opened one of the s-*s*
3, 5,7,9,12. opened the 2d s., &c.
7. 2. having the s. of the living G.
8. 1. he had opened the seventh s.
9. 4. have not the s. of God in th.
sphragizō.
Jo. 3.33. *hath set* to his s. that God is
Rev.20. 3. him up, and *set a* s. upon hi.

SEAL, [verb,]   -ed, -ing.
sphragizō.
Mat.27.66. s-*ing* the stone, and setting
Jo. 6.27. him *hath* God the Father s-*ed*
Ro. 15.28. and have s-*ed* to them this
²Co. 1.22. *Who hath* also s-*ed* us, and
Eph. 1.13. ye *were* s-*ed* with that holy
4.30. whereby ye *are* s-*ed* unto the
Rev. 7. 3. till we *have* s-*ed* the servants
4. nu. of them *which were* s-*ed*
were s-*ed* an hundred and fo.
5, 6,7,8. were s-*ed* twelve thou.
10. 4. s. *up* those things which the
22.10. s. not the sayings of the pro.
katasphragizō.
Rev. 5. 1. backside, s-*ed* with seven se.

SEAM.
arraphos.
Jo. 19.23. now the coat was *without* s.

SEARCH,   -ed, -eth, -ing.
ereunaō.
Jo. 5.39. s. the scriptures; for in th.
7.52. s., and look : for out of Gal.
Ro. 8.27. And he *that* s-*eth* the hearts
¹Co. 2.10. the Spirit s-*eth* all things
¹Pet. 1.11. s-*ing* what, or what manner

Rev. 2.23. I am he *which* s-*eth* the reins
exereunaō.
¹Pet. 1.10. enquired and s-*ed diligently*
exetazō.
Mat. 2. 8. s. diligently for the young
anakrinō.
Act.17.11. s-*ed* the scriptures daily, wh.

SEARED.
kautēriazō.
¹Ti. 4. 2. conscience s. *with a hot iron*

SEASON,   -s.
kairos.
Mat.21.41.him the fruits in their s-*s*
24.45. give them meat in due s.
Mar.12. 2. And at the s. he ; Lu. 20.10
Lu. 1.20. shall be fulfilled in their s.
4.13. he depart. from him for a s.
12.42. portion of meat in *due* s.
13. 1. were present at that s. some
Jo 5. 4. at a certain s. into the pool
Act. 1. 7. to know the times or the s-*s*
13.11. not seeing the sun for a s.
14.17. and fruitful s-*s*, filling our
24.25. when I have a *convenient* s.
Gal. 6. 9. in due s. we shall reap
¹Th. 5. 1. But of the times and the s-*s*
proskairos.
Heb.11.25. enj. the pleas. of sin *for a* s.
eukairōs.
²Ti. 4. 2. be instant *in* s., out of sea.
akairōs.
²Ti. 4. 2. be instant in season, *out of* s.
chronos.
Act.19.22. hims. stayed in Asia for a s.
20.18. have been with you at all s-*s*
Rev. 6.11. should rest yet for a little s.
20. 3. he must be loosed a little s.
hōra.
Jo. 5.35. willing for a s. to rejoice in
²Co. 7. 8. though it were but for a s.
Phile. 15. he therefore departed for a s.
oligos.
Pet. 1. 6. though now *for* a s., if need

SEASON, [verb,]   -ed.
artuō.
Mar. 9.50. wherewith *will* ye s. it
Lu. 14.34. wherewith *shall* it *be* s-*ed*
Col. 4. 6. alway with grace, s-*ed* with

SEAT, (See *Judgment*,)   -s.
thronos.
Lu. 1.52. the mighty from their s-*s*
Rev. 2.13. where Satan's s. is
4. 4. twenty s-*s*: and upon the s-*s*
11.16. sat before God on their s-*s*
13. 2. and his s., and great author.
16.10. upon the s. of the beast
kathedra.   [Mar.11.15
Mat.21.12.s-*s* of them that sold doves ;
23. 2. the Pharisees sit in Moses' s.
prōtokathedria.   [Mar.12.39
Mat.23. 6. *chief* s-*s* in the synagogues ·
Lu. 11.43. love the *uppermost* s-*s* in.
20.46. and the *highest* s-*s* in the

SECOND.
deuteros.
Mat.21.30. he came to the s., and said
22.26.Likewise the s. also, and the
39. the s. is like unto it, Thou
26.42. went away again the s. *time*
Mar.12.21.the s. took her, and died
31. the s. is like, namely this
14.72. the s. *time* the cock crew
Lu. 12.38. he shall come in the s. watch
19.18. the s. came, saying, Lord
20.30. the s. took her to wife, and
Jo. 3. 4. can he enter the s. *time into*
4.54. This is again the s. miracle
21.16. again the s. *time*; Act.10.15

Act. 7.13. at the s. time Joseph was
12.10. past the first and the **s.** war.
13.33. also written in the **s.** psalm
¹Co. 15.47. the **s.** man is the Lord
²Co. 1.15. that ye might have a **s.** bene.
13. 2. I were present, the **s.** *time*
Tit. 3.10. after the first and **s.** admon.
Heb. 8. 7. have been sought for the **s.**
9. 3. after the **s.** veil, the tabern.
7. into the **s.** went the high pr.
28. shall he appear the **s.** *time*
10. 9. he may establish the **s.**
²Pet. 3. 1. This **s.** epistle, beloved, I
Rev. 2.11. not be hurt of the **s.** death
4. 7. the **s.** beast like a calf
6. 3. the **s.** seal, I heard the **s.** be.
8. 8. the **s.** angel sounded, and as
11.14. The **s.** woe is past ; and, be.
16. 3. the **s.** angel poured out his
20. 6. the **s.** death hath no power
14. This is the **s.** death
21. 8. brimstone : which is the **s.**
9. foundation..; the **s.** sapphire
deuteroprōtos.
Lu. 6. 1. on the **s.** sabb. *after the first*

SECONDARILY.
deuteros.
¹Co. 12.28. first apostles, **s.** prophets

SECRET, -*s.*
kruptos.
Mat. 6. 4. That thine alms may be in **s.**
Fath. which seeth in **s.**; 6.18
6.18. thy Father which is in **s.**
Lu. 8.17. For nothing is **s.**, that shall
11.33. putteth it in a **s.** place
Jo. 7. 4. that doeth any thing in **s.**
10. openly, but as it were in **s.**
18.20. and in **s.** have I said nothing
Ro. 2.16. when God shall judge the **s**-*s*
¹Co. 14.25. the **s**-*s* of his heart made
kruptō.
Mat.13.35. thin. *which have been kept* **s.**
apokruphos.
Mar.4.22. neither was anything *kept* **s.**
kruphē.
Eph.5.12. which are done of them *in* **s.**
sigaō.
Ro. 16.25. mystery, *which was kept* **s.**
tameion.
Mat.24.26. beh. he is in the **s.** *chambers*

SECRETLY.
kruptō.
Jo. 19.38. but **s.** for fear of the Jews
lathra.   (a *secret* one.)
Jo. 11.28. called Mary her sister **s.**

SECT.
hairesis.
Act. 5.17. which is the **s.** of the Saddu.
15. 5. certain of the **s.** of the Phar.
24. 5. of the **s.** of the Nazarenes
26. 5. straitest **s.** of our religion
28.22. for as concerning this **s.**

SECURE.
poieō amerimnos.
Mat.28.14.will persuade him, and **s.** you

SECURITY.
hikanos.
Act.17. 9. they had taken **s.** of Jason

SEDITION, *s.*
stasis.
Lu. 23.19. for a certain **s.** made in the
25. him that for **s.** and murder
Act.24. 5. and a mover of **s.** among
dichostasia.
Gal. 5.20. emulations, wrath, strife, **s**-*s*
238

SEDUCE.
planaō.
¹Jo. 2.26. concerning them *that* **s.** you
Rev. 2.20. to teach and to **s.** my serva.
apoplanaō.
Mar.13.22.to **s.** if it were possible

SEDUCERS.
goēs.
²Ti. 3.13. evil men and **s.** shall wax

SEDUCING.
planos.
¹Tim. 4.1. giving heed to **s.** spirits, and

SEE, -*est,-eth,-ing,Seen,Saw,-est.*
eideō.
Mat. 2. 2. for we *have* **s**-*n* his star in the
9. the star, which they **sa.** in
10. *When* they **sa.** the star, they
16. Herod, *when* he **sa.** that he
3. 7. *when* he **sa.** many of the Ph.
16. he **sa.** the Spirit of God desc.
4.16. sat in darkness **sa.** great lig.
18, 21. **sa.** two brethren
5. 1. **s**-*ing* the multitudes, he went
16. that they *may* **s.** your good
8.14. he **sa.** his wife's mother laid
18. Now *when* Jesus **sa.** great
34. *when* they **sa.** him, they bes.
9. 2. Jesus, **s**-*ing* their faith, said
8. But *when* the multitudes **sa.**
9. he **sa.** a man, named Matth.
11. And *when* the Pharis. **sa.** it;
12.2 ; Lu.7.39
22. and *when* he **sa.** her, he said
23. and **sa.** the minstrels and the
36. But *when* he **sa.** the multitu.
11. 8, 9. ye out *for to* **s.**; Lu.7.25,26
12.38. Master, we would **s.** a sign
13.15. at any time they *should* **s.**
17. have desired *to* **s.** those thin.
whi. ye see, and *have not* **s**-*n*
14.14. Jesus went forth, and **sa.** a
26. And *when* the disciples **sa.**;
21.20, 26.8.; Lu. 18.15
16.28. till they **s.** the Son of man
17. 8. they **sa.** no man ; Mar.9.8
18.31. So *when* his fellow-serva. **sa.**
20. 3. and **sa.** others standing idle
21.15. *when* chief pri. and scrib. **sa.**
19. And *when* he **sa.** a fig tree in
32. ye, *when* ye *had* **s**-*n* it, rep.
38. But *when* the husbandm. **sa.**
22.11. he **sa.** there a man which
23.39. Ye *shall* not **s.** me henceforth
24.15. *shall* **s.** the abom.; Mar.13.14
33. when ye *shall* **s.** all these th.;
Mar.13.29; Lu.21.31
25.37, 44. when **sa.** we thee an hu.
38. When **sa.** we thee a stranger
39. Or when **sa.** we thee sick, or
26.58. sat with the servants, *to* **s.**
71. another maid **sa.**; Mar.14.69
27. 3. *when* he **sa.** that he was con.
24. *When* Pilate **sa.** that he cou.
49. *let* us **s.** whether E.; Mar.15.36
54. **sa.** the earthquake, and tho.
28. 6. Come, **s.** the place where the
17. And *when* they **sa.** him, they
Mar. 1.10. he **sa.** the heavens opened
16. he **sa.** Simon and Andrew
19. he **sa.** James the son of Zeb.
2. 5. *When* Je. **sa.** their ; Lu.5.20
12. saying, We never **sa.** it on
14. he **sa.** Levi the son of Alph.
16. *when* scribes and Pharis. **sa.**
5. 6. But *when* he **sa.** Jesus afar
14. they went out *to* **s.** what it
16. they *that* **sa.** it told them
22. and *when* he **sa.** him, he fell
32. he looked round about *to* **s.**

Mar. 6.33. the people **sa.** them depart.
34. Jesus, when he came out, **sa.**
38. loaves have ye? go and **s.**
48. he **sa.** them toiling in rowing
49. But *when* they **sa.** him walk.
50. For they all **sa.** him, and
7. 2. And *when* they **sa.** some of
9. 1. till they *have* **s**-*n* the kingdo.
9. what things they *had* **s**-*n*
14. he **sa.** a great multitude
20. and *when* he **sa.** him, straig.
25. *When* Jesus **sa.** that the
38. we **sa.** one casting ; Lu.9.49
10.14. But *when* Jesus **sa.** it, he
11.13. **s**-*ing* a fig tree afar off havi.
20. they **s.** the fig tree dried up
12.15. me a penny, that I *may* **s.** it
34. *when* Jesus **s.** that he answ.
14.67. *when* she **sa.** Peter warming
15.32. that we *may* **s.** and believe
39. *when* the centurion..**sa.** that
16. 5. they **sa.** a young man sitting
Lu. 1.12. *when* Zacharias **sa.** him, he
29. *when* she **sa.** him, she was
2.15. *Let* us now go..and **s.** this
17. *when* they *had* **s**-*n* it, they
20. that they *had* heard and **s**-*n*
26. **s.** death, before he *had* **s**-*n*
30. For mine eyes *have* **s**-*n* thy
48. *when* they **sa.** him, they were
5. 2. **sa.** two ships standing by
8. *When* Simon Peter **sa.** it, he
12. who **s**-*ing* Jesus fell on his
26. We *have* **s**-*n* strange things
7.13. *when* the Lord **sa.** her, he
22. Jo. what things ye *have* **s**-*n*
8.20. stand without, desiring *to* **s.**
28. *When* he **sa.** Jesus, he cried
34. *When* they that fed them **sa.**
35. they went out *to* **s.** what was
36. They also *which* **sa.** it told
47. *when* the woman **sa.** that
9. 9. he desired *to* **s.** him
27. till they **s.** the kingdom of
32. they **sa.** his glory, and the
54. *when* his disci.Jas.andJo.**sa.**
10.24. kings have desired *to* **s.** those
whi. ye see, and *have not* **s**-*n*
31. *when* he **sa.** him, he passed
33. *when* he **sa.** him, he had co.
11.38. And *when* the Pharisee,**sa.** it
12.54. When ye **s.** a cloud rise out
13.12. *when* Jesus **sa.** her, he called
35. say unto you, Ye shall not **s.**
14.18. I must needs go and **s.** it
15.20. his father **sa.** him, and had
17.14. *when* he **sa.** them, he said
15. *when* he **sa.** that he was hea.
22. ye shall desire *to* **s.** one of
18.24. *when* Jesus **sa.** that he was
43. all the people, *when* they **sa.**
19. 3. he sought *to* **s.** Jesus who he
4. up into a sycamore tree *to* **s.**
5. he looked up, and **sa.** him
7. *when* they **sa.** it, they all
37. mighty wor.that they *had* **s**-*n*
20.13. reverence him *when* they **s.**
14. *when* the husbandmen **sa.**
21. 1. And he looked up, and **sa.**
2. he **sa.** also a certain poor w.
20. *when* ye *shall* **s.** Jerusalem
22.49. *Wh*..that were about him **sa.**
58. another **sa.** him, *and* said
23. 8. And *when* Herod **sa.** Jesus
was desirous *to* **s.** him of a
he hoped *to have* **s**-*n* some
47. *when* the centurion **sa.** what
24.24. but him they **sa.** not
Jo. 1.33. Upon whom thou *shalt* **s.** the
39. myself : handle me and **s.**
39, 46. Come and **s.**
They came and **s**-*a.*

Jo. 1.47. Jesus sa. Nathanael coming
84. under the fig tree, I sa.
3. 3. he cannot s. the kingdom of
4.29. Come, s. a man, which told
48. Except ye s. signs and wond.
5. 6. When Jesus sa. him lie, and
6.14. when they had s-n the mira.
22. when the people..sa. that
24. the people therefore sa. that
26. not because ye sa. the mira.
30. that we may s., and believe
8.56. to s. my day; and he sa. it
9. 1. he sa. a man which was bli.
11.31. when they sa. Mary, that she
32. where Jes. was, and sa. him
33. When Jesus therefore sa. her
34. unto him, Lord, come and s.
12. 9. that they might s. Lazarus
21. saying, Sir, we would s. Jes.
40. that they should not s. with
41. when he sa. his glory, and
18.26. Did not I s. thee in the gar.
19. 6. priests therefore and offi. sa.
26. When Jesus therefore sa. his
33. sa. that he was dead already
20. 8. to the sepulchre, and he sa.
20. disciples glad, when they sa.
25. Except I shall s.in his hands
29. they that have not s-n, and
21.21. Peter s-ing him saith to Jes.
Act. 2.27. thine H. One to s. cor.; 13.35
31. neither his flesh did s. cor.
3. 3. Who s-ing Peter and John
9. all the people saw him walk.
12. when Peter sa. it, he answe.
4.20. things which we have s-n
6.15. sa. his face as it had been
7.24. s-ing one of them suffer wr.
31. When Moses sa. it, he won.
34. I have seen, I have s-n (the
(seeing, I have seen.)
55. sa. the glory of God, and
8.39. that the eunuch sa. him no
9.12. hath s-n in a vision a man
27. how he had s-n the Lord in
35. dwelt at Lydda and Saron sa.
40. when she saw. Peter, she sat
10. 3. He sa. in a vision evidently
17. this vision which he had s-n
11. 5. in a trance I sa. a vision
6. I considered, and sa. fourfo.
13. he had s-n an angel in his
23. when he came, and had s-n
12. 3. because he sa. it pleased the
16. had opened the door, and sa.
13.12. the deputy, when he sa. wh.
36. unto his fathers, and sa. cor.
37. God raised again, sa. no cor.
45. when the Jews sa. the multi.
14.11. when the people sa. what
16.10. after he had s-n the vision
19. And when her masters sa.
27. s-ing the prison doors open
40. when they had s-n the breth.
19.21. there, I must also s. Rome
21.32. when they sa. the chief cap.
22.14. know his will, and s. that
18. And sa. him saying unto me
26.13. I sa. in the way a light from
16. these things..thou hast s-n
28. 4. when the barbarians sa. the
15. whom when Paul sa., he th.
20. to s. you, and to speak with
27. lest they should s. with their
Ro. 1.11. For I long to s. you, that I
1Co. 2. 9. Eye hath not s-n, nor ear
8.10. if any man s. thee which ha.
16. 7. I will not s. you now by the
Gal. 1.19. other of the apostles sa. I
2. 7. when they sa. that the gospel
14. when I sa. that they walked
6.11. Ye s. how large a letter I ha.

Phi. 1.27. that whether I come and s.
30. same conflict which ye sa. in
2.28. when ye s. him again, ye may
4. 9. received, and heard, and s-n
1Th. 2.17. to s. your face with great de.
3. 6. desiring greatly to s. us, as
10. that we might s. your face
1Ti. 6.16. no man hath s-n, nor can s.
2Ti. 1. 4. Greatly desiring to s. thee
Heb. 3. 9. proved me and sa. my works
11. 5. that he should not s. death
13. having s-n them afar off, and
23. because they sa. he was a
Jas. 5.11. have s-n the end of the Lord
1Pet. 1. 8. Whom having not s-n, ye
3.10. he that will love life, and s.
1Jo. 5.16. If any man s. his brother sin
3John 14. I trust I shall shortly s. thee
Rev. 1. 2. of all things that ye sa.
12. being turned, I sa. seven
17. when I sa. him, I fell at his
19. things which thou hast s-n
20. seven stars which thou sa-est
sev. candlesticks thou sa-est
4. 4. I sa. four and twenty elders
5. 1. I sa. in the right hand of
2. I sa. a strong angel procla.
6. 1. sa. when the Lamb opened
2. I sa., and behold a white
9. I sa. under the altar the so.
7. 1. after these things I sa. four
2. I sa. another angel; 14.6
8. 2. I sa. the seven angels which
9. 1. I sa. a star fall from heaven
17. thus I sa. the horses in the
10. 1. I sa. another mighty angel
5. the angel which I sa. stand
12.17. when the dragon sa. that he
13. 1. sa. a beast rise up out of the
2. the beast which I sa. was
3. I sa. one of his heads as it
15. 1. I sa. another sign in heaven
2. I sa. as it were a sea of glass
16.13. sa. three unclean spirits like
17. 3. I sa. a woman sit upon a
6. I sa. the woman drunken
when I sa. her, I wondered
8. The beast that thou sa-est
12, 16. ten horns whi. thou sa-est
15. The waters which thou sa-est
18. The woman whi. thou sa-est
18. 1. after these things I sa. ano.
7. am no widow, and shall s.
19.11. I sa. heaven opened, and
17. I sa. an angel standing in
19. I sa. the beast, and the kings
20. 1. I sa. an angel come down
4. I sa. thrones, and they sat
11. I sa. a great white throne
12. I sa. the dead, small and
21. 1. I sa. a new heaven and a
2. I John sa. the holy city, new
22. I sa. no temple therein: for
proeideo.
Act. 2.31. He s-ing this before spake of
idou.
Lu. 17.23. s. here; or, s. there; go not
Act. 8.36. s., here is water; what doth
ide.
Mar.13. 1. s. what manner of stones
blepo.
Mat. 6. 4, 6,18. thy Father which s-th
11. 4. things whi. ye do hear and s.
12.22. and dumb both spak. and sa.
13.13. because they s-ing s. not
14. s-ing ye shall s. and shall
16. ble. are your eyes, for they s.
17. things which ye s.; Lu. 10.24.
14.30. when he sa. the wind boiste.
15.31. when they sa. the dumb to
to walk, and the blind to s
24. 2. s. ye not all these things

Mar. 4.12. That s-ing they may s. and
5.31. Thou s-st the multitude thr.
8.18. Having eyes, s. ye not? and
23. he asked him if he sa. ought
24. said, I s. men as trees, walk.
13. 2. s-st thou these great building
Lu. 7.44. Simon s-st thou this woman
8.10. that s-ing they might not s.
16. which enter in may s. the li.
10.23. eyes which s. thin. that ye s.
21.30. ye s. and know of your own
Jo. 1.29. John s-th Jesus coming unto
5.19. what he s-th the Father do
9. 7. and washed, and came s-ing
15. eyes, and I washed, and do s.
19. how then doth he now s.
21. by what means he now s-th
25. whereas I was blind, now I s.
39. they which s. not might s.
they which s. might be made
41. now ye say, We s.; therefore
11. 9. because he s-th the light of
20. 1. s-th the stone taken away
5. sa. the linen clothes lying
21. 9. they sa. a fire of coals there
s-th the disciple whom Jesus
Act. 2.33. which ye now s. and hear
8. 6. s-ing the miracles which he
9. 8. eyes were opened, he sa. no
12. 9. angel; but thought he sa.
13.11. blind, not s-ing the sun for a
28.26. s-ing ye shall s., and not
Ro. 7.23. I s. another law in my mem.
8.24. hope that is s-n is not hope
for what a man s-th, why
25. if we hope for that we s. not
11. 8. eyes that they should not s.
(of not seeing.)
10. darken., that they may not s.
1Co. 1.26. For ye s. your calling, breth.
13.12. For now we s. through a gla.
16.10. s. that he may be with you
2Co. 4.18. which are s-n, but at the thi.
which are not s-n: ..which
are s-n are temporal; but
which are not s-n are eternal
12. 6. that which he s-th me to be
Eph. 5.15. s. then that ye walk circum.
Heb.2. 9. we s. Jesus, who was made
3.19. So we s. that they could not
10.25. more, as ye s. the day appr.
11. 1. evidence of things not s-n
3. things which are s-n were
7. of things not s-n as yet, mo.
12.25. s. that ye refuse not him
Jas. 2.22. s-st thou how faith wrought
Rev. 1.11. What thou s-st, write in a
12. I turned to s. the voice that
3.18. eyesalve, that thou mayest s.
6. 1, 3, 5, 7. Come and s.
9.20. which neither can s., nor
11. 9. nations shall s. their dead
16.15. he walk naked, and they s.
18. 9. when they shall s. the smo.
22. 8. I John sa. these things, and
when I had heard and s-n
emblepo.
Mar. 8.25. and sa. every man clearly
Act.22.11. when I could not s. for the
diablepo. [Lu.6.42
Mat. 7. 5. then shalt thou s. clearly to;
anablepo.
Lu. 7.22. how that the blind s., the
horao.
Mat. 8. 4. s. thou tell no man; but go
9.30. s. that no man know it
24. 6. s. that ye be not troubled
Mar. 1.44. s. thou say nothing to any
Lu. 1.22. perceived that he had s-n a
9.36. those things wh. they had s-n
16.23. and s-th Abraham afar off
24.23. saying, that they had also s-n

Jo. 1.18. No man *hath* s-n God at any
34. And I *sa*., and bare record
3.11. and testify that we *have* s-n
32. what he *hath* s-*n* and heard
4.45. *having* s-n all the things
5.37. any time, nor s-*n* his shape
6. 2. because they *sa*. his miracles
36. ye also *have* s-n me, and be.
46. Not that any man *hath* s-n
he *hath* s-n the Father
8.38. I speak that which I *have* s-n
ye do that which ye *have* s-n
57. and *hast* thou s-n Abraham
9.37. Thou *hast* both s-n him, and
14. 7. ye know him, and *have* s-n
9. he that *hath* s-n me *hath* s-n
15.24. now *have* they both s-n and
19.35. And he *that sa*. it bare reco.
20.18. that she *had* s-n the Lord
25. We *have* s-n the Lord
29. because thou *hast* s-n me
Act. 7.44. to the fashion that he *had* s-n
22.15. of what thou *hast* s-n and
¹Co. 9. 1. *have* I not s-n Jesus Christ
Col. 2. 1. as many as *have* not s-n
18. things which he *hath* not s-n
¹Th. 5.15. s. that none render evil for
Heb. 2. 8. But now we s. not yet all
8. 5. s., saith he, that thou make
11.27. as s-*ing* him who is invisible
Jas. 2.24. Ye s. then how that by wor.
¹Pet. 1. 8. *though* now ye s. him not
¹Jo. 1. 1. which we *have* s-n with our
2. we *have* s-n it, and bear wit.
3. That which we *have* s-n and
3. 6. *hath* not s-n him, neither
4.20. his bro. whom he *hath* s-n
love G. whom he *hath* not s-n
³John 11. that doeth evil *hath* not s-n
Rev.18.18. *when* they *sa*. the smoke of
19.10. s. thou do it not: I am thy
22. 9. saith he unto me, s. thou do

prooraō.
Act.21.29. For they had s-n *before* with

kathoraō.
Ro. 1.20. *are* clearly s-*n*, being underst.

theōreō.
Mat.28. 1. Mary *to* s. the sepulchre
Mar. 3.11. unclean spir., when they *sa*.
5.15. and s. him that was possessed
38. and s-*th* the tumult, and th.
16. 4. when they looked, they *sa*.
Lu. 24.37. supposed *that* they had s-n
39. and bones, as ye s. me have
Jo. 2.23. *when* they *sa*. the miracles
6.19. they s. Jes. walking on the
40. every one *which* s-*th* the Son
62. What and if ye *shall* s. the
7. 3. that thy disciples also *may* s.
8.51. saying, he *shall* never s. dea.
9. 8. they *which* before *had* s-n
10.12. s-*th* the wolf coming, and
12.45. And he *that* s-*th* me s-*th*
14.17. because it s-*th* him not, neit.
19. s-*th* me no more; but ye s.
16.10. and ye s. me no more
16, 17, 19.and ye *shall* not s. me
20. 6. and s-*th* the linen clothes lie
12. And s-*th* two angels in white
14. *sa*. Jesus standing, and kne.
Act. 3.16. this man strong, whom ye s.
4.13. Now *when* they *sa*. the bold.
7.56. I s. the heavens opened, an
9. 7. hearing a voice, but s-*ing* no
10.11. And *sa*. heaven opened, and
17.16. *when* he *sa*. the city wholly
19.26. ye s. and hear, that not alone
20.38. that they should s. his face
21.20. Thou s-*st*, brother, how many
25.24. ye s. this man, about whom
28. 6. and *sa*. no harm come to
¹Jo. 3.17. this world's good, and s-*th*
240

Rev.11.11.fear fell upon them *which sa*.

optomai.
Mat.5. 8. for they *shall* s. God
24.30. they *shall* s. the Son of man;
Mar.13.26 ; Lu.21.27
26.64. *shall* ye s. the So.; Mar.14.62
27. 4. that to us? s. thou to that
24. of this just person : s. ye to
28. 7. there *shall* ye s.; Mat.16.7
10. and there *shall* they s. me
Lu. 3. 6. all flesh *shall* s. the salvation
13.28. when ye *shall* s. Abraham
17.22. and ye *shall* not s. it
Jo. 1.50. thou *shalt* s. greater things
51. Hereafter ye *shall* s. heaven
3.36. not the Son *shall* not s. life
11.40. thou shouldest s. the glory
16.16, 17,19. and ye *shall* s. me
22. but I *will* s. you again
Act. 2.17. your young men *shall* s. vis.
13.31. he *was* s-n many days of th.
20.25. shall s. my face no more
Ro. 15.21. not spoken of, they *shall* s.
¹Co.15. 5. And that he *was* s-n of Ceph.
6, 7. After that, he *was* s-n of
8. And last of all he *was* s-n of
¹Ti. 3.16. s-n of angels, preached unto
Heb.12.14.with. which no man *shall* s.
13.23. if he come shortly, I *will* s.
¹Jo. 3. 2. for we *shall* s. him as he is
Rev. 1. 7. and every eye *shall* s. him
11.19. there *was* s-n in his temple
22. 4. And they *shall* s. his face

optanō.
Act. 1. 3. *being* s-n of them forty days

theaomai.
Mat. 6. 1. to be s-n of them : otherwise
11. 7. to s.? A reed shaken ; Lu.7.24
22.11. the king came in to s. the
23. 5. for *to be* s-n of men : they
Mar.16.11.alive, and *had been* s-n of
14. beli. not them *which had* s-n
Lu. 5.27. and *sa*. a publican, named
Jo. 1.32. I *sa*. the Spirit descending
38. *sa*. them following, *and*
6. 5. *sa*. a great company come
8.10. and *sa*. none but the woman
11.45. and *had* s-n the things which
Act. 1.11. in like manner as ye *have* s-n
8.18. And *when* Simon *sa*. that
21.27. *when* they *sa*. him in the
22. 9. that were with me *sa*. indeed
Ro. 15.24. *to* s. you in my journey, and
¹Jo. 4.12. No man *hath* s-n God at any
14. And we *have* s-n and do tes.

phainō.
Mat.6. 5. that they *may be* s-n of men
9.33. It *was* never so s-n in Israel

heuriskō.
Mat. 2.11. they *sa*. the young child

historeō.
Gal. 1.18. up to Jerusalem *to* s. Peter

phōtizō.
Eph. 3. 9. And *to make* all men s. what

muopazō.
²Pet.1. 9. blind, *and cannot* s. *afar off*

SEED, (See *Mustard-Seed*,) -s.
sperma.
Mat.13.24. a man which sowed good s.
27. didst not thou sow good s.
32. the least of all s-*s*; Mar.4.31
37. He that soweth the good s.
38. the good s. are the children
22.24. and raise up s. unto his bro.;
Mar.12.19 ; Lu.20.28
Mar.12.20.wife, and dying left no s.
21. neither left he any s.: and
22. seven had her, and left no s.
Lu. 1.55. to Abraham, and to his s. for
Jo. 7.42. That Christ cometh of the s.
8.33. We be Abraham's s., and

Jo. 8.37. I know that ye are Abra.'s s.
Act. 3.25. And in thy s. shall all the
7. 5. and to his s. after him, whe.
6. That his s. should sojourn in
13.23. Of this man's s. hath God
Ro. 1. 3. which was made of the s. of
4.13. not to Abraham, or to his s.
16. might be sure to all the s.
18. was spoken, So shall thy s.
9. 7. because they are the s. of A.
In Isaac shall thy s. be called
8. promise are counted for the s.
29. of Sabaoth had left us a s.
11. 1. an Israelite, of the s. of Abr.
¹Co. 15.38. and to every s. his own body
²Co. 9.10. Now he that ministereth s.
11.22. Are they the s. of Abraham
Gal. 3.16. Now to Abraham and his s.
to s-s, as of many ; but as of
one, And to thy s., which
19. till the s. should come to
29. then are ye Abraham's s.
²Ti. 2. 8. Jesus Christ of the s. of Dav.
Heb. 2.16. took on him the s. of Abra.
11.11. received strength to conc. s.
18. That in Isaac shall thy s. be
¹Jo. 3. 9. for his s. remaineth in him
Rev.12.17.war with the remna. of her s.

sporos.
Mar. 4.26. as if a man should cast s. in.
27. and the s. should spring and
Lu. 8. 5. sower went out to sow his s.
11. The s. is the word of God
²Co. 9.10. and multiply your s. *sown*

speirō.
Mat.13.19.is he *which received* s. by
20. he *that received* the s.; 22,23

spora.
¹Pet.1.23. not of corruptible s., but of

SEEING, [noun.]
blemma.
²Pet. 2. 8. among them, in s. and hear.

SEEING, [*in as much as.*]
epei.
Lu. 1.34. this be, s. I know not a man
²Co. 11.18. s. *that* many glory after the
Heb. 4. 6. s. therefore it remaineth th.
5.11. s. ye are dull of hearing

epeidē.
Act.13.46. but s. ye put it from you
¹Co. 14.16. s. he understandeth not

epeiper.
Ro. 3.30. s. it is one God, which shall

eiper.
²Th. 1. 6. s. it is a righteous thing with

gar.
Act. 2.15. s. it is but the third hour

SEEK, -est, -eth, -ing, Sought.
zēteō.
Mat. 2.13. for Herod will s. the young
20. they are dead *which* so. the
6.33. But s. ye first the kingdom
7. 8. and ye shall find ; Lu.11.9
8. *that* s-*eth* findeth ; Lu.11.10
12.43. s-*ing* rest, and findeth none
13.45. unto a merchant man, s-*ing*
28.12. and s-*eth* that which is gone
21.46. *when* they so. to lay hands on
26.16. he so. opportunity to betray
59. and all the council, so. fals s
28. 5. ye s. Jesus which was cruci.
Mar. 1.37. All men s. *for* thee
3.32. brethren without s. *for* thee
8.11. s-*ing* of him a sign from he.
11.18. so. how they might destroy
12.12. they so. to lay hold on him
14. 1. pr.and the scrib. so.; Lu.22.2
11. he so. how he might conven.
55. so. *for* witness against Jesus
16. 6. Ye s. Jesus of Nazareth

Lu. 2.45. back again to Jerusa., s-*ing*
48. *have* so. thee sorrowing
49. How is it that ye so. me
4.42. and the people so. him
5.18. they so. *means* to bring him
6.19. multitude so. to touch him
11.16. so. of him a sign from heav.
24. through dry places, s-*ing* re.
54. s-*ing* to catch something out
12.29. s. not ye what ye shall eat
31. s. ye the kingdom of God
13. 6. *and* so. fruit thereon, and
7. the. three years I come s-*ing*
24. many, I say unto you,*will* s.
15. 8. and s. diligently till she find
17.33. Whosoever *shall* s. to save
19. 3. he so. to see Jesus who he
10. is come *to* s. and to save that
47. people so. to destroy him
20.19. scribes the same hour so. to
22. 6. he promised, and so. opport.
24. 5. Why s. ye the living among
Jo. 1.38. and sai. unto them, What s.
4.23. the Father s-*cth* such to wo.
27. said, What s-*cst* thou? or
5.16. and s-*o* to slay him, because
18. the Jews s-*o*. the more to kill
30. I s. not mine own will
44. and s. not the honour that
6.24. came to Capernaum s-*ing for*
26. Ye s., not because ye saw
7. 1. because the Jews so. to kill
4. he himself s-*eth* to be known
11. so. him at the feast, and
18. s-*eth* his own glory : but he
that s-*eth* his glory that sent
25. this he, whom they s. to kill
30. Then they so. to take him
34, 36. Ye *shall* s. me, and ; 8.21
8.37, 40. but ye s. to kill me
50. I s. not mine own glory : th.
is one *that* s-*eth* and judgeth
10.39. Therefore they so. again to
11. 8. the Jews of late so. to stone
56. Then so. they for Jesus, and
13.33. Ye *shall* s. me ; and as I sa.
18. 4, 7. said unto them, Whom s.
8. if therefore ye s. me, let the.
19.12. thenceforth Pilate so. to rel.
20.15. why weepest thou? why s-*est*
Act.10.19. Behold, three men s. thee
21. I am he whom ye s.: what is
13. 8. s-*ing* to turn away the depu.
11. s-*ing* some to lead him by
17. 5. and so. to bring them out
27. *That* they should s. the Lord
Ro. 2. 7. To them who..s. *for* glory
10/20. I was found of them *that* so.
11. 3. am left alone, and they s.my
1Co. 1.22. and the Greeks s. *after* wisd.
7.27. s. not to be loosed. Art thou
from a wife? s. not a wife
10.24. *Let* no man s. his own
33. not s-*ing* mine own profit
13. 5. s-*eth* not her own, is not ea.
14.12. s. that ye may excel to the
2Co.12.14. for I s. not your's, but you
13. 3. ye s. a proof of Christ speak.
Gal. 1.10. or *do* I s. to please men
2.17. But if, *while* we s. to be jus.
Phi. 2.21. all s. their own, not the thi.
Col. 3. 1. s. those things which are ab.
1Th. 2. 6. Nor of men so. we glory
Ti. 1.17. he so. me *out* very diligently
Heb. 8. 7. should no place *have been* so.
1Pet. 3.11. *let* him s. peace, and ensue
5. 8. s-*ing* whom he may devour
Rev. 9. 6. in those days *shall* men s.
epizēteō.
Mat. 6.32. *after* these things *do* Gent. s.
12.39. generation s-*eth after* a ; 16.4
Mar. 8.12. *doth* this generation s. *after*

Lu. 11.29. they s. a sign ; and there sh.
12.30. *do* the nat. of the wo. s. *after*
Act.12.19. *when* Herod had so. *for* him
Ro. 11. 7. obta. that which he s-*eth for*
Heb.11.14.plainly that they s.a country
13.14. city, but we s. one to come
ekzēteō.
Act.15.17. men *might* s. *after* the Lord
Ro. 3.11. none *that* s-*eth after* God
Heb.11. 6. them *that diligently* s. him
12.17. though he so. it *carefully*
anazēteō.
Lu. 2.44. they so. him among their
Act.11.25. Barnabas to Tarsus, for *to* s.

SEEM,   -ed, -eth.
dokeō.
Lu. 1. 3. It s-*ed good* to me also, hav.
8.18. even that which he s-*eth* to
Act.15.25. It s-*ed good* unto us, being
28. For it s-*ed good* to the Holy
17.18. He s-*eth* to be a setter forth
25.27. For it s-*eth* to me unreasona.
1Co. 3.18. s-*eth* to be wise in this world
11.16. if any man s. to be contenti.
12.22. memb. of the body, *which* s.
2Co. 10. 9. That I *may* not s. as if I wo.
Gal. 2. 6. of those *who* s-*ed* to be som.
for they *who* s-*ed* to be some.
9. *who* s-*ed* to be pillars, perce.
Heb. 4. 1. any of you *should* s. to come
12.11. the present s-*eth* to be joyous
Jas. 1.26. If any man among you s. to
ginomai eudokia.
Mat.11.26. for so it s-*ed good* ; Lu.10.21
phainō.
Lu. 24.11. their words s-*ed* to them as

SEIZE.
katechō.
Mat.21.38.*let* us s. *on* his inheritance

SELF.   (*See connected words.*)
autos.
1Pet. 2.24. Who his own s. bare our sins

SELFSAME.
houtos autos.
2Co. 5. 5. wrought us for *the* s. *thing*

SELFWILLED.
authadēs.
Tit. 1. 7. not s., not soon angry, not
2Pet. 2.10. Presumptuous are they, s.

SELL,   -eth, Sold.
pōleō.   [Lu.12.6
Mat.10.29. *Are* not two sparrows so. for;
13.44. and s-*eth* all that he hath
19.21. go and s. that thou hast;
Mar.10.21 ; Lu.12.33,18.22
21.12. cast out all them *that* so. and ;
Mar.11.15 ; Lu.19.45
of them *that* s. ; Mar. 11.15
25. 9. go ye rather to them *that* s.
Lu. 17.28. they bought, they so., they
22.36. *let* him s. his garment, and
Jo. 2.14. those *that* so. oxen and sheep
16. said unto them *that* so.doves
Act. 4.34. so. them, *and* brought the
37. Having land, so. it, *and* bro.
5. 1. Sapph. his wife, so. a posses.
1Co.10.25. *Whatsoever is* so. in the sha.
Rev.13.17. that no man might buy or s.
pipraskō.
Mat.13.46.went and so. all that he had
18.25. lord command. him *to be* so.
26. 9. might *have been* so.; Mar.14.5
Jo. 12. 5. Why *was* not this ointme. so.
Act. 2.45. And so.their possessions and
4.34. of the things *that were* so.
5. 4. and *after* it *was* so., was it
Ro. 7.14. but I am carnal, so. under

---

apodidōmi.
Act. 5. 8. whether ye so. the land for
7. 9. with envy, so. Joseph into
Heb.12.16. morsel of meat so. his birth.
emporeuomai.
Jas. 4.13. *buy and* s., and get gain

SELLER,   (See *Purple*.)

SENATE.
gerousia.
Act.5.21. all the s. of the children of Is.

SEND,   -eth, Sent.
apostellō.
Mat. 2.16. s-*t forth, and* slew all the chi.
10. 5. These twelve Jesus s-*t forth*
16. I s. you *forth* as sheep in the
40. receiveth him *that* s-*t* me
11.10. I s. my messenger ; Lu. 7.27
13.41. The Son of man *shall* s. *forth*
14.35. they s-*t out* into all that cou.
15.24. I *am* not s-*t* but unto the
20. 2. he s-*t* them into his vineyard
21. 1. then s-*t* Jesus two ; Lu.19.29
3. straightway he *will* s. them
34. he s-*t* his servants to receive
36. he s-*t* other servants more
37. last of all he s-*t* ; Mar.12.6
22. 3. s-*t forth* his servants to call
4. Again, he s-*t forth* other ser.
16. they s-*t out* unto him their
23.34. I s. unto you prophets, and
37. them *which are* s.; Lu. 13.34
24.31. he *shall* s. his angels with
27.19. his wife s-*t* unto him, saying
Mar. 1. 2. I s. my messenger before thy
3.14. that he *might* s. them *forth*
31. standing without, s-*t* unto
5.10. he *would* not s. them *away*
6. 7. began to s. them *forth* by two
17. *had* s-*t forth* and laid hold
27. king s-*t* an executioner, *and*
8.26. he s-*t* him *away* to his house
9.37. not me, but*him that* s-*t* me
11. 1. he s-*eth forth* two ; Mar.14.13
3. straightway he *will* s. him
12. 2. he s-*t* to the husbandmen a
3. beat him, and s-*t* him *away*
4. 5. he s-*t* unto them another
s-*t* him *away* shamefully
13. they s. unto him certain
13.27. then *shall* he s. his angels
Lu. 1.19. *am* s-*t* to speak unto thee
26. the angel Gabriel *was* s-*t*
4.18. he *hath* s-*t* me to heal the
43. for therefore *am* I s-*t*
7. 3. he s-*t* unto him the elders of
20 John Baptist *hath* s-*t* us unto
9. 2 he s-*t* them to preach the ki.
48. receiveth him *that* s-*t* me
52. s-*t* messengers before his face
10. 1. s-*t* them two and two before
3. I s. you *forth* as lambs amo.
16. despiseth him *that* s-*t* me
11.49. I *will* s. them prophets and
14.17. s-*t* his servant at supper time
32. he s-*eth* an ambassage, *and*
19.14. s-*t* a message after him, say.
32. they *that were* s-*t* went their
20.10. he s-*t* a servant to the husb.
20. s-*t forth* spies, which should
22. 8. he s-*t* Peter and John, saying
35. When I s-*t* you without pur.
24.49. I s. the promise of my Fath.
Jo. 1. 6. There was a man s-*t* from G.
19. when the Jews s-*t* priests and
24. they *which were* s-*t* were of
3.17. For God s-*t* not his Son into
28. but that I am s-*t* before him
34. he whom God *hath* s-*t* spea.
4.38. I s-*t* you to reap that where.
5.33. Ye s-*t* unto John, and he

241

   5.36. that the Father *hath* s-*t* me
    38. for whom he *hath* s-*t*, him
   6.29. be. on him whom he *hath* s-*t*
    57. As the living Father *hath* s-*t*
   7.29. from him, and he *hath* s-*t*
    32. chief priests s-*t* officers to ta.
   8.42. came I of myself, but he s-*t*
   9. 7. which is by interpretati., s-*t*
  10.36. sanctified, and s-*t* into the
  11. 3. Therefore his sisters s-*t* unto
    42. th.thou *hast* s-*t*; 17.21,23,25
  17. 3. Christ, whom thou *hast* s-*t*
    8. believed that thou *didst* s.
    18. As thou *hast* s-*t* me into the
      so *have* I also s-*t* them into
  18.24. Now Annas *had* s-*t* him bou.
  20.21. as my Father *hath* s-*t* me
Act. 3.20. he *shall* s. Jesus Christ, wh.
    26. s-*t* him to bless you, in turn.
   5.21. s-*t* to the prison to have th.
   7.14. Then s-*t* Joseph, *and* called
    34. I *will* s. them into Egypt
    35. the same *did* God s. to be
   8.14. they s-*t* unto them Peter and
   9.17. *hath* s. me, that thou migh.
    38. they s-*t* unto him two men
  10. 8. them he s-*t* them to Joppa
    17. the men *which were* s-*t* from
    20. nothing: for I *have* s-*t* them
    21. to the men *which were* s-*t*
    36. The word which God s-*t* un.
  11.11. s-*t* from Cæsarea unto me
    13. s. men to Joppa, and call for
    30. *and* s-*t* it to the elders by
  13.15. rulers of the synagogue s-*t*
    26. *is* the word of this salvat. s-*t*
  15.27. We *have* s-*t* therefore Judas
    35. the magistrates s-*t* the serje.
    36. The magistrates *have* s-*t* to
  19.22. So he s-*t* into Macedonia two
  26.17. unto whom now I s. thee
  28.28. salvation of God *is* s-*t* unto
Ro. 10.15. preach, except they *be* s-*t*
¹Co. 1.17. For Christ s-*t* me not to bap.
⁴Co. 12.17. of them whom I s-*t* unto you
¹Ti. 4.12. Tychicus *have* I s-*t* to Ephes.
Heb. 1.14. s-*t forth* to minister for th.
¹Pet. 1.12. Holy Ghost s-*t* down from
¹Jo. 4. 9. God s-*t* his only begotten S.
    10. he loved us, and s-*t* his Son
    14. that the Father s-*t* the Son
Rev. 1. 1. he s-*t and* signified it by his
   5. 6. s-*t forth* into all the earth
  22. 6. s-*t* his angel to shew unto
     exapostellō.
Lu. 1.53. rich he *hath* s-*t* empty *away*
  20,10, 11. and s-*t* him *away* empty
Act. 7.12. he s-*t out* our fathers first
   9.30. and s-*t* him *forth* to Tarsus
  11.22. they s-*t forth* Barnabas, that
  12.11. the Lord *hath* s-*t* his angel
  17.14. the brethren s-*t away* Paul
  22.21. for I *will* s. thee far hence
Gal. 4. 4. God s-*t forth* his Son, made
   6. God *hath* s-*t forth* the Spirit
     sunapostellō.
²Co. 12.18. *with* him I s-*t* a brother
     apostolos.
Jo. 13.16. neither *he that is* s-*t* greater
     pempō.
Mat. 2. 8. he s-*t* them to Bethleh., *and*
   11. 2. he s-*t* two of his disciples
  14.10. he s-*t*, *and* beheaded John
  22. 7. he s-*t* forth his armies, *and*
Mar. 5.12. s. us into the swine
Lu. 4.26. *was* Elias s-*t*, save unto Sar.
   7. 6. the centurion s-*t* friends to
    10. And they *that were* s-*t*, retu.
    19. s-*t* them to Jesus, saying
  15.15. and he s-*t* him into his fields
  16.24. and s. Lazarus, that he may
    27. that thou *wouldest* s. him to
242

Lu. 20.11, 12. again he s-*t* another serv.
    13. I *will* s. my beloved son
Jo. 1.22. an answer to them *that* s-*t*
    33. but he *that* s-*t* me to baptize
   4.34. will of him *that* s-*t*; 6.38,40
   5.23. the Father *which hath* s-*t* hi.
    24. on him *that* s-*t* me; 12.44
    30, 37, the Fat. *which hath* s-*t*.;
       6.44; 8.16,18; 12,49
   6.39. Father's will *which hath* s-*t*
   7.16. not mine, but his *that* s-*t* me
    18. his glory *that* s-*t* him, the sa.
    28. but he *that* s-*t* me is ; 8.26
    33. I go unto him *that* s-*t* me
   8.29. And he *that* s-*t* me is with
   9. 4. the works of him *that* s-*t*
  12.45. me seeth him *that* s-*t* me
  13.16. greater than he *that* s-*t* him
    20. whomsoever I s. receiveth
      receiveth him *that* s-*t* me
  14.24. but the Father's *which* s-*t*
    26. whom the Father *will* s. in
  15.21. they know not him *that* s-*t*
    26. whom I *will* s. unto you fro.
  16. 5. I go my way to him *that* s-*t*
    7. I *will* s. him unto you
  20.21. sent me, even so s. I you
Act. 10. 5. now s. men to Joppa, and
    32. s. therefore to Joppa, and
    33. therefore I s-*t* to thee ; and
  11.29. determined *to* s. relief unto
  15.22. *to* s. chosen men of their ow.
    25. *to* s. chosen men unto you
  19.31. s-*t* unto him, desiring him
  20.17. he s-*t* to Ephesus, *and* called
  23.30. I s-*t* straightway to thee
  25.21. till I *might* s. him to Cesar
    25. I have determined *to* s. him
    27. *to* s. a prisoner, *and* not wit.
Ro. 8. 3. God s-*ing* his own Son in the
¹Co. 4.17. *have* I s-*t* unto you Timothe.
    16. 3. them *will* I s. to bring your
²Co. 9. 3. Yet *have* I s-*t* the brethren
Eph. 6.22. Whom I *have* s-*t* unto you
Phi. 2.19. *to* s. Timotheus shortly unto
    23. hope to s. presently, so soon
    25. necessary *to* s. to you Epaph.
    28. I s-*t* him therefore the more
    4.16. ye s-*t* once and again unto
Col. 4. 8. Whom I *have* s-*t* unto you
¹Th. 3. 2. and s-*t* Timotheus, our brot.
    5. I s-*t* to know your faith, lest
²Th. 2.11. God *shall* s. them strong de.
Tit. 3.12. When I *shall* s. Artemas
¹Pet. 2.14. as unto them *that are* s-*t* by
Rev. 1.11. and s. it unto the seven chu.
  11.10. and *shall* s. gifts one to ano.
  22.16. I Jesus *have* s-*t* mine angel
     metapempō.
Act. 10.22. *to* s. *for* thee into his house
    29. *as soon as I was* s-*t for:* I
      what intent ye *have* s-*t for*
  24.24. he s-*t for* Paul; and heard
    26. he s-*t for* him the ofte., *and*
    25. 3. that he *would* s. *for* him to
     anapempō.
Lu. 23. 7. he s-*t* him to Herod, who hi.
    11. and s-*t* him *again* to Pilate
    15. nor yet Herod: for I s-*t* you
Phile. 12. Whom I *have* s-*t again* : th.
     ekpempō.
Act.13. 4. *being* s-*t forth* by the Holy
  17.10. s-*t away* Paul and Silas by
     sumpempō.
²Co. 8.18, 22. And we *have* s-*t with*
     apoluō.
Mat.14.15. s. the multitude *away*, that ;
      Mar.6.36; Lu.9.12.
    22. while he s-*t* the multi.*away*;
      15.39.; Mar.6.45.
    23. *when* he *had* s-*t* multi. *away*
  15.23. saying, s. her *away* ; for she

Mat.15.32. I will not s. them *away* fast
Mar. 8. 3. if I s. them *away* fasting
      and he s-*t* them *away*
Lu. 8.38. Jesus s-*t* him *away*, saying
Act.13. 3. on them, they s-*t* them *away*
     ekballō.
Mat. 9.38. that he will s. *forth* ; Lu.10.2
    12.20. till he s. *forth* judgment un.
Mar. 1.43. and forthwith s-*t* him *away*
Jas. 2. 25. and *had* s-*t* them *out* anoth.
     ballō.
Mat.10.34. that I am come *to* s. peace
      I come not *to* s. peace
Lu. 12.49. I am come *to* s. fire on the
     aphiēmi.
Mat.13.36.Jesus s-*t* the multitude *away*
Mar. 4.36. *when* they *had* s-*t away* the
     apotassomai.
Mar. 6.46. *when* he *had* s-*t* them *away*
     bruō.
Jas. 3.11. *Doth* a fountain s. *forth* at
     brechō.
Mat. 5.45. s-*eth* rain on the just and on
   SENSES.
     aisthētērion.
Heb. 5.14. have their s. exercised to
   SENSUAL.
     psuchikos.
Jas. 3.15. but is earthly, s., devilish
Jude 19. s., having not the spirit
   SENTENCE.
     epikrinō.
Lu. 23.24. Pilate *gave* s. that it should
     egōkrinō.
Act.15.19. Wherefore *my* s. *is*, that we
     apokrima.
²Co. 1. 9. we had the s. of death in
   SEPARATE,   -*ed.*
     aphorizō.
Mat.25.32. he *shall* s. them one from
Lu. 6.22. when they *shall* s. you from
Act.13. 2. s. me Barnabas and Saul for
  19. 9. from them, and s-*ed* the dis.
Ro. 1. 1. s-*ed* unto the gospel of God
²Co. 6.17. *be* ye s., saith the Lord, and
Gal. 1.15. *who* s-*ed* me from my moth.
  2.12. he withdrew and s-*ed* himself
     chōrizō.
Ro. 8.35. Who *shall* s. us from the love
    39. shall be able *to* s. us from
Heb. 7.26. undefiled, s. from sinners
     apodiorizō.
Jude 19. be they *who* s. them*selves*
   SEPULCHRE,   -*s.*
     mnēmeion.
Mat.23.29. and garnish the s-*s* of the
    27.60. door of the s.; Mar.15.46,16.3.
    28. 8. departed quickly from the s.
Mar.15.46. laid him in a s.; Act.13.29
    16. 2. they came unto the s. at the
      5. And entering into the s.
      8. and fled from the s.: for they
Lu. 11.47. for ye build the s-*s* of the
     48. and ye build their s-*s*
  23.55. beheld the s., and how
  24. 2. away from the s.; Jo.20.1.
     9. and returned from the s.
    12. and ran unto the s.; and
    22. which were early at the s.
    24. were with us went to the s.
Jo. 19.41. and in the garden a new s.
    42. for the s. was nigh at hand
  20. 1. unto the s., and seeth the st.
    2. away the Lord out of the s
    3. and came to the s.
    4. 8. came first to the s.
    6. and went into the s., and
    11. Mary stood without at thes.
      and looked into the s.

taphos.
Mat.23.27. ye are like unto whited s-s
 27.61. sitting over against the s.
  64. that the s. be made sure
  66. went, and made the s. sure
 28. 1. the other Mary to see the s.
Ro. 3.13. Their throat is an open s.
muēma.
Lu. 23.53. laid it in a s. that was hewn
 24. 1. they came unto the s., bring.
Act. 2.29. his s. is with us unto this
 7.16. laid in the s. that Abraham

SERJEANTS.
rabdouchos.
Act.16.35. the magistrates sent the s.
  38. And the s. told these words

SERPENT, -s.
ophis.
Mat. 7.10. will he give him a s.;Lu.11.11
 10.16. be ye therefore wise as s-s
 23.33. Ye s-s, ye generation of vip.
Mar.16.18.They shall take up s-s; and
Lu. 10.19. power to tread on s-s and
Co. 3.14. And as Moses lifted up the s.
1Co.10. 9. and were destroyed of s-s
2Co.11. 3. as the s. beguiled Eve throu.
Rev. 9.19. their tails were like unto s-s
 12. 9. that old s.,called the D.; 20.2
  14. time, from the face of the s.
  15. And the s. cast out of his m.
herpeton.
Jas. 3. 7. and of s-s, and of things in

SERVANT, (See *Hire*,) -s.
doulos.   [Lu.7.8
Mat. 8. 9. to my s., Do this, and he ;
 10.24. nor the s. above his lord
  25. as his master, and the s. as
 13.27. the s-s of the householder
  28. The s-s said unto him, Wilt
 18.23. would take account of his s-s
  26. The s. therefore fell down
  27. the lord of that s. was moved
  28. the same s. went out, and
  32. O thou wicked s., I forgave
 20.27. among you, let him be your s.
 21.34. sent his s-s to the husband.
  35. the husbandmen took his s-s
  36. Aga., he sent other s-s; 22.4
 22. 3. sent forth his s-s to call
  6. the remnant took his s-s
  8. Then saith he to his s-s
  10. those s-s went out into the
 24.45. then is a faithful and wise s.
  46. Blessed is that s., whom his
  48. that evil s. sh. say; Lu.12.45
  50. The lord of that s. shall co.
 25.14. called his own s-s, and deliv.
  19. the lord of those s-s cometh
 21, 23. thou good and faithful s.
  26. Thou wicked and slothful s.
  30. cast ye the unprofitable s.
 26.51. his sword, and struck a s.;
   Mar.14.47; Lu.22.50; Jo.18.10
Mar.10.44.the chiefest, shall be s. of all
 12. 2. sent to the husbandmen a s.;
   Lu.2o.10   [Lu.20.11
  4. sent unto them another s.;
 13.34. gave authority to his s-s
Lu. 2.29. now lettest thou thy s. depa.
 7. 2. a certain centurion's s., who
  3. would come and heal his s.
  10. found the s. whole that had
 12.37, 38. Blessed are those s-s
  43. Blessed is that s., whom his
  46. The lord of that s. will come
  47. that s.,which knew his lord's
 14.17. sent his s. at supper time
  21. So that s. came, and shewed
   said to his s., Go out quickly
  22. the s. said, Lord, it is done

Lu. 14.23. the lord said unto the s.
 15.22. the father said to his s-s
 17. 7. which of you, having a s.
  9. Doth he thank that s. beca.
  10. say, We are unprofitable s-s
 19.13. he called his ten s-s, and
  15. commanded these s-s to be
  17. unto him, Well, thou good s.
  22. I judge thee, thou wicked s.
Jo. 4.51. going down, his s-s met him
 8.34. committeth sin is the s. of sin
  35. the s. abideth not in the ho.
 13.16. The s. is not greater ; 15.20
 15.15. I call you not s-s ; for the s.
 18.10. The s-s name was Malchus
  18. the s-s and officers stood the.
  26. One of the s-s of the high pr.
Act. 2.18. on my s-s and on my handm.
 4.29. grant unto thy s-s, that with
 16.17. the s-s of the most high God
Ro. 1. 1. Paul, a s. of Jesus Christ
 6.16. s-s to obey, his s-s ye are to
 17, 20. ye were the s-s of sin
1Co. 7.21. Art thou called being a s.
  22. being a s., is the Lord's free.
   being free, is Christ's s.
  23. be not ye the s-s of men
2Co. 4. 5. ourselves your s-s for Jesus'
Gal. 1.10. I should not be the s. of Ch.
 4. 1. differeth nothing from a s.
  7. Wherefo...art no more a s.
Eph. 6. 5. s-s, be obedient to them th.
  6. as the s-s of Christ, doing
Phi. 1. 1. the s-s of Jesus Christ, to all
  2. upon him the form of a s.
Col. 3.22. s-s, obey in all things your
 4. 1. give unto your s-s that which
  12. a s. of Christ, saluteth you
1Ti. 6. 1. many s-s as are under the
2Ti. 2.24. the s. of the Lord must not
Tit. 1. 1. Paul, a s. of God, and an
 2. 9. Exhort s-s to be obedient
Phile. 16. now as a s., but above a s.
Jas. 1. 1. a s. of God and of the Lord
1Pet. 2.16. but as the s-s of God
2Pet. 1. 1. a s. and an apostle of Jesus
 2.19. themselves are the s-s of cor.
Jude 1. Jude, the s. of Jesus Christ
Rev. 1. 1. to shew unto his s-s things
   by his angel unto his s. John
 2.20. to teach and to seduce my s-s
 7. 3. have sealed the s-s of our G.
 10. 7. declared to his s-s the proph.
 11.18. give reward unto thy s-s
 15. 3. the song of Moses the s. of
 19. 2. avenged the blood of his s-s
  5. Praise our God, all ye his s-s
 22. 3. and his s-s shall serve him
  6. to shew unto his s-s the thi.
doulos, [*adject.*]
Ro. 6.19. yielded your members s-s to
   your members s-s to righteo.
douloō.
Ro. 6.18. ye became the s-s of righteo.
  22. (being) and become s-s to God
1Co. 9.19. I made myself s. unto all
pais.
Mat. 8. 6. Lord, my s. lieth at home
  8. my s. shall be healed ; Lu.7.7
  13. And his s. was healed in the
 12.18. Behold my s., whom I have
 14. 2. And said unto his s-s, This
Lu. 1.54. He hath holpen his s. Israel
  69. in the house of his s. David
 15.26. and he called one of the s-s
Act. 4.25. Who by the mouth of thy s.
Mat.22.13.Then said the king to the s-s
 23.11. among you shall be your s.
Mar. 9.35. be last of all, and s. of all
Jo. 2. 5. His mother saith unto the s-s
  9. the s-s which drew the water

Jo. 12.26. there shall also my s. be
Ro. 16. 1. Phebe our sister, whi. is a s.
oiketēs.
Lu. 16.13. No. s. can serve two masters
Act.10. 7. call. two of his *household* s-s
Ro. 14. 4. that judgest another man's s.
1Pet. 2.18. s-s, be subject to your mast.
hupēretēs.
Mat. 26.58. sat with the s-s; Mar.14.54
Mar.14.65. and the s-s did strike him
Jo. 18.36. world, then would my s-s fi
therapōn.
Heb. 3. 5. in all his house, as a s., for

SERVE, -ed, -eth, -ing.
douleuō.   [Lu.16.13
Mat. 6.24. No man can s. two masters ;
   Ye cannot s. God ; Lu. 16.13
Lu. 15.29. these many years *do* I s. thee
Act.20.19. s-ing the Lord with all hu.
Ro. 6. 6. henceforth we *should* not s.
 7. 6. we *should* s. in newness of
  25. I myself s. the law of God
 9.12. The elder *shall* s. the young.
 12.11. fervent in spirit; s-ing the
 14.18. *that* in these things s-eth Ch.
 16.18. such s. not our Lord Jesus
Gal. 5.13. by love s. one another
Phi. 2.22. he *hath* s-ed with me in the
Col. 3.24. for ye s. the Lord Christ
1Th. 1. 9. *to* s. the living and true God
Tit. 3. 3. s-ing divers lusts and pleas.
latreuō.
Mat. 4.10. and him only *shalt* thou s.
Lu. 1.74. *might* s. him without fear
 2.37. *but* s-ed God with fastings
 4. 8. and him only *shalt* thou s.
Act. 7. 7. *shall* they come forth, and s.
 26. 7. instantly s-ing God day and
 27.23. whose I am, and whom I s.
Ro. 1. 9. whom I s. with my spirit
  25. and s-ed the creature more
2Ti. 1. 3. I thank God, whom I s. from
Heb. 8. 5. Who is unto the example
 9.14. works *to* s. the living God
 12.28. we *may* s. God acceptably
 13.10. *which* s. the tabernacle
Rev. 7.15. and s. him day and night
 22. 3. and his servants *shall* s. him
diakoneō.
Lu. 10.40. my sister hath left me *to* s.
 12.37. will come forth and s. them
 17. 8. and gird thyself, and s. me
 22.26. is chief, as he *that doth* s.
  27. sitt. at meat, or he *that* s-eth
   among you as he *that* s-eth
Jo. 12. 2. a supper; and Martha s-ed
  26. If any man s. me, let him
   if any man s. me, him will
Act. 6. 2. the word of God, and s. tab.
hupēreteō.
Act.13.36. *after* he had s-ed his own

SERVICE.
latreia.
Jo. 16. 2. think that he doeth God s.
Ro. 9. 4. and the s. of God, and the
 12. 1. which is your reasonable s.
Heb 9. 1. ordinances of *divine* s.
  6. accomplishing the s. of God
latreuō.
Heb. 9. 9. make him *that did the* s. per.
diakonia.
Ro. 15.31. that my s. which I have
2Co.11. 8. of them, to *do* you s.
Rev. 2.19. works, and charity, and s.
leitourgia.
2Co. 9.12. the administration of this s.
Phi. 2.17. the sacrifice and s. of your
  30. supply your lack of s. toward
douleuō.
Gal. 4. 8. ye *did* s. unto them which

243

Eph. 6, 7. With good will *dbing* s., as
¹Ti. 6. 2. *let* them..rather *do* them s.

SERVING, [*noun.*]
diakonia.

Lu. 10.40. was cumbered about much s.

SET,   -*eth*, -*ing.*
histēmi.

Mat. 4. 5. and s-*eth* him on a; Lu. 4.9
18. 2. and s. him in the; Mar. 9.36
25.33. he *shall* s. the sheep on his
Lu. 9.47. took a child, and s. him by
Jo. 8. 3. *when* they *had* s. her in the
Act. 4. 7. *when* they *had* s. them in the
5.27. they s. them before the cou.
6. 6. Whom they s. before the ap.
13. And s. *up* false witnesses
22.30. Paul down, and s. him befo.
kathistēmi.

Heb. 2. 7. *didst* s. him over the works
tithēmi.

Jo. 2.10. at the beginning *doth* s. *forth*
Act.13.47. I *have* s. thee to be a light
¹Co.12,18. But now *hath* God s. the m.
28. And God *hath* s. some in the
Rev.10. 2. he s. his right foot upon the
paratithēmi.   [Lu.9.16

Mar. 6.41. disc. to s. *before* them ; 8.6;
8. 6. they *did* s. them *before* the
7. *to* s. them also *before* them
Ln. 10. 8. eat such thin. *as are* s. *before*
11. 6. I have nothing to s. *before*
Act.16.34. he s. meat *before* them
¹Co. 10.27. *whatsoever* is s. *before* you
epitithēmi.

Mat.27.37.And s. *up* over his head his
Mar. 4.21. and not to *be* s. on a candle.
Lu. 8.16. but s-*eth* it on a candlestick
Act.18.10. no man *shall* s. on thee
peritithēmi.

Mar.12. 1. and s. an hedge *about* it, and
protithēmi.

Ro. 3.25. Whom God *hath* s. *forth* to
keimai.

Mat. 5.14. A city *that is* s. on an hill
Lu. 2.34. Behold, this child *is* s.for the
Jo. 2. 6. And there were s. there six
19.29. Now there *was* s. a vessel
Phi. 1.17. I am s. for the defence of the
Rev. 4. 2. a throne *was* s. in heaven
prokeimai.

Heb. 6.18. hold upon the hope s. *before*
12. 1. the race *that is* s. *before* us
2. for the joy *that was* s. *before*
Jude 7. *are* s. *forth* for an example
kathizō.

Mat. 5. 1. and *when* he *was* s., his disc.
¹Co. 6. 4. s. them to judge who are lea.
Eph. 1.20. and s. him at his own right
Heb. 8. 1. who *is* s. on the right hand
12. 2. *is* s. *down* at the right hand
Rev. 3.21. and am s. *down* with my Fa.
epikathizō.

Mat.21. 7. and they s. him thereon
tassō.

Lu. 7. 8. am a man s. under authority
anatassomai.

Lu. 1. 1. to s. *forth in order* a declar.
diatassō.

¹Co. 11.34. the rest *will* I s. *in order*
taktos.

Act.12.21. And upon a s. day Herod
exoutheneō.

Lu. 23.11. s. him *at nought*, and mock.
Act. 4.11. stone *which was* s. *at nought*
Ro. 14.10. why *dost* thou s. *at nought*
epibibazō.

Ln. 10.34. s. him *on* his own beast, *and*
19.35. and they s. Jesus thereon
Act.23.24. they may s. Paul *on, and*
dunō.

Mar. 1.32. even, when the sun *did* s.
244

Lu. 4.40. Now *when* the sun *was* s-*ing*
meta, [*gen.*]

Mat.27.66. the stone, *and* s-*ing* a watch
exoudenoō.

Mar. 9.12. things, and be s. *at nought*
apostellō.

Lu. 4.18. *to* s. at liberty them that are
bēma pous, [*gen.*]

Act. 7. 5. so much as *to* s. *his foot on*
sunelaunō eis eirēnē.

Act. 7.26. *have* s. them *at one again*
atenizō.

Act.13. 9. *Then..*s.*his eyes on* him *and*
anorthoō.

Act.15.16. thereof, and I *will* s. it *up*
erchomai eis apelegmos.

Act.19.27. in danger to be s. *at nought*
anagō.

Act.21. 2. we went aboard, and s. *forth*
apodeiknumi.

¹Co. 4. 9. *hath* s. *forth* us the apostles
epidiorthoō.

Tit. 1. 5. th. thou *shouldest* s. *in order*
didōmi.

Rev. 3. 8. I *have* s. before thee an open
(See *Affection, Evidently, Fire, Liberty,
Seal, Steadfastly, Uproar, Variance.*)

SETTER,
kataggeleus.

Act.17.18. seemeth to be a s. *forth* of

SETTLE,   -*ed.*
themelioō.

¹Pet. 5.10. stablish, strengthen, s. you
tithēmi.

Lu. 21.14. s. it therefore in your hearts
hedraios.

Col. 1.23. the faith grounded and s-*ed*

SEVEN.
hepta.

Mat.12.45. s. other spirits more wicked
15.34. And they said, s.; Mar. 8.5
36. took the s. loaves ; Mar.8.5
37. left s. baskets full ; Mar.8.8
16.10. Neither the s. loaves of
18.22. but, Until seventy times s.
22.25. there were with us s. breth.;
Mar.21.20 ; Lu.20.29
28. wh.wife shall she be of the s.
Mar. 8.20. And when the s. among four
ye up? And they said, s.
12.22. And the s. had her, and left
23. the s. had her to w.; Lu.20.33
16. 9. out of whom he had cast s.
Lu. 2.36. lived with an husband s.years
8. 2. out of whom went s. devils
11.26. s. other spirits more wicked
20.31. in like manner the s. also
Act. 6. 3. s. men of honest report
13.19. destroyed s. nations in the
19.14. there were s. sons of one Sc.
20. 6. where we abode s. days ; 21.4
21. 8. which was one of the s.
27. And when the s. days were
28.14. to tarry with them s. days
Heb.11.30.were compassed about s. days
Rev. 1. 4. John to the s. churches wh.
and from the s. spirits which
12. s. golden candlesticks ; 20,2.1
13. in the midst of the s. candle.
16. in his right hand s. stars
20. The mystery of the s. stars
s. stars are the angels of the
and the s. candlesticks which
thou sawest are the s. churc.
2. 1. he that holdeth the s. stars
3. 1. s. Spirits of God, and the s.
4. 5. there were s. lamps of fire
which are the s. Spirits of G.
5. 1. sealed with s. seals
5. to loose the s. seals thereof

Rev. 5. 6. having s. horns and s. eyes
which are the s. Spirits
8. 2. I saw the s. angels which st.
to them were given s. trum.
6. s. angels which had s. trum.
10. 3, 4. s. thunders uttered their
which the s. thunders utter.
11.13. were slain of men s. thousa.
12. 3. 13.1,17.3,7. hav. s. heads and
ten horns, and s. crowns up.
15. 1. s. angels having the s. last
6. the s. angels came out of the
temple, having the s. plagues
7. the s. angels s. golden vials
8. s. plagues of the s. angels
16. 1. saying to the s. angels, Go
17. 1. s. ang. which had the s.; 21.9
9. The s. heads are s. mountai.
10. there are s. kings : five are
11. and is of the s., and goeth
21. 9. full of the s. last plagues
heptakis.

Mat.18.21. I forgive him ? till s. *times*
22. unto thee, Until s. *times*
Lu. 17. 4. against thee s. *times* in a day
and s. *times* in a day turn
heptakischilioi.

Ro.11. 4. reserved to myself s. *thousand*

SEVENTH.
hebdomos.

Jo. 4.52. Yesterday at the s. hour the
Heb. 4. 4. of the s. day on this wise
and God did rest the s. day
Jude 14. Enoch also, the s. from Ad.
Rev. 8. 1. when he had opened the s.
10. 7. of the voice of the s. angel
11.15. the s. angel sounded ; and
16.17. the s. angel poured out his
21.20. the s. chrysolite ; the eighth
hepta.

Mat.22.26.and the third, unto the s.

SEVENTY.
hebdomēkonta.

Lu. 10. 1. the Lord appointed other s.
17. the s. returned again with
hebdomēkontakis.

Mat.18.22.but until s. *times* seven

SEVER.
aphorizō.

Mat. 13.49.s. the wicked from among

SEVERAL.
ana heis hekastos.

Rev.21.21. *every* s. gate was of one

SEVERALLY.
idios.

¹Co.12.11. dividing to every man s.

SEVERITY.
apotomia.

Ro. 11.22. the goodness and s. of God
on them which fell, s. but

SEWETH.
epirraptō.

Mar.2.21. s. a piece of new cloth *on*

SHADOW.
skia.

Mat. 4.16. sat in the region and s. of
Mar. 4.32. may lodge under the s. of it
Lu. 1.79. and in the s. of death, to
Act. 5.15. the s. of Peter passing by
Col. 2.17. Which are a s. of things to
Heb. 8. 5. the example and s. of heav.
10. 1. the law having a s. of good
aposkiasma.

Jas. 1.17. variableness, neither s. of

SHADOWING.
kataskiazō.

Heb.9. 5. of glory s. the mercyseat

SHAKE, -en, Shook.
saleuō. [Lu.7.24
Mat.11. 7. A reed s-en with the wind;
24.29 of the heavens shall be s-en;
Mar.13.25; Lu.21.26
Lu. 6.38. pressed down, and s-en toge.
48. and could not s. it: for it
Act. 4.31. the place was s-en where th.
16.26. founda. of the pri. were s-en
²Th. 2. 2. That ye be not soon s-en in
Heb.12.26.Whose voice then sho. the
27. of those things that are s-en
things which cannot be s-en
ektinassō. [Mar.6.11
Mat. 10.14.s. off the dust of your feet;
Act.13.51. they sho. off the dust of their
18. 6. he sho. his raiment, and said
apotinassō.
Lu. 9. 5. s. off the very dust from yo.
Act.28. 5. he sho. off the beast into the
seiō.
Mat.28. 4. the keepers did s., and beca.
Heb.12.26.I s. not the earth only
Rev. 6.13. when she is s-en of a mighty

SHALL, -lt.
(An auxilary verb, excepting)
mellō.
Mat.16.27. the Son of man s. come in
17.12. Likewise s. also the Son of
22. The Son of man s. be betray.
20.22. that I s. drink of, and to be
24. 6. And ye s. hear of wars and
Mar.13. 4. when all these things s. be
Lu. 9.44. the Son of man s. be deliver.
21. 7. when these things s. come
36. that s. come to pass, and to
Act.23. 3. God s. smite thee, thou
24.15. that there s. be a resurrection
26. 2. because I s. answer for myse.
Ro. 4.24. to whom it s. be imputed
8.13. after the flesh, ye s. die
18. glory which s. be revealed
²Ti. 4. 1. who s. judge the quick and
Heb.1.14. who s. be heirs of salvation
10.27. which s. devour the adversa.
Jas. 2.12. as they that s. be judged
¹Pet. 1. 7. glory that s. be revealed
Rev. 1.19. the things which s. be here.
2.10. which thou s-t suffer: behold
the devil s. cast some of you
3.10. which s. come upon all the
17. 8. and s. ascend out of the
hosios.
Rev.16. 5. art, and wast, and s-t be

SHAMBLES.
makellon.
¹Co.10.25. Whatsoever is sold in the s.

SHAME, [noun.]
aischunē.
Lu. 14. 9. thou begin with s. to take
Phil. 3.19. whose glory is in their s.
Heb.12. 2. the cross, despising the s.
Jude 13. foaming out their own s.
Rev. 3.18. the s. of thy nakedness do
aischros.
¹Co.11. 6. if it be a s. for a woman
14.35. for it is a s. for women to
Eph. 5.12. For it is a s. even to speak
aischēmosunē.
Rev.16.15. naked, and they see his s.
atimazō.
Act. 5.41. worthy to suffer s. for his
entropē.
¹Co. 6. 5. I speak to your s.; 15.34
atimia.
¹Co.11.14. long hair, it is a s. unto him
paradeigmatizō.
Heb. 6. 6. and put him to an open s.

SHAME, [verb.]
kataischunō.
¹Co. 11.22. and s. them that have not
entrepō.
¹Co. 4.14. write not these things to s.

SHAMEFACEDNESS.
aidōs.
¹Ti. 2. 9. with s. and sobriety; not

SHAMEFULLY.
atimaō.
Mar.12. 4.sent him away s. handled
atimazō.
Lu. 20.11. entreated him s. and

SHAPE, -s.
eidos.
Lu. 3.22. in a bodily s. like a dove
Jo. 5.37. at any time, nor seen his s.
homoiōma.
Rev. 9. 7. the s-s of the locusts were

SHARP.
oxus.
Rev. 1.16. went a s. twoedged sword
2.12. which hath the s. sword
14.14. and in his hand a s. sickle
17. he also having a s. sickle
18. to him that had the s. sickle
saying, Thrust in thy s. sick.
19.15. his mouth goeth a s. sword

SHARPER.
tomōteros.
Heb. 4.12. s. than any two-edged sword

SHARPLY.
apotomōs.
Tit. 1.13. Wherefore rebuke them s.

SHARPNESS.
apotomōs. (deal sharply.)
²Co.13.10. being present I should use s.

SHAVE, -en.
xuraō.
Act.21.24. that they may s. their heads
¹Co. 11. 5. all one as if she were s-en
6. woman to be shorn or s-en

SHE.
autos [fem.] is generally so translated. The following are exceptions:—
hautos, [fem.]
Mat.26.12. in that s. hath poured this
Mar.12.44.s. of her want did; Lu.21.4
14. 8. She hath done what s. could
9. that s. hath done shall be
Lu. 2.36. s. was of a great age, and
37. s. was a widow of about
38. s. coming in that instant
7.44 s. hath washed my feet with
8.42. of age, and s. lay a dying
Ro. 16. 2. for s. hath been a succourer
ekeinos, [fem.]
Mar.16.10.s. went and told them that
Jo. 11.29. As soon as s. heard that
20.15. s., supposing him to be
16. s. turned herself, and saith
hode, [fem.]
Lu. 10.39. s. had a sister called Mary

SHEARER.
keirō.
Act. 8.32. like a lamb dumb bef. his s.

SHEATH.
thēkē.
Jo. 18.11. Put up thy sword into the s.

SHED.
ekcheō.
Act. 2.33. he hath s. forth this, which
22.20. thy martyr Stephen was s.
Ro. 3.15. Their feet are swift to s. blo.

Tit. 3. 6. Which he s. on us abundant
Rev.16. 6. they have s. the blood of sai.
ekchunō.
Mat. 23.35.righteous blood s. upon tho
26.28. which is s. for ma.; Mar.14.24
Lu. 11.50. prophets, which was s. from
22.20. my blood, which is s. for you
Ro. 5. 5. the love of God is s. abroad

SHEDDING, [noun.]
haimatekchusia.
Heb. 9.22. without s. of blood is no re.

SHEEP.
probaton.
Mat. 7.15. come to you in s.'s clothing
9.36. as s. having no shepherd;
Mar.6.34; [15.24
10. 6. rather to the lost s. of the;
16. I send you forth as s. in the
12.11. that shall have one s., and if
12. then is a man better than a s.
18.12. have an hundred s.; Lu.15.4
25.32. divideth his s. from the goats
33. he shall set the s. on his
26.31. the s. of the flock shall be
Mar.14.27.and the s. shall be scattered
Lu. 15. 6. for I have found my s. which
Jo. 2.14. that sold oxen and s. and do.
15. and the s., and the oxen, and
10. 2. door is the shepherd of the s.
3. and the s. hear his voice
calleth his own s. by name
4. he putteth forth his own s.
before them, and the s. foll.
7. I am the door of the s.
8. but the s. did not hear them
11. giveth his life for the s.
12. whose own the s. are not
leaveth the s., and fleeth
them, and scattereth the s.
13. and careth not for the s.
15. I lay down my life for the s.
16. And other s. I have, which
26. ye are not of my s., as I said
27. My s. hear my voice, and I
21.16, 17.unto him, Feed my s.
Act. 8.32. He was led as a s. to the
Ro. 8.36. accounted as s. for the slau
Heb.13.20.that great Shepherd of the s.
¹Pet. 2.25. For ye were as s. going astr.
Rev.18.13. beasts, and s., and horses
probatikos.
Jo. 5. 2. by the s. market a pool which

SHEEP-FOLD.
aulē probaton, [gen.]
Jo. 10. 1. not by the door into the s.

SHEEPSKINS.
mēlōtē.
Heb.11.37. they wandered about in s.

SHEET.
othonē.
Act.10.11. as it had been a great s.; 11.5

SHEPHERD, -s.
poimēn.
Mat. 9.36. as sheep having no s.; Mar.
25.32. as a s. divideth his sheep
26.31. I will smite the s.; Mar.14.27
Lu. 2. 8. s-s abiding in the field, keep.
15. the s-s said one to another
18. wh. were told them by the s-s
20. And the s-s returned, glorif.
Jo. 10. 2. door is the s. of the sheep
11, 14. I am the good s.
12. and not the s., whose own
16. shall be one fold, and one s.
Heb.13.20.that great s. of the sheep
¹Pet. 2.25. returned unto the s. and
245

archipoimēn.
¹Pet. 5. 4. when the *chief* s. shall appe.

SHEW, [noun.]
prophasis.
Lu. 20.47. for a s. make long prayers
euprosōpeō.
Gal. 6.12. *to make a fair* s. in the flesh
deigmatizō.
Col. 2.15. he *made a* s. of them openly
logos.
Col. 2.23. have indeed a s. of wisdom

SHEW, [verb,] -ed, -est, -eth, -ing.
deiknumi. [Lu.4.5
Mat. 4. 8. s-*eth* him all the kingdoms ;
8. 4. s. thyself to the priest ; Mar.
1.44 ; Lu.5.14
16.21. began Jesus *to* s. unto his di.
Mar.14.15.he *will* s.you a larg.; Lu.22.12
Jo. 2.18. What sign s-*est* thou unto us
5.20. s-*eth* him all things that hi.
and he *will* s. him greater
10.32. Many good works *have* I s-*ed*
14. 8. Lord, s. us the Father, and
9. sayest thou then, s. us the
20.20. he s-*ed* unto them his hands
Act. 7. 3. into the land which I *shall* s.
10.28. God *hath* s-*ed* me that I sho.
¹Co.12.31. s. I unto you a more excelle.
¹Ti. 6.15. Whi. in his times he *shall* s.
Heb. 8. 5. the pattern s-*ed* to thee in
Jas. 2.18. s. me thy faith without thy
and I *will* s. thee my faith
3.13. *let* him s. out of a good con.
Rev. 1. 1. *to* s. unto his servants things
4. 1. I *will* s. thee things which
17. 1. I *will* s. unto thee the judg.
21. 9. I *will* s. thee the bride, the
10. s-*ed* me that great city, the
22. 1. he s-*ed* me a pure river of w.
6. *to* s. unto his servants the th.
8. the angel *which* s-*ed* me the.
endeiknumi.
Ro. 2.15. Which s. the work of the la.
9.17. that I *might* s. my power
22. willing *to* s. his wrath
²Co. 8.24. Wherefore s. ye to them
Eph. 2. 7. he *might* s. the exceeding
¹Ti. 1.16. Jesus Christ *might* s. *forth*
Tit. 2.10. but s-*ing* all good fidelity
3. 2. s-*ing* all meekness unto all
Heb. 6.10. ye *have* s-*ed* toward his name
11. *that* every one of you *do* s.
epideiknumi.
Mat.16. 1. that he *would* s. them a sign
22.19. s. me the tribute money
24. 1. *to* s. him the buildings
Lu. 17.14. s. yourselves unto the priests
20.24. s. me a penny. Whose ima.
24.40. he s-*ed* them his hands and
Act. 9.39. s-*ing* the coats and garments
18.28. s-*ing* by the scriptures that
Heb. 6.17. *to* s. unto the heirs of prom.
hupodeiknumi.
Lu. 6.47. I *will* s. you to whom he is
Act. 9.16. I *will* s. him how great
20.35. I *have* s-*ed* you all things
anadeiknumi.
Act. 1.24. s. whether of these two thou
apodeiknumi.
²Th. 2. 4. s-*ing* himself that he is God
didōmi ginomai emphanēs.
Act.10.40. and s-*ed him openly*
apanggellō.
Mat.11. 4. Go and s. John *again* those
12.18. he *shall* s. judgment to the
28.11. s-*ed* unto the chief priests all
Lu. 7.18. s-*ed* him of all these things
14.21. came, and s-*ed* his lord these
Act.11.13. he s-*ed* us how he had seen
12.17. Go s. these things unto Jam.
26.20. s-*ed* first unto them of Dam.
246

Act.28.21. that came s-*ed* or spake any
¹Th. 1. 9. themselves s. of us what
¹Jo. 1. 2. bear witness, and s. unto you
ananggellō.
Jo. 16.13. he *will* s. you things to come
14, 15. and *shall* s. it unto you
25. I *shall* s. you plainly of the
Act.19.18. confessed, and s-*ed* their de.
20.20. *have* s-*ed* you, and have tau.
katanggellō.
Act.16.17. which s. unto us the way of
26.23. and should s. light unto
¹Co.11.26. ye do s. the Lord's death
prokatanggellō.
Act. 3.18. which God *before had* s-*ed*
7.52. slain them *which* s-*ed before*
exanggellō.
¹Pet. 2. 9. ye *should* s. *forth* the praises
poieō.
Lu. 1.51. He *hath* s-*ed* strength with
10.37. He *that* s-*ed* mercy on him
Jo. 6.30. What sign s-*est* thou then
Act. 7.36. *after* that he *had* s-*ed* wond.
Jas. 2.13. *that hath* s-*ed* no mercy
phaneroō.
Jo. 7. 4. s. thyself to the world
21. 1. Jesus s-*ed* himself again unto
on this wise s-*ed* he himself
Ro. 1.19. for God *hath* s-*ed* it unto th.
mēnuō.
Lu. 20.37. even Moses s-*ed* at the bush
Jo. 11.57. he *should* s. it, that they mi.
¹Co.10.28. not for his sake *that* s-*ed* it
didōmi. [Mar.13.22
Mat.24.24. *shall* s. great signs and won.;
Act. 2.19. I *will* s. wonders in heaven
paristēmi.
Act. 1. 3. To whom also he s-*ed* hims.
²Ti. 2.15. Study *to* s. thyself approved
parechō.
Act.28. 2. s-*ed* us no little kindness
Tit. 2. 7. s-*ing* thyself a pattern of go.
energeō. [Mar.6.14
Mat.14. 2. works *do* s. *forth themselves;*
megalunō.
Lu. 1.58. *had* s-*ed great* mercy upon
diēgeomai.
Lu. 8.39. s. how great things God hath
ginomai.
Act. 4.22. miracle of healing *was* s-*ed*
optomai.
Act. 7.26. he s-*ed himself* unto them as
emphanizō.
Act.23.22. thou *hast* s-*ed* these things to
katatithēmi.
Act.24.27. willing *to* s. the Jews a plea.
legō.
¹Co.15.51. Behold, I s. you a mystery
dēloō.
²Pet. 1.14. our L. Jes. Ch. *hath* s-*ed* me
(See *Glad, Mercy, Piety.*)

SHEWBREAD.
artos prothesis, [gen.] [6.4
Mat.12. 4. did eat the s.; Mar.2.26; Lu.
Heb. 9. 2. and the table, and the s.

SHEWING, [noun.]
anadeixis.
Lu. 1.80. till the day of his s. unto Is.

SHIELD.
thureos.
Eph. 6.16. taking the s. of faith, where.

SHINE, -ed, -eth, -ing, Shone.
phainō.
Mat.24.27. and s-*eth* even unto the west
Jo. 1. 5. And the light s-*eth* in darkn.
5.35. was a burning and a s-*ing* li.
Phi. 2.15. among whom ye s. as lights
²Pet. 1.19. as unto a light *that* s-*eth* in a
¹Jo. 2. 8. and the true light now s-*eth*
Rev. 1.16. as the sun s-*eth* in his streng.
8.12. and the day s-*o.* not for a thi.

Rev.18.23. the light of a candle *shall* s.
21.23. neither of the moon, to s. in
lampō.
Mat. 5.16. *Let* your light so s. before
17. 2. and his face *did* s. as the
Lu. 17.24. s-*eth* unto the other part.
Act.12. 7. a light s-*ed* in the prison
²Co. 4. 6. commanded the light *to* s.
out of darkness, *hath* s-*ed* in
perilampō.
Lu. 2. 9. of the Lord s-*o. round about*
Act.26.13. s-*ing round about* me and
eklampō.
Mat.13.43. *shall* the righteous s. *forth*
periastraptō.
Act. 9. 3. there s-*ed round about* him
22. 6. there s-*o.* from heav...*round*
astraptō.
Lu. 24. 4. stood by them in s-*ing* garm.
stilbō.
Mar. 9. 3. And his raiment beca. s-*ing*
augazō.
²Co. 4. 4. of God, *should* s. unto them

SHINING, [noun.]
astrapē.
Lu. 11.36. as when the *bright* s. of a

SHIP, -s.
ploion.
Mat. 4.21. in a s. with Zebedee their fa.
22. they immediately left the s.
8.23. when he was entered into a s.
24. insomuch that the s. was co.
9. 1. entered into a s.; Mar.4.1.
8.10 ; Jo.6.17; 21.3
13. 2. he went into a s.; Mar.4.1.
14.13. depar. thence by s.;Mar.6.32
22. dis. to get into a s.; Mar.6.45
24. But the s. was now ; Mar.6.45
29. was come down out of the s.
32. they were come into the s.
33. they that were in the s. came
15.39. and took s., and came into
Mar. 1.19. in the s. mending their nets
20. their father Zebedee in the s.
4.36. him even as he was in the s.
37. the waves beat into the s.
5. 2. when he was come out of s.
18. when he was come into the s.
21. by s. unto the other side
51. up unto them into the s.
54. they were come out of the s.
8.13. and entering into the s. again
14. neither had they in the s.
Lu. 5. 2. And saw two s-s standing by
3. he entered into one of the s-s
taught the peop. out of the s.
7. which were in the other s.
came, and filled both the s-s
11. when they had bro. their s-s
8.37. he went up into the s., and
Jo. 6.19. and drawing nigh unto the s.
21. received him into the s.
and immediately the s. was
21. 6. net on the right side of the s.
Act.20.13. And we went before to s.
38. they accom. him unto the s.
21. 2. And finding a s. sailing
3. for there the s. was to un.
6. we took s.; and they retur.
27. 2. And entering into a s. of
6. there the centuri. found a s.
10. not only of the lading and s.
15. And when the s. was caught
17. undergirding the s.; and
19. hands the tackling of the s.
22. among you, but of the s.
30. about to flee out of the s.
31. Except these abide in the s.
37. and we were in all in the s.
38. they lightened the s., and ca.
39. possible to thrust in the s.

Act. 27.44. on broken pieces of the s.
    28.11. we departed in a s. of Alexa.
Jas. 3. 4. Behold also the s-s, which
Rev. 8. 9. the third part of the s-s were
    18.17. and all the company in s-s
    19. all that had s-s in the sea
    ploiarion.
Mar. 3. 9. that a *small* s. should wait
    4.36. also with him other *little* s-s
Jo. 21. 8. disciples came in a *little* s.
    nauklēros.
Act.27.11. and the *owner of the* s. more
    naus.
Act.27.41. they ran the s. aground

SHIPMASTER.
    kubernētēs.
Rev.18.17. every s., and all the compa.

SHIPMEN.
    nautēs.
Act.27.27. the s. deemed that they drew
    30. as the s. were about to flee

SHIPPING.
    embainō ploion.
Jo. 6.24. they also *took* s., and came

SHIPWRECK.
    nauageō.
2Co.11.25. thrice I *suffered* s., a night
1Ti. 1.19. concerni. faith *have made* s.

SHIVERS. (See *Break.*)
SHOD.
    hupodeomai.
Mar. 6. 9. But *be* s. with sandals; and
Eph. 6.15. your feet s. with the prepar.

SHOES.
    hupodēma.
Mat. 3.11. whose s-s I am not worthy;
    Mar.1.7 ; Lu.3.16
    10.10. neither two coats, neither s-s
Lu. 10. 4. purse, nor scrip, nor s-s; 22.35
    15.22. a ring on his hand, and s-s
Jo. 1.27. whose s.'s latchet I am not
Act. 7.33. Put off thy s-s from thy feet
    13.25. whose s-s of his feet I am not

SHOOT,   -eth.
    poieō.
Mar. 4.32. and s-*eth* out great branches
    proballō.
Lu. 21.30. when they now s. *forth*, ye

SHORE.
    aigialos.
Mat.13. 2. whole multit. stood on the s.
    48. was full, they drew to s.
Jo. 21. 4. Jesus stood on the s.: but
Act.21. 5. kneeled down on the s., and
    27.39. a certain creek with a s.
    40. wind, and made toward s.
    prosormizō.
Mar. 6.53. Gennesa., and *drew to the* s.
    cheilos.
Heb. 11.12. sand which is by the sea s.

SHORN.
    keirō.
Act.18.18. *having* s. his head in Cench.
1Co.11. 6. *let* her also *be* s.: but if it be
    a shame for a woman *to be* s.

SHORT.
    oligos.
Rev.12.12. that he hath but a s. time
    17.10. he must continue a s. *space*
    hustereō.
Ro. 3.23. *come* s. of the glory of God
Heb. 4. 1. should seem *to come* s. of it
    suntemnō.
Ro. 9.28. and *cut* it s. in righteousness
    because a s. work will the

---

    sustellō.
1Co. 7.29. I say, brethren, the time is s.
    kairos hōra.
1Th. 2.17. taken from you for a s. *time*

SHORTENED.
    koloboō.
Mat.24.22. except those days *shou. be* s.
    sake those days *shall be* s.
Mar.13.20. except that the Lord *had* s.
    chosen, he *hath* s. the days

SHORTLY.
    tacheōs.
1Co. 4.19. But I will come to you s.
Phi. 2.19. to send Timotheus s. unto
    24. I also myself shall come s.
2Ti. 4. 9. Do thy diligence to come s.
    en tachos.
Act.25. 4. would depart s. thither
Ro. 16.20. Satan under your feet s.
Rev. 1. 1. things which must s.; 22.6
    tachion.
1Ti. 3.14. hoping to come unto thee s.
Heb.13.23.with whom, if he come s.
    tachinos.
2Pet.1.14. that s. I must put off this
    eutheōs.
3John 14. I trust I shall s. see thee

SHOULD,   -est.
    (*An auxiliary verb, excepting*)
    mellō.
Mar.10.32.*what* things s. happen unto
Lu. 9.31. which he s. accomplish
    19.11. of God s. immediately appe.
    22.23. it was *that* s. do this thing
    24.21. he *which* s. have redeemed
Jo. 6.71. that s. betray him ; 12.4
    7.39. that believe on him s. recei.
    11.51. that Jesus s. die for that
    12.33. what death he s. die ; 18.32
Act.11.28. *that there* s. be great dearth
    19.27. magnificence s. be destroyed
    20.38. that they s. see his face no
    22.29. *which* s. have examined him
    23.27. and s. have been killed of
    26.22. and Moses did say s. come
    23. and s. shew light unto the
    28. 6. they looked *when* he s. have
Gal. 3.23. *which* s. *afterwards* be reve.
1Th. 3. 4. that we s. suffer tribulation
1Ti. 1.16. *which* s. *hereafter* believe
Heb.11.8. which he s. *after* receive
2Pet.2. 6. that *after* s. live ungodly
Rev. 6.11. *that* s. be killed as they were
    dei.
Mat.18.33. s-*est* not thou also have had
    26.35. I s. die with thee ; Mar.14.31
    opheilō.
1Co. 9.10. that ploweth s. plow in hope

SHOULDERS.
    ōmos.
Mat.23. 4. and lay them on men's s.
Lu. 15. 5. he layeth it on his s.

SHOUT.
    epiphōneō.
Act.12.22. the people *gave a* s., saying
    keleusma.
1Th. 4.16. descend from heav. with a s.

SHOWER.
    ombros.
Lu. 12.54. ye say, There cometh a s.

SHRINES.
    naos.
Act.19.24. which made silver s. for Dia.

SHUN,   -ed.
    hupostellō.
Act.20.27. For I *have* not s-*ed* to declare

---

    periistēmi.
2Ti. 2.16. s. profane and vain babblings

SHUT,   -eth.
    kleiō.
Mat. 6. 6. *when* thou *hast* s. thy door
    23.13. ye s. *up* the kingdom of hea.
    25.10. marriage, and the door *was* s.
Lu. 4.25. when the heaven *was* s. *up*
    11. 7. the door *is* now s., and my
Jo. 20.19. *when* the doors *were* s. where
    26. the doors *being* s., and stood
Act. 5.23. The prison truly found we s.
    21.30. forthwith the doors *were* s.
1Jo. 3.17. and s-*eth up* his bowels
Rev. 3. 7. and no man s-*eth ;* and s-*eth*
    8. door, and no man can s. it
    11. 6. These have power *t^* s. heav.
    20. 3. bottomless pit, and s. him *up*
    21.25. the gates of it *shall* not *be* s.
    katakleiō.
Lu. 3. 20. that he s. *up* John in prison
Act. 26.10.saints *did* I s. *up* in prison
    apokleiō.
Lu. 13.25. up, and *hath* s. *to* the door
    sungkleiō.
Gal. 3.23. s. *up* unto the faith which

SICK, (See *Fever, Palsy.*)
    astheneō.
Mat.10. 8. Heal the s., cleanse the lep
    25.36. I *was* s., and ye visited me
Mar. 6.56. they laid the s. in the streets
Lu. 4.40. all they that had any s. with
    7.10. serva. whole *that had been* s.
    9. 2. king. of G., and to heal the s.
Jo. 4.46. whose son *was* s. at Caperna.
    11. 1. Now a certain man was s.
    2. whose brother Lazarus *was* s.
    3. he whom thou lovest *is* s.
    6. heard therefo. that he *was* s.
Act. 9.37. that she *was* s., *and* died
    19.12. were brought unto the s.
Phil. 2.26. heard that he *had been* s.
    27. he *was* s. nigh unto death
2Ti. 4.20. Trophi. I left at Miletum s.
Jas. 5.14. *Is* any s. among you ? let
    asthenēs.
Mat.25.39. Or when saw we thee s., or
    43. s., and in prison, and ye vis.
    44. naked, or s., or in prison
Lu. 10. 9. heal the s. that are therein
Act. 5.15. brought forth the s. into the
    16. bringing s. *folks*, and them
    echō kakōs.
Mat. 4.24. unto him all s. *people*
    8.16. and healed all *that were* s.
    9.12. but they that *are* s.; Mar.2.17
    Lu.5.31
Mar. 1.34. he healed many *that were* s.
    6.55. in beds those *that were* s.
Lu. 7. 2. him, was s., *and* ready to die
    arrōstos.
Mat.14.14.them, and he healed their s.
Mar. 6. 5. hands upon a few s. *folk*
    13. with oil many *that were* s.
    16.18. shall lay hands on the s.
    sunechō.
Act.28. 8. of Publius lay s. *of* a fever.
    kamnō.
Jas. 5.15. prayer of fa. shall save the s.

SICKLE.
    drepanon.
Mar. 4.29. immedi. he putteth in the
Rev.14.14. and in his hand a sharp s
    15. Thrust in thy s., and reap
    16. thrust in his s., on the earth
    17. he also having a sharp s.
    18. to him that had the sharp s.
    saying, Thru. in thy sharp s.
    19. the angel thrust in his s.

247

SICKLY.
  arrōstos.
¹Co. 11.30. many are weak and s. among

SICKNESS,   -es.
  nosos.
Mat. 4.23. healing all manner of s.; 9.35
  8.17. infirmities, and bare our s-es
  10. 1. to heal all manner of s. and
Mar. 3.15. to have power to heal s-es
  astheneia.
Jo. 11. 4. This s. is not unto death

SIDE. (See *Pass, Right.*)
  peran.
Mat. 8.18. to depart unto the *other* s.
  28. come to the *other* s.; 16.5
  14.22. before him unto the *other* s.
Mar. 4.35. pass over unto the *other* s.
  5. 1. unto the *other* s. of the sea
  21. by ship unto the *other* s.
  6.45. to go to the *other* s. before
  8.13. departed to the *other* s.
  10. 1. by the *farther* s. of Jordan
Lu. 8.22. unto the *other* s. of the lake
Jo. 6.22, 25. *on the other* s. of the sea
  para, [*accu.*]
Mat. 13. 1. house and sat *by* the sea s.
  4. fell *by* the way s.; Mar. 4.4;
    Lu.8.5
  19. received seed *by* the way s.
  20.30. sitting *by* the way s., when
Mar. 2.13. went forth again *by* the sea s.
  4. 1. to teach *by* the sea s.: and
  15. these are they *by* the way s.
  10.46. *by* the highway s.; Lu.18.35.
Lu. 8.12. Those *by* the way s. are they
Act.10. 6, 32. wh. house is *by* the sea s.
  16.13. out of the city *by* a river s.
  pleura.
Jo. 19.34. with a spear pierced his s.
  20.20. them his hands and his s.
  25. and thr. my hand into his s.
  27. and thrust it into my s.
Act.12. 7. and he smote Peter on the s.
  enteuthen kai enteuthen.
Jo. 19.18. other with him, *on either* s.
Rev.22. 2. *on either* s. of the river was
  meros.
Jo. 21. 6. Cast the net on the right s.
  pantothen.
Lu. 19.43. keep thee in *on every* s.

SIFT.
  siniazō.
Lu. 22.31. he *may* s. you as wheat

SIGHED.
  stenazō.
Mar.7.34. he s., and saith unto him
  anastenazō.
Mar. 8.12. s. *deeply* in his spirit, *and*

SIGHT, (See *Fearful, Vanish.*)
  enōpion.
Lu. 1.15. great *in the* s. of the Lord
  15.21. against heaven, and *in* thy s.
  16.15. abomination *in the* s. of God
Act. 4.19. right *in the* s. of God; 8.21
  10.31. remembrance *in the* s. of God
Ro. 3.20. no flesh be justified *in* his s.
  12.17. honest *in the* s. of all men
²Co. 4. 2. conscience *in the* s. of God
  7.12. for you *in the* s. of God mig.
  8.21. only *in the* s. of the Lord
    but also *in the* s. of men
¹Ti. 2. 3. *in the* s. of God our Saviour
  6.13. charge *in the* s. of God, who
Heb. 4.13. that is not manifest *in* his s.
  13.21 is well pleasing *in* his s. thro.
Jas. 4.10. *in the* s. of the Lord, and he
¹Pet. 3. 4. which is *in the* s. of God
¹Jo. 3.22. that are pleasing in his s.
248

Rev.13.13. on the earth *in the* s. *of* men¹
  14. to do *in the* s. *of* the beast
  katenōpion.
²Co. 2.17. *in the* s. *of* God speak we
Col. 1.22. unreprovable *in* his s.
  anablepō.
Mat.11. 5. The blind *receive* their s. and
  20.34. their eyes *received* s., and
Mar.10.51.Lo.,that I *might receive* my s.
  52. im. he *received* his s.;Lu.18.43
Lu. 18.41. Lord, that I *may receive* my s.
  42. said unto him, *Receive* thy s.
Jo. 9.11. and washed, and I *received* s.
  15. how he *had received* his s.
  18. been blind, and *received* his s
   of him *that had received* his s.
Act. 9.12. that he *might receive* his s.
  17. thou *mightest receive* thy s.
  18. he *received* s. forthwith, and
  22.13. Brother Saul, *receive* thy s.
  anablepsis.
Lu. 4.18. *recovering* of s. to the blind
  blepō, [*participle.*]
Act. 9. 9. he was three days without s.
  emprosthen.   [10.21.
Mat.11.26.it seemed good *in* thy s.; Lu.
¹Th. 1. 3. *in the* s. *of* God and our Fat.
  theōria.
Lu. 23.48. came together to that s.: and
  ophthalmos.
Act. 1. 9. received him out of their s.
  enantion.
Act. 7.10. wisdom *in the* s. *of* Pharaoh
  horama.
Act. 7.31. he wondered at the s. and
  eidos.
²Co. 5. 7. we walk by faith, not by s.
  para., [*dat.*]
Gal. 3.11. by the law *in the* s. *of* God
  phantazomai, [*participle.*]
Heb.12.21. And so terrible was *the* s.
  horasis.
Rev. 4. 3. in s. like unto an emerald

SIGN,   -s.
  sēmeion.
Mat.12.38.we would see a s. from thee
  39. seeketh after a s.; and there
   16.4 ; Lu.11.29   [Lu.11.29
   s. given..but the s. of ; 16.4
  16. 1. would shew them a s. from
  3. discern the s-s of the times
  24. 3. what shall be the s. of thy
  24. and shall shew great s-s
  30. shall appear the s. of the Son
  26.48. him gave them a s., saying
Mar. 8.11. a s. from heaven ; Lu.11.16
  12. this generation seek after a s.
   no s. be given unto this gen.
  13. 4. and what shall be the s. when
  22. and shall shew s-s and wond.
  16.17. And these s-s shall follow
  20. confirming the word with s-s
Lu. 2.12. And this shall be a s. unto
  34. and for a s. which shall be
  11.30. For as Jonas was a s. unto
  21. 7. what s. will there be when
  11. and great s-s shall there be
  25. And there shall be s-s in the
Jo. 2.18. What s. shewest thou ; 6.30
  4.48. Except ye see s-s and wonde.
  20.30. And many other s-s truly did
Act. 2.19. and s-s in the earth beneath
  22. by miracles and wond. and s-s
  43. many wonders and s-s were
  4.30. that s-s and wonders may be
  5.12. were many s-s and wonders
  7.36. had shewed wonders and s-s
  8.13. beholding the mirac. and s-s
  14. 3. and granted s-s and wonders
Ro. 4.11. And he received the s. of cir.
  15.19. Through mighty s-s and wo.

Co. 1.22. For the Jews require a s.
  14.22. Wheref. tongues are for a s.
²Co.12.12. Truly the s-s of an apostle
  in s-s, and wonders, and mi.
²Th. 2. 9. all power and s-s and lying
Heb. 2. 4. witness, both with s-s and
Rev.15. 1. And I saw another s. in hea.
  enneuō.
Lu. 1.62. they *made* s-s to his father
  parasēmos. [(*by sign,* Castor.
Act.28.11. *whose* s. *was* Castor and Pol

SIGNIFICATION.
  aphōnos.
²Co.14.10. none of them is *without* s.

SIGNIFY.   -ed, -eth, -ing.
  sēmainō.   [17.32; 21.19
Jo. 12.33. s-*ing* what death he should
Act.11.28. and s-*ed* by the spirit that
  25.27. to s. the crimes laid against
Rev. 1. 1. and s-*ed* it by his angel unto
  dēloō.
Heb. 9. 8. The Holy Ghost this s-*ing*
  12.27. s-*eth* the removing of those
¹Pet. 1.11. which was in them *did* s.
  dianggellō.
Act.21.26. *to* s. the accomplishment of
  emphanizō.
Act.23.15. s. to the chief captain that he

SILENCE.
  sigē.
Act.21.40. when there was made a gr. s.
Rev. 8. 1. there was s. in heaven about
  sigaō.
Act.15.12. Then all the multitude *kept* s.
¹Co.14.28. *let* him *keep* s. in the church
  34. *Let* your women *keep* s. in
  hēsuchia.
Act.22. 2. they kept the more s.: and
¹Ti. 2.11. Let the women learn in s.
  12. over the man, but to be in s.
  phimoō.
Mat.22.34.*had* put the Sadducees *to* s.
¹Pet. 2.15. *may* put *to* s. the ignorance

SILK.
  sērikon.
Rev.18.12.purple, and s., and scarlet

SILLY.
  gunaikarion.
²Ti. 3. 6. lead captive s. *women* laden

SILVER, (See *Piece.*)
  argurion.
Mat.26.15. thirty *pieces of* s.; 27.3,9
  27. 5. he cast down the *pieces of* s.
  6. chief priests took the s. *pieces*
Act.19.19. fifty thousand *pieces of* s.
  20.33. I have coveted no man's s.
¹Pet. 1.18. corruptible things, as s. and
  arguros.
Mat.10. 9. Provide neither gold, nor s.
Act.17.29. like unto gold, or s. or stone
¹Co. 3.12. this foundation gold, s.
Jas. 5. 3. Your gold and s. is cankered
Rev.18.12. merchandise of gold, and s.
  argureos.
Act.19.24.which made s. shrines for
²Ti. 2.20. vessels of gold, and of s.
Rev. 9.20. idols *of* gold, and s., and br.

SILVERSMITH.
  argurokopos.
Act.19.24.man named Demetrius, a s.

SIMILITUDE.
  homoiōma.
Ro. 5.14. after the s. of Adam's trans.
  homoiotēs.
Heb. 7.15. after the s. of Melchizedec

homoiōsis.
Jas. 3. 9. are made after the s. of God

SIMPLE.
akakos.
Ro. 16.18. deceive the hearts of the s.
akeraios.
Ro. 16.19. good, and s. concerning evil

SIMPLICITY.
haplotēs.
Ro. 12. 8. giveth, let him do it with s.
²Co. 1.12. that in s. and godly sincerity
11. 3. from the s. that is in Christ

SIN, [noun,]   -s.
hamartia.
Mat. 1.21. save his people from their s-s
3. 6. confessing their s-s; Mar.1.5
9. 2, 5. thy s-s..forgiven thee;
Mar.2.5,9; Lu.5.20,23; 7.48
6. pow. on earth to forgive s-s;
Mar.2.10; Lu.5.24
12.31. All manner of s. and blasph.
26.28. for the remission of s-s; Mar.
1.4; Lu.3.3; Act.2.38
2. 7. who can forgive s-s; Lu.5.21
Lu. 1.77. by the remission of their s-s
7.47. Her s-s, which are many, are
49. this that forgiveth s-s also
11. 4. forgive us our s-s; for we al.
24.47. repenta. and remission of s-s
Jo. 1.29. which taketh away the s. of
8.21, 24. and shall die in your s-s
34. committeth s. is servant of s.
46. Which of you convi. me of s.
9.34. wast altogether born in s-s
41. ye should have no s. but now
therefore your s. remaineth
15.22, 24. they had not had s.: but
th. have no cloke for their s.
16. 8. will reprove the world of s.
9. Of s., because they believe
19.11. unto thee hath the greater s.
20.23. Whose soever s-s ye remit
Act. 5.19. that your s. may be blotted
5.31. Israel, and forgiveness of s-s
7.60. lay not this s. to their charge
10.43. shall receive remission of s-s
13.38. the forgiven. of s-s; Col.1.14
22.16. and wash away thy s-s
26.18. may recei. forgiveness of s-s
Ro. 3. 9. that they are all under s.
20. law is the knowledge of s.
4. 7. forgiven, and whose s-s are
8. The Lord will not impute s.
5.12. by one man s. entered into
and death by s.; and so dea.
13. until the law s. was in the
but s. is not imputed when
20. where s. abounded, grace did
21. That as s. hath reigned
6. 1. Shall we continue in s., that
2. shall we, that are dead to s.
6. the body of s. might be des.
henc. we should not serve s.
7. that is dead is freed from s.
10. he died unto s. once: but in
11. to be dead indeed unto s., but
12. Let not s. therefore reign in
13. of unrighteousness unto s.
14. For s. shall not have domin.
16. whether of s. unto death
17, 20. ye were the servants of s.
18. Being then made free from s.
22. now being made free from s.
23. For the wages of s. is death
7. 5. the motions of s-s, which w.
7. we say then? Is the law s.
I had not known s., but by
8. s., taking occasion by the
For without the law s. was

Ro. 7. 9. came, s. revived, and I died
11. For s.,taking occasion by the
13. s., that it might appear s.
that s. by the commandment
14. I am carnal, sold under s.
17, 20. s. that dwelleth in me
23. to the law of s. which is in
25. with the flesh the law of s.
8. 2. free from the law of s. and
3. for s., condemned s. in the
10. body is dead because of s.
11.27. I shall take away their s-s
14.23. whatsoe. is not of faith is s.
¹Co. 15. 3. that Christ died for our s-s
17. vain; ye are yet in your s-s
56. is s.; and the strength of s.
²Co. 5.21. be s. for us, who knew no s.
Gal. 1. 4. Who gave himself for our s-s
2.17. ther. Christ the minister of s.
3.22. hath concluded all under s.
Eph. 2. 1. were dead in trespas. and s-s
Col. 2.11. the body of the s-s of the fle.
¹Th. 2.16. to fill up their s-s alway: for
²Th. 2. 3. that man of s. be revealed
¹Ti. 5.22. partaker of other men's s-s
24. Some men's s-s are open bef.
²Ti. 3. 6. silly women laden with s-s
Heb. 1. 3. had by hims. purged our s-s
2.17. reconciliation for the s-s of
3.13. thro. the deceitfulness of s.
4.15. like as we are, yet without s.
5. 1. both gifts and sacrifi. for s-s
3. for himself, to offer for s-s
7.27. sacrifice, first for his own s-s
8.12. their s-s and their iniquities
9.26. to put away s. by the sacrifi.
28. offered to bear the s-s of ma.
second time without s. unto
10. 2. had no more conscience of s-s
3. again made of s-s every year
4. of goats should take away s-s
6. sacrifices for s. thou hast
8. offering for s. thou wouldest
11. whi. can never take away s-s
12. offered one sacrifice for s-s
17. their s-s and iniquities will I
18. th. is no more offering for s.
26. rem. no more sacrifice for s-s
11.25. the pleasures of s. for a sea.
12. 1. the s. which doth so easily
4. unto blood, striving agai. s.
13.11. by the high priest for s., are
Jas. 1.15. it bringeth forth s.: and s.
2. 9. res. to persons, ye commit s.
4.17. doeth it not, to him it is s.
5.15. if he have committed s-s
20. shall hide a multitude of s-s
¹Pet. 2.22. Who did no s., neither was
24. his own self bare our s-s in
that we, being dead to s-s
3.18. hath once suffered for s-s
4. 1. the flesh hath ceased from s.
8. shall cover the multi. of s-s
²Pet. 1. 9. was purged from his old s-s
2.14. that cannot cease from s.
¹Jo. 1. 7. Son cleanseth us from all s.
8. If we say that we have no s.
9. If we confess our s-s, he is
and just to forgive us our s-s
2. 2. is the propitiation for our s-s
12. because your s-s are forgiven
3. 4. Whosoever committeth s.
s. is the transgression of the
5. our s-s; and in him is no s.
8. He that committeth s. is of
9. of God doth not commit s
4.10. the propitiation for our s-s
5.16. see his brother sin a s. which
There is a s. unto death: I
17. is s.: and there is a s. not
Rev. 1. 5. washed us from our s-s in his
18. 4. ye be not partakers of her s-s

Rev.18.5. For her s-s have reached un.
hamartēma.
Mar. 3.28. All s-s shall be forgiven unto
4.12. their s-s should be forgiven
Ro. 3.25. for the remission of s-s that
¹Co. 6.18. Every s. that a man doeth
paraptōma.
Eph. 1. 7. the forgiveness of s-s, accor.
2. 5. Ev. when we were dead in s-s
Col. 2.13. you, being dead in your s-s

SIN, [verb,]   -ed, -eth.
hamartanō.
Mat.18.21. how oft shall my brother s.
27. 4. I have s-ed in that I have
Lu. 15.18, 21. Father, I have s-ed agai.
Jo. 5.14. art made whole: s. no more
8.11. thee: go, and s. no more
9. 2. Master, who did s., this man
3. Neither hath this man s-ed
Ro. 2.12. as many as have s-ed without
as many as have s-ed in the
3.23. For all have s-ed, and come
5.12. men, for that all have s-ed
14. them that had not s-ed after
16. as it was by one that s-ed
6.15. shall we s., because we are
¹Co. 6.18. fornication s-eth against his
7.28. marry, thou hast not s-ed
virg. marry, she hath not s-ed
36. do what he will, he s-eth not
8.12. ye s. so against the brethren
weak conscience, ye s. again.
15.34. to righteousness, and s. not
Eph. 4.26. Be ye angry, and s. not
¹Ti. 5.20. Them that s. rebuke before
Tit. 3.11. and s-eth, being condemned
Heb. 3.17. with them that had s-ed
10.26. For if we s. wilfully after th.
²Pet. 2. 4. spa. not the angels that s-ed
¹Jo. 1.10. we say that we have not s-ed
2. 1. ye s. not. And if any man s.
3. 6. Whoso. abideth in him s-eth
whosoever s-eth hath not
8. for the devil s-eth from the
9. he cannot s., because he is
5.16. see his brother s. a sin which
them that s. not unto death
18. is born of God s-eth not
proamartanō.
²Co. 12.21. ma. which have s-ed already
13. 2. th.which heretofore have s-ed
anamartētos.
Jo. 8. 7. He that is without s. among

SINCE.
apo.
Mat.24.21. not s. the beginning of the
Lu. 1.70. which have been s. the world
7.45. this woman, s. the time I
16.16. s. that time the kingdom of
24.21. third day s. these things
Act. 3.21. holy prophets s. the world
Col. 1. 6, 9. s. the day..heard of it
Heb. 9.26. s. the foundation of the wo.
hōs.
Mar. 9.21. How long is it ago s. this ca.
ek.
Jo. 9.32. s. the world began was it not
epeidē.
¹Co. 15.21. For s. by man came death
epei.
²Co. 13. 3. s. ye seek a proof of Christ
meta, [accu.]
Heb. 7.28. which was s. the law, make

SINCERE.
eilikrinēs.
Phi. 1.10. that ye may be s. and witho.
adolos.
¹Pet. 2. 2. desire the s. milk of the word

SINCERELY.
hagnōs.
Phi. 1.16. preach..of contention,not s.

SINCERITY.
eilikrineia.
¹Co. 5. 8. with the unleav. bread of s.
²Co. 1.12. th. in simplicity and godly s.
2.17. as of s., but as of God, in the
gnēsios, [neut.]
²Co. 8. 8. to prove the s. of your love
aphtharsia.
Eph. 6.24. love our Lord Jes. Chr. in s.
Tit. 2.7. uncorruptness, gravity, s.

SINFUL.
hamartōlos.
Mar. 8.38. this adulterous and s. gener.
Lu. 5. 8. for I am a s. man, O Lord
24. 7. into the hands of s. men
Ro. 7.13. might become exceeding s.
hamartia, [gen.]
Ro. 8. 3. likeness of s. flesh, and for

SING, -ing, Sung.
adō.
Eph. 5.19. s-ing and making melody
Col. 3.16. s-ing with grace in your
Rev. 5. 9. they su. a new song; 14.3
15. 3. they s. the song of Moses
psallō.
Ro. 15. 9. I will confess..and s. unto
¹Co.14.15. I will s. with the spirit, and
I will s. with the understan.
Jas. 5.13. any merry? let him s. psalms
humneō.
Mat.26.30. when they had su. an hymn
Act.16.25. and sa. praises unto God
Heb. 2.12. will I s. praise unto thee

SINGLE.
haploos.
Mat. 6.22. if therefore thine eye be s.
Lu. 11.34. therefore when thine eye is s

SINGLENESS.
aphelotēs.
Act. 2.46. with gladness and s. of heart
haplotēs.
Eph. 6. 5. in s. of your heart, as unto
Col. 3.22. in s. of heart, fearing God

SINK, Sunk.
katapontizomai.
Mat.14.30.and beginning to s., he cried
buthizō.
Lu. 5. 7.'ships, so that they began to s.
tithēmi.
Lu. 9.44. Let these sayings s. down in
katapherō.
Act.20. 9. he su. down with sleep, and

SINNER, -s.
hamartōlos. [2.15
Mat. 9.10. many publicans and s-s; Mar.
11. Mast. with publicans and s-s
13. righteous, but s-s to repent.;
Mar.2.17; Lu.5.32 [7.34
11.19. fri. of publicans and s-s; Lu.
26.45. the hands of s-s; Mar.14.41
Mar. 2.16. eat with publicans and s-s
with public. and s-s; Lu.5.30
Lu. 6.32. for s-s also love those that
33. for s-s also do even the same
34. for s-s also lend to s-s
7.37. woman in city, which was a s.
39. toucheth him: for she is a s.
13. 2. were s-s above all the Galile.
15. 1. the publicans and s-s for to
2. This man receiveth s-s, and
7. 10. over one s. that repenteth
18.13. God be merciful to me a s.
19. 7. guest with a man that is a s.
Jo. 9.16. can a man that is a s. do
250

Jo. 9.24. know that this man is a s.
25. Whether he be a s. or no, I
31. that God heareth not s-s
Ro. 3. 7. am I also judged as a s.
5. 8. that, while we were yet s-s
19. disobedience many..made s-s
Gal. 2.15. Jews by nature, and not s-s
17. ourselves also are found s-s
¹Ti. 1. 9. for the ungodly and for s-s
15. into the world to save s-s
Heb. 7.26. undefiled, separate from s-s
12. 3. contradiction of s-s against
Jas. 4. 8. Cleanse your hands, ye s-s
5.20. which converteth the s.
¹Pet. 4.18. ungodly and the s. appear
Jude 15. which ungodly s-s have
opheiletēs.
Lu. 13. 4. ye that they were s-s above

SIR, -s.
kurios.
Mat.13.27.s., didst not thou sow good
21.30. said, I go, s.; and went not
27.63. s., we remember that that
Jo. 4.11. s., thou hast nothing to draw
15. s., give me this water, that I
19. s., I perceive that thou art a
49. s., come down ere my child
5. 7. s., I have no man, when the
12.21. saying, s., we would see Jes.
20.15. s., if thou have borne him
Act.16.30. s-s, what must I do to be sa.
Rev. 7.14. unto him, s., thou knowest
anēr.
Act. 7.26. saying, s-s, ye are brethren
14.15. s-s, why do ye these things
19.25. s-s, ye know that by this
27.10. s-s, I perceive that this voya.
21. s-s, ye should have hearken.
25. Wherefore, s-s, be of good

SISTER, -s.
adelphē. [3.35
Mat. 12.50.is my brother, and s.; Mar.
13.56. his s-s, are they not; Mar.6.3
19.29. houses, or brethren, or s-s;
Mar.10.29,30
Lu. 10.39. she had a s. called Mary
40. not care that my s. hath left
14.26. children, and breth., and s-s
Jo. 11. 1. town of Mary and her s. Ma.
3. Therefore his s-s sent unto
5. loved Martha, and her s.
28. called Mary her s. secretly
39. the s. of him that was dead
19.25. his moth., and his mother's s.
Act.23.16. when Paul's s.'s son heard of
Ro. 16. 1. comme. to you Phebe our s.
15. and Julia, Nereus, and his s.
¹Co. 7.15. A brother or a s. is not under
9. 5. to lead about a s., a wife
¹Ti. 5. 2. as moth.; the younger as s-s
Jas. 2.15. If a brother or a s. be naked
²John 13. The children of thy elect s.
anepsios.
Col. 4.10. Marcus, s.'s son to Barnabas

SIT, -est, -eth, -ing, Sat, Set.
kathēmai.
Mat. 4.16. The people which sa. in dar
to them which sa. in the regi.
9. 9. s-ing at the receipt of cust.
Mar.2.14; Lu.5.27
11.16. unto children s-ing; Lu.7.32
13. 1. and sa. by the sea side
2. into a ship, and sa.; Mar.4.1
15.29. moun.; and sa. down there
20.30. s-ing by the way side, when
22.44. s. thou on my right hand;
Mar.12.36; Lu.20.42
23.22. by him that s-eth thereon

Mat. 24. 3. as he sa. upon the; Mar.13.3
26.58. and sa. with the servants
64. Son of man s-ing on the right.
Mar.14.62; Lu.22.69
69. Peter sa. without in the pal.
27.36. And s-ing down they watched
61. s-ing over against the sepul.
28. 2. the door, and sa. upon it
Mar. 2. 6. certain of the scribes s-ing
3.32. the multitude sa. about him
34. on them which sa. about him
5.15. had the legion, s-ing, and
10.46. sa. by the highway side beg.
16. 5. they saw a young man s-ing
Lu. 1.79. to them that s. in darkness
5.17. doctors of the law s-ing by
8.35. s-ing at the feet of Jesus
10.13. repented, s-ing in sackcloth
18.35. blind man sa. by the wayside
22.55. Peter sa. down among them
56. maid beheld him as he sa.
Jo. 2.14. the changers of money s-ing
6. 3. and there he sa. with his
9. 8. Is not this he that sa. and
12.15. cometh, s-ing on an ass's colt
Act. 2. 2. house where they were s-ing
3.10. he which sa. for alms at the
8.28. and s-ing in his chariot read
14. 8. there sa. a certain man at
20. 9. And there sa. in a window
23. 3. for s-est thou to judge me
¹Co.14.30. to another that s-eth by
Col. 3. 1. where Christ s-eth on the rig.
Jas. 2. 3. s. thou here in a good place
s. here under my footstool
Rev. 4. 2. and one sa. on the throne
3. And he that sa. was to look
4. four and twenty elders s-ing
9, 10. that sa. on the throne;
5.1,7,21.5 [6.16,7.10,15
5.13. that s-eth upon the throne;
6. 2. he that sa. on him had a bow
4. to him that sa. thereon to
5. he that sa. on him had a pair
8. his name that sa. on him
9.17. and them that sa. on them
11.16. elders, which sa. before God
14.14. one sa. like unto the Son of
15, 16. to him that sa. on the cl.
17. 1. that s-eth upon many waters
3. saw a woman s. upon a scar.
9. on which the woman s-eth
15. where the whore s-eth, are
18. 7. I s. a queen, and am no wid.
19. 4. worshipped God that sa. on
11. he that sa. upon him was
18. and of them that sa. on them
19. against him that sa. on the
21. with the swo. of him that sa.
20.11. throne, and him that sa. on
sungkathēmai.
Mar.14.34. and he sa. with the servants
Act.26.30. and they that sa. with them
kathezomai.
Mat.26.55.I sa. daily with you teaching
Lu. 2.46. s-ing in the midst of the doc.
Jo. 4. 6. sa. thus on the well; and it
11.20. but Mary sa. still in the ho.
20.12. seeth two ang. in white s-ing
Act. 6.15. And all that sa. in the coun.
kathizō.
Mat. 13.48.to shore, and sa. down, and
19.28. Son of man shall s. in the
of his glory, ye also shall s.
20.21. my two sons may s., the one
23. but to s. on my; Mar.10.40
23. 2. the Pharisees s. in Moses' se.
25.31. then shall he s. upon the
26.36. s. ye here, while I go and pr.
Mar. 9.35. And he sa. down, and called
10.37. Grant unto us that we may s.
11. 2. never man sa.; Lu.19.30

Mar.11. 7. on him, and he sa. upon him
12.41. Jesus sa. over against the
14.32. s. ye here, while I shall pray
16.19. and sa. on the right hand of
Lu. 4.20. to the minister, and sa.down
5. 3. And he sa. down, and taught
14.28. s-eth not down first, and
31. s-eth not down first, and con.
16. 6. s. down quickly, and write
22.30. and s. on thrones judging
Jo. 8. 2. and he sa. down, and taught
12.14. found a young ass, sa. there.
19.13. and sa. down in the judgme.
Act. 2. 3. and it sa. upon each of them
30. Christ to s. on his throne
8.31. that he would come up and s.
12.21. sa. upon his throne, and
13.14. sabbath-day, and sa. down
16.13. we sa. down, and spake unto
25. 6. s-ing on the judgment seat
17. I sa. on the judgment seat
1Co. 10. 7. The people sa. down to eat
2Th. 2. 4. s-eth in the temple of God
Heb. 1. 3. sa. down on the right; 10.12
12. 2. is se. down at the right hand
Rev. 3.21. will I grant to s. with me on
20. 4. and they sa. upon them
anakathizō.
Lu. 7.15. he that was dead sa. up, and
Act. 9.40. when she saw P., she sa. up
parakathizō.
Lu. 10.39. also sa. at Jesus' feet, and
sungkathizō.
Eph. 2. 6. and made us s. together in
anapiptō.
Mat. 15.35.the multitude to s. down on
Mar. 6.40. they sa. down in ranks, by
8. 6. the people to s. down on the
Lu. 11.37. went in, and sa. down to meat
14.10. go and s. down in the lowest
17. 7. Go and s. down to meat
22.14. he sa. down, and the twelve
Jo. 6.10. said, Make the men s. down
So the men sa. down, in nu.
13.12. garments, and was se. down
anakeimai.
Mat. 9.10. as Jesus sa. at meat in the
26. 7. his head, as he sa. at meat
20. he sa. down with the twelve
Mar.14.18.as they sa. and did eat, Jes.
16.14. the eleven as they sa. at meat
Lu. 7.37. knew that Jesus sa. at meat
22.27. greater, he that s-eth at meat
is not he that s-eth at meat
sunanakeimai.
Mat. 9.10. came and sa. down with him
14. 9. which sa. with him at meat;
Lu.14.10,15
Mar. 2.15. sinners sa. also together with
6.22. Herod and them that sa.with
26. their sakes which sa. with
Lu. 7.49. And they that sa. at meat wi.
Jo. 12. 2. that sa. at the table with him
katakeimai.
Mar. 2.15. as Jesus sa. at meat in his
14. 3. as he sa. at meat, there came
Lu. 5.29. of others that sa. down with
1Co. 8.10. s. at meat in the idol's temple
anaklinō.
Mat. 8.11. shall s. down with Abraham
14.19. com.the multitude to s. down
Mar. 6.39. to make all s. down by com.
Lu. 7.36. house, and sa. down to meat
9.15. and made them all s. down
12.37. make them to s. down to me.
13.29. shall s. down in the kingdom
kataklinō.
Lu. 9.14. Make them s. down by fifties
14. 8. s. not down in the highest
24.30. as he sa. at meat with them
epibainō.
Mat.21. 5. meek, and s-ing upon an ass

SIX, (See *Hundred*.)
hex.   [Mar.9.2
Mat.17. 1. after s. days Jesus taketh;
Lu. 4.25. shut up three years and s.
13.14. There are s. days in which
Jo. 2. 6. were set there s. waterpots
20. Forty and s. years was this
12. 1. s. days before the passover
Act.11.12. these s. brethren accompan.
18.11. continued there a year and s.
Jas. 5.17. space of three years and s.
Rev. 4. 8. each of them s. wings about
13.18. Six hundr. threescore and s.

SIXTEEN.
hebdomēkonta hex.
Act.27.37. two hundred *threescore and* s.

SIXTH.
hektos.
Mat.20. 5. about the s. and ninth hour
27.45. from the s. hour there was
Mar.15.33.when the s. hour was come
Lu. 1.26. in the s. month the angel
36. this is the s. month with her
23.44. it was about the s. h.; Jo.4.6
Jo. 19.14. about the s. hour: and he
Act.10. 9. to pray about the s. hour
Rev. 6.12. he had opened the s. seal
9.13. And the s. angel sounded
14. Saying to the s. angel which
16.12. the s. angel poured out his
21.20. fifth, sardonyx; the s., sard.

SIXTY.
hexēkonta.
Mat.13. 8.some s. fold, some thirtyfold
23. some an hundredfold, some s.
Mar.4. 8, 20. some thirty, and some s.

SKIN,   -s.
dermatinos.
Mar. 1. 6. with a girdle of a s. about
derma.
Heb.11.37.in sheepskins and goat s-s

SKULL.
kranion.   [19.17
Mat.27.33. place of a s.; Mar.15.22; Jo.

SKY.
ouranos.
Mat.16. 2. weather: for the s. is red
3. for the s. is red and lowring
the face of the s.; Lu.12.56
Heb.11.12.many as the stars of the s.

SLACK.
bradunō.
2Pet. 3. 9. The Lord *is* not s. concerning

SLACKNESS.
bradutēs.
2Pet. 3. 9. prom., as some men count s.

SLANDERERS.
diabolos.
1Ti. 3.11. wives be grave, not s., sober

SLANDEROUSLY.
(See *Report*.)

SLAUGHTER.
sphagē.
Act. 8.32. was led as a sheep to the s.
Ro. 8.36. accounted as sheep for the s.
Jas. 5. 5. hearts, as in a day of s.
phonos.
Act. 9. 1. breath. out threaten. and s.
kopē.
Heb. 7. 1. from the s. of the kings and

SLAVES.
sōma.
Rev.18.13. and s. and souls of men

SLAY, *Slain, Slew,* (See *Beast.*)
apokteinō.
Mat.21.39. out of the vineyard, and s-10
22. 6. entreated them spit. and s-w
Lu. 9.22. be s-n and be raised the third
11.49. some of them they *shall* s.
13. 4. fell, and s-w them, think ye
Jo. 5.16. perse. Jesus, and sought to s.
Act. 7.52. they *have* s-n them which
23.14. nothing until we *have* s-n P.
Ro. 7.11. deceived me, and by it s-w
Eph. 2.16. *having* s-n the enmity there.
Rev. 2.13. who *was* s-n among you
9.15. for to s. the third part of
11.13. *were* s-n of men seven thou.
19.21. the remnant *were* s-n with
sphattō.
1Jo. 3.12. and s-w his brother. And wh.
s-w he him? Because his
Rev. 5. 6. st. a Lamb as it *had been* s-n
9. for thou *wast* s-n, and hast
12. is the Lamb *that was* s-n
6. 9. souls of them *that were* s-n
13. 8. book of life of the Lamb s-n
18.24. and of all *that were* s-n upon
katasphattō.
Lu. 19.27. and s. them before me
anaireō.
Mat. 2.16. sent forth, and s-w all the
Act. 2.23. hands *have* crucified and s-n
5.33. took counsel to s. him
36. who *was* s-n; and all, as ma.
9.29. they went about to s. him
10.39. whom they s-w and hanged
13.28. Pilate *that* he *should be* s-n
22.20. the raiment of them *that* s-w
phoneuō.
Mat.23.35. whom ye s-w between the
apothnēskō en phonos.
Heb.11.37.they *were* s-n *with* the sword
(*died by the death of.*)
diacheirizomai.
Act. 5.30. Jesus, whom ye s-w and han
thuō.
Act.11. 7. Arise, Peter; s. and eat

SLEEP, [*noun.*] (See *Awake.*)
hupnos.
Mat. 1.24. Joseph being raised from s.
Lu. 9.32. with him were heavy with s.
Jo. 11.13. spoken of taking of rest in s.
Act.20. 9. being fallen into a deep s.
he sunk down with s., and
Ro. 13.11. high time to awake out of s.
koimaomai.
Act.13.36. *fell on* s., and was laid unto

SLEEP, *-est, -eth, -ing, Slept.*
katheudō.
Mat. 9.24. maid is not dead, but s-eth;
Mar 5.39; Lu. 8.52
13.25. But while men s-t, his enemy
25. 5. they all slumbered and s-t
26.45. s. on now, and ta.; Mar.14.41.
Mar. 4.27. And *should* s., and rise night
13.36. suddenly he find you s-ing
14.37. and findeth them s-ing, and
unto Peter, Simon, s-est th.
Lu. 22.46. Why s. ye? rise and pray
Eph. 5.14. Awake thou that s-est, and
1Th. 5. 6. *let* us not s., as do others
7. For they that s. s. in the ni.
10. whether we wake or s., we
koimaomai.
Mat.27.52. bodies of the saints *which* s-t
28.13. stole him away *while* we s-t
Lu. 22.45. he found them s-ing for sor.
Jo. 11.11. Our friend Lazarus s-eth
12. Lord, if he s., he shall do
Act.12. 6. Peter was s-ing between two
1Co.11.30. sickly among you, and ma. s.
15.20. first fruits of them *that* s-t

¹Co. 15.51. We *shall* not all s., but we
Th. 4.14. them also *which* s. in Jesus

SLEIGHT.
kubeia.
Eph. 4.14. by the s. of men, and cunni.

SLIP.
pararreō.
Heb. 2. 1. time we *should let* them s.

SLOTHFUL.
oknēros.
Mat. 25.26. Thou wicked and s. servant
Ro. 12.11. Not s. in business; fervent
nōthros.
Heb. 6.12. That ye be not s., but follow.

SLOW.
bradus.
Lu. 24.25. O fools, and s. of heart to
Jas. 1.19. s. to speak, s. to wrath
argos.
Tit. 1.12. liars, evil beasts, s. bellies

SLOWLY. (See *Sail*.)

SLUMBER, [*noun*.]
katanuxis.
Ro. 11. 8. given them the spirit of s.

SLUMBER, [*verb*,] -*ed*, -*eth*.
nustazō.
Mat. 25. 5. tarried, they all s-*ed* and sl.
²Pet. 2. 3. and their damnation s-*eth* not

SMALL.
oligos.
Act. 12.18. there was no s. stir among
    15. 2. no s. dissension and disputa.
    19.23. there arose no s. stir about
    24. no s. gain unto the craftsm.
    27.20. and no s. tempest lay on us
mikros.
Act. 26.22. witnessing both to s. and gr.
Rev. 11.18. that fear thy name, s. and
    13.16. both s. and great; 19.5,18
    20.12. I saw the dead, s. and great
elachistos.
¹Co. 4. 3. with me, it is a *very* s. thing
Jas. 3. 4. about with a *very* s. helm
(See *Cord, Fish, Ship*.)

SMALLEST.
elachistos.
¹Co. 6. 2. unworthy to judge the s. ma.

SMELL.
euōdia.
Phi. 4.18. odour of a *sweet* s., a sacrifi.

SMELLING, [*noun*.]
osphrēsis.
¹Co.12.17. hearing, where were the s.

SMITE, -*est*, -*eth*, -*ten*, *Smote*.
patassō.
Mat. 26.31. I *will* s. the shep.; Mar. 14.27
Lu. 22.49. Lord, *shall* we s. with the
    50. s-*o* the servant of the high
Act. 7.24. oppressed, *and* s-*o* the Egyp.
    12. 7. he s-*o* Peter on the side, *and*
    23. the angel of the Lord s-*o* him
Rev. 11. 6. and *to* s. the earth with
    19.15. with it he *should* s. the nati.
tuptō.
Mat. 24.49. And shall begin *to* s. his
    27.30. s-*o* him on the he.; Mar. 15.19
Lu. 6.29. And unto him *that* s-*eth* thee
    18.13. but s-*o* upon his breast, sayi.
Act. 23. 2. by him *to* s. him on the mo.
    3. God shall s. thee, thou whit.
commandest me *to be* s-*en*
derō.
Lu. 22.63. mocked him, *and* s-*o* him
252

Jo. 18.23. if well, why s-*est* thou me
²Co.11.20. if a man s. you on the face
paiō.   [22.64
Mat. 26.68. Who is he *that* s-*o* thee; Lu.
Mar. 14.47. s-*o* a serva. of the ; Jo.18.10
rapizō.
Mat. 5.39. whosoever *shall* s. thee on
didōmi rapisma.
Jo. 19. 3. they s-*o* him *with their hands*
aphaireō.
Mat. 26.51. priest's, and s-*o off* his ear.
plēssō.
Rev. 8.12. third part of the sun *was* s-*en*
(See *Palm*.)

SMOKE, [*noun*.]
kapnos.
Act. 2.19. blood, and fire, and va. of s.
Rev. 8. 4. And the s. of the incense
    9. 2. there arose a s. out of the
as the s. of a great furnace
by reason of the s. of the pit
    3. there came out of the s. loc.
    17. issued fire and s. and brims.
    18. kil., by the fire, and by the s.
    14.11. And the s. of their torment
    15. 8. was filled with s. from the
    18. 9, 18. see the s. of her burning
    19. 3. And her s. rose up for ever

SMOKING, [*verb*.]
tuphomai.
Mat.12.20. and s. flax shall he not que.

SMOOTH.
leios.
Lu. 3. 5. rough ways shall be made s.

SNARE.
pagis.
Lu. 21.35. as a s. shall it come on all
Ro. 11. 9. Let their table be made a s.
¹Ti. 3. 7. the s. of the devil.; ²Ti.2.26
    6. 9. fall into temptation and a s.
brochos.
¹Co. 7.35. not that I may cast a s. upon

SNOW.
chiōn.
Mat. 28. 3. and his raiment white as s.
Mar. 9. 3. shining, exceedi. white as s.
Rev. 1.14. white like wool, as whi. as s.

SO.
houtō, *or* houtōs.
Mat. 5.12. for s. persecuted they the
    16. Let your light s. shine befo.
    19. and shall teach men s.
    47. do not even the publicans s.
    6.30. s. clothe the grass; Lu.12.28
    9.33. It was never s. seen in Israel
    11.26. for s. it seemed go.; Lu.10.21
    12.40. s. shall the Son of man be;
Lu.11.30 ; 17.24
    13.40, 49, s. shall it be in the end of
    18.35. s. likewise shall my heaven.
    19. 8. the beginning it was not s.
    10. If the case of the man be s.
    12. which were s. born from the.
    20.16. s. the last shall be first
    26. But it shall not be s. among
    24.27, 37, 39. s. shall also the com.
    33. s. likewise ye, when ye sha.;
Lu.17.10 ; 21.31
    46. shall find s. doing ; Lu.12.43
Mar. 2. 8. that they s. reasoned within
    4.26. s. is the kingdom of God
    40. Why are ye s. fearful
    7.18. Are ye s. without understa.
    10.43. But s. shall it not be among
    14.59. But neither s. did their wit.
    15.39. saw that he s. cried out
Lu. 6.10. And he did s.; and his hand
    9.15. And they did s., and made

Lu. 12.21. s. is he that layeth up treas.
    38. and find them s., blessed are
    54. cometh a shower ; and s. it is
    17.26. s. shall it be also in the days
    22.26. But ye shall not be s.
    24.24. and found it even s. as the
Jo. 3. 8. s. is every one that is born
    16. For God s. loved the world
    5.26. s. hath he given to the Son to
    8.59. of them, and s. passed by
    12.50. said unto me, s. I speak
    18.22. Answ. thou the high priest s.
Act. 1. 11. shall s. come in like manner
    3.18. suffer, he hath s. fulfilled
    7. 1. Are these things s.
    8. and s. Abraham begat Isaac
    8.32. s. opened he not his mouth
    12. 8. And s. he did. And he saith
    13. 8. for s. is his name by interpr.
    47. For s. hath the Lord comma.
    14. 1. and s. spake, that a great
    17.11. whether those things were s.
    33. s. Paul departed from among
    19.20. s. mightily grew the word of
    20.11. till break of day, s. he depar.
    13. for s. had he appointed
    35. how that s. labouring ye ou.
    21.11. s. shall the Jews at Jerusale.
    22.24. wherefore they cried s. agai.
    23.11. s. must thou bear witness al.
    24. 9. saying that these thi. were s.
    14. s. worship I the God of my
    27.17. strake sail, and s. were driv.
    44. And s. it came to pass, that
    28.14. and s. we went toward Rome
Ro. 1.15. s., as much as in me is, I am
    4.18. s. shall thy seed be
    5.12. and s. death passed upon all
    15. s. also is the free gift
    19. s. by the obedience of one
    11.26. And s. all Israel shall be sav
    12. 5. s. we, being many, are one
    15.20. Yea, s. have I strived to pr.
¹Co. 3.15. saved ; yet s. as by fire
    4. 1. Let a man s. account of us
    5. 3. that hath s. done this deed
    6. 5. Is it s., that there is not a
    7.17. s. let him walk. And s. ord.
    26. good for a man s. to be
    36. and need s. require, let him
    40. But she is happier if she s.
    8.12. when ye sin s. against the
    9.15. that it should be s. done un.
    24. s. run, that ye may obtain
    26. s. run, not as uncertainly ; s.
    11.28. and s. let him eat of that
    12.12. one body : s. also is Christ
    14. 9. s. likewise ye, except ye utt.
    25. manifest ; and s. falling down
    15.11. s. we preach, and s. ye belie.
    42. s. also is the resurrection of
    45. And s. it is written, The first
    16. 1. chu. of Galatia *even* s. do ye
²Co. 1. 5. s. our consolation also abou.
    7. 8. shall ye be also of the con.
    8. 6. s. he would also finish
    11. s. there may be a performan.
    11. 3. s. your minds should be cor.
Gal. 1. 6. marvel that ye are s. soon
    3. 3. Are ye s. foolish ? having
    6. 2. and s. fulfil the law of Christ
Eph. 4.20. But ye have not s. learned C.
    5.24. s. let the wives be to their
    28. s. ought men to love their
    33. s. love his wife even as hims.
Phi. 3.17. and mark them which walk s.
    4. 1. s. stand fast in the Lord
Col. 3.13. forgave you, s. also do ye
¹Th. 2. 8. s. being affectionately desir.
    4.17. and s. shall we ever be with
    5. 2. the day of the Lord s. come
²Th. 3.17. token in every epistle ; s

Ti. 3. 8. s. do these also resist the tr.
Heb. 5. 3. s. also for himself, to offer
     5. s. also Christ glorified not
     6.15. And s., after he had patient.
     9.28. s. Christ was once offered
    10.33. compa. of them that were s.
    12.21. And s. terrible was the sight
Jas. 1.11. s. also shall the rich man fa.
     2.12. s. speak ye, and s. do, as th.
     26. s. faith without works is de.
    3. 6. s. is the tongue among our
     10. these things ought not s. to
     12. s. can no fountain both yield
1Pet. 2.15. For s. is the will of God
2Pet. 1.11. For s. an entrance shall be
1Jo. 2. 6. ought himself also s. to walk
     4.11. Beloved, if God s. loved us
Rev. 2.15. s. hast thou also them that
     3.16. s. then because thou art luk.
    16.18. an earthquake, and s. great
    houtō kai.
Mar.13.29. s. ye *in like manner,* when
    houtōs oun.
Lu. 14.33. s. *likewise,* whosoever he be
    houtos.
Jo. 11.28. And when..had s. said;
     20.20; Act.23.7
Act.19.14. of one Sceva..which did s.
Ro. 12.20. for in s. doing thou shalt
1Co. 7.37. hath s. decreed in his heart
    hōste.
Mat.8.28. s. *that* no man might pass
    13. 2. s. *that* he went into; Mar.4.1
     32. s. *that* the birds of; Mar.4.32
Mar. 3.20. s. *that* they could not so mu.
     4.37. s. *that* it was now full
    10. 8. s. *then* they are no more tw.
    15. 5. s. *that* Pilate marvelled
Lu. 5. 7. s. *that* they began to sink
Act.16.26. s. *that* the foundations of the
    19.10. s. *that* all they which dwelt
     12. s. *that* from his body were
     16. s. *that* they fled out of that
Ro. 15.19. s. *that* from Jerusalem, and
1Co. 1. 7. s. *that* ye come behind in no
    3. 7. s. *then* neither is he that pl.
    7.38. s. *then* he that giveth her in
    13. 2. s. *that* I could remove mou.
2Co. 2. 7. s. *that* contrariwise ye ought
    3. 7. s. *that* the children of Israel
    4.12. s. *then* death worketh in us
    7. 7. s. *that* I rejoiced the more
Gal. 3. 9. s. *then* they which be of faith
Phi. 1.13. s. *that* my bonds in Christ
1Th. 1. 7. s. *that* ye were ensamples
     8. s. *that* we need not to speak
1Th. 1. 4. s. *that* we ourselves glory in
    2. 4. s. *that* he as God sitteth in
Heb.13.6. s. *that* we may boldly say
    hoios.
Mar. 9. 3. s. *as* no fuller on earth can
    homoiōs.
Lu. 5.10. And s. was also James, and J.
    kata [*accus.*] **houtos** [*plu.neu.*]
Lu. 6.26. s. did their fathers to the fa.
    oun.
Mat.1.17. s. all the generations from A.
Jo. 4.40. s. when the Samaritans were
     46. s. Jesus came again into Cana
     53. s. the father knew that it was
    6.10. s. the men sat down
     19. s. when they had rowed abo.
    7.43. s. there was a division among
    13.12. s. after he had washed their
    21.15. s. when they had dined
Act.13. 4. s. they, being sent forth by
    15.30. s. when they were dismissed
    16. 5. *And* s. were the churches
    23.18. s. he took him, and brought
     22. s. the chief captain then
    28. 9. s. when this was done
Ro. 7. 3. s. then if, while her husband

Ro. 7.25. s. then with the mind I mys.
    9.16. s. then it is not of him thatl
    14.12. s. then every one of us shal
    ean.
Mat.18.13. *if* s. be that he find it, verily
    oun men.
Mar.16.19. s. *then* after the Lord had
    ara.
1Co. 15.15. if s. *be* that the dead rise not
    eis.
Lu. 20.20. *that* s. they might deliver
Ro. 1.20. s. *that* they are without excu.
Heb.11. 3. s. *that* things which are seen
    mēte.
Mar. 3.20. could *not* s. *much as* eat
    hopōs.
Lu. 16.26. s. *that* they which would pa.
    hōs.
Act.20.24. s. *that* I might finish my
Heb. 3.11. s. I sware in my wrath
    hina.
Gal. 5.17. s. *that* ye cannot do the thin.
       ([*or*], *in order that.*)
Rev. 8.12. s. *as* the third part of them
    13.13. s. *that* he maketh fire come
    (*See words in connection.*)

SOBER.   (See *Minded.*)
    nēphō.
1Th. 5. 6. but let us watch and *be* s.
     8. us, who are of the day, *be* s.
1Pet. 1.13. be s., and hope to the end
    5. 8. *Be* s., be vigilant
    nēphalios.
1Ti. 3.11. s., faithful in all things
Tit. 2. 2. That the aged men be s., gr.
    sōphrōn.
1Ti. 3. 2. vigilant, s., of good behavio.
Tit. 1. 8. s., just, holy, temperate
    sōphroneō.
2Co. 5.13. or whether we *be* s., it is for
1Pet. 4. 7. *be* ye therefore s., and watch
    sōphronizō.
Tit. 2. 4. *may teach* the.. wo. *to be* s.

SOBERLY.
    sōphronōs.
Tit. 2.12. we should live s., righteous.
    eis sōphroneō [*infin.*]
Ro. 12. 3. but to think s., according as

SOBERNESS.
    sōphrosunē.
Act.26.25. fo. the words of truth and s.

SOBRIETY.
    sōphrosunē.
1Ti. 2. 9. with shamefacedness and s.
    15. charity and holiness with s.

SOEVER.
    ean.
Mar. 6.10. In what place s. ye enter
    hosos an.
Mar.3. 28. *wherewith* s. they shall blas.
    pas [*plu. neut.*] **hosos an.**
Mar.11.24. *what* things s. ye desire
    hosos [*plu. neut.*]
Ro. 3.19. *what* things s. the law saith

SOFT.
    malakos.   [Lu.7.25
Mat.11. 8. man clothed in s. raiment;
     they that wear s. clothing

SOFTLY.   (See *Blow.*)

SOJOURN,   -ed.
    eimi paroikos.
Act. 7. 6. his seed *should* s. in a stran.
    paroikeō.
Heb.11. 9. he s-*ed* in the land of prom.

SOJOURNING.
    paroikia.
1Pet. 1.17. pass the time of your s. here

SOLDIER,   -s.
    stratiōtēs.
Mat. 8. 9. having s-s under me ; Lu.7.8
    27.27. Then the s-s of the governor
    28.12. gave large mon. unto the s-s
Mar.15.16. And the s-s led him away
Lu. 23.36. And the s-s also mocked him
Jo. 19. 2. And the s-s platted a crown
     23. Then the s-s, when they had
      four parts, to every s. a part
     24. These things therefore the s-s
     32. Then came the s-s, and brake
     34. But one of the s-s with a sp.
Act.10. 7. and a devout s. of them that
    12. 4. him to fo. quaternions of s-s
     6. P. was sleep. between two s-s
     18. no small stir among the s-s
    21.32. Who immediately took s-s
      the chief captain and the s-s
     35. he was borne of the s-s for
    23.23. Make ready two hundred s-s
     31. Then the s-s, as it was com.
    27.31. to the centuri. and to the s-s
     32. Then the s-s cut off the ropes
     42. And the s-s' counsel was to
    28.16. by himself with a s. that kep.
2Ti. 2. 3. endure hardness, as a good s.
    strateuomai.
Lu. 3.14. the s-s likewise demanded of
    strateuma.
Act.23.10. commanded the s-s to go do.
    stratologeō.
2Ti. 2. 4. *who hath chosen* him *to be a* s.

SOLITARY.
    erēmos.
Mar. 1.35. departed into a s. place

SOME.   (See *Lest.*)
    tis.   [Mar.9.1 ; Lu.9.27
Mat.16.28. There be s. standing here ;
    27.47. s. of them that stood there
    28.11. s. of the watch came into the
Mar. 7. 2. when they saw s. of his
    14. 4. were s. that had indignation
     65. And s. began to spit on him
    15.35. And s, of them that stood by
Lu. 9. 7. because that it was said of s.
     8. And of s., that Elias had
    11.15. But s. of them said, He cast.
    13. 1. s. that told him of the Galil.
    19.39. s. of the Pharisees ; Jo.9.16
    21. 5. And as s. spake of the temp.
    23. 8. to have seen s. miracle done
Jo. 6.64. But there are s. of you that
    7.25. Then said s. of them of Jeru.
     44. s. of them would have taken
    11.37. And s. of them said, Could
     46. s. of them went their ways
    13.29. For s. of them thought, bec.
Act. 5.15. might overshadow s. of them
    8. 9. that himself was s. great one
    31. except s. *man* should guide
    34. of himself, or of s. other *man*
    11.20. And s. of them were men of
    15.36. And s. days after Paul said
    17. 4. And s. of them believed
     18. s. said, What will this babb.
     21. or to hear s. new thing
    18.23. after he had spent s. time
    27.27. they drew near to s. country
Ro. 1.11. impart unto you s. spiritual
     13. that I might have s. fruit
    3. 3. For what if s. did not believe
     8. and as s. affirm that we say
    5. 7. s. would even dare to die
    11.14. and might save s. of them
     17. if s. of the branches be brok
1Co. 4.18. Now s. are puffed up, as
    6.11. And such were s. of you
    8. 7. for s. with conscience of the
    9.22. I might by all means save s,
    10. 7. be ye idolaters, as were s. of

¹Co. 10. 8. as **s.** of them committed
9. as **s.** of them also tempted
10. as **s.** of them also murmured
15. 6. but **s.** are fallen asleep
12. how say **s.** among you that
34. for **s.** have not the knowledge
35. But **s.** man will say, How are
37. chance of wheat, or of **s.** oth.
²Co. 3. 1. or need we, as **s.** others, epis.
10. 2. against **s.**, which think of us
12. with **s.** that commend them.
Gal. 1. 7. but there be **s.** that trouble
Phi. 1.15. s. indeed preach Christ even
of envy and strife ; and **s.** also
²Th. 3 11. For we hear that there are **s.**
¹Ti. 1. 3. thou mightest charge **s.** that
6. From which **s.** have swerved
19. which **s.** having put away
4. 1. **s.** shall depart from the faith
5.15. For **s.** are already turned
24. **s.** men's sins are open before.
and **s.** men they follow after
6.10. which while **s.** coveted after
21. Which **s.** professing have
²Ti. 2.18. and overthrow the faith of **s.**
Heb. 3. 4. house is builded by **s.** *man*
4. For **s.**, when they had heard
4. 6. it remaineth that **s.** must
10.25. as the manner of **s.** is
11.40. having provided **s.** better th.
13. 2. for thereby **s.** have entertai.
²Pet. 3. 9. as **s.** men count slackness
16. **s.** things hard to be underst.

allos.

Mat.13. 5. **s.** fell upon stony ; Mar. 4.5
7. **s.** fell among thor.; Mar. 4.7
16.14. **s.**, Elias ; and others ; Mar.
8.28; Lu.9.19
Jo. 7.41. But **s.** said, Shall Christ come
9. 9. **s.** said, This is he : others sa.
Act.19.32. **s.** …cried one thing ; 21.34

ho, [*accu. plu.*]

Eph. 4.11. he gave **s.**, apostles : **s.** pro.
s. evangelists ; **s.** pastors

heteros.

Lu. 8. 6. And **s.** fell upon a rock
7. And **s.** fell among thorns

heis.

Mar. 4. 8, 20. **s.** thir., and **s.** six.,and **s.**

apo meros.

Ro. 15.15. boldly unto you *in* **s.** *sort*

pote.

Col. 3. 7. ye also walked **s.** *time,* when

SOMEBODY.
tis.

Lu. 8.46. **s.** hath touched me; for I
Act. 5.36. Theudas, boas. hims. to be **s.**

SOMETHING.
tis, [*neut.*]

Lu. 11.54. seeking to catch **s.** out of his
Jo. 13.29. he should give **s.** to the poor
Act. 3. 5. expecting to receive **s.** of th.
23.18. who hath **s.** to say unto thee
Gal. 6. 3. man think himself to be **s.**

SOMETIME,   -*s.*
pote.

Eph. 2.13. ye who **s**-*s* were far off are
5. 8. For ye were **s**-*s* darkness, but
Col. 1.21. that were **s.** alienated and
Tit. 3. 3. ourselves also were **s**-*s* foolish
¹Pet. 3.20. Which **s.** were disobedient

SOMEWHAT.
tis, [*neut.*]

Lu. 7.40. I have **s.** to say unto thee
Act.23.20. would enquire **s.** of him
25.26. I might have **s.** to write
²Co. 10. 8. For though I should boast **s.**
Gal. 2. 6. these who seemed to be **s.**
Heb. 8. 3. that this man have **s.** also

254

meros.

Ro. 15.24. be **s.** filled with your comp.

SON, (See *Bear, Sister,*)   -*s.*
huios.

Mat. 1. 1. the **s.** of David, the **s.** of, &c.
20. Joseph, thou **s.** of David, fe.
21, 23. bring forth a **s.**; Lu.1.31
25. brought forth her firstborn **s.**
2.15. Egypt have I called my **s.**
3.17. This is my beloved **s.**; 17.5;
Mar.1.11,9.7; Lu.3.22; 9.35
²Pet.1.17
4. 3, 6. If thou be the **s.** of God ;
27.40 ; Lu.4,3,9
7. 9. if his **s.** ask bread ; Lu.11.11
8.29. with thee, Jesus, thou **s.** of
9.27. Thou **s.** of David, have mer.;
Mar.10.47,48 ; Lu.18.38,39
10.37. he that loveth **s.** or daughter
11.27. man know. the **s.**; Lu.10.22
save the **s.**, and he ; Lu.10.22
s. will reveal him ; Lu.10.22
12.23. Is not this the **s.** of David
13.55. Is not this the carpenter's **s.**
14.33. thou art the **s.** of God ; Mar.
3.11 ; Jo.1.49
15.22. O Lord, thou **s.** of ; 20.30,31
16.16. Thou art the Christ, the **s.**
17.15. Lord, have mercy on my **s.**
20.20. Zebedee's childr. with her **s**-*s*
21. Grant that these my two **s**-*s*
21. 9, 15. Hosanna to the **s.** of Da.
37. he sent unto them his **s.**, sa.
reverence my **s.**; Mar. 12.6
38. the husbandmen saw the **s.**
22. 2. made a marriage for his **s.**
42. think ye of Christ ? whose **s.**
45. him Lord, how is he his **s.**;
Mar.12.37 ; Lu.20.44
23.35. blood of Zacharias **s.** of Bar.
26.37. Peter and the two **s**-*s* of Ze.
63. be the Christ, the **s.** of God
27.43. for he said, I am the **s.** of G.
54. was the **s.** of God; Mar.15.39
28.19. of the Father, and of the **s.**
Mar. 1. 1. of Jesus Christ, the **s.** of God
3.17. Boanerges, which is, The **s**-*s*
28. forgiven unto the **s**-*s* of men
5. 7. **s.** of the most high ; Lu.8.28
6. 3. the carpenter, the **s.** of Mary
9.17. have broug. unto thee my **s.**
10.35. J.and John, the **s**-*s* ; Lu.5.10
46. Bartimeus, the **s.** of Timeus
12. 6. Having yet therefore one **s.**
35. that Christ is the **s.** of David
13.32. neither the **s.**, but the Fath.
14.61. Art thou the Christ, the **s.** of
Lu. 1.13. Elisabeth shall bear thee a **s.**
32. be called the **s.** of the Highe.
35. shall be called the **s.** of God
36. she hath also conceived a **s.**
57. and she brought forth a **s.**
2. 7. brought forth her firstborn **s.**
3. 2. came unto John the **s.** of Za.
23. being, as was suppos., the **s.**
4.22. Is not this Joseph's **s.**
41. Thou art Christ the **s.** of God
7.12. the only **s.** of his mother,and
9.38. beseech thee,look upon my **s.**
41. Bring thy **s.** hither
10. 6. And if the **s.** of peace be th.
11.19. by whom do your **s**-*s* cast th.
12.53. shall be divided agai. the **s.**
and the **s.** against the father
15.11. A certain man had two **s**-*s*
13. the younger **s.** gathered all
19, 21. worthy to be called thy **s.**
21. And the **s.** said unto him, F.
24. For this my **s.** was dead, and
25. Now his elder **s.** was in the
30. But as soon as this thy **s.** was
19. 9 as he also is a **s.** of Abraham

Lu. 20.13. I will send my beloved **s.**
41. they that Christ is David's **s.**
22.70. Art thou then the **s.** of God
Jo. 1.18. the only begotten **s.**, which
34. that this is the **s.** of God
42. Thou art Simon the **s.** of Jo.
45. Jesus of Nazareth, the **s.** of
3.16. he gave his only begotten **s.**
17. God sent not his **s.** into the
18. the only begotten **s.** of God
35. The Father loveth the **s.**,and
36. He that believeth on the **s.**
he that believeth not the **s.**
4. 5. gro.that Jacob gave to his **s.**
46. whose **s.** was sick at Capern.
47. come down, and heal his **s.**
50. Go thy way ; thy **s.** liveth
53. Jesus said unto him, Thy **s.**
5.19. The **s.** can do nothing of hi.
these also doeth the **s.** like.
20. For the Father loveth the **s.**
21. even so the **s.** quickeneth w.
22. all judgment unto the **s.**
23. men should honour the **s.**
He that honoureth not the **s.**
25. shall hear the voice of the **s.**
26. hath he given to the **s.** to
6.40. every one which seeth the **s.**
42. Is not this Jesus, the **s.** of
69. thou art that Christ, the **s.** of
8.35. but the **s.** abideth ever
36. If the **s.** therefore shall make
9.19. Is this your **s.**, who ye say
20. We know that this is our **s.**
35. Dost thou believe on the **s.**
10.36. because I said, I am the **s.** of
11. 4. that the **s.** of God might be
27. the Christ, the **s.** of ; 20.31
14.13. Fa. may be glorified in the **s.**
17. 1. hour is come : glorify thy **s.**
thy **s.** also may glorify thee
12. is lost, but the **s.** of perdition
19. 7. bec. he made himself the **s.**
26. Woman, behold thy **s.**
Act. 2.17. your **s**-*s* and your daughters
4.36. interpreted, the **s.** of consol.
7.16. for a sum of money of the **s**-*s*
21. nourished him for her own **s.**
29. Mad., where he begat two **s**-*s*
8.37. Jesus Christ is the **s.** of God
9.20. that he is the **s.** of God
13.21. gave unto them Saul the **s.** of
33. Thou art my **s.**, this day ha.
16. 1. Timotheus, the **s.** of a certa.
19.14. there were seven **s**-*s* of one S.
23. 6. I am a Pharisee, the **s.** of a
16. And when Paul's sister's **s.**
Ro. 1. 3. Concerning his **s.** Jesus Chr.
4. declared to be the **s.** of God
9. spirit in the gospel of his **s.**
5.10. to God by the death of his **s**
8. 3. God sending his own **s.** in
14. they are the **s**-*s* of God
19. manifestation of the **s**-*s* of
29. confor. to the image of his **s.**
32. He that spared not his own **s.**
9. 9. and Sarah shall have a **s.**
¹Co. 1. 9. the fellowship of his **s.** Jesus
15.28. then shall the **s.** also himself
²Co. 1.19. For the **s.** of God, Jesus Ch.
6.18. and ye shall be my **s**-*s* and
Gal. 1.16. To reveal his **s.** in me, that
2.20. I live by the faith of the **s.** of
4. 4. God sent forth his **s.**, made
6. because ye are **s**-*s*, God hath
7. but a **s.**; and if a **s.**, then an
22. that Abraham had two **s**-*s*
30. out the bondwom. and her **s**
for the **s.** of the bondwoman
be heir with the **s.** of the fre.
Eph. 3. 5. not made known unto the **s**-*s*

Eph. 4.13. and of the knowled. of the s.
Col. 1.13. the kingdom of his dear s.
¹Th. 1.10. And to wait for his s. from
²Th. 2. 3. man of sin be revealed, the s.
Heb. 1. 2. spoken unto us by his s.
     5. Thou art my s., this day; 5.5
       and he shall be to me a s.
     8. But unto the s. he saith, Th.
   2. 6. or the s. of man, that thou
     10. in bringing many s-s unto
   3. 6. But Christ as a s. over his
   4.14. Jesus the s. of God, let us
   5. 8. Though he were a s., yet lea.
   6. 6. themselves the s. of God afr.
   7. 3. made like unto the s. of God
     5. that are of the s-s of Levi
     28. the s., who is consecrated
   10.29. trodden under foot the s. of
   11.21. blessed both the s-s of Jose.
     24. to be called the s. of Phara.
   12. 5. My s., despise not thou the
     6. scourgeth every s. whom he
     7. with s-s; for what s. is he
     8. are ye bastards, and not s-s
Jas. 2.21. offered Isaac his s. upon the
¹Pet. 5.13. and so doth Marcus my s.
¹Jo. 1. 3. and with his s. Jesus Christ
     7. blood of Jesus Christ his s.
   2.22. denie. the Father and the s.
     23. Whosoever denieth the s.
     24. shall continue in the s., and
   3. 8. For this purpose the s. of G.
     23. believe on the name of his s.
   4. 9. God sent his only begotten s.
     10. sent his s. to be the propiti.
     14. the Father sent the s. to be
     15. confess that Jesus is the s. of
   5. 5. believeth that Jesus is the s.
     9. wh. he hath testified of his s.
     10. He that believeth on the s. of
      reco. that God gave of his s.
     11. and this life is in his s.
     12. He that hath the s. hath life
      that hath not the s. of God
     13. believe on the name of the s.
     20. we know that the s. of God
      is true, even in his s. Jesus
²John 3. Lord Jesus Christ, the s. of
     9. both the Father and the s.
Rev. 2.18. These things saith the s. of
   21. 7. God, and he shall be my s.
     huiothesia.
Gal. 4. 5. might rec. the *adoption of* s-s
     teknon.
Mat. 9. 2. s., be of good cheer; thy si.
   21.28. A certain man had two s-s
     5. go work to day in my vi.
Mar. 2. 5. s., thy sins be forgiven thee
   13.12. to dea., and the father the s.
Lu. 2.48. s., why hast thou thus dealt
   15.31. s., thou art ever with me
   16.25. s., remember that thou in
Jo. 1.12. power to become the s-s of
¹Co. 4.14. but as my beloved s-s I warn
     17. Timo., who is my beloved s.
Phi. 2.15. the s-s of God, without reb.
     22. that, as a s. with the father
¹Ti. 1. 2. Unto Timothy, my own s.
     18. I commit unto thee, s. Tim.
²Ti. 1. 2. Tim., my dearly beloved s.
   2. 1. Thou therefore, my s., be st.
Tit. 1. 4. To Titus, mine own s. after
Phile. 10. I beseech thee for my s. On.
¹Jo. 3. 1. we should be called the s-s
     2. now are we the s-s of God
     pais.
Jo. 4.51. him, saying, Thy s. liveth
Act. 3.13. hath glorified his s. Jesus
   26. having raised up his s. Jesus
SON of man.
     huios ho anthropos, [*gen.*]
Mat. 8.20. but the s. *of man;* Lu.9.58

Mat. 9. 6. the s. *of man* hath power;
      Mar.2.10; Lu.5.24
   10.23. till the s. *of man* be come
   11.19. The s. *of man* came; Lu.7.34
   12. 8. For the s. *of man* is Lord;
      Mar.2.28; Lu.6.5
     32. agai. the s. *of man*; Lu.12.10
     40. so shall the s. *of man* be thr.
   13.37. the good seed is the s. *of man*
     41. The s. *of man* shall send for.
   16.13. say that I the s. *of man* am
     27. For the s. *of man* shall come
     28. till they see the s. *of man* co.
   17. 9. until the s. *of man;* Mar.9.9
     12. the s. *of man* suffer; Mar.
      8.31; Lu.9.22
     22. The s. *of man* shall be; 20.18
   18.11. the s. *of man* is.; Lu. 19.10
   19.28. when the s. *of man* shall sit
   20.28. s. *of man* came; Mar. 10.45
   24.27, 37, 39. comi. of the s. *of man*
     30. the sign of the s. *of man* in
      shall see the s. *of man;* 26.64
      Mar.13.26,14,62; Lu.21.27
     44. the s. *of man* cometh; 25.13;
      Lu. 12.40
   25.31. When the s. *of man* shall
   26. 2, 24,45. the s. *of man* is betra.;
      Mar.14.21,41 [Mar.14.21
     24. The s. *of man* goeth as it is;
Mar. 8.38. shall the s. *of man;* Lu.9.26
   9.12. it is written of the s. *of man*
     31. The s. *of man* is delivered
   10.33. the s. *of man* shall; Lu.9.44
Lu. 6.22. for the s. *of man's* sake
   9.56. For the s. *of man* is not co.
   11.30. sh. also the s. *of man;* 17.24
   12. 8. him shall the s. *of man* also
   17.22. of the days of the s. *of man*
     26. in the days of the s. *of man*
     30. the day when the s. *of man*
   18. 8. when the s. *of man* cometh
     31. concerning the s. *of man*
   21.36. to stand before the s. *of man*
   22.22. And truly the s. *of man* goe.
     48. betrayest thou the s. *of man*
     69. Hereafter shall the s. *of man*
   24. 7. The s. *of man* must be deliv.
Jo. 1.51. descend. upon the s. *of man*
   3.13. the s. *of man* which is in he.
     14. must the s. *of man* be lifted
   5.27. because he is the s. *of man*
   6.27. which the s. *of man* shall gi.
     53. eat the flesh of the s. *of man*
     62. if ye shall see the s. *of man*
   8.28. have lifted up the s. *of man*
   12.23. that the s. *of man* should be
     34. The s. *of man* must be lifted
      up? who is this s. *of man*
   13.31. Now is the s. *of man* glorifi.
Act. 7.56. opened, and the s. *of man*
Rev. 1.13. like unto the s. *of man*
   14.14. like unto the s. *of man,* hav.

SONG,   -s.
     ōdē.
Eph. 5.19. and spiritual s-s; Col. 3.16
Rev. 5. 9. And they sung a new s., say.
     14. 3. they sung as it were a new s.
      no man could learn that s.
   15. 3. they sing the s. of Moses the
      God, and the s. of the Lamb

SOON.   (See *Angry, As.*)
     parachrēma.
Mat.21.20. How s. is the fig tree wither
     ginomai.   (day *having come.*)
Act.12.18. as s. as *it was* day, there was
     tacheōs.
Gal. 1. 6. that ye are so s. removed fr.
²Th. 2. 2. be not s. shaken in mind

SOONER.
     tachion.
Heb.13.19. be restored to you *the* s.
SOOTHSAYING.
     manteuomai.
Act.16.16. her masters much gain *by* s
SOP.
     psōmion.
Jo. 13.26. to whom I shall give a s.
      when he had dipped the s.
     27. after the s. Satan entered
     30. He then having recei. the s.
SORCERER,   -s
     magos.
Act.13. 6. found a certain s., a false
     8. But Elymas the s…withsto.
     pharmakeus.
Rev.21. 8. whoremongers, and s-s, and
     pharmakos.
Rev.22.15. For witho. are dogs, and s-s
SORCERY,   -ies.
     mageia.
Act. 8.11. had bewitched them with s-s
     mageuō.
Act. 8. 9. *which*..*used* s., and bewitch.
     pharmakeia.
Rev. 9.21. nor of their s-s, nor of their
   18.23. for by thy s-s were all natio.
SORE.
     kakōs.
Mat.17.15. and s. vexed: for oftimes
     sphodra.
Mat.17. 6. their face, and were s. afraid
     lian.
Mar. 6.51. and they were s. amazed
     polus.
Mar. 9.26. spirit cried, and rent him s.
     hikanos.
Act.20.37. they all wept s., and fell on
   (See *Afraid, Amaze, Displease.*)
SORE,   -s.
     helkos.
Lu. 16.21. dogs came and licked his s-s
Rev.16. 2. fell a noisome and grievous s.
     11. of their pains and their s-s
     helkoomai.
Lu. 16.20. laid at his gate, *full of* s-s
SORER.
     cheirōn.
Heb.10.29. Of how much s. punishment
SORROW, [*noun,*]   -s.
     lupē.
Lu. 22.45. found them sleeping for s.
Jo. 16. 6. s. hath filled your heart
     20. but your s. shall be turned
     21. in travail hath s., because
     22. ye now therefore have s.
²Co. 2. 3. I should have s. from them
     7. swallow. up with overmuch s.
   7.10. For godly s. worketh repent.
     the s. of the world worketh
Phi. 2.27. lest I should have s. upon s.
     penthos.
Rev.18. 7. much torment and s. give
     no widow, and shall see no s.
   21. 4. neither s., nor crying, neith.
     odunē.
Ro. 9. 2. continual s. in my heart
¹Ti. 6.10. them. through with many s-s
     ōdin.   [Mar.13.8
Mat.24. 8. are the beginning of s-s;
SORROW, [*verb,*]   -ed, -ing.
     lupeō.
²Co. 7. 9. but that ye s-ed to repentan.
     11. that ye s-ed after a godly
¹Th. 4.13. that ye s. not even as others

255

odunaomai.

Lu. 2.48. and i have sought thee s-*ing*

Act.20.38. s-*ing* most of all for the wo.

SORROWFUL.

lupeō.

Mat. 19.22. he went away s.: for he had

26.22. they *were* exceeding s., *and*

37. began *to be* s.; Mar.14.19

Jo. 16.20. and ye *shall* be s., but your

2Co. 6.10. As s., yet alway rejoicing

perilupos.   [14.34

Mat.26.38. My soul is *exceeding* s.; Mar.

Lu. 18.23, 24. he was *very* s.

alupoteros.

Phi. 2.28. and that I may be the *less* s.

SORRY.

perilupos.

Mar. 6.26. the king was *exceeding* s.

lupeō.

Mat.14. 9. the king *was* s.: nevertheless

17.23. And they *were* exceeding s.

18.31. was done, they *were* very s.

2Co. 2. 2. For if I *make* you s., who is same *which is made* s. by me

7. 8. though I *made* you s. with a epistle *hath made* you s.

9. not that ye *were made* s., but repent.: for ye *were made* s.

SORT, (See *Baser, Godly.*)

apo meros.

Ro. 15.15. boldly unto you *in some* s.

hopoios.

1Co. 3.13. every man's work *of what* s.

ek houtos, [*plur.*]

2Ti. 3. 6. *of this* s. are they which cre.

axiōs.   [*worthily* of God.

3John 6. their journey *after* a godly s.

SOUL,   -s.

psuchē.

Mat. 10.28. but are not able to kill the s. to destroy both s. and body

11.29. shall find rest unto your s-s

12.18. in whom my s. is well pleas.

16.26. world, and lose his own s.;

Mar.8.36   {Mar.8.37

give in exchange for his s.;

22.37. thy heart, and with all thy s.; Mar.12.30; Lu.10.27

26.38. My s. is exceed.; Mar.14.34

Mar.12.33. understa., and with all the s.

Lu. 1.46. My s. doth magnify the Lord

2.35. pierce through thy own s.

12.19. will say to my s., s., thou

20. night thy s. shall be required

21.19. patience possess ye your s-s

Jo. 12.27. Now is my s. : troubled

Act. 2.27. wilt not leave my s. in hell

31. that his s. was not left in he.

41. about three thousand s-s

43. fear came upon every s.

3.23. every s., which will not hear

4.32. of one heart and of one s.

7.14. threescore and fifteen s-s

14.22. Confirming the s-s of the dis.

15.24. subverting your s-s, saying

27.37. hund. threescore and six. s-s

Ro. 2. 9. upon every s. of man that

13. 1. Let every s. be subject unto

1Co. 15.45. Adam was made a living s.

2Co. 1.23. God for a record upon my s.

1Th. 2. 8. G. only, but also our own s-s

5.23. your whole spirit and s. and

Heb. 4.12. the dividing asunder of s.

6.19 have as an anchor of the s.

10.38. my s. shall have no pleasure

39. beli. to the saving of the s.

13.17. for they watch for your s-s, as

Jas. 1.21. which is able to save your s-s

256

Jas. 5.20. shall save a s. from death

1Pet. 1. 9. the salvation of your s-s

22. ye have purified your s-s in

2.11. which war against the s.

25. and Bishop of your s-s

3.20. few, that is, eight s-s were

4.19. com. the keeping of their s-s

2Pet. 2. 8. vexed his righteous s. from

14. beguiling unstable s-s; an

3John 2. even as thy s. prospereth

Rev. 6. 9. I saw under the altar the s-s

16. 3. every living s. died in the

18.13. and slaves, and s-s of men

14. the fruits that thy s. lusted

20. 4. the s-s of them that were be.

SOUND, [*noun,*]   -s.

phōnē.

Mat.24.31. with a great s. of a trumpet

Jo. 3. 8. and thou hearest the s. there.

1Co. 14. 7. things without life giving s.

8. trumpet give an uncertain s.

Rev. 1.15. and his voice as the s. of ma.

9. 9. and the s. of their wings was as the s. of chariots of many

18.22. and the s. of a millstone

ēchos.

Act. 2. 2. there came a s. from heaven

Heb.12.19. And the s. of a trumpet

phthonggos.

Ro. 10.18. Yes, verily, their s. went in.

1Co.14. 7. they give a distinc. in the s-s

SOUND, [*adjec.*] (See *Safe.*)

hugiainō.

1Ti. 1.10. that is contrary to s. doctrine

2Ti. 1.13. Hold fast the form of s. wor.

4. 3. will not endure s. doctrine

Tit. 1. 9. he may be able by s. doctrine

13. that they *may be* s. in the fa.

2. 1. things which become s. doc.

2. s. in faith, in charity, in

hugiēs.

Tit. 2. 8. s. speech, that cannot be co.

sōphronismos.

2Ti. 1. 7. and of love, and of a s. mind

SOUND, [*verb,*]   -ed, -ing.

salpizō.

Mat. 6. 2. do not s. *a trumpet* before

1Co. 15.52. for the *trumpet shall* s.

Rev. 8. 6. prepared themselves to s.

7. first angel s-ed, &c.; 8,10,12

13. angels, which are yet to s.

9. 1. the fifth angel s-ed, &c.; 13

10. 7. when he shall begin to s.

11.15. And the seventh angel s-ed

ginomai.

Lu. 1.44. as soon as the voice..s-ed in

ēcheō.

1Co. 13. 1. I am become as s-*ing* brass

exēcheomai.

1Th. 1. 8. from you s-ed *out* the word

SOUNDED, (to measure depth.)

bolizō.

Act.27.28. s., *and* found it twenty fath. they s. again, *and* found it

SOUNDNESS.

holoklēria.

Act. 3.16. ha. given him this *perfect* s.

SOUTH.

notos.

Mat.12.42. The que. of the s.; Lu. 11.31

Lu. 12.55. when ye see the s. *wind* blow

13.29. and from the s., and shall

Act.27.13. And when the s. *wind* blew

28.13. the s. *wind* blew, and we ca.

Rev.21.13. on the s. three gates

mesēmbria.

Act. 8.26. Arise, and go toward the s.

SOUTHWEST.

lips.

Act.27.12. and lieth toward the s.

SOW, [*noun.*]

hus.

2Pet. 2.22. the s. that was washed to

SOW, [*verb,*]   -ed, -est, -eth, Sown.

speirō.

Mat. 6.26. fowls of the air : for they s.

13. 3. a sower went forth *to* s.; Mar.4.3 ; Lu.8.5

4. And when he s-ed some see.; Mar.4.4 ; Lu.8.5

19. that *which was* s-n in his he.

24. liken. unto a man *which* s-ed

25. and s-ed tares among the wh.

27. *didst* not thou s. good seed

31. a man took, and s-ed in his

37. He *that* s-eth the good seed

39. The enemy *that* s-ed them is

25.24. rea. where thou *hast* not s-n

26. I reap where I s-ed not

Mar. 4.15. The sower s-eth the word

14. where the word is s-n away the word *that was* s-n

16. *which are* s-n on stony grou.

18. they *which* are s-n among th.

20. they *which* are s. on good

31. when it *is* s-n in the earth

32. But when it *is* s-n, it growe.

Lu. 12.24. for they neither s. nor reap

19.21. reap. that thou *didst* not s.

22. and reaping that I *did* not s.

Jo. 4.36. that both he *that* s-eth and

37. One s-eth, and another reap.

1Co. 9.11. If we *have* s-n unto you spi.

15.36. that which thou s-est is not

37. thou s-est, thou s-est not that

42. It *is* s-n in corruption

43. It *is* s-n in dishonour it *is* s-n in weakness

44. It *is* s-n a natural body

2Co. 9. 6. He *which* s-eth sparingly sh. and he *which* s-eth bountifu.

Gal. 6. 7. for whatsoever a man s-eth

8. For he *that* s-eth to his flesh but he *that* s-eth to the Spir.

Jas. 3.18. fruit of righteousness *is* s-n

SOWER.

speirō, [*participle.*]   [Lu.8.5

Mat.13. 3. a s. went forth to; Mar.4.3 ;

18. Hear ye..the para. of the s.

Mar. 4.14. The s. soweth the word

2Co. 9.10. ministereth seed to the s.

SOWN. (See *Seed.*)

SPACE. (See *Three.*)

epi, [*accu.*]

Act.19. 8. *for the* s. *of* three months

10. *by the* s. *of* two years

34. about *the* s. *of* two hours

chronos.

Act.15.33. they had tarried there a s.

Rev. 2.21. I gave her s. to repent of

diastēma.

Act. 5. 7. was about the s. of three ho.

diistēmi, [*partic.*]

Lu. 22.59. about *the* s.*of* one hour *after*

brachus, [*neut.*]

Act. 5.34. the apostles forth a *little* s.

apo.

Rev.14.20. *by the* s. *of* a thousand and

SPARE, (See *Enough,*)-ed, -ing.

pheidomai.

Act.20.29. among you, not s-*ing* the flo.

Ro. 8.32. He that s-ed not his own Son

11.21. if God s-ed not the natural take heed lest he also s. not

¹Co. 7.28. trouble in the flesh : but I s.
²Co. 1.23. to s. you I came notas yet
13. 2. if I come again, I will not s.
¹Pet. 2. 4. if God s-ed not the angels
5. And s-ed not the old world

SPARINGLY.
pheidomenōs.
²Co. 9. 6. soweth s. shall reap also s.

SPARROWS.
strouthion.
Mat.10.29. Are not two s. sold for a fa.
31. value than many s.; Lu.12.7
Lu. 12. 6. not five s. sold for two farth.

SPEAK, -est, -eth, -ing, Spake, Spoken.
laleō.
Mat. 9.18. While he s-a these things
33. was cast out, the dumb s-a
10.19. or what ye shall s.
same hour what ye shall s.
20. it is not ye that s., but the
of your Father which s-eth
12.22. blind and dumb both s-a
34. how can ye, being evil, s.
of the heart the mouth s-eth
36. idle word that men shall s.
46, 47. desiring to s. with
13. 3. And he s-a many things unto
10. Why s-est thou unto them in
13. Therefore s. I to them in
33. Another parable s-a he unto
34. All these things s-a Jesus
with. a parable s-a ; Mar.4.34
14.27. Jesus s-a unto them ; 28.18
15.31. the dumb to s.; Mar.7.37
17. 5. While he yet s-a; 26.47 ; Mar.
5.35,14.43; Lu.8.49,22.47,60
23. 1. Then s-a Jesus to the multi.
Mar.1.34. not the devils to s.;Lu.4.41
2. 7. doth this man thus s. blasph.
4.33. many such parables s-a he
5.36. heard the word that was s-en
7.35. and he s-a plain
8.32. he s-a that saying openly
13.11. beforehand what ye shall s.
s. ye: for it is not ye that s.
14. 9 shall be s-en of for a memor.
16.17. they shall s. with new tong.
19. after the Lord had s-en
Lu. 1.19. and am sent to s. unto thee
20. and not able to s., until
22. he could not s. unto them
55. As he s-a to our fathers
64. and he s-a, and praised God
70. As he s-a by the mouth of
2.33. things which were s-en of him
38. and s-a of him to all them
50. which he s-a unto them
5. 4. when he had left s-ing
21. Who is this which s-eth bla.
6.45. of the heart his mouth s-eth
7.15. sat up, and began to s.
9.11. s-a unto them of the kingd.
11.14. was gone out, the dumb s-a
37. as he s-a, a certain Pharisee
12. 3. ye have s-en in the ear in
24. 6. remember how he s-a unto
25. that the prophets have s-en
36. And as they thus s-a, Jesus
44. Th.are the words which I s-a
Jo. 1.37. two disciples heard him s.
3.11. We s. that we do know
31. and s-eth of the earth : he
34. s-eth the words of God : for
4.26. I that s. unto thee am he
6.63. the words that I s. unto you
7.13. no man s-a openly of him
17. or whether I s. of myself
18. He that s-eth of himself
26. lo, he s-eth boldly, and they

Jo. 7. 46. Never man s-a like this man
8.12. Then s-a Jesus again unto
20. These words s-a Jesus in the
28. hath taught me, I s. these
30. As he s-a these words, many
38. I s. that which I have seen
44. When he s-eth a lie, he s-eth
9.21. he shall s. for himself
29. We know that God s-a unto
10. 6. which he s-a unto them
12.29. said, An angel s-a to him
36. These things s-a Jesus
41. he saw his glory, and s-a of
48. the word that I have s-en
49. For I have not s-en of myself
say, and what I should s.
50. whatsoever I s. therefore
Father said unto me, so I s.
14.10. I s. unto you I s. not of my.
25. have I s-en ; 15.11,16.1,33
15. 3. which I have s-en unto you
22. If I had not come and s-en
16.13. he shall not s. of himself
shall hear, that shall he s.
25. have I s-en unto you in pro.
when I shall no more s. unto
29. now s-est thou plainly
17. 1. These words s-a Jesus
13. these things I s. in the world
18.20. I s-a openly to the world
23. If I have s-en evil, bear witn.
19.10. s-est thou not unto me
Act. 2. 4. began to s. with other
6. heard them s. in his own lan.
7. are not all these which s.
11. we do hear them s. in our
31. s-a of the resurrection of
3.21. God hath s-en by the mouth
24. as many as have s-en, have
4. 1. And as they s-a unto the
17. that they s. henceforth to no
20. For we cannot but s.
29. all boldness they may s
31. they s-a the word of God
5.20. Go, stand and s. in the tem.
40. that they should not s. in
6.10. and the spirit by whi. he s-a
11. We have heard him s. blas.
13. This man ceaseth not to s.
7. 6. God s-a on this wise
38. with the angel which s-a to
44. s-ing unto Moses, that he
8.26. the angel of the Lord s-a
9.27. and that he had s-en to him
29. he s-a boldly in the name
10. 7. the angel which s-a unto Co.
32. he cometh, shall s. unto thee
44. While Peter yet s-a these
46. For they heard them s. with
11.15. as I began to s., the Holy G.
20. s-a unto the Grecians, prea.
13.46. should first have been s-en
14. 1. and so s-a, that a great
9. The same heard Paul s.
16.13. and s-a unto the women
14. the things which were s-en of
32. they s-a unto him the word
17.19. doctrine, whereof thou s-est
18. 9. but s., and hold not thy
25. he s-a and taught diligently
19. 6. they s-a with tongues, and
20.30. s-ing perverse things
21.39. suffer me to s. unto the peo.
22. 9. the voice of him that s-a to
23. 9. or an angel hath s-en to
26.14. I heard a voice s-ing unto
26. before whom also I s. freely
28.21. or s-a any harm of thee
25. Well s-a the Holy Ghost by
Ro. 7. 1. I s. to them that know the
15.18. I will not dare to s. of any
¹Co. 2. 6. we s. wisdom among them

¹Co. 2. 7. we s. the wisdom of God in
13. Which things also we s.
3. 1. I, brethren, could not s. unto
12. 3. no man s-ing by the Spirit
30. do all s. with tongues
13. 1. Though I s. with the tongues
11. When I was a child, I s-a as
14. 2, 4,13,27.that s-eth in an unkn.
tongue s-eth not unto men
in the spirit he s-eth myster.
3. prophesieth s-eth unto men
5. I would that ye all s-a witn
than he that s-eth with ton.
6. if I come unto you s-ing with
I profit you, except I shall s.
9. it be known what is s-en
for ye shall s. into the air
11. shall be unto him that s-eth
barbarian, and he that s-eth
18. I s. with tongues more than
19. I had rather s. five words
21. will I s.unto this people ; and
23. and all s. with tongues, and
28. let him s. to himself, and to
29. Let the prophets s. two or
34. not permit. unto them to s.
35. a shame for women to s. in
39. and forbid not to s. with
²Co. 2.17. sight of God s. we in Christ
4.13. and therefore have I s-en
believe, and therefore s.
7.14. as we s-a all things to you in
11.17. That which I s., I s. it
23. I s. as a fool, I am more
12.19. we s. before God in Christ
13. 3. a proof of Christ s-ing in me
Eph. 4.25. s. every man truth with his
5.19. s-ing to yourselves in psalms
6.20. boldly as I ought to s.
Phi. 1.14. more bold to s. the word
Col. 4. 3. to s. the mystery of Christ
4. it manifest, as I ought to s.
¹Th. 1. 8. we need not to s. any thing
2. 2. bold in our God to s. unto
4. even so we s.; not as pleasi.
16. Forbidding us to s. to the
¹Ti. 5.13. s-ing things which they oug.
Tit. 2. 1. But s. thou the things
15. These things s., and exhort
Heb. 1. 1. God, who..s-a in time past
2. Hath in these last days s-en
2. 2. if the word s-en by angels
3. began to be s-en by the Lord
5. world to come, whereof we s
3. 5. which were to be s-en after
4. 8. he not afterward have s-en
6. 9. salvation, though we thus s.
7.14. of which tribe Moses s-a no.
9.19. when Moses had s-en every
(having been spoken by Moses.)
11. 4. being dead yet s-eth
12.24. that s-eth better things than
25. refuse not him that s-eth
13. 7. who have s-en unto you
Jas. 1.19. slow to s., slow to wrath
2.12. So s. ye, and so do
5.10. who have s-en in the name
¹Pet. 3.10. that they s. no guile
4.11. If any man s., let him speak
²Pet.1.21. s-a as they were moved
3.16. s-ing in them of these things
¹Jo. 4. 5. therefore s. they of the world
²John 12. and s. face to face ; ³John 14
Jude 15. ungodly sinners have s-en
16. mouth s-eth great swelling
Rev. 1.12. to see the voice that s-a
10. 8. s-a unto me again, and said
13. 5. a mouth s-ing great things
11. and he s-a as a dragon
15. image of the beast should..s.
katalaleō.
Jas. 4.11. s. not evil one of anoth
257

Jas. 4.11. He that s-*eth evil of* his
   s-*eth evil of* the law, and
1Pet. 2.12. they s. *against* you as evildo.
  3.16. whereas they s. *evil of* you
   proslaleō.
Act. 13.43. s-*ing to* them, persuaded
  28.20. see you, and *to* s. *with* you
   sullaleō.
Lu. 4.36. and s-*a* among themselves
   legō.
Mat. 21.45. perceived that he s-*a* of th.
Mar. 12. 1. And he began *to* s.: Lu.7.24
  14.31. But he s-*a* the more veheme.
   71. not this man of whom ye s.
Lu. 5.36. he s-*a* a para.; Lu.13.6,18.1
  9.31. and s-*a* of his decease which
   34. *While* he thus s-*a*, there
  11.27. as he s-*a* these things, a cer.
  12.41. s-*est* thou this parable
  18.34. the things *which were* s-*en*
  20. 9. Then began he *to* s. to the
  21. 5. *as* some s-*a* of the temple
  22.65. blasphemously s-*a* they aga.
Jo. 2.21. But he s-*a* of the temple of
  6.71. He s-*a of* Judas Iscariot
  8.26. I s. to the world those things
  11.13. they thought that he had s-*en*
   56. and s-*a* among themselves
  13.18. I s. not of you all
   22. doubting of whom he s-*a*
   ~4. it should be **of whom he s-*a***
  16.29. speakest..plainly, and s-*est*
Act. 1. 3. s-*ing* of the things pertaining
  2.25. For David s-*eth* concerning
  8. 6. those things which Philip s-*a*
  4. of whom s-*eth* the prophet
  13.45. things *which were* s-*en* by ;
   27.11,28.24
  24.10. beckoned unto him *to* s.
  26. 1. Thou art permitted *to* s.
Ro. 3. 5. vengeance? I s. as a man
  6.19. I s. after the man.: Gal. 3.15
  10. 6. of faith s-*eth* on this wise
  11.13. For I s. to you Gentiles
1Co. 1.10. that ye all s. the same
  6. 5. But I s. to your shame ; 15.34
  7. 6. But I s. this by permission
   12. But to the rest s. I, not the
   35. And this I s. for your own
  10.15. I s. as to wise men ; judge
2Co. 6.13. I s. as unto my children
  7. 3. I s. not this to condemn
  8. 8. I s. not by commandment
  11.21. I s. as concerning reproach
   I s. foolishly, I am bold
Eph. 5.12. even *to* s. of those things
   32. but I s. concerning Christ
Phi. 4.11. Not that I s. in respect of
1Ti. 2. 7. I s. the truth in Christ
  4. 1. the Spirit s-*eth* expressly
Heb. 7.13. whom these things *are* s-*en*
  8. 1. *things which* we *have* s-*en*
  9. 5. we cannot now s. particular.
Rev. 2.24. depths of Satan, as they s.
   antilegō.
Lu. 2.34. sign *which shall be* s-*en aga.*
Jo. 19.12. a king s-*eth against* Cesar
Act. 13.45. s-*a against* those things wh.
  28.19. when the Jews s-*a against* it
  22. every where it *is* s-*en against*
   dialegomai.
Heb. 12.5. which s-*eth* unto you as unto
   epō.
Mat. 8. 8. but s. the word only, and
  10.27. that s. ye in light: and
  12.32. And whosoever s-*eth* a word
   but whosoever s-*eth* against
  16.11. that I s-*a* it not to you con.
  17.13. he s-*a* unto them of John
  22. 1. and s-*a* unto them again by
Mar. 1.42. And *as soon as* he had s-*en*
  3. 9. he s-*a* to his disciples
253

Mar. 9.18. and I s-*a* to thy disciples
  12.12. that he *had* s-*en*; Lu.20.19
   26. how in the bush God s-*a* un.
  14.39. prayed, *and* s-*a* the same
Lu. 6.26. when all men *shall* s. well of
   39. And he s-*a* a parable ; Lu.
   12,16,19.11,21.29
  7.39. he s-*a within* himself, saying
  8. 4. every city, he s-*a* by a parab.
  12. 3. whatsoever ye *have* s-*en* in
   13. Master, s. to my brother
  14. 3. s-*a* unto the lawyers and
  15. 3. And he s-*a* this parable; 18.9
  19.28. And *when* he *had* thus s-*en* ;
   24.40; Jo.9.6,11.43,18.22 ;
   Act.19.41,20,36.26,30,27.35
  20. 2. s-*a* unto him, saying, Tell
Jo. 1.15. This was he *of* whom I s-*a*
  4.50. the word that Jesus *had* s-*en*
  7.39. But this s-*a* he of the Spirit
  9.22. These words s-*a* his parents
  10. 6. s-*a* Jesus unto them ; but
   41. all things that John s-*a*
  11.51. this s-*a* he not of himself
  12.38. which he s-*a*, Lord, who hath
  13.28. for what intent he s-*a* this
  18. 1. *When* Jesus *had* s-*en* these
   9. be fulfilled, which he s-*a*
   16. and s-*a* unto her that kept
   32. whi. he s-*a*, signifying ; 21.19
  20.18. and that he *had* s-*en* these
  21.19. And *when* he *had* s-*en* this
Act. 1. 9. And *when* he *had* s-*en* these
  2.29. let me freely s. unto you
  18. 9. Then s-*a* the Lord to Paul
  21.37. May I s. unto thee
  25.25. *after that* Paul *had* s-*en* one
   proepō.
Act. 1.16. s-*a before* concerning Judas
   ereō.
Lu. 12.10. whosoever *shall* s. a word
Jo. 11.13. Howbeit Jesus s-*a* of his de.
Act. 2.16. this is that *which was* s-*en*
  8.24. these things wh. ye *have* s-*en*
  13.40. *which is* s-*en* of in the prop.
  20.38. for the words which he s-*a*
  23. 5. Thou *shalt* not s. evil *of* the
Ro. 4.18. accor. to that *which was* s-*en*
Heb. 4. 4. For he s-*a* in a certain place
   proereō.   [Jude 17
2Pet. 3. 2. words *which were* s-*en before ;*
   reō.
Mat. 1.22. *which was* s-*en* of the L.;2.15
  2.17, 23. *which was* s-*en* by ; 4.14,
   8.17,12.17,13.35,21,4,27.9,35
  3. 3. is he *that was* s-*en of* by the
  22.31. *which was* s-*en* unto you by
  24.15. s-*en of* by Daniel ; Mar.13.14
   kakologeō.
Mar. 9.39. that can lightly s. *evil of* me
Act. 19. 9. but sa. *evil of* that way
   apologeomai.
Act. 26.24. *as* he thus s-*a for* himself
   pseudologos.
1Ti. 4. 2. s-*ing* lies in hypocrisy ; hav.
   phthenggomai.
Act. 4.18. not *to* s. at all nor teach in
2Pet. 2.16. the dumb ass s-*ing* with
   18. *when* they s. great swelling
   apophthenggomai.
Act. 26.25. s. *forth* the words of truth
   prosphōneō.
Lu. 23.20. release Jesus, s-*a* again *to*
Act. 21.40. he s-*a unto* them in the Heb.
  22. 2. s-*a* in the Hebrew tongue *to*
   anaphōneō.
Lu. 1.42. she s-*a out* with a loud voice
   anantirrētos.
Act. 19.36. things *cannot be* s-*en* against
   ginōskō.
Act. 21.37. Who said, *Canst* thou s. Gr.

   prostithēmi.
Heb. 12.19. *that* the wo. sho. not *be* s-*en to*
   katanggellō. [them *any more*
Ro. 1. 8. your faith *is* s-*en of* through.
   ananggellō.
Ro. 15.21. To whom he *was* not s-*en* of
   chrēmatizō.
Heb. 12.25. Who refused him *that* s-*a*
   blasphēmeō.
Mat. 26.65. saying, He *hath* s-*en* blasph.
Ro. 14.16. Let not..good *be* evil s-*en of*
1Co. 10.30. why *am* I evil s-*en of* for that
Tit. 3. 2. *To* s. *evil of* no man, to be no
1Pet. 4. 4. excess of riot, s-*ing evil of*
   14. their part he *is evil* s-*en of*
2Pet. 2. 2. of truth *shall be* evil s-*en of*
   10. are not afraid *to* s. *evil of*
   12. s. *evil of* the things that they
Jude 8. despise domi.., and s. *evil of*
   10. these s. *evil of* those things
(See *Boldly, Provoke, Truth.*)

SPEAKING, [*noun*,]   -s.
   pololugia.
Mat. 6. 7. be heard for their *much* s.
   blasphēmia.
Eph. 4.31. clamour, and *evil* s., be put
   katalalia.
1Pet. 2. 1. and envies, and all *evil* s-s

SPEAKER.
   logos.
Act. 14.12. was the chief s. (*in speech.*)

SPEAR.
   longchē.
Jo. 19.34. with a s. pierced his side

SPEARMEN.
   dexiolabos.
Act. 23.23. s. two hundred, at the third

SPECIAL.
   ouk tungchanō, [*participle.*]
Act. 19.11. God wrought s. miracles

SPECIALLY.
   malista.
Act. 25.26. and s. before thee, O king
1Ti. 4.10. s. of those that believe
  5. 8. and s. for those of his own
Tit. 1.10. s. they of the circumcision
Phile. 16 a brother beloved, s. to me

SPECTACLE.
   theatron.
1Co. 4. 9. for we are made a s. unto the

SPEECH, (See *Impediment*,) -*es.*
   logos.
Act. 20. 7. continued his s. until midn.
1Co. 2. 1. not with excellency of s.
  4. And my s. and my preach.
  4.19. not the s. of them which are
2Co. 10.10. and his s. contemptible
  11. 6. But though I be rude in s.
Col. 4. 6. Let your s. be alway
Tit. 2. 8. Sound s., that cannot be con.
   lalia.
Mat. 26.73. for thy s. bewrayeth
Mar. 14.70. and thy s. agreeth thereto
Jo. 8.43. do ye not understand my s.
   eulogia.
Ro. 16.18. words and *fair* s-es deceive
   parrēsia.
2Co. 7. 4. Great is my *boldness of* s. to.
   Lukaonisti.
Act. 14.11. saying in the s. of *Lycaonia*

SPEECHLESS.
   phimoō.
Mat. 22.12. wed.garment. And he *was* s.
   kōphos.
Lu. 1.22. unto them, and remained s.
   enneos.
Act. 9. 7. stood s., hearing a voice

SPEED.
chairō.
²John 10. neither bid him *God* s.
11. he that biddeth him *God* s.
hōs tachista.
Act.17.15. to come to him *with all* s.

SPEEDILY.
en tachos.
Lu. 18. 8. he will avenge them s.

SPEND,   -est, *Spent.*
dapanaō.
Mar. 5.26. *had* s-t all that she had, and
Lu..15.14. *when* he *had* s-t all, there
²Co. 12.15. I *will* very gladly s. and be
prosdapanaō.
Lu. 10.35. whatsoever thou s-*est more*
ekdapanaō.   [*be* s-t
²Co. 12.15. *will* very gladly spend and
polus.
Mar 6.35. when the day was now *far* s-t
prosanaliskō.
Lu. 8.43. which *had* s-t all her living
klinō.
Lu. 24.29. and the day *is far* s-t
eukaireō.
Act.17.21. s-t their *time* in nothing else
poieō.
Act.18.23. *after* he *had* s-t some time
chronotribeō.
Act.20.16. he would not s. the *time* in
diaginomai.
Act.27. 9. Now *when* much time *was* s-t
prokoptō.
Ro. 13.12. The night *is far* s-t, the day

SPICES.
arōma.
Mar.16. 1. bought *sweet* s., that they
Lu. 23.56. prepared s. and ointments
24. 1. bringing the s. which they
Jo. 19.40. in linen clothes with the s.

SPIES.
engkathetos.
Lu. 20.20. watch. him and sent forth s.
kataskopos.
Heb.11.31. when she had received the s.

SPIKENARD.
nardos pistikos.
Mar.14. 3. of ointme. of s. very; Jo.12.3

SPILLED.
ekcheō.
Mar. 2.22. and the wine *is* s., and the
ekchunō.
Lu. 5.37. burst the bottles, and *be* s.

SPIN.
nēthō.   [Lu.12.27
Mat. 6.28. toil not, neither *do* they s.;

SPIRIT,   s.
pneuma.
Mat. 3.16. he saw the s. of God descen.
4. 1. led up of the s. into ; Lu. 4.1
5. 3. Blessed are the poor in s.
8.16. he cast out the s-s with his
10. 1. against unclean s-s ; Mar.6.7
20. but the s. of your Father
12.18. I will put my s. upon him
28. if I cast out devils by the s.
43. When the uncle. s.; Lu.11.24
45. sev. other s-s more; Lu.11.26
22.43. How then doth David in s.
26.41. the s. indeed is willing
Mar. 1.10. the s. like a dove descending
12. immediately the s. driveth
23. a man with an unclean s.; 5.2
26. when the unclean s. had torn
27. even the unclean s-s and they
2. 8. perceived in his s. that they

Mar. 3.11. And unclean s-s, when they
30. said, He hath an unclean s.
5. 8. of the man, thou unclean s.
13. And the unclean s-s went
7.25. daughter had an unclean s.
8.12. he sighed deeply in his s.
9.17. my son, whi. hath a dumb s.
20. the s. tare him ; and he fell
25. he rebuked the foul s.,saying
Thou dumb and deaf s., I ch.
14.38. The s. truly is ready, but the
Lu. 1.17. in the s. and power of Elias
47. my s. hath rejoiced in God
80. and waxed strong in s., and
2.27. he came by the s. into the
40. and waxed strong in s., filled
4.14. in the power of the s. into
18. The s. of the Lord is upon
33. which had a s. of an unclean
36. commandeth the unclean s-s
6.18. were vexed with unclean s-s
7.21. and of evil s-s; and unto
8. 2. had been healed of evil s-s
29. commanded the unclean s.to
55. And her s. came again, and
9.39. lo, a s. taketh him, and he
42. Jesus rebuked the unclean s.
55. what manner of s. ye are of
10.20. that the s-s are subject unto
21. Jesus rejoiced in s., and said
11.13. give the Holy s. to them th.
13.11. which had a s. of infirmity
23.46. thy hands I commend my s.
24.37. that they had seen a s.
39. a s. hath not flesh and bones
Jo. 1.32. I saw the s. descending from
33. thou shalt see the s. descend.
3. 5. of water and of the s.
6. is born of the s. is s.
8. eve.one that is born of the s.
34. for God giveth not the s. by
4.23. worship the Father in s.,and
24. God is a s.; and they that
must worship him in s. and
6.63. It is the s. that quickeneth
they are s., and they are life
7.39. this spake he of the s.,which
11.33. he groaned in the s.,and was
13.21. said, he was troubled in s.
14.17. the s. of truth ; whom the
15.26. even the s. of truth, which
16.13. when he, the s. of truth, is
Act. 2. 4. as the s.gave them utterance
17. I will pour out of my s. up.
18. out in those days of my s.
5. 9. to tempt the s. of the Lord
16. were vexed with unclean s-s
6.10. the wisdom and the s.by wh.
7.59. Lord Jesus, receive my s.
8. 7. For unclean s-s, crying with
29. Then the s. said unto Philip
39. the s. of the Lord caught
10.19. the s. said unto him, Behold
11.12. And the s. bade me go
28. signified by the s. that there
16. 7. but the s. suffered them not
16. possessed with a s. of divina.
18. turned and said to the s.
17.16. his s. was stirred in him
18. 5. Paul was pressed in the s.
25. being fervent in the s., he
19.12. the evil s-s went out of them
13. which had evil s-s the name
15. And the evil s. answered
16. man in whom the evil s. was
21. Paul purposed in the s., wh.
20.22. I go bound in the s. unto Je.
21. 4. said to Paul through the s.
23. 8. neither angel, nor s.; but
9. but if a s. or an angel
Ro. 1. 4. according to the s. of holin
9. whom I serve with my s.

Ro. 2.29. in the s., and not in the let.
7. 6. in newness of s., and not
8. 1, 4. the flesh, but after the s.
2. For the law of the s. of life
5. the s. the things of the s.
9. s., if so be that the s. of God
have not the s. of Christ
10. but the s. is life because
11. But if the s. of him that rai.
by his s. that dwelleth in
13. if ye through the s. do mor.
14. as are led by the s. of God
15. received the s. of bondage
received the s. of adoption
16. The s. itself beareth witness
with our s., that we are
23. the first fruits of the s., even
26. Likewise the s. also helpeth
the s. itself maketh interces.
27. what is the mind of the s.
11. 8. hath given them the s. of sl.
12.11. fervent in s.; serving the L.
15.19. by the power of the s. of G.
30. for the love of the s., that
¹Co. 2. 4. in demonstration of the s.
10. by his s.: for the s.searcheth
11. save the s. of man which is
no man, but the s. of God
12. not the s. of the world, but
the s. which is of God
14. the things of the s. of God
3.16. and that the s. of God dwel.
4.21. and in the s. of meekness
5. 3. but present in s., have judg.
4. and my s., with the power
5. that the s. may be saved
6.11. and by the s. of our God
17. join. unto the Lord is one s.
20. and in your s., which are G.
7.34. both in body and in s.
40. also that I have the s. of G.
12. 3. no man speaking by the s. of
4. of gifts, but the same s.
7. the manifestation of the s.
8. to one is given by the s.
knowledge by the same s.
9. faith by the same s.; to ano.
of healing by the same s.
10. to another discerning of s-s
11. that one and the self-same s.
13. For by one s. are we all bap.
all made to drink into one s.
14. 2. howbeit in the s.he speaketh
14. an unknown tongue, my s.
15. I will pray with the s.
I will sing with the s.
16. thou shalt bless with the s.
32. the s-s of the prophets are
15.45. Adam was made a quicken.s.
16.18. they have refreshed my s.
²Co. 1.22. given the earnest of the s.
2.13. I had no rest in my s.
3. 3. but with the s. of the living
6. not of the letter,but of the s.
but the s. giveth life
8. the ministration of the s.
17. Now the Lord is that s.: and
where the s. of the Lord is
18. as by the s. of the Lord
4.13. We having the same s. of fa.
5. 5. unto us the earnest of the s.
7. 1. filthiness of the flesh and s.
13. because his s. was refreshed
11. 4. or if ye receive another s.
12.18. walked we not in the same s.
Gal. 3. 2. Received ye the s. by the w.
3. having begun in the s.
5. th. ministereth to you the s.
14. the promise of the s.through
4. 6. sent forth the s. of his Son
29. that was born after the s.
5. 5. For we through the s. wait

Gal. 5.16. Walk in the s.., and ye shall
17. against the s.. and the s. ag.
18. if ye be led of the s., ye are
22. the fruit of the s. is love
25. s., let us also walk in the s.
6. 1. restore such an one in the s.
8. to the s. shall of the s. reap
18. be with your s.; ²Ti. 4.22;
  Phile.25
Eph. 1.13. sealed with that holy s. of
17. give unto you the s. of wisd.
2. 2. the s. that now worketh
18. access by one s. unto the Fa.
22. habita. of God through the s.
3. 5. and prophets by the s.
16. by his s. in the inner man
4. 3. the unity of the s. in the
4. one body, and one s., even
23. be renewed in the s. of your
30. grieve not the Holy s.of God
5. 9. For the fruit of the s. is
18. but be filled with the s.
6.17. the sword of the s., which
18. pr. and supplication in the s.
Phi. 1.19. supply of the s. of Jesus Ch.
27. that ye stand fast in one s.
2. 1. if any fellowship of the s.
3. 3. which worship God in the s.
Col. 1. 8. unto us your love in the s.
2. 5. yet am I with you in the s.
¹Th. 4. 8. also given unto us his holy s.
5.19. Quench not the s.
23. your whole s. and soul and
²Th. 2. 2. neither by s., nor by word
8. with the s. of his mouth
13. thro. sanctification of the s.
¹Ti. 3.16. justified in the s., seen of
4. 1. Now the s. speaketh expres.
  giving heed to seducing s-s
12. in charity, in s., in faith
²Ti. 1. 7. God hath not given us the s.
Heb. 1. 7. Who maketh his angels s-s
14. they not all ministering s-s
4.12. divid. asunder of soul and s.
9.14. who through the eternal s.
10.29. despite unto the s. of grace
12. 9. unto the Father of s-s
23. and to the s-s of just men
Jas. 2.26. as the body without the s. is
4. 5. The s. that dwelleth in us
¹Pet. 1. 2. thro. sanctification of the s.
11. the s. of Christ which was in
22. obeying the truth thro. the s.
3. 4. of a meek and quiet s.
18. but quickened by the s.
19. preached unto the s-s in pri.
4. 6. according to God in the s.
14. for the s. of glory and of God
¹Jo. 3.24. by the s. which he hath giv.
4. 1. every s., but try the s-s wh.
2. the s. of God. Every s. that
3. every s. that confesseth not
6. the s. of truth, and the s. of
13. he hath given us of his s.
5. 6. it is the s. that beareth
  witness, because the s. is tr.
8. the s., and the water, and
Jude 19. sensual, having not the s.
Rev. 1. from the seven s-s which are
10. I was in the s. on the Lord's
2. 7, 11,17,29. hear what the s. sa.;
  3.6,13,22
3. 1. the seven s-s of God ; 4.5,5.6
4. 2. immediately I was in the s.
11.11. the s. of life from God ente.
14.13. Yea, saith the s., that they
16.13. I saw three unclean s-s like
14. For they are the s-s of devils
17. 3. car. me away in the s.; 21.10
18. 2. and the hold of every foul s.
19.10. of Jesus is the s. of prophecy
22.17. And the s. and the bride say

phantasma.
Mat.14.26.It is a s.; and they cried out
Mar. 6.49. supposed it had been a s.

SPIRITUAL.
pneumatikos.
Ro. 1.11. unto you some s. gift, to the
7.14. we know that the law is s.
15.27. partakers of their s. things
¹Co. 2.13. comparing s. things with s.
15. But he that is s. judgeth all
3. 1. as unto s., but as unto carn.
9.11. have sown unto you s. things
10. 3. did all eat the same s. meat
4. the same s. drink : for they
  drank of that s. Rock that
12. 1. Now concerning s. gifts
14. 1. and desire s. gifts, but rath.
37. to be a prophet, or s., let hi.
15.44. it is raised a s. body. There
  body, and there is a s. body
46. not first which is s., but that
  and afterwa. that which is s.
Gal. 6. 1. ye which are s., restore such
Eph. 1. 3. blessed us with all s. blessin.
5.19. and hymns and s. songs, sin.
6.12. against s. wickedness in high
Col. 1. 9. wisdom and s. understanding
3.16. psalms and hymns and s. so.
¹Pet. 2. 5. are built up a s. house, an
  priesthood, to offer up s. sa.
pneuma.
¹Co.14.12. ye are zealous of s. gifts

SPIRITUALLY.
pneumatikōs.
¹Co. 2.14. because they are s. discerned
Rev.11. 8. which s. is called Sodom and
phronēma pneuma, [gen.]
Ro. 8. 6. to be s. minded is life and

SPIT,   -ed, Spat.
ptuō.
Mar. 7.33. he s., and touched his tong.
8.23. when he had s. on his eyes
Jo. 9. 6. he s-a on the ground, and
emptuō.
Mat.26.67.Then did they s. in his face
27.30. they s. upon him, and took
Mar.10.34.scour. him, and shall s. upon
14.65. some began to s. on him
15.19. did s. upon him, and bowing
Lu. 18.32. shall be..entre., and s-ed on

SPITEFULLY. (See Entreat.)

SPITTLE.
ptusma.
Jo. 9. 6. and made clay of the s., and

SPOIL, [verb,]   -ed.
diarpazō.   [Mar.3.27
Mat.12.29. man's house, and s. his go.;
  then he will s. his; Mar.3.27
sulagōgeō.
Col. 2. 8. Beware lest any man s. you
apekduomai.
Col. 2.15. having s-ed principalities

SPOILING.
harpagē.
Heb.10.34. took joyfully the s. of your

SPOILS.
skulon.
Lu. 11.22. trusted, and divideth his s.
akrothinion.
Heb. 7. 4. gave the tenth of the s.

SPORTING.
entruphaō.
²Pet. 2.13. s. themselves with their own

SPOT,   -ed, -s.
spilos.
Eph. 5.27. not having s. or wrinkle

²Pet. 2.13. s-s they are and blemishes
aspilos.
¹Ti. 6.14. this commandme. without s.
¹Pet. 1.19. wit. blemish and without s.
²Pet. 3.14. in peace, without s. and bl.
spilas.
Jude 12. These are.s-s in your feasts
spiloō.
Jude 23. the garment s-ed by the flesh
amōmos.
Heb. 9.14. offered himself without s. to

SPREAD.
diaphēmizō.
Mat. 9.31. s.abroad his fame in all that
strōnnumi.   [Mar.11.8
Mat.21. 8. s. their garments in the way;
hupostrōnnumi.
Lu. 19.36. they s. their clothes in the
exerchomai.
Mar. 1.28. his fame s. abroad through.
¹Th. 1. 8. fai. to God-ward is s. abroad
dianemomai.
Act. 4.17. that it s. no further among

SPRING,   -ing, Sprang, Sprung.
anatellō.
Mat. 4.16. shad. of death light is s-u up
Heb. 7.14. our Lord s-a out of Juda; of
anatolē.
Lu. 1.78. the day s. from on high
exanatellō.
Mat.13. 5. forthwith they s-u up, beca.
Mar. 4. 5. and immediately it s-a up
phuō.
Lu. 8. 6. as soon as it was s-u up, it
8. and s-a up, and bare fruit
Heb.12.15.any root of bitterness s-ing
sumphuomai.
Lu. 8. 7. the thor. s-a up with it, and
blastanō.
Mat.13.26. when the blade was s-u up
Mar. 4.27. the seed should s. and grow
anabainō.
Mat.13. 7. the thorns s-u up, and chok.
Mar. 4. 8. fruit that s-a up and increa.
hallomai.
Jo. 4.14. water s-ing up into everlast.
gennaō.
Heb.11.12. Therefore s-a there even of
eispēdaō.
Act.16.29. called for a light, and s-a in

SPRINKLE,   -ed, -ing.
rantizō.
Heb. 9.13. of an heifer, s-ing the uncle.
19. and s-ed both the book, and
21. Moreover he s-ed with blood
10.22. having our hearts s-ed from

SPRINKLING.
rantismos.
Heb.12.24.to the blood of s., that speak.
¹Pet. 1. 2. unto obedience and s. of the
proschusis.
Heb.11.28.passover, and the s. of blood

SPUE.
emeō.
Rev. 3.16. I will s. thee out of my mou.

SPUNGE.
sponggos.
Mat. 27.48.took a s.; and filled it with
Mar.15.36.And one ran and filled a s.
Jo. 19.29. they filled a s. with vinegar

SPY, [verb.]
kataskopeō.
Gal. 2. 4. privily to s. out our liberty

STABLISH,   -ed, -eth.
stērizō.
Ro. 16.25. to s. you according to my go.
¹Th. 3.13. To the end he may s. vour
²Th. 2.17. and s. you in every good wo.

²Th. 3. 3. who *shall* s. you, and keep
Jas. 5. 8. Be ye also patient; s. your
¹Pet. 5.10. make you perfect, s., streng.

bebaioō.

²Co. 1.21. he *which* s-eth us with you
Col. 2. 7. s-ed in the faith, as ye

STAFF,   *Staves.*
rabdos.

Mat. 10.10.neither shoes, nor yet s-*ves*
Mar. 6. 8. save a s. only; no scrip, no
Lu. 9. 3. neither s-*ves*, nor scrip, neit.
Heb. 11.21.leaning upon the top of his s.

xulon.

Mat. 26.47, 55.with swords and s-*es*;
    Mar.14.43,48; Lu.22.52

STAGGERED.
diakrinō.

Ro. 4.20. he s. not at the promise of

STAIRS.
anabathmos.

Act.21.35. when he came upon the s.
   40. Paul stood on the s., and be.

STALL.
phatnē.

Lu. 13.15. his ox or his ass from the s.

STANCHED.
histēmi.

Lu. 8.44. inmediate. her issue of..s.

STAND, -est, -eth, -ing, Stood.
histēmi.

Mat. 2. 9. came and s-o over where the
   6. 5. they love to pray s-*ing* in the
12.25. divi. against itself *shall* not s.
   26. *shall*..his kingd. s.; Lu.11.18
   46. his mother and his breth. s-o
   47. and thy brethren s.; Lu.8.20
13. 2. multitude s-o on the shore
16.28. There be some s-*ing* here;
   Mar. 9.1.; Lu. 9.27
20. 3, 6. others s-*ing* idle in the
   6. Why s. ye here all the day
   32. And Jesus s-o *still, and* call.
24.15. Daniel the prophet, s. in the
26.73. unto him they *that* s-o by
27.11. Jesus s-o before the governor
   47. Some of them *that* s-o there
Mar.3. 24. that kingdom cannot s.
   25. itself, that house cannot s.
   31. and, s-*ing* without, sent unto
10.49. Jesus s-o *still, and*; Lu. 18.40
11. 5. certain of them *that* s-o there
13.14. s-*ing* where it ought not
Lu. 1.11. an angel of the Lord s-*ing* on
   5. 1. he s-o by the lake of Gennesa.
   2. saw two ships s-*ing* by the
   6. 8. Rise up, and s. *forth* in the
   And he arose and s-o *forth*
   17. and s-o in the plain, and the
   7.14. they that bare him s-o *still*
   38. s-o at his feet behi. him..*and*
13.25. ye begin *to* s. without, and to
17.12. lepers, which s-o afar off
18.11. The Pharisee s-o *and* prayed
   13. the publican, s-*ing* afar off
19. 8. Zacchæus s-o, *and* said unto
21.36. *to* s. before the Son of man
23.10. priests and scribes s-o and
   35. the people s-o beholding
   49. s-o afar off, beholding these
24.36. Jesus himself s-o in the midst
Jo. 1.26. but there s-*eth* one among you
   35. the next day after John s-o
3.29. *which* s-*eth* and heareth him
6.22. the people *which* s-o on the
7.37. Jesus s-o and cried, saying
8. 9. the woman s-*ing* in the midst
11.56. themselves, *as* they s-o in the
12.29. people therefore, *that* s-o by
18. 5. which betrayed him, s-o with

Jo. 18.16. Peter s-o at the door without
   18. the servants and officers s-o
   and Peter s-o with them
   25. Simon Peter s-o and warmed
19.25. Now there s-o by the cross of
20.11. Mary s-o without at the sepu.
   14. saw Jesus s-*ing*, and knew not
19, 26. Jesus and s-o in the midst
21. 4. Jesus s-o on the shore
Act. 1.11. why s. ye gazing up into hea.
   2.14. Peter, s-*ing* up with the elev.
   3. 8. he leaping up s-o, and walked
   4.14. which was healed s-*ing* with
   5.20. Go, s. *and* speak in the temp.
   23. and the keepers s-*ing* without
   25. ye put in prison are s-*ing* in
   7.33. the place where thou s-*est* is
   55. and Jesus s-*ing* on the right
   56. the Son of man s-*ing* on the
   8.38. comma. the chariot *to* s. *still*
   9. 7. journeyed with him s-o spee.
10.30. a man s-o before me in bright
11.13. *which* s-o and said unto him
12.14. told how Peter s-o before the
16. 9. There s-o a man of Macedonia
17.22. Paul s-o in the midst of Mars'
21.40. Paul s-o on the stairs, *and*
22.25. the centurion *that* s-o by
24.20. *while* I s-o before the council
   21. that I cried s-*ing* among them
25.10. I s. at Cæsar's judgment seat
   18. *when* the accusers s-o up
26. 6. now I s. and am judged for
   16. rise, and s. upon thy feet
27.21. Paul s-o *forth* in the midst of
Ro. 5. 2. into this grace wherein we s.
11.20. and thou s-*est* by faith
14. 4. God is able *to make* him s.
¹Co. 7.37. he that s-*eth* stedfast in his
10.12. him that thinketh he s-*eth*
15. 1. received, and wherein ye s.
²Co. 1.24. your joy; for by faith ye s.
Eph. 6.11. that ye may be able *to* s. aga.
   13. and having done all, *to* s.
   14. s. therefore, having your loi.
Col. 4.12. that ye *may* s. perfect and
²Ti. 2. 19. the foundation of God s-*eth*
Heb.10.11. And every priest s-*eth* daily
Jas. 2. 3. say to the poor, s. thou there
   5. 9. the judge s-*eth* before the do.
¹Pet. 5.12. grace of God wherein ye s.
Rev. 3.20. Behold, I s. at the door
   5. 6. s-o a Lamb as it had been sla.
   6.17. and who shall be able *to* s.
   7. 1. saw four angels s-*ing* on the
   9. a great multitude,..s-o before
   11. the angels s-o round about the
   8. 2. seven angels which s-o before
   3. another angel came and s-o
10. 5. angel which I saw s. upon
   8. the angel *which* s-*eth* upon
11. 4. two candlesticks s-*ing* before
   11. and they s-o upon their feet
12. 4. the dragon s-o before the wo.
13. 1. I s-o upon the sand of the
14. 1. lo, a Lamb s-o on the moun*t*.
15. 2. s. on the sea of glass
18.10. s-*ing* afar off for the fear of
   15. *shall* s. afar off for the fear
   17. as trade by sea, s-o afar off
19.17. I saw an angel s-*ing* in the
20.12. dead, small and great, s. bef.

paristēmi.

Mar.14.47.of them *that* s-o by; 15.35
   69. to them that s-o by; Lu.19.24
   70. they *that* s-o by sa.; Act.23.4
15.39. centurion, *which* s-o over
Lu. 1.19. Gabriel, *that* s. in the pers.
Jo. 18.22. of the officers *which* s-o by
19.26. and the disciple s-*ing* by
Act. 1.10. two men s-o by them in white
   4.10. *doth* this man s. *here* before

Act. 4 26. The kings of the earth s-o *up*
   9.39. all the widows s-o *by* him
   23. 2. them *that* s-o *by* him to smi.
   27.23. For there s-o *by* me this night
Ro. 14.10. we *shall* all s. *before* the
²Ti. 4.17. the Lord s-o *with* me, and

anistēmi.

Mar.14.60.priest s-o *up* in the midst, *and*
Lu. 4.16. sabbath day, and s-o *up* for
10.25. beh., a certain lawyer s-o *up*
Act. 1.15. Peter s-o *up* in the midst of
   5.34. Then s-o there *up* one in the
10.26. saying, s. *up*; I myself also
11.28. s-o *up* one of them..*and*
13.16. Then Paul s-o *up, and* beck.
14.10. s. upright on thy feet

ephistēmi.

Lu. 4.39. he s-o over her, and rebuked
24. 4. two men s-o *by* them in shi.
Act.10.17. and s-o *before* the gate
22.13. Came unto me, and s-o, *and*
   20. I also was s-*ing by*, and con.
23.11. the Lord s-o *by* him, *and* s.1.

periistēmi.

Jo. 11.42. of the people *which* s. *by*
Act.25. 7. Jerusalem s-o *round about*

sunistaō.

Lu. 9.32. two men *that* s-o *with* him
²Pet. 3. 5. s-*ing* out of the water and

stēkō.

Mar.11.25.when ye s. praying, forgive
Ro. 14. 4. to his own master he s-*eth* or
¹Co. 16.13. s. *fast* in the faith, quit you
Gal. 5. 1. s. *fast* therefore in the liber.
Phi. 1.27. that ye s. *fast* in one spirit
   4. 1. s. *fast* in the Lord; ¹Th.3.8
²Th. 2.15. brethren, s. *fast,* and hold

egeirō.

Mar. 3. 3. the withered hand, s. forth

kukloō.

Act.14.20. *as* the disciples s-o *round ab.*

menō.

Ro. 9.11. according to election *might* s.

eimi.

¹Co. 2. 5. *should* not s. in the wisdom

sumparaginomai.

²Ti. 4.16. no man s-o *with* me, but all

echō stasis.

Heb. 9. 8. the first taberna. *was* yet s.

(See *Doubt, Jeopardy, World.*)

STAR,   -s.
astēr.

Mat. 2. 2. we have seen his s. in the
   7. what time the s. appeared
   9. lo, the s., which they saw in
   10. When they saw the s., they
24.29. the s-s shall fall from heaven
Mar.13.25.the s-s of heaven shall fall
¹Co. 15.41. glory of the s-s: for one s.
   differeth from another s. in
Jude 13. wandering s-s, to whom is
Rev. 1.16. in his right hand seven s-s
   20. The mystery of the seven s-s
   The seven s-s are the angels
2. 1. that holdeth the seven s-s in
   28. will give him the morning s.
3. 1. Sp. of God, and the seven s-s
6.13. the s-s of heaven fell unto
8.10. there fell a great s. from he.
   11. the name of the s. is called
   12. the third part of the s-s; 12.4
9. 1. I saw a s. fall from heaven
12. 7 head a crown of twelve s-s
22.16. the bright and morning s.

astron.

Lu. 21.25. in the moon, and in the s-s
Act. 7.43. the s. of your god Remphan
27.20. when neither sun nor s-s in
Heb.11.12.as the s-s of the sky in mult.

phōsphoros.

²Pet. 1.19. and the *day* s. arise in your
       261

STATE.
ho [*plu. neut.*] **peri su**, [*gen.*]
Phi. 2.19. comf., when I know *your* s.
  20. naturally care for *your* s.

STATURE.
hēlikia.   [Lu.12.25
Mat. 6.27. can add one cubit unto his s.;
Lu. 2.52. in wisdom and s., and in fa.
  19. 3. because he was little of s.
Eph. 4.13. unto the measure of the s. of

STAYED.
katechō.
Lu. 4.42. and s. him, that he should
  epechō.
Act.19.22. he himself s. in Asia for a

STEAD.
huper, [*gen.*]
2Co. 5.20. we pray you *in* Christ's s.
Phile. 13. that *in* thy s. he might have

STEAL,
kleptō.   *Stole.*
Mat. 6.19. thieves break through and s.
  20. *do* not break through nor s.
  19.18. Thou *shalt* not s.; Ro.13.9
  27.64. lest his disciples..and s.him
  28.13. and s-o him away while we
Mar.10.19.*Do* not s., Do not; Lu.18.20
Jo. 10.10. but for to s., and to kill
Ro. 2.21. *should* not s., *dost* thou s.
Eph. 4.28. Let him *that* s-o s. no more

STEDFAST.
bebaios.
2Co. 1. 7. our hope of you is s., knowi.
Heb. 2. 2. word spoken by angels was s.
  3.14. our confidence s. unto the
  6.19. of the soul, both sure and s.
  hedraios.
1Co. 7.37. that standeth s. in his heart
  15.58. my beloved brethr., be ye s.
  stereos.
1Pet. 5. 9. Whom resist s. in the faith

STEDFASTLY.
atenizō.
Act. 1.10. they *looked* s. toward heaven
  6.15. *looking* s. on him, saw his
  7.55. *looked up* s. into heaven,*and*
  14. 9. who s. *beholding* him, and
2Co. 3. 7. could not s. *behold* the face
  13. could not s. *look* to the end
  stērizō.
Lu. 9.51. he s. *set* his face to go to Je.
(See *Continue.*)

STEDFASTNESS.
stereōma.
Col. 2. 5. and the s. of your faith in C.
  stērigmos.
2Pet. 3.17. wicked, fall from your own s.

STEEP.
krēmnos.   [Mar.5.13; Lu.8.33
Mat. 8.32. ran violently down a s.*place;*

STEP, [*verb,*]   -ed, -eth.
embainō.
Jo. 5. 4. *whosoever* then first..s-ed *in*
  katabainō.
Jo. 5. 7. another s-*eth down* before

STEP, [*noun,*]   -s.
ichnos.
Ro. 4.12. who also walk in the s-s of
2Co.12.18. walked we not in the same s-s
1Pet. 2.21. that ye should follow his s-s

STERN.
prumna.
Act.27.29. four anchors out of the s.
262

STEWARD,   -s.
oikonomos.
Lu. 12.42. that faithful and wise s.
  16. 1. rich man, which had a s.
  3. the s. said within himself
  8. commended the unjust s.
1Co. 4. 1. and s-s of the mysteries of
  2. it is required in s-s, that
Tit. 1. 7. blameless, as the s. of God
1Pet. 4.10. as good s-s of the manifold
  oikonomeō.
Lu. 16. 2. thou mayest *be* no longer s.
  epitropos.
Mat.20. 8. saith unto his s., Call the
Lu. 8. 3. the wife of Chuza, Herod's s.

STEWARDSHIP.
oikonomia.
Lu. 16. 2. give an account of thy s.
  3. taketh away from me the s.
  4. when I am put out of the s.

STICKS.
phruganon.
Act.28. 3. had gathered a bundle of s.

STIFFNECKED.
sklērotrachēlos.
Act. 7.51. ye s. and uncircumcised in

STILL, [*adjec.*]
phimoō.
Mar. 4.39. unto the sea, Peace, *be* s.
(See *Abide, Stand.*)

STILL, [*conjunc.*]
eti.
Rev.22.11. him be unjust s.: and he
  let him be filthy s.: and he
  let him be righteous s.: and
  is holy, let him be holy s.

STING,   -s.
kentron.
1Co.15.55. O death, where is thy s.
  56. The s. of death is sin
Rev. 9.10. there were s-s in their tails

STINKETH.
ozō.
Jo. 11.39. Lord, by this time he s.

STIR, [*verb,*]   -ed, -eth.
diegeirō.
2Pet. 1.13. this tabernacle, *to* s. you *up*
  3. 1. I s. *up* your pure minds by
  epegeirō.
Act.14. 2. Jews s-ed *up* the Gentiles
  anaseiō.
Lu. 23. 5. saying, He s-*eth up* the peo.
  sungkineō.
Act. 6.12. they s-ed *up* the people, and
  parotrunō.
Act.13.50. the Jews s-ed *up* the devout
  saleuō.
Act.17.13. also, and s-ed *up* the people
  paroxunomai.
Act.17.16. his spirit *was* s-ed in him
  sungchueō.
Act.21.27. s-ed *up* all the people, and
  anazōpureō.
2Ti. 1. 6. thou s. *up* the gift of God

STIR, [*noun.*]
tarachos.
Act.12.18. no small s. among the soldi.
  19.23. there arose no small s. about

STOCK,   -s.
genos.
Act.13.26. children of the s.of Abraham
Phi. 3. 5. of the s. of Israel, of the tri.
  xulon.
Act.16.24. made their feet fast in the s-s

STOMACH.
stomachos.
1Ti. 5.23. a little wine for thy s.'s aako

STONE, [*noun,*]   -s.
lithos.   [Lu.3.8
Mat. 3. 9. God is able of these s-s to;
  4. 3. comm. that these s-s ; Lu.4.3
  6. thy foot against a s.; Lu.4.11
  7. 9. wi.he give him a s.; Lu.11.11
  21.42. The s. which the buil.; Mar.
  12.10; Lu.20.17; 1Pet.2.7
  44. fall on this s. shall be
  24. 2. not be left here one s. upon;
  Mar.13.2 ; Lu.19.44, 21.6
  27.60. rolled a great s.; Mar.15.46
  66. sealing the s., and setting a
  28. 2. and rolled back the s.
Mar. 5. 5. cutting himself with s-s
  13. 1. what manner of s-s and what
  16. 3. Who shall roll us away the s.
  4. they saw that the s. was rol.
Lu. 19.40. the s-s would immediately
  20.18. shall fall upon that s. shall
  21. 5. adorned with goodly s-s and
  22.41. about a s.'s cast,and kneeled
  24. 2. they found the s.rolled away
Jo. 8. 7. let him first cast a s. at her
  59. Then took they up s-s to cast
  10.31. Jews took up s-s again to st.
  11.38. cave, and a s. lay upon it
  39. Take ye away the s.; Martha
  41. they took away the s. from
  20. 1. and seeth the s. taken away
Act. 4.11. This is the s. which was
  17.29. unto gold, or silver, or s.
1Co. 3.12. silv., precious s-s; Rev.18.12
2Co. 3. 7. engraven in s-s, was glorious
1Pet. 2. 4. as unto a living s., disallow.
  5. Ye also, as lively s-s, are
  6. I lay in Sion a chief corner s.
  8. And a s. of stumbling
Rev. 4. 3. like a jasper and a sardine s.
  17. 4. with gold and precious s-s
  18.16. gold, and precious s-s, and
  21. angel took up a s. like a gre.
  21.11. like unto a s. most precious
  a jasper s., clear as crystal
  19. all manner of precious s-s
  lithinos.
Jo. 2. 6. there six waterpots *of* s.
2Co. 3. 3. not in tables *of* s., but in
Rev. 9.20. *of* gold, and silver,..and s.
  petros.
Jo. 1.42. which is by interpretat.,A s.
  psēphos.
Rev. 2.17. a white s., and in the s. a n.
(See *Cast, Hewn.*)

STONE, [*verb,*]   -ed, -est.
lithazō.
Jo. 10.31. took up stones again to s.him
  32. of those works *do* ye s. me
  33. For a good work we s. thee
  11. 8. of late sought *to* s. thee
Act. 5.26. they should have been s-ed
  14.19. *having* s-ed Paul, drew him
2Co.11.25. once *was* I s-ed, thrice I
Heb.11.37.They *were* s-ed, they were
  lithoboleō.
Mat.21.35.killed another, and s-ed ano.
  23.37. and s-*est* them which are se.
Lu. 13.34. and s-*est* them that are sent
Jo. 8. 5. *that* such *should* be s-ed
Act. 7.58. him out of the city, and s-ed
  59. And they s-ed Stephen
  14. 5. them despitefully, and *to* s.
Heb.12.20.the mountain, it *shall be* s-ed
  katalithazō.
Lu. 20. 6. all the people *will* s. us

STONY.

petrōdēs. [Mar.4.5]
Mat.13. 5. Some fell upon s. places;
20. receiv. the seed into s. places
Mar. 4.16. which are sown on s. ground

STOOP, -ed, -ing.

kuptō.
Mar. 1. 7. not worthy to s. down and
Jo. 8. 6. But Jesus s-ed down, and
8. again he s-ed down, and wr.
katakuptō.
Lu. 24.12. and s-ing down, he beheld
Jo. 20. 5. he s-ing down, and looking
11. as she wept, she s-ed down

STOP, (See Mouth,) -ed.

phrassō.
Ro. 3.19. that every mouth may be s-ed
²Co. 11.10. no man shall s. me of this
(shall not be stopped to me.)
Heb.11.33. s-ed the mouths of lions
Act. 7.57. s-ed their ears, and ran upon

STORE.

thēsaurizō.
¹Co. 16. 2. lay by him in s. (treasuring)
²Pet. 3. 7. are kept in s. (treasured)
apothēsaurizō.
¹Ti. 6.19. Laying up in s. for themse.

STOREHOUSE.

tameion.
Lu. 12.24. which neither have s. nor

STORM.

lailaps.
Mar. 4.37. there arose a great s.of wind
Lu. 8.23. came down a s. of wind

STRAIGHT.

euthus. [Lu.3.4]
Mat. 3. 3. make his paths s.; Mar.1.3;
Lu. 3. 5. the crooked shall be made s.
Act. 9.11. the street which is called s.
euthudromeō. [21.1]
Act. 16.11. we came with a s. course;
euthunō.
Jo. 1.23. Make s. the way of the Lord
anorthoō.
Lu. 13.13. she was made s., and glorifi.
orthos.
Heb.12.13. make s. paths for your feet

STRAIGHTWAY.

eutheōs.
Mat. 4.20. they s... their nets; Mar.1.18
14.22. s. Jesus constr. his; Mar.6.45
27. But s. Jesus spake unto them
21. 2. ye shall find an ass tied
3. and s. he will send them
25.15. and s. took his journey
27.48. s. one of them ran, and took
Mar. 1.10. s. coming up out of the water
20. And s. he called them : and
21. and s. on the sabbath day he
2. 2. s. many were gathered toget.
3. 6. s. took counsel with the Her.
5.29. s. the fountain of her blood
42. s. the damsel arose, and wal.
6.25. she came in s. with haste
54. the ship, s. they knew him
7.35. s. his ears were opened, and
8.10. s. he entered into a ship with
9. 15. s. all the people, when they
20. s. the spirit tare him; and
24. s. the father of the child cried
11. 3. s. he will send him hither
14.45. he goeth s. to him, and saith
15. 1. s. in the morning the chief
Lu. 5.39. s. desireth new: for he saith
12.54. s. ye say, There cometh a sh.
14. 5. will not s. pull him out

Act. 9.20. And s. he preached Christ
22.29. Then s. they departed from
Jas. 1.24. s. forgetteth what manner
euthus.
Mat. 3.16. went up s. out of the water
Jo. 13.32. and shall s. glorify him
parachrēma.
Lu. 8.55. came again, and she arose s.
Act. 5.10. Then fell she down s. at his
16.33. baptized, he and all his, s.
exautēs.
Act.23.30. I sent s. to thee, and gave

STRAIN.

diulizō.
Mat.23.24. guides, which s. at a gnat

STRAIT.

stenos. [Lu. 13.24]
Mat. 7.13. Enter ye in at the s. gate;
14. Because s. is the gate, and
sunechō.
Phi. 1.23. For I am in a s. betwixt two

STRAITEN, -ed.

sunechō.
Lu. 12.50. how am I s-ed till it be acco.
²Co. 6.12. are not s-ed in us, ..ye are s-ed

STRAITEST.

akribestatos.
Act.26. 5. after the most s. sect of our

STRAITLY. (See Charge.)

polus.
Mar. 3.12. he s. charged them that; 5.43
apeileō apeilē.
Act. 4.17. let us s. threaten them, that

STRANGE.

xenos.
Act.17.18. a setter forth of s. gods
Heb.13. 9. with divers and s. doctrines
¹Pet. 4.12. as though some s. thing
xenizō.
Act.17.20. bringest certain s. things
¹Pet. 4. 4. they think it s. that ye run
12. Beloved, think it not s.
allotrios.
Act. 7. 6. should sojourn in a s. land
Heb.11. 9. promise, as in a s. country
paradoxos.
Lu. 5.26. We have seen s. things to-day
exō.
Act.26.11. them, even unto s. cities
heteros.
Jude 7. and going after s. flesh, are

STRANGER, -s.

xenos.
Mat.25.35,43. was a s., and ye took me
38. When saw we thee a s., and
44. or a s., or naked, or sick
27. 7. the potter's field, to bury s-s
Act.17.21. the Athenians and s-s which
Eph. 2.12. and s-s from the covenants
19. ye are no more s-s and forei.
Heb.11.13.confessed that they were s-s
³John 5. to the brethren, and to s-s
allotrios.
Mat.17.25. their own children, or of s-s
26. Peter saith unto him, Of s-s
Jo. 10. 5. a s. will they not follow
they know not the voice of s-s
allogenēs.
Lu. 17.18. give glory to God, save this s.
paroikos.
Act. 7.29. and was a s. in the land of
¹Pet. 2.11. beloved, I beseech you as s-s
paroikeō.
Lu. 24.18. Art thou only a s. in Jerusa.
en ho paroikia.
Act.13.17. when they dwelt as s-s in the

epidēmeō.
Act. 2.10. and s-s of Rome, Jews and
(Romans dwelling)
parepidēmos.
¹Pet. 1. 1. to the s-s scattered through.
(See Entertain, Lodge.)

STRANGLED.

pniktos.
Act.15.20, 29. from things s., and from
21.25. from blood, and from s., and

STRAWED.

diaskorpizō.
Mat.25.24. gather where thou hast not s.
26. gather where I have not s.
strōnnumi.
Mat.21. 8. trees, and s. them; Mar.11.8

STREAM.

potamos.
Lu. 6.48. when the flood arose, the s.
49. against which the s. did beat

STREET, -s.

plateia.
Mat. 6. 5. and in the corners of the s-s
12.19. hear his voice in the s-s
Lu. 10.10. out into the s-s of the same
13.26. and thou hast taught in our s-s
14.21. Go out quickly into the s-s
Act. 5.15. the sick into the s-s, and
Rev.11. 8. dead bodies lie in the s.
21.21. and the s. of the city was
22. 2. In the midst of the s. of it
rumē.
Mat. 6. 2. and in the s-s, that they may
Act. 9.11. Arise, and go into the s. whi.
12.10. passed on through one s.
agora.
Mar.6. 56. they laid the sick in the s-s

STRENGTH. (See Increase.)

dunamis.
¹Co.15.56. the s. of sin is the law
²Co. 1. 8. out of measure, above s.
12. 9. for my s. is made perfect
Heb.11.11. received s. to conceive seed
Rev. 1.16. as the sun shineth in his s.
3. 8. for thou hast a little s.
12.10. Now is come salvation, and s.
ischus.
Mar.12.30.and with all thy s.; Lu. 10.27
33. with all the s., and to love
Rev. 5.12. and riches, and wisdom, and s.
ischuō.
Heb. 9.17. otherwise it is of no s. at all
kratos.
Lu. 1.51. He hath shewed s. with his
exousia.
Rev.17.13. shall give their power and s.
stereoō.
Act. 3. 7. feet and ancle bones received s.
asthenēs.
Ro. 5. 6. when we were yet without s.

STRENGTHEN, -ed, -eth, -ing.

dunamoō.
Col. 1.11. s-ed with all might, according
endunamoō.
Phi. 4.13. through Christ, which s-eth
²Ti. 4.17. stood with me, and s-ed me
stērizō.
Lu. 22.32. art converted, s. thy breth.
Rev. 3. 2. s. the things which remain
epistērizō.
Act.18.23. in order, s-ing all the discip.
enischuō.
Lu. 22.43. him from heaven, s-ing him
Act. 9.19. received meat, he was s-ed
krataioō.
Eph. 3.16. to be s-ed with might by his
sthenoō.
¹Pet.5.10. stablish, s., settle you

STRETCH,   *-ed, -ing.*
ekteinō.   [3.5; Lu.6.10
Mat.12.13. s. *forth* thine hand; Mar.
   he s-*ed* it *forth;* and it was
   49. he s-*ed forth* his hand; 14.31
26.51. s-*ed out* his hand, *and* drew
Mar. 3. 5. And he s-*ed* it *out;* and his
Lu. 22.53. ye s-*ed forth* no hands agai.
Jo. 21.18. thou *shalt* s. *forth* thy hands
Act. 4.30. By s-*ing forth* thine hand
   26. 1. Paul s-*ed forth* the hand,*and*
   huperekteinō.
²Co. 10.14. we s. not ourselves *beyond*
   epiballō.
Act.12. 1. the king s-*ed forth* his hands
   ekpetannumi.
Ro. 10.21. I *have* s-*ed forth* my hands

STRICKEN.
probainō.
Lu. 1. 7. were now *well* s. in years
   18. and my wife *well* s. in years

STRIFE,   *-s.*
eritheia.
²Co.12.20. envyings, wraths, s-s, back.
Gal. 5.20. emulations, wrath, s., sedit.
Phi. 2. 3. nothing be done through s.
Jas. 3.14. envying and s. in your hear.
   16. For where envying and s.
   eris.
Ro. 13.13. not in s. and envying
¹Co. 3. 3. s., and divisions, are ye not
Phi. 1.15. Christ even of envy and s.
¹Ti. 6. 4. cometh envy, s., railings
   philoneikia.
Lu. 22.24. there was also a s. among th.
   machē.
²Ti. 2.23. kno. that they do gender s-s
   antilogia.
Heb. 6.16. is to them an end of all s.
   logomachia.
¹Ti. 6. 4. about ques. and s-s *of words*

STRIKE,   *-eth, Strake, Struck.*
patassō.
Mat.26.51. s-*u* a servant of the high pr.
   ballō.
Mar.14.65.the servants *did* s. him
   tuptō.
Lu. 22.64. they s-*u* him on the face
   didōmi rapisma.   [*hand*
Jo. 18.22. s-*u* Jesus *with the palm of his*
   chalaō.
Act.27.17. s-*a* sail, *and* so were driven
   paiō.
Rev. 9. 5. scorpion, when he s-*eth* a m.

STRIKER.
plēktēs.
¹Ti. 3. 3. Not given to wine, no s.
Tit. 1. 7. no s., not given to filthy

STRING.
desmos.
Mar. 7.35. the s. of his tongue was loos.

STRIPE,   *-s.*
plēgē.
Lu. 12.48. commit things worthy of s-s
Act.16.23. when they had laid many s-s
   33. and washed their s-s; and
²Co. 6. 5. In s-s, in imprisonments, in
   11.23. in s-s above measure, in pri.
   mōlōps.
¹Pet. 2.24. by whose s-s ye were healed

STRIPPED.
ekduō.
Mat.27.28. they s. him, *and* put on him
Lu. 10.30. s. him *of his raiment and*

STRIVE, *-ed, -eth, -ing, Strove.*
machomai.
Jo. 6.52. The Jews therefore s-*o* amo.
264

Act. 7.26. himself unto them *as* they s-*o*
²Ti. 2.24. serv. of the Lord must not s.
   diamachomai.
Act.23. 9. part arose, and s-*o*, saying
   agōnizomai.
Lu. 13.24. s. to enter in at the strait
¹Co. 9.25. every man *that* s-*eth* for the
Col. 1.29. s-*ing* according to his work.
   sunagōnizomai.
Ro. 15.30. that ye s. *together with* me
   antagōnizomai.
Heb.12. 4. unto blood, s-*ing against*
   athleō.
²Ti. 2. 5. if a man also s. for masteries
   crowned except he s. lawfully
   sunathleō.
Phi. 1.27. s-*ing together for* the faith of
   erizō.
Mat.12.19. He *shall* not s., nor cry
   philotimeomai.
Ro. 15.20. so *have* I s-*ed* to preach the
   (See *Words.*)

STRIVINGS, [*noun.*]
machē.
Tit. 3. 9. content., and s. about the

STRONG, (See *Drink.*)
ischuros.   [Mar.3.27
Mat.12.29. enter into a s. *man's* house;
   first bind the s. *man;* Mar.3.27
Lu. 11.21. a s. *man* armed keepeth his
¹Co. 4.10. we are weak, but ye are s.
Heb. 5. 7. with s. crying and tears
   6.18. we might have a s. consola.
¹Jo. 2.14. young men, because ye are s.
Rev. 5. 2. I saw a s. angel proclaiming
   18. 8. s. is the Lord God who judg.
   endunamoō.
Ro. 4.20. *was* s. in faith, giving glory
Eph. 6.10. brethren, *be* s. in the Lord
²Ti. 2. 1. my son, *be* s. in the grace
Heb.11.34. of weakness *were made* s.
   dunatos.
Ro. 15. 1. We then that are s. ought
²Co.12.10. I am weak, then am I s.
   13. 9. we are weak, and ye are s.
   stereos.
Heb. 5.12. of milk, and not of s. meat
   14. but s. meat belongeth to
   stereoō.
Act. 3.16. name *hath made* this man s.
   krataioō.
Lu. 1.80. *waxed* s. in spirit; 2.40
¹Co.16.13. quit you like men, *be* s.
   energeia planē, [*gen.*]
²Th. 2.11. shall send them s. *delusion*
   megas.
Rev.18. 2. cried mightily with a s. voice

STRONGER.
ischuroteros.
Lu. 11.22. when a s. than he shall come
¹Co. 1.25. the weakness of God is s.
   10.22. jealousy? are we s. than he

STRONGHOLDS.
ochurōma.
²Co. 10. 4. to the pulling down of s.

STUBBLE.
kalamē.
¹Co. 3.12. preci. stones, wood, hay, s.

STUCK.
ereidō.
Act.27.41. the forepart s. *fast, and* re.

STUDY.
spoudazō.
²Ti. 2.15. s. to shew thyself approved
   philotimeomai.
¹Th. 4.11. *That* ye s. to be quiet, and

STUFF.
skeuos.
Lu.17.31. and his s. in the house, let

STUMBLE,   *-ed, -eth, -ing*
proskoptō.
Jo. 11. 9. walk in the day, he s-*eth* not
   10. walk in the night, he s-*eth*
Ro. 9.32. they s-*ed at* that stumblings.
   14.21. whereby thy brother s-*eth*
¹Pet. 2. 8. which s. *at* the word
   proskomma.
¹Pet. 2. 8. a stone of s-*ing*, and a rock
   ptaiō.
Ro. 11.11. *Have* they s-*ed* that they
   (See *Occasion.*)

STUMBLINGBLOCK.
skandalon.
Ro. 11. 9. a s., and a recompence unto
¹Co. 1.23. unto the Jews a s., and untl
Rev. 2.14. to cast a s. before the childr.
   proskomma.
Ro. 14.13. that no man put a s. or an
¹Co. 8. 9. become a s. to them that are

STUMBLINGSTONE.
lithos proskomma.
Ro. 9.32. they stumbled at that s.
   33. I lay in Sion a s. and rock

SUBDUE,   *-ed*
hupotassō.
¹Co. 15.28. things shall *be* s. *unto* him
Phi. 3.21. to s. all things *unto* himself
   katagōnizomai.
Heb.11.33. through faith s. kingdoms

SUBJECT.
hupotassō.
Lu. 2.51. and was s. *unto* them
   10.17. even the devils *are* s. *unto* us
   20. that the spirits *are* s. *unto* you
Ro. 8. 7. for it *is* not s. to the law of
   20. the creature *was made* s. to
   13. 1. *Let* every soul *be* s. *unto* the
   5. Wherefore ye must needs *be* s.
¹Co. 14.32. *are* s. to the prophets
   15.28. *shall* the Son also himse. *be* s.
Eph. 5.24. as the church *is* s. *unto* Christ
Tit. 3. 1. to *be* s. to principalities and
¹Pet. 2.18. Servants be s. *to* your masters
   3.22. and powers *being made* s. *unto*
   5. 5. you *be* s. one *to* another *and*
   enochos.
Heb. 2.15. their lifetime s. *to* bondage
   (See *Ordinances, Passions.*)

SUBJECTED.
hupotassō.
Ro. 8.20. by reason of him *who hath* s.

SUBJECTION.
hupotassō.
Heb. 2. 5. *hath* he not *put* in s. the wo.
   8. Thou *hast put* all things *in* s.
   that he *put* all *in* s. *under*
   12. 9. *shall* we not. .*be in* s. *unto*
¹Pet. 3. 1. *in* s. *to* your own husbands
   5. *being in* s. *unto* their own
   hupotagē.
²Co. 9.13. for your professed s. unto the
Gal. 2. 5. we gave place by s., no, not
¹Ti. 2.11. learn in silence with all s.
   3. 4. having his children in s.
   doulagōgeō.
¹Co. 9.27. my body, and *bring* it *into* s.

SUBMIT,   *-ed, -ing.*
hupotassō.
Ro. 10. 3. *have* not s-*ed* themselves *unto*
¹Co. 16.16. That ye s. *yourselves unto*
Eph. 5.21. s-*ing yourselves* one *to* anot.

Eph. 5.22. Wives s. yours. *unto* ; Col.3.18
Jas. 4. 7. s. yourselves therefore *to* God
¹Pet. 2.13. s. yourselves to every ordina.
  5. 5. younger, s. yourselves *unto*
    hupeikō.
Heb.13.17. s. your*selves :* for they watch

SUBORNED.
    hupoballō.
Act. 6.11. Then they s. men, which sa.

SUBSTANCE.
    huparchonta.
Lu. 8. 3. ministe. unto him of their s.
    huparxis.
Heb.10.34. better and an enduring s.
    hupostasis.
Heb.11. 1. faith is the s. of things hoped
    ousia.
Lu. 15.13. wasted his s. with riotous

SUBTILLY. (See *Deal.*)
SUBTILTY.
    dolos.
Mat.26. 4. they might take Jesus by s.
Act.13.10. O full of all s. and all misc.
    panourgia.
²Co.11. 3. beguiled Eve through his s.

SUBVERT,   *-ed, -ing.*
    anaskeuazō.
Act.15.24. with words, s-*ing* your souls
    anatrepō.
Tit. 1.11. who s. whole houses, teachi.
    ekstrephō.
Tit. 3.11. that he that is such *is* s-*ed*

SUBVERTING, [*noun.*]
    katastrophē.
¹Ti. 2.14. to the s. of the hearers

SUCCOUR,   *-ed.*
    boētheō.
²Co. 6. 2. the day of salva. have I s-*ed*
Heb. 2.18. he is able *to* s. them that are

SUCCOURER.
    prostatis.
Ro. 16. 2. she hath been a s. of many

SUCH, (See *Manner.*)
    toioutos.
Mat. 9. 8. which had given s. power
  18. 5. shall receive one s. little ch.
  19.14. for of s. is the kingdom ;
     Mar.10.14 ; Lu.18.16
Mar. 4.33. And with many s. parables
  6. 2. that even s. mighty works
  7. 8, 13. and many other s. like
  9.37. one of s. children in my na.
  13.19. s. as was not from the beg.
Lu. 9. 9. of whom I hear s. things
  13. 2. because they suffered s. thi.
Jo. 4.23. the Father seeketh s. to wor.
  8. 5. that s. should be stoned
  9.16. a man that is a sinner do s.
Act.16.24. Who, having received s. a
  21.25. that they observe no s. thi.
  22.22. Away with s. a fellow from
  26.29. and altogether s. as I am
Ro. 1.32. which commit s. thi.; 2.2,3
  16.18. For they that are s. serve
¹Co. 5. 1. and s. fornication as is not
  5. To deliver s. an one unto
  11. with s. an one no not to eat
  7.15. is not under bondage in s.
  28. s. shall have trouble in the
  11.16. we have no s. custom
  15.48. s. are they also that are
    s. are they also that are hea.
  16.16. submit yourselves unto s.
  18. ackno. ye them that are s.
²Co. 2. 6. Sufficient to s. a man is this
  7. s. a *one* should be swallowed
  8. 4. And s. trust have we through

²Co. 3.12. Seeing then that we have s.
  10.11. Let s. an *one* think this
    s. will we be also in deed
  11.13. For s. are false apostles
  12. 2. s. an *one* caught up to the
  3. And I knew s. a man, whe.
  5. Of s. an one will I glory
Gal. 5.21. that they which do s. things
  23. against s. there is no law
  6. 1. restore s. an one in the spi.
Eph. 5.27. or wrinkle, or any s. thing
Phi. 2.29. and hold s. in reputation
²Th. 3.12. Now them that are s. we
¹Ti. 6. 5. from s. withdraw thyself
Tit. 3.11. he that is s. is subverted
Phile. 9. being s. an one as Paul the
Heb. 7.26. For s. an high priest beca.
  8. 1. We have s. an high priest
  11.14. For they that say s. things
  12. 3. him that endured s. contra.
  13.16. with s. sacrifices God is well
Jas. 4.16. all s. rejoicing is evil
³John 8. We there. ought to receive s.
    hoios.
Mat.24.21.tribulation, s. *as* was not
Mar.13.19.affliction, s. *as* was not from
²Co. 10.11. s. *as* we are in word by
  12.20. I shall not find you s. *as* I
    unto you s. *as* ye would not
Rev.16.18. s. *as* was not since men were
    houtos.
Mar. 4.18. s. *as* hear the word
Act.18.15. be no judge of s. matters
Gal. 5.21. revellings, and s. like : of
¹Th. 4. 6. is the avenger of all s.
²Ti. 3. 5. power thereof ; from s. turn
Rev.20. 6. on s. the second death hath
    hostis.
Mar. 4.20. s. *as* hear the word, and
    deina.
Mat.26.18. into the city to s. *a* man
    hode.
Jas. 4.13. we will go into s. a city
    toiosde.
²Pet. 1.17. when there came s. a voice

SUCK,   *-ed.*
    thēlazō.   [13.17 ; Lu.21.23
Mat.24.19.to them *that give* s.; Mar.
Lu. 11.27. the paps which thou *hast* s-*ed*
  23.29. the paps which never *gave* s.

SUCKLINGS.
    thēlazō, [*participle.*]
Mat.21.16. the mouths of babes and s.

SUDDEN.
    aiphnidios.
¹Th. 5. 3. then s. destruction cometh

SUDDENLY.
    exaiphnēs.
Mar.13.36.Lest coming s. he find you
Lu. 2.13. s. there was with the angel
  9.39. he s. crieth out ; and it
Act. 9. 3. s. their shined round about
  22. 6. s. there shone from heaven
    aphnō.
Act. 2. 2. s. there came a sound from
  16.26. s. there was a great earthqu.
  28. 6. swol., or fallen down dead s.
    exapina.
Mar. 9. 8. s., when they had looked
    tacheōs.
¹Ti. 5.22. Lay hands s. on no man

SUE.
    krinō.
Mat. 5.40. man will s. thee *at the* law

SUFFER, *-ed, -est, -eth, -ing.*
    paschō.
Mat.16.21. and s. many things of the el.
  17.12. shall also the Son of man s.

Mat.27.19. for I *have* s-*ed* many things
Mar. 5.26. And *had* s-*ed* many things of
  8.31. s. many things ; 9.12 ; Lu.9.2
Lu. 13. 2. because they s-*ed* such things
  17.25. But first must he s. many
  22.15. passover with you before I s.
  24.26. Ought not Christ *to have* s-*ed*
  46. it behoved Christ *to* s., and to
Act. 3.18. *that* Christ *should* s., he hath
  9.16. how great things he must s.
  17. 3. Christ must needs *have* s-*ed*
¹Co.12.26. one member s., all the mem.
²Co. 1. 6. sufferings which we also s.
Gal. 3. 4. *Have* ye s-*ed* so many things
Phi. 1.29. but also *to* s. for his sake
¹Th. 2.14. for ye also *have* s-*ed* like thi.
²Th. 1. 5. of God, for which ye also s.
²Ti. 1.12. For the which cause I also s.
Heb. 2.18. he himself *hath* s-*ed* being
  5. 8. by the things which he s-*ed*
  9.26. then must he often *have* s-*ed*
  13.12. blood, s-*ed* without the gate
¹Pet. 2.19. endure grief, s-*ing* wrongfu.
  20. when ye do well, and s. for
  21. Christ also s-*ed* for us, leavi.
  23. *when* he s-*ed*, he threatened
  3.14. But and if ye s. for righteou.
  17. *that* ye s. for well doing
  18. Christ also *hath* once s-*ed* for
  4. 1. *Forasmuch* then *as. hath* s-*ed*
    for he *that hath* s-*ed* in the
  15. But *let* none of you s. as a
  19. Wherefore let them *that* s.
  5.10. *after that* ye *have* s-*ed* a wh.
Rev. 2.10. th.things which thou shalt s.
    sumpaschō.
Ro. 8.17. if so be that we s. *with* him
¹Co.12.26. all the members s. *with* it
    propaschō.
¹Th. 2. 2. *after that* we *had* s-*ed* before
    aphiēmi.
Mat. 3.15. s. it to be so now : for thus
    Then he s-*ed* him
  19.14. s. little children, and forbid
  23.13. neither s. ye them that
Mar. 1.34. s-*ed* not the devils to speak
  5.19. Howbeit Jesus s-*ed* him not
  37. he s-*ed* no man to follow
  7.12. ye s. him no more to do
  10.14. s. the little childr.; Lu.18.16
  11.16. *would* not s. that any man
Lu. 8.51. he s-*ed* no man to go in
  12.39. not *have* s-*ed* his house to be
Rev.11. 9. *shall* not s. their dead
    eaō.
Mat.24.43.would not *have* s-*ed* his hou.
Lu. 4.41. s-*ed* them not to speak : for
  22.51. s. ye thus far. And he tou.
Act.14.16. s-*ed* all nations to walk in
  16. 7. the Spirit s-*ed* them not
  19.30. the disciples s-*ed* him not
  28. 4. yet vengeance s-*eth* not to
¹Co.10.13. who *will* not s. you to be te.
Rev. 2.20. because thou s-*est* that wom.
    epitrepō.   [Lu.9.59
Mat. 8.21. s. me first to go and bury ;
  31. s. us to go away into the
  19. 8. s-*ed* you to put away your
Mar.10. 4. Moses s-*ed* to write a bill
Lu. 8.32. that he *would* s. them to ent
    into them. And he s-*ed* them
Act.21.39. s. me to speak unto the peo.
  28.16. but Paul *was* s-*ed* to dwell
¹Ti. 2.12. I s. not a woman to teach
    anechomai.
Mat.17.17. how long *shall* I s.; Mar.9.19
Lu. 9.41. I be with you, and s. you
¹Co. 4.12. being persecuted, we s. it
²Co.11.19. For ye s. fools gladly, seeing
  20. For ye s., if a man bring
Heb.13.22.brethren, s. the word of exh.
265

didōmi.

Act. 2.27. neither *wilt* thou s. thine
13.35. *shalt* not s. thine Holy One

pathētos.

Act.26.23. That Christ should s., and

proseaō.

Act.27. 7. the wind not s-*ing* us, we

stegō.

¹Co. 9.12. but s. all things, lest we

makrothumeō.

¹Co.13. 4. Charity s-*eth* long, and is

koluō.

Heb.7.23. because they *were not* s-*ed* to

sungkakoucheomai.

Heb.11.25. rather to s. *affliction with*

kakouchoumenos.

Heb.13. 3. and them *which* s. *adversity*

kakopatheō.

²Ti. 2. 9. Wherein I s. *trouble*, as an

hupomenō.

²Ti. 2.12. If we s., we shall also reign

hupechō.

Jude 7. s-*ing* the vengeance of etern.
(See *Loss, Manners, Need, Persecution, Reproach, Shame, Shipwreck, Tribulation, Violence, Wrong.*)

SUFFERING,   -s.

pathēma.

Ro. 8.18. I reckon that the s-*s* of this
²Co. 1. 5. For as the s-*s* of Christ abou.
6. the enduring of the same s-*s*
7. as ye are partakers of the s-*s*
Phi. 3.10. the fellowship of his s-*s*
Col. 1.24. Who now rejoice in my s-*s*
Heb.2. 9. for the s. of death, crowned
10. salvation perfect through s-*s*
¹Pet. 1.11. the s-*s* of Christ, and the
4.13. are partakers of Christ's s-*s*
5. 1. a witness of the s-*s* of Christ
(See *Affliction.*)

SUFFICE,   -cth.

arkeō.

Jo. 14. 8. shew us the Fa., and it s-*eth*

arketos.

¹Pet. 4. 3. past of our life *may* s. us

SUFFICIENCY.

hikanotēs.

²Co. 3. 5. of ourselves ; but our s. is

autarkeia.

²Co. 9. 8. having all s. in all things

SUFFICIENT.

hikanos.

²Co. 2. 6. 8. to such a man is this
16. who is s. for these things
3. 5. Not that we are s. of ourselv.

arkeō.

Jo. 6. 7. of bread *is* not s. for them
²Co. 12. 9. My grace *is* s. for thee

arketos.

Mat. 6.34. s. unto the day is the evil

SUM.

kephalaion.

Act.22.28. With a great s. obtained I
Heb. 8. 1. have spoken this is the s.

timē.

Act. 7.16. bought for a s. of money

SUMMER.

theros.   [Lu.21.30
Mat.24.32. kn. that s. is nigh; Mar.13.28;

SUMPTUOUSLY.

lamprōs.

Lu. 16.19. and fared s. every day.

SUN.

hēlios.

Mat. 5.45. he maketh his s. to rise
266

Mat.13. 6. And when the s. was up
43. the righ. shine forth as the s.
17. 2. his face did shine as the s.
24.29. the s. be darken. ; Mar.13.24
Mar. 1.32. when the s. did set, they
4. 6. But when the s. was up
16. 2. sepulc. at the rising of the s.
Lu. 4.40. Now when the s. was setting
21.25. there shall be signs in the s.
23.45. the s. was darkened, and the
Act. 2.20. The s. shall be turned into
13.11. be blind, not seeing the s.
26.13. the brightness of the s.
27.20. And when neither s. nor stars
¹Co.15.41. There is one glory of the s.
Eph. 4.26. let not the s. go down on yo.
Jas. 1.11. For the s. is no sooner risen
Rev. 1.16. as the s. shineth in his stren.
6.12. the s. became black as sackcl.
7.16. shall the s. light on them
8.12. the third part of the s. was
9. 2. the s. and the air were darke.
10. 1. his face was as it were the s.
12. 1. woman clothed with the s.
16. 8. pour. out his vial upon the s.
19.17. an angel standing in the s.
21.23. had no need of the s., neither
22. 5. neither light of the s.; for the

SUNDRY.

polumerōs.

Heb. 1. 1. God who *at* s. *times* and in

SUP,   -ed.

deipneō.

Lu. 17. 8. Make ready where I *may* s.
¹Co.11.25. the cup when he *had* s-*ed*
Rev. 3.20. *will* s. with him, and he

SUPERFLUITY.

perisseia.

Jas. 1.21. and s. of naughtiness

SUPERFLUOUS.

perissos.

²Co. 9. 1. it is s. for me to write to you

SUPERSCRIPTION.

epigraphē.   [Lu. 20.24
Mat.22.20. is this image and s.;Mar.12.16;
Mar.15.26.the s. of his accusation
Lu. 23.38. a s. also was writte over

SUPERSTITION.

deisidaimonia.

Act.25.19. against him of their own s.

SUPERSTITIOUS.

deisidaimonesteros.

Act.17.22. in all things ye are *too* s.

SUPPER.

deipnon.

Mar. 6.21. made a s. to his lords, high
Lu. 14.12. thou makest a dinner or a s.
16. A certa. man made a great s.
17. sent his servant at s. time
24. were bid. shall taste of my s.
Jo. 12. 2. There they made him a s.
13. 2. s. being ended, the devil hav.
4. He riseth from s., and laid
21.20. also leaned on his breast at s.
¹Co.11.20. this is not to eat the Lord's s.
21. taketh before other his own s.
Rev.19. 9. unto the marriage s. of the
17. unto the s. of the great God

deipneō. *[participle.]*

Lu. 22.20. Likewise also the cup after s.

SUPPLICATION,   -s.

deēsis.

Act. 1.14. one accord in prayer and s.
Eph. 6.18. always with all prayer and s.
perseverance and s. for all
Phi. 4. 6. every thing by prayer and s.

---

¹Ti. 2. 1. that, first of all, s-s, prayers
5. continueth in s-s and praye.

hiketēria.

Heb. 5. 7. offered up prayers and s-s

SUPPLY, *[noun.]*

epichorēgia.

Phi. 1.19. the s. of the spirit of Jesus

SUPPLY, *[verb,]*   -ed, -eth.

anaplēroō.

¹Co.16.17. on your part they *have* s-*ed*
Phi. 2.30. to s. your lack of service

prosanaplēroō.

²Co. 9.12. not only s-*eth* the want of
11. 9. the brethr. which came..s-*ed*

epichorēgia.

Eph. 4.16. that which every joint s-*eth*
(by every joint of *supply*.)

plēroō.

Phi. 4.19. my God *shall* s. all your need

SUPPORT.

antilambanomai.

Act.20.35. ye ought to s. the weak, and

antechomai.

¹Th. 5.14. s. the weak, be patient

SUPPOSE,   -ed, -ing.

nomizō.

Mat.20.10. they s-*ed* that they should
Lu. 2.44. s-*ing* him to have been in
3.23. being as *was* s-*ed* the son of
Act. 7.25. For he s-*ed* his brethren
14.19. he had been dead
16.27. s-*ing* that the prisoners had
21.29. whom they s-*ed* that Paul
¹Co. 7.26. I s. therefore that this is
¹Ti. 6. 5. s-*ing* that gain is godliness

dokeō.

Mar. 6.49. they s-*ed* it had been a spirit
Lu. 12.51. s. ye that I am come to give
13. 2. ye that these Galilæans
24.37. s-*ed* that they had seen a
Jo. 20.15. She, s-*ing* him to be the
Act.27.13. s-*ing* that they had obtained
Heb.10.29. much sorer punishment, s.

hupolambanō.

Lu. 7.43. I s. that he, to whom he
Act. 2.15. these are not drunk. as ye s.

logizomai.

²Co.11. 5. For I s. I was not a whit
¹Pet.5.12. brother unto you, as I s.

huponoeō.

Act.25.18. of such things as I s-*ed*

oimai.

Jo. 21.25. I s. that even the world

oiomai.

Phi. 1.16. s-*ing* to add affliction to my

hēgeomai.

Phi. 2.25. yet I s-*ed* it necessary to sen l

SUPREME.

huperechō, *[participle.]*

¹Pet. 2.13. wheth. it be to the king, as s-

SURE.

asphalēs.

Heb. 6.19. the soul, both s. and stedfast

asphalizō.

Mat. 27.64.the sepulchre *be made* s.
65. *make* it as s. as ye can
66. and *made* the sepulchre s.

bebaios.

Ro. 4.16. promise might be s. to all
²Pet. 1.10. your calling and election s.

bebaioteros.

²Pet.1.19. a *more* s. word of prophecy

ginōskō.

Lu. 10.11. *be* ye s. of this, that the kin
Jo. 6.69. we believe and *are* s. that

eideō.

Ro. 2. 2. we *are* s. that the judgment
15.29. I am s. that, when I come

pistos.
Act.13.34. the s. mercies of David
stereos.
¹Ti. 2.19. the founda. of G. standeth s.

SURELY.
alēthōs.   [Mar.14.70
Mat.26.73.s. thou also art one of them ;
Jo. 17. 8. have known s. that I came
plērophoreō.
Lu. 1. 1. which are most s. believed
pantōs.
Lu. 4.23. Ye will s. say unto me this
ē mēn.
Heb. 6.14. s. blessing I will bless thee
nai.
Rev.22.20. s. I come quickly ; Amen

SURETY.
alēthōs.
Act.12.11. I know of a s., that the Lord
engguos.
Heb. 7.22. Jesus made a s. of a better

SURFEITING.
kraipalē.
Lu. 21.34. hearts be overcharged with s.

SURMISINGS.
huponoia.
¹Ti. 6. 4. strife, railings, evil s.

SURNAME, [noun.]
epikaleomai.
Mat.10. 3. whose s. was Thaddeus
Act.10. 5, 32. whose s. is Peter ; 11.13
12.12, 25. John whose s. was Mark
kaleō.
Act.15.37. John, whose s. was Mark

SURNAME, [verb,]   -ed.
epikaleomai.
Lu. 22. 3. into Judas s-ed Iscariot
Act. 1.23. who was s-ed Justus
4.36. who by the apostles was s-ed
10.18. Simon, which was s-ed Peter
15.22. Judas s. Barnabas
epitithēmi onoma.
Mar.3.16.And Simon he s-ed Peter
17. he s-ed them Boanerges, whi.

SUSTENANCE.
chortasma, [plu.]
Act. 7.11. and our fathers found no s.

SWADDLING CLOTHES.
sparganoō.
Lu. 2. 7. and wrapped him in s. clothes
12. babe wrapped in s. clothes

SWALLOW.
katapinō.
Mat. 23.24.at a gnat, and s. a camel
¹Co. 15.54. Death is s-ed up in victory
²Co. 2. 7. should be s-ed up with over.
5. 4. mortality might be s-ed up of
Rev.12.16. and s-ed up the flood which

SWEAR,   -eth, Sware, Sworn.
omnumi.
Mat. 5.34. s. not at all ; neither by hea.
36. Neither shalt thou s. by thy
23.16, 18. Whosoever shall s. by the
18. but whosoever s-eth by the
20, 21. Whoso therefore shall s.
by the altar, s-eth by it ; 22
22. he that shall s. by hea., s-eth
26.74. to curse and to s.; Mar.14.71
Mar. 6.23. And he s-a unto her, What.
Lu. 1.73. which he s-a to our father
Act. 2.30. that God had s-o with an oa.
7.17. which God had s-o to Abra.
Heb. 3.11. So I s-a in my wrath, They
18. to whom s-a he that they
4. 3. As I have s-o in my wrath

Heb. 6.13. could s. by no greater, he s-a
16. For men verily s. by the gre.
7.21. The Lord s-a and will not
Jas. 5.12. all things, my brethren, s.
Rev.10. 6. And s-a by him that liveth

SWEAT.
hidrōs.
Lu. 22.44. his s. was as it were great

SWEEP,   Swept.
saroō.
Mat.12.44. s-t and garnished ; Lu. 11.25
Lu. 15. 8. light a candle, and s. the

SWEET, (See Spices.)
glukus.
Jas. 3.11. same place s. water and bitter
Rev.10. 9, 10. mouth s. as honey
euōdia.
²Co. 2.15. we are..a s. savour of Christ
Eph. 5. 2. for a s. smelling savour
Phi. 4.18. odour of a s. smell, a sacrifice

SWELLING.
huperongkos.
²Pet. 2.18. they speak great s. words
Jude. 16. mouth speaketh great s. wor.

SWELLINGS.
phusiōsis.
²Co. 12.20. backbitings, whisperings, s.

SWERVE,   -ed.
astocheō.
¹Ti. 1. 6. From which some having s-ed

SWIFT.
oxus.
Ro. 3.15. Their feet are s. to shed blood
tachus.
Jas. 1.19. let every man be s. to hear
tachinos.
²Pet. 2. 1. upon themselves s. destruct.

SWIM.
kolumbaō.
Act.27.43. that they which could s.
ekkolumbaō.
Act.27.42. of them should s. out, and

SWINE.
choiros.
Mat. 7. 6. cast ye your pearls before s.
8.30. an herd of many s. feeding ;
Mar.5.11 ; Lu.8.32
31. go away into the herd of s.
32. went into the herd of s.: and
the whole herd of s. ran
Mar. 5.12. Send us into the s., that we
13. entered into the s.; Lu.8.33
14. they that feed the s. fled
16. and also concerning the s.
Lu. 15.15. him into his fields to feed s.
16. the husks that the s. did eat

SWOLLEN.
pimpramai.
Act.28. 6. when he should have s.

SWORD,   -s.
machaira.
Mat.10.34. not to send peace, but a s.
26.47, 55. with s-s and staves ; Mar.
14.43,48 ; Lu.22.52
51. and drew his s., and struck
52. up aga. thy s. into ; Jo.18.11
the s. shall perish with the s.
Mar.14.47.drew a s., and smote a serv.
Lu. 21.24. sh. fall by the edge of the s.
22.36. he that hath no s., let him
38. behold, here are two s-s
49. shall we smite with the s-s
Jo. 18.10. Peter having a s. drew it
Act.12. 2. brother of John with the s.

Act.16.27. he drew out his s., and wou.
Ro. 8.35. nakedness, or peril, or s.
13. 4. beareth not the s. in vain
Eph. 6.17. s. of the Spirit, which is the
Heb. 4.12. sharp. than any twoedged s.
11.34. escaped the edge of the s.
37. were slain with the s.
Rev. 6. 4. given unto him a great s.
13.10. he that killeth with the s.
must be killed with the s.
14. which had the wound by a s.
romphaia.
Lu. 2.35. Yea, a s. shall pierce throu.
Rev. 1.16. a sharp twoedged s.
2.12. which hath the sharp s.
16. with the s. of my mouth
6. 8. to kill with s., and with
19.15. his mouth goeth a sharp s.
21. slain with the s. of him that

SYCAMINE.
sukaminos.
Lu. 17. 6. might say unto this s. tree

SYCAMORE.
sukomōraia.
Lu. 19. 4. climbed up into a s. tree

SYNAGOGUE,   -s.
sunagōgē.
Mat. 4.23. teaching in their s-s ; 9.35
6. 2. as the hypocrites do in the s-s
5. love to pray standi. in the s-s
10.17. will scourge you in their s-s
12. 9. he went into their s.;Lu.4.16.;
Act.13.14,19.8
13.54. tau. them in their s.; Lu.4.15
23. 6. ch. seats in the s-s ; Mar.12.39
34. shall ye scourge in your s-s
Mar. 1.21. he entered into the s.; 3.1 ;
Lu.6.6; Act.18.19
23. And there was in their s.
29. they were come out of the s.
39. he preac. in their s-s ; Lu.4.44
6. 2. he began to teach in the s.
13. 9. in the s-s ye shall be beaten
Lu. 4.20, 28. all them that were in the s.
33. in the s. there was a man
38. And he arose out of the s.
7. 5. and he hath built us a s.
8.41. he was a ruler of the s.
11.43. the uppermo. seats in the s-s
12.11. they bring you unto the s-s
13.10. was teaching in one of the s-s
20.46. the highest seats in the s-s
21.12. delivering you up to the s-s
Jo. 6.59. These things said he in the s.
18.20. I ever taught in the s.
Act. 6. 9. certain of the s., which is
9. 2. letters to Damascus to the s-s
20. he preached Christ in the s-s
13. 5. the word of God in the s-s
42. Jews were gone out of the s.
14. 1. went both together into the s.
15.21. being read in the s-s every
17. 1. where was a s. of the Jews
10. went into the s. of the Jews
17. disputed he in the s. with
18. 4. And he reasoned in the s.
7. house joined hard to the s.
26. to speak boldly in the s.
22.19. and beat in every s. them
24.12. neither in the s-s, nor in
26.11. punished them oft in every s.
Rev. 2. 9. but are the s. of Satan
3. 9. them of the s. of Satan
archisunagōgos.
Mar. 5.22. one of the rulers of the s.
35. from the ruler of the s.'s hou.
36. unto the ruler of the s.
38. house of the ruler of the s.
Lu. 8.49. from the ruler of the s.'s house

TAB TAK TAK

Lu. 13.14. the *ruler of the* s. answered
Act.13.15. the *rulers of the* s. sent
  18. 8. Crisp., the *chief ruler of the* s.
     17. the *chief ruler of the* s., and
  aposunagōgos.
Jo. 9.22. sho. be *put out of the* s.; 12.42
  16. 2. shall put you *out of the* s-s

TABERNACLE, -s.
  skēnē.
Mat.17. 4. make here three *t-s*; Mar.9.
     5; Lu.9.33
Act. 7.43. took up the t. of Moloch
     44. Our fathers had the t. of wit.
  15.16. build again the t. of David
Heb. 8. 2. of the true t. which the Lord
     5. he was about to make the t.
  9. 2. there was a t. made; the first
     3. after the second veil, the t.
     6. went always into the first t.
     8. as the first t. was yet standi.
     11. by a greater and more perf. t.
     21. with blood both the t., and
  11. 9. dwelling in t-s with Isaac
  13.10. to eat which serve the t.
Rev.13. 6. blasphe. his name, and his t.
  15. 5. the temple of the t. of the
  21. 3. the t. of God is with men
  skēnōma.
Act. 7.46. to find a t. for the God of Ja.
²Pet. 1.13. as long as I am in this t.
     14. I must put off this my t.
  skēnos.
²Co. 5. 1. our earthly house of this t.
     4. we that are in this t. do gro.
  skēnopēgia.
Jo. 7. 2. the Jews' feast *of t-s* was at

TABLE, (See *Sit*,) -s.
  trapeza.
Mat.15.27. wh. fall from their masters' t.
  21.12. t-s of the moneyc.; Mar.11.15
Mar. 7.28. yet the dogs under the t. eat
Lu. 16.21. wh. fell from the rich man's t.
  22.21. betr. me is with me on the t.
     30. at my t. in my kingdom, and
Jo. 2.15. money, and overthrew the t-s
Act. 6. 2. the word of God, and serve t-s
Ro. 11. 9. Let their t. be made a snare
¹Co. 10.21. be partakers of the Lord's t.
     and of the t. of devils
Heb. 9. 2. and the t., and the shewbre.
  plax.
²Co. 3. 3. not in t-s of stone, but in
     fleshy t-s of the heart
Heb. 9. 4. and the t-s of the covenant
  klinē.
Mar. 7. 4. brasen vessels, and of t-s
  pinakidion.
Lu. 1.63. he asked for a *writing* t.
  anakeimai, [*partic.*]
Jo. 13.28. no man *at the* t. knew for

TACKLING.
  skeuē.
Act.27.19. we cast out..the t. of the sh.

TAIL, -s.
  oura.
Rev. 9.10. they had t-s like unto scorpi.
     there were stings in their t-s
     19. in their t-s: for their t-s were
  12. 4. his t. drew the third part
TAKE, (See *Thought.*)
  lambanō.
Mat. 5.40. and t. *away* thy coat, let him
  8.17. Himself to. our infirmities
  10.38. And he that t-eth not his cr.
  13.31. which a man to., *and* sowed
     33. which a woman to.; Lu.13.21
  14.19. and to. the five loa.; Lu.9.16
  15.26. It is not meet to ta. the chil.
     36. And he to. the sev.; Mar.8.6
268

Mat. 16. 5. had forgotten to t.; Mar.8.14
     7. because we *have* t-en no bre.
     9, 10. many baskets ye to. up
  17.25. *do* the kings of the earth t.
     27. that t. *and* give unto them
  21 35. husband. to. his servants, *and*
  22.15. and to. counsel how they
  25. 1. which to. their lamps, *and*
     3. to. their lamps, *and* to. no
     4. But the wise to. oil in their
  26.26. to. bread, and blessed it, *and*
     t., eat; this is my body;
     Mar.14.22; ¹Co.11.24
     27. And he to. the; Mar.14.23
     52. all they *that* t. the sword sh.
  27. 1. elders of the people to. coun.
     6. pri. to. the silver pieces, *and*
     7. And they to. counsel, *and*
     9. And they to. the thirty piec.
     24. he to. water, *and* washed his
     30. and to. the reed, and smote
     48. and to. a spunge, *and* filled
     59. *when* Joseph had t-en the
  28.12. and had t-en counsel, they
     15. So they to. the money, *and*
Mar. 6.41. And *when* he had t-en the
  9.36. And he to. a child, *and* set
  12. 8. And they to. him, *and* killed
     19. his brother *should* t. his wife
     20. the first to. a wife; Lu.20.29
     21. And the second to.; Lu.20.30
  14.22. Jesus to. bread, *and* blessed
Lu. 5. 5. night, *and* have t-en nothing
     6. 4. *did* t. and eat the shewbread
  9.39. And, lo, a spirit t-eth him
  13.19. which a man to., *and* cast in.
  20.28. that his brother *should* t. his
     31. And the third to. her; and
  22.17. and said, t. this, and divide
     19. he to. bread, *and*; Act.27.35
     24.30. he to. bread, *and* blessed it
     43. And he to. it, *and* did eat
Jo. 6. 7. th. every one of them *may* t.
     11. And Jesus to. the loaves
  10.17. that I *might* t. it again
     18. I have power to t. it again
  12. 3. Then to. Mary a pound of oi.
     13. to. branches of palm trees
  13. 4. and to. a towel, *and* girded
     12. and had t-en his garments
  16.15. he *shall* t. of mine, and shall
  18.31. t. ye him, and judge him
  19. 1. Pilate therefore to. Jesus
     6. t. ye him, and crucify him
     23. to. his garments, and made
     27. that disciple to. her unto
     40. Then to. they the body of J.
  21.13. and t-eth bread, and giveth
Act. 1.20. bishoprick *let* another t.
     25. *That* he may t. part of this
     2.23. ye have t-en, *and* by wicked
     9.25. disciples to. him by night, *and*
  15.14. to t. out of them a people
     16. 3. and to. *and* circumcised
     17. 9. And *when* they had t-en sec.
  28.15. thanked God, and to. coura.
Ro. 7. 8, 11. sin, t-*ing* occasion by the
¹Co. 10.13. There *hath* no tempta. t-en
     11.23. in which he was betrayed to.
²Co. 11. 8. t-*ing* wages of them, to do
     20. if a man t. of you, if a man
Phi. 2. 7. *and* to. upon him the form
Heb. 5. 1. every high priest t-en from
     4. no man t-*eth* this honour
     9.19. he to. the blood of calves
Jas. 5.10. t., my brethren, the prophets
³John 7. t-*ing* nothing of the Gentiles
Rev. 3.11. that no man t. thy crown
     5. 7. he came and to. the book
     8. when he had t-en the book
     9. Thou art worthy to t. the bo.
     6. 4. *to* t. peace from the earth

Rev. 8. 5. the angel to. the censer
  10. 8. Go and t. the little book
     9. t. it, and eat it up; and
     10. I to. the little book out of
  11.17. because thou *hast* t-en to th.
  22.17. whosoever will, *let* him t. the
  paralambanō.
Mat. 1.20. fear not to t. unto thee Mary
     24. and to. *unto* him his wife
  2.13, 20. Arise, and t. the young ch.
     14, 21. to. the young child and his
  4. 5, 8. Then the devil t-eth him
  12.45. Then goeth he, and t-eth with
  17. 1. Jes. t-eth Peter, James, and;
     Mar.9.2,14.33; Lu.9.28
  18.16. t. with thee one or two
  20.17. to. the twelve disciples apart
  24.40, 41. the one *shall be* t-en, and;
     Lu.17.34,35
  26.37. And he to. *with* him Peter
  27.27. to. Jesus into the co. hall *and*
Mar. 4.36. they to. him even as he was
     5.40. he t-eth the father and the
  10.32. he to. again the twelve, *and*
Lu. 9.10. And he to. them, *and* went
  11.26. and t-eth to him seven other
  18.31. he to. unto him the twe., *and*
Jo. 19.16. And they to. Jesus, and led
Act.15.39. so Barnabas to. Mark, and
  16.33. And he to. them the same
  21.24. Them t., *and* purify thyself
     26. Then Paul to. the men, *and*
     32. Who immediately to. soldiers
  23.18. So he to. him, *and* brought
  epilambanō.
Mar. 8.23. to. the blind man *by the*.. *and*
Lu. 9.47. to. a child, *and* set him by
  14. 4. he to. him, *and* healed him
  20.20. that they *might* t. hold *of* his
     26. they could not t. hold *of* his
Act. 9.27. to. him, *and* brought; 17.19
  18.17. Then all the Greeks to. Sost.
  21.30. and they to. Paul, *and* drew
     33. and to. him, and command.
  23.19. the chief captain to. him *by*
Heb. 2.16. he to. not *on* him the nature
     but he to. *on* him the seed of
     8. 9. *when* I to. them *by* the hand
  analambanō.
Act. 1. 2, 22. in which he *was* t-en up
     11. Jesus, *which is* t-en up from
     7.43. Yea, ye to. *up* the tabernacle
  20.13. there intending to t. *in* Paul
     14. we to. him *in*, *and* came to
  23.31. to. Paul, *and* brought him by
Eph. 6.13. t. *unto* you the whole armour
     16. t-*ing* the shield of faith, wh.
²Ti. 4.11. t. Mark, *and* bring him with
     [Mar.14.48
Mat.26.55. swords and staves *for* to t.;
Lu. 5. 9. the fishes wh. they *had* t-en
  22.54. Then to. they him, and led
Jo. 18.12. and officers of the Jews to.
Act. 1.16. guide to them *that* to. Jesus
     12. 3. he proceeded further to t.
  23.27. This man *was* t-en of the
  proslambanō. [Mar.8.32
Mat.16.22. Then Peter to. him, *and*;
Act.17. 5. to. *unto* them certain lewd
  18.26. they to. him *unto* them
  27.33. fasting, *having* t-en nothing
     34. I pray you to t. some meat
     36. and they also to. some meat
  sumparalambanō.
Act.12.25. and to. *with* them John
  15.37. determined to t. *with* them
     38. thou. not good to t. him *with*
Gal. 2. 1. *and* to. Titus *with* me also
  katalambanō.
Mar. 9.18. wheresoever he t-eth him
Jo. 8. 3. a woman t-en in adultery
     4. this woman *was* t-en in adu.

apolambanō.
Mar. 7.33. *to.* him *aside* from the mult.
metalambanō.
Act.27.33. besought them all *to* **t.** meat
prolambanō.
1Co. 11.21. every one **t**-*eth before other*
airō.
Mat. 9. 6. Arise, **t.** *up* thy bed ; Mar.
     2.9,11 ; Lu.5.24 ; Jo.5.8
   16. fill it up **t**-*eth* from the gar.
  11.29. **t.** my yoke upon you, and
  13.12. from him *shall be* **t**-*en away;*
     Mar.4.25 ; Lu.8.18
  14.12. came, and *to. up* the body
  20. they *to. up* of the fragments
  15.37. they *to. up* of the ; Mar.8.8
  16.24. deny himself, and **t.** *up* his ;
     Mar.8.34, 10.21 ; Lu.9.23
  17.27. **t.** *up* the fish that first
  20.14. **t.** that thine is, and go thy
  21.43. of God *shall be* **t**-*en* from you
  22.13. and foot and **t.** him *away*
  24.17. *to* **t.** any thing ; Mar.13.15
   18. return back *to* **t.** his clothes
   39. came, and *to.* them all *away*
  25.28. **t.** therefore the talent from
   29. hath not *shall be* **t**-*en away*
Mar. 2.12. he arose, *to. up* the bed, *and*
   21. filled it up **t**-*eth away* from
  4.15. **t**-*eth away* the word that
  6. 8. they *should* **t.** nothing for
   29. they came and **t.** *up* his cor.
   43. they *to. up* twelve baskets
  8.19, 20. full of fragmen.*to.* ye *up*
  13.16. *for to* **t.** *up* his garment
  15.24. what every man *should* **t.**
  16.18. They *shall* **t.** *up* serpents
Lu. 5.25. before them, and *to. up* that
  6.29. him *that* **t**-*eth away* thy clo.
   30. of him *that* **t**-*eth away* thy
  8.12. the devil, and **t**-*eth away* the
  9. 3. **t.** nothing for your journey
   17. there *was* **t**-*en up* of fragme.
  11.22. he **t**-*eth* from him all his ar.
   52. ye *have* **t**-*en away* the key of
  17.31. not come down to **t.** it *away*
  19.21. thou **t**-*est up* that thou laye.
   22. **t**-*ing up* that I laid not down
   24. **t.** from him the pound, *and*
   26. he hath *shall be* **t**-*en away*
  22.36. th.hath a purse, *let* him **t.** it
Jo. 1.29. L. of God, *which* **t**-*eth away*
  2.16. **t.** these things hence ; make
  5. 9. made whole, and *to. up* his
   11, 12. said unto . . **t.** *up* thy bed
  8.59. Then *to.* they *up* stones to
  10.18. No man **t**-*eth* it from me¸l·at
  11.39. Jesus said, **t.** ye *away* the
   41. Then they *to. away* the stone
   48. Rom. *shall* come and **t.***away*
  15. 2. bear. not fruit he **t**-*eth away*
  16.22. your joy no man **t**-*eth* from
  17.15. that thou *shouldest* **t.** them
  10.31. that they *might be* **t**-*en away*
   38. *might* **t.** *away* the body of
   and *to.* the body of Jesus
  20. 1. the stone **t**-*en away* from the
   2. They *have* **t**-*en away* the Lo.
   13. they *have* **t**-*en away* my Lord
   15. him, and I *will* **t.** him *away*
Act. 8.33. his judgment *was* **t**-*en away*
   his life *is* **t**-*en* from the earth
   20. 9. third loft, and *was* **t**-*en up*
  21.11. come unto us, he *to.* Paul's
  27.17. Whi. *when* they *had* **t**-*en up*
1Co. 6.15. shall I then **t.** the members
Col. 2.14. to us, and *to.* it out of the
1Jo. 3. 5. was manifested to **t.** *away*
Rev.18.21 a mighty angel *to. up* a stone
apairō.
Mat. 9.15. bridegroom *shall be* **t**-*en*
Mar. 2.20. *shall be* **t**-*en away; Lu.*5.35

sunairō.
Mat. 18.23. which would **t.** account of
epairō.
Act. 1. 9. he *was* **t**-*en up ;* and a cloud
exairō.
1Co. 5. 2. *might be* **t**-*en away* from you
aphaireō.
Lu. 1.25. *to* **t.** *away* my reproach am.
  10.42. *shall* not *be* **t**-*en away* from
  16. 3. my lord **t**-*eth away* from me
Ro. 11.27. when I *shall* **t.** *away* their
Heb.10. 4. of goats should **t.** *away* sins
Rev.22.19. if any man *shall* **t.** *away*
   God *shall* **t.** *away* his part
periaireō.
Act.27.20. be saved *was* then **t**-*en away*
   40. And *when* they *had* **t**-*en up*
2Co. 3.16. the vail shall *be* **t**-*en away*
Heb.10.11.which can never **t.** *away* sins
kathaireō.
Mar.15.36.will come to **t.** him *down*
   46. *to.* him *down* and ; Lu.23.53
Act.13.29. *to.* him *down* from the tree
anaireō.
Act. 7.21. Pharaoh's daugh. *to.* him *up*
Heb.10. 9. He **t**-*eth away* the first, that
krateō.
Mat. 9.25. and *to.* her *by* the hand
  22. 6. remnant *to.* his servants, *and*
  26. 4. consulted that they *might* **t.**
   50. laid hands on Jesus, and *to.*
Mar. 1.31. and *to.* her *by* the ; Lu.8.54
  5.41. he *to.* the damsel *by* the
  9.27. J. *to.* him *by* the hand, *and*
  14. 1. sought how they might **t.**
   44. **t.** him, and lead him away
   46. their hands on him, and *to.*
   49. and ye *to.* me not ; but the
Act.24. 6. whom we *to.,* and would
piazō.
Jo. 7.30. Then they sought *to* **t.** him
   32. priests sent officers to **t.** him
   44. some of them would*have* **t**-*en*
  10.39. they sought again *to* **t.** him
  11.57. that they *might* **t.** him
Act. 3. 7. *to.* him *by* the ri. hand, *and*
Rev.19.20.And the beast *was* **t**-*en,* and
sunagō.
Mat.25.35.a stranger and ye *to.* me *in*
   38. a stranger, and *to.* thee *in*
   43. a stra., and ye *to.* me not *in*
anagō.
Lu. 4. 5. the devil, **t**-*ing* him *up* into
apagō.
Act.24. 7. *to.* him *away* out of our
dechomai.
Lu. 2.28. Then *to.* he him up in his
  16. 6, 7. he said unto him, **t.** thy bill
  22.17. he *to.* the cup, *and* gave
Eph. 6.17. **t.** the helmet of salvation
sunechō.
Mat. 4.24. people *that were* **t**-*en with*
Lu. 4.38. wife's mother was **t**-*en with*
  8.37. they *were* **t**-*en with* great
echō.
Mat.21.46. they *to.* him *for* a prophet
katechō.
Lu. 14. 9. with shame *to* **t.** the lowest
embainō eis.
Mat.15.39. *to.* ship, and came into the
Jo. 6.24. they also *to.* shipping and
epibainō eis.
Act.21. 6. we *to.* ship ; and they retur.
ekduō.
Mat.27.31. they *to.* the robe *off from*
Mar.15.20. *to. off* the purple *from* him
epicheireō.
Lu. 1. as many *have* **t**-*en in* hand
Act.19.13. *to. upon* them to call over
hupomenō.
1Pet. 2.20. ye shall **t.** it *patiently*
   t. it *patiently,* this is accept.

poieō.
Mar. 3. 6. *to.* counsel with the Herod.
ekballō.
Lu. 10.35. he *to. out* two pence, *and*
bastazō.
Jo. 10.31. the Jews *to. up* stones again
egeirō.
Act.10.26. Peter *to.* him *up,* saying
aporphanizomai.
1Th. 2.17. *being* **t**-*en* from you for a sh.
didōmi.
1Th. 1. 8. **t**-*ing* vengeance on them that
ginomai.
2Th. 2. 7. until he *be* **t**-*en* out of the
eis halōsis.
2Pet. 2.12. beasts, made *to be* **t**-*en* and
prosdechomai.
Heb.10.34. *to.* joyfully the spoiling of
drassomai.
1Co. 3.19. He **t**-*eth* the wise in their
epipherō.
Ro. 3. 5. unrighteous *who* **t**-*eth* veng.
parapherō.
Mar.14.36.**t.** *away* this cup from me
   (*See words in connection.*)

TALENT,   -*s.*
talanton.
Mat.18.24. which owed him ten thou.*t*-s
  25.15. And unto one he gave five *t*-s
   16, 20. he that had re. the five *t*-s
   and made them other five *t*-s
   came and broug. other five *t*-s
   thou deliver. unto me five *t*-s
   gained beside them five *t*-s
   22. He also that had rec. two *t*-s
   thou deliver. unto me two *t*-s
   gained two other *t*-s beside
   24. he which had rece. the one **t.**
   25. and hid thy **t.** in the earth
   28. Take therefore the **t.** from
   unto him which hath ten *t*-s
talantiaios.
Rev.16.21. about *the weight of a* **t.**

TALES.
lēros.
Lu. 24.11. seemed to them as *idle* t

TALITHA.
talitha.
Mar. 5.41. **t.** cumi ; which is, being into.

TALK, [*noun.*]
logos.
Mat.22.15. entangle him in his **t.**

TALK, [*verb,*] -*ed, -est, -eth, -ing.*
laleō.
Mat.12.46. *While* he yet **t**-*ed* to the peo.
Mar. 6.50. immediately he **t**-*ed* with
Lu. 24.32. while he **t**-*ed* with us by the
Jo. 4.27. marvelled that he **t**-*ed* with
   Why **t**-*est* thou with her
   9.37. it is he *that* **t**-*eth* with thee
  14.30. I *will* not **t.** much with you
Act.26.31. they **t**-*ed* between themselves
Rev. 4. 1. of a trumpet **t**-*ing* with me
   17. 1. and **t**-*ed* with me, sayi.; 21.9
   21.15. And he *that* **t**-*ed* with me had
sullaleō.
Mat.17. 3. and Elias **t**-*ing* with him
Mar. 9. 4. they were **t**-*ing with* Jesus
Lu. 9.30. there **t**-*ed* with him two men
homileō.
Lu. 24.14. they **t**-*ed* together of all these
Act.20.11. *when* he..**t**-*ed* a long while
sunomileō.
Act.10.27. *as* he **t**-*ed with* him, he went

TALKERS.
mataiologos.
Tit. 1.10. many unruly and *vain* **t.**

TALKING, [noun.]
mōrologia.

Eph. 5. 4. nor *foolish* t. nor jesting

TAME,   -ed.
damazō.

Mar. 5. 4. neither could any man t. him
Jas. 3. 7. *is* t-ed, and *hath been* t-ed of
 8. the tongue can no man t.

TANNER.
burseus.

Act. 9.43. with one Simon a t.; 10.6
10.32. house of one Simon a t.

TARES.
zizanion.

Mat.13.25. his enemy came and sowed t.
 26. then appeared the t. also
 27. from whence then hath it t.
 29. while ye gather up the t.
 30. Gather ye together first the t.
 36. the parable of the t. of the
 38. but the t. are the children of
 40. As therefore the t. are gathe.

TARRY,   -ed, -est.
menō.

Mat.26.38. t. ye here, and wa.; Mar.14.34
Lu. 24.29. And he went in to t. with th.
Jo. 4.40. *that* he *would* t. with them
 21.22, 23. If I will that he t. till I
Act. 9.43. he t-ed many days in Joppa
 18.20. When they desired him to t.
 20. 5. going before t-ed *for* us at
 15. and t-ed at Trogyllium; *and*
 epimenō.
Act.10.48. prayed they him to t. certain
 21. 4. we t-ed there seven days
 10. And *as we* t-ed there many
 28.12. we t-ed there three days
 14. to t. with them seven days
1Co. 16. 7. I trust to t. a while with you
 8. But I *will* t. at Ephesus.
 hupomenō.
Lu. 2.43. the child Jesus t-ed *behind* in
 prosmenō.
Act.18.18. Paul after this t-ed there
 chronizō.
Mat.25. 5. *While* the bridegroom t-ed
Lu. 1.21. marvell. that he t-ed *so long*
Heb.10.37. will come, and *will* not t.
 diatribō.
Jo. 3.22. there he t-ed with them, and
Act.25. 6. *when* he *had* t-ed among them
 kathizō.
Lu. 24.49. but t. ye in the city of
 poieō.
Act.15.33. *after* they *had* t-ed there a
 mellō.
Act.22.16. And now why t-est thou
 prosdokaō.
Act.27.33. day that ye *have* t-ed *and*
 ekdechomai.
1Co. 11.33. to eat, t. one *for* another
 bradunō.
1Ti. 3.15. if I t. long, that thou mayest

TASTE,   -ed.
geuomai. [Mar.9.1; Lu.9.27

Mat.16.28. which *shall* not t. of death;
 27.34. *when* he *had* t-ed thereof he
Lu. 14.24. were bidden *shall* t. of my
Jo. 2. 9. ruler of the feast *had* t-ed the
 8.52. saying, he *shall* never t. of
Col. 2.21. Touch not; t. not; handle
Heb. 2. 9. *should* t. death for every man
 6. 4. *who have* t-ed of the heavenly
 5. *have* t-ed the good word of G.
Pet. 2. 3. If so be ye *have* t-ed that the

TATLERS.
phluaros.

1Ti. 5.13. but t. also and busybodies

270

TAVERNS.
tabernai.

Act.28.15. Appii forum, and The three t.

TAX,   -ed, -ing.
apographō.

Lu. 2. 1. all the world should *be* t-ed
 3. all went to *be* t-ed, every one
 5. *To be* t-ed with Mary his
 apographē.
Lu. 2. 2. this t-*ing* was first made wh.
Act. 5.37. in the days of the t-*ing* and

TEACH, -est, -eth, -ing, Taught.
didaskō.

Mat. 4.23. t-*ing* in their synago.; 9.35
 5. 2. he opened his mouth and t-t
 19. *shall* t. men so, he shall be
 whosoever *shall* do and t.
 11. 1. to t. and to preach in their
 13.54. he t-t them in their synago.
 15. 9. t-*ing* for doctrines; Mar.7.7
 21.23. unto him *as he was* t-*ing*
 22.16. and t-est the way of God in
 26.55. with you t-*ing* in; Mar.14.49
 28.15. did as they *were* t-t : and
 20. t-*ing* them to observe all th.
Mar. 1.21. the synagog., and t-t; Lu.6.6
 2.13. restored unto him, and he t-t
 4. 1. he began again to t. by the
 2. he t-t them many things
 6. 2. began to t. in the synagogue
 6. the villages t-*ing*; Lu.13.22
 30. done, and what they *had* t-t
 34. began to t. them many thi.
 8.31. he began to t. them, that the
 9.31. for he t-t his disciples, and
 10. 1. as he was wont, he t-t them
 11.17. he t-t, saying unto them
 12.14. but t-est the way of God in
 35. *while* he t-t in the temple
Lu. 4.15. he t-t in their synagogues
 5. 3. t-t the people out of the
 17. certain day, as he was t-*ing*
 11. 1. said unto him, Lord, t. us to
 John also t-t his disciples
 12.12. the Holy Ghost *shall* t. you
 13.10. he was t-*ing* in one of the
 26. thou hast t-t in our streets
 20. 1. *as* he t-t. .in the tem.;Jo.8.20
 21. thou sayest and t-est rightly
 t-est the way of God truly
 21.37. in the day time he was t-*ing*
 23. 5. t-*ing* throughout all Jewry
Jo. 6.59. as he t-t in Capernaum
 7.14. up into the temple, and t-t
 28. Jesus in the temple *as* he t-t
 35. among the Gentiles, and t.
 8. 2. he sat down, and t-t them
 28. as my Father *hath* t-t me
 9.34. born in sins, and *dost* thou t.
 14.26. he *shall* t. you all things
 18.20. I ever t-t in the synagogue
Act. 1. 1. Jes. began both *to* do and t.
 4. 2. grieved that they t-t the peo.
 18. not *to* speak at all nor t. in
 5.21. early in the morning, and t-t
 25. in the temple, and t-*ing* the
 28. *that* ye *should* not t. in this
 42. they ceased not *to* t. and
 11.26. with the church, and t-t
 15. 1. down from Judea t-t the bre.
 35. t-*ing* and preaching the
 18.11. t-*ing* the word of God amo.
 25. he spake and t-t diligently
 20.20. have shew. you, and *have* t-t
 21.21. thau thou t-est all the Jews
 28. This is the man, *that* t-eth
 28.31. t-*ing* those things which
Ro. 2.21. Thou therefore *which* t-est
 another, t-est thou not thy.
 12. 7. or he *that* t-eth, on teaching

1Co. 4.17. as I t. everywhere in every
 11.14. *Doth* not even nat. itself t.
Gal. 1.12. neither *was* I t-t it, but by
Eph. 4.21. heard him, and *have been* t-t
Col. 1.28. t-*ing* every man in all wisd.
 2. as ye *have been* t-t, abound
 3.16. t-*ing* and admonishing one
2Th. 2.15. which ye *have been* t-t
1Ti. 2.12. I suffer not a woman *to* t.
 4.11. These things com. and t.
 6. 2. These things t. and exhort
2Ti. 2. 2. who shall be able *to* t. others
Tit. 1.11. t-*ing* things which they oug
Heb. 5.12. ye have need *that* one t. you
 8.11. they *shall* not t. every man
1Jo. 2.27. need not that any man t.
 the same anointing t-eth you
 even as it *hath* t-t you, ye
Rev. 2.14. who t-t Balac to cast a stum.
 20. *to* t. and to seduce my serv.
 eimi didaskōn, [*was teaching.*
Mat. 7.29. t-t them as one; Mar.1.22
Lu. 4.31. t-t them on the Sabbath
 19.47. he t-t daily in the temple
 didaktos.
Jo. 6.45. they shall be all t-t of God
1Co. 2.13. *which* man's wisdom t-eth
 which the Holy Ghost t-eth
 heterodidaskaleō.
1Ti. 1. 3. they t. no *other* doctrine
 6. 3. If any man t. *otherwise*
 theodidaktos.
1Th. 4. 9. are t-t *of* God to love one
 didaskalia.
Ro. 12. 7. or he that teacheth on t-*ing*
 kata [*acc.*] **ho didachē.**
Tit. 1. 9. word *as he hath been* t-t
 katēcheō.
1Co. 14.19. I *might* t. others also, than
Gal. 6. 6. Let him *that* is t-t in the
 commun. unto him *that* t-eth
 mathēteuō.
Mat.28.19.and t. all nations, baptizing
Act.14.21. and *had* t-t **many,** they ret.
 paideuō.
Act.22. 3. t-t according to the perfect
Tit. 2.12. t-*ing* us that, denying ungo.
 katanggellō.
Act.16.21. And t. customs, which are
 (See *Sober.*)

TEACHER,   -s.
didaskalos.

Jo. 3. 2. we know that thou art a t.
Act.13. 1. certain prophets and t-s
Ro. 2.20. a t. of babes, which hast the
1Co.12.28. second. prophets, thirdly t-s
 29. are all prophets? are all t-s
Eph. 4.11. and some, pastors and t-s
1Ti. 2. 7. a t. of the Gentiles; 2Ti.1.11
2Ti. 4. 3. they heap to themselves t-s
Heb. 5.12. the time ye ought to be t-s
 nomodidaskalos.
1Ti. 1. 7. Desiring to be t-s *of the law*
 kalodidaskalos.
Tit. 2. 3. much wine, t-s *of good things*
 pseudodidaskalos.
2Pet. 2. 1. be *false* t-s among you

TEAR,   -eth, Tare, Torn.
sparassō.

Mar. 1.26. *when* the..spirit *had* t-n
 9.20. straightway the spirit ta. him
Lu. 9.39. it t-eth him that he foameth
 susparassō.
Lu. 9.42. threw him down, and ta. him
 rēgnumi.
Mar. 9.18. he taketh him, he t-eth him

TEARS.
dakru.

Mar. 9.24. said with t., Lord, I believe

Lu. 7.38. beg. to wash his feet with **t.**
   44. hath washed my feet with **t.**
Act.20.19. of mind, and with many **t.**
   31. ev. one night and day with **t.**
²Co. 2. 4. wrote unto you with many **t.**
²Ti. 1. 4. being mindful of thy **t.**, that
Heb. 5. 7. supplic. with .. crying and **t.**
  12.17. he sought it carefully with **t.**
Rev. 7.17. shall wipe away all **t.**; 21.4

TEDIOUS.
engkoptō.
Act.24. 4. I be not further **t.** *unto* thee

TELL,   *Told.*
epō.
Mat. 8. 4. See thou **t.** no man
  12.48. and said unto him that *to.*
  16.20. that they *should* **t.** no man;
        Mar.7.36; Lu.8.56
  17. 9. **t.** the vision to no man
  18.17. **t.** it unto the church : but if
  21. 5. **t.** ye the daughter of Sion
  24. which if ye **t.** me, I in like
  22. 4. **t.** them which are bidden
  17. **t.** us therefore, What thinke.
  24. 3. **t.** us, when shall th.; Mar.13.4
  26.63. that thou **t.** us whether thou
  28. 7. **t.** his disciples that he is risen
    see him : lo, I *have* **t.** you
Mar. 5.33. and *to.* him all the truth
  8.26. nor **t.** it to any in the town
  9.12. he answered and *to.* them
  16. 7. go your way, **t.** his disciples
Lu. 5.14. charged him *to* **t.** no man
  7.42. **t.** me therefore, which of the.
  9.21. *to* **t.** no man that thing
  13.32. Go ye, and **t.** that fox, Beho.
  20. 2. saying, **t.** us, by what autho.
  22.67. **t.** us. And he said unto them
    If I **t.** you, ye will not
Jo 3.12. If I *have* **to.** you earthly thi.
  if I **t.** you of heavenly things
  4.29. a man, which *to.* me all thin.
  39. He *to.* me all that ever I did
  9.27. I *have* **to.** you already
  10.24. Be the Christ, **t.** us plainly
  25. I *to.* you, and ye believed not
  11.46. and *to.* them what things Je.
  14. 2. I would *have* **to.** you. I go to
  16. 4. that I *to.* you of them
  18. 8. I *have* **to.** you that I am he
  34. or *did* others **t.** it thee of me
  20.15. **t.** me where thou hast laid
Act. 5. 8. **t.** me whether ye sold the la.
proepō.
Gal. 5.21. *have* also **to.** you *in time past*
legō.
Mat.10.27. What I **t.** you in darkness
  21.27. Neither **t.** I you by what;
    Mar.11.33; Lu.20.8
Mar. 1.30. and anon they **t.** him of her
  8.30. that they *should* **t.** no man
  10.32. and began to **t.** them
Lu. 4.25. But I **t.** you of a truth ; 9.27
  10.24. For I **t.** you, that many pro.
  12.51. I **t.** you, Nay ; but rather di.
  59. I **t.** thee, thou shalt not depa.
  13. 3, 5. I **t.** you, Nay ; but, except
  27. But he shall say, I **t.** you
  17.34. I **t.** you, in that night there
  18. 8. I **t.** you that he will avenge
  14. I **t.** you, this man went down
  19.40. and said unto them, I **t.** you
  22.34. And he said, I **t.** thee, Peter
  24.10. which *to.* these things unto
Jo. 8.45. I **t.** you the truth ; 16.7
  12.22. Philip cometh and **t.**-*eth* And.
    again Andrew and Philip **t.** J.
  13.19. Now I **t.** you before it come
Act.17.21. either *to* **t.**, or to hear some
  22.27. **t.** me, art thou a Roman

Gal. 4.21. **t.** me, ye that desire to be
Phi. 3.18. of whom I *have* **to.** you often
  and now **t.** you even weeping
²Th. 2. 5. I *to.* you these things
Jude 18. How that they *to.* you there
prolegō.
Gal. 5.21. of the which I **t.** you *before*
¹Th. 3. 4. we *to.* you *before* that we
apanggellō.
Mat. 8.33. into the city, and *to.* everyth.
  14.12. buried it, and went and *to.* J.
  28. 9. And as they went *to* **t.** his
  10. go **t.** my brethren that they
Mar. 6.30. to. him all things, both what
  16.10. she went and *to.* them that
  13. they went and *to.* it unto the
Lu. 7.22. Go your way, and **t.** John
  8.20. it *was to.* him by certain whi.
  34. went and *to.* it in the city and
  36. which saw it *to.* them by wh.
  9.36. kept it close, and *to.* no man
  13. 1. some *that* to. him of the Gal.
  18.37. they *to.* him, that Jesus of
  24. 9. *to.* all these things unto the
Jo. 4.51. servants met him, and *to.* him
  20.18. came *and to.* the disciples th.
Act. **5.**22. prison, they returned, and *to.*
  25. Then came one and *to.* them
  12.14. ran in, and *to.* how Peter st.
  15 27. *who shall* also **t.** you the same
  16.36. keeper of the prison *to.* this
  22.26. he went and *to.* the chief ca.
  23.16. enter. into the castle, and *to.*
  17. he hath a certain thing *to* **t.**
  19. What is that thou hast *to* **t.**
ananggellō.
Mar. 5.14. *to.* it in the city, and in the
  19. **t.** them how great things the
Jo. 4.25. he *will* **t.** us all things
  5.15. *to.* the Jews that it was J.
Act.16.38. the serjeants *to.* these words
²Co. 7. 7. *when* he *to.* us your earnest
laleō.
Mat.26.13. *shall* also this, .. *be to.* for a
Lu. 1.45. *which were* **to.** her from the
  2.17. the saying *which was to.* the.
  18. at those things *which were to.*
  20. as it *was to.* unto them
Jo. 8.40. a man that *hath* **to.** you the
  16. 4. these things *have* I **to.** you
Act. 9. 6. it *shall be to.* thee what thou
  10. 6. he *shall* **t.** thee what thou
  11.14. Who *shall* **t.** thee words
  22.10. there it *shall be to.* thee of
  27.25. it shall be even as it *was to.*
eklaleō.
Act.23.22. **t.** no man that thou hast
eideō.
Mat.21.27. said, We *cannot* **t.**; Mar.11.33
Lu. 20. 7. that they *could* not **t.** whence
Jo. 3. 8. *canst* not **t.** whence it cometh
  8.14. I go ; but ye *can* not **t.** when.
  16.18. we *can* not **t.** what he saith
²Co.12. 2. in the body, I *can* not **t.**: or
  3. body, I *can* not **t.**: God kno.
diēgeomai.
Mar. 5.16. they that saw it *to.* them how
  9. 9. that they *should* **t.** no man
Lu. 9.10. *to.* him all that they had done
Heb.11.32.the time would fail me to **t.**
exēgeomai.
Lu. 24.35. they *to.* what things were do. [11.29
ereō.   [11.29
Mat.21.24. *will* **t.** you by what ; Mar.
Jo. 14.29. I *have* **to.** you before it
Rev.17. 7. I *will* **t.** thee the mystery
proereō.
Mat.24.25. I *have* **to.** you *before*
²Co.13. 2. I *to.* you *before*, and foretell
diasapheō.
Mat.18.31. came and *to. unto* their

mēnuō.
Act.23.30. *when it was to.* me how that
  (See *Fault, Truth.*)

TEMPERANCE.
engkrateia.
Act.24.25. reasoned of righteousness, **t.**
Gal. 5.23. Meekness, **t.**: against such
²Pet. 1. 6. to knowledge **t.**; and to **t.**

TEMPERATE.
engkrateuomai.
¹Co. 9.25. striveth for the mastery *is* **t.**
engkratēs.
Tit. 1. 8. go. men, sober, just, holy, **t.**
sōphrōn.
Tit. 2. 2. **t.**, sound in faith, in charity

TEMPERED.
sungkerannumi.
¹Co.12.24. G. *hath* **t.** the body *together*

TEMPEST.
seismos.
Mat. 8.24. there arose a great **t.** in the
cheimazomai.
Act.27.18. *being* exceed. *tossed with a* **t**
cheimōn.
Act.27.20. no small **t.** lay on us
thuella.
Heb.12.18.black., and darkness, and **t**
lailaps.
²Pet. 2.17. that are carried with a **t.**

TEMPESTUOUS.
tuphōnikos.
Act.27.14. a **t.** wind, called Euroclydon

TEMPLE,   (See *Idol,*)   -*s.*
hieron.
Mat. 4. 5. a pinnacle of the **t.**; Lu.4.9
  12. 5. in the **t.** profane the sabbath
  6. is one greater than the **t.**
  21.12. went into the **t.**; Mar.11.15 ;
    Lu.18.10,19.45; Jo.7.14 ;
    bought in the **t.** ; Mar.11.15
  14. lame came to him in the **t.**
  15. children crying in the **t.**
  23. when he was come into the **t.**
  24. 1. and departed from the **t.**
  the buildings of the **t.**
  26.55. teaching in the **t.**; Mar.14.49
    Lu.21.37
Mar.11.11.and into the **t.**; and when
  16. any vessel through the **t.**
  27. as he was walking in the **t.**
  12.35. he taught in the **t.**; Jo.8.20
  13. 1. went out of the **t.**; Jo.8.59
  3. of Olives over against the **t.**
Lu. 2.27. by the Spirit into the **t.**
  37. departed not from the **t.**
  46. they found him in the **t.**
  19.47. daily in the **t.**; Act.5.42
  20. 1. taught the people in the **t.**
  21. 5. spake of the **t.**, how it was
  38. in the **t.**, for to hear him
  22.52. and captains of the **t.**, and
  53. daily with you in the **t.**
  24.53. were continually in the **t.**
Jo. 2.14. found in the **t.** those that
  15. drove them all out of the **t.**
  5.14. Jesus findeth him in the **t.**
  7.28. Jesus in the **t.** as he taught
  8. 2. he came again into the **t.**
  10.23. Jesus walked in the **t.**
  11.56. as they stood in the **t.**
  18.20. and in the **t.**, whither the
Act. 2.46. with one accord in the **t.**
  3. 1. went up together into the **t.**
  2. at the gate of the **t.** which
  them that entered into the **t.**
  3. about to go into the **t.**
  8. entered with them into the **t**

Act. 3.10. the Beautiful gate of the t.
   4. 1. the captain of the t.; 5.24
   5.20. and speak in the t. to the
   21. into the t. early in the mor.
   25. are standing in the t., and
   19.27. the t. of the great goddess
   21.26. entered into the t., to signify
   27. when they saw him in the t.
   28. brou. Greeks also into the t.
   29. had brought into the t.
   30. and drew him out of the t.
   22.17. while I prayed in the t.
   24. 6. gone about to profane the t.
   12. neither found me in the t.
   18. found me purified in the t.
   25. 8. neither against the t., nor
   26.21. caught me in the t., and
1Co. 9.13. live of the things of the t.
   naos.
Mat. 23.16, 21. shall swear by the t.
   swear by the gold of the t.
   17. or the t. that sanctifieth
   35. between the t. and the altar
   26.61. to destroy the t. of God, and
   27. 5. the pieces of silver in the t.
   40. Thou that destroyest the t.
   51. the veil of the t. was rent ;
   Mar.15.38 ; Lu.23.45
Mar.14.58.I will destroy this t. that is
   15.29. thou that destroyest the t.
Lu. 1. 9. when he went into the t.
   '21. he tarried so long in the t.
   22. had seen a vision in the t.
Jo. 2.19. Destroy this t., and in three
   20. For. and six years was this t.
   21. But he spake of the t. of his
Act. 7.48. High dwelleth not in t-s
   17.24. dwelleth not in t-s made
1Co. 3.16. are the t. of God ; 2Co.6.16
   17. If any man defile the t. of
   for the t. of God is holy
   6.19. your body is the t. of the H.
2Co. 6.16. hath the t. of God with idols
Eph. 2.21. groweth unto an holy t. in
2Th. 2. 4. sitteth in the t. of God
Rev. 3.12. make a pillar in the t. of my
   7.15. him day and night in his t.
   11. 1. and measure the t. of God
   2. which is without the t.
   19. the t. of God was opened in
   there was seen in his t. the
   14.15, 17. came out of the t.; 15.6
   15. 5. the t. of the tabernacle of
   8. And the t. was filled with
   was able to enter into the t.
   16. 1. a great voice out of the t.
   17. voice out of the t. of heaven
   21.22. And I saw no t. therein
   and the Lamb are the t. of it
   oikos.
Lu. 11.51. between the altar and the t.

TEMPORAL.
   proskairos.
2Co. 4.18. things which are seen are t.

TEMPT,   -ed, -eth, -ing.
   peirazō.
Mat. 4. 1. wilderness to be t-ed of the
   16. 1. and t-ing desired him that
   19. 3. t-ing him, and saying ; 22.35
   22.18. Why t. ye me; Mar.12.15 ;
   Lu.20.23
Mar. 1.13. forty days, t-ed of Satan
   8.11. a sign from heaven, t-ing
   10. 2. to put away his wife? t-ing
Lu. 4. 2. Being forty days t-ed of the
   11.16. And others, t-ing him, sou.
Jo. 8. 6. This they said, t-ing him
Act. 5. 9. agreed together to t. the Sp.
   15.10. Now therefore why t. ye G.
1Co. 7. 5. that Satan t. you not for
   10. 9. as some of them also t-ed
272

1Co. 10.13. will not suffer you to be t-ed
Gal. 6. 1. thyself, lest thou also be t-ed
1Th. 3. 5. means the tempter have t-ed
Heb. 2.18. hath suffered being t-ed, he
   succour them that are t-ed
   3. 9. When your fathers t-ed me
   4.15. but was in all points t-ed
   11.37. sawn asunder, were t-ed
Jas. 1.13. when he is t-ed, I am t-ed of
   evil, neither t-eth he any
   14. But every man is t-ed, when
   ekpeirazō.   [Lu.4.12
Mat. 4. 7. Thou shalt not t. the Lord ;
Lu. 10.25. stood up, and t-ed him
1Co.10. 9. Neither let us t. Christ
   apeirastos.
Jas. 1.13. for God cannot be t-ed with

TEMPTATION,   -s.
   peirasmos.   [11.4
Mat. 6.13.*And lead us not into t.; Lu.
   26.41. enter not into t.; Lu.22.40
Mar.14.38.ye enter into t.; Lu.22.46
Lu. 4.13. the devil had ended all the t.
   8.13. and in time of t. fall away
   22.28. continued with me in my t-s
Act.20.19. and t-s, which befell me by
1Co.10.13. There hath no t. taken you
   will with the t. also make
Gal. 4.14. And my t. which was in my
1Ti. 6. 9. fall into t. and a snare
Heb. 3. 8. in the day of t. in the wild.
Jas. 1. 2. when ye fall into divers t-s
   12. Bless. is the man that end. t.
1Pet. 1. 6. heaviness thro. manifold t-s
2Pet. 2. 9. deliv. the godly out of t-s
Rev. 3.10. from the hour of t., which

TEMPTER.
   peirazō, [participle.]
Mat. 4. 3. when the t. came to him
1Th. 3. 5. lest by some means the t.

TEN.
   deka.   [10.41
Mat. 20.24.when the t. heard it; Mar.
   25. 1. heaven be likened unto t.
   28. unto him which hath t. tal.
Lu. 14.31. be able with t. thousand to
   15. 8. what woman having t. pieces
   17.12. there met him t. men that
   17. said, Were there not t. clea.
   19.13. he called his t. servants, and
   delivered them t. pounds
   16. thy pound hath gained t.
   17. have thou authority over t.
   24. give it to him that hath t.
   25. said unto him, L., he hath t.
Act.25. 6. among them more than t.
Rev. 2.10. ye shall have tribulation t.
   12. 3. and t. horns ; 13.1,17.3,7
   13. 1. and upon his horns t. crowns
   17.12, 16. t. horns thou sawest are
   t. kings, which have received
   murioi.
Mat. 18.24.which owed him t. thousand
1Co. 4.15. have t. thousand instructers
   14.19. than t. thousand words in an
   hagios murias [(holy myriads.)
Jude 14. with t.thousands of his saints

TENDER.
   hapalos.   [Mar.13.28
Mat.24.32. When..branch is yet t.;
   splangchna eleos [gen.]
Lu. 1.78. Through the t. mercy of our
   eusplangchnos.
Eph. 4.32. t. hearted, forgiving one an.
   oiktirmōn.
Jas. 5.11. very pitiful, and of t. mercy

TENTH.
   dekatos.
Jo. 1.39. it was about the t. hour

Rev.11.13. the t. part of the city fell
   21.20. topaz ; the t.,a chrysoprasus
   dekatē.
Heb. 7. 2. Abraham gave a t. part of
   4. gave the t. of the spoils

TENTMAKERS.
   skēnopoios.
Act.18. 3. their occupation they were t.

TERRESTRIAL.
   epigeios.
1Co. 15.40. and bodies t.: but the glory
   the glory of the t. is another

TERRIBLE.
   phoberos.
Heb.12.21.And so t. was the sight

TERRIFY,   -ed.
   ptoeomai.
Lu. 21. 9. be not t-ed ; for these things
   24.37. But they were t-ed..and
   ekphobeō.
2Co. 10. 9. as if I would t. you by lette.
   pturomai.
Phi. 1.28. in nothing t-ed by your adv.

TERROR.
   phobos.
Ro. 13. 3. rulers are not a t. to good
2Co. 5.11. knowing therefore the t. of
1Pet. 3.14. and be not afraid of their t.

TESTAMENT.
   diathēkē.
Mat.26.28. blo. of the new t.; Mar.14.24
Lu. 22.20. cup is the new t.; 1Co.11.25
2Co. 3. 6. able ministers of the new t.
   14. in the reading of the old t.
Heb. 7.22. made a surety of a better t.
   9.15. the mediator of the new t.
   that were under the first t.
   16. For where a t. is, there mu.
   17. For a t. is of force after
   20. This is the blood of the t.
Rev.11.19. his temple the ark of his t.

TESTATOR.
   diatithemai [part.]
Heb. 9.16. of nec. be the death of the t
   17. at all while the t. liveth

TESTIFY,   -ed, -eth, -ing.
   martureō.
Jc. 2.25. that any should t. of man
   3.11. and t. that we have seen
   32. seen and heard, that he t-eth
   4.39. of the woman which t-ed, He
   44. For Jesus himself t-ed
   5.39. are they which t. of me
   7. 7. because I t. of it, that the
   13.21. in spirit, and t-ed, and said
   15.26. from the Father he shall t.
   21.24. which t-eth of these things
Act.26. 5. if they would t., that after
1Co. 15.15. we have t-ed of God
Heb. 7.17. For he t-eth, Thou art a pri.
   11. 4. righteous, God t-ing of his
1Jo. 4.14. and do t. that the Father
   5. 9. he hath t-ed of his Son
3John 3. and t-ed of the truth that
Rev.22.16. sent mine angel to t. unto
   20. the which t-eth these things
   marturomai.
Gal. 5. 3. For I t. again to every man
Eph. 4.17. and t. in the Lord, that ye
   diamartyromai.
Lu. 16.28. that he may t. unto them
Act. 2.40. words did he t. and preached
   8.25. when they had t-ed and pre.
   10.42. to t. that it is he which was
   18. 5. and t-ed to the Jews that Je.
   20.21. t-ing both to the Jews, and

Act.20.24. *to t.* the gospel of the grace
23.11. for as thou *hast t-ed* of me
28.23. expounded *and t-ed* the kin.
1Th. 4. 6. *have* forewarn. you and *t-ed*
Heb. 2. 6. one in a certain place *t-ed*
epimartureō.
1Pet. 5.12. exhorting and *t-ing* that this
ho marturion.
1Ti. 2. 6. for all, *to be t-ed* in due time
promarturomai.
1Pet. 1.11. *when it t-ed beforehand* the
summartureō.
Rev.22.18. For I *t. unto* every man

TESTIMONY.
marturia.
Jo. 3.32. and no man receiveth his *t.*
33. that hath received his *t.* ha.
5.34. I receive not *t.* from man
8.17. that the *t.*of two men is true
21.24. we know that his *t.* is true
Act.22.18. they will not receive thy *t.*
Rev. 1. 2, 9. the *t.* of Jesus Chr.; 12.17
6. 9. and for the *t.* which they he.
11. 7. shall have finished their *t.*
12.11. and by the word of their *t.*
19.10. thy brethren that have the *t.*
for the *t.* of Jesus is the spi.
marturion. [Lu.5.14
Mat. 8. 4. for a *t.* unto th.; Mar.1.44;
10.18. for a *t.* against them ; Mar.
6.11,13.9 ; Lu.9.5
Lu. 21.13. shall turn to you for a *t.*
1Co. 1. 6. Even as the *t.* of Christ was
2. 1. unto you the *t.* of God
2Co. 1.12. the *t.* of our conscience
2Th. 1.10. because our *t.* among you
1Ti. 1. 8. ashamed of the *t.* of our Lord
Heb. 3. 5. for a *t.* of those things
Rev.15. 5. of the tabernacle of the *t.* in
martureō.
Act.13.22. to whom also he *gave t. and*
14. 3. in the Lord, *which gave t.*
Heb.11. 5. he *had* this *t.*, that he plea.

TETRARCH.
tetrarchēs.
Mat.14. 1. Herod the *t.* heard; Lu.9.7
Lu. 3.19. Herod the *t.*, being reproved
Act.13. 1. brought up with Herod the *t.*
tetrarcheō.
Lu. 3. 1. and Herod *being t.* of Galilee
and his brother Philip *t.* of
Lysanias the *t.* of Abilene

THAN. (*See connected words.*)
ē. [22, 24; Mar.6.11
Mat.10.15. day of judgment *t.* for ; 11.
18. 8, 9.*rather t.* having two;
Mar.9.43,45,47
13. *t.* of the ninety and; Mar.15.7
19.24. *t.* for a rich man to enter in.:
Mar.10.25; Lu.18.25
26.53. more *t.* twelve legions of an.
Lu. 10.12. day for Sodom, *t.* for that ci.
14. at the judgment, *t.* for you
16.17. *t.* one tittle of the law
17. 2. *t.* that he should offend
18.14. house justified rather *t.* the
Jo. 3.19. loved darkness rather *t.* light
4. 1. baptized more disciples *t.* Jo.
Act. 4.19. hearken unto you more *t.* un.
5.29. to obey God rather *t.* men
25. 6. among them more *t.* ten days
27.11. more *t.* those things which
Ro. 13.11. *t.* when we believed
1Co. 7. 9. it is better to marry *t.* to bu.
9.15. *t.* that any man should make
14. 5. *t.* he that speaketh with ton.
19. *t.* ten thousand words in an
2Co. 1 13. *t.* what ye read or acknowle.
Gal. 4.27. more children *t.* she which
1Ti. 1. 4. rather *t.* godly edifying

2Ti. 3. 4. lovers of pleasures more *t.*
Heb. 11.25.*t.* to enjoy the pleasures of
1Pet. 3.17. well doing *t.* for evil doing
2Pet. 2.21. *t.*, after they have known it
1Jo. 4. 4. *t.* he that is in the world
para, [accus.]
Lu. 3.13. no more *t.* that which is
1Co. 3.11. *t.* that is laid, which is
Gal. 1. 8. *t.* that which we have prea.
9. *t.* that ye have received
Heb. 1. 4. a more excellent name *t.*
2, 7, 9. a little lower *t.* the angels
3. 3. worthy of more glory *t.*
9.23. with better sacrifices *t.* these
11. 4. a more excellent sacrifice *t.*
12.24. better things *t.* that of Abel
huper, [accu.]
Lu. 16. 8. wiser *t.* the children of light
Heb. 4.12. sharper *t.* any twoedged sw.
ēper.
Jo. 12.43. more *t.* the praise of God
Act.15.28. *t.* these necessary things
THANK, [*noun.*]
charis.
Lu. 6.32, 33, 34. what *t.* have ye
THANK, [*verb,*]   -ed.
eucharisteō.
Lu. 18.11. God, I *t.* thee, that I am not
Jo. 11.41. Father, I *t.* thee that thou
Act.28.15. he *t-ed* God, *and* took coura.
Ro. 1. 8. I *t.* my God through J.; 7.25
1Co. 1. 4. I *t.* my God always on your
14. I *t.*God that I baptized none
14.18. I *t.* my God, I speak with
Phi. 1. 3. I *t.* my God upon every re.
1Th. 2.13. For this cause also *t.* we God
2Th. 1. 3. We are bound *to t.* God alw.
Phile. 4. I *t.* my God,making mention
echō charis.
Lu. 17. 9. *Doth* he *t.* that servant
1Ti. 1.12. I *t.* Christ Jesus our Lord
2Ti. 1. 3. I *t.* God, whom I serve from
exomologeomai. [Lu.10.21
Mat.11.25. said, I *t.* thee, O Father ;
THANKFUL.
eucharistos.
Col. 3.15. in one body ; and be ye *t.*
eucharisteō.
Ro. 1.21. not as God, neither *were t.*
THANKFULNESS.
eucharistia.
Act.24. 3. most noble Felix, with all *t.*
THANKS.
eucharisteō. [8.6 ; Lu.22.19
Mat.15.36. and *gave t.*, *and* brake ; Mar.
26.27. the cup, and *gave t.*, and ga.
Mar.14.23.and *when he had given t.* he ;
Jo.6.11 ; 1Co.11.24
Lu. 17.16. *giving* him *t.*: and he was
22.17. and *gave t.*, and said, Take
Jo. 6.23. *after that* the Lo. *had given t.*
Act.27.35. *gave t.* to God in presence of
Ro. 14. 6. for he *giveth* God *t.*; and he
eateth not, and *giveth* God *t.*
16. 4. not only I *give t.*, but also all
1Co. 10.30. for that for which I *give t.*
14.17. thou verily *givest t.* well
2Co. 1.11. *t. may be given* by many on
Eph. 1.16. Cease not *to give t.* for you
5.20. *Giving t.* always for all thin.
Col. 1. 3. We *give t.* to God and the
12. *Giving t.* unto the Father
3.17. *giving t.* to God and the Fath.
1Th. 1. 2. We *give t.* to God always for
5.18. In every thing *give t.*
2Th. 2.13. are bound *to give t.* alway
Rev.11.17. We *give* thee *t.*, O Lord God
eucharistia.
1Co. 14.16. say Amen at thy *giving of t.*

Eph. 5. 4. but rather *giving of t.*
1Th. 3. 9. For what *t.* can we render to
1Ti. 2. 1. intercessions, and *giving of t.*
Rev. 4. 9. and *t.* to him that sat on the
charis.
1Co. 15.57. *t.* he to G.; 2Co.2.14,8.16,9.15
anthomologeomai.
Lu. 2.38. *gave t.* likewise unto the
homologeō.
Heb.13.15.our lips *giving t.* to his name
THANKSGIVING,   -s.
eucharistia.
2Co. 4.15. might through the *t.* of many
9.11. causeth through us *t.* to
12. by many *t-s* unto God
Phi. 4. 6. prayer and supplicati. with *t.*
Col. 2. 7. abounding therein with *t.*
4. 2. watch in the same with *t.*
1Ti. 4. 3, 4. be received with *t.*
Rev. 7.12. and *t.*, and honour, and pow.
THANKWORTHY.
charis.
1Pet. 2. 19. For this is *t.*, if a man for
THAT, [*pronoun.*]
ekeinos.
Mat.7.22. Many will say to me in *t.* day
25, 27. and beat upon *t.* house
8.28. no man might pass by *t.* way
9.22. was made whole from *t.* hour
26. went abroad into all *t.* land
31. abroad his fame in all *t.* cou.
10.14. depart out of *t.* house or city
15. than for *t.* city ; Mar.6.11
Lu.10.12
11.25. At *t.* time Jesus; 12.1
12.45. the last state of *t.* man
13.44. that he hath, and buyeth *t.*
14. 1. At *t.* time Herod the tetrarch
35. when the men of *t.* place
sent out into all *t.* country
17.27. *t.* take and give unto them
18. 7. woe to *t.* man by whom ; 26.
24 ; Mar.14.21 ; Lu.22.22
27. the lord of *t.* servant ; 24.50
32. I forgave thee all *t.* debt
22.46. from *t.* day forth ask him
24.36. of *t.* day and hour; Mar.13.32
46. Blessed is *t.* serva.; Lu.12.43
48. if *t.* evil servant sh.; Lu.12.45
26.24. good for *t.* man ; Mar.14.21
29. until *t.* day when; Mar.14.25
27. 8. Wherefore *t.* field was called
19. nothing to do with *t.* just man
63. we remember that *t.* deceiver
Mar.3.24. *t.* kingdom cannot stand
25. *t.* house cannot stand
6.55. ran through *t.* whole region
7.20. of the man, it defileth the
13.11. shall be given you in *t.* hour
24. in those days, after *t.* tribula.
Lu. 6.23. Rejoice ye in *t.* day, and leap
48. beat vehemently upon *t.* ho.
49. the ruin of *t.* house was great
9. 5. when ye go out of *t.* city
10.12. *t.* day for Sodom than for *t.*
31. came down a certain priest *t.*
11.26. the last state of *t.* man
12.46. The lord of *t.* servant will
47. *t.* servant, which knew his
14.21. So *t.* servant came, and she.
15.14. a mighty famine in *t.* land
15. to a citizen of *t.* country
17. 9. Doth he thank *t.* servant
31. In *t.* day, he which shall be
18. 3. there was a widow in *t.* city
19. 4. for he was to pass .*way*
20.18. Whosoever shall,fall upon *t.*
35. worthy to obtain *t.* world
21.34. so *t.* day come upon you un.
Jo. 1.39. abode with him *t.* day

Jo. 4.39. the Samaritans of **t.** city
6.22. save **t.** one whereinto his
11.51. being high priest **t.** year
53. Then from **t.** day forth they
14.20. At **t.** day ye shall know
16.23, 26. in **t.** day ye shall ask me
18.15. **t.** disciple was known unto
19.27. from **t.** hour that disciple to
31. for **t.** sabbath day was an hi.
21. 3. **t.** night they caught nothing
7. **t.** disciple whom Jesus loved
23. that **t.** disciple should not die
Act. 1.19. **t.** field is called in their
3.23. which will not hear **t.** prophet
8. 1. at **t.** time there was a great
8. there was great joy in **t.** city
12. 1. Now about **t.** time Herod
14.21. preached the gospel to **t.** city
19.16. they fled out of **t.** house
22.11. for the glory of **t.** light, being
Eph. 2.12. That at **t.** time ye were
²Th. 1.10. was believed in **t.** day
²Ti. 1.12. unto him against **t.** day
18. mercy of the Lord in **t.** day
4. 8. shall give me at **t.** day
Heb. 3.10. I was grieved with **t.** genera.
4.11. to enter into **t.** rest, lest
8. 7. if **t.** first covenant had been
11.15. if they had been mindful of **t.**
Jas. 1. 7. let not **t.** man think that
4.15. we sh. live, and do this, or **t.**
Rev.16.14.to the battle of **t.** great day

ho.
Mat. 1.20. for **t.** which is conceived in
13.12. taken away even **t.** he hath;
Mat.25.29; Mar.4.25
Mar. 7.20. **t.** which cometh out of a
Lu. 8.18. taken, even **t.** he seemeth to
11.40. **t.** which is without, **t.** which
16.12. **t.** which is another man's
15. **t.** which is highly esteemed
17.10. **t.** which was our duty to do
24.12. at **t.** which was come to pass
Jo. 1. 8. *He was not* **t.** light, but was
21. Art thou **t.** prophet
3. 6. **t.** wh. is born of the fl. : **t.** wh.
11. **t.** we do know,..testify **t.** we
5.12. what man is **t.** which said
6.27. but for **t.** meat which endu.
32. Moses gave you not **t.** bread
48, 58. I am **t.** bread of life
8.38. I speak **t.** I have seen
ye do **t.** *which* ye have
13.27. **t.** thou doest, do quickly
Act. 4.21. glorified God for **t.** *which*
7.37. this is **t.** Moses which
10.37. **t.** word ye know which
Ro. 1.19. **t.** *which* may be known
4.18. according to **t.** *which* was
7. 6. **t.** being dead wherein we
[*or*] being dead *to that*)
13. was then **t.** *which* is good
15. **t.** I do I allow not
19. to perform **t.** *which* is good
¹Co. 5.13. put away from you **t.** wicked
10. 4. **t.** rock was Christ
11.23. **t.** *which* also I delivered
28. of **t.** bread..of **t.** cup
13.10. **t.** *which* is perfect, **t.** *which*
15.37. **t.** *which* thou sowest
t. body which shall be
46. **t.** was not first..but **t.** *which*
²Co. 3.11. if **t.** *which* is done away
¹Th. 3.10. perfect **t.** *which* is lacking
5.21. hold fast **t.** *which* is good
²Th. 2. 3. **t.** man of sin be revealed
¹Ti. 6.20. keep **t.** *which* is committed
Heb. 6.19. into **t.** within the vail
12.20. endure **t.** *which* was comm.
¹Pet. 3.13. followers of **t.** *which* is good
¹Jo. 1. 1. **t.** *which* was from the begin.
3. **t.** *which* we have seen and
274

---

¹Jo. 2.24. let **t.** abide in you which
if **t.** which ye have heard
³John 11. **t.** which is evil, but **t.** *which*
Rev. 2.25. **t.** *which* ye have, hold fast

houtos.
Mar.13.11. in that hour, **t.** speak ye
16.12. After **t.** he appeared in ano.
Lu. 9.21. to tell no man **t.** *thing*
12. 4. after **t.** have no more
13.32. Go and tell **t.** fox, Behold
17.34. I tell you in **t.** night
23. 7. was at Jerusalem at **t.** time
48. came together to **t.** sight
Jo. 3.32. and heard, **t.** he testifieth
4.18. in **t.** saidst thou truly
6.66. From **t.** *time* many of his
11. 7, 11. after **t.** saith he to
14.13. **t.** will I do, that the Father
16.19. among yourselves of **t.** I said
19. 8, 13. Pilate therefore heard **t.**
Act. 2.36. **t.** *same* Jesus, whom ye have
7. 7. after **t.** shall they come forth.
13.20. after **t.** he gave unto them
16.12. we were in **t.** city abiding
Ro. 1.12. **t.** is, that I may be comforted
7.15. **t.** do I not ; but wh. I hate, **t.**
16, 20. If then I do **t.** which I
19. which I would not, **t.** I do
10. 6. **t.** is, to bring Christ down
7. **t.** is, to bring up Christ
8. **t.** is, the word of faith
11. 7. Israel hath not obtained **t.**
13.11. And **t.**, knowing the time
¹Co. 6. 6. and **t.** before the unbelievers
8. defraud, and **t.** your brethren
Gal. 6. 7. soweth, **t.** shall he also reap
Eph. 2. 8. and **t.** not of yourselves
Phi. 1.28. of salvation, and **t.** of God
²Th. 3.14. note **t.** *man*, and have no.
¹Ti. 5. 4. for **t.** is good and acceptable
Phile. 18. put **t.** on mine account
Heb.13.17.for **t.** is unprofitable for you
Rev.15. 5. after **t.** I looked, and, behold
20. 3. after **t.** he must be loosed

hosos.
Mat.13.44. goeth and selleth all **t.** he
46. went and sold all **t.** he had
18.25. all **t.** he had, and payment
Mar.12.44.did cast in all **t.** she had
Lu. 4.40. all they **t.** had any sick
18.12. I give tithes of all **t.** I possess
22. sell all **t.** thou hast, and
Jo. 10.41. but all things **t.** John spake
16.15. All things **t.** the Father hath

hostis.
Mat. 2. 6. a Governor, **t.** shall rule my
18.28. Pay me **t.** thou owest
27.62. **t.** followed the day of the
Lu. 7.39. woman this is **t.** toucheth hi.
Jo. 8.25. even the same **t.** I said unto
Ro. 6. 2. How shall we, **t.** are dead to
Rev. 1.12. to see the voice **t.** spake with
17. 8. the beast **t.** was, and is not

ho autos.
Lu. 2.38. she coming in **t.** instant

THAT, [*conjunc.*]
hina.   [4.14
Mat. 1.22. **t.** it might be fulfilled ; 2.15,
4. 3. command **t.** these stones be
5.29, 30. **t.** one of thy members sh.
(Also) **Mat.**7.1,12; 8.8.; 9.6; 10.25; 12.
10,16; 14.15,36; 16.20; 18.6,14,16; 19.13,
16; 20.21,33; 21.4; 23.26; 24.20; 26.4,41,
56,63 ; 27.20,35 ; 28.10.   **Mar.**1.38 ; 2.
10 ; 3.2,9,12,14, *bis* ; 4.12,22 ; 5.10,12,
18,43 ; 6.8,12,25,36,56 ; 7.9,26,36 ; 8.30;
9.9,12,18,30 ; 10.13,17,35,37,48,51 ; 11.
16,25; 12.2,15,19 ; 13.18 ; 14.12,35 ; 15.
11,32 ; 16.1.   **Lu.**1.4,43; 4.3; 5.24; 6.7,
31; 7.6,36; 8.10,16,31,32; 9.12,45; 10.
40; 11.33,50,54; 12.36. 14.10,23; 15.29.

16.4,9,24,27 ; 17.2 ; 18.15,39,41 ; **19.**15 ;
20.10,14,20,28 ; 21.36 ; 22.8,30,32. **Jo.**
1.7,22,31; 2.25; 3.15,16,17,21; 4.15,36,47;
5.20,23,34,40; 6.5,7,12,28,29,30,39,40,50;
7.3,23; 8.6; 9.2,3,22,36,39; 10.10,17,38;
11.4,11, 16,37,42, 50, 52, 57; 12.9,10,23,
36,38,40,46; 13.1,15,18,19,29,34, *bis* ; 14.
3,13,16,29,31; 15.2,8,11,12,13,16, *bis*,17,
25; 16.1,2,4,7,24,30,32,33; 17.1,2,3,11,12,
13,15, *bis*, 19,21, *bis*, 22,23, *bis*, 24, *bis*,
26; 18.9,28,32,36,37,39; 19.4,24,28,31,*bis*,
35,36,38; 20.31,*bis*. **Act.**2.25; 4.17; 5.
15; 8.19; 9.21; 19.4; 21.24; 22.24; 23.
24; 24.4. **Ro.**1.11,13; 3.8,19; 4.16; 5.
20,21; 6.1,4,6; 7.4,13, *bis*; 8.4,17,; 9.
11,23; 11.11,19,31,32; 14.9; 15.4,6,16,
31, *bis*, 32; 16.2. **Co.**1.10,31 ; 2.5,12 ;
3.18 ; 4.2,3,6,*bis*,8 ; 5.2,5,7 ; 7.5,*bis*,29,
34,35; 9.15, *bis*, 18,19,20, *bis*, 21,22, *bis*,
23,24 ; 10.33 ; 11.19,32,34 ; 12.25 ; 14.1,5,
bis,12,13,19,31 ; 15.28 ; 16.2,6,10,11,16.
²**Co.**1.9,11,15,17;2.4,*bis*,5,9; 4.7,10,11,15;
5.4,10,12,15,21; 6.3 ; 7.9 ; 8.6,7,9,13,14;
9.3,4,5,8; 10.9 ; 11.7,12,*bis*,16 ; 12.8,9;
13.7,*bis*. **Gal.**1.16 ; 2.4,5,9,10,16,19;
3.14,*bis*,22,24; 4.5,17; 6.13. **Eph.**1.17; 2.
7,10 ; 3.16,17,19 ; 4.10,14,28,29 ; 5.26,27,
bis,33 ; 6.3,13,19,20,21,22. **Phi.**1.9,10,
26,27 ; 2.2,10,15,19,28 ; 3.8   **Col.**1.9,18,
28; 2.2 ; 4.3,4,8,12,16,*bis*,17. ¹**Th.**2.16;
4.1,12,13 ; 5.4,10. ²**Th.**1.11; 2.12 ; 3.1,
2,12,14. **Ti.**1.3,16,18,20; 2.2 ; 3.15 ;
4.15; 5.7,16,20,21 ; 6.1,19. ²**Ti.**1.4; 2.4,
10 ; 3.17 ; 4.17. **Tit.**1.5,9,13 ; 2.4,5,8,
10,12,14; 3.7,8,13,14. **Phile.**13,14,15.
Heb.2.14,17; 4.16 ; 5.1 ; 6.12,18 ; 9.25;
10.9,36 ; 11.35,40; 12.27 ; 13.12,17,19.
Jas.1.4; 4.3. ¹**Pet.**1.7; 2.2,12,21,24;
3.1,9,16,18 ; 4.6,11,13 ; 5.6. ²**Pet.**1.4.
¹**John**1.3,4 ; 2.1,19,27,28 ; 3.1,8,11,23 ;
4.9,17,21 ; 5.3,13,*bis*,16,20. ²**John** 5,6,
bis,8,12. ³**John**8. **Rev.**2.10; 3.11,18,
bis; 6.4,11 ; 7.1; 8.3; 9.4,5,20; 11.6;
12.6,14,15 ; 13.15,*bis*,17 ; 14.13,*bis* ; 16.
12 ; 18.4,*bis* ; 19.8,15,18 ; 20.3 ; 22.14.

hoti.
Mat. 2.16. when he saw **t.** he was moc.
22. But when he heard **t.** Arche.
3. 9. I say unto you, **t.** God is ab.
4.12. Now when Jes. had heard **t.**
5.17. Think not **t.** I am come to
20. **t.** except your righteousness
21. Ye have heard **t.** ; 27,33,38,43
22. But I say unto you, **t.**; 28,32;
Mar.11.23
23. **t.** thy brother hath ought ag.
6.29. And yet I say unto you, **t.**
32. knoweth **t.** ye have; Lu.12.30
(Also) **Mat.** 8.11,27; 9.6,28; 10.34;
11.24; 12.6,36 ; 13.17 ; 15.12,17; 16.11,
12,18,20; 17.10,12,13; 18.10,19; 19.4,
23,28 ; 20.10,25,30 ; 21.31,45; 22.16,34;
23.31; 24.32,33,43,47 ; 25.24,26 ; 26.2,21,
34,53,54; 27.3,18,24,63 ; 28.5,7. **Mar.**
2.1,8,10,16; 4.38,41; 5.29; 6.2,14,15, *bis*;
7.18; 8.31 ; 9.1,11,13,25 ; 10.42,47 ; 11.3,
23,24,32 ; 12.12,14,26,28,34,35,43; 13.28,
29,30; 14.30; 15.10,39; 16.4,7,11. **Lu.**
1.22 ; 2.49, *bis* ; 3.8; 4.4; 5.24 ; 6.5 ; 7.4,
16, *bis*,37,43 ; 8.47,53 ; 9.7,8, *bis*, 19 ;
10.11,12,20,21,24,40 ; 11.38 ; 12.37,39,40,
44,51; 13.2,4, ; 14.24; 15.7 ; 16.25; 17.15;
18.8,9,11,37 ; 19.7,22,26,40; 20.19,21,37;
21.3,20,30,31 ; 22.37,70; 23.7 ; 24.21,39,
44. **Jo.**1.34; 2.17,18,22,25 ; 3.2,7,19,21,
28,*bis*,33 ; 4.1,19,20,25,27,42,44,47,53 ;
5.6,15,32,36,42,45 ; 6.15,22, *bis*, 24,36,46,
61,65,69; 7.7,26,35,42 ; 8.17,24,*bis*,27,28,
37,48,52,54 ; 9.8,17,18,20,24,25,29,30,
31,32,35 ; 10.38 ; 11.6,13,15,20,22,24,27,
31, 40, 41,42, *bis*, 50,51,56 ; 12.6,9,12,16,
34,50 ; 13.1,3,*bis*, 19,21,29,35 ; 14.10,11,

20,22,31 ; 15.18 ; 16.4,15,19,20,21,26,27, 30,*bis* ; 17.7,8, *bis*, 21,23,25 ; 18.8,14,37 ; 19.4,10,21,28,35 ; 20.9,14,18,31 ; 21.4,7, 12,15,16,17,23,24 Act. 2.29,30,31,36 ; 3.10,17 ; 4.10,13,*bis*,16 ; 5.9,41 ; 6.14 ; 7.6 ; 8.14,18 ; 9.20,22,26,27,38 ; 10.34,42 ; 11.1 ; 12.9,11 ; 13.38 ; 14.9,22 ; 15.5,24 ; 16.3,10,19,38 ; 17.3,*bis*,13 ; 19.25,26,*bis*, 34 ; 20.23,*bis*,25,26,29,31,34,38 ; 21,21, 22,24,29,31 ; 22.2,19,29; 23.5,6,22,27,34; 24.11,14,26 ; 26.5,27 ; 27.10,25 ; 28.1,22, 28. Ro.1.8,13,32 ; 2.2,3,4 ; 3.2,19 ; 4.9, 21,23 ; 5.3 ; 6.3,6,8,9,16,17 ; 7.14,16,18, 21 ; 8.16,18,22,28,38 ; 9.2,30; 10.2,5,9, *bis* ; 11.25; 13.11 ; 14.14 ; 15.14,29. ¹Co. 1.5,11,12,14,15 ; 3.16,20 ; 4.9 ; 5.6 ; 6.2, 3,9,15,16,19; 7.26; 8.1,4,*bis* ; 9.10,13,24; 10,19,20; 11.2,3,14,17,23 ; 12.2,3 ; 14.23, 25,37 ; 15.4, *bis*, 5,12, *bis*, 15,27,50,58 ; 16.15. ²Co.1.7,8,10,12,14,23; 2.3 ; 3.5; 4.14; 5.1,6,14,19; 7.3,8,9,*bis*,16 ; 8.9; 9.2; 10.7,11; 11.31 ; 12.13,19; 13.2,6,*bis*, Gal.1.6,11,23 ; 2.7,14,16 ; 3.7,8,11 ; 4.15, 22 ; 5.2,3,10,21. Eph.2.11,12 ; 4.9 ; 5.5 ; 6.8,9 ; Phi.1.6,12,17,19,20,25,27 ; 2.11,16,22,24,26 ; 4.10,11,15. Col.3.24 ; 4.1,13. ¹Th.2.1 ; 3.3,4,6 ; 4.14,15 ; 5.2. ²Th.2.2,4,5 ; 3.4,10. Ti.1.8,9,15 ; 4.1. ²Ti.1.5,12,15 ; 2.23 ; 3.1,15. Tit.3.11. Phile.21,22. Heb.2.6,*bis* ; 3.19 ; 7.8, 14 ; 11.6,13,14,18,19. Jas.1.3,7 ; 2.19, 20 ; 3.1 ; 4.4,5 ; 5.11,20. ¹Pet. 1.12 ; 2.3 ; 3.9. ²Pet. 1.14,20 ; 3.3,5,8. ¹Jo. 1.5,6,8,10 ; 2.3,5,18,*bis*,19,21,22,29,*bis* ; 3.2,5,14,15,19,24 ; 4.3,10, *bis*, 13,14,15 ; 5.1,2,5,11,13,14,15,*bis*,18,19,20. ²Jo.4. ³Jo.12. Rev.2.6,23 ; 3.1, *bis*, 9,15,17 ; 10.6 ; 12.12,13.

hopōs.

Mat. 2. 8. t. I may come and worship
     23. t. it might be fulfilled ; 8.17, 12.17,13.35
     5.16. t. they may see your good
     45. t. ye may be the children
     6. 2. t. they may have glory of m.
     4. t. thine alms may be in secr.
     5. t. they may be seen of men
     16. t. they may appear unto men
     18. t. thou appear not unto men
     8.34. t. he would depart out of th.
     9.38. t. he will send forth; Lu.10.2
     23.35. t. upon you may come all the
Mar. 5.23. t. she may be healed
Lu. 2.35. t. the thoughts of many hea.
     7. 3. t. he would come and heal
     16.28. t. he may testify unto them
Jo. 11.57. t. they might take him
Act. 8.15. t. they might receive the Ho.
     24. t. none of these things which
     9. 2. t. if he found any of this w.
     12. t. he might receive his sight
     17. t. thou mightest receive thy
     15.17. t. the residue of men might
     23.15. t. he bring him down unto
     20. t. thou wouldest bring down
     24.26. t. he might loose him
     25. 3. t. he would send for him to
     26. t., after examination had, I
Ro. 3. 4. t. thou mightest be justified
     9.17. t. I might shew my power
         and t. my name might be
¹Co. 1.29. t. no flesh should glory in
²Co. 8.11. t. as there was a readiness
     14. t. there may be equality
Gal. 1. 4. t. he might deliver us from
²Th. 1.12. t. the name of our Lord Jes.
Phile. 6. t. the communication of thy
Heb. 2. 9. t. he by the grace of God sh.
     9.15. t. by means of death, for the
Jas. 5.16. t. ye may be healed
¹Pet. 2. 9. t. ye should shew forth the

eis ho, [*with infinitive.*]

Ro. 1.20. *so* t. they are without excuse
¹Co. 9.18. t. I abuse not my power
Eph. 1.18. t. ye may know what is
Phi. 1.10. t. ye may approve all things
¹Th. 3.10. t. we might see your face
²Th. 1. 5. t. ye may be counted
     2. 2. t. ye be not soon shaken
     6. t. he might be revealed
     11. t. they should believe a lie
Heb.11. 3. *so* t. things which are seen
     12.10. t. we might be partakers
Jas. 1.18. t. we should be a kind of
¹Pet. 3. 7. t. your prayers be not
     4. 2. t. he no longer should live

hōste.

Jo. 3.16. t. he gave his only begotten
Act.14. 1. and so spake, t. a great
     15.39. t. they departed asunder
Ro. 7. 6. t. we should serve in newness
¹Co. 5. 1. t. one should have his fath.
¹Pet. 1.21. t. your faith and hope might

pros ho, [*with infinitive.*]

²Co. 3.13. t. the children of Israel
Eph. 6.11. t. ye may be able to stand
²Th. 3. 8. t. we might not be chargeab.
Jas. 3. 3. t. they may obey us

ei.   [Lu.17.2

Mar. 9.42. t. a millstone were hanged;
Act.26. 8. incredible with you t. God
     23. t.Christ should suffer, and t.

hōs.

Act.28.19. not t. I had ought to accuse
Ro. 1. 9. t. without ceasing I ; ²Ti.1.3

ē.

Lu. 22.34. before t. thou shalt thrice
Act.25.16. before t. he which is accused

hote.

Mar. 6.21. day was come, t. Herod on

hotan.

Mar.14.25.until that day t. I drink

en ho, [*with infinitive.*]

Lu. 1.21. t. he tarried so long

heneka.

²Co. 7.12. but t. our care for you

pōs.

Eph. 5.15. See then t. ye walk circumsp.
(*See words connected.*)

THE

Is generally (not always necessarily)
represented by the Greek article **ho.**
The following are exceptions :—

houtos.

Lu. 24.21. to day is t. third day
Gal. 2.18. if I build again t. things
     5.17. ye cannot do t. things

hautou.

Act. 7.54. were cut to t. heart (*their* hea.)

THEATRE.

theatron.

Act.19.29. with one accord into the t.
     31. with adventure himself into the t.

THEE.

su.

Mat. 2. 6. for out of t. shall come a
     3.14. have need to be bapti. of t.
     4. 6. angels charge con. t.;Lu.4.10
     5.23. brother have ought against t.
     29, 30. and cast it from t. ; 18.8,9
     42. that would borrow of t.
     6. 2. sound a trumpet before t.
     11.10. prepare thy way before t. ;
         Mar.1.2 ; Lu.7.27
     12.38. we would see a sign from t.
     17.27. unto them for me and t.
     18.15. between t. and him alone
         if he shall hear t., thou hast
     16. take with t. one or two more
     21.19. Let no fruit grow on t. hen.

Mat.26.62.witness against t.; 27.13 ;
         Mar.14.60 ; 15.4
Mar.11.14.eat fruit of t. hereafter
Lu. 1.28. the Lord is with t.
     35. which shall be born of t-
     8.28. I beseech t., torment me **not**
     9.38. Master, I beseech t., look
     12.20. thy soul shall be req. *of* t.
     15.18. against hea. and before t.
     16. 2. is it that I hear this of t.
     22.32. But I have prayed for t.
     33. I am ready to go with t.
Jo. 3.26. he that was with t. beyond
     9.37. it is he that talketh with t.
     17. 7. thou hast given me are of t.
     8. that I came out from t.
Act. 8.34. I pray t., of whom speaketh
     10.22. and to hear words of t.
     17.32. We will hear t. again of this
     18.10. For I am with t.
     21.21. And they are informed of t.
     24. were informed concerning t.
     39. and I beseech t., suffer me to
     23.21. looking for a promise from t.
     30. to say before t. what they
     35. I will hear t., said he, when
     24. 2. by t. we enjoy great quietness
     19. to have been here before t.
     25.26. specially before t., O king
     26. 2. myself this day before t.
     3. I beseech t. to hear me pati.
     27.24. all them that will sail with t.
     28.21. out of Judea concerning t.
         spake any harm of t.
     22. But we desire to hear of t.
Ro. 10. 8. The word is nigh t., even in
     11.21. lest he also spare not t.
¹Co. 12.21. I have no need of t.
²Co. 6. 2. I have heard t. in a time
¹Ti. 4.16. and them that hear t.
     6.21. Grace be with t. Amen
²Ti. 1. 3. I have remembrance of t.
Tit. 2.15. Let no man despise t.
Phile. 4. making mention of t. always
     7. the saints are refreshed by t.
     20. let me have joy of t. in the
³John 3. of the truth that is in t.
Rev. 2. 4. I have somewhat against t.
     14, 20. have a few things aga.t.
     3. 8. set before t. an open door
     15. 4. come and worship before t.
     18.14. after are departed from t.
(*And all others except the following*) :—

hautou.   [Lu.13.34

Mat.23.37.them which are sent unto t.;

seautou.

²Ti. 4.11. Mark, and bring him with t.

THEFTS.

klopē.

Mat.15.19. fornications, t., false witness
Mar. 7.22. t., covetousness, wickedness

klemma.

Rev. 9.21. Neit. repented 'they . . their t.

THEIR, (See *Own*,)   *Theirs.*

autos.

Mat. 5. 3, 10. for t-s is the kingdom
Mar.12.44.cast in of t. abundance
¹Pet. 4.14. on t. part he is evil spoken
(*And all others except the following*):—

hautou.

Mat. 2.11. they had opened t. treasures
     3. 6. Jordan, conf. t. sins; Mar.1.5
     4.21. in a ship with Zebedee t.
     22. left the ship and t. father
     6. 2, 5, 16. They have t. reward
     16. for they disfigure t. faces
     7. 6. trample them under t. feet
     10.17. scourge you in t. synagogues
     11.16. calling unto t. fellows
     13.15. t. eyes they have closed ; lest
     43. in the kingdom of t. Father

Mat. 15.2. they wash not **t.** hands
  8. nigh unto me with **t.** mouth
  27. fall from **t.** master's table
17. 6. they fell on **t.** face, and were
  8. they had lifted up **t.** eyes
18.31. came and told unto **t.** lord
21. 7. put on them **t.** clothes, and
22.16. sent out unto him **t.** discip.
23. 4. move them with one of **t.**
  5. all **t.** works they do for to
    they make broad **t.** phylac.
    the borders of **t.** garments
25. 1. ten virgins, which took **t.** la.
  4. oil in **t.** vessels with **t.** lamps
  7. virgins arose, and trimmed **t.**
27.39. reviled him, wagging **t.** heads
Mar. 1.18. straightway they forsook **t.**
  20. they left **t.** father Zebedee
2. 6. reasoning in **t.** hearts
8. 3. fasting to **t.** own houses
11. 7. cast **t.** garments on him
  8. many spread **t.** garments in
14.46. they laid **t.** hands on him
15.29. railed on him, wagging **t.** he.
Lu. 1.66. laid them up in **t.** hearts
2. 8. keeping watch over **t.** flock
3.15. all men mused in **t.** hearts
5.15. healed by him of **t.** infirmi.
6.17. and to be healed of **t.** diseas.
19.36. spread **t.** clothes in the way
21. 1. casting **t.** gifts into the trea.
  12. shall lay **t.** hands on you
Jo. 15.22. have no cloke for **t.** sin
Act. 5.18. laid **t.** hands on the apostles
7.19. cast out **t.** young children
  39. in **t.** hearts turned back aga.
  57. stopped **t.** ears, and ran upon
  58. witnesses laid down **t.** clot.
13.50. expelled them out of **t.** coa.
  51. shook off the dust of **t.** feet
14.11. lifted up **t.** voices; 22.22
  14. they rent **t.** clothes, and ran
15.26. hazarded **t.** lives for the name
16.19. the hope of **t.** gains was
19.18. confessed, and shewed **t.**deeds
28.27. **t.** eyes have they closed; lest
Ro 1.21. became vain in **t.** imaginat.
  27. burned in **t.** lust one toward
    recompence of **t.** error which
2.15. the law written in **t.** hearts
3.13. with **t.** tongues they have
Eph. 4.17. in the vanity of **t.** mind
1Th. 2.16. to fill up **t.** sins alway
Heb. 7. 5. to the law, that is, of **t.** bre.
11.35. Women received **t.** dead
1Pet. 2.12. perish in **t.** *own* corruption
  13. with **t.** *own* deceivings while
3. 3. walking after **t.** own lusts
  16. unto **t.** own destruction
Rev. 2.22. except they repent of **t.** deeds
3. 4. have not defiled **t.** garments
4. 4. had on **t.** heads crowns of
  10. cast **t.** crowns before the thr.
6.14. were moved out of **t.** places
7.11. before the throne on **t.** faces
  14. have washed **t.** robes, and
9. 4. seal of God in **t.** foreheads
  20. not of the works of **t.** hands
  21. Neither repented they of **t.**
    murders, nor of **t.** sorceries
    nor of **t.** fornic. nor of **t.** th.
11. 7. shall have finished **t.** testi.
  11. they stood upon **t.** feet; and
  16. on **t.** seats, fell upon **t.** faces
12.11. by the word of **t.** testimony
    and they loved not **t.** lives
14. 1. name written in **t.** foreheads
  2. harpers harping with **t.** harps
  13. they may rest from **t.** labours
16.10. they gnawed **t.** tongues for
  11. because of **t.** pains, and **t.** so.
    and repented not of **t.** deeds
276

Rev.17.17. give **t.** kingdom unto the
18.19. they cast dust on **t.** heads
20. 4. upon **t.** fore., or in **t.** hands
21.24. bring **t.** glory and honour
  heautou.   [Lu.9.60
Mat. 8.22. let the dead bury **t.** dead ;
21. 8. spread **t.** garments in the
25. 3. that were foolish took **t.**
Lu. 12.36. men that wait for **t.** lord
16. 8. are in **t.** generation wiser
19.35. they cast **t.** garments upon
22.66. led them into **t.** council
23.48. smote **t.** breasts, and return.
Eph. 5.28. ought men to love **t.** wives
1Pet. 4.19. commit the keeping of **t.** so.
Jude 6. angels which kept not **t.**
Rev. 10.3, 4. seven thunders uttered **t.**
17.13. shall give **t.** power and str.
  ekeinos.
2Co. 8.14. be a supply for **t.** want
    t. abundance also may be
2Ti. 3. 9. all men, as **t**-s also was
  idios.
1Co. 14.35. let them ask **t.** husbands
1Ti. 4. 2. having **t.** conscience seared
  houtos, [*gen.*]
Ro. 11.30. mercy through **t.** unbelief

THEM.
  autos.
Mat. 2. 4. he demanded of **t.** where Ch.
  7. enquired of **t.** diligently
  8. and sent **t.** to Bethlehem
(And all other passages except the
* following)* :—
  ekeinos.
Mat.13.11.to **t.** it is not given.
20. 4. And said unto **t.**; Go ye
Mar. 4.11. unto **t.** that are without
16.13. neither believed they **t.**
Lu. 8.32. suffer them to enter into **t.**
Jo. 10.16. **t.** *also* I must bring, and
  35. If he called **t.** gods, unto
Act.18.19. Ephesus, and left **t.** there
1Co. 10.11. things happened unto **t.**
Heb. 4. 2. preached as well as unto **t.**
    preached did not profit **t.**
6. 7. herbs meet for **t.** by whom
  houtos.
Lu. 13.14. in **t.** therefore come and be
Act.21.24. **t.** take, and purify thyself
Ro. 8.30. **t.** he also called : and whom
    he called **t.** he also justified
    he justified **t.** he also glorified
1Co. 6. 4. set **t.** to judge who are least
  13. shall destroy both it and **t.**
16.13. **t.** will I send to bring your
1Ti. 4.15. give thyself wholly to **t.**
Heb. 2.15. deliver **t.** who through fear
Rev.10. 4. uttered, and write **t.** not
  heautou.
Mat.15.30.having with **t.** those that
25. 3. and took no oil with **t.**
27.35. garments among **t** ; Jo.19.24
Mar. 2.19. have the bridegroom with **t.**
8.14. with **t.** more than one loaf
Act.21.23. men which have a vow on **t.**
Rev. 4. 8. beasts..each of **t.** (by *itself*)
  hautou.
Mar. 9.16. What question ye with **t.**
Act.13.42. might be preached to **t.**
20.30. draw away disciples after **t.**
Rev. 7.14. made **t.** white in the blood
9.11. they had a king over **t.**

THEMSELVES, (See *Cast.*)
  heautou.
Mat. 9. 3. the scribes said within **t.**
14.15. villages, and buy **t.** victuals
16. 7. reasoned among **t.** ; 21.15 ;
    Mar.2.8,11,31 ; Lu.20.5,14
19.12. have made **t.** eunuchs for

Mat.21.38.they said among **t.**, This
Mar. 4.17. have no root in **t.**, and so
6.36. villages, and buy **t.** bread
  51. they were sore amazed in **t.**
9. 8. more, save Jesus only with **t.**
  10. they kept that saying with **t.**
10.26. saying among **t.**, Who then
12. 7. husbandmen said among **t.**
14. 4. had indignation within **t.**
16. 3. they said among **t.**, Who sh.
Lu. 7.30. counsel of God against **t.**
  49. began to say within **t.**
18. 9. certain which trusted in **t.**
20.20. which should feign **t.** just
22.23. began to enquire among **t.**
23.12. were at enmity between **t.**
Jo. 7.35. Then said the Jews among **t.**
11.55. the passover, to purify **t.**
12.19. therefore said among **t.**
Act.23.12. and bound **t.** under a curse
  21. which have bound **t.** with
28.29. great reasoning among **t.**
Ro. 1.24. their own bodies between **t.**
  27. receiving in **t.** that recomp.
2.14. not the law, are a law unto **t.**
13. 2. shall receive to **t.** damnation
1Co.16.15. they have addicted **t.** to the
2Co. 5.15. not henceforth live unto **t.**
10.12. that commend **t.**: but they
    measuring **t.** by **t.**, and
    comparing **t.** among **t.**
Eph. 4.19. have given **t.** over unto
Phi. 2. 3. esteem other better than **t**,
1Ti. 2. 9. women adorn **t.** in modest
3.13. purchase to **t.** a good degree
6.10. pierced **t.** through with
  19. Laying up in store for **t.**
2Ti. 4. 3. they heap to **t.** teachers
Heb. 6. 6. crucify to **t.** the Son of God
1Pet. 1.12. that not unto **t.**, but unto
3. 5. adorned **t.**, being in subject.
2Pet. 2. 1. upon **t.** swift destruction
Jude 12. feeding **t.** without fear
  19. be they who separate **t.**
Rev. 6.15. hid **t.** in the dens and in
8. 6. trumpets prepared **t.** to sou.
  hautou.
Mar. 1.27. they questioned among **t.**
Jo. 17.13. have my joy fulfilled in **t.**
  monos.
Mar. 9. 2. high mountain apart *by* **t.**
Lu. 24.12. the linen clothes laid *by* **t.**

THEN, [*adverb.*]
  tote.
Mat. 2. 7, **t.** Herod, when he had priv.
  16. **t.** Herod, when he saw that
  17. **t.** was fulfilled that which
3. 5. **t.** went out to him Jerusalem
  13. **t.** cometh Jesus from Galilee
  15. **t.** he suffered him
4. 1. **t.** was Jesus led up of the
  5. **t.**,the devil taketh him up
  10. **t.** saith Jes. unto him ; 26.52
  11. **t.** the devil leaveth him, and
5.24. and **t.** come and offer thy gi.
7. 5. and **t.** shalt thou see clearly
  23. And **t.** will I profess unto
8.26. **t.** he arose, and rebuked the
9. 6. **t.** saith he to the sick of the
  14. **t.** came to him the disciples
  15. and **t.** shall they fast
  29. **t.** touched he their eyes, sa.
  37. **t.** saith he unto his dis.; 16.24
11.20. **t.** began he to upbraid the
12.13. **t.** saith he to the man, Stret.
  22. **t.** was brought unto him one
  29. and **t.** he will spoil his house
  38. **t.** certain of the scribes and
  44. **t.** he saith, I will return into
  45. **t.** goeth he, and taketh with
13.26. **t.** appeared the tares also

Mat.13.36.**t.** Jesus sent the multitude
43. **t.** shall the righteous shine
15. 1. **t.** came to Jesus scribes and
12. **t.** came his disciples, and
28. **t.** Jesus answered and said
16.12. **t.** understood they how that
20. **t.** charged he his disciples
27. and **t.** he shall reward every
17.13. **t.** the disciples understood
19. **t.** came the disciples to Jes.
18.21. **t.** came Peter to him, and
32. **t.** his lord, after that he had
19.13.**t.** were there brought unto
27. **t.** answered Peter and said
20.20. **t.** came to him the mother of
21. 1. **t.** sent Jesus two disciples
22. 8. **t.** saith he to his servants
13. **t.** said the king to the serva.
15. **t.** went the Pharisees, and
21. **t.** saith he unto them; 26.31,
38; Lu.21.10; Jo.11.14
23. 1. **t.** spake Jesus to the multit.
24. 9. **t.** shall they deliver you up
10. And **t.** shall many be offen.
14. and **t.** shall the end come
16. **t.** let them which be in Jud.
21. For **t.** shall be great tribula.
23. **t.** if any man shall say unto
30. And **t.** shall appear the sign
and **t.** shall all the tribes of
40. **t.** shall two be in the field
25. 1. **t.** shall the kingdom of hea.
7. **t.** all those virgins arose, and
31. **t.** shall he sit upon the thro.
34. **t.** shall the King say unto,
37. **t.** shall the righteous answer
41. **t.** shall he say also unto th.
44. **t.** shall they also answer him
45. **t.** shall he answer them, sa.
26. 3. **t.** assembled together the
14. **t.** one of the twelve, called
36. **t.** cometh Jesus with them
45. **t.** cometh he to his disciples
50. **t.** came they, and laid hands
56. **t.** all the disciples forsook
65. **t.** the high priest rent his
67. **t.** did they spit in his face
74. **t.** began he to curse and to
27. 3. **t.** Judas, which had betrayed
9. **t.** was fulfilled that which
13. **t.** said Pilate unto him, He.
16. And they had **t.** a notable
26. **t.** released he Barabbas unto
27. **t.** the soldiers of the gover.
38. **t.** were two thieves crucified
58. **t.** Pilate commanded the
Mar. 2.20. and **t.** shall they fast in tho.
3.27. and **t.** he will spoil his hou.
13.14. **t.** let them that be; Lu.21.21
21. And **t.** if any man shall say
26. And **t.** shall they; Lu.21.27
27. And **t.** he shall send his an.
Lu. 5.35. **t.** shall they fast in those
6.42. and **t.** shalt thou see clearly
11.26. **t.** goeth he, and taketh to
13.26. **t.** shall ye begin to say, We
14.10. **t.** shalt thou have worship
21. **t.** the master of the house
21.20. **t.** know that the desolation
23.30. **t.** shall they begin to say to
24.45. **t.** opened he their understa.
Jo. 2.10. **t.** that which is worse: but
7.10. **t.** went he also up unto the
8.28. **t.** shall ye know that I am
12.16. **t.** remembered they that
19. 1. **t.** Pilate therefore took Jes.
16. **t.** delivered he him therefore
20. 8. **t.** went in also that other
Act. 1.12. **t.** returned they unto Jeru.
4. 8. **t.** Peter, filled with the Holy
5.26. **t.** went the captain with the
6.11. **t.** they suborned men, which

Act. 7. 4. **t.** came he out of the land
8.17. **t.** laid they their hands on
10.46. magnify God. **t.** answered
48. **t.** prayed they him to tarry
13.12. **t.** the deputy, when he saw
15.22. **t.** pleased it the apostles
17.14. And **t.** immediately the bre.
21.26. **t.** Paul took the men, and
33. **t.** the chief captain came
23. 3. **t.** said Paul unto him, God
25.12. **t.** Festus, when he had con.
26. 1. **t.** Paul stretched forth the
27.32. **t.** the soldiers cut off the
28. 1. **t.** they knew that the island
Ro. 6.21. What fruit had ye **t.** in those
¹Co. 4. 5. and **t.** shall every man have
13.10. **t.** that which is in part shall
12. but **t.** face to face : now I
but **t.** shall I know even as
15.28. **t.** shall the Son also himself
54. **t.** shall be brought to pass
²Co. 12.10. when I am weak, **t.** am I
Gal. 4. 8. Howbeit **t.**, when ye knew
29. But as **t.** he that was born
6. 4. **t.** shall ye have rejoicing in
Col. 3. 4. **t.** shall ye also appear with
¹Th. 5. 3. **t.** sudden destruction cometh
²Th. 2. 8. And **t.** shall that Wicked be
Heb.10. 7. **t.** said I, Lo, I come to do
9. **t.** said he, Lo, I come to do
12.26. Whose voice **t.** shook the
²Pet. 3. 6. Whereby the world that **t.**

eita.
Mar. 4.28. **t.** the ear, after that the
Lu. 8.12. **t.** cometh the devil, and tak.
Jo. 19.27. **t.** saith he to the disciple
20.27. **t.** saith he to Thomas, Reach
¹Co. 12.28. **t.** gifts of healings, helps
15. 5. seen of Cephas, **t.** of the twe.
7. of James ; **t.** of all the apos.
24. **t.** cometh the end, when he
¹Ti. 2.13. Adam was first formed, **t.** E.
3.10. **t.** let them use the office of
Jas. 1.15. **t.** when lust hath conceived

epeita.
Mar. 5. 7. **t.** the Pharisees and scribes
Lu. 16. 7. **t.** said he to another, And
Jo. 11. 7. **t.** after that saith he to his
Gal. 1.18. **t.** after three years I went
2. 1. **t.** fourteen years after I went
¹Th. 4.17. **t.** we which are alive and
Heb. 7.27. for his own sins, and **t.** for
Jas. 3.17. is first pure, **t.** peaceable
4.14. a little time, and **t.** vanish.

loipon.
Act.27.20. should be saved was **t.** taken

THEN, [*conjunction.*]
oun. [Lu.11.13
Mat. 7.11. If ye **t.**, being evil, know ;
12.12. How much **t.** is a man better
26. how shall **t.** his kingdom
13.27. from whence **t.** hath it tares
28. Wilt thou **t.** that we go and
56. Whence **t.** hath this man all
(Also) Mat.17.10; 19.7; 21.25; 22.43,
45; 26.54; 27.22. Mar.3.31; 11.31; 15.12.
Lu.3.7,10; 6.9; 7.31; 10.37; 12.26; 13.
15; 20.5,17; 22.36,70. Jo.1.21,22,25; 2.
18,20; 3.25; 4.5,9,11,28,30,45,48,52; 5.4,
12,19; 6.5,14,21,28,30,32,34,41,42,53,67,
68; 7.6,11,25,28,30,33,35,45,47; 8.12,19,
21,22,25,28,31,41,48,52,57,59; 9.12,15,19,
24,28; 10.7,24,31; 11.12,14,16,17,20,21,
31,32,36,41,45,47,53,56; 12.1,3,4,7,28,35;
13.6,14,22,27,30; 16.17; 18.3,6,7,10,11,
12,16,17,19,27,28,29,31,33,40; 19.5,10,
20,21,23,32,40; 20.2,6,10,19,20,21; 21.5,
9,13,23. Act.2.41; 9.31; 10.23; 11.17;
17.29; 19.3,36; 22.29; 23.31. Ro.3.1,9,
27,31; 4.1,9,10; 5.9; 6.1,15,21; 7.7,13;
8.31; 9.14,19,30; 10.14; 11.1,5,7,11,19;

4.16. ¹Co.3.5 ; 6.4,15 ; 9.18 ; 10.19 ; 14.
15,26. ²Co.3.12. Gal.3.19,21 ; 4.15.
Eph.5.15. Col.3.1. ¹Th.4.1. ¹T1.3.2.
Heb.2.14; 4.14; 9.1. ¹Pet.4.1. ²Pet.
3.11.

ara.
Mat. 12.28.**t.** the kingdom of God is
17.26. unto him, **t.** are the children
19.25. saying, Who **t.** can be saved
24.45. Who **t.** is a faithful and wise
Lu. 12.42. Who **t.** is that faithful and
Act.11.18. **t.** hath God also to the Gen.
Ro. 7. 3. So **t.** if, while her husband
21. I find **t.** a law, that, when
25. So **t.** with the mind I myself
9.16. So **t.** it is not of him that
10.17. So **t.** faith cometh by hear.
14.12. So **t.** every one of us shall
¹Co. 5.10. for **t.** must ye needs go out
15.14. **t.** is our preaching vain, and
18. **t.** they also which are fallen
²Co. 5.14. died for all, **t.** were all dead
Gal. 2.21. **t.** Christ is dead in vain
3.29. **t.** are ye Abraham's seed
4.31. So **t.**, brethren, we are not
5.11. **t.** is the offence of the cross
Heb.12. 8. **t.** are ye bastards, and not

oude.
¹Co.15.13. dead, **t.** is Christ *not* risen
16. not, **t.** is *not* Christ raised

oukoun. [*not a king then.*)
Jo. 18.37. Art thou a king **t.** (Art thou

te.
Act.23. 5. **t.** said Paul, I wist not
27.29. **t.** fearing lest we should

toinun.
Jas. 2.24. Ye see **t.** how that by works
(*See words connected.*)

THENCE.
ekeithen.
Mat. 4.21. going on *from* **t.**, he saw
5.26. by no means come out **t.**
9. 9. as Jesus passed forth *from* **t.**
27. when Jesus departed **t.**
11. 1. he departed **t.**; 13.53,14.13;
Jo.4.43; Act.18.7
12. 9. when he was departed **t.**
15. he withdrew himself *from* **t.**
15.21. went **t.**, and departed into
29. Jesus departed *from* **t.**, and
19.15. hands on them, and depa. **t.**
Mar. 1.19. had gone a little farther **t.**
6. 1. he went out *from* **t.**, and ca.
11. when ye depart **t.**, shake
7.24. *from* **t.** he arose, and went
9.30. they departed **t.**, and passed
10. 1. And he arose *from* **t.**
Lu. 9. 4. there abide, and **t.** depart
12.59. thou shalt not depart **t.**
16.26. that would come *from* **t.**
Jo. 11.54. went **t.** unto a country near
Act. 7. 4. and *from* **t.**, when his father
13. 4. *from* **t.** they sailed to Cyprus
14.26. And **t.** sailed to Antioch, fr.
16.12. *from* **t.** to Philippi, which
20.15. And we sailed **t.**, and came
21. 1. and *from* **t.** unto Patara
27. 4. And when we had. .*from* **t.**
12. advised to depart **t.** *also*
28.15. And *from* **t.**, when the bret.
(*See words in connection.*)

THENCEFORTH.
eti.
Mat. 5.13. it is **t.** good for nothing
ek houtos.
Jo. 19.12. And *from* **t.** Pilate sought

THERE.
ekei.
Mat. 2.13. be thou **t.** until I bring thee
277

Mat. 2.15. was **t.** until the death of He.
5.23. and **t.** rememberest that thy
24. Leave **t.** thy gift before the.
6.21. **t.** will your heart; Lu.12.34
8.12. **t.** shall be weeping; 13.42,50,
22.13,24.51,25.30; Lu.13.28
10.11. and **t.** abide till ye go thence
12.45. they enter in and dwell **t.**
13.58. not many mighty works **t.**
14.23. evening was come, he was **t.**
15.29. mountain, and sat down **t.**
18.20. **t.** am I in the midst of them
19. 2. and he healed them **t.**
21.17. Bethany; and he lodged **t.**
22.11. he saw **t.** a man which had
24.28. **t.** will the eagles be gathered
26.71. said unto them that were **t.**
27.36. down there watched him **t.**
47. Some of them that stood **t.**
55. many women were **t.** behold.
61. **t.** was Mary Magdalene
28. 7. **t.** shall ye see him; Mar.16.7
10. and **t.** shall they see me
Mar. 1.13. he was **t.** in the wilderness
35. a solitary place, and **t.** pra.
38. that I may preach **t.** also
2. 6. cert. of the scribes sitting **t.**
3. 1. there was a man **t.** which
5.11. Now there was **t.** nigh unto
6. 5. could **t.** do no mighty work
10. **t.** abide till ye depart from
11. 5. them that stood **t.** said
13.21. is Christ; **or,** lo, he is **t.**
14.15. **t.** make ready for; Lu.22.12
Lu. 2. 6. that, while they were **t.**
6. 6. **t.** was a man whose right
8.32. there was **t.** an herd of many
9. 4. **t.** abide, and thence depart
10. 6. if the son of peace be **t.**
11.26. they enter in, and dwell **t.**
12.18. **t.** will I bestow all my
15.13. **t.** wasted his substance
17.21. Lo here ! **or,** lo **t.!** for beho.
23. See here; **or,** see **t.**
23.33. **t.** they crucified him
Jo. 2. 1. the mother of Jesus was **t.**
6. were set **t.** six waterpots
12. they continued **t.** not many
3.22. **t.** he tarried with them
23. there was much water **t.**
4. 6. Now Jacob's well was **t.**
40. he abode **t.** two days
5. 5. a certain man was **t.**
6. 3. **t.** he sat with his disciples
22. was none other boat **t.**
24. saw that Jesus was not **t.**
10.40. first baptized; and **t.** he ab.
42. many believed on him **t.**
11.15. that I was not **t.,** to the
31. unto the grave to weep **t.**
54. and **t.** continued with his
12. 2. **t.** they made him a supper
9. knew that he was **t.**
26. **t.** shall also my servant be
19.42. **t.** laid they Jesus therefore
Act. 9.33. **t.** he found a certain man
14. 7. And **t.** they preached the go.
28. **t.** they abode long time with
16. 1. a certain disciple was **t.**
17.14. Timotheus abode **t.** still
19.21. After I have been **t.**
22.10. and **t.** it shall be told thee
25. 9. **t.** be judged of these things
14. they had been **t.** many days
20. and **t.** be judged of these
27. 6. And **t.** the centurion found
Ro. 9.26. **t.** shall they be called the
2Co. 3.17. Spirit of the Lord is, **t.** is
Tit. 3.12. I have determined **t.** to win.
Heb. 7. 8. he receiveth them, of wh.
Jas. 2. 3. to the poor, Stand thou **t.**
3.16. **t.** is confusion and every evil
278

Jas. 4.13. continue **t.** a year, and buy
Rev. 2.14. thou hast **t.** them that hold
12. 6. they should feed her **t.**
21.25. th. shall be no night **t.**; 22.5
autou.
Act.15.34. pleased Silas to abide **t.** still
18.19. to Ephesus, and left them **t.**
21. 4. we tarried **t.** seven days
en autos.
Lu. 24.18. come to pass **t.** in these
Act. 9.38. heard that Peter was **t.**
20.22. that shall befall me **t.**
ekeise.
Act.21. 3. for **t.** the ship was to unlade
22. 5. to bring them which were **t.**
hōde.
Mat.24.23. Lo, here is Christ, or **t.**
enthade.
Act.10.18. whet. Simon..were lodged **t.**
ekeithen.
Act.20.13. **t.** intending to take in Paul

THEREABOUT.
peri [*gen.*] **houtos.**
Lu. 24. 4. were much perplexed **t.**

THEREAT.
dia [*gen.*] **autos.**
Mat. 7.13. many there be that go in **t.**

THEREBY.
en autos.
Eph. 2.16. having slain the enmity **t.**
1Pet. 2. 2. that ye may grow **t.**
dia [*gen.*] **houtos.**
Heb.12.11.them who are exercised **t.**
15. and **t.** many be defiled
13. 2. some have entertained
dia [*gen.*] **autos.**
Jo. 11. 4. might be glorified **t.**

THEREFORE.
oun.
Mat.10.31. Fear ye not **t.,** ye are of more
19. 6. What **t.** God hath joined
24.42. Watch **t.**: for ye know; 25.13;
Mar.13.35
28.19. Go ye **t.**, and teach all
Mar.12. 9. shall **t.** the lord of; Lu.20.15
37. David **t.** himself calleth him
Lu. 6.36. Be ye **t.** merciful, as your
20.33. **t.** in the resurrection whose
Jo. 3.29. this my joy **t.** is fulfilled
9.41. we see, **t.** yoursin remaineth
12.50. whatsoever I speak **t.** even
Act. 3.19. Repent ye **t.**, and be conver.
Ro. 12.20. **t.** if thine enemy hunger
Eph. 5. 7. Be not ye **t.** partakers with
2Ti. 1. 8. Be not thou **t.** ashamed of
(*And all other passages in which it
occurs, except the following*):—
dia [*accu.*] **houtos.**
Mat. 6.25. **t.** I say unto you; 21.43;
Mar.11.24; Lu.12.22
12.27. **t.** they shall be your judges
13.13. **t.** speak I to them in parabl.
52. **t.** every scribe which is instr.
14. 2. **t.** mighty works; Mar.6.14
18.23. **t.** is the kingdom of heaven
23.14. **t.** ye shall receive the greater
24.44. **t.** be ye also ready : for in
Lu. 11.19. **t.** shall they be your judges
49. **t.** also said the wisdom of G.
14.20. a wife, and **t.** I cannot come
Jo. 1.31. **t.** am I come baptizing with
5.16. **t.** did the Jews persecute Je.
18. **t.** the Jews sought the more
6.65. **t.** said I unto you, that no
7.22. Moses **t.** gave unto you circ.
8.47. ye **t.** hear them not, because
9.23. **t.** said his parents, He is of
10.17. **t.** doth my Father love me

Jo. 12.39. **t.** they could not believe
13.11. **t.** said he, Ye are not all cle.
15.19. **t.** the world hateth you
16.15. **t.** said I, that'he shall take
19.11. **t.** he that delivered me unto
Act. 2.26. **t.** did my heart rejoice
Ro. 4.16. **t.** it is of faith, that it might
2Co. 4. 1. **t.** seeing we have this minis.
7.13. **t.** we were comforted in your
13.10. **t.** I write these things being
1Th. 3. 7. **t.**, brethren, we were comfo.
2Ti. 1. **t.** I endure all things for the
Phile. 15. For perhaps he **t.** departed
Heb. 1. 9. **t.** God, even thy God, hath
2. 1. **t.** we ought to give the more
1Jo. 3. 1. **t.** the world knoweth us
4. 5. **t.** speak they of the world
Rev. 7.15. **t.** are they before the throne
12.12. **t.** rejoice, ye heavens, and ye
18. 8. **t.** shall her plagues come
ara.
Mat.19.27. what shall we have **t.**
Ro. 5.18. **t.** as by the offence of one
8. 1. There is **t.** now no condemn.
12. **t.**, brethren, we are debtors
9.18. **t.** hath he mercy on whom
14.19. Let us **t.** follow after the th.
Gal. 2.17. is **t.** Christ the minister of
3. 7. Know ye **t.** that they which
6.10. As we have **t.** opportunity
Eph. 2.19. Now **t.** ye are no more stra.
1Th. 5. 6. **t.** let us not sleep, as do oth.
2Th. 2.15. **t.**, brethren, stand fast, and
Heb. 4. 9. There remaineth **t.** a rest to
dio.
Lu. 1.35. **t.** also that holy thing which
Act.10.29. **t.** came I unto you without
20.31. **t.** watch, and remember, that
Ro. 2. 1. **t.** thou art inexcusable, O
4.22. **t.** it was imputed to him
2Co. 4.13. I believed, *and* **t.** have I sp.
we also believe, and **t.** speak
12.10. **t.** I take pleasure in infirmi
Heb.11.12. **t.** sprang there even of one
hōste.
Mar. 2.28. **t.** the Son of man is Lord
Ro. 13. 2. Whosoever **t.** resisteth the
1Co. 3.21. **t.** let no man glory in men
4. 5. **t.** judge nothing before the
5. 8. **t.** let us keep the feast
15.58. **t.**, my beloved brethren
2Co. 5.17. **t.** if any man be in Christ
Gal. 4.16. Am I **t.** become your enemy
Phi. 4. 1. **t.**, my brethren dearly belo.
eis houtos.
Mar.1. 38. for **t.** came I forth
Lu. 4.43. for **t.** am I sent
1Ti. 4.14. **t.** we both labour and
toinun.
Lu. 20.25. Render **t.** unto Cæsar the
1Co. 9.26. I **t.** so run, not as uncertain.
Heb.13.13.Let us go forth **t.** unto him
alla.
Act.10.20. Arise **t.**, and get thee down
2Co. 3. 1. **t.**, as ye abound in every th.
Eph. 5.24. **t.** as the church is subject
gar.
Mar. 8.38. Whosoever **t.** shall be asha.
dioti.
Ro. 3.20. **t.** by the deeds of the law
dē.
1Co. 6.20. **t.** glorify God in your body
para [*accu.*] **houtos.**
1Co.12.15, 16. is it **t.** not of the body
toigaroun.
1Th. 4. 8. He **t.** that despiseth, despis.

THEREIN
en autos.
Lu. 10. 9. heal the sick that are **t.**
19.45. cast out them that sold **t.**
Act. 1.20. and let no man dwell **t.**

Act.14.15. all things that are **t.**; 17.24
Ro. 1.17. For **t.** is the righteousness
    6. 2. live any longer **t.**
Eph. 6.20. that **t.** I may speak boldly
Col. 2. 7. abounding **t.** with thanksgiv.
²Pet. 3.10. the works that are **t.**
Rev.10. 6. that **t.** are, and the ear, &c.
    11. 1. them that worship **t.**
    13.12. them which dwell **t.**
    21.22. I saw no temple **t.**

     eis autos.
Mar.10.15.child, he shall not enter **t.**
Lu. 18.17. shall in no wise enter **t.**
Heb.4. 6. that some must enter **t.**

     en houtos.
¹Co. 7.24. wherein he is called, **t.** abide
Phi. 1.18. I **t.** do rejoice, yea, and will
     houtos.
²Pet. 2.20. are again entangled **t.**

     en hos.
Heb.13. 9. that have been occupied **t.**
(by which they that, &c., have not pro.)

THEREINTO.
     eis autos.
Lu. 21.21. in the countries enter **t.**

THEREOF.
     peri *[gen.]* **autos.**
Mat.12.36.They shall give account **t.** in

THEREON.
     blepō autos.
Rev. 5. 3, 4. the book, neither *to look* **t.**
     epanō autos.
Mat.21. 7. they set him **t.**
     epi *[accu.]* **autos.**
Jo. 12.14. sat **t.** as it is written
Rev. 6. 4. was given to him that sat **t.**
     en autos.   Lu.13.6
Mat.21.19. found nothing **t.**;Mar.11.13;
    (See connected words.)

THERETO. (See *Add, Agree.*)
THEREUNTO. (See *Comers.*)
     eis autos houtos.
Eph. 6.18. watching **t.** with all persever.
     eis houtos.
¹Th. 3. 3. that we are appointed **t.**
¹Pet. 3. 9. knowing that ye are **t.** called

THEREUPON. (See *Build.*)
THEREWITH.
     epi *[dat.]* **houtos.**
¹Ti. 6. 8. raiment let us be **t.** content
³John 10. and not content **t.**, neither
     en autos.
Jas. 3. 9. **t.** bless we God and **t.** curse

THESE.
     houtos.
Mat. 3. 9. God is able of **t.** stones to
    4. 3. command that **t.** stones
    5.19. one of **t.** least commandm.
    37. for whatsoev. is more than **t.**
    6.29. not arrayed like one of **t.**
(And all other passages in which it occurs, except the following):—
     hode, *[plur. neut.]*   [7,14
Rev. 2. 1. **t.** *things* saith ; 8,12,18;3,1,
    (See *Many, Move, Things.*)

THEY
Is frequently represented only by the inflection of the verb. In other passages the plural of **autos** or **ho** is the word used. Except the following :—
     ekeinos.
Mat. 15.18.and **t.** defile the man
Mar.16.11.And **t.**, when they had heard
    13. And **t.** went and told it
    20. **t.** went forth, and preached
Lu 9.34. as **t.** entered into the cloud

Jo. 5.39. **t.** are they which testify of
    7.45. **t.** said unto them
    10. 6. **t.** understood not what
    11.13. **t.** thought that he had spok.
    17.24. I will that **t.** also
    20.13. **t.** say unto her, Woman
Act.10. 9. as **t.** went on their journey
    10. while **t.** made ready, he
    15.11. shall be saved, even as **t.**
    21. 6. **t.** returned home again
Ro. 11.23. **t.** also, if they abide not in
¹Co. 9.25. **t.** do it to obtain a corrupt.
    10. 6. as **t.** also lusted
    15.11. whether it were I or **t.**, so
Heb. 12.25.For if **t.** escaped not who
     houtos.
Mat. 11.7. And as **t.** departed, Jesus
Lu. 8.14. are **t.**, which, when **t.** have
    15. are **t.**, which in an honest
    13. 4. think ye that **t.** were sinners
Jo. 6. 9. but what are **t.** among so
    10.25. **t.** bear witness of me
    18.21. behold, **t.** know what I said
Act.13. 4. So **t.**, being sent forth by
    24.15. which **t.** themselves also
Ro. 8.14. of God, **t.** are the sons of
    9. 6. For **t.** are not all Israel, wh.
Gal. 6.12. **t.** constrain you to be circu.
     hostis.
Mat.25. 3. **t.** *that* were foolish took
Act. 5.16. and **t.** were healed every one
    17.11. in *that* **t.** rec. (being *such as*)
    23.14. And **t.** came to the chief pr.
Rev. 1. 7. and **t.** *also which* pierced him
     hautou.
Act.27.27. **t.** drew near to some country
     heautou.
Rev. 2. 9. which say **t.** are Jews ; 3.9

THICK. (See *Gathered.*)

THIEF,   *Thieves.*
     kleptēs.
Mat. 6.19. where **t-ves** break through
    20. where **t-ves** do not break th.
    24.43. in what watch the **t.** would
Lu. 12.33. where no **t.** approacheth
    39. what hour the **t.** would come
Jo. 10. 1. the same is a **t.** and a robber
    8. came before me are **t-ves** and
    10. The **t.** cometh not, but for
    12. 6. but because he was a **t.**, and
¹Co. 6.10. Nor **t-ves**, nor covetous, nor
¹Th. 5. 2. Lord so cometh as a **t.** in
    4. should overtake you as a **t.**
¹Pet. 4.15. or as a **t.**, or as an evildoer
²Pet. 3.10. the Lord will come as a **t.**
Rev. 3. 3. I will come on thee as a **t.**
    16.15. Behold, I come as a **t.**
     lēstēs.   [Mar.11.17; Lu.19.46
Mat. 21.13.have made it a den of **t-ves**;
    26.55. ye come out as against a **t.**;
        Mar.14.48 ; Lu.22.52
    27.38. two **t-ves** crucified with him
    44. The **t-ves** also, which were
Mar.15.27.him they crucify two **t-ves**
Lu. 10.30, 36. and fell among **t-ves**

THIGH.
     mēros.
Rev. 19.16. on his **t.** a name written

THINE. (See *Own.*)
     su. *[gen.]*
Mat. 5.25. Agree with **t.** adversary
    33. perform unto the Lord **t.** oa.
    43. neighbour, and hate **t.** enemy
(And all others, except the following) :—
     sos.
Mat. 7. 3. the beam that is in **t.** *own*
    20.14. Take that **t.** is, and go thy
    25.25. lo, there thou hast that is **t.**
Lu. 5.33. but **t.** eat and drink

Lu. 15.31. and all that I have is **t.**
    22.42. not my will, but **t.**, be done
Jo. 17. 6, 9, 10. **t.** they were, and **t.** &c.
    18.35. **t.** *own* nation and the chief
Act. 5. 4. was it not in **t.** *own* power
     menō su, *[dat.]*
Act. 5. 4. remained, *was* it not **t.** *own*

THING,   -s.
The neuter of **ho,** *and adjectives without nouns, is often so translated :—Also*
     houtos, *[plu. neut.]*
Mat. 1.20. But wh. he thou. on *these* **t-s**
    4. 9. All *these* **t-s** will I give thee
    6.32. after all *these* **t-s** do the Ge.
      ye have need of all *these* **t-s**
    33. and all *these* **t-s** shall be add.
    9.18. While he spake *these* **t-s** un.
    11.25. hast hid *these* **t-s** from the
    13.34. All *these* **t-s** spake Jesus unto
    51. ye understood all *these* **t-s**
    56. hath this man all *these* **t-s**
    15.20. *These* are the **t-s** which defile
    19.20. All *these* **t-s** have I kept from
    21.23. authority doest thou *these* **t-s**;
        Mar.11.28 ; Lu.20.2
    24, 27. what author. I do *these* **t-s**;
        Mar.11.29,33 ; Lu.20.8
    23.36. All *these* **t-s** shall come upon
    24. 2. See ye not all *these* **t-s**
    3. wh. shall *these* **t-s** be;Mar.13.4
    33. when ye shall see all *these* **t-s**
    34. till all *these* **t-s** be ; Mar.13.4
Mar. 2. 8. Why reason ye *these* **t-s** in
    6. 2. wh. hath this man *these* **t-s**
    7.23. *these* evil **t-s** come from wit.
    11.28. this authority to do *these* **t-s**
    13.29. shall see *these* **t-s** come to
    30. not pass, till all *these* **t-s**
Lu 1.20. that *these* **t-s** shall be perfor.
    2.19. But Mary kept all *these* **t-s**
    4.28. they heard *these* **t-s** ; 19.11;
        Act.17.8
    5.27. And after *these* **t-s** he went
    7. 9. Jesus heard *these* **t-s** ; 18.22
    18. shewed him of all *these* **t-s**
    8. 8. when he had said *these* **t-s**
    10. 1. After *these* **t-s** the Lord app.
    21. that thou hast hid *these* **t-s**
    11.27. as he spake *these* **t-s**
    53. And as he had said *these* **t-s** unto
    12.30. For all *these* **t-s** do the nati.
    that ye have need of *these* **t-s**
    31. all *these* **t-s** shall be added
    13.17. when he had said *these* **t-s**
    14. 6. answer him again to *these* **t-s**
    15. heard *these* **t-s**, he said unto
    21. and shewed his lord *these* **t-s**
    15.26. asked what *these* **t-s** meant
    16.14. covetous, heard all *these* **t-s**
    18.34. they under. none of *these* **t-s**
    21. 6. As for *these* **t-s** which ye
    7. but when shall *these* **t-s** be
    these **t-s** sh. come to pass ; 31
    9. *these* **t-s** must first come to
    28. And when *these* **t-s** begin to
    36. worthy to escape all *these* **t-s**
    23.31. if they do *these* **t-s** in a green
    49. afar off, beholding *these* **t-s**
    24. 9, 10. told all *these* **t-s** unto the
    14. talked together of all *these* **t-s**
    21. third day since *these* **t-s** were
    26. to have suffered *these* **t-s**
    48. ye are witnesses of *these* **t-s**
Jo. 1.28. *These* **t-s** were done in Beth.
    2.16. Take *these* **t-s** hence
    18. that thou doēst *these* **t-s**
    3. 9. How can *these* **t-s** be
    10. and knowest not *these* **t-s**
    22. After *these* **t-s** came Jesus
    5.16. because he had done *these* **t-s**
    34. *these* **t-s** I say, that ye might
    6 1. after *these* **t-s** Jesus went

Jo. 6.59. *These* **t-s** said he in the syn.
  7. 1. After *these* **t-s** Jesus walked
    4. If thou do *these* **t-s**, shew th.
    32. the people murmured *such* **t-s**
  8.26. *those* **t-s** which I have heard
    28. hath taught me, I sp. *these* **t-s**
  11.11. *These* **t-s** said he : and after
  12.16. *These* **t-s** understood not his
    that *these* **t-s** were written of
    they had done *these* **t-s** unto
    36. *These* **t-s** spake Jesus, and
    41. *These* **t-s** said Esaias, when
  13.17. If ye know *these* **t-s**
  14.25. *These* **t-s** have I spoken un.;
    15.11 ; 16.1,25,33
  15.17. *These* **t-s** I command you
    21. But all *these* **t-s** will they do
  16. 3. And *these* **t-s** will they do
    4. But *these* **t-s** have I told you
    And *these* **t-s** I said not unto
    6. because I have said *these* **t-s**
  17.13. and *these* **t-s** I speak in the
  19.24. *These* **t-s** therefore the soldi.
    36. For *these* **t-s** were done, that
  20.18. he had spoken *these* **t-s** unto
  21. 1. After *these* **t-s** Jesus shewed
    24. which testifieth of *these* **t-s**
    and wrote *these* **t-s** : and we
Act. 1. 9. And when he had sp. *these* **t-s**
   5. 5. all them that heard *these* **t-s**
    11. as many as heard *these* **t-s**
    32. are his witnesses of *these* **t-s**
  7. 1. the high priest, Are *these* **t-s**
    50. my hand made all *these* **t-s**
    54. When they..*these* **t-s** ; 11.18
  12.17. Go shew *these* **t-s** unto James
  14.15. Sirs, why do ye *these* **t-s**
  15.17. Lord, who doeth all *these* **t-s**
  17.11. daily, whether *those* **t-s** were
    20. therefore what *these* **t-s** mean
  18. 1. After *these* **t-s** Paul departed
  19.21. After *these* **t-s** were ended
    36. Seeing then that *these* **t-s**
  21.12. And we heard *these* **t-s**
  23.22. thou hast shewed *these* **t-s**
  24. 8. knowledge of all *these* **t-s**
    9. saying that *these* **t-s** were so
    22. when Felix heard *these* **t-s**
  25. 9. be judged of *these* **t-s** before
  26.26. the king knoweth of *these* **t-s**
    that none of *these* **t-s** are hid.
Ro. 8.31. shall we then say to *these* **t-s**
    37. in all *these* **t-s** we are more
  14.18. For he that in *these* **t-s** serv.
1Co. 4. 6. And *these* **t-s**, brethren, I ha.
    14. I write not *these* **t-s** to shame
  9. 8. Say I *these* **t-s** as a man
    15. I have used none of *these* **t-s**
    neither have I wri. *these* **t-s**
  10. 6. *these* **t-s** were our examples
    11. Now all *these* **t-s** happened
2Co. 2.16. who is sufficient for *these* **t-s**
  13.10. I write *these* **t-s** being absent
Eph. 5. 6. because of *these* **t-s** cometh
Phi. 4. 8. think on *these* **t-s**
    9. *Those* **t-s**, which ye have both
Col. 3. 14. And above all *these* **t-s** put
2Th. 2. 5. with you, I told you *these* **t-s**
1Ti. 3.14. *These* **t-s** write I unto thee
  4. 6. in remembrance of *these* **t-s**
    11. *These* **t-s** command and teach
    15. Meditate upon *these* **t-s**
  5. 7. And *these* **t-s** give in charge
    21. that thou observe *these* **t-s**
  6. 2. *These* **t-s** teach and exhort
    11. O man of God, flee *these* **t-s**
2Ti. 1.12. I also suffer *these* **t-s**
  2.14. Of *these* **t-s** put them in rem.
Tit. 2.15. *These* **t-s** speak, and exhort
  3. 8. *these* **t-s** I will that thou
    These **t-s** are good and profit.
Heb. 7.13. he of whom *these* **t-s** are spo.
280

Heb. 9. 6. Now when *these* **t-s** were
Jas. 3.10. *these* **t-s** ought not so to be
2Pet.1. 8. For if *these* **t-s** be in you
    9. But he that lacketh *these* **t-s**
    10. for if ye do *these* **t-s**
    12. in remembrance of *these* **t-s**
    15. to have *these* **t-s** always in
  3.11. all *these* **t-s** shall be dissolved
    16. speaking in them of *these* **t-s**
1Jo. 1. 4. And *these* **t-s** write we unto
  2. 1. *these* **t-s** write I unto you
    26. *These* **t-s** have I writt.; 5.13
Jude 10. in *those* **t-s** they corrupt th.
Rev. 7. 1. after *these* **t-s** I saw four ang.
  18. 1. And after *these* **t-s** I ; 19.1
    15. The merchants of *these* **t-s**
  22. 8. And I John saw *these* **t-s**
    which shewed me *these* **t-s**
    16. to testify unto you *these* **t-s**
    18. man shall add unto *these* **t-s**
    20. He which testifieth *these* **t-s**

pragma.
Mat.18.19. touching any **t.** that they
Lu. 1. 1. a declaration of those **t-s**
Act. 5. 4. hast thou conceived this **t.**
Heb. 6.18. That by two immutable **t-s**
    10. 1. not the very image of the **t-s**
    11. 1. is the substance of **t-s** hoped

logos. [20.3
Mat. 21.24.also will ask you one **t.** ; Lu.
Lu. 1. 4. the certainty of those **t-s**
Act. 5.24. chief priests heard these **t-s**

rēma.
Lu. 2.15. and see this **t.** which is come
    19. But Mary kept all these **t-s**
Act. 5.32. are his witnesses of these **t-s**

autos.
1Pet.1.12. they did minister *the* **t-s**
(See words in connection.)

THINK,   *-est, -eth, Thought.*
dokeō.
Mat. 3. 9. **t.** not to say within yoursel.
  6. 7. for they **t.** that they shall be
  17.25. saying, What **t-est** thou, Si.
  18.12. How **t.** ye? if a man have
  21.28. what **t.** ye? A certain man
  22.17. Tell us therefore, What **t-est**
    42. Saying, What **t.** ye of Christ
  24.44. hour as ye **t.** not ; Lu.12.40
  26.53. **t-est** thou that I cannot now
    66. What **t.** ye? They answered
Lu. 10.36. Which of these three, **t-est**
  13. 4. **t.** ye that they were sinners
  19.11. they **t-o** that the kingdom
Jo. 5.39. in them ye **t.** ye have eternal
    45. *Do* not **t.** that I will accuse
  11.13. they **t-o** that he had spoken
    56. What **t.** ye, that he will
  13.29. For som° of them **t-o**, bec.
  16. 2. *will* **t.** that he doeth God
Act.12. 9. by the angel ; but **t-o** he saw
  26. 9. I verily **t-o** with myself
1Co. 4. 9. For I **t.** that God hath set
  7.40. I **t.** also that I have the Spi.
  8. 2. if any man **t.** that he know.
  10.12. let him *that* **t-eth** he stand.
  12.23. which we **t.** to be less hono.
  14.37. If any man **t.** himself to be
2Co. 11.16. *Let* no man **t.** me a fool
  12.19. **t.** ye that we excuse ourselv.
Gal. 6. 3. if a man **t.** himself to be
Phi. 3. 4. If any other man **t-eth** that
Jas. 4. 5. *Do* ye **t.** that the scripture

eudokeō.
1Th. 3. 1. we **t-o** it *good* to be left

logizomai.
Ro. 2. 3. And **t-est** thou this, O man
1Co. 13. 5. not easily provoked, **t-eth**
    11. I **t-o** as a child : but when
2Co. 3. 5. *to* **t.** any thing as of ourselv.
    10. 2. I **t.** to be bold against some

2Co. 10. 2. *which* **t.** *of* us as if we **walked**
    7. *let* him of himself **t.** this
    11. *Let* such an one **t.** this, that
  12. 6. lest any man *should* **t.** of me
Phi. 4. 8. any praise, **t.** *on* these things

dialogizomai.
Lu. 12.17. he **t-o** within himself, say.

phroneō.
Act.28.22. hear of thee what thou **t-est**
Ro. 12. 3. than he ought *to* **t.** ; but *to* **t.**
1Co. 4. 6. not *to* **t.** of men above that
Phi. 1. 7. meet for me *to* **t.** this of you

nomizō.
Mat. 5.17. **t.** not that I am come ; 10.34
Act. 8.20. because thou *hast* **t-o** that
    17.29. we ought not *to* **t.** that the
1Co. 7.36. if any man **t.** that he behav.

hēgeomai.
Act.26. 2. I **t.** myself happy, king Ag.
2Co. 9. 5. Therefore I **t-o** it necessary
Phi. 2. 6. **t-o** it not robbery to be
2Pet.1.13. Yea, I **t.** it meet, as long as

enthumeomai.
Mat. 1.20. *while* he **t-o** on these things
    9. 4. Wherefore **t.** ye evil in your
Act.10.19. *While* Peter **t-o** on the vis.

axioō.
Lu. 7. 7. neither **t-o** I myself *worthy*
Act.15.38. Paul **t-o** not *good* to take
Heb. 10.29.*shall* he be **t-o** *worthy*, who

epiballō.
Mar.14.72.*when* he **t-o** thereon, he wept

phainō.   [*seems to you*
Mar.14.64. the blasphemy, What **t.** ye

huponoeō.
Act.13.25. Whom **t.** ye that I am

krinō.
Act.26. 8. Why *should* it be **t-o** a thing

noeō.
Eph. 3.20. above all that we ask or **t.**

oiomai.
Jas. 1. 7. *let* not that man **t.** that he
    (See *Highly, Strange.*)

THIRD.
tritos.   [Lu.9.22
Mat.16.21. and be raised again the **t.** ;
  17.23. and the **t.** day he sh.; 20.19 ;
    Mar.10.34 ; Lu.18.33
  20. 3. he went out about the **t.** ho
  22.26. also, and the **t.**, unto the se
  26.44. and prayed the **t.** time
  27.64. be made sure until the **t.**day
Mar. 9.31. he shall rise the **t.** day
  12.21. and the **t.** likewise ; Lu.20.31
  14.41. And he cometh the **t.** time
  15.25. And it was the **t.** hour
Lu. 12.38. or come in the **t** watch
  13.32. and the **t.** day I shall be per.
  20.12. And again he sent a **t.** ; and
  23.22. he said unto them the **t.** ti.
  24. 7. and the **t.** day rise again
    21. to day is the **t.** day since
    46. to rise from the dead the **t.**
Jo. 2. 1. And the **t.** day there was
  21.14. This is now the **t.** time that
    17. He saith unto him the **t.** ti.
    he said unto him the **t.** time
Act. 2.15. it is but the **t.** hour of the
  10.40. Him God raised up the **t.**
  23.23. at the **t.** hour of the night
  27.19. And the **t.** day we cast out
1Co. 15. 4. he rose again the **t.** day
2Co. 12. 2. caught up to the **t.** heaven
    14. Behold, the **t.** time I am re.
    13. 1. This is the **t.** time I am com.
Rev. 4. 7. and the **t.** beast had a face
  6. 5. opened the **t.** seal, I heard
    the **t.** beast say
  8. 7. the **t.** part of trees was bur.
    8. the **t.** part of the sea became
    9. the **t** part of the creatures

Rev. 8. 9. and the t. part of the ships
    10. And the t. angel sounded
       upon the t. part of the rivers
    11. the t. part of the waters bec.
    12. the t. part of the sun was
       and the t. part of the moon
       the t. part of the stars ; so as
       t.part of them was darkened
       the day shone not for a t.
   9.15. for to slay the t.part of men
    18. was the t. part of men killed
  11.14. the t. woe cometh quickly
  12. 4. drew the t. part of the stars
  14. 9. And the t. angel followed
  16. 4. And the t. angel poured out
  21.19. the t., a chalcedony

tristegon.

Act.20. 9. fell down from the t. loft

THIRDLY.
triton.

1Co. 12.28. t. teachers, after that mirac.

THIRST.
dipsaō.

Mat. 5. 6. which do hunger and t. after
Jo. 4.13. drinke. of this water shall t.
    14. shall give him shall never t.
    15. give me this water, that I t.
   6.35. believe. on me shall never t.
   7.37. If any man t., let him come
  19.28. might be fulfilled, saith, I t.
Ro. 12.20. feed him ; if he t., give him
1Co. 4.11. both hunger, and t., and are
Rev. 7.16. shall hu. no more, neither t.

dipsos.

2Co. 11.27. often, in hunger and t.

THIRSTY.
dipsaō.

Mat.25.35, 42. I was t., and ye gave me
    37. fed thee? or t.,and gave thee

THIRTY.
triakonta.

Mat.13.23.some sixty, some t.; Mar.4.8
  26.15. t. pieces of silver ; 27.3,9
Lu. 3.23. to be about t. years of age
Jo. 5. 5. an infirmity t. and eight ye.
   6.19. five and twenty or t. furlon.
Gal. 3.17. four hundred and t. years

THIRTYFOLD.
triakonta.   [Mar.4.20

Mat.13. 8. some sixtyfold, some t.;

THIS. (See words connected.)
houtos.

Mat. 3.17. t. is my beloved Son ; 17.5
   7.12. for t. is the law and the pro.
  27.37. t. IS JESUS THE KING
    54. Truly t. was the Son of God
Mar. 9. 7. t. is my beloved Son : hear ;
       9.35; 2Pet.1.17
  12. 7. t. is the heir ; come, let us
  23.38. t. IS THE KING OF THE
Jo. 1.34. that t. is the Son of God
   4.29. is not t. the Christ
    42. t. is indeed the Christ, the
   6.14. t. is of a truth that prophet
    42. Is not t. Jesus
    58. t. is that bread which came
   7.26. that t. is the very Christ
    41. t. is the Christ
    46. Never man spake like t.man
   9. 9. Some said, t. is he
  21.24. t. is the disciple which
Act. 7.37. t. is that Moses, which said
    38. t. is he, that was in the chu.
    40. for as for t. Moses, which
  19.26. t. Paul hath persuaded and
1Jo. 5. 6. t. is he that came by water
    20. t. is the true God
2John 7. t. is a deceiver and an anti.

Rev.20.14. t. is the second death
   (And all other passages in which it
occurs, except the following) :—
autos.
Jo. 12. 7. burying hath she kept t.
Act. 3.12. had made t. man to walk
autos houtos.
2Pet. 1. 5. And beside t. giving all
nun.
Mat.24.21. begin.of the world to t. time
Mar.13.19.unto t. time, neither shall
Act.24.25. Go thy way for t. time
1Co.16.12. not at all to come at t. time
ekeinos.
Mat.24.43. know t., that if the goodm.

THISTLES.
tribolos.

Mat. 7.16. of thorns, or figs of t.

THITHER.   (See Run.)
ekei.

Mat. 2.22. he was afraid to go t.
Mar. 6.33. ran afoot t. out of all cities
Lu. 17.37. t. will the eagles be gathered
   21. 2. casting in t. two mites
Jo. 11. 8. goest thou t. again
    18. 2. Jesus ofttimes resorted t.
     3. cometh t. with lanterns
Act.17.13. they came t. also, and stirred

THITHERWARD.
ekei.

Ro. 15.24. to be brought on my way t.

THONGS.
himas.

Act.22.25. as they bound him with t.

THORN,   -s.
akantha.

Mat. 7.16. Do men gather grapes of t-s
  13. 7. among t-s ; and the t-s ;
       Mar.4.7; Lu.8.7.
    22. seed among the t-s is he that
  27.29. had platted a crown of t-s
Mar. 4.18. which are sown among t-s
Lu. 6.44. For of t-s men do not gather
   8.14. that which fell among t-s
Jo. 19. 2. soldiers platted a crown of t-s
Heb. 6. 8. that which beareth t-s and
akanthinos.
Mar.15.17.platted a crown of t-s, and
Jo. 19. 5. wearing the crown of t-s, and
skolops.
2Co. 12. 7. given to me a t. in the flesh

THOSE.
ekeinos.

Mat. 3. 1. In t. days came John the B.
  21.40. do unto t. husbandmen
  22. 7. destroyed t. murderers
    10. So t. servants went out
  24.19. them that give suck in t.;
       Mar.13.17 ; Lu.21.23
    22. except t. days should be sho.
       elect's sake t. days shall be
    29. the tribulation of t. days
  25. 7. Then all t. virgins arose
    19. the lord of t. servants come.
Mar. 1. 9. it came to pass in t. days ;
       Lu.2.1 ; Act.9.37
   2.20. shall they fast in t.; Lu.5.35
   7.15. t. are they that defile the
   8. 1. In t. days the multitude be.
  12. 7. t. husbandmen said among
  13.19. in t. days shall be affliction
    24. in t. days, after that tribula.
Lu. 4. 2. in t. days he did eat nothing
   9.36. told no man in t. days
  12.37, 38. Blessed are t. servants
  13. 4. Or t. eighteen, upon whom
  14.24. none of t. men which were
  19.27. t. mine enemies, which
  20. 1. on one of t. days, as he tau.

Jo. 8.10. where are t. thine accusers
Act. 2.18. I will pour out in t. days
   7.41. they made a calf in t. days
  16. 3. which were in t. quarters
    35. saying, Let t. men go
  20. 2. he had gone over t. parts
Ro. 6.21. the end of t. things is death
Heb. 8.10. after t. days, saith the ; 10.16
Rev. 9. 6. in t. days shall men seek
houtos.
Lu. 1.24. after t. days his wife
    39. And Mary arose in t. days
   6.12. it came to pass in t. days
Jo. 8.26. t. things which I have heard
Act. 1.15. in t. days Peter stood up
   6. 1. in t. days, when the number
  18.17. cared for none of t. things
  21.15. after t. days we took up our
Phi. 3. 7. I counted loss for Christ
   4. 9. t. things, which ye have
Heb.13.11.For the bodies of t. beasts
Jude 10. in t. things they corrupt
autos.
Mat.21.41.destroy t. wicked men
Jo. 17.11. t. whom thou hast given me
hosos.
Jude 10. of t. things which they

THOU.
su.

Mat. 6. 6. But t., when thou prayest
    17. But t., when thou fastest
  16.16. t. art the Christ, the Son of:
       Mar.8.29; Lu.4.41; Jo.11.27
  26.39. not as I will, but as t. wilt
    69. t. also wast with ; Mar.14.67
Lu. 1.28. blessed are t. among women
   7.19, 20. Art t. he that should
  14. 8. a more honourable than t.
  15.31. Son, t. art ever with me
  16. 5, 7. And how much owest t.
    25. remember that t. in thy
       and t. art tormented
  19.42. If thou hadst known, even t.
Jo. 1.19, 22. Who art t. ; 8.25 ; 21.12
    21. What then ? Art t. Elias
       Art t. that prophet ? And he
    25. if t. be not that Christ, nor
    42. t. art Simon the son of Jona
       t. shalt be called Cephas
  3.10. Art t. a master of Israel
  4. 9. How is it that t., being a
  7.52. Art t. also of Galilee
  8. 5. stoned ; but what sayest t.
    13. t. bearest record of thyself
  9.28. and said, t. art his disciple
    37. t. hast seen him, and
  17.23. I in them, and t. in me
  18.17. Art not t. also one of this
Act. 1.24. t., Lord, which knowest the
   8.23. that t. art in the gall of bitt.
  11.14. whereby t. and all thy hou.
  13.10. t. child of the devil, t.
    33. t. art my Son, this day have
  21.38. Art not t. that Egyptian
  22.27. Tell me, art t. a Roman
  26.29. not only t. but all that hear
Ro. 2.21. t. therefore which teachest
1Ti. 4.12. be t. an example of the beli.
   6.11. But t., O man of God, flee
2Ti. 1.18. at Ephesus, t. knowest very
   2. 1. t. therefore, my son, be str.
Phile. 12. t. therefore receive him
Heb. 1.10. And, t., Lord, in the begin.
    12. but t. art the same, and thy
Jas. 4.12. who art t. that judgest ano.
Rev. 4.11. for t. hast created all things
   5. 2. t. art worthy to take the book
  (And all others in which it occurs.)

THOUGH.
ean.

Lu. 16.31. t. one rose from the dead

Act. 13.41. t. a man declare it unto you
Ro. 9.27. t. the number of the children
¹Co. 4.15. t. ye have ten thousand inst.
9.16. t. I preach the gospel, I have
13. 1. t. I speak with the tongues
2. t. I have the gift of prophe.
t. I have all faith, so that I
3. t. I bestow all my goods
t. I give my body to be bur.
²Co. 10. 8. For t. I should boast some.
12. 6. For t. I would desire to glo.
Gal. 1. 8. t. we, or an angel from hea.
Jas. 2.14. t. a man say he hath faith
ei kai.
Mat. 26.33. t. all men shall be offended
Lu. 11. 8. t. he will not rise and give
18. 4. t. I fear not God, nor regard
²Co. 4.16. t. our outward man perish
5.16. yea, t. we have known Chri.
7. 8. For t. I made you sorry with
I do not repent, t. I did repe.
t. it were but for a season
12. Wherefore, t. I wrote unto
11. 6. t. I be rude in speech, yet
12.11. chiefest apostles, t. I be no.
15. t. the more abundantly I
Col. 2. 5. For t. I be absent in the fle.
Heb. 6. 9. accompany salvation, t. we
ei per.
¹Co. 8. 5. For t. there be that are
kaiper.
Phi. 3. 4. t. I might also have confide.
Heb. 5. 8. t. he were a Son, yet learned
7. 5. t. they come out of the loins
12.17. t. he sought it carefully
²Pet. 1.12. t. ye know them, and be
kai toige.
Jo. 4. 2. t. Jesus himself baptized
Act. 17.27. t. he be not far from every
kan.
Mat. 26.35. t. I should die with thee
Jo. 8.14. t. I bear record of myself
10.38. t. ye believe not me
11.25. t. he were dead, yet shall
hoti.
Ro. 9. 6. Not as t. the word of God
²Co. 11.21. as t. we had been weak
Phi. 3.12. Not as t. I had already
dia [gen.] akrobustia.
Ro. 4.11. t. they be not circumcised
ei.
²Co. 13. 4. For t. he was crucified thr.
homōs.
Gal. 3.15. t. it be but a man's covenant

THOUGHT, -s.
dialogismos. [Mar.7.21
Mat. 15.19. of the heart proceed evil t-s ;
Lu. 2.35. that the t-s of many hearts
5.22. when Jesus percei. their t-s
6. 8. he knew their t-s, and said
9.47. perceiving the t. of their
24.38. why do t-s arise in your
¹Co. 3.20. The Lord knoweth the t-s of
Jas. 2. 4. become judges of evil t-s
logismos.
Ro. 2.15. bearing witness, and their t-s
merimnaō. [Lu.12.22
Mat. 6.25. Take no t. for your life ;
27. you by taking t.; Lu.12.25
28. why take ye t. for ; Lu.12.26
31, 34. Therefore take no t.
for the morrow shall take t.
10.19. take no t. how or ; Lu.12.11
promerimnaō.
Mar. 13.11. take no t. beforehand what
Mat. 9. 4. Jesus knowing their t-s
12.25. Jesus knew their t-s
Heb. 4.12. a discerner of the t-s and
dianoēma.
Lu. 11.17. he, knowing their t-s, said
282

epinoia.
Act. 8.22. the t. of thine heart may
noēma.
²Co. 10. 5. bringing into captiv. every t.

THOUSAND, -s.
chilioi.
²Pet. 3. 8. as a t. years, and a t. years
Rev. 11. 3. prophesy a t. 200 and
12. 6. feed her there a t. 200 and
14.20. a t. and 600 furlongs
20. 2. and bound him a t. years
3. till the t. years should be
4. reigned with Christ a t. yea.
20. 5. until the t. years were
6. shall reign with him a t. ye.
7. when the t. years are expired
chilias, [plu.]
Lu. 14.31. able with ten t. to meet him
against him with twenty t.
Act. 4. 4. of the men was about five t.
¹Co. 10. 8. one day three and twenty t.
Rev. 5.11. thousand, and t-s of t-s
7. 4. and forty and four t.; 14.1,3
5, 6, 7, 8. sealed twelve t.
11.13. were slain of men seven t.
21.16. the reed, twelve t. furlongs
dischilioi.
Mar. 5.13. they were about two t.
trischilioi.
Act. 2.41. unto them about three t. so.
tetrakischilioi.
Mat. 15.38. four t. men, beside women
16.10. loav. of the four t.; Mar.8.20
Mar. 8. 9. were about four t.; and he
Act. 21.38. four t. men that were murd.
pentakischilioi. [Lu.9.14
Mat. 14.21. about five t. men ; Mar.6.44;
16. 9. loaves of the five t.; Mar.8.19
Jo. 6.10. in number about five t.
heptakischilioi.
Ro. 11. 4. reserved to myself seven t.
murioi.
Mat. 18.24. owed him ten t. talents
¹Co. 4.15. though we have ten t. instr.
14.19. than ten t. words in an
murias.
Act. 21.20. how many t-s of Jews there
Jude 14. Lord cometh with ten t-s of
Rev. 9.16. two hundred t.
(myriads of myriads)
pente murias.
Act. 19.19. fifty t. pieces of silver

THREATEN, -ed.
apeileō.
Act. 4.17. let us straitly t. them, that
¹Pet. 2.23. when he suffered, he t-ed not
prosapeileomai.
Act. 4. 21. when they had further t-ed

THREATENING, -s.
apeilē.
Act. 4.29. And now, Lord, beh. their t.
9. 1. breathing out t-s and slaugh.
Eph. 6. 9. forbearing t.; knowing that

THREE.
treis.
Mat. 12.40. as Jonas was t. days and t.
be t. days and t. nights in
13.33. and hid in t. measures of m.
15.32. with me now t. da.; Mar.8.2
17. 4. make here t. tabernacles;
Mar.9.5 ; Lu.9.33
18.16. of two or t. witnesses every
20. where two or t. are gathered
26.61. and to build it in t. days
27.40. buildest it in t.; Mar.15.29
63. After t. days I will ; Mar.8.31
Mar. 14.58. and within t. days I will bu.
Lu. 1.56. abode with her about t. mo.
2.46. after t. days they found him
4.25. was shut up t. years and six

Lu. 10.36. Which now of these t., thin.
11. 5. Friend, lend me t. loaves
12.52. t. against two, . .against t.
13. 7. these t. years I come seeking
21. and hid in t. measures of m.
Jo. 2. 6. two or t. firkins apiece
19. in t. days I will raise it up
20. thou rear it up in t. days
21.11. an hundred and fifty and t.
Act. 5. 7. the space of t. hours after
7.20. in his father's house t.
9. 9. And he was t. days without
10.19. Behold, t. men seek thee
11.11. there were t. men already
17. 2. and t. sabbath days reasoned
19. 8. for the space of t. months
20. 3. And there abode t. months
25. 1. after t. days he ascended fr.
28. 7. lodged us t. days courteously
11. And after t. months we dep.
12. we tarried there t. days
17. that after t. days Paul called
¹Co. 10. 8. in one day t. and twenty th.
13.13. faith, hope, charity, these t.
14.27. or at the most by t., and
29. the prophets speak two or t.
²Co. 13. 1. two or t. witnesses; ¹Ti.5.19;
Heb.10.28
Gal. 1.18. Then after t. years I went up
Jas. 5.17. by the space of t. years and
¹Jo. 5. 7. For there are t. that bear re.
and these t. are one
8. are t. that bear witness in
and these t. agree in one
Rev. 6. 6. t. measures of barley for a
8.13. of the trumpet of the t. ang.
9.18. By these t. was the third pa.
11. 9, 11. t. days and an half
16.13. And I saw t. unclean spirits
19. great city was divided into t.
21.13. On the east t. gates ; on the
t. gates ; on the south t. ga.
and on the west t. gates
tris.
Act. 11.10. And this was done t. times
trietia.
Act. 20.31. by the space of t. years I
(See Hundred, Months, Thousand.)

THREESCORE.
hexēkonta.
Lu. 24.13. Jerusalem about t. furlongs
¹Ti. 5. 9. number under t. years old
Rev. 11. 3. two hundred and t.: 12.6
13.18. Six hundred t. and six
hebdomēkonta.
Act. 7.14. t. and fifteen souls ; (70 & 5)
23.23. horsemen t. and ten, and
27.37. t. and sixteen souls; (70 & 6)

THRESHETH.
aloaō.
¹Co. 9.10. that he that t. in hope shou.

THRICE.
tris.
Mat. 26.34,75. thou shalt deny me t.;
Mar.14.30,72 ; Lu.22.34,61;
Jo.13.38
Act. 10.16. this was done t.; and the
²Co. 11.25. t. was I beaten with rods
t. I suffered shipwreck
12. 8. I besought the Lord t., that

THROAT.
larungx.
Ro. 3.13. Their t. is an op'n sepulchre
pnigō.
Mat. 18.28. took him by the t., saying

THRONE, -s.
thronos.
Mat. 5.34. by heaven ; for it is God's t.
19.28. the t. of his glory ye ; 25.13

Mat.**19.28.** shall sit upon twelve *t-s*
  23.22. sweareth by the **t.** of God
Lu. **1.32.** the **t.** of his father David
  22.30. sit on *t-s* judging the twelve
Act. **2.30.** up Christ to sit on his **t.**
  7.49. Heaven is my **t.**, and earth
Col. **1.16.** whether they be *t-s*, or dom.
Heb.**1.** **8.** Thy **t.**, O God, is for ever
  4.16. boldly unto the **t.** of grace
  8. **1.** the right hand of the **t.**; **12.2**
Rev.**1.** **4.** spirits which are before his **t.**
  3.21. to sit with me in my **t.**
    with my Father in his **t.**
  4. **2.** and, behold, a **t.** was set in
    heaven, and one sat on the **t.**
  3. a rainbow round about the **t.**
  4. round about the **t.** were four
  5. out of the **t.** proceeded lightn.
    burning before the **t.**, which
  6. before the **t.** there was a sea
    t., and round about the **t.**
  9. **10.** that sat on the **t.**; **5.1,7**;
    19.4; **21.5**
  10. cast their crowns before the **t.**
  5. **6.** the midst of the **t.**; **7.17**
  11. round about the **t.** and ; **7.11**
  13. that sitteth upon the **t.**;
    6.16; **7.10,15**
  7. **9.** stood before the **t.**, and
  11. fell before the **t.** on their
  15. before the **t.** of God ; **14.5**
  8. **3.** which was before the **t.**
  12. **5.** unto God, and to his **t.**
  14. **3.** a new song before the **t.**
  16.17. from the **t.**, saying, It is done
  19. **5.** a voice came out of the **t.**
  20. **4.** And I saw *t-s*, and they
  11. a great white **t.**, and him
  22. **1.** out of the **t.** of God and
  3. the **t.** of God and of the La.
  bēma.
Act.**12.21.** sat upon his **t.**, and made

THRONG,   *-ed, -ing.*
  sunthlibō.
Mar. **5.24.** peop. followed him, and *t-ed*
  31. seest the multitude *t-ing* th.
  thlibō.
Mar. **3.** **9.** lest they *should* **t.** him
  sumpnigō.
Lu. **8.42.** as he went the people *t-ed*
  sunechō.
Lu. **8.45.** Master, the multitude **t.** thee

THROUGH.
  dia, *[gen.]*
Mat.**12.** **1.** on the sabbath day **t.** the co.
  43. he walked **t.** dry ; Lu.**11.24**
  19.24. a camel to go **t.** the eye of ;
    Mar.**10.25** ; Lu.**18.25**
Mar. **2.23.** that he went **t.** the ; Lu.**6.1**
  9.30. thence, and passed **t.** Galilee
  11.16. carry any vessel **t.** the temple
Lu. **4.30.** passing **t.** the midst ; Jo.**8.59**
  5.19. let him down **t.** the tiling
  17. **1.** woe unto him, **t.** whom they
  11. passed **t.** the midst of Sama.
Jo. **1.** **7.** all men **t.** him might believe
  3.17. the world **t.** him might be
  4. **4.** he must needs go **t.** Samaria
  17.20. believe on me **t.** their word
Act. **1.** **2.** he **t.** the Holy Ghost had gi.
  8.18. **t.** laying on of the apostles'
  10.43. **t.** his name whosoever belie.
  13.38. **t.** this man is preached unto
  14.22. we must **t.** much tribulation
  15.11. **t.** the grace of the Lord Jes.
  18.27. which had believed **t.** grace
  20. **3.** purposed to return **t.** Maced.
  21. **4.** who said to Paul **t.** the Spir.
Ro. **1.** **8.** I thank my God **t.** Jesus Ch.
  2.23. **t.** breaking the law dishono.
  3.24. **t.** the redemption that is in

Ro. **3.25.** **t.** faith in his blood
  30. uncircumcision **t.** faith
  31. make void the law **t.** faith
  4.13. seed, **t.** the law, but **t.** the
  5. **1, 11. t.** our Lord Jesus Christ ;
    7.25 ; **1Co.15.57**
  9. shall be saved from wrath **t.**
  21. **t.** righteousness unto eternal
  8. **3.** that it was weak **t.** the flesh
  37. conquerors **t.** him that loved
  11.36. For of him, and **t.** him, and
  12. **3.** **t.** the grace given unto me
  15. **4.** that we **t.** patience and com.
  16.27. be glory **t.** Jesus Christ for
1Co. **1.** **1. t.** the will of God
  4.15. I have begotten you **t.** the
  10. **1.** all passed **t.** the sea
  13.12. For now we see **t.** a glass
2Co. **3.** **4.** such trust have we **t.** Christ
  4.15. t. the thanksgiving of many
  9.11. causeth **t.** us thanksgiving
  11.33. t. a window in a basket was I
Gal. **2.19.** For I **t.** the law am dead to
  3.14. the promise of the Spirit **t.**
  4. **7.** then an heir of God **t.** Christ
Eph. **1.** **7.** we have redempt. **t.** ; Col.**1.14**
  2. **8.** by grace are ye saved **t.** faith
  18. For **t.** him we both have
  4. **6.** who is above all, and **t.** all
Phi. **1.19.** to my salvation **t.** your pra.
  3. **9.** which is **t.** the faith of Chri.
Col. **1.20.** peace **t.** the blood of his cro.
  22. In the body of his flesh **t.**
  2. **8.** lest any man spoil you **t.** ph.
  12. t. the faith of the operation
2Ti. **1.10.** immortality to light **t.** the
  3.15. t. faith which is in Christ J.
Tit. **3.** **6.** Jesus Christ our Saviour
Phile. **22.** I trust that **t.** your prayers
Heb. **2.10.** their salvation perfect **t.** su.
  14. that **t.** death he might destr.
  6.12. them who **t.** faith and patie.
  9.14. who **t.** the eternal Spirit
  10.10. t. the offering of the body of
  20. consecrated for us, **t.** the veil
  11.33. Who **t.** faith subdued kingd.
  39. obtained a good report **t.** fa.
  13.21. in his sight, **t.** Jesus Christ
1Pet.**1.** **5. t.** faith unto salvation
  22. obeying the truth **t.** the Spi.
  4.11. may be glorified **t.** Jesus Ch.
2Pet.**1.** **3. t.** the knowledge of him
1Jo. **4.** **9.** that we might live **t.** him
  dia, *[accu.]*
Lu. **1.78. t.** the tender mercy of our G.
Jo. **15.** **3.** Now ye are clean **t.** the word
Ro. **2.24.** among the Gentiles **t.** you
Gal. **4.13.** Ye know how **t.** infirmity of
Eph. **4.18. t.** the ignorance that is in
  en.
Mat. **9.34. t.** the prince of the devils
Lu. **10.17.** subject unto us **t.** thy name
  11.15. t. Beelzebub the chief of the
  18. I cast out devils **t.** Beelzebub
Jo. **17.11.** keep **t.** thine own name
  17. sanctify them **t.** thy truth
  19. be sanctified **t.** the truth
  20.31. have life **t.** his name
Act. **4.** **2. t.** Jesus the resurrection
Ro. **1.24. t.** the lusts of their own
  3. **7. t.** my lie unto his glory
  25. t. the forbearance of God
  6.11, 23. t. Jesus Christ our Lord
  15.13. abound in hope, **t.** the power
  17. I may glory **t.** Jesus Christ
  19. t. mighty signs and wonders
2Co.**11.** **3.** beguiled Eve **t.** his subtilty
Gal. **3.14.** on the Gentiles **t.** Jesus Ch.
  5.10. confidence in you **t.** the Lo.
Eph. **2.** **7.** in his kindness toward us **t.**
  22. habitation of God **t.** the Spi.
Phi. **4.** **7.** hearts and minds **t.** Christ

2Th. **2.13. t.** sanctification of ; 1Pet.**1.2**
  16. consolation and good hope **t.**
Tit. **1.** **3.** manifested his word **t.** prea.
Heb.**13.20. t.** the blood of the everlast.
1Pet.**1.** **6.** in heaviness **t.** manifold
2Pet.**1.** **1. t.** the righteousness of God
  2. t. the knowledge of God
  4. that is in the world **t.** lust
  2. **3. t.** covetousness shall they
  18. they allure **t.** the lusts of the
  20. t. the knowledge of the Lord
Rev. **8.13.** flying **t.** the midst of heaven
  kata, *[accu.]*
Lu. **9.** **6.** and went **t.** the towns
  13.22. And he went **t.** the cities
Act. **3.17.** I wot that **t.** ignorance ye
Phi. **2.** **3.** nothing be done **t.** strife
  kata, *[gen.]*
Lu. **4.14. t.** all the region round
  ek.
2Co.**13.** **4.** he was crucified **t.** weakness
Gal. **3.** **8.** justify the heathen **t.** faith
Rev.**18.** **3. t.** the abundance of her
  epi, *[dat.]*
Act. **3.16. t.** faith in his name
1Co. **8.11. t.** thy knowledge shall
  ana.
Mar. **7.31. t.** the midst of the coasts
  (See words in connection.)

THROUGHLY.
  en pas.
2Co.**11.** **6.** have been **t.** made manifest
  (See *Furnish, Purge.*)

THROUGHOUT.
  eis.
Mat. **4.24.** his fame went **t.** all Syria
Mar. **1.28. t.** all the region round about
  39. t. all Galilee, and cast out
  14. **9.** preached **t.** the whole world
Act.**26.20. t.** all the coasts of Judæa
Eph. **3.21. t.** all ages, world without
  kata, *[accu.]*
Lu. **8.** **1.** that he went **t.** *every city*
  39. published **t.** the whole city
Act. **8.** **1. t.** the regions of Judæa
  24. **5.** among all the Jews **t.** the
  kata, *[gen.]*
Lu. **23.** **5.** teaching **t.** all Jewry
Act. **9.31.** the churches rest **t.** all Jud.
  42. it was known **t.** all Joppa
  10.37. was published **t.** all Judæa
  en.
Lu. **1.65. t.** all the hill country of
  7.17. t. all Judæa, and **t.** all the
Ro. **1.** **8.** spoken of **t.** the whole wor.
  9.17. declared **t.** all the earth
  dia, *[gen.]*
Act. **9.32.** Peter passed **t.** all quarters
  13.49. published **t.** all the region
2Co. **8.18.** the gospel **t.** all the churches
  epi, *[accu.]*
Lu. **4.25.** famine was **t.** all the land
Act.**11.28.** dearth **t.** all the world
  dia *[gen.]* **holos.**
Jo. **19.23.** seam, woven from the top **t.**
  (See *Go, Pass.*)

THROW,   *Threw, Thrown.*
  ballō.
Mar.**12.42.** she *t-e* in two mites, which
Act.**22.23.** *as* they.. *t-e* dust into the
Rev.**18.21.** city Babylon be *t-n* down
  kataluō. [Mar.**13.2** ; Lu.**21.6**
Mat.**24.** **2.** that *shall* not be *t-n* down;
  riptō.
Lu. **4.35.** *when* the devil *had t-n* him

THRUST
  ballō.
Jo. **20.25.** and **t.** my hand into his side
  27. t. **t** into my side : and be
              233

Act.16.24. t. them into the inner prison
Rev.14.16. t. *in* his sickle on the earth
　19. the angel t. *in* his sickle
　ekballō.
Lu. 4.29. t. him out of the city, and
　13.28. you yourselves t. out
Act.16.37. do they t. us *out* privily
　epanagō.
Lu. 5. 3. that he *would* t. out a little
　katabibazō.
Lu.10.15. shalt be t. *down* to hell
　apōthomai.
Act. 7.27. neigh. wrong t. him *away*
　39. not obey, but t. him *from*
　exōthō.
Act.27.39. possible, *to* t. *in* the ship
　katatoxeuō.
Heb.12.20. *shall be* ston., or t. *through*
　pempō.
Rev.14.15. t. *in* thy sickle, and reap
　18. t. *in* thy sharp sickle

THUNDER,   -s.
　brontē.
Mar. 3.17. which is, The sons of t.
Rev. 6. 1. as it were the noise of t.
　10. 3, 4. seven t-s uttered their voi.
　14. 2. as the voice of a great t.
　16.18. were voices, and t-s, and

THUNDERED.
　brontē. [(there was *thunder*.)
Jo. 12.29. heard it, said that it t.

THUNDERINGS.
　brontē.
Rev. 4. 5. lightnings and t., and voices
　19. 6. as the voice of mighty t.

THUS.
　houtō.
Mat. 2. 5. for t. it is written by the
　3.15. for t. it becometh us to ful.
　26.54. be fulfilled, that t. it must
Mar. 2. 7. Why doth this man t. speak
Lu. 1.25. t. hath the Lord dealt with
　2.48. why hast thou t. dealt with
　19.31. t. shall ye say unto him
　24.46. t. it is written, and t. it be.
Jo. 4. 6. sat t. on the well: and it
　11.48. If we let him t. alone
Ro. 9.20. Why hast thou made me t.
¹Co.14.25. And t. are the secrets of his
Heb. 6. 9. salvation, though we t. spe.
　9. 6. when these things were t. or.
Rev. 9.17. And t. I saw the horses
　18.21. t. with violence shall that
　houtos.
Lu. 9.34. While he t. spake, there
　11.45. t. saying thou reproachest
　18.11. prayed t. with himself
　19.28. when he had t. spoken; Lu.
　24.40; Jo.9.6,11.43,18.22;
　Act.19.41,20.36,26.30,27.35
　23.46. having said t., he gave up
　24.36. And as they t. spake
Jo. 13.21. When Jesus had t. said
　20.14. And when she had t. said
Act.26.24. And as he t. spake for hims.
¹Co. 1.17. When I therefore was t. mi.
　5.14. because we t. judge
Phi. 3.15. many as be perfect, be t.
Rev.16. 5. because thou hast judged t.
　heōs houtos. [(*these things*.)
Lu. 22.51. and said, Suffer ye t. far
　kata [*accu.*] houtos.
Lu. 17.30. *Even* t. shall it be in the day
　hode.
Act.21.11. t. saith the Holy Ghost

THY. (See *Friends, House.*)
　su.
Mat. 1.20. unto thee Mary t. wife
284

Mat. 4. 6. dash t. foot against a stone
　7. not tempt the Lord t. God
　10. worship the Lord t. God
(*And all other passages in which it oc-*
curs, except the following) :—
　sos.
Mat. 7.22. in t. name? and in t. name
　out devils? and in t. name
　13.27. sow good seed in t. field
　24. 3. shall be the sign of t. coming
Mar. 2.18. but t. disciples fast not
Lu. 6.30. of him that taketh away t.
Jo. 4.42. believe, not because of t. say.
　17.17. thy truth : t. word is truth
Act.24. 2. done unto this nation by t.
　4. hear us of t. clemency a few
¹Co. 8.11. And through t. knowledge
　14.16. at t, giving of thanks, seeing
Phile. 14. But without t. mind would
　seautou. [(*for thyself.*)
Act. 9.34. arise, and make t. bed

THYINE.
　thuinos.
Rev.18.12. t. wood, and all manner

THYSELF.
　seautou *and* sautou.
Mat. 4. 6. cast t. down ; Lu.4.9
　8. 4. shew t. to the priest ; Mar.
　1.44 ; Lu.5.14
　19.19. thy neighbour as t.; 22.39 ;
　Mat.12.31; Lu.10.27; Jas.2.8
　27.40. save t. : Mar.15.30; Lu.23.37
Lu. 4.23. proverb, Physician, heal t.
　23.39. be Christ, save t. and us
Jo. 1.22. What sayest thou of t.
　7. 4. shew t. to the world
　8.13. Thou bearest record of t.
　53. whom makest thou t.
　10.33. a man, makest t. God
　14.22. manifest t. unto us, and not
　21.18. thou girdest t., and walkedst
Act.16.28. Do t. no harm : for we are
　26. 1. permitted to speak for t.
Ro. 2. 1. thou condemnest t.; for
　5. treasurest up unto t. wrath
　19. that *thou* t. art a guide of
　21. teachest thou not t.? thou
　14.22. have it to t. before God
Gal. 6. 1. considering t., lest thou also
¹Ti. 4. 7. exercise t. rather unto godli.
　16. Take heed unto t., and unto
　thou shalt both save t., and
　5.22. men's sins : keep t. pure
²Ti. 2.15. Study to shew t. approved
Tit. 2. 7. In all things shewing t. a
　heautou.
Jo. 18.34. Sayest thou this thing of t.
Ro. 13. 9. love thy neigh. as t.; Gal.5.14

TIDINGS.
　euanggelizō.
Lu. 1.19. to *shew* thee these glad t.
　2.10. I *bring* you *good* t. of great
　8. 1. and *shewing* the glad t.
Act.13.32. we *declare* unto you glad t.
Ro. 10.15. *bring* glad t. of good things
¹Th. 3. 6. and *brought* us *good* t. of your
　logos.
Act.11.22. Then t. of these things came
　phasis.
Act.21.31. t. came unto the chief capt.

TIED.
　deō. [Mar.11.2. ; Lu.19.30
Mat.21. 2. ye shall find an ass t.;
Mar.11. 4. found the colt t. by the door

TILING.
　keramos, [*plu.*]
Lu. 5.19. let him down through the t.

TILL.
　heōs.
Mat. 1.25. t. she had brought forth her
　2. 9. t. it came and stood over
　13.33. t. the whole was leavened
　18.21. forgive him? t. seven times
　30. t. he should pay the debt
　34. t. he should pay all that was
Lu. 1.80. t. the day of his shewing
　12.50. t. it be accomplished
　59. t. thou hast paid the very
　13. 8. t. I shall dig about it, and
　21. t. the whole was leavened
　15. 8. and seek diligently t. she find
　17. 8. t. I have eaten and drunken
　19.13. unto them, Occupy t. I come
Jo. 13.38. t. thou hast denied me thrice
　21.22. if I will that he tarry t. I co.
　23. tarry t. I come, what is that
Act. 8.40. t. he came to Cæsarea
　21. 5. t. we were out of the city
　23.12. t. they had killed Paul
　21. t. they have killed him
　25.21. t. I might send him to Cæs.
　28.23. from morning t. evening
¹Ti. 4.13. t. I come, give attendance
Heb.10.13. t. his enemies be made
　heōs an.
Mat. 5.18. t. heaven and earth pass
　the law, t. all be fulfilled
　26. t. thou hast paid the utterm.
　10.11. and there abide t. ye go he.
　23. t. the Son of man be come
　12.20. t. he send forth judgment
　16.28. t. they see the Son of man
　22.44. t. I make thine enemies;
　Mar.12.36 ; Lu.20.43
　23.39. henceforth, t. ye shall say
　24.34. t. all these things ; Lu.21.32
Mar. 6.10. there abide t. ye depart from
　9. 1. t. they have seen the kingd.
Lu. 9.27. t. they see the kingdom
　achri *and* achris.
Act. 7.18. t. another king arose, which
　20.11. even t. break of day, so he
Gal. 3.19. t. the seed should come to
Rev. 7. 3. t. we have sealed the servan.
　15. 8. t. the seven plagues of the
　20. 3. t. the thousand years should
　achris hos an.
¹Co.11.26. the Lord's death t. he come
　15.25. t. he hath put all enemies
Rev. 2.15. hold fast t. I come
　mechri.
Mar.13.30. t. all these things be done
Eph. 4.13. t. we all come in the unity
　ei mē hotan.
Mar. 9. 9. t.the S. of man(*except when.*)
　eis.
Phi. 1.10. offence t. the day of Christ

TIME,   -s.
　kairos.
Mat. 8.29. to torment us before the t.
　11.25. At that t. Jesus answered
　12. 1. At that t. Jesus went on the
　13.30. and in the t. of harvest
　14. 1. At that t. Herod the tetrarch
　16. 3. discern the signs of the t-s
　21.34. when the t. of the fruit
　26.18. My t. is at hand ; I will keep
Mar. 1.15. The t. is fulfilled, and the
　10.30. now in this t., houses, and
　11.13. for the t. of figs was not
　13.33. ye know not when the t. is
Lu. 8.13. for a while believe, and in t
　12.56. that ye do not discern this t.
　18.30. mani. more in this present t.
　19.44. the t. of thy visitation
　21. 8. and the t. draweth near
　24. until the t-s of the Gentiles

Jo. 7. 6, 8. My t. is not yet come: but
your t. is alway ready
Act. 3.19. when the t-s of refreshing
7.20. In which t. Moses was born
12. 1. about that t. Herod the king
17.26. hath determined the t-s
19.23. And the same t. there arose
Ro. 3.26. To declare, I say, at this t.
8.18. the sufferings of this pres. t.
9. 9. At this t. will I come, and
11. 5. at this present t. also there
13.11. And that, knowing the t.
1Co. 4. 5. judge nothing before the t.
7. 5. with consent for a t., that
29. the t. is short: it remaineth
2Co. 6. 2. heard thee in a t. accepted
now is the accepted t.
8.14. now at this t. your abundan.
Gal. 4.10. months, and t-s, and years
Eph. 1.10. dispensation of the ful. of t-s
2.12. at that t. ye were without C.
5.16. Redeeming the t.; Col.4.5
1Th. 2.17. from you for a short t. in
2Th. 2. 6. might be revealed in his t.
1Ti. 2. 6. to be testified in due t.
4. 1. that in the latter t-s some
6.15. Which in his t-s he shall
2Ti. 3. 1. days perilous t-s shall come
4. 3. For the t. will come when
6. the t. of my departure is at
Tit. 1. 3. But hath in due t-s manifest.
Heb. 9. 9. a figure for the t. then prese.
10. until the t. of reformation
1Pet. 1. 5. to be revealed in the last t.
11. or what manner of t. the Sp.
4.17. For the t. is come that judg.
5. 6. he may exalt you in due t.
Rev. 1. 3. for the t. is at hand; 22.10
11.18. is come, and the t. of the
12.12. that he hath but a short t.
14. a t., and t-s, and half a t.
kata [accu.] kairos.
Ro. 5. 6. in due t. Christ died for
chronos.
Mat. 2. 7. of them diligently what t.
16. according to the t. which he
25.19. After a long t. the lord of
Lu. 1.57. Now Elisabeth's full t. came
4. 5. in a moment of t.
8.27. which had devils long t.
20. 9. in. a far country for a long t.
Jo. 5. 6. he had been now a long t.
14. 9. Have I been so long t. with
Act. 1. 6. wilt thou at this t. restore
7. to know the t-s or the seaso.
21. companied with us all the t.
3.21. until the t-s of restitution
7.17. t. of the promise drew nigh
8.11. long t. he had bewitched th.
13.18. about the t. of forty years
14. 3, 28.Long t. theref. abode they
17.30. the t-s of this ignorance God
18.20. to tarry longer t. with them
23. he had spent some t. there
27. 9. Now when much t. was spe.
Gal. 4. 4. the fulness of the t. was co.
1Th. 5. 1. But of the t-s and the seaso.
Heb. 4. 7. To day, after so long a t.
5.12. when for the t. ye ought to
11.32. for the t. would fail me to
1Pet. 1.17. pass the t. of your sojourning
20. manifest in these last t-s for
4. 2. live the rest of his t. in
3. For the t. past of our life m.
Jude 18. be mockers in the last t.
Rev.10. 6. there should be t. no longer
hōra.
Mat.14.15. the t. is now past; Mar.6.35
18. 1. At the same t. came the dis.
Lu. 1.10. without at the t. of incense
14.17. sent his servant at supper t.
16. 2. the t. cometh, that whosoev.

Lu. 16. 4. that when the t. shall come
25. the t. cometh, when I shall
Ro. 13.11. it is high t. to awake
1Jo. 2.18. it is the last t.
Rev.14.15. the t. is come for thee to re.
hēmera.
Lu. 9.51. when the t. was come that
21.37. in the day t.he was teaching
23. 7. was at Jerusalem at that t.
Act. 8. 1. at that t. there was a great
pote.
Ro. 11.30. For as ye in t-s past have no
1Co. 9. 7. Who goeth a warfare any t.
Gal. 1.13. of my conversation in t. past
23. wh. persecuted us in t-s past
Eph. 2. 2. Wherein in t. past ye walked
3. in t-s past in the lusts of our
11. that ye being in t. past Gen.
1Th. 2. 5. neither at any t. used we
Phile. 11. Which in t. past was to thee
Heb. 1. 5, 13. angels said he at any t.
2. 1. lest at any t. we should let
1Pet. 2.10. Which in t. past were not a
3. 5. aft. this manner in the old t.
2Pet. 1.21. prophecy came not in old t.
tote.
Mat. 4.17. From that t. Jesus began to
16.21. From that t. forth began Je.
26.16. And from that t. he sought
Lu. 16.16. since that t. the kingdom of
genea.
Act.14.16. Who in t-s past suffered all
15.21. For Moses of old t. hath in
pōpote.
Jo. 1.18. hath seen God at any t.; [1Jo.4.12
5.37. heard his voice at any t.
ekpalai.
2Pet. 2. 3. judgment now of a long t.
ēdē.
Jo. 11.39. by this t. he stinketh
(See words in connection.)

TINKLING.
alalazō.
1Co.13. 1. sounding brass, or a t. cym.

TIP.
akron.
Lu. 16.24. dip the t. of his finger

TITHE, -s.
apodekatoō.
Mat.23.23. for ye pay t. of mint and
Lu. 18.12. I give t-s of all that I possess
Heb. 7. 5. to take t-s of the people
dekatoō.
Heb. 7. 6. received t-s of Abraham, and
9. receiveth tithes, payed t-s
dekatē.
Heb. 7. 8. here men that die, receive t-s
9. Levi also, who receiveth t-s

TITHE, [verb.]
apodekatoō.
Lu. 11.42. ye t. mint and rue, and all

TITLE.
titlos.
Jo. 19.19. Pilate wrote a t., and put
20. This t. then read many

TITTLE.
keraia.
Mat. 5.18. one jot or one t. shall in no
Lu. 16.17. than one t. of the law

TO.
(Besides representing the Infinitive of
the verb, and Dative of the noun, to is
used to translate the following:)—
eis.
Mat. 2. 1. wise men from the east t. J.
8. he sent them t. Bethlehem
7.13. the way, that leadeth t. des.

Mat.8.34. the whole city came out t.
9. 7. departed t. his; Lu.1.23,5.25
13. but sinners t. repentance;
Mar.2.17; Lu.5.32
10.17. you up t. the cou.; Mar.13.9
21. up the brother t.; Mar.13.12
22. he that endureth t. the end
14.19. up t. heaven, he blessed;
Mar.6.41; Lu.9.16
16. 5. t. the other side; Mar.6.45
17.24. were come t. Cap.;Mar.9.33
27. go thou t. the sea, and cast
20.17,18.up t. Jerus.; Mar.10.32,33;
Jo.2.13,5.1,11.55; Act.15.2,21.4,
12,15,25.9; Gal.1.17,18,2.1
21. 1. were come t. Beth.; Lu.19.29
22. 3. that were bidden t. the
5. one t. his farm, another t.
9. as ye shall find, bid t. the
23.34. persecute them from city t.
24. 9. deliver you up t. be afflicted
25. 1. went forth t. meet the bride.
6. forth t. meet (for meeting.)
10. went in with him t. the ma.
26. 2. Son of man is betrayed t. be
8. t. what purpose is this waste
27. 7. the potter's field, t. bury
Mar. 5.19. Go home t. thy friends, and
38. he cometh t. the house of
7.30. when she was come t. her
34. looking up t. heaven, he
8. 3. away fasting t. their own
22. he cometh t. Bethsaida; and
26. t. his house, saying, Neither
10.46. they came t. Jericho: and
11. 1, 15, 27. they came nigh t.
13.14. in Judea flee t.; Lu.21.21
14. 8. to anoint my body t. the.
32. they came t. a place which
Lu. 1.23, 56. returned t. her own
50. from generation t. generati.
(to generations of genera.)
2.22. brought him t. Jer.; Lu.4.9
39. Galilee, t. their own city
41. his parents went t. Jerus.
45. they turned back again t.
51. with them, and came t. Jer.
4.16. he came t. Nazareth, where
31. came down t.; Jo.2.12, 6.24
5.17. present t. heal (for healing.)
7.10. returning t. the house, fou.
8.39. Return t. thine own house
9.51, 53.go t. Jer.; 17.11; Act.19.21
56. they went t. another village
10. 7. Go not from house t. house
30. down from Jerusalem t. Jer.
34. brought him t. an inn
14. 8. bidden of any man t. a wed.
31. t. make war (to enter on war)
15.17. when he came t. himself
16.27. send him t. my father's hou.
18.14. this man went down t. his
21.12. t. the synagogues, and into
22.39. t. the mount of Olives
24. 5. down their faces t. the earth
13. went that same day t. a
20. delivered him t. be condem.
33, 52. returned t. Jerusalem;
Act.8.25,13.13
50. led them out as far as t. Bet.
Jo. 2. 2. and his disciples, t. the
3.13. no man hath ascended up t.
4. 5. Then cometh he t. a city of
8.26. I speak t. the world those
9.11. Go. t. the pool of Siloam
11.38. himself cometh t. the grave
56. that he will not come t. the
12. 1. before the passover came t.
12. people that were come t. the
that Jesus was coming t.
13. t. meet him (for meeting.)

Jo. 16.32. scattered, every man t. his
17. 1. lifted up his eyes t. heaven
18.37. t. this end was I born, and
20. 3. other disciple, and came t.
  4, 8. came first t. the sepulchre
21. 9. then as they were come t.
Act. 1.25. he might go t. his own place
4.30. forth thine hand t. heal
5.21. sent t. the prison t. have
36. scattered, and brought t. no.
6.12. brought him t. the council
8. 3. committed them t. prison
5. Philip went down t. the city
27. come t. Jerusalem for to wo.
'40. till he came t. Cæsarea
9. 2. letters t. Dam.; 26. t. Jeru.
30. t. Cæsarea, and sent him t.
10. 5. now send men t.; 11.13
8. unto them, he sent them t.
32. Send therefore t. Joppa
11. 2. t. Jer.; 11. t.Jop.; 20.t.Anti.
25. Then departed Barnabas t.
12.19. went down from Judea t.
13. 4. thence they sailed t. Cyprus
13. they came t. Perga in Pam.
14. they came t. Antioch ; 15.30
22. unto them David t. be their
31. with him from Galilee t. Je.
34. no more to return t. corrup.
46. lo, we turn t. the Gentiles
47. I have set thee t. be a light
48. as were ordained t. eternal
14.20. he departed with Barnab. t.
21. they returned again t. Lyst.
24. they came t. Pamphylia
26. thence sailed t. Antioch
15. 4. when they were come t. Jer.
22. of their own company t. An.
38. went not with them t. the
16. 1. t. Derbe ; 8. t. Troas
11. straight course t. Samoth.
and the next day t. Neapol.
12. from thence t. Philippi
16. came to pass, as we went t.
17. 1. they came t. Thessalonica
5. to bring them out t. the
20. certain strange things t. our
18. 1. from Athens, and came t.
19, 24. he came t. Eph.; 19.1
22. he went down t. Antioch
19. 1. upper coasts came t. Ephes.
27. t. be set at nought
20. 6. came unto them t. Troas
14. came t. Mitylene ; 15.t.Milet.
17. from Miletus he sent t.
21. 7. t. Ptolemais ; 17. t. Jerusa.
22. 5. t. Damascus ; 17. t. Jerusa.
23.31. t.Antipatris ; 32. t. the castle
33. when they came t. Cæsarea
24.17. to bring alms t. my nation
25. 1. ascended from Cæsarea t.
3. send for him t. Jerusalem
6. deliver any man t. die
20. whether he would go t. Jer.
26.12. as I went t. Damascus with
14. we were all fallen t. the
18. turn them from darkness t.
27. 5. we came t. Myra, a city of
12. they might attain t. Phenice
28. 6. saw no harm come t. him
13. a compass, and came t.
we came the next day t.
15. ca. t. meet us (for meeting.)
16. when we came t. Rome
Ro. 1.17. revealed from faith t. faith
24. gave them up t. uncleanness
28. over t. a reprobate mind
2. 4. God leadeth thee t. repent.
3.25. t. declare his righteousness
5.16. was by one t. condemnation
18. upon all men t. condemna
6.16. servants t. obey, his servants

Ro. 7. 4. should be married t. anoth.
5. t. bring forth fruit unto
10. which was ordained t. life
8.15. spirit of bondage again t.
9.22. of wrath fitted t. destruct.
31. t. the law of righteousness
11.36. through him, and t. him
12. 3. t. think soberly (unto sobrie.)
10. kindly affectioned one t.
13. 4. a revenger t. execute wrath
14. for the flesh t. fulfil the lusts
14. 1. not t. doubtful disputations
15. 7. received us t. the glory of
8. t. confirm the promises
16. of Jesus Christ t. the Gent.
18. t. make the Gentiles obed.
1Co. 4. 6. transferred t. myself and to
8.10. t. eat those things which
10.31. do all t. the glory of God
11.22. houses t. eat and to drink
33. when ye come together t. eat
14. 8. prepare himself t. the battle
16.15. t. the ministry of the saints
2Co. 2.12. when I came t. Troas to
3.13. t. the end of that which is
18. same image from glory t.
4.15. redound t. the glory of God
7. 3. t. die and live with you
9. that ye sorrowed t. repent.
10. worketh repentance t. salv.
8. 4. the ministering t. the; 9.1
24. t. them, and before the
9. 8. may abound t. every good
11. every thing t. all bountiful.
10. 5. t. the obedience of Christ
12. 1. I will come t. visions and
13. 3. which t. you-ward is and
10. t. edification, and not t. des.
Gal. 2. 8. in Peter t. the apostleship
11. when Peter was come t. An.
4.24. which gendereth t. bondage
6. 8. he that soweth t. his flesh
he that soweth t. the Spirit
Eph. 1. 5. the adoption of children..t.
6. t. the praise of the glory of
12. should be t. the praise of
19. great. of his power t. us-ward
3. 2. wh. is given me t. you-ward
4.19. t. work all uncleanness
32. be ye kind one t. another
Phi. 1.19. this shall turn t. my salva.
23. having a desire t. depart
2.11. t. the glory of God the Fa.
4.17. that may abound t. your
Col. 1. 4. love which ye have t. all
12. t. be partakers (for partaki.)
2. 2. t. the acknowledgment of
3. 9. Lie not one t. another, see.
15. t. the which also ye are
1Th. 2.16. t. fill up their sins
come upon them t. the utte.
3. 2. t. establish you, and to com.
5. I sent t. know your faith
4. 9. taught of God t. love one
17. t. meet the Lord in the air
5. 9. appointed us t. wrath, but
15. both among your. and t.
2Th. 2.13. chosen you t. salvation thr.
14. t. the obtaining of the glory
3. 9. an ensample unto you t.
1Ti. 1.16. believe on him t. life everla.
4. 3. created t. be received with
5.24. going before t. judgment
6.17. giveth us richly all things t.
2Ti. 2.14. strive not about words t. no
20. t. honour, and some t. dish.
25. t. the acknowledging of the
3. 7. never able to come t. the
4.10. Crescens t. Galatia, Titus
12. Tychicus have I sent t. Eph.
Tit. 3.12. to come unto me t. Nicop.
Heb. 1.14. sent forth t. minister

Heb. 2.17. t. make reconciliation
4.16. grace t. help in time of need
6. 8. end is t. be burned
7.25. to save them t. the uttermo.
t. make intercession for them
8. 3. high priest is ordained t.
9.14. t. serve the living God
26. t. put away sin
28. offered t. bear the sins of
10.19. boldness t. enter into the
24. t. provoke unto love and
39. believe t. the saving of the
11. 7. an ark t. the saving of his
11. received strength t. conceive
13.21. every good work t. do his
Jas. 1.19. t. hear, slow t. speak, slow t.
4. 9. t. mourning, joy t. heaviness
1Pet. 1. 4. t. an inheritance incorrupt.
4. 4. run not with them t. the
9. Use hospitality one t. ano.
10. minister the same one t. an.
2Pet. 2.12. made t. be taken and dest.
22. t. her wallowing in the mire
3. 9. is longsuffering t. us-ward
that all should come t. rep.
3John 5. doest t. the brethren, and t.
Jude 4. ordained t.this condemnation
Rev. 9. 6. of many horses running t.
10. 5. lifted up his hand t. heaven
11. 6. over waters to turn them t.
12. they ascended up t. heaven
12. 4. did cast them t. the earth
13. 3. as it were wounded t. death
16.14. t. the battle of that great
20. 8. gather them together t. bat.
pros, [accu.]
Mat. 2.12. they should not return t. He.
3. 5. Then went out t. him Jerus.
14. and comest thou t. me
5.28. on a woman t. lust after her
6. 1. t. be seen of them : otherwise
7.15. which come t. you in sheep's
10. 6. But go rather t. the lost she.
13. let your peace return t. you
13.30. bind them in bundles t. burn
14.29. on the water, to go t. Jesus
17.14. they were come t. the multi.
21.34. t. the husbandm. ; Mar.12.2
25. 9. but go ye rather t. them that
26.18. Go into the city t. such a man
45. Then cometh he t. his disci.
57. led him away t. Caiaphas
27. 4. What is that t. us
14. he answered him t. never a
Mar. 1.40. And there came a leper t.
45. and they came t. him from
3. 7. with his disciples t. the sea
4.41. and said one t. another
5.15. And they come t. Jesus
19. Go home t. thy friends
9.14. when he came t. his disciples
10. 7. and cleave t. his wife
50. and came t. Je.; Lu.7.4,8.35
11. 7. And they brought the colt t.
27. there come t. him the chief
13.22. t. seduce, if it were possible
14.53. Jesus away t. the high priest
Lu. 1.27. t. a virgin espoused to a man
43. of my Lord should come t.
55. As he spake t. our fathers
73. which he sware t. our father
2.15. the shepherds said one t. an.
6.47. Whosoever cometh t. me
7. 6. the centurion sent friends t.
19. sent them t. Jesus, saying
44. he turned t. the woman
50. And he said t. the woman
8. 4. and were come t. him out of
19. Then came t. him his moth.
25. saying one t. another ; Lu.
24.32 ; Act.2.7,12
9.14. he said t. his disciples

La. 9.23. And he said t them all, If
11. 6. in his journey is come t. me
12.41. parable unto us, or even t. all
 8. lest he hale thee t. the judge
14. 6. answer him again t. these
 7. a parable t. those which were
26. If any man come t. me, and
15.13. I will arise and go t. my fath.
20. and came t. his father
22. But the father said t. his se.
16.26. pass from thence t. you can.
  neither can they pass t. us
19.35. they brou. him t. J.; Jo.1.42
20. 9. began he to speak t. the peo.
10. sent a servant t. the husban.
21.38. came early in the morning t.
22.45. and was come t. his disciples
23. 4. said Pilate t. the chief pries.
 7. he sent him t. Herod, who
15. for I sent you t. him ; and
24.17. that ye have one t. another
Jo. 1.47. saw Nathanael coming t. him
 3. 2. The same came t. Jesus by
20, 21. cometh t. the light
26. and all men come t. him
 4.33. the disciples one t. another
35. are white already t. harvest
 5.40. And ye will not come t. me
45. I will accuse you t. the Fath.
 6.17. Jesus was not come t. them
35. he that cometh t. me shall
37. shall come t. me ; and him
  that cometh t. me I will
44. No man can come t. me, exc.
68. t. whom shall we go
 7.45. Then came the officers t. the
50. he that came t. Jesus ; 19.39
 8.31. Then said Jesus t. those Je.
 9.13. They brought t. the Pharise.
11.19. many of the Jews came t.
45. which came t. Mary, and had
46. went their ways t. the Phar.
13. 3. from God, and went t. God
 6. Then cometh he t. Simon Pe.
14.18. I will come t. you ; Ro.15.24
16. 5. I go my way t. him that sent
10, 16, 17, 28. I go t...Father
17.11, 13. and I come t. thee
18.13. And led him away t. Annas
20. 2. t. Simon Peter, and t. the
17. I am not yet ascended t. my
  Father ; but go t. my brethr.
21.22, 23. what is that t. thee
Act. 4.23. they went t. their own com.
24. lifted up their voice t. God
 8.24. Pray ye t. the Lord for me
 9. 2. letters to Damascus t. the
10. t. him said the Lord in a vi.
27. and brought him t. the apos.
32. came down also t. the saints
40. and turning him t. the body
10. 3. coming in t. him
13. And there came a voice t. him
21. Peter went down t. the men
33. therefore I sent t. thee
11. 3. Thou wentest in to men unci.
30. and sent it t. the elders
12.20. they came with one accord t.
14.11. The gods are come down t.
16.36. told this saying t. Paul
17.15. Timotheus for to come t. him
20.18. when they were come t. him
23.18. and brought him t. the chief
22. hast shewed these things t.
30. I sent straightway t. thee
25.16. t. whom I answered
21. till I might send him t. Cæs.
26. 9. contrary t. the name of Jesus
27.12. was not commodious t. wint.
28. 8. t. whom Paul entered in
23. there came many t. him
Ro. 3.26. t. declare, I say, at this time

Ro. 8.31. What shall we then say t.
10. 1. and prayer t. God for Israel
21. But t. Israel he saith
15. 2. for his good t. edification
22. hindered from coming t. you
30. in your prayers t. God for
1Co. 2. 1. when I came t. you, came
 4.18. though I would not come t.
19. But I will come t. you shortly
 6. 5. I speak t. your shame ; 15.34
12. 7. to every man t. profit withal
13.12. but then face t. face
14.12. t. the edifying of the church
2Co. 1.12. and more abund. t. you-ward
 2. 1. not come again t. you in he.
 3. 1. epistles of commendation t.
 4. we through Chr. t. God-ward
16. when it shall turn t. the Lo.
 4. 2. commending ourselves t. ev.
 6. t. give the light of the kno.
 5.10. according t. that he hath do.
12. somewhat t. answer them
 7. 3. I speak not this t. condemn
 8.19. administered by us t. the gl.
10. 4. mighty through God t. the
11. 8. then, t. do you service
12.14. I am ready to come t. you
13. 1. time I am coming t. you
 7. I pray t. God that ye do no
Gal. 1.17. t. them which were apostles
Eph. 4.29. good t. the use of edifying
Phi. 1.26. by my coming t. you again
 2.25. supposed necessary to send t.
Col. 2.23. t. the satisfying of the flesh
1Th. 1. 8. your faith t. God-ward
 9. turned t. God from idols
Tit. 3. 1. to be ready t. every good wo.
Heb. 1.13. But t. which of the angels
 2.17. in things pertai. t. God ; 5.1
 5.14. exercised t. discern both go.
 6.11. diligence t. the full assurance
 9.13. sanctifieth t. the purifying of
Jas. 4. 5. in us lusteth t. envy
1Pet. 2. 4. t. whom coming, as unto
 3.15. ready always t. give an ans.
2John 12. speak face t. face ; 3John 14
Rev. 3.20. I will come in t. him, and
hina.
Mat.26.16. opportunity t. betray him
27.26. delivered him t. be crucified
32. compelled t. bear his cross
Mar. 4.21. t. be put under a bushel
 t. be set on a candlestick
 6.41. to his disciples t. set be.; 8.6
 7.32. beseech him t. put his hand
 8.22. and besought him t. touch
 9.22. and into the waters, t. dest.
11.28. gave thee this authority t. do
12.13. t. catch him in his words
13.34. and commanded the porter t.
14.10. t. betray him ; Jo.13.2
15.15. t. be crucified ; Jo.19.16
20. led him out t. crucify him
21. and Rufus t. bear his cross
Lu. 6.34. lend to sinners, t. receive as
 9.40. I besought thy disciples t.
19. 4. into a sycomore tree t. see
Jo. 1. 7, 8. t. bear witness of the Lig.
19. from Jerusalem t. ask him
27. I am not worthy t. unloose
 3.17. into the world t. condemn
 4. 8. unto the city t. buy meat
34. My meat is t. do the will of
 5. 7. t. put me into the pool
36. given me t. finish, the same
 6.15. t. make him a king
38. not t. do mine own will
 7.32. priests sent officers t. take
 8.56. rejoiced t. see my day
59. took they up stones t. cast
10.31. stones again t. stone him
11.19. t. comfort them concerning

Jo. 11.31. unto the grave t. weep
53. for t. put him to death
55. the passover t. purify them.
12.20. that came up t. worship at
47. for I came not t. judge the
  but t. save the world
17. 4. thou gavest me t. do
Act.16.30. Sirs, what must I do t. be
36. magistrates have sent t. let
27.42. counsel was t. kill the priso.
1Co. 1.27. t. confound the wise
  t. confound the things which
28. t. bring to nought things th.
 9.25. they do it t. obtain a corru.
13. 3. though I give my body t. be
16.12. I greatly desired him t. come
  his will was not at all t. co.
2Co. 12. 7. the messenger of Satan t.
Gal. 4. 5. t. redeem them that were
Phi. 2.30. t. supply your lack of service
2Th. 3. 9. but t. make ourselves an en.
1Jo. 1. 9. faithful and just t. forgive
 3. 5. was manifested t. take away
3John 4. than t. hear that my children
Rev. 2.21. space t. repent of her
 3. 9. I will make them t. come
 6. 2. conquering, and t. conquer
 8. 6. prepared themselves t. soun.
13.12. t. worship the first beast
16. t. receive a mark in their
21.15. t. measure the city, and the
23. of the moon, t. shine in it
epi, [accus.]
Mat. 3. 7. Sadducees come t. his bapti
13. cometh Jesus from Galilee t.
 5.23. bring thy gift t. the altar
13.48. they drew t. shore, and sat
21.19. he came t. it ; Mar.11.13
Lu. 1.16. shall he turn t. the Lord th.
17. hearts of the fathers t. the
 5.11. had brought their ships t.
 8.27. when he went forth t. land
 9.62. put his hand t. the plough
10. 6. it shall turn t. you again
12.25. can add t. his stature one
58. thine adversary t. the magis.
17. 4. turn again t. thee, saying
19. 5. when Jesus came t. the place
22.44. falling down t. the ground
52. which were come t. him
23.33. when they were come t. the
48. came together t. that sight
24.24. with us went t. the sepulch.
Jo. 19.33. when they came t. Jesus
Act. 8.32. as a sheep t. the slaughter
 9. 4. he fell t. the earth
35. turned t. the Lord
12.12. he came t. the house of Ma.
15.19. are turned t. God
17.14. to go as it were t. the sea
18.12. brought him t. the judgment
20.13. we went before t. ship
26.20. should repent and turn t. G.
27.43. into the sea, and get t. land
44. they escaped all safe t. land
Gal. 4. 9. turn ye again t. the weak
Jas. 2. 3. ye have respect t. him that
2Pet. 2.22. turned t. his own vomit aga.
Rev.21.10. t. a great and high mountain
22.14. may have right t. the tree of
epi, [gen.]
Mat. 28.14. if this come t. the governor's
Jo. 21.11. drew the net t. land full
Act.10.11. and let down t. the earth
epi, [dat.]
2Ti. 2.14. t. the subverting of the
en.
Lu. 1.17. disobedient t. the wisdom of
Jo. 13.35. if ye have love one t. anoth.
Act.12.11. when Peter was come t. him
24.11. since I went up t. Jerusalem
1Co. 7.15. God hath called us t. peace

²Co. 4. 3. it is hid t. them that are lost
    8. 7. in your love t. us, see that
Col. 1.23. was preached t. every creat.
¹Ti. 4.15. give thyself wholly t. them
¹Th. 4.15. thy profiting may appear t.
²Pet. 1. 5. t. your faith virtue ; and t.
    6. t. knowledge temperance
      t. tempera. patience ; and t.
    7. t. godliness brotherly kind.
      and t. brotherly kindness ch.
¹Jo. 4.16. the love that God hath t. us

heōs.

Mat. 1.17. from Abraham t. David, &c.
    11.23. be brou. down t. ; Lu.10.15
    24.21. beginning of the world t.this
    31. one end of heaven t. the ot.
    27.51. from the top t. ; Mar.15.38
Mar.13.27.t. the uttermost part of hea.
Lu. 10.15. art exalted t. heaven, shalt
    23. 5. beginning from Galilee t.this
Jo. 2. 7. they filled them up t. the br.
Act. 8.10. from the least t. the greatest
    9.38. not delay to come t. them
    23.23. soldiers to go t. Cesarea
²Co. 1.13. acknowledge even t. the end
    12. 2. caught up t.the third heaven
Heb. 8.11. from the least t. the greatest

kata, [accu.]

Act.16. 7. they were come t. Mysia
    20.20. from house t. ho. (by houses)
    25.16. face t. face, and have
Ro. 14.22. have it t. thyself before
²Co. 8. 3. For t. their power
Gal. 2.11. I withstood him t. the face

hopōs.

Mat.26.59.Jesus, t. put him to death
Act. 9.24. day and night t. kill him
    23.15. soldiers t. go to Cæsarea

hōste.

Mat.10. 1. spirits t. cast them out
    27. 1. t. put him to death
Lu. 9.52. t. make ready for him

meta, [gen.]

Lu. 1.72. the mercy promised t. our

enōpion.

Lu. 24.11. their words seemed t. them

mechri.

Ro. 5.14. reigned from Adam t. Moses

huper, [accu.]

²Co. 12.13. inferior t. other churches

dia. [gen.]

²Pet. 1. 3. called us t. glory and

TO-DAY.   (See Appendix.)

TOGETHER.

epi [accu.] ho autos.

Mat.22.34.silence, they were gather. t.
Lu. 17.35. women shall be grinding t.
Act. 1.15. the number of the names t.
    2.44. all that believed were t.
    3. 1. Peter and John went up t.
    4.26. the rulers were gathered t.
¹Co. 7. 5. and come t. again that Satan

meta [gen.] allēlōn.

Lu. 23.12. Herod were made friends t.

pros [accu.] allēlōn.

Lu. 24.14. they talked t. of all these

allēlōn.

¹Th. 5.11. Wheref. comfort yourselves t.

hama.

Ro. 3.12. they are t. become unprofit.
¹Th. 4.17. shall be caught up t. with
    5.10. we should live t. with him

homou.

Jo. 4.36. that reapeth may rejoice t.
    20. 4. so they ran both t.
    21. 2. There were t. Simon Peter

kata, [accu.]

Act.14. 1. they went both t. into the
    (See words in connection.)

288

TOIL,   -ed, -ing.

kopiaō.   [Lu.12.27

Mat. 6.28. they t. not, neither do they ;
Lu. 5. 5. we have t-ed all the night

basanizō.

Mar. 6.48. he saw them t-ing in rowing

TOKEN.   (See Evident.)

sussēmon.

Mar.14.44.had given them a t., saying

endeigma.

²Th. 1. 5. a manifest t. of the righteous

sēmeion.

²Th. 3.17. which is the t. in every

TOLERABLE.

anektoteros.

Mat.10.15. It shall be more t.; 11.22,24;
      Mar.6.11 ; Lu.10.12,14

TOMB,   -s.

mnēmeion.

Mat. 8.28. coming out of the t-s, excee.
    27.60. laid it in his own new t.
Mar. 5. 2. there met him out of the t-s
    3. his dwelling among the t-s
    6.29. his corpse, and laid it in a t.

mnēma.

Mar. 5. 5. and in the t-s, crying and
Lu. 8.27. in any house, but in the t-s

taphos.

Mat.23.29. ye build the t-s of the prop.

TONGUE,   -s.

glōssa.

Mar. 7.33. he spit, and touched his t.
    35. the string of his t.was loosed
    16.17. they shall speak with new t-s
Lu. 1.64. his t. loosed, and he spake
    16.24. fin. in water, and cool my t.
Act. 2. 3. appe. unto them cloven t-s
    4. began to speak with other t-s
    11. hear them speak in our t-s
    26. heart rejoice, and my t. was
    10.46. heard them speak with t-s
    19. 6. they spake with t-s, and pr.
Ro. 3.13. with their t-s they have used
    14.11. every t. shall confess to God
¹Co. 12.10. divers kinds of t-s ; to anot.
      the interpretation of t-s
    28. governme., diversities of t-s
    30. do all speak with t-s ? do all
    13. 1. I speak with the t-s of men
    8. whether there be t-s, they
    14. 2, 4, in an unknown t. ; 13,27
    5. that ye all spake with t-s
      th. he that speaketh with t-s
    6. unto you speaking with t-s
    9. except ye utter by the t. wo.
    14. if I pray in an unknown t.
    18. I speak with t-s more than
    19. words in an unknown t.
    22. Wherefore t-s are for a sign
    23. all speak with t-s, and there
    26. hath a doctrine, hath a t.
    39. forbid not to speak with t-s
Phi. 2.11. that every t. should confess
Jas. 1.26. bridleth not his t., but
    3. 5. so the t. is a little member
    6. the t. is a fire, a world of in.
      so is the t. among our mem.
    8. the t. can no man tame
¹Pet. 3.10. let him refrain his t. from
¹Jo. 3.18. love in word, neither in t.
Rev. 5. 9. every kindred, and t.; 14.6
    7. 9. kindreds, and people, and t-s
    10.11. peoples, and nations, and t-s
    11. 9. kindreds and t-s and ; 13.7
    16.10. they gnawed their t-s for pa.
    17.15. multit., and nations, and t-s

heteroglōssos.

¹Co. 14.21. With men of other t-s and

dialektos.

Act. 1.19. called in their proper t.

Act. 2. 8. we every man in our own t.
    21.40. in the Hebrew t.; 22.2, 26.14
hebraisti.   [16.16
Jo. 5. 2. in the Hebrew t.; Rev. 9.11,

TOOTH, (See Cast,)   Teeth.

odous.

Mat. 5.38. for an eye, and a t. for a t.
    8.12. weeping and gnashing of te.;
      22.13,24.51,25.30; Lu.13.28
    13.42, 50. wail. and gnashing of te.
Mar. 9.18. and gnasheth with his te.
Act. 7.54. gnashed on him with their te.
Rev. 9. 8. their te. were as the teeth of

TOP.

anōthen.   [Mar.15.38

Mat.27.51. from the t. to the bottom ;
Jo. 19.23. woven from the t. througho.

akron.

Heb.11.21. leaning upon the t. of his

TOPAZ.

topazion.

Rev.21.20. the ninth, a t.; the tenth

TORCHES.

lampas.

Jo. 18. 3. with lanterns and t. and

TORMENT, [noun,]   -s.

basanismos.

Rev. 9. 5. their t. was as the t. of
    14.11. the smoke of their t. ascen.
    18. 7. so much t. and sorrow give
    10, 15. for the fear of her t.

basanos.

Mat. 4.24. with divers diseases and t-s
Lu. 16.23. lift up his eyes being in t-s
    28. come into this place of t.

kolasis.

¹Jo. 4.18. because fear hath t.

TORMENT, [verb,]   -ed.

basanizō.

Mat. 8. 6. sick of palsy, grievously t-ed
    29. art thou come hither to t.
Mar. 5. 7. that thou t. me not ; Lu.8.28
Rev. 9. 5. should be t-ed five months
    11.10. these two prophets t-ed them
    14.10. he shall be t-ed with fire
    20.10. shall be t-ed day and night

odunaomai.

Lu. 16.24. for I am t-ed in this flame
    25. comforted, and thou art t-ed

kakouchoumenos.

Heb.11.37.being destitute, afflicted,t-ed

TORMENTORS.

basanistēs.

Mat.18.34. and delivered him to the t.

TORTURED.

tumpanizomai.

Heb.11.35.others were t. not accepting

TOSSED. (See Tempest.)

basanizō.

Mat.14.24. of the sea, t. with waves

kludōnizomai.

Eph. 4.14. t. to and fro, and carried

ripizomai.

Jas. 1. 6. driven with the wind and t.

TOUCH, (See Feeling,) -ed, -eth.

haptomai. [Mar.1.41; Lu.5.13

Mat. 8. 3. forth his hand, and t-ed him ;
    15. he t-ed her hand, and the
    9.20. t-ed the hem of his ; Lu.8.44
    21. If I may but t. his ; Mar.5.28
    29. Then t-ed he their eyes ; 20.34
    14.36. might only t. the ; Mar.6.56
      as many as t-ed ; Mar.6.56
    17. 7. Jesus came and t-ed them
Mar. 3.10. upon him for to t. him
    5.27. behind, and t-ed his garment
    30. said, Who t-ed my ; Lu.5.45

Mar. 5.31. say. thou, Who t-ed; Lu.8.45
    7.33. he spit, and t-ed his tongue
    8.22. besought him to t. him
    10.13. that he should t.; Lu.18.15
Lu.   6.19. multitude sought to t. him
    7.14. he came and t-ed the bier
    39. woman this is that t-eth him
    8.46. Jesus said, Someb. hath t-ed
    47. what cause she had t-ed him
    22.51. he t-ed his ear, and healed
Jo. 20.17. t. me not ; for I am not
¹Co.   7. 1. for a man not to t. a woman
²Co.   6.17. t. not the unclean thing
Col.   2.21. t. not ; taste not ; handle
¹Jo.   5.18. that wicked one t-eth him
    prospsauō.
Lu.11.46. ye yourselves t. not the burd.
    katagō.
Act.27. 3. next day we t-ed at Sidon
    thigō.
Heb.11.28.destroyed the firstb. should t.
    12.20. so much as a beast t. the
    psēlaphaō.
Heb.12.18.mount that might be t-ed

TOUCHING. (See As.)
    peri, [gen.]
Act.24.21. t. the resurrection of the
    26. 2. t. all the things whereof
Col.   4.10. t. whom ye received comma.
    kata, [accu.]
Ro. 11.28. but as t. the election
Phi.   3.   5. as t. the law, a Pharisee
    6. t. the righteousness which
    epi, [accu.]
²Th.   3.   4. confidence in the Lord t.

TOWARD.
    eis.
Mat.28. 1. as it began to dawn t. the
Lu. 12.21. and is not rich t. God
    13.22. teaching, and journeying t.
Jo.   6.17. over the sea t. Capernaum
Act.   1.10. looked stedfastly t. heaven
    20.21. repentance t. God, and faith
    24.15. have hope t. God, which
    27.40. to the wind, and made t.
    28.14. and so we went t. Rome
Ro.   1.27. in their lust one t. another
    5. 8. commendeth his love t. us
    12.16. the same mind one t. anoth.
²Co.   1.16. brought on my way t. Judea
    2. 8. confirm your love t. him
    7.15. affection is more abundant t.
    9. 8. make all grace abound t.
    10. 1. being absent am bold t. you
    13. 4. by the power of God t. you
Gal.   2. 8. mighty in me t. the Gentiles
Eph. 1. 8. hath abounded t. us in all
¹Th.   3.12. one t. another, and t. all
    men, even as we do t. you
    4.10. do it t. all the brethren
²Th.   1. 3. of you all t. each other abo.
Phile.   5. the Lord Jesus, and t.
Heb. 6.10. ye have shewed t. his name
¹Pet. 3.21. of a good conscience t. God
    pros, [accu.]
Lu. 24.29. for it is t. evening, and the
Act.24.16. void of offence t. God, and
²Co.   1.18. our word t. you was not yea
    7. 4. my boldness of speech t. you
Phi.   2.30. your lack of service t. me
Col.   4.   5. Walk in wisdom t. them th.
¹Th. 4.12. t. them that are without
    5.14. be patient t. all men
Phile.   5. hast t. the Lord Jesus
¹Jo.   3.21. have we confidence t. God
    epi, [accu.]
Mat.12.49.forth his hand t. his discip.
    14.14. with compassion t. them
Ro. 11.22. but t. thee, goodness
¹Co.   7.36. uncomely t. his virgin
Eph. 2. 7. in his kindness t. us

Heb. 6.   1. works, and of faith t. God
    epi, [dat.]
Mar. 6.34. with compassion t. them
    en.
Lu.   2.14. peace, good will t. men
Ro. 15. 5. likeminded one t. another
¹Jo.   4. 9. manifest. the love of God t.
    kata, [accu.]
Act. 8.26. Arise and go t. the south
    27.12. t. the south west and
Phi. 3.14. I press t. the mark, for
    huper, [gen.]
²Co.   7. 7. your fervent mind t. me

TOWEL.
    lention.
Jo. 13. 4. took a t., and girded himself
    5. to wipe them with the t.

TOWER.
    purgos.
Mat.21.33. winepre. in it, and built a t.
Mar.12. 1. the winefat, and built a t.
Lu. 13. 4. upon whom the t. in Siloam
    14.28. intending to build a t., sitte.

TOWN, -s.
    kōmē.
Mat.10.11. city or t. ye shall enter
Mar. 8.23. and led him out of the t.
    26. Neither go into the t., nor
    tell it to any in the t.
    27. into the t-s of Cesarea Phil.
Lu.   5.17. were come out of every t. of
    9. 6. went through the t-s, preac.
    12. that they may go into the t-s
Jo.   7.42. out of the t. of Bethlehem
    11. 1. Bethany, the t. of Mary and
    30. was not yet come into the t.
    kōmopolis.
Mar. 1.38. Let us go into the next t-s

TOWNCLERK.
    grammateus.
Act.19.35. when the t. had appeased the

TRADE, -ed.
    ergazomai.
Mat.25.16. went and t-ed with the same
Rev.18.17. as many as t. by sea, stood

TRADING. (See Gain.)

TRADITION,(SeeFathers,) -s.
    paradosis.   [7.3,5
Mat.15. 2. the t. of the elders ; Mar.
    3. command. of God by your t.
    6. effect by your t.; Mar.7.13
Mar. 7. 8. ye hold the t. of men
    9. th. ye may keep your own t.
Gal.   1.14. zealous of the t-s of my fath.
Col.   2. 8. after the t. of men, after
²Th.   2.15. and hold the t-s which
    3. 6. not after the t. which he

TRAITOR, -s.
    prodotēs.
Lu. 6.16. Iscar., which also was the t.
²Ti.   3. 4. t-s, heady, highminded

TRAMPLE.
    katapateō.
Mat. 7. 6. lest they t. them under their

TRANCE.
    ekstasis.
Act.10.10. made ready, he fell into a t.
    11. 5. and in a t. I saw a vision
    22.17. in the temple, I was in a t.

TRANSFER. (See Figure.)

TRANSFIGURED.
    metamorphoomai.
Mat.17. 2. was t. before them ; Mar.9.2

TRANSFORM, -ed, -ing.
    metaschēmatizō.
²Co. 11.13. t-ing themselves into the ap.
    14. Satan himself is t-ed into an
    15. if his ministers also be t-ed
    metamorphoomai.
Ro. 12. 2. be ye t-ed by the renewing

TRANSGRESS, -ed, -eth.
    parabainō.
Mat.15. 2. Why do thy disciples t. the
    3. Why do ye also t. the
²John   9. Whosoever t-eth, and abideth
    parabatēs.
Ro. 2.27. judge thee, who..dost t. the
    parerchomai.
Lu. 15.29. neither t-ed I at any time
    poieō anomia.
¹Jo. 3. 4. commi. sin t-eth also the law

TRANSGRESSION, -s.
    parabasis.
Ro. 4.15. where no law is, there is no t.
    5.14. after the simili. of Adam's t.
Gal. 3.19. It was added because of t-s
¹Ti.   being deceived was in the t.
Heb. 2. 2. and every t. and disobedien.
    9.15. for the redemption of the t-s
    parabainō.
Act. 1.25. from which Judas by t. fell
    anomia.
¹Jo. 3. 4. for sin is the t. of the law

TRANSGRESSOR, -s.
    parabatēs.
Gal. 2.18. destroyed, I make myself a t.
Jas. 2. 9. are convinc. of the law as t-s
    11. art become a t. of the law
    anomos.   [22.37
Mar.15.28. numbered with the t-s; Lu.

TRANSLATED.
    methistanō.
Col. 1.13. and hath t. us into the
    metatithēmi.
Heb.11. 5. By faith Enoch was t. that
    because God had t. him

TRANSLATION.
    metathesis.
Heb.11. 5. for before his t. he had this

TRANSPARENT.
    diaphanēs.
Rev.21.21. gold, as it were t. glass

TRAP.
    thēra.
Ro. 11. 9. be made a snare, and a t., and

TRAVAIL, [noun.]
    mochthos.
¹Th. 2. 9. brethren our labour and t.
²Th. 3. 8. wrought with labour and t.
    tiktō.
Jo. 16.21. A woman when she is in t.
    ōdin.
¹Th. 5. 3. as t. upon a woman with

TRAVAIL, [verb,] -est, -eth, -ing.
    ōdinō.
Gal. 4.19. of whom I t. in birth again
    27. and cry, thou that t-est not.
Rev.12. 2. cried, t-ing in birth, and
    sunōdinō.
Ro. 8.22. t-eth in pain together until

TRAVEL, [noun.]
    sunekdēmos.
Act.19.29. Paul's companions in t.

TRAVEL, [verb,] -ed, -ing.
    apodēmeō.
Mat.25.14.man t-ing into a far country
    dierchomai.
Act.11.19. t-ed as far as Phenice, and
    sunekdēmos.   [trav.)
²Co. 8.19. churches to t. with (a fellow-

TREAD, *-eth, Trode, Trodden.*
  pateō.
Lu. 10.19. power *to* **t**. on serpents
  21.24. Jerusalem shall be *t-n down*
Rev.11. 2. city *shall* they **t**. *under foot*
  14.20. And the winepress *was* **t***-n*
  19.15. and he *t-eth* the winepress of
    katapateō.
Mat. 5.13. and *to be* **t***-n under foot* of
Lu. 8. 5. and it *was* **t***-n down*, and
  12. 1. that they **t***-o* one upon ano.
Heb.10.29.*who hath* **t***-n under foot* the
    aloaō.   [¹Ti.5.18
¹Co. 9. 9. ox *that* **t***-eth out the corn;*

TREASURE, *-s, Treasurest.*
  thēsauros.
Mat. 2.11. when they had open. th. **t***-s*
  6.19. yourselves *t-s* upon earth
  20. *t-s* in heaven, where neither
  21. For where your **t**.; Lu.12.34
  12.35. out of the good **t**.; Lu.6.45
    out of the evil **t**.; Lu.6.45
  13.44. is like unto **t**. hid in a field
  52. out of his **t**. things new and
  19.21. thou shalt have **t**. in hea.;
    Mar.10.21; Lu.18.22
Lu. 12.33. a **t**. in the heavens that fail.
²Co. 4. 7. we have this **t**. in earthen
Col. 2. 3. all the *t-s* of wisdom and
Heb.11.26.riches than the *t-s* in Egypt
  thēsaurizō.
Lu. 12.21. he *that layeth up* **t**. for him.
Ro. 2. 5. *t-est* up unto thyself wrath
Jas. 5. 3. ye *have heaped* **t**. *together*
  gaza.
Act. 8.27. had the charge of all her **t**.

TREASURY.
  gazophulakion.
Mar.12.41.Jesus sat over against the **t**.
    people cast money into the **t**.
  43. which have cast into the **t**.
Lu. 21. 1. casting their gifts into the **t**.
Jo. 8.20. words spake Jesus in the **t**.
  korbanas.
Mat.27. 6. to put them into the **t**.

TREATISE.
  logos.
Act. 1. 1. The former **t**. have I made

TREE, (See *Palm,*)   *-s.*
  dendron.
Mat. 3.10. the root of the *t-s*; Lu.3.9
  every **t**. which bringeth not;
    7.19; Lu.3.9
  7.17. every good **t**. bringeth forth
    but a corrupt **t**. bringeth fo.
  18. A good **t**. cannot; Lu.6.43
    neither can a cor. **t**.; Lu.6.43
  12.33. Either make the **t**. good, and
    good; or else make the **t**. co.
    for the **t**. is known; Lu.6.44
  13.32. among herbs, and beco. a **t**.
  21. 8. bran. from the *t-s*; Mar.11.8
Mar. 8.24. said, I see men as *t-s* walki.
Lu. 13.19. it grew, and waxed a great **t**.
  21.29. Behold the fig tree, and..*t-s*
Jude 12. *t-s* whose fruit withereth
Rev. 7. 1. nor on the sea, nor on any **t**.
  3. earth, neither sea, nor the *t-s*
  8. 7. the third part of *t-s* was bu.
  9. 4. any green thing, neit. any **t**.
  xulon.
Lu. 23.31. do these things in a green **t**.
Act. 5.30. slew and hang. on a **t**.; 10.39
  13.29. took him down from the **t**.
Gal. 3.13. every one that hange. on a **t**.
¹Pet. 2.24. sins in his own body on the **t**.
Rev. 2. 7. will I give to eat of the **t**. of
  22. 2. was there the **t**. of life
    and the leaves of the **t**
290

Rev.22.14. may have right to the **t**. of

TREMBLE,   *-ed, -ing.*
  tremō.
Mar. 5.33. the woman fearing and **t***-ing*
Lu. 8.47. she came **t***-ing*, and falling
Act. 9. 6. he **t***-ing* and astonished
  ginomai entromos.
Act. 7.32. Then Moses **t***-ed* and durst
  16.29. sprang in, and *came* **t***-ing*
  echō tromos.
Mar.16. 8. for they **t***-ed* and were amaz.
  ginomai emphobos.
Act.24.25. Felix **t***-ed*, and answered
  phrissō.
Jas. 2.19. devils also believe and **t**.

TREMBLING.
  tromos.
¹Co. 2. 3. in fear, and in much **t**.
²Co. 7.15. how with fear and **t**. ye

TRENCH.
  charax.
Lu. 19.43. enemies shall cast a **t**. about

TRESPASS, [*noun*,]   *-es.*
  paraptōma.
Mat. 6.14. if ye forgive men their *t-es*
  15. not men their *t-es*, neither
    your Father forgive your *t-es*
  18.35. ev. one his brother their *t-es*
Mar.11.25.may forgive you your *t-es*
  26. in heaven forgive your *t-es*
²Co. 5.19. not imputing their *t-es*
Eph. 2. 1. were dead in *t-es* and sins
Col. 2.13. having forgiven you all *t-es*

TRESPASS, [*verb*.]
  hamartanō.
Mat.18.15. thy brother *shall* **t**.; Lu.17.3
Lu. 17. 4. if he **t**. against thee seven

TRIAL.   (See *Fiery*.)
  dokimē.
²Co. 8. 2. that in a great **t**.of affliction
  dokimion.
¹Pet. 1. 7. That the **t**. of your faith
  peira.
Heb.11.36.had **t**. of cruel mockings

TRIBE,   *-s.*
  phulē.   [Lu.22.30
Mat.19.28. judging the twelve *t-s* of Is.;
  24.30. and then shall all the *t-s* of
Lu. 2.36. daugh. of Phanuel, of the **t**.
Act.13.21. of the **t**. of Benjamin; Ro.
    11.1; Phi.3.5; Rev.7.8
Heb. 7.13. pertaineth to another **t**., of
  14. of which **t**. Moses spake not.
Jas. 1. 1. to the twelve *t-s* which are
Rev. 5. 5. the Lion of the **t**. of Juda
  7. 4. of all the *t-s* of the children
    5, 6,7,8. Of the **t**. of
  21.12. the names of the twelve *t-s*
  dōdekaphulon.
Act.26. 7. which promise our *twelve* *t-s*

TRIBULATION,   *-s.*
  thlipsis.
Mat.13.21. for when **t**. or persecution
  24.21. For then shall be great **t**.
  29. after the **t**. of those days
Mar.13.24.after that **t**., the sun shall
Jo. 16.33. In the world ye shall have **t**.
Act.14.22. we must through much **t**.
Ro. 2. 9. **t**. and anguish, upon every
  5. 3. in *t-s* also: knowing that **t**.
  8.35. shall **t**., or distress, or
  12.12. patient in **t**.; continuing
²Co. 1. 4. in all our **t**.; 7.4
Eph. 3.13. faint not at my *t-s* for you
²Th. 1. 4. and *t-s* that ye endure
  6. **t**. to them that trouble you
Rev.1. 9. broth., and companion in **t**.

Rev. 2. 9. and **t**., and poverty,but thou
  10. ye shall have **t**. ten days
  22. with her into great **t**.
  7.14. which came out of great **t**.
  thlibō.
¹Th. 3. 4. that we should *suffer* **t**.

TRIBUTE.
  phoros.
Lu. 20.22. Is it lawful for us to give **t**.
  23. 2. and forbidding to give **t**. to
Ro. 13. 6. For this cause pay ye **t**.
  7. **t**. to whom **t**.is due; custom
  kēnsos.
Mat.17.25. of the earth take custom or **t**.
  22.17. it lawful to give **t**.; Mar.12.14
  19. Shew me the **t**. money
  didrachmon.
Mat.17.24. they that received **t**. money
    Doth not your master pay **t**.

TRIMMED.
  kosmeō.
Mat.25. 7. arose and **t**. their lamps

TRIUMPH,   *-ing.*
  thriambeuō.
²Co. 2.14. *which..causeth* us to **t**. in
Col. 2.15. openly, **t***-ing* over them in it

TROUBLE, [*noun*,]   *-s.*
  thlipsis.
¹Co. 7.28. shall have **t**. in the flesh
²Co. 1. 4. them which are in any **t**.
  8. of our **t**. which came
  tarachē.
Mar.13. 8. there shall be famines and *t-s*
    (See *Suffer*.)

TROUBLE, [*verb*,]*-ed,-est,-eth.*
  tarassō.
Mat. 2. 3. he *was* **t***-ed*, and all Jerus.
  14.26. *were* **t***-ed*, saying, It is a sp.
Mar. 6.50. all saw him, and *were* **t***-ed*
Lu. 1.12. Zacha. saw him, he *was* **t***-ed*
  24.38. Why are ye **t***-ed?* and why
Jo. 5. 4. into the pool, and **t***-ed* the
  7. man, when the water *is* **t***-ed*
  12.27. Now *is* my soul **t***-ed*
  13.21. he *was* **t***-ed* in spirit, and
  14. 1, 27. *Let* not your heart *be* **t***-ed*
Act.15.24. out from us *have* **t***-ed* you
  17. 8. And they **t***-ed* the people
Gal. 1. 7. there be some *that* **t**. you
  5.10. he *that* **t***-eth* you shall bear
¹Pet. 3.14. their terror, neither *be* **t***-ed*
  tarassō heautos.
Jo. 11.33. in the spirit, and *was* **t***-ed*
  ektarassō.
Act.16.20. *do exceedingly* **t**. our city
  diatarattō.
Lu. 1.29. she *was* **t***-ed* at his saying
  parechō kopos.
Mat.26.10. Why **t**. ye the; Mar.14.6
Lu. 11. 7. **t**. me not: the door is
  18. 5. this widow **t***-eth* me
Gal. 6.17. henceforth *let* no man **t**. me
  throeomai.
Mat.24. 6. see that ye *be* not **t***-ed*
Mar.13. 7. of wars *be* ye not **t***-ed*: for
²Th. 2. 2. or *be* **t***-ed*, neither by spirit
  skullō.
Mar. 5.35. why **t***-est* thou the Master
Lu. 7. 6. Lord, **t**. not thou thy*self*
  8.49. is dead: **t**. not the Master
  thlibō.
²Co. 4. 8. **t***-ed* on every side; 7.5
²Th. 1. 6. tribulation to them *that* **t**.
  7. to you *who are* **t***-ed* rest
  parenochleō.
Act.15.19. *that we* **t**. not them, which
  enochleō.
Heb.12.15.bitterness springing up **t**.
  turbazomai.
Lu. 10.41. thou art careful and **t***-ed*

thorubeomai.
Act.20.10. t. not *yourselves*, for his life

anastatoō.
Gal. 5.12. even cut off *which* t. you

TROUBLING.
tarachē.
Jo. 5. 4. after the t. of the water

TROW.
dokeō.
Lu. 17. 9. commanded him? I t. not

TRUCEBREAKERS.
aspondos.
²Ti. 3. 3. Without natural affection, t.

TRUE.
alēthēs. [Mar.12.14
Mat. 22.16. Mas. we know that th. art t.;
Jo. 3.33. set to his seal that God is t.
  5.31. of myself, my witn. is not t.
   32. which he witness. of me is t.
  7.18. that sent him, the same is t.
  8.13. of thyse.; thy record is not t.
   14. of my., yet my record is t.
   16. if I judge, my judgme. is t.
   17. the testimo. of two men is t.
   26. he that sent me is t.; and I
  10.41. John sp. of this man were t.
  19.35. he knoweth that he saith t.
  21.24. know that his testimony is t.
Act.12. 9. wist not that it was t. which
Ro. 3. 4. yea, let God be t., but every
²Co. 6. 8. as deceivers, and yet t.
Phi. 4. 8. whatsoever things are t.
Tit. 1.13. This witness is t. Where.
¹Pet. 5.12. this is the t. grace of God
²Pet. 2.22. according to the t. proverb
¹Jo. 2. 8. which thing is t. in him and
³John 12. know that our record is t.
alēthinos.
Lu. 16.11. commit to your trust the t.
Jo. 1. 9. That was the t. Light which
  4.23. when the t. worshippers sh.
   37. herein is that saying t., One
  6.32. Father giveth you the t. bre.
  7.28. he that sent me is t., whom
  15. 1. I am the t. vine, and my F.
  17. 3. know thee the only t. God
  19.35. record, and his record is t.
¹Th. 1. 9. to serve the living and t. G.
Heb.8. 2. sanctuary, and of the t. tab.
  9.24. wh. are the figures of the t.
  10.22. Let us draw near with a t.
¹Jo. 2. 8. darkness is past, and the t.
  5.20. we may know him that is t.
   we are in him that is t.
   This is the t. God, and eter.
Rev. 3. 7. he that is holy, he that is t.
   14. the faithful and t. witness
  6.10. long, O Lord, holy and t.
  15. 3. just and t. are thy ways
  16. 7. t. and righteous are; 19.2
  19. 9. These are the t. sayings of
   11. was called Faithful and t.
  21. 5. words are t. and; 22.6
pistos
²Co. 1.18. But as God is t., our word
¹Ti. 3. 1. This is a t. saying, If a man
gnēsios.
Phi. 4. 3. I entreat thee also, t. yoke.

TRULY.
men. [Lu.10.2
Mat. 9.37. the harvest t. is plenteous;
  17.11. Elias t. shall first come
Mar.14.38.The spirit t. is ready, but the
Lu. 22.22. And t. the Son of man goeth
Act. 1. 5. For John t. baptized with
  3.22. For Moses t. said unto the
  5.23. The prison t. found we shut
²Co. 12.12. t. the signs of an apostle
Heb. 7.23. And they t. were many prie.

Heb. 11.15.And t., if they had been mi.
men oun.
Jo. 20.30. other signs t. did Jesus
ara.
Lu. 11.48. t. ye bear witness that ye
alēthōs. [Mar.15.39
Mat.27.54. t. this was the Son of God;
epi [gen.] alētheia.
Lu. 20.21. teachest the way of God t.
alēthēs.
Jo. 4.18. in that saidst thou t.

TRUMP.
salpingx.
¹Co. 15.52. of an eye, at the last t.
¹Th. 4.16. and with the t. of God

TRUMPET, (See *Sound*,) -s.
salpingx.
Mat.24.31. with a great sound of a t.
¹Co.14. 8. if the t. give an uncertain
Heb.12.19.And the sound of a t., and
Rev. 1.10. a great voice, as of a t.
  /4. 1. as it were of a t. talking
  8. 2. to them were given seven t-s
  6. which had the seven t-s
  13. the other voices of the t.
  9.14. sixth angel which had the t.

TRUMPETERS.
salpistēs.
Rev.18.22. and of pipers, and t. shall

TRUST, [noun.]
pisteuō.
Lu. 16.11. who *will commit* to your t.
¹Th. 2. 4. *to be put in* t. *with* the
pepoithēsis.
²Co. 3. 4. And such t. have we through

TRUST, [verb,] -ed.
elpizō. [Ro.15.12
Mat.12.21. his name *shall* the Gentiles t.;
Lu. 24.21. we t-ed that it had been
Jo. 5.45. even Moses, in whom ye t.
Ro. 15.24. for I t. to see you in my
¹Co.16. 7. I t. to tarry a while with you
²Co. 1.10. in whom we t. that he will
  13. I t. ye shall acknowledge
  5.11. I t. also are made manifest
  13. 6. I t. that ye shall know that
Phi. 2.19. I t.in the Lord Jesus to send
¹Ti. 4.10. because we t. in the living
  5. t-eth in God, and continueth
  6.17. nor t. in uncertain riches
Phile. 22. for I t. that through your
¹Pet. 3. 5. women also, *who* t-ed in God
³John 12. I t. to come unto you
³John 14. I t. I shall shortly see thee
peithō.
Mat.27.43. He t-ed in God; let him de.
Mar.10.24.for them *that* t. in riches
Lu. 11.22. his armour wherein he t-ed
  18. 9. certain *which* t-ed in themse.
²Co. 1. 9. that we should not t. in our.
  10. 7. If any man t. to himself that
Phi. 2.24. But I t. in the Lord that I
  3. 4. hath whereof he *might* t.
  (thinketh *to trust*.)
Heb. 2.13. I will *put my* t. in him
  13.18. for we t. we have a good co.
proelpizō.
Eph. 1.12. *who first* t-ed in Christ

TRUTH.
alētheia.
Mat.22.16. way of God in t.; Mar.12.14
Mar. 5.33. him, and told him all the t.
  12.32. Master, thou hast said the t.
Lu. 4.25. I tell you of a t. many wido.
  22.59. Of a t. this fellow also was
Jo. 1.14. Father, full of grace and t.
  17. grace and t. came by Jesus

Jo. 3.21. he that doeth t. cometh to
  4.23, 24. Father in spirit and in t.
  5.33. he bare witness unto the t.
  8.32. know the t., and the t. shall
  40. man that hath told you the t.
  44. t., because there is no t. in
  45. I tell you the t., ye; 16.7
  46. if I say the t., why do ye not
  14. 6. I am the way, the t., and
  17. Even the Spirit of t.; 15.26
  16.13. when he, the Spirit of t., is
   he will guide you into all t.
  17.17. through thy t.: thy word is t.
  19. be sanctified through the t.
  18.37. bear witness unto the t.
   Every one that is of the t.
  38. Pi. saith unto him, What is t.
Act. 4.27. For of a t. against thy holy
  10.34. said, Of a t. I perceive that
  26.25. the words of t. and soberness
Ro. 1.18. hold the t. in unrighteousne.
  25. changed the t. of God into
  2. 2. of God is according to t.
  8. and do not obey the t.
  20. and of the t. in the law
  3. 7. For if the t. of God hath
  9. 1. I say the t. in Christ. I lie
  15. 8. circumcision for the t. of G.
¹Co. 5. 8. bread of sincerity and t.
  13. 6. iniquity, but rejoice. in the t.
²Co. 4. 2. by manifestation of the t.
  6. 7. the word of t., by the power
  7.14. we spake all thi. to you in t.
   before Titus, is found a t.
  11.10. As the t. of Christ is in me
  12. 6. for I will say the t.: but now
  13. 8. against the t., but for the t.
Gal. 2. 5. that the t. of the gospel mi.
  14. according to the t. of the
  3. 1. ye should not obey the t.; 5.7
Eph. 1.13. that ye heard the word of t.
  4.21. by him, as the t. is in Jesus
  25. every man t. with his neigh.
  5. 9. goodn. and righteousn. and t.
  6.14. your loins girt about with t.
Phi. 1.18. whether in pretence, or in t.
Col. 1. 5. the word of the t. of the gos.
  6. knew the grace of God in t.
²Th. 2.10. receiv. not the love of the t.
  12. dam. who believed not the t.
  13. Spirit and belief of the t.
¹Ti. 2. 4. unto the knowledge of the t.
  7. I speak the t. in Christ, and
  3.15. the pillar and grou. of the t.
  4. 3. which believe and kn. the t.
  6. 5. minds, and destitute of the t.
²Ti. 2.15. rightly dividi. the word of t.
  18. concerning the t. have erred
  25. the acknowledging of the t.
  3. 7. come to knowledge of the t.
  8. so do these also resist the t.
  4. 4. away their ears from the t.
Tit. 1. 1. acknowledging of the t. whi.
  14. men, that turn from the t.
Heb.10.26.received knowledge of the t.
Jas. 1.18. begat he us with word of t.
  3.14. not, and lie not against the t.
  5.19. any of you do err from the t.
¹Pet. 1.22. your souls in obeying the t.
²Pet. 1.12. be established in the pres. t.
  2. 2. the way of t. shall be evil
¹Jo. 1. 6. we lie, and do not the t.
  8. ourselves, and the t. is not
  2. 4. is a liar, and the t. is not in
  21. the t., but because ye know
   and that no lie is of the t.
  3.18. but in deed and in t.
  19. we know that we are of the t.
  4. 6. Hereby know we the Sp. of t.
  5. 6. witness, because the Spi. is t.
²John 1. child., whom I love in the t.
  they that have known the t.

¹John   2. For the t.'s sake, which dwe.
    3. Son of the Father, in t. and
    4. of thy children walking in t.
¹John   1. Gaius, whom I love in the t.
    3. testified of the t. that is in
    even as thou walkest in the t.
    4. that my children walk in t.
    8. be fellowhelpers to the t.
    12. and of the t. itself

alēthōs.

Mat.14.33. *Of a t.* thou art the Son of
Lu.   9.27. I tell you *of a t.,* there be
    12.44. *Of a t.* I say unto you; 21.3
Jo.   6.14. This is *of a t.* that prophet
    7.40. *Of a t.* this is the prophet
¹Th. 2.13. as it is in t. the word of God

alētheuō, [*partic.*]

Gal. 4.16. *because* I tell you the t.
Eph. 4.15. *speaking* the t. in love

alēthēs.

¹Jo. 2.27. of all things, and is t., and
    nai.
Mat.15.27. And she said, t., Lord : yet
    ontōs.
Co. 14.25. that God is in you *of a t.*

TRY,   *-ied, -eth.*
    peirazō.

Heb.11.17.*when* he *was* t-ed, offered up
Rev. 2. 2. and thou *hast* t-ed them wh.
    10. prison that ye *may be* t-ed
    3.10. *to* t. them that dwell upon
    pros [*accu.*] **peirasmos.**
¹Pet. 4.12. trial which is *to* t. you

    dokimazō   (*for trial* to you)
¹Co. 3.13. the fire *shall* t. every man's
¹Th. 2. 4. God, *which* t-eth our hearts
¹Pet. 1. 7. *though* it *be* t-ed with fire
¹Jo. 4. 1. t. the spirits whether they

    dokimos.
Jas. 1.12. for when he is t-ed, he shall
    puroomai.
Rev. 3.18. of me gold t-ed in the fire

TRYING, [*noun.*]
    dokimion.
Jas. 1. 3. the t. of your faith worketh

TUMULT,   *-s.*
    thorubos.
Mat.27.24.that rather a t. was made
Mar. 5.38. and seeth the t.
Act.21.34. the certainty for the t.
    24.18. multitude, nor with t.
    akatastasia.
Co. 6. 5. in imprisonments, in t-s, in
    12.20. whisperings, swellings, t-s

TURN,   *-ed, -ing.*
    strephō.
Mat. 5.39. t. to him the other also
    7. 6. and t. *again and* rend you
    16.23. But he t-ed, *and* said unto
Lu.   7. 9. and t-ed *him about, and* said
    44. t-ed to the woman, *and* said
    9.55. But he t-ed, *and* rebuked
    10.23. he t-ed *him* unto his discipl.
    14.25. and he t-ed, *and* said unto
    22.61. And the Lord t-ed, *and* loo.
    23.28. But Jesus t-ing unto them
Jo.   1.38. Then Jesus t-ed, and saw th.
    20.14. she t-ed *herself* back, and saw
    16. She t-ed *herself, and* saith
Act. 7.39. hearts t-ed *back again* into
    42. Then God t-ed, and gave th.
    13.46. lo, we t. to the Gentiles
Rev.11. 6. power over waters *to* t. them
    epistrephō .   [Mar.5.30
Mat. 9.22. But Jesus t-ed him *about*;
Mar. 8.33. But *when* he *had* t-ed about
    13.16. *let* him. .not t. back *again*
Lu.   1.16. children of Israel *shall* he t.
292

Lu.   1.17. *to* t. the hearts of the fathers
    17. 4. t. *again* to thee, saying
Jo.   21.20. Then Peter t-*ing about*
Act. 9.35. saw him, and t-ed to the L.
    40. t-*ing* him to the body, said
    11.21. believed, and t-ed unto the
    14.15. *that ye should* t. from these
    15.19. among the Gentiles *are* t-ed
    16.18. Paul, being grieved, t-ed *and*
    26.18. *to* t. them from darkness
    20. should repent and t. to God
²Co. 3.16. Nevertheless when it *shall* t.
Gal. 4. 9. how t. ye again to the weak
¹Th. 1. 9. how ye t-ed to God from ido.
²Pet. 2.21. they have known it *to* t.
    22. t-ed to his own vomit *again*
Rev. 1.12. I t-ed to see the voice that
    me. And *being* t-ed, I saw
    apostrephō.
Mat. 5.42. bo. of thee t. not thou *away*
Act. 3.26. in t-*ing away* every one of
Ro. 11.26. *shall* t. *away* ungodliness fr.
²Ti.   1.15. in Asia *be* t-ed *away from*
    4. 4. they *shall* t. *away* their ears
Tit. 1.14. men, *that* t. *from* the truth
Heb.12.25.if we t. *away from* him that
    hupostrephō.
Lu.   2.45. they t-ed *back again* to
    17.15. t-ed back, and with a loud
    metastrephō.
Act. 2.20. sun *shall be* t-ed into
Jas. 4. 9. *let* your laughter *be* t-ed to
    ektrepomai.
²Ti. 4. 4. and *shall be* t-ed unto fables
Heb.12.13.is lame *be* t-ed *out of the way*
    apobainō.
Lu. 21.13. it *shall* t. to you for a
Phi. 1.19. this *shall* t. to my salvation
    apotrepomai.
²Ti. 3. 5. thereof : from such t. *away*
    metagō.
Jas. 3. 3. we t. *about* their whole body
    4. yet *are* they t-ed *about* with
    anachōreō.
Mat. 2.22. he t-ed *aside* into the parts
    anakamptō.
Lu. 10. 6. it *shall* t. to you *again*
    ginomai eis.
Jo. 16.20. sorrow *shall be* t-ed *into* joy
    diastrephō.
Act.13. 8. seeking *to* t. *away* the depu.
    anastatoō.
Act.17. 6. *that have* t-ed. .*upside down*
    methistēmi.
Act.19.26. and t-ed *away* much people
    metatithēmi.
Jude   4. t-*ing* the grace of our God
    (See *Ashes, Aside.*)

TURNING.
    tropē.
Jas. 1.17. neither shadow of t.

TURTLEDOVES.
    trugōn.
Lu. 2.24. A pair of t. or two young

TUTORS.
    epitropos.
Gal. 4. 2. is under t. and governors

TWAIN.
    duo.
Mat. 5.41. to go a mile, go with him t.
    19. 5. they t. shall be one flesh
    6. Wheref. they are no more t.
    21.31. Whether of them t. did the
    27.21. Whether of the t. will ye th.
    51. te. was rent in t.; Mar.15.38
Mar.10. 8. they t. shall be one flesh
    so then they are no more t.
Eph. 2.15. make in himself of t. one

TWELFTH.
    dōdekatos.
R ev.21.20. jacinth ; the t. an amethyst

TWELVE. (See *Tribes.*)
    dōdeka.   [Mar.5.25 ; Lu.8.43
Mat. 9.20. with an issue of blood t. ye.:
    10. 1. called unto him his t.; Mar.
    6.7 ; Lu.9.1.
    2. the names of the t. apostles
    5. These t. Jesus sent forth
    11. 1. of commanding his t. disci.
    14.20. that remained t. baskets ;
    Mar.6.43; Lu.9.17 ; Jo.6.13
    19.28. ye also shall sit upon t. thr.
    judging the t. trib.; Lu.22.30
    20.17. took the t. disciples apart
    26.14. Then one of the t., called
    20. down with the t.; Lu.22.14
    47. Judas, one of the t.; Mar.
    14.10,43 ; Lu.22.47
    53. more than t. legions of ange.
Mar. 3.14. he ordained t., that they
    4.10. were about him with the t.
    5.42. was of the age of t.; Lu.8.42
    8.19. They say unto him, t.
    9.35. he sat down, and called the t.
    10.32. he took again the t., and be.
    11.11. unto Bethany with the t.
    14.17. even. he cometh with the t.
    20. It is one of the t., that dip.
Lu.   2.42. when he was t. years old
    6.13. of them he chose t., whom
    8. 1. the t. were with him
    9.12. then came the t., and said
    18.31. Then he took unto him the t.
    22. 3. being of the number of the t.
Jo.   6.67. Then said Jesus unto the t.
    70. Have not I chosen you t.
    71. bet. him, being one of the t.
    11. 9. Are there not t. hours in the
    20.24. Thomas, one of the t., called
Act. 6. 2. Then the t. called the multi.
    7. 8. Jacob begat the t. patriarchs
¹Co.15. 5. seen of Cephas, then of the t.
Jas. 1. 1. to the t. tribes which are
Rev. 7. 5, 6,7,8. were sealed t.thousand
    12. 1. her head a crown of t. stars
    21.12. high, and had t. gates, and
    at the gates t. angels, and
    the t. tribes of the children
    14. wall of the city had t. found.
    the names of the t. apostles
    16. with the reed, t. thousand
    21. the t. gates were t. pearls
    22. 2. which bare t. manner of fru.
    dekaduo.
Act.19. 7. all the men were about t.
    24.11. t. days since I went up

TWENTY.
    eikosi.
Lu. 14.31. against him with t. thous.
Jo.   6.19. about five and t. or thirty
Act. 1.15. about an hundred and t.
    27.28. sounded, and found it t. fa.
¹Co. 10. 8. in one day three and t. tho.
Rev. 4. 4. the throne were four and t.
    four and t. elders ; 5.8,14
    11.16,19.4

TWICE.
    dis.
Mar.14.30,72. before the cock crow t.
Lu. 18.12. I fast t. in the week
Jude   12. without fruit, t. dead

TWINKLING.
    ripē.
¹Co. 15.52. in the t. of an eye, at the

TWO.
    duo.
Mat. 4.18. saw t. brethren, Simon

Mat. 4.21. he saw other **t.** brethren
6.24. No man can ser. **t.**;Lu.16.13
8.28. there met him **t.** possessed
9.27. **t.** blind men followed him
10.10. neither **t.** coats, neither sh.
29. Are not **t.** sparrows; Lu.12.6
11. 2. he sent **t.** of his disciples;
Mar.11.1,14.13; Lu.19.29
14.17, 19. five loaves, and **t.** fishes ;
Mar.6.38,41;Lu.9.13,16;Jo.6.9
18. 8. having **t.** hands or **t.** feet ;
Mar.9.43,45
9. having **t.** eyes to ; Mar.9.47
16. take with thee one or **t.** mo.
that in the mouth of **t.** or
19. if **t.** of you shall agree on
20. where **t.** or three are gather.
20.21. Grant that these my **t.** sons
24. indignation against the **t.**
30. **t.**.blind men sitting by the
21. 1. then sent Jesus his **t.** disciples
28. certain man had **t.**;Lu.15.11
22.40. On these **t.** commandments
24.40. Then shall **t.** be in the field
41. **t.** woman shall be ; Lu.17.35
25.15. to another **t.**, and to another
17. **t.**, he also gained other **t.**
22. that had received **t.** talents
deliveredst unto me **t.** talen.
I have gained **t.** other talen.
26. 2. Ye know that after **t.** days is
37. Peter and the **t.** sons of Zeb.
60. at the last came **t.** false wit.
27.38. **t.** thieves crucified,Mar.15.27
Mar. 6. 7. send them forth by **t.** and **t.**
9. and not put on **t.** coats
41. the **t.** fishes divided he amo.
12.42. threw in **t.** mites ;Lu.21.2
14. 1. After **t.** days was the feast
16.12. in another form unto **t.** of
Lu. 2.24. pair of turtledoves, or **t.** yo.
3.11. He that hath **t.** coats, let
5. 2. saw **t.** ships standing by the
7.19. unto him **t.** of his disciples
41. certain creditor which had **t.**
9. 3. neither have **t.** coats apiece
30. there talked with him **t.**
32. the **t.** men that stood with
10. 1. sent them **t.** and two before
35. he departed, he took out **t.**
12.52. three against **t.**, and **t.** aga.
17.34. there shall be **t.** men in one
36. **t.** men shall be in the field
18.10. **t.** men went up into the
22.38. Lord, behold, here are **t.** sw.
23.32. there were also **t.** other
24. 4. **t.** men stood by ; Act.1.10
13. **t.** of them went that same
Jo. 1.35. John stood, and **t.** of his di.
37. the **t.** disciples heard him
40. One of the **t.** which
2. 6. containing **t.** or three firkins
4.40. them ; and he abo. there **t.**
43. after **t.** days he departed
8.17. that the testimony of **t.** men
11. 6. he abode **t.** days still in the
19.18. crucified him, and **t.** other
20.12. seeth **t.** angels in white
21. 2. Zebedee, and **t.** other of his
Act. 1.23. they appointed **t.**, Joseph
24. whether of these **t.** thou hast
7.29. of Madian, where he begat **t.**
9.38. they sent unto him **t.** men
10. 7. called **t.** of his household
12. 6. **t.** soldiers, bound with **t.**
19.10. continued by the space of **t.**
22. sent into Macedonia **t.** of
34. about the space of **t.** hours
21.33. to be bound with **t.** chains
23.23. called unto him **t.** centurions
1Co. 6.16. for **t.**, saith he, shall be one
14.27. let it be by **t.**, or at the

1Co. 14.29. the prophets speak **t.** or th.
2Co. 13. 1. In the mouth of **t.** or three
Gal. 4.22. that Abraham had **t.** sons
24. for these are the **t.** covenan.
Eph. 5.31. they **t.** shall be one flesh
Phi. 1.23. For I am in a strait bet. **t.**
1Ti. 5.19. before **t.** or three witnesses
Heb. 6.18. That by **t.** immutable things
10.28. without mercy under **t.** or
Rev. 9.12. there come **t.**.woes more
16. **t.** hundred thousand thous.
11. 2. under foot forty and **t.** mo.
3. power unto my **t.** witnesses
4. **t.** olive trees, and the **t.** ca.
10. these **t.** prophets tormented
12.14. woman were given **t.** wings
13. 5. to continue forty and **t.** mo.
11. he had **t.** horns like a lamb
Act.24.27. after **t.** years Porcius Festus
28.30. Paul dwelt **t.** whole years
Mat. 2.16. from **t.** years old and
(See *Edge, Edged, Hundred, Meeting,
Thousand.*)

TWOFOLD.
diplous.
Mat.23.15.**t.** more the child of hell

UNAWARES.
aiphnidios.
Lu. 21.34. that day come upon you **u.**
lanthanō.
Heb.13. 2. *have* entertained angels **u.**
(See *Brought, Creep.*)

UNBELIEF.
apistia.
Mat.13.58. because of their **u.**; Mar.6.6
17.20. un. them, Because of your **u.**
Mar. 9.24. believe ; help thou mine **u.**
16.14. upbraided them with their **u.**
Ro. 3. 3. shall their **u.** make the
4.20. promise of God through **u.**
11.20. because of **u.** they were bro.
23. if they abide not in **u.**
1Ti. 1.13. I did it ignorantly in **u.**
Heb. 3.12. you an evil heart of **u.**
19. not enter in because of **u.**
apeitheia.
Ro. 11.30. mercy through their **u.**
32. concluded them all in **u.**
Heb. 4. 6. entered not in because of **u.**
11. the same example of **u.**

UNBELIEVERS.
apistos.
Lu. 12.46. his portion with the **u.**
1Co. 6. 6. and that before the **u.**
14.23. that are unlearned, or **u.**
2Co. 6.14. yoked together with **u.**

UNBELIEVING.
apistos.
1Co. 7.14. For the **u.** husband is sanc.
the **u.** wife is sanctified by
15. if the **u.** depart, let him
Tit. 1.15. defiled and **u.** is nothing
Rev.21. 8. But the fearful, and **u.**, and
apeitheō.
Act.14. 2. the **u.** Jews stirred up the

UNBLAMEABLE.
amōmos.
Col. 1.22. to present you holy and **u.**
amemptos.
1Th. 3.13. stablish your hearts **u.** in

UNBLAMEABLY.
amemptōs.
1Th. 2.10. justly and **u.** we behaved

UNCERTAIN.
adēlos.
1Co. 14.8. trumpet give an **u.** sound
adēlotēs.
1Ti. 6.17. nor trust in **u.** riches
UNCERTAINLY.
adēlōs.
1Co. 9.26. so run, not as **u.** ; so fight
UNCHANGEABLE.
aparabatos.
Heb. 7.24. ever, hath an **u.** priesthood
UNCIRCUMCISED.
aperitmētos.
Act. 7.51. stiffnecked and **u.** in heart
echō akrobustia.
Act.11. 3. thou wentest in to men **u.**
(men *having uncircumcision*)
en akrobustia.
Ro. 4.11. which he had *being yet* **u.**
(*in uncircumcision*)
epispaomai.
1Co. 7.18. *let* him not *become* **u.**
UNCIRCUMCISION.
akrobustia.
Ro. 2.25. thy circumcision is made **u.**
26. if the **u.** keep the righteous.
shall not his **u.** be counted
27. shall not **u.** which is by nat.
3.30. by faith, and **u.** through
4. 9. or upon the **u.** also ? for we
10. in circumcision, or in **u.**
Not in circumcis., but in **u.**
1Co. 7.18. Is any called in **u.**? let him
19. **u.** is nothing, but the keepi.
Gal. 2. 7. gospel of the **u.** was commi.
5. 6. any thing, nor **u.**; but faith
6.15. nor **u.**, but a new creature
Eph. 2.11. who are called **u.** by that
Col. 2.13. the **u.** of your flesh, hath he
3.11. nor Jew, circumcision nor **u.**

UNCLEAN.
akathartos.   [Mar.6.7
Mat.10. 1. power against **u.** spirits ;
12.43. When the **u.** spirit; Lu.11.24
Mar. 1.23. a man with an **u.**; Mar.5.2
26. when the **u.** spirit had torn
27. command. he the **u.**; Lu.4.36
3.11. **u.** spirits, when they saw
30. said, He hath an **u.** spirit
5. 8. of the man, thou **u.** spirit
13. the **u.** spirits went out
7.25. daughter had an **u.** spirit
Lu. 4.33. had a spirit of an **u.** devil
6.18. were vexed with **u.**; Act.5.16
8.29. commanded the **u.** spirit
9.42. Jesus rebuked the **u.** spirit
Act. 8. 7. For **u.** spirits, crying with
10.14. thing that is common or **u.**
28. call any man common or **u.**
11. 8. nothing common or **u.** hath
1Co. 7.14. else were your children **u.**
2Co. 6.17. touch not the **u.** thing
Eph. 5. 5. nor **u.** person, nor covetous.
Rev.16.13. I saw three **u.** spirits like
18. 2. cage of every **u.** and hateful
koinos.
Ro. 14.14. thi. to be **u.**; to him it is **u.**
koinoō, [partic.]
Heb. 9.13. of an heifer sprinkling the **u.**
UNCLEANNESS.
akatharsia.
Mat.23.27. men's bones, and of all **u.**
Ro. 1.24. gave them up to **u.** through
6.19. your members servants to **u.**
2Co.12.21. have not repented of the **u.**
Gal. 5.19. Adultery, fornication, **u.**
Eph. 4.19. to work all **u.** with greedine.
5. 3. fornication, and all **u.**, or

293

Col. 3. 5. the earth ; fornication, **u.**
Th. 2. 3. nor of deceit, nor of u., nor
    4. 7. hath not called us unto **u.**
    miasmos.
²Pet. 2.10. the flesh in the lust of **u.**

UNCLOTHED.
    ekduō.
²Co. 5. 4. not for that we would be **u.**

UNCOMELY. (See *Behave.*)
    aschēmōn.
¹Co. 12.23. our **u.** *parts* have more

UNCONDEMNED.
    akatakritos.
Act.16.37. have beaten us openly **u.**
    22.25. man that is a Roman, and **u.**

UNCORRUPTIBLE.
    aphthartos.
Ro. 1.23. the glory of the **u.** God

UNCORRUPTNESS.
    adiaphthoria.
Tit. 2. 7. in doctrine shewing **u.**

UNCOVERED.
    apostegazō.
Mar. 2. 4. they **u.** the roof where
    akatakaluptos.
¹Co. 11. 5. prophesieth with her head **u.**
    13. a woman pray unto God **u.**

UNCTION.
    chrisma.
¹Jo. 2.20. have an **u.** from the Holy O.

UNDEFILED.
    amiantos.
Heb. 7.26. who is holy, harmless, **u.**
    13. 4. in all, and the bed **u.**
Jas. 1.27. Pure religion and **u.** before
¹Pet. 1. 4. inheritance incorrup., and **u.**

UNDER.
    hupo, [*accu.*]   [11.33
Mat. 5.15. and put it **u.** a bushel; Lu.
    8. 8. thou should. come **u.**; Lu.7.6
    9. **u.** authority,..**u.** me; Lu.7.8
    23.37. chickens **u.** her wi.; Lu.13.34
Mar. 4.21. put **u.** a bushel, or **u.** a bed
    32. may lodge **u.** the shadow of
Lu. 17.24. out of the one part **u.** heav.
    the other part **u.** heaven
Jo. 1.48. when thou wast **u.** the fig
Act. 2. 5. out of every nation **u.** heav.
    4.12. none other name **u.** heaven
Ro. 3. 9. that they are all **u.** sin
    13. the poison of asps is **u.** their
    6.14, 15. ye are **u.** the law, but **u.** grace
    7.14. but I am carnal, sold **u.** sin
    16.20. shall bruise Satan **u.** your
¹Co. 9.20. that are **u.** the law, as **u.**
    gain them that are **u.** the law
    10. 1. all our fathers were **u.** the
    15.25, 27. put . . **u.** his fe.; Eph.1.22
Gal. 3.10. are **u.** the curse : for it is
    22. hath concluded all **u.** sin
    23. we were kept **u.** the law
    25. no longer **u.** a schoolmaster
    4. 2. But is **u.** tutors and govern.
    3. **u.** the elements of the world
    4. of a woman, made **u.** the law
    5. them that were **u.** the law
    21. that desire to be **u.** the law
    5.18. ye are not **u.** the law
Col. 1.23. creature which is **u.** heaven
¹Ti. 6. 1. servants as are **u.** the yoke
Jas. 2. 3. or sit here **u.** my footstool
¹Pet. 5. 6. **u.** the mighty hand of God
Jude 6. in everlasting chains **u.** dar.
    hupokatō.
Mar. 6.11. shake off the dust **u.** your
    7.28. yet the dogs **u.** the table eat
Lu. 8.16. or putteth it **u.** a bed
294

Jo. 1.50. I saw thee **u.** the fig tree
Heb. 2. 8. all things in subjection **u.** his
Rev. 5. 3. in earth, neither **u.** the earth
    13. on the earth, and **u.** the ear.
    6. 9. I saw **u.** the altar the souls
    12. 1. and the moon **u.** her feet
    epi, [*dat.*]
Heb. 7.11. for **u.** it the people received
    9.15. **u.** the first testament
    10.28. **u.** two or three witnesses
    en.
Mat. 7. 6. trample them **u.** their feet
Ro. 3.19. them who are **u.** the law
    katōterō.
Mat. 2.16. from two years old and **u.**
    ennomos.
¹Co. 9.21. but **u.** *the law* to Christ
    elassōn.
¹Ti. 5. 9. into the number **u.** threesc.
(See *Bondage, Curse, Earth, Keep, Obe-dience, Put, Run, Sail.*)

UNDERGIRDING.
    hupozōnnumi.
Act.27.17. they used helps **u.** the ship

UNDERSTAND, *-est, -eth,*
    -ing, Understood.
    suniēmi.
Mat.13.13.hear not, neither do they **u.**
    14. hear, and *shall* not **u.**; Mar.
    4.12; Act.28.26
    15. and *should* **u.** with their he.
    19. and **u-***eth* it not, then
    23. heareth the word, and **u-***eth*
    51. *Have* ye **u-***o* all these things
    15.10. said unto them, Hear and **u.**
    16.12. Then **u-***o* they how that he
    17.13. Then the disciples **u-***o* that
Mar. 7.14. me every one of you, and **u.**
    8.17. perceive ye neit yet, neit. **u.**
    21. How is it that ye *do* not **u.**
Lu. 2.50. And they **u-***o* not the saying
    8.10. and hear. they *might* not **u.**
    18.34. And they **u-***o* none of these
    24.45. they *might* **u.** the scriptures
Act. 7.25. his brethren *would have* **u-***o*
    deliver them : but they **u-***o*
    28.27. and **u.** with their heart
Ro. 3.11. There is none *that* **u-***eth*
    15.21. that have not heard *shall* **u.**
Eph. 5.17. but **u-***ing* what the will of
    noeō.
Mat.15 17. *Do* not ye yet **u.**; 16.9
    16.11. How is it that ye *do* not **u.**
    24.15. reade., *let* him **u.**; Mar.13.14
Jo. 12.40. nor **u.** with their heart
Ro. 1.20. *being* **u-***o* by the things that
Eph. 3. 4. ye may **u.** my knowledge in
¹Ti. 1. 7. **u-***ing* neither what they say
Heb.11. 3. Through faith we **u.** that
    ginoskō.
Mat.26.10. *When* Jesus **u-***o* it, he said
Jo. 8.27. They **u-***o* not that he spake
    43. Why *do* ye not **u.** my speech
    10. 6. they **u-***o* not what things
    12.16. These things **u-***o* not his dis.
Act. 8.30. **u-***est* thou what thou readest
    24.11. Because that thou mayest **u.**
Phi. 1.12. But I would ye *should* **u.**
    agnoeō.   [Lu.9.45
Mar. 9.32. they **u-***o* not that saying ;
²Pet. 2.12. things that they **u.** not
    epistamai.
Mar.14.68.neither **u.** I what thou saye.
    manthanō.
Act.23.27. *having* **u-***o* that he was a
    punthanomai.
Act.23.34. *when* he **u-***o* that he was of
    gnōrizō.
¹Co. 12. 3 Wherefore I *give* you *to* **u.**

---

    eideō.
¹Co. 13. 2. prophecy, and **u.** all myste.
    14.16. **u-***eth* not what thou sayest
    phroneō.
¹Co. 13.11. I **u-***o* as a child
    akouō.
¹Co. 14. 2. for no man **u-***eth* him
    eusēmos.
¹Co. 14. 9. ye utter..words *easy to be* **u-***o*
    (See *Hard.*)

UNDERSTANDING.
    nous.
Lu. 24.45. Then opened he their **u.**
¹Co. 14.14. but my **u.** is unfruitful
    15. I will pray with the **u.** also
    I will sing with the **u.** also
    19. five words with my **u.**
Phi. 4. 7. which passeth all **u.**
Rev.13.18. Let him that hath **u.**
    sunesis.
Mar.12.33.and with all the **u.** and with
Lu. 2.47. were astonished at his **u.**
¹Co. 1.19. bring to nothing the **u.** of
Col. 1. 9. wisdom and spiritual **u.**
    2. 2. of the full assurance of **u.**
²Ti. 2. 7. the Lord give thee **u.** in all
    dianoia.
Eph 1.18. The eyes of your **u.** being
    4.18. Having the **u.** darkened
¹Jo. 5.20. hath given us an **u.**, that
    asunetos.   [Mar.7.18
Mat.15.16.Are ye also yet *without* **u.** ;
Ro. 1.31. *without* **u.**, covenant break.
    phrēn, [*plur.*]
    4.20. Breth., be not children n **u.**
    but in **u.** be men
    parakoloutheō.
Lu. 1. 3. *having had* perfect **u.** of all

UNEQUALLY. (See *Yoked.*)
UNFEIGNED.
    anupokritos.
²Co. 6. 6. by the Holy Gh., by love **u.**
¹Ti. 1. 5. conscience, and of faith **u.**
²Ti. 1. 5. the **u.** faith that is in thee
¹Pet. 1.22. unto **u.** love of the brethren

UNFRUITFUL.
    akarpos.   [Mar.4.19
Mat.13.22.word, and he becometh **u.**;
¹Co. 14.14. my understanding is **u.**
Eph. 5.11. with the **u.** works of darkn.
Tit. 3.14. uses, that they be not **u.**
²Pet. 1. 8. neither be barren nor **u.** in

UNGODLINESS
    asebeia.
Ro. 1.18. against all **u.** and unrighteo.
    11.26. shall turn away **u.** from Ja.
²Ti. 2.16. will increase unto more **u.**
Tit. 2.12. denying **u.** and worldly

UNGODLY.
    asebēs.
Ro. 4. 5. him that justifieth the **u.**
    5. 6. Christ died for the **u.**
¹Ti. 1. 9. for the **u.** and for sinners
¹Pet. 4.18. where shall the **u.** and the
²Pet. 2. 5. upon the world of the **u.**
    3. 7. judgment and perdition of **u.**
Jude 4. **u.** *men*, turning the grace
    15. convince all *that are* **u.**
    which **u.** sinners have
    asebeō.
²Pet. 2. 6. thereafter should *live* **u.**
Jude 15. which they *have* **u.** commi.
    asebeia.   [*godliness*
Jude 15. their **u.** deeds (deeds *of un-*
    18. after their own **u.** lusts

UNHOLY.
    anosios.
¹Ti. 1. 9. for **u.** and profane, for

Ti. 3. 2. to parents, unthankful, **u.**
koinos.
Heb.10.29.an **u.** thing, and hath done

UNITY.
henotēs.
Eph. 4. 3. to keep the **u.** of the spirit
13. come in the **u.** of the faith

UNJUST.
adikos.
Mat. 5.45. ra. on the just and on the **u.**
Lu. 16.10. is **u.** in the least is **u.**
18.11. extortioners, **u.**, adulterers
Act.24.15. both of the just and **u.**
1Co. 6. 1. go to law before the **u.**, and
1Pet. 3.18. for sins, the just for the **u.**
1Pet. 2. 9. to reserve the **u.** unto the
adikia.
Lu. 16. 8. commended the **u.** steward
18. 6. Hear what the **u.** judge saith
adikeō.
Rev.22.11. He *that is* **u.**, *let him be* **u.**

UNKNOWN.
agnōstos.
Act.17.23. inscription, To the **u.** God
agnoeō, [partic.]
2Co. 6. 9. As **u.**, and yet well known
Gal. 1.22. was **u.**, by face unto the ch.

UNLADE.
apophortizomai.
Act.21. 3. the ship was *to* **u.** her burd.

UNLAWFUL.
athemitos.
Act.10.28. it is an **u.** *thing* for a man
anomos.
2Pet. 2. 8. to day with their **u.** deeds

UNLEARNED.
agrammatos.
Act.4.13. were **u.** and ignorant men
idiōtēs.
1Co. 14.16. occupieth the room of the **u.**
23. those that are **u.**, or unbelie.
24. that believeth not, or one **u.**
apaideutos.
2Ti. 2.23. foolish and **u.** questions
amathēs.
2Pet. 3.16. which they *that are* **u.** and

UNLEAVENED.
azumos.
Mat.26.17. the feast of **u.** *bread;* Lu.22.1
Mar.14. 1. passover, and of **u.** *bread*
12. day of **u.** *bread;* Lu.22.7
Act.12. 3. the days of **u.** *bread;* 20.6.
1Co. 5. 7. be a new lump, as ye are **u.**
8. **u.** bread of sincerity and tr.

UNLESS.
ektos ei mē.
1Co.15. 2. **u.** ye have believed in vain

UNLOOSE.
luō. [Lu.3.16; Jo.1.27
Mar. 1. 7. worthy to stoop down and **u.**

UNMARRIED.
agamos.
1Co. 7. 8. say therefore to the **u.** and
11. she depart, let her remain **u.**
32. He that is **u.** careth for the
34. The **u.** woman careth for the

UNMERCIFUL.
aneleēmōn.
Ro. 1.31. nat. affection, implacable, **u.**

UNMOVEABLE.
asaleutos.
Act.27.41. stuck fast, and remained **u**

ametakinētos.
1Co. 15.58. be ye steadfast, **u.**, always

UNPREPARED.
aparaskeuastos.
2Co. 9. 4. with me, and find you **u.**

UNPROFITABLE.
achreios.
Mat.25.30. cast ye the **u.** servant
Lu. 17.10. say, We are **u.** servants
achrēstos.
Phile. 11. in time past was to thee **u.**
achreioomai.
Ro. 3.12. they *are* together *become* **u.**
anōphelēs.
Tit. 3. 9. for they are **u.** and vain
alusitelēs.
Heb.13.17.for that is **u.** for you

UNPROFITABLENESS.
anōphelēs.
Heb. 7.18. the weakness and **u.** thereof

UNQUENCHABLE.
asbestos. [Lu.3.17
Mat. 3.12. up the chaff with **u.** fire;

UNREASONABLE.
alogos.
Act.25.27. For it seemeth to be **u.**
atopos.
2Th. 3. 2. from **u.** and wicked men

UNREBUKABLE.
anepilēptos.
1Ti. 6.14. without spot, **u.**, until the

UNREPROVEABLE.
anegklētos.
Col. 1.22. holy and unblameable and **u.**

UNRIGHTEOUS.
adikos.
Lu. 16.11. faithful in the **u.** mammon
Ro. 3. 5. Is God **u.** who taketh
1Co. 6. 9. the **u.** shall not inherit the
Heb. 6.10. God is not **u.** to forget

UNRIGHTEOUSNESS.
adikia.
Lu. 16. 9. friends of the mammon of **u.**
Jo. 7.18. and no **u.** is in him
Ro. 1.18. ungodliness and **u.** of men
who hold the truth in **u.**
29. filled with all **u.**, fornication
2. 8. obey the truth, but obey **u.**
3. 5. if our **u.** commend the
6.13. instruments of **u.** unto
9.14. Is there **u.** with God
2Th. 2.10. deceivableness of **u.**
12. but had pleasure in **u.**
Heb. 8.12. will be merciful to their **u.**
2Pet. 2.13. receive the reward of **u.**
15. who loved the wages of **u.**
1Jo. 1. 9. and to cleanse us from all **u.**
5.17. All **u.** is sin; and there is
anomia.
2Co. 6.14. hath righteousness with **u.**

UNRULY.
ataktos.
1Th. 5.14. warn them that are **u.**
anupotaktos.
Tit. 1. 6. not accused of riot, or **u.**
10. there are many **u.** and vain
akatascheton.
Jas. 3. 8. an **u.** evil, full of deadly

UNSEARCHABLE.
anexereunētos.
Ro. 11.33. how **u.** are his judgments
anexichniastos.
Eph. 3. 8. the **u.** riches of Christ

UNSEEMLY, (See *Behave*.)
aschēmosunē.
Ro. 1.27. men working *that which is* **u.**

UNSKILFUL.
apeiros.
Heb. 5.13. is **u.** in the word of righteo.

UNSPEAKABLE.
anekdiēgētos.
2Co. 9.15. unto God for his **u.** gift
arrētos.
2Co. 12. 4. into paradise, and heard **u.**
aneklalētos.
1Pet. 1. 8. with joy **u.** and full of glory

UNSPOTTED.
aspilos.
Jas. 1.27. to keep himself **u.** from the

UNSTABLE.
akatastatos.
Jas. 1. 8. A double minded man is **u.**
astēriktos.
2Pet. 2.14. beguiling **u.** souls; an
3.16. that are unlearned and **u.**

UNTAKEN.
mē anakaluptō, [partic.]
2Co. 3.14. the same vail **u.** *away*

UNTHANKFUL.
acharistos.
Lu. 6.35. is kind unto the **u.** and to
2Ti. 3. 2. disobedient to parents, **u.**

UNTIL.
heōs.
Mat. 1.17. and from David **u.** the
2.15. there **u.** the death of Herod
11.12. of John the Baptist **u.** now
13. the law prophesied **u.** John
17. 9. **u.** the Son of man be risen
18.22. I say not unto thee, **u.** seven
u. seventy times seven
24.39. knew not **u.** the flood came
26.29. this fruit of the vine, **u.** that
27.64. be made sure **u.** the third
Mar.14.25.**u.** that day that I drink it
15.33. the whole land **u.** the ninth
Lu. 15. 4. which is lost, **u.** he find it
16.16. prophets were **u.** John
22.16. **u.** it be fulfilled in the king.
18. **u.** the kingdom of God
23.44. the earth **u.** the ninth hour
24.49. **u.** ye be endued with power
Jo. 2.10. hast kept the good wine **u.**
9.18. **u.** they called the parents
Act.13.20. **u.** Samuel the prophet
21.26. **u.** that an offering should be
23.14. eat nothing **u.** we have slain
1Co. 16. 8. will tarry at Ephesus **u.** Pen.
2Th. 2. 7. **u.** he be taken out of the way
2Pet. 1.19. **u.** the day dawn, and the
1Jo. 2. 9. is in darkness *even* **u.** now
Rev. 6.11. their fellowservants also
20. 5. **u.** the thousand years were
heōs an.
Mat. 2.13. thou there **u.** I bring thee
Lu. 13.35. **u.** the time come when ye
Act. 2.35. **u.** I make thy foes; Heb.1.13
1Co. 4. 5. **u.** the Lord come who both
Jas. 5. 7. **u.** he receive the early and
achri.
Mat.24.38. **u.** the day that Noe; Lu.17.27
Lu. 1.20. **u.** the day that these things
21.24. **u.** the times of the Gentiles
Act. 1. 2. **u.** the day in which he was
3.21. **u.** the times of restitution of
23. 1. conscience before God **u.** this
Ro. 5.13. For **u.** the law sin was in
8.22. travaileth in pain together **u.**
11.25. **u.** the fulness of the Gentiles
2Co. 3.14. for **u.** this day remaineth the

Gal. 4. 2. u. the time appointed of the
 19. u. Christ be formed in you
Phi. 1. 5. from the first day u. now
 6. u. the day of Jesus Christ
Rev.17.17. u. the words of God shall

mechri.

Mat.11.23. have remained u. this day
 13.30. grow together u. the harvest
 28.15. reported among the Jews u.
Act.10.30. I was fasting u. this hour
 20. 7. continued his speech u. mid.
¹Ti. 6.14. u. the appearing of our Lord
Heb. 9.10. u. the time of reformation

eis.

Eph. 1.14. u. the redemption of the

UNTIMELY. (See *Figs.*)

UNTO

*Represents the dative case, except in the
  following:—*

pros, [*accu.*]   [Lu.3.9

Mat. 3.10. the axe is laid u. the root;
 13. 2. were gathered together u.
Mar. 1.32. they brought u. him all that
 2.13. the multitude resorted u.
 4. 1. there was gathered u. him
 6.30. themselves together u. Jesus
 9.17. I have brought u. thee my
 19. bring him u. me
 20. and they brought him u. him
 10. 1. the people resort u. him aga.
Lu. 1.80. till the day of his shewing u.
 3. 9. the axe is laid u. the root
 4.40. brought them u. him
 10.23. he turned him u. his discip.
 18. 7. which cry day and night u.
 40. to be brought u. him
 19.42. things which belong u. thy
 23.28. But Jesus turning u. them
Jo. 8. 3. brought u. him a woman ta.
 10.41. many resorted u. him
 11. 4. This sickness is not u. death
 12.32. will draw all men u. me
 14. 3. and receive you u. myself
 20.10. u. their own home
 17. I ascend u. my Father, and
Act. 3.11. the people ran together u.
 12. he answered u. the people
 12. 5. prayer was made..u. God for
 21. and made an oration u. them
 13.31. his witnesses u. the people
 32. which was made u. the fath.
 36. and was laid u. his fathers
 18.21. I will return again u. you, if
 22. 1. which I make now u. you
 5. I received letters u. the bret.
 15. thou shalt be his witness u.
 23.15. that he bring him down u.
 17. Bring this young man u. the
 18. to bring this young man u.
 24. bring him safe u. Felix
 26. 6. made of God u. our fathers
Ro. 10.21. u. a disobedient and gainsa.
¹Co. 11. 2. carried away u. these dumb
 14.26. Let all things be done u. ed.
²Co. 1.20. u. the glory of God by us
 6.11. our mouth is open u. you
 7.12. might appear u. you
Gal. 6.10. let us do good u. all men
 especially u. them who are of
Eph. 2.18. by one Spirit u. the Father
 3.14. I bow my knees u. the Fath.
 5.31. shall be joined u. his wife
 6. 9. do the same thing u. them
Phi. 4. 6. requests be made known u.
¹Th. 1. 9. entering in we had u. you
 2. 1. our entrance in u. you
 3.11. direct our way u. you
¹Ti. 4. 7. exercise thyself rather u.
 8. godliness is profitable u. all
²Ti. 2.24. but be gentle u. all
 3.17. furnished u. all good works
296

Tit. 1.16. u. every good work reprobate
 3. 2. all meekness u. all men
Heb. 5. 7. u. him that was able to save
 9.20. which God hath injoined u.
²Pet. 1. 3. all things that pertain u.
 3.16. u. their own destruction
¹Jo. 5.16. a sin which is not u. death
 for them that sin not u. dea.
 There is a sin u. death
 17. and there is a sin not u. dea.
Rev.12. 5. child was caught up u. God
 22.18. If any man shall add u. these

(Said, Speak, Tell, &c., unto.)

(Also)Mat. 3.15. Lu.1.13,18,19,34,61;
2.20,34, 48,49; 3.12, 13,14; 4.21, 23, 43;
5.4,10,22,31,33,34,36; 6.9;7.24,40;8.21,22;
9.3,13,33,43,50,57,59,62; 10.2,26,29; 11.
1,5,39,53; 12.1,15,16,22,41; 13.7,23; 14.
3,7,23,25; 15.3; 16.1; 17.1,22; 18.9,31;
19.5,8,9,13,33,39; 20.2,3,23,41; 22.15,52,
70; 23.14,22; 24.5, 10,17, 18,25, 44. Jo.
2.3; 3.4; 4.15,48,49; 6.5,28,34; 7.3,50;
8. 2, 7, 57; 11.21. Act.1.7; 2.29, 37,
38; 3. 22, *bis*; 4. 1, 8, 19, 23; 5.9,
35; 7.3; 8.20,26; 9.6,11,15; 10.15,28; 11.
20; 12.8,15; 15.7,36; 16.37; 18.6,14; 19.
2, *bis*, 3; 21.37,39; 22.8,10,21,25; 23.3;
25.22; 26.1,14,28; 28.17,21,25. ¹Th.2.
2. Heb.1.8; 5.5; 7.21.

(Go, Come, Send, &c., unto.)

(Also) Mat.3.13; 11.28; 14.25,28; 19.
14; 21,1,32,37; 23.34,37; 25.36,39; 26.
14,40; 27.19,62. Mar.1.5; 2.3; 3.8,13,
31; 6.25,33,45,48,51; 7.1,31; 10.14; 12.
4,6,13,18; 14.10; 15.43. Lu.1.28; 4.26,
bis; 7.3,7,20, *bis*; 13.12; 16.30; 18.3,16.
Jo.1.29; 3.26; 4.30,40,47; 5.33; 6.5,45,
65; 7.33,37; 10.35; 11.3,15,29; 13.1; 14.
6,12,23,28,*bis*; 16.7,*bis*; 18.24,29,38; 20.
10. Act.7.31; 8.14; 9.38; 10.21, *bis*;
11.11; 15.2,25,33; 19.31; 20.6; 21.11,18;
22.13; 27.3; 28.26,30. Ro.1.10,13; 15.
23,29,32. ¹Co.4.21; 14.6; 16.5,11,12.
²Co.1.15,16; 8.17; 12.17. Eph.6.22.
Col.4.8, 10. ¹Th.2.18; 3.6. ¹Ti.3.14.
²Ti.4.9. Tit.3.12,*bis*. ³Jo.10,12. Rev.
10.9; 12.12; 21.9.

eis.

Mat. 3.11. baptise you with water u.
 7.14. the way, which leadeth u.
 8.18. u. the other side; 14.22
 9. 6. take up thy bed, and go u.
 12.20. forth judgment u. victory
 13.52. instructed u. the kingdom
 15.24. I am not sent but u. the lost
 16.21. that he must go u.Jerusalem
 21. 1. they drew nigh u. Jerusalem
 22. 4. ready; come u. the marriage
 24.13. shall endure u.; Mar.13.13

(Also) Mat. 26.3,36; 27.33. Mar.
4.35; 5.1,21; 11.1,11; 13.13; 15.41.
Lu.1.26; 2.4; 4.26; 5.24; 8.22; 11.24;
17.24; 18.13,35; 21.4; 24.28. Jo.1.11;
4.8,36,45; 5.24,29,*bis*; 6.27; 7.8,*bis*,10,
35,53; 8.1; 11.31,54; 12.25,27; 13.1;
18.28; 19.27; 20.1. Act.1.12; 4.3;
5.16; 8.26; 9.2; 11.18,22,26,27; 12.10;
13.4,51; 14.6; 15.39; 17.10; 18.6;
19.3,*bis*;20.13,22,38; 21.1,*ter*,2,8; 22.5,7,
21; 25.6,13,21; 26.7,11,17; 27.8,40.
Ro. 1.1,16,26; 3.7,22; 5.15,16,18,21;
6.16,*bis*,19,*bis*,22; 9.21,23; 10.10,*bis*,12,
18; 15.25; 16.5,19,*bis*. ¹Co. 1.9;
2.7; 10.2; 11.34; 14.36; 16.3. ²Co.
1.23; 2.4,16,*bis*; 4.11; 8.2; 9.5,13,*bis*;
10.14. Gal.1.6,17; 2.9,*bis*; 3.23,24.
Eph.1.5,14,15; 2.21; 4.13,*bis*,16,30. Phi.
1.11,12; 3.11; 4.16. Col. 1.6,10,11,
20; 2.2; 4.11. ¹Th. 1.5; 2.9,12; 4.8,
15. ¹Ti.1.6; 2.4. ²Ti. 2.21,*bis*; 3.15;
4.10,*bis*,18. Heb. 2.3,10; 6.6; 9.28;

10.39; 11.26; 12.2. Jas. 2.2. ¹Pet.
1.2,3,5,7,10,22,25; 3.12; 4.7; 5.10.
²Pet.2.4,9. ¹Jo 3.14. Jude 6,21. Rev.
1.11,*sept.*; 6.13; 9.1,7; 12.13; 19.9,17.

epi, [*accus.*]

Mat. 6.27. add one cubit u. his stature
 12.28. kingdom of God is come u.
 27.27. gathered u. him the whole
Mar. 5.21. much people gathered u.
 15.22. u. the place Golgotha
 46. u. the door of the sepulchre
 16. 2. they came u. the sepulchre
Lu. 6.35. he is kind u. the unthankful
 10. 9. 11. is come nigh u. you
 12.11. bring you u. the synagogues
 23. 1. led him u. Pilate
 24. 1, 12. u. the sepulchre
Jo. 6.16. went down u. the sea
Act. 8.26. u. the way that goeth down
 36. they came u. a certain water
 9.21. bound u. the chief priests
 10.11. vessel descending u. him
 11.11. already come u. the house
 21. turned u. the Lord
 12.10. they came u. the iron gate
 14.13. oxen and garlands u. the
 15. u. the living God.
 16.19. marketplace u. the rulers
 17. 6. u. the rulers of the city
 19. brought him u. Areopagus
 19.12. were brought u. the sick
 21.32. ran down u. them
 24. 8. his accusers to come u. thee
 25.12. u. Cesar shalt thou go
 26.18. from the power of Satan u.
²Th. 2. 1. gathering together u. him
²Ti. 2.16. will increase u. more ungod.
 4. 4. shall be turned u. fables
Heb. 6. 1. let us go on u. perfection
¹Pet. 2.25. now returned u. the Sheph.
Rev. 7.17. u. living fountains of wat.
 16.14. the kings of the earth
 22.18. God shall add u. him

epi, [*dat.*]

Mat. 9.16. new cloth u. an old garm.
Gal. 5.13. have been called u. liberty
Eph. 2.10. in Ch. Jes. u. good works
¹Th. 4. 7. not called us u. uncleanness

heōs.

Mat. 1.17. u. Christ are fourteen gener.
 11.23. art exalted u. heaven, shalt
 20. 8. beginning from the last u.
 22.26. also, and the third, u. the
 23.35. u. the blood of Zac.; Lu.11.51
 24.27. shineth even u. the west
 26.38. sorrowful, *even* u.; Mar.14.34
 58. u. the high priest's palace
 27. 8. field of blood, u. this day
 45. over all the land u. the ninth
 28.20. even u. the end of the world
Mar. 6.23. u. the half of my kingdom
 13.19. which God created u. this
Lu. 2.15. Let us now go even u. Beth.
 4.29. and led him u. the brow of
 42. sought him, and came u. him
Jo. 8. 9. even u. the last
Act. 1. 8. u. the uttermost part of the
 22. u. that same day that
 7.45. u. the days of David
 13.47. u. the ends of the earth
 17.15. brought him u. Athens
 26.11. even u. strange cities
Ro. 11. 8. should not hear; u. this day
¹Co. 1. 8. shall also confirm you u. the
 4.13. of all things u. this day
 8. 7. u. this hour eat it as a thing
 15. 6. the greater part remain u.
²Co. 3.15. But *even* u. this day
Jas. 5. 7. u. the coming of the Lord

achri, *or* **achris**

Act. 2.29. his sepulchre is with us u.
 13. 6. through the isle u. Paphos

Act.22. 4. I persecuted this way **u.** the
   22. gave him audience **u.** this
   26.22. I continue **u.** this day, witn.
¹Co. 4.11. Even **u.** this present hour we
²Co. 10.13. a measure to reach even **u.**
Heb. 6.11. full assurance of hope **u.** the
Rev. 2.10. be thou faithful **u.** death
   26. keepeth my works **u.** the end
   12.11. loved not their lives **u.** the
   14.20. even **u.** the horse bridles
   18. 5. her sins have reached **u.** hea.
en.
Mat.17.12. have done **u.** him whatsoev.
Ro. 5.21. as sin hath reigned **u.** death
¹Co. 9.15. that it should be so done **u.**
   14.11. shall be a barbarian **u.** me
²Co. 5.19. hath committed **u.** us the
¹Th. 4. 7. unto uncleanness, but **u.** ho.
   5.23. **u.** the coming of our Lord
¹Ti. 3.16. preached **u.** the Gentiles, be.
mechri, *or* **mechris.**
Ro. 15.19. and round about **u.** Illyricum
Phi. 2. 8. became obedient **u.** death
   30. he was nigh **u.** death
²Ti. 2. 9. as an evil doer, even **u.** bonds
Heb. 3. 6. rejoicing of the hope firm **u.**
   14. confidence stedfast **u.** the end
   12. 4. Ye have not yet resisted **u.**
ek.
Lu. 23. 7. belonged **u.** Herod's jurisdic.
kata, [*accus.*]
Phi. 1.12. *things wh. happened* **u.** me
hōs.
Rev. 2.18. his eyes *like* **u.** a flame of
meta, [*gen.*]
Rev. 10. 8. heaven spake **u.** me again
(See words in connection.)

UNTOWARD.
skolios.
Act. 2.40. yourselves from this **u.** gene.

UNUTTERABLE.
alalētos.
Ro. 8.26. groanin. *which cannot be* **u.**

UNWASHEN.
aniptos.
Mat.15.20. to eat with **u.** hands defileth
Mar. 7. 2. with **u.** hands, they found
   5. but eat bread with **u.** hands

UNWISE.
anoētos.
Ro. 1.14. to the wise, and to the **u.**
aphrōn.
Eph. 5.17. Wherefore be ye not **u.**

UNWORTHILY.
anaxiōs.
¹Co.11.27. cup of the Lord **u.** shall
   29. that eateth and drinketh **u.**

UNWORTHY.
ouk axios.
Act.13.46. judge yourselves **u.** of ever.
anaxios.
¹Co. 6. 2. are ye **u.** to judge the small.

UP.
anatellō.
Mat.13. 6. *when* the sun *was* **u.**;Mar.4.6
heōs.
Jo. 2. 7. filled them **u.** *to* the brim
anō.
Jo. 11.41. Jesus lifted **u.** his eyes, and
Heb.12.15.springing **u.** trouble you
(See words in connection.)

UPBRAID,   -ed, -eth.
oneidizō.
Mat.11.20.Then began he *to* **u.** the

Mar.16.14.and **u-**ed them with their
Jas. 1. 5. liberally, and **u-**eth not

UPHOLDING.
pherō.
Heb. 1. 3. **u.** all things by the word of

UPON.
epi, [*accus.*] [Mar.1.10; Lu.3.22
Mat. 3.16. dove and lighting **u.** him ;
   7.24. built his house **u.** a rock
   25. for it was found. **u.**; Lu.6.48
   26. built his house **u.**; Lu.6.49
   9.18. lay thy hand **u.** her, and
   10.13. let your peace come **u.** it
   11.29. Take my yoke **u.** you, and
   12.18. I will put my spirit **u.** him
   13. 5. Some fell **u.** stony places
   19.28. also shall sit **u.** twelve thr.
   21. 5. meek, and sitting **u.** an ass
   23.35. That **u.** you may come all
   36. shall come **u.** this generation
   24. 2. one stone **u.** another
   27.29. they put it **u.** his head
   35. **u.** my vesture did they cast
Mar. 8.25. put his hands again **u.** his
   10.16. put his hands **u.** them
   15.24. casting lots **u.** them
Lu. 1.12. troubled, and fear fell **u.** him
   35. Holy Ghost shall come **u.**
   2.25. the Holy Ghost was **u.** him
   40. the grace of God was **u.** him
   4.18. Spirit of the Lord is **u.** me
   5.19. they went **u.** the housetop
   36. a new garment **u.** an old
   8. 6. some fell **u.** a rock
   9.38. I beseech thee, look **u.** my
   10. 6. peace shall rest **u.** it ; if not
   11.20. kingdom of God is come **u.**
   13. 4. **u.** whom the tower in Siloam
   19.35. cast their garments **u.** the
   43. the days shall come **u.** thee
   20.18. siall fall **u.** that stone
   21.34. that day come **u.** you unaw.
   24.49. promise of my Father **u.** you
Jo. 1.32. it abode **u.** him
   33. **u.** whom thou shalt see the
   51. descending **u.** the Son of m.
   9.15. He put clay **u.** mine eyes
   18. 4. that should come **u.** him
Act. 1. 8. Holy Ghost is come **u.** you
   26. the lot fell **u.** Matthias
   2. 3. it sat **u.** each of them
   17. my Spirit **u.** all flesh
   4.33. great grace was **u.** them all
   5.11. great fear came **u.** all the ch.
   u. as many as heard these
   28. this man's blood **u.** us
   7.57. ran **u.** him with one accord
   8.24. have spoken come **u.** me
   10. 9. Peter went up **u.** the house
   13.11. hand of the Lord is **u.** thee
   15.10. to put a yoke **u.** the neck
   17. **u.** whom my name is called
   18. 6. **u.** your own heads
   21.35. when he came **u.** the stairs
   26.16. stand **u.** thy feet
Ro. 2. 9. **u.** every soul of man that
   12. **u.** all them that believe
   4. 9. **u.** the circumcision only
   or **u.**the uncircumcision also
   15.20. build **u.** another man's foun.
¹Co. 3.12. build **u.** this foundation
²Co. 1.23. for a record **u.** my soul
   3.15. the vail is **u.** their heart
   12. 9. power of Christ may rest **u.**
Gal. 6.16. and **u.** the Israel of God
Eph. 5. 6. wrath of God **u.** the children
¹Th. 2.16. wrath is come **u.** them
Heb.11.21.*leaning* **u.** the top of his staff
Jas. 2.21. offered Isaac his son **u.** the
¹Pet. 4.14. of God resteth **u.** you

---

¹Pet. 5. 7. Casting all your care **u.** him
Rev. 1.17. laid his right hand **u.** me
   2.24. I will put **u.** you none
   3. 3. what hour I will come **u.** th.
   12. I will write **u.** him the name
   4. 4. **u.** the seats I saw four
   8. 3. of all saints **u.** the golden
   10. **u.** third part of rivers, and
   u. the fountains of waters
   10. 2. **u.** sea, and his left foot on
   11.11. they stood **u.** their feet ; and
   fear fell **u.** them which saw
   16. seats, fell **u.** their faces
   12. 3. seven crowns **u.** his heads
   13. 1. I stood **u.** the sand of the
   u. his heads the name
   14.14. **u.** the cloud one sat like
   16. 2. poured out his vial **u.** the
   8. his vial **u.** the sun
   10. **u.** the seat of the beast
   12. **u.** the great river Euphrates
   21. there fell **u.** men a great ha.
   17. 3. sit **u.** a scarlet coloured bea.
   5. **u.** her forehead was a name
   16. which thou sawest **u.** the
   19.11. he that sat **u.** him
   20. 4. thrones, and they sat **u.** th.
   u. their foreheads

epi, [*gen.*]
Mat. 6.19. for yourselves treasures **u.**
   10.27. preach ye **u.** the housetops
   23. 9. call no man your father **u.**
   35. blood shed **u.** the earth
   24. 3. sat **u.** the mount of Olives
   25.31. sit **u.** the throne of his glory
Mar. 6.48, 49. walking **u.** the sea
   7.30. her daughter laid **u.** the bed
Lu. 5.24. hath power **u.** earth to
   12. 3. proclaimed **u.** the housetops
   17.31. shall be **u.** the housetop
   21.25. **u.** the earth distress of nati.
Jo. 19.31. not remain **u.** the cross
Act.12.21. sat **u.** his throne
Ro. 9.28. the Lord make **u.** the earth
Col. 3. 5. which are **u.** the earth
Heb. 6. 7. rain that cometh oft **u.** it
Rev. 3.10. come **u.** all the world, to try
   them that dwell **u.** the earth
   5. 7. him that sat **u.** the ; 7.10
   10. 1. a rainbow was **u.** his head
   5, 8. stand **u.** the sea and the
   11.10. **u.** the earth shall rejoice
   12. 1. **u.** her head a crown
   13. 1. **u.** his horns ten crowns
   16.18. since men were **u.** the earth
   17. 1. whore that sitteth **u.** many
   18.24. that were slain **u.** the earth
   19.21. of him that sat **u.** the house
   21. 5. he that sat **u.** the throne

epi, [*dat.*]
Mat.16.18.**u.** this rock I will build
Mar. 6.39. by companies **u.** the green
   11. 7. and he sat **u.** him
   13. 2. one stone **u.** another ;
            Lu.19.44 ; 21.6
Jo. 4.27. **u.** this came his disciples
   11.38. a stone lay **u.** it
Act. 8.16. was fallen **u.** none of them
   13.40. lest that come **u.** you
Eph. 2.20. built **u.** the foundation of
   4.26. go down **u.** your wrath
Phi. 1. 3. **u.** every remembrance of
   2.17. offered **u.** the sacrifice
   27. should have sorrow **u.** sorr.
Heb. 8. 6. established **u.** better promis.
Rev.19.14. followed him **u.** white horses
eis.
Mat.26.10. wrought a good work **u.** me
   27.30. they spit **u.** him, and took
Mar.13. 3. as he sat **u.** the mount of Ol
Lu. 8.43. spent all her living **u.** phys.

Lu. 18.13. smote **u.** his breast, saying
Act. 3. 4. fastening his eyes **u.** him wi.
  11. 6. **u.** the which when I had fa.
  22.13. same hour I look. up **u.** him
  27.26. must be cast **u.** a certain isl.
    29. should have fallen **u.** rocks
Ro. 5.12. so death passed **u.** all men
    18. **u.** all men to condemnation
        u. all men unto justification
  13. 6. attending continually **u.** this
¹Co.10.11. **u.** whom the ends of the wo.
  15.10. which was bestowed **u.** me
²Co. 1.11. **u.** us by the means of many
Gal. 4.11. bestowed **u.** you labour in
Rev. 8. 7. they were cast **u.** the earth
  9. 3. of the smoke locusts **u.** the
  16. 1. the wrath of God **u.** the
    2. grievous sore **u.** the men
    3, 4. poured out his vial **u.** the
    en.
Mat.12. 2. to do **u.** the sabbath day
Lu. 21.23. wrath **u.** this people
Act.20. 7. **u.** the first day of the week
Jas. 4. 3. consume it **u.** your lusts
    epanō.
Mat.23.18. by the gift that is **u.** it
    28. 2. from the door, and sat **u.** it
Rev.20. 3. and set a seal **u.** him, that
    meta, [*gen.*]
Lu. 1.58. shewed great mercy **u.** her
    apo.
Act.11.19. were scattered abroad **u.** the
    kata, [*accus.*]
¹Co. 16. 2. **u.** the first day of the
    kata, [*gen.*]
Jude   15. to execute judgment **u.** all
  (*See words in connection.*)

UPPER.
huperōon.
Act. 1.13. went up into an **u.** *room*
  9.37. laid her in an **u.** *chamber*
    39. bro. him into the **u.** *chamber*
  20. 8. many lights in the **u.***chamber*
    anōgeon.   [Lu.22.12
Mar.14.15. a large **u.** *room* furnished ;
    anōterikos.
Act.19. 1. passed through the **u.** coasts

UPPERMOST. (See*Room, Seat.*)

UPRIGHT.
orthos.
Act.14.10. Stand **u.** on thy feet

UPRIGHTLY.   (See *Walk.*)

UPROAR.
thorubos.
Mat.26. 5. lest there be an **u.**; Mar.14.2
Act.20. 1. And after the **u.** was ceased
    thorubeō.
Act.17.5. *set* all the city *on an* **u.**
    stasis.
Act.19.40. in question for this day's **u.**
    sungchunō.
Act.21.31. all Jerusalem *was in an* **u.**
    anastatoō.
Act.21.38. before th. days *madest an* **u.**

UPSIDE.   (See *Turn.*)

URGE.
enechō.
Lu. 11.53. began *to* **u.** him vehemently

US.
ego.
Mat.1. 23. interpreted is, God with **u.**
  3.15. it becometh **u.** to fulfil all
  6.11. give **u.** this day our daily
    12. forgive **u.** our debts as we
    13. lead **u.** not into temptation
298

Mat. 6.13. but deliver **u.** from evil
  (*And all other passages except*)
    psuchē egō.   (*our soul*)
Jo. 10.24. thou make **u.** to doubt

USE, [*noun,*]   -*s.*
chrēsis.
Ro. 1.26. did change the natural **u.**
    27. leaving the natural **u.** of
    hexis.
Heb. 5.14. those who by reason of **u.**
    chreia.
Eph. 4.29. which is good to the **u.** of
Tit. 3.14. good works for necessary **u**-*s*

USE, [*verb,*]   -ed, -eth, -ing.
chraomai.
Act.27.17. they **u**-*ed* helps, undergirding
¹Co. 7.21. mayest be made free, **u.** it
    31. they *that* **u.** this world, as
  9.12. Neverthel. we *have* not **u**-*ed*
    15. But I *have* **u**-*ed* none of the.
²Co. 1.17. thus minded, *did* I **u.** light.
  3.12. we **u.** great plainness of spe.
  13.10. present I *should* **u.** sharpne.
¹Tt. 1. 8. the law is good, if a man **u.**
  5.23. but **u.** a little wine for thy
    eimi.   [(*were* fasters)
Mar. 2.18. of the Pharisees **u**-*ed* to fast
    metechō.
Heb. 5.13. For every one *that* **u**-*eth* mi.
    anastrephō.
Heb.10.33.co. of them *that were* so **u**-*ed*
    echō.
¹Pet. 2. 6. **u**-*ing* your liberty for a clo.
    ginomai en.
¹Th. 2. 5. at any time **u**-*ed* we flatteri.
    (*were we in* word of flattery)
  (See *Arts. Deacon, Deceit, Despitefully,*
  Hospitality, Repetitions, Sorcery.)

USING.
apochrēsis.
Col. 2.22. all are to perish with the **u.**

USURP.
authenteō.
¹Ti. 2.12. nor *to* **u.** *authority over* the

USURY.
tokos.
Mat.25.27. mine own with **u.**; Lu.19.23

UTMOST.
peras.
Lu. 11.31. from the **u.** *parts* of the ear.

UTTER, (See *Hard,*)   -ed.
laleō.
²Co. 12. 4. not lawful for a man *to* **u.**
Rev.10. 3. seven thunders **u**-*ed* their
    4. thunders *had* **u**-*ed* their voi.
    which the seven thund. **u**-*ed*
    alalētos.
Ro. 8.26. groan. *which cannot be* **u**-*ed*
    ereugomai.
Mat.13.35. I *will* **u.** things which have
    didōmi.
¹Co.14. 9. except ye **u.** by the tongue
    legō.
Heb. 5.11. hard *to be* **u**-*ed*, seeing ye

UTTERANCE.
logos.
¹Co. 1. 5. enriched by him in all **u.**
²Co. 8. 7. in faith, and **u.**, and knowl.
    apophthenggomai, [*infin.*]
Act. 2. 4. as the spirit gave them **u.**

UTTERLY. (See*Burn, Perish.*)
holōs.
¹Co. 6. 7. there is **u.** a fault among

UTTERMOST. (See *Know.*)
eschatos.
Mat. 5.26. thou hast paid the **u.** farth.

Act .1. 8. unto the **u.** *part of the earth.*
    peras.
Mat.12.42.from the **u.** *parts* of the
    akron.
Mar.13.27.from the **u.** *part* of the ear.
    to the **u.** *part* of heaven
    telos.
¹Th. 2.16. is come upon them to the **u.**
    panteles.
Heb. 7.25. also to save them to the **u.**

VAGABOND.
perierchomai, [*partic.*]
Act.19.13. Then certain of the **v.** Jews

VAIL *or* VEIL.
kalumma.
²Co. 3.13. which put a **v.** over his face
    14. the same **v.** untaken away
    15. the **v.** is upon their heart
    16. the **v.** shall be taken away
    katapetasma. [15.38; Lu.23.4⁵
Mat.27.51. the **v.** of the temple ; Mar.
Heb. 6.19. into that within the **v.**
  9. 3. And after the second **v.**
  10.20. through the **v.**, that is to

VAIN.
kenos.
Act. 4.25. the people imagine **v.** things
¹Co.15.10. upon me was not *in* **v.**
    14. then is our preaching **v.**
    and your faith is also **v.**
    58. your labour is not *in* **v.** in
²Co. 6. 1. not the grace of God in **v.**
Gal. 2. 2. should run, or had run, in **v.**
Eph. 5. 6. no man deceive you with **v.**
Phi. 2.16. **v.**, neither laboured in **v.**
Col. 2. 8. through philosophy and **v.**
¹Th. 2. 1. that it was not *in* **v.**
    3. 5. and our labour be in **v.**
Jas. 2.20. O **v.** man, that faith without
    kenophōnia.   [²Ti.2.16
¹Ti. 6.20. profane and **v.** *babblings*;
    mataios.
¹Co. 3.20. of the wise, that they are **v.**
  15.17. your faith is **v.**; ye are
Tit. 3. 9. they are unprofitable and **v.**
Jas. 1.26. this man's religion is **v.**
¹Pet. 1.18. from your **v.** conversation
    mataioomai.
Ro. 1.21. but *became* **v.** in their ima.
    eikē.
Ro. 13. 4. beareth not the sword *in* **v.**
¹Co.15. 2. unless ye have believed *in* **v.**
Gal. 3. 4. thin. *in* **v.**? if it be yet *in* **v.**
    4.11. besto. upon you labour *in* **v.**
    kenoō.
²Co. 9. 3. boast. of you *should be in* **v.**
    matēn.   [Mar.7.7
Mat.15. 9. *in* **v.** they do worship me ;
    dōrean.
Gal. 2.21. then Christ is dead *in* **v.**
    kenōs.
Jas. 4. 5. that the scripture saith *in* **v.**
  (See *Glory, Jangling, Repetitions,*
  Talker.)

VAINLY.
eikē.
Col. 2.18. **v.** puffed up by his fleshly

VALIANT.
ischuros.
Heb.11.34.waxed **v.** in fight, turned to

VALLEY.
pharangx.
Lu. 3. 5. Every **v.** shall be filled, and

VALUE,   -ed
diapherō   [Lu.12.7
Mat.10.31. ye *are of more* **v.** *than* ma.;

timaō.
Mat.27. 9. price of him *that was* v-ed
    the children of Israel *did* v.

VANISH,   *-ed, -eth.*
ginomai aphantos.
Lu. 24.31. he v-*ed out of* their *sight*
    (*became invisible* to them.)
katargeō.
¹Co. 13. 8. knowledge, it shall v. away
enggus aphanismos.
Heb. 8.13. old is *ready to* v. *away*
aphanizō.
Jas. 4.14. time, and then v-*eth away*

VANITY,   *-ies.*
mataiotēs.
Ro. 8.20. was made subject to v.
Eph. 4.17. in the v. of their mind
²Pet. 2.18. swelling words of v.
mataios, [*neu. plu.*]
Act.14.15. turn from these v-*s* unto

VAPOUR.
atmis.
Act. 2.19. and fire, and v. of smoke
Jas. 4.14. It is even a v., that appear.

VARIABLENESS.
parallagē.
Jas. 1.17. with whom is no v., neither

VARIANCE.
dichazō.
Mat.10.35. *to set* a man *at* v. against
eris.
Gal. 5.20. v., emulations, wrath

VAUNTETH.
perpereuomai.
¹Co. 13. 4. charity v. not it*self*, is not

VEHEMENT. (See *Desire.*)
VEHEMENTLY. (See *Beat.*)
ek perissos.
Mar.14.31.But he spake the more v.
deinōs.
Lu. 11.53. Pharis. began to urge him v.
eutonōs.
Lu. 23.10. stood and v. accused him

VENEMOUS.
thērion.
Act.28. 4. the v. *beast* ħang on his

VENGEANCE.
ekdikēsis.
Lu. 21.22. these be the days of v.
Ro. 12.19. it is written, v. is mine
²Th. 1. 8. taking v. on them that
Heb.10.30.said, v. belongeth unto me
dikē.
Act.28. 4. yet v. suffereth not to live
Jude   7. suffering the v. of eternal
orgē.
Ro. 3. 5. God unright. who taketh v.

VERILY.
amēn.
Mat. 5.18. v. I say unto you ; 6.2,5,16 ;
8.10 ; 10.15,23,42 ; 11.11 ; 13.17 ; 16.28 ;
17.20 ; 18.3,13,18 ; 19.23,28 ; 21.21,31 ;
23.36 ; 24.2,34,47 ; 25.12,40,45 ; 26.13,21.
Mar.3.28 ; 6.11 ; 8.12 ; 9.1,41 ; 10.15,29 ;
11.23 ; 12.43 ; 13.30 ; 14.9,18,25.   Lu.4.
24 ; 12.37 ; 13.35 ; 18.17,29 ; 21.32
Mat. 5.26. v. I say unto thee ; 26.34 ;
      Mar.14.30 ; Lu.23.43
Jo.   1.51. v., v., I say unto you ; 5.19,
24 ; 6.26,32,47,53 ; 8.34,51,58 ; 10.1,7,
12.24 ; 13.16,20,21,38 ; 14.12 ; 16.20,23
Jo.   3. 3. v., v., I say unto thee ; 5,11 ;
      21.18
men.
Mar. 9.12. Elias v. cometh first, and

Act.19. 4. John v. baptized with the
22. 3. I am v. a man which am a
Ro.   2.25. circumcision v. profiteth, if
¹Co. 5. 3. For I v., as absent in body
14.17. thou v. givest thanks well
Heb. 3. 5. And Moses v. was faithful
6.16. For men v. swear by the
7. 5. And v. they that are of the
18. For there is v. a disannulling
9. 1. Then v. the first covenant
12.10. For they v. for a few days
¹Pet. 1.20. Who v. was foreordained
gar.
Act.16.37. nay v. ; but let them come
Ro. 15.27. It hath pleased them v.
nai.
Lu. 11.51. v. I say unto you, It shall
men oun.
Act.26. 9. I v. thought with myself
ontōs.
Gal. 3.21. v. righteousness should have
depou.
Heb. 2.16. For v. he took not on him
alēthōs.
¹Jo. 2. 5. in him v. is the love of God

VERITY.
alētheia.
¹Ti. 2. 7. the Gentiles in faith and v.

VERY.
sphodra.
Mat.18.31.they were v. sorry, and came
Mar.16. 4. away : for it was v. great
Lu. 18.23. sorrowful : for he was v. rich
autos.
Ro. 13. 6. continually upon this v. thi.
¹Th. 5.23. And the v. God of peace
Heb.10. 1. not the v. image of the thi.
lian.
Mar.16. 2. v. early in the morning
²Co. 11. 5. the v. chiefest apos.; 12.11
ekeinos.
Mat.15.28.from *that* v. hour ; 17.18
alēthōs.
Jo. 7.26. that this is the v. Christ
huper.
¹Th. 5.13. esteem them v. highly in
(*See words in connection.*)

VESSEL, (See *Brazen,*)   *-s.*
skeuos.
Mar.11.16.carry any v. through the
Lu. 8.16. candle, covereth it with a v.
Jo. 19.29. there was set a v. full of
Act. 9.15. he is a chosen v. unto me
10.11. and a certain v. des.; 11.5
16. and the v. was received up
Ro. 9.21. to make one v. unto honour
22. the v-*s* of wrath fitted to
23. on the v-*s* of mercy, which
²Co. 4. 7. this treasure in earthen v-*s*
¹Th. 4. 4. possess his v. in sanctification
²Ti. 2.20. not only v-*s* of gold and of
21. he shall be a v. unto honour
Heb. 9.21. and all the v-*s* of the minis.
¹Pet. 3. 7. as unto the weaker v.
Rev. 2.27. as the v-*s* of a potter shall
18.12. all manner v-*s* of ivory, and
    all manner v-*s* of most preci.
anggeion.
Mat.13.48.gathered the good into v-*s*
25. 4. wise took oil in their v-*s*

VESTURE.
himatismos.   Jo.19.24
Mat.27.35.my v. did they cast lots ;
peribolaion.
Heb. 1.12. And as a v. shalt thou fold
himation.
Rev.19.13.clothed with a v. dipped in
16. hath on his v. and on his

VEX,   *-ed.*
daimonizomai.
Mat.15.22. *is* grievou. v-*ed with a devil*
paschō.
Mat.17.15. he is lunatick, and sore v-*ed*
ochleomai.   [Act.5.16
Lu. 6.18. they *that were* v-*ed* with un.
kakoō.
Act.12. 1. *to* v. certain of the church
kataponeomai.
²Pet. 2. 7. v-*ed* with the filthy convers.
basanizō.
²Pet. 2. 8. v-*ed* his righteous soul from

VIAL,   *-s.*
phialē.
Rev. 5. 8. and golden v-*s* full of odours
15. 7. seven angels seven golden v-*s*
16. 1. pour out the v-*s* of the wra.
2. poured out his v.; 3,4,8,10,
             12,17
17. 1. which had the seven v-*s*; 21.9

VICTORY.
nikos.
Mat.11.20. send forth judgment unto v.
¹Co. 15.54. Death is swallowed up in v.
55. O grave, where is thy v.
57. which giveth us the v. thro.
nikē.
¹Jo. 5. 4. this is the v. that overcome.
nikaō.
Rev.15. 2. them *that had* gotten the v.

VICTUALS.
brōma.
Mat.14.15. and buy themselves v.
episitismos.
Lu. 9.12. and lodge, and get v. : for we

VIGILANT.
grēgoreō.
¹Pet. 5. 8. Be sober, *be* v.; because your

VILE.
atimia.   [tions (*of vileness.*)
Ro. 1.26. gave them up unto v. affec.
tapeinōsis.   [(of *humiliation*)
Phi. 3.21. who shall change our v. body
ruparos.
Jas. 2. 2. a poor man in v. raiment

VILLAGE,   *-s*
kōmē.
Mat. 9.35. about all the cities and v-*s*
14.15. that they may go into the v-*s*
21. 2. Go into the v. over against ;
      Mar.11.2 ; Lu.19.30
Mar. 6. 6. he went round about the v-*s*
36. and into the v-*s*, and buy
56. into v-*s*, or cities, or country
Lu. 8. 1. every city and v., preaching
9.52. and entered into a v. of the
56. they went to another v.
10.38. into a certain v. ; 17.12
13.22. the cities and v-*s*, teaching
24.13. that same day to a v. called
28. they drew nigh unto the v.
Act. 8.25. the gospel in many v-*s* of the

VINE.
ampelos.   [14.25 ; Lu.22.18
Mat.26.29. of this fruit of the v. ; Mar.
Jo. 15. 1. I am the true v., and my
4. except it abide in the v. ; no
5. I am the v., ye are the bran.
Jas. 3.12. olive berries? either a v., figs
Rev.14.19. gathered the v. of the earth
botrus.
Rev.14.18. gather the *clusters of the* v.

VINEGAR.
oxos.
Mat.27.34. gave him v. to drink mingl.

Mat.27.48.and filled it with **v.**
Mar.15.36.a spunge full of **v.**; Jo.19.29
Lu. 23.36. and offering him **v.**
Jo. 19.29. a vessel full of **v.**: and they
    30. had received the **v.**, he said

VINEYARD. (See *Dresser*.)
ampelōn.
Mat.20. 1. hire labourers into his **v.**
    2. he sent them into his **v.**
    4, 7. Go ye also into the **v.**
    8. the lord of the **v.** saith unto
  21.28. son, go work to day in my **v.**
    33. householder, which pla. a **v.**
    39. cast him out of the **v.**; Mar.
      12.8 ; Lu.20.15
    40. the lord therefore of the **v.**;
      Mar.12.9; Lu.20.15
    41. will let out his **v.** unto;
      Mar.12.9; Lu.20.16
Mar.12. 1. man planted a **v.**; Lu.20.9
    2. the fruit of the **v.**; Lu.20.10
Lu. 13. 6. fig tree planted in his **v.**
    20.13. Then said the lord of the **v.**
1Co. 9. 7. who planted a **v.**, and eateth

VIOLENCE.
bia.
Act. 5.26. brought them without **v.**
    21.35. for the **v.** of the people
    24. 7. with great **v.** took him
    27.41. with the **v.** of the waves
biazomai.
Mat.11.12. kingdom of hea. *suffereth* **v.**
diaseiō.
Lu. 3.14. *Do* **v.** *to* no man, neither
dunamis.
Heb.11.34.Quenched the **v.** of fire
hormēma.
Rev.18.21. Thus with **v.** shall that gre.

VIOLENT.
biastēs.
Mat.11.12.the **v.** take it by force

VIOLENTLY. (See *Run*.)

VIPER, -s.
echidna.   [23.33 ; Lu.3.7
Mat. 3. 7. O generation of **v-**s ; 12.34 ;
Act.28. 8. came a **v.** out of the heat

VIRGIN, -s.
parthenos.
Mat. 1.23. Behold, a **v.** shall be with
    25. 1. ten **v-**s, which took their
    7. Then all those **v-**s arose
    11. came also the other **v-**s
Lu. 1.27. To a **v.** espoused to a man
    and the **v.**'s name was Mary
Act.21. 9. had four daughters, **v-**s
1Co. 7.25. Now concerning **v-**s I have
    28. and if a **v.** marry, she hath
    34. between a wife and a **v.**
    36. uncomely toward his **v.**
    37. will keep his **v.**, doeth well
2Co. 11. 2. you as a chaste **v.** to Christ
Rev.14. 4. women, for they are **v-**s

VIRGINITY.
parthenia.
Lu. 2.36. seven years from her **v.**

VIRTUE.
dunamis.   [Lu.8.46
Mar.5.30. that **v.** had gone out of him ;
Lu. 6.19. for there went **v.** out of him
aretē.
Phi. 4. 8. if there be any **v.**, and if
1Pet. 1. 3. hath call. us to glory and **v.**
    5. to your faith **v.**; and to **v.**

VISIBLE.
horatos.
Col. 1.16. **v.** and invisible, whether
308

VISION, -s.
horama.
Mat.17. 9. Tell the **v.** to no man
Act. 9.10. to him said the Lord in a **v.**
    12. And hath seen in a **v.** a man
  10. 3. He saw in a **v.** evidently
    17. what this **v.** which he had
    19. Wh. Peter thought on the **v.**
  11. 5. and in a trance I saw a **v.**
  12. 9. but thought he saw a **v.**
  16. 9. a **v.** appeared to Paul in the
    10. And after he had seen the **v.**
  18. 9. to Paul in the night by a **v.**
optasia.
Lu. 1.22. that he had seen a **v.** in the
  24.23. they had also seen a **v.** of
Act.26.19. disobedient unto the hea. **v.**
2Co.12. 1. I will come to **v-**s and revel.
horasis.
Act. 2.17. your young men shall see **v-**s
Rev. 9.17. I saw the horses in the **v.**

VISIT, -ed, -est.
episkeptomai.
Mat.25.36.was sick, and ye **v-**ed me
    43. prison, and ye **v-**ed me not
Lu. 1.68. for he *hath* **v-**ed and redeem.
    78. days. from on high *hath* **v-**ed
  7.16. That God *hath* **v-**ed his peo.
Act. 7.23. *to* **v.** his brethren the child.
  15.14. how God at the first *did* **v.**
    36. *Let* us go again and **v.** our
Heb. 2. 6. of man, that thou **v-**est him
Jas. 1.27. *To* **v.** the fatherless and wid.

VISITATION.
episkopē.
Lu. 19.44. knew. not the time of thy **v.**
1Pet. 2.12. glorify God in the day of **v.**

VOCATION.
klēsis.
Eph. 4. 1. walk worthy of the **v.** where.

VOICE, -s.
phōnē.
Mat. 2.18. In Rama was there a **v.** hea.
  3. 3. The **v.** of one crying in the ;
    Mar.1.3 ; Lu.3.4; Jo.1.23;11.43
    17. a **v.** from heaven ; Mar.1.11;
    Lu.3.22 ; Jo.12.28; Rev.10.
    4 ; 14.2,13
  12.19. hear his **v.** in the streets
  17. 5. a **v.** out of the cloud ;
    Mar.9.7 ; Lu.9.35
  27.46. cried with a loud **v.**;Mar.1.26
    5.7 ; 15.34,37 ; Lu.4.33 ;
    23.46; Act.7.57,60 ; 16.28 ;
    Rev.6.10; 7.2,10;10.3; 19.17
Lu. 1.42. she spake out with a loud **v.**
    44. as soon as the **v.** of thy salu.
  8.28. and with a loud **v.** said
  9.36. And when the **v.** was past
  11.27. cer. woman. .lift. up her **v.**;
  17.13; lifted up their **v-**s; Act.14.11;
    22.22
    15. with a loud **v.** glorified God
  19.37. and praise God with a loud
  23.23. were instant with loud **v-**s
    And the **v-**s of them and of
Jo. 3.29. because of the bridegr.'s **v.**
  5.25. shall hear the **v.** of the Son
    28. in the graves sh. hear his **v.**
    37. Ye have neither heard his **v.**
  10. 3. and the sheep hear his **v.**
    4. for they know his **v.**
    5. they know not the **v.** of str.
    16. and they shall hear my **v.**
    27. My sheep hear my **v.**, and
  12.30. This **v.** came not because of
  18.37. of the truth heareth my **v.**
Act. 2.14. lifted up his **v.**, and said

Act. 4.24. they lifted up their **v.** to G.
  7.31. the **v.** of the Lord came
  8. 7. crying with loud **v.**;Rev.14.15
  9. 4. heard a **v.** saying unto ;11.7;
    22.7
    7 hearing a **v.**, but seeing no
  10.13. there came a **v.** to him
    15. And the **v.** spake unto him
  11. 9. But the **v.** answered me aga.
  12.14. And when she kn. Peter's **v.**
    22. the **v.** of a god, and not of a
  13.27. nor yet the **v-**s of the prop.
  14.10. Said with a loud **v.**, Stand
  19.34. all with one **v.** about the
  22. 9. but they heard not the **v.** of
    14. shouldest hear the **v.** of his
  24.21. Except it be for this one **v.**
  26.14. I heard a **v.** speaking unto
    24. Festus said with a loud **v.**
1Co.14.10. so many kinds of **v-**s in the
    11. not the meaning of the **v.**
    to and to change my **v.**
1Th. 4.16. with the **v.** of the archangel
Heb. 3. 7, 15. if ye will hear his **v.** ; 4.7
  12.19. trumpet, and the **v.** of words
    26. Whose **v.** then shook the ea.
2Pet. 1.17. when there came such a **v.** to
    18. this **v.** which came from he.
  2.16. ass speaking with man's **v.**
Rev. 1.10. heard behind me a great **v.**
    12. and I turned to see the **v.**
    15. his **v.** as the sound of many
  3.20. if any man hear my **v.**, and
  4. 1. the first **v.** which I heard
    5. thunderin. and **v-**s ; 8.5;11.19
  5. 2. proclaiming with a loud **v.**
    11. and I heard the **v.** of many
    12. Say. with a loud **v.**;8.13;14.7,9
  6. 6. And I heard a **v.** in the mid.
    7. I heard the **v.** of the fourth
  8.13. by reason of the other **v-**s of
  9.13. I heard a **v.** from the four
  10. 3. seven thunders utt. their **v-**s
    4. thund. had uttered their **v-**s
    7. But in the days of the **v.** of
    8. and the **v.** which I heard fr.
  11.12. they heard a great **v.** from
    15. and there were great **v-**s in
  12.10. I heard a loud **v.** saying in
  14. 2. as the **v.** of many wat. ; 19.6
    the **v.** of a great thunder
    the **v.** of harpers harping wi.
  16. 1. I heard a great **v.**; 19.1 ; 21.3
    17. came a great **v.** out of the
    18. And there were **v-**s and thn.
  18. 2. mightily with a strong **v.**
    4. I heard another **v.** from
    22. And the **v.** of harpers, and
    23. the **v.** of the bridegroom
  19. 5. And a **v.** came out of the
    6. as it were the **v.** of a great
    the **v.** of mighty thunderings
psēphos.
Act.26.10. I gave my **v.** against them

VOID. (See *Offence*.)
kenoō.
Ro. 4.14. law be heirs, faith *is made* **v.**
1Co. 9.15. *should make* my glorying **v.**
katargeō.
Ro. 3.31. *Do* we then *make* **v.** the law

VOLUME.
kephalis.
Heb.10. 7. in the **v.** of the book it is

VOLUNTARY.
thelō, [*partic.*]
Col. 2.18. in a **v.** humility, and worsh.

VOMIT.
exerama.
2Pet. 2.22. turned to his own **v.** again

VOW.
euchē.
Act.18.18. in Cenchra. ; for he had a **v.**
21.23. which have a **v.** on them
VOYAGE.
ploos.
Act.27.10. I perceive that this **v.** will
WAGES.
opsōnion.
Lu. 3.14. be content with your **w.**
Ro. 6.23. the **w.** of sin is death
²Co.11. 8. taking **w.** of them to do you
misthos.
Jo. 4.36. receiveth **w.**, and gathereth
²Pet. 2.15. who loved the **w.** of unrigh.
WAGGING.
kineō.   [15.29
Mat.27.39. him, **w.** their heads ; Mar.
WAIL,   -ed, -ing.
alalazō.
Mar. 5.38. that wept and **w**-ed greatly
koptomai.
Rev. 1. 7. shall **w.** because of him
pentheō.
Rev.18.15. torment, weeping and **w**-ing
19. cried, weeping and **w**-ing
WAILING, [noun.]
klauthmos.
Mat.13.42,50. shall be **w.** and gnashing
WAIT,   -ed, -eth, -ing.
apekdechomai.
Ro. 8.19. **w**-eth for the manifestation
23. ourselves, **w**-ing for the ad.
25. we with patience **w.** for it
¹Co. 1. 7. **w**-ing for the coming of our
Gal. 5. 5. **w.** for the hope of righteou.
prosdechomai.
Mar.15.43.which also **w**-ed for the kin.
Lu. 2.25. **w**-ing for the consolation of
12.36. unto men that **w.** for their
23.51. **w**-ed for the kingdom of God
ekdechomai.
Jo. 5. 3. withered, **w**-ing for the mo.
Act.17.16. while Paul **w**-ed for them at
Jas. 7. 2. the husbandman **w**-eth for
¹Pet. 3.20. **w**-ed in the days of Noah
prosdokaō.
Lu. 1.21. the people **w**-ed for Zachari.
8.40. they were all **w**-ing for him
Act.10.24. Cornelius **w**-ed for them
proskartereō.
Mar. 3. 9. small ship should **w.** on him
Act.10. 7. that **w**-ed on him continually
perimenō.
Act. 1. 4. but **w.** for the promise of
prosedreuō.
¹Co. 9.13. they which **w.** at the altar
anamenō.
¹Th. 1.10. to **w.** for his Son from heav.
(See Lay, Lying.)
WAITING. (See Patient.)
WAKE.
grēgoreō.
¹Th. 5.10. whether we **w.** or sleep, we
WALK, -ed, -edst, -est, -eth, -ing.
peripateō.
Mat. 4.18. **w**-ing by the sea of Galilee
9. 5. or to say, Arise, and **w.**
11. 5. the lame **w.**; 15.31 ; Lu.7.22
14.25, 26. **w**-ing on the sea; Mar.
6.48,49; Jo.6.19
29. he **w**-ed on the water, to go
Mar. 1.16. Now as he **w**-ed by the sea
2. 9. thy bed, and **w.**; Jo.5.8,11,12
5.42. the damsel arose, and **w**-ed
7. 5. Why **w.** not thy disciples

Mar. 8.24. I see men as trees, **w**-ing
11.27. and as he was **w**-ing in the
16.12. two of them, as they **w**-ed
Lu. 5.23. Rise up and **w.**; Act.3.6
11.44. the men that **w.** over them
20.46. which desire to **w.** in long
24.17. another, as ye **w.**, and are
Jo. 1.36. look. upon Jesus as he **w**-ed
5. 9. took up his bed, and **w**-ed
6.66. and **w**-ed no more with him
7. 1. Jesus **w**-ed in Galilee : for
would not **w.** in Jewry
8.12. shall not **w.** in darkness
10.23. Jesus **w**-ed in the temple in
11. 9. If any man **w.** in the day
10. But if a man **w.** in the night
54. **w**-ed no more openly among
12.35. **w.** while ye have the light
for he that **w**-eth in darkne.
21.18. and **w**-edst whither thou
Act. 3. 8. leaping up stood, and **w**-ed
into and the temple, **w**-ing, and
9. saw him **w**-ing and praising
12. we had made this man to **w.**
14. 8. who never had **w**-ed
10. And he leaped and **w**-ed
21.21. neither to **w.** after the cust.
Ro. 6. 4. we also should **w.** in newness
8. 1, 4. who **w.** not after the flesh
13.13. Let us **w.** honestly, as in the
14.15. now **w**-est thou not charita.
¹Co. 3. 3. are ye not carnal, and **w.** as
7.17. every one, so let him **w.**
²Co. 4. 2. not **w**-ing in craftiness, nor
5. 7. we **w.** by faith, not by sight
10. 2. as if we **w**-ed (as walking)
3. For though we **w.** in the fle.
12.18. **w**-ed we not in the same sp.
Gal. 5.16. **w.** in the Spirit, and ye shall
Eph. 2. 2. in time past ye **w**-ed accord.
10. that we should **w.** in them
4. 1. that ye **w.** worthy of the vo.
17. **w.** not as other Gentiles **w.**
5. 2. And **w.** in love, as Christ
8. as children of light
15. See then that ye **w.** circum.
Phi. 3.17. mark them which **w.** so as
18. For many **w.**, of whom I
Col. 1.10. That ye might **w.** worthy
2. 6. the Lord, so **w.** ye in him
3. 7. In the which ye also **w**-ed
4. 5. **w.** in wisdom toward them
¹Th. 2.12. That ye would **w.** worthy of
4. 1. how ye ought to **w.** and to
12. That ye may **w.** honestly
²Th. 3. 6. every brother that **w**-eth dis.
11. some which **w.** among you
¹Pet. 5. 8. **w**-eth about, seeking whom
¹Jo. 1. 6. and **w.** in darkness, we lie
7. But if we **w.** in the light
2. 6. so to **w.**, even as he **w**-ed
11. **w**-eth in darkness, and kno.
²John 4. found of thy children **w**-ing
6. that we **w.** after his comma.
the beginning, ye should **w.**
³John 3. even as thou **w**-est in the
4. that my children **w.** in truth
Rev. 2. 1. who **w**-eth in the midst of
3. 4. they shall **w.** with me in w.
9.20. can see, nor hear, nor **w.**
16.15. lest he **w.** naked, and they
21.24. shall **w.** in the light of it
emperipateō.
²Co. 6.16. dwell in them, and **w.** in th.
poreuomai.
Lu. 1. 6. **w**-ing in all the command.
13.33. I must **w.** to day, and
Act. 9.31. and **w**-ing in the fear of the
14.16. suffered all nations to **w.** in
¹Pet. 4. 3. when we **w**-ed in lascivious.
²Pet. 2.10. them that **w.** after the flesh
3. 3. **w**-ing after their ; Jude 16

Jude 18. who should **w.** (walking)
stoicheō.
Act.21.24. **w**-est orderly, and keepest
Ro. 4.12. but who also **w.** in the steps
Gal. 5.25. let us also **w.** in the Spirit
6.16. as many as **w.** (shall walk)
Phi. 3.16. let us **w.** by the same rule
dierchomai.   [Lu.11.24
Mat.12.43. he **w**-eth through dry places;
orthopodeō.
Gal. 2.14. that they **w**-ed not uprightly
WALL,   -s.
teichos.
Act. 9.25. down by the **w.** in; ²Co.11.33
Heb.11.30.By faith the **w**-s of Jericho
Rev.21.12. And had a **w.** great and high
14. And the **w.** of the city had
15. gates thereof, and the **w.**
17. And he measured the **w.**
18. And the building of the **w.**
19. And the foundati. of the **w.**
toichos.
Act.23. 3. smite thee, thou whited **w.**
WALLOW,   -ed, -ing.
kuliomai.
Mar. 9.20. fell on the ground, and **w**-ed
kulisma.
²Pet. 2.22. to her **w**-ing in the mire
WANDER,   -ed, -ing.
perierchomai.
¹Ti. 5.13. **w**-ing about from house to
Heb.11.37.they **w**-ed about in sheepsk.
planaō.
Heb.11.38.they **w**-ed in deserts, and in
planētēs.
Jude 13. **w**-ing stars, to whom is res.
WANT, [noun,]   -s.
husterēsis.
Mar.12.44 she of her **w.** did cast in
Phi. 4.11. I speak in respect of **w.**
husterēma.
²Co. 8.14. be a supply for their **w.**
for your **w.**: that there may
9.12. not only supplieth the **w.** of
hustereō.
Lu. 15.14. and he began to be in **w.**
chreia.
Phi. 2.25. he that minister. to my **w**-s
WANT, [verb,]   -ed, -ing.
husтereō.
Jo. 2. 3. And when they **w**-ed wine
(the wine having failed)
²Co.11. 9. present with you, and **w**-ed
leipō.
Tit. 1. 5. the things that are **w**-ing
3.13. that nothing be **w**-ing unto
Jas. 1. 4. and entire, **w**-ing nothing
WANTON.
katastrēniazō.
¹Ti. 5.11. have begun to wax **w.** against
WANTONNESS.
aselgeia.
Ro. 13.13. not in chambering and **w.**
²Pet. 2.18. through much **w.**, those
WAR, [noun,]   -s.
polemos.   [Mar.13.7
Mat.24. 6. **w**-s and rumours of **w**-s;
Lu. 14.31. going to make **w.** against
21. 9. shall hear of **w**-s and comm.
Jas. 4. 1. From whence come **w**-s and
Rev.11. 7. shall make **w.** against them
12. 7. And there was **w.** in heaven
17. went to make **w.** with the
13. 7. to make **w.** with the saints
19.19. to make **w.** against him that
polemeō.
Rev.13. 4. who is able to make **w.** with
17.14. These shall make **w.** with the
19.11. he doth judge and make **w.**

strateuma.

Lu. 23.11. Herod with his *men of* w.

WAR, [*verb*,]   -*eth*,-*ing*.
strateuomai.

²Co. 10. 3. we *do* not w. after the flesh
¹Ti. 1.18. by them *mightest* w. a good
²Ti. 2. 4. No man *that* w-*eth* entangl.
Jas. 4. 1. of your lusts *that* w. in your
¹Pet. 2.11. lusts, which w. against the
polemeō.

Jas. 4. 2. ye fight and w., yet ye have
antistrateuomai.

Ro. 7.23. w-*ing against* the law of my

WARD.
phulakē.

Act.12.10. the first and second w.

WARE.
suneideō.

Act 14. 6. They *were* w. of it, *and* fled

WARFARE.
strateia.

²Co. 10. 4. weapons of our w. are not
¹Ti. 1.18. mightest war a good w.
strateuomai.

¹Co. 9. 7. Who *goeth a* w. any time at

WARM,   -*ed*, -*ing*.
thermainomai.   [Jo.18.25

Mar.14.54.w-*ed* himself at the fire ;
   67. saw Peter w-*ing* himself,she
Jo. 18.18. and they w-*ed* them*selves*
     with them, and w-*ed* him*self*
Jas. 2.16. peace, *be* ye w-*ed* and filled

WARN,   -*ed*, -*ing*.
noutheteō.

Act.20.31. I ceased not *to* w. every one
¹Co. 4.14. as my beloved sons I w. you
Col. 1.28. w-*ing* every man, and teach.
¹Th. 5.14. w. them that are unruly
chrēmatizō.

Mat. 2.12, 22. *being* w-*ed of God* in a
Act.10.22. *was* w-*ed from God* by an
Heb.11. 7. Noah, *being* w-*ed of God* of
hupodeiknumi.   [Lu.3.7
Mat. 3. 7. who *hath* w-*ed* you to flee ;

WASH,   -*ed*, -*ing*.
niptō.

Mat. 6.17. thine head, and w. thy face
   15. 2. for they w. not their hands
Mar. 7. 3. except they w. their hands
Jo. 9. 7. Go, w. in the pool of Siloam
     and w-*ed*, and came seeing
   11. to the pool of Siloam, and w.
     I went and w-*ed*, *and* I rece.
   15. eyes, and I w-*ed*, and do see
   13. 5. and began *to* w. the discipl.
     6. Lord, *dost* thou w. my feet
     8. Thou *shalt* never w. my feet
     If I w. thee not, thou hast
   10. needeth not save *to* w. his
   12. So after he *had* w-*ed* their
   14. and Master, *have* w-*ed* your
     also ought *to* w.one another's
¹Ti. 5.10. if she *have* w-*ed* the saints'
aponiptō.

Mat.27.24. w-*ed* his hands before the
louō.

Jo. 13.10. He *that is* w-*ed* needeth not
Act. 9.37. whom *when* they *had* w-*ed*
   16.33. and w-*ed* their stripes
Heb.10.22.our bodies w-*ed* with pure
     (*washed* in the body.)
²Pet. 2.22. the sow *that was* w-*ed* to her
Rev. 1. 5. *that* loved us, and w-*ed* us
apolouō.

Act.22.16. baptized, and w. *away* thy
¹Co. 6.11. ye *are* w-*ed*, but ye are san.
baptizō.

Mar. 7. 4. except they w., they eat not
302

Lu. 11.38. *had* not first w-*ed* before di.
brechō.

Lu. 7.38. began *to* w. his feet with
   44. she *hath* w-*ed* my feet with
plunō.

Rev. 7.14. and *have* w-*ed* their robes
apoplunō.

Lu. 5. 2. and *were* w-*ing* their nets

WASHING, [*noun*,]   -*s*.
baptismos.

Mar. 7. 4, 8. the w. of cups, and pots
Heb. 9.10. and drinks, and divers w-*s*
loutron.

Eph. 5.26. cleanse it with the w. of wa.
Tit. 3. 5. by the w. of regeneration

WASTE, [*noun*.]
apōleia.

Mat.26. 8. To what purpose is this w.
Mar.14. 4. Why was this w. of the

WASTE, [*verb*,]   -*ed*.
diaskorpizō.

Lu. 15.13. there w-*ed* his substance
   16. 1. that he *had* w-*ed* his substa.
portheō.

Gal. 1.13. church of God, and w-*ed* it

WATCH, [*noun*.]
phulakē.

Mat.14.25. w. of the night ; Mar.6.48
   24.43. in what w. the thief would
Lu. 2. 8. keeping w. over their flock
   12.38. w., or come in the third w.
koustōdia.

Mat.27.65. ye have a w.: go your way
   66. stone, and setting a w.
   28.11. some of the w. came into

WATCH, [*verb*,]   -*ed*,-*eth*,-*ing*.
grēgoreō.   [25.13 ; Mar.13.35
Mat.24.42. w. therefore : for ye know ;
   43. he would *have* w-*ed*, and
   26.38. ye here, and w. ; Mar.14.34
   40. could ye not w. ; Mar.14.37
   41. w.and pray, that; Mar.14.38
Mar.13.34.commanded the porter to w.
   37. unto you I say unto all, w.
Lu. 12.37. he cometh shall find w-*ing*
   39. come, he would *have* w-*ed*
Act.20.31. Therefore w., and remember
¹Co.16.13. w. ye, stand fast in the faith
Col. 4. 2. *and* w. in the same with th.
¹Th. 5. 6. *let* us w. and be sober
Rev. 3. 3. therefore thou *shalt* not w.
   16.15. Blessed is he *that* w-*eth*,and
agrupneō.

Mar.13.33.Take ye heed, w. and pray
Lu. 21.36. w. ye therefore, and pray
Eph. 6.18. and w-*ing* thereunto with
Heb.13.17.for they w. for your souls
tēreō.

Mat.27.36. down they w-*ed* him there
   54. were with him w-*ing* Jesus
paratēreō.

Mar. 3. 2. w-*ed* him ; Lu.6.7,14.1,20.20
Act. 9.24. they w-*ed* the gates day and
nēphō.

²Ti. 4. 5. But w. thou in all things
¹Pet. 4. 7. ye therefore sober, and w.

WATCHFUL.
grēgoreō.

Rev. 3. 2. *Be* w., and strengthen the

WATCHINGS.
agrupnia.

²Co. 6. 5. in tumults, in labours, in w.
   11.27. painfulness, in w. often

WATER, [*noun*,]   -*s*.
hudōr.

Mat. 3.11. indeed baptize you with w.;
     Mar.1.8 ; Lu.3.16 ; Jo.1.26

Mat. 3.16. up straightway out of the w.
   8.32. and perished in the w-*s*
   14.28. come unto thee on the w.
   29. he walked on the w., to go
   17.15. and oft into the w.
   27.24. he took w., and washed his
Mar. 1.10. coming up out of the w., he
   9.22. into the fire,and into the w-*s*
   41. a cup of w. to drink in my
   14.13. be. a pitcher of w.; Lu.22.10
Lu. 7.44. thou gavest me no w. for
   8.24. and the raging of the w.
   25. com. even the winds and w.
   16.24. the tip of his finger in w.
Jo. 1.31. am I come baptizing with w.
   33. sent me to baptize with w.
   2. 7. Fill the waterpots with w.
   9. tasted the w. that was made
     servants which drew the w.
   3. 5. Except a man be born of w.
   23. there was much w. there
   4. 7. wom. of Samaria to draw w.
   10. have given thee living w.
   11. then hast thou that living w.
   13, 14. Who. drinketh of this w.
     but the w. that I shall give
     shall be in him a well of w.
   15. Sir, give me this w., that I
   46. where he made the w. wine
   5. 3. for the moving of the w.
   4. and troubled the w.: whos.
     after the troubling of the w.
   7. when the w. is troubled
   7.38. shall flow rivers of living w.
   13. 5. After that he poureth w.
   19.34. came thereout blood and w.
Act. 1. 5. truly baptiz. with w.; 11.16
   8.36. they came unto a certain w.
     See, here is w.: what doth
   38. went down both into the w.
   39. were come up out of the w.
   10.47. Can any man forbid w.,that
Eph. 5.26. with the washing of w. by
Heb. 9.19. with w., and scarlet wool
   10.22. bodies washed with pure w.
Jas. 3.12. both yield salt w. and fresh
¹Pet. 3.20. eight souls were saved by w.
²Pet. 3. 5. out of the w. and in the w.
   6. being overflowed with w.
¹Jo. 5. 6. that came by w. and blood
     w. only, but by w. and blo.
   8. the spirit, and the w., and
Rev. 1.15. as the sound of many w-*s*
   7.17. fount.of w-*s*; 8.10 ; 14.7; 16.4
   8.11. the third part of the w-*s* be.
     many men died of the w-*s*
   11. 6. and have power over w-*s* to
   12.15. out of his mouth w. as a flo.
   14. 2. the voice of many w-*s*; 19 6
   16. 5. heard the angel of the w-*s*
   12. and the w. thereof was dried
   17. 1. that sitteth upon many w-*s*
   15. The w-*s* which thou sawest
   21. 6. of the fountain of the w. of
   22. 1. a pure river of w. of life
   17. let him take the w. of life
hudropoteō.

¹Ti. 5.23. *Drink* no longer w., but
anudros.

²Pet. 2.17. These are wells *without* w.
Jude 12. clouds they are *without* w.
potamos.

²Co. 11.26. in perils of w-*s*, in perils of

WATER, [*verb*,] -*ed*,-*eth*,-*ing*.
potizō [(leading away, *watereth*

Lu. 13.15. and lead him away *to* w-*ing*
¹Co. 3. 6. have planted, Apollos w-*ed*
   7. neither he *that* w-*eth*
   8. and he *that* w-*eth* are one

WATERPOT, -s.
hudria.
Jo. 2. 6. there were set there six w-s
    7. Fill the w-s with water
   4.28. woman then left her w.

WAVE, -s.
kuma.
Mat. 8.24. sh.was covered with the w-s
   14.24. tossed with w-s: for the wi.
Mar. 4.37. the w-s beat into the ship
Act.27.41. with the violence of the w-s
Jude 13. Raging w-s of the sea, foam.
salos.
Lu. 21.25. the sea and the w-s roaring
kludōn.
Jas. 1. 6. is like a w. of the sea driven

WAVER, -eth, -ing.
diakrinō.
Jas. 1. 6. w-ing. For he that w-eth
aklinēs.
Heb.10.23.pro. of our fa. without w-ing

WAX, -ed.
ginomai.
Lu. 13.19. grew, and w-ed a great tree
Heb.11.34.strong, w-ed valiant in fight
prokoptō.
2Ti. 3.13. shall w. worse and worse
(See Bold, Cold, Confident, Gross, Old,
   Rich, Strong, Wanton.)

WAY, -s.
hodos.
Mat. 2.12. their own country ano. w.
   3. 3. Prepare ye the w. of the ;
     Mar.1.3 ; Lu.3.4
   4.15. by the w. of the sea, beyond
   5.25. whiles thou art in the w. wi.
   7.13. and broad is the w., that
    14. and narrow is the w. which
   8.28. man might pass by that w.
  10. 5. Go not into the w. of the
  11.10. which shall prepare thy w.;
    Mar.1.2 ; Lu.7.27
  13. 4. some seeds fell by the w.;
    Mar.4.4 ; Lu.8.5
   19. received seed by the w. side
  15.32. they faint in the w.; Mar.8.3
  20.17. disciples apart in the w.
   30. sitting by the w. side
  21. 8. spread their garm.in the w.;
    Mar.11.8; Lu.19.36
    them in the w.; Mar.11.8
   19. he saw a fig tree in the w.
   32. came unto you in the w. of
  22.16. and teachest the w. of God
Mar. 4.15. are they by the w.; Lu.8.12
  8.27. by the w. he asked his disci.
  9.33. among yourselves by the w.
   34. for by the w. they had disp.
  10.17. was gone forth into the w.
   32. they were in the w. going up
  52. followed Jesus in the w.
  12.14. teachest the w. of God in
Lu. 1.76. the Lord to prepare his w-s
   79. to guide our feet into the w.
  3. 5. the rough w-s shall be made
  9.57. as they went in the w.
  10. 4. and salute no man by the w.
   31. a certain priest that w.
  12.58. as thou art in the w., give
  18.35. sat by the w. side begging
  20.21. but teachest the w. of God
  24.32. he talked with us by the w.
   35. things were done in the w.
Jo. 1.23. Make straight the w. of the
  14. 4. and the w. ye know
   5. and how can we know the w.
   6. I am the w., the truth, and
Act. 2.28. made known to me the w-s
  8.26. unto the w. that goeth down

Act. 8.36. as they went on their w.
   39. he went on his w. rejoicing
  9. 2. if he found any of this w.
   17. appeared unto thee in the w
   27. had seen the Lord in the w.
  13.10. cease to pervert the right w-s
  14.16. to walk in their own w-s
  16.17. shew unto us the w. of salv.
  18.25. in the w. of the Lord
   26. the w. of God more perfectly
  19. 9. but spake evil of that w.
   23. no small stir about that w.
  22. 4. And I persecuted this w.
  24.14. that after the w. which
   22. perfect knowledge of that w.
  25. 3. laying wait in the w. to kill
  26.13. I saw in the w. a light from
Ro. 3.16. and misery are in their w-s
   17. the w. of peace have they
  11.33. and his w-s past finding out
1Co. 4.17. of my w-s which be in Christ
    a more excellent w.
1Th. 3.11. direct our w. unto you
Heb. 3.10. they have not known my w-s
  9. 8. the w. into the holiest of all
  10.20. By a new and living w.
Jas. 1. 8. is unstable in all his w-s
  2.25. sent them out another w.
  5.20. from the error of his w.
2Pet. 2. 2. the w. of truth shall be evil
   15. have forsaken the right w.
    following the w. of Balaam
   21. not to have known the w. of
Jude 11. they have gone in the w. of
Rev.15. 3. just and true are thy w-s
  16.12. that the w. of the kings of
en parodos.
1Co.16. 7. not see you now by the w.
mesos, [neut.]
Col. 2.14. and took it out of the w.
2Th. 2. 7. he be taken out of the w.
poreia.
Jas. 1.11. man fade away in his w-s
tropos.
Ro. 3. 2. Much every w.: chiefly, bec.
Phi. 1.18. every w., whether in prete.
propempō.
Act.15. 3. being brought on their w.
  21. 5. and..brought us on our w.
Ro. 15.24. to be brought on my w.; 2Co.
porrō. [1.16
Lu. 14.32. other is yet a great w. off
makran.
Mat. 8.30. there was a good w. off
Lu. 15.20. he was yet a great w. off
ekbasis.
1Co. 10.13. also make a w. to escape
planaō.
Heb. 5. 2. them that are out of the w.
en.
2Pet. 3. 1. minds, by w. of remembran.
(See Go, Other, Pernicious, Turn.)

WEAK.
astheneō.
Act.20.35. ye ought to support the w.
Ro. 4.19. being not w. in faith, he
  8. 3. that it was w. through the
  14. 1. Him that is w. in the faith
   2. another, who is w., eateth
   21. is offended, or is made w.
1Co. 8. 9. stumbli. to them that are w
   11. shall the w. brother perish
   12. wound their w. conscience
2Co.11.21. as though we had been w.
   29. Who is w., and I am not w.
  12.10. for when I am w., then am
  13. 3. to you-ward is not w., but
   4. For we also are w. in him
   9. we are glad, when we are w.
adunatos.
Ro. 15. 1. bear the infirmities of the w.

    asthenēs.
Mat.26.41. but the fle. is w.; Mar.14.38
1Co. 1.27. the w. things of the world
  4.10. we are w., but ye are strong
  8. 7. their conscience being w.
   10. conscience of him which is w.
  9.22. To the w. became I as w.
    that I might gain the w.
  11.30. many are w. and sickly amo.
2Co. 10.10. his bodily presence is w.
Gal. 4. 9. to the w. and beggarly elem.
1Th. 5.14. support the w., be patient

WEAKER.
asthenesteros.
1Pet. 3. 7. as unto the w. vessel, and

WEAKNESS.
astheneia.
1Co. 2. 3. I was with you in w., and in
  15.43. it is sown in w.; it is raised
2Co. 12. 9. is made perfect in w.
   13. 4. he was crucified through w.
Heb.11.34.out of w. were made strong
    asthenēs, [neut.]
1Co. 1.25. the w. of God is stronger
Heb. 7.18. for the w. and unprofitable.

WEALTH.
euporia.
Act.19.25. by this craft we have our w.

WEAPONS.
hopla.
Jo. 18. 3. lanterns and torches and w.
2Co. 10. 4. For the w. of our warfare

WEAR, -eth, -ing, Ware.
phoreō.
Mat.11. 8. they that w. soft clothing
Jo. 19. 5. w-ing the crown of thorns
Jas. 2. 3. to him that w-eth the gay
endiduskomai.
Lu. 8.27. time, and w-a no clothes
klinō.
Lu. 9.12. the day began to w. away
perithesis.
1Pet. 3. 3. hair, and of w-ing of gold

WEARINESS.
kopos.
2Co. 11.27. In w. and painfulness, in

WEARY, -ied.
ekkakeō.
Gal. 6. 9. let us not be w. in well doing
2Th. 3.13. be not w. in well doing
hupōpiazō.
Lu. 18. 5. continual coming she w. me.
kopiaō.
Jo. 4. 6. Jesus therefore, being w-ied
kamnō.
Heb.12. 3. lest ye be w-ied and faint in

WEATHER, (See Fair, Foul.)

WEDDING.
gamos.
Mat.22. 3. that were bidden to the w.
   8. The w. is ready, but they
   10. the w. was furnished with
   11. which had not on a w. gar
   12. not having a w. garment
Lu. 12.36. he will return from the w.
  14. 8. bidden of any man to a w.

WEEK.
sabbata.
Mat.28. 1. the first day of the w.; Mar.
    16.2; Lu.24.1; Jo.20.1,19,
    Act.20.7 ; 1Co.16.2
sabbaton.
Mar.16. 9. the first day of the w.
Lu. 18.12. I fast twice in the w.
303

WEEP,   *-est, -ing, Wept.*
klaiō.
Mat. 2.18. Rachael **w**-*ing* for her childr.
26.75. went out, and **w**-*t*; Lu.22.62
Mar. 5.38. and them *that* **w**-*t* and wa.
39. make ye this ado, and **w**.
14.72. when he thought the., he **w**-*t*
16.10. as they mourned and **w**-*t*
Lu. 6.21. Blessed are ye *that* **w**. now
25. for ye *shall* mourn and **w**.
7.13. and said unto her, **w**. not
32. to you, and ye *have* not **w**-*t*
38. at his feet behind him **w**-*ing*
8.52. And all **w**-*t*, and bewailed
but he said, **w**. not
19.41. behe. the city, and **w**-*t* over
23.28. **w**. not for me, but **w**. for
Jo. 11.31. She goeth unto the gr. to **w**.
33. **w**-*ing*, and the Jews..**w**-*ing*
16.20. ye *shall* **w**. and lament
20.11. sepu. **w**-*ing* : and as she **w**-*t*
13, 15. Woman, why **w**-*est* thou
Act. 9.39. widows stood by him **w**-*ing*
21.13. What mean ye *to* **w**. and to
Ro. 12.15. and **w**. with them *that* **w**.
1Co. 7.30. *that* **w**., as though they **w**-*t*
Phi. 3.18. and now tell you even **w**-*ing*
Jas. 4. 9. afflicted, and mourn, and **w**.
5. 1. ye rich men, **w**. and howl
Rev. 5. 4. And I **w**-*t* much, because
5. **w**. not : behold, the Lion of
18.11. *shall* **w**. and mourn over her
15. of her torment, **w**-*ing* and
19. cried, **w**-*ing* and wailing, sa.
dakruō.
Jo. 11.35. Jesus **w**-*t*
hikanos klauthmos ginomai.
Act.20.37. *they* all **w**-*t* sore (of all)

WEEPING.
klauthmos.
Mat. 2.18. lamentation, and **w**., and
8.12. shall be **w**. and gnashing; 22.
13; 24.51; 25.30; Lu.13.28

WEIGHT. (See *Talent.*)
baros.
2Co. 4.17. and eternal **w**. of glory
ongkos.
Heb.12. 1. let us lay aside every **w**.

WEIGHTIER.
baruteros.
Mat.23.23. omitted the **w**. matters of

WEIGHTY.
barus.
2Co. 10.10. say they, are **w**. and powerf.

WELL, [*adverb.*
kalōs.
Mat.12.12. it is lawful to do **w**. on the
15. 7. **w**. did Esaias prop.; Mar.7.6
Mar. 7. 9. *Full* **w**. ye reject the comm.
37. He hath done all things **w**.
12.28. that he had answer. them **w**.
32. **w**., Master, thou hast said
Lu. 6.26. when all men shall speak **w**.
20.39. thou hast **w**. said; Jo.4.17
Jo. 8.48. Say we not **w**. that thou art
13.13. ye say **w**.; for so I am
18.23. but if **w**., why smitest thou
Act.10.33. thou hast **w**. done that thou
28.25. **w**. spake the Holy Ghost
Ro. 11.20. **w**.; because of unbelief
1Co. 7.37. will keep his virgin, doeth **w**.
38. her in marriage doeth **w**.
14.17. thou verily givest thanks **w**.
2Co. 11. 4. ye might **w**. bear with him
Gal. 4.17. affect you, but not **w**.
5. 7. Ye did run **w**.; who did hin.
Phi. 4.14. ye have **w**. done, that ye did
1Ti. 3. 4. One that ruleth **w**. his own
12. and their own houses **w**.

804

1Ti. 3.13. used the office of a deacon **w**
5.17. Let the elders that rule **w**.
Jas. 2. 8. neighbo. as thyself, ye do **w**.
19. one God ; thou doest **w**.
2Pet. 1.19. ye do **w**. that ye take heed
3John 6. godly sort, thou shalt do **w**.
kalos.
Gal. 6. 9. not be weary *in* **w**. doing
kallion.
Act.25.10. as thou *very* **w**. knowest
eu.
Mat.25.21, 23. **w**. *done,* thou good and
Lu. 19.17. **w**., thou good servant
Act.15.29. ye shall do **w**.   Fare ye well
Eph. 6. 3. That it may be **w**. with thee
agathos.
Ro. 2. 7. continuance in **w**. doing
agathopoieō. [*partic.*]
1Pet. 2.15. *with* **w**. *doing* ye may put to
20. *when* ye do **w**., and suffer for
3. 6. *as long as ye do* **w**., and are
17. ye suffer *for* **w**. *doing,* than
agathopoios.
1Pet. 2.14. praise of them *that do* **w**.
agathopoiia.
1Pet. 4.19. souls to him in **w**. doing
kalopoieō, [*parti.*]
2Th. 3.13. be not weary *in* **w**. doing
sōzō.
Jo. 11.12. if he sleep, he *shall* do **w**.
beltion.
2Ti. 1.18. Ephesus, thou know. *very* **w**.
epiginōskō.
2Co. 6. 9. unknown, and yet **w**. *known*
(See *As, Drink, Please, Report, Stricken.*)

WELL, [*noun,*]   *-s.*
pēgē.
Jo. 4. 6. Now Jacob's **w**. was there
sat thus on the **w**.: and it
14. shall be in him a **w**.of water
2Pet. 2.17. These are **w**-*s* without water
phrear.
Jo. 4.11. draw with, and the **w**. is de.
12. Jacob, which gave us the **w**.

WELLBELOVED.
agapētos.
Mar.12. 6. one son, his **w**., he sent him
Ro. 16. 5. Salute my **w**. Epenetus
3John 1. The elder unto the **w**. Gaius

WELLPLEASING.
euarestos.
Phi. 4.18. acceptable, **w**. to God
Col. 3.20. this is **w**. unto the Lord
Heb.13.21.which is **w**. in his sight, thr.

WENT, (See *Go.*)

WEST.
dusmē.   [Lu.13.29
Mat. 8.11. come from the east and **w**.;
24.27. shineth even unto the **w**.
Lu. 12.54. see a cloud rise out of the **w**.
Rev.21.13. and on the **w**. three gates

WHALE.
kētos.
Mat.12.40. three nights in the **w**.'s belly

WHAT.
tis, [*interrog.*]
Mat. 5.46. **w**. reward have ye? do not
47. **w**. do ye more than others
6. 3. **w**. thy right hand doeth
25. **w**. ye shall eat, or **w**. ye sh.
w. ye shall put on
31. **w**. shall we eat? or, **w**. shall
(Also) Mat. 7.9; 8.29; 9.13; 10.19,
bis; 11.7,8,9; 12.3,7,11; 16.26, *bis*; 17.
25; 19.16,20,27; 20.21,22,32; 21.16,28,40;
22.17,42; 24.3; 26.8,15,62,65,66,70; 27.4.
22,23. Mar. 1.24,27,*bis*;2.25;4.24,41; 5.
7,9,14; 6.2,24; 8.36,37; 9.6,10,16,33; 10.

3,17,36,38,51; 11.5; 12.9; 13.4,11 ; 14.36
40,60,63,64,68; 15.12,14,24. Lu.1.66; 3,
10,12,14; 4.34,36; 5.22; 6.11; 7.24,25,26,
31;8.9,25,28,30; 9.25;10.25,26; 12.11,*bis*,
17,22, *bis*, 29,*bis*,49; 13.18;14.31; 15.4,8,
26; 16.3,4; 18.6,18,36,41; 19.48; 20.13,
15,17; 21.7; 22.71; 23.22,31,34; 24.17.
Jo. 1.21,22,38; 2.4,18,25; 4.27; 5.12; 6.
6,9,28,30, *bis*; 7.36,51; 8.5; 9.17,26; 10.
6; 11.47,56; 12.27,49,*bis*; 13.12,28; 15.15;
16.17,18, *bis*; 18.21,29,35,38; 21.21,22,
23. Act.2.12,37; 4.9,16; 5.35; 7.40,49;8.
36; 9.6,*bis*; 10.4,6,17,21,29; 11.17; 12.8;
16.30; 17.18,19,20; 19.3,35; 21.13,22,33;
22.10,26; 23.19. Ro.3.1,*bis*,3,5,9; 4.1,
3; 6.1,15,21; 7.7; 8.26,27,31; 9.14,30; 10.
8; 11.2,4,7,15; 12.2. 1Co. 2.11; 4.7,21;
5.12; 7.16; 9.18; 10.19; 11.22; 14.6,15,
16; 15.2,29,32. 2Co. 6.14, *bis*, 15, *bis*,
16; 12.13. Gal.4.30. Eph.1.18,*bis*,19; 3.
9,18; 4.9; 5.10,17. Phi. 1.18,22. Col.
1.27. 1Th. 2.19; 3.9; 4.2. Heb.2.6;
7.11; 11.32; 12.7; 13.6. Jas. 2.14,16.
1Pet.1.11; 4.17. 1Jo. 3.2. Rev. 2.7,
11,17,29; 3.6,13,22; 7.13; 18.18
tis, [*indefinite.*]
Jo. 5.19. but **w**. he seeth the Father
tis ara.
Act.12.18. **w**. was become of Peter
hostis, [*plu. neut.*]
Phi. 8. 7. **w**. things were gain to me
poios.   [Mar.11.28; Lu.20.2
Mat.21.23. By **w**. authority doest thou;
24, 27. by **w**. authority I do th.:
Mar.11.29,33
24.42. for ye know not **w**. hour
43. known in **w**. watch; Lu.12.39
Mar. 4.30. or with **w**. comparison shall
Lu. 5.19. by **w**. way they might bring
6.32, 33, 34. **w**. thank have ye? for
20. 8. Neither tell I you by **w**. aut.
24.19. he said unto them, **w**. things
Jo. 12.33. **w**. death he should die; 18.32
21.19. by **w**. death he should glorify
Act. 4. 7. By **w**. power, or by **w**. name
7.49. **w**. house will ye build me
23.34. he asked of **w**. province he
Ro. 3.27. By **w**. law? of works? Nay
1Co. 15.35. and with **w**. body do they
Jas. 4.14. For **w**. is your life? It is
1Pet.1.11. what, or **w**. manner of tim
2.20. For **w**. glory is it, if when
Rev. 3. 3. thou shalt not know **w**. hou.
hopoios.
1Co. 3.13. man's work *of* **w**. sort it is
1Th. 1. 9. **w**. *manner of* entering in
Jas. 1.24. forgetteth **w**. *manner of* ma
potapos.
Mat. 8.27. **w**. *manner of* man is this
Mar.13. 1. Master, see **w**. *manner of* st.
and **w**. buildings are here
Lu. 1.29. **w**. *manner of* salutation this
7.39. and **w**. *manner of* woman
2Pet. 3.11. **w**. *manner of* persons ought
1Jo. 3.1. Behold, **w**. *manner of* love
hosos, [*plu. neut.*]
Mar. 6.30. **w**. they had done, and **w**.
Act.15.12. declaring **w**. miracles and
Ro. 3.19. that **w**. *things soever* the la♦
Jude 10. but **w**. they know naturally
pas [*plu. neut.*] hosos an.
Mar.11.24.**w**. *things soever* ye desire
posos.
2Co. 7.11. **w**. carefulness it wrought in
hoios.
Lu. 9.55. know not **w**. *manner of* spirit
1Th. 1. 5. know **w**. *manner of* men we
2Ti. 3.11. **w**. persecutions I endured
ē.
1Co. 6.16, 19. **w**.? know ye not that
14.36. **w**.? came the word of God

houtōs, [(so, ye have not been able)
Mat.26.40. w., could ye not watch with
gar.
¹Co. 11.22. w.? have ye not houses to

WHATSOEVER.
hos ean.
Mat.14. 7. to give her w. she would ask
15. 5. by w. thou mightest be pro.
16.19. w. thou shalt bind on earth
   w. thou shalt loose on earth
20. 4. w. is right I will give you
7. w. is right, that shall ye rec.
Mar. 6.22. Ask of me w. thou wilt
23. w. thou shalt ask of me
7.11. by w. thou mightest be pro.
10.35. do for us w. we shall desire
11.23. he shall have w. he saith
13.11. w. shall be given you in
Gal. 6. 7. w. a man soweth, that shall
¹Jo. 3.22. w. we ask, we receive of him
³John 5. w. thou doest to the brethren
hosos, [plu. neut.]
Mat.17.12. done unto him w.; Mar.9.13
28.20. w. I have commanded you
Mar.10.21.sell w. thou hast, and give
Lu. 4.23. w. we have heard done in
12. 3. w. ye have spoken in darkn.
Jo. 15.14. if ye do w. I command you
17. 7. that all things w. thou hast
Act. 4.28. For to do w. thy hand and
Ro. 15. 4. For w. things were written
Phi. 4. 8. w. things are true w.
   w. things are just, w.
   w. things are lovely, w.
hosos [plu. neut.] an.
Mat. 7.12. all things w. ye would that
21.22. w. ye shall ask in prayer
23. 3. w. they bid you observe
Jo. 11.22. w. thou wilt ask of God
16.13. w. he shall hear, that shall
23. w. ye shall ask the Father
Act. 3.22. in all things w. he shall
hosos [plu. neut.] ean.
Mat.18.18. w. ye shall bind on earth
   w. ye shall loose on earth
hostis [neu.] an.
Lu. 10.35. and w. thou spendest more
Jo. . 5. w. he saith unto you, do
14.13. w. ye shall ask in my name
15.16. that w. ye shall ask of the
pas hostis [neu.] an.
Col. 3.17. And w. ye do in word or
23. w. ye do, do it heartily, as
pas, [neu.]
Mat.15.17. w. entereth in at the mouth
Mar. 7.18. that w. thing from without
Ro. 14.23. w. is not of faith is sin
¹Co. 10.25. w. is sold in the shambles
27. w. is set before you, eat, ask.
Eph. 5.13. for w. doth make manifest
¹Jo. 5. 4. w. is born of God overcome.
Rev.18.22. craftsman, of w. craft he be
tis, [neu.]
¹Co. 10.31. or w. ye do, do all to the
hos [neu.] ean tis.
Eph. 6. 8. w. good thing any man doeth
hopoios.
Gal. 2. 6. w. they were, it maketh

WHEAT.
sitos.
Mat. 3.12. his w. into the gar.; Lu.3.17
13.25. sowed tares among the w.
29. ye root up also the w. with
30. gather the w. into my barn
Lu. 16. 7. An hundred measures of w.
22.31. that he may sift you as w.
Jo. 12.24. Except a corn of w. fall into
Act.27.38. cast out the w. into the sea
¹Co. 15.37. it may chance of w. or of
Rev. 6. 6. A measure of w. for a penny

Rev.18.13. and fine flour, and w.

WHEN.
hotan.
Mat. 5.11. w. men shall revile you
6. 2. w. thou doest thine alms
5, 6. w. thou prayest
16. w. ye fast, be not, as the
9.15. w. the bridegroom shall be ;
   Mar.2.20; Lu.5.35
10.19. But w. they deliver you up
23. But w. they persecute you
12.43. w. the unclean spi.; Lu.11.24
13.32. w. it is grown, it is the gre.
15. 2. w. they eat bread
19.28. w. the Son of man sh.; 25.31
21.40. w. the lord therefore of the
23.15. w. he is made, ye make him
24.15. w. ye therefore shall see the
32. w. his bran. is yet; Mar.13.28
33. w. ye shall see all; Mar.13.29
26.29. until that day w. I drink it
Mar. 3.11. unclean spirits, w. they saw
4.15. but w. they have heard, Sat.
16. w. they have heard the word
29. w. the fruit is brought forth
31. w. it is sown in the earth
32. But w. it is sown, it groweth
8.38. w. he cometh in the glory of
11.25. w. ye stand praying, forgive
12.23, 25. w. they shall rise
13. 4. w. all these things shall be
7. w. ye shall hear of ; Lu.21.9
11. But w. they shall lead you
14. But w. ye shall see the abo.
Lu. 6.22. w. men shall hate you, and
   w. they shall separate you
26. Woe unto you, w. all men
8.13. which, w. they hear, receive
9.26. w. he shall come in his own
11. 2. w. ye pray, say, Our Father
21. w. a strong man armed kee.
34. w. thine eye is single
36. as w. the bright shining of a
12.11. w. they bring you unto the
54. w. ye see a cloud rise out of
55. w. ye see the south wind bl.
13.28. w. ye shall see Abraham
14. 8, 10. w. thou art bidden
10. that w. he that bade thee
12, 13. w. thou makest a
16. 4. w. I am put out of the stew.
9. that, w. ye fail, they may
17.10. w. ye shall have done all th.
21. 7. w. these things shall come
20. And w. ye shall see Jerusal.
30. w. they now shoot forth
31. w. ye see these things come
23.42. w. thou comest into thy kin.
Jo. 2.10. and w. men have well drunk
4.25. w. he is come, he will tell us
5. 7. I have no man, w. the water
7.27. but w. Christ cometh
31. w. Christ cometh, will he do
8.28. w. ye have lifted up the Son
44. w. he speaketh a lie
10. 4. And w. he putteth forth his
13.19. w. it is come to pass ; 14.29
15.26. But w. the Comforter is co.
16. 4. that w. the time shall come
13. w. he, the Spirit of truth, is
21. A woman w. she is in travail
21.18. but w. thou shalt be old
Act.23.35. w. thine accusers are also
24.22. w. Lysias the chief captain
Ro. 2.14. For w. the Gentiles
11.27. w. I shall take away their
¹Co. 13.10. But w. that which is perfect
14.26. w. ye come together
15.24. w. he shall have delivered up
   w. he shall have put down
27. But w. he saith, All things

Co. 15.28. and w. all things shall be
54. So w. this corruptible shall
16. 2. be no gatherings w. I come
3. And w. I come, whomsoever
5. w. I shall pass through Mac.
12. w. he shall have convenient
²Co. 10. 6. w. your obedience is fulfilled
12.10. for w. I am weak, then am I
13. 9. we are glad, w. we are weak
Col. 3. 4. w. Christ, who is our life
4.16. And w. this epistle is read
¹Th. 5. 3. For w. they shall say, Peace
²Th. 1.10. w. he shall come to be glor.
¹Ti. 5.11. for w. they have begun to
Tit. 3.12. w. I shall send Artemas
Heb. 1. 6. w. he bringeth in the first.
Jas. 1. 2. w. ye fall into divers tempt.
¹Jo. 2.28. that, w. he shall appear, we
5. 2. w. we love God and keep his
Rev. 4. 9. w. those beasts give glory
9. 5. of a scorpion, w. he striketh
10. 7. w. he shall begin to sound
11. 7. w. they shall have finished
17.10. and w. he cometh, he must
18. 9. w. they shall see the smoke
20. 7. w. the thousand years are
hote.
Mat. 7.28. w. Jesus had ended these
9.25. But w. the people were put
11. 1. w. Jesus had made an end
12. 3. did, w. he was an hungred
13.26. w. the blade was sprung up
40. Which, w. it was full, they
53. w. Jesus had finished these ;
   19.1 ; 26.1
17.25. And w. he was come into the
21. 1. And w. they drew nigh unto
34. And w. the time of the fruit
Mar. 1.32. w. the sun did set
2.25. w. he had need, and was an
4.10. And w. he was alone
7.17. And w. he was entered into
8.19. w. I brake the five loaves
20. And w. the seven among
11. 1. And w. they came nigh to
19. And w. even was come
14.12. w. they killed the passover
15.20. And w. they had mocked
41. w. he was in Galilee
Lu. 2.21. And w. eight days were acc.
22. And w. the days of her pur.
42. And w. he was twelve years
4.25. w. the heaven was shut up
6.13. And w. it was day, he called
13.35. come w. ye shall say, Blessed
17.22. w. ye shall desire to see one
22.14. And w. the hour was come
35. w. I sent you without purse
23.33. And w. they were come to
Jo. 1.19. w. the Jews sent priests and
2.22. w. therefore he was risen fr.
4.21. w. ye shall neither in this
23. w. the true worshippers sh.
45. Then w. he was come into
5.25. w. the dead shall hear the
6.24. w. the people therefore saw
9. 4. night cometh, w. no man can
14. w. Jesus made the clay
12.16. but w. Jesus was glorified
17. w. he called Lazarus out of
41. w. he saw his glory, and
13.31. w. he was gone out
16.25. the time cometh, w. I shall
19. 6. w. the chief priests therefore
8. w. Pilate therefore heard the
23. w. they had crucified Jesus
30. w. Jesus therefore had rece.
20.24. was not with them w. Jesus
21.15. So w. they had dined
18. w. thou wast young
Act. 1.13. And w. they were come in
8.12. But w. they believed Philip

305

Act. 8.39. And **w.** they were come up
11. 2. And **w.** Peter was come up
12. 6. And **w.** Herod would have
21. 5. And **w.** we had accomplish.
35. And **w.** he came upon the
22.20. And **w.** the blood of thy ma.
27.39. And **w.** it was day, theykn.
28.16. And **w.** we came to Rome
Ro. 2.16. In the day **w.** God shall jud.
6.20. For **w.** ye were the servants
7. 5. For **w.** we were in the flesh
13.11. nearer than **w.** we believed
¹Co. 13.11. **w.** I was a child
    but **w.** I became a man
Gal. 1.15. But **w.** it pleased God, who
2.11. But **w.** Peter was come to
12. **w.** they were come, he with.
14. But **w.** I saw that they wal.
4. 3. **w.** we were children, were in
4. But **w.** the fulness of the ti.
Phi. 4.15. **w.** I departed from Macedo.
Col. 3. 7. **w.** ye lived in them
¹Th. 3. 4. **w.** we were with you
²Th. 3.10. For even **w.** we were with
²Ti. 4. 3. **w.** they will not endure sou.
Heb. 7.10. **w.** Melchisedec met him
¹Pet. 3.20. **w.** once the long suffering of
Jude 9. **w.** contending with the devil
Rev. 1.17. And **w.** I saw him, I fell at
5. 8. And **w.** he had taken the bo.
6. 1. And I saw **w.** the Lamb ope.
3. **w.** he had opened the ; 5,7,
    9,12 ; 8.1
10. 3. and **w.** he had cried, seven
4. And **w.** the seven thunders
12.13. And **w.** the dragon saw that
22. 8. And **w.** I had heard and seen
hōs.
Lu. 1.41. that, **w.** Elizabeth heard the
2.39. And **w.** they had performed
4.25. **w.** great famine was throug.
5. 4. Now **w.** he had left speaking
7.12. **w.** he came nigh to; 19.29
11. 1. **w.** he ceased, one of his
12.58. **w.** thou goest with thine
19. 5. And **w.** Jesus came to the pl.
41. **w.** he was come near, he
20.37. **w.** he called the Lord the G.
Jo. 2. 9. **w.** the ruler of the feast had
23. Now **w.** he was in Jerusalem
4. 1. **w.** therefore the Lord knew
40. So **w.** the Samaritans were
6.12. **w.** they were filled, he
16. And **w.** even was now come
7.10. **w.** his brethren were gone
8. 7. So **w.** they continued asking
11. 6. **w.** he had heard therefore
32. Then **w.** Mary was come wh.
33. **w.** Jesus therefore saw her
19.33. **w.** they came to Jesus, and
Act. 5.24. Now **w.** the high priest
7.23. And **w.** he was full forty ye.
10. 7. **w.** the angel which spake
13.29. And **w.** they had fulfilled all
14. 5. And **w.** there was an assault
16.15. And **w.** she was baptized
17.13. But **w.** the Jews of Thessalo.
18. 5. And **w.** Silas and Timotheus
19. 9. But **w.** divers were hardened
20.14. And **w.** he met with us at
18. And **w.** they were come to
21.12. And **w.** we heard these thin.
27. And **w.** the seven days were
22.11. And **w.** I could not see for
25.14. **w.** they had been there many
27. 1. And **w.** it was determined
27. But **w.** the fourteenth night
28. 4. And **w.** the barbarians saw
¹Co. 11.34. will I set in order **w.** I come
en ho, [*with infinitive.*]
Mat. 13. 4. **w.** he sowed (*in* his sowing)
27.12. **w.** he was accused of the
306

Lu. 2.27. **w.** the parents brought
8.21. **w.** all the people were
5.12. to pass, **w.** he was in
8.40. that, **w.** Jesus was returned
9.36. **w.** the voice was past
    (*on* the voice being past)
51. **w.** the time was come
10.35. **w.** I come again I will
19.15. that **w.** he was returned
22. 7. **w.** the passover must be
Act. 2. 1. **w.** the day of Pentecost was
Ro. 3. 4. overcome **w.** thou art judged
Gal. 4.18. **w.** I am present with you
¹Pet. 4.13. **w.** his glory shall be
en ho, *or* **hos.**
Jo. 4.52. **w.** he began to (*in which* he)
Act. 13.17. **w.** *they* dwelt (*in the* dwelli.)
²Th. 1. 7. **w.** the Lo. Je. *sh. be* revealed
    (*in the* revealing of the L. Je.)
pōte.   [Mar. 13.4; Lu. 21.7
Mat. 24. 3. **w.** shall these things be ;
25.37, 44. **w.** saw we thee an hung.
38. **w.** saw we thee a stranger
39. Or **w.** saw we thee sick
Mar. 13.33,35. for ye know not **w.** the
Lu. 12.36. **w.** he will return from the
17.20. **w.** the kingdom of God sho.
Jo. 6.25. Rabbi, **w.** camest thou hith.
pote, [*indefinite.*]
Lu. 22.32. **w.** thou art converted
epan.
Mat. 2. 8. **w.** ye have found him
Lu. 11.22. **w.** a stronger than he shall
34. **w.** thine eye is evil, thy
ean.
¹Co. 14.16. **w.** thou shalt bless with the
¹Jo. 3. 2. know that, **w.** he shall appe.
hēnika.
²Co. 3.15. **w.** Moses is read, the vail
16. Nevertheless, **w.** it shall turn
hopote.
Lu. 6. 3. **w.** himself was an hungred
epei.
Lu. 7. 1. **w.** he had ended all his
hopōs.
Act. 3.19. **w.** the times of refreshing
    (*that* the times..may come)
meta, [*accu.*]
Act. 7. 4. **w.** his father was dead
kathōs.
Act. 7.17. **w.** the time of the promise
hou.
Heb. 3. 9. **w.** your fathers tempted
    (See *Alone, Call.*)

WHENCE.
pothen.
Mat. 13.27. *from* **w.** then hath it tares
54. **w.** hath this man this wisd.
56. **w.** then hath this man all
15.33. **w.** should we have so much
21.25. **w.** was it? from heaven, or
Mar. 6. 2. *From* **w.** hath this man the
8. 4. *From* **w.** can a man satisfy
12.37. and **w.** is he then his son
Lu. 1.43. And **w.** is this to me
13.25, 27. I know you not **w.** ye
20. 7. they could not tell **w.** it was
Jo. 1.48. **w.** knowest thou me
2. 9. and knew not **w.** it was
3. 8. but canst not tell **w.** it com.
4.11. *from* **w.** then hast thou that
6. 5. **w.** shall we buy bread, that
7.27. we know this man **w.** he is
    no man knoweth **w.** he is
28. and ye know **w.** I am
8.14. for I know **w.** I came and
    ye cannot tell **w.** I come
9.29. we know not *from* **w.** he is
30. that ye know not *from* **w.** he
19. 9. **w.** art thou? But Jesus

Jas. 4. 1. *From* **w.** come wars and
Rev. 2. 5. *from* **w.** thou art fallen
7.13. and **w.** came they
hothen.
Mat. 12.44. *from* **w.** I came out
Lu. 11.24. unto my house **w.** I came
Act. 14.26. *from* **w.** they had been reco.
Heb. 11.19. *from* **w.** also he received

WHENSOEVER.
hotan.
Mar. 14. 7. **w.** ye will ye may do them
hōs ean.
Ro. 15.24. **w.** I take my journey into

WHERE. (See *Every*.)
hopou.
Mat. 6.19. **w.** moth and rust doth corr.
    w. thieves break through
20. **w.** neither moth nor rust
    and **w.** thieves do not break
21. For **w.** your treas.; Lu. 12.34
13. 5. **w.** they had not much earth
25.24. reaping **w.** thou hast not so.
26. that I reap **w.** I sowed not
26.57. **w.** the scribes and the elders
28. 6. Come, see the place **w.** the
Mar. 2. 4. uncovered the roof **w.** he
4. 5. **w.** it had not much earth
15. **w.** the word is sown
5.40. entereth in **w.** the damsel
6.55. **w.** they heard he was
9.44, 46, 48. **w.** their worm dieth
13.14. standing **w.** it ought not
14.14. **w.** I shall eat the passover
16. 6. behold the place **w.** they laid
Lu. 12.33. **w.** no thief approacheth
22.11. **w.** I shall eat the passover
Jo. 1.28. **w.** John was baptizing
3. 8. The wind bloweth **w.** it list.
4.20. **w.** men ought to worship
46. **w.** he made the water wine
6.23. unto the place **w.** they did
62. ascend up **w.** he was before
7.34, 36. **w.** I am, thither ye can.
42. of Bethlehem, **w.** David was
10.40. **w.** John at first baptized
11.30. was in that place **w.** Martha
32. when Mary was come **w.** Je.
12. 1. **w.** Lazarus was which had
26. **w.** I am, there shall also my
14. 3. that **w.** I am, there ye may
17.24. be with me **w.** I am
18. 1. **w.** was a garden, into the
19.18. **w.** they crucified him, and
20. for the place **w.** Jesus was
41. in the place **w.** he was
20.12. **w.** the body of Jesus had la.
19. **w.** the disciples were assem.
Act. 17. 1. **w.** was a synagogue of the
Ro. 15.20. not **w.** Christ was named, le.
Col. 3.11. **w.** there is neither Greek nor
Heb. 9.16. For **w.** a testament is, there
10.18. Now **w.** remission of these is
Jas. 3.16. For **w.** envying and strife is
Rev. 2.13. even **w.** Satan's seat
    among you, **w.** Satan dwell.
11. 8. **w.** also our Lord was cruci.
12. 6. **w.** she hath a place prepared
14. **w.** she is nourished for a ti.
20.10. **w.** the beast and the false
pou.
Mat. 2. 2. **w.** is he that is born King of
4. **w.** Christ should be born
8.20. hath not **w.** to lay ; Lu. 9.58
26.17. **w.** wilt th. that we; Lu. 22.9
Mar. 14.12. **w.** wilt thou that we go and
14. **w.** is the guestcha.; Lu. 22.11
15.47. beheld **w.** he was laid
Lu. 8.25. **w.** is your faith
12.17. **w.** to bestow my fruits
17.17. but **w.** are the nine

Lu. 17.37. w. Lord? And he said
Jo. 1.38. Master, w. dwellest thou
39. They came and saw w. he
7.11. at the feast, and said, w. is
8.10. w. are those thine accusers
19. unto him, w. is thy Father
9.12. w. is he? He said, I know
11.34. w. have ye laid him
57. if any man knew w. he were
20. 2, 13. know not w. they have la.
15. tell me w. thou hast laid hi.
Ro. 3.27. w. is boasting then
1Co. 1.20. w. is the wise? w. is the
w. is the disputer of this
12.17. w. were the hearing
w. were the smelling
19. w. were the body
15.15. O death, w. is thy sting
O grave, w. is thy victory
1Pet. 4.18. w. shall the ungodly and
2Pet. 3. 4. w. is the promise of his co.
Rev. 2.13. and w. thou dwellest
hou.
Mat. 2. 9. and stood over w. the young
18.20. For w. two or three are gat.
28.16. w. Jesus had appointed them
Lu. 4.16. w. he had been brought up
17. found the place w. it was
22.10. into the house w. he entereth
Jo. 11.41. w. the dead was laid
Act. 1.13. w. abode both Peter, and Ja.
2. 2. filled all the house w. they
7.29. w. he begat two sons
12.12. w. many were gathered
16.13. w. prayer was wont to be
20. 6. w. we abode seven days
8. w. they were gathered toget.
25.10. w. I ought to be judged
28.14. w. we found brethren, and
Ro. 4.15. for w. no law is, there is no
5.20. But w. sin abounded, grace
9.26. in the place w. it was said
2Co. 3.17. and w. the Spirit of the Lo.
Col. 3. 1. w. Christ sitteth on the right
Rev.17.15. w. the whore sitteth
en hos.
Act. 4.31. w. they were assembled
7.33. place w. thou standest
11.11. unto the house w. I
15.36. every city w. we have
en pas. (in every [place])
Phi. 4.12. every w. and in all things
en pas topos.
1Ti. 2. 8. that men pray every w.
hothen.
Mat.25.24. gathering w. thou hast not
26. gather w. I have not strawed
kata, [accus.]
Lu. 10.33. ca. w. he was (c.toward him)
tis? [(what was)
Gal. 4.15. w. is then the blessedness
WHEREAS.
hopou.
1Co. 3. 3. for w. there is among you
2Pet. 2.11. w. angels, which are greater
en hos. (in that which)
1Pet. 2.12. that w. they speak against
3.16. w. they speak evil of you
hostis. [such as]
Jas. 4.14. w. ye know not what (being
WHEREBY.
en hos.
Lu. 1.78. w. the day spring from on
Act. 4.12. given among men, w. we
11.14. w. thou and all thy house
Ro. 8.15. w. we cry, Abba, Father
14.21. w. thy brother stumbleth
Eph. 4.30. w. ye are sealed unto
dia [gen.] hos.
Heb.12.28.grace, w. we may serve
2Pet. 1. 4. w. are given unto us

2Pet. 3. 6. w. the world that then
peri [gen.] hos.
Act.19.40. no cause w. we may give
kata [accus.] tis.
Lu. 1.18. w. shall I know this
hothen.
1Jo. 2.18. w. we know that it is the
WHEREFORE.
dio.
Mat.27. 8. w. that field was called
Lu. 7. 7. w. neither thought I myself
Act.13.35. w. he saith also in another
15.19. w. my sentence is, that we
20.26. w. I take you to record this
24.26. w. he sent for him the ofte.
25.26. w. I have brought him
26. 3. w. I beseech thee to hear me
27.25. w., sirs, be of good cheer
34. w. I pray you to take some
Ro. 1.24. w. God also gave them up to
13. 5. w. ye must needs be subject
15. 7. w. receive ye one another
1Co. 12. 3. w. I give you to understand
2Co. 2. 8. w. I beseech you that ye
5. 9. w. we labour, that, whether
6.17. w. come out from among th.
Eph. 2.11. w. remember, that ye being
3.13. w. I desire that ye faint not
4. 8. w. he saith, When he
25. w. putting away lying
5.14. w. he saith, Awake thou that
Phi. 2. 9. w. God also hath highly
1Th. 2.18. w. we would have come unto
3. 1. w. when we could no longer
5.11. w. comfort yourselves
Phile. 8. w., though I might be much
Heb.3. 7. w. as the Holy Ghost saith
10. w. I was grieved with that
10. 5. w. when he cometh into
11.16. w. God is not ashamed to
12.12. w. lift up the hands which
28. w. we receiving a kingdom
13.12. w. Jesus also, that he might
Jas. 1.21. w. lay apart all filthiness
4. 6. w. he saith, God resisteth
1Pet. 1.13. w. gird up the loins of your
2. 6. w. also it is contained in
2Pet. 1.10. w. the rather, brethren
12. w. I will not be negligent
3.14. w., beloved, seeing that ye
hoste.
Mat.12.12. w. it is lawful to do well on
19. 6. w. they are no more twain
23.31. w. ye be witnesses unto
Ro. 7. 4. w., my brethren, ye also are
12. w. the law is holy
1Co.10.12. w. let him that thinketh he
11.27. w. whosoever shall eat this
33. w., my brethren, when ye
14.22. w. tongues are for a sign
39. w., brethren, covet to
2Co. 5.16. w. henceforth know we no
Gal. 3.24. w. the law was our schoolm.
4. 7. w. thou art no more a serva.
Phi. 2.12. w., my beloved, as ye have
1Th. 4.18. w. comfort one another with
Jas. 1.19. w., my beloved brethren, let
1Pet. 4.19. w. let them that suffer acco.
dia houtos, [neu.]
Mat.12.31. w. I say unto you, All
23.34. w., behold I send unto
Ro. 5.12. w. as by one man sin
Eph. 1.15. w. I also, after I heard
5.17. w. be ye not unwise
6.13. w. take unto you the whole
3John 10. w., if I come, I will remem.
dia hos.
Act.10.21. what is the cause w. ye
22.24. know w. they cried so
23.28. the cause w. they accused
2Ti. 1. 6. w. I put thee in remembra.

Tit. 1.13. w. rebuke them sharply
oun.
Mat.24.26. w. if they shall say unto you
Act. 1.21. w. of these men which have
6. 3. w., brethren, look ye out
1Co. 4.16. w. I beseech you, be ye
2Co. 8.24. w. shew ye to them, and
Col. 2.20. w. if ye be dead with Christ
1Pet. 2. 1. w. laying aside all malice
hothen.
Heb. 2.17. w. in all things it behoved
3. 1. w., holy brethren, partakers
7.25. w. he is able also to save
8. 3. w. it is of necessity that
diati.
Lu. 19.23. w. then gavest not thou my
Ro. 9.32. w.? Because they sought it
2Co.11.11. w.? because I love you not
Rev.17. 7. w. didst thou marvel
dioper.
1Co. 8.13. w. if meat make my
10.14. w., my dearly beloved, flee
14.13. w. let him that speaketh
tis, [neu.]
Jo. 9.27. w. would ye hear it again
Act.22.30. w. he was accused of the Je.
Gal. 3.19. w. then serveth the law
tis heneken
Act.19.32. knew not w. they were come
tis charin.
1Jo. 3.12. And w. slew he him
hina tis, [neu.]
Mat. 9. 4. w. think ye evil in your
eis tis, [neu.]
Mat.14.31. w. didst thou doubt
ara.
2Co. 7.12. w., though I wrote unto you
arage.
Mat. 7.20. w. by their fruits ye shall
men oun.
Act.19.38. w. if Demetrius, and
eis hos, [neu.]
2Th. 1.11. w. also we pray always
toigaroun.
Heb.12. 1. w. seeing we also are comp.
WHEREIN.
en hos.
Mat.11.20. w. most of his mighty
25.13. w. the Son of man cometh
Jo. 19.41. w. was never man yet
Act. 2. 8. w. we were born
10.12. w. were all manner of
Ro. 2. 1. w. thou judgest another
5. 2. this grace w. we stand
7. 6. dead w. we were held
1Co. 7.20. calling w. he was called
24. w. he is called, therein
15. 1. received, and w. ye stand
2Co.11.12. that w. they glory
Eph. 1. 6. w. he hath made us accepta.
2. 2. w. in time past ye walked
5.18. with wine, w. is excess
Col. 2.12. with him in baptism, w.
2Ti. 2. 9. w. I suffer trouble
Heb. 6.17. w. God, willing more
9. 2. w. was the candlestick
4. w. was the golden pot
1Pet. 1. 6. w. ye greatly rejoice, though
4. 4. w. they think it strange
2Pet. 3.13. w. dwelleth righteousness
Rev.18.19. w. were made rich all
eis hos.
Act. 7. 4. land, w. ye now dwell
1Pet. 3.20. w. few, that is, eight souls
5.12. grace of God w. ye stand
peri [gen.] hos [plu.]
Lu. 1. 4. w. thou hast been instructed
dia hos.
2Pet. 3.12. w. the heavens being on
hou.
Lu. 23.53. w. never man before was

WHEREINSOEVER.
en hos an.
Co. 11.21. w. any is bold I speak fooli.

WHEREINTO.
eis hos.
Jo. 6.22. w. his disciples were entered

WHEREOF.
peri hos.
¹Co. 7. 1. *concerning the things* w. ye
Heb. 2. 5. world to come w. we speak
peri tis, [*plu. neu.*]
¹Ti. 1. 7. they say, nor w. they affirm

WHERESOEVER.
hopou.
Lu. 17.37. w. the body is, thither
hopou an.
Mar. 9.18. w. he taketh him, he teareth
14. 9. w. this gospel shall be prea.
hopou ean.
Mat.24.28. For w. the carcase is, there
26.13. w. this gospel shall be preac.
Mar.14.14. w. he shall go in, say ye

WHEREUNTO.
eis hos.
Col. 1.29. w. I also labour, striving
²Th. 2.14. w. he called you by our
¹Ti. 2. 7. w. I am ordained a preacher
4. w. thou art also called
¹Pet. 2. 8. w. also they were appointed
tis, [*dat.*]
Mat.11.16. w. shall I liken (*to what*);
Mar.4.30; Lu.7.31 ; 13.18,20
tis. [(*what* this might become)]
Act. 5.24. w. this would grow

WHEREUPON.
hothen.
Mat.14. 7. w. he promised with an oath
Act.26.19. w., O king Agrippa, I was
Heb. 9.18. w. neither the first testame.
en hos, [*plu. neu.*]
Act.24.18. w. certain Jews from Asia
26.12. w. as I went to Damascus

WHEREWITH. (See *Edify*.)
en tis.
Mat. 5.13. w. shall it be salted
Mar. 9.50. w. will ye season it ; Lu.14.34
en hos.
Eph. 6.16. w. ye shall be able to
Heb.10.29. w. he was sanctified
hosos an.
Mar. 3.28. w. *soever* they shall blasphe.
tis.
Lu. 17. 8. make ready w. I may sup

WHEREWITHAL.
tis.
Mat. 6.31. or, w. shall we be clothed

WHETHER.
eite.
Ro. 12. 6. w. prophecy, let us prophesy
¹Co. 3.22. w. Paul, or Apollos, or Cep.
8. 5. w. in heaven or in earth
10.31. w. therefore ye eat, or drink
12.13. w. we be Jews or Gentiles
w. we be bond or free
26. w. one member suffer, all the
13. 8. w. there be prophecies, they
w. there be tongues, they
w. there be knowledge, it sh.
14. 7. w. pipe or harp, except they
15.11. Therefore w. it were I or th.
²Co. 1. 6. And w. we be afflicted, it is
or w. we be comforted, it is
5. 9. w. present or absent, we may
10. done, w. it be good or bad
13. w. we be beside ourselves, it is
God, or w. we be sober
308

²Co. 8.23. w. any do enquire of Titus
12. 2. w. in the body, I cannot tell
w. out of the body, I
3. w. in the body, or out of the
Eph. 6. 8. w. he be bond or free
Phi. 1.18. w. in pretence, or in truth
20. w. it be by life, or by death
27. w. I come and see you, or
Col. 1.16. w. they be thrones, or domi.
20. w. things in earth, or things
¹Th. 5.10. w. we wake or sleep, we wo.
²Th. 2.15. taught, w. by word, or our
¹Pet. 2.13. w. it be to the king, as supr.
ei.
Mat.26.63. tell us w. thou be the Christ
27.49. see w. Elias will come ; Mar.
15.36
Mar. 3. 2. w. he wou. heal him; Lu.6.7
Lu. 14.28. w. he have sufficient to fini.
31. w. he be able with ten thou.
23. 6. w. the man were a Galilæan
Jo. 9.25. w. he be a sinner or no
Act. 4.19. w. it be right in the sight of
5. 8. w. ye sold the land for so
10.18. w. Simon, which was surna.
17.11. w. those things were so
19. 2. w. there be any Holy Ghost
25.20. w. he would go to Jerusalem
¹Co. 1.16. I know not w. I baptized
7.16. w. thou shalt save thy husb.
thou, O man, w. thou shalt
²Co. 2. 9. w. ye be obedient in all thi.
13. 5. Examine yourselves, w. ye
¹Jo. 4. 1. the spirits w. they are of God
tis. [Lu.5.23
Mat. 9. 5. w. is easier, to say; Mar.2.8;
21.31. w. of them twain did the will
23.17. for w. is greater, the gold
19. for w. is greater, the gift
27.21. w. of the twain will ye that
Lu. 22.27. For w. is greater, he that si.
ean.
Ro. 14. 8. w. we live,..w. we die, &c.
mēpote.
Lu. 3.15. w. he were the Christ *or not*
poteron.
Jo. 7.17. w. it be of God, or whether
te kai.
Act. 9. 2. w. they were men or women
ētoi.
Ro. 6.16. w. of sin unto death, or

WHICH.
The relatives which *and* that *are*
generally represented by hos *and* ho ;
the following are exceptions :—
hostis.
Mat. 7.15. w. come to you in sheep's
24, 26. w. built his house upon
13.52. w. bringeth forth out of his
16.28. w. shall not taste ; Mar.9.1
19.12. w. were so born from their
w. were made eunuchs for
w. have made themselves
20. 1. w. went out early in the mo.
21.33. w. planted a vineyard
41. w. shall render him the fru.
22. 2. w. made a marriage for his
23.27. w. indeed appear beautiful
25. 1. w. took their lamps, and
27.55. w. followed Jesus from Gal.
Mar.12.18.w. say there is no resurrect.
Lu. 1.20. w. shall be fulfilled in
2. 4. w. is called Bethlehem
10. w. shall be to all people
7.37. w. was a sinner, when she
8. 3. w. ministered unto him
15. w. in an honest and good he.
26. w. is over against Galilee
43. w. had spent all her living
9.30. w. were Moses and Elias
10.42. w. shall not be taken away

Lu. 12. 1. leaven of the Pharisees, w. is
15. 7. w. need no repentance
23.55. w. came with him from Galⁱ.
Jo. 8.53. father, Abraham, w. is dead
21.25. *the* w., if they should be wri.
Act.10.47. w. have received the Holy G.
11.20. w., when they were come to
28. w. came to pass in the days
12.10. w. opened to them of his own
16.12. w. is the chief city of that
16. w. brought her masters much
17. w. shew unto us the way of
23.21. w. have bound themselves
Ro. 2.15. w. shew the work of the law
16.12. w. laboured much in the Lo.
¹Co. 3.17. is holy, w. temple ye are
6.20. in your spirit, w. are God's
7.13. woman w. hath an husband
²Co. 3.14. w. vail is done away in Chri.
9.11. w. causeth through us thank.
Gal. 4.24. w. things are an allegory
gendereth to bondage, w. is
26. is free, w. is the mother of us
5.19. w. are these; Adultery
Eph. 1.23. w. is his body, the fulness of
3.13. for you, w. is your glory
6. 2. w. is the first commandment
Phi. 1.28. w. is to them an evident tok.
4. 3. women w. laboured with me
Col. 2.23. w. things have indeed a shew
3. 5. and covetousness, w. is idol.
14. w. is the bond of perfectness
4.11. w. have been a comfort unto
¹Ti. 1. 4. w. minister questions, rather
3.15. w. is the church of the living
6. 9. w. drown men in destruction
²Ti. 1. 5. w. dwelt first in thy grandm.
Heb. 2. 3. w. at the first began to be sp.
8. 6. w. was established upon bet.
9. 2. w. is called the sanctuary
9. w. was a figure for the time
10. 8. w. are offered by the law
11. w. can never take away sins
35. w. hath great recompence of
12. 5. w. speaketh unto you as unto
¹Pet. 2.11. w. war against the soul
¹Jo. 1. 2. w. was with the Father
Rev. 1. 7. *they also* w. pierced him
2.24. and w. have not known the
9. 4. w. have not the seal of God
11. 8. w. spiritually is called Sodom
12.13. w. brought forth the man ch.
17.12. w. have received no kingdom
19. 2. w. did corrupt the earth
20. 4. and w. had not worshipped
hostis an.
Act. 3.23. every soul, w. will not hear
houtos.
Act. 8.26. unto Gaza, w. is desert
tis. [Lu.12.25
Mat. 6.27. w. of you by taking thought;
Lu. 7.42. w. of them will love him mo.
9.46. w. of them should be greate.
10.36. w. now of these three, think.
11. 5. w. of you shall have a friend
14. 5. w. of you shall have an ass
28. For w. of you, intending to
17. 7. But w. of you, having a serv.
22.23. w. of them it was that shou.
24. w. of them should be accou.
Jo. 8.46. w. of you convinceth me of
21.20. Lord, w. is he that betrayeth
Act. 7.52. w. of the prophets have not
Heb. 1. 5, 13. For unto w. of the angels
5.12. w. be the first principles of
hos eimi.
Mar. 3.17. Boanerges, w. *is*, The sons
12.42. two mites, w. *make* a farthi.
Eph. 6.17. the sword of the Spirit, w. *is*
Col. 1.24. for his body's sake, w. *is* th;
Heb. 7. 2. King of Salem, w. *is*, King
Rev.21. 8. w. *is* the second death

hos en.

Jas. 1.1. tribes w. are scattered
(those in the dispersion)

hosos.

Jo. 21.25. other things w. Jesus did
Act. 9.39. garments w. Dorcas made

hoios.

Phi. 1.30. Having the same conflict w.
²Ti. 3.11. afflictions, w. came unto me

poios.

Mat.19.18. He saith unto him, w.
22.36. w. is the great commandme.
Mar.12.28.w. is the first commandment
Jo. 10.32. for w. of those works do ye

ei tis.

Eph. 4.29. but that w. is good to the
(See words in connection.)

WHILE.
en.

Mat.13.25. w. men slept his enemy
Mar. 2.19. w. the bridegro. is ; Lu.5.34
Lu. 1. 8. w. he executed the priest's
24.15. that, w. they communed
51. to pass, w. he blessed
Jo. 5. 7. w. I am coming
Act.19. 1. that, w. Apollos was at
Heb. 3.15. w. it is said, To day if ye

heōs.

Mat.14.22. w. he sent the multitudes
26.36. w. I go and pray yonder
Mar. 6.45. w. he sent away the people
14.32. here, w. I shall pray
Jo. 9. 4. that sent me, w. it is day
12.35, 36. w. ye have the light

hōs.

Lu. 24.32. w. he talked with us by the
and w. he opened to us the
Act. 1.10. And w. they looked stedfas.
10.17. Now w. Peter doubted in

hote.

Jo. 17.12. w. I was with them in the
Heb. 9.17. w. the testator liveth

achris, hos [neu.]

Heb. 3.13. w. it is called To day

achri, hos [neu.]

Act.27.33. w. the day was coming on

hotan.

¹Co. 3. 4. For w. one saith, I am of

chronos.

Lu. 18. 4. he would not for a w.
Jo. 7.33. yet a little w. am I with
12.35. a little w. is the light with

tis chronos.

¹Co. 16. 7. trust to tarry a w. with you

oligos.

Mar. 6.31. desert place, and rest a w.
¹Pet. 5.10. that ye have suffered a w.

hēmera.

Act.15. 7. a good w. ago God made
18.18. tarried there yet a good w.

kairos.

Lu. 8.13. which for a w. believe

proskairos.

Mat.13.21. but dureth for a w.

palai.

Mar.15.44.he had been any w. dead
Lu. 10.13. a great w. ago repented

mikron.

Mat.26.73. And after a w. came unto

hosos hosos [neu.]

Heb.10.37.For yet a little w., and he
(See Great, Little, Long.)

WHILES.
heōs hotou.

Mat. 5.25. w. thou art in the way with

WHISPERERS.
psithuristēs.

Ro. 1.29. full of..deceit, malig...; w.

WHISPERINGS.
psithurismos.

²Co.12.20. w., swellings, tumults

WHIT. (See Every.)
mēdeis.

²Co. 11. 5. I was not a w. behind the

WHITE.
leukos.

Mat. 5.36. not make one hair w. or bla.
17. 2. raime. was w.; 28.3; Mar.9.3
Mar.16. 5. clothed in a long w. garment
Lu. 9.29. his raiment was w. and glis.
Jo. 4.35. they are w. already to harvest
20.12. And seeth two angels in w.
Act. 1.10. stood by them in w. apparel
Rev. 1.14. were w. like wool, as w. as
2.17. will give him a w. stone
3. 4. they shall walk with me in w.
5. clothed in w. raiment ; 4.4
18. and w. raiment, that thou
6. 2. behold a w. horse ; 19.11
11. And w. robes were given unto
7. 9. clothed with w. robes, and
13. which are arrayed in w. robes
14.14. and behold a w. cloud, and
19.14. followed him upon w. horses
in fine linen, w. and clean
20.11. I saw a great w. throne

leukainō.

Rev. 7.14. made them w. in the blood

lampros.

Rev.15. 6. clothed in pure and w. linen
19. 8. in fine linen, clean and w.

WHITE, [verb,]   -ed.
koniaō.

Mat.23.27. like unto w-ed sepulchres
Act.23. 3. smite thee, thou w-ed wall

leukainō.

Mar. 9. 3. fuller on earth can w. them

WHITHER.
pou.

Jo. 3. 8. cometh and w. it goeth
7.35. w. will he go, that we shall
8.14. whence I came, and w. I go
whence I come, and w. I go
12.35. knoweth not w. he ; ¹Jo.2.11
13.36. Lord, w. goest thou ; 16.5
14. 5. we know not w. thou goest
Heb.11. 8. not knowing w. he went

hopou.

Jo. 8.21, 22. w. I go, ye can.; 13.33,36
14. 4. And w. I go ye know, and
18.20. w. the Jews always resort
21.18. walkedst w. thou wouldest
carry thee w. thou wouldest
Heb. 6.20. w. the forerunner is for us

hou.

Lu. 10. 1. w. he himself would come
24.28. the village, w. they went

WHITHERSOEVER.
hopou an.

Mar. 6.56. And w. he entered, into vill.
Lu. 9.57. follow thee w. thou goest
Jas. 3. 4. w. the governor listeth
Rev.14. 4. follow the Lamb w. he goeth

hopou ean.

Mat. 8.19. follow thee w. thou goest

hou ean.

¹Co.16. 6. me on my journey w. I go

WHO,   Whom.
The relative is usually represented by
hos or ho.

tis.

at 3. 7. w. hath warned you; Lu.3.7
10.11. enquire w. in it is worthy
12.27. by w-m do your children cast

Mat.12.48. w. is my mother? and w.
16.13. w-m do men say that I the:
Mar.8.27 ; Lu.9.18
15. But w-m say ye that I am ;
Mar.8.29; Lu.9.20; Act.13.25
17.25. w-m do the kings of the earth
18. 1. w. is the greatest in the kin.
19.25. w. then can be saved ; Mar.
10.26; Lu.18.26
21.10. was moved, saying, w. is this
23. w. gave thee this ; Mar.11.28
24.45. w. then is a faithful; Lu.12.42
26.68. w. is he that smo. ; Lu.22.64
27.17. w-m will ye that I release un.
Mar. 1.24. I know thee w. thou; Lu.4.34
2. 7. w. can forgive sins; Lu.5.21
3.33. w. is my mother, or my bret.
5.30. said, w. touched my; Lu.8.45
31. w. touched me ; Lu.8.45
9.34. w. should be the greatest
16.. 3. w. shall roll us away the sto.
Lu. 5.21. w. is this which speaketh
6.47. shew you to w-m he is like
7.39. w. and what manner of wo.
49. w. is this that forgiveth sins
9. 9. but w. is this, of whom I he.
10.22. no man knoweth w. the Son
Father; and w. the Father is
29. And w. is my neighbour
11.19. by w-m do your sons cast th.
12. 5. I will forewarn you w-m ye
14. Man, w. made me a judge or
16.11. w. will commit to your trust
12. w. shall give you that which
19. 3. he sought to see Jesus w. he
20. 2. or w. is he that gave thee
Jo. 1.19, 22. him, w. art thou; Jo.21.12
4.10. and w. it is that saith to thee
5.13. wist not w. it was: for Jesus
6.60. an hard saying ; w. can hear
64. w. they were that believed
and w. should betray him
68. Lord, to w-m shall we go
7.20. w. goeth about to kill thee
8.25. Then said they unto him, w.
53. w-m makest thou thyself
9. 2. w. did sin, this man, or his
21. or w. hath opened his eyes
36. w. is he, Lord, that I might
12.34. w. is this Son of man
38. Lord w. hath believed our
to w-m hath the arm of the
13.22. doubting of w-m he spake
24. w. it should be of whom he
25. saith unto him, Lord, w. is it
18. 4, 7. unto them, w-m seek ye
20.15. w-m seekest thou
Act. 7.27, 35. w. made thee a ruler and
8.33. and w. shall declare his gene.
34. of w-m speaketh the prophet
9. 5. w. art thou, Lord; 22.8; 26.15
19.15. and Paul I know; but w. are
21.33. and demanded w. he was
Ro. 7.24. w. shall deliver me from the
8.31. w. can be against us
33. w. shall lay anything to the
34. w. is he that condemneth
35. w. shall separate us from the
9.19. w. hath resisted his will
20. w. art thou that repliest aga.
10. 6. w. shall ascend into heaven
7. Or, w. shall descend into the
16. w. hath believed our report
11.34. For w. hath known the mind
or w. hath been his counsel.
35. Or w. hath first given to him
14. 4. w. art thou that judgest ano.
¹Co. 2.16. For w. hath known the mind
3. 5. w. then is Paul, and w. is
4. 7. For w. maketh thee to differ
9. 7. w. goeth a warfare any time
w. planteth a vineyard, and

¹Co. 9. 7. or **w.** feedeth a flock, and
   14. 8. **w.** shall prepare himself to
²Co. 2. 2. **w.** is he then that maketh
   16. And **w.** is sufficient for these
  11.29. **w.** is weak, and I am not we.
   w. is offended, and I burn
Gal. 3. 1. **w.** hath bewitched you, that
   5. 7. **w.** did hinder you that ye
²Ti. 3.14. knowing of **w-**m thou hast
Heb. 3.17. But with **w-**m was he grieved
   18. And to **w-**m sware he that
Jas. 3.13. **w.** is a wise man and endued
  4.12. **w.** art thou that judgest ano.
¹Pet. 3.13. And **w.** is he that will harm
   5. 8. seeking **w-**m he may devour
¹Jo. 2.22. **w.** is a liar but he that deni.
   5. 5. **w.** is he that overcometh the
Rev. 5. 2. **w.** is worthy to open the book
   6.17. and **w.** shall be able to stand
  13. 4. **w.** is like unto the beast
   w. is able to make war with
  15. 4. **w.** shall not fear thee, O Lo.

   hostis.

Mar.15. 7. **w.** had committed murder
Lu. 23.19. **w.** for a certain sedition ma.
Act. 7.53. **w.** have received the law by
   8.15. **w.**, when they were come
  10.41. to us, **w.** did eat and drink
  13.31. **w.** are his witnesses unto the
   43. **w.**, speaking to them, persu.
  17.10. **w.** coming thither went into
  21. 4. **w.** said to Paul through the
  23.33. **w.**, when they came to Cæsa.
  24. 1. **w.** informed the governor ag.
  28.18. **w.**, when they had examined
Ro. 1.25. **w.** changed the truth of God
   32. **w.** knowing the judgment of
  9. 4. **w.** are Israelites ; to whom
  11. 4. **w.** have not bowed the knee
  16. 4. **w.** have for my life laid down
   6. **w.** bestowed much labour on
   7. **w.** are of note among the apo.
²Co. 8.10. **w.** have begun before, not on.
Gal. 2. 4. **w.** came in privily to spy out
Eph. 4.19. **w.** being past feeling
Phi. 2.20. **w.** will naturally care for
²Th. 1. 9. **w.** shall be punished with
²Ti. 2. 2. **w.** shall be able to teach oth.
   18. **w.** concerning the truth have
Tit. 1.11. **w.** subvert whole houses
Heb. 8. 5. **w.** serve unto the example
   13. 7. **w.** have spoken unto you the
²Pet. 2. 1. **w.** privily shall bring in dam.

   houtos.

Act.13. 7. **w.** called for Barnabas and

   hosos.

Heb. 2.15. **w.** through fear of death

WHOLE. (See *Armour, Burnt.*)

   holos.

Mat. 5.29, 30. that thy **w.** body should
   6.22. thy **w.** body sh. be; Lu.11.36
  13.33. till the **w.** was lea.; Lu.13.21
  16.26. if he shall gain the **w.** world;
   Mar.8.36 ; Lu.9.25
  26.13. be preached in the **w.** world
  27.27. gathered unto him the **w.** ba.
Mar. 6.55. ran through that **w.** region
  14. 9. throughout the **w.** world
  15. 1. and the **w.** council
   16. they called together the **w.**
   33. darkness over the **w.** land
Lu. 8.39. published throughout the **w.**
  11.34. thy **w.** body also is full of
   36. If thy **w.** body therefore be
Jo. 4.53. believed, and his **w.** house
  11.50. that the **w.** nation perish not
Act 11.26. that a **w.** year they assembl.
  15.22. and elders, with the **w.** chu.
  19.29. the **w.** city was filled with
  28.30. Paul dwelt two **w.** years in
Ro. 1. 8. spoken of throughout the **w.**
310

Ro. 16.23. mine host, and of the **w.** ch.
¹Co. 5. 6. leaveneth the **w.** lump
  12.17. If the **w.** body were an eye
   If the **w.** were hearing
  14.23. If therefore the **w.** church
Gal. 5. 3. he is a debtor to do the **w.**
   9. leaveneth the **w.** lump
Tit. 1.11. who subvert **w.** houses
Jas. 2.10. whosoever shall keep the **w.**
  3. 2. able also to bridle the **w.** bo.
   3. and we turn about their **w.**
   6. that it defileth the **w.** body
¹Jo. 2. 2. for the sins of the **w.** world
  5.19. the **w.** world lieth in wicked.
Rev.12. 9. which deceiveth the **w.** world
  16.14. of the **w.** world, to gather th.

   pas.

Mat. 8.32. and, behold, the **w.** herd of
   34. the **w.** city came out to meet
  13. 2. the **w.** multitude ; Mar.4.1 ;
   Lu.1.10 ; 6.19 ; Act.6.5
Lu. 21.35. on the face of the **w.** earth
Act.13.44. came almost the **w.** city
Ro. 8.22. the **w.** creation groaneth
Eph. 3.15. Of whom the **w.** family in
  4.16. From whom the **w.** body fitly

   hapas.

Lu. 8.37. the **w.** multit. of; 19.37; 23.1

   holokleros.

¹Th. 5.23. I pray God your **w.** spirit

WHOLE, [*Healthy.*]

   hugies.   [Mar.3.5 ; Lu.6.10

Mat.12.13. it was restored **w.**, like as
  15.31. maimed to be **w.**, the lame
Mar. 5.34. and be **w.** of thy plague
Jo. 5. 4. was made **w.** of whatsoever
   6. Wilt thou be made **w.**
   9. was made **w.**, and took up
   11. He that made me **w.**, the
   14. thou art made **w.** : sin no
   15. which had made him **w.**
  7.23. every whit **w.** on the sabba.
Act. 4.10. stand here before you **w.**

   hugiaino.

Lu. 5.31. They *that are* **w.** need not a
  7.10. found the servant **w.** that

   sozo.   [Mar.5.28

Mat. 9.21. his garment, I *shall be* **w.** ;
   22. thy faith *hath made* thee **w.** ;
   Mar.5.34; 10.52; Lu.8.48;17.19
   And the wom. *was made* **w.**
Mar. 6.56. as touched him *were made* **w.**
Lu. 8.50. and she *shall be made* **w.**
Act. 4. 9. by what means he *is made* **w.**

   diasozo.

Mat.14.36. touch. *were made perfectly* **w.**

   iaomai.

Mat.15.28. her daughter *was made* **w.**
Act. 9.34. Jesus Chr. *maketh* thee **w.**

   ischuo.

Mat. 9.12. They *that be* **w.** need not a

WHOLESOME.

   hugiaino, [*part.*]

¹Ti. 6. 3. and consent not to **w.** words

WHOLLY. (See *Idolatry.*)

   holoteles.

¹Th. 5.23. God of peace sanctify you **w.**

   eimi en.

¹Ti. 4.15. *give* thyself **w.** *to* (*be* thou *in*)

WHOMSOEVER.

   hos ean.

Mat. 11.27. to **w.** the Son will reveal
Lu. 4. 6. to **w.** I will I give it
¹Co. 16. 3. **w.** ye shall approve by

   ean tis.

Jo. 13.20. He that receiveth **w.** I send

   pas hos.

Lu. 12.48. For unto **w.** much is given

WHORE.

   porne.

Rev.17. 1. the judgment of the great **w.**
   15. where the **w.** sitteth, are peo.
   16. these shall hate the **w.**
  19. 2. he hath judged the great **w.**

WHOREMONGER,   -s.

   pornos.

Eph. 5. 5. that no **w.**, nor unclean
¹Ti. 1.10. For **w-**s, for them that defile
Heb.13. 4. but **w-**s and adulterers God
Rev.21. 8. and **w-**s, and sorcerers, and
  22.15. and **w-**s, and murderers, and

WHOSE.

The relative is represented by **hos** [*gen.*]
   tis, [*gen. or dat.*]   [Lu.20.24

Mat. 22.20. **w.** is this image ; Mar.12.16;
   28. **w.** wife shall she be ; Mar.
   12.23 ; Lu.20.33
Lu. 12.20. then **w.** shall those things
Jo. 19.24. lots for it, **w.** it shall be

   an tis.

Jo. 20.23. **w.** *soever* sins ye remit
   and **w.** *soever* sins ye retain

WHOSOEVER.

   pas ho *or* **hos.**

Mat.5.22. That **w.** is angry with his
   28. **w.** looketh on a woman to
Lu. 6.47. **w.** cometh to me, and hear.
  12. 8. **w.** shall confess me before
   10. And **w.** shall speak a word
  14.11. For **w.** exalteth himself sha.
   33. **w.** he be of you that forsak.
  16.18. **w.** putteth away his wife
   and **w.** marrieth her that is
  20.18. **w.** shall fall upon that stone
Jo. 3.15,16. That **w.** believeth in him ;
   Act.10.45 ; Ro.9.33,10.11
  4.13. **w.** drinketh of this water
  8.34. **w.** committeth sin is the
  11.26. And **w.** liveth and believeth
  12.46. that **w.** believeth on me sh.
  16. 2. that **w.** killeth you will thi.
  19.12. **w.** maketh himself a king
Act. 2.21. **w.** shall call on ; Ro. 10.13
Ro. 2. 1. O man, **w.** thou art that
¹Jo. 2.23. **w.** denieth the Son, the same
  3. 4. **w.** committeth sin transgres.
   6. **w.** abideth in him sinneth
   w. sinneth hath not seen him
   9. **w.** is born of God doth not
   10. **w.** doeth not righteousness
   15. **w.** hateth his brother is a
  5. 1. **w.** believeth that Jesus is
   18. **w.** is born of God sinneth
²John 9. **w.** transgresseth, and abidet.
Rev.22.15. and **w.** loveth and maketh

   pas hostis.

Mat. 7.24. **w.** heareth these sayings of
  10.32. **w.** therefore shall confess

   hostis.

Mat. 5.39. but **w.** shall smite thee on
   41. And **w.** shall compel thee to
  13.12. **w.** hath, to him shall be giv.
   but **w.** hath not, from him
  18. 4. **w.** therefore shall humble
  23.12. **w.** shall exalt himself shall
Mar. 8.34. **w.** will come after me, let
Lu. 14.27. **w.** doth not bear his cross
Gal. 5. 4. **w.** of you are justified by
Jas. 2.10. For **w.** shall keep the whole

   hostis an.

Mat. 10.33. **w.** shall deny me before
  12.50. **w.** shall do the will of my
Gal. 5.10. bear his judgment, **w.** he

   hosos an.   [Lu. 9.5

Mar. 6.11. **w.** shall not receive you ;

   ei tis.

Rev.14.11. **w.** receiveth the mark of his
  20.15. **w.** was not found written

WHY.
tis, [neu.]

Mat. 6.28. w. take ye thought for raim.
  7. 3. And w. beholdest; Lu.6.41
  8.26. w. are ye fearful; Mar.4.40
 16. 8. w. reason ye among yoursel.
 17.10. w. then say the scribes that
 19. 7. w. did Moses then command
   17. w. callest thou me good ;
            Mar.10.18 ; Lu.18.19
 20. 6. w. stand ye here all the day
 22.18. w. tempt ye me ; Mar.12.15 ;
            Lu.20.23
 26.10. w. trouble ye the woman
Mar. 2. 7. w. doth this man thus speak
  8. w. reason ye; 3.17.
 24. w. do they on the sabbath
 5.35. w. troublest thou the Master
 39. w. make ye this ado, and
 8.12. w. doth this generation seek
 11. 3. w. do ye this? say ye that
 14. 6. Let her alone ; w. trouble ye
Lu. 2.48. w. hast thou thus dealt with
 6. 2. w. do ye that which is not
 46. And w. call ye me, Lord
 12.26. w. take ye thought for the
 57. Yea, and w. even of yoursel.
 19.33. w. loose ye the colt
 22.46. w. sleep ye? rise and pray
 24. 5. w. seek ye the living among
 38. w. are ye troubled
Jo. 1.25. w. baptizest thou then, if
 4.27. w. talkest thou with her
 7.19. w. go ye about to kill me
 10.20. and is mad ; w. hear ye him
 18.21. w. askest thou me? ask them
  23. but if well, w. smitest thou
 20.13, 15. Woman, w. weepest thou
Act. 1.11. w. stand ye gazing up into
 3.12. w. marvel ye at this ? or w.
 5. 4. w. hast thou conceived this
 9. 4. Saul, Saul, w. persecutest ;
         22.7,26.14
 14.15. Sirs, w. do ye these things
 15.10. Now therefore w. tempt ye
 22.16. And now w. tarriest thou
 26. 8. w. should it be thought a
Ro. 3. 7. w. yet am I also judged as a
 8.24. for what a man seeth, w.
 9.19. w. doth he yet find fault
 20. w. hast thou made me thus
 14.10. w. dost thou judge thy bro.
 w. dost thou set at nought
1Co. 4. 7. w. dost thou glory, as if thou
 10.29. for w. is my liberty judged
 30. w. am I evil spoken of for
 15.29. w. are they then baptized
 30. And w. stand we in jeopardy
Gal. 2.14. w. compellest thou the Gen.
 5.11. w. do I yet suffer persecuti.
Col. 2.20. w., as though living in the
eis tis.
Mar.14. 4. w. was this waste of ointm.
 15.34. w. hast thou forsaken me
diati.
Mat. 9.11. w. eateth your Master with
 14. w. do we and the Pharisees
 13.10. w. speakest thou unto them
 15. 2. w. do thy disciples transgre.
 3. w. do ye also transgress the
 17.19. w. could not we cast him
 21.25. w. did ye not then believe
Mar. 2.18. w. do the disciples : Lu.5.33
 7. 5. w. walk not thy disciples
 11.31. w. then did ye not ; Lu.20.5
Lu. 5.30. w. do ye eat and drink with
 19.31. ask you, w. do ye loose him
 24.38. w. do thoughts arise in your
Jo. 7.45. w. have ye not brought him
 8.43. w. do ye not understand my
 46. w. do ye not believe me

Jo. 12. 5. w. was not this ointment
 13.37. Lord, w. cannot I follow
Act. 5. 3. w. hath Satan filled thine
1Co. 6. 7. w. do ye not rather take
 w. do ye not rather suffer
hinati.
Mat.27.46. w. hast thou forsaken me
Lu. 13. 7. w. cumbereth it the ground
Act. 4.25. w. did the heathen rage
 7.26. w. do ye wrong one to anot.
1Co. 10.29. w. is my liberty judged of
hoti.
Mar. 9.11. w. say the scribes that Elias
 28. w. could not we cast him
gar.   [Mar.15.14; Lu.23.22
Mat. 27.23. w. what evil hath he done ;
Jo. 9.30. w. herein is a marvellous

WICKED.
ponēros.
Mat.12.45. unto this w. generation
 13.19. then cometh the w. one
 38. tares are the child. of the w.
 49. and sever the w. from among
 16. 4. A w. and adulterous gener.
 18.32. thou w. servant ; Lu. 19.22
 25.26. Thou w. and slothful serva.
Act.18.14. of wrong or w. lewdness
1Co. 5.13. put away..that w. person
Eph. 6.16. the fiery darts of the w.
Col. 1.21. in your mind by w. works
2Th. 3. 2. from unreasonable and w.
1Jo. 2.13, 14. ye have overcome the w.
 3.12. who was of that w. one
 5.18. and that w. one toucheth
ponēroteros.   [Lu.11.26
Mat.12.45.spirits more w. than himself;
anomos.
Act. 2.23. by w. hands have crucified
2Th. 2. 8. shall that w. be revealed
athesmos.
2Pet. 2. 7. filthy conversation of the w.
 3.17. with the error of the w.
kakos.
Mat. 21.41. miserably destroy those w.

WICKEDNESS.
ponēria.
Mat.22.18.Jesus perceived their w.
Mar. 7.22. covetousness, w., (plural)
Lu. 11.39. full of ravening and w.
Ro. 1.29. w., covetousness, malicious.
1Co. 5. 8. leaven of malice and w.
Eph. 6.12. against spiritual w. (the
 spirituals [or spirits] of ickedness)
ponēros.
1Jo. 5.19. whole world lieth in w.
kakia.   (in the wicked one)
Act. 8.22. Repent there. of this thy w.

WIDE.
platus.
Mat. 7.13. for w. is the gate, and broad

WIDOW.   -s.
chēra.
Mat.23.14.for ye devour w-s' houses
Mar.12.40. Which devour w-s' houses
 42. there came a certain poor w.
 43. this poor w. hath cast more
Lu. 2.37. she was a w. of about foursc.
 4.25. many w-s were in Israel in
 26. unto a woman that was a w.
 7.12. his mother, and she was a w.
 18. 3. And there was a w. in that
 5. Yet because this w. troubleth
 20.47. Which devour w-s' houses
 21. 2. a certain poor w. casting in
 3. this poor w. hath cast in mo.
Act. 6. 1. because their w-s were negl.
 9.39. all the w-s stood by him we.
 41. had called the saints and w-s
1Co. 7. 8. to the unmarried and w-s

1Ti. 5. 3. Honour w-s that are w-s in.
 4. if any w. have children or
 5. she that is a w. indeed, and
 9. Let not a w. be taken into
 11. But the younger w-s refuse
 16. wo. that believeth have w-s
 relieve them that are w-s in.
Jas. 1.27. visit the fatherless and w-s
Rev.18. 7. sit a queen, and am no w.

WIFE, (See Marry),   Wives.
gunē.
Mat. 1.20. take unto thee Mary thy w.
 24. and took unto him his w.
 5.31, 32. shall put away his w.;
      19.9 ; Mar.10.11 ; Lu.16.18
 14. 3. his brother Philip's w.; Mar.
       6.17 ; Lu.3.19
 18.25. to be sold, and his w. and
 19. 3. a man to put away his w.;
      Mar.10.2   [Mar.10.7
 5. shall cleave to his w.;
 8. you to put away your w-ves
 10. the man be so with his w.
 29. father, or mother, or w. , or ;
      Mar.10.29; Lu.14.26
 22.24. brother shall marry his w.;
      Mar.12.19; Lu.20.28
 25. left his w. unto his brother
 28. whose w. shall she be of ;
      Mar.12.23; Lu.20.33
 27.19. his w. sent unto him, saying
Mar. 6.18. to have thy brother's w.
 12.19. die, and leave his w. behind
 20. the first took a w.; Lu.20.29
 23. sev. had her to w.; Lu.20.33
Lu. 1. 5. his w. was of the daughters
 13. thy w. Elisabeth shall bear
 18. man, and my w. well strick
 24. those days his w. Elisabeth
 2. 5. taxed with Mary his espo.w.
 8. 3. Joanna the w. of Chuza
 14.20. said, I have married a w.
 17.32. Remember Lot's w.
 18.29. parents, or brethren, or w.
 20.28. man's brot. die, having a w
 30. the second took her to w.
Act. 5. 1. Anan., with Sapphira his w.
 2. his w. also being privy to it
 7. his w., not knowing what
 18. 2. from Italy, with his w. Pris.
 21. 5. on our way, with w-ves and
 24.24. Felix came with his w. Dru.
1Co. 7. 1. should have his father's w.
 2. every man have his own w.
 3. the hus. render unto the w.
 also the w. unto the husba.
 4. The w. hath not power of
 of his own body, but the w.
 10. Let not the w. depart from
 11. the husband put away his w.
 12. If any brother hath a w.
 14. husband is sancti. by the w
 and the unbelieving w. is
 16. For what know. thou, O w.
 whet. thou shalt save thy w
 27. Art thou bound unto a w.
 from a w.? seek not a w.
 29. they that have w-ves be as
 33. how he may please his w.
 34. difference between a w. and
 39. The w. is bound by the law
 9. 5. to lead about a sister, a w.
Eph. 5.22. w-ves, submit your.;Col.3.17
 23. husba. is the head of the w.
 24. so let the w-ves be to their
 25. H., love your w-ves ; Col.3.18
 28. oug. men to love their w-ves
 He that loveth his w. loveth
 31. shall be joined unto his w.
 33. w. even as him.; and the w.
1Ti. 3. 2. the husband of one w., vigi.

311

1Ti. 3. 11. Even so must their w-*ves* be
12. deacons be husba. of one w.
5. 9. having been the w. of one
Tit. 1. 6. blameless, the husb. of one w.
1Pet. 3. 1. ye w-*ves* be in subjection to
won by conver. of the w-*ves*
Rev.19. 7. his w. hath made herself
21. 9. thee the bride, the Lamb's w.

gunaikeios.
1Pet. 3. 7. giving honour unto the w.

graōdēs.
1Ti. 4. 7. profane and old w-*ves* fables

penthera.
Mat. 8. 14. he saw his w.'s *mother* laid
Mar. 1.30. Simon's w.'s *moth.*; Lu.4.38

WILD.

agrios.
Mat. 3. 4. locusts and w. hon.; Mar.1.6
(See *Beard*, *Olive Tree*.)

WILDERNESS.

erēmos.
Mat. 3. 1. preaching in the w. of Judæa
3. crying in the w., Prepare ye;
Mar.1.3; Lu.3.4; Jo.1.23
4. 1. of the sp. into the w.; Lu.4.1
11. 7. ye out into the w. to; Lu.7.24
Mar. 1. 4. John did baptize in the w.
12. driveth him into the w.
13. he was there in the w. forty
Lu. 3. 2. son of Zacharias in the w.
5.16. withdrew himself into the w.
8.29. driven of the devil into the w.
15. 4. ninety and nine in the w.
Jo. 3.14. lifted up the serpent in the w.
6.49. did eat manna in the w.
11.54. unto a country near to the w.
Act. 7.30. in the w. of mount Sina
36, 42. in the w. forty years
38. in the church in the w. with
44. taberna. of witness in the w.
13.18. their manners in the w.
21.38. leddest out into the w.
1Co. 10. 5. were overthrown in the w.
Heb. 3. 8. day of temptation in the w.
17. whose carcases fell in the w.
Rev.12. 6. fled into the w., where she
14. she might fly into the w.
17. 3. away in the spirit into the w.

erēmia.
Mat.15.33. so much bread in the w., as
Mar. 8. 4. with bread here in the w.
2Co. 11.26. in perils in the w., in perils

WILES.

methodeia.
Eph. 6.11. stand against the w. of the

WILFULLY.

hekousiōs.
Heb.10.26. For if we sin w. after that

WILL, [*noun.*]

thelēma.
Mat. 6.10. Thy w. be done in; Lu.11.2
7.21. but he that doeth the w.
12.50. whosoever shall do the w.
18.14. it is not the w. of your Father
21.31. of them twain did the w. of
26.42. except I drink it, thy w. be
Mar.3.35. shall do the w. of God, the
Lu. 12.47. which knew his lord's w.
neither did accordi. to his w.
22.42. nevertheless not my w., but
23.25. he delivered Jesus to their w.
Jo. 1.13. nor of the w. of the flesh
nor of the w. of man
4.34. the w. of him that sent; 6.40
5.30. mi. own w., but the w.; 6.38
6.39. the Father's w. which hath
7.17. do his w. he shall know of
9.31. doeth his w., him he heareth
Act.13.22. shall fulfil all my w. [*plural*]
Act.21.14. The w. of the Lord be done
22.14. that thou shoul. know his w.
Ro. 1.10. by the w. of God; 15.32; 2Co.
1.1; 8.5; Eph.1.1.; Col.1.1;
2Ti.1.1
2.18. knowest his w., and approve.
12. 2. acceptable, and perfect, w. of
1Co. 1. 1. of Jesus Ch. through the w.
7.37. hath power over his own w.
16.12. his w. was not at all to come
Gal. 1. 4. acco. to the w. of; 1Pet.4.19
Eph. 1. 5. to the good pleasure of his w.
9. unto us the myste. of his w.
11. after the coun. of his own w.
5.17. what the w. of the Lord is
6. 6. doing the w. of God from the
Col. 1. 9. the knowledge of his w. in all
4.12. complete in all the w. of God
1Th. 4. 3. this is the w. of God; 5.18
2Ti. 2.26. taken capti. by him at his w.
Heb.10. 7, 9. to do thy w., O God
10. By the which w. we are sanc.
36. after he have done the w. of
13.21. every good work to do his w.
1Pet. 2.15. so is the w. of God, that with
3.17. if the w. of God be so, that
4. 2. of men, but to the w. of God
3. wrought the w. of the Genti.
2Pet. 1.21. not in old time by the w. of
1Jo. 2.17. that doeth the w. of God abi.
5.14. according to his w., he hearet.

thelēsis.
Heb. 2. 4. according to his own w.

boulē.
Act.13.36. by the w. of God, fell on sleep

boulēma.
Ro. 9.19. For who hath resisted his w.

boulomai. [he begat)
Jas. 1.18. *Of* his *own* w. (*having willed*

eudokia.
Lu. 2.14. peace, *good* w. toward men
Phi. 1.15. and some also of *good* w.

eunoia.
Eph. 6. 7. With *good* w. doing service

gnōmē.
Rev.17.17. hearts to fulfil his w.

akōn.
1Co. 9.17. if *against* my w., or dispens.

WILL, [*verb*], *-eth, -ing, Wilt.*

An auxiliary verb, representing generally the future tense of the Greek verbs. The following are exceptions:—

thelō.
Mat. 1.19. not w-*ing* to make her a
5.40. *if* any man w. sue thee at
8. 2. thou w-*t*, thou canst; Mar.
1.40: Lu.5.12 [41; Lu.5.13
3. I w.; be thou clean; Mar.1.
9.13. I w. *have* mercy (*wish*); 12.7
11.14. if ye w. receive it, this is
13.28. w-*t* thou then that we go
15.28. it unto thee even as thou w-*t*
32. I w. not send them away
16.24. If any man w. co.; Lu.9.23
25. For whosoever w. save his;
Mar.8.35; Lu.9.24
17. 4. if thou w-*t*, let us make here
19.17. but if thou w-*t* enter into
21. If thou w-*t* be perfect, go
20.14. I w. give unto this last, even
15. to do what I will with mine
21. said unto her, What w-*t*
26, 27. whosoever w. be great;
Mar.10.43,44 [Lu.18.41
32. What w. ye that; Mar.10.51;
21.29. answered and said, I w. not
23. 4. w. not move them with one
26.15. What w. ye give me, and I
17. Where w-*t* thou that we;
Mar.14.12; Lu.22.9
39. nevertheless not as I w.
Mat.27.17, 21. Whom w. ye that I rele.
43. him now, if he w. *have* him
Mar. 6.22. of me whatsoever thou w-*t*
25. I w. that thou give me by
8.34. Whosoever w. come after
14. 7. and whensoever ye w. ye
36. not what I w., but what
15. 9. w. ye that I release unto you
12. What w. ye then that I shall
Lu. 4. 6. to whomsoever I w. I give it
9.54. Lord, w-*t* thou that we
10.29. w-*ing* to justify himself
12.49. what w. I, if it be already
13.31. for Herod w. kill thee
19.14. We w. not have this man to
23.20. w-*ing* to release Jesus
Jo. 5. 6. w-*t* thou be made whole
21. quickeneth whom he w.
35. ye *were* w-*ing* for a season to
40. ye w. not come to me
6.67. w. ye also go away
7.17. If any man w. do his will
8.44. lusts of your father ye w. do
9.27. w. ye also be his disciples
15. 7. ye shall ask what ye w.
17.24. I w. that they also, whom
21.22, 23. If I w. that he tarry till
Act. 7.28. w-*t* thou kill me
9. 6. what w-*t* thou *have* me to do
17.18. What w. this babbler say
18.21. again unto you, *if* God w.
24.27. w-*ing* to shew the Jews; 25.9
25. 9. w-*t* thou go up to Jerusalem
Ro. 7.18. for *to* w. is present with me
9.16. it is not of him *that* w-*eth*
18. mercy on whom he w. have
and whom he w. he harden.
22. What if God, w-*ing* to shew
13. 3. w-*t* thou then not be afraid
1Co. 4.19. to you shortly, if the Lord w.
21. What w. ye?..with a rod
7.36. let him do what he w.
39. be married to whom she w.
14.35. And if they w. learn anyth.
16. 7. For I w. not see you now
2Co. 8.11. a readiness *to* w., so there
Phi. 2.13. worketh in you both *to* w.
1Ti. 2. 4. Who w. *have* all men to be
5.11. against Christ, they w. marry
2Ti. 3.12. all *that* w. live godly in Ch.
Heb.13.18. in all things w-*ing* to live
Jas. 2.20. But w-*t* thou know, O vain
4.15. If the Lord w., we shall live
1Pet. 3.10. For he *that* w. love life
3John 13. but I w. not with ink and
Rev.11. 5. if any man w. hurt them
6. plagues, as often as they w.
22.17. whosoever w., let him take

boulomai.
Mat. 11.27. the Son w. reveal; Lu.10.22
Mar.15.15. Pilate, w-*ing* to content the
Lu. 22.42. Father, if thou *be* w-*ing*, re.
Jo. 18.39. w. ye therefore that I release
Act.18.15. for I w. be no judge of such
27.43. the centurion, w-*ing* to save
1Co. 12.11. every man severally as he w.
1Ti. 2. 8. I w. therefore that men pray
5.14. I w. therefore that the youn.
6. 9. they *that* w. be rich fall into
Tit. 3. 8. these things I w. that thou
Heb. 6.17. God, w-*ing* more abundant.
Jas. 4. 4. whosoever therefore w. be
2Pet. 3. 9. not w-*ing* that any should
Jude 5. I w. therefore put you in

mellō.
Mat. 2.13. Herod w. seek the young
Jo. 7.35. Whither w. he go, that we
not find him? w. he go unto
14.22. that thou w-*t* manifest thys.
Act.17.31. in the which he w. judge
27.10. w. be with hurt and much
Rev. 3.16. I w. spue thee out of my

WILLING. (See *Communicate*.)
 eudokeō.
²Co. 5. 8. *are* confident, I say, and **w.**
¹Th. 2. 8. we *were* **w.** to have impart.
 prothumos.
Mat. 26.41. the spirit indeed is **w.**, but
 prothumia.
²Co. 8.12. if there be first a **w.** *mind*
 authairetos.
²Co. 8. 3. they were **w.** *of* themselves

WILLINGLY
 thelō.   (they *willed to*)
Jo. 6.21. Then they **w.** received him
⁸Pet. 3. 5. For this they **w.** are ignora.
 hekōn.
Ro. 8.20. subject to vanity, not **w.**
·Co. 9.17. if I do this thing **w.**, I have
 hekousiōs.
¹Pet. 5. 2. not by constraint, but **w.**
 kata [*accus.*] hekousios.
Phile. 14. it were of necessity, but **w.**

WILL-WORSHIP.
 ethelothrēskeia.
Col. 2.23. indeed a shew of wisd. in **w.**

WIN,   *Won.*
 kerdainō.
Phi. 3. 8. that I *may* **w.** Christ
¹Pet. 3. 1. they also *may*..*be* wo. by the

WIND, (See *Drive, South*,) *-s.*
 anemos.
Mat. 7.25, 27. floods came, and the **w-s**
 8.26. rebuked the **w-s** and the sea;
  Mar.4.39; Lu.8.24
 27. that even the **w-s**; Mar.4.41
 11. 7. shaken with the **w.**; Lu.7.24
 14.24. for the **w.** was co.; Mar.6.48
 30. when he saw the **w.** boisterou.
 32. sh., the **w.** ceased; Mar.6.51
 24.31. fro. the four **w-s**; Mar.13.27
Mar. 4.37. there arose a great sto. of **w.**
 39. the **w.** ceased, and there was
Lu. 8.23. there came down a sto. of **w.**
 25. commandeth even the **w-s**
Jo. 6.18. by reason of a great **w.** that
Act.27. 7. because the **w-s** were contra.
 7. the **w.** not suffering us, we
 14. arose against it a tempes. **w.**
 15. could not bear up into the **w.**
Eph. 4.14. carried about with every **w.**
Jas. 3. 4. are driven of fierce **w-s**, yet
Jude 12. water, carried about of **w-s**
Rev. 6.13. she is shaken of a mighty **w.**
 7. 1. **w-s** of the earth, that the **w.**
 pneuma.
Jo. 3. 8. The **w.** bloweth where it list.
 pnoē.
Act. 2. 2. as of a rushing mighty **w.**
 pneō, [*partic.*]
Act.27.40. up the mainsail to the **w.**

WIND, [*verb*,] *Wound.*
 deō.
Jo. 19.40. and **wo.** it in linen clothes
 sustellō.
Act. 5. 6. men arose, **wo.** him *up*

WINDOW.
 thuris.
Act.20. 9. there sat in a **w.** a certain
²Co. 11.33. through a **w.** in a basket

WINE.
 oinos.   [Mar.2.22; Lu.5.37
Mat. 9.17. Neither do men put new **w.**;
 and the **w.** runneth out
 but they put new **w.** into;
Mar. 2.22. else the new **w.** do.; Lu.5.37
 botties, and the **w.** is
 15.23. they gave him to drink **w.**

Lu. 1.15. shall drink neither **w.** nor
 7.33. eating bread nor drinking **w.**
 10.34. pouring in oil and **w.**, and
Jo. 2. 3. And when they wanted **w.**
 unto him, They have no **w.**
 9. the water that was made **w.**
 10. doth set forth good **w.**
 has kept the good **w.** until
 4.46. where he made the water **w.**
Ro. 14.21. nor to drink **w.**, nor any
Eph. 5.18. be not drunk with **w.**
¹Ti. 3. 8. not given to much **w.**; Tit.2.3
 5.23. but use a little **w.** for thy
Rev. 6. 6. hurt not the oil and the **w.**
 14. 8, 10. the **w.** of the wrath; 18.3
 16.19. unto her the cup of the **w.** of
 17. 2. drunk with the **w.** of her
 18.13. and **w.**, and oil, and fine
 gleukos.
Act. 2.13. These men are full of *new* **w.**
 paroinos.
¹Ti. 3. 3. Not *given to* **w.**, no striker
Tit. 1. 7. not soon ang., not *given to* **w.**
 oinophlugia.
¹Pet. 4. 3. excess of **w.**, revellings

WINEBIBBER.
 oinopotēs.
Mat.11.19. man gluttonous, and a **w.**

WINEFAT.
 hupolēnion.
Mar.12. 1. digged a place for the **w.**

WINEPRESS.
 lēnos.
Mat.21.33. and digged a **w.** in it
Rev.14.19. cast it into the great **w.**
 20. And the **w.** was trodden wit.
 blood came out of the **w.**
 lēnos oinos.
Rev.19.15. he treadeth the **w.** of the

WINGS.
 pterux.
Mat.23.37. her chickens under her **w.**
Lu. 13.34. her brood under her **w.**
Rev. 4. 8. beasts had each of th. six **w.**
 9. 9. the sound of their **w.** was as
 12.14. two **w.** of a great eagle

WINKED.
 hupereidō.
Act.17.30. of this ignorance God **w.** *at*

WINTER,   *-ed.*
 paracheimazō.
Act.27.12. to Phenice, and there *to* **w.**
 28.11. *which had* **w-ed** in the isle
¹Co. 16. 6. yea, and **w.** with you, that
Tit. 3.12. I have determin. there *to* **w.**
 paracheimazia.
Act.27.12. not commodious to **w.** *in*
 cheimōn.   [13.18
Mat.24.20. flight be not in the **w.**; Mar.
Jo. 10.22. dedication, and it was **w.**
²Ti. 4.21. diligence to come before **w.**

WIPE,   *-ed.*
 ekmassō.
Lu. 7.38, 44. *did* **w.** th. with the hairs
Jo. 11. 2. **w-ed** his feet with her; 12.3
 13. 5. *to* **w.** them with the towel
 apomassō.
Lu.10.11. we do **w.** *off* against you
 exaleiphō.
Rev. 7.17. God *shall* **w.** away all; 21.4

WISDOM.
 sophia.   [Lu.7.35
Mat. 11.19.But **w.** is justified of her;
 12.42. to hear the **w.** of S.; Lu.11.31
 13.54. Whe. hath this man this **w.**
Mar. 6. 2. what **w.** is this which is giv.
Lu. 2.40. filled with **w.**: and the grace

Lu. 2. 52. Jesus increased in **w.** and
 11.49. Therefore also said the **w.** of
 21.15. give you a mouth and **w.**
Act. 6. 3. of the Holy Ghost and **w.**
 10. were not able to resist the **w.**
 7.10. and gave him favour and **w.**
 22. in all the **w.** of the Egyptia.
Ro. 11.33. of the riches both of the **w.**
¹Co. 1.17. not with **w.** of words, lest
 19. I will destroy the **w.** of the
 20. made foolish the **w.** of this
 21. **w.** of God the world by **w.**
 22. the Greeks seek after **w.**
 24. the power of God, and the **w.**
 30. of God is made unto us **w.**
 2. 1. excellency of speech or of **w.**
 4. enticing words of man's **w.**
 5. not stand in the **w.** of men
 6. Howbeit we speak **w.** among
 yet not the **w.** of this world
 . 7. we speak the **w.** of God in a
 13. words which man's **w.** teach.
 3.19. the **w.** of this world is fool.
 12. 8. by the Spirit the word of **w.**
²Co. 1.12. not with fleshly **w.**, but by
Eph. 1. 8. abounded towa. us in all **w.**
 17. the spirit of **w.** and revelat.
 3.10. the manifold **w.** of God
Col. 1. 9. in all **w.** and spiritual unde.
 28. teaching every man in all **w.**
 2. 3. treasures of **w.** and knowle.
 23. a shew of **w.** in will-worship
 3.16. dwell in you richly in all **w.**
 4. 5. Walk in **w.** toward them
Jas. 1. 5. If any of you lack **w.**, let
 3.13. works with meekness of **w.**
 15. This **w.** descendeth not from
 17. But the **w.** that is from abo.
²Pet. 3.15. according to the **w.** given
Rev. 5.12. and **w.**, and strength, and
 7.12. Blessing, and glory, and **w.**
 13.18. Here is **w.** Let him that
 17. 9. is the mind which hath **w.**
 phronēsis.
Lu. 1.17. to the **w.** of the just

WISE. (See *No*, ou mē)
 sophos.   [Lu.10.21
Mat.11.25. these things from the **w.**;
 23.34. send..proph., and **w.** *men*
Ro. 1.14. both to the **w.**, and to the
 16.19. **w.** unto that which is good
 27. To God only **w.**, be glory
¹Co. 1.19. destroy the wisdo. of the **w.**
 20. Where is the **w.**? where is
 26. not many **w.** *men* after the
 27. world to confound the **w.**
 3.10. as a **w.** masterbuilder, I ha.
 18. seemeth to be **w.** in this
 a fool, that he may be **w.**
 19. He taketh the **w.** in their
 20. kno. the thoughts of the **w.**
 6. 5. that there is not a **w.** *man*
Eph. 5.15. not as fools, but as **w.**
¹Ti. 1.17. the only **w.** God, be honour
Jas. 3.13. Who is a **w.** *man* and endu.
Jude 25. To the only **w.** God our Sa.
 sophizō.
²Ti. 3.15. are able *to make* thee **w.**
 phronimos.
Mat. 7.24. I will liken him unto a **w.**
 10.16. be ye therefore **w.** as serpen.
 24.45. faithf. and **w.** ser.; Lu.12.42
 25. 2. And five of them were **w.**
 4. the **w.** took oil in their vess.
 8. the foolish said unto the **w.**
 9. But the **w.** answered, saying
Ro. 11.25. lest ye should be **w.** in your
 12.16. Be not **w.** in your own con.
¹Co. 4.10. but ye are **w.** in Christ
 10.15. I speak as to **w.** *men*; judge
       313

ᵇCo. 11.19. seeing ye yourselves are **w**.

magos.

Mat. 2. 1. there came **w**. *men* from the
     7. had privily call. the **w**. *men*
     16. was mocked of the **w**. *men*
       inquired of the **w**. *men*

suniĕmi.

²Co. 10.12. among themsel. *are* not **w**.

houtō *or* **houtōs.**

Mat. 1.18. birth of J. Ch. was *on this* **w**.
Jo. 21. 1. and *on this* **w**. shewed he
Act. 7. 6. And God spake *on this* **w**.
     13.34. he said *on this* **w**., I will give
Ro. 10. 6. speaketh *on this* **w**., Say not
Heb. 4. 4. the seventh day *on this* **w**.

mē eis ho panteles.

Lu. 13.11. could *in no* **w**. lift up herself

ou pantōs.

Ro. 3. 9. *No, in no* **w**.; for we have

WISELY.

phronimōs.

Lu. 16. 8. because he had done **w**.

WISER.

phronimōteros.

Lu. 16. 8. **w**. than the children of light

sophōteros.

²Co. 1.25. foolishness of God is **w**. than

WISH,   -ed.

euchomai.

Act.27.29. and **w**-ed for the day
Ro. 9. 3. For I *could* **w** (or *was wishing*)
²Co. 13. 9. this also we **w**., even your
³John 2. I **w**. above all things that

WIST.

pluper of **eideō.**

Mar. 9. 6. For he **w**. not what to say
     14.40. neither w. they what to ans.
Lu. 2.49. **w**. ye not that I must be ab.
Jo. 5.13. he that was healed **w**. not
Act.12. 9. **w**. not that it was true which
     23. Then said Paul, I **w**. not

WIT.

hōs.

²Co. 5.19. *To* **w**. that God was in Chri.

gnōrizō. (*make known to* you.)

²Co. 8. 1. we *do you to* **w**. *of* the grace

WITCHCRAFT.

pharmakeia.

Gal. 5.20. Idolatry, **w**., hatred, varian.

WITH.

meta, [*gen.*]

Mat. 1.23. being interpreted is, God **w**.
     2. 3. and all Jerusalem **w**. him
       11. young child **w**. Mary his
     4.21. ship **w**. Zebedee their father
     5.25. thou art in the way **w**. him
     41. a mile, go **w**. him twain
     8.11. and shall sit down **w**. Abra.
     9.11. eateth your Master **w**. pub.
       15. bridegroom is **w**. them
     12. 3, 4. they that were **w**. him
       30. He that is not **w**. me is aga.
       he that gathereth not **w**, me
     41, 42. in judgment **w**. this gen.
     45. and taketh **w**. himself seven
     18.20. **w**. joy receiveth it
     14. 7. promised **w**. an oath to give
     15.30. having **w**. them those that
     16.27. in the glory of his Fath. **w**.
     17. 3. Moses and Elias talking **w**.
       17. how long shall I be **w**. you
     (Also) **Mat.** 18.16; 19,10; 20.2,20;
21.2; 22.16; 24.30,31,49,51 25 3,4,10,19,
31; 26.11,18,20,23,29,36,38,40,47,*bis*,51,
55,58,69,71,72; 27.34,41,54; 28.8,12,20,
Mar.1.13,20,29,36; 2.16, *bis*, 19, *bis*,25;
3.5,6,7,14; 4.16,24 * 5.18,24,40; 6.25,50,

8.10,14,38; 9.8,24; 10.30; 11.11; 13.26; 14.
7,14,17,18,20,33,43,*bis*,48,54,67; 15,17,28,
31;16.10. **Lu.**1.28,39,66; 2.36,51; 5.29,31,
34; 6.3,4,17; 7.36; 8.13,45; 9.49; 10.
17; 11.7,23,*bis*,31,32; 12.13,46,58; 13.1;
14.9,31; 15.29,30,31; 17.15,20; 21.27
22.11,15,21,28,33,52,53,59; 23.43; 24.29,
30, 52. **Jo.** 3.2, 22, 26; 4. 27, *bis*; 6.3,
66; 7.33; 8.29; 9.37,40; 11.16,31,54;
12.8,17,35; 13.8.18,33; 14.9,16,30; 15.
27; 16.4,32; 17.12,24; 18.2,3,5,18,26;
19.18,40; 20.7,24,26. **Act.**1.26; 2.28;4.29,
31; 7.9,38,45; 9.19,28,39; 10.38; 11.21;
13.17; 14.23,27; 15.4,35; 17.11; 18.10; 20.
18,19,24,31,34; 24. 1, 3,7,18,*bis*; 25.12,23;
26. 12; 27.10, 24; 28. 31. **Ro.** 12. 15,
bis,18 ; 15.10,33 ; 16.20,24. ¹**Co.**6.6,7 ;
7.12,13 ; 16.11,12,23,24. ²**Co.**6.15,16 ;
7.15 ; 8.4,18 ; 13.11,14. **Gal.**2.1,12 ; 4.
25,30;6.18. **Eph.**4.2,*bis*,25; 6.5,7,23,24.
Phi.1.4 ; 2.12,29;4.3,6,9,23. **Col.**1.11 ;
4.18. ¹**Th.**1.6; 3.13; 5.28. ³**Th.**1.7,*bis*;
3.12,16,18. ¹**Ti.**1.14; 2.9,15;3.4; 4.3,4,14;
6.6,21. ²**Ti.**2.10,22; 4.11,*bis*,22,*bis*. **Tit.**
2.15; 3.15,*bis*. **Phile.**25. **Heb.**5.7; 7.21;
9.19; **10**.22; 11.9,31; 12.14,17,28; 13.17,
23,25. ¹**Pet.**3.11. ²**Jo.**1.3,*ter*,6,7; 2.19.
²**Jo.**2,3. **Rev.**1.7,12; 2.22; 3.4,20,21,
bis; 4.1; 9.8; 12.9,17; 13.4,7; 14.1,4;
17.1,2,12,14,*bis*; 18.3,9; 19.20; 20.4,6;
21.3,*ter*, 9,15; 22.12,21

sun.

Mat. 25.27.have received mine own **w**.
     26.35. Though I should die **w**. thee
     27.38. there two thieves crucifi. **w**.
Mar. 2.26. also to them which were **w**.
     4.10. that were about him **w**. the
     8.34. called the peo. unto him **w**.
     9. 4. appeared unto them Elias **w**.
     15.27. And **w**. him they crucify two
Lu. 1.56. And Mary abode **w**. her abo.
     2. 5. To be taxed **w**. Mary his es.
       13. And suddenly there was **w**.
     5. 9. and all that were **w**. him
       19. **w**. his couch into the midst
     7. 6. Then Jesus went **w**. them
       12. people of the city was **w**. her
     8. 1. and the twelve were **w**. him
       38. bes. him that he might be **w**.
     9.32. Peter and they that were **w**.
     19.23. required mine own **w**. usury
     20. 1. the scrib. came upon him **w**.
     (Also) **Lu**.22.14,56; 23.11,32,35; 24.1,
10,24,29,33,44. **Jo**.18.1; 21.3. **Act.**1.
14, *bis*, 17,22; 2.14; 3.4,8; 4.13,14,27; 5.
1,17,21,26; 8.20,31; 10.2,20,23; 13.7; 14.
4, *bis*, 5,13,20,28; 15.22, *bis*, 25; 16.3;
17.34; 18.8,18; 19.38, 20.36; 21.5,16,18,
24,26,29; 22.9; 23.15,27,32; 24.24; 25.23;
26.13; 27.2; 28.16. **Ro.** 6. 8; 8. 32; 16.
14,15. ¹**Co.**1.2; 5.4; 10.13; 11.32; 15.
10; 16.4,19. ²**Co.**1.1,21 ; 4.14; 8.19; 9.
4; 13.4. **Gal.**1.2; 2.3; 3.9; 5.24. **Eph.**
3.18; 4.31. **Phi.**1.1,23; 2.22; 3.21. **Col.**
2.5,13,20; 3.3,4,9; 4.9. ¹**Th.**4.14,17,*bis*;
5.10. **Jas.**1.11. ²**Pet.**1.18.

en.

Mat. 3.11. I indeed baptize you **w**. wa.
       baptize you **w**. the Holy Gh.
     7. 2. **w**. what judgment ye judge
       w. what measure ye mete
     20.15. what I will **w**. mine own
     22.37. **w**. all thy heart, and **w**. all
       thy soul, and **w**. all thy mind
     25.16. went and traded **w**. the same
     26.52. shall perish **w**. the sword
Mar 1 8. **w**. water…**w**. the Holy Gh.
     23. a man **w**. an unclean spirit
     4.24. **w**. what measure ye mete
       30. or **w**. what comparison shall
     5 2. a man **w**. an unclean spirit
     9 1. kingdom of God come **w**.

Mar. 9.50. have peace one **w**. another
Lu. 1.51. hath shewed strength **w**. his
     3.16. w. the Holy Ghost and with
     4.32. for his word was **w**. power
     36. for **w**. authority and power
     8.15. bring forth fruit **w**. patience
     (Also) **Lu**. 11.20; 14.31; 21.25,34; 22,
49. **Jo**.1.26,31,33,*bis*. **Act.**1.5; 2.29,
46; 5.23; 11.16,26. **Ro**.1.4,9,12,27; 9.
22; 10.9; 12.8, *ter*, 21; 15.32; 16.16.
¹**Co**.1.17; 2.4; 4.21; 5.8, *ter*; 10.5; 14.21;
16.14,20. ²**Co**.1.12; 7.8; 13.12. **Eph.**1.
3; 3.12; 4.19; 5.18; 6.2,14,15,18. **Phi.**
1.20. **Col.**1.11; 2.4,7; 3.16,22; 4.2,6.
¹**Th.** 2.2,17; 4.16,*ter*,18; 5.26. ²**Th.**1.11;
2.9,10; 3.8. ¹**Ti.**2.9,11; 5.2. ²**Ti.**1.3; 4.
2. **Heb.**9.22,25; 11.37. **Jas.**1.21;2.1;
3.13. ¹**Pet.**1.12; 2.18; 3.2; 5.14. ²**Pet.**
2.7,13,16. **Jude** 14,23,24. **Rev.**2.16,
23,27; 6.8, *ter*, 9.19; 12.5; 13.10, *bis* ; 14.
2,7,9,10,15; 16.8; 17.16; 18.8.16; 19.2,15,
bis,20, *bis*, 21.

para, [*dat.*]

Mat.19.26. **w**. men this is impo. but **w**.
     21.25. reasoned **w**. themselves
     22.25. there were **w**. us seven bret.
Mar.10.27.**w**. men it is impossible, but
       not **w**. God ; for **w**. God all
Lu. 1.30. thou hast found favour **w**. G.
     37. For **w**. God nothing shall be
     2.52. and in favour **w**. God and
     11.37. besought him to dine **w**. him
     18.27. **w**. men are possible **w**. God
     19. 7. guest **w**. a man that is a sin.
Jo. 1.39. and abode **w**. him that day
     4.40. that he would tarry **w**. them
     8.38. which I have seen **w**. my Fa.
       which ye have seen **w**. your
     14.17. for he dwelleth **w**. you
     23. and make our abode **w**. him
     25. being yet present **w**. you
     17. 5. **w**. thine own self with the
       glory which I had **w**. thee
Act. 9.43. **w**. one Simon a tanner ; 10.6
     18. 3. he abode **w**. them ; 21.7
     20. to tarry longer time **w**. them
     21. 8. and abode **w**. him
     16. whom we should lodge
     26. 8. a thing incredible **w**. you
Ro. 2.11. no respect of persons **w**. God
     9.14. Is there unrightousness **w**.
¹**Co**. 3.19. is foolishness **w**. God
     7.24. therein abide **w**. God
²**Co**. 1.17. that **w**. me there should be
Eph. 6. 9. respect of persons **w**. him
²**Th**. 1. 6. a righteous thing to **w**. God
²**Ti**. 4.13. that I left at Troas **w**. Carp.
Jas. 1.17. **w**. whom is no variableness
¹**Pet**. 2.20. this is acceptable **w**. God
²**Pet**. 3. 8. one day is **w**. the Lord

pros, [*accu.*]

Mat.13.56. are they not all **w**. us
     26.55. I sat daily **w**. you teaching
Mar. 6. 3. are not his sisters here **w**. us
     9.10. kept but saying **w**. themse.
     16. What question ye **w**. them
       19. lo. shall I be **w**. you;Lu.9.41
     11.31. they reas. **w**. them.; Lu.20.5
     14.49. I was daily **w**. you in the
Lu. 6.11. and communed one **w**. anot.
     18.11. and prayed thus **w**. himself
Jo. 1. 1. and the Word was **w**. God
     2. was in the beginning **w**. God
Act. 2.47. having favour **w**. all the pe.
     3.25. which God made **w**. our
     11. 2. of the circum. contended **w**.
     15. 2. and disputation **w**. them
     17.17. **w**. them that met with him
     24.12. disputing **w**. any man
Ro. 5. 1. we have peace **w**. God thro.
     8.18. to be compared **w**. the glory
¹**Co**. 2. 3. And I was **w**. you in weakn

'Co.16. 6. will abide, yea, and wint. **w.**
    7. I trust to tarry a while **w.** you
  10. he may be **w.** you without
²Co. 5. 8. and to be present **w.** the Lo.
  6.14. hath light **w.** darkness
    15. what concord hath Christ **w.**
  11. 9. And when I was present **w.**
Gal. 1.18. and abode **w.** him fifteen
  2. 5. might continue **w.** you
  4.18. when I am present **w.** you
  20. desire to be present **w.** you
¹Th. 3. 4. when we were **w.** you
²Th. 2. 5. when I was yet **w.** you, I to.
  1. glorified, even as it is **w.** you
  10. For even when we were **w.**
Phile. 13. I would have retained **w.** me
Heb. 4.13. **w.** whom we have to do
  10.16. That I will make **w.** them
¹Jo. 1. 2. which was **w.** the Father
  2. 1. have an advocate **w.** the Fa.

ek.
Mat.27. 7. bought **w.** them the potter's
Mar.12.30.Lord thy G. **w.** all thy heart
    w. ..soul, &c.; Lu.10.27
  33. to love him **w.** all the heart
    w. all the understa., and **w.**
    the soul, and **w.** all the stre.
Jo. 4. 6. being wearied **w.** his journey
Act. 1.18. **w.** the reward of iniquity
  8.37. believest **w.** all thine heart
¹Co. 7. 5. except it be **w.** consent for a
¹Pet. 1.22. love one another **w.** a pure
Rev. 8. 5. filled it **w.** fire of the altar
  17. 2. **w.** the wine of her fornicati.
    6. **w.** the blood of the saints
    w. the blood of the martyrs
  18. 1. was lightened **w.** his glory
  19.21. were filled **w.** their flesh

dia, [gen.]
Mar.16.20.confirming the word **w.** signs
Act. 8.20. may be purchased **w.** money
  15.32. exhorted the brethren **w.**
  19.26. no gods, which are made **w.**
  20.28. hath purchased **w.** his own
Ro. 14.20. that man who eateth **w.** offe.
²Co. 2. 4. I wrote unto you **w.** many
Eph. 6.18. Praying always **w.** all prayer
¹Ti. 2.10. professing godliness **w.** good
Heb.12. 1. let us run **w.** patience the
  13.12. sanctify the people **w.** his
¹Pet. 1. 7. though it be tried **w.** fire
²John 12. write **w.** paper and ; ³John13

dia, [accus.]
Ro. 14.15. thy brother be grieved **w.** thy

hupo, [gen.]
Mat. 8.24. that the ship was covered **w.**
  11. 7. A reed shaken **w.**; Lu.7.24
  14.24. of the sea, tossed **w.** waves
Lu. 6.18. vexed **w.** unclean ; Act.5.16
  8.14. are choked **w.** cares and ric.
  21.20. Jerusalem compassed **w.** ar.
Act.17.25. Neither is worshipped **w.**
  27.41. broken **w.** the violence of
Jas. 3. 4. turned about **w.** a very small
²Pet. 2. 7. vexed **w.** the filthy conversa.
  17. clouds that are carried **w.** a
Rev. 6. 8. with death, and **w.** the beas.

epi, [dat.]
Mat.18.26, 29. have patience **w.** me
Lu. 18. 7. he bear long **w.** them
Act.21.24. be at charges **w.** them
  28.14. desired to tarry **w.** them
Rev.12.17. was wroth **w.** the woman

epi, [accus.]
Heb. 8. 8 **w.** the house of Israel
    and **w.** the house of Judah

apo.
Lu. 14.18. **w.** one consent began to ma.
  15.16. filled his belly **w.** the husks
  16.21. **w.** the crumbs that fell
Act.20. 9. **w.** sleep, and fell down

kata, [accus.]
Mar. 1.27. for **w.** authority command.
¹Co. 2. 1. came not **w.** excellency of
Eph. 6. 6. Not **w.** eyeservice, as menp.

hama.
Mat.13.29. also the wheat **w.** them

eis.
Eph. 3.19. **w.** all the fulness of God

peri, [gen.]
Mar.10.41. displeased **w.** James and

ho peri [accus.] **ego.**
Phi. 2.23. see *how it will go* **w.** *me*
    (the things concerning me)
(See words in connection.)

WITHAL.
hama.
Col. 4. 3. **w.** praying also for us, that
¹Ti. 5.13. **w.** they learn to be idle
Phile. 22. **w.** prepare me also a lodging

WITHDRAW, *-drew, -drawn.*
anachōreō.
Mat.12.15. he **w-e** him *self* from thence
Mar. 3. 7. Jesus **w-e** him *self* with his

hupochōreō.
Lu. 5.16. **w-e** him *self* into the wilder.

apospaō.
Lu. 22.41. he *was* **w-n** from them about

hupostellō.
Gal. 2.12. he **w-e** and separated himself

stellō.
²Th. 3. 6. that ye **w.** your *selves* from

aphistēmi.
¹Ti. 6. 5. from such **w.** *thyself*

WITHER, *-ed, -eth.*
xērainō. [Mar.4.6
Mat.13. 6. no root, they **w-ed** *away* ;
  21.19. pres. the fig tree **w-ed** *away*
  20. soon *is* the fig tree **w-ed** *awa.*
Mar. 3. 1, 3. which had a **w-ed** hand
  11.21. thou cursedst *is* **w-ed** *away*
Lu. 8. 6. it **w-ed** *away*, because it
Jo. 15. 6. as a branch, and *is* **w-ed**
Jas. 1.11. but it **w-eth** the grass, and
¹Pet. 1.24. The grass **w-eth**, and the

xēros. [Lu.6.6,8
Mat.12.10. which had his hand **w-ed**;
Jo. 5. 3. of blind, halt, **w-ed**, waiting

phthinopōrinos.
Jude 12. trees *whose fruit* **w-eth**

WITHHOLDETH.
katechō, [partic.]
²Th. 2. 6. ye know *what* **w.** that he

WITHIN.
en. [Lu.3.8
Mat. 3. 9. not to say **w.** yourselves ;
  9. 3. the scribes said **w.** themsel.
  21. For she said **w.** herself
Mar. 2. 8. they so reasoned **w.** themse.
Lu. 7.39. he spake **w.** himself, saying
  49. began to say **w.** themselves
  12.17. he thought **w.** himself, say.
  16. 3. the steward said **w.** himself
  18. 4. afterward he said **w.** himself
  19.44. thy children **w.** thee ; and
  24.32. our heart burn **w.** us, while
Ro. 8.23. ourselves groan **w.** ourselves

esōthen.
Mat.23.25.but **w.** they are full of exto.
  27. but are **w.** full of dead
  28. but **w.** ye are full of hypocr.
Mar. 7.21. For *from* **w.**, out of the hea.
  come *from* **w.**,and defile the
Lu. 11. 7. And he *from* **w.** shall answ.
  40. make that *which is* **w.** also
²Co. 7. 5. without were fightings, **w.**
Rev. 4. 8. were full of eyes **w.**
  5. 1. a book written **w.** and on

esō.
Jo. 20.26. his disciples were **w.**, and

Act. 5.23. opened, we found no man **w.**
¹Co. 5.12. ye judge them that are **w.**

entos.
Mat.23.26. that which is **w.** the cup
Lu. 17.21. kingdom of God is **w.** you

pros, [accu.]
Mar.14. 4. had indignation **w.** themsel.

esōteros.
Heb.6. 19. entereth into *that* **w.** the

dia, [gen.]
Mar.14.58. **w.** three days I will build

WITHOUT.
chōris. [Mar.4.34
Mat.13.34. **w.** a parable spake he not ;
Lu. 6.49. a man that **w.** a foundation
Jo. 1. 3. **w.** him was not any thing
  15. 5. **w.** me ye can do nothing
Ro. 3.21. righteousness of God **w.** the
  28. faith **w.** the deeds of the law
  4. 6. righteousness **w.** works
  7. 8. For **w.** the law sin was dead
  9. I was alive **w.** the law once
  10.14. shall they hear **w.** a preacher
¹Co. 4. 8. ye have reigned as kings **w.**
  11.11. neither is the man **w.** the
  neither the woman **w.** the
Eph. 2.12. at that time ye were **w.** Chr.
Phi. 2.14. Do all things **w.** murmurin
¹Ti. 2. 8. **w.** wrath and doubting
  5.21. **w.** preferring one before
Phile. 14. **w.** thy mind would I do
Heb. 4.15. like as we are, yet **w.** sin
  7. 7. **w.** all contradiction the less
  20. inasmuch as not **w.** an oath
  21. priests were made **w.** an
  9. 7. not **w.** blood, which he offer.
  18. was dedicated **w.** blood
  22. and **w.** shedding of blood
  28. the second time **w.** sin unto
  10.28. died **w.** mercy under two or
  11. 6. But **w.** faith it is impossible
  40. that they **w.** us should not
  12. 8. But if ye be **w.** chastisement
  14. **w.** which no man shall see
Jas. 2.20, 26. that faith **w.** works is de.
  26. as the body **w.** the spirit is

aneu.
Mat.10.29. on the ground **w.** your Fath.
¹Pet. 3. 1. may **w.** the word be won
  4. 9. hospitality one to anoth. **w.**

ater.
Lu. 22.35. when I sent you **w.** purse

ou meta, [gen.]
Act. 5.26. brought them **w.** violence

mē blepō, [partic.]
Act. 9. 9. he was three days **w.** sight

poieō medeis.
Act.25.17. **w.** *any* delay on the morrow

ektos.
¹Co. 6.18. that a man doeth is **w.** the

parektos.
²Co. 11.28. Beside those thi. *that are* **w.**

chōris *or* **ek.**
Jas. 2.18. me thy faith **w.** thy works

WITHOUT, [adverb.]
exō.
Mat.12.46. his brethren stood **w.**
  47. thy breth. stand **w.**; Lu.8.2
  26.69. Peter sat **w.** in the palace
Mar. 1.45. was **w.** in desert places
  3.31. standing **w.**, sent unto him
  32. thy brethren **w.** seek for thee
  4.11. unto them that are **w.**
  11. 4. tied by the door **w.** in a pla.
Lu. 1.10. the people were praying **w.**
  13.25. ye begin to stand **w.**, and to
Jo. 18.16. Peter stood at the door **w.**
  20.11. Mary stood **w.** at the supulc.
Act. 5.23. the keepers standing **w.**
¹Co. 5.12. judge them also *that are* **w.**
  13. them *that are* **w.** God judge.

Col. 4. 5. them *that are* w. ; ¹Th.4.12
Heb.13.11.are burned w. the camp
Heb.13.12.blood,suffered w. the gate
    13. unto him w. the camp
Rev.14.20.was trodden w. the city
    22.15. For w. are dogs, and

exōthen.
Mar. 7.15. nothing *from* w. a man
    18 whatsoever being *from* w.
Lu. 11.40. made that *which is* w.
²Co. 7. 5. w. were fightings, within
¹Ti. 3. 7. report of them *which are* w.
Rev.11. 2. the court which is w. the
    (*See words in connection.*)

WITHSTAND,   Withstood.
anthistēmi.
Act.13. 8. wo. them, seeking to turn
Gal. 2.11. I wo. him to the face
Eph. 6.13. able *to* w. in the evil day
²Ti. 3. 8. Jannes and Jambres wo. M.
    4.15. hath greatly w-o our words

kōluō.
Act.11.17. was I, that I could w. God

WITNESS, [*noun,*]   -es.
martureō.
Mat.23.31. ye *be* w-es unto yourselves
Lu. 4.22. all *bare* him w., and wonde.
    11.48. Truly ye *bear* w. that ye all.
Jo. 1. 7, 8. to bear w. of the Light
    15. John *bare* w. of him, and
    3.26. to whom thou *barest* w., be.
    28. yourselves *bear* me w., that
    5.31. If I *bear* w. of myself, my
    32. another *that beareth* w. of
    33. and he *bare* w. unto the tru.
    36. works that I do, *bear* w. of
    37. sent me, *hath borne* w. of me
    8.18. I am one *that bear* w. of my.
    sent me, *beareth* w. of me
    10.25. name, they *bear* w. of me
    15.27. ye also shall *bear* w., because
    18.23. bear w. of the evil : but if
    37. I *should bear* w. unto the tr.
Act.10.43. *give* all the prophets w.
    15. 8. *bare* them w., giving them
    22. 5. *doth bear* me w., and all
    23.11. so must thou *bear* w. also
Heb.10.15.the Holy Ghost also *is* a w.
    11. 4. he *obtained* w. that he
¹Jo. 1. 2, and *bear* w., and shew unto
    5. 6. it is the Spi. *that beareth* w.
    8. three *that bear* w. in earth
³John 6. Which *have borne* w of thy.

martur.
Mat.18.16. of two or thr. w-es ; ²Co.13.1
    26.65. further need have we of w-es
Mar.14.63. What need we any furt. w-es
Lu. 24.48. ye are w-es of these things
Act. 1. 8. and ye shall be w-es unto me
    22. to be a w. with us of his res.
    2.32. whereof we all are w-es; 3.15
    5.32. we are his w-es of these thin.
    6.13. And set up false w-es which
    7.58. the w-es laid down their clo.
    10.39. we are w-es of all things wh.
    41. unto w-es chosen before God
    13.31. who are his w-es unto the
    22.15. thou shalt be his w. unto all
    26.16. and a w. both of these things
Ro. 1. 9. For God is my w., whom I
¹Th. 2. 5. of covetousness; God is w.
    10. Ye are w-es, and God also
¹Ti. 5.19. but before two or three w-es
    6.12. profession before many w-es
²Ti. 2. 2. heard of me amo. many w-es
Heb.10.28.mercy under two or thr. w-es
    12. 1. with so great a cloud of w-es
¹Pet.5. 1. a w. of the sufferings of Chri.
Rev. 1. 5. Christ, who is the faithful w.
316

Rev. 3.14. the faithful and true w., the
    11. 3. give power unto my two w-es
marturia.
Mar.14.55.sought for w. against Jesus
    56. but their w. agreed not toge.
    59. neither so did their w. agree
Lu. 22.71. What need we any furth. w.
Jo. 1. 7. The same came for a w., to
    3.11. and ye receive not our w.
    5.31. of myself my w. is not true
    32. and I know that the w. whi.
    36. I have greater w. than that
Tit. 1.13. This w. is true Wherefore
¹Jo. 5. 9. the w. of men, the w. of G.
    for this is the w. of God
    10. hath the w. in himself ; he
Rev.20. 4. beheaded for the w. of Jesus
marturion.
Mat.24.14.for a w. unto all nations
Act. 4.33. gave the apostles w. of the
    7.44. had the tabernacle of w. in
Jas. 5. 3. the rust of them shall be a w.
summartureō.
Ro. 2.15. conscie. *also bearing* w.; 9.1
    8.16. Spirit itself *beareth* w. *with*
sunepimartureō.
Heb. 2. 4. God *also bearing* them w.
pseudomarturia.
Mat.15.19.thefts, *false* w., blasphemies
    26.59. sought *false* w. against Jesus
pseudomartureō.
Mat.19.18. sh. not *bear false* w.; Ro.13.9
Mar.10.19.*Do* not *bear false* w.; Lu.18.20
    14.56, 57. *bare false* w. against him
pseudomartur.
Mat.26.60. though many *false* w-es came
    At the last ca. two *false* w-es
¹Co. 15.15. we are found *false* w-es of
amarturos.
Act.14.17. left not himself *without* w

WITNESS, [*verb,*] -ed, -eth, -ing.
martureō.
Jo. 5.32. which he w-eth of me is true
Act.26.22. w-ing both to small and
Ro. 3.21. being w-ed by the law and
¹Ti. 6.13. *who* bef. Pontius Pilate w-ed
Heb.7. 8. whom it is w-ed that he liv.
katamartureō.
Mat.26.62. these w. *against* thee ; 27.13;
    Mar.14.60; 15.4
diamarturomai.
Act.20.23. Holy Ghost w-eth in every

WOE,   -s.
ouai.
Mat.11.21. w. unto thee Chorazin! w.
    18. 7. w. unto the world because
    but w. to that man by who.;
    26.24; Mar.14.21; Lu.22.22
    23.13. w. unto you scribes, and; 14,
    15,23,25,27,29; Lu.11.44
    16. w. unto you, ye blind guides
    24.19. w. unto them that are with;
    Mar.13.17; Lu.21.23
Lu. 6.24. w. unto you that are rich
    25. w. unto you that are full
    w. unto you that laugh now
    26. w. unto you, when all men
    10.13. w. unto thee, Chorazin! w.
    11.42, 43. w. unto you, Pharisees
    46, 52. w. unto you also, ye law.
    47. w. unto you! for ye build
    17. 1. w. unto him, through whom
¹Co. 9.16. w. is unto me, if I preach
Jude 11. w. unto them! for they have
Rev. 8.13. w., w., w., to the inhabiters
    9.12. One w. is past; and, behold
    there come two w-s more
    11.14. The second w. is past; and,
    behold, the third w. cometh
    12.12. w. to the inhabiters of the

WOLF,   Wolves.
lukos.
Mat. 7.15. inwardly they are raven. w-s
    10.16. as sheep in the midst of w-s
Lu. 10. 3. forth as lambs among w-s
Jo. 10.12. seeth the w. coming, and le
    and the w. catcheth them
Act.20.29. shall grievous w-s enter in

WOMAN,   Women.
gunē.
Mat. 5.28. whosoever looketh on a w.
    9.20. a w., which was diseased
    22. the w. was made whole from
    11.11. them that are born of we.
    13.33. leaven, which a w. took, and
    14.21. five thousand men, besi. we.
    15.22. behold, a w. of Canaan came
    28. O w., great is thy faith
    38. four thousand men besi. we.
    22.27. last of all the w. died also;
    Mar.12.22; Lu.20.32
    26. 7. There came unto him a w.
    10. Why trouble ye the w.? for
    27.55. many we. were there behold.
    28. 5. answe. and said unto the we.
Mar. 5.25. a certain w., which; Lu.8.43
    33. the w. fearing and trembling
    7.25. For a certain w., whose you.
    26. The w. was a Greek, a Syro.
    10.12. if a w. shall put away her
    14. 3. there came a w. having an
    15.40. There were also we. looking
Lu. 1.28, 42. blessed art thou amo. w.
    4.26. unto a w. that was a widow
    7.28. Among those that are .. w.
    37. behold, a w. in the city
    39. who and what manner of w.
    44. he turned to the w., and sa.
    Simon, Seest thou this w.
    50. he said to the w., Thy faith
    8. 2. certain we., which had been
    47. when the w. saw that she
    10.38. a certain w. named Martha
    11.27. a certain w. of the company
    13.11. there was a w. which had a
    12. w., thou art loosed from thi.
    21. like leaven, which a w. took
    15. 8. what w. having ten pieces
    22.57. saying, w., I know him not
    23.27. compa. of people, and of we.
    49. the we. that followed him
    55. the we. also, which came with
    24.22. certain we. also of our comp.
    24. even so as the we. had said
Jo. 2. 4. w., what have I to do with
    4. 7, 9. a w. of Samaria
    11. The w. saith unto him, Sir ;
    15,19,21,25
    17. The w. answered and said, I
    27. that he talked with the w.
    28. The w. then left her waterp.
    39. the saying of the w., which
    42. said unto the w., Now we
    8. 3. brought unto him a w. taken
    4. this w. was taken in adulte.
    9. the w. standing in the midst
    10. and saw none but the w., he
    w., where are those thine ac.
    16.21. A w. when she is in travail
    19.26. his mother, w., behold thy
    20.13, 15. w., why weepest thou
Act. 1.14. and supplicati. with the we.
    5.14. multit. both of men and we.
    8. 3. haling men and we. commit.
    12. were bap., both men and we.
    9. 2. whet. they were men or we.
    13.50. the devout and honoura. wa
    16. 1. the son of a certain w.
    13. spake unto the we. which
    14. a certain w. named Lydia
    17. 4. of the chief we. not a few

Act.17.12. also of honourable **we**. which
    34. a **w**. named Damaris, and
  22. 4. into pris. both men and **we**.
Ro. 7. 2. the **w**. which hath an husba.
¹Co. 7. 1. for a man not to touch a **w**.
    13. the **w**. which hath an husba.
  11. 3. the head of the **w**. is the man
    5. every **w**. that prayeth or
    6. if the **w**. be not covered
      a shame for a **w**. to be shorn
    7. the **w**. is the glory of the man
    8. of the **w**.; but the **w**. of the
    9. created for **w**., but the **w**.
    10. For this cause ought the **w**.
    11. the **w**., neither the **w**. with.
    12. as the **w**. is of the man, even
      so is the man also by the **w**.
    13. that a **w**. pray unto God un.
    15. if a **w**. have long hair, it is
  14.34. Let your **we**. keep silence in
    35. a shame for **we**. to speak in
Gal. 4. 4. forth his Son, made of a **w**.
¹Ti. 2. 9. that **we**. adorn themselves in
    10. which becometh **we**. profess.
    11. Let the **w**. learn in silence
    12. I suffer not a **w**. to teach
    14. the **w**. being deceived was
Heb.11.35. **we**. received their dead raised
¹Pet. 3. 5. the holy **we**. also, who trust.
Rev. 2.20. thou sufferest that **w**. Jeze.
  9. 8. had hair as the hair of **we**.
  12. 1. a **w**. clothed with the sun
    4. the dragon stood bef. the **w**.
    6. the **w**. fled into the wildern.
    13. he persecuted the **w**. which
    14. to the **w**. were given two
    15. water as a flood after the **w**.
    16. the earth helped the **w**., and
    17. dragon was wroth wi. the **w**.
  14. 4. wh. were not defiled with **we**.
  17. 3. I saw a **w**. sit upon a scarlet
    4. the **w**. was arrayed in purple
    6. I saw the **w**. drunken with
    7. tell thee the myst. of the **w**.
    9. mountains, on which the **w**.
    18. the **w**. which thou sawest
   houtos, [*fem.*]
Mat.26.13. that *this* **w**. hath done, be
Lu. 7.45. *this* **w**. since the time
    46. *this* **w**. hath anointed my
Act. 9.36. *this* **w**. was full of good wor.
   thēleia.
Ro. 1.26. even their **we**. did change
    27. the natural use of the **w**.
   hekastos, [*fem.*]
¹Co. 7. 2. *every* **w**. have her own husb.
   (See *Aged, Silly*.)

WOMB,   -s.
   koilia.
Mat.19.12. born from their mother's **w**.
Lu. 1.15. even from his mother's **w**.
    41, 44. the babe leaped in her **w**.
    42. blessed is the fruit of thy **w**.
  2.21. he was conceived in the **w**.
  11.27. Blessed is the **w**. that bare
  23.29. and the **w**-s that never bare
Jo. 3. 4. seco. time into his moth. **w**.
Act. 3. 2. lame from his mother's **w**.
    14. 8. cripple from his mother's **w**.
Gal. 1.15. sep. me from my mother's **w**.
   gastēr.
Lu. 1.31. shalt conceive in thy **w**.
   mētra.
Lu. 2.23. male that openeth the **w**.
Ro. 4.19. yet the deadne. of Sarah's **w**.

WONDER, [*noun,*]   -s.
   teras.   [Mar.13.22
Mat.24.24. shew great signs and **w**-s ;
Jo. 4.48. Except ye see signs and **w**-s
Act. 2.19. And I will shew **w**-s in hea.

Act. 2.22. by miracles and **w**-s and
    43. many **w**-s and signs ; 5.12
    4.30. that signs and **w**-s may be
    6. 8. did great **w**-s and miracles
    7.36. after that he had shewed **w**-s
    14. 3. granted signs and **w**-s to be
    15.12. declaring what mira. and **w**-s
Ro. 15.19. Thro. mighty signs and **w**-s
²Co. 12.12. in signs, and **w**-s, and migh.
⁷Th. 2. 9. po. and signs and lying **w**-s
Heb. 2. 4. both with signs and **w**-s
   sēmeion.
Rev.12. 1. a great **w**. in heaven
    3. appeared another **w**. in hea.
  13.13. And he doeth great **w**-s
   thambos.
Act. 3.10. they were filled with **w**. and

WONDER, [*verb*],   -ed, -ing.
   thaumazō.
Mat.15.31. that the multitude **w**-ed
Mar. 6.51. beyond measure, and **w**-ed
Lu. 2.18. they that heard it **w**-ed
    4.22. and **w**-ed at the gracious
    8.25. And they being afraid **w**-ed
    9.43. But while they **w**-ed every
    11.14. and the people **w**-ed
    24.12. **w**-ing in himself at that
    41. believ. not for joy, and **w**-ed
Act. 7.31. he **w**-ed at the sight
    13.41. ye despisers, and **w**., and
Rev.13. 3. world **w**-ed after the beast
    17. 6. when I saw her, I **w**-ed
    8. dwell on the earth *shall* **w**.
   existēmi.
Act. 8.13. **w**-ed, beholding the miracles
   ekthambos.
Act. 3.11. Solomon's, *greatly* **w**-ing

WONDERFUL. (See *Work*.)
   thaumasios.
Mat.21.15. the **w**. *things* that he did

WONT.
   ethō.
Mat.27.15. governor *was* **w**. to release
Mar.10. 1. as he *was* **w**., he taught
   kata ho ethos.
Lu. 22.39. and went, *as he was* **w**.
   nomizō.
Act.16.13. where prayer *was* **w**. to be

WOOD.
   xulon.
¹Co. 3.12. stones, **w**., hay, stubble
Rev.18.12. and all thyine **w**., and all
   xulinos.
²Ti. 2.20. but also *of* **w**. and of earth
Rev. 9.20. and *of* **w**.: which neither

WOOL.
   erion.
Heb. 9.19. scarlet **w**., and hyssop
Rev. 1.14. hairs were white like **w**.

WORD, (See *Enticing, Few*,) -s.
   logos.
Mat. 8. 8. but speak the **w**. only
    16. out the spirits with his **w**.
  10.14. nor hear your **w**-s, when ye
  12.32. speaketh a **w**. against the
    37. For by thy **w**-s thou shalt be
    justified, and by thy **w**-s
  13.19. heareth the **w**. of the kingd.
  20, 22, 23. is he that hea. the **w**.
    21. ariseth because of the **w**.
    22. choke the **w**.; Mar.4.19
  15.23. answered her not a **w**.
  22.46. able to answer him a **w**.
  24.35. my **w**-s shall not pass away;
    Mar.13.31 ; Lu.21.33
  26.44. time, saying the same **w**-s
Mar. 2. 2. preached the **w**. unto them
  4.14. The sower soweth the **w**.

Mar. 4.15. wayside, where the **w**. is
    taketh away the **w**.; Lu.8.12
    16. have heard the **w**.; Lu.8.15
    17. ariseth for the **w**.'s sake
    18, 20. such as hear the **w**.
    33. spake he the **w**. unto·them
    5.36. soon as Jesus heard the **w**.
  7.13. Making the **w**. of God of
  8.38. and of my **w**-s in this
  10.24. were astonished at his **w**-s
  12.13. to catch him in his **w**-s
  14.39. and spake the same **w**-s
  16.20. confirming the **w**. with
Lu. 1. 2. and ministers of the **w**.
    20. thou believest not my **w**-s
  3. 4. the book of the **w**-s of
  4.22. wondered at the gracious **w**-s
    32. for his **w**. was with power
    36. What a **w**. is this ! for with
  5. 1. to hear the **w**. of God, he
  7. 7. but say in a **w**., and my
  8.11. The seed is the **w**. of God
    13. receive the **w**. with joy
    21. whi. hear the **w**. of G.; 11.28
  9.26. asham. of me and of my **w**-s
  10.39. Jesus' feet, and heard his **w**.
  12.10. shall speak a **w**. against the
  20.20. might take hold of his **w**-s
  22.61. Peter remembered the **w**.
  23. 9. quest. with him in many **w**-s
  24.19. mighty in deed and in **w**.
    44. These are the **w**-s which I
Jo. 1. 1. In the beginning was the **w**.
    and the **w**. was with God
    and the **w**. was God
    14. And the **w**. was made flesh
  2.22. and the **w**. which Jesus
  4.41. believed beca. of his own **w**.
    50. the man believed the **w**.
  5.24. He that heareth my **w**.
    38. ye have not his **w**. abiding
  8.31. If ye continue in my **w**.
    37. my **w**. hath no place in you
    43. ye cannot hear my **w**.
  10.35. unto whom the **w**. of God
  12.48. the **w**. that I have spoken
  14.23. he will keep my **w**-s
    24. and the **w**. which ye hear
  15. 3. are clean through the **w**.
    20. Remember the **w**. that I said
    25. that the **w**. might be fulfilled
  17. 6. and they have kept thy **w**.
    14. I have given them thy **w**.
    17. thy truth: thy **w**. is truth
    20. believe on me thro. their **w**.
Act. 2.22. men of Israel, hear these **w**-s
    40. With many other **w**-s
    41. that gladly received his **w**.
  4. 4. which heard the **w**.; 10.44
    29. they may speak thy **w**.
    31. and they spake the **w**. of
  5. 5. Ananias hearing these **w**-s
  6. 2. should leave the **w**. of God
    4. the ministry of the **w**.
    7. the **w**. of God increased
  7.22. mighty in **w**-s and in deeds
  8. 4. preach. the **w**.; 11.19; 15.35
    14. had received the **w**. of God
    25. and preached the **w**.; 13.5
  10.36. The **w**. which God sent
    44. had also received the **w**. of
  12.24. But the **w**. of God grew
  13. 7, 44. to hear the **w**. of God
    15. if ye have any **w**. of exhort.
    26. to you is the **w**. of this salv.
    46. It was necessary that the **w**.
    48. glorified the **w**. of the Lord
    49. the **w**. of the Lord was pub.
  14. 3. gave testimony unto the **w**.
  15. 7. should hear the **w**. of the
    15. to this agree the **w**-s of the
    24. troubled you with **w**-s

Act.15.32. the brethren with many **w-s**
16. 6. to preach the **w.** in Asia
   32. spake unto him the **w.** of
17.11. received the **w.** with all
   13. had knowledge that the **w.**
18.11. teaching the **w.** of God
   15. if it be a question of **w-s**
19.10. heard the **w.** of the Lord
20. So mightily grew the **w.** of
20.32. and to the **w.** of his grace
   35. and to remember the **w-s**
   38. for the **w-s** which he spake
22.22. audience unto this **w.**
Ro. 9. 6. Not as though the **w.** of G.
   9. For this is the **w.** of promi.
15.18. obedient by **w.** and deed
1Co. 1.17. not with wisdom of **w-s**
2. 4. was not with enticing **w-s**
   13. not in the **w-s** which man's
4.20. not in **w.**, but in power
12. 8. the **w.** of wisdom ; to anoth.
   the **w.** of knowledge
14. 9. **w-s** easy to be understood
   19. I had rather speak five **w-s**
   than ten thousand **w-s** in an
   36. came the **w.** of God out
1Co. 1.18. our **w.** toward you was not
2.17. which corrupt the **w.** of God
4. 2. nor handling the **w.** of God
5.19. the **w.** of reconciliation
6. 7. By the **w.** of truth, by the
10.11. such as we are in **w.** by lett.
Gal. 5.14. law is fulfilled in one **w.**
6. 6. him that is taught in the **w.**
Eph. 1.13. after that ye heard the **w.** of
5. 6. deceive you with vain **w-s**
Phi. 1.14. to speak the **w.** without
2.16. Holding forth the **w.** of life
Col. 1. 5. in the **w.** of the truth
   25. to fulfil the **w.** of God
3.16. Let the **w.** of Christ dwell
   17. whatsoever ye do in **w.** or
1Th. 1. 5. came not unto you in **w.**
6. having received the **w.** in
8. sounded out the **w.** of the
2. 5. used we flattering **w-s**
   13. the **w.** of God which ye hea.
   not as the **w.** of men, but ..**w.**
   but as it is in truth, the **w.**
4.15. unto you by the **w.**, of the
   18. one another with these **w-s**
2Th. 2. 2. neither by spirit, nor by **w.**
   15. whether by **w.**, or our epistle
   17. in every good **w.** and work
3. 1. the **w.** of the Lord may have
   14. if any man obey not our **w.**
1Ti. 4. 5. sanctified by the **w.** of God
6. nourished up in the **w-s** of
12. in **w.**, in conversation, in
5.17. they who labour in the **w.**
6. 3. to wholesome **w-s**, even the
2Ti. 1.13. Hold fast the form of so. **w-s**
2. 9. the **w.** of God is not bound
   15. rightly dividing the **w.** of
   17. And their **w.** will eat as doth
4. 2. Preach the **w.**; be instant
   15. greatly withstood our **w-s**
Tit. 1. 3. manifested his **w.** through
9. Holding fast the faithful **w.**
2. 5. that the **w.** of God be not
Heb. 2. 2. For if the **w.** spoken by an.
4. 2. but the **w.** preached did not
12. For the **w.** of God is quick
5.13. unskilful in the word of rig.
7.28. but the **w.** of the oath
12.19. the **w.** should not be spoken
13. 7. have spoken unto you the **w.**
   22. suffer the **w.** of exhortation
Jas. 1.18. begat he us with the **w.** of
   21. with meek. the engrafted **w.**
   22. be ye doers of the **w.**
   23. if any be a hearer of the **w.**
818

Jas. 3. 2. If any man offend not in **w.**
1Pet. 1.23. of incorruptible, by the **w.**
2. 8. which stumble at the **w.**
3. 1. if any obey not the **w.**, they
   also may without the **w.** be
2Pet. 1.19. We have also a more sure **w.**
2. 3. with feigned **w-s** make mer.
3. 5. by the **w.** of God the heave.
7. by the same **w.** are kept in
1Jo. 1. 1. have handled, of the **w.** of
   10. and his **w.** is not in us
2. 5. But whoso keepeth his **w.**
7. The old command. is the **w.**
14. the **w.** of God abideth in
3.18. let us not love in **w.**
5. 7. the Father, the **w.**, and the
3John 10. against us with malicio. **w-s**
Rev. 1. 2. bare record of the **w.** of God
3. that hear the **w-s** of this pro.
9. for the **w.** of God, and for
3. 8. and hast kept my **w.**
   10. hast kept the **w.** of my pat.
6. 9. were slain for the **w.** of God
12.11. and by the **w.** of their testi.
19.13. is called The **w.** of God
20. 4. and for the **w.** of God
21. 5. for these **w-s** are true and
22.18. the **w-s** of the prophecy of
   19. take away from the **w-s** of

logikos.

1Pet. 2. 2. the sincere milk *of the* **w.**

rēma.

Mat. 4. 4. but by every **w.** that proce.
12.36. That every idle **w.** that men
18.16. every **w.** may be established
26.75. Peter remembered the **w.**
27.14. answered him to never a **w.**
Mar.14.72.the **w.** that Jesus said unto
Lu. 1.38. according to thy **w.**; 2.29
3. 2. the **w.** of God came unto
4. 4. but by every **w.** of God
5. 5. at thy **w.** I will let down the
20.26. could not take hold of his **w-s**
24. 8. And they remember. his **w-s**
   11. their **w-s** seemed to them as
Jo. 3.34. speaketh the **w-s** of God
5.47. how shall ye believe my **w-s**
6.63. **w-s** that I speak unto ; 14.10
68. thou hast the **w-s** of eternal
8.20. These **w-s** spake Jesus in the
47. is of G. heareth God's **w-s**
10.21. These are not the **w-s** of
12.47. if any man hear my **w-s**
48. and receiveth not my **w-s**
15. 7. and my **w-s** abide in you
17. 8. given unto them the **w-s** wh.
Act. 2.14. and hearken to my words
5.20. all the **w-s** of this life
6.11, 13. blasphemous **w-s** against
10.22. and to hear **w-s** of thee
37. That **w.**, I say, ye know
44. Peter yet spake these **w-s**
11.14. Who shall tell thee **w-s**
13.42. besought that these **w-s**
16.38. the serjeants told these **w-s**
26.25. but speak forth the **w-s** of
28.25. that Paul had spoken one **w.**
Ro. 10. 8. The **w.** is nigh thee, even in
the **w.** of faith, which we
   17. and hearing by the **w.** of
   18. and their **w-s** unto the end
2Co.12. 4. and heard unspeakable **w-s**
13. 1. shall every **w.** be established
Eph. 5,26. washing of water by the **w.**
6.17. of the Spirit, which is the **w**
Heb. 1. 3. all things by the **w.** of his
6. 5. have tasted the good **w.** of
11. 3. were framed by the **w.** of
12.19. and the voice of the **w.** of
1Pet. 1.25. But the **w.** of the Lord end.
   And this is the **w.** which

2Pet. 3. 2. may be mindful of the **w-s**
Jude 17. remember ye the **w-s** which
Rev.17.17. until the **w-s** of God shall

apaʊggellō.

Mat. 2. 8. *bring* me **w.** *again*, that I
epō.
Mat.2.13. there until I *bring* thee **w.**
chrēstologia.
Ro. 16.18. by *good* **w-s** and fair speech.
didaktos.
1Co. 2.13. **w.** *which* man's wis. *teacheth*
(in *words taught by* human wis.)
logomacheō.
2Ti. 2.14. *that they strive* not about **w-s**

WORK [*noun*],   -s.
   ergon.

Mat. 5.16. they may see your good **w-s**
   11. 2. heard in the prison the **w.** s
   23. 3. but do not ye after their **w-s**
5. But all their **w-s** they do
26.10. wrought a good **w.**; Mar.14.6
Mar.13.34.to every man his **w.**, and
Jo. 4.34. sent me, and to finish his **w.**
5.20. shew him greater **w-s** than
36. for the **w-s** which the Father
the same **w-s** that I do
6.28. that we might work the **w-s**
29. This is the **w.** of God, that
7. 3. see the **w-s** that thou doest
7. that the **w-s** thereof are evil
21. I have done one **w.**, and ye
8.39. do the **w-s** of Abraham
9. 3. the **w-s** of God should be
4. work the **w-s** of him that
10.25. the **w-s** that I do ; 14.12
32. Many good **w-s** have I shew.
Fa.; for which of those **w-s**
33. For a good **w.** we stone thee
37. If I do not the **w-s** of my
38. believe not me, beli. the **w-s**
14.10. in me, he doeth the **w-s**
11. believe me for the very **w-s**
15.24. done among them the **w-s**
17. 4. I have finished the **w.**
Act. 5.38. this **w.** be of men, it will
7.41. in the **w-s** of their own han.
9.36. this wo. was full of good **w-s**
13. 2. for the **w.** whereunto I have
41. **w.** in your days, a **w.** which
14.26. for the **w.** which they fulfil.
15.18. unto God are all his **w-s**
38. not with them to the **w.**
26.20. **w-s** meet for repentance
Ro. 2.15. shew the **w.** of the law
3.17. By what law? of **w-s**
4. 2. were justified by **w-s**, he hath
6. righteousness without **w-s**
9.11. not of **w-s**, but of him that
32. but as it were by the **w-s** of
11. 6. then is it no more of **w-s**
But if it be of **w-s**, then is
otherwise **w.** is no more **w.**
13. a terror to good **w-s**, but to
12. cast off the **w-s** of darkness
14.20. destroy not the **w.** of God
1Co. 3.13. Every man's **w.** shall be
every man's **w.** of what sort
14. If any man's **w.** abide which
15. If any man's **w.** shall be
9. 1. are not ye my **w.** in the Lo.
15.58. abounding in the **w.** of the
16.10. for he worketh the **w.** of the
2Co. 9. 8. abound to every good **w.**
11.15. according to their **w-s**
Gal. 2.16. **w-s** of the law ; 3.2,5,10
5.19. the **w-s** of the flesh are man.
6. 4. every man prove his own **w.**
Eph. 2. 9. Not of **w-s**, lest any man
in Christ Jes. unto good **w-s**
4.12. for the **w.** of the ministry
5.11. with the unfruitful **w-s** of

Phi. 1. 6. hath begun a good **w**. in you
   2.30. for the **w**. of Christ he was
Col. 1.10. fruitful in every good **w**.
   21. in your mind by wicked **w-s**
¹Th. 1. 3. your **w**. of faith and labour
   5.13. in love for their **w**.'s sake
²Th. 1.11. the **w**. of faith with power
   2.17. in every good word and **w**.
¹Ti. 2.10. godliness with good **w-s**
   3. 1. he desireth a good **w**.
   5.10. Well report. of for good **w-s**
      followed every good **w**.
   25. also the good **w-s** of some
   6.18. that they be rich in good **w-s**
²Ti. 1. 9. not according to our **w-s**
   2.21. prepared unto every good **w**.
   3.17. furnished unto all good **w-s**
   4. 5. do the **w**. of an evangelist
   14. according to his **w-s**
   18. me from every evil **w**.
Tit. 1.16. but in **w-s** they deny him
      unto every good **w**. reprobate
   2. 7. a pattern of good **w-s**: in
   14. people zealous of good **w-s**
   3. 1. to be ready to every good **w**.
   5. Not by **w-s** of righteousness
   8, 14. to maintain good **w-s**
Heb. 1.10. the **w-s** of thine hands ; 2.7
   3. 9. and saw my **w-s** forty years
   4. 3. although the **w-s** were finis.
   4. seventh day from all his **w-s**
   10. hath ceas. from his own **w-s**
   6. 1. of repentance from dead **w-s**
   10. your **w**. and labour of love
   9.14. your conscie. from dead **w-s**
   10.24. unto love and to good **w-s**
   13.21. you perfect in every good **w**.
Jas. 1. 4. patience have her perfect **w**.
   25. but a doer of the **w**.
   2.14. hath faith, and have not **w-s**
   17. faith, if it hath not **w-s**
   18. and I have **w-s** ? shew me
      faith without thy **w-s**, and I
      thee my faith by my **w-s**
   20, 26. faith without **w-s** is dead
   21. Abra. our father justi. by **w-s**
   22. with his **w-s**, and by **w-s**
   24. that by **w-s** a man is justi.
   25. the harlot justified by **w-s**
   3.13. his **w-s** with meekness of
¹Pet. 1.17. according to every man's **w**.
   2.12. by your good **w-s**, which
²Pet. 3.10. and the **w-s** that are therein
¹Jo. 3. 8. might destroy the **w-s** of
   12. his own **w-s** were evil
Rev. 2. 2. I know thy **w-s**, and thy
   5. repent, and do the first **w-s**
   9, 13,19, kn. thy **w-s** ; 3.1,8,15
   19. thy patience, and thy **w-s**
   23. of you according to your **w-s**
   26. keepeth my **w-s** unto the
   3. 2. for I have not found thy **w-s**
   9.20. repented not of the **w-s** of
   14.13. and their **w-s** do follow them
   15. 3. and marvellous are thy **w-s**
   18. 6. double according to her **w-s**
   20.12, 13, according to their **w-s**
   22.12. according as his **w**. shall be
   dunamis.
Mat. 7.22. done many *wonderful* **w-s**
   11.20. most of his *mighty* **w-s** were
   21, 23. the *mighty* **w-s** ; Lu.10.13
   13.54. wisd., and these *mighty* **w-s**
   58. did not many *mighty* **w-s**
Mar. 6. 2. even such *mighty* **w-s** are
   5. could there do no *mighty* **w**.
Lu. 19.37. the *mighty* **w-s** that they
   logos.
Ro. 9.28. will finish the **w**.
      a short **w**. will the Lord
   molis ischuō.
Act.27.16. we *had* much **w**. to come

pragma
Jas. 3.16. confusion and every evil **w**.
   praxis.
Mat.16.27. according to his **w-s**
   megaleia, [*plu.*]
Act. 2.11. the *wonderful* **w-s** c. God
WORK, [*vb.*], -eth,-ing, *Wrought.*
   energeō.
Ro. 7. 5. *did* **w**. in our members
¹Co. 12. 6. God *which* **w-eth** all in all
   11. all these **w-eth** that one and
²Co. 4.12. So then death **w-eth** in us
Gal. 2. 8. For he *that* **w-t** *effectually in*
   3. 5. and **w-eth** miracles among
   5. 6. faith *which* **w-eth** by love
Eph. 1.11. of him *who* **w-eth** all things
   20. Which he **w-t** in Christ
   2. 2. the spirit *that* now **w-eth** in
   3.20. the power *that* **w-eth** in us
Phi. 2.13. God *which* **w-eth** *in* you both
Col. 1.29. *which* **w-eth** in me mightily
¹Th. 2.13. which *effectually* **w-eth** also
²Th. 2. 7. of iniquity *doth* already **w**.
   ergasia.   [(*working of*)
Eph. 4.19. to **w**. all uncleanness (to *the*
   ergazomai.
Mat. 7.23. from me, ye *that* **w**. iniquity
   21.28. go **w**. to-day in my vineyard
   26.10. *hath* **w-t** a go. wo.; Mar.14.6
Lu. 13.14. in which men ought to **w**.
Jo. 3.21. that they are **w-t** in God
   5.17. Father **w-eth** hith., and I **w**.
   6.28. that we *might* **w**. the works
   30. beli. thee ? what *dost* thou **w**.
   9. 4. I must **w**. the works of him
      cometh, when no man can **w**.
Act.10.35. and **w-eth** righteousness, is
   13.41. I **w**. a work in your days
   18. 3. abode with them, and **w-t**
Ro. 2.10. to every man *that* **w-eth**
   4. 4. Now to him *that* **w-eth** is
   5. But to him *that* **w-eth** not
   13.10. Love **w-eth** no ill to his nei.
¹Co. 4.12. **w-ing** with our own hands
   9. 6. to forbear **w-ing** (*to work*)
   16. he **w-eth** the work of the Lo.
Eph. 4.28. **w-ing** with his hands the
¹Th. 4.11. and *to* **w**. with your own
²Th. 3. 8. **w-t** (*working*) with labour
   10. if any would not **w**., neither
   11. **w-ing** not at all, but are
   12. with quietness they **w**. *and*
Heb.11.33.**w-t** righteousness, obtained
²John 8. things which we *have* **w-t**
   katergazomai.
Ro. 1.27. **w-ing** that which is unseem.
   4.15. Because the law **w-eth** wrath
   5. 3. that tribulation **w-eth** patie.
   7. 8. **w-t** in me all manner of
   13. **w-ing** death in me by that
   15.18. which Christ *hath* not **w-t** by
²Co. 4.17. **w-eth** for us a far more exce.
   5. 5. he *that hath* **w-t**. us for the
   7.10. godly sorrow **w-eth** repent.
      sorrow of the world **w-eth**
   11. what carefulness it **w-t** in
   12.12. signs of an apostle *were* **w-t**
Phi. 2.12. **w**. *out* your own salvation
Jas. 1. 3. trying of your faith **w-eth**
   20. the wrath of man **w-eth** not
¹Pet. 4. 3. suffice us *to have* **w-t** the
   poieō
Mat. 20.12.These last *have* **w-t** but one
Act.15.12. *had* **w-t** among the G.; 21.19
   19.11. God **w-t** special miracles by
Heb.13.21.to do his will, **w-ing** in you
Rev.16.14. spirits of devils, **w-ing** mira.
   19.20. false prophet *that* **w-t** mira.
   21.27. whatsoever **w-eth** abomina.
   ginomai.
Mar. 6. 2. mighty works *are* **w-t** by
Act. 5.12. *were* many signs ...**w-t**

   sunergeō.
Mar.16.20.the Lord **w**-*ing with* them
Ro. 8.28. all things **w**. *together* for
Jas. 2.22. how faith **w-t** *with* his works
WORKERS.
   ergatēs.
Lu. 13.27. from me, all ye **w**. of iniqui.
²Co. 11.13. false apostles, deceitful **w**.
Phi. 3. 2. beware of evil **w**., beware
   dunamis.
¹Co. 12.29. are all **w**. *of miracles*
   sunergeō, [*participle.*]
²Co. 6. 1. We then as **w**. *together* with
WORKFELLOW.
   sunergos.
Ro. 16.21. Timotheus my **w**., and Luc.
WORKING, [*noun.*]
   energeia.
Eph. 1.19. the **w**. of his mighty power
   3. 7. by the *effectual* **w**. of his
   4.16. the *effectual* **w**. in the meas.
Phi. 3.21. according to the **w**. whereby
Col. 1.29. striving according to his **w**.
²Th. 2. 9. is after the **w**. of Satan
   energēma.
¹Co.12.10. To another the **w**. of miracl.
WORKMAN,   -men.
   ergatēs.
Mat.10.10. for the **w**. is worthy of his
Act.19.25. the **w-e** of like occupation
²Ti. 2.15. **w**. that needeth not to be
WORKMANSHIP.
   poiēma.
Eph. 2.10. For we are his **w**.,created in
WORLD,   -s.
   kosmos.
Mat. 4. 8. all the kingdoms of the **w**.
   5.14. Ye are the light of the **w**.
   13.35. the foundation of the **w**. ;
      25.34 ; Lu.11.50 ; Jo.17.24;
      Eph.1.4 ; Heb.4.3 ; 9.26 ;
      ¹Pet.1.20 ; Rev.13.8; 17.8
   38. The field is the **w**. ; the good
   16.26. gain the whole **w**.; Mar.8.36;
      Lu.9.25
   18. 7. Woe unto the **w**. because of
   24.21. since the beginning of the **w**.
   26.13. preached in the whole **w**.
Mar.14. 9. throughout the whole **w**.
   16.15. Go ye into all the **w**.
Lu. 12.30. do the nations of the **w**. seek
Jo. 1. 9. that cometh into the **w**.
   10. in the **w**., and the **w**. was
      made by him, and the **w**.
   29. taketh away the sin of the **w**.
   3.16. For God so loved the **w**.
   17. the **w**. to condemn the **w**.
      that the **w**. through him mi.
   19. light is come into the **w**.
   4.42. the Savi. of the **w**.;¹Jo.4.14
   6.14. sh. come into the **w**.; 11.27
   33. and giveth life unto the **w**.
   51. give for the life of the **w**.
   7. 4. shew thyself to the **w**.
   7. The **w**. cannot hate you
   8.12. I am the light of the **w**.
   23. this **w**.; I am not of this **w**.
   26. I speak to the **w**. those thi.
   9. 5. As long as I am in the **w**.,
      I am the light of the **w**.
   39. I am come into this **w**., that
   10.36. sancti., and sent into the **w**.
   11. 9. he seeth the light of this **w**.
   12.19. behold, the **w**. is gone after
   25. that hateth his life in this **w**.
   31. Now is the judg. of this **w**.
      shall the prince of this **w**.
   46. I am come a light into the **w**.
   47. the **w**., but to save the **w**.

Jo. 13. 1. he should dep. out of this **w.**
   own which were in the **w.**
14.17. whom the **w.** cannot receive
  19. and the **w.** seeth me no more
  22. unto us and not unto the **w.**
  27. not as the **w.** giveth, give I
  30. the prince of this **w.** cometh
  31. But that the **w.** may know
15.18. If the **w.** hate you, ye know
  19. were of the **w.**, the **w.** would
  are not of the **w.**; 17.14,16
  have chosen you out of the **w.**
  therefore the **w.** hateth you
16. 8. he will reprove the **w.** of sin
  11. the prince of this **w.** is judg.
  20. but the **w.** shall rejoice
  21. a man is born into the **w.**
  28. and am come into the **w.**
  again, I leave the **w.**, and go
  33. In the **w.** ye shall have tri.
  I have overcome the **w.**
17. 5. with thee before the **w.**
  6. gavest me out of the **w.**
  9. I pray not for the **w.** but for
  11. **w.**, but these are in the **w.**
  12. I was with them in the **w.**
  13. these things I speak in the **w.**
  14. and the **w.** hath hated them
  even as I am not of the **w.**; 16
  15. take them out of the **w.**
  18. hast sent me into the **w.**
  I also sent them into the **w.**
  21. that the **w.** may believe that
  23. that the **w.** may know that
  25. the **w.** hath not known thee
18.20. I spake openly to the **w.**
  36. My kingd. is not of this **w.**
  kingdom were of this **w.**
  37. this cause came I into the **w.**
21.25. I suppose that even the **w.**
Act.17.24. God that made the **w.** and
Ro. 1. 8. throughout the whole **w.**
  20. from the creation of the **w.**
3. 6. how shall God judge the **w.**
  19. all the **w.** may become guilty
4.13. should be the heir of the **w.**
5.12. sin entered into the **w.**
  13. the law sin was in the **w.**
11.12. be the riches of the **w.**
  15. be the reconciling of the **w.**
1Co. 1.20. the wisdom of this **w.**
  21. the **w.** by wisdom knew not
  27. the foolish things of the **w.**
  the weak things of the **w.**
  28. And base things of the **w.**
2.12. not the spirit of the **w.**, but
3.19. For the wisdom of this **w.**
  22. or the **w.**, or life, or death
4. 9. a spectacle unto the **w.**, and
  13. as the filth of the **w.**, and
5.10. with the fornic. of this **w.**
  ye needs go out of the **w.**
6. 2. the **w.?** and if the **w.** shall
7.31. and they that use this **w.**
  for the fashion of this **w.**
  33, 34. things that are of the **w.**
8. 4. an idol is nothing in the **w.**
11.32. not be condemn. with the **w.**
14.10. kinds of voices in the **w.**
2Co. 1.12. our conversation in the **w.**
5.19. reconciling the **w.** unto
7.10. but the sorrow of the **w.**
Gal. 4. 3. under the elements of the **w.**
6.14. by whom the **w.** is crucified
  unto me, and I unto the **w.**
Eph. 2. 2. acc. to the course of this **w.**
  12. without God in the **w.**
Phi. 2.15. ye shine as lights in the **w.**
Col. 1. 6. as it is in all the **w.**
2 8, 20. the rudiments of the **w.**
  20, though living in the **w.**
1Ti. 1.15. came into the **w.** to save
820

1Ti. 3.16. believed on in the **w.**
6. 7. brought noth. into this **w.**
Heb.10. 5. when he cometh into the **w.**
  11. 7. which he condemned the **w.**
  38. Of whom the **w.** was not
Jas. 1.27. hims. unspotted from the **w.**
2. 5. the poor of this **w.**, rich in
3. 6. a fire, a **w.** of iniquity
4. 4. the friendship of the **w.** is
  will be a friend of the **w.**
1Pet. 5. 9. brethren that are in the **w.**
2Pet. 1. 4. corruption that is in the **w.**
2. 5. And spared not the old **w.**
  flood upon the **w.** of the un.
  20. esca.the pollutions of the **w.**
3. 6. Whereby the **w.** that then
1Jo. 2. 2. for the sins of the whole **w.**
  15. Love not the **w.**, neither the
  things that are in the **w.**
  If any man love the **w.**, the
  16. For all that is in the **w.**, the
  of the Fath., but is of the **w.**
  17. And the **w.** passeth away
3. 1. therefore the **w.** knoweth us
  13. brethren, if the **w.** hate you
  17. whoso hath this **w.**'s good
4. 1. are gone out into the **w.**
3. now already is it in the **w.**
4. than he that is in the **w.**
5. They are of the **w.** : therefo.
  they of the **w.**, and the **w.**
9. only begot. Son into the **w.**
14. to be the saviour of the **w.**
17. as he is, so are we in this **w.**
5. 4. overcometh the **w.** : and this
5. that overcometh the **w.**
19. and the whole **w.** lieth in
2John 7. dec. are entered into the **w.**
Rev.11.15. The kingdoms of this **w.**
aiōn.
Mat.12.32. forgiven him nei. in this **w.**
13.22. and the care of this **w.**
  39, 40, 49 the end of the **w.**;
  24,3; 28.20
Mar. 4.19. the cares of this **w.**, and the
10.30. in the **w.** to come; Lu.18.30
Lu. 16. 8. the children of this **w.** are
20.34. The children of this **w.** mar.
  35. worthy to obtain that **w.**
Ro. 12. 2. be not conformed to this **w.**
1Co. 1.20. is the disputer of this **w.**
2. 6. yet not the wisdom of this **w.**
  nor of the princes of this **w.**
7. God ordained before the **w.**
8. none of the prin. of this **w.**
3.18. seemeth to be wise in this **w.**
2Co. 4. 4. the god of this **w.** hath blin.
Gal. 1. 4. us from this present evil **w.**
Eph. 1.21. named not only in this **w.**
6.12. of the darkness of this **w.**
1Ti. 6.17. that are rich in this **w.**
2Ti. 4.10. having loved this present **w.**
Tit. 2.12. godly, in this present **w.**
Heb. 1. 2. whom also he made the **w-s**
6. 5. the powers of the **w.** to co.
11. 3. the **w-s** were framed by the
apo aiōn,
Lu. 1.70. have been since the **w.** began
Act. 3.21. prophets since the **w.** began
15.18. fr. the beg. of the **w.**; Eph.3.9
ho aiōn, [plu.]
1Co. 2. 7. God ordained before the **w.**
10.11. the ends of the **w.** are come
Heb. 9.26. once in the end of the **w.**
pro aiōnios chronos, [plu.]
2Ti. 1. 9. Ch. Jes. before the **w.** began
Tit. 1. 1. prom. before the **w.** began
ek ho aiōn.
Jo. 9.32. since the **w.** began was it
aiōnios chronos, [dat. plu.]
Ro. 16.25. secret since the **w.** began
  (from eternal ages.)

eis ho aiōn, [plu.]
1Co. 8.13. flesh while the **w.** standeth
ho aiōn [ge. si.] ho aiōn[ge.pl.]
Eph. 3.21. all ages, **w.** without end
oikoumenē.
Mat.24.14. sh. be preached in all the **w.**
Lu. 2. 1. that all the **w.** should be
4. 5. all the kingdoms of the **w.**
Act.11.28. dearth throughout all the **w.**
17. 6. have turned the **w.** upside
  31. which he will judge the **w.**
19.27. whom all Asia and the **w.**
24. 5. the Jews throughout the **w.**
Ro. 10.18. unto the ends of the **w.**
Heb. 1. 6. firstbegotten into the **w.**
2. 5. not put in subjection the **w.**
Rev. 3.10. shall come upon all the **w.**
12. 9. wh. deceiveth the whole **w.**
16.14. earth and of the whole **w.**
gē.
Rev.13. 3. all the **w.** wondered after

WORLDLY.
kosmikos.
Tit. 2.12. denying ungodliness and **w.**
Heb. 9. 1. service, and a **w.** sanctuary

WORM, -s.
skōlēx.
Mar. 9.44. Where their **w.** dieth; 46,48
skōlēkobrōtos.
Act.12.23. and he was eaten of **w-s**

WORMWOOD.
apsinthos.
Rev. 8.11. part of the waters became **w.**

WORSE.
cheirōn.
Mat. 9.16. rent is made **w.**; Mar.2.21
12.45. of that man is **w.**; Lu.11.26
27.64. last error shall be **w.** than
Mar. 5.26. bettered, but rather grew **w.**
Jo. 5.14. lest a **w.** thing come unto
1Ti. 5. 8. and is **w.** than an infidel
2Ti. 3.13. sedu. shall wax worse and **w.**
2Pet. 2.20. the latter end is **w.** with th.
elassōn.
Jo. 2.10, then that which is **w.**
hustereō.
1Co. 8. 8. if we eat not, are we the **w.**
hēttōn.
1Co. 11.17. for the better, but for the **w.**

WORSHIP, [noun.]
doxa.
Lu. 14.10. then shalt thou have **w.** in

WORSHIP, [ver.] -ed, -eth, -ing.
proskuneō.
Mat. 2. 2. and are come to **w.** him
8. that I may come and **w.** him
11. fell down, and **w-ed** ; 18.26
4. 9. fall down and **w.** me ; Lu.4.7
10. Thou shalt **w.** the L.; Lu.4.8
8. 2. a leper and **w-ed** him
9.18. a certain ruler, and **w-ed** him
14.33. and **w-ed** him, saying; 15.25
20.20. with her sons, **w-ing** him
28. 9. by the feet, and **w-ed** him
17. they **w-ed** him; but some dou.
Mar. 5. 6. afar off, he ran and **w-ed** him
15.19. bowing their knees **w-ed** him
Lu. 24.52. And they **w-ed** him, and
Jo. 4.20. Our fathers **w-ed** in this mo.
  place where men ought to **w.**
21. ye shall neither in this..**w.**
22. Ye **w.** ye know not what
  we know what we **w.**
23. shall **w.** the Father in spirit
  Father seeketh such to **w.**
24. they that **w.** him must **w.**
9.38. I believe. And he **w-ed** him
12.20. that came up to **w.** at the fea.

Act. 7.43. which ye made *to* **w.** them
   8.27. to Jerusalem *for to* **w.**; 24.11
  10.25. at his feet, and **w**-*ed* him
¹Co. 14.25. on his face, he *will* **w.** God
Heb. 1. 6. *let* all the angels of God **w.**
  11.21. and **w**-*ed*, leaning upon
Rev. 3. 9. to come and **w.** before thy
  4.10. and **w.** him that liveth ; 5.14
  7.11. on their fa., and **w**-*ed*; 11.16
  9.20. that they *should* not **w.** dev.
  11. 1. and them *that* **w.** therein
  13. 4. they **w**-*ed* the dragon which
       and they **w**-*ed* the beast, sa.
   8. *shall* **w.** him, whose names
  12. to **w.** the first beast, whose
  15. as many as *would* not **w.** the
  14. 7. **w.** him that made heaven
   9. If any man **w.** the beast
  11. *who* **w.** the beast and his im.
  15. 4. *sh.* come and **w.** before thee
  16. 2. them *which* **w**-*ed* his image
  19. 4. fell down and **w**-*ed* God
  10. I fell at his feet *to* **w.** him
      w. God ; 22.9
  20. and them *that* **w**-*ed* his ima.
  20. 4. which *had* not **w**-*ed* the bea.
  22. 8. fell down *to* **w.** before the
    proskuneō enōpion.
Lu. 4. 7. if thou therefore wilt **w.** me
    sebomai.
Mat.15. 9. in vain they *do* **w.**; Mar.7.7
Act.16.14. *which* **w**-*ed* God, heard us
  18. 7. Justus, one *that* **w**-*ed* God
  13. persuaded men *to* **w.** God
  19.27. Asia and the world **w**-*eth*
    sebazomai.
Ro. 1.25. **w**-*ed* and served the creature
    sebasma.
²Th. 2. 4. is called God, or *that is* **w**-*ed*
    latreuō.
Act. 7.42. gave them up *to* **w.** the host
  24.14. so **w.** I the God of my fath.
Phi. 3. 3. *which* **w.** God in the spirit
    eusebeō.
Act.17.23. therefore ye ignorantly **w.**
    therapeuō.
Act.17.25. neither *is* **w**-*ed* with men's
    thrēskeia.
Col. 2.18. humility and **w**-*ing* of angels

WORSHIPPER,   -*s.*
proskunētēs.
Jo. 4.23. when the true **w**-*s* shall
    theosebēs.
Jo. 9.31. if any man be *a* **w.** *of God*
    neōkoros.
Act.19.35. is a **w.** of the great goddess
    latreuō, [*participle*.]
Heb.10. 2. because that the **w**-*s* once

WORTHY.
axios.
Mat.10.10. the workman is **w.** of his
  11. enquire who in it is **w.**; and
  13. if the house be **w.**, let your
     if it be not **w.**, let your peace
  37, 38. me is not **w.** of me
  22. 8. were bidden were not **w.**
Lu. 3. 8. therefore fruits **w.** of repent.
  7. 4. That he was **w.** for whom he
  10. 7. the labourer is **w.**; ¹Ti.5.18
  12.48. did commit things **w.** of str.
  15.19, 21. am no more **w.** to be ca.
  23.15. nothing **w.** of death is done
Jo. 1.27. shoe's latchet I am not **w.** to
Act.13.25. of his feet I am not **w.** to lo.
  23.29. laid to his charge **w.** of death
  25.11, 25.commi. any thing **w.**;26.31
Ro. 1.32. such things are **w.** of death
  8.18. present time are not **w.** to
¹Ti. 1.15. and **w.** of all accepta; 4.9
 6. 1. their own masters **w.** of all

Heb.11.38.Of whom the wo. was not **w**
Rev. 3. 4. in white ; for they are **w.**
  4.11. Thou art **w.**, O Lord, to rec.
  5. 2. Who is **w.** to open the book
  4. no man was fou. **w.** to open
  9. Thou art **w.** to take the book
  12. **w.** is the Lamb that was sla.
  16. 6. bl. to drink ; for they are **w.**
    axioō.
Lu. 7. 7. neither *thought* I myself **w.**
²Th. 1.11. God *would* count you **w.** of
¹Ti. 5.17. *be counted* **w.** of double hon.
Heb. 3. 3. *was counted* **w.** of more glo.
  10.29. *shall* he *be thought* **w.** who
    axiōs.
Eph. 4. 1. ye walk **w.** of the vocation
Col. 1.10. might walk **w.** of the Lord
¹Th. 2.12. That ye would walk **w.** of G.
    kataxioōmai.
Lu. 20.35. *which shall be accounted* **w.**
  21.36. *that ye may be accounted* **w.**
Act. 5.41. *that they were counted* **w.** to
²Th. 1. 5. *that ye may be counted* **w.** of
    hikanos.   [Lu.3.16
Mat. 3.11. shoes I am not **w.**; Mar.1.7;
  8. 8. I am not **w.** that th.; Lu.7.6
    katorthōma.
Act.24. 2. that *very* **w.** *deeds* are done
    kalos.
Jas. 2. 7. that **w.** name by the which

WOT, (See *Wist*.)
eideō. [*perfect tense*]
Act. 3.17. I **w.** that through ignorance
  7.40. we **w.** not what is become of
Ro. 11. 2. **w.** ye not what the scripture
    gnōrizō.
Phi. 1.22. I shall choose I **w.** not

WOULD,   -*est.*
*An auxiliary verb representing generally
various inflections of the Greek verb.
The following are exceptions :*—
    thelō.
Mat. 2.18. and **w.** not be comforted, be.
  5.42. him *that* **w.** borrow of thee
  7.12. whatsoever ye **w.** that men
  12.38. we **w.** see a sign from thee
  14. 5. *when* he **w.** have put him to
  18.23. which **w.** take account
    30. And he **w.** not : but went
  22. 3. and they **w.** not come
  23.37. how often **w.** I ha. ; Lu.13.34
    and ye **w.** not ; Lu.13.34
  27.15. a prisoner, whom they **w.**
    34. tasted thereof, he **w.** not dri.
Mar. 3.13. calleth unto him whom he **w.**
  6.19. and **w.** have killed him
  26. he **w.** not reject her
  48. **w.** have passed by them
  7.24. and **w.** have no man know it
  9.30. he **w.** not that any man sho.
  10.35. we **w.** that thou shouldest do
  36. What **w.** ye that I should do
Lu. 1.62. how he **w.** have him called
  6.31. and as ye **w.** that men
  15.28. he was angry, and **w.** not go
  16.26. they *which* **w.** pass from he.
  18. 4. And he **w.** not for a while
    13. **w.** not lift up so much as his
  19.27. mine enemies, *which* **w.** not
Jo. 1.43. Jesus **w.** go forth into
  6.11. the fishes as much as they **w.**
  7. 1. for he **w.** not walk in Jewry
  44. And some of them **w.** have
  9.27. wherefore **w.** ye hear it again
  12.21. Sir, we **w.** see Jesus
  21.18. walkedst whither thou **w**-*est*
    carry thee whith. thou **w**-*est*
Act. 7.39. To whom our fathers **w.** not
  10.10. hungry and **w.** have eaten
  14.13. and **w.** have done sacrifice

Act.16. 3. Him **w.** Paul *have* to go
  19.33. and **w.** have made his defen.
  24. 6. and **w.** have judged accordi.
  26. 5. if they **w.** testify, that
Ro. 1.13. Now I **w.** not *have* you igno.
  7.15. for what I **w.**, that do I not
  16. If then I do that which I **w.**
  19. For the good that I **w.** I do
    the evil which I **w.** not
  20. Now if I do that I **w.** not
  21. *when* I **w.** do good, evil is
  11.25. For I **w.** not, brethren, that
  16.19. but yet I **w.** have you wise
¹Co. 7. 7. For I **w.** that all men were
  32. but I **w.** *have* you without
  10. 1, 20. I **w.** not that ye shoul'l
  11. 3. I **w.** *have* you know
  12. 1. I **w.** not *have* you ignorant
  14. 5. I **w.** that ye all spake with
²Co. 1. 8. For we **w.** not, brethren, ha.
  5. 4. not for that we **w.** be unclo.
  12.20. sh. not find you such as I **w.**
    such as ye **w.** not
Gal. 1. 7. that trouble you, and **w.** pe.
  3. 2. This only **w.** I learn of you
  4.17. they **w.** exclude you, that
  5.17. can. do the things that ye **w.**
Col. 1.27. To whom God **w.** make kno.
  2. 1. For I **w.** that ye knew
¹Th. 2.18. we **w.** have come unto you
  4.13. But I **w.** not *have* you to be
²Th. 3.10. if any **w.** not work, neither
Phile. 14. thy mind **w.** I do nothing
Heb.10. 5. offering thou **w**-*est* not
  8. thou **w**-*est* not, neither hadst
  12.17. *when* he **w.** have inherited
    mellō.
Jo. 10. 1. whither he himself **w.** come
  6. 6. he himself knew what he **w.**
  15. that they **w.** come and take
Act.12. 6. when Herod **w.** have broug.
  16.27. and **w.** have killed himself
  23.15, 20. as though ye **w.** enquire
  25. **w.** he himself **w.** depart shortly
  27.30. as though they **w.** *have* cast
    ophelon.
¹Co. 4. 8. and I **w.** *to God* ye did reign
²Co. 11. 1. **w.** *to God* ye could bear
Gal. 5.12. I **w.** they were even cut off
Rev. 3.15. I **w.** thou wert cold or hot
    ginomai.
Act.20.16. he **w.** not spend the time
    euchomai.
Act.26.29. I **w.** to God, that not only

WOUND, [*noun*,]   -*s.*
trauma.
Lu. 10.34. and bound up his **w**-*s*
    plēgē.
Rev.13. 3, 12. deadly **w.** was healed
  14. which had the **w.** by a sword

WOUND, [*vb.*],(See *Head*,)-*ed.*
traumatizō.
Lu. 20.12. they **w**-*ed* him also, *and* cast
Act.19.16. of that house naked and **w**-*ed*
    epitithēmi plēgē, [*plu.*]
Lu. 10.30. **w**-*ed* him, *and* departed
    tuptō.
¹Co. 8.12. and **w.** their weak conscience
    sphattō.
Rev.13. 3. as it were **w**-*ed* to death

WOVEN.
huphantos.
Jo. 19.23. **w.** from the top throughout

WRAPPED. (See *Clothes*.)
entulittō.   [Lu.23.53
Mat.27.59. **w.** it *in* a clean linen cloth ;
Jo. 20. 7. **w.** *together* in a place by
    eneileō.
Mar.15.46. and **w.** him *in* the linen
321

WRATH, -s.
orgē.
Mat. 3. 7. to flee from the **w.** ; Lu.3.7
Lu. 21.23. and **w.** upon this people
Jo. 3.36. but the **w.** of God abideth
Ro. 1.18. For the **w.** of God is reveal.
2. 5. **w.** against the day of **w.**
8. unrig., indignation and **w.**
4.15. Because the law worketh **w.**
5. 9. be saved from **w.** through
9.22. God, willing to shew his **w.**
the vessels of **w.**fitted to des.
12.19. but rather give place unto **w.**
13. 4. to execute **w.** upon him that
5. not only for **w.**, but also
Eph. 2. 3. by nature the children of **w.**
5. 6. these things cometh the **w.**
Col. 3. 6. things' sake the **w.** of God
¹Th. 1.10. wh. delivered us from the **w.**
2.16. for the **w.** is come upon
5. 9. hath not appointed us to **w.**
¹Ti. 2. 8. without **w.** and doubting
Heb. 3.11. So I sware in my **w.**
4. 3. As I have sworn in my **w.**
Jas. 1.19. slow to speak, slow to **w.**
20. For the **w.** of man worketh
Rev. 6.16. and from the **w.** of the Lamb
17. For the great day of his **w.**
11.18. and thy **w.** is come, and
16.19. of the fierceness of his **w.**
19.15. and **w.** of Almighty God
thumos.
Lu. 4.28. things, were filled with **w.**
Act.19.28. they were full of **w.**, and
²Co. 12.20. debates, envyings, **w.-s**, stri.
Gal. 5.20. variance, emulations, **w.**
Eph. 4.31. Let all bitterness, and **w.**
Col. 3. 8. anger, **w.**, malice, blasphe.
Heb.11.27.fearing the **w.** of the king
Rev.12.12.having great **w.**, because
14. 8, 10. wine of the **w.** of ; 18.3
19. winepress of the **w.** of God
15. 1. is filled up the **w.** of G.
7. full of the **w.** of God, who
16. 1. the vials of the **w.** of God
parorgismos.
Eph. 4.26. sun go down upon your **w.**
parorgizō.
Eph. 6. 4. provoke not your chil. to **w.**
WREST.
strebloō.
²Pet. 3.16. unlearned and unstable **w.**
WRESTLE.
ho palē eimi.
Eph. 6.12. We **w.** not against flesh and
(the wrestling for us is not.)
WRETCHED.
talaipōros.
Ro. 7.24. O **w.** man that I am
Rev. 3.17. know. not that thou art **w.**
WRINKLE.
rutis.
Eph. 5.27. or **w.**, or any such thing
WRITE, Wrote.
graphō.
Mar.10. 4. to **w.** a bill of divorcement
5. he **w.-o** you this precept
12.19. Master, Moses **w.-o** ; Lu.20.28
Lu. 1. 3. from the very first to **w.** unto
63. **w.-o**, saying, His name is Jo.
16. 6. sit down quickly, and **w.** fif.
7. Take thy bill, and **w.** foursc.
Jo. 1.45. law, and the prophets, did **w.**
5.46. have believ. me : for he **w.-o**
8. with his finger **w.-o** on the
8. stooped down, and **w.-o** on
19.19. Pilate **w.-o** a title, and put it
21. **w.** not, The King of the Jews
21.24. and **w.-o** these things : and
322

Act.15.23. And they **w.-o** letters by the
18.27. the brethren **w.-o**, exhorting
23.25. And he **w.-o** a letter after this
25.26. I have no certain things to **w.**
I might have somewh. to **w.**
Ro. 16.22. Tertius, who **w.-o** this epistle
¹Co. 4.14. I **w.** not these things to sha.
5. 9. I **w.-o** unto you in an epistle
7. 1. things whereof ye **w.-o** unto
14.37. the things that I **w.** unto ;
Gal.1.20 ; ¹Ti.3.14; ¹Jo.2.1
²Co. 1.13. we **w.** none other things unto
2. 3. I **w.-o** this same unto you, le.
4. I **w.-o** unto you with many
9. to this end also did I **w.**, th.
7.12. Wherefore, though I **w.-o** un.
9. 1. superfluous for me to **w.** to
13. 2. being absent now I **w.** to th.
10. I **w.** these things being abse.
Phi. 3. 1. To **w.** the same things to you
¹Th. 4. 9. need not that I **w.** unto ; 5.1
²Th. 3.17. token in every epist.: so I **w.**
Phile. 21. I **w.-o** unto thee, knowing th.
²Pet. 3. 1. beloved, I now **w.** unto you
¹Jo. 1. 4. these things **w.** we unto you
2. 7. I **w.** no new commandment
8. a new commandment I **w.**
12, 13. I **w.** unto you, little chil.
13. I **w.** unto you, fathers, bec.
I **w.** unto you, young men
²John 5. s though I **w.-o** a new com.
12. Having many things to **w.**
³John 9. I **w.-o** unto the church : but
13. I had many things to **w.**
with ink and pen **w.** unto
Jude 3. to **w.** unto you of the com.
needful for me to **w.** unto
Rev. 1.11. What thou seest, **w.** in a
19. **w.** the things which thou
2. 1. of the church of Ephesus **w.**
8. of the church in Smyrna **w.**
12. of the church in Pergam. **w.**
18. of the church in Thyatira **w.**
3. 1. of the church in Sardis **w.**
7. of the church in Philad. **w.**
12. I will **w.** upon him the name
14. church of the Laodicea. **w.**
10. 4. th. voices, I was about to **w.**
thunders uttered, and **w.** th.
14.13. **w.**, Blessed are the dead wh.
19. 9. he saith unto me, **w.**, bless.
21. 5. he said unto me, **w.**: for th.
prographō.
Eph. 3. 3. as I **w.-o** afore in few words
epigraphō.
Heb. 8.10. will **w.** them in their hearts
10.16. in their minds will...I **w.** th.
epistellō.
Act.15.20. But that we **w.** unto them
WRITING, -s.
biblion.
Mat.19. 7. to give a **w.** of divorcement
gramma.
Jo. 5.47. if ye believe not his **w.-s**
graphō, [partic.]
Jo. 19.19. on the cross. And the **w.**
(See Divorcement, Table.)
WRITTEN.
graphō.
Mat. 2. 5. for thus it is **w.** by ; Mar.1.2
4. 4. It is **w.**, Man shall ; Lu.4.4
6. for it is **w.**, He sha.; Lu.4.10
7. unto him, It is **w.** again
10. hence, Satan ; for it is **w.**
11.10. he, of whom it is **w.**; Lu.7.27
21.13. It is **w.**, My house shall be
26.24. as it is **w.** of him : but woe
31. for it is **w.**, I will ; Mar.14.27
27.37. his head his accusation **w.**
Mar. 7. 6. of you hypocrites, as it is **w.**

Mar. 9.12. how it is **w.** of the Son of
13. what. they listed, as it is **w.**
11.17. sayi. unto them, Is it not **w.**
14.21. indeed goeth, as it is **w.** of
Lu. 2.23. it is **w.** in the law of the Lo.
3. 4. is **w.** in the ; Act.1.20; 7.42
4. 8. it is **w.**, Thou shalt worship
17. the place where it was **w.**
10.20. your names are **w.** in heaven
26. What is **w.** in the law? how
18.31. all things that are **w.** by the
19.46. Saying unto them, It is **w.**
20.17. What is this then that is **w.**
21.22. things which are **w.** ; Act.24.
41 ; Rev.1.3; 22.19
22.37. this that is **w.**, must yet be
23.38. a superscription also was **w.**
24.44. must be fulfil. which were **w.**
46. said unto them, Thus it is **w.**
Jo. 2.17. remembered that it was **w.**
6.31. as it is **w.**, He gave them
45. It is **w.** in the prophets, And
8.17. It is also **w.** in your ; 10.34
12.14. sat thereon ; as it is **w.**
16. these things were **w.** of him
15.25. fulfilled that is **w.** in their
19.20. it was **w.** in Hebrew, and
22. What I have **w.** I have **w.**
20.30. which are not **w.** in this bo.
31. these are **w.**, that ye might
21.25. if they should be **w.** every
the books that should be **w.**
Act.13.29. all that was **w.** of him
33. it is also **w.** in the second
15.15. words of prophe.; as it is **w.**
23. 5. for it is **w.**, Thou shalt not
Ro. 1.17. as it is **w.**, The just shall live
2.24. through you, as it is **w.**
3. 4. every man a liar ; as it is **w.**
10. as it is **w.**, There is none
4.17. as it is **w.**, I have made thee
23. it was not **w.** for his sake
8.36. as it is **w.**, For thy sake we
9.13. as it is **w.**, Jacob have I lov.
33. as it is **w.**, Behold, I lay in
10.15. as it is **w.**, How beautiful
11. 8. Accordi. as it is **w.**; ²Co.4.13
26. as it is **w.**, There shall come
12.19. it is **w.**, Vengeance is mine
14.11. For it is **w.**, As I live, saith
15. 3. as it is **w.**, The reproaches of
9. as it is **w.**,For this cause I
15. I have **w.** the more boldly
21. as it is **w.**, To whom he was
¹Co. 1.19. For it is **w.**, I will destroy
31. according as it is **w.**, He that
2. 9. as it is **w.**, Eye hath not seen
3.19. For it is **w.**, He taketh the
4. 6. above that which is **w.**, that
5.11. now I have **w.** unto you
9. 9. it is **w.** in the law of Moses
10. sakes, no doubt, this is **w.**
15. neither have I **w.** these thin.
10. 7. as it is **w.**, The people sat
11. they are **w.** for our admonit.
14.21. In the law it is **w.**, With
15.45. so it is **w.**, The first man
54. to pass the saying that is **w.**
²Co. 8.15. As it is **w.**, He that had gat.
9. 9. As it is **w.**, He hath dispers.
Gal. 3.10. for it is **w.**, Cursed is every
things which are **w.** in the
13. for it is **w.**, Cursed is every
4.22. For it is **w.**, that Abraham
27. For it is **w.**, Rejoice, thou
6.11. I have **w.** unto you with
Phile. 19. I Paul have **w.** it with
Heb.10. 7. volume of the book it is **w.**
¹Pet. 1.16. Because it is **w.**, Be ye holy
2. I have **w.** briefly, exhorting
²Pet. 3.15. given unto him hath **w.** unto
¹Jo. 2.14. I have **w.** unto you, fathers

Jo. 2.14. I *have* w. unto you, young
21. I *have* not w. unto you, bec.
26. These things *have* I w.; 5.13
Rev. 2.17. in the stone a new name w.
5. 1. a book w. within and on the
13. 8. names are not w. in the book
14. 1. his Father's name w. in the.
17. 5. her forehead *was* a name w.
8. whose names *were* not w.
19.12. he had a name w., that no
16. on his thigh a name w.
20.12. of those things *which were* w.
15. not found w. in the book of
21.27. they *which are* w. in the
22.18. plagues *that are* w. in this

graptos.
Ro. 2.15. the work of the law w. in th.

enggraphō.
²Co. 3. 2. our epistle w. in our hearts
3. by us, w. not with ink

en gramma, [*plu.*]
²Co. 3. 7. w. and engraven

prographō.
Ro. 15. 4. *were* w. aforetime were w.

apographō.
Heb.12.23.*which are* w. in heaven

epigraphō.
Mar.15.26.of his accusation was w. over
Rev.21.12. and names w. there on

epistellō.
Act.21.25. we *have* w. and concluded
Heb.13.22.I *have* w. a letter unto you

WRONG,   -ed.
adikeō.
Mat.20.13.Friend, I *do* thee no w.
Act. 7.24. seeing one of them *suffer* w.
26. why *do* ye w. one to anoth.
27. he *that did* his neighbour w.
25.10. to the Jews *have* I *done* no w.
¹Co. 6. 7. Why *do* ye not rather *take* w.
8. Nay, ye *do* w., and defraud
²Co. 7. 2. we *have* w-ed no man, we
12. cause *that had done the* w.
for his cause *that suffered* w.
Col. 3.25. he *that doeth* w. shall receive
the w. *which he hath done*
Phile. 18. If he *hath* w-ed thee, or ow.

adikēma.
Act.18.14. If it were a *matter of* w.' or

adikia.
²Co.12.13. to you? forgive me this w.

WRONGFULLY.
adikōs.
¹Pet. 2.19. endure grief, suffering w.

WROTH.
orgizomai.
Mat.18.34. his lord *was* w., *and* delive.
22. 7. he *was* w.: and he sent forth
Rev.12.17. the dragon *was* w. with the

thumoōmai.
Mat. 2.16. *was* exceeding w., and sent

YE,
*Is represented, either by the inflection of
the verb (as are the other personal pronouns), or by the pronoun* su, *which
occurs too frequently for citation.*

YEA.
nai.
Mat. 5.37. let your commun. be, y., y.
9.28. They said unto him, y.;13.51
11. 9. A prophet? y. I; Lu.7.26
21.16. y.; have ye never read out
Lu. 12. 5. y., I say unto you, Fear him
Jo. 11.27. y., Lord: I believe that thou
21,15. He saith unto him, y., Lord
16. y., Lord; thou knowest that
Act. 5. 8. And she said, y., for so mu.
22.27. thou a Roman? He said, y.

²Co. 1.17. shou. be y., y., and nay, nay
18, 19 was not y. and nay
19. but in him was y.
20. promis. of God in him are y.
Phile. 20. y., brother, let me have joy
Jas. 5.12. but let your y. be y.; and
Rev.14.13. y., saith the Spirit, that

alla.
Lu. 24.22. y., and certain women also
Jo. 16. 2. y., the time cometh, that
Ro. 3.31. God forbid: y., we establish
¹Co. 4. 3. y., I judge not mine own
²Co. 7.11. y., what clearing of your.,
what indignation, y. what
fear, y., what vehement des.
y., what zeal, y., what rev.
Gal. 4.17. y., they would exclude you
Phi. 1.18. do rejoice, y., and will rej.
2.17. y., and if I be offered upon
3. 8. y. doubtless, and I count

menounge.
Jas. 2.18. y., a man may say, Thou

menounge.
Lu. 11.28. y. *rather*, blessed are they

ē kai.   [*even*]
¹Co. 16. 6. y., *and* winter with you [(*or*

YEAR,   -s.
etos.   [Mar.5.25; Lu.8.43
Mat. 9.20. with an issue of blood tw.y-s;
Mar. 5.42. the age of twelve y-s;Lu.8.42
Lu. 2.36. with an husband seven y-s
37. about fourscore and four y-s
41. went to Jerusalem every y.
42. when he was twelve y-s old
3. 1. Now in the fifteenth y. of
23. began to be about thirty y-s
4.25. three y-s and six months
12.19. laid up for many y-s; take
13. 7. these three y-s I come seek.
8. Lord, let it alone this y. also
11. of infirmity, eighteen y-s
16. bound, lo, these eighteen y-s
15.29. these many y-s do I serve
Jo. 2.20. Forty and six y-s was this
5. 5. infirmity thirty and eight y-s
8.57. Thou art not yet fifty y-s
Act. 4.22. the man was above forty y-s
7. 6. them evil four hundred y-s
30. when forty y-s were expired
36, 42. in the wilder. forty y-s
9.33. had kept his bed eight y-s
13.20. four hundred and fifty y-s
21. by the space of forty y-s
19.10. cont. by the space of two y-s
24.10. thou hast been of many y-s
17. now after many y-s I came
Ro. 15.23. great desire these many y-s
²Co.12. 2. about fourteen y-s ago
Gal. 1.18. Then after three y-s I went
2. 1. Then fourteen y-s after I
3.17. four hundred and thirty y-s
¹Ti. 5. 9. number under threescore y-s
Heb. 1.12. and thy y-s shall not fail
3. 9. and saw my works forty y-s
17. whom was he grie. forty y-s
²Pet. 3. 8. y-s, and a thousand y-s as
Rev.20. 2. bound him a thousand y-s
3. the thousand y-s should be
4. with Christ a thousand y-s
5. until the thousand y-s were
6. reign with him a thous. y-s
7. when the thousand y-s are

eniautos.
Lu. 4.19. the acceptable y. of the Lord
Act.11.26. a whole y. they assembled
18.11. continued there a y. and six
Gal. 4.10. months, and times, and y-s
Heb. 9. 7. priest alone once every y.
25. into the holy place every y.
10. 1. they offered year by y.
3. again made of sins every y.

Jas. 4.13. continue there a y., and buy
5.17. by the space of three y-e
Rev. 9.15. day, and a month, and a y.

hēmera.
Lu. 1. 7, 18. well stricken in y-s

perusi.
²Co. 8.10. to be forward *a* y. ago
9. 2. Achaia was ready *a* y. ago

ginomai [*part.*] **megas.**
Heb.11.24.Mo., *when he was come to* y-s
(See *Forty, Hundred, Three, Two.*)

YES.
nai.
Mat.17.25.He saith, y. And when
Mar. 7.28. y., Lord: yet the dogs
Ro. 3.29. y., of the Gentiles also

menounge.
Ro. 10.18. y. verily, their sound went

YESTERDAY.
chthes.
Jo. 4.52. y. at the seventh hour the
Act. 7.28. thou diddest the Egyptian y.
Heb.13. 8. Jesus Christ the same y.

YET.
eti.
Mat.12.46.While he y. talked to the
17. 5. While he y. spake, behold, a
19.20. youth up: what lack I y.
26.47. while he y. spake;Mar.5.35;
Lu.8.49; 22.47,60
27.63. said, while he y. alive
Mar. 8.17. have ye your heart y. hard.
12. 6. Having y. therefore one son
14.43. immediately, while he y. sp.
Lu. 9.42. And as he was y. a coming
14.22. and y. there is room
32. is y. a great way off; 15.20
18.22. y. lackest thou one thing
22.37. that is written must y. be
24. 6. when he was y. in Galilee
41. And while they y. believed
44. while I was y. with you
Jo. 4.35. There are y. four months
7.33. y. a little while am I with
12.35. y. a little while is the light
13.33. y. a little while I am with
14.19. y. a little while, and the
16.12. I have y. many things to
20. 1. when it was y. dark unto
Act. 9. 1. y. breathing out threatening
10.44. While Peter y. spake these
18.18. after this tarried there y. a
Ro. 3. 7. why y. am I also judged as
5. 6. For when we were y. without
8. while we were y. sinners
9.19. Why doth he y. find fault
¹Co. 3. 2. neither y. now are ye able
3. ye are y. carnal: for whereas
12.31. and y. shew I unto you a
15.17. ye are y. in your sins
²Co. 1.10. that he will y. deliver us
Gal. 1.10. for if I y. pleased men
2.20. nevertheless I live; y. not I
5.11. if I y. preach circumcision
do I y. suffer persecution
Phi. 1. 9. your love may abound y.
²Th. 2. 5. when I was y. with you
Heb. 7.10. he was y. in the loins of his
15. it is y. far more evident
9. 8. the first tabernacle was y.
10.37. For y. a little while, and he
11. 4. he being dead y. speaketh
12.26. saying, y. once more I shake
27. And this word, y. once more
Rev. 6.11. they should rest y. for a

alla.
Mar.14.29.all shall be offended, y. will
Co. 4. 4. y. am I not hereby justified
15. instructers in Christ, y. have

323

¹Co. 9. 2. unto others, **y.** doubtless I
   14.19. **y.** in the church I had rath.
Co. 4. 8. on every side, **y.** not distres.
   16. outward man perish, **y.** the
   5.16. **y.** now henceforth know we
   11. 6. rude in speech, **y.** not in
   13. 4. cruci. through weakness, **y.**
Col. 2. 5. absent in the flesh, **y.** am I
   oute.
Lu. 14.35. neith. fit for the land *nor* **y.**
Jo. 4.21. in this mountain, *nor* **y.**
Act.19.37. robbers of churches, *nor* **y.**
   25. 8. against the temple, *nor* **y.**
Rev. 9.20. **y.** repented *not* of the works
   oudepō.
Jo. 7.39. Jesus was *not* **y.** glorified
   19.41. wherein was *never* man **y.**
   20. 9. For *as* **y.** they knew *not* the
¹Co. 8. 2. he knoweth *no* thing **y.** as he
   ouketi.
Mar.15. 5. Jesus **y.** answered *no* thing
²Co. 1.23. I came *not as* **y.** unto Cori.
Gal. 2.20. **y.** *not* I, but Christ liveth
   gar.   [Mar.7.28
Mat.15.27.**y.** the dogs eat of the crum.;
Ro. 5. 7. **y.** peradventure for a good
   akmēn.
Mat.15.16. Are ye also **y.** without und.
   ēdē.
Mat.24.32.bran. is **y.** tender; Mar.13.28
   ge.
Lu. 11. 8. **y.** because of his importun.
   18. 5. **y.** because this widow troub.
   oudeis pōpote.
Lu. 19.30. whereon **y.** *never* man sat
Jo. 4.27. **y.** no man said, What seek.
   20. 5. lying ; **y.** went he not in
   pleiōn ouk.
Act.24.11. there are **y.** *but* twelve days
   kan.
²Co. 11.16. if otherwise, **y.** as a fool
   mellō.
Rev.8.13. angels *which are* **y.** to sound
   (*See words in connection.*)

YIELD, (See *Ghost,*) -ed, -eth.
   didōmi.
Mar. 4. 7. choked it, and it **y-**ed no
   8. *did* **y.** fruit that sprang
   apodidōmi.
Heb.12.11.afterward it **y-**eth the peacea.
Rev.22. 2. **y-**ed her fruit every month
   paristēmi.
Ro. 6.13. but **y.** yourselves unto God
   19. as ye *have* **y-**ed your members
   so now **y.** your members
   paristanō.
Ro. 6.13. Neither **y.** ye your members
   16. that to whom ye **y.** yourselv.
   aphiēmi.
Mat.27.50. loud voice **y-**ed *up* the ghost
   peithō.
Act.23.21. *do* not thou **y.** unto them
   poieō.
Jas. 3.12. no fountain both **y.** salt

YOKE,   -ed.
   zugos.
Mat.11.29. Take my **y.** upon you, and
   30. For my **y.** is easy, and my
Act.15.10. to put a **y.** upon the neck of
Gal. 5. 1. entangled again with the **y.**
¹Ti. 6. 1. servants as are under the **y.**
   zeugos.
Lu. 11.29. I have bought five **y.** of oxen
   heterozugeō.
²Co. 6.14. *unequally* **y-**ed together with

YOKEFELLOW.
   suzugos.
Phi. 4. 3. I entreat thee also, true **y.**
324

YONDER.
   ekei.
Mat.17.20. Remove hence *to* **y.** *place*
   26.36. while I go and pray **y**

YOU,
Is represented by the pronoun su. *The*
   following are exceptions :—
   heautou.   [Mar.14.7; Jo.12.8
Mat.26.11. the poor always with **y.**;
Jo. 5.42. not the love of God in **y.**
   6.53. blood, ye have no life in **y.**
   psuchē su, [ge. pl.] [(your souls)
²Co. 12.15. spend and be spent for **y.**

YOUNG.
   neaniskos.
Mat.19.20. The **y.** *man* saith unto him
   22. when the **y.** *man* heard that
Mar.14.51.follow. him a certain **y.** *man*
   the **y.** *men* laid hold on him
   16. 5. they saw a **y.** *man* sitting
Lu. 7.14. **y.** *man,* I say unto thee, Ari.
Act. 2.17. your **y.** *men* shall see visions
   5.10. the **y.** *men* came in and found
¹Jo. 2.13, 14. I write unto you **y.** *men*
   neanias.
Act. 7.58. their clothes at a **y.** *man's*
   20. 9. a certain **y.** *man* named Eut.
   23.17, 18. Bring this **y.** *man* unto
   22. then let the **y.** *man* depart
   neos.
Tit. 2. 4. teach the **y.** *women* to be
   neoteros.
Jo. 21.18. When thou wast **y.,** thou
Act. 5. 6. And the **y.** *men* arose, wound
Tit. 2. 6. **y.** *men* likewise exhort to be
   neossos.
Lu. 2.24. turtle doves, or two **y.** pigeo.
   brephos.
Act. 7.19. cast out their **y.** *children*
   pais.
Act.20.12. brought the **y.** *man* alive
   (See *Ass, Child, Daughter.*)

YOUNGER.
   neos.
Lu. 15.12, 13. the **y.** of them said
   22.26. let him be as the **y.**; and he
¹Ti. 5. 1. and the **y.** men as brethren
   2. the **y.** as sisters, with all pu.
   11. But the **y.** widows refuse
   14. that the **y.** women marry
¹Pet.5. 5. Likewise, ye **y.,** submit
   elassōn.
Ro. 9.12. The elder shall serve the **y.**

YOUR,   -s.
Is generally represented by the gen. plu.
  of su. *The following are exceptions :—*
   humeteros.
Lu. 6.20. for **y.**'s is the gingdom of G.
   16.12. give you that which is **y.** own
Jo. 7. 6. but **y.** time is alway ready
   8.17. It is also written in **y.** law
   15.20. they will keep **y.**'s also
Act.27.34. for this is for **y.** health
Ro. 11.31. that through **y.** mercy
¹Co. 15.31. I protest by **y.** rejoicing
²Co. 8. 8. to prove the sincerity of **y.**
Gal. 6.13. that they may glory in **y.**
   dia [ac.] **su** [pl.]
Jo. 11.15. I am glad *for* **y.** sakes
   kata [accu.] **su** [plu.]
Act.17.28. certain also of **y.** *own* poets
   18.15. names, and of **y.** law
   24.22. the uttermost of **y.** matter
   heautou, [plu.]
Eph. 5.25. Husbands love **y.** wives
   (See *Business, Conceit, Conversation,*
     Own.)

YOURSELVES.
   heautou, [plu.]
Mat. 3. 9. think not to say within **y.**
   16. 8. why reason ye among **y.**
   23.31. ye be witnesses unto **y.**, that
   25. 9. that sell, and buy for **y.**
Mar. 9.33. that ye disputed among **y.**
   50. Have salt in **y.**, andh ave
   13. 9. take heed to **y.**: for they
Lu. 3. 8. begin not to say within **y.**
   12.33. provide **y.** bags which
   57. why even of **y.** judge ye
Lu. 16. 9. Make to **y.** friends of the
   15. Ye are they which justify **y.**
   17. 3. Take heed to **y.**: If thy bro.
   14. Go shew **y.** unto the priests
   21.34. take heed to **y.**, lest at any
   22.17. divide it among **y.**
   23.28. weep for **y.**, and for your
Act. 5.35. take heed to **y.** what ye
   13.46. judge **y.** unworthy of ever.
   15.29. from which if ye keep **y.**
   20.28. Take heed therefore unto **y.**
Ro. 6.11. reckon ye also **y.** to be dead
   13. yield **y.** unto God, as
   16. to whom ye yield **y.** servants
   12.19. beloved avenge not **y.**
²Co. 7.11. ye have approved **y.** to be
   13. 5. Examine **y.**, whether ye be
Eph. 5.19. Speaking to **y.** in psalms
¹Th. 5.13. be at peace among **y.**
Heb.10.34.knowing in **y.** that ye
Jas. 2. 4. Are ye not then partial in **y.**
¹Pet. 4. 8. fervent charity among **y.**
¹Jo. 5.21. Little children, keep **y.**
²John 8. Look to **y.**, that we lose not
Jude 20. building up **y.** on your
   21. Keep **y.** in the love of God
   su, [plu.]
Mat. 6.19, 20. up for **y.** treasures
   23.15. the child of hell than **y.**
Eph. 2. 8. and that not of **y.** it is
   su autos, [plu.]
¹Co. 5.13. put away from among **y.**

YOUTH.
   neotēs.
Mat.19.20. I kept from my **y.** up;
     Mar.19.20; Lu.18.21
Act.26. 4. manner of life from my **y.**
¹Ti. 4.12. Let no man despise thy **y.**

YOUTHFUL.
   neōterikos.
²Ti. 2.22. Flee also **y.** lusts : but fol.

ZEAL.
   zēlos.
Jo. 2.17. The **z.** of thine house hath
Ro. 10. 2. they have a **z.** of God, but
²Co. 7.11. yea, what **z.**, yea, what reve.
   9. 2. your **z.** hath provoked very
Phi. 3. 6. Concerning **z.**, persecuting
Col. 4.13. he hath a great **z.** for you

ZEALOUS.
   zēlōtēs.
Act.21.20. and they are all **z.** of the law
   22. 3. and was **z.** toward God
¹Co.14.12. as ye are **z.** of spiritual gifts
Gal. 1.14. **z.** of the traditions of my
Tit. 2.14. a peculiar people, **z.** of good
   zēloō.
Rev. 3.19. *be* **z.** therefore, and repent

ZEALOUSLY.
   zēloō.
Gal. 4.17. they **z.** affect you, but not
   18. good *to be* **z.** affected always

PROPER NAMES.

THE GREEK FORMS, WHEN THEY DIFFER FROM THE ENGLISH, ARE GIVEN WITHIN BRACKETS.

AAR	ALE	ASI

Aaron [Aărŏn]
Lu. 1. 5. wife was of the daug. of A.
Act. 7.40. say. unto A., make us gods
Heb. 5. 4. called of God as was A.
7.11. called after the order of A.
9. 4. and A.'s rod that budded

Abaddon [Abaddŏn], Rev.9.11

Abel
Mat.23.35. fr. the blo. of A.; Lu.11.51
Heb.11. 4. By faith A. offered unto G.
12.24. bet. things than that of A.

Abia, Mat.1.7; Lu.1.5

Abiathar, Mar.2.26

Abilene [Abilēnē], Lu.3.1

Abiud [Abioud], Mat.1.13

Abraham [Abraăm]
Mat. 1. 1. son of David, son of A.
2. A. begat Isaac
17. all the generations from A.
3. 9. We have A. to our father
raise up children unto A.
8.11. shall sit down with A.
22.32. the God of A.; Mar.12.26;
Act.3.13; 7.32
Lu. 1.55. spake to our fathers, to A.
73. he sware to our father A.
3. 8. We have A. to our father
raise up children unto A.
34. which was the son of A.
13.16. being a daughter of A.
28. when ye shall see A.
16.22. car. by the angels into A.'s
23. and seeth A. afar off; 29,30
24. Father A., have mercy on
25. But A. said, Son, rememb.
19. 9. as he also is a son of A.
20.37. the Lord the God of A.
Jo. 8.33. We be A.'s seed; 37,39,40,
52,57
53. greater than our father A.
56. A. rejoiced to see my day
58. Before A. was, I am
Act. 3.25. saying unto A., And in thy
7. 2. appea. unto our father A.
16, 17. the sepulchre that A.
13.26. children of the stock of A.
Ro. 4. 12. if A. were justified by wo.
9. faith was reckoned to A.
16. which is of the faith of A.
9. 7. the seed of A.; 11.1; 2Co.
11.22; Gal.3.16,29;
Heb.2.6
Gal. 3. 6. Even as A. believed God
9. blessed with faithful A.
4.22. A. had two sons, the one
Heb. 6.13. God made promise to A.
7. 1. met A. returning from the
6. received tithes of A.
11. 8, 17. By faith A., when he
Jas. 2.21. A. our father justified
23. A. believed God, and it
1Pet. 3. 6. Sara obeyed A., calling

Aceldama [Akeldama], Act.1.19

Achaia [Achaĭa]
Act.18.12. Gallio was the deputy of A.
27. to pass into A.

Act.19.21. Macedonia and A.
Ro. 15.26. them of Macedonia and A.
16. 5. who is the first fruits of A.
1Co. 16.15. first fruits of A.
2Co. 1. 1. saints which are in all A.
9. 2. A. was ready a year ago
11.10. the regiohs of A.
1Th. 1. 7, 8. in Macedonia and A.

Achaicus [Achaĭkos], 1Co.16.17

Achaz, Mat.1.9

Adam
Lu. 3.38. which was the son of A.
Ro. 5.14. death reigned from A. to
similitude of A's transgr.
1Co. 15.22. For as in A. all die, even
45. The first man A. was
1Ti. 2.14. And A. was not deceived
Jude 14. also, the seventh from A.

Adramyttium of [Adramuttēnos]
Act. 27.2

Adria [Adrias], Act.27.27

Æneas [Aineas], Act.9.33,34

Ænon [Ainŏn], Jo.3.23

Agabus [Agabos], Act.11.28; 21.10

Agar, Gal.4.24,25

Agrippa [Agrippas]
Act.25.13. King A. and Bernice came;
22,23,24,26
26. 1. Then A. said unto Paul;
2,7,19,27,28,32

Alexander [Alexandros]
Mar.15.21.father of A. and Rufus
Act. 4. 6. John and A. and as many
19.33. drew A. out of the multit.
1Ti. 1.20. Hymenæus and A. whom
2Ti. 4.14. A. the coppersmith did me

Alexandria [Alexandreus],
Act.18.24. born at A.
[Alexandrinos]
Act.27. 6. a ship of A.; 88.11

Alexandrians [Alexandreus], Act.6.9

Alphæus [Alphaios]   [Act.1.13
Mat.10. 3. James son of A.; Lu.6.15;
Mar. 2.14. Levi the son of A. sitting

Aminadab, Mat.1.4; Lu.3.33

Amphipolis, Act.17.1

Amplias, Ro.16.8

Ananias
Act. 5. 1, 3, 5. a cert. man named A.
9.10, 12, 13, 17. Dam. named A.
22.12. one A. a devout man
23. 2. high priest A. commanded
24. 1. after five days A. the high

Andrew [Andreas]
Mat. 4.18. Peter and A. his bro.; 10.2
Mar.1.16; Lu.6.14
Mar. 1.29. house of Simon and A.
3.18. And A. and Philip
13. 3. A. asked him privately
Jo. 1.40. A. Simon Peter's brother
44. city of A. and Peter
6. 8. One of his disciples A.
12.22. telleth A., and A. and P.
Act.1. 13. A. Philip and Thomas

Andronicus [Andronikos], Ro.16.7

Anna, Lu.2.36

Annas
Lu. 3. 2. A. and Caiaphas being the
Jo. 18.13. And led him away to A.
24. Now A. had sent him bou.
Act. 4. 6. And A. the high priest, and

Antioch [Antiocheia]
Act.11.19. Cyprus and A.; 20,22,26
26. called christi.first in A.; 27
13. 1. in the church that was at A.
14. they came to A. in Pisidia
14.19. Jews from A.; 21,26
15.22. own compa.to A.; 23,30,35
18.22. he went down to A.
Gal. 2.11. when Peter was come to A.
2Ti. 3.11. which came unto me at A.
[Antiocheus]
Act. 6. 5. Nicolas a proselyte of A.

Antipas, Rev.2.13

Antipatris, Act.23.31

Apelles [Apellēs], Ro.16.10

Apollonia [Apollōnia], Act.17.1

Apollos [Apollōs]
Act.18.24. a certain Jew named A.
19. 1. while A. was at Corinth
1Co. 1.12. and I of A.; 3,4,5,6,22
4. 6. to myself and to A. for
16.12. touching our brother A.
Tit. 3.13. Zenas the lawyer and A.

Apollyon [Apolluŏn], Rev.9.11

Apphia, Phile.2

Appii forum [Appiou Phoron], Act.

Aquila [Akulas]   [28.15
Act.18. 2, 18, 26. cert. Jew named A.
Ro. 16. 3. Greet Priscilla and A.
1Co.16.19. A. and Priscilla salute you
2Ti. 4.19. Salute Prisca and A.

Arabia, Gal.1.17; 4.25

Arabians [Ara. pln. Arabes], Act.2.11

Aram, Mat.1.3,4; Lu.3.33

Archelaus [Archelaos], Mat.2.22   [2

Archippus [Archippos],Col.4.17;Phile.

Areopagite [Areopagitēs], Act.17.34

Areopagus [Areios-Pagos], Act.17.17

Aretas, 2Co.11.32

Arimathæa [Arimatheia], Mat.27.57
Mar.15.43; Lu.23.51; Jo.19.38

Aristarchus [Aristarchos]
Act.19.29. caught Gaius and A., men
20. 4. Thessalonians A. and Secu.
27. 2. one A. a Macedonian
Col. 4.10. A. my fellow-prisoner
Phile. 24. Marcus, A., Demas

Aristobulus [Aristoboulos], Ro.16.10

Armageddon [Armageddŏn], Rev.16
16

Arphaxad, Lu.3.36

Artemas, Tit.3.12

Asa, Mat.1.7,8

Aser [Asēr], Lu.2.36; Rev.7.6

Asia
Act. 2. 9. Cappado. in Pontus and A.
325

Act. 6. 2. them of Cilicia and of A.
16. 6. to preach the word in A.
19.10. they which dwelt in A. he.
22, 26. stay. in A. for a season
27. A. and the world worship.
20. 4. there accomp. him into A.
16. spend the time in A.; 18
21.27. the Jews which were of A.
24.18. certain Jews from A. found
27. 2. to sail by the coasts of A.
1Co. 16.19. The churches of A. salute
2Co. 1. 8. which came to us in A.
2Ti. 1.15. they which are in A. are
1Pet. 1. 1. scattered in A. and Bithyn.
Rev. 1. 4, 11. churches which are in A.
[Asiarchēs]
Act.19.31. certain of the *chief of* A.
[Asianos]
Act.20. 4. *of* A., Tychichus and Tro.
Assos [Assos], Act.20.13,14
Asyncritus [Asungkritos], Ro.16.14
Athenians [Athēnaios], Act.17.21
Athens [Athēnai]
Act.17.15. brought him to A.; 16
22. ye men of A. I perceive
18. 1. Paul departed from A. and
1Th. 3. 1. good to be left at A. alone
Attalia [Attaleia], Act.14.25
Augustus [Augoustos],Lu.2.1
[Sebastos], Act.25,21,25; 27.1
Azor [Azōr], Mat.1.13,14
Baal [Baàl], Ro.11.4
Babylon [Babulōn]
Mat. 1.11. carried away to B.; 12.17
Act. 7.43. carry you away beyond B.
1Pet. 5.13. the church that is at B.
Rev.14. 8. angel saying B. is fallen
16.19. great B. came in remembr.
17. 5. B. the great, the mother of
18. 2. B. the great is fallen; 10.21
Balaam [Balaäm]
2Pet. 2.15. following the way of B.
Jude 11. after the error of B.
Rev. 2.14. hold the doctrine of B.
Balac [Balak], Rev.2.14
Barabbas [Barabbas]
Mat.27.16. notable prisoner called B.
17,20,21,26
Mar.15. 7. there was one named B.
11. rather release B.; 15
Lu. 23.18. and release unto us B.
Jo. 18.40. Not this man but B.
Barachias, Mat.23.35
Barak, Heb.11.32
Bar-Jesus [Bar-Iēsous], Act.13.6
Bar-Jona [Bar-Iōna], Mat.16.17
Barnabas [Barnabas],
Act. 4.36. And Joses, surnamed B.
9.27. But B. took him
11.22. and they sent forth B.
25. Then departed B. to Tars.
30. elders by the hands of B.
12.25. B. and Saul returned from
13. 1. teachers as B. and Simeon
2. Separate me B. and Saul
7. who called for B. and Saul
43. followed Paul and B.
46. Paul and B. waxed bold
50. against Paul and B.
14.12. And they called B. Jupiter
14. the apostles, B. and Paul
20. next day departed with B.
15. 2. Paul and B. had no small
determi. that Paul and B.
12. audience to B. and Paul
22. to Antio. with Paul and B.
25. with our beloved B. and
326

Act.15.35. B. continued in Antioch
36. Paul said unto B.
37. B. determined to take with
39. and so B. took Mark
1Co. 9. 6. Or I only and B., have
Gal. 2. 1. to Jerusalem with B.
9. gave to me and B.
13. B. also was carried away
Col. 4.10. Marcus, sister's son to B.
Barsabas [Barsabas], Act.1.23: 15.22
Bartholomew [Bartholomaios], Mat.
10.3; Mar.3.18; Lu.6.14; Act.1.13
Bartimeus [Bartimaios], Mar.10.46
Beelzebub [Beelzeboul]
Mat.10.25. called master of house B.
12.24. B. the prince of the devils
27. if I by B. cast out devils
Mar. 3.22. said, He hath B. [18,19
Lu. 11.15. casteth out devils thro. B.;
Belial [Belial], 2Co.6.15
Benjamin [Beniamin]
Act.13.21. of the tribe of B.
Ro.11.1; Phi.3.5; Rev.7.8
Berea [Beroia], Act.17.10,13;
Act.19.22; 2Ti.4.20
[Beraios]
Act.20. 4. Sopater *of* B.
Bernice [Bernikē]
Act.25.13. B. came into Cæsarea ; 23
26.30. B. and they that sat with
Bethabara [Bēthabara], Jo.1.28
Bethany [Bēthania]
Mat.21.17. went out of the city into B.
26. 6. when Jesus was in B.
Mar.11. 1. Bethphage and B.; 11,12
14. 3. B. in the house of Simon
Lu. 19.29. nigh to Bethphage and B.
24.50. led them out as far as B.
Jo. 11. 1. named Lazarus, of B.
18. B. was nigh unto Jerusalem
12. 1. to B., where Lazarus was
Bethesda [Bēthesda], Jo.5.2
Bethlehem [Bēthleēm]
Mat. 2. 1. Jesus was born in B.; 5
6. thou B., in the land of
8. And he sent them to B.
16. slew all the children in B.
Lu. 2. 4. which is called B.
15. Let us now go even unto B.
Jo. 7.42. and out of the town of B.
Bethphage [Bēthphagē]
Mat.21. 1. come to B.; Mar.11.1
Lu. 19.29. come nigh to B. and Beth.
Bethsaida [Bēthsaida *or* -an]
Mat.11.21. woe unto thee B.; Lu.10.13
Mar. 6.45. the other side unto B.
8.22. And he cometh to B.
Lu. 9.10. belon. to the city called B.
Jo. 1.44. Now Philip was of B.
12.21. which was of B. of Galilee
Bithynia [Bithunia], Act.16.7; 1Pet.1.1
Blastus [Blastos], Act.12.20
Boanerges [Boanerges], Mar.3.17
Booz [Boōz], Mat.1.5
Bosor [Bosor], 2Pet.2.15
Cæsar [Kaisar]
Mat.22.17. to give tribute to C. or not;
Mar.12.14; Lu.20.22
21. render unto C. the things
Mar.12.17; Lu.20.25
Lu. 2. 1. a decree from C. Augustus
3. 1. in the reign of Tiberius C.
23. 2. forbid. to give tribute to C.
Jo. 19.12. thou art not C.'s friend
15. We have no king but C.
Act.11.28. in the days of Claudius C.
17. 7. contrary to the decrees of C.

Act.25. 8. nor yet against C. have I
10, 11. stand at C.'s judgment
12. Hast thou appealed unto C.
21. till I might send him to C.
26.32. he had not appeal. unto C.
27.24. must be brought before C.
28.19. constrai. to appeal unto C.
Phi. 4.22. they that are of C.'s house.
Caiphas [Kaïaphas]
Mat.26. 3. who was called C.
57. led him away to C.
Lu. 3. 2. C. being the high priest's
Jo. 11.49. one of them, named C.
18.13. he was father in law to C.
14. Now C. was he, which gave
24. unto C. the high priest
28. Then led they Jes. from C.
Act. 4. 6. high priest and C., and Jo.
Cain [Kaïn]
Heb.11. 4. more exce. sacrifice than C.
1Jo. 3.12. Not as C., who was of that
Jude 11. gone in the way of C., and
Cainan [Kaïnan], Lu.3.36,37
Cæsarea [Kaisareia]
Mat.16.23. the coasts of C. Philippi
8.27. the town of C. Philippi
Act. 8.40. ca. to C.; 21.8; 23.33; 25.13
9.30. they brou. him down to C.
10. 1. a certain man in C.
24. they entered into C.
11.11. sent from C. unto me
12.19. from Judæa to C.
18.22. he had landed at C.
21.16. of the disciples of C.
23.23. soldiers to go to C.
25. 1. from C. to Jerusalem
4. Paul should be kept at C.
6. he went down unto C.
Calvary [Kranion], Lu.23.33
Cana [Kana],Jo.2.1,11.C. of Galilee; 4.
46; 21.2
Canaan *of* [Chananaios], Mat.15.22
Canaanite [Kananitēs], Mat.10.4;
Mar.3.18
Candace [Kandakē], Act.8.27
Capernaum [Kapernaoum]
Mat. 4.13. he came and dwelt in C.
8. 5. entered into C.; Mar.21.1;
Lu.7.1
11.23. and thou C.; Lu.10.15
17.24. when they were come to C.
Mar. 1.21. And they went into C.
9.33. came to C.; Jo.6.24
Lu. 4.23. done in C. do also here
31. And came down to C.
Jo. 2.12. he went down to C.
4.46. whose son was sick at C.
6.17. went over the sea towar. C.
59. as he taught in C.
Cappadocia [Kappadokia], Act.2.9
1Pet.1.1
Carpus [Karpos], 2Ti.4.13
Castor and **Pollux** [Dioskouroi], Act.
28.11
Cedron [Kedros *or* Kedrōn], Jo.18.1
Cenchrea [Kengchreai], Act.18.18;
Ro.16.1
Cephas [Kēphas]
Jo. 1.42. thou shalt be called C.
1Co. 1.12. I of C.; and I of Christ
3.22. Paul, or Apollos, or C.
9. 5. brethren of the Lo. and C.
15. 5. was seen of C., then of the
Gal. 2. 9. when James, C., and John
Chaldæans [Chaldaios], Act.7.4
Chanaan *of* [Chananaios], Act.7.1
13.19; 15.9

Er [Er], Lu.3.28
Erastos [Erastos]
  Ro. 16.23. E. chamberlain of the city
Esaias [Hēsaīas]
  Mat. 3. 3. sp. of by E.;4.14;8.17;12.17
    13.14. fulfilled the prophecy of E.
    15. 7. well did E. prop.; Mar.7.6
  Lu. 3. 4. book of the words of E.
    4.17. book of the prophet E.
  Jo. 1.23. as said the prophet E.
    12.38. That the saying of E.
    39. because that E. said
    41. These things said E. when
  Act. 8.28, 30. read E. the prophet
    28.25. the Holy Ghost by E.
  Ro. 9.27, 29. E. crieth concerning
    10.16. For E. saith, Lord, who
    20. E. is very bold, and saith
    15.12. And again, E. saith
Esau [Ēsau]
  Ro. 9.13. Jacob have I loved but E.
  Heb.11.20.Isaac blessed Jacob and E.
    12.16. or profane person as E.
Esli, Lu.3.25
Esrom [Esrōm], Mat.1.3; Lu.3.33
Ethiopia *of* [Aithiops], Act.8.27
Ethiopians [Aithiops], Act.8.27
Eubulus [Euboulos], ²Ti.4.21
Eve [Eua], ²Co.11.3; ¹Ti.2.13
Eunice [Euneikē], ²Ti.1.5
Euodias [Euŏdia], Phi.4.2
Euphrates [Euphratēs],Rev.9.14;16.12
Euroclydon [Eurokludōn], Act.27.14
Eutychus [Eutuchos], Act.20.9
Ezekias, Mat.1.9,10
Felix [Phelix]
  Act.23.24. safe unto F. the governor
    26. the most exce. governor F.
  24. 3. all places, most noble F.
    22. And when F. heard these
    24. when F. came with his wife
    25. F. trembled, and answered
    27. came into F.' room and F.
  25.14. left in bonds by F.
Festus [Phēstos]
  Act.24.27. Porcius F. came into Felix
  25. 1. Now when F. was come in.
    4. But F. answered, that Paul
    9. But F., willing to do the
    12. Then F. when he had conf.
    13. unto Cæsarea to salute F.
    14. F. declared Paul's cause
    22. Then Agrippa said unto F.
    23. at F.' commandment Paul
    24. And F. said, King Agrippa
  26.24. F. said with a loud voice
    25. am not mad, most noble F.
    32. Then said Agrippa unto F.
Fortunatus [Phortounatos],¹Co.16.17
Gabbatha, Jo.19.13
Gabriel [Gabriēl], Lu.1.19,26
Gad, Rev.7.5   [8.26,37
Gadarenes [Gadarēnos], Mar.5.1; Lu.
Gaius [Gaios]
  Act.19.29. having caught G.; 20.4
  Ro. 16.23. G. mine host and of the
  ²Co. 1.14. but Crispus and G.
  ³John 1. unto the well-beloved G.
Galatia
  ¹Co.16. 1. churches of G.; Gal.1.2
  ²Ti. 4.10. Crescens to G. Titus unto
  ¹Pet.1. 1. throughout Pontus G.
Galatians [Galatikos], Act.16.6; 18.23
    [Galatai], Gal.3.1
Galilee [Galilaia, Galilaios]
  Mat. 4.15. G. of the Gentiles
326

Mat. 4.18. sea of G.; 15.29; Mar.1.16;
    7.31; Jo.6.1
Mar. 1.28. round about G.
  9.30. throughout G.
Lu. 8.26. over against G.
    All Galilee.
Mat.4.23; Mar.1.39
    And Galilee.
Lu.17.11; Act.9.31
    In Galilee.
Mat.17.22; 15.41; Lu.24.6; Jo.7.1,
  9; 21.2
    From Galilee.
Mat. 3.13; 4.25; 19.1;37,55; Mar.3.7;
  Lu.3.4; 23.5,23; 49.55; Act.10.37;
  13.31
    Into Galilee.
Mat. 4.12; 26.32; 28.7, 19, 16; Mar.
  1.14; 14.28; 16.7; Lu. 2.39; 4.14;
  Jo.1.43; 4.43,45,47,54
    (*See* Nazareth.)
Galilean [Galilaios]
  Mar. 14.70. thou art a G.; Lu.22.59
  Lu. 13. 1. so. that told him of the G-s
    2. suppose ye that these G-s
    23. 6. whether the man were a G.
  Jo. 4.45. the G-s received him
  Act. 2. 7. all these which speak G-s
    5.37. rose up Judas of G. in the
Gallio [Galliōn], Act.18.12,14,17
Gamaliel [Gamaliēl], Act.5.34; 22.3
Gaza, Act.8.26
Gennesaret
  Mat.14.34.the land of G.; Mar.6.53
  Lu. 5. 1. stood by the lake of G.
Gergesenes [Gergesēnos], Mat.8.28
Gethsemane [Gethsēmanē], Mat.26.
  36; Mar.14.32
Gideon [Gedeōn], Heb.11.32
Gog [Gōg], Rev.20.8
Golgotha
  Mat.27.33.place called G.;Mar.15.22
  Jo. 19.17. called in the Hebrew G.
Gommorrha [Gomorra]
  Mat.10.15.Sodom and G.; Mar.6.11;
    ²Pet.2.6 ; Jude 7
  Ro. 9.29. been made like unto G.
Grecians [Hellēnistēs]
  Act. 6. 1. murmuring among the G.
    9.29. disputed against the G.
    11.20. spake unto the G. preach.
Greece [Hellas], Act.20.2
Greek [Hellēn]
  Jo. 12.20. there were certain G-s
  Act.14. 1. Jews and also of the G-s
    16. 1, 3. his father was a G.
    17. 4. the devout G-s a great
    18. 4. persuad. the J. and the G-s
    17. all the G-s took Sosthenes
  19.10, 17. both Jews and G-s ;
    ¹Co.1.24
    20.21. Jews and also to the G-s
    21.28. brought G-s also into the
  Ro. 1.14. am debtor both to the G-s
    16. J. first,and also to the G.
    10.12. betw. the Jew and the G.
  ¹Co. 1.22. the G-s seek after wisdom
    23. unto the G-s foolishness
  Gal. 2. 3. was with me, being a G.
    3.28. nei. Jew nor G. ; Col.3.11
    [Hellēnikos], Lu.23.38;Rev.9.11
    [Hellēnes], Mar.7.26; Act.17.12
    [Hellēnisti]
  Jo. 19.20. Hebrew and G. and Latin
  Act.21.37. Who said,Canst thou sp.G.
Heber, Lu.3.35

Hebrew [Hebraios]
  Act. 6. 1. Grecians against the H-s
  ²Co. 11.22. Are they H-s? so am I
  Phi. 3. 5. an H. of the H-s
    [Hebraikos]
  Lu. 23.38. of Greek and Latin and H.
    [Hebrais]
  Act.21.40. spake in H. tongue ; 22.2
    26.14. saying in the H. tongue
    [Hebraisti]
  Jo. 5. 2. in the H. tongue Bethesda
    19.13. but in the H. Gabbatha
    17. called in the H. Golgotha
    20. in H., and Greek, and La.
  Rev. 9.11. in the H. tongue is Abad.
    16.16. in H. tongue Armageddon
Heli [Hēli], Lu.3.23
Hermas, Ro.16.14
Hermes [Hermēs], Ro.16.14
Hermogenes [Hermogenēs], ²Ti.1.15
Herod [Hērōdēs]
  Mat. 2. 1. in the days of H. the king
    3. H. the king heard these
    7. H..had privily called
    12. should not return to H.
    13. H. will seek the young ch.
    15. there until the death of H.
    16. Then H., when he saw
    19. when H. was dead, behold
    22. room of his father H., he
  14. 1. H. the tetrarch h.; Lu.9.7
    3. H. had laid hold on John
    6. when H.'s birth.;Mar.6.21
    and pleased H.; Mar.6.22
  Mar. 6.14. H. heard of him; 16
    18. John had said unto H.
    20. For H. feared John
    8.15. and of the leaven of H.
  Lu. 1. 5. in the days of H. the king
    3. 1. H. tetrarch of Galilee
    19. H. the tetrarch, being
    the evils which H. had do.
    8. 3. of Chuza H.'s steward
    9. 9. H. said, John have I
    13.31. depart, H. will kill thee
    23. 7. belonged unto H.'s jurisdi.
    8. when H. saw J., he was
    11. H. with his men of war; 12
    15. nor yet H.; for I sent you
  Act. 4. 27. H., and Pontius with the
  12. 1. H. the king stretched
    6. when H. would have
    11. out of the hand of H.
    19. when H. had sought for
    20. H. was highly displeased
    21. on a set day H., arrayed in
  13. 1. brought up with H.
    23.35. kept in H.'s judgment hall
Herodians [Hērōdianos], Mat.22.16;
  Mar.3.6; 12.13
Herodias [Hērōdias]
  Mat.14. 3, 6. prison for H.' sake; Mar.
    6.17,19,22
  Lu. 3.19. reproved for H. his brother
Herodion [Hērōdiōn], Ro.16.11
Hierapolis, Col.4.13
Hymeneus [Humenaios],¹Ti.1.20; ²Ti.
  2.17
Iconium [Ikonion]
  Act.13.51. and came unto I.; 14.21
    14. 1. It came to pass in I.
    19. Jews from Antioch and I.
    16. 2. that were at Lystra and I.
  ²Ti. 3.11. at Antioch, at I., at Lystra
  (*Rest of letter* I, *see* p. 32, *Appendix*).
Jacob [Jacŏb]
  Mat. 1. 2. begat J.; 15,16; Act.7.8
    8.11. Isaac, and J.; Lu.13.28
    22.32. the God of J.; Mar.12.26

Lu. 1.33. over the house of J.
3.34. Which was the son of J.
20.37. God of J.; Act.7.32,46
Jo. 4. 5. that J. gave to his son
6. J.'s well was there ; 12
Act. 3.13. and of Isaac, and of J
7.12. But when J. heard; 14,15
Ro. 9.13. J. have I loved
11.26. away ungodliness from J.
Heb.11. 9. with Isaac and J.
20. Isaac blessed J. and Esau
21. J., when he was a dying

Jairus [Jäeiros], Mar.5.22 ; Lu.8.41
Jambres [Jambres], ²Ti.3.8
James [Jakōbos], (*See Peter*)
Mat. 4.21. J. the son of Zebedee; 10.2
Mar.1.19; 3.17
10. 3. J. the son of Alpheus;Mar.
8.18; Lu.6.15 ; Act.1.13
13.55. J. and Joses and Simon
17. 1. J. and John his brother ;
Mar.1.29; 3.17; 5.37; 6.3;
9.2; 10.35,41; 13.3; 14.33.
Lu.5.10; 6.14; 8.51; 9.28,
54. Act.1.13
27.56. Mary the mother of J.;
Mar.15.40 · 16.1 ; Lu.
24.10
Mar.15.40.J. the less   [Jude 1.
Lu. 6.16. Jud. brother of J.; Act.1.13;
Act.12. 2. And killed J. the brother
17. shew them unto J., and
15.13. J. answered, men and
21.18. went in with us unto J.
¹Co.15. 7. Aft. that he was seen of J.
Gal. 1. 19. save J. the Lord's brother
2. 9. J., Cephas, and John
12. that certain came from J.
Jas. 1. 1. J...servant of God

Jannes [Jannēs], ²Ti.3.8
Jason [Jasōn], Act.17.5, 6, 7, 9;
Ro.16.21
Jephtha [Jephthae], Heb. 11.32
Jeremiah [Hieremias]
Mat. 2.17. by J. the prophet ; 27.9
16.14. and others J., or one

Jericho [Hiericho]
Mat.20.29. As they departed from J.
Mar.10.46.they came to J., and as he
Lu. 10.30. from Jerusalem to J.
18.35. as he was come nigh unto J.
19. 1. and passed through J.
Heb.11.30.the walls of J. fell down

Jerusalem[HierosolumaHierousalēm]
Mat. 2. 1. there came wise m. to J-*a*
3. and all J-*a* with him
8. 5. to him J-*a*, and all Judea
5.35. neither by J-*a*, for it is the
15. 1. which were of J-*a*
21.10. when he was come into J-*a*
23.37. O. J-*m*, J-*m* that; Lu.13.34
Mar.11. 1. they came nigh to J-*m*
11. and Jesus entered into J-*a*
15. they come to J-*a*
Lu. 2.22. they brought him to J-*a*
45. turned back again to J-*m*
5.17. Galilee,and Judea, and J-*m*
6.17. out of all Judea, and J-*m*
9.51. set his face to go to J-*m*
53. as tho. he would go to J-*m*
13.22. journey toward J-*m*
33. a prophet perish out of J-*m*
17.11. as he went to J-*m*, that he
19.11. he was nigh to J-*m*
21.20. J-*m*compassed with armies
24. and J-*m* shall be trodden
23.28. Daughters of J-*m* weep not
24.33, 52 and returned to J-*m*
49. tarry ye in the city of J-*m*
52. and returned to J-*m*.

•Jo. 11.55. many went..to J-*a*
12.12. Jesus was coming to J-*a*
Act. 4.16. all them that dwell in J-*m*
5.28. ye have filled J-*m* with
8.25. returned to J-*m*, and prea.
27. to J-*m* for to worship
9.26. Paul was come to J-*m*
13.13. from them, returned to J-*a*
31. with him, fr. Galilee to J-*m*
15. 4. wh. they were come to J-*m*
19.21. Achaia, to go to J-*m*
21.17. we were come to J-*a*
31. all J-*m* was in an uproar
22. 17. I was come again to J-*m*
18. quickly out of J-*m*
25. 1. ascended from C. to J-*a*
3. would send for him to J-*m*
20. wheth. he would go to J-*m*
Ro. 15.31. serv. which I have for J-*m*
Gal. 2. 1. I went up again to J-*a*
4.25. and answereth to J-*a*
26. J-*m* which is above is free
Heb.12.22. living God the hea. J-*m*
Rev. 3.12. which is new J-*m* ; 21.2
21.10. great city the holy J-*m*
at J. [Hierosoluma]
Lu. 23. 7; Jo. 4.21, 45; 5.2; 10.22;
Act.8.1,14; 20.16; 25.15,24; 26.4,20.
at J. [Hierousalēm]
Lu. 9.31; 24.47 ; Act. 1.19; 2.5,14;4.6;
9.13,28; 13.27; 16.4; 21.11,13; Rev.15.26.
from J. [Hierosoluma]
Mat.4.25;Mar.3.8,22;7.1;Jo.1.19; Act.
1.4; 11.27; 25.7; 28.17.
from J. [Hierousalēm]
Lu.10.30; 24.13; Act.1.12; 8.26; Ro.
15.19.
in J. [Hierosoluma]
Jo.2.23; 4.20; Act. 11.22;18.21; 26.10.
in J. [Hierousalem]
Lu. 2.25,38,43;13.4; 24.18; Act.1.8;6.7;
9.21; 10.39; 23.11.
up to J. [Hierosoluma]
Mat.20.17,18; 10.32; 2.42; 18.31;19.28;
Jo.2.13; 5.1;Act.11.2;25.9; Gal.1.17,18.
up to J. [Hierousalem]
Lu.2.41; Act.15.2; 21.4,12,15; 24.11.
Hierosolumitēs
Mar. 1. 5. of Judea and *they* of J.
Jo. 7.25. said some of *them* of J.
Jesse [Jessai]
Mat.1.5,6. Obed begat J., and J.begat
Lu. 3.32. the son of J. ; Act. 13.22.
Ro. 15.12. There shall be a root of J.

Jesus [Iēsous]
Mat. 1.21, 25. call his name J.;Lu.1.31
16.20. no man that he was J.
21.11. This is J. the prophet of
26.26. J. took bread ; Mar.14.52
69, 71. wast with Jesus ; Mar.
27.17. Barabbas, or J.   [14.67
37. J. the King of the Jews ;
Jo.19.19
58. begged the body of J. ;
Mar.15.43 ; Lu.23.52
Mar. 1.24. thou J. of Nazareth
10.47. J., thou son of ; Lu.18.36
16. 6. Ye seek J. of Nazareth
Lu. 2.27. brought in the child J.
43. the child J. tarried
52. J. increased in wisdom
Jo. 2. 1, 3. the moth. of J.; Act.1.14
11.35. J. wept
13.23. whom Jesus loved; 21.7,20
20.31. that J. is the Christ, the
Act. 4.27, 30. thy holy child J.
9. 5. I am J. whom
17. 7. another king, one J.
19.13. adjure you by J. whom
15. J. I know
22. 8. I am J.; 26.15

Act.25.19. one J., which was dead
¹Co. 12. 3. calleth J. accursed : and
can say that J.
²Co. 4.10. that the life also of J.
11. 4. preacheth another J.
Eph. 4.21. truth is in J.
Phi. 2.10. at the name of J.
¹Th. 4.14. which sleep in J.
Heb. 6.20. J., made an high priest
10.19. by the blood of J.
12. 2. J. the author
24. J. the mediator
¹Jo. 4.15. J. is the son of God; 5.1,5
Rev.22.16. I J. have sent mine angel
(Also)**Mat.**2.1;3.13,16;4.1,12,17,18,23;
7.28; 8.3,5,10,14,18,29,34; 9.2,4,9,10, 12,
22,23,27,30,35; 10.5; 11.1,7; 12.1,15,25;
13.1,34,36,53; 14.1,12,13,14,22,25,27,29,
31; 15.1,21,29,30,32; 16.8,13,21; 17.1,4,
7,8,9,18,19,25; 18.1,2; 19.1,26; 20.17,25,
30,32,34; 21.1,6,12,16,27; 22.18,41; 23.1;
24.1; 26.1,4,6,10,17,19,36,49,50,51,57,59,
63,75; 27.1,11,20,22,26,27,46,50,54,55,57;
28.5,9,18. **Mar.**1.1,9,14,25,41; 2.5,8,15,
17,19; 3.7; 5.6,7,13,15,19,20,21,27,30,36;
6.30,34; 8.1,17,27; 9.2,4,5,8,25,27; 10.14,
21,23,27,32,42,47,49,50,52 ; 11.6,7,11,15,
33;12.34,41;14.22,53,55,60,72;15.1,15,34,
37,43. **Lu.**2.21; 3.21,23; 4.1,14,34,35;
5.8,12,19,22; 6.11; 7.3,4,6,9,19; 8.28, *bis*,
30,35, *bis*, 38,39,40,41,50; 9.33,36,42,43,
47; 10.21,29,39; 13.12,14; 17.13; 18.16,
22,24,37,38,40; 19.3,5,35, *bis*; 22.47,63;
23.8,20,25,26,28,42,46,52; 24.3,15,19,36;
Jo.1.29,36,37,38,42,43,45,47,48; 2.2, 11,
13,19,22,24; 3.2,22; 4.1,2,6,44,46,47,50;
54; 5.1,6,13,14,15,16; 6.1,3,5,11,14,15,17,
19,22,24, *bis*,42,61,64; 7.1, 14,28,37,39; 8.
1,6,9,10,12,20,59; 9.11,14,35; 10.6; 11.4,
13,17,20, 21, 30, 32,33,38,41,45,46,51,54,
56; 12.1,3,9,11,12,14,16,21,22,36,44;13.1,
3,21,23,25,29; 17.1; 18.1,2,4,5,7, 12,15,
bis,19,22,28, 32,33; 19.1,5,9, 13,16,18,20,
23,25,26,28,30,33, 38, *ter*, 39,40,42; 20.2,
12, 14, 19,24, 26,30; 21.1,4,7,13,14,21,25.
Act.1.1,11,14;2.32,36;3.13,26; 4.2,13,18;
5.30,40; 7.55;28.23. **Ro.**3.26; 8.11. ²**Co.**
4.5,11,14. **Heb.**2.9; 4.14; 13.12. **Rev.**
17.6; 19.10, *bis*; 20.4

Jesus said.
Mat.4.7;8.13,22;9.15;13.57;14.16;15.16
16.6,24;17.20,22; 19.14,18,21,23,28;22.37;
24.2; 26.34, 50, 52, 55; 27.11; 28.10,16.
Mar.1-17; 2.19; 6.4;7.27; 9.23,39; 10.18,
38,39,52; 14.6,18,62. **Lu.**5.10; 6.9;8.45,
46; 9.50,58,60,62; 10.37; 18.19,42; 19.
20.8; 22.48,52; 23.34,43. **Jo.**4.17,48;53;
6.10,32,35,53,67; 7.6,33; 8.11,21,28,31,
42,58; 9.37,39,41; 10.7; 11.14,25,39; 12.7,
35; 13.27,31; 18.11; 20.21; 21.23
Jesus saith.
Mat.4.10; 8.4,7,20; 9.28; 13. 51; 15.34;
17.26; 18.22;21.16,31,42;26.31,64. **Mar.**
14.27,30. **Jo.**2.4;7. 4.7,16,21,26,34,50;
5.8; 8.25,39; 11.23,40,44; 13.10; 14.6,9;
18.5; 20.15,16,17,29; 21.5,10,12,15,17,22.
Jesus answered.
Mat.11.4,25; 15.28; 16.17;17.11,17,20.
22; 21.21,24; 22.1,29; 24.4. **Mar.**10.5,24,
29,51; 11.14,29; 12.29,35; 14.48; 15.5.
Lu.4,4,8; 10.41; 22.51. **Jo.**1.50; 2.19; 3.
3,5,10; 4.10,13; 5.17,19; 6.26,29,43,70; 7.
16,21; 8.14,19,34,49,54; 9.3; 10.25,32,34;
11.9; 12.23,30; 13.7,8,26,36,38; 14.23; 16.
31; 18.8,20,23,34,36; 19.11
Jesus answering.
Mat.3.15. **Mar.**11.22,33; 12.17,24;
13.2,5. **Lu.**4.12; 5.31; 6.3; 7.22,40;9. 41;
10.30; 13.2; 14.3; 17.17; 20.34
Jesus Christ [Christos]
Mat. 1. 1. the generation of J. C.
329

Mat. 1.16. born J., who is called C.
18. birth of J. C. was on
Jo. 1.17. gr. and truth came by J.C.
17. 3. only true God, and J. C.
20.31. that J. is the C., the Son
Act. 2.38. in the name of J. C.; 3.6; 4.10; 8.12
3.20. shall send J. C., which be.
5.42. teach and preach J. C.
8.12. and the name of J. C.
37. that J. C. is the Son
10.36. peace by J. C.
18. 5, 28. that J. was C.
Ro. 1. 1. a servant of J. C., called
6. ye also the called of J. C.
8. God through J. C.; Gal. 3.14; Heb.13.21; 1Pet. 4.11
3.22. which is by faith of J. C.
6.11, 23. through J. C. our Lord
7.25. I thank God through J. C.
15.16. minis. of J. C.; 1Ti.4.6
17. I may glory throu. J. C.
16.27. be glory through J. C.
1Co. 1. 1. apostle of J. C.; 2Co.1.1; Eph.1.1; Col.1.1; 1Ti. 1.1; 2Ti.1.1; Tit.1.1; 1Pet.1.1; 2Pet.1.1
2. call upon the name of J.C.
2. J. C. and him crucified
3.11. laid, which is J. C.
2Co. 4. 6. in the face of J. C.
13. 5. that J. C. is in you
Gal. 1.12. by the revelation of J. C.
3.14. the Gentiles throu. J. C.
Eph. 2.20. J. C. himself being the
3. 1. the prisoner of J. C.
Phi. 1. 6. until the day of J. C.
8. in the bowels of J. C.
19. of the spirit of J. C.
1Ti. 4. 6. a good minister of J. C.
2Ti. 1.10. appearing of our Sav. J. C.
2. 3. good soldier of J. C.
Tit. 1. 4. through J. C. our Saviour
Phile. 1. prisoner of J. C.; 9
Heb.13. 8. J. C. the same yesterday
1Pet. 1. 2. of the blood of J. C.
3. resurrection of J. C.; 3.21
7. appearing of J. C.
13. revelation of J. C.;Rev.1.1
1Jo. 1. 3. and with his Son J. C.
7. the blood of J. C. his Son
2. 1. J. C. the righteous
22. denieth that J. is the C.
4. 2, 3. J. C. is co. in the; 2Jo.7
Jude 1. Jude, the servant of J. C. and preserved in J. C.
Rev. 1. 1. The Revelation of J. C.
2, 9. testimony of J. C.
(Also) Act.9.34. Ro.1.3; 2.16; 5.15, 17,21; 6.3; 15.8:16.25. 1Co.1.4. 2Co. 1.19;5.18. Gal.1.1; 2.16; 3.1,22; 5.6. Eph.1.5; 3.9. Phi.1.1, 11, 26; 2.21. 1Ti.1.16. 2Ti.2.8. Tit.2.13. Heb.10. 10. 1Pet.2.5. 1Jo.3.23; 5.6,20. Jude 1 Rev.1.5,9; 12.17; 14.12

Christ Jesus.

Act.19. 4. after him, that is on C. J.
Ro. 3.24. redemption that is in C. J.
8. 1. in C. J., who walk not
2. Spirit of life in C. J.
39. love of God, wh. is in C. J.
15. 5. another according to C. J.
16. 3. my helpers in C. J.
1Co. 1. 2. that are sanctified in C. J.
30. But of him are ye in C. J.
4.15. for in C. J. I have begotten
16.24. be with you all in C. J.
2Co. 4. 5. but C. J. the Lord
Gal. 2. 4. which we have in C. J.
3.26. by faith in C. J.
330

Gal. 3.28. for ye are all one in C. J.
4.14. angel of God, even as C. J.
6.15. For in C.J. neither circum.
Eph. 1. 1. and to the faithful in C. J.
2. 6. in heavenly places in C. J.
7. towards us through. C. J.
10. created in C. J. unto good
13. But now in C. J.
3.11. purposed in C. J. our Lord
21. by C. J. throughout all
Phi. 1. 1. to all the saints in C. J.
2. 5. which was only in C. J.
3. 3. and rejoice in C. J.
8. of the knowledge of C. J.
12. I am apprehended of C. J.
14. high calling of God in C. J.
4. 7. hearts and minds thro.C.J.
19. his riches in glory by C. J.
21. Salute every saint in C. J.
Col. 1. 4. heard of your faith in C. J.
28. every man perfect in C. J.
2. 6. therefore received C. J. the
1Th. 2.14. which in Judea are in C. J.
5.18. is the will of God in C. J.
1Ti. 1. 14. and love which is in C. J.
15. that C. J. came into the
2. 5. the man C. J.
3.13. the faith which is in C. J.
6.13. and before C. J.
2Ti. 1. 1. of life which is in C. J.
2. the Father and C. J. our
9. which was given us in C. J.
13. and love which is in C. J.
2. 1. the grace that is in C. J.
10. the salvation wh. is in C. J.
3.12. all will live godly in C. J.
15. through faith wh. is in C.J.
Phile. 6. which is in C. J.
23. my fellowprisoner in C. J.
Heb. 3. 1. of our profession, C. J.
1Pet. 5.10. eternal glory by C. J.
14. you all that are in C. J.

Jesus with Lord [Kurios]

Act. 7.59. Lord J. receive my spirit
8.16. name of the Lord J.; 9.29; 19.5,13,17;20.24,35;21.13. 10.C.6.11. Col.3.17
9.17. the Lord, even J., that
Ro. 4.24. raised up J. our Lord
1Co. 5. 5. day of the Lord J.; 2Co.1.14
11.23. Lord J. the same night
2Co. 4.10. dying of the Lord J.; 10.14
Gal. 6.17. marks of the Lord J.
Phi. 2.19. trust in the Lord J.
1Th. 2.15. killed the Lord J.
2Th. 1. 7. Lord J. shall be revealed
Rev.22.20. Even so, come, Lord J.
(Also) Act.1.21; 4.33; 11.20; 19.10. Ro.10.9; 14.14. 2Co.4.14. Eph.1.15. 1Th.4.1, 2. Phile. 5. Heb. 13.20. 2Pet.1.2

Jesus with Lord and Christ

Act.15.11. grace of the Lord J.Christ; Ro.16.20; 1Co.16.23; 2Co.8.9; 13.14; Gal.6.18 Phi.4.23; 1Th.5.28; 2Th. 3.18; Phile.25; Rev.21.21
16.31. on the Lord J. Christ
Ro. 13.14. ye on the Lord J. Christ
15. 6. Fa. of our Lord J. Christ; 2Co.1.3; 11.31; Eph.1.3; 3.14; Col.1.3; 1Pet.1.3
1Co. 1. 7. com. of our Lord J. Christ
8. day of our Lord J. Christ
8. 6. and one Lord J. Christ
16.22. love not the Lord J. Christ
Gal. 6.14. cross of our Lord J. Christ
Eph. 1.17. God of our Lord J. Christ
6.24. love our Lord J. Christ
Phi. 2.11. confess that J. C. is Lord
Col. 1. 3. of our Lord J. Christ

1Th. 2. 6. received Christ J. the Lord
3.13. com. of our Lord J. Christ 5.23; 2Th.2.1; 2Pet.1.16
2Th. 1. 8. gospel of our Lord J. Christ
2.14. glory of our Lord J. Christ
3. 6. name of our Lord J. Christ
1Ti. 6. 3. words of our Lord J. Christ
14. of our Lord J. Christ
2Ti. 1. 2. and Christ J. our Lord
4.22. Lord J. Christ be with thy
Phil. 1.23. grace of our Lord J. Christ
1Pet. 1. 5. of our Lord J. Christ
2Pet. 1. 8. of our Lord J. Christ
Jude 17. apost. of our Lord J. Christ
21. mercy of our Lord J.Christ
(Also) Act.11.17; 15.26; 20.21; 28.31. Ro.1.7; 5.1,11; 15.30; 16.18. 1Co.1.3,9, 10;5.4; 9,1; 15.31,57. 2Co.1.2. Gal.1.3. Eph.1.2; 5.20;6.23. Phi.1.2; 2.11; 3.20. Col.1.2. 1Th.1.1,3; 2.19; 3.11; 5.9. 2Th.1.2,12; 2.16;3.12. 1Ti.1.1,2,12; 5. 21. 2Ti.4.1. Tit.1.4. Phile. 3. Jas. 1.1; 2.1. 2Pet.1.11, 14; 2.20; 3.18. 3John 3. Jude 4.

Jesus [Iēsous], *(not the Lord)*; Act. 7.45; Heb.4.8; Col.4.11

Jew [Ioudaios]
Mat. 2. 2. is born King of the J-s; 27.11,29,37; Mar. 15.2,9, 12,18,26; Lu.23.3,37,38 Jo.18,33,39; 19,3,19,21.
28.15. reported among the J-s
Mar. 7. 3. Pharisees, and all the J-s
Lu. 7. 3. him the elders of the J-s
23.51. Arimathæa, city of the J-
Jo. 3. 1. Nicodemus ruler of the J-s
4. 9. J-s have no dealings with
22. salvation is of the J-s
18.35. Pilate ans., Am I a J.
Act.18. 2. all J-s to depart from Ro.
19.14. Sceva, a J. and chief of
34. they knew that he was a J.
21.39. which am a J.; 22.3
24.27. to shew the J-s; 25.9
Ro. 1.16. J. first, and also; 2.9,10
2.17. thou art called a J.
28. J., which is one outwar y
29. J., which is one inwaru
3. 1. What advantage..the J.
Gal. 2.14. If thou, being a J.
15. We who are J-s by nature
(Also) Jo. 1.19; 2.6,13, 18,20; 3.25; 4.9;5.1,10,15,16,18; 6.4,41,52;7.1,2,11, 1, 15,35; 8.22,31,48,52,57; 9.18,22; 10.19, 24,31, 33; 11.8,19, 31, 33, 36, 45, 54, 55; 12.9, 11; 13.33; 18.12, 14, 20,31, 36, 38, 19.3, 7,12,14,20, 21, 31, 38, 40, 42; 20.19. Act.2.5, 10, 14; 9.22, 23; 10.22, 28, 39; 11.19; 12.3, 11; 13.5,6,42,43, 45, 50; 14. 1, bis, 2,4,5,19; 16.3,20; 17.1, 5,10, 13, 17; 18.2,4,5,12,14,bis,19,24,28; 19.10,13, 17,33; 20.3,19,21; 21.11,20, 21, 27, 39; 22.12,30; 23. 12,20,27,30; 24.5,9,18, 27; 25.2,7,8,9,10,15,24; 26.2,3,4, 7, 21; 28.17, 19,29. Ro. 3.9,29; 9.24; 10.12. 1Co. 1.22,23,24; 9.20, bis; 10.32; 12.13. 2Co. 11.24. Gal. 2.13,14,15; 3.28. Col. 3.11. 1Th.2.14. Rev. 2.9; 3.9.

Jewess [Ioudaia], Act. 16.1; 24.24.

Jewry [Ioudaia], Lu. 23.5; Jo. 7.1

Jezebel [Iezabel], Rev. 2.20

Joanna [Iōanna], Lu.8.3; 24.10 [Iōannas], Lu.3.27

Job [Iōb], Jas.5.11

Joel [Iōel], Act.2.16

John (*Baptist*) [Iōannēs],
Mat. 3.1. J. the Baptist; 11.11,12; 14. 2,8; 16.14; 17.13; Mar. 6.14,24,25; 8.28,33; 9.19
4. J. had his raiment; Mar.1.6

Mat. 3.13, 14. J. to be baptised of hi.
4.12. J. cast into prison; Mar.1.
14; Lu.3.20; Jo.3.24
9.14. came..disciples of J.; Mar.
2.18; Lu.5.33; 7.18; Jo.
1.35; 3.25
11. 2, 4, 7, 13. J. had heard in the
18. J. came neither eating
14. 3, 4. Her. had laid hold on J.
10. beheaded J.; Mar.6.16;
Lu.9.9.
21.25. The baptism of J.; Mar.11.
30; Lu.7.29; 20.4; Act.1.
22; 10.37; 18.25; 19.3
26. hold J. as a pr.; Mar.11.32
32. J. came unto you
Mar. 1. 4. J. did baptize; Jo.1.28; 3.
23; 10.40; Act.1.5; 11.16;
19.4
9. was baptized of J. in Jord.
Lu. 7.20. J. Baptist hath sent us
11. 1. as J. also taught his discip.
Jo. 1.40. of the two which heard J.
4. 1. more disciples than J.
10.41. J. did no miracle
(Also) **Mar.**6.17,18,20. **Lu.**1.13,60,
63; 3.2,15,16; 7.18,19,22,24, bis; 9.7; 16.
16; 20.6. **Jo.**1.6,15,19,26,29,32; 3.26,27;
4.1. 5.33,36; 10.41. **Act.**13.24,25
John (*Beloved*) [Iōannēs]   [1.19
Mat. 4.21. J. his brother; 10.2; Mar.
17. 1. Peter, James, and J.; Mar.
9.2; 13.3; 14.33; Lu.8.51;
9.28; Act.1.13
Act. 3. 1. Peter and J. went up toge.
4.13, 19. boldness of Peter and J.
8.14. sent..Peter and J.
12. 2. slew the brother of J.
12. Mary mother of J.
Gal. 2. 9. James, Cephas, and J.
Rev. 1. 1, 4, 9. unto his servant J.
21. 2. And I J. saw; 22.8
(Also) **Mar.**1.29; 3.17; 5.37; 9.38; 10.
35,41. **Lu.**5.10;6.14; 9.49,54; 22.8. **Act.**3.
3,4,11
John(*others*) [Iōannēs], Act.4.6; 12.15;
13.5,13; 15.37
Jonan [Iōnan], Lu.3.30
Jona [Iōnas], Jo.1.42
Jonas [Iōnas], Mat.12.39,40,41; 16.4;
Lu.11.29,30,32; Jo.21.15,16,17
Joppa [Ioppē], Act.9.36,38,42,43; 10.5,
8,23.32; 11,5,13
Joram [Iōram], Mat.1.8
Jorim [Iōreim], Lu.3.29
Jordan [Iordanēs]
Mat. 3. 5. re. round about J.; Lu.3.3
6. ba. of him in J.; Mar.1.5,9
13. from Galilee to J.
4.15, 25. beyond J.; 19.1;3.8; Jo.
3.26; 10.40
Mar.10. 1. by the farther side of J.
Lu. 4. 1. returned from J., and was
Josaphat [Iōsaphat], Mat.1.8
Jose or **Joses** [Iōsēs]
Mat.13.55. James and J.;27.56; Mar.6.
3; 15.40
Mar.15.47.Mary the mother of J.
Lu. 3.29. Which was the son of J.
Act. 4.36. And J., who by the apostl.
Joseph (*patriarch*) [Iōsēph], Jo.4.5;
Act.7.9,13,14,18; Heb.11.21,22;
Rev.7.8
Joseph (*others*) [Iōsēph]
Mat. 1.16. And Jacob begat J.
18. Ma. was esp. to J.; 19,20,24
2.13, 19. appeareth to J.
27.57. of Arimathæa named J.
Mar.15.43 ; Jo.19.38
59. when J. had ; Mar.15.45

Lu. 1.27. man whose name was J.
2. 4. J. also went up from
16. found Mary and J.
33, 43. J. and his mother
3.23. the son of J.; 24,26,30
23.50. man named J. a counsellor
Act. 1.23. J. called Barsabas
Josias [Iōsias], Mat. 1.10, 11
Jotham [Iōatham], Mat. 1.9
Juda [*land*] [Ioudas], Mat. 2.6; Lu.1.39
Juda [Ioudas], Mat.2.6; Mar.6.3; Lu.3.
26,30,33; Heb.7.14; Rev.5.5; 7.5.
Judah [Ioudas], Heb.8.8
Judas [Ioudas] [*See Iscariot.*]
Jo. 13.29. J. had the bag
14.22. J.., not Iscariot
Act. 1.13. J., brother of James
5.37. After rose up J.
9.11. enquire in the house of J.
15.22. J. surnamed Barsabas
27. We have sent..J.
(Also) **Mat.**1.2, 3; 13.55; 26.14, 25,
47; 27.3. **Mar.**3.19 ; 14.10,43. **Lu.**6.16,
bis, 22.3,47,48. **Jo.**6.71;12.4; 13.2,26,29;
14,22; 18.2,3,5. **Act.**1.16,25; 15.32.
Jude [Ioudas], Jude 1
Judea [Ioudaia]
Mat.2.1,5,22; 3.1, 5; 4.25;19.1; 24.16.
Mar.1.5; 3.7; 10.1; 13.14. **Lu.**1.5,65 ;
2.4; 3.1; 5.17; 6.17; 7.17; 21.21 ;
Jo.3.22 ; 4.3,47,54; 7.3; 11.7. **Act.**
1.8; 2.9; 8.1; 9.31; 10.37; 11.1,29 ; 12.19;
15.1 ; 21.10 ; 26.20 ; 28.21. Ro.15.31.
[2]Co.1.16. **Gal.**1.22; [1]Th.2.14
[Ioudaios]
Mar. 1.5; Jo. 3.22; Act. 2.14
Julia [Ioulia], Ro. 16.15
Julius [Ioulios], Act.27.1,3
Junia [Iounias], Ro.16.7
Jupiter [Zeus], Act.14,12,13
[Diopetēs]
Act.19.35. *which fell down from* J.
Justus [Ioustos],Act.1.23; 18.7;Col.4.11
Lamech, Lu.3.36
Laodicea [Laodikeia]
Col. 2. 1. for them at L.; 4.13,15
4.16. read the epistle from L.
Rev. 1.11. Philadelphia, and unto L.
Laodiceans[Laodikeus],Col.4.16,Rev.
3.14
Lasea [Lasaia], Act.27.8
Latin [Rōmaïkos], Lu.23.38
[Rōmaïsti], Jo.19.20
Lazarus [Lazaros]
Lu. 16.20. certain beggar named L. ;
23,24,25
Jo. 11. 1. La. of Bethany;2.5,11,14,43
12. 1. where L. was ; 2,9,10,17
Lebbæus [Lebbaios], Mat.10.3
Levi[Leui],Lu.3.24,29; Heb.7.5,9; Rev.
7.7
[Leuis], Mar. 2.14; Lu.5.27,29
Levite [Leuitēs],Lu.10.32; J o.1.19;Act
4.36
Levitical [Leuitikos], Heb.7.11
Libertines [Libertinos], Act.6.9
Libya [Libua], Act.2.10
Linus [Linos], [2]Ti.4.21
Lois [Lōïs], [2]Ti.1.5
Lot [Lōt]
Lu. 17.28. in the days of L.
29. day that L. went out of
32. Remember L.'s wife
[2]Pet. 2. 7. delivered just L.
Lucas [Loukas], Phile.24

Lucius [Loukios], Act.13.1; Ro.16.21
Luke [Loukas], Col.4.14; [2]Ti.4.11
Lycaonia [Lukaonia], Act.14.6
[*See Speech.*]
Lycia [Lukia], Act.27.5
Lydda [Ludda], Act.9.32 ; 35.38
Lydia [Ludia], Act.16.14,40
Lysanias [Lusanias], Lu.3.1
Lysias [Lysias]
Act.23.26. Claudius L. unto the most
24. 7, 22. the chief captain L.
Lystra [Lustra]
Act.14. 6. fled unto L. and Derbe;
8,21; 16.1,2; [2]Ti.3.11
Maath, Lu.3.26
Macedonia [Makedōn]
Act.16. 9. There stood a man of M.;
19.29; [2]Co.9.2,4
[Makedonia]
Act.16.12. of that part of M.
Ro. 15.26. it hath pleased them of M.
[2]Co. 1.16. come again out of M.
8. 1. bestowed on the chu. of M.
[1]Th. 1. 7. all that believe in M.; 8
4.10. brethr. which are in all M.
Into Macedonia
Act.16.9,10; 19.22; 20.1; [2]Co.1.16; 2.13;
7.5; [2]Ti.1.3
From Macedonia
Act.18.5; [2]Co.11.9; Phi.4.15
Through Macedonia
Act.19.21; 20.3; [1]Co.16.5
Macedonian [Makedōn], Act.27.2
Madian [Madian], Act.7.29
Magdala [Magdala], Mat.15.39
Magdalene [Magdalēnē]
Mat.27.56, 61. Mary M.; 28.1; Mar.15.
40,47; 16.1,9; Lu.8.2; 24.
10; Jo.19.25; 20.1,18
Magog [Magōg], Rev.20.8
Malchus [Malchos], Jo.18.10
Maleleel [Maleleēl], Lu.3.37
Manaen, Act.13.1
Manasses [Manassēs], Mat.1.10; Rev
7.6
Marcus [Markos], Col.4.10; Phile.24;
[1]Pet.5.13
Mark [Markos], Act.12.12,15; 15.37,39;
[2]Ti.4.11
Mars-hill [Areios-Pagos], Act.17.22
Martha
Lu. 10.38. certain woman named M.
40. M. was cumbered about
41. said unto her, M., M.
Jo. 11. 1. town of Mary and..M.;
5,19,20,21,24,30,39
12. 2. made him a supper; and M.
Mary [Maria or Mariam]
Mat. 1.16, 18, 20. the husband of M.
2.11. the young child with M.
13.55. his mother called M.
27.56. M. mother of James; Mar.
16.1; Lu.24.10
61. the other M.; 28.1
Mar. 6. 3. carpenter, the son of M.
15.40. and M. the mother of Jam
47. M. the mother of Joses
Lu. 1.27. virgin's name was M.
30. Fear not, M.; 34,38,39,41,
46,56
2. 5, 16. M. his espoused wife
19. M. kept all these things
34. M. his mother; Act.1.14
10.39. a sister called M.
42. M. hath chosen that good
Jo. 11. 1, 2, 19. the town of M.

331

Jo. 11.20. M. sat still in the house;
28,31,32,45
12. 3. took M. a pound of ointm.
19.25. M. the wife of Cleophas
20.16. Jesus saith unto her, M.
Act.12.12. came to the house of M.
Ro. 16. 6. Greet M., who bestowed

Mathusala [Mathousala], Lu.3.37
Mattatha, Lu.3.31
Mattathias, Lu.3.25,26
Matthan, Mat.1.15
Matthat, Lu.3.24,29
Matthias, Act.1.23,26
Matthew [Matthaios], Mat.9.9; 10.3;
Mar.3.18; Lu.6.15; Act.1.13
Medes [Mēdos], Act.2.9
Melchi, Lu.3.24,28
Melchisedec [Melchisedek],
Heb.5.6. after the order of M.; 10;
6.21; 7.1,10,11,15,17,21
Melea [Meleas], Lu.3.31
Melita [Melitē], Act.28.1
Menan [Mainan], Lu.3.31
Mercurius [Hermēs], Act.14.12
Mesopotamia, Act.2.9; 7.2
Messias, Jo.1.41; 4.25
Michael [Michaēl], Jude 9 ; Rev.12.7
Miletum [Milētos], 2Ti.4.20
Miletus [Milētos], Act.20.15,17
Mitylene [Mitulēnē], Act.20.14
Mnason [Mnasōn], Act.21.16
Moloch, Act.7.43
Moses [Mōseus Mōūsēs Mōsēs]
Mat. 8. 4. M.commanded; 19.7; Mar.
1.44; 10.3; Lu.5.14; Jo.8.5r.
17. 3. unto them M. and ; Mar.9.
4,5; Lu.9.30
4. one for M. ; Lu.9.33
23. 2. Pharisees sit in M-s seat
Mar.12.26. in the book of M.
Lu. 2.22. law of M.;Lu.24.44;Jo.7.23;
Act.13.39 ; 15.5 ; 28.23 ;
1Co.9.9 ; Heb.10.28
16.29, 31. M. and the ; Act.26.22
Jo. 1.17. law was given by M.
3.14. M. lifted up the serpent
5.45, 46. M. in whom ye trust
Ro. 5.14. death..from Adam to M.
2Co. 3. 7. behold the face of M.
3.13, 15. M. which put a vail
Heb.11.23, 24. By faith Moses, when
Jude   9. about the body of M.
Rev.15. 3. the song of M.
(Also) **Mat.**19.8; 22.24. **Mar.**7.10;
10.4 ; 12.19. **Lu.**20.28,37 ; 24.27. **Jo.**
1.45 ; 6.32 ; 7.19,22 ; 9.28,29. **Act.**3.22;
6.11,14;7.20,22,29,31,32,35,37,40,44;15.1,
21; 21,21. **Ro.**9.15; 10.5,19. 1Co.10.2 ;
2Ti.3.8. **Heb.**3.2,3,5,16;7.14; 8.5 ; 9.19 ;
21.21.
Naaman [Neēman], Lu.4.27
Naasson [Naassōn], Mat.1.4 ; Lu.3.32
Nachor [Nachōr], Lu.3.34
Nagge [Nanggai], Lu.3.25
Nain [Nain], Lu.7.11
Narcissus [Narkissos], Ro.16.11
Nathan, Lu.3.31
Nathaniel [Nathanaēl], Jo.1.45,46,47,
48,49; 21.2
Naum [Naoum], Lu.3.25
Nazarene [Nazōraios], Mat.2.23; Act.
24.5.
Nazareth
Mat. 2.23. a city call. N.; Lu.1.24,26
332

Mat. 4.13. leaving N. he; Mar.1.9
21.11. prophetof N.; Jo.1.45; Act
10.38
Lu. 2.39. their own city N.
51. came to N.: 4.16
Jo. 1.46. good thing come out of N.
[Nazōraios]
Mat.26.71. Jesus of N.; Mar.10.47; Lu.
18.37 ; 24.19 ; Jo.18.5,7 ;
19.9; Act.2.22 ; 3.6; 4.10;
6.14; 22.8; 26.9
[Nazarēnos]
Mar. 1.24. Jesus of N.; 14.67;16.6; Lu.
4.34
Neapolis, Act.16.11
Nephthalim[Nephthaleim],Mat.4.13,
15; Rev.7.6
Nereus [Nēreus], Ro.16.15
Neri [Nēri], Lu.3.27
Nicanor [Nikanōr], Act.6.5
Nicodemus [Nikodēmos], Jo.3.1,4,9;
7.50; 19.39
Nicolaitanes [Nikolaites], Rev.2.6,15
Nicolas [Nikolaos], Act.6.5
Nicopolis [Nikopolis], Tit.3.12
Niger, Act.13.1
Nineve [Nineui], Lu.11.32
[Ninueitēs], Mat.12.41
Ninevites [Nineuites], Lu.11.30
Noah [Nōe], Heb.11.7; 1Pet.3.20; 2Pet.
2.5
Noe [Nōe], Mat.24.37,38; Lu.3.36; 17.
26,27
Nymphas [Numphas], Col.4.15
Obed [Obēd], Mat.1.5; Lu.3.32
Olympas [Olumpas], Ro.16.15
Onesimus[Onēsimos],Col.4.9; Phile.10
Onesiphorus [Onēsiphoros], 2Ti.1.16;
4.19
Osee [Osēe], Ro.9.25
Ozias, Mat.1.8,9
Pamphylia[Pamphulia],Act.2.10;13.13
14.24 ; 15.38 ; 27.5
Paphos, Act.13.6,13
Parmenas, Act.6.5
Parthians [Parthos], Act.2.9
Patara, Act.21.1
Patmos, Rev.1.9
Patrobas, Ro.16.14
Paul [Paulos]
Act.13. 9. Saul, who also is called P.
14.12. called P. Mercurius, beca.
14. apostles, Barnabus and P.
19. and having stoned P., drew
15.40. P. chose Silas, and depart.
16. 3. Him would P. have to go
9. a vision appeared to P. in
25. at midnight P. and Silas
17.22. Then P. stood in the midst
19.15. Jesus I know, and P. I
21.11. he took P.'s girdle, and
40. P. stood on the stairs, and
22.28. P. said, but I was free born
23.11. Be of good cheer, P.
24.27. left P. bound
26. 1. Agrippa said unto P.
24. P., thou art beside thyself
28. 3. P. had gathered a bundle
16. P. was suffered to dwell
1Co. 1.12. I am of P., and I ; 3.4
13. was P. crucified for you
(Also) **Act.**13.13,16,43,45,46,50 ; 14.9,
11; 15.2, bis, 12, 22, 25,35,36,38 ; 16.14,

17,18,19,28,29,36,37 ; 17.2,4,10, 13,14,
15, 16, 33; 18.1, 5,9, 12, 14, 18; 19.1, 4,
6,11,13,21,26,29,30; 20.1,7,9,10,13,16,37;
21.4,8,13,18,26,29,30,32,37,39 ; 22.25,30 ;
23.1,3,5,6,10,12,14,16,bis,17,18,20,24,31,
33 ; 24.1,10,23,24,26 ; 25.2, 4, 6, 7, 9, 10,
14,19, 21, 23 ; 26.1, 28, 29 ; 27.1, 3,
9,11,21,24,31,33,43 ; 28.8,15, 17, 25, 30 ;
Ro.1.1. 1Co.1.1 ; 3.4,5, 22 ; 16.21 ;
2Co.1.1: 10.1. **Gal.**1.1; 5.2. **Eph.**1.1;
3.1. **Phi.**1.1. **Col.**1.1,23; 4.18. 1Th.
1.1; 2.18. 2Th.1.1 ; 3.17. 1Ti.1.1
2Ti.1.1. **Tit.**1.1. **Phile.**1,9,19. 2Pet.
3.15.
Perga [Pergē], Act.13.13,14; 14.25
Persis, Ro.16.12
Peter [Petros]
Mat. 4.18. Simon called P.; 10.2 Mar.
3.16 ; Lu.6.14
8.14. was come into P.'s house
16.18. That thou art P.
17. 1. P., James, and John; Mar.
9.2; 13.3; 14.33; Lu.8.21;
9.28. Act.1.13
26.69. Now P. sat without ; Mar.
14.66 ; Lu 22.35
75. And P. remembered; Mar.
14 72 ; Lu.22.61
Mar. 8.32, 33. P. to rebuke him
14.67. when she saw P. warming
16. 7. tell his disciples and P.
Jo. 18.10. Simon P. having a sword
26. whose ear P. cut off
Act. 1.15. in those days P. stood up
3. 1. P. and John went up
4.13. the boldness of P. & John
5.15. the shadow of P. passing
10.13. Rise, P. : kill, and eat
12. 3. proceeded furth. to take P.
7. smote P. on the side
14. she knew P.'s voice
Gal. 1.18. to Jerusalem to see P.
2. 7. circumcision was unto P.
8. wrought effectually in P.
10. P. was come to Antioch
14. before them all
(Also) **Mat.**14.28,29; 15.15; 16 16,22,
23 ; 17.4,24,26 ; 18.21 ; 19.27; 26.33,35,
37,40,58,73. **Mar.**5.37; 8.29; 10.28;
11.21; 14.29,37,54,70. **Lu.**5.8; 8.45;
9.20,32,33 ; 12.41; 18.28 ; 22.8,34,54,58,
60,61,62; 24.12. **Jo.**1.40,44; 6.8,68; 13.6,
8,9,24,36,37;18.11,15,16,bis,17,18,25,27;
20.2, 3, 4, 6; 21.2, 3, 7, bis, 11, 15, 17, 20,
21. **Act.** 2.14, 37,38 ; 3.3,4, 6, 11, 12 ;
4.8,19; 5.3,8,9,29; 8.14,20; 9.32,34,38,
39, 40, bis; 10.5, 9, 14,17,18,19,21,23,25,
26,32, 34,44,45,46; 11.2,4,7,13 ; 12.5,6,
11,13,16,18; 15.7. 1Pet.1.1. 2Pet.1.1
Phalec [Phalek], Lu.3.35
Phanuel [Phanouēl], Lu.2.36
Pharaoh [Pharaō], Act.7.10,13,21;Ro.
9.17 ; Heb.11.24
Phares, Mat.1.3; Lu.3.33
Pharisee [Pharisaios] (See Sadducees)
Mat. 9.14. the P. fast oft ; 2.18
23. 2. The scribes and the P-s sit
13. woe unto you, scr.and P-s;
14,15,23,25,27,29,Lu.11.42,43,44
26. Thou blind ,P., cleanse
Mar. 8.15. the leav. of the P.;Lu.12.1
Lu. 7.36. he went into the P.'s hou.
11.39. ye P-s make clean the out.
53. the P-s began to urge him
Jo. 1.24. sent were of the P-s
3. 1. of the P-s, named Nicod.
Act. 5.34. a P., named Gamaliel
15. 5. the P-s which believed
23. 6, 7, 8, 9. Sad. and other P-s

Act 23. 6. I am a P., the son of a P.
  26. 5. our religion I lived a P.
Phi. 3. 5. touching the law, a P.
(Also) **Mat**.5.20; 9.11,34; 12.2,14,24,
38; 15 1, 12; 19.3; 21.45; 22.15,34, 41;
27.62. **Mar**.2.16, 24; 3.6; 7.1,3,5; 8.11;
10.2; 12.13. **Lu**.5.17, 21, 30,33; 6.2,7;
7.30,36,39; 11.37,53; 13.31; 14.1,3; 15.2;
16.14; 17.10; 19.39. **Jo**.4.1; 7.32, *bis,*
45,47,48; 8.3,13; 9.13, 15, 16, 40; 11.46,
47,57; 12.19,42; 18.3

Phebe [Phoibe], Ro.16.1
Phenice [Phoinike] Act.11.19 ; 15.3
    [Phoinix], Act.27.12
Phenicia [Phoinike], Act.21.2
Philadelphia, Rev. 1.11 ; 3.7
Philemon [Philemon], Phile.1
Philetus [Philetos], ²Ti.2.17
Philip [Philippos]
  Mat.10. 3. P., and Barth.; Lu.6.14
    14. 3. brother P.'s wife ;Mar.6.17
              Lu.3.19
  Lu. 3. 1. P. tetrarch of Ituræa
  Jo. 1.43, 44, 45, 46, 48. findeth P.
    6. 5, 7. he saith unto P., When.
    12.21, 22. came therefore to P.
    14. 8, 9. P. saith unto him
  Act. 1.13. and Andrew, P. and; 6.5
    8. 5, 6. Then P. went down to
    29. Then the Spi. said unto P.
    30. And P. ran thither to
         31, 34, 35, 37, 38, 39, 40
    21. 8. house of P. the evangelist
(Also) **Mar**.3.18. **Act**.8.6,12,13,26

Philippi [Philippos]. Mat.16.13; Mar.
  8.27; Act.16.12; 20.6; Phi.1.1 ; ¹Th.
  2.2
Philippians [Philippesios], Phi.4.15.
Philologus [Philologos], Ro.16.15
Phlegon [Phlegon], Ro.16.14
Phrygia [Phrugia],Act.2.10; 16.6;18.23
Phygellus [Phugellos], ²Ti.1.15
Pilate [Pilatos]   [Mar.15.1
  Mat.27. 2. delivered him to Pont. P.
    24. When P. saw that he cou.
    58. to P., and begged the body
  Mar.15. 2. P. asked him, Art thou
  Lu. 13. 1. whose blood P. had ming.
    23.12. P. and Herod were made
    24. And P. gave sentence that
  Jo. 18.35. P. answered, Am I a Jew
    38. P. saith unto him,What is
    19.19. And P. wrote a title, and
  Act. 3.13. the presence of P.; 4.27
    13.28. yet desired they P.
  ¹Ti. 6.13. before PontiusP.witnessed
(Also) Mat.27.13, 17,22,62,65. Mar.
16.4,5,9,12,14,15, 43, 44. **Lu**.3.1; 23.1,
3,4,6,11, 13,20,52. **Jo**.18.29,31,33, 37,
19.1,4,6,8,10,12,13,15,21,22,31,38

Pisidia, Act.13.14 ; 14.24
Pollux, see *Castor*
Pontius, see *Pilate*
Pontus [Pontos], Act. 2.9; ¹Pet.1.1
    [Pontikos],*born in* P.;Act.18.2
Porcius [Porkios], Act.24.27
Prisca [Priska], ²Ti.4.19
Priscilla [Priskilla], Act.18.1,18,26;
  Ro.16.3; ¹Co.16.19
Prochorus [Prochoros], Act.6.5
Ptolemais [Ptolemais], Act.21.7
Publius [Poplios], Act.28.7,8
Pudens [Poudes], ²Ti.4.21
Puteoli [Putioloi], Act.28.13

Quartus [Kouartos], Ro.16.23
Rachab, Mat.1.5
Rachel [Rachel], Mat. 2.18
Ragau, Lu.3.35
Rahab [Raab], Heb.11.31 ; Jas. 2.25
Rama, Mat.2.18
Rebecca [Rebekka], Ro. 9.10
Red Sea [Eruthra Thalassa], Act.7.36;
  Heb.11.29
Remphan, Act.7.43
Reuben [Rouben], Rev.7.5
Rhegium [Region], Act.28.13
Rhesa [Resa], Lu.3.27
Rhoda [Rode], Act.12.13
Rhodes [Rodos], Act.21.1
Roboam, Mat.1.7
Roman [Romaios]
  Jo. 11.48. the R-s shall come and take
  Act.16.21. neither to obser., being R-s
    37. uncondemned, being R-s
    38. that they were R-s; 23.27
    22.25. 26, 27, 29, that is a R.
    25.16. not the manner of the R-s
    28.17. into the hands of the R-s
Rome [Rome]
  Act. 2.10. strangers of R., Jews
    18. 2. all Jews to depart from R.
    19.21. I must also see R.
    23.11. thou bear witn. also at R.
    28.14. and so we went toward R.
    16. And when we came to R.
(Also) **Ro**. 1.7,15. **²Ti**.1.17

Rufus [Rouphos], Mar.15.21; Ro.16.13
Ruth [Routh], Mat.1.5
Sadducees [Saddoukaios]
  Mat. 3. 7. Phari. and S.;16.1;Act.23.7
    16. 6, 11, 12.the leaven of the..S.
    22.23, 34. came to him the S.;
           Mar.12.18; Lu.20.27
  Act. 4. 1. S. came upon them; 5.17
    23. 6, 7, 8. the one part were S.
Sadoc [Sadok], Mat.1.14
Sala, Lu.3.35
Salathiel [Salathiel],Mat.1.12;Lu.3.27
Salamis, Act.13.5
Salem [Salem], Heb.7.1,2
Salim [Saleim], Jo.3.23
Salmon [Salmon], Mat.1.4,5; Lu.3.32
Salmone [Salmone], Act.27.7
Salome [Salome], Mar.15.40; 16.1
Samaria [Samareia]
  Lu. 17.11. midst of S. and Galilee
  Jo. 4. 4, 5. needs go through S.
    7, 9. a woman of S.
  Act. 1. 8. and in S.; 8.1; 9.31; 15.3
    8. 5. Philip went..city of S.
    9. bewitched the people of S.
    14. S. had received the word
      [Samareitis], Jo.4.9
Samaritan [Samareites]
  Mat.10. 5. city of the S-s
  Lu. 9.52. village of the S-s ; Act.8.25
    10.33. But a certain S.
    17.16. and he was a S.
  Jo. 4.39, 40. And many of the S-s
    8.48. thou art a S., and hast a
Samothracia [Samothrake],Act.16.11
Samos, Act.20.15
Samson [Sampson], Heb.11.32
Samuel [Samouel], Act.3.24; 13.20;
  Heb.11.32
Sapphira [Sappheira], Act.5.1.

Sara, *or* **Sarah** [Sarra], Ro.4.19 ; **9.9.**
  Heb.11.11. ¹Pet.3.6
Sardis [Sardeis], Rev.1.11
Sarepta, Lu.4.26
Saron [Saron], Act.9.35
Saruch [Sarouch], Lu.3.35
Satan, ²Co.12.7
  [Satanas.]
  Mat. 4.10. Get thee hence, S.
    12.26. S. cast out S. ; Mar.3.23;
           Lu.11.18
    16.13. behind me, S. ; Mar.8.33 ;
           Lu.4.8
  Mar. 1.13. forty days, tempted of S.
    26. And if S. rise up against
    4.15. S. cometh immediately
  Lu. 10.18. I beheld S. as lightning
    13.16. whom S. hath bound
    22. 3. entered S. into ; Jo.13.27
    31. S. hath desired to have you
  Act. 5. 3. Ananias, why hath S.
    26.18. from the power of S.
  Ro. 16.20. bruise S. under your feet
  ¹Co. 5. 5. unto S. for the destruction
    7. 5. that S. tempt you; ²Co.2.11
  ²Co. 11.14. S. himself is transformed
  ¹Th. 2.18. but S. hindered us
  ²Th. 2. 9. after the working of S.
  ¹Ti. 1.20. I have delivered unto S,
    5.15. turned aside after S.
  Rev. 2. 9. the synagogue of S. ; 3.9
    13. S.'s seat is..S. dwelleth
    24. known the depths of S.
    12. 9. the Devil, and S. ; 20.2
    20. 7. S. shall be loosed
Saul [Saoul]
  Act. 9. 4. S., S., why prosecutest
          22.7 ; 26.14
    17. Brother S. ; 22.13
    13.21. S. the son of Cis.
    [Saulos.]
  Act. 7.58. whose name was S.
    8. 1. And S.was consenting unto
    3. As for S., he made havock
    9. 1. S., yet breathing out threa.
    8. S. arose from the earth; 11,
        19,22,24,26
    11.25. for to seek S. ; 30
    12.25. And Barnabas and S.
    13. 1. Herod the tetrarch, and S.
    2, 7. me Barnabas and S.
    9. S., who also is called Paul
Sceva [Skeuas], Act.19.14
Scythian [Skuthes], Col.3.11
Secundus [Sekoundos], Act.20.4
Selucia [Seleukia], Act.13.4
Semei, Lu.3.26
Sergius Paulus [Sergios Paulos],Act.
Sem [Sem], Lu.3.36   [13.7
Seth [Seth], Lu.3.38
Sidon [Sidon]
  Mat.11.21. in Tyre and S.; Lu.10.13
    22. to. for Tyre and S.; Lu.10.4
    15.21. the coasts of Tyre and S.;
           Mar.3.8; 7.24
  Mar. 7.31. co. of Tyre and S.; Lu.6.17
  Lu. 4.26. Sarepta, a city of S.
  Act.27. 3. we touched at S.
    [Sidonios], *of* S. ; Act.12.20
Silas
  Act.15.22. Barsabas and S., chief
    27, 32, 34. Judas and S., who
    40. And Paul chose S., and
    16.19. they caught Paul and S.
    25, 29. Paul and S. prayed, and
    17. 4. consort. with Paul and S.
    10, 14, 15. away Paul and S.
    18. 5. when S. and Timotheus

Siloam [Silōam], Lu.13.4; Jo.9.7,11
Silvanus [Silouanos], ²Co.1.19; ¹Th.1.1; ²Th.1.1; ¹Pet.5.12
Simeon [Sumeōn]
  Lu. 2.25, 34. whose name was S.
    3.30. the son of S.; Rev.7.7
  Act.13. 1. and S. that was called Ni.
    15.14. S. hath declared how God
Simon [Simōn]
  Mat. 4.18. S. called Peter ; 10.2; Mar. 3.16; Lu.6.14
    10. 4. S. the Canaanîte; Mar.3.18
    16.17. Blessed art thou, S. Bar-J.
    17.25. What thinkest thou, S.
    26. 6. house of S. the; Mar.14.3
    27.32. S. by name; Mar.15.21; Lu. 23.26
  Mar.1.30. But S.'s wife's mo.; Lu.4.38.
    6. 3. of Juda, and S.
    14.37. S., sleepest thou
  Lu. 5. 3. ships, which was S.'s
    4. said unto S., Launch out
    6.15. S. called Zelotes ; Act.1.13
    7.40. S., I have somewhat to say
    22.31. S., S., Satan hath de.
  Jo. 6.71. Judas son of S.; 21.15,16,17
    13.36. S. Peter said unto him, Lo.
    18.10. S. Peter having a sword
    15. And S. Peter followed Jes.
  Act. 8. 9, 13, 18, 24. man, called S.
    9.43. S. a tanner; 10.5,6,17,18, 32; 11.13
  (Also) Mat.13.55; 16.16. Mar.1.16, 29,36; 6.3. Lu.5.5,8,10,*bis*; 6.14; 7.43, 44; 24.34. Jo.1.40,41,42; 6.8,68; 12.4; 13.2,6,9,24,26,36; 18.25; 20.2,6;21.2,3,7, 11
    [Sumeōn], ²Pet.1.1
Sina *or* **Sinai** [Sina], Act.7.30,38; Gal. 4.24,25
Sion [Siōn]
  Mat.21. 5. ye the dau. of S.; Jo.12.15
  Ro. 9.33. I lay in S. a; ¹Pet.2.6
    11.26. come out of S. the Deliver.
  Heb.12.22.come unto mount S.
  Rev.14. 1. Lamb stood on mount S.
Smyrna [Smurna], Rev.1.11
    [Smurnaios], *in* S. ; Rev.2.8
Sodom [Sodoma]
  Mat.10.15. tolerab. for the land of S.;
    11.23,24; Mar.6.11; Lu.10.12
  Lu. 17.29. day that Lot went out of S.
  ²Pet. 2. 6. S. and Gomorrha; Jude 7
  Rev.11. 8. spiritually is called S. and
Sodoma, Ro.9.29
Solomon [Solomōn]
  Mat. 1. 6. and Dav. the king begat S.
    7. And S. begat Roboam
    6.29. even S. in all his; Lu.12.27
    12.42. the wisdom of S.; Lu.11.31
  Jo. 10.23. in S.'s por.; Act.3.11; 5.12
  Act. 7.47. S. built him an house
Sopater [Sōpatros], Act.20.4
334

Sosipater [Sōsipatros], Ro.16.21
Sosthenes [Sōsthenēs], Act .18.17; ¹Co.1.1
Spain [Spania], Ro.15.24,28
Stachys [Stachus], Ro.16.9
Stephanas, ¹Co.1.16; 16.15,17
Stephen [Stephanos]
  Act. 6. 5, 8, 9. and they chose S.
    7.59. And they stoned S.; 8.2
    11.19. persec. that arose about S.
    22.20. the blood of thy martyr S.
Stoicks [Stōikos], Act.17.18
Susanna [Sousanna],Lu.8.3
Sychar [Suchar], Jo.4.5
Sychem [Suchem], Act.7.16
Syntyche [Suntuchē], Phi.4.2
Syria [Suria]
  Mat. 4.24. throughout all S.;Act.15.23
  Lu. 2. 2. Cyren. was governor of S.
  Act.15.41. went through S.; 18.18 ; 20.3; 21.3; Gal.1.21
Syrian [Suros], Lu.4.27
Syrophenician [Surophonnissa], Mar.7.26
Syracuse [Surakousai], Act.28.12
Tabitha [Tabitha], Act.9.36,40
Tarsus [Tarsos], Act.9.30 ; 11.25; 22.3
    [Tarseus], Act.9.11 ; 21.39
Tertius [Tertios], Ro.16.22
Tertullus [Tertullos], Act.24.1,2
Thaddeus [Thaddaios], Mat.10.3 ; Mar.3.18
Thamar, Mat.1.3
Thara, Lu.3.34
Theophilus [Theophilos], Lu.1.3 ; Act.1.1
Thessalonica [Thessalonikē]
  Act.17.1,11,13; Phi.4.16; ²Ti.4.10
    [Thessalonikeus], Act.27.2
Thessalonian [Thessalonikeus]
  Act.20.4 ; ¹Th.1.1; ²Th.1.1
Theudas [Theudas], Act.5.36
Thomas [Thōmas]
  Mat.10. 3. T., and Matthew ; Lu.6.15
  Mar. 3.18. T., and James the son of
  Jo. 20.29. T., beccause thou hast
  (Also) Jo.11.16; 14.5; 20.24,26,27,28; 21.2 ; Act.1.13
Thyatira [Thuateira],Act.16.14; Rev. 1.11 ; 2.18,24
Tiberias, Jo.6.1,23 ; 21.1
Tiberius [Tiberaios], Lu.3.1
Timeus [Timaios], Mar.10.46
Timon [Timōn], Act.6.5
Timotheus
  Act.16. 1. disciple was there nam. T.;
    17.14,15; 18.5; 19.22; 20.4
  Ro. 16.21. T. my workfellow

¹Co. 4.17. sent unto you T.; 16.10.
²Co. 1.19. by me and Silvanus and T.
Phi. 1. 1. Paul and T.; Col.1.1; ¹Th. 1.1; 3.2,6; ²Th.1.1
    2.19. to send T. shortly unto
Timothy [Timotheus]
  ²Co. 1. 1. and T. our brother; ²Ti.1.2 Phile. 1
  ¹Ti. 1. 2, 18. Unto T. my own ; 6.20
  Heb.13.23.T. is set at liberty
Titus [Titos]
  ²Co. 2.13. I found not T.; 7.6
    7.13. joyed we for the joy of T.; 14 ; 8.6,16,23 ; 12.18
    12.18. Did T. make a gain of you
  (Also), Gal.2.1,3. ²Ti.4.10. Tit.1.4
Trachonitis [Trachōnitis], Lu.3.1
Troas [Trōas]
  Act.16. 8, 11. came down to T.; 20.6; ²Co.2.12
    20. 5. tarried for us at T.
  ²Ti. 4.13. cloke that I left at T.
Trogyllium [Trogullion], Act.20.15
Trophimus [Trophimos], Act.20.4 ; 21.29; ²Ti.4.20
Tryphena [Truphaina], Ro.16.12
Tryphosa [Truphōsa], Ro.16.12
Tychicus [Tuchikos], Act.20.4
Tyrannus [Turannos], Act.19.9; Eph. 6.21; Col.4.7 ; ²Ti.4.12 ; Tit.3.12
Tyre [Turos], Lu.6.17 ; Act.21.3,7
    [Turios], of Tyre, Act.12.20
    (See *Sidon*.)
Urbane [Ourbanos], Ro.16.9
Urias [Ouraios], Mat.1.6
Wormwood [Apsinthos], Rev.8.11
Zabulon [Zaboulōn], Mat.4.13,15 ; Rev.7.8
Zaccheus [Zakchaios], Lu.19,2,5,8
Zacharias
  Mat.23.35.unto the blood of Z.
  Lu. 1. 5. priest named Z.; 12,13
    18. Z. said unto the angel
    21. the people waited for Z.
    40. entered into the hou. of Z.
    59. they called him Z.
    67. his father Z. was filled
    3. 2. son of Z. in the wilderness
    11.51. unto the blood of Z.
Zara, Mat.1.3
Zebedee [Zebedaios]
  Mat. 4.21. the son of Z.; 10.2; 26.37; Mar.1.19,20; 3.17; 10.35
  Lu.5.10 ; Jo.21.2
    ship with Z. their father
  0.20. mother of Z.'s child.;27.56
Zelotes [Zēlōtēs], Lu.6.15 ; Act.1.13
Zenas [Zēnas], Tit.3.13
Zerobabel [Zorobabel], Mat.1.12,13; Lu.3.27

GREEK-ENGLISH DICTIONARY
OR
GLOSSARY

NOTICE

The explanations given after every Greek word consist of a collection of all the renderings which are given to it in our English authorised translation, omitting, of course, mere varieties of form, which, if wanted, may be found grouped together in the Concordance, and which, were they reprinted in the Glossary, would only encumber its pages. By turning up in the Concordance, therefore, the English words enumerated in the Glossary, the student may pass under his review every passage in the New Testament in which any Greek word is to be found.

It will be observed that the English explanations are partly in Roman, and partly in italic characters, and that (within parentheses) reference is frequently made to other words which are not true equivalents of the Greek. The explanation is this:—Wherever our authorised version supplies one or more true equivalents, nothing more is needed; but as it frequently happens that the Greek idiom is such as to render it impossible to translate the words literally in English; and as in such cases the English representative of the Greek word cannot be a correct translation; to meet this difficulty, the true equivalent is supplied or interpolated *in italic;* and the abnormal translations are referred to (within parentheses) under the English words in the Concordance, where they are to be found. The Roman words, therefore, are those used in the authorised translation, and found in the Concordance; the italic words are those that are unathorised, being found in neither.

It has not been thought necessary to offer a philologically precise analysis and etymology of the Greek vocables, but as much has been done in that direction as seemed necessary to determine their character and genealogy. The composite words are divided into parts by hyphens, and each of these parts may be found in its place in the Glossary, though perhaps not exactly in the same form; or, when one or more of the parts is so changed as not to be easily recognisable, the normal form is added within brackets. In most cases the root-words and their branches follow each other so closely that no reference is needed from one to the other. It is chiefly when they **are** isolated that this has been supplied.

GLOSSARY

A, α, (*alpha*)=a.

a-, *a prefix generally signifying* "not"
a-barēs [-baros], not burdensome
abba, *a Syriac word, signifying* father
a-bussos [bussos, *bottom*], *an abyss*, the deep. (*See* bottomless)
a-charistos [-charis], unthankful
a-cheiropoiētos, made without hands
achlus, mist
a-chreioō, to make unprofitable
a-chreios [-chreia], unprofitable
a-chrēstos, unprofitable
achri *or* **achris**, until, till, while, as far as, even to, unto. (*See* for, into, in, to)
achthos, *grief. pain*
achuron, chaff.
a-dapanos, without charge
a-dēlos, uncertain. (*See* appear)
a-dēlōs, uncertainly
a-dēlotēs, *uncertainty.* (*See* uncertain)
adelphē, a sister
adelphos, a brother
adelphotēs, brotherhood, the brethren
adēmoneō, to be full of heaviness, to be very heavy
a-diakritos [-diakrinō], without partiality
a-dialeiptos, continual, without ceasing
a-dialeiptōs, *uninterruptedly*, without ceasing
a-diaphthoria, uncorruptness
a-dikēma, *an act of iniquity*, evil-doing, a matter of wrong
a-dikeō, to do wrong, to hurt, to injure, to be an offender, *or* unjust. PAS., to suffer wrong
a-dikia, unrighteousness, wrong, iniquity. (*See* unjust)
a-dikos [-dikē], unjust, unrighteous
a-dikōs, *unjustly*, wrongfully
adō, to sing
a-dokimos, *that has not stood the test*, reprobate, rejected ; a castaway
a-dolos, *without guile*, sincere
a-dunateō, to be impossible
a-dunatos, impotent, weak ; impossible. (*See* possible, can)
aei, ever, always
aēr, the air
aetos, an eagle
agalliaō, to rejoice, rejoice greatly, to be exceeding glad. (*See* joy)
agalliasis, exceeding joy, gladness
a-gamos, unmarried
agan, *very, much, very much*
agan-akteō [-achthos], to be moved with indignation, to be much, *or* sore displeased
agan-aktēsis, indignation
agapaō, to love. PAS. (*also*,) to be beloved, dear [loved, dear
agapē, love, charity, feast of charity. (*See* charitably)
agapētos, beloved, dearly *or* well beloved, dear
agatho-ergeō [-ergon], to do good
agatho-poieō. to do good, to do well
agatho-poiia, well-doing
agatho-poios, one that does well
agathos, good. (*See* benefit, well)
agathōsunē, goodness
age [*imperat. of* agō], go to !
ageirō, *to gather together*
agelē, a herd
a-genealogētos, without descent
a-genēs [-genos], *vulgar*, base

a-gnaphos, new (*spoken of cloth*)
a-gnoēma [agnoeō], an error
a-gnoeo [-ginōskō], not to know, not to understand, to be ignorant. (*See* ignorantly.) PAS., to be unknown
a-gnoia, ignorance
a-gnōsia, ignorance. (*See* knowledge)
a-gnōstos, unknown
agnumi, *to break*
agō, to lead, lead away, bring, carry, bring forth. (*See* go, keep, open, be)
agōgē [agō], manner of life
agōn, a conflict, fight, contention, race
agōnia, *violent effort*, agony
agōnizomai, to strive, fight, labour fervently [a law court
agora, a market place, market, street, [See baser, law)
agoraios, *a lounger*. (*See* baser, law)
agorazō, to buy. (*See* redeem)
agoreuō, *to relate, to make a speech*
agra, *hunting*, a draught of fishes
a-grammatos, unlearned [the fields
agrauleō [agros-aulizomai], to abide in
agreuō, *to hunt*, to catch [tree
agri-elaios, *a field olive*, a wild olive
agrios, wild ; raging
agros, land, a field, country, piece of ground, farm
agrupneō, *to want sleep*, to watch
agrupnia, *sleeplessness*, watching
aichmalōsia, captivity
aichmalōteuō, to lead captive
aichmalōtizō, to bring into captivity (*See* captive)
aichmalōtos, a captive
aïdios [aei], eternal, everlasting
aidōs, reverence, shamefacedness
aigeios, *belonging to a goat*
aigialos, the shore
aineō [ainos], to praise
ainigma, *an enigma.* (*See* darkly)
ainos, praise
aiōn, *duration.* PLU. ages. (*See* world, ever, course, eternal, never, evermore)
aiōnios, eternal, everlasting. (*See* world, ever)
aiphnidios [a-phainō], *unforeseen*, sudden. (*See* unawares)
airō, to take away, carry, remove, bear up, lift. (*See* loose, put, doubt, away)
aischro-kerdēs, greedy of filthy lucre
aischro-kerdōs, for filthy lucre's sake
aischro-logia, filthy communication
aischron, *filthiness*, shame
aischros, filthy
aischrotēs, filthiness
aischunē, shame, dishonesty
aischunomai, to be ashamed
aisthanomai, to perceive
aisthēsis, *perception*, judgment
aisthētērion, the senses
aiteō, to ask, require, crave, beg, desire, call for
aitēma, a request, petition. (*See* require)
aitia, accusation, crime, fault ; cause, case. (*See* wherefore)
aitiama, a complaint
aitiaomai, to accuse
aition, a cause, a fault
aitios, *the prime mover*, author
a-kaireomai, to lack opportunity
a-kairos, out of season
a-kakos, harmless, simple
akantha, a thorn

akanthinos, *made* of thorns
a-karpos, unfruitful, without fruit
a-katagnōstos [-kataginōskō], that cannot be condemned
a-katakaluptos, uncovered
a-katakritos [-katakrinō], uncondemned [endless
a-katalutos [-kataluō], *indissoluble*,
a-katapaustos, that cannot be made *to* cease
a-kataschetos [-katechō], unruly
a-katastasia [-kathistēmi], tumult, commotion, confusion
a-katastatos, unstable
a-katharsia, uncleanness
a-kathartēs, filthiness
a-kathartos [-kathairō], unclean, foul
a-keraios [-kerannumi], *unmixed*, simple, harmless
a-klinēs, *unbending*, without wavering
akmazō, to be fully ripe
akmē, *a point*
akmēn, *at this point of time*, yet
akoē [akouō], hearing, audience ; fame, rumour, report. (*See* hear, preach, ears)
akoloutheō, to follow. (*See* reach)
a-kōlutōs [kōluō], *without hindrance*, no man forbidding
a-kōn [a-hekōn], against the will
akouō, to hear, hearken, give audience, to understand. PAS. (*also*,)to be noised, reported. (*See* audience, hearer, come, ear)
a-krasia, incontinency, excess
a-kratēs [-krateō], incontinent [ture
a-kratos [-kerannumi], without mix-
akribeia, *accuracy*, the perfect manner
akribēs, *exact*
akribestatos, most straitest
akribesteron, more perfectly. (*See* perfect) [gently
akriboō, to inquire *accurately*, diligently
akribōs, *exactly*, perfectly, diligently, circumspectly. (*See* perfect)
akris, a locust
akroaomai, *to hear*
akroatērion, a place of hearing
akroatēs [akroaomai], a hearer
akrobustia, *uncircumcision.* (*See* uncircumcised, circumcise)
akro-gōniaios, chief corner
akron, the tip, uttermost part, top, end
akrothinion, *chief of the heap*, spoil
a-kuroō, to disannul, make of none effect
alabastron, an alabaster box, a box
alalazō, *to shout*, to tinkle, wail
a-lalētos [-laleō], *unutterable.* (*See* utter)
a-lalos [-laleō], dumb
alazōn, a boaster
alazoneia, boasting, pride
aleiphō, to anoint
alektōr, a cock
alektoro-phōnia, cock-crowing
alētheia, truth, verity. (*See* true, truly)
alēthēs, true. (*See* truth, truly)
alētheuō, to speak *or* tell the truth
alēthinos, *genuine*, true
alēthō, to grind
alēthōs [alēthēs], truly, verily, surely, indeed. (*See* surety, truth, very)
aleuron, meal
algos, *pain, distress*

alisgēma, pollution
alla, but, howbeit, nevertheless, save, notwithstanding, yet, moreover. (*See* and, indeed, nay, no, therefore, yea)
allachothen, *from another place*, some other way
allattō *or* **allassō** [allos], to change
allēgoreō [allos-agoreuō], *to allegorise.* *PAS.* to be an allegory
allēlōn [allos], one another, each other, (*See* mutual, together, themselves, other, yourselves)   [alleluia
allēlouia [Hebrew],*praise ye Jehovah,*
allo-genēs [-genos], a stranger
allo-phulos [-phulē],of another nation
allos another, other. (See more, one,
allōs, otherwise   [otherwise, some)
allotrio-episkopos, a busybody in other men's matters
allotrios, another man's, strange, a stranger, an alien. (*See* other)
aloaō, to thresh, tread out corn
aloē, aloes
a-logos, *irrational*, brute; unreason-**alōpex**, a fox   [able
a-lupos, *without grief*
a-lupoteros, less sorrowful
a-lusitelēs, unprofitable
a-machos [-machomai], not a brawler
amaō, to reap down
a-marantinos [-marainō], that fadeth not away
a-marantos, that fadeth not away
a-marturos [-martur], without witness
a-mathēs [-manthanō], unlearned
ameibō, *to exchange*
a-meleō, to make light of, neglect, be negligent. (*See* regard.)
a-memptos [-meinphomai], blameless, unblameable, faultless   [less]
a-memptōs, unblameably. (*See* blame-**amēn** [Hebrew], *truth*, amen, verily
a-merimnos, *without anxiety*, without carefulness. (*See* care, secure)
a-metakinētos [-metakineō],unmove-able
a-metamelētos [-metamelomai],without repentance, not to be repented of
a-metanoētos, impenitent
a-metathetos [-metatithēmi], *unre-moveable*, immutable. *NEU.* immuta-**amethustos**, an amethyst   [bility
a-mētōr [-mētēr], without mother
a-metros [-metron], without measure
a-miantos [-miainō], undefiled
ammos, sand
amnos, a lamb   [quite)
amoibē [ameibō], *a requital.* (*See* a-**a-mōmētos**, blameless, without rebuke
a-mōmos, faultless, without fault, blame, blemish, *or* spot; unblameable
ampelōn, a vineyard
ampelos, a vine
ampel-ourgos [-ergon], a dresser of a vineyard
amphi, *on both sides, round*
amphi-blēstron [-ballō], a net
amphi-ennumi [-hennumi], to clothe
amph-odon [-hodos], *a place* where two ways meet
amphoteros, both
amunomai, to defend
an, *a conditional particle joined to verbs; [distributive when joined to pronouns and adverbs] seldom separately translated.* (*See* wheresoever, whithersoever, if)
an-. (*See* **ana-**
ana, *up to, among;* through, by, in. (*See* a piece, and, every, each)
ana- *or* **an-**, *up to, back, again, strongly*

2

ana-bainō, to go up, ascend, climb, arise, come up, spring up, grow up, enter, rise
ana-ballō, *to put back.* *MID.* to defer
ana-bathmos [anabainō], stairs
ana-bibazō, to *lift up*, to draw
ana-blepō, to look up, to see *again.* (*See* sight)
ana-blepsis, the recovering of sight
ana-boaō, to cry aloud, to cry out
ana-bolē [anaballō], delay
ana-chōreō, to give place, to turn *or* go aside, withdraw, depart
ana-chusis [-cheō], excess
ana-dechomai, to receive
ana-deiknumi, to shew, appoint
ana-deixis, *a manifestation*, shewing
ana-didōmi, *to give up*, to deliver
ana-gennaō, to beget again. *PAS.*, to be born again
ana-ginōskō, *to know well*, to read
ana-gnōrizō, *to recognise.* *PAS.*, to be made known
ana-gnōsis [anaginōskō], a reading
an-agō, to bring up again, to bring, bring forth, lead up, lead, take up. (*See* depart, launch, loose, offer, sail, set)
an-aideia [a-aidōs], *impudence*, importunity
an-aireō [-haireō], to take up *or* away, to put to death, kill, slay
an-airesis [anaireō], *a putting to* death
an-aitios [a-aitia], blameless, guiltless
ana-kainizō, *to make new again*, to
ana-kainoō, to renew   [renew
ana-kainōsis, a renewing
ana-kaluptō, *to uncover*, to open. (*See* take, untaken)
ana-kamptō, to return, turn
ana-kathizō, *to set up;* to sit up
ana-keimai, to sit at meat, to lie, to lean. *PART.*, a guest. (*See* table)
ana-kephalaioō, to gather together in one. *PAS.,* to be briefly comprehended.   [*PAS.* to sit down
ana-klinō, to lay, to make sit down.
ana-koptō, to hinder
ana-krazō, to cry out
ana-krinō, to search, examine, judge, discern, ask questions
ana-krisis [anakrinō], examination
ana-kuptō, to lift up, look up
ana-lambanō, to take, to receive up, to take up, in, *or* unto   [ceived up
analēpsis [analambanō], being re-**an-aliskō** [-haliskō], to consume
ana-logia [-logos], *analogy*, proportion
ana-logizomai,to consider *attentively*
analos [a-hals], that has lost its saltness
ana-lusis, *dissolution*, departure
ana-luō, to dissolve, to depart, return
anamartētos [a-hamartanō], without
ana-menō, to wait for   [sin
ana-mimnēskō, to put in remembrance, to bring *or* call to remembrance. *MID.*, to call to mind, to remember
ana-mnēsis [anamimnēskō], remembrance again
ana-neoō [-neos], to renew
ana-nēphō, *to be sober again*, to recover one's self
an-anggellō [ana-], *to announce*, to declare, tell, rehearse, report, shew. (*See* spoken)
anangkaios [anangkē], necessary. (*See* necessity, near)
anangkaioteros, more needful
anangkastōs, by constraint
anangkazō, to compel, constrain
anangkē, necessity, distress. (*See* necessary, needful, needeth, needs)

anantirrētos [a-anti-ereō], that cannot be spoken against
anantirrētōs, without gainsaying
ana-pauō, to give rest, refresh. *MID.* and *PAS.*, to take rest or ease, to rest
ana-pausis [anapauō], rest
ana-peithō, to persuade
ana-pempō, to send again, to send
anapēros, maimed
ana-phainō, *to shew forth.* *PAS.*, to appear. (*See* discover)
ana-pherō, to bring, carry *or* lead up; to bear, to offer up, to offer
ana-phōneō, to cry out, speak out
ana-piptō, *to lie back*, lean, sit down, sit down to meat   [occupy
ana-plēroō, to fill up, fulfil, supply,
an-apologētos [a-apologeomai], without excuse, inexcusable
ana-psuchō, to refresh
ana-psuxis [anapsuchō], a refreshing
an-aptō [ana-haptō], to kindle
ana-ptussō, *to unroll*, to open
an-arithmētos [a-], innumerable
ana-seio, to stir up, to move   [subvert
ana-skeuazō, *to pack up things*, to
ana-spaō, to draw up, to pull out
ana-stasis [anistēmi], resurrection, rising again from the dead. (*See* rise, raise)
ana-statoō, *to raise sedition*, to turn upside down, make an uproar, to trouble
ana-stauroō, to crucify afresh
ana-stenazō, to sigh deeply
ana-strephō, to overthrow, to return. *MID.*, to live, abide. *PAS.*, to be used, to behave one's self, to have conversation [*i.e. conduct.*] (*See* pass)
anastrophē [anastrephō], *conduct*, conversation
ana-tassomai, to set forth in order
ana-tellō, to make to rise, to arise, to spring. (*See* up, rising)
ana-thallō, to flourish again
ana-thema [anatithēmi], a curse, ana-thema. (*See* accursed)
ana-thēma [anatithēmi], *an offering up*, a gift
ana-thematizō, to curse, to bind under *or* with a curse *or* oath
ana-theōreō, to consider *attentively*, to behold
ana-tithēmi, to communicate, declare
ana-tolē [anatellō], rising, east, day-spring
ana-trephō, to bring up, nourish up
ana-trepō, to overthrow, subvert
an-axios [a-axios], unworthy
an-axiōs [a-axiōs], unworthily
ana-zaō, to live again, be alive again,
ana-zēteō, to seek *earnestly*   [revive
ana-zōnnumi, to gird up   [stir up
ana-zō-pureō, *to kindle up again*, to
andrapodistēs, a man-stealer
andrizomai [anēr], to quit one's self like a man
andro-phonos [anēr-], a manslayer
an-echomai [ana-echō], to bear with endure, suffer, forbear   [speakable
an-ekdiēgētos [a-ekdiēgeomai], un-**an-eklalētos** [a-eklaleō], unspeakable
an-ekleiptos [a-], that faileth not
an-ēkō [-hēkō], to be fit, convenient
anektos [anechomai], *tolerable*
anektoteros, more tolerable
an-eleēmōn [a-], unmerciful
an-ēmeros [a-hēmeros], fierce
anemizomai, *PAS.*, to be driven with the wind
anemos, the wind   [sible
an-endektos [a-endechomai], impos-

an-engklētos [a-engkaleō], unreprovable, blameless   [be ashamed

an-epaischuntos [a-], that need not

an-epilēptos [a-epilambanō], unrebukeable, blameless

anepsios, *a nephew*, a sister's son

anēr, a man, husband. (*See* fellow, sir)

an-erchomai, to go up

an-esis [aniēmi], liberty, rest. (*See* eased)

an-etazō [-hetazō], to examine *by torture* [ture

anēthon, anise

aneu, without

an-euriskō [ana-heuriskō], to find

an-euthetos [a-euthetos], not commodious

an-exereunētos [a-], unsearchable

an-exichniastos [a-exichneuō], past finding out, unsearchable [tient

anexi-kakos [anechomai-kakos], paanggareuō [anggaros], to compel to go

anggaros, *a Persian courier who could* [*compel service*

anggeion, a vessel

anggelia, a message

anggellō, *to announce*

anggelos, a messenger, an angel

angkalē, an arm

angkistron, a hook

angkura, an anchor [bear

an-iēmi [-hiēmi], to loose, leave, forgive

an-ileōs [a-hileōs], without mercy

a-niptos [a-nipto], unwashen

an-istēmi [-histēmi], to raise up, to raise up again, lift up. *ACT. & MID.*, to rise, arise, stand upright

anō, above, up. (*See* brim, high)

an-ochē [an-echomai], forbearance

a-noētos [-noēō], unwise, foolish, a fool

anōgeon, an upper room

a-noia [-noēō], folly, madness

anoigō, to open

an-oikodomeō, to build again

anoixis [anoigō], *an opening*. (*See* open)

a-nomia, transgression of the law, unrighteousness, iniquity. (*See* transgress)

a-nomos, unlawful ; lawless, without law, transgressor, wicked

a-nomōs, without law

an-ōphelēs [a-ōpheleō], unprofitable. *NEU.* unprofitableness

an-orthoō [ana-orthos], to set up, lift up, make straight

an-osios [a-hosios], unholy

anōterikos [anō], upper

anōteron [anō], higher, above

anōthen, from above, from the beginning. (*See* first, top, again)

ant-. (*See* anti)

ant-agōnizomai, to strive against

ant-allagma [-allattō], an exchange

ant-anaplēroō, to fill up

antaō [anti], *to come opposite to*

ant-apodidōmi, to recompense, repay ; to render

ant-apodoma, a recompense

ant-apodosis, reward

ant-apokrinomai, to reply against, to answer again [support

ant-echomai, to hold to, hold fast,

ant-epō, *or* ant-eipon, to say against, gainsay

anth-. (*See* anti-) [stand

anth-istēmi [-histēmi], to resist, with-

anth-omologeō [-homologeō], to give thanks

anthos, a flower [thanks

anthrakia, a fire of coals

anthrax, a coal

anthrōp-areskos, a man pleaser

anthrōpinos, human, man's ; what is common to man. (*See* manner, mankind)

anthrōpo-ktonos[kteinō],a murderer

anthrōpos, *one of mankind*, man. (*See* certain)

anthupateuō, *to fill the office of proconsul.* (*See* deputy)

anthupatos, *proconsul*, deputy

anti, *against, opposite, in exchange for*, in the room of, for

anti-, ant-, anth-, *against, in place of*

anti-ballō, *to exchange.* (*See* have)

anti-christos, antichrist

anti-diatithēmi, to oppose

anti-dikos [-dikē], an adversary

anti-kaleō, *to invite in return*, to bid

anti-kathistēmi, to resist [again

anti-keimai, to oppose, be contrary. *PART.*, adversary

antikru [anti], over against

anti-lambanō *to take in turn. MID.*, to help, support. *PART.*, partaker

anti-legō, to speak against, contradict, answer again, gainsay, deny. *PART.*, gainsayers

anti-lēpsis [anti-lambanō], help

anti-logia, contradiction, gainsaying,

anti-loidoreō, to revile again [strife

anti-lutron, a ransom

anti-metreō, to measure again

anti-misthia, a recompense

anti-parerchomai, to pass by on the

anti-peran, over against [other side

anti-piptō, to resist

anti-strateuomai, to war against

anti-tassomai [-tassō], *MID.*, to oppose one's self, to resist.

anti-thesis [-tithēmi], opposition

anti-tupon, *what corresponds to the type.* (*See* figure)

antlēma, *a bucket*, a thing to draw water with

antleō, to draw, [*as from a well*]

ant-ophthalmeō, *to look in the face*, to bear up into

an-udros [a-hudōr], without water, dry

anuō, *to perform*

an-upokritos [ā-hupokrinō], without hypocrisy *or* dissimulation, unfeigned

an-upotaktos [a-hupotassō], that is not put under, unruly, disobedient

a-oratos [-horaō], invisible

ap-. (*See* apo-)

ap-agō, to lead away, take *or* carry away ; to bring. (*See* death)

a-paideutos [-paideuō], *uneducated*,

ap-airō, to take away, take [unlearned

ap-aiteō, to ask *back* again, to require

ap-algeō [-algos], to be past feeling

ap-allassō [-allatto], *to dismiss*, to deliver. *PAS.*, to depart [an alien

ap-allotrioō, to alienate. *PAS.*, to be

apangchomai, *to strangle one's self*, to hang one's self

ap-anggellō, to bring word again, to report, shew again, tell, declare

ap-antaō, to meet

ap-antēsis, a meeting (*See* meet) [able

a-parabatos [-parabainō], unchange-

a-paraskeuastos [-paraskeuazō], unprepared

ap-archē, first fruits

ap-arneomai, to deny

ap-arti, from henceforth [ing

ap-artismos [-artios],*perfection*,finish-

apataō, to deceive

apatē, deceit, deceitfulness, deceivableness, deceiving. (*See* deceitful)

a-patōr [a-patēr], without father

ap-augasma [apo-augazō], brightness

ap-echei [*impers.*], it is enough

ap-echō, to have, receive, to be

ap-echomai. *MID.*, to have one's self *away*, to abstain

ap-eideō, *or* ap-eidō, to see

apeilē, a threatening. (*See* straitly)

apeileō [apeilē], to threaten

ap-eimi, to be absent

ap-eimi, *to go away*, to go

ap-eipon, *to forbid. MID.*, to renounce

a-peirastos [-peirazō], that cannot be tempted

a-peiros [-peira], *inexperienced*, unskilful

a-peitheia, unbelief, disobedience

a-peitheō, to be unbelieving, *or* disobedient, not to believe, not to obey

a-peithēs [-peithō], *obstinate*, disobedient

ap-ekdechomai, to wait *or* look for

ap-ekduomai, to put off, to spoil

ap-ekdusis, the putting off

ap-elaō [-elaunō], to drive *away*

ap-elegmos [-elengchō], *refutation.* (*See* nought)

ap-eleutheros, a freeman

ap-elpizō, to hope for again

ap-enanti, over against, in presence of, before, contrary

ap-erchomai, to go away, back *or* aside ; to depart, pass away. (*See* come, go, past) [traction

a-perispastōs [-perispaō], without dis-

a-peritmētos [-peritemnō], uncircumcised

aph-. (*See* apo-) [smite off, cut off

aph-aireō [-haireō], to take away,

a-phanēs [-phainō],that is not manifest

a-phanismos [aphanēs], *a disappearing.* (*See* vanish)

a-phanizō, *to make to disappear*, to disfigure, corrupt. *PAS.* to perish, to vanish away [sight

a-phantos, that has vanished out of

aphedrōn, the draught

a-pheidia [-pheidomai], a neglecting

a-phelotēs [-phelleus], *not rough*, singleness

aph-esis [aphiēmi],deliverance,liberty ; forgiveness, remission

aph-iēmi [-hiēmi], to send away, let go, let alone, let be, let have, put away, forgive, remit, lay aside, leave, forsake, omit, suffer, yield up. (*See* cry)

aph-ikneomai [-hikneomai], *to get away from*, to come abroad

a-philagathos, a despiser of the good

a-philarguros, without covetousness, not greedy of filthy lucre

aph-istēmi [-histēmi], to draw away. *ACT. and MID.*, to fall away, withdraw, refrain, depart

aph-ixis [aphikneomai], departure

a-phnō [-phainō], *unexpectedly*, suddenly

a-phobōs, without fear [denly

aph-omoioō [-homoioō], to make like

a-phōnos, dumb, without signification

aph-oraō [-horaō], to look *away*

aph-orizō [-horizō], to divide, sever, separate

aph-ormē, *opportunity*, occasion

aphrizō [aphros], *to froth*, to foam

a-phrōn, unwise, foolish ; a fool

aphros, *foam.* (*See* foam [*verb*])

a-phrosunē [aphrōn], folly, foolishness. (*See* foolishly)

a-phtharsia [aphthartos],immortality, incorruption, sincerity

aphthartos [-phtheirō], incorruptible, uncorruptible, immortal. (*See* corruptible)

aph-upnoō [-hupnos], to fall asleep

a-pisteō [-pisteuō], not to believe

a-pistia, unbelief

a-pistos, unbelieving, faithless, infidel ; incredible, an unbeliever. (*See* believe)

3

apo, from, out of, of, since, after, because of, for. (See ago, at, before, by, forth, hereafter, in, off, on, once, space, upon, with)
apo-, ap-, aph-, from, back, asunder
apo-bainō, to go from, to go out ; to come, turn
apo-ballō, to cast away
apo-blepō, to have respect
apo-blētos [apoballō], cast away, that which is to be refused
apobolē [apoballō], a casting away, loss
apo-chōreō, to depart
apo-chōrizō, to separate. PAS., to depart, depart asunder
apo-chrēsis [-chraomai], the using
apo-dechomai, to accept, receive, receive gladly [prove, approve
apo-deiknumi, to set forth, shew,
apo-deixis [-deiknumi], demonstration
apo-dekatoō, to tythe ; to give, pay, or take tithes
apo-dektos [-dechomai], acceptable
apo-dēmeō, to take a journey, to go or travel into a far country
apo-dēmos, one taking a far journey
apo-didōmi, to repay, restore, requite, recompense, reward, render, deliver again ; pay, give again, perform, sell, yield. (See payment)
apo-diorizō [-dia-horizō], to separate
apo-dochē [-dechomai], acceptation
apo-dokimazō, to reject, disallow
apo-ginomai, to be absent, to be dead
apo-graphē, a catalogue, a taxing
apo-graphō, to write, to tax
apo-kalupsis, manifestation, revelation, appearing. (See coming, lighten,
apo-kaluptō, to reveal [reveal]
apo-karadokia, earnest expectation
apo-katallattō [-katallassō], to reconcile
apo-katastasis [apokathistēmi], restitution [again
apo-kathistēmi, to restore, restore
apo-keimai, to be appointed, laid up. (See appoint, lay)
apo-kephalizō, to behead
apo-kleiō, to shut up
apo-koptō, to cut off
apo-krima [apokrinomai], a judicial answer, a sentence
apo-krinomai, to answer
apo-krisis [apokrinomai], an answer
apo-kruphos, hid, kept secret
apo-kruptō, to hide
apo-kteinō, to kill, slay, put to death
apokueō, to bring forth, beget [back
apo-kulizō [-kuliō], to roll away or
apo-lambanō, to take, receive
apolausis, enjoyment. (See enjoy)
ap-ōleia [apollumi], destruction, perdition, damnation. (See damnable, die, perish, pernicious, waste)
apoleichō, to lick
apo-leipō, to leave. PAS., to remain
ap-ollumi [-ollumi], to destroy. 2. PERF. and MID. and PAS., to perish, to be lost, marred
apolluōn, the destroyer, Apollyon
apo-logeomai [-logos], to make a defence, to answer or speak for one's self, to answer, to excuse
apo-logia, a defence, an answer for or clearing of one's self
apo-louō, to wash away, to wash
apo-luō, to release, set at liberty, loose, let go or depart ; to forgive, dismiss, divorce ; to send or put away. MID., to depart
apo-lutrōsis, redemption, deliverance
apo-massō, MID., to wipe off

apo-nemō, to allot, to give
apo-niptō, to wash [bring
apo-pherō, to carry away, to carry,
apo-pheugō, to escape
apo-phortizomai, to unlade
apo-phthenggomai, to speak forth, to say, to give utterance
apo-piptō, to fall from
apo-planaō, seduce. PAS., to err
apo-pleō, to sail from
apo-plunō, to wash
apo-pnigō, to choke
apo-psuchō [-psuchē], to swoon, to have the heart failing
a-poreomai [-poros], to be without resource, to be perplexed, to doubt, to stand in doubt
a-poria [aporeomai], perplexity
ap-orphanizomai, PAS., to be bereaved, to be taken
apo-rriptō [-riptō], to cast away
apo-skeuazomai, to take away luggage, to take up carriages
apo-skiasma [-skia], a shadow
apo-spaō, to draw away, to draw, withdraw. PAS., to be withdrawn or gotten
apo-stasia [aphistēmi], apostasy, a falling away. (See forsake)
apo-stasion, divorcement, a writing of divorcement
apo-stegazō [-stegē], to uncover
apo-stellō, to send out, forth, or away. (See set, put)
apo-stereō, to keep back by fraud, to defraud. PAS. partic., destitute
apo-stolē, [apostellō], apostleship
apo-stolos [apostellō], he that is sent, a messenger, an apostle
apo-stomatizō [-stoma], to provoke to speak [on the spur of the moment]
apo-strephō, to turn away from, to pervert. (See bring, put)
apo-stugeō, to abhor [gogue
apo-sunagōgos, put out of the synagogue
apo-tassō, to set apart. MID., to bid farewell, to take leave, send away,
apo-teleō, to finish [forsake
apo-thēkē, a barn, a garner
ap-ōtheomai [-ōtheō], to put from
ap-ōthomai [-ōtheō], to thrust away or from ; to put or cast away
apo-thēsaurizō, to lay up in store
apo-thesis [-tithēmi], a putting away or off [to press
apo-thlibō, to press hard on all sides,
apo-thnēskō, to die, to lie a dying,[in a past tense] to be dead or slain. (See death, perish)
apo-tinassō, to shake off
apo-tiō, to repay
apo-tithēmi, to put off or away, to cast off ; to lay down, apart, or aside
apo-tolmaō, to be very bold
apo-tomia [apotemnō], severity
apo-tomōs, sharply. (See sharpness)
apo-trepomai, MID., to turn away
ap-ousia [apo-eimi], absence
a-prositos [-proseimi], which no man can approach
a-proskopos [-proskopē], giving none offence, void of or without offence
a-prosōpolēptōs, without respect of persons
a-pseudēs, that cannot lie [persons
apsinthos, worn wood
a-psuchos [-psuchē], without life
a-ptaistos [-ptaiō], not falling
ara, an imprecation, a cursing
ara, therefore, wherefore, then, so, truly, no doubt, haply, perhaps. (See manner)
ara-ge, wherefore, then, haply

arch-, (See archi-
arch-anggelos [arch-], an archangel
archaios [arch-], old, of old time
archē, the beginning, first, first estate, principles, a principality ; a magistrate ; rule, power ; a corner
arch-ēgos[-hēgeomai], a prince, a captain, an author [chief
archi- or **arch-** [archē], a ruler of, a
arch-ieratikos [archiereus], of the high priest
arch-iereus [arch-hiereus], the high or chief priest, the chief of the priests
archi-poimēn, a chief shepherd
archi-sunagōgos, the ruler or chief ruler of the synagogue
archi-tektōn, a master builder [cans
archi-telōnēs, chief among the publi-
archi-trichlinos, the ruler or governor of the feast
archō, to reign or rule over. MID., to begin, to rehearse from the beginning
archōn, a prince, a ruler, chief, a chief
arēn, a lamb [ruler, a magistrate
areskeia [areskō], a pleasing
areskō, to please [reason
arestos [areskō], pleasing. (See please,
aretē, excellence, courage, virtue, praise
argeō [argos], to loiter, to linger
argos [a-ergon], idle, slow ; barren
argurion, silver, money, a piece of silver
arguro-kopos [-koptō], a silversmith
arguros, silver
argureos [arguros], made of silver,
aristaō [ariston], to dine [silver
aristeros, the left
ariston, dinner
arithmeō, to number
arithmos, a number
arkeō, to suffice, to be sufficient or enough. PAS., to be content
arketos, sufficient, enough. (See suffice)
arktos, a bear
arneomai, to deny, to refuse
arnion, a young lamb, a lamb
arōma, PLU., sweet spices, spices
arotriaō [arotron], to plough
arotron, a plough
arrabōn, a pledge, an earnest
a-rraphos [-raptō], without seam
arrēn, a man
a-rrētos [-reō], unspeakable
a-rrōstos [-rōnnumi], sick, sickly
arsēn, a male, a man
arseno-koitēs, an abuser of himself with mankind. (See defile)
artemōn, a mainsail
arti, now, even now, this present, this hour, this day. (See present, hereafter, hitherto, henceforth)
arti-gennētos, new born
artios, perfect
artizō, to complete
artos, bread, a loaf. (See shewbread)
artuō, to arrange, to season
a-saleutos [-saleuō], which cannot be moved, unmoveable
a-sbestos [-sbennumi], unquenchable. (See quench)
a-schēmōn [-schēma], uncomely
a-schēmoneō, to behave unseemly or uncomely [shame
a-schēmosunē, what is unseemly,
a-sebeia, ungodliness. (See ungodly)
a-sebeō, to live ungodly. (See commit)
a-sebēs [-sebomai], ungodly, an ungodly man [(See filthy)
aselgeia, lasciviousness, wantonness.
a-sēmos [-sēma], undistinguished,
a-sitia, abstinence [mean
a-sitos, without food, fasting

4

askeō, to exercise
askos, *a skin bottle*, a bottle
asmenōs, gladly
a-sophos, *unwise; a fool*
asōtia, excess of riot
asōtōs, *in a riotous manner*
aspasmos, a salutation, greeting
aspazomai, to embrace, salute, greet; to take leave
asphaleia, safety, certainty
asphalēs, safe, sure, certain. *NEU.* certainty
asphalizō, to make fast or sure
asphalōs, safely, assuredly
a-spilos, without spot, unspotted
aspis, an asp
a-spondos [-spondē], implacable, a truce-breaker
assarion, a farthing [worth nearly 1d.]
asson, close by
a-stateō [-histēmi], to have no certain dwelling-place
asteios [astu], elegant, polite, proper, [fair
astēr, a star
a-stēriktos [-stērizō], unstable
a-stheneia, weakness, infirmity, disease, sickness
asthenēma, infirmity
a-stheneō, to be weak, impotent, sick, diseased; to be made weak
a-sthenēs, weak, impotent, feeble, without strength, sick. (*See* weaker, weakness)
astocheō, to swerve, to err
a-storgos, without natural affection
astrapē, lightning, a bright shining
astraptō, *to flash*, to lighten, shine
astron, a star
astu, *a city* [agreeing
a-sumphōnos, *inharmonious*, not
a-sunetos, without understanding, foolish [breaker
a-sunthetos [-suntithēmi], a covenant
a-takteō, to behave disorderly
a-taktos [-tassō], unruly
a-taktōs, disorderly [childless
a-teknos [-teknon], without children,
atenizō, to behold or look steadfastly or earnestly; to fasten or set the eyes, to look
ater, without, in the absence of
a-thanasia [-thanatos], immortality
a-themitos [-themis], unlawful, abo-
a-theos, without God [minable
a-thesmos, wicked
a-theteō [-tithēmi], to cast off, reject; to despise, disannul, frustrate, bring to nothing
athleō, to strive in a contest
athlēsis, a struggle, a fight
a-thetēsis, a disannulling. (*See* put)
athōos, innocent
athroizō, *to gather together*, to collect
a-thumeō [-thumos], to discourage
a-timaō, to handle shamefully
a-timazō, to dishonour, to entreat shamefully, to despise. *PAS.*, to suffer shame
a-timia, dishonour, reproach, shame. (*See* vile)
a-timos, without honour, despised. (*See* honourable)
atmis, vapour [ment
a-tomos [-temnō], *indivisible*; a mo-
a-topos, out of place; unreasonable; [amiss; harm
aucheō, *to boast*
auchmēros, *squalid*, dark
augazō, to shine
augē, break of day [sheepfold
aulē, a court, hall, palace; a fold,
auleō [aulos], to pipe
aulētēs [auleō], a piper, a minstrel

aulizomai [aulē], to lodge, to abide
aulos, a *musical* pipe
aurion, to-morrow, morrow, next day
austēros, austere
aut-, auth-, auto-, *self*. (*See* autos)
aut-arkeia [autarkēs], contentment, sufficiency
aut-arkēs [-arkeō], *having sufficient for one's self*, content [willed
auth-adēs [-hadeō, *to please*], self-
auth-airetos [-haireomai], of his own accord, willing of himself
authenteō, to usurp authority over
auto-cheir, with his own hands
auto-katakritos [-katakrinō], self-condemned
automatos, *self-moved;* of one's self, of one's own accord
aut-optēs [-optomai], an eye-witness
autos, same, he, she, it, that, self, myself, &c.; own, very, self-same. (*See* mine, other, said, things, together, [which]
autou, here, there
auxanō, *ACT.*, to increase, to give increase. *PAS.*, to grow, be increased, to grow up
auxēsis [auxanō], increase
axinē, an axe
axioō, to count or think worthy. (*See* good, desire)
axios, worthy, meet. (*See* reward, unworthy)
axiōs, worthily, as becometh. (*See* worthy, godly sort)
a-zumos, unleavened, unleavened bread

B, β, Ϭ, (*beta*)=b.

bainō, *to go*
baion, a *palm* branch
balantion [ballō], a purse, a bag
ballō, to throw, throw down, cast, put, lay; to thrust, strike; to pour. *PAS. part.*, dung. (*See* send, lie, arise)
baptisma [baptizō], baptism [tism
baptismos [baptizō], a washing, bap-
baptistēs [baptizō], a baptist
baptizō [baptō], to baptise, to wash; *PART.*, baptist
baptō, to dip
barbaros, barbarous, a barbarian
bareō [baros], *to weigh down*, to press. *PAS.* to be burdened, heavy, charged
bareōs, *heavily*. (*See* dull)
baros, a weight, a burden. (*See* burdensome)
barunō, *to weigh down*, to overcharge
barus, heavy, grievous
baruteros [comp. of barus], weightier
baru-timos [-timē], very precious
basanismos, torment
basanistēs, a tormentor
basanizō [basanos], to torment, vex, toss. (*See* pain, toil)
basanos, *torture*, torment
basileia, a kingdom. (*See* reign)
basileion, *a palace*, a king's court
basileios, royal
basileuō, to reign. *PART.*, a king
basileus, a king
basilikos, royal, *noble; a* nobleman. (*See* king)
basilissa, a queen
basis [bainō], *a base*, the foot
baskainō, to bewitch
bastazō, to bear, to carry, to take up
bathmos [bainō], *a step*, a degree
bathos, depth, deepness, deep, a deep thing
bathunō [bathus], *to deepen*. (*See* deep)
bathus, deep. (*See* early)
batos, a measure

batos, a bush, a bramble bush
batrachos, a frog
battologeō, to use vain repetitions
bdelugma [bdelussomai], an abomina- [tion
bdeluktos, abominable
bdelussomai, to abhor. *PAS. part.*, abominable
bebaioō, to confirm, establish, stablish
bebaios, firm, steadfast, sure, of force
bebaiōsis, confirmation
bebaioteros, more sure
bebēloō, to profane
bebēlos [bēlos], *open to all, not sacred, profane; a* profane person
belos, a dart
bēlos, a *threshold*
beltion, *better*, very well
bēma [bainō], *a step*, a judgment-seat, a throne. (*See* set)
bērullos, a beryl
bia, *force*, violence
biaios [bia], mighty
biastēs [biazō], violent
biazō, *to force*. *MID.*, to press. *PAS.*, to suffer violence
bibazō, *to lift up*, raise, exalt
biblaridion [biblos], a little book
biblion, a book, a scroll, a writing, a bill
biblos, a book
bibrōskō. (*See* brōskō)
bioō [bios], to live
bios, a living, goods, life
biōsis [bioō], the manner of life
biōtikos, of this life. (*See* pertain)
blaberos, hurtful
blaptō, to hurt
blasphēmeō [blapto-phēmi], to revile, defame, rail on, speak evil, blaspheme. (*See* blasphemer, blasphemy, blasphemously, slanderously)
blasphēmia, blasphemy, railing, evil speaking [blasphemer
blasphēmos, blasphemous, railing, a
blastanō, to bud, to spring up, to bring forth [seeing
blemma [blepō], *sight, an object seen*
blepō, to behold, see, look on, perceive; to take heed to, to regard, beware of. (*See* sight, lie)
blēteos [ballō], *to be cast*. (*See* put)
boaō [boē], to cry
boē, a cry
boētheia, help
boētheō, to help, succour
boēthos, a helper
bolē [ballō], *a cast [of a stone]*
bolis [ballō], a dart
bolizō [bolis], *to heave the lead*, to sound
bōmos, an altar
borboros, mire
borras, *the north wind*, north
boskō, to feed, to keep
botanē, an herb
bothunos, a ditch, a pit.
botrus, a vine cluster
boulē, a counsel, a will. (*See* advise)
boulēma, a purpose, a will
bouleuomai, to consult, to take counsel, purpose, determine, be minded
bouleutēs, a counsellor
boulomai [boulē], to will or be willing; to intend, to be disposed, to list, to be minded. (*See* will [nn.])
bounos, a hill
bous, an ox
brabeion [brabeus], a prize
brabeus, *a judge at public games*
brabeuō, *to preside at games*, to rule
brachiōn, an arm
brachu [neut. of brachus], little a little space or while.

5

brachus, little. *PLU.*, few
bradunō, to be *slow or* slack; to tarry
bradu-ploeō [-pleō], to sail slowly
bradus, slow
bradutēs, *slowness*, slackness
brechō, to rain; to send rain; to wash
brephos, a babe, an infant, child, a young child
brimaomai, *to be wrathful or furious*
broche [brechō], rain
brochos, a snare
brontē, thunder, thundering
brōma [brōskō], meat, victuals
brōsimos [brōskō], *eatable.* (See meat)
brōsis, food, meat, eating; rust. (See
brōtos [brōskō], *eaten* [morsel)
brōskō, to eat
bruchō, to gnash
brugmos, a gnashing
bruō, to send forth
burseus, a tanner
bussinos, *made of fine linen. NEUT.*, fine linen
bussos, fine linen
buthizō, *to sink. PAS.*, to drown, to
buthos, the deep [begin to sink

X, χ, (*chi*)=ch.

chairō, to joy, rejoice, to be glad; to greet, to hail. (See joyfully, speed, farewell)
chalaō, to let down. (*Seé* strike)
chalaza, hail [ous
chalepos, *hard to bear;* fierce, peril-
chalin-agōgeō [-agō], to bridle
chalinos, a bridle, a bit
chalkēdōn, chalcedony
chalkeos, of brass
chalkeus, a coppersmith
chalkion, a brasen vessel
chalkolibanon, fine brass
chalkos, brass; money
chamai, on, *or* to the ground
chara, joy, gladness, joyfulness. (See joyous, joyfully, joyful, greatly)
charagma, *a graving*, a mark. (See grave) [image
charactēr,*a print, stamp;* the express
charax, *a wooden stake, fence;* a trench
charin [charis], for the sake of, because of. (See cause, reproachfully, wherefore)
charis, grace, favour; gift, benefit, liberality; pleasure, joy, thanks. (See acceptable, gracious, thank, thankworthy)
charisma [charizomai], a free gift,a gift
charitoō [charis], to make accepted. *PAS.*, to be highly favoured
charizomai, to give freely, to give, to grant; to forgive frankly. (See deliver)
chartēs, paper
chasma, a gulf
cheilos, a lip, a shore
cheimarros, a brook [tossed
cheimazomai, *PAS.*, to be tempest-
cheimōn, a tempest, foul weather, [winter
cheir, the hand [winter
cheir-agōgeō [-agō], to lead by the hand [the hand
cheir-agōgos [-agō], one who leads by
cheiro-graphon, handwriting
cheirōn, worse, sorer [hands
cheiro-poiētos [-poieō], made by
cheiro-toneō [-teinō], to choose, **cheō**, to pour [ordain
chēra, a widow
chilias, a thousand [a captain
chili-archos, a chief *or* high captain,
chilioi, *PLU.*, a thousand
chiōn, snow [garment, *PLU.*,clothes
chitōn, *an under garment,* a coat, a
chlamus, a robe
6

chleuazō, to mock
chliaros, lukewarm
chlōros, green, pale
choïkos, earthy
choinix, a measure [= *about a quart*]
choiros, a sow. *PLU.* swine
cholaō, to be angry
cholē, gall
chōlos, lame, cripple, halt
choös, dust [ground, a field, coast
chōra, a country, region; a land,
chorēgeō, to minister, to give
chōreō, *to make room for,* to receive, to contain. (See place, come, go, room)
chōrion, land, a possession, a parcel of ground, a field, a place (See itself)
chōris, *apart from,* without, beside.
chōrizō, to separate, to put asunder. *MID. and PAS.*, to depart
choros, *a dance. PLU.*, dancing [west
chōros, *the north-west wind,* north-
chortasma [chortazō], sustenance
chortazō [chortos], to feed, to fill, to satisfy
chortos, *fodder,* grass, hay, a blade
chraō, to lend
chraomai, to use; to entreat
chrē, *it ought,* ought
chreia, need, want, lack, necessity; use, business. (See needful, necessary)
chrēma [chraomai], money, riches
chrēmatismos, *a response,* an answer of God
chrēmatizō, *to transact business;* to reveal, speak, warn, admonish. (See
chreōs, debt [call)
chreō-pheiletēs [-opheilō], a debtor
chrēsimos [chraomai], *useful.* (See
chrēsis, use [profit)
chrēsteuomai [chrēstos], to be kind
chresto-logia [-logos], good words
chrēstos, *obliging,* kind, gracious, good. (See better, easy, goodness)
chrēstotēs, kindness, goodness, gentleness. (See good)
chrēzō, to need, to have need of
chriō, to anoint
chrisma [chriō], anointing, unction
christos, *one anointed,* Christ
chronizō, to delay, to tarry
chronos, time, a season, a while. (See space, old, oftentimes)
chrono-tribeō [-tribō], to spend time
chrōs, *the skin,* the body
chruseos [chrusos], golden, of gold
chrusion, gold
chruso-daktulios, with a gold ring
chruso-lithos, chrysolite
chrusoō, *to gild,* to deck
chrusoprasos, chrysoprasos
chrusos, gold
chthes, yesterday
chunō [cheō], to pour

Δ, δ, (*delta*)=d.

daimōn, *a heathen god,* a devil
daimoniōdēs, *demoniacal,* devilish
daimonion, a devil, a *heathen* god
daimonizomai, *PAS.*, to have *or* be possessed *or* vexed with a devil
daknō, to bite
dakru *and* **dakruon**, a tear
dakruō [dakru], to weep
daktulios, a ring
daktulos, a finger
damalis, a heifer
damazō, to tame
daneion, *a loan,* a debt
daneistēs, a creditor [borrow
daneizō [daneion], to lend. *MID.*, to
dapanaō, to spend, to be at charges.
dapanē, *expense,* cost [(See consume)

de, but, and. (See now, moreover)
dē, now, doubtless; therefore, also, and
dechomai, to receive, to accept. to take [prayer
deēsis [deomai],a request, supplication,
dei, *it behoves,*it is meet.is needful; *must needs,* should, must, ought. (See need)
deidō, *to fear*
deigma[deiknumi],an example [sure
deigmatizō, to make a shew *or* expo-
deiknuō *and* **deiknumi**, to snew
deilia, *timidity,* fear
deiliaō, *to be timid,* to be afraid
deilos, *timid,* fearful
deina, such a man. [mently
deinōs, *dreadfully,* grievously, vehe-
deipneō, to sup. (See supper
deipnon, a supper, a feast
deisi-daimonesteros, [deidō-], *venerating many deities,* too superstitious
deisi-daimonia, superstition
deixis [deiknumi], a shewing
deka, ten
deka-duo, twelve.
deka-pente, fifteen
dekatē, a tenth part, a tenth, a tithe
deka-tessares, fourteen
dekatoō [dekatē], to receive tithes.
dekatos, tenth [*PAS.*, to pay tithes
dektos[dechomai],accepted, acceptable
deleazō [delear, *a bait*], to entice, to allure, to beguile
dēloō, *to shew evidently,* to shew, to declare, to signify [bewray)
dēlos, evident, manifest, certain. (See
dēmēgoreō [dēmos-agoreuo], to make an oration
dēmiourgos [dēmos-ergazō]. *one who works for the public,* a maker
dēmos, the *common* people
dēmosios, *public,* common. (See publicly, openly)
dēnarion, a penny [= *sevenpence three farthings.*] (See pennyworth)
dendron, a tree [bonds)
deō, to bind, tie; to knit; wind. (See
deomai, to beseech, to make request, to pray; *to need*
dē-pote, soever. (See whatsoever)
dē-pou, verily
derma, the skin
dermatinos, of skin, leathern
derō, to beat, to smite
desmē [deō], a bundle
desmeō, to bind. *PAS.*, to be bound
desmeuō, to bind
desmios, a prisoner, one in bonds
desmo-phulax [-phuiassō], a jailor, the keeper of the prison
desmos,a bond, band, chain, string
desmōtērion, a prison
desmōtēs, a prisoner
despotēs, a master, a lord
deuro[*sing.*],come hither. (See hitherto)
deute [*plural of* deuro], come. (See follow)
deuteraios [deuteros], on the next day
deutero-prōtos, second after the first
deuteros, second; a second time, again, afterward, secondarily
dexio-labos [-lambano], a spearman
dexios, the right hand *or* side, right
di-, *or* **dia-,** through, thoroughly
dia [*gen.*], *by means of,* by, through. (See after, always, among, at, briefly from, in, occasion, of, thereat, thereby though, through,throughout, to,wherein, whereby, with, within)
dia [*accu.*], *on account of,* for, because, because of, for the sake of, through, by reason of. (See avoid, cause, therefore, wherefore, with)

dia-bainō, to pass through, to pass,
dia-ballō, to accuse   [to come over
dia-bebaioō, to affirm constantly, to
dia-blepō, to see clearly   [affirm
dia-bolos [diaballō], a false accuser, slanderer, the devil
dia cheirizomai [-cheir], *to handle thoroughly*, to kill, to slay
dia-chōrizomai, MID., to depart
dia-dechomai, *to receive in succession*, to come after
diadēma, a crown
dia-didōmi, to divide, to distribute, give. (See distribution)
dia-dochos [-dechomai], *a successor.* (See room)   [after]
dia-ginomai], to be past, spent. (See
dia-ginōskō, to inquire, to know to the uttermost
dia-gnōrizō. to make known   [ing
dia-gnōsis, *thorough knowledge*, hear-
di-agō, to lead *constantly*. (See living)
dia-gongguzō, to murmur
dia-grēgoreō, to be *thoroughly* awake
di-aireō [-haireō], to divide
diairesis [diaireō], difference, diversity
dia-kat-elengchomai, to convince of falsehood
dia-katharizō, to purge thoroughly
dia-kōluō, *to hinder*, to forbid
diakoneō, to minister, administer, serve; to use the office of a deacon
diakonia, service, ministry, ministration, administration, office. (See serving, relief, minister)
diakonos, a servant, a minister, a [deacon
diakosioi, two hundred
di-akouō, to hear
dia-krinō, to make *or* put a difference, to make to differ. MID. *or* PAS., to doubt, waver, stagger; to contend; to be partial
dia-krisis, a discerning. (See discern, disputation)
dia-laleō, to commune. PAS., to be noised abroad
dia-legomai, to reason, reason with, dispute; to preach, speak
dia-leipō, *to intermit*, to cease
dia-lektos [dialegomai], language, tongue   [be reconciled
di-allattō, *to exchange.* PAS. (also), to
dia-logismos, reasoning, thought, imagination, disputing. (See doubt, doubtful)
dia-logizomai, to reason, dispute, consider; to muse, think. (See mind)
dia-luō, *to dissolve*, to scatter. [strive
dia-machomai, *to fight fiercely*, to
dia-marturomai, to testify, to witness; to charge
dia-menō, to remain, to continue
dia-merismos, division
dia-merizō, to divide, to part. PAS., (also) to be cloven
dia-nemō, *to spread abroad.* PAS., *to be spread*, to spread
dia-neuō, to beckon   [signify
di-anggellō, to preach, to declare, to
dia-noēma, thought
dia-noia, the mind, understanding, [imagination
di-anoigō, to open
dia-nuktereuō [-nux], to continue all night
di-anuō [-anuō, *to perform*], to finish
dia-pantos [-pas], always, alway, continually
dia-peraō, to pass *or* go over. (See sail)
dia-phanēs [-phainō], transparent
dia-phēmizō, to blaze *or* spread abroad to commonly report. (See fame)

dia-pherō, to drive up and down, to carry, publish; to differ, matter, to be better, excellent, of value
dia-pheugō, to escape
dia-phoros [diapherō], differing, diverse; more excellent
dia-phtheirō, to corrupt, destroy. PAS., to perish.
dia-phthora, corruption   [carefully
dia-phulattō [-phulassō], to keep
dia-pleō, to sail over
dia-poneomai [-ponos], *to be fatigued or distressed*, to be grieved.
di-aporeō [-aporia], to be perplexed, much perplexed, to doubt
dia-poreuomai, to go through, to pass by, to journey   [trading
dia-pragmateuomai, to gain by
dia-priō, to cut to the heart   [spoil
di-arpazō [-harpazō], *to plunder*, to
dia-rrēssō *or* **dia-rrēgnumi** [-rēgnumi], to break, to rend
dia-saphēō [-saphēs], to tell
dia-seiō, to do violence to
dia-skorpizō, to scatter abroad, to disperse, to strew, to waste
dia-sōzō, to bring safe *or* safely *through*, to make perfectly whole, save, heal. PAS., to escape
dia-spaō, to pull in pieces, to pluck
dia-speirō, to scatter abroad [asunder
dia-spora [dia-speirō], *dispersion.* (See disperse, scattered)
dia-stellō, to charge, command, to give commandment
dia-stēma [-histēmi], *distance*, space
dia-stolē [diastellō], distinction, difference
dia-strephō, to pervert, to turn away. (See perverse)   [position
dia-tagē [diatassō], an ordinance, dis-
dia-tagma [-tassō], a commandment
dia-taratteō [-tarassō], *to disturb much*; to trouble
dia-tassō, to set in order, appoint, to give order; to ordain, command
dia-teleō, *to complete*, to continue
dia-tēreō, *to guard carefully*, to keep
dia-thēkē [diatithēmi], a covenant, a [testament
dia-ti [-tis], wherefore, why
dia-tithēmi, *to make over*, to appoint. PARTIC., a testator. (See make)
dia-tribō, to tarry, abide, continue; to [be
dia-trophē, food
di-augazō, *to shine through*, to dawn
dia-zōnnumi, to gird
dicha [dis], *severally*
dichazō, to set at variance
dicho-stasia [-stasis], division, sedition
dicho-tomeō [-temnō], to cut asunder or in sunder   [doctrine
didachē [didaskō], *a thing taught*,
didaktikos [didaskō], apt to teach
didaktos [didaskō], taught. (See teach)
didaskalia, learning, doctrine, teaching
didaskalos, a teacher, a master; a doctor   [teaching
didaskō, to teach. PART., **didaskōn**,
didōmi, to give, grant, bestow; to deliver, deliver up, yield; to offer, bring, set, put, make. (See adventure, commit, hinder, minister, number, power, receive, shew, smite, strike, suffer, take, utter)
di-drachmon [dis-drachmē], tribute
di-egeirō, to raise, to stir up. MID. and PAS., to arise, to awake
di-ēgeomai [-hēgeomai], to declare, to tell or shew
di-ēgēsis [diēgeomai], declaration
diēnekes, *perpetual;* continually, ever

di-ermēneuō [-hermēneuō], to interpret, expound. (See interpretation)
di-ermēneutēs, an interpreter
di-erōtaō, to make inquiry for
di-etēs [-etos], two years old
di-etia [dietēs], *the space of* two years
di-exodos, *a thoroughfare*, a highway
di-ikneomai [-hikneomai], to pierce through
di-ischurizomai [-ischuros], to affirm confidently *or* constantly
di-istēmi [-histēmi], to be parted, to go farther. (See space)   [ment
dikaio-krisia [-krinō], righteous judg-
dikaiōma, judgment, justification, righteousness, ordinance
dikaioō, to justify. PAS., to be freed, to be right eous. PART., justifier
dikaios [dikē], just, righteous, right, meet
dikaiōs, justly, righteously. (See righ-
dikaiōsis, justification   [teousness)
dikaiosunē, righteousness
dikastēs [dikē], a judge
dikē, *penalty*, judgment, vengeance. (See punish)
diktuon, [dikō, *to cast*], a net
di-logos [dis-], double-tongued
di-o [dia-hos], for which cause, wherefore, therefore   [go throughout
di-odeuō [-hodeuō], to pass through, to
diōgmos [diōkō], persecution
diōkō, to follow after, follow, press towards; to ensue; persecute. (See given, persecution)
diōktēs [diōkō], a persecutor
dio-per [-per], wherefore
dio-petēs [dios-, *of Jupiter*, -piptō], which fell down from Jupiter
di-orthōsis, reformation
di-orussō, to break through *or* up
di-oti [-hoti], because, for. (See therefore)
diploō [diploos], to double
di-ploūs *or* **di-plous** [dis-], double, twofold, more
dipsaō, to thirst, to be thirsty *or* athirst
dipsos, thirst   [ed
di-psuchos [dis-psuchē], double-mind-
dis, twice, again
dis-chilioi, two thousand   [doubt
di-stazō, [dis-histēmi], *to waver*, to
di-stomos [dis-], with two edges, two-edged   [meet
di-thalassos [dis-], where two seas
di-ulizō [-hulē], *to filter*, to strain
dochē, [dechomai], *an entertainment*,
dō-deka [duo-deka], twelve   [a feast
dōdeka-phulon [-phulē], the twelve
dōdekatos, twelfth   [tribes
dogma [dokeō], *a thing decreed or judged*, a decree, an ordinance
dogmatizō, *to impose a law.* MID., to be subject to ordinances
dokeō, to suppose, to think, to account; to trow, to seem. (See please, pleasure, reputation)
dokimazō [dokimos], to prove, try, examine; to discern, approve, allow. (See like)   [perience
dokimē, trial, proof, experiment, ex-
dokimion, *a test*, a trying, trial
dokimos, tried, approved
dokos, a beam
dolioō [dolos], to use deceit
dolios, deceitful
doloō, to handle deceitfully
dolos, deceit, guile, subtilty. (See crafty)
doma [didōmi], a gift
dōma, *a house*, a housetop
dōrea [dōron], a gift
dōrean [dōrea], *gratuitously*, for nought, freely, without a cause; in vain

dŏrēma [dōreō], a gift
dŏreō [dōron], to give
dŏron, a gift, an offering
dosis [didōmi], a gift, a giving
dotĕs, [didōmi], a giver   [jection
doul-agōgeō [-agō], to bring into sub-
doulē, a handmaid, a handmaiden
douleia [doulos], bondage   [service
douleuō, to be in bondage, to serve, do
doulon [neut. of doulos], servant
douloō, to bring into bondage, to make
  servants. PAS., to become a servant;
  to be under bondage. (See given)
doulos, a bondman, servant. (See bond)
doxa [dokeō]. favourable opinion, glory,
  praise, honour, worship, dignity. (See
  glorious)
doxazō, to glorify, to honour, to make
  glorious, to magnify. PAS., to be full
  of glory, to have glory
drachmē, a piece of silver [= 7¾d.]
drakōn, a dragon
drassomai [drax, the fist], to seize, to
drepanon, a sickle   [take
dromos, a race-course, a course
dunamai, to be able, to be of power.
  (See can, cannot, may, might, possible)
dunamis, power, ability, strength,
  might, violence, virtue. (See abundance, mightily, mighty, wonderful,
  miracle, meaning)
dunamoō [dunamis], to strengthen
dunastēs, a potentate; mighty, of great
dunateō, to be mighty   [authority
dunatos, able, mighty, strong, possible.
  NEU., power. (See could)
dunō, dumi, or duō, to put on, enter,
duo, two, twain, both   [to set
dus-, grievously, difficultly, hardly, un-
  favourably   [be borne
dus-bastaktos [-bastazō], grievous to
dus-enteria [-enteron, an intestine],
  dysentery, a bloody flux
dus-ermĕneutos [-hermĕneuō], difficult of interpretation, hard to be
duskolos, difficult, hard   [uttered
duskolōs, hardly
dusmē [dunō], sunset, the west [stood
dus-noētos [-noeō], hard to be under-
dus-phēmia [-phēmē], evil report

E, ι, (epsilon) = e. H, η, (ēta) = ē.

ē, or, either, or else. (See and, neither,
  nor, rather, what, yea)
ē, than. (See but, either, save, except,
ĕ mĕn, surely   [that)
ea [imper. of eaō], let alone
ean [ei-an], if, though, whether. (See
  before, but, except, when)
ean [= an], soever. (See whatsoever,
  whensoever, wheresoever, whithersoever, whoso, whosoever, whomsoever)
eaō, to let alone, let, suffer, leave.
  (See commit)
ĕcheō, make a noise, to roar. PART.,
echidna, a viper   [sounding
echō, to Have, hold, possess; to take,
  retain, keep; to be. (See able, accompany, amend, bold, can, cannot,
  conceive, count, deceased, do, eat,
  enjoy, fear, follow, lack, law, lie,
  needs, necessity, next, recover, reign,
  rest, sick, tremble, uncircumcised,
ĕchos, sound, fame   [use]
echthra, hostility, enmity, hatred
echthros, an enemy, a foe
edaphizō, to lay even with the ground
edaphos, a site, the ground
ēdē, already, even now, by this time
egeirō, to raise, lift, take or rear up,
  to raise again. MID. and PAS., to
  arise, rise up, rise again, stand, awake
8

egersis [egeirō], resurrection
egō, I, me. GEN., my
ei, if, whether, though; since, although,
  forasmuch as. (See that)
ei de mē, else, otherwise, if otherwise,
  if not, or else
ei-ge, if so be that, if yet, if
ei kai, if that, though, if
ei mē, if not, except, saving, save only
  that, but. (See till, more, than, that)
ei mē ti [tis], except
ei per, if so be, seeing, though
ei-te, whether, if, or
eideō or eidō, to see, behold, look on,
  perceive. Per. act. to know, to understand, consider, be aware, be sure,
  wist. (See can, tell, knowledge)
eidōleion [eidōlon], an idol's temple
eidōlo-latreia, idolatry
eidōlo-latrēs [-latreuō], an idolater
eidōlon [eidos], an idol
eidōlo-thuton [-thuō], a thing offered
  in sacrifice to idols. (See idols)
eidos, an appearance, a sight, a shape,
  fashion
eikē, without a cause, in vain, vainly
eikō, to yield, to give place
eikō, to be like
eikōn [eikō], an image
eikos, like truth, reasonable, fair
eikosi, twenty
eileō, to roll, twist, shut up
eili-krineia [heilē-sunshine], sincerity
eili-krinēs, judged in sunlight, pure,
  sincere
eimi, to be, to consist. (See agree,
  belong, call, come, dure, follow, have,
  live, lust, make, mean, must, profit,
  remain, say, sojourn, wrestle.)
eitha. PERF of ethō
eipō. (See epō)
eirēnē, peace, quietness, rest. (See
  one
eirēneuō, to have peace, be at peace,
  to live in peace or peaceably
eirēnikos, peaceable
eirēno-poieō, to make peace
eirēno-poios, a peacemaker
eis, towards, to, unto, into, till, until,
  against, for. (See abundantly, among,
  as, at, before, by, concerning, continual, end, exceeding, forth, hereunto,
  in, insomuch, intent, never, of, on,
  perish, set, so, therefore, thereinto,
  thereunto, throughout, with)
eis-agō, to lead or bring in or into
eis-akouō, to hearken to, to hear
eis-dechomai, to receive with favour
eis-eimi, to go or enter into
eis-erchomai, to come in, to enter
  into, to go. (See arise)
eis-kaleō, to call in
eis-odos [-hodos], an entrance or entering in. (See come, nter)
eis-pēdaō [-pēdaō, to leap], to spring
  in, run in
eis-pherō, to bring or lead in
eis-poreuomai, to go, come, or enter
eis-trechō, to run in   [in
eita, then, after that, afterward, furthermore
ek, out of, from, by, of, since. (See
  after, among, at, because, betwixt,
  beyond, means, exceedingly, for, forth,
  hereby, highly, in, off, on, over, reason,
  thenceforth, thereof, through, unto,
  vehemently, whereof, with, without)
ek- or ex-, out of, from, away, utterly
ek-ballō, to cast, put, drive, or thrust
  out; to expel, to bring or send forth,
  to pull or pluck out. (See leave) [end
ek-basis [-bainō], a way to escape, an

ek-bolē [ekballō], a casting out. (See
  lighten)   [spill. (See run)
ek-cheō, to pour out, to shed forth, to
ek-chōreō, to depart out
ek-chunō, to pour out, shed abroad,
  spill. PAS., to gush out. (See greedily)
ek-dapanaō, to spend entirely
ek-dechomai, to wait, tarry, or look
ek-dēlos, manifest   [for, to expect
ek-dēmeō [-dēmos], to be an exile, to
  emigrate, to be absent   [deliver up
ek-didōmi, to let out, to let forth; to
ek-diēgeomai, to declare thoroughly
ek-dikeō [ekdikos], to revenge, avenge
ek-dikēsis, vengeance, revenge, punishment. (See avenge)
ek-dikos [-dikē], an avenger, a revenger
ek-diōkō, to persecute
ek-dochē [ekdechomai], a looking for
ek-dotos [ekdidōmi], delivered up
ek-duō [-duno], to unclothe, to strip
  to take off from
ekei, there, thither, yonder, thitherward
ekeinos, that, that same, that very
  selfsame, he, she, it, this, selfsame
ekeise, there   [(See there)
ekeithen, from that place, thence.
ek-gamiskō or ek-gamizō, to give
  in marriage   [phews
ek-gona [-ginomai], descendants, ne-
ek-kaiō, to set on fire. PAS., to burn
ek-kakeō, to faint, to be weary
ek-kathairō, to purge out, to purge
ek-kenteō, to pierce
ek-klazō, to break off
ek-kleiō, to shut out, to exclude
ek-klēsia [-kaleō], an assembly, a
  church   [avoid, to eschew
ek-klinō, to go out of the way, to
ek-kolumbaō, to swim out
ek-komizō, to carry out
ek-koptō, to cut out, off, or down; to
  hew down. (See hinder)
ek-kremamai [-kremannumi.] MID,
  to be very attentive
ek-laleō, to speak forth, to tell
ek-lampō, to shine forth
ek-lanthanomai, PAS., to forget
ek-legomai [-legō], to choose out, to
  make choice
ek-leipō, to leave off, to fail
ek-lektos [eklegomai], chosen, elect
ek-logē [eklegomai], election. (See
  choose)
ek-luō, to relax. PAS., to be faint
ek-massō [-massō, to wipe], to wipe
  thoroughly
ek-muktērizō, to deride greatly
ek-nēphō, to awake from stupor
ek-neuō, to convey one's self away
ek-palai, of old, of a long time
ek-peirazō, to try out, to tempt
ek-pempō, to send away, to send forth
ek-petannumi, to stretch forth
ek-pherō, to carry out, to bring or
  carry forth, to bear
ek-pheugō, to flee, to escape
ek-phobeō, to terrify greatly
ek-phobos, sore afraid. (See fear)
ek-phuō, to shoot forth, to put forth
ek-piptō, to fall away or off, to be cast,
  to fail. (See effect)
ek-pleō, to sail away   (See thence)
ek-plēroō, to fill out, to fulfil
ek-plērōsis, accomplishment
ek-plēssō. PAS., to be greatly struck,
  to be amazed or astonished
ek-pneō, to expire, to give up the ghost
ek-poreuomai, to go or come out or
  forth; to depart, issue, proceed out of
ek-porneuō, to give one's self over to
  fornication

ek-psuchō [-psuchē], to yield or give up the ghost
ek-ptuō, to spit out, to reject
ek-rizoō, to root up, to pluck up by the roots
ek-stasis, amazement, astonishment, trance. (See amazed)
ek-strephō, to subvert
ek-tarassō, to trouble exceedingly
ek-teinō, to stretch or put forth, to stretch out, to cast
ek-teleō, to finish quite [instantly
ek-teneia [ektenēs], earnestness. (See
ek-tenēs [ektenō], on the stretch, fervent, without ceasing [nestly
ek-tenesteron [ektenēs], more ear-
ek-tenōs [ektenēs], fervently
ek-thambeō [ekthambos], to be greatly or sore amazed, to be affrighted
ek-thambos, utterly astonished, greatly wondering
ek-thetos [ektithēmi], cast out
ek-tinassō [-tinassō], to shake off
ek-tithēmi, to cast out; to expound
ektos, without, on the outside, out of. (See but, except, other, unless)
ek-trephō, to nourish, to bring up
ek-trepō, to turn out of the way, to turn. MID., to turn aside from, to avoid
ektrōma, one born out of due time
ek-zēteō, to seek after, to seek carefully or diligently, to inquire, require
elachistos, least, smallest, very little or small
elachistoteros, less than the least
elaia, an olive tree, an olive berry
elaion, oil
claiōn [elaia], of olives; Olivet
elaphria, lightness [in weight], levity
elaphros, not heavy, light
elassōn or **elattōn**, less, younger, worse. (See under)
elattoneō, to have less, to have lack
elattoō, to make less, to make lower. PAS., to decrease
elaunō, to drive, to carry; to row
eleeinos [eleos], miserable
eleēmōn [eleeō], merciful
eleēmosunē, alms, alms deeds [pity
eleēō, to have compassion, mercy, or
elengchō, to convict, convince; to rebuke, reprove; to tell a fault
elengchos, conviction, refutation, evidence, reproof,
elengxis [elengchō], a rebuke
eleos, mercy
elephantinos, made of ivory
eleusis [erchomai], the act of coming
eleutheria, liberty
eleutheroō, to deliver, to make free
eleutheros, free, at liberty; a free man or woman
Eli [Hebrew], my God, Eli [to impute
el-logeō [en-logos], to put on account,
elōi [Syriac], my God, Eloi
elpis, hope; (faith, Heb.10.23)
elpizō, to hope, hope for; to trust
em-. See en- [own self
emautou, myself, mine own, mine
em-bainō, to go, come, or enter into; to step in; to take ship
em-ballō, to cast into
em-baptō, to dip into
em-bateuō [-baino], to intrude into
em-bibazō, to set on, to put in
m-blepō, to look upon, behold, see. (See gaze)
m-brimaomai, to murmur against, to groan; to charge straitly
emeō, to vomit, to spue
am-mainomai, to be mad against

em-menō, to continue in
emos, mine, my
empaigmos [empaizō], a mocking
empaiktēs, a mocker, a scoffer
em-paizō, to play or jest on, to mock
em-peripateō, to walk about in
em-phanēs [-phainō], manifest. (See openly)
em-phanizō, to manifest, shew, declare plainly; to inform, signify. PAS., to appear [tremble
em-phobos, afraid, affrighted. (See
em-phusaō [-phusaō], to blow into, to breathe on
em-phutos [-phuō], engrafted
em-piplaō [-pimplēmi], to fill
em-piptō, to fall into or among
em-plekō, MID., to entangle one's self with. PAS., to be entangled in
em-plēthō, to fill. PAS., to be full
em-plokē [emplekō], plaiting
em-pneō, to breathe
em-poreuomai [emporos], to buy and sell, to make merchandise
em-poria, merchandise [dise
em-porion, a trading-place, merchan-
em-poros [-poros], a passenger, a merchant
em-prēthō [-pimprēmi], to burn up
em-prosthen, in presence of, in sight of, before. (See against, at, of)
em-ptuō, to spit on, to spit
en, IN, within; among, with; on, at, by. (See after, about, against, altogether, as, because, before, between, child, for, hereby, herein, into, inwardly, means, mightily, of, outwardly, over, quickly, shortly, therein, throughout, to, toward, under, unto, upon, when, where, wherewith, while, with)
en-, eng-, or **em-**, in, into, among, very much
en-angkalizomai [angkalē], to take up in the arms
en-alios [-hals], NEUT. plu., things belonging to or in the sea
en-anti, over against, before
en-antion, before, in the sight of
en-antios [enanti], contrary. (See against, over against)
en-archomai, to begin
en-dechetai [endechomai], it can be. (See cannot) [admitted
en-dechomai, PAS., to be accepted or
en-deēs [-deomai, to need], needy; one that lacks [manifest token
en-deigma, indication, evidence, a
en-deiknumi, to shew forth, to shew. (See do) [(See declare)
en-deixis, proof, an evident token.
en-dēmeō, to be among one's own people, to be present or at home
en-diduskomai [enduō], MID., to be clothed in, to wear
en-dikos [-dikē], just [building
en-domēsis [-domeō, to build], a
en-doxazō [endoxos], to glorify
en-doxos, glorious, honourable. (See gorgeously) [garment
en-duma [enduō], clothing, raiment, a
en-dunamoō, to strengthen, make strong; to enable. PAS., to be strong, increase in strength
en-dunō, to creep in
en-duō, to put on, to clothe with. PAS., to be arrayed, have on, be clothed, endued
en-dusis [enduō], a putting on
en-echō, to hold in [a place]; to have a quarrel against, to urge. PAS., to be held in, or entangled with [in wait.
en-edra or **en-edron** [-hedra], lying

en-edreuō, to lay wait for (See wait)
en-eileō, to wrap in
en-eimi, to be in or present. (See have)
en-ergeia [energēs], effectual working, operation, working. (See strong) [tion
en-ergēma [energeō], working, opera-
en-ergeō [energēs], to work, to work effectually in, be effectual, be mighty in. (See shew, do)
energēs [-ergon], powerful, effectual
en-eulogeō, to bless in
eng-chriō [en-], to anoint
enggizō [enggus], to come or draw near or nigh, to approach, to be at hand or nigh
eng-graphō [en-], to engrave, to write in, to write
engguos [engguē, a pledge], a surety
enggus, near, nigh, at hand. (See
engguteron, nearer [ready, from
eng-kainia [en-kainos], initiation, the feast of the Dedication [to dedicate
eng-kainizō, to initiate, to consecrate,
eng-kaleō, to call in question, implead, accuse; to lay to the charge
eng-kataleipō, to forsake, to leave
eng-kathetos [en-kathēmai], a sitter in ambush, a spy
eng-katoikeō, to dwell among
eng-kentrizō [en-kenteō], to graff into
eng-klēma [engkaleō], an accusation, what is laid to one's charge, a crime laid against one
eng-komboōmai [en-kombos, a knot]. MID., to be clothed with
eng-kopē [engkoptō], a hindrance. (See hinder) [unto
eng-koptō [en-], to hinder, to be tedious
eng-krateia [engkratēs], temperance
eng-kratēs [en-], holding self in, temperate
eng-krateuomai [engkratēs], to have power over one's self, to be able to contain, to be temperate
eng-krinō [en-], to reckon among, to make of the number
eng-kruptō [en-], to hide in
engkuos, great with child
eniautos, one year, a year
en-ischuō, to strengthen
en-istēmi [-histemi], to be present or at hand, to come
ennatos, ninth [at hand, to come
ennea, nine
ennenēkonta, ninety
ennenēkonta-ennea, ninety-nine
enneos, speechless
en-neuō, to make signs
en-noia [-nous], mind, intent
en-nomos, lawful, under law
en-nuchon [-nux], at night, before day
en-ochleō, to excite a tumult, to trouble
en-ochos [-echō], amenable to, subject to; in danger of, guilty
en-oikeō, to dwell in
enōpion, before, in presence of, in sight of. (See to)
en-ōtizomai [-ous], to hearken to
entalma [entellomai], a commandment
en-taphiasmos, a burying
en-taphiazō, to bury. (See burial)
en-tellomai [-tellō], to charge or give charge, to command or give commandments, to enjoin
enteuthen, hence, on either side
en-teuxis [entungchanō], access, prayer, intercession
enthade, here, hither, there
en-thumeomai [-thumos], to think
en-thumēsis [enthumeomai], thought, device [cious; dear
en-timos [-timē], in reputation, precious;
en-timoteros, more honourable

9

en-tolē [entellomai], a commandment, precept

en-topios [-topos], of that place

entos, within

en-trephō, to nourish up in

en-trepō, to shame. *MID. and PAS.*, to reverence, regard

en-tromos, *terrified.* (See quake, [tremble]

en-tropē [-trepō], shame

en-truphaō, *to live in riot*, to sport one's self [to deal with

en-tungchanō, to make intercession,

entulittō, to wrap in *or* together

en-tupoō [-tupos], *to stamp*, to engrave

en-ubrizō [-hubrizō],to do despite unto

en-upniazomai, to dream. (See dreamer)

en-upnion [-hupnos], a dream

ep-, *See* epi-

ep-agō, to bring upon [for

ep-agōnizomai, to contend earnestly

ep-aineō, to praise, laud, commend

ep-ainos, praise

ep-airō, to lift *or* take up, to hoise up, exalt

ep-aischunomai, *PAS.*, to be ashamed

ep-aiteō, to beg [low

ep-akoloutheō, to follow after, to fol-

ep-akouō, *to listen to*, to hear

ep-akroaomai, to hear

ep-an [epei-an], *whenever*, when

ep-anagō, *to lead out to*, to launch *or* thrust out ; to return

ep-anamimnēskō, to put in mind

ep-anangkes, *of necessity.* (See necessary)

ep-anapauomai, *MID.*, to rest *one's self* in *or* upon [again

ep-anerchomai, to return, to come

ep-anggelia, a promise ; a message

ep-angellomai, *MID.*, to declare one's *self;* to promise, to profess

ep-angelma, a promise

ep-anistamai [-anistēmi], *MID.*, to rise up against [than

ep-anō, above, over ; upon, on ; more

ep-anorthōsis [-anorthoō], correction

ep-aphrizō, to foam out *upon*

ep-archia [-archē], a province

ep-arkeō,*to ward off,protect;* to relieve

ep-athroizomai [-athroizō, *to collect*], *MID.*, *to collect themselves together*, to gather thick together

ep-aulis [-aulis, *a tent*], a habitation

ep-aurion, the day following, the morrow, next day [very act

ep-auto-phōrō [-phōr], [*adv.*], in the

ep-echō, to hold forth ; *to hold one's self to*, to take *or* give heed to, to mark; to stay

ep-egeirō, to raise *up*, to stir up

epei,when,since, seeing that, forasmuch as. (See because, for, else, otherwise)

epei-dē, after that, seeing, since, because, forasmuch as, for that

epeidē-per, forasmuch as

ep-eimi, *See* epiousa

epei-per, seeing that

ep-eisagōgē [-eisagō], the bringing in

ep-eita, after that, then, afterward

epekeina, beyond

ep-ekteinomai, *to stretch one's self out towards*, to reach forth

ep-enduomai, *to clothe one's self with*, to be clothed upon [coat

ep-endutēs, *an upper tunic*, a fisher's ē-per, than [come

ep-erchomai, to come on *or* upon, to

epēreazō, *to use despitefully*, to accuse falsely

ep-erōtaō, to ask questions, to ask after, to demand, to question; to desire

10

---

ep-erōtēma, *a question*, an answer

eph-, *See* epi-

eph-allomai [epi-hallomai], to leap on

eph-apax [-hapax], at once,once for all

eph-ēmeria, *a daily service*, a course

eph-ēmeros [-hēmera], daily

eph-euretēs [-heuriskō], an inventor

eph-ikneomai [-hikneomai], to reach

eph-istemi [-histēmi], to stand before, over, *or* by ; to stand ; to be at hand *or* present ; to be instant. (See come, assault)

eph-oraō [-horaō],to look on, to behold

ephphatha [*Syriac*], *be thou opened*, Ephphatha

epi [*gen.*], at, in, upon, before, over. (See about, above, charge, for, of, place, to)

epi [*dat.*], at, upon, for, over. (See about, above, after, against, before, behalf, beside, by, of, through, to, toward, under, unto, with)

epi [*accu.*], on, upon ; unto to ; over. (See at, above, about, after, among, because, before, charge, for, inasmuch, into, long, of, space, throughout, touching, toward, with)

epi-, **ep-**, *or* **eph-**, on, upon, above, at

epi-ballō, to cast *or* lay on, stretch forth, to put unto, to think on, to beat into. (See fall)

epi-bainō, *to go upon*, to come *or* enter into ; to sit upon. (See aboard ship)

epi-bareō, *to lay a burden on*, to be chargeable to, to overcharge

epi-bibazō, to set on

epi-blēma [epiballō], *a patch*, a piece

epi-blepō, to look upon, to regard, have respect to

epi-boaō, to cry

epi-boulē, *a conspiracy against* lying in wait, laying await

epi-cheireō, to take in hand, to take upon one's self, to go about

epi-cheō, *to pour upon*, to pour in

epi-chorēgeō, to minister nourishment, to minister unto ; to add

epi-chorēgia [epichorēgeō], a supply

epi-chriō, to anoint

epi-dechomai, to receive

epi-deiknumi, to shew

epi-dēmeō, *to dwell at. PART.*, a stranger. (See there)

epi-dēmos, a sojourner

epi-diatassomai, to add to. *MID.,to enjoin in addition*

epi-didōmi, to give *or* deliver unto, to offer, to let [*a ship*] drive

epi-diorthoō, to set in order

epi-duō [-dunō], to go down on [mency

epi-eikeia [epieikēs], gentleness, clemency

epi-eikēs [-eikos], gentle, patient. *NEUT.*, moderation

epi-gambreuō, to marry

epi-geios [-gē], earthly, terrestrial. (See earth)

epi-ginomai, *to come on.* (See blow)

epi-ginōskō, to know well ; to have *or* take knowledge ; acknowledge, perceive

epi-gnōsis, knowledge, acknowledgment, acknowledging [scription

epi-graphē, *an inscription*, a super-

epi-graphō, to write on, over, *or* in. (See inscription)

epi-kaleomai, *MID.*, to call, to call upon ; to appeal unto. (See surname)

epi-kalumma [epikaluptō], a cloke

epi-kaluptō, to cover

epi-kataratos, cursed

epi-kathizō, to set on, to set

---

epi-keimai, to lie on, to be laid upon; to be instant, to press upon, to be im-

epikouria, *a defence*, a help [posed

epi-krinō, to give sentence

epi-lambanō, to lay hold on, to take hold of, to catch [forgetful

epi-lanthanomai, to forget, to be

epi-legō, to call. *MID.*, to choose

epi-leipō, to fail

epi-lēsmonē [epilanthanomai], *forgetfulness.* (See forgetful)

epi-loipos, *remaining;* the rest [mine

epi-luō, *to set loose;* to expound, determine

epi-lusis, *a solution*, interpretation

epi-martureō, to testify

epi-meleia [epimeleomai], *attention.* (See refresh)

epi-meleomai[-melei], to take care of

epi-melōs, *carefully*, diligently

epi-menō, to continue in, abide in ; to tarry

epi-neuō, *to nod upon*, to consent

epi-noia [-nous], thought

epi-orkeo, to forswear one's self

epi-orkos [-horkos], a perjured person

ētios, gentle [ing, next

epi-ousa [*partic. of* epeimi], follow-

epi-ousios [-ousia, *existence*], daily

epi-phainō, to appear *unto*, to give light

epi-phaneia, an appearing, brightness

epi-phanēs [epiphainō], *illustrious*, notable [light to

epi-phauō [-phaō], *to shine on*, to give

epi-pherō, to bring against, to bring, add. (See take) [to give a shout

epi-phōneō, to cry against, to cry to,

epi-phōskō, to dawn *upon*, to begin to dawn [or lie on

epi-piptō, to fall upon *or* into,to press

epi-plēttō [-plēssō], to rebuke

epi-pnigō, to choke

epi-poreuomai, *to go to ;* to come

epi-potheō, to long after greatly, to desire earnestly *or* greatly, to lust

epi-pothēsis, earnest *or* vehement desire [sire

epi-pothētos, longed for

epi-pothia, great desire

epi-rraptō [-raptō], to sew on

epi-rriptō [-riptō], to cast upon [fierce

ep-ischuō, *to add force*, to be the more

epi-sēmos [-sēma], notable, of note

epi-sitismos [-sitos],victuals

epi-skēnoō, *to come and dwell upon*, to rest upon

epi-skeptomai, to look out, to visit

epi-skiazō [-skia], to overshadow

epi-skopē [episkopos], visitation, the office of bishop, bishoprick

epi-skopeō, to take the oversight, to look diligently

epi-skopos, an overseer, a bishop

epi-sōreuō, to heap [cumcised

epi-spaomai, *MID.*, to become uncir-

epi-sphalēs [-sphallō], *nearly falling*, dangerous

epistamai, to know, to understand

epi-statēs [ephistēmi], *one set over*, a master

epi-stellō, *to send to*, to write a letter to, to write

epi-stēmōn [epistamai], endued with knowledge

epi-stērizō, to confirm, to strengthen

epi-stolē [epistellō], an epistle, a letter

epi-stomizō [-stoma],to stop the mouth

epi-strephō, to turn [*trans. and intr.*], to turn again [*int.*], to convert [*tr.*], to return *or* go again. *MID. and PAS.*, to turn about [*int.*], to return

epi-strophē [epistrephō], conversion

epi-sunagō, to gather together

epi-sunagōgē, a gathering or assembling together [gether
epi-suntrechō, to come running to-
epi-sustasis, *a coming together upon a person.* (See come, raise)
epi-sphalēs [-sphallō], dangerous
epi-tagē, [epitassō], a commandment, authority [enjoin
epi-tassō, to charge, to command, to
epitēdeios, *suitable*, needful
epi-teleō, to perfect, make perfect, finish, accomplish, perform ; to do. (See performance)
epi-thanatios, appointed to death
epi-thesis [epitithēmi], a laying or putting on [(See fain)
epi-thumeō, to covet, lust after, desire.
epi-thumētēs, one who lusts after
epi-thumia, concupiscence, lust, desire. (See to lust)
epi-timaō, to rebuke, to charge straitly, to charge
epi-timia [epitimaō], punishment
epi-tithēmi, to put, lay, or set upon ; to add unto ; to set up ; to lade. (See surname, wound)
epi-trepō, to give license, leave, or liberty ; to permit, suffer, let
epi-tropē, *a charge*, a commission
epi-tropos [epitrepō], a steward, tutor
epi-tungchanō, to obtain
epi-zeteō, to seek for or after, to inquire, desire
epō or **eipō**, to say, speak, tell ; to answer, bid, call, command, bring word. (See grant) [up
ep-oikodomeō, to build upon, to build
epokellō, *to force upon*, to run aground
ep-onomazō, to put a name upon, to call
ep-optēs [-optomai], an eye-witness
ep-opteuō [epoptēs], *to look upon*, to
epos [epō], *a word.* (See say) [behold
ep-ouranios, heavenly, celestial, high. NEU. plu., things in heaven
erchomai, to come, enter, resort; to go, pass. (See accompany, appear, bring, fall, grow, light, next, set)
ereidō, *to fix firmly*, to stick fast
erēmia, a desert, a wilderness
erēmoō, to make desolate, to bring to desolation. (See nought)
erēmos, desert, desolate, solitary ; a
ēremos, quiet [desert, a wilderness
erēmōsis, desolation
ereō, to speak, say, tell. (See call)
eretēs, *a rower*
erethizō [eris], to provoke
ereugomai, *to belch*, to utter
ereunaō, to search
ergasia, *working; craft*, diligence ; gain. (See to work)
ergatēs, a workman, a worker, a labourer
ergazomai [ergon], to work, labour ; to trade. (See commit, do, minister)
ergon, a work, deed, a labour. (See well-**erion**, wool [doing)
eriphion, a young kid, a goat
eriphos, a goat, a kid
eris, strife, contention, variance, debate
eritheia, strife, contention. (See con
erizō [eris], to strive [tentious)
erōtaō, to ask, entreat, beseech ; to desire, to pray [latter end, ends
eschatos, last, uttermost, lowest. NEU.
eschatōs, at the end, at the point of death [(See into)
esō, within, in [adv.]; inner, inward.
esoptron [eis-optomai], a mirror, glass
esōteros, inner ; within
esōthen, from within, within ; inward, inwardly. (See without)

---

esthēs [hennumi], apparel, raiment, clothing, a robe
esthēsis, *clothing*, a garment
esthiō, to eat, devour. (See live)
ethelo-thrēskeia [ethelo-, to choose], will-worship
ethizō [ethos], to accustom. (See custom)
ethn-archēs [ethnos-], governor
ethnikos [ethnos], heathen ; a Gentile, a heathen man [of Gentiles
ethnikōs [ethnikos], after the manner
ethnos, a nation, people. PLU., heathen, Gentiles [ner or custom
ethō [ethos], to be wont, to be the man-**ethos**, *what is* wont, a custom, manner
ēthos, *custom*. PLU., manners
eti, yet, still, even ; moreover, further, also. (See after, henceforth, hereafter, longer, more, now, thenceforth)
ē-toi, whether
etos, a year
eu, well, well-done. (See good)
eu-, *pleasing, joyful, good, well*
eu-anggelion [-anggellō], *good tidings*, the gospel
eu-anggelistēs, an evangelist
eu-anggelizō, to declare, bring, or shew glad tidings ; to bring good tidings ; to preach the gospel [to please
eu-aresteō [euarestos], to p'ease well,
eu-arestos, well-pleasing, acceptable, accepted
eu-arestōs, acceptably. (See please)
eu-charisteō, to give thanks, to thank, be thankful [thankfulness
eu-charistia, thanksgiving, thanks,
eu-charistos [-charizomai], thankful
euchē, a prayer, a vow
euchomai, to pray, to wish. (See would)
eu-chrēstos, *very useful*, profitable.
eudia, fair weather [meet for use
eu-dokeō, to be well pleased, to have or take pleasure in, to think good, to be willing
eu-dokia, good pleasure, good will, desire. (See please, seem)
eu-ergesia [euergetēs], good deed done, a benefit [tually
eu-ergeteō [-ergon], to do good habi-**eu-ergetēs**, a benefactor
eugenēs, *well-born*, noble; a nobleman
eu-kaireō [eukairos], to have a convenient time or opportunity, to have leisure ; to spend time
eu-kairia, *a fit time*, opportunity
eu-kairos, *well-timed*, convenient, in time of need
eu-kairōs, conveniently, in season
eu-kopōteros [-kopos], easier
eu-labeia [eulabēs], godly fear. (See fear)
eu-labeomai, to fear, to be moved with *godly* fear [fearing, devout
eu-labēs [-lambanō], circumspect, God-**eu-logeō** [-logos], to bless, to praise
eu-logētos, *to be blessed*, blessed
eu-logia, blessing, fair speech, bounty. (See bountifully) [distribute
eu-metadotos [metadidōmi], ready to
eu-noeō [nous], *to be reconciled*, to agree
eu-noia [eunoeō], benevolence, good will
eunouchizō, to make a eunuch
eunouchos [eunē, *a bed*; echō], *a lord of the bedchamber*, a eunuch
eu-ōdia [-ozō], a sweet smell or savour. (See sweetsmelling)
eu-odoumai [-hodos], to have a prosperous journey, to prosper [hand
euōnumos, the left. NEU., on the left
eu-peithēs [-peithomai], easy to be entreated
eu-peristatos [-peri'stēmi], *well circumstanced*, easily besetting

---

eu-phēmia, a good report
eu-phēmos [-phēmi], of good report
eu-phoreō [-pherō], to bring forth plentifully
eu-phrainō, -omai [-phrēn], to make glad or merry. MID. and PAS., to be merry, to rejoice. (See fare)
eu-phrosunē [euphrōn, *glad*], gladness, joy
eu-poiïa [-poiëō], *the doing of* good
eu-poreomai [euporos, *prosperous*], *to be prosperous.* (See ability)
eu-poria [euporeomai], wealth [grace
eu-prepeia [-prepei], *becomingness*,
eu-prosdektos [-prosdechomai], acceptable, accepted
eu-prosedros [-prosedreuō], *applying diligently to.* NEU., devotedness. (See attend) [fair shew
eu-prosōpeō [-prosōpon], to make a
eu-psucheō [-psuchē], to be of good comfort
euru-chōros, *spacious, roomy*, broad
eurus, *wide, broad* [ourable
eu-schēmōn [-schēma], comely, honest
eu-schēmonōs, *becomingly*, decently, honestly [ness
eu-schēmosunē [euschēmōn], comeliness
eu-sebeia [eusebēs], godliness, holiness
eu-sebeō [eusebēs], to worship, to shew piety
eu-sebēs [-sebomai], devout, godly
eu-sebōs [eusebēs], *piously*, godly
eu-sēmos [-sēma], *well-marked*, easy to be understood [ful
eu-splangchnos, tender-hearted, piti-**eutheōs** [euthus], immediately, straight-way, forthwith ; anon, shortly, by-and-by ; as soon as
eu-thetos [-tithēmi], fit, meet
euthu-dromeō [-dromos], *to run in a direct line*, to come with a straight course. (See come)
eu-thumeō, to be of good cheer ; to be
eu-thumos, of good cheer [merry
eu-thumoteron, more cheerfully
euthunō, to direct, to make straight. (See list)
enthus, [adjec.], straight, right
euthus [adverb], straightway, immediately, forthwith ; by and by, anon
euthutēs [euthus], *rectitude*, righteousness [ly, mightily
eu-tonōs [-teinō], *intensely*, vehemently
eu-trapelia [-trepō], *polite ; wit*, jesting
ex-, See ek-
ex-agō, to lead, fetch, or bring out ; to
ex-agorazō, to redeem [bring forth
ex-aiphnēs, *unforeseen*, suddenly
ex-aireō [-haireō], to pluck out, rescue,
ex-airō, to take or put away [deliver
ex-aiteomai, to demand or entreat for one's self, to desire
ex-akoloutheō, to follow
ex-aleiphō, to wipe away, to blot out
ex-allomai [-hallomai], to leap up
ex-anastasis, resurrection
ex-anatellō, to spring up
ex-anggellō [-anggellō], to shew forth
ex-anistēmi, to raise up ; to rise up
ex-apataō, to deceive, to beguile
ex-apina [exaiphnēs], suddenly
ex-aporeomai, *to be wholly without resource*, to despair, to be in despair
ex-apostellō, to send out, forth, or away [furnish throughly
ex-artizō [-artios], to accomplish, to
ex-astraptō, *to shine out*, to be glistering [presently ; by and by
ex-autēs, straightway, immediately,
ex-ēcheomai, *to be sounded abroad*,
ex-egeirō, to raise up [to sound out

11

ex-ēgeomai [-hēgeomai], *to lead out,* to tell, to declare
ex-eimi, *to be given out,* to be lawful, to go out, to depart, to get to land, go out. (See get)   [convince
ex-elengchō, *to convict perfectly,* to
ex-elkō [-helkō], to draw away
exerama, *what is vomited,* a vomit
ex-erchomai, to come *or* go out, to come *or* go forth, to go thence *or* away, to go *or* spread abroad, to depart *or* get out, to proceed forth, to escape
ex-ereunaō, to search *out* diligently
ex-esti [-eimi, to be], it is lawful. (See let, may)
ex-etazō [-hetazo],to search,inquire,ask
ex-ichneuō [-ichnos], *to trace out*
ex-ischuō, to be *fully* able
ex-istēmi [-histēmi], ACT., to astonish, bewitch. ACT. and MID., to be beside one's self, amazed *or* astonished; to wonder
exō, without, outward, out; away, forth. (See strange)   [principal]
ex-ochē [execho], prominence. (See
ex-odos [-hodos], a departing; decease
ex-olothreuō [-olethros], to destroy utterly
ex-omologeomai [-homologeō], to confess *publicly ;* to promise, thank
ex-orkistēs [exorkizō], an exorcist
ex-orkizō [-horkizō], to adjure
ex-oruttō [-orussō], to pluck out ; to break up
exōteros, outer
exōthen, outwardly, from without, outward, outside
ex-ōthō [-ōtheō], to drive out, to thrust
ex-oudenoō, to set at nought
ex-ousia [exeimi], authority ; jurisdiction ; power, strength ; right, liberty
ex-ousiazō [exousia], to exercise authority upon, to bring under the power of, to have power of *or* over
ex-outheneō [exoudenoō], to set at nought, despise. (See esteem, contemptible   [out of sleep
ex-upnizō [exupnos], to *make to* awake
ex-upnos [-hupnos], *awake,* out of, sleep

Γ, , (gamma) = g.

gala, milk
galēnē, a calm
gambros, *a relation by marriage*
gameō, to marry
gamiskō, to give in marriage
gamos, marriage, a wedding
ganggraina [graō, *to devour*], a canker
gar, for, because. (See as, but, doubt, even, indeed, seeing, then, therefore, verily, what, why, yet)
gastēr, the belly, the womb. (See child)
gaza, a treasure
gazo-phulakion, a treasury
ge [often not expressed in English], at least, yet. (See and, beside, doubtless)
gē, the earth, the ground, country, land, world. (See earthly)
geënna [the valley of Hinnom], hell
geitōn, a neighbour
gelaō, to laugh
gelōs, laughter
gemizō, to fill. PAS. (also) to be full
gemō, to be full
genea [genō], a generation; a nation, a time. PLU., ages
genea-logeō, to count one's descent
genea-logia, a genealogy
genesia [genō], a birth-day *festival*
genesis, nativity, generation. (See nature, natural)

12

genetō [genō], *a birth*
gennaō, to beget, to gender, conceive ; to bring forth, bear. (See born, deliver, spring, make)
gennēma, a generation ; *production,*
gennēsis, birth   [fruit
gennētos, born
genō [obsolete], to generate
genos, offspring, stock, generation, kind, kindred, country, nation. (See born, countryman, diversity)
geōrgeō [geōrgos], to dress *or* till the
geōrgion, husbandry   [ground
geōrgos [gē-ergon], husbandman
gēras, old age
gēraskō, to wax old, to be old
gerōn, an old man   [senate
gerousia [gerōn], *a council of elders,* a
geuomai, to taste. (See eaten)
ginomai, to become, to be ; to happen, befall, come to pass, be fulfilled, to be made *or* performed ; to grow, wax. (See arise, assemble, behave, come, continue, divide, do, draw, ended, fall, finish, follow, find, forbid, have, keep, make, marry, ordain, partake, past, publish, require, seem, shew, soon, sound, take, turn, use, will, work]
ginōskō, to know, perceive, understand, be aware of, to be sure. (See allow, feel, knowledge, resolve, speak)
gleukos, *grape juice,* new wine
glōssa, a tongue
glōssokomon, a bag
glukus, sweet,fresh. NEU.,sweet water
gnapheus, *a dresser of cloth,* a fuller
gnēsios [genō], *legitimate by birth,* true, own. (See sincerity)
gnēsiōs, genuinely, naturally
gnōmē [ginōskō], judgment, mind, advice ; will, purpose. (See agree)
gnophos [nephos], darkness
gnōrizō, to make known, give to understand, to certify, declare. (See wit, wot)
gnōsis [ginōskō], knowledge, science
gnōstēs, *one who knows,* expert
gnōstos, known, notable ; an acquaintance,which may be known
goēs, *a juggler, a cheat ;* a seducer
gomos [gemō], *a ship's cargo,* or burden, merchandise
goneus [genō], a parent
gonggusmos, murmuring, grudging
gonggustēs, a murmurer
gongguzō, to murmur
gōnia, *an angle,* a corner
gonos [genō], *an offspring, progeny*
gonu, the knee. (See kneel)
gonu-peteō [-piptō], to kneel down, to bow the knee
gramma [graphō],a letter; a bill. PLU., learning, scriptures. (See write, written)
grammateus, a scribe, a town-clerk
graōdēs, *belonging to old wives, silly*
graphē, scripture
graphō, to write ; to describe. (See writing)
graptos [graphō], written
grēgoreō,to wake,be watchful, watch, to be vigilant
gumnasia [gumnos], *bodily exercise*
gumnazō, *to train by exercise [as for games]*, to exercise
gumnēteuō, to be naked
gumnos, naked, bare
gumnotēs, nakedness
gunaikarion [diminutive of gunē], a silly woman
gunaikeios, womanly. (See wife)
gunē, a woman, a wife

(ʽ) *Greek aspirate* = h.

hadēs [a-eidō], *the unseen world;* hell
hadrotēs, abundance   [the grace
hagiasmos, sanctification, holiness
hagiazō, to sanctify, hallow. PAS. (also) to be holy
hagion, a sanctuary. PLU., holy places or place, [gen. pl. of holies], holiest of all, holiest
hagios, holy ; a holy one, a saint
hagiōsunē, holiness
hagiōtatos, most holy
hagiōtēs, holiness
hagneia [hagnos], chastity, purity
hagnismos, purification
hagnizō, to purify
hagnos, pure, chaste, clear
hagnōs, purely, sincerely
hagnotēs, pureness
haima, blood
haimat-ekchusia [-ekcheō], shedding of blood   [of blood
haimo-rreō [haima-], to have an issue
haireō, to seize, to carry off. MID., to choose
hairesis, *a choosing,* a sect ; a heresy
hairetikos [hairesis],heretical,a heretic
hairetizō [haireomai], to choose
halas, salt
halēs, thronged, in a mass
halieuō, to go a-fishing
halieus [hals], a fisher, fisherman
haliskō, *to catch*
halizō [halas], to salt
hallomai, to leap, to spring up
halōn, *a threshing floor*
halōsis [haliskō],a catching. (See taken)
hals, *the sea,* salt
halukos [hals], salt [adjec.]
halusis [a-luō], a chain ; bonds
hama, with, together *with.* (See and, also, withal)
hamartanō, to sin, to trespass, offend.
hamartēma, sin   [(See fault]
hamartia, sin, offence. (See sinful)
hamartōlos, sinful ; a sinner
hapalos, tender
hapas [pas], the whole ; all, every one. PLU., all things
hapax, once (and once only)
haphē, a joint
haploōs or **haplous**, single
haplōs, *with simplicity ;* liberally
haplotēs, simplicity, singleness ; liberality, bountifulness. (See liberal)
haptō, to light, kindle
haptomai, MID., to touch
harma, a chariot
harmos, a joint
harmozō [harmos], *to join,* to espouse
harpagē [harpazō], extortion, raven-
harpagmos, robbery   [ing, spoiling
harpax, ravening; an extortioner
harpazō, to take by force, to catch away, to take, pull, pluck. PAS., to be caught up
hautou [no nominative],[heautou], his, his own, her, her own, their, their own, him, himself, them, themselves (See him, it, thee, they)
heautou [no nominative], [hos-autos] his, his own, her, her own, their, their own, their ownselves, thine own, our own, your, your own, he himself, herself, &c.   [score]
hebdomēkonta, seventy. (See three-
hebdomēkontakis, seventy times
hebdomos, seventh
hēdeōs [hēdus, sweet], gladly
hēdista, very *or* most gladly
hēdomai,to enjoy,take pleasure, be glad

hēdonē [hēdomai], *gratification*, pleahedra, *a seat* [sure, lust
hedraiōma [hedra], the ground
hedraios [hedra], settled, stedfast
hēdu-osmon [hēdus, *sweet*, -osmē], mint [nor, prince
hēgemōn [-hēgeomai], a ruler, gover-
hēgemoneuō, to be a governor
hēgemonia, *government*, reign
hēgeomai, to rule over, be chief; to judge, account, count, esteem, think, suppose. (*See* governor)
heilissō [helissō] to roll together
heis, one. (*See* a, another, any, certain,
hekastos, each, every, each *or* every one. (*See* both, any, particularly)
hekastote, always
hekaton, a hundred [years old
hekatonta-etēs [-etos], an hundred
hekatonta-plasion, a hundredfold
hekatont-archēs *or* -os, *a captain of a hundred*, a centurion
hēkō, *to be arrived*, to come
hekōn, *consenting*. (*See* willingly)
hekousios, willing. (*See* willingly)
hekousiōs, willingly, wilfully
hektos, sixth
hēlikia, *maturity*; age, stature
hēlikos, how great, what great
hēlios, the sun. (*See* east)
helissō, to fold up
helkoōmai, PAS., to be full of sores
helkos, a sore
helkō *or* **helkuō**, to draw
hēlos, a nail
hēmera, a day, daytime; time. (*See* midday, day, alway, daily, ever, judgment, while, years)
hēmeros, *tame, gentle*
hēmeteros [hēmeis, *we*], our
hēmi-, *a half*
hēmi-ōrion [-hōra], half-an-hour
hēmisu, half
hēmi-thanēs [-thnēskō], half dead
hen- [*neut.* of **heis**], *one*
hen-deka, *one and ten*, eleven
hen-dekatos, eleventh
heneka, *or* **heneken**, *or* **heineken**, for the sake of, for, by reason of, for cause of. (*See* because, wherefore, that)
hēnika, when
hennumi, *to clothe*
henotēs [hen], unity
heortazō, to keep a feast
heortē, *a sacred feast*, a holiday
heōs, until, till, unto, to, even, unto, as far as, up to. (*See* even, hitherto, how long, far, not, while, whiles)
hepta, seven. (*See* seventh)
heptakis, seven times
heptakis-chilioi, seven thousand
hermēneia, interpretation
hermēneuō, to interpret. (*See* interpretation)
herpeton, a creeping thing, a serpent
hespera, the evening, eventide
hēsuchazō, to be quiet, hold one's peace; to rest, cease
hēsuchia, quietness, silence
hēsuchios, quiet, peaceable
hetairos, *a comrade*, fellow, friend
hetazō, *to examine*, to test
hetero-didaskaleō [-didaskalos], to teach otherwise *or* other doctrine
hetero-glōssos, *one who speaks another language*, of other tongues
heteros, other, another; strange. (*See* altered, else, next, one, some)
heterōs, otherwise [unequally
hetero-zugeō, to be yoked together
hetoimasia, preparation [provide
hetoimazō, to prepare, make ready,

hetoimos, prepared, ready, ready to one's hand. (*See* readiness)
hetoimōs, *preparedly*. (*See* ready)
hēttaomai [hettōn], PAS., to be inferior, to be overcome [a fault
hēttēma, *a being worse*, a diminishing,
hēttōn, less, worse
heuriskō, to find, get, obtain. (*See* [perceive, see]
hex, six
hexakosioi [-hekaton], six hundred
hexēkonta, sixty, threescore, sixtyfold
hexēs, *successively*, following, after, next, morrow
hexis [echō], *habit, practice*, use
hidrōs, sweat
hiēmi, to send
hierateia [hieros], the office of priesthood. (*See* priest)
hierateuma, priesthood
hierateuō, to execute a priest's office
hiereus, a priest; a high priest
hieron, a temple
hiero-prepēs [-prepei], as becometh
hieros, *sacred*, holy [holiness
hiero-suleō, to commit sacrilege
hiero-sulos, *a temple-robber*, a robber of churches
hierōsunē, the priesthood
hierourgeō [hieros-ergon], *to officiate in the temple*, to minister [meet *or* able
hikanoō, *to make sufficient*, to make
hikanos, sufficient, worthy, meet, able. (*See* content, enough, good, great, large, long, many, much, security, sore)
hikanotēs, sufficiency
hiketēria, supplication
hikneomai, *to come, go, or arrive at*
hilaros, cheerful
hilarotēs, cheerfulness
hilaskomai [hileōs], MID., to make reconciliation. PAS., to be merciful
hilasmos, propitiation [seat
hilastērion, a propitiation; the mercy
hileōs, merciful. (*See* be it far)
himas, a thong, a latchet
himation, *an outer garment*, a garment, vesture, a robe, cloke, clothes. PLU., raiment, apparel, clothes
himatismos, apparel, vesture, raiment, array. (*See* apparelled)
himatizō, to clothe [sirous of
himeiromai, to be affectionately desirous of
hina, to the intent that, so that, that. (*See* albeit, for, lest, so, to, because)
hina-ti [-tis], why, wherefore
hippeus, a horseman
hippikon, *cavalry*, horsemen
hippos, a horse
histēmi, to set, set up, establish, appoint, present; to stand, stanch. (*See* abide, bring, continue, covenant, hold,
historeō, *to find out*, to see [lay
ho, the. (*See* who, which, that)
ho-de, *this*; he, she. PLU., these. (*See* such, thus, after this manner) [there
hōde, here, hither, in this place. (*See*
hod-ēgeō [hodēgos], to lead, to guide
hod-ēgos [-hēgeomai], a guide; a leader
hodeuō [hodos], to journey
hodoi-poreō [hodos-poreuomai], to go on a journey
hodoi-poria, a journey, a journeying
hodos, a way, a highway; a journey
hoios, what manner of; such as, so as, as. (*See* what, which) [burnt offering
holo-kautōma [holos-kaiō], a whole
holo-klēria [holoklēros], *completeness in all parts*, perfect soundness
holo-klēros, *complete in all parts*, whole, entire.
holos [*adi.*], *the whole*; all, every whit, altogether, throughout

holōs, *completely*, utterly, commonly; [*after a negative*], at all
holo-telēs [-teleō], *wholly finished*, wholly
homileō, *to converse*, to commune, talk
homilia, *intercourse*, communication
homilos, company [agree to
homoiazō, [homoios] *to resemble*, to
homoiōma, likeness, similitude, shape. (*See* like)
homoioō, to make like, liken. PAS., to resemble, be like. (*See* likeness)
homoio-pathēs, of, *or* subject to like
homoios, like. (*See* manner) [passions
homoiōs, likewise; so
homoiōsis, similitude [like]
homoiotēs, *likeness*, similitude. (*See*
homo-logeō [-logos], *to make the same declaration*, to confess, make confession; to give thanks, profess, promise
homo-logia, confession, profession. (*See* profess) [out controversy
homo-logoumenōs, *confessedly*, with-
homo-phrōn [-phrēn], of one mind
omos, *one and the same* [but
homōs, nevertheless; and even, though
homo-technos, of the same craft
homo-thumadon [-thumos], with one accord, with one mind
homou, together [struments
hopla [*plural*], armour, weapons, in-
hoplizō [hopla], *to equip*, to arm
ho-poios, of what sort, what manner of, whatsoever
ho-pōs, so that, that, how. (*See* because, when)
ho-pote [hos-], *at what time*, when
ho-pou, in what place, where, whither, whithersoever, wheresoever. (*See* whereas)
hōra, an hour, a season. (*See* day, eventide, instant, time, short)
hōraios [hōra], *seasonable*, beautiful
horama [horaō], a sight, a vision
horaō, to see, behold, perceive; to take heed
horasis, a vision. (*See* sight, to look)
horatos, visible [coast
horia [horos], *boundaries*, borders,
horizō [horia], *to set limits*, to limit; *to define*, to determine, ordain, declare. (*See* determinate)
horkizō [horkos], *to administer an oath*, to adjure, to charge *on oath*
hork-ōmosia [-omnumi], *the act of swearing*, an oath
horkos, an oath [violently
hormaō [hormē], to rush, to run, to run
hormē, *a rushing*, an assault
hormēma [hormaō], violence
horos, *a border, boundary, landmark*
horo-thesia [-tithēmi], *the setting of a bound*
hos, who, which. (*See* whosoever, whatsoever, when, where, whereas, whereby, &c.)
hōs, as, even as, even like, like as, according as, as it had been, as it were; so that, that, how, how greatly; to wit, since, when, while. (*See* speed)
hosakis [hosos], as oft as, as often as
hōsanna [Hebrew], *save us*, hosanna
hōs-autōs, even so
hōs-ei, as it had been, as it were, like, as, like as, about
hosios, *hallowed*, holy. NEU. *plu.* mercies. (*See* be)
hosiōs, *piously*, holily
hosiotēs, *religiousness*, holiness
hosos, how great, what great. NEUT. how much, as long as, as much as, (*See* whosoever, whatsoever, all.) PLU.

(also) how many, as many as, so many as. *(See* ever, more, so, things, while, wherewith)

hōs-per, like as, even as, as

hōs-per-ei, as

hōs-te, so that, in so much that, that, as, inasmuch as. *(See* to, therefore, wherefore)

hos-tis, such as; whosoever, whatsoever; who, which, what, that. *(See* and, as, he, in, they, whereas)

hot-an [hote-], whensoever, when, while, as long as; as soon as. *(See* that, till)

hote, when, after that, after, as soon as, while. *(See* that)

hothen [hos], from whence ; wherefore, from thence, whereupon; whereby. *(See* where)

ho-ti [hostis], because, for, that, as concerning that, as though, in that, how that. *(See* for, how, that, though, why)   [whiles]

hotou [*gen. of* hostis], *what time. (See*

hou [*gen. of* hos], where; wherein, whither

houtō *or* **houtōs,** in *or* after this manner, in like manner, so, on this wise, on this fashion, likewise, even so, thus, so, like. *(See* as, more)

houtos [ho-autos], this, the same; he, she, it, &c. *PLU.,* these, they, &c. (See hereof, which)

houtōs. *(See* houtō)

huakinthinos, of jacinth

huakinthos, jacinth

hualinos, of glass

hualos, glass

hubris, *an insult, outrage;* a hurt, harm, reproach

hubristēs, *abusive,* injurious, despiteful

hubrizō, to use despitefully, to entreat shamefully *or* despitefully, to reproach

hudōr, water

hudria, a water pot

hudrōpikos, having the dropsy

hudro-poteō [-pinō], to drink water

huetos, rain

hugiainō, to be sound, whole, in health, to be safe and sound ; wholesome

hugiēs, *healthy,* whole, sound

hugros, *moist,* green

huios, a son ; a child ; a foal

huio-thesia [-tithēmi], adoption of sons *or* children

hulē, *a wood ; (combustible)* matter

humeteros [humeis, *ye*], your own

humneō, to sing a hymn, sing praise

humnos, a hymn   [unto

hup-, *See* hupo-

hup-agō, to go away, depart. *(See* get)   [dient]

hup-akoē, obedience. *(See* obey, obedient to

hup-akouō, to hearken, obey, be obedient to

hup-andros [-anēr], that hath an husband

hup-antaō, to meet, to go and meet

hupantēsis, *a meeting. (See* meet)

hup-archō, to begin imperceptibly to *be ;* to be, to live. *(See* after, have)

hup-archonta [*partic. plu. of* huparchō], what one has *or* possesses, goods, substance

hup-arxis [huparchō], substance, goods

hup-echō, to suffer

hup-eikō, to retire, to submit one's self

hup-ēkoös [hupakouō], obedient. *(See* obey)

hup-enantios, contrary; an adversary

huper [*gen.*], for, for the sake of, on behalf of, instead of, on the part of. *(See* concerning, of, by, toward)

14

huper [*accus*], above, more than, over beyond. *(See* more, to, very)

huper-, *over, above, in excess, in behalf of, in defence of*

huper-airō, *to lift up over. MID.,* to exalt one's self. *PAS or MID.,* to be above measure exalted

huper-akmos, past the flower of age

huper-anō, far above, over

huper-auxanō, to grow exceedingly

huper-bainō, to go beyond

huper-ballō, *to overshoot,* to pass, excel. *(See* exceeding)

huper-ballontōs, above measure

huper-bolē, *-excess,* abundance, excellency. *(See* exceeding, excellent, measure)

huper-echō, *to surpass,* to pass. *(See* better, higher, supreme, excellency)

huper-eidō, *to overlook,* to wink at

huper-ekchunō, *to pour over. PAS.,* to run over   [yond

huper-ekeina, *beyond those parts,* be-

huper-ekteinō, to stretch beyond

huper-entungchanō, to make intercession for

huperē-phania, pride   [proud

huperēphanos [-phainō], *arrogant,*

hupēreteō [hupēretēs], to minister unto, to serve   [officer, minister

hup-ēretēs, *an attendant,* a servant,

huper-nikaō, to be more than conqueror   [authority

huper-ochē [huperechō], excellency,

huperongkos, *much swollen. NEU. plu.,* great swelling words of vanity

huperōon, an upper room *or* chamber

huper-perisseuō, to abound much more. *(See* exceeding)

huper-perissōs, *beyond superabundance,* beyond measure

huper-phroneō, to think more highly

huper-pleonazō, to be exceeding abundant   [highly

huper-upsoō [-hupsoō], to exalt

huphantos, woven

hupnos, sleep

hupo [*gen.*], by. *(See* of, with, from,

hupo [*accus.*], under   [among]

hupo-, hup-, huph-, *under, a little, secretly*

hupo-ballō, *to thrust under,* to suborn

hupo-chōreō, to withdraw one's self, to go aside   [ensample

hupo-deigma, a pattern, example,

hupo-deiknumi, to shew *secretly,* to warn, forewarn

hupo-dechomai, to receive

hupo-dēma [hupodeō], a shoe

hupo-deō. *MID.,* to bind on, to have *or* get shod. *PAS.,* to be shod

hupo-dikos [-dikē], guilty

hupo-grammos [-graphō], *a writing copy,* an example

hupo-katō, under

hupo-krinomai, *to act a part,* to feign

hupo-krisis, hypocrisy, dissimulation. *(See* condemnation)

hupo-kritēs, *a play-actor,* a hypocrite

hupo-lambanō, *to take up,* to receive; to answer, suppose

hupo-leipō, *to leave behind,* to leave

hupo-lēnion, *the under wine-press,* the wine-fat

hupo-limpanō [hupoleipō], to leave

hupo-menō, to endure, be patient, to suffer *or* take patiently, to abide, tarry behind

hupo-mimneskō, to put in mind *or* remembrance, to bring to remembrance. *PAS.,* to remember

hupo-mnēsis, remembrance

hupo-monē [hupomenō], patient continuance *or* waiting, patience, the enduring

hupo-noēō, to suppose, think, deem

hupo-noia, an *under-thought, suspicion,* a surmising

hupo-pherō, to endure, bear

hup-ōpiazō [-ops], *to strike under the eye,* to keep under, to weary

hupo-pleō, to sail under

hupo-pneō, to blow softly

hupo-podion [-pous], a footstool

hupo-stasis [-histēmi], confidence ; substance, person. *(See* confident)

hupo-stellō, *ACT. or MID.,* to keep, *or* draw back, to withdraw, shun   [back

hupo-stolē [hupostellō], a drawing

hupo-strephō, to return back again, turn back, to come again

hupo-strōnnumi, to spread *under*

hupo-tagē [hupotassō], subjection

hupo-tassō, to put under, make subject, to subdue unto, to put in subjection. *MID. and PAS.,* to be subject, obedient, under obedience *or* subjection

hupo-tithēmi, *to put under,* to lay down, put in remembrance

hupo-trechō, to run under

hupo-tupōsis [-tupoō, *to print*], a pattern, a form

hup-ourgeō [-ergon], *to render service or help*

hupo-zōnnumi, to undergird   [ass

hupo-zugion, *a beast of burden,* an

hupsēlos [hupsos], high, highly esteemed   [teemed

hupsēloteros, higher

hupsēlo-phroneō, to be high minded

hupsistos, highest, most high

hupsoō [hupsos], to lift up, to exalt

hupsōma, a high thing, a height

hupsos, height. *(See* high, on high, exalted

hus, a sow   [exalted

hussōpos, hyssop *(a plant)*

husterēma, a want, that which is behind *or* lacking, lack, penury

hustereō [husteros], to be lacking, to fail, to lack, to be behind. *(See* want) *PAS.,* to be in want *or* destitute, to want, to be the worse, to come *or* be behind, to come short

husterēsis, *deficiency ;* want

husteron, last, at the last, last of all, afterward

husteros, *the last,* the latter

I, i, *(iota)*=i.

iama, healing

iaomai, *MID.,* to heal, to make whole. *PAS.,* to be healed

iasis, healing, cure. *(See* heal)

iaspis, jasper

iatros, a physician

ichnos, *a footmark,* a step

ichthudion, a little *or* small fish

ichthus, a fish   [hold, lo, see

ide, *and* **idou** [*imper. of* eidō], be-

idea [eideō], *appearance,* countenance

idios, one's own, proper, private; due. *(See* acquaintance, alone, apart, aside, business, home, privately, several, severally)

idiōtes, unlearned, ignorant, rude

idou, *See* ide

ikmas, moisture

ios, poison, rust

iōta, *the small Hebrew letter* Iod, a jot

ioudaios, *Jewish,* a Jew

ioudaïsmos, the Jews' religion

ioudaïzō, to live as a Jew

iris, a rainbow

is-anggelos [isos-], equal to the angels

ischuō [ischus], to be able, to be of strength, to prevail, avail. (See can, cannot, good, might, whole, work)

ischuros, powerful, mighty, strong, valiant, boisterous

ischuroteros [comparat. of ischuros], mightier, stronger

ischus, power, strength, might, ability. (See mightily)

isēmi, to know

iso-psuchos [-psuchē], likeminded

isos, equal ; ike, as much. (See agree)

isōs, equally, possibly, it may be

isotēs, equality. (See equal)

iso-timos [-timē], like precious

K, κ, (kappa) = k.

kagō [kai-egō], and I

kai, and ; even, also

kainos, new

kainotēs, newness   [to burn

kaiō, to cause to burn, to light. PAS.,

kai-per, and yet, although

kairos, a season, opportunity, time. (See always, while)

kai-toi, though, although, nevertheless

kakei [kai-ekei], and there, there also, thither also

kakeinos [kai-ekeinos], he also, and he, even he. PLU., they also. (See other)

kakeithen [kai-ekeithen], and from thence, thence also, and afterward

kakia [kakos], evil, malice, maliciousness, wickedness, naughtiness

kako-ētheia [-ēthos], malignity [curse

kako-logeō [-logos], to speak evil, to

kakoō, to harm, hurt, evil entreat, vex ; to make to be evil affected

kako-patheia, suffering of affliction

kako-patheō [-paschō], to suffer trouble, endure hardness or afflictions, to be afflicted

kako-poieō, to do evil. (See evil-doer)

kako-poios, an evil-doer, a malefactor

kakos, evil, bad, wicked, noisome. NEU., evil, ill, harm

kakōs, badly, amiss ; grievously, miserably, sore. (See evil, sick, diseased)

kakōsis, affliction

kakoucheomai [kakos-echō], to be afflicted. PAS. part., **kakouchoumenos**, suffering adversity, tormented

kakourgos [kakos-ergon], an evil-[doer, a malefactor

kalamē, stubble

kalamos, a reed, a pen

kaleō, to call, call forth ; to bid. (See name, surname)

kalli-elaios [kalos], a good olive tree

kallion [kalos], better ; very well

kalo-didaskalos, a teacher of good things

kalo-poieō, to do well. (See well-doing)

kalos, good, goodly, fair, honest ; worthy, meet. (See better, well)

kalōs, well, very well, full well ; honestly. (See good, recover)

kalumma [kaluptō], a vail or veil

kaluptō, to cover, hide

kamēlos, a camel

kaminos, a furnace

kammuō, to shut, to close

kamnō, to be wearied, sick, or faint

kamptō, to bend, to bow

kan [kai-ean], and if, also if, but if, and if so much as. (See least, yet, but, though)

kanōn, a standard, a rule, a line

kapēleuō, to corrupt

kapnos, smoke

---

karadokeō, to watch eagerly

kardia, the heart. (See broken-hearted)

kardia-gnōstēs [-ginōskō], that knows the heart

karphos, a mote

karpo-phoreō [-pherō], to bear or bring forth fruit ; to be fruitful

karpo-phoros, fruitful

karpos, fruit

kartereō, to endure

kata [genit.], against ; to the charge of, down. (See on, through, throughout, of)

kata [accusative], according to ; in respect of, as touching, as pertaining to, as concerning. (See about, before, over against, in, upon, through, throughout, among, to, into, at, toward, from, by, for, out of, according as every, exceeding, excellent, divers, inasmuch, like, manner, measure, part, so, thus, unto, together)

kata-, or **kat-**, or **kath-**, down, against, downright, in an increased degree

kata-bainō, to go down, to get, come, step, or fall down ; to descend

kata-ballō, to cast down, to lay

kata-bareō, to weigh down, to burden

kata-basis [katabainō], a going down, a descent

kata-bibazō, to bring or thrust down

kata-bolē [kataballō], a casting down, foundation. (See conceive)

kata-brabeuō, to beguile of reward

kata-cheō, to pour down

kata-chraomai, to over-use, to abuse

kata-chthonios [-chthōn, the earth], under the earth

kata-dēlos, very evident

kata-deō, to bind up

kata-dikazō [-dikē], to condemn

kata-diōkō, to pursue, to follow after

kata-douloō, to bring into bondage

kata-dunasteuō, to use power against, to oppress

kata-gelaō, to laugh to scorn

kata-ginōskō, to blame, to condemn

kat-agnumi, to break

kat-agō, to bring down or forth, to bring to land. PAS., to land, to touch

kat-agōnizomai, to subdue

kat-aischunō, to make ashamed, to shame, confound, dishonour. PAS., (also) to be ashamed

kata-kaiō, to burn up, to burn utterly

kata-kaluptō, to veil, to cover

kata-kauchaomai, to boast or rejoice against, to boast, to glory

kata-keimai, to recline, to sit down, to sit at meat, to lie. (See keep)

kata-klaō or **kataklazō**, to break

kata-kleiō, to shut up

kata-klēro-doteō [-klēros-didōmi], to divide by lot

kata-klinō, to make sit down. PAS., to sit down, to sit at meat

kata-klusmos, a flood

kata-kluzō, to overflow   [after

kat-akoloutheō, to follow, to follow

kata-koptō, to cut down, to cut

kata-krēmnizō, to cast headlong

kata-krima [katakrinō], condemnation

kata-krinō, to condemn. PAS., also, to be damned   [demn]

kata-krisis, condemnation. (See con

kata-kurieuō, to exercise lordship or dominion over, to be lords over, to overcome

kata-laleō, to speak evil of or against

kata-lalia, evilspeaking, backbiting

kata-lalos, a backbiter

kata-lambanō, to take, attain, find,

---

overtake, come upon ; to comprehend, perceive, apprehend, obtain

kata-legō, to take into the number

kata-leimma [kataleipō], a remnant

kata-leipō, to leave, forsake ; to re-

kata-lithazō, to stone   [serve

kat-allagē [katallattō], a favourable exchange, reconciliation ; a reconciling, an atonement (at-one-ment)

kat-allattō or **kat-allassō**, to change from enmity to friendship, to reconcile

kata-loipos, one left behind. PLU., the residue   [ber, an inn

kata-luma [kataluō], a guest-cham-

kata-luō, to dissolve, throw down, destroy, overthrow ; to lodge, be a guest. PAS., (also) to come to nought

kata-manthanō, to learn thoroughly, to consider

kata-martureō, to witness against

kata-menō, to abide

kata-monas [-monos], [adverb], alone

kat-analiskō, to consume

kata-narkaō, to be torpid against, to be burdensome or chargeable

kat-anathema, a curse

kat-anathematizō, to anathematise,

kata-neuō, to beckon   [to curse

kat-anggeleus [katanggellō], a setter forth

kat-anggellō, to declare, preach, teach, shew, speak of

kata-noeō, to perceive distinctly, to consider, to behold, discover

kat-antaō, to arrive, to come, to attain

kata-nussō [nuttō], to stab or pierce through, to prick

kata-nuxis [-nux], slumber

kata-pateō, to tread down or underfoot, to trample

kata-pauō, to cause to cease, to restrain, to give rest ; to cease, to rest.

kata-pausis, rest   [a vail

kata-petasma [-petànnumi, to spread],

kata-phagō, to devour, to eat up

kata-pherō, to bring down, to give. PAS., to be sunk down. (See fall into)

kata-pheugō, to flee down

kata-phileō, to kiss tenderly

kata-phroneō, to think against, to despise   [spiser

kata-phronētēs [kataphroneō], a de-

kata-phtheirō, to corrupt utterly. PAS., to be corrupt, to perish utterly

kata-pinō, to swallow up, swallow, devour. PAS., (also) to be drowned

kata-piptō, to fall down, to fall

kata-pleō, to arrive by sailing

kata-poneō [-ponos], to work down, to oppress, to vex   [be drowned

kata-pontizō, PAS., to sink down, to

kata-psuchō, to cool

kat-ara, a curse, a cursing. (See cursed)

kat-araomai, MID., to curse. PAS., to be cursed

kat-argeō, to make void, to bring to nought, to do away, abolish, loose, destroy, put down or away, cumber. PAS., (also) to cease, fail, vanish away, come to nought. (See delivered, effect)

kat-arithmeō, to number

kat-artisis, perfection in all parts

kat-artismos, the act of perfecting

kat-artizō, to join perfectly together, to make perfect, to frame, fit ; to prepare, mend, restore

kataschesis [katechō], a possession

kata-seiō, to beckon

kata-skaptō, to dig down. (See ruins)

kata-skēnoō, to pitch a tent, to lodge, rest

kata-skēnōsis a nest

kata-skeuazō, *to furnish*, to prepare, make, build, *to put in order*, to ordain

kata-skiazō, *to overshadow*, to shadow

kata-skopeō, *to spy out*

kata-skopos [kataskopeō], a spy

kata-sophizomai, to deal subtilly with

kata-sphattō, to slay

kata-sphragizō, to seal

kata-stellō, *to put down;* to appease. *PAS.*, to be quiet   [haviour

kata-stēma [-histēmi], *position*, be-

kata-stolē [katastellō], *drapery*, apparel   [wanton against

kata-strēniazō, to begin to wax

kata-strephō, to overturn, to overthrow   [overthrow

kata-strōnnumi, *to strew down*, to

kata-strophē [katastrephō], an overthrow, a subverting

kata-surō, *to drag*, to hale

kata-tithēmi, *to put down ;* to lay, shew, do   [cision

kata-tomē [-temnō],*a cutting off*, con-

kata-toxeuō, *to shoot down*, to thrust

kata-trechō, to run down   [through

kat-axioō, to ac:ount or count worthy

kat-ēchō, *to sound forth;* to instruct, teach, inform

kat-echō, to hold fast, hold, seize on, take; to keep, retain, possess, have; to withhold, to stay or let [*in the sense of hindering*]. (*See* make, memory)

kat-ēgoreō [-agoreuō], *to harangue against*, to accuse, object

kat-ēgoria [katēgoreō], accusation. (*See* accuse)

kat-ēgoros [katēgoreō], an accuser

kat-eidōlos, wholly given to idolatry

kat-elengchō [-elengchō], *to convict*

kat-enanti, over against, before

kat-enōpion, before the presence of, in the sight of, before

kat-ephtheia [-phaos, *the eye*], *dejection*, heaviness

kat-ephistēmi, *to rush down on*, to make insurrection against

kat-erchomai, to come or go down, to descend, to land, to depart

kat-ergazomai, *MID.*, to work out, to work, perform, to cause. *PAS.*, to be wrought. (*See* do)

kat-esthiō, to devour

kat-euthunō, to direct, to guide

kat-exousiazō, to exercise authority

kath-, *See* **kata-**   [over

kath-a [kata-hos], *according to what things ;* as

kath-aireō [-haireō], to take down, to put or pull down, to cast down, destroy

kath-airesis [kathaireō], a pulling down, destruction

kathairō [katharos], *to cleanse*, to

katha-per, as well as, even as   [purge

kath-aptō [-haptō], to fasten on

katharismos [katharos], cleansing, purification, purifying. (*See* purge)

katharizō, to cleanse, purge, purify, make clean

katharma [kathairō], *the offscouring*, filth

katharos, clean, pure, clear

katharotēs, *pureness*, a purifying

kath-edra [-hedra], a seat   [master

kath-ēgētēs [-hēgeomai], *a leader*, a

kath-eis [-heis], every one

kath-ēkei [-hēkō], *it is becoming*. *PART.*, **kathēkōn**, fit, convenient

kathēmai, to sit down or by, to sit, to dwell

kath hēmeran [kata-hēmera], day by day, daily, every day
16

kath-ēmerinos [kath hēmeran], daily

kath-eudō [-heudō, *to sleep*], to sleep, to be *deeply asleep*

kath-exēs [-hexēs], in or by order. (*See* after, afterward)

kathezomai, to sit

kath-iēmi [-hiēmi], to let down

kath-istēmi or **kathistaō** [-histēmi], to appoint, ordain, set, conduct, make. *PAS.*, (*also*) to be   [to continue

kathizō, to sit down, to sit, to tarry, to set down

kath-o [-hos], according to that *which*, as, inasmuch as

kath-olou [-holos], *wholly ;* at all (*after a negative*)

kath-oplizō [-hoplizō],*to equip*, to arm

kath-oraō [-horaō], to see clearly

kath-ōs [-hōs], according as, even as, (*See* according, how, when)

kath-oti [-hoti], *according to what ;* according as, forasmuch as, because that, as

kat-idian [kata-idios], *by themselves;* apart, aside, alone, privately

kat-ioōmai [-ios], *PAS.* to be *rusted*, to be cankered

kat-ischuō, to prevail against, prevail

kat-oikeō, *to dwell fixedly*, to dwell. *PART.*, a dweller, inhabiter, inhabitant

kat-oikēsis [katoikeō], a dwelling

kat-oikētērion, *a place of dwelling*, a habitation   [a habitation

kat-oikia, a habitation

kat-optrizomai [katoptron], to behold as in a glass

kat-optron [-optomai], *a mirror*

kat-orthōma [katorthoō, *to set upright*], a very worthy deed

katō, down, beneath. (*See* bottom)

katōterō, *further down*, under

katōteros, lower

kauchaomai, to boast, make a boast, glory ; to joy, rejoice

kauchēma, a boasting, glorying, rejoicing. (*See* rejoice, glory)

kauchēsis, a boasting, glorying, rejoicing. (*See* glory)

kauma [kaiō], heat

kaumatizō [kauma], to scorch

kausis [kaiō], *a burning*. (*See* burned)

kausoō, to set on fire. (*See* fervent)

kausōn, a burning heat, heat

kautēriazō [kautērion, *a branding iron ;* kaiō], to scar with a hot iron

keimai, to lie, to be laid, be laid up, be set, appointed, or made ; to be

keiria [keirō], *a bandage*. *PLU.*, grave clothes

keirō,*to clip*,to shear. *PART.*,a shearer

keleuō, to command, bid. (*See* commandment)

keleusma, *a command*, a shout

keno-doxia, vain glory   [glory

keno-doxos [-doxa], desirious of vain

kenoō, to make void, or of none effect, or of no reputation. *PAS.*, to be in

keno-phōnia, vain babbling   [vain

kenos, empty, vain. (*See* vain)

kenōs, in vain

kēnsos, *a census*, tribute

kenteō, *to prick or pierce*

kentron, a sting, a prick

kenturiōn [*Latin*, centurio, *an officer over 100 soldiers*], a centurion

kephalaion [kephalē], *the chief thing*, the sum

kephalaioō, to wound in the head

kephalē, the head

kephalis, a volume

kēpos, a garden

kēp-ouros, a gardener

keraia [keras], *one of the horn-like points of some Hebrew letters*, a tittle

kerameus, a potter

keramikos, of a potter

keramion, *an earthenware pitcher*

keramos, *potter's clay*, tiling

kerannumi, *to mingle, mix ;* to pour out, to fill

keras, a horn

keration, *a carob-pod shaped like a little horn*, a husk

kerdainō, to win, to get gain, to gain

kerdos, gain, lucre

kērion, *honey* comb

kerma [keirō], *small*, money

kermatistēs, a changer of money

kērugma [kērussō], *a proclamation*, preaching   [*PART.*, a preacher

kērussō, to proclaim, preach, publish.

kērux, *a public crier*, *a herald*, a   [preacher

kētos, a whale

kibōtos, an ark

kinamōmon, cinnamon

kinduneuō, to be in danger, to stand or be in jeopardy

kindunos, *danger*, peril   [mover

kineō,to move,wag; to remove. *PART.*,

kinēsis, a moving

kithara, a harp

kitharizō, *to play on a harp*, to harp

kitharōdos, a harper

klados, a branch

klaiō, to weep, to bewail

klaō or **klazō**, to break

klasis, a breaking   [meat

klasma, a fragment. *PLU.*, broken

klauthmos [klaiō], weeping, wailing

kleiō, to shut, to shut up

kleis [kleiō], a key   [branch

klēma [klaō], *a slip for grafting*, a

klemma [kleptō], theft

kleos [kaleō], *fame*, glory

kleptēs [kleptō], a thief

kleptō, to steal

klēro-nomeō[klēro-nomos],to inherit, obtain by inheritance, to be an heir

klēro-nomia, an inheritance

klēro-nomos [klēros-nemō], *one who enjoys an inheritance*, an heir

klēroōmai, *PAS.*, *to be made an inheritance [for God];* to obtain an inheritance

klēros, a lot, heritage, inheritance,part

klēsis [kaleō], a calling, a vocation

klētos [kaleō], one called ; *invited*, applied   [pointed

klibanos, an oven

klima, a *clime*, a region, a part

klinē [klinō], a bed, a table

klinidion, *a little bed*, a couch

klinō, to recline, to bow, to bow down, lay ; to turn to flight,wear away. (*See* spent)

klisia [klinō], a company (*reclining*)

klopē [kleptō], theft

kludōn [kluzō], a wave, the raging

kludōnizomai,to be tossed to and fro

kluzō, *to dash against*, inundate

knēthomai, *PAS.*, *to be tickled*,to itch

kodrantēs, *a quarter of an assarion*, a farthing

koilia, the belly, the womb

koimaomai, to sleep, be asleep, fall asleep or on sleep ; to be dead

koimēsis, *a sleeping*, the taking of rest

koinōneō [koinōnos], *to be partner ;* (1.) to be partaker of,(2.) to distribute, communicate

koinōnia, *partnership ;* fellowship, communion,distribution,contribution, communication. (*See* communicate)

koinōnikos, willing to communicate

koinōnos [koinos], *one who holds property with another*, a partner, partaker, companion. (*See* fellowship)

koinoō [koinos], (1.) to call *what is sacred* common ; (2.) to pollute,defile. PAS., to be unclean   [filed

koinos, common ; unholy, unclean, defiled

koitē, a bed ; chambering. (See conceive)

koitōn, a bed-chamber. (See chamberlain)

kokkinos, scarlet, scarlet coloured

kokkos, a seed, a grain, a corn

kolakeia, flattery. (See flatter)

kolaphizō [kolaphos,*the fist*], to buffet

kolasis, punishment, torment

kolazomai, MID., to punish. PAS., to be punished

kollaomai, MID. and PAS., to join one's self, to be joined, to keep company, to cleave to

kollourion, eye-salve

kollubistēs, a money changer, a koloboō, to shorten   [changer

kōlon, a carcase

kolōnia [Latin, colonia], a colony

kolpos, the bosom, a creek

kolumbaō, to swim

kolumbēthra, a pool

kōluō, to hinder, withstand, forbid ; not to suffer, to keep from, to let *or* cease

komaō, to have long hair   [hinder

komē, hair

kōmē, a village, a town

komeō, to take care of, to tend

komizō, MID., to receive, to bring

kōmo-polis [kōmē], a village-city, a kōmos, revelling, rioting   [town

kompsoteron, in better condition. (See amend)

koniaō, to whiten

koniortos, dust

kōnōps, a gnat

kopazō [kopos], to work one's self out, to cease

kopē [koptō], slaughter

kopetos, lamentation

kophinos, a basket

kōphos, deaf, dumb, speechless

kopiaō, to toil, labour, to bestow labour, to be wearied

kopos, toil, labour, weariness. (See kopria, dung ; dunghill [trouble [vb.])

koptō, to strike ; to cut down. MID., to mourn, wail, lament, bewail

korasion, a damsel, a maid

korax, a raven   [ban

korban [Hebrew], a gift (to God), Corkorbanas, the treasury

korennumi, to satiate. PAS., to eat enough, to be full

koros, a measure (= about 15 bushels)

kosmeō, to adorn, garnish, trim

kosmikos [kosmos], worldly

kosmios [kosmos], orderly ; of good behaviour, modest   [ruler

kosmo-kratōr,the world-governor,the kosmos, regularity, adorning ; the world

koumi [Syriac], arise, cumi

kouphizō [kouphos, light], to lighten

koustōdia [Latin, custodia], custody, a guard, a watch

krabbatos, a bed, a couch

kraipalē, surfeiting

kranion, a skull ; Calvary

kraspedon, a fringe, a border, a hem

krataios [kratos], mighty

krataioō, PAS., to be strengthened, to wax *or* be strong

krateō, to lay hand *or* hold on, take, hold fast, hold by, keep, retain ; to obtain

kratistos, most noble, most excellent

kratos, power, strength, dominion. (See mightily)

---

kraugazō, to cry, to cry out

kraugē, clamour, cry, a crying

krazō, to cry, to cry out

kreas, flesh

kreisson [adverb], better   [(See best)

kreissōn [comp. of agathos], better.

kremamai, MID., to hang. PAS., to krēmnos, a steep place   [be hanged

krima [krinō], judgment, condemnation, damnation. (See avenge, condemn, law)

krinō, to judge, determine, think, decree, ordain, conclude, esteem ; to condemn, damn. PAS. (also), to go to *or* sue at law. (See avenge, question, sentence)

krinon, a lily

krisis [krinō], judgment ; condemnation, damnation ; accusation

kritērion, a rule of judging, a judgment seat. (See judgment, judge)

kritēs [krinō], a judge

krithē, barley

krithinos, of barley

kritikos, skilled in judging; a discerner

krouō, to knock

kruphē [kruptō], in secret

kruptō, to hide, keep secret. (See secretly)

kruptos, hidden, hid, secret. (See inwardly)

krustallizō, to be clear as crystal

krustallos, crystal   [purchase

ktaomai, to obtain, possess, provide, kteinō, to kill

ktēma [ktaomai], possession

ktēnos, property in cattle ; a beast

ktētōr [ktaomai], a possessor

ktisis [ktizō], the creature, creation ; building ; ordinance

ktisma, a creature

ktistēs, the Creator

ktizō, to create, make. PART. Creator

kubeia [kubeuō, to handle dice], craft, sleight

kubernēsis [kubernaō, to steer (a ship), to govern], government

kubernētēs, steersman, shipmaster, master

kuklō [kuklos],in a circle ; round about

kukloō [kuklos], to stand or come round about, to compass, compass

kuklos, a circle   [about

kuklothen, round about, about

kuliō, to roll. MID. or PAS., to wallow

kulisma [kuliō], a wallowing

kullos, maimed

kuma, a wave   [bal

kumbalon [kumbos, a hollow], a cymkuminon, cummin

kunarion [kuōn], a little dog, a dog

kuneō, to kiss

kuōn, a dog

kuptō, to stoop, stoop down

kureō, to hit, to light upon, to reach

kuria [fem. of kurios], a lady   [Lord's

kuriakos, belonging to a lord, the

kurieuō, to exercise lordship, or have dominion over, to be lord of. PART., lord

kurios, lord, Lord, master, sir. (See God, Act.19.2o)

kuriotēs, dominion, government

kuroō, to confirm

Λ, λ, (lambda)=l.

lachanon, an herb

lailaps, a storm, a tempest

lakeō, or laskō, to burst asunder

laktizō, to kick   [(See preach)

laleō, to speak, talk, utter, tell, say.

---

lalia [laleō], a saying, speech

lama [Hebrew], wherefore, lama

lambanō, to take, catch, bring ; to receive, accept, obtain, attain, hold. (See assay, call, come, have)

lampas [lampō], lamp, torch, light

lampō, to give light, to shine

lampros [lampō], bright, clear ; gorgeous, white, gay, goodly   [tuously

lamprōs [lampros], gorgeously, sumplamprotēs [lampros], brightness [lot)

langchanō, to obtain, cast lots. (See

lanthanō, to be hid, to be hid from. (See ignorant, unawares)

laos, a people

larungx, the throat

lathra [lanthanō], privately, secretly

latomeō, to hew

latreia [latreuō], divine service, service

latreuō, to worship, serve ; to do [sacred] service to. PART.,a worshipper

laxeutos, hewn in stone

legeōn [Latin, legio], a division of the Roman army,=3000 or 4000 men, a legion

legō, to lay together, to say, tell, speak, utter, describe, call. (See ask, bid, boast, give, name [vb.], put, saying [nn.])

leichō, to lick

leimma [leipō], a remnant

leios, level, smooth.

leipō, to leave. PAS., to be wanting ; to be destitute. (See lack)

leitourgeō [leitourgos], to do the work of a leitourgos, to minister

leitourgia, public service, ministration, ministry

leitourgikos [leitourgos], ministering

leitourgos [leitos, public ; ergon], a minister, one that ministers

lēnos, a wine-press

lention, an apron, a towel

leōn, a lion

lepis, an incrustation, a scale

lepra [lepis], leprosy

lepros, a leper

lepsis [lambanō], a receiving

lepton, a mite (the smallest coin)

lēros, an idle tale

lēstēs, a robber, a thief   [forget)

lēthē [lanthanō], forgetfulness. (See

leukainō [leukos], to make white, to leukos, white   [white

lian, greatly, very, exceeding. (See great, chiefest, sore)

libanos, frankincense

libanōton, a censer

likmaō, to grind to powder

limēn, a haven

limnē, a lake

limos, a famine, dearth ; hunger

linon, linen, a wick of flax

liparos, sumptuous, dainty

lips, south-west

lithazō [lithos], to stone

lithinos [lithos], made of stone

litho-boleō [-ballō], to cast stones, to stone   [blingstone)

lithos, a stone. (See millstone, stumlitra, a pound (= about 12 oz. avoir.)

logia [legō], a collection, a gathering

logikos [logos], reasonable, of the word

logion [legō], a divine utterance, an logios, eloquent   [oracle

logismos [logizomai], thought, imagination

logizomai [logos], to account, to reckon, esteem ; to suppose, think on, reason, impute, count, conclude, to number. (See lay, despise)

17

logo-macheō [-machomai], to strive about words

logo-machia, strife of words

logos, a word, a speech, talk, utterance, saying, communication ; account, reason, doctrine ; a treatise. (See cause, concerning, fame, do, intent, matter, mouth, things, preaching, question, rumour, say, shew, speaker, thing, tidings, work, reckon)

loidoreō [loidoros], to revile

loidoria, railing. (See reproachfully)

loidoros, a railer, a reviler

loimos, a pestilence, a pestilent fellow

loipon, finally, besides, furthermore, moreover, henceforth ; it remaineth. (See then, now)

loipos [leipō], PLU., the rest, or remnant, or residue, other, others. NEU. PLU., things which remain

loipou [gen. of loipos with ho], from

longchē, a spear   [henceforth

louō, to wash

loutron [louō], a washing

luchnia [luchnos], a candlestick

luchnos, a candle, a light

lukos, a wolf

lumainomai, to make havoc

luō, to loose, unloose ; put off ; dissolve, break, destroy. PAS., (also) to melt

lupē, grief, sorrow, heaviness. (See grievous, grudgingly)

lupeō [lupē], to cause grief, to make sorry, to grieve. PAS., to be grieved or sorry or sorrowful or in heaviness, to be made sorry ; to sorrow

lusis, [luō], a loosing. (See loose [vb.])

lusitelei, it is better

lutron [luō], a ransom

lutroō, to redeem by a ransom

lutrōsis [lutroō], redemption. (See

lutrōtēs, a deliverer   [redeem)

M, μ, (mu) = m.

machaira, a sword

machē, strife, fighting, striving

machomai, to fight, strive

mageia [magos], sorcery

mageuō, to use sorcery   [a sorcerer

magos, one of the magi, a wise man,

mainomai, to be mad or beside one's

makarios, happy, blessed   [self

makariōteros, happier

makarismos, blessedness

makarizō [makarios], to count happy, to call blessed

makellon, a flesh-market, the shambles

makran [makros], far, afar off, a good or great way off

makro-chronios [chronos], long lived

makros, long, far

makrothen, from far, afar off

makro-thumeō [-thumos], to be long suffering, to suffer or bear long, to endure patiently, to have patience or long patience, to be patient

makro-thumia, longsuffering, patience

makro-thumōs, patiently

malakia, a weakness, a disease

malakos, soft, effeminate

malista, especially, chiefly, most of all, specially

mallon, more, rather ; so much the more, more and more. (See better, far, [much)

mammē, a grandmother

mammōnas, wealth, mammon

mania, madness. (See mad)

manna, manna   [soothsaying)

manteuomai, to be a soothsayer. (See

manthanō, to learn, to understand

marainomai. PAS., to be dried up, to fade away

18

maran atha [Syriac], = our Lord

margaritēs, a pearl   [cometh

marmaron, marble   [martyr

martur, a witness, a record [= witness],

martureō [martur], to be a witness, to bear witness or record, to testify, give testimony. (See give.) MID., to witness, to charge. PAS., to be well reported of, to have or obtain a good report, to be of good or honest report, to be witnessed   [record = testimony

marturia, testimony, report, witness,

marturion, testimony, witness. (See testify)

marturomai, to testify, to take to

massaomai, to gnaw   [record

massō, to handle, to knead ; to wipe

mastigoō, to scourge

mastix, a scourging, a plague

mastizō, to scourge

mastos, a pap

mataio-logia [-logos], vain jangling

mataio-logos, a vain talker

mataioōmai, PAS., to become vain

mataios, vain. PLU. NEU., vanities

mataiotēs [mataios], vanity

matēn, in vain   [disciple

mathētēs [manthanō], a learner, a

mathēteuō, to make a disciple ; to be a disciple ; to instruct, teach

mathētria a female disciple

mē (1.), not, lest. (See but, neither, never, none, nor, nothing, without)

ean mē, if not, except,' but. (See before, whosoever, not)

hina mē, lest, that not. (See albeit, no, nothing)

mē (2.), a sign of interrogation, changing what would otherwise be an affirmation into a question

mechri or **mechris**, till, until, to, unto

mēdamōs, by no means, not so

mē-de, nor, neither ; not even ; not so muh as ; not once, nor yet, no not

mēdeis [mēde-heis], no man, not any man, none, no. NEU., (also) nothing. (See any, at all, whit)

mēde-pō, not yet

mēde-pote, not at any time, never

megal-aucheō [megas-aucheō, to boast], to boast great things

megaleios, PLU. neu., great things, wonderful works

megaleiotēs, greatness, magnificence, mighty power, majesty

megalo-prepēs [-prepei], excellent

megalōs, greatly

megalōsunē, majesty   [shew, great)

megalunō, to magnify, enlarge. (See

megas, great, large, mighty ; greatest ; strong, loud, high. (See sore, exceed-

megethos, greatness   [ingly years)

megistanes [megistos], PLU., chiefs, great men, lords

megistos [super. of megas], greatest, exceeding great

meizon, the more

meizōn [comp. of megas], more, greater, greatest. (See elder) [greater, greater

meizoteros [comp. of meizōn], still

mēketi, no more, no longer, not henceforth or hereafter. (See room)

mēkos, length   [up

mēkunō, to lengthen. MID., to grow

melan [neut. of melas], ink

melas, black

melei [impersonal], it is an object of care to. (See care)

meletaō [melei], to bestow care upon, to meditate, imagine, premeditate

meli, honey

melissios, of honey, honey comb

mellō, to be about to do something expressed by a following verb ; to intend, mind, mean ; to be ready, to be yet or at the point ; to begin ; to tarry ; shall, will, should. (See after, afterwards, almost, hereafter, time.) PART., (also) to come = coming

melos, a member

mēlōtē, a sheepskin

membrana, a membrane, parchment

memphomai, to find fault

mempsimoiros, a repiner at one's lot, a complainer

men, truly, indeed, verily, even. (See

mēn, a month   [so, some)

menō, to remain, abide, continue, tarry, endure, dwell ; to stand, be present. (See own)

men-oun-ge, yea verily, yea rather, yea doubtless (See nay but)

men-toi, howbeit, yet, but. (See also)

mēnuō, to shew, tell

mē-pō, not yet   [perhaps, lest

mē-pōs, lest by any means, lest haply or

mē-pote, lest haply, lest at any time ; if peradventure ; whether or not. (See all)

merimna [merizō], distracting thought, anxiety, care

merimnaō, to be anxiously careful, to take thought, to care

meris, a share, a part. (See partaker)

merismos [merizō], a dividing asunder ;

meristēs, a divider   [a gift

merizō, to divide, deal, distribute, to give a part. (See difference)

meros, a part, piece, portion ; the coast, side. (See course, craft, sort, partly, particular, particularly, somewhat,

mēros, the thigh   [behalf, respect)

mes-ēmbria [mesos-hēmera], mid-day, noon ; the south

mesitēs [mesos], a mediator   [firm

mesiteuō [mesitēs], to mediate, to con-

meso-nuktion [mesos-nux], midnight

mesoō, to be in the midst. (See midst)

mesos, the middle, in the midst of ; (See midst, among, way, midday, midnight, forth, before)

meso-toichon, a middle wall

mes-ouranēma [-ouranos], mid-heaven, the midst of heaven

mestoō, to fill. PAS., to be full

mestos, full

meta [gen.], with, among. (See of, in, upon, on, unto, against)

meta [accus.], after. (See afterward, hereafter, hence, since)

meta-, met-, meth-, indicates a change from one state to another ; (also), with ; after

meta-bainō, to go from one place to another ; to pass, remove, depart

meta-ballomai, MID., to change one's mind

meta-didōmi, to transfer ; to impart,

met-agō, to turn about   [to give

met-airō, to remove one's self, to depart   [hither ; to call

meta-kaleō, MID., to call for or

meta-kineō, PAS., to be moved away

meta-lambanō, to share with ; to be a partaker of, to take, receive. (See eat, have)

meta-lēpsis [metalambanō], a partaking. (See receive)

met-allattō [-allattō], to exchange, to change

meta-melomai [-melei], to be sorry, to repent, repent one's self

meta-morphoōmai, PAS., to be transformed, transfigured, changed

MET　MOR　OH

meta-noeō. *to change one's mind, to repent*

meta-noia, *change of mind,* repentance

meta-pempō, to send for, call for

meta-schēmatizō, to transform; to change, to transfer in a figure

meta-strephō, to turn *into*; to pervert

meta-thesis [metatithēmi], *transference*, a translation, removing, a change

meta-tithēmi, to carry over, translate, remove; to change, turn

metaxu, between, meanwhile, next

mē-te, neither, nor, not so much as. (See or)

met-echō, to be partaker of, take part of; to use. (See pertain)

met-epeita, afterward

meteōrizomai [meteōros, *lofty*], *to be unsettled,* to be of doubtful mind

mētēr [mētēr], a mother　[ness

methē [methu, *mulled wine*], drunken-

meth-ermēneuō [-hermēneuō], to interpret. (See interpretation)

meth-istanō or meth-istēmi [-histēmi], *to transfer,* to translate, remove; to put out, turn away

meth-odeia [-hodos], *a stratagem,* a wile　[border

meth-orion [-horion], *a boundary,* a

methuō, to make drunk; to be drunken. PAS., (also) to drink well

methuskomai, *to make one's self drunk,* to be drunk *or* drunken

methusos, a drunkard

mē-ti has usually, like mē, *simply interrogative power.* In Mat.12.23, it is *a negative interrogative. With ge, it is rendered,* how much more　[any?

mē-tis [mē?-tis], hath any man? [have

met-ochē [metechō], *participation,* fellowship　[ner, fellow

met-ochos [metechō], a partaker, part-

met-oikesia [-oikos], *a change of abode,* a carrying away. (See carry, bring)

met-oikizō, *to make to change one's abode;* to carry away, to remove *into*

met-ōpen [meta-ōps], the forehead

mētra [mētēr], the womb　[mother

mētralōēs [mētēr], the murderer of a

metreō [metron], to measure, mete

metrētēs, a firkin (=*about* 13½ *gallons*)

metrio-patheō, *to feel kindness towards;* to have compassion on

metriōs, *by measure,* a little

metron, a measure

miainō, to defile

miasma, pollution

miasmos, uncleanness

migma, a mixture

mignumi, *to mix,* to mingle

mikron, a little; a little while, a while

mikros, little, small; least

mikroteros, less; [*with* ho], the least

milion, a mile

mimeomai, *to imitate,* to follow

mimētēs, a follower　[mindful

mimnēskomai, to remember, be

miseō, to hate. PAS., (also) to be hateful

misth-apodosia [-apodidōmi], a recompence of reward

misth-apodotēs, a rewarder

misthios [misthos], a hired servant

misthōma, *a thing hired,* a hired house

misthoōmai, to hire　[house

misthos, wages, hire, reward

misthōtos, a hireling, a hired servant

mna, a pound (=*about* £3, 4s. 7d)

mnaomai, to remember, be mindful. (See remembrance)

mneia, remembrance; mention

---

mnēma, a sepulchre, a tomb, a grave

mnēmē, remembrance

mnēmeion, a sepulchre, tomb, grave

mnēmoneuō, to remember, be mindful, make mention

mnēmosunon, a memorial

mnēsteuō, to espouse　[fulness

mochthos [mogos], *toil, travail,* painfulness

modios, a bushel (=*about a peck*)

mogi-lalos, *hardly able to speak,* having an impediment in speech

mogis, *with difficulty,* hardly

mogos, *labour*

moichalis [*fem.*], adulterous; an adulteress; adultery

moichaomai, to commit adultery

moicheia, adultery

moicheuō, to commit adultery with. PAS. part., in adultery

moichos, an adulterer　[work]

molis, hardly, scarcely, scarce. (See

mōlōps, stripes

molunō, to defile

molusmos, filthiness

mōmaomai, *to find fault,* to blame

mōmos, *a fault,* a blemish

momphē [memphomai], *a cause of complaint,* a quarrel　[mansion

monē [menō], *a home,* an abode, a

mono-genēs, only-begotten; an only

monon [*adv.*], only, alone; but　[child

monoōmai, PAS., to be desolate

mon-ophthalmos, with one eye

monos [*adj.*], alone, only. (See themselves)

mōrainō, to make foolish. PAS., to become a fool; *to become insipid,* to lose savour

mōria, foolishness

mōro-logia, foolish talking

mōros, foolish; a fool. NEU.,foolishness

morphē, form

morphoō, to form

morphōsis, *formation,* form

moscho-poieō, to make a calf

moschos, a calf

mousikos, a musician

muelos, marrow

mueō, *to initiate,* to instruct

mukaomai, to roar

muktērizō, to mock

mulikos, *of a mill.* (See millstone)

mulōn, a mill

mulos, a millstone

muō, *to close,* to be shut　[(See afar)

muōpazō [muō-ōps], *to be near sighted.*

murias, ten thousand. (See thousand,

murioi, ten thousand　[innumerable)

murizō [muron], to anoint

muron, *myrrh,* ointment

musterion [muō], *a secret rite revealed to a select few,* a mystery

mutheomai, *to speak, talk, tell*

muthos, a fable

N, ν, (nu)=n.

nai, yes, yea, even so; verily, surely. (See truth)

naos, a temple; a *heathen* shrine

nardos, nard. (See spikenard)

narkaō, *to grow stiff or numb*

nau-ageō [-agnumi, *to break*], to make shipwreck, to be shipwrecked

nau-klēros, the owner of a ship

naus, a ship

nautēs, a shipman, sailor　[by

nē [*a particle of swearing*], by, I protest

neanias [neos], a young man

neaniskos, a young man

neikos, *a quarrel,* strife

nekroō, to mortify. PAS., to be dead

nekros, dead

nekrōsis, a dying; deadness

---

nemō, *to distribute,* to possess. MID., *to enjoy, to feed on*

neōkoros, *a temple-keeper,* a worshipper

neo-phutos, *newly planted, a neophyte,*

neos, new, young　[a novice

neōteros [*comp. of* neos], *newer,* younger

neossos, a young *bird*

neōterikos, youthful

neotēs, youth

nēphalios, sober

nephelē, a cloud

nēphō, *to abstain,* to be sober; to watch

nephos, a cloud

nephros, PLU., the reins

nēpiazō, to be a child

nēpios, a child, babe. (See childish)

nēsion, an island

nēsos, an isle, island

nēsteia, a fast, fasting

nēsteuō, to fast

nēstis, fasting [*adj.*]

nēthō, to spin

neuō, *to nod,* to beckon

nikaō, to conquer, overcome, get the

nikē, victory　[victory, prevail

nikos, victory

niptēr, a bason

niptō, to wash　[the mind

noēma, a perception, thought, device;

noeō, to perceive, understand, think, consider

nomē [nemō], pasture. (See eat)　[sider

nomikos [nomos], about the law; a

nomimōs, lawfully　[lawyer

nomisma [nomizō], money

nomizō, *to judge,* to think, suppose. PAS., to be wont　[tor of the law

nomo-didaskalos, a teacher *or* doctor

nomos, law　[the law

nomo-thesia [-tithēmi], the giving of

nomo-theteō [-tithēmi], PAS., to be established *as law;* to be legislated for. (See receive)

nomo-thetēs [nomotheteō], a lawgiver

noōs, See nous

nosēma, a disease

noseō, *to be sick;* to dote

nosos, a disease, sickness, infirmity

nosphizomai, MID., to keep back, to purloin

nossia [neossos], a brood　[purloin

nossion [neossos], a chicken

nothos, a bastard

nōthros, slothful, dull

notos, the south wind, the south

nōtos, the back (*of an animal*)

nou-mēnia [neos], the new moon

noun-echōs [nous-echō], *having sound judgment,* discreetly

nous *or* noōs, *the perceptive faculty,* the mind, understanding

nou-thesia [noutheteō], *putting in mind,* admonition

nou-theteō [nous-tithēmi], *to put in mind,* to admonish, warn

nuchth-ēmeron [nux-hēmera], a night and a day

numphē, a bride, a daughter-in-law

numphios, a bridegroom

numphōn, a bridechamber

nun, now, at this time, at present. (See late, henceforth, hereafter)

ta nun [ta *the neu. plu. of* ho], *in present circumstances,* now but now

nuni [nun], now

nustazō [neuō], *to nod,* to slumber

nuttō *or* nussō, to pierce

nux, the night, midnight

O, o, (*omikron*)=o.

Ω, ω, (*omega*) =ō.

ō, Omega, the last letter of the Greek

ō, oh!　[alphabet
19

ochleō [ochlos], *to mob*, to vex
ochlo-poieō, *to make a mob*,to gather a company
ochlos, *a crowd*, a multitude, a company, number of people, press
ochtheō, *to be burdened or grieved*
echurōma, a stronghold
ōdē, a song
ōdin, travail; pain, sorrow
ōdinō, to travail in birth
odous, a tooth
odunaomai, *PAS.*, to be tormented, to sorrow
odunē, *pain*, sorrow
odurmos, mourning
ogdoēkonta [okto], *eighty*, fourscore
ogdoös [oktō], the eighth
oikeios, of the house or household
oikēma, *a dwelling;* a prison
oikeō, to dwell
oikētērion, a habitation, a house
oiketēs, a household servant, a servant
oikia, a house, a home, a household
oikiakos, one of a household
oiko-despoteō, *to be ruler of a house*, to guide the house
oiko-despotēs, the master or goodman of the house, a householder
oiko-domē, a building; edification, edifying. *(See* edify*)*
oiko-domeō,to build up,edify. *PART.*, a builder. *PAS.*, *(also)* to be in building; to be emboldened
oiko-nomeō, to be a steward
oiko-nomia, stewardship; *economy*, dispensation. *(See edifying)*
oiko-nomos, a steward, chamberlain, governor
oikos, a house,home, household,temple
oikoumenē [*pas. part. of* oikeō], *the inhabited land*, the earth, the world
oik-ouros, a keeper at home
oikteirō, to have compassion on
oiktirmōn, merciful, of tender mercy
oiktirmos, mercy
oimai [oiomai], to suppose
oino-phlugia [phluō, *to overflow*], excess of wine
oino-potēs [-pinō], a wine-bibber
oinos, wine. *(See* wine-press*)*
oiomai, to suppose, think
okellō, *to run* (a ship) *aground*
okneō, to delay
oknēros, slothful, grievous
okta-ēmeros [-hemera] [*adj.*], on the eighth day
oktō, eight. *(See* eighteen*)*
olethros [ollumi], destruction
oligo-pistos, of little faith
oligo-psuchos, feeble-minded
oligōreō, *to care little for*, to despise
oligos, little, small, short. *PLU.*, few. *(See* almost, briefly,long, season, while*)*
ollumi, *to destroy*. *MID.*, *to perish*
ololuzō, to howl
olothreuō [olethros], to destroy
olothreutēs [olethros], a destroyer
olunthos, an untimely fig
ombros, a shower
omma, the eye
omnumi, to swear
ōmos, the shoulder   [come]
ōn [*partic. of* eimi], *being*. *(See* be,have,
onar, a dream
onarion [onos], a young ass
oneidismos, reproach
oneidizō, to reproach, revile, upbraid, to cast in one's teeth
oneidos, reproach
onēmi, *MID.*, to have joy
ōneomai, to buy
ongkos, a weight
20

onikos [onos], *of an ass, i.e., turned by an ass*. *(See* millstone*)*
onoma, a name. *(See* call, name [*vb.*], surname [*vb.*]*)*
onomazō, to name, to call
onos, an ass
ontōs [*adv. from* ōn], indeed, certainly,of a truth,verily. *(See* clean[*adv.*]*)*
ōon, an egg
opē, a cave, a place
opheilē, a debt, what is due
opheilēma, a debt   [sinner
opheiletēs, a debtor, one who owes, a
opheilō, to be a debtor, to owe, to be indebted,'to be bound, to behove. *PAS.*, to be due. *(See* debt, duty, guilty, need, needs, ought, should.,
ōpheleia, profit, advantage
ōpheleō, to profit, to prevail. *PAS.*, to be profited, advantaged, or bettered
ōphelimos, profitable. *(See* profit [*vb.*]*)*
ophelon [opheilō], *oh that*, I would that, I would to God
ophelos, *an advantage*, profit. *(See* advantage [*vb.*], profit [*vb.*]*)*
ophis, a serpent
ophrus, a brow
ophthalmo-douleia, eye-service
ophthalmos, the eye. *PLU.*, *(also)* sight
opisō, *at the back of*, behind, back, after, backward. *(See* follow.*)*
opisthen, *from behind*, behind, after, backside
opōra, *PLU.*, autumn fruits
ōps, *the countenance*
opsarion, a small fish, a fish
opse, *late*, at even, in the end
opsia [opse] evening, eventide, even
opsimos, *late*, latter   [face, appearance
opsis, [optomai], the countenance, the
opsōnion, wages, charges
optanō, to see
optasia, a vision
optomai, to see, look. *PAS.*, to appear,
optos, broiled   [shew one's self
orcheomai, to dance
oregō, *to stretch out*. *MID.*, *to stretch one's self towards*, to covet
oreinos [oros], *mountainous*, hill [*adj.*]
orexis [oregomai], lust   [geance
orgē, wrath, anger, indignation, ven-
orgilos, *prone to anger*, soon angry
orgizomai, to be angry or wroth
orguia [oregō], a fathom (=6 *feet*)
orneon, a fowl, a bird
ornis, a hen
oros, a mountain, hill, mount
orphanos, fatherless, comfortless
ortho-podeō [-pous], to walk uprightly
orthos, erect, upright, straight
orthōs, rightly, right [*adv.*], plain [*adv.*]
ortho-tomeō [-temnō],to divide rightly
orthrinos [orthros], *of* the morning
orthrios, early
orthrizō [orthros], *to rise early*, to come early in the morning
orthros, *morning*, early in the morning
ōruomai, to roar
orussō or oruttō, to dig
osmē, *smell*, odour, savour
osphrēsis, smelling
osphus, the loins
osteon, a bone
ostrakinos [ostrakon, *burnt clay*], earthen, of earth
ōtheō, *to push, shove, thrust*
othonē, a linen sheet
othonion, a linen cloth
ōtion, the ear
ou, *See* ouk
oua, ah

ouai, alas, woe
ouch, *See* ouk
ouchi, not? not, not so, nay
oudamōs, by no means, not
ou-de neither, nor; not even, **not.** *(See* also, even, then, more, much, yet, then*)*
oud-eis [oude-heis], no man, none, nought, not any, nothing, neither any. *(See* any, never, ought*)*
oudenoō [oudeis], *to bring to nought*
oude-pō, not yet, never yet, never before, as yet not. *(See* yet*)*
oude-pote, never, neither at any time. *(See* time*)*
ouk or ouch, or **ou**, not, no, nay, neither, nor, never. *(See* none, nothing*)*
ouk mē or **ou mē** [*an intense negative*], *not not, no never*, not at all, in no wise, by no means, *not*, by any means, never; neither. *(See* more, nor, no, nothing, case*)*
ouk-eti, no longer, no more, now no more, not any more, not after that, henceforth, not, not as yet, now not, hereafter not, yet not
ouk-oun, *not then*. *(See* then*)*
oun, therefore, then; so then, now then, wherefore, truly, verily, and so. *(See* likewise*)*
ou-pō, not yet, *not* as yet, hitherto not
oura, a tail
ouranios, heavenly
ouranothen, from heaven
ouros, *a watcher*
ous, the ear
ousia [eimi], substance, goods
ou-te, neither, nor; no not, nor yet, yet not. *(See* nothing, none*)*
oxos, vinegar
oxus, sharp, swift
ozō, *to emit a smell*, to stink

Π, π, (*pi*) =p.
Φ, φ, (*phi*) =ph.
Ψ, ψ, (*psi*) =ps.

pachunomai [pachus, *thick*], to wax gross
pagideuō, *to ensnare*, to entangle
pagis, a snare
paid-agōgos [pais-agōgos], an instructer of *children*, a schoolmaster
paidarion [*dim. of* pais], a child, a lad
paideia, instruction, nurture; chastisement, chastening
paideuō, to teach, instruct; to chasten, chastise. *PAS.*, *(also)* to learn
paideutēs [paideuō], an instructer, one who corrects   [a damsel
paidion, a child, a young or little child;
paidiothen, *from childhood*, of a child
paidiskē, a maid, maiden, damsel; bondmaid, bondwoman
paiō, to strike, to smite
pais, a child; son, young man; maid, maiden; a servant, man-servant
paizō [pais], *to sport like children;* to play *idolatrously*
palai, of old, long ago, in time past, a great while ago; any while
palaioō, to make old. *PAS.*, to wax old, to decay
palaios, *ancient*, old
palaiotēs, oldness
palē, *a wrestling*. *(See* wrestle*)*
palin, again   [neration
palinggenesia [palin-genesis], rege-
pam-plēthei [pan-plēthos], all at once
pam-puos [-pan-], very great

pan- [neuter of pas], See **pas**

pau-docheion [-dechomai], an inn

pan-docheus, an innkeeper, a host

pan-ēguris [-aguris, an assembly], a general or universal assembly

pan-oiki, with all one's house

pan-oplia [-hoplon], a complete suit of armour, all armour, whole armour

pan-ourgia [panourgos], craftiness, cunning, subtilty

pan-ourgos [-ergon], skilful, crafty

pantachothen [pas], from every quarter

pantachou, every where, in all places

pantē, always

pan-teles [-telos], the uttermost. (See wise, [nn.])

panto-kratŏr [pas-krateō], almighty, omnipotent

pantōs, altogether, by all means, no doubt, surely; at all. (See needs, wise [nn.])

pantote, alway, always, evermore, ever

pantothen, from all quarters, on every side, round about

para-, **par-**, alongside, beyond, contrary to

para, [gen.], from. (See of)

para, [dative], near, with, among, before, by. (See of, in sight)

para [accus.], by, nigh unto; beyond, past, contrary to, against, more than, above. (See at, save, than)

para-bainō, to transgress. (See transgression)

para-ballō, to compare; to arrive

para-basis [parabainō], transgression. (See break)

para-batēs[parabainō], a transgressor, breaker of a law. (See transgress)

para-biazomai, to constrain

para-bolē [paraballō], comparison, parable, figure, proverb

para-bouleuomai, not to regard

para-cheimasia, wintering. (See winter)

para-cheimazŏ [-cheimon], to winter

para-chrēma, on the spot, immediately, straightway, presently, forthwith; soon

para-dechomai, to receive

para-deigmatizō, to make a public example, to put to an open shame

paradeisos, a pleasure park, garden, or grove; paradise

para-diatribē [-diatribē, employment], perverse disputing

para-didōmi, to give or deliver up, to give over; to bring forth, betray, cast or put into prison; to commit, recommend. (See hazard, prison)

para-dosis [paradidōmi], delivery; tradition; ordinance

para-doxos, contrary to opinion, strange

para-ginomai, to come, to be present. (See go)

par-agō, to lead one's self by, to pass in or away, to depart, to pass forth; to be past

par-aineō, to exhort, to admonish

par-aiteomai, to intreat, to make excuse; to avoid, reject. PAS., to be excused

para-kaleō, to call for; to exhort or give exhortation; to comfort, beseech, intreat, pray, desire

para-kaluptō, to hide

para-katathēkē [-katatithēmi], a trust, that which is committed to one's trust

para-kathizō, to sit alongside

para-keimai, to lie near, to be present

para-klēsis, exhortation, intreaty; comfort, consolation

para-klētos, a comforter; an advocate

par-akoē [parakouō], the neglecting to hear, disobedience

par-akoloutheō, to follow, attain; to know fully, to have understanding

par-akouō, to neglect to hear

para-kuptō, to stoop down and look, to look

para-lambanō, to take with or unto, to take, to receive

para-legomai, to pass by, to sail by

par-alios [-hals], the sea coast

par-allagē [-allattō], variableness

para-logizomai, to mislead by false reasoning, to deceive, beguile

para-luomai [-luō], PAS., to be feeble, to be sick of the palsy

para-lutikos, one sick of the palsy

para-menō, to abide, continue

para-mutheomai, to comfort

para-muthia, comfort

para-muthion, comfort

par-anggelia, a command, a charge

par-anggellō, to command, charge, give commandment; to declare

para-nomeō, to act contrary to law

para-nomia, a violation of law, iniquity

para-pherō, to take away, to remove

para-phroneō, to be foolish, to be as

para-phronia, folly, madness [a fool

para-pikrainō, to provoke

para-pikrasmos, provocation

para-piptō, to fall away

para-pleō, to sail by

para-plēsion, nigh unto

para-plēsiōs, likewise [to go

para-poreuomai, to pass by, to pass,

para-ptōma [-piptō], a fall, offence, trespass, sin, fault

para-rreō [-reō], PAS., to be carried away from, to let slip

para-sēmos, marked; whose sign was

para-skeuazō, to make ready. MID., to prepare one's self. PAS., to be ready

para-skeuē, preparation

para-teinō, to stretch out, to continue

para-tēreō, to watch, to observe

para-tērēsis [paratēreō], a watching, observation

para-thalassios, upon the sea-coast

para-thēkē [paratithēmi], a deposit, something committed in trust

para-theoreō, to neglect

para-tithēmi, to put alongside, to put forth, set before, allege. MID., to commend, commit the keeping of

para-tungchanō, to meet with

parautika, but for a moment

para-zēloō, to provoke to emulation or jealousy

pardalis, a leopard

par-echō, to bring, give, offer, minister; to shew, keep. (See do, trouble [vb.])

par-ēgoria [-agoreuō], comfort

par-eimi, to be here, to be present; to be come. PART., present. (See lack, have)

par-eisagō, to bring in privil,

par-eisaktos [pareisagō], brought in unawares

par-eis-dunō [-eisdunō, to enter into], to creep in unawares

par-eiserchomai, to come in privily, to enter

par-eispherō, to bring in alongside, to give

par-ektos, except, saving; without

par-embolē [-emballō], an interposition, a camp, a castle, an army

par-enochleō, to create disturbance to trouble

par-epidēmos, a pilgrim, a stranger

par-erchomai, to pass by, or away, or over; to come forth; to transgress. (See go) [mission

par-esis [pariēmi], a letting pass, re-

par-iĕmi[-hiĕmi], PAS., to be let down, to hang down

paristanō, See **paristēmi**

par-istēmi [-histĕmi], to bring before, to present, provide, yield, shew, prove; to commend; to bring one's self before, to stand by, before, up, with, or here; to assist; to stand, be come. (See presently)

par-odos [-hodos], a way

par-oichomai [-oichomai, to go], te go past. PART., past

par-oikia, sojourning. (See stranger)

par-oikeō, to sojourn in, to be a stranger

par-oikos, a stranger, a foreigner. (See sojourn)

par-oimia [oimos, a way], a word by the way, a proverb, a parable

par-oinos, given to wine

par-omoiazō [-homoiazō], to liken. PAS., to be like unto

par-omoios [-homoios], like

par-opsis [-opson], a side dish, a platter

parthenia, virginity

parthenos, a virgin

par-orgismos [parorgizō], wrath

par-orgizō, to provoke to wrath, to

parotrunō, to stir up [anger

par-ousia [pareimi], presence, a coming

par-oxunomai, PAS., to be easily provoked, stirred

par-oxusmos, excitement, a sharp contention. (See provoke)

parrēsia [pas-rēsis, speech], plainness of speech, boldness, confidence. (See bold, boldly, freely, openly, plainly)

parrēsiazomai, to be bold, wax bold; to speak or preach boldly. (See freely)

pas, all, every one, the whole, any: **pas ho**, or **hos**, whosoever, whatsoever. (See always, many, daily, throughly)

pascha, the passover, Easter

paschō, to suffer, to be vexed, to feel. (See passion)

patassō, to smite, to strike

pateō, to tread down or under foot

patĕr, a father; a parent

pathēma, suffering, affliction; emotion, affection. (See motion)

pathētos, liable to suffering. (See suffer)

pathos, passion, inordinate affection, lust, affection

patralōēs, the murderer of a father

patria, family, kindred, lineage

patri-archēs, a patriarch

patrikos [patĕr], of the fathers

patris, one's own country

patrōos, paternal, of one's fathers

patro-paradotos [-paradidōmi], received by tradition from one's fathers

pauō, to cause to cease, to make to refrain. MID. and PAS., to cease. (See leave)

pēchus, a cubit (= about 18 inches)

pēdalion, a helm, a rudder

pēdaō, to leap or spring

pedē [pezē], a fetter

pedinos, level. (See plain [nn.])

pēganon, the plant rue

pēgē, a fountain, a well

pēgnumi, to fix, to pitch a tent

peinaō, to hunger or be hungry, to be an hungered

21

petra, an experiment, a trial. (See assay)
peiraō, to try, to assay, to go about
peirasmos, a temptation. (See try)
peirazō, to try, examine, prove; to tempt; to assay. PART., a tempter. (See go)
peismonē [peithō], persuasion
peith-archeō, to obey magistrates, to obey, to hearker
peithō, to persuade, assure, to make a friend. PERF. [with present meaning], to trust, have confidence, to be or wax confident. (See trust [nn.]) PAS., to be persuaded; believe, agree, yield,
peithos, enticing   [obey
pelagos, a sea, a depth
pelekizō [pelekus, an axe], to behead
pēlikos, how large, how great
pēlos, mire, clay
pempō, to send, to thrust in
pemptos, the fifth
penēs, poor
penichros, poor
pentakis, five times
pentakis-chilioi, five thousand
pentakosioi, five hundred
pente, five. (See thousand)
pente-kai-dekatos, fifteenth
pentēkonta, fifty
pentēkostē [pentēkonta], Pentecost, a feast celebrated on the fiftieth day, counting from the second day of the Passover
pentheō, to bewail, to wail, to mourn
penthera, a wife's mother, a mother-
pentheros, a father-in-law   [in-law
penthos, mourning, sorrow
pepoithēsis [peithō], trust, confidence
per, soever, indeed. (See whosoever)
pēra, a satchel, a scrip
peran, beyond, over; the other side, the further side
peraō, to pass across   [the end
peras, the utmost or uttermost part,
peri [gen.], concerning, about, pertaining to, which concern, as touching, on behalf of, over, at, on, with, against. (See of, for)
peri [accus.], about. (See of)
peri-, round about, wholly, exceedingly
peri-agō, to lead about; to go about or round about, to compass [to take up
peri-aireō [-haireō], to take wholly away,
peri-astraptō, to shine round about
peri-ballō, to cast about, to put on, to array; to clothe
peri-blepō, to look round about on
peri-bolaion [periballō], covering, vesture
peri-chōros, the country or region round about
peri-deomai, PAS., to be bound about
peri-echō, to possess wholly; to have one's self contained. (See astonish, manner)
peri-erchomai, to fetch a compass, to wander about. PART., a vagabond
peri-ergazomai, to be a busybody
peri-ergos, curious art: a busy-body
peri-istēmi [-histēmi], to stand round about, to stand by; to shun, avoid
peri-kaluptō, to cover, overlay; to
peri-katharma, filth   [blindfold
peri-keimai, to be hanged about, to be compassed with, to be bound with
peri-kephalaia, a helmet
peri-kratēs [-krateō], having complete power of. (See come}
peri-kruptō, to hide completely
peri-kukloō, to compass round
peri-lambanō, to throw the arms around
peri-lampō, to shine round about
22

peri-leipō, to leave over. PAS., to remain
peri-lupos, very sorrowful, exceeding
peri-menō, to wait for   [sorry
peri-ochē [periechō], a context, a place
peri-oikeō, to dwell round about
peri-oikos, a neighbour
peri-ousios, valuable, peculiar
peri-pateō, to walk about, walk, to go, to be occupied
peri-peirō, to pierce through.
peri-pherō, to carry about, to bear
peri-phroneō, to despise   [about
peri-piptō, to fall among or into
peri-poieomai, MID., to purchase for one's self
peri-poiēsis, an obtaining, saving; a purchased possession. (See peculiar)
peri-psēma [-psaō, to wipe], offscouring
peri-rrēgnumi [-rēgnumi], to rend off
peri-spaō, to distract. PAS., to be cumbered
perisseia, superfluity, abundance. (See abundantly)
perisseuma, superabundance, abundance, what is left
perisseuō [perissos], to make abound; to abound or be abundant, to redound, to abound more, to exceed, increase, excel, be better; to remain, remain over and above, to be left. (See abundance.) PAS., to be made to have more abundance
perissos, superfluous, beyond measure, more. (See advantage.) NEU., more abundantly, vehemently. **huper ek perissos**, exceedingly, very highly, exceeding abundantly above
perissōs, exceedingly, out of measure, the more
perissoteron, more abundantly, far more, a great deal more
perissoteros [comp. of perissos], more, greater, much more, more abundant, overmuch
perissoterōs, more abundantly, more exceedingly, much more, the rather. (See abundant, earnest, frequent)
peristera, a dove, a pigeon
peri-temnō, to circumcise
peri-thesis [perithēmi], the putting around a person, the wearing of dress
peri-tithēmi, to put about or on, to set about, to bestow upon
peri-tomē [peritemnō], circumcision. (See circumcise)
peri-trechō, to run round, to run through
peri-trepō, to turn about. (See make)
perix, round about .
peri-zōnnumi, MID., to gird one's self about. PAS. part., girt, girded
perpereuomai, to vaunt one's self
perusi, a year ago
petannumi, to spread or stretch out
petaomai, to fly
peteinon [petomai], a bird, a fowl
petomai, to spread the wing, to fly
petra, a rock
petrōdēs, stony
petros, a piece of rock, a stone
pezē [pous], on foot, afoot
pezeuō [pezē], to go afoot
phagō, to eat. (See meat)
phagos, gluttonous
phailonēs, a cloke
phainō, to give light, to shine. MID. and PAS., to appear, be seen, shine; to seem. (See think)
phaneroō, to make manifest, manifest forth, declare, shew. PAS., (also) to be manifest to, to appear

phaneros, manifest, known, outward. (See abroad, appear, openly, outwardly)
phanerōs, openly, evidently
phanerōsis, manifestation
phanos [phainō], a lantern
phantasia, display, pomp
phantasma, an appearance, a spirit
phantazomai, PAS., to be made to appear. PART., a sight
phaō [phōs], to shine
pharangx, a ravine, a valley
pharmakeia, sorcery, witchcraft
pharmakeus, a drug administrator, a sorcerer   [sorcerer
pharmakos, a dealer in drugs, a
phasis [phēmi], a report, tidings
phaskō, to affirm, say, profess
phatnē, a manger, a stall
phaulos, evil
pheidomai, to spare, forbear
pheidomenōs [pheidomai], sparingly
phelleus, stony ground or soil
phēmē [phēmi], fame
phēmi, to say, affirm
phenggos, light
pherō, to bear, carry, uphold; to endure; to bring, lay, lead, reach; to move, drive. MID., to go on. PART., rushing. PAS., (also) to come, to be
pheugō, to flee away, escape
phialē, a vase, or large phial, a vial
phil-adelphia, brotherly love, love to the brethren, brotherly kindness
phil-adelphos, loving as brethren. (See love [vb.])
phil-agathos, a lover of good men
phil-andros, loving one's husband. (See love [vb.])   [kindness
phil-anthrōpia, love toward man,
phil-anthrōpōs, philanthropically, courteously
phil-arguria, love of money
phil-arguros, covetous
phil-autos, a lover of one's self
phil-ēdonos [-hēdonē], a lover of pleasure   [sure
philēma, a kiss
phileō [philos], to love; to kiss
philia [philos], friendship
philo-neikia, love of strife, strife
philo-neikos, contentious
philo-phrōn [-phrēn], courteous
philo-phronōs, courteously
philo-prōteuō, to love to have preeminence
philos, a friend   [eminence
philo-sophia, love of wisdom, philosophy
philo-sophos, a philosopher   [phy
philo-storgos, kindly affectioned
philo-teknos, loving one's children
philo-theos, a lover of God
philo-timeomai, to be emulous, to study, strive, labour
philo-xenia, the entertaining of strangers, hospitality. (See entertain)
philo-xenos, given to or a lover of hospitality
phimoō, to gag, to muzzle, put to silence. PAS., to be speechless, to hold one's peace, be still
phlogizō [phlox], to set on fire
phlox, flame. (See flaming)
phluareō, to prate against
phluaros, a tattler
phobeomai [phobos], to fear, be afraid, to reverence
phoberos, fearful, terrible
phobētron, a fearful sight
phobos, fear, a terror. (See fear [vb.])
phoinix, a palm tree, a palm [afraid]
phōleos, a den, a hole
phōnē, a voice, a sound, a noise
phōneō, to cry, call, call for; to crow
phoneuō, to kill, to slay, to do murder

phoneus, a murderer
phonos, murder, slaughter. (See slain)
phōr, a thief
phoreō, to carry frequently, to bear,
    [wear
phoros, tribute
phortion, a burden
phortizō, to lade. PAS. part., heavy
phortos, lading   [laden
phōs [phaō], light, fire
phōs-phoros[-pherō], the light bringer,
    the day star
phōster, a light-giver, a light
phōteinos, full of light, bright
phōtismos, an enlightening, light
phōtizō, to illuminate, light, lighten,
    enlighten, give light, bring to light ; to
    make see
phragellion, a scourge
phragelloō, to scourge
phragmos, a partition, hedge. (See to
    hedge)
phrassō, to enclose or fortify, to stop
phrazō, to declare
phrear, a well, a pit
phrēn the mind, the understanding.
    PLU.,, the understanding
phren-apataō, to deceive the mind
phren-apatēs, a deceiver
phrissō, to tremble   [be minded
phronēma, a minding, the mind, to
phroneō, to mind, be minded, think, re-
    gard, savour, care, set affection on, to
    be careful. (See likeminded, mind [nn.])
phronēsis, prudence, wisdom
phronimos, wise
phronimōs, wisely
phronimōteros[comp. of phronimos],
    wiser
phrontizō, to be careful
phroureō, to keep with a garrison, to
    keep
phruassō, to be noisy, to rage
phruganon, a dry stick
phthanō, to prevent or get before, to
    come ; to attain already
phthartos [phtheirō], corruptible
phtheirō, to corrupt, defile, destroy
phthenggomai, to articulate, to speak
phthinopōrinos, late, autumnal,
    whose fruit withereth. (See wither.)
phthoneō [phthonos], to envy
phthonggos [phthenggomai], sound
phthonos, envy
phthora [phtheirō], corruption. (See
    perish, destroy)
phugē, flight
phulakē, a prison, ward, cage, hold ;
    imprisonment ; a watch of the night
phulakizō, to imprison
phulaktērion, a preservative, a phy-
    lactery
phulassō, to keep, observe, save. MID.,
    to keep one's self, to beware
phulax, a keeper
phulē, a tribe, kindred
phullon, a leaf
phuō, to make grow, to produce ; to
    spring up. PAS., to spring up
phurama, a lump
phusaō, to breathe or blow into
phusikos [phusis], natural
phusikōs, naturally
phusioō, to puff up
phusiōsis [phusioō], a swelling
phusis [phuō], nature, kind. (See natural,
    mankind)
phuteia [phuteuō], a plant
phuteuō [phuton, a plant], to plant
piazō, to lay hands on, to catch, appre-
    hend, take
piezō, to press down   [bitter
pikrainō, to make bitter. PAS., to be

pikria, bitterness
pikros, bitter
pikrōs, bitterly
pimplēmi, to fill
pimprēmi, to burn. PAS., **pimpra-**
    mai, to be burned, to swell   [table
pinakidion, a small table, a writing
pinax, a board, a platter, a charger
pinō, to drink
piotēs, fatness
pipraskō, to sell
piptō, to fall, fall down, light ; to fail
pisteuō [pistis], to believe ; to trust, to
    commit. PAS., (also) to be entrusted
    with, to be put in trust with. (See
    commit)
pistikos, unadulterated, genuine, spike.
    —(See spike-nard)
pistis, belief, faith ; assurance ; fidelity.
    (See believe)
pistoō, to make assured of. PAS., to be
    assured of
pistos, believing, faithful ; sure, true ; a
    believer. (See faithfully)
pithano-logia [peithō-], persuasive
    talk, enticing words
planaō, to cause to wander, to seduce,
    deceive. PAS., (also), to wander, go
    astray, err, be out of the way
planē, error, delusion, deceit. (See de-
    ceive)
planētēs, a wanderer ; wandering
planos, seducing ; a deceiver
-plasiōn, ply, fold,
plasma [plassō], a thing formed
plassō, to form
plastos, formed, feigned
plateia [platus], a street
platos, breadth
platunō, to make broad, enlarge
platus, wide
plax, a tablet, a table   [wounded]
plēgē, a wound, stripe ; plague. (See
    plegma [plekō], broidered hair
pleiōn [comp. of polus], more, greater,
    longer, most, more excellent. PLU.,
    (also) many, very many, more or
    greater part. (See exceed, yet, above)
pleion or **pleon** [neut. of pleiōn],
    most, **epi-pleion** further, long.
pleistos [sup. of polus], most, very
    great. NEU., [adv.] at most
plekō, to weave, to plait
plēktēs [plēssō], a striker
plēmmura, a flood
plēn, except, save, but, but rather,
    nevertheless, notwithstanding. (See
pleō, to sail   [than]
pleon, See pleion
pleon-, more
pleonazō [pleon], to abound, to have
    over, to make to increase. PART.,
    abundant
pleon-ekteō [pleonektēs], to make a
    gain, defraud. PAS., to be taken advan-
    tage of
pleon-ektēs [-echō], one who will
    have more, covetous
pleon-exia [pleonektēs], covetousness,
    greediness. PLU., covetous practices
plērēs, full
plērōma, fulness, fulfilling, what is
    put in to fill up. (See full)
plēroō, to fill, fulfil, complete, fill up,
    perfect ; to end, accomplish, supply.
    PAS., (also) to be full, be full come,
    expire. (See fully, old, after)
plēro-phoreō[-phoreō], to bring fully,
    to make full proof of. PAS., to be
    fully persuaded ; to be fully known, to
    be most surely believed   [surance
plēro-phoria [plērophoreō], full as-

plēsion, near : **ho plēsion**, one's
    neighbour
plēsmonē [plēthō], a filling up, a sa-
    plēssō, to smite   [tisfying
plēthō, to fill, accomplish, furnish.
    (See full)   [bundle
plēthos, a multitude, company, a large
plēthunō, to multiply ; [act.] to abound.
    PAS., to multiply or be multiplied
pleura, the side
ploiarion, a small or little ship, a boat
ploion, a ship. (See shipping)
ploōs, a voyage, a sailing, a course
plousios [ploutos], rich
plousiōs, richly, abundantly
plouteō [ploutos], to be or wax rich,
    to be increased with goods. PART., rich
ploutizō, to make rich, to enrich
ploutos, wealth, riches
plunō, to wash
pneō, to breathe, to blow. (See wind)
pneuma [pneō], the wind ; a spirit,
    ghost ; Ghost ; breath, life. (See
    spiritual, spiritually)
pneumatikos, spiritual
pneumatikōs, spiritually
pnigō, to choke, to take by the throat
pniktos [pnigō], choked. NEUT. sing.,
    things strangled
pnoē [pneō], breath, wind
podērēs [pous], reaching to the feet ; a
    garment down to the foot   [ship
poiēma, a thing that is made, workman-
poieō, to make ; do, deal, perform, exe-
    cute, work, fulfil, commit ; to cause,
    bear, bring, bring forth, provide, yield,
    gain ; to appoint, ordain, give, put,
    exercise, shew, keep, observe. (See
    abide, agree, avenge, band [vb.], be,
    bewray, cast, content, continue, have,
    hold, journey [vb.], lay, lighten, mean,
    move, provide, purge, purpose [vb.],
    raise, redeem, secure, shoot, spend,
    take, tarry, transgress)
poiēsis, a deed
poiētēs, a doer ; a maker, a poet
poikilos, various, divers, manifold
poimainō [poimēn], to feed, feed cattle ;
    to rule
poimēn, a shepherd, a pastor ; a ruler
poimnē, a flock ; a fold
poimnion, a little flock
poios, what manner of ; what, which
polemeō [polemos], to war, to make
    war, to fight
polemos, war, a battle, a fight
pōleō, to sell
polis, a city
polit-archēs [polis-], a ruler of the city
politeia [polis-], the commonwealth ;
    freedom
politēs [polis], a citizen
politeuma [politeuomai], citizenship,
    conversation [i.e. conduct]
politeuomai [politēs], PAS., to be a
    citizen, to be regulated, to live. (See
    conversation)
pollakis [polus], often, oftentimes,
    oft, ofttimes
polla-plasiōn, manifold, more
pōlos, a young animal, a colt
polu-logia[polus-logos], much speaking
polu-merōs, in many parts, at sundry
    times
polu-poikilos, of many varieties,
    manifold
polus, much, abundant, plenteous ;
    great, long. PLU., (also) many. (See
    altogether, common, far.) NEUT. (ad-
    verb), much, a great deal, greatly ; oft,
    oftentimes. (See straitly, sore)
polu-splangchnos, very pitiful

23

polu-telēs, very precious, of great price, costly

polu-timos, very costly, of great price

polu-tropōs, in many ways, in divers manners

poma [pinō], drink

poneō [ponos], to cause toil or distress

ponēria [ponēros], iniquity, wickedness

ponēros [poneō], wicked, bad, evil; malicious, lewd; grievous; the wicked one. NEUT., wickedness, evil, moral harm   [wicked

ponēroteros [comp. of ponēros], more

ponos, severe toil, pain

pontos, the sea: **pontizō,** to plunge

pō-pote [pōs-], ever, at any time. (See never)

poreia, a journey, a way. (See journey [vb.])

poreuomai [poros], to go, to go forth, up, or away; to depart, to walk, to journey or make a journey

porismos, gain

pornē, a harlot, a whore

porneia, fornication

porneuō, to commit fornication

pornos, a fornicator, a whoremonger

poros, a passage, a way; a means

pōroō, to harden. PAS., (also) to be

pōrōsis, hardness, blindness [blinded

porphura, purple [noun]

porphureos, purple [adjec.] [purple

porphuro-pōlis [-pōleō], a seller of

porrō, forward, further, far, a great way off

porrōthen, from a distance, afar off

portheō, to lay waste, to waste, destroy

-pōs, by any or some means, haply, perhaps

pōs, how? by what means, after what manner. (See that)

posakis, how oft, how often

posis [pinō], the act of drinking, drink

posos, how great, how much, how long. PLU., how many, what

potamos, a river, stream, flood; water

potamo-phorētos, carried away of a flood

potapos, what manner of, what

pote, (1.) when? when. (See long)

pote, (2.) at any time, some time or sometimes, once; in time or times past, aforetime; in the old time. (See ever, last, length, never)

potērion [potos], a cup

poteron, whether

pothen, whence, from whence

potheō, to long for, to yearn after

potizō, to make to drink, to give to drink, to water. (See feed)

potos, a drinking, a banqueting

pou, (1.) where? whither? [about

pou, (2.) somewhere, in a certain place,

pous, a foot. (See footstool)

pragma [prassō], a business; work, a matter, a thing

pragmateia, an affair

pragmateuomai, [pragma], to do business; to occupy

praitōrion, the general's tent, Prætorium, a judgment hall; a common hall, a palace

praktōr [prassō], an agent, an officer

praüs, meek

praütēs, meekness

prasia, a garden bed, a rank

prassō, to practise to do; to commit. (See deed, exact, keep, require, use [vb.])

praütēs, meekness

praxis [prassō], a deed, work; an office

prēnēs, with face downward, headlong

24

prepō, to be comely; **prepei** [impersonal], it becometh

presbeia [presbeuō], an ambassage, message   [sador

presbeuō, to act as, or be an ambas-

presbuterion [presbuteros], a council of elders, the estate of the elders, a presbytery, the elders [(See old

presbuteros, elder, eldest, an elder.

presbutēs, an old or aged man

presbutis, an aged woman [before

prin, before, ere; **prin ē,** before that,

priō or **prizō,** to saw asunder [ever]

pro, before, in front of, above. (See ago,

pro-, before, forth, forward

pro-agō, to bring forth or out; to bring one's self before, to go before [purpose

pro-aireomai [-haireō], to prefer, to

pro-aitiaomai, to charge previously, to prove before

pro-akouō, to hear before

pro-amartanō [-hamartanō], to sin heretofore or already

pro-aulion, a porch

pro-bainō, to go on or further. (See age, stricken)   [forth

pro-ballō, to put forward, to shoot

probatikos, of sheep, sheep—(See sheep-market)   [sheepfold]

probaton, a sheep. PLU., sheep. (See

pro-bibazō, to push forward, to instruct before; to draw forward

pro-blepō, to provide

pro-cheirizomai [-cheir], to cause to be at hand, to choose, to make

pro-cheirotoneō, to choose before

pro-dēlos, manifest beforehand, open beforehand; evident

pro-didōmi, to give first; to betray

pro-dotēs [prodidōmi], a betrayer, a traitor

pro-dromos [pro-trechō], a forerunner

pro-echomai [-echō], to have one's self before, to excel, to be better than

pro-ēgeomai [-hēgeomai], to prefer

pro-eideō, to see before, to foresee

pro-elpizō, to hope before, to trust first

pro-enarchomai, to begin before, to begin

pro-epanggellomai, to promise afore

pro-epō, to speak before, to tell in time past, to forewarn

pro-erchomai, to go before, forward, or farther; to pass on, to outgo

pro-ereō, to speak, tell, or say before; to foretell [afore, ordain before

pro-etoimazō [-hetoimazō], to prepare

pro-euanggelizomai, to preach the gospel before

pro-ginomai, to be before. PERF. tense, to be past

pro-ginōskō, to know before, to foreknow; to foreordain, to know

pro-gonos, a forefather, a parent

pro-graphō, to write afore or aforetime, to set forth evidently, to ordain before. (See write)

prōi, early in the morning, early

prōïa, the morning. (See early)

pro-gnōsis [proginōskō], foreknowledge

prōïmos, early [adjec.]

prōïnos, morning [adjec.]

pro-istēmi [-histēmi], ACT. and MID., to stand forward, to be over, to rule, to maintain

pro-kaleomai, to provoke

pro-katanggellō, to foretell, shew before. (See notice)

pro-katartizō, to make up beforehand

pro-keimai, to be first, to be set before or forth

pro-kērussō, to preach before or first

pro-kopē [prokoptō], furtherance, profiting

pro-koptō, to drive forward, to progress; to proceed, increase, wax; to profit. (See spend)

pro-krima, a preference. (See prefer)

pro-kuroō, to confirm before

pro-lambanō, to take before, overtake; to anticipate, to come beforehand

pro-legō, to foretell, tell before

pro-marturomai, to testify beforehand

pro-meletaō, to meditate before

pro-merimnaō, to take thought beforehand

pro-noeō, to provide, to provide for

pro-noia, provident care, provision for, providence   [before

pro-oraō [-horaō], to foresee, to see

pro-orizō [-horizō], to determine before, predestinate, ordain

pro-paschō, to suffer before

pro-pempō, to send on before, to conduct forth, to bring forward on a journey; to accompany [rashly]

pro-petēs [-piptō], rash, heady. (See

pro-phasis [-phainō], a pretence, a shew. (See colour, cloke)

pro-pherō, to bring forth

pro-phēteia (-phēmi], prophecy, prophesying

pro-phētēs [-phēmi], a prophet

pro-phēteuō [prophētēs], to prophesy

prophētikos, of the prophet; prophetic, of prophecy

prophētis, a prophetess

pro-phthanō, to come before, to prevent or anticipate

pro-poreuomai, to go before [part

prōra, the prow, the foreship, the fore-

pros [with genitive], for

pros [with dative], near, at, about

pros [with accusative], with reference to, toward, unto, to. (See about, against, among, at, because, by, end, for, necessary, nigh, of, together, with, within)

pros-, to, towards, besides, in addition

pro-sabbaton, the day before the Sabbath

pros-agō, to bring near. MID., to draw near

pros-agōgē, access

pros-agoreuō, to speak to, to call [beg

pros-aiteō, to ask in continuance, to

pros-anabainō, to go up farther

pros-analiskō, to consume upon, to spend upon or besides

pros-anaplēroō, to supply so as to fill

pros-anatithēmi, MID., to lay on in addition, to add in conference; to confer with

pros-apeileomai, to threaten further

pros-dapanaō, to spend more

pros-dechomai, to receive, accept, take; to wait for, look for; to allow

pros-deomai, to need in addition

pros-dokaō, to look for, to expect, to wait for, to tarry. (See expectation)

pros-dokia, a looking after, expecta-

pros-eaō, to allow, to suffer [tion

pros-echō, to take or give heed to, to have regard to, to attend unto; to give attendance at or to; to beware. (See give)

pros-edreuō [-hedra], to sit near, to

pros-ēloō [hēlos], to nail to [wait at

pros-ēlutos [proserchomai], one who has come to embrace the Jewish religion, a proselyte

pros-enggizō, to come nigh

pros-erchomai, to come unto, to go to, to draw near. (See comer, consent

pros-ergazomai, *to produce in addition*, to gain
pros-euchē, prayer. (*See* pray)
pros-euchomai, to pray, pray for, make prayers [(*See* dure, endure)
pros-kairos, for a season, temporal.
pros-kaleomai, to call unto *or* for; to call
pros-kartereō, to continue with, to attend continually on, to wait on, to continue instant *or* stedfastly. (*See* continually)
pros-karterēsis, perseverance
pros-kephalaion, a pillow
pros-klēroō, *PAS.*, *to be associated with*, to consort with
pros-klisis [-klinō],*a leaning towards*, partiality
pros-kollaomai, *PAS.*, to cleave to, to join one's self to
pros-komma [proskoptō], a stumbling, a stumbling-block, an offence. (*See* stumbling-stone)
pros-kopē [proskoptō], an offence
pros-koptō, to stumble at; to beat upon, to dash
pros-kuliō, to roll to, to roll
pros-kuneō, to worship [shipper
proskunētēs [proskuneō], a wor-
pros-laleō, to speak to *or* with [ceive
pros-lambanō, to take unto, to re-
pros-lēpsis [proslambanō], a receiving
pres-menō, to continue in *or* with, to be with, to abide still, tarry, cleave unto [with
pros-ochthizō[-ochtheō],to be grieved
pros-opheilō, to owe besides
prosōpo-lēpsia [-lambanō], respect of persons [respect of persons
prosōpo-lēpteō [-lambanō], to have
prosōpo-lēptēs,a respecter of persons
pros-ōpon [-ops], the face, the countenance; the person, presence; outward appearance. (*See* before)
pros-ormizō [-hormizō], *to bring* [a ship] *to anchorage. PAS.*, to draw to the shore
pros-pēgnumi, *to fix to*, to crucify
pros-peinos [-peinaō], very hungry
pros-phagion, *what is eaten in addition to bread, animal food*, meat
prosphatos, *newly killed*, new
prosphatōs [prosphatos], lately
pros-pherō, to bring unto, to offer up, to present unto;to put to. (*See* deal,do)
pros-philēs, *kindly, friendly*, lovely
pros-phōneō, to call *or* speak to
pros-phora [prospherō],an offering, an offering up [to beat upon
pros-piptō, to fall down before *or* at;
pros-poieō, *MID.*, *to claim to one's self, to assume the appearance of*, to make as though
pros-poreuomai, to come unto
pros-psauō, to touch
pros-rēgnumi, *to break upon*, to beat vehemently upon [tion
pros-tassō, to bid *or* command in addi-
pro-statis [proïstēmi], *a patroness, a* succourer
pros-tithēmi, to add, to lay unto, to give more, to increase. *MID.*, to proceed farther. (*See* speak, send)
pros-trechō, to run to
pro-tassō, to appoint before
pro-teinō,*to hold out,to expose*; to bind
proteros, before, first, at first. [former]
prōteuō [prōtos],to have the pre-eminence
pro-thesis [protithēmi],*a setting before, exhibition*, purpose. (*See* shew-bread)

pro-thesmia [protithēmi], *before appointed*, a time appointed
pro-thumia, readiness *or* forwardness of mind, a ready *or* willing mind
pro-thumos, ready, willing [lingly
pro-thumōs, *of a ready mind*, willingly
pro-tithēmi, to set forth ; to purpose
prōto-kathedria, the highest, uppermost, *or* chief seat
prōto-klisia, *the best place at a feast ;* the highest, uppermost, *or* chief room
prōton, first, at first, chiefly, at the beginning. (*See* before)
prōtos, first, former, chief, chiefest, best. (*See* before, beginning)
prōto-statēs [-stasis], a ringleader
prōto-tokia [prōtotokos], a birthright
prōto-tokos [-tiktō], the first born, first begotten
pro-trechō, to run before, to outrun
pro-trepō, *MID.*, *to incite*, to exhort
pro-uparchō [-huparchō],to be before *or* beforetime
prumna, the stern, the hinder part
psallō, *to play on the psaltery*, to make melody, to sing psalms
psalmos, a psalm
psauō, *to touch, handle, feel*
psēlaphaō, to feel after, to handle. *PAS. part.*, that might be touched
psēphizō [psēphos], *to give one's vote with a pebble*, to count [(*See* voice)
psēphos, a stone *used in voting, a vote.*
pseud-adelphos, a false brother
pseud-apostolos, a false apostle
pseudēs [pseudomai], false ; a liar
pseudo-christos, a false Christ
pseudo-didaskalos, a false teacher
pseudo-logos, speaking lies
pseudomai, to lie. (*See* falsely)
pseudo-martur, a false witness [ness
pseudo-martureō, to bear false wit-
pseudo-marturia, false witness *or* testimony [called
pseud-ōnumos [-onoma], falsely so
pseudo-prophētēs, a false prophet
pseudos, a lie, lying [*nn.*]
pseusma [pseudomai], a lie
pseustēs, a liar
psichion, a crumb
psithurismos, whispering
psithuristēs, a whisperer
psōchō, to rub
psōmion, a sop
psōmizō, to feed. (*See* bestow)
psuchē [psuchō], *animal life*, life; the soul; the mind ; *the emotional nature*, the heart. (*See* heartily, us, you)
psuchikos, *of the animal or emotional nature*, sensual ; natural
psuchō, *to breathe, blow ; to cool. PAS.*, to wax cold
psuchos, coolness, cold
psuchros, cold [*adj.*] [offend
ptaiō [piptō], to fall, to stumble, to
ptēnon [petomai], a bird
pterna, the heel [pinnacle
pterugion [pterux], *a little wing*, a
pterux, a wing
ptōcheia, poverty
ptōcheuō, to become poor
ptōchos, poor, beggarly, a beggar
ptoeō, to terrify
ptoēsis, *terrifiedness, amazement*
ptōma [piptō], a carcase, a corpse, a dead body
ptōsis [piptō], a fall
ptuō, to spit
ptuon, a fan
pturō, to terrify
ptusma [ptuō], a spittle

ptussō, *to fold or roll up*, to close
pugmē, *the fist*. (*See* oft)
puknos, [*adj.*] compact, frequent, often
puknoteron [*comp. neut. of* puknos], oftener
pukteuō [pugmē], *to box*, to fight
pulē, a gate
pulōn, a gate, a porch
punthanomai, to inquire, to ask, to demand. (*See* understand)
pur, fire. (*See* fiery)
pura, a fire
puressō [pur], *to be in a burning heat*, to be sick of a fever
puretos [pur], a fever
purgos, a tower
purinos [pur], of fire
puroōmai, *PAS.*, to be on fire, to burn. *PART.*, burned, fiery. (*See* try)
purōsis, a burning ; a fiery trial
purrazō [purros], to be red
purros [pur], *of a fiery colour*, red

P, ϱ, (rho) = r.

rabbi [*Syriac*], Rabbi, master
rabboni [*Syriac*], Rabboni, lord
rabdizō [rabdos], to beat with rods
rabdos, a rod, a staff, a sceptre
rabdouchos [rabdos-echō], *a rod-bearer*, a serjeant
radios, *easy*
radiourgēma [radios-ergon], *a reckless action*, lewdness [chief
radi-ourgia [-ergon], *recklessness*, mis-
raka [*Syriac, meaning an empty person, a fop*], Raka
rakos, *a ragged garment*, a cloth
rantismos [rantizō], a sprinkling
rantizō, to sprinkle
raphis, a needle
rapisma [rapizō], *a blow with the palm of the hand*. (*See* smite, strike)
rapizō, to smite with the palm of the hand [hand
raptō [raphis], *to sew* [ruin
reda, a chariot
rēgma [rēgnumi], *a fracture, a crash*,
rēgnumi *or* **rēssō**, to break, burst, tear, rend ; to break forth
rēma [reō], a saying, a word. (*See* nothing, evil)
reō [ereō], to speak, say, command.
reō, to flow [(*See* make)
rēssō, *See* rēgnumi
rētōr [reō], *a public speaker*, an orator
rētōs [reō], *in express terms*, expressly
ripē [riptō], *a swift motion*, a twinkling
ripizō, to toss *to and fro*
riptō, to hurl, to throw, cast, scatter abroad, to cast off, down, *or* out
riza, a root
rizoōmai [riza], *PAS.*, to be rooted
roizēdon, with a great *rushing* noise
romphaia, *a large* sword [farewell !
rōnnumi, *PAS., to be strong. IMPER.*,
rumē, a street, a lane
ruomai, to rescue, to deliver. *PART.*, a
ruparia [rupos], filthiness [deliverer
ruparos, *dirty*, vile
rupoō [rupos], to be filthy
rupos, filth
rusis [reō], an issue
rutis, a wrinkle

Σ, σ, ς, (sigma) = s.

sabachthani [*Syriac*], sabachthani? *hast thou forsaken me*
sabaōth [*Hebrew, of hosts*], Sabaoth
sabbatismos [sabbaton], rest
sabbaton, sabbath day, a week. *PLU.*, **sabbata**, sabbath days, the week ; the sabbath
sagēnē, a net

25

saino, *to wag the tail.* MID., to be
sakkos, sackcloth   [moved
saleuo [salos], *to toss* [act.], to shake,
   to move, to stir up
salos, *the surging of the sea ;* waves
salpingx [salpizō], a trumpet, a trump
salpistēs, a trumpeter
salpizō, to sound a trumpet, to sound.
   IMPERS., a trumpet sounds
sandalion, a sandal
sanis, *a plank,* a board
saphēs, distinct, plain, certain
sappheiros, a sapphire
sapros, rotten, corrupt, bad
sardinos, *of a sardius,* sardine
sardios, a sardius
sardonux, a sardonyx
sarganē, a basket
sarkikos, [sarx], carnal, fleshly
sarkinos, fleshy
saroō, to sweep (*with a besom*)
sarx, flesh. (*See* carnal, carnally, fleshly)
saton, a measure [= *about* 1½ *pecks*]
sbennumi, to quench. PAS., (*also*) to
   go out
schedon, almost   [fashion
schēma, *the outward appearance,*
schisma [schizō], a schism, a division,
   a rent   [make a rent
schizō, to rend, divide, open, break,
schoinion, a small cord, a rope
scholazō [scholē], *to have leisure for,*
   to give one's self to. (*See* empty)
scholē, *leisure,* a school
seautou, thyself, thou thyself, thine
   ownself, thyself. (*See* thy, thee)
sebasma [sebazomai], that which is
   worshipped. (*See* devotion)
sebastos, *august,* Augustus
sebazomai [sebomai], to worship
sebomai, *to feel awe,* to worship. PART.,
   devout, religious
seio, to shake, move *to and fro.* PAS.
seira, a chain   [(*also*) to quake
seismos [seiō], *a shaking,* an earthquake, a tempest
selēnē, the moon
selēniazomai, to be lunatic
sēma, *a sign, a mark*   [signify
sēmainō [sēma], *to shew by a sign,* to
sēmeion [sēma], a sign, a token ; a
   miracle, a wonder
sēmeioō, MID., *to mark for one's self,*
sēmeron, to-day, this day   [to note
semidalis, fine flour
semnos [sebomai], revered, grave, honest
semnotēs [semnos], solemnity, dignity,
   gravity, honesty
sēpō, *to make rotten ;* to be corrupted
sērikon, silk
sēs, a moth
sēto-brōtos [sēs-brōskō], moth-eaten
siagōn, *the jawbone,* the cheek
sidēreos, of iron, iron [adj.]
sidēros, iron
sigaō [sigē], to keep silence, to hold
   one's peace, to keep secret *or* close
sigē, silence
sikarios [*Latin,* sicarius], a murderer
sikera, strong drink
simikinthion [*Latin,* semicinctium],
   a handkerchief, an apron
sinapi, mustard-seed
sindōn, fine linen, linen cloth, linen
siniazō, *to winnow,* to sift
siōpaō, to hold one's peace, to be dumb.
   IMPER., peace !
siteutos [sitos], fatted
sitistos [sitos], a fatling
sito-metrion, a portion of meat
sitos, wheat, corn ; *food*
skandalizō [skandalon], *to cause to*
26

stumble, *fall, or sin ;* to make to offend,
   to offend
skandalon, a stumblingblock ; an occasion of stumbling, an occasion to fall ;
   offence, a thing that offends
skaphē [skaptō], a boat
skaptō, to dig
skelos, the leg
skēnē, *a moveable tent,* a tabernacle, a
skēnōma, a tabernacle   [habitation
skēnoō [skēnē], *to live in a tent,* to
   dwell   [*feast of tabernacles*
skēno-pēgia, *a pitching of tents, the*
skēno-poios [-poieō], a tent-maker
skēnos, *a tent,* a tabernacle
skepasma, *a covering,* raiment
skeptomai, *to look about, to watch, to*
skeuazō, *to prepare, to furnish*   [spy
skeuē, *equipment,* tackling
skeuos, *a vessel, an implement,* a sail.
   PLU., *furniture,* stuff, goods
skia, a shadow
skiazō [skia], *to shade, overshadow*
skirtaō, to leap, to leap for joy
sklēro-kardia, hardness of heart
sklēros, hard, fierce
sklērotes, hardness
sklēro-trachēlos, stiff-necked
sklērunō, to harden   [worms
skōlēko-brōtos [-brōskō], eaten of
skōlēx, a worm
skolios, crooked, froward, untoward
skolops, a thorn
skopeō [skopos], to look at *or* on, to
   take heed, mark, consider
skopos [skeptomai], a mark ; *a senti-*
   nel, a scout   [perse abroad
skorpizō, to scatter, to scatter *or* dis-
skorpios, a scorpion   [ness
skoteinos [skotos], dark, full of dark-
skotia, darkness. (*See* dark)
skotizō, to darken   [darkness
skotoō, *to darken.* PAS., to be full of
skotos, darkness
skubalon, dung
skullō, *to flay, annoy,* to trouble.
   PAS. part., scattered abroad
skulon [skullō], spoil, *stripped from*
   an enemy
skuthrōpos [skuthros, sullen, -ōps], of
   a sad countenance
smaragdinos, *of an emerald*
smaragdos, an emerald
smurna, myrrh
smurnizō, to mingle with myrrh
sōma, a body. (*See* bodily, slave)
sōmatikos, *of the body,* bodily
sōmatikōs [adv.], bodily
sōos *or* sōs, sound, *healthy*
sophia [sophos], wisdom
sophizō, to make wise. PAS. part.,
   cunningly devised
sophos, wise
sophōteros, wiser
sōphrōn [sōos-phrēn], *of sound mind,*
   sober, temperate, discreet
sōphroneō, to be in a right mind, to
   be sober *or* sober minded (*See* soberly)
sōphronismos [sōphronizō], a sound
   mind
sōphronizō, *to train to right minded-*
   ness, to teach to be sober
sōphronōs, *temperately,* soberly
sōphrosunē, *right-mindedness,* sobriety, soberness
sōreuō, to heap. PAS. part., laden
soros, *a coffin,* a bier   [friends
sos, thine, thy, thine own. PLU., thy
sōtēr [sōzō], a saviour   [deliver)
sōtēria, salvation, health. (*See* save,
sōtērion [*neu. of* sōtērios], salvation
sōtērios, that bringeth salvation

sondarion, a napkin, a handkerchief
sōzō, to save, preserve ; to heal, make
   whole. PAS., (*also*) to be whole, to
   do well, to save one's self
sparassō, to rend, to tear   [clothes
sparganoō, to wrap in swaddling
spaō, MID., to draw out, to draw
spatalaō, to live in pleasure
speira, *a coil ;* a band
speirō, to sow. PART., sower PAS.,
   (*also*) to receive seed
spekoulatōr, *one of a body guard,*
   an executioner
spēlaion, a cave, a den
spendō, *to pour out as a drink offering.*
   MID., to pour out one's self, to be
   offered, to be ready to be offered ; *to*
   make a treaty
sperma [speirō], seed ; offspring, issue
spermo-logos [-legō], *one who gathers*
   scraps
speudō [spoudē], to make haste, to
   haste unto. PART., with haste
sphagē [sphattō], slaughter
sphagion [sphattō], a slain beast
sphallō, to trip up. PAS. t *o* fall
spattō, to slay, kill, wound
sphodra, exceedingly, greatly, very.
   (*See* sore, exceeding)
sphodrōs, exceedingly
sphragis, a seal   [stop)
sphragizō, to seal, to set a seal. (*See*
sphuron, the ancle bone
spilas [spilos], *a rock ;* a spot   [file
spiloō [spilos], *to stain,* to spot, to de-
spilos, *a stain,* a spot
splangchna, bowels, bowels of compassion, inward affection. (*See* tender)
splangchnizomai, PAS., to have *or*
   be moved with compassion
spodos, ashes
spondē [spendomai], *a drink-offering,*
   a treaty or truce
sponggos, a sponge
spora [speirō], seed
sporima [sporos], PLU., cornfields, the
sporos, seed sown, seed   [corn
spoudaios [spoudē], diligent
spoudaiōs, diligently, instantly
spoudaioteros [*comp. of* spoudaios],
   more diligent *or* forward. NEU.,
   spoudaioteron, very diligently
spoudaioterōs [*comp. of* spoudaiōs]
   the more carefully
spoudazō, *to make haste,* to be diligent *or* give diligence, to be forward,
   to endeavour, labour, study
spoudē, haste, diligence, forwardness,
   earnest care, care, carefulness. (*See*
spuris, a basket   [business)
stadios, a furlong ; *a race-course,* a
stachus, an ear of corn   [race
stamnos, *an earthen* jar, a pot
staphulē, a grape, *a cluster of grapes*
stasis [histēmi], *a standing, a faction* ;
   sedition, insurrection, dissension, uproar. (*See* stand)
statēr, a piece of money [= *about* 2s. 6d.]
-statos [histēmi], *placed, standing*
stauroō [stauros], to crucify
stauros, a cross
stegē [stegō], a roof
stegō, *to cover closely,* to forbear, bear,
steira [*feminine*], barren
stēkō [histēmi], to stand fast, to stand,
   suffer
stellō, to set, to send, to equip and send.
   MID., to take one's self back from, to
   withdraw one's self, to avoid
stemma [stephō], a garland
stenagmos, a groan, groaning   [grief
stenazō, to sigh, groan, grudge. (*See*

steno-chōreomai, PAS., to be straitened or distressed
steno-chōria, straitenedness, distress,
stenos, narrow, strait [anguish
stephanoō, to crown
stephanos [stephō], a crown
stephō, to surround, to crown
stereō, to deprive, bereave
stereōma [stereoō], stedfastness
stereoō [stereos], to establish, make strong. PAS.,(also) to receive strength
stereos, stable, stedfast, strong, sure
stērigmos [stērizō], stedfastness
stērizō, to fix, set stedfastly, establish, stablish, strengthen
stēthos, the breast
sthenos, strength
sthenoō [sthenos], to strengthen [ing
stigma, a mark by wounding or branding
stigmē, a puncture, a point, a moment
stilbō, to glitter, to shine
stoa, a colonnade, a porch [branches
stoibas, a thing trodden. PLU.,strewed
stoicheion, an elementary part or principle, an element, principle, rudiment
stoicheō [stoichos, a row], to stand in a line, to walk orderly
stolē [stellō], a long robe or garment, a robe. PLU., (also) clothing
stoma, the mouth; the face, the edge
stomachos, the stomach
storgē, natural affection
stratēgos [stratos-agō], the leader of an army; a captain; a magistrate
strateia, warfare [war
strateuma, an army; soldiers, men of
strateuomai [stratos], to go a warfare to war. PART., a soldier
stratia, an army; a host
stratiōtēs, a soldier [soldier
strato-logeō, to choose one to be a
stratoped-archēs, a captain of the guard [army
stratopedon, an encampment, an
stratos, an army; a host
strebloō [strephō], to screw up, to strain, to wrest [liciously
strēniaō [strēnos], to revel, to live de-
strēnos, revelling; delicacies
strephō, to turn anything. MID., to turn one's self. PAS., (also) to turn about or back again, to be converted.
strōnnumi, to strew, spread; to make a bed, furnish
strophē [strephō], a turning
strouthion, a sparrow
stugeō, to hate, to loathe
stugētos, hateful [be lowering
stugnazō, to be gloomy, to be sad, to
stulos, a pillar
su, thou
su-, See sun-
sukon, a fig
suko-phanteō [sukophantēs, an accuser of illegal exporters of figs from Attica], to accuse falsely, to take by false accusation
sukaminos, a sycamine tree
sukē [sukon], a fig tree
sukomōraia, a sycamore tree
sul-, See sun-
sul-agōgeō, to spoil [sulē-ago]
sulaō [sulē], to spoil, to rob
sulē or **sulon**, the right of seizure
sul-laleō,to talk, confer, or commune with; to speak among
sul-lambanō, to take; to conceive. MID., to take to one's self; to catch, to help; to conceive
sul-legō, to gather together or up
sul-logizomai, to reason with

sul-lupeomai, to be grieved with
sum-, See sun- [to be so
sum-baino, to happen unto, to befall,
sum-ballō, to put together, ponder, confer; to encounter, meet with. MID., to help. (See make)
sum-basileuō, to reign with
sum-bibazō, to knit together, to compact; to gather assuredly, to prove; to instruct
sum-bouleuō [sumboulos], to give counsel, to counsel. MID., to take counsel together, to consult
sum-boulion, a counsel, consultation; a council
sum-boulos [-boulē], a counsellor
sum-martureō, to bear witness with or also, to testify unto
sum-mathētēs, a fellow-disciple
sum-merizomai, to be partaker with
sum-metochos, a fellow partaker
sum-mimētēs, a joint-imitator, a follower together
sum-morphoō, to make conformable unto [like unto, conformed to
sum-morphos [-morphē], fashioned
sum-paraginomai, to come together, to stand with
snm-parakaleō, to comfort together
sum-paralambanō, to take with
sum-paramenō, to continue with
sum-pareimi, to be present with
sum-paschō, to suffer with
sum-patheō [sumpathēs], to sympathise with, to be touched with a fellow feeling, to have compassion
sum-pathēs [-pathos], sympathising, having compassion one of another
sum-pempō, to send with
sum-perilambanō, to embrace
sum-phēmi, to assent to, to consent unto
sum-pherō, to bring together, to be expedient, good or profitable,or for the better. (See profit·
sum-phōneō,to agree together or with
sum-phōnēsis, harmony, concord
sum-phōnia, symphony, music
sum-phōnos [-phōnē], harmonious. NEU., consent
sum-phuletēs [-phulē], a compatriot, a countryman
sum-phuō, to make grow together. PAS., to spring up with
sum-phutos [sumphuō], united in one stock; planted together
sum-pinō, to drink with
sum-plēroō, PAS., to be filled; to become or fully come
sum-pnigō, to choke; to throng
sum-politēs, a fellow citizen
sum-poreuomai,to go with, to resort together
sum-posion [sumpinō], a banqueting party, a company
sum-presbuteros, a fellow elder
sum-psēphizō, to reckon together, to count
sum-psuchos [-psuchē], like minded
sun, with; together with, beside
sun-, **su-**, **sul-**, **sum-**, **sung-**, or **sus-**, with, together, completely
sun-agō, to gather together or up, to take in, to lead unto, to bestow. MID., to come or gather-selves together. PAS., (also) to assemble, gather or come together, to be assembled, to resort [gregation, synagogue
sun-agōgē [sunagō], an assembly, con-
sun-agōnizomai, to strive together with
sun-aichmalōtos, a fellow prisoner

sun-airō, to take up together, to take, reckon [pany
sun-akoloutheō, to follow in company
sun-alizomai [-halēs], to be assembled together
sun-anabainō, to come up with
sun-anakeimai, to sit at meat or at the table with, to sit down or together with
sun-ana-mignumi, to intermingle with, to keep company with, to company [freshed with
sun-anapauomai, MID., to be re
sun-antaō, to meet together, to befall
sun-antēsis [sunantaō], a meeting. (See meet) [with
sun-antilambanomai, to help along
sun-apagō, to lead or carry away with. MID., (also) to condescend
sun-apollumi, MID., to perish with
sun-apostellō, to send with
sun-apothnēskō, to die with. PAST., to be dead with [i.e., to have died]
sun-armologeō[-harmologeō, to join], to frame or join fitly together
sun-arpazō [-harpazō], to catch
sun-athleō, to labour with, to strive together for
sun-athroizō,to gather or call together
sun-auxanomai, to grow together
sun-deō, PAS., to be bound with
sun-desmos [sundeō], a bond, a band
sun-doxazō, to glorify together
sun-doulos, a fellow servant
sun-dromē [suntrechō], a running together. (See run)
sun-echō, to hold together, to keep in, hold,stop; to press,straiten,constrain, throng. PAS., (also) to be taken with, to lie sick of, to be in a strait
sun-ēdomai[-hēdomai], to rejoice with, to delight in [Sanhedrim
sun-edrion [-hedra], a council, the
sun-egeirō, to raise up together. PAS., to rise with
sun-eideō, to be conscious of, to be ware of, or privy to, to know, consider
sun-eidēsis, consciousness, conscience
sun-eimi, to be with [together
sun-eimi, to go with, to be gathered
sun-eiserchomai, to go in with, to go with
sun-ekdēmos, a companion in travel. (See travel)
sun-eklektos, elected together with
sun-elaunō, to set together. (See set)
sun-ēlikiōtēs [-hēlikia], one of equal age, an equal
sun-ephistēmi, to rise up together
sun-epimartureō, to bear witness also [pany
sun-epomai, to follow close, to accom-
sun-erchomai, to come together or with, to be assembled with, to resort, go with, accompany, to company with
sun-ergeō [sunergos], to work together or with, to help with. PART., a worker together with
sun-ergos [-ergon], a work-fellow, a fellow-worker, fellow-labourer, companion in labour, a labourer together with, fellow-helper, a helper
sun-esis [suniēmi], understanding, knowledge
sun-esthiō, to eat with [a custom
sun-ētheia [ēthos], a common practice,
sun-etos [suniēmi], prudent
sun-eudokeō, to be pleased with,have pleasure in, consent, allow
sun-euōcheomai, to feast with
sung-, See sun-
sung-chairō, to rejoice with or in

sung-cheŏ, to stir up

sung-chraomai, to have dealings with

sung-chunŏ or **sungcheŏ**, *to pour together*, to confound. *PAS.*, (*also*) to be confused, be in an uproar

sung-chusis [sungchunŏ], confusion

sung-geneia [sunggenēs], kindred

sung-genēs [-genos], kin ; a kinsman ; *a kinswoman*, a cousin. *PLU.*, kinsfolk

sung-gnŏmē [sungginōskŏ, *to agree*], permission

sung-kakopatheŏ, to be partaker of afflictions   [tion with

sung-kakoucheomai, to suffer afflic-

sung-kaleŏ, to call together

sung-kaluptŏ, to cover *completely*

sung-kamptŏ, to bow down

sung-katabainŏ, to go down with

sung-kata-psēphizŏ, to number *along* with

sung-katatithemai, *to set one's self along with*, to consent   [agreement

sung-katathesis [sungkatatithemai],

sung-kathēmai, to sit with

sung-kathizŏ, to make sit together ; to be set down together   [together

sung-kerannumi, *PAS.*, to temper

sung-kineŏ, *to move together*, to stir up

sung-kleiŏ, to shut up together, to inclose ; to conclude

sung-klēronomos, a joint-heir, *or* fellow-heir, an heir together *or* with

sung-koinŏneŏ, to communicate, to have fellowship with, to be partaker of

sung-koinŏnos, a partaker with, a companion. (*See* partake)

sung-komizŏ, *to join in carrying*, to carry

sung-krinŏ, to compare with *or* among

sung-kuptŏ, to be bowed together

sung-kuria [-kureŏ], *a coincidence*, chance

sun-iēmi or **sunieŏ** [-hiēmi], *to bring together*, to understand, consider ; to be wise   [to commend

sun-istanŏ [-histēmi], *to bring together*,

sun-istaŏ or **sun-istēmi** [-histēmi], *to make to stand with*, to approve, commend, make ; to stand with, consist   [anguish

sun-ochē [sunechŏ], *pressure*, distress,

sun-odeuŏ [-hodeuŏ], to journey with

sun-odia [-hodos], a company [*on a journey*]

sun-ŏdinŏ, to travail in pain together

sun-oikeŏ, to dwell with

sun-oikodomeŏ, to build together

sun-omileŏ [-homileŏ], to talk with

sun-om-oreŏ [-homoreŏ, *to border*], to have the same borders, to join hard to

sun-ŏmosia [-omnumi], a conspiracy

sun-tassŏ, *to arrange*, to appoint

sun-teleia, a complete end

sun-teleŏ [*to complete*, to end, finish, fulfil. (*See* make)

sun-temnŏ, to cut short. (*See* short)

sun-tēreŏ, to keep *with one's self*, to preserve, to observe

sun-thaptŏ, to bury with

sun-thlaŏ, to break *completely*

sun-thlibŏ, to throng *very much*

sun-thruptŏ, to break *completely*

sun-tithēmi, to agree, assent, to covenant   [few words

sun-tomŏs [suntemnŏ], *concisely*, in

sun-trechŏ, to run together, to run with

sun-tribŏ, to break in pieces *or* to shivers, to bruise, break. (*See* broken hearted)

sun-trimma [suntribŏ], destruction

sun-trophos [-trephŏ], brought up with

28

---

sun-tungchanŏ, *to meet with*, to come at   [to dissemble with

sun-upokrinomai [-hupokrinomai],

sun-upourgeŏ [-hupourgeŏ], to help together

surŏ, to drag, hale, draw

surtis, a sandbank, quicksands

su-schēmatizŏ [-schēma, *MID.*, to fashion one's self according to, to be conformed to

su-sparassŏ, *to rend severely*, to tear

sus-sēmon [-sēma], *a concerted sign*, a token

sus-sōmos, of the same body

su-stasiastēs [sustasis], *a fellow-rebel*, one that makes insurrection with another   [ance

su-stasis, *a setting together*, an alliance

su-statikos [sunistēmi], *commendatory*, of commendation

su-stauroŏ, to crucify with

su-stellō, to wind up. (*See* to wound) *PAS. part.*, contracted, short

su-stenazŏ, to groan together

su-stoicheŏ, to rank *with*, to answer to

su-stratiōtēs, a fellow soldier

su-strephŏ, *to roll together*, to gather

su-strophē [sustrephŏ], *a combining*, a concourse. (*See* band [*vb.*])

su-zaŏ, to live with

su-zēteŏ, to question *or* dispute with, to inquire, to reason together

su-zētēsis, disputation, disputing, reasoning

su-zētētēs, a disputer   [soning

su-zeugnumi, to join together

su-zōopoieŏ, to quicken together with

su-zugos, a'yoke fellow

Τ, σ,   (*tau*) = t.

Θ, ϑ, ϑ, (*theta*) = th.

tabernē, a tavern   [perhaps

tacha [tachus], readily, peradventure

tacheōs, quickly, shortly, hastily, suddenly, soon

tachinos, speedy, swift. (*See* shortly)

tachion [*comp.* of tachus], sooner, shortly, quickly. (*See* outrun)

tachista [*super.* of tacheōs], *very quickly*, with all speed

tachos, *speed :* **en tachos**, *in speed*, speedily, shortly, quickly

tachu [*neu.* of tachus], quickly, lightly

tachus, swift

tagma [tassŏ], *an arrangement*, order

taktos [tassŏ], *ordered*, set

talaipōreŏ [talaipōros], *to be afflicted*

talaipōria, *wretchedness*, misery

talaipōros, *miserable*, wretched

talantiaios, of the weight of a talent [*about 56 lb.*]

talanton [talaŏ, *to bear*], a talent ; *a measure of weight*, (*probably a man's burden*), at least 56 lb.; *also of money*, at least £200. It varied at different places and times

talitha [*Syriac word signifying* "*damsel*"], Talitha

tameion, a closet, secret chamber, storehouse   [humble, abase

tapeinoŏ [tapeinos], to bring low,

tapeino-phrosunē [-phrēn], lowliness, humbleness *or* humility of mind ; humility

tapeinos, lowly, humble, of low estate *or* degree ; base, cast down

tapeinōsis, humiliation, low estate. (*See* low, vile)

taphē [thaptŏ], *burial*. (*See* bury)

taphos [thaptŏ], a sepulchre, a tomb

tarachē [tarassŏ], trouble, a troubling

tarachos [tarassŏ], a stir

---

tarassō, to trouble

tartaroō, to cast down to hell

tassō, *to arrange*, set, appoint, addict, ordain, determine

tauros, a bull, an ox

taxis [tassō], *an arrangement*, order

te, and, both, also, even, then, whether

technē [teuchō], an art, an occupation, a craft

technitēs, a craftsman *;* an artificer

teichos, a wall   [builder

teinō, *to stretch*

tekmērion, *a sure sign*, infallible proof

teknion [teknon], a little *or* dear child

tekno-goneŏ [-genō], to bear children

tekno-gonia, child-bearing

teknon [tiktō], a child ; a son, daughter

tekno-tropheŏ [-trephŏ], to bring up children

tēkŏ, *to liquify*. *PAS.*, to melt

tektōn [teuchō], *a builder*, a carpenter

tēl-augōs [tēle-, *far*], *far shining*, clearly

teleioō [teleios], to make perfect, to finish, perfect, fulfil. (*See* consecrate)

teleios [telos], perfect, of full age. (*See* [man]

teleiōs, *perfectly*, to the end   [man]

teleiōsis, perfection, performance

teleiotēs [teleios], perfection, perfect-

teleiōtēs [teleioŏ], a finisher   [ness

teleŏ [telos], to make an end of, to finish ; to go over, fulfil, accomplish, fill up, perform, pay. *PAS.*, (*also*) to expire

teles-phoreŏ [telos-], to bring fruit to perfection

teleutaŏ, to decease, to die, to be dead [*i.e.*, *to have died*]

teleutē [teleŏ], *the finale*, death

tēlikoutos, so great, so mighty

tellō, *to make to arise*

telōnēs [telos-ōneomai], *one who buys or farms the taxes*, a publican

telōnion [telōnēs], *the tax office*, the receipt of custom

telos, the end, ending, the uttermost ; *a tax*, custom. (*See* finally, continual)

temnŏ, *to cut*

tephroŏ, to turn into ashes

teras, a wonder

tēreŏ, to keep, hold fast, preserve, reserve, watch, observe. *PART.*, a keeper

tērēsis [tēreŏ], a keeping, a hold, a prison

tessarakonta, forty

tessarakonta-etēs [-etos], of forty years. (*See* forty)

tessares, four   [years. (*See* forty)

tessares-kai-dekatos, fourteenth

tetartaios, of four days. (*See* four)

tetartos, fourth. (*See* four)

tetr-, **tetra-** [tessares], *four*

tetradion [tetras, *a set of four*], a quaternion

tetra-gōnos [-gōnia], *four-cornered*, four-square   [four thousand

tetrakis-chilioi [tetrakis-*four times*],

tetra-kosioi, four hundred

tetra-mēnon, *the space of* four months

tetraploös, four fold   [beasts

tetra-pous, *NEU. plu.*, fourfooted

tetr-archeŏ, to be a tetrarch

tetr-archēs, *a ruler of a fourth part of a province*, a tetrarch

teuchō, *to prepare*, *to make*

thalassa, the sea

thallō, *to grow luxuriantly*, to blossom

thalpŏ, to cherish

thambeŏ, *ACT. and PAS.*, to be amazed *or* astonished   [amazed

thambos, wonder. (*See* astonish)

thanasimos [thanatos], deadly

thanatē-phoros [-pherŏ], *causing death*, deadly.

thanatoō, to kill, put to death, to cause to be put to death, mortify. *PAS.* (also) to become dead

thanatos [thnēskō],death. (See deadly)

thaptō, to bury

tharreō [tharseō], to be bold or confident, to have confidence. (See boldly)

tharseō [tharsos], to be of good cheer

tharsos, courage   [or comfort

thauma, wonder, admiration, [i. e. astonishment]

thaumasios, wonderful   [marvel

thaumastos, marvellous. (*NEU.* a

thaumazō,to wonder, marvel, admire, have in admiration

thea [theos], a goddess

theaomai, *MID. and perf. of PAS.*, to see, look upon, behold

theatrizō [theatron], to make one a gazing stock   [theatre

theatron [theaomai], a spectacle, a

theiōdēs, sulphurous, of brimstone

theion, sulphur, brimstone

theios [Theos], divine : **ho theion** [neu.], the Godhead

theiotēs [theios], Godhead

thēkē [tithēmi], a receptacle ; a sheath

thēlazō [thēlē], to give suck ; to suck. *PAS. part.*, suckling

thēlē, the breast

thēleia [thēlē], a female, a woman

thelēma [thelō], will, pleasure, desire

thelēsis [thelō], a choosing, will

thelō, to choose, to will, to be willing or desirous, to desire, love, list ; to be disposed or forward ; to intend, mean. (See rather, please, voluntary, within, would)   [female

thēlu [neut. of thēleia], the female sex,

themelioō, to lay the foundation ; to found, settle, ground

themelios, a foundation

themis, law, right, justice   [God

theo-didaktos [-didaskō], taught of

theo-macheō, to fight against God

theo-machos, one who fights against God. (See fight)   [ration of God

theo-pneustos [-pneō],given by inspi-

theōreō [theōros], to be a spectator, to behold, look on, see, consider, perceive

theōria, a spectacle, a sight

theōros [theaomai], a spectator

Theos, God. (See godly, Godward, exceeding): **theos**, a heathen deity, a god. *PLU.*, goda

theo-sebeia [theosebēs], the worship of God, godliness   [of God

theo-sebēs [-sebomai], a worshipper

theo-stugēs [-stugeō], a hater of God

theotēs [Theos], Godhead

thēr, a wild beast

thēra [thēr], a trap ; hunting

therapeia [therapeuō], healing; attendants, a household

therapeuō, to attend upon ; to heal, to cure ; to worship   [dant, a servant

therapōn [therō], a voluntary atten-

thēreuō [thēr], to hunt, to catch

thērio-macheō, to fight with beasts

thērion [thēr], a wild beast ; a venomous beast

therismos [therizō], the harvest

theristēs [therizō], a reaper

therizō [theros], to reap

thermainomai [thermē], to warm one's self, to be warmed

thermē [therō], heat

therō, to warm, cherish, nurse

theros, the warm season, summer

thēsaurizō [thēsauros], to treasure, lay or heap up treasure, to keep in rest, to lay up

thēsauros, a treasure   [lished

thesmos, a law, that which is estab-

thigō, to touch, to handle

thlaō, to crush, or bruise

thlibō, to press upon, to afflict, trouble, throng. *PAS.*, (also) to suffer tribulation. (See narrow)

thlipsis, pressure, affliction, trouble, persecution, tribulation, anguish. (See afflict, burdened)   [i.e., to have died

thnēskō, to die. Past., to be dead, **thnētos**, mortal. *NEUT.*, mortality

thōrax, a breastplate

thorubeō, *ACT. and MID.*, to set on an uproar ; to make an ado or noise, to trouble one's self

thorubos, an uproar, a tumult

thrauō, to bruise   [cattle

thremma [trephō], what is reared,

thrēneō, to lament, to mourn

thrēnos, lamentation   [worshipping)

thrēskeia, worship, religion. (See

thrēskos, religious   [triumph over

thriambeuō, to cause to triumph ; to

thrix, hair

throeō, to frighten, alarm ; to trouble

thrombos, a great drop

thronos, a seat, a throne

thuella, a tempest

thugatēr, a daughter

thugatrion, a little or young daughter

thuinos [thuia, a fragrant wood], fragrant, thyine

thumiama [thumiaō], incense, odour

thumiaō [thuō], to burn incense

thumiatērion, a censer

thumo-macheō [thumos-], to fight fiercely, to be highly displeased [wroth

thumoōmai [thumos]. *PAS.*, to be

thumos, wrath, indignation, fierceness

thō, to sacrifice, slay in sacrifice ; kill

thura, a door, a gate

thureos, a shield [oblong in form]

thuris, a window

thur-ōros [thura-ouros], one that keeps the door, a porter

thusia [thuō], sacrifice

thusiastērion, an altar

tiktō, to bring forth, bear, be delivered, to be in travail. *PAS.*, to be born

tillō, to pluck

timaō, to honour, to value

timē, honour, esteem ; a price, a sum. (See precious)

timios [timē], precious, honourable, dear, had in reputation

timiotēs, costliness

tim-ōreō, to avenge, to punish

tim-ōria, retribution, punishment

tim-ōros [timē-ouros], watchful of one's honour, a helper, an avenger

tinassō, to swing, to shake

tiō, to pay, to endure. (See punish)

tis, a certain, one, any, some. (See a, every, kind, divers, he, thing, man, ought, nothing, what, whose, whatsoever, whosoever, wherewith)

tis, who ? which ? what ? how ? why ? (See every, no, none, nothing, manner, where ? whereby, whose ? wherefore, whereunto, wherewith, wherewithal, whither)

tithēmi, to put, lay, lay down or aside, to set forth, make, ordain, appoint. *MID.*, to set, put, appoint, settle, make, lay up, conceive, purpose. (See advise, bow, commit, give, kneel, sink)

titlos, a title   [sink]

to, the neuter of **ho**

toi, therefore, in truth, nevertheless

toichos, a wall

toi-gar-oun, therefore, wherefore

toi-nun, moreover, then, therefore

toios-de [toios-, such], such indeed

toioutos, such, such an one. (See like,

tokos [tiktō], offspring, gain, usury

tolmaō, to be bold, to dare. (See boldly]

tolmēroteron, the more boldly

tolmētēs, audacious, presumptuous

tomē [temnō], a cutting

tomōteros [temnō], more cutting, sharper

topazion, a topaz

topos, a place, a room, a quarter. (See coasts, license, plain, rock, where)

tosoutos, so great, so much, as large, so long. *PLU.*, (also) so many, these many

tote, then, at that time. (See when)

tounantion [to-enantion],contrariwise

tounoma [to-onoma], by name. (See named)   [to say

tout-esti [houtos-esti], that is, that is

toxon, a bow

trachēlizō, to take by the throat, lay bare. *PAS.*, to be open

trachēlos, the neck

trachus, rough. (See rock)

tragos, a goat

trapeza, a table ; a banker's table, a bank. (See meat)   [exchanger

trapezitēs [trapeza], a banker, an

trauma, a wound

traumatizō, to wound

trechō, to run, to have course

treis, three

tremō, to tremble, to be afraid

trephō, to feed, nourish, bring up

trepō, to turn

tri-, See **tris**

triakonta, thirty, thirtyfold

triakosioi, three hundred

tribō, to rub, wear, spend

tribolos, a brier, a thistle

tribos [tribō], a path

trichinos [thrix], of hair

tri-etia [-etos], the space of three years

tri-mēnon, the space of three months

tri-klinos, a dining room with three couches [tris [treis], thrice, three times

tris- or tri-, three, three times

tris-chilioi, three thousand   [floor

tris-tegon [-stegē], the third loft or

tritos [treis], third. *NEU.*, **triton**, thirdly, the third time

trizō, to make a grating noise, to gnash

trochia [trochos], the track of wheels, a path

trochos [trechō], a wheel, a course

trōgō, to chew, to eat   [tremble]

tromos [tremō], a trembling. (See

tropē [trepō], a turning   [meat

trophē [trephō], nourishment, food,

trophos [trephō], a nurse

tropo-phoreō, to suffer the manners

tropos, a manner, a way. (See as, conversation, means)

trublion, a bowl, a dish

trugaō, to harvest, to gather in

trugōn, a turtle dove

trumalia, a hole, the eye of a needle

trupēma, a bored hole, the eye of a needle

truphaō, to live in pleasure

truphē, luxurious living. (See delicately, to riot)

tuchon [tungchanō], perhaps, it may be

tumpanizō, *PAS.*, to be beaten as a drum, to be tortured

tungchanō, to hit, to chance, may be; to obtain, to enjoy. (See refresh, little,

tuphloō [tuphlos], to blind   [special]

tuphlos, blind

tuphomai, to smoke

tuphōnikos [tuphōn, *a whirlwind*], tempestuous

tuphoōmai, *PAS.*, to be wrapped in smoke, to be high-minded, proud, *or* lifted up with pride

tupos, *a type*, figure, form, pattern; a print, fashion; example, ensample. (*See* manner)

tuptō, to strike, smite, beat, wound

turbazomai, *MID. or PAS.*, to trouble one's self, to be troubled

Ξ, ξ, (xi)=x.

xenia [xenos], a lodging

xenizō, to lodge *or* entertain *as a guest*. *MID.*, to think strange. *PAS.*, to be lodged, to lodge. (*See* stranger)

xeno-docheō [-dechomai], to lodge strangers

xenos, strange; a stranger; a host

xestēs, a pot (= *about* 1½ *pints*)

xērainō [xēros], to dry up, to wither. *PAS.*, (*also*) to wither away, to be ripe, to pine away. *PART.*, withered

xēros, dry, withered; dry land

xulinos [xulon], of wood

xulon, wood; a tree, a staff, the stocks

xuraō [xuros, *a razor*], to shave

Z, ζ, ζ, (zeta)=z.

zaō, to live, be alive. *PART.*, (*also*) lively, quick [*i.e.*, living]. (*See* life, lifetime)

zēloō, to covet earnestly, desire to have, to be zealous; to be jealous, to envy, to be moved with envy. (*See* affect.) *MID. or PAS.*, to be zealously affected

zēlos, zeal, fervent mind, emulation, envying, envy, jealousy, indignation

zēlōtēs [zēloō], *a zealot*; zealous

zēmia, damage, loss

zēmioō [zēmia], *PAS.*, to receive damage, suffer loss, to lose, be a cast-away

zeō, *to be hot*, to be fervent

zestos [zeō], hot

zētēma [zēteō], *a subject of inquiry*, a question

zēteō, *to seek*, to seek for *or* after, en-quire for; to desire, require, endeavour to seek means, to go *or* be about

zētēsis, *a questioning*, a question

zeugnumi, *to yoke*, to join

zeugos [zeugnumi], a yoke, a pair

zeuktēria [zeugnumi], *a fastening*, a band

zizanion, *a deleterious plant like wheat*, a tare, tares

zōē [zaō], life; a lifetime

zōgreō [zōos-agreuō], *to take alive*, to take captive, catch

zōnē, a girdle, purse

zōnnuō [zōnē], to gird

zōo-goneō [zōos-gonos], *to bring forth alive*, to preserve. (*See* live) [beast

zōon [*neut. of* zōos], *a living creature*, a

zōo-poieō, to make alive, give life, quicken

zōos [zaō], *alive, living*

zophos, darkness, blackness, mist

zugos [zeugnumi], a yoke; a pair of balances

zumē, leaven

zumoō, to leaven

CHARACTERISTIC TERMINATIONS.

I. VERBS.

1. The usual terminations of Verbs in the active voice are -ō and -mi. In the middle and passive voices the -ō is changed into -omai, and the -mi into -mai. The following are the characteristic forms of the voices:—

Active, **tuptō**, *to strike*
Middle, **tuptomai**, *to strike one's self*
Passive, **tuptomai**, *to be struck*

Active, **tithēmi**, *to place*
Middle, **tithemai**, *to place one's self*
Passive, **tithemai**, *to be placed*

But from these there are many deviations. Some verbs are used only in the middle or passive voices, and yet have active significations.

2. Verbs ending in -zō, derived from other verbs, are generally causative.

sōphron, *sober*
sōphroneō, *to be sober*
sōphronizō, *to make sober*

3. When derived from a noun, they generally imply its application.

lithos, *a stone*; **lithazō**, *to stone*
potos, *drink*; **potizō**, *to give drink*

4. Verbs ending in -skō are causative.

methuō, *to be drunk*
methuskō, *to make drunk*

II. NOUNS.

1. Nouns have a great variety of terminations. -eus and -os are masculine.

basileus, *a king*
adelphos, *a brother*

-a and -ē are feminine terminations.

basilissa, *a queen*
adelphē, *a sister*

-on is a neuter termination.

2. Nouns in -tēs, -sis, and -ma, *derived from verbs*, have usually the following significations:—

-tēs, the person who acts
-sis, the doing of the act
-ma, the act when completed

poieō, *to make*
poiētēs, *the maker* (poet)
poiēsis, *the making* (poesy)
poiēma, *the thing made* (poem)

3. Nouns in -tēs, *derived from adjectives or nouns*, signify the quality of the adjective or the character of the noun.

hagios, *holy*
hagiotēs, *holiness*
adelphos, *a brother*
adelphotēs, *brotherhood*

4. Nouns in -tērion, signify the place of that from which they are derived.

krinō, *to judge*
kritērion, *the judgment-seat*

5. The active present participle ending in -ōn is frequently used also as a noun.

archō, *to rule*; **archōn**, *ruling*
archōn, *a ruler*

6. Nouns in -ion, *or* -arion, derived from other nouns, are diminutives.

kuōn, *a dog*
kunarion, *a little dog*

III. ADJECTIVES.

1. Adjectives in -ios, derived from nouns, denote their *belonging to* the noun.

basileus, *a king*
basileios, *belonging to a king*

2. Adjectives in -ikos, derived from nouns, denote their being invested with the qualities *essential* to the nouns.

basileus, *a king*
basilikos, *kingly*

3. Adjectives in -ikos, derived from verbs, denote capability or fitness.

krinō, *to judge*
kritikos, *one fit to judge*

4. Adjectives ending in -tos, derived from verbs, often denote a passive state; in -teos, a passive state future.

kruptō, *to hide*; **kruptos**, *hidden*
ballō, *to cast*; **blēteos**, *to be cast*

5. Adjectives in -teros and -iōn, denote the comparative degree.

bathus, *deep*
bathuteros *or* **bathiōn**, *deeper*

6. Adjectives in -tatos and -istos, denote the superlative degree.

bathus, *deep*
bathutatos *or* **bathistos**, *deepest*

IV. ADVERBS.

1. The most frequent termination of Adverbs is -ōs.

lampros, *bright*; **lamprōs**, *brightly*

2. The neuter of an adjective frequently becomes an adverb.

prōtos, *first*; **prōton**, *firstly*

3. The adverbial terminations -then, -thi, and -de, denote motion *from* a place, location *in* a place, and motion *to* a place.

ouranothen, *from heaven*
ouranothi, *in heaven*
ouranonde, *to heaven*

THE following Prefixes are those most commonly used in the formation of compounds.

a-, kata-, sun-, epi- apo-, ek-, dia-, en-, ana-, pro-, pros-, hupo-, para-, meta-, peri-, anti-, huper-, eis-.

APPENDIX.

The Greek Article.

The Greek **ho** *does very much, but not altogether, represent the English* **the**. *They both give definiteness to the object, but the one is often used where the other is inadmissible. Moreover the absence of* **the** *in English is not always equivalent to the presence of* **a** *or* **an**, *and therefore, plural nouns are less capable of precise treatment.*

Nevertheless **ho** *does always indicate a certain amount of definiteness, and is worthy of notice. Under* **A** *or* **AN** *in the Concordance there will be found a list of cases in which the authorised version translates* **ho** *by* **a** *or* **an**. *The following are additional instances of an indefinite translation where the Greek is definite. The parentheses indicate the presence of the Greek article :—*

Mat. 5.37. whats. cometh of ( ) evil [one]
6.13. deliver us from ( ) evil [one]
8.12. unto ( ) outer ( ) darkness
(the darkness, which is outer)
( ) weep. and ( ) gnash.; 13.42
12.20. send forth ( ) judg., (ver. 18)
13.42. cast them into ( ) a furnace
14. 2. therefore ( ) mighty works do
17.24. ( ) tribute money..pay ( )trib.
25, 26. of ( ) strangers
18. 7. beca. of ( ) offences..that ( )
Mat. 18.8. cast into ( ) everlast. ( ); 25.41
(the fire which is everlasting)
24.15. abomination of ( ) desolation
26.51. struck a ( ) servant of the
Mar. 6.33. ran .. out of all ( ) cities
Lu. 16. 9. into ( ) everlasting habitation
23.39. If thou be ( ) Christ save
Jo. 1. 4. in him was ( ) life, and the life
5. shineth in ( ) darkness, and
17. ( ) grace and ( ) truth came
3.12. ( ) earthly things..of ( ) hea.
19. that ( ) light is come into
loved ( ) dark. rather than ( )
21. he that doeth ( ) truth
8.12. shall not walk in ( ) darkness
12.36. while ye have ( ) light believe
46. should not abide in ( ) dark.
13.13. call me ( ) master and ( ) lord
16.13. spirit of ( ) truth..unto all ( )
Act.17. 3. alleging that ( ) Christ must
27.26. until that an ( ) offering sho.
Ro. 3.30. seeing it is ( ) one God which
uncircumc. through faith ( )
4. 9. that ( ) faith was reckoned to
14. ( ) faith is made void, and the
6. 4. buried with him by ( ) bapti.
into ( ) death
9.27. a ( ) remnant shall be saved
13.12. put on the armour of ( ) light
1Co. 11.13. for such are ( ) false apostles
12.18. with him I send a ( ) brother
Gal. 3.16. not to ( ) seeds, as of many
19. added because of ( ) transgr.
Eph. 1 3. 20. in ( ) heavenly pl.; 2.6;3.10

Eph. 2.12. from the covenants of ( ) pr.
6.12. ( ) principaliti...( ); Col.2.15
Col. 2.14. the handwriting of ( ) ordna.
17. a shadow of ( ) things to com;
18. worshipping of ( ) angels
2Pet. 1. 4. unto us ( ) exceeding great
19. we have a ( ) more sure word
1Jo. 5.19. lieth in ( ) wick. (wicked one)

The following are selected from passages which are definite in English but indefinite in Greek : —

Mat. 1.20. behold t. [an] angel of the;
2.13; 28.2; Lu.2.9; Act.5.
19; 8.26; 12.7,23
3. 3. saying t. [a] voice of one
8. 8. speak t. [a] word only, and
Mat.15. 9. teach. for doct. t. ; Mar.7.7
22.30. as t. angels of God; Mar.12.25
Mar. 1.45. openly enter unto t. [a] city
2. 1. that he was in t. [a] house
Lu. 1.78. where. t. day spr. [a dawn]
2.12. ye shall find t. [a] babe
7. 3. sent unto him t. elders of the
22.17. he took t. [a] cup, and gave
37. reckoned among t. transgres.
Act. 7.35. by the hands of t. [an] angel
38. who received t. lively oracles
9. 5. hard.. to kick against t. pric.
10.22. Cornelius t. [a] centurion, a
27.23. by me this night t. [an] an.
Ro. 2.12. sinned in t. law (under law)
shall be judged by t. law
14. when t. Gen. wh. have not t.
do..contained in t. law..
having not t. law, are a law
3.20. therefore by t. deeds of t. law
21. without t. law..by the law
27. Nay, but by t. [a] law of fai.
28. Is he the God of t. Jews only
is he not also of t. Gentiles
31. do we make void t. law
4.13. but through t. [a] righteous.
14. if they which are of t. law
6.14, 15. not under t. law but un.
9.22. endured..t. vessels of wrath
23. on t. vessels of mercy
11. 5. according to t. [an] election
13. 4. he is t. [a] minister of God
1Co. 2.14. But t. [a] natural man recei.
3.16. ye are t. [a]temple of G.; 6.19
6.15. t. mem. of Ch...t. [a] mem.
10. 4. drank of that spirit. rock th.
(of a spiritual following rock)
16. is it not t. communion of the
(a participation of the body)
12.15. not t. [a] hand..t. [an] eye
15.47. the first man is of t. earth
2Co. 3. 3. declared to be t. [an] epistle
6.16. agreement hath t. [a] temple
17. touch not t. [an] unclean th.
11.13. transf...into t. apostles of
15. transf...as t. ministers of ri.
12. 7. the abundance of t. revelati.
1Th. 2. 6. burdensome as t. apostles of
1Ti. 5.11. But t. younger widows refuse
(very young widows refuse)
Heb. 1. 6. Let all t. angels of God wors.
2John 3. when t. brethren came and

Italic Words

In the Authorised Version.

The Translators have indicated those words for which there is no corresponding Greek, by printing them in italic; but there are many others which are not so printed, and having no Greek headings under which they could appear, they have been omitted in the present Concordance.

The following should have appeared in their places:—

Addenda.

A, heis
1Co. 15.45. a living soul..a quick.

ABUNDANTLY, perissoteros
2Co. 12.15. the more a. I love you
1Th. 2.17. endeavoured the more a.

ACCORDING, pros
2Co. 5.10. a. to that he hath done

AFTER, hōs
Act. 21. 1. a. we were gotten from

AGAINST, meta, [gen.]
Rev. 2.16. will fight a. them with

ANY, oudeis, [without another neg.]
Mar. 5. 4. neither could a. man tame

BE, hōs
Act.17.22. ye are too superstitious
ginomai
Lu. 19.17. because thou hast b-n
Act. 15. 7. th. had b-n much disput.

BEFORE, enantion
Mar. 2.12. went forth b. them all
Lu. 20.26. his words b. the people
24.19. b. God and all the people
Act. 8.32. like a lamb dumb b. his

COME, erchomai
Jo. 12.46. I am c. a light unto the

EVERY, kata, [accu.]
Act. 5.42. in the temple and in e.
Eph. 5.33. let e. one of you in part.

FROM, kata, [accu.]
Act. 20.20. publicly and f. house to

HE, houtos
Act. 25.25. that h. himself hath appea

HIMSELF, autos
Act. 25.25. that he h. hath appealed

HOLY, hagiotatos
Jude 20. on your most h. faith

HOME, pros [accu.] heautos [plu.]
Jo. 20.10. discip...unto their own h.

MEAN-time, ho [dat. plu.]
Lu. 12. 1. In the m. t. when there

MEN. *This word is used when adjectives appear in the plural masculine without nouns.*

31

APPENDIX.

MOREOVER, kai.
Act.19.26. **m.** ye see and hear
  de kai.
²Pet. 1.15. **m.** I will endeavour
  de.
Ro. 8.30. **m.** whom he did
¹Co. 15. 1. **m.** brethren I declare
²Co. 1.23. **m.** I call God for a
  8. 1. **m.** brethren we do you
Heb. 9.21. **m.** he sprinkled

ONE, ho krinō, [partic.]
Jo. 12.48. hath **o.** *that judgeth* him

PUT, didōmi.
Rev.17.11. God hath **p.** in their hearts

QUARTERS, dia [gen.] pas [plu.]
Act. 9.32. Peter passed *throug.* all **q.**

READY, prothumōs.
¹Pet. 5. 2. filthy lucre but of a **r.**

SAME, autos.
Mat. 5.46. do not even the pub. the **s.**
  12.50. *the* **s.** in my brother and
  25.26. went and traded with the **s.**
  26.48. *that* **s.** is he ; Mar.14.44
  27.44. also cast *the* **s.** in his teeth
Mar.13.13.*the* **s.** shall be saved
Lu. 6.33. sinners also do even the **s.**
  38. for with the **s.** measure ye
  7.21. in that **s.** hour he cured
  12.12. shall teach you in the **s.**
  20.17. the **s.** is become the head
  19. the **s.** hour sought to lay
  23.12. the **s.** day Pilate and Her.
  40. thou art in the **s.** condem.
  24.33. they rose up the **s.** hour
Jo. 1.33. *the* **s.** is he which baptiseth
  5.36. the **s.** works that I do
Act.16.18. he came out the **s.** hour
  22.13. not only do the **s.** but have
  24.20. the **s.** hour I looked up
Ro. 1.32. or else let these **s.** here
  2. 3. doest *the* **s.** that thou sha.
  10.12. the **s.** Lord over all
  12. 4. members have not the **s.**
  13. 3. shalt have praise of *the* **s**
¹Co.10. 3. all eat the **s.**spiritual meat
  4. drink the **s.** spiritual drink
  12. 4. div. of gifts but the **s.** sp.
  5. administrations, but the **s.**
  6. the **s.** God which worketh
  15.39. All flesh is not the **s.** flesh
²Co. 2. 3. I wrote this **s.** unto you
  4.13. having the **s.** spirit of fai.
  8.19. to the glory of the **s.** Lord
  12.18. walked we not in the **s.**
Eph. 4.10. *the* **s.** also that ascended
Phi. 1.30. having the **s.** conflict wh.
  2. 2. likeminded having the **s.**
  3.16. by the **s.** rule..mind the **s.**
Col. 4. 2. watch in *the* **s.** with
Heb. 1.12. thou art the **s.** and thy
  2.14. like. took part of the **s.**

32

Heb. 11.9. with him of the **s.** prom.
  13. 8. Jesus Christ, the **s.** yester.
¹Pet. 4.10. minister the **s.** one to ano.
²Pet. 3. 7. by the **s.** word are kept in
¹Jo. 2.27. the **s.** anointing teacheth
  ho.
Lu. 17.29. *the* **s.** day that Lot went
Act. 1.22. *that* **s.** day that he was
  houtos ho.
Act. 2.36. God hath made *that* **s.** J.
  ho ti kai.
Jo. 8.25. *even the* **s.** *that* I said unto

THAT, ho.
Jo. 1. 8. to bear witness of **t.** light
  21. art thou **t.** prophet
  25. if thou be not **t.** Christ
  6.32. Moses gave you not **t.** bre.
  48. I am **t.** bread of life
  58. This is **t.** bread which
  69. sure that thou art **t.** Chr.
  7.37. last day, **t.** great day of
Act. 2.2c. before **t.** great and notab.
  7.37. this is **t.** Moses which
  21.38. Art not thou **t.** Egyptian
  22.14. and see **t.** just one
Ro. 1.27. she is free from **t.** law

THINGS. *This word generally represents the plural neuter of adjectives without nouns.*

TO-DAY, sēmeron.
Mat. 6.30. **t.** is, and tomorrow Lu.
  12.28
  16. 3. it will be foul weather **t.**
  21.28. go work **t.** in my vineyard
Lu. 5.26. seen strange things **t.**
  13.32. do cures **t.** and tomorrow
  33. I must walk **t.** and
  19. 5. **t.** I must abide at thy
  house
  23.43. **t.** shalt thou be with me
  24.21. **t.** is the third day since
Heb. 3. 7. **t.** if ye will hear his
  voice
  13. daily, while it is called **t.**
  15. **t.** if ye will hear his
  voice
  4. 7. **t.** after so long a time **t.**
  5. 5. **t.** have I begotten thee
  13. 8. yesterday, and **t.** and
Ja. 4.13. ye that say **t.** or to-
  morrow.

VERY, ho.
Act. 9.22. proving that this is **v.** Ch.

PROPER NAMES.

Idumea [Idoumaia] Mar. 3.8.

Illyricum [Illurikon] Ro. 15.19.

Isaac [Isaäc] *Mat.* 1.2; 8.11; 22.32.
Mar. 12.26. *Lu.* 3.34; 13.28; 20.37.
Acts 3.13; 7.8,32. *Ro.* 9.7,10. *Gal.*
4.28. *Heb.* 11.9,17,18,20. *Ja.* 2.21.

Iscariot [Iskariōtēs] *Mat.* 10.4;
26.14. *Mar.* 3.19; 14.10. *Lu.* 6.16;
22.3. *Joh.* 6.71; 12.4; 13.2,26; 14.22.

Israel [Israēl] *Mat.* 2.20,21; 8.10;
9.33; 10.23; 19.28. *Mar.* 12.29.
Lu. 1.54,80; 2.25,34; 4.25,27; 22.30;
24.21. *Joh.* 1.31; 3.10. *Act.* 1.6;
4.8; 5.31; 13.23; 28.20. *Rom.* 9.6,
27,31; 10.1,19,21; 11.2,7,25,26. 1
Cor. 10.18. *Gal.* 6.16. *Eph.* 2.12.
Phi. 3.5.
(See also. *Children, House, King,
God, People.*)

Israelite. [Israēlitēs] *Joh.* 1.47. *Ro.*
9.4; 11.1. 2 *Cor.* 11.22. (See *Men.*)

Issachar [Isachar] Rev. 7.7.

Italian [Italikos] Act. 10.1.

Italy [Italia] *Act.* 18.2; 27.1,6. *Heb.*
13.24.

Ituræa [Itouraia] Lu. 3.1.